BELLAMY & CHILD

MATERIALS ON EUROPEAN UNION LAW OF COMPETITION

2014 Edition

Edited by

ANDREW MACNAB
Barrister, Monckton Chambers

OXFORD
UNIVERSITY PRESS

OXFORD
UNIVERSITY PRESS

Great Clarendon Street, Oxford, OX2 6DP,
United Kingdom

Oxford University Press is a department of the University of Oxford.
It furthers the University's objective of excellence in research, scholarship,
and education by publishing worldwide. Oxford is a registered trade mark of
Oxford University Press in the UK and in certain other countries

© Oxford University Press, 2014

The moral rights of the authors have been asserted

First Edition published in 2008
Seventh Edition published in 2014

Impression: 1

Published in the United States of America by Oxford University Press
198 Madison Avenue, New York, NY 10016, United States of America

British Library Cataloguing in Publication Data
Data available

ISBN 978–0–19–968947–7

Printed in Italy by
L.E.G.O. S.p.A.—Lavis TN

CONTENTS

C. SUBSTANTIVE ANTITRUST MATTERS

Regulations

Notice etc

D. MERGERS AND CONCENTRATIONS

Regulations, etc

Notices, etc

E. SECTORAL REGIMES

Electronic Communications

Legislation

Information and Notices

Insurance

Postal services

Agriculture

Transport

Rail, road, inland waterway

Maritime transport

Air transport

F. PUBLIC UNDERTAKINGS

Legislation

G. STATE AIDS

Procedure/Implementation

Regulations

Notices, etc

Block Exemptions

Horizontal Rules

Specific Aid Instruments

Reference/Discount Rates and Recovery Interest Rates

INTRODUCTION TO MATERIALS ON EUROPEAN UNION LAW OF COMPETITION 2014 EDITION

Welcome to *Bellamy & Child Materials on European Union Law of Competition*, 2014 Edition.

This work started life as the volume of Appendices to *Bellamy & Child, European Community Law of Competition*. This work serves three aims:

- First, it acts as the volume of Appendices to *Bellamy & Child, European Union Law of Competition* (7th edition, 2013). A copy of the current Materials volume will be bundled with the main work.
- Second, it acts as a companion to *Faull and Nikpay, The EU Law of Competition* (3rd edition).
- Third, it is intended to be a self-standing volume of EU competition law materials.

Readers' attention is drawn to the following features, which have been incorporated into the work to optimise utility and ease of use:

- The work is divided into seven main Parts (Treaty provisions, procedural matters, substantive antitrust matters, mergers and concentrations, sectoral regimes, public undertakings and State aids) and are indicated by headings and thumb-tabs.
- Within each Part, materials are, in the main, sub-divided into legislation and notices and are, in the main, arranged chronologically within each sub-division.
- The arrangement of the seven main Parts broadly follows the structure of *Bellamy & Child* and the Parts and Chapter headings cross-refer to *Bellamy & Child* (7th edition).
- In addition, documents include pinpoint cross-references to paragraphs in *Bellamy & Child* (7th edition) and *Faull & Nikpay* (3rd edition).
- Helpful tables of contents and page-headings throughout aim to optimise accessibility of content and to ensure easy navigation.
- Documents are reproduced with details of their publication in the Official Journal, Celex numbers and EUR-Lex website permanent links (where available).
- Original Official Journal footnotes are reproduced,[1] together with editorial annotations regarding amendments, etc.
- Where applicable, details of instruments' EEA application are included.

Selection of materials for inclusion in this work is dictated largely by the content of *Bellamy & Child* (7th edition). Unfortunately, continuing pressure on space means that we have had to limit our ambitions in respect of our third aim. We have not been able to include every document we would have wished, principally in the sections on sectoral regimes and State

---

[1] Although some original footnotes have been renumbered because of the differences between the format of the original and the format of this work.

aids. Documents reproduced in this work are up to date as at 30 September 2013, although it has been possible to incorporate some later changes during the production process.

The 2014 edition of this volume has been fully updated to take account of the publication of the 7th edition of *Bellamy & Child*, mainly in the form of renumbering the index and renumbering the various Treaty articles to reflect the changes made by the Treaty of Lisbon (below). We have also taken into account the various changes and developments since the 2013 edition. The new materials include:

- The Communication from the Commission on quantifying harm in actions for damages based on breaches of Article 101 or 102 TFEU
- The Commission staff working document accompanying that Communication, containing a Practical Guide to quantifying harm in actions for damages based on breaches of Article 101 or 102 TFEU
- The 2012 Communication applying Articles 107 and 108 TFEU to short-term export-credit insurance (which was published too late for inclusion in the last edition).

On 1 December 2009, the Treaty of Lisbon came into force and replaced the Treaty on European Union and the EC Treaty with a new Treaty on European Union ('TEU') and a Treaty on the Functioning of the European Union ('TFEU'), referred together as 'the Treaties'. With it, the 'European Community' and the 'Community' passed into history. The Lisbon Treaty also resulted in a renumbering of the articles of the former EC Treaty, most of which are now incorporated into the TFEU and some of which have migrated to the TEU. We have renamed and renumbered the Treaty recitals, articles, sections, chapters, titles and parts so that all numbering, etc is (we hope) now shown as current TFEU and TEU article numbers. References to the 'Community' in pre-Lisbon instruments remain. A separate note to this effect appears (Note on the Lisbon Treaty at p.xvii).

Legislation included in this work is © European Union, <http://eur-lex.europa.eu/>. Before 1 July 2013, only European Union legislation printed in the paper edition of the *Official Journal of the European Union* is deemed authentic. Since 1 July 2013, only the Official Journal published in electronic form ('the electronic edition of the Official Journal') shall be authentic and shall produce legal effects: see Council Regulation (EU) No 216/2013 of 7 March 2013 on the electronic publication of the *Official Journal of the European Union*, OJ L 69, 13/03/2013, p. 1, Article 1(2).

For reasons of space, the following materials are no longer reproduced in this volume. These materials remain available within the online service *Oxford Competition Law*: <http://oxcat.ouplaw.com/>

- Regulation 17 (implementation of the rules on competition)
- Joint statement of the Council and the Commission on the functioning of the Network of Competition Authorities (2002)
- Leniency Application
- Authorisation to conduct an inspection
- Explanatory note to an authorisation to conduct an inspection (2013)
- Merger notification and procedures template (2008)

- US–EU Merger working group: Best practices on cooperation in merger investigations (2011)
- Regulation 487/2009 (Council enabling regulation – the air transport sector)
- Notice on the determination of the applicable rules for the assessment of unlawful State aid (2002)
- Criteria for the compatibility analysis of training State aid (2009)
- Criteria for the analysis of the compatibility of State aid for the employment of disadvantaged and disabled workers subject to individual notification (2009)
- The new Guidelines on regional State aid for 2014–2020

NOTE ON THE LISBON TREATY

The Treaty of Lisbon came into force on 1 December 2009 and replaced the Treaty on European Union and the EC Treaty with a new Treaty on European Union ('TEU') and a Treaty on the Functioning of the European Union ('TFEU'). The 'European Community' has now passed into history.

The Lisbon Treaty also resulted in a renumbering of the articles of the former EC Treaty (now abbreviated, confusingly, to 'TEC' rather than the former 'EC'), most of which are now incorporated into the TFEU or which in some cases have been moved to the new TEU. Article 5 of the Lisbon Treaty and the 'Tables of Equivalences' referred to in that Article are reproduced at A1.

With the publication of the 7th edition of *Bellamy & Child, European Union Law of Competition*, we have (at last) renamed and renumbered the Treaty recitals, articles, sections, chapters, titles and parts. Thus all article numbers have been updated post-Treaty of Amsterdam and post-Treaty of Lisbon and are shown in their current TFEU or TEU form. For example, Article 85 EEC (in pre-Treaty of Amsterdam documents) and Article 81 EC (in post-Treaty of Amsterdam documents) are now shown as 'Article [101]' or 'Article [101 TFEU]'. Similarly, references to the 'EEC Treaty' and the 'EC Treaty' are shown as the '[Treaty on the Functioning of the European Union]' or as '[TFEU]' (or, where appropriate, '[TEU]' – mainly in relation to the former Articles 3(1)(g) and 10 TEC). In an attempt to keep changes to a minimum, references to 'the Treaty' *simpliciter* are not amended but are to be read as references to the TFEU.

PART A

TREATY PROVISIONS[*]

* Ed note: please see the Note on the Lisbon Treaty at p.xvii.

A1

ARTICLE 5 OF THE LISBON TREATY AND TABLES OF EQUIVALENCES

(CONDENSED)

(2012/C 326/01)

Official Journal C 326, 26.10.2012, p.1 at 363–390

Celex No: C2012/326/01

EUR-Lex permanent link: <http://eur-lex.europa.eu/LexUriServ/LexUriServ.do?uri=CELEX:C2012/326/01:EN:NOT>

Article 5 of the Treaty of Lisbon (OJ C 306, 17.12.2007, p.134) provides:

1. The articles, sections, chapters, titles and parts of the Treaty on European Union and of the Treaty establishing the European Community, as amended by this Treaty, shall be renumbered in accordance with the tables of equivalences set out in the annex to this Treaty, and which form an integral part of this Treaty.

2. The cross-references to the articles, sections, chapters, titles and parts of the Treaty on European Union and of the Treaty on the Functioning of the European Union, as well as between them, shall be adapted pursuant to paragraph 1 and the references to paragraphs of the said articles as renumbered or re-ordered by the provisions of this treaty shall be adapted in accordance with those provisions.

   References to the articles, sections, chapters, titles and parts of the Treaty on European Union and of the Treaty establishing the European Community contained in the other treaties and acts of primary legislation on which the Union is founded shall be adapted pursuant to paragraph 1 of this article. References to recitals of the Treaty on European Union or to paragraphs or articles of the Treaty on European Union or of the Treaty establishing the European Community as renumbered or re-arranged by the provisions of this Treaty shall be adapted pursuant to this latter.

   Such adaptations shall, where necessary, also apply in the event that the provision in question has been repealed.

3. The references to the recitals, articles, sections, chapters, titles and parts of the Treaty on European Union and of the Treaty establishing the European Community, as amended by this Treaty, contained in other instruments or acts shall be understood as referring to the recitals, articles, sections, chapters, titles and parts of those Treaties as renumbered pursuant to paragraph 1 and, respectively, to the paragraphs of the said articles, as renumbered or re-arranged by certain provisions of this Treaty.

TABLES OF EQUIVALENCES(*)

Treaty on European Union

Old numbering of the Treaty on European Union	New numbering of the Treaty on European Union
TITLE I — COMMON PROVISIONS	TITLE I — COMMON PROVISIONS
Article 1	Article 1
	Article 2
Article 2	Article 3
Article 3 (repealed)(¹)	
	Article 4
	Article 5 (²)
Article 4 (repealed) (³)	
Article 5 (repealed) (⁴)	
Article 6	Article 6
Article 7	Article 7
	Article 8
TITLE II — PROVISIONS AMENDING THE TREATY ESTABLISHING THE EUROPEAN ECONOMIC COMMUNITY WITH A VIEW TO ESTABLISHING THE EUROPEAN COMMUNITY	TITLE II — PROVISIONS ON DEMOCRATIC PRINCIPLES
Article 8 (repealed) (⁵)	Article 9
	Article 10 (⁶)

(*) Tables of equivalences as referred to in Article 5 of the Treaty of Lisbon. The original centre column, which set out the intermediate numbering as used in that Treaty, has been omitted.

(¹) Replaced, in substance, by Article 7 of the Treaty on the Functioning of the European Union ('TFEU') and by Articles 13(1) and 21, paragraph 3, second subparagraph of the Treaty on European Union ('TEU').

(²) Replaces Article 5 of the Treaty establishing the European Community ('TEC').

(³) Replaced, in substance, by Article 15.

(⁴) Replaced, in substance, by Article 13, paragraph 2.

(⁵) Article 8 TEU, which was in force until the entry into force of the Treaty of Lisbon (hereinafter 'current'), amended the TEC. Those amendments are incorporated into the latter Treaty and Article 8 is repealed. Its number is used to insert a new provision.

(⁶) Paragraph 4 replaces, in substance, the first subparagraph of Article 191 TEC.

Old numbering of the Treaty on European Union	New numbering of the Treaty on European Union
	Article 11
	Article 12
TITLE III — PROVISIONS AMENDING THE TREATY ESTABLISHING THE EUROPEAN COAL AND STEEL COMMUNITY [Ed note: omitted for reasons of space]	TITLE III — PROVISIONS ON THE INSTITUTIONS
TITLE IV — PROVISIONS AMENDING THE TREATY ESTABLISHING THE EUROPEAN ATOMIC ENERGY COMMUNITY [Ed note: omitted for reasons of space]	TITLE IV — PROVISIONS ON ENHANCED COOPERATION

[Ed note: footnotes 7 to 24 are omitted.]

Treaty on the Functioning of the European Union

Old numbering of the Treaty establishing the European Community	New numbering of the Treaty on the Functioning of the European Union
PART ONE — PRINCIPLES	PART ONE — PRINCIPLES
Article 1 (repealed)	
	Article 1
Article 2 (repealed) (^{25})	
	Title I — Categories and areas of union competence
	Article 2
	Article 3
	Article 4
	Article 5
	Article 6
	Title II — Provisions having general application
	Article 7
Article 3, paragraph 1 (repealed) (^{26})	
Article 3, paragraph 2	Article 8
Article 4 (moved)	Article 119
Article 5 (replaced) (^{27})	
	Article 9
	Article 10
Article 6	Article 11
Article 153, paragraph 2 (moved)	Article 12
	Article 13 (^{28})
Article 7 (repealed) (^{29})	
Article 8 (repealed) (^{30})	
Article 9 (repealed)	
Article 10 (repealed) (^{31})	
Article 11 (replaced) (^{32})	Articles 326 to 334
Article 11a (replaced) (^{32})	Articles 326 to 334
Article 12 (repealed)	Article 18
Article 13 (moved)	Article 19

(^{25}) Replaced, in substance, by Article 3 TEU.
(^{26}) Replaced, in substance, by Articles 3 to 6 TFEU.
(^{27}) Replaced, in substance, by Article 5 TEU.
(^{28}) Insertion of the operative part of the protocol on protection and welfare of animals.
(^{29}) Replaced, in substance, by Article 13 TEU.
(^{30}) Replaced, in substance, by Article 13 TEU and Article 282, paragraph 1, TFEU.
(^{31}) Replaced, in substance, by Article 4, paragraph 3, TEU.
(^{32}) Also replaced by Article 20 TEU.
[Ed note: footnotes 33 to 39 are omitted]

Old numbering of the Treaty establishing the European Community	New numbering of the Treaty on the Functioning of the European Union
Article 14 (moved)	Article 26
Article 15 (moved)	Article 27
Article 16	Article 14
Article 255 (moved)	Article 15
Article 286 (moved)	Article 16
	Article 17
PART TWO — CITIZENSHIP OF THE UNION [Ed note: omitted for reasons of space]	PART TWO — NON-DISCRIMINATION AND CITIZENSHIP OF THE UNION
PART THREE — COMMUNITY POLICIES	PART THREE — POLICIES AND INTERNAL ACTIONS OF THE UNION
	Title I — The internal market
Article 14 (moved)	Article 26
Article 15 (moved)	Article 27
Title I — Free movement of goods	Title II — Free movement of goods
Article 23	Article 28
Article 24	Article 29
Chapter 1 — The customs union	Chapter 1 — The customs union
Article 25	Article 30
Article 26	Article 31
Article 27	Article 32
Part Three, Title X, Customs cooperation (moved)	Chapter 2 — Customs cooperation
Article 135 (moved)	Article 33
Chapter 2 — Prohibition of quantitative restrictions between Member States	Chapter 3 — Prohibition of quantitative restrictions between Member States
Article 28	Article 34
Article 29	Article 35
Article 30	Article 36
Article 31	Article 37
Title II — Agriculture	Title III — Agriculture and fisheries
Article 32	Article 38
Article 33	Article 39
Article 34	Article 40
Article 35	Article 41
Article 36	Article 42
Article 37	Article 43
Article 38	Article 44
Title III — Free movement of persons, services and capital	Title IV — Free movement of persons, services and capital

Old numbering of the Treaty establishing the European Community	New numbering of the Treaty on the Functioning of the European Union
Chapter 1 — Workers	Chapter 1 — Workers
Article 39	Article 45
Article 40	Article 46
Article 41	Article 47
Article 42	Article 48
Chapter 2 — Right of establishment	Chapter 2 — Right of establishment
Article 43	Article 49
Article 44	Article 50
Article 45	Article 51
Article 46	Article 52
Article 47	Article 53
Article 48	Article 54
Article 294 (moved)	Article 55
Chapter 3 — Services	Chapter 3 — Services
Article 49	Article 56
Article 50	Article 57
Article 51	Article 58
Article 52	Article 59
Article 53	Article 60
Article 54	Article 61
Article 55	Article 62
Chapter 4 — Capital and payments	Chapter 4 — Capital and payments
Article 56	Article 63
Article 57	Article 64
Article 58	Article 65
Article 59	Article 66
Article 60 (moved)	Article 75
Title IV — Visas, asylum, immigration and other policies related to free movement of persons [Ed note: omitted for reasons of space]	Title V — Area of freedom, security and justice
Title V — Transport	Title VI — Transport
Article 70	Article 90
Article 71	Article 91
Article 72	Article 92
Article 73	Article 93
Article 74	Article 94
Article 75	Article 95

Old numbering of the Treaty establishing the European Community	New numbering of the Treaty on the Functioning of the European Union
Article 76	Article 96
Article *77*	Article 97
Article 78	Article 98
Article 79	Article 99
Article 80	Article 100
Title VI — Common rules on competition, taxation and approximation of laws	Title VII — Common rules on competition, taxation and approximation of laws
Chapter 1 — Rules on competition	Chapter 1 — Rules on competition
Section 1 — Rules applying to undertakings	Section 1 — Rules applying to undertakings
Article 81	Article 101
Article 83	Article 103
Article 84	Article 104
Article 85	Article 105
Article 86	Article 106
Section 2 — Aids granted by States	Section 2 — Aids granted by States
Article 87	Article 107
Article 88	Article 108
Article 89	Article 109
Chapter 2 — Tax provisions	Chapter 2 — Tax provisions
Article 90	Article 110
Article 91	Article 111
Article 92	Article 112
Article 93	Article 113
Chapter 3 — Approximation of laws	Chapter 3 — Approximation of laws
Article 95 (moved)	Article 114
Article 94 (moved)	Article 115
Article 96	Article 116
Article 97	Article 117
	Article 118
Title VII — Economic and monetary policy	Title VIII — Economic and monetary policy
Article 4 (moved)	Article 119
Chapter 1 — Economic policy	Chapter 1 — Economic policy
Article 98	Article 120
Article 99	Article 121
Article 100	Article 122
Article 101	Article 123
Article 102	Article 124
Article 103	Article 125

Old numbering of the Treaty establishing the European Community	New numbering of the Treaty on the Functioning of the European Union
Article 104	Article 126
Chapter 2 — monetary policy	Chapter 2 — monetary policy
Article 105	Article 127
Article 106	Article 128
Article 107	Article 129
Article 108	Article 130
Article 109	Article 131
Article 110	Article 132
Article 111, paragraphs 1 to 3 and 5 (moved)	Article 219
Article 111, paragraph 4 (moved)	Article 138
	Article 133
Chapter 3 — Institutional provisions	Chapter 3 — Institutional provisions
Article 112 (moved)	Article 283
Article 113 (moved)	Article 284
Article 114	Article 134
Article 115	Article 135
	Chapter 4 — Provisions specific to Member States whose currency is the euro
	Article 136
	Article 137
Article 111, paragraph 4 (moved)	Article 138
Chapter 4 — Transitional provisions	Chapter 5 — Transitional provisions
Article 116 (repealed)	
	Article 139
Article 117, paragraphs 1, 2, sixth indent, and 3 to 9 (repealed)	
Article 117, paragraph 2, first five indents (moved)	Article 141, paragraph 2
Article 121, paragraph 1 (moved) Article 122, paragraph 2, second sentence (moved) Article 123, paragraph 5 (moved)	Article 140 (40)
Article 118 (repealed)	
Article 123, paragraph 3 (moved) Article 117, paragraph 2, first five indents (moved)	Article 141 (41)

(40) — Article 140, paragraph 1 takes over the wording of paragraph 1 of Article 121.
    — Article 140, paragraph 2 takes over the second sentence of paragraph 2 of Article 122.
    — Article 140, paragraph 3 takes over paragraph 5 of Article 123.
(41) — Article 141, paragraph 1 takes over paragraph 3 of Article 123.
    — Article 141, paragraph 2 takes over the first five indents of paragraph 2 of Article 117.
[Ed note: footnotes 42 to 48 are omitted.]

Old numbering of the Treaty establishing the European Community	New numbering of the Treaty on the Functioning of the European Union
Article 124, paragraph 1 (moved)	Article 142
Article 119	Article 143
Article 120	Article 144
Article 121, paragraph 1 (moved)	Article 140, paragraph 1
Article 121, paragraphs 2 to 4 (repealed)	
Article 122, paragraphs 1, 2, first sentence, 3, 4, 5 and 6 (repealed)	
Article 122, paragraph 2, second sentence (moved)	Article 140, paragraph 2, first subparagraph
Article 123, paragraphs 1, 2 and 4 (repealed)	
Article 123, paragraph 3 (moved)	Article 141, paragraph 1
Article 123, paragraph 5 (moved)	Article 140, paragraph 3
Article 124, paragraph 1 (moved)	Article 142
Article 124, paragraph 2 (repealed)	
Title VIII — Employment [Ed note: omitted for reasons of space]	Title IX — Employment
Title IX — Common commercial policy (moved)	Part Five, Title II, common commercial policy
Article 131 (moved)	Article 206
Article 132 (repealed)	
Article 133 (moved)	Article 207
Article 134 (repealed)	
Title X — Customs cooperation (moved)	Part Three, Title II, Chapter 2, Customs cooperation
Article 135 (moved)	Article 33
Title XI — Social policy, education, vocational training and youth [Ed note: omitted for reasons of space]	Title X — Social policy
Title XII — Culture [Ed note: omitted for reasons of space]	Title XIII — Culture
Title XIII — Public health [Ed note: omitted for reasons of space]	Title XIV — Public health
Title XIV — Consumer protection [Ed note: omitted for reasons of space]	Title XV — Consumer protection
Title XV — Trans-European networks [Ed note: omitted for reasons of space]	Title XVI — Trans-European networks
Title XVI — Industry [Ed note: omitted for reasons of space]	Title XVII — Industry
Title XVII — Economic and social cohesion [Ed note: omitted for reasons of space]	Title XVIII — Economic, social and territorial cohesion

Old numbering of the Treaty establishing the European Community	New numbering of the Treaty on the Functioning of the European Union
Title XVIII — Research and technological development [Ed note: omitted for reasons of space]	Title XIX — Research and technological development and space
Title XIX — Environment [Ed note: omitted for reasons of space]	Title XX — Environment
Title XX — Development cooperation (moved) [Ed note: omitted for reasons of space]	Part Five, Title III, Chapter 1, Development cooperation
Title XXI — Economic, financial and technical cooperation with third countries (moved) [Ed note: omitted for reasons of space]	Part Five, Title III, Chapter 2, Economic, financial and technical cooperation with third countries
PART FOUR — ASSOCIATION OF THE OVERSEAS COUNTRIES AND TERRITORIES [Ed note: omitted for reasons of space]	PART FOUR — ASSOCIATION OF THE OVERSEAS COUNTRIES AND TERRITORIES
	PART FIVE — EXTERNAL ACTION BY THE UNION [Ed note: omitted for reasons of space]
PART FIVE — INSTITUTIONS OF THE COMMUNITY	PART SIX — INSTITUTIONAL AND FINANCIAL PROVISIONS
Title I — Institutional provisions	Title I — Institutional provisions
Chapter 1 — The institutions	Chapter 1 — The institutions
Section 1 — The European Parliament [Ed note: omitted for reasons of space]	Section 1 — The European Parliament
Section 2 — The Council	Section 3 — The Council
Article 202 (repealed) [49]	
Article 203 (repealed) [50]	
Article 204	Article 237
Article 205, paragraphs 2 and 4 (repealed) [51]	
Article 205, paragraphs 1 and 3	Article 238
Article 206	Article 239
Article 207	Article 240
Article 208	Article 241
Article 209	Article 242

[49] Replaced, in substance, by Article 16, paragraph 1, TEU and by Articles 290 and 291 TFEU.
[50] Replaced, in substance, by Article 16, paragraphs 2 and 9 TEU.
[51] Replaced, in substance, by Article 16, paragraphs 4 and 5 TEU.

Old numbering of the Treaty establishing the European Community	New numbering of the Treaty on the Functioning of the European Union
Article 210	Article 243
Section 3 — The Commission	Section 4 — The Commission
Article 211 (repealed) ([52])	
	Article 244
Article 212 (moved)	Article 249, paragraph 2
Article 213	Article 245
Article 214 (repealed) ([53])	
Article 215	Article 246
Article 216	Article 247
Article 217, paragraphs 1, 3 and 4 (repealed) ([54])	
Article 217, paragraph 2	Article 248
Article 218, paragraph 1 (repealed) ([55])	
Article 218, paragraph 2	Article 249
Article 219	Article 250
Section 4 — The Court of Justice	Section 5 — The Court of Justice of the European Union
Article 220 (repealed) ([56])	
Article 221, first paragraph (repealed) ([57])	
Article 221, second and third paragraphs	Article 251
Article 222	Article 252
Article 223	Article 253
Article 224 ([58])	Article 254
	Article 255
Article 225	Article 256
Article 225a	Article 257
Article 226	Article 258
Article 227	Article 259
Article 228	Article 260
Article 229	Article 261
Article 229a	Article 262

[52] Replaced, in substance, by Article 17, paragraph 1 TEU.
[53] Replaced, in substance, by Article 17, paragraphs 3 and 7 TEU.
[54] Replaced, in substance, by Article 17, paragraph 6, TEU.
[55] Replaced, in substance, by Article 295 TFEU.
[56] Replaced, in substance, by Article 19 TEU.
[57] Replaced, in substance, by Article 19, paragraph 2, first subparagraph, of the TEU.
[58] The first sentence of the first subparagraph is replaced, in substance, by Article 19, paragraph 2, second subparagraph of the TEU.

Old numbering of the Treaty establishing the European Community	New numbering of the Treaty on the Functioning of the European Union
Article 230	Article 263
Article 231	Article 264
Article 232	Article 265
Article 233	Article 266
Article 234	Article 267
Article 235	Article 268
	Article 269
Article 236	Article 270
Article 237	Article 271
Article 238	Article 272
Article 239	Article 273
Article 240	Article 274
	Article 275
	Article 276
Article 241	Article 277
Article 242	Article 278
Article 243	Article 279
Article 244	Article 280
Article 245	Article 281
	Section 6 — The European Central Bank
	Article 282
Article 112 (moved)	Article 283
Article 113 (moved)	Article 284
Section 5 — The Court of Auditors	Section 7 — The Court of Auditors
Article 246	Article 285
Article 247	Article 286
Article 248	Article 287
Chapter 2 — Provisions common to several institutions	Chapter 2 — Legal acts of the Union, adoption procedures and other provisions
	Section 1 — The legal acts of the Union
Article 249	Article 288
	Article 289
	Article 290 ([59])
	Article 291 ([59] [SIC])

([59]) Replaces, in substance, the third indent of Article 202 TEC.
[Ed note: footnotes 60 to 64 are omitted]

Old numbering of the Treaty establishing the European Community	New numbering of the Treaty on the Functioning of the European Union
	Article 292
	Section 2 — Procedures for the adoption of acts and other provisions
Article 250	Article 293
Article 251	Article 294
Article 252 (repealed)	
	Article 295
Article 253	Article 296
Article 254	Article 297
	Article 298
Article 255 (moved)	Article 15
Article 256	Article 299
	Chapter 3 — The Union's advisory bodies
	Article 300
Chapter 3 — The Economic and Social Committee [Ed note: omitted for reasons of space]	Section 1 — The Economic and Social Committee
Chapter 4 — The Committee of the Regions [Ed note: omitted for reasons of space]	Section 2 — The Committee of the Regions
Chapter 5 — The European Investment Bank [Ed note: omitted for reasons of space]	Chapter 4 — The European Investment Bank
Title II — Financial provisions [Ed note: omitted for reasons of space]	Title II — Financial provisions
PART SIX — GENERAL AND FINAL PROVISIONS	PART SEVEN — GENERAL AND FINAL PROVISIONS
Article 281 (repealed) [65]	
Article 282	Article 335
Article 283	Article 336
Article 284	Article 337
Article 285	Article 338
Article 286 (replaced)	Article 16
Article 287	Article 339
Article 288	Article 340
Article 289	Article 341
Article 290	Article 342
Article 291	Article 343

[65] Replaced, in substance, by Article 47 TEU.

Old numbering of the Treaty establishing the European Community	New numbering of the Treaty on the Functioning of the European Union
Article 292	Article 344
Article 293 (repealed)	
Article 294 (moved)	Article 55
Article 295	Article 345
Article 296	Article 346
Article 297	Article 347
Article 298	Article 348
Article 299, paragraph 1 (repealed) [66]	
Article 299, paragraph 2, second, third and fourth subparagraphs	Article 349
Article 299, paragraph 2, first subparagraph, and paragraphs 3 to 6 (moved)	Article 355
Article 300 (replaced)	Article 218
Article 301 (replaced)	Article 215
Article 302 (replaced)	Article 220
Article 303 (replaced)	Article 220
Article 304 (replaced)	Article 220
Article 305 (repealed)	
Article 306	Article 350
Article 307	Article 351
Article 308	Article 352
	Article 353
Article 309	Article 354
Article 310 (moved)	Article 217
Article 311 (repealed) [67]	
Article 299, paragraph 2, first subparagraph, and paragraphs 3 to 6 (moved)	Article 355
Article 312	Article 356
Final Provisions	
Article 313	Article 357
	Article 358
Article 314 (repealed) [68]	

[66] Replaced, in substance by Article 52 TEU.
[67] Replaced, in substance by Article 51 TEU.
[68] Replaced, in substance by Article 55 TEU.

A2

TREATY ON THE FUNCTIONING OF THE EUROPEAN UNION: RULES ON COMPETITION

(Articles 101 to 109 TFEU; formerly Articles 81 to 89 TEC*)

Notes

References to former Article numbers are to the former Article numbers in the Treaty establishing the European Community (TEC), Amsterdam consolidated version).

* Ed note: please see the Note on the Lisbon Treaty at p.xvii in regard to article renumbering introduced by the Lisbon Treaty.

Commentary

Arts 101–106 (ex Arts 81–86 TEC): B&C: 1.114, 12.154
Arts 101–109 (ex Arts 81–89 TEC): B&C: 1.021, 2.022, 11.009, 12.148, 17.071 F&N: 6.09, 6.50

Section i

Rules Applying to Undertakings

Article 101 (ex Article 81 TEC)

1. The following shall be prohibited as incompatible with the internal market: all agreements between undertakings, decisions by associations of undertakings and concerted practices which may affect trade between Member States and which have as their object or effect the prevention, restriction or distortion of competition within the internal market, and in particular those which:

(a) directly or indirectly fix purchase or selling prices or any other trading conditions;
(b) limit or control production, markets, technical development, or investment;
(c) share markets or sources of supply;
(d) apply dissimilar conditions to equivalent transactions with other trading parties, thereby placing them at a competitive disadvantage;
(e) make the conclusion of contracts subject to acceptance by the other parties of supplementary obligations which, by their nature or according to commercial usage, have no connection with the subject of such contracts.

2. Any agreements or decisions prohibited pursuant to this Article shall be automatically void.

3. The provisions of paragraph 1 may, however, be declared inapplicable in the case of:

— any agreement or category of agreements between undertakings;
— any decision or category of decisions by associations of undertakings;
— any concerted practice or category of concerted practices,

which contributes to improving the production or distribution of goods or to promoting technical or economic progress, while allowing consumers a fair share of the resulting benefit, and which does not:

(a) impose on the undertakings concerned restrictions which are not indispensable to the attainment of these objectives;
(b) afford such undertakings the possibility of eliminating competition in respect of a substantial part of the products in question.

Commentary

Art 101 (ex Art 81 TEC): B&C: see Chapters 2 and 3 F&N: see Chapter 3, 6.04, 6.05, 6.06
Art 101(1) (ex Art 81(1) TEC): B&C: see Chapter 2 F&N: see Chapter 3
Art 101(1)(a) (ex Art 81(1)(a) TEC): B&C: 2.121, 5.038, 7.040 F&N: 11.193
Art 101(1)(b) (ex Art 81(1)(b) TEC): B&C: 2.113, 2.121, 5.060, 6.112 F&N: 3.314

17

Art 101(1)(c) (ex Art 81(1)(c) TEC): **B&C:** 2.121, 5.060, 5.065
Art 101)(1)(d) (ex Art 81(1)(d) TEC): **B&C:** 1.034, 2.132
Art 101(1)(e) (ex Art 81(1)(e) TEC): **B&C:** 7.145
Art 101(2) (ex Art 81(2) TEC): **B&C:** 1.022 **F&N:** 3.442, 3.443, 3.444, 3.489
Art 101(3) (ex Art 81(3) TEC): **B&C:** see Chapter 3
Art 101(3)(b) (ex Art 81(3)(b) TEC): **B&C:** 2.088

Article 102 (ex Article 82 TEC)

Any abuse by one or more undertakings of a dominant position within the internal market or in a substantial part of it shall be prohibited as incompatible with the internal market in so far as it may affect trade between Member States.

Such abuse may, in particular, consist in:

(a) directly or indirectly imposing unfair purchase or selling prices or other unfair trading conditions;
(b) limiting production, markets or technical development to the prejudice of consumers;
(c) applying dissimilar conditions to equivalent transactions with other trading parties, thereby placing them at a competitive disadvantage;
(d) making the conclusion of contracts subject to acceptance by the other parties of supplementary obligations which, by their nature or according to commercial usage, have no connection with the subject of such contracts.

Commentary

Art 102 (ex Art 82 TEC): **B&C** see Chapter 10 **F&N:** see Chapter 4
Art 102(a)–(d) (ex Art 82(a)–(d) TEC): **B&C:** 10.053, 10.055
Art 102(a) (ex Art 82(a) TEC): **B&C:** 9.092, 10.089, 10.106, 10.143 **F&N:** 4.22, 4.259, 4.844, 14.126, 14.131
Art 102(b) (ex Art 82(b) TEC): **B&C:** 9.056, 10.089, 10.148, 10.150 **F&N:** 4.22, 4.259, 4.418, 4.607, 4.935, 4.936, 6.66
Art 102(c) (ex Art 82(c) TEC): **B&C:** 10.082, 10.083, 10.084, 10.085, 10.086, 10.089, 10.152, 11.022
    F&N: 4.260, 4.895, 4.896, 4.900, 4.907, 4.908, 4.915, 4.916, 4.920, 4.921, 4.923, 4.924, 4.926, 7.935, 15.372
Art 102(d) (ex Art 82(d) TEC): **B&C:** 10.126, 12.146

Article 103 (ex Article 83 TEC)

1. The appropriate regulations or directives to give effect to the principles set out in Articles 101 and 102 shall be laid down by the Council, on a proposal from the Commission and after consulting the European Parliament.

2. The regulations or directives referred to in paragraph 1 shall be designed in particular:

(a) to ensure compliance with the prohibitions laid down in Article 101(1) and in Article 102 by making provision for fines and periodic penalty payments;
(b) to lay down detailed rules for the application of Article 101(3), taking into account the need to ensure effective supervision on the one hand, and to simplify administration to the greatest possible extent on the other;
(c) to define, if need be, in the various branches of the economy, the scope of the provisions of Articles 101 and 102;
(d) to define the respective functions of the Commission and of the Court of Justice of the European Union in applying the provisions laid down in this paragraph;
(e) to determine the relationship between national laws and the provisions contained in this Section or adopted pursuant to this Article.

Commentary

Art 103 (ex Art 83 TEC): **B&C:** 1.024, 1.025, 1.026, 1.045, 8.268, 8.270, 11.027, 16.006 **F&N:** 2.182
Art 103(2)(a) (ex Art 83(2)(a) TEC): **F&N:** 2.76
Art 103(2)(b) (ex Art 83(2)(b) TEC): **F&N:** 2.20
Art 103(2)(e) (ex Art 83(2)(e) TEC): **B&C:** 15.055 **F&N:** 2.31

Article 104 (ex Article 84 TEC)

Until the entry into force of the provisions adopted in pursuance of Article 103, the authorities in Member States shall rule on the admissibility of agreements, decisions and concerted practices and on abuse of a dominant position in the internal market in accordance with the law of their country and with the provisions of Article 101, in particular paragraph 3, and of Article 102.

Commentary
Art 104 (ex Art 84 TEC): B&C: 1.026, 8.271

Article 105 (ex Article 85 TEC)

1. Without prejudice to Article 104, the Commission shall ensure the application of the principles laid down in Articles 101 and 102. On application by a Member State or on its own initiative, and in cooperation with the competent authorities in the Member States, which shall give it their assistance, the Commission shall investigate cases of suspected infringement of these principles. If it finds that there has been an infringement, it shall propose appropriate measures to bring it to an end.

2. If the infringement is not brought to an end, the Commission shall record such infringement of the principles in a reasoned decision. The Commission may publish its decision and authorise Member States to take the measures, the conditions and details of which it shall determine, needed to remedy the situation.

3. The Commission may adopt regulations relating to the categories of agreement in respect of which the Council has adopted a regulation or a directive pursuant to Article 103(2)(b).

Commentary
Art 105 (ex Art 85 TEC): B&C: 1.026, 1.047, 8.271, 13.002 F&N: 15.12, 15.179
Art 105(1) (ex Art 85(1) TEC): F&N: 2.97

Article 106 (ex Article 86 TEC)

1. In the case of public undertakings and undertakings to which Member States grant special or exclusive rights, Member States shall neither enact nor maintain in force any measure contrary to the rules contained in the Treaties, in particular to those rules provided for in Article 18 and Articles 101 to 109.

2. Undertakings entrusted with the operation of services of general economic interest or having the character of a revenue-producing monopoly shall be subject to the rules contained in the Treaties, in particular to the rules on competition, in so far as the application of such rules does not obstruct the performance, in law or in fact, of the particular tasks assigned to them. The development of trade must not be affected to such an extent as would be contrary to the interests of the Union.

3. The Commission shall ensure the application of the provisions of this Article and shall, where necessary, address appropriate directives or decisions to Member States.

Commentary
Art 106 (ex Art 86 TEC): B&C: 1.017, 1.027, 1.094, 2.022, 2.046, 10.013, 10.086, 10.152, 11.003, 11.009, 11.011, 11.013, 11.015, 11.018, 11.020, 11.027, 11.053, 12.003, 12.005, 12.033, 12.086, 12.135, 12.145 F&N: 2.68, 2.111, see Chapter 6, 12.147, 17.409
Art 106(1) (ex Art 86(1) TEC): B&C: 10.013, 11.001, 11.002, 11.007, 11.008, 11.009, 11.010, 11.012, 11.013, 11.014, 11.015, 11.016, 11.017, 11.018, 11.020, 11.021, 11.022, 11.023, 11.024, 11.025, 11.046, 12.092, 16.086 F&N: 6.02, 6.09, 6.10, 6.11, 6.13, 6.15, 6.16, 6.17, 6.26, 6.29, 6.30, 6.34, 6.36, 6.38, 6.39, 6.42, 6.43, 6.44, 6.45, 6.46, 6.47, 6.48, 6.49, 6.50, 6.51, 6.52, 6.53, 6.54, 6.55, 6.56, 6.57, 6.58, 6.59, 6.60, 6.61, 6.62, 6.63, 6.66, 6.67, 6.70, 6.72, 6.75, 6.76, 6.77, 6.79, 6.80, 6.81, 6.82, 6.84, 6.85, 6.88, 6.89, 6.90, 6.92, 6.94, 6.95, 6.97, 6.98, 6.99, 6.100, 6.103, 6.111, 6.127, 6.133, 6.134, 6.135, 6.136, 6.139, 6.142, 6.151, 6.164, 6.176, 6.194, 6.195, 6.220, 6.228, 6.231, 6.233, 6.234, 6.235, 6.238, 6.241, 6.246, 6.255, 6.257, 6.262, 15.370
Art 106(2) (ex Art 86(2) TEC): B&C: 1.027, 2.022, 10.013, 11.001, 11.020, 11.023, 11.046, 11.047, 11.048, 11.049, 11.053, 11.054, 11.056, 11.057, 11.058, 11.059, 11.060, 12.041, 12.092, 12.107, 17.003, 17.011, 17.043, 17.071, 17.072, 17.073, 17.083 F&N: 6.22, 6.66, 6.79, 6.84, 6.90, 6.136, 6.137, 6.138, 6.139, 6.140, 6.141, 6.142, 6.144, 6.145, 6.146, 6.149, 6.155, 6.157, 6.158, 6.159, 6.163, 6.164, 6.165, 6.166, 6.167, 6.168,

6.169, 6.170, 6.171, 6.174, 6.175, 6.176, 6.177, 6.182, 6.183, 6.184, 6.190, 6.191, 6.194, 6.195, 6.198, 6.200, 6.202, 6.203, 6.204, 6.205, 6.207, 6.208, 6.209, 6.212, 6.213, 6.214, 6.215, 6.216, 6.217, 6.218, 6.221, 6.223, 6.224, 6.226, 6.227, 6.255, 6.258, 12.05, 15.361, 15.363, 17.338, 17.339, 17.348

Art 106(3) (ex Art 86(3) TEC): B&C: 1.027, 11.015, 11.024, 11.025, 11.026, 11.027, 11.060, 12.086, 13.131
F&N: 6.99, 6.104, 6.166, 6.211, 6.228, 6.229, 6.230, 6.231, 6.234, 6.235, 6.237, 6.243, 6.244, 6.245, 6.246, 6.247, 6.248, 6.250, 6.252, 6.253, 6.254, 6.255, 6.256, 6.257, 6.258, 6.260, 6.261, 6.262, 6.263, 6.264, 6.265, 6.267, 6.268, 6.269, 6.270, 6.271, 14.155

SECTION 2

AIDS GRANTED BY STATES

Article 107 (ex Article 87 TEC)

1. Save as otherwise provided in the Treaties, any aid granted by a Member State or through State resources in any form whatsoever which distorts or threatens to distort competition by favouring certain undertakings or the production of certain goods shall, in so far as it affects trade between Member States, be incompatible with the internal market.

2. The following shall be compatible with the internal market:

(a) aid having a social character, granted to individual consumers, provided that such aid is granted without discrimination related to the origin of the products concerned;

(b) aid to make good the damage caused by natural disasters or exceptional occurrences;

(c) aid granted to the economy of certain areas of the Federal Republic of Germany affected by the division of Germany, in so far as such aid is required in order to compensate for the economic disadvantages caused by that division. Five years after the entry into force of the Treaty of Lisbon, the Council, acting on a proposal from the Commission, may adopt a decision repealing this point.

3. The following may be considered to be compatible with the internal market:

(a) aid to promote the economic development of areas where the standard of living is abnormally low or where there is serious underemployment, and of the regions referred to in Article 349, in view of their structural, economic and social situation;

(b) aid to promote the execution of an important project of common European interest or to remedy a serious disturbance in the economy of a Member State;

(c) aid to facilitate the development of certain economic activities or of certain economic areas, where such aid does not adversely affect trading conditions to an extent contrary to the common interest;

(d) aid to promote culture and heritage conservation where such aid does not affect trading conditions and competition in the Union to an extent that is contrary to the common interest;

(e) such other categories of aid as may be specified by decision of the Council on a proposal from the Commission.

Commentary
Art 107 (ex Art 87 TEC): B&C 1.028, 1.120, 1.122, 11.003, 11.009, 11.027, 11.047, 11.048, 17.003, 17.004, 17.011, 17.017, 17.025, 17.029, 17.046, 17.080, 17.096, 17.114, 17.128 **F&N:** 6.08, 6.165, 6.198, 6.229, 17.35, 17.36, 17.49, 17.50, 17.58, 17.121, 17.130, 17.520
Art 107(1) (ex Art 87(1) TEC): B&C: 1.028, 17.001, 17.003, 17.006, 17.007, 17.008, 17.010, 17.011, 17.016, 17.017, 17.022, 17.023, 17.024, 17.025, 17.027, 17.029, 17.030, 17.033, 17.034, 17.072, 17.073, 17.077, 17.086, 17.114, 17.115, 17.126, 17.128 **F&N:** 6.44, 6.101, 6.165, 17.01, 17.18, 17.20, 17.29, 17.58, 17.89, 17.95, 17.147, 17.172, 17.173, 17.203, 17.204, 17.245, 17.348, 17.351, 17.353, 17.409
Art 107(2) (ex Art 87(2) TEC): B&C: 17.001, 17.006, 17.038, 17.039, 17.070, 17.114 **F&N:** 17.184, 17.201, 17.203, 17.409
Art 107(2)(a) (ex Art 87(2)(a) TEC): B&C: 17.040 **F&N:** 17.204, 17.205
Art 107(2)(b) (ex Art 87(2)(b) TEC): B&C: 17.041 **F&N:** 17.207, 17.208, 17.209
Art 107(2)(c) (ex Art 87(2)(c) TEC): B&C: 17.004, 17.042, 17.044 **F&N:** 17.214

Art 107(3) (ex Art 87(3) TEC): **B&C:** 17.001, 17.006, 17.008, 17.033, 17.038, 17.039, 17.044, 17.045, 17.046, 17.049, 17.058, 17.067, 17.070, 17.128 **F&N:** 17.184, 17.215, 17.217, 17.220, 17.224, 17.409
Art 107(3)(a)–(d) (ex Art 87(3)(a)–(d) TEC): **B&C:** 17.043
Art 107(3)(a) (ex Art 87(3)(a) TEC): **B&C:** 17.044, 17.046, 17.047, 17.048, 17.051, 17.056, 17.058, 17.059, 17.061 **F&N:** 17.221, 17.223, 17.229, 17.235
Art 107(3)(b) (ex Art 87(3)(b) TEC): **B&C:** 17.055, 17.056, 17.057, 17.058 **F&N:** 17.235, 17.237, 17.239, 17.242, 17.244
Art 107(3)(c) (ex Art 87(3)(c) TEC): **B&C:** 17.044, 17.047, 17.048, 17.052, 17.056, 17.058, 17.059, 17.060, 17.063, 17.067 **F&N:** 17.223, 17.229, 17.235, 17.246, 17.248, 17.251, 17.257, 17.326, 17.514
Art 107(3)(d) (ex Art 87(3)(d) TEC): **B&C:** 4.008, 17.004, 17.058, 17.067 **F&N:** 17.245
Art 107(3)(e) (ex Art 87(3)(d) TEC): **B&C:** 17.043, 17.068, 17.069 **F&N** 17.327

Article 108 (ex Article 88 TEC)

1. The Commission shall, in cooperation with Member States, keep under constant review all systems of aid existing in those States. It shall propose to the latter any appropriate measures required by the progressive development or by the functioning of the internal market.

2. If, after giving notice to the parties concerned to submit their comments, the Commission finds that aid granted by a State or through State resources is not compatible with the internal market having regard to Article 107, or that such aid is being misused, it shall decide that the State concerned shall abolish or alter such aid within a period of time to be determined by the Commission.

If the State concerned does not comply with this decision within the prescribed time, the Commission or any other interested State may, in derogation from the provisions of Articles 258 and 259, refer the matter to the Court of Justice of the European Union direct.

On application by a Member State, the Council may, acting unanimously, decide that aid which that State is granting or intends to grant shall be considered to be compatible with the internal market, in derogation from the provisions of Article 107 or from the regulations provided for in Article 109, if such a decision is justified by exceptional circumstances. If, as regards the aid in question, the Commission has already initiated the procedure provided for in the first subparagraph of this paragraph, the fact that the State concerned has made its application to the Council shall have the effect of suspending that procedure until the Council has made its attitude known.

If, however, the Council has not made its attitude known within three months of the said application being made, the Commission shall give its decision on the case.

3. The Commission shall be informed, in sufficient time to enable it to submit its comments, of any plans to grant or alter aid. If it considers that any such plan is not compatible with the internal market having regard to Article 107, it shall without delay initiate the procedure provided for in paragraph 2. The Member State concerned shall not put its proposed measures into effect until this procedure has resulted in a final decision.

4. The Commission may adopt regulations relating to the categories of Stateaid that the Council has, pursuant to Article 109, determined may be exempted from the procedure provided for by paragraph 3 of this Article.

Commentary
Art 108 (ex Art 88 TEC): **B&C:** 1.028, 1.094, 17.003, 17.046, 17.074, 17.096, 17.111, 17.114 **F&N:** 6.08, 6.165, 6.166, 6.258
Art 108(1) (ex Art 88(1) TEC): **B&C:** 17.062, 17.080, 17.118 **F&N:** 17.337, 17.511, 17.517
Art 108(2) (ex Art 88(2) TEC): **B&C:** 13.131, 17.001, 17.043, 17.069, 17.079, 17.086, 17.087, 17.088, 17.089, 17.090, 17.091, 17.092, 17.094, 17.098, 17.099, 17.116, 17.118, 17.119, 17.120, 17.122, 17.123, 17.125, 17.131 **F&N:** 17.329, 17.334, 17.335, 17.336, 17.424, 17.450, 17.511, 17.517, 17.522, 17.537, 17.566
Art 108(3) (ex Art 88(3) TEC): **B&C:** 17.039, 17.061, 17.071, 17.080, 17.081, 17.083, 17.088, 17.096, 17.097, 17.098, 17.103, 17.111, 17.113, 17.118, 17.127, 17.131 **F&N:** 17.348, 17.368, 17.387, 17.401, 17.402, 17.403, 17.409, 17.416, 17.447, 17.475, 17.479, 17.517, 17.519, 17.525, 17.527, 17.554

Article 109 (ex Article 89 TEC)

The Council, on a proposal from the Commission and after consulting the European Parliament, may make any appropriate regulations for the application of Articles 107 and 108 and may in particular determine the conditions in which Article 108(3) shall apply and the categories of aid exempted from this procedure.

Commentary
Art 109 (ex Art 89 TEC): B&C: 1.028, 11.027, 17.069, 17.096 F&N: 17.173, 17.185

A3

THE TREATIES: GENERAL PRINCIPLES

Notes
'TEU' refers to the Treaty on European Union.
'TFEU' refers to the Treaty on the Functioning of the European Union.
'TEC' refers to the Treaty establishing the European Community.
* Ed note: please see the Note on the Lisbon Treaty at p.xvii in regard to article renumbering introduced by the Lisbon Treaty.

Commentary
General principles: F&N: 16.10
Arts 2–6 TEC: B&C: 12.148

Article 1 TEU (ex Article 1 TEU)

By this Treaty, the HIGH CONTRACTING PARTIES establish among themselves a EUROPEAN UNION, hereinafter called 'the Union', on which the Member States confer competences to attain objectives they have in common.

This Treaty marks a new stage in the process of creating an ever closer union among the peoples of Europe, in which decisions are taken as openly as possible and as closely as possible to the citizen.

The Union shall be founded on the present Treaty and on the Treaty on the Functioning of the European Union (hereinafter referred to as 'the Treaties'). Those two Treaties shall have the same legal value. The Union shall replace and succeed the European Community.

Article 3 TEU (ex Article 2 TEU and Article 2 TEC)

1. The Union's aim is to promote peace, its values and the well-being of its peoples.

2. The Union shall offer its citizens an area of freedom, security and justice without internal frontiers, in which the free movement of persons is ensured in conjunction with appropriate measures with respect to external border controls, asylum, immigration and the prevention and combating of crime.

3. The Union shall establish an internal market. It shall work for the sustainable development of Europe based on balanced economic growth and price stability, a highly competitive social market economy, aiming at full employment and social progress, and a high level of protection and improvement of the quality of the environment. It shall promote scientific and technological advance.

It shall combat social exclusion and discrimination, and shall promote social justice and protection, equality between women and men, solidarity between generations and protection of the rights of the child.

It shall promote economic, social and territorial cohesion, and solidarity among Member States.

It shall respect its rich cultural and linguistic diversity, and shall ensure that Europe's cultural heritage is safeguarded and enhanced.

4. The Union shall establish an economic and monetary union whose currency is the euro.

5. In its relations with the wider world, the Union shall uphold and promote its values and interests and contribute to the protection of its citizens. It shall contribute to peace, security, the sustainable development of the Earth, solidarity and mutual respect among peoples, free and fair trade, eradication of poverty and the protection of human rights, in particular the rights of the child, as well as to the strict observance and the development of international law, including respect for the principles of the United Nations Charter.

6. The Union shall pursue its objectives by appropriate means commensurate with the competences which are conferred upon it in the Treaties.

Commentary

Art 3: F&N: 3.02, 3.389, 6.04, 17.250
Art 3(3): F&N: 6.04, 6.05, 6.07, 6.96
Art 3(4): F&N: 2.85, 2.86, 2.161, 2.168, 2.169, 2.204, 2.274, 2.275, 2.280, 2.283

Article 4 TEU (ex Article 10 TEC)

1. In accordance with Article 5, competences not conferred upon the Union in the Treaties remain with the Member States.

2. The Union shall respect the equality of Member States before the Treaties as well as their national identities, inherent in their fundamental structures, political and constitutional, inclusive of regional and local self-government. It shall respect their essential State functions, including ensuring the territorial integrity of the State, maintaining law and order and safeguarding national security. In particular, national security remains the sole responsibility of each Member State.

3. Pursuant to the principle of sincere cooperation, the Union and the Member States shall, in full mutual respect, assist each other in carrying out tasks which flow from the Treaties.

The Member States shall take any appropriate measure, general or particular, to ensure fulfilment of the obligations arising out of the Treaties or resulting from the acts of the institutions of the Union.

The Member States shall facilitate the achievement of the Union's tasks and refrain from any measure which could jeopardise the attainment of the Union's objectives.

Commentary

Art 4(3) (ex Art 10 TEC): B&C: 1.070, 2.046, 2.051, 2.137, 8.289, 11.001, 11.005, 11.007, 11.008, 11.009, 11.029, 11.030, 11.031, 11.032, 11.033, 11.034, 11.035, 12.042, 13.034, 13.103, 15.011, 15.033, 15.043, 15.047, 15.048, 15.055, 15.056, 16.005, 16.010, 16.043 F&N: 3.159, 6.04, 6.05, 6.06, 6.07, 6.96, 8.242, 12.214, 14.35, 15.28, 17.462

Article 5 TEU (ex Article 5 TEC)

1. The limits of Union competences are governed by the principle of conferral. The use of Union competences is governed by the principles of subsidiarity and proportionality.

2. Under the principle of conferral, the Union shall act only within the limits of the competences conferred upon it by the Member States in the Treaties to attain the objectives set out therein. Competences not conferred upon the Union in the Treaties remain with the Member States.

3. Under the principle of subsidiarity, in areas which do not fall within its exclusive competence, the Union shall act only if and in so far as the objectives of the proposed action cannot be sufficiently achieved by the Member States, either at central level or at regional and local level, but can rather, by reason of the scale or effects of the proposed action, be better achieved at Union level.

The institutions of the Union shall apply the principle of subsidiarity as laid down in the Protocol on the application of the principles of subsidiarity and proportionality. National Parliaments ensure compliance with the principle of subsidiarity in accordance with the procedure set out in that Protocol.

4. Under the principle of proportionality, the content and form of Union action shall not exceed what is necessary to achieve the objectives of the Treaties.

The institutions of the Union shall apply the principle of proportionality as laid down in the Protocol on the application of the principles of subsidiarity and proportionality.

Commentary
Art 5 (ex Art 5 TEC): B&C: 1.032, 1.042
Art 5(1) (ex Art 5(1) TEC): B&C: 1.030, 1.031, 1.033
Art 5(2) (ex Art 5(2) TEC): B&C: 1.030
Art 5(3) (ex Art 5(3) TEC): B&C: 1.031 F&N: 5.217
Art 5(4) (ex Art 5(4) TEC): B&C: 1.033

Article 13 TEU (ex Article 7 TEC)

1. The Union shall have an institutional framework which shall aim to promote its values, advance its objectives, serve its interests, those of its citizens and those of the Member States, and ensure the consistency, effectiveness and continuity of its policies and actions.

The Union's institutions shall be:
— the European Parliament,
— the European Council,
— the Council,
— the European Commission (hereinafter referred to as "the Commission"),
— the European Central Bank,
— the Court of Auditors.

2. Each institution shall act within the limits of the powers conferred on it in the Treaties, and in conformity with the procedures, conditions and objectives set out in them. The institutions shall practice mutual sincere cooperation.

3. The provisions relating to the European Central Bank and the Court of Auditors and detailed provisions on the other institutions are set out in the Treaty on the Functioning of the European Union.

4. The European Parliament, the Council and the Commission shall be assisted by an Economic and Social Committee and a Committee of the Regions acting in an advisory capacity.

Commentary
Art 13(1) (ex Art 7(1) TEC): B&C: 1.040

Article 3 TFEU

1. The Union shall have exclusive competence in the following areas:

(a) customs union;
(b) the establishing of the competition rules necessary for the functioning of the internal market;
(c) monetary policy for the Member States whose currency is the euro;
(d) the conservation of marine biological resources under the common fisheries policy;
(e) common commercial policy.

2. The Union shall also have exclusive competence for the conclusion of an international agreement when its conclusion is provided for in a legislative act of the Union or is necessary to enable the Union to exercise its internal competence, or in so far as its conclusion may affect common rules or alter their scope.

Article 4 TFEU

1. The Union shall share competence with the Member States where the Treaties confer on it a competence which does not relate to the areas referred to in Articles 3 and 6.

2. Shared competence between the Union and the Member States applies in the following principal areas:

(a) internal market;
(b) social policy, for the aspects defined in this Treaty;

(c) economic, social and territorial cohesion;
(d) agriculture and fisheries, excluding the conservation of marine biological resources;
(e) environment;
(f) consumer protection;
(g) transport;
(h) trans-European networks;
(i) energy;
(j) area of freedom, security and justice;
(k) common safety concerns in public health matters, for the aspects defined in this Treaty.

3. In the areas of research, technological development and space, the Union shall have competence to carry out activities, in particular to define and implement programmes; however, the exercise of that competence shall not result in Member States being prevented from exercising theirs.

4. In the areas of development cooperation and humanitarian aid, the Union shall have competence to carry out activities and conduct a common policy; however, the exercise of that competence shall not result in Member States being prevented from exercising theirs.

Commentary
Art 4(3) F&N: 17.517

Article 5 TFEU

1. The Member States shall coordinate their economic policies within the Union. To this end, the Council shall adopt measures, in particular broad guidelines for these policies.

Specific provisions shall apply to those Member States whose currency is the euro.

2. The Union shall take measures to ensure coordination of the employment policies of the Member States, in particular by defining guidelines for these policies.

3. The Union may take initiatives to ensure coordination of Member States' social policies.

Article 6 TFEU

The Union shall have competence to carry out actions to support, coordinate or supplement the actions of the Member States. The areas of such action shall, at European level, be:

(a) protection and improvement of human health;
(b) industry;
(c) culture;
(d) tourism;
(e) education, vocational training, youth and sport;
(f) civil protection;
(g) administrative cooperation.

Article 8 TFEU (ex Article 3(2) TEC)

In all its activities, the Union shall aim to eliminate inequalities, and to promote equality, between men and women.

Notes
The foregoing provisions have replaced Article 3 TEC in substance.

Commentary
Art 3 TEC: B&C: 1.030, 1.034
Art 4 TEC: B&C: 1.006, 1.030
Art 4(2) TEC: B&C: 12.088
Art 4(2)(d) TEC: B&C: 12.148
Art 4(2)(e) TEC: B&C: 1.038
Art 4(3) TEC: B&C: 17.109

Article 11 TFEU (ex Article 6 TEC)

Environmental protection requirements must be integrated into the definition and implementation of the Union's policies and activities, in particular with a view to promoting sustainable development.

Commentary
Art 11 (ex Art 6 TEC): B&C: 12.118 F&N: 3.12, 3.13, 3.458

Article 14 TFEU (ex Article 16 TEC)

Without prejudice to Article 4 of the Treaty on European Union or to Articles 93, 106 and 107 of this Treaty, and given the place occupied by services of general economic interest in the shared values of the Union as well as their role in promoting social and territorial cohesion, the Union and the Member States, each within their respective powers and within the scope of application of the Treaties, shall take care that such services operate on the basis of principles and conditions, particularly economic and financial conditions, which enable them to fulfil their missions. The European Parliament and the Council, acting by means of regulations in accordance with the ordinary legislative procedure, shall establish these principles and set these conditions without prejudice to the competence of Member States, in compliance with the Treaties, to provide, to commission and to fund such services.

Commentary
Art 14 (ex Art 16 TEC): B&C 10.013, 11.003 F&N: 6.137, 6.222, 6.223, 6.224, 6.269, 6.270, 17.338

A4

TREATY ON THE FUNCTIONING OF THE EUROPEAN UNION: FREE MOVEMENT OF GOODS

(Articles 28–30; 34–37 TFEU (ex Articles 23–25; 28–31 TEC*))

Notes
* Ed note: please see the Note on the Lisbon Treaty at p.xvii in regard to article renumbering introduced by the Lisbon Treaty.

Commentary
Arts 28–32 (ex Arts 23–27 TEC): B&C: 1.036
Arts 34–36 (ex Arts 28–30 TEC): B&C: 9.008

Article 28 (ex Article 23 TEC)

1. The Union shall comprise a customs union which shall cover all trade in goods and which shall involve the prohibition between Member States of customs duties on imports and exports and of all charges having equivalent effect, and the adoption of a common customs tariff in their relations with third countries.

2. The provisions of Article 30 and of Chapter 2 of this Title shall apply to products originating in Member States and to products coming from third countries which are in free circulation in Member States.

Commentary
Art 28 (ex Art 23 TEC): F&N: 6.101, 6.109, 6.124, 6.125, 6.135

Article 29 (ex Article 24 TEC)

Products coming from a third country shall be considered to be in free circulation in a Member State if the import formalities have been complied with and any customs duties or charges having equivalent effect which are payable have been levied in that Member State, and if they have not benefited from a total or partial drawback of such duties or charges.

CHAPTER 1
THE CUSTOMS UNION

Article 30 (ex Article 25 TEC)

Customs duties on imports and exports and charges having equivalent effect shall be prohibited between Member States. This prohibition shall also apply to customs duties of a fiscal nature.

CHAPTER 2
PROHIBITION OF QUANTITATIVE RESTRICTIONS BETWEEN MEMBER STATES

Article 34 (ex Article 28 TEC)

Quantitative restrictions on imports and all measures having equivalent effect shall be prohibited between Member States.

Commentary

Art 34 (ex Art 28 TEC): B&C: 1.036, 3.021, 6.088, 9.003, 9.008, 9.010, 9.011, 9.013, 9.025, 9.027, 9.035, 9.046, 9.100, 11.009, 11.010, 11.038, 16.092 **F&N:** 6.51, 6.105, 6.106, 6.107, 6.108, 6.163, 6.257, 10.10, 10.17, 10.38, 10.175, 16.155

Article 35 (ex Article 29 TEC)

Quantitative restrictions on exports, and all measures having equivalent effect, shall be prohibited between Member States.

Commentary

Art 35 (ex Art 29 TEC): B&C: 1.036, 1.089, 9.008 **F&N:** 6.108, 10.17, 10.19

Article 36 (ex Article 30 TEC)

The provisions of Articles 34 and 35 shall not preclude prohibitions or restrictions on imports, exports or goods in transit justified on grounds of public morality, public policy or public security; the protection of health and life of humans, animals or plants; the protection of national treasures possessing artistic, historic or archaeological value; or the protection of industrial and commercial property. Such prohibitions or restrictions shall not, however, constitute a means of arbitrary discrimination or a disguised restriction on trade between Member States.

Commentary

Art 36 (ex Art 30 TEC): B&C: 1.036, 9.001, 9.003, 9.009, 9.010, 9.011, 9.012, 9.013, 9.014, 9.015, 9.016, 9.017, 9.018, 9.021, 9.025, 9.036, 9.037, 9.043, 9.044, 9.045, 9.046, 9.047, 9.048, 16.092 **F&N:** 6.171, 6.172, 6.174, 6.175, 10.17, 10.38, 16.155

Article 37 (ex Article 31 TEC)

1. Member States shall adjust any State monopolies of a commercial character so as to ensure that no discrimination regarding the conditions under which goods are procured and marketed exists between nationals of Member States.

The provisions of this Article shall apply to any body through which a Member State, in law or in fact, either directly or indirectly supervises, determines or appreciably influences imports or exports between Member States. These provisions shall likewise apply to monopolies delegated by the State to others.

2. Member States shall refrain from introducing any new measure which is contrary to the principles laid down in paragraph 1 or which restricts the scope of the articles dealing with the prohibition of customs duties and quantitative restrictions between Member States.

3. If a State monopoly of a commercial character has rules which are designed to make it easier to dispose of agricultural products or obtain for them the best return, steps should be taken in applying the rules contained in this article to ensure equivalent safeguards for the employment and standard of living of the producers concerned.

Commentary
Art 37 (ex Art 31 TEC): B&C: 1.037, 11.036, 11.037, 11.038, 11.039, 11.040, 11.042, 11.055, 12.092, 12.107
  F&N: 6.105, 6.109, 6.110, 6.111, 6.112, 6.114, 6.115, 6.117, 6.120, 6.121, 6.122, 6.123, 6.124, 6.125, 6.135, 6.139, 6.140, 6.164, 6.176, 6.257
Art 37(1) (ex Art 31(1) TEC): B&C: 11.036, 11.039, 11.041, 11.042, 11.043, 11.044, 11.045 **F&N:** 6.110, 6.111, 6.118, 6.119, 12.05
Art 37(2) (ex Art 31(2) TEC): B&C: 11.043, 11.044, 11.045 **F&N:** 6.110, 6.116
Art 37(3) (ex Art 31(3) TEC): B&C: 11.044 **F&N:** 6.110

A5

TREATY ON THE FUNCTIONING OF THE EUROPEAN UNION: AGRICULTURE AND FISHERIES

(Articles 38 to 44 TFEU; ex Articles 32–38 TEC*)

Notes
* Ed note: Please see the Note on the Lisbon Treaty at p.xvii in regard to article renumbering introduced by the Lisbon Treaty.

Commentary
Arts 38 to 44 (ex Arts 32–38 TEC): B&C: 1.038
Arts 39 to 44 (ex Arts 33–38 TEC): B&C: 12.150

Article 38 (ex Article 32 TEC)

1. The Union shall define and implement a common agriculture and fisheries policy.

The internal market shall extend to agriculture, fisheries and trade in agricultural products. "Agricultural products" means the products of the soil, of stockfarming and of fisheries and products of first-stage processing directly related to these products. References to the common agricultural policy or to agriculture, and the use of the term "agricultural", shall be understood as also referring to fisheries, having regard to the specific characteristics of this sector.

2. Save as otherwise provided in Articles 39 to 44, the rules laid down for the establishment and functioning of the internal market shall apply to agricultural products.

3. The products subject to the provisions of Articles 39 to 44 are listed in Annex I.

4. The operation and development of the internal market for agricultural products must be accompanied by the establishment of a common agricultural policy.

Commentary
Art 38 (ex Art 32(1) TEC) B&C: 12.148

Article 39 (ex Article 33 TEC)

1. The objectives of the common agricultural policy shall be:

(a) to increase agricultural productivity by promoting technical progress and by ensuring the rational development of agricultural production and the optimum utilisation of the factors of production, in particular labour;

(b) thus to ensure a fair standard of living for the agricultural community, in particular by increasing the individual earnings of persons engaged in agriculture;

(c) to stabilise markets;

(d) to assure the availability of supplies;

(e) to ensure that supplies reach consumers at reasonable prices.

2. In working out the common agricultural policy and the special methods for its application, account shall be taken of:

(a) the particular nature of agricultural activity, which results from the social structure of agriculture and from structural and natural disparities between the various agricultural regions;

(b) the need to effect the appropriate adjustments by degrees;

(c) the fact that in the Member States agriculture constitutes a sector closely linked with the economy as a whole.

Commentary

Art 39 (ex Art 33 TEC): **B&C:** 12.001, 12.148, 12.156, 12.157, 12.159 **F&N:** 3.03

Article 40 (ex Article 34 TEC)

1. In order to attain the objectives set out in Article 39, a common organisation of agricultural markets shall be established.

This organisation shall take one of the following forms, depending on the product concerned:

(a) common rules on competition;

(b) compulsory coordination of the various national market organisations;

(c) a European market organisation.

2. The common organisation established in accordance with paragraph 1 may include all measures required to attain the objectives set out in Article 39, in particular regulation of prices, aids for the production and marketing of the various products, storage and carryover arrangements and common machinery for stabilising imports or exports.

The common organisation shall be limited to pursuit of the objectives set out in Article 39 and shall exclude any discrimination between producers or consumers within the Union.

Any common price policy shall be based on common criteria and uniform methods of calculation.

3. In order to enable the common organisation referred to in paragraph 1 to attain its objectives, one or more agricultural guidance and guarantee funds may be set up.

Commentary

Art 40 (ex Art 34 TEC)

Article 41 (ex Article 35 TEC)

To enable the objectives set out in Article 39 to be attained, provision may be made within the framework of the common agricultural policy for measures such as:

(a) an effective coordination of efforts in the spheres of vocational training, of research and of the dissemination of agricultural knowledge; this may include joint financing of projects or institutions;

(b) joint measures to promote consumption of certain products.

Article 42 (ex Article 36 TEC)

The provisions of the Chapter relating to rules on competition shall apply to production of and trade in agricultural products only to the extent determined by the European Parliament and the Council within the framework of Article 43(2) and in accordance with the procedure laid down therein, account being taken of the objectives set out in Article 39.

The Council, on a proposal from the Commission, may authorise the granting of aid:

(a) for the protection of enterprises handicapped by structural or natural conditions;
(b) within the framework of economic development programmes.

Commentary
Art 42 (ex Art 36 TEC): B&C: 12.148, 12.149 F&N: 3.03

Article 43 (ex Article 37 TEC)

1. The Commission shall submit proposals for working out and implementing the common agricultural policy, including the replacement of the national organisations by one of the forms of common organisation provided for in Article 40(1), and for implementing the measures specified in this Title.

These proposals shall take account of the interdependence of the agricultural matters mentioned in this Title.

2. The European Parliament and the Council, acting in accordance with the ordinary legislative procedure and after consulting the Economic and Social Committee, shall establish the common organisation of agricultural markets provided for in Article 40(1) and the other provisions necessary for the pursuit of the objectives of the common agricultural policy and the common fisheries policy.

3. The Council, on a proposal from the Commission, shall adopt measures on fixing prices, levies, aid and quantitative limitations and on the fixing and allocation of fishing opportunities.

4. In accordance with paragraph 2, the national market organisations may be replaced by the common organisation provided for in Article 40(1) if:

(a) the common organisation offers Member States which are opposed to this measure and which have an organisation of their own for the production in question equivalent safeguards for the employment and standard of living of the producers concerned, account being taken of the adjustments that will be possible and the specialisation that will be needed with the passage of time;
(b) such an organisation ensures conditions for trade within the Union similar to those existing in a national market.

5. If a common organisation for certain raw materials is established before a common organisation exists for the corresponding processed products, such raw materials as are used for processed products intended for export to third countries may be imported from outside the Union.

Commentary
Art 43 (ex Art 37 TEC): F&N: 3.03
Art 43(2) (ex Art 37(2) TEC): B&C: 12.148, 12.151 F&N: 3.03
Art 43(3) (ex Art 37(3) TEC): B&C: 12.151

Article 44 (ex Article 38 TEC)

Where in a Member State a product is subject to a national market organisation or to internal rules having equivalent effect which affect the competitive position of similar production in another Member State, a countervailing charge shall be applied by Member States to imports of this product coming from the Member State where such organisation or rules exist, unless that State applies a countervailing charge on export.

The Commission shall fix the amount of these charges at the level required to redress the balance; it may also authorise other measures, the conditions and details of which it shall determine.

A6

TREATY ON THE FUNCTIONING OF THE EUROPEAN UNION: THE COURT OF JUSTICE OF THE EUROPEAN UNION

(Article 19 TEU and Articles 251–252, 256–267, 278–279 TFEU; ex Articles 220–222; 225–234; 242–243 TEC*)

Notes
* Ed note: please see the Note on the Lisbon Treaty at p.xvii in regard to article renumbering introduced by the Lisbon Treaty.

Article 19 TEU (ex Article 220 TEC)

1. The Court of Justice of the European Union shall include the Court of Justice, the General Court and specialised courts. It shall ensure that in the interpretation and application of the Treaties the law is observed.

Member States shall provide remedies sufficient to ensure effective legal protection in the fields covered by Union law.

2. The Court of Justice shall consist of one judge from each Member State. It shall be assisted by Advocates-General.

The General Court shall include at least one judge per Member State.

The Judges and the Advocates-General of the Court of Justice and the Judges of the General Court shall be chosen from persons whose independence is beyond doubt and who satisfy the conditions set out in Articles 253 and 254 of the Treaty on the Functioning of the European Union. They shall be appointed by common accord of the governments of the Member States for six years. Retiring Judges and Advocates-General may be reappointed.

3. The Court of Justice of the European Union shall, in accordance with the Treaties:

(a) rule on actions brought by a Member State, an institution or a natural or legal person;
(b) give preliminary rulings, at the request of courts or tribunals of the Member States, on the interpretation of Union law or the validity of acts adopted by the institutions;
(c) rule in other cases provided for in the Treaties.

Commentary
Art 19 TEU (ex Art 220 TEC): B&C: 1.050, 1.051, 1.053

Article 251 (ex Article 221 TEC)

The Court of Justice shall sit in chambers or in a Grand Chamber, in accordance with the rules laid down for that purpose in the Statute of the Court of Justice of the European Union.

When provided for in the Statute, the Court of Justice may also sit as a full Court.

Article 252 (ex Article 222 TEC)

The Court of Justice shall be assisted by eight Advocates-General. Should the Court of Justice so request, the Council, acting unanimously, may increase the number of Advocates-General.

It shall be the duty of the Advocate-General, acting with complete impartiality and independence, to make, in open court, reasoned submissions on cases which, in accordance with the Statute of the Court of Justice of the European Union, require his involvement.

Commentary
Art 252 (ex Art 222 TEC): B&C: 1.053, 1.058

Article 256 (ex Article 225 TEC)

1. The General Court shall have jurisdiction to hear and determine at first instance actions or proceedings referred to in Articles 263, 265, 268, 270 and 272, with the exception of those assigned to a specialised court set up under Article 257 and those reserved in the Statute for the Court of Justice. The Statute may provide for the General Court to have jurisdiction for other classes of action or proceeding.

Decisions given by the General Court under this paragraph may be subject to a right of appeal to the Court of Justice on points of law only, under the conditions and within the limits laid down by the Statute.

2. The General Court shall have jurisdiction to hear and determine actions or proceedings brought against decisions of the specialised courts.

Decisions given by the General Court under this paragraph may exceptionally be subject to review by the Court of Justice, under the conditions and within the limits laid down by the Statute, where there is a serious risk of the unity or consistency of Union law being affected.

3. The General Court shall have jurisdiction to hear and determine questions referred for a preliminary ruling under Article 267, in specific areas laid down by the Statute.

Where the General Court considers that the case requires a decision of principle likely to affect the unity or consistency of Union law, it may refer the case to the Court of Justice for a ruling.

Decisions given by the General Court on questions referred for a preliminary ruling may exceptionally be subject to review by the Court of Justice, under the conditions and within the limits laid down by the Statute, where there is a serious risk of the unity or consistency of Union law being affected.

Note

The Court of First Instance has been renamed the General Court.

Commentary

Art 256 (ex Art 225 TEC): B&C: 13.122, 13.170 F&N: 5.1126, 5.1179
Art 256(1) (ex Art 225(1) TEC): B&C: 1.054, 13.122
Art 256(3) (ex Art 225(3) TEC): B&C: 1.052

Article 257 (ex Article 225a TEC)

The European Parliament and the Council, acting in accordance with the ordinary legislative procedure, may establish specialised courts attached to the General Court to hear and determine at first instance certain classes of action or proceeding brought in specific areas. The European Parliament and the Council shall act by means of regulations either on a proposal from the Commission after consultation of the Court of Justice or at the request of the Court of Justice after consultation of the Commission.

The regulation establishing a specialised court shall lay down the rules on the organisation of the court and the extent of the jurisdiction conferred upon it.

Decisions given by specialised courts may be subject to a right of appeal on points of law only or, when provided for in the regulation establishing the specialised court, a right of appeal also on matters of fact, before the General Court.

The members of the specialised courts shall be chosen from persons whose independence is beyond doubt and who possess the ability required for appointment to judicial office. They shall be appointed by the Council, acting unanimously.

The specialised courts shall establish their Rules of Procedure in agreement with the Court of Justice. Those Rules shall require the approval of the Council.

Unless the regulation establishing the specialised court provides otherwise, the provisions of the Treaties relating to the Court of Justice of the European Union and the provisions of the Statute of the Court of Justice of the European Union shall apply to the specialised courts. Title I of the Statute and Article 64 thereof shall in any case apply to the specialised courts.

Commentary

Art 257 (ex Art 225a TEC): B&C: 1.050

Article 258 (ex Art 226 TEC)

If the Commission considers that a Member State has failed to fulfil an obligation under the Treaties, it shall deliver a reasoned opinion on the matter after giving the State concerned the opportunity to submit its observations.

If the State concerned does not comply with the opinion within the period laid down by the Commission, the latter may bring the matter before the Court of Justice of the European Union.

Commentary

Art 258 (ex Art 226 TEC): **B&C:** 1.054, 8.104, 11.007, 11.024, 11.045, 12.093, 12.094, 12.107, 13.162, 17.094, 17.119 **F&N:** 2.53, 3.07, 5.1126, 6.229, 6.230, 6.234, 6.235, 6.241, 6.250, 12.05, 13.36, 17.448

Article 259 (ex Article 227 TEC)

A Member State which considers that another Member State has failed to fulfil an obligation under the Treaties may bring the matter before the Court of Justice of the European Union.

Before a Member State brings an action against another Member State for an alleged infringement of an obligation under the Treaties, it shall bring the matter before the Commission.

The Commission shall deliver a reasoned opinion after each of the States concerned has been given the opportunity to submit its own case and its observations on the other party's case both orally and in writing.

If the Commission has not delivered an opinion within three months of the date on which the matter was brought before it, the absence of such opinion shall not prevent the matter from being brought before the Court.

Commentary

Art 259 (ex Art 227 TEC): **B&C:** 17.054 **F&N:** 3.07

Article 260 (ex Article 228 TEC)

A Member State which considers that another Member State has failed to fulfil an obligation under the Treaties may bring the matter before the Court of Justice of the European Union.

Before a Member State brings an action against another Member State for an alleged infringement of an obligation under the Treaties, it shall bring the matter before the Commission.

The Commission shall deliver a reasoned opinion after each of the States concerned has been given the opportunity to submit its own case and its observations on the other party's case both orally and in writing.

If the Commission has not delivered an opinion within three months of the date on which the matter was brought before it, the absence of such opinion shall not prevent the matter from being brought before the Court.

Commentary

Art 260 (ex Art 228 TEC): **B&C:** 17.108 **F&N:** 5.1126
Art 260(2) (ex Art 228(2) TEC)

Article 261 (ex Article 229 TEC)

Regulations adopted jointly by the European Parliament and the Council, and by the Council, pursuant to the provisions of the Treaties, may give the Court of Justice of the European Union unlimited jurisdiction with regard to the penalties provided for in such regulations.

Commentary

Art 261 (ex Art 229 TEC): **B&C:** 1.052, 13.053, 13.122, 13.123, 13.124, 13.151, 13.153, 13.160, 13.176, 14.003, 14.007 **F&N:** 5.1195

Article 262 (ex Article 229a TEC)

Without prejudice to the other provisions of the Treaties, the Council, acting unanimously in accordance with a special legislative procedure and after consulting the European Parliament, may adopt provisions to confer jurisdiction, to the extent that it shall determine, on the Court of Justice of the European Union in disputes relating to the application of acts adopted on the basis of the Treaties which create European intellectual property rights. These provisions shall enter into force after their approval by the Member States in accordance with their respective constitutional requirements

Article 263 (ex Article 230 TEC)

The Court of Justice of the European Union shall review the legality of legislative acts, of acts of the Council, of the Commission and of the European Central Bank, other than recommendations and opinions, and of acts of the European Parliament and of the European Council intended to produce legal effects vis-à-vis third parties. It shall also review the legality of acts of bodies, offices or agencies of the Union intended to produce legal effects vis-à-vis third parties.

It shall for this purpose have jurisdiction in actions brought by a Member State, the European Parliament, the Council or the Commission on grounds of lack of competence, infringement of an essential procedural requirement, infringement of the Treaties or of any rule of law relating to their application, or misuse of powers.

The Court shall have jurisdiction under the same conditions in actions brought by the Court of Auditors, by the European Central Bank and by the Committee of the Regions for the purpose of protecting their prerogatives.

Any natural or legal person may, under the conditions laid down in the first and second paragraphs, institute proceedings against an act addressed to that person or which is of direct and individual concern to them, and against a regulatory act which is of direct concern to them and does not entail implementing measures.

Acts setting up bodies, offices and agencies of the Union may lay down specific conditions and arrangements concerning actions brought by natural or legal persons against acts of these bodies, offices or agencies intended to produce legal effects in relation to them.

The proceedings provided for in this Article shall be instituted within two months of the publication of the measure, or of its notification to the plaintiff, or, in the absence thereof, of the day on which it came to the knowledge of the latter, as the case may be.

Commentary

Art 263 (ex Art 230 TEC): **B&C:** 1.052, 8.248, 8.250, 8.251, 8.252, 8.258, 12.020, 13.025, 13.031, 13.043, 13.048, 13.049, 13.053, 13.057, 13.060, 13.122, 13.123, 13.128, 13.129, 13.131, 13.133, 13.139, 13.140, 13.151, 13.153, 13.162, 13.164, 15.065, 17.090, 17.094, 17.116, 17.118, 17.120, 17.121, 17.123, 17.124, 17.127 **F&N:** 2.144, 2.150, 4.68, 4.78, 5.337, 5.1126, 5.1129, 5.1151, 5.1165, 6.233, 6.239, 6.241, 6.249, 8.399, 8.708, 17.550

Art 263(2) (ex Art 230(2) TEC): **F&N:** 5.1138

Art 263(3) (ex Art 230(3) TEC): **F&N:** 5.1138

Art 263(4) (ex Art 230(4) TEC): **B&C:** 13.132, 17.121 **F&N:** 5.1139, 5.1141

Art 263(5) (ex Art 230(5) TEC)

Article 264 (ex Article 231 TEC)

If the action is well founded, the Court of Justice of the European Union shall declare the act concerned to be void.

However, the Court shall, if it considers this necessary, state which of the effects of the act which it has declared void shall be considered as definitive.

Commentary

Art 264 (ex Article 231 TEC): **B&C:** 17.114

Article 265 (ex Article 232 TEC)

Should the European Parliament, the European Council, the Council, the Commission or the European Central Bank, in infringement of the Treaties, fail to act, the Member States and the other institutions of the Union may bring an action before the Court of Justice of the European Union to have the infringement established. This Article shall apply, under the same conditions, to bodies, offices and agencies of the Union which fail to act.

The action shall be admissible only if the institution, body, office or agency concerned has first been called upon to act. If, within two months of being so called upon, the institution, body, office or agency concerned has not defined its position, the action may be brought within a further period of two months.

Any natural or legal person may, under the conditions laid down in the preceding paragraphs, complain to the Court that an institution, body, office or agency of the Union has failed to address to that person any act other than a recommendation or an opinion.

Commentary
Art 265 (ex Art 232 TEC): **B&C**: 1.054, 8.248, 8.251, 13.047, 13.048, 13.122, 13.130, 13.161, 13.162, 13.163, 13.164, 17.118, 17.119, 17.122, 17.127 **F&N**: 5.1126, 6.239, 17.532, 17.533, 17.559

Article 266 (ex Article 233 TEC)

The institution whose act has been declared void or whose failure to act has been declared contrary to the Treaties shall be required to take the necessary measures to comply with the judgment of the Court of Justice of the European Union.

This obligation shall not affect any obligation which may result from the application of the second paragraph of Article 340.

Commentary
Art 266 (ex Art 233 TEC): **B&C**: 13.064, 13.157, 13.158, 13.160, 14.086, 17.119

Article 267 (ex Article 234 TEC)

The Court of Justice of the European Union shall have jurisdiction to give preliminary rulings concerning:

(a) the interpretation of the Treaties;
(b) the validity and interpretation of acts of the institutions, bodies, offices or agencies of the Union.

Where such a question is raised before any court or tribunal of a Member State, that court or tribunal may, if it considers that a decision on the question is necessary to enable it to give judgment, request the Court to give a ruling thereon.

Where any such question is raised in a case pending before a court or tribunal of a Member State against whose decisions there is no judicial remedy under national law, that court or tribunal shall bring the matter before the Court.

If such a question is raised in a case pending before a court or tribunal of a Member State with regard to a person in custody, the Court of Justice of the European Union shall act with the minimum of delay.

Commentary
Art 267 (ex Art 234 TEC): **B&C**: 1.050, 1.057, 1.072, 5.061, 5.087, 9.052, 13.109, 15.065, 16.003, 16.073, 16.100, 16.101, 17.116 **F&N**: 2.150, 2.151, 2.237, 2.255, 2.256, 2.284, 3.314, 5.1126, 9.01, 10.247
Art 267(2) (ex Art 234(2) TEC): **B&C**: 16.100
Art 267(3) (ex Art 234(3) TEC): **F&N**: 2.272

Article 278 (ex Article 242 TEC)

Actions brought before the Court of Justice of the European Union shall not have suspensory effect. The Court may, however, if it considers that circumstances so require, order that application of the contested act be suspended.

Commentary
Art 278 (ex Art 242 TEC): B&C: 1.052, 8.250, 13.122, 13.164, 13.165, 13.177 **F&N:** 5.1170, 8.393, 8.399, 17.471, 17.561

Article 279 (ex Article 243 TEC)

The Court of Justice of the European Union may in any cases before it prescribe any necessary interim measures.

Commentary
Art 279 (ex Art 243 TEC): B&C: 8.250, 13.122, 13.164, 13.165, 13.168, 13.177 **F&N:** 5.1170, 17.561

A7

TREATY ON THE FUNCTIONING OF THE EUROPEAN UNION: ART 346 AND LIST

*Article 346 TFEU (ex Article 296 TEC)**

1. The provisions of the Treaties shall not preclude the application of the following rules:

(a) no Member State shall be obliged to supply information the disclosure of which it considers contrary to the essential interests of its security;

(b) any Member State may take such measures as it considers necessary for the protection of the essential interests of its security which are connected with the production of or trade in arms, munitions and war material; such measures shall not adversely affect the conditions of competition in the common market regarding products which are not intended for specifically military purposes.

2. The Council may, acting unanimously on a proposal from the Commission, make changes to the list, which it drew up on 15 April 1958, of the products to which the provisions of paragraph 1(b) apply.

Notes
* Ed note: please see the Note on the Lisbon Treaty at p.xvii in regard to article renumbering introduced by the Lisbon Treaty.

LIST OF PRODUCTS REFERRED TO IN ARTICLE 346 OF THE TREATY

The provisions of Article [346] paragraph 1(b) of the [Treaty on the Functioning of the European Union] are applicable to the arms, munition and war material specified below, including nuclear arms:

1. Portable and automatic firearms, such as rifles, carbines, revolvers, pistols, sub-machine guns and machine guns, except for hunting weapons, pistols and other low calibre weapons of the calibre less than 7mm.
2. Artillery, and smoke, gas and flame throwing weapons such as:
    (a) cannon, howitzers, mortars, artillery, anti-tank guns, rocket launchers, flame-throwers, recoilless guns;
    (b) military smoke and gas guns.
3. Ammunition for the weapons at 1 and 2 above.
4. Bombs, torpedoes, rockets and guided missiles:
    (a) bombs, torpedoes, grenades, including smoke grenades, smoke bombs, rockets, mines, guided missiles, underwater grenades, incendiary bombs;
    (b) military apparatus and components specially designed for the handling, assembly, dismantling, firing or detection of the articles at (a) above.

5. Military fire control equipment:
   (a) firing computers and guidance systems in infra-red and other night guidance devices;
   (b) telemeters, position indicators, altimeters;
   (c) electronic tracking components, gyroscopic, optical and acoustic;
   (d) bomb sights and gun sights, periscopes for the equipment specified in this list.
6. Tanks and specialist fighting vehicles:
   (a) tanks;
   (b) military type vehicles, armed or armoured including amphibious vehicles;
   (c) armoured cars;
   (d) half-tracked military vehicles;
   (e) military vehicles with tank bodies;
   (f) trailers specially designed for the transportation of ammunition specified at paragraphs 3 and 4.
7. Toxic and radioactive agents:
   (a) toxic, biological or chemical agents and radioactive agents adapted for destructive use in war against persons, animals or crops;
   (b) military apparatus for the propagation, detection and identification of substances at paragraph (a) above;
   (c) counter-measures material related to paragraph (a) above.
8. Powders, explosives and liquid or solid propellants:
   (a) powders and liquid or solid propellants specially designed and constructed for use with the material at paragraphs 3, 4 and 7 above;
   (b) military explosives;
   (c) incendiary and freezing agents for military use.
9. Warships and their specialist equipment:
   (a) warships of all kinds;
   (b) equipment specially designed for laying, detecting and sweeping mines;
   (c) underwater cables.
10. Aircraft and equipment for military use.
11. Military electronic equipment.
12. Camera equipment specially designed for military use.
13. Other equipment and material:
    (a) parachutes and parachute fabric;
    (b) water purification plant specially designed for military use;
    (c) military command relay electrical equipment.
14. Specialised parts and items of material included in this list in so far as they are of a military nature.
15. Machines, equipment and items exclusively designed for the study, manufacture, testing and control of arms, munitions and apparatus of an exclusively military nature included in this list.

Commentary
Art 346 (ex Art 296 TEC): B&C: 1.038, 8.103, 8.105, 8.183, 11.001, 11.046, 11.061, 11.063 F&N: 3.07, 3.11, 5.294
Art 346(1) (ex Art 296(1) TEC): F&N: 3.06
Art 346(1)(a) (ex Art 296(1)(a) TEC): F&N: 5.295
Art 346(1)(b) (ex Art 296(1)(b) TEC): B&C: 8.105, 11.061, 11.062, 11.063 F&N: 5.296, 5.297
Art 346(2) (ex Art 296(2)) TEC: B&C: 11.062 F&N: 3.06, 3.08

A8

AGREEMENT ON THE EUROPEAN ECONOMIC AREA

(As amended: Articles 1, 2, 53–65 and 108–109)

Notes
For information regarding the EEA Agreement, see the website of the EFTA Secretariat at <http: www.efta.int/>
EEA Agreement legal texts are available in full at: <http://www.efta.int/legal-texts/eea.aspx>

Commentary
EEA Agreement: B&C: 1.002, 1.018, 1.036, 1.090, 1.091, 1.110, 2.003, 7.003, 7.024, 8.085, 8.089, 8.292, 12.137

PART I
OBJECTIVES AND PRINCIPLES

Article 1

1. The aim of this Agreement of association is to promote a continuous and balanced strengthening of trade and economic relations between the Contracting Parties with equal conditions of competition, and the respect of the same rules, with a view to creating a homogeneous European Economic Area, hereinafter referred to as the EEA.

2. In order to attain the objectives set out in paragraph 1, the association shall entail, in accordance with the provisions of this Agreement:

(a) the free movement of goods;
(b) the free movement of persons;
(c) the free movement of services;
(d) the free movement of capital;
(e) the setting up of a system ensuring that competition is not distorted and that the rules thereon are equally respected; as well as
(f) closer cooperation in other fields, such as research and development, the environment, education and social policy.

Article 2

For the purposes of this Agreement:

(a) the term "Agreement" means the main Agreement, its Protocols and Annexes as well as the acts referred to therein;
[(b) the term "EFTA States" means the []² Iceland, the Principality of Liechtenstein and the Kingdom of Norway;]¹
(c) the term "Contracting Parties" means, concerning the Community and the EC Member States, the Community and the EC Member States, or the Community, or the EC Member States. The meaning to be attributed to this expression in each case is to be deduced from the relevant provisions of this Agreement and from the respective competences of the Community and the EC Member States as they follow from the Treaty establishing the European Economic Community [. . .];³
[(d) the term "Act of Accession of 16 April 2003" shall mean the Act concerning the conditions of Accession of the Czech Republic, the Republic of Estonia, the Republic of Cyprus, the Republic of Latvia, the Republic of Lithuania, the Republic of Hungary, the Republic of Malta, the Republic of Poland, the Republic of Slovenia and the Slovak Republic and the adjustments to the Treaties on which the European Union is founded, adopted in Athens on 16 April 2003.]⁴
[(e) the term "Act of Accession of 25 April 2005" shall mean the Act concerning the conditions of accession of the Republic of Bulgaria and Romania and the adjustments to the Treaties on which the European Union is founded, adopted in Luxembourg on 25 April 2005;

(f) the term "Protocol of Accession of 25 April 2005" shall mean the Protocol concerning the conditions and arrangements for admission of the Republic of Bulgaria and Romania to the European Union, adopted in Luxembourg on 25 April 2005][5]

Notes

[1] As replaced by the Adjusting Protocol and subsequently by the EEA Enlargement Agreement (OJ L 130, 29.4.2004, p.3 and EEA Supplement No 23, 29.4.2004, p.1), with effect from 1 May 2004.

[2] Words "Republic of" deleted by the 2007 EEA Enlargement Agreement (OJ No L 221, 25.8.2007, p.15; EEA supplement No 39, 26.6.2008, p.10), provisionally applicable as of 1.8.2007, entry into force 9 November 2011.

[3] Words "and the Treaty establishing the European Coal and Steel Community" deleted by the EEA Enlargement Agreement (OJ L 130, 29.4.2004, p.3 and EEA Supplement No 23, 29.4.2004, p.1), with effect from 1 May 2004, entry into force 6 December 2005.

[4] Point added by the EEA Enlargement Agreement (OJ L 130, 29.4.2004, p.3 and EEA Supplement No 23, 29.4.2004, p. 1), with effect from 1 May 2004.

[5] Paragraphs (e) and (f) were added by the 2007 EEA Enlargement Agreement (OJ No L 221, 25.8.2007, p.15; EEA supplement No 39, 26.6.2008, p.1), provisionally applicable as of 1 August 2007, entry into force 9 November 2011.

[Articles 3 to 52]

Notes

Articles 3 to 52 are not reproduced in this volume. They are available at:
<http://www.efta.int/legal-texts/EEA/main-text-of-the-agreement.aspx>.

Part IV
Competition and Other Common Rules
Chapter 1
Rules Applicable to Undertakings
Article 53

1. The following shall be prohibited as incompatible with the functioning of this Agreement: all agreements between undertakings, decisions by associations of undertakings and concerted practices which may affect trade between Contracting Parties and which have as their object or effect the prevention, restriction or distortion of competition within the territory covered by this Agreement, and in particular those which:

(a) directly or indirectly fix purchase or selling prices or any other trading conditions;
(b) limit or control production, markets, technical development, or investment;
(c) share markets or sources of supply;
(d) apply dissimilar conditions to equivalent transactions with other trading parties, thereby placing them at a competitive disadvantage;
(e) make the conclusion of contracts subject to acceptance by the other parties of supplementary obligations which, by their nature or according to commercial usage, have no connection with the subject of such contracts.

2. Any agreements or decisions prohibited pursuant to this Article shall be automatically void.

3. The provisions of paragraph 1 may, however, be declared inapplicable in the case of:
— any agreement or category of agreements between undertakings;
— any decision or category of decisions by associations of undertakings;
— any concerted practice or category of concerted practices;

which contributes to improving the production or distribution of goods or to promoting technical or economic progress, while allowing consumers a fair share of the resulting benefit, and which does not:

(a) impose on the undertakings concerned restrictions which are not indispensable to the attainment of these objectives;

(b) afford such undertakings the possibility of eliminating competition in respect of a substantial part of the products in question.

Commentary
Art 53: B&C: 1.094, 1.095, 2.051, 8.005, 13.003 **F&N:** 2.198, 5.459, 8.155, 11.57
Art 53(1): B&C: 2.036, 3.095, 6.036, 7.054, 7.153 **F&N:** 3.336
Art 53(3): B&C: 3.001, 3.093–3.096

Article 54

Any abuse by one or more undertakings of a dominant position within the territory covered by this Agreement or in a substantial part of it shall be prohibited as incompatible with the functioning of this Agreement in so far as it may affect trade between Contracting Parties.

Such abuse may, in particular, consist in:

(a) directly or indirectly imposing unfair purchase or selling prices or other unfair trading conditions;
(b) limiting production, markets or technical development to the prejudice of consumers;
(c) applying dissimilar conditions to equivalent transactions with other trading parties, thereby placing them at a competitive disadvantage;
(d) making the conclusion of contracts subject to acceptance by the other parties of supplementary obligations which, by their nature or according to commercial usage, have no connection with the subject of such contracts.

Commentary
Art 54: B&C: 1.094, 1.095, 8.005, 13.003 **F&N:** 2.198, 5.459, 8.155, 11.57

Article 55

1. Without prejudice to the provisions giving effect to Articles 53 and 54 as contained in Protocol 21 and Annex XIV of this Agreement, the EC Commission and the EFTA Surveillance Authority provided for in Article 108(1) shall ensure the application of the principles laid down in Articles 53 and 54.

The competent surveillance authority, as provided for in Article 56, shall investigate cases of suspected infringement of these principles, on its own initiative, or on application by a State within the respective territory or by the other surveillance authority. The competent surveillance authority shall carry out these investigations in cooperation with the competent national authorities in the respective territory and in cooperation with the other surveillance authority, which shall give it its assistance in accordance with its internal rules. If it finds that there has been an infringement, it shall propose appropriate measures to bring it to an end.

2. If the infringement is not brought to an end, the competent surveillance authority shall record such infringement of the principles in a reasoned decision.

The competent surveillance authority may publish its decision and authorize States within the respective territory to take the measures, the conditions and details of which it shall determine, needed to remedy the situation. It may also request the other surveillance authority to authorize States within the respective territory to take such measures.

Notes
Protocol 21 and Annex XIV are not reproduced in this volume.
Protocol 21 is available at:
<http://www.efta.int/legal-texts/EEA/protocols-to-the-agreement.aspx>.
Annex XIV is available at:
<http://www.efta.int/legal-texts/EEA/annexes-to-the-agreement.aspx>.

Commentary
Art 55(1): B&C: 1.095

Article 56

1. Individual cases falling under Article 53 shall be decided upon by the surveillance authorities in accordance with the following provisions:

(a) individual cases where only trade between EFTA States is affected shall be decided upon by the EFTA Surveillance Authority;

(b) without prejudice to subparagraph (c), the EFTA Surveillance Authority decides, as provided for in the provisions set out in Article 58, Protocol 21 and the rules adopted for its implementation, Protocol 23 and Annex XIV, on cases where the turnover of the undertakings concerned in the territory of the EFTA States equals 33 per cent or more of their turnover in the territory covered by this Agreement;

(c) the EC Commission decides on the other cases as well as on cases under (b) where trade between EC Member States is affected, taking into account the provisions set out in Article 58, Protocol 21, Protocol 23 and Annex XIV.

2. Individual cases falling under Article 54 shall be decided upon by the surveillance authority in the territory of which a dominant position is found to exist. The rules set out in paragraph 1(b) and (c) shall apply only if dominance exists within the territories of both surveillance authorities.

3. Individual cases falling under subparagraph (c) of paragraph 1, whose effects on trade between EC Member States or on competition within the Community are not appreciable, shall be decided upon by the EFTA Surveillance Authority.

4. The terms "undertaking" and "turnover" are, for the purposes of this Article, defined in Protocol 22.

Notes
Protocols 21, 22, and 23 and Annex XIV are not reproduced in this volume.
Protocols 21, 22, and 23 are available at:
<http://www.efta.int/legal-texts/EEA/protocols-to-the-agreement.aspx>.
Annex XIV is available at:
<http://www.efta.int/legal-texts/EEA/annexes-to-the-agreement.aspx>.

Commentary
Art 56: **B&C:** 1.095

Article 57

1. Concentrations the control of which is provided for in paragraph 2 and which create or strengthen a dominant position as a result of which effective competition would be significantly impeded within the territory covered by this Agreement or a substantial part of it, shall be declared incompatible with this Agreement.

2. The control of concentrations falling under paragraph 1 shall be carried out by:

(a) the EC Commission in cases falling under Regulation (EEC) No 4064/89 in accordance with that Regulation and in accordance with Protocols 21 and 24 and Annex XIV to this Agreement. The EC Commission shall, subject to the review of the EC Court of Justice, have sole competence to take decisions on these cases;

(b) the EFTA Surveillance Authority in cases not falling under subparagraph (a) where the relevant thresholds set out in Annex XIV are fulfilled in the territory of the EFTA States in accordance with Protocols 21 and 24 and Annex XIV. This is without prejudice to the competence of EC Member States.

Notes
Protocols 21 and 24 and Annex XIV are not reproduced in this volume.
Protocols 21 and 24 are available at:
<http://www.efta.int/legal-texts/EEA/protocols-to-the-agreement.aspx>.
Annex XIV is available at:
<http://www.efta.int/legal-texts/EEA/annexes-to-the-agreement.aspx>.

Commentary
Art 57: **B&C:** 1.094, 8.011, 8.062, 8.119, 8.191, 8.294 **F&N:** 2.198, 5.312, 5.459, 8.155
Art 57(1): **F&N:** 5.310
Art 57(2): **F&N:** 5.313
Art 57(2)(a): **B&C:** 8.282, 8.293
Art 57(2)(b): **B&C:** 8.292

Article 58

With a view to developing and maintaining a uniform surveillance throughout the European Economic Area in the field of competition and to promoting a homogeneous implementation, application and interpretation of the provisions of this Agreement to this end, the competent authorities shall cooperate in accordance with the provisions set out in Protocols 23 and 24.

Notes
Protocols 23 and 24 are not reproduced in this volume.
Protocols 23 and 24 are available at: <http://www.efta.int/legal-texts/EEA/protocols-to-the-agreement.aspx>.

Commentary
Art 58: B&C: 1.097

Article 59

1. In the case of public undertakings and undertakings to which EC Member States or EFTA States grant special or exclusive rights, the Contracting Parties shall ensure that there is neither enacted nor maintained in force any measure contrary to the rules contained in this Agreement, in particular to those rules provided for in Articles 4 and 53 to 63.

2. Undertakings entrusted with the operation of services of general economic interest or having the character of a revenue-producing monopoly shall be subject to the rules contained in this Agreement, in particular to the rules on competition, in so far as the application of such rules does not obstruct the performance, in law or in fact, of the particular tasks assigned to them. The development of trade must not be affected to such an extent as would be contrary to the interests of the Contracting Parties.

3. The EC Commission as well as the EFTA Surveillance Authority shall ensure within their respective competence the application of the provisions of this Article and shall, where necessary, address appropriate measures to the States falling within their respective territory.

Commentary
Art 59: B&C: 1.094, 11.014

Article 60

Annex XIV contains specific provisions giving effect to the principles set out in Articles 53, 54, 57 and 59.

Notes
Annex XIV is not reproduced in this volume.
Annex XIV is available at:
<http://www.efta.int/legal-texts/EEA/annexes-to-the-agreement.aspx>.

Commentary
Art 60: B&C: 1.094, 8.117

CHAPTER 2
STATE AID

Article 61

1. Save as otherwise provided in this Agreement, any aid granted by EC Member States, EFTA States or through State resources in any form whatsoever which distorts or threatens to distort competition by favouring certain undertakings or the production of certain goods shall, in so far as it affects trade between Contracting Parties, be incompatible with the functioning of this Agreement.

2. The following shall be compatible with the functioning of this Agreement:

(a) aid having a social character, granted to individual consumers, provided that such aid is granted without discrimination related to the origin of the products concerned;

(b) aid to make good the damage caused by natural disasters or exceptional occurrences;

(c) aid granted to the economy of certain areas of the Federal Republic of Germany affected by the division of Germany, in so far as such aid is required in order to compensate for the economic disadvantages caused by that division.

3. The following may be considered to be compatible with the functioning of this Agreement:

(a) aid to promote the economic development of areas where the standard of living is abnormally low or where there is serious underemployment;

(b) aid to promote the execution of an important project of common European interest or to remedy a serious disturbance in the economy of an EC Member State or an EFTA State;

(c) aid to facilitate the development of certain economic activities or of certain economic areas, where such aid does not adversely affect trading conditions to an extent contrary to the common interest;

(d) such other categories of aid as may be specified by the EEA Joint Committee in accordance with Part VII.

Commentary
Art 61: **B&C:** 1.094, 17.004
Art 61(2): **B&C:** 17.004, 17.042
Art 61(3): **B&C:** 17.004

Article 62

1. All existing systems of State aid in the territory of the Contracting Parties, as well as any plans to grant or alter State aid, shall be subject to constant review as to their compatibility with Article 61. This review shall be carried out:

(a) as regards the EC Member States, by the EC Commission according to the rules laid down in Article 93 of the Treaty establishing the European Economic Community;[1]

(b) as regards the EFTA States, by the EFTA Surveillance Authority according to the rules set out in an agreement between the EFTA States establishing the EFTA Surveillance Authority which is entrusted with the powers and functions laid down in Protocol 26.

2. With a view to ensuring a uniform surveillance in the field of State aid throughout the territory covered by this Agreement, the EC Commission and the EFTA Surveillance Authority shall cooperate in accordance with the provisions set out in Protocol 27.

Notes
[1] Now Art 88 of the EC Treaty.
Protocols 26 and 27 are not reproduced in this volume.
Protocols 26 and 27 are available at:
<http://www.efta.int/legal-texts/EEA/protocols-to-the-agreement.aspx>.

Commentary
Art 62: **B&C:** 1.094, 17.004
Art 62(1)(a): **B&C:** 17.004
Art 62(1)(b): **B&C:** 17.004
Art 62(2): **B&C:** 17.004

Article 63

Annex XV contains specific provisions on State aid.

Notes
Annex XV is not reproduced in this volume.
Annex XV is available at:
<http://www.efta.int/legal-texts/EEA/annexes-to-the-agreement.aspx>.

Article 64

1. If one of the surveillance authorities considers that the implementation by the other surveillance authority of Articles 61 and 62 of this Agreement and Article 5 of Protocol 14 is not in conformity with the maintenance of equal conditions of competition within the territory covered by this

Agreement, exchange of views shall be held within two weeks according to the procedure of Protocol 27, paragraph (f).

If a commonly agreed solution has not been found by the end of this two-week period, the competent authority of the affected Contracting Party may immediately adopt appropriate interim measures in order to remedy the resulting distortion of competition.

Consultations shall then be held in the EEA Joint Committee with a view to finding a commonly acceptable solution.

If within three months the EEA Joint Committee has not been able to find such a solution, and if the practice in question causes, or threatens to cause, distortion of competition affecting trade between the Contracting Parties, the interim measures may be replaced by definitive measures, strictly necessary to offset the effect of such distortion. Priority shall be given to such measures that will least disturb the functioning of the EEA.

2. The provisions of this Article will also apply to State monopolies, which are established after the date of signature of the Agreement.

Notes
Protocols 14 and 27 are not reproduced in this volume.
Protocols 14 and 27 are available at:
<http://www.efta.int/legal-texts/EEA/protocols-to-the-agreement.aspx>.

CHAPTER 3
OTHER COMMON RULES

Article 65

1. Annex XVI contains specific provisions and arrangements concerning procurement which, unless otherwise specified, shall apply to all products and to services as specified.

2. Protocol 28 and Annex XVII contain specific provisions and arrangements concerning intellectual, industrial and commercial property, which, unless otherwise specified, shall apply to all products and services.

Notes
Protocol 28 and Annexes XVI and XVII are not reproduced in this volume.
Protocol 28 is available at: <http://www.efta.int/legal-texts/EEA/protocols-to-the-agreement.aspx>.
Annexes XVI and XVII are available at:
<http://www.efta.int/legal-texts/EEA/annexes-to-the-agreement.aspx>.

[Articles 66 to 107]

Notes
Articles 66 to 107 are not reproduced in this volume. They are available at:
<http://www.efta.int/legal-texts/EEA/main-text-of-the-agreement.aspx>.

PART VII

INSTITUTIONAL PROVISIONS

CHAPTER 3
HOMOGENEITY, SURVEILLANCE PROCEDURE AND SETTLEMENT OF DISPUTES

Section 2
Surveillance procedure

Article 108

1. The EFTA States shall establish an independent surveillance authority (EFTA Surveillance Authority) as well as procedures similar to those existing in the Community including procedures for ensuring the fulfilment of obligations under this Agreement and for control of the legality of acts of the EFTA Surveillance Authority regarding competition.

2. The EFTA States shall establish a court of justice (EFTA Court).

The EFTA Court shall, in accordance with a separate agreement between the EFTA States, with regard to the application of this Agreement be competent, in particular, for:

(a) actions concerning the surveillance procedure regarding the EFTA States;

(b) appeals concerning decisions in the field of competition taken by the EFTA Surveillance Authority;

(c) the settlement of disputes between two or more EFTA States.

Commentary
Art 108: B&C: 1.092

Article 109

1. The fulfilment of the obligations under this Agreement shall be monitored by, on the one hand, the EFTA Surveillance Authority and, on the other, the EC Commission acting in conformity with the Treaty establishing the European Economic Community [. . .].[1]

2. In order to ensure a uniform surveillance throughout the EEA, the EFTA Surveillance Authority and the EC Commission shall cooperate, exchange information and consult each other on surveillance policy issues and individual cases.

3. The EC Commission and the EFTA Surveillance Authority shall receive any complaints concerning the application of this Agreement. They shall inform each other of complaints received.

4. Each of these bodies shall examine all complaints falling within its competence and shall pass to the other body any complaints which fall within the competence of that body.

5. In case of disagreement between these two bodies with regard to the action to be taken in relation to a complaint or with regard to the result of the examination, either of the bodies may refer the matter to the EEA Joint Committee which shall deal with it in accordance with Article 111.

Notes
[1] Words "and the Treaty establishing the European Coal and Steel Community" deleted by the EEA Enlargement Agreement (OJ L 130, 29.4.2004, p.3 and EEA Supplement No 23, 29.4.2004, p.1), with effect from 1 May 2004.

Commentary
Art 109: B&C: 1.097

[Articles 110 to 129]

Notes
Articles 110 to 129 are not reproduced in this volume. They are available on the EFTA Secretariat's website at: <http://www.efta.int/legal-texts/eea.aspx>.

Part B

PROCEDURAL MATTERS

B1

REGULATION NO 17

First Regulation implementing Articles [101 and 102] of the [Treaty on the Functioning of the European Union]*

NOTE

Official Journal P 13, 21.2.1962, p.204

Celex No: 31962R0017

EUR-Lex permanent link: <http://eur-lex.europa.eu/LexUriServ/LexUriServ.do?uri=CELEX:31962R0017:EN:NOT>

Notes

* Ed note: please see the Note on the Lisbon Treaty at p.xvii in regard to article renumbering introduced by the Lisbon Treaty. Regulation No 17 was repealed and superseded with effect from 1 May 2004 (with the exception of Article 8(3), which continues to apply to decisions adopted pursuant to Article 101(3) TFEU prior to 1 May 2004 until the date of expiration of those decisions) by Council Regulation 1/2003/EC (OJ L 1, 4.1.2003, p.1), Article 43. For reasons of space, Regulation No 17 is no longer reproduced in this volume. It remains available on Oxford Competition Law, in the form in which it stood immediately before repeal.

Commentary
Reg 17/62: B&C: 1.006, 1.022, 1.049, 1.066, 1.067, 3.003, 3.006, 3.010, 3.014, 3.020, 12.162, 12.163, 12.165, 13.001, 13.034, 13.101, 13.117, 14.123, 15.073, 15.074, 15.075, 16.006 **F&N:** 2.02, 2.03, 2.07, 2.09, 2.30, 2.41, 2.57, 2.116, 2.147, 2.151, 2.261, 3.223, 3.445, 3.473, 4.54, 7.51, 7.123, 8.107, 8.253, 8.353, 8.362, 8.364, 8.412, 9.12, 9.13, 9.19, 12.231, 15.07, 15.10, 16.106, 17.395

B2

COUNCIL REGULATION (EC) NO 1/2003

of 16 December 2002 on the implementation of the rules on competition laid down in Articles [101 and 102] of the [Treaty on the Functioning of the European Union]*

(Text with EEA relevance)

Official Journal L 1, 4.1.2003, p.1

Celex No: 32003R0001

EUR-Lex permanent link: <http://eur-lex.europa.eu/LexUriServ/LexUriServ.do?uri=CELEX: 3200 3R0001:EN:NOT>

Notes

* Ed note: please see the Note on the Lisbon Treaty at p.xvii in regard to article renumbering introduced by the Lisbon Treaty. **EEA application:** see the Surveillance and Court Agreement, Protocol 4, Part I, Chapter II, as amended by the Agreement of 24 September 2004 (entry into force 20 May 2005). See also EEA Agreement, Protocol 21, Article 3(1), Point 1 (as replaced by EEA Joint Committee Decision No 130/2004 of 24 September 2004 (OJ L 64, 10.3.2005, p.57 and EEA Supplement No 12, 10.2.3005, p.42) with effect from 19 May 2005.

Commentary

Reg 1/2003/EC: B&C: 1.004, 1.020, 1.022, 1.025, 1.026, 1.027, 1.029, 1.049, 1.067, 1.070, 1.071, 1.094, 1.096, 1.118, 1.121, 2.053, 2.063, 3.003, 3.004, 3.006, 3.093, 5.036, 7.026, 7.061, 7.138, 8.247, 8.270, 8.273, 10.012, 11.024, 11.025, 12.040, 12.163, 12.165, 12.191, 13.002, 13.061, 13.169, 15.001, 15.006, 15.015, 15.016, 15.017, 15.025, 15.026, 15.029, 15.031, 15.035, 15.041, 15.055, 15.056, 15.075, 16.001, 16.006, 16.009, 16.013, 16.098 **F&N:** see Chapter 2, 3.458, 4.29, 4.36, 5.31, 6.242, 7.09, 7.38, 7.48, 8.103, 8.225, 8.233, 8.235, 8.250, 8.253, 8.254, 8.316, 8.317, 8.352, 8.353, 8.358, 8.446, 8.482, 8.557, 9.12, 9.19, 11.189, 11.190, 12.230, 14.81, 15.05, 15.14, 15.15, 15.41, 15.156, 15.179, 15.242, 15.243, 15.314, 16.176
Arts 4–6: B&C: 3.003
Arts 7–10: B&C: 1.068, 13.090 **F&N:** 2.24, 2.96
Arts 9–11: F&N: 17.459, 17.467, 17.469
Arts 11–14: F&N: 2.154
Arts 11–16: F&N: 8.429
Arts 17–22: B&C: 13.033, 15.031
Arts 18–21: F&N: 2.96, 8.249
Arts 20–22: F&N: 8.430
Arts 36–38: B&C: 12.163
Arts 36–43: F&N: 8.2542
Chap III: B&C: 1.068, 3.007, 13.002 **F&N:** 2.215, 2.229, 2.231, 5.338
Chap IV: B&C: 15.002 **F&N:** 2.202, 8.429
Chap V: B&C: 1.068
Chap VII: F&N: 8.300
Recitals 1–4: B&C: 3.003

THE COUNCIL OF THE EUROPEAN UNION,

Having regard to the Treaty [on the Functioning of the European Union], and in particular Article [103] thereof,

Having regard to the proposal from the Commission,[1]

Having regard to the opinion of the European Parliament,[2]

Having regard to the opinion of the European Economic and Social Committee,[3]

Notes
[1] OJ C 365 E, 19.12.2000, p.284.
[2] OJ C 72 E, 21.3.2002, p.305.
[3] OJ C 155, 29.5.2001, p.73.

Commentary
Preamble: F&N: 8.259, 8.316, 8.446

Whereas:

(1) In order to establish a system which ensures that competition in the common market is not distorted, Articles [101] and [102] of the Treaty must be applied effectively and uniformly in the Community. Council Regulation No 17 of 6 February 1962, First Regulation implementing Articles [101] and [102][1] of the Treaty,[2] has allowed a Community competition policy to develop that has helped to disseminate a competition culture within the Community. In the light of experience, however, that Regulation should now be replaced by legislation designed to meet the challenges of an integrated market and a future enlargement of the Community.

Notes
[1] The title of Regulation No 17 has been adjusted to take account of the renumbering of the Articles of the EC Treaty, in accordance with Article 12 of the Treaty of Amsterdam; the original reference was to Articles 85 and 86 of the Treaty. [Ed note: the title has subsequently been adjusted to take account of the renumbering introduced by Article 5 of the Treaty of Lisbon. See the Note on the Lisbon Treaty at p.xvii.]
[2] OJ 13, 21.2.1962, p. 204/62. Regulation as last amended by Regulation (EC) No 1216/1999 (OJ L 148, 15.6.1999, p. 5).

(2) In particular, there is a need to rethink the arrangements for applying the exception from the prohibition on agreements, which restrict competition, laid down in Article [101](3) of the Treaty. Under Article [103](2)(b) of the Treaty, account must be taken in this regard of the need to ensure effective supervision, on the one hand, and to simplify administration to the greatest possible extent, on the other.

(3) The centralised scheme set up by Regulation No 17 no longer secures a balance between those two objectives. It hampers application of the Community competition rules by the courts and competition authorities of the Member States, and the system of notification it involves prevents the Commission from concentrating its resources on curbing the most serious infringements. It also imposes considerable costs on undertakings.

Commentary
Recital 3: F&N: 2.92

(4) The present system should therefore be replaced by a directly applicable exception system in which the competition authorities and courts of the Member States have the power to apply not only Article [101](1) and Article [102] of the Treaty, which have direct applicability by virtue of the case-law of the Court of Justice of the European Communities, but also Article [101](3) of the Treaty.

Commentary
Recital 4: B&C: 15.001 F&N: 2.92

(5) In order to ensure an effective enforcement of the Community competition rules and at the same time the respect of fundamental rights of defence, this Regulation should regulate the burden of proof under Articles [101] and [102] of the Treaty. It should be for the party or the authority alleging an infringement of Article [101](1) and Article [102] of the Treaty to prove the existence thereof to the required legal standard. It should be for the undertaking or association of undertakings invoking the benefit of a defence against a finding of an infringement to demonstrate to the required legal standard that the conditions for applying such defence are satisfied. This Regulation affects neither national rules on the standard of proof nor obligations of competition authorities and courts of the Member States to ascertain the relevant facts

of a case, provided that such rules and obligations are compatible with general principles of Community law.

Commentary
Recital 5: B&C: 16.009 F&N: 2.25, 2.26, 2.28, 2.29, 8.466

(6) In order to ensure that the Community competition rules are applied effectively, the competition authorities of the Member States should be associated more closely with their application. To this end, they should be empowered to apply Community law.

Commentary
Recital 6: F&N: 2.154

(7) National courts have an essential part to play in applying the Community competition rules. When deciding disputes between private individuals, they protect the subjective rights under Community law, for example by awarding damages to the victims of infringements. The role of the national courts here complements that of the competition authorities of the Member States. They should therefore be allowed to apply Articles [101] and [102] of the Treaty in full.

Commentary
Recital 7: B&C: 16.002, 16.006 F&N: 2.154

(8) In order to ensure the effective enforcement of the Community competition rules and the proper functioning of the cooperation mechanisms contained in this Regulation, it is necessary to oblige the competition authorities and courts of the Member States to also apply Articles [101] and [102] of the Treaty where they apply national competition law to agreements and practices which may affect trade between Member States. In order to create a level playing field for agreements, decisions by associations of undertakings and concerted practices within the internal market, it is also necessary to determine pursuant to Article [103](2)(e) of the Treaty the relationship between national laws and Community competition law. To that effect it is necessary to provide that the application of national competition laws to agreements, decisions or concerted practices within the meaning of Article [101](1) of the Treaty may not lead to the prohibition of such agreements, decisions and concerted practices if they are not also prohibited under Community competition law. The notions of agreements, decisions and concerted practices are autonomous concepts of Community competition law covering the coordination of behaviour of undertakings on the market as interpreted by the Community Courts. Member States should not under this Regulation be precluded from adopting and applying on their territory stricter national competition laws which prohibit or impose sanctions on unilateral conduct engaged in by undertakings. These stricter national laws may include provisions which prohibit or impose sanctions on abusive behaviour toward economically dependent undertakings. Furthermore, this Regulation does not apply to national laws which impose criminal sanctions on natural persons except to the extent that such sanctions are the means whereby competition rules applying to undertakings are enforced.

Commentary
Recital 8: B&C: 15.024, 15.057, 15.058, 15.059, 15.060, 15.062 F&N: 2.22, 2.40, 2.45, 2.46, 2.72, 2.73, 2.74, 2.75, 2.76

(9) Articles [101] and [102] of the Treaty have as their objective the protection of competition on the market. This Regulation, which is adopted for the implementation of these Treaty provisions, does not preclude Member States from implementing on their territory national legislation, which protects other legitimate interests provided that such legislation is compatible with general principles and other provisions of Community law. In so far as such national legislation pursues predominantly an objective different from that of protecting competition on the market, the competition authorities and courts of the Member States may apply such legislation on their territory. Accordingly, Member States may under this Regulation implement

on their territory national legislation that prohibits or imposes sanctions on acts of unfair trading practice, be they unilateral or contractual. Such legislation pursues a specific objective, irrespective of the actual or presumed effects of such acts on competition on the market. This is particularly the case of legislation which prohibits undertakings from imposing on their trading partners, obtaining or attempting to obtain from them terms and conditions that are unjustified, disproportionate or without consideration.

Commentary
Recital 9: B&C: 2.086, 15.060 F&N: 2.46, 2.60, 2.62, 2.63, 2.72, 3.452, 12.63

(10)   Regulations such as 19/65/EEC,[1] (EEC) No 2821/71,[2] (EEC) No 3976/87,[3] (EEC) No 1534/91,[4] or (EEC) No 479/92[5] empower the Commission to apply Article [101](3) of the Treaty by Regulation to certain categories of agreements, decisions by associations of undertakings and concerted practices. In the areas defined by such Regulations, the Commission has adopted and may continue to adopt so called "block" exemption Regulations by which it declares Article [101](1) of the Treaty inapplicable to categories of agreements, decisions and concerted practices. Where agreements, decisions and concerted practices to which such Regulations apply nonetheless have effects that are incompatible with Article [101](3) of the Treaty, the Commission and the competition authorities of the Member States should have the power to withdraw in a particular case the benefit of the block exemption Regulation.

Notes

[1] Council Regulation No 19/65/EEC of 2 March 1965 on the application of Article [101](3) (the titles of the Regulations have been adjusted to take account of the renumbering of the Articles of the EC Treaty, in accordance with Article 12 of the Treaty of Amsterdam; the original reference was to Article 85(3) of the Treaty) of the Treaty to certain categories of agreements and concerted practices (OJ 36, 6.3.1965, p.533). Regulation as last amended by Regulation (EC) No 1215/1999 (OJ L 148, 15.6.1999, p.1). [Ed note: the title has subsequently been adjusted to take account of the renumbering introduced by Article 5 of the Treaty of Lisbon. See the Note on the Lisbon Treaty at p.xvii.]

[2] Council Regulation (EEC) No 2821/71 of 20 December 1971 on the application of Article [101](3) (the titles of the Regulations have been adjusted to take account of the renumbering of the Articles of the EC Treaty, in accordance with Article 12 of the Treaty of Amsterdam; the original reference was to Article 85(3) of the Treaty) of the Treaty to categories of agreements, decisions and concerted practices (OJ L 285, 29.12.1971, p.46). Regulation as last amended by the Act of Accession of 1994. [Ed note: the title has subsequently been adjusted to take account of the renumbering introduced by Article 5 of the Treaty of Lisbon. See the Note on the Lisbon Treaty at p.xvii.]

[3] Council Regulation (EEC) No 3976/87 of 14 December 1987 on the application of Article [101](3) (the titles of the Regulations have been adjusted to take account of the renumbering of the Articles of the EC Treaty, in accordance with Article 12 of the Treaty of Amsterdam; the original reference was to Article 85(3) of the Treaty) of the Treaty to certain categories of agreements and concerted practices in the air transport sector (OJ L 374, 31.12.1987, p.9). Regulation as last amended by the Act of Accession of 1994. [Ed note: the title has subsequently been adjusted to take account of the renumbering introduced by Article 5 of the Treaty of Lisbon. See the Note on the Lisbon Treaty at p.xvii.]

[4] Council Regulation (EEC) No 1534/91 of 31 May 1991 on the application of Article [101](3) (the titles of the Regulations have been adjusted to take account of the renumbering of the Articles of the EC Treaty, in accordance with Article 12 of the Treaty of Amsterdam; the original reference was to Article 85(3) of the Treaty) of the Treaty to certain categories of agreements, decisions and concerted practices in the insurance sector (OJ L 143, 7.6.1991, p.1). [Ed note: the title has subsequently been adjusted to take account of the renumbering introduced by Article 5 of the Treaty of Lisbon. See the Note on the Lisbon Treaty at p.xvii.]

[5] Council Regulation (EEC) No 479/92 of 25 February 1992 on the application of Article [101](3) (the titles of the Regulations have been adjusted to take account of the renumbering of the Articles of the EC Treaty, in accordance with Article 12 of the Treaty of Amsterdam; the original reference was to Article 85(3) of the Treaty) of the Treaty to certain categories of agreements, decisions and concerted practices between liner shipping companies (Consortia) (OJ L 55, 29.2.1992, p.3). Regulation amended by the Act of Accession of 1994. [Ed note: the title has subsequently been adjusted to take account of the renumbering introduced by Article 5 of the Treaty of Lisbon. See the Note on the Lisbon Treaty at p.xvii.]

Commentary
Recital 10: F&N: 7.272

(11)   For it to ensure that the provisions of the Treaty are applied, the Commission should be able to address decisions to undertakings or associations of undertakings for the purpose of bringing to an end infringements of Articles [101] and [102] of the Treaty. Provided there is a legitimate interest in doing so, the Commission should also be able to adopt decisions which

find that an infringement has been committed in the past even if it does not impose a fine. This Regulation should also make explicit provision for the Commission's power to adopt decisions ordering interim measures, which has been acknowledged by the Court of Justice.

Commentary
Recital 11: **B&C:** 13.085 **F&N:** 5.362

(12) This Regulation should make explicit provision for the Commission's power to impose any remedy, whether behavioural or structural, which is necessary to bring the infringement effectively to an end, having regard to the principle of proportionality. Structural remedies should only be imposed either where there is no equally effective behavioural remedy or where any equally effective behavioural remedy would be more burdensome for the undertaking concerned than the structural remedy. Changes to the structure of an undertaking as it existed before the infringement was committed would only be proportionate where there is a substantial risk of a lasting or repeated infringement that derives from the very structure of the undertaking.

Commentary
Recital 12: **F&N:** 2.110, 2.111, 4.49, 5.454, 12.172, 12.229

(13) Where, in the course of proceedings which might lead to an agreement or practice being prohibited, undertakings offer the Commission commitments such as to meet its concerns, the Commission should be able to adopt decisions which make those commitments binding on the undertakings concerned. Commitment decisions should find that there are no longer grounds for action by the Commission without concluding whether or not there has been or still is an infringement. Commitment decisions are without prejudice to the powers of competition authorities and courts of the Member States to make such a finding and decide upon the case. Commitment decisions are not appropriate in cases where the Commission intends to impose a fine.

Commentary
Recital 13: **B&C:** 13.102, 15.071 **F&N:** 2.122, 2.127, 2.153, 5.458, 8.715, 12.235

(14) In exceptional cases where the public interest of the Community so requires, it may also be expedient for the Commission to adopt a decision of a declaratory nature finding that the prohibition in Article [101] or Article [102] of the Treaty does not apply, with a view to clarifying the law and ensuring its consistent application throughout the Community, in particular with regard to new types of agreements or practices that have not been settled in the existing case-law and administrative practice.

Commentary
Recital 14: **B&C:** 3.007, 13.110 **F&N:** 2.146, 2.147, 2.151

(15) The Commission and the competition authorities of the Member States should form together a network of public authorities applying the Community competition rules in close cooperation. For that purpose it is necessary to set up arrangements for information and consultation. Further modalities for the cooperation within the network will be laid down and revised by the Commission, in close cooperation with the Member States.

Commentary
Recital 15: **B&C:** 15.002, 15.005 **F&N:** 2.154, 2.211

(16) Notwithstanding any national provision to the contrary, the exchange of information and the use of such information in evidence should be allowed between the members of the network even where the information is confidential. This information may be used for the application of Articles [101] and [102] of the Treaty as well as for the parallel application of national competition law, provided that the latter application relates to the same case and does not

lead to a different outcome. When the information exchanged is used by the receiving authority to impose sanctions on undertakings, there should be no other limit to the use of the information than the obligation to use it for the purpose for which it was collected given the fact that the sanctions imposed on undertakings are of the same type in all systems. The rights of defence enjoyed by undertakings in the various systems can be considered as sufficiently equivalent. However, as regards natural persons, they may be subject to substantially different types of sanctions across the various systems. Where that is the case, it is necessary to ensure that information can only be used if it has been collected in a way which respects the same level of protection of the rights of defence of natural persons as provided for under the national rules of the receiving authority.

Commentary
Recital 16: **B&C**: 15.028, 15.033, 15.035 **F&N**: 2.180

(17) If the competition rules are to be applied consistently and, at the same time, the network is to be managed in the best possible way, it is essential to retain the rule that the competition authorities of the Member States are automatically relieved of their competence if the Commission initiates its own proceedings. Where a competition authority of a Member State is already acting on a case and the Commission intends to initiate proceedings, it should endeavour to do so as soon as possible. Before initiating proceedings, the Commission should consult the national authority concerned.

Commentary
Recital 17: **F&N**: 2.230, 2.249, 2.277, 5.1029

(18) To ensure that cases are dealt with by the most appropriate authorities within the network, a general provision should be laid down allowing a competition authority to suspend or close a case on the ground that another authority is dealing with it or has already dealt with it, the objective being that each case should be handled by a single authority. This provision should not prevent the Commission from rejecting a complaint for lack of Community interest, as the case-law of the Court of Justice has acknowledged it may do, even if no other competition authority has indicated its intention of dealing with the case.

Commentary
Recital 18: **B&C**: 15.023 **F&N**: 2.11, 2.157, 2.159

(19) The Advisory Committee on Restrictive Practices and Dominant Positions set up by Regulation No 17 has functioned in a very satisfactory manner. It will fit well into the new system of decentralised application. It is necessary, therefore, to build upon the rules laid down by Regulation No 17, while improving the effectiveness of the organisational arrangements. To this end, it would be expedient to allow opinions to be delivered by written procedure. The Advisory Committee should also be able to act as a forum for discussing cases that are being handled by the competition authorities of the Member States, so as to help safeguard the consistent application of the Community competition rules.

Commentary
Recital 19: **F&N**: 5.497

(20) The Advisory Committee should be composed of representatives of the competition authorities of the Member States. For meetings in which general issues are being discussed, Member States should be able to appoint an additional representative. This is without prejudice to members of the Committee being assisted by other experts from the Member States.

(21) Consistency in the application of the competition rules also requires that arrangements be established for cooperation between the courts of the Member States and the Commission. This is relevant for all courts of the Member States that apply Articles [101] and [102] of the Treaty, whether applying these rules in lawsuits between private parties, acting as public enforcers or as review courts. In particular, national courts should be able to ask the

Commission for information or for its opinion on points concerning the application of Community competition law. The Commission and the competition authorities of the Member States should also be able to submit written or oral observations to courts called upon to apply Article [101] or Article [102] of the Treaty. These observations should be submitted within the framework of national procedural rules and practices including those safeguarding the rights of the parties. Steps should therefore be taken to ensure that the Commission and the competition authorities of the Member States are kept sufficiently well informed of proceedings before national courts.

Commentary
Recital 21: F&N: 2.289

(22) In order to ensure compliance with the principles of legal certainty and the uniform application of the Community competition rules in a system of parallel powers, conflicting decisions must be avoided. It is therefore necessary to clarify, in accordance with the case-law of the Court of Justice, the effects of Commission decisions and proceedings on courts and competition authorities of the Member States. Commitment decisions adopted by the Commission do not affect the power of the courts and the competition authorities of the Member States to apply Articles [101] and [102] of the Treaty.

Commentary
Recital 22: B&C: 15.063, 15.071

(23) The Commission should be empowered throughout the Community to require such information to be supplied as is necessary to detect any agreement, decision or concerted practice prohibited by Article [101] of the Treaty or any abuse of a dominant position prohibited by Article [102] of the Treaty. When complying with a decision of the Commission, undertakings cannot be forced to admit that they have committed an infringement, but they are in any event obliged to answer factual questions and to provide documents, even if this information may be used to establish against them or against another undertaking the existence of an infringement.

Commentary
Recital 23: F&N: 8.259, 8.475

(24) The Commission should also be empowered to undertake such inspections as are necessary to detect any agreement, decision or concerted practice prohibited by Article [101] of the Treaty or any abuse of a dominant position prohibited by Article [102] of the Treaty. The competition authorities of the Member States should cooperate actively in the exercise of these powers.

Commentary
Recital 24: F&N: 8.322, 8.403

(25) The detection of infringements of the competition rules is growing ever more difficult, and, in order to protect competition effectively, the Commission's powers of investigation need to be supplemented. The Commission should in particular be empowered to interview any persons who may be in possession of useful information and to record the statements made. In the course of an inspection, officials authorised by the Commission should be empowered to affix seals for the period of time necessary for the inspection. Seals should normally not be affixed for more than 72 hours. Officials authorised by the Commission should also be empowered to ask for any information relevant to the subject matter and purpose of the inspection.

Commentary
Recital 25: F&N: 8.316

(26) Experience has shown that there are cases where business records are kept in the homes of directors or other people working for an undertaking. In order to safeguard the effectiveness of inspections, therefore, officials and other persons authorised by the Commission should be empowered to enter any premises where business records may be kept, including private homes. However, the exercise of this latter power should be subject to the authorisation of the judicial authority.

Commentary
Recital 26: B&C: 13.023 F&N: 8.412

(27) Without prejudice to the case-law of the Court of Justice, it is useful to set out the scope of the control that the national judicial authority may carry out when it authorises, as foreseen by national law including as a precautionary measure, assistance from law enforcement authorities in order to overcome possible opposition on the part of the undertaking or the execution of the decision to carry out inspections in non-business premises. It results from the case-law that the national judicial authority may in particular ask the Commission for further information which it needs to carry out its control and in the absence of which it could refuse the authorisation. The case-law also confirms the competence of the national courts to control the application of national rules governing the implementation of coercive measures.

(28) In order to help the competition authorities of the Member States to apply Articles [101] and [102] of the Treaty effectively, it is expedient to enable them to assist one another by carrying out inspections and other fact-finding measures.

Commentary
Recital 28: F&N: 2.160

(29) Compliance with Articles [101] and [102] of the Treaty and the fulfilment of the obligations imposed on undertakings and associations of undertakings under this Regulation should be enforceable by means of fines and periodic penalty payments. To that end, appropriate levels of fine should also be laid down for infringements of the procedural rules.

(30) In order to ensure effective recovery of fines imposed on associations of undertakings for infringements that they have committed, it is necessary to lay down the conditions on which the Commission may require payment of the fine from the members of the association where the association is not solvent. In doing so, the Commission should have regard to the relative size of the undertakings belonging to the association and in particular to the situation of small and medium-sized enterprises. Payment of the fine by one or several members of an association is without prejudice to rules of national law that provide for recovery of the amount paid from other members of the association.

(31) The rules on periods of limitation for the imposition of fines and periodic penalty payments were laid down in Council Regulation (EEC) No 2988/74,[1] which also concerns penalties in the field of transport. In a system of parallel powers, the acts, which may interrupt a limitation period, should include procedural steps taken independently by the competition authority of a Member State. To clarify the legal framework, Regulation (EEC) No 2988/74 should therefore be amended to prevent it applying to matters covered by this Regulation, and this Regulation should include provisions on periods of limitation.

Notes

[1] Council Regulation (EEC) No 2988/74 of 26 November 1974 concerning limitation periods in proceedings and the enforcement of sanctions under the rules of the European Economic Community relating to transport and competition (OJ L 319, 29.11.1974, p.1).

(32) The undertakings concerned should be accorded the right to be heard by the Commission, third parties whose interests may be affected by a decision should be given the opportunity of submitting their observations beforehand, and the decisions taken should be widely

publicised. While ensuring the rights of defence of the undertakings concerned, in particular, the right of access to the file, it is essential that business secrets be protected. The confidentiality of information exchanged in the network should likewise be safeguarded.

(33) Since all decisions taken by the Commission under this Regulation are subject to review by the Court of Justice in accordance with the Treaty, the Court of Justice should, in accordance with Article [261] thereof be given unlimited jurisdiction in respect of decisions by which the Commission imposes fines or periodic penalty payments.

(34) The principles laid down in Articles [101] and [102] of the Treaty, as they have been applied by Regulation No 17, have given a central role to the Community bodies. This central role should be retained, whilst associating the Member States more closely with the application of the Community competition rules. In accordance with the principles of subsidiarity and proportionality as set out in [Article 5 of the Treaty on European Union], this Regulation does not go beyond what is necessary in order to achieve its objective, which is to allow the Community competition rules to be applied effectively.

(35) In order to attain a proper enforcement of Community competition law, Member States should designate and empower authorities to apply Articles [101] and [102] of the Treaty as public enforcers. They should be able to designate administrative as well as judicial authorities to carry out the various functions conferred upon competition authorities in this Regulation. This Regulation recognises the wide variation which exists in the public enforcement systems of Member States. The effects of Article 11(6) of this Regulation should apply to all competition authorities. As an exception to this general rule, where a prosecuting authority brings a case before a separate judicial authority, Article 11(6) should apply to the prosecuting authority subject to the conditions in Article 35(4) of this Regulation. Where these conditions are not fulfilled, the general rule should apply. In any case, Article 11(6) should not apply to courts insofar as they are acting as review courts.

Commentary
Recital 35: B&C: 15.020 **F&N:** 8.360

(36) As the case-law has made it clear that the competition rules apply to transport, that sector should be made subject to the procedural provisions of this Regulation. Council Regulation No 141 of 26 November 1962 exempting transport from the application of Regulation No 17[1] should therefore be repealed and Regulations (EEC) No 1017/68,[2] (EEC) No 4056/86[3] and (EEC) No 3975/87[4] should be amended in order to delete the specific procedural provisions they contain.

Notes
[1] OJ 124, 28.11.1962, p.2751/62; Regulation as last amended by Regulation No 1002/67/EEC (OJ 306, 16.12.1967, p.1).
[2] Council Regulation (EEC) No 1017/68 of 19 July 1968 applying rules of competition to transport by rail, road and inland waterway (OJ L 175, 23.7.1968, p.1). Regulation as last amended by the Act of Accession of 1994.
[3] Council Regulation (EEC) No 4056/86 of 22 December 1986 laying down detailed rules for the application of Articles [101] and [102] (the title of the Regulation has been adjusted to take account of the renumbering of the Articles of the EC Treaty, in accordance with Article 12 of the Treaty of Amsterdam; the original reference was to Articles 85 and 86 of the Treaty) of the Treaty to maritime transport (OJ L 378, 31.12.1986, p.4). Regulation as last amended by the Act of Accession of 1994. [Ed note: the title has subsequently been adjusted to take account of the renumbering introduced by Article 5 of the Treaty of Lisbon. See the Note on the Lisbon Treaty at p.xvii.]
[4] Council Regulation (EEC) No 3975/87 of 14 December 1987 laying down the procedure for the application of the rules on competition to undertakings in the air transport sector (OJ L 374, 31.12.1987, p.1). Regulation as last amended by Regulation (EEC) No 2410/92 (OJ L 240, 24.8.1992, p.18).

Commentary
Recital 36: F&N: 8.252

(37) This Regulation respects the fundamental rights and observes the principles recognised in particular by the Charter of Fundamental Rights of the European Union. Accordingly, this Regulation should be interpreted and applied with respect to those rights and principles.

Commentary
Recital 37: **B&C:** 13.006, 14.104 **F&N:** 8.255

---

(38) Legal certainty for undertakings operating under the Community competition rules contributes to the promotion of innovation and investment. Where cases give rise to genuine uncertainty because they present novel or unresolved questions for the application of these rules, individual undertakings may wish to seek informal guidance from the Commission. This Regulation is without prejudice to the ability of the Commission to issue such informal guidance,

---

Commentary
Recital 38: **B&C:** 13.004, 15.072

HAS ADOPTED THIS REGULATION:

CHAPTER I
PRINCIPLES

Article 1
Application of Articles [101] and [102] of the Treaty

1. Agreements, decisions and concerted practices caught by Article [101](1) of the Treaty which do not satisfy the conditions of Article [101](3) of the Treaty shall be prohibited, no prior decision to that effect being required.

2. Agreements, decisions and concerted practices caught by Article [101](1) of the Treaty which satisfy the conditions of Article [101](3) of the Treaty shall not be prohibited, no prior decision to that effect being required.

3. The abuse of a dominant position referred to in Article [102] of the Treaty shall be prohibited, no prior decision to that effect being required.

Commentary
Art 1: **F&N:** 2.23, 2.57, 2.77
Art 1(1): **B&C:** 2.002 **F&N:** 2.22, 2.45, 2.93
Art 1(2): **B&C:** 3.003, 16.005 **F&N:** 2.03, 2.22, 3.445
Art 1(3): **F&N:** 2.22

Article 2
Burden of proof

In any national or Community proceedings for the application of Articles [101] and [102] of the Treaty, the burden of proving an infringement of Article [101](1) or of Article [102] of the Treaty shall rest on the party or the authority alleging the infringement. The undertaking or association of undertakings claiming the benefit of Article [101](3) of the Treaty shall bear the burden of proving that the conditions of that paragraph are fulfilled.

Commentary
Art 2: **B&C:** 1.067, 2.108, 2.150, 3.014, 3.077, 13.054, 13.138 **F&N:** 2.26, 2.27, 2.28, 2.252, 3.449, 4.15, 5.403, 5.410, 8.446, 8.466, 10.135, 15.95
Art 2(3): **F&N:** 5.403

Article 3
Relationship between Articles [101] and [102] of the Treaty and national competition laws

1. Where the competition authorities of the Member States or national courts apply national competition law to agreements, decisions by associations of undertakings or concerted practices within the meaning of Article [101](1) of the Treaty which may affect trade between Member States within the meaning of that provision, they shall also apply Article [101] of the Treaty to such agreements,

decisions or concerted practices. Where the competition authorities of the Member States or national courts apply national competition law to any abuse prohibited by Article [102] of the Treaty, they shall also apply Article [102] of the Treaty.

2. The application of national competition law may not lead to the prohibition of agreements, decisions by associations of undertakings or concerted practices which may affect trade between Member States but which do not restrict competition within the meaning of Article [101](1) of the Treaty, or which fulfil the conditions of Article [101](3) of the Treaty or which are covered by a Regulation for the application of Article [101](3) of the Treaty. Member States shall not under this Regulation be precluded from adopting and applying on their territory stricter national laws which prohibit or sanction unilateral conduct engaged in by undertakings.

3. Without prejudice to general principles and other provisions of Community law, paragraphs 1 and 2 do not apply when the competition authorities and the courts of the Member States apply national merger control laws nor do they preclude the application of provisions of national law that predominantly pursue an objective different from that pursued by Articles [101] and [102] of the Treaty.

Commentary
Art 3: B&C: 1.067, 1.070, 5.036, 15.024, 15.055, 15.060, 15.061, 15.124 **F&N:** 2.31, 2.32, 2.44, 2.52, 2.56, 2.57, 2.59, 2.61, 2.64, 2.65, 2.67, 2.68, 2.69, 2.70, 2.71, 2.72, 2.73, 2.77, 2.87, 2.183, 2.184, 2.230, 2.281, 3.387, 3.391, 5.410, 8.234, 8.243
Art 3(1): B&C: 1.022, 1.070, 1.121, 15.004, 15.019, 15.057 **F&N:** 2.05, 2.32, 2.33, 2.34, 2.35, 2.36, 2.37, 2.39, 2.40, 2.41, 2.42, 2.44, 2.48, 2.52, 2.53, 2.54, 2.58, 2.70, 2.74, 2.93, 2.94, 2.253, 3.386, 5.523, 8.429, 17.411
Art 3(2): B&C: 1.121, 6.006, 15.004, 15.019, 15.034, 15.058, 15.059 **F&N:** 2.32, 2.38, 2.44, 2.45, 2.46, 2.47, 2.48, 2.51, 2.52, 2.53, 2.54, 2.56, 2.57, 2.58, 2.59, 2.70, 2.93, 2.184, 2.281, 3.386, 3.405
Art 3(3): B&C: 15.019, 15.060 **F&N:** 2.57, 2.58, 2.60, 2.62, 2.69, 2.70, 2.71, 2.73, 2.76

Chapter II
Powers

Article 4
Powers of the Commission

For the purpose of applying Articles [101] and [102] of the Treaty, the Commission shall have the powers provided for by this Regulation.

Commentary
Art 4: F&N: 2.96, 2.156, 17.419, 17.508
Art 4(1): F&N: 5.404, 8.368
Art 4(2): F&N: 5.380, 5.403, 8.368

Article 5
Powers of the competition authorities of the Member States

The competition authorities of the Member States shall have the power to apply Articles [101] and [102] of the Treaty in individual cases. For this purpose, acting on their own initiative or on a complaint, they may take the following decisions:

— requiring that an infringement be brought to an end,
— ordering interim measures,
— accepting commitments,
— imposing fines, periodic penalty payments or any other penalty provided for in their national law.

Where on the basis of the information in their possession the conditions for prohibition are not met they may likewise decide that there are no grounds for action on their part.

Commentary
Art 5: B&C: 1.070, 3.008, 15.010, 15.020, 15.053, 15.057, 16.002, 16.005 **F&N:** 2.05, 2.23, 2.24, 2.70, 2.77, 2.78, 2.83, 2.84, 2.85, 2.87, 2.88, 2.89, 2.91, 2.92, 2.94, 2.156, 2.184, 2.187, 2.219, 2.234, 2.235, 2.242, 2.282, 3.468, 5.411

Art 5(2): **F&N:** 5.414, 5.526
Art 5(3): **F&N:** 5.413
Art 5(4): **F&N:** 2.277
Art 5(5): **F&N:** 5.416

Article 6
Powers of the national courts

National courts shall have the power to apply Articles [101] and [102] of the Treaty.

Commentary
Art 6: **B&C:** 16.005, 16.006 **F&N:** 2.05, 2.23, 2.252

CHAPTER III
COMMISSION DECISIONS

Article 7
Finding and termination of infringement

1. Where the Commission, acting on a complaint or on its own initiative, finds that there is an infringement of Article [101] or of Article [102] of the Treaty, it may by decision require the undertakings and associations of undertakings concerned to bring such infringement to an end. For this purpose, it may impose on them any behavioural or structural remedies which are proportionate to the infringement committed and necessary to bring the infringement effectively to an end. Structural remedies can only be imposed either where there is no equally effective behavioural remedy or where any equally effective behavioural remedy would be more burdensome for the undertaking concerned than the structural remedy. If the Commission has a legitimate interest in doing so, it may also find that an infringement has been committed in the past.

2. Those entitled to lodge a complaint for the purposes of paragraph 1 are natural or legal persons who can show a legitimate interest and Member States.

Commentary
Art 7: **B&C:** 1.033, 1.068, 13.043, 13.049, 13.052, 13.055, 13.057, 13.071, 13.085, 13.106, 13.115, 13.117, 13.120, 13.130, 14.133 **F&N:** 2.99, 2.107, 2.114, 2.117, 2.118, 2.122, 2.126, 2.127, 2.128, 2.129, 2.132, 2.134, 2.140, 2.144, 2.218, 3.471, 4.29, 4.48, 4.50, 4.51, 5.437, 8.446, 8.472, 8.592, 8.704, 8.715, 8.722, 12.169, 12.171, 12.229, 12.231, 12.235
Art 7(1): **B&C:** 2.049, 13.102, 13.111, 13.112, 13.117, 13.118 **F&N:** 2.100, 2.103, 2.107, 2.108, 2.109, 12.60, 12.175, 12.176, 12.177
Art 7(2): **B&C:** 13.041, 13.042, 13.043, 13.045, 13.074, 13.132 **F&N:** 2.114

Article 8
Interim measures

1. In cases of urgency due to the risk of serious and irreparable damage to competition, the Commission, acting on its own initiative may by decision, on the basis of a prima facie finding of infringement, order interim measures.

2. A decision under paragraph 1 shall apply for a specified period of time and may be renewed in so far this is necessary and appropriate.

Commentary
Art 8: **B&C:** 13.055, 13.071, 13.085, 13.104, 13.105, 13.106, 13.130, 16.059 **F&N:** 2.116, 2.117, 4.52, 8.296
Art 8(1): **F&N:** 2.116
Art 8(2): **F&N:** 2.116
Art 8(3): **F&N:** 8.297

Article 9
Commitments

1. Where the Commission intends to adopt a decision requiring that an infringement be brought to an end and the undertakings concerned offer commitments to meet the concerns expressed to them by the Commission in its preliminary assessment, the Commission may by decision make those commitments binding on the undertakings. Such a decision may be adopted for a specified period and shall conclude that there are no longer grounds for action by the Commission.

2. The Commission may, upon request or on its own initiative, reopen the proceedings:

    (a) where there has been a material change in any of the facts on which the decision was based;

    (b) where the undertakings concerned act contrary to their commitments; or

    (c) where the decision was based on incomplete, incorrect or misleading information provided by the parties.

Commentary

Art 9: B&C: 1.033, 1.068, 1.069, 3.007, 3.090, 4.042, 6.086, 6.107, 9.060, 10.034, 12.060, 13.001, 13.057, 13.100, 13.101, 13.103, 13.130, 14.133, 15.071, 15.074 **F&N:** 2.107, 2.118, 2.120, 2.121, 2.122, 2.123, 2.124, 2.126, 2.127, 2.128, 2.129, 2.130, 2.132, 2.133, 2.139, 2.140, 2.144, 2.145, 2.152, 2.153, 2.218, 2.268, 3.471, 4.53, 4.54, 4.55, 4.60, 4.61, 4.62, 4.64, 4.66, 4.795, 5.338, 5.340, 5.420, 5.441, 7.351, 8.296, 8.317, 8.715, 11.133, 11.143, 12.169, 12.231, 12.235, 12.236, 15.110
Art 9(1): B&C: 10.098, 12.103, 13.057, 13.102 **F&N:** 2.119, 2.122, 2.132, 2.135, 2.143, 4.54
Art 9(1)(b): F&N: 5.420
Art 9(2): B&C: 13.102, 13.103 **F&N:** 2.137, 2.138, 2.144, 15.112
Art 9(2)(a): F&N: 2.139
Art 9(2)(b): F&N: 2.140

Article 10
Finding of inapplicability

Where the Community public interest relating to the application of Articles [101] and [102] of the Treaty so requires, the Commission, acting on its own initiative, may by decision find that Article [101] of the Treaty is not applicable to an agreement, a decision by an association of undertakings or a concerted practice, either because the conditions of Article [101](1) of the Treaty are not fulfilled, or because the conditions of Article [101](3) of the Treaty are satisfied.

The Commission may likewise make such a finding with reference to Article [102] of the Treaty.

Commentary

Art 10: B&C: 1.068, 3.007, 13.001, 13.065, 15.069, 15.074 **F&N:** 2.57, 2.84, 2.145, 2.147, 2.148, 2.149, 2.150, 2.151, 2.152, 2.153, 2.219, 2.268

CHAPTER IV
COOPERATION

Article 11
Cooperation between the Commission and the competition authorities of the Member States

1. The Commission and the competition authorities of the Member States shall apply the Community competition rules in close cooperation.

2. The Commission shall transmit to the competition authorities of the Member States copies of the most important documents it has collected with a view to applying Articles 7, 8, 9, 10 and Article 29(1). At the request of the competition authority of a Member State, the Commission shall provide it with a copy of other existing documents necessary for the assessment of the case.

3. The competition authorities of the Member States shall, when acting under Article [101] or Article [102] of the Treaty, inform the Commission in writing before or without delay after commencing the first formal investigative measure. This information may also be made available to the competition authorities of the other Member States.

4. No later than 30 days before the adoption of a decision requiring that an infringement be brought to an end, accepting commitments or withdrawing the benefit of a block exemption Regulation, the competition authorities of the Member States shall inform the Commission. To that effect, they shall provide the Commission with a summary of the case, the envisaged decision or, in the absence thereof, any other document indicating the proposed course of action. This information may also be made available to the competition authorities of the other Member States. At the request of the Commission, the acting competition authority shall make available to the Commission other documents it holds which are necessary for the assessment of the case. The information supplied to the Commission may be made available to the competition authorities of the other Member States. National competition authorities may also exchange between themselves information necessary for the assessment of a case that they are dealing with under Article [101] or Article [102] of the Treaty.

5. The competition authorities of the Member States may consult the Commission on any case involving the application of Community law.

6. The initiation by the Commission of proceedings for the adoption of a decision under Chapter III shall relieve the competition authorities of the Member States of their competence to apply Articles [101] and [102] of the Treaty. If a competition authority of a Member State is already acting on a case, the Commission shall only initiate proceedings after consulting with that national competition authority.

Commentary
Art 11: **B&C:** 13.033, 13.074, 15.026, 15.036, 15.039, 16.043 **F&N:** 2.43, 2.170, 2.203, 5.47, 5.440, 5.458, 5.480, 8.236, 8.237
Art 11(1): **B&C:** 15.011 **F&N:** 2.161, 2.211
Art 11(1)(a): **F&N:** 5.345
Art 11(1)(b): **F&N:** 5.347
Art 11(1)(c): **F&N:** 5.356
Art 11(2): **B&C:** 14.123, 15.014, 15.037 **F&N:** 2.43, 2.157, 2.213, 8.237
Art 11(3): **B&C:** 15.014, 15.025, 15.037, 15.039 **F&N:** 2.43, 2.157, 2.212, 2.213, 2.239, 2.248, 8.237, 8.306
Art 11(4): **B&C:** 15.025 **F&N:** 2.05, 2.43, 2.53, 2.202, 2.212, 2.214, 2.215, 2.216, 2.218, 2.220, 2.221, 2.222, 2.224, 2.225, 2.226, 2.228, 2.230
Art 11(5): **B&C:** 15.041 **F&N:** 2.219
Art 11(6): **B&C:** 13.057, 13.162, 14.124, 15.006, 15.014, 15.017, 15.018, 15.019, 15.020, 15.022, 15.025 **F&N:** 2.43, 2.44, 2.53, 2.157, 2.212, 2.215, 2.222, 2.223, 2.229, 2.230, 2.231, 2.232, 2.234, 2.235, 2.236, 2.237, 2.238, 2.240, 2.241, 2.246, 2.248, 2.256, 2.264, 8.234, 8.243, 8.706

Article 12
Exchange of information

1. For the purpose of applying Articles [101] and [102] of the Treaty the Commission and the competition authorities of the Member States shall have the power to provide one another with and use in evidence any matter of fact or of law, including confidential information.

2. Information exchanged shall only be used in evidence for the purpose of applying Article [101] or Article [102] of the Treaty and in respect of the subject-matter for which it was collected by the transmitting authority. However, where national competition law is applied in the same case and in parallel to Community competition law and does not lead to a different outcome, information exchanged under this Article may also be used for the application of national competition law.

3. Information exchanged pursuant to paragraph 1 can only be used in evidence to impose sanctions on natural persons where:

— the law of the transmitting authority foresees sanctions of a similar kind in relation to an infringement of Article [101] or Article [102] of the Treaty or, in the absence thereof,

— the information has been collected in a way which respects the same level of protection of the rights of defence of natural persons as provided for under the national rules of the receiving authority. However, in this case, the information exchanged cannot be used by the receiving authority to impose custodial sanctions.

Commentary

Art 12: B&C: 13.033, 13.035, 13.074, 13.090, 14.123, 15.028, 15.029, 15.032, 15.033, 15.034, 15.035, 15.036, 15.038, 15.039, 16.043 **F&N:** 2.72, 2.160, 2.162, 2.163, 2.165, 2.166, 2.167, 2.168, 2.169, 2.173, 2.174, 2.177, 2.180, 2.181, 2.191, 2.203, 2.204, 2.282, 8.100, 8.238, 8.239, 8.240, 8.259, 8.320, 8.426, 8.430, 8.431, 8.446, 8.483, 12.10

Art 12(1): B&C: 15.028, 15.029, 15.033 **F&N:** 2.182, 2.184, 2.282, 5.395

Art 12(2): B&C: 13.035, 15.031, 15.032, 15.034 **F&N:** 2.42, 2.182, 2.183, 2.184, 2.185, 2.276, 2.278, 2.279, 2.280, 2.281, 8.483

Art 12(3): B&C: 13.035, 15.035 **F&N:** 2.177, 2.187, 2.189, 2.190, 2.191, 2.278, 2.282, 8.240, 8.367, 8.431

Article 13
Suspension or termination of proceedings

1. Where competition authorities of two or more Member States have received a complaint or are acting on their own initiative under Article [101] or Article [102] of the Treaty against the same agreement, decision of an association or practice, the fact that one authority is dealing with the case shall be sufficient grounds for the others to suspend the proceedings before them or to reject the complaint. The Commission may likewise reject a complaint on the ground that a competition authority of a Member State is dealing with the case.

2. Where a competition authority of a Member State or the Commission has received a complaint against an agreement, decision of an association or practice which has already been dealt with by another competition authority, it may reject it.

Commentary

Art 13: B&C: 13.045, 13.050, 15.014, 15.023 **F&N:** 2.115, 2.128, 2.156, 2.157, 2.158, 2.159, 5.459, 17.469

Art 13(1): B&C: 15.017 **F&N:** 2.158

Art 13(2): B&C: 15.023, **F&N:** 5.454, 5.457, 5.478

Art 13(3): F&N: 5.478

Article 14
Advisory Committee

1. The Commission shall consult an Advisory Committee on Restrictive Practices and Dominant Positions prior to the taking of any decision under Articles 7, 8, 9, 10, 23, Article 24(2) and Article 29(1).

2. For the discussion of individual cases, the Advisory Committee shall be composed of representatives of the competition authorities of the Member States. For meetings in which issues other than individual cases are being discussed, an additional Member State representative competent in competition matters may be appointed. Representatives may, if unable to attend, be replaced by other representatives.

3. The consultation may take place at a meeting convened and chaired by the Commission, held not earlier than 14 days after dispatch of the notice convening it, together with a summary of the case, an indication of the most important documents and a preliminary draft decision. In respect of decisions pursuant to Article 8, the meeting may be held seven days after the dispatch of the operative part of a draft decision. Where the Commission dispatches a notice convening the meeting which gives a shorter period of notice than those specified above, the meeting may take place on the proposed date in the absence of an objection by any Member State. The Advisory Committee shall deliver a written opinion on the Commission's preliminary draft decision. It may deliver an opinion even if some members are absent and are not represented. At the request of one or several members, the positions stated in the opinion shall be reasoned.

4. Consultation may also take place by written procedure. However, if any Member State so requests, the Commission shall convene a meeting. In case of written procedure, the Commission shall determine a time-limit of not less than 14 days within which the Member States are to put forward their observations for circulation to all other Member States. In case of decisions to be taken pursuant to Article 8, the time-limit of 14 days is replaced by seven days. Where the Commission determines

a time-limit for the written procedure which is shorter than those specified above, the proposed time-limit shall be applicable in the absence of an objection by any Member State.

5. The Commission shall take the utmost account of the opinion delivered by the Advisory Committee. It shall inform the Committee of the manner in which its opinion has been taken into account.

6. Where the Advisory Committee delivers a written opinion, this opinion shall be appended to the draft decision. If the Advisory Committee recommends publication of the opinion, the Commission shall carry out such publication taking into account the legitimate interest of undertakings in the protection of their business secrets.

7. At the request of a competition authority of a Member State, the Commission shall include on the agenda of the Advisory Committee cases that are being dealt with by a competition authority of a Member State under Article [101] or Article [102] of the Treaty. The Commission may also do so on its own initiative. In either case, the Commission shall inform the competition authority concerned.

A request may in particular be made by a competition authority of a Member State in respect of a case where the Commission intends to initiate proceedings with the effect of Article 11(6).

The Advisory Committee shall not issue opinions on cases dealt with by competition authorities of the Member States. The Advisory Committee may also discuss general issues of Community competition law.

Commentary
Art 14: **B&C:** 1.075, 8.005, 13.021, 13.033, 13.055, 13.134, 15.042 **F&N:** 2.203
Art 14(1): **B&C:** 13.017, 13.032, 13.088, 13.101, 13.106 **F&N:** 5.480
Art 14(2): **B&C:** 13.088 **F&N:** 5.480, 8.297
Art 14(3): **B&C:** 13.088
Art 14(4): **B&C:** 13.088
Art 14(5): **B&C:** 13.088
Art 14(6): **B&C:** 13.088 **F&N:** 2.202
Art 14(7): **F&N:** 2.250

Article 15
Cooperation with national courts

1. In proceedings for the application of Article [101] or Article [102] of the Treaty, courts of the Member States may ask the Commission to transmit to them information in its possession or its opinion on questions concerning the application of the Community competition rules.

2. Member States shall forward to the Commission a copy of any written judgment of national courts deciding on the application of Article [101] or Article [102] of the Treaty. Such copy shall be forwarded without delay after the full written judgment is notified to the parties.

3. Competition authorities of the Member States, acting on their own initiative, may submit written observations to the national courts of their Member State on issues relating to the application of Article [101] or Article [102] of the Treaty. With the permission of the court in question, they may also submit oral observations to the national courts of their Member State. Where the coherent application of Article [101] or Article [102] of the Treaty so requires, the Commission, acting on its own initiative, may submit written observations to courts of the Member States. With the permission of the court in question, it may also make oral observations.

For the purpose of the preparation of their observations only, the competition authorities of the Member States and the Commission may request the relevant court of the Member State to transmit or ensure the transmission to them of any documents necessary for the assessment of the case.

4. This Article is without prejudice to wider powers to make observations before courts conferred on competition authorities of the Member States under the law of their Member State.

Commentary
Art 15: B&C: 3.009, 13.033, 13.034, 13.102, 15.003, 15.036, 15.040, 15.047, 15.049, 15.053 F&N: 2.154, 2.203,
 2.252, 2.257, 2.268, 2.272, 2.273, 2.285, 5.480, 5.482, 5.485
Art 15(1): B&C: 1.072, 13.034, 15.0, 15.047, 15.050, 16.041, 16.042 F&N: 2.151, 2.274, 2.278, 2.280, 2.282,
 2.283, 8.235, 8.242, 14.137
Art 15(2): B&C: 1.072, 15.044 F&N: 2.263, 2.286
Art 15(3): B&C: 1.072, 1.143, 5.062, 7.120, 15.051, 15.054 F&N: 2.237, 2.285

Article 16
Uniform application of Community competition law

1. When national courts rule on agreements, decisions or practices under Article [101] or Article [102] of the Treaty which are already the subject of a Commission decision, they cannot take decisions running counter to the decision adopted by the Commission. They must also avoid giving decisions which would conflict with a decision contemplated by the Commission in proceedings it has initiated. To that effect, the national court may assess whether it is necessary to stay its proceedings. This obligation is without prejudice to the rights and obligations under Article [267] of the Treaty.

2. When competition authorities of the Member States rule on agreements, decisions or practices under Article [101] or Article [102] of the Treaty which are already the subject of a Commission decision, they cannot take decisions which would run counter to the decision adopted by the Commission.

Commentary
Art 16: B&C: 15.003, 15.004, 15.055, 15.063, 15.064, 15.067, 15.068, 15.069, 15.073, 15.074, 16.038, 16.091
F&N: 2.57, 2.98, 2.122, 2.126, 2.150, 2.151, 2.153, 2.233, 5.356, 5.458, 5.480
Art 16(1): B&C: 3.006, 3.007, 15.053, 15.065 F&N: 2.154, 2.264, 2.267, 5.458, 5.478
Art 16(2): B&C: 3.006, 3.007, 15.066 F&N: 2.154

Chapter V
Powers of Investigation

Article 17
Investigations into sectors of the economy and into types of agreements

1. Where the trend of trade between Member States, the rigidity of prices or other circumstances suggest that competition may be restricted or distorted within the common market, the Commission may conduct its inquiry into a particular sector of the economy or into a particular type of agreements across various sectors. In the course of that inquiry, the Commission may request the undertakings or associations of undertakings concerned to supply the information necessary for giving effect to Articles [101] and [102] of the Treaty and may carry out any inspections necessary for that purpose.

The Commission may in particular request the undertakings or associations of undertakings concerned to communicate to it all agreements, decisions and concerted practices.

The Commission may publish a report on the results of its inquiry into particular sectors of the economy or particular types of agreements across various sectors and invite comments from interested parties.

2. Articles 14, 18, 19, 20, 22, 23 and 24 shall apply *mutatis mutandis.*

Commentary
Art 17: B&C: 6.102, 12.090, 13.021 F&N: 2.48, 8.99, 12.12, 16.25
Art 17(1): B&C: 13.021 F&N: 5.459, 5.461, 8.99
Art 17(2): B&C: 13.021
Art 17(3): F&N: 5.462

Article 18
Requests for information

1. In order to carry out the duties assigned to it by this Regulation, the Commission may, by simple request or by decision, require undertakings and associations of undertakings to provide all necessary information.

2. When sending a simple request for information to an undertaking or association of undertakings, the Commission shall state the legal basis and the purpose of the request, specify what information is required and fix the time-limit within which the information is to be provided, and the penalties provided for in Article 23 for supplying incorrect or misleading information.

3. Where the Commission requires undertakings and associations of undertakings to supply information by decision, it shall state the legal basis and the purpose of the request, specify what information is required and fix the time-limit within which it is to be provided. It shall also indicate the penalties provided for in Article 23 and indicate or impose the penalties provided for in Article 24. It shall further indicate the right to have the decision reviewed by the Court of Justice.

4. The owners of the undertakings or their representatives and, in the case of legal persons, companies or firms, or associations having no legal personality, the persons authorised to represent them by law or by their constitution shall supply the information requested on behalf of the undertaking or the association of undertakings concerned. Lawyers duly authorised to act may supply the information on behalf of their clients. The latter shall remain fully responsible if the information supplied is incomplete, incorrect or misleading.

5. The Commission shall without delay forward a copy of the simple request or of the decision to the competition authority of the Member State in whose territory the seat of the undertaking or association of undertakings is situated and the competition authority of the Member State whose territory is affected.

6. At the request of the Commission the governments and competition authorities of the Member States shall provide the Commission with all necessary information to carry out the duties assigned to it by this Regulation.

Commentary
Art 18: B&C: 1.098, 13.011, 13.013, 13.016, 13.021, 13.033 F&N: 5.371, 8.268, 8.286, 8.289, 8.291, 8.298,
8.300, 8.302, 8.303, 8.304, 8.305, 8.306, 8.312, 8.313, 8.314, 8.317, 8.321, 8.365, 8.423
Art 18(1): B&C: 13.011, 13.015 F&N: 8.287, 8.288
Art 18(2): B&C: 13.012 F&N: 5.470, 8.263, 8.305, 8.306, 8.308, 8.309, 8.313, 8.321
Art 18(3): B&C: 13.011, 13.013, 15.026 F&N: 5.470, 8.263, 8.305, 8.306, 8.308, 8.313, 8.315
Art 18(4): B&C: 13.013 F&N: 8.284, 8.315
Art 18(5): B&C: 13.012, 13.013, 15.026
Art 18(6): B&C: 13.018, 13.074, 15.026 F&N: 2.162, 2.168

Article 19
Power to take statements

1. In order to carry out the duties assigned to it by this Regulation, the Commission may interview any natural or legal person who consents to be interviewed for the purpose of collecting information relating to the subject-matter of an investigation.

2. Where an interview pursuant to paragraph 1 is conducted in the premises of an undertaking, the Commission shall inform the competition authority of the Member State in whose territory the interview takes place. If so requested by the competition authority of that Member State, its officials may assist the officials and other accompanying persons authorised by the Commission to conduct the interview.

Commentary
Art 19: B&C: 13.021 F&N: 5.338, 8.104, 8.284, 8.316, 8.317, 8.318, 8.319, 8.320, 8.321, 8.362, 8.499, 8.508
Art 19(1): B&C: 13.019 F&N: 5.419, 5.1022
Art 19(2): B&C: 13.019, 15.026 F&N: 5.438, 5.498, 8.321

Article 20
The Commission's powers of inspection

1. In order to carry out the duties assigned to it by this Regulation, the Commission may conduct all necessary inspections of undertakings and associations of undertakings.

2. The officials and other accompanying persons authorised by the Commission to conduct an inspection are empowered:

(a) to enter any premises, land and means of transport of undertakings and associations of undertakings;

(b) to examine the books and other records related to the business, irrespective of the medium on which they are stored;

(c) to take or obtain in any form copies of or extracts from such books or records;

(d) to seal any business premises and books or records for the period and to the extent necessary for the inspection;

(e) to ask any representative or member of staff of the undertaking or association of undertakings for explanations on facts or documents relating to the subject-matter and purpose of the inspection and to record the answers.

3. The officials and other accompanying persons authorised by the Commission to conduct an inspection shall exercise their powers upon production of a written authorisation specifying the subject matter and purpose of the inspection and the penalties provided for in Article 23 in case the production of the required books or other records related to the business is incomplete or where the answers to questions asked under paragraph 2 of the present Article are incorrect or misleading. In good time before the inspection, the Commission shall give notice of the inspection to the competition authority of the Member State in whose territory it is to be conducted.

4. Undertakings and associations of undertakings are required to submit to inspections ordered by decision of the Commission. The decision shall specify the subject matter and purpose of the inspection, appoint the date on which it is to begin and indicate the penalties provided for in Articles 23 and 24 and the right to have the decision reviewed by the Court of Justice. The Commission shall take such decisions after consulting the competition authority of the Member State in whose territory the inspection is to be conducted.

5. Officials of as well as those authorised or appointed by the competition authority of the Member State in whose territory the inspection is to be conducted shall, at the request of that authority or of the Commission, actively assist the officials and other accompanying persons authorised by the Commission. To this end, they shall enjoy the powers specified in paragraph 2.

6. Where the officials and other accompanying persons authorised by the Commission find that an undertaking opposes an inspection ordered pursuant to this Article, the Member State concerned shall afford them the necessary assistance, requesting where appropriate the assistance of the police or of an equivalent enforcement authority, so as to enable them to conduct their inspection.

7. If the assistance provided for in paragraph 6 requires authorisation from a judicial authority according to national rules, such authorisation shall be applied for. Such authorisation may also be applied for as a precautionary measure.

8. Where authorisation as referred to in paragraph 7 is applied for, the national judicial authority shall control that the Commission decision is authentic and that the coercive measures envisaged are neither arbitrary nor excessive having regard to the subject matter of the inspection. In its control of the proportionality of the coercive measures, the national judicial authority may ask the Commission, directly or through the Member State competition authority, for detailed explanations in particular on the grounds the Commission has for suspecting infringement of Articles [101] and [102] of the Treaty, as well as on the seriousness of the suspected infringement and on the nature of the involvement of the undertaking concerned. However, the national judicial authority may not call into question the necessity for the inspection nor demand that it be provided with the information in the Commission's file. The lawfulness of the Commission decision shall be subject to review only by the Court of Justice.

Commentary

Art 20: B&C: 1.098, 13.010, 13.012, 13.021, 13.022, 13.025, 13.027, 13.090, 15.026, 15.027, 15.032 F&N: 2.170, 8.171, 8.252, 8.268, 8.278, 8.286, 8.301, 8.312, 8.322, 8.334, 8.386, 8.403, 8.411, 8.414, 8.415, 8.418, 8.423

Art 20(1): F&N: 8.287

Art 20(2): B&C: 13.027, 13.030 F&N: 8.291, 8.339, 8.342, 8.351, 8.411

Art 20(2)(a): F&N: 8.397

Art 20(2)(c): F&N: 8.397

Art 20(2)(d): F&N: 8.360

Art 20(2)(e): B&C: 13.019 F&N: 8.318, 8.362, 8.363, 8.508

Art 20(3): B&C: 13.022, 13.024 F&N: 8.324, 8.327, 8.328, 8.330, 8.338, 8.397, 8.398

Art 20(4): B&C: 13.022, 13.025, 13.032, 15.026 F&N: 8.134, 8.171, 8.250, 8.263, 8.324, 8.327, 8.329, 8.330, 8.331, 8.338, 8.388, 8.391, 8.393, 8.395, 8.397, 8.404, 8.409, 8.419, 8.425

Art 20(5): B&C: 13.027, 15.026 F&N: 8.375, 8.398, 8.403, 8.411, 8.424, 8.425

Art 20(6): B&C: 13.027, 15.026 F&N: 8.333, 8.343, 8.380, 8.388, 8.404, 8.406, 8.424, 8.425

Art 20(7): B&C: 13.027, 15.043 F&N: 8.333, 8.405

Art 20(8): B&C: 13.029, 15.026, 15.043 F&N: 8.331, 8.333, 8.399, 8.405, 8.420

Article 21
Inspection of other premises

1. If a reasonable suspicion exists that books or other records related to the business and to the subject-matter of the inspection, which may be relevant to prove a serious violation of Article [101] or Article [102] of the Treaty, are being kept in any other premises, land and means of transport, including the homes of directors, managers and other members of staff of the undertakings and associations of undertakings concerned, the Commission can by decision order an inspection to be conducted in such other premises, land and means of transport.

2. The decision shall specify the subject matter and purpose of the inspection, appoint the date on which it is to begin and indicate the right to have the decision reviewed by the Court of Justice. It shall in particular state the reasons that have led the Commission to conclude that a suspicion in the sense of paragraph 1 exists. The Commission shall take such decisions after consulting the competition authority of the Member State in whose territory the inspection is to be conducted.

3. A decision adopted pursuant to paragraph 1 cannot be executed without prior authorisation from the national judicial authority of the Member State concerned. The national judicial authority shall control that the Commission decision is authentic and that the coercive measures envisaged are neither arbitrary nor excessive having regard in particular to the seriousness of the suspected infringement, to the importance of the evidence sought, to the involvement of the undertaking concerned and to the reasonable likelihood that business books and records relating to the subject matter of the inspection are kept in the premises for which the authorisation is requested. The national judicial authority may ask the Commission, directly or through the Member State competition authority, for detailed explanations on those elements which are necessary to allow its control of the proportionality of the coercive measures envisaged.

However, the national judicial authority may not call into question the necessity for the inspection nor demand that it be provided with information in the Commission's file. The lawfulness of the Commission decision shall be subject to review only by the Court of Justice.

4. The officials and other accompanying persons authorised by the Commission to conduct an inspection ordered in accordance with paragraph 1 of this Article shall have the powers set out in Article 20(2)(a), (b) and (c). Article 20(5) and (6) shall apply *mutatis mutandis*.

Commentary

Art 21: B&C: 13.023, 13.030, 15.026, 15.032 F&N: 2.170, 8.78, 8.284, 8.286, 8.324, 8.412, 8.413, 8.414, 8.416, 8.417, 8.418, 8.419, 8.421, 8.423, 8.425, 8.426, 8.427

Art 21(1): B&C: 13.026 F&N: 8.419

Art 21(2): B&C: 13.026

Art 21(3): B&C: 13.026, 13.027, 13.029, 15.026 F&N: 8.417, 8.420, 8.423, 8.424

Art 21(4): B&C: 13.027, 13.030 F&N: 8.425

Article 22
Investigations by competition authorities of Member States

1. The competition authority of a Member State may in its own territory carry out any inspection or other fact-finding measure under its national law on behalf and for the account of the competition authority of another Member State in order to establish whether there has been an infringement of Article [101] or Article [102] of the Treaty. Any exchange and use of the information collected shall be carried out in accordance with Article 12.

2. At the request of the Commission, the competition authorities of the Member States shall undertake the inspections which the Commission considers to be necessary under Article 20(1) or which it has ordered by decision pursuant to Article 20(4). The officials of the competition authorities of the Member States who are responsible for conducting these inspections as well as those authorised or appointed by them shall exercise their powers in accordance with their national law.

If so requested by the Commission or by the competition authority of the Member State in whose territory the inspection is to be conducted, officials and other accompanying persons authorised by the Commission may assist the officials of the authority concerned.

Commentary
Art 22: B&C: 13.021, 15.027 F&N: 2.154, 2.162, 2.170, 2.181, 2.191, 2.202, 5.338, 8.326, 8.407, 8.408, 8.410, 8.424, 8.433
Art 22(1): B&C: 13.027, 15.027, 15.038 F&N: 2.160, 2.161, 2.162, 8.407, 8.409
Art 22(2): B&C: 13.027, 15.027 F&N: 2.160, 2.162, 8.325, 8.407, 8.408, 8.409, 8.410, 8.411

CHAPTER VI
PENALTIES

Article 23
Fines

1. The Commission may by decision impose on undertakings and associations of undertakings fines not exceeding 1% of the total turnover in the preceding business year where, intentionally or negligently:

(a) they supply incorrect or misleading information in response to a request made pursuant to Article 17 or Article 18(2);

(b) in response to a request made by decision adopted pursuant to Article 17 or Article 18(3), they supply incorrect, incomplete or misleading information or do not supply information within the required time-limit;

(c) they produce the required books or other records related to the business in incomplete form during inspections under Article 20 or refuse to submit to inspections ordered by a decision adopted pursuant to Article 20(4);

(d) in response to a question asked in accordance with Article 20(2)(e),

— they give an incorrect or misleading answer,

— they fail to rectify within a time-limit set by the Commission an incorrect, incomplete or misleading answer given by a member of staff, or

— they fail or refuse to provide a complete answer on facts relating to the subject-matter and purpose of an inspection ordered by a decision adopted pursuant to Article 20(4);

(e) seals affixed in accordance with Article 20(2)(d) by officials or other accompanying persons authorised by the Commission have been broken.

2. The Commission may by decision impose fines on undertakings and associations of undertakings where, either intentionally or negligently:

(a) they infringe Article [101] or Article [102] of the Treaty; or

(b) they contravene a decision ordering interim measures under Article 8; or

(c) they fail to comply with a commitment made binding by a decision pursuant to Article 9.

For each undertaking and association of undertakings participating in the infringement, the fine shall not exceed 10% of its total turnover in the preceding business year.

Where the infringement of an association relates to the activities of its members, the fine shall not exceed 10% of the sum of the total turnover of each member active on the market affected by the infringement of the association.

3. In fixing the amount of the fine, regard shall be had both to the gravity and to the duration of the infringement.

4. When a fine is imposed on an association of undertakings taking account of the turnover of its members and the association is not solvent, the association is obliged to call for contributions from its members to cover the amount of the fine.

Where such contributions have not been made to the association within a time-limit fixed by the Commission, the Commission may require payment of the fine directly by any of the undertakings whose representatives were members of the decision-making bodies concerned of the association.

After the Commission has required payment under the second subparagraph, where necessary to ensure full payment of the fine, the Commission may require payment of the balance by any of the members of the association which were active on the market on which the infringement occurred.

However, the Commission shall not require payment under the second or the third subparagraph from undertakings which show that they have not implemented the infringing decision of the association and either were not aware of its existence or have actively distanced themselves from it before the Commission started investigating the case.

The financial liability of each undertaking in respect of the payment of the fine shall not exceed 10% of its total turnover in the preceding business year.

5. Decisions taken pursuant to paragraphs 1 and 2 shall not be of a criminal law nature.

Commentary
Art 23: B&C: 8.187, 8.189, 13.021, 13.055, 13.071, 13.085, 13.130, 14.008, 14.044, 14.133 F&N: 2.88, 2.104,
　　2.124, 2.140, 2.187, 4.35, 5.410, 8.298, 8.306, 8.309, 8.310, 8.312, 8.332, 8.343, 8.349, 8.350, 8.374, 8.392,
　　8.397, 8.425, 8.515, 8.549, 8.710
Art 23(1): B&C: 14.001 F&N: 8.283, 8.370, 8.392
Art 23(1)(a): B&C: 13.007, 14.045 F&N: 8.308, 8.309
Art 23(1)(b): B&C: 13.017 F&N: 8.308, 8.309
Art 23(1)(c): B&C: 13.025, 13.032 F&N: 8.380, 8.406
Art 23(1)(d): B&C: 13.019, 13.032 F&N: 8.363, 8.371, 8.373
Art 23(1)(e): B&C: 13.032 F&N: 8.358, 8.361
Art 23(2): B&C: 14.001, 14.078 F&N: 8.308, 8.550, 8.621, 8.674, 8.675, 8.676, 8.682
Art 23(2)(a): B&C: 14.001, 14.009, 14.132 F&N: 2.88, 4.37
Art 23(2)(b): B&C: 14.001
Art 23(2)(c): B&C: 13.103, 14.001 F&N: 4.54
Art 23(3): B&C: 14.001, 14.002, 14.003, 14.016, 14.032, 14.035 F&N: 8.570
Art 23(4): B&C: 14.083, 14.084, 14.133 F&N: 8.549
Art 23(5): B&C: 5.036, 14.006 F&N: 4.36

Article 24
Periodic penalty payments

1. The Commission may, by decision, impose on undertakings or associations of undertakings periodic penalty payments not exceeding 5% of the average daily turnover in the preceding business year per day and calculated from the date appointed by the decision, in order to compel them:

(a) to put an end to an infringement of Article [101] or Article [102] of the Treaty, in accordance with a decision taken pursuant to Article 7;

(b) to comply with a decision ordering interim measures taken pursuant to Article 8;

(c) to comply with a commitment made binding by a decision pursuant to Article 9;

(d) to supply complete and correct information which it has requested by decision taken pursuant to Article 17 or Article 18(3);

(e) to submit to an inspection which it has ordered by decision taken pursuant to Article 20(4).

2. Where the undertakings or associations of undertakings have satisfied the obligation which the periodic penalty payment was intended to enforce, the Commission may fix the definitive amount of the periodic penalty payment at a figure lower than that which would arise under the original decision. Article 23(4) shall apply correspondingly.

Commentary
Art 24: B&C: 8.189, 13.021, 13.130, 14.133, 14.134 **F&N:** 2.88, 2.104, 2.140, 2.187, 5.338, 5.361, 8.298, 8.310, 8.312, 8.332, 8.343, 8.349, 8.350, 8.374, 8.392, 8.397, 8.425
Art 24(1): B&C: 13.032, 14.133 **F&N:** 4.54
Art 24(1)(a): B&C: 13.120
Art 24(1)(b): B&C: 14.133
Art 24(1)(c): B&C: 13.103, 14.133
Art 24(1)(d): B&C: 13.017 **F&N:** 8.308
Art 24(1)(e): B&C: 13.025 **F&N:** 8.329, 8.380, 8.394
Art 24(2): B&C: 13.017, 13.032, 13.055, 13.071, 13.085, 13.120, 14.134, 14.135 **F&N:** 8.308

Chapter VII
Limitation Periods

Article 25
Limitation periods for the imposition of penalties

1. The powers conferred on the Commission by Articles 23 and 24 shall be subject to the following limitation periods:

(a) three years in the case of infringements of provisions concerning requests for information or the conduct of inspections;
(b) five years in the case of all other infringements.

2. Time shall begin to run on the day on which the infringement is committed. However, in the case of continuing or repeated infringements, time shall begin to run on the day on which the infringement ceases.

3. Any action taken by the Commission or by the competition authority of a Member State for the purpose of the investigation or proceedings in respect of an infringement shall interrupt the limitation period for the imposition of fines or periodic penalty payments. The limitation period shall be interrupted with effect from the date on which the action is notified to at least one undertaking or association of undertakings which has participated in the infringement. Actions which interrupt the running of the period shall include in particular the following:

(a) written requests for information by the Commission or by the competition authority of a Member State;
(b) written authorisations to conduct inspections issued to its officials by the Commission or by the competition authority of a Member State;
(c) the initiation of proceedings by the Commission or by the competition authority of a Member State;
(d) notification of the statement of objections of the Commission or of the competition authority of a Member State.

4. The interruption of the limitation period shall apply for all the undertakings or associations of undertakings which have participated in the infringement.

5. Each interruption shall start time running afresh. However, the limitation period shall expire at the latest on the day on which a period equal to twice the limitation period has elapsed without the Commission having imposed a fine or a periodic penalty payment. That period shall be extended by the time during which limitation is suspended pursuant to paragraph 6.

6. The limitation period for the imposition of fines or periodic penalty payments shall be suspended for as long as the decision of the Commission is the subject of proceedings pending before the Court of Justice.

Article 26
Limitation period for the enforcement of penalties

1. The power of the Commission to enforce decisions taken pursuant to Articles 23 and 24 shall be subject to a limitation period of five years.

2. Time shall begin to run on the day on which the decision becomes final.

3. The limitation period for the enforcement of penalties shall be interrupted:

(a) by notification of a decision varying the original amount of the fine or periodic penalty payment or refusing an application for variation;

(b) by any action of the Commission or of a Member State, acting at the request of the Commission, designed to enforce payment of the fine or periodic penalty payment.

4. Each interruption shall start time running afresh.

5. The limitation period for the enforcement of penalties shall be suspended for so long as:

(a) time to pay is allowed;

(b) enforcement of payment is suspended pursuant to a decision of the Court of Justice.

CHAPTER VIII
HEARINGS AND PROFESSIONAL SECRECY

Article 27
Hearing of the parties, complainants and others

1. Before taking decisions as provided for in Articles 7, 8, 23 and Article 24(2), the Commission shall give the undertakings or associations of undertakings which are the subject of the proceedings conducted by the Commission the opportunity of being heard on the matters to which the Commission has taken objection. The Commission shall base its decisions only on objections on which the parties concerned have been able to comment. Complainants shall be associated closely with the proceedings.

2. The rights of defence of the parties concerned shall be fully respected in the proceedings. They shall be entitled to have access to the Commission's file, subject to the legitimate interest of undertakings

in the protection of their business secrets. The right of access to the file shall not extend to confidential information and internal documents of the Commission or the competition authorities of the Member States. In particular, the right of access shall not extend to correspondence between the Commission and the competition authorities of the Member States, or between the latter, including documents drawn up pursuant to Articles 11 and 14. Nothing in this paragraph shall prevent the Commission from disclosing and using information necessary to prove an infringement.

3. If the Commission considers it necessary, it may also hear other natural or legal persons. Applications to be heard on the part of such persons shall, where they show a sufficient interest, be granted. The competition authorities of the Member States may also ask the Commission to hear other natural or legal persons.

4. Where the Commission intends to adopt a decision pursuant to Article 9 or Article 10, it shall publish a concise summary of the case and the main content of the commitments or of the proposed course of action. Interested third parties may submit their observations within a time limit which is fixed by the Commission in its publication and which may not be less than one month. Publication shall have regard to the legitimate interest of undertakings in the protection of their business secrets.

Commentary
Art 27: **B&C:** 13.033, 13.077, 13.081, 13.106 **F&N:** 2.203, 8.286, 8.308, 8.312, 8.476, 8.508, 9.27
Art 27(1): **B&C:** 13.017, 13.032, 13.055, 13.085 **F&N:** 2.209, 8.705
Art 27(2): **B&C:** 13.052, 13.068, 13.072, 13.073, 13.074, 13.077, 15.029 **F&N:** 2.202, 2.207, 9.164
Art 27(3): **B&C:** 13.085 **F&N:** 2.144
Art 27(4): **B&C:** 13.065, 13.101 **F&N:** 2.88, 2.120, 2.133, 2.134, 2.144, 2.145, 2.202, 2.268

Article 28
Professional secrecy

1. Without prejudice to Articles 12 and 15, information collected pursuant to Articles 17 to 22 shall be used only for the purpose for which it was acquired.

2. Without prejudice to the exchange and to the use of information foreseen in Articles 11, 12, 14, 15 and 27, the Commission and the competition authorities of the Member States, their officials, servants and other persons working under the supervision of these authorities as well as officials and civil servants of other authorities of the Member States shall not disclose information acquired or exchanged by them pursuant to this Regulation and of the kind covered by the obligation of professional secrecy. This obligation also applies to all representatives and experts of Member States attending meetings of the Advisory Committee pursuant to Article 14.

Commentary
Art 28: **B&C:** 1.097, 12.174, 13.034, 13.035 **F&N:** 2.176, 2.193, 8.102, 8.238, 8.291, 8.443
Art 28(1): **B&C:** 13.033, 15.031 **F&N:** 8.367
Art 28(2): **B&C:** 13.033, 15.029, 15.031 **F&N:** 2.176, 2.192, 2.193, 2.195, 2.202, 2.203, 2.204, 2.207

CHAPTER IX
EXEMPTION REGULATIONS

Article 29
Withdrawal in individual cases

1. Where the Commission, empowered by a Council Regulation, such as Regulations 19/65/EEC, (EEC) No 2821/71, (EEC) No 3976/87, (EEC) No 1534/91 or (EEC) No 479/92, to apply Article [101](3) of the Treaty by regulation, has declared Article [101](1) of the Treaty inapplicable to certain categories of agreements, decisions by associations of undertakings or concerted practices, it may, acting on its own initiative or on a complaint, withdraw the benefit of such an exemption Regulation when it finds that in any particular case an agreement, decision or concerted practice to which the exemption Regulation applies has certain effects which are incompatible with Article [101](3) of the Treaty.

2. Where, in any particular case, agreements, decisions by associations of undertakings or concerted practices to which a Commission Regulation referred to in paragraph 1 applies have effects which are incompatible with Article [101](3) of the Treaty in the territory of a Member State, or in a part thereof, which has all the characteristics of a distinct geographic market, the competition authority of that Member State may withdraw the benefit of the Regulation in question in respect of that territory.

Commentary
Art 29: **B&C:** 6.051, 7.061, 7.063, 13.050 **F&N:** 2.22, 7.153, 7.165, 7.226, 7.272
Art 29(1): **B&C:** 3.089, 7.061 **F&N:** 3.471, 9.164
Art 29(2): **B&C:** 3.090, 7.062, 9.173 **F&N:** 3.471

CHAPTER X
GENERAL PROVISIONS

Article 30
Publication of decisions

1. The Commission shall publish the decisions, which it takes pursuant to Articles 7 to 10, 23 and 24.

2. The publication shall state the names of the parties and the main content of the decision, including any penalties imposed. It shall have regard to the legitimate interest of undertakings in the protection of their business secrets.

Commentary
Art 30: **B&C:** 13.013, 13.025, 13.094
Art 30(1): **B&C:** 13.101, 13.112
Art 30(2): **F&N:** 2.202

Article 31
Review by the Court of Justice

The Court of Justice shall have unlimited jurisdiction to review decisions whereby the Commission has fixed a fine or periodic penalty payment. It may cancel, reduce or increase the fine or periodic penalty payment imposed.

Commentary
Art 31: **B&C:** 1.052, 13.017, 13.053, 13.123 **F&N:** 4.78

[Article 32]

Notes
Article 32(c) was repealed by Council Regulation 411/2004/EC of 26 February 2004 (OJ L 68, 6.3.2004, p.1), Article 3, with effect from 1 May 2004.
Article 32 was deleted by Council Regulation 1419/2006/EC of 28 September 2006 (OJ L 269, 28.9.2006, p.1), Article 2, with effect from 18 October 2006.

Commentary
Art 32: **B&C:** 12.163, 14.079 **F&N:** 8.252

Article 33
Implementing provisions

1. The Commission shall be authorised to take such measures as may be appropriate in order to apply this Regulation. The measures may concern, inter alia:

Part B Procedural Matters

(a) the form, content and other details of complaints lodged pursuant to Article 7 and the procedure for rejecting complaints;

(b) the practical arrangements for the exchange of information and consultations provided for in Article 11;

(c) the practical arrangements for the hearings provided for in Article 27.

2. Before the adoption of any measures pursuant to paragraph 1, the Commission shall publish a draft thereof and invite all interested parties to submit their comments within the time-limit it lays down, which may not be less than one month. Before publishing a draft measure and before adopting it, the Commission shall consult the Advisory Committee on Restrictive Practices and Dominant Positions.

CHAPTER XI
TRANSITIONAL, AMENDING AND FINAL PROVISIONS

Article 34
Transitional provisions

1. Applications made to the Commission under Article 2 of Regulation No 17, notifications made under Articles 4 and 5 of that Regulation and the corresponding applications and notifications made under Regulations (EEC) No 1017/68, (EEC) No 4056/86 and (EEC) No 3975/87 shall lapse as from the date of application of this Regulation.

2. Procedural steps taken under Regulation No 17 and Regulations (EEC) No 1017/68, (EEC) No 4056/86 and (EEC) No 3975/87 shall continue to have effect for the purposes of applying this Regulation.

Commentary
Art 34: B&C: 15.073
Art 34(1): B&C: 3.006, 15.073

Article 35
Designation of competition authorities of Member States

1. The Member States shall designate the competition authority or authorities responsible for the application of Articles [101] and [102] of the Treaty in such a way that the provisions of this regulation are effectively complied with. The measures necessary to empower those authorities to apply those Articles shall be taken before 1 May 2004. The authorities designated may include courts.

2. When enforcement of Community competition law is entrusted to national administrative and judicial authorities, the Member States may allocate different powers and functions to those different national authorities, whether administrative or judicial.

3. The effects of Article 11(6) apply to the authorities designated by the Member States including courts that exercise functions regarding the preparation and the adoption of the types of decisions foreseen in Article 5. The effects of Article 11(6) do not extend to courts insofar as they act as review courts in respect of the types of decisions foreseen in Article 5.

4. Notwithstanding paragraph 3, in the Member States where, for the adoption of certain types of decisions foreseen in Article 5, an authority brings an action before a judicial authority that is separate and different from the prosecuting authority and provided that the terms of this paragraph are complied with, the effects of Article 11(6) shall be limited to the authority prosecuting the case which shall withdraw its claim before the judicial authority when the Commission opens proceedings and this withdrawal shall bring the national proceedings effectively to an end.

Commentary

Art 35: **B&C:** 1.070, 15.053

Art 35(1): **B&C:** 15.001, 15.008 **F&N:** 2.23, 2.78, 2.79, 2.86, 2.220, 2.282

Art 35(2): **F&N:** 2.79, 2.220

Art 35(3): **B&C:** 15.020, 15.053 **F&N:** 2.234, 2.235, 2.236, 2.264

Art 35(4): **B&C:** 15.020, 15.053 **F&N:** 2.234, 2.235, 2.236, 2.264

[*Articles 36 to 42*]

Notes

Articles 36 to 42 amend Regulations 1017/68/EEC, 2988/74/EEC, 4056/86/EEC, 3975/87/EEC, 19/65/EEC, 2821/71/EEC, 1534/91/EEC, 3976/87/EEC and 479/92/EEC.

Article 43
Repeal of Regulations No 17 and No 141

1. Regulation No 17 is repealed with the exception of Article 8(3) which continues to apply to decisions adopted pursuant to Article [101](3) of the Treaty prior to the date of application of this Regulation until the date of expiration of those decisions.

2. Regulation No 141 is repealed.

3. References to the repealed Regulations shall be construed as references to this Regulation.

Commentary

Art 43: **B&C:** 14.133

Article 44
Report on the application of the present Regulation

Five years from the date of application of this Regulation, the Commission shall report to the European Parliament and the Council on the functioning of this Regulation, in particular on the application of Article 11(6) and Article 17.

On the basis of this report, the Commission shall assess whether it is appropriate to propose to the Council a revision of this Regulation.

Article 45
Entry into force

This Regulation shall enter into force on the 20th day following that of its publication in the *Official Journal of the European Communities*.

It shall apply from 1 May 2004.

Notes

Date of entry into force: 24 January 2003.

Commentary

Art 45: **B&C:** 15.075

This Regulation shall be binding in its entirety and directly applicable in all Member States.
Done at Brussels, 16 December 2002.

B3

COMMISSION REGULATION (EC) NO 773/2004

of 7 April 2004

relating to the conduct of proceedings by the Commission pursuant to Articles [101 and 102] of the [Treaty on the Functioning of the European Union]*

(Text with EEA relevance)

Official Journal L 123, 27.4.2004, p.18

Celex No: 32004R0773

EUR-Lex permanent link: <http://eur-lex.europa.eu/LexUriServ/LexUriServ.do?uri=CELEX:3200 4R0773:EN:NOT>

Notes

* Ed note: please see the Note on the Lisbon Treaty at p.xvii in regard to article renumbering introduced by the Lisbon Treaty. **EEA application:** see the Surveillance and Court Agreement, Protocol 4, Part I, Chapter III, as replaced by the Agreement amending Protocol 4 of 3 December 2004 with effect from 1 July 2005. See also the EEA Agreement, Protocol 21, Article 3(1), point 4 (as amended).

Commentary

Reg 773/2004/EC: B&C: 1.069, 3.005, 5.023, 13.061 **F&N:** 8.103, 8.250, 8.270, 8.329, 8.358, 8.360, 8.418
Arts 5–9: F&N: 8.103

THE COMMISSION OF THE EUROPEAN COMMUNITIES,

Having regard to the Treaty [on the Functioning of the European Union],

Having regard to the Agreement on the European Economic Area,

Having regard to Council Regulation (EC) No 1/2003 of 16 December 2002 on the implementation of the rules on competition laid down in Articles [101] and [102] of the Treaty,[1] and in particular Article 33 thereof,

---

Notes

[1] OJ L 1, 4.1.2003, p.1. Regulation as amended by Regulation (EC) No 411/2004 (OJ L 68, 6.3.2004, p.1).

After consulting the Advisory Committee on Restrictive Practices and Dominant Positions,

Whereas:

(1) Regulation (EC) No 1/2003 empowers the Commission to regulate certain aspects of proceedings for the application of Articles [101] and [102] of the Treaty. It is necessary to lay down rules concerning the initiation of proceedings by the Commission as well as the handling of complaints and the hearing of the parties concerned.

(2) According to Regulation (EC) No 1/2003, national courts are under an obligation to avoid taking decisions which could run counter to decisions envisaged by the Commission in the same case. According to Article 11(6) of that Regulation, national competition authorities are relieved from their competence once the Commission has initiated proceedings for the adoption of a decision under Chapter III of Regulation (EC) No 1/2003. In this context, it is important that courts and competition authorities of the Member States are aware of the initiation of proceedings by the Commission. The Commission should therefore be able to make public its decisions to initiate proceedings.

(3) Before taking oral statements from natural or legal persons who consent to be interviewed, the Commission should inform those persons of the legal basis of the interview and its voluntary nature. The persons interviewed should also be informed of the purpose of the interview and of any record which may be made. In order to enhance the accuracy of the statements, the persons interviewed should also be given an opportunity to correct the statements recorded. Where information gathered from oral statements is exchanged pursuant to Article 12 of Regulation (EC) No 1/2003, that information should only be used in evidence to impose sanctions on natural persons where the conditions set out in that Article are fulfilled.

(4) Pursuant to Article 23(1)(d) of Regulation (EC) No 1/2003 fines may be imposed on undertakings and associations of undertakings where they fail to rectify within the time limit fixed by the Commission an incorrect, incomplete or misleading answer given by a member of their staff to questions in the course of inspections. It is therefore necessary to provide the undertaking concerned with a record of any explanations given and to establish a procedure enabling it to add any rectification, amendment or supplement to the explanations given by the member of staff who is not or was not authorised to provide explanations on behalf of the undertaking. The explanations given by a member of staff should remain in the Commission file as recorded during the inspection.

Commentary
Recital 4: F&N: 8.718

(5) Complaints are an essential source of information for detecting infringements of competition rules. It is important to define clear and efficient procedures for handling complaints lodged with the Commission.

(6) In order to be admissible for the purposes of Article 7 of Regulation (EC) No 1/2003, a complaint must contain certain specified information.

(7) In order to assist complainants in submitting the necessary facts to the Commission, a form should be drawn up. The submission of the information listed in that form should be a condition for a complaint to be treated as a complaint as referred to in Article 7 of Regulation (EC) No 1/2003.

(8) Natural or legal persons having chosen to lodge a complaint should be given the possibility to be associated closely with the proceedings initiated by the Commission with a view to finding an infringement. However, they should not have access to business secrets or other confidential information belonging to other parties involved in the proceedings.

(9) Complainants should be granted the opportunity of expressing their views if the Commission considers that there are insufficient grounds for acting on the complaint. Where the Commission rejects a complaint on the grounds that a competition authority of a Member State is dealing with it or has already done so, it should inform the complainant of the identity of that authority.

(10) In order to respect the rights of defence of undertakings, the Commission should give the parties concerned the right to be heard before it takes a decision.

Commentary
Recital 10: F&N: 8.219

(11) Provision should also be made for the hearing of persons who have not submitted a complaint as referred to in Article 7 of Regulation (EC) No 1/2003 and who are not parties to whom a statement of objections has been addressed but who can nevertheless show a sufficient interest. Consumer associations that apply to be heard should generally be regarded as having a sufficient interest, where the proceedings concern products or services used by the end-consumer or products or services that constitute a direct input into such products or services. Where it considers this to be useful for the proceedings, the Commission should also be able to invite other persons to express their views in writing and to attend the oral hearing of the parties to whom a statement of objections has been addressed. Where appropriate, it should also be able to invite such persons to express their views at that oral hearing.

(12) To improve the effectiveness of oral hearings, the Hearing Officer should have the power to allow the parties concerned, complainants, other persons invited to the hearing, the Commission services and the authorities of the Member States to ask questions during the hearing.

(13) When granting access to the file, the Commission should ensure the protection of business secrets and other confidential information. The category of "other confidential information" includes information other than business secrets, which may be considered as confidential, insofar as its disclosure would significantly harm an undertaking or person. The Commission should be able to request undertakings or associations of undertakings that submit or have submitted documents or statements to identify confidential information.

Commentary
Recital 13: F&N: 2.201

(14) Where business secrets or other confidential information are necessary to prove an infringement, the Commission should assess for each individual document whether the need to disclose is greater than the harm which might result from disclosure.

Commentary
Recital 14: F&N: 2.206

(15) In the interest of legal certainty, a minimum time-limit for the various submissions provided for in this Regulation should be laid down.

(16) This Regulation replaces Commission Regulation (EC) No 2842/98 of 22 December 1998 on the hearing of parties in certain proceedings under Articles [101] and [102] of the [Treaty on the Functioning of the European Union],[1] which should therefore be repealed.

Notes
[1] OJ L 354, 30.12.1998, p.18.

(17) This Regulation aligns the procedural rules in the transport sector with the general rules of procedure in all sectors. Commission Regulation (EC) No 2843/98 of 22 December 1998 on the form, content and other details of applications and notifications provided for in Council Regulations (EEC) No 1017/68, (EEC) No 4056/86 and (EEC) No 3975/87 applying the rules on competition to the transport sector[1] should therefore be repealed.

Notes
[1] OJ L 354, 30.12.1998, p.22.

(18) Regulation (EC) No 1/2003 abolishes the notification and authorisation system. Commission Regulation (EC) No 3385/94 of 21 December 1994 on the form, content and other details of applications and notifications provided for in Council Regulation No 17[1] should therefore be repealed,

Notes
[1] OJ L 377, 31.12.1994, p.28.

HAS ADOPTED THIS REGULATION:

CHAPTER I
SCOPE

Article 1
Subject-matter and scope

This regulation applies to proceedings conducted by the Commission for the application of Articles [101] and [102] of the Treaty.

Chapter II
Initiation of Proceedings

Article 2
Initiation of proceedings

[1. The Commission may decide to initiate proceedings with a view to adopting a decision pursuant to Chapter III of Regulation (EC) No 1/2003 at any point in time, but no later than the date on which it issues a preliminary assessment as referred to in Article 9(1) of that Regulation, a statement of objections or a request for the parties to express their interest in engaging in settlement discussions, or the date on which a notice pursuant to Article 27(4) of that Regulation is published, whichever is the earlier.]

2. The Commission may make public the initiation of proceedings, in any appropriate way. Before doing so, it shall inform the parties concerned.

3. The Commission may exercise its powers of investigation pursuant to Chapter V of Regulation (EC) No 1/2003 before initiating proceedings.

4. The Commission may reject a complaint pursuant to Article 7 of Regulation (EC) No 1/2003 without initiating proceedings.

Notes

Article 2(1) was substituted as shown in square brackets by Commission Regulation (EC) No 622/2008 (OJ L 171, 1.7.2008), Article 1(1), with effect from 1 July 2008.

Commentary

Art 2(1): B&C: 13.057, 13.101 F&N: 2.130, 8.719
Art 2(2): B&C: 13.057, 15.053
Art 2(3): B&C: 13.057
Art 2(4): B&C: 13.057

Chapter III
Investigations by the Commission

Article 3
Power to take statements

1. Where the Commission interviews a person with his consent in accordance with Article 19 of Regulation (EC) No 1/2003, it shall, at the beginning of the interview, state the legal basis and the purpose of the interview, and recall its voluntary nature. It shall also inform the person interviewed of its intention to make a record of the interview.

2. The interview may be conducted by any means including by telephone or electronic means.

3. The Commission may record the statements made by the persons interviewed in any form. A copy of any recording shall be made available to the person interviewed for approval. Where necessary, the Commission shall set a time-limit within which the person interviewed may communicate to it any correction to be made to the statement.

Commentary

Art 3: F&N: 8.318, 8.446, 8.472
Art 3(1): B&C: 13.019 F&N: 8.321
Art 3(2): F&N: 8.321
Art 3(3): B&C: 13.019 F&N: 8.321

Article 4
Oral questions during inspections

1. When, pursuant to Article 20(2)(e) of Regulation (EC) No 1/2003, officials or other accompanying persons authorised by the Commission ask representatives or members of staff of an undertaking or of an association of undertakings for explanations, the explanations given may be recorded in any form.

2. A copy of any recording made pursuant to paragraph 1 shall be made available to the undertaking or association of undertakings concerned after the inspection.

3. In cases where a member of staff of an undertaking or of an association of undertakings who is not or was not authorised by the undertaking or by the association of undertakings to provide explanations on behalf of the undertaking or association of undertakings has been asked for explanations, the Commission shall set a time-limit within which the undertaking or the association of undertakings may communicate to the Commission any rectification, amendment or supplement to the explanations given by such member of staff. The rectification, amendment or supplement shall be added to the explanations as recorded pursuant to paragraph 1.

Commentary
Art 4: F&N: 8.292, 8.363, 8.364, 8.367, 8.446, 8.472, 8.718
Art 4(1): B&C: 13.031
Art 4(3): F&N: 8.373

CHAPTER IV
HANDLING OF COMPLAINTS

Article 5
Admissibility of complaints

1. Natural and legal persons shall show a legitimate interest in order to be entitled to lodge a complaint for the purposes of Article 7 of Regulation (EC) No 1/2003.

Such complaints shall contain the information required by Form C, as set out in the Annex. The Commission may dispense with this obligation as regards part of the information, including documents, required by Form C.

2. Three paper copies as well as, if possible, an electronic copy of the complaint shall be submitted to the Commission. The complainant shall also submit a non-confidential version of the complaint, if confidentiality is claimed for any part of the complaint.

3. Complaints shall be submitted in one of the official languages of the Community.

Commentary
Art 5: B&C: 13.042, 13.132 F&N: 2.114, 2.144

Article 6
Participation of complainants in proceedings

[1. Where the Commission issues a statement of objections relating to a matter in respect of which it has received a complaint, it shall provide the complainant with a copy of the non-confidential version of the statement of objections, except in cases where the settlement procedure applies, where it shall inform the complainant in writing of the nature and subject matter of the procedure. The Commission shall also set a time limit within which the complainant may make known its views in writing.]

2. The Commission may, where appropriate, afford complainants the opportunity of expressing their views at the oral hearing of the parties to which a statement of objections has been issued, if complainants so request in their written comments.

Notes
Article 6(1) was substituted as shown in square brackets by Commission Regulation (EC) No 622/2008 (OJ L 171, 1.7.2008), Article 1(2), with effect from 1 July 2008.

Commentary
Art 6: F&N: 2.114
Art 6(1): B&C: 13.051
Art 6(2): B&C: 13.051

Article 7
Rejection of complaints

1. Where the Commission considers that on the basis of the information in its possession there are insufficient grounds for acting on a complaint, it shall inform the complainant of its reasons and set a time-limit within which the complainant may make known its views in writing. The Commission shall not be obliged to take into account any further written submission received after the expiry of that time-limit.

2. If the complainant makes known its views within the time-limit set by the Commission and the written submissions made by the complainant do not lead to a different assessment of the complaint, the Commission shall reject the complaint by decision.

3. If the complainant fails to make known its views within the time-limit set by the Commission, the complaint shall be deemed to have been withdrawn.

Commentary
Art 7: B&C: 13.045, 13.050, 13.130, 13.162
Art 7(1): B&C: 13.047, 13.081
Art 7(3): B&C: 13.047

Article 8
Access to information

1. Where the Commission has informed the complainant of its intention to reject a complaint pursuant to Article 7(1) the complainant may request access to the documents on which the Commission bases its provisional assessment. For this purpose, the complainant may however not have access to business secrets and other confidential information belonging to other parties involved in the proceedings.

2. The documents to which the complainant has had access in the context of proceedings conducted by the Commission under Articles [101] and [102] of the Treaty may only be used by the complainant for the purposes of judicial or administrative proceedings for the application of those Treaty provisions.

Commentary
Art 8: B&C: 13.047 F&N: 2.209
Art 8(2): F&N: 8.708

Article 9
Rejections of complaints pursuant to Article 13
of Regulation (EC) No 1/2003

Where the Commission rejects a complaint pursuant to Article 13 of Regulation (EC) No 1/2003, it shall inform the complainant without delay of the national competition authority which is dealing or has already dealt with the case.

Commentary
Art 9: B&C: 13.045

Chapter V
Exercise of the Right to be Heard

Article 10
Statement of objections and reply

[1. The Commission shall inform the parties concerned of the objections raised against them. The statement of objections shall be notified in writing to each of the parties against whom objections are raised.]

2. The Commission shall, when notifying the statement of objections to the parties concerned, set a time-limit within which these parties may inform it in writing of their views. The Commission shall not be obliged to take into account written submissions received after the expiry of that time-limit.

3. The parties may, in their written submissions, set out all facts known to them which are relevant to their defence against the objections raised by the Commission. They shall attach any relevant documents as proof of the facts set out. They shall provide a paper original as well as an electronic copy or, where they do not provide an electronic copy, [31] paper copies of their submission and of the documents attached to it. They may propose that the Commission hear persons who may corroborate the facts set out in their submission.

Notes

Article 10(1) was substituted as shown in square brackets by Commission Regulation (EC) No 622/2008 (OJ L 171, 1.7.2008), Article 1(3), with effect from 1 July 2008.

Article 10(3) was amended as shown in square brackets by Commission Regulation (EU) No 519/2013 of 21 February 2013 adapting certain regulations and decisions by reason of the accession of Croatia (OJ L 158, 10.6.2013, p. 74), with effect from 1 April 2013.

Commentary

Art 10(1): B&C: 13.055, 13.057, 13.060
Art 10(2): B&C: 13.064
Art 10(3): B&C: 13.055, 13.064 F&N: 8.506

[*Article 10a*
Settlement procedure in cartel cases

1. After the initiation of proceedings pursuant to Article 11(6) of Regulation (EC) No 1/2003, the Commission may set a time limit within which the parties may indicate in writing that they are prepared to engage in settlement discussions with a view to possibly introducing settlement submissions. The Commission shall not be obliged to take into account replies received after the expiry of that time limit.

If two or more parties within the same undertaking indicate their willingness to engage in settlement discussions pursuant to the first subparagraph, they shall appoint a joint representation to engage in discussions with the Commission on their behalf. When setting the time limit referred to in the first subparagraph, the Commission shall indicate to the relevant parties that they are identified within the same undertaking, for the sole purpose of enabling them to comply with this provision.

2. Parties taking part in settlement discussions may be informed by the Commission of:

(a) the objections it envisages to raise against them;
(b) the evidence used to determine the envisaged objections;
(c) non-confidential versions of any specified accessible document listed in the case file at that point in time, in so far as a request by the party is justified for the purpose of enabling the party to ascertain its position regarding a time period or any other particular aspect of the cartel; and
(d) the range of potential fines.

This information shall be confidential vis-à-vis third parties, save where the Commission has given a prior explicit authorisation for disclosure.

Should settlement discussions progress, the Commission may set a time limit within which the parties may commit to follow the settlement procedure by introducing settlement submissions reflecting the results of the settlement discussions and acknowledging their participation in an infringement of Article [101] of the Treaty as well as their liability. Before the Commission sets a time limit to introduce their settlement submissions, the parties concerned shall be entitled to have the information specified in Article 10a(2), first subparagraph disclosed to them, upon request, in a timely manner. The Commission shall not be obliged to take into account settlement submissions received after the expiry of that time limit.

3. When the statement of objections notified to the parties reflects the contents of their settlement submissions, the written reply to the statement of objections by the parties concerned shall, within a time limit set by the Commission, confirm that the statement of objections addressed to them reflects the contents of their settlement submissions. The Commission may then proceed to the adoption of a Decision pursuant to Article 7 and Article 23 of Regulation (EC) No 1/2003 after consultation of the Advisory Committee on Restrictive Practices and Dominant Positions pursuant to Article 14 of Regulation (EC) No 1/2003.

4. The Commission may decide at any time during the procedure to discontinue settlement discussions altogether in a specific case or with respect to one or more of the parties involved, if it considers that procedural efficiencies are not likely to be achieved.]

Notes

Article 10a was inserted by Commission Regulation (EC) No 622/2008 (OJ L 171, 1.7.2008), Article 1(4), with effect from 1 July 2008.

Commentary
Art 10a(1): **B&C:** 13.055, 13.057, 13.060 **F&N:** 8.719
Art 10a(2): **B&C:** 13.097 **F&N:** 8.720, 8.722
Art 10a(3): **B&C:** 13.064

Article 11
Right to be heard

[1. The Commission shall give the parties to whom it addresses a statement of objections the opportunity to be heard before consulting the Advisory Committee referred to in Article 14(1) of Regulation (EC) No 1/2003.]

2. The Commission shall, in its decisions, deal only with objections in respect of which the parties referred to in paragraph 1 have been able to comment.

Notes

Article 11(1) was substituted as shown in square brackets by Commission Regulation (EC) No 622/2008 (OJ L 171, 1.7.2008), Article 1(5), with effect from 1 July 2008.

Commentary
Art 11(1): **B&C:** 13.055 **F&N:** 8.710
Art 11(2): **B&C:** 13.055, 13.061 **F&N:** 8.476, 8.705

[*Article 12*

1. The Commission shall give the parties to whom it addresses a statement of objections the opportunity to develop their arguments at an oral hearing, if they so request in their written submissions.

2. However, when introducing their settlement submissions the parties shall confirm to the Commission that they would only require having the opportunity to develop their arguments at an oral hearing, if the statement of objections does not reflect the contents of their settlement submissions.]

Notes

Article 12 was substituted as shown in square brackets by Commission Regulation (EC) No 622/2008 (OJ L 171, 1.7.2008), Article 1(6), with effect from 1 July 2008.

Commentary
Art 12: **B&C:** 13.055, 13.082 **F&N:** 8.710

Article 13
Hearing of other persons

1. If natural or legal persons other than those referred to in Articles 5 and 11 apply to be heard and show a sufficient interest, the Commission shall inform them in writing of the nature and subject matter of the procedure and shall set a time-limit within which they may make known their views in writing.

2. The Commission may, where appropriate, invite persons referred to in paragraph 1 to develop their arguments at the oral hearing of the parties to whom a statement of objections has been addressed, if the persons referred to in paragraph 1 so request in their written comments.

3. The Commission may invite any other person to express its views in writing and to attend the oral hearing of the parties to whom a statement of objections has been addressed. The Commission may also invite such persons to express their views at that oral hearing.

Commentary
Art 13: B&C: 13.051
Art 13(1): B&C: 13.085
Art 13(2): B&C: 13.085 F&N: 8.710
Art 13(3): B&C: 13.085

Article 14
Conduct of oral hearings

1. Hearings shall be conducted by a Hearing Officer in full independence.

2. The Commission shall invite the persons to be heard to attend the oral hearing on such date as it shall determine.

3. The Commission shall invite the competition authorities of the Member States to take part in the oral hearing. It may likewise invite officials and civil servants of other authorities of the Member States.

4. Persons invited to attend shall either appear in person or be represented by legal representatives or by representatives authorised by their constitution as appropriate. Undertakings and associations of undertakings may also be represented by a duly authorised agent appointed from among their permanent staff.

5. Persons heard by the Commission may be assisted by their lawyers or other qualified persons admitted by the Hearing Officer.

6. Oral hearings shall not be public. Each person may be heard separately or in the presence of other persons invited to attend, having regard to the legitimate interest of the undertakings in the protection of their business secrets and other confidential information.

7. The Hearing Officer may allow the parties to whom a statement of objections has been addressed, the complainants, other persons invited to the hearing, the Commission services and the authorities of the Member States to ask questions during the hearing.

8. The statements made by each person heard shall be recorded. Upon request, the recording of the hearing shall be made available to the persons who attended the hearing. Regard shall be had to the legitimate interest of the parties in the protection of their business secrets and other confidential information.

Commentary
Art 14(1): F&N: 8.710
Art 14(3): B&C: 13.082
Art 14(4): B&C: 13.082
Art 14(5): B&C: 13.082
Art 14(6): B&C: 13.084 F&N: 8.710
Art 14(8): B&C: 13.084

Chapter VI
Access to the File and Treatment of Confidential Information

Article 15
Access to the file and use of documents

1. If so requested, the Commission shall grant access to the file to the parties to whom it has addressed a statement of objections. Access shall be granted after the notification of the statement of objections.

[1a. After the initiation of proceedings pursuant to Article 11(6) of Regulation (EC) No 1/2003 and in order to enable the parties willing to introduce settlement submissions to do so, the Commission shall disclose to them the evidence and documents described in Article 10a(2) upon request and subject to the conditions established in the relevant subparagraphs. In view thereof, when introducing their settlement submissions, the parties shall confirm to the Commission that they will only require access to the file after the receipt of the statement of objections, if the statement of objections does not reflect the contents of their settlement submissions.]

2. The right of access to the file shall not extend to business secrets, other confidential information and internal documents of the Commission or of the competition authorities of the Member States. The right of access to the file shall also not extend to correspondence between the Commission and the competition authorities of the Member States or between the latter where such correspondence is contained in the file of the Commission.

3. Nothing in this Regulation prevents the Commission from disclosing and using information necessary to prove an infringement of Articles [101] or [102] of the Treaty.

4. Documents obtained through access to the file pursuant to this Article shall only be used for the purposes of judicial or administrative proceedings for the application of Articles [101] and [102] of the Treaty.

Notes

Article 15(1a) was inserted by Commission Regulation (EC) No 622/2008 (OJ L 171, 1.7.2008), Article 1(7), with effect from 1 July 2008.

Commentary

Art 15: B&C: 13.051 F&N: 8.708
Art 15(1): B&C: 13.068, 13.071
Art 15(2): B&C: 13.072, 13.074, 13.077 F&N: 2.207
Art 15(3): B&C: 15.029 F&N: 2.205
Art 15(4): F&N: 8.155, 8.218, 8.219, 8.220, 8.708

Article 16
Identification and protection of confidential information

1. Information, including documents, shall not be communicated or made accessible by the Commission in so far as it contains business secrets or other confidential information of any person.

2. Any person which makes known its views pursuant to Article 6(1), Article 7(1), Article 10(2) and Article 13(1) and (3) or subsequently submits further information to the Commission in the course of the same procedure, shall clearly identify any material which it considers to be confidential, giving reasons, and provide a separate non-confidential version by the date set by the Commission for making its views known.

3. Without prejudice to paragraph 2 of this Article, the Commission may require undertakings and associations of undertakings which produce documents or statements pursuant to Regulation (EC) No 1/2003 to identify the documents or parts of documents which they consider to contain business secrets or other confidential information belonging to them and to identify the undertakings with regard to which such documents are to be considered confidential. The Commission may likewise require undertakings or associations of undertakings to identify any part of a statement of objections, a case summary drawn up pursuant to Article 27(4) of Regulation (EC) No 1/2003 or a decision adopted by the Commission which in their view contains business secrets.

The Commission may set a time-limit within which the undertakings and associations of undertakings are to:

(a) substantiate their claim for confidentiality with regard to each individual document or part of document, statement or part of statement;

(b) provide the Commission with a non-confidential version of the documents or statements, in which the confidential passages are deleted;

(c) provide a concise description of each piece of deleted information.

4. If undertakings or associations of undertakings fail to comply with paragraphs 2 and 3, the Commission may assume that the documents or statements concerned do not contain confidential information.

Commentary
Art 16: **B&C:** 13.076 **F&N:** 8.708
Art 16(1): **B&C:** 13.072, 13.075 **F&N:** 2.207
Art 16(2): **B&C:** 13.078
Art 16(3): **B&C:** 13.078
Art 16(4): **B&C:** 13.078

Chapter VII
General and Final Provisions

Article 17
Time-limits

[1. In setting the time limits provided for in Article 3(3), Article 4(3), Article 6(1), Article 7(1), Article 10(2), Article 10a(1), Article 10a(2), Article 10a(3) and Article 16(3), the Commission shall have regard both to the time required for preparation of the submission and to the urgency of the case.]

2. The time-limits referred to in Article 6(1), Article 7(1) and Article 10(2) shall be at least four weeks. However, for proceedings initiated with a view to adopting interim measures pursuant to Article 8 of Regulation (EC) No 1/2003, the time-limit may be shortened to one week.

[3. The time limits referred to in Article 4(3), Article 10a(1), Article 10a(2) and Article 16(3) shall be at least two weeks. The time limit referred to in Article 3(3) shall be at least two weeks, except for settlement submissions, for which corrections shall be made within one week. The time limit referred to in Article 10a(3) shall be at least two weeks.]

4. Where appropriate and upon reasoned request made before the expiry of the original time-limit, time-limits may be extended.

Commentary
Art 17: **B&C:** 13.099
Art 17(2): **B&C:** 13.107

Article 18
Repeals

Regulations (EC) No 2842/98, (EC) No 2843/98 and (EC) No 3385/94 are repealed.

References to the repealed regulations shall be construed as references to this Regulation.

Article 19
Transitional provisions

Procedural steps taken under Regulations (EC) No 2842/98 and (EC) No 2843/98 shall continue to have effect for the purpose of applying this Regulation.

Commentary
Art 19(1): **F&N:** 5.419
Art 19(2): **B&C:** 5.983

Article 20
Entry into force

This Regulation shall enter into force on 1 May 2004.

This Regulation shall be binding in its entirety and directly applicable in all Member States.

Done at Brussels, 7 April 2004.

ANNEX
FORM C
COMPLAINT PURSUANT TO ARTICLE 7 OF REGULATION (EC) NO 1/2003

I. INFORMATION REGARDING THE COMPLAINANT AND THE UNDERTAKING(S) OR ASSOCIATION OF UNDERTAKINGS GIVING RISE TO THE COMPLAINT

1. Give full details on the identity of the legal or natural person submitting the complaint. Where the complainant is an undertaking, identify the corporate group to which it belongs and provide a concise overview of the nature and scope of its business activities. Provide a contact person (with telephone number, postal and e-mail-address) from which supplementary explanations can be obtained.

2. Identify the undertaking(s) or association of undertakings whose conduct the complaint relates to, including, where applicable, all available information on the corporate group to which the undertaking(s) complained of belong and the nature and scope of the business activities pursued by them. Indicate the position of the complainant vis-à-vis the undertaking(s) or association of undertakings complained of (e.g. customer, competitor).

II. DETAILS OF THE ALLEGED INFRINGEMENT AND EVIDENCE

3. Set out in detail the facts from which, in your opinion, it appears that there exists an infringement of Article [101] or [102] of the Treaty and/or Article 53 or 54 of the EEA agreement. Indicate in particular the nature of the products (goods or services) affected by the alleged infringements and explain, where necessary, the commercial relationships concerning these products. Provide all available details on the agreements or practices of the undertakings or associations of undertakings to which this complaint relates. Indicate, to the extent possible, the relative market positions of the undertakings concerned by the complaint.

4. Submit all documentation in your possession relating to or directly connected with the facts set out in the complaint (for example, texts of agreements, minutes of negotiations or meetings, terms of transactions, business documents, circulars, correspondence, notes of telephone conversations...). State the names and address of the persons able to testify to the facts set out in the complaint, and in particular of persons affected by the alleged infringement. Submit statistics or other data in your possession which relate to the facts set out, in particular where they show developments in the marketplace (for example information relating to prices and price trends, barriers to entry to the market for new suppliers etc.).

5. Set out your view about the geographical scope of the alleged infringement and explain, where that is not obvious, to what extent trade between Member States or between the Community and one or more EFTA States that are contracting parties of the EEA Agreement may be affected by the conduct complained of.

III. FINDING SOUGHT FROM THE COMMISSION AND LEGITIMATE INTEREST

6. Explain what finding or action you are seeking as a result of proceedings brought by the Commission.

7. Set out the grounds on which you claim a legitimate interest as complainant pursuant to Article 7 of Regulation (EC) No 1/2003. State in particular how the conduct complained of affects you and explain how, in your view, intervention by the Commission would be liable to remedy the alleged grievance.

IV. PROCEEDINGS BEFORE NATIONAL COMPETITION AUTHORITIES OR NATIONAL COURTS

8. Provide full information about whether you have approached, concerning the same or closely related subject-matters, any other competition authority and/or whether a lawsuit has been brought

before a national court. If so, provide full details about the administrative or judicial authority contacted and your submissions to such authority.

Declaration that the information given in this form and in the Annexes thereto is given entirely in good faith.

Date and signature

B4

DECISION OF THE PRESIDENT OF THE EUROPEAN COMMISSION OF 13 OCTOBER 2011

on the function and terms of reference of the hearing officer in certain competition proceedings

(Text with EEA relevance) (2011/695/EU)

Official Journal L 275, 20.10.2010, p.29

Celex No: 32011D0695

EUR-Lex permanent link: <http://eur-lex.europa.eu/LexUriServ/LexUriServ.do?uri=CELEX:3201 1D0695:EN:NOT>

Notes

Date of entry into force: 21 October 2011 (Article 19)
EEA application: the EFTA Surveillance Authority has adopted a parallel notice on the function and terms of reference of the hearing officer in certain competition proceedings: see Decision No 442/12/COL of 29 November 2012 (OJ L 190, 11.7.2013, p.93).

Commentary
Arts 10–13 B&C: 13.082
Chap.4: F&N: 5.459

THE PRESIDENT OF THE EUROPEAN COMMISSION,

Having regard to the Treaty on European Union,

Having regard to the Treaty on the Functioning of the European Union,

Having regard to the Agreement on the European Economic Area,

Having regard to the Rules of Procedure of the Commission[1], and in particular Article 22 thereof,

---

Notes
[1] OJ L 308, 8.12.2000, p.26.

Whereas:

(1) Under the system for competition law enforcement established under the Treaty on the Functioning of the European Union (hereinafter 'the Treaty'), the Commission investigates and decides on cases by administrative decision, subject to judicial review by the Court of Justice of the European Union (hereinafter 'the Court of Justice').

(2) The Commission has to conduct its competition proceedings fairly, impartially and objectively and must ensure respect of the procedural rights of the parties concerned as set out in Council

Regulation (EC) No 1/2003 of 16 December 2002 on the implementation of the rules on competition laid down in Articles [101] and [102] of the Treaty[1]*, Council Regulation (EC) No 139/2004 of 20 January 2004 on the control of concentrations between undertakings (the EC Merger Regulation)[2], Commission Regulation (EC) No 773/2004 of 7 April 2004 relating to the conduct of proceedings by the Commission pursuant to Articles [101] and [102] of the [Treaty on the Functioning of the European Union][3], and Commission Regulation (EC) No 802/2004 of 7 April 2004 implementing Council Regulation (EC) No 139/2004 on the control of concentrations between undertakings[4], as well as in the relevant case-law of the Court of Justice. In particular, the right of the parties concerned to be heard before the adoption of any individual decision adversely affecting them is a fundamental right of European Union law recognised by the Charter of Fundamental Rights, and in particular Article 41 thereof[5].

Notes

* Ed note: please see the Note on the Lisbon Treaty at p.xvii in regard to article renumbering introduced by the Lisbon Treaty.
[1] OJ L 1, 4.1.2003, p.1.
[2] OJ L 24, 29.1.2004, p.1.
[3] OJ L 123, 27.4.2004, p.18.
[4] OJ L 133, 30.4.2004, p.1.
[5] OJ C 303, 14.12.2007, p.1.

---

(3) In order to ensure the effective exercise of the procedural rights of the parties concerned, other involved parties within the meaning of Article 11(b) of Regulation (EC) No 802/2004 (hereinafter 'other involved parties'), complainants within the meaning of Article 7(2) of Regulation (EC) No 1/2003 (hereinafter 'complainants') and persons other than those referred to in Articles 5 and 11 of Regulation (EC) No 773/2004 and third persons within the meaning of Article 11 of Regulation (EC) No 802/2004 (hereinafter 'third persons') involved in competition proceedings, responsibility for safeguarding the observance of such rights should be entrusted to an independent person experienced in competition matters who has the integrity necessary to contribute to the objectivity, transparency and efficiency of those proceedings.

(4) The Commission created the function of hearing officer for these purposes in 1982, revised it in Commission Decision 94/810/ECSC, EC of 12 December 1994 on the terms of reference of hearing officers in competition procedures before the Commission[1] and in Commission Decision 2001/462/EC, ECSC of 23 May 2001 on the terms of reference of hearing officers in certain competition proceedings[2]. It is now necessary to clarify and further strengthen the role of the hearing officer and to adapt the terms of reference of the hearing officer in the light of developments in Union competition law.

Notes
[1] OJ L 330, 21.12.1994, p.67.
[2] OJ L 162, 19.6.2001, p.21.

---

(5) The function of the hearing officer has been generally perceived as an important contribution to the competition proceedings before the Commission due to the independence and expertise that hearing officers have brought to these proceedings. In order to ensure the continued independence of the hearing officer from the Directorate-General for Competition, he or she should be attached, for administrative purposes, to the member of the Commission with special responsibility for competition.

(6) The hearing officer should be appointed in accordance with the rules laid down in the Staff Regulations of Officials and the Conditions of Employment of Other Servants of the European Union. In accordance with those rules, consideration may also be given to candidates who are not officials of the Commission. Transparency as regards the appointment, termination of appointment and transfer of hearing officers should be ensured.

(7) The Commission may appoint one or more hearing officers and should provide for their supporting staff. Where the hearing officer perceives a conflict of interests in the performance of his or her functions, the hearing officer should cease from acting on a case. If the hearing officer is unable to act, his or her role should be carried out by another hearing officer.

(8) The hearing officer should operate as an independent arbiter who seeks to resolve issues affecting the effective exercise of the procedural rights of the parties concerned, other involved parties, complainants or interested third persons where such issues could not be resolved through prior contacts with the Commission services responsible for the conduct of competition proceedings, which must respect these procedural rights.

(9) The terms of reference of the hearing officer in competition proceedings should be framed in such a way as to safeguard the effective exercise of procedural rights throughout proceedings before the Commission pursuant to Articles 101 and 102 of the Treaty and Regulation (EC) No 139/2004, in particular the right to be heard.

(10) In order to strengthen this role, the hearing officer should be attributed with the function of safeguarding the effective exercise of procedural rights of undertakings and associations of undertakings in the context of the Commission's powers of investigation under Chapter V of Regulation (EC) No 1/2003, as well as pursuant to Article 14 of Regulation (EC) No 139/2004 which empowers the Commission to impose fines on undertakings and associations of undertakings. The hearing officer should also be attributed with specific functions during this investigative phase in relation to claims for legal professional privilege, the privilege against self-incrimination, deadlines for replying to decisions requesting information pursuant to Article 18(3) of Regulation (EC) No 1/2003, as well as with regard to the right of undertakings and associations of undertakings subject to an investigative measure by the Commission under Chapter V of Regulation (EC) No 1/2003 to be informed of their procedural status, namely whether they are subject to an investigation and, if so, the subject matter and purpose of that investigation. In assessing claims made in relation to privilege against self-incrimination, the hearing officer may consider whether undertakings make clearly unfounded claims for protection merely as a delaying tactic.

(11) The hearing officer should be able to facilitate the resolution of claims that a document is covered by legal professional privilege. To this end, if the undertaking or association of undertakings making the claim agrees, the hearing officer will be allowed to examine the document concerned and make an appropriate recommendation, referring to the applicable case-law of the Court of Justice.

(12) The hearing officer should be responsible for deciding whether a third person shows a sufficient interest to be heard. Consumer associations that apply to be heard should be generally regarded as having a sufficient interest, where the proceedings concern products or services used by end-consumers or products or services that constitute a direct input into such products or services.

(13) The hearing officer should decide whether to admit complainants and interested third persons to the oral hearing, taking into account the contribution they can make to the clarification of the relevant facts of the case.

(14) The right of the parties concerned to be heard before a final decision adversely affecting their interests is taken is guaranteed through their right to reply in writing to the preliminary position of the Commission, as set out in the statement of objections and their right to develop their arguments, if they so request, at the oral hearing. In order to exercise these rights effectively, parties to whom a statement of objections has been addressed have the right of access to the Commission's investigation file.

(15) In order to safeguard the effective exercise of the rights of defence of parties to whom a statement of objections has been addressed, the hearing officer should be responsible for ensuring that disputes about access to the file or about the protection of business secrets and other confidential information between those parties and the Commission's Directorate-General for Competition are resolved. In exceptional circumstances, the hearing officer may suspend the running of the time period in which an addressee of a statement of objections should reply to that statement until a dispute about access to file has been resolved, if the addressee would not be in a position to reply within the deadline granted and an extension would not be an adequate solution at that point in time.

(16) In order to safeguard the effective exercise of procedural rights while respecting the legitimate interests of confidentiality, the hearing officer should, where appropriate, be able to order specific measures for access to the Commission's file. In particular, the hearing officer should have the power to decide that parts of the file are made accessible to the party requesting access in a

restricted manner, for example by limiting the number or category of persons having access, and the use of the information being accessed.

(17) The hearing officer should be responsible for deciding on requests for the extension of time limits set for the reply to a statement of objections, a supplementary statement of objections or a letter of facts or time limits within which other involved parties, complainants or interested third persons may make comments, in case of disagreement between any such person and the Directorate-General for Competition.

(18) The hearing officer should promote the effectiveness of the oral hearing, by, inter alia, taking all appropriate preparatory measures, including the circulation, in due time before the hearing, of a provisional list of participants and a provisional agenda.

(19) The oral hearing allows the parties to whom the Commission has addressed a statement of objections and other involved parties to further exercise their right to be heard by developing their arguments orally before the Commission, which should be represented by the Directorate-General for Competition as well as other services that contribute to the further preparation of a decision to be taken by the Commission. It should provide an additional opportunity to ensure that all relevant facts — whether favourable or unfavourable to the parties concerned, including the factual elements relating to the gravity and duration of the alleged infringement — are clarified as much as possible. The oral hearing should also allow the parties to present their arguments as to the matters that may be of importance for the possible imposition of fines.

(20) To ensure the effectiveness of oral hearings, the hearing officer may allow the parties to whom a statement of objections has been addressed, other involved parties, complainants, other persons invited to the hearing, the Commission services and the authorities of the Member States to ask questions during the hearing. The oral hearing should not be public so as to guarantee that all participants can express themselves freely. Therefore, information disclosed during the oral hearing should not be used for a purpose other than judicial and/or administrative proceedings for the application of Articles 101 and 102 of the Treaty. Where justified to protect business secrets and other confidential information, the hearing officer should be able to hear persons in a closed session.

(21) Parties to the proceedings which offer commitments pursuant to Article 9 of Regulation (EC) No 1/2003, as well as parties which engage in settlement procedures in cartel cases pursuant to Article 10a of Regulation (EC) No 773/2004, should be able to call upon the hearing officer in relation to the effective exercise of their procedural rights.

(22) The hearing officer should report on the respect for the effective exercise of procedural rights throughout competition proceedings. Moreover, and separately from his or her reporting function, the hearing officer should also be able to make observations on the further progress and objectivity of the proceedings and thereby contribute to ensuring that competition proceedings are concluded on the basis of a sound assessment of all relevant facts.

(23) When disclosing information about natural persons, the hearing officer should have regard, in particular, to Regulation (EC) No 45/2001 of the European Parliament and of the Council of 18 December 2000 on the protection of individuals with regard to the processing of personal data by the Community institutions and bodies and on the free movement of such data[1].

Notes
[1] OJ L 8, 12.1.2001, p.1.

---

(24) Decision 2001/462/EC, ECSC should be repealed,

HAS DECIDED AS FOLLOWS:

CHAPTER 1
ROLE, APPOINTMENT AND DUTIES OF THE HEARING OFFICER

Article 1
The Hearing Officer

1. There shall be one or more hearing officers for competition proceedings, whose powers and functions are laid down in the present decision.

2. The hearing officer shall safeguard the effective exercise of procedural rights throughout competition proceedings before the Commission for the implementation of Articles 101 and 102 of the Treaty, and under Regulation (EC) No 139/2004 (hereinafter 'competition proceedings').

Article 2
Appointment, Termination of Appointment and Deputising

1. The Commission shall appoint the hearing officer. The appointment shall be published in the *Official Journal of the European Union*. Any interruption, termination or transfer of the hearing officer shall be the subject of a reasoned decision of the Commission. That decision shall be published in the *Official Journal of the European Union*.

2. The hearing officer shall be attached, for administrative purposes, to the member of the Commission with special responsibility for competition (hereinafter 'the competent member of the Commission').

3. Where the hearing officer is unable to act, his or her role shall be carried out by another hearing officer. If no hearing officer is able to act, the competent member of the Commission, where appropriate after consultation of the hearing officer, shall designate another competent Commission official, who is not involved in the case in question, to carry out the hearing officer's duties.

4. In case of an actual or potential conflict of interests, the hearing officer shall refrain from acting on a case. Paragraph 3 shall apply.

Commentary
Art 2(1): B&C: 13.083
Art 2(2): B&C: 13.083

Article 3
Method of Operation

1. In exercising his or her functions, the hearing officer shall act independently.

2. In exercising his or her functions, the hearing officer shall take account of the need for effective application of the competition rules in accordance with Union legislation in force and the principles laid down by the Court of Justice.

3. In exercising his or her functions, the hearing officer shall have access to any files relating to competition proceedings.

4. The hearing officer shall be kept informed by the director responsible for investigating the case in the Directorate-General for Competition (hereinafter 'the director responsible') about the development of the procedure.

5. The hearing officer may present observations on any matter arising out of any Commission competition proceeding to the competent member of the Commission.

6. If the hearing officer makes reasoned recommendations to the competent member of the Commission or takes decisions as foreseen in this decision, the hearing officer shall provide a copy of these documents to the director responsible and the Legal Service of the Commission.

7. Any issue regarding the effective exercise of the procedural rights of the parties concerned, other involved parties within the meaning of Article 11(b) of Regulation (EC) No 802/2004 (hereinafter 'the other involved parties'), complainants within the meaning of Article 7(2) of Regulation (EC) No 1/2003 (hereinafter 'complainants') and interested third persons within the meaning of Article 5 of this Decision involved in such proceedings shall first be raised by those persons with the Directorate-General for Competition. If the issue is not resolved, it may be referred to the hearing officer for independent review. Requests related to a measure for which a time limit applies must be made in due time, within the original time limit.

Commentary
Art 3(1): B&C: 13.083
Art 3(4): B&C: 13.083
Art 3(5): B&C: 13.083

Chapter 2
INVESTIGATION

Article 4
Procedural rights in the investigation phase

1. The hearing officer shall safeguard the effective exercise of procedural rights which arise in the context of the exercise of the Commission's powers of investigation under Chapter V of Regulation (EC) No 1/2003 and in proceedings that can result in the imposition of fines pursuant to Article 14 of Regulation (EC) No 139/2004.

2. In particular, the hearing officer shall have the following functions, subject to Article 3(7):

(a) The hearing officer may be asked by undertakings or associations of undertakings to examine claims that a document required by the Commission in the exercise of powers conferred on it pursuant to Article 18, 20 or 21 of Regulation (EC) No 1/2003, in inspections pursuant to Article 13 of Regulation (EC) No 139/2004 or in the context of investigatory measures in proceedings that can result in the imposition of fines pursuant to Article 14 of Regulation (EC) No 139/2004 and which was withheld from the Commission is covered by legal professional privilege, within the meaning of the case-law of the Court of Justice. The hearing officer may only review the matter if the undertaking or association of undertakings making the claim consent to the hearing officer viewing the information claimed to be covered by legal professional privilege as well as related documents that the hearing officer considers necessary for his or her review. Without revealing the potentially privileged content of the information, the hearing officer shall communicate to the director responsible and the undertaking or association of undertakings concerned his or her preliminary view, and may take appropriate steps to promote a mutually acceptable resolution. Where no resolution is reached, the hearing officer may formulate a reasoned recommendation to the competent member of the Commission, without revealing the potentially privileged content of the document. The party making the claim shall receive a copy of this recommendation.

(b) Where the addressee of a request for information pursuant to Article 18(2) of Regulation (EC) No 1/2003 refuses to reply to a question in such a request invoking the privilege against self-incrimination, as determined by the case-law of the Court of Justice, it may refer the matter, in due time following the receipt of the request, to the hearing officer. In appropriate cases, and having regard to the need to avoid undue delay in proceedings, the hearing officer may make a reasoned recommendation as to whether the privilege against self-incrimination applies and inform the director responsible of the conclusions drawn, to be taken into account in case of any decision taken subsequently pursuant to Article 18(3) of Regulation (EC) No 1/2003. The addressee of the request shall receive a copy of the reasoned recommendation.

(c) Where the addressee of a decision requesting information pursuant to Article 18(3) of Regulation (EC) No 1/2003 considers that the time limit imposed for its reply is too short, it may refer the matter to the hearing officer, in due time before the expiry of the original time limit set. The hearing officer shall decide on whether an extension of the time limit should be granted, taking account of the length and complexity of the request for information and the requirements of the investigation.

(d) Undertakings or associations of undertakings subject to an investigative measure by the Commission under Chapter V of Regulation (EC) No 1/2003 shall have the right to be informed of their procedural status, namely whether they are subject to an investigation and, if so, the subject matter and purpose of that investigation. If such an undertaking or association of undertakings considers that it has not been properly informed by the Directorate-General for Competition of its procedural status, it may refer the matter to the hearing officer for resolution. The hearing officer shall take a decision that the Directorate-General for Competition will inform the undertaking or association of undertakings that made the request of their procedural status. This decision shall be communicated to the undertaking or association of undertakings that made the request.

Commentary
Art 4(2)(a): B&C: 13.038, 13.085
Art 4(2)(b): B&C: 13.039
Art 4(2)(c): B&C: 13.013

CHAPTER 3
APPLICATIONS TO BE HEARD

Article 5
Interested third persons

1. Applications to be heard from persons other than those referred to in Articles 5 and 11 of Regulation (EC) No 773/2004 and third persons within the meaning of Article 11 of Regulation (EC) No 802/2004 (hereinafter 'third persons') shall be made in accordance with Article 13(1) of Regulation (EC) No 773/2004 and Article 16 of Regulation (EC) No 802/2004. Applications shall be submitted in writing and explain the applicant's interest in the outcome of the procedure.

2. The hearing officer shall decide as to whether third persons are to be heard after consulting the director responsible. In assessing whether a third person shows a sufficient interest, the hearing officer shall take into account whether and to what extent the applicant is sufficiently affected by the conduct which is the subject of the competition proceedings or whether the applicant fulfils the requirements of Article 18(4) of Regulation (EC) No 139/2004.

3. Where the hearing officer considers that an applicant has not shown a sufficient interest to be heard, he or she shall inform the applicant in writing of the reasons thereof. A time limit shall be fixed within which the applicant may make known its views in writing. If the applicant makes known its views in writing within the time limit set by the hearing officer and the written submission does not lead to a different assessment, that finding shall be stated in a reasoned decision which shall be notified to the applicant.

4. The hearing officer shall inform parties to competition proceedings as from the initiation of proceedings pursuant to Article 11(6) of Regulation (EC) No 1/2003 or Article 6(1)(c) of Regulation (EC) No 139/2004 of the identities of interested third persons to be heard, unless such disclosure would significantly harm a person or undertaking.

Commentary
Art 5: F&N: 5.458

Article 6
Right to an oral hearing; participation of complainants and third persons in the oral hearing

1. At the request of parties to whom the Commission has addressed a statement of objections or other involved parties, the hearing officer shall conduct an oral hearing so that such parties can further develop their written submissions.

2. The hearing officer may, where appropriate and after consulting the director responsible, decide to afford complainants and interested third persons within the meaning of Article 5 the opportunity to express their views at the oral hearing of the parties to which a statement of objections has been issued, provided they so request in their written comments. The hearing officer may also invite representatives from competition authorities from third countries to attend the oral hearing as observers in accordance with agreements concluded between the Union and third countries.

Commentary
Art 6: F&N: 5.480
Art 6(1): F&N: 5.480

CHAPTER 4
ACCESS TO FILE, CONFIDENTIALITY AND BUSINESS SECRETS

Article 7
Access to File and Access to Documents and Information

1. Where a party which has exercised its right of access to the file has reason to believe that the Commission has in its possession documents which have not been disclosed to it and that those documents are necessary for the proper exercise of the right to be heard, it may make a reasoned request for access to these documents to the hearing officer, subject to Article 3(7).

2. Subject to Article 3(7), other involved parties, complainants and interested third persons within the meaning of Article 5 may make a reasoned request to the hearing officer in the circumstances listed hereafter:

(a) Other involved parties who have reason to believe that they have not been informed of the objections addressed to the notifying parties in accordance with Article 13(2) of Regulation (EC) No 802/2004.

(b) A complainant who has been informed by the Commission of its intention to reject a complaint pursuant to Article 7(1) of Regulation (EC) No 773/2004 and has reason to believe that the Commission has in its possession documents which have not been disclosed to it and that those documents are necessary for the proper exercise of its rights in accordance with Article 8(1) of Regulation (EC) No 773/2004.

(c) A complainant who considers that it has not received a copy of the non-confidential version of the statement of objections in accordance with Article 6(1) of Regulation (EC) No 773/2004 or that the non-confidential version of the statement of objections has not been established in a manner which enables it to exercise its rights effectively, with the exception of cases where the settlement procedure applies.

(d) An interested third person within the meaning of Article 5 of this Decision who has reason to believe that it has not been informed of the nature and subject matter of a procedure in accordance with Article 13(1) of Regulation (EC) No 773/2004 and Article 16(1) of Regulation (EC) No 802/2004. The same applies to a complainant in a case to which the settlement procedure applies who has reason to believe that it has not been informed of the nature and subject matter of the procedure in accordance with Article 6(1) of Regulation (EC) No 773/2004.

3. The hearing officer shall take a reasoned decision on a request addressed to him or her under paragraph 1 or 2 and communicate such decision to the person that made the request and to any other person concerned by the procedure.

Commentary
Art 7: F&N: 5.476

Article 8
Business secrets and other confidential information

1. Where the Commission intends to disclose information which may constitute a business secret or other confidential information of any undertaking or person, the latter shall be informed in writing of this intention and the reasons thereof by the Directorate-General for Competition. A time limit shall be fixed within which the undertaking or person concerned may submit any written comments.

2. Where the undertaking or person concerned objects to the disclosure of the information it may refer the matter to the hearing officer. If the hearing officer finds that the information may be disclosed because it does not constitute a business secret or other confidential information or because there is an overriding interest in its disclosure that finding shall be stated in a reasoned decision which shall be notified to the undertaking or person concerned. The decision shall specify the date after which the information will be disclosed. This date shall not be less than 1 week from the date of notification.

3. Paragraphs 1 and 2 shall apply *mutatis mutandis* to the disclosure of information by publication in the *Official Journal of the European Union*.

4. Where appropriate in order to balance the effective exercise of a party's rights of defence with legitimate interests of confidentiality, the hearing officer may decide that parts of the file which are indispensable for the exercise of the party's rights of defence will be made accessible to the party requesting access in a restricted manner, the details of which shall be determined by the hearing officer.

Commentary
Art 8: B&C: 13.078 F&N: 5.435, 5.473
Art 8(3) F&N: 5.503

CHAPTER 5
EXTENSION OF TIME LIMITS

Article 9
Requests for extension of time limits

1. If an addressee of a statement of objections considers that the time limit imposed for its reply to the statement of objections is too short, it may seek an extension of that time limit by means of a reasoned request addressed to the director responsible. Such a request must be made in due time before the expiry of the original time limit in proceedings pursuant to Articles 101 and 102 of the Treaty and at least 5 working days before the expiry of the original time limit in proceedings under Regulation (EC) No 139/2004. If such a request is not granted or the addressee of the statement of objections making the request disagrees with the length of the extension granted, it may refer the matter to the hearing officer for review before the expiry of the original time limit. After hearing the director responsible, the hearing officer shall decide on whether an extension of the time limit is necessary to allow the addressee of a statement of objections to exercise its right to be heard effectively, while also having regard to the need to avoid undue delay in proceedings. In proceedings pursuant to Articles 101 and 102 of the Treaty, the hearing officer shall take into account, among others, the following elements:

  (a) the size and complexity of the file;
  (b) whether the addressee of the statement of objections making the request has had prior access to information;
  (c) any other objective obstacles which may be faced by the addressee of the statement of objections making the request in providing its observations.

For the purposes of assessing point (a) of the first subparagraph, the number of infringements, the alleged duration of the infringement(s), the size and number of documents and the size and complexity of expert studies may be taken into consideration.

2. If other involved parties, a complainant or an interested third person within the meaning of Article 5 considers that the time limit to make its views known is too short, it may seek an extension of that time limit by means of a reasoned request addressed to the director responsible in due time before the expiry of the original time limit. If such a request is not granted or the other involved party, complainant or interested third person disagrees with this decision, it may refer the matter to the hearing officer for review. After hearing the director responsible, the hearing officer shall decide on whether an extension of the time limit should be granted.

Commentary
Art 9: F&N: 5.478
Art 9(1): B&C: 13.064

CHAPTER 6
THE ORAL HEARING

Article 10
Organisation and function

1. The hearing officer shall organise and conduct the hearings provided for in the provisions implementing Articles 101 and 102 of the Treaty and Regulation (EC) No 139/2004.

2. The oral hearing shall be conducted by the hearing officer in full independence.

3. The hearing officer shall ensure that the hearing is properly conducted and shall contribute to the objectivity of the hearing itself and of any decision taken subsequently.

4. The hearing officer shall ensure that the oral hearing provides addressees of the statement of objections, other involved parties, as well as complainants and interested third persons within the meaning of Article 5 which have been admitted to the oral hearing, with sufficient opportunity to develop their views as to the preliminary findings of the Commission.

Commentary
Art 10: F&N: 5.485

Article 11
Preparation of the oral hearing

1. The hearing officer shall be responsible for the preparation of the oral hearing and shall take all appropriate measures in that regard. In order to ensure the proper preparation of the oral hearing, the hearing officer may, after consulting the director responsible, supply in advance to the persons invited to the hearing a list of questions on which they are invited to make known their views. The hearing officer may also indicate to the persons invited to the hearing the focal areas for debate, having regard, in particular, to the facts and issues that the addressees of a statement of objections who have requested an oral hearing want to raise.

2. For this purpose, after consulting the director responsible, the hearing officer may hold a meeting with the persons invited to the hearing and, where appropriate, the Commission services, in order to prepare for the hearing itself.

3. The hearing officer may also ask for prior written notification of the essential contents of the intended statements of persons invited to the hearing.

4. The hearing officer may set a time limit for all persons invited to the oral hearing to provide a list of participants who will attend on their behalf. The hearing officer shall make this list available to all persons invited to the oral hearing in due time before the date of the hearing.

Commentary
Art 11: B&C: 13.084 F&N: 5.481

Article 12
Timing and conduct

1. After consulting the director responsible, the hearing officer shall determine the date, the duration and the place of the hearing. Where a postponement is requested, the hearing officer shall decide whether or not to allow it.

2. The hearing officer shall decide whether new documents should be admitted during the hearing and which persons should be heard on behalf of a party.

3. The hearing officer may allow the parties to whom a statement of objections has been addressed, other involved parties, complainants, other persons invited to the hearing, the Commission services and the authorities of the Member States to ask questions during the hearing. To the extent that, exceptionally, a question cannot be answered in whole or in part at the oral hearing, the hearing officer may allow the reply to be given in writing within a set time limit. Such written reply shall be distributed to all participants in the oral hearing, unless the hearing officer decides otherwise in order to protect the rights of defence of an addressee of a statement of objections or the business secrets or other confidential information of any person.

4. Where required by the need to ensure the right to be heard, the hearing officer may, after consulting the director responsible, afford the parties concerned, other involved parties, complainants or interested third persons within the meaning of Article 5 the opportunity to submit further written comments after the oral hearing. The hearing officer shall fix a date by which such submissions may be made. The Commission shall not be obliged to take into account written comments received after that date.

Commentary
Art 12: B&C: 13.084 F&N: 5.481, 5.486
Art 12(4): B&C: 13.084

Article 13
Protection of business secrets and confidentiality at the oral hearing

Each person shall normally be heard in the presence of all other persons invited to attend the oral hearing. The hearing officer may also decide to hear persons separately in a closed session, having regard to their legitimate interest in the protection of their business secrets and other confidential information.

Commentary
Art 13: F&N: 5.485

Chapter 7
Interim Report and Right to Make Observations

Article 14
Interim report and observations

1. The hearing officer shall submit an interim report to the competent member of the Commission on the hearing and the conclusions he or she draws with regard to the respect for the effective exercise of procedural rights. The observations in this report shall concern procedural issues including the following:

    (a) disclosure of documents and access to the file;
    (b) time limits for replying to the statement of objections;
    (c) the observance of the right to be heard;
    (d) the proper conduct of the oral hearing.

A copy of the report shall be given to the Director-General for Competition, to the director responsible and to the other competent services of the Commission.

2. In addition to, and separately from, the report referred to in paragraph 1, the hearing officer may make observations on the further progress and impartiality of the proceedings. In so doing, the hearing officer shall seek to ensure in particular that, in the preparation of draft Commission decisions, due account is taken of all the relevant facts, whether favourable or unfavourable to the parties concerned, including the factual elements relevant to the gravity and duration of any infringement. Such observations may relate to, inter alia, the need for further information, the withdrawal of certain objections, the formulation of further objections or suggestions for further investigative measures pursuant to Chapter V of Regulation (EC) No 1/2003.

The Director-General for Competition, the director responsible and the Legal Service shall be informed of such observations.

Commentary
Art 14: B&C: 13.083 F&N: 5.486
Art 14(2): B&C: 13.083

Chapter 8
Commitments and Settlements

Article 15
Commitments and settlements

1. Parties to the proceedings which offer commitments to meet the concerns expressed to them by the Commission in its preliminary assessment pursuant to Article 9 of Regulation (EC) No 1/2003 may call upon the hearing officer at any stage in the procedure pursuant to Article 9, in order to ensure the effective exercise of their procedural rights.

2. Parties to proceedings in cartel cases which engage in settlement discussions pursuant to Article 10a of Regulation (EC) No 773/2004 may call upon the hearing officer at any stage during the settlement procedure in order to ensure the effective exercise of their procedural rights.

CHAPTER 9
FINAL REPORT

Article 16
Content and transmission prior to the adoption of a decision

1. The hearing officer shall, on the basis of the draft decision to be submitted to the Advisory Committee in the case in question, prepare a final report in writing on the respect for the effective exercise of procedural rights, as referred to in Article 14(1), at any stage of the proceedings. That report will also consider whether the draft decision deals only with objections in respect of which the parties have been afforded the opportunity of making known their views.

2. The final report shall be submitted to the competent member of the Commission, the Director-General for Competition, the director responsible and the other competent services of the Commission. It shall be communicated to the competent authorities of the Member States and, in accordance with the provisions on cooperation laid down in Protocols 23 and 24 of the EEA Agreement, to the EFTA Surveillance Authority.

Commentary
Art 16: B&C: 13.083 F&N: 5.486

Article 17
Submission to the Commission and publication

1. The hearing officer's final report shall be presented to the Commission together with the draft decision submitted to it, in order to ensure that, when it reaches a decision on an individual case, the Commission is fully apprised of all relevant information as to the course of the procedure and that the effective exercise of procedural rights has been respected throughout the proceedings.

2. The final report may be modified by the hearing officer in the light of any amendments to the draft decision prior to its adoption by the Commission.

3. The Commission shall communicate the hearing officer's final report, together with the decision, to the addressees of the decision. It shall publish the hearing officer's final report in the *Official Journal of the European Union*, together with the decision, having regard to the legitimate interest of undertakings in the protection of their business secrets.

Commentary
Art 17: F&N: 5.486
Art 17(3): F&N: 5.503

CHAPTER 10
FINAL PROVISIONS

Article 18
Repeal and transitional provision

1. Decision 2001/462/EC, ECSC is repealed.

2. Procedural steps already taken under Decision 2001/462/EC, ECSC shall continue to have effect. In relation to investigatory measures that were taken before the entry into force of this Decision, the hearing officer may decline to exercise his or her powers pursuant to Article 4.

In cases where the initiation of proceedings pursuant to Article 11(6) of Regulation (EC) No 1/2003 or the initiation of proceedings pursuant to Article 6(1)(c) of Regulation (EC) No 139/2004 took place before the entry into force of the present Decision, the interim report pursuant to Article 14 of the present Decision and the final report pursuant to Article 16 shall not cover the investigation phase, unless the hearing officer decides otherwise.

Article 19
Entry into force

This Decision shall enter into force on the day following its publication in the *Official Journal of the European Union.*

Done at Brussels, 13 October 2011.

B5

JOINT STATEMENT OF THE COUNCIL AND THE COMMISSION ON THE FUNCTIONING OF THE NETWORK OF COMPETITION AUTHORITIES (10 DECEMBER 2002)

NOTE

Notes

For reasons of space, this document is no longer reproduced in this volume. It remains available on Oxford Companion Law and on the Commission's website at: <http://ec.europa.eu/competition/ecn/joint_statement_en.pdf>

B6

COMMISSION NOTICE ON COOPERATION WITHIN THE NETWORK OF COMPETITION AUTHORITIES

(2004/C 101/03)

(Text with EEA relevance)

Official Journal C 101, 27.4.2004, p.43

Celex No: 52004XC0427(02)

EUR-Lex permanent link: <http://eur-lex.europa.eu/LexUriServ/LexUriServ.do?uri=CELEX:5200 4XC0427(02):EN:NOT>

Notes

EEA application: the EFTA Surveillance Authority has adopted a parallel notice on cooperation within the EFTA Network of Competition Authorities under Article 5(2)(b) of the Surveillance and Court Agreement: OJ C 227, 12.9.2006, p.7 and EEA Supplement No 47, 21.9.2006, p.1.

Commentary
Notice: B&C: 1.071, 3.004, 14.123, 15.005, 15.007, 15.032

1. Introduction

1. Council Regulation (EC) No 1/2003 of 16 December 2002 on the implementation of the rules on competition laid down in Articles [101] and [102]* of the Treaty[1] (hereafter the "Council Regulation") creates a system of parallel competences in which the Commission and the Member States' competition authorities (hereafter the "NCAs")[2] can apply Article [101] and Article [102] of the [Treaty on the Functioning of the European Union] (hereafter the "Treaty"). Together the NCAs and the Commission form a network of public authorities: they act in the public interest and cooperate closely in order to protect competition. The network is a forum for discussion and cooperation in the application and enforcement of EC competition policy. It provides a framework for the cooperation of European competition authorities in cases where Articles [101] and [102] of the Treaty are applied and is the basis for the creation and maintenance of a common competition culture in Europe. The network is called "European Competition Network" (ECN).

Notes

* Ed note: please see the Note on the Lisbon Treaty at p.xvii in regard to article renumbering introduced by the Lisbon Treaty.
[1] OJ L 1, 4.1.2003, p.1.
[2] In this notice, the European Commission and the NCAs are collectively referred to as "the competition authorities".

2. The structure of the NCAs varies between Member States. In some Member States, one body investigates cases and takes all types of decisions. In other Member States, the functions are divided between two bodies, one which is in charge of the investigation of the case and another, often a college, which is responsible for deciding the case. Finally, in certain Member States, prohibition decisions and/or decisions imposing a fine can only be taken by a court: another competition authority acts as a prosecutor bringing the case before that court. Subject to the general principle of effectiveness, Article 35 of the Council Regulation allows Member States to choose the body or bodies which will be designated as national competition authorities and to allocate functions between them. Under general principles of Community law, Member States are under an obligation to set up a sanctioning system providing for sanctions which are effective, proportionate and dissuasive for infringements of EC law.[3] The enforcement systems of the Member States differ but they have recognised the standards of each other's systems as a basis for cooperation.[4]

Notes

[3] Cf. ECJ Case 68/88 *Commission v Greece* [1989] ECR 2965 (Recitals 23 to 25).
[4] See paragraph 8 of the Joint Statement of the Council and the Commission on the functioning of the network available from the Council register at <http://register.consilium.eu.int (document No 15435/02 ADD 1)>.

Commentary
para 2: B&C: 15.008

3. The network formed by the competition authorities should ensure both an efficient division of work and an effective and consistent application of EC competition rules. The Council Regulation together with the joint statement of the Council and the Commission on the functioning of the European Competition Network sets out the main principles of the functioning of the network. This notice presents the details of the system.

Commentary
para 3: B&C: 15.012, 15.021

4. Consultations and exchanges within the network are matters between public enforcers and do not alter any rights or obligations arising from Community or national law for companies. Each competition authority remains fully responsible for ensuring due process in the cases it deals with.

2. Division of Work

2.1 Principles of allocation

5. The Council Regulation is based on a system of parallel competences in which all competition authorities have the power to apply Articles [101] or [102] of the Treaty and are responsible for an efficient division of work with respect to those cases where an investigation is deemed to be necessary. At the same time each network member retains full discretion in deciding whether or not to investigate a case. Under this system of parallel competences, cases will be dealt with by:

— a single NCA, possibly with the assistance of NCAs of other Member States; or
— several NCAs acting in parallel; or
— the Commission.

Commentary
para 5: B&C: 15.009 **F&N:** 2.156, 2.157

6. In most instances the authority that receives a complaint or starts an *ex-officio* procedure[5] will remain in charge of the case. Re-allocation of a case would only be envisaged at the outset of a procedure (see paragraph 18 below) where either that authority considered that it was not well placed to act or where other authorities also considered themselves well placed to act (see paragraphs 8 to 15 below).

Notes
[5] In this Notice the term "procedure" is used for investigations and/or formal proceedings for the adoption of a decision pursuant to the Council Regulation conducted by an NCA or the Commission, as the case may be.

7. Where re-allocation is found to be necessary for an effective protection of competition and of the Community interest, network members will endeavour to re-allocate cases to a single well placed competition authority as often as possible.[6] In any event, re-allocation should be a quick and efficient process and not hold up ongoing investigations.

Notes
[6] See Recital 18 of the Council Regulation.

8. An authority can be considered to be well placed to deal with a case if the following three cumulative conditions are met:

1. the agreement or practice has substantial direct actual or foreseeable effects on competition within its territory, is implemented within or originates from its territory;
2. the authority is able to effectively bring to an end the entire infringement, i.e. it can adopt a cease-and-desist order the effect of which will be sufficient to bring an end to the infringement and it can, where appropriate, sanction the infringement adequately;
3. it can gather, possibly with the assistance of other authorities, the evidence required to prove the infringement.

Commentary
para 8: B&C: 15.013 **F&N:** 2.157

9. The above criteria indicate that a material link between the infringement and the territory of a Member State must exist in order for that Member State's competition authority to be considered well placed. It can be expected that in most cases the authorities of those Member States where competition is substantially affected by an infringement will be well placed provided they are capable of effectively bringing the infringement to an end through either single or parallel action unless the Commission is better placed to act (see below paragraphs 14 and 15).

10. It follows that a single NCA is usually well placed to deal with agreements or practices that substantially affect competition mainly within its territory.

> Example 1: *Undertakings situated in Member State A are involved in a price fixing cartel on products that are mainly sold in Member State A.*
>
> *The NCA in A is well placed to deal with the case.*

11. Furthermore single action of an NCA might also be appropriate where, although more than one NCA can be regarded as well placed, the action of a single NCA is sufficient to bring the entire infringement to an end.

> Example 2: *Two undertakings have set up a joint venture in Member State A. The joint venture provides services in Member States A and B and gives rise to a competition problem. A cease-and-desist order is considered to be sufficient to deal with the case effectively because it can bring an end to the entire infringement. Evidence is located mainly at the offices of the joint venture in Member State A.*
>
> *The NCAs in A and B are both well placed to deal with the case but single action by the NCA in A would be sufficient and more efficient than single action by NCA in B or parallel action by both NCAs.*

12. Parallel action by two or three NCAs may be appropriate where an agreement or practice has substantial effects on competition mainly in their respective territories and the action of only one NCA would not be sufficient to bring the entire infringement to an end and/or to sanction it adequately.

> Example 3: *Two undertakings agree on a market sharing agreement, restricting the activity of the company located in Member State A to Member State A and the activity of the company located in Member State B to Member State B.*
>
> *The NCAs in A and B are well placed to deal with the case in parallel, each one for its respective territory.*

Commentary
para 12: **B&C:** 15.013, 15.021 **F&N:** 2.157

13. The authorities dealing with a case in parallel action will endeavour to coordinate their action to the extent possible. To that effect, they may find it useful to designate one of them as a lead authority and to delegate tasks to the lead authority such as for example the coordination of investigative measures, while each authority remains responsible for conducting its own proceedings.

Commentary
para 13: **B&C:** 15.013, 15.021

14. The Commission is particularly well placed if one or several agreement(s) or practice(s), including networks of similar agreements or practices, have effects on competition in more than three Member States (cross-border markets covering more than three Member States or several national markets).

Commentary
para 14: **B&C:** 14.124, 15.013 **F&N:** 2.157, 8.100, 8.243, 8.245, 14.19

> Example 4: *Two undertakings agree to share markets or fix prices for the whole territory of the Community. The Commission is well placed to deal with the case.*

> Example 5: *An undertaking, dominant in four different national markets, abuses its position by imposing fidelity rebates on its distributors in all these markets. The Commission is well placed to deal with the case. It could also deal with one national market so as to create a "leading" case and other national markets could be dealt with by NCAs, particularly if each national market requires a separate assessment.*

15. Moreover, the Commission is particularly well placed to deal with a case if it is closely linked to other Community provisions which may be exclusively or more effectively applied by the Commission, if the Community interest requires the adoption of a Commission decision to develop Community competition policy when a new competition issue arises or to ensure effective enforcement.

Commentary
para 15: B&C: 15.013 **F&N:** 2.157

2.2. Mechanisms of cooperation for the purpose of case allocation and assistance

2.2.1. Information at the beginning of the procedure (Article 11 of the Council Regulation)

16. In order to detect multiple procedures and to ensure that cases are dealt with by a well placed competition authority, the members of the network have to be informed at an early stage of the cases pending before the various competition authorities.[7] If a case is to be re-allocated, it is indeed in the best interest both of the network and of the undertakings concerned that the re-allocation takes place quickly.

Notes
[7] For cases initiated following a leniency application see paragraphs 37 *et subseq.*

Commentary
para 16: F&N: 8.100

17. The Council Regulation creates a mechanism for the competition authorities to inform each other in order to ensure an efficient and quick re-allocation of cases. Article 11(3) of the Council Regulation lays down an obligation for NCAs to inform the Commission when acting under Article [101] or [102] of the Treaty before or without delay after commencing the first formal investigative measure. It also states that the information may be made available to other NCAs.[8] The rationale of Article 11(3) of the Council Regulation is to allow the network to detect multiple procedures and address possible case re-allocation issues as soon as an authority starts investigating a case. Information should therefore be provided to NCAs and the Commission before or just after any step similar to the measures of investigation that can be undertaken by the Commission under Articles 18 to 21 of the Council Regulation. The Commission has accepted an equivalent obligation to inform NCAs under Article 11(2) of the Council Regulation. Network members will inform each other of pending cases by means of a standard form containing limited details of the case, such as the authority dealing with the case, the product, territories and parties concerned, the alleged infringement, the suspected duration of the infringement and the origin of the case. They will also provide each other with updates when a relevant change occurs.

Notes
[8] The intention of making any information exchanged pursuant to Article 11 available and easily accessible to all network members is however expressed in the Joint Statement on the functioning of the network mentioned above in footnote 4.

Commentary
para 17: B&C: 15.014 **F&N:** 2.157

18. Where case re-allocation issues arise, they should be resolved swiftly, normally within a period of two months, starting from the date of the first information sent to the network pursuant to Article 11 of the Council Regulation. During this period, competition authorities will endeavour to reach an agreement on a possible re-allocation and, where relevant, on the modalities for parallel action.

Commentary
para 18: B&C: 15.012, 15.016

19. In general, the competition authority or authorities that is/are dealing with a case at the end of the re-allocation period should continue to deal with the case until the completion of the proceedings. Re-allocation of a case after the initial allocation period of two months should only occur where the facts known about the case change materially during the course of the proceedings.

Commentary
para 19: B&C: 15.012

2.2.2. Suspension or termination of proceedings (Article 13 of the Council Regulation)

20. If the same agreement or practice is brought before several competition authorities, be it because they have received a complaint or have opened a procedure on their own initiative, Article 13 of the Council Regulation provides a legal basis for suspending proceedings or rejecting a complaint on the grounds that another authority is dealing with the case or has dealt with the case. In Article 13 of the Council Regulation, "dealing with the case" does not merely mean that a complaint has been lodged with another authority. It means that the other authority is investigating or has investigated the case on its own behalf.

Commentary
para 20: B&C: 15.023 **F&N:** 2.159

21. Article 13 of the Council Regulation applies when another authority has dealt or is dealing with the competition issue raised by the complainant, even if the authority in question has acted or acts on the basis of a complaint lodged by a different complainant or as a result of an *ex-officio* procedure. This implies that Article 13 of the Council Regulation can be invoked when the agreement or practice involves the same infringement(s) on the same relevant geographic and product markets.

Commentary
para 21: F&N: 2.159

22. An NCA may suspend or close its proceedings but it has no obligation to do so. Article 13 of the Council Regulation leaves scope for appreciation of the peculiarities of each individual case. This flexibility is important: if a complaint was rejected by an authority following an investigation of the substance of the case, another authority may not want to re-examine the case. On the other hand, if a complaint was rejected for other reasons (e.g. the authority was unable to collect the evidence necessary to prove the infringement), another authority may wish to carry out its own investigation and deal with the case. This flexibility is also reflected, for pending cases, in the choice open to each NCA as to whether it closes or suspends its proceedings. An authority may be unwilling to close a case before the outcome of another authority's proceedings is clear. The ability to suspend its proceedings allows the authority to retain its ability to decide at a later point whether or not to terminate its proceedings. Such flexibility also facilitates consistent application of the rules.

Commentary
para 22: F&N: 2.158

23. Where an authority closes or suspends proceedings because another authority is dealing with the case, it may transfer — in accordance with Article 12 of the Council Regulation — the information provided by the complainant to the authority which is to deal with the case.

24. Article 13 of the Council Regulation can also be applied to part of a complaint or to part of the proceedings in a case. It may be that only part of a complaint or of an *ex-officio* procedure overlaps with a case already dealt or being dealt with by another competition authority. In that case, the competition authority to which the complaint is brought is entitled to reject part of the complaint on the basis of Article 13 of the Council Regulation and to deal with the rest of the complaint in an appropriate manner. The same principle applies to the termination of proceedings.

Commentary
para 24: B&C: 15.023 **F&N:** 2.158, 2.232

25. Article 13 of the Council Regulation is not the only legal basis for suspending or closing *ex-officio* proceedings or rejecting complaints. NCAs may also be able to do so according to their national

procedural law. The Commission may also reject a complaint for lack of Community interest or other reasons pertaining to the nature of the complaint.[9]

Notes
[9] See Commission Notice on complaints.

Commentary
para 25: F&N: 2.158

2.2.3. Exchange and use of confidential information (Article 12 of the Council Regulation)

26. A key element of the functioning of the network is the power of all the competition authorities to exchange and use information (including documents, statements and digital information) which has been collected by them for the purpose of applying Article [101] or Article [102] of the Treaty. This power is a precondition for efficient and effective allocation and handling of cases.

Commentary
para 26: F&N: 8.259, 8.230

---

27. Article 12 of the Council Regulation states that for the purpose of applying Articles [101] and [102] of the Treaty, the Commission and the competition authorities of the Member States shall have the power to provide one another with and use in evidence any matter of fact or of law, including confidential information. This means that exchanges of information may not only take place between an NCA and the Commission but also between and amongst NCAs. Article 12 of the Council Regulation takes precedence over any contrary law of a Member State. The question whether information was gathered in a legal manner by the transmitting authority is governed on the basis of the law applicable to this authority. When transmitting information the transmitting authority may inform the receiving authority whether the gathering of the information was contested or could still be contested.

Commentary
para 27: B&C: 15.028 F&N: 2.181, 8.259, 8.320

---

28. The exchange and use of information contains in particular the following safeguards for undertakings and individuals.
   (a) First, Article 28 of the Council Regulation states that "the Commission and the competition authorities of the Member States, their officials, servants and other persons working under the supervision of these authorities (…) shall not disclose information acquired or exchanged by them pursuant to the" Council Regulation which is "of the kind covered by the obligation of professional secrecy". However, the legitimate interest of undertakings in the protection of their business secrets may not prejudice the disclosure of information necessary to prove an infringement of Articles [101] and [102] of the Treaty. The term "professional secrecy" used in Article 28 of the Council Regulation is a Community law concept and includes in particular business secrets and other confidential information. This will create a common minimum level of protection throughout the Community.
   (b) The second safeguard given to undertakings relates to the use of information which has been exchanged within the network. Under Article 12(2) of the Council Regulation, information so exchanged can only be used in evidence for the application of Articles [101] and [102] of the Treaty and for the subject matter for which it was collected.[10] According to Article 12(2) of the Council Regulation, the information exchanged may also be used for the purpose of applying national competition law in parallel in the same case. This is, however, only possible if the application of national law does not lead to an outcome as regards the finding of an infringement different from that under Articles [101] and [102] of the Treaty.
   (c) The third safeguard given by the Council Regulation relates to sanctions on individuals on the basis of information exchanged pursuant to Article 12(1). The Council Regulation only provides for sanctions on undertakings for violations of Articles [101] and [102] of the Treaty.

Some national laws also provide for sanctions on individuals in connection with violations of Articles [101] and [102] of the Treaty. Individuals normally enjoy more extensive rights of defence (e.g. a right to remain silent compared to undertakings which may only refuse to answer questions which would lead them to admit that they have committed an infringement.[11]) Article 12(3) of the Council Regulation ensures that information collected from undertakings cannot be used in a way which would circumvent the higher protection of individuals. This provision precludes sanctions being imposed on individuals on the basis of information exchanged pursuant to the Council Regulation if the laws of the transmitting and the receiving authorities do not provide for sanctions of a similar kind in respect of individuals, unless the rights of the individual concerned as regards the collection of evidence have been respected by the transmitting authority to the same standard as they are guaranteed by the receiving authority. The qualification of the sanctions by national law ("administrative" or "criminal") is not relevant for the purpose of applying Article 12(3) of the Council Regulation. The Council Regulation intends to create a distinction between sanctions which result in custody and other types of sanctions such as fines on individuals and other personal sanctions. If both the legal system of the transmitting and that of the receiving authority provide for sanctions of a similar kind (e.g. in both Member States, fines can be imposed on a member of the staff of an undertaking who has been involved in the violation of Article [101] or [102] of the Treaty), information exchanged pursuant to Article 12 of the Council Regulation can be used by the receiving authority. In that case, procedural safeguards in both systems are considered to be equivalent. If on the other hand, both legal systems do not provide for sanctions of a similar kind, the information can only be used if the same level of protection of the rights of the individual has been respected in the case at hand (see Article 12(3) of the Council Regulation). In that latter case however, custodial sanctions can only be imposed where both the transmitting and the receiving authority have the power to impose such a sanction.

Notes

10 See ECJ Case 85/87 *Dow Benelux* [1989] ECR 3137 (Recitals 17–20).

11 See ECJ Case 374/87 *Orkem* [1989] ECR 3283 and CFI Case T-112/98 *Mannesmannröhren-Werke AG* [2001] ECR II-729.

Commentary

para 28: F&N: 8.259, 8.320
para 28(a): B&C: 15.029
para 28(b): F&N: 2.179, 2.185
para 28(c): F&N: 2.189

2.2.4. Investigations (Article 22 of the Council Regulation)

29. The Council Regulation provides that an NCA may ask another NCA for assistance in order to collect information on its behalf. An NCA can ask another NCA to carry out fact-finding measures on its behalf. Article 12 of the Council Regulation empowers the assisting NCA to transmit the information it has collected to the requesting NCA. Any exchange between or amongst NCAs and use in evidence by the requesting NCA of such information shall be carried out in accordance with Article 12 of the Council Regulation. Where an NCA acts on behalf of another NCA, it acts pursuant to its own rules of procedure, and under its own powers of investigation.

Commentary

para 29: B&C: 15.027 F&N: 2.162

30. Under Article 22(2) of the Council Regulation, the Commission can ask an NCA to carry out an inspection on its behalf. The Commission can either adopt a decision pursuant to Article 20(4) of the Council Regulation or simply issue a request to the NCA. The NCA officials will exercise their powers in accordance with their national law. The agents of the Commission may assist the NCA during the inspection.

Commentary
para 30: B&C: 15.027

2.3. Position of undertakings

2.3.1. General

31. All network members will endeavour to make the allocation of cases a quick and efficient process. Given the fact that the Council Regulation has created a system of parallel competences, the allocation of cases between members of the network constitutes a mere division of labour where some authorities abstain from acting. The allocation of cases therefore does not create individual rights for the companies involved in or affected by an infringement to have the case dealt with by a particular authority.

Commentary
para 31: B&C: 15.015

32. If a case is re-allocated to a given competition authority, it is because the application of the allocation criteria set out above led to the conclusion that this authority is well placed to deal with the case by single or parallel action. The competition authority to which the case is re-allocated would have been in a position, in any event, to commence an *ex-officio* procedure against the infringement.

33. Furthermore, all competition authorities apply Community competition law and the Council Regulation sets out mechanisms to ensure that the rules are applied in a consistent way.

34. If a case is re-allocated within the network, the undertakings concerned and the complainant(s) are informed as soon as possible by the competition authorities involved.

Commentary
para 34: B&C: 15.012

2.3.2. Position of complainants

35. If a complaint is lodged with the Commission pursuant to Article 7 of the Council Regulation and if the Commission does not investigate the complaint or prohibit the agreement or practice complained of, the complainant has a right to obtain a decision rejecting his complaint. This is without prejudice to Article 7(3) of the Commission implementing regulation.[12] The rights of complainants who lodge a complaint with an NCA are governed by the applicable national law.

Notes
[12] Commission Regulation (EC) No 773/2004, OJ L 123, 27.4.2004.

36. In addition, Article 13 of the Council Regulation gives all NCAs the possibility of suspending or rejecting a complaint on the ground that another competition authority is dealing or has dealt with the same case. That provision also allows the Commission to reject a complaint on the ground that a competition authority of a Member State is dealing or has dealt with the case. Article 12 of the Council Regulation allows the transfer of information between competition authorities within the network subject to the safeguards provided in that Article (see paragraph 28 above).

2.3.3. Position of applicants claiming the benefit of a leniency programme

37. The Commission considers[13] that it is in the Community interest to grant favourable treatment to undertakings which co-operate with it in the investigation of cartel infringements. A number of Member States have also adopted leniency programmes[14] relating to cartel investigations. The aim of these leniency programmes is to facilitate the detection by competition authorities of cartel activity and also thereby to act as a deterrent to participation in unlawful cartels.

Notes

13 OJ C 45, 19.2.2002, p.3, at paragraph 3.

14 In this Notice, the term "leniency programme" is used to describe all programmes (including the Commission's programme) which offer either full immunity or a significant reduction in the penalties which would otherwise have been imposed on a participant in a cartel, in exchange for the freely volunteered disclosure of information on the cartel which satisfies specific criteria prior to or during the investigative stage of the case. The term does not cover reductions in the penalty granted for other reasons. The Commission will publish on its website a list of those authorities that operate a leniency programme.

38. In the absence of a European Union-wide system of fully harmonised leniency programmes, an application for leniency to a given authority is not to be considered as an application for leniency to any other authority. It is therefore in the interest of the applicant to apply for leniency to all competition authorities which have competence to apply Article [101] of the Treaty in the territory which is affected by the infringement and which may be considered well placed to act against the infringement in question.15 In view of the importance of timing in most existing leniency programmes, applicants will also need to consider whether it would be appropriate to file leniency applications with the relevant authorities simultaneously. It is for the applicant to take the steps which it considers appropriate to protect its position with respect to possible proceedings by these authorities.

Notes

15 See paragraphs 8 to 15 above.

Commentary

para 38: B&C: 14.124

39. As for all cases where Articles [101] and [102] of the Treaty are applied, where an NCA deals with a case which has been initiated as a result of a leniency application, it must inform the Commission and may make the information available to other members of the network pursuant to Article 11(3) of the Council Regulation (cf. paragraphs 16 *et subseq.*). The Commission has accepted an equivalent obligation to inform NCAs under Article 11(2) of the Council Regulation. In such cases, however, information submitted to the network pursuant to Article 11 will not be used by other members of the network as the basis for starting an investigation on their own behalf whether under the competition rules of the Treaty or, in the case of NCAs, under their national competition law or other laws.16 This is without prejudice to any power of the authority to open an investigation on the basis of information received from other sources or, subject to paragraphs 40 and 41 below, to request, be provided with and use information pursuant to Article 12 from any member of the network, including the network member to whom the leniency application was submitted.

Notes

16 Similarly, information transmitted with a view to obtaining assistance from the receiving authority under Articles 20 or 21 of the Council Regulation or of carrying out an investigation or other fact-finding measure under Article 22 of the Council Regulation may only be used for the purpose of the application of the said Articles.

Commentary

para 39: F&N: 2.170, 8.237

40. Save as provided under paragraph 41, information voluntarily submitted by a leniency applicant will only be transmitted to another member of the network pursuant to Article 12 of the Council Regulation with the consent of the applicant. Similarly other information that has been obtained during or following an inspection or by means of or following any other fact-finding measures which, in each case, could not have been carried out except as a result of the leniency application will only be transmitted to another authority pursuant to Article 12 of the Council Regulation if the applicant has consented to the transmission to that authority of information it has voluntarily submitted in its application for leniency. The network members will encourage leniency applicants to give such consent, in particular as regards disclosure to authorities in respect of which it would be open to the applicant to obtain lenient treatment. Once the leniency applicant has given consent to the transmission of information to another

111

authority, that consent may not be withdrawn. This paragraph is without prejudice, however, to the responsibility of each applicant to file leniency applications to whichever authorities it may consider appropriate.

Commentary
para 40: B&C: 15.038, 15.039 **F&N:** 2.170, 2.276, 8.238, 8.483

41. Notwithstanding the above, the consent of the applicant for the transmission of information to another authority pursuant to Article 12 of the Council Regulation is not required in any of the following circumstances:

    1. No consent is required where the receiving authority has also received a leniency application relating to the same infringement from the same applicant as the transmitting authority, provided that at the time the information is transmitted it is not open to the applicant to withdraw the information which it has submitted to that receiving authority.

    2. No consent is required where the receiving authority has provided a written commitment that neither the information transmitted to it nor any other information it may obtain following the date and time of transmission as noted by the transmitting authority, will be used by it or by any other authority to which the information is subsequently transmitted to impose sanctions:

       (a) on the leniency applicant;

       (b) on any other legal or natural person covered by the favourable treatment offered by the transmitting authority as a result of the application made by the applicant under its leniency programme;

       (c) on any employee or former employee of any of the persons covered by (a) or (b).

       A copy of the receiving authority's written commitment will be provided to the applicant.

    3. In the case of information collected by a network member under Article 22(1) of the Council Regulation on behalf of and for the account of the network member to whom the leniency application was made, no consent is required for the transmission of such information to, and its use by, the network member to whom the application was made.

Commentary
para 41: B&C: 15.038, 15.039 **F&N:** 2.170, 2.276, 8.238, 8.483
para 41(2): B&C: 15.038 **F&N:** 2.172

42. Information relating to cases initiated as a result of a leniency application and which has been submitted to the Commission under Article 11(3) of the Council Regulation[17] will only be made available to those NCAs that have committed themselves to respecting the principles set out above (see paragraph 72). The same principle applies where a case has been initiated by the Commission as a result of a leniency application made to the Commission. This does not affect the power of any authority to be provided with information under Article 12 of the Council Regulation, provided however that the provisions of paragraphs 40 and 41 are respected.

Notes
[17] See paragraph 17.

Commentary
para 42: B&C: 15.039 **F&N:** 8.240

3. CONSISTENT APPLICATION OF EC COMPETITION RULES[18]

Notes
[18] Article 15 of the Council Regulation empowers NCAs and the Commission to submit written and, with the permission of the Court, oral submissions in court proceedings for the application of Articles [101] and [102] of the Treaty. This is a very important tool for ensuring consistent application of Community rules. In exercising this power NCAs and the Commission will cooperate closely.

3.1. Mechanism of Cooperation (Article 11(4) and 11(5) of the Council Regulation)

43. The Council Regulation pursues the objective that Articles [101] and [102] of the Treaty are applied in a consistent manner throughout the Community. In this respect NCAs will respect the convergence rule contained in Article 3(2) of the Council Regulation. In line with Article 16(2) they cannot — when ruling on agreements, decisions and practices under Article [101] or Article [102] of the Treaty which are already the subject of a Commission decision — take decisions, which would run counter to the decisions adopted by the Commission. Within the network of competition authorities the Commission, as the guardian of the Treaty, has the ultimate but not the sole responsibility for developing policy and safeguarding consistency when it comes to the application of EC competition law.

44. According to Article 11(4) of the Council Regulation, no later than 30 days before the adoption of a decision applying Articles [101] or [102] of the Treaty and requiring that an infringement be brought to an end, accepting commitments or withdrawing the benefit of a block-exemption regulation, NCAs shall inform the Commission. They have to send to the Commission, at the latest 30 days before the adoption of the decision, a summary of the case, the envisaged decision or, in the absence thereof, any other document indicating the proposed course of action.

45. As under Article 11(3) of the Council Regulation, the obligation is to inform the Commission, but the information may be shared by the NCA informing the Commission with the other members of the network

Commentary
para 45: B&C: 15.041

46. Where an NCA has informed the Commission pursuant to Article 11(4) of the Council Regulation and the 30 days deadline has expired, the decision can be adopted as long as the Commission has not initiated proceedings. The Commission may make written observations on the case before the adoption of the decision by the NCA. The NCA and the Commission will make the appropriate efforts to ensure the consistent application of Community law (cf. paragraph 3 above).

Commentary
para 46: F&N: 2.223

47. If special circumstances require that a national decision is taken in less than 30 days following the transmission of information pursuant to Article 11(4) of the Council Regulation, the NCA concerned may ask the Commission for a swifter reaction. The Commission will endeavour to react as quickly as possible.

Commentary
para 47: F&N: 2.217

48. Other types of decisions, i.e. decisions rejecting complaints, decisions closing an *ex-officio* procedure or decisions ordering interim measures, can also be important from a competition policy point of view, and the network members may have an interest in informing each other about them and possibly discussing them. NCAs can therefore on the basis of Article 11(5) of the Council Regulation inform the Commission and thereby inform the network of any other case in which EC competition law is applied.

Commentary
para 48: B&C: 15.041

49. All members of the network should inform each other about the closure of their procedures which have been notified to the network pursuant to Article 11(2) and (3) of the Council Regulation.[19]

Notes
[19] See paragraph 24 of the Joint Statement on the functioning of the network mentioned above in footnote 4.

Commentary
para 49: B&C: 15.041

3.2. The Initiation of Proceedings by the Commission Under Article 11(6) of the Council Regulation

50. According to the case law of the Court of Justice, the Commission, entrusted by Article [105](1) of the Treaty with the task of ensuring the application of the principles laid down in Articles [101] and [102] of the Treaty, is responsible for defining and implementing the orientation of Community competition policy.[20] It can adopt individual decisions under Articles [101] and [102] of the Treaty at any time.

Notes

[20] See ECJ Case C-344/98 *Masterfoods Ltd* [2000] ECR I-11369.

51. Article 11(6) of the Council Regulation states that the initiation by the Commission of proceedings for the adoption of a decision under the Council Regulation shall relieve all NCAs of their competence to apply Articles [101] and [102] of the Treaty. This means that once the Commission has opened proceedings, NCAs cannot act under the same legal basis against the same agreement(s) or practice(s) by the same undertaking(s) on the same relevant geographic and product market.

52. The initiation of proceedings by the Commission is a formal act[21] by which the Commission indicates its intention to adopt a decision under Chapter III of the Council Regulation. It can occur at any stage of the investigation of the case by the Commission. The mere fact that the Commission has received a complaint is not in itself sufficient to relieve NCAs of their competence.

Notes

[21] The ECJ has defined that concept in Case 48/72 *SA Brasserie de Haecht* [1973] ECR 77: "the initiation of a procedure within the meaning of Article 9 of Regulation No 17 implies an authoritative act of the Commission, evidencing its intention of taking a decision."

Commentary
para 52: B&C: 15.017 F&N: 2.231

53. Two situations can arise. First, where the Commission is the first competition authority to initiate proceedings in a case for the adoption of a decision under the Council Regulation, national competition authorities may no longer deal with the case. Article 11(6) of the Council Regulation provides that once the Commission has initiated proceedings, the NCAs can no longer start their own procedure with a view to applying Articles [101] and [102] of the Treaty to the same agreement(s) or practice(s) by the same undertaking(s) on the same relevant geographic and product market.

54. The second situation is where one or more NCAs have informed the network pursuant to Article 11(3) of the Council Regulation that they are acting on a given case. During the initial allocation period (indicative time period of two months, see paragraph 18 above), the Commission can initiate proceedings with the effects of Article 11(6) of the Council Regulation after having consulted the authorities concerned. After the allocation phase, the Commission will in principle only apply Article 11(6) of the Council Regulation if one of the following situations arises:

   (a) Network members envisage conflicting decisions in the same case.
   (b) Network members envisage a decision which is obviously in conflict with consolidated case law; the standards defined in the judgements of the Community courts and in previous decisions and regulations of the Commission should serve as a yardstick; concerning the assessment of the facts (e.g. market definition), only a significant divergence will trigger an intervention of the Commission;
   (c) Network member(s) is (are) unduly drawing out proceedings in the case;

(d) There is a need to adopt a Commission decision to develop Community competition policy in particular when a similar competition issue arises in several Member States or to ensure effective enforcement;

(e) The NCA(s) concerned do not object.

Commentary
para 54: F&N: 2.240
para 54(b): B&C: 15.068 **F&N:** 2.244

55. If an NCA is already acting on a case, the Commission will explain the reasons for the application of Article 11(6) of the Council Regulation in writing to the NCA concerned and to the other members of the Network.[22]

Notes
[22] See paragraph 22 of the Joint Statement mentioned in footnote 4.

56. The Commission will announce to the network its intention of applying Article 11(6) of the Council Regulation in due time, so that Network members will have the possibility of asking for a meeting of the Advisory Committee on the matter before the Commission initiates proceedings.

57. The Commission will normally not — and to the extent that Community interest is not at stake — adopt a decision which is in conflict with a decision of an NCA after proper information pursuant to both Article 11(3) and (4) of the Council Regulation has taken place and the Commission has not made use of Article 11(6) of the Council Regulation.

Commentary
para 57: B&C: 15.025

4. The Role and the Functioning of the Advisory Committee in the New System

58. The Advisory Committee is the forum where experts from the various competition authorities discuss individual cases and general issues of Community competition law.[23]

Notes
[23] In accordance with Article 14(2) of the Council Regulation, where horizontal issues such as block-exemption regulations and guidelines are being discussed, Member States can appoint an additional representative competent in competition matters and who does not necessarily belong to the competition authority.

4.1. Scope of the Consultation

4.1.1. Decisions of the Commission

59. The Advisory Committee is consulted prior to the Commission taking any decision pursuant to Articles 7, 8, 9, 10, 23, 24(2) or 29(1) of the Council Regulation. The Commission must take the utmost account of the opinion of the Advisory Committee and inform the Committee of the manner in which its opinion has been taken into account.

60. For decisions adopting interim measures, the Advisory Committee is consulted following a swifter and lighter procedure, on the basis of a short explanatory note and the operative part of the decision.

4.1.2. Decisions of NCAs

61. It is in the interest of the network that important cases dealt with by NCAs under Articles [101] and [102] of the Treaty can be discussed in the Advisory Committee. The Council Regulation enables the Commission to put a given case being dealt with by an NCA on the agenda of the Advisory Committee. Discussion can be requested by the Commission or by any Member State. In either case, the Commission will put the case on the agenda after having informed the

NCA(s) concerned. This discussion in the Advisory Committee will not lead to a formal opinion.

62. In important cases, the Advisory Committee could also serve as a forum for the discussion of case allocation. In particular, where the Commission intends to apply Article 11(6) of the Council Regulation after the initial allocation period, the case can be discussed in the Advisory Committee before the Commission initiates proceedings. The Advisory Committee may issue an informal statement on the matter.

Commentary
para 62: B&C: 15.016

4.1.3. Implementing measures, block-exemption regulations, guidelines and other notices (Article 33 of the Council Regulation)

63. The Advisory Committee will be consulted on draft Commission regulations as provided for in the relevant Council Regulations.

64. Beside regulations, the Commission may also adopt notices and guidelines. These more flexible tools are very useful for explaining and announcing the Commission's policy, and for explaining its interpretation of the competition rules. The Advisory Committee will also be consulted on these notices and guidelines.

4.2. Procedure

4.2.1. Normal procedure

65. For consultation on Commission draft decisions, the meeting of the Advisory Committee takes place at the earliest 14 days after the invitation to the meeting is sent by the Commission. The Commission attaches to the invitation a summary of the case, a list of the most important documents, i.e. the documents needed to assess the case, and a draft decision. The Advisory Committee gives an opinion on the Commission draft decision. At the request of one or several members, the opinion shall be reasoned.

66. The Council Regulation allows for the possibility of the Member States agreeing upon a shorter period of time between the sending of the invitation and the meeting.

4.2.2. Written procedure

67. The Council Regulation provides for the possibility of a written consultation procedure. If no Member State objects, the Commission can consult the Member States by sending the documents to them and setting a deadline within which they can comment on the draft. This deadline would not normally be shorter than 14 days, except for decisions on interim measures pursuant to Article 8 of the Council Regulation. Where a Member State requests that a meeting takes place, the Commission will arrange for such a meeting.

4.3. Publication of the Opinion of the Advisory Committee

68. The Advisory Committee can recommend the publication of its opinion. In that event, the Commission will carry out such publication simultaneously with the decision, taking into account the legitimate interest of undertakings in the protection of their business secrets.

5. FINAL REMARKS

69. This Notice is without prejudice to any interpretation of the applicable Treaty and regulatory provisions by the Court of First Instance and the Court of Justice.

70. This Notice will be the subject of periodic review carried out jointly by the NCAs and the Commission. On the basis of the experience acquired, it will be reviewed no later than at the end of the third year after its adoption.

71. This notice replaces the Commission notice on cooperation between national competition authorities and the Commission in handling cases falling within the scope of Articles [101] and [102] of the Treaty published in 1997.[24]

Notes
[24] OJ C 313, 15.10.1997, p.3.

6. Statement by Other Network Members

72. The principles set out in this notice will also be abided by those Member States' competition authorities which have signed a statement in the form of the Annex to this Notice. In this statement they acknowledge the principles of this notice, including the principles relating to the protection of applicants claiming the benefit of a leniency programme[25] and declare that they will abide by them. A list of these authorities is published on the website of the European Commission. It will be updated if appropriate.

Notes
[25] See paragraphs 37 *et subseq.*

Annex
Statement Regarding the Commission Notice on Cooperation within the Network of Competition Authorities

In order to cooperate closely with a view to protecting competition within the European Union in the interest of consumers, the undersigned competition authority:

Acknowledges the principle set out in the Commission Notice on Cooperation within the Network of Competition Authorities; and

Declares that it will abide by those principles, which include principles relating to the protection of applicants claiming the benefit of a leniency programme, in any case in which it is acting or may act and to which those principles apply.

(place)   (date)

Commentary
Annex: B&C: 1.076

B7

COMMISSION NOTICE ON THE COOPERATION BETWEEN THE COMMISSION AND THE COURTS OF THE EU MEMBER STATES IN THE APPLICATION OF ARTICLES [101] AND [102] [TFEU]*

(2004/C 101/04)

(Text with EEA relevance)

Official Journal C 101, 27.4.2004, p.54

Celex No: 52004XC0427(03)

EUR-Lex permanent link: <http://eur-lex.europa.eu/LexUriServ/LexUriServ.do?uri=CELEX:5200
4XC0427(03):EN:NOT>

Note

* Ed note: please see the Note on the Lisbon Treaty at p.xvii in regard to article renumbering introduced by the Lisbon Treaty.
EEA application: the EFTA Surveillance Authority has adopted a parallel notice on the co-operation between the EFTA Surveillance Authority and the courts of the EFTA States in the application of Articles 53 and 54 of the EEA Agreement under Article 5(2)(b) of the Surveillance and Court Agreement: OJ C 305, 14.12.2006, p.19 and EE Supplement No 62, 14.12.2006, p.21.

Commentary
Notice: B&C: 1.072, 3.004, 8.272, 15.043, 16.013
points 11–14: B&C: 8.272
points 21–26: B&C: 15.053 F&N: 2.204
points 21–30: B&C: 3.009, 15.050
points 23–26: B&C: 15.048
points 31–35: B&C: 15.051

I. THE SCOPE OF THE NOTICE

1. The present notice addresses the co-operation between the Commission and the courts of the EU Member States, when the latter apply Articles [101] and [102] [TFEU]. For the purpose of this notice, the "courts of the EU Member States" (hereinafter "national courts") are those courts and tribunals within an EU Member State that can apply Articles [101] and [102] [TFEU] and that are authorised to ask a preliminary question to the Court of Justice of the European Communities pursuant to Article [267 TFEU].[1]

Notes

[1] For the criteria to determine which entities can be regarded as courts or tribunals within the meaning of Article [267 TFEU], see e.g. Case C-516/99 *Schmid* [2002] ECR I-4573, 34:"The Court takes account of a number of factors, such as whether the body is established by law, whether it is permanent, whether its jurisdiction is compulsory, whether its procedure is inter partes, whether it applies rules of law and whether it is independent".

Commentary
point 1: F&N: 2.257

2. The national courts may be called upon to apply Articles [101] or [102] [TFEU] in lawsuits between private parties, such as actions relating to contracts or actions for damages. They may also act as public enforcer or as review court. A national court may indeed be designated as a competition authority of a Member State (hereinafter "the national competition authority") pursuant to Article

35(1) of Regulation (EC) No 1/2003 (hereinafter "the regulation").[2] In that case, the co-operation between the national courts and the Commission is not only covered by the present notice, but also by the notice on the co-operation within the network of competition authorities.[3]

Notes

[2] Council Regulation (EC) No 1/2003 of 16 December 2002 on the implementation of the rules on competition laid down in Articles [101] and [102] of the Treaty (OJ L 1, 4.1.2003, p.1).

[3] Notice on co-operation within the network of competition authorities (OJ C 101, 27.4.2004, p.43). For the purpose of this notice, a "national competition authority" is the authority designated by a Member State in accordance with Article 35(1) of the regulation.

II. The Application of EC Competition Rules by National Courts

A. The Competence of National Courts to Apply EC Competition Rules

3. To the extent that national courts have jurisdiction to deal with a case[4], they have the power to apply Articles [101] and [102] [TFEU].[5] Moreover, it should be remembered that Articles [101] and [102] [TFEU] are a matter of public policy and are essential to the accomplishment of the tasks entrusted to the Community, and, in particular, for the functioning of the internal market.[6] According to the Court of Justice, where, by virtue of domestic law, national courts must raise of their own motion points of law based on binding domestic rules which have not been raised by the parties, such an obligation also exists where binding Community rules, such as the EC competition rules, are concerned. The position is the same if domestic law confers on national courts a discretion to apply of their own motion binding rules of law: national courts must apply the EC competition rules, even when the party with an interest in application of those provisions has not relied on them, where domestic law allows such application by the national court. However, Community law does not require national courts to raise of their own motion an issue concerning the breach of provisions of Community law where examination of that issue would oblige them to abandon the passive role assigned to them by going beyond the ambit of the dispute defined by the parties themselves and relying on facts and circumstances other than those on which the party with an interest in application of those provisions bases his claim.[7]

Notes

[4] The jurisdiction of a national court depends on national, European and international rules of jurisdiction. In this context, it may be recalled that Council Regulation (EC) No 44/2001 of 22 December 2000 on jurisdiction and the recognition and enforcement of judgements in civil and commercial matters (OJ L 12, 16.1.2001, p.1) is applicable to all competition cases of a civil or commercial nature.

[5] See Article 6 of the regulation.

[6] See Articles 2 and 3 EC [Ed note: now Article 3 TEU and Articles 3 to 6 and 8 TFEU], Case C-126/97 *Eco Swiss* [1999] ECR I-3055, 36; Case T-34/92 *Fiatagri UK and New Holland Ford* [1994] ECR II-905, 39 and Case T-128/98 *Aéroports de Paris* [2000] ECR II-3929, 241.

[7] Joined Cases C-430/93 and C-431/93 *van Schijndel* [1995] ECR I-4705, 13 to 15 and 22.

Commentary

point 3: B&C: 16.032

4. Depending on the functions attributed to them under national law, national courts may be called upon to apply Articles [101] and [102] [TFEU] in administrative, civil or criminal proceedings.[8] In particular, where a natural or legal person asks the national court to safeguard his individual rights, national courts play a specific role in the enforcement of Articles [101] and [102] [TFEU], which is different from the enforcement in the public interest by the Commission or by national competition authorities.[9] Indeed, national courts can give effect to Articles [101] and [102] [TFEU] by finding contracts to be void or by awards of damages.

Notes

[8] According to the last sentence of Recital 8 of Regulation (EC) No 1/2003, the regulation does not apply to national laws which impose criminal sanctions on natural persons except to the extent that such sanctions are the means whereby competition rules applying to undertakings are enforced.

[9] Case T-24/90 *Automec* [1992] ECR II-2223, 85.

5. National courts can apply Articles [101] and [102] [TFEU], without it being necessary to apply national competition law in parallel. However, where a national court applies national competition law to agreements, decisions by associations of undertakings or concerted practices which may affect trade between Member States within the meaning of Article [101](1) [TFEU][10] or to any abuse prohibited by Article [102] [TFEU], they also have to apply EC competition rules to those agreements, decisions or practices.[11]

Notes
[10] For further clarification of the effect on trade concept, see the notice on this issue (OJ L 101, 27.4.2004, p.81).
[11] Article 3(1) of the regulation.

6. The regulation does not only empower the national courts to apply EC competition law. The parallel application of national competition law to agreements, decisions of associations of undertakings and concerted practices which affect trade between Member States may not lead to a different outcome from that of EC competition law. Article 3(2) of the regulation provides that agreements, decisions or concerted practices which do not infringe Article [101](1) [TFEU] or which fulfil the conditions of Article [101](3) [TFEU] cannot be prohibited either under national competition law.[12] On the other hand, the Court of Justice has ruled that agreements, decisions or concerted practices that violate Article [101](1) and do not fulfil the conditions of Article [101](3) [TFEU] cannot be upheld under national law.[13] As to the parallel application of national competition law and Article [102] [TFEU] in the case of unilateral conduct, Article 3 of the regulation does not provide for a similar convergence obligation. However, in case of conflicting provisions, the general principle of primacy of Community law requires national courts to disapply any provision of national law which contravenes a Community rule, regardless of whether that national law provision was adopted before or after the Community rule.[14]

Notes
[12] See also the notice on the application of Article [101](3) [TFEU] (OJ L 101, 27.4.2004, p.2).
[13] Case 14/68 *Walt Wilhelm* [1969] ECR 1 and Joined Cases 253/78 and 1 to 3/79 *Giry and Guerlain* [1980] ECR 2327, 15 to 17.
[14] Case 106/77 *Simmenthal* [1978] ECR 629, 21 and Case C-198/01 *Consorzio Industrie Fiammiferi (CIF)* [2003] ECR I-49.

7. Apart from the application of Articles [101] and [102] [TFEU], national courts are also competent to apply acts adopted by EU institutions in accordance with the [Treaty on the Functioning of the European Union] or in accordance with the measures adopted to give the Treaty effect, to the extent that these acts have direct effect. National courts may thus have to enforce Commission decisions[15] or regulations applying Article [101](3) [TFEU] to certain categories of agreements, decisions or concerted practices. When applying these EC competition rules, national courts act within the framework of Community law and are consequently bound to observe the general principles of Community law.[16]

Notes
[15] E.g. a national court may be asked to enforce a Commission decision taken pursuant to Articles 7 to 10, 23, and 24 of the regulation.
[16] See e.g. Case 5/88 *Wachauf* [1989] ECR 2609, 19.

8. The application of Articles [101] and [102] [TFEU] by national courts often depends on complex economic and legal assessments.[17] When applying EC competition rules, national courts are bound by the case law of the Community courts as well as by Commission regulations applying Article [101](3) [TFEU] to certain categories of agreements, decisions or concerted practices.[18] Furthermore, the application of Articles [101] and [102] [TFEU] by the Commission in a specific case binds the national courts when they apply EC competition rules in the same case in parallel with or subsequent to the Commission.[19] Finally, and without prejudice to the ultimate

interpretation of the [Treaty on the Functioning of the European Union] by the Court of Justice, national courts may find guidance in Commission regulations and decisions which present elements of analogy with the case they are dealing with, as well as in Commission notices and guidelines relating to the application of Articles [101] and [102] [TFEU][20] and in the annual report on competition policy.[21]

Notes

[17] Joined Cases C-215/96 and C-216/96 *Bagnasco* [1999] ECR I-135, 50.

[18] Case 63/75 *Fonderies Roubaix* [1976] ECR 111, 9 to 11 and Case C-234/89 *Delimitis* [1991] ECR I-935, 46.

[19] On the parallel or consecutive application of EC competition rules by national courts and the Commission, see also points 11 to 14.

[20] Case 66/86 *Ahmed Saeed Flugreisen* [1989] ECR 803, 27 and Case C-234/89 *Delimitis* [1991] ECR I-935, 50. A list of Commission guidelines, notices and regulations in the field of competition policy, in particular the regulations applying Article [101](3) [TFEU] to certain categories of agreements, decisions or concerted practices, [is] annexed to this notice. For the decisions of the Commission applying Articles [101] and [102] [TFEU] (since 1964), see <http://www.europa.eu.int/comm/competition/antitrust/cases/>.

[21] Joined Cases C-319/93, C-40/94 and C-224/94 *Dijkstra* [1995] ECR I-4471, 32.

Commentary
point 8: B&C: 8.272, 15.068

B. Procedural Aspects of the Application of EC Competition Rules by National Courts

9. The procedural conditions for the enforcement of EC competition rules by national courts and the sanctions they can impose in case of an infringement of those rules, are largely covered by national law. However, to some extent, Community law also determines the conditions in which EC competition rules are enforced. Those Community law provisions may provide for the faculty of national courts to avail themselves of certain instruments, e.g. to ask for the Commission's opinion on questions concerning the application of EC competition rules[22] or they may create rules that have an obligatory impact on proceedings before them, e.g. allowing the Commission and national competition authorities to submit written observations.[23] These Community law provisions prevail over national rules. Therefore, national courts have to set aside national rules which, if applied, would conflict with these Community law provisions. Where such Community law provisions are directly applicable, they are a direct source of rights and duties for all those affected, and must be fully and uniformly applied in all the Member States from the date of their entry into force.[24]

Notes

[22] On the possibility for national courts to ask the Commission for an opinion, see further in points 27 to 30.

[23] On the submission of observations, see further in points 31 to 35.

[24] Case 106/77 *Simmenthal* [1978] ECR 629, 14 and 15.

10. In the absence of Community law provisions on procedures and sanctions related to the enforcement of EC competition rules by national courts, the latter apply national procedural law and — to the extent that they are competent to do so — impose sanctions provided for under national law. However, the application of these national provisions must be compatible with the general principles of Community law. In this regard, it is useful to recall the case law of the Court of Justice, according to which:

   (a) where there is an infringement of Community law, national law must provide for sanctions which are effective, proportionate and dissuasive;[25]

   (b) where the infringement of Community law causes harm to an individual, the latter should under certain conditions be able to ask the national court for damages; [26]

   (c) the rules on procedures and sanctions which national courts apply to enforce Community law

   — must not make such enforcement excessively difficult or practically impossible (the principle of effectiveness)[27] and they

   — must not be less favourable than the rules applicable to the enforcement of equivalent national law (the principle of equivalence).[28]

On the basis of the principle of primacy of Community law, a national court may not apply national rules that are incompatible with these principles.

Notes

25 Case 68/88 *Commission v Greece* [1989] ECR 2965, 23 to 25.

26 On damages in case of an infringement by an undertaking, see Case C-453/99 *Courage v Crehan* [2001] ECR 6297, 26 and 27. On damages in case of an infringement by a Member State or by an authority which is an emanation of the State and on the conditions of such State liability, see e.g. Joined Cases C-6/90 and C-9/90 *Francovich* [1991] ECR I-5357, 33 to 36; Case C-271/91 *Marshall v Southampton and South West Hampshire Area Health Authority* [1993] ECR I-4367, 30 and 34 to 35; Joined Cases C-46/93 and C-48/93 *Brasserie du Pêcheur and Factortame* [1996] ECR I-1029; Case C-392/93 *British Telecommunications* [1996] ECR I-1631, 39 to 46 and Joined Cases C-178/94, C-179/94 and C-188/94 to 190/94 *Dillenkofer* [1996] ECR I-4845, 22 to 26 and 72.

27 See e.g. Case 33/76 *Rewe* [1976] ECR 1989, 5; Case 45/76 *Comet* [1976] ECR 2043, 12 and Case 79/83 *Harz* [1984] ECR 1921, 18 and 23.

28 See e.g. Case 33/76 *Rewe* [1976] ECR 1989, 5; Case 158/80 *Rewe* [1981] ECR 1805, 44; Case 199/82 *San Giorgio* [1983] ECR 3595, 12 and Case C-231/96 *Edis* [1998] ECR I-4951, 36 and 37.

Commentary
point 10: B&C: 15.056, 16.010

C. Parallel or Consecutive Application of EC Competition Rules by the Commission and by National Courts

11. A national court may be applying EC competition law to an agreement, decision, concerted practice or unilateral behaviour affecting trade between Member States at the same time as the Commission or subsequent to the Commission.[29] The following points outline some of the obligations national courts have to respect in those circumstances.

Notes

29 Article 11(6), juncto Article 35(3) and (4) of the regulation prevents a parallel application of Articles [101] or [102] [TFEU] by the Commission and a national court only when the latter has been designated as a national competition authority.

Commentary
point 11: B&C: 15.053

12. Where a national court comes to a decision before the Commission does, it must avoid adopting a decision that would conflict with a decision contemplated by the Commission.[30] To that effect, the national court may ask the Commission whether it has initiated proceedings regarding the same agreements, decisions or practices[31] and if so, about the progress of proceedings and the likelihood of a decision in that case.[32] The national court may, for reasons of legal certainty, also consider staying its proceedings until the Commission has reached a decision.[33] The Commission, for its part, will endeavour to give priority to cases for which it has decided to initiate proceedings within the meaning of Article 2(1) of Commission Regulation (EC) No 773/2004 and that are the subject of national proceedings stayed in this way, in particular when the outcome of a civil dispute depends on them. However, where the national court cannot reasonably doubt the Commission's contemplated decision or where the Commission has already decided on a similar case, the national court may decide on the case pending before it in accordance with that contemplated or earlier decision without it being necessary to ask the Commission for the information mentioned above or to await the Commission's decision.

Notes

30 Article 16(1) of the regulation.

31 The Commission makes the initiation of its proceedings with a view to adopting a decision pursuant to Articles 7 to 10 of the regulation public (see Article 2(2) of Commission Regulation (EC) No 773/2004 of 7 April relating to proceedings pursuant to Articles [101] and [102] of the [Treaty on the Functioning of the European Union] (OJ C 101, 27.4.2004). According to the Court of Justice, the initiation of proceedings implies an authoritative act of the Commission, evidencing its intention of taking a decision (Case 48/72 *Brasserie de Haecht* [1973] ECR 77, 16).

[32] Case C-234/89 *Delimitis* [1991] ECR I-935, 53, and Joined Cases C-319/93, C-40/94 and C-224/94 *Dijkstra* [1995] ECR I-4471, 34. See further on this issue point 21 of this notice.

[33] See Article 16(1) of the regulation and Case C-234/89 I [1991] ECR I-935, 47 and Case C-344/98 *Masterfoods* [2000] ECR I-11369, 51.

Commentary

point 12: B&C: 15.053 F&N: 2.268

13. Where the Commission reaches a decision in a particular case before the national court, the latter cannot take a decision running counter to that of the Commission. The binding effect of the Commission's decision is of course without prejudice to the interpretation of Community law by the Court of Justice. Therefore, if the national court doubts the legality of the Commission's decision, it cannot avoid the binding effects of that decision without a ruling to the contrary by the Court of Justice.[34] Consequently, if a national court intends to take a decision that runs counter to that of the Commission, it must refer a question to the Court of Justice for a preliminary ruling (Article [267 TFEU]). The latter will then decide on the compatibility of the Commission's decision with Community law. However, if the Commission's decision is challenged before the Community courts pursuant to Article [263 TFEU] and the outcome of the dispute before the national court depends on the validity of the Commission's decision, the national court should stay its proceedings pending final judgment in the action for annulment by the Community courts unless it considers that, in the circumstances of the case, a reference to the Court of Justice for a preliminary ruling on the validity of the Commission decision is warranted.[35]

Notes

[34] Case 314/85 *Foto-Frost* [1987] ECR 4199, 12 to 20.

[35] See Article 16(1) of the regulation and Case C-344/98 *Masterfoods* [2000] ECR I-11369, 52 to 59.

Commentary

point 13: B&C: 15.065

14. When a national court stays proceedings, e.g. awaiting the Commission's decision (situation described in point 12 of this notice) or pending final judgement by the Community courts in an action for annulment or in a preliminary ruling procedure (situation described in point 13), it is incumbent on it to examine whether it is necessary to order interim measures in order to safeguard the interests of the parties.[36]

Notes

[36] Case C-344/98 *Masterfoods* [2000] ECR, I-11369, 58.

III. The Co-operation Between the Commission and National Courts

15. Other than the co-operation mechanism between the national courts and the Court of Justice under Article [267 TFEU], the [Treaty on the Functioning of the European Union] does not explicitly provide for co-operation between the national courts and the Commission. However, in its interpretation of Article [4, paragraph 3, TEU], which obliges the Member States to facilitate the achievement of the Community's tasks, the Community courts found that this Treaty provision imposes on the European institutions and the Member States mutual duties of loyal co-operation with a view to attaining the objectives of the [Treaty on the Functioning of the European Union]. Article [4, paragraph 3 TEU] thus implies that the Commission must assist national courts when they apply Community law.[37] Equally, national courts may be obliged to assist the Commission in the fulfilment of its tasks.[38]

Notes

[37] Case C-2/88 *Imm Zwartveld* [1990] ECR I-3365, 16 to 22 and Case C-234/89 *Delimitis* [1991] I-935, 53.

[38] C-94/00 *Roquette Frères* [2002] ECR 9011, 31.

Commentary

point 15: B&C: 15.043 F&N: 2.280

16. It is also appropriate to recall the co-operation between national courts and national authorities, in particular national competition authorities, for the application of Articles [101] and [102] [TFEU]. While the co-operation between these national authorities is primarily governed by national rules, Article 15(3) of the regulation provides for the possibility for national competition authorities to submit observations before the national courts of their Member State. Points 31 and 33 to 35 of this notice are *mutatis mutandis* applicable to those submissions.

A. The Commission as *Amicus Curiae*

17. In order to assist national courts in the application of EC competition rules, the Commission is committed to help national courts where the latter find such help necessary to be able to decide on a case. Article 15 of the regulation refers to the most frequent types of such assistance: the transmission of information (points 21 to 26) and the Commission's opinions (points 27 to 30), both at the request of a national court and the possibility for the Commission to submit observations (points 31 to 35). Since the regulation provides for these types of assistance, it cannot be limited by any Member States' rule. However, in the absence of Community procedural rules to this effect and to the extent that they are necessary to facilitate these forms of assistance, Member States must adopt the appropriate procedural rules to allow both the national courts and the Commission to make full use of the possibilities the regulation offers.[39]

Notes

[39] On the compatibility of such national procedural rules with the general principles of Community law, see points 9 and 10 of this notice.

18. The national court may send its request for assistance in writing to

    European Commission
    Directorate General for Competition
    B-1049 Brussels
    Belgium
    or send it electronically to comp-amicus@cec.eu.int

19. It should be recalled that whatever form the co-operation with national courts takes, the Commission will respect the independence of national courts. As a consequence, the assistance offered by the Commission does not bind the national court. The Commission has also to make sure that it respects its duty of professional secrecy and that it safeguards its own functioning and independence.[40] In fulfilling its duty under Article [4, paragraph 3 TEU], of assisting national courts in the application of EC competition rules, the Commission is committed to remaining neutral and objective in its assistance. Indeed, the Commission's assistance to national courts is part of its duty to defend the public interest. It has therefore no intention to serve the private interests of the parties involved in the case pending before the national court. As a consequence, the Commission will not hear any of the parties about its assistance to the national court. In case the Commission has been contacted by any of the parties in the case pending before the court on issues which are raised before the national court, it will inform the national court thereof, independent of whether these contacts took place before or after the national court's request for co-operation.

Notes

[40] On these duties, see e.g. points 23 to 26 of this notice.

Commentary
point 19: B&C: 15.046 F&N: 2.272, 2.288

20. The Commission will publish a summary concerning its co-operation with national courts pursuant to this notice in its annual Report on Competition Policy. It may also make its opinions and observations available on its website.

1. The Commission's duty to transmit information to national courts

21. The duty for the Commission to assist national courts in the application of EC competition law is mainly reflected in the obligation for the Commission to transmit information it holds to national courts. A national court may, e.g., ask the Commission for documents in its possession or for information of a procedural nature to enable it to discover whether a certain case is pending before the Commission, whether the Commission has initiated a procedure or whether it has already taken a position. A national court may also ask the Commission when a decision is likely to be taken, so as to be able to determine the conditions for any decision to stay proceedings or whether interim measures need to be adopted.[41]

Notes
[41] Case C-234/89 *Delimitis* [1991] ECR I-935, 53, and Joined Cases C-319/93, C-40/94 and C-224/94 *Dijkstra* [1995] ECR I-4471, 34.

22. In order to ensure the efficiency of the co-operation with national courts, the Commission will endeavour to provide the national court with the requested information within one month from the date it receives the request. Where the Commission has to ask the national court for further clarification of its request or where the Commission has to consult those who are directly affected by the transmission of the information, that period starts to run from the moment that it receives the required information.

Commentary
point 22: **B&C:** 15.047, 16.041

23. In transmitting information to national courts, the Commission has to uphold the guarantees given to natural and legal persons by Article [339 TFEU].[42] Article [339 TFEU] prevents members, officials and other servants of the Commission from disclosing information covered by the obligation of professional secrecy. The information covered by professional secrecy may be both confidential information and business secrets. Business secrets are information of which not only disclosure to the public but also mere transmission to a person other than the one that provided the information might seriously harm the latter's interests.[43]

Notes
[42] Case C-234/89 *Delimitis* [1991] I-935, 53.
[43] Case T-353/94 *Postbank* [1996] ECR II-921, 86 and 87 and Case 145/83 *Adams* [1985] ECR 3539, 34.

24. The combined reading of Articles [4, paragraph 3 TEU and 339 TFEU] does not lead to an absolute prohibition for the Commission to transmit information which is covered by the obligation of professional secrecy to national courts. The case law of the Community courts confirms that the duty of loyal co-operation requires the Commission to provide the national court with whatever information the latter asks for, even information covered by professional secrecy. However, in offering its co-operation to the national courts, the Commission may not in any circumstances undermine the guarantees laid down in Article [339 TFEU].

25. Consequently, before transmitting information covered by professional secrecy to a national court, the Commission will remind the court of its obligation under Community law to uphold the rights which Article [339 TFEU] confers on natural and legal persons and it will ask the court whether it can and will guarantee protection of confidential information and business secrets. If the national court cannot offer such guarantee, the Commission shall not transmit the information covered by professional secrecy to the national court.[44] Only when the national court has offered a guarantee that it will protect the confidential information and business secrets, will the Commission transmit the information requested, indicating those parts which are covered by professional secrecy and which parts are not and can therefore be disclosed.

Notes
[44] Case C-2/88 *Zwartveld* [1990] ECR I-4405, 10 and 11 and Case T-353/94 *Postbank* [1996] ECR II-921, 93.

Commentary
point 25: **B&C:** 13.034

26. There are further exceptions to the disclosure of information by the Commission to national courts. Particularly, the Commission may refuse to transmit information to national courts for overriding reasons relating to the need to safeguard the interests of the Community or to avoid any interference with its functioning and independence, in particular by jeopardising the accomplishment of the tasks entrusted to it.[45] Therefore, the Commission will not transmit to national courts information voluntarily submitted by a leniency applicant without the consent of that applicant.

Notes

[45] Case C-2/88 *Zwartveld* [1990] ECR I-4405, 10 and 11; Case C-275/00 *First and Franex* [2002] ECR I-10943, 49 and Case T-353/94 *Postbank* [1996] ECR II-921, 93.

Commentary

point 26: **B&C:** 15.049 **F&N:** 2.276, 8.242

2. Request for an opinion on questions concerning the application of EC competition rules

27. When called upon to apply EC competition rules to a case pending before it, a national court may first seek guidance in the case law of the Community courts or in Commission regulations, decisions, notices and guidelines applying Articles [101] and [102] [TFEU].[46] Where these tools do not offer sufficient guidance, the national court may ask the Commission for its opinion on questions concerning the application of EC competition rules. The national court may ask the Commission for its opinion on economic, factual and legal matters.[47] The latter is of course without prejudice to the possibility or the obligation for the national court to ask the Court of Justice for a preliminary ruling regarding the interpretation or the validity of Community law in accordance with Article [267 TFEU].

Notes

[46] See point 8 of this notice.

[47] Case C-234/89 *Delimitis* [1991] ECR I-935, 53, and Joined Cases C-319/93, C-40/94 and C-224/94 *Dijkstra* [1995] ECR I-4471, 34.

28. In order to enable the Commission to provide the national court with a useful opinion, it may request the national court for further information.[48] In order to ensure the efficiency of the co-operation with national courts, the Commission will endeavour to provide the national court with the requested opinion within four months from the date it receives the request. Where the Commission has requested the national court for further information in order to enable it to formulate its opinion, that period starts to run from the moment that it receives the additional information.

Notes

[48] Compare with Case 96/81 *Commission v The Netherlands* [1982] ECR 1791, 7 and Case 272/86 *Commission v Greece* [1988] ECR 4875, 30.

29. When giving its opinion, the Commission will limit itself to providing the national court with the factual information or the economic or legal clarification asked for, without considering the merits of the case pending before the national court. Moreover, unlike the authoritative interpretation of Community law by the Community courts, the opinion of the Commission does not legally bind the national court.

30. In line with what has been said in point 19 of this notice, the Commission will not hear the parties before formulating its opinion to the national court. The latter will have to deal with the Commission's opinion in accordance with the relevant national procedural rules, which have to respect the general principles of Community law.

3. The Commission's submission of observations to the national court

31. According to Article 15(3) of the regulation, the national competition authorities and the Commission may submit observations on issues relating to the application of Articles [101] or [102] [TFEU] to a national court which is called upon to apply those provisions. The regulation distinguishes between written observations, which the national competition authorities and the

Commission may submit on their own initiative, and oral observations, which can only be submitted with the permission of the national court.[49]

Notes

[49] According to Article 15(4) of the regulation, this is without prejudice to wider powers to make observations before courts conferred on national competition authorities under national law.

32. The regulation specifies that the Commission will only submit observations when the coherent application of Articles [101] or [102] [TFEU] so requires. That being the objective of its submission, the Commission will limit its observations to an economic and legal analysis of the facts underlying the case pending before the national court.

Commentary
point 32: B&C: 15.046

33. In order to enable the Commission to submit useful observations, national courts may be asked to transmit or ensure the transmission to the Commission of a copy of all documents that are necessary for the assessment of the case. In line with Article 15(3), second subparagraph, of the regulation, the Commission will only use those documents for the preparation of its observations.[50]

Notes

[50] See also Article 28(2) of the regulation, which prevents the Commission from disclosing the information it has acquired and which is covered by the obligation of professional secrecy.

34. Since the regulation does not provide for a procedural framework within which the observations are to be submitted, Member States' procedural rules and practices determine the relevant procedural framework. Where a Member State has not yet established the relevant procedural framework, the national court has to determine which procedural rules are appropriate for the submission of observations in the case pending before it.

35. The procedural framework should respect the principles set out in point 10 of this notice. That implies amongst others that the procedural framework for the submission of observations on issues relating to the application of Articles [101] or [102] [TFEU]

  (a) has to be compatible with the general principles of Community law, in particular the fundamental rights of the parties involved in the case;
  (b) cannot make the submission of such observations excessively difficult or practically impossible (the principle of effectiveness);[51] and
  (c) cannot make the submission of such observations more difficult than the submission of observations in court proceedings where equivalent national law is applied (the principle of equivalence).

Notes

[51] Joined Cases 46/87 and 227/88 *Hoechst* [1989] ECR, 2859, 33. See also Article 15(3) of the regulation.

Commentary
point 35: F&N: 2.289

B. The National Courts Facilitating the Role of the Commission in the Enforcement of EC Competition Rules

36. Since the duty of loyal co-operation also implies that Member States' authorities assist the European institutions with a view to attaining the objectives of the [Treaty on the Functioning of the European Union],[52] the regulation provides for three examples of such assistance: (1) the transmission of documents necessary for the assessment of a case in which the Commission would like to submit observations (see point 33), (2) the transmission of judgements applying Articles [101] or [102] [TFEU], and (3) the role of national courts in the context of a Commission inspection.

Notes

[52] Case C-69/90 *Commission v Italy* [1991] ECR 6011, 15.

1. The transmission of judgements of national courts applying Articles [101] or [102] [TFEU]

37. According to Article 15(2) of the regulation, Member States shall send to the Commission a copy of any written judgement of national courts applying Articles [101] or [102] [TFEU] without delay after the full written judgement is notified to the parties. The transmission of national judgements on the application of Articles [101] or [102] [TFEU] and the resulting information on proceedings before national courts primarily enable the Commission to become aware in a timely fashion of cases for which it might be appropriate to submit observations where one of the parties lodges an appeal against the judgement.

2. The role of national courts in the context of a Commission inspection

38. Finally, national courts may play a role in the context of a Commission inspection of undertakings and associations of undertakings. The role of the national courts depends on whether the inspections are conducted in business premises or in non-business premises.

39. With regard to the inspection of business premises, national legislation may require authorisation from a national court to allow a national enforcement authority to assist the Commission in case of opposition of the undertaking concerned. Such authorisation may also be sought as a precautionary measure. When dealing with the request, the national court has the power to control that the Commission's inspection decision is authentic and that the coercive measures envisaged are neither arbitrary nor excessive having regard to the subject matter of the inspection. In its control of the proportionality of the coercive measures, the national court may ask the Commission, directly or through the national competition authority, for detailed explanations in particular on the grounds the Commission has for suspecting infringement of Articles [101] and [102] [TFEU], as well as on the seriousness of the suspected infringement and on the nature of the involvement of the undertaking concerned.[53]

Notes

[53] Article 20(6) to (8) of the regulation and Case C-94/00 *Roquette Frères* [2002] ECR 9011.

40. With regard to the inspection of non-business premises, the regulation requires the authorisation from a national court before a Commission decision ordering such an inspection can be executed. In that case, the national court may control that the Commission's inspection decision is authentic and that the coercive measures envisaged are neither arbitrary nor excessive having regard in particular to the seriousness of the suspected infringement, to the importance of the evidence sought, to the involvement of the undertaking concerned and to the reasonable likelihood that business books and records relating to the subject matter of the inspection are kept in the premises for which the authorisation is requested. The national court may ask the Commission, directly or through the national competition authority, for detailed explanations on those elements that are necessary to allow its control of the proportionality of the coercive measures envisaged.[54]

Notes

[54] Article 21(3) of the regulation.

41. In both cases referred to in points 39 and 40, the national court may not call into question the lawfulness of the Commission's decision or the necessity for the inspection nor can it demand that it be provided with information in the Commission's file.[55] Furthermore, the duty of loyal co-operation requires the national court to take its decision within an appropriate timeframe that allows the Commission to effectively conduct its inspection.[56]

Notes

[55] Case C-94/00 *Roquette Frères* [2002] ECR 9011, 39 and 62 to 66.
[56] See also *ibidem*, 91 and 92.

IV. Final Provisions

42. This notice is issued in order to assist national courts in the application of Articles [101] and [102] [TFEU]. It does not bind the national courts, nor does it affect the rights and obligations of the EU Member States and natural or legal persons under Community law.

43. This notice replaces the 1993 notice on co-operation between national courts and the Commission in applying Articles [101 and 102 TFEU].[57]

Notes

[57] OJ C 39, 13.2.93, p.6.

Commentary

point 43: B&C: 15.058

Annex
Commission Block Exemption Regulations, Notices and Guidelines

This list is also available and updated on the website of the Directorate General for Competition of the European Commission:

<http://europa.eu.int/comm/competition/antitrust/legislation/>

A. Non-sector Specific Rules

1. *Notices of a general nature*
   — Notice on the definition of the relevant market for the purposes of Community competition law (OJ C 372, 9.12.1997, p.5)
   — Notice on agreements of minor importance which do not appreciably restrict competition under Article [101](1) of the [Treaty on the Functioning of the European Union] (*de minimis*) (OJ C 368, 22.12.2001, p.13)
   — Notice on the effect on trade concept contained in Articles [101] and [102] of the Treaty (OJ C 101, 27.4.2004, p.81)
   — Guidelines on the application of Article [101](3) of the Treaty (OJ C 101, 27.4.2004, p.2)

2. *Vertical agreements*
   — Regulation (EC) No 2790/1999 of 22 December 1999 on the application of Article [101](3) of the Treaty to categories of vertical agreements and concerted practices (OJ L 336, 29.12.1999, p.21)
   — Guidelines on Vertical Restraints (OJ C 291, 13.10.2000, p.1)

3. *Horizontal co-operation agreements*
   — Regulation (EC) No 2658/2000 of 29 November 2000 on the application of Article [101](3) of the Treaty to categories of specialisation agreements (OJ L 304, 5.12.2000, p.3)
   — Regulation (EC) No 2659/2000 of 29 November 2000 on the application of Article [101] (3) of the Treaty to categories of research and development agreements (OJ L 304, 5.12.2000, p.7)
   — Guidelines on the applicability of Article [101] to horizontal co-operation agreements (OJ C 3, 6.1.2001, p.2)

4. *Licensing agreements for the transfer of technology*
   — Regulation (EC) No 773/2004 of 27 April 2004 on the application of Article [101](3) of the Treaty to categories of technology transfer agreements (OJ L 123, 27.4.2004)
   — Guidelines on the application of Article [101] of the [Treaty on the Functioning of the European Union] to technology transfer agreements (OJ C 101, 27.4.2004, p.2)

B. Sector Specific Rules

1. Insurance

— Regulation (EC) No 358/2003 of 27 February 2003 on the application of Article [101](3) of the Treaty to certain categories of agreements, decisions and concerted practices in the insurance sector (OJ L 53, 28.2.2003, p.8)

2. Motor vehicles

— Regulation (EC) No 1400/2002 of 31 July 2002 on the application of Article [101](3) of the Treaty to categories of vertical agreements and concerted practices in the motor vehicle sector (OJ L 203, 1.8.2002, p.30)

3. Telecommunications and postal services

— Guidelines on the application of EEC competition rules in the telecommunications sector (OJ C 233, 6.9.1991, p.2)
— Notice on the application of the competition rules to the postal sector and on the assessment of certain State measures relating to postal services (OJ C 39, 6.2.1998, p.2)
— Notice on the application of the competition rules to access agreements in the telecommunications sector—Framework, relevant markets and principles (OJ C 265, 22.8.1998, p.2)
— Guidelines on market analysis and the assessment of significant market power under the Community regulatory framework for electronic communications networks and services (OJ C 165, 11.7.2002, p.6)

4. Transport

— Regulation (EEC) No 1617/93 on the application of Article [101](3) of the Treaty to certain categories of agreements and concerted practices concerning joint planning and co-ordination of schedules, joint operations, consultations on passenger and cargo tariffs on scheduled air services and slot allocation at airports (OJ L 155, 26.6.1993, p.18)
— Communication on clarification of the Commission recommendations on the application of the competition rules to new transport infrastructure projects (OJ C 298, 30.9.1997, p.5)
— Regulation (EC) No 823/2000 of 19 April 2000 on the application of Article [101](3) of the Treaty to certain categories of agreements, decisions and concerted practices between liner shipping companies (consortia) (OJ L 100, 20.4.2000, p.24)

B8

COMMISSION NOTICE ON THE HANDLING OF COMPLAINTS BY THE COMMISSION UNDER ARTICLES [101 AND 102] OF THE [TREATY ON THE FUNCTIONING OF THE EUROPEAN UNION]*

(2004/C 101/05)

(Text with EEA relevance)

Official Journal C 101, 27.4.2004, p.65

Celex No: 52004XC0427(04)

EUR-Lex permanent link: <http://eur-lex.europa.eu/LexUriServ/LexUriServ.do?uri=CELEX:5200 4XC0427(04):EN:NOT>

Notes

* Ed note: please see the Note on the Lisbon Treaty at p.xvii in regard to article renumbering introduced by the Lisbon Treaty.
EEA application: the EFTA Surveillance Authority has adopted a parallel notice under Article 5(2)(b) of the Surveillance and Court Agreement: see College Decision No 175/05/COL of 15 July 2005, OJ C 287, 29.11.2007, p.12 and EEA Supplement No. 57, 29.11.2007, p.1.

Commentary
Notice: F&N: 8.103
Part III: B&C: 13.041

I. Introduction and Subject-matter of the Notice

1. Regulation 1/2003[1] establishes a system of parallel competence for the application of Articles [101] and [102] of the [Treaty on the Functioning of the European Union] by the Commission and the Member States' competition authorities and courts. The Regulation recognises in particular the complementary functions of the Commission and Member States' competition authorities acting as public enforcers and the Member States' courts that rule on private lawsuits in order to safeguard the rights of individuals deriving from Articles [101] and [102].[2]

Notes

[1] Council Regulation (EC) No 1/2003 of 16 December 2002 on the implementation of the rules on competition laid down in Articles [101] and [102] of the Treaty (OJ L 1, 4.1.2003, p.1–25).
[2] Cf. in particular Recitals 3–7 and 35 of Regulation 1/2003.

2. Under Regulation 1/2003, the public enforcers may focus their action on the investigation of serious infringements of Articles [101] and [102] which are often difficult to detect. For their enforcement activity, they benefit from information supplied by undertakings and by consumers in the market.

Commentary
point 2: B&C: 13.041

3. The Commission therefore wishes to encourage citizens and undertakings to address themselves to the public enforcers to inform them about suspected infringements of the competition rules. At the level of the Commission, there are two ways to do this, one is by lodging a complaint pursuant

to Article 7(2) of Regulation 1/2003. Under Articles 5 to 9 of Regulation 773/2004,[3] such complaints must fulfil certain requirements.

Notes
3 Commission Regulation (EC) No 773/2004 of 7 April 2004 relating to the conduct of proceedings by the Commission pursuant to Articles [101] and [102] of the [Treaty on the Functioning of the European Union] (OJ 123, 27.4.2004).
Commentary
para 3: **B&C:** 13.041 **F&N:** 8.103

4. The other way is the provision of market information that does not have to comply with the requirements for complaints pursuant to Article 7(2) of Regulation 1/2003. For this purpose, the Commission has created a special website to collect information from citizens and undertakings and their associations who wish to inform the Commission about suspected infringements of Articles [101] and [102]. Such information can be the starting point for an investigation by the Commission.[4] Information about suspected infringements can be supplied to the following address:

<http://europa.eu.int/dgcomp/info-on-anti-competitivepractices>

or to:

Commission européenne/Europese Commissie
Competition DG
B-1049 Bruxelles/Brussel

Notes
4 The Commission handles correspondence from informants in accordance with its principles of good administrative practice.
Commentary
para 4: **B&C:** 13.042 **F&N:** 8.103

5. Without prejudice to the interpretation of Regulation 1/2003 and of Commission Regulation 773/2004 by the Community Courts, the present Notice intends to provide guidance to citizens and undertakings that are seeking relief from suspected infringements of the competition rules. The Notice contains two main parts:

— Part II gives indications about the choice between complaining to the Commission or bringing a lawsuit before a national court. Moreover, it recalls the principles related to the work-sharing between the Commission and the national competition authorities in the enforcement system established by Regulation 1/2003 that are explained in the Notice on cooperation within the network of competition authorities.[5]

— Part III explains the procedure for the treatment of complaints pursuant to Article 7(2) of Regulation 1/2003 by the Commission.

Notes
5 Notice on cooperation within the Network of competition authorities (OJ C 81, 27.4.2004, p.43).

6. This Notice does not address the following situations:

— complaints lodged by Member States pursuant to Article 7(2) of Regulation 1/2003,
— complaints that ask the Commission to take action against a Member State pursuant to Article [106](3) in conjunction with Articles [101] or [102] of the Treaty,
— complaints relating to Article [107] of the Treaty on state aids,
— complaints relating to infringements by Member States that the Commission may pursue in the framework of Article [258] of the Treaty.[6]

Notes
6 For the handling of such complaints, cf. Commission communication of 10 October 2002, COM(2002) 141.

II. Different Possibilities for Lodging Complaints about Suspected Infringements of Articles [101] or [102]

A. Complaints in the New Enforcement System Established by Regulation 1/2003

7. Depending on the nature of the complaint, a complainant may bring his complaint either to a national court or to a competition authority that acts as public enforcer. The present chapter of this Notice intends to help potential complainants to make an informed choice about whether to address themselves to the Commission, to one of the Member States' competition authorities or to a national court.

8. While national courts are called upon to safeguard the rights of individuals and are thus bound to rule on cases brought before them, public enforcers cannot investigate all complaints, but must set priorities in their treatment of cases. The Court of Justice has held that the Commission, entrusted by Article [105](1) of the [Treaty on the Functioning of the European Union] with the task of ensuring application of the principles laid down in Articles [101] and [102] of the Treaty, is responsible for defining and implementing the orientation of Community competition policy and that, in order to perform that task effectively, it is entitled to give differing degrees of priority to the complaints brought before it.[7]

Notes

[7] Case C-344/98 *Masterfoods v HB Ice Cream* [2000] ECR I-11369, para 46; Case C-119/97 P *Union française de l'express (Ufex) and Others v Commission of the European Communities* [1999] ECR I-1341, para 88; Case T-24/90 *Automec v Commission of the European Communities* [1992] ECR II-2223, paras 73–77.

9. Regulation 1/2003 empowers Member States' courts and Member States' competition authorities to apply Articles [101] and [102] in their entirety alongside the Commission. Regulation 1/2003 pursues as one principal objective that Member States' courts and competition authorities should participate effectively in the enforcement of Articles [101] and [102].[8]

Notes

[8] Cf. in particular Articles 5, 6, 11, 12, 15, 22, 29, 35 and Recitals 2 to 4 and 6 to 8 of Regulation 1/2003.

10. Moreover, Article 3 of Regulation 1/2003 provides that Member States' courts and competition authorities have to apply Articles [101] and [102] to all cases of agreements or conduct that are capable of affecting trade between Member States to which they apply their national competition laws. In addition, Articles 11 and 15 of the Regulation create a range of mechanisms by which Member States' courts and competition authorities cooperate with the Commission in the enforcement of Articles [101] and [102].

11. In this new legislative framework, the Commission intends to refocus its enforcement resources along the following lines:

— enforce the EC competition rules in cases for which it is well placed to act,[9] concentrating its resources on the most serious infringements;[10]

— handle cases in relation to which the Commission should act with a view to define Community competition policy and/or to ensure coherent application of Articles [101] or [102].

Notes

[9] Cf. Notice on cooperation within the network of competition authorities [OJ C 101, 27.4.2004, p 43], points 5 [ff].
[10] Cf. Recital 3 of Regulation 1/2003.

Commentary
point 11: B&C: 13.005

B. The Complementary Roles of Private and Public Enforcement

12. It has been consistently held by the Community Courts that national courts are called upon to safeguard the rights of individuals created by the direct effect of Articles [101](1) and [102].[11]

Part B Procedural Matters

Notes

11 Settled case law, cf. Case 127/73 *Belgische Radio en Televisie (BRT) v SABAM and Fonior* [1974] ECR 51, para 16; Case C-282/95 P *Guérin automobiles v Commission of the European Communities* [1997] ECR I-1503, para 39; Case C-453/99 *Courage v Bernhard Crehan* [2001] ECR I-6297, para 23.

13. National courts can decide upon the nullity or validity of contracts and only national courts can grant damages to an individual in case of an infringement of Articles [101] and [102]. Under the case law of the Court of Justice, any individual can claim damages for loss caused to him by a contract or by conduct which restricts or distorts competition, in order to ensure the full effectiveness of the Community competition rules. Such actions for damages before the national courts can make a significant contribution to the maintenance of effective competition in the Community as they discourage undertakings from concluding or applying restrictive agreements or practices.[12]

Notes

12 Case C-453/99 *Courage v Bernhard Crehan* [2001] ECR I-6297, paras 26 and 27; the power of national courts to grant damages is also underlined in Recital 7 of Regulation 1/2003.

14. Regulation 1/2003 takes express account of the fact that national courts have an essential part to play in applying the EC competition rules.[13] By extending the power to apply Article [101](3) to national courts it removes the possibility for undertakings to delay national court proceedings by a notification to the Commission and thus eliminates an obstacle for private litigation that existed under Regulation No 17.[14]

Notes

13 Cf Articles 1, 6 and 15 as well as Recital 7 of Regulation 1/2003.
14 Regulation No 17: First Regulation implementing Articles [101] and [102] of the Treaty; OJ P 13 of 21 February 1962, p.204–211; English special edition: Series I Chapter 1959–1962, p.87. Regulation No 17 is repealed by Article 43 of Regulation 1/2003 with effect from 1 May 2004.

15. Without prejudice to the right or obligation of national courts to address a preliminary question to the Court of Justice in accordance with Article [267 TFEU], Article 15(1) of Regulation 1/2003 provides expressly that national courts may ask for opinions or information from the Commission. This provision aims at facilitating the application of Articles [101] and [102] by national courts.[15]

Notes

15 For more detailed explanations of this mechanism, cf. Notice on co-operation between the Commission and the courts of the EU Member States in the application of Articles [101] and [102] [TFEU] [OJ C 101, 27.4.2004, p 54].

16. Action before national courts has the following advantages for complainants:

— National courts may award damages for loss suffered as a result of an infringement of Article [101] or [102].

— National courts may rule on claims for payment or contractual obligations based on an agreement that they examine under Article [101].

— It is for the national courts to apply the civil sanction of nullity of Article [101](2) in contractual relationships between individuals.[16] They can in particular assess, in the light of the applicable national law, the scope and consequences of the nullity of certain contractual provisions under Article [101](2), with particular regard to all the other matters covered by the agreement.[17]

— National courts are usually better placed than the Commission to adopt interim measures.[18]

— Before national courts, it is possible to combine a claim under Community competition law with other claims under national law.

— Courts normally have the power to award legal costs to the successful applicant. This is never possible in an administrative procedure before the Commission.

Notes

16 Case T-24/90 *Automec v Commission of the European Communities* [1992] ECR II-2223, para 93.

[17] Case C-230/96 *Cabour and Nord Distribution Automobile v Arnor "SOCO"* [1998] ECR I-2055, para 51; Joined Cases T-185/96, T-189/96 and T-190/96 *Dalmasso and Others v Commission of the European Communities* [1999] ECR II-93, para 50.
[18] Cf. Article 8 of Regulation 1/2003 and [point] 80 below. Depending on the case, Member States' competition authorities may equally be well placed to adopt interim measures.

17. The fact that a complainant can secure the protection of his rights by an action before a national court, is an important element that the Commission may take into account in its examination of the Community interest for investigating a complaint.[19]

Notes
[19] Cf. points 41 [ff] below.

18. The Commission holds the view that the new enforcement system established by Regulation 1/2003 strengthens the possibilities for complainants to seek and obtain effective relief before national courts.

C. WORK-SHARING BETWEEN THE PUBLIC ENFORCERS IN THE EUROPEAN COMMUNITY

19. Regulation 1/2003 creates a system of parallel competence for the application of Articles [101] and [102] by empowering Member States' competition authorities to apply Articles [101] and [102] in their entirety (Article 5). Decentralised enforcement by Member States' competition authorities is further encouraged by the possibility to exchange information (Article 12) and to provide each other assistance with investigations (Article 22).

20. The Regulation does not regulate the work-sharing between the Commission and the Member States' competition authorities but leaves the division of case work to the cooperation of the Commission and the Member States' competition authorities inside the European Competition Network (ECN). The Regulation pursues the objective of ensuring effective enforcement of Articles [101] and [102] through a flexible division of case work between the public enforcers in the Community.

21. Orientations for the work sharing between the Commission and the Member States' competition authorities are laid down in a separate Notice.[20] The guidance contained in that Notice, which concerns the relations between the public enforcers, will be of interest to complainants as it permits them to address a complaint to the authority most likely to be well placed to deal with their case.

Notes
[20] Notice on cooperation within the Network of competition authorities (p.43).

22. The Notice on cooperation within the Network of Competition Authorities states in particular:[21]

> "An authority can be considered to be well placed to deal with a case if the following three cumulative conditions are met:
> — the agreement or practice has substantial direct actual or foreseeable effects on competition within its territory, is implemented within or originates from its territory;
> — the authority is able effectively to bring to an end the entire infringement, i.e. it can adopt a cease-and desist order, the effect of which will be sufficient to bring an end to the infringement and it can, where appropriate, sanction the infringement adequately;
> — it can gather, possibly with the assistance of other authorities, the evidence required to prove the infringement.
> The above criteria indicate that a material link between the infringement and the territory of a Member State must exist in order for that Member State's competition authority to be considered well placed. It can be expected that in most cases the authorities of those Member States where competition is substantially affected by an infringement will be well placed provided they are capable of effectively bringing the infringement to an end through either single or parallel action unless the Commission is better placed to act (see below […]).
> It follows that a single NCA is usually well placed to deal with agreements or practices that substantially affect competition mainly within its territory […].

Part B Procedural Matters

Furthermore single action of an NCA might also be appropriate where, although more than one NCA can be regarded as well placed, the action of a single NCA is sufficient to bring the entire infringement to an end [...].

Parallel action by two or three NCAs may be appropriate where an agreement or practice has substantial effects on competition mainly in their respective territories and the action of only one NCA would not be sufficient to bring the entire infringement to an end and/or to sanction it adequately [...].

The authorities dealing with a case in parallel action will endeavour to coordinate their action to the extent possible. To that effect, they may find it useful to designate one of them as a lead authority and to delegate tasks to the lead authority such as for example the coordination of investigative measures, while each authority remains responsible for conducting its own proceedings.

The Commission is particularly well placed if one or several agreement(s) or practice(s), including networks of similar agreements or practices, have effects on competition in more than three Member States (crossborder markets covering more than three Member States or several national markets) [...].

Moreover, the Commission is particularly well placed to deal with a case if it is closely linked to other Community provisions which may be exclusively or more effectively applied by the Commission, if the Community interest requires the adoption of a Commission decision to develop Community competition policy when a new competition issue arises or to ensure effective enforcement".

Notes

[21] Notice on cooperation within the Network of competition authorities [OJ C 101, 27.4.2004, p 43], points 8–15.

23. Within the European Competition Network, information on cases that are being investigated following a complaint will be made available to the other members of the network before or without delay after commencing the first formal investigative measure.[22] Where the same complaint has been lodged with several authorities or where a case has not been lodged with an authority that is well placed, the members of the network will endeavour to determine within an indicative time-limit of two months which authority or authorities should be in charge of the case.

Notes

[22] Article 11(2) and (3) of Regulation 1/2003; Notice on cooperation within the Network of Competition Authorities [OJ C 101, 27.4.2004, p 43], points 16 and 17.

24. Complainants themselves have an important role to play in further reducing the potential need for reallocation of a case originating from their complaint by referring to the orientations on work sharing in the network set out in the present chapter when deciding on where to lodge their complaint. If nonetheless a case is reallocated within the network, the undertakings concerned and the complainant(s) are informed as soon as possible by the competition authorities involved.[23]

Notes

[23] Notice on cooperation within the Network of Competition Authorities [OJ C 101, 27.4.2004, p 43], point 34.

25. The Commission may reject a complaint in accordance with Article 13 of Regulation 1/2003, on the grounds that a Member State competition authority is dealing or has dealt with the case. When doing so, the Commission must, in accordance with Article 9 of Regulation 773/2004, inform the complainant without delay of the national competition authority which is dealing or has already dealt with the case.

III. The Commission's Handling of Complaints Pursuant to Article 7(2) of Regulation 1/2003

A. General

26. According to Article 7(2) of Regulation 1/2003 natural or legal persons that can show a legitimate interest[24] are entitled to lodge a complaint to ask the Commission to find an infringement of Articles [101] and [102] [TFEU] and to require that the infringement be brought to an end in accordance with Article 7(1) of Regulation 1/2003. The present part of this Notice explains the requirements applicable to complaints based on Article 7(2) of Regulation 1/2003, their assessment and the procedure followed by the Commission.

Notes

[24] For more extensive explanations on this notion in particular, cf. points 33 [ff] below.

27. The Commission, unlike civil courts, whose task is to safeguard the individual rights of private persons, is an administrative authority that must act in the public interest. It is an inherent feature of the Commission's task as public enforcer that it has a margin of discretion to set priorities in its enforcement activity.[25]

Notes

[25] Case C-119/97 P *Union française de l'express (Ufex) and Others v Commission of the European Communities* [1999] ECR I-1341, para 88; Case T-24/90 *Automec v Commission of the European Communities* [1992] ECR II-2223, paras 73–77 and 85.

28. The Commission is entitled to give different degrees of priority to complaints made to it and may refer to the Community interest presented by a case as a criterion of priority.[26] The Commission may reject a complaint when it considers that the case does not display a sufficient Community interest to justify further investigation. Where the Commission rejects a complaint, the complainant is entitled to a decision of the Commission[27] without prejudice to Article 7(3) of Regulation 773/2004.

Notes

[26] Settled case law since Case T-24/90 *Automec v Commission of the European Communities* [1992] ECR II-2223, para 85.

[27] Case C-282/95 P *Guérin automobiles v Commission of the European Communities* [1997] ECR I-1503, para 36.

B. Making a Complaint pursuant to Article 7(2) of Regulation 1/2003

(a) Complaint form

29. A complaint pursuant to Article 7(2) of Regulation 1/2003 can only be made about an alleged infringement of Articles [101] or [102] with a view to the Commission taking action under Article 7(1) of Regulation 1/2003. A complaint under Article 7(2) of Regulation 1/2003 has to comply with Form C mentioned in Article 5(1) of Regulation 773/2004 and annexed to that Regulation.

30. Form C is available at <http://europa.eu.int/dgcomp/complaints-form> and is also annexed to this Notice. The complaint must be submitted in three paper copies as well as, if possible, an electronic copy. In addition, the complainant must provide a non-confidential version of the complaint (Article 5(2) of Regulation 773/2004). Electronic transmission to the Commission is possible via the website indicated, the paper copies should be sent to the following address:

Commission européenne/Europese Commissie
Competition DG
B-1049 Bruxelles/Brussel

31. Form C requires complainants to submit comprehensive information in relation to their complaint. They should also provide copies of relevant supporting documentation reasonably available to them and, to the extent possible, provide indications as to where relevant information and

documents that are unavailable to them could be obtained by the Commission. In particular cases, the Commission may dispense with the obligation to provide information in relation to part of the information required by Form C (Article 5(1) of Regulation 773/2004). The Commission holds the view that this possibility can in particular play a role to facilitate complaints by consumer associations where they, in the context of an otherwise substantiated complaint, do not have access to specific pieces of information from the sphere of the undertakings complained of.

32. Correspondence to the Commission that does not comply with the requirements of Article 5 of Regulation 773/2004 and therefore does not constitute a complaint within the meaning of Article 7(2) of Regulation 1/2003 will be considered by the Commission as general information that, where it is useful, may lead to an own-initiative investigation (cf. point 4 above).

(b) Legitimate interest

33. The status of formal complainant under Article 7(2) of Regulation 1/2003 is reserved to legal and natural persons who can show a legitimate interest.[28] Member States are deemed to have a legitimate interest for all complaints they choose to lodge.

Notes
[28] Cf. Article 5(1) of Regulation 773/2004.

Commentary
point 33: B&C: 13.043

34. In the past practice of the Commission, the condition of legitimate interest was not often a matter of doubt as most complainants were in a position of being directly and adversely affected by the alleged infringement. However, there are situations where the condition of a "legitimate interest" in Article 7(2) requires further analysis to conclude that it is fulfilled. Useful guidance can best be provided by a non-exhaustive set of examples.

35. The Court of First Instance has held that an association of undertakings may claim a legitimate interest in lodging a complaint regarding conduct concerning its members, even if it is not directly concerned, as an undertaking operating in the relevant market, by the conduct complained of, provided that, first, it is entitled to represent the interests of its members and secondly, the conduct complained of is liable to adversely affect the interests of its members.[29] Conversely, the Commission has been found to be entitled not to pursue the complaint of an association of undertakings whose members were not involved in the type of business transactions complained of.[30]

Notes
[29] Case T-114/92 *Bureau Européen des Médias et de l'Industrie Musicale (BEMIM) v Commission of the European Communities* [1995] ECR II-147, para 28. Associations of undertakings were also the complainants in the cases underlying the judgments in Case 298/83 *Comité des industries cinématographiques des Communautés Européennes (CICCE) v Commission of the European Communities* [1985] ECR 1105 and Case T-319/99 *Federacion Nacional de Empresas (FENIN) v Commission of the European Communities* [2003] ECR II-357 [and see, on appeal, Case C-205/03 P *FENIN v Commission of the European Communities* [2006] ECR, judgment of 11 July 2006].
[30] Joined Cases T-133/95 and T-204/95 *International Express Carriers Conference (IECC) v Commission of the European Communities* [1998] ECR II-3645, paras 79–83.

36. From this case law, it can be inferred that undertakings (themselves or through associations that are entitled to represent their interests) can claim a legitimate interest where they are operating in the relevant market or where the conduct complained of is liable to directly and adversely affect their interests. This confirms the established practice of the Commission which has accepted that a legitimate interest can, for instance, be claimed by the parties to the agreement or practice which is the subject of the complaint, by competitors whose interests have allegedly been damaged by the behaviour complained of or by undertakings excluded from a distribution system.

37. Consumer associations can equally lodge complaints with the Commission.[31] The Commission moreover holds the view that individual consumers whose economic interests are directly and adversely affected insofar as they are the buyers of goods or services that are the object of an infringement can be in a position to show a legitimate interest.[32]

Notes

31 Case T-37/92 *Bureau Européen des Unions des Consommateurs (BEUC) v Commission of the European Communities* [1994] ECR II-285, para 36.
32 This question is currently raised in a pending procedure before the Court of First Instance (Joined Cases T-213 and 214/01). The Commission has also accepted as complainant an individual consumer in its Decision of 9 December 1998 in Case IV/D-2/34.466, Greek Ferries, OJ L 109/24 of 27 April 1999, para 1.

Commentary
point 37: B&C: 13.043

38. However, the Commission does not consider as a legitimate interest within the meaning of Article 7(2) the interest of persons or organisations that wish to come forward on general interest considerations without showing that they or their members are liable to be directly and adversely affected by the infringement (*pro bono publico*).
39. Local or regional public authorities may be able to show a legitimate interest in their capacity as buyers or users of goods or services affected by the conduct complained of. Conversely, they cannot be considered as showing a legitimate interest within the meaning of Article 7(2) of Regulation 1/2003 to the extent that they bring to the attention of the Commission alleged infringements *pro bono publico*.
40. Complainants have to demonstrate their legitimate interest. Where a natural or legal person lodging a complaint is unable to demonstrate a legitimate interest, the Commission is entitled, without prejudice to its right to initiate proceedings of its own initiative, not to pursue the complaint. The Commission may ascertain whether this condition is met at any stage of the investigation.[33]

Notes

33 Joined Cases T-133/95 and T-204/95 *International Express Carriers Conference (IECC) v Commission of the European Communities* [1998] ECR II-3645, para 79.

Commentary
point 40: B&C: 13.043

C. Assessment of Complaints

(a) Community interest

41. Under the settled case law of the Community Courts, the Commission is not required to conduct an investigation in each case[34] or, *a fortiori*, to take a decision within the meaning of Article [288 TFEU] on the existence or non-existence of an infringement of Articles [101] or [102],[35] but is entitled to give differing degrees of priority to the complaints brought before it and refer to the Community interest in order to determine the degree of priority to be applied to the various complaints it receives.[36] The position is different only if the complaint falls within the exclusive competence of the Commission.[37]

Notes

34 Case T-24/90 *Automec v Commission of the European Communities* [1992] ECR II-2223, para 76; Case C-91/95 P *Roger Tremblay and Others v Commission of the European Communities* [1996] ECR I-5547, para 30.
35 Case 125/78 *GEMA v Commission of the European Communities* [1979] ECR 3173, para 17; Case C-119/97/P *Union française de l'express (Ufex) and Others v Commission of the European Communities* [1999] ECR I-1341, para 87.
36 Settled case law since Case T-24/90 *Automec v Commission of the European Communities* [1992] ECR II-2223, paras 77 and 85; Recital 18 of Regulation 1/2003 expressly confirms this possibility.
37 Settled case law since Case T-24/90 *Automec v Commission of the European Communities* [1992] ECR II-2223, para 75. Under Regulation 1/2003, this principle may only be relevant in the context of Article 29 of that Regulation.

42. The Commission must however examine carefully the factual and legal elements brought to its attention by the complainant in order to assess the Community interest in further investigation of a case.[38]

Notes

38 Case 210/81 *Oswald Schmidt, trading as Demo-Studio Schmidt v Commission of the European Communities* [1983] ECR 3045, para 19; Case C-119/97 P *Union française de l'express (Ufex) and Others v Commission of the European Communities* [1999] ECR I-1341, para 86.

43. The assessment of the Community interest raised by a complaint depends on the circumstances of each individual case. Accordingly, the number of criteria of assessment to which the Commission may refer is not limited, nor is the Commission required to have recourse exclusively to certain criteria. As the factual and legal circumstances may differ considerably from case to case, it is permissible to apply new criteria which had not before been considered.[39] Where appropriate, the Commission may give priority to a single criterion for assessing the Community interest.[40]

Notes

39 Case C-119/97 P *Union française de l'express (Ufex) and Others v Commission of the European Communities* [1999] ECR I-1341, paras 79–80.
40 Case C-450/98 P *International Express Carriers Conference (IECC) v Commission of the European Communities* [2001] ECR I-3947, paras 57–59.

Commentary
point 43: B&C: 13.050

44. Among the criteria which have been held relevant in the case law for the assessment of the Community interest in the (further) investigation of a case are the following:

   — The Commission can reject a complaint on the ground that the complainant can bring an action to assert its rights before national courts.[41]
   — The Commission may not regard certain situations as excluded in principle from its purview under the task entrusted to it by the Treaty but is required to assess in each case how serious the alleged infringements are and how persistent their consequences are. This means in particular that it must take into account the duration and the extent of the infringements complained of and their effect on the competition situation in the Community.[42]
   — The Commission may have to balance the significance of the alleged infringement as regards the functioning of the common market, the probability of establishing the existence of the infringement and the scope of the investigation required in order to fulfil its task of ensuring that Articles [101] and [102] of the Treaty are complied with.[43]
   — While the Commission's discretion does not depend on how advanced the investigation of a case is, the stage of the investigation forms part of the circumstances of the case which the Commission may have to take into consideration.[44]
   — The Commission may decide that it is not appropriate to investigate a complaint where the practices in question have ceased. However, for this purpose, the Commission will have to ascertain whether anticompetitive effects persist and if the seriousness of the infringements or the persistence of their effects does not give the complaint a Community interest.[45]
   — The Commission may also decide that it is not appropriate to investigate a complaint where the undertakings concerned agree to change their conduct in such a way that it can consider that there is no longer a sufficient Community interest to intervene.[46]

Notes

41 Case T-24/90 *Automec v Commission of the European Communities* [1992] ECR II-2223, paras 88 [ff]; Case T-5/93 *Roger Tremblay and Others v Commission of the European Communities* [1995] ECR II-185, paras 65 [ff]; Case T-575/93 *Casper Koelman v Commission of the European Communities* [1996] ECR II-1, paras 75–80; see also Part II above, where more detailed explanations concerning this situation are given.
42 Case C-119/97 P *Union française de l'express (Ufex) and Others v Commission of the European Communities* [1999] ECR I-1341, paras 92 and 93.
43 Settled case law since Case T-24/90 *Automec v Commission of the European Communities* [1992] ECR II-2223, para 86.
44 Case C-449/98 P *International Express Carriers Conference (IECC) v Commission of the European Communities* [2001] ECR I-3875, para 37.

45 Case T-77/95 *Syndicat français de l'Express International and Others v Commission of the European Communities* [1997] ECR II-1, para 57; Case C-119/97 P *Union française de l'express (Ufex) and Others v Commission of the European Communities* [1999] ECR I-1341, para 95. Cf. also Case T-37/92 *Bureau Européen des Unions des Consommateurs (BEUC) v Commission of the European Communities* [1994] ECR II-285, para 113, where an unwritten commitment between a Member State and a third county outside the common commercial policy was held not to suffice to establish that the conduct complained of had ceased.

46 Case T-110/95 *International Express Carriers (IECC) v Commission of the European Communities and Others* [1998] ECR II-3605, para 57, upheld by Case 449/98 P *International Express Carriers (IECC) v Commission of the European Communities and Others* [2001] ECR I-3875, paras 44–47.

Commentary
point 44: B&C: 13.050

45. Where it forms the view that a case does not display sufficient Community interest to justify (further) investigation, the Commission may reject the complaint on that ground. Such a decision can be taken either before commencing an investigation or after taking investigative measures.[47] However, the Commission is not obliged to set aside a complaint for lack of Community interest.[48]

Notes
47 Case C-449/98 P *International Express Carriers (IECC) v Commission of the European Communities e.a.* [2001] ECR I-3875, para 37.
48 Cf. Case T-77/92 *Parker Pen v Commission of the European Communities* [1994] ECR II-549, paras 64/65.

Commentary
point 45: B&C: 13.046

(b) Assessment under Articles [101] and [102]

46. The examination of a complaint under Articles [101] and [102] involves two aspects, one relating to the facts to be established to prove an infringement of Articles [101] or [102] and the other relating to the legal assessment of the conduct complained of.

47. Where the complaint, while complying with the requirements of Article 5 of Regulation 773/2004 and Form C, does not sufficiently substantiate the allegations put forward, it may be rejected on that ground.[49] In order to reject a complaint on the ground that the conduct complained of does not infringe the EC competition rules or does not fall within their scope of application, the Commission is not obliged to take into account circumstances that have not been brought to its attention by the complainant and that it could only have uncovered by the investigation of the case.[50]

Notes
49 Case 298/83 *Comité des industries cinématographiques des Communautés Européennes (CICCE) v Commission of the European Communities* [1985] ECR 1105, paras 21–24; Case T-198/98 *Micro Leader Business v Commission of the European Communities* [1999] ECR II-3989, paras 32–39.
50 Case T-319/99 *Federación Nacional de Empresas (FENIN) v Commission of the European Communities* [2003] ECR II-357, para 43 [and see, on appeal, Case C-205/03 P *FENIN v Commission of the European Communities* [2006] ECR I-6295, judgment of 11 July 2006].

48. The criteria for the legal assessment of agreements or practices under Articles [101] and [102] cannot be dealt with exhaustively in the present Notice. However, potential complainants should refer to the extensive guidance available from the Commission,[51] in addition to other sources and in particular the case law of the Community Courts and the case practice of the Commission. Four specific issues are mentioned in the following points with indications on where to find further guidance.

Notes
51 Extensive guidance can be found on the Commission's website at <http://europa.eu.int/comm/competition/index_en.html>.

49. Agreements and practices fall within the scope of application of Articles [101] and [102] where they are capable of affecting trade between Member States. Where an agreement or practice does

not fulfil this condition, national competition law may apply, but not EC competition law. Extensive guidance on this subject can be found in the Notice on the effect on trade concept.[52]

Notes

[52] Notice on the effect on trade concept contained in Articles [101] and [102] of the Treaty [OJ C 101, 27.4.2004, p.81].

50. Agreements falling within the scope of Article [101] may be agreements of minor importance which are deemed not to restrict competition appreciably. Guidance on this issue can be found in the Commission's *de minimis* Notice.[53]

Notes

[53] Commission Notice on agreements of minor importance which do not appreciably restrict competition under Article [101](1) of the [Treaty on the Functioning of the European Union] (*de minimis*), OJ C 368 of 22 December [2001], p.13.

51. Agreements that fulfil the conditions of a block exemption regulation are deemed to satisfy the conditions of Article [101](3).[54] For the Commission to withdraw the benefit of the block exemption pursuant to Article 29 of Regulation 1/2003, it must find that upon individual assessment an agreement to which the exemption regulation applies has certain effects which are incompatible with Article [101](3).

Notes

[54] The texts of all block exemption regulations are available on the Commission's website at <http://europa.eu.int/comm/competition/index_en.html>.

52. Agreements that restrict competition within the meaning of Article [101](1) [TFEU] may fulfil the conditions of Article [101](3) [TFEU]. Pursuant to Article 1(2) of Regulation 1/2003 and without a prior administrative decision being required, such agreements are not prohibited. Guidance on the conditions to be fulfilled by an agreement pursuant to Article [101](3) can be found in the Notice on Article [101](3).[55]

Notes

[55] Commission Notice — Guidelines on the application of Article [101](3) of the Treaty [OJ C101, 27.4.2004, p.97].

D. The Commission's Procedures when Dealing with Complaints

(a) Overview

53. As recalled above, the Commission is not obliged to carry out an investigation on the basis of every complaint submitted with a view to establishing whether an infringement has been committed. However, the Commission is under a duty to consider carefully the factual and legal issues brought to its attention by the complainant, in order to assess whether those issues indicate conduct which is liable to infringe Articles [101] and [102].[56]

Notes

[56] Case 210/81 *Oswald Schmidt, trading as Demo-Studio Schmidt v Commission of the European Communities* [1983] ECR 3045, para 19; Case T-24/90 *Automec v Commission of the European Communities* [1992] ECR II-2223, para 79.

54. In the Commission's procedure for dealing with complaints, different stages can be distinguished.[57]

Notes

[57] Cf. Case T-64/89 *Automec v Commission of the European Communities* [1990] ECR II-367, paras 45–47; Case T-37/92 *Bureau Européen des Unions des Consommateurs (BEUC) v Commission of the European Communities* [1994] ECR II-285, para 29.

55. During the first stage, following the submission of the complaint, the Commission examines the complaint and may collect further information in order to decide what action it will take on the complaint. That stage may include an informal exchange of views between the Commission and the complainant with a view to clarifying the factual and legal issues with which the complaint is

concerned. In this stage, the Commission may give an initial reaction to the complainant allowing the complainant an opportunity to expand on his allegations in the light of that initial reaction.

Commentary
point 55: B&C: 13.046

56. In the second stage, the Commission may investigate the case further with a view to initiating proceedings pursuant to Article 7(1) of Regulation 1/2003 against the undertakings complained of. Where the Commission considers that there are insufficient grounds for acting on the complaint, it will inform the complainant of its reasons and offer the complainant the opportunity to submit any further comments within a time-limit which it fixes (Article 7(1) of Regulation 773/2004).

Commentary
point 56: B&C: 13.047

57. If the complainant fails to make known its views within the time-limit set by the Commission, the complaint is deemed to have been withdrawn (Article 7(3) of Regulation 773/2004). In all other cases, in the third stage of the procedure, the Commission takes cognisance of the observations submitted by the complainant and either initiates a procedure against the subject of the complaint or adopts a decision rejecting the complaint.[58]

Notes
[58] Case C-282/95 P, *Guérin automobiles v Commission of the European Communities* [1997] ECR I-1503, para 36.

Commentary
point 57: B&C: 13.047

58. Where the Commission rejects a complaint pursuant to Article 13 of Regulation 1/2003 on the grounds that another authority is dealing or has dealt with the case, the Commission proceeds in accordance with Article 9 of Regulation 773/2004.

59. Throughout the procedure, complainants benefit from a range of rights as provided in particular in Articles 6 to 8 of Regulation 773/2004. However, proceedings of the Commission in competition cases do not constitute adversarial proceedings between the complainant on the one hand and the companies which are the subject of the investigation on the other hand. Accordingly, the procedural rights of complainants are less far-reaching than the right to a fair hearing of the companies which are the subject of an infringement procedure.[59]

Notes
[59] Joined Cases 142 and 156/84 *British American Tobacco Company and R. J. Reynolds Industries v Commission of the European Communities* [1987] ECR 249, paras 19 and 20.

(b) Indicative time limit for informing the complainant of the Commission's proposed action

60. The Commission is under an obligation to decide on complaints within a reasonable time.[60] What is a reasonable duration depends on the circumstances of each case and in particular, its context, the various procedural steps followed by the Commission, the conduct of the parties in the course of the procedure, the complexity of the case and its importance for the various parties involved.[61]

Notes
[60] Case C-282/95 P *Guérin automobiles v Commission of the European Communities* [1997] ECR I-1503, para 37.
[61] Joined Cases T-213/95 and T-18/96 *Stichting Certificatie Kraanverhuurbedrijf (SCK) and Federatie van Nederlandse Kraanbedrijven (FNK) v Commission of the European Communities* [1997] ECR 1739, para 57.

61. The Commission will in principle endeavour to inform complainants of the action that it proposes to take on a complaint within an indicative time frame of four months from the reception of the complaint. Thus, subject to the circumstances of the individual case and in particular the possible need to request complementary information from the complainant or third parties, the Commission will in principle inform the complainant within four months whether or not it

intends to investigate its case further. This time-limit does not constitute a binding statutory term.

Commentary
point 61: B&C: 13.046

62. Accordingly, within this four month period, the Commission may communicate its proposed course of action to the complainant as an initial reaction within the first phase of the procedure (see point 55 above). The Commission may also, where the examination of the complaint has progressed to the second stage (see point 56 above), directly proceed to informing the complainant about its provisional assessment by a letter pursuant to Article 7(1) of Regulation 773/2004.
63. To ensure the most expeditious treatment of their complaint, it is desirable that complainants cooperate diligently in the procedures,[62] for example by informing the Commission of new developments.

Notes
[62] The notion of "diligence" on the part of the complainant is used by the Court of First Instance in Case T-77/94 *Vereniging van Groothandelaren in Bloemkwekerijprodukten and Others v Commission of the European Communities* [1997] ECR II-759, para 75.

(c) Procedural rights of the complainant

64. Where the Commission addresses a statement of objections to the companies complained of pursuant to Article 10(1) of Regulation 773/2004, the complainant is entitled to receive a copy of this document from which business secrets and other confidential information of the companies concerned have been removed (non-confidential version of the statement of objections; cf. Article 6(1) of Regulation 773/2004). The complainant is invited to comment in writing on the statement of objections. A time-limit will be set for such written comments.

Commentary
point 64: B&C: 13.051

65. Furthermore, the Commission may, where appropriate, afford complainants the opportunity of expressing their views at the oral hearing of the parties to which a statement of objections has been addressed, if the complainants so request in their written comments.[63]

Notes
[63] Article 6(2) of Commission Regulation 773/2004.

Commentary
point 65: B&C: 13.051 F&N: 8.452

66. Complainants may submit, of their own initiative or following a request by the Commission, documents that contain business secrets or other confidential information. Confidential information will be protected by the Commission.[64] Under Article 16 of Regulation 773/2004, complainants are obliged to identify confidential information, give reasons why the information is considered confidential and submit a separate non-confidential version when they make their views known pursuant to Article 6(1) and 7(1) of Regulation 773/2004, as well as when they subsequently submit further information in the course of the same procedure. Moreover, the Commission may, in all other cases, request complainants which produce documents or statements to identify the documents or parts of the documents or statements which they consider to be confidential. It may in particular set a deadline for the complainant to specify why it considers a piece of information to be confidential and to provide a non-confidential version, including a concise description or non-confidential version of each piece of information deleted.

Notes
[64] Article [339 TFEU], Article 28 of Regulation 1/2003 and Articles 15 and 16 of Regulation 773/2004.

67. The qualification of information as confidential does not prevent the Commission from disclosing and using information where that is necessary to prove an infringement of Articles [101] or [102].[65] Where business secrets and confidential information are necessary to prove an infringement, the Commission must assess for each individual document whether the need to disclose is greater than the harm which might result from disclosure.

Notes
[65] Article 27(2) of Regulation 1/2003.

68. Where the Commission takes the view that a complaint should not be further examined, because there is no sufficient Community interest in pursuing the case further or on other grounds, it will inform the complainant in the form of a letter which indicates its legal basis (Article 7(1) of Regulation 773/2004), sets out the reasons that have led the Commission to provisionally conclude in the sense indicated and provides the complainant with the opportunity to submit supplementary information or observations within a time-limit set by the Commission. The Commission will also indicate the consequences of not replying pursuant to Article 7(3) of Regulation 773/2004, as explained below.

69. Pursuant to Article 8(1) of Regulation 773/2004, the complainant has the right to access the information on which the Commission bases its preliminary view. Such access is normally provided by annexing to the letter a copy of the relevant documents.

Commentary
point 69: B&C: 13.047

70. The time-limit for observations by the complainant on the letter pursuant to Article 7(1) of Regulation 773/2004 will be set in accordance with the circumstances of the case. It will not be shorter than four weeks (Article 17(2) of Regulation 773/2004). If the complainant does not respond within the time-limit set, the complaint is deemed to have been withdrawn pursuant to Article 7(3) of Regulation 773/2004. Complainants are also entitled to withdraw their complaint at any time if they so wish.

Commentary
point 70: B&C: 13.047

71. The complainant may request an extension of the time-limit for the provision of comments. Depending on the circumstances of the case, the Commission may grant such an extension.

Commentary
point 71: B&C: 13.047

72. In that case, where the complainant submits supplementary observations, the Commission takes cognisance of those observations. Where they are of such a nature as to make the Commission change its previous course of action, it may initiate a procedure against the companies complained of. In this procedure, the complainant has the procedural rights explained above.

73. Where the observations of the complainant do not alter the Commission's proposed course of action, it rejects the complaint by decision.[66]

Notes
[66] Article 7(2) of Regulation 773/2004; Case C-282/95 P *Guérin automobiles v Commission of the European Communities* [1997] ECR I-1503, para 36.

(d) The Commission decision rejecting a complaint

74. Where the Commission rejects a complaint by decision pursuant to Article 7(2) of Regulation 773/2004, it must state the reasons in accordance with Article [296 TFEU], i.e. in a way that is appropriate to the act at issue and takes into account the circumstances of each case.

75. The statement of reasons must disclose in a clear and unequivocal fashion the reasoning followed by the Commission in such a way as to enable the complainant to ascertain the reasons for the

decision and to enable the competent Community Court to exercise its power of review. However, the Commission is not obliged to adopt a position on all the arguments relied on by the complainant in support of its complaint. It only needs to set out the facts and legal considerations which are of decisive importance in the context of the decision.[67]

Notes

[67] Settled case law, cf. i.a. Case T-114/92 *Bureau Européen des Médias et de l'Industrie Musicale (BEMIM) v Commission of the European Communities* [1995] ECR II-147, para 41.

76. Where the Commission rejects a complaint in a case that also gives rise to a decision pursuant to Article 10 of Regulation 1/2003 (Finding of inapplicability of Articles [101] or [102]) or Article 9 of Regulation 1/2003 (Commitments), the decision rejecting a complaint may refer to that other decision adopted on the basis of the provisions mentioned.

77. A decision to reject a complaint is subject to appeal before the Community Courts.[68]

Notes

[68] Settled case law since Case 210/81 *Oswald Schmidt, trading as Demo-Studio Schmidt v Commission of the European Communities* [1983] ECR 3045.

78. A decision rejecting a complaint prevents complainants from requiring the reopening of the investigation unless they put forward significant new evidence. Accordingly, further correspondence on the same alleged infringement by former complainants cannot be regarded as a new complaint unless significant new evidence is brought to the attention of the Commission. However, the Commission may re-open a file under appropriate circumstances.

Commentary
point 78: B&C: 13.048

79. A decision to reject a complaint does not definitively rule on the question of whether or not there is an infringement of Articles [101] or [102], even where the Commission has assessed the facts on the basis of Articles [101] and [102]. The assessments made by the Commission in a decision rejecting a complaint therefore do not prevent a Member State court or competition authority from applying Articles [101] and [102] to agreements and practices brought before it. The assessments made by the Commission in a decision rejecting a complaint constitute facts which Member States' courts or competition authorities may take into account in examining whether the agreements or conduct in question are in conformity with Articles [101] and [102].[69]

Notes

[69] Case T-575/93 *Casper Koelman v Commission of the European Communities* [1996] ECR II-1, paras 41–43.

(e) Specific situations

80. According to Article 8 of Regulation 1/2003 the Commission may on its own initiative order interim measures where there is the risk of serious and irreparable damage to competition. Article 8 of Regulation 1/2003 makes it clear that interim measures cannot be applied for by complainants under Article 7(2) of Regulation 1/2003. Requests for interim measures by undertakings can be brought before Member States' courts which are well placed to decide on such measures.[70]

Notes

[70] Depending on the case, Member States' competition authorities may equally be well placed to adopt interim measures.

Commentary
point 80: B&C: 13.104

81. Some persons may wish to inform the Commission about suspected infringements of Articles [101] or [102] without having their identity revealed to the undertakings concerned by the allegations. These persons are welcome to contact the Commission. The Commission is bound to respect an informant's request for anonymity,[71] unless the request to remain anonymous is manifestly unjustified.

Notes
[71] Case 145/83 *Stanley George Adams v Commission of the European Communities* [1985] ECR 3539.

Commentary
point 81: F&N: 8.103

ANNEX
FORM C
COMPLAINT PURSUANT TO ARTICLE 7 OF REGULATION (EC) NO 1/2003

I. INFORMATION REGARDING THE COMPLAINANT AND THE UNDERTAKING(S) OR ASSOCIATION OF UNDERTAKINGS GIVING RISE TO THE COMPLAINT

Commentary
Annex F&N: 8.473

1. Give full details on the identity of the legal or natural person submitting the complaint. Where the complainant is an undertaking, identify the corporate group to which it belongs and provide a concise overview of the nature and scope of its business activities. Provide a contact person (with telephone number, postal and e-mail-address) from which supplementary explanations can be obtained.
2. Identify the undertaking(s) or association of undertakings whose conduct the complaint relates to, including, where applicable, all available information on the corporate group to which the undertaking(s) complained of belong and the nature and scope of the business activities pursued by them. Indicate the position of the complainant vis-à-vis the undertaking(s) or association of undertakings complained of (e.g. customer, competitor).

II. DETAILS OF THE ALLEGED INFRINGEMENT AND EVIDENCE

3. Set out in detail the facts from which, in your opinion, it appears that there exists an infringement of Article [101] or [102] of the Treaty and/or Article 53 or 54 of the EEA agreement. Indicate in particular the nature of the products (goods or services) affected by the alleged infringements and explain, where necessary, the commercial relationships concerning these products. Provide all available details on the agreements or practices of the undertakings or associations of undertakings to which this complaint relates. Indicate, to the extent possible, the relative market positions of the undertakings concerned by the complaint.
4. Submit all documentation in your possession relating to or directly connected with the facts set out in the complaint (for example, texts of agreements, minutes of negotiations or meetings, terms of transactions, business documents, circulars, correspondence, notes of telephone conversations...). State the names and address of the persons able to testify to the facts set out in the complaint, and in particular of persons affected by the alleged infringement. Submit statistics or other data in your possession which relate to the facts set out, in particular where they show developments in the marketplace (for example information relating to prices and price trends, barriers to entry to the market for new suppliers etc.).
5. Set out your view about the geographical scope of the alleged infringement and explain, where that is not obvious, to what extent trade between Member States or between the Community and one or more EFTA States that are contracting parties of the EEA Agreement may be affected by the conduct complained of.

III. FINDING SOUGHT FROM THE COMMISSION AND LEGITIMATE INTEREST

6. Explain what finding or action you are seeking as a result of proceedings brought by the Commission.

Part B Procedural Matters

7. Set out the grounds on which you claim a legitimate interest as complainant pursuant to Article 7 of Regulation (EC) No 1/2003. State in particular how the conduct complained of affects you and explain how, in your view, intervention by the Commission would be liable to remedy the alleged grievance.

IV. Proceedings before National Competition Authorities or National Courts

8. Provide full information about whether you have approached, concerning the same or closely related subject-matters, any other competition authority and/or whether a lawsuit has been brought before a national court. If so, provide full details about the administrative or judicial authority contacted and your submissions to such authority.

Declaration that the information given in this form and in the Annexes thereto is given entirely in good faith.

Date and signature.

B9

COMMISSION NOTICE ON INFORMAL GUIDANCE RELATING TO NOVEL QUESTIONS CONCERNING ARTICLES [101] AND [102] OF THE [TREATY ON THE FUNCTIONING OF THE EUROPEAN UNION]* THAT ARISE IN INDIVIDUAL CASES (GUIDANCE LETTERS)

(2004/C 101/06)

(Text with EEA relevance)

Official Journal C 101, 27.04.2004, p.78

Celex No: 52004XC0427(05)

EUR-Lex permanent link: <http://eur-lex.europa.eu/LexUriServ/LexUriServ.do?uri=CELEX:5200 4XC0427(05):EN:NOT>

Notes

* Ed note: please see the Note on the Lisbon Treaty at p.xvii in regard to article renumbering introduced by the Lisbon Treaty.
EEA application: the EFTA Surveillance Authority has adopted a parallel notice on informal guidance relating to novel questions concerning Articles 53 and 54 of the EEA Agreement that arise in individual cases (guidance letters) under Article 5(2)(b) of the Surveillance and Court Agreement: OJ C 305, 14.12.2006, p.34 and EEA Supplement No 62, 14.12.2006, p.17.

Commentary
Notice: F&N: 2.13, 2.16, 2.17, 2.19

I. Regulation 1/2003

1. Regulation 1/2003[1] sets up a new enforcement system for Articles [101] and [102] of the Treaty. While designed to restore the focus on the primary task of effective enforcement of the competition rules, the Regulation also creates legal certainty inasmuch as it provides that agreements[2] which fall under Article [101](1) but fulfil the conditions in Article [101](3) are valid and fully enforceable *ab initio* without a prior decision by a competition authority (Article 1 of Regulation 1/2003).

Notes

[1] Council Regulation (EC) No 1/2003 of 16 December 2002 on the implementation of the rules on competition laid down in Articles [101] and [102] of the Treaty (OJ L 1, 4.1.2003, p.1–25).

[2] In this notice, the term "agreement" is used for agreements, decisions by associations of undertakings and concerted practices. The term "practices" refers to the conduct of dominant undertakings. The term "undertakings" equally covers "associations of undertakings".

2. The framework of Regulation 1/2003, while introducing parallel competence of the Commission, Member States' competition authorities and Member States' courts to apply Article [101] and [102] in their entirety, limits risks of inconsistent application by a range of measures, thereby ensuring the primary aspect of legal certainty for companies as reflected in the case law of the Court of Justice, i.e. that the competition rules are applied in a consistent way throughout the Community.

3. Undertakings are generally well placed to assess the legality of their actions in such a way as to enable them to take an informed decision on whether to go ahead with an agreement or practice and in what form. They are close to the facts and have at their disposal the framework of block exemption regulations, case law and case practice as well as extensive guidance in Commission guidelines and notices.[3]

Notes

[3] All texts mentioned are available at <http://ec.europa.eu./comm/competition/index_en.html>.

4. Alongside the reform of the rules implementing Articles [101] and [102] brought about by Regulation 1/2003, the Commission has conducted a review of block exemption regulations, Commission notices and guidelines, with a view to further assist self-assessment by economic operators. The Commission has also produced guidelines on the application of Article [101](3).[4] This allows undertakings in the vast majority of cases to reliably assess their agreements with regard to Article [101]. Furthermore, it is the practice of the Commission to impose more than symbolic fines[5] only in cases where it is established, either in horizontal instruments or in the case law and practice that a certain behaviour constitutes an infringement.

Notes

[4] Commission Notice — Guidelines on the application of Article [101](3) of the Treaty [OJ C 101, 27.4.2004, p.97].

[5] Symbolic fines are normally set at 1000 EUR; cf. Commission Guidelines on the method of setting fines imposed pursuant to Article 15(2) of Regulation No 17 and Article 65(5) of the ECSC Treaty (OJ C 9, 14.1.1998).

Commentary
point 4: B&C: 14.067

5. Where cases, despite the above elements, give rise to genuine uncertainty because they present novel or unresolved questions for the application of Articles [101] and [102], individual undertakings may wish to seek informal guidance from the Commission.[6] Where it considers it appropriate and subject to its enforcement priorities, the Commission may provide such guidance on novel questions concerning the interpretation of Articles [101] and/or [102] in a written statement (guidance letter). The present Notice sets out details of this instrument.

Notes

[6] Cf. Recital 38 of Regulation 1/2003.

II. Framework for Assessing Whether to Issue a Guidance Letter

6. Regulation 1/2003 confers powers on the Commission to effectively prosecute infringements of Articles [101] and [102] and to impose sanctions.[7] One major objective of the Regulation is to ensure efficient enforcement of the EC competition rules by removing the former notification system and thus allowing the Commission to focus its enforcement policy on the most serious infringements.[8]

Notes
[7] Cf. in particular Articles 7 to 9, 12, 17–24, 29 of Regulation 1/2003.
[8] Cf. in particular Recital 3 of Regulation 1/2003.

7. While Regulation 1/2003 is without prejudice to the ability of the Commission to issue informal guidance to individual undertakings,[9] as set out in this Notice, this ability should not interfere with the primary objective of the Regulation, which is to ensure effective enforcement. The Commission may therefore only provide informal guidance to individual undertakings in so far as this is compatible with its enforcement priorities.

Notes
[9] Cf. Recital 38 of Regulation 1/2003.

8. Subject to point 7, the Commission, seized of a request for a guidance letter, will consider whether it is appropriate to process it. Issuing a guidance letter may only be considered if the following cumulative conditions are fulfilled:

(a) The substantive assessment of an agreement or practice with regard to Articles [101] and/or [102] of the Treaty, poses a question of application of the law for which there is no clarification in the existing EC legal framework including the case law of the Community Courts, nor publicly available general guidance or precedent in decision-making practice or previous guidance letters.
(b) A prima facie evaluation of the specificities and background of the case suggests that the clarification of the novel question through a guidance letter is useful, taking into account the following elements:
— the economic importance from the point of view of the consumer of the goods or services concerned by the agreement or practice, and/or
— the extent to which the agreement or practice corresponds or is liable to correspond to more widely spread economic usage in the marketplace, and/or
— the extent of the investments linked to the transaction in relation to the size of the companies concerned and the extent to which the transaction relates to a structural operation such as the creation of a non-full function joint venture.
(c) It is possible to issue a guidance letter on the basis of the information provided, i.e. no further fact-finding is required.

Commentary
point 8: B&C: 13.004

9. Furthermore, the Commission will not consider a request for a guidance letter in either of the following circumstances:
— the questions raised in the request are identical or similar to issues raised in a case pending before the European Court of First Instance or the European Court of Justice;
— the agreement or practice to which the request refers is subject to proceedings pending with the Commission, a Member State court or Member State competition authority.

Commentary
point 9: B&C: 13.004

10. The Commission will not consider hypothetical questions and will not issue guidance letters on agreements or practices that are no longer being implemented by the parties. Undertakings may however present a request for a guidance letter to the Commission in relation to questions raised

by an agreement or practice that they envisage, i.e. before the implementation of that agreement or practice. In this case the transaction must have reached a sufficiently advanced stage for a request to be considered.

11. A request for a guidance letter is without prejudice to the power of the Commission to open proceedings in accordance with Regulation 1/2003 with regard to the facts presented in the request.

III. Indications on How to Request Guidance

12. A request can be presented by an undertaking or undertakings which have entered into or intend to enter into an agreement or practice that could fall within the scope of Articles [101] and/or [102] of the Treaty with regard to questions of interpretation raised by such agreement or practice.

13. A request for a guidance letter should be addressed to the following address:

Commission européenne/Europese Commissie
Competition DG
B-1049 Bruxelles/Brussel.

14. There is no form. A memorandum should be presented which clearly states:
   — the identity of all undertakings concerned as well as a single address for contacts with the Commission;
   — the specific questions on which guidance is sought;
   — full and exhaustive information on all points relevant for an informed evaluation of the questions raised, including pertinent documentation;
   — a detailed reasoning, having regard to point 8 a), why the request presents (a) novel question(s);
   — all other information that permits an evaluation of the request in the light of the aspects explained in points 8–10 of this Notice, including in particular a declaration that the agreement or practice to which the request refers is not subject to proceedings pending before a Member State court or competition authority;
   — where the request contains elements that are considered business secrets, a clear identification of these elements;
   — any other information or documentation relevant to the individual case.

IV. Processing of the Request

15. The Commission will in principle evaluate the request on the basis of the information provided. Notwithstanding point 8 c), the Commission may use additional information at its disposal from public sources, former proceedings or any other source and may ask the applicant(s) to provide supplementary information. The normal rules on professional secrecy apply to the information supplied by the applicant(s).

16. The Commission may share the information submitted to it with the Member States' competition authorities and receive input from them. It may discuss the substance of the request with the Member States' competition authorities before issuing a guidance letter.

17. Where no guidance letter is issued, the Commission shall inform the applicant(s) accordingly.

18. An undertaking can withdraw its request at any point in time. In any case, information supplied in the context of a request for guidance remains with the Commission and can be used in subsequent procedures under Regulation 1/2003 (cf. point 11 above).

V. Guidance Letters

19. A guidance letter sets out:
   — a summary description of the facts on which it is based;
   — the principal legal reasoning underlying the understanding of the Commission on novel questions relating to Articles [101] and/or [102] raised by the request.

20. A guidance letter may be limited to part of the questions raised in the request. It may also include additional aspects to those set out in the request.

Part B Procedural Matters

21. Guidance letters will be posted on the Commission's [web-site], having regard to the legitimate interest of undertakings in the protection of their business secrets. Before issuing a guidance letter, the Commission will agree with the applicants on a public version.

VI. The Effects of Guidance Letters

22. Guidance letters are in the first place intended to help undertakings carry out themselves an informed assessment of their agreements and practices.

23. A guidance letter cannot prejudge the assessment of the same question by the Community Courts.

24. Where an agreement or practice has formed the factual basis for a guidance letter, the Commission is not precluded from subsequently examining that same agreement or practice in a procedure under Regulation 1/2003, in particular following a complaint. In that case, the Commission will take the previous guidance letter into account, subject in particular to changes in the underlying facts, to any new aspects raised by a complaint, to developments in the case law of the European Courts or wider changes of the Commission's policy.

25. Guidance letters are not Commission decisions and do not bind Member States' competition authorities or courts that have the power to apply Articles [101] and [102]. However, it is open to Member States' competition authorities and courts to take account of guidance letters issued by the Commission as they see fit in the context of a case.

Commentary
point 25: B&C: 15.072

B10

COMMISSION NOTICE ON THE RULES FOR ACCESS TO THE COMMISSION FILE IN CASES PURSUANT TO ARTICLES [101 AND 102] OF THE [TREATY ON THE FUNCTIONING OF THE EUROPEAN UNION]*, ARTICLES 53, 54 AND 57 OF THE EEA AGREEMENT AND COUNCIL REGULATION (EC) NO 139/2004

(2005/C 325/07)

(Text with EEA relevance)

Official Journal C 325, 22.12.2005, p.7

Celex No: 52005XC1222(03)

EUR-Lex permanent link: <http://eur-lex.europa.eu/LexUriServ/LexUriServ.do?uri=CELEX:52005XC1222(03):EN:NOT>

Notes

* Ed note: please see the Note on the Lisbon Treaty at p.xvii in regard to article renumbering introduced by the Lisbon Treaty.
EEA application: the EFTA Surveillance Authority has adopted a parallel notice on the rules for access to the EFTA Surveillance Authority file in cases pursuant to Articles 53, 54 and 57 of the EEA Agreement under Article 5(2)(b) of the Surveillance and Court Agreement: see OJ C 250, 25.10.2007, p.16.

Commentary

Notice: B&C: 8.008, 13.063, 13.068, 13.072, 16.040 F&N: 5.1161, 8.250, 8.347, 8.348
paras 8–10: F&N: 5.462
paras 29–32: B&C: 13.079
paras 35–38: F&N: 5.470
paras 35–49: F&N: 5.341
paras 40–42: F&N: 5.473
section 3.1.1: F&N: 8.446, 8.473

I. Introduction and Subject-matter of the Notice

1. Access to the Commission file is one of the procedural guarantees intended to apply the principle of equality of arms and to protect the rights of the defence. Access to the file is provided for in Article 27(1) and (2) of Council Regulation (EC) No 1/2003,[1] Article 15(1) of Commission Regulation (EC) No 773/2004 ("the Implementing Regulation"),[2] Article 18(1) and (3) of the Council Regulation (EC) No 139/2004 ("Merger Regulation")[3] and Article 17(1) of Commission Regulation (EC) No 802/2004 ("the Merger Implementing Regulation").[4] In accordance with these provisions, before taking decisions on the basis of Articles 7, 8, 23 and 24(2) of Regulation (EC) No 1/2003 and Articles 6(3), 7(3), 8(2) to (6), 14 and 15 of the Merger Regulation, the Commission shall give the persons, undertakings or associations of undertakings, as the case may be, an opportunity of making known their views on the objections against them and they shall be entitled to have access to the Commission's file in order to fully respect their rights of defence in the proceedings. The present notice provides the framework for the exercise of the right set out in these provisions. It does not cover the possibility of the provision of documents in the context of other proceedings. This notice is without prejudice to the interpretation of such provisions by the Community Courts. The principles set out in this Notice apply also when the Commission enforces Articles 53, 54 and 57 of the EEA Agreement.[5]

Notes

[1] Council Regulation (EC) No 1/2003 of 16 December 2002 on the implementation of the rules on competition laid down in Articles [101] and [102] of the Treaty, OJ L 1, 4.1.2003, p.1–25.
[2] Commission Regulation (EC) No 773/2004 of 7 April 2004 relating to the conduct of proceedings by the Commission pursuant to Articles [101] and [102] of the [Treaty on the Functioning of the European Union], OJ L 123, 27.4.2004, pp.18–24.
[3] Council Regulation (EC) No 139/2004 of 20 January 2004 on the control of concentrations between undertakings, OJ L 24, 29.1.2004, pp.1–22.
[4] Commission Regulation (EC) No 802/2004 of 21 April 2004 implementing Council Regulation (EC) No 139/2004 on the control of concentrations between undertakings, OJ L 133, 30.4.2004, pp.1–39. Corrected in the OJ L 172, 6.5.2004, p.9.
[5] References in this Notice to Articles [101] and [102] therefore apply also to Articles 53 and 54 of the EEA Agreement.

2. This specific right outlined above is distinct from the general right to access to documents under Regulation (EC) No 1049/2001,[1] which is subject to different criteria and exceptions and pursues a different purpose.

Notes

[1] Regulation (EC) No 1049/2001 of the European Parliament and of the Council of 30 May 2001 regarding public access to European Parliament, Council and Commission documents, OJ L 145, 31.5.2001, p.43. See for instance Case T-2/03, *Verein für Konsumenteninformation v Commission*, judgment of 13 April 2005 [[2005] ECR II-1121].

Commentary
para 2: F&N: 5.478

3. The term access to the file is used in this notice exclusively to mean the access granted to the persons, undertakings or association of undertakings to whom the Commission has addressed a statement of objections. This notice clarifies who has access to the file for this purpose.

4. The same term, or the term access to documents, is also used in the above-mentioned regulations in respect of complainants or other involved parties. These situations are, however, distinct from that of the addressees of a statement of objections and therefore do not fall under the definition of access to the file for the purposes of this notice. These related situations are dealt with in a separate section of the notice.

5. This notice also explains to which information access is granted, when access takes place and what are the procedures for implementing access to the file.

6. As from its publication, this notice replaces the 1997 Commission notice on access to the file.[1] The new rules take account of the legislation applicable as of 1 May 2004, namely the above referred Regulation (EC) No 1/2003, Merger Regulation, Implementing Regulation and Merger Implementing Regulation, as well as the Commission Decision of 23 May 2001 on the terms of reference of Hearing Officers in certain competition proceedings.[2] It also takes into account the recent case law of the Court of Justice and the Court of First Instance of the European Communities[3] and the practice developed by the Commission since the adoption of the 1997 notice.

Notes

[1] Commission notice on the internal rules of procedure for processing requests for access to the file in cases under Articles [101] and [102] of the [Treaty on the Functioning of the European Union], Articles 65 and 66 of the ECSC Treaty and Council Regulation (EEC) No 4064/89, OJ C 23, 23.1.1997, p.3.

[2] OJ L 162, 19.6.2001, p.21.

[3] In particular Joint Cases T-25/95 et al., *Cimenteries CBR SA et al. v Commission* [2000] ECR II-0491.

II. Scope of Access to the File

A. Who is entitled to access to the file?

7. Access to the file pursuant to the provisions mentioned in paragraph 1 is intended to enable the effective exercise of the rights of defence against the objections brought forward by the Commission. For this purpose, both in cases under Articles [101] and [102] [TFEU] and in cases under the Merger Regulation, access is granted, upon request, to the persons, undertakings or associations of undertakings,[1] as the case may be, to which the Commission addresses its objections[2] (hereinafter, "the parties").

Notes

[1] In the remainder of this Notice, the term "undertaking" includes both undertakings and associations of undertakings. The term "person" encompasses natural and legal persons. Many entities are legal persons and undertakings at the same time; in this case, they are covered by both terms. The same applies where a natural person is an undertaking within the meaning of Articles [101] and [102]. In Merger proceedings, account must also be taken of persons referred to in Article 3(1)(b) of the Merger Regulation, even when they are natural persons. Where entities without legal personality which are also not undertakings become involved in Commission competition proceedings, the Commission applies, where appropriate, the principles set out in this Notice mutatis mutandis.

[2] Cf. Article 15(1) of the Implementing Regulation, Article 18(3) of the Merger Regulation and Article 17(1) of the Merger Implementing Regulation.

Commentary
para 7: B&C: 13.071 F&N: 2.207

B. To which documents is access granted?

1. The content of the Commission file

8. The "Commission file" in a competition investigation (hereinafter also referred to as "the file") consists of all documents,[1] which have been obtained, produced and/or assembled by the Commission Directorate General for Competition, during the investigation.

Notes

[1] In this notice the term "document" is used for all forms of information support, irrespective of the storage medium. This covers also any electronic data storage device as may be or become available.

Commentary
para 8: **B&C:** 8.149, 13.072 **F&N:** 8.708

---

9. In the course of investigation under Articles 20, 21 and 22(2) of Regulation (EC) No 1/2003 and Articles 12 and 13 of the Merger Regulation, the Commission may collect a number of documents, some of which may, following a more detailed examination, prove to be unrelated to the subject matter of the case in question. Such documents may be returned to the undertaking from which those have been obtained. Upon return, these documents will no longer constitute part of the file.

Commentary
para 9: **B&C:** 13.030, 13.072 **F&N:** 8.347, 8.708

---

2. Accessible documents

10. The parties must be able to acquaint themselves with the information in the Commission's file, so that, on the basis of this information, they can effectively express their views on the preliminary conclusions reached by the Commission in its objections. For this purpose they will be granted access to all documents making up the Commission file, as defined in paragraph 8, with the exception of internal documents, business secrets of other undertakings, or other confidential information.[1]

Notes

[1] Cf. Article 27(2) of Regulation (EC) No 1/2003, Articles 15(2) and 16(1) of the Implementing Regulation, and Article 17(3) of the Merger Implementing Regulation. Those exceptions are also mentioned in Case T-7/89, *Hercules Chemicals v Commission* [1991] ECR II-1711, para 54. The Court has ruled that it does not belong to the Commission alone to decide which documents in the file may be useful for the purposes of the defence. (Cf. Case T-30/91 *Solvay v Commission* [1995] ECR II-1775, paragraphs 81–86, and Case T-36/91 *ICI v Commission* [1995] ECR II-1847, paragraphs 91–96.)

Commentary
para 10: **B&C:** 8.149, 13.072 **F&N:** 8.708

---

11. Results of a study commissioned in connection with proceedings are accessible together with the terms of reference and the methodology of the study. Precautions may however be necessary in order to protect intellectual property rights.

Commentary
para 11: **B&C:** 13.073

---

3. Non-accessible documents

3.1. Internal documents

3.1.1. General principles

12. Internal documents can be neither incriminating nor exculpatory.[1] They do not constitute part of the evidence on which the Commission can rely in its assessment of a case. Thus, the parties will not be granted access to internal documents in the Commission file.[2] Given their lack of evidential value, this restriction on access to internal documents does not prejudice the proper exercise of the parties" right of defence.[3]

Notes

1 Examples of internal documents are drafts, opinions, memos or notes from the Commission departments or other public authorities concerned.
2 Cf. Article 27(2) of Regulation (EC) No 1/2003, Article 15(2) of the Implementing Regulation, and Article 17(3) of the Merger Implementing Regulation.
3 Cf. paragraph 1 above.

Commentary
para 12: B&C: 13.073 F&N: 5.463, 8.708

13. There is no obligation on the Commission departments to draft any minutes of meetings[1] with any person or undertaking. If the Commission chooses to make notes of such meetings, such documents constitute the Commission's own interpretation of what was said at the meetings, for which reason they are classified as internal documents. Where, however, the person or undertaking in question has agreed the minutes, such minutes will be made accessible after deletion of any business secrets or other confidential information. Such agreed minutes constitute part of the evidence on which the Commission can rely in its assessment of a case.[2]

Notes

1 Cf. judgment of 30.9.2003 in Joined Cases T-191/98 and T-212/98 to T-214/98 *Atlantic Container Line and others v Commission (TACA)* [2003] ECR II-3275, paragraphs 349–359.
2 Statements recorded pursuant to Article 19 or Article 20(2)(e) of Regulation 1/2003 or Article 13(2)(e) of the Merger Regulation will also normally belong to the accessible documents (see paragraph 10 above).

Commentary
para 13: B&C: 13.073 F&N: 5.465, 8.708

14. In the case of a study commissioned in connection with proceedings, correspondence between the Commission and its contractor containing evaluation of the contractor's work or relating to financial aspects of the study, are considered internal documents and will thus not be accessible.

Commentary
para 14: B&C: 13.073

3.1.2. Correspondence with other public authorities

15. A particular case of internal documents is the Commission's correspondence with other public authorities and the internal documents received from such authorities (whether from EC Member States ("the Member States') or non-member countries). Examples of such non-accessible documents include:

— correspondence between the Commission and the competition authorities of the Member States, or between the latter;[1]
— correspondence between the Commission and other public authorities of the Member States;[2]
— correspondence between the Commission, the EFTA Surveillance Authority and public authorities of EFTA States;[3]
— correspondence between the Commission and public authorities of non-member countries, including their competition authorities, in particular where the Community and a third country have concluded an agreement governing the confidentiality of the information exchanged.[4]

Notes

1 Cf. Article 27(2) of Regulation (EC) No 1/2003, Article 15(2) of the Implementing Regulation, Article 17(3) of the Merger Implementing Regulation.
2 Cf. Order of the Court of First Instance in Cases T-134/94 et al. *NMH Stahlwerke and Others v Commission* [1997] ECR II-2293, paragraph 36, and Case T-65/89 *BPB Industries and British Gypsum* [1993] ECR II-389, paragraph 33.
3 In this notice the term "EFTA States" includes the EFTA States that are parties to the EEA Agreement.

[4] For example, Article VIII.2 of the Agreement between the European Communities and the Government of the United States of America regarding the application of their competition laws (OJ No L 95, 27.4.1995, p.47) stipulates that information provided to it in confidence under the Agreement must be protected "to the fullest extent possible". That Article creates an international-law obligation binding the Commission.

Commentary
para 15: **B&C:** 13.074

16. In certain exceptional circumstances, access is granted to documents originating from Member States, the EFTA Surveillance Authority or EFTA States, after deletion of any business secrets or other confidential information. The Commission will consult the entity submitting the document prior to granting access to identify business secrets or other confidential information.

This is the case where the documents originating from Member States contain allegations brought against the parties, which the Commission must examine, or form part of the evidence in the investigative process, in a way similar to documents obtained from private parties. These considerations apply, in particular, as regards:

— documents and information exchanged pursuant to Article 12 of Regulation (EC) No 1/2003, and information provided to the Commission pursuant to Article 18(6) of Regulation (EC) No 1/2003;
— complaints lodged by a Member State under Article 7(2) of Regulation (EC) No 1/2003.

Access will also be granted to documents originating from Member States or the EFTA Surveillance Authority in so far as they are relevant to the parties' defence with regard to the exercise of competence by the Commission.[1]

Notes
[1] In the merger control area, this may apply in particular to submissions by a Member State under Article 9(2) of the Merger Regulation with regard to a case referral.

Commentary
para 16: **B&C:** 13.074 **F&N:** 5.464

3.2. Confidential information

17. The Commission file may also include documents containing two categories of information, namely business secrets and other confidential information, to which access may be partially or totally restricted.[1] Access will be granted, where possible, to non-confidential versions of the original information. Where confidentiality can only be assured by summarising the relevant information, access will be granted to a summary. All other documents are accessible in their original form.

Notes
[1] Cf. Article 16(1) of the Implementing Regulation and Article 17(3) of the Merger Implementing Regulation; Case T-7/89, *Hercules Chemicals NV v Commission* [1991] ECR II-1711, paragraph 54; Case T-23/99, *LR AF 1998 A/S v Commission* [2002] ECR II-1705, paragraph 170.

Commentary
para 17: **B&C:** 8.183, 13.075

3.2.1. Business secrets

18. In so far as disclosure of information about an undertaking's business activity could result in a serious harm to the same undertaking, such information constitutes business secrets.[1] Examples of information that may qualify as business secrets include: technical and/or financial information relating to an undertaking's know-how, methods of assessing costs, production secrets and processes, supply sources, quantities produced and sold, market shares, customer and distributor lists, marketing plans, cost and price structure and sales strategy.

Notes
[1] Judgement of 18.9.1996 in Case T-353/94 *Postbank NV v Commission* [1996] ECR II-921, paragraph 87.

Commentary
para 18: B&C: 8.183, 13.033, 13.075 **F&N:** 2.198, 5.467

3.2.2. Other confidential information

19. The category "other confidential information" includes information other than business secrets, which may be considered as confidential, insofar as its disclosure would significantly harm a person or undertaking. Depending on the specific circumstances of each case, this may apply to information provided by third parties about undertakings which are able to place very considerable economic or commercial pressure on their competitors or on their trading partners, customers or suppliers. The Court of First Instance and the Court of Justice have acknowledged that it is legitimate to refuse to reveal to such undertakings certain letters received from their customers, since their disclosure might easily expose the authors to the risk of retaliatory measures.[1] Therefore the notion of other confidential information may include information that would enable the parties to identify complainants or other third parties where those have a justified wish to remain anonymous.

Notes
[1] The Community Courts have pronounced upon this question both in cases of alleged abuse of a dominant position (Article [102] of the [Treaty on the Functioning of the European Union]) (Case T-65/89, *BPB Industries and British Gypsum* [1993] ECR II-389; and Case C-310/93P, *BPB Industries and British Gypsum* [1995] ECR I-865), and in merger cases (Case T-221/95 *Endemol v Commission* [1999] ECR II-1299, paragraph 69; and Case T-5/02 *Laval v Commission* [2002] ECR II-4381, paragraph 98 et seq.).

Commentary
para 19: B&C: 8.183, 13.076 **F&N:** 2.201, 5.468

20. The category of other confidential information also includes military secrets.

Commentary
para 20: B&C: 8.183 **F&N:** 5.473

3.2.3. Criteria for the acceptance of requests for confidential treatment

21. Information will be classified as confidential where the person or undertaking in question has made a claim to this effect and such claim has been accepted by the Commission.[1]

Notes
[1] See paragraph 40 below.

Commentary
para 21: B&C: 13.078

22. Claims for confidentiality must relate to information which is within the scope of the above descriptions of business secrets or other confidential information. The reasons for which information is claimed to be a business secret or other confidential information must be substantiated.[1] Confidentiality claims can normally only pertain to information obtained by the Commission from the same person or undertaking and not to information from any other source.

Notes
[1] See paragraph 35 below.

Commentary
para 22: B&C: 13.078

23. Information relating to an undertaking but which is already known outside the undertaking (in case of a group, outside the group), or outside the association to which it has been communicated by that undertaking, will not normally be considered confidential.[1] Information that has lost its commercial importance, for instance due to the passage of time, can no longer be regarded as confidential. As a general rule, the Commission presumes that information pertaining to the

parties' turnover, sales, market-share data and similar information which is more than 5 years old is no longer confidential.[2]

24. In proceedings under Articles [101] and [102] of the Treaty, the qualification of a piece of information as confidential is not a bar to its disclosure if such information is necessary to prove an alleged infringement ("inculpatory document") or could be necessary to exonerate a party ("exculpatory document"). In this case, the need to safeguard the rights of the defence of the parties through the provision of the widest possible access to the Commission file may outweigh the concern to protect confidential information of other parties.[1] It is for the Commission to assess whether those circumstances apply to any specific situation. This calls for an assessment of all relevant elements, including:

— the relevance of the information in determining whether or not an infringement has been committed, and its probative value;
— whether the information is indispensable;
— the degree of sensitivity involved (to what extent would disclosure of the information harm the interests of the person or undertaking in question);
— the preliminary view of the seriousness of the alleged infringement.

Similar considerations apply to proceedings under the Merger Regulation when the disclosure of information is considered necessary by the Commission for the purpose of the procedure.[2]

25. Where the Commission intends to disclose information, the person or undertaking in question shall be granted the possibility to provide a non-confidential version of the documents where that information is contained, with the same evidential value as the original documents.[1]

C. When is access to the file granted?

26. Prior to the notification of the Commission's statement of objections pursuant to the provisions mentioned in paragraph 1, the parties have no right of access to the file.

1. In antitrust proceedings under Articles [101] and [102] of the Treaty

27. Access to the file will be granted upon request and, normally, on a single occasion, following the notification of the Commission's objections to the parties, in order to ensure the principle of equality of arms and to protect their rights of defence. As a general rule, therefore, no access will be granted to other parties' replies to the Commission's objections.

Part B Procedural Matters

A party will, however, be granted access to documents received after notification of the objections at later stages of the administrative procedure, where such documents may constitute new evidence — whether of an incriminating or of an exculpatory nature —, pertaining to the allegations concerning that party in the Commission's statement of objections. This is particularly the case where the Commission intends to rely on new evidence.

Commentary
para 27: **B&C:** 8.149, 13.071, 13.078 **F&N:** 8.708

2. In proceedings under the Merger Regulation

28. In accordance with Article 18(1) and (3) of the Merger Regulation and Article 17(1) of the Merger Implementing Regulation, the notifying parties will be given access to the Commission's file upon request at every stage of the procedure following the notification of the Commission's objections up to the consultation of the Advisory Committee. In contrast, this notice does not address the possibility of the provision of documents before the Commission states its objections to undertakings under the Merger Regulation.[1]

Notes

[1] This question is dealt with in the Directorate General Competition document "DG COMP Best Practices on the conduct of EC merger control proceedings" available on the web-site of the Directorate General for Competition:<http://europa.eu.int/comm/competition/index_en.html>.

Commentary
para 28: **B&C:** 8.149

III. Particular Questions Regarding Complainants and Other Involved Parties

29. The present section relates to situations where the Commission may or has to provide access to certain documents contained in its file to the complainants in antitrust proceedings and other involved parties in merger proceedings. Irrespective of the wording used in the antitrust and merger implementing regulations,[1] these two situations are distinct — in terms of scope, timing, and rights — from access to the file, as defined in the preceding section of this notice.

Notes

[1] Cf. Article 8(1) of the Implementing Regulation, which speaks about "access to documents" to complainants and Article 17(2) of the Merger Implementing Regulation, which speaks about "access to file" to other involved parties "in so far as this is necessary for the purposes of preparing their comments".

A. Provision of documents to complainants in antitrust proceedings

30. The Court of First Instance has ruled[1] that complainants do not have the same rights and guarantees as the parties under investigation. Therefore complainants cannot claim a right of access to the file as established for parties.

Notes

[1] See Case T-17/93 *Matra-Hachette SA v Commission* [1994] ECR II-595, paragraph 34. The Court ruled that the rights of third parties, as laid down by Article 19 of the Council Regulation No 17 of 6.2.1962 (now replaced by Article 27 of Regulation (EC) No 1/2003), were limited to the right to participate in the administrative procedure.

31. However, a complainant who, pursuant to Article 7(1) of the Implementing Regulation, has been informed of the Commission's intention to reject its complaint,[1] may request access to the documents on which the Commission has based its provisional assessment.[2] The complainant will be provided access to such documents on a single occasion, following the issuance of the letter informing the complainant of the Commission's intention to reject its complaint.

Notes

[1] By means of a letter issued in accordance with Article 7(1) of the Implementing Regulation.
[2] Cf. Article 8(1) of the Implementing Regulation.

32. Complainants do not have a right of access to business secrets or other confidential information which the Commission has obtained in the course of its investigation.[1]

Notes

[1] Cf. Article 8(1) of the Implementing Regulation.

B. Provision of documents to other involved parties in merger proceedings

33. In accordance with Article 17(2) of the Merger Implementing Regulation, access to the file in merger proceedings shall also be given, upon request, to other involved parties who have been informed of the objections in so far as this is necessary for the purposes of preparing their comments.

Commentary
para 33: **B&C:** 8.150 **F&N:** 5.462

34. Such other involved parties are parties to the proposed concentration other than the notifying parties, such as the seller and the undertaking which is the target of the concentration.[1]

Notes

[1] Cf. Article 11(b) of the Merger Implementing Regulation.

Commentary
para 34: **B&C:** 15.039

IV. Procedure for Implementing Access to the File

A. Preparatory procedure

35. Any person which submits information or comments in one of the situations listed hereunder, or subsequently submits further information to the Commission in the course of the same procedures, has an obligation to clearly identify any material which it considers to be confidential, giving reasons, and provide a separate non-confidential version by the date set by the Commission for making its views known:[1]

(a) In antitrust proceedings
   — an addressee of a Commission's statement of objections making known its views on the objections;[2]
   — a complainant making known its views on a Commission statement of objections;[3]
   — any other natural or legal person, which applies to be heard and shows a sufficient interest, or which is invited by the Commission to express its views, making known its views in writing or at an oral hearing;[4]
   — a complainant making known his views on a Commission letter informing him on the Commission's intention to reject the complaint.[5]

(b) In merger proceedings
   — notifying parties or other involved parties making known their views on Commission objections adopted with a view to take a decision with regard to a request for a derogation from suspension of a concentration and which adversely affects one or more of those parties, or on a provisional decision adopted in the matter;[6]
   — notifying parties to whom the Commission has addressed a statement of objections, other involved parties who have been informed of those objections or parties to whom the Commission has addressed objections with a view to inflict a fine or a periodic penalty payment, submitting their comments on the objections;[7]

— third persons who apply to be heard, or any other natural or legal person invited by the Commission to express their views, making known their views in writing or at an oral hearing;[8]

— any person which supplies information pursuant to Article 11 of the Merger Regulation.

Notes

[1] Cf. Article 16(2) of the Implementing Regulation and Article 18(2) of the Merger Implementing Regulation.
[2] pursuant to Article 10(2) of the Implementing Regulation.
[3] pursuant to Article 6(1) of the Implementing Regulation.
[4] pursuant to Article 13(1) and (3) of the Implementing Regulation.
[5] pursuant to Article 7(1) of the Implementing Regulation.
[6] Article 12 of the Merger Implementing Regulation.
[7] Article 13 of the Merger Implementing Regulation.
[8] pursuant to Article 16 of the Merger Implementing Regulation.

Commentary
para 35 B&C: 13.078

36. Moreover, the Commission may require undertakings,[1] in all cases where they produce or have produced documents, to identify the documents or parts of documents, which they consider to contain business secrets or other confidential information belonging to them, and to identify the undertakings with regard to which such documents are to be considered confidential.[2]

Notes

[1] In merger proceedings the principles set out in the present and subsequent paragraphs also apply to the persons referred to in Article 3(1)(b) of Merger Regulation.
[2] Cf. Article 16(3) of the Implementing Regulation and Article 18(3) of the Merger Implementing Regulation. This also applies to documents gathered by the Commission in an inspection pursuant to Article 13 of the Merger Regulation and Articles 20 and 21 of Regulation (EC) No 1/2003.

37. For the purposes of quickly dealing with confidentiality claims referred to in paragraph 36 above, the Commission may set a time-limit within which the undertakings shall: (i) substantiate their claim for confidentiality with regard to each individual document or part of document; (ii) provide the Commission with a non-confidential version of the documents, in which the confidential passages are deleted.[1] In antitrust proceedings the undertakings in question shall also provide within the said time-limit a concise description of each piece of deleted information.[2]

Notes

[1] Cf. Article 16(3) of the Implementing Regulation and Article 18(3) of the Merger Implementing Regulation.
[2] Cf. Article 16(3) of the Implementing Regulation.

38. The non-confidential versions and the descriptions of the deleted information must be established in a manner that enables any party with access to the file to determine whether the information deleted is likely to be relevant for its defence and therefore whether there are sufficient grounds to request the Commission to grant access to the information claimed to be confidential.

Commentary
para 38: B&C: 13.079

B. Treatment of confidential information

39. In antitrust proceedings, if undertakings fail to comply with the provisions set out in paragraphs 35 to 37 above, the Commission may assume that the documents or statements concerned do not contain confidential information.[1] The Commission may consequently assume that the undertaking has no objections to the disclosure of the documents or statements concerned in their entirety.

Notes

[1] Cf. Article 16 of the Implementing Regulation.

Commentary
para 39: B&C: 13.078

40. In both antitrust proceedings and in proceedings under the Merger Regulation, should the person or undertaking in question meet the conditions set out in paragraphs 35 to 37 above, to the extent they are applicable, the Commission will either:

   — provisionally accept the claims which seem justified; or
   — inform the person or undertaking in question that it does not agree with the confidentiality claim in whole or in part, where it is apparent that the claim is unjustified.

Commentary
para 40: B&C: 13.078

41. The Commission may reverse its provisional acceptance of the confidentiality claim in whole or in part at a later stage.
42. Where the Directorate General for Competition does not agree with the confidentiality claim from the outset or where it takes the view that the provisional acceptance of the confidentiality claim should be reversed, and thus intends to disclose information, it will grant the person or undertaking in question an opportunity to express its views. In such cases, the Directorate General for Competition will inform the person or undertaking in writing of its intention to disclose information, give its reasons and set a time-limit within which such person or undertaking may inform it in writing of its views. If, following submission of those views, a disagreement on the confidentiality claim persists, the matter will be dealt with by the Hearing Officer according to the applicable Commission terms of reference of Hearing Officers.[1]

Notes
[1] Cf. Article 9 of the Commission Decision of 23.5.2001 on the terms of reference of hearing officers in certain competition proceedings, OJ L 162, 19.6.2001, p.21.

Commentary
para 42: B&C: 8.183

43. Where there is a risk that an undertaking which is able to place very considerable economic or commercial pressure on its competitors or on its trading partners, customers or suppliers will adopt retaliatory measures against those, as a consequence of their collaboration in the investigation carried out by the Commission,[1] the Commission will protect the anonymity of the authors by providing access to a non-confidential version or summary of the responses in question.[2] Requests for anonymity in such circumstances, as well as requests for anonymity according to point 81 of the Commission Notice on the handling of complaints[3] will be dealt with according to paragraphs 40 to 42 above.

Notes
[1] Cf. paragraph 19 above.
[2] Cf. Case T-5/02, *Tetra Laval vs Commission* [2002] ECR II-4381, paragraph 98, 104 and 105.
[3] Commission Notice on the handling of complaints by the Commission under Articles [101] and [102] of the [Treaty on the Functioning of the European Union], OJ C 101, 27.4.2004, p.65.

Commentary
para 43: B&C: 8.183, 13.078

C. Provision of access to file

44. The Commission may determine that access to the file shall be granted in one of the following ways, taking due account of the technical capabilities of the parties:

   — by means of a CD-ROM(s) or any other electronic data storage device as may become available in future;
   — through copies of the accessible file in paper form sent to them by mail;
   — by inviting them to examine the accessible file on the Commission's premises.

The Commission may choose any combination of these methods.

Commentary
para 44: **B&C:** 8.149, 13.079 **F&N:** 5.461, 8.708

45. In order to facilitate access to the file, the parties will receive an enumerative list of documents setting out the content of the Commission file, as defined in paragraph 8 above.

Commentary
para 45: **B&C:** 13.079

46. Access is granted to evidence as contained in the Commission file, in its original form: the Commission is under no obligation to provide a translation of documents in the file.[1]

Notes
[1] Cf Case T-25/95 et al. *Cimenteries*, paragraph 635.

Commentary
para 46: **B&C:** 13.079

47. If a party considers that, after having obtained access to the file, it requires knowledge of specific non-accessible information for its defence, it may submit a reasoned request to that end to the Commission. If the services of the Directorate General for Competition are not in a position to accept the request and if the party disagrees with that view, the matter will be resolved by the Hearing Officer, in accordance with the applicable terms of reference of Hearing Officers.[1]

Notes
[1] Cf. Article 8 of the Commission Decision of 23.5.2001 on the terms of reference of hearing officers in certain competition proceedings, OJ L 162, 19.6.2001, p.21.

Commentary
para 47: **F&N:** 8.475, 8.708

48. Access to the file in accordance with this notice is granted on the condition that the information thereby obtained may only be used for the purposes of judicial or administrative proceedings for the application of the Community competition rules at issue in the related administrative proceedings.[1] Should the information be used for a different purpose, at any point in time, with the involvement of an outside counsel, the Commission may report the incident to the bar of that counsel, with a view to disciplinary action.

Notes
[1] Cf. Articles 15(4) and 8(2) of the Implementing Regulation, respectively, and Article 17(4) of the Merger Implementing Regulation.

Commentary
para 48: **B&C:** 15.049, 16.040 **F&N:** 5.476, 8.218, 8.708

49. With the exception of paragraphs 45 and 47, this section C applies equally to the grant of access to documents to complainants (in antitrust proceedings) and to other involved parties (in merger proceedings).

B11

GUIDELINES ON THE METHOD OF SETTING FINES IMPOSED PURSUANT TO ARTICLE 23(2)(A) OF REGULATION NO 1/2003

(2006/C 210/02)

(Text with EEA relevance)

Official Journal C 210, 1.9.2006, p.2

Celex No: 52006XC0901(01)

EUR-Lex permanent link: <http://eur-lex.europa.eu/LexUriServ/LexUriServ.do?uri=CELEX:5200 6XC0901(01):EN:NOT>

Notes

EEA application: the EFTA Surveillance Authority has adopted a parallel notice on the method of setting fines imposed pursuant to Article 23(2)(a) of Chapter II of Protocol 4 to the Surveillance and Court Agreement under Article 5(2)(b) of the Surveillance and Court Agreement: see College Decision 343/06/COL of 15 November 2006 OJ C 314, 21.12.2006, p.84 and EEA Supplement No 63, 14.12.2006, p.44.

Commentary

Guidelines: B&C: 5.034, 13.124, 14.003, 14.005, 14.027, 14.030, 14.031, 14.040, 14.063 **F&N:** 8.44, 8.86, 8.549, 8.561, 8.562, 8.567, 8.579, 8.580, 8.585, 8.589, 8.590, 8.595, 8.596, 8.598, 8.599, 8.618, 8.622, 8.624, 8.627, 8.631, 8.632, 8.643, 8.650, 8.661, 8.662, 8.663, 8.667, 8.673, 8.683, 8.697, 8.698
points 15–17: F&N: 8.553
section C: F&N: 8.350, 8.589, 8.684

INTRODUCTION

1. Pursuant to Article 23(2)(a) of Regulation No 1/2003,[1] the Commission may, by decision, impose fines on undertakings or associations of undertakings where, either intentionally or negligently, they infringe Article [101] or [102] of the Treaty.*

Notes

[1] Council Regulation (EC) No 1 of 16 December 2002 on the implementation of the rules on competition laid down in Articles [101] and [102] of the Treaty (OJ L 1, 4.1.2003, p.1).

* Ed note: please see the Note on the Lisbon Treaty at p.xvii in regard to article renumbering introduced by the Lisbon Treaty.

Commentary
point 1: F&N: 4.37

---

2. In exercising its power to impose such fines, the Commission enjoys a wide margin of discretion[1] within the limits set by Regulation No 1/2003. First, the Commission must have regard both to the gravity and to the duration of the infringement. Second, the fine imposed may not exceed the limits specified in Article 23(2), second and third subparagraphs, of Regulation No 1/2003.

Notes

[1] See, for example, Case C-189/02 P, C-202/02 P, C-205/02 P to C-208/02 P and C-213/02 P, *Dansk Rørindustri A/S and others v Commission* [2005] ECR I-5425, paragraph 172.

---

3. In order to ensure the transparency and impartiality of its decisions, the Commission published on 14 January 1998 guidelines on the method of setting fines.[1] After more than eight years of implementation, the Commission has acquired sufficient experience to develop further and refine its policy on fines.

Notes
[1] Guidelines on the method of setting fines imposed pursuant to Article 15(2) of Regulation No 17 and Article 65(5) of the ECSC Treaty (OJ C 9, 14.1.1998, p.3).

4. The Commission's power to impose fines on undertakings or associations of undertakings which, intentionally or negligently, infringe Article [101] or [102] of the Treaty is one of the means conferred on it in order for it to carry out the task of supervision entrusted to it by the Treaty. That task not only includes the duty to investigate and sanction individual infringements, but it also encompasses the duty to pursue a general policy designed to apply, in competition matters, the principles laid down by the Treaty and to steer the conduct of undertakings in the light of those principles.[1] For this purpose, the Commission must ensure that its action has the necessary deterrent effect.[2] Accordingly, when the Commission discovers that Article [101] or [102] of the Treaty has been infringed, it may be necessary to impose a fine on those who have acted in breach of the law. Fines should have a sufficiently deterrent effect, not only in order to sanction the undertakings concerned (specific deterrence) but also in order to deter other undertakings from engaging in, or continuing, behaviour that is contrary to Articles [101] and [102] of the [Treaty on the Functioning of the European Union] (general deterrence).

Notes
[1] See, for example, *Dansk Rørindustri A/S and others v Commission*, cited above, paragraph 170.
[2] See Joined Cases 100/80 to 103/80 *Musique Diffusion française and others v Commission* [1983] ECR 1825, paragraph 106.

5. In order to achieve these objectives, it is appropriate for the Commission to refer to the value of the sales of goods or services to which the infringement relates as a basis for setting the fine. The duration of the infringement should also play a significant role in the setting of the appropriate amount of the fine. It necessarily has an impact on the potential consequences of the infringement on the market. It is therefore considered important that the fine should also reflect the number of years during which an undertaking participated in the infringement.
6. The combination of the value of sales to which the infringement relates and of the duration of the infringement is regarded as providing an appropriate proxy to reflect the economic importance of the infringement as well as the relative weight of each undertaking in the infringement. Reference to these factors provides a good indication of the order of magnitude of the fine and should not be regarded as the basis for an automatic and arithmetical calculation method.

Commentary
point 6: F&N: 8.551

7. It is also considered appropriate to include in the fine a specific amount irrespective of the duration of the infringement, in order to deter companies from even entering into illegal practices.
8. The sections below set out the principles which will guide the Commission when it sets fines imposed pursuant to Article 23(2)(a) of Regulation No 1/2003.

METHOD FOR THE SETTING OF FINES

9. Without prejudice to point 37 below, the Commission will use the following two-step methodology when setting the fine to be imposed on undertakings or associations of undertakings.
10. First, the Commission will determine a basic amount for each undertaking or association of undertakingts (see Section 1 below).

Commentary
point 10: B&C: 14.016

11. Second, it may adjust that basic amount upwards or downwards (see Section 2 below).

1. Basic amount of the fine

12. The basic amount will be set by reference to the value of sales and applying the following methodology.

A. Calculation of the value of sales

13. In determining the basic amount of the fine to be imposed, the Commission will take the value of the undertaking's sales of goods or services to which the infringement directly or indirectly[1] relates in the relevant geographic area within the EEA. It will normally take the sales made by the undertaking during the last full business year of its participation in the infringement (hereafter "value of sales").

Notes

[1] Such will be the case for instance for horizontal price fixing arrangements on a given product, where the price of that product then serves as a basis for the price of lower or higher quality products.

Commentary
point 13: **B&C:** 14.019, 14.025 **F&N:** 8.552, 8.554, 8.560

14. Where the infringement by an association of undertakings relates to the activities of its members, the value of sales will generally correspond to the sum of the value of sales by its members.

Commentary
point 14: **F&N:** 8.552

15. In determining the value of sales by an undertaking, the Commission will take that undertaking's best available figures.
16. Where the figures made available by an undertaking are incomplete or not reliable, the Commission may determine the value of its sales on the basis of the partial figures it has obtained and/or any other information which it regards as relevant and appropriate.
17. The value of sales will be determined before VAT and other taxes directly related to the sales.
18. Where the geographic scope of an infringement extends beyond the EEA (e.g. worldwide cartels), the relevant sales of the undertakings within the EEA may not properly reflect the weight of each undertaking in the infringement. This may be the case in particular with worldwide market-sharing arrangements. In such circumstances, in order to reflect both the aggregate size of the relevant sales within the EEA and the relative weight of each undertaking in the infringement, the Commission may assess the total value of the sales of goods or services to which the infringement relates in the relevant geographic area (wider than the EEA), may determine the share of the sales of each undertaking party to the infringement on that market and may apply this share to the aggregate sales within the EEA of the undertakings concerned. The result will be taken as the value of sales for the purpose of setting the basic amount of the fine.

Commentary
point 18: **F&N:** 8.559

B. Determination of the basic amount of the fine

19. The basic amount of the fine will be related to a proportion of the value of sales, depending on the degree of gravity of the infringement, multiplied by the number of years of infringement.

Commentary
point 19: **F&N:** 8.551

20. The assessment of gravity will be made on a case-by-case basis for all types of infringement, taking account of all the relevant circumstances of the case.

Commentary
point 20: **F&N:** 8.551

21. As a general rule, the proportion of the value of sales taken into account will be set at a level of up to 30% of the value of sales.

Commentary
point 21: **B&C:** 14.027 **F&N:** 8.561, 8.699

22. In order to decide whether the proportion of the value of sales to be considered in a given case should be at the lower end or at the higher end of that scale, the Commission will have regard to a number of factors, such as the nature of the infringement, the combined market share of all the undertakings concerned, the geographic scope of the infringement and whether or not the infringement has been implemented.

Commentary
point 22: B&C: 4.008, 5.032, 14.031, 14.054, 14.064 **F&N:** 8.561

23. Horizontal price-fixing, market-sharing and output-limitation agreements,[1] which are usually secret, are, by their very nature, among the most harmful restrictions of competition. As a matter of policy, they will be heavily fined. Therefore, the proportion of the value of sales taken into account for such infringements will generally be set at the higher end of the scale.

Notes
[1] This includes agreements, concerted practices and decisions by associations of undertakings within the meaning of Article [101] of the Treaty.

Commentary
point 23: B&C: 14.036 **F&N:** 8.319, 8.416, 8.563, 8.564

24. In order to take fully into account the duration of the participation of each undertaking in the infringement, the amount determined on the basis of the value of sales (see points 20 to 23 above) will be multiplied by the number of years of participation in the infringement. Periods of less than six months will be counted as half a year; periods longer than six months but shorter than one year will be counted as a full year.

Commentary
point 24: B&C: 14.032 **F&N:** 8.574

25. In addition, irrespective of the duration of the undertaking's participation in the infringement, the Commission will include in the basic amount a sum of between 15% and 25% of the value of sales as defined in Section A above in order to deter undertakings from even entering into horizontal price-fixing, market-sharing and output-limitation agreements. The Commission may also apply such an additional amount in the case of other infringements. For the purpose of deciding the proportion of the value of sales to be considered in a given case, the Commission will have regard to a number of factors, in particular those referred in point 22.

Commentary
point 25: B&C: 14.008, 14.037 **F&N:** 8.578

26. Where the value of sales by undertakings participating in the infringement is similar but not identical, the Commission may set for each of them an identical basic amount. Moreover, in determining the basic amount of the fine, the Commission will use rounded figures.

Commentary
point 26: F&N: 8.581

2. Adjustments to the basic amount

27. In setting the fine, the Commission may take into account circumstances that result in an increase or decrease in the basic amount as determined in Section 1 above. It will do so on the basis of an overall assessment which takes account of all the relevant circumstances.

Commentary
point 27: B&C: 14.038 **F&N:** 8.550, 8.582

A. Aggravating circumstances

28. The basic amount may be increased where the Commission finds that there are aggravating circumstances, such as:

— where an undertaking continues or repeats the same or a similar infringement after the Commission or a national competition authority has made a finding that the undertaking infringed Article [101] or [102]: the basic amount will be increased by up to 100% for each such infringement established;

— refusal to cooperate with or obstruction of the Commission in carrying out its investigations;

— role of leader in, or instigator of, the infringement; the Commission will also pay particular attention to any steps taken to coerce other undertakings to participate in the infringement and/or any retaliatory measures taken against other undertakings with a view to enforcing the practices constituting the infringement.

Commentary
point 28: B&C: 14.039 **F&N:** 8.588

B. Mitigating circumstances

29. The basic amount may be reduced where the Commission finds that mitigating circumstances exist, such as:

— where the undertaking concerned provides evidence that it terminated the infringement as soon as the Commission intervened: this will not apply to secret agreements or practices (in particular, cartels);

— where the undertaking provides evidence that the infringement has been committed as a result of negligence;

— where the undertaking provides evidence that its involvement in the infringement is substantially limited and thus demonstrates that, during the period in which it was party to the offending agreement, it actually avoided applying it by adopting competitive conduct in the market: the mere fact that an undertaking participated in an infringement for a shorter duration than others will not be regarded as a mitigating circumstance since this will already be reflected in the basic amount;

— where the undertaking concerned has effectively cooperated with the Commission outside the scope of the Leniency Notice and beyond its legal obligation to do so;

— where the anti-competitive conduct of the undertaking has been authorized or encouraged by public authorities or by legislation.[1]

Notes
[1] This is without prejudice to any action that may be taken against the Member State concerned.

Commentary
point 29: B&C: 11.006, 14.051, 14.052, 14.122 **F&N:** 6.60, 8.617

C. Specific increase for deterrence

30. The Commission will pay particular attention to the need to ensure that fines have a sufficiently deterrent effect; to that end, it may increase the fine to be imposed on undertakings which have a particularly large turnover beyond the sales of goods or services to which the infringement relates.

Commentary
para 30: B&C: 5.033, 14.071 **F&N:** 8.661, 8.665

31. The Commission will also take into account the need to increase the fine in order to exceed the amount of gains improperly made as a result of the infringement where it is possible to estimate that amount.

Commentary
point 31: B&C: 14.074 **F&N:** 8.661

D. Legal maximum

32. The final amount of the fine shall not, in any event, exceed 10% of the total turnover in the preceding business year of the undertaking or association of undertakings participating in the infringement, as laid down in Article 23(2) of Regulation No 1/2003.

Commentary
point 32: F&N: 8.674, 8.676

33. Where an infringement by an association of undertakings relates to the activities of its members, the fine shall not exceed 10% of the sum of the total turnover of each member active on the market affected by that infringement.

Commentary
point 33: F&N: 8.674, 8.685

E. Leniency Notice

34. The Commission will apply the leniency rules in line with the conditions set out in the applicable notice.

Commentary
point 34: F&N: 8.684

F. Ability to pay

35. In exceptional cases, the Commission may, upon request, take account of the undertaking's inability to pay in a specific social and economic context. It will not base any reduction granted for this reason in the fine on the mere finding of an adverse or loss-making financial situation. A reduction could be granted solely on the basis of objective evidence that imposition of the fine as provided for in these Guidelines would irretrievably jeopardise the economic viability of the undertaking concerned and cause its assets to lose all their value.

Commentary
point 35: B&C: 5.058, 14.075, 14.077, 14.107 F&N: 8.686, 8.690, 8.691, 8.695

FINAL CONSIDERATIONS

36. The Commission may, in certain cases, impose a symbolic fine. The justification for imposing such a fine should be given in its decision.

Commentary
point 36: B&C: 14.067, 14.069 F&N: 8.699

37. Although these Guidelines present the general methodology for the setting of fines, the particularities of a given case or the need to achieve deterrence in a particular case may justify departing from such methodology or from the limits specified in point 21.

Commentary
point 37: B&C: 14.084 F&N: 8.550, 8.683, 8.690, 8.699

38. These Guidelines will be applied in all cases where a statement of objections is notified after their date of publication in the Official Journal, regardless of whether the fine is imposed pursuant to Article 23(2) of Regulation No 1/2003 or Article 15(2) of Regulation 17/62.[1]

Notes
[1] Article 15(2) of Regulation 17/62 of 6 February 1962: First Regulation implementing Articles [101 and 102] of the Treaty (OJ 13, 21.2.1962, p.204).

B12

COMMISSION NOTICE ON IMMUNITY FROM FINES AND REDUCTION OF FINES IN CARTEL CASES

(Text with EEA relevance)

(2006/C 298/11)

Official Journal C 298, 8.12.2006, p.17

Celex No: 52006XC1208(04)

EUR-Lex permanent link: <http://eur-lex.europa.eu/LexUriServ/LexUriServ.do?uri=CELEX: 5200 6XC1208(04):EN:NOT>

Notes

EEA application: the EFTA Surveillance Authority has adopted a parallel Notice on Immunity from fines and reduction of fines in cartel cases (OJ C 294, 3.12.2009, p.7).

Commentary

Notice: B&C: 5.022, 14.054, 14.109, 14.119, 15.036, 16.085 **F&N:** 8.95, 8.105, 8.111, 8.129, 8.130, 8.131, 8.133, 8.191, 8.196, 8.197, 8.200, 8.201, 8.214, 8.250, 8.251, 8.320, 8.387, 8.416, 8.489, 8.503, 8.562, 8.632, 8.633, 8.636, 8.685

points 31–35: F&N: 8.110

section II: F&N: 8.132, 8.175

section III: F&N: 8.132, 8.150, 8.175, 8.177, 8.183, 8.192, 8.203, 8.205

section IV: F&N: 8.155, 8.708

I. INTRODUCTION

(1) This notice sets out the framework for rewarding cooperation in the Commission investigation by undertakings which are or have been party to secret cartels affecting the Community. Cartels are agreements and/or concerted practices between two or more competitors aimed at coordinating their competitive behaviour on the market and/or influencing the relevant parameters of competition through practices such as the fixing of purchase or selling prices or other trading conditions, the allocation of production or sales quotas, the sharing of markets including bid-rigging, restrictions of imports or exports and/or anticompetitive actions against other competitors. Such practices are among the most serious violations of Article [101]* [TFEU].[1]

Notes

[1] Reference in this text to Article [101] [TFEU] also covers Article 53 EEA when applied by the Commission according to the rules laid down in Article 56 of the EEA Agreement.

* Ed note: please see the Note on the Lisbon Treaty at p.xvii in regard to article renumbering introduced by the Lisbon Treaty.

Commentary

point 1: B&C: 5.003 **F&N:** 8.139

(2) By artificially limiting the competition that would normally prevail between them, undertakings avoid exactly those pressures that lead them to innovate, both in terms of product development and the introduction of more efficient production methods. Such practices also lead to more expensive raw materials and components for the Community companies that purchase from such producers. They ultimately result in artificial prices and reduced choice for the consumer. In the long term, they lead to a loss of competitiveness and reduced employment opportunities.

(3) By their very nature, secret cartels are often difficult to detect and investigate without the cooperation of undertakings or individuals implicated in them. Therefore, the Commission considers that it is in the Community interest to reward undertakings involved in this type of illegal practices which are willing to put an end to their participation and co-operate in the Commission's investigation. The interests of consumers and citizens in ensuring that secret cartels are detected and punished outweigh the interest in fining those undertakings that enable the Commission to detect and prohibit such practices.

Commentary
point 3: F&N: 8.108

(4) The Commission considers that the collaboration of an undertaking in the detection of the existence of a cartel has an intrinsic value. A decisive contribution to the opening of an investigation or to the finding of an infringement may justify the granting of immunity from any fine to the undertaking in question, on condition that certain additional requirements are fulfilled.

(5) Moreover, co-operation by one or more undertakings may justify a reduction of a fine by the Commission. Any reduction of a fine must reflect an undertaking's actual contribution, in terms of quality and timing, to the Commission's establishment of the infringement. Reductions are to be limited to those undertakings that provide the Commission with evidence that adds significant value to that already in the Commission's possession.

(6) In addition to submitting pre-existing documents, undertakings may provide the Commission with voluntary presentations of their knowledge of a cartel and their role therein prepared specially to be submitted under this leniency program. These initiatives have proved to be useful for the effective investigation and termination of cartel infringements and they should not be discouraged by discovery orders issued in civil litigation. Potential leniency applicants might be dissuaded from cooperating with the Commission under this Notice if this could impair their position in civil proceedings, as compared to companies who do not cooperate. Such undesirable effect would significantly harm the public interest in ensuring effective public enforcement of Article [101] [TFEU] in cartel cases and thus their subsequent or parallel effective private enforcement.

Commentary
point 6: B&C: 5.022, 14.126 **F&N:** 8.218

(7) The supervisory task conferred on the Commission by the Treaty in competition matters does not only include the duty to investigate and punish individual infringements, but also encompasses the duty to pursue a general policy. The protection of corporate statements in the public interest is not a bar to their disclosure to other addressees of the statement of objections in order to safeguard their rights of defence in the procedure before the Commission, to the extent that it is technically possible to combine both interests by rendering corporate statements accessible only at the Commission premises and normally on a single occasion following the formal notification of the objections. Moreover, the Commission will process personal data in the context of this notice in conformity with its obligations under Regulation (EC) No 45/2001.[1]

Notes
[1] OJ L 8, 12.1.2001, p.1.
Commentary
point 7: F&N: 8.218

II. Immunity from Fines

A. Requirements to qualify for immunity from fines

(8) The Commission will grant immunity from any fine which would otherwise have been imposed to an undertaking disclosing its participation in an alleged cartel affecting the Community if that undertaking is the first to submit information and evidence which in the Commission's view will enable it to:

(a) carry out a targeted inspection in connection with the alleged cartel;[1] or

(b) find an infringement of Article [101] [TFEU] in connection with the alleged cartel.

Notes

[1] The assessment of the threshold will have to be carried out *ex ante*, *i.e.* without taking into account whether a given inspection has or has not been successful or whether or not an inspection has or has not been carried out. The assessment will be made exclusively on the basis of the type and the quality of the information submitted by the applicant.

Commentary
point 8: B&C: 14.116 F&N: 8.133, 8.139
point 8(a): B&C: 14.110, 14.111, 14.112, 14.115 F&N: 8.133, 8.134, 8.138, 8.150, 8.154, 8.158, 8.161, 8.169, 8.170, 8.171, 8.186
point 8(b): B&C: 5.022, 14.110, 14.112, 14.115 F&N: 8.133, 8.138, 8.150, 8.154, 8.158, 8.161, 8.169, 8.186

---

(9) For the Commission to be able to carry out a targeted inspection within the meaning of point (8)(a), the undertaking must provide the Commission with the information and evidence listed below, to the extent that this, in the Commission's view, would not jeopardize the inspections:

(a) A corporate statement[1] which includes, in so far as it is known to the applicant at the time of the submission:
  — A detailed description of the alleged cartel arrangement, including for instance its aims, activities and functioning; the product or service concerned, the geographic scope, the duration of and the estimated market volumes affected by the alleged cartel; the specific dates, locations, content of and participants in alleged cartel contacts, and all relevant explanations in connection with the pieces of evidence provided in support of the application;
  — The name and address of the legal entity submitting the immunity application as well as the names and addresses of all the other undertakings that participate(d) in the alleged cartel;
  — The names, positions, office locations and, where necessary, home addresses of all individuals who, to the applicant's knowledge, are or have been involved in the alleged cartel, including those individuals which have been involved on the applicant's behalf;
  — Information on which other competition authorities, inside or outside the EU, have been approached or are intended to be approached in relation to the alleged cartel; and

(b) Other evidence relating to the alleged cartel in possession of the applicant or available to it at the time of the submission, including in particular any evidence contemporaneous to the infringement.

Notes

[1] Corporate statements may take the form of written documents signed by or on behalf of the undertaking or be made orally.

Commentary
point 9: B&C: 14.111, 14.116 F&N: 8.136
point 9(a): F&N: 8.137, 8.138, 8.166

---

(10) Immunity pursuant to point (8)(a) will not be granted if, at the time of the submission, the Commission had already sufficient evidence to adopt a decision to carry out an inspection in connection with the alleged cartel or had already carried out such an inspection.

(11) Immunity pursuant to point (8)(b) will only be granted on the cumulative conditions that the Commission did not have, at the time of the submission, sufficient evidence to find an infringement of Article [101] [TFEU] in connection with the alleged cartel and that no undertaking had been granted conditional immunity from fines under point (8)(a) in connection with the alleged cartel. In order to qualify, an undertaking must be the first to provide contemporaneous, incriminating evidence of the alleged cartel as well as a corporate statement containing the kind of information specified in point (9)(a), which would enable the Commission to find an infringement of Article [101] [TFEU].

Commentary
point 11: F&N: 8.138, 8.140

(12) In addition to the conditions set out in points (8)(a), (9) and (10) or in points (8)(b) and 11, all the following conditions must be met in any case to qualify for any immunity from a fine:

(a) The undertaking cooperates genuinely,[1] fully, on a continuous basis and expeditiously from the time it submits its application throughout the Commission's administrative procedure. This includes:

— providing the Commission promptly with all relevant information and evidence relating to the alleged cartel that comes into its possession or is available to it;

— remaining at the Commission's disposal to answer promptly to any request that may contribute to the establishment of the facts;

— making current (and, if possible, former) employees and directors available for interviews with the Commission;

— not destroying, falsifying or concealing relevant information or evidence relating to the alleged cartel; and

— not disclosing the fact or any of the content of its application before the Commission has issued a statement of objections in the case, unless otherwise agreed;

(b) The undertaking ended its involvement in the alleged cartel immediately following its application, except for what would, in the Commission's view, be reasonably necessary to preserve the integrity of the inspections;

(c) When contemplating making its application to the Commission, the undertaking must not have destroyed, falsified or concealed evidence of the alleged cartel nor disclosed the fact or any of the content of its contemplated application, except to other competition authorities.

Notes

[1] This requires in particular that the applicant provides accurate, not misleading, and complete information. [Cf] judgment of the European Court of Justice of 29 June 2006 in case C-301/04 P, *Commission v SGL Carbon AG a.o.*, at paragraphs 68–70, and judgment of the European Court of Justice of 28 June 2005 in cases C-189/02 P, C-202/02 P, C-205/02 P, C-208/02 P and C-213/02 P, *Dansk Rørindustri A/S a.o. v Commission* [[2005] ECR I-5425], at paragraphs 395–399.

Commentary
point 12: B&C: 5.022 F&N: 8.141, 8.142, 8.164, 8.165, 8.181, 8.188, 8.194, 8.221, 8.232, 8.320, 8.321
point 12(a): B&C: 14.113 F&N: 8.183, 8.194
point 12(b): B&C: 14.113 F&N: 8.146
point 12(c): B&C: 14.113 F&N: 8.147, 8.148, 8.149

(13) An undertaking which took steps to coerce other undertakings to join the cartel or to remain in it is not eligible for immunity from fines. It may still qualify for a reduction of fines if it fulfils the relevant requirements and meets all the conditions therefor.

Commentary
point 13: B&C: 5.022, 14.113 **F&N:** 8.141, 8.164

B. Procedure

(14) An undertaking wishing to apply for immunity from fines should contact the Commission's Directorate General for Competition. The undertaking may either initially apply for a marker or immediately proceed to make a formal application to the Commission for immunity from fines in order to meet the conditions in points (8)(a) or (8)(b), as appropriate. The Commission may disregard any application for immunity from fines on the ground that it has been submitted after the statement of objections has been issued.

Commentary
point 14: B&C: 14.114 **F&N:** 8.150, 8.152

(15) The Commission services may grant a marker protecting an immunity applicant's place in the queue for a period to be specified on a case-by-case basis in order to allow for the gathering of the necessary information and evidence. To be eligible to secure a marker, the applicant must provide the Commission with information concerning its name and address, the parties to the alleged cartel, the affected product(s) and territory(-ies), the estimated duration of the alleged cartel and the nature of the alleged cartel conduct. The applicant should also inform the Commission on other past or possible future leniency applications to other authorities in relation to the alleged cartel and justify its request for a marker. Where a marker is granted, the Commission services determine the period within which the applicant has to perfect the marker by submitting the information and evidence required to meet the relevant threshold for immunity. Undertakings which have been granted a marker cannot perfect it by making a formal application in hypothetical terms. If the applicant perfects the marker within the period set by the Commission services, the information and evidence provided will be deemed to have been submitted on the date when the marker was granted.

Commentary
point 15: B&C: 14.115, 14.116 **F&N:** 8.153

(16) An undertaking making a formal immunity application to the Commission must:
   (a) provide the Commission with all information and evidence relating to the alleged cartel available to it, as specified in points (8) and (9), including corporate statements; or
   (b) initially present this information and evidence in hypothetical terms, in which case the undertaking must present a detailed descriptive list of the evidence it proposes to disclose at a later agreed date. This list should accurately reflect the nature and content of the evidence, whilst safeguarding the hypothetical nature of its disclosure. Copies of documents, from which sensitive parts have been removed, may be used to illustrate the nature and content of the evidence. The name of the applying undertaking and of other undertakings involved in the alleged cartel need not be disclosed until the evidence described in its application is submitted. However, the product or service concerned by the alleged cartel, the geographic scope of the alleged cartel and the estimated duration must be clearly identified.

Commentary
point 16(b): B&C: 14.116 **F&N:** 8.154

(17) If requested, the Directorate General for Competition will provide an acknowledgement of receipt of the undertaking's application for immunity from fines, confirming the date and, where appropriate, time of the application.

Commentary
point 17: F&N: 8.158

Part B Procedural Matters

(18) Once the Commission has received the information and evidence submitted by the undertaking under point (16)(a) and has verified that it meets the conditions set out in points (8)(a) or (8)(b), as appropriate, it will grant the undertaking conditional immunity from fines in writing.

(19) If the undertaking has presented information and evidence in hypothetical terms, the Commission will verify that the nature and content of the evidence described in the detailed list referred to in point (16)(b) will meet the conditions set out in points (8)(a) or (8)(b), as appropriate, and inform the undertaking accordingly. Following the disclosure of the evidence no later than on the date agreed and having verified that it corresponds to the description made in the list, the Commission will grant the undertaking conditional immunity from fines in writing.

Commentary
point 19: F&N: 8.154

(20) If it becomes apparent that immunity is not available or that the undertaking failed to meet the conditions set out in points (8)(a) or (8)(b), as appropriate, the Commission will inform the undertaking in writing. In such case, the undertaking may withdraw the evidence disclosed for the purposes of its immunity application or request the Commission to consider it under section III of this notice. This does not prevent the Commission from using its normal powers of investigation in order to obtain the information.

Commentary
point 20: B&C: 14.114, 14.116 F&N: 8.150

(21) The Commission will not consider other applications for immunity from fines before it has taken a position on an existing application in relation to the same alleged infringement, irrespective of whether the immunity application is presented formally or by requesting a marker.

Commentary
point 21: F&N: 8.157

(22) If at the end of the administrative procedure, the undertaking has met the conditions set out in point (12), the Commission will grant it immunity from fines in the relevant decision. If at the end of the administrative procedure, the undertaking has not met the conditions set out in point (12), the undertaking will not benefit from any favourable treatment under this Notice. If the Commission, after having granted conditional immunity ultimately finds that the immunity applicant has acted as a coercer, it will withhold immunity.

Commentary
point 22: B&C: 14.128

III. Reduction of a Fine

A. Requirements to qualify for reduction of a fine

(23) Undertakings disclosing their participation in an alleged cartel affecting the Community that do not meet the conditions under section II above may be eligible to benefit from a reduction of any fine that would otherwise have been imposed.

Commentary
point 23: B&C: 14.119

(24) In order to qualify, an undertaking must provide the Commission with evidence of the alleged infringement which represents significant added value with respect to the evidence already in

the Commission's possession and must meet the cumulative conditions set out in points (12)(a) to (12)(c) above.

Commentary
point 24: F&N: 8.181, 8.188, 8.194, 8.196, 8.320, 8.321

(25) The concept of "added value" refers to the extent to which the evidence provided strengthens, by its very nature and/or its level of detail, the Commission's ability to prove the alleged cartel. In this assessment, the Commission will generally consider written evidence originating from the period of time to which the facts pertain to have a greater value than evidence subsequently established. Incriminating evidence directly relevant to the facts in question will generally be considered to have a greater value than that with only indirect relevance. Similarly, the degree of corroboration from other sources required for the evidence submitted to be relied upon against other undertakings involved in the case will have an impact on the value of that evidence, so that compelling evidence will be attributed a greater value than evidence such as statements which require corroboration if contested.

Commentary
point 25: F&N: 8.177, 8.178, 8.180, 8.181, 8.188, 8.197, 8.199, 8.202, 8.203, 8.446

(26) The Commission will determine in any final decision adopted at the end of the administrative procedure the level of reduction an undertaking will benefit from, relative to the fine which would otherwise be imposed. For the:

— first undertaking to provide significant added value: a reduction of 30–50%,
— second undertaking to provide significant added value: a reduction of 20–30%,
— subsequent undertakings that provide significant added value: a reduction of up to 20%.

In order to determine the level of reduction within each of these bands, the Commission will take into account the time at which the evidence fulfilling the condition in point (24) was submitted and the extent to which it represents added value.

If the applicant for a reduction of a fine is the first to submit compelling evidence in the sense of point (25) which the Commission uses to establish additional facts increasing the gravity or the duration of the infringement, the Commission will not take such additional facts into account when setting any fine to be imposed on the undertaking which provided this evidence.

Commentary
point 26: B&C: 14.120 F&N: 8.140, 8.176, 8.178, 8.179, 8.181, 8.183, 8.188

B. Procedure

(27) An undertaking wishing to benefit from a reduction of a fine must make a formal application to the Commission and it must present it with sufficient evidence of the alleged cartel to qualify for a reduction of a fine in accordance with point (24) of this Notice. Any voluntary submission of evidence to the Commission which the undertaking that submits it wishes to be considered for the beneficial treatment of section III of this Notice must be clearly identified at the time of its submission as being part of a formal application for a reduction of a fine.

Commentary
point 27: F&N: 8.181, 8.184, 8.221, 8.232, 8.374

(28) If requested, the Directorate General for Competition will provide an acknowledgement of receipt of the undertaking's application for a reduction of a fine and of any subsequent submissions of evidence, confirming the date and, where appropriate, time of each submission. The Commission will not take any position on an application for a reduction of a fine before it has taken a position on any existing applications for conditional immunity from fines in relation to the same alleged cartel.

Commentary
point 28: F&N: 8.185, 8.310

(29) If the Commission comes to the preliminary conclusion that the evidence submitted by the undertaking constitutes significant added value within the meaning of points (24) and (25), and that the undertaking has met the conditions of points (12) and (27), it will inform the undertaking in writing, no later than the date on which a statement of objections is notified, of its intention to apply a reduction of a fine within a specified band as provided in point (26). The Commission will also, within the same time frame, inform the undertaking in writing if it comes to the preliminary conclusion that the undertaking does not qualify for a reduction of a fine. The Commission may disregard any application for a reduction of fines on the grounds that it has been submitted after the statement of objections has been issued.

Commentary
point 29: B&C: 14.119 F&N: 8.189

(30) The Commission will evaluate the final position of each undertaking which filed an application for a reduction of a fine at the end of the administrative procedure in any decision adopted. The Commission will determine in any such final decision:

(a) whether the evidence provided by an undertaking represented significant added value with respect to the evidence in the Commission's possession at that same time;

(b) whether the conditions set out in points (12)(a) to (12)(c) above have been met;

(c) the exact level of reduction an undertaking will benefit from within the bands specified in point (26). If the Commission finds that the undertaking has not met the conditions set out in point (12), the undertaking will not benefit from any favourable treatment under this Notice.

Commentary
point 30(b): F&N: 8.206

IV. Corporate Statements Made to Qualify under this Notice

(31) A corporate statement is a voluntary presentation by or on behalf of an undertaking to the Commission of the undertaking's knowledge of a cartel and its role therein prepared specially to be submitted under this Notice. Any statement made vis-à-vis the Commission in relation to this notice, forms part of the Commission's file and can thus be used in evidence.

(32) Upon the applicant's request, the Commission may accept that corporate statements be provided orally unless the applicant has already disclosed the content of the corporate statement to third parties. Oral corporate statements will be recorded and transcribed at the Commission's premises. In accordance with Article 19 of Council Regulation (EC) No 1/2003[1] and Articles 3 and 17 of Commission Regulation (EC) No 773/2004,[2] undertakings making oral corporate statements will be granted the opportunity to check the technical accuracy of the recording, which will be available at the Commission's premises and to correct the substance of their oral statements within a given time limit. Undertakings may waive these rights within the said time limit, in which case the recording will from that moment on be deemed to have been approved. Following the explicit or implicit approval of the oral statement or the submission of any corrections to it, the undertaking shall listen to the recordings at the Commission's premises and check the accuracy of the transcript within a given time limit. Non-compliance with the last requirement may lead to the loss of any beneficial treatment under this Notice.

Notes
[1] OJ L 1 of 4.1.2003, p.1.
[2] OJ L 123 of 27.4.2004, p.18.

Commentary
point 32: B&C: 14.116, 15.049 F&N: 8.156

(33) Access to corporate statements is only granted to the addressees of a statement of objections, provided that they commit, — together with the legal counsels getting access on their behalf —, not to make any copy by mechanical or electronic means of any information in the corporate statement to which access is being granted and to ensure that the information to be obtained from the corporate statement will solely be used for the purposes mentioned below. Other parties such as complainants will not be granted access to corporate statements. The Commission considers that this specific protection of a corporate statement is not justified as from the moment when the applicant discloses to third parties the content thereof.

Commentary
point 33: F&N: 8.219, 8.220, 8.708

(34) In accordance with the Commission Notice on rules for access to the Commission file,[1] access to the file is only granted to the addressees of a statement of objections on the condition that the information thereby obtained may only be used for the purposes of judicial or administrative proceedings for the application of the Community competition rules at issue in the related administrative proceedings. The use of such information for a different purpose during the proceeding may be regarded as lack of cooperation within the meaning of points (12) and (27) of this Notice. Moreover, if any such use is made after the Commission has already adopted a prohibition decision in the proceeding, the Commission may, in any legal proceedings before the Community Courts, ask the Court to increase the fine in respect of the responsible undertaking. Should the information be used for a different purpose, at any point in time, with the involvement of an outside counsel, the Commission may report the incident to the bar of that counsel, with a view to disciplinary action.

Notes
[1] OJ C 325, 22.12.2005, p.7.

Commentary
point 34: F&N: 8.218, 8.219, 8.708

(35) Corporate statements made under the present Notice will only be transmitted to the competition authorities of the Member States pursuant to Article 12 of Regulation No 1/2003, provided that the conditions set out in the Network Notice[1] are met and provided that the level of protection against disclosure awarded by the receiving competition authority is equivalent to the one conferred by the Commission.

Notes
[1] Commission Notice on cooperation within the Network of Competition Authorities, OJ C 101, 27.4.2004, p.43.

Commentary
point 35: B&C: 14.123, 15.039

V. GENERAL CONSIDERATIONS

(36) The Commission will not take a position on whether or not to grant conditional immunity, or otherwise on whether or not to reward any application, if it becomes apparent that the application concerns infringements covered by the five years limitation period for the imposition of penalties stipulated in Article 25(1)(b) of Regulation 1/2003, as such applications would be devoid of purpose.

Commentary
point 36: F&N: 8.168

(37) From the date of its publication in the Official Journal, this notice replaces the 2002 Commission notice on immunity from fines and reduction of fines in cartel cases for all cases in which no undertaking has contacted the Commission in order to take advantage of the favourable treatment set out in that notice. However, points (31) to (35) of the current notice will be

applied from the moment of its publication to all pending and new applications for immunity from fines or reduction of fines.

Commentary
point 37: F&N: 8.110, 8.156

(38) The Commission is aware that this notice will create legitimate expectations on which undertakings may rely when disclosing the existence of a cartel to the Commission.

Commentary
point 38: B&C: 14.129

(39) In line with the Commission's practice, the fact that an undertaking cooperated with the Commission during its administrative procedure will be indicated in any decision, so as to explain the reason for the immunity or reduction of the fine. The fact that immunity or reduction in respect of fines is granted cannot protect an undertaking from the civil law consequences of its participation in an infringement of Article [101] [TFEU].

Commentary
point 39: F&N: 8.218

(40) The Commission considers that normally public disclosure, at any time, of documents or written or recorded statements received in the context of this notice would undermine certain public or private interests, for example the protection of the purpose of inspections and investigations, within the meaning of Article 4 of Regulation (EC) No 1049/2001,[1] even after the decision has been taken.

Notes
[1] OJ L 145, 31.5.2001, p.43.

Commentary
point 40: F&N: 8.222

B13

LENIENCY APPLICATION

NOTE

Note
For reasons of space, this document is no longer reproduced in this volume. It remains available on Oxford Competition Law and on the Commission's website at: <http://ec.europa.eu/comm/competition/cartels/leniency/leniency.html>

B14

COMMISSION NOTICE ON THE CONDUCT OF SETTLEMENT PROCEDURES IN VIEW OF THE ADOPTION OF DECISIONS PURSUANT TO ARTICLE 7 AND ARTICLE 23 OF COUNCIL REGULATION (EC) NO 1/2003 IN CARTEL CASES

(Text with EEA relevance)

(2008/C 167/01)

Official Journal C 167, 2.7.2008, p.1

Celex No: 52008XC0702(01)

Eur-Lex permanent link: <http://eur-lex.europa.eu/LexUriServ/LexUriServ.do?uri=CELEX:52008 XC0702(01):EN:NOT>

Commentary
Notice: F&N: 8.250, 8.685, 12.235
points 8–13: F&N: 8.719
points 35–40: B&C: 13.099, 15.049

1. Introduction

1. This Notice sets out the framework for rewarding cooperation in the conduct of proceedings commenced in view of the application of Article [101]* of the [Treaty on the Functioning of the European Union][1] to cartel cases.[2] The settlement procedure may allow the Commission to handle more cases with the same resources, thereby fostering the public interest in the Commission's delivery of effective and timely punishment, while increasing overall deterrence. The cooperation covered by this Notice is different from the voluntary production of evidence to trigger or advance the Commission's investigation, which is covered by the Commission Notice on Immunity from fines and reduction of fines in cartel cases[3] (the Leniency Notice). Provided that the cooperation offered by an undertaking qualifies under both Commission Notices, it can be cumulatively rewarded accordingly.[4]

Notes

[*] Ed note: please see the Note on the Lisbon Treaty at p.xvii in regard to article renumbering introduced by the Lisbon Treaty.

[1] References in this text to Article [101] also cover Article 53 EEA when applied by the Commission in accordance with the rules laid down in Article 56 of the EEA Agreement.

[2] Cartels are agreements and/or concerted practices between two or more competitors aimed at coordinating their competitive behaviour on the market and/or influencing the relevant parameters of competition through practices such as the fixing of purchase or selling prices or other trading conditions, the allocation of production or sales quotas, the sharing of markets including bid-rigging, restrictions of imports or exports and/or anti-competitive actions against other competitors. Such practices are among the most serious violations of Article [101] [TFEU].

[3] OJ C 298, 8.12.2006, p.17.

[4] See point 33.

Commentary
point 1: F&N: 8.723

---

2. When parties to the proceedings are prepared to acknowledge their participation in a cartel violating Article [101] of the Treaty and their liability therefore, they may also contribute to expediting the proceedings leading to the adoption of the corresponding decision pursuant to Article 7 and Article 23 of Council Regulation (EC) No 1/2003 of 16 December 2002 on the implementation of the rules on competition laid down in Articles [101] and [102] of the Treaty[1] in the way and with the safeguards specified in this Notice. Whilst the Commission, as the investigative authority and the guardian of the Treaty empowered to adopt enforcement decisions subject to judicial control by the Community Courts, does not negotiate the question of the existence of an infringement of Community law and the appropriate sanction, it can reward the cooperation described in this Notice.

Notes
[1] OJ L 1, 4.1.2003, p.1. Regulation as last amended by Regulation (EC) No 1419/2006 (OJ L 269, 28.9.2006, p.1).

3. Commission Regulation (EC) No 773/2004 of 7 April 2004 relating to the conduct of proceedings by the Commission pursuant to Articles [101] and [102] of the [Treaty on the Functioning of the European Union][1] lays down the core practical rules concerning the conduct of proceedings in antitrust cases including those applicable in the variant for settlement. In this regard, Regulation (EC) No 773/2004 bestows on the Commission the discretion whether to explore the settlement procedure or not in cartel cases, while ensuring that the choice of the settlement procedure cannot be imposed on the parties.

Notes
[1] OJ L 123, 27.4.2004, p.18. Regulation as last amended by Regulation (EC) No 622/2008 (OJ L 171, 1.7.2008, p.3).

4. Effective enforcement of Community competition law is compatible with full respect of the parties' rights of defence, which constitutes a fundamental principle of Community law to be respected in all circumstances, and in particular in antitrust procedures which may give rise to penalties. It follows that the rules established to conduct the Commission proceedings to enforce Article [101] of the Treaty should ensure that the undertakings and associations of undertakings concerned are afforded the opportunity effectively to make known their views on the truth and relevance of the facts, objections and circumstances put forward by the Commission,[1] throughout the administrative procedure.

Notes
[1] Case 85/76, *Hoffmann-La Roche* v *Commission* [1979] ECR 461, at paragraphs 9 and 11.

2. PROCEDURE

5. The Commission retains a broad margin of discretion to determine which cases may be suitable to explore the parties' interest to engage in settlement discussions, as well as to decide to engage in them or discontinue them or to definitely settle. In this regard, account may be taken of the probability of reaching a common understanding regarding the scope of the potential objections with the parties involved within a reasonable timeframe, in view of factors such as number of parties involved, foreseeable conflicting positions on the attribution of liability, extent of contestation of the facts. The prospect of achieving procedural efficiencies in view of the progress made overall in the settlement procedure, including the scale of burden involved in providing access to non-confidential versions of documents from the file, will be considered. Other concerns such as the possibility of setting a precedent might apply. The Commission may also decide to discontinue settlement discussions if the parties to the proceedings coordinate to distort or destroy any evidence relevant to the establishment of the infringement or any part thereof or to the calculation of the applicable fine. Distortion or destruction of evidence relevant to the establishment of the infringement or any part thereof may also constitute an aggravating circumstance within the meaning of point 28 of the Commission Guidelines on the method of setting fines imposed

pursuant to Article 23(2)(a) of Regulation (EC) No 1/2003[1] (the Guidelines on fines), and may be regarded as lack of cooperation within the meaning of points 12 and 27 of the Leniency Notice. The Commission may only engage in settlement discussions upon the written request of the parties concerned.

Notes
[1] OJ C 210, 1.9.2006, p.2.
Commentary
point 5: **B&C:** 5.023, 13.097 **F&N:** 8.718, 8.721

6. While parties to the proceedings do not have a right to settle, should the Commission consider that a case may, in principle, be suitable for settlement, it will explore the interest in settlement of all parties to the same proceedings.

Commentary
point 6: **B&C:** 5.023 **F&N:** 8.718

7. The parties to the proceedings may not disclose to any third party in any jurisdiction the contents of the discussions or of the documents which they have had access to in view of settlement, unless they have a prior explicit authorization by the Commission. Any breach in this regard may lead the Commission to disregard the undertaking's request to follow the settlement procedure. Such disclosure may also constitute an aggravating circumstance, within the meaning of point 28 of the Guidelines on fines and may be regarded as lack of cooperation within the meaning of points 12 and 27 of the Leniency Notice.

Commentary
point 7: **F&N:** 8.232, 8.721

2.1. Initiation of proceedings and exploratory steps regarding settlement

8. Where the Commission contemplates the adoption of a decision pursuant to Article 7 and/or Article 23 of Regulation (EC) No 1/2003, it is required in advance to identify and recognize as parties to the proceedings the legal persons on whom a penalty may be imposed for an infringement of Article [101] of the Treaty.

9. To this end, the initiation of proceedings pursuant to Article 11(6) of Regulation (EC) No 1/2003 in view of adopting such a decision can take place at any point in time, but no later than the date on which the Commission issues a statement of objections against the parties concerned. Article 2(1) of Regulation (EC) No 773/2004 further specifies that, should the Commission consider it suitable to explore the parties' interest in engaging in settlement discussions, it will initiate proceedings no later than the date on which it either issues a statement of objections or requests the parties to express in writing their interest to engage in settlement discussions, whichever is the earlier.

Commentary
point 9: **F&N:** 8.719

10. After the initiation of proceedings pursuant to Article 11(6) of Regulation (EC) No 1/2003, the Commission becomes the only competition authority competent to apply Article [101] of the Treaty to the case in point.

11. Should the Commission consider it suitable to explore the parties' interest to engage in settlement discussions, it will set a time-limit of no less than two weeks pursuant to Articles 10a(1) and 17(3) of Regulation (EC) No 773/2004 within which parties to the same proceedings should declare in writing whether they envisage engaging in settlement discussions in view of possibly introducing settlement submissions at a later stage. This written declaration does not imply an admission by the parties of having participated in an infringement or of being liable for it.

12. Whenever the Commission initiates proceedings against two or more parties within the same undertaking, the Commission will inform each of them of the other legal entities which it identifies within the same undertaking and which are also concerned by the proceedings. In such a case, should the concerned parties wish to engage in settlement discussions, they must appoint joint representatives duly empowered to act on their behalf by the end of the time-limit referred to in point 11. The appointment of joint representatives aims solely to facilitate the settlement discussions and it does not prejudge in any way the attribution of liability for the infringement amongst the different parties.

13. The Commission may disregard any application for immunity from fines or reduction of fines on the ground that it has been submitted after the expiry of the time-limit referred to in point 11.

Commentary
point 12: F&N: 8.725

2.2. Commencing the settlement procedure: settlement discussions

14. Should some of the parties to the proceedings request settlement discussions and comply with the requirements referred to in points 11 and 12, the Commission may decide to pursue the settlement procedure by means of bilateral contacts between the Commission Directorate- General for Competition and the settlement candidates.

15. The Commission retains discretion to determine the appropriateness and the pace of the bilateral settlement discussions with each undertaking. In line with Article 10a(2) of Regulation (EC) No 773/2004, this includes determining, in view of the progress made overall in the settlement procedure, the order and sequence of the bilateral settlement discussions as well as the timing of the disclosure of information, including the evidence in the Commission file used to establish the envisaged objections and the potential fine.[1] Information will be disclosed in a timely manner as settlement discussions progress.

Notes

[1] Reference to the 'potential fine' in Article 10a(2) of Regulation (EC) No 773/2004 affords the Commission services the possibility to inform the parties concerned by settlement discussions of an estimate of their potential fine in view of the guidance contained in the Guidelines on fines, the provisions of this Notice and the Leniency Notice, where applicable.

Commentary
point 15: F&N: 8.718

16. Such an early disclosure in the context of settlement discussions pursuant to Article 10a(2) and Article 15(1a) of Regulation (EC) No 773/2004 will allow the parties to be informed of the essential elements taken into consideration so far, such as the facts alleged, the classification of those facts, the gravity and duration of the alleged cartel, the attribution of liability, an estimation of the range of likely fines, as well as the evidence used to establish the potential objections. This will enable the parties effectively to assert their views on the potential objections against them and will allow them to make an informed decision on whether or not to settle. Upon request by a party, the Commission services will also grant it access to non-confidential versions of any specified accessible document listed in the case file at that point in time, in so far as this is justified for the purpose of enabling the party to ascertain its position regarding a time period or any other aspect of the cartel.[1]

Notes

[1] For that purpose, the parties will be provided with a list of all accessible documents in the case file at that point in time.

Commentary
point 16: F&N: 8.720

17. When the progress made during the settlement discussions leads to a common understanding regarding the scope of the potential objections and the estimation of the range of likely fines to be imposed by the Commission, and the Commission takes the preliminary view that procedural efficiencies are likely to be achieved in view of the progress made overall, the Commission may grant a final time-limit of at least 15 working days for an undertaking to introduce a final settlement submission pursuant to Articles 10a(2) and 17(3) of Regulation (EC) No 773/2004. The time-limit can be extended following a reasoned request. Before granting such time-limit, the parties will be entitled to have the information specified in point 16 disclosed to them upon request.

18. The parties may call upon the Hearing Officer at any time during the settlement procedure in relation to issues that might arise relating to due process. The Hearing Officer's duty is to ensure that the effective exercise of the rights of defence is respected.

Commentary
point 18: B&C: 13.083

19. Should the parties concerned fail to introduce a settlement submission, the procedure leading to the final decision in their regard will follow the general provisions, in particular Articles 10(2), 12(1) and 15(1) of Regulation (EC) No 773/2004, instead of those regulating the settlement procedure.

2.3. Settlement submissions

20. Parties opting for a settlement procedure must introduce a formal request to settle in the form of a settlement submission. The settlement submission provided for in Article 10a(2) of Regulation (EC) No 773/2004 should contain:

    (a) an acknowledgement in clear and unequivocal terms of the parties' liability for the infringement summarily described as regards its object, its possible implementation, the main facts, their legal qualification, including the party's role and the duration of their participation in the infringement in accordance with the results of the settlement discussions;

    (b) an indication[1] of the maximum amount of the fine the parties foresee to be imposed by the Commission and which the parties would accept in the framework of a settlement procedure;

    (c) the parties' confirmation that, they have been sufficiently informed of the objections the Commission envisages raising against them and that they have been given sufficient opportunity to make their views known to the Commission;

    (d) the parties' confirmation that, in view of the above, they do not envisage requesting access to the file or requesting to be heard again in an oral hearing, unless the Commission does not reflect their settlement submissions in the statement of objections and the decision;

    (e) the parties' agreement to receive the statement of objections and the final decision pursuant to Articles 7 and 23 of Regulation (EC) No 1/2003 in an agreed official language of the European Community.

Notes
[1] This would result from the discussions as set out in points 16 and 17.

Commentary
point 20: B&C: 13.098 **F&N:** 8.722

21. The acknowledgments and confirmations provided by the parties in view of settlement constitute the expression of their commitment to cooperate in the expeditious handling of the case following the settlement procedure. However, those acknowledgments and confirmations are conditional upon the Commission meeting their settlement request, including the anticipated maximum amount of the fine.

22. Settlement requests cannot be revoked unilaterally by the parties which have provided them unless the Commission does not meet the settlement requests by reflecting the settlement submissions first in a statement of objections and ultimately, in a final decision (see in this regard

points 27 and 29). The statement of objections would be deemed to have endorsed the settlement submissions if it reflects their contents on the issues mentioned in point 20(a). Additionally, for a final decision to be deemed to have reflected the settlement submissions, it should also impose a fine which does not exceed the maximum amount indicated therein.

2.4. Statement of objections and reply

23. Pursuant to Article 10(1) of Regulation (EC) No 773/2004, the notification of a written statement of objections to each of the parties against whom objections are raised is a mandatory preparatory step before adopting any final decision. Therefore, the Commission will issue a statement of objections also in a settlement procedure.[1]

Notes

[1] In the context of settlement procedures, statements of objections should contain the information necessary to enable the parties to corroborate that it reflects their settlement submissions.

24. For the parties' rights of defence to be exercised effectively, the Commission should hear their views on the objections against them and supporting evidence before adopting a final decision and take them into account by amending its preliminary analysis, where appropriate.[1] The Commission must be able not only to accept or reject the parties' relevant arguments expressed during the administrative procedure, but also to make its own analysis of the matters put forward by them in order to either abandon such objections because they have been shown to be unfounded or to supplement and reassess its arguments both in fact and in law, in support of the objections which it maintains.

Notes

[1] In line with settled case-law, the Commission shall base its decisions only on objections on which the parties concerned have been able to comment and, to this end, they shall be entitled to have access to the Commission's file, subject to the legitimate interest of undertakings in the protection of their business secrets.

25. By introducing a formal settlement request in the form of a settlement submission prior to the notification of the statement of objections, the parties concerned enable the Commission to effectively take their views into account[1] already when drafting the statement of objections, rather than only before the consultation of the Advisory Committee on Restrictive Practices and Dominant Positions (hereinafter the 'Advisory Committee') or before the adoption of the final decision.[2]

Notes

[1] In this regard, recital 2 of Regulation (EC) No 622/2008 states: '(...) *Such early disclosure should enable the parties concerned to put forward their views on the objections which the Commission intends to raise against them as well as on their potential liability*'.
[2] As required by Article 11(1) of Regulation (EC) No 773/2004 and Article 27(1) of Regulation (EC) No 1/2003, respectively.

26. Should the statement of objections reflect the parties' settlement submissions, the parties concerned should within a time-limit of at least two weeks set by the Commission in accordance with Articles 10a(3) and 17(3) of Regulation (EC) No 773/2004, reply to it by simply confirming (in unequivocal terms) that the statement of objections corresponds to the contents of their settlement submissions and that they therefore remain committed to follow the settlement procedure. In the absence of such a reply, the Commission will take note of the party's breach of its commitment and may also disregard the party's request to follow the settlement procedure.

27. The Commission retains the right to adopt a statement of objections which does not reflect the parties' settlement submission. If so, the general provisions in Articles 10(2), 12(1) and 15(1) of Regulation (EC) No 773/2004 will apply. The acknowledgements provided by the parties in the settlement submission would be deemed to be withdrawn and could not be used in evidence against any of the parties to the proceedings. Hence, the parties concerned would no longer be bound by their settlement submissions and would be granted a time-limit allowing them,

upon request, to present their defence anew, including the possibility to access the file and to request an oral hearing.

Commentary
point 27: B&C: 13.099 **F&N:** 8.722

2.5. Commission decision and settlement reward

28. Upon the parties' replies to the statement of objections confirming their commitment to settle, Regulation (EC) No 773/2004 allows the Commission to proceed, without any other procedural step, to the adoption of the subsequent final decision pursuant to Articles 7 and/or 23 of Regulation (EC) No 1/2003, after consultation of the Advisory Committee pursuant to Article 14 of Regulation (EC) No 1/2003. In particular, this implies that no oral hearing or access to the file may be requested by those parties once their settlement submissions have been reflected by the statement of objections, in line with Articles 12(2) and 15(1a) of Regulation (EC) No 773/2004.

Commentary
point 28: B&C: 13.099

29. The Commission retains the right to adopt a final position which departs from its preliminary position expressed in a statement of objections endorsing the parties' settlement submissions, either in view of the opinion provided by the Advisory Committee or for other appropriate considerations in view of the ultimate decisional autonomy of the Commission to this effect. However, should the Commission opt to follow that course, it will inform the parties and notify to them a new statement of objections in order to allow for the exercise of their rights of defence in accordance with the applicable general rules of procedure. It follows that the parties would then be entitled to have access to the file, to request an oral hearing and to reply to the statement of objections. The acknowledgments provided by the parties in the settlement submissions would be deemed to have been withdrawn and could not be used in evidence against any of the parties to the proceedings.

Commentary
point 29: B&C: 13.009 **F&N:** 8.722

30. The final amount of the fine in a particular case is determined in the decision finding an infringement pursuant to Article 7 and imposing a fine pursuant to Article 23 of Regulation (EC) No 1/2003.

31. In line with the Commission's practice, the fact that an undertaking cooperated with the Commission under this Notice during the administrative procedure will be indicated in the final decision, so as to explain the reason for the level of the fine.

32. Should the Commission decide to reward a party for settlement in the framework of this Notice, it will reduce by 10 % the amount of the fine to be imposed after the 10% cap has been applied having regard to the Guidelines on the method of setting fines imposed pursuant to Article 23(2)(a) of Regulation (EC) No 1/2003.[1] Any specific increase for deterrence[2] used in their regard will not exceed a multiplication by two.

Notes
[1] OJ C 210, 1.9.2006, p.2.
[2] Point 30 of the Guidelines on fines.

Commentary
point 32: B&C: 13.099, 14.132 **F&N:** 8.665, 8.725

33. When settled cases involve also leniency applicants, the reduction of the fine granted to them for settlement will be added to their leniency reward.

Commentary
point 33: B&C: 13.099, 14.132 **F&N:** 8.230

Part B Procedural Matters

3. GENERAL CONSIDERATIONS

34. This Notice applies to any case pending before the Commission at the time of or after its publication in the Official Journal of the European Union.

Commentary
point 34: B&C: 13.051

35. Access to settlement submissions is only granted to those addressees of a statement of objections who have not requested settlement, provided that they commit — together with the legal counsels getting access on their behalf — not to make any copy by mechanical or electronic means of any information in the settlement submissions to which access is being granted and to ensure that the information to be obtained from the settlement submission will solely be used for the purposes of judicial or administrative proceedings for the application of the Community competition rules at issue in the related proceedings. Other parties such as complainants will not be granted access to settlement submissions.

Commentary
point 35: F&N: 8.721

36. The use of such information for a different purpose during the proceeding may be regarded as lack of cooperation within the meaning of points 12 and 27 of the Leniency Notice. Moreover, if any such use is made after the Commission has already adopted a prohibition decision in the proceedings, the Commission may, in any legal proceedings before the Community Courts, ask the Court to increase the fine in respect of the responsible undertaking. Should the information be used for a different purpose, at any point in time, with the involvement of an outside counsel, the Commission may report the incident to the bar of that counsel, with a view to disciplinary action.

Commentary
point 36: F&N: 8.721

37. Settlement submissions made under this Notice will only be transmitted to the competition authorities of the Member States pursuant to Article 12 of Regulation (EC) No 1/2003, provided that the conditions set out in the Network Notice[1] are met and provided that the level of protection against disclosure awarded by the receiving competition authority is equivalent to the one conferred by the Commission.

Notes
[1] Commission Notice on cooperation within the Network of Competition Authorities (OJ C 101, 27.4.2004, p.43).

38. Upon the applicant's request, the Commission may accept that settlement submissions be provided orally. Oral settlement submissions will be recorded and transcribed at the Commission's premises. In accordance with Article 19 of Regulation (EC) No 1/2003 and Articles 3(3) and 17(3) of Regulation (EC) No 773/2004 undertakings making oral settlement submissions will be granted the opportunity to check the technical accuracy of the recording, which will be available at the Commission's premises and to correct the substance of their oral settlement submissions and the accuracy of the transcript without delay.

39. The Commission will not transmit settlement submissions to national courts without the consent of the relevant applicants, in line with the provisions in the Commission Notice on the co-operation between the Commission and the courts of the EU Member States in the application of Articles [101] and [102] [TFEU].[1]

Notes
[1] OJ C 101, 27.4.2004, p.54; point 26.

40. The Commission considers that normally public disclosure of documents and written or recorded statements (including settlement submissions) received in the context of this Notice would

undermine certain public or private interests, for example the protection of the purpose of inspections and investigations, within the meaning of Article 4 of Regulation (EC) No 1049/2001 of the European Parliament and of the Council of 30 May 2001 regarding public access to European Parliament, Council and Commission documents,[1] even after the decision has been taken.

Notes

[1] OJ C 101, 27.4.2004, p.54; point 26.

Commentary
point 40: B&C: 16.048

41. Final decisions taken by the Commission under Regulation (EC) No 1/2003 are subject to judicial review in accordance with Article [263] of the Treaty. Moreover, as provided in Article [261] of the Treaty and Article 31 of Regulation (EC) No 1/2003, the Court of Justice has unlimited jurisdiction to review decisions on fines adopted pursuant to Article 23 of Regulation (EC) No 1/2003.

Commentary
point 41: F&N: 8.716

Overview of the procedure leading to the adoption of a (settlement) Decision pursuant to Articles 7 and 23 of Regulation No (EC) 1/2003

I. Investigation as usual

— Parties may express their interest in a hypothetical settlement.

II. Exploratory steps regarding settlement

— Letter to all companies (and MS) informing of the decision to initiate proceedings in view of settlement (Article 11(6)) and requesting them to express their interest in settlement.

III. Bilateral rounds of settlement discussions

— Disclosure and exchange of arguments on potential objections, liability, fines range.
— Disclosure of evidence used to establish potential objections, liability, fines.
— Disclosure of other non-confidential versions of documents in the file, when justified.

IV. Settlement

— Conditional settlement submissions by the companies, jointly represented where applicable.
— DG COMP sends acknowledgement of receipt.

V. 'Settled' statement of objections

— Notification of streamlined SO endorsing company's settlement submissions, where appropriate.
— Company's reply to SO confirming clearly that it reflects its settlement submission.

VI. 'Settlement' Decision Pursuant to Articles 7 and 23 of Regulation No (EC) 1/2003

— Advisory Committee on a draft streamlined final decision.

If College of Commissioners agrees:

— Adoption of streamlined final decision.

B15

AUTHORISATION TO CONDUCT AN INSPECTION

NOTE

Note

For reasons of space, this document is no longer reproduced in this volume. It remains available on Oxford Competition Law and on the Commission's website at: <http://ec.europa.eu/competition/antitrust/information_en.html>

B16

EXPLANATORY NOTE TO AN AUTHORISATION TO CONDUCT AN INSPECTION IN EXECUTION OF A COMMISSION DECISION UNDER ARTICLE 20(4) OF COUNCIL REGULATION NO 1/2003 (2013)

NOTE

Note

For reasons of space, this document is no longer reproduced in this volume. It remains available on Oxford Competition Law and on the Commission's website at: <http://ec.europa.eu/competition/antitrust/information_en.html>

B17

DG COMPETITION
BEST PRACTICES FOR THE SUBMISSION OF ECONOMIC EVIDENCE AND DATA COLLECTION IN CASES CONCERNING THE APPLICATION OF ARTICLES 101 AND 102 TFEU AND IN MERGER CASES STAFF WORKING PAPER

SEC/2011/1216 final

Celex No: 52011SC1216

EUR-Lex link: <http://eur-lex.europa.eu/LexUriServ/LexUriServ.do?uri=CELEX:52011SC1216:EN:NOT>

Notes

This document was originally published for consultation on 6 January 2010. An amended staff working paper was published on 17 October 2011. A final form of the document has not yet been adopted. The version reproduced here is available on the Commission's website at the following address: <http://ec.europa.eu/competition/antitrust/legislation/legislation.html>.

Commentary

Notice: B&C: 1.019, 2.129, 3.031, 4.044, 8.008, 8.155, 13.014 F&N: 5.375, 5.449

1. Scope and Purpose

1. Economic analysis plays a central role in competition enforcement. Economics as a discipline provides a framework to think about the way in which each particular market operates and how competitive interactions take place. This framework further allows formulating the possible consequences of the practices under review, whether a merger, an agreement between firms, or single firm conduct. In certain cases it may also provide tools to identify the direction and magnitude of these effects empirically, if appropriate and relevant. In a number of cases, economic analysis may involve the production, handling and assessment of voluminous sets of quantitative data, including, when appropriate, the development of econometric models[1].

Notes

[1] The assessment of mergers and potential infringements "by effect" often requires a complex economic assessment by the Commission, as well as the use of statistical or econometric analysis.

---

2. Economic analysis needs to be framed in such a way that the Commission and the EU Courts can understand and evaluate its relevance and significance. As an administrative authority the Commission is required to take a decision within an appropriate or sometimes a statutory time limit. It is therefore necessary to: (i) ensure that economic analysis meets certain minimum technical standards at the outset, (ii) facilitate the effective gathering and exchange of facts and evidence, in particular any underlying quantitative data, and (iii) use in an effective way reliable and relevant evidence obtained during the administrative procedure, whether quantitative or qualitative.

3. In order to determine the relevance and significance of an economic analysis for a particular case, it is first necessary to assess its intrinsic quality from a technical perspective, i.e. whether it has been generated and presented in a way that meets adequate technical requirements prevalent in the profession. This involves, in particular, an evaluation of whether the hypothesis to be tested is formulated without ambiguity and clearly related to facts, whether the assumptions of the economic model are consistent with the institutional features and other relevant facts of the industry, whether economic models are well established in the relevant literature, whether the empirical methods and the data are appropriate, whether the results are properly interpreted and robust and whether counterarguments have been given adequate consideration.

4. Second, one must assess the congruence and consistency of the economic analysis with other pieces of quantitative and qualitative evidence (such as customer responses, or documentary evidence)[2].

Notes

[2] Economic models or econometric analysis, as is the case with other types of evidence will rarely, if ever, prove conclusive by themselves. The Commission can always take into account different items of evidence. The General Court has held that "*It is the Commission's task to make an overall assessment of what is shown by the set of indicative factors used to evaluate the competitive situation. It is possible, in that regard, for certain items of evidence to be prioritised and other evidence to be discounted. That examination and the associated reasoning are subject to a review of legality which the Court carries out in relation to Commission decisions on concentrations*". See Case T-342/07, Ryanair v Commission, [2010] paragraph 136.

---

5. The present document formulates best practices concerning the generation as well as the presentation of relevant economic and empirical evidence that may be taken into account in the assessment of a case concerning the application of Articles 101 and 102 of the Treaty on the Functioning of the European Union (TFEU)[3] or merger case[4]. These Best Practices are organised along two themes.

   i)   First of all, it provides recommendations regarding the content and presentation of economic or econometric analysis. This is meant to facilitate its assessment and the replication of any empirical results by the Commission and/or other parties.

   ii) Second, the document provides guidance to respond to Commission requests for quantitative data[5] to ensure that timely and relevant input for the investigation can be provided.

Notes

[3] Proceedings before the European Commission concerning Articles 101 and 102 TFEU, in accordance with Council Regulation (EC) No 1/2003 of 16 December 2002 on the implementation of the rules on competition laid down in Articles 81 and 82 of the Treaty (OJ L 1, 4.1.2003, p.1, as amended).

[4] Proceedings under the Council Regulation (EC) No 139/2004 of 20 January 2004 on the control of concentrations between undertakings (OJ L 24, 29.1.2004, p.1).

[5] Quantitative data means, generally, observations or measurements, expressed as numbers. For the purposes of these Best Practices, this concept is used to refer to large sets of quantitative data submitted and/or obtained for the purposes of the conduct of an assessment of an economic (and often econometric) nature.

6. The desire to ensure transparency and accountability, these Best Practices apply to all parties involved in proceedings concerning the application of Articles 101 and 102 TFEU and mergers, that is the parties to the case and interested third parties (including complainants), as well as the Commission.

7. These Best Practices do not create any new rights or obligations, nor alter the rights and obligations which arise from the TFEU, secondary EU law and the case-law of the Court of Justice of the European Union. The Best Practices also do not alter the Commission's interpretative notices and established decisional practice.

Notes

Commentary
Para 7: B&C: 2.129

8. The principles contained here may be further developed and refined by the Commission in individual cases when appropriate in light of future developments. The specificity of an individual case or particular circumstances may require an adaptation of, or deviation from, these Best Practices. The recommendations contained in this document should be interpreted in light of procedural and resource constraints.

2. Best Practices Regarding the Content and Presentation of Economic and Econometric Submissions

9. Economic reasoning is employed in competition cases notably in order to develop in a consistent manner or, conversely, to rebut because of its inconsistency, the economic evidence and arguments in a given case.

10. Any economic model which explicitly or implicitly supports a theoretical claim must rely on assumptions that are consistent with the facts of the industry under consideration. These assumptions should be carefully laid out and the sensitivity of its predictions to changes to the assumptions should be made explicit. While it is not necessary for economic submissions to actually formalize verbal arguments in a model, this will sometimes be helpful to clearly spell out the assumptions underlying an argument, to check its logic consistency, to assess effects of a high degree of complexity, or to use the model as the theoretical basis for an empirical estimation[6].

Notes

[6] If an economic submission is well-reasoned, then the fact that a particular argument is "theoretical" or "general" is often a strength rather than a weakness of the submission. This is the case when one has deduced a general conclusion (which holds irrespective of the precise magnitudes of the parameters of the analysis) from a set of assumptions that are considered consistent with the facts of the case. For instance, an economic submission may try to substantiate that irrespective of the size or existence of efficiencies, a particular conduct cannot possibly harm consumers.

11. An economic analysis may support an assessment of the anticompetitive or pro-competitive effects of a merger. Such analysis usually involves a comparison of the actual or likely future situation in the relevant market with the absence of the proposed merger.

12. By their very nature, economic models and arguments are based on simplifications of reality. It is therefore normally not sufficient to disprove a particular argument or model, to point out that it is "based on seemingly unrealistic assumptions". It is also necessary to explicitly identify which

aspects of reality should be better reflected in the model or argumentation, and to indicate why this would alter the conclusions.

13. In many cases, economic theory is used to develop a testable hypothesis that is later checked against the data. In that case, the economic analysis makes predictions about reality that can be tested by observations and potentially rejected or verified. Thus, whenever feasible, an economic model should be accompanied by an appropriate empirical model — i.e. a model which is capable of testing the relevant hypotheses given the data available.

14. Very often simple but well focused measurement of economic variables (prices, cost, margins, capacity constraints, R&D intensity) will provide important insights into the significance of particular factors. Occasionally, more advanced statistical and econometric techniques may provide more useful evidence[7]. In any case, otherwise valid economic analysis may not always produce unambiguous results when applied to the facts of a competition or merger case. Contradictions may result from differences in the data, differences in the approach to economic modelling or in the assumptions used to interpret the data or differences in the empirical techniques and methodologies.

Notes

[7] For instance, an econometric analysis of the extent to which prices of an undertaking have been affected by the observed entry of a competitor may provide evidence of the competitive constraint exercised by that entrant. In turn this could provide insights with respect to the likely degree of harm, that would result if an incumbent dominant undertaking were to engage in practices resulting in anticompetitive foreclosure in that or related markets.

15. The following sections provide practical advice on the generation and communication of economic and econometric analyses. The goal of these recommendations is to ensure that every economic or econometric analysis developed by any party involved submitted for consideration in a case states to the largest possible extent the economic reasoning and the observations on which it relies and explains the relevance of its findings and the robustness of the results. This should allow the Commission and all interested parties to scrutinise the economic evidence submitted during the proceedings so as to avoid that empirical results that are not robust be disguised as such and key assumptions in theoretical reasoning be presented as innocuous. Economic or econometric analysis that does not strictly meet the standards set out in these Best Practices will normally be attached less probative value than otherwise and may not be taken into consideration.

2.1. Formulating the relevant question

16. The first step in any economic analysis, theoretical or empirical, is the formulation of a question that is relevant to the case at hand.

17. The question of interest should be:
    (a) precisely formulated so that its answer can be interpreted without ambiguity,
    (b) properly motivated taking into account the nature of the competition or merger case, the institutional features of the markets under consideration and the relevant economic theory[8].

Notes

[8] Occasionally the parties might submit a literature survey or review regarding an economic question of particular relevance for the case. A literature review may be useful when it is accompanied by an explanation on the merits and shortcomings, of the existing studies and explains how the party's own reasoning or analysis relates to past research, academic or otherwise.

18. An economic or econometric report should explicitly formulate not only the hypothesis to be tested (the "null hypothesis"[9]) but also the alternative hypothesis (or hypotheses) under consideration, so that rejection of the null hypothesis can be properly interpreted[10].

Notes

[9] The null hypothesis is generally that which is presumed to be true initially. A null hypothesis is a hypothesis set up to be nullified or refuted in order to support an alternative hypothesis.

[10] For example, consider an empirical project aimed at testing whether certain conduct would lead to higher prices. One could define as the null hypothesis that prices did not increase in which case a rejection of the null hypothesis would imply that the agreement had a positive price impact. Alternatively, one could have defined as the null hypothesis that prices did not change as a result of the agreement. A rejection of the null hypothesis in that case would be harder to interpret: did prices rise or fall as a result of the specific relationship between buyer and seller?

19. Sometimes, an empirical exercise which is being carried out may provide only partial verification of an accompanying economic model or theory of competitive effects. This evidence may be nonetheless useful but should be properly qualified[11].

Notes

[11] For example, the analysis of scanner data (retail prices and quantities) may provide valuable evidence in the context of a merger between producers of fast moving consumption goods, even when the direct impact of the transaction would be felt at the wholesale level and not at the consumer level.

2.2. Data relevance and reliability

20. The intrinsic quality of an economic theory depends on the extent to which the underlying assumptions match the corresponding economic facts. Likewise, empirical analysis depends on the relevance and the reliability of the underlying data.
21. First, it is necessary to identify the relevant facts to validate the theoretical assumptions and employ data which is appropriate to respond to the empirical question under investigation[12].

Notes

[12] For example when discounts are important, the analysis of the price impact of a merger, agreement or practice must focus on prices paid by consumers rather than on list prices.

22. Second, not all facts can be observed or measured with high accuracy and most datasets are incomplete or otherwise imperfect. Hence, parties and/or the Commission should become familiar with the facts and data and acknowledge its limitations explicitly. As regards quantitative data, for example, this requires (i) a thorough inspection of the data, including summary statistics and graphs, and (ii) a sufficient understanding of how the data were gathered, the sample selection process, the measurement of the variables and whether they bear a close relationship with their theoretical counterparts. Quantitative data may contain anomalies because of miscoding or other errors, which should be discussed with the data providers to decide how to best adjust the data to address these problems.
23. Failure to observe and validate all key assumptions or deficiencies in the data should not prevent an economic analysis to be given weight, though caution must be exercised before relying on its conclusions[13]. Furthermore, statistical techniques have been developed to deal with measurement errors, missing observations and sample selection problems. While these techniques may not be able to improve the data, they may help to deal with some of its imperfections.

Notes

[13] For example, assumptions regarding firms' expectations regarding the identity of the market leader may be inferred indirectly through observation of which firm first announces its future prices.

2.3. Choice of empirical methodology

24. The choice of methodology to empirically test a hypothesis or to validate the predictions of an economic model should be properly motivated, and its pros and cons should be made explicit, including potential identification problems[14].

Notes

[14] Problems of inference can be separated into statistical and identification problems. Studies of identification seek to characterize the conclusions that could be drawn if one could use the sampling process to obtain an unlimited number of observations. Studies of statistical inference seek to characterize the generally weaker conclusions that can be drawn from a finite number of observations.

25. Identification can be understood as clarifying the basis upon which one theory can be preferred to another. Similarly, the term can be used to refer to any situation where an econometric model will invariably have more than one set of parameters which generate the same distribution of observations.

26. One should explain how the chosen methodology exploits the variation in the data, to at least partially discriminate between the tested (or null) hypothesis and the alternative hypotheses. At the very least, an economic model or argument should generate predictions that are consistent with a significant number of relevant observed facts.

27. The choice of methodology must take due account of (a) the dataset and its potential limitations, (b) the features of the market under investigation, and (c) the economic issues under consideration—i.e., it should be designed to test the hypothesis of interest (see also section 2.1 above).

28. If statistical and/or econometric methods are used, it is strongly recommended that important methodological choices are explicitly justified, in particular:
    i)   specification (what is the range of sensible general forms for the relationship under evaluation, including the relevant variables, the way they could interact, and the nature of errors or uncertainty?).
    ii) observation (how well do the measurements approximate the variables they are intended to represent?).
    iii) estimation (what do the data in the sample suggest as to the range of plausible relationships among variables?).

29. Moreover, a reasoned justification should be given when applying statistical techniques that deviate from generally accepted methods commonly used to assess the question of interest. In particular, one should motivate the changes, describe the modified technique or model, and document the likely biases, if any, that the new or adapted method is likely to introduce.

30. In general, it is recommended to follow a "bottom-up" approach. In the context of multiple regression analysis, this would mean estimating simple models first and then engage in more refined estimation exercises if necessary in order to avoid bias[15]. Large-scale surveys of final consumers may usefully supplement qualitative or other documentary evidence obtained from targeted requests of information to market participants. Whilst the evidential value of replies to information requests from market participants lies in the substance of the information provided by players with intrinsic industry or market knowledge, the specific purpose of large-scale surveys of final consumers is to obtain statistically relevant data in order to estimate the characteristics, behaviour and views of a larger group of final consumers from the responses received from a smaller sample. The objectives of a high quality sample survey should be specific, clear-cut and unambiguous. Further, the definition of the relevant population of consumers (and the associated sampling frame) is crucial because there may be systematic differences in the responses of various differentiated consumer segments. Identification of a survey population must be followed by selection of a sample that accurately represents that population. The researcher can apply probability sampling in large-scale surveys of final consumers to some aspects of respondent selection to reduce the likelihood of biased selection[16].

Notes

[15] For example, it is sound practice to estimate an Ordinary Least Squares (OLS) regression first and then, to the extent endogeneity is suspected to be a problem in the case at hand, move on to an instrumental variable (IV) estimation.
[16] Probability samples range from simple random samples to complex multistage sampling designs that use stratification, clustering of population elements into various groupings, or both. In simple random sampling, the most basic type of probability sampling, every element in the population has a known, equal probability of being included in the sample, and all possible samples of a given size are equally likely to be selected. In all forms of probability sampling, each element in the relevant population has a known, nonzero probability of being included in the sample.

31. The use of probability sampling techniques in large-scale surveys of final consumers enhances both the reliability and representativeness of the survey results and the ability to assess the accuracy of quantitative estimates obtained from the survey as regards the relevant population of consumers. Probability sampling in large-scale surveys of final consumers offers two important advantages over other types of sampling. First, the sample can provide an unbiased quantitative estimate of the responses of the relevant consumers from which the sample was drawn; that is, the

expected value of the sample estimate is the population value being estimated. Second, the researcher can calculate a confidence interval that describes explicitly how reliable the sample estimate of the population is likely to be.

32. If possible, given time and data constraints, conducting multiple empirical analyses relying on different methodologies would help determine whether the conclusions of the empirical investigation are robust to different tests or models (see also section 2.5 below).

2.4. Reporting and interpreting the results

33. The results of economic and econometric analysis must be presented clearly, taking the reader through each step of the reasoning[17]. All empirical analysis, even descriptive statistics of relevant variables (e.g. price series) should be accompanied by all the documentation needed to allow timely replication, as well as a deep understanding of the methodology of any prior data management efforts. Reports which do not allow for replication and in particular econometric analysis not including the code and data in electronic form will receive less consideration and are consequently unlikely to be given much weight.

Notes

[17] Any mathematical notation should either (a) follow the standard notation in the literature or (b) be very self-explanatory.

34. An empirical submission should not only discuss the statistical significance of the results but also their practical relevance. In general, with very large samples coefficients may be statistically significant even if they are of trivial magnitude[18]. This creates the potentially misleading impression that certain variables are important. Therefore, the magnitude of the coefficients must always be examined and discussed. This requires interpreting the results in connection with the hypothesis that is being tested, so as to draw implications for the case under investigation.

Notes

[18] Statistical significance is determined, in part, by the number of observations in the data set. The more observations used to calculate the regression coefficients, the smaller the standard error of each coefficient. A smaller standard error reflects less random variability in the estimated coefficient (or estimate). Other things being equal, the statistical significance of a regression coefficient increases as the sample size increases. If the data set is sufficiently large, results that are economically significant are often also statistically significant. However, when the sample size is small it is not uncommon to obtain results that are economically significant but statistically insignificant.

35. Commonly, results from economic analysis and statistical information are presented in tables. Although it is not necessary to comment on or restate every piece of information that a table contains an interpretation of the data in it must be provided.

36. The results of the empirical analyses should be reported in the standard format found in academic papers. For example, when reporting multiple regression results, one should report on the statistical significance[19] of the parameter estimates by following the convention of reporting coefficients, p-values, standard errors and the size of the sample. Where the coefficient of interest is economically significant, the emphasis should be on statistically significant findings, for example to the 5% or 10% level (i.e. p-value<0.05 or 0.10). However, just because some hypothesis cannot be rejected in a statistical sense does not necessarily mean that the empirical analysis has no evidentiary value.

Notes

[19] A statistically significant result is one that is unlikely to have occurred by chance. In hypothesis testing, the significance level is the criterion used for rejecting the null hypothesis. The p-value is the probability of obtaining a test statistic at least as extreme as the one that was actually observed, assuming that the null hypothesis is true. If the obtained p-value is smaller than or equal to the significance level, then the null hypothesis is rejected and the outcome is said to be statistically significant.

37. It may be that a particular analysis can be criticized in terms of its accuracy. However, it is often possible to evaluate that inaccuracy, for example by providing confidence intervals around an estimate. Also, depending on the question of interest, an approximate economic or econometric result can be informative if, for example, it is the direction of the effects rather than its magnitude

that are most relevant. Similarly a particular estimate may be criticized because some facet of the methodology introduces bias. However, it is often the case that an estimate is biased in a particular direction; if this is the case it may be known that the estimate is too large, or too small. This may not matter in the context of a particular case. If it is known that the estimate is too large, and yet it is insufficient in size to reach some critical value, then the bias does not invalidate the conclusion that the critical value will not be reached. Detailed information should also be provided on all other specification tests and statistical diagnoses (see also section 2.5 on robustness).

38. The results of any statistical or econometric analysis should also be assessed with respect to the relevant economic theory[20]. When discussing the results of a multiple regression analysis, this requirement includes assessing not only the coefficient(s) of direct interest, but also the coefficients of all other explanatory variables, as they often provide a signal on the reliability of the analysis. For example, a finding that the sign of a particular coefficient is counter to what would be expected by economic theory[21] may be an indication of an omitted-variable problem[22], a selection bias[23], or some other identification problem[24].

Notes

[20] For example, econometric estimates of the elasticity of demand for a given product implying an upward sloping demand curve should be discarded in almost all cases, unless the product in question can be shown to be a Giffen good— i.e., a product for which a rise in price of this product makes people buy even more of the product.

[21] For example, a study showing that an increase in the marginal costs of production of a given good is associated with lower prices for that product should, ceteris paribus, be discarded automatically.

[22] That is, when a relevant explanatory variable, which is correlated with the dependent variable has been omitted from the analysis, so that the coefficients of some or all other explanatory variables suffer from a bias of a priori unknown sign or magnitude.

[23] The bias that arises when the selection process influences the availability of data in a way that is related to the dependent variable.

[24] See note 13 *supra*.

---

39. In the case of large-scale surveys of final consumers the report should disclose essential information about how the research was conducted to allow judging the reliability and validity of the results. All data must be fully documented and made available (subject to appropriate safeguards to maintain privacy and confidentiality). Non-sampling error, in particular the non-response rate and response bias[25] should also be taken into account in the analysis. Conclusions from large-scale surveys of final consumers should be carefully distinguished from the factual findings.

Notes

[25] Response bias refers to situations where, for a host of reasons, respondents fail to answer questions truthfully, fully and/or were influenced by the interviewer.

2.5. Robustness (non implemented proposal: place robustness before reporting)

40. Economic and econometric analysis should to the greatest possible extent be accompanied by a thorough robustness analysis, except where its absence is appropriately justified. In any event, any formal economic model or econometric analysis needs to be generally consistent and reasonably predict observed past outcomes and behaviour.

41. Other common robustness checks that may be appropriate include assessing whether empirical results are sensitive to changes in (a) the data, (b) the choice of empirical method, and (c) the precise modelling assumptions[26]. Similarly, the relevance and credibility of an economic model can be significantly enhanced if accompanied by a sensitivity analysis with respect to the key variables.

Notes

[26] For example, in a multiple regression analysis, one should indicate whether the results are severely affected by how the variables were defined, by the set of explanatory variables incorporated to the analysis, or the functional form.

---

42. It is strongly recommended to address explicitly (i) to what extent, the results of the analysis are in line with past results using similar methods, and whether the results can be generalised[27].

Congruent and convergent results based on methods supported by academic and practitioners' are likely to be given greater significance than widely divergent results.

Notes

[27] For example, if the elasticity of demand for a given product has been estimated for a given country, where data is available, but the case at hand would require estimates of the elasticity of demand for various countries, one should consider whether or not, and under which assumptions, her results for one country apply to the others. Similarly, if an economic model assumes that firms make take-it-or-leave- it offers when interacting with intermediate buyers with certain characteristics, it may be necessary to assess whether such assumption extends to all types of intermediate buyers.

2.6. Further recommendations

43. The credibility of an economic submission may be enhanced when the limitations with regards to accuracy or explanatory power of the underlying data and methodology are explicitly acknowledged. In this regard it is often advisable to address rather than minimize uncertainty.

44. The parties rely sometimes on data that they do not have the means to audit and verify. Hence, they should be careful not to misleadingly present economic opinions as statements of fact. The sources of information should be carefully acknowledged, and the facts properly documented and described without ambiguity. This applies whether the economic or econometric analysis is a stand alone report or part of a broader submission.

45. It is advisable that the parties consult DG Competition regarding the types of empirical analyses that they consider useful in testing the anticompetitive and/or efficiencies theories. In particular, the parties can suggest potential analyses which may be easier for DG Competition to conduct, given its access to data from third parties. DG Competition, in turn, may propose analyses it believes might be useful for the parties to conduct. Similarly, it is recommended that the parties consult the DG Competition regarding the most suitable robustness checks for a given methodology. Experience suggests that such consultation can be most effective if the parties are prepared to share any relevant preliminary results in advance of a formal submission.

46. Where economic submissions rely on quantitative data the parties should provide the data and codes timely, in an appropriate format and in accordance with the criteria laid down in section 3 of this document. In particular, the absence of all the necessary elements needed for replication and assessment of an economic submission can constitute grounds for not taking it further into consideration.

47. When granting access to the file, the Commission may provide upon request the data and codes underlying its final economic analysis or, to the extent that they have been made available to the Commission, that of third parties on which it intends to rely or take into account. Where necessary to protect the confidentiality of other parties' data, access to the data and codes will be granted only at Commission premises in a so-called data room procedure[28], subject to strict confidentiality obligations and secure procedures[29]. Third parties or complainants are equally expected to submit all the underlying data used in the analysis. They are also expected to authorise the Commission, where appropriate, to offer data room access to the parties upon request.

Notes

[28] See Commission Notice on Best Practices for the conduct of proceedings concerning Articles 101 and 102, paragraphs 97 and 98.

[29] Similarly, the Commission will endeavour to organise access to a data room, normally to the parties' economic advisors and external counsel, if necessary to ensure their rights of defence are fully respected.

---

48. When conducting large-scale surveys of final consumers to address a case-specific issue the parties might want to involve the Commission in the questionnaire development and design[30]. Subject to time and resource constraints it is often desirable to conduct a pre-test or pilot[31].

Notes

[30] Occasionally, the Commission may take the initiative to commission its own large scale consumer survey. In that case, it will normally consult the parties and interested third parties on the questionnaire design and instruments of data collection, subject to confidentiality safeguards and to the extent such consultation does not delay or otherwise jeopardize the investigation.

[31] All questions should be pretested to ensure that (i) questions are understood by respondents, (ii) can be properly administered by interviewers, and (iii) do not adversely affect survey cooperation.

3. Best Practices on Responding to Requests for Quantitative Data

49. Pursuant to Article 18 of Regulation 1/2003 and Article 11 of the Merger Regulation, the Commission is empowered, in order to carry out its duties, to require undertakings and associations of undertakings to provide it with all necessary information. It is the Commission that defines the scope and the format of requests for information.

50. Most competition or merger investigations involve (1) collecting data, (2) analyzing data, and (3) drawing inferences from data. In most antitrust and merger cases, the Commission will gather evidence by sending targeted requests for information pursuant to Article 11 of the Merger Regulation and Article 18 of Regulation 1/2003 to the main players in the market (e.g. competitors, direct customers and other parties with specific knowledge of the market). This document, however, provides specific guidance to respond to a request for quantitative data[32]. However, many of the principles here identified apply, more generally, to responses to any request for economic information, quantitative or qualitative.

Notes

[32] For statistical purposes, "quantitative data" means a series of observations or measurements, expressed as numbers. A statistic may refer to a particular numerical value, derived from the data. For example, an HHI measure and a correlation coefficient are statistics.

---

51. Quantitative data may help the Commission to conduct statistical analysis to define markets, establish a counterfactual, assess the potential anti-competitive effects of a notified merger, validate efficiency claims or predict the impact of remedies. In order to do that the Commission needs to get accurate data, with sufficient time to analyze it.

52. The Commission is aware of the costs that its procedures may impose on undertakings. An important objective of this section is, therefore, to provide recommendations to reduce the burden on the involved parties and on the Commission posed by the production and processing of quantitative data, while at the same time ensuring and enhancing the effectiveness of the Commission's substantive review.

53. These best practices are intended as general guidance and do not supersede any specific instructions in any Data Request issued by the Commission in specific cases.

3.1. General motivation for Data Requests

54. The primary objective of a Data Request is to obtain accurate information concerning quantitative variables such as prices, turnover, capacity and entry or exit decisions within the possible relevant markets over a reasonable period. Quantitative data may be necessary to understand current market conditions and competitive dynamics. In some cases, reliable quantitative data may allow to conduct statistical or econometric analysis to be submitted as evidence in an antitrust or merger investigation.

55. The Commission will endeavour to ask for the appropriate amount of data to carry out the required analyses. The Commission is mindful of time constraints and must balance the usefulness of each request against the time left before any legal or procedural deadline. In appropriate cases, DG Competition may discuss in advance with the addressees or other affected parties the scope and the format of the Data Request. DG Competition may also explain the analysis that it intends to perform with the requested data in order to improve the efficiency of the data collecting process and to ensure the data is of adequate quality. This is particularly the case in the later stages of an investigation as early requests could be of a more general nature and aimed primarily at better understanding the functioning of the market in question.

56. The Commission will carefully consider what the proper sample to characterize a population is. Inferences from the part to the whole are justified only when the sample is representative[33].

Notes

[33] For example, in certain circumstances it may be appropriate to limit the data request to a certain representative subset of the involved firms' customers, or to a particular geographic market which stands out for a valid given reason.

---

57. A further issue that may influence the scope of the Data Request is whether third party data will be necessary and available to conduct any meaningful analysis.

3.2. Common elements of a Data Request

58. Examples of data necessary for a competition investigation include data on costs, output, sales, prices, capacity, product characteristics, delivery flows, customer characteristics, tender details, entry barriers, business strategies, and market shares of the parties involved and of the other participants in the relevant market.

59. The source of the information can be the parties involved in the procedure, third parties, trade associations, trade press, independent consultants, survey information or government sources.

60. Data may be costly to collect or hardly accessible in the relevant time frame. Often, however, requests for quantitative data in merger proceedings seek data that is readily available to the involved parties. Readily available data refers to data that is routinely collected and maintained for a reasonable period as part of the firm's normal business operations, for example to inform business strategy or for internal reporting. Readily available data also includes data that is regularly purchased from third parties, such as scanner data or survey data[34]. In any event, in its investigations, the Commission is not limited to request only data that is readily available to the parties (see point 77 below). Deadlines for submitting data which is difficult or costly to retrieve will be decided by the Commission on a case-by-case basis.

Notes

[34] Where econometric analyses are to be conducted, the sample needs to be of sufficient size for meaningful inference. For instance, in the absence of cross-section variability, requests would generally cover at least a three year period of monthly observations.

61. A Data Request often includes the following sections, but each request will be tailored to the specific information needs and circumstances of the case:
    (i) a glossary of terms, in particular key variables;
    (ii) a list of the variables;
    (iii) for each variable: the units of measurement; the level of aggregation over time (e.g. monthly); the time range (e.g. the last three fiscal years) and the geographic scope (e.g. countries, regions or cities);
    (iv) the preferred electronic format (stata file, excel file, etc);
    (v) suggestions or specific requests on data formatting, variable classification and tests to detect data inconsistencies;
    (vi) deadline for compliance with the request.

62. In some instances, particularly where data is requested from different parties, DG Competition may provide a template to ensure all submissions are compatible and can be efficiently combined with minimal risk of error.

3.3. Main criteria to consider when responding to a Data Request

63. Responses to a Data Request must be: (i) complete, (ii) correct, and (iii) timely.

64. The Commission may impose on undertakings and associations of undertakings fines where, intentionally or negligently, they supply incorrect or misleading information or when, in response to a request made by decision, they supply incomplete information or do not supply information within the required time-limit[35]. Furthermore, in merger cases, the relevant time limits for initiating proceedings and for the adoption of decisions may exceptionally be suspended where, owing to circumstances for which one of the undertakings involved in the concentration is responsible, the Commission has had to request information by decision or to order an inspection[36].

Notes

[35] Article 23(1)(a) and (b) of Regulation 1/2003 and Article 14(1)(a), (b) and (c) of the Merger Regulation.
[36] Article 10(4) of the Merger Regulation, but see also Article 8(6) thereof.

3.3.1. *Completeness*

65. The parties should provide all data requested, in any of the stated formats and follow indications regarding presentation and consistency checks. Subsidiary data that is necessary to construct or to understand any variable requested should also be provided, except when adequately justified and with prior approval by the Commission.

66. It is strongly encouraged that problems of missing data are flagged to the Commission well in advance of the deadline for compliance with the Data Request to allow, if appropriate, for either a modification of the request or an extension of the deadline. Any data missing from the original Data Request must be adequately justified. In any event, a response to a Data Request may not be considered complete unless accompanied by a memo:

    (i) describing the data compilation process: from raw data through aggregation and merging operations to the final database submitted. How was the sample selected and was it necessary to eliminate certain kinds of observations;

    (ii) identifying all relevant sources;

    (iii) labelling and thoroughly describing all variables;

    (iv) reporting on the reasons for potential measurement error such as missing information or any changes in the collection process;

    (v) describing any assumptions and estimations used to fill incomplete data; and

    (vi) reporting on consistency checking and all data cleaning operations.

3.3.2. *Correctness*

67. It is up to interested parties to ensure the correctness of the data submitted. Tests for accuracy of all variables should always be undertaken and reported[37].

Notes

[37] For example, negative sales volumes or zero transaction prices are normally inaccurate and are often indicative of data extraction errors, systematic measurement errors or inadequate accounting of rebates or taxes.

---

68. In order to detect incorrectness in data it will be expected that consistency checks are performed and documented prior to submission. In particular:

    i) Responses to the Data Request should be consistent with responses provided to other requests for information (e.g. turnover, market shares, etc);

    ii) Individual values within a variable must be consistent with the economic reality[38];

    iii) When aggregation of raw data is necessary, one needs to ensure the aggregation algorithm is sensible and applied consistently;

    iv) Coherence between different variables is necessary[39];

    v) Over time consistency across and within variables must also be ensured.

Notes

[38] For example, transaction prices (net of discounts) should generally be positive, missing or unexpected values (i.e. sales not in line with historical levels) should be checked.

[39] For example, shipments of one product must be related to shipments of any by-products. Also, charged prices should generally remain above transportation costs (i.e. ex-works negative prices cast doubts on either the correctness of the charged price and/or the transportation cost).

3.3.3. *Timely submission*

69. Deadlines for responses to Data Requests must be strictly respected. Where parties plan to submit data in connection with an empirical analysis conducted at their own initiative, it is useful to warn in advance DG Competition of the planned timing and scope of such a submission. Results that the parties intend to rely upon or discuss in a meeting with DG Competition should be submitted, including data and code to facilitate replication, at least 2 working days before the said meeting.

3.4. Other Recommendations

70. This section sets down further recommended best practices concerning responses to a Data Request.

3.4.1. *Cooperation in good-faith*

71. Data production is an area where cooperation between the parties and the Commission is especially important. The parties will need to explain clearly the complexities that can be associated with requests that the Commission may regard as simple[40]. The Commission endeavours to define its requests as specifically and quickly as possible so the parties can understand what is

being sought. This dialogue may help both sides deal more efficiently with data issues. In any event, it is for the Commission to decide the scope, format and timing of the Data Request.

Notes

[40] Why, for example, it may be difficult, impossible or useless to simply "turn over" a "database," or the burdens and costs associated with providing data in the manner the Commission seeks.

72. It is important to emphasise in that regard that the integrity and efficiency of the process are undermined if, inter alia, the parties make representations about what data exist without reasonably diligent efforts to confirm their accuracy, if they ignore a carefully drafted and limited Data Request and produce large amounts of data points disregarding the submission format, scope, or data processing requirements, if they use non-obvious "definitions" of common terms in construing requests, or if they make unilateral and undisclosed inferences about what the Commission is effectively seeking.

3.4.2. Early consultation with the Commission to inform about what type of data is available

73. In some cases, the burden of compliance with Data Requests may be significantly reduced if the parties inform the Commission at the earliest opportunity on the availability of quantitative data. Early consultation allows to determine not only what data is available and its suitability, but also in what form it can be provided, thereby making it easier and faster for the parties to provide the data, in the event the Commission makes a Data Request. However, the Commission is not limited to request only data that is readily available to the parties.

74. To make these early discussions fruitful, parties must be prepared to thoroughly explain their information management systems and should be prepared to discuss certain issues such as: every field of information captured, how the underlying data is collected and formatted, the frequency of collection, what software is used, the size of the data set, what reports are routinely generated from that database, etc. It is recommended that the involved firms provide any written documentation and/or training materials to the Commission in advance of any discussion. It is also generally useful that parties create a diagram to show how the relevant data is distributed throughout the organization. In any event, as a general rule, parties should provide relevant documents to support their contentions concerning the availability, scope and production time of quantitative data.

75. Preliminary meetings or telephone conversations with those responsible for data collection or analysis in the firms are often quite useful. Parties are advised to make such personnel available as early as possible. These discussions should involve descriptions of the type of electronic (or other) data that the parties maintain (both in the ordinary course of business and what is archived, and in what form).

76. In the case of mergers, pre-notification discussions should routinely deal with data issues. Although, the Commission will endeavour to identify all issues that may require a Data Request as soon as possible, certain issues may not be identified until later in the proceedings.

3.4.3. Consultation on a Draft Data Requests and data samples

77. When appropriate and useful, DG Competition will send a "draft" Data Request for quantitative data in order to facilitate a better identification of the format, and to allow for basic consistency checks (see section 3.3.2). The purpose of the draft Data Request is to invite parties to propose any modifications that could alleviate the compliance burden while producing the necessary information. Any reduction on the scope of the Data Request can only be accepted if it does not risk harming the investigation and may trigger, particularly in merger cases, a reduction in the deadline for response initially anticipated.

78. In this connection, providing samples of the data is generally very helpful as it helps the Commission to determine what data is available and would be useful. As a result, on the basis of the sample it may be possible to draft a more focused Data Request, limiting the eventual burden on the parties.

3.4.4. Transparency regarding data collection, formatting and submission

79. A transparent process allows for all parties involved to be aware of any incidences during the data collection process and thus react more rapidly and effectively.

Part B   Procedural Matters

80. The parties are advised to submit quantitative data in a format that minimises the time and manipulation required to process the data for analysis. Parties should always be able to answer all the following questions:
    i) How applicable is the data to the analyses under consideration;
    ii) How reliable or "clean" is the data;
    iii) Is it enough to conduct a meaningful analysis;
    iv) What institutional factors specific to the industry setting and/or company may impact the proper interpretation of the data?

81. The involved parties should draw the Commission's attention early on to any limitations in the data. They should make clear how raw data has been compiled and what steps have been taken to ensure its reliability[41].

Notes

[41] For example, if the raw data is based on a sample of individual customer accounts, an explanation of how these accounts have been chosen and why they are representative of all customers should also be provided.

82. The involved parties are also strongly encouraged to conduct their own descriptive analysis to detect data problems before submitting the data to the Commission. Also the Commission may sometimes welcome efforts by the involved parties to deal with any remaining data imperfections using statistical analysis. In some cases statistics allow in various ways to average out errors in measurement and yield statistically sound estimates. All such statistical analysis should be adequately reported. In any event, raw data should be provided wherever possible because the aggregation and cleaning of data may have a significant impact on the outcome of statistical or econometric analysis. Also parties should provide the program files that manipulate, clean and complete the raw data in preparation for the analysis.

3.4.5. Direct access

83. In some instances, the Commission will accept that as part of its response to a Data Request the involved parties provide direct electronic access to the underlying data. This alternative can provide an inexpensive and fast way to provide access to large amounts of data. Limited direct access can also provide a means to assess the value of certain corporate information.

84. The terms and conditions for direct access can be discussed in advance, addressing issues such as the availability of technical assistance, the ability to print or otherwise retrieve the data, the number of log-ins the company should provide, assurances that the activities of the services of the Commission will not be tracked, that underlying data will not be removed without agreement of the Commission and, most importantly, continued access throughout the entire course of the investigation. In limited instances, when providing direct access to corporate resources is unworkable, the Commission may submit a set of queries to the firm so that reports can be generated.

ANNEX I

STRUCTURE AND BASIC ELEMENTS OF A SOUND EMPIRICAL SUBMISSION

This Annex briefly describes how to structure an empirical submission in a competition or merger case according with the principles set out in the preceding sections (esp. section 2 above). A sound economic or econometric submission should contain the following sections and elements:

A. THE RELEVANT QUESTION

— The research question must be: (i) formulated unambiguously and (ii) properly motivated, taking into account both the nature of the competition issue, the institutional features of the markets and industries under consideration, and the relevant economic theory.

— The hypothesis to be tested (or null hypothesis) must be clearly spelled out as well as the alternative hypothesis or hypotheses under consideration.

B. The data

— A clear description of data sources must be provided as well as hard copies of the databases employed in the analysis. Normally, an accompanying memo would describe how previous intermediate data sets and programs were employed to create the final dataset as well as the software code employed to generate the final dataset. All efforts made to correct for anomalies in the data should be clearly explained.

— One should also report how the data were gathered, the sample selection process, the measurement of the variables and whether they match with their theoretical counterparts, etc.

— In addition, the data should be thoroughly described. This includes reporting the sample time frame and the statistical population under consideration, the units of observation, a clear definition of each variable, any data cleaning procedures, etc. This information should be accompanied by descriptive statistics (including means, standard errors, maximums, minimums, correlations, and histograms, residual plots, etc) of all relevant variables.

C. Methodology

— The choice of empirical methodology should be properly motivated. One should discuss their methodological choices in light of: (a) their data limitations, (b) the features of the market under investigation, and (c) the economic issues under consideration (the relevant question).

— Alternative methodologies should also be discussed and if possible, given time and data constraints, employed to verify the robustness of the results to the choice of model. An economic model or argument must generate predictions that are consistent with a significant number of relevant observed facts.

D. Results and implications

— Parties should explain the details of their models, and share any documentation needed to allow timely replication (e.g. the programming code used to run the analysis).

— The results of the empirical analyses should be reported in the standard format found in academic papers. For example, when reporting multiple regression results, one should report both the estimated coefficients and their standard errors for all relevant variables. They should also provide detailed information on all other specification tests and statistical diagnoses.

— One should discuss not only the statistical significance of their results but also their practical relevance. This requires interpreting the results in connection with the hypothesis that is being tested, so as to draw implications for the case under investigation. The results of the statistical and econometric analyses should also be assessed with respect to the relevant economic theory.

E. Robustness tests

— All empirical work should be accompanied by a thorough robustness analysis that (i) checks whether the empirical results are sensitive to changes in the data, the choice of empirical method, and the precise modelling assumptions; (ii) tests whether the results of the analysis can be generalised; and (iii) compares the results of the empirical work in question with previous results in the relevant literature.

— An economic model should generally be accompanied by a sensitivity analysis with respect to the key variables, to the extent only the plausible but not the exact value of each variable can be determined. All results from the sensitivity analysis conducted should also be reported and not only those that support the argument.

B18

COMMISSION NOTICE ON BEST PRACTICES FOR THE CONDUCT OF PROCEEDINGS CONCERNING ARTICLES 101 AND 102 TFEU

(Text with EEA relevance)

(2011/C 308/06)

Official Journal: C308, 20.10.2011, p.6

Celex number: 52011XC1020(02)

EUR-Lex permanent link: <http://eur-lex.europa.eu/legal-content/EN/TXT/?qid=1395758963115&uri=CELEX:52011XC1020(02)>

TABLE OF CONTENTS

Commentary
Notice: B&C: 1.074, 13.002, 13.041 F&N: 8.103, 8.250, 8.317, 17.259
points 95–98: B&C: 13.068 F&N: 5.474
points 109–112: B&C: 13.066
points 115–113: B&C: 13.101

---

1. Scope and Purpose of the Notice

1. The principal purpose of this notice is to provide practical guidance on the conduct of proceedings before the European Commission (Commission) concerning Articles 101 and 102 of the Treaty on the Functioning of the European Union (TFEU)[1] in accordance with Regulation (EC) No 1/2003[2], its Implementing Regulation[3] and the case law of the Court of Justice of the European Union. In this regard, the notice seeks to increase understanding of the Commission's investigation process[4] and thereby enhance the efficiency of investigations and ensure a high degree of transparency and predictability in the process. The notice covers the main proceedings[5] concerning alleged infringements of Articles 101 and 102 TFEU.

Notes

[1] With effect from 1 December 2009, Articles 81 and 82 of the EC Treaty have become Articles 101 and 102 respectively of the TFEU. The two sets of provisions are in substance identical. For the purposes of this document, references to Articles 101 and 102 TFEU should be understood as references to Articles 81 and 82 of the EC Treaty when appropriate. [Ed note: please see the Note on the Lisbon Treaty at p.xvii in regard to article renumbering introduced by the Lisbon Treaty.]

[2] Council Regulation (EC) No 1/2003 of 16 December 2002 on the implementation of the rules on competition laid down in Articles [101] and [102] of the Treaty (OJ L 1, 4.1.2003, p.1), as amended by Council Regulation (EC) No 411/2004 of 26 February 2004 repealing Regulation (EEC) No 3975/87 and amending Regulations (EEC) No 3976/87 and (EC) No 1/2003, in connection with air transport between the Community and third countries (OJ L 68, 6.3.2004, p.1) and Council Regulation (EC) No 1419/2006 of 25 September 2006 repealing Regulation (EEC) No 4056/86 laying down detailed rules for the application of Articles 85 and 86 of the Treaty to maritime transport, and amending Regulation (EC) No 1/2003 as regards the extension of its scope to include cabotage and international tramp services (OJ L 269, 28.9.2006, p.1).

[3] Commission Regulation (EC) No 773/2004 of 7 April 2004 relating to the conduct of proceedings by the Commission pursuant to Articles [101] and [102] of the [Treaty on the Functioning of the European Union] (OJ L 123, 27.4.2004, p.18), as amended by Commission Regulation (EC) No 622/2008 of 30 June 2008 amending Regulation (EC) No 773/2004, as regards the conduct of settlement procedures in cartel cases (OJ L 171, 1.7.2008, p.3).

[4] This notice applies exclusively to the Commission's procedures for the enforcement of Articles 101 and 102 TFEU and does not concern the national competition authorities when they apply these provisions.

[5] This notice does not deal with specific procedures, for example for imposing fines on undertakings having provided misleading information, refused to submit to inspections or breached seals affixed by officials (see Article 23(1) of Regulation (EC) No 1/2003). It covers neither decisions on interim measures pursuant to Article 8 of Regulation (EC) No 1/2003 nor decisions on finding of inapplicability pursuant to Article 10 of Regulation (EC) No 1/2003.

2. Infringement proceedings against Member States based notably on Article 106 TFEU in conjunction with Articles 101 and 102 TFEU fall outside the scope of this notice. Nor does it apply to proceedings under the Merger Regulation[6] or to State aid proceedings[7].

Commentary
para 2: B&C: 13.039

Notes
[6] See Council Regulation (EC) No 139/2004 of 20 January 2004 on the control of concentrations between undertakings (OJ L 24, 29.1.2004, p.1). See in this respect the Directorate-General for Competition's Best Practices on the conduct of EC Merger Proceedings of 20 January 2004, published on the Directorate-General for Competition's website (http://ec.europa.eu/competition/mergers/legislation/proceedings.pdf).
[7] See Council Regulation (EC) No 659/1999 of 22 March 1999 laying down detailed rules for the application of Article 93 (now Article 108 TFEU) of the EC Treaty (OJ L 83, 27.3.1999, p.1). See in this respect the Commission notice on a Code of Best Practice for the conduct of State aid control procedures (OJ C 136, 16.6.2009, p.13).

3. Proceedings concerning the application of Articles 101 and 102 TFEU (hereafter generally referred to as 'proceedings') are in particular regulated by Regulation (EC) No 1/2003 and the Implementing Regulation. The Commission's notices on access to file[8] and handling of complaints[9], as well as the terms of reference of the hearing officer[10] are also relevant for the conduct of proceedings. As regards submissions of reports of economic experts and submission of quantitative data, reference is made to the Best Practices on the submission of economic evidence[11]. This notice should therefore not be taken as an exhaustive account of all measures governing proceedings before the Commission. The notice should be read in conjunction with other such instruments and any relevant jurisprudence.

Notes
[8] Commission notice on the rules for access to the Commission file in cases pursuant to Articles [101] and [102] of the [Treaty on the Functioning of the European Union], Articles 53, 54 and 57 of the EEA Agreement and Council Regulation (EC) No 139/2004 (OJ C 325, 22.12.2005, p.7).
[9] Commission notice on the handling of complaints by the Commission under Articles [101] and [102] of the [Treaty on the Functioning of the European Union] (OJ C 101, 27.4.2004, p.65).
[10] Decision C(2011) 5742 of the President of the European Commission of 13 October 2011 on the function and terms of reference of the hearing officer in certain competition proceedings.
[11] Staff working paper on Best Practices for the submission of economic evidence and data collection in cases concerning the application of Articles 101 and 102 TFEU and merger cases, http://ec.europa.eu/competition/index_en.html

4. The investigation of cartels, as defined in the Leniency Notice[12], may also be subject to the specific procedures on applications for leniency and on settlements[13]. These specific procedures are not covered by this notice. Moreover, the particular nature of cartel proceedings in some circumstances requires special provisions, in order not to interfere with possible leniency applications[14] or settlement discussions[15]. These special provisions are indicated where applicable.

Notes
[12] Commission notice on immunity from fines and reduction of fines in cartel cases (OJ C 298, 8.12.2006, p.17) (Leniency Notice), i.e. secret 'agreements and/or concerted practices between two or more competitors aimed at coordinating their competitive behaviour on the market and/or influencing the relevant parameters of competition through practices such as the fixing of purchase or selling prices or other trading conditions, the allocation of production or sales quotas, the sharing of markets including bid-rigging, restrictions of imports or exports and/or anti-competitive actions against other competitors. Such practices are among the most serious violations of (Article 101 TFEU)'.
[13] Commission Regulation (EC) No 622/2008 of 30 June 2008 amending Regulation (EC) No 773/2004, as regards the conduct of settlement procedures in cartel cases (OJ L 171, 1.7.2008, p.3); Commission notice on the conduct of settlement procedures in view of the adoption of Decisions pursuant to Article 7 and Article 23 of Council Regulation (EC) No 1/2003 in cartel cases OJ C 167, 2.7.2008, p.1.

[14] It should be noted that the Commission may disregard any application for immunity from fines on the ground that it has been submitted after the statement of objections has been issued (see paragraphs 14 and 29 of the Leniency Notice).

[15] The Commission may disregard any application for immunity from fines or reductions of fines under the Leniency Notice on the ground that it has been submitted after the expiry of the time limit set for parties to declare in writing whether they envisage engaging in settlement discussions (see paragraph 13 of the Settlement Notice).

5. This notice is structured in the following way. Section 2 sets out the procedure followed during the investigative phase. This part is relevant for any investigation regardless of whether it leads to a prohibition decision (Article 7 of Regulation (EC) No 1/2003), a commitment decision (Article 9 of Regulation (EC) No 1/2003) or a rejection of complaint decision (Article 7 of the Implementing Regulation). Section 3 describes the main procedural steps and rights of defence in the context of procedures leading to prohibition decisions. Section 4 describes the specific features of the commitment procedure. Section 5 covers rejection of complaints. The remaining sections are of general application: Section 6 describes the limits to use of information, Section 7 deals with the adoption, notification and publication of decisions and Section 8 with future revisions.

6. This notice is notably built upon the experience to date in the application of Regulation (EC) No 1/2003 and the Implementing Regulation. It reflects the views of the Commission at the time of publication and will be applied as from the date of publication for pending[16] and future cases. The specific features of an individual case may however require an adaptation of, or deviation from this notice, depending on the case at issue.

Notes

[16] With regard to cases which are pending at the time of the publication of this document, the latter will apply to any procedural steps that remain to be taken after publication.

7. This notice does not create any new rights or obligations, nor alter, the rights or obligations which arise from the Treaty on the Functioning of the European Union (TFEU), Regulation (EC) No 1/2003, the Implementing Regulation and the case law of the Court of Justice of the European Union.

8. The Commission encourages the use of electronic information (e-mails or digital devices) for any case- related correspondence.

2. The Investigative Phase

2.1. Origin of cases

9. A case concerning an alleged infringement of Article 101 or 102 TFEU may be based on a complaint by undertakings, other natural and legal persons and even Member States.

10. Information from citizens and undertakings is important in triggering investigations by the Commission. The Commission therefore encourages citizens and undertakings to inform it about suspected infringements of the competition rules[17]. This can be done either by lodging a formal complaint[18] or by simply providing market information to the Commission. Anyone who is able to show a legitimate interest as a complainant, and who submits a complaint in compliance with form C[19], enjoys certain procedural rights. The details of the procedure to be followed are set out in the Implementing Regulation and in the notice on the handling of complaints. Natural and legal persons, other than complainants, which show a sufficient interest to be heard and which are admitted to the proceedings by the hearing officer also enjoy certain procedural rights in accordance with Article 13 of the Implementing Regulation.

Notes

[17] Or, when appropriate, the relevant national competition authority.

[18] Pursuant to Article 7(2) of Regulation (EC) No 1/2003. Under Articles 5 to 9 of the Implementing Regulation, formal complaints have to fulfil certain requirements. Information contained in submissions that do not respect these requirements may nevertheless be taken into account as market information.

[19] See Article 5(1) of the Implementing Regulation.

11. The Commission may also open a case on its own initiative (*ex officio*). It may do so when certain facts have been brought to its attention, or further to information gathered in the context of sector enquiries, informal meetings with industry, monitoring of markets or on the basis of information exchanged within the European Competition Network (ECN) or with competition authorities of third countries. Cartel cases can also be initiated on the basis of an application for leniency by one of the cartel members.

2.2. Initial assessment and case allocation

12. All cases, irrespective of their origin, are subject to an initial assessment phase. During this phase the Commission examines whether the case merits further investigation[20] and, if so, provisionally defines its focus, in particular with regard to the parties, the markets and the conduct to be investigated. During this phase, the Commission may make use of investigative measures such as requests for information in accordance with Article 18(2) of Regulation (EC) No 1/2003.

Notes

[20] The Court of Justice of the European Union has recognised that the Commission is entitled to give differing degrees of priority to the complaints that it receives. This is settled case law since Case T-24/90, *Automec v Commission* (hereinafter 'Automec II') (1992) ECR II-2223, para 85.

13. In practice, the system of initial assessment means that some cases will be discarded at a very early stage because they are not deemed to merit further investigation. In this regard, the Commission focuses its enforcement resources on cases where it appears likely that an infringement may be found, in particular on cases with the most significant impact on the functioning of competition in the internal market and risk of consumer harm, as well as on cases which are likely to contribute to defining EU competition policy and/or to ensuring the coherent application of Articles 101 and/or 102 TFEU?[21].

Notes

[21] The Commission has made public a non-exhaustive list of criteria which it intends to use when examining whether or not complaints show a sufficient 'European Union interest'. The criteria were published in the Annual Report on Competition Policy 2005, adopted in June 2006. See as well paragraph 44 of the notice on handling of complaints.

14. This initial assessment phase also attempts to address, at an early stage, the allocation of cases within the ECN. Regulation (EC) No 1/2003 introduced the possibility of reallocating cases to other network members if they are well placed to deal with them. Accordingly, the Commission may reallocate a case to a national competition authority and vice versa[22].

Notes

[22] See paragraphs 5 to 15 of the Commission notice on cooperation within the Network of Competition Authorities (OJ C 101, 27.4.2004, p.43).

15. When the first investigative measure is addressed to them (normally a request for information[23] or an inspection), addressees are informed of the fact that they are subject to a preliminary investigation and about the subject matter and purpose of such investigation. In the context of requests for information, they will further be reminded that if the behaviour under investigation is confirmed to have taken place this might constitute an infringement of Articles 101 and/or 102 TFEU. After having received a request for information or being subject to an inspection, parties[24] may at any time inquire with the Directorate-General for Competition about the status of the investigation, including before the opening of proceedings. If such an undertaking considers that it has not been properly informed by the Directorate-General for Competition of its procedural status, it may refer the matter to the hearing officer for resolution, after having raised the matter with the Directorate-General for Competition[25]. The hearing officer shall take a decision that the Directorate-General for Competition will inform the undertaking or association of undertakings that made the request of their procedural status. This decision shall be communicated to the undertaking or association of undertakings that made the request. If at any stage during the initial assessment phase, the Commission decides not to investigate the case further (and thus not to open proceedings), the Commission will, at its own initiative, inform the party subject to the preliminary investigation thereof.

Part B Procedural Matters

Notes

[23] See Case T-99/04 *AC Treuhand* v *Commission* [2008] ECR II-1501, para 56.

[24] In this notice, 'parties' are defined as the parties subject to the investigation. If not explicitly mentioned, 'parties' does not include complainants and admitted third persons (also referred to as 'third parties' in this notice).

[25] Article 4(2)(d) of the terms of reference of the hearing officer.

Commentary

point 15: F&N: 8.317

16. In cases based on a complaint, the Commission will endeavour to inform complainants within four months from the receipt of the complaint of the action that it proposes to take with regard to the complaint[26]. This time frame is indicative and will depend on the circumstances of the individual case and whether the Directorate-General for Competition has received sufficient information from the complainant or third parties, notably in response to its requests for information, in order for it to decide whether or not to investigate the case further.

Notes

[26] Notice on the handling of complaints, paragraph 61.

2.3. Opening of proceedings

17. The Commission will open proceedings[27] under Article 11(6) of Regulation (EC) No 1/2003 when the initial assessment leads to the conclusion that the case merits further investigation and where the scope of the investigation has been sufficiently defined.

Notes

[27] According to Article 2 of the Implementing Regulation, the Commission may decide to initiate proceedings with a view to adopting a decision (e.g. a decision finding an infringement or a commitment decision) at any point in time, but no later than the date on which it issues a statement of objections, a preliminary assessment (as referred to in Article 9(1) of Regulation (EC) No 1/2003) or a notice pursuant to Article 27(4) of Regulation (EC) No 1/2003, whichever is the earlier.

18. The opening of proceedings determines the allocation of the case within the ECN[28] and in relation to the parties and the complainant, if applicable. It also signals a commitment on the part of the Commission to further investigate the case. The Commission will thus allocate resources to the case and will endeavour to deal with the case in a timely manner.

Notes

[28] The opening of proceedings relieves the national competition authorities of their competence to apply Articles 101 and 102 TFEU, see Article 11(6) of Regulation (EC) No 1/2003.

19. The decision to open proceedings identifies the parties subject to the proceedings and briefly describes the scope of the investigation. In particular, it sets out the behaviour constituting the alleged infringement of Articles 101 and/or 102 TFEU to be covered by the investigation and normally identifies the territory and sector(s) where that behaviour takes place.

20. Pursuant to Article 2 of the Implementing Regulation, the Commission may make the opening of proceedings public. The Commission's policy is to publish the opening of proceedings on the website of the Directorate-General for Competition and issue a press release, unless such publication may harm the investigation.

21. The parties subject to the investigation are informed orally or in writing of the opening of proceedings sufficiently in advance before the opening of proceedings is made public so as to enable them to prepare their own communication (in particular in relation to shareholders, the financial institutions and the press).

22. It should be emphasised that the opening of proceedings does not prejudge in any way the existence of an infringement. It merely indicates that the Commission will further pursue the case. This important clarification will be mentioned in the decision opening the proceedings (notified to the parties), as well as in all public communications concerning the opening of the case.

23. The opening of proceedings does not limit the right of the Commission to extend the scope and/ or the addressees of the investigation at a later point in time. In case of such an extension of the scope of the investigation, the measures in paragraphs (20) to (21) apply.

24. In cartel cases, the opening of proceedings normally takes place simultaneously with the adoption of the Statement of Objections (see paragraph (4) above), though it may take place earlier.

2.4. Languages

25. Pursuant to Article 3 of Regulation No 1[29], documents which the Commission sends to an undertaking based in the European Union will be drafted in the language of the Member State in which the undertaking is based.

Notes

[29] EEC Council: Regulation No 1 determining the languages to be used by the European Economic Community (OJ 17, 6.10.1958, p.385; Consolidated version of 1.1.2007).

---

26. Pursuant to Article 2 of that same Regulation, documents which an undertaking sends to the Commission may be drafted in any one of the official languages of the European Union selected by the sender. The reply and subsequent correspondence will be drafted in the same language.

27. In order to avoid delays due to translation, the addressees may waive their right to receive the text in the language resulting from the above rule and opt for another language. Duly authorised language waivers can be given for some specific documents and/or for the whole procedure.

28. As regards simple requests for information it is standard practice to send the cover letter in the language of the addressee's location or in English (including a reference to Article 3 of Regulation No 1) and to attach the questionnaire in English. The addressee is also clearly informed — in the language of the addressee's location — of its right to obtain a translation of the cover letter and/ or questionnaire into the language of the addressee's location, as well as the right to reply in that language. This practice allows for more expeditious treatment of information requests, while preserving the rights of addressees.

Commentary
para 28: B&C: 13.012

---

29. The Statement of Objections, Preliminary Assessment and decisions pursuant to Articles 7, 9 and 23(2) of Regulation (EC) No 1/2003 are notified in the authentic language of the addressee unless it has signed the above mentioned language waiver.

Commentary
para 29: B&C: 13.084

---

30. Pursuant to Article 2 of Regulation No 1, the reply and the subsequent correspondence addressed to the complainant will be in the language of their complaint.

31. Participants in the oral hearing may request to be heard in an EU official language other than the language of proceedings. In that case, interpretation will be provided during the oral hearing, as long as sufficient advance notice of this requirement is given to the hearing officer.

2.5. Information requests

32. Pursuant to Article 18 of Regulation (EC) No 1/2003, the Commission is empowered to require undertakings and associations of undertakings to provide it with all necessary information. Information can be requested by letter ('simple request' (Article 18(2)) or by decision (Article 18(3))[30]. It should be underlined that requests for information are regularly sent not only to the undertakings under investigation, but also to other undertakings or associations of undertakings which may have information relevant for the case.

Notes

[30] Non-respect of an Article 18(3) decision requesting information (supplying incomplete information or not respecting the time limit set out) can lead to fines and periodic penalties, see Articles 23 and 24 of Regulation (EC) No 1/2003.

Submitting incorrect or misleading information may lead to fines being imposed both in case of an Article 18(2) letter and an Article 18(3) decision (see Article 23 of Regulation (EC) No 1/2003).

Commentary
para 32: B&C: 13.012

2.5.1. Scope of request for information

33. Pursuant to Article 18 of Regulation (EC) No 1/2003, the Commission may require undertakings and associations of undertakings to provide all necessary information. Information is necessary, in particular, if it may enable the Commission to verify the existence of the alleged infringement referred to in the request. The Commission enjoys a margin of appreciation in this respect[31].

Notes
[31] As regards the Commission's discretion in shaping the enquiry, see Case T-141/94 *Thyssen Stahl* v *Commission* [1999] ECR II-347, paragraph 110; Case T-9/99 *HFB and Others* v *Commission* [2002] ECR II-1487, paragraph 384; Case T-48/00 *Corus UK* v *Commission* [2004] ECR II-2325, paragraph 212. In exercising its discretion, the Commission is bound by the principle of proportionality and, in relation to Article 18(3) decisions, must respect the privilege against self-incrimination.

34. It is for the Commission to define the scope and the format of the request for information. Where appropriate, the Directorate-General for Competition might however discuss with the addressees the scope and the format of the request for information. This may be particularly useful in cases of requests concerning quantitative data[32].

Notes
[32] See the Best Practices on the submission of economic evidence.

35. When, in a reply to a request for information, undertakings submit manifestly irrelevant information (in particular documents which are clearly not related to the subject matter of the investigation), the Directorate-General for Competition may, in order not to unnecessarily burden the often voluminous administrative file, return such information to the addressee of the request as early as possible after having received the reply. A short notice reporting this fact will be put in the file.

2.5.2. Self-incrimination

36. Where the addressee of a request for information pursuant to Article 18(2) of Regulation (EC) No 1/2003 refuses to reply to a question in such a request invoking the privilege against self-incrimination, as defined by the case law of the Court of Justice of the European Union[33], it may refer the matter in due time following the receipt of the request to the hearing officer, after having raised the matter with the Directorate-General for Competition before the expiry of the original time limit set[34]. In appropriate cases, and having regard to the need to avoid undue delay in proceedings, the hearing officer may make a reasoned recommendation as to whether the privilege against self- incrimination applies and inform the director responsible of the conclusions drawn, to be taken into account in case of any decision taken subsequently pursuant to Article 18(3) of Regulation (EC) No 1/2003. The addressee of the request shall receive a copy of the reasoned recommendation. The addressee of an Article 18(3) decision will be reminded of the privilege against self-incrimination as defined by case law of the Court of Justice of the European Union[35].

Notes
[33] See for example Case C-301/04 P *Commission* v *SGL*, [2006] ECR I-5915, which specifies that addressees of an Article 18(3) decision may be required to provide pre-existing documents, such as minutes of cartel meetings, even if those documents may incriminate the party providing them.
[34] Article 4(2)(b) of the terms of reference of the hearing officer.
[35] See footnote 33.

2.5.3. Time limits

37. The request for information specifies which information is required and fixes the time limit within which the information is to be provided.

38. Addressees are given a reasonable time limit to reply to the request, according to the length and complexity of the request taking into account the requirements of the investigation. In general, this time limit will be at least two weeks from the receipt of the request. If from the outset, it is considered that a longer period is required, the time limit to reply to the request will be set accordingly. When the scope of the request is limited, for example if it only covers a short clarification of information previously provided or information readily available to the addressee of the request, the time limit will normally be shorter (one week or less).

39. If they have difficulties responding within the time limit set, addressees may ask for it to be extended. A reasoned request should be made or confirmed in writing (letter or e-mail), sufficiently in advance of the expiry of the time limit. If the Commission considers the request to be justified, additional time (depending on the complexity of the information asked and other factors) will be granted. The Commission may also agree with the addressee of the request that certain parts of the requested information that are of particular importance or easily available for the addressee will be supplied within a shorter time limit, whereas additional time will be granted for supplying the remaining information.

40. Where the addressee of a decision requesting information pursuant to Article 18(3) Regulation (EC) No 1/2003 is unable to resolve its concerns about the time limit through the procedure outlined above, it may refer the matter to the hearing officer. Such a request should be made in due time before the expiry of the original time limit set[36]. The hearing officer shall decide on whether an extension of the time limit should be granted, taking account of the length and complexity of the request for information and the requirements of the investigation.

Notes

[36] Article 4(2)(c) of the terms of reference of the hearing officer.

2.5.4. Confidentiality

41. The cover letter of the request for information also requires the addressee to indicate whether it considers that information provided in the reply is confidential. In that case, in accordance with Article 16(3) of the Implementing Regulation, the addressee must substantiate its claims individually with regard to each item of information and provide a non-confidential version of the information. Such a non-confidential version shall be provided in the same format as the confidential information, replacing deleted passages by summaries thereof. Unless otherwise agreed, a non-confidential version should be provided at the same time as the original submission. If undertakings fail to comply with these requirements, the Commission may assume that the documents or statements concerned do not contain confidential information pursuant to Article 16(4) of the Implementing Regulation.

2.5.5. Meetings and other contacts with the parties and third parties

42. During the investigative phase, the Directorate-General for Competition may hold meetings (or conduct phone calls) with the parties subject to the proceedings, complainants, or third parties. In particular, it will hold State of Play meetings or may hold triangular meetings as outlined in Sections 2.9 or 2.10 below.

Commentary
para 42: B&C: 13.019

43. When a meeting takes place at the request of the parties, complainants or third parties, they should as a general rule submit in advance a proposed agenda of topics to be discussed at the meeting, as well as a memorandum or a presentation which covers these issues in more detail. After meetings or phone calls on substantive issues, the parties, complainants or third parties may substantiate their statements or presentations in writing.

44. Any written documentation prepared by the undertakings which attended a meeting that is communicated to the Directorate-General for Competition will be put on the file. A non-confidential

version of such documentation, together with a brief note prepared by the Directorate-General for Competition, will be made accessible to the parties subject to the investigation during their access to the file, if the case is further pursued. Subject to any anonymity requests[37] this note will mention the undertaking(s) attending the meeting (or participating in the phone call relating to substantive issues) and the timing and topic(s) covered by the meeting (or phone call)[38]. Such a brief note will also be prepared when the meeting takes place on the Commission's initiative (e.g. State of Play meetings).

Notes

[37] See paragraph 143 below.

[38] The provisions of this section also apply to State of Play meetings and triangular meetings (see Section 2.10 below).

45. The Commission may, after a meeting or other informal contact with the parties, complainants or third parties, request that they provide information in writing pursuant to Article 18 of Regulation (EC) No 1/2003 or invite them to make a statement pursuant to Article 19 of that Regulation.

2.5.6. Power to take statements (interviews)

46. Regulation (EC) No 1/2003 and the Implementing Regulation establish a specific procedure for taking statements from natural or legal persons who may be in possession of useful information concerning an alleged infringement of Articles 101 and 102 TFEU (see Article 19 of Regulation (EC) No 1/2003 and Article 3 of the Implementing Regulation)[39].

Notes

[39] This power to take statements pursuant to Article 19 of Regulation (EC) No 1/2003 should be distinguished from the power of the Commission, during an inspection, to ask any representative or member of staff of the undertaking or association of undertakings for explanations on facts or documents relating to the subject matter and purpose of the inspection and to record the answers, pursuant to Article 20(2)(e) of Regulation (EC) No 1/2003.

47. The Commission may, under this procedure, interview by any means, such as by telephone or video conference, any natural or legal person who consents to be interviewed for the purpose of collecting information relating to the subject matter of an investigation.

48. Before taking such statements, the Directorate-General for Competition will inform the interviewee of the legal basis of the interview, its voluntary nature and the right of the interviewee to consult a lawyer. The Directorate-General for Competition will further inform the interviewee of the purpose of the interview and of its intention to make a record of the interview. In practice this will be done by providing a document explaining the procedure to be signed by the interviewee. In order to enhance the accuracy of the statements, a copy of any recording will be made available shortly thereafter to the person interviewed for approval.

Commentary

point 48: F&N: 8.321

49. The procedure for taking statements pursuant to Article 19 of Regulation (EC) No 1/2003 and Article 3 of the Implementing Regulation applies only when it is expressly agreed between the interviewee and the Directorate-General for Competition that the conversation will be recorded as a formal interview under Article 19. It is within the discretion of the Commission to decide when to propose interviews. A party may however also make a request to the Directorate-General for Competition to have its statement recorded as an interview. Such a request will in principle be accepted, subject to the needs and requirements of the proper conduct of the investigation.

2.6. Inspections

50. In the context of an investigation the Commission has the power to conduct inspections at the premises of an undertaking and in certain circumstances at other premises, including private premises. The Commission's practice in relation to inspections at the premises of an undertaking

is currently described in an explanatory note available on the website of the Directorate-General for Competition[40].

Notes
[40] See: http://ec.europa.eu/competition/antitrust/legislation/legislation.html

2.7. Legal professional privilege

51. According to the case law of the Court of Justice of the European Union[41], the main features of which are summarised below, certain communications between lawyer and client may, subject to strict conditions, be protected by legal professional privilege (also referred to as 'LPP') and thus be confidential as regards the Commission, as an exception to the latter's powers of investigation and examination of documents[42]. Communications between lawyer and client are protected by legal professional privilege provided that they are made for the purpose and interest of the exercise of the client's rights of defence in competition proceedings and that they emanate from independent lawyers[43].

Notes
[41] The exclusion of certain communications between lawyers and clients from the Commission's powers of enquiry derives from the general principles of law common to the laws of the Member States as clarified by the Court of Justice of the European Union: Case 155/79 *AM&S Europe Limited* v *Commission* (hereinafter 'AM&S') [1982] ECR 1575; Order in Case T-30/89 *Hilti* v *Commission* (hereinafter 'Hilti') [1990] ECR II-163; Joined Cases T-125/03 and T-253/03 *Akzo Nobel Chemicals and Akcros Chemicals* v *Commission* (hereinafter 'Akzo') [2007] ECR II-3523, as confirmed by Case C-550/07 P, *Akzo Nobel Chemicals and Akcros Chemicals* v *Commission*, judgment of 14 September 2010.
[42] The Court of Justice of the European Union has considered that the protection of the confidentiality of communications between lawyer and client is an essential corollary to the full exercise of the rights of defence (*AM&S*, paragraphs 18 and 23). In any event, the principle of legal professional privilege does not prevent a lawyer's client from disclosing the written communications between them if the client considers that it is in his interest to do so (*AM&S*, paragraph 28).
[43] *AM&S*, paragraphs 21, 22 and 27. According to the case law, the substantive scope of the protection of legal professional privilege covers also, further to written communications with an independent lawyer made for the purposes of the exercise of the client's rights of defence, (i) internal notes circulated within an undertaking which are confined to reporting the text or the content of communications with independent lawyers containing legal advice (*Hilti*, paragraphs 13, 16 to 18) and (ii) preparatory documents prepared by the client, even if not exchanged with a lawyer or not created for the purpose of being sent physically to a lawyer, provided that they were drawn up exclusively for the purpose of seeking legal advice from a lawyer in exercise of the rights of the defence (*Akzo*, paragraphs 120 to 123). As for the personal scope of the protection of legal professional privilege, it only applies to the extent that the lawyer is independent (i.e. not bound to his client by a relationship of employment); in-house lawyers are explicitly excluded from legal professional privilege, irrespective of their membership of a Bar or Law Society or their subjection to professional discipline and ethics or protection under national law: *AM&S*, paragraphs 21, 22, 24 and 27; *Akzo*, paragraphs 166 to 168; confirmed by ECJ in its judgment of 14 September 2010, Case C-550/07 P, paragraphs 44 to 51. Moreover, according to the case law, protection under legal professional privilege applies only to lawyers entitled to practise their profession in one of the EU Member States, regardless of the country in which the client lives (*AM&S*, paragraphs 25 and 26), and does not extend to other professional advisers such as patent attorneys, accountants, etc. Finally, it shall be observed that the protection of legal professional privilege covers, in principle, written communications exchanged after the initiation of the administrative procedure that may lead to a decision on the application of Articles 101 and/or 102 TFEU or to a decision imposing a pecuniary sanction on the undertaking; this protection can also extend to earlier written communications made for the purpose of exercising rights of the defence and which have a relationship to the subject matter of that procedure (*AM&S*, paragraph 23).

52. It is for the undertaking claiming the protection of legal professional privilege with regard to a given document to provide the Commission with appropriate justification and relevant material to substantiate its claim, while not being bound to disclose the contents of such document[44]. Redacted versions removing the parts covered by legal professional privilege should be submitted. Where the Commission considers that such evidence has not been provided, it may order production of the document in question and, if necessary, impose on the undertaking fines or periodic penalty payments for its refusal either to supply such additional necessary evidence or to produce the contested document[45].

Notes
[44] Hence, the mere fact that an undertaking claims that a document is protected by legal professional privilege is not sufficient to prevent the Commission from reading that document if the undertaking produces no relevant material of

such a kind (*Akzo*, paragraph 80; see below). In order to substantiate its claim, the undertaking concerned may, in particular, inform the Directorate-General for Competition of the author of the document and for whom it was intended, explain the respective duties and responsibilities of each, and refer to the objective and the context in which the document was drawn up. Similarly, it may also mention the context in which the document was found, the way in which it was filed and any related documents (*Akzo*, paragraph 80).

[45] *AM&S*, paragraphs 29 to 31. The undertaking may subsequently bring an action for the annulment of such a decision, where appropriate, coupled with a request for interim relief (*AM&S*, paragraphs 32; see below).

53. In many cases, a mere cursory look by Commission officials, normally during an inspection, at the general layout, heading, title or other superficial features of a document will enable them to confirm or not the accuracy of the reasons invoked by the undertaking. However, an undertaking is entitled to refuse to allow the Commission officials to take even a cursory look, provided that it gives appropriate reasons to justify why such a cursory look would be impossible without revealing the content of the document[46].

Notes

[46] *Akzo*, paragraphs 81 and 82.

54. Where, in the course of an inspection, the Commission officials consider that the undertaking has: (i) not substantiated its claim that the document concerned is covered by legal professional privilege; (ii) has only invoked reasons that, according to the case law, cannot justify such protection; or (iii) bases itself on factual assertions that are manifestly wrong, the Commission officials may immediately read the contents of the document and take a copy of it (without using the sealed envelope procedure). However, where, in the course of an inspection, the Commission officials consider that the material presented by the undertaking is not of such a nature as to prove that the document in question is protected by legal professional privilege as defined by the case law of the Court of Justice of the European Union, in particular where that undertaking refuses to give the Commission officials a cursory look at a document, but where it cannot be excluded that the document may be protected, the officials may place a copy of the contested document in a sealed envelope and bring it to the Commission's premises, with a view to a subsequent resolution of the dispute.

Commentary
para 54: B&C: 13.058

55. The hearing officer may be asked by undertakings or associations of undertakings to examine claims that a document required by the Commission in the exercise of Articles 18, 20 or 21 of Regulation (EC) No 1/2003 and which was withheld from the Commission is covered by legal professional privilege, within the meaning of the case law, if the undertaking has been unable to resolve the matter with the Directorate-General for Competition[47]. The undertaking making the claim may refer the matter to the hearing officer if they consent to the hearing officer viewing the information claimed to be covered by legal professional privilege and any other material necessary for the hearing officer's assessment. Without revealing the potentially privileged content of the information, the hearing officer shall communicate to the director responsible and the undertaking or association of undertakings concerned his or her preliminary view, and may take appropriate steps to promote a mutually acceptable resolution.

Notes

[47] Article 4(2)(a) of the terms of reference of the hearing officer.

56. Where no resolution is reached, the hearing officer may formulate a reasoned recommendation to the competent member of the Commission, without revealing the potentially privileged content of the document. The party making the claim shall receive a copy of this recommendation. If the matter is not resolved on this basis, the Commission will examine the matter further. Where appropriate, it may adopt a decision rejecting the claim.

57. In cases where the undertaking has claimed the protection of legal professional privilege and has provided reasons substantiating its claims, the Commission (with the exception of the hearing officer if a claim has been referred to him or her on the basis of Article 4(2)(a) of the terms of reference of the hearing officer) will not read the contents of the document before it has adopted a decision rejecting this claim and allowed the undertaking concerned to refer the matter to the

Court of Justice of the European Union. Thus, if the company brings an action for annulment and applies for interim relief within the specified time limit, the Commission will not open the sealed envelope and will not read the documents until the Court of Justice of the European Union has decided on this application for interim measures[48].

Notes

[48] Thus, the Commission will wait until the time limit for bringing an action against the rejection decision has expired before reading the contents of the contested document. However, since such an action does not have suspensory effect, it is for the undertaking concerned to make a prompt application for interim relief seeking suspension of operation of the decision rejecting the request for legal professional privilege.

58. Undertakings making clearly unfounded claims for protection under legal professional privilege merely as delaying tactics or opposing, without objective justification, any cursory look at the documents during an investigation may be subject to fines pursuant to Article 23(1) of Regulation (EC) No 1/2003, if the other conditions of this provision are met. Similarly, such actions may be taken into account as aggravating circumstances in any decision imposing a fine for infringement of Articles 101 and/or 102 TFEU[49].

Notes

[49] *Akzo*, paragraph 89.

2.8. Information exchange between competition authorities

59. In the context of an investigation the Commission may also exchange information with national competition authorities pursuant to Article 12 of Regulation (EC) No 1/2003. The Commission's practice in relation to these exchanges is currently described in the Commission notice on cooperation within the Network of Competition Authorities[50].

Notes

[50] OJ C 101, 27.4.2004, p.43.

2.9. State of Play meetings

60. Throughout the procedure the Directorate-General for Competition endeavours to give, on its own initiative or upon request, parties subject to the proceedings ample opportunity for open and frank discussions — taking into account the stage of the investigation — and to make their points of view known.

Commentary
para 60: B&C: 13.058

61. In this respect the Commission will offer State of Play meetings at certain stages of the procedure. State of Play meetings, which are completely voluntary in nature for the parties, can contribute to the quality and efficiency of the decision making process and to ensure transparency and communication between the Directorate-General for Competition and the parties, notably to inform them of the status of the proceedings at key points in the procedure. State of Play meetings will only be offered to the parties being investigated and not to the complainant (except where the Commission has opened proceedings pursuant to Article 11(6) of Regulation (EC) No 1/2003 and intends to inform the complainant that it will reject its complaint by formal letter under Article 7(1) of the Implementing Regulation) nor to third parties. Where several parties are investigated, State of Play meetings will be offered to each party separately. In cartel proceedings, a State of Play meeting will be offered as provided for in paragraph (65).

2.9.1. Format of the State of Play meetings

62. State of Play meetings are normally conducted at the Commission's premises, but if appropriate, they may also be held by telephone or videoconference. Senior management of the Directorate-General for Competition (Director or Deputy Director-General) will normally

chair the meeting. However, in cases involving multiple parties, the meeting may be chaired by the responsible head of unit.

2.9.2. Timing of the State of Play meetings

63. The Directorate-General for Competition will offer State of Play meetings at several key stages of the case. These correspond, in principle (although not normally in the context of cartel proceedings), to the following events:
    1) Shortly after the opening of proceedings: the Directorate-General for Competition will inform the parties subject to the proceedings of the issues identified at this stage and of the anticipated scope of the investigation. This meeting provides the parties with an opportunity to react initially to the issues identified and may also serve to assist the Directorate-General for Competition in deciding on the appropriate framework for its further investigation. This meeting may also be used to discuss with the parties any relevant language waivers that may be appropriate for the conduct of the investigation. The Directorate-General for Competition will normally at this stage indicate a tentative timetable for the case. Such tentative timetable will, if appropriate, be updated at following State of Play meetings.
    2) At a sufficiently advanced stage in the investigation: this meeting gives the parties subject to the proceedings an opportunity to understand the Commission's preliminary views on the status of the case following its investigation and on the competition concerns identified. The meeting may also be used by the Directorate-General for Competition and by the parties to clarify certain issues and facts relevant for the outcome of the case.
64. Where a Statement of Objections is issued, the parties will also be offered a State of Play meeting after their reply to the Statement of Objections or after the Oral Hearing, should one be held: the parties will at this meeting normally be informed of the Commission's preliminary view on how it intends to pursue the case further.

Commentary
para 64: B&C: 13.058

65. In the context of cartel proceedings one State of Play meeting will be offered after the oral hearing. Furthermore, two specific State of Play Meetings will be offered in the context of procedures leading to commitment decisions (see Section 4 below) and to complainants where the Commission has opened proceedings under Article 11(6) of Regulation (EC) No 1/2003 and intends to inform the complainant that it will reject its complaint by formal letter under Article 7(1) of the Implementing Regulation (see Section 5 below).
66. State of Play meetings do not in any way preclude discussions between the parties, complainants or third parties and the Directorate-General for Competition on substance or on timing issues on other occasions throughout the procedure as appropriate.

2.10. Triangular meetings

67. In addition to bilateral meetings between the Directorate-General for Competition and each individual party such as the State of Play meetings, the Commission may exceptionally decide to invite the parties subject to the proceedings, and possibly also the complainant and/or third parties, to a so-called 'triangular' meeting. Such a meeting will be organised if the Directorate-General for Competition believes it to be in the interests of the investigation to hear the views on, or to verify the accuracy of, factual issues of all the parties in a single meeting. Such a meeting could be useful to the investigation, for example, where two or more opposing views or information have been put forward as to key data or evidence.
68. Any triangular meeting would normally take place at the initiative of the Commission and on a voluntary basis. Triangular meetings are normally chaired by senior management of the Directorate-General for Competition (Director or Deputy Director-General). A triangular meeting does not replace the formal Oral Hearing.
69. Where triangular meetings are held, this should be done as early as possible during the investigatory phase (after the opening of proceedings and before any issuing of Statement of Objections) in order to help the Commission reach a conclusion on substantive issues before the Commission decides whether to issue a Statement of Objections, although the holding of such meetings after

the issue of the Statement of Objections in appropriate cases is not excluded. Triangular meetings should be prepared on the basis of an agenda established by the Directorate-General for Competition after consulting all parties that agree to attend the meeting. The preparation of the meeting may include a mutual exchange of non-confidential submissions between the attending parties sufficiently in advance of the meeting.

2.11. Meetings with the Commissioner or the Director-General

70. If the parties so request, it is normal practice to offer senior officers of the parties subject to the proceedings and the complainant an opportunity to discuss the case either with the Director-General for competition, the Deputy Director-General for antitrust, or if appropriate, with the Commissioner responsible for Competition. The senior officers may be accompanied by their legal and/or economic advisors.

2.12. Review of key submissions

71. In the spirit of encouraging an open exchange of views the Commission will, in cases based on formal complaints, provide the parties subject to the proceedings, at an early stage (unless such is considered to likely prejudice the investigation) and at the latest shortly after the opening of proceedings, with the opportunity of commenting on a non-confidential version of the complaint[51]. However, this may not be the case where the complaint is rejected at an early stage without further in-depth investigation (e.g. based on 'insufficient grounds for acting', also known as 'lack of European Union interest').

Notes

[51] A non-confidential version of the reply of the party subject to the investigation to the complaint may thereafter be provided to the complainant.

---

72. Early access to the complaint may allow the parties to provide useful information at an early stage of the procedure and facilitate the assessment of the case.

73. In the same spirit, the Commission's objective will be to provide the parties subject to the proceedings shortly after the opening of proceedings with the opportunity to review non-confidential versions of other 'key submissions' already submitted to the Commission. This would include significant submissions of the complainant or interested third parties, but not, for example, replies to requests for information. After this early stage, other such submissions will only be shared with the parties if this is in the interest of the investigation and would not risk unduly slowing down the investigative phase. The Commission will respect justified requests by the complainant or interested third parties for non-disclosure of their submissions prior to the issuing of a Statement of Objections where they have genuine concerns regarding confidentiality, including fears of retaliation and the protection of business secrets.

74. The review of key submissions will not be offered in the context of cartel proceedings (see paragraph (4) above).

2.13. Possible outcomes of the investigation phase

75. Once the Commission has reached a preliminary view of the main issues raised by a case, different procedural paths may be envisaged.
    — The Commission may decide to proceed towards the adoption of a Statement of Objections with a view to adopting a prohibition decision relating to all or some of the issues identified at the opening of proceedings (see Section 3 below).
    — The parties subject to the investigation may consider offering commitments which address the competition concerns arising from the investigation, or at least show their willingness to discuss such a possibility; in that case, the Commission may decide to engage in discussion with a view to a commitment decision (see Section 4 below).
    — The Commission may decide that there are no grounds to continue the proceedings with regard to all or some of the parties and close the proceedings accordingly. If the case originated via a complaint, the Commission shall, before closing the case, give the complainant the possibility to express its views (see Section 5 on rejection of complaints).

76. When closing a case in relation to one or several parties in multi-party proceedings at an early stage after proceedings have been formally opened, the Commission will normally not only notify the decision to those parties but also in those cases where the opening of proceedings has been made public, note the closure on its website and/or issue a press release. The same applies in cases where proceedings have not been formally opened but the Commission has already made public its investigation (e.g. by having confirmed that inspections have taken place).

3. Procedures Leading To A Prohibition Decision

77. An important procedural step in procedures which may lead to a prohibition decision is the adoption of a Statement of Objections. However, the adoption of a Statement of Objections does not prejudge the final outcome of the investigation. It may well lead to the closing of the case without the adoption of a prohibition decision or a commitment decision.

3.1. Right to be heard

78. The right of the parties to the proceedings to be heard before a final decision adversely affecting their interests is taken is a fundamental principle of EU law. The Commission is committed to ensuring that the effective exercise of the right to be heard is respected in its proceedings[52].

Notes
[52] Article 27 of Regulation (EC) No 1/2003, mentioned above.

79. The hearing officers have the function of safeguarding the effective exercise of procedural rights, in particular the right to be heard, in competition proceedings[53]. The hearing officers carry out their tasks in full independence from the Directorate-General for Competition, and disputes arising between the latter and any party subject to the proceedings can be brought before the relevant hearing officer for resolution.

Notes
[53] Article 1 of terms of reference of the hearing officer.

80. The hearing officer is directly involved throughout antitrust proceedings, including in particular the organisation and conduct of the oral hearing, if one is held. After the oral hearing, and taking into account the parties' written replies to the Statement of Objections, the hearing officer reports to the Commissioner responsible for Competition on the hearing and the conclusions to be drawn from it. Moreover, prior to a final decision being taken by the College of Commissioners, the hearing officer informs it whether the right to exercise procedural rights effectively has been respected throughout the administrative proceedings. The final report is sent to the parties subject to the proceedings, together with the Commission's final decision, and is published in the *Official Journal of the European Union*.

3.1.1. Statement of Objections

81. Before adopting a decision adversely affecting the interests of an addressee, in particular, a decision finding an infringement of Article 101 and 102 TFEU and ordering its termination (Article 7 of Regulation (EC) No 1/2003) and/or imposing fines (Article 23 of Regulation (EC) No 1/2003), the Commission will give the parties subject to the proceedings the opportunity to be heard on the matters to which the Commission has objected[54]. The Commission will do this by adopting a Statement of Objections, which is notified to each of the parties subject to the proceedings.

Notes
[54] Article 27 of Regulation (EC) No 1/2003.

3.1.1.1. Purpose and content of the Statement of Objections

82. The Statement of Objections sets out the preliminary position of the Commission on the alleged infringement of Articles 101 and/or 102 TFEU, after an in-depth investigation. Its purpose is to

inform the parties concerned of the objections raised against them with a view to enabling them to exercise their rights of defence in writing and orally (at the hearing). It thus constitutes an essential procedural safeguard which ensures that the right to be heard is observed. The parties concerned will be provided with all the information they need to defend themselves effectively and to comment on the allegations made against them.

3.1.1.2. *Possible imposition of remedies and arguments of the parties*

83. If the Commission intends to impose remedies on the parties, in accordance with Article 7(1) of Regulation (EC) No 1/2003, the Statement of Objections will indicate the remedies envisaged that may be necessary to bring the suspected infringement to an end. The information given should be sufficiently detailed to allow the parties to defend themselves as to the necessity and proportionality of the remedies envisaged. If structural remedies are envisaged, in accordance with Article 7(1) of Regulation (EC) No 1/2003, the Statement of Objections will spell out why there is no equally effective behavioural remedy or why the Commission considers any equally effective behavioural remedy would be more burdensome for the undertaking concerned than the structural remedy.

3.1.1.3. *Possible imposition of fines and arguments of the parties*

84. The Statement of Objections will clearly indicate whether the Commission intends to impose fines on the undertakings, should the objections be upheld (Article 23 of Regulation (EC) No 1/2003). In such cases, the Statement of Objections will refer to the relevant principles laid down in the Guidelines on setting fines[55]. In the Statement of Objections the Commission will indicate the essential facts and matters of law which may result in the imposition of a fine, such as the duration and gravity of the infringement and that the infringement was committed intentionally or by negligence. The Statement of Objections will also mention in a sufficiently precise manner that certain facts may give rise to aggravating circumstances and, to the extent possible, to attenuating circumstances.

Notes

[55] Guidelines on the method of setting fines imposed pursuant to Article 23(2)(a) of Regulation (EC) No 1/2003 (OJ C 210, 1.9.2006, p.2).

85. Although under no legal obligation in this respect, in order to increase transparency, the Commission will endeavour to include in the Statement of Objections (using information available) further matters relevant to any subsequent calculation of fines, including the relevant sales figures to be taken into account and the year(s) that will be considered for the value of such sales. Such information may also be provided to the parties after the Statement of Objections. In both cases, the parties will be provided with an opportunity to comment.

Commentary
para 85: B&C: 13.062

86. Should the Commission intend to depart in its final decision from the elements of fact or of law set out in the Statement of Objections to the disadvantage of one or more parties or should the Commission intend to take account of additional inculpatory evidence, the party or parties concerned will always be given the opportunity to make their views known thereon in an appropriate manner.

87. In the Statement of Objections the Commission will also inform parties that in exceptional cases, it may, upon request, take account of the undertaking's inability to pay and reduce or cancel the fine that might otherwise be imposed if that fine would irretrievably jeopardise the economic viability of the undertaking, according to point 35 of the Guidelines on setting fines[56].

Notes
[56] See footnote 55.

Commentary
para 87: B&C: 14.077

88. The undertakings making such a request should be prepared to provide, detailed and up-to-date financial information to support their request. Usually, the Directorate-General for Competition will be in contact with the parties in order to collect additional information and/or clarify the information obtained, which will allow the parties to bring further relevant information to the attention of the Commission. When assessing an undertaking's claim that it is unable to pay, the Commission looks in particular at the financial statements for recent years and forecasts for the current and coming years; at ratios measuring the financial strength, profitability, solvency and liquidity; and the undertaking's relations with outside financial partners and with shareholders. The Commission also examines the specific social and economic context of each undertaking and assesses whether the fine would likely cause its assets to lose significantly their value[57].

Notes
[57] See Note SEC(2010) 737/2 of 12 June 2010.

Commentary
point 88: F&N 8.693

89. The assessment of the financial situation is carried out for all undertakings that have made an inability to pay request close to the adoption of the decision and on the basis of up-to-date information, irrespective of when the request was submitted.
90. The parties may also present their arguments as to the matters that may be of importance for the possible imposition of fines at the oral hearing[58].

Notes
[58] See paragraph 107 below.

3.1.1.4. Transparency

91. In order to enhance the transparency of the proceedings, the Commission will, as a general rule, publish a press release setting out the key issues in the Statement of Objections shortly after it is received by its addressees. This press release will explicitly state that the Statement of Objections does not predetermine the final outcome of the proceedings, once the parties have been heard.

3.1.2. Access to file

92. The addressees of the Statement of Objections are granted access to the Commission's file, in accordance with Article 27(2) of Regulation (EC) No 1/2003 and Articles 15 and 16 of the Implementing Regulation, so as to allow them to effectively express their views on the preliminary conclusions reached by the Commission in its Statement of Objections.
93. The practicalities of access to the file, as well as detailed indications on the type of documents that will be accessible and confidentiality issues, are covered by a separate notice on access to file[59]. Granting access to the Commission file is primarily the responsibility of the Directorate-General for Competition. The hearing officers will decide disputes between the parties, the information providers and the Directorate-General for Competition over access to information contained in the Commission's file in accordance with the notice on access to file, the applicable regulations and the principles laid down in the relevant case law. Lastly, special rules govern access to corporate statements in cartel cases and settlement procedures[60].

Notes
[59] Notice on the rules for access to the Commission file, mentioned above.
[60] Commission Notice on Immunity from fines and reduction of fines in cartel cases (mentioned above), paragraphs 31 to 35 and Commission Notice on the conduct of settlement procedures (mentioned above), paragraphs 35 to 40.

94. Efficient access to file depends to a large extent on the cooperation of the parties and other undertakings having provided information included in the file. As noted in paragraph (41) above, information providers must, in accordance with Article 16(3) of the Implementing Regulation, substantiate their confidentiality claims and provide a non-confidential version of the information. Such a non-confidential version must be provided in the same format as the confidential information, replacing deleted passages with summaries thereof. Unless otherwise agreed, a non-confidential version should be provided at the same time as the original submission. In the

case of a failure to provide a non-confidential version, it may be assumed that the documents do not contain confidential information[61].

Notes
[61] See Article 16(4) of the Implementing Regulation.

3.1.3. *Procedures for facilitating the exchange of confidential information between parties to the proceedings*

95. Further to the possibilities contemplated in the notice on access to the file, two additional procedures may be used for the purpose of alleviating the burden of drawing up non-confidential versions of submissions: the negotiated disclosure to a restricted circle of persons and the data room procedure.

Commentary
para 95: B&C: 13.080

96. First, the Directorate-General for Competition may accept in certain cases, especially those with a very voluminous file that the parties agree voluntarily to use a negotiated disclosure procedure. Under this procedure, the party entitled to access to file agrees bilaterally with the information providers claiming confidentiality to receive all or some of the information which the latter have provided to the Commission, including confidential information. The party being granted access to file limits access to the information to a restricted circle of persons (to be decided by the parties on a case-by-case basis, if requested, under the supervision of the Directorate-General for Competition). To the extent that such negotiated access to the file would amount to restricting a party's right to have access to the investigation file, that party must waive its right to access to the file vis-à-vis the Commission. Normally, the party would receive the information subject to the negotiated disclosure procedure directly from the information provider. However, if the information that is subject to such an agreement would, exceptionally, be provided to the restricted circle of persons by the Commission, the information providers must waive their rights to confidentiality vis-à-vis the Commission.

97. Second, the Directorate-General for Competition may organise the so-called data room procedure. This procedure is typically used for the disclosure of quantitative data relevant for econometric analysis. Under this procedure, part of the file, including confidential information, is gathered in a room, at the Commission's premises (the data room). Access to the data room is granted to a restricted group of persons, i.e. the external legal counsel and/or the economic advisers of the party (collectively known as the 'advisers'), under the supervision of a Commission official. The advisers may make use of the information contained in the data room for the purpose of defending their client but may not disclose any confidential information to their client. The data room is equipped with several PC workstations and the necessary software (and if relevant the necessary data sets and a log of the regressions used to support the Commission's case). There is no network connection and no external communication is allowed. The advisers are permitted to remain in the data room during normal working hours and, if justified, access may be provided for several days. The advisers are strictly prohibited from taking copies, notes or summaries of the documents and may only remove a final report from the data room, which is to be verified by the case team in order to ensure that it does not contain any confidential information. Each adviser will sign a confidentiality agreement and will be presented with the conditions of special access to the data room before entering. To the extent that the use of such a data room procedure would restrict a party's right to have full access to the investigation file, the procedural guarantees provided for in Article 8 of the terms of reference of the hearing officer apply.

98. The hearing officer may decide pursuant to Article 8(4) of the terms of reference of the hearing officer that the data room procedure shall be used in those limited cases where access to certain confidential information is indispensable for a party's rights of defence and where the hearing officer considers that, on balance, the conflict between respect for confidentiality and the rights of defence is best solved in this way. The hearing officer will not take such decisions if he or she considers that the data room is not appropriate and that access to the information should be given in a different form (e.g. a non-confidential version).

3.1.4. *Written reply to the Statement of Objections*

99. Pursuant to Article 27(1) of Regulation (EC) No 1/2003, the Commission shall give the addressees of a Statement of Objections the opportunity of being heard on matters to which the Commission has taken objection. The written reply gives the parties subject to the proceedings the opportunity to set out their views on the objections raised by the Commission.

100. The time limit for the reply to the Statement of Objections will take into account both the time required for the preparation of the submission and the urgency of the case[62]. The addressees of the Statement of Objections have the right to a minimum period of four weeks to reply in writing[63]. A longer period (normally, a period of two months, although this may be longer or shorter depending on the circumstances of the case) will be granted by the Directorate-General for Competition taking into account, inter alia, the following elements:
    — the size and complexity of the file (e.g. the number of infringements, the alleged duration of the infringement(s), the size and number of documents and/or the size and complexity of expert studies); and/or
    — whether the addressee of the statement of objection making the request has had prior access to information (e.g. key submissions, leniency applications); and/or
    — any other objective obstacles which may be faced by the addressee of the Statement of Objections making the request in providing its observations.

Notes
[62] See Case T-44/00 *Mannesmannröhren-Werke AG* v *Commission* [2004] ECR II-2223, para 65.
[63] See Article 17(2) of the Implementing Regulation. For the rule applicable to settlement procedures, see Article 10(a) of the Implementing Regulation.

Commentary
para 100: B&C: 13.064

101. An addressee of a Statement of Objections may, within the original time limit, seek an extension of the time limit to reply by means of a reasoned request to the Directorate-General for Competition at least 10 working days before the expiry of the original time limit. If such a request is not granted or the addressee of the Statement of Objections disagrees with the length of the extension granted, it may refer the matter to the hearing officer for review before the expiry of the original time limit.

102. The time limit will start to run from the date when access to the main documents of the file has been granted[64]. In particular, time limits will normally not start running before the addressee of the Statement of Objections has been offered access to documents which are only accessible on Commission premises, e.g. corporate statements. The fact that access to the entire file has not been granted does not have the automatic consequence that a time limit has not started running[65].

Notes
[64] In most cases, parties will be given access to the complete file by means of a CD-Rom containing all documents in the file.
[65] See Case T-44/00, *Mannesmannröhren-Werke AG* v *Commission*, [2004] ECR II-2223, para 65. See also recital 15 of the terms of reference of the hearing officer which states 'In exceptional circumstances, the hearing officer may suspend the running of the time period in which an addressee of a statement of objections should reply to that statement until a dispute about access to file has been resolved, if the addressee would not be in a position to reply within the deadline granted and an extension would not be an adequate solution at that point in time.'

103. Where required by the rights of defence[66], or where it may in the Commission's view help to further clarify factual and legal issues relevant for the case, the Commission may give parties a copy of the non-confidential version (or specific parts thereof) of other parties' written replies to the Statement of Objections. This would normally be done prior to the oral hearing, so as to allow parties to comment on them at the oral hearing. The Commission may also decide to do so in appropriate cases with respect to complainants and admitted third parties. If access to other parties' replies is granted because it is required for the rights of the defence parties are also entitled to have sufficient additional time to comment on these replies.

Notes
[66] See Joined Cases T-191/98 and T-212/98 to T-214/98 *Atlantic Container Line and Others* v *Commission* [2003] ECR II- 3275; Case T-54/03 *Lafarge* v *Commission* [2008] ECR II-120, paras 69–73; Case T-52/03 *Knauf* v *Commission* [2008] ECR II-115, paras 41–47, 67–79; Case C-407/08P *Knauf* v *Commission*, judgment of 1 July 2010 (not yet reported), paras 23–28.

3.1.5. *Rights of complainants and interested third persons*

104. Complainants are closely associated with the proceedings. Pursuant to Article 6(1) of the Implementing Regulation, they are entitled to receive a non-confidential version of the Statement of Objections, and the Commission shall set a time limit in which the complainant may make its views known in writing. A request for an extension of this time limit may be made by way of a reasoned request to the Commission in due time before the expiry of the original time limit. If such a request is not granted or the Directorate-General for Competition and the complainant disagree about a requested extension, the complainant may refer the matter to the hearing officer, by means of a reasoned request[67].

Notes
[67] Article 9(2) of the terms of reference of the hearing officer.

105. Upon application, the Commission shall also hear other natural or legal persons which can demonstrate a sufficient interest in the outcome of the procedure in accordance with Article 13 of the Implementing Regulation. The hearing officer takes the decision on whether such third persons are admitted to the proceedings. Persons who have been admitted shall be informed in writing of the nature and subject matter of the procedure and a time limit shall be set by the Commission in which they may make their views known in writing. A request for an extension of this time limit may be made by way of a reasoned request to the Directorate-General for Competition in due time before the expiry of the original time limit. If such a request is not granted or the Directorate-General for Competition and the third person admitted to the proceedings disagree about a requested extension the third person may refer the matter to the hearing officer, by means of a reasoned request[68].

Notes
[68] See footnote 67.

3.1.6. *Oral hearing*

106. Every party to which a Statement of Objections has been addressed has the right to an oral hearing. An oral hearing may be requested within the time limit set for their written reply to the Statement of Objections.

107. The oral hearing allows the parties to develop orally the arguments that they submitted in writing and to supplement, where appropriate, the written evidence, or to inform the Commission of other matters that may be relevant. The oral hearing also allows the parties to present their arguments as to the matters that may be of importance for the possible imposition of fines. The fact that the hearing is not public guarantees that all attendees can express themselves freely. Any information disclosed during the hearing shall only be used for the purposes of judicial and/or administrative proceedings for the application of Articles 101 and 102 TFEU and shall not be disclosed or used for any other purpose by any participant in a hearing. This restriction also applies to the recording of the oral hearing, as well as any visual presentations. Should information disclosed during the oral hearing be used for a purpose other than judicial and/or administrative proceedings for the application of Articles 101 and 102 TFEU at any point in time with the involvement of outside counsel, the Commission may report the incident to the bar of that counsel, with a view to disciplinary action.

108. In view of the importance of the oral hearing, it is the practice of the Directorate-General for Competition to ensure the continuous presence of senior management of the Directorate-General for Competition (Director or Deputy Director-General), together with the case team of Commission officials responsible for the investigation. The competition authorities of the Member

States, the Chief Economist's team, and associated Commission services[69], including the Legal Service, are also invited to attend by the hearing officer.

Notes

[69] See further the document 'Key actors and checks and balances', available on the Directorate-General for Competition's website.

Commentary
para 108: B&C: 13.084

3.1.7. Supplementary Statement of Objections and letter of facts

109. If, after the Statement of Objections has been issued, new evidence is identified which the Commission intends to rely upon or if the Commission intends to change its legal assessment to the disadvantage of the undertakings concerned, the undertakings in question shall be given an opportunity to present their observations on these new aspects.

110. If additional objections are issued or the intrinsic nature of the infringement with which an undertaking is charged is modified[70], the Commission shall notify this to the parties in a Supplementary Statement of Objections. Before doing so, a State of Play meeting will normally be offered to the parties. The rules on setting the time limit for the reply to a Statement of Objections apply (see above), although a shorter time limit will typically be set in this context.

Notes

[70] For example a supplementary Statement of Objections would be issued if the new evidence allows the Commission to extend the duration of the infringement, the geographic scope or the nature or scope of the infringement.

111. If, however, the objections already raised against the undertakings in the Statement of Objections are only corroborated by new evidence that the Commission intends to rely on, it will bring this to the attention of the parties concerned by a simple letter (letter of facts)[71]. The letter of facts gives undertakings the opportunity to provide written comments on the new evidence within a fixed time limit. A request for an extension of this time limit may be made by way of a reasoned request to the Commission. If the Directorate-General for Competition and the addressee disagree about a requested extension, the addressee may refer the matter to the hearing officer, by means of a reasoned request.

Notes

[71] When the Commission merely communicates to a party a non-confidential version (or specific excerpts thereof) of the other parties' written replies to the Statement of Objections and gives it the opportunity to submit its comments (see paragraph 103 above), this does not constitute a letter of facts.

112. The procedural rights which are triggered by the sending of the Statement of Objections apply *mutatis mutandis* where a Supplementary Statement of Objections is issued, including the right of the parties to request an oral hearing. Access to all evidence gathered between the initial Statement of Objections and the Supplementary Statement of Objections will also be provided. If a letter of facts is issued, access will in general be granted to evidence gathered after the Statement of Objections up to the date of the said letter of facts. However, in cases where the Commission only intends to rely upon specific evidence that concerns one or a limited number of parties and/or isolated issues (in particular those regarding the determination of the amount of the fine or issues of parental liability), access will be provided only to the parties directly concerned and to the evidence relating to the issue(s) in question.

3.2. Possible outcomes of this phase

113. If, having regard to the parties' replies given in writing and/or at the oral hearing and on the basis of a thorough assessment of all information obtained up to this stage the objections are substantiated, the Commission will proceed towards adopting a decision finding an infringement of the relevant competition rules. The Commission can also decide to withdraw certain objections and to continue towards a decision finding an infringement for the remaining part.

114. If, however, the objections at this stage are not substantiated, the Commission will close the case. In this case, the information measures described above in paragraph (76) would also apply.

4. COMMITMENT PROCEDURES

115. Article 9 of Regulation (EC) No 1/2003 provides the possibility for undertakings to offer commitments that are intended to address the competition concerns identified by the Commission. If the Commission accepts these commitments, it may adopt a decision which makes them binding on the parties subject to the proceedings. It is at the discretion of the Commission whether or not to accept commitments. In light of the principle of proportionality, the Commission must verify that the commitments address the identified competition concerns and that the commitments offered do not manifestly go beyond what is necessary to address these concerns. When carrying out that assessment, the Commission will take into consideration the interests of third parties. However, it is not obliged to compare such voluntary commitments with measures it could impose under Article 7 of Regulation (EC) No 1/2003 and to regard as disproportionate any commitments which go beyond such measures[72].

Notes
[72] Case C-441/07 P *Commission* v *Alrosa*, judgment of 29 June 2010, paragraph 120.

116. Commitment decisions are not appropriate in cases where the Commission considers that the nature of the infringement calls for the imposition of a fine[73]. Consequently, the Commission does not apply the Article 9 procedure to secret cartels that fall under the Notice on immunity from fines and reduction of fines in cartel cases.

Notes
[73] See recital 13 of Regulation (EC) No 1/2003.

117. The main difference between a prohibition decision pursuant to Article 7 and a commitment decision pursuant to Article 9 of Regulation (EC) No 1/2003 is that the former contains a finding of an infringement while the latter makes the commitments binding without concluding whether there was or still is an infringement. A commitment decision concludes that there are no longer grounds for action by the Commission. Moreover, commitments are offered by undertakings on a voluntary basis. Conversely, by an Article 7 decision, the Commission can impose remedies which are necessary to bring the infringement to an end (and/or fines) on undertakings.

4.1. Initiation of commitment discussions

118. Undertakings may contact the Directorate-General for Competition at any time to explore the Commission's readiness to pursue the case with the aim of reaching a commitment decision. The Commission encourages undertakings to signal at the earliest possible stage their interest in discussing commitments.

119. A State of Play meeting will be offered to the parties at that point. The Directorate-General for Competition will indicate to the undertaking the timeframe within which the discussions on potential commitments should be concluded and will present to them the preliminary competition concerns arising from the investigation.

120. In order to avoid delays due to translation, that meeting and the following steps of the procedure may be conducted in an agreed language on the basis of a duly provided 'language waiver' by which the parties accept to receive and submit documents in a language other than the language of the Member State in which they are located (see above Section 2.4).

4.2. Preliminary Assessment

121. Once the Commission is convinced of the undertakings' genuine willingness to propose commitments which will effectively address the competition concerns, a Preliminary Assessment will be issued. Pursuant to Article 9 of Regulation (EC) No 1/2003 the Preliminary Assessment summarises the main facts of the case and identifies the competition concerns that would war-

rant a decision requiring that the infringement is brought to an end. Prior to issuing the Preliminary Assessment, the parties will also be offered a State of Play meeting.

122. The Preliminary Assessment will serve as a basis for the parties to formulate appropriate commitments addressing the competition concerns expressed by the Commission, or to better define previously discussed commitments.

123. If a Statement of Objections has already been sent to the parties, commitments may nevertheless still be accepted, in appropriate cases. In these circumstances, a Statement of Objections fulfils the requirements of a Preliminary Assessment, as it contains a summary of the main facts as well as an assessment of the competition concerns identified.

124. Parties to the proceedings which offer commitments to meet the concerns expressed to them by the Commission in its Preliminary Assessment may call upon the hearing officer at any time during which the procedure under Article 9 is followed in relation to the effective exercise of their procedural rights[74].

Notes
[74] Article 15(1) of the terms of reference of the hearing officer.

125. The Commission or the undertaking(s) concerned may decide at any moment during the commitment procedure to discontinue their discussions. The Commission can then normally continue formal proceedings pursuant to Article 7 of Regulation (EC) No 1/2003[75].

Notes
[75] See Section 3 of this notice.

4.3. Submission of the commitments

126. After receiving the Preliminary Assessment, the parties will normally have one month to formally submit their commitments. If the parties have received a Statement of Objections and subsequently decide to submit commitments, the time limit to reply to the Statement of Objections will generally not be extended. The submission of commitments does not necessarily imply that the parties agree with the Commission's Preliminary Assessment.

127. The parties can offer commitments of a behavioural or structural nature that address adequately the competition concerns identified. Commitments which do not adequately remedy these concerns will not be accepted by the Commission.

128. Commitments must be unambiguous and self-executing[76]. If need be, a trustee can be appointed to assist the Commission in their implementation (monitoring and/or divestiture trustee). Furthermore, when commitments cannot be implemented without the agreement of third parties (e.g. where a third party that would not be a suitable buyer under the commitments holds a pre-emption right), the undertaking should submit evidence of the third party's agreement.

Notes
[76] That is, their implementation must not be dependant on the will of a third party which is not bound by the commitments.

4.4. The 'market test' and subsequent discussions with the parties

129. In accordance with Article 27(4) of Regulation (EC) No 1/2003 the Commission must conduct a market test of the commitments before making them binding by decision. The Commission will only conduct a market test if it considers that the commitments offered prima facie address the competition concerns identified. The Commission must publish in the *Official Journal of the European Union* a notice (market test notice) containing a concise summary of the case and the main content of the commitments, whilst respecting the obligations of professional secrecy[77]. It will also publish on the Directorate-General for Competition's website the full text of the commitments[78] in the authentic language[79]. In order to enhance the transparency of the process, the Commission will also publish a press release setting out the key issues of the case and the proposed commitments. If the case is based on a complaint, the Commission will at this stage also

inform the complainant about the market test and invite the complainant to submit comments. Similarly, third parties admitted to the procedure will be informed and invited to submit comments. At the Commission's discretion, triangular meetings with the parties and the complainant and/or admitted third parties may be held.

Notes
[77] Article 28 of Regulation (EC) No 1/2003.
[78] Non-confidential version.
[79] Without translation.

Commentary
para 129: B&C: 13.101

130. Interested third parties are invited to submit their observations within a fixed time limit of not less than one month in accordance with Article 27(4) of Regulation (EC) No 1/2003.

131. The Commission may send the market test document to other parties that may be potentially concerned by the outcome of the case (e.g. consumer associations).

132. After receipt of the replies to the market test, a State of Play meeting will be organised with the parties. The Commission will inform the parties orally or in writing of the substance of the replies.

133. Where the Commission is of the view, on the basis of the results of the market test (and any other information available) that the competition concerns identified have not been addressed or that changes in the text of the commitments are necessary to make them effective, this will be brought to the attention of the undertakings offering the commitments. If the latter are willing to address the problems identified by the Commission, they should submit an amended version of the commitments. If the amended version of the commitments alters the very nature or scope of the commitments, a new market test will be conducted. If the undertakings are unwilling to submit an amended version of the commitments, where this is required by the Commission's assessment of the result of the market test, the Commission can revert to the Article 7 procedure.

5. Procedure for Rejection of Complaints

134. Formal complaints are an important tool in the implementation of the competition rules and are therefore carefully examined by the Commission. However, after appropriate assessment of the factual and legal circumstances of the individual case, the Commission may reject a complaint pursuant to the grounds and procedure set out below[80].

Notes
[80] See also Commission notice on the handling of complaints (mentioned above).

Commentary
para 134: B&C: 13.049

5.1. Grounds for rejection

135. The rejection of complaints can be based on 'insufficient grounds for acting' (also known as 'lack of European Union interest'), lack of competence or lack of evidence to establish the existence of an infringement.

136. Rejections based on 'insufficient grounds for acting'[81] concern in particular complaints where, given the limited likelihood of establishing the proof of the alleged infringements and the substantial investigatory resources which the Commission would have to invest in order to verify their existence, allocating the resources necessary to further investigate the case would be disproportionate, in light of its expected limited impact on the functioning of the internal market and/or the possibility of the complainant to have recourse to other means[82].

Notes
[81] Cf. in particular Case T-24/90, *Automec II*, [1992] ECR II-2223 and Case C-119/97 P, *Ufex*, [1999] ECR I-1341.
[82] The Commission notice on the handling of complaints lists in paragraph 44 certain criteria that can be used in isolation or combination for rejections on the grounds of lack of 'European Union interest'. Moreover, the Commission

identified in its Report on Competition Policy 2005 some criteria that it could use to decide whether or not there is 'European Union interest'. See also Case T-427/08, *Confédération européenne des associations d'horlogeurs-réparateurs (CEAHR)* v *Commission*, not yet reported.

137. The Commission may also reject complaints for lack of substantiation (when the complainant fails to submit even a minimum of prima facie evidence necessary to substantiate an infringement of Articles 101 and/or 102 TFEU) or on substantive grounds (absence of an infringement).

138. If a national competition authority is dealing or has already dealt with the same case[83], the Commission shall inform the complainant accordingly. In such a situation, the complainant may withdraw the complaint. If the complainant maintains the complaint, the Commission may reject it by decision pursuant to Article 13 of Regulation (EC) No 1/2003 and in accordance with Article 9 of the Implementing Regulation[84]. If a national court is dealing or has already dealt with the same case, the Commission may reject the complaint based on 'insufficient grounds for acting'[85].

Notes

[83] The notion of same case essentially implies: infringement of the same nature, same product market, same geographic market, at least one of the same undertakings, same period of time.
[84] Paragraph 25 of the Commission's notice on the handling of complaints.
[85] See Annual Report on Competition Policy 2005, adopted in June 2006, p.25 ff.

5.2. Procedure

139. If the Commission, after careful examination of the case, comes to the preliminary conclusion that it should not pursue the case for any of the reasons mentioned above, it will first inform the complainant in a meeting or by phone that it has come to the preliminary view that the case may be rejected. Once informed, the complainant may decide to withdraw the complaint. Otherwise, the Commission will inform the complainant by a formal letter pursuant to Article 7(1) of the Implementing Regulation of its preliminary conclusion that there are insufficient grounds for acting and set a time limit for its written observations[86]. In this context, the complainant has the right to request access to the documents on which the Commission bases its provisional assessment[87]. If in the course of its examination of the complaint, the Commission has opened proceedings pursuant to Article 11(6) of Regulation (EC) No 1/2003 a State of Play meeting will be offered to the complainant prior to sending such a formal letter. The time limit set in the formal letter shall be at least four weeks[88]. The time limit will start to run from the date when access to the main documents on which the assessment was made has been granted. Where appropriate and upon reasoned request to the Directorate-General for Competition made before the expiry of the original time limit, the time limit may be extended[89]. If such a request is not granted or the Directorate-General for Competition and the complainant disagree about the extension requested, the addressee may refer the matter to the hearing officer, by means of a reasoned request[90].

Notes

[86] Article 7(1) of the Implementing Regulation; paragraph 68 of the Commission's notice on the handling of complaints.
[87] Article 8 of Regulation of the Implementing Regulation; paragraph 69 of the Commission's notice on the handling of complaints.
[88] Article 17(2) of the Implementing Regulation.
[89] Article 17(4) of the Implementing Regulation.
[90] See footnote 67.

140. If the complainant does not react to the above mentioned letter of the Commission within the time limit, the complaint shall be deemed to have been withdrawn pursuant to Article 7(3) of the Implementing Regulation. The complainant will be informed accordingly about the administrative closure of the case.

141. If the submissions of the complainant in response to the above mentioned letter of the Commission, does not lead the Commission to a different assessment of the complaint, it will reject the complaint by formal decision pursuant to Article 7(2) of the Implementing Regulation.

If the submissions of the complainant lead to a different assessment of the complaint, the Commission will continue its investigation.

6. Limits On The Use of Information

142. Information exchanged in the course of these procedures, in particular in the context of access to file and review of key submissions, shall only be used for the purposes of judicial or administrative proceedings for the application of Articles 101 and 102 TFEU[91].

Notes
[91] Cf. Article 15(4) of the Implementing Regulation.

143. At all stages of the proceedings, the Commission will respect genuine and justified requests from complainants or from information providers regarding the confidential nature of their submissions or contacts with the Commission, including, where appropriate, their identity, in order to protect their legitimate interests (in particular in case of possible retaliation) and to avoid discouraging them from coming forward to the Commission[92].

Notes
[92] See Article 16(1) of Regulation (EC) No 1/2003.

144. Commission officials and the members of the Advisory Committee are bound by the obligation of professional secrecy set out in Article 28 of Regulation (EC) No 1/2003. They are therefore prohibited from disclosing any information of the kind covered by this obligation which they have acquired or exchanged in the context of the investigation and the preparation of, and the deliberations in, the Advisory Committee. As regards the Advisory Committee, its members also must not reveal the opinion of the Advisory Committee prior to its publication, if any, or any information concerning the deliberations which led to the formulation of the opinion.

7. Adoption, Notification and Publication of Decisions

145. All decisions pursuant to Articles 7, 9, 23 and 24 of Regulation (EC) No 1/2003 are adopted by the Commission, on a proposal of the Commissioner responsible for competition policy.

146. Immediately after the decision has been adopted, the addressees will be informed of the decision. The Directorate-General for Competition endeavours to send a courtesy copy to the parties. A certified copy of the full text of the decision as well as a copy of the final report of the hearing officer will then be notified to the addressees by express courier service.

Commentary
para 146: B&C: 13.094

147. A press release will be published after the adoption of the decision by the Commission. The press release describes the scope of the case and the nature of the infringement. It also indicates (where appropriate) the amount of fines for each undertaking concerned and/or the remedies imposed or, in decisions pursuant to Article 9 of Regulation (EC) No 1/2003, the commitments rendered binding.

Commentary
para 147: B&C: 13.094

148. The summary of the decision, the hearing officer's final report as well as the Opinion of the Advisory Committee will be published shortly after the adoption of the decision in the *Official Journal of the European Union* in all official languages[93].

Notes
[93] With the exception of Irish (see Article 2 of Council Regulation (EC) No 920/2005 of 13 June 2005).

Commentary
para 148: B&C: 13.094

149. In addition to the requirements set out in Article 30(1) of Regulation (EC) No 1/2003, the Directorate- General for Competition will endeavour to publish as soon as possible on its website a non-confidential version of the decision in the authentic languages as well as in additional languages, if such versions are available. A non-confidential version of the decision will also be sent to the complainant. The addressees of the decision will normally be asked to provide the Commission within two weeks with a non-confidential version of the decision and to approve the summary. Should disputes arise regarding the deletion of business secrets, a provisional version of the decision excluding all information for which confidentiality has been requested will be made available on the website of the Directorate-General for Competition in any of the official languages in anticipation of a final version after resolution of the disputed parts.

150. In the interest of transparency, the Commission intends to make public on its website its decisions rejecting complaints (pursuant to Article 7 of the Implementing Regulation) or a summary thereof. If required for the protection of legitimate interests of the complainant, the published version of the decision will not identify the complainant. Decisions adopted pursuant to Article 7 of Regulation (EC) No 1/2003 or modifying commitments that have been made binding under Article 9 of that Regulation will also be made public on the website. Other types of decisions may also be published in appropriate cases.

8. FUTURE REVISION

151. This notice may be revised to reflect changes in the applicable legislation, significant developments in the case law of the Court of Justice of the European Union, or further experience gained in applying the competition rules. The Commission intends to engage in regular dialogue with the business and legal community and other interested parties on the experience gained through the application of this notice, of Regulation (EC) No 1/2003, the Implementing Regulation and its various notices and guidelines.

ANNEX I

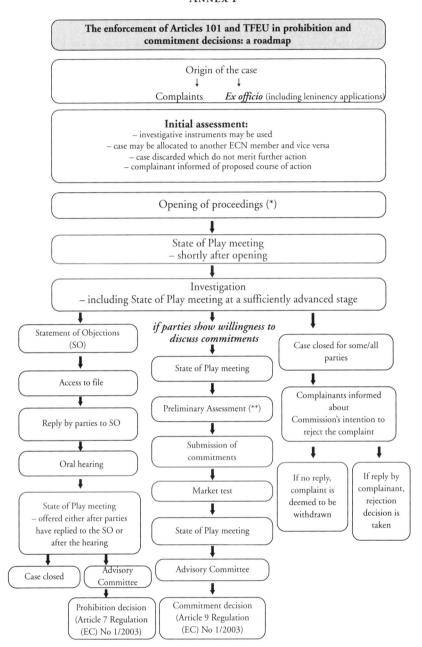

The enforcement of Articles 101 and TFEU in prohibition and commitment decisions: a roadmap

Origin of the case

Complaints   *Ex officio* (including leniency applications)

Initial assessment:
– investigative instruments may be used
– case may be allocated to another ECN member and vice versa
– case discarded which do not merit further action
– complainant informed of proposed course of action

Opening of proceedings (*)

State of Play meeting
– shortly after opening

Investigation
– including State of Play meeting at a sufficiently advanced stage

Statement of Objections (SO)

if parties show willingness to discuss commitments

Case closed for some/all parties

Access to file

State of Play meeting

Complainants informed about Commission's intention to reject the complaint

Reply by parties to SO

Preliminary Assessment (**)

Oral hearing

Submission of commitments

If no reply, complaint is deemed to be withdrawn

If reply by complainant, rejection decision is taken

State of Play meeting – offered either after parties have replied to the SO or after the hearing

Market test

State of Play meeting

Case closed

Advisory Committee

Advisory Committee

Prohibition decision (Article 7 Regulation (EC) No 1/2003)

Commitment decision (Article 9 Regulation (EC) No 1/2003)

(*) With the exception of cartel proceedings, where the opening of proceeding normally takes place simultaneously with the adoption of the Statement of Objections.

(**) If an SO has already been issued, a Preliminary Assessment is not required.

B19

COMMUNICATION FROM THE COMMISSION ON QUANTIFYING HARM IN ACTIONS FOR DAMAGES BASED ON BREACHES OF ARTICLE 101 OR 102 OF THE TREATY ON THE FUNCTIONING OF THE EUROPEAN UNION

(Text with EEA relevance)

(2013/C 167/07)

Official Journal: C 167, 13.6.2013, p.19

Celex No: 52013XC0613(04)

EUR-Lex permanent link: <http://eur-lex.europa.eu/LexUriServ/LexUriServ.do?uri=CELEX:5201 3XC0613(04):EN:NOT>

Notes

The 'Practical Guide' referred to in this Communication (ie the Commission Staff Working Document – Practical Guide – Quantifying harm in actions for damages based on breaches of Article 101 or 102 of the Treaty on the Functioning of the European Union, accompanying this Communication {C(2013) 3440}) is reproduced at B20.

---

1. Compensation for Victims of Competition law Infringements: The Challenge of Quantifying the Harm Suffered

1. Infringements of Article 101 or 102 of the Treaty on the Functioning of the European Union ('TFEU'), hereafter the 'EU competition rules', cause great harm to the economy as a whole and hamper the proper functioning of the internal market. In order to prevent such harm, the Commission has the power to impose fines on undertakings and associations of undertakings for infringing EU competition rules[1]. The objective of the fines imposed by the Commission is deterrence, i.e. sanctioning the undertakings concerned (specific deterrence) and deterring other undertakings from engaging in, or continuing, behaviour that is contrary to Articles 101 and 102 TFEU (general deterrence)[2].

Notes

[1] See Article 23(2) of Council Regulation (EC) No 1/2003 on the implementation of the rules on competition laid down in Articles 81 and 82 of the Treaty, OJ L 1, 4.1.2003, p.1. With effect from 1 December 2009, Articles 81 and 82 of the EC Treaty have become Articles 101 and 102 TFEU. Their substance has not been changed.

[2] Commission Guidelines on the method of setting fines imposed pursuant to Article 23(2) of Regulation (EC) No 1/2003, OJ C 210, 1.9.2006, p.2, at paragraph 4.

---

2. Moreover, infringements of Article 101 or 102 TFEU cause great harm to consumers and undertakings. Anyone who has suffered harm through an infringement of EU competition rules has a right to compensation. This is guaranteed by EU law, as the Court of Justice has repeatedly emphasised[1]. While the objective of the fines is deterrence, the point of damages claims is to repair the harm suffered because of an infringement. More effective remedies for consumers and undertakings to obtain damages would, inherently, also produce beneficial effects in terms of deterring future infringements and ensuring greater compliance with those rules[2].

Notes

[1] Case C-453/99, *Courage and Crehan* [2001] ECR I-6297; Joined Cases C-295-298/04, *Manfredi* [2006] ECR I-6619; Case C-360/09, *Pfleiderer* [2011] ECR I-5161 and Case C-199/11, *European Community* v *Otis NV and others* [2012], not yet reported.

3. A major difficulty encountered by courts, tribunals and parties in damages actions is how to quantify the harm suffered. Quantification is based on comparing the actual position of claimants with the position they would find themselves in had the infringement not occurred. In any hypothetical assessment of how market conditions and the interactions of market participants would have evolved without the infringement, complex and specific economic and competition law issues often arise. Courts and parties are increasingly confronted with these matters and with considering the methods and techniques available to address them.

2. Interplay of Rules and Principles of EU Law and National Law

2.1. Acquis communautaire

4. Articles 101 and 102 TFEU are a matter of public policy[1] and are central to the functioning of the internal market, which includes a system to ensure that competition is not distorted[2]. These Treaty provisions create rights and obligations for individuals, be they undertakings or consumers. Such rights become part of the legal assets of these individuals[3] and are protected under the Charter of Fundamental Rights of the European Union[4]. National courts have a duty under EU law to enforce such rights and obligations fully and effectively in any proceedings brought before them.

Notes
[1] Joined Cases C-295-298/04, *Manfredi* [2006] ECR I-6619, 31.
[2] Protocol (No 27) to the Treaty on European Union, on the internal market and competition.
[3] Case C-453/99, *Courage and Crehan* [2001] ECR I-6297, 19 and 23; Joined Cases C-295-298/04, *Manfredi* [2006] ECR I-6619, 39.
[4] See Article 17 of the Charter for the protection of an individual's assets; the right to an effective remedy for breaches of rights guaranteed by the law of the Union is set out in Article 47 of the Charter.

5. Amongst the rights guaranteed by EU law is the right to compensation for harm suffered because of an infringement of Article 101 or 102 TFEU: the full effectiveness of EU competition rules would be put at risk if injured parties were not able to claim damages for losses caused to them by an infringement of these rules. Anyone can claim compensation for the harm suffered where there is a causal relationship between that harm and an agreement or practice prohibited by the EU competition rules[1].

Notes
[1] Case C-360/09, *Pfleiderer* [2011] ECR I-5161, 28; Case C-199/11, *European Community* v *Otis NV and others* [2012], not yet reported, 43.

6. Compensation for harm suffered means placing the injured parties in the position they would have been in had there been no infringement of Article 101 or 102 TFEU. Parties injured by an infringement of directly effective EU rules should therefore have the full real value of their losses restored: the entitlement to full compensation covers the actual loss (damnum emergens), as well as compensation for loss of profit (lucrum cessans) suffered as a result of the infringement[1]; and entitlement to interest from the time the damage occurred[2].

Notes
[1] Joined Cases C-295-298/04, *Manfredi* [2006] ECR I-6619, 95-96 and Joined Cases C-46/93 and C-48/93, *Brasserie du Pêcheur and Factortame* [1996] ECR I-1029, 87.
[2] Joined Cases C-295-298/04, *Manfredi* [2006] ECR I-6619, 97, referring to Case C-271/91, *Marshall* [1993] ECR I-4367, 31.

7. In so far as there are no EU rules governing damages actions for breaches of Article 101 or 102 TFEU, it is for the domestic legal system of each Member State to lay down the detailed rules governing the exercise of the right to compensation guaranteed by EU law. Such rules must not,

however, render the exercise of rights conferred by EU law excessively difficult or practically impossible (principle of effectiveness). Nor may they be less favourable than those governing damages actions for breaches of similar rights conferred by domestic law (principle of equivalence)[1].

Notes
[1] Case C-453/99, *Courage and Crehan* [2001] ECR I-6297, 29; Joined Cases C-295-298/04, *Manfredi* [2006] ECR I-6619, 62.

2.2. National law and its interaction with the principles of EU law

8. On the question of quantifying harm, to the extent that such exercise is not governed by EU law, the legal rules of the Member States determine the appropriate standard of proof and the required degree of precision in showing the amount of harm suffered. National rules will also assign the burden of proof and of the respective responsibilities of the parties to make factual submissions to the court. National law may provide for the burden of proof to shift once the claimant has proved a certain set of factors, and may provide for simplified rules of calculation and presumptions of a rebuttable or irrefutable nature. National law further determines to what extent and how courts are empowered to quantify the harm suffered on the basis of approximate best estimates or to make use of equitable considerations. All these national rules and procedures governing the quantification of harm should be laid down and applied in individual cases in a way that allows parties injured by EU competition law infringements to obtain full compensation for the harm suffered without any disproportionate difficulties; in no circumstances may they be less effective than in similar actions based on domestic law.

9. One consequence of the principle of effectiveness is that applicable national legal rules and their interpretation should reflect the difficulties and limits inherent to quantifying harm in competition cases. The quantification of such harm requires comparing the actual position of the injured party with the position this party would have been in without the infringement. This is something that cannot be observed in reality; it is impossible to know with certainty how market conditions and the interactions between market participants would have evolved in the absence of the infringement. All that is possible is an estimate of the scenario likely to have existed without the infringement. Quantification of harm in competition cases has always, by its very nature, been characterised by considerable limits to the degree of certainty and precision that can be expected. Sometimes only approximate estimates are possible[1].

Notes
[1] The limits of such assessments of a hypothetical situation have been recognised by the Court of Justice in the context of quantifying the loss of earnings in an action for damages against the European Community, see Joined Cases C-104/89 and C-37/90, *Mulder and others* v *Council* [2000] ECR I-203, 79.

3. Guidance on the Quantification of Harm

2.1. Acquis communautaire

10. Against this background, the Commission's services have drawn up a practical guide on the quantification of harm in actions for damages based on breaches of Article 101 or 102 TFEU (the 'practical guide').

11. The aim of the practical guide is to offer assistance to national courts and parties involved in actions for damages by making information on quantifying harm caused by infringements of the EU competition rules more widely available. It therefore provides insights into various forms of harm typically caused by anticompetitive practices and, in particular, sets out information on the methods and techniques available to quantify such harm. Giving such information wider circulation will enhance the effectiveness of actions for damages. It should also make such actions more foreseeable, thereby increasing legal certainty for all parties involved. The practical guide can also help parties find a consensual resolution of their disputes, be it within or outside the context of judicial or alternative dispute resolution proceedings.

12. This practical guide is purely informative and does not bind national courts or parties. It does not therefore alter the legal rules of the Member States governing actions for damages and does not affect the rights and obligations of Member States or of natural or legal persons under EU law.

13. In particular, the practical guide should not be seen as raising or lowering the standard of proof or the level of detail of the factual submissions required from the parties in the legal systems of the Member States. Nor should it be seen as affecting the rules and practices in the Member States regarding the burden of proof. National courts have often adopted, within their legal systems, pragmatic approaches to determining the amount of damages to be awarded, including the use of presumptions, shifts in the burden of proof, or the power of courts to make approximate best estimate assessments. The practical guide is intended to provide information that can be used within the framework of national legal rules and practices, not instead of them. Depending on the legal rules applicable and on the specific features of each case, it may therefore well be sufficient for the parties to provide facts and evidence on the damages quantum which are less detailed than those required by some of the methods and techniques mentioned in the practical guide.

14. The practical guide explains the particular features, including the strengths and weaknesses, of various methods and techniques available to quantify antitrust harm. It is up to the applicable law to determine which approach to quantification can be considered appropriate in the specific circumstances of a given case. Relevant considerations include — alongside the standard and burden of proof under applicable law — the availability of data, the costs and time involved and their proportionality in relation to the value of the damages claim.

15. The practical guide also presents and discusses a range of practical examples. These illustrate the typical effects that infringements of EU competition rules tend to have, and how the abovementioned methods and techniques for quantifying harm can be applied in practice.

16. Economic insights into the harm caused by antitrust infringements and methods and techniques for quantifying it can evolve over time in line with the theoretical and empirical economic research and judicial practice in this area. The practical guide should therefore not be seen as a comprehensive or definitive account of the insights, methods and techniques available.

B20

COMMISSION STAFF WORKING DOCUMENT PRACTICAL GUIDE QUANTIFYING HARM IN ACTIONS FOR DAMAGES BASED ON BREACHES OF ARTICLE 101 OR 102 OF THE TREATY ON THE FUNCTIONING OF THE EUROPEAN UNION

Accompanying the

Communication from the Commission on quantifying harm in actions for damages based on breaches of Article 101 or 102 of the Treaty on the Functioning of the European Union

{C(2013) 3440}

Notes

This document is available at the following locations:

<http://ec.europa.eu/competition/antitrust/actionsdamages/quantification_guide_en.pdf>

<http://ec.europa.eu/competition/antitrust/actionsdamages/documents.html>

The Communication on quantifying harm in actions for damages based on breaches of Article 101 or 102 TFEU, which this document accompanies, is reproduced at B19.

OVERVIEW OF CONTENTS

<table>
<tr><td>TABLE OF ILLUSTRATIVE EXAMPLES</td></tr>
<tr><td>*The flour cartel [32], [147]*</td></tr>
<tr><td>*Refusal to supply an essential input for commercial solvents [194],[195],[196], [208]*</td></tr>
<tr><td>*The medical equipment case [203], [205]*</td></tr>
<tr><td>*Recoupment in a predatory case [211],[214]*</td></tr>
</table>

PART 1 CONTEXT AND GENERAL APPROACH TO QUANTIFYING HARM IN COMPETITION CASES

I. LEGAL CONTEXT

A. The right to compensation

1. Everyone who has suffered harm because of an infringement of Article 101 or 102 of the Treaty on the Functioning of the European Union (TFEU) has a right to be compensated for that harm. The Court of Justice of the EU held that this right is guaranteed by primary EU law.[1] Compensation means placing the injured party in the position it would have been in had there been no infringement. Therefore, compensation includes reparation not only for actual loss suffered (*damnum emergens*), but also for loss of profit (*lucrum cessans*) and the payment of interest.[2] Actual loss means a reduction in a person's assets; loss of profit means that an increase in those assets, which would have occurred without the infringement, did not happen.[3]

Notes

[1] Case C-453/99 *Courage* [2001] ECR I-6297, 26; joined cases C-295/04 to C-298/04 *Manfredi* [2006] ECR I-6619, 60; case C-360/09 *Pfleiderer* [2011] ECR I-5161, 36 and case C-199/11, *European Community v. Otis NV and others* [2012], not yet reported. These cases concern Article 101 TFEU (ex Article 81 EC Treaty); the same principles apply however also to Article 102 TFEU (ex Article 82 EC Treaty) – case C-360/09 *Pfleiderer* [2011] ECR I-5161, 36.
[2] Joined cases C-295/04 to C-298/04 *Manfredi* [2006] ECR I-6619, 95.
[3] Opinion of Advocate General Capotorti in case 238/78 *Ireks-Arkady GmbH* v *Council and Commission* [1979] ECR 2955, 9.

---

2. Civil actions for compensation are generally adjudicated by national courts.[4] In so far as there are no EU rules governing the matter, it is for the domestic legal system of each Member State to lay down detailed rules on the exercise of the right to compensation guaranteed by EU law. Such rules, however, must not render excessively difficult or practically impossible the exercise of rights conferred on individuals by EU law (principle of effectiveness), and must not be less favourable than those governing damages actions for breaches of similar rights conferred by domestic law (principle of equivalence).[5]

Notes

[4] The international jurisdiction of the national court is often determined by Council Regulation (EC) No 44/2001 of 22 December 2000 on jurisdiction and the recognition and enforcement of judgments in civil and commercial matters, OJ L 12, 16.1.2001, p.1. This Regulation has been recently replaced by Regulation (EU) No 1215/2012 of 12 December 2012 on jurisdiction and the recognition and enforcement of judgments in civil and commercial matters, OJ L 351, 20.12.2012, p.1, which for the most part will enter into force on 10 January 2015. The substantive law applicable in a given individual case will often be determined by EU Regulations, in particular Article 6 of Regulation 864/2007 on the law applicable to non-contractual obligations, OJ L 199, 31.7.2007, p.40. The applicable procedural rules will usually be those in force in the country of the court hearing the action (*lex fori*). Actions for damages can also be decided by arbitration tribunals and by courts of non-EU states.
[5] Case C-453/99 *Courage* [2001] ECR I-6297, 29; joined cases C-295/04 to C-298/04 *Manfredi* [2006] ECR I-6619, 62.

B. National rules on quantification and this Practical Guide

3. In an action for compensation of harm suffered because of an infringement of Article 101 or 102 TFEU, national courts have to determine whether the claimant suffered a harm because of the

infringement, and, if that is the case, the amount to be awarded to the claimant as compensation for that harm.[6] This determination – assessing and proving the quantum of damages – is often difficult.[7] Normally, this determination is only necessary once the national court has made a finding concerning the other legal requirements for a damages claim, in particular a finding of an infringement and the causal link between this infringement and the harm suffered by the claimant.[8]

Notes

[6] This Practical Guide is only concerned with the assessment of harm in the context of claims for financial (monetary) compensation. While the present paper does not specifically cover the determination of the award in other civil law remedies, its insights may also be used in making such determination, in particular with regard to actions for restitution.

[7] See in more detail paragraphs 11 ff. in Section II below.

[8] Art. 16 of Reg. 1/2003. This paper does not specifically deal with the question whether a certain practice infringes Articles 101 or 102 TFEU.

4. The legal framework in which courts deal with the quantification of harm is defined by EU and national law, including rules on:

- the heads of damages to be compensated and general rules of liability governing claims for compensation;
- requirements such as causality or proximity that link the illegal act and the harm. The Court of Justice has clarified in this respect that in so far as there are no rules at EU level on this matter, it is for national law to prescribe the rules on the application of the concept of 'causal relationship', provided that the principles of equivalence and effectiveness are observed;[9]
- the procedural framework in which claims for damages are adjudicated. National rules typically provide for an allocation of the burden of proof and of the respective responsibilities of the parties to make factual submissions to the court;[10]
- the appropriate standard of proof, which may vary between different stages of the proceedings, and may also be different for questions of liability for damages and those of the quantum of damages;
- to what extent and how courts are empowered to quantify the harm suffered on the basis of approximate best estimates or equitable considerations; and
- the admissibility and the role of evidence in civil litigation and its evaluation (and in particular of expert evidence).

Notes

[9] Joined cases C-295/04 to C-298/04 *Manfredi* [2006] ECR I-6619, 61, 64; case C-453/99 *Courage* [2001] ECR I-6297, 29.

[10] See, for an example of distribution of this burden in competition cases, *Kammergericht Berlin* (Higher Regional Court, Berlin), decision of 1 October 2009, case No 2 U 10/03 Kart *(Vitaminpreise)*.

5. Within their respective legal frameworks, legislators and courts have often adopted pragmatic approaches in determining the amount of damages to be awarded, for instance, by establishing presumptions. The burden of proof may shift, for example once a party has provided a certain amount of facts and evidence. Also, the law of the Member States may provide that the illicit profit made by the infringing undertaking(s) plays a role — either directly or indirectly — in estimating the harm suffered by injured parties.[11]

Notes

[11] See paragraph 146 in Part 3 below.

6. The purpose of this Practical Guide is to place at the disposal of courts and parties to damages actions economic and practical insights that may be of use when national rules and practices are applied. To this end, the Practical Guide gives insights into the harm caused by anticompetitive practices prohibited by the Treaty and information on the main methods and techniques available to quantify such harm.[12] Such guidance may help the claimant make factual submissions to the court concerning the amount of damages claimed and may assist the defendant in pleading his position

vis-à-vis these submissions by the claimant. The guidance may also help parties in finding a consensual resolution of their disputes, be it within or outside the context of judicial proceedings or alternative dispute resolution mechanisms.

Notes

12 The Commission has found useful assistance in preparing this Practical Guide in various studies it commissioned as well as in the comments received from external experts; see http://ec.europa.eu/competition/antitrust/actionsdamages/index.html.

7. This Practical Guide is purely informative, does not bind national courts and does not alter the legal rules applicable in the Member States to damages actions based on infringements of Article 101 or 102 TFEU.[13]

Notes

13 Neither does it affect the rights and obligations of Member States and natural or legal persons under EU law.

8. In particular, whether the use of any and, if so, which of the methods and techniques described in this Practical Guide are considered appropriate in a given case depends on national law applied in accordance with the above-mentioned EU law principles of effectiveness and equivalence. Relevant considerations in this respect are likely to include

- whether a certain method or technique meets the standard required under national law;
- whether sufficient data are available to the party charged with the burden of proof to apply the method or technique; and
- whether the burden and costs involved are proportionate to the value of the damages claim at stake.

Excessive difficulties in exercising the right to damages guaranteed by EU law and therefore concerns in view of the principle of effectiveness could arise, for instance, through disproportionate costs or through overly demanding requirements regarding the degree of certainty and precision of a quantification of the harm suffered.[14]

Notes

14 See also paragraphs 16 and 17 below.

9. Nothing in this Practical Guide should be understood as arguing against the use of more pragmatic approaches, or as raising or lowering the standard of proof or the level of detail of the factual submissions required from the parties in the legal systems of the Member States. Indeed, it may well be sufficient for the parties to provide facts and evidence on the quantum of damages that are less detailed than the methods and techniques discussed in this Practical Guide.

10. It should also be noted that the economic insights into the harm caused by antitrust infringements and methods and techniques to quantify such harm can evolve over time along with theoretical and empirical research and the judicial practice in this area. The present paper should therefore not be seen as exhaustive.

II. GENERAL APPROACH TO QUANTIFYING HARM IN COMPETITION CASES

11. Compensation for harm suffered aims to place the injured party in the position in which it would have been had the infringement of Article 101 or 102 TFEU not occurred: the actual position of the injured party has to be compared with the position in which this party would have been but for the infringement. This assessment is sometimes called 'but-for analysis'.

12. The central question in antitrust damages quantification is hence to determine what is likely to have happened without the infringement. This hypothetical situation cannot be observed directly and some form of estimation is necessary to construct a reference scenario with which the actual situation can be compared. This reference scenario is referred to as the 'non-infringement scenario' or the 'counterfactual scenario'.

13. In a specific case, the starting point for determining if the infringement has in fact harmed the claimant and, if so, the quantum of that harm, are the specificities of the case at hand and the evidence at the disposal of the court (including decisions by competition authorities). The concrete (alleged) infringement in question and how it could affect a particular market stand at the beginning of any determination of the quantum of harm caused by that infringement.

14. National courts can, in a particular case, use pieces of direct evidence relevant for the quantification of harm, such as documents produced by an infringing undertaking regarding agreed price increases and their implementation or assessing the development of its market position. Oral evidence given by witnesses can be used as well. The availability of such evidence may play an important role when a court decides whether any, and if so which, of the methods and techniques set out below can be used by a party to meet the required standard of proof under applicable law.

15. The type of harm for which the claimant seeks compensation determines which kind of economic variables (such as prices, sales volumes, profits, costs or market shares) need to be considered. For example, in a cartel leading to higher prices for customers of the cartelists, a non-infringement price will need to be estimated in order to establish a reference point for comparing it with the price actually paid by these customers. In an abuse of dominance case leading to the market foreclosure of competitors, the profits lost by these competitors may be measured by comparing their actual turnover and profit margins with the turnover and profit margins they were likely to have generated without the infringement.

16. It is impossible to know with certainty how a market would have exactly evolved in the absence of the infringement of Article 101 or 102 TFEU. Prices, sales volumes, and profit margins depend on a range of factors and complex, often strategic interactions between market participants that are not easily estimated. Estimation of the hypothetical non-infringement scenario will thus by definition rely on a number of assumptions.[15] In practice, the unavailability or inaccessibility of data will often add to this intrinsic limitation.

Notes

[15] The limits and implications of such assessment of a hypothetical situation have been recognised by the Court of Justice (in the context of quantifying loss of earnings in an action for damages against the European Community in the agricultural sector): 'the loss of earnings is the result not of a simple mathematical calculation but of an evaluation and assessment of complex economic data. The Court is thus called upon to evaluate economic activities which are of a largely hypothetical nature. Like a national court, it therefore has a broad discretion as to both the figures and the statistical data to be chosen and also, above all, as to the way in which they are to be used to calculate and evaluate the damage', see joined cases C-104/89 and C-37/90 *Mulder and others* v *Council and Commission* [2000] ECR I-203, 79.

17. For these reasons, quantification of harm in competition cases is, by its very nature, subject to considerable limits as to the degree of certainty and precision that can be expected. There cannot be a single 'true' value of the harm suffered that could be determined, but only best estimates relying on assumptions and approximations.[16] Applicable national legal rules and their interpretation should reflect these inherent limits in the quantification of harm in damages actions for breaches of Articles 101 and 102 TFEU in accordance with the EU law principle of effectiveness so that the exercise of the right to damages guaranteed by the Treaty is not made practically impossible or excessively difficult.

Notes

[16] For an example of the reconstruction of a counterfactual by a national court and the issues arising from the underlying assumptions see for instance *Competition Appeal Tribunal*, decision of 28 March 2013, case No 1166/5/7/10 (*Albion Water Limited v Dŵr Cymru Cyfyngedig*).

18. This Practical Guide outlines a number of methods and techniques that have been developed in economics and legal practice to establish a suitable reference scenario and to estimate the value of the economic variable of interest (for example, in a price cartel the likely price that would have been charged for the product had the infringement not occurred).[17] The methods and techniques are based on different approaches and vary in terms of the underlying assumptions and the variety and detail of data needed. They also differ in the extent to which they control for factors other than the infringement that may have affected the situation of the claimant. As a result, these methods and techniques may be more or less difficult, time-consuming and cost-intensive to apply.

Notes
[17] See Part 2 below.

19. Once a value for the relevant economic variable (such as prices, profit margins, or sales volumes) in the hypothetical non-infringement scenario has been estimated, a comparison with the actual circumstances (e.g. the price actually paid by the injured party) is necessary to quantify the harm caused by the infringement of Article 101 or 102 TFEU.

20. Addition of interest will also need to be considered. The award of interest is an essential component of compensation. As the Court of Justice has emphasised, full compensation for the harm suffered must include the reparation of the adverse effects resulting from the lapse of time since the occurrence of the harm caused by the infringement.[18] These effects are monetary devaluation[19] and the lost opportunity for the injured party to have the capital at its disposal.[20] National law may account for these effects in the form of statutory interest or other forms of interest, as long as they are in accordance with the above-mentioned principles of effectiveness and equivalence.

Notes
[18] Case C-271/91 *Marshall* [1993] ECR I-4367, 31; joined cases C-295/04 to C-298/04 *Manfredi* [2006] ECR I-6619, 97; European Commission, White Paper on damages actions for breach of the EC antitrust rules (COM(2008) 165), section 2.5 and the accompanying Commission Staff Working Paper (SEC(2008) 404), paragraph 187.
[19] Case C-308/87 *Grifoni II* [1994] ECR I-341, 40; Opinion of Advocate General Tesauro in Case C-308/87 *Grifoni II* [1994] ECR I-341, 25; joined cases C-104/89 and C-37/90 *Mulder and others* v *Council and Commission* [2000] ECR I-203, 51. In the context of loss of purchasing power, see joined cases T-17/89, T-21/89 and T-25/89 *Brazzelli Lualdi* [1992] ECR II-293, 40.
[20] Opinion of Advocate General Saggio in joined cases C-104/89 and C-37/90 *Mulder and others* v *Council and Commission* [2000] ECR I-203, 105.

III. Structure of the Practical Guide

21. The basis of a claim for damages is the submission that an infringement of Article 101 or 102 TFEU adversely affected the situation of the claimant. Broadly speaking, two principal categories of harmful effects of such infringements can be distinguished:

(a) Infringements can result in a raise in the prices paid by customers of infringing undertakings.[21] Among the infringements having such effect are cartel infringements of Article 101 TFEU, such as price fixing, market sharing or output limitation cartels. Also, exploitative abuses within the meaning of Article 102 TFEU can have the same effect.

   Increased prices mean that the customers who purchase the affected product or service[22] pay an overcharge. Moreover, a rise in prices may also lead to less demand and may entail a loss of profits for customers who use the product for their own commercial activities.[23]

(b) Undertakings can also infringe Articles 101 and 102 TFEU by illegal practices which exclude competitors from a market or reduce their market share.[24] Typical examples are abuses of a dominant position through margin squeeze, predatory pricing or tying, or certain vertical exclusivity agreements between suppliers and distributors that infringe competition law.[25] Such practices have a significant effect on competitors, who suffer harm as they forego business opportunities and profit in this market. Where foreclosure of competitors is successful and competitive pressure in a market diminishes, customers will be harmed too, typically by a rise in prices.

Notes
[21] Where the infringement affects the buying activity of the infringing undertakings, the corresponding effect will be the decrease in the purchase prices that these undertakings have to pay to their suppliers. See paragraph 134 in Part 3, Section 1 for more details.
[22] For ease of presentation, in the following reference will only be made to 'products' affected by an infringement, which should however be understood as also referring to the 'services' affected.
[23] See paragraphs 128 ff. in Part 3, Section I for more details.
[24] Case C-209/10 *Post Danmark*, not yet reported, 22, 23 and 24.
[25] Vertical agreements are those concluded between undertakings from different levels of the supply chain.

22. Infringements of Articles 101 and 102 TFEU can also have further harmful effects, for example adverse impacts on product quality and innovation. The Practical Guide focuses on the two principal categories of harm and the categories of injured parties[26] described in paragraph 21. The methods and techniques described in the Practical Guide may, nonetheless, also be relevant in damages actions concerning other types of harm and other injured parties.

Notes

[26] The Practical Guide does not specifically address the situation of persons other than those mentioned in points (a) and (b) of paragraph 21, although other persons (such as suppliers of the infringers or customers of law-abiding competitors of the infringers) may also be harmed by infringements leading to price overcharges or the exclusion of competitors; see also footnote 107.

23. Part 3 of the Practical Guide addresses specifically the quantification of the kind of harm referred to in paragraph 21(a). This part includes a description of the basic effects on the market of price increases resulting from an infringement and illustrates how these types of harm (in particular the harm resulting from the payment of an overcharge and the harm associated with a reduction in demand) can be quantified.

24. Part 4 of the Practical Guide addresses specifically the quantification of the kind of harm referred to in paragraph 21(b). This part includes a description of the possible effects of the exclusion of competitors from a market and illustrates through examples how these types of harm (namely the loss of profit of the excluded competitor and the harm to customers) can be quantified.

25. The main methods and techniques available to quantify the harm resulting from infringements of Article 101 or 102 TFEU are common to all kinds of harm caused by such infringements. Part 2 of the Practical Guide therefore provides a general overview of these methods and techniques, and it gives more information on the basic assumptions on which these methods rely and explains their application in practice.

PART 2 METHODS AND TECHNIQUES

I. OVERVIEW

26. Various methods are available to construct a non-infringement scenario for the purposes of quantifying the harm in damages actions in competition cases.

27. The methods most widely used by parties and courts estimate what would have happened without the infringement by looking at the time periods before or after the infringement or at other markets that have not been affected by the infringement. Such comparator-based methods take the data (prices, sales volumes, profit margins or other economic variables) observed in the unaffected period or on the unaffected markets as an indication of the hypothetical scenario without the infringement. The implementation of these methods is sometimes refined by the use of econometric techniques, which combine economic theory with statistical or quantitative methods to identify and measure economic relationships between variables. Various comparator-based methods and techniques to implement these methods are described in Section II below (paras 32 to 95).

28. Methods other than comparator-based are addressed in Section III below (paras 96 to 121). One of these methods uses economic models fitted to the actual market to simulate the likely market outcome that would have occurred without the infringement. These models draw on economic theory to explain the likely functioning of a market in view of its main features (e.g. the number of competitors, the way they compete with each other, the degree of product differentiation, entry barriers). Further methods include the cost-based method, which uses production costs for the affected product and a mark-up for a 'reasonable' profit margin to estimate the hypothetical non-infringement scenario or finance-based approaches that take the financial performance of the claimant or the defendant as a starting point.

29. Each of these methods and techniques has particular features, strengths and weaknesses that may make them more or less suitable to estimate the harm suffered in a given set of circumstances. In particular, they differ in the degree to which they rely on data that are the outcome of actual market interactions or on assumptions based on economic theory and in the extent to which they control

for factors other than the infringement that may have affected the claimant for damages. Moreover, the methods and techniques differ in the degree to which they are simple to use and in the kind and amount of data required.

30. While these methods seek to construct how the market in question would have evolved absent the infringement, more direct evidence available to the parties and to the court (for instance, internal documents of the infringing undertakings on agreed price increases) may also provide, under applicable national legal rules, useful information for assessing quantum of damages in a given case.[27]

Notes
[27] See for an example of such an approach *Oberlandesgericht Karlsruhe* (Higher Regional Court, Karlsruhe), decision of 11 June 2010, case No 6 U 118/05, where specifically agreed price increases of the infringing undertakings of a cartel were used, under applicable legal rules on the distribution of fact pleading and the establishment of *prima facie* evidence, to determine the damages award. This part of the decision was confirmed on appeal by the *Bundesgerichtshof* (Federal Court of Justice), decision of 28 June 2011, case no KZR 75/10.

31. Section IV below sets out considerations on the choice of method, which will usually depend on the specific features of that case and on the requirements under applicable law.

II. COMPARATOR-BASED METHODS

32. In order to appreciate how comparator-based methods work in practice, it is useful to consider a (entirely fictitious) example of a damages action based on a hypothetical cartel infringing Article 101 TFEU.[28]

Notes
[28] This example is further developed at paragraph 147.

> ### The flour cartel
>
> Assume that all of the milling companies in a particular Member State have been found, by the national competition authority, to have fixed among themselves the prices for the grinding of cereals and the production of flour.
>
> A bakery that regularly purchased flour in recent years brings a damages claim against one of the milling companies. The bakery submits that the infringement has led to an illegal rise in prices for the flour it purchased from that milling company. The bakery asks for compensation for this price overcharge it paid over the past years.

33. The key question regarding the quantification of harm in the aforementioned example is to find out what price the claimant bakery would have paid for flour had there been no infringement. If a comparator-based method is used to do so, these methods compare the price in the infringement scenario with a non-infringement scenario that is established on the basis of price data observed either:

- on the same market at a time before and/or after the infringement (1); or
- on a different but similar geographic market (2); or
- on a different but similar product market (3).

It is also possible to combine a comparison over time with a comparison across different geographic or product markets (4).

34. In the example of the flour cartel, the application of the methods focuses on prices. It is, however, likewise possible to use these methods to estimate other economic variables such as market shares, profit margins, rate of return on capital, value of assets, or the level of costs of an undertaking. Which economic variable can be usefully considered for the purposes of damages quantification depends on the circumstances of the case at hand.

35. The data used in such a comparison across markets or over time can be data that relate to the entire market (i.e. the average of the price for flour charged to all bakeries operating in a

neighbouring geographic market) or data that relate to certain specific market participants only (i.e. the price charged for flour to certain customer groups such as wholesale purchasers operating in a neighbouring market).

36. It could also be appropriate, in particular in cases concerning exclusionary practices, to compare data relating to only one market participant. An example for such a comparison between individual companies, i.e. the injured party and a sufficiently similar comparator firm, may be the comparison between the profits achieved by a company trying to enter a new market where it faced exclusionary practices in breach of the EU competition rules and the profits that a comparable new entrant achieved on a different but similar geographic market without being affected by anticompetitive practices. Sections A.1 to 4 below cover the comparison with aggregated market data and firm-level data alike.[29]

Notes

[29] The comparison with firm-level data of another company could, theoretically, be made not only for companies that operate in another geographic or product market as discussed in Sections 2–4 below, but also for data of companies operating in the same product and geographic market as the injured party. In practice, such intra-market comparisons do not play a significant role, possibly because within the same market it can be difficult to find a sufficiently comparable other company that was not affected by the infringement. The following sections therefore do not further discuss such comparisons within a market.

37. The strength of all comparator-based methods lies in the fact that they use real-life data that are observed on the same or a similar market.[30] The comparator-based methods rely on the premise that the comparator scenario can be considered representative of the likely non-infringement scenario and that the difference between the infringement data and the data chosen as a comparator is due to the infringement. Important market characteristics which can play a role in considering whether two markets are sufficiently similar are the degrees of competition and concentration on those markets, cost and demand characteristics and barriers to entry. Whether the level of similarity between infringement and comparator markets or time periods is considered sufficient in order for the results of such comparison to be used in quantifying harm depends on national legal systems.[31] Where significant differences exist between the time periods or markets considered, various techniques are available to account for such differences.[32]

Notes

[30] This aspect is emphasised, for instance, by the *Bundesgerichtshof* (Federal Court of Justice, Germany), decision of 19 June 2007, case No KRB 12/07 (*Paper Wholesale Cartel*).
[31] See for more detail paragraph 94. For an example of issues that may arise when assessing comparability of data see for instance *Tribunal Administratif de Paris* (Administrative Court of Paris), decision of 27 March 2009, (*SNCF* v *Bouygues*).
[32] See for more detail paragraphs 59–95 in Section B below.

A. Methods for establishing a non-infringement scenario

(1) Comparison over time on the same market

38. One frequently used method consists in comparing the actual situation during the period when the infringement produced effects with the situation on the same market before the infringement produced effects or after they ceased.[33] For instance, where an undertaking abused its dominant position by foreclosing a competitor from the market during 2004 and 2005, the method could look at e.g. the competitor's profits during the infringement period and its profits in 2002 and 2003 when there was not yet an infringement.[34] Another example would be a price fixing cartel (such as the flour cartel example mentioned above) that lasted from 2005 to 2007 where the method could compare the price paid by the cartel customers during the infringement period with the price paid by customers in a period after the infringement, e.g. in 2008 and 2009.[35]

Notes

[33] See, for example, *Corte d'Appello di Milano* (Court of Appeal, Milan), decision of 11 July 2003, (*Bluvacanze*) and *Corte d'Appello di Milano* (Court of Appeal, Milan), decision of 3 February 2000, case No I, 308 (*Inaz Paghe* v *Associazione Nazionale Consulenti del Lavoro*) (in both cases, comparison before, during and after); *Landgericht Dortmund* (Regional Court, Dortmund), decision of 1 April 2004, case No 13 O 55/02 Kart (*Vitaminpreise*) (during and after comparison);

Landesgericht für Zivilrechtssachen Graz (Regional Civil Court of Graz), decision of 17 August 2007, case No 17 R 91/07 p (*Driving school*) (accepting a comparison during and after).

[34] For more detailed examples of the method's application in cases of exclusionary practices, see Part 4 below.

[35] For more detailed examples of the method's application in cases of infringements that lead to a price overcharge, see Part 3 below.

39. There are, in principle, three different points of reference that can be used for the comparison over time:[36]

- an unaffected *pre*-infringement period (comparison 'before and during' — in the flour cartel example: comparison of the prices paid for flour in the same market *before* the infringement had effects with those affected by the infringement);
- an unaffected *post*-infringement period (comparison 'during and after' — in the flour cartel example: comparison of the prices affected by the infringement with prices paid in the same market *after* the infringement ended); and
- both an unaffected *pre-* and *post*-infringement period (comparison 'before, during and after').

Notes

[36] The comparison over time method is also referred to as the 'before-after method' or 'benchmark method'.

40. Making an informed choice of reference period and type of data will usually require good knowledge of the industry in question and will have to take the specific case at hand as a starting point. The choice will also be influenced by the availability of data and the requirements of applicable rules regarding the standard and burden of proof.

41. An advantage of all methods comparing, over time, data from the *same* geographic and product market is that market characteristics such as the degree of competition, market structure, costs and demand characteristics may be more comparable than in a comparison with different product or geographic markets.

42. However, also in comparisons over time it happens that some differences between the two data sets are not only due to the infringement. In such cases, it may be appropriate to make adjustments to the data observed in the comparator period to account for differences with the infringement period[37] or to choose a different comparator period or market. For instance, in the case of a long-lasting infringement, the assumption that e.g. prices of 10 years ago would have remained unchanged over time absent the infringement is probably overly strong and may lead to opting e.g. for a comparison with the pre-infringement period *and* the post-infringement period. In cases of long infringement periods, it may also be appropriate to address practical issues of comparability of data that result from changes in the way that data have been recorded by companies (e.g. changes in accounting practices or changes in the data organisation software).

Notes

[37] On such adjustments and, in particular, the possibility to use regression analysis, see paragraphs 59–95 in Section B below.

43. Where data are available, the choice between a comparison 'before and during', 'during and after' or 'before, during and after' can be determined by a range of factors. It is highly unlikely to find any reference period where market circumstances exactly represent what would have happened in the infringement period had the infringement not occurred. It is only possible to identify a sufficiently similar time period that allows a likely non-infringement scenario to be reasonably approximated. Factors to be considered in this context may include uncertainties as to which time periods were actually not affected by the infringement. Some infringements start, or cease, gradually; and often doubts exist regarding the exact beginning of an infringement and, in particular, the effects it produces. Indeed, decisions of competition authorities regularly mention evidence suggesting that the infringement may have started earlier than the period established as the infringement period for the purposes of the decision.[38] Econometric analysis of observed data can be a way to identify when the infringement's effects started or ceased.

[38] It is possible that a competition authority limits the finding of an infringement to a certain period, while in fact the infringement may have had a longer duration.

44. The ending of an infringement and its effects may be more easily established than its beginning, but here too uncertainties could arise as to whether the period immediately after the infringement's end is unaffected by the anticompetitive behaviour.[39] For example, when there is some delay until market conditions return to a non-infringement level, using data from the period immediately after the infringement could lead to an underestimation of the effect of the infringement. It may also occur that prices are, for a short period after the end of a cartel, particularly low as companies might temporarily engage in aggressive pricing strategies until the 'normal', i.e. non-infringement, equilibrium on the market is reached.

Notes

[39] See the decision of the *Oberlandesgericht Karlsruhe* (Higher Regional Court, Karlsruhe) of 11 June 2010 in case No 6 U 118/05, for an example where a national court ruled that the prices charged in the five months after the infringement ended were still influenced by the cartel.

45. Specifically in oligopolistic markets another issue may arise, namely that the participants in a cartel can use the knowledge gained through the operation of the cartel to coordinate their behaviour afterwards without infringing Article 101. In such a situation, post-infringement prices are likely to be higher than without the infringement and can only serve to make a lower-bound estimate of the harm suffered. The pre-infringement period may be a more suitable reference point where central market characteristics changed radically towards the end of the infringement period due to exogenous factors (e.g. a steep increase in raw material costs or an increase in demand for the product).[40]

Notes

[40] For the short period of the infringement after such a change, post-infringement data can be the more appropriate comparator as they may better reflect the market characteristics after the change. However, where the change in market characteristics was caused by the infringement itself (e.g. where due to anticompetitive foreclosure several competitors exited the market), the post-infringement period is obviously not a suitable comparator to estimate the situation that would have existed without the infringement.

46. Nonetheless, even when there are doubts as to whether or not a certain period before or after the infringement was affected by the infringement, this period could, in principle, still serve as a reference period in order to obtain a safe estimate of the harm that will at least have been suffered ('lower-bound' estimate or 'minimum damage').[41]

Notes

[41] If during the infringement exogenous factors lead to a decrease in prices (e.g. a sharp fall in input costs of the infringer), the inference of a lower bound could be rebutted.

47. In certain circumstances, the non-infringement scenario may be appropriately estimated on the basis of two reference periods (before and after the infringement), for example, by using the average from these periods or by using other techniques to reflect a trend in the development of market circumstances during the infringement.[42] Pre-infringement data could also be used as the reference period up to a certain point during the infringement when a significant change in market circumstances occurred, and post-infringement data as the reference period for the time thereafter.

Notes

[42] For example, interpolation or regression analysis. For these different techniques to implement comparator-based methods, see paragraphs 59–95 in Section B below.

48. Also the choice of data can contribute to building a sufficiently similar basis for the comparison: there can be situations where aggregated data such as industry price averages (or averages for certain groups of firms) are sufficiently representative,[43] whilst in other situations it would be more appropriate to use only data from pre- or post-infringement transactions by the injured

Part B Procedural Matters

company or average data that relate to similar companies. For example, where the injured party belongs to a specific group of market players such as wholesale customers (as opposed to end customers), pre- or post-infringement prices charged to wholesale customers may be an appropriate reference point.

Notes

[43] For further detail on the use of averages in implementing comparator-based approaches, see paragraph 70 in Part 2, Section II below.

(2) Comparison with data from other geographic markets

49. Another comparator-based method consists in looking at data observed in a different geographic market[44] for the purpose of estimating a non-infringement scenario.[45] These may be data observed across the entire geographic comparator market or data observed in relation to certain market participants only. For instance, in the example of a flour cartel mentioned above at paragraph 32, the prices paid by the claimant bakery during the infringement period could be compared with the prices paid on average by similar bakeries, in a different geographic market untouched by the infringement. The same type of comparison can be undertaken with regard to any other economic variable, e.g. the market shares, profit margins, rate of return on capital, value of assets, or level of costs of an undertaking. A comparison with the commercial performance of firms active on another geographic market that is unaffected by the infringement[46] will be particularly relevant in cases of exclusionary behaviour.

Notes

[44] For the concepts of relevant (geographic and product) market, see Commission Notice on the definition of the relevant market for the purposes of Community competition law, OJ C 372, 9.12.1997, p.5.

[45] This method is also referred to as 'yardstick method' or 'cross-sectional method'. These terms are also used to refer to the comparator-based method that looks at data observed in different but similar product markets, see paragraphs 54–55 in Section 3 below. For examples of the use of the comparator-based method looking at different geographic markets see, for instance, *Cour d'Appel de Paris* (Court of Appeal, Paris), decision of 23 June 2003 (*Lescarcelle-De Memoris* v *OGF*); *Juzgado Mercantil numero 5 de Madrid* (Commercial Court, Madrid), decision of 11 November 2005, case No 85/2005 (*Conduit-Europe, S.A.* v *Telefónica de España S.A.*), confirmed by *Audiencia Provincial de Madrid* (Court of Appeal, Madrid), decision of 25 May 2006, case No 73/2006; *Bundesgerichtshof* (Federal Court of Justice, Germany), decision of 19 June 2007, case No KBR 12/07 (*Paper Wholesale Cartel*) (in the context of assessing the illicit gain by cartelists for the purpose of calculating a fine).

[46] The comparator firm might, in principle, also be a firm active on the infringement market provided that its performance was not significantly influenced by the exclusionary behaviour. Even if the comparator firm was not directly affected by the infringement, it may still have been indirectly affected, e.g. by gaining market shares from a foreclosed competitor. The risk of being directly or indirectly influenced by the infringement is lower if the comparison is carried out in relation to a similar firm active on another geographic market. Characteristics that could be relevant when considering the sufficient similarity of firms include their size, cost structure, customers and features of the product they sell.

50. The more a geographic market is similar (except for the infringement effects) to the market affected by the infringement, the more it is likely to be suitable as a comparator market. This means that the products traded in the two geographic markets compared should be the same or, at least, sufficiently similar. Also the competitive characteristics of the geographic comparator market should be similar to the characteristics of the affected market except for the infringement. This may well be a market that is not perfectly competitive.

51. The method of using geographic comparator markets for deriving a non-infringement scenario is, in practice, mainly used when the infringement concerns geographic markets that are local, regional or national in scope.[47] Where the infringement market and the geographic comparator market are neighbouring areas, possibly within one country, there may be an increased likelihood that they are sufficiently similar for the purpose of a comparison.[48]

Notes

[47] It might, however, also be used when the relevant market is wider than national provided that a sufficiently similar comparator market can be identified.

[48] See, however, paragraph 53 below.

52. The comparator market does not always need to be sufficiently similar in its entirety. Where, for instance, the prices paid by one customer group (e.g. wholesalers) or the profits earned by one competitor company (e.g. a new entrant) in the comparator market are used as a reference, it is important that the market position of this customer group or this competitor is sufficiently similar to that of the injured party on the infringement market.

53. The choice of a geographic comparator market may also be influenced by uncertainties about the geographic scope of an infringement. Geographic markets on which the same or a similar infringement occurred are, in principle, not good candidates for being used as comparator markets. Also neighbouring markets on which no similar infringement occurred may still have been influenced by the anticompetitive practices on the infringement market (e.g. because prices on the neighbouring market were raised in view of the increased prices on the infringement market and lesser competitive pressure emanating from this market). A comparison with such markets will not show the full extent of the harm suffered, but they may, nonetheless, constitute a useful basis to establish a lower-bound estimate of the harm caused on the infringement market. This means that a party to an action for damages could, in principle, safely choose to rely on the comparison with a geographic market that was influenced by the same or a similar infringement, in particular where such influence is likely to have been rather small.

(3) Comparison with data from other product markets

54. Similar to the comparison across geographic markets is the approach to look at a different product market[49] with similar market characteristics.[50] For example, in a case of exclusionary behaviour partially foreclosing a company selling one product, the profit margin earned by that company in the infringement market could be compared with the profit margin for another product that is traded (by a similar or the same company) in a distinct but similar product market.

Notes

[49] For the concepts of the relevant (geographic and product) market, see Commission Notice on the definition of the relevant market for the purposes of Community competition law, OJ C 372, 9.12.1997, p.5.

[50] This method is sometimes also referred to as 'yardstick method' or 'cross-sectional method' (as is the comparator-based method looking at different geographic markets).

---

55. The considerations discussed in the context of geographic comparator markets are, *mutatis mutandis*, also likely to be relevant for the choice of a suitable comparator product market. They will often relate to the degree of similarity between the two product markets. In particular, the comparator product should be carefully chosen with a view to the nature of the products compared, the way they are traded and the characteristics of the market e.g. in terms of number of competitors, their cost structure and the buying power of customers.[51] Uncertainties as to whether a potential comparator product market was affected by the infringement or a similar infringement of Article 101 or 102 TFEU can also play a role.

Notes

[51] Similarity of market characteristics may be more likely if the two products compared are traded in the same geographic market. However, the circumstances may also be sufficiently similar where the same or similar products from different geographic markets are compared.

---

(4) Combining comparisons over time and across markets

56. Where sufficient data are available, it may be possible to combine comparisons over time and comparisons across markets. This approach is sometimes called the 'difference in differences' method because it looks at the development of the relevant economic variable (e.g. the price for flour) in the infringement market during a certain period (difference over time on the infringement market) and compares it to the development of the same variable during the same time period on an unaffected comparator market (difference over time on the non-infringement market).[52] The comparison shows the difference between these two differences over time. This gives an estimate of the change in the variable produced by the infringement and excludes all those factors that affected both the infringement and the comparator market in the same way. The method is thus a way to isolate the effects of the infringement from other influences on the relevant variable common to both markets.

57. A simple example derived from the flour cartel mentioned above may illustrate the method: assume that a before, during and after comparison reveals an increase in price of € 40 per 100 kg bag of flour in the Member State where the cartel occurred between 2005 and 2008. Looking at an unaffected geographic market over the same period may show that prices for flour rose by € 10 per 100 kg bag due to increased costs for an input product (cereals). Assuming that the increased input costs also concerned the infringement market, a comparison of the different development of prices on the infringement and the comparator market would indicate the price difference caused by the flour cartel. In the example, this would be € 30 per unit.

58. The strength of the 'difference in differences' method is therefore that it can subtract out changes unrelated to the infringement that occurred during the same time period as the infringement.[53] It rests, however, to a large extent on the assumption that these other changes affected both markets similarly.[54] The considerations regarding the application of the comparison over time and across market methods, in particular the need for sufficient similarity of the markets in question, are also relevant for the difference in differences method. From a practical point of view, this method usually requires a range of data from different markets and periods of time that may not always be easy to obtain; lesser amounts of data may, however, still allow lower-bound or approximate estimates to be derived.[55]

Notes
[53] Compared to a simple comparison across markets, the 'difference in differences' method also has the advantage of filtering out fixed differences between markets (such as differences due to constantly lower input costs in one of the markets).
[54] If, for example, price increases unrelated to the infringement were higher in the affected market than in the comparator market during the infringement period, application of the difference in differences method using simple averages would overestimate the amount of damages. An econometric implementation of the difference in differences technique may help control for such factors.
[55] See, for an example of a national court establishing a lower bound in the course of estimating the quantum of damages (although not using the difference-in-differences method, but the comparison over time method), *Kammergericht Berlin* (Higher Regional Court, Berlin), decision of 1 October 2009, case No 2 U 10/03 Kart.

B. Implementing the method in practice: techniques for estimating the price or other economic variable in the non-infringement scenario

59. Once a suitable comparator-based method for establishing a non-infringement scenario has been chosen, various techniques are available to implement this method in practice. These techniques differ mainly in the degree to which they rely on individual or average data (e.g. price observations), and in the degree to which the data observed in the comparator market[56] or period are subject to further adjustment. As a consequence, these techniques differ in the amount of data they require in order to be carried out.

Notes
[56] As mentioned in paragraph 35, the data used in such comparison across markets or over time can be data that relate to the entire market or data that relate to certain specific market participants only.

60. One possibility in implementing comparator-based methods is to use comparator data directly in the form they are observed and to estimate on this basis a value for the economic variable under consideration in the non-infringement scenario (e.g., in the above example, the price of flour). Where more than one data observation is available (e.g. the price of flour in a range of transactions on a geographic comparator market), they can be combined through a calculation of averages into one or more values for the non-infringement scenario. Such average value(s) for the non-infringement scenarios could then be compared to the average value(s) actually observed during the infringement, e.g. the prices really paid for flour (see in more detail in Section (1) below).

61. Where certain factors (such as an increase in raw material prices) have influenced only the comparator or only the infringement market or period, it should be considered, depending on the standard of proof required and depending on applicable rules regarding causality, whether adjustments

need to be made to the observed data in order to account for such influences. These could be simple adjustments to the data in cases where the influencing factor and the magnitude of its effects can be relatively easily ascertained and accounted for (see Section (1) below). More sophisticated adjustments of observed comparator data can be obtained on the basis of econometric techniques, in particular through the use of regression analysis, which is described in Section (2) below. Whether it is for the defendant or the claimant to plead, substantiate and prove such adjustments is a matter of applicable law.[57]

Notes

[57] See, for instance, *Kammergericht Berlin* (Higher Regional Court, Berlin), decision of 1 October 2009, case No 2 U 10/03 Kart., as an example of the distribution of fact pleading obligations in the quantification of harm.

62. In a given case, the choice between these different techniques depends on the specific circumstances of the case and applicable legal rules, taking account of the different advantages and disadvantages of these techniques, for instance with regard to their accuracy and precision and the data requirements they entail (see Section (3) below).

(1) Simple techniques: individual data observations, averages, interpolation and simple adjustments

63. Depending on the requirements under applicable national law and on the circumstances of the case, especially the degree of similarity between the infringement market and the comparator market or period, the data observed may be compared directly, i.e. without further adjustments, with the data observed in the infringement market.[58]

Notes

[58] For instance, time-based comparison could be based on the simple observation of prices before and during the infringement. For an example of the legal implications of such method see *Corte Suprema di Cassazione* (Supreme Court of Cassation, Italy), decision of 2 February 2007, case No 2305 (*Fondiaria SAI SpA v Nigriello*).

64. The amount of data observed for the variable of interest (e.g., in the flour cartel example, the price for flour) in the comparator markets or comparator time periods may range from only one or very few data observations (i.e. the price observed in a small number of transactions) to a large number of data observations. In bidding markets, for example, auctions may occur very infrequently and at the time of the damages estimation only the price observed in the one tender after the infringement may be available. A similar situation could occur in industries where long-term contracts are common. It may be appropriate to use damages estimations based on single data observations where these are sufficiently representative for the period of interest.

65. Where looking at comparator markets or time periods produces a greater number of data observations, e.g. the prices paid by the injured party in a series of post-infringement transactions, or the prices paid by a number of customers in another geographic market, these data observations can be used either individually or in the form of averages.[59]

Notes

[59] For the purposes of this Practical Guide, the term 'average' is used as referring to the mean, i.e. the average calculated by dividing the sum of observations by the number of observations. There may, however, be situations where it may be more appropriate to use other descriptive statistics (i.e. the median or the mode). For example, where in a market of 25 companies, 21 charge a price of € 50 and four a price of € 75, the modal price of € 50 (the price most observed in the sample) may be the more meaningful representation of the market price than the mean of € 54 (in this example, the modal price equals the median price, which is the price charged by the middle-ranked company).

66. The use of various forms of averages or other forms of data aggregation can be appropriate, provided that like with like is compared. For example, where a wholesaler claims damages for having purchased a product in January, May, July and October 2009 from the participants in a price cartel and where the chosen method is comparison with another geographic market, the monthly average prices paid in that market by the *same type of customer* (wholesaler) during the *same months* may be the appropriate reference point (i.e. comparing January data with January data, May data with May data,

and so forth). Comparing data from the same months will, for instance, account for seasonal differences over a year and thus make the comparison more reliable. If, however, little monthly price variation exists, the average price on the comparator market for the entire year of 2009 may be considered an appropriate indicator. It may also be the case that yearly data or other average data (e.g. aggregated industry data) are simply the only information available. Legal systems in the Member States may generally allow parties to rely on average data whilst granting the defendant the opportunity to show that significant differences exist, and they may require the use of more disaggregated data where available.

67. Another simple technique for deriving a comparator value from a range of data observations is linear interpolation. Where a comparison over time has produced price series from before and after the infringement, the 'non-infringement' or 'counterfactual' price during the infringement period can be estimated by drawing a line between the pre-infringement price and the post-infringement price, as shown in the illustration below. From this line, a comparator value can be read for each relevant point in time during the infringement period. Compared with the calculation of a single average value for price during the entire infringement period, interpolation therefore allows to some degree to account for trends in price developments over time that are not due to the infringement. Reading comparator data from the interpolated line will, therefore, produce more accurate results than using an average value for the period, e.g. in cases where damages are claimed that result from transactions (or other events) which occurred only towards the beginning or the end of the infringement period.[60] The following illustration gives a simple example of linear interpolation (the dotted line shows the interpolated non-infringement price, the full line the actually observed prices):

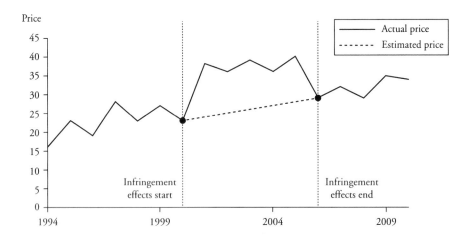

Linear extrapolation works similarly to interpolation except that the line is continued from either only pre- or only post-infringement data.[61]

Notes

[60] Interpolation likewise has advantages over using averages where the number of transactions (or other events) is unevenly distributed during the infringement period.

[61] Extrapolation thus extends a trend existing in a time series either before or after the infringement. For example, if in the three years before a cartel prices were € 12, € 13.20, and € 14.52 respectively (reflecting a 10% increase each year), a simple technique would be to estimate that prices during the two-year duration of a cartel were € 15.97 and € 17.57 respectively; a more accurate estimation of the underlying trend could be obtained through using regression analysis.

68. There may be situations where it is quite straightforward to identify a differentiating factor between an infringement market (or period) and a comparator market (or period) and to make the corresponding adjustment to the value of the observed comparator data. For example, certain seasonal effects occurring on a market or effects stemming from changes in input prices or exchange rates may

have a pattern and a magnitude that can in some cases be rather easily understood from internal business records of a party or from other sources, such as expert statements. In these cases, for example, the straight line obtained in a simple linear interpolation should be adjusted to reflect such patterns.[62]

Notes

[62] Such adjustment, could, data permitting, be done in a more sophisticated way by using regression analysis as explained in the following section.

(2) Regression analysis

a. Concept and purpose of regression analysis

69. Regression analysis is a statistical technique which helps to investigate patterns in the relationship between economic variables and to measure to what extent a certain variable of interest[63] (e.g., in the flour cartel example, the price for flour[64]) is influenced by the infringement as well as by other variables that are not affected by the infringement[65] (e.g. raw material costs, variations in customer demand, product characteristics, the level of market concentration)[66]. Regression analysis therefore makes it possible to assess whether, and by how much, observable factors other than the infringement have contributed to the difference between the value of the variable of interest observed on the infringement market during the infringement period and the value observed in a comparator market or during a comparator time period. Regression analysis is thus a way to account for alternative causes for the difference between the compared data sets. All comparator-based methods are, in principle, capable of being implemented through regression analysis provided that sufficient data observations are available.[67]

Notes

[63] Also referred to as an 'explained variable' or 'dependent variable'.

[64] Possible other variables of interest for which regression analysis may be applied include, for instance, sales volumes, market shares or profit margins (e.g. those of an excluded competitor who claims damages for loss of profits through a reduction of sales or a decrease in its margins), costs of production (which may also be relevant in the context of a loss of profits estimation).

[65] Also referred to as 'explanatory variable(s)' or 'influencing variable(s)'.

[66] Other factors influencing the variable of interest may, for example, include customer and order sizes, the technology used for production, the size and cost structure of the firms offering the product, or advertising expenditure.

[67] A sufficient number of data observations is, however, required to apply statistical methods in a meaningful manner. Such sets of data observations could be obtained (in comparisons over time) from time series of observations, or (in comparisons at one point in time) from a range of comparator markets or from a range of firms or a range of transactions, or a combination of both (observations over time from a range of markets, firms or transactions).

70. In a regression analysis, a number of data observations for the variable of interest and the likely influencing variables are examined by means of statistical techniques. The relationship identified is usually described in the form of an equation (referred to as a 'regression equation' or 'regression model'). This equation makes it possible to estimate the effects of influencing variables on the variable of interest and to isolate them from the effects of the infringement. Regression analysis estimates how closely the relevant variables are correlated[68] with each other, which may in some instances be suggestive of a causal influence of one variable on the other.[69]

Notes

[68] In multivariate regression analysis (see in more detail below), the correlation established is a conditional correlation, i.e. one where the effect of other variables is controlled for.

[69] Provided this is consistent with a coherent economic framework and with other pieces of qualitative and quantitative evidence.

71. There are two main approaches to carrying out a regression analysis for damages estimation, depending on whether only data from non-infringement periods (markets) are used to build the regression equation or whether, in addition to non-infringement data, also data from within the infringement period (market) are used. If only data from non-infringement periods are used to estimate the regression, the regression equation would be used to 'forecast' the effect on the variable of

interest during the infringement period on the basis of the pattern identified outside this period ('forecasting approach').[70] Where, in addition, also data from the infringement period (market) are used to estimate the regression, the effect of the infringement would be accounted for in the regression equation through a separate indicator variable (called 'dummy variable').[71]

Notes

[70] This 'forecasting approach' is sometimes also referred to as a 'residual model approach'. This approach is illustrated in the graph in paragraph 79 below.

[71] Such a 'dummy variable' measures whether there has been an upward shift in the variable of interest during the infringement period.

72. Whether it is more appropriate to apply the forecasting or the dummy variable approach will depend on the circumstances of the case: In particular, while the forecasting method has the advantage of allowing the choice of a regression model that is only based on data observations from the non-infringement period (and hence, untainted by the effects of the infringement), using data from both periods/markets may allow a more precise and accurate estimation of the parameters of interest, in particular if the available non-infringement data are limited or do not allow the dynamics of the industry at hand to be fully captured. In practice, both methods can often be combined, e.g. by selecting the model on the basis of the pre-infringement period and estimating a dummy-variable regression using data from both periods (and allowing, if appropriate, the effects of the other influencing variables to vary in the infringement and non-infringement periods).

b. Examples and illustrations

73. A simple example that, for illustrative purposes, looks only at one potential influencing variable may show the basic steps in regression analysis. Assume that, in the above-mentioned example of a flour cartel, the prices paid by bakeries during the cartel period to the milling companies are compared with the prices paid by bakeries to the milling companies in the pre-infringement period, and that this comparison shows a price increase during the infringement period of 20%. Assume further that there are indications that this increase is not exclusively due to the cartel but that during the infringement period costs for an important input material (e.g. cereals) also increased significantly. It is therefore not clear how much of the increase in price for flour is due to the infringement and how much is due to the increased input costs (the rise in cereals prices).

74. One option to address this uncertainty could be to use data from another period or market where input costs (price for cereals) were more similar and no infringement existed, but there may be situations where this is not possible.[72] Regression analysis can offer a tool to account for the variation in input costs, by showing the statistical relationship between input costs and price for flour. To this end, a range of data observations on input costs (cereal prices) and on prices for flour during the period not affected by the infringement could be examined.[73] Through applying statistical techniques to these data observations, it is possible to establish a pattern of how the prices for cereals influenced the price for flour in a period where the flour prices were not influenced by the infringement. It is then possible to deduce a statistical relationship between the price for flour and the price for cereals from this period. By applying the insight on this relationship to the prices for flour from the infringement period, it is possible to eliminate the part of the increase of prices for flour not imputable to the infringement, but to the change in input costs. This allows to 'forecast' prices for flour without the cartel overcharge but including the price increase caused by higher input costs.

Notes

[72] For instance, because reliable data from other periods (or markets) are not available or because in such other periods (or markets) market characteristics differed significantly.

[73] On the possibility of whether or not to also consider data from the infringement period (market), see paragraph 82 below.

75. The following graph gives a simple illustration of how such a statistical relationship is deduced. The chart shows several data observations of the input costs (cereals prices) and the corresponding price for flour at the same point in time during a non-infringement period. For instance, when at one particular moment the price for cereals was 60, the price for flour was 128. It is possible to calculate the

coordinates of the line that best fits all data observations in order to represent the statistical relationship (correlation) between the price for cereals and the price for flour. This relationship is expressed in the graph below as a line and can be, and usually is, also expressed as an equation.[74] The steepness of this line shows what increase in the price for flour is associated with a certain increase in the price for cereals. In the example shown in the graph, the identified relationship indicates that e.g. a rise in the price for cereals from 50 to 60 relates to a rise in price for flour from 120 to 130. As an increase in input costs (cereals) by € 10 is associated with a flour price increase of € 10, the statistical relationship thus shows that an increase in this input cost is fully passed on.

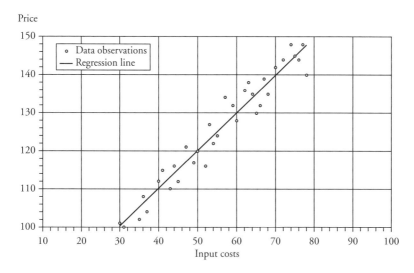

Notes

[74] Estimating a regression of price (as the variable of interest) over input costs (as the influencing variable) provides the coordinates of this line. In this example, the ordinary least squares (OLS) technique is used to calculate the coordinates of a straight line that is located at a minimal distance ('least squares') from the set of data points on the graph. The OLS technique is a common statistical method to estimate the parameters of a linear regression model.

76. Knowing the pattern of how the input cost (cereals prices) influenced prices for flour outside the infringement period makes it possible to estimate ('forecast') how much the observed higher values of these costs (cereals prices) during the infringement period influenced prices for flour. Excluding these effects from the price comparison allows the price overcharge caused by the infringement to be estimated on a more reliable basis than without the regression analysis. In the above example, if during the infringement period the price for flour was 140 instead of 120 during the non-infringement period, but the input cost (cereals prices) increased from 50 to 60, the likely price for flour without the cartel would not be 120 but 130.

77. Whilst the example described so far concerned only the influence of a *single* other variable (cereals price as input cost) on the variable of interest (flour price), regression analysis in competition practice usually has to account for *several* other factors influencing the variable of interest (*multiple* regression analysis[75]). In this situation, data need to be observed for all additional relevant influencing variables and a regression equation needs to be deduced from these data that reflects their relationship to the variable of interest. For instance, in the above-mentioned flour cartel example, it may be the case that during the infringement period the milling companies not only had to pay higher prices for cereals, but were also subject to an increase in energy and labour costs and introduced a more efficient milling and packaging technology, all of which may have had an impact on the price of the flour they sold to bakeries during the cartel period. To identify the statistical pattern of how these factors influenced the flour price, series of data observations for each of these influencing variables need to be analysed.

Notes

75 Also referred to as 'multivariate regression analysis' as opposed to 'single variable ('univariate') regression analysis' as used in the above example.

78. When undertaking a regression analysis, it is important to consider all variables that are relevant in the specific case. Suppose that either the defendant or the claimant uses, in a comparison of the flour prices charged by a mill before and during an infringement, a multiple regression analysis to control for the potential influence on the flour price of the above-mentioned factors (i.e. the cereal prices, energy and labour costs and milling and packaging technology). If, however, a significant demand change took place during the cartel (e.g. higher demand by bakeries for flour due to an increased demand by end customers for bread and cake) and if the influence of this event on the price for flour is not accounted for in the regression equation, the estimate of the infringement effect is likely to be biased, despite the otherwise comprehensive regression analysis.[76] It is for the applicable national law to determine, in accordance with the principle of effectiveness, the party on which the burden falls to invoke and prove facts, such as the above-mentioned change in demand or the completeness of the variables considered in a regression analysis.

Notes

76 It is, however, important not only to include all relevant factors in the regression model, but also to refrain from including variables that appear clearly irrelevant (on the basis of industry knowledge). In fact, damages estimates could be wrongly lowered (even down to zero) if irrelevant variables are included in order to explain the price variation in the model.

79. The basis of each damages quantification using regression analysis is thus the statistical relationship between the variable of interest (e.g. price) and the relevant explanatory variable(s) expressed in a regression equation. When the forecasting approach is used,[77] the estimation of a regression equation using data from the non-infringement period constitutes the first step. In a second step, using this regression equation and the observed values of these relevant variables during the infringement period, the price injured parties are likely to have paid without the infringement can then be estimated. In a third step, the difference between this likely non-infringement price and the price actually paid by the injured parties gives an estimate of the overcharge resulting from the infringement. The graph below illustrates the second and the third step. When the dummy variable approach is used, the regression analysis combines the three steps described above.[78]

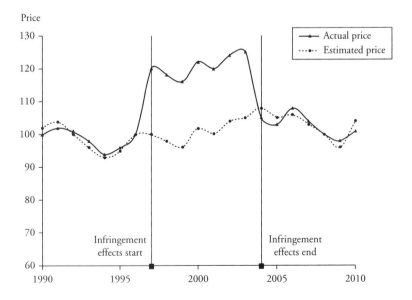

Part B Procedural Matters

Notes

77 The alternative approach is the dummy variable approach; see paragraph 71 above. Unlike the forecasting approach, the dummy variable approach estimates the effect of the infringement in a single step, by carrying out a regression analysis using data from both the infringement and non-infringement periods. In the case of the example above, this approach would estimate the effect of the cartel as the upward shift in price that is observed during the cartel period (i.e. the coefficient of the dummy variable in the regression equation) and is not explained by changes in other influencing variables, such as raw material costs.

78 In this case, the regression equation is estimated using data from both the infringement and non-infringement periods and directly indicates how much the variable of interest changed during the infringement period after accounting for the effect of other explanatory variables.

80. The regression analysis illustrated in this graph is based on the forecasting approach, in which a regression is carried out on pre- and post-infringement data to establish in an equation the statistical relationship between price and various relevant explanatory variables (input costs and other relevant factors). Using this equation and the observed values of the relevant explanatory variables, an estimated price can be derived that is likely to have prevailed absent the infringement (dotted line). The continuous line is the actually observed price. The difference between the continuous and the dotted line during the infringement period is the estimated overcharge. The dotted line outside the infringement period is also derived from the regression equation and can serve, through comparison with the actually observed non-infringement prices (continuous line), to assess the predictive power of the regression model.

c. Requirements for applying regression analysis

81. Carrying out a regression analysis requires knowledge of various statistical techniques to measure the relationship between variables, to construct an appropriate regression equation and to calculate the precision of the parameters in this equation. In addition, it is necessary to have a good understanding of the industry concerned, in the first place, to formulate the right hypotheses when constructing the regression equation and to make the right choice as to the factors that are likely to have significantly influenced the variable of interest (and which should therefore be included in the analysis). Industry understanding is furthermore necessary to make informed choices about which statistical techniques to use in a given situation, for instance, to account for unusual observations (outliers) or other specific features in data sets. In particular, where the influencing variables were themselves affected by the infringement, biased results may occur if this aspect is not taken into account, e.g. through applying specific statistical techniques[79] or through using data observations that lie outside the infringement period or market.[80]

Notes

79 For example, the use of instrumental variables, an econometric technique that may be applied to correct such bias.

80 In particular, by using the forecasting approach described above, where the value of the influencing variables included in the model to predict the counterfactual are corrected for the infringement effect on these variables.

82. Without a sufficient number of data observations, statistical analysis cannot identify relationships between economic variables. To identify the effect of influencing variables on the variable of interest therefore requires that a sufficient range of data observations is available for all variables considered. Regression analysis therefore typically requires extensive data. However, statistical techniques may help to overcome some gaps in data or biases in their interpretation[81] and there can be situations where also the analysis of a smaller number of data observations is meaningful.

Notes

81 E.g. where a sample of data observations is not fully representative.

83. Data observations can, in principle, be gathered at different levels of aggregation. For example, where the relationship between price and input cost is to be analysed, data series either for the prices charged in individual transactions, for annual industry average prices or — in between — monthly data at firm level could be examined next to data series either for individual input costs per unit or for industry cost averages respectively. Using disaggregated data makes it possible to analyse a greater number of observations and therefore to obtain more precise estimates. Where such disaggregated

data do not exist or are not accessible to the party carrying out the regression analysis, the analysis of aggregated data may still produce informative results, in particular if the aggregated data have a high frequency.

84. Having a sufficient range of data observations and the level of data aggregation are examples of the importance of data reliability and data relevance for economic analysis. However, most datasets are incomplete, and not all relevant facts may be observed or measured with high accuracy. It is therefore proper to explicitly acknowledge those imperfections. Deficiencies in the data should not prevent an economic analysis from being given proper weight, though conclusions should be drawn with caution.[82]

Notes

[82] See for a further explanation on the importance of data reliability and data relevance: DG COMP Best Practices for the submission of economic evidence and data collection in cases concerning the application of Articles 101 and 102 TFEU and in merger cases, at http://ec.europa.eu/competition/antitrust/legislation/best_practices_submission_en.pdf. [Ed note: this document is reproduced at B17 above.]

---

85. Where used appropriately and on the basis of sufficient data observations, regression analysis can considerably refine the damages estimation through comparator-based methods. It should be stressed, however, that even very sophisticated regression equations rely on a range of assumptions and will (like any technique to predict a hypothetical situation) only be able to deliver estimates. It is good practice to consider the assumptions underlying a regression equation, because some assumptions may be more appropriate than others in a given situation and may lead to significantly different results.

86. One way to deal with the uncertainty of the estimate is to indicate the results not as a point estimate ('the price in the non-infringement scenario is 10 €'), but as an interval ('the price in the non-infringement scenario is between 9 € and 11 €'). The notion of 'confidence interval' – which is standard in statistics – is used to describe how likely it is that the true value is contained in an interval. By convention in economics, a 95% likelihood that a specific interval does in fact contain the true value is regarded as a high degree of certainty.

87. A similar way of dealing with the uncertainty of estimates is to refer to the notion of 'statistical significance', which is a standard way of testing whether the results obtained in a regression analysis are due to a coincidence or whether they reflect in fact a genuine correlation. For this, a certain hypothesis is tested: in the field of damages actions, such a hypothesis could for instance be whether the cartel infringement did in fact have an actual effect on prices or not. The hypothesis that the infringement did *not* have an effect (and that therefore the non-infringement price does not differ from the price in the infringement scenario) is called the 'null hypothesis'. Regression analysis is then used to test this null hypothesis. A result of a regression analysis is said to be statistically significant when it is possible to reject the null hypothesis, because it would be very unlikely that the results observed are due to chance. By convention, a likelihood of at least 95% that the null hypothesis is rejected is regarded in economics as allowing to judge that the results are 'statistically significant'.

88. As described above, it is a convention in economic science for both the notion of 'confidence interval' and 'statistical significance' to use a 95% threshold of probability. It should be stressed that this represents a pure convention and that more as well as less stringent thresholds (for instance: 99%, or 90% probability) may likewise provide useful information. This is because statistical significance is determined, in part, by the number of observations in the data set: other things being equal, the statistical significance increases as the sample size increases. It is good practice to indicate the probability threshold chosen. In a damages action, it is then for the court, under applicable law to decide, the probative value of such regression analysis and the procedural consequences (in particular with regard to the burden of fact-pleading and proof) which such analysis may entail.

89. Whether, by which party and at which stage of the proceedings a regression analysis is carried out in a court case will *inter alia* depend on the existence or accessibility of data and the rules under applicable law regarding fact pleading requirements, disclosure of evidence, the standard of proof and the allocation of the burden of proof between the claimant and the defendant.

90. The different forms of regression analysis mentioned above (paragraphs 71 ff.) are sometimes referred to as 'reduced form' approaches, as they directly estimate parameters of an equation that are themselves derived from other economic relationships (e.g. the interaction of supply and demand), without modelling these explicitly. Alternatively, econometric models can be built to estimate these underlying economic relationships. Although such econometric models, which are usually referred to as 'structural', often rely on particularly strong assumptions, they may bring a deeper understanding of the market concerned and form an integral part of simulation exercises to estimate damages (as further detailed in section III.A).

(3) Choice of techniques

91. Sections 1 and 2 above have described different techniques whereby comparator-based methods can be implemented in practice. In a given case, the choice of technique will usually depend on a range of aspects, in particular the legal requirements and the factual circumstances of the case. Considerations relating to the standard and burden of proof are likely to be very relevant in practice.

92. Econometric techniques can increase the degree of accuracy of a damages estimate and may thus help in meeting a higher standard of proof if required under applicable rules. Whether regression analysis is required (possibly in addition to other evidence available) to meet such a standard, and on which party the burden of proof falls in this respect are questions of applicable law, including the EU law principle of effectiveness. It should be considered that carrying out an econometric analysis usually requires a significant number of data observations, which may not always be accessible. Moreover, it may also be that in a given procedural situation the applicable standard of proof does not require the party charged with the burden of proof to go further than the techniques mentioned in Section 1 above. This could be because the national legal system concerned considers the markets or periods compared as sufficiently similar and the estimate of damages resulting from the simple comparison as sufficiently accurate for what the party has to show in the given procedural situation. It may also be that the legal system, in view of the damages estimation presented by a claimant and the data that are reasonably accessible to him, provides for a shift of the burden of proof from the claimant to the defendant. In such a situation, the defendant may consider carrying out a regression analysis to rebut the submission of the claimant.

93. Considerations of proportionality may also play an important role, as the gathering of data and their econometric analysis can entail considerable costs (including those of third parties) that may be disproportionate to or even exceed the value of the damages claim at hand. Such considerations may also become relevant with a view to the principle of effectiveness.[83]

Notes
[83] See above paragraph 2 in Part 1, Section 1.

94. Courts in the EU have mainly used straightforward implementations of comparator-based methods without regression analysis, often on the basis of averages.[84] They have also accepted simple adjustments to the value of observed data when it is quite straightforward to identify a differentiating factor between an infringement market (or period) and a comparator market (or period). To date, little experience exists with econometric analysis in actions for antitrust damages before courts in the EU,[85] although such techniques can, as described above, provide valuable help in quantifying the harm suffered through infringements of Article 101 or 102 TFEU.

Notes
[84] The use of averages was accepted in e.g. *Landgericht Dortmund* (Regional Court, Dortmund), decision of 1 April 2004, Case No 13 O 55/02 Kart (*Vitaminpreise*); WuW/DE-R 1352.
[85] For a recent example concerning lost profits in an exclusionary case see *Juzgado Mercantil numero 2 de Barcelona* (Commercial Court, Barcelona), decision of 20 January 2011, case No 45/2010 (Céntrica Energìa S.L.U./Endesa Distribuciòn Eléctrica S.A.).

95. Courts in the EU sometimes also apply a 'safety discount', i.e. they deduct from the observed data values an amount sufficient, under the standards of applicable law, to take account of uncertainties in a damages estimate.[86] Regression analysis can also be considered to account for these other possible influencing factors, and to obtain a 'lower bound estimate' of the damages incurred.[87]

Part B Procedural Matters

Notes

86 For instance, to exclude the effects on the variable of interest of possible other factors. See e.g. *Kammergericht Berlin* (Higher Regional Court, Berlin), decision of 1 October 2009, case No 2 U 10/03 Kart.; *Oberlandesgericht Karlsruhe* (Higher Regional Court, Karlsruhe) of 11 June 2010 in case No 6 U118/05.

87 Indeed, in addition to providing damages estimates that already control for the influence of other factors, regression analysis also measures the precision of these estimates (in the form of 'standard errors'), from which lower (and upper) bounds on the estimated damages can be obtained.

III. Simulation Models, Cost-Based and Finance-Based Analysis and Other Methods

96. Alongside comparator-based methods, other methods exist to establish an estimate for the hypothetical non-infringement situation. Such other methods include, in particular, the simulation of market outcomes on the basis of economic models (A), and the approach to estimate a likely non-infringement scenario on the basis of costs of production and a reasonable profit margin (B).

A. Simulation models

97. Simulation methods draw on economic models of market behaviour. Economic studies on how markets function and how firms compete with each other have shown that markets with certain characteristics may allow the likely outcomes of market interaction to be predicted, for instance the likely price or production levels or profit margins. The branch of economics known as industrial organisation has developed models of competition for various types of markets that can simulate such outcomes. These models range from monopoly models to, at the other end of the spectrum, perfect competition models.

98. Intermediate models designed to reflect firm behaviour in oligopolistic markets are, in particular, those designed originally in the 19th century by the economists Augustin Cournot and Joseph Bertrand. The Bertrand oligopoly model of competition describes a market with a relatively small number of firms (and high barriers to entry) that compete on price, not output quantity. Firms set their price simultaneously, based on their beliefs about the prices their competitors will charge. In this model, prices increase with the degree of product differentiation. The Cournot oligopoly model of competition describes a market with a relatively small number of firms (and high barriers to entry) that compete on the amount of output they will produce. Before they choose prices, they set their quantity (or capacity) simultaneously on the basis of how much they each believe the other firms will produce. Numerous extensions and variations of the Cournot and Bertrand models exist. These include, in particular, dynamic oligopoly models based on game theory[88] that take into account the repeated interaction between firms in the market.[89]

Notes

88 Game theory is the study of how people and firms behave in strategic situations in which they must consider how others respond to their action.

89 Taking into account the repeated interaction between firms in the market can be useful to explain, for instance, coordinated behaviour between firms or market entry of a new competitor.

99. Prices are likely to be highest (and sales volumes lowest) in a monopoly and prices are likely to be lowest (and sales volumes highest) in a situation of perfect competition. Bertrand oligopolies in markets with differentiated goods[90] and Cournot oligopolies will normally lead to prices and volumes somewhere between perfect competition and monopoly levels; the exact outcome depends inter alia on the number of firms in the market and barriers to entry, on the degree of differentiation between them and their products and on other characteristics of the market at hand, such as demand characteristics (especially, how sensitive customers are to changes in price), and the capacities and cost structure of producers.

Notes

90 In a market with homogeneous goods with no capacity constraints, Bertrand price competition will, in contrast, lead to very competitive outcomes. Homogenous goods are goods that have little differences in terms of quality or features.

100.   Based on such theoretical insights that link the market outcome e.g. in terms of prices to a given set of market characteristics, simulation models can be built to estimate the prices (or other variables) that are likely to have prevailed in the market had an infringement of Article 101 or 102 TFEU not occurred. The simulation model should be constructed in such a way that it replicates (a) the most significant factors influencing supply (in particular, the way competition takes place between firms ('competitive interactions')[91] and the cost structure of firms) and (b) demand conditions (in particular, the extent to which customers respond to price changes). These factors would be expressed as a set of equations in which a number of parameter values need to be included. These values may be known, estimated econometrically or assumed so that the output of the model matches some observed variables. When using simulation models to generate a non-infringement scenario, the relevant market structure and other characteristics must be those that would have existed without the infringement; these may correspond to the structure and other characteristics of the market observed in the infringement scenario, but they may also differ to some extent.[92]

Notes

[91] The term 'competitive interactions' is used to indicate how competition between firms takes place, e.g. (but not limited to) Bertrand or Cournot competition, or how firms refrain from competing between each other (in the case of collusive behaviour infringing competition rules). Markets on which price formation occurs through auctions or other bidding processes may also be conducive to modelling as interaction between competitors often follows fixed rules (prices or output quantities likely to result from an auction or other bidding process not affected by the infringement could, in particular, be estimated by oligopoly models that incorporate game theory to simulate the likely bidding behaviour of competitors in a non-infringement scenario).

[92] As the infringement may have led to a change in the market structure or may have prevented changes in the market that would otherwise have occurred (e.g. the exit of an inefficient competitor), the (hypothetical) market characteristics in the non-infringement scenario are not necessarily the same as those that could be observed in the infringement scenario. In addition, market shares observed during an infringement may significantly differ from those that would have prevailed in the absence of the infringement as cartel members may allocate markets between themselves.

101.   An example may illustrate the use of simulation modelling to estimate damages. In the example of a cartel on a differentiated product market (e.g. confectionary chocolates), non-infringement prices could be estimated as follows, using data from the non-infringement period. First, one would estimate how the demand for each chocolate product varies with its own price (own-price elasticity) and with the price of competing products (cross-price elasticity).[93] Second, one would decide which model appropriately reflects the competitive interaction between firms in the non-infringement period (e.g. the Bertrand model of competition in the confectionary chocolates example). On this basis, it can be calculated at which prices the profits of the firms are maximised in view of the cost parameters (e.g. marginal costs) and demand parameters (e.g. the level of demand).[94] The value of some of these parameters can then be adapted to reflect the relevant conditions during the infringement period (e.g. supposing the cost of cocoa increases by 10%). With all this information expressed in equations, it can be simulated (under the assumption that firms strive for maximised profits) what prices these firms are likely to have charged during the infringement period. The cartel overcharge can then be estimated by taking the difference between the observed prices and the simulated non-infringement prices.

Notes

[93] Technically, this would involve estimating a demand system, which is an example of the structural econometric analysis mentioned in paragraph 90.

[94] The value of these parameters (e.g. the value for marginal costs used in the calculation) in the non-infringement period can be determined so that the derived prices and volumes match the observed data.

102.   This example is particularly demanding in terms of data requirements and assumptions. Simpler simulation models may be envisaged to estimate damages but they rely even more heavily on crucial assumptions that are difficult to verify. For example, damages following a cartel infringement could be calculated by comparing monopoly prices (aimed at reflecting prices during the cartel) with prices expected under a Cournot model (aimed at reflecting prices in the non-infringement scenario), using data such as market shares, costs, and market price elasticity. However, such a method crucially depends on the assumed competitive interactions in the infringement and non-infringement scenarios and entails the risk that these do not mirror sufficiently closely the way in which the cartel

operates during the infringement period and the way in which competition on the market would have operated absent the infringement.

103. Simulation models can be used to estimate market outcomes not only in cartel cases (or other price raising infringements), but also in cases of exclusionary behaviour. For example, an oligopoly model could be used to simulate the sales volume and the market share a foreclosed competitor would have attained had the infringement not taken place.

104. Each model simulating market outcomes is an approximation of reality and relies on theoretical and often also factual assumptions regarding market characteristics and the likely behaviour of producers and customers. Although, by their very nature, models rely on simplification of reality, even simple models may in certain cases provide useful insights regarding the likely damages. Therefore, pointing out that a model relies on seemingly simplifying assumptions should therefore on its own not be sufficient to dismiss it; rather, one should consider how some of the simplifying assumptions are likely to affect its results. Building a comprehensive model that replicates a range of specific features of the market in question, if it can be properly solved and evaluated, can increase the likelihood that the result of the simulation is a reasonable estimate for the hypothetical non-infringement scenario. Even very comprehensive models, though, still depend very much on the right assumptions being made, in particular regarding the central questions of what is the likely mode of competition and the likely customer demand in the non-infringement scenario. Moreover, the development of complex simulation models can be technically demanding and may require significant amounts of data that may not always be accessible to the party concerned or possible to be estimated with sufficient reliability.

105. Nonetheless, both simple and more complex simulation models could provide useful insights when estimating the outcomes that a market would have produced absent an infringement of Article 101 or 102 TFEU. Whether and in which procedural situation legal systems will consider that the use of an economic simulation is appropriate and its results are sufficiently reliable will depend on the specific circumstances of the case in point and the requirements under applicable legal rules.

B. Cost-based and finance-based methods

106. Other approaches to estimating the likely prices that would have emerged absent the infringement is provided by the cost-based method[95] or by methods based on the financial performance of claimant or defendant undertakings (finance-based methods).

Notes

[95] This method is also referred to as the 'cost plus method' or 'bottom-up costing method'. It is mentioned, as a subsidiary approach in cases where comparator-based methods are not appropriate, by the *Bundesgerichtshof* (Federal Court of Justice, Germany), decision of 19 June 2007, case No KBR 12/07 (*Paper Wholesale Cartel*).

107. The cost-based method consists in using some measure of production costs per unit, and adding a mark-up for a profit that would have been 'reasonable' in the non-infringement scenario. The resulting estimate for a per unit non-infringement price can be compared to the per unit price actually charged by the infringing undertaking(s) to obtain an estimate of the overcharge.[96]

Notes

[96] Usually, the cost-based method is considered for quantifying price overcharges. The method, or elements of it, may, however, also be used for quantifying other forms of harm such as the profits lost by foreclosed competitors. For instance, the *Oberlandesgericht Düsseldorf* (Higher Regional Court, Düsseldorf), decision of 16 April 2008, case No VI-2 U (kart) 8/06, 2 U 8/06 (*Stadtwerke Düsseldorf*), estimated the lost profits of a foreclosed competitor by considering the costs of the competitor and the likely profit margin expressed as a proportion of these costs.

108. Different types of production costs may be suitable for implementing the cost-based method, depending on the characteristics of the industry concerned. It is, however, essential to ensure that the treatment of costs and margins is consistent. For example, if variable costs (i.e. costs that vary with the level of production) are considered as the basis of this exercise, a gross margin (i.e. the margin earned once variable costs have been deducted) should be added to calculate the price. It should also be noted that the relevant cost for determining prices may be not only the cost of the infringer, but also the cost of one of its competitors (e.g. if the price in the market is determined by the least efficient producer).

109. The first step of the cost-based method is to determine the production cost per unit. Per unit costs can be estimated by dividing the actual relevant production costs incurred by the infringer(s) for the relevant business activity by the total number of products produced. This approach can be rather straightforward where companies or separate business divisions of companies produce only one main product. Such companies or business divisions sometimes publish their major cost data or file this information as part of their audited accounts with public registries. In other situations, the access to data and the allocation of costs to the product affected by the infringement is more difficult. Where accounting data are available, adjustments may be necessary given that the notions of costs in accounting terms can differ from the notions of costs in economic terms.

110. It may occur that the observed production costs during the infringement are not representative of the production costs that would have been likely without the infringement. This could mainly be for two reasons: first, in the event of infringements of Article 101, companies which due to their collusive behaviour are not subject to the competitive pressure that would exist in the non-infringement scenario may operate less efficiently and therefore generate higher production costs than under competitive pressure. Second, infringers may restrict output and may therefore, during the infringement, forego economies of scale that would have led to lower production costs. Where indications for such situations exist, adjustments to the observed costs data of the infringer(s) may be appropriate. Where such adjustments are not made, the observed costs may still contribute, under the cost-based method, to a lower-bound estimate of the possible price overcharge.

111. The second step of the cost-based method requires a 'reasonable' profit margin to be estimated and added to the per unit production costs. Various approaches exist to estimate a 'reasonable' profit margin. They are based either on a comparison over time or across markets, or on economic models, and thus have commonalities with the methods described in the preceding Sections. For instance, an estimate for the profit margin that could reasonably be expected in a non-infringement scenario may be derived from the profit margins made by similar undertakings in a comparable geographic market not affected by the infringement or in comparable product markets.[97] Similarly, the profit margins of the infringing (or a similar) undertaking during the pre- or post infringement periods could be used as a basis for the estimate. Both these comparator-based methods rest on the assumption that the reference period, market or firm are sufficiently similar,[98] in particular with respect to market characteristics that are relevant for profit margins such as the level of competition in the market,[99] the cost structure of producers (including costs of innovation), capacity utilisation and capacity constraints. These assumptions are not always easily verified, as a large number of factors and strategic decisions are likely to determine a firm's price and margin setting.

Notes

[97] *Bundesgerichtshof* (Federal Court of Justice, Germany), decision of 19 June 2007, case No KBR 12/07 (*Paper Wholesale Cartel*), referring to the profit margins generated in 'comparable industries'.

[98] For relevant considerations regarding sufficient similarity see above paragraphs 38–58 in Part 2, Section II.

[99] E.g. whether competition would have been so strong as to drive the price downwards towards marginal costs (as assumed in the model of perfect competition) or whether profit margins, due to an oligopolistic structure, would have been higher even without the infringement.

112. Another approach to estimating a 'reasonable' profit margin is to consider the nature of competition and the characteristics of the market absent the infringement and to derive a likely profit margin from the insights from industrial organisation models.[100] For instance, absent the infringement, prices may be likely to tend towards costs due to relative homogeneity of goods and overcapacities in the market; in such cases, the likely profit margin of producers would be relatively low.[101]

Notes

[100] See above paragraphs 97 ff. in Part 2, Section III.

[101] The cost of capital (i.e. the cost at which a firm can obtain capital on the market) is sometimes considered as an approximation of a 'reasonable' profit margin in such cases. However, margins in the absence of an infringement may significantly differ from the cost of capital, for example in the absence of perfect competition or in the presence of firm-specific cost advantages for certain firms, or demand and supply shocks.

113. It is clear from the above that both the estimation of likely non-infringement costs and the estimation of a 'reasonable' profit margin can, in practice, require a range of difficult issues to be considered. In addition, the cost-based method supposes access to data that may be in the possession of the opposing party or a third party. Nonetheless, depending on the circumstances of the particular case and on the requirements under applicable legal rules, it may provide useful insights to support an estimation of the harm suffered through an antitrust infringement.

114. Methods based on financial analysis take the financial performance of the claimant or the defendant undertaking as the starting point for estimating whether the claimant has suffered harm and the amount of that harm.

115. Where the claimant in an action for damages is an undertaking and the infringement has caused harm to that undertaking, it is possible that an analysis of the financial situation of that undertaking (and in particular its profitability) may give useful insights into that harm. This may be particularly useful in instances where loss of profits is claimed, for example in the case of a competitor illegally foreclosed from a market.

116. On this basis, standard methods to assess the profitability of an undertaking (such as for instance the 'net present value' method, which calculates the present value of future cash flows of an undertaking) may be used to give insights into the amount of harm. Likewise, methods of business valuations, including accounting methods, may yield useful insights.

117. For all of these methods, the appropriate counterfactual scenario has to be determined: once the actual profitability of the claimant undertaking has been calculated, it must be assessed how that profitability would have been had there been no infringement. It is possible to build this counterfactual by using profitability data from a comparator market – this approach is then similar to the comparator-based methods discussed above.[102] For instance, the profitability of the claimant before and after the infringement could be used to construct a non-infringement scenario. It is also possible to use an alternative standard to construct the counterfactual. One possibility in this regard is to use the cost of capital as a benchmark: this measure describes the minimal profit margin necessary in a particular industry to attract capital and it can therefore be appropriate to presume that the undertaking in question would at least have obtained that minimum profit in the non-infringement scenario.

Notes

[102] See in more detail at paragraph 32 ff.

---

118. One advantage of financial methods is that in some case, the information necessary to apply them may be held by undertakings because of accounting requirements, or may even be publicly available, as may be the case of publicly traded companies.

C. Other methods

119. The methods described in this Practical Guide are those that have received most consideration so far in legal practice and academic scholarship. They should, however, not be seen as an exhaustive list, firstly, as the methods described could further evolve or others could be developed in practice.

120. Secondly, there are methods *not* discussed in this Practical Guide could nonetheless prove useful, in particular, in order to establish an upper- or lower-bound[103] or approximate estimate[104] for the harm suffered. Especially where the legal systems provide for the possibility of an approximate estimation, national courts have opted for pragmatic techniques rather than a sophisticated implementation of the methods set out in Sections A and B above to establish the amount of damages to be awarded to injured parties. For instance, in cases where a new entrant has been foreclosed in breach of Article 101 or 102 TFEU, business plans have sometimes been used[105] as a source of information on the likely profits of a business, albeit in some instances adjusted depending on the market circumstances or through the use of data from a comparator market or undertaking.

Notes

[103] For example, an upper-bound estimation could be obtained through critical loss analysis. This technique assesses for a price increase what loss in quantities would make that price increase unprofitable.

[104] For instance, counterfactual profits could be *prima facie* identified by taking as a benchmark the cost of capital, on the assumption that, absent the infringement, the undertaking would have earned the cost of capital, which represents the minimum return required by providers of capital to an undertaking. On the limitations of this approach, see footnote 101.

[105] See for instance *Højesteret* (Danish Supreme Court), judgment of 20 April 2005, case UFR 2005.217H (*GT Linien A/S* v *De Danske Statsbaner DSB and Scandlines A/S*).

121. It is for national courts to establish whether, under the applicable rules, a method can be accepted for the quantification of harm in a given case, provided that the principles of effectiveness and equivalence of EU law are observed.

IV. Choice of methods

122. Each of the methods described in Sections II and III above can, in principle, provide useful insights in relation to all infringements of Article 101 or 102 TFEU and the different types of harm such infringements tend to produce. In particular, they make it possible to estimate not only the amount of illegal price overcharge in a price fixing cartel but also, for example, the sales volume or the profit lost by a company suffering harm through an exclusionary abuse by a dominant competitor.

123. It should be stressed that it is only possible to estimate, not to measure with certainty and precision, what the hypothetical non-infringement scenario is likely to have looked like. There is no method that could be singled out as the one that would in all cases be more appropriate than others. Each of the methods described above has particular features, strengths and weaknesses that may make it more or less suitable to estimate the harm suffered in a given set of circumstances. In particular, the methods differ in the degree to which they are simple to apply, in the degree to which they rely on data that are the outcome of actual market interactions or on assumptions based on economic theory and in the extent to which they take into account factors other than the infringement that may have affected the situation of the parties.

124. In the specific circumstances of any given case, the appropriate approach to quantification must be determined under the applicable rules of law. Relevant considerations may include, alongside the standard and burden of proof under applicable legal rules, the availability of data, the costs and time involved and their proportionality in relation to the value of the damages claim at stake. The costs to be considered in this context may not only be those incurred when the party bearing the burden of proof applies the method, but also include the costs for the other party to rebut its submissions and the costs to the judicial system when the court assesses the results produced by the method, possibly with the help of a court-appointed expert. The costs and burden for an injured party and their proportionality may become particularly relevant with a view to the principle of effectiveness.[106] Moreover, the decision under applicable law as to whether and, if so, which of the methods and techniques described in this Practical Guide should be used may also depend on the availability of other evidence, for instance documentary evidence produced by the undertakings on the course of business showing that an illegally agreed price increase was actually implemented at a certain amount.

Notes

[106] See above paragraph 2 in Part 1, Section 1.

125. It may be that in a given case the application of *several* methods (e.g. comparison over time and comparison across geographic markets) is envisaged, either alternatively or cumulatively. Where two different methods yield results that are similar, such findings may lead a legal system to attribute stronger evidentiary value to the damages estimate, possibly a lower bound, based on these methods. Where, however, the application of two methods produces apparently contradictory results (especially when two opposing parties each rely on a different method), it is normally not appropriate to simply take the average of the two results, nor would it be appropriate to consider that the contradictory results cancel each other out in the sense that both methods should be disregarded. In such a scenario it would rather be appropriate to examine the reasons for the diverging results and to carefully consider the strengths and weaknesses of each method and its implementation in the case at hand.

PART 3 QUANTIFYING HARM CAUSED BY A RISE IN PRICES

I. EFFECTS OF INFRINGEMENTS LEADING TO A RISE IN PRICES

126. Anticompetitive practices can have the effect of raising the prices that direct and often also indirect customers[107] of the infringing undertakings pay for the product concerned. The direct customers of the infringing undertakings are those who purchase a product directly from one of the infringing undertakings; indirect customers are those who purchase a product affected by the infringement from such direct customers or from other indirect customers.

Notes

[107] In some instances, undertakings that do not infringe the competition rules themselves can raise their prices, as market prices are higher because of the infringement. Customers who purchase from these undertakings are sometimes referred to as 'umbrella customers'. To what extent such customers can claim compensation for the harm from the infringing undertakings depends on the applicable legal rules.

---

127. Typical examples of infringements leading to such increases are price cartels, or excessive pricing by a dominant undertaking. Customers can also be affected by practices that limit output or allocate customers or markets — distortions of competition which in turn normally lead to a rise in prices. A different type of harm is caused where infringements adversely affect the market position of competitors; the quantification of such harm and its consequences for customers is discussed in Part 4 below.

128. In so far as infringements lead to a rise in prices for the products concerned, two main kinds[108] of harm caused by such infringement can be distinguished:

(a) the harm resulting from the fact that direct and indirect customers of the infringing undertakings have to pay more for each product they purchase than without the infringement (the 'overcharge'). This type of harm is further discussed in Section II; and

(b) the harm resulting from the so-called 'volume effect', which is caused by the fact that fewer of the products in question are bought due to the rise in prices. This type of harm is further discussed in Section III. The following figure represents in a stylised way these two main effects:

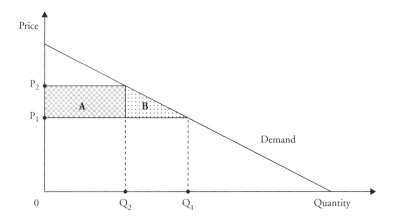

Notes

[108] For other kinds of harm, see above paragraph 22 in Part 1, Section III.

---

129. P_1 is the price charged if no infringement of Article 101 or 102 TFEU affects the market. In a perfectly competitive market, this price will equal the supplier's cost of producing one more unit ('the marginal cost'). Many markets are in fact not perfectly competitive and non-infringement prices on these markets will be above the level of marginal costs. At price P_1, Q_1 is the quantity of the product bought by customers.

130. P_2 is the higher price resulting from an infringement having an effect on price. This in turn leads to lower demand (Q_2) because some customers will consider that the higher price they have to pay

exceeds the value of owning the product or of benefiting from the service. This effect is referred to as the 'volume effect' or the 'quantity effect'. The degree to which a rise in prices affects demand depends on demand elasticity: Demand elasticity measures by what percentage the quantity sold of a product in a given market varies in response to a one percent price change for a particular demand level, and provides a useful indication of the magnitude of the volume effect for small price changes.

131. Rectangle A represents the value transferred from the customers to the infringers due to the infringement: the customers who buy at the higher price P_2 have to transfer more money to the infringing undertaking(s) in order to obtain the product. They can demand compensation for having had to pay more and Section II below will explain how to quantify this harm.

132. Triangle B represents the volume effect and thus the value foregone by those who would have bought the product for price P_1, but refrain from doing so when the price rises to P_2.[109]

Notes

[109] For the economy as a whole, this triangle therefore represents the loss in value for customers due to a reduction in output: while the overcharge affects the distribution of assets within the economy, triangle B means welfare not created because of the infringement. This is referred to in economics as 'deadweight loss'.

133. Some customers use the product in question for their own commercial activities — for example to sell it on or to manufacture other goods. When they do not buy at price P_2 (or buy less), they forego the profit they would have made had they been able to purchase at price P_1. They can claim reparation for this loss of profit and Section III below will illustrate how to quantify this harm. Other customers are end consumers. If these do not purchase at price this means that they fail to enjoy the utility of these products or services, for which they would have been prepared to pay price P_1.[110] Applicable legal rules may provide that some or all of such harm should be compensated for such failure to enjoy the usefulness of the product. At a minimum, end-consumers who have to bear higher costs (for example for the purchase of a substitute good) and who therefore have suffered an actual loss[111] must be able to obtain compensation.

Notes

[110] It is also possible that customers would have been prepared to pay a price higher than P_1, but lower than P_2.
[111] See, for this legal term, joined cases C-295/04 to C-298/04 *Manfredi* [2006] ECR I-6619, 95.

134. The foregoing summarises the basic effects on the market of infringements that lead to a *higher* selling price. Infringements of Article 101 or 102 TFEU can also affect the demand side and lead to lower purchasing prices paid by infringers in their own supply with products, for example in the case of a buyers' cartel or in the abuse of market power exercised by a dominant buyer vis-à-vis its suppliers. In such a case, the price effects would consist in an 'undercharge' for the supplier of the infringer, and often also an overcharge on the downstream markets, i.e. for the direct and indirect customers of the infringer.[112] The same methods used to quantify an overcharge can, in principle, also be used to quantify the undercharge, e.g. the lower prices paid by the members of a buyers' cartel vis-à-vis their suppliers.

Notes

[112] In order to drive down input prices, the cartel members/dominant buyers with downstream market power are likely to restrict their input purchases, hence also reducing output sales and increasing downstream prices.

135. The same methods can, in principle, also be used[113] where at first sight no overcharge is visible, because the infringement served to artificially stabilise prices over a certain period of time in which prices would under normal market circumstances (i.e. without infringement) have declined. In the following, the term 'overcharge' designates also these situations.

Notes

[113] Only the method based on comparison between time periods in the variant of 'before and during' comparison (i.e. comparing the infringement prices with pre-infringement prices) would obviously be unsuitable, unless regression analysis or simple adjustments are applied to account for the factors that would lead to a price decrease under normal market circumstances (e.g. decreased raw material costs).

II. Quantifying the Overcharge

136. Different types of infringements lead directly or indirectly to overcharges. Antitrust damages actions often deal with overcharges caused by cartels, which will be addressed in Section A below. The quantification of overcharges caused by other types of infringements will be addressed in Section B below.

A. *Quantifying overcharges caused by cartels*

137. In an action for compensation, it will be necessary — within the framework of applicable legal rules — to quantify the overcharge paid by the claimant(s). Economic and legal studies have analysed the effects of cartels; some insights from these studies are set out below in Section 1.

138. In actions for damages, it is useful to distinguish between the initial overcharge paid by the direct customer of the infringing undertaking (see below Section 2) and the possible harm that such overcharge causes to indirect customers at different levels of the supply chain (Section 3).

(1) Effects of cartels

139. Cartels are agreements and concerted practices between two or more undertakings aimed at influencing the parameters of competition through practices such as fixing the purchase or selling price or other trading conditions, allocating production or sales quotas or sharing markets (including bid-rigging). For the purpose of finding whether such practices infringe Article 101 TFEU, there is no need to quantify the concrete effects of such a practice, because the object of the cartel agreement is the prevention, restriction or distortion of competition.[114]

Notes

[114] Judgments of the General Court in joined cases T-25/95 etc. *Cimenteries CBR SA* v *Commission* [2000] ECR II-491, 837, 1531, 2589; case T-202/98 *Tate & Lyle v Commission* [2001] ECR II-2035, 72–74; Communication from the Commission: Guidelines on the application of Article [101](3) of the Treaty, OJ C 101, 27.4.2004, p.97, 20–23. [Ed note: the Guidelines are reproduced at C13.]

140. Infringing the competition rules exposes the cartel members to the risk of being discovered and thus subject to a decision finding an infringement and imposing fines. The fact alone that undertakings nonetheless engage in such illegal activity suggests that they expect to reap substantial benefits from their actions, i.e. that they expect the cartel to have effects on the market and, hence, on their customers.[115]

Notes

[115] See also the decision of the *Kammergericht Berlin* (Higher Regional Court, Berlin) of 1 October 2009 in case No 2 U 10/03, where the court referred to a similar argument.

141. A study undertaken for the Commission examined the empirical evidence on the existence of overcharge effects and on their magnitude.[116] This study draws on a range of existing empirical studies on the effects of cartels. In particular, it refines the sample of cartels examined in the most comprehensive existing study by considering only cartels (a) that started after 1960 (thus taking into account only more recent cartels), (b) for which an estimate of the average overcharge was available (rather than only an estimate of the highest or lowest overcharge), (c) for which the relevant background study explicitly explained the method for calculating the average overcharge estimate, and (d) which were discussed in peer-reviewed academic articles or chapters in books.[117] While some care is required in interpreting the results of this exercise,[118] the study undertaken for the Commission contains some useful information as to the effects of cartels.

Notes

[116] External study prepared for the Commission 'Quantifying antitrust damages' (2009), pages 88 ff., available at http://ec.europa.eu/competition/antitrust/actionsdamages/index.html.

[117] In all, the study considers 114 cartels based on different types of collusion, including bid-rigging. The sample includes international and national cartels that affected a wide range of different industries. The geographic spread of the sample extends to the US and Canada as well as cartels from Europe and other regions.

[118] In particular, it seems possible that cartels that do have an effect on the market receive more attention in empirical studies than those that have no effects, which may lead to a certain bias in the findings; see the study 'Quantifying antitrust damages', page 89 (ref. in footnote 116), for further details about the interpretation of the data used in the study.

142. On the basis of the data observed, this study found that in 93% of all cartel cases considered, cartels do lead to an overcharge. As to the magnitude of the cartel overcharge, this study made the following findings:[119]

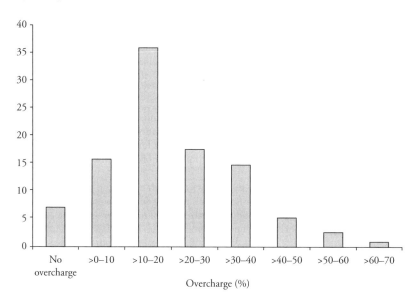

Notes

[119] Study 'Quantifying antitrust damages', page 91 (ref. in footnote 116). That magnitude is expressed as a percentage of the actual price. This means that if the actual price (meaning the price paid as influenced by the infringement) is € 100 and the overcharge is said to be 10%, the price absent the infringement is deemed to be € 90.

143. According to this study, there is thus a considerable spread of the overcharges observed (with some cartels even having an overcharge of more than 50%). About 70% of all cartels considered in this study have an overcharge of between 10% and 40%. The average overcharge observed in these cartels is around 20%.

144. The insights of this study concord with those of other available empirical studies, namely that (a) the vast majority of cartels do in fact lead to an overcharge, and (b) there is considerable variance in the overcharges observed. Also, all of these other empirical studies come largely to a similar estimate of the magnitude of the average overcharges as described above.[120]

Notes

[120] For details and further references see the study 'Quantifying antitrust damages', pages 89 ff. (ref. in footnote 116).

145. These insights into the effects of cartels do not replace the quantification of the specific harm suffered by claimants in a particular case. However, national courts have, on the basis of such empirical knowledge, asserted that it is likely that cartels normally do lead to an overcharge and that the longer and more sustainable a cartel was, the more difficult it would be for a defendant to argue that no adverse impact on price did take place in a concrete case.[121] Such inferences, however, are a matter for the applicable legal rules.

Notes

[121] See for example *Bundesgerichtshof* (Federal Court of Justice, Germany), decision of 28 June 2005, case No KRB 2/05 (*Transportable concrete*) (in the context of assessing the illicit gain by cartelists for the purpose of calculating a fine).

(2) The initial overcharge paid by the direct customer

146. All of the methods and techniques described above in Part 2 can, in principle, be used to quantify the initial overcharge paid by the direct customers of the infringing undertakings. Other types of evidence (such as, for instance, a specific agreement on the rise in prices as shown by internal documents) may also provide valuable insights into the scope of the overcharge. As the initial overcharge is a transfer of money from the direct customer to the infringing undertaking(s), any information that may exist on the illicit profits made by infringers can also serve to quantify this overcharge, although this will likely underestimate the amount of overcharge paid.[122]

Notes

[122] See also Section 33(3)(3) of the German Act against restraints on competition (*Gesetz gegen Wettbewerbsbeschränkungen*), which states that the proportion of the profit which the infringing undertaking made from the infringement may be taken into account when estimating damages.

147. In order to illustrate how methods and techniques can be used to estimate prices in a non-infringement scenario and, based on this estimate, to determine the overcharge paid by the customers of infringing undertakings, it is useful to consider the stylised example of a flour cartel already mentioned in Part 2.[123]

The flour cartel

In this example, all the flour in a certain Member State is produced by four milling companies (Mill A, Mill B, Mill C and Mill D). These mills purchase cereals from various farmers, grind the cereals and apply the appropriate treatments, package the flour and sell it on to bakers. These bakers use the flour to bake bread, which they sell on to consumers as well as to supermarkets. The national competition authority investigates the market on suspicion of price-fixing and in January 2008 carries out unannounced inspections on the premises of the milling companies.

In July 2010 the competition authority adopts a decision in which it establishes that all four milling companies infringed Article 101 TFEU by participating, during the period from 1 January 2005 till 31 December 2007, in a single and continuous infringement regarding the production of flour, covering the whole Member State, which consisted of fixing prices.

A bakery company having purchased flour from one of the milling companies (Mill A) sues this company for compensation of the harm suffered because of the infringement of Article 101 TFEU.[124] The bakery claims that the infringement has led to a rise in prices for the flour and demands compensation for the payment of this overcharge for all purchases made in 2005, 2006 and 2007.

Notes

[123] Any resemblance of this fictitious example to real events would be purely coincidental; the example cannot be seen as reflecting the Commission's views regarding any specific undertaking or sector or the market definition in such a sector.

[124] National law might well provide that all members of a cartel are jointly and severally liable for the entire harm caused by the cartel. The present example has no implications for these rules.

---

148. The bakery is a direct customer of one of the infringing undertakings. If the infringement caused higher prices, the bakery paid an overcharge for each of the units of flour purchased while price was affected. Application of the methods and techniques described will yield an estimate of the price which the bakery would have paid for the flour had there been no infringement. By subtracting that non-infringement price from the price actually paid by the bakery, the cartel overcharge per unit purchased can be determined. That figure has to be multiplied by the number of units bought by the bakery in order to determine the actual direct overcharge loss (assuming that there were no significant changes in the overcharge during the infringement period). For the estimation of the overcharge paid by the bakery in the present example, the use of comparator-based methods will be illustrated as these are most often used in practice and will often yield helpful results in quantifying the initial overcharge.

a. Comparison over time

149. In the present example, the claimant bakery company bought flour from Mill A before, during and after the time for which the national competition authority found an infringement. As described above, using the prices actually paid before or after the infringement to reconstruct the prices as they would have been without the infringement makes it necessary, first, to determine which prices were affected by the infringement and which were not. This means finding out at which point the cartel infringement began to have an effect on the flour market and at which point that effect ended.

150. In the present case, the national competition authority has determined the duration of the infringement. In fact, the decision details the evidence the authority had, which indicates that the milling companies met in January 2005 to discuss prices and thereafter continued to meet on a monthly basis, adjusting their pricing arrangements. The last meeting was held in December 2007. The authority found no evidence of meetings after it inspected the companies in January 2008. In a first step, therefore, the prices before January 2005 and after December 2007 appear to be suitable material for a time-based comparison. However, as described in Part 2, further consideration should be given to the extent to which these figures are useful to serve as comparators.

151. As mentioned above, the decision by a competition authority might limit the finding of an infringement to a certain period for which solid evidence is available to the authority, while indicating that the infringement might have had a longer duration.[125] It may then be appropriate not to use the relevant price data for the period that might have been affected by the infringement (and thus include an overcharge), although such data may nonetheless be used to determine a lower bound for the damages estimation, i.e. a safe estimate of what the harm suffered has been at least.

Notes
[125] See paragraph 43 in Part 2, Section II.

152. Also, the timing of the cartel infringement may be different from the timing of the effects of the infringement: the milling companies infringed Article 101 TFEU by entering into an anticompetitive agreement. For the purpose of determining which prices observed could be regarded as unaffected by the infringement, it is necessary to look at the timing of the effects of that agreement, not its conclusion. If it can be shown that the companies met in January 2005 for the first time, but that their agreement was implemented from March 2005 onwards, prices before March 2005 would not be tainted by the infringement.

153. As regards the suitability of using post-infringement price observations, it is possible that the cartel produced effects on the market even after the cartel members had ceased to engage in the kind of cooperation forbidden by Article 101 TFEU.[126] This may, in particular, be the case in oligopoly markets, where the information gathered because of the cartel might allow cartel members to adopt on a sustainable basis — after the cartel infringement has ended — a course of action aimed at selling at a price higher than the price likely associated with absence of the cartel infringement, without engaging in the sort of practices forbidden by Article 101 TFEU.[127] It is also possible that, after the end of the cartel, former cartel members resort to another type of infringement of the competition rules that raises prices for their customers. In these cases any time comparison based on the prices observed after the infringement ceased might lead to an underestimation of the overcharge paid by the customers of the infringers, as the post-infringement prices might still be influenced by an infringement. Where in the present example, the claimant bakery has reasons to believe that this might be the case for the prices paid in 2008 and thereafter, it could only use these prices in its submission to the court to estimate a lower bound of the overcharge harm suffered.

Notes
[126] See also paragraph 44 in Part 2, Section II.
[127] For further insights into the workings of such 'coordinated effects', see Commission, Guidelines on the assessment of horizontal mergers under the Council Regulation on the control of concentrations between undertakings, OJ C 31, 5.2.2004, p.5, paragraph 39.

154. In the present example, the claimant bakery finds that the prices paid before the infringement are well suited to estimate the likely hypothetical price. If the bakery compares infringement and non-infringement prices as they are observed, it implicitly assumes that the entire difference between

Part B Procedural Matters

the prices paid in the non-infringement years 2003 and 2004 and the prices paid in the infringement years 2005, 2006 and 2007 is due to the infringement. It is possible, however, that causes other than the infringement had a significant influence on the development of prices during the infringement period. Changes in grain prices, for instance, might be an alternative cause that influenced price developments, and they may be accounted for by using the techniques set out in Part 2, Section II B above. In so far as significant other influences can be identified and the price data are adjusted for their effects, the submission that the remaining difference between the prices in the non-infringement and the infringement periods is due to the infringement gains additional strength.[128] The circumstances in which such adjustments would be required from claimants or defendants will depend on the rules of applicable law.

Notes

[128] This is without implications for the application of national rules allowing the claimant to use the basic, unadjusted comparisons between prices charged in infringement and non-infringement periods to make an initial pleading, or to fulfil the duties incumbent upon him under national legal rules with regard to fact-pleading (in particular where national law allows a court to determine the damages award by way of approximate estimation or determination on an *ex-aequo-et-bono* basis). Also, rules on the standard and the burden of proof remain unaffected.

---

b. Other comparator-based methods

155. Besides comparisons over time, other comparator-based methods as described above in Part 2 may also be useful in quantifying the amount of the initial overcharge paid by the direct customer. In the example of the flour cartel, the claimant bakery could alternatively use a comparison with prices from another geographic market or another product market to show what the prices in its own market are likely to have been without the infringement.

156. One possibility would be the comparison with price data observed on a different geographic market for flour. On the assumption that the flour cartel as described above covered a national market, price data from another Member State could be used to construct the non-infringement price. In the case of markets with a sub-national regional scope, sales prices for flour from a different regional market could be a suitable reference point.

157. In order to be a suitable indicator for the prices as they would have been absent the infringement, the comparator prices should themselves not be influenced by the same or a similar infringement of the competition rules. If in the example of the flour cartel price data from a neighbouring geographic market are used and there is evidence that the anticompetitive agreement also covered that neighbouring market, prices from that market would lead to an underestimation of the overcharge. Also, in the case of neighbouring markets, the infringement in one market may have had an influence on that neighbouring market (for example through a rise in demand in the market without infringement), which might therefore not reflect non-infringement prices either.

158. Where the comparator market has different market characteristics, price data from that market might likewise not be sufficiently indicative of the prices as they would have been had there been no infringement. In the present example, the market concerned by the infringement is supplied by four milling companies. For instance, if it can be shown that prior to entering into the infringing practices, vigorous competition existed, price data from a neighbouring market characterised by the presence of a dominant milling company might not adequately reflect the prices as they would have been had there been no cartel and may only serve as a basis for a lower-bound estimate.

159. If the claimant bakery uses price data from a different geographic market in the form in which they are observed, it makes the implicit assumption that the remaining differences between the prices actually paid to the infringers and the prices prevailing on that comparator market are due to the infringement. Depending on the circumstances of the case and requirements under applicable law, the techniques described in Part 2 Section II B above may be used to identify and account for possible alternative influences on prices.

160. A further possibility to estimate the non-infringement price is comparison with price data observed on other product markets. In the case of flour, it may, however, be difficult to find a sufficiently similar product market not affected by the same or a similar infringement.

(3) The pass-on of overcharges

161. Direct customers of the infringing undertakings who pay an overcharge caused by the cartel may themselves sell on the affected products (or use them as input for their own production of other goods or services). In the example of the flour cartel discussed above, the bakeries are the direct customers of the infringing undertakings and they use the purchased flour to bake bread, which they then sell on either directly to final customers or to supermarkets. These direct customers (bakeries), in reaction to the price increase they face, may raise the prices for their own goods or services (the bread they sell on), thereby passing on some or the entire initial overcharge to their own customers (the consumers or supermarkets). The same effect exists where it is *indirect* customers (such as the supermarkets in the present example) who themselves raise their own selling prices in their business deals with their customers, thereby passing on an overcharge which was first passed on to them.

162. Such pass-on of overcharges normally entails a volume effect: as described above in paragraphs 128 ff., a rise in prices normally leads to a decrease in demand. In the example of the flour cartel, in so far as the bakery passes on the overcharge by raising the prices it charges for the bread to the supermarkets and end customers, it may reduce the adverse financial impact of the overcharge on itself, but it will suffer decreased demand.[129] This decrease in demand means, for the bakery, less sales and a loss of profit — harm that is also caused by the infringement and should be compensated (see Section III below).

Notes

[129] This connection between a company passing on an overcharge and its own sales volume has, in a different context, also been emphasised by the Court of Justice in case C-147/01 *Weber's Wine World* [2003] ECR I-11365, 98-99: 'even where it is established that the (…) charge (…) has been passed on in whole or in part to third parties (…) the person may suffer as a result of a fall in the volume of his sales'.

163. The price increase through pass-on and the reduction in sales are thus intrinsically connected. In fact, both pass-on and volume effects are determined by the same factors, in particular, the elasticity of demand from downstream customers. This is because the market conditions regarding downstream demand affect both the sales price and the corresponding sales volumes at which the bakery would maximise its profits.

164. In the context of a claim for compensation of overcharges in an antitrust damages action, the pass-on of overcharges can become relevant in two different types of situations:

(a) In an action brought by the direct customer claiming reparation for the initial overcharge paid by him (in the present example: the claim by the bakery against Mill A), the defendant cartel infringer might argue that the direct customer should not, in fact, be compensated for the overcharge harm to the extent that he raised his own prices and thus passed on the overcharge. This is commonly referred to as the 'passing-on defence'. Pass-on by the purchaser may, as mentioned above, lead to a loss of sales and therefore a loss of profit for him.

(b) An action brought by an indirect customer against the infringer (for example, a supermarket or a consumer who purchased bread from the bakery and who brings a claim against the milling companies) will also depend on a pass-on argument. Indeed, the indirect purchaser can claim compensation for an overcharge only where the initial overcharge paid by the direct customer has been passed on partially or entirely to him. This can be of relevance for claimants situated at different levels of the supply chain, including end customers.

165. Different legal rules exist concerning the availability of the passing-on defence and the burden of proof in this context.[130] The economic insights into the quantification of pass-on set out in paragraphs 168 ff. below can be of use no matter how these rules are designed.

Notes

[130] See Commission White Paper on damages actions for breach of the EC antitrust rules (COM(2008) 165 final, 2.4.2008) for policy proposals concerning the treatment of pass-on in antitrust damages actions.

166. In both situations considered above, claimants and defendants could rely on two different approaches to substantiate their claim that the overcharge was passed on to the indirect customer: they could either

   (a) quantify the initial overcharge and determine the pass-on rate to the indirect customer, possibly at several levels of the supply chain and using the econometric techniques outlined above, or

   (b) use the methods and techniques outlined above to determine whether the indirect customer concerned paid an overcharge. This second approach will often be easier to implement.

167. For instance, where an indirect customer brings a claim for compensation of an overcharge caused by a cartel, that indirect customer can either show that there was an initial overcharge and that this overcharge was passed on to him[131] or he may quantify the overcharge passed on to his level in the same manner as a direct customer would quantify an initial overcharge, namely by comparing the actual price he paid with the likely price in a non-infringement scenario: comparator-based methods can provide useful insights into the amount of overcharge paid by indirect customers, without it being necessary to identify the degree of pass-on. By using a time comparison, for instance, for the prices paid by the indirect customer before and during the infringement, it can be possible to ascertain how much those prices rose because of the infringement, without having to make a finding concerning the pass-on rate.

Notes

131 Where the indirect customer substantiates his claim with reference to a pass-on rate and the infringement concerns a cost factor which is small compared to the entire cost of the product, the pass-on rates of other, more important cost factors that may be more easily estimated might serve as a useful indicator.

168. It is not possible to establish a typical pass-on rate that would apply in most situations. Rather, careful examination of all the characteristics of the market in question will be necessary to assess pass-on rates. In a specific case, the existence and degree of pass-on is determined by a range of different criteria and can therefore only be assessed having regard to the conditions of the market in question.

169. Where the direct customer of the infringing undertakings uses the cartelised goods to compete in a downstream market, it is likely that the direct customer will normally not be able to pass on this increase in cost (or only to a very limited degree) if his own competitors in that downstream market are not subject to the same or a similar overcharge (for example, where they receive their input from a market that is not subject to the cartel). In the example of the flour cartel, the claimant bakery is in competition with other bakeries for the production and supply of bread. In so far as these other bakeries do not obtain their flour from the cartel members, but are able to buy it at a lower price elsewhere, the bakery having to buy from the cartel is placed at a competitive disadvantage vis-à-vis its own competitors that prevents it from passing on the extra cost of the overcharge.

170. Where all the undertakings in that downstream market are hit by the cartel and are thus similarly exposed to the payment of the direct overcharge, it is likely that the direct customer will be able to pass on at least part of that overcharge. The degree of such pass-on is influenced by the intensity of competition in the downstream market: if the downstream market is perfectly competitive, the pass-on rate in this case will be virtually 100%. This reflects the fact that in perfectly competitive markets, price equals marginal costs and a rise in prices for the input will therefore directly lead to an equal rise in cost/output price. For less than perfectly competitive markets, it is likely that affected firms will pass on at least part of the overcharge, though not necessarily 100%. For example, if the direct customer is a monopolist on the downstream market, he will choose a pass-on rate that reflects — for him — a profit-maximising price in view of the decrease in demand that the pass-on of the overcharge is likely to generate.[132]

Notes

132 The exact extent of this pass-on will depend on the demand the direct customer faces and his cost structure. For example, in the simple case of a monopolist facing linear demand (meaning that the relationship between the quantity and price can be represented by a straight line) and constant marginal costs, the pass-on will be 50% of the direct overcharge.

171. The other characteristics that may also have an influence on the degree of pass-on in such situations (everything else being constant) include:

   • The price elasticity of demand and the question whether customers become more or less sensitive to price as prices rise. In particular, pass-on is generally more likely if customers do not easily switch to other products following a price increase (inelastic demand) and if customers become less sensitive to price increases when prices are higher.

- The variation of marginal cost with output changes. For instance, a substantial pass-on is less likely if marginal cost significantly decreases following a reduction in output, because the lower output would become less costly to produce (e.g. in the presence of capacity constraints). Conversely, a substantial pass-on is more likely if marginal cost does not significantly decrease following a reduction in output (e.g. due to the absence of capacity constraints).
- The impact of the infringement on different types of costs. Where the infringement impacts on variable costs, this renders pass-on more likely than if the impact is on fixed costs.
- The duration of the infringement and the frequency of business exchanges. Where infringements last for a long time, it is more likely that some level of pass-on occurs; the same applies to sectors where business exchanges and price adjustments are frequent.

B. *Quantifying overcharges caused by other types of infringements leading to overcharge harm*

172. Cartels are but one of the infringements leading to a rise in prices for customers of the infringing undertakings and thus to overcharge harm (or, in the case of infringements pertaining to the supply to the infringing undertakings, to an 'undercharge'). Other examples of behaviour that can lead to overcharge harm include infringements of Article 101 TFEU by way of certain anti-competitive joint ventures and the abusive charging of excessive prices by a dominant undertaking within the meaning of Article 102 TFEU.

173. A common feature of these infringements is the fact that they may directly or indirectly allow the infringing undertaking(s) to raise the prices for their customers.[133] The payment of such overcharge in turn leads to a decrease in demand and thus to a volume effect as described above.

Notes

[133] Or, if the infringement relates to the supply to the infringing undertakings, to lower the price these suppliers obtain from their customers.

174. The methods and techniques whose application to the case of cartel overcharge has been described above[134] can in principle be used to quantify the overcharge harm caused by other infringements. The starting point is the question how the position of the claimant would have been had the specific infringement in question not taken place.

Notes

[134] See paragraphs 149 and following, and 155 and following.

III. QUANTIFYING THE HARM CAUSED BY THE VOLUME EFFECT

175. A rise in prices for a particular product leads to less demand. The degrees to which both prices rise and quantities decrease following an infringement depend on the same cost and demand parameters, and are determined jointly. Hence, the overcharge and volume effects are intrinsically linked.

176. For an overcharge to an intermediate customer (as discussed above in paragraphs 161 ff.), the volume effect is also closely linked to the pass-on of overcharges along the supply chain to the final customer: where a customer of the infringing undertakings does not pass on the overcharge and thus absorbs it entirely, his own sales will not decrease because of the infringement as his customers will not experience a rise in prices due to the infringement. Where, however, the overcharge is passed on partly or entirely to the final customer, that customer will be subject to the rise in prices described in paragraph 128 and will reduce his demand. This in turn will reduce demand upstream in the supply chain.

177. As explained above, for those direct or indirect customers of the infringing undertakings who use the product in question for their own commercial activities, this decrease in demand ('volume effect') means that they sell less because of the infringement and therefore forego the profit they would have made on the units they failed to sell because of this effect. This loss of profit is harm for which compensation may be awarded[135] and, in principle, the methods and techniques described above in Part 2 could be used to quantify it.[136]

Notes
135 Joined cases C-295/04 to C-298/04 *Manfredi* [2006] ECR I-6619, 95.
136 Except for the cost-based method.

178. In particular, the comparator-based methods and techniques, whose application to the quantification of the initial overcharge paid by the direct customer is discussed above, can provide the claimant with useful insights in determining the decrease in his turnover and profits. For instance, a comparison over time or across markets can be used to reconstruct the sales volume in the non-infringement scenario, i.e. how many units the claimant would have been able to sell had there been no infringement. Likewise, the application of these methods and techniques can be used to arrive at the hypothetical profit margin in a non-infringement scenario. In some instances, a court may also agree to these methods being used in a simplified fashion, for instance by determining an average profit margin per transaction and then multiplying it by the units that were not sold because of the infringement.[137]

Notes
137 See also below, paragraph 191.

179. Loss of profit is a form of harm often associated with infringements that have the effect of excluding competitors from the market. Part 4 of the Practical Guide discusses the quantification of such harm in more detail. The insights presented in that part can also be relevant when it comes to quantifying the loss of profit caused by a rise in prices.

Part 4 Quantifying Harm from Exclusionary Practices

I. Effects of Exclusionary Practices

180. Infringements of Article 101 or 102 TFEU can have the effect of completely excluding competitors from a market or of reducing their market shares. Such effects of infringements on competitors are commonly referred to as 'foreclosure'. Examples of these practices are abuses of a dominant position prohibited by Article 102 TFEU through, for instance, predation, exclusive dealing, refusal to supply, tying, bundling, or margin squeeze.[138] Such abuses are called 'exclusionary abuses'. Foreclosure of a competitor can also be the object or effect of a practice prohibited by Article 101 TFEU. It is therefore possible to refer to 'exclusionary practices', covering both infringements of Article 101 and of Article 102 TFEU.

Notes
138 For a description of these practices see also Communication from the Commission — Guidance on the Commission's enforcement priorities in applying Article [102 TFEU] to abusive exclusionary conduct by dominant undertakings, OJ C 45, 24.2.2009, p.7. [Ed note: the Guidance is reproduced at C14.]

181. Through exclusionary practices prohibited by the Treaty's competition rules, infringers distort competition in order to improve or artificially maintain their position on the market. This immediately affects their competitors by deteriorating their position in a market, driving them out of a market or preventing them from entering a market. Exclusionary practices can affect the costs borne by a competitor, the price it is able to charge for its products, or the quantities it is capable of producing and selling. They typically lead to a loss of profit for the competitors concerned.

182. Moreover, by illegally affecting the market position of competitors and thereby the level of competition in the market, such practices lead to harm to customers in the form of higher prices or reduced choice, quality or innovation. However, the detrimental effects of exclusionary practices on customers may not always manifest themselves immediately, as these practices target competitors in the first place, thereby reducing the competitive constraints exerted by them on the infringer(s). Whereas infringements of the kind described in Part 3 normally produce an immediate illegal profit for the infringers and immediate harm for their customers, exclusionary practices could result in an initial disadvantage for the infringers and in better prices for customers in the short run, as typically occurs in predatory pricing. The following sections will separately approach the issues of quantifying harm suffered by competitors (Section II) and harm suffered by customers (Section III).

183. The Treaty guarantees consumers and undertakings that have suffered harm caused by an exclusionary practice a right to compensation regardless of whether they are customers or competitors of the infringers. As already stated, the Court of Justice has specified that such compensation encompasses the actual loss suffered (*damnum emergens*), compensation for the profit they have lost due to the infringement (*lucrum cessans*), and the payment of interest.[139] For the purposes of quantifying harm from exclusionary practices, the following Sections will primarily refer to the concept of 'loss of profit', in line with the case-law of the Court of Justice. The concept of 'loss of profit' will be used in a broad sense, as meaning any difference between the actual profits generated by an undertaking and the profits it would have generated in the absence of the infringement. The approaches to quantifying such loss of profit described in the following are without prejudice to the possibility of injured parties to claim compensation under other heads of damage under national law. Indeed, some elements of lost profits in a broad sense may be classified under different legal concepts under the law of Member States (such as loss of chance[140] or loss of reputation) and there may also be heads of damage caused by exclusionary behaviour that go beyond the notion of lost profits.

Notes

[139] Joined cases C-295/04 to 298/04 *Manfredi* [2006] ECR I-6619, 95.
[140] Loss of a chance identifies the business opportunities forgone by an undertaking due to the illegal exclusionary practice.

II. Quantifying harm to competitors

184. Loss of profit to competitors can be caused by reduced revenues (e.g. through the reduction in the quantity that such competitors can sell) or increased costs (e.g. when the infringement affects the price of an input). The overall situation can be reflected in a decrease in the competitor's market share. In the following Sections, after a short description of how exclusionary practices affect competitors over time (A), and an outline of the general approach to the quantification of lost profits (B), some typical situations in the quantification of exclusionary practices will be addressed, namely in cases where they affect existing competitors (C) and new entrants (D) and when the harm they produce extends also to the future (E).

A. The time dimension of exclusionary practices

185. Depending on the period considered, exclusionary practices can affect competitors in different ways. When an exclusionary practice starts, competitors typically face difficulties in selling their products or (where the practice concerns the upstream market) obtaining supplies. This translates into a deterioration of their profit through higher costs or reduced revenues. Competitors may typically suffer a drop in their market shares, or a lower market share than they could have expected absent the infringement (for instance where their expansion is prevented). This phase may coincide with an increase in profits for infringers. This is, however, not necessarily so, since infringers may have to bear costs due to the implementation of the exclusionary practice (e.g. by lowering their price, by not supplying a competitor and thus reducing their own sales, or by offering rebates or other advantages to customers that could lower profits in the short term). Competitors may eventually be forced out of the market.

186. Once competitors have been successfully prevented from entering a market, or once their market presence has been reduced or eliminated, infringers usually recoup and benefit from increased profits to the detriment of customers and foreclosed competitors. When this occurs (either very soon after the infringement started or after a certain period of time), customers may have to pay a higher price and suffer a loss of quality or choice. The full exclusion of a competitor from a market is not a prerequisite for these effects on customers. Such effects may occur also from the very beginning of the exclusionary practice, and even if competitors are still on the market, provided the competitive pressure they exercise is weakened.

187. When the exclusionary practice is detected by public enforcers or brought to an end as a result of private actions, competitive conditions could be progressively restored. It is important to stress that the restoration of market conditions as if the infringement had not occurred is factually impossible in many cases. This depends mainly on structural effects of the infringement that may be difficult and

lengthy to undo (existing contractual obligations, network effects, or other barriers to the re-entry of a foreclosed competitor). Therefore, in some instances full convergence between the non-infringement scenario and the actual market development cannot take place.

B. General approach to the quantification of lost profits

188. In order to determine whether and to what extent competitors have suffered a loss of profits, it is necessary to compare the profit obtained by competitors during the infringement in the market affected by it with the profit they would have obtained from those products in a non-infringement scenario (i.e. the counterfactual scenario).[141] Whenever it can be shown that the foreclosed competitor would have earned higher profits in a non-infringement scenario, and that the difference is caused by the infringement, the competitor has suffered harm, even if its market share is unchanged or profits increased due to other factors.[142]

Notes

[141] This does not concern claims aimed at recovering only part of that loss, e.g. only the additional costs incurred. Such claims arise in practice also because of the availability of more straightforward approaches to quantifying the harm suffered. See below, paragraph 192.

[142] For instance, a new entrant with high potential for growth may maintain its profit levels but would have increased them absent the infringement.

---

189. The actual profits earned by the undertaking in question are normally determined by deducting the actual costs incurred from the actual revenues earned. Similarly, profits that would have been obtained in a non-infringement scenario (counterfactual profits) can be determined by deducting the estimated costs in a non-infringement scenario (counterfactual costs)[143] from the revenues expected in the absence of the infringement (counterfactual revenues).[144] The amount of profits lost is the difference between counterfactual and actual profits. In the case of prevented entry, the actual profits are normally zero, or can even be a negative number if the foreclosed competitor incurred costs (e.g. investment to enter the market) that did not return any revenue.

Notes

[143] When estimating the profit lost by the undertaking in question, it is necessary to take into account the additional costs it would have naturally faced to increase production. In this respect, the cost per unit incurred by the undertaking does not necessarily correspond to its cost per unit in the counterfactual scenario. For instance, in the case of increasing returns to scale, the cost per unit in the counterfactual scenario would be lower than the observed cost as the undertaking's production would be higher in the counterfactual scenario (i.e. had it not been affected by the infringement).

[144] E.g. *Stockholms tingsrätt* (Stockholm District Court), judgment of 20 November 2008, joined cases T 32799-05 and T 34227-05 (*Europe Investor Direct AB and others* v *VPC Aktiebolag*), appeal pending.

---

190. This basic approach to calculating lost profits can be put into practice in different ways. For instance, it is possible to compare the revenues of the foreclosed competitor in the non-infringement scenario with actual revenues from the market as affected by the infringement. Once the lost revenues have been established, it is possible to deduct the costs that the undertaking has avoided due to the lower volumes produced, in order to obtain a value of lost profits. This approach to assessing lost profits does not make it necessary to quantify the entire costs that would have been incurred by the company, but only an estimate of those costs that have not been incurred because of the infringement.

191. There are also some further pragmatic approaches to assessing lost profits that may be suitable in certain specific cases. For instance, an average profit margin per unit of the product traded in the non-infringement scenario could be estimated and then multiplied by the number of units that have not been sold due to the infringement.[145] Such an estimate of the average per unit profit may be based on one or more transactions that can be considered as sufficiently representative of the claimant's business for the product concerned. It is worth noting that in this calculation the avoided costs would implicitly be included.[146]

Notes

[145] For an example of a pragmatic approach based on real data on costs and revenues implemented through regression techniques, see *Juzgado Mercantil numero 2 de Barcelona* (Commercial Court, Barcelona), decision of 20 January 2011, case No 45/2010 (Céntrica Energìa S.L.U./Endesa Distribuciòn Eléctrica S.A.).

---

[146] In order to estimate the average profit margin, it could be still appropriate to consider how costs and revenues in the counterfactual scenario would have evolved without the infringement. For example, profit margins observed in a pre-infringement period could have been reduced during the infringement period for reasons unrelated to the infringement, due to a reduction in demand or an increase in input costs that are caused by other factors. In addition, the reduction in the output of the excluded competitor could affect its unit cost, hence also affecting the margin on the units it continues to sell.

192. Practice of antitrust damages actions shows that foreclosed competitors sometimes choose to claim damages only for part of the harm, for instance the costs incurred in order to respond to an exclusionary practice,[147] the non recoverable costs ('sunk costs') incurred with a view to entering a market from which they have been foreclosed[148] or the amount judged excessive in cases of margin squeeze or of discriminatory pricing[149] that infringe EU competition law. This choice is sometimes prompted by the consideration that quantifying such heads of damage is more straightforward or may require less data, and that evidence is more easily available. Also when claimants seek compensation for loss of profits, quantification of harm on the basis of additional costs incurred (sunk and non-sunk) will generally constitute a lower bound when estimating the full loss of profit.

Notes

[147] E.g. additional marketing expenses necessary to retain the market position.
[148] E.g. the costs of building a new factory on that market.
[149] See for instance *Lietuvos apeliacinis teismas* (Lithuanian Court of Appeal), decision of 26 May 2006, case No 2A-41/2006 (*Stumbras*); *Højesteret* (Supreme Court, Denmark), decision of 20 April 2005, case No 387/2002 (*GT Linien A/S v DSB*).

193. Whichever the method or technique chosen, quantifying lost profits may entail evaluating complex data referring to a hypothetical non-infringement situation against which the actual position of the foreclosed competitor needs to be assessed, often with a view at likely future developments. Assessing the profits that a company would have made, including future profits, may depend on such a number of factors that it could be appropriate to provide for less demanding requirements when it comes to quantification. Therefore, legal systems may allow courts to exercise some discretion as to the figures and statistical method to be chosen, and the way in which they are to be used to evaluate the damage.[150]

Notes

[150] See for instance Joined cases C-104/89 and C-37/90 *Mulder and others v Council and Commission* [2000] ECR I-203, 79.

C. Existing competitors

194. In order to quantify the harm they suffered because of an exclusionary practice, competitors may choose to rely on the methods or techniques described in Part 2. The non-infringement scenario could be reconstructed by comparison with the performance of the same undertaking in a time period that was not affected by an infringement, a similar undertaking on the same market, aggregated industry profits[151] or the performance of the same or a similar undertaking in a market other than the one in which the exclusionary practice occurred. Alternatively, methods based on simulations may provide an estimate of the non-infringement scenario, i.e. simulating on the basis of a number of assumptions (regarding e.g. the type of competitive interactions among firms) what the likely situation would have been if the excluded competitor could have been active on the market and unaffected by the exclusionary practice. The use of other methods is also possible, e.g. financial data from the undertakings involved could provide useful insights on the likely returns of companies had they not been affected by an infringement.

Notes

[151] See above at paragraphs 35, 48 and 66.

Refusal to supply an essential input for commercial solvents

Worldco is a leading international producer of raw materials that are an essential input in the manufacturing of commercial solvents. Eusolv is a company that has been active on the market for commercial solvents since 1995, and most of its turnover is made from sales of Betanol. In order to produce Betanol, Eusolv purchases Rawbeta from Worldco. Worldco is dominant in the production of Rawbeta, which is the only raw material suitable for producing Betanol on an industrial scale and at prices that enable Betanol to be marketed. Worldco also supplies Rawbeta to its subsidiary Subco, which since 2004 has been producing Betanol and competes with Eusolv.

In 2006, Worldco decides to stop supplying Rawbeta to companies selling Betanol in the European Union, with the exception of its own subsidiary Subco. Eusolv initially tries to acquire sufficient Rawbeta from alternative suppliers or to replace its Rawbeta input with other raw materials produced through experimental processes, which are significantly more costly and produce sharp rises in the sales price of Betanol, together with a decrease in its quality and suitability for commercial purposes. As a consequence, Eusolv suffers a progressive decline in its sales and finally discontinues the production of Betanol in 2010. In the same year, Eusolv brings a damages action against Worldco and its subsidiary Subco in order to recover the profits it lost due to the refusal to supply. The court holds that Worldco's practice amounted to an abuse of a dominant position prohibited by Article 102 TFEU.

---

(1) Comparison over time

195. When an exclusionary practice affects existing competitors, it is likely that data from the same undertaking in an unaffected period are available. In such cases, the profits lost by the harmed competitor could be estimated by means of a comparison over time. The non-infringement scenario could, for example, be constructed by reference to data on revenues and costs of the harmed undertaking before the exclusionary infringement produced effects.[152] In many exclusionary practices cases, data from after the infringement may not be available or would not be equally suitable, particularly if the infringement produced effects that may alter the structure of a market and are unlikely to disappear in the short term, for instance when the competitor is excluded from the market and there are barriers to re-entry in the short term, or when the competitor has lost market shares that could be difficult to regain because of network effects.[153]

In the Betanol example, reliable data from after the infringement are not available, since Eusolv, the harmed undertaking, is no longer active on the market, and its effective re-entry into the market may not occur promptly after the termination of the infringement. Eusolv thus decides to construct a likely non-infringement scenario by using data from before 2006, when the exclusionary practice was initiated.

Notes

[152] For an example of the application of a before and during comparison to estimate the harm from an exclusionary practice prohibited by Article 101 TFEU see *Corte d'Appello di Milano* (Court of Appeal, Milan), decision of 3 February 2000, case No I, 308 (*Inaz Paghe* v *Associazione Nazionale Consulenti del Lavoro*).
[153] A product is subject to network effects if its value for each user increases as the number of users increases.

---

196. Under some circumstances, the pre-infringement revenue and cost data used for the comparison could be refined. For instance, and depending on applicable national rules on evidence and on the burden of proof, a defendant may challenge the amount estimated by the claimant by indicating other elements that may have adversely influenced the performance of an undertaking and are not related to the infringement, such as a drop in marketing investment, a loss of competitiveness of the product, or an increase in the cost of inputs that is specific to the competitor claiming damages. Conversely, it could be shown that the harmed competitor's situation in the non-infringement scenario would have been better than it was before the infringement, for instance because it had a potential for growth. Generally, the reference to an earlier unaffected time period on the same market is likely to be more

reliable the longer the competitor has been on that market and the more stable its market position has been. In other words, the reference to a pre-infringement scenario could benefit more from adjustments[154] if the harmed competitor was a recent entrant on the market, since its market share could have been more likely subject to fluctuations.

In the example, Eusolv provides data on its overall actual revenues and costs from the production and sale of Betanol, as set out in the following chart:

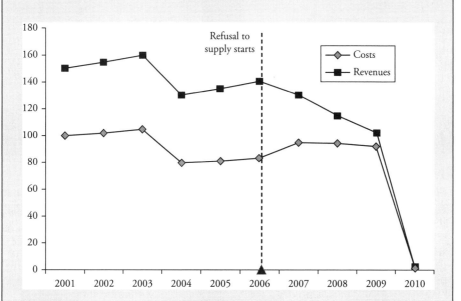

In order to establish a reliable non-infringement scenario, data from before 2004 are not taken into account because Subco, the most significant competitor of Eusolv, was not yet active on the market, whereas after 2004 and until 2006 Eusolv held a stable share of the market.

Eusolv, in accordance with national rules on the burden and the standard of proof, provides figures on the 'counterfactual' quantities, revenues and costs that would have occurred in the absence of the infringement.

Due to increasing industrial applications of Betanol, it is observed that the total demand for this product (thus, the size of the market) has grown steadily. The stability of Eusolv's market share after Subco's entry into the Betanol market is used by Eusolv to rely on the assumption that, absent the infringement, it would have maintained a similar market share. On this assumption Eusolv provides figures on its 'counterfactual' revenues for the years 2006–2010, calculated on the basis of the total value of the market and Eusolv's share of it. From its internal accounts, Eusolv provides figures on its unit costs for the years 2004 to 2006.[155] It is shown that costs closely followed the prices of the inputs for the production of Betanol, i.e. that, for instance, a rise in the input prices directly leads to a corresponding increase in costs. Using available industry data on input prices, Eusolv's experts estimate 'counterfactual' unit costs and, e.g. through regression analysis, account for the evolution in input prices and efficiencies related to the production of higher volumes. The figure for overall 'counterfactual' costs in the years 2006–2010 is then obtained by multiplying the estimated 'counterfactual' unit cost by the number of units it would have sold in the absence of the infringement.

Part B Procedural Matters

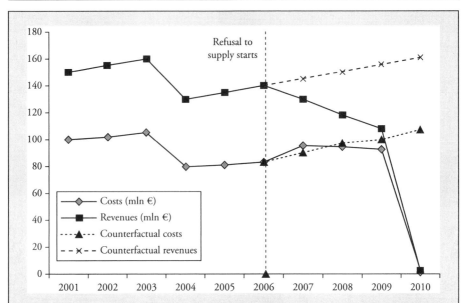

The figures obtained are compared with the actual revenues and costs faced by Eusolv as follows: the actual profits (actual revenues minus actual costs) are deducted from counterfactual profits (counterfactual revenues minus counterfactual costs). This constitutes the final estimate of the damages claimed by Eusolv.

However, Worldco and Subco argue that in order to be able to supply the expected increasing number of units in 2006-2010, Eusolv would have needed to expand its capacity, facing extra sunk costs that have not been included in the calculation. The defence is accepted by the court, and the compensation for lost profits is reduced accordingly (by deducting the expected extra sunk costs for the years in question, on a pro-rata basis, from the figure submitted by Eusolv).

Notes

[154] Such adjustments could be performed through the techniques described above at paragraphs 59 ff.

[155] These include sunk costs, distributed over time.

197. In exclusionary practices cases, market shares can play an important role as an indicator in the calculation of lost profits through comparator-based methods such as time comparisons. For instance, a comparator-based method could be used to obtain the likely market share of the foreclosed competitor absent the infringement. Lost profits could then be quantified by multiplying the observed data on actual per-unit costs and revenues (or the actual average profit margin) by the extra quantities corresponding to the higher 'counterfactual' market share expected in the absence of the infringement. This relies on the assumption that costs and revenues per unit would not have significantly changed in the non-infringement scenario, and could be accepted by a legal system as an estimate of the harm suffered, possibly as *prima facie* evidence or as sufficient to shift the burden of proof.[156] A more refined estimate would assess the evolution of costs and revenues in the non-infringement scenario, provided that sufficient data are available.

Notes

[156] For an example of a court estimation based on multiplying the total number of contracts concluded by the infringer by the market share held by claimants before the exclusionary practice started, see *Corte d'Appello di Roma* (Court of Appeal, Rome), decision of 20 January 2003, case No I, 2474 (*Albacom S.p.A.* v *Telecom Italia S.p.A.*).

198. When the market share is taken as an indicator in the estimation of lost profits, consideration should be given to the fact that it may be subject to fluctuations due to factors other than the infringement, such as the 2004 fall in Eusolv's market share in the Betanol example due to the entry of Subco as a competitor.[157] It may also be the case that if the infringement shrank the total size of the market,

revenues for the excluded competitor estimated on the basis of actual market shares would result in an underestimate.

Notes

[157] For this reason, in the example the market share considered for the quantification is the stable market share held by Eusolv after 2004.

(2) Other comparator-based methods

199.   Other geographic or product markets may also be used as a comparator in order to construct the non-infringement scenario.[158] Thus, costs and revenues of the same or a similar undertaking on a different market could be taken as a reference to estimate the costs and revenues that would have been yielded by the harmed competitor had the infringement not occurred. These methods can also be used as a means to assess the reliability of an estimation obtained by a comparison over time or other methods. For instance, if the pre-infringement performance of the sole competitor of a historically monopolistic undertaking indicates that it would have held a certain market share absent the infringement, the estimation could be comforted by the finding that the same or a similar undertaking which competes with the formerly monopolistic incumbent on a comparable geographic market actually holds a similar market share, taking into account possible differences between the undertakings or the markets concerned.

Notes

[158] *Juzgado Mercantil numero 5 de Madrid* (Commercial Court, Madrid), decision of 11 November 2005, case No 85/2005 (*Conduit-Europe, S.A.* v *Telefónica de España S.A.*), confirmed by *Audiencia Provincial de Madrid* (Court of Appeal, Madrid), decision of 25 May 2006, case No 73/2006.

D. Prevented entry of competitors

200.   Exclusionary practices can not only lead to the deterioration of the market position of an existing competitor, but also prevent the entry of a potential competitor that was not already active on the market. The foreclosure of new entrants can cause them a very significant harm for which they are entitled to compensation. Legal systems should take account of the inherent difficulties of quantifying such harm and should ensure that damages actions by prevented market entrants are not made practically impossible or excessively difficult.[159]

Notes

[159] In some cases it is possible under applicable legal rules to quantify this harm through pragmatic approaches, such as calculation of the total value of the lost market in terms of profits, multiplied by a percentage expressing the share of the market that the foreclosed undertaking would have been likely to acquire. For instance if the total profits generated by undertakings active on the relevant market after the infringement amount to 200 million euros, and it is estimated that, in the absence of the infringement, the foreclosed competitor would have held a market share of 30 per cent, the lost profit could be estimated, under this approach, at 60 million euros.

201.   The situation of prevented entry presents some peculiar circumstances that can be taken into account when quantifying the harm. In particular, if the harmed undertaking was willing to enter a market where it was not active before, there is an inherent lack of observable data on its performance on that market.

202.   The general approach to quantifying the profits lost by competitors in such situations is not essentially different from the situation of foreclosure of competitors that see their existing market position deteriorate, as it also involves an assessment of the profits that could have been yielded by the excluded competitor absent the infringement. These can then be compared with the actual situation. In cases of prevented entry, it is likely that the excluded competitor made no profits or even sustained losses (for instance where the competitor had to bear costs it did not recover through not being able to enter the market).

203.   As mentioned above, foreclosed competitors may decide to seek damages only in relation to the costs borne in order to enter the market rather than the whole of the profits foregone. This approach

can be more straightforward than claiming compensation for loss of profits as it only involves quantifying the sunk costs incurred by the claimant.

The medical equipment case

Newco is an undertaking that was committed to entering the market for a particular type of medical device in a Member State where Medco has a dominant position. In order to be profitable, Newco would have needed to achieve a minimum size on the market to take advantage of economies of scale.

Fearing to lose substantial sales to Newco, Medco concluded exclusive purchasing agreements with a number of customers in order to prevent Newco from achieving this minimum scale. As a result, Newco could not compete with Medco for these customers and was unable to profitably enter the market, which led to higher average prices for consumers than if Newco had entered the market. As Medco's conduct was considered to infringe Article 102 TFEU, Newco would be entitled to claim compensation for the profits it lost as a result of the infringement. However, in order to avoid carrying out a full loss of profit analysis, Newco only claimed compensation for the sunk costs it had already incurred to set up a new plant and enter the market (including e.g. financial costs and non-recoverable losses on purchased input material).

---

204. In cases where entry of competitors is prevented, there are no pre-infringement revenue and cost data for the market concerned, while post-infringement data could equally not lend themselves to be a reference for a time comparison because of the effects of the infringement. In such instances, reference to a comparable geographic or product market where the same or a comparable undertaking is active could prove a better means to construct a non-infringement scenario. Product or geographic markets concerned should offer a sufficient degree of similarity, although it may be possible to adjust for some differences between the markets.[160]

Notes

[160] This could be done, for instance, through regression analysis, provided that sufficient data are available. See above, paragraph 69 ff. For an example of an exclusionary practice where the use of a different geographic market was, in principle, accepted as a comparator see *Juzgado Mercantil numero 5 de Madrid* (Commercial Court, Madrid), decision of 11 November 2005, case No 85/2005 (*Conduit Europe, S.A. v Telefónica de España S.A.*), confirmed by *Audiencia Provincial de Madrid* (Court of Appeal, Madrid), decision of 25 May 2006, case No 73/2006.

205. In some cases, assessment of the competitor's financial performance may suffice to find data in order to estimate the profits in the non-infringement scenario.[161]

In the situation referred to in the example above, assume that Newco is willing to supply the three biggest private health centres in a Member State with an innovative type of films for X-ray machines. Assume that normally the market for this type of medical equipment for private health centres is a bidding market. Thanks to a technological improvement, Newco is capable of offering its products at a lower price than Medco. However, Medco, which holds a dominant position in the market for X-ray machines, ties the products by applying a higher price for X-ray machines to centres that do not purchase films from it. As a result, Newco does not obtain any contract. In such circumstances, Newco showed that it was actually capable of supplying the quantities demanded by the centres for the price offered, and provided detailed data on its own costs. On the basis of these data, and on the assumption that Newco would have been chosen as a contractor in those instances where it offered the lowest price, expected profit margins could be estimated without resorting to a comparison in time or with other geographic or product markets.

Notes

[161] For an illustration of the quantification of harm to a foreclosed new entrant in a bidding market see *Oberlandesgericht Düsseldorf* (Higher Regional Court, Düsseldorf), decision of 16 April 2008, case No VI-2 U (kart) 8/06, 2 U 8/06 (*Stadtwerke Düsseldorf*).

E. Compensation for future loss

206.   When foreclosed competitors claim compensation, they may seek compensation not only for the profits lost during the infringement period, but also for the profits foregone after its termination.[162] This is relevant, in particular, where they could not re-enter the market or fully recover their market share because of lasting effects of the terminated infringement. Compensation would then be asked for future profits, i.e. profits that are likely to be lost after the claim for compensation is brought and adjudicated.

Notes

[162] For an example of a damages award also for the period subsequent to the end of an infringement see *Østre landsrets* (Eastern High Court, Denmark), decision of 20 May 2009, case No B-3355-06 (*Forbruger-Kontakt a-s v Post Danmark A/S*).

---

207.   The challenges for quantifying such loss not only lie in the techniques to be deployed, but also have to do with the time frame during which a lost profit can still be identified and compensated. National law plays an important role in this context, for instance by determining under which circumstances a future loss can be recovered, or by establishing pragmatic rules to address this issue on a case-by-case basis.[163]

Notes

[163] When future profits are estimated, it is normally appropriate to discount their value in order to reflect the loss in the value of money over time.

---

208.   Factors likely to affect the choice of the relevant limit in time for claiming loss of future profit may encompass, for instance, the likely time needed to re-enter the market in question. In other cases, this assessment could be easier because of the circumstances of the case. For instance, in the X-ray machine example above, the duration of the contracts Newco was bidding for could constitute a reasonable lapse of time over which loss of future profits should be compensated under applicable national rules. In other cases, the time over which the undertaking could reasonably have continued producing goods or providing services in the absence of new investments could also be considered.

Part B Procedural Matters

In the Betanol example, Eusolv may claim compensation also for the profits it could have obtained after 2010, when it was driven out of the market and brought an action for damages.

In such a case, it would be possible to use the same techniques employed to reconstruct the non-infringement scenario in the years 2006–2010 and project it further into the future. Of course, lost profits for the future cannot be claimed for an indefinite duration. Eusolv decided to take as a benchmark the likely lapse of time that would be needed for Eusolv to re-enter the market once the infringement was brought to an end.

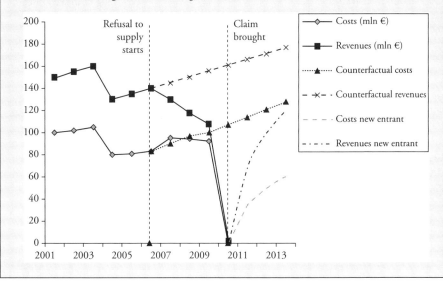

III. QUANTIFYING HARM TO CUSTOMERS

209.   Undertakings that collude or abuse their dominant position in order to foreclose a competitor might face costs or a temporary reduction in their profits in order to implement the infringement. This sacrifice is borne in order to achieve a distortion of the competitive process that will eventually place the infringers in a position where they gain higher profits thanks to the distorted market conditions achieved, thus allowing them to recoup, at the expense of their customers, the temporary loss or reduction in profits borne in order to attain that position. The following sections will address two typical situations of harm to customers caused by exclusionary practices. For the purposes of quantification, the harm caused to customers by exclusionary practices can be analogous to that caused by infringements leading to a rise in prices, which is discussed in more detail in Part 3 of the Practical Guide.

A. Recoupment

210.   The most straightforward example of the harm caused to customers in the recoupment phase of exclusionary practices is price predation, where an undertaking abuses its dominant position by setting its prices at an artificially low level that cannot be matched by its competitors, who will eventually leave the market or suffer a reduction in their market share. Once the competitors have been excluded from the market, or once a higher market share has been achieved, infringers can enjoy higher profits due to the weaker competitive constraints.

211.   Recoupment can be seen as a complementary phase of the infringement that can result in overcharge effects for the customers of the infringers. These overcharge effects constitute harm caused by the exclusionary practice, and compensation for them can be sought by customers.

Recoupment in a predatory pricing case

Consider, for example, the market for flights on a particular route between two cities. Operating on this market in a dominant position is Titan Airlines, an established undertaking which offers high quality in-flight service for a standard fare of 1000 euros. Another player on this specific market is the smaller Bluesky Airlines, which recently started operating on the same route with prices of 800 euros.

Titan Airlines engages in predatory pricing by strategically lowering its fares to a standard price of 500 euros. Bluesky Airlines experiences difficulties in meeting these predatory fares, as a result of which it fails to remain profitable, and is eventually driven out of the market. The dominant Titan Airlines will in that case take advantage of the reduction of competition and increase its profits by raising fares to a level beyond pre-predation fares, i.e. exceeding its initial standard price of 1000 euros. If Titan Airlines, until re-entry of a competitor, were to charge a price of 1100 euros, its customers would, due to the infringement, pay an overcharge of 100 euros.

---

212.   When overcharges resulting from recoupment are to be quantified, the conceptual framework that applies is in principle not different from that discussed in Part 3, namely regarding infringements leading more directly to a rise in prices. Since the harm caused by an exclusionary practice is not confined to competitors of the infringer but extends to all customers in a specific market, the issues discussed in the framework of overcharge harm are thus relevant also in this scenario.

213.   The position achieved by an undertaking on the market due to an exclusionary infringement does not lead in all cases to a rise in price for customers of the infringing undertaking. However, also in such cases customers may still be harmed by the infringement, for instance if it results in reduced quality. In the example, it could happen that the dominant undertaking Titan Airlines reinstates the same standard price of 1000 euros, not exceeding the fares it charged prior to the exclusion of Bluesky Airlines. Passengers travelling on this particular route are nevertheless adversely affected, for instance, if Titan Airlines seizes the opportunity of less competitive constraints to lower the standard of its in-flight service.

214.   Customers of the foreclosed competitor could be in a different situation than customers of the infringers, because they may have to switch to the products sold by the infringing undertaking

as the competitor is driven out of the market. Apart from the possibility of reduced quality, they may also have to pay to the infringing undertaking prices that are higher than the prices paid for the products sold by the foreclosed undertaking. Depending on applicable legal rules, they could be allowed to show that, in the absence of the infringement, they would have purchased from the foreclosed competitor at a lower price. In such case, the effect to be considered is, in principle, similar to an overcharge. The overcharge can be calculated by comparing the price of the product sold by the infringing undertaking in the actual scenario with that charged by the foreclosed undertaking in the non-infringement scenario.

> For instance, passengers travelling with Bluesky Airlines prior to its foreclosure may face an overcharge when, due to Bluesky Airlines' exclusion from the market, they are forced to fly at more expensive fares with Titan Airlines. The overcharge could be estimated as the difference between the actual price of 1000 euros paid to Titan Airlines and the price of 800 euros which Bluesky Airlines would have charged, had it not been driven out of the market. In such case, the overcharge suffered by passengers constrained to switch from Bluesky Airlines to Titan Airline could be estimated at 200 euros.

B. Harm to competitors as customers of the infringers

215.   In cases where a competitor is also a customer of the infringer, the exclusionary practice could damage the competitor in so far as it purchases from the infringer. In these situations, the foreclosed competitor can not only claim compensation for the increase in costs produced by the infringement, but also choose to claim compensation for the profits lost because the resulting volumes produced or sold are lower than if the infringement had not occurred.[164]

Notes

[164] For an example of the estimation of damages in a discriminatory pricing affecting a competitor as a customer of the infringer, see *Højesteret* (Supreme Court, Denmark), decision of 20 April 2005, case No 387/2002 (*GT Linien A/S v DSB*).

216.   It can be observed that for the purposes of quantification, competitors that suffer an overcharge are in a position analogous to that of customers of the members of a cartel or another infringement leading to an overcharge. In order to explain this, it is possible to take the example of Betanol, and assume that rather than refusing to supply Rawbeta to Eusolv, the dominant firm Worldco decides to increase the price of Rawbeta charged to Eusolv so as to squeeze its profit margins. In such a situation, similar considerations arise as in the case of an increase in price generated by other types of infringements. In the example Eusolv would claim compensation for the overcharge represented by the difference between the price it paid as a result of the exclusionary practice and the price it would have paid in the absence of the infringement. If the overcharge has been passed on, claims for damages could be also brought by Eusolv's own customers, and Eusolv itself could claim compensation for the volumes lost because of the price increase.

Table of Cases Cited

Court of Justice of the EU

Case 238/78 *Ireks-Arkady GmbH* v *Council and Commission* [1979] ECR 2955.

Case C-271/91 *Marshall* [1993] ECR I-4367.

Case C-308/87 *Grifoni II* [1994] ECR I-341.

Joined Cases C-104/89 and C-37/90 *Mulder and others* v *Council and Commission* [2000] ECR I-203.

Case C-453/99 *Courage* [2001] ECR I- 6297.

Case C-147/01 *Weber's Wine World* [2003] ECR I-11365.

Joined Cases C-295/04 to 298/04 *Manfredi* [2006] ECR I-6619.

Case C-360/09 *Pfleiderer* [2011] ECR I-5161.

Case C-199/11, *European Community* v. *Otis NV and others* [2012], not yet reported.

General Court

Joined Cases T-25/95 etc. *Cimenteries CBR SA v Commission* [2000] ECR II-491.

Case T-202/98 *Tate & Lyle v Commission* [2001] ECR II-2035.

Courts of the Member States

Corte d'Appello di Milano (Court of Appeal, Milan), decision of 3 February 2000, case No I, 308 (*Inaz Paghe v Associazione Nazionale Consulenti del Lavoro*).

Corte d'Appello di Roma (Court of Appeal, Rome), decision of 20 January 2003, case No I, 2474 (*Albacom S.p.A. v Telecom Italia S.p.A.*).

Corte d'Appello di Milano (Court of Appeal, Milan), decision of 11 July 2003, (*Bluvacanze*).

Cour d'Appel de Paris (Court of Appeal, Paris), decision of 23 June 2003 (*Lescarcelle-De Memoris v OGF*).

Landgericht Dortmund (Regional Court, Dortmund), decision of 1 April 2004, Case No 13 O 55/02 Kart (*Vitaminpreise*).

Højesteret (Supreme Court, Denmark), decision of 20 April 2005, case No 387/2002 (*GT Linien A/S v DSB*).

Bundesgerichtshof (Federal Court of Justice, Germany), decision of 28 June 2005, case No KRB 2/05 (*Transportable concrete*).

Juzgado Mercantil numero 5 de Madrid (Commercial Court, Madrid), decision of 11 November 2005, case No 85/2005 (*Conduit-Europe, S.A. v Telefónica de España S.A.*).

Audiencia Provincial de Madrid (Court of Appeal, Madrid), decision of 25 May 2006, case No 73/2006.

Lietuvos apeliacinis teismas (Lithuanian Court of Appeal), decision of 26 May 2006, case No 2A-41/2006 (*Stumbras*).

Corte Suprema di Cassazione (Supreme Court of Cassation, Italy), decision of 2 February 2007, case No 2305 (*Fondiaria SAI SpA v Nigriello*).

Bundesgerichtshof (Federal Court of Justice, Germany), decision of 19 June 2007, case No KBR 12/07 (*Paper Wholesale Cartel*).

Landesgericht für Zivilrechtssachen Graz (Regional Civil Court of Graz), decision of 17 August 2007, case No 17 R 91/07 p (*Driving school*).

Oberlandesgericht Düsseldorf (Higher Regional Court, Düsseldorf), decision of 16 April 2008, case No VI-2 U (kart) 8/06, 2 U 8/06 (*Stadtwerke Düsseldorf*).

Stockholms tingsrätt (Stockholm District Court), judgment of 20 November 2008, joined cases T 32799-05 and T 34227-05 (*Europe Investor Direct AB and others v VPC Aktiebolag*), appeal pending.

Tribunal Administratif de Paris (Administrative Court of Paris), decision of 27 Mars 2009, (*SNCF v Bouygues*).

Østre landsrets (Eastern High Court, Denmark), decision of 20 May 2009, case No B-3355-06 (*Forbruger- Kontakt a-s v Post Danmark A/S*).

Kammergericht Berlin (Higher Regional Court, Berlin), decision of 1 October 2009, case No 2 U 10/03 Kart.

Oberlandesgericht Karlsruhe (Higher Regional Court, Karlsruhe), decision of 11 June 2010, case No 6 U 118/05; appealed to the Federal Court of Justice (see below).

Juzgado Mercantil numero 2 de Barcelona (Commercial Court, Barcelona), decision of 20 January 2011, case No 45/2010 (*Céntrica Energìa S.L.U./Endesa Distribuciòn Eléctrica S.A.*).

Bundesgerichtshof (Federal Court of Justice), decision of 28 June 2011, case KZR 75/10.

Competition Appeal Tribunal, decision of 28 March 2013, case No 1166/5/7/10 (*Albion Water Limited v Dŵr Cymru Cyfyngedig*).

PART C

SUBSTANTIVE ANTITRUST MATTERS

C1

REGULATION NO 19/65/EEC
OF THE COUNCIL

of 2 March 1965

on application of Article [101](3)* of the [Treaty on the Functioning of the European Union] to certain categories of agreements and concerted practices

Official Journal P 36, 6.3.1965, p.533

Celex No: 31965R0019

EUR-Lex permanent link: <http://eur-lex.europa.eu/LexUriServ/LexUriServ.do?uri=CELEX:31965R0019:EN:NOT>

Notes

* Ed note: please see the Note on the Lisbon Treaty at p.xvii in regard to article renumbering introduced by the Lisbon Treaty.

Commentary

Regulation 19/65/EEC: B&C: 1.025, 1.073, 3.079, 3.092, 7.002 **F&N:** 3.468, 9.14, 9.18, 9.20, 9.22, 9.28, 10.68

THE COUNCIL OF THE EUROPEAN ECONOMIC COMMUNITY,

Having regard to the [Treaty on the Functioning of the European Union], and in particular Article [103] thereof;

Having regard to the proposal from the Commission;

Having regard to the Opinion of the European Parliament;[1]

Having regard to the Opinion of the Economic and Social Committee;[2]

Notes

[1] OJ No [81], 27.5.1964, p.1275/64.
[2] OJ No 197, 30.11.1964, p.3320/64.

---

[1] Whereas Article [101](1) of the Treaty may in accordance with Article [101](3) be declared inapplicable to certain categories of agreements, decisions and concerted practices which fulfil the conditions contained in Article [101](3);

[2] Whereas the provisions for implementation of Article [101](3) must be adopted by way of regulation pursuant to Article [103];

[3] Whereas in view of the large number of notifications submitted in pursuance of Regulation No 17[1] it is desirable that in order to facilitate the task of the Commission it should be enabled to declare by way of regulation that the provisions of Article [101](1) do not apply to certain categories of agreements and concerted practices;

Notes

[1] OJ No 13, 21.2.1962, p.204/62 (Regulation No 17 as amended by Regulation No 59 — OJ No 58, 10.7.1962, p.1655/62 — and Regulation No 118/63/ EEC — OJ No 162, 7.11.1963, p.2696/63.

---

[4] Whereas it should be laid down under what conditions the Commission, in close and constant liaison with the competent authorities of the Member States, may exercise such powers after sufficient

experience has been gained in the light of individual decisions and it becomes possible to define categories of agreements and concerted practices in respect of which the conditions of Article [101](3) may be considered as being fulfilled;

[5] Whereas the Commission has indicated by the action it has taken, in particular by Regulation No 153,[1] that there can be no easing of the procedures prescribed by Regulation No 17 in respect of certain types of agreements and concerted practices that are particularly liable to distort competition in the common market;

Notes
[1] OJ No 139, 24.12.1962, p.2918/62.

[6] Whereas under Article 6 of Regulation No 17 the Commission may provide that a decision taken pursuant to Article [101](3) of the Treaty shall apply with retroactive effect; whereas it is desirable that the Commission be also empowered to adopt, by regulation, provisions to the like effect;

[7] Whereas under Article 7 of Regulation No 17 agreements, decisions and concerted practices may, by decision of the Commission, be exempted from prohibition in particular if they are modified in such manner that they [satisfy] the requirements of Article [101](3); whereas it is desirable that the Commission be enabled to grant like exemption by regulation to such agreements and concerted practices if they are modified in such manner as to fall within a category defined in an exempting regulation;

[8] Whereas, since there can be no exemption if the conditions set out in Article [101](3) are not satisfied, the Commission must have power to lay down by decision the conditions that must be satisfied by an agreement or concerted practice which owing to special circumstances has certain effects incompatible with Article [101](3);

HAS ADOPTED THIS REGULATION:

Article 1

[1. Without prejudice to the application of Regulation No 17 and in accordance with Article [101](3) of the Treaty the Commission may by regulation declare that Article [101](1) shall not apply to:

(a) categories of agreements which are entered into by two or more undertakings, each operating, for the purposes of the agreement, at a different level of the production or distribution chain, and which relate to the conditions under which the parties may purchase, sell or resell certain goods or services,

(b) categories of agreements to which only two undertakings are party and which include restrictions imposed in relation to the acquisition or use of industrial property rights, in particular of patents, utility models, designs or trade marks, or to the rights arising out of contracts for assignment of, or the right to use, a method of manufacture or knowledge relating to the use or to the application of industrial processes.]

2. The regulation shall define the categories of agreements to which it applies and shall specify in particular:

(a) the restrictions or clauses which must not be contained in the agreements;

(b) [...] the other conditions which must be satisfied.

3. Paragraphs 1 and 2 shall apply by analogy to categories of concerted practices [...]

Notes
The amendments in square brackets were made by Council Regulation (EC) No 1215/1999 of 10 June 1999 (OJ L 148, 15.6.1999, p.1) with effect from 18 June 1999.

[Article 1a

A regulation pursuant to Article 1 may stipulate the conditions which may lead to the exclusion from its application of certain parallel networks of similar agreements or concerted practices operating on particular market; when these circumstances are fulfilled the Commission may establish this by means of regulation and fix a period at the expiry of which the Regulation pursuant to Article 1 would no longer be applicable in respect of the relevant agreements or concerted practices on that market; such period must not be shorter than six months.]

Notes
Article 1a was added by Council Regulation (EC) No 1215/1999 of 10 June 1999 (OJ L 148, 15.6.1999, p.1) with effect from 18 June 1999.
Commentary
Art 1(a): B&C: 3.092, 7.063 F&N: 9.24

Article 2

1. A regulation pursuant to Article 1 shall be made for a specified period.

2. It may be repealed or amended where circumstances have changed with respect to any factor which was basic to its being made; in such case, a period shall be fixed for modification of the agreements and concerted practices to which the earlier regulation applies.

Article 3

A regulation pursuant to Article 1 may stipulate that it shall apply with retroactive effect to agreements and concerted practices to which, at the date of entry into force of that regulation, a decision issued with retroactive effect in pursuance of Article 6 of Regulation No 17 would have applied.

Article 4

1. A regulation pursuant to Article 1 may stipulate that the prohibition contained in Article [101](1) of the Treaty shall not apply, for such period as shall be fixed by that regulation, to agreements and concerted practices already in existence on 13 March 1962 which do not satisfy the conditions of Article [101](3)[; or]

[A regulation pursuant to Article 1 may stipulate that the prohibition contained in Article [101](1) of the Treaty shall not apply, for such period as shall be fixed by that regulation, to agreements and concerted practices already in existence at the date of accession to which Article [101] applies by virtue of accession and which do not satisfy the conditions of Article [101](3), where:][1]

— within three months from the entry into force of the Regulation, they are so modified as to satisfy the said conditions in accordance with the provisions of the regulation; and
— the modifications are brought to the notice of the Commission within the time limit fixed by the regulation.

[The provisions of the preceding subparagraph shall apply in the same way in the case of the accession of the Hellenic Republic, the Kingdom of Spain and of the Portuguese Republic.][2]

[The provisions of the preceding subparagraphs shall apply in the same way in the case of the accession of Austria, Finland and Sweden.][3]

2. Paragraph 1 shall apply to agreements and concerted practices which had to be notified before 1 February 1963, in accordance with Article 5 of Regulation No 17, only where they have been so notified before that date.

[Paragraph 1 shall not apply to agreements and concerted practices to which Article [101](1) of the Treaty applies by virtue of accession and which must be notified before 1 July 1973, in accordance with Articles 5 and 25 of Regulation No 17, unless they have been so notified before that date.][1]

[Paragraph 1 shall not apply to agreements and concerted practices to which Article [101](1) of the Treaty applies by virtue of the accession of the Hellenic Republic and which must be notified before 1 July 1981, in accordance with Articles 5 and 25 of Regulation No 17, unless they have been so notified before that date.][4]

[Paragraph 2 shall not apply to agreements and concerted practices to which Article [101](1) of the Treaty applies by virtue of the accession of the Kingdom of Spain and the Portuguese Republic and which must be notified before 1 July 1986, in accordance with Articles 5 and 25 of Regulation No 17, unless they have been so notified before that date.][5]

[Paragraph 1 shall not apply to agreements and concerted practices to which Article [101](1) of the Treaty applies by virtue of the accession of Austria, Finland and Sweden and which must be notified within six months of accession, in accordance with Articles 5 and 25 of Regulation No 17, unless they have been so notified within that period. The present paragraph shall not apply to agreements and concerted practices which at the date of accession already fall under Article 53 (1) of the EEA Agreement.][(3)]

3. The benefit of the provisions laid down pursuant to paragraph 1 may not be claimed in actions pending at the date of entry into force of a regulation adopted pursuant to Article 1; neither may it be relied on as grounds for claims for damages against third parties.

Notes

[(1)] The words in square brackets were added by the Act of Accession of Denmark, Ireland and the United Kingdom of Great Britain and Northern Ireland (OJ L 73, 27.3.1972, p.14).
[(2)] The words in square brackets were added by the Act of Accession of Greece (OJ L 291, 19.11.1979, p.17); subsequently amended by the Act of Accession of Spain and Portugal (OJ L 302, 15.11.1985, p.23).
[(3)] The words in square brackets were added by the Act of Accession of Austria, Sweden and Finland (OJ C 241, 29.8.1994, p.21), as amended by Council Decision 95/1/EC (OJ L 1, 1.1.1995, p.1).
[(4)] The words in square brackets were added by the Act of Accession of Greece (OJ L 291, 19.11.1979, p.17).
[(5)] The words in square brackets were added by the Act of Accession of Spain and Portugal (OJ L 302, 15/11/1985, p.23).

Article 5

Before adopting a regulation, the Commission shall publish a draft thereof and invite all persons concerned to submit their comments within such time limit, being not less than one month, as the Commission shall fix.

Article 6

1. The Commission shall consult the [Advisory] Committee on Restrictive Practices and Monopolies:

(a) [with regard to a regulation pursuant to Article 1 before publishing a draft regulation and before adopting a regulation;

(b) with regard to a regulation pursuant to Article 1a before publishing a draft regulation if requested by a Member State, and before adopting a regulation.]

2. Article 10(5) and (6) of Regulation No 17, relating to consultation with the Advisory Committee, shall apply by analogy, it being understood that joint meetings with the Commission shall take place not earlier than one month after dispatch of the notice convening them.

Notes

The amendments in square brackets were made by Council Regulation (EC) No 1215/1999 of 10 June 1999 (OJ L 148, 15.6.1999, p.1) with effect from 18 June 1999.

Article 7

[. . .]

Notes

Article 7 was repealed by Council Regulation (EC) No 1/2003 of 16 December 2002 (OJ L 1, 4.1.2003, p.1), Article 40, with effect from 1 May 2004.

Commentary
Art 7: **F&N**: 9.27

Article 8

The Commission shall, before 1 January 1970, submit to the Council a proposal for a Regulation for such amendment of this Regulation as may prove necessary in the light of experience.

This Regulation shall be binding in its entirety and directly applicable in all Member States.

Done at Brussels, 2 March 1965

C2

REGULATION (EEC) NO 2821/71 OF THE COUNCIL

of 20 December 1971

on application of Article [101](3)* of the [Treaty on the Functioning of the European Union] to categories of agreements, decisions and concerted practices

Official Journal L 281, 29.12.1971, p.46

Celex No: 31971R2821

EUR-Lex permanent link: <http://eur-lex.europa.eu/LexUriServ/LexUriServ.do?uri=CELEX:31971R2821:EN:NOT>

Notes

* Ed note: please see the Note on the Lisbon Treaty at p.xvii in regard to article renumbering introduced by the Lisbon Treaty.

Commentary

Regulation 2821/71/EEC: **B&C:** 1.025, 3.079 **F&N:** 3.468, 7.163, 7.269

THE COUNCIL OF THE EUROPEAN COMMUNITIES,

Having regard to the [Treaty on the Functioning of the European Union], and in particular Article [103] thereof;

Having regard to the proposal from the Commission;

Having regard to the Opinion of the European Parliament;

Having regard to the Opinion of the Economic and Social Committee;

[1] Whereas Article [101](1) of the Treaty may in accordance with Article [101](3) be declared inapplicable to categories of agreements, decisions and concerted practices which fulfil the conditions contained in Article [101](3);

[2] Whereas the provisions for implementation of Article [101](3) must be adopted by way of regulation pursuant to Article [103];

[3] Whereas the creation of a common market requires that undertakings be adapted to the conditions of the enlarged market and whereas co-operation between undertakings can be a suitable means of achieving this;

[4] Whereas agreements, decisions and concerted practices for co-operation between undertakings which enable the undertakings to work more rationally and adapt their productivity and competitiveness to the enlarged market may, in so far as they fall within the prohibition contained in Article [101] (1), be exempted therefrom under certain conditions; whereas this measure is necessary in particular as regards agreements, decisions and concerted practices relating to the application of standards and types, research and development of products or processes up to the stage of industrial application, exploitation of the results thereof and specialisation;

[5] Whereas it is desirable that the Commission be enabled to declare by way of regulation that the provisions of Article [101](1) do not apply to those categories of agreements, decisions and concerted practices, in order to make it easier for undertakings to co-operate in ways which are economically desirable and without adverse effect from the point of view of competition policy;

[6] Whereas it should be laid down under what conditions the Commission, in close and constant liaison with the competent authorities of the Member States, may exercise such powers;

[7] Whereas under Article 6 of Regulation No 17[1] the Commission may provide that a decision taken in accordance with Article [101](3) of the Treaty shall apply with retroactive effect; whereas it is desirable that the Commission be empowered to issue regulations whose provisions are to the like effect;

Notes
[1] OJ No 13, 21.2.1962, p.204/62.

[8] Whereas under Article 7 of Regulation No 17 agreements, decisions and concerted practices may by decision of the Commission be exempted from prohibition, in particular if they are modified in such manner that Article [101](3) applies to them; whereas it is desirable that the Commission be enabled to grant by regulation like exemption to such agreements, decisions and concerted practices if they are modified in such manner as to fall within a category defined in an exempting regulation;

[9] Whereas the possibility cannot be excluded that, in a specific case, the conditions set out in Article [101](3) may not be fulfilled; whereas the Commission must have power to regulate such a case in pursuance of Regulation No 17 by way of decision having effect for the future;

HAS ADOPTED THIS REGULATION:

Article 1

1. Without prejudice to the application of Regulation No 17 the Commission may, by regulation and in accordance with Article [101](3) of the Treaty, declare that Article [101](1) shall not apply to categories of agreements between undertakings, decisions of associations of undertakings and concerted practices which have as their object:

(a) the application of standards or types;
(b) the research and development of products or processes up to the stage of industrial application, and exploitation of the results, including provisions regarding industrial property rights and confidential technical knowledge;
(c) specialisation, including agreements necessary for achieving it.

2. Such regulation shall define the categories of agreements, decisions and concerted practices to which it applies and shall specify in particular:

(a) the restrictions or clauses which may, or may not, appear in the agreements, decisions and concerted practices;
(b) the clauses which must be contained in the agreements, decisions and concerted practices or the other conditions which must be satisfied.

Article 2

1. Any regulation pursuant to Article 1 shall be made for a specified period.

2. It may be repealed or amended where circumstances have changed with respect to any of the facts which were basic to its being made; in such case, a period shall be fixed for modification of the agreements, decisions and concerted practices to which the earlier regulation applies.

Article 3

A regulation pursuant to Article 1 may provide that it shall apply with retroactive effect to agreements, decisions and concerted practices to which, at the date of entry into force of that regulation, a decision issued with retroactive effect in pursuance of Article 6 of Regulation No 17 would have applied.

Article 4

1. A regulation pursuant to Article 1 may provide that the prohibition contained in Article [101](1) of the Treaty shall not apply, for such period as shall be fixed by that regulation, to agreements, decisions and concerted practices already in existence on 13 March 1962 which do not satisfy the conditions of Article [101](3), where:

— within six months from the entry into force of the regulation, they are so modified as to satisfy the said conditions in accordance with the provisions of the regulation; and
— the modifications are brought to the notice of the Commission within the time limit fixed by the regulation.

[A Regulation adopted pursuant to Article 1 may lay down that the prohibition referred to in Article [101](1) of the Treaty shall not apply, for the period fixed in the same Regulation, to agreements and concerted practices which existed at the date of accession and which, by virtue of accession, come within the scope of Article [101] and do not fulfil the conditions set out in Article [101](3).](1)

[The provisions of the preceding subparagraph shall apply in the same way in the case of the accession of the Hellenic Republic, the Kingdom of Spain and of the Portuguese Republic.](2)

[The provisions of the preceding subparagraphs shall apply in the same way in the case of the accession of Austria, Finland and Sweden.](3)

2. Paragraph 1 shall apply to agreements, decisions and concerted practices which had to be notified before 1 February 1963, in accordance with Article 5 of Regulation No 17, only where they have been so notified before that date.

[Paragraph 1 shall be applicable to those agreements and concerted practices which, by virtue of the accession, come within the scope of Article [101](1) of the Treaty and for which notification before 1 July 1973 is mandatory, in accordance with Articles 5 and 25 of Regulation No 17, only if notification was given before that date.](1)

[Paragraph 1 shall not apply to agreements and concerted practices to which Article [101](1) of the Treaty applies by virtue of the accession of the Hellenic Republic and which must be notified before 1 July 1981, in accordance with Articles 5 and 25 of Regulation No 17, unless they have been so notified before that date.](5)

[Paragraph 1 shall not apply to agreements and concerted practices to which Article [101](1) of the Treaty applies by virtue of the accession of the Kingdom of Spain and of the Portuguese Republic and which must be notified before 1 July 1986, in accordance with Articles 5 and 25 of Regulation No 17, unless they have been so notified before that date.](5)

[Paragraph 1 shall not apply to agreements and concerted practices to which Article [101](1) of the Treaty applies by virtue of the accession of Austria, Finland and Sweden and which must be notified within six months of accession, in accordance with Articles 5 and 25 of Regulation No 17, unless they have been so notified within that period. The present paragraph shall not apply to agreements and concerted practices which at the date of accession already fall under Article 53(1) of the EEA Agreement.](4)

3. The benefit of the provisions laid down pursuant to paragraph 1 may not be claimed in actions pending at the date of entry into force of a regulation adopted pursuant to Article 1; neither may it be relied on as grounds for claims for damages against third parties.

Notes

(1) The words in square brackets were added by the Regulation (EEC) No 2743/72 of the Council of 19 December 1972 (OJ L 291, 28.12.1972, p.144).
(2) The words in square brackets were added by the Act of Accession of Greece (OJ L 291, 19.11.1979, p.17); subsequently amended by the Act of Accession of Spain and Portugal (OJ L 302, 15.11.1985, p.23).
(3) The words in square brackets were added by the Act of Accession of Austria, Sweden and Finland (OJ C 241, 29.8.1994, p.21) as amended by Council Decision 95/1/EC (OJ L 1, 1.1.1995, p.1).
(4) The words in square brackets were added by the Act of Accession of Greece (OJ L 291, 19.11.1979, p.17).
(5) The words in square brackets were added by the Act of Accession of Spain and Portugal (OJ L 302, 15.11.1985, p.23).

Article 5

Before making a regulation, the Commission shall publish a draft thereof to enable all persons and organisations concerned to submit their comments within such time limit, being not less than one month, as the Commission shall fix.

Article 6

1. The Commission shall consult the Advisory Committee on Restrictive Practices and Monopolies:

(a) before publishing a draft regulation;
(b) before making a regulation.

2. Paragraphs 5 and 6 of Article 10 of Regulation No 17, relating to consultation with the Advisory Committee, shall apply by analogy, it being understood that joint meetings with the Commission shall take place not earlier than one month after dispatch of the notice convening them.

Article 7

[...]

Notes

Article 7 was repealed by Council Regulation (EC) No 1/2003 (OJ L 4.1.2003, p.1), Article 40, with effect from 1 May 2004.

This Regulation shall be binding in its entirety and directly applicable in all Member States.

Done at Brussels, 20 December 1971.

C3

COMMISSION REGULATION (EC) NO 772/2004

of [7] April 2004

on the application of Article [101](3)* of the [Treaty on the Functioning of the European Union] to categories of technology transfer agreements

(Text with EEA relevance)

Official Journal L 123, 27.4.2004, p.11

Celex No: 32004R0772

EUR-Lex permanent link: <http://eur-lex.europa.eu/LexUriServ/LexUriServ.do?uri=CELEX:3200 4R0772:EN:NOT>

Notes

* Ed note: please see the Note on the Lisbon Treaty at p.xvii in regard to article renumbering introduced by the Lisbon Treaty. The date of this Regulation is shown as corrected by the Corrigendum at OJ L 127, 29.4.2004, p.158.

This Regulation is due to expire on 30 April 2014. Its successor was adopted on 21 March 2014. It is available at <http:// ec.europa.eu/competition/antitrust/legislation/transfer.html>, but is not included in this volume.

EEA application: this instrument was adopted with appropriate adaptations by EEA Joint Committee Decision No 42/2005 of 11 March 2005, OJ L 198, 28.7.2005, p.42 and EEA Supplement No 38, 28.7.2005, p.24: see EEA Agreement, Annex XIV, Chapter C, Point 5.

Commentary

Regulation 772/2004/EC: B&C: 3.096, 5.081, 6.044, 9.004, 9.007, 9.049, 9.069, 9.072, 9.083, 9.090, 9.101, 9.110, 9.120, 9.127, 9.131, 9.132, 9.133, 9.134, 9.135, 9.175 **F&N:** 2.12, 7.186, 8.103, 9.87, 10.71, 10.72, 10.73, 10.74, 10.77, 10.86, 10.87, 10.96, 10.113, 10.136, 10.139, 10.144, 14.83

THE COMMISSION OF THE EUROPEAN COMMUNITIES,

Having regard to the [Treaty on the Functioning of the European Union],

Having regard to Council Regulation No 19/65/EEC of 2 March 1965 on application of Article [101]1(3) of the Treaty to certain categories of agreements and concerted practices,[1] and in particular Article 1 thereof,

Having published a draft of this Regulation,[2]

After consulting the Advisory Committee on Restrictive Practices and Dominant Positions,

---

Notes

1 OJ 36, 6.3.1965, 533/65. Regulation as last amended by Regulation (EC) No 1/2003 (OJ L 1, 4.1.2003, p.1).
2 OJ C 235, 1.10.2003, p.10.

Whereas:

(1) Regulation No 19/65/EEC empowers the Commission to apply Article [101](3) of the Treaty by Regulation to certain categories of technology transfer agreements and corresponding concerted practices to which only two undertakings are party which fall within Article [101](1).

(2) Pursuant to Regulation No 19/65/EEC, the Commission has, in particular, adopted Regulation (EC) No 240/96 of 31 January 1996 on the application of Article [101](3) of the Treaty to certain categories of technology transfer agreements.[1]

Notes

1 OJ L 31, 9.2.1996, p.2. Regulation as amended by the 2003 Act of Accession.

---

(3) On 20 December 2001 the Commission published an evaluation report on the transfer of technology block exemption Regulation (EC) No 240/96.[1] This generated a public debate on the application of Regulation (EC) No 240/96 and on the application in general of Article [101](1) and (3) of the Treaty to technology transfer agreements. The response to the evaluation report from Member States and third parties has been generally in favour of reform of Community competition policy on technology transfer agreements. It is therefore appropriate to repeal Regulation (EC) No 240/96.

Notes

1 COM(2001) 786 final.

---

(4) This Regulation should meet the two requirements of ensuring effective competition and providing adequate legal security for undertakings. The pursuit of these objectives should take account of the need to simplify the regulatory framework and its application. It is appropriate to move away from the approach of listing exempted clauses and to place greater emphasis on defining the categories of agreements which are exempted up to a certain level of market power and on specifying the restrictions or clauses which are not to be contained in such agreements. This is consistent with an economics-based approach which assesses the impact of agreements on the relevant market. It is also consistent with such an approach to make a distinction between agreements between competitors and agreements between non-competitors.

Commentary
Recital 4: B&C: 9.130

---

(5) Technology transfer agreements concern the licensing of technology. Such agreements will usually improve economic efficiency and be pro-competitive as they can reduce duplication of research and development, strengthen the incentive for the initial research and development, spur incremental innovation, facilitate diffusion and generate product market competition.

(6) The likelihood that such efficiency-enhancing and pro-competitive effects will outweigh any anti-competitive effects due to restrictions contained in technology transfer agreements depends on the degree of market power of the undertakings concerned and, therefore, on the extent to which those undertakings face competition from undertakings owning substitute technologies or undertakings producing substitute products.

(7) This Regulation should only deal with agreements where the licensor permits the licensee to exploit the licensed technology, possibly after further research and development by the licensee, for the production of goods or services. It should not deal with licensing agreements for the purpose of subcontracting research and development. It should also not deal with licensing agreements to set up technology pools, that is to say, agreements for the pooling of technologies with the purpose of licensing the created package of intellectual property rights to third parties.

Commentary
Recital 7: B&C: 9.142

(8) For the application of Article [101](3) by regulation, it is not necessary to define those technology transfer agreements that are capable of falling within Article [101](1). In the individual assessment of agreements pursuant to Article [101](1), account has to be taken of several factors, and in particular the structure and the dynamics of the relevant technology and product markets.

(9) The benefit of the block exemption established by this Regulation should be limited to those agreements which can be assumed with sufficient certainty to satisfy the conditions of Article [101](3). In order to attain the benefits and objectives of technology transfer, the benefit of this Regulation should also apply to provisions contained in technology transfer agreements that do not constitute the primary object of such agreements, but are directly related to the application of the licensed technology.

(10) For technology transfer agreements between competitors it can be presumed that, where the combined share of the relevant markets accounted for by the parties does not exceed 20% and the agreements do not contain certain severely anti-competitive restraints, they generally lead to an improvement in production or distribution and allow consumers a fair share of the resulting benefits.

(11) For technology transfer agreements between non-competitors it can be presumed that, where the individual share of the relevant markets accounted for by each of the parties does not exceed 30% and the agreements do not contain certain severely anti-competitive restraints, they generally lead to an improvement in production or distribution and allow consumers a fair share of the resulting benefits.

(12) There can be no presumption that above these market-share thresholds technology transfer agreements do fall within the scope of Article [101](1). For instance, an exclusive licensing agreement between non-competing undertakings does often not fall within the scope of Article [101](1). There can also be no presumption that, above these market-share thresholds, technology transfer agreements falling within the scope of Article [101](1) will not satisfy the conditions for exemption. However, it can also not be presumed that they will usually give rise to objective advantages of such a character and size as to compensate for the disadvantages which they create for competition.

Commentary
Recital 12: B&C: 9.131, 9.144

(13) This Regulation should not exempt technology transfer agreements containing restrictions which are not indispensable to the improvement of production or distribution. In particular, technology transfer agreements containing certain severely anti-competitive restraints such as the fixing of prices charged to third parties should be excluded from the benefit of the block exemption established by this Regulation irrespective of the market shares of the undertakings concerned. In the case of such hardcore restrictions the whole agreement should be excluded from the benefit of the block exemption.

(14) In order to protect incentives to innovate and the appropriate application of intellectual property rights, certain restrictions should be excluded from the block exemption. In particular exclusive grant back obligations for severable improvements should be excluded. Where such a restriction is included in a licence agreement only the restriction in question should be excluded from the benefit of the block exemption.

(15) The market-share thresholds, the non-exemption of technology transfer agreements containing severely anti-competitive restraints and the excluded restrictions provided for in this Regulation will normally ensure that the agreements to which the block exemption applies do not enable the participating undertakings to eliminate competition in respect of a substantial part of the products in question.

(16) In particular cases in which the agreements falling under this Regulation nevertheless have effects incompatible with Article [101](3), the Commission should be able to withdraw the benefit of the block exemption. This may occur in particular where the incentives to innovate are reduced or where access to markets is hindered.

(17) Council Regulation (EC) No 1/2003 of 16 December 2002 on the implementation of the rules on competition laid down in Articles [101] and [102] of the Treaty[1] empowers the competent authorities of Member States to withdraw the benefit of the block exemption in respect of technology transfer agreements having effects incompatible with Article [101](3), where such effects are felt in their respective territory, or in a part thereof, and where such territory has the characteristics of a distinct geographic market. Member States must ensure that the exercise of this power of withdrawal does not prejudice the uniform application throughout the common market of the Community competition rules or the full effect of the measures adopted in implementation of those rules.

Notes

[1] OJ L 1, 4.1.2003, p.1. Regulation as amended by Regulation (EC) No 411/2004 (OJ L 68, 6.3.2004, p.1).

(18) In order to strengthen supervision of parallel networks of technology transfer agreements which have similar restrictive effects and which cover more than 50% of a given market, the Commission should be able to declare this Regulation inapplicable to technology transfer agreements containing specific restraints relating to the market concerned, thereby restoring the full application of Article [101] to such agreements.

(19) This Regulation should cover only technology transfer agreements between a licensor and a licensee. It should cover such agreements even if conditions are stipulated for more than one level of trade, by, for instance, requiring the licensee to set up a particular distribution system and specifying the obligations the licensee must or may impose on resellers of the products produced under the licence. However, such conditions and obligations should comply with the competition rules applicable to supply and distribution agreements. Supply and distribution agreements concluded between a licensee and its buyers should not be exempted by this Regulation.

Commentary
Recital 19: F&N: 10.78

(20) This Regulation is without prejudice to the application of Article [102] of the Treaty,

HAS ADOPTED THIS REGULATION:

Article 1
Definitions

1. For the purposes of this Regulation, the following definitions shall apply:

(a) "agreement" means an agreement, a decision of an association of undertakings or a concerted practice;

(b) "technology transfer agreement" means a patent licensing agreement, a know-how licensing agreement, a software copyright licensing agreement or a mixed patent, know-how or software copyright licensing agreement, including any such agreement containing provisions which relate to the sale and purchase of products or which relate to the licensing of other intellectual property rights or the assignment of intellectual property rights, provided that those provisions do not constitute the primary object of the agreement and are directly related to the production of the contract products; assignments of patents, know-how, software copyright or a combination thereof where part of the risk associated with the exploitation of the technology remains with the assignor, in particular where the sum payable in consideration of the assignment is dependent on the turnover obtained by the assignee in respect of products produced with the assigned technology, the quantity of such products produced or the number of operations carried out employing the technology, shall also be deemed to be technology transfer agreements;

(c) "reciprocal agreement" means a technology transfer agreement where two undertakings grant each other, in the same or separate contracts, a patent licence, a know-how licence, a software copyright licence or a mixed patent, know-how or software copyright licence and where these licences concern competing technologies or can be used for the production of competing products;

(d) "non-reciprocal agreement" means a technology transfer agreement where one undertaking grants another undertaking a patent licence, a know-how licence, a software copyright licence or a mixed patent, know-how or software copyright licence, or where two undertakings grant each other such a licence but where these licences do not concern competing technologies and cannot be used for the production of competing products;

(e) "product" means a good or a service, including both intermediary goods and services and final goods and services;

(f) "contract products" means products produced with the licensed technology;

(g) "intellectual property rights" includes industrial property rights, know-how, copyright and neighbouring rights;

(h) "patents" means patents, patent applications, utility models, applications for registration of utility models, designs, topographies of semiconductor products, supplementary protection certificates for medicinal products or other products for which such supplementary protection certificates may be obtained and plant breeder's certificates;

(i) "know-how" means a package of non-patented practical information, resulting from experience and testing, which is:

    (i) secret, that is to say, not generally known or easily accessible,

    (ii) substantial, that is to say, significant and useful for the production of the contract products, and

    (iii) identified, that is to say, described in a sufficiently comprehensive manner so as to make it possible to verify that it fulfils the criteria of secrecy and substantiality;

(j) "competing undertakings" means undertakings which compete on the relevant technology market and/or the relevant product market, that is to say:

    (i) competing undertakings on the relevant technology market, being undertakings which license out competing technologies without infringing each others' intellectual property rights (actual competitors on the technology market); the relevant technology market includes technologies which are regarded by the licensees as interchangeable with or substitutable for the licensed technology, by reason of the technologies' characteristics, their royalties and their intended use,

    (ii) competing undertakings on the relevant product market, being undertakings which, in the absence of the technology transfer agreement, are both active on the relevant product and geographic market(s) on which the contract products are sold without infringing each others' intellectual property rights (actual competitors on the product market) or would, on realistic grounds, undertake the necessary additional investments or other necessary switching costs so that they could timely enter, without infringing each others' intellectual property rights, the(se) relevant product and geographic market(s) in response to a small and permanent increase in relative prices (potential competitors on the product market); the relevant product market comprises products which are regarded by the buyers as interchangeable with or substitutable for the contract products, by reason of the products' characteristics, their prices and their intended use;

(k) "selective distribution system" means a distribution system where the licensor undertakes to license the production of the contract products only to licensees selected on the basis of specified criteria and where these licensees undertake not to sell the contract products to unauthorised distributors;

(l) "exclusive territory" means a territory in which only one undertaking is allowed to produce the contract products with the licensed technology, without prejudice to the possibility of allowing within that territory another licensee to produce the contract products only for a particular customer where this second licence was granted in order to create an alternative source of supply for that customer;

(m) "exclusive customer group" means a group of customers to which only one undertaking is allowed actively to sell the contract products produced with the licensed technology;

(n) "severable improvement" means an improvement that can be exploited without infringing the licensed technology.

2. The terms "undertaking", "licensor" and "licensee" shall include their respective connected undertakings.

"Connected undertakings" means:

(a) undertakings in which a party to the agreement, directly or indirectly:

   (i) has the power to exercise more than half the voting rights, or
   (ii) has the power to appoint more than half the members of the supervisory board, board of management or bodies legally representing the undertaking, or
   (iii) has the right to manage the undertaking's affairs;

(b) undertakings which directly or indirectly have, over a party to the agreement, the rights or powers listed in (a);

(c) undertakings in which an undertaking referred to in (b) has, directly or indirectly, the rights or powers listed in (a);

(d) undertakings in which a party to the agreement together with one or more of the undertakings referred to in (a), (b) or (c), or in which two or more of the latter undertakings, jointly have the rights or powers listed in (a);

(e) undertakings in which the rights or the powers listed in (a) are jointly held by:

   (i) parties to the agreement or their respective connected undertakings referred to in (a) to (d), or
   (ii) one or more of the parties to the agreement or one or more of their connected undertakings referred to in (a) to (d) and one or more third parties.

Commentary
Art 1(1): **B&C:** 9.136
Art 1(1)(a): **B&C:** 9.137
Art 1(1)(b): **B&C:** 3.005, 3.084, 6.044, 9.112, 9.137, 9.138, 9.139, 9.140 **F&N:** 10.76
Art 1(1)(c): **B&C:** 9.082
Art 1(1)(d): **B&C:** 9.082
Art 1(1)(e): **B&C:** 9.082, 9.138
Art 1(1)(f): **B&C:** 9.138
Art 1(1)(h): **B&C:** 9.137
Art 1(1)(i): **B&C:** 9.079
Art 1(1)(j): **B&C:** 9.079 **F&N:** 10.85, 10.89
Art 1(1)(j)(i): **B&C:** 9.079 **F&N:** 10.87
Art 1(1)(j)(ii): **F&N:** 10.88
Art 1(1)(n): **B&C:** 9.119, 9.170
Art 1(2): **B&C:** 9.141

Article 2
Exemption

Pursuant to Article [101](3) of the Treaty and subject to the provisions of this Regulation, it is hereby declared that Article [101](1) of the Treaty shall not apply to technology transfer agreements entered into between two undertakings permitting the production of contract products.

This exemption shall apply to the extent that such agreements contain restrictions of competition falling within the scope of Article [101](1). The exemption shall apply for as long as the intellectual property right in the licensed technology has not expired, lapsed or been declared invalid or, in the case of know-how, for as long as the know-how remains secret, except in the event where the know-how becomes publicly known as a result of action by the licensee, in which case the exemption shall apply for the duration of the agreement.

Commentary
Art 2: **B&C:** 2.025, 3.005, 3.084, 9.087, 9.136, 9.141, 9.143, 9.144, 9.150
Art 2(1): **F&N:** 10.68, 10.69

Article 3
Market-share thresholds

1. Where the undertakings party to the agreement are competing undertakings, the exemption provided for in Article 2 shall apply on condition that the combined market share of the parties does not exceed 20% on the affected relevant technology and product market.

2. Where the undertakings party to the agreement are not competing undertakings, the exemption provided for in Article 2 shall apply on condition that the market share of each of the parties does not exceed 30% on the affected relevant technology and product market.

3. For the purposes of paragraphs 1 and 2, the market share of a party on the relevant technology market(s) is defined in terms of the presence of the licensed technology on the relevant product market(s). A licensor's market share on the relevant technology market shall be the combined market share on the relevant product market of the contract products produced by the licensor and its licensees.

Commentary
Art 3: B&C: 3.084 F&N: 3.380, 10.119
Art 3(1): B&C: 6.044, 9.150
Art 3(2): B&C: 9.150
Art 3(3): B&C: 4.065 F&N: 10.120

Article 4
Hardcore restrictions

1. Where the undertakings party to the agreement are competing undertakings, the exemption provided for in Article 2 shall not apply to agreements which, directly or indirectly, in isolation or in combination with other factors under the control of the parties, have as their object:

(a) the restriction of a party's ability to determine its prices when selling products to third parties;

(b) the limitation of output, except limitations on the output of contract products imposed on the licensee in a non-reciprocal agreement or imposed on only one of the licensees in a reciprocal agreement;

(c) the allocation of markets or customers except:

　(i) the obligation on the licensee(s) to produce with the licensed technology only within one or more technical fields of use or one or more product markets,

　(ii) the obligation on the licensor and/or the licensee, in a non-reciprocal agreement, not to produce with the licensed technology within one or more technical fields of use or one or more product markets or one or more exclusive territories reserved for the other party,

　(iii) the obligation on the licensor not to license the technology to another licensee in a particular territory,

　(iv) the restriction, in a non-reciprocal agreement, of active and/or passive sales by the licensee and/or the licensor into the exclusive territory or to the exclusive customer group reserved for the other party,

　(v) the restriction, in a non-reciprocal agreement, of active sales by the licensee into the exclusive territory or to the exclusive customer group allocated by the licensor to another licensee provided the latter was not a competing undertaking of the licensor at the time of the conclusion of its own licence,

　(vi) the obligation on the licensee to produce the contract products only for its own use provided that the licensee is not restricted in selling the contract products actively and passively as spare parts for its own products,

　(vii) the obligation on the licensee, in a non-reciprocal agreement, to produce the contract products only for a particular customer, where the licence was granted in order to create an alternative source of supply for that customer;

(d) the restriction of the licensee's ability to exploit its own technology or the restriction of the ability of any of the parties to the agreement to carry out research and development, unless such latter restriction is indispensable to prevent the disclosure of the licensed know-how to third parties.

2. Where the undertakings party to the agreement are not competing undertakings, the exemption provided for in Article 2 shall not apply to agreements which, directly or indirectly, in isolation or in combination with other factors under the control of the parties, have as their object:

(a) the restriction of a party's ability to determine its prices when selling products to third parties, without prejudice to the possibility of imposing a maximum sale price or recommending a sale price, provided that it does not amount to a fixed or minimum sale price as a result of pressure from, or incentives offered by, any of the parties;

(b) the restriction of the territory into which, or of the customers to whom, the licensee may passively sell the contract products, except:

  (i) the restriction of passive sales into an exclusive territory or to an exclusive customer group reserved for the licensor,

  (ii) the restriction of passive sales into an exclusive territory or to an exclusive customer group allocated by the licensor to another licensee during the first two years that this other licensee is selling the contract products in that territory or to that customer group,

  (iii) the obligation to produce the contract products only for its own use provided that the licensee is not restricted in selling the contract products actively and passively as spare parts for its own products,

  (iv) the obligation to produce the contract products only for a particular customer, where the licence was granted in order to create an alternative source of supply for that customer,

  (v) the restriction of sales to end-users by a licensee operating at the wholesale level of trade,

  (vi) the restriction of sales to unauthorised distributors by the members of a selective distribution system;

(c) the restriction of active or passive sales to end-users by a licensee which is a member of a selective distribution system and which operates at the retail level, without prejudice to the possibility of prohibiting a member of the system from operating out of an unauthorised place of establishment.

3. Where the undertakings party to the agreement are not competing undertakings at the time of the conclusion of the agreement but become competing undertakings afterwards, paragraph 2 and not paragraph 1 shall apply for the full life of the agreement unless the agreement is subsequently amended in any material respect.

Commentary

Art 4: B&C: 3.084, 9.074, 9.151, 16.057 F&N: 10.92, 10.93, 10.94, 10.95, 10.169
Art 4(1): B&C: 9.110, 9.151 F&N: 10.93, 10.94, 10.100
Art 4(1)(a): B&C: 9.111, 9.153 F&N: 10.95, 10.97, 10.98
Art 4(1)(b): B&C: 9.155 F&N: 10.95, 10.99, 10.141
Art 4(1)(c): B&C: 9.096, 9.106, 9.156 F&N: 10.95, 10.106
Art 4(1)(c)(i): B&C: 9.157 F&N: 10.95, 10.104
Art 4(1)(c)(ii): B&C: 9.094, 9.107, 9.157, 9.158 F&N: 10.95, 10.103, 10.104
Art 4(1)(c)(iii): B&C: 9.158 F&N: 10.95, 10.105
Art 4(1)(c)(iv): B&C: 9.158, 9.159 F&N: 10.95, 10.103
Art 4(1)(c)(v): B&C: 9.158, 9.159 F&N: 10.95
Art 4(1)(c)(vi): B&C: 9.159 F&N: 10.95, 10.107, 12.69
Art 4(1)(c)(vii): B&C: 9.159 F&N: 10.95, 10.107
Art 4(1)(d): B&C: 6.044, 9.160, 9.172 F&N: 10.95, 10.98, 10.104, 10.105, 10.112, 10.118
Art 4(2): B&C: 9.151, 9.161 F&N: 10.93, 10.94, 10.100
Art 4(2)(a): B&C: 9.109, 9.111, 9.162 F&N: 10.95, 10.97
Art 4(2)(b): B&C: 9.165 F&N: 10.95, 10.108, 10.109, 10.111
Art 4(2)(b)(i): B&C: 9.114, 9.164 F&N: 10.95, 10.111
Art 4(2)(b)(ii): B&C: 2.099, 9.100, 9.114, 9.164 F&N: 10.95, 10.111
Art 4(2)(b)(iii): B&C: 9.166 F&N: 10.94, 10.105, 10.111, 12.69
Art 4(2)(b)(iv): B&C: 9.166 F&N: 10.95, 10.111
Art 4(2)(b)(v): B&C: 9.167, 9.168 F&N: 10.95, 10.106, 10.111
Art 4(2)(b)(vi): B&C: 9.168 F&N: 10.95, 10.111
Art 4(2)(c): B&C: 9.164, 9.168 F&N: 10.95, 10.108, 10.110, 10.111
Art 4(3): B&C: 9.081, 9.151, 9.161 F&N: 10.91, 10.95

Article 5
Excluded restrictions

1. The exemption provided for in Article 2 shall not apply to any of the following obligations contained in technology transfer agreements:

(a) any direct or indirect obligation on the licensee to grant an exclusive licence to the licensor or to a third party designated by the licensor in respect of its own severable improvements to or its own new applications of the licensed technology;

(b) any direct or indirect obligation on the licensee to assign, in whole or in part, to the licensor or to a third party designated by the licensor, rights to its own severable improvements to or its own new applications of the licensed technology;

(c) any direct or indirect obligation on the licensee not to challenge the validity of intellectual property rights which the licensor holds in the common market, without prejudice to the possibility of providing for termination of the technology transfer agreement in the event that the licensee challenges the validity of one or more of the licensed intellectual property rights.

2. Where the undertakings party to the agreement are not competing undertakings, the exemption provided for in Article 2 shall not apply to any direct or indirect obligation limiting the licensee's ability to exploit its own technology or limiting the ability of any of the parties to the agreement to carry out research and development, unless such latter restriction is indispensable to prevent the disclosure of the licensed know-how to third parties.

Commentary
Art 5: B&C: 9.130, 9.169, 9.170, 16.057 F&N: 10.61, 10.92, 10.112, 10.114
Art 5(1): F&N: 10.115
Art 5(1)(a): B&C: 9.119, 9.170 F&N: 10.115, 10.116
Art 5(1)(b): B&C: 9.170 F&N: 10.115, 10.116
Art 5(1)(c): B&C: 9.124, 9.171 F&N: 7.223, 10.115, 10.117
Art 5(2): B&C: 9.172 F&N: 10.118

Article 6
Withdrawal in individual cases

1. The Commission may withdraw the benefit of this Regulation, pursuant to Article 29(1) of Regulation (EC) No 1/2003, where it finds in any particular case that a technology transfer agreement to which the exemption provided for in Article 2 applies nevertheless has effects which are incompatible with Article [101](3) of the Treaty, and in particular where:

(a) access of third parties' technologies to the market is restricted, for instance by the cumulative effect of parallel networks of similar restrictive agreements prohibiting licensees from using third parties' technologies;

(b) access of potential licensees to the market is restricted, for instance by the cumulative effect of parallel networks of similar restrictive agreements prohibiting licensors from licensing to other licensees;

(c) without any objectively valid reason, the parties do not exploit the licensed technology.

2. Where, in any particular case, a technology transfer agreement to which the exemption provided for in Article 2 applies has effects which are incompatible with Article [101](3) of the Treaty in the territory of a Member State, or in a part thereof, which has all the characteristics of a distinct geographic market, the competition authority of that Member State may withdraw the benefit of this Regulation, pursuant to Article 29(2) of Regulation (EC) No 1/2003, in respect of that territory, under the same circumstances as those set out in paragraph 1 of this Article.

Commentary
Art 6: B&C: 9.173 F&N: 10.124
Art 6(1)(a): B&C: 9.173 F&N: 10.125
Art 6(1)(b): B&C: 9.173 F&N: 10.125, 10.126
Art 6(1)(c): B&C: 9.173 F&N: 10.125
Art 6(2): B&C: 9.173

Article 7
Non-application of this Regulation

1. Pursuant to Article 1a of Regulation No 19/65/EEC, the Commission may by regulation declare that, where parallel networks of similar technology transfer agreements cover more than 50% of a relevant market, this Regulation is not to apply to technology transfer agreements containing specific restraints relating to that market.

2. A regulation pursuant to paragraph 1 shall not become applicable earlier than six months following its adoption.

Commentary
Art 7: B&C: 3.092 **F&N:** 10.127
Art 7(1): B&C: 9.174
Art 7(2): B&C: 9.174

Article 8
Application of the market-share thresholds

1. For the purposes of applying the market-share thresholds provided for in Article 3 the rules set out in this paragraph shall apply.

The market share shall be calculated on the basis of market sales value data. If market sales value data are not available, estimates based on other reliable market information, including market sales volumes, may be used to establish the market share of the undertaking concerned.

The market share shall be calculated on the basis of data relating to the preceding calendar year.

The market share held by the undertakings referred to in point (e) of the second subparagraph of Article 1(2) shall be apportioned equally to each undertaking having the rights or the powers listed in point (a) of the second subparagraph of Article 1(2).

2. If the market share referred to in Article 3(1) or (2) is initially not more than 20% respectively 30% but subsequently rises above those levels, the exemption provided for in Article 2 shall continue to apply for a period of two consecutive calendar years following the year in which the 20% threshold or 30% threshold was first exceeded.

Commentary
Art 8: B&C: 9.150
Art 8(1): B&C: 9.150

Article 9
Repeal

Regulation (EC) No 240/96 is repealed.

References to the repealed Regulation shall be construed as references to this Regulation.

Article 10
Transitional period

The prohibition laid down in Article [101](1) of the Treaty shall not apply during the period from 1 May 2004 to 31 March 2006 in respect of agreements already in force on 30 April 2004 which do not satisfy the conditions for exemption provided for in this Regulation but which, on 30 April 2004, satisfied the conditions for exemption provided for in Regulation (EC) No 240/96.

Commentary
Art 10: B&C: 9.130, 9.151

Article 11
Period of validity

This Regulation shall enter into force on 1 May 2004.

It shall expire on 30 April 2014.

Part C Substantive Antitrust Matters

Commentary
Art 11: B&C: 3.084

This Regulation shall be binding in its entirety and directly applicable in all Member States.
Done at Brussels, [7] April 2004.

Notes
The date of this Regulation is shown as corrected by the Corrigendum at OJ L 127, 29.4.2004, p.158.

C4

COMMISSION REGULATION (EU) NO 330/2010

of 20 April 2010

on the application of Article 101(3) of the Treaty on the Functioning of the European Union to categories of vertical agreements and concerted practices

(Text with EEA relevance)

Official Journal L 102, 23.4.2010, p.1

Celex No: 32010R0330

EUR-Lex permanent link: <http://eur-lex.europa.eu/LexUriServ/LexUriServ.do?uri=CELEX:3201 0R0330:EN:NOT>

Notes
EEA application: see the EEA Agreement, Annex XIV, Chapter B, Point 2, as amended by EEA Joint Decision No 77/2010 of 11 June 2010 (OJ L, 244, 16.9.2010, p.35) with effect from 12 June 2010.

Commentary
Regulation 330/2010/EU: B&C: 2.074, 2.167, 3.005, 3.073, 3.074, 3.082, 3.092, 3.096, 4.007, 5.079, 6.073, 7.002, 7.003, 7.004, 7.011, 7.024, 7.025, 7.026, 7.027, 7.036, 7.046, 7.058, 7.066, 7.068, 7.077, 7.078, 7.079, 7.112, 7.114, 7.116, 7.118, 7.119, 7.124, 7.125, 7.126, 7.133, 7.134, 7.135, 7.136, 7.137, 7.149, 7.154, 7.155, 7.167, 7.176, 7.178, 7.179, 7.180, 7.181, 7.192, 7.196, 7.197, 9.133, 9.134, 12.133, 16.057 **F&N:** 2.12, 3.380, 4.477, 7.17, 7.241, 7.297, 7.316, 9.11, 9.28, 9.29, 9.30, 9.31, 9.33, 9.64, 9.67, 9.69, 9.70, 9.75, 9.76, 9.98, 9.136, 9.138, 9.158, 9.160, 9.163, 9.164, 9.165, 9.166, 9.172, 9.179, 9.183, 9.185, 9.188, 9.245, 9.251, 9.252, 9.255, 9.256, 9.291, 10.62, 10.64, 10.78, 10.79, 10.94, 14.83

THE EUROPEAN COMMISSION,

Having regard to the Treaty on the Functioning of the European Union,

Having regard to Regulation No 19/65/EEC of the Council of 2 March 1965 on the application of Article [101(3)] of the Treaty to certain categories of agreements and concerted practices,[1] and in particular Article 1 thereof,

Having published a draft of this Regulation,

After consulting the Advisory Committee on Restrictive Practices and Dominant Positions,

Notes
[1] OJ 36, 6.3.1965, p.533.

Whereas:

(1) Regulation No 19/65/EEC empowers the Commission to apply Article 101(3) of the Treaty on the Functioning of the European Union[1] by regulation to certain categories of vertical agreements and corresponding concerted practices falling within Article 101(1) of the Treaty.

Notes

[1] With effect from 1 December 2009, Article 81 of the EC Treaty has become Article 101 of the Treaty on the Functioning of the European Union. The two Articles are, in substance, identical. For the purposes of this Regulation, references to Article 101 of the Treaty on the Functioning of the European Union should be understood as references to Article 81 of the EC Treaty where appropriate.

Commentary
Recital 1: B&C: 7.002

(2) Commission Regulation (EC) No 2790/1999 of 22 December 1999 on the application of Article [101](3) of the Treaty to categories of vertical agreements and concerted practices[1] defines a category of vertical agreements which the Commission regarded as normally satisfying the conditions laid down in Article 101(3) of the Treaty. In view of the overall positive experience with the application of that Regulation, which expires on 31 May 2010, and taking into account further experience acquired since its adoption, it is appropriate to adopt a new block exemption regulation.

Notes
[1] OJ L 336, 29.12.1999, p.21.

Commentary
Recital 3: B&C: 2.069

(3) The category of agreements which can be regarded as normally satisfying the conditions laid down in Article 101(3) of the Treaty includes vertical agreements for the purchase or sale of goods or services where those agreements are concluded between non-competing undertakings, between certain competitors or by certain associations of retailers of goods. It also includes vertical agreements containing ancillary provisions on the assignment or use of intellectual property rights. The term "vertical agreements" should include the corresponding concerted practices.

(4) For the application of Article 101(3) of the Treaty by regulation, it is not necessary to define those vertical agreements which are capable of falling within Article 101(1) of the Treaty. In the individual assessment of agreements under Article 101(1) of the Treaty, account has to be taken of several factors, and in particular the market structure on the supply and purchase side.

Commentary
Recital 4: F&N: 9.64

(5) The benefit of the block exemption established by this Regulation should be limited to vertical agreements for which it can be assumed with sufficient certainty that they satisfy the conditions of Article 101(3) of the Treaty.

Commentary
Recital 5: F&N: 9.64

(6) Certain types of vertical agreements can improve economic efficiency within a chain of production or distribution by facilitating better coordination between the participating undertakings. In particular, they can lead to a reduction in the transaction and distribution costs of the parties and to an optimisation of their sales and investment levels.

Commentary
Recital 6: B&C: 7.011

Part C Substantive Antitrust Matters

(7) The likelihood that such efficiency-enhancing effects will outweigh any anti-competitive effects due to restrictions contained in vertical agreements depends on the degree of market power of the parties to the agreement and, therefore, on the extent to which those undertakings face competition from other suppliers of goods or services regarded by their customers as inter-changeable or substitutable for one another, by reason of the products' characteristics, their prices and their intended use.

(8) It can be presumed that, where the market share held by each of the undertakings party to the agreement on the relevant market does not exceed 30%, vertical agreements which do not contain certain types of severe restrictions of competition generally lead to an improvement in production or distribution and allow consumers a fair share of the resulting benefits.

Commentary
Recital 8: **B&C:** 7.031 **F&N:** 9.64

(9) Above the market share threshold of 30%, there can be no presumption that vertical agreements falling within the scope of Article 101(1) of the Treaty will usually give rise to objective advantages of such a character and size as to compensate for the disadvantages which they create for competition. At the same time, there is no presumption that those vertical agreements are either caught by Article 101(1) of the Treaty or that they fail to satisfy the conditions of Article 101(3) of the Treaty.

Commentary
Recital 9: **B&C:** 2.105, 2.128, 7.026, 7.031 **F&N:** 9.36

(10) This Regulation should not exempt vertical agreements containing restrictions which are likely to restrict competition and harm consumers or which are not indispensable to the attainment of the efficiency-enhancing effects. In particular, vertical agreements containing certain types of severe restrictions of competition such as minimum and fixed resale-prices, as well as certain types of territorial protection, should be excluded from the benefit of the block exemption established by this Regulation irrespective of the market share of the undertakings concerned.

Commentary
Recital 10: **B&C:** 7.024, 7.178

(11) In order to ensure access to or to prevent collusion on the relevant market, certain conditions should be attached to the block exemption. To this end, the exemption of non-compete obligations should be limited to obligations which do not exceed a defined duration. For the same reasons, any direct or indirect obligation causing the members of a selective distribution system not to sell the brands of particular competing suppliers should be excluded from the benefit of this Regulation.

(12) The market-share limitation, the non-exemption of certain vertical agreements and the conditions provided for in this Regulation normally ensure that the agreements to which the block exemption applies do not enable the participating undertakings to eliminate competition in respect of a substantial part of the products in question.

(13) The Commission may withdraw the benefit of this Regulation, pursuant to Article 29(1) of Council Regulation (EC) No 1/2003 of 16 December 2002 on the implementation of the rules on competition laid down in Articles [101] and [102] of the Treaty,[1] where it finds in a particular case that an agreement to which the exemption provided for in this Regulation applies nevertheless has effects which are incompatible with Article 101(3) of the Treaty.

Notes
[1] OJ L 1, 4.1.2003, p.1.

Commentary
Recital 13: **B&C:** 7.061, 7.154 **F&N:** 9.164

(14) The competition authority of a Member State may withdraw the benefit of this Regulation pursuant to Article 29(2) of Regulation (EC) No 1/2003 in respect of the territory of that Member State, or a part thereof where, in a particular case, an agreement to which the exemption provided for in this Regulation applies nevertheless has effects which are incompatible with Article 101(3) of the Treaty in the territory of that Member State, or in a part thereof, and where such territory has all the characteristics of a distinct geographic market.

Commentary
Recital 14: B&C: 7.061, 7.062 **F&N:** 9.164

---

(15) In determining whether the benefit of this Regulation should be withdrawn pursuant to Article 29 of Regulation (EC) No 1/2003, the anti-competitive effects that may derive from the existence of parallel networks of vertical agreements that have similar effects which significantly restrict access to a relevant market or competition therein are of particular importance. Such cumulative effects may for example arise in the case of selective distribution or non compete obligations.

(16) In order to strengthen supervision of parallel networks of vertical agreements which have similar anti-competitive effects and which cover more than 50% of a given market, the Commission may by regulation declare this Regulation inapplicable to vertical agreements containing specific restraints relating to the market concerned, thereby restoring the full application of Article 101 of the Treaty to such agreements,

HAS ADOPTED THIS REGULATION:

Article 1
Definitions

1. For the purposes of this Regulation, the following definitions shall apply:

(a) "vertical agreement" means an agreement or concerted practice entered into between two or more undertakings each of which operates, for the purposes of the agreement or the concerted practice, at a different level of the production or distribution chain, and relating to the conditions under which the parties may purchase, sell or resell certain goods or services;

(b) "vertical restraint" means a restriction of competition in a vertical agreement falling within the scope of Article 101(1) of the Treaty;

(c) "competing undertaking" means an actual or potential competitor; "actual competitor" means an undertaking that is active on the same relevant market; "potential competitor" means an undertaking that, in the absence of the vertical agreement, would, on realistic grounds and not just as a mere theoretical possibility, in case of a small but permanent increase in relative prices be likely to undertake, within a short period of time, the necessary additional investments or other necessary switching costs to enter the relevant market;

(d) "non-compete obligation" means any direct or indirect obligation causing the buyer not to manufacture, purchase, sell or resell goods or services which compete with the contract goods or services, or any direct or indirect obligation on the buyer to purchase from the supplier or from another undertaking designated by the supplier more than 80% of the buyer's total purchases of the contract goods or services and their substitutes on the relevant market, calculated on the basis of the value or, where such is standard industry practice, the volume of its purchases in the preceding calendar year;

(e) "selective distribution system" means a distribution system where the supplier undertakes to sell the contract goods or services, either directly or indirectly, only to distributors selected on the basis of specified criteria and where these distributors undertake not to sell such goods or services to unauthorised distributors within the territory reserved by the supplier to operate that system;

(f) "intellectual property rights" includes industrial property rights, know how, copyright and neighbouring rights;

(g) "know-how" means a package of non-patented practical information, resulting from experience and testing by the supplier, which is secret, substantial and identified: in this context, "secret" means that the know-how is not generally known or easily accessible; "substantial" means that the know-how is significant and useful to the buyer for the use, sale or resale of the contract goods or services; "identified" means that the know-how is described in a sufficiently comprehensive manner so as to make it possible to verify that it fulfils the criteria of secrecy and substantiality;

(h) "buyer" includes an undertaking which, under an agreement falling within Article 101(1) of the Treaty, sells goods or services on behalf of another undertaking;

(i) "customer of the buyer" means an undertaking not party to the agreement which purchases the contract goods or services from a buyer which is party to the agreement.

2. For the purposes of this Regulation, the terms "undertaking", "supplier" and "buyer" shall include their respective connected undertakings.

"Connected undertakings" means:

(a) undertakings in which a party to the agreement, directly or indirectly:
   (i) has the power to exercise more than half the voting rights, or
   (ii) has the power to appoint more than half the members of the supervisory board, board of management or bodies legally representing the undertaking, or
   (iii) has the right to manage the undertaking's affairs;

(b) undertakings which directly or indirectly have, over a party to the agreement, the rights or powers listed in point (a);

(c) undertakings in which an undertaking referred to in point (b) has, directly or indirectly, the rights or powers listed in point (a);

(d) undertakings in which a party to the agreement together with one or more of the undertakings referred to in points (a), (b) or (c), or in which two or more of the latter undertakings, jointly have the rights or powers listed in point (a);

(e) undertakings in which the rights or the powers listed in point (a) are jointly held by:
   (i) parties to the agreement or their respective connected undertakings referred to in points (a) to (d), or
   (ii) one or more of the parties to the agreement or one or more of their connected undertakings referred to in points (a) to (d) and one or more third parties.

Commentary

Art 1: **B&C:** 3.082
Art 1(1)(a): **B&C:** 2.069, 7.027, 7.080, 7.196 **F&N:** 9.68
Art 1(1)(c): **B&C:** 5.079, 7.028 **F&N:** 9.66, 9.73
Art 1(1)(d): **B&C:** 7.090, 7.113, 7.127, 7.143 **F&N:** 9.155, 9.215, 12.74
Art 1(1)(e): **B&C:** 7.093, 7.106, 7.178 **F&N:** 9.126, 9.127, 9.248
Art 1(1)(f): **B&C:** 7.093, 7.197 **F&N:** 9.81
Art 1(1)(g): **B&C:** 7.179, 7.197 **F& N:** 9.160
Art 1(1)(h): **B&C:** 7.190
Art 1(2) **F&N:** 9.175
Art 1(2)(e): **F&N:** 9.175

Article 2
Exemption

1. Pursuant to Article 101(3) of the Treaty and subject to the provisions of this Regulation, it is hereby declared that Article 101(1) of the Treaty shall not apply to vertical agreements.

This exemption shall apply to the extent that such agreements contain vertical restraints.

2. The exemption provided for in paragraph 1 shall apply to vertical agreements entered into between an association of undertakings and its members, or between such an association and its suppliers, only if all its members are retailers of goods and if no individual member of the association, together with its connected undertakings, has a total annual turnover exceeding EUR 50 million. Vertical agreements entered into by such associations shall be covered by this Regulation without prejudice to the application of Article 101 of the Treaty to horizontal agreements concluded between the members of the association or decisions adopted by the association.

3. The exemption provided for in paragraph 1 shall apply to vertical agreements containing provisions which relate to the assignment to the buyer or use by the buyer of intellectual property rights, provided that those provisions do not constitute the primary object of such agreements and are directly related to the use, sale or resale of goods or services by the buyer or its customers. The exemption applies on condition that, in relation to the contract goods or services, those provisions do not contain restrictions of competition having the same object as vertical restraints which are not exempted under this Regulation.

4. The exemption provided for in paragraph 1 shall not apply to vertical agreements entered into between competing undertakings. However, it shall apply where competing undertakings enter into a non-reciprocal vertical agreement and:

(a) the supplier is a manufacturer and a distributor of goods, while the buyer is a distributor and not a competing undertaking at the manufacturing level; or

(b) the supplier is a provider of services at several levels of trade, while the buyer provides its goods or services at the retail level and is not a competing undertaking at the level of trade where it purchases the contract services.

5. This Regulation shall not apply to vertical agreements the subject matter of which falls within the scope of any other block exemption regulation, unless otherwise provided for in such a regulation.

Commentary
Art 2: B&C: 7.024, 7.124 F&N: 9.64
Art 2(1): B&C: 4.007
Art 2(2): B&C: 7.029 F&N: 9.72, 9.78
Art 2(3): B&C: 7.030, 7.176, 7.197, 9.134 F&N: 9.81, 14.83
Art 2(4): B&C: 5.079, 6.002, 7.028, 7.080, 7.196 F&N: 7.17, 9.72, 9.74
Art 2(5) F&N: 9.72, 9.87, 14.83

Article 3
Market share threshold

1. The exemption provided for in Article 2 shall apply on condition that the market share held by the supplier does not exceed 30% of the relevant market on which it sells the contract goods or services and the market share held by the buyer does not exceed 30% of the relevant market on which it purchases the contract goods or services.

2. For the purposes of paragraph 1, where in a multi party agreement an undertaking buys the contract goods or services from one undertaking party to the agreement and sells the contract goods or services to another undertaking party to the agreement, the market share of the first undertaking must respect the market share threshold provided for in that paragraph both as a buyer and a supplier in order for the exemption provided for in Article 2 to apply.

Commentary
Art 3: B&C: 3.082, 3.083, 4.064, 7.024, 7.031, 7.124, 7.137, 16.053 F&N: 3.380, 9.65, 9.173
Art 3(1): B&C: 4.007, 7.177 F&N: 9.174
Art 3(2): B&C: 7.034 F&N: 9.66, 9.174

Article 4
Restrictions that remove the benefit of the block exemption — hardcore restrictions

The exemption provided for in Article 2 shall not apply to vertical agreements which, directly or indirectly, in isolation or in combination with other factors under the control of the parties, have as their object:

(a) the restriction of the buyer's ability to determine its sale price, without prejudice to the possibility of the supplier to impose a maximum sale price or recommend a sale price, provided that they do not amount to a fixed or minimum sale price as a result of pressure from, or incentives offered by, any of the parties;

(b) the restriction of the territory into which, or of the customers to whom, a buyer party to the agreement, without prejudice to a restriction on its place of establishment, may sell the contract goods or services, except:

   (i) the restriction of active sales into the exclusive territory or to an exclusive customer group reserved to the supplier or allocated by the supplier to another buyer, where such a restriction does not limit sales by the customers of the buyer,

  (ii) the restriction of sales to end users by a buyer operating at the wholesale level of trade,

 (iii) the restriction of sales by the members of a selective distribution system to unauthorised distributors within the territory reserved by the supplier to operate that system, and

 (iv) the restriction of the buyer's ability to sell components, supplied for the purposes of incorporation, to customers who would use them to manufacture the same type of goods as those produced by the supplier;

(c) the restriction of active or passive sales to end users by members of a selective distribution system operating at the retail level of trade, without prejudice to the possibility of prohibiting a member of the system from operating out of an unauthorised place of establishment;

(d) the restriction of cross-supplies between distributors within a selective distribution system, including between distributors operating at different level of trade;

(e) the restriction, agreed between a supplier of components and a buyer who incorporates those components, of the supplier's ability to sell the components as spare parts to end-users or to repairers or other service providers not entrusted by the buyer with the repair or servicing of its goods.

Commentary

Art 4: **B&C:** 2.120, 3.082, 7.024, 7.108, 7.124, 7.130, 7.178 **F&N:** 9.35, 9.82, 9.88, 9.89, 9.90, 9.93, 9.133

Art 4(a): **B&C:** 7.016, 7.038, 7.108, 7.132, 7.180, 7.190 **F&N:** 9.94, 9.97

Art 4(b): **B&C:** 7.016, 7.046, 7.047, 7.053, 7.068, 7.071, 7.101, 7.107, 7.130, 7.131, 7.133, 7.178 **F&N:** 9.112, 9.113, 9.114, 9.116, 9.126, 9.127, 9.140, 9.142, 9.143, 10.64, 12.69

Art 4(b)(i): **B&C:** 7.131, 7.133, 7.178 **F&N:** 9.117, 9.119, 9.121

Art 4(b)(ii): **B&C:** 7.048, 7.069, 7.108, 7.131, 7.197 **F&N:** 9.122, 9.123, 9.129

Art 4(b)(iii): **B&C:** 7.107, 7.131 **F&N:** 9.122, 9.127

Art 4(b)(iv): **B&C:** 7.050, 7.131 **F&N:** 9.122, 9.124

Art 4(c): **B&C:** 7.037, 7.079, 7.094, 7.108, 7.110, 7.130, 7.133 **F&N:** 9.128, 9.129, 9.131, 9.133, 9.140, 9.236, 9.246, 9.251

Art 4(d): **B&C:** 7.037, 7.108, 7.130, 7.133 **F&N:** 9.128, 9.130, 9.131

Art 4(e): **B&C:** 7.057, 7.136, 7.198 **F&N:** 9.115, 9.145

Article 5
Excluded restrictions

1. The exemption provided for in Article 2 shall not apply to the following obligations contained in vertical agreements:

(a) any direct or indirect non-compete obligation, the duration of which is indefinite or exceeds five years;

(b) any direct or indirect obligation causing the buyer, after termination of the agreement, not to manufacture, purchase, sell or resell goods or services;

(c) any direct or indirect obligation causing the members of a selective distribution system not to sell the brands of particular competing suppliers.

For the purposes of point (a) of the first subparagraph, a non-compete obligation which is tacitly renewable beyond a period of five years shall be deemed to have been concluded for an indefinite duration.

2. By way of derogation from paragraph 1(a), the time limitation of five years shall not apply where the contract goods or services are sold by the buyer from premises and land owned by the supplier or leased by the supplier from third parties not connected with the buyer, provided that the duration of the non-compete obligation does not exceed the period of occupancy of the premises and land by the buyer.

3. By way of derogation from paragraph 1(b), the exemption provided for in Article 2 shall apply to any direct or indirect obligation causing the buyer, after termination of the agreement, not to manufacture, purchase, sell or resell goods or services where the following conditions are fulfilled:

(a) the obligation relates to goods or services which compete with the contract goods or services;

(b) the obligation is limited to the premises and land from which the buyer has operated during the contract period;

(c) the obligation is indispensable to protect know-how transferred by the supplier to the buyer;

(d) the duration of the obligation is limited to a period of one year after termination of the agreement.

Paragraph 1(b) is without prejudice to the possibility of imposing a restriction which is unlimited in time on the use and disclosure of know-how which has not entered the public domain.

Commentary
Art 5: **B&C:** 7.024, 7.059, 7.124, 7.126, 16.057 **F&N:** 9.35, 9.82, 9.153, 9.154, 9.157, 9.215, 9.218
Art 5(1) **F&N:** 9.156, 12.78
Art 5(1)(a): **B&C:** 7.113, 7.126, 7.137, 7.155, 7.179 **F&N:** 9.154, 9.155
Art 5(1)(b): **B&C:** 7.060, 7.179 **F&N:** 9.154, 9.160
Art 5(1)(c): **B&C:** 7.113, 7.133 **F&N:** 9.154, 9.162
Art 5(2): **B&C:** 7.155 **F&N:** 9.154, 9.159
Art 5(3): **B&C:** 7.060, 7.179 **F&N:** 9.154

Article 6
Non-application of this Regulation

Pursuant to Article 1a of Regulation No 19/65/EEC, the Commission may by regulation declare that, where parallel networks of similar vertical restraints cover more than 50% of a relevant market, this Regulation shall not apply to vertical agreements containing specific restraints relating to that market.

Commentary
Art 6: **B&C:** 3.092, 7.063, 7.105, 7.154 **F&N:** 9.169, 9.170, 9.171

Article 7
Application of the market share threshold

For the purposes of applying the market share thresholds provided for in Article 3 the following rules shall apply:

(a) the market share of the supplier shall be calculated on the basis of market sales value data and the market share of the buyer shall be calculated on the basis of market purchase value data. If market sales value or market purchase value data are not available, estimates based on other reliable market information, including market sales and purchase volumes, may be used to establish the market share of the undertaking concerned;

(b) the market shares shall be calculated on the basis of data relating to the preceding calendar year;

(c) the market share of the supplier shall include any goods or services supplied to vertically integrated distributors for the purposes of sale;

(d) if a market share is initially not more than 30% but subsequently rises above that level without exceeding 35%, the exemption provided for in Article 2 shall continue to apply for a period of two consecutive calendar years following the year in which the 30% market share threshold was first exceeded;

(e) if a market share is initially not more than 30% but subsequently rises above 35%, the exemption provided for in Article 2 shall continue to apply for one calendar year following the year in which the level of 35% was first exceeded;

(f) the benefit of points (d) and (e) may not be combined so as to exceed a period of two calendar years;

(g) the market share held by the undertakings referred to in point (e) of the second subparagraph of Article 1(2) shall be apportioned equally to each undertaking having the rights or the powers listed in point (a) of the second subparagraph of Article 1(2).

Article 8
Application of the turnover threshold

1. For the purpose of calculating total annual turnover within the meaning of Article 2(2), the turnover achieved during the previous financial year by the relevant party to the vertical agreement and the turnover achieved by its connected undertakings in respect of all goods and services, excluding all taxes and other duties, shall be added together. For this purpose, no account shall be taken of dealings between the party to the vertical agreement and its connected undertakings or between its connected undertakings.

2. The exemption provided for in Article 2 shall remain applicable where, for any period of two consecutive financial years, the total annual turnover threshold is exceeded by no more than 10%.

Article 9
Transitional period

The prohibition laid down in Article 101(1) of the Treaty shall not apply during the period from 1 June 2010 to 31 May 2011 in respect of agreements already in force on 31 May 2010 which do not satisfy the conditions for exemption provided for in this Regulation but which, on 31 May 2010, satisfied the conditions for exemption provided for in Regulation (EC) No 2790/1999.

Article 10
Period of validity

This Regulation shall enter into force on 1 June 2010.

It shall expire on 31 May 2022.

This Regulation shall be binding in its entirety and directly applicable in all Member States.

Done at Brussels, 20 April 2010.

C5

COMMISSION REGULATION (EU)
NO 461/2010

of 27 May 2010

on the application of Article 101(3) of the Treaty on the Functioning of the European Union to categories of vertical agreements and concerted practices in the motor vehicle sector

Official Journal L 129, 28.5.2010, p.52

Celex No: 32010R0461

EUR-Lex permanent link: <http://eur-lex.europa.eu/LexUriServ/LexUriServ.do?uri=CELEX:32010R0461:EN:NOT>

Notes

EEA application: Regulation 461/2010/EU was incorporated into the EEA Agreement, Annex XIV, point 4(b), with adaptations, by EEA Joint Committee Decision No 91/2010 (OJ L 277, 21.10.2010, p.44), with effect from 3 July 2010.

Commentary

Regulation 461/2010/EU: B&C: 3.005, 3.083, 3.092, 3.096, 7.004, 7.058, 7.117, 7.120, 7.134, 7.135, 7.136, 7.139, 7.198 **F&N:** 2.12, 9.87
Recitals 10–15: B&C: 7.117
Recitals 14–18: B&C: 7.198

THE EUROPEAN COMMISSION,

Having regard to the Treaty on the Functioning of the European Union,

Having regard to Regulation No 19/65/EEC of the Council of 2 March 1965 on the application of Article [101](3) of the Treaty to certain categories of agreements and concerted practices,[1] and in particular Article 1 thereof,

Having published a draft of this Regulation,

After consulting the Advisory Committee on Restrictive Practices and Dominant Positions,

---

Notes
[1] OJ 36, 6.3.1965, p.533/65.

Whereas:

(1) Regulation No 19/65/EEC empowers the Commission to apply Article 101(3) of the Treaty on the Functioning of the European Union* by regulation to certain categories of vertical agreements and corresponding concerted practices falling within Article 101(1) of the Treaty. Block exemption regulations apply to vertical agreements which fulfil certain conditions and may be general or sector-specific.

Notes

* With effect from 1 December 2009, Article 81 of the EC Treaty has become Article 101 of the Treaty on the Functioning of the European Union. The two Articles are, in substance, identical. For the purposes of this Regulation, references to Article 101 of the Treaty on the Functioning of the European Union should be understood as references to Article 81 of the EC Treaty where appropriate.

---

(2) The Commission has defined a category of vertical agreements which it regards as normally satisfying the conditions laid down in Article 101(3) of the Treaty and to this end has adopted Commission Regulation (EU) No 330/2010 of 20 April 2010 on the application of Article 101(3) of the

Treaty on the Functioning of the European Union to categories of vertical agreements and concerted practices[1], which replaces Commission Regulation (EC) No 2790/1999. [2]

Notes
[1] OJ L 102, 23.4.2010, p.1.
[2] OJ L 336, 29.12.1999, p.21.

(3) The motor vehicle sector, which includes both passenger cars and commercial vehicles, has been subject to specific block exemption regulations since 1985, the most recent being Commission Regulation (EC) No 1400/2002 of 31 July 2002 on the application of Article [101](3) of the Treaty to categories of vertical agreements and concerted practices in the motor vehicle sector.[1] Regulation (EC) No 2790/1999 expressly stated that it did not apply to vertical agreements the subject matter of which fell within the scope of any other block exemption regulation. The motor vehicle sector therefore fell outside the scope of that Regulation.

Notes
[1] OJ L 203, 1.8.2002, p.30.

Commentary
Recital 3: B&C: 3.074, 7.122

(4) Regulation (EC) No 1400/2002 expires on 31 May 2010. However, the motor vehicle sector should continue to benefit from a block exemption in order to simplify administration and reduce compliance costs for the undertakings concerned, while ensuring effective supervision of markets in accordance with Article 103(2)(b) of the Treaty.

(5) Experience acquired since 2002 regarding the distribution of new motor vehicles, the distribution of spare parts and the provision of repair and maintenance services for motor vehicles, makes it possible to define a category of vertical agreements in the motor vehicle sector which can be regarded as normally satisfying the conditions laid down in Article 101(3) of the Treaty.

(6) This category includes vertical agreements for the purchase, sale or resale of new motor vehicles, vertical agreements for the purchase, sale or resale of spare parts for motor vehicles and vertical agreements for the provision of repair and maintenance services for such vehicles, where those agreements are concluded between non-competing undertakings, between certain competitors, or by certain associations of retailers or repairers. It also includes vertical agreements containing ancillary provisions on the assignment or use of intellectual property rights. The term "vertical agreements" should be defined accordingly to include both such agreements and the corresponding concerted practices.

(7) Certain types of vertical agreements can improve economic efficiency within a chain of production or distribution by facilitating better coordination between the participating undertakings. In particular, they can lead to a reduction in the transaction and distribution costs of the parties and to an optimisation of their sales and investment levels.

(8) The likelihood that such efficiency-enhancing effects will outweigh any anticompetitive effects due to restrictions contained in vertical agreements depends on the degree of market power of the parties to the agreement and, therefore, on the extent to which those undertakings face competition from other suppliers of goods or services regarded by their customers as interchangeable or substitutable for one another, by reason of the products' characteristics, their prices and their intended use. Vertical agreements containing restrictions which are likely to restrict competition and harm consumers, or which are not indispensable to the attainment of the efficiency-enhancing effects, should be excluded from the benefit of the block exemption.

(9) In order to define the appropriate scope of a block exemption regulation, the Commission must take into account the competitive conditions in the relevant sector. In this respect, the conclusions of the in-depth monitoring of the motor vehicle sector set out in the Evaluation Report on the operation of Commission Regulation (EC) No 1400/2002 of 28 May 2008[1] and in the Commission Communication on The Future Competition Law Framework applicable to the Motor Vehicle sector of 22 July 2009[2] have shown that a distinction should be drawn between agreements for the distribution of new motor vehicles and agreements for the provision of repair and maintenance services and distribution of spare parts.

Notes
1 SEC(2008) 1946.
2 COM(2009) 388.

(10) As regards the distribution of new motor vehicles, there do not appear to be any significant competition shortcomings which would distinguish this sector from other economic sectors and which could require the application of rules different from and stricter than those set out in Regulation (EU) No 330/2010. The market-share threshold, the non-exemption of certain vertical agreements and the other conditions laid down in that Regulation normally ensure that vertical agreements for the distribution of new motor vehicles comply with the requirements of Article 101(3) of the Treaty. Therefore, such agreements should benefit from the exemption granted by Regulation (EU) No 330/2010, subject to all the conditions laid down therein.

(11) As regards agreements for the distribution of spare parts and for the provision of repair and maintenance services, certain specific characteristics of the motor vehicle aftermarket should be taken into account. In particular, the experience acquired by the Commission in applying Regulation (EC) No 1400/2002 shows that price increases for individual repair jobs are only partially reflected in increased reliability of modern cars and lengthening of service intervals. These latter trends are linked to technological evolution and to the increasing complexity and reliability of automotive components that the vehicle manufacturers purchase from original equipment suppliers. Such suppliers sell their products as spare parts in the aftermarket both through the vehicle manufacturers' authorised repair networks and through independent channels, thereby representing an important competitive force in the motor vehicle aftermarket. The costs borne on average by consumers in the Union for motor vehicle repair and maintenance services represent a very high proportion of total consumer expenditure on motor vehicles.

(12) Competitive conditions in the motor vehicle aftermarket also have a direct bearing on public safety, in that vehicles may be driven in an unsafe manner if they have been repaired incorrectly, as well as on public health and the environment, as emissions of carbon dioxide and other air pollutants may be higher from vehicles which have not undergone regular maintenance work.

(13) In so far as a separate aftermarket can be defined, effective competition on the markets for the purchase and sale of spare parts, as well as for the provision of repair and maintenance services for motor vehicles, depends on the degree of competitive interaction between authorised repairers, that is to say those operating within repair networks established directly or indirectly by vehicle manufacturers, as well as between authorised and independent operators, including independent spare parts suppliers and repairers. The latters' ability to compete depends on unrestricted access to essential inputs such as spare parts and technical information.

(14) Having regard to those specificities, the rules in Regulation (EU) No 330/2010, including the uniform market share threshold of 30%, are necessary but are not sufficient to ensure that the benefit of the block exemption is reserved only to those vertical agreements for the distribution of spare parts and for the provision of repair and maintenance services for which it can be assumed with sufficient certainty that the conditions of Article 101(3) of the Treaty are satisfied.

(15) Therefore, vertical agreements for the distribution of spare parts and for the provision of repair and maintenance services should benefit from the block exemption only if, in addition to the conditions for exemption set out in Regulation (EU) No 330/2010, they comply with stricter requirements concerning certain types of severe restrictions of competition that may limit the supply and use of spare parts in the motor vehicle aftermarket.

Commentary
Recital 15: B&C: 3.074

(16) In particular, the benefit of the block exemption should not be granted to agreements that restrict the sale of spare parts by members of the selective distribution system of a vehicle manufacturer to independent repairers, which use them for the provision of repair or maintenance services. Without access to such spare parts, independent repairers would not be able to compete effectively with authorised repairers, since they could not provide consumers with good quality services which contribute to the safe and reliable functioning of motor vehicles.

(17) Moreover, in order to ensure effective competition on the repair and maintenance markets and to allow repairers to offer end users competing spare parts, the block exemption should not cover vertical agreements which, although they comply with Regulation (EU) No 330/2010, nonetheless restrict the ability of a producer of spare parts to sell such parts to authorised repairers within the distribution system of a vehicle manufacturer, independent distributors of spare parts, independent repairers or end users. This does not affect the liability of producers of spare parts under civil law, or the ability of vehicle manufacturers to require the authorised repairers within their distribution system to only use spare parts that match the quality of the components used for the assembly of a certain motor vehicle. Moreover, in view of the vehicle manufacturers' direct contractual involvement in repairs under warranty, free servicing, and recall operations, agreements containing obligations on authorised repairers to use only spare parts supplied by the vehicle manufacturer for those repairs should be covered by the exemption.

Commentary
Recital 17: B&C: 7.137

(18) Finally, in order to allow authorised and independent repairers and end users to identify the manufacturer of motor vehicle components or of spare parts and to choose between alternative parts, the block exemption should not cover agreements by which a manufacturer of motor vehicles limits the ability of a manufacturer of components or original spare parts to place its trade mark or logo on those parts effectively and in a visible manner.

(19) In order to allow all operators time to adapt to this Regulation, it is appropriate to extend the period of application of the provisions of Regulation (EC) No 1400/2002 relating to vertical agreements for the purchase, sale and resale of new motor vehicles until 31 May 2013. As regards vertical agreements for the distribution of spare parts and for the provision of repair and maintenance services, this Regulation should apply from 1 June 2010 so as to continue to ensure adequate protection of competition on the motor vehicle aftermarkets.

Commentary
Recital 19: B&C: 7.122

(20) The Commission will, on a continuous basis, monitor developments in the motor vehicle sector and will take appropriate remedial action if competition shortcomings arise which may lead to consumer harm on the market for the distribution of new motor vehicles or the supply of spare parts or after-sales services for motor vehicles.

(21) The Commission may withdraw the benefit of this Regulation, pursuant to Article 29(1) of Council Regulation (EC) No 1/2003 of 16 December 2002 on the implementation of the rules on competition laid down in Articles [101] and [102] of the Treaty,[1] where it finds in a particular case that an agreement to which the exemption provided for in this Regulation applies nevertheless has effects which are incompatible with Article 101(3) of the Treaty.

Notes
[1] OJ L 1, 4.1.2003, p.1.

Commentary
Recital 21: B&C: 7.138

(22) The competition authority of a Member State may withdraw the benefit of this Regulation pursuant to Article 29(2) of Regulation (EC) No 1/2003 in respect of the territory of that Member State, or a part thereof where, in a particular case, an agreement to which the exemption provided for in this Regulation applies nevertheless has effects which are incompatible with Article 101(3) of the Treaty in the territory of that Member State, or in a part thereof, and where such territory has all the characteristics of a distinct geographic market.

Commentary
Recital 22: B&C: 7.138

(23) In determining whether the benefit of this Regulation should be withdrawn pursuant to Article 29 of Regulation (EC) No 1/2003, the anti-competitive effects that may derive from the existence of parallel networks of vertical agreements that have similar effects which significantly restrict access to a relevant market or competition therein are of particular importance. Such cumulative effects may, for example, arise in the case of selective distribution or non-compete obligations.

(24) In order to strengthen supervision of parallel networks of vertical agreements which have similar anti-competitive effects and which cover more than 50% of a given market, the Commission may by regulation declare this Regulation inapplicable to vertical agreements containing specific restraints relating to the market concerned, thereby restoring the full application of Article 101 of the Treaty to such agreements.

(25) In order to assess the effects of this Regulation on competition in motor vehicle retailing, in the supply of spare parts and in after sales servicing for motor vehicles in the internal market, it is appropriate to draw up an evaluation report on the operation of this Regulation,

HAS ADOPTED THIS REGULATION:

CHAPTER I
COMMON PROVISIONS

Article 1
Definitions

1. For the purposes of this Regulation, the following definitions shall apply:

(a) "vertical agreement" means an agreement or concerted practice entered into between two or more undertakings each of which operates, for the purposes of the agreement or the concerted practice, at a different level of the production or distribution chain, and relating to the conditions under which the parties may purchase, sell or resell certain goods or services;

(b) "vertical restraint" means a restriction of competition in a vertical agreement falling within the scope of Article 101(1) of the Treaty;

(c) "authorised repairer" means a provider of repair and maintenance services for motor vehicles operating within the distribution system set up by a supplier of motor vehicles;

(d) "authorised distributor" means a distributor of spare parts for motor vehicles operating within the distribution system set up by a supplier of motor vehicles;

(e) "independent repairer" means:
   (i) a provider of repair and maintenance services for motor vehicles not operating within the distribution system set up by the supplier of the motor vehicles for which it provides repair or maintenance;
   (ii) an authorised repairer within the distribution system of a given supplier, to the extent that it provides repair or maintenance services for motor vehicles in respect of which it is not a member of the respective supplier's distribution system;

(f) "independent distributor" means:
   (i) a distributor of spare parts for motor vehicles not operating within the distribution system set up by the supplier of the motor vehicles for which it distributes spare parts;
   (ii) an authorised distributor within the distribution system of a given supplier, to the extent that it distributes spare parts for motor vehicles in respect of which it is not a member of the respective supplier's distribution system;

(g) "motor vehicle" means a self-propelled vehicle intended for use on public roads and having three or more road wheels;

(h) "spare parts" means goods which are to be installed in or upon a motor vehicle so as to replace components of that vehicle, including goods such as lubricants which are necessary for the use of a motor vehicle, with the exception of fuel;

(i) "selective distribution system" means a distribution system where the supplier undertakes to sell the contract goods or services, either directly or indirectly, only to distributors selected on the basis of specified criteria and where these distributors undertake not to sell such goods or services to unauthorised distributors within the territory reserved by the supplier to operate that system.

2. For the purposes of this Regulation, the terms "undertaking", "supplier", "manufacturer" and "buyer" shall include their respective connected undertakings.

"Connected undertakings" means:

(a) undertakings in which a party to the agreement, directly or indirectly:
    (i) has the power to exercise more than half the voting rights; or
    (ii) has the power to appoint more than half the members of the supervisory board, board of management or bodies legally representing the undertaking; or
    (iii) has the right to manage the undertaking's affairs;
(b) undertakings which directly or indirectly have, over a party to the agreement, the rights or powers listed in point (a);
(c) undertakings in which an undertaking referred to in point (b) has, directly or indirectly, the rights or powers listed in point (a);
(d) undertakings in which a party to the agreement together with one or more of the undertakings referred to in points (a), (b) or (c), or in which two or more of the latter undertakings, jointly have the rights or powers listed in point (a);
(e) undertakings in which the rights or the powers listed in point (a) are jointly held by:
    (i) parties to the agreement or their respective connected undertakings referred to in points (a) to (d); or
    (ii) one or more of the parties to the agreement or one or more of their connected undertakings referred to in points (a) to (d) and one or more third parties.

Commentary
Art 1(1)(a): **B&C:** 7.120
Art 1(1)(g): **B&C:** 7.120
Art 1(1)(h): **B&C:** 7.120
Art 1(1)(i): **B&C:** 7.129

Chapter II
Vertical Agreements Relating to the Purchase, Sale or Resale of New Motor Vehicles

Article 2
Application of Regulation (EC) No 1400/2002

Pursuant to Article 101(3) of the Treaty, from 1 June 2010 until 31 May 2013, Article 101(1) of the Treaty shall not apply to vertical agreements relating to the conditions under which the parties may purchase, sell or resell new motor vehicles, which fulfil the requirements for an exemption under Regulation (EC) No 1400/2002 that relate specifically to vertical agreements for the purchase, sale or resale of new motor vehicles.

Commentary
Art 2: **B&C:** 7.119, 7.122

Article 3
Application of Regulation (EU) No 330/2010

With effect from 1 June 2013, Regulation (EU) No 330/2010 shall apply to vertical agreements relating to the purchase, sale or resale of new motor vehicles.

Chapter III
Vertical Agreements Relating to the Motor Vehicle Aftermarket

Article 4
Exemption

Pursuant to Article 101(3) of the Treaty and subject to the provisions of this Regulation Article 101(1) of the Treaty shall not apply to vertical agreements relating to the conditions under which the parties may purchase, sell or resell spare parts for motor vehicles or provide repair and maintenance services for motor vehicles, which fulfil the requirements for an exemption under Regulation (EU) No 330/2010 and do not contain any of the hardcore clauses listed in Article 5 of this Regulation.

This exemption shall apply to the extent that such agreements contain vertical restraints.

Article 5
Restrictions that remove the benefit of the block exemption — hardcore restrictions

The exemption provided for in Article 4 shall not apply to vertical agreements which, directly or indirectly, in isolation or in combination with other factors under the control of the parties, have as their object:

(a) the restriction of the sales of spare parts for motor vehicles by members of a selective distribution system to independent repairers which use those parts for the repair and maintenance of a motor vehicle;

(b) the restriction, agreed between a supplier of spare parts, repair tools or diagnostic or other equipment and a manufacturer of motor vehicles, of the supplier's ability to sell those goods to authorised or independent distributors or to authorised or independent repairers or end users;

(c) the restriction, agreed between a manufacturer of motor vehicles which uses components for the initial assembly of motor vehicles and the supplier of such components, of the supplier's ability to place its trade mark or logo effectively and in an easily visible manner on the components supplied or on spare parts.

Commentary
Art 5(a): **B&C:** 7.136
Art 5(b): **B&C:** 7.136, 7.198
Art 5(c): **B&C:** 7.136, 7.198

CHAPTER IV
FINAL PROVISIONS

Article 6
Non-application of this Regulation

Pursuant to Article 1a of Regulation No 19/65/EEC, the Commission may by regulation declare that, where parallel networks of similar vertical restraints cover more than 50% of a relevant market, this Regulation shall not apply to vertical agreements containing specific restraints relating to that market.

Commentary
Art 6: **B&C:** 3.092, 7.139

Article 7
Monitoring and evaluation report

The Commission will monitor the operation of this Regulation and draw up a report on its operation by 31 May 2021 at the latest, having regard in particular to the conditions set out in Article 101(3) of the Treaty.

Article 8
Period of validity

This Regulation shall enter into force on 1 June 2010.

It shall expire on 31 May 2023.

This Regulation shall be binding in its entirety and directly applicable in all Member States.

Done at Brussels, 27 May 2010.

Commentary
Art 8: **B&C:** 3.083, 7.117, 7.119

Part C Substantive Antitrust Matters

C6

COMMISSION REGULATION (EU) NO 1217/2010

of 14 December 2010

on the application of Article 101(3) of the Treaty on the Functioning of the
European Union to certain categories of research and development agreements

(Text with EEA relevance)

Official Journal L 335, 18.12.2010, p.36

Celex No: 32010R1217

EUR-Lex permanent link: <http://eur-lex.europa.eu/LexUriServ/LexUriServ.do?uri=CELEX:32010
R1217:EN:NOT>

Notes

EEA application: Regulation 1217/2010/EU was incorporated into the EEA Agreement (Annex XIV, Chapter D, point 7) by EEA Joint Committee Decision No 3/2011 of 11 February 2011 (OJ L 93, 7.4.2011, p.32).

Commentary

Regulation 1217/2010/EU: B&C: 3.081, 3.096, 5.064, 5.073, 6.006, 6.011, 6.039, 6.049, 7.179, 9.133, 12.061, 12.062 **F&N:** 2.12, 3.380, 7.10, 7.162–7.234, 7.271, 7.297, 7.315, 10.62, 10.81, 10.94, 11.205

THE EUROPEAN COMMISSION,

Having regard to the Treaty on the Functioning of the European Union,

Having regard to Regulation (EEC) No 2821/71 of the Council of 20 December 1971 on application of Article [101](3) of the Treaty to categories of agreements, decisions and concerted practices,[1]

Having published a draft of this Regulation,

After consulting the Advisory Committee on Restrictive Practices and Dominant Positions,

---

Notes

[1] OJ L 285, 29.12.1971, p.46.

Whereas:

(1) Regulation (EEC) No 2821/71 empowers the Commission to apply Article 101(3) of the Treaty on the Functioning of the European Union (*) by regulation to certain categories of agreements, decisions and concerted practices falling within the scope of Article 101(1) of the Treaty which have as their object the research and development of products, technologies or processes up to the stage of industrial application, and exploitation of the results, including provisions regarding intellectual property rights.

Notes

(*) With effect from 1 December 2009, Article 81 of the EC Treaty has become Article 101 of the Treaty on the Functioning of the European Union (TFEU). The two articles are, in substance, identical. For the purposes of this Regulation, references to Article 101 of the TFEU should be understood as references to Article 81 of the EC Treaty where appropriate. The TFEU also introduced certain changes in terminology, such as the replacement of "Community" by "Union" and "common market" by "internal market". The terminology of the TFEU will be used throughout this Regulation.

---

(2) Article 179(2) of the Treaty calls upon the Union to encourage undertakings, including small and medium- sized undertakings, in their research and technological development activities of high quality, and to support their efforts to cooperate with one another. This Regulation is intended to facilitate research and development while at the same time effectively protecting competition.

(3) Commission Regulation (EC) No 2659/2000 of 29 November 2000 on the application of Article [101](3) of the Treaty to categories of research and development agreements[1] defines categories of research and development agreements which the Commission regarded as normally satisfying the conditions laid down in Article 101(3) of the Treaty. In view of the overall positive experience with the application of that Regulation, which expires on 31 December 2010, and taking into account further experience acquired since its adoption, it is appropriate to adopt a new block exemption regulation.

Notes

1 OJ L 304, 5.12.2000, p.7.

(4) This Regulation should meet the two requirements of ensuring effective protection of competition and providing adequate legal security for undertakings. The pursuit of those objectives should take account of the need to simplify administrative supervision and the legislative framework to as great an extent as possible. Below a certain level of market power it can in general be presumed, for the application of Article 101(3) of the Treaty, that the positive effects of research and development agreements will outweigh any negative effects on competition.

(5) For the application of Article 101(3) of the Treaty by regulation, it is not necessary to define those agreements which are capable of falling within Article 101(1) of the Treaty. In the individual assessment of agreements under Article 101(1) of the Treaty, account has to be taken of several factors, and in particular the market structure on the relevant market.

(6) Agreements on the joint execution of research work or the joint development of the results of the research, up to but not including the stage of industrial application, generally do not fall within the scope of Article 101(1) of the Treaty. In certain circumstances, however, such as where the parties agree not to carry out other research and development in the same field, thereby forgoing the opportunity of gaining competitive advantages over the other parties, such agreements may fall within Article 101(1) of the Treaty and should therefore be included within the scope of this Regulation.

(7) The benefit of the exemption established by this Regulation should be limited to those agreements for which it can be assumed with sufficient certainty that they satisfy the conditions of Article 101(3) of the Treaty.

(8) Cooperation in research and development and in the exploitation of the results is most likely to promote technical and economic progress if the parties contribute complementary skills, assets or activities to the co-operation. This also includes scenarios where one party merely finances the research and development activities of another party.

(9) The joint exploitation of results can be considered as the natural consequence of joint research and development. It can take different forms such as manufacture, the exploitation of intellectual property rights that substantially contribute to technical or economic progress, or the marketing of new products.

(10) Consumers can generally be expected to benefit from the increased volume and effectiveness of research and development through the introduction of new or improved products or services, a quicker launch of those products or services, or the reduction of prices brought about by new or improved technologies or processes.

(11) In order to justify the exemption, the joint exploitation should relate to products, technologies or processes for which the use of the results of the research and development is decisive. Moreover, all the parties should agree in the research and development agreement that they will all have full access to the final results of the joint research and development, including any arising intellectual property rights and know-how, for the purposes of further research and development and exploitation, as soon as the final results become available. Access to the results should generally not be limited as regards the use of the results for the purposes of further research and development. However, where the parties, in accordance with this Regulation, limit their rights of exploitation, in particular where they specialise in the context of exploitation, access to the results for the purposes of exploitation may be limited accordingly. Moreover, where academic bodies, research institutes or undertakings which supply research and development as a

commercial service without normally being active in the exploitation of results participate in research and development, they may agree to use the results of research and development solely for the purpose of further research. Depending on their capabilities and commercial needs, the parties may make unequal contributions to their research and development cooperation. Therefore, in order to reflect, and to make up for, the differences in the value or the nature of the parties' contributions, a research and development agreement benefiting from this Regulation may provide that one party is to compensate another for obtaining access to the results for the purposes of further research or exploitation. However, the compensation should not be so high as to effectively impede such access.

(12) Similarly, where the research and development agreement does not provide for any joint exploitation of the results, the parties should agree in the research and development agreement to grant each other access to their respective pre-existing know-how, as long as this know-how is indispensable for the purposes of the exploitation of the results by the other parties. The rates of any licence fee charged should not be so high as to effectively impede access to the know-how by the other parties.

(13) The exemption established by this Regulation should be limited to research and development agreements which do not afford the undertakings the possibility of eliminating competition in respect of a substantial part of the products, services or technologies in question. It is necessary to exclude from the block exemption agreements between competitors whose combined share of the market for products, services or technologies capable of being improved or replaced by the results of the research and development exceeds a certain level at the time the agreement is entered into. However, there is no presumption that research and development agreements are either caught by Article 101(1) of the Treaty or that they fail to satisfy the conditions of Article 101(3) of the Treaty once the market share threshold set out in this Regulation is exceeded or other conditions of this Regulation are not met. In such cases, an individual assessment of the research and development agreement needs to be conducted under Article 101 of the Treaty.

(14) In order to ensure the maintenance of effective competition during joint exploitation of the results, provision should be made for the block exemption to cease to apply if the parties' combined share of the market for the products, services or technologies arising out of the joint research and development becomes too great. The exemption should continue to apply, irrespective of the parties' market shares, for a certain period after the commencement of joint exploitation, so as to await stabilisation of their market shares, particularly after the introduction of an entirely new product, and to guarantee a minimum period of return on the investments involved.

(15) This Regulation should not exempt agreements containing restrictions which are not indispensable to the attainment of the positive effects generated by a research and development agreement. In principle, agreements containing certain types of severe restrictions of competition such as limitations on the freedom of parties to carry out research and development in a field unconnected to the agreement, the fixing of prices charged to third parties, limitations on output or sales, and limitations on effecting passive sales for the contract products or contract technologies in territories or to customers reserved for other parties should be excluded from the benefit of the exemption established by this Regulation irrespective of the market share of the parties. In this context, field of use restrictions do not constitute limitations of output or sales, and also do not constitute territorial or customer restrictions.

(16) The market share limitation, the non-exemption of certain agreements and the conditions provided for in this Regulation normally ensure that the agreements to which the block exemption applies do not enable the parties to eliminate competition in respect of a substantial part of the products or services in question.

(17) The possibility cannot be ruled out that anti-competitive foreclosure effects may arise where one party finances several research and development projects carried out by competitors with regard to the same contract products or contract technologies, in particular where it obtains the exclusive right to exploit the results vis-à-vis third parties. Therefore the benefit of this Regulation should be conferred on such paid-for research and development agreements only if the combined market share of all the parties involved in the connected agreements, that is to say, the financing party and all the parties carrying out the research and development, does not exceed 25%.

(18) Agreements between undertakings which are not competing manufacturers of products, technologies or processes capable of being improved, substituted or replaced by the results of the research and development will only eliminate effective competition in research and development in exceptional circumstances. It is therefore appropriate to enable such agreements to benefit from the exemption established by this Regulation irrespective of market share and to address any exceptional cases by way of withdrawal of its benefit.

(19) The Commission may withdraw the benefit of this Regulation, pursuant to Article 29(1) of Council Regulation (EC) No 1/2003 of 16 December 2002 on the implementation of the rules on competition laid down in Articles [101] and [102] of the Treaty,[1] where it finds in a particular case that an agreement to which the exemption provided for in this Regulation applies nevertheless has effects which are incompatible with Article 101(3) of the Treaty.

Notes
[1] OJ L 1, 4.1.2003, p.1.

---

(20) The competition authority of a Member State may withdraw the benefit of this Regulation pursuant to Article 29(2) of Regulation (EC) No 1/2003 in respect of the territory of that Member State, or a part thereof where, in a particular case, an agreement to which the exemption established by this Regulation applies nevertheless has effects which are incompatible with Article 101(3) of the Treaty in the territory of that Member State, or in a part thereof, and where such territory has all the characteristics of a distinct geographic market.

(21) The benefit of this Regulation could be withdrawn pursuant to Article 29 of Regulation (EC) No 1/2003, for example, where the existence of a research and development agreement substantially restricts the scope for third parties to carry out research and development in the relevant field because of the limited research capacity available elsewhere, where because of the particular structure of supply, the existence of the research and development agreement substantially restricts the access of third parties to the market for the contract products or contract technologies, where without any objectively valid reason, the parties do not exploit the results of the joint research and development vis-à-vis third parties, where the contract products or contract technologies are not subject in the whole or a substantial part of the internal market to effective competition from products, technologies or processes considered by users as equivalent in view of their characteristics, price and intended use, or where the existence of the research and development agreement would restrict competition in innovation or eliminate effective competition in research and development on a particular market.

Commentary
Recital 21: B&C: 6.051

---

(22) As research and development agreements are often of a long-term nature, especially where the cooperation extends to the exploitation of the results, the period of validity of this Regulation should be fixed at 12 years,

HAS ADOPTED THIS REGULATION:

Article 1
Definitions

1. For the purposes of this Regulation, the following definitions shall apply:

(a) 'research and development agreement' means an agreement entered into between two or more parties which relate to the conditions under which those parties pursue:
   (i) joint research and development of contract products or contract technologies and joint exploitation of the results of that research and development;
   (ii) joint exploitation of the results of research and development of contract products or contract technologies jointly carried out pursuant to a prior agreement between the same parties;
   (iii) joint research and development of contract products or contract technologies excluding joint exploitation of the results;

(iv) paid-for research and development of contract products or contract technologies and joint exploitation of the results of that research and development;

(v) joint exploitation of the results of paid-for research and development of contract products or contract technologies pursuant to a prior agreement between the same parties; or

(vi) paid-for research and development of contract products or contract technologies excluding joint exploitation of the results;

(b) 'agreement' means an agreement, a decision by an association of undertakings or a concerted practice;

(c) 'research and development' means the acquisition of know-how relating to products, technologies or processes and the carrying out of theoretical analysis, systematic study or experimentation, including experimental production, technical testing of products or processes, the establishment of the necessary facilities and the obtaining of intellectual property rights for the results;

(d) 'product' means a good or a service, including both intermediary goods or services and final goods or services;

(e) 'contract technology' means a technology or process arising out of the joint research and development;

(f) 'contract product' means a product arising out of the joint research and development or manufactured or provided applying the contract technologies;

(g) 'exploitation of the results' means the production or distribution of the contract products or the application of the contract technologies or the assignment or licensing of intellectual property rights or the communication of know-how required for such manufacture or application;

(h) 'intellectual property rights' means intellectual property rights, including industrial property rights, copyright and neighbouring rights;

(i) 'know-how' means a package of non-patented practical information, resulting from experience and testing, which is secret, substantial and identified;

(j) 'secret', in the context of know-how, means that the know-how is not generally known or easily accessible;

(k) 'substantial', in the context of know-how, means that the know-how is significant and useful for the manufacture of the contract products or the application of the contract technologies;

(l) 'identified', in the context of know-how, means that the know-how is described in a sufficiently comprehensive manner so as to make it possible to verify that it fulfils the criteria of secrecy and substantiality;

(m) 'joint', in the context of activities carried out under a research and development agreement, means activities where the work involved is:

(i) carried out by a joint team, organisation or undertaking;

(ii) jointly entrusted to a third party; or

(iii) allocated between the parties by way of specialisation in the context of research and development or exploitation;

(n) 'specialisation in the context of research and development' means that each of the parties is involved in the research and development activities covered by the research and development agreement and they divide the research and development work between them in any way that they consider most appropriate; this does not include paid-for research and development;

(o) 'specialisation in the context of exploitation' means that the parties allocate between them individual tasks such as production or distribution, or impose restrictions upon each other regarding the exploitation of the results such as restrictions in relation to certain territories, customers or fields of use; this includes a scenario where only one party produces and distributes the contract products on the basis of an exclusive licence granted by the other parties;

(p) 'paid-for research and development' means research and development that is carried out by one party and financed by a financing party;

(q) 'financing party' means a party financing paid-for research and development while not carrying out any of the research and development activities itself;

(r) 'competing undertaking' means an actual or potential competitor;

(s) 'actual competitor' means an undertaking that is supplying a product, technology or process capable of being improved, substituted or replaced by the contract product or the contract technology on the relevant geographic market;

(t) 'potential competitor' means an undertaking that, in the absence of the research and development agreement, would, on realistic grounds and not just as a mere theoretical possibility, in case of a small but permanent increase in relative prices be likely to undertake, within not more than 3 years, the necessary additional investments or other necessary switching costs to supply a product, technology or process capable of being improved, substituted or replaced by the contract product or contract technology on the relevant geographic market;

(u) 'relevant product market' means the relevant market for the products capable of being improved, substituted or replaced by the contract products;

(v) 'relevant technology market' means the relevant market for the technologies or processes capable of being improved, substituted or replaced by the contract technologies.

2. For the purposes of this Regulation, the terms 'undertaking' and 'party' shall include their respective connected undertakings.

'Connected undertakings' means:

(a) undertakings in which a party to the research and development agreement, directly or indirectly:
   (i) has the power to exercise more than half the voting rights;
   (ii) has the power to appoint more than half the members of the supervisory board, board of management or bodies legally representing the undertaking; or
   (iii) has the right to manage the undertaking's affairs;

(b) undertakings which directly or indirectly have, over a party to the research and development agreement, the rights or powers listed in point (a);

(c) undertakings in which an undertaking referred to in point (b) has, directly or indirectly, the rights or powers listed in point (a);

(d) undertakings in which a party to the research and development agreement together with one or more of the undertakings referred to in points (a), (b) or (c), or in which two or more of the latter undertakings, jointly have the rights or powers listed in point (a);

(e) undertakings in which the rights or the powers listed in point (a) are jointly held by:

   (i) parties to the research and development agreement or their respective connected undertakings referred to in points (a) to (d); or
   (ii) one or more of the parties to the research and development agreement or one or more of their connected undertakings referred to in points (a) to (d) and one or more third parties.

Commentary

Art 1(1)(a): **B&C:** 6.047 **F&N:** 7.163, 7.170, 7.185
Art 1(1)(a)(i)): **B&C:** 6.050
Art 1(1)(a)(i)–(iii) : **B&C:** 6.052
Art 1(1)(a)(ii): **B&C:** 6.050, 6.079
Art 1(1)(a)(iii): **B&C:** 6.050 **F&N:** 7.179
Art 1(1)(a)(iv): **B&C:** 6.050
Art 1(1)(a)(iv)–(vi): **B&C:** 6.052 **F&N:** 7.167
Art 1(1)(a)(v): **B&C:** 6.050, 6.079
Art 1(1)(a)(vi): **B&C:** 6.050
Art 1(1)(b): **B&C:** 6.055 **F&N:** 7.170, 7.172
Art 1(1)(c): **B&C:** 6.050, 6.055 **F&N:** 7.170, 7.173
Art 1(1)(g): **B&C:** 6.079 **F&N:** 7.167, 7.170, 7.171, 7.175, 7.190
Art 1(1)(i) : **B&C:** 6.051 **F&N:** 7.189
Art 1(1)(k): **B&C:** 7.179 **F&N:** 7.173, 7.189
Art 1(1)(m): **B&C:** 6.050, 6.051, 6.053 **F&N:** 7.170, 7.171, 7.172, 7.176, 7.178, 7.180, 7.186, 7.202
Art 1(1)(n): **B&C:** 2.097 **F&N:** 7.170, 7.176, 7.177, 7.180, 7.202
Art 1(1)(p): **B&C:** 6.050 **F&N:** 7.156, 7.157, 7.170, 7.180, 7.202
Art 1(1)(s)–(v): **B&C:** 6.041
Art 1(1)(s)(t): **B&C:** 6.052
Art 1(1)(t): **B&C:** 2.097, 4.020 **F&N:** 7.167, 7.183, 7.198
Art 1(1)(v): **B&C:** 6.041 **F&N:** 7.184
Art 1(2): **B&C:** 6.052

Part C Substantive
Antitrust Matters

Article 2
Exemption

1. Pursuant to Article 101(3) of the Treaty and subject to the provisions of this Regulation, it is hereby declared that Article 101(1) of the Treaty shall not apply to research and development agreements.

This exemption shall apply to the extent that such agreements contain restrictions of competition falling within the scope of Article 101(1) of the Treaty.

2. The exemption provided for in paragraph 1 shall apply to research and development agreements containing provisions which relate to the assignment or licensing of intellectual property rights to one or more of the parties or to an entity the parties establish to carry out the joint research and development, paid-for research and development or joint exploitation, provided that those provisions do not constitute the primary object of such agreements, but are directly related to and necessary for their implementation.

Commentary
Art 2: **B&C:** 6.047 **F&N:** 7.185
Art 2(1): **B&C:** 6.079 **F&N:** 7.163, 7.167, 7.185
Art 2(2): **B&C:** 6.050, 9.135 **F&N:** 7.186, 7.187

Article 3
Conditions for exemption

1. The exemption provided for in Article 2 shall apply subject to the conditions set out in paragraphs 2 to 5.

2. The research and development agreement must stipulate that all the parties have full access to the final results of the joint research and development or paid-for research and development, including any resulting intellectual property rights and know-how, for the purposes of further research and development and exploitation, as soon as they become available. Where the parties limit their rights of exploitation in accordance with this Regulation, in particular where they specialise in the context of exploitation, access to the results for the purposes of exploitation may be limited accordingly. Moreover, research institutes, academic bodies, or undertakings which supply research and development as a commercial service without normally being active in the exploitation of results may agree to confine their use of the results for the purposes of further research. The research and development agreement may foresee that the parties compensate each other for giving access to the results for the purposes of further research or exploitation, but the compensation must not be so high as to effectively impede such access.

3. Without prejudice to paragraph 2, where the research and development agreement provides only for joint research and development or paid-for research and development, the research and development agreement must stipulate that each party must be granted access to any pre-existing know-how of the other parties, if this know-how is indispensable for the purposes of its exploitation of the results. The research and development agreement may foresee that the parties compensate each other for giving access to their pre-existing know-how, but the compensation must not be so high as to effectively impede such access.

4. Any joint exploitation may only pertain to results which are protected by intellectual property rights or constitute know-how and which are indispensable for the manufacture of the contract products or the application of the contract technologies.

5. Parties charged with the manufacture of the contract products by way of specialisation in the context of exploitation must be required to fulfil orders for supplies of the contract products from the other parties, except where the research and development agreement also provides for joint distribution within the meaning of point (m)(i) or (ii) of Article 1(1) or where the parties have agreed that only the party manufacturing the contract products may distribute them.

Commentary
Art 3(2): **B&C:** 6.048, 6.051 **F&N:** 7.167, 7.190, 7.191, 7.193
Art 3(3): **B&C:** 6.051 **F&N:** 7.171, 7.179, 7.192, 7.193, 7.194
Art 3(4): **B&C:** 6.047, 6.051, 6.079, 12.062 **F&N:** 7.195

Article 4
Market share threshold and duration of exemption

1. Where the parties are not competing undertakings, the exemption provided for in Article 2 shall apply for the duration of the research and development. Where the results are jointly exploited, the exemption shall continue to apply for 7 years from the time the contract products or contract technologies are first put on the market within the internal market.

2. Where two or more of the parties are competing undertakings, the exemption provided for in Article 2 shall apply for the period referred to in paragraph 1 of this Article only if, at the time the research and development agreement is entered into:

(a) in the case of research and development agreements referred to in point (a)(i), (ii) or (iii) of Article 1(1), the combined market share of the parties to a research and development agreement does not exceed 25% on the relevant product and technology markets; or

(b) in the case of research and agreements referred to in point (a)(iv), (v) or (vi) of Article 1(1), the combined market share of the financing party and all the parties with which the financing party has entered into research and development agreements with regard to the same contract products or contract technologies, does not exceed 25% on the relevant product and technology markets.

3. After the end of the period referred to in paragraph 1, the exemption shall continue to apply as long as the combined market share of the parties does not exceed 25% on the relevant product and technology markets.

Commentary
Art 4: B&C: 3.081 **F&N:** 3.380, 7.184, 7.185, 7.197, 7.227, 7.229
Art 4(1): B&C: 6.052 **F&N:** 7.153, 7.157, 7.181, 7.183, 7.197, 7.203, 7.204, 7.231
Art 4(2): B&C: 6.052 **F&N:** 7.161, 7.177, 7.181, 7.183, 7.197, 7.200, 7.201, 7.202, 7.203, 7.231
Art 4(2)(b): B&C: 6.052 **F&N:** 7.180, 7.200, 7.202, 7.204
Art 4(3): B&C: 6.052 **F&N:** 7.153, 7.157, 7.200, 7.204, 7.231, 7.232

Article 5
Hardcore restrictions

The exemption provided for in Article 2 shall not apply to research and development agreements which, directly or indirectly, in isolation or in combination with other factors under the control of the parties, have as their object any of the following:

(a) the restriction of the freedom of the parties to carry out research and development independently or in cooperation with third parties in a field unconnected with that to which the research and development agreement relates or, after the completion of the joint research and development or the paid-for research and development, in the field to which it relates or in a connected field;

(b) the limitation of output or sales, with the exception of:
   (i) the setting of production targets where the joint exploitation of the results includes the joint production of the contract products;
   (ii) the setting of sales targets where the joint exploitation of the results includes the joint distribution of the contract products or the joint licensing of the contract technologies within the meaning of point (m)(i) or (ii) of Article 1(1);
   (iii) practices constituting specialisation in the context of exploitation; and
   (iv) the restriction of the freedom of the parties to manufacture, sell, assign or license products, technologies or processes which compete with the contract products or contract technologies during the period for which the parties have agreed to jointly exploit the results;

(c) the fixing of prices when selling the contract product or licensing the contract technologies to third parties, with the exception of the fixing of prices charged to immediate customers or the fixing of licence fees charged to immediate licensees where the joint exploitation of the results includes the joint distribution of the contract products or the joint licensing of the contract technologies within the meaning of point (m)(i) or (ii) of Article 1(1);

(d) the restriction of the territory in which, or of the customers to whom, the parties may passively sell the contract products or license the contract technologies, with the exception of the requirement to exclusively license the results to another party;

(e) the requirement not to make any, or to limit, active sales of the contract products or contract technologies in territories or to customers which have not been exclusively allocated to one of the parties by way of specialisation in the context of exploitation;

(f) the requirement to refuse to meet demand from customers in the parties' respective territories, or from customers otherwise allocated between the parties by way of specialisation in the context of exploitation, who would market the contract products in other territories within the internal market;

(g) the requirement to make it difficult for users or resellers to obtain the contract products from other resellers within the internal market.

Commentary
Art 5: **B&C:** 6.053 **F&N:** 7.164, 7.176, 7.179, 7.185, 7.206, 7.207, 7.209, 7.213, 7.219, 7.222
Art 5(a): **B&C:** 6.053 **F&N:** 7.208
Art 5(b): **B&C:** 6.053 **F&N:** 7.210, 7.212, 7.213, 7.214, 7.215
Art 5(b)(iii): **B&C:** 6.079 **F&N:** 7.213, 7.214
Art 5(c): **B&C:** 6.053, 6.079 **F&N:** 7.216
Art 5(d): **B&C:** 6.053 **F&N:** 7.167, 7.217, 7.218
Art 5(e): **B&C:** 6.053 **F&N:** 7.167, 7.219
Art 5(f): **B&C:** 6.053 **F&N:** 7.220
Art 5(g): **B&C:** 6.053 **F&N:** 7.221

Article 6
Excluded restrictions

The exemption provided for in Article 2 shall not apply to the following obligations contained in research and development agreements:

(a) the obligation not to challenge after completion of the research and development the validity of intellectual property rights which the parties hold in the internal market and which are relevant to the research and development or, after the expiry of the research and development agreement, the validity of intellectual property rights which the parties hold in the internal market and which protect the results of the research and development, without prejudice to the possibility to provide for termination of the research and development agreement in the event of one of the parties challenging the validity of such intellectual property rights;

(b) the obligation not to grant licences to third parties to manufacture the contract products or to apply the contract technologies unless the agreement provides for the exploitation of the results of the joint research and development or paid-for research and development by at least one of the parties and such exploitation takes place in the internal market vis-à-vis third parties.

Commentary
Art 6(a): **B&C:** 6.054 **F&N:** 7.167, 7.223
Art 6(b): **B&C:** 6.054 **F&N:** 7.167, 7.225

Article 7
Application of the market share threshold

For the purposes of applying the market share threshold provided for in Article 4 the following rules shall apply:

(a) the market share shall be calculated on the basis of the market sales value; if market sales value data are not available, estimates based on other reliable market information, including market sales volumes, may be used to establish the market share of the parties;

(b) the market share shall be calculated on the basis of data relating to the preceding calendar year;

(c) the market share held by the undertakings referred to in point (e) of the second subparagraph of Article 1(2) shall be apportioned equally to each undertaking having the rights or the powers listed in point (a) of that subparagraph;

(d) if the market share referred to in Article 4(3) is initially not more than 25% but subsequently rises above that level without exceeding 30%, the exemption provided for in Article 2 shall continue to apply for a period of two consecutive calendar years following the year in which the 25% threshold was first exceeded;

(e) if the market share referred to in Article 4(3) is initially not more than 25% but subsequently rises above 30%, the exemption provided for in Article 2 shall continue to apply for a period of one calendar year following the year in which the level of 30% was first exceeded;

(f) the benefit of points (d) and (e) may not be combined so as to exceed a period of two calendar years.

Commentary

Art 7: B&C: 6.052 **F&N:** 7.200, 7.227, 7.230, 11.208

Art 7(c): B&C: 6.052 **F&N:** 7.227

Article 8
Transitional period

The prohibition laid down in Article 101(1) of the Treaty shall not apply during the period from 1 January 2011 to 31 December 2012 in respect of agreements already in force on 31 December 2010 which do not satisfy the conditions for exemption provided for in this Regulation but which satisfy the conditions for exemption provided for in Regulation (EC) No 2659/2000.

Article 9
Period of validity

This Regulation shall enter into force on 1 January 2011.

It shall expire on 31 December 2022.

This Regulation shall be binding in its entirety and directly applicable in all Member States.

Done at Brussels, 14 December 2010.

Commentary

Art 9: B&C: 3.081

C7

COMMISSION REGULATION (EU) NO 1218/2010

of 14 December 2010

on the application of Article 101(3) of the Treaty on the Functioning of the European Union to certain categories of specialisation agreements

(Text with EEA relevance)

Official Journal L 335, 18.12.2010, p.43

Celex No: 32010R1218

EUR-Lex permanent link: <http://Teur-lex.europa.eu/LexUriServ/LexUriServ.do?uri=CELEX: 32010 R1218:EN:NOT>

Notes

EEA application: Regulation 1218/2010/EU was incorporated into the EEA Agreement (Annex XIV, Chapter D, point 6) by EEA Joint Committee Decision No 3/2011 of 11 February 2011 (OJ L 93, 7.4.2011, p.32).

Commentary
Regulation 1218/2010/EU: B&C: 3.080, 3.096, 5.063, 5.074, 6.006, 6.011, 6.055, 6.062, 9.133, 9.135
F&N: 2.12, 3.379, 3.380, 7.10, 7.241, 7.264, 7.270, 7.271, 7.272, 7.273, 7.274, 7.275, 8.22, 10.62, 10.80, 10.94

THE EUROPEAN COMMISSION,

Having regard to the Treaty on the Functioning of the European Union,

Having regard to Regulation (EEC) No 2821/71 of the Council of 20 December 1971 on application of Article [101] (3) of the Treaty to categories of agreements, decisions and concerted practices,[1]

Having published a draft of this Regulation,

After consulting the Advisory Committee on Restrictive Practices and Dominant Positions,

---

Notes
[1] OJ L 285, 29.12.1971, p.46.

Whereas:

(1) Regulation (EEC) No 2821/71 empowers the Commission to apply Article 101(3) of the Treaty on the Functioning of the European Union (*) by regulation to certain categories of agreements, decisions and concerted practices falling within the scope of Article 101(1) of the Treaty which have as their object specialisation, including agreements necessary for achieving it.

Notes

(*) With effect from 1 December 2009, Article 81 of the EC Treaty has become Article 101 of the Treaty on the Functioning of the European Union (TFEU). The two Articles are, in substance, identical. For the purposes of this Regulation, references to Article 101 of the TFEU should be understood as references to Article 81 of the EC Treaty where appropriate. The TFEU also introduced certain changes in terminology, such as the replacement of "Community" by "Union" and "common market" by "internal market". The terminology of the TFEU will be used throughout this Regulation.

---

(2) Commission Regulation (EC) No 2658/2000 of 29 November 2000 on the application of Article [101](3) of the Treaty to categories of specialisation agreements[1] defines categories of specialisation agreements which the Commission regarded as normally satisfying the conditions laid down in Article 101(3) of the Treaty. In view of the overall positive experience with the application of

that Regulation, which expires on 31 December 2010, and taking into account further experience acquired since its adoption, it is appropriate to adopt a new block exemption regulation.

Notes
1 OJ L 304, 5.12.2000, p.3.

(3) This Regulation should meet the two requirements of ensuring effective protection of competition and providing adequate legal security for undertakings. The pursuit of those objectives should take account of the need to simplify administrative supervision and the legislative framework to as great an extent as possible. Below a certain level of market power it can in general be presumed, for the application of Article 101(3) of the Treaty, that the positive effects of specialisation agreements will outweigh any negative effects on competition.

(4) For the application of Article 101(3) of the Treaty by regulation, it is not necessary to define those agreements which are capable of falling within Article 101(1) of the Treaty. In the individual assessment of agreements under Article 101(1) of the Treaty, account has to be taken of several factors, and in particular the market structure on the relevant market.

(5) The benefit of the exemption established by this Regulation should be limited to those agreements for which it can be assumed with sufficient certainty that they satisfy the conditions of Article 101(3) of the Treaty.

(6) Agreements on specialisation in production are most likely to contribute to improving the production or distribution of goods if the parties have complementary skills, assets or activities, because they can concentrate on the manufacture of certain products and thus operate more efficiently and supply the products more cheaply. The same can generally be said about agreements on specialisation in the preparation of services. Given effective competition, it is likely that consumers will receive a fair share of the resulting benefits.

(7) Such advantages can arise from agreements whereby one party fully or partly gives up the manufacture of certain products or preparation of certain services in favour of another party (unilateral specialisation), from agreements whereby each party fully or partly gives up the manufacture of certain products or preparation of certain services in favour of another party (reciprocal specialisation) and from agreements whereby the parties undertake to jointly manufacture certain products or prepare certain services (joint production). In the context of this Regulation, the concepts of unilateral and reciprocal specialisation do not require a party to reduce capacity, as it is sufficient if they reduce their production volumes. The concept of joint production, however, does not require the parties to reduce their individual production activities outside the scope of their envisaged joint production arrangement.

(8) The nature of unilateral and reciprocal specialisation agreements presupposes that the parties are active on the same product market. It is not necessary for the parties to be active on the same geographic market. Consequently, the application of this Regulation to unilateral and reciprocal specialisation agreements should be limited to scenarios where the parties are active on the same product market. Joint production agreements can be entered into by parties who are already active on the same product market but also by parties who wish to enter a product market by way of the agreement. Therefore, joint production agreements should fall within the scope of this Regulation irrespective of whether the parties are already active in the same product market.

Commentary
Recital 8: B&C: 6.055

(9) To ensure that the benefits of specialisation will materialise without one party leaving the market downstream of production entirely, unilateral and reciprocal specialisation agreements should only be covered by this Regulation where they provide for supply and purchase obligations or joint distribution. Supply and purchase obligations may, but do not have to, be of an exclusive nature.

Commentary
Recital 9: B&C: 6.058

(10) It can be presumed that, where the parties' share of the relevant market for the products which are the subject matter of a specialisation agreement does not exceed a certain level, the agreements will, as a general rule, give rise to economic benefits in the form of economies of scale or scope or better production technologies, while allowing consumers a fair share of the resulting benefits. However, where the products manufactured under a specialisation agreement are intermediary products which one or more of the parties fully or partly use as an input for their own production of certain downstream products which they subsequently sell on the market, the exemption conferred by this Regulation should also be conditional on the parties' share on the relevant market for these downstream products not exceeding a certain level. In such a case, merely looking at the parties' market share at the level of the intermediary product would ignore the potential risk of foreclosing or increasing the price of inputs for competitors at the level of the downstream products. However, there is no presumption that specialisation agreements are either caught by Article 101(1) of the Treaty or that they fail to satisfy the conditions of Article 101(3) of the Treaty once the market share threshold set out in this Regulation is exceeded or other conditions of this Regulation are not met. In such cases, an individual assessment of the specialisation agreement needs to be conducted under Article 101 of the Treaty.

Commentary
Recital 10: B&C: 6.058 **F&N:** 7.271, 7.305

(11) This Regulation should not exempt agreements containing restrictions which are not indispensable to the attainment of the positive effects generated by a specialisation agreement. In principle, agreements containing certain types of severe restrictions of competition relating to the fixing of prices charged to third parties, limitation of output or sales, and allocation of markets or customers should be excluded from the benefit of the exemption established by this Regulation irrespective of the market share of the parties.

(12) The market share limitation, the non-exemption of certain agreements and the conditions provided for in this Regulation normally ensure that the agreements to which the block exemption applies do not enable the parties to eliminate competition in respect of a substantial part of the products or services in question.

(13) The Commission may withdraw the benefit of this Regulation, pursuant to Article 29(1) of Council Regulation (EC) No 1/2003 of 16 December 2002 on the implementation of the rules on competition laid down in Articles [101] and [102] of the Treaty,[1] where it finds in a particular case that an agreement to which the exemption provided for in this Regulation applies nevertheless has effects which are incompatible with Article 101(3) of the Treaty.

Notes
[1] OJ L 1, 4.1.2003, p.1.

(14) The competition authority of a Member State may withdraw the benefit of this Regulation pursuant to Article 29(2) of Regulation (EC) No 1/2003 in respect of the territory of that Member State, or a part thereof where, in a particular case, an agreement to which the exemption established by this Regulation applies nevertheless has effects which are incompatible with Article 101(3) of the Treaty in the territory of that Member State, or in a part thereof, and where such territory has all the characteristics of a distinct geographic market.

(15) The benefit of this Regulation could be withdrawn pursuant to Article 29 of Regulation (EC) No 1/2003 where, for example, the relevant market is very concentrated and competition is already weak, in particular because of the individual market positions of other market participants or links between other market participants created by parallel specialisation agreements.

Commentary
Recital 15: F&N: 7.273

(16) In order to facilitate the conclusion of specialisation agreements, which can have a bearing on the structure of the parties, the period of validity of this Regulation should be fixed at 12 years,

HAS ADOPTED THIS REGULATION:

Article 1
Definitions

1. For the purposes of this Regulation, the following definitions shall apply:

(a) 'specialisation agreement' means a unilateral specialisation agreement, a reciprocal specialisation agreement or a joint production agreement;

(b) 'unilateral specialisation agreement' means an agreement between two parties which are active on the same product market by virtue of which one party agrees to fully or partly cease production of certain products or to refrain from producing those products and to purchase them from the other party, who agrees to produce and supply those products;

(c) 'reciprocal specialisation agreement' means an agreement between two or more parties which are active on the same product market, by virtue of which two or more parties on a reciprocal basis agree to fully or partly cease or refrain from producing certain but different products and to purchase these products from the other parties, who agree to produce and supply them;

(d) 'joint production agreement' means an agreement by virtue of which two or more parties agree to produce certain products jointly;

(e) 'agreement' means an agreement, a decision by an association of undertakings or a concerted practice;

(f) 'product' means a good or a service, including both intermediary goods or services and final goods or services, with the exception of distribution and rental services;

(g) 'production' means the manufacture of goods or the preparation of services and includes production by way of subcontracting;

(h) 'preparation of services' means activities upstream of the provision of services to customers;

(i) 'relevant market' means the relevant product and geographic market to which the specialisation products belong, and, in addition, where the specialisation products are intermediary products which one or more of the parties fully or partly use captively for the production of downstream products, the relevant product and geographic market to which the downstream products belong;

(j) 'specialisation product' means a product which is produced under a specialisation agreement;

(k) 'downstream product' means a product for which a specialisation product is used by one or more of the parties as an input and which is sold by those parties on the market;

(l) 'competing undertaking' means an actual or potential competitor;

(m) 'actual competitor' means an undertaking that is active on the same relevant market;

(n) 'potential competitor' means an undertaking that, in the absence of the specialisation agreement, would, on realistic grounds and not just as a mere theoretical possibility, in case of a small but permanent increase in relative prices be likely to undertake, within not more than 3 years, the necessary additional investments or other necessary switching costs to enter the relevant market;

(o) 'exclusive supply obligation' means an obligation not to supply a competing undertaking other than a party to the agreement with the specialisation product;

(p) 'exclusive purchase obligation' means an obligation to purchase the specialisation product only from a party to the agreement;

(q) 'joint', in the context of distribution, means that the parties:
   (i) carry out the distribution of the products by way of a joint team, organisation or undertaking; or
   (ii) appoint a third party distributor on an exclusive or non-exclusive basis, provided that the third party is not a competing undertaking;

(r) 'distribution' means distribution, including the sale of goods and the provision of services.

2. For the purposes of this Regulation, the terms 'undertaking' and 'party' shall include their respective connected undertakings.

'Connected undertakings' means:

(a) undertakings in which a party to the specialisation agreement, directly or indirectly:
   (i) has the power to exercise more than half the voting rights;

341

    (ii) has the power to appoint more than half the members of the supervisory board, board of management or bodies legally representing the undertaking; or

    (iii) has the right to manage the undertaking's affairs;

(b) undertakings which directly or indirectly have, over a party to the specialisation agreement, the rights or powers listed in point (a);

(c) undertakings in which an undertaking referred to in point (b) has, directly or indirectly, the rights or powers listed in point (a);

(d) undertakings in which a party to the specialisation agreement together with one or more of the undertakings referred to in points (a), (b) or (c), or in which two or more of the latter undertakings, jointly have the rights or powers listed in point (a);

(e) undertakings in which the rights or the powers listed in point (a) are jointly held by:

    (i) parties to the specialisation agreement or their respective connected undertakings referred to in points (a) to (d); or

    (ii) one or more of the parties to the specialisation agreement or one or more of their connected undertakings referred to in points (a) to (d) and one or more third parties.

Commentary

Art 1: B&C: 3.080 F&N: 7.277
Art 1(1)(a): B&C: 6.055, 6.062 F&N: 7.278, 7.298
Art 1(1)(a)–(d): F&N: 7.292, 7.293, 7.297, 7.298
Art 1(1)(a)–(f): F&N: 7.288
Art 1(1)(b): B&C: 6.062 F&N: 7.275, 7.278, 7.279, 7.282
Art 1(1)(c): B&C: 6.062 F&N: 7.269, 7.275, 7.278, 7.281, 7.282, 7.294
Art 1(1)(d): B&C: 6.055, 6.062 F&N: 7.278, 7.282
Art 1(1)(e): F&N: 7.283
Art 1(1)(g): F&N: 7.282, 7.285, 7.294
Art 1(1)(h): F&N: 7.285, 7.286
Art 1(1)(i): B&C: 6.058 F&N: 7.275, 7.287, 7.304, 7.321
Art 1(1)(i)–(k): B&C: 6.063
Art 1(1)(k): F&N: 7.289
Art 1(1)(l): F&N: 7.290, 7.292
Art 1(1)(m): F&N: 7.290, 7.294
Art 1(1)(m)(iii): F&N: 7.315
Art 1(1)(n): B&C: 4.020 F&N: 7.275, 7.287, 7.290
Art 1(1)(o): F&N: 7.290, 7.291, 7.292, 7.300, 7.312, 7.315
Art 1(1)(p): F&N: 7.293, 7.300
Art 1(1)(q): B&C: 6.062 F&N: 7.282, 7.290, 7.291, 7.294, 7.300, 7.310, 7.314, 7.315
Art 1(1)(r): F&N: 7.290, 7.291, 7.295, 7.300, 7.314, 7.315
Art 1(2): B&C: 6.063 F&N: 7.296, 7.297
Art 1(2)(a)–(d): F&N: 7.296
Art 1(2)(e): F&N: 7.296, 7.318

Article 2
Exemption

1. Pursuant to Article 101(3) of the Treaty and subject to the provisions of this Regulation, it is hereby declared that Article 101(1) of the Treaty shall not apply to specialisation agreements.

This exemption shall apply to the extent that such agreements contain restrictions of competition falling within the scope of Article 101(1) of the Treaty.

2. The exemption provided for in paragraph 1 shall apply to specialisation agreements containing provisions which relate to the assignment or licensing of intellectual property rights to one or more of the parties, provided that those provisions do not constitute the primary object of such agreements, but are directly related to and necessary for their implementation.

3. The exemption provided for in paragraph 1 shall apply to specialisation agreements whereby:

    (a) the parties accept an exclusive purchase or exclusive supply obligation; or

    (b) the parties do not independently sell the specialisation products but jointly distribute those products.

Commentary
Art 2: F&N: 7.298
Art 2(1): B&C: 6.062 F&N 7.298, 7.315
Art 2(2): B&C: 6.062 F&N 7.301, 7.302
Art 2(2)(b): F&N 7.279
Art 2(3): F&N 7.290, 7.300
Art 2(3)(a): B&C: 6.072, 6.079 F&N 7.281, 7.292, 7.293
Art 2(3)(b): F&N 7.281, 7.288, 7.294, 7.315

Article 3
Market share threshold

The exemption provided for in Article 2 shall apply on condition that the combined market share of the parties does not exceed 20% on any relevant market.

Commentary
Art 3(1): B&C: 3.080, 6.063 F&N: 7.270, 7.275, 7.287, 7.289, 7.299, 7.303, 7.304, 7.307, 7.316, 7.319
Art 3(3): B&C: 6.062

Article 4
Hardcore restrictions

The exemption provided for in Article 2 shall not apply to specialisation agreements which, directly or indirectly, in isolation or in combination with other factors under the control of the parties, have as their object any of the following:

(a) the fixing of prices when selling the products to third parties with the exception of the fixing of prices charged to immediate customers in the context of joint distribution;
(b) the limitation of output or sales with the exception of:
  (i) provisions on the agreed amount of products in the context of unilateral or reciprocal specialisation agreements or the setting of the capacity and production volume in the context of a joint production agreement; and
  (ii) the setting of sales targets in the context of joint distribution;
(c) the allocation of markets or customers.

Commentary
Art 4: B&C: 6.064 F&N: 7.278, 7.299, 7.308, 7.309, 12.100
Art 4(a): F&N: 7.310, 12.117
Art 4(b): B&C: 6.064 F&N: 7.311, 7.312, 7.314, 12.98, 12.99
Art 4(b)(i): F&N: 7.312, 7.313
Art 4(b)(ii): F&N: 7.314
Art 4(c): B&C: 6.064 F&N: 7.315, 12.49

Article 5
Application of the market share threshold

For the purposes of applying the market share threshold provided for in Article 3 the following rules shall apply:

(a) the market share shall be calculated on the basis of the market sales value; if market sales value data are not available, estimates based on other reliable market information, including market sales volumes, may be used to establish the market share of the parties;
(b) the market share shall be calculated on the basis of data relating to the preceding calendar year;
(c) the market share held by the undertakings referred to in point (e) of the second subparagraph of Article 1(2) shall be apportioned equally to each undertaking having the rights or the powers listed in point (a) of that subparagraph;
(d) if the market share referred to in Article 3 is initially not more than 20% but subsequently rises above that level without exceeding 25%, the exemption provided for in Article 2 shall continue to apply for a period of 2 consecutive calendar years following the year in which the 20% threshold was first exceeded;

(e) if the market share referred to in Article 3 is initially not more than 20% but subsequently rises above 25%, the exemption provided for in Article 2 shall continue to apply for a period of 1 calendar year following the year in which the level of 25% was first exceeded;

(f) the benefit of points (d) and (e) may not be combined so as to exceed a period of 2 calendar years.

Commentary
Art 5: F&N: 7.316, 7.318
Art 5(a): B&C: 6.063 F&N: 7.303, 7.316, 7.317
Art 5(b): B&C: 6.063 F&N: 7.303, 7.316, 7.317, 7.319
Art 5(c): B&C: 6.063 F&N: 7.303, 7.316, 7.317
Art 5(d): B&C: 6.063 F&N: 7.316, 7.319, 7.320
Art 5(e): B&C: 6.063 F&N: 7.316, 7.320
Art 5(f): B&C: 6.063 F&N: 7.316

Article 6
Transitional period

The prohibition laid down in Article 101(1) of the Treaty shall not apply during the period from 1 January 2011 to 31 December 2012 in respect of agreements already in force on 31 December 2010 which do not satisfy the conditions for exemption provided for in this Regulation but which satisfy the conditions for exemption provided for in Regulation (EC) No 2658/2000.

Commentary
Art 6: B&C: 6.055

Article 7
Period of validity

This Regulation shall enter into force on 1 January 2011.

It shall expire on 31 December 2022.

This Regulation shall be binding in its entirety and directly applicable in all Member States.

Done at Brussels, 14 December 2010.

Commentary
Art 7: B&C: 3.080 F&N: 7.322

C8

COMMISSION NOTICE

of 18 December 1978
concerning its assessment of certain subcontracting agreements in relation to
Article [101](1) of the [Treaty on the Functioning of the European Union]*

Official Journal C 1, 3.1.1979, p.2

Celex No: 31979Y0103(01)

EUR-Lex permanent link: <http://eur-lex.europa.eu/LexUriServ/LexUriServ.do?uri=CELEX:3197
9Y0103(01):EN:NOT>

Notes

* Ed note: please see the Note on the Lisbon Treaty at p.xvii in regard to article renumbering introduced by the Lisbon Treaty.
EEA application: the EFTA Surveillance Authority has adopted a parallel notice concerning its assessment of certain subcontracting agreements in relation to Article 53(1) of the EEA Agreement under Article 5(2)(b) of the Surveillance and Court Agreement: OJ L 153, 18.6.1994, p.30 and EEA Supplement No 15, 18.6.1994, p.29.

Commentary
Notice: **B&C:** 2.151, 7.136, 7.192, 7.193, 9.142 **F&N:** 3.31, 7.241, 9.60

---

1. In this notice the Commission of the European Communities gives its view as to subcontracting agreements in relation to Article [101](1) of the [Treaty on the Functioning of the European [...] Union]. This class of agreement is at the present time a form of work distribution which concerns firms of all sizes, but which offers opportunities for development in particular to small and medium sized firms.

   The Commission considers that agreements under which one firm, called the "contractor", whether or not in consequence of a prior order from a third party, entrusts to another, called "the subcontractor", the manufacture of goods, the supply of services or the performance of work under the contractor's instructions, to be provided to the contractor or performed on his behalf, are not of themselves caught by the prohibition in Article [101](1).

   To carry out certain subcontracting agreements in accordance with the contractor's instructions, the subcontractor may have to make use of particular technology or equipment which the contractor will have to provide. In order to protect the economic value of such technology or equipment, the contractor may wish to restrict their use by the subcontractor to whatever is necessary for the purpose of the agreement. The question arises whether such restrictions are caught by Article [101](1). They are assessed in this notice with due regard to the purpose of such agreements, which distinguishes them from ordinary patent and know-how licensing agreements.

2. In the Commission's view, Article [101](1) does not apply to clauses whereby:

   — technology or equipment provided by the contractor may not be used except for the purposes of the subcontracting agreement,
   — technology or equipment provided by the contractor may not be made available to third parties,
   — the goods, services or work resulting from the use of such technology or equipment may be supplied only to the contractor or performed on his behalf,

   provided that and in so far as this technology or equipment is necessary to enable the subcontractor under reasonable conditions to manufacture the goods, to supply the services or to carry out the work in accordance with the contractor's instructions. To that extent the subcontractor is providing goods, services or work in respect of which he is not an independent supplier in the market.

The above proviso is satisfied where performance of the subcontracting agreement makes necessary the use by the subcontractor of:

— industrial property rights of the contractor or at his disposal, in the form of patents, utility models, designs protected by copyright, registered designs or other rights, or
— secret knowledge or manufacturing processes (know-how) of the contractor or at his disposal, or of
— studies, plans or documents accompanying the information given which have been prepared by or for the contractor, or
— dies, patterns or tools, and accessory equipment that are distinctively the contractor's,

which, even though not covered by industrial property rights nor containing any element of secrecy, permit the manufacture of goods which differ in form, function or composition from other goods manufactured or supplied on the market.

However, the restrictions mentioned above are not justifiable where the subcontractor has at his disposal or could under reasonable conditions obtain access to the technology and equipment needed to produce the goods, provide the services or carry out the work. Generally, this is the case when the contractor provides no more than general information which merely describes the work to be done. In such circumstances the restrictions could deprive the subcontractor of the possibility of developing his own business in the fields covered by the agreement.

Commentary
para 2: B&C: 7.193

---

3. The following restrictions in connection with the provision of technology by the contractor may in the Commission's view also be imposed by subcontracting agreements without giving grounds for objection under Article [101](1):

— an undertaking by either of the parties not to reveal manufacturing processes or other know-how of a secret character, or confidential information given by the other party during the negotiation and performance of the agreement, as long as the know-how or information in question has not become public knowledge,
— an undertaking by the subcontractor not to make use, even after expiry of the agreement, of manufacturing processes or other know-how of a secret character received by him during the currency of the agreement, as long as they have not become public knowledge,
— an undertaking by the subcontractor to pass on to the contractor on a non-exclusive basis any technical improvements which he has made during the currency of the agreement, or, where a patentable invention has been discovered by the subcontractor, to grant non-exclusive licences in respect of inventions relating to improvements and new applications of the original invention to the contractor for the term of the patent held by the latter.

This undertaking by the subcontractor may be exclusive in favour of the contractor in so far as improvements and inventions made by the subcontractor during the currency of the agreement are incapable of being used independently of the contractor's secret know-how or patent, since this does not constitute an appreciable restriction of competition.

However, any undertaking by the subcontractor regarding the right to dispose of the results of his own research and development work may restrain competition, where such results are capable of being used independently. In such circumstances, the subcontracting relationship is not sufficient to displace the ordinary competition rules on the disposal of industrial property rights or secret know-how.

Commentary
para 3: F&N: 9.60, 10.71
para 3(1): B&C: 7.194
para 3(2): B&C: 7.194
para 3(3): B&C: 7.194, 7.195

---

4. Where the subcontractor is authorized by a subcontracting agreement to use a specified trade mark, trade name or get up, the contractor may at the same time forbid such use by the sub-contractor in the case of goods, services or work which are not to be supplied to the contractor.

Commentary

para 4: **B&C:** 7.195

5. Although this notice should in general obviate the need for firms to obtain a ruling on the legal position by an individual Commission Decision, it does not affect the right of the firms concerned to apply for negative [clearance] as defined by Article 2 of Regulation No 17 or to notify the agreement to the Commission under Article 4(1) of that Regulation.[1]

Notes

[1] First Regulation implementing Articles [101] and [102] of the [Treaty on the Functioning of the European Union] (OJ No 13, 21.2.1962, p.204/62).

The 1968 notice on cooperation between enterprises,[2] which lists a number of agreements that by their nature are not to be regarded as anti-competitive, is thus supplemented in the subcontracting field. The Commission also reminds firms that, in order to promote cooperation between small and medium sized businesses, it has published a notice concerning agreements of minor importance which do not fall under Article [101](1) of the [Treaty on the Functioning of the European Union].[3]

Notes

[2] Notice concerning agreements, decisions and concerted practices relating to cooperation between enterprises (OJ No C 75, 29.7.1968, p.3). [Ed note: see now Commission Notice 2011/C 11/01, Guidelines on the applicability of Article 101 of the Treaty on the Functioning of the European Union to horizontal co-operation agreements (OJ C 11, 14.1.2011, p.1), reproduced at C17 below.]

[3] OJ C 313, 29.12.1977, p.3. [Ed note: see now Commission Notice on agreements of minor importance which do not appreciably restrict competition under Article [101](1) of the [Treaty on the Functioning of the European Union] (*de minimis*) (OJ C 368, 22.12.2001 p.13), reproduced at C10 below.]

This notice is without prejudice to the view that may be taken of subcontracting agreements by the Court of Justice of the European Communities.

Part C Substantive Antitrust Matters

C9

COMMISSION NOTICE

on the definition of relevant market for the purposes of Community competition law

(97/C 372/03)

(Text with EEA relevance)

Official Journal C 372, 9.12.1997, p.5

Celex No: 31997Y1209(01)

EUR-Lex permanent link: <http://eur-lex.europa.eu/LexUriServ/LexUriServ.do?uri=CELEX:3199 7Y1209(01):EN:NOT>

Notes

EEA application: the EFTA Surveillance Authority has adopted a parallel notice on the definition of the relevant market for the purpose of competition law in the EEA under Article 5(2)(b) of the Surveillance and Court Agreement: OJ L 200, 16.7.1998, p.48 and EEA Supplement No 28, 16.7.1998, p.3.

Commentary

Notice: B&C: 1.132, 2.164, 4.002, 4.010, 4.048, 4.051, 4.063, 4.087, 6.052, 7.032, 8.008, 8.083, 8.195, 9.145, 12.045, 12.176 **F&N:** 1.136, 2.260, 4.145, 5.589, 5.683, 7.242, 7.365, 7.366, 9.180, 11.182, 15.45, 15.57, 15.182, 15.259, 16.30
paras 10–12: F&N: 16.31
paras 28–30: B&C: 4.069
paras 28–31: B&C: 10.032

I. Introduction

1. The purpose of this notice is to provide guidance as to how the Commission applies the concept of relevant product and geographic market in its ongoing enforcement of Community competition law, in particular the application of Council Regulation No 17 and (EEC) No 4064/89, their equivalents in other sectoral applications such as transport, coal and steel, and agriculture, and the relevant provisions of the EEA Agreement.[1] Throughout this notice, references to Articles [101] and [102]* of the Treaty and to merger control are to be understood as referring to the equivalent provisions in the EEA Agreement and the ECSC Treaty.

Notes

[1] The focus of assessment in State aid cases is the aid recipient and the industry/sector concerned rather than identification of competitive constraints faced by the aid recipient. When consideration of market power and therefore of the relevant market are raised in any particular case, elements of the approach outlined here might serve as a basis for the assessment of State aid cases.

* Please see the Note on the Lisbon Treaty at p.xvii in regard to article renumbering introduced by the Lisbon Treaty.

---

2. Market definition is a tool to identify and define the boundaries of competition between firms. It serves to establish the framework within which competition policy is applied by the Commission. The main purpose of market definition is to identify in a systematic way the competitive constraints that the undertakings involved[2] face. The objective of defining a market in both its product and geographic dimension is to identify those actual competitors of the undertakings involved that are capable of constraining those undertakings' behaviour and of preventing them from behaving independently of effective competitive pressure. It is from this perspective that the market definition makes it possible inter alia to calculate market shares that would convey meaningful information regarding market power for the purposes of assessing dominance or for the purposes of applying Article [101].

Notes

2 For the purposes of this notice, the undertakings involved will be, in the case of a concentration, the parties to the concentration; in investigations within the meaning of Article [102] of the Treaty, the undertaking being investigated or the complainants; for investigations within the meaning of Article [101], the parties to the Agreement.

Commentary
para 2: B&C: 4.001

3. It follows from point 2 that the concept of "relevant market" is different from other definitions of market often used in other contexts. For instance, companies often use the term "market" to refer to the area where it sells its products or to refer broadly to the industry or sector where it belongs.

4. The definition of the relevant market in both its product and its geographic dimensions often has a decisive influence on the assessment of a competition case. By rendering public the procedures which the Commission follows when considering market definition and by indicating the criteria and evidence on which it relies to reach a decision, the Commission expects to increase the transparency of its policy and decision-making in the area of competition policy.

5. Increased transparency will also result in companies and their advisers being able to better anticipate the possibility that the Commission may raise competition concerns in an individual case. Companies could, therefore, take such a possibility into account in their own internal decision-making when contemplating, for instance, acquisitions, the creation of joint ventures, or the establishment of certain agreements. It is also intended that companies should be in a better position to understand what sort of information the Commission considers relevant for the purposes of market definition.

6. The Commission's interpretation of "relevant market" is without prejudice to the interpretation which may be given by the Court of Justice or the Court of First Instance of the European Communities.

II. Definition of Relevant Market

Definition of relevant product market and relevant geographic market

7. The Regulations based on Article [101] and [102] of the [EC] Treaty, in particular in section 6 of Form A/B with respect to Regulation No 17, as well as in section 6 of Form CO with respect to Regulation (EEC) No 4064/89 on the control of concentrations having a Community dimension have laid down the following definitions, "Relevant product markets" are defined as follows:
   "A relevant product market comprises all those products and/or services which are regarded as interchangeable or substitutable by the consumer, by reason of the products' characteristics, their prices and their intended use".

Commentary
para 7: B&C: 2.109, 8.195, 8.198 F&N: 5.591

8. "Relevant geographic markets" are defined as follows:
   "The relevant geographic market comprises the area in which the undertakings concerned are involved in the supply and demand of products or services, in which the conditions of competition are sufficiently homogeneous and which can be distinguished from neighbouring areas because the conditions of competition are appreciably different in those areas".

Commentary
para 8: B&C: 2.129 F&N: 1.169, 5.602, 5.610

9. The relevant market within which to assess a given competition issue is therefore established by the combination of the product and geographic markets. The Commission interprets the definitions in paragraphs 7 an 8 (which reflect the case-law of the Court of Justice and the Court of First Instance as well as its own decision-making practice) according to the orientations defined in this notice.

Commentary
para 9: B&C: 4.010

Concept of relevant market and objectives of Community competition policy

10. The concept of relevant market is closely related to the objectives pursued under Community competition policy. For example, under the Community's merger control, the objective in controlling structural changes in the supply of a product/service is to prevent the creation or reinforcement of a dominant position as a result of which effective competition would be significantly impeded in a substantial part of the common market. Under the Community's competition rules, a dominant position is such that a firm or group of firms would be in a position to behave to an appreciable extent independently of its competitors, customers and ultimately of its consumers.[3] Such a position would usually arise when a firm or group of firms accounted for a large share of the supply in any given market, provided that other factors analysed in the assessment (such as entry barriers, customers' capacity to react, etc.) point in the same direction.

Notes

[3] Definition given by the Court of Justice in its judgment of 13 February 1979 in Case 85/76, *Hoffmann-La Roche* [1979] ECR 461, and confirmed in subsequent judgments.

11. The same approach is followed by the Commission in its application of Article [102] of the Treaty to firms that enjoy a single or collective dominant position. Within the meaning of Regulation No 17, the Commission has the power to investigate and bring to an end abuses of such a dominant position, which must also be defined by reference to the relevant market. Markets may also need to be defined in the application of Article [101] of the [EC] Treaty, in particular, in determining whether an appreciable restriction of competition exists or in establishing if the condition pursuant to Article [101](3)(b) for an exemption from the application of Article [101](1) is met.

12. The criteria for defining the relevant market are applied generally for the analysis of certain types of behaviour in the market and for the analysis of structural changes in the supply of products. This methodology, though, might lead to different results depending on the nature of the competition issue being examined. For instance, the scope of the geographic market might be different when analysing a concentration, where the analysis is essentially prospective, from an analysis of past behaviour. The different time horizon considered in each case might lead to the result that different geographic markets are defined for the same products depending on whether the Commission is examining a change in the structure of supply, such as a concentration or a cooperative joint venture, or examining issues relating to certain past behaviour.

Commentary
para 12: B&C: 4.014 F&N: 5.657, 16.31

Basic principles for market definition

Competitive constraints

13. Firms are subject to three main sources or competitive constraints: demand substitutability, supply substitutability and potential competition. From an economic point of view, for the definition of the relevant market, demand substitution constitutes the most immediate and effective disciplinary force on the suppliers of a given product, in particular in relation to their pricing decisions. A firm or a group of firms cannot have a significant impact on the prevailing conditions of sale, such as prices, if its customers are in a position to switch easily to available substitute products or to suppliers located elsewhere. Basically, the exercise of market definition consists in identifying the effective alternative sources of supply for the customers of the undertakings involved, in terms both of products/services and of geographic location of suppliers.

Commentary
para 13: B&C: 4.012. 4.028, 6.066

14. The competitive constraints arising from supply side substitutability other than those described in paragraphs 20 to 23 and from potential competition are in general less immediate and in any case require an analysis of additional factors. As a result such constraints are taken into account at the assessment stage of competition analysis.

Commentary
para 14: B&C: 6.066

Demand substitution

15. The assessment of demand substitution entails a determination of the range of products which are viewed as substitutes by the consumer. One way of making this determination can be viewed as a speculative experiment, postulating a hypothetical small, lasting change in relative prices and evaluating the likely reactions of customers to that increase. The exercise of market definition focuses on prices for operational and practical purposes, and more precisely on demand substitution arising from small, permanent changes in relative prices. This concept can provide clear indications as to the evidence that is relevant in defining markets.

Commentary
para 15: B&C: 4.010 F&N: 5.593

16. Conceptually, this approach means that, starting from the type of products that the undertakings involved sell and the area in which they sell them, additional products and areas will be included in, or excluded from, the market definition depending on whether competition from these other products and areas affect or restrain sufficiently the pricing of the parties' products in the short term.

Commentary
para 16: B&C: 4.020

17. The question to be answered is whether the parties' customers would switch to readily available substitutes or to suppliers located elsewhere in response to a hypothetical small (in the range 5% to 10%) but permanent relative price increase in the products and areas being considered. If substitution were enough to make the price increase unprofitable because of the resulting loss of sales, additional substitutes and areas are included in the relevant market. This would be done until the set of products and geographical areas is such that small, permanent increases in relative prices would be profitable. The equivalent analysis is applicable in cases concerning the [concentration] of buying power, where the starting point would then be the supplier and the price test serves to identify the alternative distribution channels or outlets for the supplier's products. In the application of these principles, careful account should be taken of certain particular situations as described within paragraphs 56 and 58.

18. A practical example of this test can be provided by its application to a merger of, for instance, soft-drink bottlers. An issue to examine in such a case would be to decide whether different flavours of soft drinks belong to the same market. In practice, the question to address would be whether consumers of flavour A would switch to other flavours when confronted with a permanent price increase of 5% to 10% for flavour A. If a sufficient number of consumers would switch to, say, flavour B, to such an extent that the price increase for flavour A would not be profitable owing to the resulting loss of sales, then the market would comprise at least flavours A and B. The process would have to be extended in addition to other available flavours until a set of products is identified for which a price rise would not induce a sufficient substitution in demand.

19. Generally, and in particular for the analysis of merger cases, the price to take into account will be the prevailing market price. This may not be the case where the prevailing price has been determined in the absence of sufficient competition. In particular for the investigation of abuses of dominant positions, the fact that the prevailing price might already have been substantially increased will be taken into account.

Commentary
para 19: **B&C:** 4.026 **F&N:** 4.146, 5.660

Supply substitution

20. Supply-side substitutability may also be taken into account when defining markets in those [situations] in which its effects are equivalent to those of demand substitution in terms of effectiveness and immediacy. This means that suppliers are able to switch production to the relevant products and market them in the short term[4] without incurring significant additional costs or risks in response to small and permanent changes in relative prices. When these conditions are met, the additional production that is put on the market will have a disciplinary effect on the competitive behaviour of the companies involved. Such an impact in terms of effectiveness and immediacy is equivalent to the demand substitution effect.

Notes

[4] That is such a period that does not entail a significant adjustment of existing tangible and intangible assets (see paragraph 23).

Commentary
para 20: **B&C:** 4.020, 4.048, 4.082 **F&N:** 1.161, 5.599

21. These situations typically arise when companies market a wide range of qualities or grades of one product; even if, for a given final customer or group of consumers, the different qualities are not substitutable, the different qualities will be grouped into one product market, provided that most of the suppliers are able to offer and sell the various qualities immediately and without the significant increases in costs described above. In such cases, the relevant product market will encompass all products that are substitutable in demand and supply, and the current sales of those products will be aggregated so as to give the total value or volume of the market. The same reasoning may lead to group different geographic areas.

Commentary
para 21: **F&N:** 1.164, 5.596

22. A practical example of the approach to supply-side substitutability when defining product markets is to be found in the case of paper. [Paper] is usually supplied in a range of different qualities, from standard writing paper to high quality papers to be used, for instance, to publish art books. From a demand point of view, different qualities of paper cannot be used for any given use, i.e. an art book or a high quality publication cannot be based on lower quality papers. However, paper plants are prepared to manufacture the different qualities, and production can be adjusted with negligible costs and in a short time-frame. In the absence of particular difficulties in distribution, paper manufacturers are able therefore, to compete for orders of the various qualities, in particular if orders are placed with sufficient lead time to allow for modification of production plans. Under such circumstances, the Commission would not define a separate market for each quality of paper and its respective use. The various qualities of paper are included in the relevant market, and their sales added up to estimate total market [value] and volume.

Commentary
para 22: **B&C:** 4.047 **F&N:** 1.162, 5.599

23. When supply-side substitutability would entail the need to adjust significantly existing tangible and intangible assets, additional investments, strategic decisions or time delays, it will not be considered at the stage of market definition. Examples where supply-side substitution did not induce the Commission to enlarge the market are offered in the area of consumer products, in particular for branded beverages. Although bottling plants may in principle bottle different beverages, there are costs and lead times involved (in terms of advertising, product testing and distribution) before the products can actually be sold. In these cases, the effects of supply-side substitutability and other forms of potential competition would then be examined at a later stage.

Commentary
para 23: **B&C:** 4.048

Potential competition

24. The third source of competitive constraint, potential competition, is not taken into account when defining markets, since the conditions under which potential competition will actually represent an effective competitive constraint depend on the analysis of specific factors and circumstances related to the conditions of entry. If required, this analysis is only carried out at a subsequent stage, in general once the position of the companies involved in the relevant market has already been ascertained, and when such position gives rise to concerns from a competition point of view.

Commentary
para 24: **B&C:** 4.003, 4.013, 10.032

III. Evidence Relied on to Define Relevant Markets

The process of defining the relevant market in practice

Product dimension

25. There is a range of evidence permitting an assessment of the extent to which substitution would take place. In individual cases, certain types of evidence will be determinant, depending very much on the characteristics and specificity of the industry and products or services that are being examined. The same type of evidence may be of no importance in other cases. In most cases, a decision will have to be based on the consideration of a number of criteria and different items of evidence. The Commission follows an open approach to empirical evidence, aimed at making an effective use of all available information which may be relevant in individual cases. The Commission does not follow a rigid hierarchy of different sources of information or types of evidence.

Commentary
para 25: **F&N:** 4.148, 5.627

26. The process of defining relevant markets may be summarized as follows: on the basis of the preliminary information available or information submitted by the undertakings involved, the Commission will usually be in a position to broadly establish the possible relevant markets within which, for instance, a concentration or a restriction of competition has to be assessed. In general, and for all practical purposes when handling individual cases, the question will usually be to decide on a few alternative possible relevant markets. For instance, with respect to the product market, the issue will often be to establish whether product A and product B belong or do not belong to the same product market. it is often the case that the inclusion of product B would be enough to remove any competition concerns.

Commentary
para 26: **B&C:** 4.022

27. In such situations it is not necessary to consider whether the market includes additional products, or to reach a definitive conclusion on the precise product market. If under the conceivable alternative market definitions the operation in question does not raise competition concerns, the question of market definition will be left open, reducing thereby the burden on companies to supply information.

Commentary
para 27: **B&C:** 8.195 **F&N:** 5.590

Geographic dimension

28. The Commission's approach to geographic market definition might be summarized as follows: it will take a preliminary view of the scope of the geographic market on the basis of broad indications as to the distribution of market shares between the parties and their competitors, as well as a preliminary analysis of pricing and price differences at national and Community or EEA level. This initial view is used basically as a working hypothesis to focus the Commission's enquiries for the purposes of arriving at a precise geographic market definition.

Commentary
para 28: B&C: 4.076 **F&N:** 5.604

---

29. The reasons behind any particular configuration of prices and market shares need to be explored. Companies might enjoy high market shares in their domestic markets just because of the weight of the past, and conversely, a homogeneous presence of companies throughout the EEA might be consistent with national or regional geographic markets. The initial working hypothesis will therefore be checked against an analysis of demand characteristics (importance of national or local preferences, current patterns of purchases of customers, product differentiation/brands, other) in order to establish whether companies in different areas do indeed constitute a real alternative source of supply for consumers. The theoretical experiment is again based on substitution arising from changes in relative prices, and the question to answer is again whether the customers of the parties would switch their orders to companies located elsewhere in the short term and at a negligible cost.

Commentary
para 29: B&C: 4.081 **F&N:** 1.170

---

30. If necessary, a further check on supply factors will be carried out to ensure that those companies located in differing areas do not face impediments in developing their sales on competitive terms throughout the whole geographic market. This analysis will include an examination of requirements for a local presence in order to sell in that area the conditions of access to distribution channels, costs associated with setting up a distribution network, and the presence or absence of regulatory barriers arising from public procurement, price regulations, quotas and tariffs limiting trade or production, technical standards, monopolies, freedom of establishment, requirements for administrative authorizations, packaging regulations, etc. In short, the Commission will identify possible obstacles and barriers isolating companies located in a given area from the competitive pressure of companies located outside that area, so as to determine the precise degree of market interpenetration at national, European or global level.

31. The actual pattern and evolution of trade flows offers useful supplementary indications as to the economic importance of each demand or supply factor mentioned above, and the extent to which they may or may not constitute actual barriers creating different geographic markets. The analysis of trade flows will generally address the question of transport costs and the extent to which these may hinder trade between different areas, having regard to plant location, costs of production and relative price levels.

Market integration in the Community

32. Finally, the Commission also takes into account the continuing process of market integration, in particular in the Community, when defining geographic markets, especially in the area of concentrations and structural joint ventures. The measures adopted and implemented in the internal market programme to remove barriers to trade and further integrate the Community markets cannot be ignored when assessing the effects on competition of a concentration or a structural joint venture. A situation where national markets have been [artificially] isolated from each other because of the existence of legislative barriers that have now been removed will generally lead to a cautious assessment of past evidence regarding prices, market shares or trade patterns. A process of market integration that would, in the short term, lead to wider geographic markets may therefore be taken into consideration when defining the geographic market for the purposes of assessing concentrations and joint ventures.

Commentary
para 32: **B&C:** 4.070

The process of gathering evidence

33. When a precise market definition is deemed necessary, the Commission will often contact the main customers and the main companies in the industry to enquire into their views about the [boundaries] of product and geographic markets and to obtain the necessary factual evidence to reach a conclusion. The Commission might also contact the relevant professional associations, and companies active in upstream markets, so as to be able to define, in so far as necessary, separate product and geographic markets, for different levels of production or distribution of the products/services in question. It might also request additional information to the undertakings involved.

34. Where appropriate, the Commission will address written requests for information to the market players mentioned above. These requests will usually include questions relating to the perceptions of companies about reactions to hypothetical price increases and their views of the boundaries of the relevant market. They will also ask for provision of the factual information the Commission deems necessary to reach a conclusion on the extent of the relevant market. The Commission might also discuss with marketing directors or other officers of those companies to gain a better understanding on how negotiations between suppliers and customers take place and better understand issues relating to the definition of the relevant market. Where appropriate, they might also carry out visits or inspections to the premises of the parties, their customers and/or their competitors, in order to better understand how products are manufactured and sold.

35. The type of evidence relevant to reach a conclusion as to the product market can be categorized as follows:

Evidence to define markets — product dimension

36. An analysis of the product characteristics and its intended use allows the Commission, as a first step, to limit the field of investigation of possible substitutes. However, product characteristics and intended use are insufficient to show whether two products are demand substitutes. Functional interchangeability or similarity in characteristics may not, in themselves, provide sufficient criteria, because the responsiveness of customers to relative price changes may be [determined] by other considerations as well. For example, there may be different competitive [constraints] in the original equipment market for car components and in spare parts, thereby leading to a separate delineation of two relevant markets. Conversely, differences in product characteristics are not in themselves sufficient to exclude demand substitutability, since this will depend to a large extent on how customers value different characteristics.

Commentary
para 36: **B&C:** 4.029

37. The type of evidence the Commission considers relevant to assess whether two products are demand substitutes can be categorized as follows:

38. *Evidence of substitution in the recent past.* In certain cases, it is possible to analyse evidence relating to recent past events or shocks in the market that offer actual examples of [substitution] between two products. When available, this sort of information will normally be fundamental for market definition. If there have been changes in relative prices in the past (all else being equal), the reactions in terms of quantities demanded will be determinant in establishing substitutability. Launches of new products in the past can also offer useful information, when it is possible to precisely analyse which products have lost sales to the new product.

Commentary
para 38: **B&C:** 4.035

39. There are a number of *quantitative tests* that have specifically been designed for the purpose of delineating markets. These tests consist of various econometric and statistical approaches estimates of elasticities and cross-price elasticities[5] for the demand of a product, tests

based on similarity of price movements over time, the analysis of causality between price series and similarity of price levels and/or their convergence. The Commission takes into account the available quantitative evidence capable of withstanding rigorous scrutiny for the purposes of establishing patterns of substitution in the past.

Notes

5 Own-price elasticity of demand for product X is a measure of the responsiveness of demand for X to percentage change in its own price. Cross-price elasticity between products X and Y is the responsiveness of demand for product X to percentage change in the price of product Y.

Commentary
para 39: B&C: 4.038

40. *Views of customers and competitors.* The Commission often contacts the main customers and competitors of the companies involved in its enquiries, to gather their views on the boundaries of the product market as well as most of the factual information it requires to reach a conclusion on the scope of the market. Reasoned answers of customers and competitors as to what would happen if relative prices for the candidate products were to increase in the candidate geographic area by a small amount (for instance of 5% to 10%) are taken into account when they are sufficiently backed by factual evidence.

Commentary
para 40: B&C: 4.044

41. *Consumer preferences.* In the case of consumer goods, it may be difficult for the Commission to gather the direct views of end consumers about substitute products. Marketing studies that companies have commissioned in the past and that are used by companies in their own decision-making as to pricing of their products and/or marketing actions may provide useful information for the Commission's delineation of the relevant market. Consumer surveys on usage patterns and attitudes, data from consumer's purchasing patterns, the views expressed by retailers and more generally, market research studies submitted by the parties and their competitors are taken into account to establish whether an economically significant proportion of consumers consider two products as substitutable, also taking into account the importance of brands for the products in question. The methodology followed in consumer surveys carried out ad hoc by the undertakings involved or their competitors for the purposes of a merger procedure or a procedure pursuant to Regulation No 17 will usually be scrutinized with utmost care. Unlike pre-existing studies, they have not been prepared in the normal course of business for the adoption of business decisions.

Commentary
para 41: B&C: 4.045

42. *Barriers and costs associated with switching demand to potential substitutes.* There are a number of barriers and costs that might prevent the Commission from considering two prima facie demand substitutes as belonging to one single product market. It is not possible to provide an exhaustive list of all the possible barriers to substitution and of switching costs. These barriers or obstacles might have a wide range of origins, and in its decisions, the Commission has been confronted with regulatory barriers or other forms of State intervention, constraints arising in downstream markets, need to incur specific capital investment or loss in current output in order to switch to alternative inputs, the location of customers, specific investment in production process, learning and human capital investment, retooling costs or other investments, uncertainty about quality and reputation of unknown suppliers, and others.

Commentary
para 42: B&C: 4.020, 4.033

43. *Different categories of customers and price discrimination.* The extent of the product market might be narrowed in the presence of distinct groups of customers. A distinct group of customers for the

relevant product may constitute a narrower, distinct market when such a group could be subject to price discrimination. This will usually be the case when two conditions are met: (a) it is possible to identify clearly which group an individual customer belongs to at the moment of selling the relevant products to him, and (b) trade among customers or arbitrage by third parties should not be feasible.

Commentary
para 43: **B&C:** 4.041 **F&N:** 5.619, 5.623

Evidence for defining markets — geographic dimension

44. The type of evidence the Commission considers relevant to reach a conclusion as to the geographic market can be categorized as follows:

45. *Past evidence of diversion of orders to other areas.* In certain cases, evidence on changes in prices between different areas and consequent reactions by customers might be available. Generally, the same quantitative tests used for product market definition might as well be used in geographic market definition, bearing in mind that international comparisons of prices might be more complex due to a number of factors such as exchange rate movements, taxation and product differentiation.

Commentary
para 45: **B&C:** 4.077, 4.083

46. *Basic demand characteristics.* The nature of demand for the relevant product may in itself determine the scope of the geographical market. Factors such as national preferences or preferences for national brands, language, culture and life style, and the need for a local presence have a strong potential to limit the geographic scope of competition.

Commentary
para 46: **B&C:** 4.074

47. *Views of customers and competitors.* Where appropriate, the Commission will contact the main customers and competitors of the parties in its enquiries, to gather their views on the boundaries of the geographic market as well as most of the factual information it requires to reach a conclusion on the scope of the market when they are sufficiently backed by factual evidence.

Commentary
para 47: **B&C:** 4.080

48. *Current geographic pattern of purchases.* An examination of the customers' current geographic pattern of purchases provides useful evidence as to the possible scope of the geographic market. When customers purchase from companies located anywhere in the Community or the EEA on similar terms, or they procure their supplies through effective tendering procedures in which companies from anywhere in the Community or the EEA submit bids, usually the geographic market will be considered to be Community-wide.

Commentary
para 48: **B&C:** 4.075

49. *Trade flows/pattern of shipments.* When the number of customers is so large that it is not possible to obtain through them a clear picture of geographic purchasing patterns, information on trade flows might be used alternatively, provided that the trade statistics are available with a sufficient degree of detail for the relevant products. Trade flows, and above all, the rationale behind trade flows provide useful insights and information for the purpose of establishing the scope of the geographic market but are not in themselves conclusive.

Commentary
para 49: **B&C:** 4.075

50. *Barriers and switching costs associated to divert orders to companies located in other areas.* The absence of trans-border purchases or trade flows, for instance, does not necessarily mean that the market is at most national in scope. Still, barriers isolating the national market have to identified before it is concluded that the relevant geographic market in such a case is national. Perhaps the clearest obstacle for a customer to divert its orders to other areas is the impact of transport costs and transport restrictions arising from legislation or from the nature of the relevant products. The impact of transport costs will usually limit the scope of the geographic market for bulky, low-value products, bearing in mind that a transport disadvantage might also be compensated by a comparative advantage in other costs (labour costs or raw materials). Access to distribution in a given area, regulatory barriers still existing in certain sectors, quotas and custom tariffs might also constitute barriers isolating a geographic area from the competitive pressure of companies located outside that area. Significant switching costs in procuring supplies from companies located in other countries constitute additional sources of such barriers.

Commentary
para 50: B&C: 4.074

51. On the basis of the evidence gathered, the Commission will then define a geographic market that could range from a local dimension to a global one, and there are examples of both local and global markets in past decisions of the Commission.
52. The paragraphs above describe the different factors which might be relevant to define markets. This does not imply that in each individual case it will be necessary to obtain evidence and assess each of these factors. Often in practice the evidence provided by a [subset] of these factors will be sufficient to reach a conclusion, as shown in the past decisional practice of the Commission.

IV. Calculation of Market Share

53. The definition of the relevant market in both its product and [geographic] dimensions allows the identification the suppliers and the customers/consumers active on that market. On that basis, a total market size and market shares for each supplier can be calculated on the basis of their sales of the relevant products in the relevant area. In practice, the total market size and market shares are often available from market sources, i.e. companies' estimates, studies commissioned from industry consultants and/or trade associations. When this is not the case, or when available estimates are not reliable, the Commission will usually ask each supplier in the relevant market to provide its own sales in order to calculate total market size and market shares.
54. If sales are usually the reference to calculate market shares, there are nevertheless other indications that, depending on the specific products or industry in question, can offer useful information such as, in particular, capacity, the number of players in bidding markets, units of fleet as in aerospace, or the reserves held in the case of sectors such as mining.

Commentary
para 54: F&N: 4.150

55. As a rule of thumb, both volume sales and value sales provide useful information. In cases of differentiated products, sales in value and their associated market share will usually be considered to better reflect the relative position and strength of each supplier.

Commentary
para 55: F&N: 4.150

V. Additional Considerations

56. There are certain areas where the application of the principles above has to be undertaken with care. This is the case when considering primary and secondary markets, in particular, when the behaviour of undertakings at a point in time has to b\e analysed pursuant to Article [102]. The method of defining markets in these cases is the same, i.e. assessing the responses of customers

based on their purchasing decisions to relative price changes, but taking into account as well, constraints on substitution imposed by conditions in the connected markets. A narrow definition of market for secondary products, for instance, spare parts, may result when compatibility with the primary product is important. Problems of finding compatible secondary products together with the existence of high prices and a long lifetime of the primary products may render relative price increases of secondary products profitable. A different market definition may result if significant substitution between secondary products is possible or if the characteristics of the primary products make quick and direct consumer responses to relative price increases of the secondary products feasible.

Commentary
para 56: F&N: 9.184

57. In certain cases, the existence of chains of substitution might lead to the definition of a relevant market where products or areas at the extreme of the market are not directly substitutable. An example might be provided by the geographic dimension of a product with significant transport costs. In such cases, deliveries from a given plant are limited to a certain area around each plant by the impact of transport costs. In principle, such an area could constitute the relevant geographic market. However, if the distribution of plants is such that there are considerable overlaps between the areas around different plants, it is possible that the pricing of those products will be constrained by a chain substitution effect, and lead to the definition of a broader geographic market. The same reasoning may apply if product B is a demand substitute for products A and C. Even if products A and C are not direct demand substitutes, they might be found to be in the same relevant product market since their respective pricing might be constrained by substitution to B.

Commentary
para 57: B&C: 4.063

58. From a practical perspective, the concept of chains of substitution has to be corroborated by actual evidence, for instance related to price interdependence at the extremes of the chains of substitution, in order to lead to an extension of the relevant market in an individual case. Price levels at the extremes of the chains would have to be of the same magnitude as well.

Commentary
para 58: B&C: 4.063, 4.085

C10

COMMISSION NOTICE

on agreements of minor importance which do not appreciably
restrict competition under Article [101](1)* of the [Treaty on the
Functioning of the European Union] (*de minimis*)[1]

(Text with EEA relevance)

(2001/C 368/07)

Official Journal C 368, 22.12.2001, p.13

Celex No: 52001XC1222(03)

EUR-Lex permanent link: <http://eur-lex.europa.eu/LexUriServ/LexUriServ.do?uri=CELEX:5200
1XC1222(03):EN:NOT>

Notes

* Ed note: please see the Note on the Lisbon Treaty at p.xvii in regard to article renumbering introduced by the Lisbon Treaty.
On 11 July 2013 the Commission launched a consultation on a proposal to revise the *de minimis* notice: see <http://
ec.europa.eu/competition/consultations/2013_de_minimis_notice/index_en.html>

[1] This notice replaces the notice on agreements of minor importance published in OJ C 372, 9.12.1997.

EEA application: the EFTA Surveillance Authority has adopted a parallel notice under Article 5(2)(b) of the Surveillance
and Court Agreement: OJ C 67, 20.3.2003, p.20 and EEA Supplement No 15, 20.3.2003, p.11.

Commentary

Notice: B&C: 1.077, 1.130, 2.128, 2.158, 2.164, 2.166, 4.007, 5.032, 7.020 **F&N:** 3.215, 3.216, 3.295, 3.374,
3.378, 3.381, 7.63, 8.111, 9.28, 9.37, 9.39, 9.66, 9.226
points 8–11: F&N: 9.38

I

1. Article [101](1) prohibits agreements between undertakings which may affect trade between
Member States and which have as their object or effect the prevention, restriction or distortion
of competition within the common market. The Court of Justice of the European Communities
has clarified that this provision is not applicable where the impact of the agreement on intra-
Community trade or on competition is not appreciable.

2. In this notice the Commission quantifies, with the help of market share thresholds, what is not an
appreciable restriction of competition under Article [101] of the [Treaty on the Functioning of
the European Union]. This negative definition of appreciability does not imply that agreements
between undertakings which exceed the thresholds set out in this notice appreciably restrict competition. Such agreements may still have only a negligible effect on competition and may therefore
not be prohibited by Article [101](1).[1]

Notes

[1] See, for instance, the judgment of the Court of Justice in Joined Cases C-215/96 and C-216/96 *Bagnasco (Carlos) v Banca
Popolare di Novara and Casa di Risparmio di Genova e Imperia* [1999] ECR I-135, points 34–35. This notice is also without
prejudice to the principles for assessment under Article [101](1) as expressed in the Commission notice "Guidelines on the
applicability of Article [101] of the [Treaty on the Functioning of the European Union] to horizontal cooperation agreements", OJ C 3, 6.1.2001, in particular points 17–31 inclusive, and in the Commission notice "Guidelines on vertical
restraints", OJ C 291, 13.10.2000, in particular points 5–20 inclusive. [Ed note: see now Commission Notice 2011/C
11/01, Guidelines on the applicability of Article 101 of the Treaty on the Functioning of the European Union to horizontal
co-operation agreements (OJ C 11, 14.1.2011, p.1), reproduced at C17 below, and Commission Notice 2010/C 130/01,
Guidelines on Vertical Restraints (OJ C 130, 19.5.2010, p.1), reproduced at C15 below.]

Commentary

point 2: F&N: 3.297, 3.384

3. Agreements may in addition not fall under Article [101](1) because they are not capable of appreciably affecting trade between Member States. This notice does not deal with this issue. It does not quantify what does not constitute an appreciable effect on trade. It is however acknowledged that agreements between small and medium-sized undertakings, as defined in the Annex to Commission Recommendation 96/280/EC,[1] are rarely capable of appreciably affecting trade between Member States. Small and medium-sized undertakings are currently defined in that recommendation as undertakings which have fewer than 250 employees and have either an annual turnover not exceeding EUR 40 million or an annual balance-sheet total not exceeding EUR 27 million.

Notes

[1] OJ L 107, 30.4.1996, p.4. This recommendation will be revised. It is envisaged to increase the annual turnover threshold from EUR 40 million to EUR 50 million and the annual balance-sheet total threshold from EUR 27 million to EUR 43 million. [See now Commission Recommendation of 6 May 2003 concerning the definition of micro, small and medium-sized enterprises (notified under document number C(2003) 1422) OJ L 124, 20.5.2003, p.36.]

4. In cases covered by this notice the Commission will not institute proceedings either upon application or on its own initiative. Where undertakings assume in good faith that an agreement is covered by this notice, the Commission will not impose fines. Although not binding on them, this notice also intends to give guidance to the courts and authorities of the Member States in their application of Article [101].

Commentary
point 4: F&N: 3.295, 3.381

5. This notice also applies to decisions by associations of undertakings and to concerted practices.

6. This notice is without prejudice to any interpretation of Article [101] which may be given by the Court of Justice or the Court of First Instance of the European Communities.

II

7. The Commission holds the view that agreements between undertakings which affect trade between Member States do not appreciably restrict competition within the meaning of Article [101](1):

  (a) if the aggregate market share held by the parties to the agreement does not exceed 10% on any of the relevant markets affected by the agreement, where the agreement is made between undertakings which are actual or potential competitors on any of these markets (agreements between competitors);[1] or

  (b) if the market share held by each of the parties to the agreement does not exceed 15% on any of the relevant markets affected by the agreement, where the agreement is made between undertakings which are not actual or potential competitors on any of these markets (agreements between non-competitors).

  In cases where it is difficult to classify the agreement as either an agreement between competitors or an agreement between non-competitors the 10% threshold is applicable.

Notes

[1] On what are actual or potential competitors, see the Commission notice "Guidelines on the applicability of Article [101] of the [Treaty on the Functioning of the European Union] to horizontal cooperation agreements", OJ C 3, 6.1.2001, paragraph 9. A firm is treated as an actual competitor if it is either active on the same relevant market or if, in the absence of the agreement, it is able to switch production to the relevant products and market them in the short term without incurring significant additional costs or risks in response to a small and permanent increase in relative prices (immediate supply-side substitutability). A firm is treated as a potential competitor if there is evidence that, absent the agreement, this firm could and would be likely to undertake the necessary additional investments or other necessary switching costs so that it could enter the relevant market in response to a small and permanent increase in relative prices.

[Ed note: see now Commission Notice 2011/C 11/01, Guidelines on the applicability of Article 101 of the Treaty on the Functioning of the European Union to horizontal co-operation agreements (OJ C 11, 14.1.2011, p.1), reproduced at C17 below.]

Commentary
point 7: B&C: 6.003, 6.012, 7.020
point 7(a): F&N: 3.215
point 7(b): F&N: 3.215

8. Where in a relevant market competition is restricted by the cumulative effect of agreements for the sale of goods or services entered into by different suppliers or distributors (cumulative foreclosure effect of parallel networks of agreements having similar effects on the market), the market share thresholds under point 7 are reduced to 5%, both for agreements between competitors and for agreements between non-competitors. Individual suppliers or distributors with a market share not exceeding 5% are in general not considered to contribute significantly to a cumulative foreclosure effect.[1] A cumulative foreclosure effect is unlikely to exist if less than 30% of the relevant market is covered by parallel (networks of) agreements having similar effects.

Notes
[1] See also the Commission notice "Guidelines on vertical restraints", OJ C 291, 13.10.2000, in particular paragraphs 73, 142, 143 and 189. While in the guidelines on vertical restraints in relation to certain restrictions reference is made not only to the total but also to the tied market share of a particular supplier or buyer, in this notice all market share thresholds refer to total market shares. [Ed note: see now Commission Notice 2010/C 130/01, Guidelines on Vertical Restraints (OJ C 130, 19.5.2010, p.1), reproduced at C15 below.]

Commentary
point 8: B&C: 7.018

9. The Commission also holds the view that agreements are not restrictive of competition if the market shares do not exceed the thresholds of respectively 10%, 15% and 5% set out in points 7 and 8 during two successive calendar years by more than 2 percentage points.

Commentary
point 9: B&C: 2.165 F&N: 3.295

10. In order to calculate the market share, it is necessary to determine the relevant market. This consists of the relevant product market and the relevant geographic market. When defining the relevant market, reference should be had to the notice on the definition of the relevant market for the purposes of Community competition law.[1] The market shares are to be calculated on the basis of sales value data or, where appropriate, purchase value data. If value data are not available, estimates based on other reliable market information, including volume data, may be used.

Notes
[1] OJ C 372, 9.12.1997, p.5.

11. Points 7, 8 and 9 do not apply to agreements containing any of the following hardcore restrictions:
    (1) as regards agreements between competitors as defined in point 7, restrictions which, directly or indirectly, in isolation or in combination with other factors under the control of the parties, have as their object:[1]
        (a) the fixing of prices when selling the products to third parties;
        (b) the limitation of output or sales;
        (c) the allocation of markets or customers;
    (2) as regards agreements between non-competitors as defined in point 7, restrictions which, directly or indirectly, in isolation or in combination with other factors under the control of the parties, have as their object:
        (a) the restriction of the buyer's ability to determine its sale price, without prejudice to the possibility of the supplier imposing a maximum sale price or recommending a sale price,

provided that they do not amount to a fixed or minimum sale price as a result of pressure from, or incentives offered by, any of the parties;

(b) the restriction of the territory into which, or of the customers to whom, the buyer may sell the contract goods or services, except the following restrictions which are not hardcore:

— the restriction of active sales into the exclusive territory or to an exclusive customer group reserved to the supplier or allocated by the supplier to another buyer, where such a restriction does not limit sales by the customers of the buyer,

— the restriction of sales to end users by a buyer operating at the wholesale level of trade,

— the restriction of sales to unauthorised distributors by the members of a selective distribution system, and

— the restriction of the buyer's ability to sell components, supplied for the purposes of incorporation, to customers who would use them to manufacture the same type of goods as those produced by the supplier;

(c) the restriction of active or passive sales to end users by members of a selective distribution system operating at the retail level of trade, without prejudice to the possibility of prohibiting a member of the system from operating out of an unauthorised place of establishment;

(d) the restriction of cross-supplies between distributors within a selective distribution system, including between distributors operating at different levels of trade;

(e) the restriction agreed between a supplier of components and a buyer who incorporates those components, which limits the supplier's ability to sell the components as spare parts to end users or to repairers or other service providers not entrusted by the buyer with the repair or servicing of its goods;

(3) as regards agreements between competitors as defined in point 7, where the competitors operate, for the purposes of the agreement, at a different level of the production or distribution chain, any of the hardcore restrictions listed in paragraph (1) and (2) above.

Notes

[1] Without prejudice to situations of joint production with or without joint distribution as defined in Article 5, paragraph 2, of Commission Regulation (EC) No 2658/2000 and Article 5, paragraph 2, of Commission Regulation (EC) No 2659/2000, OJ L 304, 5.12.2000, p. 3 and 7 respectively.

Commentary
point 11: B&C: 5.032 F&N: 3.215, 3.295, 3.381
point 11(2): B&C: 7.020
point 11(2)(a): B&C: 7.041

12.(1) For the purposes of this notice, the terms "undertaking," "party to the agreement," "distributor," "supplier" and "buyer" shall include their respective connected undertakings.

(2) "Connected undertakings" are:

(a) undertakings in which a party to the agreement, directly or indirectly:

— has the power to exercise more than half the voting rights, or

— has the power to appoint more than half the members of the supervisory board, board of management or bodies legally representing the undertaking, or

— has the right to manage the undertaking's affairs;

(b) undertakings which directly or indirectly have, over a party to the agreement, the rights or powers listed in (a);

(c) undertakings in which an undertaking referred to in (b) has, directly or indirectly, the rights or powers listed in (a);

(d) undertakings in which a party to the agreement together with one or more of the undertakings referred to in (a), (b) or (c), or in which two or more of the latter undertakings, jointly have the rights or powers listed in (a);

(e) undertakings in which the rights or the powers listed in (a) are jointly held by:

— parties to the agreement or their respective connected undertakings referred to in (a) to (d), or

363

    — one or more of the parties to the agreement or one or more of their connected under-takings referred to in (a) to (d) and one or more third parties.

(3) For the purposes of paragraph 2(e), the market share held by these jointly held undertakings shall be apportioned equally to each undertaking having the rights or the powers listed in paragraph 2(a).

Commentary
point 12: B&C: 2.165
point 12(2): F&N: 3.416

C11

COMMISSION NOTICE

Guidelines on the application of Article [101]* of the [Treaty on the Functioning of the European Union] to technology transfer agreements (2004/C 101/02)

(Text with EEA relevance)

Official Journal C 101, 27.4.2004, p.2

Celex No: 52004XC0427(01)

EUR-Lex permanent link: <http://eur-lex.europa.eu/LexUriServ/LexUriServ.do?uri=CELEX:52004XC0427(01):EN:NOT>

Notes

* Ed note: please see the Note on the Lisbon Treaty at p.xvii in regard to article renumbering introduced by the Lisbon Treaty. Regulation 772/2004/EC is due to expire on 30 April 2014. The successor regulation and guidelines were adopted on 21 March 2014. They are available at <http://ec.europa.eu/competition/antitrust/legislation/transfer.html> but are not reproduced in this volume.
EEA application: the EFTA Surveillance Authority has adopted a parallel notice on the application of Article 53 of the EEA Agreement to technology transfer agreements under Article 5(2)(b) of the Surveillance and Court Agreement: see College Decision 228/05/COL of 21 September 2005, OJ L 259, 4.10.2007, p.1 and EEA Supplement No 46, 4.10.2007, p.1.

Commentary
Notice: B&C: 1.074, 3.005, 4.065, 9.049, 9.065, 9.066, 9.084, 9.131, 9.151, 9.152 F&N: 2.12, 3.357, 3.424, 3.478, 3.499, 7.297, 7.301, 7.302, 7.316, 9.66, 10.70, 10.74, 10.75, 10.82, 10.84, 10.86, 10.102, 10.131, 10.165, 10.166, 10.171, 14.83
paras 7–8: B&C: 9.001
paras 19–25: B&C: 9.145
paras 41–46: B&C: 9.142
paras 49–53: B&C: 9.112
paras 79–81: F&N: 10.98
paras 114–116: B&C: 9.172 F&N: 10.118
paras 156–160: B&C: 3.039
paras 161–174: B&C: 3.039
paras 162–167: B&C: 9.093
paras 162–174: B&C: 9.102
paras 175–178: B&C: 3.039
paras 177–178: B&C: 9.103
paras 179–183: B&C: 9.157
paras 179–185: B&C: 3.039
paras 186–190: B&C: 3.039, 9.159, 9.166

I. Introduction

1. These guidelines set out the principles for the assessment of technology transfer agreements under Article [101] of the Treaty. Technology transfer agreements concern the licensing of technology where the licensor permits the licensee to exploit the licensed technology for the production of goods or services, as defined in Article 1(1)(b) of Commission Regulation (EC) No 773/2004 on the application of Article [101](3) of the Treaty to categories of technology transfer agreements (the TTBER).[1]

Notes

[1] OJ L 123, 27.4.2004. The TTBER replaces Commission Regulation (EC) No 240/96 of 31 January 1996 on the application of Article [101](3) of the Treaty to certain categories of technology transfer agreements (OJ L 31, 9.2.1996, p.2).

2. The purpose of the guidelines is to provide guidance on the application of the TTBER as well as on the application of Article [101] to technology transfer agreements that fall outside the scope of the TTBER. The TTBER and the guidelines are without prejudice to the possible parallel application of Article [102] of the Treaty to licensing agreements.[2]

Notes

[2] See Joined Cases C-395/96 P and C-396/96 P, *Compagnie Maritime Belge*, [2000] ECR I-1365, paragraph 130, and paragraph 106 of the Commission Guidelines on the application of Article [101](3) of the Treaty, [OJ C 101, 27.4.2004, p.97].

Commentary
para 2: **B&C:** 4.065

3. The standards set forth in these guidelines must be applied in light of the circumstances specific to each case. This excludes a mechanical application. Each case must be assessed on its own facts and the guidelines must be applied reasonably and flexibly. Examples given serve as illustrations only and are not intended to be exhaustive. The Commission will keep under review the functioning of the TTBER and the guidelines in the new enforcement system created by Regulation 1/2003[3] to consider whether changes need to be made.

Notes

[3] Council Regulation (EC) No 1/2003 on the implementation of the rules on competition laid down in Articles [101] and [102] of the Treaty (OJ L 1, 4.1.2003, p.1).

4. The present guidelines are without prejudice to the interpretation of Article [101] and the TTBER that may be given by the Court of Justice and the Court of First Instance.

II. General Principles

1. Article [101] and intellectual property rights

5. The aim of Article [101] as a whole is to protect competition on the market with a view to promoting consumer welfare and an efficient allocation of resources. Article [101](1) prohibits all agreements and concerted practices between undertakings and decisions by associations of undertakings[4] which may affect trade between Member States[5] and which have as their object or effect the prevention, restriction or distortion of competition.[6] As an exception to this rule Article [101] (3) provides that the prohibition contained in Article [101](1) may be declared inapplicable in the case of agreements between undertakings which contribute to improving the production or distribution of products or to promoting technical or economic progress, while allowing consumers

a fair share of the resulting benefits and which do not impose restrictions which are not indispensable to the attainment of these objectives and do not afford such undertakings the possibility of eliminating competition in respect of a substantial part of the products concerned.

Notes

4 In the following the term "agreement" includes concerted practices and decisions of associations of undertakings.
5 See Commission Notice on the concept of effect on trade between Member States contained in Articles [101] and [102] of the Treaty [OJ C 101, 27.04.2004, p.81].
6 In the following the term "restriction" includes the prevention and distortion of competition.

6. Intellectual property laws confer exclusive rights on holders of patents, copyright, design rights, trademarks and other legally protected rights. The owner of intellectual property is entitled under intellectual property laws to prevent unauthorised use of his intellectual property and to exploit it, *inter alia*, by licensing it to third parties. Once a product incorporating an intellectual property right has been put on the market inside the EEA by the holder or with his consent, the intellectual property right is exhausted in the sense that the holder can no longer use it to control the sale of the product[7] (principle of Community exhaustion). The right holder has no right under intellectual property laws to prevent sales by licensees or buyers of such products incorporating the licensed technology.[8] The principle of Community exhaustion is in line with the essential function of intellectual property rights, which is to grant the holder the right to exclude others from exploiting his intellectual property without his consent.

Notes

7 This principle of Community exhaustion is for example enshrined in Article 7(1) of Directive 104/89/EEC to approximate the laws of the Member States relating to trade marks (OJ L 40, 11.2.1989, p.1), which provides that the trade mark shall not entitle the proprietor to prohibit its use in relation to goods which have been put on the market in the Community under that trade mark by the proprietor or with his consent.
8 On the other hand, the sale of copies of a protected work does not lead to the exhaustion of performance rights, including rental rights, in the work, see in this respect Case 158/86, *WarnerBrothers and Metronome Video*, [1988] ECR 2605, and Case C-61/97, *Foreningen af danskevideogramdistributører*, [1998] ECR I-5171.

7. The fact that intellectual property laws grant exclusive rights of exploitation does not imply that intellectual property rights are immune from competition law intervention. Articles [101] and [102] are in particular applicable to agreements whereby the holder licenses another undertaking to exploit his intellectual property rights.[9] Nor does it imply that there is an inherent conflict between intellectual property rights and the Community competition rules. Indeed, both bodies of law share the same basic objective of promoting consumer welfare and an efficient allocation of resources. Innovation constitutes an essential and dynamic component of an open and competitive market economy. Intellectual property rights promote dynamic competition by encouraging undertakings to invest in developing new or improved products and processes. So does competition by putting pressure on undertakings to innovate. Therefore, both intellectual property rights and competition are necessary to promote innovation and ensure a competitive exploitation thereof.

Notes

9 See e.g. Joined Cases 56/64 and 58/64, *Consten and Grundig*, [1966] ECR 429.

Commentary
para 7: B&C: 2.086 F&N: 10.60

8. In the assessment of licence agreements under Article [101] it must be kept in mind that the creation of intellectual property rights often entails substantial investment and that it is often a risky endeavour. In order not to reduce dynamic competition and to maintain the incentive to innovate, the innovator must not be unduly restricted in the exploitation of intellectual property rights that turn out to be valuable. For these reasons the innovator should normally be free to seek compensation for successful projects that is sufficient to maintain investment incentives, taking failed projects into account. Technology licensing may also require the licensee to make significant sunk investments in the licensed technology and production assets necessary to exploit it. Article [101] cannot

be applied without considering such *ex ante* investments made by the parties and the risks relating thereto. The risk facing the parties and the sunk investment that must be committed may thus lead to the agreement falling outside Article [101](1) or fulfilling the conditions of Article [101](3), as the case may be, for the period of time required to recoup the investment.

Commentary
para 8: **B&C:** 9.075 **F&N:** 10.64

9. In assessing licensing agreements under Article [101], the existing analytical framework is sufficiently flexible to take due account of the dynamic aspects of technology licensing. There is no presumption that intellectual property rights and licence agreements as such give rise to competition concerns. Most licence agreements do not restrict competition and create pro-competitive efficiencies. Indeed, licensing as such is pro-competitive as it leads to dissemination of technology and promotes innovation. In addition, even licence agreements that do restrict competition may often give rise to pro-competitive efficiencies, which must be considered under Article [101] (3) and balanced against the negative effects on competition.[10] The great majority of licence agreements are therefore compatible with Article [101].

Notes
[10] The methodology for the application of Article [101](3) is set out in the Commission Guidelines on the application of Article [101](3) of the Treaty [OJ C 101, 27.4.2004, p.97].

Commentary
para 9: **B&C:** 9.001, 9.075 **F&N:** 10.64, 10.129

2. The general framework for applying Article [101]

10. Article [101](1) prohibits agreements which have as their object or effect the restriction of competition. Article [101](1) applies both to restrictions of competition between the parties to an agreement and to restrictions of competition between any of the parties and third parties.

11. The assessment of whether a licence agreement restricts competition must be made within the actual context in which competition would occur in the absence of the agreement with its alleged restrictions.[11] In making this assessment it is necessary to take account of the likely impact of the agreement on inter-technology competition (i.e. competition between undertakings using competing technologies) and on intra-technology competition (i.e. competition between undertakings using the same technology).[12] Article [101](1) prohibits restrictions of both inter-technology competition and intra-technology competition. It is therefore necessary to assess to what extent the agreement affects or is likely to affect these two aspects of competition on the market.

Notes
[11] See Case 56/65, *Société Technique Minière*, [1966] ECR 337, and Case C-7/95 P, *John Deere*, [1998] ECR I-3111, paragraph 76.
[12] See in this respect e.g. judgment in *Consten and Grundig* cited in note 9.

Commentary
para 11: **B&C:** 9.077, 9.078 **F&N:** 10.130

12. The following two questions provide a useful framework for making this assessment. The first question relates to the impact of the agreement on inter-technology competition while the second question relates to the impact of the agreement on intra-technology competition. As restraints may be capable of affecting both inter-technology competition and intra-technology competition at the same time, it may be necessary to analyse a restraint in the light of both questions before it can be concluded whether or not competition within the meaning of Article [101] (1) is restricted:

(a) Does the licence agreement restrict actual or potential competition that would have existed without the contemplated agreement? If so, the agreement may be caught by Article [101](1). In making this assessment it is necessary to take into account competition between the parties and competition from third parties. For instance, where two undertakings established in different Member States cross licence competing technologies and undertake not to sell products in each other's home markets, (potential) competition that existed prior to the agreement is restricted. Similarly, where a licensor imposes obligations on his licensees not to use competing technologies and these obligations foreclose third party technologies, actual or potential competition that would have existed in the absence of the agreement is restricted.

(b) Does the agreement restrict actual or potential competition that would have existed in the absence of the contractual restraint(s) If so, the agreement may be caught by Article [101](1). For instance, where a licensor restricts its licensees from competing with each other, (potential) competition that could have existed between the licensees absent the restraints is restricted. Such restrictions include vertical price fixing and territorial or customer sales restrictions between licensees. However, certain restraints may in certain cases not be caught by Article [101](1) when the restraint is objectively necessary for the existence of an agreement of that type or that nature.[13] Such exclusion of the application of Article [101](1) can only be made on the basis of objective factors external to the parties themselves and not the subjective views and characteristics of the parties. The question is not whether the parties in their particular situation would not have accepted to conclude a less restrictive agreement, but whether, given the nature of the agreement and the characteristics of the market, a less restrictive agreement would not have been concluded by undertakings in a similar setting. For instance, territorial restraints in an agreement between non-competitors may fall outside Article [101](1) for a certain duration if the restraints are objectively necessary for a licensee to penetrate a new market. Similarly, a prohibition imposed on all licensees not to sell to certain categories of end users may not be restrictive of competition if such a restraint is objectively necessary for reasons of safety or health related to the dangerous nature of the product in question. Claims that in the absence of a restraint the supplier would have resorted to vertical integration are not sufficient. Decisions on whether or not to vertically integrate depend on a broad range of complex economic factors, a number of which are internal to the undertaking concerned.

Notes

13 See in this respect the judgment in *Société Technique Minière* cited in note 11 and Case 258/78, *Nungesser*, [1982] ECR 2015.

Commentary
para 12: B&C: 9.078 F&N: 10.67, 10.130
para 12(b): F&N: 10.67, 10.140

---

13. In the application of the analytical framework set out in the previous paragraph it must be taken into account that Article [101](1) distinguishes between those agreements that have a restriction of competition as their object and those agreements that have a restriction of competition as their effect. An agreement or contractual restraint is only prohibited by Article [101](1) if its object or effect is to restrict inter-technology competition and/or intra-technology competition.

14. Restrictions of competition by object are those that by their very nature restrict competition. These are restrictions which in light of the objectives pursued by the Community competition rules have such a high potential for negative effects on competition that it is not necessary for the purposes of applying Article [101](1) to demonstrate any actual effects on the market.[14] Moreover, the conditions of Article [101](3) are unlikely to be fulfilled in the case of restrictions by object. The assessment of whether or not an agreement has as its object a restriction of competition is based on a number of factors. These factors include, in particular, the content of the agreement and the objective aims pursued by it. It may also be necessary to consider the context in which it is (to be) applied or the actual conduct and behaviour of the parties on the market.[15] In other words, an examination of the facts underlying the agreement and the specific circumstances in which it operates may be required before it can be concluded whether a particular restriction constitutes a hardcore restriction of competition. The way in which an agreement is actually implemented may reveal a restriction by object even where the formal agreement does not contain an express provision to that effect. Evidence of subjective intent on the part of the parties to

restrict competition is a relevant factor but not a necessary condition. For licence agreements, the Commission considers that the restrictions covered by the list of hardcore restrictions of competition contained in Article 4 of the TTBER are restrictive by their very object.

Notes

14 See in this respect e.g. Case C-49/92 P, *Anic Partecipazioni*, [1999] ECR I-4125, paragraph 99.

15 See Joined Cases 29/83 and 30/83, *CRAM and Rheinzink*, [1984] ECR 1679, paragraph 26, and Joined Cases 96/82 and others, *ANSEAU-NAVEWA*, [1983] ECR 3369, paragraphs 23–25.

Commentary

para 14: F&N: 10.93

15. If an agreement is not restrictive of competition by object it is necessary to examine whether it has restrictive effects on competition. Account must be taken of both actual and potential effects.16 In other words the agreement must have likely anti-competitive effects. For licence agreements to be restrictive of competition by effect they must affect actual or potential competition to such an extent that on the relevant market negative effects on prices, output, innovation or the variety or quality of goods and services can be expected with a reasonable degree of probability. The likely negative effects on competition must be appreciable.17 Appreciable anti-competitive effects are likely to occur when at least one of the parties has or obtains some degree of market power and the agreement contributes to the creation, maintenance or strengthening of that market power or allows the parties to exploit such market power. Market power is the ability to maintain prices above competitive levels or to maintain output in terms of product quantities, product quality and variety or innovation below competitive levels for a not insignificant period of time. The degree of market power normally required for a finding of an infringement under Article [101](1) is less than the degree of market power required for a finding of dominance under Article [102].

Notes

16 See the judgment in *John Deere*, [1998] cited in note 11.

17 Guidance on the issue of appreciability can be found in Commission notice on agreements of minor importance which do not appreciably restrict competition under Article [101](1) of the Treaty (OJ C 368, 22.12.2001, p.13). The notice defines appreciability in a negative way. Agreements, which fall outside the scope of the de minimis notice, do not necessarily have appreciable restrictive effects. An individual assessment is required.

16. For the purposes of analysing restrictions of competition by effect it is normally necessary to define the relevant market and to examine and assess, inter alia, the nature of the products and technologies concerned, the market position of the parties, the market position of competitors, the market position of buyers, the existence of potential competitors and the level of entry barriers. In some cases, however, it may be possible to show anti-competitive effects directly by analysing the conduct of the parties to the agreement on the market. It may for example be possible to ascertain that an agreement has led to price increases.

17. Licence agreements, however, also have substantial pro-competitive potential. Indeed, the vast majority of licence agreements are pro-competitive. Licence agreements may promote innovation by allowing innovators to earn returns to cover at least part of their research and development costs. Licence agreements also lead to a dissemination of technologies, which may create value by reducing the production costs of the licensee or by enabling him to produce new or improved products. Efficiencies at the level of the licensee often stem from a combination of the licensor's technology with the assets and technologies of the licensee. Such integration of complementary assets and technologies may lead to a cost/output configuration that would not otherwise be possible. For instance, the combination of an improved technology of the licensor with more efficient production or distribution assets of the licensee may reduce production costs or lead to the production of a higher quality product. Licensing may also serve the pro-competitive purpose of removing obstacles to the development and exploitation of the licensee's own technology. In particular in sectors where large numbers of patents are prevalent licensing often occurs in order to create design freedom by removing the risk of infringement claims by the licensor. When the licensor agrees not to invoke his intellectual property rights to prevent the sale of the licensee's

products, the agreement removes an obstacle to the sale of the licensee's product and thus generally promotes competition.

Commentary
para 17: B&C: 9.075 F&N: 10.64

18. In cases where a licence agreement is caught by Article [101](1) the pro-competitive effects of the agreement must be balanced against its restrictive effects in the context of Article [101](3). When all four conditions of Article [101](3) are satisfied, the restrictive licence agreement in question is valid and enforceable, no prior decision to that effect being required.[18] Hardcore restrictions of competition only fulfil the conditions of Article [101](3) in exceptional circumstances. Such agreements generally fail (at least) one of the first two conditions of Article [101](3). They generally do not create objective economic benefits or benefits for consumers. Moreover, these types of agreements generally also fail the indispensability test under the third condition. For example, if the parties fix the price at which the products produced under the licence must be sold, this will generally lead to a lower output and a misallocation of resources and higher prices for consumers. The price restriction is also not indispensable to achieve the possible efficiencies resulting from the availability to both competitors of the two technologies.

Notes
[18] See Article 1(2) of Council Regulation No 1/2003 cited in note 3.

Commentary
para 18: F&N: 10.67, 10.93

3. Market definition

19. The Commission's approach to defining the relevant market is laid down in its market definition guidelines.[19] The present guidelines only address aspects of market definition that are of particular importance in the field of technology licensing.

Notes
[19] Commission notice on the definition of the relevant market for the purposes of Community competition law (OJ C 372, 9.12.1997, p.5).

20. Technology is an input, which is integrated either into a product or a production process. Technology licensing can therefore affect competition both in input markets and in output markets. For instance, an agreement between two parties which sell competing products and which cross license technologies relating to the production of these products may restrict competition on the product market concerned. It may also restrict competition on the market for technology and possibly also on other input markets. For the purposes of assessing the competitive effects of licence agreements it may therefore be necessary to define relevant goods and service markets (product markets) as well as technology markets.[20] The term "product market" used in Article 3 of the TTBER refers to relevant goods and service markets in both their geographic and product dimension. As is clear from Article 1(1)(j) of the TTBER, the term is used merely to distinguish relevant goods and service markets from relevant technology markets.

Notes
[20] As to these distinctions see also Commission Guidelines on the applicability of Article [101] of the [Treaty on the Functioning of the European Union] to horizontal cooperation agreements (OJ C 3, 6.1.2001, p.2, paragraphs 44 to 52). [Ed note: see now Commission Notice 2011/C 11/01, Guidelines on the applicability of Article 101 of the Treaty on the Functioning of the European Union to horizontal co-operation agreements (OJ C 11, 14.1.2011, p.1), reproduced at C17 below.]

Commentary
para 20: B&C: 9.145 F&N: 3.422

21. The TTBER and these guidelines are concerned with effects both on product markets for final products and on product markets for intermediate products. The relevant product market includes products which are regarded by the buyers as interchangeable with or substitutable for

the contract products incorporating the licensed technology, by reason of the products' characteristics, their prices and their intended use.

22. Technology markets consist of the licensed technology and its substitutes, i.e. other technologies which are regarded by the licensees as interchangeable with or substitutable for the licensed technology, by reason of the technologies' characteristics, their royalties and their intended use. The methodology for defining technology markets follows the same principles as the definition of product markets. Starting from the technology which is marketed by the licensor, one needs to identify those other technologies to which licensees could switch in response to a small but permanent increase in relative prices, i.e. the royalties. An alternative approach is to look at the market for products incorporating the licensed technology (cf. paragraph [23] below).

Commentary
para 22: **B&C:** 9.079, 9.147 **F&N:** 3.422

23. Once relevant markets have been defined, market shares can be assigned to the various sources of competition in the market and used as an indication of the relative strength of market players. In the case of technology markets one way to proceed is to calculate market shares on the basis of each technology's share of total licensing income from royalties, representing a technology's share of the market where competing technologies are licensed. However, this may often be a mere theoretical and not a practical way to proceed because of lack of clear information on royalties etc. An alternative approach, which is the one used in Article 3(3) of the TTBER, is to calculate market shares on the technology market on the basis of sales of products incorporating the licensed technology on downstream product markets (see paragraph 70 below). Under this approach all sales on the relevant product market are taken into account, irrespective of whether the product incorporates a technology that is being licensed. In the case of technology markets the approach of Article 3(3) to take into account technologies that are (only) being used in-house, is justified. Indeed, this approach is in general a good indicator of the strength of the technology. First, it captures any potential competition from undertakings that are producing with their own technology and that are likely to start licensing in the event of a small but permanent increase in the price for licenses. Secondly, even where it is unlikely that other technology owners would start licensing, the licensor does not necessarily have market power on the technology market even if he has a high share of licensing income. If the downstream product market is competitive, competition at this level may effectively constrain the licensor. An increase in royalties upstream affects the costs of the licensee, making him less competitive, causing him to lose sales. A technology's market share on the product market also captures this element and is thus normally a good indicator of licensor market power. In individual cases outside the safe harbour of the TTBER it may be necessary, where practically possible, to apply both of the described approaches in order to assess more accurately the market strength of the licensor.

Commentary
para 23: **B&C:** 4.065

24. Moreover, outside the safe harbour of the TTBER it must also be taken into account that market share may not always be a good indication of the relative strength of available technologies. The Commission will therefore, inter alia, also have regard to the number of independently controlled technologies available in addition to the technologies controlled by the parties to the agreement that may be substitutable for the licensed technology at a comparable cost to the user (see paragraph 131 below).

25. Some licence agreements may affect innovation markets. In analysing such effects, however, the Commission will normally confine itself to examining the impact of the agreement on competition within existing product and technology markets.[21] Competition on such markets may be affected by agreements that delay the introduction of improved products or new products that over time will replace existing products. In such cases innovation is a source of potential competition which must be taken into account when assessing the impact of the agreement on product markets and technology markets. In a limited number of cases, however, it may be useful and necessary to also define innovation markets. This is particularly the case where the agreement

affects innovation aiming at creating new products and where it is possible at an early stage to identify research and development poles.[22] In such cases it can be analysed whether after the agreement there will be a sufficient number of competing research and development poles left for effective competition in innovation to be maintained.

Notes
[21] See to that effect paragraphs 50 to 52 of the Guidelines on horizontal cooperation agreements, cited in the previous note.
[22] Idem, paragraph 51.

Commentary
para 25: B&C: 4.066 F&N: 10.85

4. The distinction between competitors and non-competitors

26. In general, agreements between competitors pose a greater risk to competition than agreements between non-competitors. However, competition between undertakings that use the same technology (intra-technology competition between licensees) constitutes an important complement to competition between undertakings that use competing technologies (inter-technology competition). For instance, intra-technology competition may lead to lower prices for the products incorporating the technology in question, which may not only produce direct and immediate benefits for consumers of these products, but also spur further competition between undertakings that use competing technologies. In the context of licensing it must also be taken into account that licensees are selling their own product. They are not re-selling a product supplied by another undertaking. There may thus be greater scope for product differentiation and quality-based competition between licensees than in the case of vertical agreements for the resale of products.

Commentary
para 26: F&N: 10.82, 10.83

27. In order to determine the competitive relationship between the parties it is necessary to examine whether the parties would have been actual or potential competitors in the absence of the agreement. If without the agreement the parties would not have been actual or potential competitors in any relevant market affected by the agreement they are deemed to be non-competitors.

Commentary
para 27: B&C: 2.097 F&N: 10.84

28. Where the licensor and the licensee are both active on the same product market or the same technology market without one or both parties infringing the intellectual property rights of the other party, they are actual competitors on the market concerned. The parties are deemed to be actual competitors on the technology market if the licensee is already licensing out his technology and the licensor enters the technology market by granting a license for a competing technology to the licensee.

Commentary
para 28: F&N: 10.87, 10.88

29. The parties are considered to be potential competitors on the product market if in the absence of the agreement and without infringing the intellectual property rights of the other party it is likely that they would have undertaken the necessary additional investment to enter the relevant market in response to a small but permanent increase in product prices. In order to constitute a realistic competitive constraint entry has to be likely to occur within a short period. Normally a period of one to two years is appropriate. However, in individual cases longer periods can be taken into account. The period of time needed for undertakings already on the market to adjust their capacities can be used as a yardstick to determine this period. For instance, the parties are likely to be considered potential competitors on the product market where the licensee produces on the

basis of its own technology in one geographic market and starts producing in another geographic market on the basis of a licensed competing technology. In such circumstances, it is likely that the licensee would have been able to enter the second geographic market on the basis of its own technology, unless such entry is precluded by objective factors, including the existence of blocking patents (see paragraph 32 below).

30. The parties are considered to be potential competitors on the technology market where they own substitutable technologies if in the specific case the licensee is not licensing his own technology, provided that he would be likely to do so in the event of a small but permanent increase in technology prices. However, for the application of the TTBER potential competition on the technology market is not taken into account (see paragraph 66 below).

31. In some cases the parties may become competitors subsequent to the conclusion of the agreement because the licensee develops and starts exploiting a competing technology. In such cases it must be taken into account that the parties were non-competitors at the time of conclusion of the agreement and that the agreement was concluded in that context. The Commission will therefore mainly focus on the impact of the agreement on the licensee's ability to exploit his own (competing) technology. In particular, the list of hardcore restrictions applying to agreements between competitors will not be applied to such agreements unless the agreement is subsequently amended in any material respect after the parties have become competitors (cf. Article 4(3) of the TTBER). The undertakings party to an agreement may also become competitors subsequent to the conclusion of the agreement where the licensee was already active on the product market prior to the licence and where the licensor subsequently enters the product market either on the basis of the licensed technology or a new technology. Also in this case the hardcore list relevant for agreements between non-competitors will continue to apply to the agreement unless the agreement is subsequently amended in any material respect (cf. article 4(3) of the TTBER).

32. If the parties own technologies that are in a one-way or two-way blocking position, the parties are considered to be non-competitors on the technology market. A one-way blocking position exists when a technology cannot be exploited without infringing upon another technology. This is for instance the case where one patent covers an improvement of a technology covered by another patent. In that case the exploitation of the improvement patent pre-supposes that the holder obtains a licence to the basic patent. A two-way blocking position exists where neither technology can be exploited without infringing upon the other technology and where the holders thus need to obtain a licence or a waiver from each other. In assessing whether a blocking position exists the Commission will rely on objective factors as opposed to the subjective views of the parties. Particularly convincing evidence of the existence of a blocking position is required where the parties may have a common interest in claiming the existence of a blocking position in order to be qualified as non-competitors, for instance where the claimed two-way blocking position concerns technologies that are technological substitutes. Relevant evidence includes court decisions including injunctions and opinions of independent experts. In the latter case the Commission will, in particular, closely examine how the expert has been selected. However, also other convincing evidence, including expert evidence from the parties that they have or had good and valid reasons to believe that a blocking position exists or existed, can be relevant to substantiate the existence of a blocking position.

Part C Substantive Antitrust Matters

33. In some cases it may also be possible to conclude that while the licensor and the licensee produce competing products, they are non-competitors on the relevant product market and the relevant technology market because the licensed technology represents such a drastic innovation that the technology of the licensee has become obsolete or uncompetitive. In such cases the licensor's technology either creates a new market or excludes the licensee's technology from the market. Often, however, it is not possible to come to this conclusion at the time the agreement is concluded. It is usually only when the technology or the products incorporating it have been available to consumers for some time that it becomes apparent that the older technology has become obsolete or uncompetitive. For instance, when CD technology was developed and players and discs were put on the market, it was not obvious that this new technology would replace LP technology. This only became apparent some years later. The parties will therefore be considered to be competitors if at the time of the conclusion of the agreement it is not obvious that the licensee's technology is obsolete or uncompetitive. However, given that both Articles [101](1) and Article [101](3) must be applied in light of the actual context in which the agreement occurs, the assessment is sensitive to material changes in the facts. The classification of the relationship between the parties will therefore change into a relationship of non-competitors, if at a later point in time the licensee's technology becomes obsolete or uncompetitive on the market.

Commentary
para 33: B&C: 9.081 F&N: 10.90

III. Application of the Block Exemption Regulation

1. The effects of theBlock Exemption Regulation

34. Technology transfer agreements that fulfil the conditions set out in the TTBER are block exempted from the prohibition rule contained in Article [101](1). Block exempted agreements are legally valid and enforceable. Such agreements can only be prohibited for the future and only upon withdrawal of the block exemption by the Commission or a Member State competition authority. Block exempted agreements cannot be prohibited under Article [101] by national courts in the context of private litigation.

35. Block exemption of categories of technology transfer agreements is based on the presumption that such agreements — to the extent that they are caught by Article [101](1) — fulfil the four conditions laid down in Article [101](3). It is thus presumed that the agreements give rise to economic efficiencies, that the restrictions contained in the agreements are indispensable to the attainment of these efficiencies, that consumers within the affected markets receive a fair share of the efficiency gains and that the agreements do not afford the undertakings concerned the possibility of eliminating competition in respect of a substantial part of the products in question. The market share thresholds (Article 3), the hardcore list (Article 4) and the excluded restrictions (Article 5) set out in the TTBER aim at ensuring that only restrictive agreements that can reasonably be presumed to fulfil the four conditions of Article [101](3) are block exempted.

36. As set out in section IV below, many licence agreements fall outside Article [101](1), either because they do not restrict competition at all or because the restriction of competition is not appreciable.[23] To the extent that such agreements would anyhow fall within the scope of the TTBER, there is no need to determine whether they are caught by Article [101](1).[24]

Notes
[23] See in this respect the Notice on agreements of minor importance cited in note 17.
[24] According to Article 3(2) of Regulation 1/2003, agreements which may affect trade between Member States but which are not prohibited by Article [101] cannot be prohibited by national competition law.

Commentary
para 36: B&C: 9.075

37. Outside the scope of the block exemption it is relevant to examine whether in the individual case the agreement is caught by Article [101](1) and if so whether the conditions of Article [101](3) are satisfied. There is no presumption that technology transfer agreements falling outside the

block exemption are caught by Article [101](1) or fail to satisfy the conditions of Article [101] (3). In particular, the mere fact that the market shares of the parties exceed the market share thresholds set out in Article 3 of the TTBER is not a sufficient basis for finding that the agreement is caught by Article [101](1). Individual assessment of the likely effects of the agreement is required. It is only when agreements contain hardcore restrictions of competition that it can normally be presumed that they are prohibited by Article [101].

Commentary
para 37: **B&C**: 3.011, 3.074 **F&N**: 3.470, 10.63

2. Scope and duration of the Block Exemption Regulation

2.1. Agreements between two parties

38. According to Article 2(1) of the TTBER, the Regulation covers technology transfer agreements "between two undertakings." Technology transfer agreements between more than two undertakings are not covered by the TTBER.[25] The decisive factor in terms of distinguishing between agreements between two undertakings and multiparty agreements is whether the agreement in question is concluded between more than two undertakings.

Notes
[25] Under Council Regulation 19/65, OJ Special Edition Series I 1965–1966, 35, the Commission is not empowered to block exempt technology transfer agreements concluded between more than two undertakings.

39. Agreements concluded by two undertakings fall within the scope of the TTBER even if the agreement stipulates conditions for more than one level of trade. For instance, the TTBER applies to a licence agreement concerning not only the production stage but also the distribution stage, stipulating the obligations that the licensee must or may impose on resellers of the products produced under the licence.[26]

40. Licence agreements concluded between more than two undertakings often give rise to the same issues as licence agreements of the same nature concluded between two undertakings. In its individual assessment of licence agreements which are of the same nature as those covered by the block exemption but which are concluded between more than two undertakings, the Commission will apply by analogy the principles set out in the TTBER.

Notes
[26] See recital 19 of the TTBER and further section 2.5 below.

Commentary
para 40: **B&C**: 9.141 **F&N**: 10.68

2.2. Agreements for the production of contract products

41. It follows from Article 2 that for licence agreements to be covered by the TTBER they must concern "the production of contract products", i.e. products incorporating or produced with the licensed technology. In other words, to be covered by the TTBER the licence must permit the licensee to exploit the licensed technology for production of goods or services (see recital 7 of the TTBER). The TTBER does not cover technology pools. The notion of technology pools covers agreements whereby two or more parties agree to pool their respective technologies and license them as a package. The notion of technology pools also covers arrangements whereby two or more undertakings agree to license a third party and authorise him to license on the package of technologies. Technology pools are dealt with in section IV.4 below.

Commentary
para 41: **F&N**: 10.161

42. The TTBER applies to licence agreements for the production of contract products whereby the licensee is also permitted to sublicense the licensed technology to third parties provided, however, that the production of contract products constitutes the primary object of the agreement.

Conversely, the TTBER does not apply to agreements that have sublicensing as their primary object. However, the Commission will apply by analogy the principles set out in the TTBER and these guidelines to such "master licensing" agreements between licensor and licensee. Agreements between the licensee and sub-licensees are covered by the TTBER.

Commentary
para 42: B&C: 9.142 F&N: 10.69

43. The term "contract products" encompasses goods and services produced with the licensed technology. This is the case both where the licensed technology is used in the production process and where it is incorporated into the product itself. In these guidelines the term "products incorporating the licensed technology" covers both situations. The TTBER applies in all cases where technology is licensed for the purposes of producing goods and services. It is sufficient in this respect that the licensor undertakes not to exercise his intellectual property rights against the licensee. Indeed, the essence of a pure patent licence is the right to operate inside the scope of the exclusive right of the patent. It follows that the TTBER also covers so-called non-assertion agreements and settlement agreements whereby the licensor permits the licensee to produce within the scope of the patent.

Commentary
para 43: F&N: 10.72

44. The TTBER covers "subcontracting" whereby the licensor licenses technology to the licensee who undertakes to produce certain products on the basis thereof exclusively for the licensor. Subcontracting may also involve the supply of equipment by the licensor to be used in the production of the goods and services covered by the agreement. For the latter type of subcontracting to be covered by the TTBER, the licensed technology and not the supplied equipment must constitute the primary object of the agreement. Subcontracting is also covered by the Commission's Notice concerning the assessment of certain subcontracting agreements in relation to Article [101](1) of the Treaty.[27] According to this notice, which remains applicable, subcontracting agreements whereby the subcontractor undertakes to produce certain products exclusively for the contractor generally fall outside Article [101](1). However, other restrictions imposed on the subcontractor such as the obligation not to conduct or exploit his own research and development may be caught by Article [101].[28]

Notes
[27] OJ C 1, 3.1.1979, p.2.
[28] See paragraph 3 of the subcontracting notice.

Commentary
para 44: B&C: 9.142

45. The TTBER also applies to agreements whereby the licensee must carry out development work before obtaining a product or a process that is ready for commercial exploitation, provided that a contract product has been identified. Even if such further work and investment is required, the object of the agreement is the production of an identified contract product. On the other hand, the TTBER and the guidelines do not cover agreements whereby a technology is licensed for the purpose of enabling the licensee to carry out further research and development in various fields. For instance, the TTBER and the guidelines do not cover the licensing of a technological research tool used in the process of further research activity. The framework of the TTBER and the guidelines is based on the premise that there is a direct link between the licensed technology and an identified contract product. In cases where no such link exists the main object of the agreement is research and development as opposed to bringing a particular product to the market; in that case the analytical framework of the TTBER and the guidelines may not be appropriate. For the same reasons the TTBER and the guidelines do not cover research and development sub-contracting whereby the licensee undertakes to carry out research and development in the field of the licensed technology and to hand back the improved technology package to the licensor. The main object of such agreements is the provision of research and development services aimed at

improving the technology as opposed to the production of goods and services on the basis of the licensed technology.

Commentary
para 45: F&N: 10.70

2.3. The concept of technology transfer agreements

46. The TTBER and these guidelines cover agreements for the transfer of technology. According to Article 1(1)(b) and (h) of the TTBER the concept of "technology" covers patents and patent applications, utility models and applications for utility models, design rights, plant breeders rights, topographies of semiconductor products, supplementary protection certificates for medicinal products or other products for which such supplementary protection certificates may be obtained, software copyright, and know-how. The licensed technology should allow the licensee with or without other inputs to produce the contract products.

Commentary
para 46: B&C: 9.137

47. Know-how is defined in Article 1(1)(i) as a package of non-patented practical information, resulting from experience and testing, which is secret, substantial and identified. "Secret" means that the know-how is not generally known or easily accessible. "Substantial" means that the know-how includes information which is significant and useful for the production of the products covered by the licence agreement or the application of the process covered by the licence agreement. In other words, the information must significantly contribute to or facilitate the production of the contract products. In cases where the licensed know-how relates to a product as opposed to a process, this condition implies that the know-how is useful for the production the contract product. This condition is not satisfied where the contract product can be produced on the basis of freely available technology. However, the condition does not require that the contract product is of higher value than products produced with freely available technology. In the case of process technologies, this condition implies that the know-how is useful in the sense that it can reasonably be expected at the date of conclusion of the agreement to be capable of significantly improving the competitive position of the licensee, for instance by reducing his production costs. "Identified" means that it is possible to verify that the licensed know-how fulfils the criteria of secrecy and substantiality. This condition is satisfied where the licensed know-how is described in manuals or other written form. However, in some cases this may not be reasonably possible. The licensed know-how may consist of practical knowledge possessed by the licensor's employees. For instance, the licensor's employees may possess secret and substantial knowledge about a certain production process which is passed on to the licensee in the form of training of the licensee's employees. In such cases it is sufficient to describe in the agreement the general nature of the know-how and to list the employees that will be or have been involved in passing it on to the licensee.

Commentary
para 47: B&C: 9.137

48. The concept of "transfer" implies that technology must flow from one undertaking to another. Such transfers normally take the form of licensing whereby the licensor grants the licensee the right to use his technology against payment of royalties. It can also take the form of sub-licensing, whereby a licensee, having been authorised to do so by the licensor, grants licenses to third parties (sub-licensees) for the exploitation of the technology.

Commentary
para 48: B&C: 9.137

49. The TTBER only applies to agreements that have as their primary object the transfer of technology as defined in that Regulation as opposed to the purchase of goods and services or the licensing

Part C Substantive Antitrust Matters

of other types of intellectual property. Agreements containing provisions relating to the purchase and sale of products are only covered by the TTBER to the extent that those provisions do not constitute the primary object of the agreement and are directly related to the application of the licensed technology. This is likely to be the case where the tied products take the form of equipment or process input which is specifically tailored to efficiently exploit the licensed technology. If, on the other hand, the product is simply another input into the final product, it must be carefully examined whether the licensed technology constitutes the primary object of the agreement. For instance, in cases where the licensee is already manufacturing a final product on the basis of another technology, the licence must lead to a significant improvement of the licensee's production process, exceeding the value of the product purchased from the licensor. The requirement that the tied products must be related to the licensing of technology implies that the TTBER does not cover the purchase of products that have no relation with the products incorporating the licensed technology. This is for example the case where the tied product is not intended to be used with the licensed product, but relates to an activity on a separate product market.

Commentary
para 49: B&C: 9.138, 9.141, 9.142 **F&N:** 10.77

50. The TTBER only covers the licensing of other types of intellectual property such as trademarks and copyright, other than software copyright, to the extent that they are directly related to the exploitation of the licensed technology and do not constitute the primary object of the agreement. This condition ensures that agreements covering other types of intellectual property rights are only block exempted to the extent that these other intellectual property rights serve to enable the licensee to better exploit the licensed technology. The licensor may for instance authorise the licensee to use his trademark on the products incorporating the licensed technology. The trademark licence may allow the licensee to better exploit the licensed technology by allowing consumers to make an immediate link between the product and the characteristics imputed to it by the licensed technology. An obligation on the licensee to use the licensor's trademark may also promote the dissemination of technology by allowing the licensor to identify himself as the source of the underlying technology. However, where the value of the licensed technology to the licensee is limited because he already employs an identical or very similar technology and the main object of the agreement is the trademark, the TTBER does not apply.[29]

Notes
[29] See in this respect Commission Decision in *Moosehead/Whitbread* (OJ L 100, 20.4.1990, p.32).

Commentary
para 50: B&C: 9.139

51. The licensing of copyright for the purpose of reproduction and distribution of the protected work, i.e. the production of copies for resale, is considered to be similar to technology licensing. Since such licence agreements relate to the production and sale of products on the basis of an intellectual property right, they are considered to be of a similar nature as technology transfer agreements and normally raise comparable issues. Although the TTBER does not cover copyright other than software copyright, the Commission will as a general rule apply the principles set out in the TTBER and these guidelines when assessing such licensing of copyright under Article [101].

Commentary
para 51: B&C: 9.139

52. On the other hand, the licensing of rights in performances and other rights related to copyright is considered to raise particular issues and it may not be warranted to assess such licensing on the basis of the principles developed in these guidelines. In the case of the various rights related to performances value is created not by the reproduction and sale of copies of a product but by each individual performance of the protected work. Such exploitation can take various forms

including the performance, showing or the renting of protected material such as films, music or sporting events. In the application of Article [101] the specificities of the work and the way in which it is exploited must be taken into account.[30] For instance, resale restrictions may give rise to less competition concerns whereas particular concerns may arise where licensors impose on their licensees to extend to each of the licensors more favourable conditions obtained by one of them. The Commission will therefore not apply the TTBER and the present guidelines by way of analogy to the licensing of these other rights.

Notes
[30] See in this respect Case 262/81, *Coditel (II)*, [1982] ECR 3381.

Commentary
para 52: **B&C:** 9.139 **F&N:** 10.74

53. The Commission will also not extend the principles developed in the TTBER and these guidelines to trademark licensing. Trademark licensing often occurs in the context of distribution and resale of goods and services and is generally more akin to distribution agreements than technology licensing. Where a trademark licence is directly related to the use, sale or resale of goods and services and does not constitute the primary object of the agreement, the licence agreement is covered by Commission Regulation (EC) No 2790/1999 on the application of Article [101](3) of the Treaty to categories of vertical agreements and concerted practices.[31]

Notes
[31] OJ L 336, 29.12.1999, p.21.

Commentary
para 53: **B&C:** 9.094, 9.139

2.4. Duration

54. Subject to the duration of the TTBER, the block exemption applies for as long as the licensed property right has not lapsed, expired or been declared invalid. In the case of know-how the block exemption applies as long as the licensed know-how remains secret, except where the know-how becomes publicly known as a result of action by the licensee, in which case the exemption shall apply for the duration of the agreement (cf. Article 2 of the TTBER).

Commentary
para 54: **B&C:** 9.087

55. The block exemption applies to each licensed property right covered by the agreement and ceases to apply on the date of expiry, invalidity or the coming into the public domain of the last intellectual property right which constitutes "technology" within the meaning of the TTBER (cf. paragraph above).

Commentary
para 55: **B&C:** 9.143

2.5. Relationship with other block exemption regulations

56. The TTBER covers agreements between two undertakings concerning the licensing of technology for the purpose of the production of contract products. However, technology can also be an element of other types of agreements. In addition, the products incorporating the licensed technology are subsequently sold on the market. It is therefore necessary to address the interface between the TTBER and Commission Regulation (EC) No 2658/2000 on the application of Article [101](3) of the Treaty to categories of specialisation agreements,[32] Commission Regulation 2659/2000 on the application of Article [101](3) to categories of research and development agreements[33] and Commission Regulation (EC) No 2790/1999 on the application of Article [101](3) of the Treaty to categories of vertical agreements and concerted practices.[34]

Commentary
para 56: B&C: 9.133

2.5.1. The Block Exemption Regulations on specialisation and R&D agreements

57. According to Article 1(1)(c) of Regulation 2658/2010 on specialisation agreements, that Regulation covers, inter alia, joint production agreements by virtue of which two or more undertakings agree to produce certain products jointly. The Regulation extends to provisions concerning the assignment or use of intellectual property rights, provided that they do not constitute the primary object of the agreement, but are directly related to and necessary for its implementation.

58. *Where undertakings establish a production joint venture and license the joint venture to exploit technology, which is used in the production of the products produced by the joint venture, such licensing is subject to Regulation 2658/2000 and not the TTBER. Accordingly, licensing in the context of a production joint venture normally falls to be considered under Regulation 2658/2000. However, where the joint venture engages in licensing of the technology to third parties, the activity is not linked to production by the joint venture and therefore not covered by that Regulation. Such licensing arrangements, which bring together the technologies of the parties, constitute technology pools, which are dealt with in section IV.4 below.*

Commentary
para 58: B&C: 9.135 **F&N:** 7.302

59. Regulation 2659/2000 on research and development agreements covers agreements whereby two or more undertakings agree to jointly carry out research and development and to jointly exploit the results thereof. According to Article 2(11), research and development and the exploitation of the results are carried out jointly where the work involved is carried out by a joint team, organisation or undertakings, jointly entrusted to a third party or allocated between the parties by way of specialisation in research, development, production and distribution, including licensing.

Commentary
para 59: F&N: 7.187

60. It follows that Regulation 2659/2000 covers licensing between the parties and by the parties to a joint entity in the context of a research and development agreement. In the context of such agreements the parties can also determine the conditions for licensing the fruits of the research and development agreement to third parties. However, since third party licensees are not party to the research and development agreement, the individual licence agreement concluded with third parties is not covered by Regulation 2659/2000. Such licence agreements are block exempted by the TTBER where they fulfil the conditions of that Regulation.

Commentary
para 60: B&C: 9.135

2.5.2. The Block Exemption Regulation on vertical agreements

61. Commission Regulation (EC) No 2790/1999 on vertical agreements covers agreements entered into between two or more undertakings each operating, for the purposes of the agreement, at different levels of the production or distribution chain, and relating to the conditions under which the parties may purchase, sell or resell certain goods or services. It thus covers supply and distribution agreements.[35]

Notes

35 See the guide "Competition policy in Europe — The competition rules for supply and distribution agreements", 2002.

62. Given that the TTBER only covers agreements between two parties and that a licensee, selling products incorporating the licensed technology, is a supplier for the purposes of Regulation 2790/1999, these two block exemption regulations are closely related. The agreement between licensor and licensee is subject to the TTBER whereas agreements concluded between a licensee and buyers are subject to Regulation 2790/1999 and the Guidelines on Vertical Restraints.[36]

Notes

36 OJ C 291, 13.10.2000, p.1, and note 31. [Ed note: see now Commission Notice 2010/C 130/01, Guidelines on Vertical Restraints (OJ C 130, 19.5.2010, p.1), reproduced at C15 below.]

63. The TTBER also block exempts agreements between the licensor and the licensee where the agreement imposes obligations on the licensee as to the way in which he must sell the products incorporating the licensed technology. In particular, the licensee can be obliged to establish a certain type of distribution system such as exclusive distribution or selective distribution. However, the distribution agreements concluded for the purposes of implementing such obligations must, in order to be block exempted, comply with Regulation 2790/1999. For instance, the licensor can oblige the licensee to establish a system based on exclusive distribution in accordance with specified rules. However, it follows from Article 4(b) of Regulation 2790/1999 that distributors must be free to make passive sales into the territories of other exclusive distributors.

64. Furthermore, distributors must in principle be free to sell both actively and passively into territories covered by the distribution systems of other licensees producing their own products on the basis of the licensed technology. This is because for the purposes of Regulation 2790/1999 each licensee is a separate supplier. However, the reasons underlying the block exemption contained in that Regulation may also apply where the products incorporating the licensed technology are sold by the licensees under a common brand belonging to the licensor. When the products incorporating the licensed technology are sold under a common brand identity there may be the same efficiency reasons for applying the same types of restraints between licensees' distribution systems as within a single vertical distribution system. In such cases the Commission would be unlikely to challenge restraints where by analogy the requirements of Regulation 2790/1999 are fulfilled. For a common brand identity to exist the products must be sold and marketed under a common brand, which is predominant in terms of conveying quality and other relevant information to the consumer. It does not suffice that in addition to the licensees' brands the product carries the licensor's brand, which identifies him as the source of the licensed technology.

Commentary
para 64: F&N: 10.79

3. The safe harbour established by the Block Exemption Regulation

65. According to Article 3 of the TTBER the block exemption of restrictive agreements is subject to market share thresholds, confining the scope of the block exemption to agreements that although they may be restrictive of competition can generally be presumed to fulfil the conditions of Article [101](3). Outside the safe harbour created by the market share thresholds individual assessment is required. The fact that market shares exceed the thresholds does not give rise to any presumption either that the agreement is caught by Article [101](1) or that the agreement does not fulfil the conditions of Article [101](3). In the absence of hardcore restrictions, market analysis is required.

Commentary
para 65: B&C: 9.131, 9.144 F&N: 10.63

66. The market share threshold to be applied for the purpose of the safe harbour of the TTBER depends on whether the agreement is concluded between competitors or non-competitors. For

the purposes of the TTBER undertakings are competitors on the relevant technology market when they license competing technologies. Potential competition on the technology market is not taken into account for the application of the market share threshold or the hardcore list. Outside the safe harbour of the TTBER potential competition on the technology market is taken into account but does not lead to the application of the hardcore list relating to agreements between competitors (see also paragraph 31 above).

Commentary
para 66: B&C: 9.079 F&N: 10.86

67. Undertakings are competitors on the relevant product market where both undertakings are active on the same product and geographic market(s) on which the products incorporating the licensed technology are sold (actual competitors). They are also considered competitors where they would be likely, on realistic grounds, to undertake the necessary additional investments or other necessary switching costs to enter the relevant product and geographic market(s) within a reasonably short period of time[37] in response to a small and permanent increase in relative prices (potential competitors).

Notes
[37] See paragraph 29 above.

68. It follows from paragraphs 66 and 67 that two undertakings are not competitors for the purposes of the TTBER where the licensor is neither an actual nor a potential supplier of products on the relevant market and the licensee, already present on the product market, is not licensing out a competing technology even if he owns a competing technology and produces on the basis of that technology. However, the parties become competitors if at a later point in time the licensee starts licensing out his technology or the licensor becomes an actual or potential supplier of products on the relevant market. In that case the hardcore list relevant for agreements between non-competitors will continue to apply to the agreement unless the agreement is subsequently amended in any material respect, see Article 4(3) of the TTBER and paragraph 31 above.

69. In the case of agreements between competitors the market share threshold is 20% and in the case of agreements between non-competitors it is 30% (cf. Article 3(1) and (2) of the TTBER). Where the undertakings party to the licensing agreement are not competitors the agreement is covered if the market share of neither party exceeds 30% on the affected relevant technology and product markets. Where the undertakings party to the licensing agreement are competitors the agreement is covered if the combined market shares of the parties do not exceed 20% on the relevant technology and product markets. The market share thresholds apply both to technology markets and markets for products incorporating the licensed technology. If the applicable market share threshold is exceeded on an affected relevant market, the block exemption does not apply to the agreement for that relevant market. For instance, if the licence agreement concerns two separate product markets or two separate geographic markets, the block exemption may apply to one of the markets and not to the other.

Commentary
para 69: F&N: 10.122

70. In the case of technology markets, it follows from Article 3(3) of the TTBER that the licensor's market share is to be calculated on the basis of the sales of the licensor and all his licensees of products incorporating the licensed technology and this for each relevant market separately.[38] Where the parties are competitors on the technology market, sales of products incorporating the licensee's own technology must be combined with the sales of the products incorporating the licensed technology. In the case of new technologies that have not yet generated any sales, a zero market share is assigned. When sales commence the technology will start accumulating market share.

Notes
[38] The reasons for this calculation rule are explained in paragraph 23 above.

71. In the case of product markets, the licensee's market share is to be calculated on the basis of the licensee's sales of products incorporating the licensor's technology and competing products, i.e. the total sales of the licensee on the product market in question. Where the licensor is also a supplier of products on the relevant market, the licensor's sales on the product market in question must also be taken into account. In the calculation of market shares for product markets, however, sales made by other licensees are not taken into account when calculating the licensee's and/ or licensor's market share.

72. Market shares should be calculated on the basis of sales value data where such data are available. Such data normally provide a more accurate indication of the strength of a technology than volume data. However, where value based data are not available, estimates based on other reliable market information may be used, including market sales volume data.

73. The principles set out above can be illustrated by the following examples:

Licensing between non-competitors

Example 1

Company A is specialised in developing bio-technological products and techniques and has developed a new product Xeran. It is not active as a producer of Xeran, for which it has neither the production nor the distribution facilities. Company B is one of the producers of competing products, produced with freely available non-proprietary technologies. In year 1, B was selling EUR 25 million worth of products produced with the freely available technologies. In year 2, A gives a licence to B to produce Xeran. In that year B sells EUR 15 million produced with the help of the freely available technologies and EUR 15 million of Xeran. In year 3 and the following years B produces and sells only Xeran worth EUR 40 million annually. In addition in year 2, A is also licensing to C. C was not active on that product market before. C produces and sells only Xeran, EUR 10 million in year 2 and EUR 15 million in year 3 and thereafter. It is established that the total market of Xeran and its substitutes where B and C are active is worth EUR 200 million in each year.

In year 2, the year the licence agreement is concluded, A's market share on the technology market is 0% as its market share has to be calculated on the basis of the total sales of Xeran in the preceding year. In year 3 A's market share on the technology market is 12,5%, reflecting the value of Xeran produced by B and C in the preceding year 2. In year 4 and thereafter A's market share on the technology market is 27,5%, reflecting the value of Xeran produced by B and C in the preceding year.

In year 2 B's market share on the product market is 12,5%, reflecting B's EUR 25 million sales in year 1. In year 3 B's market share is 15% because its sales have increased to EUR 30 million in year 2. In year 4 and thereafter B's market share is 20% as its sales are EUR 40 million annually. C's market share on the product market is 0% in year 1 and 2,5% in year 3 and 7,5% thereafter. As the licence agreements are between non-competitors and the individual market shares of A, B and C are below 30% each year, the agreements fall within the safe harbour of the TTBER.

Example 2

The situation is the same as in example 1, however now B and C are operating in different geographic markets. It is established that the total market of Xeran and its substitutes is worth EUR 100 million annually in each geographic market.

In this case, A's market share on the technology market has to be calculated for each of the two geographic markets. In the market where B is active A's market share depends on the sale of Xeran by B. As in this example the total market is assumed to be EUR 100 million, i.e. half the size of the market in example 1, the market share of A is 0% in year 2, 15% in year 3 and 40% thereafter. B's market share is 25% in year 2, 30% in year 3 and 40% thereafter. In year 2 and 3 both A's and B's market share does not exceed the 30% threshold. The threshold is however

---

> exceeded from year 4 and this means that, in line with Article 8(2) of the TTBER, after year 6 the licence agreement between A and B can no longer benefit from the safe harbour but has to be assessed on an individual basis.
>
> *In the market where C is active A's market share depends on the sale of Xeran by C. A's market share on the technology market, based on C's sales in the previous year, is therefore 0% in year 2, 10% in year 3 and 15% thereafter. The market share of C on the product market is the same: 0% in year 2, 10% in year 3 and 15% thereafter. The licence agreement between A and C therefore falls within the safe harbour for the whole period.*

Licensing between competitors

> Example 3
>
> Companies A and B are active on the same relevant product and geographic market for a certain chemical product. They also each own a patent on different technologies used to produce this product. In year 1 A and B sign a cross licence agreement licensing each other to use their respective technologies. In year 1 A and B produce only with their own technology and A sells EUR 15 million of the product and B sells EUR 20 million of the product. From year 2 they both use their own and the other's technology. From that year onward A sells EUR 10 million of the product produced with its own technology and EUR 10 million of the product produced with B's technology. B sells from year 2 EUR 15 million of the product produced with its own technology and EUR 10 million of the product produced with A's technology. It is established that the total market of the product and its substitutes is worth EUR 100 million in each year.
>
> To assess the licence agreement under the TTBER, the market shares of A and B have to be calculated both on the technology market and the product market. The market share of A on the technology market depends on the amount of the product sold in the preceding year that was produced, by both A and B, with A's technology. In year 2 the market share of A on the technology market is therefore 15%, reflecting its own production and sales of EUR 15 million in year 1. From year 3 A's market share on the technology market is 20%, reflecting the EUR 20 million sale of the product produced with A's technology and produced and sold by A and B (EUR 10 million each). Similarly, in year 2 B's market share on the technology market is 20% and thereafter 25%.
>
> The market shares of A and B on the product market depend on their respective sales of the product in the previous year, irrespective of the technology used. The market share of A on the product market is 15% in year 2 and 20% thereafter. The market share of B on the product market is 20% in year 2 and 25% thereafter.
>
> As the agreement is between competitors, their combined market share, both on the technology and on the product market, has to be below the 20% market share threshold in order to benefit from the safe harbour. It is clear that this is not the case here. The combined market share on the technology market and on the product market is 35% in year 2 and 45% thereafter. This agreement between competitors will therefore have to be assessed on an individual basis.

Commentary
para 73: **B&C:** 9.149. 9.150 **F&N:** 10.122

4. Hardcore restrictions of competition under the Block Exemption Regulation

4.1. General principles

74. Article 4 of the TTBER contains a list of hardcore restrictions of competition. The classification of a restraint as a hardcore restriction of competition is based on the nature of the restriction and experience showing that such restrictions are almost always anti-competitive. In line with the case

law of the Community Courts[39] such a restriction may result from the clear objective of the agreement or from the circumstances of the individual case (cf. paragraph 14 above).

Notes
[39] See e.g. the case law cited in note 15.

75. When a technology transfer agreement contains a hardcore restriction of competition, it follows from Article 4(1) and 4(2) of the TTBER that the agreement as a whole falls outside the scope of the block exemption. For the purposes of the TTBER hardcore restrictions cannot be severed from the rest of the agreement. Moreover, the Commission considers that in the context of individual assessment hardcore restrictions of competition will only in exceptional circumstances fulfil the four conditions of Article [101](3) (cf. paragraph 18 above).

Commentary
para 75: F&N: 10.93

76. Article 4 of the TTBER distinguishes between agreements between competitors and agreements between non-competitors.

4.2. Agreements between competitors

77. Article 4(1) lists the hardcore restrictions for licensing between competitors. According to Article 4(1), the TTBER does not cover agreements which, directly or indirectly, in isolation or in combination with other factors under the control of the parties, have as their object:

(a) The restriction of a party's ability to determine its prices when selling products to third parties;

(b) The limitation of output, except limitations on the output of contract products imposed on the licensee in a non-reciprocal agreement or imposed on only one of the licensees in a reciprocal agreement;

(c) The allocation of markets or customers except

(i) the obligation on the licensee(s) to produce with the licensed technology only within one or more technical fields of use or one or more product markets;

(ii) the obligation on the licensor and/or the licensee, in a non-reciprocal agreement, not to produce with the licensed technology within one or more technical fields of use or one or more product markets or one or more exclusive territories reserved for the other party;

(iii) the obligation on the licensor not to license the technology to another licensee in a particular territory;

(iv) the restriction, in a non-reciprocal agreement, of active and/or passive sales by the licensee and/or the licensor into the exclusive territory or to the exclusive customer group reserved for the other party;

(v) the restriction, in a non-reciprocal agreement, of active sales by the licensee into the exclusive territory or to the exclusive customer group allocated by the licensor to another licensee provided that the latter was not a competing undertaking of the licensor at the time of the conclusion of its own licence;

(vi) the obligation on the licensee to produce the contract products only for its own use provided that the licensee is not restricted in selling the contract products actively and passively as spare parts for its own products;

(vii) the obligation on the licensee in a non-reciprocal agreement to produce the contract products only for a particular customer, where the licence was granted in order to create an alternative source of supply for that customer;

(d) The restriction of the licensee's ability to exploit its own technology or the restriction of the ability of any of the parties to the agreement to carry out research and development, unless such latter restriction is indispensable to prevent the disclosure of the licensed know-how to third parties.

78. For a number of hardcore restrictions the TTBER makes a distinction between reciprocal and non-reciprocal agreements. The hardcore list is stricter for reciprocal agreements than for

Part C Substantive Antitrust Matters

non-reciprocal agreements between competitors. Reciprocal agreements are cross-licensing agreements where the licensed technologies are competing technologies or can be used for the production of competing products. A non-reciprocal agreement is an agreement where only one of the parties is licensing its technology to the other party or where in case of cross-licensing the licensed technologies are not competing technologies and cannot be used for the production of competing products. An agreement is not reciprocal merely because the agreement contains a grant back obligation or because the licensee licenses back own improvements of the licensed technology. In case at a later point in time a non-reciprocal agreement becomes a reciprocal agreement due to the conclusion of a second licence between the same parties, they may have to revise the first licence in order to avoid that the agreement contains a hardcore restriction. In the assessment of the individual case the Commission will take into account the time lapsed between the conclusion of the first and the second licence.

Commentary
para 78: B&C: 9.082 F&N: 10.96

79. The hardcore restriction of competition contained in Article 4(1)(a) concerns agreements between competitors that have as their object the fixing of prices for products sold to third parties, including the products incorporating the licensed technology. Price fixing between competitors constitutes a restriction of competition by its very object. Price fixing can for instance take the form of a direct agreement on the exact price to be charged or on a price list with certain allowed maximum rebates. It is immaterial whether the agreement concerns fixed, minimum, maximum or recommended prices. Price fixing can also be implemented indirectly by applying disincentives to deviate from an agreed price level, for example, by providing that the royalty rate will increase if product prices are reduced below a certain level. However, an obligation on the licensee to pay a certain minimum royalty does not in itself amount to price fixing.

Commentary
para 79: B&C: 9.086, 9.111, 9.153

80. When royalties are calculated on the basis of individual product sales, the amount of the royalty has a direct impact on the marginal cost of the product and thus a direct impact on product prices.[40] Competitors can therefore use cross licensing with reciprocal running royalties as a means of co-ordinating prices on downstream product markets.[41] However, the Commission will only treat cross licences with reciprocal running royalties as price fixing where the agreement is devoid of any pro-competitive purpose and therefore does not constitute a bona fide licensing arrangement. In such cases where the agreement does not create any value and therefore has no valid business justification, the arrangement is a sham and amounts to a cartel.

Notes
40 See in this respect paragraph 98 of the Guidelines on the application of Article [101](3) of the Treaty cited in note 2.
41 This is also the case where one party grants a licence to the other party and accepts to buy a physical input from the licensee. The purchase price can serve the same function as the royalty.

Commentary
para 80: B&C: 9.086, 9.091, 9.154

81. The hardcore restriction contained in Article 4(1)(a) also covers agreements whereby royalties are calculated on the basis of all product sales irrespective of whether the licensed technology is being used. Such agreements are also caught by Article 4(1)(d) according to which the licensee must not be restricted in his ability to use his own technology (see paragraph 95 below). In general such agreements restrict competition since the agreement raises the cost of using the licensee's own competing technology and restricts competition that existed in the absence of the agreement.[42] This is so both in the case of reciprocal and non-reciprocal arrangements. Exceptionally, however, an agreement whereby royalties are calculated on the basis of all product sales may fulfil the conditions of Article [101](3) in an individual case where on the basis of objective factors it can be concluded that the restriction is indispensable for pro-competitive licensing to occur. This may

be the case where in the absence of the restraint it would be impossible or unduly difficult to calculate and monitor the royalty payable by the licensee, for instance because the licensor's technology leaves no visible trace on the final product and practicable alternative monitoring methods are unavailable.

Notes
[42] See in this respect Case 193/83, *Windsurfing International*, [1986] ECR 611, paragraph 67.

Commentary
para [81]: B&C: 9.153

82. The hardcore restriction of competition set out in Article 4(1)(b) concerns reciprocal output restrictions on the parties. An output restriction is a limitation on how much a party may produce and sell. Article 4(1)(b) does not cover output limitations on the licensee in a non-reciprocal agreement or output limitations on one of the licensees in a reciprocal agreement provided that the output limitation only concerns products produced with the licensed technology. Article 4(1)(b) thus identifies as hardcore restrictions reciprocal output restrictions on the parties and output restrictions on the licensor in respect of his own technology. When competitors agree to impose reciprocal output limitations, the object and likely effect of the agreement is to reduce output in the market. The same is true of agreements that reduce the incentive of the parties to expand output, for example by obliging each other to make payments if a certain level of output is exceeded.

Commentary
para 82: B&C: 9.155 F&N: 10.99

83. The more favourable treatment of non-reciprocal quantity limitations is based on the consideration that a one-way restriction does not necessarily lead to a lower output on the market while also the risk that the agreement is not a bona fide licensing arrangement is less when the restriction is non-reciprocal. When a licensee is willing to accept a one-way restriction, it is likely that the agreement leads to a real integration of complementary technologies or an efficiency enhancing integration of the licensor's superior technology with the licensee's productive assets. In a reciprocal agreement an output restriction on one of the licensees is likely to reflect the higher value of the technology licensed by one of the parties and may serve to promote pro-competitive licensing.

Commentary
para 83: B&C: 9.155 F&N: 10.99

84. The hardcore restriction of competition set out in Article 4(1)(c) concerns the allocation of markets and customers. Agreements whereby competitors share markets and customers have as their object the restriction of competition. It is a hardcore restriction where competitors in a reciprocal agreement agree not to produce in certain territories or not to sell actively and/or passively into certain territories or to certain customers reserved for the other party.

85. Article 4(1)(c) applies irrespective of whether the licensee remains free to use his own technology. Once the licensee has tooled up to use the licensor's technology to produce a given product, it may be costly to maintain a separate production line using another technology in order to serve customers covered by the restrictions. Moreover, given the anti-competitive potential of the restraint the licensee may have little incentive to produce under his own technology. Such restrictions are also highly unlikely to be indispensable for pro-competitive licensing to occur.

Commentary
para 85: F&N: 10.102

86. Under Article 4(1)(c)(ii) it is not a hardcore restriction for the licensor in a non-reciprocal agreement to grant the licensee an exclusive licence to produce on the basis of the licensed technology in a particular territory and thus agree not to produce himself the contract products in or provide

387

the contract products from that territory. Such exclusive licences are block exempted irrespective of the scope of the territory. If the licence is world-wide, the exclusivity implies that the licensor abstains from entering or remaining on the market. The block exemption also applies where the licence is limited to one or more technical fields of use or one or more product markets. The purpose of agreements covered by Article 4(1)(c)(ii) may be to give the licensee an incentive to invest in and develop the licensed technology. The object of the agreement is therefore not necessarily to share markets.

Commentary
para 86: B&C: 9.157, 9.158

87. According to Article 4(1)(c)(iv) and for the same reason, the block exemption also applies to non-reciprocal agreements whereby the parties agree not to sell actively or passively[43] into an exclusive territory or to an exclusive customer group reserved for the other party.

88. According to Article 4(1)(c)(iii) it is also not a hardcore restriction if the licensor appoints the licensee as his sole licensee in a particular territory, implying that third parties will not be licensed to produce on the basis of the licensor's technology in the territory in question. In the case of such sole licences the block exemption applies irrespective of whether the agreement is reciprocal or not given that the agreement does not affect the ability of the parties to fully exploit their own technology in the respective territories.

Notes
[43] For a general definition of active and passive sales, reference is made to paragraph 50 of the Guidelines on vertical restraints cited in note 36.

Commentary
para 88: B&C: 9.158 **F&N:** 10.105

89. Article 4(1)(c)(v) excludes from the hardcore list and thus block exempts up to the market share threshold restrictions in a non-reciprocal agreement on active sales by a licensee into the territory or to the customer group allocated by the licensor to another licensee. It is a condition, however, that the protected licensee was not a competitor of the licensor when the agreement was concluded. It is not warranted to hardcore such restrictions. By allowing the licensor to grant a licensee, who was not already on the market, protection against active sales by licensees which are competitors of the licensor and which for that reason are already established on the market, such restrictions are likely to induce the licensee to exploit the licensed technology more efficiently. On the other hand, if the licensees agree between themselves not to sell actively or passively into certain territories or to certain customer groups, the agreement amounts to a cartel amongst the licensees. Given that such agreements do not involve any transfer of technology they fall outside the scope of the TTBER.

Commentary
para 89: B&C: 9.158, 9.159

90. According to Article 4(1)(c)(i) restrictions in agreements between competitors that limit the licence to one or more product markets or technical fields of use[44] are not hardcore restrictions. Such restrictions are block exempted up to the market share threshold of 20% irrespective of whether the agreement is reciprocal or not. It is a condition for the application of the block exemption, however, that the field of use restrictions do not go beyond the scope of the licensed technologies. It is also a condition that licensees are not limited in the use of their own technology (see Article 4(1)(d)). Where licensees are limited in the use of their own technology the agreement amounts to market sharing.

Notes
[44] Field of use restrictions are further dealt with in section IV.2.4 below.

Commentary
para 90: B&C: 9.157 **F&N:** 10.104

91. The block exemption applies irrespective of whether the field of use restriction is symmetrical or asymmetrical. An asymmetrical field of use restriction in a reciprocal licence agreement implies that both parties are allowed to use the respective technologies that they license in only within different fields of use. As long as the parties are unrestricted in the use of their own technologies, it is not assumed that the agreement leads the parties to abandon or refrain from entering the field(s) covered by the licence to the other party. Even if the licensees tool up to use the licensed technology within the licensed field of use, there may be no impact on assets used to produce outside the scope of the licence. It is important in this regard that the restriction relates to distinct product markets or fields of use and not to customers, allocated by territory or by group, who purchase products falling within the same product market or technical field of use. The risk of market sharing is considered substantially greater in the latter case (see paragraph 85 above). In addition, field of use restrictions may be necessary to promote pro-competitive licensing (see paragraph 182 below).

Commentary
para 91: F&N: 10.104

92. Article 4(1)(c)(vi) contains a further exception, namely captive use restrictions, i.e. a requirement whereby the licensee may produce the products incorporating the licensed technology only for his own use. Where the contract product is a component the licensee can thus be obliged to produce that component only for incorporation into his own products and can be obliged not to sell the components to other producers. The licensee must be able, however, to sell the components as spare parts for his own products and must thus be able to supply third parties that perform after sale services on these products. Captive use restrictions as defined may be necessary to encourage the dissemination of technology, particularly between competitors, and are covered by the block exemption. Such restrictions are also dealt with in section IV.2.5 below.

Commentary
para 92: B&C: 9.159

93. Finally, Article 4(1)(c)(vii) excludes from the hardcore list an obligation on the licensee in a non-reciprocal agreement to produce the contract products only for a particular customer with a view to creating an alternative source of supply for that customer. It is thus a condition for the application of Article 4(1)(c)(vii) that the licence is limited to creating an alternative source of supply for that particular customer. It is not a condition, however, that only one such licence is granted. Article 4(1)(c)(vii) also covers situations where more than one undertaking is licensed to supply the same specified customer. The potential of such agreements to share markets is limited where the licence is granted only for the purpose of supplying a particular customer. In particular, in such circumstances it cannot be assumed that the agreement will cause the licensee to cease exploiting his own technology.

94. The hardcore restriction of competition set out in Article 4(1)(d) covers firstly restrictions on any of the parties' ability to carry out research and development. Both parties must be free to carry out independent research and development. This rule applies irrespective of whether the restriction applies to a field covered by the licence or to other fields. However, the mere fact that the parties agree to provide each other with future improvements of their respective technologies does not amount to a restriction on independent research and development. The effect on competition of such agreements must be assessed in light of the circumstances of the individual case. Article 4(1)(d) also does not extend to restrictions on a party to carry out research and development with third parties, where such restriction is necessary to protect the licensor's know-how against disclosure. In order to be covered by the exception, the restrictions imposed to protect the licensor's know-how against disclosure must be necessary and proportionate to ensure such protection. For instance, where the agreement designates particular employees of the licensee to be trained in and responsible for the use of the licensed know-how, it may be sufficient to oblige the licensee not to allow those employees to be involved in research and development with third parties. Other safeguards may be equally appropriate.

Commentary
para 94: B&C: 9.108, 9.160 F&N: 10.112

95. According to Article 4(1)(d) the licensee must also be unrestricted in the use of his own competing technology provided that in so doing he does not make use of the technology licensed from
the licensor. In relation to his own technology the licensee must not be subject to limitations in
terms of where he produces or sells, how much he produces or sells and at what price he sells. He
must also not be obliged to pay royalties on products produced on the basis of his own technology
(cf. paragraph 81 above). Moreover, the licensee must not be restricted in licensing his own technology to third parties. When restrictions are imposed on the licensee's use of his own technology
or to carry out research and development, the competitiveness of the licensee's technology is
reduced. The effect of this is to reduce competition on existing product and technology markets
and to reduce the licensee's incentive to invest in the development and improvement of his
technology.

Commentary
para 95: B&C: 9.160 F&N: 10.105

4.3. Agreements between non-competitors

96. Article 4(2) lists the hardcore restrictions for licensing between non-competitors. According to
this provision, the TTBER does not cover agreements which, directly or indirectly, in isolation or
in combination with other factors under the control of the parties, have as their object:

(a) the restriction of a party's ability to determine its prices when selling products to third parties,
without prejudice to the possibility to impose a maximum sale price or recommend a sale
price, provided that it does not amount to a fixed or minimum sale price as a result of pressure
from, or incentives offered by, any of the parties;

(b) the restriction of the territory into which, or of the customers to whom, the licensee may passively sell the contract products, except:

(i) the restriction of passive sales into an exclusive territory or to an exclusive customer
group reserved for the licensor;

(ii) the restriction of passive sales into an exclusive territory or to an exclusive customer
group allocated by the licensor to another licensee during the first two years that this
other licensee is selling the contract products in that territory or to that customer group;

(iii) the obligation to produce the contract products only for its own use provided that the
licensee is not restricted in selling the contract products actively and passively as spare
parts for its own products;

(iv) the obligation to produce the contract products only for a particular customer, where
the licence was granted in order to create an alternative source of supply for that
customer;

(v) the restriction of sales to end users by a licensee operating at the wholesale level of trade;

(vi) the restriction of sales to unauthorised distributors by the members of a selective distribution system;

(c) the restriction of active or passive sales to end users by a licensee which is a member of a selective distribution system and which operates at the retail level, without prejudice to the possibility of prohibiting a member of the system from operating out of an unauthorised place of
establishment.

97. The hardcore restriction of competition set out in Article 4(2)(a) concerns the fixing of prices
charged when selling products to third parties. More specifically, this provision covers restrictions
which have as their direct or indirect object the establishment of a fixed or a minimum selling
price or a fixed or minimum price level to be observed by the licensor or the licensee when selling
products to third parties. In the case of agreements that directly establish the selling price, the
restriction is clear-cut. However, the fixing of selling prices can also be achieved through indirect
means. Examples of the latter are agreements fixing the margin, fixing the maximum level of
discounts, linking the sales price to the sales prices of competitors, threats, intimidation,

warnings, penalties, or contract terminations in relation to observance of a given price level. Direct or indirect means of achieving price fixing can be made more effective when combined with measures to identify price-cutting, such as the implementation of a price monitoring system, or the obligation on licensees to report price deviations. Similarly, direct or indirect price fixing can be made more effective when combined with measures that reduce the licensee's incentive to lower his selling price, such as the licensor obliging the licensee to apply a most-favoured-customer clause, i.e. an obligation to grant to a customer any more favourable terms granted to any other customer. The same means can be used to make maximum or recommended prices work as fixed or minimum selling prices. However, the provision of a list of recommended prices to or the imposition of a maximum price on the licensee by the licensor is not considered in itself as leading to fixed or minimum selling prices.

Commentary
para 97: B&C: 9.111, 9.123, 9.162 F&N: 10.98

98. Article 4(2)(b) identifies as hardcore restrictions of competition agreements or concerted practices that have as their direct or indirect object the restriction of passive sales by licensees of products incorporating the licensed technology.[45] Passive sales restrictions on the licensee may be the result of direct obligations, such as the obligation not to sell to certain customers or to customers in certain territories or the obligation to refer orders from these customers to other licensees. It may also result from indirect measures aimed at inducing the licensee to refrain from making such sales, such as financial incentives and the implementation of a monitoring system aimed at verifying the effective destination of the licensed products. Quantity limitations may be an indirect means to restrict passive sales. The Commission will not assume that quantity limitations as such serve this purpose. However, it will be otherwise where quantity limitations are used to implement an underlying market partitioning agreement. Indications thereof include the adjustment of quantities over time to cover only local demand, the combination of quantity limitations and an obligation to sell minimum quantities in the territory, minimum royalty obligations linked to sales in the territory, differentiated royalty rates depending on the destination of the products and the monitoring of the destination of products sold by individual licensees. The general hardcore restriction covering passive sales by licensees is subject to a number of exceptions, which are dealt with below.

Notes
[45] This hardcore restriction applies to licence agreements concerning trade within the Community. As regards agreements concerning exports outside the Community or imports/re-imports from outside the Community see Case C-306/96, *Javico*, [1998] ECR I-1983.

Commentary
para 98: B&C: 9.165 F&N: 10.109, 10.143

99. Article 4(2)(b) does not cover sales restrictions on the licensor. All sales restrictions on the licensor are block exempted up to the market share threshold of 30%. The same applies to all restrictions on active sales by the licensee, with the exception of what is said on active selling in paragraphs 105 and 106 below. The block exemption of restrictions on active selling is based on the assumption that such restrictions promote investments, non-price competition and improvements in the quality of services provided by the licensees by solving free rider problems and hold-up problems. In the case of restrictions of active sales between licensees' territories or customer groups, it is not a condition that the protected licensee has been granted an exclusive territory or an exclusive customer group. The block exemption also applies to active sales restrictions where more than one licensee has been appointed for a particular territory or customer group. Efficiency enhancing investment is likely to be promoted where a licensee can be ensured that he will only face active sales competition from a limited number of licensees inside the territory and not also from licensees outside the territory.

Commentary
para 99: B&C: 9.163, 9.164 F&N: 10.110

100. Restrictions on active and passive sales by licensees into an exclusive territory or to an exclusive customer group reserved for the licensor do not constitute hardcore restrictions of competition (cf. Article 4(2)(b)(i)). Indeed, they are block exempted. It is presumed that up to the market share threshold such restraints, where restrictive of competition, promote pro-competitive dissemination of technology and integration of such technology into the production assets of the licensee. For a territory or customer group to be reserved for the licensor, it is not required that the licensor is actually producing with the licensed technology in the territory or for the customer group in question. A territory or customer group can also be reserved by the licensor for later exploitation.

Commentary
para 100: **B&C:** 9.165 **F&N:** 10.111, 14.83

101. Restrictions on passive sales by licensees into an exclusive territory or customer group allocated to another licensee are block exempted for two years calculated from the date on which the protected licensee first markets the products incorporating the licensed technology inside his exclusive territory or to his exclusive customer group (cf. Article 4(2)(b)(ii)). Licensees often have to commit substantial investments in production assets and promotional activities in order to start up and develop a new territory. The risks facing the new licensee are therefore likely to be substantial, in particular since promotional expenses and investment in assets required to produce on the basis of a particular technology are often sunk, i.e. they cannot be recovered if the licensee exits the market. In such circumstances, it is often the case that licensees would not enter into the licence agreement without protection for a certain period of time against (active and) passive sales into their territory by other licensees. Restrictions on passive sales into the exclusive territory of a licensee by other licensees therefore often fall outside Article [101](1) for a period of up to two years from the date on which the product incorporating the licensed technology was first put on the market in the exclusive territory by the licensee in question. However, to the extent that in individual cases such restrictions are caught by Article [101](1) they are block exempted. After the expiry of this two-year period restrictions on passive sales between licensees constitute hardcore restrictions. Such restrictions are generally caught by Article [101](1) and are unlikely to fulfil the conditions of Article [101](3). In particular, passive sales restrictions are unlikely to be indispensable for the attainment of efficiencies.[46]

Notes
[46] See in this respect paragraph 77 of the judgment in *Nungesser* cited in note 13.

Commentary
para 101: **B&C:** 9.165 **F&N:** 3.357, 3.465, 10.66, 10.111, 14.83

102. Article 4(2)(b)(iii) brings under the block exemption a restriction whereby the licensee is obliged to produce products incorporating the licensed technology only for his own (captive) use. Where the contract product is a component the licensee can thus be obliged to use that product only for incorporation into his own products and can be obliged not to sell the product to other producers. The licensee must however be able to actively and passively sell the products as spare parts for his own products and must thus be able to supply third parties that perform after sale services on these products. Captive use restrictions are also dealt with in section IV.2.5 below.

Commentary
para 102: **B&C:** 9.166

103. As in the case of agreements between competitors (cf. paragraph 93 above) the block exemption also applies to agreements whereby the licensee is obliged to produce the contract products only for a particular customer in order to provide that customer with an alternative source of supply (cf. Article 4(2)(b)(iv)). In the case of agreements between non-competitors, such restrictions are unlikely to be caught by Article [101](1).

Commentary
para 103: B&C: 9.166

104. Article 4(2)(b)(v) brings under the block exemption an obligation on the licensee not to sell to end users and thus only to sell to retailers. Such an obligation allows the licensor to assign the wholesale distribution function to the licensee and normally falls outside Article [101](1).[47]

Notes
[47] See in this respect Case 26/76, *Metro (I)*, [1977] ECR 1875.

Commentary
para 104: B&C: 9.167

105. Finally Article 4(2)(b)(vi) brings under the block exemption a restriction on the licensee not to sell to unauthorised distributors. This exception allows the licensor to impose on the licensees an obligation to form part of a selective distribution system. In that case, however, the licensees must according to Article 4(2)(c) be permitted to sell both actively and passively to end users, without prejudice to the possibility to restrict the licensee to a wholesale function as foreseen in Article 4(2)(b)(v) (cf. the previous paragraph).

106. It is recalled (cf. paragraph 39 above) that the block exemption covers licence agreements whereby the licensor imposes obligations which the licensee must or may impose on his buyers, including distributors. However, these obligations must comply with the competition rules applicable to supply and distribution agreements. Since the TTBER is limited to agreements between two parties the agreements concluded between the licensee and his buyers implementing such obligations are not covered by the TTBER. Such agreements are only block exempted when they comply with Regulation 2790/1999 (cf. section 2.5.2 above).

Commentary
para 106: B&C: 9.168

5. *Excluded restrictions*

107. Article 5 of the TTBER lists four types of restrictions that are not block exempted and which thus require individual assessment of their anti-competitive and pro-competitive effects. It follows from Article 5 that the inclusion in a licence agreement of any of the restrictions contained in these provisions does not prevent the application of the block exemption to the rest of the agreement. It is only the individual restriction in question that is not block exempted, implying that individual assessment is required. Accordingly, the rule of severability applies to the restrictions set out in Article 5.

108. Article 5(1) provides that the block exemption shall not apply to the following three obligations:
    (a) Any direct or indirect obligation on the licensee to grant an exclusive licence to the licensor or to a third party designated by the licensor in respect of its own severable improvements to or its new applications of the licensed technology.
    (b) Any direct or indirect obligation on the licensee to assign to the licensor or to a third party designated by the licensor rights to severable improvements to or new applications of the licensed technology.
    (c) Any direct or indirect obligation on the licensee not to challenge the validity of intellectual property rights held by the licensor in the common market. However, the TTBER does cover the possibility for the licensor to terminate the licence agreement in the event that the licensee challenges the validity of the licensed technology.

The purpose of Article 5(1)(a), (b) and (c) is to avoid block exemption of agreements that may reduce the incentive of licensees to innovate.

109. Article 5(1)(a) and 5(1)(b) concerns exclusive grant backs or assignments to the licensor of severable improvements of the licensed technology. An improvement is severable if it can be exploited without infringing upon the licensed technology. An obligation to grant the licensor an exclusive licence to severable improvements of the licensed technology or to assign such

improvements to the licensor is likely to reduce the licensee's incentive to innovate since it hinders the licensee in exploiting his improvements, including by way of licensing to third parties. This is the case both where the severable improvement concerns the same application as the licensed technology and where the licensee develops new applications of the licensed technology. According to Article 5(1)(a) and (b) such obligations are not block exempted. However, the block exemption does cover non-exclusive grant back obligations in respect of severable improvements. This is so even where the grant back obligation is non-reciprocal, i.e. only imposed on the licensee, and where under the agreement the licensor is entitled to feed-on the severable improvements to other licensees. A non-reciprocal grant back obligation may promote innovation and the dissemination of new technology by permitting the licensor to freely determine whether and to what extent to pass on his own improvements to his licensees. A feed-on clause may also promote the dissemination of technology because each licensee knows at the time of contracting that he will be on an equal footing with other licensees in terms of the technology on the basis of which he is producing. Exclusive grant backs and obligations to assign non-severable improvements are not restrictive of competition within the meaning of Article [101](1) since non-severable improvements cannot be exploited by the licensee without the licensor's permission.

Commentary
para 109: B&C: 9.119, 9.170 **F&N:** 10.116

110. The application of Article 5(1)(a) and (b) does not depend on whether or not the licensor pays consideration in return for acquiring the improvement or for obtaining an exclusive licence. However, the existence and level of such consideration may be a relevant factor in the context of an individual assessment under Article [101]. When grant backs are made against consideration it is less likely that the obligation creates a disincentive for the licensee to innovate. In the assessment of exclusive grant backs outside the scope of the block exemption the market position of the licensor on the technology market is also a relevant factor. The stronger the position of the licensor, the more likely it is that exclusive grant back obligations will have restrictive effects on competition in innovation. The stronger the position of the licensor's technology the more likely it is that the licensee will be an important source of innovation and future competition. The negative impact of grant back obligations can also be increased in case of parallel networks of licence agreements containing such obligations. When available technologies are controlled by a limited number of licensors that impose exclusive grant back obligations on licensees, the risk of anti-competitive effects is greater than where there are a number of technologies only some of which are licensed on exclusive grant back terms.

Commentary
para 110: B&C: 9.170 **F&N:** 10.116

111. The risk of negative effects on innovation is higher in the case of cross licensing between competitors where a grant back obligation on both parties is combined with an obligation on both parties to share with the other party improvements of his own technology. The sharing of all improvements between competitors may prevent each competitor from gaining a competitive lead over the other (see also paragraph 208 below). However, the parties are unlikely to be prevented from gaining a competitive lead over each other where the purpose of the licence is to permit them to develop their respective technologies and where the licence does not lead them to use the same technological base in the design of their products. This is the case where the purpose of the licence is to create design freedom rather than to improve the technological base of the licensee.

112. The excluded restriction set out in Article 5(1)(c) concerns non-challenge clauses, i.e. obligations not to challenge the validity of the licensor's intellectual property. The reason for excluding non-challenge clauses from the scope of the block exemption is the fact that licensees are normally in the best position to determine whether or not an intellectual property right is invalid. In the interest of undistorted competition and in conformity with the principles underlying the protection of intellectual property, invalid intellectual property rights should be eliminated.

Invalid intellectual property stifles innovation rather than promoting it. Article [101](1) is likely to apply to non-challenge clauses where the licensed technology is valuable and therefore creates a competitive disadvantage for undertakings that are prevented from using it or are only able to use it against payment of royalties.[48] In such cases the conditions of Article [101](3) are unlikely to be fulfilled.[49] However, the Commission takes a favourable view of non-challenge clauses relating to know-how where once disclosed it is likely to be impossible or very difficult to recover the licensed know-how. In such cases, an obligation on the licensee not to challenge the licensed know-how promotes dissemination of new technology, in particular by allowing weaker licensors to license stronger licensees without fear of a challenge once the know-how has been absorbed by the licensee.

Notes

[48] If the licensed technology is outdated no restriction of competition arises, see in this respect Case 65/86, *Bayer v Süllhofer*, [1988] ECR 5249.

[49] As to non-challenge clauses in the context of settlement agreements see point 209 below.

Commentary
para 112: **B&C**: 9.124, 9.171 **F&N**: 10.117

113. The TTBER covers the possibility for the licensor to terminate the licence agreement in the event of a challenge of the licensed technology. Accordingly, the licensor is not forced to continue dealing with a licensee that challenges the very subject matter of the licence agreement, implying that upon termination any further use by the licensee of the challenged technology is at the challenger's own risk. Article 5(1)(c) ensures, however, that the TTBER does not cover contractual obligations obliging the licensee not to challenge the licensed technology, which would permit the licensor to sue the licensee for breach of contract and thereby create a further disincentive for the licensee to challenge the validity of the licensor's technology. The provision thereby ensures that the licensee is in the same position as third parties.

Commentary
para 113: **F&N**: 10.117

114. Article 5(2) excludes from the scope of the block exemption, in the case of agreements between non-competitors, any direct or indirect obligation limiting the licensee's ability to exploit his own technology or limiting the ability of the parties to the agreement to carry out research and development, unless such latter restriction is indispensable to prevent the disclosure of licensed know-how to third parties. The content of this condition is the same as that of Article 4(1)(d) of the hardcore list concerning agreements between competitors, which is dealt with in paragraphs 94 and 95 above. However, in the case of agreements between non-competitors it cannot be considered that such restrictions generally have negative effects on competition or that the conditions of Article [101](3) are generally not satisfied.[50] Individual assessment is required.

Notes
[50] See paragraph 14 above.

115. In the case of agreements between non-competitors, the licensee normally does not own a competing technology. However, there may be cases where for the purposes of the block exemption the parties are considered non-competitors in spite of the fact that the licensee does own a competing technology. This is the case where the licensee owns a technology but does not license it and the licensor is not an actual or potential supplier on the product market. For the purposes of the block exemption the parties are in such circumstances neither competitors on the technology market nor competitors on the product market.[51] In such cases it is important to ensure that the licensee is not restricted in his ability to exploit his own technology and further develop it. This technology constitutes a competitive constraint in the market, which should be preserved. In such a situation restrictions on the licensee's use of his own technology or on research and development are normally considered to be restrictive of competition and not to satisfy the conditions of Article [101](3). For instance, an obligation on the licensee to pay royalties not only on the basis of products it produces with the licensed technology but also on the basis of

Part C Substantive Antitrust Matters

products it produces with its own technology will generally limit the ability of the licensee to exploit its own technology and thus be excluded from the scope of the block exemption.

Notes

51 See paragraphs 66 and 67 above.

116. In cases where the licensee does not own a competing technology or is not already developing such a technology, a restriction on the ability of the parties to carry out independent research and development may be restrictive of competition where only a few technologies are available. In that case the parties may be an important (potential) source of innovation in the market. This is particularly so where the parties possess the necessary assets and skills to carry out further research and development. In that case the conditions of Article [101](3) are unlikely to be fulfilled. In other cases where several technologies are available and where the parties do not possess special assets or skills, the restriction on research and development is likely to either fall outside Article [101](1) for lack of an appreciable restrictive effect or satisfy the conditions of Article [101](3). The restraint may promote the dissemination of new technology by assuring the licensor that the licence does not create a new competitor and by inducing the licensee to focus on the exploitation and development of the licensed technology. Moreover, Article [101](1) only applies where the agreement reduces the licensee's incentive to improve and exploit his own technology. This is for instance not likely to be the case where the licensor is entitled to terminate the licence agreement once the licensee commences to produce on the basis of his own competing technology. Such a right does not reduce the licensee's incentive to innovate, since the agreement can only be terminated when a commercially viable technology has been developed and products produced on the basis thereof are ready to be put on the market.

6. *Withdrawal and disapplication of the Block Exemption Regulation*

6.1. Withdrawal procedure

117. According to Article 6 of the TTBER, the Commission and the competition authorities of the Member States may withdraw the benefit of the block exemption in respect of individual agreements that do not fulfil the conditions of Article [101](3). The power of the competition authorities of the Member States to withdraw the benefit of the block exemption is limited to cases where the relevant geographic market is no wider than the territory of the Member State in question.

118. The four conditions of Article [101](3) are cumulative and must all be fulfilled for the exception rule to be applicable.52 The block exemption can therefore be withdrawn where a particular agreement fails one or more of the four conditions.

Notes

52 See in this respect paragraph 42 of the Guidelines on the application of Article [101](3) of the Treaty, cited in note 2.

119. Where the withdrawal procedure is applied, the withdrawing authority bears the burden of proving that the agreement falls within the scope of Article [101](1) and that the agreement does not satisfy all four conditions of Article [101](3). Given that withdrawal implies that the agreement in question restricts competition within the meaning of Article [101](1) and does not fulfil the conditions of Article [101](3), withdrawal is necessarily accompanied by a negative decision based on Articles 5, 7 or 9 of Regulation 1/2003.

Commentary

para 119: B&C: 9.173

120. According to Article 6, withdrawal may in particular be warranted in the following circumstances:

   1. access of third parties' technologies to the market is restricted, for instance by the cumulative effect of parallel networks of similar restrictive agreements prohibiting licensees from using third party technology;

2. access of potential licensees to the market is restricted, for instance by the cumulative effect of parallel networks of similar restrictive agreements preventing licensors from licensing to other licensees;

3. without any objectively valid reason the parties refrain from exploiting the licensed technology.

121. Articles 4 and 5 of the TTBER, containing the list of hardcore restrictions of competition and excluded restrictions, aim at ensuring that block exempted agreements do not reduce the incentive to innovate, do not delay the dissemination of technology, and do not unduly restrict competition between the licensor and licensee or between licensees. However, the list of hardcore restrictions and the list of excluded restrictions do not take into account all the possible impacts of licence agreements. In particular, the block exemption does not take account of any cumulative effect of similar restrictions contained in networks of licence agreements. Licence agreements may lead to foreclosure of third parties both at the level of the licensor and at the level of the licensee. Foreclosure of other licensors may stem from the cumulative effect of networks of licence agreements prohibiting the licensees from exploiting competing technologies, leading to the exclusion of other (potential) licensors. Foreclosure of licensors is likely to arise in cases where most of the undertakings on the market that could (efficiently) take a competing licence are prevented from doing so as a consequence of restrictive agreements and where potential licensees face relatively high barriers to entry. Foreclosure of other licensees may stem from the cumulative effect of licence agreements prohibiting licensors from licensing other licensees and thereby preventing potential licensees from gaining access to the necessary technology. The issue of foreclosure is examined in more detail in section IV.2.7 below. In addition, the Commission is likely to withdraw the benefit of the block exemption where a significant number of licensors of competing technologies in individual agreements impose on their licensees to extend to them more favourable conditions agreed with other licensors.

122. The Commission is also likely to withdraw the benefit of the block exemption where the parties refrain from exploiting the licensed technology, unless they have an objective justification for doing so. Indeed, when the parties do not exploit the licensed technology, no efficiency enhancing activity takes place, in which case the very rationale of the block exemption disappears. However, exploitation does not need to take the form of an integration of assets. Exploitation also occurs where the licence creates design freedom for the licensee by allowing him to exploit his own technology without facing the risk of infringement claims by the licensor. In the case of licensing between competitors, the fact that the parties do not exploit the licensed technology may be an indication that the arrangement is a disguised cartel. For these reasons the Commission will examine very closely cases of non-exploitation.

Commentary
para 122: B&C: 9.173

6.2. Disapplication of the Block Exemption Regulation

123. Article 7 of the TTBER enables the Commission to exclude from the scope of the TTBER, by means of regulation, parallel networks of similar agreements where these cover more than 50% of a relevant market. Such a measure is not addressed to individual undertakings but concerns all undertakings whose agreements are defined in the regulation disapplying the TTBER.

124. Whereas withdrawal of the benefit of the TTBER by the Commission under Article 6 implies the adoption of a decision under Articles 7 or 9 of Regulation 1/2003, the effect of a Commission disapplication regulation under Article 7 of the TTBER is merely to remove, in respect of the restraints and the markets concerned, the benefit of the TTBER and to restore the full application of Article [101](1) and (3). Following the adoption of a regulation declaring the TTBER inapplicable for a particular market in respect of agreements containing certain restraints, the criteria developed by the relevant case law of the Community Courts and by notices and previous decisions adopted by the Commission will give guidance on the application of Article [101] to individual agreements. Where appropriate, the Commission will take a decision in an individual case, which can provide guidance to all the undertakings operating on the market concerned.

125. For the purpose of calculating the 50% market coverage ratio, account must be taken of each individual network of licence agreements containing restraints, or combinations of restraints, producing similar effects on the market.

126. Article 7 does not entail an obligation on the part of the Commission to act where the 50% market-coverage ratio is exceeded. In general, disapplication is appropriate when it is likely that access to the relevant market or competition therein is appreciably restricted. In assessing the need to apply Article 7, the Commission will consider whether individual withdrawal would be a more appropriate remedy. This may depend, in particular, on the number of competing undertakings contributing to a cumulative effect on a market or the number of affected geographic markets within the Community.

Commentary
para 126: B&C: 9.174

127. Any regulation adopted under Article 7 must clearly set out its scope. This means, first, that the Commission must define the relevant product and geographic market(s) and, secondly, that it must identify the type of licensing restraint in respect of which the TTBER will no longer apply. As regards the latter aspect, the Commission may modulate the scope of its regulation according to the competition concern which it intends to address. For instance, while all parallel networks of non-compete arrangements will be taken into account for the purpose of establishing the 50% market coverage ratio, the Commission may nevertheless restrict the scope of the disapplication regulation only to non-compete obligations exceeding a certain duration. Thus, agreements of a shorter duration or of a less restrictive nature might be left unaffected, due to the lesser degree of foreclosure attributable to such restraints. Where appropriate, the Commission may also provide guidance by specifying the market share level which, in the specific market context, may be regarded as insufficient to bring about a significant contribution by an individual undertaking to the cumulative effect. In general, when the market share of the products incorporating a technology licensed by an individual licensor does not exceed 5%, the agreement or network of agreements covering that technology is not considered to contribute significantly to a cumulative foreclosure effect.[53]

Notes
53 See in this respect paragraph 8 of the Commission Notice on agreements of minor importance, cited in note 17.

Commentary
para 127: B&C: 9.174

128. The transitional period of not less than six months that the Commission will have to set under Article 7(2) should allow the undertakings concerned to adapt their agreements to take account of the regulation disapplying the TTBER.

129. A regulation disapplying the TTBER will not affect the block exempted status of the agreements concerned for the period preceding its entry into force.

IV. Application of Article [101](1) and [101](3) Outside the Scope of the Block Exemption Regulation

1. The general framework for analysis

130. Agreements that fall outside the block exemption, for example because the market share thresholds are exceeded or the agreement involves more than two parties, are subject to individual assessment. Agreements that either do not restrict competition within the meaning of Article [101](1) or which fulfil the conditions of Article [101](3) are valid and enforceable. It is recalled that there is no presumption of illegality of agreements that fall outside the scope of the block exemption provided that they do not contain hardcore restrictions of competition. In particular, there is no presumption that Article [101](1) applies merely because the market share thresholds are exceeded. Individual assessment based on the principles described in these guidelines is required.

Commentary
para 130: F&N: 10.63

131. In order to promote predictability beyond the application of the TTBER and to confine detailed analysis to cases that are likely to present real competition concerns, the Commission takes the view that outside the area of hardcore restrictions Article [101] is unlikely to be infringed where there are four or more independently controlled technologies in addition to the technologies controlled by the parties to the agreement that may be substitutable for the licensed technology at a comparable cost to the user. In assessing whether the technologies are sufficiently substitutable the relative commercial strength of the technologies in question must be taken into account. The competitive constraint imposed by a technology is limited if it does not constitute a commercially viable alternative to the licensed technology. For instance, if due to network effects in the market consumers have a strong preference for products incorporating the licensed technology, other technologies already on the market or likely to come to market within a reasonable period of time may not constitute a real alternative and may therefore impose only a limited competitive constraint. The fact that an agreement falls outside the safe harbour described in this paragraph does not imply that the agreement is caught by Article [101](1) and, if so, that the conditions of Article [101](3) are not satisfied. As for the market share safe harbour of the TTBER, this additional safe harbour merely creates a negative presumption that the agreement is not prohibited by Article [101]. Outside the safe harbour individual assessment of the agreement based on the principles developed in these guidelines is required.

Commentary
para 131: B&C: 1.074, 9.075, 9.076 **F&N:** 10.123

1.1. The relevant factors

132. In the application of Article [101] to individual cases it is necessary to take due account of the way in which competition operates on the market in question. The following factors are particularly relevant in this respect:

   (a) the nature of the agreement;
   (b) the market position of the parties;
   (c) the market position of competitors;
   (d) the market position of buyers of the licensed products;
   (e) entry barriers;
   (f) maturity of the market; and
   (g) other factors.

   The importance of individual factors may vary from case to case and depends on all other factors. For instance, a high market share of the parties is usually a good indicator of market power, but in the case of low entry barriers it may not be indicative of market power. It is therefore not possible to provide firm rules on the importance of the individual factors.

Commentary
para 132: B&C: 9.077

133. Technology transfer agreements can take many shapes and forms. It is therefore important to analyse the nature of the agreement in terms of the competitive relationship between the parties and the restraints that it contains. In the latter regard it is necessary to go beyond the express terms of the agreement. The existence of implicit restraints may be derived from the way in which the agreement has been implemented by the parties and the incentives that they face.

134. The market position of the parties provides an indication of the degree of market power, if any, possessed by the licensor, the licensee or both. The higher their market share the greater their market power is likely to be. This is particularly so where the market share reflects cost advantages or other competitive advantages vis-à-vis competitors. These competitive advantages may for instance result from being a first mover in the market, from holding essential patents or from having superior technology.

135. In analysing the competitive relationship between the parties it is sometimes necessary to go beyond the analysis set out in the above sections II.3 on market definition and II.4 on the distinction between competitors and non-competitors. Even where the licensor is not an actual or potential supplier on the product market and the licensee is not an actual or potential competitor on the technology market, it is relevant to the analysis whether the licensee owns a competing technology, which is not being licensed. If the licensee has a strong position on the product market, an agreement granting him an exclusive licence to a competing technology can restrict competition significantly compared to the situation where the licensor does not grant an exclusive licence or licences other undertakings.

Commentary
para 135: F&N: 16.114

---

136. Market shares and possible competitive advantages and disadvantages are also used to assess the market position of competitors. The stronger the actual competitors and the greater their number the less risk there is that the parties will be able to individually exercise market power. However, if the number of competitors is rather small and their market position (size, costs, R & D potential, etc.) is rather similar, this market structure may increase the risk of collusion.

137. The market position of buyers provides an indication of whether or not one or more buyers possess buyer power. The first indicator of buying power is the market share of the buyer on the purchase market. This share reflects the importance of his demand for possible suppliers. Other indicators focus on the position of the buyer on his resale market, including characteristics such as a wide geographic spread of his outlets, and his brand image amongst final consumers. In some circumstances buyer power may prevent the licensor and/or the licensee from exercising market power on the market and thereby solve a competition problem that would otherwise have existed. This is particularly so when strong buyers have the capacity and the incentive to bring new sources of supply on to the market in the case of a small but permanent increase in relative prices. Where the strong buyers merely extract favourable terms from the supplier or simply pass on any price increase to their customers, the position of the buyers is not such as to prevent the exercise of market power by the licensee on the product market and therefore not such as to solve the competition problem on that market.[54]

Notes
[54] See in this respect Case T-228/97, *Irish Sugar*, [1999] ECR II-2969, paragraph 101.

---

138. Entry barriers are measured by the extent to which incumbent companies can increase their price above the competitive level without attracting new entry. In the absence of entry barriers, easy and quick entry would render price increases unprofitable. When effective entry, preventing or eroding the exercise of market power, is likely to occur within one or two years, entry barriers can, as a general rule, be said to be low. Entry barriers may result from a wide variety of factors such as economies of scale and scope, government regulations, especially where they establish exclusive rights, state aid, import tariffs, intellectual property rights, ownership of resources where the supply is limited due to for instance natural limitations, essential facilities, a first mover advantage or brand loyalty of consumers created by strong advertising over a period of time. Restrictive agreements entered into by undertakings may also work as an entry barrier by making access more difficult and foreclosing (potential) competitors. Entry barriers may be present at all stages of the research and development, production and distribution process. The question whether certain of these factors should be described as entry barriers depends particularly on whether they entail sunk costs. Sunk costs are those costs which have to be incurred to enter or be active on a market but which are lost when the market is exited. The more costs are sunk, the more potential entrants have to weigh the risks of entering the market and the more credibly incumbents can threaten that they will match new competition, as sunk costs make it costly for incumbents to leave the market. In general, entry requires sunk costs, sometimes minor and sometimes major. Therefore, actual competition is in general more effective and will weigh more heavily in the assessment of a case than potential competition.

139. A mature market is a market that has existed for some time, where the technology used is well known and widespread and not changing very much and in which demand is relatively stable or declining. In such a market restrictions of competition are more likely to have negative effects than in more dynamic markets.

140. In the assessment of particular restraints other factors may have to be taken into account. Such factors include cumulative effects, i.e. the coverage of the market by similar agreements, the duration of the agreements, the regulatory environment and behaviour that may indicate or facilitate collusion like price leadership, pre-announced price changes and discussions on the "right" price, price rigidity in response to excess capacity, price discrimination and past collusive behaviour.

Commentary
para 140: B&C: 9.077

1.2. Negative effects of restrictive licence agreements

141. The negative effects on competition on the market that may result from restrictive technology transfer agreements include the following:

    1. reduction of inter-technology competition between the companies operating on a technology market or on a market for products incorporating the technologies in question, including facilitation of collusion, both explicit and tacit;
    2. foreclosure of competitors by raising their costs, restricting their access to essential inputs or otherwise raising barriers to entry; and
    3. reduction of intra-technology competition between undertakings that produce products on the basis of the same technology.

Commentary
para 141: B&C: 9.072

142. Technology transfer agreements may reduce inter-technology competition, i.e. competition between undertakings that license or produce on the basis of substitutable technologies. This is particularly so where reciprocal obligations are imposed. For instance, where competitors transfer competing technologies to each other and impose a reciprocal obligation to provide each other with future improvements of their respective technologies and where this agreement prevents either competitor from gaining a technological lead over the other, competition in innovation between the parties is restricted (see also paragraph 208 below).

Commentary
para 142: B&C: 9.078

143. Licensing between competitors may also facilitate collusion. The risk of collusion is particularly high in concentrated markets. Collusion requires that the undertakings concerned have similar views on what is in their common interest and on how the co-ordination mechanisms function. For collusion to work the undertakings must also be able to monitor each other's market behaviour and there must be adequate deterrents to ensure that there is an incentive not to depart from the common policy on the market, while entry barriers must be high enough to limit entry or expansion by outsiders. Agreements can facilitate collusion by increasing transparency in the market, by controlling certain behaviour and by raising barriers to entry. Collusion can also exceptionally be facilitated by licensing agreements that lead to a high degree of commonality of costs, because undertakings that have similar costs are more likely to have similar views on the terms of coordination.[55]

Notes
[55] See in this respect paragraph 23 of the Guidelines on horizontal cooperation agreements, cited in note 20.

144. Licence agreements may also affect inter-technology competition by creating barriers to entry for and expansion by competitors. Such foreclosure effects may stem from restraints that

Part C Substantive
Antitrust Matters

prevent licensees from licensing from third parties or create disincentives for them to do so. For instance, third parties may be foreclosed where incumbent licensors impose non-compete obligations on licensees to such an extent that an insufficient number of licensees are available to third parties and where entry at the level of licensees is difficult. Suppliers of substitutable technologies may also be foreclosed where a licensor with a sufficient degree of market power ties together various parts of a technology and licenses them together as a package while only part of the package is essential to produce a certain product.

145. Licence agreements may also reduce intra-technology competition, i.e. competition between undertakings that produce on the basis of the same technology. An agreement imposing territorial restraints on licensees, preventing them from selling into each other's territory reduces competition between them. Licence agreements may also reduce intra-technology competition by facilitating collusion between licensees. Moreover, licence agreements that reduce intra-technology competition may facilitate collusion between owners of competing technologies or reduce inter-technology competition by raising barriers to entry.

Commentary
para 145: B&C: 9.078

1.3. Positive effects of restrictive licence agreements and the framework for analysing such effects

146. Even restrictive licence agreements mostly also produce pro-competitive effects in the form of efficiencies, which may outweigh their anti-competitive effects. This assessment takes place within the framework of Article [101](3), which contains an exception from the prohibition rule of Article [101](1). For this exception to be applicable the licence agreement must produce objective economic benefits, the restrictions on competition must be indispensable to attain the efficiencies, consumers must receive a fair share of the efficiency gains, and the agreement must not afford the parties the possibility of eliminating competition in respect of a substantial part of the products concerned.

147. The assessment of restrictive agreements under Article [101](3) is made within the actual context in which they occur[56] and on the basis of the facts existing at any given point in time. The assessment is sensitive to material changes in the facts. The exception rule of Article [101](3) applies as long as the four conditions are fulfilled and ceases to apply when that is no longer the case.[57] However, when applying Article [101](3) in accordance with these principles it is necessary to take into account the initial sunk investments made by any of the parties and the time needed and the restraints required to commit and recoup an efficiency enhancing investment. Article [101] cannot be applied without considering the *ex ante* investment and the risks relating thereto. The risk facing the parties and the sunk investment that must be committed to implement the agreement can thus lead to the agreement falling outside Article [101](1) or fulfilling the conditions of Article [101](3), as the case may be, for the period of time required to recoup the investment.

Notes
56 See Joined Cases 25/84 and 26/84, *Ford*, [1985] ECR 2725.
57 See in this respect for example Commission Decision in TPS (OJ L 90, 2.4.1999, p.6). Similarly, the prohibition of Article [101](1) also only applies as long as the agreement has a restrictive object or restrictive effects.

148. The first condition of Article [101](3) requires an assessment of what are the objective benefits in terms of efficiencies produced by the agreement. In this respect, licence agreements have the potential of bringing together complementary technologies and other assets allowing new or improved products to be put on the market or existing products to be produced at lower cost. Outside the context of hardcore cartels, licensing often occurs because it is more efficient for the licensor to licence the technology than to exploit it himself. This may particularly be the case where the licensee already has access to the necessary production assets. The agreement allows the licensee to gain access to a technology that can be combined with these assets, allowing him to exploit new or improved technologies. Another example of potentially efficiency enhancing licensing is where the licensee already has a technology and where the combination of this

technology and the licensor's technology gives rise to synergies. When the two technologies are combined the licensee may be able to attain a cost/output configuration that would not otherwise be possible. Licence agreements may also give rise to efficiencies at the distribution stage in the same way as vertical distribution agreements. Such efficiencies can take the form of cost savings or the provision of valuable services to consumers. The positive effects of vertical agreements are described in the Guidelines on Vertical Restraints.[58] A further example of possible efficiency gains is agreements whereby technology owners assemble a technology package for licensing to third parties. Such pooling arrangements may in particular reduce transaction costs, as licensees do not have to conclude separate licence agreements with each licensor. Pro-competitive licensing may also occur to ensure design freedom. In sectors where large numbers of intellectual property rights exist and where individual products may infringe upon a number of existing and future property rights, licence agreements whereby the parties agree not to assert their property rights against each other are often pro-competitive because they allow the parties to develop their respective technologies without the risk of subsequent infringement claims.

Notes

[58] Cited in note 36. See in particular paragraphs 115 et seq.

149. In the application of the indispensability test contained in Article [101](3) the Commission will in particular examine whether individual restrictions make it possible to perform the activity in question more efficiently than would have been the case in the absence of the restriction concerned. In making this assessment the market conditions and the realities facing the parties must be taken into account. Undertakings invoking the benefit of Article [101](3) are not required to consider hypothetical and theoretical alternatives. They must, however, explain and demonstrate why seemingly realistic and significantly less restrictive alternatives would be significantly less efficient. If the application of what appears to be a commercially realistic and less restrictive alternative would lead to a significant loss of efficiencies, the restriction in question is treated as indispensable. In some cases, it may also be necessary to examine whether the agreement as such is indispensable to achieve the efficiencies. This may for example be so in the case of technology pools that include complementary but non-essential technologies,[59] in which case it must be examined to what extent such inclusion gives rise to particular efficiencies or whether, without a significant loss of efficiencies, the pool could be limited to technologies for which there are no substitutes. In the case of simple licensing between two parties it is generally not necessary to go beyond an examination of the indispensability of individual restraints. Normally there is no less restrictive alternative to the licence agreement as such.

Notes

[59] As to these concepts see section IV.4.1 below.

150. The condition that consumers must receive a fair share of the benefits implies that consumers of the products produced under the licence must at least be compensated for the negative effects of the agreement.[60] This means that the efficiency gains must fully off-set the likely negative impact on prices, output and other relevant factors caused by the agreement. They may do so by changing the cost structure of the undertakings concerned, giving them an incentive to reduce price, or by allowing consumers to gain access to new or improved products, compensating for any likely price increase.[61]

Notes

[60] See paragraph 85 of the Guidelines on the application of Article [101](3) of the Treaty, cited in note 2.
[61] Idem, paragraphs 98 and 102.

151. The last condition of Article [101](3), according to which the agreement must not afford the parties the possibility of eliminating competition in respect of a substantial part of the products concerned, presupposes an analysis of remaining competitive pressures on the market and the impact of the agreement on such sources of competition. In the application of the last condition of Article [101](3) the relationship between Article [101](3) and Article [102] must be taken

into account. According to settled case law, the application of Article [101](3) cannot prevent the application of Article [102] of the Treaty.[62] Moreover, since Articles [101] and [102] both pursue the aim of maintaining effective competition on the market, consistency requires that Article [101](3) be interpreted as precluding any application of the exception rule to restrictive agreements that constitute an abuse of a dominant position.[63]

Notes

[62] See paragraph 130 of the judgment cited in note 2. Similarly, the application of Article [101](3) does not prevent the application of the Treaty rules on the free movement of goods, services, persons and capital. These provisions are in certain circumstances applicable to agreements, decisions and concerted practices within the meaning of Article [101](1), see to that effect Case C-309/99, *Wouters*, [2002] ECR I-1577, paragraph 120.

[63] See in this respect Case T-51/89, *Tetra Pak (I)*, [1990] ECR II-309. See also paragraph 106 of the Guidelines on the application of Article [101](3) of the Treaty cited in note 2 above.

152. The fact that the agreement substantially reduces one dimension of competition does not necessarily mean that competition is eliminated within the meaning of Article [101](3). A technology pool, for instance, can result in an industry standard, leading to a situation in which there is little competition in terms of the technological format. Once the main players in the market adopt a certain format, network effects may make it very difficult for alternative formats to survive. This does not imply, however, that the creation of a de facto industry standard always eliminates competition within the meaning of the last condition of Article [101](3). Within the standard, suppliers may compete on price, quality and product features. However, in order for the agreement to comply with Article [101](3), it must be ensured that the agreement does not unduly restrict competition and does not unduly restrict future innovation.

2. The application of Article [101] to various types of licensing restraints

153. This section deals with various types of restraints that are commonly included in licence agreements. Given their prevalence it is useful to provide guidance as to how they are assessed outside the safe harbour of the TTBER. Restraints that have already been dealt with in the preceding parts of these guidelines, in particular sections III.4 and III.5, are only dealt with briefly in the present section.

154. This section covers both agreements between non-competitors and agreements between competitors. In respect of the latter a distinction is made — where appropriate — between reciprocal and non-reciprocal agreements. No such distinction is required in the case of agreements between non-competitors. When undertakings are neither actual nor potential competitors on a relevant technology market or on a market for products incorporating the licensed technology, a reciprocal licence is for all practical purposes no different from two separate licences. Arrangements whereby the parties assemble a technology package, which is then licensed to third parties, are technology pools, which are dealt with in section 4 below.

155. This section does not deal with obligations in licence agreements that are generally not restrictive of competition within the meaning of Article [101](1). These obligations include but are not limited to:

(a) confidentiality obligations;

(b) obligations on licensees not to sub-license;

(c) obligations not to use the licensed technology after the expiry of the agreement, provided that the licensed technology remains valid and in force;

(d) obligations to assist the licensor in enforcing the licensed intellectual property rights;

(e) obligations to pay minimum royalties or to produce a minimum quantity of products incorporating the licensed technology; and

(f) obligations to use the licensor's trade mark or indicate the name of the licensor on the product.

Commentary

para 155: **B&C:** 9.125, 9.127
para 155(d): **B&C:** 9.122
para 155(e): **B&C:** 9.086, 9.109
para 155(f): **B&C:** 9.112

2.1. Royalty obligations

156. The parties to a licence agreement are normally free to determine the royalty payable by the licensee and its mode of payment without being caught by Article [101](1). This principle applies both to agreements between competitors and agreements between non-competitors. Royalty obligations may for instance take the form of lump sum payments, a percentage of the selling price or a fixed amount for each product incorporating the licensed technology. In cases where the licensed technology relates to an input which is incorporated into a final product it is as a general rule not restrictive of competition that royalties are calculated on the basis of the price of the final product, provided that it incorporates the licensed technology. In the case of software licensing royalties based on the number of users and royalties calculated on a per machine basis are generally compatible with Article [101](1).

Commentary
para 156: B&C: 9.085, 9.089 F&N: 10.133

157. In the case of licence agreements between competitors it is recalled, see paragraphs and above, that in a limited number of circumstances royalty obligations may amount to price fixing, which is a hardcore restriction (cf. Article 4(1)(a)). It is a hardcore restriction under Article 4(1)(a) if competitors provide for reciprocal running royalties in circumstances where the licence is a sham, in that its purpose is not to allow an integration of complementary technologies or to achieve another pro-competitive aim. It is also a hardcore restriction under Article 4(1)(a) and 4(1)(d) if royalties extend to products produced solely with the licensee's own technology.

Commentary
para 157: B&C: 9.086, 9.090, 9.091

158. Other types of royalty arrangements between competitors are block exempted up to the market share threshold of 20% even if they restrict competition. Outside the safe harbour of the block exemption Article [101](1) may be applicable where competitors cross license and impose running royalties that are clearly disproportionate compared to the market value of the licence and where such royalties have a significant impact on market prices. In assessing whether the royalties are disproportionate it is relevant to have regard to the royalties paid by other licensees on the product market for the same or substitute technologies. In such cases it is unlikely that the conditions of Article [101](3) are satisfied. Article [101](1) may also apply where reciprocal running royalties per unit increase as output increases. If the parties have a significant degree of market power, such royalties may have the effect of limiting output.

Commentary
para 158: B&C: 9.091 F&N: 10.135

159. Notwithstanding the fact that the block exemption only applies as long as the technology is valid and in force, the parties can normally agree to extend royalty obligations beyond the period of validity of the licensed intellectual property rights without falling foul of Article [101](1). Once these rights expire, third parties can legally exploit the technology in question and compete with the parties to the agreement. Such actual and potential competition will normally suffice to ensure that the obligation in question does not have appreciable anti-competitive effects.

Commentary
para 159: B&C: 9.087

160. In the case of agreements between non-competitors the block exemption covers agreements whereby royalties are calculated on the basis of both products produced with the licensed technology and products produced with technologies licensed from third parties. Such arrangements may facilitate the metering of royalties. However, they may also lead to foreclosure by increasing the cost of using third party inputs and may thus have similar effects as a non-compete obligation. If royalties are paid not just on products produced with the licensed technology but also on products produced with third party technology, then the royalties will increase the

cost of the latter products and reduce demand for third party technology. Outside the scope of the block exemption it must therefore be examined whether the restriction has foreclosure effects. For that purpose it is appropriate to use the analytical framework set out in section 2.7 below. In the case of appreciable foreclosure effects such agreements are caught by Article [101] (1) and unlikely to fulfil the conditions of Article [101](3), unless there is no other practical way of calculating and monitoring royalty payments.

Commentary
para 160: B&C: 9.088

2.2. Exclusive licensing and sales restrictions

161. For the present purposes it is useful to distinguish between restrictions as to production within a given territory (exclusive or sole licences) and restrictions on the sale of products incorporating the licensed technology into a given territory and to a given customer group (sales restrictions).

2.2.1. Exclusive and sole licences

162. A licence is deemed to be exclusive if the licensee is the only one who is permitted to produce on the basis of the licensed technology within a given territory. The licensor thus undertakes not to produce itself or license others to produce within a given territory. This territory may cover the whole world. Where the licensor undertakes only not to licence third parties to produce within a given territory, the licence is a sole licence. Often exclusive or sole licensing is accompanied by sales restrictions that limit the parties in where they may sell products incorporating the licensed technology.

163. Reciprocal exclusive licensing between competitors falls under Article 4(1)(c), which identifies market sharing between competitors as a hardcore restriction. Reciprocal sole licensing between competitors is block exempted up to the market share threshold of 20%. Under such an agreement the parties mutually commit not to license their competing technologies to third parties. In cases where the parties have a significant degree of market power such agreements may facilitate collusion by ensuring that the parties are the only sources of output in the market based on the licensed technologies.

Commentary
para 163: B&C: 9.096, 9.106

164. Non-reciprocal exclusive licensing between competitors is block exempted up to the market share threshold of 20%. Above the market share threshold it is necessary to analyse what are the likely anti-competitive effects of such exclusive licensing. Where the exclusive licence is worldwide it implies that the licensor leaves the market. In cases where exclusivity is limited to a particular territory such as a Member State the agreement implies that the licensor abstains from producing goods and services inside the territory in question. In the context of Article [101](1) it must in particular be assessed what is the competitive significance of the licensor. If the licensor has a limited market position on the product market or lacks the capacity to effectively exploit the technology in the licensee's territory, the agreement is unlikely to be caught by Article [101](1). A special case is where the licensor and the licensee only compete on the technology market and the licensor, for instance being a research institute or a small research based undertaking, lacks the production and distribution assets to effectively bring to market products incorporating the licensed technology. In such cases Article [101](1) is unlikely to be infringed.

Commentary
para 164: B&C: 9.094 F&N: 10.126, 10.137

165. Exclusive licensing between non-competitors — to the extent that it is caught by Article [101] (1)[64] — is likely to fulfil the conditions of Article [101](3). The right to grant an exclusive licence is generally necessary in order to induce the licensee to invest in the licensed technology and to bring the products to market in a timely manner. This is in particular the case where the

licensee must make large investments in further developing the licensed technology. To intervene against the exclusivity once the licensee has made a commercial success of the licensed technology would deprive the licensee of the fruits of his success and would be detrimental to competition, the dissemination of technology and innovation. The Commission will therefore only exceptionally intervene against exclusive licensing in agreements between non-competitors, irrespective of the territorial scope of the licence.

Notes
64 See the judgment in *Nungesser* cited in note 13.

Commentary
para 165: **B&C:** 9.094 **F&N:** 10.126, 10.138

166. The main situation in which intervention may be warranted is where a dominant licensee obtains an exclusive licence to one or more competing technologies. Such agreements are likely to be caught by Article [101](1) and unlikely to fulfil the conditions of Article [101](3). It is a condition however that entry into the technology market is difficult and the licensed technology constitutes a real source of competition on the market. In such circumstances an exclusive licence may foreclose third party licensees and allow the licensee to preserve his market power.

Commentary
para 166: **B&C:** 9.094 **F&N:** 10.138

167. Arrangements whereby two or more parties cross licence each other and undertake not to licence third parties give rise to particular concerns when the package of technologies resulting from the cross licences creates a de facto industry standard to which third parties must have access in order to compete effectively on the market. In such cases the agreement creates a closed standard reserved for the parties. The Commission will assess such arrangements according to the same principles as those applied to technology pools (see section 4 below). It will normally be required that the technologies which support such a standard be licensed to third parties on fair, reasonable and non-discriminatory terms.[65] Where the parties to the arrangement compete with third parties on an existing product market and the arrangement relates to that product market a closed standard is likely to have substantial exclusionary effects. This negative impact on competition can only be avoided by licensing also to third parties.

Notes
65 See in this respect the Commission's Notice in the *Canon/Kodak Case* (OJ C 330, 1.11.1997, p.10) and the *IGR Stereo Television* Case mentioned in the XI Report on Competition Policy, paragraph 94.

2.2.2. Sales restrictions

168. Also as regards sales restrictions there is an important distinction to be made between licensing between competitors and between non-competitors.

169. Restrictions on active and passive sales by one or both parties in a reciprocal agreement between competitors are hardcore restrictions of competition under Article 4(1)(c). Sales restrictions on either party in a reciprocal agreement between competitors are caught by Article [101](1) and are unlikely to fulfil the conditions of Article [101](3). Such restrictions are generally considered market sharing, since they prevent the affected party from selling actively and passively into territories and to customer groups which he actually served or could realistically have served in the absence of the agreement.

170. In the case of non-reciprocal agreements between competitors the block exemption applies to restrictions on active and passive sales by the licensee or the licensor into the exclusive territory or to the exclusive customer group reserved for the other party (cf. Article 4(1)(c)(iv)). Above the market share threshold of 20% sales restrictions between licensor and licensee are caught by Article [101](1) when one or both of the parties have a significant degree of market power. Such restrictions, however, may be indispensable for the dissemination of valuable technologies and therefore fulfil the conditions of Article [101](3). This may be the case where the licensor has a

relatively weak market position in the territory where he exploits himself the technology. In such circumstances restrictions on active sales in particular may be indispensable to induce the licensor to grant the licence. In the absence thereof the licensor would risk facing active competition in his main area of activity. Similarly, restrictions on active sales by the licensor may be indispensable, in particular, where the licensee has a relatively weak market position in the territory allocated to him and has to make significant investments in order to efficiently exploit the licensed technology.

Commentary
para 170: **B&C:** 9.097 **F&N:** 3.465, 10.139

171. The block exemption also covers restrictions on active sales into the territory or to the customer group allocated to another licensee, who was not a competitor of the licensor at the time when he concluded the licence agreement with the licensor. It is a condition, however, that the agreement between the parties in question is non-reciprocal. Above the market share threshold such active sales restrictions are likely to be caught by Article [101](1) when the parties have a significant degree of market power. However, the restraint is likely to be indispensable within the meaning of Article [101](3) for the period of time required for the protected licensee to penetrate a new market and establish a market presence in the allocated territory or vis-à-vis the allocated customer group. This protection against active sales allows the licensee to overcome the asymmetry, which he faces due to the fact that some of the licensees are competing undertakings of the licensor and thus already established on the market. Restrictions on passive sales by licensees into a territory or to a customer group allocated to another licensee are hardcore restrictions under Article 4(1)(c) of the TTBER.

Commentary
para 171: **B&C:** 9.100

172. In the case of agreements between non-competitors sales restrictions between the licensor and a licensee are block exempted up to the market share threshold of 30%. Above the market share threshold restrictions on active and passive sales by licensees to territories or customer groups reserved for the licensor may fall outside Article [101](1) where on the basis of objective factors it can be concluded that in the absence of the sales restrictions licensing would not occur. A technology owner cannot normally be expected to create direct competition with himself on the basis of his own technology. In other cases sales restrictions on the licensee may be caught by Article [101](1) both where the licensor individually has a significant degree of market power and in the case of a cumulative effect of similar agreements concluded by licensors which together hold a strong position on the market.

Commentary
para 172: **B&C:** 9.098 **F&N:** 3.357, 10.140

173. Sales restrictions on the licensor, when caught by Article [101](1), are likely to fulfil the conditions of Article [101](3) unless there are no real alternatives to the licensor's technology on the market or such alternatives are licensed by the licensee from third parties. Such restrictions and in particular restrictions on active sales are likely to be indispensable within the meaning of Article [101](3) in order to induce the licensee to invest in the production, marketing and sale of the products incorporating the licensed technology. It is likely that the licensee's incentive to invest would be significantly reduced if he would face direct competition from the licensor whose production costs are not burdened by royalty payments, possibly leading to sub-optimal levels of investment.

Commentary
para 173: **B&C:** 9.096

174. As regards restrictions on sales between licensees in agreements between non-competitors, the TTBER block exempts restrictions on active selling between territories or customer groups.

Above the market share threshold restrictions on active sales between licensees' territories and customer groups limit intra-technology competition and are likely to be caught by Article [101] (1) when the individual licensee has a significant degree of market power. Such restrictions, however, may fulfil the conditions of Article [101](3) where they are necessary to prevent free riding and to induce the licensee to make the investment necessary for efficient exploitation of the licensed technology inside his territory and to promote sales of the licensed product. Restrictions on passive sales are covered by the hardcore list of Article 4(2)(b), cf. paragraph 101 above, when they exceed two years from the date on which the licensee benefiting from the restrictions first put the product incorporating the licensed technology on the market inside his exclusive territory. Passive sales restrictions exceeding this two-year period are unlikely to fulfil the conditions of Article [101](3).

Commentary
para 174: B&C: 9.100 **F&N:** 10.140

2.3. Output restrictions

175. Reciprocal output restrictions in licence agreements between competitors constitute a hardcore restriction covered by Article 4(1)(b) of the TTBER (cf. point [102] above). Article 4(1)(b) does not cover output restrictions imposed on the licensee in a non-reciprocal agreement or on one of the licensees in an reciprocal agreement. Such restrictions are block exempted up to the market share threshold of 20%. Above the market share threshold, output restrictions on the licensee may restrict competition where the parties have a significant degree of market power. However, Article [101](3) is likely to apply in cases where the licensor's technology is substantially better than the licensee's technology and the output limitation substantially exceeds the output of the licensee prior to the conclusion of the agreement. In that case the effect of the output limitation is limited even in markets where demand is growing. In the application of Article [101](3) it must also be taken into account that such restrictions may be necessary in order to induce the licensor to disseminate his technology as widely as possible. For instance, a licensor may be reluctant to license his competitors if he cannot limit the licence to a particular production site with a specific capacity (a site licence). Where the licence agreement leads to a real integration of complementary assets, output restrictions on the licensee may therefore fulfil the conditions of Article [101](3). However, this is unlikely to be the case where the parties have substantial market power.

Commentary
para 175: B&C: 9.103 **F&N:** 10.65, 10.141, 10.142

176. Output restrictions in licence agreements between non-competitors are block exempted up to the market share threshold of 30%. The main anti-competitive risk flowing from output restrictions on licensees in agreements between non-competitors is reduced intra-technology competition between licensees. The significance of such anti-competitive effects depends on the market position of the licensor and the licensees and the extent to which the output limitation prevents the licensee from satisfying demand for the products incorporating the licensed technology.

177. When output restrictions are combined with exclusive territories or exclusive customer groups, the restrictive effects are increased. The combination of the two types of restraints makes it more likely that the agreement serves to partition markets.

178. Output limitations imposed on the licensee in agreements between non-competitors may also have pro-competitive effects by promoting the dissemination of technology. As a supplier of technology, the licensor should normally be free to determine the output produced with the licensed technology by the licensee. If the licensor were not free to determine the output of the licensee, a number of licence agreements might not come into existence in the first place, which would have a negative impact on the dissemination of new technology. This is particularly likely to be the case where the licensor is also a producer, since in that case the output of the licensees may find their way back into the licensor's main area of operation and thus have a direct impact

on these activities. On the other hand, it is less likely that output restrictions are necessary in order to ensure dissemination of the licensor's technology when combined with sales restrictions on the licensee prohibiting him from selling into a territory or customer group reserved for the licensor.

Commentary
para 178: **B&C:** 9.103 **F&N:** 10.143

2.4. Field of use restrictions

179. Under a field of use restriction the licence is either limited to one or more technical fields of application or one or more product markets. There are many cases in which the same technology can be used to make different products or can be incorporated into products belonging to different product markets. A new moulding technology may for instance be used to make plastic bottles and plastic glasses, each product belonging to separate product markets. However, a single product market may encompass several technical fields of use. For instance a new engine technology may be employed in four cylinder engines and six cylinder engines. Similarly, a technology to make chipsets may be used to produce chipsets with up to four CPUs and more than four CPUs. A licence limiting the use of the licensed technology to produce say four cylinder engines and chipsets with up to four CPUs constitutes a technical field of use restriction.

Commentary
para 179: **B&C:** 9.106 **F&N:** 10.144

180. Given that field of use restrictions are block exempted and that certain customer restrictions are hardcore restrictions under Articles 4(1)(c) and 4(2)(b) of the TTBER, it is important to distinguish the two categories of restraints. A customer restriction presupposes that specific customer groups are identified and that the parties are restricted in selling to such identified groups. The fact that a technical field of use restriction may correspond to certain groups of customers within a product market does not imply that the restraint is to be classified as a customer restriction. For instance, the fact that certain customers buy predominantly or exclusively chipsets with more than four CPUs does not imply that a licence which is limited to chipsets with up to four CPUs constitutes a customer restriction. However, the field of use must be defined objectively by reference to identified and meaningful technical characteristics of the licensed product.

Commentary
para 180: **B&C:** 9.102, 9.106, 9.107, 9.157

181. A field of use restriction limits the exploitation of the licensed technology by the licensee to one or more particular fields of use without limiting the licensor's ability to exploit the licensed technology. In addition, as with territories, these fields of use can be allocated to the licensee under an exclusive or sole licence. Field of use restrictions combined with an exclusive or sole licence also restrict the licensor's ability to exploit his own technology, by preventing him from exploiting it himself, including by way of licensing to others. In the case of a sole license only licensing to third parties is restricted. Field of use restrictions combined with exclusive and sole licences are treated in the same way as the exclusive and sole licenses dealt with in section 2.2.1 above. In particular, for licensing between competitors, this means that reciprocal exclusive licensing is hardcore under Article 4(1)(c).

Commentary
para 181: **B&C:** 9.106

182. Field of use restrictions may have pro-competitive effects by encouraging the licensor to license his technology for applications that fall outside his main area of focus. If the licensor could not prevent licensees from operating in fields where he exploits the technology himself or in fields

where the value of the technology is not yet well established, it would be likely to create a disincentive for the licensor to license or would lead him to charge a higher royalty. It must also be taken into account that in certain sectors licensing often occurs to ensure design freedom by preventing infringement claims. Within the scope of the licence the licensee is able to develop his own technology without fearing infringement claims by the licensor.

Commentary
para 182: F&N: 10.65, 10.145

183. Field of use restrictions on licensees in agreements between actual or potential competitors are block exempted up to the market share threshold of 20%. The main competitive concern in the case of such restrictions is the risk that the licensee ceases to be a competitive force outside the licensed field of use. This risk is greater in the case of cross licensing between competitors where the agreement provides for asymmetrical field of use restrictions. A field of use restriction is asymmetrical where one party is permitted to use the licensed technology within one product market or technical field of use and the other party is permitted to use the other licensed technology within another product market or technical field of use. Competition concerns may in particular arise where the licensee's production facility, which is tooled up to use the licensed technology, is also used to produce with his own technology products outside the licensed field of use. If the agreement is likely to lead the licensee to reduce output outside the licensed field of use, the agreement is likely to be caught by Article [101](1). Symmetrical field of use restrictions, i.e. agreements whereby the parties are licensed to use each other's technologies within the same field(s) of use, are unlikely to be caught by Article [101](1). Such agreements are unlikely to restrict competition that existed in the absence of the agreement. Article [101](1) is also unlikely to apply in the case of agreements that merely enable the licensee to develop and exploit his own technology within the scope of the licence without fearing infringement claims by the licensor. In such circumstances field of use restrictions do not in themselves restrict competition that existed in the absence of the agreement. In the absence of the agreement the licensee also risked infringement claims outside the scope of the licensed field of use. However, if the licensee without business justification terminates or scales back his activities in the area outside the licensed field of use this may be an indication of an underlying market sharing arrangement amounting to a hardcore restriction under Article 4(1)(c) of the TTBER.

Commentary
para 183: **B&C:** 9.106 **F&N:** 10.146, 10.147

184. Field of use restrictions on licensee and licensor in agreements between non-competitors are block exempted up to the market share threshold of 30%. Field of use restrictions in agreements between non-competitors whereby the licensor reserves one or more product markets or technical fields of use for himself are generally either non-restrictive of competition or efficiency enhancing. They promote dissemination of new technology by giving the licensor an incentive to license for exploitation in fields in which he does not want to exploit the technology himself. If the licensor could not prevent licensees from operating in fields where the licensor exploits the technology himself, it would be likely to create a disincentive for the licensor to licence.

Commentary
para 184: **B&C:** 9.107 **F&N:** 10.148

185. In agreements between non-competitors the licensor is normally also entitled to grant sole or exclusive licences to different licensees limited to one or more fields of use. Such restrictions limit intra-technology competition between licensees in the same way as exclusive licensing and are analysed in the same way (cf. section 2.2.1 above).

Commentary
para 185: **B&C:** 9.107

2.5. Captive use restrictions

186. A captive use restriction can be defined as an obligation on the licensee to limit his production of the licensed product to the quantities required for the production of his own products and for the maintenance and repair of his own products. In other words, this type of use restriction takes the form of an obligation on the licensee to use the products incorporating the licensed technology only as an input for incorporation into his own production; it does not cover the sale of the licensed product for incorporation into the products of other producers. Captive use restrictions are block exempted up to the respective market share thresholds of 20% and 30%. Outside the scope of the block exemption it is necessary to examine what are the pro-competitive and anti-competitive effects of the restraint. In this respect it is necessary to distinguish agreements between competitors from agreements between non-competitors.

Commentary
para 186: B&C: 9.104, 9.105 F&N: 10.149

187. In the case of licence agreements between competitors a restriction that imposes on the licensee to produce under the licence only for incorporation into his own products prevents him from being a supplier of components to third party producers. If prior to the conclusion of the agreement, the licensee was not an actual or likely potential supplier of components to other producers, the captive use restriction does not change anything compared to the pre-existing situation. In those circumstances the restriction is assessed in the same way as in the case of agreements between non-competitors. If, on the other hand, the licensee is an actual or likely component supplier, it is necessary to examine what is the impact of the agreement on this activity. If by tooling up to use the licensor's technology the licensee ceases to use his own technology on a stand alone basis and thus to be a component supplier, the agreement restricts competition that existed prior to the agreement. It may result in serious negative market effects when the licensor has a significant degree of market power on the component market.

Commentary
para 187: B&C: 9.104 F&N: 10.149

188. In the case of licence agreements between non-competitors there are two main competitive risks stemming from captive use restrictions: (a) a restriction of intra-technology competition on the market for the supply of inputs and (b) an exclusion of arbitrage between licensees enhancing the possibility for the licensor to impose discriminatory royalties on licensees.

Commentary
para 188: B&C: 9.105

189. Captive use restrictions, however, may also promote pro-competitive licensing. If the licensor is a supplier of components, the restraint may be necessary in order for the dissemination of technology between non-competitors to occur. In the absence of the restraint the licensor may not grant the licence or may do so only against higher royalties, because otherwise he would create direct competition to himself on the component market. In such cases a captive use restriction is normally either not restrictive of competition or covered by Article [101](3). It is a condition, however, that the licensee is not restricted in selling the licensed product as replacement parts for his own products. The licensee must be able to serve the after market for his own products, including independent service organisations that service and repair the products produced by him.

Commentary
para 189: F&N: 10.150

190. Where the licensor is not a component supplier on the relevant market, the above reason for imposing captive use restrictions does not apply. In such cases a captive use restriction may in principle promote the dissemination of technology by ensuring that licensees do not sell to producers that compete with the licensor on other markets. However, a restriction on the

licensee not to sell into certain customer groups reserved for the licensor normally constitutes a less restrictive alternative. Consequently, in such cases a captive use restriction is normally not necessary for the dissemination of technology to take place.

Commentary
para 190: B&C: 9.105

2.6. Tying and bundling

191. In the context of technology licensing tying occurs when the licensor makes the licensing of one technology (the tying product) conditional upon the licensee taking a licence for another technology or purchasing a product from the licensor or someone designated by him (the tied product). Bundling occurs where two technologies or a technology and a product are only sold together as a bundle. In both cases, however, it is a condition that the products and technologies involved are distinct in the sense that there is distinct demand for each of the products and technologies forming part of the tie or the bundle. This is normally not the case where the technologies or products are by necessity linked in such a way that the licensed technology cannot be exploited without the tied product or both parts of the bundle cannot be exploited without the other. In the following the term "tying" refers to both tying and bundling.

192. Article 3 of the TTBER, which limits the application of the block exemption by market share thresholds, ensures that tying and bundling are not block exempted above the market share thresholds of 20% in the case of agreements between competitors and 30% in the case of agreements between non-competitors. The market share thresholds apply to any relevant technology or product market affected by the licence agreement, including the market for the tied product. Above the market share thresholds it is necessary to balance the anti-competitive and pro-competitive effects of tying.

193. The main restrictive effect of tying is foreclosure of competing suppliers of the tied product. Tying may also allow the licensor to maintain market power in the market for the tying product by raising barriers to entry since it may force new entrants to enter several markets at the same time. Moreover, tying may allow the licensor to increase royalties, in particular when the tying product and the tied product are partly substitutable and the two products are not used in fixed proportion. Tying prevents the licensee from switching to substitute inputs in the face of increased royalties for the tying product. These competition concerns are independent of whether the parties to the agreement are competitors or not. For tying to produce likely anti-competitive effects the licensor must have a significant degree of market power in the tying product so as to restrict competition in the tied product. In the absence of market power in the tying product the licensor cannot use his technology for the anti-competitive purpose of foreclosing suppliers of the tied product. Furthermore, as in the case of non-compete obligations, the tie must cover a certain proportion of the market for the tied product for appreciable foreclosure effects to occur. In cases where the licensor has market power on the market for the tied product rather than on the market for the tying product, the restraint is analysed as non-compete or quantity forcing, reflecting the fact that any competition problem has its origin on the market for the "tied" product and not on the market for the "tying" product.[66]

Notes
[66] For the applicable analytical framework see section 2.7 below and paragraphs 138 et seq. of the Guidelines on Vertical Restraints cited in note 36.

Commentary
para 193: B&C: 9.120 F&N: 10.153

194. Tying can also give rise to efficiency gains. This is for instance the case where the tied product is necessary for a technically satisfactory exploitation of the licensed technology or for ensuring that production under the licence conforms to quality standards respected by the licensor and other licensees. In such cases tying is normally either not restrictive of competition or covered by Article [101](3). Where the licensees use the licensor's trademark or brand name or where it is otherwise obvious to consumers that there is a link between the product incorporating the

licensed technology and the licensor, the licensor has a legitimate interest in ensuring that the quality of the products are such that it does not undermine the value of his technology or his reputation as an economic operator. Moreover, where it is known to consumers that the licensees (and the licensor) produce on the basis of the same technology it is unlikely that licensees would be willing to take a licence unless the technology is exploited by all in a technically satisfactory way.

Commentary
para 194: **B&C:** 9.120, 9.111 **F&N:** 10.154

195. Tying is also likely to be pro-competitive where the tied product allows the licensee to exploit the licensed technology significantly more efficiently. For instance, where the licensor licenses a particular process technology the parties can also agree that the licensee buys a catalyst from the licensor which is developed for use with the licensed technology and which allows the technology to be exploited more efficiently than in the case of other catalysts. Where in such cases the restriction is caught by Article [101](1), the conditions of Article [101](3) are likely to be fulfilled even above the market share thresholds.

Commentary
para 195: **F&N:** 10.154

2.7. Non-compete obligations

196. Non-compete obligations in the context of technology licensing take the form of an obligation on the licensee not to use third party technologies which compete with the licensed technology. To the extent that a non-compete obligation covers a product or additional technology supplied by the licensor the obligation is dealt with in the preceding section on tying.

197. The TTBER exempts non-compete obligations both in the case of agreements between competitors and in the case of agreements between non-competitors up to the market share thresholds of 20% and 30% respectively.

198. The main competitive risk presented by non-compete obligations is foreclosure of third party technologies. Non-compete obligations may also facilitate collusion between licensors in the case of cumulative use. Foreclosure of competing technologies reduces competitive pressure on royalties charged by the licensor and reduces competition between the incumbent technologies by limiting the possibilities for licensees to substitute between competing technologies. As in both cases the main problem is foreclosure, the analysis can in general be the same in the case of agreements between competitors and agreements between non-competitors. However, in the case of cross licensing between competitors where both agree not to use third party technologies the agreement may facilitate collusion between them on the product market, thereby justifying the lower market share threshold of 20%.

199. Foreclosure may arise where a substantial part of potential licensees are already tied to one or, in the case of cumulative effects, more sources of technology and are prevented from exploiting competing technologies. Foreclosure effects may result from agreements concluded by a single licensor with a significant degree of market power or by a cumulative effect of agreements concluded by several licensors, even where each individual agreement or network of agreements is covered by the TTBER. In the latter case, however, a serious cumulative effect is unlikely to arise as long as less than 50% of the market is tied. Above this threshold significant foreclosure is likely to occur when there are relatively high barriers to entry for new licensees. If barriers to entry are low, new licensees are able to enter the market and exploit commercially attractive technologies held by third parties and thus represent a real alternative to incumbent licensees. In order to determine the real possibility for entry and expansion by third parties it is also necessary to take account of the extent to which distributors are tied to licensees by non-compete obligations. Third party technologies only have a real possibility of entry if they have access to the necessary production and distribution assets. In other words, the ease of entry depends not only on the availability of licensees but also the extent to which they have access to distribution.

In assessing foreclosure effects at the distribution level the Commission will apply the analytical framework set out in section IV.2.1 of the Guidelines on Vertical Restraints.[67]

Notes
[67] See note 36.

Commentary
para 199: F&N: 10.156

200. When the licensor has a significant degree of market power, obligations on licensees to obtain the technology only from the licensor can lead to significant foreclosure effects. The stronger the market position of the licensor the higher the risk of foreclosing competing technologies. For appreciable foreclosure effects to occur the non-compete obligations do not necessarily have to cover a substantial part of the market. Even in the absence thereof, appreciable foreclosure effects may occur where non-compete obligations are targeted at undertakings that are the most likely to license competing technologies. The risk of foreclosure is particularly high where there is only a limited number of potential licensees and the licence agreement concerns a technology which is used by the licensees to make an input for their own use. In such cases the entry barriers for a new licensor are likely to be high. Foreclosure may be less likely in cases where the technology is used to make a product that is sold to third parties; although in this case the restriction also ties production capacity for the input in question, it does not tie demand for the product incorporating the input produced with the licensed technology. To enter the market in the latter case licensors only need access to one or more licensee(s) that have suitable production capacity and unless only few undertakings possess or are able to obtain the assets required to take a licence, it is unlikely that by imposing non-compete obligations on its licensees the licensor is able to deny competitors access to efficient licensees.

Commentary
para 200: F&N: 10.156

201. Non-compete obligations may also produce pro-competitive effects. First, such obligations may promote dissemination of technology by reducing the risk of misappropriation of the licensed technology, in particular know-how. If a licensee is entitled to license competing technologies from third parties, there is a risk that particularly licensed know-how would be used in the exploitation of competing technologies and thus benefit competitors. When a licensee also exploits competing technologies, it normally also makes monitoring of royalty payments more difficult, which may act as a disincentive to licensing.

Commentary
para 201: F&N: 10.157

202. Second, non-compete obligations possibly in combination with an exclusive territory may be necessary to ensure that the licensee has an incentive to invest in and exploit the licensed technology effectively. In cases where the agreement is caught by Article [101](1) because of an appreciable foreclosure effect, it may be necessary in order to benefit from Article [101](3) to choose a less restrictive alternative, for instance to impose minimum output or royalty obligations, which normally have less potential to foreclose competing technologies.

Commentary
para 202: F&N: 10.157

203. Third, in cases where the licensor undertakes to make significant client specific investments for instance in training and tailoring of the licensed technology to the licensee's needs, non-compete obligations or alternatively minimum output or minimum royalty obligations may be necessary to induce the licensor to make the investment and to avoid hold-up problems. However, normally the licensor will be able to charge directly for such investments by way of a lump sum payment, implying that less restrictive alternatives are available.

Part C Substantive Antitrust Matters

3. Settlement and non-assertion agreements

204. Licensing may serve as a means of settling disputes or avoiding that one party exercises his intellectual property rights to prevent the other party from exploiting his own technology. Licensing including cross licensing in the context of settlement agreements and non-assertion agreements is not as such restrictive of competition since it allows the parties to exploit their technologies post agreement. However, the individual terms and conditions of such agreements may be caught by Article [101](1). Licensing in the context of settlement agreements is treated like other licence agreements. In the case of technologies that from a technical point of view are substitutes, it is therefore necessary to assess to what extent it is likely that the technologies in question are in a one-way or two-way blocking position (cf. paragraph 32 above). If so, the parties are not deemed to be competitors.

Commentary
para 204: B&C: 9.129 **F&N:** 10.158

205. The block exemption applies provided that the agreement does not contain any hardcore restrictions of competition as set out in Article 4 of the TTBER. The hardcore list of Article 4(1) may in particular apply where it was clear to the parties that no blocking position exists and that consequently they are competitors. In such cases the settlement is merely a means to restrict competition that existed in the absence of the agreement.

206. In cases where it is likely that in the absence of the licence the licensee could be excluded from the market, the agreement is generally pro-competitive. Restrictions that limit intra-technology competition between the licensor and the licensee are often compatible with Article [101], see section 2 above.

207. Agreements whereby the parties cross license each other and impose restrictions on the use of their technologies, including restrictions on the licensing to third parties, may be caught by Article [101](1). Where the parties have a significant degree of market power and the agreement imposes restrictions that clearly go beyond what is required in order to unblock, the agreement is likely to be caught by Article [101](1) even if it is likely that a mutual blocking position exists. Article [101](1) is particularly likely to apply where the parties share markets or fix reciprocal running royalties that have a significant impact on market prices.

Commentary
para 207: B&C: 9.086 **F&N:** 10.158

208. Where under the agreement the parties are entitled to use each other's technology and the agreement extends to future developments, it is necessary to assess what is the impact of the agreement on the parties' incentive to innovate. In cases where the parties have a significant degree of market power the agreement is likely to be caught by Article [101](1) where the agreement prevents the parties from gaining a competitive lead over each other. Agreements that eliminate or substantially reduce the possibilities of one party to gain a competitive lead over the other reduce the incentive to innovate and thus adversely affect an essential part of the competitive process. Such agreements are also unlikely to satisfy the conditions of Article [101](3). It is particularly unlikely that the restriction can be considered indispensable within the meaning of the third condition of Article [101](3). The achievement of the objective of the agreement, namely to ensure that the parties can continue to exploit their own technology without being blocked by the other party, does not require that the parties agree to share future innovations. However, the parties are unlikely to be prevented from gaining a competitive lead over each other where the purpose of the licence is to allow the parties to develop their respective technologies and where the licence does not lead them to use the same technological solutions. Such agreements merely create design freedom by preventing future infringement claims by the other party.

Commentary
para 208: F&N: 10.160

209. In the context of a settlement and non-assertion agreement, non-challenge clauses are generally considered to fall outside Article [101](1). It is inherent in such agreements that the parties agree not to challenge *ex post* the intellectual property rights covered by the agreement. Indeed, the very purpose of the agreement is to settle existing disputes and/or to avoid future disputes.

Commentary
para 209: F&N: 10.159

4. Technology pools

210. Technology pools are defined as arrangements whereby two or more parties assemble a package of technology which is licensed not only to contributors to the pool but also to third parties. In terms of their structure technology pools can take the form of simple arrangements between a limited number of parties or elaborate organisational arrangements whereby the organisation of the licensing of the pooled technologies is entrusted to a separate entity. In both cases the pool may allow licensees to operate on the market on the basis of a single licence.

Commentary
para 210: F&N: 10.161

211. There is no inherent link between technology pools and standards, but in some cases the technologies in the pool support (wholly or partly) a de facto or de jure industry standard. When technology pools do support an industry standard they do not necessarily support a single standard. Different technology pools may support competing standards.[68]

212. Agreements establishing technology pools and setting out the terms and conditions for their operation are not — irrespective of the number of parties — covered by the block exemption (cf. section III.2.2 above). Such agreements are addressed only by these guidelines. Pooling arrangements give rise to a number of particular issues regarding the selection of the included technologies and the operation of the pool, which do not arise in the context of other types of licensing. The individual licences granted by the pool to third party licensees, however, are treated like other licence agreements, which are block exempted when the conditions set out in the TTBER are fulfilled, including the requirements of Article 4 of the TTBER containing the list of hardcore restrictions.

Notes
[68] See in this respect the Commission's press release IP/02/1651 concerning the licensing of patents for third generation (3G) mobile services. This case involved five technology pools creating five different technologies, each of which could be used to produce 3G equipment.

Commentary
para 212: F&N: 10.161

213. Technology pools may be restrictive of competition. The creation of a technology pool necessarily implies joint selling of the pooled technologies, which in the case of pools composed solely or predominantly of substitute technologies amounts to a price fixing cartel. Moreover, in addition to reducing competition between the parties, technology pools may also, in particular when they support an industry standard or establish a de facto industry standard, result in a reduction of innovation by foreclosing alternative technologies. The existence of the standard and the related technology pool may make it more difficult for new and improved technologies to enter the market.

214. Technology pools can also produce pro-competitive effects, in particular by reducing transaction costs and by setting a limit on cumulative royalties to avoid double marginalisation. The creation of a pool allows for one-stop licensing of the technologies covered by the pool. This is particularly important in sectors where intellectual property rights are prevalent and where in order to operate on the market licences need to be obtained from a significant number of licensors. In cases where licensees receive on-going services concerning the application of the licensed technology, joint licensing and servicing can lead to further cost reductions.

4.1. The nature of the pooled technologies

215. The competitive risks and the efficiency enhancing potential of technology pools depend to a large extent on the relationship between the pooled technologies and their relationship with technologies outside the pool. Two basic distinctions must be made, namely (a) between technological complements and technological substitutes and (b) between essential and non-essential technologies.

216. Two technologies[69] are complements as opposed to substitutes when they are both required to produce the product or carry out the process to which the technologies relate. Conversely, two technologies are substitutes when either technology allows the holder to produce the product or carry out the process to which the technologies relate. A technology is essential as opposed to non-essential if there are no substitutes for that technology inside or outside the pool and the technology in question constitutes a necessary part of the package of technologies for the purposes of producing the product(s) or carrying out the process(es) to which the pool relates. A technology for which there are no substitutes, remains essential as long as the technology is covered by at least one valid intellectual property right. Technologies that are essential are by necessity also complements.

Notes

[69] The term "technology" is not limited to patents. It covers also patent applications and intellectual property rights other than patents.

217. When technologies in a pool are substitutes, royalties are likely to be higher than they would otherwise be, because licensees do not benefit from rivalry between the technologies in question. When the technologies in the pool are complements the arrangement reduces transaction costs and may lead to lower overall royalties because the parties are in a position to fix a common royalty for the package as opposed to each fixing a royalty which does not take account of the royalty fixed by others.

218. The distinction between complementary and substitute technologies is not clear-cut in all cases, since technologies may be substitutes in part and complements in part. When due to efficiencies stemming from the integration of two technologies licensees are likely to demand both technologies the technologies are treated as complements even if they are partly substitutable. In such cases it is likely that in the absence of the pool licensees would want to licence both technologies due to the additional economic benefit of employing both technologies as opposed to employing only one of them.

219. The inclusion in the pool of substitute technologies restricts inter-technology competition and amounts to collective bundling. Moreover, where the pool is substantially composed of substitute technologies, the arrangement amounts to price fixing between competitors. As a general rule the Commission considers that the inclusion of substitute technologies in the pool constitutes a violation of Article [101](1). The Commission also considers that it is unlikely that the conditions of Article [101](3) will be fulfilled in the case of pools comprising to a significant extent substitute technologies. Given that the technologies in question are alternatives, no transaction cost savings accrue from including both technologies in the pool. In the absence of the pool licensees would not have demanded both technologies. It is not sufficient that the parties remain free to license independently. In order not to undermine the pool, which allows them to jointly exercise market power, the parties are likely to have little incentive to do so.

Commentary
para 219: **B&C**: 9.067 **F&N**: 10.166

220. When a pool is composed only of technologies that are essential and therefore by necessity also complements, the creation of the pool as such generally falls outside Article [101](1) irrespective of the market position of the parties. However, the conditions on which licences are granted may be caught by Article [101](1).

Commentary
para 220: **B&C**: 9.126 **F&N**: 10.166

221. Where non-essential but complementary patents are included in the pool there is a risk of fore-closure of third party technologies. Once a technology is included in the pool and is licensed as part of the package, licensees are likely to have little incentive to license a competing technology when the royalty paid for the package already covers a substitute technology. Moreover, the inclusion of technologies which are not necessary for the purposes of producing the product(s) or carrying out the process(es) to which the technology pool relates also forces licensees to pay for technology that they may not need. The inclusion of complementary patents thus amounts to collective bundling. When a pool encompasses non-essential technologies, the agreement is likely to be caught by Article [101](1) where the pool has a significant position on any relevant market.

Commentary
para 221: B&C: 9.068 F&N: 10.167

222. Given that substitute and complementary technologies may be developed after the creation of the pool, the assessment of essentiality is an on-going process. A technology may therefore become non-essential after the creation of the pool due to the emergence of new third party technologies. One way to ensure that such third party technologies are not foreclosed is to exclude from the pool technologies that have become non-essential. However, there may be other ways to ensure that third party technologies are not foreclosed. In the assessment of tech-nology pools comprising non-essential technologies, i.e. technologies for which substitutes exist outside the pool or which are not necessary in order to produce one or more products to which the pool relates, the Commission will in its overall assessment, inter alia, take account of the following factors:
    (a) whether there are any pro-competitive reasons for including the non-essential technologies in the pool;
    (b) whether the licensors remain free to license their respective technologies independently. Where the pool is composed of a limited number of technologies and there are substitute technologies outside the pool, licensees may want to put together their own technological package composed partly of technology forming part of the pool and partly of technology owned by third parties;
    (c) whether, in cases where the pooled technologies have different applications some of which do not require use of all of the pooled technologies, the pool offers the technologies only as a single package or whether it offers separate packages for distinct applications. In the latter case it is avoided that technologies which are not essential to a particular product or process are tied to essential technologies;
    (d) whether the pooled technologies are available only as a single package or whether licensees have the possibility of obtaining a licence for only part of the package with a corresponding reduction of royalties. The possibility to obtain a licence for only part of the package may reduce the risk of foreclosure of third party technologies outside the pool, in particular where the licensee obtains a corresponding reduction in royalties. This requires that a share of the overall royalty has been assigned to each technology in the pool. Where the licence agreements concluded between the pool and individual licensees are of relatively long dura-tion and the pooled technology supports a de facto industry standard, it must also be taken into account that the pool may foreclose access to the market of new substitute technolo-gies. In assessing the risk of foreclosure in such cases it is relevant to take into account whether or not licensees can terminate at reasonable notice part of the licence and obtain a corresponding reduction of royalties.

Commentary
para 222: B&C: 9.068 F&N: 10.168

4.2. Assessment of individual restraints

223. The purpose of this section is to address a certain number of restraints that in one form or another are commonly found in technology pools and which need to be assessed in the overall

context of the pool. It is recalled, cf. paragraph 212 above, that the TTBER applies to licence agreements concluded between the pool and third party licensees. This section is therefore limited to addressing the creation of the pool and licensing issues that are particular to licensing in the context of technology pools.

224. In making its assessment the Commission will be guided by the following main principles:

1. The stronger the market position of the pool the greater the risk of anti-competitive effects.
2. Pools that hold a strong position on the market should be open and non-discriminatory.
3. Pools should not unduly foreclose third party technologies or limit the creation of alternative pools.

225. Undertakings setting up a technology pool that is compatible with Article [101], and any industry standard that it may support, are normally free to negotiate and fix royalties for the technology package and each technology's share of the royalties either before or after the standard is set. Such agreement is inherent in the establishment of the standard or pool and cannot in itself be considered restrictive of competition and may in certain circumstances lead to more efficient outcomes. In certain circumstances it may be more efficient if the royalties are agreed before the standard is chosen and not after the standard is decided upon, to avoid that the choice of the standard confers a significant degree of market power on one or more essential technologies. On the other hand, licensees must remain free to determine the price of products produced under the licence. Where the selection of technologies to be included in the pool is carried out by an independent expert this may further competition between available technological solutions.

Commentary
para 225: F&N: 10.166, 10.170

---

226. Where the pool has a dominant position on the market, royalties and other licensing terms should be fair and non-discriminatory and licences should be non-exclusive. These requirements are necessary to ensure that the pool is open and does not lead to foreclosure and other anti-competitive effects on down stream markets. These requirements, however, do not preclude different royalties for different uses. It is in general not considered restrictive of competition to apply different royalty rates to different product markets, whereas there should be no discrimination within product markets. In particular, the treatment of licensees should not depend on whether they are licensors or not. The Commission will therefore take into account whether licensors are also subject to royalty obligations.

Commentary
para 226: F&N: 10.169

---

227. Licensors and licensees must be free to develop competing products and standards and must also be free to grant and obtain licences outside the pool. These requirements are necessary in order to limit the risk of foreclosure of third party technologies and ensure that the pool does not limit innovation and preclude the creation of competing technological solutions. Where a pool supports a (de facto) industry standard and where the parties are subject to non-compete obligations, the pool creates a particular risk of preventing the development of new and improved technologies and standards.

Commentary
para 227: F&N: 10.169

---

228. Grant back obligations should be non-exclusive and be limited to developments that are essential or important to the use of the pooled technology. This allows the pool to feed on and benefit from improvements to the pooled technology. It is legitimate for the parties to ensure that the exploitation of the pooled technology cannot be held up by licensees that hold or obtain essential patents.

229. One of the problems identified with regard to patent pools is the risk that they shield invalid patents. Pooling raises the costs/risks for a successful challenge, because the challenge fails if only one patent in the pool is valid. The shielding of invalid patents in the pool may oblige licensees

to pay higher royalties and may also prevent innovation in the field covered by an invalid patent. In order to limit this risk any right to terminate a licence in the case of a challenge must be limited to the technologies owned by the licensor who is the addressee of the challenge and must not extend to the technologies owned by the other licensors in the pool.

4.3. The institutional framework governing the pool

230. The way in which a technology pool is created, organised and operated can reduce the risk of it having the object or effect of restricting competition and provide assurances to the effect that the arrangement is pro-competitive.

231. When participation in a standard and pool creation process is open to all interested parties representing different interests it is more likely that technologies for inclusion into the pool are selected on the basis of price/quality considerations than when the pool is set up by a limited group of technology owners. Similarly, when the relevant bodies of the pool are composed of persons representing different interests, it is more likely that licensing terms and conditions, including royalties, will be open and non-discriminatory and reflect the value of the licensed technology than when the pool is controlled by licensor representatives.

232. Another relevant factor is the extent to which independent experts are involved in the creation and operation of the pool. For instance, the assessment of whether or not a technology is essential to a standard supported by a pool is often a complex matter that requires special expertise. The involvement in the selection process of independent experts can go a long way in ensuring that a commitment to include only essential technologies is implemented in practice.

233. The Commission will take into account how experts are selected and what are the exact functions that they are to perform. Experts should be independent from the undertakings that have formed the pool. If experts are connected to the licensors or otherwise depend on them, the involvement of the expert will be given less weight. Experts must also have the necessary technical expertise to perform the various functions with which they have been entrusted. The functions of independent experts may include, in particular, an assessment of whether or not technologies put forward for inclusion into the pool are valid and whether or not they are essential.

234. It is also relevant to consider the arrangements for exchanging sensitive information among the parties. In oligopolistic markets exchanges of sensitive information such as pricing and output data may facilitate collusion.[70] In such cases the Commission will take into account to what extent safeguards have been put in place, which ensure that sensitive information is not exchanged. An independent expert or licensing body may play an important role in this respect by ensuring that output and sales data, which may be necessary for the purposes of calculating and verifying royalties is not disclosed to undertakings that compete on affected markets.

Notes

[70] See in this respect the judgment in *John Deere* cited in note 11.

235. Finally, it is relevant to take account of the dispute resolution mechanism foreseen in the instruments setting up the pool. The more dispute resolution is entrusted to bodies or persons that are independent of the pool and the members thereof, the more likely it is that the dispute resolution will operate in a neutral way.

C12

COMMISSION NOTICE

Guidelines on the effect on trade concept contained in Articles [101] and [102]* of the [Treaty on the Functioning of the European Union](2004/C 101/07)

(Text with EEA relevance)

Official Journal C 101, 27.4.2004, p.81

Celex No: 52004XC0427(06)

EUR-Lex permanent link: <http://eur-lex.europa.eu/LexUriServ/LexUriServ.do?uri=CELEX:5200 4XC0427(06):EN:NOT>

Notes

* Ed note: please see the Note on the Lisbon Treaty at p.xvii in regard to article renumbering introduced by the Lisbon Treaty. **EEA application:** the EFTA Surveillance Authority has adopted a parallel notice on the effect on trade concept contained in Articles 53 and 54 of the EEA Agreement under Article 5(2)(b) of the Surveillance and Court Agreement: OJ C 291, 30.11.2006, p.46 and EEA Supplement No 59, 30.11.2006, p.18.

Commentary
Notice: B&C: 1.110, 1.122, 1.130, 1.141, 1.143, 2.164 **F&N:** 2.114, 2.260, 3.387, 3.416, 3.426, 3.427, 8.453, 9.39
paras 77–99: B&C: 1.140
paras 89–92: B&C: 1.143
paras 93–96: B&C: 1.141
paras 97–99: B&C: 1.143

---

1. INTRODUCTION

1. Articles [101] and [102] of the Treaty are applicable to horizontal and vertical agreements and practices on the part of undertakings which "may affect trade between Member States".

2. In their interpretation of Articles [101] and [102], the Community Courts have already substantially clarified the content and scope of the concept of effect on trade between Member States.

3. The present guidelines set out the principles developed by the Community Courts in relation to the interpretation of the effect on trade concept of Articles [101] and [102]. They further spell out a rule indicating when agreements are in general unlikely to be capable of appreciably affecting trade between Member States (the non-appreciable affectation of trade rule or NAAT-rule). The guidelines are not intended to be exhaustive. The aim is to set out the methodology for the application of the effect on trade concept and to provide guidance on its application in frequently occurring situations. Although not binding on them, these guidelines also intend to give guidance to the courts and authorities of the Member States in their application of the effect on trade concept contained in Articles [101] and [102].

Commentary
para 3: F&N: 3.427

---

4. The present guidelines do not address the issue of what constitutes an appreciable restriction of competition under Article [101](1). This issue, which is distinct from the ability of agreements to appreciably affect trade between Member States, is dealt with in the Commission Notice on agreements of minor importance which do not appreciably restrict competition under Article [101](1) of the Treaty[1] (the *de minimis* rule). The guidelines are also not intended to provide guidance on the effect on trade concept contained in Article 87(1) of the Treaty on State aid.

Notes
1 OJ C 368, 22.12.2001, p.13.

Commentary
para 4: B&C: 1.122

5. These guidelines, including the NAAT-rule, are without prejudice to the interpretation of Articles [101] and [102] which may be given by the Court of Justice and the Court of First Instance.

2. The Effect on Trade Criterion

2.1. General principles

6. Article [101](1) provides that "the following shall be prohibited as incompatible with the common market: all agreements between undertakings, decisions of associations of undertakings and concerted practices which may affect trade between Member States and which have as their object or effect the prevention, restriction or distortion of competition within the common market". For the sake of simplicity the terms "agreements, decisions of associations of undertakings and concerted practices" are collectively referred to as "agreements".

7. Article [102] on its part stipulates that "any abuse by one or more undertakings of a dominant position within the common market or in a substantial part thereof shall be prohibited as incompat-ible with the common market insofar as it may affect trade between Member States." In what follows the term "practices" refers to the conduct of dominant undertakings.

8. The effect on trade criterion also determines the scope of application of Article 3 of Regulation 1/2003 on the implementation of the rules on competition laid down in Articles [101] and [102] of the Treaty.[2]

Notes
2 OJ L 1, 4.1.2003, p.1.

9. According to Article 3(1) of that Regulation the competition authorities and courts of the Member States must apply Article [101] to agreements, decisions by associations of undertakings or concerted practices within the meaning of Article [101](1) of the Treaty which may affect trade between Member States within the meaning of that provision, when they apply national competition law to such agreements, decisions or concerted practices. Similarly, when the competition authorities and courts of the Member States apply national competition law to any abuse prohibited by Article [102] of the Treaty, they must also apply Article [102] of the Treaty. Article 3(1) thus obliges the competition authorities and courts of the Member States to also apply Articles [101] and [102] when they apply national competition law to agreements and abusive practices which may affect trade between Member States. On the other hand, Article 3(1) does not oblige national competition authorities and courts to apply national competition law when they apply Articles [101] and [102] to agreements, decisions and concerted practices and to abuses which may affect trade between Member States. They may in such cases apply the Community competition rules on a stand alone basis.

10. It follows from Article 3(2) that the application of national competition law may not lead to the prohibition of agreements, decisions by associations of undertakings or concerted practices which may affect trade between Member States but which do not restrict competition within the meaning of Article [101](1) of the Treaty, or which fulfil the conditions of Article [101](3) of the Treaty or which are covered by a Regulation for the application of Article [101](3) of the Treaty. Member States, however, are not under Regulation 1/2003 precluded from adopting and applying on their territory stricter national laws which prohibit or sanction unilateral conduct engaged in by undertakings.

11. Finally it should be mentioned that Article 3(3) stipulates that without prejudice to general principles and other provisions of Community law, Article 3(1) and (2) do not apply when the competition authorities and the courts of the Member States apply national merger control laws,

nor do they preclude the application of provisions of national law that predominantly pursue an objective different from that pursued by Articles [101] and [102] of the Treaty.

12. The effect on trade criterion is an autonomous Community law criterion, which must be assessed separately in each case. It is a jurisdictional criterion, which defines the scope of application of Community competition law.[3] Community competition law is not applicable to agreements and practices that are not capable of appreciably affecting trade between Member States.

Notes

[3] See e.g. Joined Cases 56/64 and 58/64, *Consten and Grundig*, [1966] ECR 429, and Joined Cases 6/73 and 7/73, *Commercial Solvents*, [1974] ECR 223.

---

13. The effect on trade criterion confines the scope of application of Articles [101] and [102] to agreements and practices that are capable of having a minimum level of cross-border effects within the Community. In the words of the Court of Justice, the ability of the agreement or practice to affect trade between Member States must be "appreciable".[4]

Notes

[4] See in this respect Case 22/71, *Béguelin*, [1971] ECR 949, paragraph 16.

---

14. In the case of Article [101] of the Treaty, it is the agreement that must be capable of affecting trade between Member States. It is not required that each individual part of the agreement, including any restriction of competition which may flow from the agreement, is capable of doing so.[5] If the agreement as a whole is capable of affecting trade between Member States, there is Community law jurisdiction in respect of the entire agreement, including any parts of the agreement that individually do not affect trade between Member States. In cases where the contractual relations between the same parties cover several activities, these activities must, in order to form part of the same agreement, be directly linked and form an integral part of the same overall business arrangement.[6] If not, each activity constitutes a separate agreement.

Notes

[5] See Case 193/83, *Windsurfing*, [1986] ECR 611, paragraph 96, and Case T-77/94, *Vereniging van Groothandelaren in Bloemkwekerijprodukten*, [1997] ECR II-759, paragraph 126.
[6] See paragraphs 142 to 144 of the judgment in *Vereniging van Groothandelaren in Bloemkwekerijprodukteten* cited in the previous footnote.

Commentary
para 14: F&N: 3.392

---

15. It is also immaterial whether or not the participation of a particular undertaking in the agreement has an appreciable effect on trade between Member States.[7] An undertaking cannot escape Community law jurisdiction merely because of the fact that its own contribution to an agreement, which itself is capable of affecting trade between Member States, is insignificant.

Notes

[7] See e.g. Case T-2/89, *Petrofina*, [1991] ECR II-1087, paragraph 226.

---

16. It is not necessary, for the purposes of establishing Community law jurisdiction, to establish a link between the alleged restriction of competition and the capacity of the agreement to affect trade between Member States. Non-restrictive agreements may also affect trade between Member States. For example, selective distribution agreements based on purely qualitative selection criteria justified by the nature of the products, which are not restrictive of competition within the meaning of Article [101](1), may nevertheless affect trade between Member States. However, the alleged restrictions arising from an agreement may provide a clear indication as to the capacity of the agreement to affect trade between Member States. For instance, a distribution agreement prohibiting exports is by its very nature capable of affecting trade between Member States, although not necessarily to an appreciable extent.[8]

Notes
8 The concept of appreciability is dealt with in section 2.4 below.

17. In the case of Article [102] it is the abuse that must affect trade between Member States. This does not imply, however, that each element of the behaviour must be assessed in isolation. Conduct that forms part of an overall strategy pursued by the dominant undertaking must be assessed in terms of its overall impact. Where a dominant undertaking adopts various practices in pursuit of the same aim, for instance practices that aim at eliminating or foreclosing competitors, in order for Article [102] to be applicable to all the practices forming part of this overall strategy, it is sufficient that at least one of these practices is capable of affecting trade between Member States.9

Notes
9 See in this respect Case 85/76, *Hoffmann-La Roche*, [1979] ECR 461, paragraph 126.
Commentary
para 17: B&C: 1.136 F&N: 3.394

18. It follows from the wording of Articles [101] and [102] and the case law of the Community Courts that in the application of the effect on trade criterion three elements in particular must be addressed:
    (a) The concept of "trade between Member States",
    (b) The notion of "may affect", and
    (c) The concept of "appreciability".

2.2. The concept of "trade between Member States"

19. The concept of "trade" is not limited to traditional exchanges of goods and services across borders.10 It is a wider concept, covering all cross-border economic activity including establishment.11 This interpretation is consistent with the fundamental objective of the Treaty to promote free movement of goods, services, persons and capital.

Notes
10 Throughout these guidelines the term "products" covers both goods and services.
11 See Case 172/80, *Züchner*, [1981] ECR 2021, paragraph 18. See also Case C-309/99, *Wouters*, [2002] ECR I-1577, paragraph 95, Case C-475/99, *Ambulanz Glöckner*, [2001] ECR I-8089, paragraph 49, Joined Cases C-215/96 and 216/96, *Bagnasco*, [1999] ECR I-135, paragraph 51, Case C-55/96, *Job Centre*, [1997] ECR I-7119, paragraph 37, and Case C-41/90, *Höfner and Elser*, [1991] ECR I-1979, paragraph 33.

20. According to settled case law the concept of "trade" also encompasses cases where agreements or practices affect the competitive structure of the market. Agreements and practices that affect the competitive structure inside the Community by eliminating or threatening to eliminate a competitor operating within the Community may be subject to the Community competition rules.12 When an undertaking is or risks being eliminated the competitive structure within the Community is affected and so are the economic activities in which the undertaking is engaged.

Notes
12 See e.g. Joined Cases T-24/93 and others, *Compagnie maritime belge*, [1996] ECR II-1201, paragraph 203, and paragraph 23 of the judgment in *Commercial Solvents* cited in footnote [3].
Commentary
para 20: B&C: 1.127

21. The requirement that there must be an effect on trade "between Member States" implies that there must be an impact on cross-border economic activity involving at least two Member States. It is not required that the agreement or practice affect trade between the whole of one Member State and the whole of another Member State. Articles [101] and [102] may be applicable also in cases involving part of a Member State, provided that the effect on trade is appreciable.13

Notes
13 See e.g. Joined Cases T-213/95 and T-18/96, *SCK and FNK*, [1997] ECR II-1739, and sections 3.2.4 and 3.2.6 below.

22. The application of the effect on trade criterion is independent of the definition of relevant geographic markets. Trade between Member States may be affected also in cases where the relevant market is national or sub-national.[14]

Notes
[14] See section 3.2 below.

Commentary
para 22: F&N: 3.391

2.3. The notion "may affect"

23. The function of the notion "may affect" is to define the nature of the required impact on trade between Member States. According to the standard test developed by the Court of Justice, the notion "may affect" implies that it must be possible to foresee with a sufficient degree of probability on the basis of a set of objective factors of law or fact that the agreement or practice may have an influence, direct or indirect, actual or potential, on the pattern of trade between Member States.[15,16] As mentioned in paragraph 20 above the Court of Justice has in addition developed a test based on whether or not the agreement or practice affects the competitive structure. In cases where the agreement or practice is liable to affect the competitive structure inside the Community, Community law jurisdiction is established.

Notes
[15] See e.g. the judgment in *Züchner* cited in footnote 11 and Case 319/82 *Kerpen & Kerpen* [1983] ECR 4173, Joined Cases 240/82 and others *Stichting Sigarettenindustrie* [1985] ECR 3831, paragraph 48, and Joined Cases T-25/95 and others *Cimenteries CBR* [2000] ECR II-491, paragraph 3930.
[16] In some judgments mainly relating to vertical agreements the Court of Justice has added wording to the effect that the agreement was capable of hindering the attainment of the objectives of a single market between Member States, see e.g. Case T-62/98 *Volkswagen* [2000] ECR II-2707, paragraph 179, and paragraph 47 of the *Bagnasco* judgment cited in footnote 11, and Case 56/65 *Société Technique Minière* [1966] ECR 337. The impact of an agreement on the single market objective is thus a factor which can be taken into account.

24. The "pattern of trade"—test developed by the Court of Justice contains the following main elements, which are dealt with in the following sections:
    (a) "A sufficient degree of probability on the basis of a set of objective factors of law or fact",
    (b) An influence on the "pattern of trade between Member States",
    (c) "A direct or indirect, actual or potential influence" on the pattern of trade.

2.3.1. A sufficient degree of probability on the basis of a set of objective factors of law or fact

25. The assessment of effect on trade is based on objective factors. Subjective intent on the part of the undertakings concerned is not required. If, however, there is evidence that undertakings have intended to affect trade between Member States, for example because they have sought to hinder exports to or imports from other Member States, this is a relevant factor to be taken into account.

26. The words "may affect" and the reference by the Court of Justice to "a sufficient degree of probability" imply that, in order for Community law jurisdiction to be established, it is not required that the agreement or practice will actually have or has had an effect on trade between Member States. It is sufficient that the agreement or practice is "capable" of having such an effect.[17]

Notes
[17] See e.g. Case T-228/97 *Irish Sugar* [1999] ECR II-2969, paragraph 170, and Case 19/77 *Miller* [1978] ECR 131, paragraph 15.

27. There is no obligation or need to calculate the actual volume of trade between Member States affected by the agreement or practice. For example, in the case of agreements prohibiting exports to other Member States there is no need to estimate what would have been the level of parallel trade between the Member States concerned, in the absence of the agreement. This interpretation is consistent with the jurisdictional nature of the effect on trade criterion. Community law jurisdiction extends to categories of agreements and practices that are capable of having cross-border effects, irrespective of whether a particular agreement or practice actually has such effects.

Commentary
para 27: B&C: 1.128

28. The assessment under the effect on trade criterion depends on a number of factors that individually may not be decisive.[18] The relevant factors include the nature of the agreement and practice, the nature of the products covered by the agreement or practice and the position and importance of the undertakings concerned.[19]

Notes
[18] See e.g. Case C-250/92, *Gøttrup-Klim* [1994] ECR II-5641, paragraph 54.
[19] See e.g. Case C-306/96, *Javico*, [1998] ECR I-1983, paragraph 17, and paragraph 18 of the judgment in *Béguelin* cited in footnote 4.
Commentary
para 28: F&N: 3.398

29. The nature of the agreement and practice provides an indication from a qualitative point of view of the ability of the agreement or practice to affect trade between Member States. Some agreements and practices are by their very nature capable of affecting trade between Member States, whereas others require more detailed analysis in this respect. Cross-border cartels are an example of the former, whereas joint ventures confined to the territory of a single Member State are an example of the latter. This aspect is further examined in section 3 below, which deals with various categories of agreements and practices.

30. The nature of the products covered by the agreements or practices also provides an indication of whether trade between Member States is capable of being affected. When by their nature products are easily traded across borders or are important for undertakings that want to enter or expand their activities in other Member States, Community jurisdiction is more readily established than in cases where due to their nature there is limited demand for products offered by suppliers from other Member States or where the products are of limited interest from the point of view of cross-border establishment or the expansion of the economic activity carried out from such place of establishment.[20] Establishment includes the setting-up by undertakings in one Member State of agencies, branches or subsidiaries in another Member State.

Notes
[20] Compare in this respect the judgments in *Bagnasco* and *Wouters* cited in footnote 11.
Commentary
para 30: B&C: 1.124

31. The market position of the undertakings concerned and their sales volumes are indicative from a quantitative point of view of the ability of the agreement or practice concerned to affect trade between Member States. This aspect, which forms an integral part of the assessment of appreciability, is addressed in section 2.4 below.

32. In addition to the factors already mentioned, it is necessary to take account of the legal and factual environment in which the agreement or practice operates. The relevant economic and legal context provides insight into the potential for an effect on trade between Member States. If there are absolute barriers to cross-border trade between Member States, which are external to the agreement or practice, trade is only capable of being affected if those barriers are likely to disappear in the foreseeable future. In cases where the barriers are not absolute but merely render cross-border activities more difficult, it is of the utmost importance to ensure that agreements and practices do not further hinder such activities. Agreements and practices that do so are capable of affecting trade between Member States.

Commentary
para 32: B&C: 1.137 F&N: 3.403

2.3.2. An influence on the "pattern of trade between Member States"

33. For Articles [101] and 82 to be applicable there must be an influence on the "pattern of trade between Member States".

34. The term "pattern of trade" is neutral. It is not a condition that trade be restricted or reduced.[21] Patterns of trade can also be affected when an agreement or practice causes an increase in trade. Indeed, Community law jurisdiction is established if trade between Member States is likely to develop differently with the agreement or practice compared to the way in which it would probably have developed in the absence of the agreement or practice.[22]

35. This interpretation reflects the fact that the effect on trade criterion is a jurisdictional one, which serves to distinguish those agreements and practices which are capable of having cross-border effects, so as to warrant an examination under the Community competition rules, from those agreements and practices which do not.

Notes

[21] See e.g. Case T-141/89, *Tréfileurope*, [1995] ECR II-791, Case T-29/92, *Vereniging van Samenwerkende Prijsregelende Organisaties in de Bouwnijverheid (SPO)*, [1995] ECR II-289, as far as exports were concerned, and Commission Decision in *Volkswagen (II)* (OJ L 264, 2.10.2001, p.14).

[22] See in this respect Case 71/74, *Frubo*, [1975] ECR 563, paragraph 38, Joined Cases 209/78 and others, *Van Landewyck*, [1980] ECR 3125, paragraph 172, Case T-61/89, *Dansk Pelsdyravler Forening*, [1992] ECR II-1931, paragraph 143, and Case T-65/89, *BPB Industries and British Gypsum*, [1993] ECR II-389, paragraph 135.

2.3.3. A "direct or indirect, actual or potential influence" on the pattern of trade

36. The influence of agreements and practices on patterns of trade between Member States can be "direct or indirect, actual or potential".

37. Direct effects on trade between Member States normally occur in relation to the products covered by an agreement or practice. When, for example, producers of a particular product in different Member States agree to share markets, direct effects are produced on trade between Member States on the market for the products in question. Another example of direct effects being produced is when a supplier limits distributor rebates to products sold within the Member State in which the distributors are established. Such practices increase the relative price of products destined for exports, rendering export sales less attractive and less competitive.

38. Indirect effects often occur in relation to products that are related to those covered by an agreement or practice. Indirect effects may, for example, occur where an agreement or practice has an impact on cross-border economic activities of undertakings that use or otherwise rely on the products covered by the agreement or practice.[23] Such effects can, for instance, arise where the agreement or practice relates to an intermediate product, which is not traded, but which is used in the supply of a final product, which is traded. The Court of Justice has held that trade between Member States was capable of being affected in the case of an agreement involving the fixing of prices of spirits used in the production of cognac.[24] Whereas the raw material was not exported, the final product—cognac—was exported. In such cases Community competition law is thus applicable, if trade in the final product is capable of being appreciably affected.

Notes

[23] See in this respect Case T-86/95, *Compagnie Générale Maritime and others*, [2002] ECR II-1011, paragraph 148, and paragraph 202 of the judgment in *Compagnie maritime belge* cited in footnote 12.

[24] See Case 123/83, *BNIC v Clair*, [1985] ECR 391, paragraph 29.

Commentary
para 38: B&C: 1.129

39. Indirect effects on trade between Member States may also occur in relation to the products covered by the agreement or practice. For instance, agreements whereby a manufacturer limits warranties to products sold by distributors within their Member State of establishment create disincentives for consumers from other Member States to buy the products because they would not be able to invoke the warranty.[25] Export by official distributors and parallel traders is made

more difficult because in the eyes of consumers the products are less attractive without the manufacturer's warranty.[26]

Notes
[25] See Commission Decision in *Zanussi*, OJ L 322, 16.11.1978, p.36, paragraph 11.
[26] See in this respect Case 31/85, *ETA Fabrique d'Ébauches*, [1985] ECR 3933, paragraphs 12 and 13.
Commentary
para 39: B&C: 1.129 F&N: 3.407

40. Actual effects on trade between Member States are those that are produced by the agreement or practice once it is implemented. An agreement between a supplier and a distributor within the same Member State, for instance one that prohibits exports to other Member States, is likely to produce actual effects on trade between Member States. Without the agreement the distributor would have been free to engage in export sales. It should be recalled, however, that it is not required that actual effects are demonstrated. It is sufficient that the agreement or practice be capable of having such effects.

Commentary
para 40: F&N: 3.407

41. Potential effects are those that may occur in the future with a sufficient degree of probability. In other words, foreseeable market developments must be taken into account.[27] Even if trade is not capable of being affected at the time the agreement is concluded or the practice is implemented, Articles [101] and [102] remain applicable if the factors which led to that conclusion are likely to change in the foreseeable future. In this respect it is relevant to consider the impact of liberalisation measures adopted by the Community or by the Member State in question and other foreseeable measures aiming at eliminating legal barriers to trade.

Notes
[27] See Joined Cases C-241/91 P and C-242/91 P, *RTE (Magill)*, [1995] ECR I-743, paragraph 70, and Case 107/82, *AEG*, [1983] ECR 3151, paragraph 60.
Commentary
para 41: B&C: 1.137

42. Moreover, even if at a given point in time market conditions are unfavourable to cross-border trade, for example because prices are similar in the Member States in question, trade may still be capable of being affected if the situation may change as a result of changing market conditions.[28] What matters is the ability of the agreement or practice to affect trade between Member States and not whether at any given point in time it actually does so.

Notes
[28] See paragraph 60 of the *AEG* judgment cited in the previous footnote.

43. The inclusion of indirect or potential effects in the analysis of effects on trade between Member States does not mean that the analysis can be based on remote or hypothetical effects. The likelihood of a particular agreement to produce indirect or potential effects must be explained by the authority or party claiming that trade between Member States is capable of being appreciably affected. Hypothetical or speculative effects are not sufficient for establishing Community law jurisdiction. For instance, an agreement that raises the price of a product which is not tradable reduces the disposable income of consumers. As consumers have less money to spend they may purchase fewer products imported from other Member States. However, the link between such income effects and trade between Member States is generally in itself too remote to establish Community law jurisdiction.

Commentary
para 43: F&N: 3.412

Part C Substantive
Antitrust Matters

2.4. The concept of appreciability

2.4.1. General principle

44. The effect on trade criterion incorporates a quantitative element, limiting Community law jurisdiction to agreements and practices that are capable of having effects of a certain magnitude. Agreements and practices fall outside the scope of application of Articles [101] and [102] when they affect the market only insignificantly having regard to the weak position of the undertakings concerned on the market for the products in question.[29] Appreciability can be appraised in particular by reference to the position and the importance of the relevant undertakings on the market for the products concerned.[30]

Notes

[29] See Case 5/69, *Völk*, [1969] ECR 295, paragraph 7.

[30] See e.g. paragraph 17 of the judgment in *Javico* cited in footnote 19, and paragraph 138 of the judgment in *BPB Industries and British Gypsum* cited in footnote 22.

45. The assessment of appreciability depends on the circumstances of each individual case, in particular the nature of the agreement and practice, the nature of the products covered and the market position of the undertakings concerned. When by its very nature the agreement or practice is capable of affecting trade between Member States, the appreciability threshold is lower than in the case of agreements and practices that are not by their very nature capable of affecting trade between Member States. The stronger the market position of the undertakings concerned, the more likely it is that an agreement or practice capable of affecting trade between Member States can be held to do so appreciably.[31]

Notes

[31] See paragraph 138 of the judgment in *BPB Industries and British Gypsum* cited in footnote 22.

Commentary

para 45: F&N: 3.414

46. In a number of cases concerning imports and exports the Court of Justice has considered that the appreciability requirement was fulfilled when the sales of the undertakings concerned accounted for about 5% of the market.[32] Market share alone, however, has not always been considered the decisive factor. In particular, it is necessary also to take account of the turnover of the undertakings in the products concerned.[33]

Notes

[32] See e.g. paragraphs 9 and 10 of the *Miller* judgment cited in footnote 17, and paragraph 58 of the *AEG* judgment cited in footnote 27.

[33] See Joined Cases 100/80 and others, *Musique Diffusion Française*, [1983] ECR 1825, paragraph 86. In that case the products in question accounted for just above 3% of sales on the national markets concerned. The Court held that the agreements, which hindered parallel trade, were capable of appreciably affecting trade between Member States due to the high turnover of the parties and the relative market position of the products, compared to those of products produced by competing suppliers.

47. Appreciability can thus be measured both in absolute terms (turnover) and in relative terms, comparing the position of the undertaking(s) concerned to that of other players on the market (market share). This focus on the position and importance of the undertakings concerned is consistent with the concept "may affect", which implies that the assessment is based on the ability of the agreement or practice to affect trade between Member States rather than on the impact on actual flows of goods and services across borders. The market position of the undertakings concerned and their turnover in the products concerned are indicative of the ability of an agreement or practice to affect trade between Member States. These two elements are reflected in the presumptions set out in paragraphs and 53 below.

48. The application of the appreciability test does not necessarily require that relevant markets be defined and market shares calculated.[34] The sales of an undertaking in absolute terms may be sufficient to support a finding that the impact on trade is appreciable. This is particularly so in the

case of agreements and practices that by their very nature are liable to affect trade between Member States, for example because they concern imports or exports or because they cover several Member States. The fact that in such circumstances turnover in the products covered by the agreement may be sufficient for a finding of an appreciable effect on trade between Member States is reflected in the positive presumption set out in paragraph below.

Notes

[34] See in this respect paragraphs 179 and 231 of the *Volkswagen* judgment cited in footnote 16, and Case T-213/00, *CMA CGM and others*, [2003] ECR [II-913], paragraphs 219 and 220.

49. Agreements and practices must always be considered in the economic and legal context in which they occur. In the case of vertical agreements it may be necessary to have regard to any cumulative effects of parallel networks of similar agreements.[35] Even if a single agreement or network of agreements is not capable of appreciably affecting trade between Member States, the effect of parallel networks of agreements, taken as a whole, may be capable of doing so. For that to be the case, however, it is necessary that the individual agreement or network of agreements makes a significant contribution to the overall effect on trade.[36]

Notes

[35] See e.g. Case T-7/93, *Langnese-Iglo*, [1995] ECR II-1533, paragraph 120.
[36] See paragraphs 140 and 141 of the judgment in *Vereniging van Groothandelaren in Bloemkwekerijprodukten* cited in footnote 5.

2.4.2. *Quantification of appreciability*

50. It is not possible to establish general quantitative rules covering all categories of agreements indicating when trade between Member States is capable of being appreciably affected. It is possible, however, to indicate when trade is normally not capable of being appreciably affected. Firstly, in its notice on agreements of minor importance which do not appreciably restrict competition in the meaning of Article [101](1) of the Treaty (the de minimis rule)[37] the Commission has stated that agreements between small and medium-sized undertakings (SMEs) as defined in the Annex to Commission Recommendation 96/280/EC[38] are normally not capable of affecting trade between Member States. The reason for this presumption is the fact that the activities of SMEs are normally local or at most regional in nature. However, SMEs may be subject to Community law jurisdiction in particular where they engage in cross-border economic activity. Secondly, the Commission considers it appropriate to set out general principles indicating when trade is normally not capable of being appreciably affected, i.e. a standard defining the absence of an appreciable effect on trade between Member States (the NAAT-rule). When applying Article [101], the Commission will consider this standard as a negative rebuttable presumption applying to all agreements within the meaning of Article [101](1) irrespective of the nature of the restrictions contained in the agreement, including restrictions that have been identified as hardcore restrictions in Commission block exemption regulations and guidelines. In cases where this presumption applies the Commission will normally not institute proceedings either upon application or on its own initiative. Where the undertakings assume in good faith that an agreement is covered by this negative presumption, the Commission will not impose fines.

Notes

[37] See Commission Notice on agreements of minor importance which do not appreciably restrict competition under Article [101](1) of the Treaty (OJ C 368, 22.12.2001, p.13, paragraph 3).
[38] OJ L 107, 30.4.1996, p.4. With effect from 1.1.2005 this recommendation will be replaced by Commission Recommendation 2003/361/EC concerning the definition of micro, small and medium-sized enterprises (OJ L 124, 20.5.2003, p.36).

Commentary
para 50: B&C: 1.130 **F&N:** 3.420

51. Without prejudice to paragraph below, this negative definition of appreciability does not imply that agreements, which do not fall within the criteria set out below, are automatically capable of appreciably affecting trade between Member States. A case by case analysis is necessary.

Commentary
para 51: B&C: 1.134

52. The Commission holds the view that in principle agreements are not capable of appreciably affecting trade between Member States when the following cumulative conditions are met:
    (a) The aggregate market share of the parties on any relevant market within the Community affected by the agreement does not exceed 5%, and
    (b) In the case of horizontal agreements, the aggregate annual Community turnover of the undertakings concerned[39] in the products covered by the agreement does not exceed 40 million euro. In the case of agreements concerning the joint buying of products the relevant turnover shall be the parties' combined purchases of the products covered by the agreement.

    In the case of vertical agreements, the aggregate annual Community turnover of the supplier in the products covered by the agreement does not exceed 40 million euro. In the case of licence agreements the relevant turnover shall be the aggregate turnover of the licensees in the products incorporating the licensed technology and the licensor's own turnover in such products. In cases involving agreements concluded between a buyer and several suppliers the relevant turnover shall be the buyer's combined purchases of the products covered by the agreements.
    The Commission will apply the same presumption where during two successive calendar years the above turnover threshold is not exceeded by more than 10% and the above market threshold is not exceeded by more than 2 percentage points. In cases where the agreement concerns an emerging not yet existing market and where as a consequence the parties neither generate relevant turnover nor accumulate any relevant market share, the Commission will not apply this presumption. In such cases appreciability may have to be assessed on the basis of the position of the parties on related product markets or their strength in technologies relating to the agreement.

Notes

[39] The term "undertakings concerned" shall include connected undertakings as defined in paragraph 12.2 of the Commission's Notice on agreements of minor importance which do not appreciably restrict competition under Article [101](1) of the [Treaty on the Functioning of the European Union] (OJ C 368, 22.12.2001, p.13).

Commentary
para 52: B&C: 1.131, 1.133, 4.007 **F&N:** 3.416, 3.417
para 52(a): F&N: 3.421
para 52(b): F&N: 3.422, 3.423

53. The Commission will also hold the view that where an agreement by its very nature is capable of affecting trade between Member States, for example, because it concerns imports and exports or covers several Member States, there is a rebuttable positive presumption that such effects on trade are appreciable when the turnover of the parties in the products covered by the agreement calculated as indicated in paragraphs 52 and 54 exceeds 40 million euro. In the case of agreements that by their very nature are capable of affecting trade between Member States it can also often be presumed that such effects are appreciable when the market share of the parties exceeds the 5% threshold set out in the previous paragraph. However, this presumption does not apply where the agreement covers only part of a Member State (see paragraph 90 below).

Commentary
para 53: B&C: 1.134 **F&N:** 3.425

54. With regard to the threshold of 40 million euro (cf. paragraph 52 above), the turnover is calculated on the basis of total Community sales excluding tax during the previous financial year by the undertakings concerned, of the products covered by the agreement (the contract products). Sales between entities that form part of the same undertaking are excluded.[40]

Notes
40 See the previous footnote.

Commentary
para 54: B&C: 1.132

55. In order to apply the market share threshold, it is necessary to determine the relevant market.[41] This consists of the relevant product market and the relevant geographic market. The market shares are to be calculated on the basis of sales value data or, where appropriate, purchase value data. If value data are not available, estimates based on other reliable market information, including volume data, may be used.

Notes
41 When defining the relevant market, reference should be made to the notice on the definition of the relevant market for the purposes of Community competition law (OJ C 372, 9.12.1997, p.5).

Commentary
para 55: B&C: 1.132

56. In the case of networks of agreements entered into by the same supplier with different distributors, sales made through the entire network are taken into account.

Commentary
para 56: B&C: 1.131 F&N: 3.418, 3.424

57. Contracts that form part of the same overall business arrangement constitute a single agreement for the purposes of the NAAT-rule.[42] Undertakings cannot bring themselves inside these thresholds by dividing up an agreement that forms a whole from an economic perspective.

Notes
42 See also paragraph 14 above.

Commentary
para 57: F&N: 3.418

3. The Application of the Above Principles to Common Types of Agreements and Abuses

58. The Commission will apply the negative presumption set out in the preceding section to all agreements, including agreements that by their very nature are capable of affecting trade between Member States as well as agreements that involve trade with undertakings located in third countries (cf. section 3.3 below).

59. Outside the scope of negative presumption, the Commission will take account of qualitative elements relating to the nature of the agreement or practice and the nature of the products that they concern (see paragraphs and above). The relevance of the nature of the agreement is also reflected in the positive presumption set out in paragraph 53 above relating to appreciability in the case of agreements that by their very nature are capable of affecting trade between Member States. With a view to providing additional guidance on the application of the effect on trade concept it is therefore useful to consider various common types of agreements and practices.

60. In the following sections a primary distinction is drawn between agreements and practices that cover several Member States and agreements and practices that are confined to a single Member State or to part of a single Member State. These two main categories are broken down into further subcategories based on the nature of the agreement or practice involved. Agreements and practices involving third countries are also dealt with.

3.1. Agreements and abuse covering or implemented in several Member States

61. Agreements and practices covering or implemented in several Member States are in almost all cases by their very nature capable of affecting trade between Member States. When the relevant

turnover exceeds the threshold set out in paragraph above it will therefore in most cases not be necessary to conduct a detailed analysis of whether trade between Member States is capable of being affected. However, in order to provide guidance also in these cases and to illustrate the principles developed in section 2 above, it is useful to explain what are the factors that are normally used to support a finding of Community law jurisdiction.

Commentary
para 61: B&C: 1.126

3.1.1. Agreements concerning imports and exports

62. Agreements between undertakings in two or more Member States that concern imports and exports are by their very nature capable of affecting trade between Member States. Such agreements, irrespective of whether they are restrictive of competition or not, have a direct impact on patterns of trade between Member States. In Kerpen & Kerpen, for example, which concerned an agreement between a French producer and a German distributor covering more than 10% of exports of cement from France to Germany, amounting in total to 350000 tonnes per year, the Court of Justice held that it was impossible to take the view that such an agreement was not capable of (appreciably) affecting trade between Member States.[43]

Notes

[43] See paragraph 8 of the judgment in *Kerpen & Kerpen* cited in footnote 15. It should be noted that the Court does not refer to market share but to the share of French exports and to the product volumes involved.

63. This category includes agreements that impose restrictions on imports and exports, including restrictions on active and passive sales and resale by buyers to customers in other Member States.[44] In these cases there is an inherent link between the alleged restriction of competition and the effect on trade, since the very purpose of the restriction is to prevent flows of goods and services between Member States, which would otherwise be possible. It is immaterial whether the parties to the agreement are located in the same Member State or in different Member States.

Notes

[44] See e.g. the judgment in *Volkswagen* cited in footnote 16 and Case T-175/95, *BASF Coatings*, [1999] ECR II-1581. For a horizontal agreement to prevent parallel trade see Joined Cases 96/82 and others, *IAZ International*, [1983] ECR 3369, paragraph 27.

3.1.2. Cartels covering several Member States

64. Cartel agreements such as those involving price fixing and market sharing covering several Member States are by their very nature capable of affecting trade between Member States. Cross-border cartels harmonise the conditions of competition and affect the interpenetration of trade by cementing traditional patterns of trade.[45] When undertakings agree to allocate geographic territories, sales from other areas into the allocated territories are capable of being eliminated or reduced. When undertakings agree to fix prices, they eliminate competition and any resulting price differentials that would entice both competitors and customers to engage in cross-border trade. When undertakings agree on sales quotas traditional patterns of trade are preserved. The undertakings concerned abstain from expanding output and thereby from serving potential customers in other Member States.

65. The effect on trade produced by cross-border cartels is generally also by its very nature appreciable due to the market position of the parties to the cartel. Cartels are normally only formed when the participating undertakings together hold a large share of the market, as this allows them to raise price or reduce output.

Notes

[45] See e.g. Case T-142/89, *Usines Gustave Boël*, [1995] ECR II-867, paragraph 102.

3.1.3. Horizontal cooperation agreements covering several Member States

66. This section covers various types of horizontal cooperation agreements. Horizontal cooperation agreements may for instance take the form of agreements whereby two or more undertakings cooperate in the performance of a particular economic activity such as production and distribution.[46] Often such agreements are referred to as joint ventures. However, joint ventures that perform on a lasting basis all the functions of an autonomous economic entity are covered by the Merger Regulation.[47] At the level of the Community such full function joint ventures are not dealt with under Articles [101] and [102] except in cases where Article 2(4) of the Merger Regulation is applicable.[48] This section therefore does not deal with full-function joint ventures. In the case of non-full function joint ventures the joint entity does not operate as an autonomous supplier (or buyer) on any market. It merely serves the parents, who themselves operate on the market.[49]

Notes

[46] Horizontal cooperation agreements are dealt with in the Commission Guidelines on the applicability of Article [101] of the [Treaty on the Functioning of the European Union] to horizontal cooperation agreements (OJ C 3, 6.1.2001, p.2). Those guidelines deal with the substantive competition assessment of various types of agreements but do not deal with the effect on trade issue. [Ed note: see now Commission Notice 2011/C 11/01, Guidelines on the applicability of Article 101 of the Treaty on the Functioning of the European Union to horizontal co-operation agreements (OJ C 11, 14.1.2011, p.1), reproduced at C17 below.]

[47] See Council Regulation (EC) No 139/2004 on the control of concentrations between undertakings (OJ L 24, 29.1.2004, p.1).

[48] The Commission Notice on the concept of full-function joint ventures under the Merger Regulation (OJ C 66, 2.3.1998, p.1) gives guidance on the scope of this concept. [Ed note: see now the Commission Consolidated Jurisdictional Notice (OJ C 95, 16.4.2008, p.1), reproduced at D11 below].

[49] See e.g. the Commission Decision in *Ford/Volkswagen* (OJ L 20, 28.1.1993, p.14).

67. Joint ventures which engage in activities in two or more Member States or which produce an output that is sold by the parents in two or more Member States affect the commercial activities of the parties in those areas of the Community. Such agreements are therefore normally by their very nature capable of affecting trade between Member States compared to the situation without the agreement.[50] Patterns of trade are affected when undertakings switch their activities to the joint venture or use it for the purpose of establishing a new source of supply in the Community.

Notes

[50] See in this respect paragraph 146 of the *Compagnie Générale Maritime* judgment cited in footnote 23 above.

Commentary
para 67: B&C: 1.127

68. Trade may also be capable of being affected where a joint venture produces an input for the parent companies, which is subsequently further processed or incorporated into a product by the parent undertakings. This is likely to be the case where the input in question was previously sourced from suppliers in other Member States, where the parents previously produced the input in other Member States or where the final product is traded in more than one Member State.

Commentary
para 68: B&C: 1.127

69. In the assessment of appreciability it is important to take account of the parents' sales of products related to the agreement and not only those of the joint entity created by the agreement, given that the joint venture does not operate as an autonomous entity on any market.

3.1.4. Vertical agreements implemented in several Member States

70. Vertical agreements and networks of similar vertical agreements implemented in several Member States are normally capable of affecting trade between Member States if they cause trade to be channelled in a particular way. Networks of selective distribution agreements implemented in two or more Member States for example, channel trade in a particular way because they limit

trade to members of the network, thereby affecting patterns of trade compared to the situation without the agreement.[51]

Notes
[51] See in this respect Joined Cases 43/82 and 63/82, *VBVB and VBBB*, [1984] ECR 19, paragraph 9.

71. Trade between Member States is also capable of being affected by vertical agreements that have foreclosure effects. This may for instance be the case of agreements whereby distributors in several Member States agree to buy only from a particular supplier or to sell only its products. Such agreements may limit trade between the Member States in which the agreements are implemented, or trade from Member States not covered by the agreements. Foreclosure may result from individual agreements or from networks of agreements. When an agreement or networks of agreements that cover several Member States have foreclosure effects, the ability of the agreement or agreements to affect trade between Member States is normally by its very nature appreciable.

72. Agreements between suppliers and distributors which provide for resale price maintenance (RPM) and which cover two or more Member States are normally also by their very nature capable of affecting trade between Member States.[52] Such agreements alter the price levels that would have been likely to exist in the absence of the agreements and thereby affect patterns of trade.

Notes
[52] See in this respect Case T-66/89, *Publishers Association*, [1992] ECR II-1995.

3.1.5. *Abuses of dominant positions covering several Member States*

73. In the case of abuse of a dominant position it is useful to distinguish between abuses that raise barriers to entry or eliminate competitors (exclusionary abuses) and abuses whereby the dominant undertaking exploits its economic power for instance by charging excessive or discriminatory prices (exploitative abuses). Both kinds of abuse may be carried out either through agreements, which are equally subject to Article [101](1), or through unilateral conduct, which as far as Community competition law is concerned is subject only to Article [102].

74. In the case of exploitative abuses such as discriminatory rebates, the impact is on downstream trading partners, which either benefit or suffer, altering their competitive position and affecting patterns of trade between Member States.

Commentary
para 74: **B&C:** 1.136

75. When a dominant undertaking engages in exclusionary conduct in more than one Member State, such abuse is normally by its very nature capable of affecting trade between Member States. Such conduct has a negative impact on competition in an area extending beyond a single Member State, being likely to divert trade from the course it would have followed in the absence of the abuse. For example, patterns of trade are capable of being affected where the dominant undertaking grants loyalty rebates. Customers covered by the exclusionary rebate system are likely to purchase less from competitors of the dominant firm than they would otherwise have done. Exclusionary conduct that aims directly at eliminating a competitor such as predatory pricing is also capable of affecting trade between Member States because of its impact on the competitive market structure inside the Community.[53] When a dominant firm engages in behaviour with a view to eliminating a competitor operating in more than one Member State, trade is capable of being affected in several ways. First, there is a risk that the affected competitor will cease to be a source of supply inside the Community. Even if the targeted undertaking is not eliminated, its future competitive conduct is likely to be affected, which may also have an impact on trade between Member States. Secondly, the abuse may have an impact on other competitors. Through its abusive behaviour the dominant undertaking can signal to its competitors that it will discipline attempts to engage in real competition. Thirdly, the very fact of eliminating a competitor may be sufficient for trade between Member States to be capable of being affected. This may be the case even where the undertaking that risks being eliminated mainly engages in exports to third countries.[54] Once the effective competitive market structure inside the Community risks being further impaired, there is Community law jurisdiction.

Notes

⁵³ See in this respect the judgment in *Commercial Solvents* cited in footnote 3, in the judgment in *Hoffmann-La Roche*, cited in footnote, paragraph 125, and in *RTE and ITP* cited in footnote, as well as Case 6/72, *Continental Can*, [1973] ECR 215, paragraph 16, and Case 27/76, *United Brands*, [1978] ECR 207, paragraphs 197 to 203.

⁵⁴ See paragraphs 32 and 33 of the judgment in *Commercial Solvents* cited in footnote 3.

Commentary
para 75: B&C: 1.128

76. Where a dominant undertaking engages in exploitative or exclusionary abuse in more than one Member State, the capacity of the abuse to affect trade between Member States will normally also by its very nature be appreciable. Given the market position of the dominant undertaking concerned, and the fact that the abuse is implemented in several Member States, the scale of the abuse and its likely impact on patterns of trade is normally such that trade between Member States is capable of being appreciably affected. In the case of an exploitative abuse such as price discrimination, the abuse alters the competitive position of trading partners in several Member States. In the case of exclusionary abuses, including abuses that aim at eliminating a competitor, the economic activity engaged in by competitors in several Member States is affected. The very existence of a dominant position in several Member States implies that competition in a substantial part of the common market is already weakened.⁵⁵ When a dominant undertaking further weakens competition through recourse to abusive conduct, for example by eliminating a competitor, the ability of the abuse to affect trade between Member States is normally appreciable.

Notes

⁵⁵ According to settled case law dominance is a position of economic strength enjoyed by an undertaking which enables it to prevent effective competition being maintained on the relevant market by affording it the power to act to an appreciable extent independently of its competitors, its customers and ultimately of the consumers, see e.g. paragraph 38 of the judgment in *Hoffmann-La Roche* cited in footnote 9.

3.2. Agreements and abuses covering a single, or only part of a, Member State

77. When agreements or abusive practices cover the territory of a single Member State, it may be necessary to proceed with a more detailed inquiry into the ability of the agreements or abusive practices to affect trade between Member States. It should be recalled that for there to be an effect on trade between Member States it is not required that trade is reduced. It is sufficient that an appreciable change is capable of being caused in the pattern of trade between Member States. Nevertheless, in many cases involving a single Member State the nature of the alleged infringement, and in particular, its propensity to foreclose the national market, provides a good indication of the capacity of the agreement or practice to affect trade between Member States. The examples mentioned hereafter are not exhaustive. They merely provide examples of cases where agreements confined to the territory of a single Member State can be considered capable of affecting trade between Member States.

3.2.1. *Cartels covering a single Member State*

78. Horizontal cartels covering the whole of a Member State are normally capable of affecting trade between Member States. The Community Courts have held in a number of cases that agreements extending over the whole territory of a Member State by their very nature have the effect of reinforcing the partitioning of markets on a national basis by hindering the economic penetration which the Treaty is designed to bring about.⁵⁶

Notes

⁵⁶ See for a recent example paragraph 95 of the *Wouters* judgment cited in footnote 11.

79. The capacity of such agreements to partition the internal market follows from the fact that undertakings participating in cartels in only one Member State, normally need to take action to exclude competitors from other Member States.⁵⁷ If they do not, and the product covered by the agreement is tradable,⁵⁸ the cartel risks being undermined by competition from undertakings from

other Member States. Such agreements are normally also by their very nature capable of having an appreciable effect on trade between Member States, given the market coverage required for such cartels to be effective.

Notes

57 See e.g. Case 246/86, *Belasco*, [1989] ECR 2117, paragraph 32–38.

58 See paragraph 34 of the *Belasco* judgment cited in the previous footnote and more recently Joined Cases T-202/98 a.o., *British Sugar*, [2001] ECR II-2035, paragraph 79. On the other hand this is not so when the market is not susceptible to imports, see paragraph 51 of the *Bagnasco* judgment cited in footnote 11.

Commentary
para 79: B&C: 1.140

80. Given the fact that the effect on trade concept encompasses potential effects, it is not decisive whether such action against competitors from other Member States is in fact adopted at any given point in time. If the cartel price is similar to the price prevailing in other Member States, there may be no immediate need for the members of the cartel to take action against competitors from other Member States. What matters is whether or not they are likely to do so, if market conditions change. The likelihood of that depends on the existence or otherwise of natural barriers to trade in the market, including in particular whether or not the product in question is tradable. In a case involving certain retail banking services[59] the Court of Justice has, for example, held that trade was not capable of being appreciably affected because the potential for trade in the specific products concerned was very limited and because they were not an important factor in the choice made by undertakings from other Member States regarding whether or not to establish themselves in the Member State in question.[60]

Notes

59 Guarantees for current account credit facilities.

60 See paragraph 51 of the *Bagnasco* judgment cited in footnote 11.

Commentary
para 80: B&C: 1.140

81. The extent to which the members of a cartel monitor prices and competitors from other Member States can provide an indication of the extent to which the products covered by the cartel are tradable. Monitoring suggests that competition and competitors from other Member States are perceived as a potential threat to the cartel. Moreover, if there is evidence that the members of the cartel have deliberately fixed the price level in the light of the price level prevailing in other Member States (limit pricing), it is an indication that the products in question are tradable and that trade between Member States is capable of being affected.

Commentary
para 81: B&C: 1.128 F&N: 2.115

82. Trade is normally also capable of being affected when the members of a national cartel temper the competitive constraint imposed by competitors from other Member States by inducing them to join the restrictive agreement, or if their exclusion from the agreement places the competitors at a competitive disadvantage.[61] In such cases the agreement either prevents these competitors from exploiting any competitive advantage that they have, or raises their costs, thereby having a negative impact on their competitiveness and their sales. In both cases the agreement hampers the operations of competitors from other Member States on the national market in question. The same is true when a cartel agreement confined to a single Member State is concluded between undertakings that resell products imported from other Member States.[62]

Notes

61 See in this respect Case 45/85, *Verband der Sachversicherer*, [1987] ECR 405, paragraph 50, and Case C-7/95 P, *John Deere*, [1998] ECR I-3111. See also paragraph 172 of the judgment in *Van Landewyck* cited in footnote 22, where the Court stressed that the agreement in question reduced appreciably the incentive to sell imported products.

62 See e.g. the judgment in *Stichting Sigarettenindustrie*, cited in footnote 15, paragraphs 49 and 50.

3.2.2. *Horizontal cooperation agreements covering a single Member State*

83. Horizontal cooperation agreements and in particular non-full function joint ventures (cf. paragraph 66 above), which are confined to a single Member State and which do not directly relate to imports and exports, do not belong to the category of agreements that by their very nature are capable of affecting trade between Member States. A careful examination of the capacity of the individual agreement to affect trade between Member States may therefore be required.

84. Horizontal cooperation agreements may, in particular, be capable of affecting trade between Member States where they have foreclosure effects. This may be the case with agreements that establish sector-wide standardisation and certification regimes, which either exclude under-takings from other Member States or which are more easily fulfilled by undertakings from the Member State in question due to the fact that they are based on national rules and traditions. In such circumstances the agreements make it more difficult for undertakings from other Member States to penetrate the national market.

Commentary
para 84: F&N: 3.429

85. Trade may also be affected where a joint venture results in undertakings from other Member States being cut off from an important channel of distribution or source of demand. If, for example, two or more distributors established within the same Member State, and which account for a substantial share of imports of the products in question, establish a purchasing joint venture combining their purchases of that product, the resulting reduction in the number of distribution channels limits the possibility for suppliers from other Member States of gaining access to the national market in question. Trade is therefore capable of being affected.[63] Trade may also be affected where undertakings which previously imported a particular product form a joint venture which is entrusted with the production of that same product. In this case the agreement causes a change in the patterns of trade between Member States compared to the situation before the agreement.

Notes
[63] See in this respect Case T-22/97, *Kesko*, [1999] ECR II-3775, paragraph 109.

3.2.3. *Vertical agreements covering a single Member State*

86. Vertical agreements covering the whole of a Member State may, in particular, be capable of affecting patterns of trade between Member States when they make it more difficult for undertakings from other Member States to penetrate the national market in question, either by means of exports or by means of establishment (foreclosure effect). When vertical agreements give rise to such foreclosure effects, they contribute to the partitioning of markets on a national basis, thereby hindering the economic interpenetration which the Treaty is designed to bring about.[64]

Notes
[64] See e.g. Case T-65/98, *Van den Bergh Foods*, [2003] ECR II-[4653], and the judgment in *Langnese-Iglo*, cited in footnote 35, paragraph 120.

Commentary
para 86: F&N: 3.429

87. Foreclosure may, for example, occur when suppliers impose exclusive purchasing obligations on buyers.[65] In *Delimitis*,[66] which concerned agreements between a brewer and owners of premises where beer was consumed whereby the latter undertook to buy beer exclusively from the brewer, the Court of Justice defined foreclosure as the absence, due to the agreements, of real and concrete possibilities of gaining access to the market. Agreements normally only create significant barriers to entry when they cover a significant proportion of the market. Market share and market coverage can be used as an indicator in this respect. In making the assessment account must be taken not only of the particular agreement or network of agreements in question, but also of other parallel networks of agreements having similar effects.[67]

Part C Substantive Antitrust Matters

Notes

⁶⁵ See e.g. judgment of 7.12.2000, Case C-214/99, *Neste*, ECR I-11121.

⁶⁶ See judgment of 28.2.1991, Case C-234/89, *Delimitis*, ECR I-935.

⁶⁷ See paragraph 120 of the *Langnese-Iglo* judgment cited in footnote 35.

88. Vertical agreements which cover the whole of a Member State and which relate to tradable products may also be capable of affecting trade between Member States, even if they do not create direct obstacles to trade. Agreements whereby undertakings engage in resale price maintenance (RPM) may have direct effects on trade between Member States by increasing imports from other Member States and by decreasing exports from the Member State in question.⁶⁸ Agreements involving RPM may also affect patterns of trade in much the same way as horizontal cartels. To the extent that the price resulting from RPM is higher than that prevailing in other Member States this price level is only sustainable if imports from other Member States can be controlled.

Notes

⁶⁸ See e.g. Commission Decision in *Volkswagen (II)*, cited in footnote 21, paragraphs 81 et seq.

3.2.4. *Agreements covering only part of a Member State*

89. In qualitative terms the assessment of agreements covering only part of a Member State is approached in the same way as in the case of agreements covering the whole of a Member State. This means that the analysis in section 2 applies. In the assessment of appreciability, however, the two categories must be distinguished, as it must be taken into account that only part of a Member State is covered by the agreement. It must also be taken into account what proportion of the national territory is susceptible to trade. If, for example, transport costs or the operating radius of equipment render it economically unviable for undertakings from other Member States to serve the entire territory of another Member State, trade is capable of being affected if the agreement forecloses access to the part of the territory of a Member State that is susceptible to trade, provided that this part is not insignificant.⁶⁹

Notes

⁶⁹ See in this respect paragraphs 177 to 181 of the judgment in *SCK and FNK* cited in footnote 13.

Commentary
para 89: F&N: 3.432

90. Where an agreement forecloses access to a regional market, then for trade to be appreciably affected, the volume of sales affected must be significant in proportion to the overall volume of sales of the products concerned inside the Member State in question. This assessment cannot be based merely on geographic coverage. The market share of the parties to the agreement must also be given fairly limited weight. Even if the parties have a high market share in a properly defined regional market, the size of that market in terms of volume may still be insignificant when compared to total sales of the products concerned within the Member State in question. In general, the best indicator of the capacity of the agreement to (appreciably) affect trade between Member States is therefore considered to be the share of the national market in terms of volume that is being foreclosed. Agreements covering areas with a high concentration of demand will thus weigh more heavily than those covering areas where demand is less concentrated. For Community jurisdiction to be established the share of the national market that is being foreclosed must be significant.

Commentary
para 90: B&C: 1.143 **F&N:** 3.433

91. Agreements that are local in nature are in themselves not capable of appreciably affecting trade between Member States. This is the case even if the local market is located in a border region. Conversely, if the foreclosed share of the national market is significant, trade is capable of being affected even where the market in question is not located in a border region.

Commentary
para 91: F&N: 3.433

92. In cases in this category some guidance may be derived from the case law concerning the concept in Article [102] of a substantial part of the common market.[70] Agreements that, for example, have the effect of hindering competitors from other Member States from gaining access to part of a Member State, which constitutes a substantial part of the common market, should be considered to have an appreciable effect on trade between Member States.

Notes

[70] See as to this notion the judgment in *Ambulanz Glöckner*, cited in footnote 11, paragraph 38, and Case C-179/90, *Merci convenzionali porto di Genova*, [1991] ECR I-5889, and Case C-242/95, *GT-Link*, [1997] ECR I-4449.

Commentary
para 92: B&C: 1.143 F&N: 3.434

3.2.5. *Abuses of dominant positions covering a single Member State*

93. Where an undertaking, which holds a dominant position covering the whole of a Member State, engages in exclusionary abuses, trade between Member States is normally capable of being affected. Such abusive conduct will generally make it more difficult for competitors from other Member States to penetrate the market, in which case patterns of trade are capable of being affected.[71] In Michelin,[72] for example, the Court of Justice held that a system of loyalty rebates foreclosed competitors from other Member States and therefore affected trade within the meaning of Article [102]. In Rennet[73] the Court similarly held that an abuse in the form of an exclusive purchasing obligation on customers foreclosed products from other Member States.

Notes

[71] See e.g. paragraph 135 of the judgment in *BPB Industries and British Gypsum* cited in footnote [22].
[72] See Case 322/81, *Nederlandse Banden Industrie Michelin*, [1983] ECR 3461.
[73] See Case 61/80, *Coöperative Stremsel-en Kleurselfabriek*, [1981] ECR 851, paragraph 15.

94. Exclusionary abuses that affect the competitive market structure inside a Member State, for instance by eliminating or threatening to eliminate a competitor, may also be capable of affecting trade between Member States. Where the undertaking that risks being eliminated only operates in a single Member State, the abuse will normally not affect trade between Member States. However, trade between Member States is capable of being affected where the targeted undertaking exports to or imports from other Member States[74] and where it also operates in other Member States.[75] An effect on trade may arise from the dissuasive impact of the abuse on other competitors. If through repeated conduct the dominant undertaking has acquired a reputation for adopting exclusionary practices towards competitors that attempt to engage in direct competition, competitors from other Member States are likely to compete less aggressively, in which case trade may be affected, even if the victim in the case at hand is not from another Member State.

Notes

[74] See in this respect judgment in *Irish Sugar*, cited in footnote 17, paragraph 169.
[75] See paragraph 70 of the judgment in *RTE (Magill)* cited in footnote 27.

Commentary
para 94: B&C: 1.141

95. In the case of exploitative abuses such as price discrimination and excessive pricing, the situation may be more complex. Price discrimination between domestic customers will normally not affect trade between Member States. However, it may do so if the buyers are engaged in export activities and are disadvantaged by the discriminatory pricing or if this practice is used to prevent imports.[76] Practices consisting of offering lower prices to customers that are the most likely to import products from other Member States may make it more difficult for competitors from other Member States to enter the market. In such cases trade between Member States is capable of being affected.

Notes

[76] See the judgment in *Irish Sugar* cited in footnote 17.

Part C Substantive Antitrust Matters

Commentary
para 95: B&C: 1.141

96. As long as an undertaking has a dominant position which covers the whole of a Member State it is normally immaterial whether the specific abuse engaged in by the dominant undertaking only covers part of its territory or affects certain buyers within the national territory. A dominant firm can significantly impede trade by engaging in abusive conduct in the areas or vis-à-vis the customers that are the most likely to be targeted by competitors from other Member States. For example, it may be the case that a particular channel of distribution constitutes a particularly important means of gaining access to broad categories of consumers. Hindering access to such channels can have a substantial impact on trade between Member States. In the assessment of appreciability it must also be taken into account that the very presence of the dominant undertaking covering the whole of a Member State is likely to make market penetration more difficult. Any abuse which makes it more difficult to enter the national market should therefore be considered to appreciably affect trade. The combination of the market position of the dominant undertaking and the anti-competitive nature of its conduct implies that such abuses have normally by their very nature an appreciable effect on trade. However, if the abuse is purely local in nature or involves only an insignificant share of the sales of the dominant undertaking within the Member State in question, trade may not be capable of being appreciably affected.

Commentary
para 96: B&C: 1.142 F&N: 3.433

3.2.6. Abuse of a dominant position covering only part of a Member State

97. Where a dominant position covers only part of a Member State some guidance may, as in the case of agreements, be derived from the condition in Article [102] that the dominant position must cover a substantial part of the common market. If the dominant position covers part of a Member State that constitutes a substantial part of the common market and the abuse makes it more difficult for competitors from other Member States to gain access to the market where the undertaking is dominant, trade between Member States must normally be considered capable of being appreciably affected.

Commentary
para 97: B&C: 1.144 F&N: 3.434

98. In the application of this criterion regard must be had in particular to the size of the market in question in terms of volume. Regions and even a port or an airport situated in a Member State may, depending on their importance, constitute a substantial part of the common market.[77] In the latter cases it must be taken into account whether the infrastructure in question is used to provide cross-border services and, if so, to what extent. When infrastructures such as airports and ports are important in providing cross-border services, trade between Member States is capable of being affected.

Notes
[77] See e.g. the case law cited in footnote 70.

Commentary
para 98: B&C: 1.144

99. As in the case of dominant positions covering the whole of a Member State (cf. paragraph 95 above), trade may not be capable of being appreciably affected if the abuse is purely local in nature or involves only an insignificant share of the sales of the dominant undertaking.

Commentary
para 99: B&C: 1.144

3.3. Agreements and abuses involving imports and exports with undertakings located in third countries, and agreements and practices involving undertakings located in third countries

3.3.1. General remarks

100. Articles [101] and [102] apply to agreements and practices that are capable of affecting trade between Member States even if one or more of the parties are located outside the Community.[78] Articles [101] and [102] apply irrespective of where the undertakings are located or where the agreement has been concluded, provided that the agreement or practice is either implemented inside the Community,[79] or produce effects inside the Community.[80] Articles [101] and [102] may also apply to agreements and practices that cover third countries, provided that they are capable of affecting trade between Member States. The general principle set out in section 2 above according to which the agreement or practice must be capable of having an appreciable influence, direct or indirect, actual or potential, on the pattern of trade between Member States, also applies in the case of agreements and abuses which involve undertakings located in third countries or which relate to imports or exports with third countries.

Notes

[78] See in this respect Case 28/77, *Tepea*, [1978] ECR 1391, paragraph 48, and paragraph 16 of the judgment in *Continental Can* cited in footnote 53.

[79] See Joined Cases C-89/85 and others, *Ahlström Osakeyhtiö (Woodpulp)*, [1988] ECR 651, paragraph 16.

[80] See in this respect Case T-102/96, *Gencor*, [1999] ECR II-753, which applies the effects test in the field of mergers.

Commentary
para 100: B&C: 1.145 **F&N:** 3.435

101. For the purposes of establishing Community law jurisdiction it is sufficient that an agreement or practice involving third countries or undertakings located in third countries is capable of affecting cross-border economic activity inside the Community. Import into one Member State may be sufficient to trigger effects of this nature. Imports can affect the conditions of competition in the importing Member State, which in turn can have an impact on exports and imports of competing products to and from other Member States. In other words, imports from third countries resulting from the agreement or practice may cause a diversion of trade between Member States, thus affecting patterns of trade.

102. In the application of the effect on trade criterion to the above mentioned agreements and practices it is relevant to examine, inter alia, what is the object of the agreement or practice as indicated by its content or the underlying intent of the undertakings involved.[81]

103. Where the object of the agreement is to restrict competition inside the Community the requisite effect on trade between Member States is more readily established than where the object is predominantly to regulate competition outside the Community. Indeed in the former case the agreement or practice has a direct impact on competition inside the Community and trade between Member States. Such agreements and practices, which may concern both imports and exports, are normally by their very nature capable of affecting trade between Member States.

Notes

[81] See to that effect paragraph 19 of the judgment in *Javico* cited in footnote 19.

3.3.2. Arrangements that have as their object the restriction of competition inside the Community

104. In the case of imports, this category includes agreements that bring about an isolation of the internal market.[82] This is, for instance, the case of agreements whereby competitors in the Community and in third countries share markets, e.g. by agreeing not to sell in each other's home markets or by concluding reciprocal (exclusive) distribution agreements.[83]

105. In the case of exports, this category includes cases where undertakings that compete in two or more Member States agree to export certain (surplus) quantities to third countries with a view to co-ordinating their market conduct inside the Community. Such export agreements serve to reduce price competition by limiting output inside the Community, thereby affecting trade

between Member States. Without the export agreement these quantities might have been sold inside the Community.[84]

Notes

82 See in this respect Case 51/75, *EMI v CBS*, [1976] ECR 811, paragraphs 28 and 29.

83 See Commission Decision in *Siemens/Fanuc* (OJ L 376, 31.12.1985, p.29).

84 See in this respect Joined Cases 29/83 and 30/83, *CRAM and Rheinzinc*, [1984] ECR 1679, and Joined Cases 40/73 and others, *Suiker Unie*, [1975] ECR 1663, paragraphs 564 and 580.

3.3.3. *Other arrangements*

106. In the case of agreements and practices whose object is not to restrict competition inside the Community, it is normally necessary to proceed with a more detailed analysis of whether or not cross-border economic activity inside the Community, and thus patterns of trade between Member States, are capable of being affected.

Commentary
para 106: B&C: 1.134, 2.128

107. In this regard it is relevant to examine the effects of the agreement or practice on customers and other operators inside the Community that rely on the products of the undertakings that are parties to the agreement or practice.[85] In Compagnie maritime belge,[86] which concerned agreements between shipping companies operating between Community ports and West African ports, the agreements were held to be capable of indirectly affecting trade between Member States because they altered the catchment areas of the Community ports covered by the agreements and because they affected the activities of other undertakings inside those areas. More specifically, the agreements affected the activities of undertakings that relied on the parties for transportation services, either as a means of transporting goods purchased in third countries or sold there, or as an important input into the services that the ports themselves offered.

Notes

85 See paragraph 22 of the judgment in *Javico* cited in footnote 19.

86 See paragraph 203 of the judgment in *Compagnie maritime belge* cited in footnote 12.

108. Trade may also be capable of being affected when the agreement prevents re-imports into the Community. This may, for example, be the case with vertical agreements between Community suppliers and third country distributors, imposing restrictions on resale outside an allocated territory, including the Community. If in the absence of the agreement resale to the Community would be possible and likely, such imports may be capable of affecting patterns of trade inside the Community.[87]

Notes

87 See in this respect the judgment in *Javico* cited in footnote 19.

109. However, for such effects to be likely, there must be an appreciable difference between the prices of the products charged in the Community and those charged outside the Community, and this price difference must not be eroded by customs duties and transport costs. In addition, the product volumes exported compared to the total market for those products in the territory of the common market must not be insignificant.[88] If these product volumes are insignificant compared to those sold inside the Community, the impact of any re-importation on trade between Member States is considered not to be appreciable. In making this assessment, regard must be had not only to the individual agreement concluded between the parties, but also to any cumulative effect of similar agreements concluded by the same and competing suppliers. It may be, for example, that the product volumes covered by a single agreement are quite small, but that the product volumes covered by several such agreements are significant. In that case the agreements taken as a whole may be capable of appreciably affecting trade between Member States. It should be recalled, however (cf. paragraph 49 above), that the individual agreement or network of agreements must make a significant contribution to the overall effect on trade.

C13

COMMUNICATION FROM THE COMMISSION

Notice

Guidelines on the application of Article [101](3)* of the [Treaty on the
Functioning of the European Union]

(2004/C 101/08)

(Text with EEA relevance)

Official Journal C 101, 27.4.2004, p.97

Celex No: 52004XC0427(07)

EUR-Lex permanent link: <http://eur-lex.europa.eu/LexUriServ/LexUriServ.do?uri=CELEX: 52004
XC0427(07):EN:NOT>

1. INTRODUCTION

1. Article [101](3) of the Treaty sets out an exception rule, which provides a defence to undertakings
against a finding of an infringement of Article [101][1] of the Treaty. Agreements, decisions of associations of undertakings and concerted practices(1) caught by Article [101](1) which satisfy the
conditions of Article [101](3) are valid and enforceable, no prior decision to that effect being
required.

2. Article [101](3) can be applied in individual cases or to categories of agreements and concerted practices by way of block exemption regulation. Regulation 1/2003 on the implementation of the competition rules laid down in Articles [101] and [102]² does not affect the validity and legal nature of block exemption regulations. All existing block exemption regulations remain in force and agreements covered by block exemption regulations are legally valid and enforceable even if they are restrictive of competition within the meaning of Article [101](1).³ Such agreements can only be prohibited for the future and only upon formal withdrawal of the block exemption by the Commission or a national competition authority.⁴ Block exempted agreements cannot be held invalid by national courts in the context of private litigation.

Notes

² OJ L 1, 4.1.2003, p.1.

³ All existing block exemption regulations and Commission notices are available on the DG Competition website: <http://www.europa.eu.int/comm/%20dgs/competition>.

⁴ See paragraph 36 below.

3. The existing guidelines on vertical restraints, horizontal cooperation agreements and technology transfer agreements⁵ deal with the application of Article [101] to various types of agreements and concerted practices. The purpose of those guidelines is to set out the Commission's view of the substantive assessment criteria applied to the various types of agreements and practices.

Notes

⁵ See Commission Notice on Guidelines on vertical restraints (OJ C 291, 13.10.2000, p.1) [Ed note: see now Commission Notice 2010/C 130/01, Guidelines on Vertical Restraints (OJ C 130, 19.5.2010, p.1), reproduced at C15 below.], Commission Notice on Guidelines on the application of Article [101] of the Treaty to horizontal cooperation agreements (OJ C 3, 6.1.2001, p.2) [Ed note: see now Commission Notice 2011/C 11/01, Guidelines on the applicability of Article 101 of the Treaty on the Functioning of the European Union to horizontal co-operation agreements (OJ C 11, 14.1.2011, p.1), reproduced at C17 below.], and Commission Notice on Guidelines on the application of Article [101] of the Treaty to technology transfer agreements, [OJ C 101, 27.04.2004, p.2].

4. The present guidelines set out the Commission's interpretation of the conditions for exception contained in Article [101](3). It thereby provides guidance on how it will apply Article [101] in individual cases. Although not binding on them, these guidelines also intend to give guidance to the courts and authorities of the Member States in their application of Article [101](1) and (3) of the Treaty.

5. The guidelines establish an analytical framework for the application of Article [101](3). The purpose is to develop a methodology for the application of this Treaty provision. This methodology is based on the economic approach already introduced and developed in the guidelines on vertical restraints, horizontal co-operation agreements and technology transfer agreements. The Commission will follow the present guidelines, which provide more detailed guidance on the application of the four conditions of Article [101](3) than the guidelines on vertical restraints, horizontal co-operation agreements and technology transfer agreements, also with regard to agreements covered by those guidelines.

6. The standards set forth in the present guidelines must be applied in light of the circumstances specific to each case. This excludes a mechanical application. Each case must be assessed on its own facts and the guidelines must be applied reasonably and flexibly.

7. With regard to a number of issues, the present guidelines outline the current state of the case law of the Court of Justice. However, the Commission also intends to explain its policy with regard to issues that have not been dealt with in the case law, or that are subject to interpretation. The Commission's position, however, is without prejudice to the case law of the Court of Justice and the Court of First Instance concerning the interpretation of Article [101](1) and (3), and to the interpretation that the Community Courts may give to those provisions in the future.

Commentary
para 7: B&C: 1.074

2. The General Framework of Article [101 TFEU]

2.1. The Treaty provisions

8. Article [101](1) prohibits all agreements between undertakings, decisions by associations of undertakings and concerted practices which may affect trade between Member States[6] and which have as their object or effect the prevention, restriction or distortion of competition.[7]

Notes

[6] The concept of effect on trade between Member States is dealt with in separate guidelines.

[7] In the following the term "restriction" includes the prevention and distortion of competition.

9. As an exception to this rule Article [101](3) provides that the prohibition contained in Article [101](1) may be declared inapplicable in case of agreements which contribute to improving the production or distribution of goods or to promoting technical or economic progress, while allowing consumers a fair share of the resulting benefits, and which do not impose restrictions which are not indispensable to the attainment of these objectives, and do not afford such undertakings the possibility of eliminating competition in respect of a substantial part of the products concerned.

10. According to Article 1(1) of Regulation 1/2003 agreements which are caught by Article [101](1) and which do not satisfy the conditions of Article [101](3) are prohibited, no prior decision to that effect being required.[8] According to Article 1(2) of the same Regulation agreements which are caught by Article [101](1) but which satisfy the conditions of Article [101](3) are not prohibited, no prior decision to that effect being required. Such agreements are valid and enforceable from the moment that the conditions of Article [101](3) are satisfied and for as long as that remains the case.

Notes

[8] According to Article [101](2) such agreements are automatically void.

11. The assessment under Article [101] thus consists of two parts. The first step is to assess whether an agreement between undertakings, which is capable of affecting trade between Member States, has an anti-competitive object or actual or potential[9] anti-competitive effects. The second step, which only becomes relevant when an agreement is found to be restrictive of competition, is to determine the pro-competitive benefits produced by that agreement and to assess whether these pro-competitive effects outweigh the anti-competitive effects. The balancing of anticompetitive and pro-competitive effects is conducted exclusively within the framework laid down by Article [101](3).[10]

Notes

[9] Article [101](1) prohibits both actual and potential anti-competitive effects, see e.g. Case C-7/95 P *John Deere* [1998] ECR I-3111, paragraph 77.

[10] See Case T-65/98 *Van den Bergh Foods* [2003] ECR II-[4653], paragraph 107 and Case T-112/99 *Métropole télévision (M6) and others* [2001] ECR II-2459, paragraph 74, where the Court of First Instance held that it is only in the precise framework of Article [101](3) that the pro-and anti-competitive aspects of a restriction may be weighed.

Commentary

para 11.3: F&N: 3.511

12. The assessment of any countervailing benefits under Article [101](3) necessarily requires prior determination of the restrictive nature and impact of the agreement. To place Article [101](3) in its proper context it is appropriate to briefly outline the objective and principal content of the prohibition rule of Article [101](1). The Commission guidelines on vertical restraints, horizontal co-operation agreements and technology transfer agreements[11] contain substantial guidance on the application of Article [101](1) to various types of agreements. The present guidelines are therefore limited to recalling the basic analytical framework for applying Article [101](1).

Notes

[11] See note 5 above.

Part C Substantive Antitrust Matters

2.2. The prohibition rule of Article [101](1)

2.2.1. General remarks

13. The objective of Article [101] is to protect competition on the market as a means of enhancing consumer welfare and of ensuring an efficient allocation of resources. Competition and market integration serve these ends since the creation and preservation of an open single market promotes an efficient allocation of resources throughout the Community for the benefit of consumers.

Commentary
para 13: B&C: 2.086 F&N: 2.29, 2.65, 3.167, 3.179

14. The prohibition rule of Article [101](1) applies to restrictive agreements and concerted practices between undertakings and decisions by associations of undertakings in so far as they are capable of affecting trade between Member States. A general principle underlying Article [101](1) which is expressed in the case law of the Community Courts is that each economic operator must determine independently the policy, which he intends to adopt on the market.[12] In view of this the Community Courts have defined "agreements", "decisions" and "concerted practices" as Community law concepts which allow a distinction to be made between the unilateral conduct of an undertaking and co-ordination of behaviour or collusion between undertakings.[13] Unilateral conduct is subject only to Article [102] of the Treaty as far as Community competition law is concerned. Moreover, the convergence rule set out in Article 3(2) of Regulation 1/2003 does not apply to unilateral conduct. This provision applies only to agreements, decisions and concerted practices, which are capable of affecting trade between Member States. Article 3(2) provides that when such agreements, decisions and concerted practices are not prohibited by Article [101], they cannot be prohibited by national competition law. Article 3 is without prejudice to the fundamental principle of primacy of Community law, which entails in particular that agreements and abusive practices that are prohibited by Articles [101] and [102] cannot be upheld by national law.[14]

Notes
[12] See e.g. Case C-49/92 P *Anic Partecipazioni* [1999] ECR I-4125, paragraph 116; and Joined Cases 40/73 to 48/73 and others, *Suiker Unie* [1975] ECR page 1663, paragraph 173.
[13] See in this respect paragraph 108 of the judgment in *Anic Partecipazioni* cited in the previous note and Case C-277/87 *Sandoz Prodotti* [1990] ECR I-45.
[14] See in this respect e.g. Case 14/68 *Walt Wilhelm* [1969] ECR 1, and more recently Case T-203/01 *Michelin (II)* [2003] ECR II -[4071], paragraph 112.

15. The type of co-ordination of behaviour or collusion between undertakings falling within the scope of Article [101](1) is that where at least one undertaking vis-à-vis another undertaking undertakes to adopt a certain conduct on the market or that as a result of contacts between them uncertainty as to their conduct on the market is eliminated or at least substantially reduced.[15] It follows that co-ordination can take the form of obligations that regulate the market conduct of at least one of the parties as well as of arrangements that influence the market conduct of at least one of the parties by causing a change in its incentives. It is not required that co-ordination is in the interest of all the undertakings concerned.[16] Co-ordination must also not necessarily be express. It can also be tacit. For an agreement to be capable of being regarded as having been concluded by tacit acceptance there must be an invitation from an undertaking to another undertaking, whether express or implied, to fulfil a goal jointly.[17] In certain circumstances an agreement may be inferred from and imputed to an ongoing commercial relationship between the parties.[18] However, the mere fact that a measure adopted by an undertaking falls within the context of on-going business relations is not sufficient.[19]

Notes
[15] See Joined Cases T-25/95 and others, *Cimenteries CBR* [2000] ECR II-491, paragraphs 1849 and 1852; and Joined Cases T-202/98 and others, *British Sugar* [2001] ECR II-2035, paragraphs 58 to 60.
[16] See to that effect Case C-453/99 *Courage v Crehan* [2001] ECR I-6297, and paragraph 3444 of the judgment in *Cimenteries CBR* cited in the previous note.
[17] See in this respect Joined Cases C-2/01 P and C-3/01 P *Bundesverband der Arzneimittel-Importeure* [2004] ECR I-[23], paragraph 102.

[18] See e.g. Joined Cases 25/84 and 26/84 *Ford* [1985] ECR 2725.

[19] See in this respect paragraph 141 of the judgment in *Bundesverband der Arzneimittel-Importeure* cited in note [17].

Commentary
para 15: F&N: 3.346

16. Agreements between undertakings are caught by the prohibition rule of Article [101](1) when they are likely to have an appreciable adverse impact on the parameters of competition on the market, such as price, output, product quality, product variety and innovation. Agreements can have this effect by appreciably reducing rivalry between the parties to the agreement or between them and third parties.

2.2.2. *The basic principles for assessing agreements under Article [101](1)*

17. The assessment of whether an agreement is restrictive of competition must be made within the actual context in which competition would occur in the absence of the agreement with its alleged restrictions.[20] In making this assessment it is necessary to take account of the likely impact of the agreement on inter-brand competition (i.e. competition between suppliers of competing brands) and on intra-brand competition (i.e. competition between distributors of the same brand). Article [101](1) prohibits restrictions of both inter-brand competition and intra-brand competition.[21]

Notes

[20] See Case 56/65 *Société Technique Minière* [1966] ECR 337, and paragraph 76 of the judgment in *John Deere*, cited in note 9.

[21] See in this respect e.g. Joined Cases 56/64 and 58/66 *Consten and Grundig* [1966] ECR 429.

Commentary
para 17: B&C: 2.124 F&N: 3.181

18. For the purpose of assessing whether an agreement or its individual parts may restrict inter-brand competition and/or intra-brand competition it needs to be considered how and to what extent the agreement affects or is likely to affect competition on the market. The following two questions provide a useful framework for making this assessment. The first question relates to the impact of the agreement on inter-brand competition while the second question relates to the impact of the agreement on intra-brand competition. As restraints may be capable of affecting both inter-brand competition and intra-brand competition at the same time, it may be necessary to analyse a restraint in light of both questions before it can be concluded whether or not competition is restricted within the meaning of Article [101](1):

   (1) Does the agreement restrict actual or potential competition that would have existed without the agreement? If so, the agreement may be caught by Article [101](1). In making this assessment it is necessary to take into account competition between the parties and competition from third parties. For instance, where two undertakings established in different Member States undertake not to sell products in each other's home markets, (potential) competition that existed prior to the agreement is restricted. Similarly, where a supplier imposes obligations on his distributors not to sell competing products and these obligations foreclose third party access to the market, actual or potential competition that would have existed in the absence of the agreement is restricted. In assessing whether the parties to an agreement are actual or potential competitors the economic and legal context must be taken into account. For instance, if due to the financial risks involved and the technical capabilities of the parties it is unlikely on the basis of objective factors that each party would be able to carry out on its own the activities covered by the agreement the parties are deemed to be non-competitors in respect of that activity.[22] It is for the parties to bring forward evidence to that effect.

   (2) Does the agreement restrict actual or potential competition that would have existed in the absence of the contractual restraint(s) If so, the agreement may be caught by Article [101](1). For instance, where a supplier restricts its distributors from competing with each other, (potential) competition that could have existed between the distributors absent the restraints is restricted. Such restrictions include resale price maintenance and territorial or customer

sales restrictions between distributors. However, certain restraints may in certain cases not be caught by Article [101](1) when the restraint is objectively necessary for the existence of an agreement of that type or that nature.[23] Such exclusion of the application of Article [101](1) can only be made on the basis of objective factors external to the parties themselves and not the subjective views and characteristics of the parties. The question is not whether the parties in their particular situation would not have accepted to conclude a less restrictive agreement, but whether given the nature of the agreement and the characteristics of the market a less restrictive agreement would not have been concluded by undertakings in a similar setting. For instance, territorial restraints in an agreement between a supplier and a distributor may for a certain period of time fall outside Article [101](1), if the restraints are objectively necessary in order for the distributor to penetrate a new market.[24] Similarly, a prohibition imposed on all distributors not to sell to certain categories of end users may not be restrictive of competition if such restraint is objectively necessary for reasons of safety or health related to the dangerous nature of the product in question. Claims that in the absence of a restraint the supplier would have resorted to vertical integration are not sufficient. Decisions on whether or not to vertically integrate depend on a broad range of complex economic factors, a number of which are internal to the undertaking concerned.

Notes

[22] See in this respect e.g. Commission Decision in *Elopak/Metal Box-Odin* (OJ 1990 L 209, p.15) and in *TPS* (OJ 1999 L 90, p.6).

[23] See in this respect the judgment in *Société Technique Minière* cited in note 20 and Case 258/78 *Nungesser* [1982] ECR 2015.

[24] See rule 10 in paragraph 119 of the Guidelines on vertical restraints cited in note 5 above, according to which *inter alia* passive sales restrictions — a hardcore restraint — are held to fall outside Article [101](1) for a period of 2 years when the restraint is linked to opening up new product or geographic markets.

Commentary

para 18: F&N: 3.350
para 18(1): F&N: 3.334, 3.350, 3.352
para 18(2): B&C: 2.102 F&N: 3.274, 3.353, 3.355, 3.356, 3.357, 3.358, 9.147, 12.89

19. In the application of the analytical framework set out in the previous paragraph it must be taken into account that Article [101](1) distinguishes between those agreements that have a restriction of competition as their object and those agreements that have a restriction of competition as their effect. An agreement or contractual restraint is only prohibited by Article [101](1) if its object or effect is to restrict inter-brand competition and/or intra-brand competition.

20. The distinction between restrictions by object and restrictions by effect is important. Once it has been established that an agreement has as its object the restriction of competition, there is no need to take account of its concrete effects.[25] In other words, for the purpose of applying Article [101](1) no actual anti-competitive effects need to be demonstrated where the agreement has a restriction of competition as its object. Article [101](3), on the other hand, does not distinguish between agreements that restrict competition by object and agreements that restrict competition by effect. Article [101](3) applies to all agreements that fulfil the four conditions contained therein.[26]

Notes

[25] See e.g. paragraph 99 of the judgment in *Anic Partecipazioni* cited in note 12.

[26] See paragraph 46 below.

21. Restrictions of competition *by object* are those that by their very nature have the potential of restricting competition. These are restrictions which in light of the objectives pursued by the Community competition rules have such a high potential of negative effects on competition that it is unnecessary for the purposes of applying Article [101](1) to demonstrate any actual effects on the market. This presumption is based on the serious nature of the restriction and on experience showing that restrictions of competition by object are likely to produce negative effects on the market and to jeopardise the objectives pursued by the Community competition rules. Restrictions by object such as price fixing and market sharing reduce output and raise prices,

leading to a misallocation of resources, because goods and services demanded by customers are not produced. They also lead to a reduction in consumer welfare, because consumers have to pay higher prices for the goods and services in question.

Commentary
para 21: F&N: 3.184, 3.185, 3.186, 3.211

22. The assessment of whether or not an agreement has as its object the restriction of competition is based on a number of factors. These factors include, in particular, the content of the agreement and the objective aims pursued by it. It may also be necessary to consider the context in which it is (to be) applied and the actual conduct and behaviour of the parties on the market.[27] In other words, an examination of the facts underlying the agreement and the specific circumstances in which it operates may be required before it can be concluded whether a particular restriction constitutes a restriction of competition by object. The way in which an agreement is actually implemented may reveal a restriction by object even where the formal agreement does not contain an express provision to that effect. Evidence of subjective intent on the part of the parties to restrict competition is a relevant factor but not a necessary condition.

Notes
[27] See Joined Cases 29/83 and 30/83 *CRAM and Rheinzink* [1984] ECR 1679, paragraph 26, and Joined Cases 96/82 and others, *ANSEAU-NAVEWA* [1983] ECR 3369, paragraphs 23–25.

Commentary
para 22: B&C: 2.133 F&N: 3.186, 3.201

23. Non-exhaustive guidance on what constitutes restrictions by object can be found in Commission block exemption regulations, guidelines and notices. Restrictions that are black-listed in block exemptions or identified as hardcore restrictions in guidelines and notices are generally considered by the Commission to constitute restrictions by object. In the case of horizontal agreements restrictions of competition by object include price fixing, output limitation and sharing of markets and customers.[28] As regards vertical agreements the category of restrictions by object includes, in particular, fixed and minimum resale price maintenance and restrictions providing absolute territorial protection, including restrictions on passive sales.[29]

Notes
[28] See the Guidelines on horizontal cooperation agreements, cited in note, paragraph 25, and Article 5 of Commission Regulation 2658/2000 on the application of Article [101](3) of the Treaty to categories of specialisation agreements (OJ L 304, 5.12.2000, p.3). [Ed note: see now Commission Regulation (EU) No 1218/2010 on the application of Article 101(3) TFEU to certain categories of specialisation agreements (OJ L 335, 18.12.2010, p.43), reproduced at C7 above.]
[29] See Article 4 Commission Regulation 2790/1999 on the application of Article [101](3) of the Treaty to categories of vertical agreements and concerted practices (OJ L 336, 29.12.1999, p.21) and the Guidelines on Vertical Restraints, cited in note 5, paragraph 46 et seq. [Ed note: see now Commission Regulation (EU) No 330/2010 on the application of Article 101(3) TFEU to categories of vertical agreements and concerted practices (OJ L 102, 23.4.2010, p.1), reproduced at C4 above, and Commission Notice 2010/C 130/01, Guidelines on Vertical Restraints (OJ C 130, 19.5.2010, p.1), reproduced at C15 below.] See also Case 279/87 Tipp-Ex [1990] ECR I-261, and Case T-62/98 Volkswagen v Commission [2000] ECR II-2707, paragraph 178.

Commentary
para 23: B&C: 2.120, F&N: 3.454, 7.21

24. If an agreement is not restrictive of competition by object it must be examined whether it has restrictive effects on competition. Account must be taken of both actual and potential effects.[30] In other words the agreement must have likely anti-competitive effects. In the case of restrictions of competition by effect there is no presumption of anti-competitive effects. For an agreement to be restrictive by effect it must affect actual or potential competition to such an extent that on the relevant market negative effects on prices, output, innovation or the variety or quality of goods and services can be expected with a reasonable degree of probability.[31] Such negative effects must be appreciable. The prohibition rule of Article [101](1) does not apply when the identified anti-competitive effects are insignificant.[32] This test reflects the economic approach which the

Commission is applying. The prohibition of Article [101](1) only applies where on the basis of proper market analysis it can be concluded that the agreement has likely anti-competitive effects on the market.[33] It is insufficient for such a finding that the market shares of the parties exceed the thresholds set out in the Commission's de minimis notice.[34] Agreements falling within safe harbours of block exemption regulations may be caught by Article [101](1) but this is not necessarily so. Moreover, the fact that due to the market shares of the parties, an agreement falls outside the safe harbour of a block exemption is in itself an insufficient basis for finding that the agreement is caught by Article [101](1) or that it does not fulfil the conditions of Article [101](3). Individual assessment of the likely effects produced by the agreement is required.

Notes

[30] See paragraph 77 of the judgment in *John Deere* cited in note 9.

[31] It is not sufficient in itself that the agreement restricts the freedom of action of one or more of the parties, see paragraphs 76 and 77 of the judgment in *Métropole television (M6)* cited in note 10. This is in line with the fact that the object of Article [101] is to protect competition on the market for the benefit of consumers.

[32] See e.g. Case 5/69 *Völk* [1969] ECR 295, paragraph 7. Guidance on the issue of appreciability can be found in the Commission Notice on agreements of minor importance which do not appreciably restrict competition under Article [101](1) of the Treaty (OJ C 368, 22.12.2001, p.13) The notice defines appreciability in a negative way. Agreements, which fall outside the scope of the de minimis notice, do not necessarily have appreciable restrictive effects. An individual assessment is required.

[33] See in this respect Joined Cases T-374/94 and others, *European Night Services* [1998] ECR II-3141.

[34] See note 32.

Commentary
para 24: F&N: 2.48, 3.349, 3.454, 3.456

25. Negative effects on competition within the relevant market are likely to occur when the parties individually or jointly have or obtain some degree of market power and the agreement contributes to the creation, maintenance or strengthening of that market power or allows the parties to exploit such market power. Market power is the ability to maintain prices above competitive levels for a significant period of time or to maintain output in terms of product quantities, product quality and variety or innovation below competitive levels for a significant period of time. In markets with high fixed costs undertakings must price significantly above their marginal costs of production in order to ensure a competitive return on their investment. The fact that undertakings price above their marginal costs is therefore not in itself a sign that competition in the market is not functioning well and that undertakings have market power that allows them to price above the competitive level. It is when competitive constraints are insufficient to maintain prices and output at competitive levels that undertakings have market power within the meaning of Article [101](1).

Commentary
para 25: B&C: 2.086, 2.112, 2.128

26. The creation, maintenance or strengthening of market power can result from a restriction of competition between the parties to the agreement. It can also result from a restriction of competition between any one of the parties and third parties, e.g. because the agreement leads to fore-closure of competitors or because it raises competitors' costs, limiting their capacity to compete effectively with the contracting parties. Market power is a question of degree. The degree of market power normally required for the finding of an infringement under Article [101](1) in the case of agreements that are restrictive of competition by effect is less than the degree of market power required for a finding of dominance under Article [102].

Commentary
para 26: B&C: 2.128 F&N: 15.93

27. For the purposes of analysing the restrictive effects of an agreement it is normally necessary to define the relevant market.[35] It is normally also necessary to examine and assess, *inter alia*, the nature of the products, the market position of the parties, the market position of competitors, the market position of buyers, the existence of potential competitors and the level of entry barriers.

In some cases, however, it may be possible to show anti-competitive effects directly by analysing the conduct of the parties to the agreement on the market. It may for example be possible to ascertain that an agreement has led to price increases. The guidelines on horizontal cooperation agreements and on vertical restraints set out a detailed framework for analysing the competitive impact of various types of horizontal and vertical agreements under Article [101](1).[36]

Notes

[35] See in this respect Commission notice on the definition of the relevant market for the purposes of Community competition law (OJ C 372, 9.12.1997, p.1).

[36] For the reference in the OJ see note 5.

Commentary

para 27: **B&C:** 2.129, 4.001, 4.007 **F&N:** 3.362

2.2.3. Ancillary restraints

28. Paragraph 18 above sets out a framework for analysing the impact of an agreement and its individual restrictions on inter-brand competition and intra-brand competition. If on the basis of those principles it is concluded that the main transaction covered by the agreement is not restrictive of competition, it becomes relevant to examine whether individual restraints contained in the agreement are also compatible with Article [101](1) because they are ancillary to the main non-restrictive transaction.

Commentary

para 28: **B&C:** 6.016

29. In Community competition law the concept of ancillary restraints covers any alleged restriction of competition which is directly related and necessary to the implementation of a main non-restrictive transaction and proportionate to it.[37] If an agreement in its main parts, for instance a distribution agreement or a joint venture, does not have as its object or effect the restriction of competition, then restrictions, which are directly related to and necessary for the implementation of that transaction, also fall outside Article [101](1).[38] These related restrictions are called ancillary restraints. A restriction is directly related to the main transaction if it is subordinate to the implementation of that transaction and is inseparably linked to it. The test of necessity implies that the restriction must be objectively necessary for the implementation of the main transaction and be proportionate to it. It follows that the ancillary restraints test is similar to the test set out in paragraph 18(2) above. However, the ancillary restraints test applies in all cases where the main transaction is not restrictive of competition.[39] It is not limited to determining the impact of the agreement on intra-brand competition.

Notes

[37] See paragraph 104 of the judgment in *Métropole télévision (M6) and others*, cited in note 10.

[38] See e.g. Case C-399/93 *Luttikhuis* [1995] ECR I-4515, paragraphs 12 to 14.

[39] See in this respect paragraphs 118 et seq. of the *Métropole television* judgment cited in note 10.

Commentary

para 29: **B&C:** 6.016 **F&N:** 3.274, 3.355, 3.357

30. The application of the ancillary restraint concept must be distinguished from the application of the defence under Article [101](3) which relates to certain economic benefits produced by restrictive agreements and which are balanced against the restrictive effects of the agreements. The application of the ancillary restraint concept does not involve any weighing of pro-competitive and anticompetitive effects. Such balancing is reserved for Article [101](3).[40]

Notes

[40] See paragraph 107 of the judgment in *Métropole télévision* judgement cited in note 10.

Commentary

para 30: **F&N:** 3.357

Part C Substantive Antitrust Matters

31. The assessment of ancillary restraints is limited to determining whether, in the specific context of the main non-restrictive transaction or activity, a particular restriction is necessary for the implementation of that transaction or activity and proportionate to it. If on the basis of objective factors it can be concluded that without the restriction the main non-restrictive transaction would be difficult or impossible to implement, the restriction may be regarded as objectively necessary for its implementation and proportionate to it.[41] If, for example, the main object of a franchise agreement does not restrict competition, then restrictions, which are necessary for the proper functioning of the agreement, such as obligations aimed at protecting the uniformity and reputation of the franchise system, also fall outside Article [101](1).[42] Similarly, if a joint venture is not in itself restrictive of competition, then restrictions that are necessary for the functioning of the agreement are deemed to be ancillary to the main transaction and are therefore not caught by Article [101](1). For instance in TPS[43] the Commission concluded that an obligation on the parties not to be involved in companies engaged in distribution and marketing of television programmes by satellite was ancillary to the creation of the joint venture during the initial phase. The restriction was therefore deemed to fall outside Article [101](1) for a period of three years. In arriving at this conclusion the Commission took account of the heavy investments and commercial risks involved in entering the market for pay-television.

Notes

[41] See e.g. Commission Decision in *Elopak/Metal Box-Odin* cited in note 22.

[42] See Case 161/84 *Pronuptia* [1986] ECR 353.

[43] See note 22. The decision was upheld by the Court of First Instance in the judgment in *Métropole télévision (M6)* cited in note 10.

Commentary
para 31: **B&C:** 2.150 **F&N:** 3.357

2.3. The exception rule of Article [101](3)

32. The assessment of restrictions by object and effect under Article [101](1) is only one side of the analysis. The other side, which is reflected in Article [101](3), is the assessment of the positive economic effects of restrictive agreements.

33. The aim of the Community competition rules is to protect competition on the market as a means of enhancing consumer welfare and of ensuring an efficient allocation of resources. Agreements that restrict competition may at the same time have pro-competitive effects by way of efficiency gains.[44] Efficiencies may create additional value by lowering the cost of producing an output, improving the quality of the product or creating a new product. When the pro-competitive effects of an agreement outweigh its anti-competitive effects the agreement is on balance pro-competitive and compatible with the objectives of the Community competition rules. The net effect of such agreements is to promote the very essence of the competitive process, namely to win customers by offering better products or better prices than those offered by rivals. This analytical framework is reflected in Article [101](1) and Article [101] (3). The latter provision expressly acknowledges that restrictive agreements may generate objective economic benefits so as to outweigh the negative effects of the restriction of competition.[45]

Notes

[44] Cost savings and other gains to the parties that arise from the mere exercise of market power do not give rise to objective benefits and cannot be taken into account, cf. paragraph 49 below.

[45] See the judgment in *Consten and Grundig*, cited in note 21.

Commentary
para 33: **B&C:** 2.086, 2.125

34. The application of the exception rule of Article [101](3) is subject to four cumulative conditions, two positive and two negative:
    (a) The agreement must contribute to improving the production or distribution of goods or contribute to promoting technical or economic progress,

(b) Consumers must receive a fair share of the resulting benefits,

(c) The restrictions must be indispensable to the attainment of these objectives, and finally

(d) The agreement must not afford the parties the possibility of eliminating competition in respect of a substantial part of the products in question. When these four conditions are fulfilled the agreement enhances competition within the relevant market, because it leads the undertakings concerned to offer cheaper or better products to consumers, compensating the latter for the adverse effects of the restrictions of competition.

35. Article [101](3) can be applied either to individual agreements or to categories of agreements by way of a block exemption regulation. When an agreement is covered by a block exemption the parties to the restrictive agreement are relieved of their burden under Article 2 of Regulation 1/2003 of showing that their individual agreement satisfies each of the conditions of Article [101](3). They only have to prove that the restrictive agreement benefits from a block exemption. The application of Article [101](3) to categories of agreements by way of block exemption regulation is based on the presumption that restrictive agreements that fall within their scope[46] fulfil each of the four conditions laid down in Article [101](3).

Notes

[46] The fact that an agreement is block exempted does not in itself indicate that the individual agreement is caught by Article [101](1).

---

36. If in an individual case the agreement is caught by Article [101](1) and the conditions of Article [101](3) are not fulfilled the block exemption may be withdrawn. According to Article 29(1) of Regulation 1/2003 the Commission is empowered to withdraw the benefit of a block exemption when it finds that in a particular case an agreement covered by a block exemption regulation has certain effects which are incompatible with Article [101](3) of the Treaty. Pursuant to Article 29(2) of Regulation 1/2003 a competition authority of a Member State may also withdraw the benefit of a Commission block exemption regulation in respect of its territory (or part of its territory), if this territory has all the characteristics of a distinct geographic market. In the case of withdrawal it is for the competition authorities concerned to demonstrate that the agreement infringes Article [101](1) and that it does not fulfil the conditions of Article [101](3).

Commentary
para 36: 2.218

---

37. The courts of the Member States have no power to withdraw the benefit of block exemption regulations. Moreover, in their application of block exemption regulations Member State courts may not modify their scope by extending their sphere of application to agreements not covered by the block exemption regulation in question.[47] Outside the scope of block exemption regulations Member State courts have the power to apply Article [101] in full (cf. Article 6 of Regulation 1/2003).

Notes

[47] See e.g. Case C-234/89 *Delimitis* [1991] ECR I-935, paragraph 46.

---

3. THE APPLICATION OF THE FOUR CONDITIONS OF ARTICLE [101](3)

38. The remainder of these guidelines will consider each of the four conditions of Article [101](3).[48] Given that these four conditions are cumulative[49] it is unnecessary to examine any remaining conditions once it is found that one of the conditions of Article [101](3) is not fulfilled. In individual cases it may therefore be appropriate to consider the four conditions in a different order.

Notes

[48] Article 36(4) of Regulation 1/2003 has, *inter alia*, repealed Article 5 of Regulation 1017/68 applying rules of competition to transport by rail, road and inland waterway. However, the Commission's case practice adopted under Regulation 1017/68 remains relevant for the purposes of applying Article [101](3) in the inland transport sector.

[49] See paragraph 42 below.

39. For the purposes of these guidelines it is considered appropriate to invert the order of the second and the third condition and thus deal with the issue of indispensability before the issue of pass-on to consumers. The analysis of pass-on requires a balancing of the negative and positive effects of an agreement on consumers. This analysis should not include the effects of any restrictions, which already fail the indispensability test and which for that reason are prohibited by Article [101].

3.1. General principles

40. Article [101](3) of the Treaty only becomes relevant when an agreement between undertakings restricts competition within the meaning of Article [101](1). In the case of non-restrictive agreements there is no need to examine any benefits generated by the agreement.

41. Where in an individual case a restriction of competition within the meaning of Article [101](1) has been proven, Article [101](3) can be invoked as a defence. According to Article 2 of Regulation 1/2003 the burden of proof under Article [101](3) rests on the undertaking(s) invoking the benefit of the exception rule. Where the conditions of Article [101](3) are not satisfied the agreement is null and void, cf. Article [101](2). However, such automatic nullity only applies to those parts of the agreement that are incompatible with Article [101], provided that such parts are severable from the agreement as a whole.[50] If only part of the agreement is null and void, it is for the applicable national law to determine the consequences thereof for the remaining part of the agreement.[51]

Notes

[50] See the judgment in *Société Technique Minière* cited in note 20.
[51] See in this respect Case 319/82 *Kerpen & Kerpen* [1983] ECR 4173, paragraphs 11 and 12.

42. According to settled case law the four conditions of Article [101](3) are cumulative,[52] i.e. they must all be fulfilled for the exception rule to be applicable. If they are not, the application of the exception rule of Article [101](3) must be refused.[53] The four conditions of Article [101](3) are also exhaustive. When they are met the exception is applicable and may not be made dependant on any other condition. Goals pursued by other Treaty provisions can be taken into account to the extent that they can be subsumed under the four conditions of Article [101](3).[54]

Notes

[52] See e.g. Case T-185/00 and others, *Métropole télévision SA (M6)* [2002] ECR II-3805, paragraph 86, Case T-17/93 *Matra* [1994] ECR II-595, paragraph 85; and Joined Cases 43/82 and 63/82 *VBVB and VBBB* [1984] ECR 19, paragraph 61.
[53] See Case T-213/00 *CMA CGM and others* [2003] ECR II -[913], paragraph 226.
[54] See to that effect implicitly paragraph 139 of the *Matra* judgment cited in note 52 and Case 26/76 *Metro (I)* [1977] ECR 1875, paragraph 43.

Commentary
para 42: B&C: 3.023, 3.047 **F&N**: 3.15, 3.458, 3.479

43. The assessment under Article [101](3) of benefits flowing from restrictive agreements is in principle made within the confines of each relevant market to which the agreement relates. The Community competition rules have as their objective the protection of competition on the market and cannot be detached from this objective. Moreover, the condition that consumers[55] must receive a fair share of the benefits implies in general that efficiencies generated by the restrictive agreement within a relevant market must be sufficient to outweigh the anti-competitive effects produced by the agreement within that same relevant market.[56] Negative effects on consumers in one geographic market or product market cannot normally be balanced against and compensated by positive effects for consumers in another unrelated geographic market or product market. However, where two markets are related, efficiencies achieved on separate markets can be taken into account provided that the group of consumers affected by the restriction and benefiting from the efficiency gains are substantially the same.[57] Indeed, in some cases only consumers in a downstream market are affected by the agreement in which case the impact of the agreement on such consumers must be assessed. This is for instance so in the case of purchasing agreements.[58]

Notes

55 As to the concept of consumers see paragraph 84 below where it is stated that consumers are the customers of the parties and subsequent buyers. The parties themselves are not "consumers" for the purposes of Article [101](3).

56 The test is market specific, see to that effect Case T-131/99 *Shaw* [2002] ECR II-2023, paragraph 163, where the Court of First Instance held that the assessment under Article [101](3) had to be made within the same analytical framework as that used for assessing the restrictive effects, and Case C-360/92 P *Publishers Association* [1995] ECR I-23, paragraph 29, where in a case where the relevant market was wider than national the Court of Justice held that in the application of Article [101](3) it was not correct only to consider the effects on the national territory.

57 In Case T-86/95 *Compagnie Générale Maritime and others* [2002] ECR II-1011, paragraphs 343 to 345, the Court of First Instance held that Article [101](3) does not require that the benefits are linked to a specific market and that in appropriate cases regard must be had to benefits "for every other market on which the agreement in question might have beneficial effects, and even, in a more general sense, for any service the quality or efficiency of which might be improved by the existence of that agreement". Importantly, however, in this case the affected group of consumers was the same. The case concerned intermodal transport services encompassing a bundle of, *inter alia*, inland and maritime transportation provided to shipping companies across the Community. The restrictions related to inland transport services, which were held to constitute a separate market, whereas the benefits were claimed to occur in relation to maritime transport services. Both services were demanded by shippers requiring intermodal transport services between northern Europe and South-East and East Asia. The judgment in *CMA CGM*, cited in note 53 above, also concerned a situation where the agreement, while covering several distinct services, affected the same group of consumers, namely shippers of containerised cargo between northern Europe and the Far East. Under the agreement the parties fixed charges and surcharges relating to inland transport services, port services and maritime transport services. The Court of First Instance held (cf. paragraphs 226 to 228) that in the circumstances of the case there was no need to define relevant markets for the purpose of applying Article [101](3). The agreement was restrictive of competition by its very object and there were no benefits for consumers.

58 See paragraphs 126 and 132 of the Guidelines on horizontal co-operation agreements cited in note 5 above.

Commentary
para **43**: **B&C**: 3.024, 3.043 **F&N**: 3.461, 15.96, 15.98

44. The assessment of restrictive agreements under Article [101](3) is made within the actual context in which they occur[59] and on the basis of the facts existing at any given point in time. The assessment is sensitive to material changes in the facts. The exception rule of Article [101](3) applies as long as the four conditions are fulfilled and ceases to apply when that is no longer the case.[60] When applying Article [101](3) in accordance with these principles it is necessary to take into account the initial sunk investments made by any of the parties and the time needed and the restraints required to commit and recoup an efficiency enhancing investment. Article [101] cannot be applied without taking due account of such *ex ante* investment. The risk facing the parties and the sunk investment that must be committed to implement the agreement can thus lead to the agreement falling outside Article [101](1) or fulfilling the conditions of Article [101](3), as the case may be, for the period of time required to recoup the investment.

Notes

59 See the *Ford* judgment cited in note 18.

60 See in this respect for example Commission Decision in *TPS* (OJ L 90, 2.4.1999, p.6). Similarly, the prohibition of Article [101](1) also only applies as long as the agreement has a restrictive object or restrictive effects.

Commentary
para **44**: **B&C**: 3.017, 16.053 **F&N**: 2.48, 3.465

45. In some cases the restrictive agreement is an irreversible event. Once the restrictive agreement has been implemented the *ex ante* situation cannot be re-established. In such cases the assessment must be made exclusively on the basis of the facts pertaining at the time of implementation. For instance, in the case of a research and development agreement whereby each party agrees to abandon its respective research project and pool its capabilities with those of another party, it may from an objective point of view be technically and economically impossible to revive a project once it has been abandoned. The assessment of the anti-competitive and pro-competitive effects of the agreement to abandon the individual research projects must therefore be made as of the time of the completion of its implementation. If at that point in time the agreement is compatible with Article [101], for instance because a sufficient number of third parties have competing research and development projects, the parties' agreement to abandon their individual projects

remains compatible with Article [101], even if at a later point in time the third party projects fail. However, the prohibition of Article [101] may apply to other parts of the agreement in respect of which the issue of irreversibility does not arise. If for example in addition to joint research and development, the agreement provides for joint exploitation, Article [101] may apply to this part of the agreement if due to subsequent market developments the agreement becomes restrictive of competition and does not (any longer) satisfy the conditions of Article [101](3) taking due account of *ex ante* sunk investments, cf. the previous paragraph.

Commentary
para 45: B&C: 3.017 **F&N**: 3.466

46. Article [101](3) does not exclude *a priori* certain types of agreements from its scope. As a matter of principle all restrictive agreements that fulfil the four conditions of Article [101](3) are covered by the exception rule.[61] However, severe restrictions of competition are unlikely to fulfil the conditions of Article [101](3). Such restrictions are usually black-listed in block exemption regulations or identified as hardcore restrictions in Commission guidelines and notices. Agreements of this nature generally fail (at least) the two first conditions of Article [101](3). They neither create objective economic benefits[62] nor do they benefit consumers.[63] For example, a horizontal agreement to fix prices limits output leading to misallocation of resources. It also transfers value from consumers to producers, since it leads to higher prices without producing any countervailing value to consumers within the relevant market. Moreover, these types of agreements generally also fail the indispensability test under the third condition.[64]

Notes
[61] See paragraph 85 of the *Matra* judgment cited in note 52.
[62] As to this requirement see paragraph 49 below.
[63] See e.g. Case T-29/92 *Vereniging van Samenwerkende Prijsregelende Organisaties in deBouwnijverheid (SPO)* [1995] ECR II-289.
[64] See e.g. Case 258/78 *Nungesser* [1982] ECR 2015, paragraph 77, concerning absolute territorial protection.

Commentary
para 46: B&C: 3.013 **F&N**: 3.457, 3.470

47. Any claim that restrictive agreements are justified because they aim at ensuring fair conditions of competition on the market is by nature unfounded and must be discarded.[65] The purpose of Article [101] is to protect effective competition by ensuring that markets remain open and competitive. The protection of fair conditions of competition is a task for the legislator in compliance with Community law obligations[66] and not for undertakings to regulate themselves.

Notes
[65] See in this respect e.g. the judgment in *SPO* cited in note 63.
[66] National measures must, inter alia, comply with the Treaty rules on free movement of goods, services, persons and capital.

3.2. First condition of Article [101](3): Efficiency gains

3.2.1. General remarks

48. According to the first condition of Article [101](3) the restrictive agreement must contribute to improving the production or distribution of goods or to promoting technical or economic progress. The provision refers expressly only to goods, but applies by analogy to services.

Commentary
para 48: B&C: 3.023 **F&N**: 3.473

49. It follows from the case law of the Court of Justice that only objective benefits can be taken into account.[67] This means that efficiencies are not assessed from the subjective point of view of the parties.[68] Cost savings that arise from the mere exercise of market power by the parties cannot be

taken into account. For instance, when companies agree to fix prices or share markets they reduce output and thereby production costs. Reduced competition may also lead to lower sales and marketing expenditures. Such cost reductions are a direct consequence of a reduction in output and value. The cost reductions in question do not produce any pro-competitive effects on the market. In particular, they do not lead to the creation of value through an integration of assets and activities. They merely allow the undertakings concerned to increase their profits and are therefore irrelevant from the point of view of Article [101](3).

Notes

[67] See e.g. the judgment in *Consten and Grundig* cited in note 21.

[68] See in this respect Commission Decision in *Van den Bergh Foods* (OJ 1998 L 246, p.1).

Commentary
para 49: F&N: 3.477

50. The purpose of the first condition of Article [101](3) is to define the types of efficiency gains that can be taken into account and be subject to the further tests of the second and third conditions of Article [101](3). The aim of the analysis is to ascertain what are the objective benefits created by the agreement and what is the economic importance of such efficiencies. Given that for Article [101](3) to apply the pro-competitive effects flowing from the agreement must outweigh its anti-competitive effects, it is necessary to verify what is the link between the agreement and the claimed efficiencies and what is the value of these efficiencies.

51. All efficiency claims must therefore be substantiated so that the following can be verified:
   (a) The *nature* of the claimed efficiencies;
   (b) The *link* between the agreement and the efficiencies;
   (c) The *likelihood* and *magnitude* of each claimed efficiency; and
   (d) *How* and *when* each claimed efficiency would be achieved.

52. Letter (a) allows the decision-maker to verify whether the claimed efficiencies are objective in nature, cf. paragraph 49 above.

53. Letter (b) allows the decision-maker to verify whether there is a sufficient causal link between the restrictive agreement and the claimed efficiencies. This condition normally requires that the efficiencies result from the economic activity that forms the object of the agreement. Such activities may, for example, take the form of distribution, licensing of technology, joint production or joint research and development. To the extent, however, that an agreement has wider efficiency enhancing effects within the relevant market, for example because it leads to a reduction in industry wide costs, these additional benefits are also taken into account.

Commentary
para 53: F&N: 3.476, 3.485, 15.99

54. The causal link between the agreement and the claimed efficiencies must normally also be direct.[69] Claims based on indirect effects are as a general rule too uncertain and too remote to be taken into account. A direct causal link exists for instance where a technology transfer agreement allows the licensees to produce new or improved products or a distribution agreement allows products to be distributed at lower cost or valuable services to be produced. An example of indirect effect would be a case where it is claimed that a restrictive agreement allows the undertakings concerned to increase their profits, enabling them to invest more in research and development to the ultimate benefit of consumers. While there may be a link between profitability and research and development, this link is generally not sufficiently direct to be taken into account in the context of Article [101](3).

Notes

[69] See in this respect Commission Decision in *Glaxo Wellcome* (OJ 2001 L 302, p.1).

Commentary
para 54: F&N: 3.486

55. Letters (c) and (d) allow the decision-maker to verify the value of the claimed efficiencies, which in the context of the third condition of Article [101](3) must be balanced against the anti-competitive effects of the agreement, see paragraph 101 below. Given that Article [101](1) only applies in cases where the agreement has likely negative effects on competition and consumers (in the case of hardcore restrictions such effects are presumed) efficiency claims must be substantiated so that they can be verified. Unsubstantiated claims are rejected.

Commentary
para 55: F&N: 3.487

56. In the case of claimed cost efficiencies the undertakings invoking the benefit of Article [101](3) must as accurately as reasonably possible calculate or estimate the value of the efficiencies and describe in detail how the amount has been computed. They must also describe the method(s) by which the efficiencies have been or will be achieved. The data submitted must be verifiable so that there can be a sufficient degree of certainty that the efficiencies have materialised or are likely to materialise.

Commentary
para 56: F&N: 3.487

57. In the case of claimed efficiencies in the form of new or improved products and other non-cost based efficiencies, the undertakings claiming the benefit of Article [101](3) must describe and explain in detail what is the nature of the efficiencies and how and why they constitute an objective economic benefit.

Commentary
para 57: F&N: 3.487

58. In cases where the agreement has yet to be fully implemented the parties must substantiate any projections as to the date from which the efficiencies will become operational so as to have a significant positive impact in the market.

Commentary
para 58: F&N: 3.487

3.2.2. *The different categories of efficiencies*

59. The types of efficiencies listed in Article [101](3) are broad categories which are intended to cover all objective economic efficiencies. There is considerable overlap between the various categories mentioned in Article [101](3) and the same agreement may give rise to several kinds of efficiencies. It is therefore not appropriate to draw clear and firm distinctions between the various categories. For the purpose of these guidelines, a distinction is made between cost efficiencies and efficiencies of a qualitative nature whereby value is created in the form of new or improved products, greater product variety etc.

60. In general, efficiencies stem from an integration of economic activities whereby undertakings combine their assets to achieve what they could not achieve as efficiently on their own or whereby they entrust another undertaking with tasks that can be performed more efficiently by that other undertaking.

Commentary
para 60: F&N: 3.476

61. The research and development, production and distribution process may be viewed as a value chain that can be divided into a number of stages. At each stage of this chain an undertaking must make a choice between performing the activity itself, performing it together with (an)other undertaking(s) or outsourcing the activity entirely to (an)other undertaking(s).

Commentary
para 61: F&N: 3.476

62. In each case where the choice made involves cooperation on the market with another undertaking, an agreement within the meaning of Article [101](1) normally needs to be concluded. These agreements can be vertical, as is the case where the parties operate at different levels of the value chain or horizontal, as is the case where the firms operate at the same level of the value chain. Both categories of agreements may create efficiencies by allowing the undertakings in question to perform a particular task at lower cost or with higher added value for consumers. Such agreements may also contain or lead to restrictions of competition in which case the prohibition rule of Article [101](1) and the exception rule of Article [101](3) may become relevant.

63. The types of efficiencies mentioned in the following are only examples and are not intended to be exhaustive.

3.2.2.1. Cost efficiencies

64. Cost efficiencies flowing from agreements between undertakings can originate from a number of different sources. One very important source of cost savings is the development of new production technologies and methods. In general, it is when technological leaps are made that the greatest potential for cost savings is achieved. For instance, the introduction of the assembly line led to a very substantial reduction in the cost of producing motor vehicles.

Commentary
para 64: F&N: 3.481

---

65. Another very important source of efficiency is synergies resulting from an integration of existing assets. When the parties to an agreement combine their respective assets they may be able to attain a cost/output configuration that would not otherwise be possible. The combination of two existing technologies that have complementary strengths may reduce production costs or lead to the production of a higher quality product. For instance, it may be that the production assets of firm A generate a high output per hour but require a relatively high input of raw materials per unit of output, whereas the production assets of firm B generate lower output per hour but require a relatively lower input of raw materials per unit of output. Synergies are created if by establishing a production joint venture combining the production assets of A and B the parties can attain a high(er) level of output per hour with a low(er) input of raw materials per unit of output. Similarly, if one undertaking has optimised one part of the value chain and another undertaking has optimised another part of the value chain, the combination of their operations may lead to lower costs. Firm A may for instance have a highly automated production facility resulting in low production costs per unit whereas B has developed an efficient order processing system. The system allows production to be tailored to customer demand, ensuring timely delivery and reducing warehousing and obsolescence costs. By combining their assets A and B may be able to obtain cost reductions.

Commentary
para 65: F&N: 3.481

---

66. Cost efficiencies may also result from economies of scale, i.e. declining cost per unit of output as output increases. To give an example: investment in equipment and other assets often has to be made in indivisible blocks. If an undertaking cannot fully utilise a block, its average costs will be higher than if it could do so. For instance, the cost of operating a truck is virtually the same regardless of whether it is almost empty, half-full or full. Agreements whereby undertakings combine their logistics operations may allow them to increase the load factors and reduce the number of vehicles employed. Larger scale may also allow for better division of labour leading to lower unit costs. Firms may achieve economies of scale in respect of all parts of the value chain, including research and development, production, distribution and marketing. Learning economies constitute a related type of efficiency. As experience is gained in using a particular production process or in performing particular tasks, productivity may increase because the process is made to run more efficiently or because the task is performed more quickly.

67. Economies of scope are another source of cost efficiency, which occur when firms achieve cost savings by producing different products on the basis of the same input. Such efficiencies may arise

from the fact that it is possible to use the same components and the same facilities and personnel to produce a variety of products. Similarly, economies of scope may arise in distribution when several types of goods are distributed in the same vehicles. For instance, a producer of frozen pizzas and a producer of frozen vegetables may obtain economies of scope by jointly distributing their products. Both groups of products must be distributed in refrigerated vehicles and it is likely that there are significant overlaps in terms of customers. By combining their operations the two producers may obtain lower distribution costs per distributed unit.

68. Efficiencies in the form of cost reductions can also follow from agreements that allow for better planning of production, reducing the need to hold expensive inventory and allowing for better capacity utilisation. Efficiencies of this nature may for example stem from the use of "just in time" purchasing, i.e. an obligation on a supplier of components to continuously supply the buyer according to its needs thereby avoiding the need for the buyer to maintain a significant stock of components which risks becoming obsolete. Cost savings may also result from agreements that allow the parties to rationalise production across their facilities.

3.2.2.2. Qualitative efficiencies

69. Agreements between undertakings may generate various efficiencies of a qualitative nature which are relevant to the application of Article [101](3). In a number of cases the main efficiency enhancing potential of the agreement is not cost reduction; it is quality improvements and other efficiencies of a qualitative nature. Depending on the individual case such efficiencies may therefore be of equal or greater importance than cost efficiencies.

Commentary
para 69: F&N: 3.482

---

70. Technical and technological advances form an essential and dynamic part of the economy, generating significant benefits in the form of new or improved goods and services. By cooperating undertakings may be able to create efficiencies that would not have been possible without the restrictive agreement or would have been possible only with substantial delay or at higher cost. Such efficiencies constitute an important source of economic benefits covered by the first condition of Article [101](3). Agreements capable of producing efficiencies of this nature include, in particular, research and development agreements. An example would be A and B creating a joint venture for the development and, if successful, joint production of a cell-based tyre. The puncture of one cell does not affect other cells, which means that there is no risk of collapse of the tyre in the event of a puncture. The tyre is thus safer than traditional tyres. It also means that there is no immediate need to change the tyre and thus to carry a spare. Both types of efficiencies constitute objective benefits within the meaning of the first condition of Article [101](3).

71. In the same way that the combination of complementary assets can give rise to cost savings, combinations of assets may also create synergies that create efficiencies of a qualitative nature. The combination of production assets may for instance lead to the production of higher quality products or products with novel features. This may for instance be the case for licence agreements, and agreements providing for joint production of new or improved goods or services. Licence agreements may, in particular, ensure more rapid dissemination of new technology in the Community and enable the licensee(s) to make available new products or to employ new production techniques that lead to quality improvements. Joint production agreements may, in particular, allow new or improved products or services to be introduced on the market more quickly or at lower cost.[70] In the telecommunications sector, for example, cooperation agreements have been held to create efficiencies by making available more quickly new global services.[71] In the banking sector cooperation agreements that made available improved facilities for making crossborder payments have also been held to create efficiencies falling within the scope of the first condition of Article [101](3).[72]

Notes

[70] See e.g. Commission Decision in *GEAE/P&W* (OJ 2000 L 58, p.16); in *British Interactive Broadcasting/Open* (OJ 1999 L 312, p.1) and in *Asahi/Saint Gobain* (OJ 1994 L 354, page 87).

[71] See e.g. Commission Decision in *Atlas* (OJ 1996 L 239, p.23), and in *Phoenix/Global One* (OJ 1996 L 239, p.57).

[72] See e.g. Commission Decision in *Uniform Eurocheques* (OJ 1985 L 35, p.43).

72. Distribution agreements may also give rise to qualitative efficiencies. Specialised distributors, for example, may be able to provide services that are better tailored to customer needs or to provide quicker delivery or better quality assurance throughout the distribution chain.[73]

Notes

[73] See e.g. Commission Decision in *Cégétel + 4* (OJ 1999 L 88, p.26).

3.3. Third condition of Article [101](3): Indispensability of the restrictions

73. According to the third condition of Article [101](3) the restrictive agreement must not impose restrictions, which are not indispensable to the attainment of the efficiencies created by the agreement in question. This condition implies a two-fold test. First, the restrictive agreement as such must be reasonably necessary in order to achieve the efficiencies. Secondly, the individual restrictions of competition that flow from the agreement must also be reasonably necessary for the attainment of the efficiencies.

Commentary
para 73: F&N: 3.491

74. In the context of the third condition of Article [101](3) the decisive factor is whether or not the restrictive agreement and individual restrictions make it possible to perform the activity in question more efficiently than would likely have been the case in the absence of the agreement or the restriction concerned. The question is not wheth er in the absence of the restriction the agreement would not have been concluded, but whether more efficiencies are produced with the agreement or restriction than in the absence of the agreement or restriction.[74]

Notes

[74] As to the former question, which may be relevant in the context of Article [101](1), see paragraph 18 above.

Commentary
para 74: F&N: 3.463, 3.490

75. The first test contained in the third condition of Article [101](3) requires that the efficiencies be specific to the agreement in question in the sense that there are no other economically practicable and less restrictive means of achieving the efficiencies. In making this latter assessment the market conditions and business realities facing the parties to the agreement must be taken into account. Undertakings invoking the benefit of Article [101](3) are not required to consider hypothetical or theoretical alternatives. The Commission will not second guess the business judgment of the parties. It will only intervene where it is reasonably clear that there are realistic and attainable alternatives. The parties must only explain and demonstrate why such seemingly realistic and significantly less restrictive alternatives to the agreement would be significantly less efficient.

Commentary
para 75: B&C: 3.062 F&N: 3.463, 3.493

76. It is particularly relevant to examine whether, having due regard to the circumstances of the individual case, the parties could have achieved the efficiencies by means of another less restrictive type of agreement and, if so, when they would likely be able to obtain the efficiencies. It may also be necessary to examine whether the parties could have achieved the efficiencies on their own. For instance, where the claimed efficiencies take the form of cost reductions resulting from economies of scale or scope the undertakings concerned must explain and substantiate why the same efficiencies would not be likely to be attained through internal growth and price competition. In making this assessment it is relevant to consider, *inter alia,* what is the minimum efficient scale on the market concerned. The minimum efficient scale is the level of output required to minimise average cost and exhaust economies of scale.[75] The larger the minimum efficient scale compared to the current size of either of the parties to the agreement, the more likely it is that the efficiencies will be deemed to be specific to the agreement. In the case of agreements that produce substantial synergies through the combination of complementary assets and capabilities the very nature of the efficiencies give rise to a presumption that the agreement is necessary to attain them.

Notes

75 Scale economies are normally exhausted at a certain point. Thereafter average costs will stabilise and eventually rise due to, for example, capacity constraints and bottlenecks.

Commentary
para 76: B&C: 3.062 F&N: 3.463

77. These principles can be illustrated by the following hypothetical example: A and B combine within a joint venture their respective production technologies to achieve higher output and lower raw material consumption. The joint venture is granted an exclusive licence to their respective production technologies. The parties transfer their existing production facilities to the joint venture. They also transfer key staff in order to ensure that existing learning economies can be exploited and further developed. It is estimated that these economies will reduce production costs by a further 5%. The output of the joint venture is sold independently by A and B. In this case the indispensability condition necessitates an assessment of whether or not the benefits could be substantially achieved by means of a licence agreement, which would be likely to be less restrictive because A and B would continue to produce independently. In the circumstances described this is unlikely to be the case since under a licence agreement the parties would not be able to benefit in the same seamless and continued way from their respective experience in operating the two technologies, resulting in significant learning economies.

78. Once it is found that the agreement in question is necessary in order to produce the efficiencies, the indispensability of each restriction of competition flowing from the agreement must be assessed. In this context it must be assessed whether individual restrictions are reasonably necessary in order to produce the efficiencies. The parties to the agreement must substantiate their claim with regard to both the nature of the restriction and its intensity.

79. A restriction is indispensable if its absence would eliminate or significantly reduce the efficiencies that follow from the agreement or make it significantly less likely that they will materialise. The assessment of alternative solutions must take into account the actual and potential improvement in the field of competition by the elimination of a particular restriction or the application of a less restrictive alternative. The more restrictive the restraint the stricter the test under the third condition.[76] Restrictions that are black listed in block exemption regulations or identified as hardcore restrictions in Commission guidelines and notices are unlikely to be considered indispensable.

Notes

76 See in this respect paragraphs 392 to 395 of the judgment in *Compagnie Générale Maritime* cited in note 57.

Commentary
para 79: B&C: 3.064, 3.065 F&N: 3.494

80. The assessment of indispensability is made within the actual context in which the agreement operates and must in particular take account of the structure of the market, the economic risks related to the agreement, and the incentives facing the parties. The more uncertain the success of the product covered by the agreement, the more a restriction may be required to ensure that the efficiencies will materialise. Restrictions may also be indispensable in order to align the incentives of the parties and ensure that they concentrate their efforts on the implementation of the agreement. A restriction may for instance be necessary in order to avoid hold-up problems once a substantial sunk investment has been made by one of the parties. Once for instance a supplier has made a substantial relationship-specific investment with a view to supplying a customer with an input, the supplier is locked into the customer. In order to avoid that *ex post* the customer exploits this dependence to obtain more favourable terms, it may be necessary to impose an obligation not to purchase the component from third parties or to purchase minimum quantities of the component from the supplier.[77]

Notes

77 See for more detail paragraph 116 of the Guidelines on Vertical Restraints cited in note 5.

Commentary
para 80: F&N: 3.492

81. In some cases a restriction may be indispensable only for a certain period of time, in which case the exception of Article [101](3) only applies during that period. In making this assessment it is necessary to take due account of the period of time required for the parties to achieve the efficiencies justifying the application of the exception rule.[78] In cases where the benefits cannot be achieved without considerable investment, account must, in particular, be taken of the period of time required to ensure an adequate return on such investment, see also paragraph 44 above.

Notes

[78] See Joined Cases T-374/94 and others, *European Night Services* [1998] ECR II-3141, paragraph 230.

Commentary

para 81: B&C: 3.064

82. These principles can be illustrated by the following hypothetical examples: P produces and distributes frozen pizzas, holding 15% of the market in Member State X. Deliveries are made directly to retailers. Since most retailers have limited storage capacity, relatively frequent deliveries are required, leading to low capacity utilisation and use of relatively small vehicles. T is a wholesaler of frozen pizzas and other frozen products, delivering to most of the same customers as P. The pizza products distributed by T hold 30% of the market. T has a fleet of larger vehicles and has excess capacity. P concludes an exclusive distribution agreement with T for Member State X and undertakes to ensure that distributors in other Member States will not sell into T's territory either actively or passively. T undertakes to advertise the products, survey consumer tastes and satisfaction rates and ensure delivery to retailers of all products within 24 hours. The agreement leads to a reduction in total distribution costs of 30% as capacity is better utilised and duplication of routes is eliminated. The agreement also leads to the provision of additional services to consumers. Restrictions on passive sales are hardcore restrictions under the block exemption regulation on vertical restraints[79] and can only be considered indispensable in exceptional circumstances. The established market position of T and the nature of the obligations imposed on it indicate this is not an exceptional case. The ban on active selling, on the other hand, is likely to be indispensable. T is likely to have less incentive to sell and advertise the P brand, if distributors in other Member States could sell actively in Member State X and thus get a free ride on the efforts of T. This is particularly so, as T also distributes competing brands and thus has the possibility of pushing more of the brands that are the least exposed to free riding. S is a producer of carbonated soft drinks, holding 40% of the market. The nearest competitor holds 20%. S concludes supply agreements with customers accounting for 25% of demand, whereby they undertake to purchase exclusively from S for 5 years. S concludes agreements with other customers accounting for 15% of demand whereby they are granted quarterly target rebates, if their purchases exceed certain individually fixed targets. S claims that the agreements allow it to predict demand more accurately and thus to better plan production, reducing raw material storage and warehousing costs and avoiding supply shortages. Given the market position of S and the combined coverage of the restrictions, the restrictions are very unlikely to be considered indispensable. The exclusive purchasing obligation exceeds what is required to plan production and the same is true of the target rebate scheme. Predictability of demand can be achieved by less restrictive means. S could, for example, provide incentives for customers to order large quantities at a time by offer-ing quantity rebates or by offering a rebate to customers that place firm orders in advance for delivery on specified dates.

Notes

[79] See Commission Regulation No 2790/1999 on the application of Article [101](3) of the Treaty on categories of vertical agreements and concerted practices (OJ 1999 L 336, page 21). [Ed note: see now Commission Regulation (EU) No 330/2010 on the application of Article 101(3) TFEU to categories of vertical agreements and concerted practices (OJ L 102, 23.4.2010, p.1), reproduced at C4 above.]

Part C Substantive Antitrust Matters

3.4. Second condition of Article [101](3): Fair share for consumers

3.4.1. General remarks

83. According to the second condition of Article [101](3) consumers must receive a fair share of the efficiencies generated by the restrictive agreement.

84. The concept of "consumers" encompasses all direct or indirect users of the products covered by the agreement, including producers that use the products as an input, wholesalers, retailers and final consumers, i.e. natural persons who are acting for purposes which can be regarded as outside their trade or profession. In other words, consumers within the meaning of Article [101](3) are the customers of the parties to the agreement and subsequent purchasers. These customers can be undertakings as in the case of buyers of industrial machinery or an input for further processing or final consumers as for instance in the case of buyers of impulse ice-cream or bicycles.

Commentary
para 84: B&C: 3.056 F&N: 3.495, 3.496

---

85. The concept of *"fair share"* implies that the pass-on of benefits must at least compensate consumers for any actual or likely negative impact caused to them by the restriction of competition found under Article [101](1). In line with the overall objective of Article [101] to prevent anti-competitive agreements, the net effect of the agreement must at least be neutral from the point of view of those consumers directly or likely affected by the agreement.[80] If such consumers are worse off following the agreement, the second condition of Article [101](3) is not fulfilled. The positive effects of an agreement must be balanced against and compensate for its negative effects on consumers.[81] When that is the case consumers are not harmed by the agreement. Moreover, society as a whole benefits where the efficiencies lead either to fewer resources being used to produce the output consumed or to the production of more valuable products and thus to a more efficient allocation of resources.

Notes

[80] See in this respect the judgment in *Consten and Grundig* cited in note 21, where the Court of Justice held that the improvements within the meaning of the first condition of Article [101](3) must show appreciable objective advantages of such a character as to compensate for the disadvantages which they cause in the field of competition.

[81] It is recalled that positive and negative effects on consumers are in principle balanced within each relevant market (cf. paragraph 43 above).

Commentary
para 85: B&C: 3.057 F&N: 3.497, 15.101

---

86. It is not required that consumers receive a share of each and every efficiency gain identified under the first condition. It suffices that sufficient benefits are passed on to compensate for the negative effects of the restrictive agreement. In that case consumers obtain a fair share of the overall benefits.[82] If a restrictive agreement is likely to lead to higher prices, consumers must be fully compensated through increased quality or other benefits. If not, the second condition of Article [101](3) is not fulfilled.

Notes
[82] See in this respect paragraph 48 of the *Metro (I)* judgment cited in note 54.

Commentary
para 86: B&C: 3.057

---

87. The decisive factor is the overall impact on consumers of the products within the relevant market and not the impact on individual members of this group of consumers[83]. In some cases a certain period of time may be required before the efficiencies materialise. Until such time the agreement may have only negative effects. The fact that pass-on to the consumer occurs with a certain time lag does not in itself exclude the application of Article [101](3). However, the greater the time lag, the greater must be the efficiencies to compensate also for the loss to consumers during the period preceding the pass-on.

Notes

83 See paragraph 163 of the judgment in *Shaw* cited in note 56.

88. In making this assessment it must be taken into account that the value of a gain for consumers in the future is not the same as a present gain for consumers. The value of saving 100 euro today is greater than the value of saving the same amount a year later. A gain for consumers in the future therefore does not fully compensate for a present loss to consumers of equal nominal size. In order to allow for an appropriate comparison of a present loss to consumers with a future gain to consumers, the value of future gains must be discounted. The discount rate applied must reflect the rate of inflation, if any, and lost interest as an indication of the lower value of future gains.

89. In other cases the agreement may enable the parties to obtain the efficiencies earlier than would otherwise be possible. In such circumstances it is necessary to take account of the likely negative impact on consumers within the relevant market once this lead-time has lapsed. If through the restrictive agreement the parties obtain a strong position on the market, they may be able to charge a significantly higher price than would otherwise have been the case. For the second condition of Article [101](3) to be satisfied the benefit to consumers of having earlier access to the products must be equally significant. This may for instance be the case where an agreement allows two tyre manufacturers to bring to market three years earlier a new substantially safer tyre but at the same time, by increasing their market power, allows them to raise prices by 5%. In such a case it is likely that having early access to a substantially improved product outweighs the price increase.

90. The second condition of Article [101](3) incorporates a sliding scale. The greater the restriction of competition found under Article [101](1) the greater must be the efficiencies and the pass-on to consumers. This sliding scale approach implies that if the restrictive effects of an agreement are relatively limited and the efficiencies are substantial it is likely that a fair share of the cost savings will be passed on to consumers. In such cases it is therefore normally not necessary to engage in a detailed analysis of the second condition of Article [101](3), provided that the three other conditions for the application of this provision are fulfilled.

Commentary
para 90: F&N: 3.449, 3.488, 3.505

91. If, on the other hand, the restrictive effects of the agreement are substantial and the cost savings are relatively insignificant, it is very unlikely that the second condition of Article [101](3) will be fulfilled. The impact of the restriction of competition depends on the intensity of the restriction and the degree of competition that remains following the agreement.

92. If the agreement has both substantial anti-competitive effects and substantial pro-competitive effects a careful analysis is required. In the application of the balancing test in such cases it must be taken into account that competition is an important long-term driver of efficiency and innovation. Undertakings that are not subject to effective competitive constraints — such as for instance dominant firms — have less incentive to maintain or build on the efficiencies. The more substantial the impact of the agreement on competition, the more likely it is that consumers will suffer in the long run.

93. The following two sections describe in more detail the analytical framework for assessing consumer pass-on of efficiency gains. The first section deals with cost efficiencies, whereas the section that follows covers other types of efficiencies such as new or improved products (qualitative efficiencies). The framework, which is developed in these two sections, is particularly important in cases where it is not immediately obvious that the competitive harms exceed the benefits to consumers or *vice versa*.[84]

Notes

84 In the following sections, for convenience the competitive harm is referred to in terms of higher prices; competitive harm could also mean lower quality, less variety or lower innovation than would otherwise have occurred.

94. In the application of the principles set out below the Commission will have regard to the fact that in many cases it is difficult to accurately calculate the consumer pass-on rate and other types of

consumer pass-on. Undertakings are only required to substantiate their claims by providing estimates and other data to the extent reasonably possible, taking account of the circumstances of the individual case.

3.4.2. *Pass-on and balancing of cost efficiencies*

95. When markets, as is normally the case, are not perfectly competitive, undertakings are able to influence the market price to a greater or lesser extent by altering their output.[85] They may also be able to price discriminate amongst customers.

Notes

[85] In perfectly competitive markets individual undertakings are price-takers. They sell their products at the market price, which is determined by overall supply and demand. The output of the individual undertaking is so small that any individual undertaking's change in output does not affect the market price.

96. Cost efficiencies may in some circumstances lead to increased output and lower prices for the affected consumers. If due to cost efficiencies the undertakings in question can increase profits by expanding output, consumer pass-on may occur. In assessing the extent to which cost efficiencies are likely to be passed on to consumers and the outcome of the balancing test contained in Article [101](3) the following factors are in particular taken into account:
    (a) The characteristics and structure of the market,
    (b) The nature and magnitude of the efficiency gains,
    (c) The elasticity of demand, and
    (d) The magnitude of the restriction of competition.

    All factors must normally be considered. Since Article [101](3) only applies in cases where com-petition on the market is being appreciably restricted, see paragraph 24 above, there can be no presumption that residual competition will ensure that consumers receive a fair share of the benefits. However, the degree of competition remaining on the market and the nature of this competition influences the likelihood of pass-on.

Commentary
para 96: F&N: 3.500

97. The greater the degree of residual competition the more likely it is that individual undertakings will try to increase their sales by passing on cost efficiencies. If undertakings compete mainly on price and are not subject to significant capacity constraints, pass-on may occur relatively quickly. If competition is mainly on capacity and capacity adaptations occur with a certain time lag, pass-on will be slower. Pass-on is also likely to be slower when the market structure is conducive to tacit collusion.[86] If competitors are likely to retaliate against an increase in output by one or more parties to the agreement, the incentive to increase output may be tempered, unless the competitive advantage conferred by the efficiencies is such that the undertakings concerned have an incentive to break away from the common policy adopted on the market by the members of the oligopoly. In other words, the efficiencies generated by the agreement may turn the undertakings concerned into so-called "mavericks".[87]

Notes

[86] Undertakings collude tacitly when in an oligopolistic market they are able to coordinate their action on the market without resorting to an explicit cartel agreement.

[87] This term refers to undertakings that constrain the pricing behaviour of other undertakings in the market who might otherwise have tacitly colluded.

Commentary
para 97: F&N: 15.102

98. The nature of the efficiency gains also plays an important role. According to economic theory undertakings maximise their profits by selling units of output until marginal revenue equals marginal cost. Marginal revenue is the change in total revenue resulting from selling an additional unit of output and marginal cost is the change in total cost resulting from producing that additional unit of output. It follows from this principle that as a general rule output and pricing

decisions of a profit maximising undertaking are not determined by its fixed costs (i.e. costs that do not vary with the rate of production) but by its variable costs (i.e. costs that vary with the rate of production). After fixed costs are incurred and capacity is set, pricing and output decisions are determined by variable cost and demand conditions. Take for instance a situation in which two companies each produce two products on two production lines operating only at half their capacities. A specialisation agreement may allow the two undertakings to specialise in producing one of the two products and scrap their second production line for the other product. At the same time the specialisation may allow the companies to reduce variable input and stocking costs. Only the latter savings will have a direct effect on the pricing and output decisions of the undertakings, as they will influence the marginal costs of production. The scrapping by each undertaking of one of their production lines will not reduce their variable costs and will not have an impact on their production costs. It follows that undertakings may have a direct incentive to pass on to consumers in the form of higher output and lower prices efficiencies that reduce marginal costs, whereas they have no such direct incentive with regard to efficiencies that reduce fixed costs. Consumers are therefore more likely to receive a fair share of the cost efficiencies in the case of reductions in variable costs than they are in the case of reductions in fixed costs.

Commentary
para 98: **B&C:** 3.058 **F&N:** 3.483, 3.503, 12.103, 15.102

---

99. The fact that undertakings may have an incentive to pass on certain types of cost efficiencies does not imply that the pass-on rate will necessarily be 100%. The actual pass-on rate depends on the extent to which consumers respond to changes in price, i.e. the elasticity of demand. The greater the increase in demand caused by a decrease in price, the greater the pass-on rate. This follows from the fact that the greater the additional sales caused by a price reduction due to an increase in output the more likely it is that these sales will offset the loss of revenue caused by the lower price resulting from the increase in output. In the absence of price discrimination the lowering of prices affects all units sold by the undertaking, in which case marginal revenue is less than the price obtained for the marginal product. If the undertakings concerned are able to charge different prices to different customers, i.e. price discriminate, pass-on will normally only benefit price-sensitive consumers.[88]

Notes
[88] The restrictive agreement may even allow the undertakings in question to charge a higher price to customers with a low elasticity of demand.

Commentary
para 99: **F&N:** 3.504, 15.102

---

100. It must also be taken into account that efficiency gains often do not affect the whole cost structure of the undertakings concerned. In such event the impact on the price to consumers is reduced. If for example an agreement allows the parties to reduce production costs by 6%, but production costs only make up one third of the costs on the basis of which prices are determined, the impact on the product price is 2%, assuming that the full amount is passed-on.

101. Finally, and very importantly, it is necessary to balance the two opposing forces resulting from the restriction of competition and the cost efficiencies. On the one hand, any increase in market power caused by the restrictive agreement gives the undertakings concerned the ability and incentive to raise price. On the other hand, the types of cost efficiencies that are taken into account may give the undertakings concerned an incentive to reduce price, see paragraph 98 above. The effects of these two opposing forces must be balanced against each other. It is recalled in this regard that the consumer pass-on condition incorporates a sliding scale. When the agreement causes a substantial reduction in the competitive constraint facing the parties, extraordinarily large cost efficiencies are normally required for sufficient pass-on to occur.

3.4.3. Pass-on and balancing of other types of efficiencies

102. Consumer pass-on can also take the form of qualitative efficiencies such as new and improved products, creating sufficient value for consumers to compensate for the anticompetitive effects of the agreement, including a price increase.

Commentary
para 102: F&N: 3.483

103. Any such assessment necessarily requires value judgment. It is difficult to assign precise values to dynamic efficiencies of this nature. However, the fundamental objective of the assessment remains the same, namely to ascertain the overall impact of the agreement on the consumers within the relevant market. Undertakings claiming the benefit of Article [101](3) must substantiate that consumers obtain countervailing benefits (see in this respect paragraphs 57 and 86 above).

Commentary
para 103: B&C: 3.059

104. The availability of new and improved products constitutes an important source of consumer welfare. As long as the increase in value stemming from such improvements exceeds any harm from a maintenance or an increase in price caused by the restrictive agreement, consumers are better off than without the agreement and the consumer pass-on requirement of Article [101](3) is normally fulfilled. In cases where the likely effect of the agreement is to increase prices for consumers within the relevant market it must be carefully assessed whether the claimed efficiencies create real value for consumers in that market so as to compensate for the adverse effects of the restriction of competition.

Commentary
para 104: B&C: 3.059

3.5. Fourth condition of Article [101](3): No elimination of competition

105. According to the fourth condition of Article [101](3) the agreement must not afford the undertakings concerned the possibility of eliminating competition in respect of a substantial part of the products concerned. Ultimately the protection of rivalry and the competitive process is given priority over potentially pro-competitive efficiency gains which could result from restrictive agreements. The last condition of Article [101](3) recognises the fact that rivalry between undertakings is an essential driver of economic efficiency, including dynamic efficiencies in the shape of innovation. In other words, the ultimate aim of Article [101] is to protect the competitive process. When competition is eliminated the competitive process is brought to an end and short-term efficiency gains are outweighed by longer-term losses stemming *inter alia* from expenditures incurred by the incumbent to maintain its position (rent seeking), misallocation of resources, reduced innovation and higher prices.

Commentary
para 105: B&C: 3.067 F&N: 3.506

106. The concept in Article [101](3) of elimination of competition in respect of a substantial part of the products concerned is an autonomous Community law concept specific to Article [101](3).[89] However, in the application of this concept it is necessary to take account of the relationship between Article [101] and Article [102]. According to settled case law the application of Article [101](3) cannot prevent the application of Article [102] of the Treaty.[90] Moreover, since Articles [101] and [102] both pursue the aim of maintaining effective competition on the market, consistency requires that Article [101](3) be interpreted as precluding any application of this provision to restrictive agreements that constitute an abuse of a dominant position.[91,92] However, not all restrictive agreements concluded by a dominant undertaking constitute an abuse of a dominant position. This is for instance the case where a dominant undertaking is party to a

non-full function joint venture,[93] which is found to be restrictive of competition but at the same time involves a substantial integration of assets.

Notes

[89] See Joined Cases T-191/98, T-212/98 and T-214/98 *Atlantic Container Line (TACA)* [2003] ECR II-[3275], paragraph 939, and Case T-395/94 *Atlantic Container Line* [2002] ECR II-875, paragraph 330.

[90] See Joined Cases C-395/96 P and C-396/96 P *Compagnie maritime belge* [2000] ECR I-1365, paragraph 130. Similarly, the application of Article [101](3) does not prevent the application of the Treaty rules on the free movement of goods, services, persons and capital. These provisions are in certain circumstances applicable to agreements, decisions and concerted practices within the meaning of Article [101](1), see to that effect Case C-309/99 *Wouters* [2002] ECR I-1577, paragraph 120.

[91] See in this respect Case T-51/89 *Tetra Pak (I)* [1990] ECR II-309, and Joined Cases T-191/98, T-212/98 and T-214/98 *Atlantic Container Line (TACA)* [2003] ECR II-[3275], paragraph 1456.

[92] This is how paragraph 135 of the Guidelines on vertical restraints and paragraphs 36, 71, 105, 134 and 155 of the Guidelines on horizontal cooperation agreements, cited in note 5, should be understood when they state that in principle restrictive agreements concluded by dominant undertakings cannot be exempted.

[93] Full function joint ventures, i.e. joint ventures that perform on a lasting basis all the functions of an autonomous economic entity, are covered by Council Regulation (EEC) No 4064/89 on the control of concentrations between undertakings (OJ 1990 L 257, p.13).

Commentary
para 106: B&C: 3.058

107. Whether competition is being eliminated within the meaning of the last condition of Article [101](3) depends on the degree of competition existing prior to the agreement and on the impact of the restrictive agreement on competition, i.e. the reduction in competition that the agreement brings about. The more competition is already weakened in the market concerned, the slighter the further reduction required for competition to be eliminated within the meaning of Article [101](3). Moreover, the greater the reduction of competition caused by the agreement, the greater the likelihood that competition in respect of a substantial part of the products concerned risks being eliminated.

Commentary
para 107: F&N: 3.510

108. The application of the last condition of Article [101](3) requires a realistic analysis of the various sources of competition in the market, the level of competitive constraint that they impose on the parties to the agreement and the impact of the agreement on this competitive constraint. Both actual and potential competition must be considered.

Commentary
para 108: F&N: 15.106

109. While market shares are relevant, the magnitude of remaining sources of actual competition cannot be assessed exclusively on the basis of market share. More extensive qualitative and quantitative analysis is normally called for. The capacity of actual competitors to compete and their incentive to do so must be examined. If, for example, competitors face capacity constraints or have relatively higher costs of production their competitive response will necessarily be limited.

Commentary
para 109: B&C: 3.070 F&N: 15.107

110. In the assessment of the impact of the agreement on competition it is also relevant to examine its influence on the various parameters of competition. The last condition for exception under Article [101](3) is not fulfilled, if the agreement eliminates competition in one of its most important expressions. This is particularly the case when an agreement eliminates price competition[94] or competition in respect of innovation and development of new products.

Notes
94 See paragraph 21 of the judgment in *Metro (I)* cited in note 54.

111. The actual market conduct of the parties can provide insight into the impact of the agreement. If following the conclusion of the agreement the parties have implemented and maintained substantial price increases or engaged in other conduct indicative of the existence of a considerable degree of market power, it is an indication that the parties are not subject to any real competitive pressure and that competition has been eliminated with regard to a substantial part of the products concerned.

112. Past competitive interaction may also provide an indication of the impact of the agreement on future competitive interaction. An undertaking may be able to eliminate competition within the meaning of Article [101](3) by concluding an agreement with a competitor that in the past has been a "maverick".⁹⁵ Such an agreement may change the competitive incentives and capabilities of the competitor and thereby remove an important source of competition in the market.

Notes
95 See paragraph 97 above.

113. In cases involving differentiated products, i.e. products that differ in the eyes of consumers, the impact of the agreement may depend on the competitive relationship between the products sold by the parties to the agreement. When undertakings offer differentiated products the competitive constraint that individual products impose on each other differs according to the degree of substitutability between them. It must therefore be considered what is the degree of substitutability between the products offered by the parties, i.e. what is the competitive constraint that they impose on each other. The more the products of the parties to the agreement are close substitutes the greater the likely restrictive effect of the agreement. In other words, the more substitutable the products the greater the likely change brought about by the agreement in terms of restriction of competition on the market and the more likely it is that competition in respect of a substantial part of the products concerned risks being eliminated.

Commentary
para 113: B&C: 4.004

114. While sources of actual competition are usually the most important, as they are most easily verified, sources of potential competition must also be taken into account. The assessment of potential competition requires an analysis of barriers to entry facing undertakings that are not already competing within the relevant market. Any assertions by the parties that there are low barriers to market entry must be supported by information identifying the sources of potential competition and the parties must also substantiate why these sources constitute a real competitive pressure on the parties.

115. In the assessment of entry barriers and the real possibility for new entry on a significant scale, it is relevant to examine, *inter alia,* the following:
    (i) The regulatory framework with a view to determining its impact on new entry.
    (ii) The cost of entry including sunk costs. Sunk costs are those that cannot be recovered if the entrant subsequently exits the market. The higher the sunk costs the higher the commercial risk for potential entrants.
    (iii) The minimum efficient scale within the industry, i.e. the rate of output where average costs are minimised. If the minimum efficient scale is large compared to the size of the market, efficient entry is likely to be more costly and risky.
    (iv) The competitive strengths of potential entrants. Effective entry is particularly likely where potential entrants have access to at least as cost efficient technologies as the incumbents or other competitive advantages that allow them to compete effectively. When potential entrants are on the same or an inferior technological trajectory compared to the incumbents and possess no other significant competitive advantage entry is more risky and less effective.

(v) The position of buyers and their ability to bring onto the market new sources of competition. It is irrelevant that certain strong buyers may be able to extract more favourable conditions from the parties to the agreement than their weaker competitors.[96] The presence of strong buyers can only serve to counter a prima facie finding of elimination of competition if it is likely that the buyers in question will pave the way for effective new entry.

(vi) The likely response of incumbents to attempted new entry. Incumbents may for example through past conduct have acquired a reputation of aggressive behaviour, having an impact on future entry.

(vii) The economic outlook for the industry may be an indicator of its longer-term attractiveness. Industries that are stagnating or in decline are less attractive candidates for entry than industries characterised by growth.

(viii) Past entry on a significant scale or the absence thereof.

Notes

[96] See in this respect Case T-228/97 *Irish Sugar* [1999] ECR II-2969, paragraph 101.

Commentary
para 115(v): F&N: 3.510

---

116. The above principles can be illustrated by the following hypothetical examples, which are not intended to establish thresholds: Firm A is brewer, holding 70% of the relevant market, comprising the sale of beer through cafés and other on-trade premises. Over the past 5 years A has increased its market share from 60%. There are four other competitors in the market, B, C, D and E with market shares of 10%, 10%, 5% and 5%. No new entry has occurred in the recent past and price changes implemented by A have generally been followed by competitors. A concludes agreements with 20% of the on-trade premises representing 40% of sales volumes whereby the contracting parties undertake to purchase beer only from A for a period of 5 years. The agreements raise the costs and reduce the revenues of rivals, which are foreclosed from the most attractive outlets. Given the market position of A, which has been strengthened in recent years, the absence of new entry and the already weak position of competitors it is likely that competition in the market is eliminated within the meaning of Article [101](3). Shipping firms A, B, C, and D, holding collectively more than 70% of the relevant market, conclude an agreement whereby they agree to coordinate their schedules and their tariffs. Following the implementation of the agreement prices rise between 30% and 100%. There are four other suppliers, the largest holding about 14% of the relevant market. There has been no new entry in recent years and the parties to the agreement did not lose significant market share following the price increases. The existing competitors brought no significant new capacity to the market and no new entry occurred. In light of the market position of the parties and the absence of competitive response to their joint conduct it can reasonably be concluded that the parties to the agreement are not subject to real competitive pressures and that the agreement affords them the possibility of eliminating competition within the meaning of Article [101](3). A is a producer of electric appliances for professional users with a market share of 65% of a relevant national market. B is a competing manufacturer with 5% market share which has developed a new type of motor that is more powerful while consuming less electricity. A and B conclude an agreement whereby they establish a production joint venture for the production of the new motor. B undertakes to grant an exclusive licence to the joint venture. The joint venture combines the new technology of B with the efficient manufacturing and quality control process of A. There is one other main competitor with 15% of the market. Another competitor with 5% market share has recently been acquired by C, a major international producer of competing electric appliances, which itself owns efficient technologies. C has thus far not been active on the market mainly due to the fact that local presence and servicing is desired by customers. Through the acquisition C gains access to the service organisation required to penetrate the market. The entry of C is likely to ensure that competition is not being eliminated.

C14

COMMUNICATION FROM THE COMMISSION

Guidance on the Commission's enforcement priorities in applying Article [102]*
of the [Treaty on the Functioning of the European Union] to abusive
exclusionary conduct by dominant undertakings

(2009/C 45/02)

(Text with EEA relevance)

Official Journal C 45, 24.2.2009, p.7

Celex No: 52009XC0224(01)

EUR-Lex permanent link: <http://eur-lex.europa.eu/LexUriServ/LexUriServ.do?uri=CELEX:5200
9XC0224(01):EN:NOT>

Notes

* Ed note: please see the Note on the Lisbon Treaty at p.xvii in regard to article renumbering introduced by the Lisbon Treaty.

Commentary

Notice: **B&C:** 1.077, 4.026, 10.012, 10.026, 10.063, 10.115, 12.070, 13.005 **F&N:** 4.43, 4.99, 4.101, 4.102,
  4.104, 4.129, 4.134, 4.135, 4.266, 4.267, 4.286, 4.367, 4.368, 4.386, 4.412, 4.429, 4.443, 4.445, 4.446, 4.454,
  4.458, 4.460, 4.463, 4.467, 4.522, 4.592, 4.605, 4.730, 4.745, 9.28, 9.212, 12.140, 17.86
paras 9–18: **B&C:** 10.004
paras 10–12: **F&N:** 1.214
paras 19–22: **B&C:** 10.004, 10.064
paras 23–27: **B&C:** 10.004, 10.069
paras 28–31: **B&C:** 10.004 **F&N:** 3.508, 4.293
paras 33–36: **B&C:** 10.101
paras 39–45: **B&C:** 10.095
paras 41–45; **F&N:** 4.272
paras 43–44: **B&C:** 10.092
paras 47–62: **B&C:** 12.079
paras 59–61: **F&N:** 4.272
paras 60–63 : **F&N:** 4.351
paras 63–74: **B&C:** 10.070
paras 64–65: **F&N:** 4.350
paras 70–71: **B&C:** 10.078
paras 89–90: **B&C:** 10.063
paras 154–162: **B&C:** 9.050

I. INTRODUCTION

1. Article [102] of the [Treaty on the Functioning of the European Union] ('Article [102]') prohibits
   abuses of a dominant position. In accordance with the case-law, it is not in itself illegal for an undertaking to be in a dominant position and such a dominant undertaking is entitled to compete on the
   merits. However, the undertaking concerned has a special responsibility not to allow its conduct to
   impair genuine undistorted competition on the common market. Article [102] is the legal basis for
   a crucial component of competition policy and its effective enforcement helps markets to work
   better for the benefit of businesses and consumers. This is particularly important in the context of
   the wider objective of achieving an integrated internal market.

II. PURPOSE OF THIS DOCUMENT

2. This document sets out the enforcement priorities that will guide the Commission's action in
   applying Article [102] to exclusionary conduct by dominant undertakings. Alongside the Commission's specific enforcement decisions, it is intended to provide greater clarity and predictability

as regards the general framework of analysis which the Commission employs in determining whether it should pursue cases concerning various forms of exclusionary conduct and to help undertakings better assess whether certain behaviour is likely to result in intervention by the Commission under Article [102].

Commentary
para 2: B&C: 10.004

---

3. This document is not intended to constitute a statement of the law and is without prejudice to the interpretation of Article [102] by the Court of Justice or the Court of First Instance of the European Communities. In addition, the general framework set out in this document applies without prejudice to the possibility for the Commission to reject a complaint when it considers that a case lacks priority on grounds of lack of Community interest.

Commentary
para 3: B&C: 10.004

---

4. Article [102] applies to undertakings which hold a dominant position on one or more relevant markets. Such a position may be held by one undertaking (single dominance) or by two or more undertakings (collective dominance). This document only relates to abuses committed by an undertaking holding a single dominant position.

Commentary
para 4: B&C: 10.004

---

5. In applying Article [102] to exclusionary conduct by dominant undertakings, the Commission will focus on those types of conduct that are most harmful to consumers. Consumers benefit from competition through lower prices, better quality and a wider choice of new or improved goods and services. The Commission, therefore, will direct its enforcement to ensuring that markets function properly and that consumers benefit from the efficiency and productivity which result from effective competition between undertakings.

Commentary
para 5: F&N: 4.90

---

6. The emphasis of the Commission's enforcement activity in relation to exclusionary conduct is on safeguarding the competitive process in the internal market and ensuring that undertakings which hold a dominant position do not exclude their competitors by other means than competing on the merits of the products or services they provide. In doing so the Commission is mindful that what really matters is protecting an effective competitive process and not simply protecting competitors. This may well mean that competitors who deliver less to consumers in terms of price, choice, quality and innovation will leave the market.

Commentary
para 6: B&C: 10.002 F&N: 4.745

---

7. Conduct which is directly exploitative of consumers, for example charging excessively high prices or certain behaviour that undermines the efforts to achieve an integrated internal market, is also liable to infringe Article [102]. The Commission may decide to intervene in relation to such conduct, in particular where the protection of consumers and the proper functioning of the internal market cannot otherwise be adequately ensured. For the purpose of providing guidance on its enforcement priorities the Commission at this stage limits itself to exclusionary conduct and in, particular, certain specific types of exclusionary conduct which, based on its experience, appear to be the most common.

8. In applying the general enforcement principles set out in this Communication, the Commission will take into account the specific facts and circumstances of each case. For example, in cases involving regulated markets, the Commission will take into account the specific regulatory environment in conducting its assessment.[1] The Commission may therefore adapt the approach set out in this

Communication to the extent that this would appear to be reasonable and appropriate in a given case.

Notes

1 See for instance paragraph 82.

Commentary
para 8: F&N: 4.132

III. GENERAL APPROACH TO EXCLUSIONARY CONDUCT

A. Market power

9. The assessment of whether an undertaking is in a dominant position and of the degree of market power it holds is a first step in the application of Article [102]. According to the case-law, holding a dominant position confers a special responsibility on the undertaking concerned, the scope of which must be considered in the light of the specific circumstances of each case.[1]

Notes

1 Case 322/81, *Nederlandsche Banden Industrie Michelin (Michelin I) v Commission*, [1983] ECR 3461, paragraph 57; Case T-83/91, *Tetra Pak v Commission (Tetra Pak II)*, [1993] ECR II-755, paragraph 114; Case T-111/96, *ITT Promedia v Commission*, [1998] ECR II-2937, paragraph 139; Case T-228/97, *Irish Sugar v Commission*, [1999] ECR II-2969, paragraph 112; and Case T-203/01, *Michelin v Commission (Michelin II)*, [2003] ECR II-4071, paragraph 97.

Commentary
para 9: B&C: 10.057

10. Dominance has been defined under Community law as a position of economic strength enjoyed by an undertaking, which enables it to prevent effective competition being maintained on a relevant market, by affording it the power to behave to an appreciable extent independently of its competitors, its customers and ultimately of consumers.[1] This notion of independence is related to the degree of competitive constraint exerted on the undertaking in question. Dominance entails that these competitive constraints are not sufficiently effective and hence that the undertaking in question enjoys substantial market power over a period of time. This means that the undertaking's decisions are largely insensitive to the actions and reactions of competitors, customers and, ultimately, consumers. The Commission may consider that effective competitive constraints are absent even if some actual or potential competition remains.[2] In general, a dominant position derives from a combination of several factors which, taken separately, are not necessarily determinative.[3]

Notes

1 See Case 27/76, *United Brands Company and United Brands Continentaal v Commission*, [1978] ECR 207, paragraph 65; Case 85/76, *Hoffmann-La Roche & Co v Commission*, [1979] ECR 461, paragraph 38.
2 See Case 27/76, *United Brands Company and United Brands Continentaal v Commission* [1978] ECR 207, paragraphs 113 to 121; Case T-395/94, *Atlantic Container Line and Others v Commission*, [2002] ECR II-875, paragraph 330.
3 Case 27/76, *United Brands and United Brands Continentaal v Commission*, [1978] ECR 207, paragraphs 65 and 66; Case C-250/92, *Gøttrup-Klim e.a. Grovvareforeninger v Dansk Landbrugs Grovvareselskab*, [1994] ECR I-5641, paragraph 47; Case T-30/89, *Hilti v Commission*, [1991] ECR II-1439, paragraph 90.

Commentary
para 10: F&N: 4.128

11. The Commission considers that an undertaking which is capable of profitably increasing prices above the competitive level for a significant period of time does not face sufficiently effective competitive constraints and can thus generally be regarded as dominant.[1] In this Communication, the expression 'increase prices' includes the power to maintain prices above the competitive level and is used as shorthand for the various ways in which the parameters of competition — such as prices, output, innovation, the variety or quality of goods or services — can be influenced to the advantage of the dominant undertaking and to the detriment of consumers.[2]

Notes

[1] What is a significant period of time will depend on the product and on the circumstances of the market in question, but normally a period of two years will be sufficient.

[2] Accounting profitability may be a poor proxy for the exercise of market power. See to that effect Case 27/76, *United Brands Company and United Brands Continentaal v Commission*, [1978] ECR 207, paragraph 126.

Commentary
para 11: B&C: 4.001 F&N: 4.132, 4.268

12. The assessment of dominance will take into account the competitive structure of the market, and in particular the following factors:
    — constraints imposed by the existing supplies from, and the position on the market of, actual competitors (the market position of the dominant undertaking and its competitors),
    — constraints imposed by the credible threat of future expansion by actual competitors or entry by potential competitors (expansion and entry),
    — constraints imposed by the bargaining strength of the undertaking's customers (countervailing buyer power).

Commentary
para 12: F&N: 4.143, 4.180

(a) Market position of the dominant undertaking and its competitors

13. Market shares provide a useful first indication for the Commission of the market structure and of the relative importance of the various undertakings active on the market.[1] However, the Commission will interpret market shares in the light of the relevant market conditions, and in particular of the dynamics of the market and of the extent to which products are differentiated. The trend or development of market shares over time may also be taken into account in volatile or bidding markets.

Notes

[1] Case 85/76, *Hoffmann-La Roche & Co v Commission*, [1979] ECR 461, paragraph 39–41; Case C-62/86, *AKZO v Commission*, [1991] ECR I-3359, paragraph 60; Case T-30/89, *Hilti v Commission*, [1991] ECR II-1439, paragraphs 90, 91 and 92; Case T-340/03, *France Télécom v Commission*, [2007] ECR II-107, paragraph 100.

Commentary
para 13: B&C: 10.022 F&N: 4.166

14. The Commission considers that low market shares are generally a good proxy for the absence of substantial market power. The Commission's experience suggests that dominance is not likely if the undertaking's market share is below 40% in the relevant market. However, there may be specific cases below that threshold where competitors are not in a position to constrain effectively the conduct of a dominant undertaking, for example where they face serious capacity limitations. Such cases may also deserve attention on the part of the Commission.

Commentary
para 14: B&C: 10.028

15. Experience suggests that the higher the market share and the longer the period of time over which it is held, the more likely it is that it constitutes an important preliminary indication of the existence of a dominant position and, in certain circumstances, of possible serious effects of abusive conduct, justifying an intervention by the Commission under Article [102].[1] However, as a general rule, the Commission will not come to a final conclusion as to whether or not a case should be pursued without examining all the factors which may be sufficient to constrain the behaviour of the undertaking.

(b) Expansion or entry

16. Competition is a dynamic process and an assessment of the competitive constraints on an undertaking cannot be based solely on the existing market situation. The potential impact of expansion by actual competitors or entry by potential competitors, including the threat of such expansion or entry, is also relevant. An undertaking can be deterred from increasing prices if expansion or entry is likely, timely and sufficient. For the Commission to consider expansion or entry likely it must be sufficiently profitable for the competitor or entrant, taking into account factors such as the barriers to expansion or entry, the likely reactions of the allegedly dominant undertaking and other competitors, and the risks and costs of failure. For expansion or entry to be considered timely, it must be sufficiently swift to deter or defeat the exercise of substantial market power. For expansion or entry to be considered sufficient, it cannot be simply small-scale entry, for example into some market niche, but must be of such a magnitude as to be able to deter any attempt to increase prices by the putatively dominant undertaking in the relevant market.

17. Barriers to expansion or entry can take various forms. They may be legal barriers, such as tariffs or quotas, or they may take the form of advantages specifically enjoyed by the dominant undertaking, such as economies of scale and scope, privileged access to essential inputs or natural resources, important technologies[1] or an established distribution and sales network.[2] They may also include costs and other impediments, for instance resulting from network effects, faced by customers in switching to a new supplier. The dominant undertaking's own conduct may also create barriers to entry, for example where it has made significant investments which entrants or competitors would have to match,[3] or where it has concluded long-term contracts with its customers that have appreciable foreclosing effects. Persistently high market shares may be indicative of the existence of barriers to entry and expansion.

(c) Countervailing buyer power

18. Competitive constraints may be exerted not only by actual or potential competitors but also by customers. Even an undertaking with a high market share may not be able to act to an appreciable extent independently of customers with sufficient bargaining strength.[1] Such countervailing buying power may result from the customers' size or their commercial significance for the dominant undertaking, and their ability to switch quickly to competing suppliers, to promote new entry or to vertically integrate, and to credibly threaten to do so. If countervailing power is of a sufficient magnitude, it may deter or defeat an attempt by the undertaking to profitably increase prices. Buyer power may not, however, be considered a sufficiently effective constraint if it only ensures that a particular or limited segment of customers is shielded from the market power of the dominant undertaking.

Notes

1 See Case T-228/97, *Irish Sugar v Commission*, [1999] ECR II-2969, paragraphs 97 to 104, in which the Court of First Instance considered whether the alleged lack of independence of the undertaking *vis-à-vis* its customers should be seen as an exceptional circumstance preventing the finding of a dominant position in spite of the fact that the undertaking was responsible for a very large part of the sales recorded on the industrial sugar market in Ireland.

Commentary
para 18: F&N: 1.201, 4.216

B. Foreclosure leading to consumer harm ('anti-competitive foreclosure')

19. The aim of the Commission's enforcement activity in relation to exclusionary conduct is to ensure that dominant undertakings do not impair effective competition by foreclosing their competitors in an anti-competitive way, thus having an adverse impact on consumer welfare, whether in the form of higher price levels than would have otherwise prevailed or in some other form such as limiting quality or reducing consumer choice. In this document the term 'anti-competitive foreclosure' is used to describe a situation where effective access of actual or potential competitors to supplies or markets is hampered or eliminated as a result of the conduct of the dominant undertaking whereby the dominant undertaking is likely to be in a position to profitably increase prices[1] to the detriment of consumers. The identification of likely consumer harm can rely on qualitative and, where possible and appropriate, quantitative evidence. The Commission will address such anti-competitive foreclosure either at the intermediate level or at the level of final consumers, or at both levels.[2]

Notes

1 For the meaning of the expression 'increase price' see paragraph 11.

2 The concept of 'consumers' encompasses all direct or indirect users of the products affected by the conduct, including intermediate producers that use the products as an input, as well as distributors and final consumers both of the immediate product and of products provided by intermediate producers. Where intermediate users are actual or potential competitors of the dominant undertaking, the assessment focuses on the effects of the conduct on users further downstream.

Commentary
para 19: B&C: 2.100, 10.069 F&N: 4.101, 4.112, 4.267, 4.268

20. The Commission will normally intervene under Article [102] where, on the basis of cogent and convincing evidence, the allegedly abusive conduct is likely to lead to anti-competitive foreclosure. The Commission considers the following factors to be generally relevant to such an assessment:
    — *the position of the dominant undertaking*: in general, the stronger the dominant position, the higher the likelihood that conduct protecting that position leads to anti-competitive foreclosure,
    — *the conditions on the relevant market*: this includes the conditions of entry and expansion, such as the existence of economies of scale and/or scope and network effects. Economies of scale mean that competitors are less likely to enter or stay in the market if the dominant undertaking forecloses a significant part of the relevant market. Similarly, the conduct may allow the dominant undertaking to 'tip' a market characterised by network effects in its favour or to further entrench its position on such a market. Likewise, if entry barriers in the upstream and/or downstream market are significant, this means that it may be costly for competitors to overcome possible foreclosure through vertical integration,
    — *the position of the dominant undertaking's competitors*: this includes the importance of competitors for the maintenance of effective competition. A specific competitor may play a significant competitive role even if it only holds a small market share compared to other competitors. It may, for example, be the closest competitor to the dominant undertaking, be a particularly innovative competitor, or have the reputation of systematically cutting prices. In its assessment, the Commission may also consider in appropriate cases, on the basis of information available, whether there are realistic, effective and timely counterstrategies that competitors would be likely to deploy,

— *the position of the customers or input suppliers*: this may include consideration of the possible selectivity of the conduct in question. The dominant undertaking may apply the practice only to selected customers or input suppliers who may be of particular importance for the entry or expansion of competitors, thereby enhancing the likelihood of anti-competitive foreclosure.[1] In the case of customers, they may, for example, be the ones most likely to respond to offers from alternative suppliers, they may represent a particular means of distributing the product that would be suitable for a new entrant, they may be situated in a geographic area well suited to new entry or they may be likely to influence the behaviour of other customers. In the case of input suppliers, those with whom the dominant undertaking has concluded exclusive supply arrangements may be the ones most likely to respond to requests by customers who are competitors of the dominant undertaking in a downstream market, or may produce a grade of the product — or produce at a location — particularly suitable for a new entrant. Any strategies at the disposal of the customers or input suppliers which could help to counter the conduct of the dominant undertaking will also be considered,

— *the extent of the allegedly abusive conduct*: in general, the higher the percentage of total sales in the relevant market affected by the conduct, the longer its duration, and the more regularly it has been applied, the greater is the likely foreclosure effect,

— *possible evidence of actual foreclosure*: if the conduct has been in place for a sufficient period of time, the market performance of the dominant undertaking and its competitors may provide direct evidence of anti-competitive foreclosure. For reasons attributable to the allegedly abusive conduct, the market share of the dominant undertaking may have risen or a decline in market share may have been slowed. For similar reasons, actual competitors may have been marginalised or may have exited, or potential competitors may have tried to enter and failed,

— *direct evidence of any exclusionary strategy*: this includes internal documents which contain direct evidence of a strategy to exclude competitors, such as a detailed plan to engage in certain conduct in order to exclude a competitor, to prevent entry or to pre-empt the emergence of a market, or evidence of concrete threats of exclusionary action. Such direct evidence may be helpful in interpreting the dominant undertaking's conduct.

Notes

[1] Case T-228/97, *Irish Sugar v Commission*, [1999] ECR II-2969, paragraph 188.

Commentary
para 20: **B&C:** 10.019, 10.056 **F&N:** 4.101, 4.113, 4.269, 4.276, 4.451, 4.548

21. When pursuing a case the Commission will develop the analysis of the general factors mentioned in paragraph 20, together with the more specific factors described in the sections dealing with certain types of exclusionary conduct, and any other factors which it may consider to be appropriate. This assessment will usually be made by comparing the actual or likely future situation in the relevant market (with the dominant undertaking's conduct in place) with an appropriate counterfactual, such as the simple absence of the conduct in question or with another realistic alternative scenario, having regard to established business practices.

Commentary
para 21: **F&N:** 4.114

22. There may be circumstances where it is not necessary for the Commission to carry out a detailed assessment before concluding that the conduct in question is likely to result in consumer harm. If it appears that the conduct can only raise obstacles to competition and that it creates no efficiencies, its anti-competitive effect may be inferred. This could be the case, for instance, if the dominant undertaking prevents its customers from testing the products of competitors or provides financial incentives to its customers on condition that they do not test such products, or pays a distributor or a customer to delay the introduction of a competitor's product.

C. Price-based exclusionary conduct

23. The considerations in paragraphs 23 to 27 apply to price-based exclusionary conduct. Vigorous price competition is generally beneficial to consumers. With a view to preventing anti-competitive

foreclosure, the Commission will normally only intervene where the conduct concerned has already been or is capable of hampering competition from competitors which are considered to be as efficient as the dominant undertaking.[1]

Notes

[1] Case 62/86, *AKZO Chemie v Commission*, [1991] ECR I-3359, paragraph 72: in relation to pricing below average total cost (ATC) the Court of Justice stated: '*Such prices can drive from the market undertakings which are perhaps as efficient as the dominant undertaking but which, because of their smaller financial resources, are incapable of withstanding the competition waged against them*'. See also Judgment of 10 April 2008 in Case T-271/03, *Deutsche Telekom v Commission*, not yet reported, [now [2008] ECR II-477] paragraph 194.

Commentary
para 23: F&N: 4.116, 4.270, 4.430, 4.431

24. However, the Commission recognises that in certain circumstances a less efficient competitor may also exert a constraint which should be taken into account when considering whether particular price-based conduct leads to anti-competitive foreclosure. The Commission will take a dynamic view of that constraint, given that in the absence of an abusive practice such a competitor may benefit from demand-related advantages, such as network and learning effects, which will tend to enhance its efficiency.

Commentary
para 24: B&C: 10.069 F&N: 4.116, 4.273

25. In order to determine whether even a hypothetical competitor as efficient as the dominant undertaking would be likely to be foreclosed by the conduct in question, the Commission will examine economic data relating to cost and sales prices, and in particular whether the dominant undertaking is engaging in below-cost pricing. This will require that sufficiently reliable data be available. Where available, the Commission will use information on the costs of the dominant undertaking itself. If reliable information on those costs is not available, the Commission may decide to use the cost data of competitors or other comparable reliable data.

26. The cost benchmarks that the Commission is likely to use are average avoidable cost (AAC) and long-run average incremental cost (LRAIC).[1] Failure to cover AAC indicates that the dominant undertaking is sacrificing profits in the short term and that an equally efficient competitor cannot serve the targeted customers without incurring a loss. LRAIC is usually above AAC because, in contrast to AAC (which only includes fixed costs if incurred during the period under examination), LRAIC includes product specific fixed costs made before the period in which allegedly abusive conduct took place. Failure to cover LRAIC indicates that the dominant undertaking is not recovering all the (attributable) fixed costs of producing the good or service in question and that an equally efficient competitor could be foreclosed from the market.[2]

Notes

[1] Average avoidable cost is the average of the costs that could have been avoided if the company had not produced a discrete amount of (extra) output, in this case the amount allegedly the subject of abusive conduct. In most cases, AAC and the average variable cost (AVC) will be the same, as it is often only variable costs that can be avoided. Long-run average incremental cost is the average of all the (variable and fixed) costs that a company incurs to produce a particular product. LRAIC and average total cost (ATC) are good proxies for each other, and are the same in the case of single product undertakings. If multi-product undertakings have economies of scope, LRAIC would be below ATC for each individual product, as true common costs are not taken into account in LRAIC. In the case of multiple products, any costs that could have been avoided by not producing a particular product or range are not considered to be common costs. In situations where common costs are significant, they may have to be taken into account when assessing the ability to foreclose equally efficient competitors.

[2] In order to apply these cost benchmarks it may also be necessary to look at revenues and costs of the dominant company and its competitors in a wider context. It may not be sufficient to only assess whether the price or revenue covers the costs for the product in question, but it may be necessary to look at incremental revenues in case the dominant company's conduct in question negatively affects its revenues in other markets or of other products. Similarly, in the case of two sided markets it may be necessary to look at revenues and costs of both sides at the same time.

Commentary
para 26: B&C: 10.072 F&N: 4.352, 4.364, 17.86

27. If the data clearly suggest that an equally efficient competitor can compete effectively with the pricing conduct of the dominant undertaking, the Commission will, in principle, infer that the dominant undertaking's pricing conduct is not likely to have an adverse impact on effective competition, and thus on consumers, and will therefore be unlikely to intervene. If, on the contrary, the data suggest that the price charged by the dominant undertaking has the potential to foreclose equally efficient competitors, then the Commission will integrate this in the general assessment of anti-competitive foreclosure (see Section B above), taking into account other relevant quantitative and/or qualitative evidence.

Commentary
para 27: B&C: 10.072 F&N: 4.434

D. Objective necessity and efficiencies

28. In the enforcement of Article [102], the Commission will also examine claims put forward by a dominant undertaking that its conduct is justified.[1] A dominant undertaking may do so either by demonstrating that its conduct is objectively necessary or by demonstrating that its conduct produces substantial efficiencies which outweigh any anticompetitive effects on consumers. In this context, the Commission will assess whether the conduct in question is indispensable and proportionate to the goal allegedly pursued by the dominant undertaking.

Notes

[1] See Case 27/76, *United Brands v Commission* [1978] ECR 207, paragraph 184; Case 311/84, *Centre Belge d'études de marché — Télémarketing (CBEM) v Compagnie luxembourgeoise de télédiffusion (CLT) and Information publicité Benelux (IPB)*, [1985] ECR 3261, paragraph 27; Case T-30/89, *Hilti v Commission*, [1991] ECR II-1439, paragraphs 102 to 119; Case T-83/91, *Tetra Pak International v Commission (Tetra Pak II)*, [1994] ECR II-755, paragraphs 136 and 207; Case C-95/04 P, *British Airways v Commission*, [2007] ECR I-2331, paragraphs 69 and 86.

Commentary
para 28: F&N: 4.290

29. The question of whether conduct is objectively necessary and proportionate must be determined on the basis of factors external to the dominant undertaking. Exclusionary conduct may, for example, be considered objectively necessary for health or safety reasons related to the nature of the product in question. However, proof of whether conduct of this kind is objectively necessary must take into account that it is normally the task of public authorities to set and enforce public health and safety standards. It is not the task of a dominant undertaking to take steps on its own initiative to exclude products which it regards, rightly or wrongly, as dangerous or inferior to its own product.[1]

Notes

[1] See, for instance, Case T-30/89, *Hilti v Commission*, [1991] ECR II-1439, paragraph 118–119; Case T-83/91, *Tetra Pak International v Commission (Tetra Pak II)*, [1994] ECR II-755, paragraphs 83 and 84 and 138.

Commentary
para 29: F&N: 4.291

30. The Commission considers that a dominant undertaking may also justify conduct leading to foreclosure of competitors on the ground of efficiencies that are sufficient to guarantee that no net harm to consumers is likely to arise. In this context, the dominant undertaking will generally be expected to demonstrate, with a sufficient degree of probability, and on the basis of verifiable evidence, that the following cumulative conditions are fulfilled:[1]— the efficiencies have been, or are likely to be, realised as a result of the conduct. They may, for example, include technical improvements in the quality of goods, or a reduction in the cost of production or distribution,

— the conduct is indispensable to the realisation of those efficiencies: there must be no less anti-competitive alternatives to the conduct that are capable of producing the same efficiencies,

— the likely efficiencies brought about by the conduct outweigh any likely negative effects on competition and consumer welfare in the affected markets,

— the conduct does not eliminate effective competition, by removing all or most existing sources of actual or potential competition. Rivalry between undertakings is an essential driver of economic efficiency, including dynamic efficiencies in the form of innovation. In its absence the dominant undertaking will lack adequate incentives to continue to create and pass on efficiency gains. Where there is no residual competition and no foreseeable threat of entry, the protection of rivalry and the competitive process outweighs possible efficiency gains. In the Commission's view, exclusionary conduct which maintains, creates or strengthens a market position approaching that of a monopoly can normally not be justified on the grounds that it also creates efficiency gains.

Notes

[1] See, in the different context of Article [101], the Communication from the Commission — Notice — Guidelines on the application of Article [101](3) of the Treaty (OJ C 101, 27.4.2004, p.97).

Commentary
para 30: B&C: 10.063 F&N: 4.120, 4.293, 9.213

31. It is incumbent upon the dominant undertaking to provide all the evidence necessary to demonstrate that the conduct concerned is objectively justified. It then falls to the Commission to make the ultimate assessment of whether the conduct concerned is not objectively necessary and, based on a weighing-up of any apparent anti-competitive effects against any advanced and substantiated efficiencies, is likely to result in consumer harm.

Commentary
para 31: F&N: 4.121

IV. Specific Forms of Abuse

A. Exclusive dealing

32. A dominant undertaking may try to foreclose its competitors by hindering them from selling to customers through use of exclusive purchasing obligations or rebates, together referred to as exclusive dealing.[1] This section sets out the circumstances which are most likely to prompt an intervention by the Commission in respect of exclusive dealing arrangements entered into by dominant undertakings.

Notes

[1] The notion of exclusive dealing also includes exclusive supply obligations or incentives with the same effect, whereby the dominant undertaking tries to foreclose its competitors by hindering them from purchasing from suppliers. The Commission considers that such input foreclosure is in principle liable to result in anti-competitive foreclosure if the exclusive supply obligation or incentive ties most of the efficient input suppliers and customers competing with the dominant undertaking are unable to find alternative efficient sources of input supply.

(a) Exclusive purchasing

33. An exclusive purchasing obligation requires a customer on a particular market to purchase exclusively or to a large extent only from the dominant undertaking. Certain other obligations, such as stocking requirements, which appear to fall short of requiring exclusive purchasing, may in practice lead to the same effect.[1]

Notes

[1] Case T-65/98, *Van den Bergh Foods v Commission*, [2003] ECR II-4653. In this case the obligation to use coolers exclusively for the products of the dominant undertaking was considered to lead to outlet exclusivity.

Commentary
para 33: F&N: 4.397

34. In order to convince customers to accept exclusive purchasing, the dominant undertaking may have to compensate them, in whole or in part, for the loss in competition resulting from the

exclusivity. Where such compensation is given, it may be in the individual interest of a customer to enter into an exclusive purchasing obligation with the dominant undertaking. But it would be wrong to conclude automatically from this that all exclusive purchasing obligations, taken together, are beneficial for customers overall, including those currently not purchasing from the dominant undertaking, and the final consumers. The Commission will focus its attention on those cases where it is likely that consumers as a whole will not benefit. This will, in particular, be the case if there are many customers and the exclusive purchasing obligations of the dominant undertaking, taken together, have the effect of preventing the entry or expansion of competing undertakings.

Commentary
para 34: F&N: 4.432

35. In addition to the factors mentioned in paragraph 20, the following factors will generally be of particular relevance in determining whether the Commission will intervene in respect of exclusive purchasing arrangements.

36. The capacity for exclusive purchasing obligations to result in anti-competitive foreclosure arises in particular where, without the obligations, an important competitive constraint is exercised by competitors who either are not yet present in the market at the time the obligations are concluded, or who are not in a position to compete for the full supply of the customers. Competitors may not be able to compete for an individual customer's entire demand because the dominant undertaking is an unavoidable trading partner at least for part of the demand on the market, for instance because its brand is a 'must stock item' preferred by many final consumers or because the capacity constraints on the other suppliers are such that a part of demand can only be provided for by the dominant supplier.[1] If competitors can compete on equal terms for each individual customer's entire demand, exclusive purchasing obligations are generally unlikely to hamper effective competition unless the switching of supplier by customers is rendered difficult due to the duration of the exclusive purchasing obligation. In general, the longer the duration of the obligation, the greater the likely foreclosure effect. However, if the dominant undertaking is an unavoidable trading partner for all or most customers, even an exclusive purchasing obligation of short duration can lead to anti-competitive foreclosure.

Notes
[1] Case T-65/98, *Van den Bergh Foods v Commission*, [2003] ECR II-4653, paragraphs 104 and 156.

Commentary
para 36: F&N: 4.433

(b) Conditional rebates

37. Conditional rebates are rebates granted to customers to reward them for a particular form of purchasing behaviour. The usual nature of a conditional rebate is that the customer is given a rebate if its purchases over a defined reference period exceed a certain threshold, the rebate being granted either on all purchases (retroactive rebates) or only on those made in excess of those required to achieve the threshold (incremental rebates). Conditional rebates are not an uncommon practice. Undertakings may offer such rebates in order to attract more demand, and as such they may stimulate demand and benefit consumers. However, such rebates — when granted by a dominant undertaking — can also have actual or potential foreclosure effects similar to exclusive purchasing obligations. Conditional rebates can have such effects without necessarily entailing a sacrifice for the dominant undertaking.[1]

Notes
[1] In this regard, the assessment of conditional rebates differs from that of predation, which always entails a sacrifice.

Commentary
para 37: F&N: 4.430, 4.431

38. In addition to the factors already mentioned in paragraph 20, the following factors are of particular importance to the Commission in determining whether a given system of conditional rebates is liable to result in anti-competitive foreclosure and, consequently, will be part of the Commission's enforcement priorities.

39. As with exclusive purchasing obligations, the likelihood of anti-competitive foreclosure is higher where competitors are not able to compete on equal terms for the entire demand of each individual customer. A conditional rebate granted by a dominant undertaking may enable it to use the 'non contestable' portion of the demand of each customer (that is to say, the amount that would be purchased by the customer from the dominant undertaking in any event) as leverage to decrease the price to be paid for the 'contestable' portion of demand (that is to say, the amount for which the customer may prefer and be able to find substitutes).[1]

Notes

[1] See Case T-203/01, *Michelin v Commission (Michelin II)*, [2003] ECR II-4071, paragraphs 162 and 163. See also Case T-219/99, *British Airways v Commission*, [2003] ECR II-5917, paragraphs 277 and 278.

Commentary
para 39: F&N: 4.433

40. In general terms, retroactive rebates may foreclose the market significantly, as they may make it less attractive for customers to switch small amounts of demand to an alternative supplier, if this would lead to loss of the retroactive rebates.[1] The potential foreclosing effect of retroactive rebates is in principle strongest on the last purchased unit of the product before the threshold is exceeded. However, what is in the Commission's view relevant for an assessment of the loyalty enhancing effect of a rebate is not simply the effect on competition to provide the last individual unit, but the foreclosing effect of the rebate system.

Notes

[1] Case 322/81, *Nederlandsche Banden Industrie Michelin v Commission (Michelin I)*, [1983] ECR 3461, paragraphs 70 to 73 on (actual or potential) competitors of the dominant supplier. The higher the rebate as a percentage of the total price and the higher the threshold, the greater the inducement below the threshold and, therefore, the stronger the likely foreclosure of actual or potential competitors.

41. When applying the methodology explained in paragraphs 23 to 27, the Commission intends to investigate, to the extent that the data are available and reliable, whether the rebate system is capable of hindering expansion or entry even by competitors that are equally efficient by making it more difficult for them to supply part of the requirements of individual customers. In this context the Commission will estimate what price a competitor would have to offer in order to compensate the customer for the loss of the conditional rebate if the latter would switch part of its demand ('the relevant range') away from the dominant undertaking. The effective price that the competitor will have to match is not the average price of the dominant undertaking, but the normal (list) price less the rebate the customer loses by switching, calculated over the relevant range of sales and in the relevant period of time. The Commission will take into account the margin of error that may be caused by the uncertainties inherent in this kind of analysis.

42. The relevant range over which to calculate the effective price in a particular case depends on the specific facts of each case and on whether the rebate is incremental or retroactive. For incremental rebates, the relevant range is normally the incremental purchases that are being considered. For retroactive rebates, it will generally be relevant to assess in the specific market context how much of a customer's purchase requirements can realistically be switched to a competitor (the 'contestable share' or 'contestable portion'). If it is likely that customers would be willing and able to switch large amounts of demand to a (potential) competitor relatively quickly, the relevant range is likely to be relatively large. If, on the other hand, it is likely that customers would only be willing or able to switch small amounts incrementally, then the relevant range will be relatively small. For existing competitors their capacity to expand sales to customers and the fluctuations in those sales over time may also provide an indication of the relevant range. For potential competitors, an assessment of the scale at which a new entrant would realistically be able to enter may be undertaken, where possible. It may be possible to take the historical growth pattern of new entrants in the same or in similar markets as an indication of a realistic market share of a new entrant.[1]

Notes

1 The relevant range will be estimated on the basis of data which may have varying degrees of precision. The Commission will take this into account in drawing any conclusions regarding the dominant undertaking's ability to foreclose equally efficient competitors. It may also be useful to calculate how big a share of customers' requirements on average the entrant should capture as a minimum so that the effective price is at least as high as the LRAIC of the dominant company. In a number of cases the size of this share, when compared with the actual market shares of competitors and their shares of the customers' requirements, may make it clear whether the rebate scheme is capable to have an anti-competitive foreclosure effect.

43. The lower the estimated effective price over the relevant range is compared to the average price of the dominant supplier, the stronger the loyalty-enhancing effect. However, as long as the effective price remains consistently above the LRAIC of the dominant undertaking, this would normally allow an equally efficient competitor to compete profitably notwithstanding the rebate. In those circumstances the rebate is normally not capable of foreclosing in an anti-competitive way.

44. Where the effective price is below AAC, as a general rule the rebate scheme is capable of foreclosing even equally efficient competitors. Where the effective price is between AAC and LRAIC, the Commission will investigate whether other factors point to the conclusion that entry or expansion even by equally efficient competitors is likely to be affected. In this context, the Commission will investigate whether and to what extent competitors have realistic and effective counterstrategies at their disposal, for instance their capacity to also use a 'non contestable' portion of their buyers' demand as leverage to decrease the price for the relevant range. Where competitors do not have such counterstrategies at their disposal, the Commission will consider that the rebate scheme is capable of foreclosing equally efficient competitors.

45. As indicated in paragraph 27, this analysis will be integrated in the general assessment, taking into account other relevant quantitative or qualitative evidence. It is normally important to consider whether the rebate system is applied with an individualised or a standardised threshold. An individualised threshold — one based on a percentage of the total requirements of the customer or an individualised volume target — allows the dominant supplier to set the threshold at such a level as to make it difficult for customers to switch suppliers, thereby creating a maximum loyalty enhancing effect.[1] By contrast, a standardised volume threshold — where the threshold is the same for all or a group of customers — may be too high for some smaller customers and/or too low for larger customers to have a loyalty enhancing effect. If, however, it can be established that a standardised volume threshold approximates the requirements of an appreciable proportion of customers, the Commission is likely to consider that such a standardised system of rebates may produce anti-competitive foreclosure effects.

Notes

1 See Case 85/76, *Hoffmann-La Roche & Co v Commission*, [1979] ECR 461, paragraphs 89 and 90; Case T-288/97, *Irish Sugar v Commission*, [1999] ECR II-2969, paragraph 213; Case T-219/99, *British Airways v Commission* [2003] ECR II-5917, paragraphs 7 to 11 and 270 to 273.

Commentary
para 45: B&C: 10.092

(c) Efficiencies

46. Provided that the conditions set out in Section III D are fulfilled, the Commission will consider claims by dominant undertakings that rebate systems achieve cost or other advantages which are passed on to customers.[1] Transaction-related cost advantages are often more likely to be achieved with standardised volume targets than with individualised volume targets. Similarly, incremental rebate schemes are in general more likely to give resellers an incentive to produce and resell a higher volume than retroactive rebate schemes.[2] Under the same conditions, the Commission will consider evidence demonstrating that exclusive dealing arrangements result in advantages to particular customers if those arrangements are necessary for the dominant undertaking to make certain relationship-specific investments in order to be able to supply those customers.

Notes

1 For instance, for rebates see Case C-95/04 P, *British Airways v Commission*, [2007] ECR I-2331, paragraph 86.

[2] See, to that effect, Case T-203/01, *Michelin v Commission (Michelin II)*, [2003] ECR II-4071, paragraphs 56 to 60, 74 and 75.

Commentary
para 46: **B&C:** 10.063, 10.092, 10.099 **F&N:** 4.434, 4.456

B. Tying and bundling

47. A dominant undertaking may try to foreclose its competitors by tying or bundling. This section sets out the circumstances which are most likely to prompt an intervention by the Commission when assessing tying and bundling by dominant undertakings.

48. 'Tying' usually refers to situations where customers that purchase one product (the tying product) are required also to purchase another product from the dominant undertaking (the tied product). Tying can take place on a technical or contractual basis.[1] 'Bundling' usually refers to the way products are offered and priced by the dominant undertaking. In the case of pure bundling the products are only sold jointly in fixed proportions. In the case of mixed bundling, often referred to as a multi-product rebate, the products are also made available separately, but the sum of the prices when sold separately is higher than the bundled price.

Notes

[1] Technical tying occurs when the tying product is designed in such a way that it only works properly with the tied product (and not with the alternatives offered by competitors). Contractual tying occurs when the customer who purchases the tying product undertakes also to purchase the tied product (and not the alternatives offered by competitors).

Commentary
para 48: **F&N:** 4.475

49. Tying and bundling are common practices intended to provide customers with better products or offerings in more cost effective ways. However, an undertaking which is dominant in one product market (or more) of a tie or bundle (referred to as the tying market) can harm consumers through tying or bundling by foreclosing the market for the other products that are part of the tie or bundle (referred to as the tied market) and, indirectly, the tying market.

Commentary
para 49: **F&N:** 4.523, 4.529

50. The Commission will normally take action under Article [102] where an undertaking is dominant in the tying market[1] and where, in addition, the following conditions are fulfilled: (i) the tying and tied products are distinct products, and (ii) the tying practice is likely to lead to anti-competitive foreclosure.[2]

Notes

[1] The undertaking should be dominant in the tying market, though not necessarily in the tied market. In bundling cases, the undertaking needs to be dominant in one of the bundled markets. In the special case of tying in after-markets, the condition is that the undertaking is dominant in the tying market and/or the tied after-market.
[2] Case T-201/04, *Microsoft v Commission*, [2007] ECR II-3601, in particular paragraphs 842, 859 to 862, 867 and 869.

Commentary
para 50: **B&C:** 10.123 **F&N:** 4.524

(a) Distinct products

51. Whether the products will be considered by the Commission to be distinct depends on customer demand. Two products are distinct if, in the absence of tying or bundling, a substantial number of customers would purchase or would have purchased the tying product without also buying the tied product from the same supplier, thereby allowing stand-alone production for both the tying and the tied product.[1] Evidence that two products are distinct could include direct evidence that, when given a choice, customers purchase the tying and the tied products separately from different sources of supply, or indirect evidence, such as the presence on the market of undertakings specialised in the manufacture or sale of the tied product without the tying product[2] or of each

of the products bundled by the dominant undertaking, or evidence indicating that undertakings with little market power, particularly in competitive markets, tend not to tie or not to bundle such products.

Notes

1 Case T-201/04, *Microsoft v Commission*, [2007] ECR II-3601, paragraphs 917, 921 and 922.
2 Case T-30/89, *Hilti v Commission*, [1991] ECR II-1439, paragraph 67.

Commentary
para 51: B&C: 10.124 F&N: 4.477, 4.483

(b) Anti-competitive foreclosure in the tied and/or tying market

52. Tying or bundling may lead to anti-competitive effects in the tied market, the tying market, or both at the same time. However, even when the aim of the tying or bundling is to protect the dominant undertaking's position in the tying market, this is done indirectly through foreclosing the tied market. In addition to the factors already mentioned in paragraph 20, the Commission considers that the following factors are generally of particular importance for identifying cases of likely or actual anti-competitive foreclosure.

Commentary
para 52: F&N: 4.538

53. The risk of anti-competitive foreclosure is expected to be greater where the dominant undertaking makes its tying or bundling strategy a lasting one, for example through technical tying which is costly to reverse. Technical tying also reduces the opportunities for resale of individual components.

Commentary
para 53: F&N: 4.512, 4.525

54. In the case of bundling, the undertaking may have a dominant position for more than one of the products in the bundle. The greater the number of such products in the bundle, the stronger the likely anti-competitive foreclosure. This is particularly true if the bundle is difficult for a competitor to replicate, either on its own or in combination with others.

55. The tying may lead to less competition for customers interested in buying the tied product, but not the tying product. If there is not a sufficient number of customers who will buy the tied product alone to sustain competitors of the dominant undertaking in the tied market, the tying can lead to those customers facing higher prices.

56. If the tying and the tied product can be used in variable proportions as inputs to a production process, customers may react to an increase in price for the tying product by increasing their demand for the tied product while decreasing their demand for the tying product. By tying the two products the dominant undertaking may seek to avoid this substitution and as a result be able to raise its prices.

Commentary
para 56: F&N: 4.477, 4.525

57. If the prices the dominant undertaking can charge in the tying market are regulated, tying may allow the dominant undertaking to raise prices in the tied market in order to compensate for the loss of revenue caused by the regulation in the tying market.

Commentary
para 57: F&N: 4.525

58. If the tied product is an important complementary product for customers of the tying product, a reduction of alternative suppliers of the tied product and hence a reduced availability of that product can make entry to the tying market alone more difficult.

(c) Multi-product rebates

59. A multi-product rebate may be anti-competitive on the tied or the tying market if it is so large that equally efficient competitors offering only some of the components cannot compete against the discounted bundle.

60. In theory, it would be ideal if the effect of the rebate could be assessed by examining whether the incremental revenue covers the incremental costs for each product in the dominant undertaking's bundle. However, in practice assessing the incremental revenue is complex. Therefore, in its enforcement practice the Commission will in most situations use the incremental price as a good proxy. If the incremental price that customers pay for each of the dominant undertaking's products in the bundle remains above the LRAIC of the dominant undertaking from including that product in the bundle, the Commission will normally not intervene since an equally efficient competitor with only one product should in principle be able to compete profitably against the bundle. Enforcement action may, however, be warranted if the incremental price is below the LRAIC, because in such a case even an equally efficient competitor may be prevented from expanding or entering.[1]

Notes

[1] In principle, the LRAIC cost benchmark is relevant here as long as competitors are not able to also sell bundles (see paragraphs 23 to 27 and paragraph 61).

61. If the evidence suggests that competitors of the dominant undertaking are selling identical bundles, or could do so in a timely way without being deterred by possible additional costs, the Commission will generally regard this as a bundle competing against a bundle, in which case the relevant question is not whether the incremental revenue covers the incremental costs for each product in the bundle, but rather whether the price of the bundle as a whole is predatory.

(d) Efficiencies

62. Provided that the conditions set out in Section III D are fulfilled, the Commission will look into claims by dominant undertakings that their tying and bundling practices may lead to savings in production or distribution that would benefit customers. The Commission may also consider whether such practices reduce transaction costs for customers, who would otherwise be forced to buy the components separately, and enable substantial savings on packaging and distribution costs for suppliers. It may also examine whether combining two independent products into a new, single product might enhance the ability to bring such a product to the market to the benefit of consumers. The Commission may also consider whether tying and bundling practices allow the supplier to pass on efficiencies arising from its production or purchase of large quantities of the tied product.

Part C Substantive Antitrust Matters

C. Predation

63. In line with its enforcement priorities, the Commission will generally intervene where there is evidence showing that a dominant undertaking engages in predatory conduct by deliberately incurring losses or foregoing profits in the short term (referred to hereafter as 'sacrifice'), so as to foreclose or be likely to foreclose one or more of its actual or potential competitors with a view to strengthening or maintaining its market power, thereby causing consumer harm.[1]

Notes

[1] The Commission may also pursue predatory practices by dominant undertakings on secondary markets on which they are not yet dominant. In particular, the Commission will be more likely to find such an abuse in sectors where activities are protected by a legal monopoly. While the dominant undertaking does not need to engage in predatory conduct to protect its dominant position in the market protected by legal monopoly, it may use the profits gained in the monopoly market to cross-subsidize its activities in another market and thereby threaten to eliminate effective competition in that other market.

Commentary
para 63: B&C: 10.069, 10.121 F&N: 4.348

(a) Sacrifice

64. Conduct will be viewed by the Commission as entailing a sacrifice if, by charging a lower price for all or a particular part of its output over the relevant time period, or by expanding its output over the relevant time period, the dominant undertaking incurred or is incurring losses that could have been avoided. The Commission will take AAC as the appropriate starting point for assessing whether the dominant undertaking incurred or is incurring avoidable losses. If a dominant undertaking charges a price below AAC for all or part of its output, it is not recovering the costs that could have been avoided by not producing that output: it is incurring a loss that could have been avoided.[1] Pricing below AAC will thus in most cases be viewed by the Commission as a clear indication of sacrifice.[2]

Notes

[1] In most cases the average variable cost (AVC) and AAC will be the same, as often only variable costs can be avoided. However, in circumstances where AVC and AAC differ, the latter better reflects possible sacrifice: for example, if the dominant undertaking had to expand capacity in order to be able to predate, then the sunk costs of that extra capacity should be taken into account in looking at the dominant undertaking's losses. Those costs would be reflected in the AAC, but not the AVC.

[2] In Case 62/86, *AKZO Chemie v Commission*, [1991] ECR I-3359, paragraph 71, the Court held, in relation to pricing below average variable cost (AVC), that: '*A dominant undertaking has no interest in applying such prices except that of eliminating competitors so as to enable it subsequently to raise its price by taking advantage of its monopolistic position, since each sale generates a loss…*'.

Commentary
para 64: B&C: 10.072 F&N: 4.350, 4.352

65. However, the concept of sacrifice does not only include pricing below AAC.[1] In order to show a predatory strategy, the Commission may also investigate whether the allegedly predatory conduct led in the short term to net revenues lower than could have been expected from a reasonable alternative conduct, that is to say, whether the dominant undertaking incurred a loss that it could have avoided.[2] The Commission will not compare the actual conduct with hypothetical or theoretical alternatives that might have been more profitable. Only economically rational and practicable alternatives will be considered which, taking into account the market conditions and business realities facing the dominant undertaking, can realistically be expected to be more profitable.

Notes

[1] If the estimate of cost is based on the direct cost of production (as registered in the undertaking's accounts), it may not adequately capture whether or not there has been a sacrifice.

[2] However, undertakings should not be penalised for incurring *ex post* losses where the *ex ante* decision to engage in the conduct was taken in good faith, that is to say, if they can provide conclusive evidence that they could reasonably expect that the activity would be profitable.

Commentary
para 65: **B&C:** 10.072, 10.079 **F&N:** 4.350

66. In some cases it will be possible to rely upon direct evidence consisting of documents from the dominant undertaking which clearly show a predatory strategy,[1] such as a detailed plan to sacrifice in order to exclude a competitor, to prevent entry or to pre-empt the emergence of a market, or evidence of concrete threats of predatory action.[2]

Notes

[1] See Case T-83/91, *Tetra Pak International v Commission (Tetra Pak II)*, [1994] ECR II-755, paragraphs 151 and 171; and Case T-340/03, *France Télécom v Commission*, [2007] ECR II-107, paragraphs 198 to 215.

[2] In Case 62/86, *AKZO Chemie v Commission*, [1991] ECR I-3359, the Court accepted that there was clear evidence of AKZO threatening ECS in two meetings with below cost pricing if it did not withdraw from the organic peroxides market. In addition there was a detailed plan, with figures, describing the measures that AKZO would put into effect if ECS would not withdraw from the market (see paragraphs 76 to 82, 115, and 131 to 140).

Commentary
para 66: **B&C:** 10.077

(b) Anti-competitive foreclosure

67. If sufficient reliable data are available, the Commission will apply the equally efficient competitor analysis, described in paragraphs 25 to 27, to determine whether the conduct is capable of harming consumers. Normally only pricing below LRAIC is capable of foreclosing as efficient competitors from the market.

68. In addition to the factors already mentioned in paragraph 20, the Commission will generally investigate whether and how the suspected conduct reduces the likelihood that competitors will compete. For instance, if the dominant undertaking is better informed about cost or other market conditions, or can distort market signals about profitability, it may engage in predatory conduct so as to influence the expectations of potential entrants and thereby deter entry. If the conduct and its likely effects are felt on multiple markets and/or in successive periods of possible entry, the dominant undertaking may be shown to be seeking a reputation for predatory conduct. If the targeted competitor is dependent on external financing, substantial price decreases or other predatory conduct by the dominant undertaking could adversely affect the competitor's performance so that its access to further financing may be seriously undermined.

69. The Commission does not consider that it is necessary to show that competitors have exited the market in order to show that there has been anti-competitive foreclosure. The possibility cannot be excluded that the dominant undertaking may prefer to prevent the competitor from competing vigorously and have it follow the dominant undertaking's pricing, rather than eliminate it from the market altogether. Such disciplining avoids the risk inherent in eliminating competitors, in particular the risk that the assets of the competitor are sold at a low price and stay in the market, creating a new low cost entrant.

Commentary
para 69: **F&N:** 4.350

70. Generally speaking, consumers are likely to be harmed if the dominant undertaking can reasonably expect its market power after the predatory conduct comes to an end to be greater than it would have been had the undertaking not engaged in that conduct in the first place, that is to say, if the undertaking is likely to be in a position to benefit from the sacrifice.

Commentary
para 70: **B&C:** 10.078 **F&N:** 4.347

71. This does not mean that the Commission will only intervene if the dominant undertaking would be likely to be able to increase its prices above the level persisting in the market before the conduct. It is sufficient, for instance, that the conduct would be likely to prevent or delay a decline in prices that would otherwise have occurred. Identifying consumer harm is not a mechanical

calculation of profits and losses, and proof of overall profits is not required. Likely consumer harm may be demonstrated by assessing the likely foreclosure effect of the conduct, combined with consideration of other factors, such as entry barriers.[1] In this context, the Commission will also consider possibilities of re-entry.

Notes

[1] This was confirmed in Case T-83/91, *Tetra Pak International v Commission (Tetra Pak II)*, [1994] ECR II-755, upheld on appeal in Case C-333/94 P, *Tetra Pak International v Commission*, [1996] ECR I-5951, where the Court of First Instance stated that proof of actual recoupment was not required (paragraph 150 in fine). More in general, as predation may turn out to be more difficult than expected at the start of the conduct, the total costs to the dominant undertaking of predating could outweigh its later profits and thus make actual recoupment impossible while it may still be rational to decide to continue with the predatory strategy that it started some time ago. See also COMP/38.233 *Wanadoo Interactive*, Commission Decision of 16 July 2003, paragraphs 332 to 367.

Commentary
para 71: **B&C:** 10.078 **F&N:** 7.347

72. It may be easier for the dominant undertaking to engage in predatory conduct if it selectively targets specific customers with low prices, as this will limit the losses incurred by the dominant undertaking.

73. It is less likely that the dominant undertaking engages in predatory conduct if the conduct concerns a low price applied generally for a long period of time.

(c) Efficiencies

74. In general it is considered unlikely that predatory conduct will create efficiencies. However, provided that the conditions set out in Section III D are fulfilled, the Commission will consider claims by a dominant undertaking that the low pricing enables it to achieve economies of scale or efficiencies related to expanding the market.

Commentary
para 74: **B&C:** 10.063, 10.074, 10.079

D. Refusal to supply and margin squeeze

75. When setting its enforcement priorities, the Commission starts from the position that, generally speaking, any undertaking, whether dominant or not, should have the right to choose its trading partners and to dispose freely of its property. The Commission therefore considers that intervention on competition law grounds requires careful consideration where the application of Article [102] would lead to the imposition of an obligation to supply on the dominant undertaking.[1] The existence of such an obligation — even for a fair remuneration — may undermine undertakings' incentives to invest and innovate and, thereby, possibly harm consumers. The knowledge that they may have a duty to supply against their will may lead dominant undertakings — or undertakings who anticipate that they may become dominant — not to invest, or to invest less, in the activity in question. Also, competitors may be tempted to free ride on investments made by the dominant undertaking instead of investing themselves. Neither of these consequences would, in the long run, be in the interest of consumers.

Notes

[1] Joined Cases C-241/91 P and C-242/91, *Radio Telefis Eireann (RTE) and Independent Television Publications (ITP) v Commission (Magill)*, [1995] ECR I-743, paragraph 50; Case C-418/01, *IMS Health v NDC Health*, [2004] ECR I-5039, paragraph 35; Case T-201/04, *Microsoft v Commission*, [2007] ECR II-3601, paragraphs 319, 330, 331, 332 and 336.

Commentary
para 75: **B&C:** 9.050, 10.129, 10.135 **F&N:** 4.620, 4.621, 12.226

76. Typically competition problems arise when the dominant undertaking competes on the 'downstream' market with the buyer whom it refuses to supply. The term 'downstream market' is used to refer to the market for which the refused input is needed in order to manufacture a product or provide a service. This section deals only with this type of refusal.

77. Other types of possibly unlawful refusal to supply, in which the supply is made conditional upon the purchaser accepting limitations on its conduct, are not dealt with in this section. For instance, halting supplies in order to punish customers for dealing with competitors or refusing to supply customers that do not agree to tying arrangements, will be examined by the Commission in line with the principles set out in the sections on exclusive dealing and tying and bundling. Similarly, refusals to supply aimed at preventing the purchaser from engaging in parallel trade[1] or from lowering its resale price are also not dealt with in this section.

Notes

[1] See Judgment of 16 September 2008 in Joined Cases C-468/06 to C-478/06, *Sot. Lélos kai Sia and Others* v *GlaxoSmithKline*, not yet reported [now [2008] ECR II-7139].

Commentary
para 77: F&N: 4.564

78. The concept of refusal to supply covers a broad range of practices, such as a refusal to supply products to existing or new customers,[1] refusal to license intellectual property rights,[2] including when the licence is necessary to provide interface information,[3] or refusal to grant access to an essential facility or a network.[4]

Notes

[1] Joined Cases 6/73 and 7/73, *Istituto Chemioterapico Italiano and Commercial Solvents v Commission*, [1974] ECR 223.
[2] Joined Cases C-241/91 P and C-242/91 P, *Radio Telefis Eireann (RTE) and Independent Television Publications Ltd (ITP) v Commission (Magill)*, [1995] ECR 743; Case C-418/01, *IMS Health v NDC Health*, [2004] ECR I-5039. Those judgments show that in exceptional circumstances a refusal to license intellectual property rights is abusive.
[3] See Case T-201/04, *Microsoft v Commission*, [2007] ECR II-3601.
[4] See Commission Decision 94/19/EC of 21 December 1993 in Case IV/34.689, *Sea Containers v Stena Sealink — Interim Measures* (OJ L 15, 18.1.1994, p.8); and Commission Decision 92/213/EEC of 26 February 1992 in Case IV/33.544, *British Midland v Aer Lingus* — (OJ L 96, 10.4.1992, p.34).

79. The Commission does not regard it as necessary for the refused product to have been already traded: it is sufficient that there is demand from potential purchasers and that a potential market for the input at stake can be identified.[1] Likewise, it is not necessary for there to be actual refusal on the part of a dominant undertaking; 'constructive refusal' is sufficient. Constructive refusal could, for example, take the form of unduly delaying or otherwise degrading the supply of the product or involve the imposition of unreasonable conditions in return for the supply.

Notes

[1] Case C-418/01, *IMS Health v NDC Health*, [2004] ECR I-5039, paragraph 44.

Commentary
para 79: B&C: 10.129, 10.131 F&N: 4.593

80. Finally, instead of refusing to supply, a dominant undertaking may charge a price for the product on the upstream market which, compared to the price it charges on the downstream market,[1] does not allow even an equally efficient competitor to trade profitably in the downstream market on a lasting basis (a so-called 'margin squeeze'). In margin squeeze cases the benchmark which the Commission will generally rely on to determine the costs of an equally efficient competitor are the LRAIC of the downstream division of the integrated dominant undertaking.[2]

Notes

[1] Including a situation in which an integrated undertaking that sells a 'system' of complementary products refuses to sell one of the complementary products on an unbundled basis to a competitor that produces the other complementary product.
[2] In some cases, however, the LRAIC of a non-integrated competitor downstream might be used as the benchmark, for example when it is not possible to clearly allocate the dominant undertaking's costs to downstream and upstream operations.

Commentary
para 80: F&N: 4.274

81. The Commission will consider these practices as an enforcement priority if all the following circumstances are present:
    — the refusal relates to a product or service that is objectively necessary to be able to compete effectively on a downstream market,
    — the refusal is likely to lead to the elimination of effective competition on the downstream market, and
    — the refusal is likely to lead to consumer harm.

Commentary
para 81: B&C: 10.136 **F&N:** 4.624

82. In certain specific cases, it may be clear that imposing an obligation to supply is manifestly not capable of having negative effects on the input owner's and/or other operators' incentives to invest and innovate upstream, whether *ex ante* or *ex post*. The Commission considers that this is particularly likely to be the case where regulation compatible with Community law already imposes an obligation to supply on the dominant undertaking and it is clear, from the considerations underlying such regulation, that the necessary balancing of incentives has already been made by the public authority when imposing such an obligation to supply. This could also be the case where the upstream market position of the dominant undertaking has been developed under the protection of special or exclusive rights or has been financed by state resources. In such specific cases there is no reason for the Commission to deviate from its general enforcement standard of showing likely anti-competitive foreclosure, without considering whether the three circumstances referred to in paragraph 81 are present.

Commentary
para 82: F&N: 4.688, 13.136

(a) Objective necessity of the input

83. In examining whether a refusal to supply deserves its priority attention, the Commission will consider whether the supply of the refused input is objectively necessary for operators to be able to compete effectively on the market. This does not mean that, without the refused input, no competitor could ever enter or survive on the downstream market.[1] Rather, an input is indispensable where there is no actual or potential substitute on which competitors in the downstream market could rely so as to counter — at least in the long-term — the negative consequences of the refusal.[2] In this regard, the Commission will normally make an assessment of whether competitors could effectively duplicate the input produced by the dominant undertaking in the foreseeable future.[3] The notion of duplication means the creation of an alternative source of efficient supply that is capable of allowing competitors to exert a competitive constraint on the dominant undertaking in the downstream market.[4]

Notes

[1] Case T-201/04, *Microsoft v Commission*, [2007] ECR II-3601, paragraphs 428 and 560 to 563.

[2] Joined Cases C-241/91 P and C-242/91, *Radio Telefís Eireann (RTE) and Independent Television Publications LTD (ITP) v Commission (Magill)*, [1995] ECR 743, paragraphs 52 and 53; Case 7/97, *Oscar Bronner v Mediaprint Zeitungs-und Zeitschriftenverlag, Mediaprint Zeitungsvertriebsgesellschaft and Mediaprint Anzeigengesellschaft*, [1998] ECR I-7791, paragraphs 44 and 45; Case T-201/04, *Microsoft v Commission*, [2007] ECR II-3601, paragraph 421.

[3] In general, an input is likely to be impossible to replicate when it involves a natural monopoly due to scale or scope economies, where there are strong network effects or when it concerns so-called 'single source' information. However, in all cases account should be taken of the dynamic nature of the industry and, in particular whether or not market power can rapidly dissipate.

[4] Case 7/97, *Oscar Bronner v Mediaprint Zeitungs-und Zeitschriftenverlag, Mediaprint Zeitungsvertriebsgesellschaft and Mediaprint Anzeigengesellschaft*, [1998] ECR I-7791, paragraph 46; Case C-418/01, *IMS Health v NDC Health*, [2004] ECR I-5039, paragraph 29.

Commentary
para 83: B&C: 10.138

84. The criteria set out in paragraph 81 apply both to cases of disruption of previous supply, and to refusals to supply a good or service which the dominant company has not previously supplied to others (*de novo* refusals to supply). However, the termination of an existing supply arrangement is more likely to be found to be abusive than a *de novo* refusal to supply. For example, if the dominant undertaking had previously been supplying the requesting undertaking, and the latter had made relationship-specific investments in order to use the subsequently refused input, the Commission may be more likely to regard the input in question as indispensable. Similarly, the fact that the owner of the essential input in the past has found it in its interest to supply is an indication that supplying the input does not imply any risk that the owner receives inadequate compensation for the original investment. It would therefore be up to the dominant company to demonstrate why circumstances have actually changed in such a way that the continuation of its existing supply relationship would put in danger its adequate compensation.

Commentary
para 84: B&C: 10.136

(b) Elimination of effective competition

85. If the requirements set out in paragraphs 83 and 84 are fulfilled, the Commission considers that a dominant undertaking's refusal to supply is generally liable to eliminate, immediately or over time, effective competition in the downstream market. The likelihood of effective competition being eliminated is generally greater the higher the market share of the dominant undertaking in the downstream market. The less capacity-constrained the dominant undertaking is relative to competitors in the downstream market, the closer the substitutability between the dominant undertaking's output and that of its competitors in the downstream market, the greater the proportion of competitors in the downstream market that are affected, and the more likely it is that the demand that could be served by the foreclosed competitors would be diverted away from them to the advantage of the dominant undertaking.

(c) Consumer harm

86. In examining the likely impact of a refusal to supply on consumer welfare, the Commission will examine whether, for consumers, the likely negative consequences of the refusal to supply in the relevant market outweigh over time the negative consequences of imposing an obligation to supply. If they do, the Commission will normally pursue the case.

87. The Commission considers that consumer harm may, for instance, arise where the competitors that the dominant undertaking forecloses are, as a result of the refusal, prevented from bringing innovative goods or services to market and/or where follow-on innovation is likely to be stifled.[1] This may be particularly the case if the undertaking which requests supply does not intend to limit itself essentially to duplicating the goods or services already offered by the dominant undertaking on the downstream market, but intends to produce new or improved goods or services for which there is a potential consumer demand or is likely to contribute to technical development.[2]

88. The Commission also considers that a refusal to supply may lead to consumer harm where the price in the upstream input market is regulated, the price in the downstream market is not regulated and the dominant undertaking, by excluding competitors on the downstream market through a refusal to supply, is able to extract more profits in the unregulated downstream market than it would otherwise do.

Notes

[1] Case T-201/04, *Microsoft v Commission*, [2007] ECR II-3601, paragraphs 643, 647, 648, 649, 652, 653 and 656.

[2] Case C-418/01, *IMS Health v NDC Health*, [2004] ECR I-5039, paragraph 49; Case T-201/04, *Microsoft v Commission*, [2007] ECR II-3601, paragraph 658.

(d) Efficiencies

89. The Commission will consider claims by the dominant undertaking that a refusal to supply is necessary to allow the dominant undertaking to realise an adequate return on the investments required to develop its input business, thus generating incentives to continue to invest in the future, taking the risk of failed projects into account. The Commission will also consider claims

Part C Substantive Antitrust Matters

by the dominant undertaking that its own innovation will be negatively affected by the obligation to supply, or by the structural changes in the market conditions that imposing such an obligation will bring about, including the development of follow-on innovation by competitors.

90. However, when considering such claims, the Commission will ensure that the conditions set out in Section III D are fulfilled. In particular, it falls on the dominant undertaking to demonstrate any negative impact which an obligation to supply is likely to have on its own level of innovation.[1] If a dominant undertaking has previously supplied the input in question, this can be relevant for the assessment of any claim that the refusal to supply is justified on efficiency grounds.

Notes

[1] Case T-201/04, *Microsoft v Commission* [2007] ECR II-3601, paragraph 659.

C15

GUIDELINES ON VERTICAL RESTRAINTS

(2010/C 130/01)

(Text with EEA relevance)

Official Journal C 130, 19.5.2010, p.1

Celex No: 52010XC0519(04)

EUR-Lex permanent link: <http://eur-lex.europa.eu/LexUriServ/LexUriServ.do?uri=CELEX:5201 0XC0519(04):EN:NOT>

Notes

EEA application: the EFTA Surveillance Authority has adopted a parallel notice. See EFTA Surveillance Authority Notice—Guidelines on Vertical Restraints (2012/C 362/01), OJ C 362, 22.11.2012, p.1.

TABLE OF CONTENTS

Commentary

Guidelines: B&C: 1.074, 1.075, 2.164, 2.167, 2.168, 3.005, 3.011, 3.082, 7.003, 7.025, 7.036, 7.042, 7.083, 7.100, 7.118, 7.155, 7.168, 7.187, 7.188, 9.158 F&N: 2.12, 3.219, 3.374, 4.412, 5.132, 7.17, 7.241, 9.29, 9.30, 9.31, 9.33, 9.43, 9.54, 9.99, 9.148, 9.158, 9.170, 9.180, 9.193, 9.194, 9.197, 9.201, 9.205, 9.222, 9.225, 9.229, 9.230, 9.231, 9.237, 9.241, 9.251, 9.256, 9.258, 9.259, 9.261, 9.265, 9.272, 9.273, 9.284, 9.289, 9.291, 9.292, 10.78, 14.83
paras 12–21: F&N: 3.31, 9.44
paras 40–42: F&N: 9.84
paras 74–78: F&N: 9.167
paras 79–80: F&N: 9.169
paras 79–85: B&C: 3.092, 7.063, 7.139
paras 106–107: B&C: 7.011
paras 106–109: B&C: 3.039 F&N: 9.202
paras 110–121: B&C: 7.158
paras 111–112: F&N: 9.195
paras 111–116: B&C: 4.007
paras 111–121: B&C: 2.168
paras 132–150: B&C: 3.039
paras 136–138: B&C: 7.158
paras 151–153: F&N: 12.83
paras 153–157: B&C: 3.039
paras 170–173: B&C: 3.039

Part C Substantive Antitrust Matters

I. Introduction

1. Purpose of the Guidelines

(1) These Guidelines set out the principles for the assessment of vertical agreements under Article 101 of the Treaty on the Functioning of the European Union* (hereinafter "Article 101").[1] Article 1(1)(a) of Commission Regulation (EU) No 330/2010 of 20 April 2010 on the appli-cation of Article 101(3) of the Treaty on the Functioning of the European Union to categories of vertical agreements and concerted practices[2] (hereinafter referred to as the "Block Exemption Regula-tion") (see paragraphs (24) to (46)) defines the term "vertical agreement". These Guidelines are without prejudice to the possible parallel application of Article 102 of the Treaty on the Functioning of the European Union (hereinafter "Article 102") to vertical agreements. These Guidelines are structured in the following way:

— Section II (paragraphs (8) to (22)) describes vertical agreements which generally fall outside Article 101(1);
— Section III (paragraphs (23) to (73)) clarifies the conditions for the application of the Block Exemption Regulation;
— Section IV (paragraphs (74) to (85)) describes the principles concerning the withdrawal of the block exemption and the disapplication of the Block Exemption Regulation;
— Section V (paragraphs (86) to (95)) provides guidance on how to define the relevant market and calculate market shares;
— Section VI (paragraphs (96) to (229)) describes the general framework of analysis and the enforcement policy of the Commission in individual cases concerning vertical agreements.

Notes

* With effect from 1 December 2009, Articles 81 and 82 of the EC Treaty have become Articles 101 and, 102, respectively, of the Treaty on the Functioning of the European Union ("TFEU"). The two sets of provisions are, in substance, identical. For the purposes of these Guidelines, references to Articles 101 and 102 of the TFEU should be understood as references to Articles 81 and 82, respectively, of the EC Treaty where appropriate. The TFEU also introduced certain changes in terminology, such as the replacement of "Community" by "Union" and "common market" by "internal market". The terminology of the TFEU will be used throughout these Guidelines.

[1] These Guidelines replace the Commission Notice—Guidelines on Vertical Restraints, OJ C 291, 13.10.2000, p.1.
[2] OJ L 102, 23.4.2010, p.1.

Commentary
para 1: F&N: 4.477

(2) Throughout these Guidelines, the analysis applies to both goods and services, although certain vertical restraints are mainly used in the distribution of goods. Similarly, vertical agreements can be concluded for intermediate and final goods and services. Unless otherwise stated, the analysis and arguments in these Guidelines apply to all types of goods and services and to all levels of trade. Thus, the term "products" includes both goods and services. The terms "supplier" and "buyer" are used for all levels of trade. The Block Exemption Regulation and these Guidelines do not apply to agreements with final consumers where the latter are not undertakings, since Article 101 only applies to agreements between undertakings.

(3) By issuing these Guidelines, the Commission aims to help companies conduct their own assess-ment of vertical agreements under EU competition rules. The standards set forth in these Guidelines cannot be applied mechanically, but must be applied with due consideration for the specific circumstances of each case. Each case must be evaluated in the light of its own facts.

Commentary
para 3: B&C: 7.003

(4) These Guidelines are without prejudice to the case-law of the General Court and the Court of Justice of the European Union concerning the application of Article 101 to vertical agreements. The Commission will continue to monitor the operation of the Block Exemption Regulation and Guidelines based on market information from stakeholders and national competition authorities and may revise this notice in the light of future developments and of evolving insight.

2. Applicability of Article 101 to vertical agreements

(5) Article 101 applies to vertical agreements that may affect trade between Member States and that prevent, restrict or distort competition ("vertical restraints").[1] Article 101 provides a legal framework for the assessment of vertical restraints, which takes into consideration the distinction between anti-competitive and pro-competitive effects. Article 101(1) prohibits those agreements which appreciably restrict or distort competition, while Article 101(3) exempts those agreements which confer sufficient benefits to outweigh the anti-competitive effects.[2]

Notes

[1] See inter alia judgments of the Court of Justice in Joined Cases 56/64 and 58/64 *Grundig-Consten v Commission* [1966] ECR 299; Case 56/65 *Technique Minière v Maschinenbau Ulm* [1966] ECR 235; and judgment of the Court of First Instance in Case T-77/92 *Parker Pen v Commission* [1994] ECR II-549.

[2] See Communication from the Commission — Notice — Guidelines on the application of Article [101](3) of the Treaty, OJ C 101, 27.4.2004, p.97 for the Commission's general methodology and interpretation of the conditions for applying Article 101(1) and in particular Article 101(3).

Commentary
para 5: B&C: 9.34

(6) For most vertical restraints, competition concerns can only arise if there is insufficient competition at one or more levels of trade, that is, if there is some degree of market power at the level of the supplier or the buyer or at both levels. Vertical restraints are generally less harmful than horizontal restraints and may provide substantial scope for efficiencies.

Commentary
para 6: B&C: 9.61, 9.188, 9.192

(7) The objective of Article 101 is to ensure that undertakings do not use agreements — in this context, vertical agreements — to restrict competition on the market to the detriment of consumers. Assessing vertical restraints is also important in the context of the wider objective of achieving an integrated internal market. Market integration enhances competition in the European Union. Companies should not be allowed to re-establish private barriers between Member States where State barriers have been successfully abolished.

II. Vertical Agreements which Generally Fall Outside the Scope of Article 101(1)

1. Agreements of minor importance and SMEs

(8) Agreements that are not capable of appreciably affecting trade between Member States or of appreciably restricting competition by object or effect do not fall within the scope of Article 101(1). The Block Exemption Regulation applies only to agreements falling within the scope of application of Article 101(1). These Guidelines are without prejudice to the application of Commission Notice on agreements of minor importance which do not appreciably restrict competition under Article [101](1) of the [Treaty on the Functioning of the European Union] (*de minimis*)[1] or any future *de minimis* notice.

Notes
[1] OJ C 368, 22.12.2001, p.13.

(9) Subject to the conditions set out in the *de minimis* notice concerning hardcore restrictions and cumulative effect issues, vertical agreements entered into by non-competing undertakings whose

individual market share on the relevant market does not exceed 15% are generally considered to fall outside the scope of Article 101(1).[1] There is no presumption that vertical agreements concluded by undertakings having more than 15% market share automatically infringe Article 101(1). Agreements between undertakings whose market share exceeds the 15% threshold may still not have an appreciable effect on trade between Member States or may not constitute an appreciable restriction of competition.[2] Such agreements need to be assessed in their legal and economic context. The criteria for the assessment of individual agreements are set out in paragraphs (96) to (229).

Notes

[1] For agreements between competing undertakings the *de minimis* market share threshold is 10% for their collective market share on each affected relevant market.
[2] See judgment of the Court of First Instance in Case T-7/93 *Langnese-Iglo v Commission* [1995] ECR II-1533, paragraph 98.

Commentary
para 9: B&C: 2.128, 2.167, 7.020

(10) As regards hardcore restrictions referred to in the *de minimis* notice, Article 101(1) may apply below the 15% threshold, provided that there is an appreciable effect on trade between Member States and on competition. The applicable case-law of the Court of Justice and the General Court is relevant in this respect.[1] Reference is also made to the possible need to assess positive and negative effects of hardcore restrictions as described in particular in paragraph (47) of these Guidelines.

Notes

[1] See judgments of the Court of Justice in Case 5/69 *Völk v Vervaecke* [1969] ECR 295; Case 1/71 *Cadillon v Höss* [1971] ECR 351 and Case C-306/96 *Javico v Yves Saint Laurent* [1998] ECR I-1983, paragraphs 16 and 17.

Commentary
para 10: B&C: 12.133

(11) In addition, the Commission considers that, subject to cumulative effect and hardcore restrictions, vertical agreements between small and medium-sized undertakings as defined in the Annex to Commission Recommendation of 6 May 2003 concerning the definition of micro, small and medium-sized enterprises[1] are rarely capable of appreciably affecting trade between Member States or of appreciably restricting competition within the meaning of Article 101(1), and therefore generally fall outside the scope of Article 101(1). In cases where such agreements nonetheless meet the conditions for the application of Article 101(1), the Commission will normally refrain from opening proceedings for lack of sufficient interest for the European Union unless those undertakings collectively or individually hold a dominant position in a substantial part of the internal market.

Notes

[1] OJ L 124, 20.5.2003, p.36.

Commentary
para 11: B&C: 7.020

2. Agency agreements

2.1. Definition of agency agreements

(12) An agent is a legal or physical person vested with the power to negotiate and/or conclude contracts on behalf of another person (the principal), either in the agent's own name or in the name of the principal, for the:
— purchase of goods or services by the principal, or
— sale of goods or services supplied by the principal.

Commentary
para 12: B&C: 12.133

(13) The determining factor in defining an agency agreement for the application of Article 101(1) is the financial or commercial risk borne by the agent in relation to the activities for which it has been appointed as an agent by the principal.[1] In this respect it is not material for the assessment whether the agent acts for one or several principals. Neither is material for this assessment the qualification given to their agreement by the parties or national legislation.

Notes

[1] See judgment of the Court of First Instance in Case T-325/01 *Daimler Chrysler v Commission* [2005] ECR II-3319; judgments of the Court of Justice in Case C-217/05 *Confederación Espanola de Empresarios de Estaciones de Servicio v CEPSA* [2006] ECR I-11987; and Case C-279/06 *CEPSA Estaciones de Servicio SA v LV Tobar e Hijos SL* [2008] ECR I-6681.

Commentary
para 13: F&N: 9.46

(14) There are three types of financial or commercial risk that are material to the definition of an agency agreement for the application of Article 101(1). First, there are the contract-specific risks which are directly related to the contracts concluded and/or negotiated by the agent on behalf of the principal, such as financing of stocks. Secondly, there are the risks related to market-specific investments. These are investments specifically required for the type of activity for which the agent has been appointed by the principal, that is, which are required to enable the agent to conclude and/or negotiate this type of contract. Such investments are usually sunk, which means that upon leaving that particular field of activity the investment cannot be used for other activities or sold other than at a significant loss. Thirdly, there are the risks related to other activities undertaken on the same product market, to the extent that the principal requires the agent to undertake such activities, but not as an agent on behalf of the principal but for its own risk.

Commentary
para 14: B&C: 7.187 F&N: 9.47

(15) For the purposes of applying Article 101(1), the agreement will be qualified as an agency agreement if the agent does not bear any, or bears only insignificant, risks in relation to the contracts concluded and/or negotiated on behalf of the principal, in relation to market-specific investments for that field of activity, and in relation to other activities required by the principal to be undertaken on the same product market. However, risks that are related to the activity of providing agency services in general, such as the risk of the agent's income being dependent upon its success as an agent or general investments in for instance premises or personnel, are not material to this assessment.

Commentary
para 15: B&C: 7.187 F&N: 9.48

(16) For the purpose of applying Article 101(1), an agreement will thus generally be considered an agency agreement where property in the contract goods bought or sold does not vest in the agent, or the agent does not himself supply the contract services and where the agent:

(a) does not contribute to the costs relating to the supply/purchase of the contract goods or services, including the costs of transporting the goods. This does not preclude the agent from carrying out the transport service, provided that the costs are covered by the principal;

(b) does not maintain at its own cost or risk stocks of the contract goods, including the costs of financing the stocks and the costs of loss of stocks and can return unsold goods to the principal without charge, unless the agent is liable for fault (for example, by failing to comply with reasonable security measures to avoid loss of stocks);

(c) does not undertake responsibility towards third parties for damage caused by the product sold (product liability), unless, as agent, it is liable for fault in this respect;

(d) does not take responsibility for customers' non-performance of the contract, with the exception of the loss of the agent's commission, unless the agent is liable for fault (for example, by failing to comply with reasonable security or anti-theft measures or failing to comply with reasonable measures to report theft to the principal or police or to communicate to the principal all necessary information available to him on the customer's financial reliability);

(e) is not, directly or indirectly, obliged to invest in sales promotion, such as contributions to the advertising budgets of the principal;

(f) does not make market-specific investments in equipment, premises or training of personnel, such as for example the petrol storage tank in the case of petrol retailing or specific software to sell insurance policies in case of insurance agents, unless these costs are fully reimbursed by the principal;

(g) does not undertake other activities within the same product market required by the principal, unless these activities are fully reimbursed by the principal.

Commentary
para 16: B&C: 7.187 F&N: 9.50

(17) This list is not exhaustive. However, where the agent incurs one or more of the risks or costs mentioned in paragraphs (14), (15) and (16), the agreement between agent and principal will not be qualified as an agency agreement. The question of risk must be assessed on a case-by-case basis, and with regard to the economic reality of the situation rather than the legal form. For practical reasons, the risk analysis may start with the assessment of the contract-specific risks. If contract-specific risks are incurred by the agent, it will be enough to conclude that the agent is an independent distributor. On the contrary, if the agent does not incur contract-specific risks, then it will be necessary to continue further the analysis by assessing the risks related to market-specific investments. Finally, if the agent does not incur any contract-specific risks and risks related to market-specific investments, the risks related to other required activities within the same product market may have to be considered.

Commentary
para 17: B&C: 7.186 F&N: 9.49

2.2. The application of Article 101(1) to agency agreements

(18) In the case of agency agreements as defined in section 2.1, the selling or purchasing function of the agent forms part of the principal's activities. Since the principal bears the commercial and financial risks related to the selling and purchasing of the contract goods and services all obligations imposed on the agent in relation to the contracts concluded and/or negotiated on behalf of the principal fall outside Article 101(1). The following obligations on the agent's part will be considered to form an inherent part of an agency agreement, as each of them relates to the ability of the principal to fix the scope of activity of the agent in relation to the contract goods or services, which is essential if the principal is to take the risks and therefore to be in a position to determine the commercial strategy:

(a) limitations on the territory in which the agent may sell these goods or services;

(b) limitations on the customers to whom the agent may sell these goods or services;

(c) the prices and conditions at which the agent must sell or purchase these goods or services.

Commentary
para 18: B&C: 7.188

(19) In addition to governing the conditions of sale or purchase of the contract goods or services by the agent on behalf of the principal, agency agreements often contain provisions which concern the relationship between the agent and the principal. In particular, they may contain a provision preventing the principal from appointing other agents in respect of a given type of transaction, customer or territory (exclusive agency provisions) and/or a provision preventing the agent from acting as an agent or distributor of undertakings which compete with the principal (single branding provisions). Since the agent is a separate undertaking from the principal, the

provisions which concern the relationship between the agent and the principal may infringe Article 101(1). Exclusive agency provisions will in general not lead to anti-competitive effects. However, single branding provisions and post-term non-compete provisions, which concern inter-brand competition, may infringe Article 101(1) if they lead to or contribute to a (cumulative) foreclosure effect on the relevant market where the contract goods or services are sold or purchased (see in particular Section VI.2.1). Such provisions may benefit from the Block Exemption Regulation, in particular when the conditions provided in Article 5 of that Regulation are fulfilled. They can also be individually justified by efficiencies under Article 101(3) as for instance described in paragraphs (144) to (148).

Commentary
para 19: B&C: 7.183 F&N: 11.218

(20) An agency agreement may also fall within the scope of Article 101(1), even if the principal bears all the relevant financial and commercial risks, where it facilitates collusion. That could, for instance, be the case when a number of principals use the same agents while collectively excluding others from using these agents, or when they use the agents to collude on marketing strategy or to exchange sensitive market information between the principals.

Commentary
para 20: B&C: 7.191 F&N: 9.56

(21) Where the agent bears one or more of the relevant risks as described in paragraph (16), the agreement between agent and principal does not constitute an agency agreement for the purpose of applying Article 101(1). In that situation, the agent will be treated as an independent undertaking and the agreement between agent and principal will be subject to Article 101(1) as any other vertical agreement.

3. Subcontracting agreements

(22) Subcontracting concerns a contractor providing technology or equipment to a subcontractor that undertakes to produce certain products on the basis thereof (exclusively) for the contractor. Subcontracting is covered by Commission notice of 18 December 1978 concerning the assessment of certain subcontracting agreements in relation to Article [101](1) of the [Treaty on the Functioning of the European Union][1] (hereinafter "subcontracting notice"). According to that notice, which remains applicable, subcontracting agreements whereby the subcontractor undertakes to produce certain products exclusively for the contractor generally fall outside the scope of Article 101(1) provided that the technology or equipment is necessary to enable the subcontractor to produce the products. However, other restrictions imposed on the subcontractor such as the obligation not to conduct or exploit its own research and development or not to produce for third parties in general may fall within the scope of Article 101.[2]

Notes
[1] OJ C 1, 3.1.1979, p.2.
[2] See paragraph 3 of the subcontracting notice.

Commentary
para 22: B&C: 7.003 F&N: 3.31, 9.82

III. Application of the Block Exemption Regulation

1. Safe harbour created by the Block Exemption Regulation

(23) For most vertical restraints, competition concerns can only arise if there is insufficient competition at one or more levels of trade, that is, if there is some degree of market power at the level of the supplier or the buyer or at both levels. Provided that they do not contain hardcore restrictions of competition, which are restrictions of competition by object, the Block Exemption Regulation creates a presumption of legality for vertical agreements depending on the market share of the

supplier and the buyer. Pursuant to Article 3 of the Block Exemption Regulation, it is the supplier's market share on the market where it sells the contract goods or services and the buyer's market share on the market where it purchases the contract goods or services which determine the applicability of the block exemption. In order for the block exemption to apply, the supplier's and the buyer's market share must each be 30% or less. Section V of these Guidelines provides guidance on how to define the relevant market and calculate the market shares. Above the market share threshold of 30%, there is no presumption that vertical agreements fall within the scope of Article 101(1) or fail to satisfy the conditions of Article 101(3) but there is also no presumption that vertical agreements falling within the scope of Article 101(1) will usually satisfy the conditions of Article 101(3).

Commentary
para 23: **B&C:** 2.128, 3.072, 7.031 **F&N:** 9.90

2. Scope of the Block Exemption Regulation

2.1. Definition of vertical agreements

(24) Article 1(1)(a) of the Block Exemption Regulation defines a "vertical agreement" as "an agreement or concerted practice entered into between two or more undertakings each of which operates, for the purposes of the agreement or the concerted practice, at a different level of the production or distribution chain, and relating to the conditions under which the parties may purchase, sell or resell certain goods or services".

(25) The definition of "vertical agreement" referred to in paragraph (24) has four main elements:

(a) The Block Exemption Regulation applies to agreements and concerted practices. The Block Exemption Regulation does not apply to unilateral conduct of the undertakings concerned. Such unilateral conduct can fall within the scope of Article 102 which prohibits abuses of a dominant position. For there to be an agreement within the meaning of Article 101 it is sufficient that the parties have expressed their joint intention to conduct themselves on the market in a specific way. The form in which that intention is expressed is irrelevant as long as it constitutes a faithful expression of the parties' intention. In case there is no explicit agreement expressing the concurrence of wills, the Commission will have to prove that the unilateral policy of one party receives the acquiescence of the other party. For vertical agreements, there are two ways in which acquiescence with a particular unilateral policy can be established. First, the acquiescence can be deduced from the powers conferred upon the parties in a general agreement drawn up in advance. If the clauses of the agreement drawn up in advance provide for or authorise a party to adopt subsequently a specific unilateral policy which will be binding on the other party, the acquiescence of that policy by the other party can be established on the basis thereof.[1] Secondly, in the absence of such an explicit acquiescence, the Commission can show the existence of tacit acquiescence. For that it is necessary to show first that one party requires explicitly or implicitly the cooperation of the other party for the implementation of its unilateral policy and second that the other party complied with that requirement by implementing that unilateral policy in practice.[2] For instance, if after a supplier's announcement of a unilateral reduction of supplies in order to prevent parallel trade, distributors reduce immediately their orders and stop engaging in parallel trade, then those distributors tacitly acquiesce to the supplier's unilateral policy. This can however not be concluded if the distributors continue to engage in parallel trade or try to find new ways to engage in parallel trade. Similarly, for vertical agreements, tacit acquiescence may be deduced from the level of coercion exerted by a party to impose its unilateral policy on the other party or parties to the agreement in combination with the number of distributors that are actually implementing in practice the unilateral policy of the supplier. For instance, a system of monitoring and penalties, set up by a supplier to penalise those distributors that do not comply with its unilateral policy, points to tacit acquiescence with the supplier's unilateral policy if this system allows the supplier to implement in practice its policy. The two ways of establishing acquiescence described in this paragraph can be used jointly;

(b) The agreement or concerted practice is between two or more undertakings. Vertical agreements with final consumers not operating as an undertaking are not covered by the Block Exemption Regulation. More generally, agreements with final consumers do not fall under Article 101(1), as that article applies only to agreements between undertakings, decisions by associations of undertakings and concerted practices of undertakings. This is without prejudice to the possible application of Article 102;

(c) The agreement or concerted practice is between undertakings each operating, for the purposes of the agreement, at a different level of the production or distribution chain. This means for instance that one undertaking produces a raw material which the other undertaking uses as an input, or that the first is a manufacturer, the second a wholesaler and the third a retailer. This does not preclude an undertaking from being active at more than one level of the production or distribution chain;

(d) The agreements or concerted practices relate to the conditions under which the parties to the agreement, the supplier and the buyer, "may purchase, sell or resell certain goods or services". This reflects the purpose of the Block Exemption Regulation to cover purchase and distribution agreements. These are agreements which concern the conditions for the purchase, sale or resale of the goods or services supplied by the supplier and/or which concern the conditions for the sale by the buyer of the goods or services which incorporate these goods or services. Both the goods or services supplied by the supplier and the resulting goods or services are considered to be contract goods or services under the Block Exemption Regulation. Vertical agreements relating to all final and intermediate goods and services are covered. The only exception is the automobile sector, as long as this sector remains covered by a specific block exemption such as that granted by Commission Regulation (EC) No 1400/2002 of 31 July 2002 on the application of Article [101](3) of the Treaty to categories of vertical agreements and concerted practices in the motor vehicle sector[3] or its successor. The goods or services provided by the supplier may be resold by the buyer or may be used as an input by the buyer to produce its own goods or services.

Notes

[1] Judgment of the Court of Justice in Case C-74/04P *Commission v Volkswagen AG* [2006] ECR I-6585.

[2] Judgment of the Court of First Instance in Case T-41/96 *Bayer AG v Commission* [2000] ECR II-3383.

[3] OJ L 203, 1.8.2002, p.30.

Commentary

para 25(a): B&C: 2.040, 7.006 F&N: 9.96, 9.113

(26) The Block Exemption Regulation also applies to goods sold and purchased for renting to third parties. However, rent and lease agreements as such are not covered, as no good or service is sold by the supplier to the buyer. More generally, the Block Exemption Regulation does not cover restrictions or obligations that do not relate to the conditions of purchase, sale and resale, such as an obligation preventing parties from carrying out independent research and development which the parties may have included in an otherwise vertical agreement. In addition, Article 2(2) to (5) of the Block Exemption Regulation directly or indirectly excludes certain vertical agreements from the application of that Regulation.

Commentary

para 26: B&C: 7.027

2.2. Vertical agreements between competitors

(27) Article 2(4) of the Block Exemption Regulation explicitly excludes "vertical agreements entered into between competing undertakings" from its application. Vertical agreements between competitors are dealt with, as regards possible collusion effects, in the Commission Guidelines on the applicability of Article [101] of the [Treaty on the Functioning of the European Union] to horizontal cooperation agreements.[1] However, the vertical aspects of such agreements need to be assessed under these Guidelines. Article 1(1)(c) of the Block Exemption Regulation defines a competing undertaking as "an actual or potential competitor". Two companies are treated as

actual competitors if they are active on the same relevant market. A company is treated as a potential competitor of another company if, absent the agreement, in case of a small but permanent increase in relative prices it is likely that this first company, within a short period of time normally not longer than one year, would undertake the necessary additional investments or other necessary switching costs to enter the relevant market on which the other company is active. That assessment must be based on realistic grounds; the mere theoretical possibility of entering a market is not sufficient.[2] A distributor that provides specifications to a manufacturer to produce particular goods under the distributor's brand name is not to be considered a manufacturer of such own-brand goods.

Notes

[1] OJ C 3, 6.1.2001, p.2. A revision of those Guidelines is forthcoming.

[2] See Commission Notice on the definition of the relevant market for the purposes of Community competition law, OJ C 372, 9.12.1997, p.5, paragraphs 20 to 24, the Commission's Thirteenth Report on Competition Policy, point 55, and Commission Decision 90/410/EEC in Case No IV/32.009 — Elopak/Metal Box-Odin, OJ L 209, 8.8.1990, p.15.

Commentary
para 27: **B&C**: 5.079, 7.028 **F&N**: 9.72, 9.73

(28) Article 2(4) of the Block Exemption Regulation contains two exceptions to the general exclusion of vertical agreements between competitors. These exceptions concern non-reciprocal agreements. Non-reciprocal agreements between competitors are covered by the Block Exemption Regulation where (a) the supplier is a manufacturer and distributor of goods, while the buyer is only a distributor and not also a competing undertaking at the manufacturing level, or (b) the supplier is a provider of services operating at several levels of trade, while the buyer operates at the retail level and is not a competing undertaking at the level of trade where it purchases the contract services. The first exception covers situations of dual distribution, that is, the manufacturer of particular goods also acts as a distributor of the goods in competition with independent distributors of its goods. In case of dual distribution it is considered that in general any potential impact on the competitive relationship between the manufacturer and retailer at the retail level is of lesser importance than the potential impact of the vertical supply agreement on competition in general at the manufacturing or retail level. The second exception covers similar situations of dual distribution, but in this case for services, when the supplier is also a provider of products at the retail level where the buyer operates.

Commentary
para 28: **B&C**: 5.079, 7.028, 7.196 **F&N**: 9.75

2.3. Associations of retailers

(29) Article 2(2) of the Block Exemption Regulation includes in its application vertical agreements entered into by an association of undertakings which fulfils certain conditions and thereby excludes from the Block Exemption Regulation vertical agreements entered into by all other associations. Vertical agreements entered into between an association and its members, or between an association and its suppliers, are covered by the Block Exemption Regulation only if all the members are retailers of goods (not services) and if each individual member of the association has a turnover not exceeding EUR 50 million. Retailers are distributors reselling goods to final consumers. Where only a limited number of the members of the association have a turnover exceeding the EUR 50 million threshold and where these members together represent less than 15% of the collective turnover of all the members combined, the assessment under Article 101 will normally not be affected.

Commentary
para 29: **B&C**: 9.80

(30) An association of undertakings may involve both horizontal and vertical agreements. The horizontal agreements must be assessed according to the principles set out in the Guidelines on the applicability of Article [101] of the [Treaty on the Functioning of the European Union] to

horizontal cooperation agreements.[1] If that assessment leads to the conclusion that a cooperation between undertakings in the area of purchasing or selling is acceptable, a further assessment will be necessary to examine the vertical agreements concluded by the association with its suppliers or its individual members. The latter assessment will follow the rules of the Block Exemption Regulation and these Guidelines. For instance, horizontal agreements concluded between the members of the association or decisions adopted by the association, such as the decision to require the members to purchase from the association or the decision to allocate exclusive territories to the members must first be assessed as a horizontal agreement. Once that assessment leads to the conclusion that the horizontal agreement is not anticompetitive, an assessment of the vertical agreements between the association and individual members or between the association and suppliers is necessary.

Notes

[1] See paragraph (27).

2.4. Vertical agreements containing provisions on intellectual property rights (IPRs)

(31) Article 2(3) of the Block Exemption Regulation includes vertical agreements containing certain provisions relating to the assignment of IPRs to or use of IPRs by the buyer in its application and thereby excludes all other vertical agreements containing IPR provisions from the Block Exemption Regulation. The Block Exemption Regulation applies to vertical agreements containing IPR provisions where five conditions are fulfilled:

(a) The IPR provisions must be part of a vertical agreement, that is, an agreement with conditions under which the parties may purchase, sell or resell certain goods or services;

(b) The IPRs must be assigned to, or licensed for use by, the buyer;

(c) The IPR provisions must not constitute the primary object of the agreement;

(d) The IPR provisions must be directly related to the use, sale or resale of goods or services by the buyer or its customers. In the case of franchising where marketing forms the object of the exploitation of the IPRs, the goods or services are distributed by the master franchisee or the franchisees;

(e) The IPR provisions, in relation to the contract goods or services, must not contain restrictions of competition having the same object as vertical restraints which are not exempted under the Block Exemption Regulation.

Commentary

para 31: **B&C:** 7.197 **F&N:** 9.81

(32) Such conditions ensure that the Block Exemption Regulation applies to vertical agreements where the use, sale or resale of goods or services can be performed more effectively because IPRs are assigned to or licensed for use by the buyer. In other words, restrictions concerning the assignment or use of IPRs can be covered when the main object of the agreement is the purchase or distribution of goods or services.

Commentary

para 32: **F&N:** 9.82

(33) The first condition makes clear that the context in which the IPRs are provided is an agreement to purchase or distribute goods or an agreement to purchase or provide services and not an agreement concerning the assignment or licensing of IPRs for the manufacture of goods, nor a pure licensing agreement. The Block Exemption Regulation does not cover for instance:

(a) agreements where a party provides another party with a recipe and licenses the other party to produce a drink with this recipe;

(b) agreements under which one party provides another party with a mould or master copy and licenses the other party to produce and distribute copies;

(c) the pure licence of a trade mark or sign for the purposes of merchandising;

(d) sponsorship contracts concerning the right to advertise oneself as being an official sponsor of an event;

(e) copyright licensing such as broadcasting contracts concerning the right to record and/or broadcast an event.

Commentary
para 33: B&C: 7.030

(34) The second condition makes clear that the Block Exemption Regulation does not apply when the IPRs are provided by the buyer to the supplier, no matter whether the IPRs concern the manner of manufacture or of distribution. An agreement relating to the transfer of IPRs to the supplier and containing possible restrictions on the sales made by the supplier is not covered by the Block Exemption Regulation. That means, in particular, that subcontracting involving the transfer of know-how to a subcontractor[1] does not fall within the scope of application of the Block Exemption Regulation (see also paragraph (22)). However, vertical agreements under which the buyer provides only specifications to the supplier which describe the goods or services to be supplied fall within the scope of application of the Block Exemption Regulation.

Notes

[1] See the subcontracting notice (referred to in paragraph (22)).

Commentary
para 34: B&C: 7.030, 7.197

(35) The third condition makes clear that in order to be covered by the Block Exemption Regulation, the primary object of the agreement must not be the assignment or licensing of IPRs. The primary object must be the purchase, sale or resale of goods or services and the IPR provisions must serve the implementation of the vertical agreement.

Commentary
para 35: B&C: 7.030

(36) The fourth condition requires that the IPR provisions facilitate the use, sale or resale of goods or services by the buyer or its customers. The goods or services for use or resale are usually supplied by the licensor but may also be purchased by the licensee from a third supplier. The IPR provisions will normally concern the marketing of goods or services. An example would be a franchise agreement where the franchisor sells goods for resale to the franchisee and licenses the franchisee to use its trade mark and know-how to market the goods or where the supplier of a concentrated extract licenses the buyer to dilute and bottle the extract before selling it as a drink.

Commentary
para 36: B&C: 7.030

(37) The fifth condition highlights the fact that the IPR provisions should not have the same object as any of the hardcore restrictions listed in Article 4 of the Block Exemption Regulation or any of the restrictions excluded from the coverage of the Block Exemption Regulation by Article 5 of that Regulation (see paragraphs (47) to (69) of these Guidelines).

Commentary
para 37: B&C: 7.030

(38) Intellectual property rights relevant to the implementation of vertical agreements within the meaning of Article 2(3) of the Block Exemption Regulation generally concern three main areas: trade marks, copyright and know-how.

Trade mark

(39) A trade mark licence to a distributor may be related to the distribution of the licensor's products in a particular territory. If it is an exclusive licence, the agreement amounts to exclusive distribution.

Commentary
para 39: B&C: 7.065 F&N: 9.83

Copyright

(40) Resellers of goods covered by copyright (books, software, etc.) may be obliged by the copyright holder only to resell under the condition that the buyer, whether another reseller or the end user, shall not infringe the copyright. Such obligations on the reseller, to the extent that they fall under Article 101(1) at all, are covered by the Block Exemption Regulation.

(41) Agreements, under which hard copies of software are supplied for resale and where the reseller does not acquire a licence to any rights over the software but only has the right to resell the hard copies, are to be regarded as agreements for the supply of goods for resale for the purpose of the Block Exemption Regulation. Under that form of distribution, licensing the software only occurs between the copyright owner and the user of the software. It may take the form of a "shrink wrap" licence, that is, a set of conditions included in the package of the hard copy which the end user is deemed to accept by opening the package.

(42) Buyers of hardware incorporating software protected by copyright may be obliged by the copyright holder not to infringe the copyright, and must therefore not make copies and resell the software or make copies and use the software in combination with other hardware. Such use-restrictions, to the extent that they fall within Article 101(1) at all, are covered by the Block Exemption Regulation.

Know-how

(43) Franchise agreements, with the exception of industrial franchise agreements, are the most obvious example of where know-how for marketing purposes is communicated to the buyer.[1] Franchise agreements contain licences of intellectual property rights relating to trade marks or signs and know-how for the use and distribution of goods or the provision of services. In addition to the licence of IPR, the franchisor usually provides the franchisee during the life of the agreement with commercial or technical assistance, such as procurement services, training, advice on real estate, financial planning etc. The licence and the assistance are integral components of the business method being franchised.

Notes

[1] Paragraphs 43–45 apply by analogy to other types of distribution agreements which involve the transfer of substantial know-how from supplier to buyer.

Commentary
para 43: F&N: 9.86

---

(44) Licensing contained in franchise agreements is covered by the Block Exemption Regulation where all five conditions listed in paragraph (31) are fulfilled. Those conditions are usually fulfilled as under most franchise agreements, including master franchise agreements, the franchisor provides goods and/or services, in particular commercial or technical assistance services, to the franchisee. The IPRs help the franchisee to resell the products supplied by the franchisor or by a supplier designated by the franchisor or to use those products and sell the resulting goods or services. Where the franchise agreement only or primarily concerns licensing of IPRs, it is not covered by the Block Exemption Regulation, but the Commission will, as a general rule, apply the principles set out in the Block Exemption Regulation and these Guidelines to such an agreement.

Commentary
para 44: B&C: 7.176, 7.181 F&N: 9.86

---

(45) The following IPR-related obligations are generally considered necessary to protect the franchisor's intellectual property rights and are, where these obligations fall under Article 101(1), also covered by the Block Exemption Regulation:

  (a) an obligation on the franchisee not to engage, directly or indirectly, in any similar business;

  (b) an obligation on the franchisee not to acquire financial interests in the capital of a competing undertaking such as would give the franchisee the power to influence the economic conduct of such undertaking;

(c) an obligation on the franchisee not to disclose to third parties the know-how provided by the franchisor as long as this know-how is not in the public domain;

(d) an obligation on the franchisee to communicate to the franchisor any experience gained in exploiting the franchise and to grant the franchisor, and other franchisees, a non-exclusive licence for the know-how resulting from that experience;

(e) an obligation on the franchisee to inform the franchisor of infringements of licensed intellectual property rights, to take legal action against infringers or to assist the franchisor in any legal actions against infringers;

(f) an obligation on the franchisee not to use know-how licensed by the franchisor for purposes other than the exploitation of the franchise;

(g) an obligation on the franchisee not to assign the rights and obligations under the franchise agreement without the franchisor's consent.

Commentary
para 45: B&C: 7.180, 9.137

2.5. Relationship to other block exemption regulations

(46) Article 2(5) states that the Block Exemption Regulation does "not apply to vertical agreements the subject matter of which falls within the scope of any other block exemption regulation, unless otherwise provided for in such a regulation". The Block Exemption Regulation does not therefore apply to vertical agreements covered by Commission Regulation (EC) No 772/2004 of 27 April 2004 on the application of Article [101](3) of the Treaty to categories of technology transfer agreements,[1] Regulation 1400/2002 on the application of Article [101](3) of the Treaty to categories of vertical agreements and concerted practices in the motor vehicle sector[2] or Commission Regulation (EC) No 2658/2000 of 29 November 2000 on the application of Article [101](3) of the Treaty to categories of specialisation agreements[3] and Commission Regulation (EC) No 2659/2000 of 29 November 2000 on the application of Article [101](3) of the Treaty to categories of research and development agreements[4] exempting vertical agreements concluded in connection with horizontal agreements, or any future regulations of that kind, unless otherwise provided for in such a regulation.

Notes
[1] OJ L 123, 27.4.2004, p.11.
[2] See paragraph (25).
[3] OJ L 304, 5.12.2000, p.3.
[4] OJ L 304, 5.12.2000, p.7.

3. Hardcore restrictions under the Block Exemption Regulation

(47) Article 4 of the Block Exemption Regulation contains a list of hardcore restrictions which lead to the exclusion of the whole vertical agreement from the scope of application of the Block Exemption Regulation.[1] Where such a hardcore restriction is included in an agreement, that agreement is presumed to fall within Article 101(1). It is also presumed that the agreement is unlikely to fulfil the conditions of Article 101(3), for which reason the block exemption does not apply. However, undertakings may demonstrate pro-competitive effects under Article 101(3) in an individual case.[2] Where the undertakings substantiate that likely efficiencies result from including the hardcore restriction in the agreement and demonstrate that in general all the conditions of Article 101(3) are fulfilled, the Commission will be required to effectively assess the likely negative impact on competition before making an ultimate assessment of whether the conditions of Article 101(3) are fulfilled.[3]

Notes
[1] This list of hardcore restrictions applies to vertical agreements concerning trade within the Union. In so far as vertical agreements concern exports outside the Union or imports/re-imports from outside the Union see judgment of the Court of Justice in Case C-306/96 *Javico v Yves Saint Laurent* [1998] ECR I-1983. In that judgment the ECJ held in paragraph 20 that "an agreement in which the reseller gives to the producer an undertaking that it will sell the contractual products

on a market outside the Community cannot be regarded as having the object of appreciably restricting competition within the common market or as being capable of affecting, as such, trade between Member States".

2 See in particular paragraphs 106 to 109 describing in general possible efficiencies related to vertical restraints and Section VI.2.10 on resale price restrictions. See for general guidance on this the Communication from the Commission — Notice — Guidelines on the application of Article [101](3) of the Treaty, OJ C 101, 27.4.2004, p.97.

3 Although, in legal terms, these are two distinct steps, they may in practice be an iterative process where the parties and Commission in several steps enhance and improve their respective arguments.

Commentary

para 47: **B&C:** 2.120, 3.011, 7.036, 7.073 **F&N:** 9.90, 9.92, 12.57

(48) The hardcore restriction set out in Article 4(a) of the Block Exemption Regulation concerns resale price maintenance (RPM), that is, agreements or concerted practices having as their direct or indirect object the establishment of a fixed or minimum resale price or a fixed or minimum price level to be observed by the buyer. In the case of contractual provisions or concerted practices that directly establish the resale price, the restriction is clear cut. However, RPM can also be achieved through indirect means. Examples of the latter are an agreement fixing the distribution margin, fixing the maximum level of discount the distributor can grant from a prescribed price level, making the grant of rebates or reimbursement of promotional costs by the supplier subject to the observance of a given price level, linking the prescribed resale price to the resale prices of competitors, threats, intimidation, warnings, penalties, delay or suspension of deliveries or contract terminations in relation to observance of a given price level. Direct or indirect means of achieving price fixing can be made more effective when combined with measures to identify price-cutting distributors, such as the implementation of a price monitoring system, or the obligation on retailers to report other members of the distribution network that deviate from the standard price level. Similarly, direct or indirect price fixing can be made more effective when combined with measures which may reduce the buyer's incentive to lower the resale price, such as the supplier printing a recommended resale price on the product or the supplier obliging the buyer to apply a most-favoured-customer clause. The same indirect means and the same "supportive" measures can be used to make maximum or recommended prices work as RPM. However, the use of a particular supportive measure or the provision of a list of recommended prices or maximum prices by the supplier to the buyer is not considered in itself as leading to RPM.

Commentary

para 48: **B&C:** 7.007, 7.039, 7.043 **F&N:** 9.95

(49) In the case of agency agreements, the principal normally establishes the sales price, as the agent does not become the owner of the goods. However, where such an agreement cannot be qualified as an agency agreement for the purposes of applying Article 101(1) (see paragraphs (12) to (21)) an obligation preventing or restricting the agent from sharing its commission, fixed or variable, with the customer would be a hardcore restriction under Article 4(a) of the Block Exemption Regulation. In order to avoid including such a hardcore restriction in the agreement, the agent should thus be left free to lower the effective price paid by the customer without reducing the income for the principal.[1]

Notes

1 See, for instance, Commission Decision 91/562/EEC in Case No IV/32.737 — *Eirpage*, OJ L 306, 7.11.1991, p.22, in particular recital (6).

Commentary

para 49: **B&C:** 7.190

(50) The hardcore restriction set out in Article 4(b) of the Block Exemption Regulation concerns agreements or concerted practices that have as their direct or indirect object the restriction of sales by a buyer party to the agreement or its customers, in as far as those restrictions relate to the territory into which or the customers to whom the buyer or its customers may sell the contract goods or services. This hardcore restriction relates to market partitioning by territory or by customer group. That may be the result of direct obligations, such as the obligation not to sell to

certain customers or to customers in certain territories or the obligation to refer orders from these customers to other distributors. It may also result from indirect measures aimed at inducing the distributor not to sell to such customers, such as refusal or reduction of bonuses or discounts, termination of supply, reduction of supplied volumes or limitation of supplied volumes to the demand within the allocated territory or customer group, threat of contract termination, requiring a higher price for products to be exported, limiting the proportion of sales that can be exported or profit pass-over obligations. It may further result from the supplier not providing a Union-wide guarantee service under which normally all distributors are obliged to provide the guarantee service and are reimbursed for this service by the supplier, even in relation to products sold by other distributors into their territory.[1] Such practices are even more likely to be viewed as a restriction of the buyer's sales when used in conjunction with the implementation by the supplier of a monitoring system aimed at verifying the effective destination of the supplied goods, such as the use of differentiated labels or serial numbers. However, obligations on the reseller relating to the display of the supplier's brand name are not classified as hardcore. As Article 4(b) only concerns restrictions of sales by the buyer or its customers, this implies that restrictions of the supplier's sales are also not a hardcore restriction, subject to what is stated in paragraph (59) regarding sales of spare parts in the context of Article 4(e) of the Block Exemption Regulation. Article 4(b) applies without prejudice to a restriction on the buyer's place of establishment. Thus, the benefit of the Block Exemption Regulation is not lost if it is agreed that the buyer will restrict its distribution outlet(s) and warehouse(s) to a particular address, place or territory.

Notes

[1] If the supplier decides not to reimburse its distributors for services rendered under the Union-wide guarantee, it may be agreed with these distributors that a distributor which makes a sale outside its allocated territory, will have to pay the distributor appointed in the territory of destination a fee based on the cost of the services (to be) carried out including a reasonable profit margin. This type of scheme may not be seen as a restriction of the distributors' sales outside their territory (see judgment of the Court of First Instance in Case T-67/01 *JCB Service v Commission* [2004] ECR II-49, paragraphs 136 to 145).

Commentary
para 50: **B&C:** 7.007, 7.036, 7.046, 7.071 **F&N:** 9.113, 9.114, 9.118, 12.61

---

(51) There are four exceptions to the hardcore restriction in Article 4(b) of the Block Exemption Regulation. The first exception in Article 4(b)(i) allows a supplier to restrict active sales by a buyer party to the agreement to a territory or a customer group which has been allocated exclusively to another buyer or which the supplier has reserved to itself. A territory or customer group is exclusively allocated when the supplier agrees to sell its product only to one distributor for distribution in a particular territory or to a particular customer group and the exclusive distributor is protected against active selling into its territory or to its customer group by all the other buyers of the supplier within the Union, irrespective of sales by the supplier. The supplier is allowed to combine the allocation of an exclusive territory and an exclusive customer group by for instance appointing an exclusive distributor for a particular customer group in a certain territory. Such protection of exclusively allocated territories or customer groups must, however, permit passive sales to such territories or customer groups. For the application of Article 4(b) of the Block Exemption Regulation, the Commission interprets "active" and "passive" sales as follows:

— "Active" sales mean actively approaching individual customers by for instance direct mail, including the sending of unsolicited e-mails, or visits; or actively approaching a specific customer group or customers in a specific territory through advertisement in media, on the internet or other promotions specifically targeted at that customer group or targeted at customers in that territory. Advertisement or promotion that is only attractive for the buyer if it (also) reaches a specific group of customers or customers in a specific territory, is considered active selling to that customer group or customers in that territory.

— "Passive" sales mean responding to unsolicited requests from individual customers including delivery of goods or services to such customers. General advertising or promotion that reaches customers in other distributors' (exclusive) territories or customer groups but which is a reasonable way to reach customers outside those territories or customer groups, for instance to reach customers in one's own territory, are considered passive selling. General advertising or promotion is considered a reasonable way to reach such customers if it would be attractive for the buyer to undertake these investments also if they would not reach customers in other distributors' (exclusive) territories or customer groups.

Commentary
para 51: **B&C:** 7.100 **F&N:** 7.219, 9.11, 14.114

(52) The internet is a powerful tool to reach a greater number and variety of customers than by more traditional sales methods, which explains why certain restrictions on the use of the internet are dealt with as (re)sales restrictions. In principle, every distributor must be allowed to use the internet to sell products. In general, where a distributor uses a website to sell products that is considered a form of passive selling, since it is a reasonable way to allow customers to reach the distributor. The use of a website may have effects that extend beyond the distributor's own territory and customer group; however, such effects result from the technology allowing easy access from everywhere. If a customer visits the web site of a distributor and contacts the distributor and if such contact leads to a sale, including delivery, then that is considered passive selling. The same is true if a customer opts to be kept (automatically) informed by the distributor and it leads to a sale. Offering different language options on the website does not, of itself, change the passive character of such selling. The Commission thus regards the following as examples of hardcore restrictions of passive selling given the capability of these restrictions to limit the distributor's access to a greater number and variety of customers:

(a) an agreement that the (exclusive) distributor shall prevent customers located in another (exclusive) territory from viewing its website or shall automatically re-rout[e] its customers to the manufacturer's or other (exclusive) distributors' websites. This does not exclude an agreement that the distributor's website shall also offer a number of links to websites of other distributors and/or the supplier;

(b) an agreement that the (exclusive) distributor shall terminate consumers' transactions over the internet once their credit card data reveal an address that is not within the distributor's (exclusive) territory;

(c) an agreement that the distributor shall limit its proportion of overall sales made over the internet. This does not exclude the supplier requiring, without limiting the online sales of the distributor, that the buyer sells at least a certain absolute amount (in value or volume) of the products offline to ensure an efficient operation of its brick and mortar shop (physical point of sales), nor does it preclude the supplier from making sure that the online activity of the distributor remains consistent with the supplier's distribution model (see paragraphs (54) and (56)). This absolute amount of required offline sales can be the same for all buyers, or determined individually for each buyer on the basis of objective criteria, such as the buyer's size in the network or its geographic location;

(d) an agreement that the distributor shall pay a higher price for products intended to be resold by the distributor online than for products intended to be resold offline. This does not exclude the supplier agreeing with the buyer a fixed fee (that is, not a variable fee where the sum increases with the realised offline turnover as this would amount indirectly to dual pricing) to support the latter's offline or online sales efforts.

Commentary
para 52: **B&C:** 7.070 **F&N:** 9.133
para 52(c): **B&C:** 7.100 **F&N:** 9.136

(53) A restriction on the use of the internet by distributors that are party to the agreement is compatible with the Block Exemption Regulation to the extent that promotion on the internet or use of the internet would lead to active selling into, for instance, other distributors' exclusive territories or customer groups. The Commission considers online advertisement specifically addressed to certain customers as a form of active selling to those customers. For instance, territory-based banners on third party websites are a form of active sales into the territory where these banners are shown. In general, efforts to be found specifically in a certain territory or by a certain customer group is active selling into that territory or to that customer group. For instance, pay-

ing a search engine or online advertisement provider to have advertisements displayed specifically to users in a particular territory is active selling into that territory.

Commentary
para 53: B&C: 7.070

(54) However, under the Block Exemption the supplier may require quality standards for the use of the internet site to resell its goods, just as the supplier may require quality standards for a shop or for selling by catalogue or for advertising and promotion in general. This may be relevant in particular for selective distribution. Under the Block Exemption, the supplier may, for example, require that its distributors have one or more brick and mortar shops or showrooms as a condition for becoming a member of its distribution system. Subsequent changes to such a condition are also possible under the Block Exemption, except where those changes have as their object to directly or indirectly limit the online sales by the distributors. Similarly, a supplier may require that its distributors use third party platforms to distribute the contract products only in accordance with the standards and conditions agreed between the supplier and its distributors for the distributors' use of the internet. For instance, where the distributor's website is hosted by a third party platform, the supplier may require that customers do not visit the distributor's website through a site carrying the name or logo of the third party platform.

Commentary
para 54: B&C: 7.100

(55) There are three further exceptions to the hardcore restriction set out in Article 4(b) of the Block Exemption Regulation. All three exceptions allow for the restriction of both active and passive sales. Under the first exception, it is permissible to restrict a wholesaler from selling to end users, which allows a supplier to keep the wholesale and retail level of trade separate. However, that exception does not exclude the possibility that the wholesaler can sell to certain end users, such as bigger end users, while not allowing sales to (all) other end users. The second exception allows a supplier to restrict an appointed distributor in a selective distribution system from selling, at any level of trade, to unauthorised distributors located in any territory where the system is currently operated or where the supplier does not yet sell the contract products (referred to as "the territory reserved by the supplier to operate that system" in Article 4(b)(iii)). The third exception allows a supplier to restrict a buyer of components, to whom the components are supplied for incorporation, from reselling them to competitors of the supplier. The term "component" includes any intermediate goods and the term "incorporation" refers to the use of any input to produce goods.

Commentary
para 55: B&C: 7.048 F&N: 9.123, 9.127

(56) The hardcore restriction set out in Article 4(c) of the Block Exemption Regulation excludes the restriction of active or passive sales to end users, whether professional end users or final consumers, by members of a selective distribution network, without prejudice to the possibility of prohibiting a member of the network from operating out of an unauthorised place of establishment. Accordingly, dealers in a selective distribution system, as defined in Article 1(1)(e) of the Block Exemption Regulation, cannot be restricted in the choice of users to whom they may sell, or purchasing agents acting on behalf of those users except to protect an exclusive distribution system operated elsewhere (see paragraph (51)). Within a selective distribution system the dealers should be free to sell, both actively and passively, to all end users, also with the help of the internet. Therefore, the Commission considers any obligations which dissuade appointed dealers from using the internet to reach a greater number and variety of customers by imposing criteria for online sales which are not overall equivalent to the criteria imposed for the sales from the brick and mortar shop as a hardcore restriction. This does not mean that the criteria imposed for online sales must be identical to those imposed for offline sales, but rather that they should pursue the same objectives and achieve comparable results and that the difference between the criteria must be justified by the different nature of these two distribution modes.

For example, in order to prevent sales to unauthorised dealers, a supplier can restrict its selected dealers from selling more than a given quantity of contract products to an individual end user. Such a requirement may have to be stricter for online sales if it is easier for an unauthorised dealer to obtain those products by using the internet. Similarly, it may have to be stricter for offline sales if it is easier to obtain them from a brick and mortar shop. In order to ensure timely delivery of contract products, a supplier may impose that the products be delivered instantly in the case of offline sales. Whereas an identical requirement cannot be imposed for online sales, the supplier may specify certain practicable delivery times for such sales. Specific requirements may have to be formulated for an online after-sales help desk, so as to cover the costs of customers returning the product and for applying secure payment systems.

Commentary
para 56: **B&C:** 7.111 **F&N:** 9.137

(57) Within the territory where the supplier operates selective distribution, this system may not be combined with exclusive distribution as that would lead to a hardcore restriction of active or passive selling by the dealers under Article 4(c) of the Block Exemption Regulation, with the exception that restrictions can be imposed on the dealer's ability to determine the location of its business premises. Selected dealers may be prevented from operating their business from different premises or from opening a new outlet in a different location. In that context, the use by a distributor of its own website cannot be considered to be the same thing as the opening of a new outlet in a different location. If the dealer's outlet is mobile, an area may be defined outside which the mobile outlet cannot be operated. In addition, the supplier may commit itself to supplying only one dealer or a limited number of dealers in a particular part of the territory where the selective distribution system is applied.

Commentary
para 57: **B&C:** 7.079, 7.110, 7.133, 7.180 **F&N:** 9.129

(58) The hardcore restriction set out in Article 4(d) of the Block Exemption Regulation concerns the restriction of cross-supplies between appointed distributors within a selective distribution system. Accordingly, an agreement or concerted practice may not have as its direct or indirect object to prevent or restrict the active or passive selling of the contract products between the selected distributors. Selected distributors must remain free to purchase the contract products from other appointed distributors within the network, operating either at the same or at a different level of trade. Consequently, selective distribution cannot be combined with vertical restraints aimed at forcing distributors to purchase the contract products exclusively from a given source. It also means that within a selective distribution network, no restrictions can be imposed on appointed wholesalers as regards their sales of the product to appointed retailers.

(59) The hardcore restriction set out in Article 4(e) of the Block Exemption Regulation concerns agreements that prevent or restrict end-users, independent repairers and service providers from obtaining spare parts directly from the manufacturer of those spare parts. An agreement between a manufacturer of spare parts and a buyer that incorporates those parts into its own products (original equipment manufacturer (OEM)), may not, either directly or indirectly, prevent or restrict sales by the manufacturer of those spare parts to end users, independent repairers or service providers. Indirect restrictions may arise particularly when the supplier of the spare parts is restricted in supplying technical information and special equipment which are necessary for the use of spare parts by users, independent repairers or service providers. However, the agreement may place restrictions on the supply of the spare parts to the repairers or service providers entrusted by the original equipment manufacturer with the repair or servicing of its own goods. In other words, the original equipment manufacturer may require its own repair and service network to buy spare parts from it.

Part C Substantive Antitrust Matters

Commentary
para 59: B&C: 7.057, 7.198 F&N: 9.145

4. Individual cases of hardcore sales restrictions that may fall outside the scope of Article 101(1) or may fulfil the conditions of Article 101(3)

(60) Hardcore restrictions may be objectively necessary in exceptional cases for an agreement of a particular type or nature[1] and therefore fall outside Article 101(1). For example, a hardcore restriction may be objectively necessary to ensure that a public ban on selling dangerous substances to certain customers for reasons of safety or health is respected. In addition, undertakings may plead an efficiency defence under Article 101(3) in an individual case. This section provides some examples for (re)sales restrictions, whereas for RPM this is dealt with in section VI.2.10.

Notes
[1] See paragraph 18 of Communication from the Commission — Notice — Guidelines on the application of Article [101](3) of the Treaty, OJ C 101, 27.4.2004, p.97.

Commentary
para 60: B&C: 2.107, 7.036, 7.076, 7.086 F&N: 3.179

(61) A distributor which will be the first to sell a new brand or the first to sell an existing brand on a new market, thereby ensuring a genuine entry on the relevant market, may have to commit substantial investments where there was previously no demand for that type of product in general or for that type of product from that producer. Such expenses may often be sunk and in such circumstances the distributor may not enter into the distribution agreement without protection for a certain period of time against (active and) passive sales into its territory or to its customer group by other distributors. For example such a situation may occur where a manufacturer established in a particular national market enters another national market and introduces its products with the help of an exclusive distributor and where this distributor needs to invest in launching and establishing the brand on this new market. Where substantial investments by the distributor to start up and/or develop the new market are necessary, restrictions of passive sales by other distributors into such a territory or to such a customer group which are necessary for the distributor to recoup those investments generally fall outside the scope of Article 101(1) during the first two years that the distributor is selling the contract goods or services in that territory or to that customer group, even though such hardcore restrictions are in general presumed to fall within the scope of Article 101(1).

Commentary
para 61: B&C: 2.098, 2.102, 2.139, 3.052 F&N: 9.149

(62) In the case of genuine testing of a new product in a limited territory or with a limited customer group and in the case of a staggered introduction of a new product, the distributors appointed to sell the new product on the test market or to participate in the first round(s) of the staggered introduction may be restricted in their active selling outside the test market or the market(s) where the product is first introduced without falling within the scope of Article 101(1) for the period necessary for the testing or introduction of the product.

Commentary
para 62: F&N: 9.150

(63) In the case of a selective distribution system, cross supplies between appointed distributors must normally remain free (see paragraph (58)). However, if appointed wholesalers located in different territories are obliged to invest in promotional activities in "their" territories to support the sales by appointed retailers and it is not practical to specify in a contract the required promotional activities, restrictions on active sales by the wholesalers to appointed retailers in other wholesalers' territories to overcome possible free riding may, in an individual case, fulfil the conditions of Article 101(3).

Commentary
para 63: F&N: 9.151

(64) In general, an agreement that a distributor shall pay a higher price for products intended to be resold by the distributor online than for products intended to be resold offline ("dual pricing") is a hardcore restriction (see paragraph (52)). However, in some specific circumstances, such an agreement may fulfil the conditions of Article 101(3). Such circumstances may be present where a manufacturer agrees such dual pricing with its distributors, because selling online leads to substantially higher costs for the manufacturer than offline sales. For example, where offline sales include home installation by the distributor but online sales do not, the latter may lead to more customer complaints and warranty claims for the manufacturer. In that context, the Commission will also consider to what extent the restriction is likely to limit internet sales and hinder the distributor to reach more and different customers.

Commentary
para 64: B&C: 7.045 F&N: 9.152

5. Excluded restrictions under the Block Exemption Regulation

(65) Article 5 of the Block Exemption Regulation excludes certain obligations from the coverage of the Block Exemption Regulation even though the market share threshold is not exceeded. However, the Block Exemption Regulation continues to apply to the remaining part of the vertical agreement if that part is severable from the non-exempted obligations.

Commentary
para 65: F&N: 9.153

(66) The first exclusion is provided for in Article 5(1)(a) of the Block Exemption Regulation and concerns non-compete obligations. Non-compete obligations are arrangements that result in the buyer purchasing from the supplier or from another undertaking designated by the supplier more than 80% of the buyer's total purchases of the contract goods and services and their substitutes during the preceding calendar year (as defined by Article 1(1)(d) of the Block Exemption Regulation), thereby preventing the buyer from purchasing competing goods or services or limiting such purchases to less than 20% of total purchases. Where, in the first year after entering in the agreement, for the year preceding the conclusion of the contract no relevant purchasing data for the buyer are available, the buyer's best estimate of its annual total requirements may be used. Such non-compete obligations are not covered by the Block Exemption Regulation where the duration is indefinite or exceeds five years. Non-compete obligations that are tacitly renewable beyond a period of five years are also not covered by the Block Exemption Regulation (see the second subparagraph of Article 5(1)). In general, non-compete obligations are exempted under that Regulation where their duration is limited to five years or less and no obstacles exist that hinder the buyer from effectively terminating the non-compete obligation at the end of the five year period. If, for instance, the agreement provides for a five-year non-compete obligation and the supplier provides a loan to the buyer, the repayment of that loan should not hinder the buyer from effectively terminating the non-compete obligation at the end of the five-year period. Similarly, when the supplier provides the buyer with equipment which is not relationship-specific, the buyer should have the possibility to take over the equipment at its market asset value once the non-compete obligation expires.

Commentary
para 66: B&C: 7.161 F&N: 4.401, 9.155, 9.157, 12.74, 12.75

(67) The five-year duration limit does not apply when the goods or services are resold by the buyer "from premises and land owned by the supplier or leased by the supplier from third parties not connected with the buyer". In such cases the non-compete obligation may be of the same duration as the period of occupancy of the point of sale by the buyer (Article 5(2) of the Block Exemption Regulation). The reason for this exception is that it is normally unreasonable to expect a supplier to allow competing products to be sold from premises and land owned by the supplier without its permission. By analogy, the same principles apply where the buyer operates

Part C Substantive Antitrust Matters

from a mobile outlet owned by the supplier or leased by the supplier from third parties not connected with the buyer. Artificial ownership constructions, such as a transfer by the distributor of its proprietary rights over the land and premises to the supplier for only a limited period, intended to avoid the five-year limit cannot benefit from this exception.

Commentary
para 67: B&C: 7.155 F&N: 9.159

(68) The second exclusion from the block exemption is provided for in Article 5(1)(b) of the Block Exemption Regulation and concerns post term non-compete obligations on the buyer. Such obligations are normally not covered by the Block Exemption Regulation, unless the obligation is indispensable to protect know-how transferred by the supplier to the buyer, is limited to the point of sale from which the buyer has operated during the contract period, and is limited to a maximum period of one year (see Article 5(3) of the Block Exemption Regulation). According to the definition in Article 1(1)(g) of the Block Exemption Regulation the know-how needs to be "substantial", meaning that the know-how includes information which is significant and useful to the buyer for the use, sale or resale of the contract goods or services.

(69) The third exclusion from the block exemption is provided for in Article 5(1)(c) of the Block Exemption Regulation and concerns the sale of competing goods in a selective distribution system. The Block Exemption Regulation covers the combination of selective distribution with a non-compete obligation, obliging the dealers not to resell competing brands in general. However, if the supplier prevents its appointed dealers, either directly or indirectly, from buying products for resale from specific competing suppliers, such an obligation cannot enjoy the benefit of the Block Exemption Regulation. The objective of the exclusion of such an obligation is to avoid a situation whereby a number of suppliers using the same selective distribution outlets prevent one specific competitor or certain specific competitors from using these outlets to distribute their products (foreclosure of a competing supplier which would be a form of collective boycott).[1]

Notes

[1] An example of indirect measures having such exclusionary effects can be found in Commission Decision 92/428/EEC in Case No IV/33.542 — *Parfum Givenchy*, OJ L 236, 19.8.1992, p.11.

Commentary
para 69: B&C: 7.133

6. Severability

(70) The Block Exemption Regulation exempts vertical agreements on condition that no hardcore restriction, as set out in Article 4 of that Regulation, is contained in or practised with the vertical agreement. If there are one or more hardcore restrictions, the benefit of the Block Exemption Regulation is lost for the entire vertical agreement. There is no severability for hardcore restrictions.

Commentary
para 70: B&C: 7.059 F&N: 9.91

(71) The rule of severability does apply, however, to the excluded restrictions set out in Article 5 of the Block Exemption Regulation. Therefore, the benefit of the block exemption is only lost in relation to that part of the vertical agreement which does not comply with the conditions set out in Article 5.

Commentary
para 71: B&C: 7.059 F&N: 9.153

7. Portfolio of products distributed through the same distribution system

(72) Where a supplier uses the same distribution agreement to distribute several goods/services some of these may, in view of the market share threshold, be covered by the Block Exemption

Regulation while others may not. In that case, the Block Exemption Regulation applies to those goods and services for which the conditions of application are fulfilled.

Commentary
para 72: B&C: 7.035

(73) In respect of the goods or services which are not covered by the Block Exemption Regulation, the ordinary rules of competition apply, which means:
   (a) there is no block exemption but also no presumption of illegality;
   (b) if there is an infringement of Article 101(1) which is not exemptible, consideration may be given to whether there are appropriate remedies to solve the competition problem within the existing distribution system;
   (c) if there are no such appropriate remedies, the supplier concerned will have to make other distribution arrangements.

   Such a situation can also arise where Article 102 applies in respect of some products but not in respect of others.

Commentary
para 73: B&C: 7.035 F&N: 9.183

IV. WITHDRAWAL OF THE BLOCK EXEMPTION AND DISAPPLICATION OF THE BLOCK EXEMPTION REGULATION

1. Withdrawal procedure

(74) The presumption of legality conferred by the Block Exemption Regulation may be withdrawn where a vertical agreement, considered either in isolation or in conjunction with similar agreements enforced by competing suppliers or buyers, comes within the scope of Article 101(1) and does not fulfil all the conditions of Article 101(3).

Commentary
para 74: B&C: 7.061

(75) The conditions of Article 101(3) may in particular not be fulfilled when access to the relevant market or competition therein is significantly restricted by the cumulative effect of parallel networks of similar vertical agreements practised by competing suppliers or buyers. Parallel networks of vertical agreements are to be regarded as similar if they contain restraints producing similar effects on the market. Such a situation may arise for example when, on a given market, certain suppliers practise purely qualitative selective distribution while other suppliers practise quantitative selective distribution. Such a situation may also arise when, on a given market, the cumulative use of qualitative criteria forecloses more efficient distributors. In such circumstances, the assessment must take account of the anti-competitive effects attributable to each individual network of agreements. Where appropriate, withdrawal may concern only a particular qualitative criterion or only the quantitative limitations imposed on the number of authorised distributors.

Commentary
para 75: B&C: 7.061 F&N: 9.167

(76) Responsibility for an anti-competitive cumulative effect can only be attributed to those undertakings which make an appreciable contribution to it. Agreements entered into by undertakings whose contribution to the cumulative effect is insignificant do not fall under the prohibition provided for in Article 101(1)[1] and are therefore not subject to the withdrawal mechanism. The assessment of such a contribution will be made in accordance with the criteria set out in paragraphs (128) to (229).

Notes

1 Judgment of the Court of Justice of 28 February 1991 in Case C-234/89, *Stergios Delimitis v Henninger Bräu AG* [1991] ECR I-935.

(77) Where the withdrawal procedure is applied, the Commission bears the burden of proof that the agreement falls within the scope of Article 101(1) and that the agreement does not fulfil one or several of the conditions of Article 101(3). A withdrawal decision can only have ex nunc effect, which means that the exempted status of the agreements concerned will not be affected until the date at which the withdrawal becomes effective.

Commentary
para 77: B&C: 3.077, 7.061

(78) As referred to in recital 14 of the Block Exemption Regulation, the competition authority of a Member State may withdraw the benefit of the Block Exemption Regulation in respect of vertical agreements whose anti-competitive effects are felt in the territory of the Member State concerned or a part thereof, which has all the characteristics of a distinct geographic market. The Commission has the exclusive power to withdraw the benefit of the Block Exemption Regulation in respect of vertical agreements restricting competition on a relevant geographic market which is wider than the territory of a single Member State. When the territory of a single Member State, or a part thereof, constitutes the relevant geographic market, the Commission and the Member State concerned have concurrent competence for withdrawal.

Commentary
para 78: B&C: 3.090, 7.062

2. Disapplication of the Block Exemption Regulation

(79) Article 6 of the Block Exemption Regulation enables the Commission to exclude from the scope of the Block Exemption Regulation, by means of regulation, parallel networks of similar vertical restraints where these cover more than 50% of a relevant market. Such a measure is not addressed to individual undertakings but concerns all undertakings whose agreements are defined in the regulation disapplying the Block Exemption Regulation.

(80) Whereas the withdrawal of the benefit of the Block Exemption Regulation implies the adoption of a decision establishing an infringement of Article 101 by an individual company, the effect of a regulation under Article 6 is merely to remove, in respect of the restraints and the markets concerned, the benefit of the application of the Block Exemption Regulation and to restore the full application of Article 101(1) and (3). Following the adoption of a regulation declaring the Block Exemption Regulation inapplicable in respect of certain vertical restraints on a particular market, the criteria developed by the relevant case-law of the Court of Justice and the General Court and by notices and previous decisions adopted by the Commission will guide the application of Article 101 to individual agreements. Where appropriate, the Commission will take a decision in an individual case, which can provide guidance to all the undertakings operating on the market concerned.

Commentary
para 80: B&C: 3.092, 7.063

(81) For the purpose of calculating the 50% market coverage ratio, account must be taken of each individual network of vertical agreements containing restraints, or combinations of restraints, producing similar effects on the market. Article 6 of the Block Exemption Regulation does not entail an obligation on the part of the Commission to act where the 50% market-coverage ratio is exceeded. In general, disapplication is appropriate when it is likely that access to the relevant market or competition therein is appreciably restricted. This may occur in particular when parallel networks of selective distribution covering more than 50% of a market are liable to foreclose the market by using selection criteria which are not required by the nature of the relevant goods or which discriminate against certain forms of distribution capable of selling such goods.

(82) In assessing the need to apply Article 6 of the Block Exemption Regulation, the Commission will consider whether individual withdrawal would be a more appropriate remedy. This may depend, in particular, on the number of competing undertakings contributing to a cumulative effect on a market or the number of affected geographic markets within the Union.

Commentary
para 82: B&C: 7.063

(83) Any regulation referred to in Article 6 of the Block Exemption Regulation must clearly set out its scope. Therefore, the Commission must first define the relevant product and geographic market(s) and, secondly, must identify the type of vertical restraint in respect of which the Block Exemption Regulation will no longer apply. As regards the latter aspect, the Commission may modulate the scope of its regulation according to the competition concern which it intends to address. For instance, while all parallel networks of single-branding type arrangements shall be taken into account in view of establishing the 50% market coverage ratio, the Commission may nevertheless restrict the scope of the disapplication regulation only to non-compete obligations exceeding a certain duration. Thus, agreements of a shorter duration or of a less restrictive nature might be left unaffected, in consideration of the lesser degree of foreclosure attributable to such restraints. Similarly, when on a particular market selective distribution is practised in combination with additional restraints such as non-compete or quantity-forcing on the buyer, the disapplication regulation may concern only such additional restraints. Where appropriate, the Commission may also provide guidance by specifying the market share level which, in the specific market context, may be regarded as insufficient to bring about a significant contribution by an individual undertaking to the cumulative effect.

Commentary
para 83: F&N: 9.172

(84) Pursuant to Regulation No 19/65/EEC of 2 March 1965 of the Council on the application of Article [101](3) of the Treaty to certain categories of agreements and concerted practices,[1] the Commission will have to set a transitional period of not less than six months before a regulation disapplying the Block Exemption Regulation becomes applicable. This should allow the undertakings concerned to adapt their agreements to take account of the regulation disapplying the Block Exemption Regulation.

Notes
[1] OJ 36, 6.3.1965, p.533/65, English special edition: OJ Series I Chapter 1965–1966, p.35.

Commentary
para 84: B&C: 7.063

(85) A regulation disapplying the Block Exemption Regulation will not affect the exempted status of the agreements concerned for the period preceding its date of application.

V. Market Definition and Market Share Calculation

1. Commission Notice on definition of the relevant market

(86) The Commission Notice on definition of the relevant market for the purposes of Community competition law[1] provides guidance on the rules, criteria and evidence which the Commission uses when considering market definition issues. That Notice will not be further explained in these Guidelines and should serve as the basis for market definition issues. These Guidelines will only deal with specific issues that arise in the context of vertical restraints and that are not dealt with in that notice.

Notes
1 OJ C 372, 9.12.1997, p.5.
Commentary
para 86: B&C: 7.032

2. The relevant market for calculating the 30% market share threshold under the Block Exemption Regulation

(87) Under Article 3 of the Block Exemption Regulation, the market share of both the supplier and the buyer are decisive to determine if the block exemption applies. In order for the block exemption to apply, the market share of the supplier on the market where it sells the contract products to the buyer, and the market share of the buyer on the market where it purchases the contract products, must each be 30% or less. For agreements between small and medium-sized undertakings it is in general not necessary to calculate market shares (see paragraph (11)).

(88) In order to calculate an undertaking's market share, it is necessary to determine the relevant market where that undertaking sells and purchases, respectively, the contract products. Accordingly, the relevant product market and the relevant geographic market must be defined. The relevant product market comprises any goods or services which are regarded by the buyers as interchangeable, by reason of their characteristics, prices and intended use. The relevant geographic market comprises the area in which the undertakings concerned are involved in the supply and demand of relevant goods or services, in which the conditions of competition are sufficiently homogeneous, and which can be distinguished from neighbouring geographic areas because, in particular, conditions of competition are appreciably different in those areas.

(89) The product market definition primarily depends on substitutability from the buyers' perspective. When the supplied product is used as an input to produce other products and is generally not recognisable in the final product, the product market is normally defined by the direct buyers' preferences. The customers of the buyers will normally not have a strong preference concerning the inputs used by the buyers. Usually, the vertical restraints agreed between the supplier and buyer of the input only relate to the sale and purchase of the intermediate product and not to the sale of the resulting product. In the case of distribution of final goods, substitutes for the direct buyers will normally be influenced or determined by the preferences of the final consumers. A distributor, as reseller, cannot ignore the preferences of final consumers when it purchases final goods. In addition, at the distribution level the vertical restraints usually concern not only the sale of products between supplier and buyer, but also their resale. As different distribution formats usually compete, markets are in general not defined by the form of distribution that is applied. Where suppliers generally sell a portfolio of products, the entire portfolio may determine the product market when the portfolios and not the individual products are regarded as substitutes by the buyers. As distributors are professional buyers, the geographic wholesale market is usually wider than the retail market, where the product is resold to final consumers. Often, this will lead to the definition of national or wider wholesale markets. But retail markets may also be wider than the final consumers' search area where homogeneous market conditions and overlapping local or regional catchment areas exist.

Commentary
para 89: B&C: 7.032 F&N: 9.181, 9.182, 9.183

(90) Where a vertical agreement involves three parties, each operating at a different level of trade, each party's market share must be 30% or less in order for the block exemption to apply. As specified in Article 3(2) of the Block Exemption Regulation, where in a multi party agreement an undertaking buys the contract goods or services from one undertaking party to the agreement and sells the contract goods or services to another undertaking party to the agreement, the block exemption applies only if its market share does not exceed the 30% threshold both as a buyer and a supplier. If, for instance, in an agreement between a manufacturer, a wholesaler (or association of retailers) and a retailer, a non-compete obligation is agreed, then the market shares of the manufacturer and the wholesaler (or association of retailers) on their respective downstream markets must not exceed 30% and the market share of the wholesaler (or association of retailers)

and the retailer must not exceed 30% on their respective purchase markets in order to benefit from the block exemption.

Commentary
para 90: **B&C:** 7.027, 7.034 **F&N:** 9.174

(91) Where a supplier produces both original equipment and the repair or replacement parts for that equipment, the supplier will often be the only or the major supplier on the after-market for the repair and replacement parts. This may also arise where the supplier (OEM supplier) subcontracts the manufacturing of the repair or replacement parts. The relevant market for application of the Block Exemption Regulation may be the original equipment market including the spare parts or a separate original equipment market and after-market depending on the circumstances of the case, such as the effects of the restrictions involved, the lifetime of the equipment and importance of the repair or replacement costs.[1] In practice, the issue is whether a significant proportion of buyers make their choice taking into account the lifetime costs of the product. If so, it indicates there is one market for the original equipment and spare parts combined.

Notes

[1] See for example Commission Decision in *Pelikan/Kyocera* (1995), COM(96) 126 (not published), point 87, and Commission Decision 91/595/EEC in Case No IV/M.12 — *Varta/Bosch*, OJ L 320, 22.11.1991, p.26, Commission Decision in Case No IV/M.1094 — *Caterpillar/Perkins Engines*, OJ C 94, 28.3.1998, p.23, and Commission Decision in Case No IV/M.768 — *Lucas/Varity*, OJ C 266, 13.9.1996, p.6. See also point 56 of the Notice on the definition of the relevant market for the purposes of Community competition law (see paragraph 86).

Commentary
para 91: **B&C:** 7.032 **F&N:** 9.184

(92) Where the vertical agreement, in addition to the supply of the contract goods, also contains IPR provisions — such as a provision concerning the use of the supplier's trademark — which help the buyer to market the contract goods, the supplier's market share on the market where it sells the contract goods is relevant for the application of the Block Exemption Regulation. Where a franchisor does not supply goods to be resold but provides a bundle of services and goods combined with IPR provisions which together form the business method being franchised, the franchisor needs to take account of its market share as a provider of a business method. For that purpose, the franchisor needs to calculate its market share on the market where the business method is exploited, which is the market where the franchisees exploit the business method to provide goods or services to end users. The franchisor must base its market share on the value of the goods or services supplied by its franchisees on this market. On such a market, the competitors may be providers of other franchised business methods but also suppliers of substitutable goods or services not applying franchising. For instance, without prejudice to the definition of such market, if there was a market for fast-food services, a franchisor operating on such a market would need to calculate its market share on the basis of the relevant sales figures of its franchisees on this market.

Commentary
para 92: **B&C:** 7.032, 7.177 **F&N:** 9.186

3. Calculation of market shares under the Block Exemption Regulation

(93) The calculation of market shares needs to be based in principle on value figures. Where value figures are not available substantiated estimates can be made. Such estimates may be based on other reliable market information such as volume figures (see Article 7(a) of the Block Exemption Regulation).

(94) In-house production, that is, production of an intermediate product for own use, may be very important in a competition analysis as one of the competitive constraints or to accentuate the market position of a company. However, for the purpose of market definition and the calculation of market share for intermediate goods and services, in-house production will not be taken into account.

Commentary
para 94: B&C: 7.032

(95) However, in the case of dual distribution of final goods, that is, where a producer of final goods also acts as a distributor on the market, the market definition and market share calculation need to include sales of their own goods made by the producers through their vertically integrated distributors and agents (see Article 7(c) of the Block Exemption Regulation). "Integrated distributors" are connected undertakings within the meaning of Article 1(2) of the Block Exemption Regulation.[1]

Notes

[1] For these market definition and market share calculation purposes, it is not relevant whether the integrated distributor sells in addition products of competitors.

VI. Enforcement Policy in Individual Cases

1. The framework of analysis

(96) Outside the scope of the block exemption, it is relevant to examine whether in the individual case the agreement falls within the scope of Article 101(1) and if so whether the conditions of Article 101(3) are satisfied. Provided that they do not contain restrictions of competition by object and in particular hardcore restrictions of competition, there is no presumption that vertical agreements falling outside the block exemption because the market share threshold is exceeded fall within the scope of Article 101(1) or fail to satisfy the conditions of Article 101(3). Individual assessment of the likely effects of the agreement is required. Companies are encouraged to do their own assessment. Agreements that either do not restrict competition within the meaning of Article 101(1) or which fulfil the conditions of Article 101(3) are valid and enforceable. Pursuant to Article 1(2) of Council Regulation (EC) No 1/2003 of 16 December 2002 on the imple-mentation of the rules on competition laid down in Articles 81 and 82 of the Treaty[1] no notification needs to be made to benefit from an individual exemption under Article 101(3). In the case of an individual examination by the Commission, the latter will bear the burden of proof that the agreement in question infringes Article 101(1). The undertakings claiming the benefit of Article 101(3) bear the burden of proving that the conditions of that paragraph are fulfilled. When likely anti-competitive effects are demonstrated, undertakings may substantiate efficiency claims and explain why a certain distribution system is indispensable to bring likely benefits to consumers without eliminating competition, before the Commission decides whether the agreement satisfies the conditions of Article 101(3).

Notes

[1] OJ L 1, 4.1.2003, p.1.

Commentary
para 96: B&C: 2.128, 3.073, 3.074 F&N: 9.36, 9.90

(97) The assessment of whether a vertical agreement has the effect of restricting competition will be made by comparing the actual or likely future situation on the relevant market with the vertical restraints in place with the situation that would prevail in the absence of the vertical restraints in the agreement. In the assessment of individual cases, the Commission will take, as appropriate, both actual and likely effects into account. For vertical agreements to be restrictive of competition by effect they must affect actual or potential competition to such an extent that on the relevant market negative effects on prices, output, innovation, or the variety or quality of goods and services can be expected with a reasonable degree of probability. The likely negative effects on competition must be appreciable.[1] Appreciable anticompetitive effects are likely to occur when at least one of the parties has or obtains some degree of market power and the agreement contributes to the creation, maintenance or strengthening of that market power or allows the parties to exploit such market power. Market power is the ability to maintain prices

above competitive levels or to maintain output in terms of product quantities, product quality and variety or innovation below competitive levels for a not insignificant period of time. The degree of market power normally required for a finding of an infringement under Article 101(1) is less than the degree of market power required for a finding of dominance under Article 102.

Notes

[1] See Section II.1.

Commentary

para 97: **B&C:** 2.168, 7.010 **F&N:** 9.61, 9.62, 9.188

(98) Vertical restraints are generally less harmful than horizontal restraints. The main reason for the greater focus on horizontal restraints is that such restraints may concern an agreement between competitors producing identical or substitutable goods or services. In such horizontal relationships, the exercise of market power by one company (higher price of its product) may benefit its competitors. This may provide an incentive to competitors to induce each other to behave anti-competitively. In vertical relationships, the product of the one is the input for the other, in other words, the activities of the parties to the agreement are complementary to each other. The exercise of market power by either the upstream or downstream company would therefore normally hurt the demand for the product of the other. The companies involved in the agreement therefore usually have an incentive to prevent the exercise of market power by the other.

Commentary

para 98: **B&C:** 2.094, 7.009 **F&N:** 9.63, 10.82

(99) Such self-restraining character should not, however, be over-estimated. When a company has no market power, it can only try to increase its profits by optimising its manufacturing and distribution processes, with or without the help of vertical restraints. More generally, because of the complementary role of the parties to a vertical agreement in getting a product on the market, vertical restraints may provide substantial scope for efficiencies. However, when an undertaking does have market power it can also try to increase its profits at the expense of its direct competitors by raising their costs and at the expense of its buyers and ultimately consumers by trying to appropriate some of their surplus. This can happen when the upstream and downstream company share the extra profits or when one of the two uses vertical restraints to appropriate all the extra profits.

Commentary

para 99: **F&N:** 10.82

1.1. Negative effects of vertical restraints

(100) The negative effects on the market that may result from vertical restraints which EU competition law aims at preventing are the following:
   (a) anticompetitive foreclosure of other suppliers or other buyers by raising barriers to entry or expansion;
   (b) softening of competition between the supplier and its competitors and/or facilitation of collusion amongst these suppliers, often referred to as reduction of inter-brand competition;[1]
   (c) softening of competition between the buyer and its competitors and/or facilitation of collusion amongst these competitors, often referred to as reduction of intra-brand competition if it concerns distributors' competition on the basis of the brand or product of the same supplier;
   (d) the creation of obstacles to market integration, including, above all, limitations on the possibilities for consumers to purchase goods or services in any Member State they may choose.

Notes

[1] By collusion is meant both explicit collusion and tacit collusion (conscious parallel behaviour).

Commentary

para 100: **B&C:** 2.100, 2.125 **F&N:** 1.241, 9.191, 10.82

(101) Foreclosure, softening of competition and collusion at the manufacturers' level may harm consumers in particular by increasing the wholesale prices of the products, limiting the choice of products, lowering their quality or reducing the level of product innovation. Foreclosure, softening of competition and collusion at the distributors' level may harm consumers in particular by increasing the retail prices of the products, limiting the choice of price-service combinations and distribution formats, lowering the availability and quality of retail services and reducing the level of innovation of distribution.

Commentary
para 101: F&N: 10.82

(102) On a market where individual distributors distribute the brand(s) of only one supplier, a reduction of competition between the distributors of the same brand will lead to a reduction of intra-brand competition between these distributors, but may not have a negative effect on competition between distributors in general. In such a case, if inter-brand competition is fierce, it is unlikely that a reduction of intra-brand competition will have negative effects for consumers.

Commentary
para 102: F&N: 9.194

(103) Exclusive arrangements are generally more anti-competitive than non-exclusive arrangements. Exclusive arrangements, whether by means of express contractual language or their practical effects, result in one party sourcing all or practically all of its demand from another party. For instance, under a non-compete obligation the buyer purchases only one brand. Quantity forcing, on the other hand, leaves the buyer some scope to purchase competing goods. The degree of foreclosure may therefore be less with quantity forcing.

Commentary
para 103: F&N: 9.199

(104) Vertical restraints agreed for non-branded goods and services are in general less harmful than restraints affecting the distribution of branded goods and services. Branding tends to increase product differentiation and reduce substitutability of the product, leading to a reduced elasticity of demand and an increased possibility to raise price. The distinction between branded and non-branded goods or services will often coincide with the distinction between intermediate goods and services and final goods and services.

Commentary
para 104: F&N: 9.200

(105) In general, a combination of vertical restraints aggravates their individual negative effects. However, certain combinations of vertical restraints are less anti-competitive than their use in isolation. For instance, in an exclusive distribution system, the distributor may be tempted to increase the price of the products as intra-brand competition has been reduced. The use of quantity forcing or the setting of a maximum resale price may limit such price increases. Possible negative effects of vertical restraints are reinforced when several suppliers and their buyers organise their trade in a similar way, leading to so-called cumulative effects.

Commentary
para 105: B&C: 7.044 F&N: 9.198

1.2. Positive effects of vertical restraints

(106) It is important to recognise that vertical restraints may have positive effects by, in particular, promoting non-price competition and improved quality of services. When a company has no market power, it can only try to increase its profits by optimising its manufacturing or distribution processes. In a number of situations vertical restraints may be helpful in this respect

since the usual arm's length dealings between supplier and buyer, determining only price and quantity of a certain transaction, can lead to a sub-optimal level of investments and sales.

(107) While trying to give a fair overview of the various justifications for vertical restraints, these Guidelines do not claim to be complete or exhaustive. The following reasons may justify the application of certain vertical restraints:

(a) To solve a "free-rider" problem. One distributor may free-ride on the promotion efforts of another distributor. That type of problem is most common at the wholesale and retail level. Exclusive distribution or similar restrictions may be helpful in avoiding such free-riding. Free-riding can also occur between suppliers, for instance where one invests in promotion at the buyer's premises, in general at the retail level, that may also attract customers for its competitors. Non-compete type restraints can help to overcome free-riding.[1] For there to be a problem, there needs to be a real free-rider issue. Free-riding between buyers can only occur on pre-sales services and other promotional activities, but not on after-sales services for which the distributor can charge its customers individually. The product will usually need to be relatively new or technically complex or the reputation of the product must be a major determinant of its demand, as the customer may otherwise very well know what it wants, based on past purchases. And the product must be of a reasonably high value as it is otherwise not attractive for a customer to go to one shop for information and to another to buy. Lastly, it must not be practical for the supplier to impose on all buyers, by contract, effective promotion or service requirements. Free-riding between suppliers is also restricted to specific situations, namely to cases where the promotion takes place at the buyer's premises and is generic, not brand specific.

(b) To "open up or enter new markets". Where a manufacturer wants to enter a new geographic market, for instance by exporting to another country for the first time, this may involve special "first time investments" by the distributor to establish the brand on the market. In order to persuade a local distributor to make these investments, it may be necessary to provide territorial protection to the distributor so that it can recoup these investments by temporarily charging a higher price. Distributors based in other markets should then be restrained for a limited period from selling on the new market (see also paragraph (61) in Section III.4). This is a special case of the free-rider problem described under point (a).

(c) The "certification free-rider issue". In some sectors, certain retailers have a reputation for stocking only "quality" products. In such a case, selling through those retailers may be vital for the introduction of a new product. If the manufacturer cannot initially limit its sales to the premium stores, it runs the risk of being de-listed and the product introduction may fail. There may, therefore, be a reason for allowing for a limited duration a restriction such as exclusive distribution or selective distribution. It must be enough to guarantee introduction of the new product but not so long as to hinder large-scale dissemination. Such benefits are more likely with "experience" goods or complex goods that represent a relatively large purchase for the final consumer.

(d) The so-called "hold-up problem". Sometimes there are client-specific investments to be made by either the supplier or the buyer, such as in special equipment or training. For instance, a component manufacturer that has to build new machines and tools in order to satisfy a particular requirement of one of its customers. The investor may not commit the necessary investments before particular supply arrangements are fixed. However, as in the other free-riding examples, there are a number of conditions that have to be met before the risk of under-investment is real or significant. Firstly, the investment must be relationship-specific. An investment made by the supplier is considered to be relationship-specific when, after termination of the contract, it cannot be used by the supplier to supply other customers and can only be sold at a significant loss. An investment made by the buyer is considered to be relationship-specific when, after termination of the contract, it cannot be used by the buyer to purchase and/or use products supplied by other suppliers and can only be sold at a significant loss. An investment is thus relationship-specific because it can only, for instance, be used to produce a brand-specific component or to store a particular brand and thus cannot be used profitably to produce or resell alternatives. Secondly, it must be a long-term investment that is not recouped in the short run. And thirdly, the investment must be asymmetric, that is, one party to the contract invests more than the other party. Where these conditions are met, there is usually a good reason to have a vertical restraint for the duration it takes to depreciate the investment. The appropriate vertical restraint will be of the non-compete type or quantity-forcing type when the investment is made by the supplier and of the exclusive distribution, exclusive customer allocation or exclusive supply type when the investment is made by the buyer.

(e) The "specific hold-up problem that may arise in the case of transfer of substantial know-how". The know-how, once provided, cannot be taken back and the provider of the know-how may not want it to be used for or by its competitors. In as far as the know-how was not readily available to the buyer, is substantial and indispensable for the operation of the agreement, such a transfer may justify a non-compete type of restriction, which would normally fall outside Article 101(1).

(f) The "vertical externality issue". A retailer may not gain all the benefits of its action taken to improve sales; some may go to the manufacturer. For every extra unit a retailer sells by lowering its resale price or by increasing its sales effort, the manufacturer benefits if its wholesale price exceeds its marginal production costs. Thus, there may be a positive externality bestowed on the manufacturer by such retailer's actions and from the manufacturer's perspective the retailer may be pricing too high and/or making too little sales efforts. The negative externality of too high pricing by the retailer is sometimes called the "double marginalisation problem" and it can be avoided by imposing a maximum resale price on the retailer. To increase the retailer's sales efforts selective distribution, exclusive distribution or similar restrictions may be helpful.[2]

(g) "Economies of scale in distribution". In order to have scale economies exploited and thereby see a lower retail price for its product, the manufacturer may want to concentrate the resale of its products on a limited number of distributors. To do so, it could use exclusive distribution, quantity forcing in the form of a minimum purchasing requirement, selective distribution containing such a requirement or exclusive sourcing.

(h) "Capital market imperfections". The usual providers of capital (banks, equity markets) may provide capital sub-optimally when they have imperfect information on the quality of the borrower or there is an inadequate basis to secure the loan. The buyer or supplier may have better information and be able, through an exclusive relationship, to obtain extra security for its investment. Where the supplier provides the loan to the buyer, this may lead to non-compete or quantity forcing on the buyer. Where the buyer provides the loan to the supplier, this may be the reason for having exclusive supply or quantity forcing on the supplier.

(i) "Uniformity and quality standardisation". A vertical restraint may help to create a brand image by imposing a certain measure of uniformity and quality standardisation on the distributors, thereby increasing the attractiveness of the product to the final consumer and increasing its sales. This can for instance be found in selective distribution and franchising.

Notes

[1] Whether consumers actually benefit overall from extra promotional efforts depends on whether the extra promotion informs and convinces and thus benefits many new customers or mainly reaches customers who already know what they want to buy and for whom the extra promotion only or mainly implies a price increase.

[2] See however the previous footnote.

Commentary

para 107(a): **B&C:** 7.081 **F&N:** 9.209, 9.211
para 107(a)–(c) : **B&C:** 7.012
para 107(b) **F&N:** 3.179
para 107(c): **B&C:**.042
para 107(d): **B&C:** 7.082, 7.160, 7.161 **F&N:** 9.210
para 107(d)–(e): **B&C:** 7.013
para 107(e): **B&C:** 7.157, 7.161
para 107(f): **B&C:** 7.044
para 107(g): **B&C:** 7.081

para 107(g)–(i): B&C: 7.014
para 107(h): B&C: 7.161

(108) The nine situations listed in paragraph (107) make clear that under certain conditions, vertical agreements are likely to help realise efficiencies and the development of new markets and that this may offset possible negative effects. The case is in general strongest for vertical restraints of a limited duration which help the introduction of new complex products or protect relationship-specific investments. A vertical restraint is sometimes necessary for as long as the supplier sells its product to the buyer (see in particular the situations described in paragraph (107)(a), (e), (f), (g) and (i)).

(109) A large measure of substitutability exists between the different vertical restraints. As a result, the same inefficiency problem can be solved by different vertical restraints. For instance, economies of scale in distribution may possibly be achieved by using exclusive distribution, selective distribution, quantity forcing or exclusive sourcing. However, the negative effects on competition may differ between the various vertical restraints, which plays a role when indispensability is discussed under Article 101(3).

Commentary
para 109: B&C: 7.022

1.3. Methodology of analysis

(110) The assessment of a vertical restraint generally involves the following four steps:[1]

    (a) First, the undertakings involved need to establish the market shares of the supplier and the buyer on the market where they respectively sell and purchase the contract products.

    (b) If the relevant market share of the supplier and the buyer each do not exceed the 30% threshold, the vertical agreement is covered by the Block Exemption Regulation, subject to the hardcore restrictions and excluded restrictions set out in that Regulation.

    (c) If the relevant market share is above the 30% threshold for supplier and/or buyer, it is necessary to assess whether the vertical agreement falls within Article 101(1).

    (d) If the vertical agreement falls within Article 101(1), it is necessary to examine whether it fulfils the conditions for exemption under Article 101(3).

Notes
[1] These steps are not intended to present a legal reasoning that the Commission should follow in this order to take a decision.

1.3.1. Relevant factors for the assessment under Article 101(1)

(111) In assessing cases above the market share threshold of 30%, the Commission will undertake a full competition analysis. The following factors are particularly relevant to establish whether a vertical agreement brings about an appreciable restriction of competition under Article 101(1):

    (a) nature of the agreement;

    (b) market position of the parties;

    (c) market position of competitors;

    (d) market position of buyers of the contract products;

    (e) entry barriers;

    (f) maturity of the market;

    (g) level of trade;

    (h) nature of the product;

    (i) other factors.

Commentary
para 111: B&C: 2.128, 2.135

(112) The importance of individual factors may vary from case to case and depends on all other factors. For instance, a high market share of the parties is usually a good indicator of market

power, but in the case of low entry barriers it may not be indicative of market power. It is therefore not possible to provide firm rules on the importance of the individual factors.

Commentary
para 112: B&C: 2.168

(113) Vertical agreements can take many shapes and forms. It is therefore important to analyse the nature of the agreement in terms of the restraints that it contains, the duration of those restraints and the percentage of total sales on the market affected by those restraints. It may be necessary to go beyond the express terms of the agreement. The existence of implicit restraints may be derived from the way in which the agreement is implemented by the parties and the incentives that they face.

(114) The market position of the parties provides an indication of the degree of market power, if any, possessed by the supplier, the buyer or both. The higher their market share, the greater their market power is likely to be. This is particularly so where the market share reflects cost advantages or other competitive advantages vis-à-vis competitors. Such competitive advantages may, for instance, result from being a first mover on the market (having the best site, etc.), from holding essential patents or having superior technology, from being the brand leader or having a superior portfolio.

Commentary
para 114: B&C: 2.168

(115) Such indicators, namely market share and possible competitive advantages, are used to assess the market position of competitors. The stronger the competitors are and the greater their number, the less risk there is that the parties will be able to individually exercise market power and foreclose the market or soften competition. It is also relevant to consider whether there are effective and timely counterstrategies that competitors would be likely to deploy. However, if the number of competitors becomes rather small and their market position (size, costs, R&D potential, etc.) is rather similar, such a market structure may increase the risk of collusion. Fluctuating or rapidly changing market shares are in general an indication of intense competition.

(116) The market position of the parties' customers provides an indication of whether or not one or more of those customers possess buyer power. The first indicator of buyer power is the market share of the customer on the purchase market. That share reflects the importance of its demand for possible suppliers. Other indicators focus on the position of the customer on its resale market, including characteristics such as a wide geographic spread of its outlets, own brands including private labels and its brand image amongst final consumers. In some circumstances, buyer power may prevent the parties from exercising market power and thereby solve a competition problem that would otherwise have existed. This is particularly so when strong customers have the capacity and incentive to bring new sources of supply on to the market in the case of a small but permanent increase in relative prices. Where strong customers merely extract favourable terms for themselves or simply pass on any price increase to their customers, their position does not prevent the parties from exercising market power.

(117) Entry barriers are measured by the extent to which incumbent companies can increase their price above the competitive level without attracting new entry. In the absence of entry barriers, easy and quick entry would render price increases unprofitable. When effective entry, preventing or eroding the exercise of market power, is likely to occur within one or two years, entry barriers can, as a general rule, be said to be low. Entry barriers may result from a wide variety of factors such as economies of scale and scope, government regulations, especially where they establish exclusive rights, state aid, import tariffs, intellectual property rights, ownership of resources where the supply is limited due to for instance natural limitations,[1] essential facilities, a first mover advantage and brand loyalty of consumers created by strong advertising over a period of time. Vertical restraints and vertical integration may also work as an entry barrier by making access more difficult and foreclosing (potential) competitors. Entry barriers may be present at only the supplier or buyer level or at both levels. The question whether certain of

those factors should be described as entry barriers depends particularly on whether they entail sunk costs. Sunk costs are those costs that have to be incurred to enter or be active on a market but that are lost when the market is exited. Advertising costs to build consumer loyalty are normally sunk costs, unless an exiting firm could either sell its brand name or use it somewhere else without a loss. The more costs are sunk, the more potential entrants have to weigh the risks of entering the market and the more credibly incumbents can threaten that they will match new competition, as sunk costs make it costly for incumbents to leave the market. If, for instance, distributors are tied to a manufacturer via a non-compete obligation, the foreclosing effect will be more significant if setting up its own distributors will impose sunk costs on the potential entrant. In general, entry requires sunk costs, sometimes minor and sometimes major. Therefore, actual competition is in general more effective and will weigh more heavily in the assessment of a case than potential competition.

Notes

[1] See Commission Decision 97/26/EC (Case No IV/M.619 — *Gencor/Lonrho*), OJ L 11, 14.1.1997, p.30.

Commentary
para 117: B&C: 2.168

(118) A mature market is a market that has existed for some time, where the technology used is well known and widespread and not changing very much, where there are no major brand innovations and in which demand is relatively stable or declining. In such a market, negative effects are more likely than in more dynamic markets.

(119) The level of trade is linked to the distinction between intermediate and final goods and services. Intermediate goods and services are sold to undertakings for use as an input to produce other goods or services and are generally not recognisable in the final goods or services. The buyers of intermediate products are usually well-informed customers, able to assess quality and therefore less reliant on brand and image. Final goods are, directly or indirectly, sold to final consumers that often rely more on brand and image. As distributors have to respond to the demand of final consumers, competition may suffer more when distributors are foreclosed from selling one or a number of brands than when buyers of intermediate products are prevented from buying competing products from certain sources of supply.

(120) The nature of the product plays a role in particular for final products in assessing both the likely negative and the likely positive effects. When assessing the likely negative effects, it is important whether the products on the market are more homogeneous or heterogeneous, whether the product is expensive, taking up a large part of the consumer's budget, or is inexpensive and whether the product is a one-off purchase or repeatedly purchased. In general, when the product is more heterogeneous, less expensive and resembles more a one-off purchase, vertical restraints are more likely to have negative effects.

Commentary
para 120: F&N: 9.196

(121) In the assessment of particular restraints other factors may have to be taken into account. Among these factors can be the cumulative effect, that is, the coverage of the market by similar agreements of others, whether the agreement is "imposed" (mainly one party is subject to the restrictions or obligations) or "agreed" (both parties accept restrictions or obligations), the regulatory environment and behaviour that may indicate or facilitate collusion like price leadership, pre-announced price changes and discussions on the "right" price, price rigidity in response to excess capacity, price discrimination and past collusive behaviour.

1.3.2. Relevant factors for the assessment under Article 101(3)

(122) Restrictive vertical agreements may also produce pro-competitive effects in the form of efficiencies, which may outweigh their anti-competitive effects. Such an assessment takes place within the framework of Article 101(3), which contains an exception from the prohibition rule of Article 101(1). For that exception to be applicable, the vertical agreement must produce objective economic benefits, the restrictions on competition must be indispensable to attain

the efficiencies, consumers must receive a fair share of the efficiency gains, and the agreement must not afford the parties the possibility of eliminating competition in respect of a substantial part of the products concerned.[1]

Notes

[1] See Communication from the Commission — Notice — Guidelines on the application of Article [101](3) of the Treaty, OJ C 101, 27.4.2004, p.97.

Commentary
para 122: F&N: 9.201

(123) The assessment of restrictive agreements under Article 101(3) is made within the actual context in which they occur[1] and on the basis of the facts existing at any given point in time. The assessment is sensitive to material changes in the facts. The exception rule of Article 101(3) applies as long as the four conditions are fulfilled and ceases to apply when that is no longer the case.[2] When applying Article 101(3) in accordance with these principles it is necessary to take into account the investments made by any of the parties and the time needed and the restraints required to commit and recoup an efficiency enhancing investment.

Notes

[1] See Judgment of the Court of Justice in Joined Cases 25/84 and 26/84 *Ford* [1985] ECR 2725.
[2] See in this respect for example Commission Decision 1999/242/EC (Case No IV/36.237 — *TPS*), OJ L 90, 2.4.1999, p.6. Similarly, the prohibition of Article 101(1) also only applies as long as the agreement has a restrictive object or restrictive effects.

Commentary
para 123: B&C: 3.017

(124) The first condition of Article 101(3) requires an assessment of what are the objective benefits in terms of efficiencies produced by the agreement. In this respect, vertical agreements often have the potential to help realise efficiencies, as explained in section 1.2, by improving the way in which the parties conduct their complementary activities.

(125) In the application of the indispensability test contained in Article 101(3), the Commission will in particular examine whether individual restrictions make it possible to perform the production, purchase and/or (re)sale of the contract products more efficiently than would have been the case in the absence of the restriction concerned. In making such an assessment, the market conditions and the realities facing the parties must be taken into account. Undertakings invoking the benefit of Article 101(3) are not required to consider hypothetical and theoretical alternatives. They must, however, explain and demonstrate why seemingly realistic and significantly less restrictive alternatives would be significantly less efficient. If the application of what appears to be a commercially realistic and less restrictive alternative would lead to a significant loss of efficiencies, the restriction in question is treated as indispensable.

Commentary
para 125: B&C: 3.063 F&N: 9.208

(126) The condition that consumers must receive a fair share of the benefits implies that consumers of the products purchased and/or (re)sold under the vertical agreement must at least be compensated for the negative effects of the agreement.[1] In other words, the efficiency gains must fully off-set the likely negative impact on prices, output and other relevant factors caused by the agreement.

Notes

[1] See paragraph 85 of Communication from the Commission — Notice — Guidelines on the application of Article [101](3) of the Treaty, OJ C 101, 27.4.2004, p.97.

(127) The last condition of Article 101(3), according to which the agreement must not afford the parties the possibility of eliminating competition in respect of a substantial part of the products concerned, presupposes an analysis of remaining competitive pressures on the market and the

impact of the agreement on such sources of competition. In the application of the last condition of Article 101(3), the relationship between Article 101(3) and Article 102 must be taken into account. According to settled case law, the application of Article 101(3) cannot prevent the application of Article 102.[1] Moreover, since Articles 101 and 102 both pursue the aim of maintaining effective competition on the market, consistency requires that Article 101(3) be interpreted as precluding any application of the exception rule to restrictive agreements that constitute an abuse of a dominant position.[2] The vertical agreement may not eliminate effective competition, by removing all or most existing sources of actual or potential competition. Rivalry between undertakings is an essential driver of economic efficiency, including dynamic efficiencies in the form of innovation. In its absence, the dominant undertaking will lack adequate incentives to continue to create and pass on efficiency gains. Where there is no residual competition and no foreseeable threat of entry, the protection of rivalry and the competitive process outweighs possible efficiency gains. A restrictive agreement which maintains, creates or strengthens a market position approaching that of a monopoly can normally not be justified on the grounds that it also creates efficiency gains.

Notes

[1] See Judgment of the Court of Justice in Joined Cases C-395/96 P and C-396/96 P *Compagnie Maritime Belge* [2000] ECR I-1365, paragraph 130. Similarly, the application of Article 101(3) does not prevent the application of the Treaty rules on the free movement of goods, services, persons and capital. These provisions are in certain circumstances applicable to agreements, decisions and concerted practices within the meaning of Article 101(1), see to that effect Judgment of the Court of Justice in Case C-309/99 *Wouters* [2002] ECR I-1577, paragraph 120.

[2] See in this respect Judgment of the Court of First Instance in Case T-51/89 *Tetra Pak (I)* [1990] ECR II-309. See also paragraph 106 of Communication from the Commission — Notice — Guidelines on the application of Article [101] (3) of the Treaty, OJ C 101, 27.4.2004, p.97.

Commentary
para 127: B&C: 3.067, 7.022 **F&N:** 9.212, 9.213

2. Analysis of specific vertical restraints

(128) The most common vertical restraints and combinations of vertical restraints are analysed in the remainder of these Guidelines following the framework of analysis developed in paragraphs (96) to (127). Other restraints and combinations exist for which no direct guidance is provided in these Guidelines. They will, however, be treated according to the same principles and with the same emphasis on the effect on the market.

2.1. Single branding

(129) Under the heading of "single branding" fall those agreements which have as their main element the fact that the buyer is obliged or induced to concentrate its orders for a particular type of product with one supplier. That component can be found amongst others in non-compete and quantity-forcing on the buyer. A non-compete arrangement is based on an obligation or incentive scheme which makes the buyer purchase more than 80% of its requirements on a particular market from only one supplier. It does not mean that the buyer can only buy directly from the supplier, but that the buyer will not buy and resell or incorporate competing goods or services. Quantity-forcing on the buyer is a weaker form of non-compete, where incentives or obligations agreed between the supplier and the buyer make the latter concentrate its purchases to a large extent with one supplier. Quantity-forcing may for example take the form of minimum purchase requirements, stocking requirements or non-linear pricing, such as conditional rebate schemes or a two-part tariff (fixed fee plus a price per unit). A so-called "English clause", requiring the buyer to report any better offer and allowing him only to accept such an offer when the supplier does not match it, can be expected to have the same effect as a single branding obligation, especially when the buyer has to reveal who makes the better offer.

Commentary
para 129: B&C: 7.143, 7.147, 7.158 **F&N:** 4.403, 9.214, 12.74, 12.75

(130) The possible competition risks of single branding are foreclosure of the market to competing suppliers and potential suppliers, softening of competition and facilitation of collusion between suppliers in case of cumulative use and, where the buyer is a retailer selling to final consumers, a loss of in-store inter-brand competition. Such restrictive effects have a direct impact on inter-brand competition.

Commentary
para 130: B&C: 7.158 F&N: 9.217

(131) Single branding is exempted by the Block Exemption Regulation where the supplier's and buyer's market share each do not exceed 30% and are subject to a limitation in time of five years for the non-compete obligation. The remainder of this section provides guidance for the assessment of individual cases above the market share threshold or beyond the time limit of five years.

(132) The capacity for single branding obligations of one specific supplier to result in anticompetitive foreclosure arises in particular where, without the obligations, an important competitive constraint is exercised by competitors that either are not yet present on the market at the time the obligations are concluded, or that are not in a position to compete for the full supply of the customers. Competitors may not be able to compete for an individual customer's entire demand because the supplier in question is an unavoidable trading partner at least for part of the demand on the market, for instance because its brand is a "must stock item" preferred by many final consumers or because the capacity constraints on the other suppliers are such that a part of demand can only be provided for by the supplier in question.[1] The market position of the supplier is thus of main importance to assess possible anti-competitive effects of single branding obligations.

Notes

[1] Judgment of the Court of First Instance in Case T-65/98 *Van den Bergh Foods v Commission* [2003] ECR II-4653, paragraphs 104 and 156.

Commentary
para 132: B&C: 2.100 F&N: 9.220

(133) If competitors can compete on equal terms for each individual customer's entire demand, single branding obligations of one specific supplier are generally unlikely to hamper effective competition unless the switching of supplier by customers is rendered difficult due to the duration and market coverage of the single branding obligations. The higher its tied market share, that is, the part of its market share sold under a single branding obligation, the more significant foreclosure is likely to be. Similarly, the longer the duration of the single branding obligations, the more significant foreclosure is likely to be. Single branding obligations shorter than one year entered into by non-dominant companies are generally not considered to give rise to appreciable anti-competitive effects or net negative effects. Single branding obligations between one and five years entered into by non-dominant companies usually require a proper balancing of pro-and anti-competitive effects, while single branding obligations exceeding five years are for most types of investments not considered necessary to achieve the claimed efficiencies or the efficiencies are not sufficient to outweigh their foreclosure effect. Single branding obligations are more likely to result in anti-competitive foreclosure when entered into by dominant companies.

Commentary
para 133: B&C: 2.100, 7.157, 7.158 F&N: 9.221

(134) When assessing the supplier's market power, the market position of its competitors is important. As long as the competitors are sufficiently numerous and strong, no appreciable anti-competitive effects can be expected. Foreclosure of competitors is not very likely where they have similar market positions and can offer similarly attractive products. In such a case, foreclosure may, however, occur for potential entrants when a number of major suppliers enter into single branding contracts with a significant number of buyers on the relevant market

(cumulative effect situation). This is also a situation where single branding agreements may facilitate collusion between competing suppliers. If, individually, those suppliers are covered by the Block Exemption Regulation, a withdrawal of the block exemption may be necessary to deal with such a negative cumulative effect. A tied market share of less than 5% is not considered in general to contribute significantly to a cumulative foreclosure effect.

Commentary
para 134: **B&C:** 7.154 **F&N:** 9.226

(135) In cases where the market share of the largest supplier is below 30% and the market share of the five largest suppliers is below 50%, there is unlikely to be a single or a cumulative anti-competitive effect situation. Where a potential entrant cannot penetrate the market profitably, it is likely to be due to factors other than single branding obligations, such as consumer preferences.

Commentary
para 135: **B&C:** 7.154 **F&N:** 9.226

(136) Entry barriers are important to establish whether there is anticompetitive foreclosure. Wherever it is relatively easy for competing suppliers to create new buyers or find alternative buyers for their product, foreclosure is unlikely to be a real problem. However, there are often entry barriers, both at the manufacturing and at the distribution level.

Commentary
para 136: **B&C:** 2.100

(137) Countervailing power is relevant, as powerful buyers will not easily allow themselves to be cut off from the supply of competing goods or services. More generally, in order to convince customers to accept single branding, the supplier may have to compensate them, in whole or in part, for the loss in competition resulting from the exclusivity. Where such compensation is given, it may be in the individual interest of a customer to enter into a single branding obligation with the supplier. But it would be wrong to conclude automatically from this that all single branding obligations, taken together, are overall beneficial for customers on that market and for the final consumers. It is in particular unlikely that consumers as a whole will benefit if there are many customers and the single branding obligations, taken together, have the effect of preventing the entry or expansion of competing undertakings.

Commentary
para 137: **F&N:** 9.228

(138) Lastly, "the level of trade" is relevant. Anticompetitive foreclosure is less likely in case of an intermediate product. When the supplier of an intermediate product is not dominant, the competing suppliers still have a substantial part of demand that is free. Below the level of dominance an anticompetitive foreclosure effect may however arise in a cumulative effect situation. A cumulative anticompetitive effect is unlikely to arise as long as less than 50% of the market is tied.

Commentary
para 138: **B&C:** 2.100, 7.154, 7.164

(139) Where the agreement concerns the supply of a final product at the wholesale level, the question whether a competition problem is likely to arise depends in large part on the type of wholesaling and the entry barriers at the wholesale level. There is no real risk of anticompetitive foreclosure if competing manufacturers can easily establish their own wholesaling operation. Whether entry barriers are low depends in part on the type of wholesaling, that is, whether or not wholesalers can operate efficiently with only the product concerned by the agreement (for example ice cream) or whether it is more efficient to trade in a whole range of products (for example frozen foodstuffs). In the latter case, it is not efficient for a manufacturer selling

only one product to set up its own wholesaling operation. In that case, anti-competitive effects may arise. In addition, cumulative effect problems may arise if several suppliers tie most of the available wholesalers.

Commentary
para 139: B&C: 2.100, 7.164

(140) For final products, foreclosure is in general more likely to occur at the retail level, given the significant entry barriers for most manufacturers to start retail outlets just for their own products. In addition, it is at the retail level that single branding agreements may lead to reduced in-store inter-brand competition. It is for these reasons that for final products at the retail level, significant anti-competitive effects may start to arise, taking into account all other relevant factors, if a non-dominant supplier ties 30% or more of the relevant market. For a dominant company, even a modest tied market share may already lead to significant anti-competitive effects.

Commentary
para 140: B&C: 7.164 **F&N:** 9.232, 12.79

(141) At the retail level, a cumulative foreclosure effect may also arise. Where all suppliers have market shares below 30%, a cumulative anticompetitive foreclosure effect is unlikely if the total tied market share is less than 40% and withdrawal of the block exemption is therefore unlikely. That figure may be higher when other factors like the number of competitors, entry barriers etc. are taken into account. Where not all companies have market shares below the threshold of the Block Exemption Regulation but none is dominant, a cumulative anticompetitive foreclosure effect is unlikely if the total tied market share is below 30%.

Commentary
para 141: B&C: 2.100, 7.154, 7.164 **F&N:** 9.233

(142) Where the buyer operates from premises and land owned by the supplier or leased by the supplier from a third party not connected with the buyer, the possibility of imposing effective remedies for a possible foreclosure effect will be limited. In that case, intervention by the Commission below the level of dominance is unlikely.

Commentary
para 142: F&N: 9.223

(143) In certain sectors, the selling of more than one brand from a single site may be difficult, in which case a foreclosure problem can better be remedied by limiting the effective duration of contracts.

(144) Where appreciable anti-competitive effects are established, the question of a possible exemption under Article 101(3) arises. For non-compete obligations, the efficiencies described in points (a) (free riding between suppliers), (d), (e) (hold-up problems) and (h) (capital market imperfections) of paragraph (107), may be particularly relevant.

Commentary
para 144: B&C: 7.161 **F&N:** 9.234

(145) In the case of an efficiency as described in paragraph (107)(a), (107)(d) and (107)(h), quantity forcing on the buyer could possibly be a less restrictive alternative. A non-compete obligation may be the only viable way to achieve an efficiency as described in paragraph (107)(e), (hold-up problem related to the transfer of know-how).

Commentary
para 145: B&C: 7.161

(146) In the case of a relationship-specific investment made by the supplier (see paragraph (107)(d)), a non-compete or quantity forcing agreement for the period of depreciation of the investment will in general fulfil the conditions of Article 101(3). In the case of high relationship-specific investments, a non-compete obligation exceeding five years may be justified. A relationship-specific investment could, for instance, be the installation or adaptation of equipment by the supplier when this equipment can be used afterwards only to produce components for a particular buyer. General or market-specific investments in (extra) capacity are normally not relationship-specific investments. However, where a supplier creates new capacity specifically linked to the operations of a particular buyer, for instance a company producing metal cans which creates new capacity to produce cans on the premises of or next to the canning facility of a food producer, this new capacity may only be economically viable when producing for this particular customer, in which case the investment would be considered to be relationship-specific.

Commentary
para 146: **B&C:** 7.161 **F&N:** 10.156

(147) Where the supplier provides the buyer with a loan or provides the buyer with equipment which is not relationship-specific, this in itself is normally not sufficient to justify the exemption of an anticompetitive foreclosure effect on the market. In case of capital market imperfection, it may be more efficient for the supplier of a product than for a bank to provide a loan (see paragraph (107)(h)). However, in such a case the loan should be provided in the least restrictive way and the buyer should thus in general not be prevented from terminating the obligation and repaying the outstanding part of the loan at any point in time and without payment of any penalty.

Commentary
para 147: **B&C:** 2.100, 7.161 **F&N:** 9.234

(148) The transfer of substantial know-how (paragraph (107)(e)) usually justifies a non-compete obligation for the whole duration of the supply agreement, as for example in the context of franchising.

Commentary
para 148: **B&C:** 7.157, 7.161

(149) <u>Example of non-compete obligation</u>

The market leader in a national market for an impulse consumer product, with a market share of 40%, sells most of its products (90%) through tied retailers (tied market share 36%). The agreements oblige the retailers to purchase only from the market leader for at least four years. The market leader is especially strongly represented in the more densely populated areas like the capital. Its competitors, 10 in number, of which some are only locally available, all have much smaller market shares, the biggest having 12%. Those 10 competitors together supply another 10% of the market via tied outlets. There is strong brand and product differentiation in the market. The market leader has the strongest brands. It is the only one with regular national advertising campaigns. It provides its tied retailers with special stocking cabinets for its product.

The result on the market is that in total 46% (36% + 10%) of the market is foreclosed to potential entrants and to incumbents not having tied outlets. Potential entrants find entry even more difficult in the densely populated areas where foreclosure is even higher, although it is there that they would prefer to enter the market. In addition, owing to the strong brand and product differentiation and the high search costs relative to the price of the product, the absence of in-store inter-brand competition leads to an extra welfare loss for consumers. The possible efficiencies of the outlet exclusivity, which the market leader claims result from reduced transport costs and a possible hold-up problem concerning the stocking cabinets, are limited and do not outweigh the negative effects on competition. The efficiencies are limited, as the transport costs are linked to quantity and not exclusivity and the stocking cabinets do not contain

Part C Substantive Antitrust Matters

special know-how and are not brand specific. Accordingly, it is unlikely that the conditions of Article 101(3) are fulfilled.

(150) Example of quantity forcing

A producer X with a 40% market share sells 80% of its products through contracts which specify that the reseller is required to purchase at least 75% of its requirements for that type of product from X. In return X is offering financing and equipment at favourable rates. The contracts have a duration of five years in which repayment of the loan is foreseen in equal instalments. However, after the first two years buyers have the possibility to terminate the contract with a six-month notice period if they repay the outstanding loan and take over the equipment at its market asset value. At the end of the five-year period the equipment becomes the property of the buyer. Most of the competing producers are small, twelve in total with the biggest having a market share of 20%, and engage in similar contracts with different durations. The producers with market shares below 10% often have contracts with longer durations and with less generous termination clauses. The contracts of producer X leave 25% of requirements free to be supplied by competitors. In the last three years, two new producers have entered the market and gained a combined market share of around 8%, partly by taking over the loans of a number of resellers in return for contracts with these resellers.

Producer X's tied market share is 24% (0,75 × 0,80 × 40%). The other producers' tied market share is around 25%. Therefore, in total around 49% of the market is foreclosed to potential entrants and to incumbents not having tied outlets for at least the first two years of the supply contracts. The market shows that the resellers often have difficulty in obtaining loans from banks and are too small in general to obtain capital through other means like the issuing of shares. In addition, producer X is able to demonstrate that concentrating its sales on a limited number of resellers allows him to plan its sales better and to save transport costs. In the light of the efficiencies on the one hand and the 25% non-tied part in the contracts of producer X, the real possibility for early termination of the contract, the recent entry of new producers and the fact that around half the resellers are not tied on the other hand, the quantity forcing of 75% applied by producer X is likely to fulfil the conditions of Article 101(3).

Commentary
para 150: B&C: 7.161

2.2. Exclusive distribution

(151) In an exclusive distribution agreement, the supplier agrees to sell its products to only one distributor for resale in a particular territory. At the same time, the distributor is usually limited in its active selling into other (exclusively allocated) territories. The possible competition risks are mainly reduced intra-brand competition and market partitioning, which may facilitate price discrimination in particular. When most or all of the suppliers apply exclusive distribution, it may soften competition and facilitate collusion, both at the suppliers' and distributors' level. Lastly, exclusive distribution may lead to foreclosure of other distributors and therewith reduce competition at that level.

Commentary
para 151: B&C: 7.064, 7.075 **F&N:** 9.235

(152) Exclusive distribution is exempted by the Block Exemption Regulation where both the supplier's and buyer's market share each do not exceed 30%, even if combined with other non-hardcore vertical restraints, such as a non-compete obligation limited to five years, quantity forcing or exclusive purchasing. A combination of exclusive distribution and selective distribution is only exempted by the Block Exemption Regulation if active selling in other territories is not restricted. The remainder of this section provides guidance for the assessment of exclusive distribution in individual cases above the 30% market share threshold.

Commentary
para 152: B&C: 7.079, 7.110

(153) The market position of the supplier and its competitors is of major importance, as the loss of intra-brand competition can only be problematic if inter-brand competition is limited. The stronger the position of the supplier, the more serious is the loss of intra-brand competition. Above the 30% market share threshold, there may be a risk of a significant reduction of intra-brand competition. In order to fulfil the conditions of Article 101(3), the loss of intra-brand competition may need to be balanced with real efficiencies.

Commentary
para 153: F&N: 9.238, 12.83

(154) The position of the competitors can have a dual significance. Strong competitors will generally mean that the reduction in intra-brand competition is outweighed by sufficient inter-brand competition. However, if the number of competitors becomes rather small and their market position is rather similar in terms of market share, capacity and distribution network, there is a risk of collusion and/or softening of competition. The loss of intra-brand competition can increase that risk, especially when several suppliers operate similar distribution systems. Multiple exclusive dealerships, that is, when different suppliers appoint the same exclusive distributor in a given territory, may further increase the risk of collusion and/or softening of competition. If a dealer is granted the exclusive right to distribute two or more important competing products in the same territory, inter-brand competition may be substantially restricted for those brands. The higher the cumulative market share of the brands distributed by the exclusive multiple brand dealers, the higher the risk of collusion and/or softening of competition and the more inter-brand competition will be reduced. If a retailer is the exclusive distributor for a number of brands this may have as result that if one producer cuts the wholesale price for its brand, the exclusive retailer will not be eager to transmit this price cut to the final consumer as it would reduce its sales and profits made with the other brands. Hence, compared to the situation without multiple exclusive dealerships, producers have a reduced interest in entering into price competition with one another. Such cumulative effect situations may be a reason to withdraw the benefit of the Block Exemption Regulation where the market shares of the suppliers and buyers are below the threshold of the Block Exemption Regulation.

Commentary
para 154: B&C: 7.075 F&N: 9.239

(155) Entry barriers that may hinder suppliers from creating new distributors or finding alternative distributors are less important in assessing the possible anti-competitive effects of exclusive distribution. Foreclosure of other suppliers does not arise as long as exclusive distribution is not combined with single branding.

Commentary
para 155: B&C: 7.079

(156) Foreclosure of other distributors is not an issue where the supplier which operates the exclusive distribution system appoints a high number of exclusive distributors on the same market and those exclusive distributors are not restricted in selling to other non-appointed distributors. Foreclosure of other distributors may however become an issue where there is buying power and market power downstream, in particular in the case of very large territories where the exclusive distributor becomes the exclusive buyer for a whole market. An example would be a supermarket chain which becomes the only distributor of a leading brand on a national food retail market. The foreclosure of other distributors may be aggravated in the case of multiple exclusive dealership.

Commentary
para 156: B&C: 7.076 F&N: 9.240, 12.83

(157) Buying power may also increase the risk of collusion on the buyers' side when the exclusive distribution arrangements are imposed by important buyers, possibly located in different territories, on one or several suppliers.

Part C Substantive
Antitrust Matters

539

Commentary
para 157: **F&N:** 9.240

(158) Maturity of the market is important, as loss of intra-brand competition and price discrimination may be a serious problem in a mature market but may be less relevant on a market with growing demand, changing technologies and changing market positions.

Commentary
para 158: **B&C:** 7.076

(159) The level of trade is important as the possible negative effects may differ between the wholesale and retail level. Exclusive distribution is mainly applied in the distribution of final goods and services. A loss of intra-brand competition is especially likely at the retail level if coupled with large territories, since final consumers may be confronted with little possibility of choosing between a high price/high service and a low price/low service distributor for an important brand.

Commentary
para 159: **B&C:** 7.076

(160) A manufacturer that chooses a wholesaler to be its exclusive distributor will normally do so for a larger territory, such as a whole Member State. As long as the wholesaler can sell the products without limitation to downstream retailers there are not likely to be appreciable anti-competitive effects. A possible loss of intra-brand competition at the wholesale level may be easily outweighed by efficiencies obtained in logistics, promotion etc., especially when the manufacturer is based in a different country. The possible risks for inter-brand competition of multiple exclusive dealerships are however higher at the wholesale than at the retail level. Where one wholesaler becomes the exclusive distributor for a significant number of suppliers, not only is there a risk that competition between these brands is reduced, but also that there is foreclosure at the wholesale level of trade.

Commentary
para 160: **B&C:** 7.079, 7.110 **F&N:** 9.241

(161) As stated in paragraph (155), foreclosure of other suppliers does not arise as long as exclusive distribution is not combined with single branding. But even when exclusive distribution is combined with single branding anticompetitive foreclosure of other suppliers is unlikely, except possibly when the single branding is applied to a dense network of exclusive distributors with small territories or in case of a cumulative effect. In such a case it may be necessary to apply the principles on single branding set out in section 2.1. However, when the combination does not lead to significant foreclosure, the combination of exclusive distribution and single branding may be pro-competitive by increasing the incentive for the exclusive distributor to focus its efforts on the particular brand. Therefore, in the absence of such a foreclosure effect, the combination of exclusive distribution with non-compete may very well fulfil the conditions of Article 101(3) for the whole duration of the agreement, particularly at the wholesale level.

Commentary
para 161: **B&C:** 2.100, 7.079, 7.165

(162) The combination of exclusive distribution with exclusive sourcing increases the possible competition risks of reduced intra-brand competition and market partitioning which may facilitate price discrimination in particular. Exclusive distribution already limits arbitrage by customers, as it limits the number of distributors and usually also restricts the distributors in their freedom of active selling. Exclusive sourcing, requiring the exclusive distributors to buy their supplies for the particular brand directly from the manufacturer, eliminates in addition possible arbitrage by the exclusive distributors, which are prevented from buying from other distributors in the system. As a result, the supplier's possibilities to limit intra-brand

competition by applying dissimilar conditions of sale to the detriment of consumers are enhanced, unless the combination allows the creation of efficiencies leading to lower prices to all final consumers.

Commentary
para 162: **B&C:** 7.079, 7.141, 7.165 **F&N:** 9.243

---

(163) The nature of the product is not particularly relevant to the assessment of possible anti-competitive effects of exclusive distribution. It is, however, relevant to an assessment of possible efficiencies, that is, after an appreciable anti-competitive effect is established.

(164) Exclusive distribution may lead to efficiencies, especially where investments by the distributors are required to protect or build up the brand image. In general, the case for efficiencies is strongest for new products, complex products, and products whose qualities are difficult to judge before consumption (so-called experience products) or whose qualities are difficult to judge even after consumption (so-called credence products). In addition, exclusive distribution may lead to savings in logistic costs due to economies of scale in transport and distribution.

Commentary
para 164: **B&C:** 7.081 **F&N:** 9.244

---

(165) Example of exclusive distribution at the wholesale level
On the market for a consumer durable, A is the market leader. A sells its product through exclusive wholesalers. Territories for the wholesalers correspond to the entire Member State for small Member States, and to a region for larger Member States. Those exclusive distributors deal with sales to all the retailers in their territories. They do not sell to final consumers. The wholesalers are in charge of promotion in their markets, including sponsoring of local events, but also explaining and promoting the new products to the retailers in their territories. Technology and product innovation are evolving fairly quickly on this market, and pre-sale service to retailers and to final consumers plays an important role. The wholesalers are not required to purchase all their requirements of the brand of supplier A from the producer himself, and arbitrage by wholesalers or retailers is practicable because the transport costs are relatively low compared to the value of the product. The wholesalers are not under a non-compete obligation. Retailers also sell a number of brands of competing suppliers, and there are no exclusive or selective distribution agreements at the retail level. On the EU market of sales to wholesalers A has around 50% market share. Its market share on the various national retail markets varies between 40% and 60%. A has between 6 and 10 competitors on every national market. B, C and D are its biggest competitors and are also present on each national market, with market shares varying between 20% and 5%. The remaining producers are national producers, with smaller market shares. B, C and D have similar distribution networks, whereas the local producers tend to sell their products directly to retailers.
On the wholesale market described in this example, the risk of reduced intra-brand competition and price discrimination is low. Arbitrage is not hindered, and the absence of intra-brand competition is not very relevant at the wholesale level. At the retail level, neither intra-nor inter-brand competition are hindered. Moreover, inter-brand competition is largely unaffected by the exclusive arrangements at the wholesale level. Therefore it is likely, even if anti-competitive effects exist, that also the conditions of Article 101(3) are fulfilled.

(166) Example of multiple exclusive dealerships in an oligopolistic market
On a national market for a final product, there are four market leaders, which each have a market share of around 20%. Those four market leaders sell their product through exclusive distributors at the retail level. Retailers are given an exclusive territory which corresponds to the town in which they are located or a district of the town for large towns. In most territories, the four market leaders happen to appoint the same exclusive retailer ("multiple dealership"), often centrally located and rather specialised in the product. The remaining 20% of the national market is composed of small local producers, the largest of these producers having a market share of 5% on the national market. Those local producers sell their products in general through

other retailers, in particular because the exclusive distributors of the four largest suppliers show in general little interest in selling less well-known and cheaper brands. There is strong brand and product differentiation on the market. The four market leaders have large national advertising campaigns and strong brand images, whereas the fringe producers do not advertise their products at the national level. The market is rather mature, with stable demand and no major product and technological innovation. The product is relatively simple.

In such an oligopolistic market, there is a risk of collusion between the four market leaders. That risk is increased through multiple dealerships. Intra-brand competition is limited by the territorial exclusivity. Competition between the four leading brands is reduced at the retail level, since one retailer fixes the price of all four brands in each territory. The multiple dealership implies that, if one producer cuts the price for its brand, the retailer will not be eager to transmit this price cut to the final consumer as it would reduce its sales and profits made with the other brands. Hence, producers have a reduced interest in entering into price competition with one another. Inter-brand price competition exists mainly with the low brand image goods of the fringe producers. The possible efficiency arguments for (joint) exclusive distributors are limited, as the product is relatively simple, the resale does not require any specific investments or training and advertising is mainly carried out at the level of the producers.

Even though each of the market leaders has a market share below the threshold, the conditions of Article 101(3) may not be fulfilled and withdrawal of the block exemption may be necessary for the agreements concluded with distributors whose market share is below 30% of the procurement market.

Commentary
para 166: **B&C:** 7.076

---

(167) Example of exclusive distribution combined with exclusive sourcing

Manufacturer A is the European market leader for a bulky consumer durable, with a market share of between 40% and 60% in most national retail markets. In Member States where it has a high market share, it has less competitors with much smaller market shares. The competitors are present on only one or two national markets. A's long time policy is to sell its product through its national subsidiaries to exclusive distributors at the retail level, which are not allowed to sell actively into each other's territories. Those distributors are thereby incentivised to promote the product and provide pre-sales services. Recently the retailers are in addition obliged to purchase manufacturer A's products exclusively from the national subsidiary of manufacturer A in their own country. The retailers selling the brand of manufacturer A are the main resellers of that type of product in their territory. They handle competing brands, but with varying degrees of success and enthusiasm. Since the introduction of exclusive sourcing, A applies price differences of 10% to 15% between markets with higher prices in the markets where it has less competition. The markets are relatively stable on the demand and the supply side, and there are no significant technological changes.

In the high price markets, the loss of intra-brand competition results not only from the territorial exclusivity at the retail level but is aggravated by the exclusive sourcing obligation imposed on the retailers. The exclusive sourcing obligation helps to keep markets and territories separate by making arbitrage between the exclusive retailers, the main resellers of that type of product, impossible. The exclusive retailers also cannot sell actively into each other's territory and in practice tend to avoid delivering outside their own territory. As a result, price discrimination is possible, without it leading to a significant increase in total sales. Arbitrage by consumers or independent traders is limited due to the bulkiness of the product.

While the possible efficiency arguments for appointing exclusive distributors may be convincing, in particular because of the incentivising of retailers, the possible efficiency arguments for the combination of exclusive distribution and exclusive sourcing, and in particular the possible efficiency arguments for exclusive sourcing, linked mainly to economies of scale in transport, are unlikely to outweigh the negative effect of price discrimination and reduced intra-brand competition. Consequently, it is unlikely that the conditions of Article 101(3) are fulfilled.

2.3. Exclusive customer allocation

(168) In an exclusive customer allocation agreement, the supplier agrees to sell its products to only one distributor for resale to a particular group of customers. At the same time, the distributor is usually limited in its active selling to other (exclusively allocated) groups of customers. The Block Exemption Regulation does not limit the way an exclusive customer group can be defined; it could for instance be a particular type of customers defined by their occupation but also a list of specific customers selected on the basis of one or more objective criteria. The possible competition risks are mainly reduced intra-brand competition and market partitioning, which may in particular facilitate price discrimination. Where most or all of the suppliers apply exclusive customer allocation, competition may be softened and collusion, both at the suppliers' and the distributors' level, may be facilitated. Lastly, exclusive customer allocation may lead to foreclosure of other distributors and therewith reduce competition at that level.

Commentary
para 168: B&C: 7.064

(169) Exclusive customer allocation is exempted by the Block Exemption Regulation when both the supplier's and buyer's market share does not exceed the 30% market share threshold, even if combined with other non-hardcore vertical restraints such as non-compete, quantity-forcing or exclusive sourcing. A combination of exclusive customer allocation and selective distribution is normally a hardcore restriction, as active selling to end-users by the appointed distributors is usually not left free. Above the 30% market share threshold, the guidance provided in paragraphs (151) to (167) applies also to the assessment of exclusive customer allocation, subject to the specific remarks in the remainder of this section.

Commentary
para 169: B&C: 7.075, 7.079, 7.112

(170) The allocation of customers normally makes arbitrage by the customers more difficult. In addition, as each appointed distributor has its own class of customers, non-appointed distributors not falling within such a class may find it difficult to obtain the product. Consequently, possible arbitrage by non-appointed distributors will be reduced.

Commentary
para 170: B&C: 7.160

(171) Exclusive customer allocation is mainly applied to intermediate products and at the wholesale level when it concerns final products, where customer groups with different specific requirements concerning the product can be distinguished.

(172) Exclusive customer allocation may lead to efficiencies, especially when the distributors are required to make investments in for instance specific equipment, skills or know-how to adapt to the requirements of their group of customers. The depreciation period of these investments indicates the justified duration of an exclusive customer allocation system. In general the case is strongest for new or complex products and for products requiring adaptation to the needs of the individual customer. Identifiable differentiated needs are more likely for intermediate products, that is, products sold to different types of professional buyers. Allocation of final consumers is unlikely to lead to efficiencies.

Commentary
para 172: B&C: 7.082 F&N: 9.247

(173) <u>Example of exclusive customer allocation</u>
A company has developed a sophisticated sprinkler installation. The company has currently a market share of 40% on the market for sprinkler installations. When it started selling the sophisticated sprinkler it had a market share of 20% with an older product. The installation of the new type of sprinkler depends on the type of building that it is installed in and on the use of the building (office, chemical plant, hospital etc.). The company has appointed a number of

Part C Substantive Antitrust Matters

distributors to sell and install the sprinkler installation. Each distributor needed to train its employees for the general and specific requirements of installing the sprinkler installation for a particular class of customers. To ensure that distributors would specialise, the company assigned to each distributor an exclusive class of customers and prohibited active sales to each others' exclusive customer classes. After five years, all the exclusive distributors will be allowed to sell actively to all classes of customers, thereby ending the system of exclusive customer allocation. The supplier may then also start selling to new distributors. The market is quite dynamic, with two recent entries and a number of technological developments. Competitors, with market shares between 25% and 5%, are also upgrading their products.

As the exclusivity is of limited duration and helps to ensure that the distributors may recoup their investments and concentrate their sales efforts first on a certain class of customers in order to learn the trade, and as the possible anti-competitive effects seem limited in a dynamic market, the conditions of Article 101(3) are likely to be fulfilled.

Commentary
para 173: B&C: 7.082

2.4. Selective distribution

(174) Selective distribution agreements, like exclusive distribution agreements, restrict the number of authorised distributors on the one hand and the possibilities of resale on the other. The difference with exclusive distribution is that the restriction of the number of dealers does not depend on the number of territories but on selection criteria linked in the first place to the nature of the product. Another difference with exclusive distribution is that the restriction on resale is not a restriction on active selling to a territory but a restriction on any sales to non-authorised distributors, leaving only appointed dealers and final customers as possible buyers. Selective distribution is almost always used to distribute branded final products.

Commentary
para 174: B&C: 7.064, 7.093, 7.094

(175) The possible competition risks are a reduction in intra-brand competition and, especially in case of cumulative effect, foreclosure of certain type(s) of distributors and softening of competition and facilitation of collusion between suppliers or buyers. To assess the possible anti-competitive effects of selective distribution under Article 101(1), a distinction needs to be made between purely qualitative selective distribution and quantitative selective distribution. Purely qualitative selective distribution selects dealers only on the basis of objective criteria required by the nature of the product such as training of sales personnel, the service provided at the point of sale, a certain range of the products being sold etc.[1] The application of such criteria does not put a direct limit on the number of dealers. Purely qualitative selective distribution is in general considered to fall outside Article 101(1) for lack of anti-competitive effects, provided that three conditions are satisfied. First, the nature of the product in question must necessitate a selective distribution system, in the sense that such a system must constitute a legitimate requirement, having regard to the nature of the product concerned, to preserve its quality and ensure its proper use. Secondly, resellers must be chosen on the basis of objective criteria of a qualitative nature which are laid down uniformly for all and made available to all potential resellers and are not applied in a discriminatory manner. Thirdly, the criteria laid down must not go beyond what is necessary.[2] Quantitative selective distribution adds further criteria for selection that more directly limit the potential number of dealers by, for instance, requiring minimum or maximum sales, by fixing the number of dealers, etc.

Notes

[1] See for example judgment of the Court of First Instance in Case T-88/92 *Groupement d'achat Édouard Leclerc v Commission* [1996] ECR II-1961.

2 See judgments of the Court of Justice in Case 31/80 *L'Oréal v PVBA* [1980] ECR 3775, paragraphs 15 and 16; Case 26/76 *Metro I* [1977] ECR 1875, paragraphs 20 and 21; Case 107/82 *AEG* [1983] ECR 3151, paragraph 35; and judgment of the Court of First Instance in Case T-19/91 *Vichy v Commission* [1992] ECR II-415, paragraph 65.

Commentary
para 175: F&N: 9.132, 9.249

(176) Qualitative and quantitative selective distribution is exempted by the Block Exemption Regulation as long as the market share of both supplier and buyer each do not exceed 30%, even if combined with other non-hardcore vertical restraints, such as non-compete or exclusive distribution, provided active selling by the authorised distributors to each other and to end users is not restricted. The Block Exemption Regulation exempts selective distribution regardless of the nature of the product concerned and regardless of the nature of the selection criteria. However, where the characteristics of the product[1] do not require selective distribution or do not require the applied criteria, such as for instance the requirement for distributors to have one or more brick and mortar shops or to provide specific services, such a distribution system does not generally bring about sufficient efficiency enhancing effects to counterbalance a significant reduction in intra-brand competition. Where appreciable anti-competitive effects occur, the benefit of the Block Exemption Regulation is likely to be withdrawn. In addition, the remainder of this section provides guidance for the assessment of selective distribution in individual cases which are not covered by the Block Exemption Regulation or in the case of cumulative effects resulting from parallel networks of selective distribution.

Notes

1 See for example judgments of the Court of First Instance in Case T-19/92, *Groupement d'achat Edouard Leclerc v Commission* [1996] ECR II-1851, paragraphs 112 to 123; Case T-88/92 *Groupement d'achat Edouard Leclerc v Commission* [1996] ECR II-1961, paragraphs 106 to 117, and the case law referred to in the preceding footnote.

Commentary
para 176: F&N: 9.132, 9.252, 9.255

(177) The market position of the supplier and its competitors is of central importance in assessing possible anti-competitive effects, as the loss of intra-brand competition can only be problematic if inter-brand competition is limited. The stronger the position of the supplier, the more problematic is the loss of intra-brand competition. Another important factor is the number of selective distribution networks present in the same market. Where selective distribution is applied by only one supplier on the market, quantitative selective distribution does not normally create net negative effects provided that the contract goods, having regard to their nature, require the use of a selective distribution system and on condition that the selection criteria applied are necessary to ensure efficient distribution of the goods in question. The reality, however, seems to be that selective distribution is often applied by a number of the suppliers on a given market.

Commentary
para 177: F&N: 9.257

(178) The position of competitors can have a dual significance and plays in particular a role in case of a cumulative effect. Strong competitors will mean in general that the reduction in intra-brand competition is easily outweighed by sufficient inter-brand competition. However, when a majority of the main suppliers apply selective distribution, there will be a significant loss of intra-brand competition and possible foreclosure of certain types of distributors as well as an increased risk of collusion between those major suppliers. The risk of foreclosure of more efficient distributors has always been greater with selective distribution than with exclusive distribution, given the restriction on sales to non-authorised dealers in selective distribution. That restriction is designed to give selective distribution systems a closed character, making it impossible for non-authorised dealers to obtain supplies. Accordingly, selective distribution is particularly well suited to avoid pressure by price discounters (whether offline or online-only distributors) on the margins of the manufacturer, as well as on the margins of the authorised

dealers. Foreclosure of such distribution formats, whether resulting from the cumulative application of selective distribution or from the application by a single supplier with a market share exceeding 30%, reduces the possibilities for consumers to take advantage of the specific benefits offered by these formats such as lower prices, more transparency and wider access.

Commentary
para 178: B&C: 7.075, 7.079, 7.112

(179) Where the Block Exemption Regulation applies to individual networks of selective distribution, withdrawal of the block exemption or disapplication of the Block Exemption Regulation may be considered in case of cumulative effects. However, a cumulative effect problem is unlikely to arise when the share of the market covered by selective distribution is below 50%. Also, no problem is likely to arise where the market coverage ratio exceeds 50%, but the aggregate market share of the five largest suppliers (CR5) is below 50%. Where both the CR5 and the share of the market covered by selective distribution exceed 50%, the assessment may vary depending on whether or not all five largest suppliers apply selective distribution. The stronger the position of the competitors which do not apply selective distribution, the less likely other distributors will be foreclosed. If all five largest suppliers apply selective distribution, competition concerns may arise with respect to those agreements in particular that apply quantitative selection criteria by directly limiting the number of authorised dealers or that apply qualitative criteria, such as a requirement to have one or more brick and mortar shops or to provide specific services, which forecloses certain distribution formats. The conditions of Article 101(3) are in general unlikely to be fulfilled if the selective distribution systems at issue prevent access to the market by new distributors capable of adequately selling the products in question, especially price discounters or online-only distributors offering lower prices to consumers, thereby limiting distribution to the advantage of certain existing channels and to the detriment of final consumers. More indirect forms of quantitative selective distribution, resulting for instance from the combination of purely qualitative selection criteria with the requirement imposed on the dealers to achieve a minimum amount of annual purchases, are less likely to produce net negative effects, if such an amount does not represent a significant proportion of the dealer's total turnover achieved with the type of products in question and it does not go beyond what is necessary for the supplier to recoup its relationship-specific investment and/or realise economies of scale in distribution. As regards individual contributions, a supplier with a market share of less than 5% is in general not considered to contribute significantly to a cumulative effect.

Commentary
para 179: B&C: 7.105, 7.106 **F&N:** 9.259

(180) Entry barriers are mainly of interest in the case of foreclosure of the market to non-authorised dealers. In general, entry barriers will be considerable as selective distribution is usually applied by manufacturers of branded products. It will in general take time and considerable investment for excluded retailers to launch their own brands or obtain competitive supplies elsewhere.

Commentary
para 180: F&N: 9.260

(181) Buying power may increase the risk of collusion between dealers and thus appreciably change the analysis of possible anti-competitive effects of selective distribution. Foreclosure of the market to more efficient retailers may especially result where a strong dealer organisation imposes selection criteria on the supplier aimed at limiting distribution to the advantage of its members.

Commentary
para 181: B&C: 7.094

(182) Article 5(1)(c) of the Block Exemption Regulation provides that the supplier may not impose an obligation causing the authorised dealers, either directly or indirectly, not to sell the brands

of particular competing suppliers. Such a condition aims specifically at avoiding horizontal collusion to exclude particular brands through the creation of a selective club of brands by the leading suppliers. That kind of obligation is unlikely to be exemptible when the CR5 is equal to or above 50%, unless none of the suppliers imposing such an obligation belongs to the five largest suppliers on the market.

(183) Foreclosure of other suppliers is normally not a problem as long as other suppliers can use the same distributors, that is, as long as the selective distribution system is not combined with single branding. In the case of a dense network of authorised distributors or in the case of a cumulative effect, the combination of selective distribution and a non-compete obligation may pose a risk of foreclosure to other suppliers. In that case, the principles set out in section 2.1. on single branding apply. Where selective distribution is not combined with a non-compete obligation, foreclosure of the market to competing suppliers may still be a problem where the leading suppliers apply not only purely qualitative selection criteria, but impose on their dealers certain additional obligations such as the obligation to reserve a minimum shelf-space for their products or to ensure that the sales of their products by the dealer achieve a minimum percentage of the dealer's total turnover. Such a problem is unlikely to arise if the share of the market covered by selective distribution is below 50% or, where this coverage ratio is exceeded, if the market share of the five largest suppliers is below 50%.

Commentary
para 183: B&C: 7.094, 7.113

(184) Maturity of the market is important, as loss of intra-brand competition and possible foreclosure of suppliers or dealers may be a serious problem on a mature market but is less relevant on a market with growing demand, changing technologies and changing market positions.

(185) Selective distribution may be efficient when it leads to savings in logistical costs due to economies of scale in transport and that may occur irrespective of the nature of the product (paragraph (107)(g)). However, such an efficiency is usually only marginal in selective distribution systems. To help solve a free-rider problem between the distributors (paragraph (107)(a)) or to help create a brand image (paragraph (107)(i)), the nature of the product is very relevant. In general, the case is strongest for new products, complex products, products whose qualities are difficult to judge before consumption (so-called experience products) or whose qualities are difficult to judge even after consumption (so-called credence products). The combination of selective distribution with a location clause, protecting an appointed dealer against other appointed dealers opening up a shop in its vicinity, may in particular fulfil the conditions of Article 101(3) if the combination is indispensable to protect substantial and relationship-specific investments made by the authorised dealer (paragraph (107)(d)).

Commentary
para 185: B&C: 3.042, 7.110, 7.115 F&N: 9.263

(186) To ensure that the least anti-competitive restraint is chosen, it is relevant to see whether the same efficiencies can be obtained at a comparable cost by for instance service requirements alone.

(187) <u>Example of quantitative selective distribution</u>
On a market for consumer durables, the market leader (brand A) with a market share of 35%, sells its product to final consumers through a selective distribution network. There are several criteria for admission to the network: the shop must employ trained staff and provide pre-sales services, there must be a specialised area in the shop devoted to the sales of the product and similar hi-tech products, and the shop is required to sell a wide range of models of the supplier and to display them in an attractive manner. Moreover, the number of admissible retailers in the network is directly limited through the establishment of a maximum number of retailers per number of inhabitants in each province or urban area. Manufacturer A has 6 competitors in that market. Its largest competitors, B, C and D, have market shares of respectively 25, 15 and 10%, whilst the other producers have smaller market shares. A is the only manufacturer to use selective distribution. The selective distributors of brand A always handle a few competing brands. However, competing brands are also widely sold in shops which are not member of A's

selective distribution network. Channels of distribution are various: for instance, brands B and C are sold in most of A's selected shops, but also in other shops providing a high quality service and in hypermarkets. Brand D is mainly sold in high service shops. Technology is evolving quite rapidly in this market, and the main suppliers maintain a strong quality image for their products through advertising.

On that market, the coverage ratio of selective distribution is 35%. Inter-brand competition is not directly affected by the selective distribution system of A. Intra-brand competition for brand A may be reduced, but consumers have access to low service/low price retailers for brands B and C, which have a comparable quality image to brand A. Moreover, access to high service retailers for other brands is not foreclosed, since there is no limitation on the capacity of selected distributors to sell competing brands, and the quantitative limitation on the number of retailers for brand A leaves other high service retailers free to distribute competing brands. In this case, in view of the service requirements and the efficiencies these are likely to provide and the limited effect on intra-brand competition the conditions of Article 101(3) are likely to be fulfilled.

Commentary
para 187: B&C: 7.114

(188) <u>Example of selective distribution with cumulative effects</u>

On a market for a particular sports article, there are seven manufacturers, whose respective market shares are: 25%, 20%, 15%, 15%, 10%, 8% and 7%. The five largest manufacturers distribute their products through quantitative selective distribution, whilst the two smallest use different types of distribution systems, which results in a coverage ratio of selective distribution of 85%. The criteria for access to the selective distribution networks are remarkably uniform amongst manufacturers: the distributors are required to have one or more brick and mortar shops, those shops are required to have trained personnel and to provide pre-sale services, there must be a specialised area in the shop devoted to the sales of the article and a minimum size for this area is specified. The shop is required to sell a wide range of the brand in question and to display the article in an attractive manner, the shop must be located in a commercial street, and that type of article must represent at least 30% of the total turnover of the shop. In general, the same dealer is appointed selective distributor for all five brands. The two brands which do not use selective distribution usually sell through less specialised retailers with lower service levels. The market is stable, both on the supply and on the demand side, and there is strong brand image and product differentiation. The five market leaders have strong brand images, acquired through advertising and sponsoring, whereas the two smaller manufacturers have a strategy of cheaper products, with no strong brand image.

On that market, access by general price discounters and online-only distributors to the five leading brands is denied. Indeed, the requirement that this type of article represents at least 30% of the activity of the dealers and the criteria on presentation and pre-sales services rule out most price discounters from the network of authorised dealers. The requirement to have one or more brick and mortar shops excludes online-only distributors from the network. As a consequence, consumers have no choice but to buy the five leading brands in high service/high price shops. This leads to reduced inter-brand competition between the five leading brands. The fact that the two smallest brands can be bought in low service/low price shops does not compensate for this, because the brand image of the five market leaders is much better. Inter-brand competition is also limited through multiple dealership. Even though there exists some degree of intra-brand competition and the number of retailers is not directly limited, the criteria for admission are strict enough to lead to a small number of retailers for the five leading brands in each territory.

The efficiencies associated with these quantitative selective distribution systems are low: the product is not very complex and does not justify a particularly high service. Unless the manufacturers can prove that there are clear efficiencies linked to their network of selective distribution, it is probable that the block exemption will have to be withdrawn because of its cumulative effects resulting in less choice and higher prices for consumers.

Commentary
para 188: B&C: 7.105

2.5. Franchising

(189) Franchise agreements contain licences of intellectual property rights relating in particular to trade marks or signs and know-how for the use and distribution of goods or services. In addition to the licence of IPRs, the franchisor usually provides the franchisee during the life of the agreement with commercial or technical assistance. The licence and the assistance are integral components of the business method being franchised. The franchisor is in general paid a franchise fee by the franchisee for the use of the particular business method. Franchising may enable the franchisor to establish, with limited investments, a uniform network for the distribution of its products. In addition to the provision of the business method, franchise agreements usually contain a combination of different vertical restraints concerning the products being distributed, in particular selective distribution and/or non-compete and/or exclusive distribution or weaker forms thereof.

(190) The coverage by the Block Exemption Regulation of the licensing of IPRs contained in franchise agreements is dealt with in paragraphs (24) to (46). As for the vertical restraints on the purchase, sale and resale of goods and services within a franchising arrangement, such as selective distribution, non-compete obligations or exclusive distribution, the Block Exemption Regulation applies up to the 30% market share threshold.[1] The guidance provided in respect of those types of restraints applies also to franchising, subject to the following two specific remarks:

(a) The more important the transfer of know-how, the more likely it is that the restraints create efficiencies and/or are indispensable to protect the know-how and that the vertical restraints fulfil the conditions of Article 101(3);

(b) A non-compete obligation on the goods or services purchased by the franchisee falls outside the scope of Article 101(1) where the obligation is necessary to maintain the common identity and reputation of the franchised network. In such cases, the duration of the non-compete obligation is also irrelevant under Article 101(1), as long as it does not exceed the duration of the franchise agreement itself.

Notes

[1] See also paragraphs (86) to (95), in particular paragraph (92).

Commentary
para 190: B&C: 7.178 **F&N:** 9.264
para 190(a): B&C: 7.181
para 190(b): B&C: 7.170, 7.171, 7.179

(191) Example of franchising

A manufacturer has developed a new format for selling sweets in so-called fun shops where the sweets can be coloured specially on demand from the consumer. The manufacturer of the sweets has also developed the machines to colour the sweets. The manufacturer also produces the colouring liquids. The quality and freshness of the liquid is of vital importance to producing good sweets. The manufacturer made a success of its sweets through a number of own retail outlets all operating under the same trade name and with the uniform fun image (style of layout of the shops, common advertising etc.). In order to expand sales the manufacturer started a franchising system. The franchisees are obliged to buy the sweets, liquid and colouring machine from the manufacturer, to have the same image and operate under the trade name, pay a franchise fee, contribute to common advertising and ensure the confidentiality of the operating manual prepared by the franchisor. In addition, the franchisees are only allowed to sell from the agreed premises, to sell to end users or other franchisees and are not allowed to sell other sweets. The franchisor is obliged not to appoint another franchisee nor operate a retail outlet himself in a given contract territory. The franchisor is also under the obligation to update and further develop its products, the business outlook and the operating manual and make these improvements available to all retail franchisees. The franchise agreements are concluded for a duration of 10 years.

Sweet retailers buy their sweets on a national market from either national producers that cater for national tastes or from wholesalers which import sweets from foreign producers in addition to selling products from national producers. On that market the franchisor's products compete with other brands of sweets. The franchisor has a market share of 30% on the market for sweets sold to retailers. Competition comes from a number of national and international brands, sometimes produced by large diversified food companies. There are many potential points of sale of sweets in the form of tobacconists, general food retailers, cafeterias and specialised sweet shops. The franchisor's market share of the market for machines for colouring food is below 10%.

Most of the obligations contained in the franchise agreements can be deemed necessary to protect the intellectual property rights or maintain the common identity and reputation of the franchised network and fall outside Article 101(1). The restrictions on selling (contract territory and selective distribution) provide an incentive to the franchisees to invest in the colouring machine and the franchise concept and, if not necessary to, at least help maintain the common identity, thereby offsetting the loss of intra-brand competition. The non-compete clause excluding other brands of sweets from the shops for the full duration of the agreements does allow the franchisor to keep the outlets uniform and prevent competitors from benefiting from its trade name. It does not lead to any serious foreclosure in view of the great number of potential outlets available to other sweet producers. The franchise agreements of this franchisor are likely to fulfil the conditions for exemption under Article 101(3) in as far as the obligations contained therein fall under Article 101(1).

Commentary
para 191: B&C: 7.181

2.6. Exclusive supply

(192) Under the heading of exclusive supply fall those restrictions that have as their main element that the supplier is obliged or induced to sell the contract products only or mainly to one buyer, in general or for a particular use. Such restrictions may take the form of an exclusive supply obligation, restricting the supplier to sell to only one buyer for the purposes of resale or a particular use, but may for instance also take the form of quantity forcing on the supplier, where incentives are agreed between the supplier and buyer which make the former concentrate its sales mainly with one buyer. For intermediate goods or services, exclusive supply is often referred to as industrial supply.

Commentary
para 192: B&C: 7.064, 7.065, 7.142 **F&N:** 9.265, 16.117

(193) Exclusive supply is exempted by the Block Exemption Regulation where both the supplier's and buyer's market share does not exceed 30%, even if combined with other non-hardcore vertical restraints such as non-compete. The remainder of this section provides guidance for the assessment of exclusive supply in individual cases above the market share threshold.

Commentary
para 193: B&C: 7.105

(194) The main competition risk of exclusive supply is anticompetitive foreclosure of other buyers. There is a similarity with the possible effects of exclusive distribution, in particular when the exclusive distributor becomes the exclusive buyer for a whole market (see section 2.2, in particular paragraph (156)). The market share of the buyer on the upstream purchase market is obviously important for assessing the ability of the buyer to impose exclusive supply which forecloses other buyers from access to supplies. The importance of the buyer on the downstream market is however the factor which determines whether a competition problem may arise. If the buyer has no market power downstream, then no appreciable negative effects for consumers can be expected. Negative effects may arise when the market share of the buyer on the downstream supply market as well as the upstream purchase market exceeds 30%. Where the market share of

the buyer on the upstream market does not exceed 30%, significant foreclosure effects may still result, especially when the market share of the buyer on its downstream market exceeds 30% and the exclusive supply relates to a particular use of the contract products. Where a company is dominant on the downstream market, any obligation to supply the products only or mainly to the dominant buyer may easily have significant anti-competitive effects.

(195) It is not only the market position of the buyer on the upstream and downstream market that is important but also the extent to and the duration for which it applies an exclusive supply obligation. The higher the tied supply share, and the longer the duration of the exclusive supply, the more significant the foreclosure is likely to be. Exclusive supply agreements shorter than five years entered into by non-dominant companies usually require a balancing of pro-and anti-competitive effects, while agreements lasting longer than five years are for most types of investments not considered necessary to achieve the claimed efficiencies or the efficiencies are not sufficient to outweigh the foreclosure effect of such long-term exclusive supply agreements.

(196) The market position of the competing buyers on the upstream market is important as it is likely that competing buyers will be foreclosed for anti-competitive reasons, that is, to increase their costs, if they are significantly smaller than the foreclosing buyer. Foreclosure of competing buyers is not very likely where those competitors have similar buying power and can offer the suppliers similar sales possibilities. In such a case, foreclosure could only occur for potential entrants, which may not be able to secure supplies when a number of major buyers all enter into exclusive supply contracts with the majority of suppliers on the market. Such a cumulative effect may lead to withdrawal of the benefit of the Block Exemption Regulation.

(197) Entry barriers at the supplier level are relevant to establishing whether there is real foreclosure. In as far as it is efficient for competing buyers to provide the goods or services themselves via upstream vertical integration, foreclosure is unlikely to be a real problem. However, there are often significant entry barriers.

(198) Countervailing power of suppliers is relevant, as important suppliers will not easily allow themselves to be cut off from alternative buyers. Foreclosure is therefore mainly a risk in the case of weak suppliers and strong buyers. In the case of strong suppliers, the exclusive supply may be found in combination with non-compete obligations. The combination with non-compete obligations brings in the rules developed for single branding. Where there are relationship-specific investments involved on both sides (hold-up problem) the combination of exclusive supply and non-compete obligations that is, reciprocal exclusivity in industrial supply agreements may often be justified, in particular below the level of dominance.

(199) Lastly, the level of trade and the nature of the product are relevant for foreclosure. Anticompetitive foreclosure is less likely in the case of an intermediate product or where the product is homogeneous. Firstly, a foreclosed manufacturer that uses a certain input usually has more flexibility to respond to the demand of its customers than the wholesaler or retailer has in responding to the demand of the final consumer for whom brands may play an important role. Secondly, the loss of a possible source of supply matters less for the foreclosed buyers in the case of homogeneous products than in the case of a heterogeneous product with different grades and qualities. For final branded products or differentiated intermediate products where there

are entry barriers, exclusive supply may have appreciable anti-competitive effects where the competing buyers are relatively small compared to the foreclosing buyer, even if the latter is not dominant on the downstream market.

Commentary
para 199: **B&C:** 2.100, 7.076

(200) Efficiencies can be expected in the case of a hold-up problem (paragraph (107)(d) and (107)(e)), and such efficiencies are more likely for intermediate products than for final products. Other efficiencies are less likely. Possible economies of scale in distribution (paragraph (107)(g)) do not seem likely to justify exclusive supply.

Commentary
para 200: **B&C:** 7.082 **F&N:** 9.273

(201) In the case of a hold-up problem and even more so in the case of economies of scale in distribution, quantity forcing on the supplier, such as minimum supply requirements, could well be a less restrictive alternative.

Commentary
para 201: **B&C:** 7.082 **F&N:** 9.273

(202) <u>Example of exclusive supply</u>
On a market for a certain type of components (intermediate product market) supplier A agrees with buyer B to develop, with its own know-how and considerable investment in new machines and with the help of specifications supplied by buyer B, a different version of the component. B will have to make considerable investments to incorporate the new component. It is agreed that A will supply the new product only to buyer B for a period of five years from the date of first entry on the market. B is obliged to buy the new product only from A for the same period of five years. Both A and B can continue to sell and buy respectively other versions of the component elsewhere. The market share of buyer B on the upstream component market and on the downstream final goods market is 40%. The market share of the component supplier is 35%. There are two other component suppliers with around 20–25% market share and a number of small suppliers.
Given the considerable investments, the agreement is likely to fulfil the conditions of Article 101(3) in view of the efficiencies and the limited foreclosure effect. Other buyers are foreclosed from a particular version of a product of a supplier with 35% market share and there are other component suppliers that could develop similar new products. The foreclosure of part of buyer B's demand to other suppliers is limited to maximum 40% of the market.

Commentary
para 202: **B&C:** 7.082

2.7. Upfront access payments

(203) Upfront access payments are fixed fees that suppliers pay to distributors in the framework of a vertical relationship at the beginning of a relevant period, in order to get access to their distribution network and remunerate services provided to the suppliers by the retailers. This category includes various practices such as slotting allowances,[1] the so called pay-to-stay fees,[2] payments to have access to a distributor's promotion campaigns etc. Upfront access payments are exempted under the Block Exemption Regulation when both the supplier's and buyer's market share does not exceed 30%. The remainder of this section provides guidance for the assessment of upfront access payments in individual cases above the market share threshold.

Notes
[1] Fixed fees that manufacturers pay to retailers in order to get access to their shelf space.
[2] Lump sum payments made to ensure the continued presence of an existing product on the shelf for some further period.

(204) Upfront access payments may sometimes result in anticompetitive foreclosure of other distributors if such payments induce the supplier to channel its products through only one or a limited number of distributors. A high fee may make that a supplier wants to channel a substantial volume of its sales through this distributor in order to cover the costs of the fee. In such a case, upfront access payments may have the same downstream foreclosure effect as an exclusive supply type of obligation. The assessment of that negative effect is made by analogy to the assessment of exclusive supply obligations (in particular paragraphs (194) to (199)).

Commentary
para 204: **B&C**: 2.100 **F&N**: 9.276

(205) Exceptionally, upfront access payments may also result in anticompetitive foreclosure of other suppliers, where the widespread use of upfront access payments increases barriers to entry for small entrants. The assessment of that possible negative effect is made by analogy to the assessment of single branding obligations (in particular paragraphs (132) to (141)).

Commentary
para 205: **B&C**: 2.100, 7.145

(206) In addition to possible foreclosure effects, upfront access payments may soften competition and facilitate collusion between distributors. Upfront access payments are likely to increase the price charged by the supplier for the contract products since the supplier must cover the expense of those payments. Higher supply prices may reduce the incentive of the retailers to compete on price on the downstream market, while the profits of distributors are increased as a result of the access payments. Such reduction of competition between distributors through the cumulative use of upfront access payments normally requires the distribution market to be highly concentrated.

Commentary
para 206: **F&N**: 9.277

(207) However, the use of upfront access payments may in many cases contribute to an efficient allocation of shelf space for new products. Distributors often have less information than suppliers on the potential for success of new products to be introduced on the market and, as a result, the amount of products to be stocked may be sub-optimal. Upfront access payments may be used to reduce this asymmetry in information between suppliers and distributors by explicitly allowing suppliers to compete for shelf space. The distributor may thus receive a signal of which products are most likely to be successful since a supplier would normally agree to pay an upfront access fee if it estimates a low probability of failure of the product introduction.

Commentary
para 207: **B&C**: 7.083 **F&N**: 9.278

(208) Furthermore, due to the asymmetry in information mentioned in paragraph (207), suppliers may have incentives to free-ride on distributors' promotional efforts in order to introduce sub-optimal products. If a product is not successful, the distributors will pay part of the costs of the product failure. The use of upfront access fees may prevent such free riding by shifting the risk of product failure back to the suppliers, thereby contributing to an optimal rate of product introductions.

Commentary
para 208: **F&N**: 9.278

2.8. Category Management Agreements

(209) Category management agreements are agreements by which, within a distribution agreement, the distributor entrusts the supplier (the "category captain") with the marketing of a category of products including in general not only the supplier's products, but also the products of its competitors. The category captain may thus have an influence on for instance the product placement and product promotion in the shop and product selection for the shop. Category management agreements are exempted under the Block Exemption Regulation when both the supplier's and buyer's market share does not exceed 30%. The remainder of this section provides guidance for the assessment of category management agreements in individual cases above the market share threshold.

(210) While in most cases category management agreements will not be problematic, they may sometimes distort competition between suppliers, and finally result in anticompetitive foreclosure of other suppliers, where the category captain is able, due to its influence over the marketing decisions of the distributor, to limit or disadvantage the distribution of products of competing suppliers. While in most cases the distributor may not have an interest in limiting its choice of products, when the distributor also sells competing products under its own brand (private labels), the distributor may also have incentives to exclude certain suppliers, in particular intermediate range products. The assessment of such upstream foreclosure effect is made by analogy to the assessment of single branding obligations (in particular paragraphs (132) to (141)) by addressing issues like the market coverage of these agreements, the market position of competing suppliers and the possible cumulative use of such agreements.

Commentary
para 210: B&C: 2.100, 7.145 **F&N:** 9.281

(211) In addition, category management agreements may facilitate collusion between distributors when the same supplier serves as a category captain for all or most of the competing distributors on a market and provides these distributors with a common point of reference for their marketing decisions.

Commentary
para 211: B&C: 6.023, 7.145 **F&N:** 9.280

(212) Category management may also facilitate collusion between suppliers through increased opportunities to exchange via retailers sensitive market information, such as for instance information related to future pricing, promotional plans or advertising campaigns.[1]

Notes
[1] Direct information exchange between competitors is not covered by the Block Exemption Regulation, see Article 2(4) of that Regulation and paragraphs 27–28 of these Guidelines.

Commentary
para 212: B&C: 7.145

(213) However, the use of category management agreements may also lead to efficiencies. Category management agreements may allow distributors to have access to the supplier's marketing expertise for a certain group of products and to achieve economies of scale as they ensure that the optimal quantity of products is presented timely and directly on the shelves. As category management is based on customers' habits, category management agreements may lead to higher customer satisfaction as they help to better meet demand expectations. In general, the higher the inter-brand competition and the lower consumers' switching costs, the greater the economic benefits achieved through category management.

Commentary
para 213: B&C: 7.145 **F&N:** 9.282

2.9. Tying

(214) Tying refers to situations where customers that purchase one product (the tying product) are required also to purchase another distinct product (the tied product) from the same supplier or someone designated by the latter. Tying may constitute an abuse within the meaning of Article 102.[1] Tying may also constitute a vertical restraint falling under Article 101 where it results in a single branding type of obligation (see paragraphs (129) to (150)) for the tied product. Only the latter situation is dealt with in these Guidelines.

Notes

[1] Judgment of the Court of Justice in Case C-333/94 P *Tetrapak v Commission* [1996] ECR I-5951, paragraph 37. See also Communication from the Commission — Guidance on the Commission's enforcement priorities in applying Article [102] of the [Treaty on the Functioning of the European Union] to abusive conduct by dominant undertakings, OJ C 45, 24.2.2009, p.7.

(215) Whether products will be considered as distinct depends on customer demand. Two products are distinct where, in the absence of the tying, a substantial number of customers would purchase or would have purchased the tying product without also buying the tied product from the same supplier, thereby allowing stand-alone production for both the tying and the tied product.[1] Evidence that two products are distinct could include direct evidence that, when given a choice, customers purchase the tying and the tied products separately from different sources of supply, or indirect evidence, such as the presence on the market of undertakings specialised in the manufacture or sale of the tied product without the tying product,[2] or evidence indicating that undertakings with little market power, particularly on competitive markets, tend not to tie or not to bundle such products. For instance, since customers want to buy shoes with laces and it is not practicable for distributors to lace new shoes with the laces of their choice, it has become commercial usage for shoe manufacturers to supply shoes with laces. Therefore, the sale of shoes with laces is not a tying practice.

Notes

[1] Judgment of the Court of First Instance in Case T-201/04 *Microsoft v Commission* [2007] ECR II-3601, paragraphs 917, 921 and 922.
[2] Judgment of the Court of First Instance in Case T-30/89 *Hilti v Commission* [1991] ECR II-1439, paragraph 67.

Commentary
para 215: B&C: 7.144 F&N: 4.477, 4.483, 9.283

(216) Tying may lead to anticompetitive foreclosure effects on the tied market, the tying market, or both at the same time. The foreclosure effect depends on the tied percentage of total sales on the market of the tied product. On the question of what can be considered appreciable foreclosure under Article 101(1), the analysis for single branding can be applied. Tying means that there is at least a form of quantity-forcing on the buyer in respect of the tied product. Where in addition a non-compete obligation is agreed in respect of the tied product, this increases the possible foreclosure effect on the market of the tied product. The tying may lead to less competition for customers interested in buying the tied product, but not the tying product. If there is not a sufficient number of customers that will buy the tied product alone to sustain competitors of the supplier on the tied market, the tying can lead to those customers facing higher prices. If the tied product is an important complementary product for customers of the tying product, a reduction of alternative suppliers of the tied product and hence a reduced availability of that product can make entry onto the tying market alone more difficult.

Commentary
para 216: B&C: 2.100, 7.144 F&N: 4.477, 10.163

(217) Tying may also directly lead to prices that are above the competitive level, especially in three situations. Firstly, if the tying and the tied product can be used in variable proportions as inputs to a production process, customers may react to an increase in price for the tying product by increasing their demand for the tied product while decreasing their demand for the tying product. By tying the two products the supplier may seek to avoid this substitution and as a result

be able to raise its prices. Secondly, when the tying allows price discrimination according to the use the customer makes of the tying product, for example the tying of ink cartridges to the sale of photocopying machines (metering). Thirdly, when in the case of long-term contracts or in the case of after-markets with original equipment with a long replacement time, it becomes difficult for the customers to calculate the consequences of the tying.

Commentary
para 217: B&C: 7.162 F&N: 4.477, 9.285

(218) Tying is exempted under the Block Exemption Regulation when the market share of the supplier, on both the market of the tied product and the market of the tying product, and the market share of the buyer, on the relevant upstream markets, do not exceed 30%. It may be combined with other vertical restraints, which are not hardcore restrictions under that Regulation, such as non-compete obligations or quantity forcing in respect of the tying product, or exclusive sourcing. The remainder of this section provides guidance for the assessment of tying in individual cases above the market share threshold.

(219) The market position of the supplier on the market of the tying product is obviously of central importance to assess possible anti-competitive effects. In general, this type of agreement is imposed by the supplier. The importance of the supplier on the market of the tying product is the main reason why a buyer may find it difficult to refuse a tying obligation.

(220) The market position of the supplier's competitors on the market of the tying product is important in assessing the supplier's market power. As long as its competitors are sufficiently numerous and strong, no anti-competitive effects can be expected, as buyers have sufficient alternatives to purchase the tying product without the tied product, unless other suppliers are applying similar tying. In addition, entry barriers on the market of the tying product are relevant to establish the market position of the supplier. When tying is combined with a non-compete obligation in respect of the tying product, this considerably strengthens the position of the supplier.

Commentary
para 220: B&C: 7.162

(221) Buying power is relevant, as important buyers will not easily be forced to accept tying without obtaining at least part of the possible efficiencies. Tying not based on efficiency is therefore mainly a risk where buyers do not have significant buying power.

Commentary
para 221: F&N: 9.288

(222) Where appreciable anti-competitive effects are established, the question whether the conditions of Article 101(3) are fulfilled arises. Tying obligations may help to produce efficiencies arising from joint production or joint distribution. Where the tied product is not produced by the supplier, an efficiency may also arise from the supplier buying large quantities of the tied product. For tying to fulfil the conditions of Article 101(3), it must, however, be shown that at least part of these cost reductions are passed on to the consumer, which is normally not the case when the retailer is able to obtain, on a regular basis, supplies of the same or equivalent products on the same or better conditions than those offered by the supplier which applies the tying practice. Another efficiency may exist where tying helps to ensure a certain uniformity and quality standardisation (see paragraph (107)(i)). However, it needs to be demonstrated that the positive effects cannot be realised equally efficiently by requiring the buyer to use or resell products satisfying minimum quality standards, without requiring the buyer to purchase these from the supplier or someone designated by the latter. The requirements concerning minimum quality standards would not normally fall within the scope of Article 101(1). Where the supplier of the tying product imposes on the buyer the suppliers from which the buyer must purchase the tied product, for instance because the formulation of minimum quality standards is not possible, this may also fall outside the scope of Article 101(1), especially where

the supplier of the tying product does not derive a direct (financial) benefit from designating the suppliers of the tied product.

Commentary
para 222: **B&C:** 7.162 **F&N:** 9.290

2.10. Resale price restrictions

(223) As explained in section III.3, resale price maintenance (RPM), that is, agreements or concerted practices having as their direct or indirect object the establishment of a fixed or minimum resale price or a fixed or minimum price level to be observed by the buyer, are treated as a hardcore restriction. Where an agreement includes RPM, that agreement is presumed to restrict competition and thus to fall within Article 101(1). It also gives rise to the presumption that the agreement is unlikely to fulfil the conditions of Article 101(3), for which reason the block exemption does not apply. However, undertakings have the possibility to plead an efficiency defence under Article 101(3) in an individual case. It is incumbent on the parties to substantiate that likely efficiencies result from including RPM in their agreement and demonstrate that all the conditions of Article 101(3) are fulfilled. It then falls to the Commission to effectively assess the likely negative effects on competition and consumers before deciding whether the conditions of Article 101(3) are fulfilled.

(224) RPM may restrict competition in a number of ways. Firstly, RPM may facilitate collusion between suppliers by enhancing price transparency on the market, thereby making it easier to detect whether a supplier deviates from the collusive equilibrium by cutting its price. RPM also undermines the incentive for the supplier to cut its price to its distributors, as the fixed resale price will prevent it from benefiting from expanded sales. Such a negative effect is particularly plausible where the market is prone to collusive outcomes, for instance if the manufacturers form a tight oligopoly, and a significant part of the market is covered by RPM agreements. Second, by eliminating intra-brand price competition, RPM may also facilitate collusion between the buyers, that is, at the distribution level. Strong or well organised distributors may be able to force or convince one or more suppliers to fix their resale price above the competitive level and thereby help them to reach or stabilise a collusive equilibrium. The resulting loss of price competition seems especially problematic when the RPM is inspired by the buyers, whose collective horizontal interests can be expected to work out negatively for consumers. Third, RPM may more generally soften competition between manufacturers and/or between retailers, in particular when manufacturers use the same distributors to distribute their products and RPM is applied by all or many of them. Fourth, the immediate effect of RPM will be that all or certain distributors are prevented from lowering their sales price for that particular brand. In other words, the direct effect of RPM is a price increase. Fifth, RPM may lower the pressure on the margin of the manufacturer, in particular where the manufacturer has a commitment problem, that is, where it has an interest in lowering the price charged to subsequent distributors. In such a situation, the manufacturer may prefer to agree to RPM, so as to help it to commit not to lower the price for subsequent distributors and to reduce the pressure on its own margin. Sixth, RPM may be implemented by a manufacturer with market power to foreclose smaller rivals. The increased margin that RPM may offer distributors, may entice the latter to favour the particular brand over rival brands when advising customers, even where such advice is not in the interest of these customers, or not to sell these rival brands at all. Lastly, RPM may reduce dynamism and innovation at the distribution level. By preventing price competition between different distributors, RPM may prevent more efficient retailers from entering the market or acquiring sufficient scale with low prices. It also may prevent or hinder the entry and expansion of distribution formats based on low prices, such as price discounters.

Commentary
para 224: **B&C:** 2.098, 7.016, 7.040 **F&N:** 9.101

(225) However, RPM may not only restrict competition but may also, in particular where it is supplier driven, lead to efficiencies, which will be assessed under Article 101(3). Most notably,

Part C Substantive
Antitrust Matters

where a manufacturer introduces a new product, RPM may be helpful during the introductory period of expanding demand to induce distributors to better take into account the manufacturer's interest to promote the product. RPM may provide the distributors with the means to increase sales efforts and if the distributors on this market are under competitive pressure this may induce them to expand overall demand for the product and make the launch of the product a success, also for the benefit of consumers.[1] Similarly, fixed resale prices, and not just maximum resale prices, may be necessary to organise in a franchise system or similar distribution system applying a uniform distribution format a coordinated short term low price campaign (2 to 6 weeks in most cases) which will also benefit the consumers. In some situations, the extra margin provided by RPM may allow retailers to provide (additional) pre-sales services, in particular in case of experience or complex products. If enough customers take advantage from such services to make their choice but then purchase at a lower price with retailers that do not provide such services (and hence do not incur these costs), high-service retailers may reduce or eliminate these services that enhance the demand for the supplier's product. RPM may help to prevent such free-riding at the distribution level. The parties will have to convincingly demonstrate that the RPM agreement can be expected to not only provide the means but also the incentive to overcome possible free riding between retailers on these services and that the pre-sales services overall benefit consumers as part of the demonstration that all the conditions of Article 101(3) are fulfilled.

Notes

[1] This assumes that it is not practical for the supplier to impose on all buyers by contract effective promotion requirements, see also paragraph 107 point (a).

Commentary
para 225: **B&C:** 3.037, 7.042 **F&N:** 9.104

(226) The practice of recommending a resale price to a reseller or requiring the reseller to respect a maximum resale price is covered by the Block Exemption Regulation when the market share of each of the parties to the agreement does not exceed the 30% threshold, provided it does not amount to a minimum or fixed sale price as a result of pressure from, or incentives offered by, any of the parties. The remainder of this section provides guidance for the assessment of maximum or recommended prices above the market share threshold and for cases of withdrawal of the block exemption.

(227) The possible competition risk of maximum and recommended prices is that they will work as a focal point for the resellers and might be followed by most or all of them and/or that maximum or recommended prices may soften competition or facilitate collusion between suppliers.

(228) An important factor for assessing possible anti-competitive effects of maximum or recommended resale prices is the market position of the supplier. The stronger the market position of the supplier, the higher the risk that a maximum resale price or a recommended resale price leads to a more or less uniform application of that price level by the resellers, because they may use it as a focal point. They may find it difficult to deviate from what they perceive to be the preferred resale price proposed by such an important supplier on the market.

Commentary
para 228: **B&C:** 7.044

(229) Where appreciable anti-competitive effects are established for maximum or recommended resale prices, the question of a possible exemption under Article 101(3) arises. For maximum resale prices, the efficiency described in paragraph (107)(f) (avoiding double marginalisation), may be particularly relevant. A maximum resale price may also help to ensure that the brand in question competes more forcefully with other brands, including own label products, distributed by the same distributor.

C16

COMMISSION NOTICE

Supplementary Guidelines on Vertical Restraints in Agreements for the Sale and Repair of Motor Vehicles and for the Distribution of Spare Parts for Motor Vehicles

(2010/C 138/05)

(Text with EEA relevance)

Official Journal C 138, 28.5.2010, p.16

Celex No: 52010XC0528(01)

EUR-Lex permanent link: <http://eur-lex.europa.eu/LexUriServ/LexUriServ.do?uri=CELEX:5201 0XC0528(01):EN:NOT>

Notes

EEA application: see EFTA Surveillance Authority Notice — Supplementary guidelines on vertical restraints in agreements for the sale and repair of motor vehicles and for the distribution of spare parts for motor vehicles (2012/C 307/03), OJ C 307, 11.10.2012, p.3

Commentary
Guidelines: B&C: 7.118, 7.119, 7.126, 7.128, 7.134, 7.135 **F&N:** 2.12
paras 9–16: B&C: 3.005, 3.083
paras 18–24: B&C: 7.136
paras 33–37: B&C: 7.138

I. INTRODUCTION

1. Purpose of the Guidelines

(1) These Guidelines set out principles for assessing under Article 101 of the Treaty on the Functioning of the European Union[1] particular issues arising in the context of vertical restraints in agreements for the sale and repair of motor vehicles and for the distribution of spare parts. They accompany Commission Regulation (EU) No 461/2010 on the application of Article 101(3) of the Treaty on the Functioning of the European Union to categories of vertical agreements and concerted practices in the motor vehicle sector[2] (hereinafter "the Motor Vehicle Block Exemption Regulation") and are aimed at helping companies to make their own assessment of such agreements.

Notes

[1] With effect from 1 December 2009, Articles 81 and 82 of the EC Treaty have become Articles 101 and 102, respectively, of the Treaty on the Functioning of the European Union ("TFEU"). The two sets of provisions are in substance identical. For the purposes of these Guidelines, references to Articles 101 and 102 of the TFEU should be understood as references to Articles 81 and 82, respectively, of the EC Treaty where appropriate. The TFEU also introduced certain changes in terminology, such as the replacement of "Community" by "Union" and "common market" by "internal market". The terminology of the TFEU will be used throughout these Guidelines.

[2] OJ L 129, 28.5.2010, p.52.

---

(2) These Guidelines provide clarification on issues that are particularly relevant for the motor vehicle sector, including the interpretation of certain provisions of Commission Regulation (EU) No 330/2010 of 20 April 2010 on the application of Article 101(3) of the Treaty on the Functioning of the European Union to categories of vertical agreements and concerted practices[1] (hereinafter "the General Vertical Block Exemption Regulation"). They are without prejudice to the applicability of the Guidelines on Vertical Restraints[2] (hereinafter "the General Vertical Guidelines") and are therefore to be read in conjunction with and as a supplement to the General Vertical Guidelines.

Notes

1 OJ L 102, 23.4.2010, p.1.
2 OJ C 130, 19.5.2010, p.1.

(3) These Guidelines apply to both vertical agreements and concerted practices relating to the conditions under which the parties may purchase, sell or resell spare parts and/or provide repair and maintenance services for motor vehicles, and to vertical agreements and concerted practices relating to the conditions under which the parties may purchase, sell or resell new motor vehicles. As explained in Section II of these Guidelines, the latter category of agreements and concerted practices will remain subject to the relevant provisions of Commission Regulation (EC) No 1400/2002 of 31 July 2002 on the application of Article [101](3) of the Treaty to categories of vertical agreements and concerted practices in the motor vehicle sector[1] until 31 May 2013. Therefore, as regards vertical agreements and concerted practices for the purchase, sale or resale of new motor vehicles, these Guidelines will only apply as from 1 June 2013. These Guidelines do not apply to vertical agreements in sectors other than motor vehicles, and the principles set out herein may not necessarily be used to assess agreements in other sectors.

Notes

1 OJ L 203, 1.8.2002, p.30.

Commentary
para 3: B&C: 7.119, 7.122

(4) These Guidelines are without prejudice to the possible parallel application of Article 102 of the Treaty to vertical agreements in the motor vehicle sector, or to the interpretation that the Court of Justice of the European Union may give in relation to the application of Article 101 of the Treaty to such vertical agreements.

(5) Unless otherwise stated, the analysis and arguments set out in these Guidelines apply to all levels of trade. The terms "supplier" and "distributor"[1] are used for all levels of trade. The General Vertical Block Exemption Regulation and the Motor Vehicle Block Exemption Regulation are collectively referred to as "the Block Exemption Regulations".

Notes

1 Retail level distributors are commonly referred to in the sector as "dealers".

(6) The standards set forth in these Guidelines must be applied to each case having regard to the individual factual and legal circumstances. The Commission will apply[1] these Guidelines reasonably and flexibly, and having regard to the experience that it has acquired in the course of its enforcement and market monitoring activities.

Notes

1 Since the modernisation of the Union competition rules, the primary responsibility for such analysis lies with the parties to agreements. The Commission may however investigate the compatibility of agreements with Article 101 of the Treaty, on its own initiative or following a complaint.

(7) The history of competition enforcement in this sector shows that certain restraints can be arrived at either as a result of explicit direct contractual obligations or through indirect obligations or indirect means which nonetheless achieve the same anti-competitive result. Suppliers wishing to influence a distributor's competitive behaviour may, for instance, resort to threats or intimidation, warnings or penalties. They may also delay or suspend deliveries or threaten to terminate the contracts of distributors that sell to foreign consumers or fail to observe a given price level. Transparent relationships between contracting parties would normally reduce the risk of manufacturers being held responsible for using such indirect forms of pressure aimed at achieving anticompetitive outcomes. Adhering to a Code of Conduct is one means of achieving greater transparency in commercial relationships between parties. Such codes may inter alia provide for notice periods for contract termination, which may be determined in function of the contract duration, for compensation to be given for outstanding relationship-specific investments made by the dealer in case of early termination without just cause, as well as for arbitration as an alternative mechanism for

dispute resolution. If a supplier incorporates such a Code of Conduct into its agreements with distributors and repairers, makes it publicly available, and complies with its provisions, this will be regarded as a relevant factor for assessing the supplier's conduct in individual cases.

Commentary
para 7: **B&C:** 2.043, 7.007, 7.121

2. Structure of the Guidelines

(8) These Guidelines are structured as follows:
   (a) Scope of the Motor Vehicle Block Exemption Regulation and relationship with the General Vertical Block Exemption Regulation (Section II)
   (b) The application of the additional provisions in the Motor Vehicle Block Exemption Regulation (Section III)
   (c) The assessment of specific restraints: single branding and selective distribution (Section IV)

II. Scope of The Motor Vehicle Block Exemption Regulation and Relationship with the General Vertical Block Exemption Regulation

(9) Pursuant to Article 4 thereof, the Motor Vehicle Block Exemption Regulation covers vertical agreements relating to the purchase, sale or resale of spare parts for motor vehicles and to the provision of repair and maintenance services for motor vehicles.

(10) Article 2 of the Motor Vehicle Block Exemption Regulation extends the application of the relevant provisions of Regulation (EC) No 1400/2002 until 31 May 2013 as far as they relate to vertical agreements for the purchase, sale or resale of new motor vehicles. Pursuant to Article 3 of the Motor Vehicle Block Exemption Regulation vertical agreements for the purchase, sale and resale of new motor vehicles will be covered by the General Vertical Block Exemption Regulation, from 1 June 2013.[1]

Notes

[1] The expiry of Regulation (EC) No 1400/2002 and its replacement with the new legal framework explained in these Guidelines does not of itself require that existing contracts be terminated. See for example Case C-125/05 *Vulcan Silkeborg A/S v Skandinavisk Motor Co. A/S* [2006] ECR I-7637.

Commentary
para 10: **B&C:** 7.122

(11) The distinction that the new framework makes between the markets for the sale of new motor vehicles and the motor vehicle aftermarkets reflects the differing competitive conditions on these markets.

(12) On the basis of an in-depth market analysis set out in the Evaluation Report on the operation of Commission Regulation (EC) No 1400/2002 of 28 May 2008[1] and in the Commission Communication on The Future Competition Law Framework applicable to the Motor Vehicle Sector of 22 July 2009,[2] it appears that there are no significant competition shortcomings distinguishing the new motor vehicle distribution sector from other economic sectors and which could require the application of rules different from and stricter than those in the General Vertical Block Exemption Regulation. Consequently, the application of a market share threshold of 30%,[3] the non-exemption of certain vertical restraints and the conditions provided for in the General Vertical Block Exemption Regulation will normally ensure that vertical agreements for the distribution of new motor vehicles satisfy the conditions laid down in Article 101(3) of the Treaty without the need for any additional requirements over and above those applicable to other sectors.

Notes

[1] SEC(2008) 1946.

[2] COM(2009) 388.

3 Pursuant to Article 7 of the General Vertical Block Exemption Regulation, the calculation of this market share threshold is normally based on market sales value data or, if such data are not available, on other reliable market information, including market sales volumes. In this respect, the Commission takes note of the fact that, for the distribution of new motor vehicles, market shares are currently calculated by the industry on the basis of the volume of motor vehicles sold by the supplier on the relevant market, which includes all motor vehicles that are regarded by the buyer as interchangeable or substitutable, by reason of the products' characteristics, prices and intended use.

(13) However, in order to allow all operators time to adapt to the general regime, in particular in view of relationship-specific investments which have been made in the long term, the period of application of Regulation (EC) No 1400/2002 is extended by three years until 31 May 2013 with regard to those requirements that relate specifically to vertical agreements for the purchase, sale or resale of new motor vehicles. From 1 June 2010 until 31 May 2013, those provisions of Regulation (EC) No 1400/2002 which relate to both agreements for the distribution of new motor vehicles and agreements for the purchase, sale and resale of spare parts for motor vehicles and/or the provision of repair and maintenance services, will apply only in respect of the former. During that period these Guidelines will not be used for interpreting the provisions of Regulation (EC) No 1400/2002. Instead, reference should be made to the Explanatory Brochure on that Regulation.[1]

Notes

[1] Explanatory brochure for Commission Regulation (EC) No 1400/2002 of 31 July 2002 — Distribution and Servicing of Motor Vehicles in the European Union.

Commentary
para 13: B&C: 7.122

(14) As regards vertical agreements relating to the conditions under which the parties may purchase, sell or resell spare parts for motor vehicles and/or provide repair and maintenance services for motor vehicles, the Motor Vehicle Block Exemption Regulation applies from 1 June 2010. This means that, in order to be exempted pursuant to Article 4 of that Regulation, those agreements not only need to fulfil the conditions for an exemption under the General Vertical Block Exemption Regulation, but must also not contain any serious restrictions of competition, commonly referred to as hardcore restrictions as listed in Article 5 of the Motor Vehicle Block Exemption Regulation.

(15) Because of the generally brand-specific nature of the markets for repair and maintenance services and for the distribution of spare parts, competition on those markets is inherently less intense compared to that on the market for the sale of new motor vehicles. While reliability has improved and service intervals have lengthened thanks to technological improvement, this evolution is outpaced by an upward price trend for individual repair and maintenance jobs. On the spare parts markets, parts bearing the motor vehicle manufacturer's brand face competition from those supplied by the original equipment suppliers (OES) and by other parties. This maintains price pressure on those markets, which in turn maintains pressure on prices on the repair and maintenance markets, since spare parts make up a large percentage of the cost of the average repair. Moreover, repair and maintenance as a whole represent a very high proportion of total consumer expenditure on motor vehicles, which itself accounts for a significant slice of the average consumer's budget.

(16) In order to address particular competition issues arising on the motor vehicle aftermarkets, the General Vertical Block Exemption Regulation is supplemented with three additional hardcore restrictions in the Motor Vehicle Block Exemption Regulation applying to agreements for the repair and maintenance of motor vehicles and for the supply of spare parts. Further guidance on those additional hardcore restrictions is given in Section III of these Guidelines.

III. The Application of The Additional Provisions in the Motor Vehicle Block Exemption Regulation

(17) Agreements will not benefit from the block exemption if they contain hardcore restrictions. These restrictions are listed in Article 4 of the General Vertical Block Exemption Regulation and Article 5 of the Motor Vehicle Block Exemption Regulation. Including any such restrictions in

an agreement gives rise to the presumption that the agreement falls within Article 101(1) of the Treaty. It also gives rise to the presumption that the agreement is unlikely to satisfy the conditions laid down in Article 101(3) of the Treaty, for which reason the block exemption does not apply. However, this is a rebuttable presumption which leaves open the possibility for undertakings to plead an efficiency defence under Article 101(3) of the Treaty in an individual case.

(18) One of the Commission's objectives as regards competition policy for the motor vehicle sector is to protect access by spare parts manufacturers to the motor vehicle aftermarkets, thereby ensuring that competing brands of spare parts continue to be available to both independent and authorised repairers, as well as to parts wholesalers. The availability of such parts brings considerable benefits to consumers, especially since there are often large differences in price between parts sold or resold by a car manufacturer and alternative parts. Alternatives for parts bearing the trademark of the motor vehicle manufacturer (OEM parts) include original parts manufactured and distributed by original equipment suppliers (OES parts), while other parts matching the quality of the original components are supplied by "matching quality" parts manufacturers.

(19) "Original parts or equipment" means parts or equipment which are manufactured according to the specifications and production standards provided by the motor vehicle manufacturer for the production of parts or equipment for the assembly of the motor vehicle in question. This includes parts or equipment which are manufactured on the same production line as those parts or equipment. It is presumed unless the contrary is proven, that parts constitute original parts if the part manufacturer certifies that the parts match the quality of the components used for the assembly of the motor vehicle in question and have been manufactured according to the specifications and production standards of the motor vehicle (see Article 3(26) of Directive 2007/46/EC of the European Parliament and of the Council of 5 September 2007 establishing a framework for the approval of motor vehicles and their trailers, and of systems, components and separate technical units intended for such motor vehicles (Framework Directive)[1]).

Notes

[1] OJ L 263, 9.10.2007, p.1.

Commentary
para 19: **B&C:** 7.137

---

(20) In order to be considered as "matching quality", parts must be of a sufficiently high quality that their use does not endanger the reputation of the authorised network in question. As with any other selection standard, the motor vehicle manufacturer may bring evidence that a given spare part does not meet this requirement.

(21) Article 4(e) of the General Vertical Block Exemption Regulation describes it as a hardcore restriction for an agreement between a supplier of components and a buyer who incorporates those components, to prevent or restrict the supplier's ability to sell its components to end-users, independent repairers or other service providers not entrusted by the buyer with the repair or servicing of its goods. Article 5(a), (b) and (c) of the Motor Vehicle Block Exemption Regulation lay down three additional hardcore restrictions relating to agreements for the supply of spare parts.

(22) Article 5(a) of the Motor Vehicle Block Exemption Regulation concerns the restriction of the sale of spare parts for motor vehicles by members of a selective distribution system to independent repairers. This provision is most relevant for a particular category of parts, sometimes referred to as captive parts, which may only be obtained from the motor vehicle manufacturer or from members of its authorised networks. If a supplier and a distributor agree that such parts may not be supplied to independent repairers, this agreement would be likely to foreclose such repairers from the market for repair and maintenance services and fall foul of Article 101 of the Treaty.

(23) Article 5(b) of the Motor Vehicle Block Exemption Regulation concerns any direct or indirect restriction agreed between a supplier of spare parts, repair tools or diagnostic or other equipment and a manufacturer of motor vehicles, which limits the supplier's ability to sell these goods to authorised and/or independent distributors and repairers. So-called "tooling arrangements" between component suppliers and motor vehicle manufacturers are one example of possible indirect restrictions of this type. Reference should be made in this respect to the Commission

notice of 18 December 1978 concerning its assessment of certain subcontracting agreements in relation to Article [101](1) of the [Treaty on the Functioning of the European Union][1] (the Subcontracting Notice). Normally, Article 101(1) of the Treaty does not apply to an arrangement whereby a motor vehicle manufacturer provides a tool to a component manufacturer which is necessary for the production of certain components, shares in the product development costs, or contributes necessary[2] intellectual property rights, or know-how, and does not allow this contribution to be used for the production of parts to be sold directly in the aftermarket. On the other hand, if a motor vehicle manufacturer obliges a component supplier to transfer its ownership of such a tool, intellectual property rights, or know-how, bears only an insignificant part of the product development costs, or does not contribute any necessary tools, intellectual property rights, or know-how, the agreement at issue will not be considered to be a genuine subcontracting arrangement. Therefore, it may be caught by Article 101(1) of the Treaty and be examined pursuant to the provisions of the Block Exemption Regulations.

Notes

[1] OJ C 1, 3.1.1979, p.2.

[2] Where the motor vehicle manufacturer provides a tool, intellectual property rights (IPR) and/or know-how to a component supplier, this arrangement will not benefit from the Sub-contracting Notice if the component supplier already has this tool, IPR or know-how at its disposal, or could, under reasonable conditions obtain them, since under these circumstances the contribution would not be necessary.

(24) Article 5(c) of the Motor Vehicle Block Exemption Regulation relates to the restriction agreed between a manufacturer of motor vehicles which uses components for the initial assembly of motor vehicles and the supplier of such components, which limits the supplier's ability to place its trade mark or logo effectively and in an easily visible manner on the components supplied or on spare parts. In order to improve consumer choice, repairers and consumers should be able to identify which spare parts from alternative suppliers match a given motor vehicle, other than those bearing the car manufacturer's brand. Putting the trade mark or logo on the components and on spare parts facilitates the identification of compatible replacement parts which can be obtained from OES. By not allowing this, motor vehicle manufacturers can restrict the marketing of OES parts and limit consumers' choice in a manner that runs counter to the provisions of Article 101 of the Treaty.

IV. The Assessment of Specific Restraints

(25) Parties to vertical agreements in the motor vehicle sector should use these Guidelines as a supplement to and in conjunction with the General Vertical Guidelines in order to assess the compatibility of specific restraints with Article 101 of the Treaty. This section gives particular guidance as to single branding and selective distribution, which are two areas which may have particular relevance for assessing the category of agreements referred to in Section II of these Guidelines.

1. Single branding obligations

(i) Assessment of single-branding obligations under the Block Exemption Regulations

(26) Pursuant to Article 3 of the Motor Vehicle Block Exemption Regulation read in conjunction with Article 5(1)(a) of the General Vertical Block Exemption Regulation, a motor vehicle supplier and a distributor having a share of the relevant market that does not exceed 30% may agree on a single-branding obligation that obliges the distributor to purchase motor vehicles only from the supplier or from other firms designated by the supplier, on condition that the duration of such non-compete obligations is limited to five years or less. The same principles apply to agreements between suppliers and their authorised repairers and/or spare parts distributors. A renewal beyond five years requires explicit consent of both parties, and there should be no obstacles that hinder the distributor from effectively terminating the non-compete obligation at the end of the five-year period. Non-compete obligations are not covered by the Block Exemption Regulations when their duration is indefinite or exceeds five years, although in those circumstances the Block Exemption Regulations would continue to apply to the remaining part of the vertical agreement. The same applies to non-compete obligations that are tacitly renewable beyond a period of five

years. Obstacles, threats of termination, or intimations that single-branding will be re-imposed before a sufficient period has elapsed to allow either the distributor or the new supplier to amortise their sunk investments would amount to a tacit renewal of the single-branding obligation in question.

Commentary
para 26: B&C: 7.126

(27) Pursuant to Article 5(1)(c) of the General Vertical Block Exemption Regulation, any direct or indirect obligation causing the members of a selective distribution system not to sell the brands of particular competing suppliers, are not covered by the exemption. Particular attention should be paid to the manner in which single branding obligations are applied to existing multi-brand distributors, in order to ensure that the obligations in question do not form part of an overall strategy aimed at eliminating competition from one or more specific suppliers, and in particular from newcomers or weaker competitors. This type of concern could arise in particular if the market share thresholds indicated in paragraph 34 of these Guidelines are exceeded and if the supplier applying this type of restraint has a position on the relevant market that enables it to contribute significantly to the overall foreclosure effect.[1]

Notes

[1] Commission notice on agreements of minor importance which do not appreciably restrict competition under Article [101](1) of the [Treaty on the Functioning of the European Union] (*de minimis*), OJ C 368, 22.12.2001, p.13.

(28) Non-compete obligations in vertical agreements do not constitute hardcore restrictions, but depending on the market circumstances, can nonetheless have negative effects which may cause the agreements to fall under Article 101(1) of the Treaty.[1] One such harmful effect may arise if barriers to entry or expansion are raised that foreclose competing suppliers, and harm consumers in particular by increasing the prices or limiting the choice of products, lowering their quality or reducing the level of product innovation.

Notes

[1] As regards the relevant factors to be taken into account to carry out the assessment of non-compete obligations under Article 101(1) of the Treaty, see the relevant section in the General Vertical Guidelines, in particular paragraphs 129 to 150.

(29) However, non-compete obligations may also have positive effects which may justify the application of Article 101(3) of the Treaty. They may in particular help to overcome a "free-rider" problem, by which one supplier benefits from investments made by another. A supplier may, for instance, invest in a distributor's premises, but in doing so attract customers for a competing brand that is also sold from the same premises. The same applies to other types of investment made by the supplier which may be used by the distributor to sell motor vehicles of competing manufacturers, such as investments in training.

(30) Another positive effect of non-compete obligations in the motor vehicle sector relates to the enhancement of the brand image and reputation of the distribution network. Such restraints may help to create and maintain a brand image by imposing a certain measure of uniformity and quality standardisation on distributors, thereby increasing the attractiveness of that brand to the final consumer and increasing its sales.

(31) Article 1(d) of the General Vertical Block Exemption Regulation defines a non-compete obligation as:
"(a) any direct or indirect obligation causing the buyer not to manufacture, purchase, sell or resell goods or services which compete with the contract goods or services; or
(b) any direct or indirect obligation on the buyer to purchase from the supplier or from another undertaking designated by the supplier more than 80% of the buyer's total purchases of the contract goods or services and their substitutes on the relevant market."

(32) Apart from direct means to tie the distributor to its own brand(s), a supplier may also have recourse to indirect means having the same effect. In the motor vehicle sector, such indirect means may include qualitative standards specifically designed to discourage the distributors

from selling products of competing brands,[1] bonuses made conditional on the distributor agreeing to sell exclusively one brand, target rebates or certain other requirements such as the requirement to set up a separate legal entity for the competing brand or the obligation to display the additional competing brand in a separate showroom in a geographic location where the fulfilment of such a requirement would not be economically viable (for example sparsely populated areas).

Notes

[1] See cases *BMW*, IP/06/302 — 13.3.2006 and *Opel* 2006, IP/06/303 — 13.3.2006.

Commentary
para 32: **B&C:** 7.127

(33) The block exemption provided for in the General Vertical Block Exemption Regulation covers all forms of direct or indirect non-compete obligations provided that the market shares of both the supplier and the distributor do not exceed 30% and the duration of the non-compete obligation does not exceed five years. However, even in cases where individual agreements satisfy those conditions, the use of non-compete obligations may result in anti-competitive effects not outweighed by their positive effects. In the motor vehicle industry, such net anti-competitive effects could in particular result from cumulative effects leading to the foreclosure of competing brands.

Commentary
para 33: **B&C:** 7.128

(34) For the distribution of motor vehicles at the retail level, foreclosure of this type is unlikely to occur in markets where all suppliers have market shares below 30% and where the total percentage of all motor vehicle sales that are subject to single-branding obligations on the market in question (that is to say the total tied market share) is below 40%[1]. In a situation where there is one non-dominant supplier with a market share of more than 30% of the relevant market whereas all other suppliers' market shares are below 30%, cumulative anticompetitive effects are unlikely as long as the total tied market share does not exceed 30%.

Notes

[1] See General Vertical Guidelines at paragraph 141.

Commentary
para 34: **B&C:** 7.128

(35) If access to the relevant market for the sale of new motor vehicles and competition therein is significantly restricted by the cumulative effect of parallel networks of similar vertical agreements containing single branding obligations, the benefit of the block exemption may be withdrawn by the Commission, pursuant to Article 29 of Council Regulation (EC) No 1/2003 of 16 December 2002 on the implementation of the rules on competition laid down in Articles 81 and 82 of the Treaty.[1] A withdrawal decision may be addressed in particular to those suppliers that contribute in a significant manner to a cumulative foreclosure effect on the relevant market. Where that effect occurs on a national market, the National Competition Authorities of that Member State may also withdraw the benefit of the block exemption in respect of that territory.

Notes

[1] OJ L 1, 4.1.2003, p.1.

Commentary
para 35: **B&C:** 7.128

(36) In addition, if parallel networks of agreements containing similar vertical restraints cover more than 50% of a given market, the Commission may adopt a Regulation declaring the block exemption inapplicable to the market in question in respect of such restraints. In particular, such

a situation may arise if cumulative effects resulting from the widespread use of single-branding obligations lead to consumer harm on that market.

Commentary
para 36: **B&C:** 7.128

(37) With regard to the assessment of minimum purchasing obligations calculated on the basis of the distributor's total annual requirements, it may be justified to withdraw the benefit of the block exemption if cumulative anticompetitive effects arise even if the supplier imposes a minimum purchasing obligation that is below the 80% limit established in Article 1(d) of the General Vertical Block Exemption Regulation. The parties need to consider whether, in the light of the relevant factual circumstances, an obligation on the distributor to ensure that a given percentage of its total purchases of motor vehicles bear the supplier's brand will prevent the distributor from taking on one or more additional competing brands. From that perspective, even a minimum purchasing requirement set at a level lower than 80% of total annual purchases will amount to a single-branding obligation if it obliges a distributor wishing to take up a new brand of its choice from a competing manufacturer to purchase so many motor vehicles of the brand that it currently sells that the distributor's business is made economically unsustainable.[1] Such a minimum purchasing obligation will also amount to a single branding obligation if it forces a competing supplier to split its envisaged sales volume in a given territory over several distributors, leading to duplication of investments and a fragmented sales presence.

Notes

[1] For instance, if a dealer purchases 100 cars of brand A in a year to meet demand, and wishes to buy 100 cars of brand B, an 80% minimum purchasing obligation as regards brand A would imply that the following year, the dealer would have to buy 160 brand A cars. Given that penetration rates are likely to be relatively stable, this would likely leave the dealer with a large unsold stock of brand A. It would therefore be forced to dramatically reduce its purchases of brand B in order to avoid such a situation. Depending on the specific circumstances of the case, such a practice can be viewed as a single-branding obligation.

(ii) Assessment of single-branding obligations outside the scope of the Block Exemption Regulations

(38) Parties may also be called upon to assess the compatibility with the competition rules of single-branding obligations in respect of agreements that do not qualify for block exemption because the parties' market shares exceed 30% or the duration of the agreement exceeds five years. Such agreements will therefore be subject to individual scrutiny in order to ascertain whether they are caught by Article 101(1) of the Treaty and if so, whether efficiencies offsetting any possible anticompetitive effect can be demonstrated. If that is the case, they may be able to benefit from the exception laid down in Article 101(3) of the Treaty. For assessment in an individual case the general principles set out in Section VI.2.1 of the General Vertical Guidelines will apply.

(39) In particular, agreements entered into between a motor vehicle manufacturer or its importer, on the one hand, and spare parts distributors and/or authorised repairers, on the other, will fall outside the Block Exemption Regulations when the market shares held by the parties exceed the 30% threshold, which is likely to be the case for most such agreements. Single-branding obligations that will need to be assessed in such circumstances include all types of restriction that directly or indirectly limit authorised distributors' or repairers' ability to obtain original or matching quality spare parts from third parties. However, an obligation on an authorised repairer to use original spare parts supplied by the motor vehicle manufacturer for repairs carried out under warranty, free servicing and motor vehicle recall work would not be considered to be a single-branding obligation, but rather an objectively justified requirement.

Commentary
para 39: **B&C:** 7.137

(40) Single-branding obligations in agreements for the distribution of new motor vehicles will also need to be individually assessed where their duration exceeds five years or/and where the market share of the supplier exceeds 30%, which may be the case for certain suppliers in some Member States. In such circumstances, the parties should have regard not only to the supplier's and buyer's

Part C Substantive Antitrust Matters

market share, but also to the total tied market share taking into account the thresholds indicated in paragraph 34. Above those thresholds, individual cases will be assessed in accordance with the general principles set out in Section VI.2.1 of the General Vertical Guidelines.

(41) Outside the scope of the Block Exemption Regulations, the assessment of minimum purchasing obligations calculated on the basis of the distributor's total annual requirements will take into account all the relevant factual circumstances. In particular, a minimum purchasing requirement set at a level lower than 80% of total annual purchases will amount to a single-branding obligation if it has the effect of preventing distributors from dealing in one or more additional competing brands.

Commentary
para 41: B&C: 7.127

---

2. Selective distribution

(42) Selective distribution is currently the predominant form of distribution in the motor vehicle sector. Its use is widespread in motor vehicle distribution, as well as for repair and maintenance and the distribution of spare parts.

(43) In purely qualitative selective distribution, distributors and repairers are only selected on the basis of objective criteria required by the nature of the product or service, such as the technical skills of sales personnel, the layout of sales facilities, sales techniques and the type of sales service to be provided by the distributor.[1] The application of such criteria does not put a direct limit on the number of distributors or repairers admitted to the supplier's network. Purely qualitative selective distribution is in general considered to fall outside Article 101(1) of the Treaty for lack of anti-competitive effects, provided that three conditions are satisfied. First, the nature of the product in question must necessitate the use of selective distribution, in the sense that such a system must constitute a legitimate requirement, having regard to the nature of the product concerned, to preserve its quality and ensure its proper use. Second, distributors or repairers must be chosen on the basis of objective criteria of a qualitative nature which are laid down uniformly for all potential resellers and are not applied in a discriminatory manner. Third, the criteria laid down must not go beyond what is necessary.

Notes

[1] It should be recalled however that, in accordance with the established case law of the European Courts, purely qualitative selective distribution systems may nevertheless restrict competition where the existence of a certain number of such systems does not leave any room for other forms of distribution based on a different way of competing. This situation will generally not arise on the markets for the sale of new motor vehicles, on which leasing and other similar arrangements are a valid alternative to outright purchase of a motor vehicle, nor in the markets for repair and maintenance, as long as independent repairers provide consumers with an alternative channel for the upkeep of their motor vehicles. See for example Case T-88/92 *Groupement d'achat Édouard Leclerc v Commission* [1996] ECR II-1961.

Commentary
para 43: B&C: 7.129

---

(44) Whereas qualitative selective distribution involves the selection of distributors or repairers only on the basis of objective criteria required by the nature of the product or service, quantitative selection adds further criteria for selection that more directly limit the potential number of distributors or repairers either by directly fixing their number, or for instance, requiring a minimum level of sales. Networks based on quantitative criteria are generally held to be more restrictive than those that rely on qualitative selection alone, and are accordingly more likely to be caught by Article 101(1) of the Treaty.

(45) If selective distribution agreements are caught by Article 101(1) of the Treaty, the parties will need to assess whether their agreements can benefit from the Block Exemption Regulations, or individually, from the exception in Article 101(3) of the Treaty.

(i) The assessment of selective distribution under the Block Exemption Regulations

(46) The Block Exemption Regulations exempt selective distribution agreements, irrespective of whether quantitative or purely qualitative selection criteria are used, so long as the parties'

market shares do not exceed 30%. However, that exemption is conditional on the agreements not containing any of the hardcore restrictions set out in Article 4 of the General Vertical Block Exemption Regulation and Article 5 of the Motor Vehicle Block Exemption Regulation, or any of the excluded restrictions described in Article 5 of the General Vertical Block Exemption Regulation.

(47) Three of the hardcore restrictions in the General Vertical Block Exemption Regulation relate specifically to selective distribution. Article 4(b) describes as hardcore the restriction of the territory into which, or of the customers to whom, a buyer party to the agreement may sell the contract goods or services, except the restriction of sales by the members of a selective distribution system to unauthorised distributors in markets where such a system is operated. Article 4(c) describes as hardcore agreements restricting active or passive sales to end users by members of a selective distribution system operating at the retail level of trade, without prejudice to the possibility of prohibiting a member of the system from operating out of an unauthorised place of establishment, while Article 4(d) relates to the restriction of cross-supplies between distributors within a selective distribution system, including between distributors operating at different levels of trade. Those three hardcore restrictions have special relevance for motor vehicle distribution.

(48) The internal market has enabled consumers to purchase motor vehicles in other Member States and take advantage of price differentials between them, and the Commission views the protection of parallel trade in this sector as an important competition objective. The consumer's ability to buy goods in other Member States is especially important as far as motor vehicles are concerned, given the high value of the goods and the direct benefits in the form of lower prices accruing to consumers buying motor vehicles elsewhere in the Union. The Commission is therefore concerned that distribution agreements should not restrict parallel trade, since this cannot be expected to satisfy the conditions laid down in Article 101(3) of the Treaty.[1]

(49) The Commission has brought several cases against motor vehicle manufacturers for impeding such trade, and its decisions have been largely confirmed by the European Courts.[2] This experience shows that restrictions on parallel trade may take a number of forms. A supplier may, for instance, put pressure on distributors, threaten them with contract termination, fail to pay bonuses, refuse to honour warranties on motor vehicles imported by a consumer or cross-supplied between distributors established in different Member States, or make a distributor wait significantly longer for delivery of an identical motor vehicle when the consumer in question is resident in another Member State.

Notes

[1] The notion that cross-border trade restrictions may harm consumers has been confirmed by the Court in Case C-551/03 P, *General Motors*, [2006] ECR I-3173, paragraphs 67 and 68; Case C-338/00 P, *Volkswagen/Commission*, [2003] ECR I-9189, paragraphs 44 and 49, and Case T-450/05, *Peugeot/Commission*, judgment of 9 July 2009, not yet reported, [now [2009] ECR II-2533] paragraphs 46–49.

[2] Commission Decision 98/273/EC of 28 January 1998 in Case IV/35.733 — *VW*, Commission Decision 2001/146/EC of 20 September 2000 in Case COMP/36.653 — *Opel*, OJ L 59, 28.2.2001, p.1, Commission Decision 2002/758/EC of 10 October 2001 in Case COMP/36.264 — *Mercedes-Benz*, OJ L 257, 25.9.2002, p.1, Commission Decision 2006/431/EC of 5 October 2005 in Cases F-2/36.623/36.820/37.275 — *SEP et autres/Peugeot SA*.

(50) One particular example of indirect restrictions on parallel trade arises when a distributor is unable to obtain new motor vehicles with the appropriate specifications needed for cross-border sales. In those specific circumstances, the benefit of the block exemption may depend on whether a supplier provides its distributors with motor vehicles with specifications identical to those sold in other Member States for sale to consumers from those countries (the so-called "availability clause").[1]

Notes

[1] Joined Cases 25 and 26/84 *Ford-Werke AG and Ford of Europe Inc. v Commission of the European Communities* [1985] ECR 2725.

Commentary

para 50: B&C: 7.130

(51) For the purposes of the application of the Block Exemption Regulations, and in particular as regards the application of Article 4(c) of the General Vertical Block Exemption Regulation, the notion of "end users" includes leasing companies. This means in particular that distributors in selective distribution systems may not be prevented from selling new motor vehicles to leasing companies of their choice. However, a supplier using selective distribution may prevent its distributors from selling new motor vehicles to leasing companies when there is a verifiable risk that those companies will resell them while still new. A supplier can therefore require a dealer to check, before selling to a particular company, the general leasing conditions applied so as to verify that the company in question is indeed a leasing company rather than an unauthorised reseller. However, an obligation on a dealer to provide its supplier with copies of each leasing agreement before the dealer sells a motor vehicle to a leasing company could amount to an indirect restriction on sales.

Commentary
para 51: B&C: 7.131

(52) The notion of "end users" also encompasses consumers who purchase through an intermediary. An intermediary is a person or an undertaking which purchases a new motor vehicle on behalf of a named consumer without being a member of the distribution network. Those operators perform an important role in the motor vehicle sector, in particular by facilitating consumers' purchases of motor vehicles in other Member States. Evidence of intermediary status should as a rule be established by a valid mandate including the name and address of the consumer obtained prior to the transaction. The use of the Internet as a means to attract customers in relation to a given range of motor vehicles and collect electronic mandates from them does not affect intermediary status. Intermediaries are to be distinguished from independent resellers, which purchase motor vehicles for resale and do not operate on behalf of named consumers. Independent resellers are not to be considered as end users for the purposes of the Block Exemption Regulations.

Commentary
para 52: B&C: 7.130, 7.131

(ii) *The assessment of selective distribution outside the scope of the Block Exemption Regulations*

(53) As paragraph 175 of the General Vertical Guidelines explains, the possible competition risks brought about by selective distribution are a reduction in intra-brand competition and, especially in case of cumulative effect, foreclosure of certain type(s) of distributors and facilitation of collusion between suppliers or buyers.

(54) To assess the possible anti-competitive effects of selective distribution under Article 101(1) of the Treaty, a distinction needs to be made between purely qualitative selective distribution and quantitative selective distribution. As pointed out in paragraph 43, qualitative selective distribution is normally not caught by Article 101(1) of the Treaty.

(55) The fact that a network of agreements does not benefit from the block exemption because the market share of one or more of the parties is above the 30% threshold for exemption does not imply that such agreements are illegal. Instead, the parties to such agreements need to subject them to an individual analysis to check whether they fall under Article 101(1) of the Treaty and, if so, whether they may nonetheless benefit from the exception in Article 101(3) of the Treaty.

(56) As regards the specificities of new motor vehicle distribution, quantitative selective distribution will generally satisfy the conditions laid down in Article 101(3) of the Treaty if the parties' market shares do not exceed 40%. However, the parties to such agreements should bear in mind that the presence of particular selection standards could have an effect on whether their agreements satisfy the conditions laid down in Article 101(3) of the Treaty. For instance, although the use of location clauses in selective distribution agreements for new motor vehicles, that is to say agreements containing a prohibition on a member of a selective distribution system from operating out of an unauthorised place of establishment, will usually bring efficiency benefits in the form of more efficient logistics and predictable network coverage, those benefits may be outweighed

by disadvantages if the market share of the supplier is very high, and in those circumstances such clauses might not be able to benefit from the exception in Article 101(3) of the Treaty.

Commentary
para 56: B&C: 7.129

(57) Individual assessment of selective distribution for authorised repairers also raises specific issues. Insofar as a market exists[1] for repair and maintenance services that is separate from that for the sale of new motor vehicles, this is considered to be brand-specific. On that market, the main source of competition results from the competitive interaction between independent repairers and authorised repairers of the brand in question.

Notes

[1] In some circumstances, a system market which includes motor vehicles and spare parts together may be defined, taking into account, inter alia, the life-time of the motor vehicle as well as the preferences and buying behaviour of the users. See Commission notice on the definition of the relevant market for the purposes of Community competition law, OJ C 372, 9.12.1997, p.5, paragraph 56. One important factor is whether a significant proportion of buyers make their choice taking into account the lifetime costs of the motor vehicle or not. For instance, buying behaviour may significantly differ between buyers of trucks who purchase and operate a fleet, and who take into account maintenance costs at the moment of purchasing the motor vehicle and buyers of individual motor vehicles. Another relevant factor is the existence and relative position of part suppliers, repairers and/or parts distributors operating in the aftermarket independently from motor vehicle manufacturers. In most cases, there is likely to be a brand-specific aftermarket, in particular because the majority of buyers are private individuals or small and medium-size enterprises that purchase motor vehicles and aftermarket services separately and do not have systematic access to data permitting them to assess the overall costs of motor vehicle ownership in advance.

(58) Independent repairers in particular provide vital competitive pressure, as their business models and their related operating costs are different from those in the authorised networks. Moreover, unlike authorised repairers, which to a large extent use car manufacturer-branded parts, independent garages generally have greater recourse to other brands, thereby allowing a motor vehicle owner to choose between competing parts. In addition, given that a large majority of repairs for newer motor vehicles are currently carried out in authorised repair shops, it is important that competition between authorised repairers remains effective, which may only be the case if access to the networks remains open for new entrants.

(59) The new legal framework makes it easier for the Commission and National Competition Authorities to protect competition between independent garages and authorised repairers, as well as between the members of each authorised repairer network. In particular, the reduction in the market share threshold for exemption of qualitative selective distribution from 100% to 30% broadens the scope for competition authorities to act.

(60) When assessing the competitive impact of vertical agreements on the motor vehicle aftermarkets, the parties should therefore be aware of the Commission's determination to preserve competition both between the members of authorised repair networks and between those members and independent repairers. To this end, particular attention should be paid to three specific types of conduct which may restrict such competition, namely preventing access of independent repairers to technical information, misusing the legal and/or extended warranties to exclude independent repairers, or making access to authorised repairer networks conditional upon non-qualitative criteria.

Commentary
para 60: B&C: 7.134

(61) Although the following three subsections refer specifically to selective distribution, the same anti-competitive foreclosure effects could stem from other types of vertical agreements that limit, directly or indirectly, the number of service partners contractually linked to a motor vehicle manufacturer.

Access to technical information by independent operators

(62) Although purely qualitative selective distribution is in general considered to fall outside Article 101(1) of the Treaty for lack of anti-competitive effects,[1] qualitative selective distribution

agreements concluded with authorised repairers and/or parts distributors may be caught by Article 101(1) of the Treaty if, within the context of those agreements, one of the parties acts in a way that forecloses independent operators from the market, for instance by failing to release technical repair and maintenance information to them. In that context, the notion of independent operators includes independent repairers, spare parts manufacturers and distributors, manufacturers of repair equipment or tools, publishers of technical information, automobile clubs, roadside assistance operators, operators offering inspection and testing services and operators offering training for repairers.

Notes

[1] As pointed out in paragraph 54 above, this will generally be the case on the markets for repair and maintenance as long as independent repairers provide consumers with an alternative channel for the upkeep of their motor vehicles.

(63) Suppliers provide their authorised repairers with the full scope of technical information needed to perform repair and maintenance work on motor vehicles of their brands and are often the only companies able to provide repairers with all of the technical information that they need on the brands in question. In such circumstances, if the supplier fails to provide independent operators with appropriate access to its brand-specific technical repair and maintenance information, possible negative effects stemming from its agreements with authorised repairers and/or parts distributors could be strengthened, and cause the agreements to fall within Article 101(1) of the Treaty.

(64) Moreover, a lack of access to necessary technical information could cause the market position of independent operators to decline, leading to consumer harm, in terms of a significant reduction in choice of spare parts, higher prices for repair and maintenance services, a reduction in choice of repair outlets and potential safety problems. In those circumstances, the efficiencies that might normally be expected to result from the authorised repair and parts distribution agreements would not be such as to offset these anti-competitive effects, and the agreements in question would consequently fail to satisfy the conditions laid down in Article 101(3) of the Treaty.

(65) Regulation (EC) No 715/2007 of the European Parliament and of the Council of 20 June 2007 on type approval of motor vehicles with respect to emissions from light passenger and commercial vehicles (Euro 5 and Euro 6) and on access to vehicle repair and maintenance information[1] as well as Commission Regulation (EC) No 692/2008 of 18 July 2008 implementing and amending Regulation (EC) No 715/2007 of the European Parliament and of the Council on type-approval of motor vehicles with respect to emissions from light passenger and commercial vehicles (Euro 5 and Euro 6) and on access to vehicle repair and maintenance information[2] provide for a system for disseminating repair and maintenance information in respect of passenger cars put on the market from 1 September 2009. Regulation (EC) No 595/2009 of the European Parliament and of the Council of 18 June 2009 on type approval of motor vehicles and engines with respect to emissions from heavy duty vehicles (Euro 6) and on access to vehicle repair an maintenance information[3] and the ensuing implementing measures provide for such a system in respect of commercial vehicles put on the market from 1 January 2013. The Commission will take those Regulations into account when assessing cases of suspected withholding of technical repair and maintenance information concerning motor vehicles marketed before those dates. When considering whether withholding a particular item of information may lead the agreements at issue to be caught by Article 101(1) of the Treaty, a number of factors should be considered, including:

    (a) whether the item in question is technical information, or information of another type, such as commercial information,[4] which may legitimately be withheld;

    (b) whether withholding the technical information in question will have an appreciable impact on the ability of independent operators to carry out their tasks and exercise a competitive constraint on the market;

    (c) whether the technical information in question is made available to members of the relevant authorised repair network; if it is made available to the authorised network in whatever form, it should also be made available to independent operators on a non-discriminatory basis;

(d) whether the technical information in question will ultimately[5] be used for the repair and maintenance of motor vehicles, or rather for another purpose,[6] such as for the manufacturing of spare parts or tools.

Notes

[1] OJ L 171, 29.6.2007, p.1.

[2] OJ L 199, 28.7.2008, p.1.

[3] OJ L 188, 18.7.2009, p.1.

[4] Commercial information can be thought of as information that is used for carrying on a repair and maintenance business but is not needed to repair or maintain motor vehicles. Examples include billing software, or information on the hourly tariffs practiced within the authorised network.

[5] Such as information supplied to publishers for resupply to motor vehicle repairers.

[6] Information used for fitting a spare part to or using a tool on a motor vehicle should be considered as being used for repair and maintenance, while information on the design, production process or the materials used for manufacturing a spare part should not be considered to fall within this category, and may therefore be withheld.

(66) Technological progress implies that the notion of technical information is fluid. Currently, particular examples of technical information include software, fault codes and other parameters, together with updates, which are required to work on electronic control units with a view to introducing or restoring settings recommended by the supplier, motor vehicle identification numbers or any other motor vehicle identification methods, parts catalogues, repair and maintenance procedures, working solutions resulting from practical experience and relating to problems typically affecting a given model or batch, and recall notices as well as other notices identifying repairs that may be carried out without charge within the authorised repair network. The part code and any other information necessary to identify the correct car manufacturer-branded spare part to fit a given individual motor vehicle (that is to say the part that the car manufacturer would generally supply to the members of its authorised repair networks to repair the motor vehicle in question) also constitute technical information.[1] The lists of items set out in Article 6(2) of Regulation (EC) No 715/2007 and Regulation (EC) No 595/2009 should also be used as a guide to what the Commission views as technical information for the purposes of applying Article 101 of the Treaty.

Notes

[1] The independent operator should not have to purchase the spare part in question to be able to obtain this information.

Commentary
para 66: B&C: 7.135

(67) The way in which technical information is supplied is also important for assessing the compatibility of authorised repair agreements with Article 101 of the Treaty. Access should be given upon request and without undue delay, the information should be provided in a usable form, and the price charged should not discourage access to it by failing to take into account the extent to which the independent operator uses the information. A supplier of motor vehicles should be required to give independent operators access to technical information on new motor vehicles at the same time as such access is given to its authorised repairers and should not oblige independent operators to purchase more than the information necessary to carry out the work in question. Article 101 of the Treaty does not, however, oblige a supplier to provide technical information in a standardised format or through a defined technical system, such as the CEN/ISO standard and the OASIS format as provided for by Regulation (EC) No 715/2007 and Commission Regulation (EC) No 295/2009 of 18 March 2009 concerning the classification of certain goods in the Combined Nomenclature.[1]

Notes

[1] OJ L 95, 9.4.2009, p.7.

Commentary
para 67: B&C: 7.135

(68) The above considerations also apply to the availability of tools and training to independent operators. "Tools" in this context includes electronic diagnostic and other repair tools, together with related software, including periodic updates thereof, and after-sales services for such tools.

Commentary
para 68: B&C: 7.135

Misuse of warranties

(69) Qualitative selective distribution agreements may also be caught by Article 101(1) of the Treaty if the supplier and the members of its authorised network explicitly or implicitly reserve repairs on certain categories of motor vehicles to the members of the authorised network. This might happen, for instance, if the manufacturer's warranty vis-à-vis the buyer, whether legal or extended, is made conditional on the end user having repair and maintenance work that is not covered by warranty carried out only within the authorised repair networks. The same applies to warranty conditions which require the use of the manufacturer's brand of spare parts in respect of replacements not covered by the warranty terms. It also seems doubtful that selective distribution agreements containing such practices could bring benefits to consumers in such a way as to allow the agreements in question to benefit from the exception in Article 101(3) of the Treaty. However, if a supplier legitimately refuses to honour a warranty claim on the grounds that the situation leading to the claim in question is causally linked to a failure on the part of a repairer to carry out a particular repair or maintenance operation in the correct manner or to the use of poor quality spare parts, this will have no bearing on the compatibility of the supplier's repair agreements with the competition rules.

Commentary
para 69: B&C: 7.135

Access to authorised repairer networks

(70) Competition between authorised and independent repairers is not the only form of competition that needs to be taken into account when analysing the compatibility of authorised repair agreements with Article 101 of the Treaty. Parties should also assess the degree to which authorised repairers within the relevant network are able to compete with one another. One of the main factors driving this competition relates to the conditions of access to the network established under the standard authorised repairer agreements. In view of the generally strong market position of networks of authorised repairers, their particular importance for owners of newer motor vehicles, and the fact that consumers are not prepared to travel long distances to have their cars repaired, the Commission considers it important that access to the authorised repair networks should generally remain open to all firms that meet defined quality criteria. Submitting applicants to quantitative selection is likely to cause the agreement to fall within Article 101(1) of the Treaty.

Commentary
para 70: B&C: 7.135

(71) A particular case arises when agreements oblige authorised repairers to also sell new motor vehicles. Such agreements are likely to be caught by Article 101(1) of the Treaty, since the obligation in question is not required by the nature of the contract services. Moreover, for an established brand, agreements containing such an obligation would not normally be able to benefit from the exception in Article 101(3) of the Treaty, since the impact would be to severely restrict access to the authorised repair network, thereby reducing competition without bringing corresponding benefits to consumers. However, in certain cases, a supplier wishing to launch a brand on a particular geographic market might initially find it difficult to attract distributors willing to make the necessary investment unless they could be sure that they would not face competition from "stand-alone" authorised repairers that sought to free-ride on these initial investments. In those circumstances, contractually linking the two activities for a limited period of time would have a

pro-competitive effect on the motor vehicle sales market by allowing a new brand to launch, and would have no effect on the potential brand-specific repair market, which would in any event not exist if the motor vehicles could not be sold. The agreements in question would therefore be unlikely to be caught by Article 101(1) of the Treaty.

Commentary
para 71: B&C: 7.135

C17

COMMUNICATION FROM THE COMMISSION

Guidelines on the applicability of Article 101 of the Treaty on the Functioning of the European Union to horizontal co-operation agreements

(Text with EEA relevance)

(2011/C 11/01)

Official Journal C 11, 14.1.2011, p.1

Celex No: 52011XC0114(04)

EUR-Lex permanent link: <http://eur-lex.europa.eu/LexUriServ/LexUriServ.do?uri=CELEX:5201 1XC0114(04):EN:NOT>

Notes
This document is reproduced as corrected by the Corrigendum at OJ C 33, 2.2.2011, p.20.
EEA application: the EFTA Surveillance has adopted parallel Guidelines on the applicability of Article 53 of the EEA Agreement to horizontal cooperation agreements (OJ C 362, 12.12.2013, p.3).

Commentary
Guidelines: B&C: 1.038, 1.074, 2.097, 2.164, 3.005, 3.012, 3.048, 6.012, 6.013, 6.014, 6.031, 6.069, 8.268, 9.067, 12.064, 12.120, 12.131, 12.132, 12.174 **F&N:** 1.119, 2.12, 3.155, 3.219, 3.366, 3.375, 3.378, 3.499, 4.774, 7.01, 7.10, 7.11, 7.18, 7.20, 7.21, 7.70, 7.145–7.161, 7.234, 7.237, 7.240, 7.241, 7.242, 7.246, 7.247, 7.252, 7.253, 7.278, 7.320, 7.326, 7.327, 7.331, 7.438, 7.457, 7.474, 7.478, 7.487, 7.498, 7.510, 7.512, 7.516, 7.517, 7.527, 7.539, 7.542, 7.545, 7.546, 7.548, 7.549, 7.550, 7.551, 8.02, 8.44, 9.79, 11.202, 12.101, 12.130, 13.232, 14.31
paras 35–37: B&C: 2.125
paras 60–63: B&C: 2.057
paras 64–71: B&C: 6.025
paras 69–71: B&C: 2.100, 6.026
paras 72–74: B&C: 2.120, 2.121
paras 95–104: B&C: 3.038
paras 95–110: B&C: 6.038
paras 96–99: B&C: 3.038
paras 111–122: B&C: 9.145
paras 111–149 F&N: 7.144
paras 116–117: B&C: 4.065
paras 116–118: B&C: 6.041
paras 119–122: B&C: 6.041
paras 120–122: B&C: 6.043

TABLE OF CONTENTS

Part C Substantive Antitrust Matters

I. Introduction

1.1. Purpose and scope

1. These guidelines set out the principles for the assessment under Article 101 of the Treaty on the Functioning of the European Union (*) ("Article 101") of agreements between undertakings, decisions by associations of undertakings and concerted practices (collectively referred to as 'agreements') pertaining to horizontal co-operation. Co-operation is of a "horizontal nature" if an agreement is entered into between actual or potential competitors. In addition, these guidelines also cover horizontal co-operation agreements between non-competitors, for example, between two companies active in the same product markets but in different geographic markets without being potential competitors.

Notes

(*) With effect from 1 December 2009, Article [101] of the EC Treaty has become Article 101 of the Treaty on the Functioning of the European Union ("TFEU"). The two Articles are, in substance, identical. For the purposes of these guidelines, references to Article 101 of the TFEU should be understood as references to Article [101] of the EC Treaty where appropriate. The TFEU also introduced certain changes in terminology, such as the replacement of "Community" by "Union" and "common market" by "internal market". The terminology of the TFEU will be used throughout these guidelines.

Commentary
para 1: B&C: 6.011 F&N: 7.01

2. Horizontal co-operation agreements can lead to substantial economic benefits, in particular if they combine complementary activities, skills or assets. Horizontal co-operation can be a means to share risk, save costs, increase investments, pool know-how, enhance product quality and variety, and launch innovation faster.

Commentary
para 2: F&N: 7.05

3. On the other hand, horizontal co-operation agreements may lead to competition problems. This is, for example, the case if the parties agree to fix prices or output or to share markets, or if the co-operation enables the parties to maintain, gain or increase market power and thereby is likely to give rise to negative market effects with respect to prices, output, product quality, product variety or innovation.

Commentary
para 3: F&N: 7.06, 8.03

4. The Commission, while recognising the benefits that can be generated by horizontal co-operation agreements, has to ensure that effective competition is maintained. Article 101 provides the legal framework for a balanced assessment taking into account both adverse effects on competition and pro-competitive effects.

5. The purpose of these guidelines is to provide an analytical framework for the most common types of horizontal co-operation agreements; they deal with research and development agreements, production agreements including subcontracting and specialisation agreements, purchasing agreements, commercialisation agreements, standardisation agreements including standard contracts, and information exchange. This framework is primarily based on legal and economic criteria that help to analyse a horizontal co-operation agreement and the context in which it occurs. Economic criteria such as the market power of the parties and other factors relating to the market structure form a key element of the assessment of the market impact likely to be caused by a horizontal co-operation agreement and, therefore, for the assessment under Article 101.

Commentary
para 5: B&C: 2.169, 6.014

6. These guidelines apply to the most common types of horizontal co-operation agreements irrespective of the level of integration they entail with the exception of operations constituting a

concentration within the meaning of Article 3 of Council Regulation (EC) No 139/2004 of 20 January 2004 on the control of concentrations between undertakings[1] ("the Merger Regulation") as would be the case, for example, with joint ventures performing on a lasting basis all the functions of an autonomous economic entity ("full-function joint ventures").[2]

Notes

[1] OJ L 24, 29.1.2004, p.1.

[2] See Article 3(4) of the Merger Regulation. However, in assessing whether there is a full-function joint venture, the Commission examines whether the joint venture is autonomous in an operational sense. This does not mean that it enjoys autonomy from its parent companies as regards the adoption of its strategic decisions (see Commission Consolidated Jurisdictional Notice under Council Regulation (EC) No 139/2004 on the control of concentrations between undertakings, OJ C 95, 16.4.2008, p.1, paragraphs 91–109 ("Consolidated Jurisdictional Notice")). It also needs to be recalled that if the creation of a joint venture constituting a concentration under Article 3 of the Merger Regulation has as its object or effect the coordination of the competitive behaviour of undertakings that remain independent, then that coordination will be appraised under Article 101 of the Treaty (see Article 2(4) of the Merger Regulation).

Commentary
para 6: **B&C:** 6.005 **F&N:** 7.12, 7.17

7. Given the potentially large number of types and combinations of horizontal co-operation and market circumstances in which they operate, it is difficult to provide specific answers for every possible scenario. These guidelines will nevertheless assist businesses in assessing the compatibility of an individual co-operation agreement with Article 101. Those criteria do not, however, constitute a "checklist" which can be applied mechanically. Each case must be assessed on the basis of its own facts, which may require a flexible application of these guidelines.

8. The criteria set out in these guidelines apply to horizontal co-operation agreements concerning both goods and services (collectively referred to as "products"). These guidelines complement Commission Regulation (EU) No 1217/2010 of 14 December 2010 on the application of Article 101(3) of the Treaty on the Functioning of the European Union to certain categories of research and development agreements[1] ("the R&D Block Exemption Regulation") and Commission Regulation (EU) No 1218/2010 of 14 December 2010 on the application of Article 101(3) of the Treaty on the Functioning of the European Union to certain categories of specialisation agreements[2] ("the Specialisation Block Exemption Regulation").

Notes

[1] OJ L 335, 18.12.2010, p.36.
[2] OJ L 335, 18.12.2010, p.43.

9. Although these guidelines contain certain references to cartels, they are not intended to give any guidance as to what does and does not constitute a cartel as defined by the decisional practice of the Commission and the case-law of the Court of Justice of the European Union.

Commentary
para 9: **F&N:** 7.22, 8.03

10. The term "competitors" as used in these guidelines includes both actual and potential competitors. Two companies are treated as actual competitors if they are active on the same relevant market. A company is treated as a potential competitor of another company if, in the absence of the agreement, in case of a small but permanent increase in relative prices it is likely that the former, within a short period of time,[1] would undertake the necessary additional investments or other necessary switching costs to enter the relevant market on which the latter is active. This assessment has to be based on realistic grounds, the mere theoretical possibility to enter a market is not sufficient (see Commission Notice on the definition of the relevant market for the purposes of Community competition law)[2] ("the Market Definition Notice").

Notes

[1] What constitutes a "short period of time" depends on the facts of the case at hand, its legal and economic context, and, in particular, on whether the company in question is a party to the agreement or a third party. In the first case, that is to say, where it is analysed whether a party to an agreement should be considered a potential competitor of the other party,

the Commission would normally consider a longer period to be a "short period of time" than in the second case, that is to say, where the capacity of a third party to act as a competitive constraint on the parties to an agreement is analysed. For a third party to be considered a potential competitor, market entry would need to take place sufficiently fast so that the threat of potential entry is a constraint on the parties' and other market participants' behaviour. For these reasons, both the R&D and the Specialisation Block Exemption Regulations consider a period of not more than three years a "short period of time".

2 OJ C 372, 9.12.1997, p.5, paragraph 24; see also the Commission's Thirteenth Report on Competition Policy, point 55 and Commission Decision in Case IV/32.009 *Elopak/Metal Box-Odin* OJ L 209, 8.8.1990, p.15.

Commentary
para 10: **B&C:** 2.097, 2.127, 4.020 **F&N:** 3.282, 7.16, 7.70, 7.71, 7.183, 7.291

11. Companies that form part of the same "undertaking" within the meaning of Article 101(1) are not considered to be competitors for the purposes of these guidelines. Article 101 only applies to agreements between independent undertakings. When a company exercises decisive influence over another company they form a single economic entity and, hence, are part of the same undertaking.[1] The same is true for sister companies, that is to say, companies over which decisive influence is exercised by the same parent company. They are consequently not considered to be competitors even if they are both active on the same relevant product and geographic markets.

Notes

[1] See, for example, Case C-73/95 *Viho* [1996] ECR I-5457, paragraph 51. The exercise of decisive influence by the parent company over the conduct of a subsidiary can be presumed in case of wholly-owned subsidiaries; see, for example, Case 107/82 *AEG* [1983] ECR-3151, paragraph 50; Case C-286/98 P *Stora* [2000] ECR-I 9925, paragraph 29; or Case C-97/08 P *Akzo* [2009] ECR I-8237, paragraphs 60 et seq.

Commentary
para 11: **F&N:** 7.105, 7.122

12. Agreements that are entered into between undertakings operating at a different level of the production or distribution chain, that is to say, vertical agreements, are in principle dealt with in Commission Regulation (EU) No 330/2010 of 20 April 2010 on the application of Article 101(3) of the Treaty on the Functioning of the European Union to categories of vertical agreements and concerted practices[1] ("the Block Exemption Regulation on Vertical Restraints") and the Guidelines on Vertical Restraints.[2] However, to the extent that vertical agreements, for example, distribution agreements, are concluded between competitors, the effects of the agreement on the market and the possible competition problems can be similar to horizontal agreements. Therefore, vertical agreements between competitors fall under these guidelines.[3] Should there be a need to also assess such agreements under the Block Exemption Regulation on Vertical Restraints and the Guidelines on Vertical Restraints, this will be specifically stated in the relevant chapter of these guidelines. In the absence of such a reference, only these guidelines will be applicable to vertical agreements between competitors.

Notes

[1] OJ L 102, 23.4.2010, p.1.

[2] OJ C 130, 19.5.2010, p.1.

[3] This does not apply where competitors enter into a non-reciprocal vertical agreement and (i) the supplier is a manufacturer and a distributor of goods, while the buyer is a distributor and not a competing undertaking at the manufacturing level, or (ii) the supplier is a provider of services at several levels of trade, while the buyer provides its goods or services at the retail level and is not a competing undertaking at the level of trade where it purchases the contract services. Such agreements are exclusively assessed under the Block Exemption Regulation and the Guidelines on Vertical Restraints (see Article 2(4) of the Block Exemption Regulation on Vertical Restraints).

Commentary
para 12: **B&C:** 1.038 **F&N:** 7.17, 16.117

13. Horizontal co-operation agreements may combine different stages of co-operation, for example research and development ("R&D") and the production and/or commercialisation of its results. Such agreements are generally also covered by these guidelines. When using these guidelines for the analysis of such integrated co-operation, as a general rule, all the chapters pertaining to the different parts of the co-operation will be relevant. However, where the relevant chapters of these

guidelines contain graduated messages, for example with regard to safe harbours or whether certain conduct will normally be considered a restriction of competition by object or by effect, what is set out in the chapter pertaining to that part of an integrated co-operation which can be considered its 'centre of gravity' prevails for the entire co-operation.[1]

Notes

[1] It should be noted that this test only applies to the relationship between the different chapters of these guidelines, not to the relationship between different block exemption regulations. The scope of a block exemption regulation is defined by its own provisions.

Commentary

para 13: **B&C:** 6.013. 6.055, 6.073 **F&N:** 7.427

14. Two factors are in particular relevant for the determination of the centre of gravity of integrated co-operation: firstly, the starting point of the co-operation, and, secondly, the degree of integration of the different functions which are combined. For example, the centre of gravity of a horizontal co-operation agreement involving both joint R&D and joint production of the results would thus normally be the joint R&D, as the joint production will only take place if the joint R&D is successful. This implies that the results of the joint R&D are decisive for the subsequent joint production. The assessment of the centre of gravity would change if the parties would have engaged in the joint production in any event, that is to say, irrespective of the joint R&D, or if the agreement provided for a full integration in the area of production and only a partial integration of some R&D activities. In this case, the centre of gravity of the co-operation would be the joint production.

Commentary

para 14: **B&C:** 6.013, 6.073

15. Article 101 only applies to those horizontal co-operation agreements which may affect trade between Member States. The principles on the applicability of Article 101 set out in these guidelines are therefore based on the assumption that a horizontal co-operation agreement is capable of affecting trade between Member States to an appreciable extent.

16. The assessment under Article 101 as described in these guidelines is without prejudice to the possible parallel application of Article 102 of the Treaty to horizontal co-operation agreements.[1]

Notes

[1] See Case T-51/89 *Tetra Pak I* [1990] ECR-II 309, paragraphs 25 *et seq.* and Guidance on the Commission's enforcement priorities in applying Article [102] of the [Treaty on the Functioning of the European Union] to abusive exclusionary conduct by dominant undertakings, OJ C 45, 24.2.2009, p.7 ("Article 102 Guidance Paper").

17. These guidelines are without prejudice to the interpretation the Court of Justice of the European Union may give to the application of Article 101 to horizontal co-operation agreements.

18. These guidelines replace the Commission guidelines on the applicability of Article [101] of the [Treaty on the Functioning of the European Union] to horizontal co-operation agreements[1] which were published by the Commission in 2001 and do not apply to the extent that sector specific rules apply as is the case for certain agreements with regard to agriculture,[2] transport[3] or insurance.[4] The Commission will continue to monitor the operation of the R&D and Specialisation Block Exemption Regulations and these guidelines based on market information from stakeholders and national competition authorities and may revise these guidelines in the light of future developments and of evolving insight.

Notes

[1] OJ C 3, 6.1.2001, p.2. These guidelines do not contain a separate chapter on "environmental agreements" as was the case in the previous guidelines. Standard-setting in the environment sector, which was the main focus of the former chapter on environmental agreements, is more appropriately dealt with in the standardisation chapter of these guidelines. In general, depending on the competition issues "environmental agreements" give rise to, they are to be assessed under the relevant chapter of these guidelines, be it the chapter on R&D, production, commercialisation or standardisation agreements.

[2] Council Regulation (EC) No 1184/2006 of 24 July 2006 applying certain rules of competition to the production of, and trade in, agricultural products, OJ L 214, 4.8.2006, p.7.

3 Council Regulation (EC) No 169/2009 of 26 February 2009 applying rules of competition to transport by rail, road and inland waterway, OJ L 61, 5.3.2009, p.1; Council Regulation (EC) No 246/2009 of 26 February 2009 on the application of Article [101](3) of the Treaty to certain categories of agreements and concerted practices between liner shipping companies (consortia), OJ L 79, 25.3.2009, p.1; Commission Regulation (EC) No 823/2000 of 19 April 2000 on the application of Article [101](3) of the Treaty to certain categories of agreements, decisions and concerted practices between liner shipping companies (consortia), OJ L 100, 20.4.2000, p.24; Guidelines on the application of Article [101] of the [Treaty on the Functioning of the European Union] to maritime transport services, OJ C 245, 26.9.2008, p.2.

4 Commission Regulation (EU) No 267/2010 of 24 March 2010 on the application of Article 101(3) of the Treaty on the Functioning of the European Union to certain categories of agreements, decisions and concerted practices in the insurance sector, OJ L 83, 31.3.2010, p.1.

Commentary
para 18(a): F&N: 12.114, 12.117

19. The Commission guidelines on the application of Article [101](3) of the Treaty[1] ('the General Guidelines') contain general guidance on the interpretation of Article 101. Consequently, these guidelines have to be read in conjunction with the General Guidelines.

Notes
1 OJ C 101, 27.4.2004, p.97.

1.2. Basic principles for the assessment under Article 101

20. The assessment under Article 101 consists of two steps. The first step, under Article 101(1), is to assess whether an agreement between undertakings, which is capable of affecting trade between Member States, has an anti-competitive object or actual or potential[1] restrictive effects on competition. The second step, under Article 101(3), which only becomes relevant when an agreement is found to be restrictive of competition within the meaning of Article 101(1), is to determine the pro-competitive benefits produced by that agreement and to assess whether those pro-competitive effects outweigh the restrictive effects on competition.[2] The balancing of restrictive and pro-competitive effects is conducted exclusively within the framework laid down by Article 101(3).[3] If the pro-competitive effects do not outweigh a restriction of competition, Article 101(2) stipulates that the agreement shall be automatically void.

Notes
1 Article 101(1) prohibits both actual and potential anti-competitive effects; see for example Case C-7/95 P *John Deere* [1998] ECR I-3111, paragraph 77; Case C-238/05 *Asnef-Equifax* [2006] ECR I-11125, paragraph 50.
2 See Joined Cases C-501/06 P and others *GlaxoSmithKline* [2009] ECR I-9291, paragraph 95.
3 See Case T-65/98 *Van den Bergh Foods* [2003] ECR II-4653, paragraph 107; Case T-112/99 *Métropole télévision (M6) and others* [2001] ECR II-2459, paragraph 74; Case T-328/03 *O2* [2006] ECR II-1231, paragraphs 69 et seq., where the General Court held that it is only in the precise framework of Article 101(3) that the pro-and anti-competitive aspects of a restriction may be weighed.

Commentary
para 20: B&C: 2.108, 3.012

21. The analysis of horizontal co-operation agreements has certain common elements with the analysis of horizontal mergers pertaining to the potential restrictive effects, in particular as regards joint ventures. There is often only a fine line between full-function joint ventures that fall under the Merger Regulation and non-full-function joint ventures that are assessed under Article 101. Hence, their effects can be quite similar.

Commentary
para 21: B&C: 6.009 **F&N:** 15.75

22. In certain cases, companies are encouraged by public authorities to enter into horizontal co-operation agreements in order to attain a public policy objective by way of self-regulation. However, companies remain subject to Article 101 if a national law merely encourages or makes it easier for them to engage in autonomous anti-competitive conduct.[1] In other words, the fact that public authorities encourage a horizontal co-operation agreement does not mean that it is

permissible under Article 101.[2] It is only if anti-competitive conduct is required of companies by national legislation, or if the latter creates a legal framework which precludes all scope for competitive activity on their part, that Article 101 does not apply.[3] In such a situation, the restriction of competition is not attributable, as Article 101 implicitly requires, to the autonomous conduct of the companies and they are shielded from all the consequences of an infringement of that article.[4] Each case must be assessed on its own facts according to the general principles set out in these guidelines.

Notes

[1] See judgment of 14 October 2010 in Case C-280/08 P *Deutsche Telekom*, ECR I not yet reported, paragraph 82 and the case-law cited therein.

[2] See Case C-198/01 *CIF* [2003] ECR I-8055, paragraphs 56-58; Joined Cases T-217/03 and T-245/03 *French Beef* [2006] ECR II-4987, paragraph 92; Case T-7/92 *Asia Motor France II* [1993] ECR II-669, paragraph 71; and Case T-148/89 *Tréfilunion* [1995] ECR II-1063, paragraph 118.

[3] See Case C-280/08 P *Deutsche Telekom*, paragraphs 80–81. This possibility has been narrowly interpreted; see, for example, Joined Cases 209/78 and others *Van Landewyck* [1980] ECR 3125, paragraphs 130–134; Joined Cases 240/82 and others *Stichting Sigarettenindustrie* [1985] ECR 3831, paragraphs 27–29; and Joined Cases C-359/95 P and C-379/95 P *Ladbroke Racing* [1997] ECR I-6265, paragraphs 33 et seq.

[4] At least until a decision to disapply the national legislation has been adopted and that decision has become definitive; see Case C-198/01 *CIF* [2003] ECR I-8055, paragraphs 54 et seq.

Commentary
para 22: F&N: 3.155, 3.158

1.2.1. Article 101(1)

23. Article 101(1) prohibits agreements the object or effect of which is to restrict[1] competition.

Notes

[1] For the purpose of these guidelines, the term "restriction of competition" includes the prevention and distortion of competition.

Commentary
para 23: F&N: 3.183

(i) Restrictions of competition by object

24. Restrictions of competition by object are those that by their very nature have the potential to restrict competition within the meaning of Article 101(1).[1] It is not necessary to examine the actual or potential effects of an agreement on the market once its anti-competitive object has been established.[2]

Notes

[1] See, for example, Case C-209/07 *BIDS* [2008] ECR I-8637, paragraph 17.

[2] See, for example, Joined Cases C-501/06 P and others *GlaxoSmithKline* [2009] ECR I-9291, paragraph 55; Case C-209/07 *BIDS* [2008] ECR I-8637, paragraph 16; Case C-8/08 *T-Mobile Netherlands* [2009] ECR I-4529, paragraph 29 et seq.; Case C-7/95 P *John Deere* [1998] ECR I-3111, paragraph 77.

Commentary
para 24: F&N: 3.184, 7.21

25. According to the settled case-law of the Court of Justice of the European Union, in order to assess whether an agreement has an anti-competitive object, regard must be had to the content of the agreement, the objectives it seeks to attain, and the economic and legal context of which it forms part. In addition, although the parties' intention is not a necessary factor in determining whether an agreement has an anti-competitive object, the Commission may nevertheless take this aspect into account in its analysis.[1] Further guidance with regard to the notion of restrictions of competition by object can be obtained in the General Guidelines.

Notes

[1] See, for example, Joined Cases C-501/06 P and others *GlaxoSmithKline* [2009] ECR I-9291, paragraph 58; Case C-209/07 *BIDS* [2008] ECR I-8637, paragraphs 15 et seq.

Commentary
para 25: F&N: 3.155, 3.185, 7.21, 12.126

(ii) Restrictive effects on competition

26. If a horizontal co-operation agreement does not restrict competition by object, it must be examined whether it has appreciable restrictive effects on competition. Account must be taken of both actual and potential effects. In other words, the agreement must at least be likely to have anti-competitive effects.

27. For an agreement to have restrictive effects on competition within the meaning of Article 101(1) it must have, or be likely to have, an appreciable adverse impact on at least one of the parameters of competition on the market, such as price, output, product quality, product variety or innovation. Agreements can have such effects by appreciably reducing competition between the parties to the agreement or between any one of them and third parties. This means that the agreement must reduce the parties' decision-making independence,[1] either due to obligations contained in the agreement which regulate the market conduct of at least one of the parties or by influencing the market conduct of at least one of the parties by causing a change in its incentives.

Notes

[1] See Case C-7/95 P *John Deere* [1998] ECR I-3111, paragraph 88; Case C-238/05 *Asnef-Equifax* [2006] ECR I-11125, paragraph 51.

Commentary
para 27: F&N: 3.346, 3.365, 3.367, 7.23

28. Restrictive effects on competition within the relevant market are likely to occur where it can be expected with a reasonable degree of probability that, due to the agreement, the parties would be able to profitably raise prices or reduce output, product quality, product variety or innovation. This will depend on several factors such as the nature and content of the agreement, the extent to which the parties individually or jointly have or obtain some degree of market power, and the extent to which the agreement contributes to the creation, maintenance or strengthening of that market power or allows the parties to exploit such market power.

Commentary
para 28: F&N: 7.23, 7.24

29. The assessment of whether a horizontal co-operation agreement has restrictive effects on competition within the meaning of Article 101(1) must be made in comparison to the actual legal and economic context in which competition would occur in the absence of the agreement with all of its alleged restrictions (that is to say, in the absence of the agreement as it stands (if already implemented) or as envisaged (if not yet implemented) at the time of assessment). Hence, in order to prove actual or potential restrictive effects on competition, it is necessary to take into account competition between the parties and competition from third parties, in particular actual or potential competition that would have existed in the absence of the agreement. This comparison does not take into account any potential efficiency gains generated by the agreement as these will only be assessed under Article 101(3).

Commentary
para 29: F&N: 3.368, 3.371, 7.25, 7.27, 7.455, 15.80

30. Consequently, horizontal co-operation agreements between competitors that, on the basis of objective factors, would not be able to independently carry out the project or activity covered by the co-operation, for instance, due to the limited technical capabilities of the parties, will normally not give rise to restrictive effects on competition within the meaning of Article 101(1) unless the parties could have carried out the project with less stringent restrictions.[1]

Notes

[1] See also paragraph 18 of the General Guidelines.

Commentary

para 30: B&C: 2.091, 2.102 F&N: 7.28, 7.251

31. General guidance with regard to the notion of restrictions of competition by effect can be obtained in the General Guidelines. These guidelines provide additional guidance specific to the competition assessment of horizontal co-operation agreements.

Nature and content of the agreement

32. The nature and content of an agreement relates to factors such as the area and objective of the co-operation, the competitive relationship between the parties and the extent to which they combine their activities. Those factors determine which kinds of possible competition concerns can arise from a horizontal co-operation agreement.

33. Horizontal co-operation agreements may limit competition in several ways. The agreement may:
    — be exclusive in the sense that it limits the possibility of the parties to compete against each other or third parties as independent economic operators or as parties to other, competing agreements;
    — require the parties to contribute such assets that their decision-making independence is appreciably reduced; or
    — affect the parties' financial interests in such a way that their decision-making independence is appreciably reduced. Both financial interests in the agreement and also financial interests in other parties to the agreement are relevant for the assessment.

Commentary

para 33: B&C: 2.131, 6.015

34. The potential effect of such agreements may be the loss of competition between the parties to the agreement. Competitors can also benefit from the reduction of competitive pressure that results from the agreement and may therefore find it profitable to increase their prices. The reduction in those competitive constraints may lead to price increases in the relevant market. Factors such as whether the parties to the agreement have high market shares, whether they are close competitors, whether the customers have limited possibilities of switching suppliers, whether competitors are unlikely to increase supply if prices increase, and whether one of the parties to the agreement is an important competitive force, are all relevant for the competitive assessment of the agreement.

Commentary

para 34: B&C: 2.132

35. A horizontal co-operation agreement may also:
    — lead to the disclosure of strategic information thereby increasing the likelihood of coordination among the parties within or outside the field of the co-operation;
    — achieve significant commonality of costs (that is to say, the proportion of variable costs which the parties have in common), so the parties may more easily coordinate market prices and output.

Commentary

para 35: B&C: 6.015 F&N: 10.146

36. Significant commonality of costs achieved by a horizontal co-operation agreement can only allow the parties to more easily coordinate market prices and output where the parties have market power, the market characteristics are conducive to such coordination, the area of co-operation accounts for a high proportion of the parties' variable costs in a given market, and the parties combine their activities in the area of co-operation to a significant extent. This could, for instance,

Part C Substantive Antitrust Matters

be the case, where they jointly manufacture or purchase an important intermediate product or jointly manufacture or distribute a high proportion of their total output of a final product.

Commentary
para 36: F&N: 12.105

37. A horizontal agreement may therefore decrease the parties' decision-making independence and as a result increase the likelihood that they will coordinate their behaviour in order to reach a collusive outcome but it may also make coordination easier, more stable or more effective for parties that were already coordinating before, either by making the coordination more robust or by permitting them to achieve even higher prices.

38. Some horizontal co-operation agreements, for example production and standardisation agreements, may also give rise to anti-competitive foreclosure concerns.

Commentary
para 38: B&C: 2.100

Market power and other market characteristics

39. Market power is the ability to profitably maintain prices above competitive levels for a period of time or to profitably maintain output in terms of product quantities, product quality and variety or innovation below competitive levels for a period of time.

Commentary
para 39: B&C: 4.007 F&N: 3.365, 3.373

40. In markets with fixed costs undertakings must price above their variable costs of production in order to ensure a competitive return on their investment. The fact that undertakings price above their variable costs is therefore not in itself a sign that competition in the market is not functioning well and that undertakings have market power that allows them to price above the competitive level. It is when competitive constraints are insufficient to maintain prices, output, product quality, product variety and innovation at competitive levels that undertakings have market power in the context of Article 101(1).

Commentary
para 40: F&N: 3.376

41. The creation, maintenance or strengthening of market power can result from superior skill, foresight or innovation. It can also result from reduced competition between the parties to the agreement or between any one of the parties and third parties, for example, because the agreement leads to anti-competitive foreclosure of competitors by raising competitors' costs and limiting their capacity to compete effectively with the contracting parties.

Commentary
para 41: B&C: 2.100

42. Market power is a question of degree. The degree of market power required for the finding of an infringement under Article 101(1) in the case of agreements that are restrictive of competition by effect is less than the degree of market power required for a finding of dominance under Article 102, where a substantial degree of market power is required.

Commentary
para 42: F&N: 3.376

43. The starting point for the analysis of market power is the position of the parties on the markets affected by the co-operation. To carry out this analysis the relevant market(s) have to be defined by using the methodology of the Commission's Market Definition Notice. Where specific types

of markets, such as purchasing or technology markets, are concerned these guidelines will provide additional guidance.

Commentary
para 43: **B&C:** 9.145 **F&N:** 3.377

44. If the parties have a low combined market share, the horizontal co-operation agreement is unlikely to give rise to restrictive effects on competition within the meaning of Article 101(1) and, normally, no further analysis will be required. What is considered to be a "low combined market share" depends on the type of agreement in question and can be inferred from the "safe harbour" thresholds set out in various chapters of these guidelines and, more generally, from the Commission Notice on agreements of minor importance which do not appreciably restrict competition under Article [101](1) of the [Treaty on the Functioning of the European Union] (*de minimis*)[1] ('the *De Minimis* Notice'). If one of just two parties has only an insignificant market share and if it does not possess important resources, even a high combined market share normally cannot be seen as indicating a likely restrictive effect on competition in the market.[2] Given the variety of horizontal co-operation agreements and the different effects they may cause in different market situations, it is not possible to give a general market share threshold above which sufficient market power for causing restrictive effects on competition can be assumed.

Notes

[1] OJ C 368, 22.12.2001, p.13.

[2] If there are more than two parties, then the collective share of all co-operating competitors has to be significantly greater than the share of the largest single participating competitor.

Commentary
para 44: **B&C:** 2.128, 2.169 **F&N:** 3.378

45. Depending on the market position of the parties and the concentration in the market, other factors such as the stability of market shares over time, entry barriers and the likelihood of market entry, and the countervailing power of buyers/suppliers also have to be considered.

Commentary
para 45: **B&C:** 2.169

46. Normally, the Commission uses current market shares in its competitive analysis.[1] However, reasonably certain future developments may also be taken into account, for instance in the light of exit, entry or expansion in the relevant market. Historic data may be used if market shares have been volatile, for instance when the market is characterised by large, lumpy orders. Changes in historic market shares may provide useful information about the competitive process and the likely future importance of the various competitors, for instance, by indicating whether undertakings have been gaining or losing market shares. In any event, the Commission interprets market shares in the light of likely market conditions, for instance, if the market is highly dynamic in character and if the market structure is unstable due to innovation or growth.

Notes

[1] As to the calculation of market shares, see also Market Definition Notice, paragraphs 54–55.

47. When entering a market is sufficiently easy, a horizontal co-operation agreement will normally not be expected to give rise to restrictive effects on competition. For entry to be considered a sufficient competitive constraint on the parties to a horizontal co-operation agreement, it must be shown to be likely, timely and sufficient to deter or defeat any potential restrictive effects of the agreement. The analysis of entry may be affected by the presence of horizontal co-operation agreements. The likely or possible termination of a horizontal co-operation agreement may influence the likelihood of entry.

Commentary
para 47: **F&N:** 15.90

Part C Substantive Antitrust Matters

1.2.2. Article 101(3)

48. The assessment of restrictions of competition by object or effect under Article 101(1) is only one side of the analysis. The other side, which is reflected in Article 101(3), is the assessment of the pro-competitive effects of restrictive agreements. The general approach when applying Article 101(3) is presented in the General Guidelines. Where in an individual case a restriction of competition within the meaning of Article 101(1) has been proven, Article 101(3) can be invoked as a defence. According to Article 2 of Council Regulation (EC) No 1/2003 of 16 December 2002 on the implementation of the rules on competition laid down in Articles [101] and [102] of the Treaty,[1] the burden of proof under Article 101(3) rests on the undertaking(s) invoking the benefit of this provision. Therefore, the factual arguments and the evidence provided by the undertaking(s) must enable the Commission to arrive at the conviction that the agreement in question is sufficiently likely to give rise to pro-competitive effects or that it is not.[2]

Notes

[1] OJ L 1, 4.1.2003, p.1.

[2] See, for example, Joined Cases C-501/06 P and others *GlaxoSmithKline* [2009] ECR I-9291, paragraphs 93–95.

Commentary
para 48: B&C: 2.108

49. The application of the exception rule of Article 101(3) is subject to four cumulative conditions, two positive and two negative:
    — the agreement must contribute to improving the production or distribution of products or contribute to promoting technical or economic progress, that is to say, lead to efficiency gains;
    — the restrictions must be indispensable to the attainment of those objectives, that is to say, the efficiency gains;
    — consumers must receive a fair share of the resulting benefits, that is to say, the efficiency gains, including qualitative efficiency gains, attained by the indispensable restrictions must be sufficiently passed on to consumers so that they are at least compensated for the restrictive effects of the agreement; hence, efficiencies only accruing to the parties to the agreement will not suffice; for the purposes of these guidelines, the concept of "consumers" encompasses the customers, potential and/or actual, of the parties to the agreement;[1] and
    — the agreement must not afford the parties the possibility of eliminating competition in respect of a substantial part of the products in question.

Notes

[1] More detail on the concept of consumer is provided in paragraph 84 of the General Guidelines.

50. In the area of horizontal co-operation agreements there are block exemption regulations based on Article 101(3) for research and development[1] and specialisation (including joint production)[2] agreements. Those Block Exemption Regulations are based on the premise that the combination of complementary skills or assets can be the source of substantial efficiencies in research and development and specialisation agreements. This may also be the case for other types of horizontal co-operation agreements. The analysis of the efficiencies of an individual agreement under Article 101(3) is therefore to a large extent a question of identifying the complementary skills and assets that each of the parties brings to the agreement and evaluating whether the resulting efficiencies are such that the conditions of Article 101(3) are fulfilled.

Notes

[1] R&D Block Exemption Regulation.

[2] Specialisation Block Exemption Regulation.

Commentary
para 50: B&C: 3.030, 3.038

51. Complementarities may arise from horizontal co-operation agreements in various ways. A research and development agreement may bring together different research capabilities that

allow the parties to produce better products more cheaply and shorten the time for those products to reach the market. A production agreement may allow the parties to achieve economies of scale or scope that they could not achieve individually.

Commentary
para 51: B&C: 3.033, 3.038

52. Horizontal co-operation agreements that do not involve the combination of complementary skills or assets are less likely to lead to efficiency gains that benefit consumers. Such agreements may reduce duplication of certain costs, for instance because certain fixed costs can be eliminated. However, fixed cost savings are, in general, less likely to result in benefits to consumers than savings in, for instance, variable or marginal costs.

Commentary
para 52: B&C: 6.061

53. Further guidance regarding the Commission's application of the criteria of Article 101(3) can be obtained in the General Guidelines.

1.3. Structure of these guidelines

54. Chapter 2 will first set out some general principles for the assessment of the exchange of information, which are applicable to all types of horizontal co-operation agreements entailing the exchange of information. The subsequent chapters of these guidelines will each address one specific type of horizontal co-operation agreement. Each chapter will apply the analytical framework described in section 1.2 as well as the general principles on the exchange of information to the specific type of co-operation in question.

Commentary
para 54: F&N: 3.158

2. GENERAL PRINCIPLES ON THE COMPETITIVE ASSESSMENT OF INFORMATION EXCHANGE

2.1. Definition and scope

55. The purpose of this chapter is to guide the competitive assessment of information exchange. Information exchange can take various forms. Firstly, data can be directly shared between competitors. Secondly, data can be shared indirectly through a common agency (for example, a trade association) or a third party such as a market research organisation or through the companies' suppliers or retailers.

Commentary
para 55: B&C: 2.067, 6.020, 6.023 F&N: 8.50

56. Information exchange takes place in different contexts. There are agreements, decisions by associations of undertakings, or concerted practices under which information is exchanged, where the main economic function lies in the exchange of information itself. Moreover, information exchange can be part of another type of horizontal co-operation agreement (for example, the parties to a production agreement share certain information on costs). The assessment of the latter type of information exchanges should be carried out in the context of the assessment of the horizontal co-operation agreement itself.

57. Information exchange is a common feature of many competitive markets and may generate various types of efficiency gains. It may solve problems of information asymmetries,[1] thereby making markets more efficient. Moreover, companies may improve their internal efficiency through benchmarking against each other's best practices. Sharing of information may also help companies to save costs by reducing their inventories, enabling quicker delivery of perishable products to

consumers, or dealing with unstable demand etc. Furthermore, information exchanges may directly benefit consumers by reducing their search costs and improving choice.

Notes

[1] Economic theory on information asymmetries deals with the study of decisions in transactions where one party has more information than the other.

Commentary
para 57: B&C: 6.025 F&N: 3.158

58. However, the exchange of market information may also lead to restrictions of competition in particular in situations where it is liable to enable undertakings to be aware of market strategies of their competitors.[1] The competitive outcome of information exchange depends on the characteristics of the market in which it takes place (such as concentration, transparency, stability, symmetry, complexity etc.) as well as on the type of information that is exchanged, which may modify the relevant market environment towards one liable to coordination.

Notes

[1] See Case C-7/95 P *John Deere* [1998] ECR I-3111, paragraph 88.

Commentary
para 58: B&C: 6.025

59. Moreover, communication of information among competitors may constitute an agreement, a concerted practice, or a decision by an association of undertakings with the object of fixing, in particular, prices or quantities. Those types of information exchanges will normally be considered and fined as cartels. Information exchange may also facilitate the implementation of a cartel by enabling companies to monitor whether the participants comply with the agreed terms. Those types of exchanges of information will be assessed as part of the cartel.

Commentary
para 59: F&N: 7.409, 8.44

Concerted practice

60. Information exchange can only be addressed under Article 101 if it establishes or is part of an agreement, a concerted practice or a decision by an association of undertakings. The existence of an agreement, a concerted practice or decision by an association of undertakings does not prejudge whether the agreement, concerted practice or decision by an association of undertakings gives rise to a restriction of competition within the meaning of Article 101(1). In line with the case-law of the Court of Justice of the European Union, the concept of a concerted practice refers to a form of coordination between undertakings by which, without it having reached the stage where an agreement properly so-called has been concluded, practical cooperation between them is knowingly substituted for the risks of competition.[1] The criteria of coordination and cooperation necessary for determining the existence of a concerted practice, far from requiring an actual plan to have been worked out, are to be understood in the light of the concept inherent in the provisions of the Treaty on competition, according to which each company must determine independently the policy which it intends to adopt on the internal market and the conditions which it intends to offer to its customers.[2]

Notes

[1] See for example Case C-8/08 *T-Mobile Netherlands* [2009] ECR I-4529, paragraph 26; Joined Cases C-89/85 and others *Wood Pulp* [1993] ECR 1307, paragraph 63.
[2] See Case C-7/95 P *John Deere* [1998] ECR I-3111, paragraph 86.

Commentary
para 60: F&N: 3.136, 3.137, 7.448, 7.454, 12.117

61. This does not deprive companies of the right to adapt themselves intelligently to the existing or anticipated conduct of their competitors. It does, however, preclude any direct or indirect contact between competitors, the object or effect of which is to create conditions of competition which do not correspond to the normal competitive conditions of the market in question, regard being had to the nature of the products or services offered, the size and number of the undertakings, and the volume of the said market.[1] This precludes any direct or indirect contact between competitors, the object or effect of which is to influence conduct on the market of an actual or potential competitor, or to disclose to such competitor the course of conduct which they themselves have decided to adopt or contemplate adopting on the market, thereby facilitating a collusive outcome on the market.[2] Hence, information exchange can constitute a concerted practice if it reduces strategic uncertainty[3] in the market thereby facilitating collusion, that is to say, if the data exchanged is strategic. Consequently, sharing of strategic data between competitors amounts to concertation, because it reduces the independence of competitors' conduct on the market and diminishes their incentives to compete.

Notes

[1] Case C-7/95 P *John Deere* [1998] ECR I-3111, paragraph 87.

[2] See Cases 40/73 and others *Suiker Unie* [1975] ECR 1663, paragraph 173 et seq.

[3] Strategic uncertainty in the market arises as there is a variety of possible collusive outcomes available and because companies cannot perfectly observe past and current actions of their competitors and entrants.

Commentary

para 61: B&C: 6.020 **F&N:** 3.137

62. A situation where only one undertaking discloses strategic information to its competitor(s) who accept(s) it can also constitute a concerted practice.[1] Such disclosure could occur, for example, through contacts via mail, emails, phone calls, meetings etc. It is then irrelevant whether only one undertaking unilaterally informs its competitors of its intended market behaviour, or whether all participating undertakings inform each other of the respective deliberations and intentions. When one undertaking alone reveals to its competitors strategic information concerning its future commercial policy, that reduces strategic uncertainty as to the future operation of the market for all the competitors involved and increases the risk of limiting competition and of collusive behaviour.[2] For example, mere attendance at a meeting[3] where a company discloses its pricing plans to its competitors is likely to be caught by Article 101, even in the absence of an explicit agreement to raise prices.[4] When a company receives strategic data from a competitor (be it in a meeting, by mail or electronically), it will be presumed to have accepted the information and adapted its market conduct accordingly unless it responds with a clear statement that it does not wish to receive such data.[5]

Notes

[1] See for example Joined Cases T-25/95 and others *Cimenteries* [2000] ECR II-491, paragraph 1849: "[…] the concept of concerted practice does in fact imply the existence of reciprocal contacts […]. That condition is met where one competitor discloses its future intentions or conduct on the market to another when the latter requests it or, at the very least, accepts it".

[2] See Opinion of Advocate General Kokott, Case C-8/08 *T-Mobile Netherlands* [2009] ECR I-4529, paragraph 54.

[3] See Case C-8/08 *T-Mobile Netherlands* [2009] ECR I-4529, paragraph 59: "Depending on the structure of the market, the possibility cannot be ruled out that a meeting on a single occasion between competitors, such as that in question in the main proceedings, may, in principle, constitute a sufficient basis for the participating undertakings to concert their market conduct and thus successfully substitute practical cooperation between them for competition and the risks that that entails."

[4] See Joined Cases T-202/98 and others *Tate & Lyle v Commission* [2001] ECR II-2035, paragraph 54.

[5] See Case C-199/92 P *Hüls* [1999] ECR I-4287, paragraph 162; Case C-49/92 P *Anic Partezipazioni* [1999] ECR I-4125, paragraph 121.

Commentary

para 62: F&N: 3.138, 7.453, 8.44, 8.49

Part C Substantive Antitrust Matters

63. Where a company makes a unilateral announcement that is also genuinely public, for example through a newspaper, this generally does not constitute a concerted practice within the meaning of Article 101(1).[1] However, depending on the facts underlying the case at hand, the possibility of finding a concerted practice cannot be excluded, for example in a situation where such an announcement was followed by public announcements by other competitors, not least because strategic responses of competitors to each other's public announcements (which, to take one instance, might involve readjustments of their own earlier announcements to announcements made by competitors) could prove to be a strategy for reaching a common understanding about the terms of coordination.

Notes

[1] This would not cover situations where such announcements involve invitations to collude.

Commentary
para 63: B&C: 5.046, 6.021 **F&N:** 3.139, 7.451, 8.49

2.2. Assessment under Article 101(1)

2.2.1. Main competition concerns [1]

Notes

[1] The use of the term "main competition concerns" means that the ensuing description of competition concerns is neither exclusive nor exhaustive.

64. Once it has been established that there is an agreement, concerted practice or decision by an association of undertakings, it is necessary to consider the main competition concerns pertaining to information exchanges.

Collusive outcome

65. By artificially increasing transparency in the market, the exchange of strategic information can facilitate coordination (that is to say, alignment) of companies' competitive behaviour and result in restrictive effects on competition. This can occur through different channels.

Commentary
para 65: B&C: 6.026 **F&N:** 7.535

66. One way is that through information exchange companies may reach a common understanding on the terms of coordination, which can lead to a collusive outcome on the market. Information exchange can create mutually consistent expectations regarding the uncertainties present in the market. On that basis companies can then reach a common understanding on the terms of coordination of their competitive behaviour, even without an explicit agreement on coordination. Exchange of information about intentions concerning future conduct is the most likely means to enable companies to reach such a common understanding.

67. Another channel through which information exchange can lead to restrictive effects on competition is by increasing the internal stability of a collusive outcome on the market. In particular, it can do so by enabling the companies involved to monitor deviations. Namely, information exchange can make the market sufficiently transparent to allow the colluding companies to monitor to a sufficient degree whether other companies are deviating from the collusive outcome, and thus to know when to retaliate. Both exchanges of present and past data can constitute such a monitoring mechanism. This can either enable companies to achieve a collusive outcome on markets where they would otherwise not have been able to do so, or it can increase the stability of a collusive outcome already present on the market (see Example 3, paragraph 107).

68. A third channel through which information exchange can lead to restrictive effects on competition is by increasing the external stability of a collusive outcome on the market. Information exchanges that make the market sufficiently transparent can allow colluding companies to

monitor where and when other companies are attempting to enter the market, thus allowing the colluding companies to target the new entrant. This may also tie into the anti-competitive fore-closure concerns discussed in paragraphs 69 to 71. Both exchanges of present and past data can constitute such a monitoring mechanism.

Commentary
para 68: B&C: 2.100

Anti-competitive foreclosure

69. Apart from facilitating collusion, an exchange of information can also lead to anti-competitive foreclosure.[1]

Notes

[1] With regard to foreclosure concerns that vertical agreements can give rise to, see paragraphs 100 et seq. of the Guidelines on Vertical Restraints.

---

70. An exclusive exchange of information can lead to anti-competitive foreclosure on the same market where the exchange takes place. This can occur when the exchange of commercially sensitive information places unaffiliated competitors at a significant competitive disadvantage as compared to the companies affiliated within the exchange system. This type of foreclosure is only possible if the information concerned is very strategic for competition and covers a significant part of the relevant market.

71. It cannot be excluded that information exchange may also lead to anti-competitive foreclosure of third parties in a related market. For instance, by gaining enough market power through an information exchange, parties exchanging information in an upstream market, for instance vertically integrated companies, may be able to raise the price of a key component for a market downstream. Thereby, they could raise the costs of their rivals downstream, which could result in anti-competitive foreclosure in the downstream market.

2.2.2. *Restriction of competition by object*

72. Any information exchange with the objective of restricting competition on the market will be considered as a restriction of competition by object. In assessing whether an information exchange constitutes a restriction of competition by object, the Commission will pay particular attention to the legal and economic context in which the information exchange takes place.[1] To this end, the Commission will take into account whether the information exchange, by its very nature, may possibly lead to a restriction of competition.[2]

Notes

[1] See, for example, Joined Cases C-501/06 P and others *GlaxoSmithKline* [2009] ECR I-9291, paragraph 58; Case C-209/07 *BIDS* [2008] ECR I-8637, paragraphs 15 et seq.

[2] See also General Guidelines, paragraph 22.

Commentary
para 72: F&N: 8.03

---

73. Exchanging information on companies' individualised intentions concerning future conduct regarding prices or quantities[1] is particularly likely to lead to a collusive outcome. Informing each other about such intentions may allow competitors to arrive at a common higher price level without incurring the risk of losing market share or triggering a price war during the period of adjustment to new prices (see Example 1, paragraph 105). Moreover, it is less likely that information exchanges concerning future intentions are made for pro-competitive reasons than exchanges of actual data.

Notes

[1] Information regarding intended future quantities could for instance include intended future sales, market shares, territories, and sales to particular groups of consumers.

Commentary
para 73: B&C: 6.029 **F&N:** 7.439, 12.131

74. Information exchanges between competitors of individualised data regarding intended future prices or quantities should therefore be considered a restriction of competition by object.[1], [2] In addition, private exchanges between competitors of their individualised intentions regarding future prices or quantities would normally be considered and fined as cartels because they generally have the object of fixing prices or quantities. Information exchanges that constitute cartels not only infringe Article 101(1), but, in addition, are very unlikely to fulfil the conditions of Article 101(3).

Notes

[1] The notion of "intended future prices" is illustrated in Example 1. In specific situations where companies are fully committed to sell in the future at the prices that they have previously announced to the public (that is to say, they cannot revise them), such public announcements of future individualised prices or quantities would not be considered as intentions, and hence would normally not be found to restrict competition by object. This could occur, for example, because of the repeated interactions and the specific type of relationship companies may have with their customers, for instance since it is essential that the customers know future prices in advance or because they can already take advanced orders at these prices. This is because in these situations the information exchange would be a more costly means for reaching a collusive outcome in the market than exchanging information on future intentions, and would be more likely to be done for pro-competitive reasons. However, this does not imply that in general price commitment towards customers is necessarily pro-competitive. On the contrary, it could limit the possibility of deviating from a collusive outcome and hence render it more stable.

[2] This is without prejudice to the fact that public announcements of intended individualised prices may give rise to efficiencies and that the parties to such exchange would have a possibility to rely on Article 101(3).

Commentary
para 74: B&C: 3.030 **F&N:** 7.443, 7.447, 8.56

2.2.3. Restrictive effects on competition

75. The likely effects of an information exchange on competition must be analysed on a case-by-case basis as the results of the assessment depend on a combination of various case specific factors. The assessment of restrictive effects on competition compares the likely effects of the information exchange with the competitive situation that would prevail in the absence of that specific information exchange.[1] For an information exchange to have restrictive effects on competition within the meaning of Article 101(1), it must be likely to have an appreciable adverse impact on one (or several) of the parameters of competition such as price, output, product quality, product variety or innovation. Whether or not an exchange of information will have restrictive effects on competition depends on both the economic conditions on the relevant markets and the characteristics of information exchanged.

Notes

[1] Case C-7/95 P *John Deere* v *Commission* [1998] ECR I-3111, paragraph 76.

Commentary
para 75: B&C: 6.031 **F&N:** 7.439, 7.455

76. Certain market conditions may make coordination easier to achieve, sustain internally, or sustain externally.[1] Exchanges of information in such markets may have more restrictive effects compared to markets with different conditions. However, even where market conditions are such that coordination may be difficult to sustain before the exchange, the exchange of information may change the market conditions in such a way that coordination becomes possible after the exchange — for example by increasing transparency in the market, reducing market complexity, buffering instability or compensating for asymmetry. For this reason it is important to assess the restrictive effects of the information exchange in the context of both the initial market conditions, and how the information exchange changes those conditions. This will include an assessment of the specific characteristics of the system concerned, including its purpose, conditions of access to the system and conditions of participation in the system. It will also be

necessary to examine the frequency of the information exchanges, the type of information exchanged (for example, whether it is public or confidential, aggregated or detailed, and historical or current), and the importance of the information for the fixing of prices, volumes or conditions of service.[2] The following factors are relevant for this assessment.

Notes

[1] Information exchange may restrict competition in a similar way to a merger if it leads to more effective, more stable or more likely coordination in the market; see Case C-413/06 P *Sony* [2008] ECR I-4951, paragraph 123, where the Court of Justice endorsed the criteria established by the General Court in Case T-342/99 *Airtours* [2002] ECR II-2585, paragraph 62.

[2] Case C-238/05 *Asnef-Equifax* [2006] ECR I-11125, paragraph 54.

Commentary
para 76: F&N: 7.456

(i) Market characteristics

77. Companies are more likely to achieve a collusive outcome in markets which are sufficiently transparent, concentrated, non-complex, stable and symmetric. In those types of markets companies can reach a common understanding on the terms of coordination and successfully monitor and punish deviations. However, information exchange can also enable companies to achieve a collusive outcome in other market situations where they would not be able to do so in the absence of the information exchange. Information exchange can thereby facilitate a collusive outcome by increasing transparency in the market, reducing market complexity, buffering instability or compensating for asymmetry. In this context, the competitive outcome of an information exchange depends not only on the initial characteristics of the market in which it takes place (such as concentration, transparency, stability, complexity etc.), but also on how the type of the information exchanged may change those characteristics.[1]

Notes

[1] It should be noted that the discussion in paragraphs 78 to 85 is not a complete list of relevant market characteristics. There may be other characteristics of the market which are important in the setting of certain information exchanges.

Commentary
para 77: B&C: 6.032

78. Collusive outcomes are more likely in transparent markets. Transparency can facilitate collusion by enabling companies to reach a common understanding on the terms of coordination, or/and by increasing internal and external stability of collusion. Information exchange can increase transparency and hence limit uncertainties about the strategic variables of competition (for example, prices, output, demand, costs etc.). The lower the pre-existing level of transparency in the market, the more value an information exchange may have in achieving a collusive outcome. An information exchange that contributes little to the transparency in a market is less likely to have restrictive effects on competition than an information exchange that significantly increases transparency. Therefore it is the combination of both the pre-existing level of transparency and how the information exchange changes that level that will determine how likely it is that the information exchange will have restrictive effects on competition. The pre-existing degree of transparency, inter alia, depends on the number of market participants and the nature of transactions, which can range from public transactions to confidential bilateral negotiations between buyers and sellers. When evaluating the change in the level of transparency in the market, the key element is to identify to what extent the available information can be used by companies to determine the actions of their competitors.

79. Tight oligopolies can facilitate a collusive outcome on the market as it is easier for fewer companies to reach a common understanding on the terms of coordination and to monitor deviations. A collusive outcome is also more likely to be sustainable with fewer companies. With more companies coordinating, the gains from deviating are greater because a larger market share can be gained through undercutting. At the same time, gains from the collusive outcome are smaller

because, when there are more companies, the share of the rents from the collusive outcome declines. Exchanges of information in tight oligopolies are more likely to cause restrictive effects on competition than in less tight oligopolies, and are not likely to cause such restrictive effects on competition in very fragmented markets. However, by increasing transparency, or modifying the market environment in another way towards one more liable to coordination, information exchanges may facilitate coordination and monitoring among more companies than would be possible in its absence.

Commentary
para 79: F&N: 7.459, 7.463

---

80. Companies may find it difficult to achieve a collusive outcome in a complex market environment. However, to some extent, the use of information exchange may simplify such environments. In a complex market environment more information exchange is normally needed to reach a common understanding on the terms of coordination and to monitor deviations. For example, it is easier to achieve a collusive outcome on a price for a single, homogeneous product, than on numerous prices in a market with many differentiated products. It is nonetheless possible that to circumvent the difficulties involved in achieving a collusive outcome on a large number of prices, companies may exchange information to establish simple pricing rules (for example, pricing points).

81. Collusive outcomes are more likely where the demand and supply conditions are relatively stable.[1] In an unstable environment it may be difficult for a company to know whether its lost sales are due to an overall low level of demand or due to a competitor offering particularly low prices, and therefore it is difficult to sustain a collusive outcome. In this context, volatile demand, substantial internal growth by some companies in the market, or frequent entry by new companies, may indicate that the current situation is not sufficiently stable for coordination to be likely.[2] Information exchange in certain situations can serve the purpose of increasing stability in the market, and thereby may enable a collusive outcome in the market. Moreover, in markets where innovation is important, coordination may be more difficult since particularly significant innovations may allow one company to gain a major advantage over its rivals. For a collusive outcome to be sustainable, the reactions of outsiders, such as current and future competitors not participating in the coordination, as well as customers, should not be capable of jeopardising the results expected from the collusive outcome. In this context, the existence of barriers to entry makes it more likely that a collusive outcome on the market is feasible and sustainable.

Notes
[1] See Case T-35/92 *John Deere v Commission* [1994] ECR II-957, paragraph 78.
[2] See Commission Decision in Cases IV/31.370 and 31.446, *UK Agricultural Tractor Registration Exchange*, OJ L 68, 13.3.1992, p.19, paragraph 51 and Case T-35/92 *John Deere v Commission* [1994] ECR II-957, paragraph 78. It is not necessary that absolute stability be established or fierce competition excluded.

---

82. A collusive outcome is more likely in symmetric market structures. When companies are homogenous in terms of their costs, demand, market shares, product range, capacities etc., they are more likely to reach a common understanding on the terms of coordination because their incentives are more aligned. However, information exchange may in some situations also allow a collusive outcome to occur in more heterogeneous market structures. Information exchange could make companies aware of their differences and help them to design means to accommodate for their heterogeneity in the context of coordination.

83. The stability of a collusive outcome also depends on the companies' discounting of future profits. The more companies value the current profits that they could gain from undercutting versus all the future ones that they could gain by the collusive outcome, the less likely it is that they will be able to achieve a collusive outcome.

84. By the same token, a collusive outcome is more likely among companies that will continue to operate in the same market for a long time, as in such a scenario they will be more committed to coordinate. If a company knows that it will interact with the others for a long time, it will have a

greater incentive to achieve the collusive outcome because the stream of future profits from the collusive outcome will be worth more than the short term profit it could have if it deviated, that is to say, before the other companies detect the deviation and retaliate.

Commentary
para 84: F&N: 3.168

85. Overall, for a collusive outcome to be sustainable, the threat of a sufficiently credible and prompt retaliation must be likely. Collusive outcomes are not sustainable in markets in which the consequences of deviation are not sufficiently severe to convince coordinating companies that it is in their best interest to adhere to the terms of the collusive outcome. For example, in markets characterised by infrequent, lumpy orders, it may be difficult to establish a sufficiently severe deterrence mechanism, since the gain from deviating at the right time may be large, certain and immediate, whereas the losses from being punished small and uncertain, and only materialise after some time. The credibility of the deterrence mechanism also depends on whether the other coordinating companies have an incentive to retaliate, determined by their short-term losses from triggering a price war versus their potential long-term gain in case they induce a return to a collusive outcome. For example, companies' ability to retaliate may be reinforced if they are also interrelated by vertical commercial relationships which they can use as a threat of punishment for deviations.

(ii) Characteristics of the information exchange

Strategic information

86. The exchange between competitors of strategic data, that is to say, data that reduces strategic uncertainty in the market, is more likely to be caught by Article 101 than exchanges of other types of information. Sharing of strategic data can give rise to restrictive effects on competition because it reduces the parties' decision-making independence by decreasing their incentives to compete. Strategic information can be related to prices (for example, actual prices, discounts, increases, reductions or rebates), customer lists, production costs, quantities, turnovers, sales, capacities, qualities, marketing plans, risks, investments, technologies and R&D programmes and their results. Generally, information related to prices and quantities is the most strategic, followed by information about costs and demand. However, if companies compete with regard to R&D it is the technology data that may be the most strategic for competition. The strategic usefulness of data also depends on its aggregation and age, as well as the market context and frequency of the exchange.

Market coverage

87. For an information exchange to be likely to have restrictive effects on competition, the companies involved in the exchange have to cover a sufficiently large part of the relevant market. Otherwise, the competitors that are not participating in the information exchange could constrain any anticompetitive behaviour of the companies involved. For example, by pricing below the coordinated price level companies unaffiliated within the information exchange system could threaten the external stability of a collusive outcome.

Commentary
para 87: F&N: 7.472

88. What constitutes "a sufficiently large part of the market" cannot be defined in the abstract and will depend on the specific facts of each case and the type of information exchange in question. Where, however, an information exchange takes place in the context of another type of horizontal co-operation agreement and does not go beyond what is necessary for its implementation, market coverage below the market share thresholds set out in the relevant chapter of these guidelines, the relevant block exemption regulation[1] or the *De Minimis* Notice pertaining to the type of agreement in question will usually not be large enough for the information exchange to give rise to restrictive effects on competition.

Notes

1 Exchanges of information in the context of an R&D agreement, if they do not exceed what is necessary for implementation of the agreement, can benefit from the safe harbour of 25% set out in the R&D Block Exemption Regulation. For the Specialisation Block Exemption Regulation, the relevant safe harbour is 20%.

Aggregated/individualised data

89. Exchanges of genuinely aggregated data, that is to say, where the recognition of individualised company level information is sufficiently difficult, are much less likely to lead to restrictive effects on competition than exchanges of company level data. Collection and publication of aggregated market data (such as sales data, data on capacities or data on costs of inputs and components) by a trade organisation or market intelligence firm may benefit suppliers and customers alike by allowing them to get a clearer picture of the economic situation of a sector. Such data collection and publication may allow market participants to make better-informed individual choices in order to adapt efficiently their strategy to the market conditions. More generally, unless it takes place in a tight oligopoly, the exchange of aggregated data is unlikely to give rise to restrictive effects on competition. Conversely, the exchange of individualised data facilitates a common understanding on the market and punishment strategies by allowing the coordinating companies to single out a deviator or entrant. Nevertheless, the possibility cannot be excluded that even the exchange of aggregated data may facilitate a collusive outcome in markets with specific characteristics. Namely, members of a very tight and stable oligopoly exchanging aggregated data who detect a market price below a certain level could automatically assume that someone has deviated from the collusive outcome and take market-wide retaliatory steps. In other words, in order to keep collusion stable, companies may not always need to know who deviated, it may be enough to learn that "someone" deviated.

Commentary
para 89: B&C: 6.033, 6.034 F&N: 7.487

Age of data

90. The exchange of historic data is unlikely to lead to a collusive outcome as it is unlikely to be indicative of the competitors' future conduct or to provide a common understanding on the market.[1] Moreover, exchanging historic data is unlikely to facilitate monitoring of deviations because the older the data, the less useful it would be for timely detection of deviations and thus as a credible threat of prompt retaliation.[2] There is no predetermined threshold when data becomes historic, that is to say, old enough not to pose risks to competition. Whether data is genuinely historic depends on the specific characteristics of the relevant market and in particular the frequency of price re-negotiations in the industry. For example, data can be considered as historic if it is several times older than the average length of contracts in the industry if the latter are indicative of price re-negotiations. Moreover, the threshold when data becomes historic also depends on the data's nature, aggregation, frequency of the exchange, and the characteristics of the relevant market (for example, its stability and transparency).

Notes

1 The collection of historic data can also be used to convey a sector association's input to or analysis of a review of public policy.

2 For example, in past cases the Commission has considered the exchange of individual data which was more than one year old as historic and as not restrictive of competition within the meaning of Article 101(1), whereas information less than one year old has been considered as recent; Commission Decision in Case IV/31.370, *UK Agricultural Tractor Registration Exchange*, OJ L 68, 13.3.1992, p.19, paragraph 50; Commission Decision in Case IV/36.069, *Wirtschaftsvereinigung Stahl*, OJ L 1, 3.1.1998, p.10, paragraph 17.

Commentary
para 90: F&N: 7.494

Frequency of the information exchange

91. Frequent exchanges of information that facilitate both a better common understanding of the market and monitoring of deviations increase the risks of a collusive outcome. In more unstable markets, more frequent exchanges of information may be necessary to facilitate a collusive outcome than in stable markets. In markets with long-term contracts (which are indicative of infrequent price re-negotiations) a less frequent exchange of information would normally be sufficient to achieve a collusive outcome. By contrast, infrequent exchanges would not tend to be sufficient to achieve a collusive outcome in markets with short-term contracts indicative of frequent price re-negotiations.[1] However, the frequency at which data needs to be exchanged to facilitate a collusive outcome also depends on the nature, age and aggregation of data.[2]

Notes

[1] However, infrequent contracts could decrease the likelihood of a sufficiently prompt retaliation.

[2] However, depending on the structure of the market and the overall context of the exchange, the possibility cannot be excluded that an isolated exchange may constitute a sufficient basis for the participating undertakings to concert their market conduct and thus successfully substitute practical co-operation between them for competition and the risks that that entails; see Case C-8/08 *T-Mobile Netherlands* [2009] ECR I-4529, paragraph 59.

Commentary
para 91: B&C: 6.033 F&N: 7.497

Public/non-public information

92. In general, exchanges of genuinely public information are unlikely to constitute an infringement of Article 101.[1] *Genuinely public information* is information that is generally equally accessible (in terms of costs of access) to all competitors and customers. For information to be genuinely public, obtaining it should not be more costly for customers and companies unaffiliated to the exchange system than for the companies exchanging the information. For this reason, competitors would normally not choose to exchange data that they can collect from the market at equal ease, and hence in practice exchanges of genuinely public data are unlikely. In contrast, even if the data exchanged between competitors is what is often referred to as being "in the public domain", it is not genuinely public if the costs involved in collecting the data deter other companies and customers from doing so.[2] A possibility to gather the information in the market, for example to collect it from customers, does not necessarily mean that such information constitutes market data readily accessible to competitors.[3]

Notes

[1] Joined Cases T-191/98 and others *Atlantic Container Line (TACA)* [2003] ECR II-3275, paragraph 1154. This may not be the case if the exchange underpins a cartel.

[2] Moreover, the fact that the parties to the exchange have previously communicated the data to the public (for example through a daily newspaper or on their websites) does not imply that a subsequent non-public exchange would not infringe Article 101.

[3] See Joined Cases T-202/98 and others *Tate & Lyle v Commission* [2001] ECR II-2035, paragraph 60.

93. Even if there is public availability of data (for example, information published by regulators), the existence of an additional information exchange by competitors may give rise to restrictive effects on competition if it further reduces strategic uncertainty in the market. In that case, it is the incremental information that could be critical to tip the market balance towards a collusive outcome.

Public/non-public exchange of information

94. An *information exchange* is genuinely public if it makes the exchanged data equally accessible (in terms of costs of access) to all competitors and customers.[1] The fact that information is exchanged in public may decrease the likelihood of a collusive outcome on the market to the extent that non-coordinating

companies, potential competitors, as well as customers may be able to constrain potential restrictive effect on competition.[2] However, the possibility cannot be entirely excluded that even genuinely public exchanges of information may facilitate a collusive outcome in the market.

Notes

[1] This does not preclude that a database be offered at a lower price to customers which themselves have contributed data to it, as by doing so they normally would have also incurred costs.

[2] Assessing barriers to entry and countervailing "buyer power" in the market would be relevant for determining whether outsiders to the information exchange system would be able to jeopardise the outcomes expected from coordination. However, increased transparency to consumers may either decrease or increase scope for a collusive outcome because with increased transparency to consumers, as price elasticity of demand is higher, pay-offs from deviation are higher but retaliation is also harsher.

Commentary
para 94: B&C: 3.033

2.3. Assessment under Article 101(3)

2.3.1. Efficiency gains[1]

Notes

[1] The discussion of potential efficiency gains from information exchange is neither exclusive nor exhaustive.

95. Information exchange may lead to efficiency gains. Information about competitors' costs can enable companies to become more efficient if they benchmark their performance against the best practices in the industry and design internal incentive schemes accordingly.

Commentary
para 95: B&C: 3.044

96. Moreover, in certain situations information exchange can help companies allocate production towards high-demand markets (for example, demand information) or low cost companies (for example, cost information). The likelihood of those types of efficiencies depends on market characteristics such as whether companies compete on prices or quantities and the nature of uncertainties on the market. Some forms of information exchanges in this context may allow substantial cost savings where, for example, they reduce unnecessary inventories or enable quicker delivery of perishable products to areas with high demand and their reduction in areas with low demand (see Example 6, paragraph 110).

Commentary
para 96: B&C: 3.034

97. Exchange of consumer data between companies in markets with asymmetric information about consumers can also give rise to efficiencies. For instance, keeping track of the past behaviour of customers in terms of accidents or credit default provides an incentive for consumers to limit their risk exposure. It also makes it possible to detect which consumers carry a lower risk and should benefit from lower prices. In this context, information exchange can also reduce consumer lock-in, thereby inducing stronger competition. This is because information is generally specific to a relationship and consumers would otherwise lose the benefit from that information when switching to another company. Examples of such efficiencies are found in the banking and insurance sectors, which are characterised by frequent exchanges of information about consumer defaults and risk characteristics.

98. Exchanging past and present data related to market shares may in some situations provide benefits to both companies and consumers by allowing companies to announce it as a signal of quality of their products to consumers. In situations of imperfect information about product quality, consumers often use indirect means to gain information on the relative qualities of products such

as price and market shares (for example, consumers use best-selling lists in order to choose their next book).

99. Information exchange that is genuinely public can also benefit consumers by helping them to make a more informed choice (and reducing their search costs). Consumers are most likely to benefit in this way from public exchanges of current data, which are the most relevant for their purchasing decisions. Similarly, public information exchange about current input prices can lower search costs for companies, which would normally benefit consumers through lower final prices. Those types of direct consumer benefits are less likely to be generated by exchanges of future pricing intentions because companies which announce their pricing intentions are likely to revise them before consumers actually purchase based on that information. Consumers generally cannot rely on companies' future intentions when making their consumption plans. However, to some extent, companies may be disciplined not to change the announced future prices before implementation when, for example, they have repeated interactions with consumers and consumers rely on knowing the prices in advance or, for example, when consumers can make advance orders. In those situations, exchanging information related to the future may improve customers' planning of expenditure.

100. Exchanging present and past data is more likely to generate efficiency gains than exchanging information about future intentions. However, in specific circumstances announcing future intentions could also give rise to efficiency gains. For example, companies knowing early the winner of an R&D race could avoid duplicating costly efforts and wasting resources that cannot be recovered.[1]

Notes

[1] Such efficiencies need to be weighed against the potential negative effects of, for example, limiting competition for the market which stimulates innovation.

2.3.2. Indispensability

101. Restrictions that go beyond what is necessary to achieve the efficiency gains generated by an information exchange do not fulfil the conditions of Article 101(3). For fulfilling the condition of indispensability, the parties will need to prove that the data's subject matter, aggregation, age, confidentiality and frequency, as well as coverage, of the exchange are of the kind that carries the lowest risks indispensable for creating the claimed efficiency gains. Moreover, the exchange should not involve information beyond the variables that are relevant for the attainment of the efficiency gains. For instance, for the purpose of benchmarking, an exchange of individualised data would generally not be indispensable because information aggregated in for example some form of industry ranking could also generate the claimed efficiency gains while carrying a lower risk of leading to a collusive outcome (see Example 4, paragraph 108). Finally, it is generally unlikely that the sharing of individualised data on future intentions is indispensable, especially if it is related to prices and quantities.

102. Similarly, information exchanges that form part of horizontal co-operation agreements are also more likely to fulfil the conditions of Article 101(3) if they do not go beyond what is indispensable for the implementation of the economic purpose of the agreement (for example, sharing technology necessary for an R&D agreement or cost data in the context of a production agreement).

2.3.3. Pass-on to consumers

103. Efficiency gains attained by indispensable restrictions must be passed on to consumers to an extent that outweighs the restrictive effects on competition caused by an information exchange. The lower is the market power of the parties involved in the information exchange, the more likely it is that the efficiency gains would be passed on to consumers to an extent that outweighs the restrictive effects on competition.

Commentary
para 103: B&C: 3.057, 3.062

2.3.4. No elimination of competition

104. The criteria of Article 101(3) cannot be met if the companies involved in the information exchange are afforded the possibility of eliminating competition in respect of a substantial part of the products concerned.

2.4. Examples

105. Exchange of intended future prices as a restriction of competition by object

---

Example 1

Situation: A trade association of coach companies in country X disseminates individualised information on intended future prices only to the member coach companies. The information contains several elements, such as the intended fare and the route to which the fare applies, the possible restrictions to this fare, such as which consumers can buy it, if advanced payment or minimum stay is required, the period during which tickets can be sold for the given fare (first and last ticket date), and the time during which the ticket with the given fare can be used for travel (first and last travel dates).

Analysis: This information exchange, which is triggered by a decision by an association of undertakings, concerns pricing intentions of competitors. This information exchange is a very efficient tool for reaching a collusive outcome and therefore restricts competition by object. This is because the companies are free to change their own intended prices as announced within the association at any time if they learn that their competitors intend to charge higher prices. This allows the companies to reach a common higher price level without incurring the cost of losing market share. For example, coach Company A can announce today a price increase on the route from city 1 to city 2 for travel as of the following month. Since this information is accessible to all other coach companies, Company A can then wait and see the reaction of its competitors to this price announcement. If a competitor on the same route, say, Company B, matched the price increase, then Company A's announcement would be left unchanged and later would likely become effective. However, if Company B did not match the price increase, then Company A could still revise its fare. The adjustment would continue until the companies converged to an increased anti-competitive price level. This information exchange is unlikely to fulfil the conditions of Article 101(3). The information exchange is only confined to competitors, that is to say, customers of the coach companies do not directly benefit from it.

---

106. Exchange of current prices with sufficient efficiency gains for consumers

---

Example 2

Situation: A national tourist office together with the coach companies in small country X agree to disseminate information on current prices of coach tickets through a freely accessible website (in contrast to Example 1, paragraph 105, consumers can already purchase tickets at the prices and conditions which are exchanged, thus they are not intended future prices but present prices of current and future services). The information contains several elements, such as the fare and the route to which the fare is applied, the possible restrictions to this fare, such as which consumers can buy it, if advanced payment or minimum stay is required, and the time during which the ticket with the given fare can be used for travel (first and last travel dates). Coach travel in country X is not in the same relevant market as train and air travel. It is presumed that the relevant market is concentrated, stable and relatively non-complex, and pricing becomes transparent with the information exchange.

Analysis: This information exchange does not constitute a restriction of competition by object. The companies are exchanging current prices rather than intended future prices because they are effectively already selling tickets at these prices (unlike in Example 1, paragraph 105). Therefore, this exchange of information is less likely to constitute an efficient mechanism for reaching a focal point for coordination. Nevertheless, given the market structure and strategic nature of the data, this information exchange is likely to constitute an efficient mechanism for monitoring deviations from a collusive outcome, which would be likely to occur in this type of market setting. Therefore, this information exchange could give rise to restrictive effects on competition within the meaning of Article 101(1). However, to the extent that some restrictive effects on competition could result from the possibility to monitor deviations, it is likely that the efficiency gains stemming from the information exchange would be passed on to consumers to an extent that outweighs the restrictive effects on competition in both their likelihood and magnitude. Unlike in Example 1, paragraph 105, the information exchange is public and consumers can actually purchase tickets at the prices and conditions that are exchanged. Therefore this information exchange is likely to directly benefit consumers by reducing their search costs and improving choice, and thereby also stimulating price competition. Hence, the conditions of Article 101(3) are likely to be met.

107. Current prices deduced from the information exchanged

Example 3

Situation: The luxury hotels in the capital of country A operate in a tight, non-complex and stable oligopoly, with largely homogenous cost structures, which constitute a separate relevant market from other hotels. They directly exchange individual information about current occupancy rates and revenues. In this case, from the information exchanged the parties can directly deduce their actual current prices.

Analysis: Unless it is a disguised means of exchanging information on future intentions, this exchange of information would not constitute a restriction of competition by object because the hotels exchange present data and not information on intended future prices or quantities. However, the information exchange would give rise to restrictive effects on competition within the meaning of Article 101(1) because knowing the competitors' actual current prices would be likely to facilitate coordination (that is to say, alignment) of companies' competitive behaviour. It would be most likely used to monitor deviations from the collusive outcome. The information exchange increases transparency in the market as even though the hotels normally publish their list prices, they also offer various discounts to the list price resulting from negotiations or for early or group bookings, etc. Therefore, the incremental information that is non-publicly exchanged between the hotels is commercially sensitive, that is to say, strategically useful. This exchange is likely to facilitate a collusive outcome on the market because the parties involved constitute a tight, non-complex and stable oligopoly involved in a long-term competitive relationship (repeated interactions). Moreover, the cost structures of the hotels are largely homogeneous. Finally, neither consumers nor market entry can constrain the incumbents' anti-competitive behaviour as consumers have little buyer power and barriers to entry are high. It is unlikely that in this case the parties would be able to demonstrate any efficiency gains stemming from the information exchange that would be passed on to consumers to an extent that would outweigh the restrictive effects on competition. Therefore it is unlikely that the conditions of Article 101(3) can be met.

Commentary
para 107: F&N: 12.106

Part C Substantive Antitrust Matters

108. Benchmarking benefits — criteria of Article 101(3) not fulfilled

---

Example 4

Situation: Three large companies with a combined market share of 80% in a stable, non-complex, concentrated market with high barriers to entry, non-publicly and frequently exchange information directly between themselves about a substantial fraction of their individual costs. The companies claim that they do this to benchmark their performance against their competitors and thereby intend to become more efficient.

Analysis: This information exchange does not in principle constitute a restriction of competition by object. Consequently, its effects on the market need to be assessed. Because of the market structure, the fact that the information exchanged relates to a large proportion of the companies' variable costs, the individualised form of presentation of the data, and its large coverage of the relevant market, the information exchange is likely to facilitate a collusive outcome and thereby gives rise to restrictive effects on competition within the meaning of Article 101(1). It is unlikely that the criteria of Article 101(3) are fulfilled because there are less restrictive means to achieve the claimed efficiency gains, for example by way of a third party collecting, anonymising and aggregating the data in some form of industry ranking. Finally, in this case, since the parties form a very tight, non-complex and stable oligopoly, even the exchange of aggregated data could facilitate a collusive outcome in the market. However, this would be very unlikely if this exchange of information happened in a non-transparent, fragmented, unstable, and complex market.

Commentary
para 108: F&N: 12.106

109. Genuinely public information

Example 5

Situation: The four companies owning all the petrol stations in a large country A exchange current gasoline prices over the telephone. They claim that this information exchange cannot have restrictive effects on competition because the information is public as it is displayed on large display panels at every petrol station.

Analysis: The pricing data exchanged over the telephone is not genuinely public, as in order to obtain the same information in a different way it would be necessary to incur substantial time and transport costs. One would have to travel frequently large distances to collect the prices displayed on the boards of petrol stations spread all over the country. The costs for this are potentially high, so that the information could in practice not be obtained but for the information exchange. Moreover, the exchange is systematic and covers the entire relevant market, which is a tight, non-complex, stable oligopoly. Therefore it is likely to create a climate of mutual certainty as to the competitors' pricing policy and thereby it is likely to facilitate a collusive outcome. Consequently, this information exchange is likely to give rise to restrictive effects on competition within the meaning of Article 101(1).

Commentary
para 109: F&N: 12.133

110. Improved meeting of demand as an efficiency gain

Example 6

Situation: There are five producers of fresh bottled carrot juice in the relevant market. Demand for this product is very unstable and vary from location to location in different points in time. The juice has to be sold and consumed within one day from the date of production. The producers agree to establish an independent market research company that on a daily basis collects current information about unsold juice in each point of sale, which it publishes on its website the following week in a form that is aggregated per point of sale. The published statistics allow producers and retailers to forecast demand and to better position the product. Before the information exchange was put in place, the retailers had reported large quantities of wasted juice and therefore had reduced the quantity of juice purchased from the producers; that is to say, the market was not working efficiently. Consequently, in some periods and areas there were frequent instances of unmet demand. The information exchange system, which allows better forecasting of oversupply and undersupply, has significantly reduced the instances of unmet consumer demand and increased the quantity sold in the market.

Analysis: Even though the market is quite concentrated and the data exchanged is recent and strategic, it is not very likely that this exchange would facilitate a collusive outcome because a collusive outcome would be unlikely to occur in such an unstable market. Even if the exchange creates some risk of giving rise to restrictive effects on competition, the efficiency gains stemming from increasing supply to places with high demand and decreasing supply in places with low demand is likely to offset potential restrictive effects. The information is exchanged in a public and aggregated form, which carries lower anti-competitive risks than if it were non-public and individualised. The information exchange therefore does not go beyond what is necessary to correct the market failure. Therefore, it is likely that this information exchange meets the criteria of Article 101(3).

Commentary
para 110: B&C: 6.022

---

3. Research and Development Agreements

3.1. Definition

111. R&D agreements vary in form and scope. They range from outsourcing certain R&D activities to the joint improvement of existing technologies and co-operation concerning the research, development and marketing of completely new products. They may take the form of a co-operation agreement or of a jointly controlled company. This chapter applies to all forms of R&D agreements, including related agreements concerning the production or commercialisation of the R&D results.

Commentary
para 111: B&C: 6.039

3.2. Relevant markets

112. The key to defining the relevant market when assessing the effects of an R&D agreement is to identify those products, technologies or R&D efforts that will act as the main competitive constraints on the parties. At one end of the spectrum of possible situations, innovation may result in a product (or technology) which competes in an existing product (or technology) market. This is, for example, the case with R&D directed towards slight improvements or variations, such as new models of certain products. Here possible effects concern the market for existing products. At the other end of the spectrum, innovation may result in an entirely new product which creates its own new product market (for example, a new vaccine for a previously incurable disease). However, many cases concern situations in between those two extremes, that is to say, situations in which innovation efforts may create products (or technology) which, over time, replace existing ones (for example, CDs which have replaced records). A careful analysis of those situations may have to cover both existing markets and the impact of the agreement on innovation.

Commentary
para 112: B&C: 6.041, 6.043 F&N: 7.146

Existing product markets

113. Where the co-operation concerns R&D for the improvement of existing products, those existing products and their close substitutes form the relevant market concerned by the co-operation.[1]

Notes
[1] For market definition, see the Market Definition Notice.

Commentary
para 113: F&N: 15.88

114. If the R&D efforts aim at a significant change of existing products or even at a new product to replace existing ones, substitution with the existing products may be imperfect or long-term. It may be concluded that the old and the potentially emerging new products do not belong to the same relevant market.[1] The market for existing products may nevertheless be concerned, if the pooling of R&D efforts is likely to result in the coordination of the parties' behaviour as suppliers of existing products, for instance because of the exchange of competitively sensitive information relating to the market for existing products.

Notes
[1] See also Commission Guidelines on the application of Article [101] of the [Treaty on the Functioning of the European Union] to technology transfer agreements, OJ C 101, 27.4.2004, p.2 ("Technology Transfer Guidelines"), paragraph 33.

Commentary
para 114: B&C: 9.146 F&N: 7.147

115. If the R&D concerns an important component of a final product, not only the market for that component may be relevant for the assessment, but also the existing market for the final product. For instance, if car manufacturers co-operate in R&D related to a new type of engine, the car market may be affected by that R&D co-operation. The market for final products, however, is only relevant for the assessment if the component at which the R&D is aimed is technically or economically a key element of those final products and if the parties to the R&D agreement have market power with respect to the final products.

Commentary
para 115: B&C: 6.045

Existing technology markets

116. R&D co-operation may not only concern products but also technology. When intellectual property rights are marketed separately from the products to which they relate, the relevant technology market has to be defined as well. Technology markets consist of the intellectual property that is licensed and its close substitutes, that is to say, other technologies which customers could use as a substitute.

Commentary
para 116: B&C: 9.147

117. The methodology for defining technology markets follows the same principles as product market definition.[1] Starting from the technology which is marketed by the parties, those other technologies to which customers could switch in response to a small but non-transitory increase in relative prices need to be identified. Once those technologies are identified, market shares can be calculated by dividing the licensing income generated by the parties by the total licensing income of all licensors.

Notes

[1] See Market Definition Notice; see also Technology Transfer Guidelines, paragraphs 19 et seq.

Commentary
para 117: **B&C**: 6.041, 6.042, 9.147

118. The parties' position in the market for existing technology is a relevant assessment criterion where the R&D co-operation concerns a significant improvement to an existing technology or a new technology that is likely to replace the existing technology. The parties' market shares can, however, only be taken as a starting point for this analysis. In technology markets, particular emphasis must be placed on potential competition. If companies which do not currently license their technology are potential entrants on the technology market they could constrain the ability of the parties to profitably raise the price for their technology. This aspect of the analysis may also be taken into account directly in the calculation of market shares by basing those on the sales of the products incorporating the licensed technology on downstream product markets (see paragraphs 123 to 126).

Commentary
para 118: **B&C**: 6.042

Competition in innovation (R&D efforts)

119. R&D co-operation may not only affect competition in existing markets, but also competition in innovation and new product markets. This is the case where R&D co-operation concerns the development of new products or technology which either may — if emerging — one day replace existing ones or which are being developed for a new intended use and will therefore not replace existing products but create a completely new demand. The effects on competition in innovation are important in these situations, but can in some cases not be sufficiently assessed by analysing actual or potential competition in existing product/technology markets. In this respect, two scenarios can be distinguished, depending on the nature of the innovative process in a given industry.

Commentary
para 119: **B&C**: 6.042 **F&N**: 7.148, 7.198

120. In the first scenario, which is, for instance, present in the pharmaceutical industry, the process of innovation is structured in such a way that it is possible at an early stage to identify competing R&D poles. Competing R&D poles are R&D efforts directed towards a certain new product or technology, and the substitutes for that R&D, that is to say, R&D aimed at developing substitutable products or technology for those developed by the co-operation and having similar timing. In this case, it can be analysed whether after the agreement there will be a sufficient number of remaining R&D poles. The starting point of the analysis is the R&D of the parties. Then credible competing R&D poles have to be identified. In order to assess the credibility of competing poles, the following aspects have to be taken into account: the nature, scope and size of any other R&D efforts, their access to financial and human resources, know-how/patents, or other specialised assets as well as their timing and their capability to exploit possible results. An R&D pole is not a credible competitor if it cannot be regarded as a close substitute for the parties' R&D effort from the viewpoint of, for instance, access to resources or timing.

121. Besides the direct effect on the innovation itself, the co-operation may also affect a new product market. It will often be difficult to analyse the effects on such a market directly as by its very nature it does not yet exist. The analysis of such markets will therefore often be implicitly incorporated in the analysis of competition in innovation. However, it may be necessary to consider directly the effects on such a market of aspects of the agreement that go beyond the R&D stage. An R&D agreement that includes joint production and commercialisation on the new product market may, for instance, be assessed differently than a pure R&D agreement.

122. In the second scenario, the innovative efforts in an industry are not clearly structured so as to allow the identification of R&D poles. In this situation, in the absence of exceptional circumstances,

Part C Substantive
Antitrust Matters

the Commission would not try to assess the impact of a given R&D co-operation on innovation, but would limit its assessment to existing product and/or technology markets which are related to the R&D co-operation in question.

Commentary
para 122: F&N: 7.148

Calculation of market shares

123. The calculation of market shares, both for the purposes of the R&D Block Exemption Regulation and of these guidelines, has to reflect the distinction between existing markets and competition in innovation. At the beginning of an R&D co-operation the reference point is the existing market for products capable of being improved, substituted or replaced by the products under development. If the R&D agreement only aims at improving or refining existing products, that market includes the products directly concerned by the R&D. Market shares can thus be calculated on the basis of the sales value of the existing products.

Commentary
para 123: F&N: 7.150

124. If the R&D aims at replacing an existing product, the new product will, if successful, become a substitute for the existing products. To assess the competitive position of the parties, it is again possible to calculate market shares on the basis of the sales value of the existing products. Consequently, the R&D Block Exemption Regulation bases its exemption of those situations on the market share in the relevant market for the products capable of being improved, substituted or replaced by the contract products.[1] To fall under the R&D Block Exemption Regulation, that market share may not exceed 25%.[2]

Notes
[1] Point (u) of Article 1(1) of the R&D Block Exemption Regulation.
[2] Article 4(2) of the R&D Block Exemption Regulation.

125. For technology markets one way to proceed is to calculate market shares on the basis of each technology's share of total licensing income from royalties, representing a technology's share of the market where competing technologies are licensed. However, this may often be a mere theoretical and not very practical way to proceed because of lack of clear information on royalties, the use of royalty free cross-licensing, etc. An alternative approach is to calculate market shares on the technology market on the basis of sales of products or services incorporating the licensed technology on downstream product markets. Under that approach all sales on the relevant product market are taken into account, irrespective of whether the product incorporates a technology that is being licensed.[1] Also for that market the share may not exceed 25% (irrespective of the calculation method used) for the benefits of the R&D Block Exemption Regulation to apply.

Notes
[1] See also Technology Transfer Guidelines, paragraph 23.

Commentary
para 125: B&C: 6.042 F&N: 7.152, 7.200, 7.204, 7.229

126. If the R&D aims at developing a product which will create a completely new demand, market shares based on sales cannot be calculated. Only an analysis of the effects of the agreement on competition in innovation is possible. Consequently, the R&D Block Exemption Regulation treats those agreements as agreements between non-competitors and exempts them irrespective of market share for the duration of the joint R&D and an additional period of seven years after the product is first put on the market.[1] However, the benefit of the block exemption may be withdrawn if the agreement eliminated effective competition in innovation.[2] After the seven year period, market shares based on sales value can be calculated, and the market share threshold of 25% applies.[3]

Notes

[1] Article 4(1) of the R&D Block Exemption Regulation.

[2] See recitals 19, 20 and 21 in the preamble to the R&D Block Exemption Regulation.

[3] Article 4(3) of the R&D Block Exemption Regulation.

Commentary

para 126: **B&C:** 6.022, 6.043, 6.052 **F&N:** 7.154, 7.198

3.3. Assessment under Article 101(1)

3.3.1. *Main competition concerns*

127. R&D co-operation can restrict competition in various ways. First, it may reduce or slow down innovation, leading to fewer or worse products coming to the market later than they otherwise would. Secondly, on product or technology markets the R&D co-operation may reduce significantly competition between the parties outside the scope of the agreement or it may make anti-competitive coordination on those markets likely, thereby leading to higher prices. A foreclosure problem may only arise in the context of co-operation involving at least one player with a significant degree of market power (which does not necessarily amount to dominance) for a key technology and the exclusive exploitation of the results.

Commentary

para 127: **B&C:** 6.040 **F&N:** 3.372, 7.154

3.3.2. *Restrictions of competition by object*

128. R&D agreements restrict competition by object if they do not truly concern joint R&D, but serve as a tool to engage in a disguised cartel, that is to say, otherwise prohibited price fixing, output limitation or market allocation. However, an R&D agreement which includes the joint exploitation of possible future results is not necessarily restrictive of competition.

Commentary

para 128: **B&C:** 6.046, 6.047

3.3.3. *Restrictive effects on competition*

129. Most R&D agreements do not fall under Article 101(1). First, this can be said for many agreements relating to co-operation in R&D at a rather early stage, far removed from the exploitation of possible results.

Commentary

para 129: **B&C:** 6.044 **F&N:** 7.155

130. Moreover, R&D co-operation between non-competitors does generally not give rise to restrictive effects on competition.[1] The competitive relationship between the parties has to be analysed in the context of affected existing markets and/or innovation. If, on the basis of objective factors, the parties are not able to carry out the necessary R&D independently, for instance, due to the limited technical capabilities of the parties, the R&D agreement will normally not have any restrictive effects on competition. This can apply, for example, to companies bringing together complementary skills, technologies and other resources. The issue of potential competition has to be assessed on a realistic basis. For instance, parties cannot be defined as potential competitors simply because the co-operation enables them to carry out the R&D activities. The decisive question is whether each party independently has the necessary means as regards assets, know-how and other resources.

Notes

[1] R&D co-operation between non-competitors can, however, produce foreclosure effects under Article 101(1) if it relates to an exclusive exploitation of results and if it is concluded between companies, one of which has a significant degree of market power (which does not necessarily amount to dominance) with respect to a key technology.

Commentary
para 130: B&C: 6.045 F&N: 7.155, 7.156

131. Outsourcing of previously captive R&D is a specific form of R&D co-operation. In such a scenario, the R&D is often carried out by specialised companies, research institutes or academic bodies, which are not active in the exploitation of the results. Normally, such agreements are combined with a transfer of know-how and/or an exclusive supply clause concerning the possible results, which, due to the complementary nature of the co-operating parties in such a scenario, do not give rise to restrictive effects on competition within the meaning of Article 101(1).

Commentary
para 131: B&C: 6.045 F&N: 7.156

132. R&D co-operation which does not include the joint exploitation of possible results by means of licensing, production and/or marketing rarely gives rise to restrictive effects on competition within the meaning of Article 101(1). Those pure R&D agreements can only cause a competition problem if competition with respect to innovation is appreciably reduced, leaving only a limited number of credible competing R&D poles.

Commentary
para 132: B&C: 6.045, 6.046, 6.047 F&N: 7.155

133. R&D agreements are only likely to give rise to restrictive effects on competition where the parties to the co-operation have market power on the existing markets and/or competition with respect to innovation is appreciably reduced.

Commentary
para 133: B&C: 6.040, 6.045, 6.047 F&N: 7.157

134. There is no absolute threshold above which it can be presumed that an R&D agreement creates or maintains market power and thus is likely to give rise to restrictive effects on competition within the meaning of Article 101(1). However, R&D agreements between competitors are covered by the R&D Block Exemption Regulation provided that their combined market share does not exceed 25% and that the other conditions for the application of the R&D Block Exemption Regulation are fulfilled.

Commentary
para 134: B&C: 6.012

135. Agreements falling outside the R&D Block Exemption Regulation because the combined market share of the parties exceeds 25% do not necessarily give rise to restrictive effects on competition. However, the stronger the combined position of the parties on existing markets and/or the more competition in innovation is restricted, the more likely it is that the R&D agreement can cause restrictive effects on competition.[1]

Notes

[1] This is without prejudice to the analysis of potential efficiency gains, including those that regularly exist in publicly co-funded R&D.

136. If the R&D is directed at the improvement or refinement of existing products or technologies, possible effects concern the relevant market(s) for those existing products or technologies. Effects on prices, output, product quality, product variety or innovation in existing markets are, however, only likely if the parties together have a strong position, entry is difficult and few other innovation activities are identifiable. Furthermore, if the R&D only concerns a relatively minor input of a final product, effects on competition in those final products are, if any, very limited.

137. In general, a distinction has to be made between pure R&D agreements and agreements providing for more comprehensive co-operation involving different stages of the exploitation of results (that is to say, licensing, production or marketing). As set out in paragraph 132, pure R&D agreements

will only rarely give rise to restrictive effects on competition within the meaning of Article 101(1). This is in particular true for R&D directed towards a limited improvement of existing products or technologies. If, in such a scenario, the R&D co-operation includes joint exploitation only by means of licensing to third parties, restrictive effects such as foreclosure problems are unlikely. If, however, joint production and/or marketing of the slightly improved products or technologies are included, the effects on competition of the co-operation have to be examined more closely. Restrictive effects on competition in the form of increased prices or reduced output in existing markets are more likely if strong competitors are involved in such a situation.

138. If the R&D is directed at an entirely new product (or technology) which creates its own new market, price and output effects on existing markets are rather unlikely. The analysis has to focus on possible restrictions of innovation concerning, for instance, the quality and variety of possible future products or technologies or the speed of innovation. Those restrictive effects can arise where two or more of the few companies engaged in the development of such a new product start to co-operate at a stage where they are each independently rather near to the launch of the product. Such effects are typically the direct result of the agreement between the parties. Innovation may be restricted even by a pure R&D agreement. In general, however, R&D co-operation concerning entirely new products is unlikely to give rise to restrictive effects on competition unless only a limited number of credible alternative R&D poles exist. This principle does not change significantly if the joint exploitation of the results, even joint marketing, is involved. In those situations the issue of joint exploitation may only give rise to restrictive effects on competition where foreclosure from key technologies plays a role. Those problems would, however, not arise where the parties grant licences that allow third parties to compete effectively.

Commentary
para 138: B&C: 6.046, 6.047

139. Many R&D agreements will lie somewhere in between the two situations described in paragraphs 137 and 138. They may therefore have effects on innovation as well as repercussions on existing markets. Consequently, both the existing market and the effect on innovation may be of relevance for the assessment with respect to the parties' combined positions, concentration ratios, number of players or innovators and entry conditions. In some cases there can be restrictive effects on competition in the form of increased prices or reduced output, product quality, product variety or innovation in existing markets and in the form of a negative impact on innovation by means of slowing down the development. For instance, if significant competitors on an existing technology market co-operate to develop a new technology which may one day replace existing products that co-operation may slow down the development of the new technology if the parties have market power on the existing market and also a strong position with respect to R&D. A similar effect can occur if the major player in an existing market co-operates with a much smaller or even potential competitor who is just about to emerge with a new product or technology which may endanger the incumbent's position.

Commentary
para 139: B&C: 6.047

140. Agreements may also fall outside the R&D Block Exemption Regulation irrespective of the parties' market power. This applies for instance to agreements which unduly restrict access of a party to the results of the R&D co-operation.[1] The R&D Block Exemption Regulation provides for a specific exception to this general rule in the case of academic bodies, research institutes or specialised companies which provide R&D as a service and which are not active in the industrial exploitation of the results of R&D.[2] Nevertheless, agreements falling outside the R&D Block Exemption Regulation and containing exclusive access rights for the purposes of exploitation may, where they fall under Article 101(1), fulfil the criteria of Article 101(3), particularly where exclusive access rights are economically indispensable in view of the market, risks and scale of the investment required to exploit the results of the research and development.

Notes

[1] See Article 3(2) of the R&D Block Exemption Regulation.
[2] See Article 3(2) of the R&D Block Exemption Regulation.

Commentary
para 140: B&C: 6.048

3.4. Assessment under Article 101(3)

3.4.1. Efficiency gains

141. Many R&D agreements — with or without joint exploitation of possible results — bring about efficiency gains by combining complementary skills and assets, thus resulting in improved or new products and technologies being developed and marketed more rapidly than would otherwise be the case. R&D agreements may also lead to a wider dissemination of knowledge, which may trigger further innovation. R&D agreements may also give rise to cost reductions.

Commentary
para 141: B&C: 6.049 F&N: 7.158

3.4.2. Indispensability

142. Restrictions that go beyond what is necessary to achieve the efficiency gains generated by an R&D agreement do not fulfil the criteria of Article 101(3). In particular, the restrictions listed in Article 5 of the R&D Block Exemption Regulation may mean it is less likely that the criteria of Article 101(3) will be found to be met, following an individual assessment. It will therefore generally be necessary for the parties to an R&D agreement to show that such restrictions are indispensable to the co-operation.

Commentary
para 142: B&C: 6.049

3.4.3. Pass-on to consumers

143. Efficiency gains attained by indispensable restrictions must be passed on to consumers to an extent that outweighs the restrictive effects on competition caused by the R&D agreement. For example, the introduction of new or improved products on the market must outweigh any price increases or other restrictive effects on competition. In general, it is more likely that an R&D agreement will bring about efficiency gains that benefit consumers if the R&D agreement results in the combination of complementary skills and assets. The parties to an agreement may, for instance, have different research capabilities. If, on the other hand, the parties' skills and assets are very similar, the most important effect of the R&D agreement may be the elimination of part or all of the R&D of one or more of the parties. This would eliminate (fixed) costs for the parties to the agreement but would be unlikely to lead to benefits which would be passed on to consumers. Moreover, the higher the market power of the parties the less likely they are to pass on the efficiency gains to consumers to an extent that would outweigh the restrictive effects on competition.

Commentary
para 143: B&C: 3.057, 3.059, 6.049

3.4.4. No elimination of competition

144. The criteria of Article 101(3) cannot be met if the parties are afforded the possibility of eliminating competition in respect of a substantial part of the products (or technologies) in question.

3.4.5. Time of the assessment

145. The assessment of restrictive agreements under Article 101(3) is made within the actual context in which they occur and on the basis of the facts existing at any given point in time. The assessment is sensitive to material changes in the facts. The exception rule of Article 101(3) applies as long as the four conditions of Article 101(3) are fulfilled and ceases to apply when that is no longer the case. When applying Article 101(3) in accordance with those principles it is necessary to take into account the initial sunk investments made by any of the parties and the time needed and the restraints required to making and recouping an efficiency enhancing investment. Article 101

cannot be applied without taking due account of such *ex ante* investment. The risk facing the parties and the sunk investment that must be made to implement the agreement can thus lead to the agreement falling outside Article 101(1) or fulfilling the conditions of Article 101(3), as the case may be, for the period of time needed to recoup the investment. Should the invention resulting from the investment benefit from any form of exclusivity granted to the parties under rules specific to the protection of intellectual property rights, the recoupment period for such an investment will generally be unlikely to exceed the exclusivity period established under those rules.

Commentary
para 145: **B&C:** 3.017, 6.049 **F&N:** 7.161

146. In some cases the restrictive agreement is an irreversible event. Once the restrictive agreement has been implemented the *ex ante* situation cannot be re-established. In such cases the assessment must be made exclusively on the basis of the facts pertaining at the time of implementation. For instance, in the case of an R&D agreement whereby each party agrees to abandon its respective research project and pool its capabilities with those of another party, it may from an objective point of view be technically and economically impossible to revive a project once it has been abandoned. The assessment of the anti-competitive and pro-competitive effects of the agreement to abandon the individual research projects must therefore be made as of the time of the completion of its implementation. If at that point in time the agreement is compatible with Article 101, for instance because a sufficient number of third parties have competing R&D projects, the parties' agreement to abandon their individual projects remains compatible with Article 101, even if at a later point in time the third party projects fail. However, the prohibition of Article 101 may apply to other parts of the agreement in respect of which the issue of irreversibility does not arise. If, for example, in addition to joint R&D, the agreement provides for joint exploitation, Article 101 may apply to that part of the agreement if, due to subsequent market developments, the agreement gives rise to restrictive effects on competition and does not (any longer) satisfy the conditions of Article 101(3) taking due account of *ex ante* sunk investments.

Commentary
para 146: **B&C:** 3.017, 6.049

3.5. Examples

147. Impact of joint R&D on innovation markets/new product market

---

Example 1

Situation: A and B are the two major companies on the Union-wide market for the manufacture of existing electronic components. Both have a market share of 30%. They have each made significant investments in the R&D necessary to develop miniaturised electronic components and have developed early prototypes. They now agree to pool those R&D efforts by setting up a joint venture to complete the R&D and produce the components, which will be sold back to the parents, who will commercialise them separately. The remainder of the market consists of small companies without sufficient resources to undertake the necessary investments.

Analysis: Miniaturised electronic components, while likely to compete with the existing components in some areas, are essentially a new technology and an analysis must be made of the poles of research destined towards that future market. If the joint venture goes ahead then only one route to the necessary manufacturing technology will exist, whereas it would appear likely that A and B could reach the market individually with separate products. The agreement therefore reduces product variety. The joint production is also likely to directly limit competition between the parties to the agreement and lead them to agree on output levels, quality or other competitively important parameters. This would limit competition even though the parties will commercialise the products independently. The parties could, for instance, limit the output of the joint venture

---

compared to what the parties would have brought to the market if they had decided their output on their own. The joint venture could also charge a high transfer price to the parties, thereby increasing the input costs for the parties which could lead to higher downstream prices. The parties have a large combined market share on the existing downstream market and the remainder of that market is fragmented. This situation is likely to become even more pronounced on the new downstream product market since the smaller competitors cannot invest in the new components. It is therefore quite likely that the joint production will restrict competition.

Furthermore, the market for miniaturised electronic components is in the future likely to develop into a duopoly with a high degree of commonality of costs and possible exchange of commercially sensitive information between the parties. There may therefore also be a serious risk of anti-competitive coordination leading to a collusive outcome in the market. The R&D agreement is therefore likely to give rise to restrictive effects on competition within the meaning of Article 101(1). While the agreement could give rise to efficiency gains in the form of bringing a new technology forward quicker, the parties would face no competition at the R&D level, so their incentives to pursue the new technology at a high pace could be severely reduced. Although some of those concerns could be remedied if the parties committed to license key know-how for manufacturing miniature components to third parties on reasonable terms, it seems unlikely that this could remedy all concerns and fulfil the conditions of Article 101(3).

Example 2

Situation: A small research company (Company A) which does not have its own marketing organisation has discovered and patented a pharmaceutical substance based on new technology that will revolutionise the treatment of a certain disease. Company A enters into an R&D agreement with a large pharmaceutical producer Company B of products that have so far been used for treating the disease. Company B lacks any similar expertise and R&D programme and would not be able to build such expertise within a relevant timeframe. For the existing products Company B has a market share of around 75% in all Member States, but the patents will expire over the next five years. There exist two other poles of research with other companies at approximately the same stage of development using the same basic new technology. Company B will provide considerable funding and know-how for product development, as well as future access to the market. Company B is granted a licence for the exclusive production and distribution of the resulting product for the duration of the patent. It is expected that the product could be brought to market in five to seven years.

Analysis: The product is likely to belong to a new relevant market. The parties bring complementary resources and skills to the co-operation, and the probability of the product coming to market increases substantially. Although Company B is likely to have considerable market power on the existing market, that market power will be decreasing shortly. The agreement will not lead to a loss in R&D on the part of Company B, as it has no expertise in this area of research, and the existence of other poles of research are likely to eliminate any incentive to reduce R&D efforts. The exploitation rights during the remaining patent period are likely to be necessary for Company B to make the considerable investments needed and Company A has no marketing resources of its own. The agreement is therefore unlikely to give rise to restrictive effects on competition within the meaning of Article 101(1). Even if there were such effects, it is likely that the conditions of Article 101(3) would be fulfilled.

---

148. Risk of foreclosure

Example 3

Situation: A small research company (Company A) which does not have its own marketing organisation has discovered and patented a new technology that will revolutionise the market for a certain product for which there is a monopoly producer (Company B) worldwide as no competitors can compete with Company B's current technology. There exist two other poles of research with other companies at approximately the same stage of development using the same basic new technology. Company B will provide considerable funding and know-how for product development, as well as future access to the market. Company B is granted an exclusive licence for the use of the technology for the duration of the patent and commits to funding only the development of Company A's technology.

Analysis: The product is likely to belong to a new relevant market. The parties bring complementary resources and skills to the co-operation, and the probability of the product coming to market increases substantially. However, the fact that Company B commits to Company A's new technology may be likely to lead the two competing poles of research to abandon their projects as it could be difficult to receive continued funding once they have lost the most likely potential customer for their technology. In such a situation no potential competitors would be able to challenge Company B's monopoly position in the future. The foreclosure effect of the agreement would then be likely to be considered to give rise to restrictive effects on competition within the meaning of Article 101(1). In order to benefit from Article 101(3) the parties would have to show that the exclusivity granted would be indispensable to bring the new technology to the market.

Example 4

Situation: Company A has market power on the market of which its blockbuster medicine forms part. A small company (Company B) which is engaged in pharmaceutical R&D and active pharmaceutical ingredient ("API") production has discovered and filed a patent application for a new process that makes it possible to produce the API of Company A's blockbuster in a more economic fashion and continues to develop the process for industrial production. The compound (API) patent of the blockbuster expires in a little less than three years; thereafter there will remain a number of process patents relating to the medicine. Company B considers that the new process developed by it would not infringe the existing process patents of Company A and would allow the production of a generic version of the blockbuster once the API patent has expired. Company B could either produce the product itself or license the process to interested third parties, for example, generic producers or Company A. Before concluding its research and development in this area, Company B enters into an agreement with Company A, in which Company A makes a financial contribution to the R&D project being carried out by Company B on condition that it acquires an exclusive licence for any of Company B's patents related to the R&D project. There exist two other independent poles of research to develop a non-infringing process for the production of the blockbuster medicine, but it is not yet clear that they will reach industrial production.

Analysis: The process covered by Company B's patent application does not allow for the production of a new product. It merely improves an existing production process. Company A has market power on the existing market of which the blockbuster medicine forms part. Whilst that market power would decrease significantly with the actual market entry of generic competitors, the exclusive licence makes the process developed by Company B unavailable to third parties and is thus liable to delay generic entry (not least as the product is still protected by a number of process patents) and, consequently, restricts competition within the meaning of Article 101(1). As Company A and Company B are potential competitors, the R&D Block Exemption Regulation does not apply because Company A's market share on the market of which the blockbuster medicine forms part is above 25%. The cost savings based on the new production process for Company A are not sufficient to outweigh the restriction of competition. In any event, an exclusive licence is not indispensable to obtain the savings in the production process. Therefore, the agreement is unlikely to fulfil the conditions of Article 101(3).

149. Impact of R&D co-operation on dynamic product and technology markets and the environment

---

Example 5

Situation: Two engineering companies that produce vehicle components agree to set up a joint venture to combine their R&D efforts to improve the production and performance of an existing component. The production of that component would also have a positive effect on the environment. Vehicles would consume less fuel and therefore emit less CO2. The companies pool their existing technology licensing businesses in the area, but will continue to manufacture and sell the components separately. The two companies have market shares in the Union of 15% and 20% on the Original Equipment Manufacturer ("OEM") product market. There are two other major competitors together with several in-house research programmes by large vehicle manufacturers. On the world-wide market for the licensing of technology for those products the parties have shares of 20% and 25%, measured in terms of revenue generated, and there are two other major technologies. The product life cycle for the component is typically two to three years. In each of the last five years one of the major companies has introduced a new version or upgrade.

Analysis: Since neither company's R&D effort is aimed at a completely new product, the markets to consider are those for the existing components and for the licensing of relevant technology. The parties' combined market share on both the OEM market (35%) and, in particular, on the technology market (45%) are quite high. However, the parties will continue to manufacture and sell the components separately. In addition, there are several competing technologies, which are regularly improved. Moreover, the vehicle manufacturers who do not currently license their technology are also potential entrants on the technology market and thus constrain the ability of the parties to profitably raise prices. To the extent that the joint venture has restrictive effects on competition within the meaning of Article 101(1), it is likely that it would fulfil the criteria of Article 101(3). For the assessment under Article 101(3) it would be necessary to take into account that consumers will benefit from a lower consumption of fuel.

---

4. PRODUCTION AGREEMENTS

4.1. Definition and scope

150. Production agreements vary in form and scope. They can provide that production is carried out by only one party or by two or more parties. Companies can produce jointly by way of a joint venture, that is to say, a jointly controlled company operating one or several production facilities or by looser forms of co-operation in production such as subcontracting agreements where one party (the "contractor") entrusts to another party (the "subcontractor") the production of a good.

Commentary
para 150: B&C: 7.192

---

151. There are different types of subcontracting agreements. Horizontal subcontracting agreements are concluded between companies operating in the same product market irrespective of whether they are actual or potential competitors. Vertical subcontracting agreements are concluded between companies operating at different levels of the market.

Commentary
para 151: F&N: 7.239

---

152. Horizontal subcontracting agreements comprise unilateral and reciprocal specialisation agreements as well as subcontracting agreements with a view to expanding production. Unilateral specialisation agreements are agreements between two parties which are active on the same product market or markets, by virtue of which one party agrees to fully or partly cease production of certain products or to refrain from producing those products and to purchase them from the

other party, which agrees to produce and supply the products. Reciprocal specialisation agreements are agreements between two or more parties which are active on the same products market or markets, by virtue of which two or more parties agree, on a reciprocal basis, to fully or partly cease or refrain from producing certain but different products and to purchase those products from the other parties, which agree to produce and supply them. In the case of subcontracting agreements with a view to expanding production the contractor entrusts the subcontractor with the production of a good, while the contractor does not at the same time cease or limit its own production of the good.

Commentary
para 152: **F&N**: 7.278, 7.282

153. These guidelines apply to all forms of joint production agreements and horizontal subcontracting agreements. Subject to certain conditions, joint production agreements as well as unilateral and reciprocal specialisation agreements may benefit from the Specialisation Block Exemption Regulation.

Commentary
para 153: **F&N**: 7.239, 7.282

154. Vertical subcontracting agreements are not covered by these guidelines. They fall within the scope of the Guidelines on Vertical Restraints and, subject to certain conditions, may benefit from the Block Exemption Regulation on Vertical Restraints. In addition, they may be covered by the Commission notice of 18 December 1978 concerning its assessment of certain subcontracting agreements in relation to Article [101](1) of the [Treaty on the Functioning of the European Union][1] ("the Subcontracting Notice").

Notes
[1] OJ C 1, 3.1.1979, p.2.
Commentary
para 154: **B&C**: 2.151, 7.193

4.2. Relevant markets

155. In order to assess the competitive relationship between the co-operating parties, it is necessary first to define the relevant market or markets directly concerned by the co-operation in production, that is to say, the markets to which the products manufactured under the production agreement belong.

Commentary
para 155: **B&C**: 6.058

156. A production agreement can also have spill-over effects in markets neighbouring the market directly concerned by the co-operation, for instance upstream or downstream to the agreement (the so-called "spill-over markets").[1] The spill-over markets are likely to be relevant if the markets are interdependent and the parties are in a strong position on the spill-over market.

Notes
[1] As also referred to in Article 2(4) of the Merger Regulation.
Commentary
para 156: **F&N**: 12.118

4.3. Assessment under Article 101(1)

4.3.1. Main competition concerns

157. Production agreements can lead to a direct limitation of competition between the parties. Production agreements, and in particular production joint ventures, may lead the parties to

Part C Substantive Antitrust Matters

directly align output levels and quality, the price at which the joint venture sells on its products, or other competitively important parameters. This may restrict competition even if the parties market the products independently.

Commentary
para 157: B&C: 6.058 F&N: 3.372

158. Production agreements may also result in the coordination of the parties' competitive behaviour as suppliers leading to higher prices or reduced output, product quality, product variety or innovation, that is to say, a collusive outcome. This can happen, subject to the parties having market power and the existence of market characteristics conducive to such coordination, in particular when the production agreement increases the parties' commonality of costs (that is to say, the proportion of variable costs which the parties have in common) to a degree which enables them to achieve a collusive outcome, or if the agreement involves an exchange of commercially sensitive information that can lead to a collusive outcome.

Commentary
para 158: B&C: 6.058

159. Production agreements may furthermore lead to anti-competitive foreclosure of third parties in a related market (for example, the downstream market relying on inputs from the market in which the production agreement takes place). For instance, by gaining enough market power, parties engaging in joint production in an upstream market may be able to raise the price of a key component for a market downstream. Thereby, they could use the joint production to raise the costs of their rivals downstream and, ultimately, force them off the market. This would, in turn, increase the parties' market power downstream, which could enable them to sustain prices above the competitive level or otherwise harm consumers. Such competition concerns could materialise irrespective of whether the parties to the agreement are competitors on the market in which the co-operation takes place. However, for this kind of foreclosure to have anti-competitive effects, at least one of the parties must have a strong market position in the market where the risks of foreclosure are assessed.

Commentary
para 159: B&C: 2.100

4.3.2. Restrictions of competition by object

160. Generally, agreements which involve price-fixing, limiting output or sharing markets or customers restrict competition by object. However, in the context of production agreements, this does not apply where:
   — the parties agree on the output directly concerned by the production agreement (for example, the capacity and production volume of a joint venture or the agreed amount of out-sourced products), provided that the other parameters of competition are not eliminated; or
   — a production agreement that also provides for the joint distribution of the jointly manufac-tured products envisages the joint setting of the sales prices for those products, and only those products, provided that that restriction is necessary for producing jointly, meaning that the parties would not otherwise have an incentive to enter into the production agree-ment in the first place.

Commentary
para 160: B&C: 6.057 F&N: 3.454, 12.98, 12.103, 12.124

161. In these two cases an assessment is required as to whether the agreement gives rise to likely restrictive effects on competition within the meaning of Article 101(1). In both scenarios the agreement on output or prices will not be assessed separately, but in the light of the overall effects of the entire production agreement on the market.

Commentary
para 161: F&N: 12.98

4.3.3. Restrictive effects on competition

162. Whether the possible competition concerns that production agreements can give rise to are likely to materialise in a given case depends on the characteristics of the market in which the agreement takes place, as well as on the nature and market coverage of the co-operation and the product it concerns. These variables determine the likely effects of a production agreement on competition and thereby the applicability of Article 101(1).

Commentary
para 162: B&C: 6.058 F&N: 3.372

163. Whether a production agreement is likely to give rise to restrictive effects on competition depends on the situation that would prevail in the absence of the agreement with all its alleged restrictions. Consequently, production agreements between companies which compete on markets on which the co-operation occurs are not likely to have restrictive effects on competition if the co-operation gives rise to a new market, that is to say, if the agreement enables the parties to launch a new product or service, which, on the basis of objective factors, the parties would otherwise not have been able to do, for instance, due to the technical capabilities of the parties.

Commentary
para 163: B&C: 6.058, 6.060 F&N: 7.249, 7.250

164. In some industries where production is the main economic activity, even a pure production agreement can in itself eliminate key dimensions of competition, thereby directly limiting competition between the parties to the agreements.

Commentary
para 164: B&C: 6.058

165. Alternatively, a production agreement can lead to a collusive outcome or anti-competitive foreclosure by increasing the companies' market power or their commonality of costs or if it involves the exchange of commercially sensitive information. On the other hand, a direct limitation of competition between the parties, a collusive outcome or anti-competitive foreclosure is not likely to occur if the parties to the agreement do not have market power in the market in which the competition concerns are assessed. It is only market power that can enable them to profitably maintain prices above the competitive level, or profitably maintain output, product quality or variety below what would be dictated by competition.

Commentary
para 165: B&C: 2.100, 6.058

166. In cases where a company with market power in one market co-operates with a potential entrant, for example, with a supplier of the same product in a neighbouring geographic or product market, the agreement can potentially increase the market power of the incumbent. This can lead to restrictive effects on competition if actual competition in the incumbent's market is already weak and the threat of entry is a major source of competitive constraint.

167. Production agreements which also involve commercialisation functions, such as joint distribution or marketing, carry a higher risk of restrictive effects on competition than pure joint production agreements. Joint commercialisation brings the co-operation closer to the consumer and usually involves the joint setting of prices and sales, that is to say, practices that carry the highest risks for competition. However, joint distribution agreements for products which have been jointly produced are generally less likely to restrict competition than stand-alone joint distribution agreements. Also, a joint distribution agreement that is necessary for the joint production agreement to take place in the first place is less likely to restrict competition than if it were not necessary for the joint production.

Commentary
para 167: **B&C:** 6.058 **F&N:** 12.124

Market power

168. A production agreement is unlikely to lead to restrictive effects on competition if the parties to the agreement do not have market power in the market on which a restriction of competition is assessed. The starting point for the analysis of market power is the market share of the parties. This will normally be followed by the concentration ratio and the number of players in the market as well as by other dynamic factors such as potential entry, and changing market shares.

Commentary
para 168: **F&N:** 7.248, 12.105

169. Companies are unlikely to have market power below a certain level of market share. Therefore, unilateral or reciprocal specialisation agreements as well as joint production agreements including certain integrated commercialisation functions such as joint distribution are covered by the Specialisation Block Exemption Regulation if they are concluded between parties with a combined market share not exceeding 20% in the relevant market or markets, provided that the other conditions for the application of the Specialisation Block Exemption Regulation are fulfilled. Moreover, as regards horizontal subcontracting agreements with a view to expanding production, in most cases it is unlikely that market power exists if the parties to the agreement have a combined market share not exceeding 20%. In any event, if the parties' combined market share does not exceed 20% it is likely that the conditions of Article 101(3) are fulfilled.

Commentary
para 169: **B&C:** 6.012 **F&N:** 3.379, 7.278

170. However, if the parties' combined market share exceeds 20%, the restrictive effects have to be analysed as the agreement does not fall within the scope of the Specialisation Block Exemption Regulation or the safe harbour for horizontal subcontracting agreements with a view to expanding production referred to in sentences 3 and 4 of paragraph 169. A moderately higher market share than allowed for in the Specialisation Block Exemption Regulation or the safe harbour referred to in sentences 3 and 4 of paragraph 169 does not necessarily imply a highly concentrated market, which is an important factor in the assessment. A combined market share of the parties of slightly more than 20% may occur in a market with a moderate concentration. Generally, a production agreement is more likely to lead to restrictive effects on competition in a concentrated market than in a market which is not concentrated. Similarly, a production agreement in a concentrated market may increase the risk of a collusive outcome even if the parties only have a moderate combined market share.

Commentary
para 170: **F&N:** 7.265

171. Even if the market shares of the parties to the agreement and the market concentration are high, the risks of restrictive effects on competition may still be low if the market is dynamic, that is to say, a market in which entry occurs and market positions change frequently.

Commentary
para 171: **F&N:** 7.521

172. In the analysis of whether the parties to a production agreement have market power, the number and intensity of links (for example, other co-operation agreements) between the competitors in the market are relevant to the assessment.

Commentary
para 172: **F&N:** 12.110

173. Factors such as whether the parties to the agreement have high market shares, whether they are close competitors, whether the customers have limited possibilities of switching suppliers, whether competitors are unlikely to increase supply if prices increase, and whether one of the parties to the agreement is an important competitive force, are all relevant for the competitive assessment of the agreement.

Commentary
para 173: **B&C:** 6.058

Direct limitation of competition between the parties

174. Competition between the parties to a production agreement can be directly limited in various ways. The parties to a production joint venture could, for instance, limit the output of the joint venture compared to what the parties would have brought to the market if each of them had decided their output on their own. If the main product characteristics are determined by the production agreement this could also eliminate the key dimensions of competition between the parties and, ultimately, lead to restrictive effects on competition. Another example would be a joint venture charging a high transfer price to the parties, thereby increasing the input costs for the parties which could lead to higher downstream prices. Competitors may find it profitable to increase their prices as a response, thereby contributing to price increases in the relevant market.

Commentary
para 174: **F&N:** 7.258, 12.106

Collusive outcome

175. The likelihood of a collusive outcome depends on the parties' market power as well as the characteristics of the relevant market. A collusive outcome can result in particular (but not only) from commonality of costs or an exchange of information brought about by the production agreement.

Commentary
para 175: **F&N:** 7.78

176. A production agreement between parties with market power can have restrictive effects on competition if it increases their commonality of costs (that is to say, the proportion of variable costs which the parties have in common) to a level which enables them to collude. The relevant costs are the variable costs of the product with respect to which the parties to the production agreement compete.

Commentary
para 176: **B&C:** 6.059

177. A production agreement is more likely to lead to a collusive outcome if prior to the agreement the parties already have a high proportion of variable costs in common, as the additional increment (that is to say, the production costs of the product subject to the agreement) can tip the balance towards a collusive outcome. Conversely, if the increment is large, the risk of a collusive outcome may be high even if the initial level of commonality of costs is low.

178. Commonality of costs increases the risk of a collusive outcome only if production costs constitute a large proportion of the variable costs concerned. This is, for instance, not the case where the co-operation concerns products which require costly commercialisation. An example would be new or heterogeneous products requiring expensive marketing or high transport costs.

Commentary
para 178: **B&C:** 6.059

179. Another scenario where commonality of costs can lead to a collusive outcome could be where the parties agree on the joint production of an intermediate product which accounts for a large

proportion of the variable costs of the final product with respect to which the parties compete downstream. The parties could use the production agreement to increase the price of that common important input for their products in the downstream market. This would weaken competition downstream and would be likely to lead to higher final prices. The profit would be shifted from downstream to upstream to be then shared between the parties through the joint venture.

Commentary
para 179: F&N: 7.93, 12.105

180. Similarly, commonality of costs increases the anti-competitive risks of a horizontal subcontracting agreement where the input which the contractor purchases from the subcontractor accounts for a large proportion of the variable costs of the final product with which the parties compete.

181. Any negative effects arising from the exchange of information will not be assessed separately but in the light of the overall effects of the agreement. A production agreement can give rise to restrictive effects on competition if it involves an exchange of commercially strategic information that can lead to a collusive outcome or anti-competitive foreclosure. Whether the exchange of information in the context of a production agreement is likely to lead to restrictive effects on competition should be assessed according to the guidance given in Chapter 2.

Commentary
para 181: B&C: 2.100

182. If the information exchange does not exceed the sharing of data necessary for the joint production of the goods subject to the production agreement, then even if the information exchange had restrictive effects on competition within the meaning of Article 101(1), the agreement would be more likely to meet the criteria of Article 101(3) than if the exchange went beyond what was necessary for the joint production. In this case the efficiency gains stemming from producing jointly are likely to outweigh the restrictive effects of the coordination of the parties' conduct. Conversely, in the context of a production agreement the sharing of data which is not necessary for producing jointly, for example the exchange of information related to prices and sales, is less likely to fulfil the conditions of Article 101(3).

Commentary
para 182: F&N: 12.104

4.4. Assessment under Article 101(3)

4.4.1. Efficiency gains

183. Production agreements can be pro-competitive if they provide efficiency gains in the form of cost savings or better production technologies. By producing together companies can save costs that otherwise they would duplicate. They can also produce at lower costs if the co-operation enables them to increase production where marginal costs decline with output, that is to say, by economies of scale. Producing jointly can also help companies to improve product quality if they put together their complementary skills and know-how. Co-operation can also enable companies to increase product variety, which they could not have afforded, or would not have been able to achieve, otherwise. If joint production allows the parties to increase the number of different types of products, it can also provide cost savings by means of economies of scope.

Commentary
para 183: B&C: 3.033, 3.037, 6.061 F&N: 7.266

4.4.2. Indispensability

184. Restrictions that go beyond what is necessary to achieve the efficiency gains generated by a production agreement do not fulfil the criteria of Article 101(3). For instance, restrictions imposed in a production agreement on the parties' competitive conduct with regard to output outside the co-operation will normally not be considered to be indispensable. Similarly, setting

prices jointly will not be considered indispensable if the production agreement does not also involve joint commercialisation.

Commentary
para 184: B&C: 3.063, 6.061

4.4.3. *Pass-on to consumers*

185. Efficiency gains attained by indispensable restrictions need to be passed on to consumers in the form of lower prices or better product quality or variety to an extent that outweighs the restrictive effects on competition. Efficiency gains that only benefit the parties or cost savings that are caused by output reduction or market allocation are not sufficient to meet the criteria of Article 101(3). If the parties to the production agreement achieve savings in their variable costs they are more likely to pass them on to consumers than if they reduce their fixed costs. Moreover, the higher the market power of the parties, the less likely they will pass on the efficiency gains to consumers to an extent that would outweigh the restrictive effects on competition.

Commentary
para 185: B&C: 3.057, 3.058, 6.061

4.4.4. *No elimination of competition*

186. The criteria of Article 101(3) cannot be met if the parties are afforded the possibility of eliminating competition in respect of a substantial part of the products in question. This has to be analysed in the relevant market to which the products subject to the co-operation belong and in any possible spill-over markets.

Commentary
para 186: B&C: 3.068, 6.062

4.5. Examples

187. Commonality of costs and collusive outcomes

Example 1

Situation: Companies A and B, two suppliers of a product X decide to close their current old production plants and build a larger, modern and more efficient production plant run by a joint venture, which will have a higher capacity than the total capacity of the old plants of Companies A and B. No other such investments are planned by competitors, which are using their facilities at full capacity. Companies A and B have market shares of 20% and 25% respectively. Their products are the closest substitutes in a specific segment of the market, which is concentrated. The market is transparent and rather stagnant, there is no entry and the market shares have been stable over time. Production costs constitute a major part of Company A and Company B's variable costs for product X. Commercialisation is a minor economic activity in terms of costs and strategic importance compared to production: marketing costs are low as product X is homogenous and established and transport is not a key driver of competition.

Analysis: If Companies A and B share all or most of their variable costs, this production agreement could lead to a direct limitation of competition between them. It may lead the parties to limit the output of the joint venture compared to what they would have brought to the market if each of them had decided their output on their own. In the light of the capacity constraints of the competitors this reduction output could lead to higher prices.

Even if Companies A and B were not sharing most of their variable costs, but only a significant part thereof, this production agreement could lead to a collusive outcome between Companies A and B, thereby indirectly eliminating competition between the two parties. The likelihood of

---

this depends not only on the issue of commonality of costs (which are high in this case) but also on the characteristics of the relevant market such as, for example, transparency, stability and level of concentration.

In either of the two situations mentioned above, it is likely, in the market configuration of this example, that the production joint venture of Companies A and B would give rise to restrictive effects on competition within the meaning of Article 101(1) on the market of X.

The replacement of two smaller old production plants by the larger, modern and more efficient one may lead the joint venture to increase output at lower prices to the benefits of consumers. However, the production agreement could only meet the criteria of Article 101(3) if the parties provided substantiated evidence that the efficiency gains would be passed on to consumers to such an extent that they would outweigh the restrictive effects on competition.

Commentary
para 187: B&C: 6.058 **F&N:** 7.79, 7.256

188. Links between competitors and collusive outcomes

Example 2

Situation: Two suppliers, Companies A and B, form a production joint venture with respect to product Y. Companies A and B each have a 15% market share on the market for Y. There are 3 other players on the market: Company C with a market share of 30%, Company D with 25% and Company E with 15%. Company B already has a joint production plant with Company D.

Analysis: The market is characterised by very few players and rather symmetric structures. Co-operation between Companies A and B would add an additional link in the market, *de facto* increasing the concentration in the market, as it would also link Company D to Companies A and B. This co-operation is likely to increase the risk of a collusive outcome and thereby likely to give rise to restrictive effects on competition within the meaning of Article 101(1). The criteria of Article 101(3) could only be fulfilled in the presence of significant efficiency gains which are passed on to consumers to such an extent that they would outweigh the restrictive effects on competition.

Commentary
para 188: F&N: 7.79

189. Anti-competitive foreclosure on a downstream market

Example 3

Situation: Companies A and B set up a production joint venture for the intermediate product X which covers their entire production of X. The production costs of X account for 70% of the variable costs of the final product Y with respect to which Companies A and B compete downstream. Companies A and B each have a share of 20% on the market for Y, there is limited entry and the market shares have been stable over time. In addition to covering their own demand for X, both Companies A and B each have a market share of 40% on the market for X. There are high barriers to entry on the market for X and existing producers are operating near full capacity. On the market for Y, there are two other significant suppliers, each with a 15% market share, and several smaller competitors. This agreement generates economies of scale.

Analysis: By virtue of the production joint venture, Companies A and B would be able to largely control supplies of the essential input X to their competitors in the market for Y. This would give

Companies A and B the ability to raise their rivals' costs by artificially increasing the price of X, or by reducing the output. This could foreclose the competitors of Companies A and B in market for Y. Because of the likely anti-competitive foreclosure downstream, this agreement is likely to give rise to restrictive effects on competition within the meaning of Article 101(1). The economies of scale generated by the production joint venture are unlikely to outweigh the restrictive effects on competition and therefore this agreement would most likely not meet the criteria of Article 101(3).

Commentary

para 189: F&N: 7.262, 10.169

---

190. Specialisation agreement as market allocation

Example 4

Situation: Companies A and B each manufacture both products X and Y. Company A's market share of X is 30% and of Y 10%. B's market share of X is 10% and of Y 30%. To obtain economies of scale they conclude a reciprocal specialisation agreement under which Company A will only produce X and Company B only Y. They do not cross-supply the products to each other so that Company A only sells X and Company B sells only Y. The parties claim that by specialising in this way they save costs due to the economies of scale and by focusing on only one product will improve their production technologies, which will lead to better quality products.

Analysis: With regard to its effects on competition in the market, this specialisation agreement is close to a hardcore cartel where parties allocate the market among themselves. Therefore, this agreement restricts competition by object. Because the claimed efficiencies in the form of economies of scale and improving production technology are only linked to the market allocation, they are unlikely to outweigh the restrictive effects, and therefore the agreement would not meet the criteria of Article 101(3). In any event, if Company A or B believes that it would be more efficient to focus on only one product, it can simply take the unilateral decision to only produce X or Y without at the same time agreeing that the other company will focus on producing the respective other product.

The analysis would be different if Companies A and B supplied each other with the product they focus on so that they both continue to sell X and Y. In such a case Companies A and B could still compete on price on both markets, especially if production costs (which become common through the production agreement) did not constitute a major share of the variable costs of their products. The relevant costs in this context are the commercialisation costs. Hence, the specialisation agreement would be unlikely to restrict competition if X and Y were largely heterogeneous products with a very high proportion of marketing and distribution costs (for example, 65–70% or more of total costs). In such a scenario the risks of a collusive outcome would not be high and the criteria of Article 101(3) may be fulfilled, provided that the efficiency gains would be passed on to consumers to such an extent that they would outweigh the restrictive effects on competition of the agreement.

Commentary

para 190: B&C: 6.057 **F&N:** 10.169

---

191. Potential competitors

Example 5

Situation: Company A produces final product X and Company B produces final product Y. X and Y constitute two separate product markets, in which Companies A and B respectively have strong market power. Both companies use Z as an input for their production of X and Y and they both produce Z for captive use only. X is a low added value product for which Z is an essential input (X is quite a simple transformation of Z). Y is a high value added product, for which Z is one of many inputs (Z constitutes a small part of variable costs of Y). Companies A and B agree to jointly produce Z, which generates modest economies of scale.

Analysis: Companies A and B are not actual competitors with regard to X, Y or Z. However, since X is a simple transformation of input Z, it is likely that Company B could easily enter the market for X and thus challenge Company A's position on that market. The joint production agreement with regard to Z might reduce Company B's incentives to do so as the joint production might be used for side payments and limit the probability of Company B selling product X (as Company A is likely to have control over the quantity of Z purchased by Company B from the joint venture). However, the probability of Company B entering the market for X in the absence of the agreement depends on the expected profitability of the entry. As X is a low added value product, entry might not be profitable and thus entry by Company B could be unlikely in the absence of the agreement. Given that Companies A and B already have market power, the agreement is likely to give rise to restrictive effects on competition within the meaning of Article 101(1) if the agreement does indeed decrease the likelihood of entry of Company B into Company A's market, that is to say, the market for X. The efficiency gains in the form of economies of scale generated by the agreement are modest and therefore unlikely to outweigh the restrictive effects on competition.

Commentary
para 191: F&N: 7.71

---

192. Information exchange in a production agreement

Example 6

Situation: Companies A and B with high market power decide to produce together to become more efficient. In the context of this agreement they secretly exchange information about their future prices. The agreement does not cover joint distribution.

Analysis: This information exchange makes a collusive outcome likely and is therefore likely have as its object the restriction of competition within the meaning of Article 101(1). It would be unlikely to meet the criteria of Article 101(3) because the sharing of information about the parties' future prices is not indispensable for producing jointly and attaining the corresponding cost savings.

---

193. Swaps and information exchange

Example 7

Situation: Companies A and B both produce Z, a commodity chemical. Z is a homogenous product which is manufactured according to a European standard which does not allow for any product variations. Production costs are a significant cost factor regarding Z. Company A has a market share of 20% and Company B of 25% on the Union-wide market for Z. There are four other manufacturers on the market for Z, with respective market shares of 20%, 15%, 10% and 10%. The production plant of Company A is located in Member State X in northern Europe whereas the production plant of Company B is located in Member State Y in southern Europe. Even though the majority of Company A's customers are located in northern Europe, Company A also has a number of customers in southern Europe. The majority of Company B's customers are in southern Europe, although it also has a number of customers located in northern Europe. Currently, Company A provides its southern European customers with Z manufactured in its production plant in Member State X and transports it to southern Europe by truck. Similarly, Company B provides its northern European customers with Z manufactured in Member State Y and transports it to northern Europe by truck. Transport costs are quite high, but not so high as to make the deliveries by Company A to southern Europe and Company B to northern Europe unprofitable. Transport costs from Member State X to southern Europe are lower than from Member State Y to northern Europe.

Companies A and B decide that it would be more efficient if Company A stopped transporting Z from Member State X to southern Europe and if Company B stopped transporting the Z from Member State Y to northern Europe although, at the same time, they are keen on retaining their customers. To do so, Companies A and B intend to enter into a swap agreement which allows them to purchase an agreed annual quantity of Z from the other party's plant with a view to selling the purchased Z to those of their customers which are located closer to the other party's plant. In order to calculate a purchase price which does not favour one party over the other and which takes due account of the parties' different production costs and different savings on transport costs, and in order to ensure that both parties can achieve an appropriate margin, they agree to disclose to each other their main costs with regard to Z (that is to say, production costs and transport costs).

Analysis: The fact that Companies A and B — who are competitors — swap parts of their production does not in itself give rise to competition concerns. However, the envisaged swap agreement between Companies A and B provides for the exchange of both parties' production and transport costs with regard to Z. Moreover, Companies A and B have a strong combined market position in a fairly concentrated market for a homogenous commodity product. Therefore, due to the extensive information exchange on a key parameter of competition with regard to Z, it is likely that the swap agreement between Companies A and B will give rise to restrictive effects on competition within the meaning of Article 101(1) as it can lead to a collusive outcome. Even though the agreement will give rise to significant efficiency gains in the form of cost savings for the parties, the restrictions on competition generated by the agreement are not indispensable for their attainment. The parties could achieve similar cost savings by agreeing on a price formula which does not entail the disclosure of their production and transport costs. Consequently, in its current form the swap agreement does not fulfil the criteria of Article 101(3).

5. Purchasing Agreements

5.1. Definition

194. This chapter focuses on agreements concerning the joint purchase of products. Joint purchasing can be carried out by a jointly controlled company, by a company in which many other companies hold non-controlling stakes, by a contractual arrangement or by even looser forms of co-operation (collectively referred to as "joint purchasing arrangements"). Joint purchasing arrangements usually aim at the creation of buying power which can lead to lower prices or better quality products or services for consumers. However, buying power may, under certain circumstances, also give rise to competition concerns.

Commentary
para 194: **B&C:** 6.067 **F&N:** 14.71

195. Joint purchasing arrangements may involve both horizontal and vertical agreements. In these cases a two-step analysis is necessary. First, the horizontal agreements between the companies engaging in joint purchasing have to be assessed according to the principles described in these guidelines. If that assessment leads to the conclusion that the joint purchasing arrangement does not give rise to competition concerns, a further assessment will be necessary to examine the relevant vertical agreements. The latter assessment will follow the rules of the Block Exemption Regulation on Vertical Restraints and the Guidelines on Vertical Restraints.

Commentary
para 195: **F&N:** 7.363

196. A common form of joint purchasing arrangement is an "alliance", that is to say an association of undertakings formed by a group of retailers for the joint purchasing of products. Horizontal agreements concluded between the members of the alliance or decisions adopted by the alliance first have to be assessed as a horizontal co-operation agreement according to these guidelines. Only if that assessment does not reveal any competition concerns does it become relevant to assess the relevant vertical agreements between the alliance and an individual member thereof and between the alliance and suppliers. Those agreements are covered — subject to certain conditions — by the Block Exemption Regulation on Vertical Restraints. Vertical agreements not covered by that Block Exemption Regulation are not presumed to be illegal but require individual examination.

5.2. Relevant markets

197. There are two markets which may be affected by joint purchasing arrangements. First, the market or markets with which the joint purchasing arrangement is directly concerned, that is to say, the relevant purchasing market or markets. Secondly, the selling market or markets, that is to say, the market or markets downstream where the parties to the joint purchasing arrangement are active as sellers.

198. The definition of relevant purchasing markets follows the principles described in the Market Definition Notice and is based on the concept of substitutability to identify competitive constraints. The only difference from the definition of "selling markets" is that substitutability has to be defined from the viewpoint of supply and not from the viewpoint of demand. In other words, the suppliers' alternatives are decisive in identifying the competitive constraints on purchasers. Those alternatives could be analysed, for instance, by examining the suppliers' reaction to a small but non-transitory price decrease. Once the market is defined, the market share can be calculated as the percentage of the purchases by the parties out of the total sales of the purchased product or products in the relevant market.

Commentary
para 198: F&N: 7.365

199. If the parties are, in addition, competitors on one or more selling markets, those markets are also relevant for the assessment. The selling markets have to be defined by applying the methodology described in the Market Definition Notice.

5.3. Assessment under Article 101(1)

5.3.1. Main competition concerns

200. Joint purchasing arrangements may lead to restrictive effects on competition on the purchasing and/or downstream selling market or markets, such as increased prices, reduced output, product quality or variety, or innovation, market allocation, or anti-competitive foreclosure of other possible purchasers.

Commentary
para 200: B&C: 2.100 F&N: 7.369, 12.114

201. If downstream competitors purchase a significant part of their products together, their incentives for price competition on the selling market or markets may be considerably reduced. If the parties have a significant degree of market power (which does not necessarily amount to dominance) on the selling market or markets, the lower purchase prices achieved by the joint purchasing arrangement are likely not to be passed on to consumers.

Commentary
para 201: B&C: 6.067

202. If the parties have a significant degree of market power on the purchasing market (buying power) there is a risk that they may force suppliers to reduce the range or quality of products they produce,

which may bring about restrictive effects on competition such as quality reductions, lessening of innovation efforts, or ultimately sub-optimal supply.

Commentary
para 202: B&C: 6.067

203. Buying power of the parties to the joint purchasing arrangement could be used to foreclose competing purchasers by limiting their access to efficient suppliers. This is most likely if there are a limited number of suppliers and there are barriers to entry on the supply side of the upstream market.

Commentary
para 203: F&N: 14.76

204. In general, however, joint purchasing arrangements are less likely to give rise to competition concerns when the parties do not have market power on the selling market or markets.

Commentary
para 204: B&C: 6.067

5.3.2. Restrictions of competition by object

205. Joint purchasing arrangements restrict competition by object if they do not truly concern joint purchasing, but serve as a tool to engage in a disguised cartel, that is to say, otherwise prohibited price fixing, output limitation or market allocation.

Commentary
para 205: B&C: 6.069

206. Agreements which involve the fixing of purchase prices can have the object of restricting competition within the meaning of Article 101(1).[1] However, this does not apply where the parties to a joint purchasing arrangement agree on the purchasing prices the joint purchasing arrangement may pay to its suppliers for the products subject to the supply contract. In that case an assessment is required as to whether the agreement is likely to give rise to restrictive effects on competition within the meaning of Article 101(1). In both scenarios the agreement on purchase prices will not be assessed separately, but in the light of the overall effects of the purchasing agreement on the market.

Notes
[1] See Article 101(1)(a); Joined Cases T-217/03 and T-245/03 *French Beef* [2006] ECR II-4987, paragraphs 83 et seq.; Case C-8/08 *T-Mobile Netherlands* [2009] ECR I-4529, paragraph 37.

Commentary
para 206: B&C: 6.070 **F&N:** 7.375

5.3.3. Restrictive effects on competition

207. Joint purchasing arrangements which do not have as their object the restriction of competition must be analysed in their legal and economic context with regard to their actual and likely effects on competition. The analysis of the restrictive effects on competition generated by a joint purchasing arrangement must cover the negative effects on both the purchasing and the selling markets.

Commentary
para 207: B&C: 6.071

Market power

208. There is no absolute threshold above which it can be presumed that the parties to a joint purchasing arrangement have market power so that the joint purchasing arrangement is likely to give rise to restrictive effects on competition within the meaning of Article 101(1). However, in most cases it is unlikely that market power exists if the parties to the joint purchasing arrangement have a combined market share not exceeding 15% on the purchasing market or markets as well as a combined market share not exceeding 15% on the selling market or markets. In any event, if the parties' combined market shares do not exceed 15% on both the purchasing and the selling market or markets, it is likely that the conditions of Article 101(3) are fulfilled.

Commentary
para 208: B&C: 2.169, 6.012, 6.071, 6.072 **F&N:** 3.378, 7.379

209. A market share above that threshold in one or both markets does not automatically indicate that the joint purchasing arrangement is likely to give rise to restrictive effects on competition. A joint purchasing arrangement which does not fall within that safe harbour requires a detailed assessment of its effects on the market involving, but not limited to, factors such as market concentration and possible countervailing power of strong suppliers.

Commentary
para 209: F&N: 7.379, 7.391, 7.395

210. Buying power may, under certain circumstances, cause restrictive effects on competition. Anti-competitive buying power is likely to arise if a joint purchasing arrangement accounts for a sufficiently large proportion of the total volume of a purchasing market so that access to the market may be foreclosed to competing purchasers. A high degree of buying power may indirectly affect the output, quality and variety of products on the selling market.

Commentary
para 210: B&C: 6.067, 6.071 **F&N:** 7.380, 7.394

211. In the analysis of whether the parties to a joint purchasing arrangement have buying power, the number and intensity of links (for example, other purchasing agreements) between the competitors in the market are relevant.

212. If, however, competing purchasers co-operate who are not active on the same relevant selling market (for example, retailers which are active in different geographic markets and cannot be regarded as potential competitors), the joint purchasing arrangement is unlikely to have restrictive effects on competition unless the parties have a position in the purchasing markets that is likely to be used to harm the competitive position of other players in their respective selling markets.

Commentary
para 212: B&C: 6.067, 6.071 **F&N:** 7.367, 14.74

Collusive outcome

213. Joint purchasing arrangements may lead to a collusive outcome if they facilitate the coordination of the parties' behaviour on the selling market. This can be the case if the parties achieve a high degree of commonality of costs through joint purchasing, provided the parties have market power and the market characteristics are conducive to coordination.

Commentary
para 213: B&C: 6.071 **F&N:** 14.76

214. Restrictive effects on competition are more likely if the parties to the joint purchasing arrangement have a significant proportion of their variable costs in the relevant downstream market in common. This is, for instance, the case if retailers, which are active in the same relevant retail market or markets, jointly purchase a significant amount of the products they offer for resale. It

may also be the case if competing manufacturers and sellers of a final product jointly purchase a high proportion of their input together.

Commentary
para 214: **B&C:** 6.071 **F&N:** 7.382

215. The implementation of a joint purchasing arrangement may require the exchange of commercially sensitive information such as purchase prices and volumes. The exchange of such information may facilitate coordination with regard to sales prices and output and thus lead to a collusive outcome on the selling markets. Spill-over effects from the exchange of commercially sensitive information can, for example, be minimised where data is collated by a joint purchasing arrangement which does not pass on the information to the parties thereto.

216. Any negative effects arising from the exchange of information will not be assessed separately but in the light of the overall effects of the agreement. Whether the exchange of information in the context of a joint purchasing arrangement is likely to lead to restrictive effects on competition should be assessed according to the guidance given in Chapter 2. If the information exchange does not exceed the sharing of data necessary for the joint purchasing of the products by the parties to the joint purchasing arrangement, then even if the information exchange has restrictive effects on competition within the meaning of Article 101(1), the agreement is more likely to meet the criteria of Article 101(3) than if the exchange goes beyond what was necessary for the joint purchasing.

Commentary
para 216: **F&N:** 7.383

5.4. Assessment under Article 101(3)

5.4.1. Efficiency gains

217. Joint purchasing arrangements can give rise to significant efficiency gains. In particular, they can lead to cost savings such as lower purchase prices or reduced transaction, transportation and storage costs, thereby facilitating economies of scale. Moreover, joint purchasing arrangements may give rise to qualitative efficiency gains by leading suppliers to innovate and introduce new or improved products on the markets.

Commentary
para 217: **B&C:** 3.032, 3.037, 6.072 **F&N:** 7.404

5.4.2. Indispensability

218. Restrictions that go beyond what is necessary to achieve the efficiency gains generated by a purchasing agreement do not meet the criteria of Article 101(3). An obligation to purchase exclusively through the co-operation may, in certain cases, be indispensable to achieve the necessary volume for the realisation of economies of scale. However, such an obligation has to be assessed in the context of the individual case.

Commentary
para 218: **B&C:** 6.072

5.4.3. Pass-on to consumers

219. Efficiency gains, such as cost efficiencies or qualitative efficiencies in the form of the introduction of new or improved products on the market, attained by indispensable restrictions must be passed on to consumers to an extent that outweighs the restrictive effects of competition caused by the joint purchasing arrangement. Hence, cost savings or other efficiencies that only benefit the parties to the joint purchasing arrangement will not suffice. Cost savings need to be passed on to consumers, that is to say, the parties' customers. To take a notable example, this pass-on may occur through lower prices on the selling markets. Lower purchasing prices resulting from the mere

exercise of buying power are not likely to be passed on to consumers if the purchasers together have market power on the selling markets, and thus do not meet the criteria of Article 101(3). Moreover, the higher the market power of the parties on the selling market or markets the less likely they will pass on the efficiency gains to consumers to an extent that would outweigh the restrictive effects on competition.

Commentary
para 219: B&C: 3.057, 3.058, 6.072

5.4.4. No elimination of competition

220. The criteria of Article 101(3) cannot be fulfilled if the parties are afforded the possibility of eliminating competition in respect of a substantial part of the products in question. That assessment has to cover both purchasing and selling markets.

Commentary
para 220: B&C: 3.068, 6.072 **F&N:** 7.406

5.5. Examples

221. Joint purchasing by small companies with moderate combined market shares

---

Example 1

Situation: 150 small retailers conclude an agreement to form a joint purchasing organisation. They are obliged to purchase a minimum volume through the organisation, which accounts for roughly 50% of each retailer's total costs. The retailers can purchase more than the minimum volume through the organisation, and they may also purchase outside the co-operation. They have a combined market share of 23% on both the purchasing and the selling markets. Company A and Company B are their two large competitors. Company A has a 25% share on both the purchasing and selling markets, Company B 35%. There are no barriers which would prevent the remaining smaller competitors from also forming a purchasing group. The 150 retailers achieve substantial cost savings by virtue of purchasing jointly through the purchasing organisation.

Analysis: The retailers have a moderate market position on the purchasing and the selling markets. Furthermore, the co-operation brings about some economies of scale. Even though the retailers achieve a high degree of commonality of costs, they are unlikely to have market power on the selling market due to the market presence of Companies A and B, which are both individually larger than the joint purchasing organisation. Consequently, the retailers are unlikely to coordinate their behaviour and reach a collusive outcome. The formation of the joint purchasing organisation is therefore unlikely to give rise to restrictive effects on competition within the meaning of Article 101(1).

Commentary
para 221: F&N: 7.385

222. Commonality of costs and market power on the selling market

---

Example 2

Situation: Two supermarket chains conclude an agreement to jointly purchase products which account for roughly 80% of their variable costs. On the relevant purchasing markets for the different categories of products the parties have combined market shares between 25% and 40%. On the relevant selling market they have a combined market share of 60%. There are four other significant retailers each with a 10% market share. Market entry is not likely.

Analysis: It is likely that this purchasing agreement would give the parties the ability to coordinate their behaviour on the selling market, thereby leading to a collusive outcome. The parties have market power on the selling market and the purchasing agreement gives rise to a significant commonality of costs. Moreover, market entry is unlikely. The incentive for the parties to coordinate their behaviour would be reinforced if their cost structures were already similar prior to concluding the agreement. Moreover, similar margins of the parties would further increase the risk of a collusive outcome. This agreement also creates the risk that by the parties' withholding demand and, consequently, as a result of reduced quantity, downstream selling prices would increase. Hence, the purchasing agreement is likely to give rise to restrictive effects on competition within the meaning of Article 101(1). Even though the agreement is very likely to give rise to efficiency gains in the form of cost savings, due to the parties' significant market power on the selling market, these are unlikely to be passed on to consumers to an extent that would outweigh the restrictive effects on competition. Therefore, the purchasing agreement is unlikely to fulfil the criteria of Article 101(3).

Commentary
para 222: F&N: 7.388, 7.405, 14.76

---

223. Parties active in different geographic markets

Example 3

Situation: Six large retailers, which are each based in a different Member State, form a purchasing group to buy several branded durum wheat flour-based products jointly. The parties are allowed to purchase other similar branded products outside the co-operation. Moreover, five of them also offer similar private label products. The members of the purchasing group have a combined market share of approximately 22% on the relevant purchasing market, which is Union-wide. In the purchasing market there are three other large players of similar size. Each of the parties to the purchasing group has a market share between 20% and 30% on the national selling markets on which they are active. None of them is active in a Member State where another member of the group is active. The parties are not potential entrants to each other's markets.

Analysis: The purchasing group will be able to compete with the other existing major players on the purchasing market. The selling markets are much smaller (in turnover and geographic scope) than the Union-wide purchasing market and in those markets some of the members of the group may have market power. Even if the members of the purchasing group have a combined market share of more than 15% on the purchasing market, the parties are unlikely to coordinate their conduct and collude on the selling markets since they are neither actual nor potential competitors on the downstream markets. Consequently, the purchasing group is not likely to give rise to restrictive effects on competition within the meaning of Article 101(1).

---

224. Information exchange

Example 4

Situation: Three competing manufacturers A, B and C entrust an independent joint purchasing organisation with the purchase of product Z, which is an intermediary product used by the three parties for their production of the final product X. The costs of Z are not a significant cost factor for the production of X. The joint purchasing organisation does not compete with the parties on the selling market for X. All information necessary for the purchases (for example quality specifications, quantities, delivery dates, maximum purchase prices) is only disclosed to the joint purchasing organisation, not to the other parties. The joint purchasing organisation agrees the purchasing prices with the suppliers. A, B and C have a combined market share of 30% on each of the purchasing and selling markets. They have six competitors in the purchasing and selling markets, two of which have a market share of 20%.

Analysis: Since there is no direct information exchange between the parties, the transfer of the information necessary for the purchases to the joint purchasing organisation is unlikely to lead to a collusive outcome. Consequently, the exchange of information is unlikely to give rise to restrictive effects on competition within the meaning of Article 101(1).

6. Agreements on Commercialisation

6.1. Definition

225. Commercialisation agreements involve co-operation between competitors in the selling, distribution or promotion of their substitute products. This type of agreement can have widely varying scope, depending on the commercialisation functions which are covered by the co-operation. At one end of the spectrum, joint selling agreements may lead to a joint determination of all commercial aspects related to the sale of the product, including price. At the other end, there are more limited agreements that only address one specific commercialisation function, such as distribution, after-sales service, or advertising.

Commentary
para 225: F&N: 7.323

226. An important category of those more limited agreements is distribution agreements. The Block Exemption Regulation on Vertical Restraints and Guidelines on Vertical Restraints generally cover distribution agreements unless the parties to the agreement are actual or potential competitors. If the parties are competitors, the Block Exemption Regulation on Vertical Restraints only covers non-reciprocal vertical agreements between competitors, if (a) the supplier is a manufacturer and a distributor of goods, while the buyer is a distributor and not a competing undertaking at the manufacturing level or, (b) the supplier is a provider of services at several levels of trade, while the buyer provides its goods or services at the retail level and does not provide competing services at the level of trade where it purchases the contract services.[1]

Notes
[1] Article 2(4) of the Block Exemption Regulation on Vertical Restraints.

227. If competitors agree to distribute their substitute products on a reciprocal basis (in particular if they do so on different geographic markets) there is a possibility in certain cases that the agreements have as their object or effect the partitioning of markets between the parties or that they lead to a collusive outcome. The same can be true for non-reciprocal agreements between competitors. Reciprocal agreements and non-reciprocal agreements between competitors thus have first to be assessed according to the principles set out in this Chapter. If that assessment leads to the conclusion that co-operation between competitors in the area of distribution would in principle be acceptable, a further assessment will be necessary to examine the vertical restraints included in such agreements. That second step of the assessment should be based on the principles set out in the Guidelines on Vertical Restraints.

228. A further distinction should be drawn between agreements where the parties agree only on joint commercialisation and agreements where the commercialisation is related to another type of co-operation upstream, such as joint production or joint purchasing. When analysing commercialisation agreements combining different stages of co-operation it is necessary to determine the centre of gravity of the co-operation in accordance with paragraphs 13 and 14.

Commentary
para 228: B&C: 6.073

6.2. Relevant markets

229. To assess the competitive relationship between the parties, the relevant product and geographic market or markets directly concerned by the co-operation (that is to say, the market or markets to

634

which the products subject to the agreement belong) have to be defined. As a commercialisation agreement in one market may also affect the competitive behaviour of the parties in a neighbouring market which is closely related to the market directly concerned by the co-operation, any such neighbouring market also needs to be defined. The neighbouring market may be horizontally or vertically related to the market where the co-operation takes place.

6.3. Assessment under Article 101(1)

6.3.1. Main competition concerns

230. Commercialisation agreements can lead to restrictions of competition in several ways. First, and most obviously, commercialisation agreements may lead to price fixing.

Commentary
para 230: F&N: 3.372

---

231. Secondly, commercialisation agreements may also facilitate output limitation, because the parties may decide on the volume of products to be put on the market, therefore restricting supply.

232. Thirdly, commercialisation agreements may become a means for the parties to divide the markets or to allocate orders or customers, for example in cases where the parties' production plants are located in different geographic markets or when the agreements are reciprocal.

233. Finally, commercialisation agreements may also lead to an exchange of strategic information relating to aspects within or outside the scope of the co-operation or to commonality of costs — in particular with regard to agreements not encompassing price fixing — which may result in a collusive outcome.

6.3.2. Restrictions of competition by object

234. Price fixing is one of the major competition concerns arising from commercialisation agreements between competitors. Agreements limited to joint selling generally have the object of coordinating the pricing policy of competing manufacturers or service providers. Such agreements may not only eliminate price competition between the parties on substitute products but may also restrict the total volume of products to be delivered by the parties within the framework of a system for allocating orders. Such agreements are therefore likely to restrict competition by object.

Commentary
para 234: B&C: 6.075 F&N: 7.329, 7.342, 12.117

---

235. That assessment does not change if the agreement is non-exclusive (that is to say, where the parties are free to sell individually outside the agreement), as long as it can be concluded that the agreement will lead to an overall coordination of the prices charged by the parties.

Commentary
para 235: B&C: 6.075 F&N: 7.347, 12.117

---

236. Another specific competition concern related to distribution arrangements between parties which are active in different geographic markets is that they can be an instrument of market partitioning. If the parties use a reciprocal distribution agreement to distribute each other's products in order to eliminate actual or potential competition between them by deliberately allocating markets or customers, the agreement is likely to have as its object a restriction of competition. If the agreement is not reciprocal, the risk of market partitioning is less pronounced. It is necessary, however, to assess whether the non-reciprocal agreement constitutes the basis for a mutual understanding to avoid entering each other's markets.

Commentary
para 236: B&C: 6.075 F&N: 7.329

Part C Substantive
Antitrust Matters

6.3.3. *Restrictive effects on competition*

237. A commercialisation agreement is normally not likely to give rise to competition concerns if it is objectively necessary to allow one party to enter a market it could not have entered individually or with a more limited number of parties than are effectively taking part in the co-operation, for example, because of the costs involved. A specific application of this principle would be consortia arrangements that allow the companies involved to participate in projects that they would not be able to undertake individually. As the parties to the consortia arrangement are therefore not potential competitors for implementing the project, there is no restriction of competition within the meaning of Article 101(1).

Commentary
para 237: B&C: 6.074 F&N: 7.327, 12.118

238. Similarly, not all reciprocal distribution agreements have as their object a restriction of competition. Depending on the facts of the case at hand, some reciprocal distribution agreements may, nevertheless, have restrictive effects on competition. The key issue in assessing an agreement of this type is whether the agreement in question is objectively necessary for the parties to enter each other's markets. If it is the agreement does not create competition problems of a horizontal nature. However, if the agreement reduces the decision-making independence of one of the parties with regard to entering the other parties' market or markets by limiting its incentives to do so, it is likely to give rise to restrictive effects on competition. The same reasoning applies to non-reciprocal agreements, where the risk of restrictive effects on competition is, however, less pronounced.

Commentary
para 238: B&C: 6.076 F&N: 7.332

239. Moreover, a distribution agreement can have restrictive effects on competition if it contains vertical restraints, such as restrictions on passive sales, resale price maintenance, etc.

Market power

240. Commercialisation agreements between competitors can only have restrictive effects on competition if the parties have some degree of market power. In most cases, it is unlikely that market power exists if the parties to the agreement have a combined market share not exceeding 15%. In any event, if the parties' combined market share does not exceed 15% it is likely that the conditions of Article 101(3) are fulfilled.

Commentary
para 240: B&C: 2.169, 6.012, 6.076, 6.079 F&N: 3.379, 7.333

241. If the parties' combined market share is greater than 15%, their agreement will fall outside the safe harbour of paragraph 240 and thus the likely impact of the joint commercialisation agreement on the market must be assessed.

Commentary
para 241: B&C: 6.012, 6.076 F&N: 7.334

Collusive outcome

242. A joint commercialisation agreement that does not involve price fixing is also likely to give rise to restrictive effects on competition if it increases the parties' commonality of variable costs to a level which is likely to lead to a collusive outcome. This is likely to be the case for a joint commercialisation agreement if prior to the agreement the parties already have a high proportion of their variable costs in common as the additional increment (that is to say, the commercialisation costs of the product subject to the agreement) can tip the balance towards a collusive outcome. Conversely, if the increment is large, the risk of a collusive outcome may be high even if the initial level of commonality of costs is low.

Commentary
para 242: **B&C:** 6.076

243. The likelihood of a collusive outcome depends on the parties' market power and the characteristics of the relevant market. Commonality of costs can only increase the risk of a collusive outcome if the parties have market power and if the commercialisation costs constitute a large proportion of the variable costs related to the products concerned. This is, for example, not the case for homogeneous products for which the highest cost factor is production. However, commonality of commercialisation costs increases the risk of a collusive outcome if the commercialisation agreement concerns products which entail costly commercialisation, for example, high distribution or marketing costs. Consequently, joint advertising or joint promotion agreements can also give rise to restrictive effects on competition if those costs constitute a significant cost factor.

Commentary
para 243: **B&C:** 6.076

244. Joint commercialisation generally involves the exchange of sensitive commercial information, particularly on marketing strategy and pricing. In most commercialisation agreements, some degree of information exchange is required in order to implement the agreement. It is therefore necessary to verify whether the information exchange can give rise to a collusive outcome with regard to the parties' activities within and outside the co-operation. Any negative effects arising from the exchange of information will not be assessed separately but in the light of the overall effects of the agreement.

Commentary
para 244: **B&C:** 6.076

245. For example, where the parties to a joint advertising agreement exchange pricing information, this may lead to a collusive outcome with regard to the sale of the jointly advertised products. In any event, the exchange of such information in the context of a joint advertising agreement goes beyond what would be necessary to implement that agreement. The likely restrictive effects on competition of information exchange in the context of commercialisation agreements will depend on the characteristics of the market and the data shared, and should be assessed in the light of the guidance given in Chapter 2.

Commentary
para 245: **B&C:** 6.076

6.4. Assessment under Article 101(3)

6.4.1. Efficiency gains

246. Commercialisation agreements can give rise to significant efficiency gains. The efficiencies to be taken into account when assessing whether a commercialisation agreement fulfils the criteria of Article 101(3) will depend on the nature of the activity and the parties to the co-operation. Price fixing can generally not be justified, unless it is indispensable for the integration of other marketing functions, and this integration will generate substantial efficiencies. Joint distribution can generate significant efficiencies, stemming from economies of scale or scope, especially for smaller producers.

Commentary
para 246: **B&C:** 3.039, 6.079 **F&N:** 7.355, 7.360

247. In addition, the efficiency gains must not be savings which result only from the elimination of costs that are inherently part of competition, but must result from the integration of economic activities. A reduction of transport cost which is only a result of customer allocation without any

integration of the logistical system can therefore not be regarded as an efficiency gain within the meaning of Article 101(3).

Commentary
para 247: **B&C:** 3.039, 6.079 **F&N:** 7.356

248. Efficiency gains must be demonstrated by the parties to the agreement. An important element in this respect would be the contribution by the parties of significant capital, technology, or other assets. Cost savings through reduced duplication of resources and facilities can also be accepted. However, if the joint commercialisation represents no more than a sales agency without any investment, it is likely to be a disguised cartel and as such unlikely to fulfil the conditions of Article 101(3).

Commentary
para 248: **F&N:** 7.356

6.4.2. *Indispensability*

249. Restrictions that go beyond what is necessary to achieve the efficiency gains generated by a commercialisation agreement do not fulfil the criteria of Article 101(3). The question of indispensability is especially important for those agreements involving price fixing or market allocation, which can only under exceptional circumstances be considered indispensable.

Commentary
para 249: **B&C:** 6.079

6.4.3. *Pass-on to consumers*

250. Efficiency gains attained by indispensable restrictions must be passed on to consumers to an extent that outweighs the restrictive effects on competition caused by the commercialisation agreement. This can happen in the form of lower prices or better product quality or variety. The higher the market power of the parties, however, the less likely it is that efficiency gains will be passed on to consumers to an extent that outweighs the restrictive effects on competition. Where the parties have a combined market share of below 15%, it is likely that any demonstrated efficiency gains generated by the agreement will be sufficiently passed on to consumers.

Commentary
para 250: **B&C:** 3.057, 6.079

6.4.4. *No elimination of competition*

251. The criteria of Article 101(3) cannot be fulfilled if the parties are afforded the possibility of eliminating competition in respect of a substantial part of the products in question. This has to be analysed in the relevant market to which the products subject to the co-operation belong and in possible spill-over markets.

Commentary
para 251: **B&C:** 3.068

6.5. Examples

252. Joint commercialisation necessary to enter a market

Example 1

Situation: Four companies providing laundry services in a large city close to the border of another Member State, each with a 3% market share of the overall laundry market in that city, agree to create a joint marketing arm for the selling of laundry services to institutional customers (that is to say, hotels, hospitals and offices), whilst keeping their independence and freedom to compete

---

for local, individual clients. In view of the new segment of demand (the institutional customers) they develop a common brand name, a common price and common standard terms including, inter alia, a maximum period of 24 hours before deliveries and schedules for delivery. They set up a common call centre where institutional clients can request their collection and/or delivery service. They hire a receptionist (for the call centre) and several drivers. They further invest in vans for dispatching, and in brand promotion, to increase their visibility. The agreement does not fully reduce their individual infrastructure costs (since they are keeping their own premises and still compete with each other for the individual local clients), but it increases their economies of scale and allows them to offer a more comprehensive service to other types of clients, which includes longer opening hours and dispatching to a wider geographic coverage. In order to ensure the viability of the project, it is indispensable that all four of them enter into the agreement. The market is very fragmented, with no individual competitor having more than 15% market share.

Analysis: Although the joint market share of the parties is below 15%, the fact that the agreement involves price fixing means that Article 101(1) could apply. However, the parties would not have been in a position to enter the market for providing laundry services to institutional customers, either individually or in co-operation with a fewer number of parties than the four currently taking part in the agreement. As such, the agreement would not create competition concerns, irrespective of the price-fixing restriction, which in this case can be considered as indispensable to the promotion of the common brand and the success of the project.

Commentary
para 252: F&N: 2.12, 7.331

253. Commercialisation agreement by more parties than necessary to enter a market

---

Example 2

Situation: The same facts as in Example 1, paragraph 252, apply with one main difference: in order to ensure the viability of the project, the agreement could have been implemented by only three of the parties (instead of the four actually taking part in the co-operation).

Analysis: Although the joint market share of the parties is below 15%, the fact that the agreement involves price fixing and could have been carried out by fewer than the four parties means that Article 101(1) applies. The agreement thus needs to be assessed under Article 101(3). The agreement gives rise to efficiency gains as the parties are now able to offer improved services for a new category of customers on a larger scale (which they would not otherwise have been able to service individually). In the light of the parties' combined market share of below 15%, it is likely that they will sufficiently pass-on any efficiency gains to consumers. It is further necessary to consider whether the restrictions imposed by the agreement are indispensable to achieve the efficiencies and whether the agreement eliminates competition. Given that the aim of the agreement is to provide a more comprehensive service (including dispatch, which was not offered before) to an additional category of customers, under a single brand with common standard terms, the price fixing can be considered as indispensable to the promotion of the common brand and, consequently, the success of the project and the resulting efficiencies. Additionally, taking into account the market fragmentation, the agreement will not eliminate competition. The fact that there are four parties to the agreement (instead of the three that would have been strictly necessary) allows for increased capacity and contributes to simultaneously fulfilling the demand of several institutional customers in compliance with the standard terms (that is to say, meeting maximum delivery time terms). As such, the efficiency gains are likely to outweigh the restrictive effects arising from the reduction of competition between the parties and the agreement is likely to fulfil the conditions of Article 101(3).

Commentary
para 253: F&N: 7.361

Part C Substantive Antitrust Matters

254. Joint internet platform

Example 3

Situation: A number of small specialty shops throughout a Member State join an electronic web-based platform for the promotion, sale and delivery of gift fruit baskets. There are a number of competing web-based platforms. By means of a monthly fee, they share the running costs of the platform and jointly invest in brand promotion. Through the webpage, where a wide range of different types of gift baskets are offered, customers order (and pay for) the type of gift basket they want to be delivered. The order is then allocated to the specialty shop closest to the address of delivery. The shop individually bears the costs of composing the gift basket and delivering it to the client. It reaps 90% of the final price, which is set by the web-based platform and uniformly applies to all participating specialty shops, whilst the remaining 10% is used for the common promotion and the running costs of the web-based platform. Apart from the payment of the monthly fee, there are no further restrictions for specialty shops to join the platform, throughout the national territory. Moreover, specialty shops having their own company website are also able to (and in some cases do) sell gift fruit baskets on the internet under their own name and thus can still compete among themselves outside the co-operation. Customers purchasing over the web-based platform are guaranteed same day delivery of the fruit baskets and they can also choose a delivery time convenient to them.

Analysis: Although the agreement is of a limited nature, since it only covers the joint selling of a particular type of product through a specific marketing channel (the web-based platform), since it involves price-fixing, it is likely to restrict competition by object. The agreement therefore needs to be assessed under Article 101(3). The agreement gives rise to efficiency gains such as greater choice and higher quality service and the reduction of search costs, which benefit consumers and are likely to outweigh the restrictive effects on competition the agreement brings about. Given that the specialty stores taking part in the co-operation are still able to operate individually and to compete one with another, both through their shops and the internet, the price-fixing restriction could be considered as indispensable for the promotion of the product (since when buying through the web-based platform consumers do not know where they are buying the gift basket from and do not want to deal with a multitude of different prices) and the ensuing efficiency gains. In the absence of other restrictions, the agreement fulfils the criteria of Article 101(3). Moreover, as other competing web-based platforms exist and the parties continue to compete with each other, through their shops or over the internet, competition will not be eliminated.

---

255. Sales joint venture

Example 4

Situation: Companies A and B, located in two different Member States, produce bicycle tyres. They have a combined market share of 14% on the Union-wide market for bicycle tyres. They decide to set up a (non full-function) sales joint venture for marketing the tyres to bicycle producers and agree to sell all their production through the joint venture. The production and transport infrastructure remains separate within each party. The parties claim considerable efficiency gains stem from the agreement. Such gains mainly relate to increased economies of scale, being able to fulfil the demands of their existing and potential new customers and better competing with imported tyres produced in third countries. The joint venture negotiates the prices and allocates orders to the closest production plant, as a way to rationalise transport costs when further delivering to the customer.

Analysis: Even though the combined market share of the parties is below 15%, the agreement falls under Article 101(1). It restricts competition by object since it involves customer allocation and the setting of prices by the joint venture. The claimed efficiencies deriving from the agreement do not result from the integration of economic activities or from common investment. The joint venture would have a very limited scope and would only serve as an interface for allocating

---

orders to the production plants. It is therefore unlikely that any efficiency gains would be passed on to consumers to such an extent that they would outweigh the restrictive effects on competition brought about by the agreement. Thus, the conditions of Article 101(3) would not be fulfilled.

Commentary
para 255: F&N: 8.27

256. Non-poaching clause in agreement on outsourcing of services

Example 5

Situation: Companies A and B are competing providers of cleaning services for commercial premises. Both have a market share of 15%. There are several other competitors with market shares between 10 and 15%. A has taken the (unilateral) decision to only focus on large customers in the future as servicing large and small customers has proved to require a somewhat different organisation of the work. Consequently, Company A has decided to no longer enter into contracts with new small customers. In addition, Companies A and B enter into an outsourcing agreement whereby Company B would directly provide cleaning services to Company A's existing small customers (which represent 1/3 of its customer base). At the same time, Company A is keen not to lose the customer relationship with those small customers. Hence, Company A will continue to keep its contractual relationships with the small customers but the direct provision of the cleaning services will be done by Company B. In order to implement the outsourcing agreement, Company A will necessarily need to provide Company B with the identities of Company A's small customers which are subject to the agreement. As Company A is afraid that Company B may try to poach those customers by offering cheaper direct services (thereby bypassing Company A), Company A insists that the outsourcing agreement contain a "non-poaching clause". According to that clause, Company B may not contact the small customers falling under the outsourcing agreements with a view to providing direct services to them. In addition, Companies A and B agree that Company B may not even provide direct services to those customers if Company B is approached by them. Without the "non-poaching clause" Company A would not enter into an outsourcing agreement with Company B or any other company.

Analysis: The outsourcing agreement removes Company B as an independent supplier of cleaning services for Company A's small customers as they will no longer be able to enter into a direct contractual relationship with Company B. However, those customers only represent 1/3 of Company A's customer base, that is to say, 5% of the market. They will still be able to turn to Company A and Company B's competitors, which represent 70% of the market. Hence, the outsourcing agreement will not enable Company A to profitably raise the prices charged to the customers subject to the outsourcing agreement. In addition, the outsourcing agreement is not likely to give rise to a collusive outcome as Companies A and B only have a combined market share of 30% and they are faced with several competitors that have market shares similar to Company A's and Company B's individual market shares. Moreover, the fact that servicing large and small customers is somewhat different minimises the risk of spill-over effects from the outsourcing agreement to Company A's and Company B's behaviour when competing for large customers. Consequently, the outsourcing agreement is not likely to give rise to restrictive effects on competition within the meaning of Article 101(1).

7. Standardisation Agreements

7.1. Definition

Standardisation agreements

257. Standardisation agreements have as their primary objective the definition of technical or quality requirements with which current or future products, production processes, services or methods may comply.[1] Standardisation agreements can cover various issues, such as standardisation of different grades or sizes of a particular product or technical specifications in product or services

markets where compatibility and interoperability with other products or systems is essential. The terms of access to a particular quality mark or for approval by a regulatory body can also be regarded as a standard. Agreements setting out standards on the environmental performance of products or production processes are also covered by this chapter.

Notes

[1] Standardisation can take different forms, ranging from the adoption of consensus based standards by the recognised European or national standards bodies, through consortia and fora, to agreements between independent companies.

Commentary

para 257: **B&C:** 6.080, 12.052 **F&N:** 7.510

258. The preparation and production of technical standards as part of the execution of public powers are not covered by these guidelines.[1] The European standardisation bodies recognised under Directive 98/34/EC of the European Parliament and of the Council of 22 June 1998 laying down a procedure for the provision of information in the field of technical standards and regulations and on rules on Information Society services[2] are subject to competition law to the extent that they can be considered to be an undertaking or an association of undertakings within the meaning of Articles 101 and 102.[3] Standards related to the provision of professional services, such as rules of admission to a liberal profession, are not covered by these guidelines.

Notes

[1] See Case C-113/07 *SELEX* [2009] ECR I-2207, paragraph 92.

[2] OJ L 204, 21.7.1998, p.37.

[3] See judgment of 12 May 2010 in Case T-432/05 *EMC Development AB v Commission*, not yet reported [now [2010] ECR II-1629].

Standard terms

259. In certain industries companies use standard terms and conditions of sale or purchase elaborated by a trade association or directly by the competing companies ('standard terms').[1] Such standard terms are covered by these guidelines to the extent that they establish standard conditions of sale or purchase of goods or services between competitors and consumers (and not the conditions of sale or purchase between competitors) for substitute products. When such standard terms are widely used within an industry, the conditions of purchase or sale used in the industry may become de facto aligned.[2] Examples of industries in which standard terms play an important role are the banking (for example, bank account terms) and insurance sectors.

Notes

[1] Such standard terms might cover only a very small part of the clauses contained in the final contract or a large part thereof.

[2] This refers to a situation where (legally non-binding) standard terms in practice are used by most of the industry and/ or for most aspects of the product/service thus leading to a limitation or even lack of consumer choice.

Commentary

para 259: **B&C:** 6.081

260. Standard terms elaborated individually by a company solely for its own use when contracting with its suppliers or customers are not horizontal agreements and are therefore not covered by these guidelines.

Commentary

para 260: **B&C:** 6.081

7.2. Relevant markets

261. Standardisation agreements may produce their effects on four possible markets, which will be defined according to the Market Definition Notice. First, standard-setting may have an impact on the product or service market or markets to which the standard or standards relates. Second, where the standard-setting involves the selection of technology and where the rights to intellectual property are marketed separately from the products to which they relate, the standard can have

effects on the relevant technology market.[1] Third, the market for standard-setting may be affected if different standard-setting bodies or agreements exist. Fourth, where relevant, a distinct market for testing and certification may be affected by standard-setting.

Notes

[1] See Chapter 3 on R&D agreements.

Commentary
para 261: B&C: 6.082

262. As regards standard terms, the effects are, in general, felt on the downstream market where the companies using the standard terms compete by selling their product to their customers.

Commentary
para 262: B&C: 6.082

7.3. Assessment under Article 101(1)

7.3.1. Main competition concerns

Standardisation agreements

263. Standardisation agreements usually produce significant positive economic effects,[1] for example by promoting economic interpenetration on the internal market and encouraging the development of new and improved products or markets and improved supply conditions. Standards thus normally increase competition and lower output and sales costs, benefiting economies as a whole. Standards may maintain and enhance quality, provide information and ensure interoperability and compatibility (thus increasing value for consumers).

Notes

[1] See also paragraph 308.

Commentary
para 263: F&N: 7.499

264. Standard-setting can, however, in specific circumstances, also give rise to restrictive effects on competition by potentially restricting price competition and limiting or controlling production, markets, innovation or technical development. This can occur through three main channels, namely reduction in price competition, foreclosure of innovative technologies and exclusion of, or discrimination against, certain companies by prevention of effective access to the standard.

265. First, if companies were to engage in anti-competitive discussions in the context of standard-setting, this could reduce or eliminate price competition in the markets concerned, thereby facilitating a collusive outcome on the market.[1]

Notes

[1] Depending on the circle of participants in the standard-setting process, restrictions can occur either on the supplier or on the purchaser side of the market for the standardised product.

266. Second, standards that set detailed technical specifications for a product or service may limit technical development and innovation. While a standard is being developed, alternative technologies can compete for inclusion in the standard. Once one technology has been chosen and the standard has been set, competing technologies and companies may face a barrier to entry and may potentially be excluded from the market. In addition, standards requiring that a particular technology is used exclusively for a standard or preventing the development of other technologies by obliging the members of the standard-setting organisation to exclusively use a particular standard, may lead to the same effect. The risk of limitation of innovation is increased if one or more companies are unjustifiably excluded from the standard-setting process.

267. In the context of standards involving intellectual property rights ("IPR"),[1] three main groups of companies with different interests in standard-setting can be distinguished in the abstract.[2] First, there are upstream-only companies that solely develop and market technologies. Their only

Part C Substantive Antitrust Matters

source of income is licensing revenue and their incentive is to maximise their royalties. Secondly, there are downstream-only companies that solely manufacture products or offer services based on technologies developed by others and do not hold relevant IPR. Royalties represent a cost for them, and not a source of revenue, and their incentive is to reduce or avoid royalties. Finally, there are vertically integrated companies that both develop technology and sell products. They have mixed incentives. On the one hand, they can draw licensing revenue from their IPR. On the other hand, they may have to pay royalties to other companies holding IPR essential to the standard. They might therefore cross-license their own essential IPR in exchange for essential IPR held by other companies.

Notes

[1] In the context of this chapter IPR in particular refers to patent(s) (excluding non-published patent applications). However, in case any other type of IPR in practice gives the IPR holder control over the use of the standard the same principles should be applied.

[2] In practice, many companies use a mix of these business models.

268. Third, standardisation may lead to anti-competitive results by preventing certain companies from obtaining effective access to the results of the standard-setting process (that is to say, the specification and/or the essential IPR for implementing the standard). If a company is either completely prevented from obtaining access to the result of the standard, or is only granted access on prohibitive or discriminatory terms, there is a risk of an anti-competitive effect. A system where potentially relevant IPR is disclosed up-front may increase the likelihood of effective access being granted to the standard since it allows the participants to identify which technologies are covered by IPR and which are not. This enables the participants to both factor in the potential effect on the final price of the result of the standard (for example choosing a technology without IPR is likely to have a positive effect on the final price) and to verify with the IPR holder whether they would be willing to license if their technology is included in the standard.

269. Intellectual property laws and competition laws share the same objectives[1] of promoting innovation and enhancing consumer welfare. IPR promote dynamic competition by encouraging undertakings to invest in developing new or improved products and processes. IPR are therefore in general pro-competitive. However, by virtue of its IPR, a participant holding IPR essential for implementing the standard, could, in the specific context of standard-setting, also acquire control over the use of a standard. When the standard constitutes a barrier to entry, the company could thereby control the product or service market to which the standard relates. This in turn could allow companies to behave in anti-competitive ways, for example by "holding-up" users after the adoption of the standard either by refusing to license the necessary IPR or by extracting excess rents by way of excessive[2] royalty fees thereby preventing effective access to the standard. However, even if the establishment of a standard can create or increase the market power of IPR holders possessing IPR essential to the standard, there is no presumption that holding or exercising IPR essential to a standard equates to the possession or exercise of market power. The question of market power can only be assessed on a case by case basis.

Notes

[1] See Technology Transfer Guidelines, paragraph 7.

[2] High royalty fees can only be qualified as excessive if the conditions for an abuse of a dominant position as set out in Article 102 of the Treaty and the case-law of the Court of Justice of the European Union are fulfilled. See for example Case 27/76 *United Brands* [1978] ECR 207.

Commentary
para 269: **B&C:** 2.086 **F&N:** 7.515, 7.526

Standard terms

270. Standard terms can give rise to restrictive effects on competition by limiting product choice and innovation. If a large part of an industry adopts the standard terms and chooses not to deviate from them in individual cases (or only deviates from them in exceptional cases of strong buyer-power), customers might have no option other than to accept the conditions in the standard

terms. However, the risk of limiting choice and innovation is only likely in cases where the standard terms define the scope of the end-product. As regards classical consumer goods, standard terms of sale generally do not limit innovation of the actual product or product quality and variety.

Commentary
para 270: B&C: 6.083, 12.131

---

271. In addition, depending on their content, standard terms might risk affecting the commercial conditions of the final product. In particular, there is a serious risk that standard terms relating to price would restrict price competition.

Commentary
para 271: B&C: 6.083

---

272. Moreover, if the standard terms become industry practice, access to them might be vital for entry into the market. In such cases, refusing access to the standard terms could risk causing anti-competitive foreclosure. As long as the standard terms remain effectively open for use for anyone that wishes to have access to them, they are unlikely to give rise to anti-competitive foreclosure.

Commentary
para 272: B&C: 2.100, 6.083

7.3.2. *Restrictions of competition by object*

Standardisation agreements

273. Agreements that use a standard as part of a broader restrictive agreement aimed at excluding actual or potential competitors restrict competition by object. For instance, an agreement whereby a national association of manufacturers sets a standard and puts pressure on third parties not to market products that do not comply with the standard or where the producers of the incumbent product collude to exclude new technology from an already existing standard[1] would fall into this category.

Notes

[1] See for example Commission Decision in Case IV/35.691, *Pre-insulated pipes*, OJ L 24, 30.1.1999, p.1, where part of the infringement of Article 101 consisted in "using norms and standards in order to prevent or delay the introduction of new technology which would result in price reductions" (paragraph 147).

---

274. Any agreements to reduce competition by using the disclosure of most restrictive licensing terms prior to the adoption of a standard as a cover to jointly fix prices either of downstream products or of substitute IPR or technology will constitute restrictions of competition by object.[1]

Notes

[1] This paragraph should not prevent unilateral ex ante disclosures of most restrictive licensing terms as described in paragraph 299. It also does not prevent patent pools created in accordance with the principles set out in the Technology Transfer Guidelines or the decision to license IPR essential to a standard on royalty-free terms as set out in this Chapter.

Standard terms

275. Agreements that use standard terms as part of a broader restrictive agreement aimed at excluding actual or potential competitors also restrict competition by object. An example would be where a trade association does not allow a new entrant access to its standards terms, the use of which is vital to ensure entry to the market.

Commentary
para 275: F&N: 7.542

---

276. Any standard terms containing provisions which directly influence the prices charged to customers (that is to say, recommended prices, rebates, etc.) would constitute a restriction of competition by object.

Commentary
para 276: F&N: 7.542

7.3.3. *Restrictive effects on competition*

Standardisation agreements

Agreements normally not restrictive of competition

277. Standardisation agreements which do not restrict competition by object must be analysed in their legal and economic context with regard to their actual and likely effect on competition. In the absence of market power,[1] a standardisation agreement is not capable of producing restrictive effects on competition. Therefore, restrictive effects are most unlikely in a situation where there is effective competition between a number of voluntary standards.

Notes

[1] See by analogy paragraph 39 et seq. As regards market shares see also paragraph 296.

Commentary
para 277: B&C: 6.084 F&N: 7.519

278. For those standard-setting agreements which risk creating market power, paragraphs 280 to 286 set out the conditions under which such agreements would normally fall outside the scope of Article 101(1).

279. The non-fulfilment of any or all of the principles set out in this section will not lead to any presumption of a restriction of competition within Article 101(1). However, it will necessitate a self-assessment to establish whether the agreement falls under Article 101(1) and, if so, if the conditions of Article 101(3) are fulfilled. In this context, it is recognised that there exist different models for standard-setting and that competition within and between those models is a positive aspect of a market economy. Therefore, standard-setting organisations remain entirely free to put in place rules and procedures that do not violate competition rules whilst being different to those described in paragraphs 280 to 286.

Commentary
para 279: F&N: 7.518

280. Where participation in standard-setting is **unrestricted** and the procedure for adopting the standard in question is **transparent**, standardisation agreements which contain **no obligation to comply**[1] with the standard and provide **access to the standard on fair, reasonable and non-discriminatory terms** will normally not restrict competition within the meaning of Article 101(1).

Notes

[1] See also paragraph 293 in this regard.

281. In particular, to ensure **unrestricted participation** the rules of the standard-setting organisation would need to guarantee that all competitors in the market or markets affected by the standard can participate in the process leading to the selection of the standard. The standard-setting organisations would also need to have objective and non-discriminatory procedures for allocating voting rights as well as, if relevant, objective criteria for selecting the technology to be included in the standard.

Commentary
para 281: F&N: 7.521

282. With respect to **transparency**, the relevant standard-setting organisation would need to have procedures which allow stakeholders to effectively inform themselves of upcoming, on-going and finalised standardisation work in good time at each stage of the development of the standard.

283. Furthermore, the standard-setting organisation's rules would need to ensure effective **access to the standard on fair, reasonable and non discriminatory terms.**[1]

Notes

[1] For example effective access should be granted to the specification of the standard.

284. In the case of a standard involving IPR, **a clear and balanced IPR policy,**[1] **adapted to the particular industry** and the needs of the standard-setting organisation in question, increases the likelihood that the implementers of the standard will be granted effective access to the standards elaborated by that standard-setting organisation.

Notes

[1] As specified in paragraphs 285 and 286.

285. In order to ensure effective access to the standard, the IPR policy would need to require participants wishing to have their IPR included in the standard to provide an irrevocable commitment in writing to offer to license their essential IPR to all third parties on fair, reasonable and non-discriminatory terms ('**FRAND commitment**').[1] That commitment should be given prior to the adoption of the standard. At the same time, the IPR policy should allow IPR holders to exclude specified technology from the standard-setting process and thereby from the commitment to offer to license, providing that exclusion takes place at an early stage in the development of the standard. To ensure the effectiveness of the FRAND commitment, there would also need to be a requirement on all participating IPR holders who provide such a commitment to ensure that any company to which the IPR owner transfers its IPR (including the right to license that IPR) is bound by that commitment, for example through a contractual clause between buyer and seller.

Notes

[1] It should be noted that FRAND can also cover royalty-free licensing.

286. Moreover, the IPR policy would need to require **good faith disclosure**, by participants, of their IPR that might be essential for the implementation of the standard under development. This would enable the industry to make an informed choice of technology and thereby assist in achieving the goal of effective access to the standard. Such a disclosure obligation could be based on ongoing disclosure as the standard develops and on reasonable endeavours to identify IPR reading on the potential standard.[1] It is also sufficient if the participant declares that it is likely to have IPR claims over a particular technology (without identifying specific IPR claims or applications for IPR). Since the risks with regard to effective access are not the same in the case of a standard-setting organisation with a royalty-free standards policy, IPR disclosure would not be relevant in that context.

Notes

[1] To obtain the sought after result a good faith disclosure does not need to go as far as to require participants to compare their IPR against the potential standard and issue a statement positively concluding that they have no IPR reading on the potential standard.

FRAND Commitments

287. FRAND commitments are designed to ensure that essential IPR protected technology incorporated in a standard is accessible to the users of that standard on fair, reasonable and non-discriminatory terms and conditions. In particular, FRAND commitments can prevent IPR holders from making the implementation of a standard difficult by refusing to license or by requesting unfair or unreasonable fees (in other words excessive fees) after the industry has been locked-in to the standard or by charging discriminatory royalty fees.

Commentary
para 287: B&C: 6.087 F&N: 7.532, 13.239

288. Compliance with Article 101 by the standard-setting organisation does not require the standard-setting organisation to verify whether licensing terms of participants fulfil the FRAND commitment. Participants will have to assess for themselves whether the licensing terms and in particular the fees they charge fulfil the FRAND commitment. Therefore, when deciding whether to commit to FRAND for a particular IPR, participants will need to anticipate the implications of the FRAND commitment, notably on their ability to freely set the level of their fees.

289. In case of a dispute, the assessment of whether fees charged for access to IPR in the standard-setting context are unfair or unreasonable should be based on whether the fees bear a reasonable relationship to the economic value of the IPR.[1] In general, there are various methods available to make this assessment. In principle, cost-based methods are not well adapted to this context because of the difficulty in assessing the costs attributable to the development of a particular patent or groups of patents. Instead, it may be possible to compare the licensing fees charged by the company in question for the relevant patents in a competitive environment before the industry has been locked into the standard (*ex ante*) with those charged after the industry has been locked in (*ex post*). This assumes that the comparison can be made in a consistent and reliable manner.[2]

Notes

[1] See Case 27/76 *United Brands* [1978] ECR 207, paragraph 250; see also Case C-385/07 P *Der Grüne Punkt — Duales System Deutschland GmbH* [2009] ECR I-6155, paragraph 142.
[2] See Case 395/87 *Ministère public v Jean-Louis Tournier* [1989] ECR 2521, paragraph 38; Joined Cases 110/88, 241/88 and 242/88 *Francois Lucazeau v SACEM* [1989] ECR 2811, paragraph 33.

Commentary
para 289: B&C: 6.087

290. Another method could be to obtain an independent expert assessment of the objective centrality and essentiality to the standard at issue of the relevant IPR portfolio. In an appropriate case, it may also be possible to refer to *ex ante* disclosures of licensing terms in the context of a specific standard-setting process. This also assumes that the comparison can be made in a consistent and reliable manner. The royalty rates charged for the same IPR in other comparable standards may also provide an indication for FRAND royalty rates. These guidelines do not seek to provide an exhaustive list of appropriate methods to assess whether the royalty fees are excessive.

291. However, it should be emphasised that nothing in these Guidelines prejudices the possibility for parties to resolve their disputes about the level of FRAND royalty rates by having recourse to the competent civil or commercial courts.

Effects based assessment for standardisation agreements

292. The assessment of each standardisation agreement must take into account the likely effects of the standard on the markets concerned. The following considerations apply to all standardisation agreements that depart from the principles as set out in paragraphs 280 to 286.

293. Whether standardisation agreements may give rise to restrictive effects on competition may depend on whether the members of a standard-setting organisation remain *free to develop alternative standards or products* that do not comply with the agreed standard.[1] For example, if the standard-setting agreement binds the members to only produce products in compliance with the standard, the risk of a likely negative effect on competition is significantly increased and could in certain circumstances give rise to a restriction of competition by object.[2] In the same vein, standards only covering minor aspects or parts of the end-product are less likely to lead to competition concerns than more comprehensive standards.

Notes

[1] See Commission Decision in Case IV/29/151, *Philips/VCR*, OJ L 47, 18.2.1978, p.42, paragraph 23: "As these standards were for the manufacture of VCR equipment, the parties were obliged to manufacture and distribute only cassettes and recorders conforming to the VCR system licensed by Philips. They were prohibited from changing to manufacturing and distributing other video cassette systems…This constituted a restriction of competition under Article [101](1)(b)".
[2] See Commission Decision in Case IV/29/151, *Philips/VCR*, paragraph 23.

Commentary
para 293: B&C: 6.086 F&N: 7.529

294. The assessment whether the agreement restricts competition will also focus on **access to the standard**. Where the result of a standard (that is to say, the specification of how to comply with the standard and, if relevant, the essential IPR for implementing the standard) is not at all accessible, or only accessible on discriminatory terms, for members or third parties (that is to say, non-members of the relevant standard-setting organisation) this may discriminate or foreclose or segment markets according to their geographic scope of application and thereby is likely to restrict competition. However, in the case of several competing standards or in the case of effective competition between the standardised solution and non-standardised solution, a limitation of access may not produce restrictive effects on competition.

Commentary
para 294: B&C: 6.086

295. **If participation in the standard-setting process** is open in the sense that it allows all competitors (and/or stakeholders) in the market affected by the standard to take part in choosing and elaborating the standard, this will lower the risks of a likely restrictive effect on competition by not excluding certain companies from the ability to influence the choice and elaboration of the standard.[1] The greater the likely market impact of the standard and the wider its potential fields of application, the more important it is to allow equal access to the standard-setting process. However, if the facts at hand show that there is competition between several such standards and standard-setting organisations (and it is not necessary that the whole industry applies the same standards) there may be no restrictive effects on competition. Also, if in the absence of a limitation on the number of participants it would not have been possible to adopt the standard, the agreement would not be likely to lead to any restrictive effect on competition under Article 101(1).[2] In certain situations the potential negative effects of restricted participation may be removed or at least lessened by ensuring that stakeholders are **kept informed and consulted** on the work in progress.[3] The more transparent the procedure for adopting the standard, the more likely it is that the adopted standard will take into account the interests of all stakeholders.

Notes

[1] In Commission Decision in Case IV/31.458, *X/Open Group*, OJ L 35, 6.2.1987, p.36, the Commission considered that even if the standards adopted were made public, the restricted membership policy had the effect of preventing non-members from influencing the results of the work of the group and from getting the know-how and technical understanding relating to the standards which the members were likely to acquire. In addition, non-members could not, in contrast to the members, implement the standard before it was adopted (see paragraph 32). The agreement was therefore in these circumstances seen to constitute a restriction under Article 101(1).

[2] Or if the adoption of the standard would have been heavily delayed by an inefficient process, any initial restriction could be outweighed by efficiencies to be considered under Article 101(3).

[3] See Commission Decision of 14 October 2009 in Case 39.416, *Ship Classification*. The Decision can be found at: <http://ec.europa.eu/competition/antitrust/cases/index/by_nr_78.html#i39_416>.

296. To assess the effects of a standard-setting agreement, **the market shares of the goods or services based on the standard** should be taken into account. It might not always be possible to assess with any certainty at an early stage whether the standard will in practice be adopted by a large part of the industry or whether it will only be a standard used by a marginal part of the relevant industry. In many cases the relevant market shares of the companies having participated in developing the standard could be used as a proxy for estimating the likely market share of the standard (since the companies participating in setting the standard would in most cases have an interest in implementing the standard).[1] However, as the effectiveness of standardisation agreements is often proportional to the share of the industry involved in setting and/or applying the standard, high market shares held by the parties in the market or markets affected by the standard will not necessarily lead to the conclusion that the standard is likely to give rise to restrictive effects on competition.

Notes
[1] See paragraph 261.
Commentary
para 296: B&C: 6.086

297. Any standard-setting agreement which clearly **discriminates** against any of the participating or potential members could lead to a restriction of competition. For example, if a standard-setting organisation explicitly excludes upstream only companies (that is to say, companies not active on the downstream production market), this could lead to an exclusion of potentially better technologies.

298. As regards standard-setting agreements with **different types of IPR disclosure models** from the ones described in paragraph 286, it would have to be assessed on a case by case basis whether the disclosure model in question (for example a disclosure model not requiring but only encouraging IPR disclosure) guarantees effective access to the standard. In other words, it needs to be assessed whether, in the specific context, an informed choice between technologies and associated IPR is in practice not prevented by the IPR disclosure model.

299. Finally, standard-setting agreements providing for **ex ante disclosures of most restrictive licensing terms**, will not, in principle, restrict competition within the meaning of Article 101(1). In that regard, it is important that parties involved in the selection of a standard be fully informed not only as to the available technical options and the associated IPR, but also as to the likely cost of that IPR. Therefore, should a standard-setting organisation's IPR policy choose to provide for IPR holders to individually disclose their most restrictive licensing terms, including the maximum royalty rates they would charge, prior to the adoption of the standard, this will normally not lead to a restriction of competition within the meaning of Article 101(1).[1] Such unilateral ex ante disclosures of most restrictive licensing terms would be one way to enable the standard-setting organisation to take an informed decision based on the disadvantages and advantages of different alternative technologies, not only from a technical perspective but also from a pricing perspective.

Notes
[1] Any unilateral ex ante disclosures of most restrictive licensing terms should not serve as a cover to jointly fix prices either of downstream products or of substitute IPR/technologies which is, as outlined in paragraph 274, a restriction of competition by object.
Commentary
para 299: B&C: 6.086

Standard terms

300. The establishment and use of standard terms must be assessed in the appropriate economic context and in the light of the situation on the relevant market in order to determine whether the standard terms at issue are likely to give rise to restrictive effects on competition.

301. As long as participation in the actual establishment of standard terms is **unrestricted** for the competitors in the relevant market (either by participation in the trade association or directly), and the established standard terms are **non-binding** and **effectively accessible** for anyone, such agreements are not likely to give rise to restrictive effects on competition (subject to the caveats set out in paragraphs 303, 304, 305 and 307).

Commentary
para 301: B&C: 6.089

302. Effectively accessible and non-binding standard terms for the sale of consumer goods or services (on the presumption that they have no effect on price) thus generally do not have any restrictive effect on competition since they are unlikely to lead to any negative effect on product quality, product variety or innovation. There are, however, two general exceptions where a more in-depth assessment would be required.

303. Firstly, standard terms for the sale of consumer goods or services where the standard terms define the scope of the product sold to the customer, and where therefore the risk of limiting product

choice is more significant, could give rise to restrictive effects on competition within the meaning of Article 101(1) where their common application is likely to result in a *de facto* alignment. This could be the case when the widespread use of the standard terms *de facto* leads to a limitation of innovation and product variety. For instance, this may arise where standard terms in insurance contracts limit the customer's practical choice of key elements of the contract, such as the standard risks covered. Even if the use of the standard terms is not compulsory, they might undermine the incentives of the competitors to compete on product diversification.

Commentary
para 303: B&C: 6.089 **F&N:** 7.544

304. When assessing whether there is a risk that the standard terms are likely to have restrictive effects by way of a limitation of product choice, factors such as existing competition on the market should be taken into account. For example if there is a large number of smaller competitors, the risk of a limitation of product choice would seem to be less than if there are only a few bigger competitors.[1] The market shares of the companies participating in the establishment of the standard terms might also give a certain indication of the likelihood of uptake of the standard terms or of the likelihood that the standard terms will be used by a large part of the market. However, in this respect, it is not only relevant to analyse whether the standard terms elaborated are likely to be used by a large part of the market, but also whether the standard terms only cover part of the product or the whole product (the less extensive the standard terms, the less likely that they will lead, overall, to a limitation of product choice). Moreover, in cases where in the absence of the establishment of the standard terms it would not have been possible to offer a certain product, there would not be likely to be any restrictive effect on competition within the meaning of Article 101(1). In that scenario, product choice is increased rather than decreased by the establishment of the standard terms.

Notes

[1] If previous experience with standard terms on the relevant market shows that the standard terms did not lead to lessened competition on product differentiation, this might also be an indication that the same type of standard terms elaborated for a neighbouring product will not lead to a restrictive effect on competition.

Commentary
para 304: B&C: 6.089 **F&N:** 7.544

305. Secondly, even if the standard terms do not define the actual scope of the end-product they might be a decisive part of the transaction with the customer for other reasons. An example would be online shopping where customer confidence is essential (for example, in the use of safe payment systems, a proper description of the products, clear and transparent pricing rules, flexibility of the return policy, etc). As it is difficult for customers to make a clear assessment of all those elements, they tend to favour widespread practices and standard terms regarding those elements could therefore become a *de facto* standard with which companies would need to comply to sell in the market. Even though non-binding, those standard terms would become a *de facto* standard, the effects of which are very close to a binding standard and need to be analysed accordingly.

Commentary
para 305: B&C: 6.089

306. If the use of standard terms is binding, there is a need to assess their impact on product quality, product variety and innovation (in particular if the standard terms are binding on the entire market).

307. Moreover, should the standard terms (binding or non-binding) contain any terms which are likely to have a negative effect on competition relating to prices (for example terms defining the type of rebates to be given), they would be likely to give rise to restrictive effects on competition within the meaning of Article 101(1).

Commentary
para 307: B&C: 6.089

7.4. Assessment under Article 101(3)

7.4.1. Efficiency gains

Standardisation agreements

308. Standardisation agreements frequently give rise to significant efficiency gains. For example, Union wide standards may facilitate market integration and allow companies to market their goods and services in all Member States, leading to increased consumer choice and decreasing prices. Standards which establish technical interoperability and compatibility often encourage competition on the merits between technologies from different companies and help prevent lock-in to one particular supplier. Furthermore, standards may reduce transaction costs for sellers and buyers. Standards on, for instance, quality, safety and environmental aspects of a product may also facilitate consumer choice and can lead to increased product quality. Standards also play an important role for innovation. They can reduce the time it takes to bring a new technology to the market and facilitate innovation by allowing companies to build on top of agreed solutions.

Commentary
para 308: **B&C:** 6.091, 6.092 **F&N:** 7.534

309. To achieve those efficiency gains in the case of standardisation agreements, the information necessary to apply the standard must be effectively available to those wishing to enter the market.[1]

Notes
[1] See Commission Decision in Case IV/31.458, *X/Open Group*, paragraph 42: "The Commission considers that the willingness of the Group to make available the results as quickly as possible is an essential element in its decision to grant an exemption".

Commentary
para 309: **F&N:** 7.534

310. Dissemination of a standard can be enhanced by marks or logos certifying compliance thereby providing certainty to customers. Agreements for testing and certification go beyond the primary objective of defining the standard and would normally constitute a distinct agreement and market.

Commentary
para 310: **F&N:** 7.511

311. While the effects on innovation must be analysed on a case-by-case basis, standards creating compatibility on a horizontal level between different technology platforms are considered to be likely to give rise to efficiency gains.

Commentary
para 311: **F&N:** 7.534

Standard terms

312. The use of standard terms can entail economic benefits such as making it easier for customers to compare the conditions offered and thus facilitate switching between companies. Standard terms might also lead to efficiency gains in the form of savings in transaction costs and, in certain sectors (in particular where the contracts are of a complex legal structure), facilitate entry. Standard terms may also increase legal certainty for the contract parties.

Commentary
para 312: **B&C:** 6.093

313. The higher the number of competitors on the market, the greater the efficiency gain of facilitating the comparison of conditions offered.

7.4.2. Indispensability

314. Restrictions that go beyond what is necessary to achieve the efficiency gains that can be generated by a standardisation agreement or standard terms do not fulfil the criteria of Article 101(3).

Standardisation agreements

315. The assessment of each standardisation agreement must take into account its likely effect on the markets concerned, on the one hand, and the scope of restrictions that possibly go beyond the objective of achieving efficiencies, on the other.[1]

Notes

[1] In Case IV/29/151, *Philips/VCR*, compliance with the VCR standards led to the exclusion of other, perhaps better systems. Such exclusion was particularly serious in view of the pre-eminent market position enjoyed by Philips "…[R]restrictions were imposed upon the parties which were not indispensable to the attainment of these improvements. The compatibility of VCR video cassettes with the machines made by other manufacturers would have been ensured even if the latter had to accept no more than an obligation to observe the VCR standards when manufacturing VCR equipment" (paragraph 31).

316. Participation in standard-setting should normally be open to all competitors in the market or markets affected by the standard unless the parties demonstrate significant inefficiencies of such participation or recognised procedures are foreseen for the collective representation of interests.[1]

Notes

[1] See Commission Decision in Case IV/31.458, *X/Open Group*, paragraph 45: "[T]he aims of the Group could not be achieved if any company willing to commit itself to the Group objectives had a right to become a member. This would create practical and logistical difficulties for the management of the work and possibly prevent appropriate proposals being passed." See also Commission Decision of 14 October 2009 in Case 39.416, *Ship Classification*, paragraph 36: "the Commitments strike an appropriate balance between maintaining demanding criteria for membership of IACS on the one hand, and removing unnecessary barriers to membership of IACS on the other hand. The new criteria will ensure that only technically competent CSs are eligible to become member of IACS, thus preventing that the efficiency and quality of IACS' work is unduly impaired by too lenient requirements for participation in IACS. At the same time, the new criteria will not hinder CSs, who are technically competent and willing to do so from joining IACS".

317. As a general rule standardisation agreements should cover no more than what is necessary to ensure their aims, whether this is technical interoperability and compatibility or a certain level of quality. In cases where having only one technological solution would benefit consumers or the economy at large that standard should, be set on a non-discriminatory basis. Technology neutral standards can, in certain circumstances, lead to larger efficiency gains. Including substitute IPR[1] as essential parts of a standard while at the same time forcing the users of the standard to pay for more IPR than technically necessary would go beyond what is necessary to achieve any identified efficiency gains. In the same vein, including substitute IPR as essential parts of a standard and limiting the use of that technology to that particular standard (that is to say, exclusive use) could limit inter-technology competition and would not be necessary to achieve the efficiencies identified.

Notes

[1] Technology which is regarded by users or licensees as interchangeable with or substitutable for another technology, by reason of the characteristics and intended use of the technologies.

Commentary
para 317: B&C: 6.091

318. Restrictions in a standardisation agreement making a standard binding and obligatory for the industry are in principle not indispensable.

319. In a similar vein, standardisation agreements that entrust certain bodies with the exclusive right to test compliance with the standard go beyond the primary objective of defining the standard and may also restrict competition. The exclusivity can, however, be justified for a certain period of time, for example by the need to recoup significant start-up costs.[1] The standardisation agreement should in that case include adequate safeguards to mitigate possible risks to competition resulting

from exclusivity. This concerns, inter alia, the certification fee which needs to be reasonable and proportionate to the cost of the compliance testing.

Notes

1 In this context see Commission Decision in Cases IV/34.179, 34.202, 216, *Dutch Cranes (SCK and FNK)*, OJ L 312, 23.12.1995, p.79, paragraph 23: "The ban on calling on firms not certified by SCK as sub-contractors restricts the freedom of action of certified firms. Whether a ban can be regarded as preventing, restricting or distorting competition within the meaning of Article [101](1) must be judged in the legal and economic context. If such a ban is associated with a certification system which is completely open, independent and transparent and provides for the acceptance of equivalent guarantees from other systems, it may be argued that it has no restrictive effects on competition but is simply aimed at fully guaranteeing the quality of the certified goods or services".

Standard terms

320. It is generally not justified to make standard terms binding and obligatory for the industry or the members of the trade association that established them. The possibility cannot, however, be ruled out that making standard terms binding may, in a specific case, be indispensable to the attainment of the efficiency gains generated by them.

Commentary
para 320: B&C: 6.093

7.4.3. Pass-on to consumers

Standardisation agreements

321. Efficiency gains attained by indispensable restrictions must be passed on to consumers to an extent that outweighs the restrictive effects on competition caused by a standardisation agreement or by standard terms. A relevant part of the analysis of likely pass-on to consumers is which procedures are used to guarantee that the interests of the users of standards and end consumers are protected. Where standards facilitate technical interoperability and compatibility or competition between new and already existing products, services and processes, it can be presumed that the standard will benefit consumers.

Commentary
para 321: F&N: 7.536

Standard terms

322. Both the risk of restrictive effects on competition and the likelihood of efficiency gains increase with the companies' market shares and the extent to which the standard terms are used. Hence, it is not possible to provide any general 'safe harbour' within which there is no risk of restrictive effects on competition or which would allow the presumption that efficiency gains will be passed on to consumers to an extent that outweighs the restrictive effects on competition.

Commentary
para 322: B&C: 3.057

323. However, certain efficiency gains generated by standard terms, such as increased comparability of the offers on the market, facilitated switching between providers, and legal certainty of the clauses set out in the standard terms, are necessarily beneficial for the consumers. As regards other possible efficiency gains, such as lower transaction costs, it is necessary to make an assessment on a case-by-case basis and in the relevant economic context whether these are likely to be passed on to consumers.

7.4.4. No elimination of competition

324. Whether a standardisation agreement affords the parties the possibility of eliminating competition depends on the various sources of competition in the market, the level of competitive constraint that they impose on the parties and the impact of the agreement on that competitive constraint.

While market shares are relevant for that analysis, the magnitude of remaining sources of actual competition cannot be assessed exclusively on the basis of market share except in cases where a standard becomes a *de facto* industry standard.[1] In the latter case competition may be eliminated if third parties are foreclosed from effective access to the standard. Standard terms used by a majority of the industry might create a *de facto* industry standard and thus raise the same concerns. However, if the standard or the standard terms only concern a limited part of the product or service, competition is not likely to be eliminated.

Notes

[1] *De facto* standardisation refers to a situation where a (legally non-binding) standard, is, in practice, used by most of the industry.

Commentary
para 324: B&C: 3.068

7.5. Examples

325. Setting standards competitors cannot satisfy

> **Example 1**
>
> **Situation:** A standard-setting organisation sets and publishes safety standards that are widely used by the relevant industry. Most competitors of the industry take part in the setting of the standard. Prior to the adoption of the standard, a new entrant has developed a product which is technically equivalent in terms of the performance and functional requirements and which is recognised by the technical committee of the standard-setting organisation. However, the technical specifications of the safety standard are, without any objective justification, drawn up in such a way as to not allow for this or other new products to comply with the standard.
>
> **Analysis:** This standardisation agreement is likely to give rise to restrictive effects on competition within the meaning of Article 101(1) and is unlikely to meet the criteria of Article 101(3). The members of the standards development organisation have, without any objective justification, set the standard in such a way that products of their competitors which are based on other technological solutions cannot satisfy it, even though they have equivalent performance. Hence, this standard, which has not been set on a non-discriminatory basis, will reduce or prevent innovation and product variety. It is unlikely that the way the standard is drafted will lead to greater efficiency gains than a neutral one.

326. Non-binding and transparent standard covering a large part of the market

> **Example 2**
>
> **Situation:** A number of consumer electronics manufacturers with substantial market shares agree to develop a new standard for a product to follow up the DVD.
>
> **Analysis:** Provided that (a) the manufacturers remain free to produce other new products which do not conform to the new standard, (b) participation in the standard-setting is unrestricted and transparent, and (c) the standardisation agreement does not otherwise restrict competition, Article 101(1) is not likely to be infringed. If the parties agreed to only manufacture products which conform to the new standard, the agreement would limit technical development, reduce innovation and prevent the parties from selling different products, thereby creating restrictive effects on competition within the meaning of Article 101(1).

327. Standardisation agreement without IPR disclosure

655

Example 3

Situation: A private standard-setting organisation active in standardisation in the ICT (information and communication technology) sector has an IPR policy which neither requires nor encourages disclosures of IPR which could be essential for the future standard. The standard-setting organisation took the conscious decision not to include such an obligation in particular considering that in general all technologies potentially relevant for the future standard are covered by many IPR. Therefore the standard-setting organisation considered that an IPR disclosure obligation would, on the one hand, not lead to the benefit of enabling the participants to choose a solution with no or little IPR and, on the other, would lead to additional costs in analysing whether the IPR would be potentially essential for the future standard. However, the IPR policy of the standard-setting organisation requires all participants to make a commitment to license any IPR that might read on the future standard on FRAND terms. The IPR policy allows for opt-outs if there is specific IPR that an IPR holder wishes to put outside the blanket licensing commitment. In this particular industry there are several competing private standard-setting organisations. Participation in the standard-setting organisation is open to anyone active in the industry.

Analysis: In many cases an IPR disclosure obligation would be pro-competitive by increasing competition between technologies ex ante. In general, such an obligation allows the members of a standard-setting organisation to factor in the amount of IPR reading on a particular technology when deciding between competing technologies (or even to, if possible, choose a technology which is not covered by IPR). The amount of IPR reading on a technology will often have a direct impact on the cost of access to the standard. However, in this particular context, all available technologies seem to be covered by IPR, and even many IPR. Therefore, any IPR disclosure would not have the positive effect of enabling the members to factor in the amount of IPR when choosing technology since regardless of what technology is chosen, it can be presumed that there is IPR reading on that technology. IPR disclosure would be unlikely to contribute to guaranteeing effective access to the standard which in this scenario is sufficiently guaranteed by the blanket commitment to license any IPR that might read on the future standard on FRAND terms. On the contrary, an IPR disclosure obligation might in this context lead to additional costs for the participants. The absence of IPR disclosure might also, in those circumstances, lead to a quicker adoption of the standard which might be important if there are several competing standard-setting organisations. It follows that the agreement is unlikely to give rise to any negative effects on competition within the meaning of Article 101(1).

---

328. Standards in the insurance sector

Example 4

Situation: A group of insurance companies comes together to agree non-binding standards for the installation of certain security devices (that is to say, components and equipment designed for loss prevention and reduction and systems formed from such elements). The non-binding standards set by the insurance companies (a) are agreed in order to address a specific need and to assist insurers to manage risk and offer risk-appropriate premiums; (b) are discussed with the installers (or their representatives) and their views are taken on board prior to finalisation of the standards; (c) are published by the relevant insurance association on a dedicated section of its website so that any installer or other interested party can access them easily.

Analysis: The process for setting these standards is transparent and allows for the participation of interested parties. In addition, the result is easily accessible on a reasonable and non-discriminatory basis for anyone that wishes to have access to it. Provided that the standard does not have negative effects on the downstream market (for example by excluding certain installers through very specific and unjustified requirements for installations) it is not likely to lead to restrictive effects on competition. However, even if the standards led to restrictive effects on competition, the conditions set out in Article 101(3) would seem to be fulfilled. The standards would assist insurers

---

in analysing to what extent such installation systems reduce relevant risk and prevent losses so that they can manage risks and offer risk-appropriate premiums. Subject to the caveat regarding the downstream market, they would also be more efficient for installers, allowing them to comply with one set of standards for all insurance companies rather than be tested by every insurance company separately. They could also make it easier for consumers to switch between insurers. In addition, they could be beneficial for smaller insurers who may not have the capacity to test separately. As regards the other conditions of Article 101(3), it seems that the non-binding standards do not go beyond what is necessary to achieve the efficiencies in question, that benefits would be passed on to the consumers (some would even be directly beneficial for the consumers) and that the restrictions would not lead to an elimination of competition.

329. Environmental standards

Example 5

Situation: Almost all producers of washing machines agree, with the encouragement of a public body, to no longer manufacture products which do not comply with certain environmental criteria (for example, energy efficiency). Together, the parties hold 90% of the market. The products which will be thus phased out of the market account for a significant proportion of total sales. They will be replaced by more environmentally friendly, but also more expensive products. Furthermore, the agreement indirectly reduces the output of third parties (for example, electric utilities and suppliers of components incorporated in the products phased out). Without the agreement, the parties would not have shifted their production and marketing efforts to the more environmentally friendly products.

Analysis: The agreement grants the parties control of individual production and concerns an appreciable proportion of their sales and total output, whilst also reducing third parties' output. Product variety, which is partly focused on the environmental characteristics of the product, is reduced and prices will probably rise. Therefore, the agreement is likely to give rise to restrictive effects on competition within the meaning of Article 101(1). The involvement of the public authority is irrelevant for that assessment. However, newer, more environmentally friendly products are more technically advanced, offering qualitative efficiencies in the form of more washing machine programmes which can be used by consumers. Furthermore, there are cost efficiencies for the purchasers of the washing machines resulting from lower running costs in the form of reduced consumption of water, electricity and soap. Those cost efficiencies are realised on markets which are different from the relevant market of the agreement. Nevertheless, those efficiencies may be taken into account as the markets on which the restrictive effects on competition and the efficiency gains arise are related and the group of consumers affected by the restriction and the efficiency gains is substantially the same. The efficiency gains outweigh the restrictive effects on competition in the form of increased costs. Other alternatives to the agreement are shown to be less certain and less cost-effective in delivering the same net benefits. Various technical means are economically available to the parties in order to manufacture washing machines which do comply with the environmental characteristics agreed upon and competition will still take place for other product characteristics. Therefore, the criteria of Article 101(3) would appear to be fulfilled.

Commentary
para 329: B&C: 1.038, 3.048, 12.120

---

330. Government encouraged standardisation

Example 6

Situation: In response to the findings of research into the recommended levels of fat in certain processed food conducted by a government-funded think tank in one Member State, several major manufacturers of the processed foods in the same Member State agree, through formal discussions at an industry trade association, to set recommended fat levels for the products. Together, the parties represent 70% of sales of the products within the Member State. The parties' initiative will be supported by a national advertising campaign funded by the think tank highlighting the dangers of a high fat content in processed foods.

Analysis: Although the fat levels are recommendations and therefore voluntary, as a result of the wide publicity resulting from the national advertising campaign, the recommended fat levels are likely to be implemented by all manufacturers of the processed foods in the Member State. It is therefore likely to become a *de facto* maximum fat level in the processed foods. Consumer choice across the product markets could therefore be reduced. However, the parties will be able to continue to compete with regard to a number of other characteristics of the products, such as price, product size, quality, taste, other nutritional and salt content, balance of ingredients, and branding. Moreover, competition regarding the fat levels in the product offering may increase where parties seek to offer products with the lowest levels. The agreement is therefore unlikely to give rise to restrictive effects on competition within the meaning of Article 101(1).

331. Open standardisation of product packaging

Example 7

Situation: The major manufacturers of a fast-moving consumer product in a competitive market in a Member State - as well as manufacturers and distributors in other Member States who sell the product into the Member State ('importers') — agree with the major packaging suppliers to develop and implement a voluntary initiative to standardise the size and shape of the packaging of the product sold in that Member State. There is currently a wide variation in packaging sizes and materials within and across the Member States. This reflects the fact that the packaging does not represent a high proportion of total production costs and that switching costs for packaging producers are not significant. There is no actual or pending European standard for the packaging. The agreement has been entered into by the parties voluntarily in response to pressure from the Member State's government to meet environmental targets. Together, the manufacturers and importers represent 85% of sales of the product within the Member State. The voluntary initiative will give rise to a uniform-sized product for sale within the Member State that uses less packaging material, occupies less shelf space, has lower transport and packaging costs, and is more environmentally friendly through reduced packaging waste. It also reduces the recycling costs of producers.

The standard does not specify that particular types of packaging materials must be used. The specifications of the standard have been agreed between manufacturers and importers in an open and transparent manner, with the draft specifications having been published for open consultation on an industry website in a timely manner prior to adoption. The final specifications adopted are also published on an industry trade association website that is freely accessible to any potential entrants, even if they are not members of the trade association.

Analysis: Although the agreement is voluntary, the standard is likely to become a de facto industry practice because the parties together represent a high proportion of the market for the product in the Member State and retailers are also being encouraged by the government to reduce packaging waste. As such, the agreement could in theory create barriers to entry and give rise to potential anticompetitive foreclosure effects in the Member State market. This would in particular be a risk for importers of the product in question who may need to repackage the product to meet the de facto standard in order to sell in the Member State if the pack size used in other Member States does not meet the standard. However, significant barriers to entry and foreclosure are unlikely to occur in practice because (a) the agreement is voluntary, (b) the standard has been agreed with major importers in an open and transparent manner, (c) switching costs are low, and (d) the technical details of the standard are accessible to new entrants, importers and all packaging suppliers.

In particular, importers will have been aware of potential changes to packaging at an early stage of development and will have had the opportunity through the open consultation on the draft standards to put forward their views before the standard was eventually adopted. The agreement therefore may not give rise to restrictive effects on competition within the meaning of Article 101(1).

In any event, it is likely that the conditions of Article 101(3) will be fulfilled in this case: (i) the agreement will give rise to quantitative efficiencies through lower transport and packaging costs, (ii) the prevailing conditions of competition on the market are such that these costs reductions are likely to be passed on to consumers, (iii) the agreement includes only the minimum restrictions necessary to achieve the packaging standard and is unlikely to result in significant foreclosure effects and (iv) competition will not be eliminated in a substantial part of the products in question.

Commentary
para 331: B&C: 1.038, 3.048, 12.120

332. Closed standardisation of product packaging

Example 8

Situation: The situation is the same as in Example 7, paragraph 331, except the standard is agreed only between manufacturers of the fast-moving consumer product located within the Member State (who represent 65% of the sales of the product in the Member State), there was no open consultation on the specifications adopted (which include detailed standards on the type of packaging material that must be used) and the specifications of the voluntary standard are not published. This resulted in higher switching costs for producers in other Member States than for domestic producers.

Analysis: Similar to Example 7, paragraph 331, although the agreement is voluntary, it is very likely to become *de facto* standard industry practice since retailers are also being encouraged by the government to reduce packaging waste and the domestic manufacturers account for 65% of sales of the product within the Member State. The fact that relevant producers in other Member States were not consulted resulted in the adoption of a standard which imposes higher switching costs on them compared to domestic producers. The agreement may therefore create barriers to entry and give rise to potential anti-competitive foreclosure effects on packaging suppliers, new entrants and importers — all of whom were not involved in the standard-setting process — as they may need to repackage the product to meet the de facto standard in order to sell in the Member State if the pack size used in other Member States does not meet the standard.

Unlike in Example 7, paragraph 331, the standardisation process has not been carried out in an open and transparent manner. In particular, new entrants, importers and packaging suppliers have not been given the opportunity to comment on the proposed standard and may not even be aware of it until a late stage, creating the possibility that they may not be able to change their production methods or switch suppliers quickly and effectively. Moreover, new entrants, importers and packaging suppliers may not be able to compete if the standard is unknown or difficult to comply with. Of particular relevance here is the fact that the standard includes detailed specifications on the packaging materials to be used which, because of the closed nature of the consultation and the standard, importers and new entrants will struggle to comply with. The agreement may therefore restrict competition within the meaning of Article 101(1). This conclusion is not affected by the fact the agreement has been entered into in order to meet underlying environmental targets agreed with the Member State's government.

It is unlikely that the conditions of Article 101(3) will be fulfilled in this case. Although the agreement will give rise to similar quantitative efficiencies as arise under Example 7, paragraph 331, the closed and private nature of the standardisation agreement and the non-published detailed standard on the type of packaging material that must be used are unlikely to be indispensable to achieving the efficiencies under the agreement.

Commentary
para 332: B&C: 1.038, 3.048, 6.092, 12.120

333. Non-binding and open standard terms used for contracts with end-users

---

Example 9

Situation: A trade association for electricity distributors establishes non-binding standard terms for the supply of electricity to end-users. The establishment of the standard terms is made in a transparent and non-discriminatory manner. The standard terms cover issues such as the specification of the point of consumption, the location of the connection point and the connection voltage, provisions on service reliability as well as the procedure for settling the accounts between the parties to the contract (for example, what happens if the customer does not provide the supplier with the readings of the measurement devices). The standard terms do not cover any issues relating to prices, that is to say, they contain no recommended prices or other clauses related to price. Any company active within the sector is free to use the standard terms as it sees fit. About 80% of the contracts concluded with end-users in the relevant market are based on these standard terms.

Analysis: These standard terms are not likely to give rise to restrictive effects on competition within the meaning of Article 101(1). Even if they have become industry practice, they do not seem to have any appreciable negative impact on prices, product quality or variety.

---

334. Standard terms used for contracts between companies

Example 10

Situation: Construction companies in a certain Member State come together to establish non-binding and open standard terms and conditions for use by a contractor when submitting a quotation for construction work to a client. A form of quotation is included together with terms and conditions suitable for building or construction. Together, the documents create the construction contract. Clauses cover such matters as contract formation, general obligations of the contractor and the client and non-price related payment conditions (for example, a provision specifying the contractor's right to give notice to suspend the work for non-payment), insurance, duration, handover and defects, limitation of liability, termination, etc. In contrast to Example 9, paragraph 333, these standard terms would often be used between companies, one active upstream and one active downstream.

Analysis: These standard terms are not likely to have restrictive effects on competition within the meaning of Article 101(1). There would normally not be any significant limitation in the customer's choice of the end-product, namely the construction work. Other restrictive effects on competition do not seem likely. Indeed, several of the clauses above (handover and defects, termination, etc.) would often be regulated by law.

---

335. Standard terms facilitating the comparison of different companies' products

---

Example 11

Situation: A national association for the insurance sector distributes non-binding standard policy conditions for house insurance contracts. The conditions give no indication of the level of insurance premiums, the amount of the cover or the excesses payable by the insured. They do not impose comprehensive cover including risks to which a significant number of policyholders are not simultaneously exposed and do not require the policyholders to obtain cover from the same insurer for different risks. While the majority of insurance companies use standard policy conditions, not all their contracts contain the same conditions as they are adapted to each client's

---

individual needs and therefore there is no *de facto* standardisation of insurance products offered to consumers. The standard policy conditions enable consumers and consumer organisations to compare the policies offered by the different insurers. A consumer association is involved in the process of laying down the standard policy conditions. They are also available for use by new entrants, on a non-discriminatory basis.

Analysis: These standard policy conditions relate to the composition of the final insurance product. If the market conditions and other factors would show that there might be a risk of limitation in product variety as a result of insurance companies using such standard policy conditions, it is likely that such possible limitation would be outweighed by efficiencies such as facilitation of comparison by consumers of conditions offered by insurance companies. Those comparisons in turn facilitate switching between insurance companies and thus enhance competition. Furthermore the switching of providers, as well as market entry by competitors, constitutes an advantage for consumers. The fact that the consumer association has participated in the process could, in certain instances, increase the likelihood of those efficiencies which do not automatically benefit the consumers being passed on. The standard policy conditions are also likely to reduce transaction costs and facilitate entry for insurers on a different geographic and/or product markets. Moreover, the restrictions do not seem to go beyond what is necessary to achieve the identified efficiencies and competition would not be eliminated. Consequently, the criteria of Article 101(3) are likely to be fulfilled.

Commentary
para 335: B&C: 12.131

PART D

MERGERS AND CONCENTRATIONS

D1

COUNCIL REGULATION (EC) NO 139/2004*

of 20 January 2004
on the control of concentrations between undertakings
(the EC Merger Regulation)

(Text with EEA relevance)

Official Journal L 24, 29.1.2004, p.1

Celex No: 32004R0139

EUR-Lex permanent link: <http://eur-lex.europa.eu/LexUriServ/LexUriServ.do?uri=CELEX:
32004R0139:EN:NOT>

Notes

* Ed note: please see the Note on the Lisbon Treaty at p.xvii in regard to article renumbering introduced by the Lisbon Treaty.
EEA application: Articles 1 to 5 of the Merger Regulation were adopted with appropriate adaptations by EEA Joint
Committee Decision No 78/2004 of 8 June 2004, OJ L 219, 19.6.2004, p.13 and EEA Supplement No 32, 19.6.2004,
p.1, and EEA Joint Committee Decision No 79/2004 of 8 June 2004, OJ L 219, 19.6.2004, p.24 and EEA Supplement
No 32, 19.6.2004, p.10: see EEA Agreement, Annex XIV, Chapter A, Point 1 and Protocol 21, Article 3(1), Point 1. The
procedural provisions of Articles 4(4), 4(5) and 6 to 25 were adopted with appropriate adaptations, by agreement of 4
June 2004: see the Surveillance and Court Agreement, Protocol 4, Part III, Chapter XIII.

Commentary

Regulation 139/2004/EC: B&C: 1.018, 1.025, 1.029, 1.114, 1.116, 2.009, 2.129, 2.151, 4.045, 6.002, 6.120,
8.001, 8.003, 8.004, 8.005, 8.007, 8.009, 8.011, 8.012, 8.014, 8.015, 8.016, 8.26, 8.029, 8.041, 8.043, 8.045,
8.054, 8.061, 8.063, 8.082, 8.102, 8.104, 8.105, 8.111, 8.118, 8.122, 8.132, 8.141, 8.171, 8.172, 8.175, 8.182,
8.196, 8.197, 8.200, 8.201, 8.205, 8.211, 8.217, 8.242, 8.248, 8.249, 8.251, 8.258, 8.259, 8.260, 8.261, 8.262,
8.264, 8.266, 8.279, 8.288, 8.289, 8.292, 8.293, 10.048, 10.052, 12.016, 12.018, 12.044, 15.060, 15.063, 16.007,
16.047 **F&N:** 1.17, 1.190, 2.198, 3.269, 4.77, 4.218, 5.04, 5.09, 5.90, 5.120, 5.128, 5.196, 5.277, 5.299, 5.334,
5.559, 5.1145, 5.1153, 5.1163, 5.1206, 7.38, 7.46, 7.50, 7.140, 7.324, 7.1123, 8.155, 8.526, 11.08, 11.69, 11.70,
11.86, 11.88, 11.90, 11.204, 12.97, 12.101, 13.180, 14.101, 15.130
recitals 2–6: **F&N:** 5.22
recitals 3–5: **F&N:** 5.332
Arts 6–22: **F&N:** 5.341
Arts 7–10: **F&N:** 5.338
Arts 11–13: **F&N:** 5.334
Arts 11–15: **F&N:** 5.425

THE COUNCIL OF THE EUROPEAN UNION,

Having regard to the [Treaty on the Functioning of the European Union], and in particular Articles
[103] and [352] thereof,

Having regard to the proposal from the Commission,[1]

Having regard to the opinion of the European Parliament,[2]

Having regard to the opinion of the European Economic and Social Committee,[3]

Notes

[1] OJ C 20, 28.1.2003, p.4.
[2] Opinion delivered on 9.10.2003 (not yet published in the Official Journal).
[3] Opinion delivered on 24.10.2003 [OJ C 10, 14.1.2004].

Whereas:

(1) Council Regulation (EEC) No 4064/89 of 21 December 1989 on the control of concentrations
between undertakings[1] has been substantially amended. Since further amendments are to be
made, it should be recast in the interest of clarity.

Notes

1 OJ L 395, 30.12.1989, p.1. Corrected version in OJ L 257, 21.9.1990, p.13. Regulation as last amended by Regulation (EC) No 1310/97 (OJ L 180, 9.7.1997, p.1). Corrigendum in OJ L 40, 13.2.1998, p.17.

(2) For the achievement of the aims of the Treaty, Article 3(1)(g)* gives the Community the objective of instituting a system ensuring that competition in the internal market is not distorted. Article [119(1)] of the Treaty provides that the activities of the Member States and the Community are to be conducted in accordance with the principle of an open market economy with free competition. These principles are essential for the further development of the internal market.

(3) The completion of the internal market and of economic and monetary union, the enlargement of the European Union and the lowering of international barriers to trade and investment will continue to result in major corporate reorganisations, particularly in the form of concentrations.

Notes

* Ed note: Article 3(1)(g) EC was repealed by the Treaty of Lisbon. Article 3(1) EC was replaced in substance by Articles 3 to 6 TFEU. The nearest to an equivalent provision in the TFEU is Article 3(1)(b) ("The Union shall have exclusive competence in the following areas: ... (b) the establishing of the competition rules necessary for the functioning of the internal market").

(4) Such reorganisations are to be welcomed to the extent that they are in line with the requirements of dynamic competition and capable of increasing the competitiveness of European industry, improving the conditions of growth and raising the standard of living in the Community.

(5) However, it should be ensured that the process of reorganisation does not result in lasting damage to competition; Community law must therefore include provisions governing those concentrations which may significantly impede effective competition in the common market or in a substantial part of it.

(6) A specific legal instrument is therefore necessary to permit effective control of all concentrations in terms of their effect on the structure of competition in the Community and to be the only instrument applicable to such concentrations. Regulation (EEC) No 4064/89 has allowed a Community policy to develop in this field. In the light of experience, however, that Regulation should now be recast into legislation designed to meet the challenges of a more integrated market and the future enlargement of the European Union. In accordance with the principles of subsidiarity and of proportionality as set out in Article 5 of the [Treaty on European Union], this Regulation does not go beyond what is necessary in order to achieve the objective of ensuring that competition in the common market is not distorted, in accordance with the principle of an open market economy with free competition.

Commentary
Recital 6: **B&C:** 8.270

(7) Articles [101] and [102], while applicable, according to the case-law of the Court of Justice, to certain concentrations, are not sufficient to control all operations which may prove to be incompatible with the system of undistorted competition envisaged in the Treaty. This Regulation should therefore be based not only on Article [103] but, principally, on Article [352] of the Treaty, under which the Community may give itself the additional powers of action necessary for the attainment of its objectives, and also powers of action with regard to concentrations on the markets for agricultural products listed in Annex I to the Treaty.

Commentary
Recital 7: **B&C:** 8.268, 8.270

(8) The provisions to be adopted in this Regulation should apply to significant structural changes, the impact of which on the market goes beyond the national borders of any one Member State. Such concentrations should, as a general rule, be reviewed exclusively at Community level, in application of a "one-stop shop" system and in compliance with the principle of subsidiarity. Concentrations not covered by this Regulation come, in principle, within the jurisdiction of the Member States.

Commentary
Recital 8: B&C: 8.011 F&N: 5.31, 5.37, 5.208

(9) The scope of application of this Regulation should be defined according to the geographical area of activity of the undertakings concerned and be limited by quantitative thresholds in order to cover those concentrations which have a Community dimension. The Commission should report to the Council on the implementation of the applicable thresholds and criteria so that the Council, acting in accordance with Article 202* of the Treaty, is in a position to review them regularly, as well as the rules regarding pre-notification referral, in the light of the experience gained; this requires statistical data to be provided by the Member States to the Commission to enable it to prepare such reports and possible proposals for amendments. The Commission's reports and proposals should be based on relevant information regularly provided by the Member States.

Notes

* Ed note: Article 202 was repealed by the Treaty of Lisbon. It was replaced, in substance, by Article 16(1) TEU and by Articles 290 and 291 TFEU.

Commentary
Recital 9: F&N: 5.37, 5.164

(10) A concentration with a Community dimension should be deemed to exist where the aggregate turnover of the undertakings concerned exceeds given thresholds; that is the case irrespective of whether or not the undertakings effecting the concentration have their seat or their principal fields of activity in the Community, provided they have substantial operations there.

Commentary
Recital 10: F&N: 5.37

(11) The rules governing the referral of concentrations from the Commission to Member States and from Member States to the Commission should operate as an effective corrective mechanism in the light of the principle of subsidiarity; these rules protect the competition interests of the Member States in an adequate manner and take due account of legal certainty and the "one-stop shop" principle.

Commentary
Recital 11: B&C: 8.011

(12) Concentrations may qualify for examination under a number of national merger control systems if they fall below the turnover thresholds referred to in this Regulation. Multiple notification of the same transaction increases legal uncertainty, effort and cost for undertakings and may lead to conflicting assessments. The system whereby concentrations may be referred to the Commission by the Member States concerned should therefore be further developed.

Commentary
Recital 12: F&N: 5.219

(13) The Commission should act in close and constant liaison with the competent authorities of the Member States from which it obtains comments and information.

(14) The Commission and the competent authorities of the Member States should together form a network of public authorities, applying their respective competences in close cooperation, using efficient arrangements for information-sharing and consultation, with a view to ensuring that a case is dealt with by the most appropriate authority, in the light of the principle of subsidiarity and with a view to ensuring that multiple notifications of a given concentration are avoided to the greatest extent possible. Referrals of concentrations from the Commission to Member States and from Member States to the Commission should be made in an efficient manner avoiding, to the greatest extent possible, situations where a concentration is subject to a referral both before and after its notification.

Part D Mergers and Concentrations

(15) The Commission should be able to refer to a Member State notified concentrations with a Community dimension which threaten significantly to affect competition in a market within that Member State presenting all the characteristics of a distinct market. Where the concentration affects competition on such a market, which does not constitute a substantial part of the common market, the Commission should be obliged, upon request, to refer the whole or part of the case to the Member State concerned. A Member State should be able to refer to the Commission a concentration which does not have a Community dimension but which affects trade between Member States and threatens to significantly affect competition within its territory. Other Member States which are also competent to review the concentration should be able to join the request. In such a situation, in order to ensure the efficiency and predictability of the system, national time limits should be suspended until a decision has been reached as to the referral of the case. The Commission should have the power to examine and deal with a concentration on behalf of a requesting Member State or requesting Member States.

(16) The undertakings concerned should be granted the possibility of requesting referrals to or from the Commission before a concentration is notified so as to further improve the efficiency of the system for the control of concentrations within the Community. In such situations, the Commission and national competition authorities should decide within short, clearly defined time limits whether a referral to or from the Commission ought to be made, thereby ensuring the efficiency of the system. Upon request by the undertakings concerned, the Commission should be able to refer to a Member State a concentration with a Community dimension which may significantly affect competition in a market within that Member State presenting all the characteristics of a distinct market; the undertakings concerned should not, however, be required to demonstrate that the effects of the concentration would be detrimental to competition. A concentration should not be referred from the Commission to a Member State which has expressed its disagreement to such a referral. Before notification to national authorities, the undertakings concerned should also be able to request that a concentration without a Community dimension which is capable of being reviewed under the national competition laws of at least three Member States be referred to the Commission. Such requests for pre-notification referrals to the Commission would be particularly pertinent in situations where the concentration would affect competition beyond the territory of one Member State. Where a concentration capable of being reviewed under the competition laws of three or more Member States is referred to the Commission prior to any national notification, and no Member State competent to review the case expresses its disagreement, the Commission should acquire exclusive competence to review the concentration and such a concentration should be deemed to have a Community dimension. Such pre-notification referrals from Member States to the Commission should not, however, be made where at least one Member State competent to review the case has expressed its disagreement with such a referral.

(17) The Commission should be given exclusive competence to apply this Regulation, subject to review by the Court of Justice.

Commentary
Recital 17: F&N: 5.31

---

(18) The Member States should not be permitted to apply their national legislation on competition to concentrations with a Community dimension, unless this Regulation makes provision therefor. The relevant powers of national authorities should be limited to cases where, failing intervention by the Commission, effective competition is likely to be significantly impeded within the territory of a Member State and where the competition interests of that Member State cannot be sufficiently protected otherwise by this Regulation. The Member States concerned must act promptly in such cases; this Regulation cannot, because of the diversity of national law, fix a single time limit for the adoption of final decisions under national law.

Commentary
Recital 18: F&N: 5.31

---

(19) Furthermore, the exclusive application of this Regulation to concentrations with a Community dimension is without prejudice to Article [346] of the Treaty, and does not prevent the Member States from taking appropriate measures to protect legitimate interests other than those pursued by this Regulation, provided that such measures are compatible with the general principles and other provisions of Community law.

(20) It is expedient to define the concept of concentration in such a manner as to cover operations bringing about a lasting change in the control of the undertakings concerned and therefore in the structure of the market. It is therefore appropriate to include, within the scope of this Regulation, all joint ventures performing on a lasting basis all the functions of an autonomous economic entity. It is moreover appropriate to treat as a single concentration transactions that are closely connected in that they are linked by condition or take the form of a series of transactions in securities taking place within a reasonably short period of time.

Commentary
Recital 20: B&C: 8.014, 8.045 F&N: 5.37, 5.67, 5.112, 5.120, 5.124, 5.148

(21) This Regulation should also apply where the undertakings concerned accept restrictions directly related to, and necessary for, the implementation of the concentration. Commission decisions declaring concentrations compatible with the common market in application of this Regulation should automatically cover such restrictions, without the Commission having to assess such restrictions in individual cases. At the request of the undertakings concerned, however, the Commission should, in cases presenting novel or unresolved questions giving rise to genuine uncertainty, expressly assess whether or not any restriction is directly related to, and necessary for, the implementation of the concentration. A case presents a novel or unresolved question giving rise to genuine uncertainty if the question is not covered by the relevant Commission notice in force or a published Commission decision.

Commentary
Recital 21: B&C: 2.052, 8.273 F&N: 5.152

(22) The arrangements to be introduced for the control of concentrations should, without prejudice to Article [106](2) of the Treaty, respect the principle of non-discrimination between the public and the private sectors. In the public sector, calculation of the turnover of an undertaking concerned in a concentration needs, therefore, to take account of undertakings making up an economic unit with an independent power of decision, irrespective of the way in which their capital is held or of the rules of administrative supervision applicable to them.

Commentary
Recital 22: B&C: 8.017, 8.075 F&N: 5.37, 11.87

(23) It is necessary to establish whether or not concentrations with a Community dimension are compatible with the common market in terms of the need to maintain and develop effective competition in the common market. In so doing, the Commission must place its appraisal within the general framework of the achievement of the fundamental objectives referred to in [Article 3 of the Treaty on European Union].

Commentary
Recital 23: B&C: 8.190

(24) In order to ensure a system of undistorted competition in the common market, in furtherance of a policy conducted in accordance with the principle of an open market economy with free competition, this Regulation must permit effective control of all concentrations from the point of view of their effect on competition in the Community. Accordingly, Regulation (EEC) No 4064/89 established the principle that a concentration with a Community dimension which creates or strengthens a dominant position as a result of which effective competition in the common market or in a substantial part of it would be significantly impeded should be declared incompatible with the common market.

Commentary
Recital 24: F&N: 5.22

(25) In view of the consequences that concentrations in oligopolistic market structures may have, it is all the more necessary to maintain effective competition in such markets. Many oligopolistic markets exhibit a healthy degree of competition. However, under certain circumstances, concentrations involving the elimination of important competitive constraints that the merging parties had exerted upon each other, as well as a reduction of competitive pressure on the remaining competitors, may, even in the absence of a likelihood of coordination between the members of the oligopoly, result in a significant impediment to effective competition. The Community courts have, however, not to date expressly interpreted Regulation (EEC) No 4064/89 as requiring concentrations giving rise to such non-coordinated effects to be declared incompatible with the common market. Therefore, in the interests of legal certainty, it should be made clear that this Regulation permits effective control of all such concentrations by providing that any concentration which would significantly impede effective competition, in the common market or in a substantial part of it, should be declared incompatible with the common market. The notion of "significant impediment to effective competition" in Article 2(2) and (3) should be interpreted as extending, beyond the concept of dominance, only to the anti-competitive effects of a concentration resulting from the non-coordinated behaviour of undertakings which would not have a dominant position on the market concerned.

Commentary
Recital 25: B&C: 8.201, 8.203 F&N: 5.344, 5.583

(26) A significant impediment to effective competition generally results from the creation or strengthening of a dominant position. With a view to preserving the guidance that may be drawn from past judgments of the European courts and Commission decisions pursuant to Regulation (EEC) No 4064/89, while at the same time maintaining consistency with the standards of competitive harm which have been applied by the Commission and the Community courts regarding the compatibility of a concentration with the common market, this Regulation should accordingly establish the principle that a concentration with a Community dimension which would significantly impede effective competition, in the common market or in a substantial part thereof, in particular as a result of the creation or strengthening of a dominant position, is to be declared incompatible with the common market.

Commentary
Recital 26: B&C: 8.203, 10.014

(27) In addition, the criteria of Article [101](1) and (3) of the Treaty should be applied to joint ventures performing, on a lasting basis, all the functions of autonomous economic entities, to the extent that their creation has as its consequence an appreciable restriction of competition between undertakings that remain independent.

Commentary
Recital 27: B&C: 10.014

(28) In order to clarify and explain the Commission's appraisal of concentrations under this Regulation, it is appropriate for the Commission to publish guidance which should provide a sound economic framework for the assessment of concentrations with a view to determining whether or not they may be declared compatible with the common market.

(29) In order to determine the impact of a concentration on competition in the common market, it is appropriate to take account of any substantiated and likely efficiencies put forward by the undertakings concerned. It is possible that the efficiencies brought about by the concentration counteract the effects on competition, and in particular the potential harm to consumers, that it might otherwise have and that, as a consequence, the concentration would not significantly impede effective competition, in the common market or in a substantial part of it, in particular as a result of the creation or strengthening of a dominant position. The Commission should

publish guidance on the conditions under which it may take efficiencies into account in the assessment of a concentration.

Commentary
Recital 29: **B&C:** 8.242 **F&N:** 5.928, 15.94

(30) Where the undertakings concerned modify a notified concentration, in particular by offering commitments with a view to rendering the concentration compatible with the common market, the Commission should be able to declare the concentration, as modified, compatible with the common market. Such commitments should be proportionate to the competition problem and entirely eliminate it. It is also appropriate to accept commitments before the initiation of proceedings where the competition problem is readily identifiable and can easily be remedied. It should be expressly provided that the Commission may attach to its decision conditions and obligations in order to ensure that the undertakings concerned comply with their commitments in a timely and effective manner so as to render the concentration compatible with the common market. Transparency and effective consultation of Member States as well as of interested third parties should be ensured throughout the procedure.

Commentary
Recital 30: **B&C:** 8.168, 8.170 **F&N:** 5.980, 5.983, 8.986, 5.988, 5.1000, 5.1016, 15.112

(31) The Commission should have at its disposal appropriate instruments to ensure the enforcement of commitments and to deal with situations where they are not fulfilled. In cases of failure to fulfil a condition attached to the decision declaring a concentration compatible with the common market, the situation rendering the concentration compatible with the common market does not materialise and the concentration, as implemented, is therefore not authorised by the Commission. As a consequence, if the concentration is implemented, it should be treated in the same way as a non-notified concentration implemented without authorisation. Furthermore, where the Commission has already found that, in the absence of the condition, the concentration would be incompatible with the common market, it should have the power to directly order the dissolution of the concentration, so as to restore the situation prevailing prior to the implementation of the concentration. Where an obligation attached to a decision declaring the concentration compatible with the common market is not fulfilled, the Commission should be able to revoke its decision. Moreover, the Commission should be able to impose appropriate financial sanctions where conditions or obligations are not fulfilled.

Commentary
Recital 31: **B&C:** 8.176 **F&N:** 5.983, 5.990

(32) Concentrations which, by reason of the limited market share of the undertakings concerned, are not liable to impede effective competition may be presumed to be compatible with the common market. Without prejudice to Articles [101] and [102] of the Treaty, an indication to this effect exists, in particular, where the market share of the undertakings concerned does not exceed 25% either in the common market or in a substantial part of it.

Commentary
Recital 32: **F&N:** 5.684

(33) The Commission should have the task of taking all the decisions necessary to establish whether or not concentrations with a Community dimension are compatible with the common market, as well as decisions designed to restore the situation prevailing prior to the implementation of a concentration which has been declared incompatible with the common market.

(34) To ensure effective control, undertakings should be obliged to give prior notification of concentrations with a Community dimension following the conclusion of the agreement, the announcement of the public bid or the acquisition of a controlling interest. Notification should also be possible where the undertakings concerned satisfy the Commission of their intention to enter into an agreement for a proposed concentration and demonstrate to the Commission that

Part D Mergers and Concentrations

their plan for that proposed concentration is sufficiently concrete, for example on the basis of an agreement in principle, a memorandum of understanding, or a letter of intent signed by all undertakings concerned, or, in the case of a public bid, where they have publicly announced an intention to make such a bid, provided that the intended agreement or bid would result in a concentration with a Community dimension. The implementation of concentrations should be suspended until a final decision of the Commission has been taken. However, it should be possible to derogate from this suspension at the request of the undertakings concerned, where appropriate. In deciding whether or not to grant a derogation, the Commission should take account of all pertinent factors, such as the nature and gravity of damage to the undertakings concerned or to third parties, and the threat to competition posed by the concentration. In the interest of legal certainty, the validity of transactions must nevertheless be protected as much as necessary.

Commentary
Recital 34: **B&C:** 8.111 **F&N:** 5.32, 5.400

---

(35) A period within which the Commission must initiate proceedings in respect of a notified concentration and a period within which it must take a final decision on the compatibility or incompatibility with the common market of that concentration should be laid down. These periods should be extended whenever the undertakings concerned offer commitments with a view to rendering the concentration compatible with the common market, in order to allow for sufficient time for the analysis and market testing of such commitment offers and for the consultation of Member States as well as interested third parties. A limited extension of the period within which the Commission must take a final decision should also be possible in order to allow sufficient time for the investigation of the case and the verification of the facts and arguments submitted to the Commission.

(36) The Community respects the fundamental rights and observes the principles recognised in particular by the Charter of Fundamental Rights of the European Union.[1] Accordingly, this Regulation should be interpreted and applied with respect to those rights and principles.

Notes
[1] OJ C 364, 18.12.2000, p.1.

---

(37) The undertakings concerned must be afforded the right to be heard by the Commission when proceedings have been initiated; the members of the management and supervisory bodies and the recognised representatives of the employees of the undertakings concerned, and interested third parties, must also be given the opportunity to be heard.

Commentary
Recital 37: **B&C:** 8.131

---

(38) In order properly to appraise concentrations, the Commission should have the right to request all necessary information and to conduct all necessary inspections throughout the Community. To that end, and with a view to protecting competition effectively, the Commission's powers of investigation need to be expanded. The Commission should, in particular, have the right to interview any persons who may be in possession of useful information and to record the statements made.

(39) In the course of an inspection, officials authorised by the Commission should have the right to ask for any information relevant to the subject matter and purpose of the inspection; they should also have the right to affix seals during inspections, particularly in circumstances where there are reasonable grounds to suspect that a concentration has been implemented without being notified; that incorrect, incomplete or misleading information has been supplied to the Commission; or that the undertakings or persons concerned have failed to comply with a condition or obligation imposed by decision of the Commission. In any event, seals should only be used in exceptional circumstances, for the period of time strictly necessary for the inspection, normally not for more than 48 hours.

(40) Without prejudice to the case-law of the Court of Justice, it is also useful to set out the scope of the control that the national judicial authority may exercise when it authorises, as provided by national law and as a precautionary measure, assistance from law enforcement authorities in order to overcome possible opposition on the part of the undertaking against an inspection, including the affixing of seals, ordered by Commission decision. It results from the case-law that the national judicial authority may in particular ask of the Commission further information which it needs to carry out its control and in the absence of which it could refuse the authorisation. The case-law also confirms the competence of the national courts to control the application of national rules governing the implementation of coercive measures. The competent authorities of the Member States should cooperate actively in the exercise of the Commission's investigative powers.

Commentary
Recital 40: F&N: 5.301

(41) When complying with decisions of the Commission, the undertakings and persons concerned cannot be forced to admit that they have committed infringements, but they are in any event obliged to answer factual questions and to provide documents, even if this information may be used to establish against themselves or against others the existence of such infringements.

(42) For the sake of transparency, all decisions of the Commission which are not of a merely procedural nature should be widely publicised. While ensuring preservation of the rights of defence of the undertakings concerned, in particular the right of access to the file, it is essential that business secrets be protected. The confidentiality of information exchanged in the network and with the competent authorities of third countries should likewise be safeguarded.

Commentary
Recital 42: F&N: 5.436

(43) Compliance with this Regulation should be enforceable, as appropriate, by means of fines and periodic penalty payments. The Court of Justice should be given unlimited jurisdiction in that regard pursuant to Article [261] of the Treaty.

Commentary
Recital 43: B&C: 8.248

(44) The conditions in which concentrations, involving undertakings having their seat or their principal fields of activity in the Community, are carried out in third countries should be observed, and provision should be made for the possibility of the Council giving the Commission an appropriate mandate for negotiation with a view to obtaining non-discriminatory treatment for such undertakings.

Commentary
Recital 44: B&C: 8.298

(45) This Regulation in no way detracts from the collective rights of employees, as recognised in the undertakings concerned, notably with regard to any obligation to inform or consult their recognised representatives under Community and national law.

(46) The Commission should be able to lay down detailed rules concerning the implementation of this Regulation in accordance with the procedures for the exercise of implementing powers conferred on the Commission. For the adoption of such implementing provisions, the Commission should be assisted by an Advisory Committee composed of the representatives of the Member States as specified in Article 23,

HAS ADOPTED THIS REGULATION:

Article 1
Scope

1. Without prejudice to Article 4(5) and Article 22, this Regulation shall apply to all concentrations with a Community dimension as defined in this Article.

2. A concentration has a Community dimension where:

(a) the combined aggregate worldwide turnover of all the undertakings concerned is more than EUR 5000 million; and

(b) the aggregate Community-wide turnover of each of at least two of the undertakings concerned is more than EUR 250 million,

unless each of the undertakings concerned achieves more than two-thirds of its aggregate Community-wide turnover within one and the same Member State.

3. A concentration that does not meet the thresholds laid down in paragraph 2 has a Community dimension where:

(a) the combined aggregate worldwide turnover of all the undertakings concerned is more than EUR 2500 million;

(b) in each of at least three Member States, the combined aggregate turnover of all the undertakings concerned is more than EUR 100 million;

(c) in each of at least three Member States included for the purpose of point (b), the aggregate turnover of each of at least two of the undertakings concerned is more than EUR 25 million; and

(d) the aggregate Community-wide turnover of each of at least two of the undertakings concerned is more than EUR 100 million,

unless each of the undertakings concerned achieves more than two-thirds of its aggregate Community-wide turnover within one and the same Member State.

4. On the basis of statistical data that may be regularly provided by the Member States, the Commission shall report to the Council on the operation of the thresholds and criteria set out in paragraphs 2 and 3 by 1 July 2009 and may present proposals pursuant to paragraph 5.

5. Following the report referred to in paragraph 4 and on a proposal from the Commission, the Council, acting by a qualified majority, may revise the thresholds and criteria mentioned in paragraph 3.

Commentary

Art 1: F&N: 5.37, 5.153, 5.156, 5.160
Art 1(1): F&N: 5.498
Art 1(1)–(3): B&C: 8.061
Art 1(2): B&C: 8.062, 8.085 F&N: 5.35, 5.157, 5.158, 5.161, 5.163, 5.165, 5.166, 5.167, 5.312
Art 1(3): B&C: 8.062, 8.085 F&N: 5.35, 5.160, 5.161, 5.162, 5.163, 5.164, 5.165, 5.166, 5.167,
    5.312, 11.100
Art 1(3)(b): F&N: 5.203
Art 1(3)(c): F&N: 5.203
Art 1(4): F&N: 5.164, 7.254
Art 1(5): F&N: 5.164

Article 2
Appraisal of concentrations

1. Concentrations within the scope of this Regulation shall be appraised in accordance with the objectives of this Regulation and the following provisions with a view to establishing whether or not they are compatible with the common market.

In making this appraisal, the Commission shall take into account:

(a) the need to maintain and develop effective competition within the common market in view of, among other things, the structure of all the markets concerned and the actual or potential competition from undertakings located either within or outwith the Community;

(b) the market position of the undertakings concerned and their economic and financial power, the alternatives available to suppliers and users, their access to supplies or markets, any legal or other barriers to entry, supply and demand trends for the relevant goods and services, the interests of the intermediate and ultimate consumers, and the development of technical and economic progress provided that it is to consumers' advantage and does not form an obstacle to competition.

2. A concentration which would not significantly impede effective competition in the common market or in a substantial part of it, in particular as a result of the creation or strengthening of a dominant position, shall be declared compatible with the common market.

3. A concentration which would significantly impede effective competition, in the common market or in a substantial part of it, in particular as a result of the creation or strengthening of a dominant position, shall be declared incompatible with the common market.

4. To the extent that the creation of a joint venture constituting a concentration pursuant to Article 3 has as its object or effect the coordination of the competitive behaviour of undertakings that remain independent, such coordination shall be appraised in accordance with the criteria of Article [101](1) and (3) of the Treaty, with a view to establishing whether or not the operation is compatible with the common market.

5. In making this appraisal, the Commission shall take into account in particular:

— whether two or more parent companies retain, to a significant extent, activities in the same market as the joint venture or in a market which is downstream or upstream from that of the joint venture or in a neighbouring market closely related to this market,
— whether the coordination which is the direct consequence of the creation of the joint venture affords the undertakings concerned the possibility of eliminating competition in respect of a substantial part of the products or services in question.

Commentary
Art 2: **B&C:** 12.045 **F&N:** 5.556, 5.1162, 5.1190
Art 2(1): **B&C:** 8.190, 8.213
Art 2(1)(b): **F&N:** 5.562, 5.929, 15.94
Art 2(2): **B&C:** 2.086, 4.008, 8.191, 10.014 **F&N:** 5.583
Art 2(3): **B&C:** 2.086, 8.191, 10.014 **F&N:** 5.502, 5.556, 5.583, 5.585, 5.980, 7.38
Art 2(4): **B&C:** 6.008, 8.192, 8.246 **F&N:** 5.105, 5.115, 5.502, 5.516, 7.37, 7.108, 7.109, 7.122, 7.124, 7.126, 7.129, 7.133, 7.142
Art 2(5): **B&C:** 8.192, 8.246 **F&N:** 5.05, 7.37

Article 3
Definition of concentration

1. A concentration shall be deemed to arise where a change of control on a lasting basis results from:

(a) the merger of two or more previously independent undertakings or parts of undertakings, or
(b) the acquisition, by one or more persons already controlling at least one undertaking, or by one or more undertakings, whether by purchase of securities or assets, by contract or by any other means, of direct or indirect control of the whole or parts of one or more other undertakings.

2. Control shall be constituted by rights, contracts or any other means which, either separately or in combination and having regard to the considerations of fact or law involved, confer the possibility of exercising decisive influence on an undertaking, in particular by:

(a) ownership or the right to use all or part of the assets of an undertaking;
(b) rights or contracts which confer decisive influence on the composition, voting or decisions of the organs of an undertaking.

3. Control is acquired by persons or undertakings which:

(a) are holders of the rights or entitled to rights under the contracts concerned; or
(b) while not being holders of such rights or entitled to rights under such contracts, have the power to exercise the rights deriving therefrom.

4. The creation of a joint venture performing on a lasting basis all the functions of an autonomous economic entity shall constitute a concentration within the meaning of paragraph 1(b).

Part D Mergers and Concentrations

5. A concentration shall not be deemed to arise where:

(a) credit institutions or other financial institutions or insurance companies, the normal activities of which include transactions and dealing in securities for their own account or for the account of others, hold on a temporary basis securities which they have acquired in an undertaking with a view to reselling them, provided that they do not exercise voting rights in respect of those securities with a view to determining the competitive behaviour of that undertaking or provided that they exercise such voting rights only with a view to preparing the disposal of all or part of that undertaking or of its assets or the disposal of those securities and that any such disposal takes place within one year of the date of acquisition; that period may be extended by the Commission on request where such institutions or companies can show that the disposal was not reasonably possible within the period set;

(b) control is acquired by an office-holder according to the law of a Member State relating to liquidation, winding up, insolvency, cessation of payments, compositions or analogous proceedings;

(c) the operations referred to in paragraph 1(b) are carried out by the financial holding companies referred to in Article 5(3) of Fourth Council Directive 78/660/EEC of 25 July 1978 based on Article [50(2)(g)] of the Treaty on the annual accounts of certain types of companies[1] provided however that the voting rights in respect of the holding are exercised, in particular in relation to the appointment of members of the management and supervisory bodies of the undertakings in which they have holdings, only to maintain the full value of those investments and not to determine directly or indirectly the competitive conduct of those undertakings.

Notes

[1] OJ L 222, 14. 8. 1978, p.11. Directive as last amended by Directive 2003/51/EC of the European Parliament and of the Council (OJ L 178, 17.7.2003, p.16).

Commentary

Art 3: B&C: 8.018, 8.024, 8.066, 8.074, 8.076, 8.262, 8.270 **F&N:** 5.37, 5.139, 5.140, 5.258, 5.269, 7.12, 7.37, 7.108, 7.128, 7.254

Art 3(1): B&C: 8.014, 8.054 **F&N:** 5.33, 5.67, 5.141

Art 3(1)(a): B&C: 8.020, 8.021, 8.112, 8.140 **F&N:** 5.37, 5.43, 5.175

Art 3(1)(b): B&C: 8.020, 8.022, 8.026, 8.073, 8.140, 8.178, 8.187, 8.188, 8.189 **F&N:** 5.43, 5.48, 5.62, 5.126, 5.175, 16.112

Art 3(2): B&C: 8.023 **F&N:** 5.37, 5.50, 5.57, 5.128, 5.190, 6.27

Art 3(2)(a): B&C: 8.023 **F&N:** 5.59

Art 3(3): B&C: 8.283 **F&N:** 5.37, 5.54

Art 3(3)(a): B&C: 8.025

Art 3(3)(b): B&C: 8.025 **F&N:** 5.53

Art 3(4): B&C: 2.028, 6.005, 8.033, 8.054 **F&N:** 2.70, 5.33, 5.37, 5.115, 5.121, 7.37, 7.112, 8.531, 15.74

Art 3(5): F&N: 5.34, 5.37, 5.106

Art 3(5)(a): B&C: 8.049, 8.050, 8.051

Art 3(5)(b): B&C: 8.052

Art 3(5)(c): B&C: 8.053

Article 4
Prior notification of concentrations and pre-notification referral at the request of the notifying parties

1. Concentrations with a Community dimension defined in this Regulation shall be notified to the Commission prior to their implementation and following the conclusion of the agreement, the announcement of the public bid, or the acquisition of a controlling interest.

Notification may also be made where the undertakings concerned demonstrate to the Commission a good faith intention to conclude an agreement or, in the case of a public bid, where they have publicly announced an intention to make such a bid, provided that the intended agreement or bid would result in a concentration with a Community dimension.

For the purposes of this Regulation, the term "notified concentration" shall also cover intended concentrations notified pursuant to the second subparagraph. For the purposes of paragraphs 4 and 5 of this Article, the term "concentration" includes intended concentrations within the meaning of the second subparagraph.

2. A concentration which consists of a merger within the meaning of Article 3(1)(a) or in the acquisition of joint control within the meaning of Article 3(1)(b) shall be notified jointly by the parties to the merger or by those acquiring joint control as the case may be. In all other cases, the notification shall be effected by the person or undertaking acquiring control of the whole or parts of one or more undertakings.

3. Where the Commission finds that a notified concentration falls within the scope of this Regulation, it shall publish the fact of the notification, at the same time indicating the names of the undertakings concerned, their country of origin, the nature of the concentration and the economic sectors involved. The Commission shall take account of the legitimate interest of undertakings in the protection of their business secrets.

4. Prior to the notification of a concentration within the meaning of paragraph 1, the persons or undertakings referred to in paragraph 2 may inform the Commission, by means of a reasoned submission, that the concentration may significantly affect competition in a market within a Member State which presents all the characteristics of a distinct market and should therefore be examined, in whole or in part, by that Member State.

The Commission shall transmit this submission to all Member States without delay. The Member State referred to in the reasoned submission shall, within 15 working days of receiving the submission, express its agreement or disagreement as regards the request to refer the case. Where that Member State takes no such decision within this period, it shall be deemed to have agreed.

Unless that Member State disagrees, the Commission, where it considers that such a distinct market exists, and that competition in that market may be significantly affected by the concentration, may decide to refer the whole or part of the case to the competent authorities of that Member State with a view to the application of that State's national competition law.

The decision whether or not to refer the case in accordance with the third subparagraph shall be taken within 25 working days starting from the receipt of the reasoned submission by the Commission. The Commission shall inform the other Member States and the persons or undertakings concerned of its decision. If the Commission does not take a decision within this period, it shall be deemed to have adopted a decision to refer the case in accordance with the submission made by the persons or undertakings concerned.

If the Commission decides, or is deemed to have decided, pursuant to the third and fourth subparagraphs, to refer the whole of the case, no notification shall be made pursuant to paragraph 1 and national competition law shall apply. Article 9(6) to (9) shall apply mutatis mutandis.

5. With regard to a concentration as defined in Article 3 which does not have a Community dimension within the meaning of Article 1 and which is capable of being reviewed under the national competition laws of at least three Member States, the persons or undertakings referred to in paragraph 2 may, before any notification to the competent authorities, inform the Commission by means of a reasoned submission that the concentration should be examined by the Commission.

The Commission shall transmit this submission to all Member States without delay.
Any Member State competent to examine the concentration under its national competition law may, within 15 working days of receiving the reasoned submission, express its disagreement as regards the request to refer the case.

Where at least one such Member State has expressed its disagreement in accordance with the third subparagraph within the period of 15 working days, the case shall not be referred. The Commission shall, without delay, inform all Member States and the persons or undertakings concerned of any such expression of disagreement.

Where no Member State has expressed its disagreement in accordance with the third subparagraph within the period of 15 working days, the concentration shall be deemed to have a Community dimension and shall be notified to the Commission in accordance with paragraphs 1 and 2. In such situations, no Member State shall apply its national competition law to the concentration.

Part D Mergers and Concentrations

6. The Commission shall report to the Council on the operation of paragraphs 4 and 5 by 1 July 2009. Following this report and on a proposal from the Commission, the Council, acting by a qualified majority, may revise paragraphs 4 and 5.

Commentary
Art 4: **B&C:** 8.187 **F&N:** 5.31, 5.32, 5.303, 5.333, 5.337, 5.341
Art 4(1): **B&C:** 8.110, 8.111, 8.251 **F&N:** 5.15, 5.204, 5.275, 5.388, 5.389, 5.399, 5.401, 5.402
Art 4(2): **B&C:** 8.014, 8.112 **F&N:** 5.177, 5.345, 5.403
Art 4(3): **B&C:** 8.132, 8.133, 8.182 **F&N:** 5.411, 5.416
Art 4(4): **B&C:** 8.007, 8.010, 8.012, 8.081, 8.082, 8.083, 8.084, 8.086, 8.089, 8.110, 8.111, 8.191, 8.271, 8.288 **F&N:** 5.163, 5.209, 5.210, 5.214, 5.218, 5.219, 5.220, 5.221, 5.222, 5.224, 5.225, 5.226, 5.230, 5.232, 5.238, 5.242, 5.245, 5.261, 5.276, 5.278, 5.311, 5.334, 5.362, 5.374, 5.526
Art 4(5): **B&C:** 8.007, 8.010, 8.012, 8.085, 8.086, 8.087, 8.088, 8.089, 8.101, 8.110, 8.271, 8.290 **F&N:** 5.29, 5.162, 5.163, 5.209, 5.210, 5.214, 5.220, 5.221, 5.222, 5.224, 5.256, 5.257, 5.258, 5.259, 5.260, 5.261, 5.263, 5.265, 5.278, 5.280, 5.374, 5.374, 5.526, 11.107
Art 4(6): **B&C:** 8.090

Article 5
Calculation of turnover

1. Aggregate turnover within the meaning of this Regulation shall comprise the amounts derived by the undertakings concerned in the preceding financial year from the sale of products and the provision of services falling within the undertakings' ordinary activities after deduction of sales rebates and of value added tax and other taxes directly related to turnover. The aggregate turnover of an undertaking concerned shall not include the sale of products or the provision of services between any of the undertakings referred to in paragraph 4.

Turnover, in the Community or in a Member State, shall comprise products sold and services provided to undertakings or consumers, in the Community or in that Member State as the case may be.

2. By way of derogation from paragraph 1, where the concentration consists of the acquisition of parts, whether or not constituted as legal entities, of one or more undertakings, only the turnover relating to the parts which are the subject of the concentration shall be taken into account with regard to the seller or sellers.

However, two or more transactions within the meaning of the first subparagraph which take place within a two-year period between the same persons or undertakings shall be treated as one and the same concentration arising on the date of the last transaction.

3. In place of turnover the following shall be used:

(a) for credit institutions and other financial institutions, the sum of the following income items as defined in Council Directive 86/635/EEC,[1] after deduction of value added tax and other taxes directly related to those items, where appropriate:
  (i) interest income and similar income;
  (ii) income from securities:
      — income from shares and other variable yield securities,
      — income from participating interests,
      — income from shares in affiliated undertakings;
  (iii) commissions receivable;
  (iv) net profit on financial operations;
  (v) other operating income.

  The turnover of a credit or financial institution in the Community or in a Member State shall comprise the income items, as defined above, which are received by the branch or division of that institution established in the Community or in the Member State in question, as the case may be;

(b) for insurance undertakings, the value of gross premiums written which shall comprise all amounts received and receivable in respect of insurance contracts issued by or on behalf of the insurance undertakings, including also outgoing reinsurance premiums, and after deduction of taxes and parafiscal contributions or levies charged by reference to the amounts of individual premiums or the total volume of premiums; as regards Article 1(2)(b) and (3)(b), (c) and (d) and the final part of Article 1(2) and (3), gross premiums received from Community residents and from residents of one Member State respectively shall be taken into account.

4. Without prejudice to paragraph 2, the aggregate turnover of an undertaking concerned within the meaning of this Regulation shall be calculated by adding together the respective turnovers of the following:

(a) the undertaking concerned;
(b) those undertakings in which the undertaking concerned, directly or indirectly:
  (i) owns more than half the capital or business assets, or
  (ii) has the power to exercise more than half the voting rights, or
  (iii) has the power to appoint more than half the members of the supervisory board, the administrative board or bodies legally representing the undertakings, or
  (iv) has the right to manage the undertakings' affairs;
(c) those undertakings which have in the undertaking concerned the rights or powers listed in (b);
(d) those undertakings in which an undertaking as referred to in (c) has the rights or powers listed in (b);
(e) those undertakings in which two or more undertakings as referred to in (a) to (d) jointly have the rights or powers listed in (b).

5. Where undertakings concerned by the concentration jointly have the rights or powers listed in paragraph 4(b), in calculating the aggregate turnover of the undertakings concerned for the purposes of this Regulation:

(a) no account shall be taken of the turnover resulting from the sale of products or the provision of services between the joint undertaking and each of the undertakings concerned or any other undertaking connected with any one of them, as set out in paragraph 4(b) to (e);
(b) account shall be taken of the turnover resulting from the sale of products and the provision of services between the joint undertaking and any third undertakings. This turnover shall be apportioned equally amongst the undertakings concerned.

Notes

[1] OJ L 372, 31. 12. 1986, p.1. Directive as last amended by Directive 2003/51/EC of the European Parliament and of the Council.

Commentary

Art 5: **B&C:** 8.187, 8.188 **F&N:** 5.37, 5.184
Art 5(1): **B&C:** 8.063, 8.067 **F&N:** 5.185, 5.197, 5.202
Art 5(2): **B&C:** 8.044, 8.065, 8.066 **F&N:** 5.37, 5.140, 5.149, 5.151, 5.180, 5.181, 5.188, 5.189
Art 5(3): **B&C:** 8.068 **F&N:** 5.186, 11.71
Art 5(3)(a): **B&C:** 8.051, 8.068 **F&N:** 11.73
Art 5(3)(a)(i)–(v): **F&N:** 11.73
Art 5(4): **B&C:** 8.063, 8.069, 8.070, 8.076, 8.077, 8.078 **F&N:** 5.186, 5.190, 5.191, 5.192, 5.195
Art 5(4)(a): **F&N:** 5.191
Art 5(4)(b): **F&N:** 5.191
Art 5(4)(b)(i)–(v): **F&N:** 5.191
Art 5(4)(b)(iv): **B&C:** 8.076
Art 5(4)(c): **F&N:** 5.191
Art 5(4)(d): **F&N:** 5.191
Art 5(4)(e): **F&N:** 5.191
Art 5(5): **B&C:** 8.076, 8.078
Art 5(5)(a): **F&N:** 5.198
Art 5(5)(b): **F&N:** 5.195

Article 6
Examination of the notification and initiation of proceedings

1. The Commission shall examine the notification as soon as it is received.

(a) Where it concludes that the concentration notified does not fall within the scope of this Regulation, it shall record that finding by means of a decision.

(b) Where it finds that the concentration notified, although falling within the scope of this Regulation, does not raise serious doubts as to its compatibility with the common market, it shall decide not to oppose it and shall declare that it is compatible with the common market.

A decision declaring a concentration compatible shall be deemed to cover restrictions directly related and necessary to the implementation of the concentration.

(c) Without prejudice to paragraph 2, where the Commission finds that the concentration notified falls within the scope of this Regulation and raises serious doubts as to its compatibility with the common market, it shall decide to initiate proceedings. Without prejudice to Article 9, such proceedings shall be closed by means of a decision as provided for in Article 8(1) to (4), unless the undertakings concerned have demonstrated to the satisfaction of the Commission that they have abandoned the concentration.

2. Where the Commission finds that, following modification by the undertakings concerned, a notified concentration no longer raises serious doubts within the meaning of paragraph 1(c), it shall declare the concentration compatible with the common market pursuant to paragraph 1(b).

The Commission may attach to its decision under paragraph 1(b) conditions and obligations intended to ensure that the undertakings concerned comply with the commitments they have entered into vis-à-vis the Commission with a view to rendering the concentration compatible with the common market.

3. The Commission may revoke the decision it took pursuant to paragraph 1(a) or (b) where:

(a) the decision is based on incorrect information for which one of the undertakings is responsible or where it has been obtained by deceit, or

(b) the undertakings concerned commit a breach of an obligation attached to the decision.

4. In the cases referred to in paragraph 3, the Commission may take a decision under paragraph 1, without being bound by the time limits referred to in Article 10(1).

5. The Commission shall notify its decision to the undertakings concerned and the competent authorities of the Member States without delay.

Commentary

Art 6: F&N: 5.42, 5.336
Art 6(1): F&N: 5.1184, 5.1197
Art 6(1)(a): B&C: 8.137, 8.139, 8.251 F&N: 5.40, 5.349, 5.362, 5.373, 5.430, 5.436, 5.1131, 5.1135, 5.1149
Art 6(1)(b): B&C: 8.091, 8.137, 8.139, 8.188, 8.189, 8.273 F&N: 5.40, 5.152, 5.349, 5.362, 5.417, 5.430, 5.436, 5.980, 5.1033, 5.1118, 5.1120, 5.1130
Art 6(1)(c): B&C: 8.094, 8.137, 8.142, 8.143, 8.160, 8.168, 8.170, 8.251, 8.294, 13.131 F&N: 5.40, 5.249, 5.349, 5.362, 5.417, 5.427, 5.430, 5.434, 5.437, 5.441, 5.445, 5.446, 5.453, 5.529, 5.1016, 5.1033, 5.1038, 5.1039, 5.1045, 5.1118, 5.1134, 7.142
Art 6(2): B&C: 8.134, 8.137, 8.168, 8.175 F&N: 5.349, 5.417, 5.420, 5.430, 5.436, 5.980, 5.983, 5.988, 5.1033, 5.1130, 15.110
Art 6(3): F&N: 5.338, 5.349, 5.452, 5.543, 5.990, 5.1118
Art 6(3)(a): B&C: 8.115, 8.141 F&N: 5.996
Art 6(3)(b): B&C: 8.141, 8.176 F&N: 5.983
Art 6(4): B&C: 8.176 F&N: 5.119, 5.338, 5.1120
Art 6(5): B&C: 8.139 F&N: 5.431, 5.432

Article 7
Suspension of concentrations

1. A concentration with a Community dimension as defined in Article 1, or which is to be examined by the Commission pursuant to Article 4(5), shall not be implemented either before its notification or until it has been declared compatible with the common market pursuant to a decision under Articles 6(1)(b), 8(1) or 8(2), or on the basis of a presumption according to Article 10(6).

2. Paragraph 1 shall not prevent the implementation of a public bid or of a series of transactions in securities including those convertible into other securities admitted to trading on a market such as a stock exchange, by which control within the meaning of Article 3 is acquired from various sellers, provided that:

(a) the concentration is notified to the Commission pursuant to Article 4 without delay; and

(b) the acquirer does not exercise the voting rights attached to the securities in question or does so only to maintain the full value of its investments based on a derogation granted by the Commission under paragraph 3.

3. The Commission may, on request, grant a derogation from the obligations imposed in paragraphs 1 or 2. The request to grant a derogation must be reasoned. In deciding on the request, the Commission shall take into account inter alia the effects of the suspension on one or more undertakings concerned by the concentration or on a third party and the threat to competition posed by the concentration. Such a derogation may be made subject to conditions and obligations in order to ensure conditions of effective competition. A derogation may be applied for and granted at any time, be it before notification or after the transaction.

4. The validity of any transaction carried out in contravention of paragraph 1 shall be dependent on a decision pursuant to Article 6(1)(b) or Article 8(1), (2) or (3) or on a presumption pursuant to Article 10(6).

This Article shall, however, have no effect on the validity of transactions in securities including those convertible into other securities admitted to trading on a market such as a stock exchange, unless the buyer and seller knew or ought to have known that the transaction was carried out in contravention of paragraph 1.

Commentary

Art 7: B&C: 8.051 F&N: 5.274, 5.333, 5.361, 5.396, 5.536
Art 7(1): B&C: 8.126, 8.127 F&N: 5.15, 5.389, 5.1196, 11.96
Art 7(2): B&C: 8.128 F&N: 5.391, 5.392, 5.537
Art 7(3): B&C: 8.128, 8.188, 8.189 F&N: 5.338, 5.349, 5.362, 5.378, 5.392, 5.452, 5.511, 5.539, 5.1132, 11.96
Art 7(4): B&C: 7.130, 8.145 F&N: 5.100, 5.396

Article 8
Powers of decision of the Commission

1. Where the Commission finds that a notified concentration fulfils the criterion laid down in Article 2(2) and, in the cases referred to in Article 2(4), the criteria laid down in Article [101](3) of the Treaty, it shall issue a decision declaring the concentration compatible with the common market.

A decision declaring a concentration compatible shall be deemed to cover restrictions directly related and necessary to the implementation of the concentration.

2. Where the Commission finds that, following modification by the undertakings concerned, a notified concentration fulfils the criterion laid down in Article [101](2) and, in the cases referred to in Article 2(4), the criteria laid down in Article 2(3) of the Treaty, it shall issue a decision declaring the concentration compatible with the common market.

The Commission may attach to its decision conditions and obligations intended to ensure that the undertakings concerned comply with the commitments they have entered into vis-à-vis the Commission with a view to rendering the concentration compatible with the common market.

A decision declaring a concentration compatible shall be deemed to cover restrictions directly related and necessary to the implementation of the concentration.

3. Where the Commission finds that a concentration fulfils the criterion defined in Article 2(3) or, in the cases referred to in Article 2(4), does not fulfil the criteria laid down in Article [101](3) of the Treaty, it shall issue a decision declaring that the concentration is incompatible with the common market.

4. Where the Commission finds that a concentration:

(a) has already been implemented and that concentration has been declared incompatible with the common market, or

(b) has been implemented in contravention of a condition attached to a decision taken under paragraph 2, which has found that, in the absence of the condition, the concentration would fulfil the criterion laid down in Article 2(3) or, in the cases referred to in Article 2(4), would not fulfil the criteria laid down in Article [101](3) of the Treaty the Commission may:

— require the undertakings concerned to dissolve the concentration, in particular through the dissolution of the merger or the disposal of all the shares or assets acquired, so as to restore the situation prevailing prior to the implementation of the concentration; in circumstances where restoration of the situation prevailing before the implementation of the concentration is not possible through dissolution of the concentration, the Commission may take any other measure appropriate to achieve such restoration as far as possible,

— order any other appropriate measure to ensure that the undertakings concerned dissolve the concentration or take other restorative measures as required in its decision.

In cases falling within point (a) of the first subparagraph, the measures referred to in that subparagraph may be imposed either in a decision pursuant to paragraph 3 or by separate decision.

5. The Commission may take interim measures appropriate to restore or maintain conditions of effective competition where a concentration:

(a) has been implemented in contravention of Article 7, and a decision as to the compatibility of the concentration with the common market has not yet been taken;

(b) has been implemented in contravention of a condition attached to a decision under Article 6(1) (b) or paragraph 2 of this Article;

(c) has already been implemented and is declared incompatible with the common market.

6. The Commission may revoke the decision it has taken pursuant to paragraphs 1 or 2 where:

(a) the declaration of compatibility is based on incorrect information for which one of the undertakings is responsible or where it has been obtained by deceit; or

(b) the undertakings concerned commit a breach of an obligation attached to the decision.

7. The Commission may take a decision pursuant to paragraphs 1 to 3 without being bound by the time limits referred to in Article 10(3), in cases where:

(a) it finds that a concentration has been implemented

   (i) in contravention of a condition attached to a decision under Article 6(1)(b), or

   (ii) in contravention of a condition attached to a decision taken under paragraph 2 and in accordance with Article 10(2), which has found that, in the absence of the condition, the concentration would raise serious doubts as to its compatibility with the common market; or

(b) a decision has been revoked pursuant to paragraph 6.

8. The Commission shall notify its decision to the undertakings concerned and the competent authorities of the Member States without delay.

Commentary
Art 8: B&C: 8.106, 8.145 **F&N:** 5.336, 5.361, 5.495, 5.499, 5.501, 5.503, 5.504
Art 8(1): B&C: 8.159, 8.273 **F&N:** 5.152, 5.184, 5.349, 5.450, 5.500
Art 8(2): B&C: 8.159, 8.161, 8.164, 8.169, 8.175, 8.188, 8.189, 8.273 **F&N:** 5.152, 5.349, 5.450, 5.500, 5.502, 5.980, 5.983, 5.988, 5.1045, 5.1118, 5.1120, 5.1121, 12.236, 15.110
Art 8(3): B&C: 8.159, 8.161, 8.188 **F&N:** 5.349, 5.500, 5.502, 5.1121
Art 8(4): B&C: 8.100, 8.159, 8.161, 8.163, 8.185, 8.188, 8.189, 8.249, 13.168 **F&N:** 5.14, 5.100, 5.349, 5.396, 5.502, 5.533, 5.1119, 5.1120, 5.1121, 5.1122, 5.1145
Art 8(4)(b): F&N: 5.502, 5.983, 5.990
Art 8(5): B&C: 8.161, 8.188, 8.189, 13.168 **F&N:** 5.35, 5.349, 5.396, 5.500, 5.502, 5.534
Art 8(5)(a): B&C: 8.130
Art 8(5)(b): B&C: 8.176 **F&N:** 5.983
Art 8(5)(c): B&C: 8.163
Art 8(6): F&N: 5.349, 5.500, 5.543, 5.983, 5.1118
Art 8(6)(a): B&C: 8.115, 8.164 **F&N:** 5.996
Art 8(6)(b): B&C: 8.176 **F&N:** 5.990, 5.996
Art 8(7): B&C: 7.164, 8.176 **F&N:** 5.338, 5.1119, 5.1120
Art 8(7)(a): F&N: 5.983
Art 8(8): B&C: 8.161 **F&N:** 5.503

Article 9
Referral to the competent authorities of the Member States

1. The Commission may, by means of a decision notified without delay to the undertakings concerned and the competent authorities of the other Member States, refer a notified concentration to the competent authorities of the Member State concerned in the following circumstances.

2. Within 15 working days of the date of receipt of the copy of the notification, a Member State, on its own initiative or upon the invitation of the Commission, may inform the Commission, which shall inform the undertakings concerned, that:

(a) a concentration threatens to affect significantly competition in a market within that Member State, which presents all the characteristics of a distinct market, or

(b) a concentration affects competition in a market within that Member State, which presents all the characteristics of a distinct market and which does not constitute a substantial part of the common market.

3. If the Commission considers that, having regard to the market for the products or services in question and the geographical reference market within the meaning of paragraph 7, there is such a distinct market and that such a threat exists, either:

(a) it shall itself deal with the case in accordance with this Regulation; or

(b) it shall refer the whole or part of the case to the competent authorities of the Member State concerned with a view to the application of that State's national competition law.

If, however, the Commission considers that such a distinct market or threat does not exist, it shall adopt a decision to that effect which it shall address to the Member State concerned, and shall itself deal with the case in accordance with this Regulation.

In cases where a Member State informs the Commission pursuant to paragraph 2(b) that a concentration affects competition in a distinct market within its territory that does not form a substantial part of the common market, the Commission shall refer the whole or part of the case relating to the distinct market concerned, if it considers that such a distinct market is affected.

4. A decision to refer or not to refer pursuant to paragraph 3 shall be taken:

(a) as a general rule within the period provided for in Article 10(1), second subparagraph, where the Commission, pursuant to Article 6(1)(b), has not initiated proceedings; or

(b) within 65 working days at most of the notification of the concentration concerned where the Commission has initiated proceedings under Article 6(1)(c), without taking the preparatory steps in order to adopt the necessary measures under Article 8(2), (3) or (4) to maintain or restore effective competition on the market concerned.

5. If within the 65 working days referred to in paragraph 4(b) the Commission, despite a reminder from the Member State concerned, has not taken a decision on referral in accordance with paragraph 3 nor has taken the preparatory steps referred to in paragraph 4(b), it shall be deemed to have taken a decision to refer the case to the Member State concerned in accordance with paragraph 3(b).

6. The competent authority of the Member State concerned shall decide upon the case without undue delay.

Within 45 working days after the Commission's referral, the competent authority of the Member State concerned shall inform the undertakings concerned of the result of the preliminary competition assessment and what further action, if any, it proposes to take. The Member State concerned may exceptionally suspend this time limit where necessary information has not been provided to it by the undertakings concerned as provided for by its national competition law.

Where a notification is requested under national law, the period of 45 working days shall begin on the working day following that of the receipt of a complete notification by the competent authority of that Member State.

7. The geographical reference market shall consist of the area in which the undertakings concerned are involved in the supply and demand of products or services, in which the conditions of competition are sufficiently homogeneous and which can be distinguished from neighbouring areas because, in particular, conditions of competition are appreciably different in those areas. This assessment should

take account in particular of the nature and characteristics of the products or services concerned, of the existence of entry barriers or of consumer preferences, of appreciable differences of the undertakings' market shares between the area concerned and neighbouring areas or of substantial price differences.

8. In applying the provisions of this Article, the Member State concerned may take only the measures strictly necessary to safeguard or restore effective competition on the market concerned.

9. In accordance with the relevant provisions of the Treaty, any Member State may appeal to the Court of Justice, and in particular request the application of Article [279] of the Treaty, for the purpose of applying its national competition law.

Commentary
Art 9: **B&C:** 7.062, 8.012, 8.081, 8.083, 8.085, 8.091, 8.092, 8.094, 8.097, 8.102, 8.104, 8.106, 8.137, 8.138, 8.157, 8.191, 8.249, 8.271, 8.288, 8.293, 13.132 **F&N:** 5.31, 5.159, 5.210, 5.214, 5.218, 5.219, 5.220, 5.222, 5.224, 5.239, 5.240, 5.248, 5.249, 5.253, 5.276, 5.278, 5.303, 5.337, 5.362, 5.526, 5.580, 5.1131, 5.1149, 11.78, 13.203
Art 9(1): **B&C:** 8.091
Art 9(2): **B&C:** 7.062, 8.047, 8.094, 8.134, 8.216 **F&N:** 5.419, 5.420, 5.464, 5.511
Art 9(2)(a): **B&C:** 8.083, 8.091, 8.092 **F&N:** 5.224, 5.241, 5.242, 5.243, 5.247, 5.269, 5.580, 5.1148, 9.245
Art 9(2)(b): **B&C:** 8.091, 8.093 **F&N:** 5.224, 5.242, 5.244, 5.246, 5.315, 5.580, 9.245
Art 9(3): **B&C:** 8.092, 8.093, 8.137 **F&N:** 5.580
Art 9(3)(b): **B&C:** 8.092, 8.198
Art 9(4)(a): **B&C:** 8.094
Art 9(5): **B&C:** 8.094
Art 9(6): **B&C:** 8.084, 8.094 **F&N:** 5.251
Art 9(7): **B&C:** 7.062, 8.083, 8.095, 8.198
Art 9(8): **B&C:** 8.092, 8.094
Art 9(9): **B&C:** 8.094 **F&N:** 5.253, 5.1132, 5.1170

Article 10
Time limits for initiating proceedings and for decisions

1. Without prejudice to Article 6(4), the decisions referred to in Article 6(1) shall be taken within 25 working days at most. That period shall begin on the working day following that of the receipt of a notification or, if the information to be supplied with the notification is incomplete, on the working day following that of the receipt of the complete information.

That period shall be increased to 35 working days where the Commission receives a request from a Member State in accordance with Article 9(2) or where, the undertakings concerned offer commitments pursuant to Article 6(2) with a view to rendering the concentration compatible with the common market.

2. Decisions pursuant to Article 8(1) or (2) concerning notified concentrations shall be taken as soon as it appears that the serious doubts referred to in Article 6(1)(c) have been removed, particularly as a result of modifications made by the undertakings concerned, and at the latest by the time limit laid down in paragraph 3.

3. Without prejudice to Article 8(7), decisions pursuant to Article 8(1) to (3) concerning notified concentrations shall be taken within not more than 90 working days of the date on which the proceedings are initiated. That period shall be increased to 105 working days where the undertakings concerned offer commitments pursuant to Article 8(2), second subparagraph, with a view to rendering the concentration compatible with the common market, unless these commitments have been offered less than 55 working days after the initiation of proceedings.

The periods set by the first subparagraph shall likewise be extended if the notifying parties make a request to that effect not later than 15 working days after the initiation of proceedings pursuant to Article 6(1)(c). The notifying parties may make only one such request. Likewise, at any time following the initiation of proceedings, the periods set by the first subparagraph may be extended by the Commission with the agreement of the notifying parties. The total duration of any extension or extensions effected pursuant to this subparagraph shall not exceed 20 working days.

4. The periods set by paragraphs 1 and 3 shall exceptionally be suspended where, owing to circumstances for which one of the undertakings involved in the concentration is responsible, the

Commission has had to request information by decision pursuant to Article 11 or to order an inspection by decision pursuant to Article 13.

The first subparagraph shall also apply to the period referred to in Article 9(4)(b).

5. Where the Court of Justice gives a judgment which annuls the whole or part of a Commission decision which is subject to a time limit set by this Article, the concentration shall be re-examined by the Commission with a view to adopting a decision pursuant to Article 6(1).

The concentration shall be re-examined in the light of current market conditions.

The notifying parties shall submit a new notification or supplement the original notification, without delay, where the original notification becomes incomplete by reason of intervening changes in market conditions or in the information provided. Where there are no such changes, the parties shall certify this fact without delay.

The periods laid down in paragraph 1 shall start on the working day following that of the receipt of complete information in a new notification, a supplemented notification, or a certification within the meaning of the third subparagraph.

The second and third subparagraphs shall also apply in the cases referred to in Article 6(4) and Article 8(7).

6. Where the Commission has not taken a decision in accordance with Article 6(1)(b), (c), 8(1), (2) or (3) within the time limits set in paragraphs 1 and 3 respectively, the concentration shall be deemed to have been declared compatible with the common market, without prejudice to Article 9.

Commentary
Art 10: B&C: 13.110 F&N: 5.336, 5.338, 5.361, 5.960
Art 10(1): **B&C:** 8.094, 8.134, 8.168 **F&N:** 5.340, 5.362, 5.414, 5.418, 5.511, 5.983
Art 10(2): **B&C:** 8.143, 8.169 **F&N:** 5.443, 5.983, 5.1045
Art 10(3): **B&C:** 4.143, 8.164, 8.169 **F&N:** 5.340, 5.440, 5.441, 5.983, 5.1038, 5.1120, 5.1159
Art 10(4): **B&C:** 8.134, 8.144 **F&N:** 5.340, 5.420
Art 10(5): **B&C:** 8.018, 8.141, 8.164, 8.267 **F&N:** 5.1197, 5.1198, 5.1200, 5.1201
Art 10(6): **B&C:** 8.126, 8.138, 8.159 **F&N:** 5.338, 5.430, 5.444, 5.1126, 5.1184

Article 11
Requests for information

1. In order to carry out the duties assigned to it by this Regulation, the Commission may, by simple request or by decision, require the persons referred to in Article 3(1)(b), as well as undertakings and associations of undertakings, to provide all necessary information.

2. When sending a simple request for information to a person, an undertaking or an association of undertakings, the Commission shall state the legal basis and the purpose of the request, specify what information is required and fix the time limit within which the information is to be provided, as well as the penalties provided for in Article 14 for supplying incorrect or misleading information.

3. Where the Commission requires a person, an undertaking or an association of undertakings to supply information by decision, it shall state the legal basis and the purpose of the request, specify what information is required and fix the time limit within which it is to be provided. It shall also indicate the penalties provided for in Article 14 and indicate or impose the penalties provided for in Article 15. It shall further indicate the right to have the decision reviewed by the Court of Justice.

4. The owners of the undertakings or their representatives and, in the case of legal persons, companies or firms, or associations having no legal personality, the persons authorised to represent them by law or by their constitution, shall supply the information requested on behalf of the undertaking concerned. Persons duly authorised to act may supply the information on behalf of their clients. The latter shall remain fully responsible if the information supplied is incomplete, incorrect or misleading.

5. The Commission shall without delay forward a copy of any decision taken pursuant to paragraph 3 to the competent authorities of the Member State in whose territory the residence of the person or the seat of the undertaking or association of undertakings is situated, and to the competent authority of the Member State whose territory is affected. At the specific request of the competent authority of

a Member State, the Commission shall also forward to that authority copies of simple requests for information relating to a notified concentration.

6. At the request of the Commission, the governments and competent authorities of the Member States shall provide the Commission with all necessary information to carry out the duties assigned to it by this Regulation.

7. In order to carry out the duties assigned to it by this Regulation, the Commission may interview any natural or legal person who consents to be interviewed for the purpose of collecting information relating to the subject matter of an investigation. At the beginning of the interview, which may be conducted by telephone or other electronic means, the Commission shall state the legal basis and the purpose of the interview.

Where an interview is not conducted on the premises of the Commission or by telephone or other electronic means, the Commission shall inform in advance the competent authority of the Member State in whose territory the interview takes place. If the competent authority of that Member State so requests, officials of that authority may assist the officials and other persons authorised by the Commission to conduct the interview.

Commentary
Art 11: B&C: 8.132, 8.135, 8.143, 8.178, 8.187 F&N: 5.295, 5.425, 5.441, 5.547, 5.985
Art 11(1): B&C: 8.178
Art 11(2): B&C: 8.178
Art 11(3): B&C: 8.178, 8.181 F&N: 5.349, 5.441, 5.545
Art 11(5): B&C: 8.178
Art 11(6): B&C: 8.178 F&N: 5.302
Art 11(7): B&C: 8.179 F&N: 5.300

Article 12
Inspections by the authorities of the Member States

1. At the request of the Commission, the competent authorities of the Member States shall undertake the inspections which the Commission considers to be necessary under Article 13(1), or which it has ordered by decision pursuant to Article 13(4). The officials of the competent authorities of the Member States who are responsible for conducting these inspections as well as those authorised or appointed by them shall exercise their powers in accordance with their national law.

2. If so requested by the Commission or by the competent authority of the Member State within whose territory the inspection is to be conducted, officials and other accompanying persons authorised by the Commission may assist the officials of the authority concerned.

Commentary
Art 12: B&C: 8.180 F&N: 5.302, 5.337

Article 13
The Commission's powers of inspection

1. In order to carry out the duties assigned to it by this Regulation, the Commission may conduct all necessary inspections of undertakings and associations of undertakings.

2. The officials and other accompanying persons authorised by the Commission to conduct an inspection shall have the power:

(a) to enter any premises, land and means of transport of undertakings and associations of undertakings;
(b) to examine the books and other records related to the business, irrespective of the medium on which they are stored;
(c) to take or obtain in any form copies of or extracts from such books or records;
(d) to seal any business premises and books or records for the period and to the extent necessary for the inspection;

(e) to ask any representative or member of staff of the undertaking or association of undertakings for explanations on facts or documents relating to the subject matter and purpose of the inspection and to record the answers.

3. Officials and other accompanying persons authorised by the Commission to conduct an inspection shall exercise their powers upon production of a written authorisation specifying the subject matter and purpose of the inspection and the penalties provided for in Article 14, in the production of the required books or other records related to the business which is incomplete or where answers to questions asked under paragraph 2 of this Article are incorrect or misleading. In good time before the inspection, the Commission shall give notice of the inspection to the competent authority of the Member State in whose territory the inspection is to be conducted.

4. Undertakings and associations of undertakings are required to submit to inspections ordered by decision of the Commission. The decision shall specify the subject matter and purpose of the inspection, appoint the date on which it is to begin and indicate the penalties provided for in Articles 14 and 15 and the right to have the decision reviewed by the Court of Justice. The Commission shall take such decisions after consulting the competent authority of the Member State in whose territory the inspection is to be conducted.

5. Officials of, and those authorised or appointed by, the competent authority of the Member State in whose territory the inspection is to be conducted shall, at the request of that authority or of the Commission, actively assist the officials and other accompanying persons authorised by the Commission. To this end, they shall enjoy the powers specified in paragraph 2.

6. Where the officials and other accompanying persons authorised by the Commission find that an undertaking opposes an inspection, including the sealing of business premises, books or records, ordered pursuant to this Article, the Member State concerned shall afford them the necessary assistance, requesting where appropriate the assistance of the police or of an equivalent enforcement authority, so as to enable them to conduct their inspection.

7. If the assistance provided for in paragraph 6 requires authorisation from a judicial authority according to national rules, such authorisation shall be applied for. Such authorisation may also be applied for as a precautionary measure.

8. Where authorisation as referred to in paragraph 7 is applied for, the national judicial authority shall ensure that the Commission decision is authentic and that the coercive measures envisaged are neither arbitrary nor excessive having regard to the subject matter of the inspection. In its control of proportionality of the coercive measures, the national judicial authority may ask the Commission, directly or through the competent authority of that Member State, for detailed explanations relating to the subject matter of the inspection. However, the national judicial authority may not call into question the necessity for the inspection nor demand that it be provided with the information in the Commission's file. The lawfulness of the Commission's decision shall be subject to review only by the Court of Justice.

Commentary
Art 13: B&C: 8.135, 8.144, 8.180 F&N: 5.302, 5.441, 5.547, 5.1161
Art 13(1): F&N: 5.541
Art 13(2): B&C: 8.151
Art 13(3): B&C: 8.151, 8.181
Art 13(4): B&C: 8.180, 8.181 F&N: 5.349
Art 13(5): B&C: 8.180

Article 14
Fines

1. The Commission may by decision impose on the persons referred to in Article 3(1)(b), undertakings or associations of undertakings, fines not exceeding 1% of the aggregate turnover of the undertaking or association of undertakings concerned within the meaning of Article 5 where, intentionally or negligently:

(a) they supply incorrect or misleading information in a submission, certification, notification or supplement thereto, pursuant to Article 4, Article 10(5) or Article 22(3);

(b) they supply incorrect or misleading information in response to a request made pursuant to Article 11(2);

(c) in response to a request made by decision adopted pursuant to Article 11(3), they supply incorrect, incomplete or misleading information or do not supply information within the required time limit;

(d) they produce the required books or other records related to the business in incomplete form during inspections under Article 13, or refuse to submit to an inspection ordered by decision taken pursuant to Article 13(4);

(e) in response to a question asked in accordance with Article 13(2)(e),
   — they give an incorrect or misleading answer,
   — they fail to rectify within a time limit set by the Commission an incorrect, incomplete or misleading answer given by a member of staff, or
   — they fail or refuse to provide a complete answer on facts relating to the subject matter and purpose of an inspection ordered by a decision adopted pursuant to Article 13(4);

(f) seals affixed by officials or other accompanying persons authorised by the Commission in accordance with Article 13(2)(d) have been broken.

2. The Commission may by decision impose fines not exceeding 10% of the aggregate turnover of the undertaking concerned within the meaning of Article 5 on the persons referred to in Article 3(1)(b) or the undertakings concerned where, either intentionally or negligently, they:

(a) fail to notify a concentration in accordance with Articles 4 or 22(3) prior to its implementation, unless they are expressly authorised to do so by Article 7(2) or by a decision taken pursuant to Article 7(3);

(b) implement a concentration in breach of Article 7;

(c) implement a concentration declared incompatible with the common market by decision pursuant to Article 8(3) or do not comply with any measure ordered by decision pursuant to Article 8(4) or (5);

(d) fail to comply with a condition or an obligation imposed by decision pursuant to Articles 6(1)(b), Article 7(3) or Article 8(2), second subparagraph.

3. In fixing the amount of the fine, regard shall be had to the nature, gravity and duration of the infringement.

4. Decisions taken pursuant to paragraphs 1, 2 and 3 shall not be of a criminal law nature.

Commentary
Art 14: **B&C:** 8.178, 8.186, 8.187 **F&N:** 5.35, 5.334, 5.349, 5.414, 5.452, 5.545, 5.990, 5.1161, 5.1195
Art 14(1): **B&C:** 8.115, 8.187 **F&N:** 5.550
Art 14(1)(a): **F&N:** 5.550
Art 14(1)(b): **F&N:** 5.550
Art 14(1)(c): **F&N:** 5.550
Art 14(1)(d): **F&N:** 5.550
Art 14(1)(e): **F&N:** 5.550
Art 14(1)(f): **F&N:** 5.550
Art 14(2): **B&C:** 8.029, 8.187, 8.188 **F&N:** 5.1123
Art 14(2)(a): **F&N:** 5.390, 5.396, 5.549
Art 14(2)(b): **B&C:** 8.127, 8.130 **F&N:** 5.396, 5.537, 5.549
Art 14(2)(c): **B&C:** 8.159, 8.163 **F&N:** 5.537, 5.549
Art 14(2)(d): **B&C:** 8.176 **F&N:** 5.537, 5.549
Art 14(3): **B&C:** 8.186
Art 14(4): **B&C:** 8.186

Article 15
Periodic penalty payments

1. The Commission may by decision impose on the persons referred to in Article 3(1)(b), undertakings or associations of undertakings, periodic penalty payments not exceeding 5% of the average daily

aggregate turnover of the undertaking or association of undertakings concerned within the meaning of Article 5 for each working day of delay, calculated from the date set in the decision, in order to compel them:

(a) to supply complete and correct information which it has requested by decision taken pursuant to Article 11(3);

(b) to submit to an inspection which it has ordered by decision taken pursuant to Article 13(4);

(c) to comply with an obligation imposed by decision pursuant to Article 6(1)(b), Article 7(3) or Article 8(2), second subparagraph; or

(d) to comply with any measures ordered by decision pursuant to Article 8(4) or (5).

2. Where the persons referred to in Article 3(1)(b), undertakings or associations of undertakings have satisfied the obligation which the periodic penalty payment was intended to enforce, the Commission may fix the definitive amount of the periodic penalty payments at a figure lower than that which would arise under the original decision.

Commentary
Art 15: **B&C:** 8.178, 8.186, 8.189 **F&N:** 5.35, 5.334, 5.349, 5.390, 5.452, 5.545, 5.1195
Art 15(1)(a): **F&N:** 5.554
Art 15(1)(b): **F&N:** 5.554
Art 15(1)(c): **B&C:** 8.176 **F&N:** 5.554
Art 15(1)(d): **F&N:** 5.537, 5.554
Art 15(2): **B&C:** 8.189 **F&N:** 5.555

Article 16
Review by the Court of Justice

The Court of Justice shall have unlimited jurisdiction within the meaning of Article [261] of the Treaty to review decisions whereby the Commission has fixed a fine or periodic penalty payments; it may cancel, reduce or increase the fine or periodic penalty payment imposed.

Commentary
Art 16: **B&C:** 8.248, 13.123 **F&N:** 5.337, 5.1195

Article 17
Professional secrecy

1. Information acquired as a result of the application of this Regulation shall be used only for the purposes of the relevant request, investigation or hearing.

2. Without prejudice to Article 4(3), Articles 18 and 20, the Commission and the competent authorities of the Member States, their officials and other servants and other persons working under the supervision of these authorities as well as officials and civil servants of other authorities of the Member States shall not disclose information they have acquired through the application of this Regulation of the kind covered by the obligation of professional secrecy.

3. Paragraphs 1 and 2 shall not prevent publication of general information or of surveys which do not contain information relating to particular undertakings or associations of undertakings.

Commentary
Art 17: **F&N:** 5.337, 5.371
Art 17(1): **B&C:** 8.182
Art 17(2): **B&C:** 8.120, 8.182

Article 18
Hearing of the parties and of third persons

1. Before taking any decision provided for in Article 6(3), Article 7(3), Article 8(2) to (6), and Articles 14 and 15, the Commission shall give the persons, undertakings and associations of undertakings

concerned the opportunity, at every stage of the procedure up to the consultation of the Advisory Committee, of making known their views on the objections against them.

2. By way of derogation from paragraph 1, a decision pursuant to Articles 7(3) and 8(5) may be taken provisionally, without the persons, undertakings or associations of undertakings concerned being given the opportunity to make known their views beforehand, provided that the Commission gives them that opportunity as soon as possible after having taken its decision.

3. The Commission shall base its decision only on objections on which the parties have been able to submit their observations. The rights of the defence shall be fully respected in the proceedings. Access to the file shall be open at least to the parties directly involved, subject to the legitimate interest of undertakings in the protection of their business secrets.

4. In so far as the Commission or the competent authorities of the Member States deem it necessary, they may also hear other natural or legal persons. Natural or legal persons showing a sufficient interest and especially members of the administrative or management bodies of the undertakings concerned or the recognised representatives of their employees shall be entitled, upon application, to be heard.

Commentary
Art 18: B&C: 8.152, 8.182, 8.184, 8.255 F&N: 5.307, 5.336
Art 18(1): B&C: 8.145, 8.152, 8.164, 8.186, 13.068 F&N: 5.395, 5.452, 5.461, 5.1156
Art 18(2): B&C: 8.145, 8.176 F&N: 5.395, 5.541
Art 18(3): B&C: 8.145, 8.149, 13.068 F&N: 5.439, 5.455, 5.459, 5.461
Art 18(4): B&C: 8.131, 8.152, 8.255 F&N: 5.356, 5.458, 5.480

Article 19
Liaison with the authorities of the Member States

1. The Commission shall transmit to the competent authorities of the Member States copies of notifications within three working days and, as soon as possible, copies of the most important documents lodged with or issued by the Commission pursuant to this Regulation. Such documents shall include commitments offered by the undertakings concerned vis-à-vis the Commission with a view to rendering the concentration compatible with the common market pursuant to Article 6(2) or Article 8(2), second subparagraph.

2. The Commission shall carry out the procedures set out in this Regulation in close and constant liaison with the competent authorities of the Member States, which may express their views upon those procedures. For the purposes of Article 9 it shall obtain information from the competent authority of the Member State as referred to in paragraph 2 of that Article and give it the opportunity to make known its views at every stage of the procedure up to the adoption of a decision pursuant to paragraph 3 of that Article; to that end it shall give it access to the file.

3. An Advisory Committee on concentrations shall be consulted before any decision is taken pursuant to Article 8(1) to (6), Articles 14 or 15 with the exception of provisional decisions taken in accordance with Article 18(2).

4. The Advisory Committee shall consist of representatives of the competent authorities of the Member States. Each Member State shall appoint one or two representatives; if unable to attend, they may be replaced by other representatives. At least one of the representatives of a Member State shall be competent in matters of restrictive practices and dominant positions.

5. Consultation shall take place at a joint meeting convened at the invitation of and chaired by the Commission. A summary of the case, together with an indication of the most important documents and a preliminary draft of the decision to be taken for each case considered, shall be sent with the invitation. The meeting shall take place not less than 10 working days after the invitation has been sent. The Commission may in exceptional cases shorten that period as appropriate in order to avoid serious harm to one or more of the undertakings concerned by a concentration.

6. The Advisory Committee shall deliver an opinion on the Commission's draft decision, if necessary by taking a vote. The Advisory Committee may deliver an opinion even if some members are absent and unrepresented. The opinion shall be delivered in writing and appended to the draft decision. The

Commission shall take the utmost account of the opinion delivered by the Committee. It shall inform the Committee of the manner in which its opinion has been taken into account.

7. The Commission shall communicate the opinion of the Advisory Committee, together with the decision, to the addressees of the decision. It shall make the opinion public together with the decision, having regard to the legitimate interest of undertakings in the protection of their business secrets.

Commentary

Art 19: F&N: 5.303, 5.308, 5.337, 5.357
Art 19(1): B&C: 8.157, 8.166 F&N: 5.300, 5.305, 5.1027
Art 19(2): B&C: 8.094, 8.150, 8.157 F&N: 5.250, 5.300, 5.1027
Art 19(3): B&C: 8.158, 8.164, 8.166, 8.176, 8.186, 12.195 F&N: 5.494, 5.541
Art 19(4): B&C: 8.158
Art 19(5): B&C: 8.158 F&N: 5.497
Art 19(6): B&C: 8.158 F&N: 5.497
Art 19(7): F&N: 5.497

Article 20
Publication of decisions

1. The Commission shall publish the decisions which it takes pursuant to Article 8(1) to (6), Articles 14 and 15 with the exception of provisional decisions taken in accordance with Article 18(2) together with the opinion of the Advisory Committee in the *Official Journal of the European Union*.

2. The publication shall state the names of the parties and the main content of the decision; it shall have regard to the legitimate interest of undertakings in the protection of their business secrets.

Commentary

Art 20: B&C: 8.182 F&N: 5.337, 5.497
Art 20(1): B&C: 8.161 F&N: 5.305, 5.503
Art 20(2): B&C: 8.182

Article 21
Application of the Regulation and jurisdiction

1. This Regulation alone shall apply to concentrations as defined in Article 3, and Council Regulations (EC) No 1/2003,[1] (EEC) No 1017/68,[2] (EEC) No 4056/86[3] and (EEC) No 3975/87[4] shall not apply, except in relation to joint ventures that do not have a Community dimension and which have as their object or effect the coordination of the competitive behaviour of undertakings that remain independent.

2. Subject to review by the Court of Justice, the Commission shall have sole jurisdiction to take the decisions provided for in this Regulation.

3. No Member State shall apply its national legislation on competition to any concentration that has a Community dimension.

The first subparagraph shall be without prejudice to any Member State's power to carry out any enquiries necessary for the application of Articles 4(4), 9(2) or after referral, pursuant to Article 9(3), first subparagraph, indent (b), or Article 9(5), to take the measures strictly necessary for the application of Article 9(8).

4. Notwithstanding paragraphs 2 and 3, Member States may take appropriate measures to protect legitimate interests other than those taken into consideration by this Regulation and compatible with the general principles and other provisions of Community law.

Public security, plurality of the media and prudential rules shall be regarded as legitimate interests within the meaning of the first subparagraph.

Any other public interest must be communicated to the Commission by the Member State concerned and shall be recognised by the Commission after an assessment of its compatibility with the general principles and other provisions of Community law before the measures referred to above may be taken. The Commission shall inform the Member State concerned of its decision within 25 working days of that communication.

Notes

1 OJ L 1, 4.1.2003, p.1.

2 OJ L 175, 23. 7. 1968, p.1. Regulation as last amended by Regulation (EC) No 1/2003 (OJ L 1, 4.1.2003, p.1). [Ed note: see now Regulation 169/2009/EC, OJ L 61, 5.3.2009, p.1, reproduced at E17.]

3 OJ L 378, 31. 12. 1986, p.4. Regulation as last amended by Regulation (EC) No 1/2003. [Ed note: Regulation 4056/86/EEC was repealed by Regulation 1419/2006/EC. See also the Guidelines on the application of Article [101 TFEU] to maritime transport, C 245, 26.9.2008, p.2, which have themselves expired, and the note at E20.]

4 OJ L 374. 31. 12. 1987, p.1. Regulation as last amended by Regulation (EC) No 1/2003. [Ed note: Regulation 3975/87/EEC was repealed by Regulation 411/2004/EC, OJ L 68, 6.3.2004, p.1.]

Commentary
Art 21: **B&C:** 8.102, 8.104, 8.105 **F&N:** 5.334, 5.337, 5.1126, 5.1132, 5.1138
Art 21(1): **B&C:** 8.247, 8.270, 8.272, 16.007 **F&N:** 5.31, 5.152, 14.163
Art 21(2): **B&C:** 8.011, 8.270 **F&N:** 5.31, 5.337, 14.163
Art 21(3): **B&C:** 8.011, 8.102, 8.293 **F&N:** 5.31, 5.208, 5.281, 14.163
Art 21(4): **B&C:** 8.012, 8.102, 8.103, 8.104, 8.105, 8.251, 8.293, 13.131 **F&N:** 5.22, 5.281, 5.282, 5.283, 5.284, 5.286, 5.288, 5.292, 5.293, 5.297, 5.1126, 11.102, 14.163

Article 22
Referral to the Commission

1. One or more Member States may request the Commission to examine any concentration as defined in Article 3 that does not have a Community dimension within the meaning of Article 1 but affects trade between Member States and threatens to significantly affect competition within the territory of the Member State or States making the request.

Such a request shall be made at most within 15 working days of the date on which the concentration was notified, or if no notification is required, otherwise made known to the Member State concerned.

2. The Commission shall inform the competent authorities of the Member States and the undertakings concerned of any request received pursuant to paragraph 1 without delay.

Any other Member State shall have the right to join the initial request within a period of 15 working days of being informed by the Commission of the initial request.

All national time limits relating to the concentration shall be suspended until, in accordance with the procedure set out in this Article, it has been decided where the concentration shall be examined. As soon as a Member State has informed the Commission and the undertakings concerned that it does not wish to join the request, the suspension of its national time limits shall end.

3. The Commission may, at the latest 10 working days after the expiry of the period set in paragraph 2, decide to examine, the concentration where it considers that it affects trade between Member States and threatens to significantly affect competition within the territory of the Member State or States making the request. If the Commission does not take a decision within this period, it shall be deemed to have adopted a decision to examine the concentration in accordance with the request.

The Commission shall inform all Member States and the undertakings concerned of its decision. It may request the submission of a notification pursuant to Article 4.

The Member State or States having made the request shall no longer apply their national legislation on competition to the concentration.

4. Article 2, Article 4(2) to (3), Articles 5, 6, and 8 to 21 shall apply where the Commission examines a concentration pursuant to paragraph 3. Article 7 shall apply to the extent that the concentration has not been implemented on the date on which the Commission informs the undertakings concerned that a request has been made.

Where a notification pursuant to Article 4 is not required, the period set in Article 10(1) within which proceedings may be initiated shall begin on the working day following that on which the Commission informs the undertakings concerned that it has decided to examine the concentration pursuant to paragraph 3.

5. The Commission may inform one or several Member States that it considers a concentration fulfils the criteria in paragraph 1. In such cases, the Commission may invite that Member State or those Member States to make a request pursuant to paragraph 1.

Commentary

Art 22: B&C: 1.120, 1.127, 8.012, 8.013, 8.087, 8.097, 8.099, 8.100, 8.101, 8.102, 8.271 **F&N:** 5.19, 5.31, 5.32,
5.159, 5.209, 5.210, 5.214, 5.218, 5.219, 5.221, 5.222, 5.224, 5.266, 5.267, 5.268, 5.269, 5.271, 5.272, 5.273,
5.276, 5.278, 5.280, 5.315, 5.334, 5.337, 5.526, 5.967, 11.107
Art 22(1): B&C: 8.098, 8.099
Art 22(2): B&C: 8.099
Art 22(3): B&C: 8.099, 8.100, 8.187 **F&N:** 5.214, 5.273
Art 22(4): B&C: 8.099, 8.100
Art 22(5): B&C: 8.099

Article 23
Implementing provisions

1. The Commission shall have the power to lay down in accordance with the procedure referred to in paragraph 2:

(a) implementing provisions concerning the form, content and other details of notifications and submissions pursuant to Article 4;

(b) implementing provisions concerning time limits pursuant to Article 4(4), (5) Articles 7, 9, 10 and 22;

(c) the procedure and time limits for the submission and implementation of commitments pursuant to Article 6(2) and Article 8(2);

(d) implementing provisions concerning hearings pursuant to Article 18.

2. The Commission shall be assisted by an Advisory Committee, composed of representatives of the Member States.

(a) Before publishing draft implementing provisions and before adopting such provisions, the Commission shall consult the Advisory Committee.

(b) Consultation shall take place at a meeting convened at the invitation of and chaired by the Commission. A draft of the implementing provisions to be taken shall be sent with the invitation. The meeting shall take place not less than 10 working days after the invitation has been sent.

(c) The Advisory Committee shall deliver an opinion on the draft implementing provisions, if necessary by taking a vote. The Commission shall take the utmost account of the opinion delivered by the Committee.

Commentary
Art 23(2)(b): B&C: 13.108

Article 24
Relations with third countries

1. The Member States shall inform the Commission of any general difficulties encountered by their undertakings with concentrations as defined in Article 3 in a third country.

2. Initially not more than one year after the entry into force of this Regulation and, thereafter periodically, the Commission shall draw up a report examining the treatment accorded to undertakings having their seat or their principal fields of activity in the Community, in the terms referred to in paragraphs 3 and 4, as regards concentrations in third countries. The Commission shall submit those reports to the Council, together with any recommendations.

3. Whenever it appears to the Commission, either on the basis of the reports referred to in paragraph 2 or on the basis of other information, that a third country does not grant undertakings having their seat or their principal fields of activity in the Community, treatment comparable to that granted by the Community to undertakings from that country, the Commission may submit proposals to the

Council for an appropriate mandate for negotiation with a view to obtaining comparable treatment for undertakings having their seat or their principal fields of activity in the Community.

4. Measures taken under this Article shall comply with the obligations of the Community or of the Member States, without prejudice to Article [351] of the Treaty, under international agreements, whether bilateral or multilateral.

Commentary
Art 24: **B&C:** 8.298
Art 24(1)(b): **B&C:** 13.108

Article 25
Repeal

1. Without prejudice to Article 26(2), Regulations (EEC) No 4064/89 and (EC) No 1310/97 shall be repealed with effect from 1 May 2004.

2. References to the repealed Regulations shall be construed as references to this Regulation and shall be read in accordance with the correlation table in the Annex.

Article 26
Entry into force and transitional provisions

1. This Regulation shall enter into force on the 20th day following that of its publication in the *Official Journal of the European Union.*

It shall apply from 1 May 2004.

2. Regulation (EEC) No 4064/89 shall continue to apply to any concentration which was the subject of an agreement or announcement or where control was acquired within the meaning of Article 4(1) of that Regulation before the date of application of this Regulation, subject, in particular, to the provisions governing applicability set out in Article 25(2) and (3) of Regulation (EEC) No 4064/89 and Article 2 of Regulation (EEC) No 1310/97.

3. As regards concentrations to which this Regulation applies by virtue of accession, the date of accession shall be substituted for the date of application of this Regulation.

This Regulation shall be binding in its entirety and directly applicable in all Member States.

Done at Brussels, 20 January 2004.

Annex
Correlation Table

Regulation (EEC) No 4064/89	This Regulation
Article 1(1), (2) and (3)	Article 1(1), (2) and (3)
Article 1(4)	Article 1(4)
Article 1(5)	Article 1(5)
Article 2(1)	Article 2(1)
—	Article 2(2)
Article 2(2)	Article 2(3)
Article 2(3)	Article 2(4)
Article 2(4)	Article 2(5)
Article 3(1)	Article 3(1)
Article 3(2)	Article 3(4)
Article 3(3)	Article 3(2)
Article 3(4)	Article 3(3)
—	Article 3(4)
Article 3(5)	Article 3(5)
Article 4(1) first sentence	Article 4(1) first subparagraph
Article 4(1) second sentence	—
—	Article 4(1) second and third subparagraphs

Regulation (EEC) No 4064/89	This Regulation
Article 4(2) and (3)	Article 4(2) and (3)
—	Article 4(4) to (6)
Article 5(1) to (3)	Article 5(1) to (3)
Article 5(4), introductory words	Article 5(4), introductory words
Article 5(4) point (a)	Article 5(4) point (a)
Article 5(4) point (b), introductory words	Article 5(4) point (b), introductory words
Article 5(4) point (b), first indent	Article 5(4) point (b)(i)
Article 5(4) point (b), second indent	Article 5(4) point (b)(ii)
Article 5(4) point (b), third indent	Article 5(4) point (b)(iii)
Article 5(4) point (b), fourth indent	Article 5(4) point (b)(iv)
Article 5(4) points (c), (d) and (e)	Article 5(4) points (c), (d) and (e)
Article 5(5)	Article 5(5)
Article 6(1), introductory words	Article 6(1), introductory words
Article 6(1) points (a) and (b)	Article 6(1) points (a) and (b)
Article 6(1) point (c)	Article 6(1) point (c), first sentence
Article 6(2) to (5)	Article 6(2) to (5)
Article 7(1)	Article 7(1)
Article 7(3)	Article 7(2)
Article 7(4)	Article 7(3)
Article 7(5)	Article 7(4)
Article 8(1)	Article 6(1) point (c), second sentence
Article 8(2)	Article 8(1) and (2)
Article 8(3)	Article 8(3)
Article 8(4)	Article 8(4)
—	Article 8(5)
Article 8(5)	Article 8(6)
Article 8(6)	Article 8(7)
—	Article 8(8)
Article 9(1) to (9)	Article 9(1) to (9)
Article 9(10)	—
Article 10(1) and (2)	Article 10(1) and (2)
Article 10(3)	Article 10(3) first subparagraph, first sentence
—	Article 10(3) first subparagraph, second sentence
—	Article 10(3) second subparagraph
Article 10(4)	Article 10(4) first subparagraph
—	Article 10(4), second subparagraph
Article 10(5)	Article 10(5), first and fourth subparagraphs
—	Article 10(5), second, third and fifth subparagraphs
Article 10(6)	Article 10(6)
Article 11(1)	Article 11(1)
Article 11(2)	—
Article 11(3)	Article 11(2)
Article 11(4)	Article 11(4) first sentence
—	Article 11(4) second and third sentences
—	Article 11(5) second sentence
Article 11(3)	Article 11(6)
Article 11(5)	—
Article 11(6) and (7)	Article 12
Article 12	Article 13(1) first subparagraph
Article 13(1)	Article 13(1) second subparagraph, introductory words

Regulation (EEC) No 4064/89	This Regulation
Article 13(2) introductory words	Article 13(1) second subparagraph, point (a)
Article 13(2) point (b)	Article 13(1) second subparagraph, point (b)
Article 13(2) point (c)	Article 13(1) second subparagraph, point (c)
Article 13(2) point (e)	Article 13(1) second subparagraph, point (d)
Article 13(2) point (a)	—
Article 13(2) point (d)	Article 13(2)
Article 13(3)	Article 13(3)
Article 13(4) first and second sentences	Article 13(4)
Article 13(4) third sentence	Article 13(5)
Article 13(5), first sentence	—
Article 13(5), second sentence	Article 13(6) first sentence
Article 13(6)	Article 13(6) second sentence
—	—
Article 13(7) and (8)	Article 14(1) introductory words
Article 14(1) introductory words	Article 14(1) point (a)
Article 14(2) point (a)	Article 14(1) point (b)
Article 14(1) point (a)	Article 14(1) point (c)
Article 14(1) points (b) and (c)	Article 14(1) point (d)
Article 14(1) point (d)	—
Article 14(1) points (e) and (f)	Article 14(2) introductory words
Article 14(2) introductory words	Article 14(2) point (a)
Article 14(2) point (d)	Article 14(2) points (b) and (c)
Article 14(2) points (b) and (c)	Article 14(3)
Article 14(3)	Article 14(4)
Article 14(4)	Article 15(1) introductory words
Article 15(1) introductory words	Article 15(1) points (a) and (b)
Article 15(1) points (a) and (b)	Article 15(2) introductory words
Article 15(1) introductory words	Article 15(2) point (a)
Article 15(1) point (c)	Article 15(2) point (b)
Article 15(1) point (d)	Article 15(3)
Article 15(2)	Articles 16 to 20
Articles 16 to 20	Article 21(1)
Article 21(2)	Article 21(2)
Article 21(3)	Article 21(3)
Article 21(4)	Article 22(1)
Article 21(1)	Article 22(3)
—	—
Article 22(1) to (3)	Article 22(4)
Article 22(4)	Article 22(5)
—	—
Article 22(5)	Article 23
Article 23(1)	—
Article 23(2)	Article 24
Article 24	—
Article 25	Article 25(1)
Article 26(1), first subparagraph	—
Article 26(1), second subparagraph	Article 25(2)
Article 26(2)	Article 25(3)
Article 26(3)	—
Annex	

D2

COMMISSION REGULATION (EC) NO 802/2004

of [21] April 2004

implementing Council Regulation (EC) No 139/2004 on the control of concentrations between undertakings

(Text with EEA relevance)

Official Journal L 133, 30.4.2004, p.1

Celex No: 32004R0802

EUR-Lex permanent link: <http://eur-lex.europa.eu/LexUriServ/LexUriServ.do?uri=CELEX:3200 4R0802:EN:NOT>

Notes

The date of this Regulation is shown as corrected by the Corrigendum at OJ L 172, 6.5.2004, p.9. [Ed note: please see the Note on the Lisbon Treaty at p.xvii in regard to article renumbering introduced by the Lisbon Treaty.]

With effect from 1 January 2014, Regulation 802/2004 was amended by Commission Implementing Regulation (EU) No 1269/2013 of 5 December 2013 (OJ L 336, 14.12.2013). The amending regulation was published too late to incorporate the amendments in this edition. The amending regulation is available at: <http://eur-lex.europa.eu/ LexUriServ/LexUriServ.do?uri=CELEX:32013R1269:EN:NOT>.

EEA application: see EEA Agreement, Protocol 21, Article 3(1), point 2, as amended by Decision No 117/2009 of 22 October 2009 (OJ L 334/17.12.2009, p.20).

Commentary

Regulation 802/2004/EC: B&C: 8.007, 8.109, 8.129, 8.133, 8.149, 8.167 F&N: 5.14, 5.168, 5.299, 5.332, 5.341, 5.408, 5.410, 5.476, 5.983, 5.1023, 15.41

Arts 7–10: B&C: 8.143

THE COMMISSION OF THE EUROPEAN COMMUNITIES,

Having regard to the Treaty [on the Functioning of the European Union],

Having regard to the Agreement on the European Economic Area,

Having regard to Council Regulation (EC) No 139/2004 of 20 January 2004 on the control of concentrations between undertakings (EC Merger Regulation),[1] and in particular Article 23(1) thereof,

Having regard to Council Regulation (EEC) No 4064/89 of 21 December 1989 on the control of concentrations between undertakings,[2] as last amended by Regulation (EC) No 1310/97,[3] and in particular Article 23 thereof,

Having consulted the Advisory Committee,

Notes

[1] OJ L 24, 29.1.2004, p.1.

[2] OJ L 395, 30.12.1989, p.1.

[3] OJ L 180, 9.7.1997, p.1.

Whereas:

(1) Council Regulation (EEC) No 4064/89 of 21 December 1989 on the control of concentrations between undertakings has been recast, with substantial amendments to various provisions of that Regulation.

(2) Commission Regulation (EC) No 447/98[1] of 1 March 1998 on the notifications, time-limits and hearings provided for in Council Regulation (EEC) No 4064/89 must be modified in order to take account of those amendments. For the sake of clarity it should therefore be repealed and replaced by a new regulation.

Notes

[1] OJ L 61, 2.3.1998, p.1. Regulation as amended by the 2003 Act of Accession.

(3) The Commission has adopted measures concerning the terms of reference of hearing officers in certain competition proceedings.

(4) Regulation (EC) No 139/2004 is based on the principle of compulsory notification of concentrations before they are put into effect. On the one hand, a notification has important legal consequences which are favourable to the parties to the proposed concentration, while, on the other hand, failure to comply with the obligation to notify renders the parties liable to fines and may also entail civil law disadvantages for them. It is therefore necessary in the interests of legal certainty to define precisely the subject matter and content of the information to be provided in the notification.

(5) It is for the notifying parties to make a full and honest disclosure to the Commission of the facts and circumstances which are relevant for taking a decision on the notified concentration.

(6) Regulation (EC) No 139/2004 also allows the undertakings concerned to request, in a reasoned submission, prior to notification, that a concentration fulfilling the requirements of that Regulation be referred to the Commission by one or more Member States, or referred by the Commission to one or more Member States, as the case may be. It is important to provide the Commission and the competent authorities of the Member States concerned with sufficient information, in order to enable them to assess, within a short period of time, whether or not a referral ought to be made. To that end, the reasoned submission requesting the referral should contain certain specific information.

(7) In order to simplify and expedite examination of notifications and of reasoned submissions, it is desirable to prescribe that forms be used.

(8) Since notification sets in motion legal time-limits pursuant to Regulation (EC) No 139/2004, the conditions governing such time-limits and the time when they become effective should also be determined.

(9) Rules must be laid down in the interests of legal certainty for calculating the time-limits provided for in Regulation (EC) No 139/2004. In particular, the beginning and end of time periods and the circumstances suspending the running of such periods must be determined, with due regard to the requirements resulting from the exceptionally tight legal timeframe available for the proceedings.

(10) The provisions relating to the Commission's procedure must be framed in such a way as to safeguard fully the right to be heard and the rights of defence. For these purposes, the Commission should distinguish between the parties who notify the concentration, other parties involved in the proposed concentration, third parties and parties regarding whom the Commission intends to take a decision imposing a fine or periodic penalty payments.

(11) The Commission should give the notifying parties and other parties involved in the proposed concentration, if they so request, an opportunity before notification to discuss the intended concentration informally and in strict confidence. In addition, the Commission should, after notification, maintain close contact with those parties, to the extent necessary to discuss with them any practical or legal problems which it discovers on a first examination of the case, with a view, if possible, to resolving such problems by mutual agreement.

Commentary
Recital 11: **B&C:** 8.109, 8.136

(12) In accordance with the principle of respect for the rights of defence, the notifying parties must be given the opportunity to submit their comments on all the objections which the Commission

proposes to take into account in its decisions. The other parties involved in the proposed concentration should also be informed of the Commission's objections and should be granted the opportunity to express their views.

(13) Third parties demonstrating a sufficient interest must also be given the opportunity of expressing their views, if they make a written application to that effect.

(14) The various persons entitled to submit comments should do so in writing, both in their own interests and in the interests of sound administration, without prejudice to their right to request a formal oral hearing, where appropriate, to supplement the written procedure. In urgent cases, however, the Commission must be enabled to proceed immediately to formal oral hearings of the notifying parties, of other parties involved or of third parties.

(15) It is necessary to define the rights of persons who are to be heard, to what extent they should be granted access to the Commission's file and on what conditions they may be represented or assisted.

(16) When granting access to the file, the Commission should ensure the protection of business secrets and other confidential information. The Commission should be able to ask undertakings that have submitted documents or statements to identify confidential information.

Commentary
Recital 16: B&C: 8.149

---

(17) In order to enable the Commission to carry out a proper assessment of commitments offered by the notifying parties with a view to rendering the concentration compatible with the common market, and to ensure due consultation with other parties involved, with third parties and with the authorities of the Member States as provided for in Regulation (EC) No 139/2004, in particular Article 18(1), 18(4), Article 19(1), 19(2), 19(3) and 19(5) thereof, the procedure and time-limits for submitting the commitments referred to in Article 6(2) and Article 8(2) of that Regulation should be laid down.

(18) It is also necessary to define the rules applicable to certain time limits set by the Commission.

(19) The Advisory Committee on Concentrations must deliver its opinion on the basis of a preliminary draft decision. It must therefore be consulted on a case after the inquiry in to that case has been completed. Such consultation does not, however, prevent the Commission from reopening an inquiry if need be.

HAS ADOPTED THIS REGULATION:

CHAPTER I
SCOPE

Article 1
Scope

This Regulation shall apply to the control of concentrations conducted pursuant to Regulation (EC) No 139/2004.

CHAPTER II
NOTIFICATIONS AND OTHER SUBMISSIONS

Article 2
Persons entitled to submit notifications

1. Notifications shall be submitted by the persons or undertakings referred to in Article 4(2) of Regulation (EC) No 139/2004.

2. Where notifications are signed by representatives of persons or of undertakings, such representatives shall produce written proof that they are authorised to act.

3. Joint notifications shall be submitted by a joint representative who is authorised to transmit and to receive documents on behalf of all notifying parties.

Commentary
Art 2(1): B&C: 8.112
Art 2(2): B&C: 8.118
Art 2(3): B&C: 8.112

Article 3
Submission of notifications

1. Notifications shall be submitted in the manner prescribed by Form CO as set out in Annex I. Under the conditions set out in Annex II, notifications may be submitted in Short Form as defined therein. Joint notifications shall be submitted on a single form.

2. One original and [38] copies of the Form CO and the supporting documents shall be submitted to the Commission. The notification shall be delivered to the address referred to in Article 23(1) and in the format specified by the Commission.

3. The supporting documents shall be either originals or copies of the originals; in the latter case the notifying parties shall confirm that they are true and complete.

4. Notifications shall be in one of the official languages of the Community. For the notifying parties, this language shall also be the language of the proceeding, as well as that of any subsequent proceedings relating to the same concentration. Supporting documents shall be submitted in their original language. Where the original language is not one of the official languages of the Community, a translation into the language of the proceeding shall be attached.

5. Where notifications are made pursuant to Article 57 of the Agreement on the European Economic Area, they may also be submitted in one of the official languages of the EFTA States or the working language of the EFTA Surveillance Authority. If the language chosen for the notifications is not an official language of the Community, the notifying parties shall simultaneously supplement all documentation with a translation into an official language of the Community. The language which is chosen for the translation shall determine the language used by the Commission as the language of the proceeding for the notifying parties.

Notes
The amendment shown in square brackets in Article 3(2) was made by Commission Regulation (EU) No 519/2013 of 21 February 2013 adapting certain regulations and decisions by reason of the accession of Croatia (OJ L 158, 10.6.2013, p. 74), with effect from 1 July 2013.

Commentary
Art 3(1): B&C: 8.117, 8.121, 8.124 F&N: 5.409
Art 3(2): B&C: 8.118 F&N: 5.410
Art 3(3): B&C: 8.118
Art 3(4): B&C: 8.119
Art 3(5): B&C: 8.119

Article 4
Information and documents to be provided

1. Notifications shall contain the information, including documents, requested in the applicable forms set out in the Annexes. The information shall be correct and complete.

2. The Commission may dispense with the obligation to provide any particular information in the notification, including documents, or with any other requirement specified in Annexes I and II where the Commission considers that compliance with those obligations or requirements is not necessary for the examination of the case.

3. The Commission shall without delay acknowledge in writing to the notifying parties or their representatives receipt of the notification and of any reply to a letter sent by the Commission pursuant to Article 5(2) and 5(3).

Commentary
Art 4(1): B&C: 8.121
Art 4(2): B&C: 8.114

Article 5
Effective date of notification

1. Subject to paragraphs 2, 3 and 4, notifications shall become effective on the date on which they are received by the Commission.

2. Where the information, including documents, contained in the notification is incomplete in any material respect, the Commission shall inform the notifying parties or their representatives in writing without delay. In such cases, the notification shall become effective on the date on which the complete information is received by the Commission.

3. Material changes in the facts contained in the notification coming to light subsequent to the notification which the notifying parties know or ought to know, or any new information coming to light subsequent to the notification which the parties know or ought to know and which would have had to be notified if known at the time of notification, shall be communicated to the Commission without delay. In such cases, when these material changes or new information could have a significant effect on the appraisal of the concentration, the notification may be considered by the Commission as becoming effective on the date on which the relevant information is received by the Commission; the Commission shall inform the notifying parties or their representatives of this in writing and without delay.

4. Incorrect or misleading information shall be considered to be incomplete information.

5. When the Commission publishes the fact of the notification pursuant to Article 4(3) of Regulation (EC) No 139/2004, it shall specify the date upon which the notification has been received. Where, further to the application of paragraphs 2, 3 and 4 of this Article, the effective date of notification is later than the date specified in that publication, the Commission shall issue a further publication in which it shall state the later date.

Commentary
Art 5(1): B&C: 8.113
Art 5(2): B&C: 8.113
Art 5(3): B&C: 8.113, 8.121
Art 5(5): B&C: 8.133

Article 6
Specific provisions relating to reasoned submissions, supplements and certifications

1. Reasoned submissions within the meaning of Article 4(4) and 4(5) of Regulation (EC) No 139/2004 shall contain the information, including documents, requested in accordance with Annex III to this Regulation.

2. Article 2, Article 3(1), third sentence, 3(2) to (5), Article 4, Article 5(1), 5(2) first sentence, 5(3), 5(4), Article 21 and Article 23 of this Regulation shall apply *mutatis mutandis* to reasoned submissions within the meaning of Article 4(4) and 4(5) of Regulation (EC) No 139/2004.

Article 2, Article 3(1), third sentence, 3(2) to (5), Article 4, Article 5(1) to (4), Article 21 and Article 23 of this Regulation shall apply *mutatis mutandis* to supplements to notifications and certifications within the meaning of Article 10(5) of Regulation (EC) No 139/2004.

Commentary
Art 6: B&C: 8.089
Art 6(1)(c): B&C: 8.131
Art 6(2): B&C: 8.118

Part D Mergers and
Concentrations

CHAPTER III
TIME-LIMITS

Article 7
Beginning of time periods

Time periods shall begin on the working day, as defined in Article 24 of this Regulation, following the event to which the relevant provision of Regulation (EC) No 139/2004 refers.

Commentary
Art 7: B&C: 8.134

Article 8
Expiry of time periods

A time period calculated in working days shall expire at the end of its last working day.

A time period set by the Commission in terms of a calendar date shall expire at the end of that day.

Commentary
Art 8: B&C: 8.134

Article 9
Suspension of time limit

1. The time limits referred to in Articles 9(4), Article 10(1) and 10(3) of Regulation (EC) No 139/2004 shall be suspended where the Commission has to take a decision pursuant to Article 11(3) or Article 13(4) of that Regulation, on any of the following grounds:

(a) information which the Commission has requested pursuant to Article 11(2) of Regulation (EC) No 139/2004 from one of the notifying parties or another involved party, as defined in Article 11 of this Regulation, is not provided or not provided in full within the time limit fixed by the Commission;

(b) information which the Commission has requested pursuant to Article 11(2) of Regulation (EC) No 139/2004 from a third party, as defined in Article 11 of this Regulation, is not provided or not provided in full within the time limit fixed by the Commission owing to circumstances for which one of the notifying parties or another involved party, as defined in Article 11 of this Regulation, is responsible;

(c) one of the notifying parties or another involved party, as defined in Article 11 of this Regulation, has refused to submit to an inspection deemed necessary by the Commission on the basis of Article 13(1) of Regulation (EC) No 139/2004 or to cooperate in the carrying out of such an inspection in accordance with Article 13(2) of that Regulation;

(d) the notifying parties have failed to inform the Commission of material changes in the facts contained in the notification, or of any new information of the kind referred to in Article 5(3) of this Regulation.

2. The time limits referred to in Articles 9(4), Article 10(1) and 10(3) of Regulation (EC) No 139/2004 shall be suspended where the Commission has to take a decision pursuant to Article 11(3) of that Regulation, without proceeding first by way of simple request for information, owing to circumstances for which one of the undertakings involved in the concentration is responsible.

3. The time limits referred to in Articles 9(4), Article 10(1) and (3) of Regulation (EC) No 139/2004 shall be suspended:

(a) in the cases referred to in points (a) and (b) of paragraph 1, for the period between the expiry of the time limit set in the simple request for information, and the receipt of the complete and correct information required by decision;

(b) in the cases referred to in point (c) of paragraph 1, for the period between the unsuccessful attempt to carry out the inspection and the completion of the inspection ordered by decision;

(c) in the cases referred to in point (d) of paragraph 1, for the period between the occurrence of the change in the facts referred to therein and the receipt of the complete and correct information.

(d) in the cases referred to in paragraph 2 for the period between the expiry of the time limit set in the decision and the receipt of the complete and correct information required by decision.

4. The suspension of the time limit shall begin on the working day following the date on which the event causing the suspension occurred. It shall expire with the end of the day on which the reason for suspension is removed. Where such a day is not a working day, the suspension of the time-limit shall expire with the end of the following working day.

Commentary

Art 9(1): B&C: 8.181
Art 9(1)(a): B&C: 8.135, 8.144
Art 9(1)(c): B&C: 8.135, 8.144
Art 9(1)(d): B&C: 8.135, 8.144
Art 9(2): B&C: 8.144, 8.181
Art 9(3): B&C: 8.144
Art 9(4): B&C: 8.135, 8.144

Article 10
Compliance with the time-limits

1. The time limits referred to in Article 4(4), fourth subparagraph, Article 9(4), Article 10(1) and (3), and Article 22(3) of Regulation (EC) No 139/2004 shall be met where the Commission has taken the relevant decision before the end of the period.

2. The time limits referred to in Article 4(4), second subparagraph, Article 4(5), third subparagraph, Article 9(2), Article 22(1), second subparagraph, and 22(2), second subparagraph, of Regulation (EC) No 139/2004 shall be met by a Member State concerned where that Member State, before the end of the period, informs the Commission in writing or makes or joins the request in writing, as the case may be.

3. The time limit referred to in Article 9(6) of Regulation (EC) No 139/2004 shall be met where the competent authority of a Member State concerned informs the undertakings concerned in the manner set out in that provision before the end of the period.

CHAPTER IV
EXERCISE OF THE RIGHT TO BE HEARD; HEARINGS

Article 11
Parties to be heard

For the purposes of the rights to be heard pursuant to Article 18 of Regulation (EC) No 139/2004, the following parties are distinguished:

(a) notifying parties, that is, persons or undertakings submitting a notification pursuant to Article 4(2) of Regulation (EC) No 139/2004;

(b) other involved parties, that is, parties to the proposed concentration other than the notifying parties, such as the seller and the undertaking which is the target of the concentration;

(c) third persons, that is natural or legal persons, including customers, suppliers and competitors, provided they demonstrate a sufficient interest within the meaning of Article 18(4), second sentence, of Regulation (EC) No 139/2004, which is the case in particular

— for members of the administrative or management bodies of the undertakings concerned or the recognised representatives of their employees;

— for consumer associations, where the proposed concentration concerns products or services used by final consumers[;]

(d) parties regarding whom the Commission intends to take a decision pursuant to Article 14 or Article 15 of Regulation (EC) No 139/2004.

Commentary
Art 11: B&C: 8.112, 8.150

Article 12
Decisions on the suspension of concentrations

1. Where the Commission intends to take a decision pursuant to Article 7(3) of Regulation (EC) No 139/2004 which adversely affects one or more of the parties, it shall, pursuant to Article 18(1) of that Regulation, inform the notifying parties and other involved parties in writing of its objections and shall set a time limit within which they may make known their views in writing.

2. Where the Commission, pursuant to Article 18(2) of Regulation (EC) No 139/2004, has taken a decision referred to in paragraph 1 of this Article provisionally without having given the notifying parties and other involved parties the opportunity to make known their views, it shall without delay send them the text of the provisional decision and shall set a time limit within which they may make known their views in writing.

Once the notifying parties and other involved parties have made known their views, the Commission shall take a final decision annulling, amending or confirming the provisional decision. Where they have not made known their views in writing within the time limit set, the Commission's provisional decision shall become final with the expiry of that period.

Commentary
Art 12(1): B&C: 8.129
Art 12(2): B&C: 8.129

Article 13
Decisions on the substance of the case

1. Where the Commission intends to take a decision pursuant to Article 6(3) or Article 8(2) to (6) of Regulation (EC) No 139/2004, it shall, before consulting the Advisory Committee on Concentrations, hear the parties pursuant to Article 18(1) and (3) of that Regulation.

Article 12(2) of this Regulation shall apply *mutatis mutandis* where, in application of Article 18(2) of Regulation (EC) No 139/2004, the Commission has taken a decision pursuant to Article 8(5) of that Regulation provisionally.

2. The Commission shall address its objections in writing to the notifying parties.

The Commission shall, when giving notice of objections, set a time limit within which the notifying parties may inform the Commission of their comments in writing.

The Commission shall inform other involved parties in writing of these objections.

The Commission shall also set a time limit within which those other involved parties may inform the Commission of their comments in writing.

The Commission shall not be obliged to take into account comments received after the expiry of a time limit which it has set.

3. The parties to whom the Commission's objections have been addressed or who have been informed of those objections shall, within the time limit set, submit in writing their comments on the objections. In their written comments, they may set out all facts and matters known to them which are relevant to their defence, and shall attach any relevant documents as proof of the facts set out. They may also propose that the Commission hear persons who may corroborate those facts. They shall submit one original and 10 copies of their comments to the Commission to the address of the Commission's Directorate General for Competition. An electronic copy shall also be submitted at the same address and in the format specified by the Commission. The Commission shall forward copies of such written comments without delay to the competent authorities of the Member States.

4. Where the Commission intends to take a decision pursuant to Article 14 or Article 15 of Regulation (EC) No 139/2004, it shall, before consulting the Advisory Committee on Concentrations, hear

pursuant to Article 18(1) and (3) of that Regulation the parties regarding whom the Commission intends to take such a decision.

The procedure provided for in paragraph 2, first and second subparagraphs, and paragraph 3 shall apply, *mutatis mutandis*.

Commentary
Art 13(2): **B&C:** 8.148, 8.151

Article 14
Oral hearings

1. Where the Commission intends to take a decision pursuant to Article 6(3) or Article 8(2) to (6) of Regulation (EC) No 139/2004, it shall afford the notifying parties who have so requested in their written comments the opportunity to develop their arguments in a formal oral hearing. It may also, at other stages in the proceedings, afford the notifying parties the opportunity of expressing their views orally.

2. Where the Commission intends to take a decision pursuant to Article 6(3) or Article 8(2) to (6) of Regulation (EC) No 139/2004, it shall also afford other involved parties who have so requested in their written comments the opportunity to develop their arguments in a formal oral hearing. It may also, at other stages in the proceedings, afford other involved parties the opportunity of expressing their views orally.

3. Where the Commission intends to take a decision pursuant to Article 14 or Article 15 of Regulation (EC) No 139/2004, it shall afford parties on whom it proposes to impose a fine or periodic penalty payment the opportunity to develop their arguments in a formal oral hearing, if so requested in their written comments. It may also, at other stages in the proceedings, afford such parties the opportunity of expressing their views orally.

Commentary
Art 14(1): **B&C:** 8.152, 8.164
Art 14(2): **B&C:** 8.112, 8.152

Article 15
Conduct of formal oral hearings

1. Formal oral hearings shall be conducted by the Hearing Officer in full independence.

2. The Commission shall invite the persons to be heard to attend the formal oral hearing on such date as it shall determine.

3. The Commission shall invite the competent authorities of the Member States to take part in any formal oral hearing.

4. Persons invited to attend shall either appear in person or be represented by legal representatives or by representatives authorised by their constitution as appropriate. Undertakings and associations of undertakings may also be represented by a duly authorised agent appointed from among their permanent staff.

5. Persons heard by the Commission may be assisted by their lawyers or other qualified and duly authorised persons admitted by the Hearing Officer.

6. Formal oral hearings shall not be public. Each person may be heard separately or in the presence of other persons invited to attend, having regard to the legitimate interest of the undertakings in the protection of their business secrets and other confidential information.

7. The Hearing Officer may allow all parties within the meaning of Article 11, the Commission services and the competent authorities of the Member States to ask questions during the formal oral hearing.

The Hearing Officer may hold a preparatory meeting with the parties and the Commission services, so as to facilitate the efficient organisation of the formal oral hearing.

8. The statements made by each person heard shall be recorded. Upon request, the recording of the formal oral hearing shall be made available to the persons who attended that hearing. Regard shall be had to the legitimate interest of the undertakings in the protection of their business secrets and other confidential information.

Commentary
Art 15(3): B&C: 8.152, 8.164
Art 15(6): B&C: 8.152
Art 15(7): B&C: 8.152
Art 15(8): B&C: 8.152

Article 16
Hearing of third persons

1. If third persons apply in writing to be heard pursuant to Article 18(4), second sentence, of Regulation (EC) No 139/2004, the Commission shall inform them in writing of the nature and subject matter of the procedure and shall set a time limit within which they may make known their views.

2. The third persons referred to in paragraph 1 shall make known their views in writing within the time limit set. The Commission may, where appropriate, afford such third parties who have so requested in their written comments the opportunity to participate in a formal hearing. It may also in other cases afford such third parties the opportunity of expressing their views orally.

3. The Commission may likewise invite any other natural or legal person to express its views, in writing as well as orally, including at a formal oral hearing.

Commentary
Art 16(1): B&C: 8.131
Art 16(2): B&C: 8.131, 8.152
Art 16(3): B&C: 8.131, 8.152

CHAPTER V
ACCESS TO THE FILE AND TREATMENT OF CONFIDENTIAL INFORMATION

Article 17
Access to the file and use of documents

1. If so requested, the Commission shall grant access to the file to the parties to whom it has addressed a statement of objections, for the purpose of enabling them to exercise their rights of defence. Access shall be granted after the notification of the statement of objections.

2. The Commission shall, upon request, also give the other involved parties who have been informed of the objections access to the file in so far as this is necessary for the purposes of preparing their comments.

3. The right of access to the file shall not extend to confidential information, or to internal documents of the Commission or of the competent authorities of the Member States. The right of access to the file shall equally not extend to correspondence between the Commission and the competent authorities of the Member States or between the latter.

4. Documents obtained through access to the file pursuant to this Article may only be used for the purposes of the relevant proceeding pursuant to Regulation (EC) No 139/2004.

Commentary
Art 17(1): B&C: 8.149
Art 17(2): B&C: 8.149
Art 17(3): B&C: 8.149
Art 17(4): B&C: 8.149

Article 18
Confidential information

1. Information, including documents, shall not be communicated or made accessible by the Commission in so far as it contains business secrets or other confidential information the disclosure of which is not considered necessary by the Commission for the purpose of the procedure.

2. Any person which makes known its views or comments pursuant to Articles 12, Article 13 and Article 16 of this Regulation, or supplies information pursuant to Article 11 of Regulation (EC) No 139/2004, or subsequently submits further information to the Commission in the course of the same procedure, shall clearly identify any material which it considers to be confidential, giving reasons, and provide a separate non-confidential version by the date set by the Commission.

3. Without prejudice to paragraph 2, the Commission may require persons referred to in Article 3 of Regulation (EC) No 139/2004, undertakings and associations of undertakings in all cases where they produce or have produced documents or statements pursuant to Regulation (EC) No 139/2004 to identify the documents or parts of documents which they consider to contain business secrets or other confidential information belonging to them and to identify the undertakings with regard to which such documents are to be considered confidential.

The Commission may also require persons referred to in Article 3 of Regulation (EC) No 139/2004, undertakings or associations of undertakings to identify any part of a statement of objections, case summary or a decision adopted by the Commission which in their view contains business secrets.

Where business secrets or other confidential information are identified, the persons, undertakings and associations of undertakings shall give reasons and provide a separate non-confidential version by the date set by the Commission.

[4. If persons, undertakings or associations of undertakings fail to comply with paragraphs 2 or 3, the Commission may assume that the documents or statements concerned do not contain confidential information.]

Notes

Paragraph 4, shown in square brackets, was added by Commission Regulation (EC) No 1033/2008 (OJ L 279, 22.10.2008, p. 3), Article 1(1), with effect from 23 October 2008.

Commentary
Art 18(1): **B&C:** 8.183
Art 18(2): **B&C:** 8.120, 8.183
Art 18(3): **B&C:** 8.120, 8.139, 8.183
Art 18(4): **B&C:** 8.120

CHAPTER VI
COMMITMENTS OFFERED BY THE UNDERTAKINGS CONCERNED

Article 19
Time limits for submission of commitments

1. Commitments offered by the undertakings concerned pursuant to Article 6(2) of Regulation (EC) No 139/2004 shall be submitted to the Commission within not more than 20 working days from the date of receipt of the notification.

2. Commitments offered by the undertakings concerned pursuant to Article 8(2) of Regulation (EC) No 139/2004 shall be submitted to the Commission within not more than 65 working days from the date on which proceedings were initiated.

Where pursuant to Article 10(3), second subparagraph, of Regulation (EC) No 139/2004 the period for the adoption of a decision pursuant to Article 8(1), (2) and (3) is extended, the period of 65 working days for the submission of commitments shall automatically be extended by the same number of working days.

In exceptional circumstances, the Commission may accept commitments offered after the expiry of the time limit for their submission within the meaning of this paragraph provided that the procedure provided for in Article 19(5) of Regulation (EC) No 139/2004 is complied with.

3. Articles 7, 8 and 9 shall apply *mutatis mutandis.*

Commentary
Art 19(1): **B&C:** 8.168
Art 19(2): **B&C:** 8.169

Article 20
Procedure for the submission of commitments

1. One original and 10 copies of commitments offered by the undertakings concerned pursuant to Article 6(2) or Article 8(2) of Regulation (EC) No 139/2004 shall be submitted to the Commission at the address of the Commission's Directorate General for Competition. An electronic copy shall also be submitted at the same address and in the format specified by the Commission. The Commission shall forward copies of such commitments without delay to the competent authorities of the Member States.

[1a. In addition to the requirements set out in paragraph 1, the undertakings concerned shall, at the same time as offering commitments pursuant to Article 6(2) or Article 8(2) of Regulation (EC) No 139/2004, submit one original and 10 copies of the information and documents prescribed by the Form RM relating to remedies (Form RM) as set out in Annex IV to this Regulation. The information submitted shall be correct and complete.]

2. When offering commitments pursuant to Articles 6(2) or Article 8(2) of Regulation (EC) No 139/2004, the undertakings concerned shall at the same time clearly identify any information which they consider to be confidential, giving reasons, and shall provide a separate non-confidential version.

Notes
Paragraph 1a, shown in square brackets, was inserted by Commission Regulation (EC) No 1033/2008 (OJ L 279, 22.10.2008, p. 3), Article 1(2), with effect from 23 October 2008.

Commentary
Art 20(1): **B&C:** 8.168

[Article 20a
Trustees

1. The commitments offered by the undertakings concerned pursuant to Article 6(2) or Article 8(2) of Regulation (EC) No 139/2004 may include, at the own expense of the undertakings concerned, the appointment of an independent trustee (or trustees) assisting the Commission in overseeing the parties' compliance with the commitments or having a mandate to implement the commitments. The trustee may be appointed by the parties, after the Commission has approved its identity, or by the Commission. The trustee shall carry out its tasks under the supervision of the Commission.

2. The Commission may attach such trustee-related provisions of the commitments as conditions and obligations pursuant to Article 6(2) or Article 8(2) of Regulation (EC) No 139/2004.]

Notes
Article 20a, shown in square brackets, was inserted by Commission Regulation (EC) No 1033/2008 (OJ L 279, 22.10.2008, p. 3), Article 1(3), with effect from 23 October 2008.

Commentary
Art 20a: **B&C:** 8.175

CHAPTER VII
MISCELLANEOUS PROVISIONS

Article 21
Transmission of documents

1. Transmission of documents and invitations from the Commission to the addressees may be effected in any of the following ways:

(a) delivery by hand against receipt;
(b) registered letter with acknowledgement of receipt;
(c) fax with a request for acknowledgement of receipt;
(d) telex;
(e) electronic mail with a request for acknowledgement of receipt.

2. Unless otherwise provided in this Regulation, paragraph 1 also applies to the transmission of documents from the notifying parties, from other involved parties or from third parties to the Commission.

3. Where a document is sent by telex, by fax or by electronic mail, it shall be presumed that it has been received by the addressee on the day on which it was sent.

Commentary
Art 21: B&C: 8.139, 8.161

Article 22
Setting of time limits

In setting the time limits provided for pursuant to Article 12(1) and (2), Article 13(2) and Article 16(1), the Commission shall have regard to the time required for the preparation of statements and to the urgency of the case. It shall also take account of working days as well as public holidays in the country of receipt of the Commission's communication.

Time limits shall be set in terms of a precise calendar date.

Commentary
Art 22: B&C: 8.134, 8.151

Article 23
Receipt of documents by the Commission

1. In accordance with the provisions of Article 5(1) of this Regulation, notifications shall be delivered to the Commission at the address of the Commission's Directorate General for Competition as published by the Commission in the *Official Journal of the European Union*.

2. Additional information requested to complete notifications must reach the Commission at the address referred to in paragraph 1.

3. Written comments on Commission communications pursuant to Article 12(1) and (2), Article 13(2) and Article 16(1) of this Regulation must have reached the Commission at the address referred to in paragraph 1 before the expiry of the time limit set in each case.

Commentary
Art 23: B&C: 8.118

Article 24
Definition of working days

The expression working days in Regulation (EC) No 139/2004 and in this Regulation means all days other than Saturdays, Sundays, and Commission holidays as published in the *Official Journal of the European Union* before the beginning of each year.

Commentary
Art 24: B&C: 8.134

Article 25
Repeal and transitional provision

1. Without prejudice to paragraphs 2 and 3, Regulation (EC) No 447/98 is repealed with effect from 1 May 2004.

References to the repealed Regulation shall be construed as references to this Regulation.

2. Regulation (EC) No 447/98 shall continue to apply to any concentration falling within the scope of Regulation (EEC) No 4064/89.

3. For the purposes of paragraph 2, Sections 1 to 12 of the Annex to Regulation (EC) No 447/98 shall be replaced by Sections 1 to 11 of Annex I to this Regulation. In such cases references in those sections to the "EC Merger Regulation" and to the "Implementing Regulation" shall be read as referring to the corresponding provisions of Regulation (EEC) No 4064/89 and Regulation (EC) No 447/98, respectively.

Article 26
Entry into force

This Regulation shall enter into force on 1 May 2004.

This Regulation shall be binding in its entirety and directly applicable in all Member States.

Done at Brussels, [21] April 2004.

Notes
The date of this Regulation is shown as corrected by the Corrigendum at OJ L 172, 6.5.2004, p. 9.

Annex I
Form CO Relating to the Notification of a Concentration Pursuant to Regulation (EC) No 139/2004

Commentary
Annex I: B&C: 8.114, 8.117 F&N: 5.341, 5.404, 5.405, 5.409, 5.410

1. INTRODUCTION

1.1. The purpose of this Form

[This Form specifies the information that must be provided by notifying parties when submitting a notification to the European Commission of a proposed merger, acquisition or other concentration. The merger control system of the European Union is laid down in Council Regulation (EC) No 139/2004 (hereinafter referred to as "the EC Merger Regulation"), and in Commission Regulation (EC) No 802/2004 (hereinafter referred to as "the Implementing Regulation"), to which this Form CO is annexed.[1] The text of these regulations, as well as other relevant documents, can be found on the Competition page of the Commission's Europa web site. Your attention is drawn to the corresponding provisions of the Agreement on the European Economic Area (hereinafter referred to as "the EEA Agreement").[2]]

In order to limit the time and expense involved in complying with various merger control procedures in several individual countries, the European Union has put in place a system of merger control by which concentrations having a Community dimension (normally, where the parties to the concentration fulfil certain turnover thresholds)[3] are assessed by the European Commission in a single procedure (the "one stop shop" principle).

[Mergers which do not meet the turnover thresholds may fall within the competence of the Member States' and/or the EFTA States' authorities in charge of merger control.]

The EC Merger Regulation requires the Commission to reach a decision within a legal deadline. In an initial phase the Commission normally has 25 working days to decide whether to clear the concentration or to "initiate proceedings", i.e., to undertake an in-depth investigation.[4] If the Commission decides to initiate proceedings, it normally has to take a final decision on the operation within no more than 90 working days of the date when proceedings are initiated.[5] In view of these deadlines, and for the "one stop shop" principle to work, it is essential that the Commission is provided, in a timely fashion, with the information required to carry out the necessary investigation and to assess the impact of the concentration on the markets concerned. This requires that a certain amount of information be provided at the time of notification.

It is recognised that the information requested in this Form is substantial. However, experience has shown that, depending on the specific characteristics of the case, not all information is always necessary for an adequate examination of the proposed concentration. Accordingly, if you consider that any particular information requested by this Form may not be necessary for the Commission's examination of the case, you are encouraged to ask the Commission to dispense with the obligation to provide certain information ("waiver"). See Section 1.3(g) for more details.

Pre-notification contacts are extremely valuable to both the notifying parties and the Commission in determining the precise amount of information required in a notification and, in the majority of cases, will result in a significant reduction of the information required. Notifying parties may refer to the Commission's Best Practices on the Conduct of EC Merger Control Proceedings, which provides guidance on pre-notification contacts and the preparation of notifications.

In addition, it should be noted that certain concentrations, which are unlikely to pose any competition concerns, can be notified using a Short Form, which is attached to the Implementing Regulation, as Annex II.

Notes

[1] Council Regulation (EC) No 139/2004 of 20 January 2004 (OJ L 24, 29.1.2004, p. 1).

[2] See in particular Article 57 of the EEA Agreement, point 1 of Annex XIV to the EEA Agreement, Protocols 21 and 24 to the EEA Agreement, as well as Protocol 4 to the Agreement between the EFTA States on the establishment of a Surveillance Authority and a Court of Justice (hereinafter referred to as the 'Surveillance and Court Agreement'). Any reference to EFTA States shall be understood to mean those EFTA States which are Contracting Parties to the EEA Agreement. As of 1 May 2004, these States are Iceland, Liechtenstein and Norway.]

[3] The term "concentration" is defined in Article 3 of the EC Merger Regulation and the term "Community dimension" in Article 1 thereof. Furthermore, Article 4(5) provides that in certain circumstances where the Community turnover thresholds are not met, notifying parties may request that the Commission treat their proposed concentration as having a Community dimension.

[4] See Article 10(1) of the EC Merger Regulation.

[5] See Article 10(3) of the EC Merger Regulation.

Point 1.1 was amended as shown in square brackets by Commission Regulation (EC) No 1033/2008 (OJ L 279, 22.10.2008, p. 3) with effect from 23 October 2008.

1.2. Who must notify

In the case of a merger within the meaning of Article 3(1)(a) of the EC Merger Regulation or the acquisition of joint control of an undertaking within the meaning of Article 3(1)(b) of the EC Merger Regulation, the notification shall be completed jointly by the parties to the merger or by those acquiring joint control, as the case may be.[1]

In case of the acquisition of a controlling interest in one undertaking by another, the acquirer must complete the notification.

In the case of a public bid to acquire an undertaking, the bidder must complete the notification. Each party completing the notification is responsible for the accuracy of the information which it provides.

Notes

[1] See Article 4(2) of the EC Merger Regulation.

1.3. The requirement for a correct and complete notification

All information required by this Form must be correct and complete. The information required must be supplied in the appropriate Section of this Form.

In particular you should note that:

(a) In accordance with Article 10(1) of the EC Merger Regulation and Article 5(2) and (4) of the Implementing Regulation, the time-limits of the EC Merger Regulation linked to the notification will not begin to run until all the information that has to be supplied with the notification has been received by the Commission. This requirement is to ensure that the Commission is able to assess the notified concentration within the strict time-limits provided by the EC Merger Regulation.

(b) The notifying parties should verify, in the course of preparing their notification, that contact names and numbers, and in particular fax numbers and e-mail addresses, provided to the Commission are accurate, relevant and up-to-date.

(c) Incorrect or misleading information in the notification will be considered to be incomplete information (Article 5(4) of the Implementing Regulation).

(d) If a notification is incomplete, the Commission will inform the notifying parties or their representatives in writing and without delay. The notification will only become effective on the date on which the complete and accurate information is received by the Commission (Article 10(1) of the EC Merger Regulation, Articles 5(2) and (4) of the Implementing Regulation).

(e) Under Article 14(1)(a) of the EC Merger Regulation, notifying parties who, either intentionally or negligently, supply incorrect or misleading information, may be liable to fines of up to 1% of the aggregate turnover of the undertaking concerned. In addition, pursuant to Article 6(3)(a) and Article 8(6)(a) of the EC Merger Regulation the Commission may revoke its decision on the compatibility of a notified concentration where it is based on incorrect information for which one of the undertakings is responsible.

(f) You may request in writing that the Commission accept that the notification is complete notwithstanding the failure to provide information required by this Form, if such information is not reasonably available to you in part or in whole (for example, because of the unavailability of information on a target company during a contested bid). The Commission will consider such a request, provided that you give reasons for the unavailability of that information, and provide your best estimates for missing data together with the sources for the estimates. Where possible, indications as to where any of the requested information that is unavailable to you could be obtained by the Commission should also be provided.

(g) You may request in writing that the Commission accept that the notification is complete notwithstanding the failure to provide information required by this Form, if you consider that any particular information required, in the full or short form version, may not be necessary for the Commission's examination of the case. The Commission will consider such a request, provided that you give adequate reasons why that information is not relevant and necessary to its inquiry into the notified operation. You should explain this during your pre-notification contacts with the Commission and, submit a written request for a waiver, asking the Commission to dispense with the obligation to provide that information, pursuant to Article 4(2) of the Implementing Regulation.

1.4. How to notify

The notification must be completed in one of the official languages of the European Community. This language will thereafter be the language of the proceedings for all notifying parties. Where notifications are made in accordance with Article 12 of Protocol 24 to the EEA Agreement in an official language of an EFTA State which is not an official language of the Community, the notification must simultaneously be supplemented with a translation into an official language of the Community.

The information requested by this Form is to be set out using the sections and paragraph numbers of the Form, signing a declaration as provided in Section 11, and annexing supporting documentation. In completing Sections 7 to 9 of this Form, the notifying parties are invited to consider whether, for purposes of clarity, these sections are best presented in numerical order, or whether they can be grouped together for each individual affected market (or group of affected markets).

For the sake of clarity, certain information may be put in annexes. However, it is essential that all key substantive pieces of information, and in particular market share information for the parties and their largest competitors, are presented in the body of Form CO. Annexes to this Form shall only be used to supplement the information supplied in the Form itself.

Contact details must be provided in a format provided by the Commission's Directorate-General for Competition (DG Competition). For a proper investigatory process, it is essential that the contact details are accurate. Multiple instances of incorrect contact details may be a ground for declaring a notification incomplete.

Supporting documents are to be submitted in their original language; where this is not an official language of the Community, they must be translated into the language of the proceeding (Article 3(4) of the Implementing Regulation).

Supporting documents may be originals or copies of the originals. In the latter case, the notifying party must confirm that they are true and complete.

One original and [38] copies of the Form CO and the supporting documents shall be submitted to the Commission's Directorate-General for Competition.

The notification shall be delivered to the address referred to in Article 23 (1) of the Implementing Regulation and in the format specified by the Commission from time to time. This address is published in the *Official Journal of the European Union*. The notification must be delivered to the Commission on working days as defined by Article 24 of the Implementing Regulation. In order to enable it to be registered on the same day, it must be delivered before 17.00 hrs on Mondays to Thursdays and before 16.00 hrs on Fridays and workdays preceding public holidays and other holidays as determined by the Commission and published in the *Official Journal of the European Union*. The security instructions given on DG Competition's website must be adhered to.

Notes

The amendment shown in square brackets was made by Commission Regulation (EU) No 519/2013 of 21 February 2013 adapting certain regulations and decisions by reason of the accession of Croatia (OJ L 158, 10.6.2013, p. 74), with effect from 1 July 2013.

1.5. Confidentiality

Article [339] of the Treaty and Article 17(2) of the EC Merger Regulation as well as the corresponding provisions of the EEA Agreement[1] require the Commission, the Member States, the EFTA Surveillance Authority and the EFTA States, their officials and other servants not to disclose information they have acquired through the application of the Regulation of the kind covered by the obligation of professional secrecy. The same principle must also apply to protect confidentiality between notifying parties.

If you believe that your interests would be harmed if any of the information you are asked to supply were to be published or otherwise divulged to other parties, submit this information separately with each page clearly marked "Business Secrets". You should also give reasons why this information should not be divulged or published.

In the case of mergers or joint acquisitions, or in other cases where the notification is completed by more than one of the parties, business secrets may be submitted under separate cover, and referred to in the notification as an annex. All such annexes must be included in the submission in order for a notification to be considered complete.

Notes

[1] See, in particular, Article 122 of the EEA Agreement, Article 9 of Protocol 24 to the EEA Agreement and Article 17(2) of Chapter XIII of Protocol 4 to the Agreement between the EFTA States on the establishment of a Surveillance Authority and a Court of Justice (ESA Agreement).

1.6. Definitions and instructions for purposes of this Form

Notifying party or parties: in cases where a notification is submitted by only one of the undertakings who is a party to an operation, "notifying parties" is used to refer only to the undertaking actually submitting the notification.

Party(ies) to the concentration or parties: these terms relate to both the acquiring and acquired parties, or to the merging parties, including all undertakings in which a controlling interest is being acquired or which is the subject of a public bid.

Except where otherwise specified, the terms notifying party(ies) and party(ies) to the concentration include all the undertakings which belong to the same groups as those parties.

Affected markets: Section 6 of this Form requires the notifying parties to define the relevant product markets, and further to identify which of those relevant markets are likely to be affected by the notified operation. This definition of affected market is used as the basis for requiring information for a number of other questions contained in this Form. The definitions thus submitted by the notifying parties are referred to in this Form as the affected market(s). This term can refer to a relevant market made up either of products or of services.

Year: all references to the word year in this Form should be read as meaning calendar year, unless otherwise stated. All information requested in this Form must, unless otherwise specified, relate to the year preceding that of the notification.

The financial data requested in Sections 3.3 to 3.5 must be provided in euros at the average exchange rates prevailing for the years or other periods in question.

All references contained in this Form are to the relevant articles and paragraphs of the EC Merger Regulation, unless otherwise stated.

1.7. Provision of Information to Employees and their Representatives

The Commission would like to draw attention to the obligations to which the parties to a concentration may be subject under Community and/or national rules on information and consultation regarding transactions of a concentrative nature vis-à-vis employees and/or their representatives.

SECTION 1

Description of the concentration

1.1. Provide an executive summary of the concentration, specifying the parties to the concentration, the nature of the concentration (for example, merger, acquisition, or joint venture), the areas of activity of the notifying parties, the markets on which the concentration will have an impact (including the main affected markets),[1] and the strategic and economic rationale for the concentration.

Notes

[1] See Section 6.III for the definition of affected markets.

1.2. Provide a summary (up to 500 words) of the information provided under Section 1.1. It is intended that this summary will be published on the Commission's website at the date of notification. The summary must be drafted so that it contains no confidential information or business secrets.

SECTION 2

Information about the parties

2.1. Information on notifying party (or parties)

Give details of:

2.1.1. name and address of undertaking;

2.1.2. nature of the undertaking's business;

2.1.3. name, address, telephone number, fax number and e-mail address of, and position held by, the appropriate contact person; and

2.1.4. an address for service of the notifying party (or each of the notifying parties) to which documents and, in particular, Commission decisions may be delivered. The name, telephone number and e-mail address of a person at this address who is authorised to accept service must be provided.

2.2. Information on other parties[1] to the concentration

For each party to the concentration (except the notifying party or parties) give details of:

2.2.1. name and address of undertaking;

2.2.2. nature of undertaking's business;

2.2.3. name, address, telephone number, fax number and e-mail address of, and position held by, the appropriate contact person; and

2.2.4. an address for service of the party (or each of the parties) to which documents and, in particular, Commission Decisions may be delivered. The name, e-mail address and telephone number of a person at this address who is authorised to accept service must be provided.

Notes

[1] This includes the target company in the case of a contested bid, in which case the details should be completed as far as is possible.

2.3. Appointment of representatives

Where notifications are signed by representatives of undertakings, such representatives must produce written proof that they are authorised to act. The written proof must contain the name and position of the persons granting such authority.

Provide the following contact details of any representatives who have been authorised to act for any of the parties to the concentration, indicating whom they represent:

2.3.1. name of representative;

2.3.2. address of representative;

2.3.3. name, address, telephone number, fax number and e-mail address of person to be contacted; and

2.3.4. an address of the representative (in Brussels if available) to which correspondence may be sent and documents delivered.

Section 3
Details of the concentration

3.1. Describe the nature of the concentration being notified. In doing so, state:

(a) whether the proposed concentration is a full legal merger, an acquisition of sole or joint control, a full-function joint venture within the meaning of Article 3(4) of the EC Merger Regulation or a contract or other means of conferring direct or indirect control within the meaning of Article 3(2) of the EC Merger Regulation;

(b) whether the whole or parts of parties are subject to the concentration;

(c) a brief explanation of the economic and financial structure of the concentration;

(d) whether any public offer for the securities of one party by another party has the support of the former's supervisory boards of management or other bodies legally representing that party;

(e) the proposed or expected date of any major events designed to bring about the completion of the concentration;

(f) the proposed structure of ownership and control after the completion of the concentration;

(g) any financial or other support received from whatever source (including public authorities) by any of the parties and the nature and amount of this support; and

(h) the economic sectors involved in the concentration.

3.2. State the value of the transaction (the purchase price or the value of all the assets involved, as the case may be).

3.3. For each of the undertakings concerned by the concentration[1] provide the following data[2] for the last financial year:

    3.3.1. world-wide turnover;

    3.3.2. Community-wide turnover;

    3.3.3. EFTA-wide turnover;

    3.3.4. turnover in each Member State;

    3.3.5. turnover in each EFTA State;

    3.3.6. the Member State, if any, in which more than two-thirds of Community-wide turnover is achieved; and

    3.3.7. the EFTA State, if any, in which more than two-thirds of EFTA-wide turnover is achieved.

Notes

[1] See Commission Notice on the concept of undertakings concerned.

[2] See, generally, the Commission Notice on calculation of turnover. Turnover of the acquiring party or parties to the concentration should include the aggregated turnover of all undertakings within the meaning of Article 5(4) of the EC Merger Regulation. Turnover of the acquired party or parties should include the turnover relating to the parts subject to the transaction within the meaning of Article 5(2) of the EC Merger Regulation. Special provisions are contained in Articles 5(3), (4) and 5(5) of the EC Merger Regulation for credit, insurance, other financial institutions and joint undertakings.

3.4. For the purposes of Article 1(3) of the EC Merger Regulation, if the operation does not meet the thresholds set out in Article 1(2), provide the following data for the last financial year:

    3.4.1. the Member States, if any, in which the combined aggregate turnover of all the undertakings concerned is more than EUR 100 million; and

    3.4.2. the Member States, if any, in which the aggregate turnover of each of at least two of the undertakings concerned is more than EUR 25 million.

3.5. For the purposes of determining whether the concentration qualifies as an EFTA cooperation case,[1] provide the following information with respect to the last financial year:

    3.5.1. does the combined turnover of the undertakings concerned in the territory of the EFTA States equal 25% or more of their total turnover in the EEA territory?

    3.5.2. does each of at least two undertakings concerned have a turnover exceeding EUR 250 million in the territory of the EFTA States?

Notes

[1] See Article 57 of the EEA Agreement and, in particular, Article 2(1) of Protocol 24 to the EEA Agreement. A case qualifies as a cooperation case if the combined turnover of the undertakings concerned in the territory of the EFTA States equals 25% or more of their total turnover within the territory covered by the EEA Agreement; or each of at least two undertakings concerned has a turnover exceeding EUR 250 million in the territory of the EFTA States; or the concentration is liable to significantly impede effective competition in the territories of the EFTA States or a substantial part thereof, in particular as a result of the creation or strengthening of a dominant position.]
Footnote 1 was replaced as shown in square brackets by Commission Regulation (EC) No 1033/2008 (OJ L 279, 22.10.2008, p.3) with effect from 23 October 2008.

3.6. Describe the economic rationale of the concentration.

SECTION 4

Ownership and control[1]

Notes

[1] See Articles 3(3), 3(4) and 3(5) and Article 5(4) of the EC Merger Regulation.

4.1. For each of the parties to the concentration provide a list of all undertakings belonging to the same group.

This list must include:

    4.1.1. all undertakings or persons controlling these parties, directly or indirectly;

4.1.2. all undertakings active on any affected market[1] that are controlled, directly or indirectly:
  (a) by these parties;
  (b) by any other undertaking identified in 4.1.1.

For each entry listed above, the nature and means of control should be specified.

The information sought in this section may be illustrated by the use of organization charts or diagrams to show the structure of ownership and control of the undertakings.

Notes

[1] See Section 6 for the definition of affected markets.

4.2. With respect to the parties to the concentration and each undertaking or person identified in response to Section 4.1, provide:

  4.2.1. a list of all other undertakings which are active in affected markets (affected markets are defined in Section 6) in which the undertakings, or persons, of the group hold individually or collectively 10% or more of the voting rights, issued share capital or other securities; in each case, identify the holder and state the percentage held;

  4.2.2. a list for each undertaking of the members of their boards of management who are also members of the boards of management or of the supervisory boards of any other undertaking which is active in affected markets; and (where applicable) for each undertaking a list of the members of their supervisory boards who are also members of the boards of management of any other undertaking which is active in affected markets;
  in each case, identify the name of the other undertaking and the positions held;

  4.2.3. details of acquisitions made during the last three years by the groups identified above (Section 4.1) of undertakings active in affected markets as defined in Section 6.

Information provided here may be illustrated by the use of organization charts or diagrams to give a better understanding.

SECTION 5
Supporting documentation

Notifying parties must provide the following:

5.1. copies of the final or most recent versions of all documents bringing about the concentration, whether by agreement between the parties to the concentration, acquisition of a controlling interest or a public bid;

5.2. in a public bid, a copy of the offer document; if it is unavailable at the time of notification, it should be submitted as soon as possible and not later than when it is posted to shareholders;

5.3. copies of the most recent annual reports and accounts of all the parties to the concentration; and

5.4. copies of all analyses, reports, studies, surveys, and any comparable documents prepared by or for any member(s) of the board of directors, or the supervisory board, or the other person(s) exercising similar functions (or to whom such functions have been delegated or entrusted), or the shareholders' meeting, for the purpose of assessing or analysing the concentration with respect to market shares, competitive conditions, competitors (actual and potential), the rationale of the concentration, potential for sales growth or expansion into other product or geographic markets, and/or general market conditions.[1]

For each of these documents, indicate (if not contained in the document itself) the date of preparation, the name and title of each individual who prepared each such document.

Notes

[1] As set out in introductory Parts 1.1 and 1.3(g), in the context of pre-notification, you may want to discuss with the Commission to what extent dispensation (waivers) to provide the requested documents would be appropriate. Where waivers are sought, the Commission may specify the documents to be provided in a particular case in a request for information under Article 11 of the EC Merger Regulation.

SECTION 6
Market definitions

The relevant product and geographic markets determine the scope within which the market power of the new entity resulting from the concentration must be assessed.[1]

Notes

[1] See Commission Notice on the definition of the relevant market for the purposes of Community competition law.

The notifying party or parties must provide the data requested having regard to the following definitions:

I. Relevant product markets:

A relevant product market comprises all those products and/or services which are regarded as interchangeable or substitutable by the consumer, by reason of the products' characteristics, their prices and their intended use. A relevant product market may in some cases be composed of a number of individual products and/or services which present largely identical physical or technical characteristics and are interchangeable.

Factors relevant to the assessment of the relevant product market include the analysis of why the products or services in these markets are included and why others are excluded by using the above definition, and having regard to, for example, substitutability, conditions of competition, prices, cross-price elasticity of demand or other factors relevant for the definition of the product markets (for example, supply-side substitutability in appropriate cases).

II. Relevant geographic markets:

The relevant geographic market comprises the area in which the undertakings concerned are involved in the supply and demand of relevant products or services, in which the conditions of competition are sufficiently homogeneous and which can be distinguished from neighbouring geographic areas because, in particular, conditions of competition are appreciably different in those areas.

Factors relevant to the assessment of the relevant geographic market include inter alia the nature and characteristics of the products or services concerned, the existence of entry barriers, consumer preferences, appreciable differences in the undertakings' market shares between neighbouring geographic areas or substantial price differences.

III. Affected markets:

For purposes of information required in this Form, affected markets consist of relevant product markets where, in the EEA territory, in the Community, in the territory of the EFTA States, in any Member State or in any EFTA State:

(a) two or more of the parties to the concentration are engaged in business activities in the same product market and where the concentration will lead to a combined market share of 15% or more. These are horizontal relationships;

(b) one or more of the parties to the concentration are engaged in business activities in a product market, which is upstream or downstream of a product market in which any other party to the concentration is engaged, and any of their individual or combined market shares at either level is 25% or more, regardless of whether there is or is not any existing supplier/customer relationship between the parties to the concentration.[1] These are vertical relationships.

Notes

[1] For example, if a party to the concentration holds a market share larger than 25% in a market that is upstream to a market in which the other party is active, then both the upstream and the downstream markets are affected markets. Similarly, if a vertically integrated company merges with another party which is active at the downstream level, and the merger leads to a combined market share downstream of 25% or more, then both the upstream and the downstream markets are affected markets.

On the basis of the above definitions and market share thresholds, provide the following information:[1]

— Identify each affected market within the meaning of Section III, at:
— the EEA, Community or EFTA level;
— the individual Member States or EFTA States level.

Notes

[1] As set out in introductory Parts 1.1 and 1.3(g), in the context of pre-notification, you may want to discuss with the Commission to what extent dispensation (waivers) to provide the requested information would be appropriate for certain affected markets, or for certain other markets (as described under IV).

6.2. In addition, state and explain the parties' view regarding the scope of the relevant geographic market within the meaning of Section II that applies in relation to each affected market identified above.

Notes

There is no paragraph 6.1 in the original instrument.

IV. Other markets in which the notified operation may have a significant impact

6.3. On the basis of the above definitions, describe the product and geographic scope of markets other than affected markets identified in Section 6.1 in which the notified operation may have a significant impact, for example, where:
   (a) any of the parties to the concentration has a market share larger than 25% and any other party to the concentration is a potential competitor into that market. A party may be considered a potential competitor, in particular, where it has plans to enter a market, or has developed or pursued such plans in the past two years;
   (b) any of the parties to the concentration has a market share larger than 25% and any other party to the concentration holds important intellectual property rights for that market;
   (c) any of the parties to the concentration is present in a product market, which is a neighbouring market closely related to a product market in which any other party to the concentration is engaged, and the individual or combined market shares of the parties in any one of these markets is 25% or more. Product markets are closely related neighbouring markets when the products are complementary to each other[1] or when they belong to a range of products that is generally purchased by the same set of customers for the same end use;[2]
   where such markets include the whole or a part of the EEA.
   In order to enable the Commission to consider, from the outset, the competitive impact of the proposed concentration in the markets identified under this Section 6.3, notifying parties are invited to submit the information under Sections 7 and 8 of this Form in relation to those markets.

Notes

[1] Products (or services) are called complementary when, for example, the use (or consumption) of one product essentially implies the use (or consumption) of the other product, such as for staple machines and staples, and printers and printer cartridges.

[2] Examples of products belonging to such a range would be whisky and gin sold to bars and restaurants, and different materials for packaging a certain category of goods sold to producers of such goods.

SECTION 7
Information on affected markets

For each affected relevant product market, for each of the last three financial years:[1]

Notes

[1] Without prejudice to Article 4(2) of the Implementing Regulation.

(a) for the EEA territory;
(b) for the Community as a whole;
(c) for the territory of the EFTA States as a whole;

(d) individually for each Member State and EFTA State where the parties to the concentration do business; and

(e) where in the opinion of the notifying parties, the relevant geographic market is different;

provide the following:

7.1. an estimate of the total size of the market in terms of sales value (in euros) and volume (units).[1] Indicate the basis and sources for the calculations and provide documents where available to confirm these calculations;

Notes

[1] The value and volume of a market should reflect output less exports plus imports for the geographic areas under consideration. If readily available, please provide disaggregated information on imports and exports by country of origin and destination, respectively.

7.2. the sales in value and volume, as well as an estimate of the market shares, of each of the parties to the concentration;

7.3. an estimate of the market share in value (and where appropriate, volume) of all competitors (including importers) having at least 5% of the geographic market under consideration. On this basis, provide an estimate of the HHI index[1] pre- and post-merger, and the difference between the two (the delta).[2] Indicate the proportion of market shares used as a basis to calculate the HHI. Identify the sources used to calculate these market shares and provide documents where available to confirm the calculation;

Notes

[1] HHI stands for Herfindahl-Hirschman Index, a measure of market concentration. The HHI is calculated by summing the squares of the individual market shares of all the firms in the market. For example, a market containing five firms with market shares of 40%, 20%, 15%, 15%, and 10%, respectively, has an HHI of 2550 ($40^2 + 20^2 + 15^2 + 15^2 + 10^2 = 2,550$). The HHI ranges from close to zero (in an atomistic market) to 10000 (in the case of a pure monopoly). The post-merger HHI is calculated on the working assumption that the individual market shares of the companies do not change. Although it is best to include all firms in the calculation, lack of information about very small firms may not be important because such firms do not affect the HHI significantly.

[2] The increase in concentration as measured by the HHI can be calculated independently of the overall market concentration by doubling the product of the market shares of the merging firms. For example, a merger of two firms with market shares of 30% and 15% respectively would increase the HHI by 900 ($30 \times 15 \times 2 = 900$). The explanation for this technique is as follows: Before the merger, the market shares of the merging firms contribute to the HHI by their squares individually: $(a)^2 + (b)^2$. After the merger, the contribution is the square of their sum: $(a + b)^2$, which equals $(a)^2 + (b)^2 + 2ab$. The increase in the HHI is therefore represented by $2ab$.

7.4. the name, address, telephone number, fax number and e-mail address of the head of the legal department (or other person exercising similar functions; and in cases where there is no such person, then the chief executive) for the competitors identified under 7.3;

7.5. an estimate of the total value and volume and source of imports from outside the EEA territory and identify:

    (a) the proportion of such imports that are derived from the groups to which the parties to the concentration belong;

    (b) an estimate of the extent to which any quotas, tariffs or non-tariff barriers to trade, affect these imports; and

    (c) an estimate of the extent to which transportation and other costs affect these imports;

7.6. the extent to which trade among States within the EEA territory is affected by:

    (a) transportation and other costs; and

    (b) other non-tariff barriers to trade;

7.7. the manner in which the parties to the concentration produce, price and sell the products and/or services; for example, whether they manufacture and price locally, or sell through local distribution facilities;

7.8. a comparison of price levels in each Member State and EFTA State by each party to the concentration and a similar comparison of price levels between the Community, the EFTA States and other areas where these products are produced (e.g. Russia, the United States of America, Japan, China, or other relevant areas); and

7.9. the nature and extent of vertical integration of each of the parties to the concentration compared with their largest competitors.

Section 8
General conditions in affected markets

8.1. Identify the five largest independent[1] suppliers to the parties to the concentration and their individual shares of purchases from each of these suppliers (of raw materials or goods used for purposes of producing the relevant products). Provide the name, address, telephone number, fax number and e-mail address of the head of the legal department (or other person exercising similar functions; and in cases where there is no such person, then the chief executive) for each of these suppliers.

Notes

[1] That is, suppliers which are not subsidiaries, agents or undertakings forming part of the group of the party in question. In addition to those five independent suppliers the notifying parties can, if they consider it necessary for a proper assessment of the case, identify the intra-group suppliers. The same will apply in 8.6 in relation to customers.

Structure of supply in affected markets

8.2. Explain the distribution channels and service networks that exist in the affected markets. In so doing, take account of the following where appropriate:
   (a) the distribution systems prevailing in the market and their importance. To what extent is distribution performed by third parties and/or undertakings belonging to the same group as the parties identified in Section 4?
   (b) the service networks (for example, maintenance and repair) prevailing and their importance in these markets. To what extent are such services performed by third parties and/or undertakings belonging to the same group as the parties identified in Section 4?

8.3. Provide an estimate of the total Community-wide and EFTA-wide capacity for the last three years. Over this period what proportion of this capacity is accounted for by each of the parties to the concentration, and what have been their respective rates of capacity utilization. If applicable, identify the location and capacity of the manufacturing facilities of each of the parties to the concentration in affected markets.

8.4. Specify whether any of the parties to the concentration, or any of the competitors, have "pipeline products", products likely to be brought to market in the near term, or plans to expand (or contract) production or sales capacity. If so, provide an estimate of the projected sales and market shares of the parties to the concentration over the next three to five years.

8.5. If you consider any other supply-side considerations to be relevant, they should be specified.

Structure of demand in affected markets

8.6. Identify the five[1] largest independent customers of the parties in each affected market and their individual share of total sales for such products accounted for by each of those customers. Provide the name, address, telephone number, fax number and e-mail address of the head of the legal department (or other person exercising similar functions; and in cases where there is no such person, then the chief executive) for each of these customers.

Notes

[1] Experience has shown that the examination of complex cases often requires more customer contact details. In the course of pre-notification contacts, the Commission's services may ask for more customer contact details for certain affected markets.

8.7. Explain the structure of demand in terms of:
   (a) the phases of the markets in terms of, for example, take-off, expansion, maturity and decline, and a forecast of the growth rate of demand;
   (b) the importance of customer preferences, for example in terms of brand loyalty, the provision of pre- and after-sales services, the provision of a full range of products, or network effects;
   (c) the role of product differentiation in terms of attributes or quality, and the extent to which the products of the parties to the concentration are close substitutes;

(d) the role of switching costs (in terms of time and expense) for customers when changing from one supplier to another;

(e) the degree of concentration or dispersion of customers;

(f) segmentation of customers into different groups with a description of the "typical customer" of each group;

(g) the importance of exclusive distribution contracts and other types of long-term contracts; and

(h) the extent to which public authorities, government agencies, State enterprises or similar bodies are important participants as a source of demand.

Market entry

8.8. Over the last five years, has there been any significant entry into any affected markets? If so, identify such entrants and provide the name, address, telephone number, fax number and e-mail address of the head of the legal department (or other person exercising similar functions; and in cases where there is no such person, then the chief executive) and an estimate of the current market share of each such entrant. If any of the parties to the concentration entered an affected market in the past five years, provide an analysis of the barriers to entry encountered.

8.9. In the opinion of the notifying parties, are there undertakings (including those at present operating only outside the Community or the EEA) that are likely to enter the market? If so, identify such entrants and provide the name, address, telephone number, fax number and e-mail address of the head of the legal department (or other person exercising similar functions; and in cases where there is no such person, then the chief executive). Explain why such entry is likely and provide an estimate of the time within which such entry is likely to occur.

8.10. Describe the various factors influencing entry into affected markets, examining entry from both a geographical and product viewpoint. In so doing, take account of the following where appropriate:

(a) the total costs of entry (R& D, production, establishing distribution systems, promotion, advertising, servicing, and so forth) on a scale equivalent to a significant viable competitor, indicating the market share of such a competitor;

(b) any legal or regulatory barriers to entry, such as government authorization or standard setting in any form, as well as barriers resulting from product certification procedures, or the need to have a proven track record;

(c) any restrictions created by the existence of patents, know-how and other intellectual property rights in these markets and any restrictions created by licensing such rights;

(d) the extent to which each of the parties to the concentration are holders, licensees or licensors of patents, know-how and other rights in the relevant markets;

(e) the importance of economies of scale for the production or distribution of products in the affected markets; and

(f) access to sources of supply, such as availability of raw materials and necessary infrastructure.

Research and development

8.11. Give an account of the importance of research and development in the ability of a firm operating the relevant market(s) to compete in the long term. Explain the nature of the research and development in affected markets carried out by the parties to the concentration.

In so doing, take account of the following, where appropriate:

(a) trends and intensities of research and development[1] in these markets and for the parties to the concentration;

(b) the course of technological development for these markets over an appropriate time period (including developments in products and/or services, production processes, distribution systems, and so on);

(c) the major innovations that have been made in these markets and the undertakings responsible for these innovations; and

(d) the cycle of innovation in these markets and where the parties are in this cycle of innovation.

Notes
1 Research and development intensity is defined as research development expenditure as a proportion of turnover.

Cooperative agreements

8.12. To what extent do cooperative agreements (horizontal, vertical, or other) exist in the affected markets?

8.13. Give details of the most important cooperative agreements engaged in by the parties to the concentration in the affected markets, such as research and development, licensing, joint production, specialization, distribution, long term supply and exchange of information agreements and, where deemed useful, provide a copy of these agreements.

Trade associations

8.14. With respect to the trade associations in the affected markets:
   (a) identify those of which the parties to the concentration are members; and
   (b) identify the most important trade associations to which the customers and suppliers of the parties to the concentration belong.
   Provide the name, address, telephone number, fax number and e-mail address of the appropriate contact person for all trade associations listed above.

Section 9
Overall market context and efficiencies

9.1. Describe the world wide context of the proposed concentration, indicating the position of each of the parties to the concentration outside of the EEA territory in terms of size and competitive strength.

9.2. Describe how the proposed concentration is likely to affect the interests of intermediate and ultimate consumers and the development of technical and economic progress.

9.3. Should you wish the Commission specifically to consider from the outset[1] whether efficiency gains generated by the concentration are likely to enhance the ability and incentive of the new entity to act pro-competitively for the benefit of consumers, please provide a description of, and supporting documents relating to, each efficiency (including cost savings, new product introductions, and service or product improvements) that the parties anticipate will result from the proposed concentration relating to any relevant product.[2]
   For each claimed efficiency, provide:
   (i) a detailed explanation of how the proposed concentration would allow the new entity to achieve the efficiency. Specify the steps that the parties anticipate taking to achieve the efficiency, the risks involved in achieving the efficiency, and the time and costs required to achieve it;
   (ii) where reasonably possible, a quantification of the efficiency and a detailed explanation of how the quantification was calculated. Where relevant, also provide an estimate of the significance of efficiencies related to new product introductions or quality improvements. For efficiencies that involve cost savings, state separately the one-time fixed cost savings, recurring fixed cost savings, and variable cost savings (in euros per unit and euros per year);
   (iii) the extent to which customers are likely to benefit from the efficiency and a detailed explanation of how this conclusion is arrived at; and
   (iv) the reason why the party or parties could not achieve the efficiency to a similar extent by means other than through the concentration proposed, and in a manner that is not likely to raise competition concerns.

Notes
1 It should be noted that submitting information in response to Section 9.3 is voluntary. Parties are not required to offer any justification for not completing this section. Failure to provide information on efficiencies will not be taken to imply that the proposed concentration does not create efficiencies or that the rationale for the concentration is to increase market power. Not providing the requested information on efficiencies at the notification stage does not preclude

Part D Mergers and Concentrations

providing the information at a later stage. However, the earlier the information is provided, the better the Commission can verify the efficiency claim.

2 For further guidance on the assessment of efficiencies, see the Commission Notice on the assessment of horizontal mergers.

SECTION 10
Cooperative effects of a joint venture

10. For the purpose of Article 2(4) of the EC Merger Regulation, answer the following questions:
    (a) Do two or more parents retain to a significant extent activities in the same market as the joint venture or in a market which is upstream or downstream from that of the joint venture or in a neighbouring market closely related to this market?[1] If the answer is affirmative, please indicate for each of the markets referred to here:
        — the turnover of each parent company in the preceding financial year;
        — the economic significance of the activities of the joint venture in relation to this turnover;
        — the market share of each parent.
        If the answer is negative, please justify your answer.

    [(b) If the answer to (a) is affirmative and in your view the creation of the joint venture does not lead to coordination between independent undertakings that restricts competition within the meaning of Article [101](1) of the [Treaty on the Functioning of the European Union], and, where applicable, the corresponding provisions of the EEA Agreement,[2] give your reasons.]

    (c) [Without prejudice to the answers to (a) and (b) and in order to ensure that a complete assessment of the case can be made by the Commission, please explain how the criteria of Article [101](3) of the [Treaty on the Functioning of the European Union] and, where applicable, the corresponding provisions of the EEA Agreement[3] apply. Under Article [101](3), the provisions of Article [101](1) may be declared inapplicable if the operation:]
        (i) contributes to improving the production or distribution of goods, or to promoting technical or economic progress;
        (ii) allows consumers a fair share of the resulting benefit;
        (iii) does not impose on the undertakings concerned restrictions which are not indispensable to the attainment of these objectives; and
        (iv) does not afford such undertakings the possibility of eliminating competition in respect of a substantial part of the products in question.

Notes

1 For market definitions refer to Section 6.

[2 See Article 53(1) of the EEA Agreement.]

[3 See Article 53(3) of the EEA Agreement.]

Section 10 was amended as shown in square brackets by Commission Regulation (EC) No 1033/2008 (OJ L 279, 22.10.2008, p.3 with effect from 23 October 2008.

SECTION 11
Declaration

Article 2(2) of the Implementing Regulation states that where notifications are signed by representatives of undertakings, such representatives must produce written proof that they are authorized to act. Such written authorization must accompany the notification.

The notification must conclude with the following declaration which is to be signed by or on behalf of all the notifying parties:

The notifying party or parties declare that, to the best of their knowledge and belief, the information given in this notification is true, correct, and complete, that true and complete copies of documents required by Form CO have been supplied, that all estimates are identified as such and are their best estimates of the underlying facts, and that all the opinions expressed are sincere.

They are aware of the provisions of Article 14(1)(a) of the EC Merger Regulation.

Place and date:

Signatures:

Name/s and positions:

On behalf of:

Annex II
Short Form for the Notification of a Concentration Pursuant to Regulation (EC) No 139/2004

Commentary
Annex II: B&C: 8.114, 8.124   F&N: 5.341, 5.409, 5.410, 5.523

1. Introduction

1.1. The purpose of the Short Form

The Short Form specifies the information that must be provided by the notifying parties when submitting a notification to the European Commission of certain proposed mergers, acquisitions or other concentrations that are unlikely to raise competition concerns.

[In completing this Form, your attention is drawn to Council Regulation (EC) No 139/2004 (hereinafter referred to as "the EC Merger Regulation"), and Commission Regulation (EC) No 802/2004 (hereinafter referred to as "the Implementing Regulation"), to which this Form is annexed.[1] The text of these regulations, as well as other relevant documents, can be found on the Competition page of the Commission's Europa web site. Your attention is also drawn to the corresponding provisions of the Agreement on the European Economic Area (hereinafter referred to as "the EEA Agreement").[2]]

As a general rule, the Short Form may be used for the purpose of notifying concentrations, where one of the following conditions is met:
1. in the case of a joint venture, the joint venture has no, or negligible, actual or foreseen activities within the territory of the European Economic Area (EEA). Such cases occur where:
    (a) the turnover of the joint venture and/or the turnover of the contributed activities is less than EUR 100 million in the EEA territory; and
    (b) the total value of the assets transferred to the joint venture is less than EUR 100 million in the EEA territory;
2. none of the parties to the concentration are engaged in business activities in the same relevant product and geographic market (no horizontal overlap), or in a market which is upstream or downstream of a market in which another party to the concentration is engaged (no vertical relationship);
3. two or more of the parties to the concentration are engaged in business activities in the same relevant product and geographic market (horizontal relationships), provided that their combined market share is less than 15%; and/or one or more of the parties to the concentration are engaged in business activities in a product market which is upstream or downstream of a product market in which any other party to the concentration is engaged (vertical relationships), and provided that none of their individual or combined market shares at either level is 25% or more; or
4. a party is to acquire sole control of an undertaking over which it already has joint control.

The Commission may require a full form notification where it appears either that the conditions for using the Short Form are not met, or, exceptionally, where they are met, the Commission determines, nonetheless, that a notification under Form CO is necessary for an adequate investigation of possible competition concerns.

Examples of cases where a notification under Form CO may be necessary are concentrations where it is difficult to define the relevant markets (for example, in emerging markets or where there is no established case practice); where a party is a new or potential entrant, or an important patent holder; where it is not possible to adequately determine the parties' market shares; in markets with high entry barriers, with a high degree of concentration or known competition problems; where at least two parties to the concentration are present in closely related neighbouring markets;[3] and in concentrations where an issue of coordination arises, as referred to in Article 2(4) of the EC Merger Regulation. Similarly, a Form CO notification may be required in the case of a party acquiring sole control of a joint venture in which it currently holds joint control, where the acquiring party and the joint venture, together, have a strong market position, or the joint venture and the acquiring party have strong positions in vertically related markets.

Notes

[[1] Council Regulation (EC) No 139/2004 of 20 January 2004 (OJ L 24, 29.1.2004, p. 1).

[2] See in particular Article 57 of the EEA Agreement, point 1 of Annex XIV to the EEA Agreement, Protocols 21 and 24 to the EEA Agreement, as well as Protocol 4 to the Agreement between the EFTA States on the establishment of a Surveillance Authority and a Court of Justice (hereinafter referred to as the 'Surveillance and Court Agreement'). Any reference to EFTA States shall be understood to mean those EFTA States which are Contracting Parties to the EEA Agreement. As of 1 May 2004, these States are Iceland, Liechtenstein and Norway.]

[3] Product markets are closely related neighbouring markets when the products are complementary to each other or when they belong to a range of products that is generally purchased by the same set of customers for the same end use.

Point 1.1 was amended as shown in square brackets by Commission Regulation (EC) No 1033/2008 (OJ L 279, 22.10.2008, p. 3) with effect from 23 October 2008.

1.2. Reversion to the full Form CO notification

In assessing whether a concentration may be notified under the Short Form, the Commission will ensure that all relevant circumstances are established with sufficient clarity. In this respect, the responsibility to provide correct and complete information rests with the notifying parties.

If, after the concentration has been notified, the Commission considers that the case is not appropriate for notification under the Short Form, the Commission may require full, or where appropriate partial, notification under Form CO. This may be the case where:

— it appears that the conditions for using the Short Form are not met;
— although the conditions for using the Short Form are met, a full or partial notification under Form CO appears to be necessary for an adequate investigation of possible competition concerns or to establish that the transaction is a concentration within the meaning of Article 3 of the EC Merger Regulation;
— the Short Form contains incorrect or misleading information;
[— a Member State or an EFTA State expresses substantiated competition concerns about the notified concentration within 15 working days of receipt of the copy of the notification; or]
— a third party expresses substantiated competition concerns within the time-limit laid down by the Commission for such comments.

In such cases, the notification may be treated as being incomplete in a material respect pursuant to Article 5(2) of the Implementing Regulation. The Commission will inform the notifying parties or their representatives of this in writing and without delay. The notification will only become effective on the date on which all information required is received.

Notes

Point 1.2 was amended as shown in square brackets by Commission Regulation (EC) No 1033/2008 (OJ L 279, 22.10.2008, p. 3) with effect from 23 October 2008.

1.3. Importance of pre-notification contacts

Experience has shown that pre-notification contacts are extremely valuable to both the notifying parties and the Commission in determining the precise amount of information required in a notification. Also, in cases where the parties wish to submit a Short Form notification, they are advised to engage in pre-notification contacts with the Commission in order to discuss whether the case is one for which it is appropriate to use a Short Form. Notifying parties may refer to the Commission's Best Practices on the Conduct of EC Merger Control Proceedings, which provides guidance on pre-notification contacts and the preparation of notifications.

1.4. Who must notify

In the case of a merger within the meaning of Article 3(1)(a) of the EC Merger Regulation or the acquisition of joint control of an undertaking within the meaning of Article 3(1)(b) of the EC Merger Regulation, the notification shall be completed jointly by the parties to the merger or by those acquiring joint control, as the case may be.[1]

In the case of the acquisition of a controlling interest in one undertaking by another, the acquirer must complete the notification.

In the case of a public bid to acquire an undertaking, the bidder must complete the notification.

Each party completing the notification is responsible for the accuracy of the information which it provides.

Notes

[1] See Article 4(2) of the EC Merger Regulation.

1.5. The requirement for a correct and complete notification

All information required by this Form must be correct and complete. The information required must be supplied in the appropriate Section of this Form.

In particular you should note that:

(a) In accordance with Article 10(1) of the EC Merger Regulation and Article 5(2) and (4) of the Implementing Regulation, the time-limits of the EC Merger Regulation linked to the notification will not begin to run until all the information that must be supplied with the notification has been received by the Commission. This requirement is to ensure that the Commission is able to assess the notified concentration within the strict time-limits provided by the EC Merger Regulation.

(b) The notifying parties should verify, in the course of preparing their notification, that contact names and numbers, and in particular fax numbers and e-mail addresses, provided to the Commission are accurate, relevant and up-to-date.

(c) Incorrect or misleading information in the notification will be considered to be incomplete information (Article 5(4) of the Implementing Regulation).

(d) If a notification is incomplete, the Commission will inform the notifying parties or their representatives in writing and without delay. The notification will only become effective on the date on which the complete and accurate information is received by the Commission (Article 10(1) of the EC Merger Regulation, Article 5(2) and (4) of the Implementing Regulation).

(e) Under Article 14(1)(a) of the EC Merger Regulation, notifying parties who, either intentionally or negligently, supply incorrect or misleading information, may be liable to fines of up to 1% of the aggregate turnover of the undertaking concerned. In addition, pursuant to Article 6(3)(a) and Article 8(6)(a) of the EC Merger Regulation the Commission may revoke its decision on the compatibility of a notified concentration where it is based on incorrect information for which one of the undertakings is responsible.

(f) You may request in writing that the Commission accept that the notification is complete notwithstanding the failure to provide information required by this Form, if such information is not reasonably available to you in part or in whole (for example, because of the unavailability of information on a target company during a contested bid). The Commission will consider such a request, provided that you give reasons for the unavailability of that information, and provide your best estimates for missing data together with the sources for the estimates. Where possible, indications as to where any of the requested information that is unavailable to you could be obtained by the Commission should also be provided.

(g) You may request in writing that the Commission accept that the notification is complete notwithstanding the failure to provide information required by this Form, if you consider that any particular information required may not be necessary for the Commission's examination of the case.

Part D Mergers and Concentrations

The Commission will consider such a request, provided that you give adequate reasons why that information is not relevant and necessary to its inquiry into the notified operation. You should explain this during your pre-notification contacts with the Commission and submit a written request for a waiver, asking the Commission to dispense with the obligation to provide that information, pursuant to Article 4(2) of the Implementing Regulation.

1.6. How to notify

The notification must be completed in one of the official languages of the European Community. This language will thereafter be the language of the proceedings for all notifying parties. Where notifications are made in accordance with Article 12 of Protocol 24 to the EEA Agreement in an official language of an EFTA State which is not an official language of the Community, the notification must simultaneously be supplemented with a translation into an official language of the Community.

The information requested by this Form is to be set out using the sections and paragraph numbers of the Form, signing a declaration as provided in Section 9, and annexing supporting documentation. In completing Section 7 of this Form, the notifying parties are invited to consider whether, for purposes of clarity, this section is best presented in numerical order, or whether information can be grouped together for each individual reportable market (or group of reportable markets).

For the sake of clarity, certain information may be put in annexes. However, it is essential that all key substantive pieces of information, in particular, market share information for the parties and their largest competitors, are presented in the body of this Form. Annexes to this Form shall only be used to supplement the information supplied in the Form itself.

Contact details must be provided in a format provided by the Commission's Directorate-General for Competition (DG Competition). For a proper investigatory process, it is essential that the contact details are accurate. Multiple instances of incorrect contact details may be a ground for declaring a notification incomplete.

Supporting documents are to be submitted in their original language; where this is not an official language of the Community, they must be translated into the language of the proceeding (Article 3(4) of the Implementing Regulation).

Supporting documents may be originals or copies of the originals. In the latter case, the notifying party must confirm that they are true and complete.

One original and [38] copies of the Short Form and the supporting documents shall be submitted to the Commission's Directorate-General for Competition.

The notification shall be delivered to the address referred to in Article 23(1) of the Implementing Regulation and in the format specified by the Commission from time to time. This address is published in the *Official Journal of the European Union*. The notification must be delivered to the Commission on working days as defined by Article 24 of the Implementing Regulation. In order to enable it to be registered on the same day, it must be delivered before 17.00 hrs on Mondays to Thursdays and before 16.00 hrs on Fridays and workdays preceding public holidays and other holidays as determined by the Commission and published in the *Official Journal of the European Union*. The security instructions given on DG Competition's website must be adhered to.

Notes

The amendment shown in square brackets was made by Commission Regulation No 519/2013 of 21 February 2013 adapting certain regulations and decisions by reason of the accession of Croatia (OJ L 158, 10.6.2013, p. 74), with effect from 1 July 2013.

1.7. Confidentiality

Article [339] of the Treaty and Article 17(2) of the EC Merger Regulation as well as the corresponding provisions of the EEA Agreement[1] require the Commission, the Member States, the EFTA Surveillance Authority and the EFTA States, their officials and other servants not to disclose information they have acquired through the application of the Regulation of the kind covered by the obligation of professional secrecy. The same principle must also apply to protect confidentiality between notifying parties.

If you believe that your interests would be harmed if any of the information you are asked to supply were to be published or otherwise divulged to other parties, submit this information separately with each page clearly marked "Business Secrets". You should also give reasons why this information should not be divulged or published.

In the case of mergers or joint acquisitions, or in other cases where the notification is completed by more than one of the parties, business secrets may be submitted under separate cover, and referred to in the notification as an annex. All such annexes must be included in the submission in order for a notification to be considered complete.

Notes

[1] See, in particular, Article 122 of the EEA Agreement, Article 9 of Protocol 24 to the EEA Agreement and Article 17(2) of Chapter XIII of Protocol 4 to the Agreement between the EFTA States on the establishment of a Surveillance Authority and a Court of Justice (ESA Agreement).

1.8. Definitions and instructions for purposes of this Form

Notifying party or parties: in cases where a notification is submitted by only one of the undertakings who is a party to an operation, "notifying parties" is used to refer only to the undertaking actually submitting the notification.

Party(ies) to the concentration or parties: these terms relate to both the acquiring and acquired parties, or to the merging parties, including all undertakings in which a controlling interest is being acquired or which is the subject of a public bid.

Except where otherwise specified, the terms notifying party(ies) and party(ies) to the concentration include all the undertakings which belong to the same groups as those parties.

Year: all references to the word year in this Form should be read as meaning calendar year, unless otherwise stated. All information requested in this Form must, unless otherwise specified, relate to the year preceding that of the notification.

The financial data requested in Sections 3.3 to 3.5 must be provided in euros at the average exchange rates prevailing for the years or other periods in question.

All references contained in this Form are to the relevant articles and paragraphs of the EC Merger Regulation, unless otherwise stated.

1.9. Provision of information to employees and their representatives

The Commission would like to draw attention to the obligations to which the parties to a concentration may be subject under Community and/or national rules on information and consultation regarding transactions of a concentrative nature vis-à-vis employees and/or their representatives.

Section i

Description of the concentration

1.1. Provide an executive summary of the concentration, specifying the parties to the concentration, the nature of the concentration (for example, merger, acquisition, joint venture), the areas of activity of the notifying parties, the markets on which the concentration will have an impact (including the main reportable markets),[1] and the strategic and economic rationale for the concentration.

Notes

[1] See Section 6.III for the definition of reportable markets.

1.2. Provide a summary (up to 500 words) of the information provided under Section 1.1. It is intended that this summary will be published on the Commission's website at the date of notification. The summary must be drafted so that it contains no confidential information or business secrets.

Information about the parties

2.1. Information on notifying party (or parties)

Give details of:

2.1.1. name and address of undertaking;

2.1.2. nature of the undertaking's business;

2.1.3. name, address, telephone number, fax number and e-mail address of, and position held by, the appropriate contact person; and

2.1.4. an address for service of the notifying party (or each of the notifying parties) to which documents and, in particular, Commission Decisions may be delivered. The name, e-mail address and telephone number of a person at this address who is authorised to accept service must be provided.

2.2. Information on other parties[1] to the concentration

For each party to the concentration (except the notifying party or parties) give details of:

2.2.1. name and address of undertaking;

2.2.2. nature of undertaking's business;

2.2.3. name, address, telephone number, fax number and e-mail address of, and position held by, the appropriate contact person; and

2.2.4. an address for service of the party (or each of the parties) to which documents and, in particular, Commission Decisions may be delivered. The name, e-mail address and telephone number of a person at this address who is authorised to accept service must be provided.

Notes

[1] This includes the target company in the case of a contested bid, in which case the details should be completed as far as is possible.

2.3. Appointment of representatives

Where notifications are signed by representatives of undertakings, such representatives must produce written proof that they are authorised to act. The written proof must contain the name and position of the persons granting such authority.

Provide the following contact details of information of any representatives who have been authorised to act for any of the parties to the concentration, indicating whom they represent:

2.3.1. name of representative;

2.3.2. address of representative;

2.3.3. name, address, telephone number, fax number and e-mail address of person to be contacted; and

2.3.4. an address of the representative for service (in Brussels if available) to which correspondence may be sent and documents delivered.

Details of the concentration

3.1. Describe the nature of the concentration being notified. In doing so state:

(a) whether the proposed concentration is a full legal merger, an acquisition of sole or joint control, a full-function joint venture within the meaning of Article 3(4) of the EC Merger Regulation or a contract or other means of conferring direct or indirect control within the meaning of Article 3(2) of the EC Merger Regulation;

(b) whether the whole or parts of parties are subject to the concentration;

(c) a brief explanation of the economic and financial structure of the concentration;

(d) whether any public offer for the securities of one party by another party has the support of the former's supervisory boards of management or other bodies legally representing that party;

(e) the proposed or expected date of any major events designed to bring about the completion of the concentration;

(f) the proposed structure of ownership and control after the completion of the concentration;

(g) any financial or other support received from whatever source (including public authorities) by any of the parties and the nature and amount of this support; and

(h) the economic sectors involved in the concentration.

3.2. State the value of the transaction (the purchase price or the value of all the assets involved, as the case may be);

3.3. For each of the undertakings concerned by the concentration[1] provide the following data[2] for the last financial year:

    3.3.1. world-wide turnover;

    3.3.2. Community-wide turnover;

    3.3.3. EFTA-wide turnover;

    3.3.4. turnover in each Member State;

    3.3.5. turnover in each EFTA State;

    3.3.6. the Member State, if any, in which more than two-thirds of Community-wide turnover is achieved; and

    3.3.7. the EFTA State, if any, in which more than two-thirds of EFTA-wide turnover is achieved.

Notes

[1] See Commission Notice on the concept of undertakings concerned.

[2] See, generally, the Commission Notice on calculation of turnover. Turnover of the acquiring party or parties to the concentration should include the aggregated turnover of all undertakings within the meaning of Article 5(4) of the EC Merger Regulation. Turnover of the acquired party or parties should include the turnover relating to the parts subject to the transaction within the meaning of Article 5(2) of the EC Merger Regulation. Special provisions are contained in Articles 5(3), (4) and 5(5) of the EC Merger Regulation for credit, insurance, other financial institutions and joint undertakings.

3.4. For the purposes of Article 1(3) of the EC Merger Regulation, if the operation does not meet the thresholds set out in Article 1(2), provide the following data for the last financial year:

    3.4.1. the Member States, if any, in which the combined aggregate turnover of all the undertakings concerned is more than EUR 100 million; and

    3.4.2. the Member States, if any, in which the aggregate turnover of each of at least two of the undertakings concerned is more than EUR 25 million.

3.5. For the purposes of determining whether the concentration qualifies as an EFTA cooperation case,[1] provide the following information with respect to the last financial year:

    3.5.1. does the combined turnover of the undertakings concerned in the territory of the EFTA States equal 25% or more of their total turnover in the EEA territory?

    3.5.2. does each of at least two undertakings concerned have a turnover exceeding EUR 250 million in the territory of the EFTA States?

Notes

[[1] See Article 57 of the EEA Agreement and, in particular, Article 2(1) of Protocol 24 to the EEA Agreement. A case qualifies to be treated as a cooperation case if the combined turnover of the undertakings concerned in the territory of the EFTA States equals 25% or more of their total turnover within the territory covered by the EEA Agreement; or each of at least two undertakings concerned has a turnover exceeding EUR 250 million in the territory of the EFTA States; or the concentration is liable to significantly impede effective competition in the territories of the EFTA States or a substantial part thereof, in particular as a result of the creation or strengthening of a dominant position.]

Footnote 1 was amended as shown in square brackets by Commission Regulation (EC) No 1033/2008 (OJ L 279, 22.10.2008, p. 3) with effect from 23 October 2008.

3.6. In case the transaction concerns the acquisition of joint control of a joint venture, provide the following information:

    3.6.1. the turnover of the joint venture and/or the turnover of the contributed activities to the joint venture; and/or

    3.6.2. the total value of assets transferred to the joint venture.

3.7. Describe the economic rationale of the concentration.

SECTION 4

Ownership and control[1]

Notes

[1] See Articles 3(3), 3(4) and 3(5) and Article 5(4) of the EC Merger Regulation.

For each of the parties to the concentration provide a list of all undertakings belonging to the same group.

This list must include:

4.1. all undertakings or persons controlling these parties, directly or indirectly;

4.2. all undertakings active in any reportable market[1] that are controlled, directly or indirectly:

    (a) by these parties;

    (b) by any other undertaking identified in 4.1.

For each entry listed above, the nature and means of control should be specified.

The information sought in this section may be illustrated by the use of organisation charts or diagrams to show the structure of ownership and control of the undertakings.

Notes

[1] See Section 6.III for the definition of reportable markets.

SECTION 5

Supporting documentation

Notifying parties must provide the following:

5.1. copies of the final or most recent versions of all documents bringing about the concentration, whether by agreement between the parties to the concentration, acquisition of a controlling interest or a public bid; and

5.2. copies of the most recent annual reports and accounts of all the parties to the concentration.

SECTION 6

Market definitions

The relevant product and geographic markets determine the scope within which the market power of the new entity resulting from the concentration must be assessed.[1]

Notes

[1] See Commission Notice on the definition of the relevant market for the purposes of Community competition law.

The notifying party or parties must provide the data requested having regard to the following definitions:

I. Relevant product markets

A relevant product market comprises all those products and/or services which are regarded as interchangeable or substitutable by the consumer, by reason of the products' characteristics, their prices and their intended use. A relevant product market may in some cases be composed of a number of individual products and/or services which present largely identical physical or technical characteristics and are interchangeable.

Factors relevant to the assessment of the relevant product market include the analysis of why the products or services in these markets are included and why others are excluded by using the above definition, and having regard to, for example, substitutability, conditions of competition, prices, cross-price elasticity of demand or other factors relevant for the definition of the product markets (for example, supply-side substitutability in appropriate cases).

II. Relevant geographic markets

The relevant geographic market comprises the area in which the undertakings concerned are involved in the supply and demand of relevant products or services, in which the conditions of competition are sufficiently homogeneous and which can be distinguished from neighbouring geographic areas because, in particular, conditions of competition are appreciably different in those areas.

Factors relevant to the assessment of the relevant geographic market include inter alia the nature and characteristics of the products or services concerned, the existence of entry barriers, consumer preferences, appreciable differences in the undertakings' market shares between neighbouring geographic areas, or substantial price differences.

III. Reportable markets

For purposes of information required in this Form, reportable markets consist of all relevant product and geographic markets, as well as plausible alternative relevant product and geographic market definitions, on the basis of which:

(a) two or more of the parties to the concentration are engaged in business activities in the same relevant market (horizontal relationships);

(b) one or more of the parties to the concentration are engaged in business activities in a product market, which is upstream or downstream of a market in which any other party to the concentration is engaged, regardless of whether there is or is not any existing supplier/customer relationship between the parties to the concentration (vertical relationships).

6.1. On the basis of the above market definitions, identify all reportable markets.

SECTION 7
Information on markets

For each reportable market described in Section 6, for the year preceding the operation, provide the following:[1]

Notes

[1] In the context of pre-notification, you may want to discuss with the Commission to what extent dispensation (waivers) to provide the requested information would be appropriate for certain reportable markets.

7.1. an estimate of the total size of the market in terms of sales value (in euros) and volume (units).[1] Indicate the basis and sources for the calculations and provide documents where available to confirm these calculations;

Notes

[1] The value and volume of a market should reflect output less exports plus imports for the geographic areas under consideration.

7.2. the sales in value and volume, as well as an estimate of the market shares, of each of the parties to the concentration. Indicate if there have been significant changes to the sales and market shares for the last three financial years; and

7.3. for horizontal and vertical relationships, an estimate of the market share in value (and where appropriate, volume) of the three largest competitors (indicating the basis for the estimates). Provide the name, address, telephone number, fax number and e-mail address of the head of the legal department (or other person exercising similar functions; and in cases where there is no such person, then the chief executive) for these competitors.

SECTION 8
Cooperative effects of a joint venture

8. For the purpose of Article 2(4) of the EC Merger Regulation, please answer the following questions:

   (a) Do two or more parents retain to a significant extent activities in the same market as the joint venture or in a market which is upstream or downstream from that of the joint venture or in

Part D Mergers and Concentrations

a neighbouring market closely related to this market?[1] If the answer is affirmative, please indicate for each of the markets referred to here:

— the turnover of each parent company in the preceding financial year;
— the economic significance of the activities of the joint venture in relation to this turnover;
— the market share of each parent.

If the answer is negative, please justify your answer.

[(b) If the answer to (a) is affirmative and in your view the creation of the joint venture does not lead to coordination between independent undertakings that restricts competition within the meaning of Article [101](1) TFEU] and, where applicable, the corresponding provisions of the EEA Agreement,[2] give your reasons.]

(c) [Without prejudice to the answers to (a) and (b) and in order to ensure that a complete assessment of the case can be made by the Commission, please explain how the criteria of Article [101](3) TFEU] and, where applicable, the corresponding provisions of the EEA Agreement[3] apply. Under Article [101](3), the provisions of Article [101](1) may be declared inapplicable if the operation:]

(i) contributes to improving the production or distribution of goods, or to promoting technical or economic progress;

(ii) allows consumers a fair share of the resulting benefit;

(iii) does not impose on the undertakings concerned restrictions which are not indispensable to the attainment of these objectives; and

(iv) does not afford such undertakings the possibility of eliminating competition in respect of a substantial part of the products in question.

Notes

[1] For market definitions refer to Section 6.
[2 See Article 53(1) of the EEA Agreement.]
[3 See Article 53(3) of the EEA Agreement.]

Section 8 was amended as shown in square brackets by Commission Regulation (EC) No 1033/2008 (OJ L 279, 22.10.2008, p. 3) with effect from 23 October 2008.

SECTION 9
DECLARATION

Article 2(2) of the Implementing Regulation states that where notifications are signed by representatives of undertakings, such representatives must produce written proof that they are authorized to act. Such written authorization must accompany the notification.

The notification must conclude with the following declaration which is to be signed by or on behalf of all the notifying parties:

The notifying party or parties declare that, to the best of their knowledge and belief, the information given in this notification is true, correct, and complete, that true and complete copies of documents required by this Form have been supplied, that all estimates are identified as such and are their best estimates of the underlying facts, and that all the opinions expressed are sincere.

They are aware of the provisions of Article 14(1)(a) of the EC Merger Regulation.

Place and date:

Signatures:

Name/s and positions:

On behalf of:

ANNEX III
FORM RS
(RS = REASONED SUBMISSION PURSUANT TO ARTICLE 4(4) AND (5) OF
COUNCIL REGULATION (EC) No 139/2004)

FORM RS RELATING TO REASONED SUBMISSIONS

Pursuant to Articles 4(4) and 4(5) of Regulation (EC) No 139/2004

Commentary
Annex III: **B&C:** 8.089, 8.114 **F&N:** 5.341, 5.409

INTRODUCTION

[A. The purpose of this Form

This Form specifies the information that requesting parties should provide when making a reasoned submission for a pre-notification referral under Article 4(4) or (5) of Council Regulation (EC) No 139/2004 (hereinafter referred to as "the EC Merger Regulation").[1]

Your attention is drawn to the EC Merger Regulation and to Commission Regulation (EC) No 802/2004 (hereinafter referred to as "the EC Merger Implementing Regulation"), to which this Form RS is annexed. The text of these regulations, as well as other relevant documents, can be found on the Competition page of the Commission's Europa web site. Your attention is also drawn to the corresponding provisions of the Agreement on the European Economic Area (hereinafter referred to as "the EEA Agreement").[2]

Experience has shown that prior contacts are extremely valuable to both the parties and the relevant authorities in determining the precise amount and type of information required. Accordingly, parties are encouraged to consult the Commission and the relevant Member State/s or EFTA State/s regarding the adequacy of the scope and type of information on which they intend to base their reasoned submission.]

Notes
[1   Council Regulation (EC) No 139/2004 of 20 January 2004 (OJ L 24, 29.1.2004, p. 1).
[2   See in particular Article 57 of the EEA Agreement, point 1 of Annex XIV to the EEA Agreement, Protocols 21 and 24 to the EEA Agreement, as well as Protocol 4 to the Agreement between the EFTA States on the establishment of a Surveillance Authority and a Court of Justice (hereinafter referred to as the "Surveillance and Court Agreement"). Any reference to EFTA States shall be understood to mean those EFTA States which are Contracting Parties to the EEA Agreement. As of 1 May 2004, these States are Iceland, Liechtenstein and Norway.]

Section A was replaced as shown in square brackets by Commission Regulation (EC) No 1033/2008 (OJ L 279, 22.10.2008, p. 3) with effect from 23 October 2008.

B. The requirement for a reasoned submission to be correct and complete

All information required by this Form must be correct and complete. The information required must be supplied in the appropriate section of this Form.

Incorrect or misleading information in the reasoned submission will be considered to be incomplete information (Article 5(4) of the EC Merger Implementing Regulation).

If parties submit incorrect information, the Commission will have the power to revoke any Article 6 or 8 decision it adopts following an Article 4(5) referral, pursuant to Article 6(3)(a) or 8(6)(a) of the EC Merger Regulation. Following revocation, national competition laws would once again be applicable to the transaction. In the case of referrals under Article 4(4) made on the basis of incorrect information, the Commission may require a notification pursuant to Article 4(1). In addition, the Commission will have the power to impose fines for submission of incorrect or misleading information pursuant to Article 14(1)(a) of the EC Merger Regulation. (See point d below). [Finally, parties

Part D Mergers and Concentrations

should also be aware that, if a referral is made on the basis of incorrect, misleading or incomplete information included in Form RS, the Commission and/or the Member States and the EFTA States may consider making a post-notification referral rectifying any referral made at pre-notification.]

In particular you should note that:

(a) [In accordance with Articles 4(4) and (5) of the EC Merger Regulation, the Commission is obliged to transmit reasoned submissions to the Member States and the EFTA States without delay. The time limits for considering a reasoned submission will begin upon receipt of the submission by the relevant Member State/s or EFTA State/s.] The decision whether or not to accede to a reasoned submission will normally be taken on the basis of the information contained therein, without further investigation efforts being undertaken by the authorities involved.

(b) The submitting parties should therefore verify, in the course of preparing their reasoned submission, that all information and arguments relied upon are sufficiently supported by independent sources.

(c) Under Article 14(1)(a) of the EC Merger Regulation, parties making a reasoned submission who, either intentionally or negligently, provide incorrect or misleading information, may be liable to fines of up to 1% of the aggregate turnover of the undertaking concerned.

(d) You may request in writing that the Commission accept that the reasoned submission is complete notwithstanding the failure to provide information required by this Form, if such information is not reasonably available to you in part or in whole (for example, because of the unavailability of information on a target company during a contested bid). The Commission will consider such a request, provided that you give reasons for the non-availability of that information, and provide your best estimates for missing data together with the sources for the estimates.
[Where possible, indications as to where any of the requested information that is unavailable to you could be obtained by the Commission or the relevant Member State/s and EFTA State/s should also be provided.]

[(e) You may request that the Commission accept that the reasoned submission is complete notwithstanding the failure to provide information required by this Form, if you consider that any particular information requested by this Form may not be necessary for the Commission's or the relevant Member State/s' or EFTA State/s' examination of the case.
The Commission will consider such a request, provided that you give adequate reasons why that information is not relevant and necessary to dealing with your request for a pre-notification referral. You should explain this during your prior contacts with the Commission and with the relevant Member State/s and EFTA State/s, and submit a written request for a waiver asking the Commission to dispense with the obligation to provide that information, pursuant to Article 4(2) of the EC Merger Implementing Regulation. The Commission may consult with the relevant Member State or EFTA State authority or authorities before deciding whether to accede to such a request.]

Notes

Section B was amended as shown in square brackets by Commission Regulation (EC) No 1033/2008 (OJ L 279, 22.10.2008, p. 3) with effect from 23 October 2008.

C. Persons entitled to submit a reasoned submission

In the case of a merger within the meaning of Article 3(1)(a) of the EC Merger Regulation or the acquisition of joint control of an undertaking within the meaning of Article 3(1)(b) of the Merger Regulation, the reasoned submission must be completed jointly by the parties to the merger or by those acquiring joint control as the case may be.

In case of the acquisition of a controlling interest in one undertaking by another, the acquirer must complete the reasoned submission.

In the case of a public bid to acquire an undertaking, the bidder must complete the reasoned submission.

Each party completing a reasoned submission is responsible for the accuracy of the information which it provides.

D. How to make a reasoned submission

The reasoned submission must be completed in one of the official languages of the European Union.

[In order to facilitate treatment of Form RS by Member State and EFTA State authorities, parties are strongly encouraged to provide the Commission with a translation of their reasoned submission in a language or languages which will be understood by all addressees of the information. As regards requests for referral to (a) Member State/s or (an) EFTA State/s, the requesting parties are strongly encouraged to include a copy of the request in the language/s of the Member State/s and EFTA State/s to which referral is being requested.][1]

The information requested by this Form is to be set out using the sections and paragraph numbers of the Form, signing the declaration at the end, and annexing supporting documentation. For the sake of clarity, certain information may be put in annexes. However, it is essential that all key substantive pieces of information are presented in the body of Form RS. Annexes to this Form shall only be used to supplement the information supplied in the Form itself.

Supporting documents are to be submitted in their original language; where this is not an official language of the Community, they must be translated into the language of the proceeding.

Supporting documents may be originals or copies of the originals. In the latter case, the submitting party must confirm that they are true and complete.

One original and [38][2] copies of the Form RS and of the supporting documents must be submitted to the Commission. The reasoned submission shall be delivered to the address referred to in Article 23 (1) of the EC Merger Implementing Regulation and in the format specified by the Commission services.

The submission must be delivered to the address of the Commission's Directorate-General for Competition (DG Competition). This address is published in the *Official Journal of the European Union*. The submission must be delivered to the Commission on working days as defined by Article 24 of the EC Merger Implementing Regulation. In order to enable it to be registered on the same day, it must be delivered before 17.00 hrs on Mondays to Thursdays and before 16.00 hrs on Fridays and workdays preceding public holidays and other holidays as determined by the Commission and published in the *Official Journal of the European Union*. The security instructions given on DG Competition's website must be adhered to.

Notes

[1] The words in square brackets were substituted by Commission Regulation (EC) No 1033/2008 (OJ L 279, 22.10.2008, p. 3) with effect from 23 October 2008.

[2] The amendment shown in square brackets was made by Commission Regulation (EU) No 519/2013 of 21 February 2013 adapting certain regulations and decisions by reason of the accession of Croatia (OJ L 158, 10.6.2013, p. 74), with effect from 1 July 2013.

E. Confidentiality

[Article [339] of the Treaty and Article 17(2) of the EC Merger Regulation, as well as the corresponding provisions of the EEA Agreement[1] require the Commission, the Member States, the EFTA Surveillance Authority and the EFTA States, their officials and other servants not to disclose information they have acquired through the application of the Regulation of the kind covered by the obligation of professional secrecy. The same principle must also apply to protect confidentiality between notifying parties.]

If you believe that your interests would be harmed if any of the information supplied were to be published or otherwise divulged to other parties, submit this information separately with each page clearly marked "Business Secrets". You should also give reasons why this information should not be divulged or published.

In the case of mergers or joint acquisitions, or in other cases where the reasoned submission is completed by more than one of the parties, business secrets may be submitted in separate annexes, and referred to in the submission as an annex. All such annexes must be included in the reasoned submission.

Notes

[1 See, in particular, Article 122 of the EEA Agreement, Article 9 of Protocol 24 to the EEA Agreement and Article 17(2) of Chapter XIII of Protocol 4 to the Surveillance and Court Agreement.]
Section E was amended as shown in square brackets by Commission Regulation (EC) No 1033/2008 (OJ L 279, 22.10.2008, p. 3) with effect from 23 October 2008.

F. Definitions and instructions for the purposes of this Form

Submitting party or parties: in cases where a reasoned submission is made by only one of the undertakings who is a party to an operation, "submitting parties" is used to refer only to the undertaking actually making the submission.

Party(ies) to the concentration or parties: these terms relate to both the acquiring and acquired parties, or to the merging parties, including all undertakings in which a controlling interest is being acquired or which is the subject of a public bid.

Except where otherwise specified, the terms "submitting party(ies)" and "party(ies) to the concentration" include all the undertakings which belong to the same groups as those "parties".

Affected markets: Section 4 of this Form requires the submitting parties to define the relevant product markets, and further to identify which of those relevant markets are likely to be affected by the operation. This definition of affected market is used as the basis for requiring information for a number of other questions contained in this Form. The definitions thus submitted by the submitting parties are referred to in this Form as the affected market(s). This term can refer to a relevant market made up either of products or of services.

Year: all references to the word "year" in this Form should be read as meaning calendar year, unless otherwise stated. All information requested in this Form relates, unless otherwise specified, to the year preceding that of the reasoned submission.

The financial data requested in this Form must be provided in Euros at the average exchange rates prevailing for the years or other periods in question.

All references contained in this Form are to the relevant Articles and paragraphs of the EC Merger Regulation, unless otherwise stated.

SECTION I

Background information

1.0. Indicate whether the reasoned submission is made under Article 4(4) or (5).
    — Article 4(4) referral
    — Article 4(5) referral

1.1. Information on the submitting party (or parties)
    Give details of:
    1.1.1. the name and address of undertaking;
    1.1.2. the nature of the undertaking's business;
    1.1.3. the name, address, telephone number, fax number and electronic address of, and position held by, the appropriate contact person; and
    1.1.4. an address for service of the submitting party (or each of the submitting parties) to which documents and, in particular, Commission decisions may be delivered. The name, telephone number and e-mail address of a person at this address who is authorised to accept service must be provided.

1.2. Information on the other parties[1] to the concentration
    For each party to the concentration (except the submitting party or parties) give details of:
    1.2.1. the name and address of undertaking;
    1.2.2. the nature of undertaking's business;
    1.2.3. the name, address, telephone number, fax number and electronic address of, and position held by the appropriate contact person;

1.2.4. an address for service of the party (or each of the parties) to which documents and, in particular, Commission Decisions may be delivered. The name, e-mail address and telephone number of a person at this address who is authorised to accept service must be provided.

Notes

[1] This includes the target company in the case of a contested bid, in which case the details should be completed as far as is possible.

1.3. Appointment of representatives

Where reasoned submissions are signed by representatives of undertakings, such representatives must produce written proof that they are authorized to act. The written proof must contain the name and position of the persons granting such authority.

Provide the following contact details of any representatives who have been authorized to act for any of the parties to the concentration, indicating whom they represent:

1.3.1. the name of the representative;

1.3.2. the address of the representative;

1.3.3. the name, address, telephone number, fax number and e-mail address of the person to be contacted; and

1.3.4. an address of the representative (in Brussels if available) to which correspondence may be sent and documents delivered.

SECTION 2

General background and details of the concentration

2.1. Describe the general background to the concentration. In particular, give an overview of the main reasons for the transaction, including its economic and strategic rationale.

Provide an executive summary of the concentration, specifying the parties to the concentration, the nature of the concentration (for example, merger, acquisition, or joint venture.), the areas of activity of the submitting parties, the markets on which the concentration will have an impact (including the main affected markets[1]), and the strategic and economic rationale for the concentration.

Notes

[1] See Section 4 for the definition of affected markets.

2.2. Describe the legal nature of the transaction which is the subject of the reasoned submission. In doing so, indicate:
   (a) whether the whole or parts of the parties are subject to the concentration;
   (b) the proposed or expected date of any major events designed to bring about the completion of the concentration;
   (c) the proposed structure of ownership and control after the completion of the concentration; and
   (d) whether the proposed transaction is a concentration within the meaning of Article 3 of the EC Merger Regulation.

2.3. List the economic sectors involved in the concentration.
   2.3.1. State the value of the transaction (the purchase price or the value of all the assets involved, as the case may be).

2.4. Provide sufficient financial or other data to show that the concentration meets OR does not meet the jurisdictional thresholds under Article 1 of the EC Merger Regulation.
   2.4.1. Provide a breakdown of the Community-wide turnover achieved by the undertakings concerned, indicating, where applicable, the Member State, if any, in which more than two-thirds of this turnover is achieved.
   [2.4.2. Provide a breakdown of the EFTA-wide turnover achieved by the undertakings concerned, indicating, where applicable, the EFTA State, if any, in which more than two-thirds of this turnover is achieved.]

Part D Mergers and Concentrations

Notes
Subsection 2.4.2 was added by Commission Regulation (EC) No 1033/2008 (OJ L 279, 22.10.2008, p. 3) with effect from 23 October 2008.

SECTION 3
Ownership and control[1]

Notes
[1] See Article 3(3), 3(4) and 3(5) and Article 5(4).

For each of the parties to the concentration provide a list of all undertakings belonging to the same group.

This list must include:

3.1. all undertakings or persons controlling these parties, directly or indirectly;

3.2. all undertakings active on any affected market[1] that are controlled, directly or indirectly:
    (a) by these parties;
    (b) by any other undertaking identified in 3.1.

For each entry listed above, the nature and means of control should be specified.

The information sought in this section may be illustrated by the use of organization charts or diagrams to show the structure of ownership and control of the undertakings.

Notes
[1] See Section 4 for the definition of affected markets.

SECTION 4
Market definitions

The relevant product and geographic markets determine the scope within which the market power of the new entity resulting from the concentration must be assessed.[1]

Notes
[1] See Commission Notice on the definition of the relevant market for the purposes of Community competition law.

The submitting party or parties must provide the data requested having regard to the following definitions:

I. Relevant product markets

A relevant product market comprises all those products and/or services which are regarded as interchangeable or substitutable by the consumer, by reason of the products' characteristics, their prices and their intended use. A relevant product market may in some cases be composed of a number of individual products and/or services which present largely identical physical or technical characteristics and are interchangeable.

Factors relevant to the assessment of the relevant product market include the analysis of why the products or services in these markets are included and why others are excluded by using the above definition, and having regard to, for example, substitutability, conditions of competition, prices, cross-price elasticity of demand or other factors relevant for the definition of the product markets (for example, supply-side substitutability in appropriate cases).

II. Relevant geographic markets

The relevant geographic market comprises the area in which the undertakings concerned are involved in the supply and demand of relevant products or services, in which the conditions of competition are sufficiently homogeneous and which can be distinguished from neighbouring geographic areas because, in particular, conditions of competition are appreciably different in those areas.

Factors relevant to the assessment of the relevant geographic market include inter alia the nature and characteristics of the products or services concerned, the existence of entry barriers, consumer preferences, appreciable differences in the undertakings' market shares between neighbouring geographic areas, or substantial price differences.

III. Affected markets

[For the purposes of the information required in this Form, affected markets consist of relevant product markets where, in the EEA territory, in the Community, in the territory of the EFTA States, in any Member State or in any EFTA State:]

(a) two or more of the parties to the concentration are engaged in business activities in the same product market and where the concentration will lead to a combined market share of 15% or more. These are horizontal relationships;

(b) one or more of the parties to the concentration are engaged in business activities in a product market, which is upstream or downstream of a product market in which any other party to the concentration is engaged, and any of their individual or combined market shares at either level is 25% or more, regardless of whether there is or is not any existing supplier/customer relationship between the parties to the concentration.[1] These are vertical relationships.

On the basis of the above definitions and market share thresholds, provide the following information:

[4.1 Identify each affected market within the meaning of Section III:
 (a) at the EEA, Community or EFTA level;
 (b) in the case of a request for referral pursuant to Article 4(4) of the EC Merger Regulation, at the level of each individual Member State or EFTA State;
 (c) in the case of a request for referral pursuant to Article 4(5) of the EC Merger Regulation, at the level of each Member State or EFTA State identified at Section 6.3.1 of this Form as capable of reviewing the concentration.]

4.2. In addition, explain the submitting parties' view as to the scope of the relevant geographic market within the meaning of Section II in relation to each affected market identified at 4.1 above.

Notes

[1] For example, if a party to the concentration holds a market share larger than 25% in a market that is upstream to a market in which the other party is active, then both the upstream and the downstream markets are affected markets. Similarly, if a vertically integrated company merges with another party which is active at the downstream level, and the merger leads to a combined market share downstream of 25% or more, then both the upstream and the downstream markets are affected markets.

Section III was amended as shown in square brackets by Commission Regulation (EC) No 1033/2008 (OJ L 279, 22.10.2008, p.3) with effect from 23 October 2008.

SECTION 5

Information on affected markets

[For each affected relevant product market, for the last financial year,

(a) for the EEA Territory, for the Community as a whole and for the EFTA States as a whole;

(b) in the case of a request for referral pursuant to Article 4(4) of the EC Merger Regulation, individually for each Member State/EFTA State where the parties to the concentration do business; and

(c) in the case of a request for referral pursuant to Article 4(5) of the EC Merger Regulation, individually for each Member State/EFTA State identified at Section 6.3.1 of this Form as capable of reviewing the concentration where the parties to the concentration do business; and]

(d) where in the opinion of the submitting parties, the relevant geographic market is different;

provide the following information:

5.1. an estimate of the total size of the market in terms of sales value (in Euros) and volume (units).[1] Indicate the basis and sources for the calculations and provide documents where available to confirm these calculations;

5.2. the sales in value and volume, as well as an estimate of the market shares, of each of the parties to the concentration;

5.3. an estimate of the market share in value (and where appropriate volume) of all competitors (including importers) having at least 5% of the geographic market under consideration; On this basis, provide an estimate of the HHI index[2] pre- and post-merger, and the difference between the two (the delta).[3] Indicate the proportion of market shares used as a basis to calculate the HHI; Identify the sources used to calculate these market shares and provide documents where available to confirm the calculation;

5.4. the five largest independent customers of the parties in each affected market and their individual share of total sales for such products accounted for by each of those customers;

5.5. the nature and extent of vertical integration of each of the parties to the concentration compared with their largest competitors;

5.6. identify the five largest independent[4] suppliers to the parties;

5.7. Over the last five years, has there been any significant entry into any affected markets? In the opinion of the submitting parties are there undertakings (including those at present operating only in extra-Community markets) that are likely to enter the market? Please specify.

5.8. To what extent do cooperative agreements (horizontal or vertical) exist in the affected markets?

5.9. If the concentration is a joint venture, do two or more parents retain to a significant extent activities in the same market as the joint venture or in a market which is downstream or upstream from that of the joint venture or in a neighbouring market closely related to this market?[5]

5.10. Describe the likely impact of the proposed concentration on competition in the affected markets and how the proposed concentration is likely to affect the interests of intermediate and ultimate consumers and the development of technical and economic progress.

Notes

[1] The value and volume of a market should reflect output less exports plus imports for the geographic areas under consideration.

[2] HHI stands for Herfindahl-Hirschman Index, a measure of market concentration. The HHI is calculated by summing the squares of the individual market shares of all the firms in the market. For example, a market containing five firms with market shares of 40%, 20%, 15%, 15%, and 10%, respectively, has an HHI of 2550 ($40^2 + 20^2 + 15^2 + 15^2 + 10^2 = 2,550$). The HHI ranges from close to zero (in an atomistic market) to 10,000 (in the case of a pure mono poly). The post-merger HHI is calculated on the working assumption that the individual market shares of the companies do not change. Although it is best to include all firms in the calculation, lack of information about very small firms may not be important because such firms do not affect the HHI significantly.

[3] The increase in concentration as measured by the HHI can be calculated independently of the overall market concentration by doubling the product of the market shares of the merging firms. For example, a merger of two firms with market shares of 30% and 15% respectively would increase the HHI by 900 ($30 \times 15 \times 2 = 900$). The explanation for this technique is as follows: Before the merger, the market shares of the merging firms contribute to the HHI by their squares individually: $(a)^2 + (b)^2$. After the merger, the contribution is the square of their sum: $(a + b)^2$, which equals $(a)^2 + (b)^2 + 2ab$. The increase in the HHI is therefore represented by $2ab$.

[4] That is suppliers which are not subsidiaries, agents or undertakings forming part of the group of the party in question. In addition to those five independent suppliers the notifying parties can, if they consider it necessary for a proper assessment of the case, identify the intra-group suppliers. The same applies in relation to customers.

[5] For market definitions refer to Section 4.

Section 5 was amended as shown in square brackets by Commission Regulation (EC) No 1033/2008 (OJ L 279, 22.10.2008, p. 3) with effect from 23 October 2008.

SECTION 6
Details of the referral request and reasons why the case should be referred

6.1. Indicate whether the reasoned submission is made pursuant to Article 4(4) or 4(5) of the EC Merger Regulation, and fill in only the relevant sub-section:
  — Article 4.4. referral
  — Article 4.5 referral

Sub-section 6.2

ARTICLE 4(4) REFERRAL

[6.2.1. Identify the Member State/s and EFTA State/s which, pursuant to Article 4(4) of the EC Merger Regulation, you submit should examine the concentration, indicating whether or not you have made informal contact with this Member State/s and/or EFTA State/s.]

6.2.2. Specify whether you are requesting referral of the whole or part of the case. If you are requesting referral of part of the case, specify clearly the part or parts of the case for which you request the referral. [If you are requesting referral of the whole of the case, you must confirm that there are no affected markets outside the territory of the Member State/s and EFTA State/s to which you request the referral to be made.]

[6.2.3. Explain in what way each of the affected markets in the Member State/s and EFTA State/s to which referral is requested presents all the characteristics of a distinct market within the meaning of Article 4(4) of the EC Merger Regulation.]

6.2.4. Explain in what way competition may be significantly affected in each of the above-mentioned distinct markets within the meaning of Article 4(4).

[6.2.5. In the event of a Member State/s and/or EFTA State/s becoming competent to review the whole or part of the case following a referral pursuant to Article 4(4) of the EC Merger Regulation, do you consent to the information contained in this Form being relied upon by the Member State/s and/or EFTA State/s in question for the purpose of its/their national proceedings relating to that case or part thereof? YES or NO.]

Sub-section 6.3

ARTICLE 4(5) REFERRAL

[6.3.1. For each Member State and/or EFTA State, specify whether the concentration is or is not capable of being reviewed under its national competition law. You must tick one box for each and every Member State and/or EFTA State.

Is the concentration capable of being reviewed under the national competition law of each of the following Member States and/or EFTA States? You must reply for each Member State and/or EFTA State. Only indicate YES or NO for each Member State and/or EFTA State. Failure to indicate YES or NO for any Member State and/or EFTA State shall be deemed to constitute an indication of YES for that Member State and/or EFTA State.

Belgium:	YES	NO
Bulgaria:	YES	NO
Czech Republic:	YES	NO
Denmark:	YES	NO
Germany:	YES	NO
Estonia:	YES	NO
Ireland:	YES	NO
Greece:	YES	NO
Spain:	YES	NO
France:	YES	NO
Italy:	YES	NO
Cyprus:	YES	NO
Latvia:	YES	NO
Lithuania:	YES	NO
Luxembourg:	YES	NO
Hungary:	YES	NO
Malta:	YES	NO
Netherlands:	YES	NO

743

Austria:	YES	NO
Poland:	YES	NO
Portugal:	YES	NO
Romania:	YES	NO
Slovenia:	YES	NO
Slovakia:	YES	NO
Finland:	YES	NO
Sweden:	YES	NO
United Kingdom:	YES	NO

6.3.2. For each Member State and/or EFTA State, provide sufficient financial or other data to show that the concentration meets or does not meet the relevant jurisdictional criteria under the applicable national competition law.

6.3.3. Explain why the case should be examined by the Commission. Explain in particular whether the concentration might affect competition beyond the territory of one Member State and/ or EFTA State.]

Notes

Section 6 was amended as shown in square brackets by Commission Regulation (EC) No 1033/2008 (OJ L 279, 22.10.2008, p.3) with effect from 23 October 2008.

SECTION 7
Declaration

It follows from Articles 2(2) and 6(2) of the EC Merger Implementing Regulation that where reasoned submissions are signed by representatives of undertakings, such representatives must produce written proof that they are authorized to act. Such written authorization must accompany the submission.

The reasoned submission must conclude with the following declaration which is to be signed by or on behalf of all the submitting parties:

The submitting party or parties declare that, following careful verification, the information given in this reasoned submission is to the best of their knowledge and belief true, correct, and complete, that true and complete copies of documents required by Form RS, have been supplied, and that all estimates are identified as such and are their best estimates of the underlying facts and that all the opinions expressed are sincere.

They are aware of the provisions of Article 14(1)(a) of the EC Merger Regulation.

Place and date:

Signatures:

Name/s and positions:

On behalf of:

[ANNEX IV
FORM RM RELATING TO THE INFORMATION CONCERNING COMMITMENTS SUBMITTED PURSUANT TO ARTICLE 6(2) AND ARTICLE 8(2) OF REGULATION (EC) No 139/2004

FORM RM RELATING TO REMEDIES]

Commentary

Annex IV: **B&C:** 8.167 **F&N:** 5.341, 5.409, 5.983

Notes
Annex IV was added by Commission Regulation (EC) No 1033/2008 (OJ L 279, 22.10.2008, p. 3) with effect from 23 October 2008.

Introduction

This form specifies the information and documents to be submitted by the undertakings concerned at the same time as offering commitments pursuant to Article 6(2) or Article 8(2) of Regulation (EC) No 139/2004. The information requested is necessary to allow the Commission to examine whether the commitments are capable of rendering the concentration compatible with the common market in that they will prevent a significant impediment to effective competition. The Commission may dispense with the obligation to provide any particular information in respect of the commitments offered, including documents, or with any other requirement laid down in this form where it considers that compliance with those obligations or requirements is not necessary for the examination of the commitments offered. The level of information required will vary according to the type and structure of the remedy proposed. For example, carve-out remedies will typically require more detailed information than divestitures of stand-alone businesses. The Commission is available to discuss the scope of the information required with the parties upfront. If you consider that any particular information requested by this Form may not be necessary for the Commission's assessment, you may approach the Commission asking to dispense with certain requirements, giving adequate reasons why that information is not relevant.

Section 1
Description of the commitment

1.1. Provide detailed information on
 (i) the object of the commitments offered, and
 (ii) the conditions for their implementation.

1.2. Where the commitments offered consist in the divestiture of a business, Section 5 provides for the specific information required.

Section 2
Suitability to remove competition concerns

2. Provide information showing the suitability of the commitments offered to remove the significant impediment of effective competition identified by the Commission.

Section 3
Deviation from model texts

3. Identify any deviations of the commitments offered from the pertinent Model Commitments texts published by the Commission's services, as revised from time-to-time, and explain the reasons for the deviations.

Section 4
Summary of the commitments

4. Provide a non-confidential summary of the nature and scope of the commitments offered and why, in your view, they are suitable to remove any significant impediment to effective competition. The Commission may use this summary for the market test of the commitments offered with third parties.

Section 5
Information on a business to be divested

5. Where the commitments offered consist in the divestiture of a business, provide the following information and documents.

Part D Mergers and Concentrations

General information on the business to be divested

The following information should be provided as to the current operation of the business to be divested and changes already planned for the future:

5.1. Describe the business to be divested generally, including the entities belonging to it, their registered place of business and place of management, other locations for production or provisions of services, the general organisational structure and any other relevant information relating to the administrative structure of the business to be divested.

5.2. State whether there are and describe any legal obstacles for the transfer of the business to be divested or the assets, including third party rights and administrative approvals required.

5.3. List and describe the products manufactured or services provided, in particular their technical and other characteristics, the brands involved, the turnover generated with each of these products or services, and any innovations or new products or services planned.

5.4. Describe the level on which the essential functions of the business to be divested are operated if they are not operated on the level of the business to be divested itself, including such functions as research and development, production, marketing and sales, logistics, relations with customers, relations with suppliers, IT systems, etc. The description should contain the role performed by those other levels, the relations with the business to be divested and the resources (personnel, assets, financial resources, etc.) involved in the function.

5.5. Describe in detail the links between the business to be divested and other undertakings controlled by the notifying parties (irrespective of the direction of the link), such as:
   — supply, production, distribution, service or other contracts,
   — shared tangible or intangible assets,
   — shared or seconded personnel,
   — shared IT systems or other systems, and
   — shared customers.

5.6. Describe in general terms all relevant tangible and intangible assets used and/or owned by the business to be divested, including, in any case, IP rights and brands.

5.7. Submit an organisational chart identifying the number of personnel currently working in each of the functions of the business to be divested and a list of those employees who are indispensable for the operation of the business to be divested, describing their functions.

5.8. Describe the customers of the business to be divested, including a list of customers, a description of the corresponding records available, and provide the total turnover generated by the business to be divested with each of these customers (in EUR and as percentage of the total turnover of business to be divested).

5.9. Provide financial data for the business to be divested, including the turnover and the EBITDA achieved in the last two years, and the forecast for the next two years.

5.10. Identify and describe any changes that have occurred in the last two years, in the organisation of the business to be divested or in the links with other undertakings controlled by the notifying parties.

5.11. Identify and describe any changes, planned for the next two years, in the organisation of the business to be divested or in the links with other undertakings controlled by the notifying parties.

General information on the business to be divested as described in the commitments

5.12. Describe any areas where the business to be divested as set out in the commitments offered differs from the nature and scope of the business as currently operated.

Acquisition by a suitable purchaser

5.13. Explain the reasons why, in your view, the business will be acquired by a suitable purchaser in the time-frame proposed in the commitments offered.'

D3

BEST PRACTICE GUIDELINES: THE COMMISSION'S MODEL TEXTS FOR DIVESTITURE COMMITMENTS AND THE TRUSTEE MANDATE UNDER THE EC MERGER REGULATION

Note

This document is published on the Europa website at:
<http://ec.europa.eu/comm/competition/mergers/legislation/explanatory_note.pdf>

Commentary
Best Practice: B&C: 8.007 F&N: 5.983, 5.1018

1. The European Commission's model texts for divestiture commitments and trustee mandates are designed to serve as best practice guidelines for notifying parties submitting commitments under the EC Merger Regulation.[1] These texts are (1) the model to be used for divestiture commitments (the "*Standard Model for Divestiture Commitments*" or the "*Standard Commitments*"); and (2) the model for the mandate of the two types of trustees referred to in the Standard Commitments, that is, the mandate appointing monitoring and divestiture trustees (the "*Standard Trustee Mandate*").

Notes

[1] Council Regulation (EEC) No 4064/89 of 21 December 1989 on the control of concentrations between undertakings, as amended, OJ L 395, 30.12.1989, p.1; corrigendum OJ L 257, 21.9.1990, p.13.

2. The model texts (the "*Standard Models*") are based upon the experience the Commission has gained to date in fashioning remedies from previous merger cases and are drafted in line with the remedies policy set out in the Commission's Notice on Remedies[2] (the "*Remedies Notice*"). The Standard Models are neither intended to provide an exhaustive coverage of all issues that may become relevant in all cases, nor are they legally binding upon parties in a merger procedure. Rather, they contain the elements for all standard provisions that should be included in commitments and trustee mandates relating to divestitures. In providing a framework for commitments and trustee mandates to be submitted in concrete cases, the Standard Models leave the flexibility to adapt the texts to the specific requirements of the case in question.

Notes

[2] See Commission Notice on remedies acceptable under Council Regulation (EEC) No 4064/89 and Regulation (EC) No 447/98 at *Official Journal* C 68, 02.03.2001, pp. 3–11; published on <http://europa.eu.int/eur-lex/pri/en/oj/dat/2001/c_068/c_06820010302en00030011.pdf>. [Ed note: see now Commission Notice on remedies acceptable under Council Regulation (EC) No 139/2004 and under Commission Regulation (EC) No 802/2004 (OJ C 267, 22.10.2008, p.1), reproduced below at D13.]

3. The Standard Models are designed to apply to all remedy proceedings in both Phase I and Phase II, therefore to all Commission decisions according to Articles 6(2) and 8(2) of the Merger Regulation. The Standard Models deal specifically with divestiture commitments inasmuch as the Commission's Remedies Notice stipulates that divestiture commitments are normally the preferred form of merger remedies; they are also the most common. However, it should be underlined that the Commission will consider the acceptability of other types of commitments in appropriate circumstances, as set out in the Remedies Notice. Individual provisions contained in the Standard Models can be used in cases involving such other types of commitments.

4. Finally, it is expected that the text of these models will evolve, based on ongoing practice, and will be regularly up-dated by the Commission, taking into consideration both the developments of the Commission's remedies policy and the experience gained from working with the merging parties and trustees in future matters.

The Purpose of the Standard Models

5. The Commission recognises that timing is crucial when merging parties reach the remedies stage in merger review procedures, where they offer commitments in order to resolve the Commission's competition concerns in a given case. Through the use of standardised models, the merging parties and the Commission will be relieved of the heavy demands — both in terms of time and resources — that would otherwise be required to negotiate the standard terms and provisions for commitments and trustee mandates under tight time constraints. The use of standardised models will expedite the proceedings and allow the merging parties to concentrate more on the actual substance and implementation of the commitments.

6. The use of the standard models will ensure consistency across cases and will thereby contribute to increasing the level of transparency and legal certainty for the merging parties offering commitments to the Commission.

Overview of the Contents of the Standard Models

7. The Standard Model for Divestiture Commitments sets out all requirements for achieving full and effective compliance with divestiture commitments offered by the merging parties (the "*Parties*") to obtain a clearance decision. More specifically, this Model is designed (i) to describe clearly the business to be divested ("*Divestment Business*"), the divestiture procedure and the obligations of the parties in relation to the Divestment Business for the interim period until divestiture has been completed, (ii) to set out the various responsibilities that the merging parties will thereby have, respectively, to the Commission, the Trustee, and the Divestment Business; and (iii) to enshrine the importance which the Commission places upon requiring an acceptable purchaser for the Divestment Business in order to ensure the viability and competitiveness of the new entity in the market where the divestiture takes place.

8. The Standard Model for Trustee Mandates sets out the role and functions of the Trustee, as provided in the Standard Commitments, in a contractual relationship between the Parties responsible for the divestiture and the Trustee. As the Commitments set out the basis for the responsibilities of the Trustee, the Standard Trustee Mandate has been prepared in conformity with the requirements laid down for the Trustee in the Standard Model for Divestiture Commitments.

9. Although the Standard Trustee Mandate is a bilateral contract between the Parties responsible for the divestiture and the Trustee, this document forms the basis for a tri-partite relationship among the Commission, the Trustee, and the Parties. The relationship between the Parties and the Trustee is not a traditional trusteeship. The Trustee rather benefits from a status which makes it independent from the Parties and which is characterised by the role of the Trustee to monitor (Monitoring Trustee) or even to effectuate (Divestiture Trustee) the Parties' compliance with the commitments. Accordingly, the Parties are not entitled to give instructions to the Trustee, whereas the Commission is allowed to do so. This specific relationship is also confirmed by the fact that the Trustee Mandate requires the Commission's approval.

10. The Standard Trustee Mandate is designed (i) to facilitate the smooth and timely appointment of the Trustee and the approval of the Trustee Mandate; (ii) to clarify the relationship among the Commission, the Trustee, and the Parties; and (iii) to set out the tasks of the Trustee in the process in order to enable the Trustee to expedite compliance with the commitments. Whereas the Standard Trustee Mandate defines the role of a Monitoring and a Divestiture Trustee in one text, they can be assigned to different Trustees in practice.

11. In providing guidance for the interpretation of the Standard Texts, a certain hierarchy is established. The Standard Trustee Mandate should be interpreted in the light of the Standard Commitments, as they lay the foundation for the application of the Trustee Mandate. To the extent that they are attached as conditions and obligations, the commitments are to be interpreted in the light of the respective Commission decision. Moreover, both Standard Texts should be interpreted in the general framework of Community law, in particular in the light of the EC Merger Regulation, and by reference to the Commission's Remedies Notice setting out the Commission's remedies policy.

Description of the Provisions of the Standard Models

12. The most important provisions contained in both Standard Models are briefly set out below.

Standard Model for Divestiture Commitments

13. The Standard Model for Commitments consists of the following main elements:

14. Section A contains a definitions section.

15. Section B contains the commitment to divest and the definition of the Divestment Business. After spelling out the general obligation to divest the Divestment Business as a going concern, paragraph 1 describes the divestiture procedure, which may take two phases. The Commitments provide that in the first phase (that is, the *Divestiture Period*), the Parties have the sole responsibility for finding a suitable purchaser for the Divestment Business. If the Parties do not succeed in divesting the business on their own in the Divestiture Period, then a Divestiture Trustee will be appointed with an exclusive mandate to dispose of the Divestment Business at no minimum price, in the Extended Divestiture Period. The individual deadlines are determined in the definitions section. The experience of the Commission has shown that short divestiture periods contribute largely to the success of the divestiture as, otherwise, the Divestment Business will be exposed to an extended period of uncertainty. The Commission will normally consider a period of around 6 months for the Divestiture Period and an additional period of 3 to 6 months for the Extended Divestiture Period as appropriate. These periods may be modified according to the particular requirements of the case in question.

16. The divestiture commitment will take a special form in those cases where the Parties propose an up-front buyer. The Parties commit not to implement the proposed concentration unless and until they have entered into a binding agreement with a purchaser for the Divestment Business, approved by the Commission. The qualification of the buyer are the same as in other divestiture commitments. The up-front buyer concept has been applied in several cases[3] and will be used in the specific circumstances as described in the Notice.[4] The structure of the divestiture commitment also needs to be adapted in cases of alternative divestitures, in particular "Crown Jewels" structures, i.e. structures in which the Parties commit to divest a very attractive business if they have not divested the originally proposed business until the end of a period fixed in the commitments. The circumstances in which the Commission will accept alternative divestiture commitments are also set out in the Remedies Notice.[5]

Notes

[3] Cases COMP/M.2060 — *Bosch/Rexroth*; COMP/M.1915 — *The Post Office/TPG/SPPL*; COMP/M.2544 — *Masterfood/Royal Canin*.

[4] Paragraph 18 of the Remedies Notice.

[5] Paragraphs 22, 23 of the Remedies Notice.

---

17. The divestiture commitment includes the commitment not to re-acquire direct or indirect influence over the Divestment Business (paragraph 3). This re-acquisition prohibition is limited to ten years after the date of the decision and serves to maintain the structural effects of the Commitments. The Commission may grant a waiver if the structure of the market has changed to such an extent that the absence of influence over the Divestment Business is no longer necessary to render the concentration compatible with the common market.

18. Section B, together with the Schedule to the Commitments, defines what is included in the Divestment Business. The clear identification of the Divestment Business is of great importance as thereby the scope of the divestiture and of the hold-separate obligations are defined. As set out in the Notice, the Divestment Business is considered to be an existing entity that can operate on a stand-alone-basis.[6] The Divestment Business is the minimum which is to be divested by the Parties in order to comply with the Commitments. In order to make the package more attractive to buyers, the Parties may add, on their own initiative, other assets.[7] The Divestment Business must include all the assets and personnel necessary to ensure the viability of the divested activities. Whereas this principle is set out as an undertaking of the Parties in paragraph 3 of the Standard Commitments, the Parties have to give a detailed factual description of the Divestment Business in the Schedule to the Standard Commitments.

Notes

6 Cf. paragraph 14 of the Remedies Notice. The importance of the divestiture of an on-going business for the success of the remedy has also been underlined by the FTC in a published study entitled A Study of the Commission's Divestiture Process, prepared by the Staff of the Bureau of Competition of the Federal Trade Commission, p.10 ff.

7 Cf. paragraph 21 of the Remedies Notice.

19. The Divestment Business must comprise the Personnel and the Key Personnel retained by the Divestment Business as well as the personnel providing essential functions for the Divestment Business, such as the central R&D staff. The personnel (according to groups and functions performed) is to be listed in the Schedule to the Commitments, the Key Personnel is to be listed separately. The principle, indicated in paragraph 4(d), is that the personnel should be transferred with the Divestment Business. If the Divestment Business takes the form of a company or if the transfer of undertakings legislation applies, the personnel will normally be transferred by operation of law. In other cases, the acquirer of the business can retain and select the personnel and can make offers of employment. The transfer — whichever form it takes — is without prejudice to the application of Council Directives, where applicable, on collective redundancies;[8] on safeguarding employees rights in the event of transfers of undertakings;[9] and on informing and consulting employees,[10] as well as relevant national law on these matters.

Notes

8 Council Directive 98/59/EC of 20 July 1998 on the approximation of the laws of the Member States relating to collective redundancies (OJ L 225, 12.8.1998, p.16).

9 Council Directive 77/187/EEC on the approximation of the laws of the Member States relating to the safeguarding of employees rights in the event of transfers of undertakings, businesses or parts of a business (OJ L 61, 5.3.1977, p.26) as amended by Council Directive 98/50/EC (OJ L 201, 17.7.1998, p.88).

10 Council Directive 94/45/EC of 22 September 1994 on the establishment of a European Works Council or a procedure in Community-scale undertakings and Community-scale groups of undertakings for the purposes of informing and consulting employees (OJ L 254, 30.9.1994, p.64) as amended by Directive 97/74/EC (OJ L 10, 16.1.1998, p.22).

20. Furthermore, the Standard Commitments foresee that the Divestment Business shall be entitled to benefit from products or services provided by the Parties for a transitional period, determined on a case-by-case basis, if this is necessary to maintain the full economic viability and competitiveness of the Divestment Business (paragraph 4(e) of the Standard Commitments referring to the products or services listed in the Schedule).

21. Section C contains a number of related commitments, which are designed to maintain, pending divestiture, the viability, marketability and competitiveness of the Divestment Business. These provisions deal with the preservation of the divested entity's viability and independence, as well as the hold-separate and ring-fencing obligations. The Hold Separate Manager, to be appointed by the Parties and normally the manager of the Divestment Business, is responsible for the management of the Divestment Business as a distinct entity separate from the businesses retained by the Parties, and is supervised by the Monitoring Trustee.

22. In certain cases it may also be necessary for the hold-separate obligation to apply to the corporate structure itself. That is, in cases where the Divestment Business takes the form of a company and a strict separation of the corporate structure is necessary, the Monitoring Trustee must be given the authority to (i) exercise the Parties' rights as shareholders in the Divestment Business and (ii) to replace members of the supervisory board or non-executive directors on the board of directors who have been appointed on behalf of the Parties (cf. paragraph 8 of the Standard Commitments and paragraph 6(d) of the Standard Trustee Mandate).

23. Of particular importance is the ring-fencing of competitively sensitive information of the Divestment Business. The parties are obliged to implement all necessary measures to ensure that they do not obtain such information of the Divestment Business and, in particular, to sever its participation in a central information technology network. The Monitoring Trustee may allow the disclosure of information to the divesting party if this is reasonably necessary for the divestiture of the Divestment Business or required by law (e.g. information necessary for group accounts).

24. The related commitments further contain a non-solicitation clause for Key Personnel of the Divestment Business. According to the experience of the Commission, the non-solicitation

period, dependent on the circumstances of the case, should normally be two years. In addition, the Commission may request the inclusion of a non-compete clause in the commitments protecting the customers of the Divestment Business for a start-up period. This may be required to enable the Divestment Business to be active as a viable competitor in the market. The period for such customer protection clause will depend on the market in question.

25. During the Divestiture Phase, the divestiture lies in the hands of the divesting party. The Commission does not have a preference as to the method the parties use to select an acceptable purchaser as long as they meet the objective of the divestiture, to maintain or restore competition. However, as part of the due diligence procedure, it is foreseen that the divesting party shall provide to potential purchasers sufficient information as regards the Divestment Business and allow them access to its personnel (paragraph 11 of the Standard Commitments) in order to enable them to determine whether it will be possible to maintain and to develop the Divestment Business as active and viable competitive force in the market after the divestiture.

26. The divesting party shall further submit regular reports on potential purchasers and developments in the divestiture process to the Commission and the Monitoring Trustee (paragraph 12 of the Standard Commitments). This reporting mechanism gives the Monitoring Trustee the basis on which to assess the progress of the divestiture process as well as potential purchasers (for the Trustee's report, see paragraph 23(vi) of the Standard Commitments) and keeps the Commission informed.

27. Section D sets out the requirements to be met by the Purchaser. The aim of this section is to ensure that the Divestment Business will be sold to a suitable purchaser who is independent of and unconnected to the Parties, and who possesses the financial resources, proven expertise and incentive to maintain and develop the Divestment Business as a viable and active competitive force in the marketplace. These Purchaser Requirements can generally be met by either industrial or financial investors. The latter must demonstrate the necessary management capabilities and "proven expertise" which can in particular be met by financing a management buy-out.

28. Section D also deals with the approval process. After finalising the agreement(s), the divesting party shall submit a fully documented and reasoned proposal to the Commission. The Commission will verify that the purchaser will fulfil the requirements and that the Divestment Business is being sold in a manner consistent with the Commitments. One element for its assessment will be the report of the Monitoring Trustee according to paragraph 23(vii). The Commission may approve the sale of the Divestment Business without parts of the assets or personnel of the Divestment Business if this does not affect the viability and competitiveness of the Divestment Business, in particular if the Purchaser provides for such assets or personnel itself.

29. Section E deals with both the Monitoring and Divestiture Trustees. It identifies the terms for their appointment, as well as the content of the Trustee Mandates, and conditions for replacement of the Trustee during the divestiture periods if that becomes necessary. A Monitoring Trustee must be proposed by the Parties within one week after the adoption of the decision, whereas a Divestiture Trustee must be proposed no later than one month before the end of the Divestiture Period, (paragraph 16 of the Standard Commitments). The Commission wishes to emphasise the importance it attaches to compliance with these deadlines in practise, as otherwise the Parties are in breach of the commitments and the divestiture procedure is endangered.

30. Section E also sets out the duties and obligations of both types of Trustees. The Monitoring Trustee's responsibilities (mainly set out in paragraph 23 Standard Commitments) relate to both the management of the Divestment Business during the hold-separate period and the monitoring of the divestiture process itself. The supervision of the management shall in particular ensure the viability, marketability and competitiveness of the Divestment Business and the compliance with the hold-separate and ring-fencing obligations. The Standard Commitments further assign certain monitoring tasks concerning the divestiture process to the Monitoring Trustee in the Divestiture Period. Once the Parties have proposed a purchaser for the Divestment Business, the Monitoring Trustee assesses the independence and suitability of the proposed purchaser and the viability of the Divestment Business after the sale to the purchaser, in order to assist the Commission in assessing the suitability of the proposed purchaser.

31. In the Extended Divestiture Period, the Divestiture Trustee will have an exclusive mandate to sell the Divestment Business at no minimum price and is empowered to include in the sale and

purchase agreement such terms and conditions as it considers appropriate for an expedient sale. However, it is foreseen that the Trustee has to protect the legitimate financial interests of the divesting parties, subject to its unconditional obligation to divest at no minimum price. The Divestiture Trustee must report regularly on the progress of the divestiture process.

32. Also in Section E (paragraphs 26–30), the duties and obligations of the Parties vis-à-vis the Trustee are defined. Beside the provision of information, the Parties are in particular obliged to provide the Monitoring Trustee with all managerial and administrative support necessary for the Divestment Business and to grant to the Divestiture Trustee comprehensive powers of attorney covering all steps of the sale of the Divestment Business. An indemnification clause is included in order to reinforce the independent status of the Trustee from the Parties. Such a clause is already common practice in the trustee mandates submitted to the Commission for approval. The Trustee may further, at the expense of the Parties, retain advisors with specialised skills, in particular for corporate finance or legal advice.

33. Section E further foresees that trustees may only be removed in exceptional circumstances and with the approval of the Commission before the complete implementation of the Commitments.

34. Section F contains a review clause, which allows the Commission to extend the periods specified in the Commitments and to waive or modify the undertakings in the Commitments. The Parties must show good cause in order to be able to benefit from the exercise of the review clause. Requests for the extension of time periods shall, normally, be submitted no later than one month before the expiry of the time period in question.

Standard Model for Trustee Mandates

35. The Standard Model for Trustee Mandates sets out the duties and responsibilities of both Monitoring and Divestiture Trustee in a single text. However, the language makes clear that the Commission does not have a preference for the appointment of a single person to serve in the dual role of both Monitoring and Divestiture Trustee. Rather, the decision as to whether one or more trustees are appointed should be determined on a case-by-case basis by the Parties. If more than one trustee shall serve in these roles, only the provisions relevant for the Monitoring or Divestiture Trustee, respectively, have to be included in the individual mandate.

36. The Standard Trustee Mandate consists of the following main elements:

37. Section A contains some definitions and references the definitions included in the Standard Commitments.

38. Sections B to G contain provisions regarding the appointment of the Trustee (Section B), its general duties (Section C), the specific duties and obligations of the Monitoring and Divestiture Trustees (Sections D and E), reporting obligations identifying certain important subjects that should be discussed in each report (Section G), and duties and obligations of the Parties vis-à-vis the Trustee (Section F). These arrangements are based on the provisions established in the Standard Commitments in relation to the Trustee and described above.

39. Sections H to J cover additional trustee-related provisions, including provisions regarding the remuneration of the Trustee(s), procedures concerning the termination of the Mandate, and certain additional provisions, such as determination of applicable national law.

40. In particular, the independence of the trustee and the absence of conflicts of interests of the trustee are of great importance for the Commission in deciding on the approval of the Trustee and the respective mandate. The provisions in the Standard Trustee Mandate (paragraphs 20 to 23) ensuring the independence of the trustee from the parties and the absence of conflicts of interest foresee the following procedure: (1) The Trustee must disclose all current relationships with the Parties (paragraph 20) at the time at which the Trustee Mandate is entered into. (2) During the term of the mandate, the Trustee undertakes not to create a conflict of interest by having or accepting employment or appointment as a Member of the Board of the Parties or by having or accepting any assignments or other business relationships with, or financial interests in, the Parties. (3) As legal consequences it is foreseen that, if the Trustee becomes aware of a conflict of interest during the Mandate, the Trustee must notify the Commission and resolve the problem immediately and, if the conflict of interest cannot subsequently be resolved, the Commission may require the termination of the trustee mandate. These rules concerning conflicts of interests apply to the Trustee itself,

members of the Trustee Team and the Trustee Partner Firms as members of the same organisation. (4) For a period of one year following termination of the Mandate, the members of the Trustee Team shall not provide services to the Parties without the Commission's prior approval and must establish measures to ensure the integrity of the members of the Trustee Team.

41. In addition to the rules laid down in the Standard Trustee Mandate, it is up to the Parties and the Trustee to include provisions dealing with other potential conflicts of interests, such as conflicts of interests of the Trustee with potential purchasers.

Model Texts For Divestiture Commitments

Notes

The following texts are published on the Europa website at:
<http://ec.europa.eu/comm/competition/mergers/legislation/commitments.pdf>
All square brackets in the following document are original and not editorial.

By hand and by fax: 00 32 2 296 4301

European Commission — Merger Task Force

DG Competition

Rue Joseph II 70 Jozef-II straat

B-1000 BRUSSELS

Case M. [*No…*] — [*Title…*]
Commitments To The European Commission

Pursuant to [Article 6(2), *if Phase I Commitments*] [Article 8(2), *if Phase II Commitments*] [Articles 8(2) and 10(2), *if in Phase II Commitments prior to the sending out of the Statement of Objections*] of Council Regulation (EEC) No. 4064/89 as amended (the "***Merger Regulation***"), [*Indicate the name of the Undertakings offering the Commitments*] (the "***Parties***") hereby provide the following Commitments (the "***Commitments***") in order to enable the European Commission (the "***Commission***") to declare [*Description of the operation: e.g. the acquisition of…; the creation of a full-function joint venture between…*] compatible with the common market and the EEA Agreement by its decision pursuant to [Article 6(1)(b) of the Merger Regulation, *if Phase I Commitments*] [Article 8(2), *if Phase II Commitments*] of the Merger Regulation (the "***Decision***").

The Commitments shall take effect upon the date of adoption of the Decision.

This text shall be interpreted in the light of the Decision to the extent that the Commitments are attached as conditions and obligations, in the general framework of Community law, in particular in the light of the Merger Regulation, and by reference to the Commission Notice on remedies acceptable under Council Regulation (EEC) No 4064/89 and under Commission Regulation (EC) No 447/98.

Section A. Definitions

For the purpose of the Commitments, the following terms shall have the following meaning:

Affiliated Undertakings: undertakings controlled by the Parties and/or by the ultimate parents of the Parties, including the JV [*Only in the case when the proposed operation is a creation of a JV*], whereby the notion of control shall be interpreted pursuant to Article 3 Merger Regulation and in the light of the Commission Notice on the concept of concentration under Council Regulation (EEC) No 4064/89.

Closing: the transfer of the legal title of the Divestment Business to the Purchaser.

Divestment Business: the business or businesses as defined in Section B and the Schedule that the Parties commit to divest.

Divestiture Trustee: one or more natural or legal person(s), independent from the Parties, who is approved by the Commission and appointed by [*X*] and who has received from [*X*] the exclusive Trustee Mandate to sell the Divestment Business to a Purchaser at no minimum price.

Effective Date: the date of adoption of the Decision.

First Divestiture Period: the period of [∑] months from the Effective Date.

Hold Separate Manager: the person appointed by [*X*] for the Divestment Business to manage the day-to-day business under the supervision of the Monitoring Trustee.

Key Personnel: all personnel necessary to maintain the viability and competitiveness of the Divestment Business, as listed in the Schedule.

Monitoring Trustee: one or more natural or legal person(s), independent from the Parties, who is approved by the Commission and appointed by [*X*], and who has the duty to monitor [*X's*] compliance with the conditions and obligations attached to the Decision.

Personnel: all personnel currently employed by the Divestment Business, including Key Personnel, staff seconded to the Divestment Business, shared personnel and the additional personnel listed in the Schedule.

Purchaser: the entity approved by the Commission as acquirer of the Divestment Business in accordance with the criteria set out in Section D.

Trustee(s): the Monitoring Trustee and the Divestiture Trustee.

Trustee Divestiture Period: the period of [∑] months from the end of the First Divestiture Period.

[*X*]: [*Indicate the short name of the Undertaking Concerned that will divest its business/es*], incorporated under the laws of [∑], with its registered office at [∑] and registered with the Commercial/Company Register at [∑] under number [∑].

Section B. The Divestment Business

Commitment to divest

1. In order to restore effective competition, [*X*] commits to divest, or procure the divestiture of the Divestment Business by the end of the Trustee Divestiture Period as a going concern to a purchaser and on terms of sale approved by the Commission in accordance with the procedure described in paragraph 15. To carry out the divestiture, [*X*] commits to find a purchaser and to enter into a final binding sale and purchase agreement for the sale of the Divestment Business within the First Divestiture Period. If [*X*] has not entered into such an agreement at the end of the First Divestiture Period, [*X*] shall grant the Divestiture Trustee an exclusive mandate to sell the Divestment Business in accordance with the procedure described in paragraph 24 in the Trustee Divestiture Period. [*The following sentence should be inserted in case of an "up-front buyer"*: The proposed concentration shall not be implemented unless and until [*X*] or the Divestiture Trustee has entered into a final binding sale and purchase agreement for the sale of the Divestment Business and the Commission has approved the purchaser and the terms of sale in accordance with paragraph 15].

2. [*X*] shall be deemed to have complied with this commitment if, by the end of the Trustee Divestiture Period, [*X*] has entered into a final binding sale and purchase agreement, if the Commission approves the Purchaser and the terms in accordance with the procedure described in paragraph 15 and if the closing of the sale of the Divestment Business takes place within a period not exceeding 3 months after the approval of the purchaser and the terms of sale by the Commission.

3. In order to maintain the structural effect of the Commitments, the Parties shall, for a period of 10 years after the Effective Date, not acquire direct or indirect influence over the whole or part of the Divestment Business, unless the Commission has previously found that the structure of the market has changed to such an extent that the absence of influence over the Divestment Business is no longer necessary to render the proposed concentration compatible with the common market.

Structure and definition of the Divestment Business

4. The Divestment Business consists of [*Provide a summary description of the Divestment Business*]. The present legal and functional structure of the Divestment Business as operated to date is described in the Schedule. The Divestment Business, described in more detail in the Schedule, includes

   (a) all tangible and intangible assets (including intellectual property rights), which contribute to the current operation or are necessary to ensure the viability and competitiveness of the Divestment Business;

(b) all licences, permits and authorisations issued by any governmental organisation for the benefit of the Divestment Business;

(c) all contracts, leases, commitments and customer orders of the Divestment Business; all customer, credit and other records of the Divestment Business (items referred to under (a)–(c) hereinafter collectively referred to as "*Assets*");

(d) the Personnel; and

(e) [*To be included in cases in which the Divestment Business needs an on-going relationship with the Parties in order to be fully competitive and viable:* the benefit, for a transitional period of up to [*insert*] years after Closing and on terms and conditions equivalent to those at present afforded to the Divestment Business, of all current arrangements under which [*X*] or Affiliated Undertakings supply products or services to the Divestment Business, as detailed in the Schedule, unless otherwise agreed with the Purchaser.]

Section C. Related commitments

Preservation of Viability, Marketability and Competitiveness

5. From the Effective Date until Closing, [*X*] shall preserve the economic viability, marketability and competitiveness of the Divestment Business, in accordance with good business practice, and shall minimise as far as possible any risk of loss of competitive potential of the Divestment Business. In particular [*X*] undertakes:

(a) not to carry out any act upon its own authority that might have a significant adverse impact on the value, management or competitiveness of the Divestment Business or that might alter the nature and scope of activity, or the industrial or commercial strategy or the investment policy of the Divestment Business;

(b) to make available sufficient resources for the development of the Divestment Business, on the basis and continuation of the existing business plans;

(c) to take all reasonable steps, including appropriate incentive schemes (based on industry practice), to encourage all Key Personnel to remain with the Divestment Business.

Hold-separate obligations of Parties

6. [*X*] commits, from the Effective Date until Closing, to keep the Divestment Business separate from the businesses it is retaining and to ensure that Key Personnel of the Divestment Business – including the Hold Separate Manager – have no involvement in any business retained and vice versa. [*X*] shall also ensure that the Personnel does not report to any individual outside the Divestment Business.

7. Until Closing, [*X*] shall assist the Monitoring Trustee in ensuring that the Divestment Business is managed as a distinct and saleable entity separate from the businesses retained by the Parties. [*X*] shall appoint a Hold Separate Manager who shall be responsible for the management of the Divestment Business, under the supervision of the Monitoring Trustee. The Hold Separate Manager shall manage the Divestment Business independently and in the best interest of the business with a view to ensuring its continued economic viability, marketability and competitiveness and its independence from the businesses retained by the Parties.

8. [*The following is to be inserted in cases in which a company or a share in a company is to be divested and a strict separation of the corporate structure is necessary:* To ensure that the Divestment Business is held and managed as a separate entity the Monitoring Trustee shall exercise [*X's*] rights as shareholder in the Divestment Business (except for its rights for dividends that are due before Closing), with the aim of acting in the best interest of the business, determined on a stand-alone basis, as an independent financial investor, and with a view to fulfilling [*X's*] obligations under the Commitments. Furthermore, the Monitoring Trustee shall have the power to replace members of the supervisory board or non-executive directors of the board of directors, who have been appointed on behalf of [*X*]. Upon request of the Monitoring Trustee, [*X*] shall resign as member of the boards or shall cause such members of the boards to resign.]

Ring-fencing

9. [*X*] shall implement all necessary measures to ensure that it does not after the Effective Date obtain any business secrets, know-how, commercial information, or any other information of a confidential or proprietary nature relating to the Divestment Business. In particular, the

participation of the Divestment Business in a central information technology network shall be severed to the extent possible, without compromising the viability of the Divestment Business. [X] may obtain information relating to the Divestment Business which is reasonably necessary for the divestiture of the Divestment Business or whose disclosure to [X] is required by law.

Non-solicitation clause

10. The Parties undertake, subject to customary limitations, not to solicit, and to procure that Affiliated Undertakings do not solicit, the Key Personnel transferred with the Divestment Business for a period of [∑] after Closing.

Due Diligence

11. In order to enable potential purchasers to carry out a reasonable due diligence of the Divestment Business, [X] shall, subject to customary confidentiality assurances and dependent on the stage of the divestiture process:
    (a) provide to potential purchasers sufficient information as regards the Divestment Business;
    (b) provide to potential purchasers sufficient information relating to the Personnel and allow them reasonable access to the Personnel.

Reporting

12. [X] shall submit written reports in [*Indicate the language of the procedure or another language agreed with the Commission*] on potential purchasers of the Divestment Business and developments in the negotiations with such potential purchasers to the Commission and the Monitoring Trustee no later than 10 days after the end of every month following the Effective Date (or otherwise at the Commission's request).

13. The Parties shall inform the Commission and the Monitoring Trustee on the preparation of the data room documentation and the due diligence procedure and shall submit a copy of an information memorandum to the Commission and the Monitoring Trustee before sending the memorandum out to potential purchasers.

Section D. The Purchaser

14. In order to ensure the immediate restoration of effective competition, the Purchaser, in order to be approved by the Commission, must:
    (a) be independent of and unconnected to the Parties;
    (b) have the financial resources, proven expertise and incentive to maintain and develop the Divestment Business as a viable and active competitive force in competition with the Parties and other competitors;
    (c) neither be likely to create, in the light of the information available to the Commission, *prima facie* competition concerns nor give rise to a risk that the implementation of the Commitments will be delayed, and must, in particular, reasonably be expected to obtain all necessary approvals from the relevant regulatory authorities for the acquisition of the Divestment Business (the before-mentioned criteria for the purchaser hereafter the "***Purchaser Requirements***").

15. The final binding sale and purchase agreement shall be conditional on the Commission's approval. When [X] has reached an agreement with a purchaser, it shall submit a fully documented and reasoned proposal, including a copy of the final agreement(s), to the Commission and the Monitoring Trustee. [X] must be able to demonstrate to the Commission that the purchaser meets the Purchaser Requirements and that the Divestment Business is being sold in a manner consistent with the Commitments. For the approval, the Commission shall verify that the purchaser fulfils the Purchaser Requirements and that the Divestment Business is being sold in a manner consistent with the Commitments. The Commission may approve the sale of the Divestment Business without one or more Assets or parts of the Personnel, if this does not affect the viability and competitiveness of the Divestment Business after the sale, taking account of the proposed purchaser.

Section E. Trustee

I. <u>Appointment Procedure</u>

16. [X] shall appoint a Monitoring Trustee to carry out the functions specified in the Commitments for a Monitoring Trustee. If [X] has not entered into a binding sales and purchase agreement one month before the end of the First Divestiture Period or if the Commission has rejected a purchaser proposed by [X] at that time or thereafter, [X] shall appoint a Divestiture Trustee to carry out the functions specified in the Commitments for a Divestiture Trustee. The appointment of the Divestiture Trustee shall take effect upon the commencement of the Extended Divestment Period.

17. The Trustee shall be independent of the Parties, possess the necessary qualifications to carry out its mandate, for example as an investment bank or consultant or auditor, and shall neither have nor become exposed to a conflict of interest. The Trustee shall be remunerated by the Parties in a way that does not impede the independent and effective fulfilment of its mandate. In particular, where the remuneration package of a Divestiture Trustee includes a success premium linked to the final sale value of the Divestment Business, the fee shall also be linked to a divestiture within the Trustee Divestiture Period.

Proposal by the Parties

18. No later than one week after the Effective Date, [X] shall submit a list of one or more persons whom [X] proposes to appoint as the Monitoring Trustee to the Commission for approval. No later than one month before the end of the First Divestiture Period, [X] shall submit a list of one or more persons whom [X] proposes to appoint as Divestiture Trustee to the Commission for approval. The proposal shall contain sufficient information for the Commission to verify that the proposed Trustee fulfils the requirements set out in paragraph 17 and shall include:

    (a) the full terms of the proposed mandate, which shall include all provisions necessary to enable the Trustee to fulfil its duties under these Commitments;

    (b) the outline of a work plan which describes how the Trustee intends to carry out its assigned tasks;

    (c) an indication whether the proposed Trustee is to act as both Monitoring Trustee and Divestiture Trustee or whether different trustees are proposed for the two functions.

Approval or rejection by the Commission

19. The Commission shall have the discretion to approve or reject the proposed Trustee(s) and to approve the proposed mandate subject to any modifications it deems necessary for the Trustee to fulfil its obligations. If only one name is approved, [X] shall appoint or cause to be appointed, the individual or institution concerned as Trustee, in accordance with the mandate approved by the Commission. If more than one name is approved, [X] shall be free to choose the Trustee to be appointed from among the names approved. The Trustee shall be appointed within one week of the Commission's approval, in accordance with the mandate approved by the Commission.

New proposal by the Parties

20. If all the proposed Trustees are rejected, [X] shall submit the names of at least two more individuals or institutions within one week of being informed of the rejection, in accordance with the requirements and the procedure set out in paragraphs 16 and 19.

Trustee nominated by the Commission

21. If all further proposed Trustees are rejected by the Commission, the Commission shall nominate a Trustee, whom [X] shall appoint, or cause to be appointed, in accordance with a trustee mandate approved by the Commission.

II. <u>Functions of the Trustee</u>

22. The Trustee shall assume its specified duties in order to ensure compliance with the Commitments. The Commission may, on its own initiative or at the request of the Trustee or [X], give any

orders or instructions to the Trustee in order to ensure compliance with the conditions and obligations attached to the Decision.

Duties and obligations of the Monitoring Trustee

23. The Monitoring Trustee shall:
    (i) propose in its first report to the Commission a detailed work plan describing how it intends to monitor compliance with the obligations and conditions attached to the Decision.
    (ii) oversee the on-going management of the Divestment Business with a view to ensuring its continued economic viability, marketability and competitiveness and monitor compliance by [X] with the conditions and obligations attached to the Decision. To that end the Monitoring Trustee shall:
        (a) monitor the preservation of the economic viability, marketability and competitiveness of the Divestment Business, and the keeping separate of the Divestment Business from the business retained by the Parties, in accordance with paragraphs 5 and 6 of the Commitments;
        (b) supervise the management of the Divestment Business as a distinct and saleable entity, in accordance with paragraph 7 of the Commitments;
        (c) (i) in consultation with [X], determine all necessary measures to ensure that [X] does not after the effective date obtain any business secrets, knowhow, commercial information, or any other information of a confidential or proprietary nature relating to the Divestment Business, in particular strive for the severing of the Divestment Business' participation in a central information technology network to the extent possible, without compromising the viability of the Divestment Business, and (ii) decide whether such information may be disclosed to [X] as the disclosure is reasonably necessary to allow [X] to carry out the divestiture or as the disclosure is required by law;
        (d) monitor the splitting of assets and the allocation of Personnel between the Divestment Business and [X] or Affiliated Undertakings;
    (iii) assume the other functions assigned to the Monitoring Trustee under the conditions and obligations attached to the Decision;
    (iv) propose to [X] such measures as the Monitoring Trustee considers necessary to ensure [X]'s compliance with the conditions and obligations attached to the Decision, in particular the maintenance of the full economic viability, marketability or competitiveness of the Divestment Business, the holding separate of the Divestment Business and the non-disclosure of competitively sensitive information;
    (v) review and assess potential purchasers as well as the progress of the divestiture process and verify that, dependent on the stage of the divestiture process, (a) potential purchasers receive sufficient information relating to the Divestment Business and the Personnel in particular by reviewing, if available, the data room documentation, the information memorandum and the due diligence process, and (b) potential purchasers are granted reasonable access to the Personnel;
    (vi) provide to the Commission, sending [X] a non-confidential copy at the same time, a written report within 15 days after the end of every month. The report shall cover the operation and management of the Divestment Business so that the Commission can assess whether the business is held in a manner consistent with the Commitments and the progress of the divestiture process as well as potential purchasers. In addition to these reports, the Monitoring Trustee shall promptly report in writing to the Commission, sending [X] a non-confidential copy at the same time, if it concludes on reasonable grounds that [X] is failing to comply with these Commitments;
    (vii) within one week after receipt of the documented proposal referred to in paragraph 15, submit to the Commission a reasoned opinion as to the suitability and independence of the proposed purchaser and the viability of the Divestment Business after the Sale and as to whether the Divestment Business is sold in a manner consistent with the conditions and obligations attached to the Decision, in particular, if relevant, whether the Sale of the

Divestment Business without one or more Assets or not all of the Personnel affects the viability of the Divestment Business after the sale, taking account of the proposed purchaser.

Duties and obligations of the Divestiture Trustee

24. Within the Trustee Divestiture Period, the Divestiture Trustee shall sell at no minimum price the Divestment Business to a purchaser, provided that the Commission has approved both the purchaser and the final binding sale and purchase agreement in accordance with the procedure laid down in paragraph 15. The Divestiture Trustee shall include in the sale and purchase agreement such terms and conditions as it considers appropriate for an expedient sale in the Trustee Divestiture Period. In particular, the Divestiture Trustee may include in the sale and purchase agreement such customary representations and warranties and indemnities as are reasonably required to effect the sale. The Divestiture Trustee shall protect the legitimate financial interests of [*X*], subject to the Parties' unconditional obligation to divest at no minimum price in the Trustee Divestiture Period.

25. In the Trustee Divestiture Period (or otherwise at the Commission's request), the Divestiture Trustee shall provide the Commission with a comprehensive monthly report written in [*Please indicate the language of the procedure or a different language agreed with the Commission*] on the progress of the divestiture process. Such reports shall be submitted within 15 days after the end of every month with a simultaneous copy to the Monitoring Trustee and a non-confidential copy to the Parties.

III. Duties and obligations of the Parties

26. [*X*] shall provide and shall cause its advisors to provide the Trustee with all such cooperation, assistance and information as the Trustee may reasonably require to perform its tasks. The Trustee shall have full and complete access to any of [*X*'s] or the Divestment Business' books, records, documents, management or other personnel, facilities, sites and technical information necessary for fulfilling its duties under the Commitments and [*X*] and the Divestment Business shall provide the Trustee upon request with copies of any document. [*X*] and the Divestment Business shall make available to the Trustee one or more offices on their premises and shall be available for meetings in order to provide the Trustee with all information necessary for the performance of its tasks.

27. [*X*] shall provide the Monitoring Trustee with all managerial and administrative support that it may reasonably request on behalf of the management of the Divestment Business. This shall include all administrative support functions relating to the Divestment Business which are currently carried out at headquarters level. [*X*] shall provide and shall cause its advisors to provide the Monitoring Trustee, on request, with the information submitted to potential purchasers, in particular give the Monitoring Trustee access to the data room documentation and all other information granted to potential purchasers in the due diligence procedure. [*X*] shall inform the Monitoring Trustee on possible purchasers, submit a list of potential purchasers, and keep the Monitoring Trustee informed of all developments in the divestiture process.

28. [*X*] shall grant or procure Affiliated Undertakings to grant comprehensive powers of attorney, duly executed, to the Divestiture Trustee to effect the sale, the Closing and all actions and declarations which the Divestiture Trustee considers necessary or appropriate to achieve the sale and the Closing, including the appointment of advisors to assist with the sale process. Upon request of the Divestiture Trustee, [*X*] shall cause the documents required for effecting the sale and the Closing to be duly executed.

29. [*X*] shall indemnify the Trustee and its employees and agents (each an "***Indemnified Party***") and hold each Indemnified Party harmless against, and hereby agrees that an Indemnified Party shall have no liability to [*X*] for any liabilities arising out of the performance of the Trustee's duties under the Commitments, except to the extent that such liabilities result from the wilful default, recklessness, gross negligence or bad faith of the Trustee, its employees, agents or advisors.

30. At the expense of [X], the Trustee may appoint advisors (in particular for corporate finance or legal advice), subject to [X's] approval (this approval not to be unreasonably withheld or delayed) if the Trustee considers the appointment of such advisors necessary or appropriate for the performance of its duties and obligations under the Mandate, provided that any fees and other expenses incurred by the Trustee are reasonable. Should [X] refuse to approve the advisors proposed by the Trustee the Commission may approve the appointment of such advisors instead, after having heard [X]. Only the Trustee shall be entitled to issue instructions to the advisors. Paragraph 29 shall apply mutatis mutandis. In the Trustee Divestiture Period, the Divestiture Trustee may use advisors who served [X] during the Divestiture Period if the Divestiture Trustee considers this in the best interest of an expedient sale.

IV. Replacement, discharge and reappointment of the Trustee

31. If the Trustee ceases to perform its functions under the Commitments or for any other good cause, including the exposure of the Trustee to a conflict of interest:
    (a) the Commission may, after hearing the Trustee, require [X] to replace the Trustee; or
    (b) [X], with the prior approval of the Commission, may replace the Trustee.

32. If the Trustee is removed according to paragraph 31, the Trustee may be required to continue in its function until a new Trustee is in place to whom the Trustee has effected a full hand over of all relevant information. The new Trustee shall be appointed in accordance with the procedure referred to in paragraphs 16–21.

33. Beside the removal according to paragraph 31, the Trustee shall cease to act as Trustee only after the Commission has discharged it from its duties after all the Commitments with which the Trustee has been entrusted have been implemented. However, the Commission may at any time require the reappointment of the Monitoring Trustee if it subsequently appears that the relevant remedies might not have been fully and properly implemented.

Section F. The Review Clause

34. The Commission may, where appropriate, in response to a request from [X] showing good cause and accompanied by a report from the Monitoring Trustee:
    (i) Grant an extension of the time periods foreseen in the Commitments, or
    (ii) Waive, modify or substitute, in exceptional circumstances, one or more of the undertakings in these Commitments.

    Where [X] seeks an extension of a time period, it shall submit a request to the Commission no later than one month before the expiry of that period, showing good cause. Only in exceptional circumstances shall [X] be entitled to request an extension within the last month of any period.

....

duly authorised for and on behalf of

[*Indicate the name of each of the Parties*]

SCHEDULE

1. The Divestment Business as operated to date has the following legal and functional structure: [*Describe the legal and functional structure of the Divestment Business, including the organisational chart*].

2. Following paragraph [4] of these Commitments, the Divestment Business includes, but is not limited to:
    (a) the following main tangible assets: [*Indicate the essential tangible assets, e.g. xyz factory/warehouse/pipelines located at abc and the real estate/property on which the factory/warehouse is located; the R&D facilities*];
    (b) the following main intangible assets: [*Indicate the main intangible assets. This should in particular include (i) the brand names and (ii) all other Intellectual Property Rights used in conducting the Divestment Business.*];

(c) the following main licences, permits and authorisations: [*Indicate the main licences, permits and authorisations*];

(d) the following main contracts, agreements, leases, commitments and understandings [*Indicate the main contracts, etc.*];

(e) the following customer, credit and other records: [*Indicate the main customer, credit and other records, according to further sector specific indications, where appropriate*];

(f) the following Personnel: [*Indicate the personnel to be transferred in general, including personnel providing essential functions for the Divestment Business, such as central R&D staff*];

(g) the following Key Personnel: [*Indicate the names and functions of the Key Personnel, including the Hold Separate Manager, where appropriate*]; and

(h) the arrangements for the supply with the following products or services by [*X*] or Affiliated Undertakings for a transitional period of up to [Σ] after Closing: [*Indicate the products or services to be provided for a transitional period in order to maintain the economic viability and competitiveness of the Divestment Business*].

3. The Divestment Business shall not include:

(i) ...;

(ii) [*It is the responsibility of the Parties to indicate clearly what the Divestment Business will not encompass*].

MODELS TEXTS FOR TRUSTEE MANDATES

Notes

The following texts are published on the Europa website at:
<http://ec.europa.eu/comm/competition/mergers/legislation/trustee_mandate.pdf>
All square brackets in the following document are original and not editorial.

TRUSTEE MANDATE

BETWEEN:

1. [*X*] [*Indicate a short name(s) of the Undertaking(s) Concerned that will divest its/their businesses*] (hereafter [*X*]), a company organised under the laws of [*Indicate law of origin*], which has its registered seat at [*Indicate complete address*], represented by [*Indicate name and title of individual representing X for the Mandate*],

AND

2. [*Insert name, address, and, as the case may be, company details of the Trustee*], (the "***Trustee***").

[*X*] and the Trustee are hereafter referred to as the "***Mandate Parties***".

WHEREAS

In [*Indicate full case name and number*] and pursuant to [*Article 6(2)/Article 8(2)*] of Council Regulation (EEC) No. 4064/89 as amended (the "***Merger Regulation***"), [*X*] offered commitments (the "***Commitments***"), attached hereto as Annex 1, in order to enable the European Commission (the "***Commission***") to declare [*Description of the operation: e.g. the acquisition of...; the creation of a full-function joint venture between...*] compatible with the common market and the functioning of the EEA Agreement. The Commission approved the operation by its decision pursuant to [*Article 6(1)(b)/Article 8(2)*] of the Merger Regulation (the "***Decision***"), subject to full compliance with the conditions and obligations attached to the Decision (the "***Conditions and Obligations***").

According to the Conditions and Obligations, [*X*] undertakes to divest the [*Indicate the business to be divested*] and, in the meantime, to preserve the economic viability, marketability and competitiveness of this business. Therefore, [*X*] undertakes to appoint a Monitoring Trustee for the monitoring of the hold separate obligations and of the divestiture procedure, and to appoint a

Divestiture Trustee for the divestiture of the said business if [*X*] has not succeeded in divesting it during the First Divestiture Period. In accordance with the Conditions and Obligations, [*X*] hereby engages the Trustee and this agreement forms the mandate referred to in the Commitments (hereafter the "*Mandate*").

The appointment of the Trustee and the terms of this Mandate were approved by the Commission on [*Indicate date of approval letter*].

In case of doubt or conflict, this Mandate shall be interpreted in the light of (1) the Conditions and Obligations and the Decision, (2) the general framework of Community law, in particular in the light of the Merger Regulation, and (3) the Commission Notice on remedies acceptable under Council Regulation (EEC) No 4064/89 and under Commission Regulation (EC) No 447/98.

IT HAS BEEN AGREED AS FOLLOWS:

Section A. Definitions

Terms used in this Mandate shall have the meaning set out in Section 1 of the Commitments. For the purpose of this Mandate, the following terms shall have the following meaning:

Sale: the entering into a binding sale and purchase agreement for the selling of the Divestment Business to the Purchaser.

Trustee Partner Firms: the other firms belonging to the same organisation of individual partnerships and companies as the Trustee.

Trustee Team: The key persons responsible for carrying out the tasks assigned by the Mandate and identified in paragraph [*3*] below of the Mandate.

Work-Plan: the outline of the work-plan submitted to the Commission by the Trustee before the approval of the Trustee and attached hereto as Annex [Σ], a more detailed version of which will be prepared by the Trustee and submitted to the Commission in its first report.

Section B. Appointment of Trustee

1. [*X*] hereby appoints the Trustee to act as its exclusive trustee for fulfilling the tasks of a [Monitoring Trustee and/or Divestiture Trustee] according to the Conditions and Obligations and the Trustee hereby accepts the said appointment in accordance with the terms of this Mandate.
2. The appointment and this Mandate shall become effective on the date hereof except for the provisions specifically addressing the duties and obligations of the Divestiture Trustee which shall become effective with the beginning of the Trustee Divestiture Period.
3. The Trustee Team consists of the following key persons: [*Indicate name and title of each of the key persons (partners/leading persons)*]. The Trustee shall not replace the persons of the Trustee Team without prior approval of the Commission and [*X*].

Section C. General Duties and Obligations of the Trustee

4. The Trustee shall act on behalf of the Commission to ensure [*X's*] compliance with the Conditions and Obligations and assume the duties specified in the Conditions and Obligations for a [*Monitoring and/or Divestiture Trustee*]. The Trustee shall carry out the duties under this Mandate in accordance with the Work-Plan as well as revisions of the Work-Plan, approved by the Commission. The Commission may, on its own initiative or at the request of the Trustee or [*X*], give any orders or instructions to the Trustee in order to ensure compliance with the Conditions and Obligations. [*X*] is not entitled to give instructions to the Trustee.
5. The Trustee shall propose to [*X*] such measures as the Trustee considers necessary to ensure [*X's*] compliance with the Commitments and/or the Mandate, and the Trustee shall propose necessary measures to the Commission in the event that [*X*] does not comply with the Trustee's proposals within the timeframe set by the Trustee.

Section D. Duties and Obligations of the Monitoring Trustee

Monitoring and Management of the Divestment Business

6. The Monitoring Trustee shall, in conformity with the Conditions and Obligations, oversee the ongoing management of the Divestment Business with a view to ensuring its continued economic

viability, marketability and competitiveness and monitor the compliance of [X] with the Conditions and Obligations. To that end, the Monitoring Trustee shall until Closing in particular:

(a) monitor (i) the preservation of the economic viability, marketability and competitiveness of the Divestment Business in accordance with good business practice, (ii) the minimisation, as far as possible, of any risk of loss of competitive potential of the Divestment Business; (iii) the not carrying out by [X] or Affiliated Undertakings of any act on its own authority that might have a significant adverse impact on the value, management or competitiveness of the Divestment Business or that might to alter the nature and scope of activity, or the industrial or commercial strategy or the investment policy of the Divestment Business; and (iv) the making available by [X] of sufficient resources for the Divestment Business to develop, based on the existing business plans and their continuation, and (v) the taking of all reasonable steps by [X], including appropriate incentive schemes (based on business practice), to encourage all Key Personnel to remain with the Divestment Business;

(b) monitor (i) the holding separate of the Divestment Business from the businesses retained by [X] and Affiliated Undertakings, (ii) the absence of involvement of Key Employees of the Divestment Business — including the Hold Separate Manager — in any business retained and vice versa, and (iii) the absence of reporting of the Personnel of the Divestment Business to any individual outside the Divestment Business, except where permitted in the Commitments;

(c) seek to ensure that the Divestment Business is managed as a distinct and saleable entity separate from [X's] or Affiliated Undertakings' businesses and that the Hold Separate Manager manages the Divestment Business independently and in the best interest of the business and ensuring its continued economic viability, marketability and competitiveness as well as its independence from the businesses retained by the Parties;

[(d) *the following paragraph to be inserted in cases in which the Commitments foresee the voting of shares by the Monitoring Trustee and/or the replacement of member of the supervisory board/ board of directors*: exercise [X's] rights as shareholder in the Divestment Business (except for its rights for dividends that are due before Closing), with the aim of acting in the best interest of the business, determined on a stand-alone basis, as an independent financial investor, and with a view to fulfilling [X's] obligation under the Conditions and Obligations. Consequently, [X] grants a comprehensive and duly executed proxy to the Monitoring Trustee in Annex [Σ] for the exercise of the voting rights attached to [X's] shares in the Divestment Business. The Monitoring Trustee shall have the power to replace members of the supervisory board or non-executive directors of the board of directors of the Divestment Business, who have been appointed on behalf of [X]. Upon request of the Monitoring Trustee, [X] shall resign as a member of the boards or shall cause such members of the boards to resign. The representatives of the Monitoring Trustee to be appointed to the board shall be one or more persons of the Trustee Team. In the event that appointments outside these named individuals are envisaged the prior approval of the Commission is required;]

(e) monitor the splitting of assets and the allocation of Personnel between the Divestment Business and [X] or Affiliated Undertakings;

(f) (i) in consultation with [X], determine all necessary measures to ensure that [X] does not after the Effective Date obtain any business secrets, know-how, commercial information, or any other information of a confidential or proprietary nature relating to the Divestment Business, in particular strive for the severing of the Divestment Business' participation in a central information technology network to the extent possible, without compromising the viability of the Divestment Business, and (ii) decide whether such information may be disclosed to [X] as the disclosure is reasonably necessary to allow [X] to carry out the divestiture or as the disclosure is required by law.

Monitoring of Divestiture

7. Until the end of the First Divestiture Period, the Monitoring Trustee shall assist the Commission in reviewing the divestiture process and assessing proposed purchasers. Therefore the Monitoring Trustee shall during the First Divestiture Period:

(a) review and assess the progress of the divestiture process and potential purchasers;

   (b) verify that, dependent on the stage of the divestiture process, (i) potential purchasers receive sufficient information relating to the Divestment Business and the Personnel, in particular by reviewing, if available, the data room documentation, the information memorandum and the due diligence process, and (ii) potential purchasers are granted reasonable access to the Personnel;

8. Once [X] has submitted to the Commission a proposal for a purchaser, the Trustee shall, within one week after receipt of the documented proposal by the Parties, submit to the Commission a reasoned opinion as to the suitability and independence of the proposed purchaser and the viability of the Divestment Business after the Sale and as to whether the Divestment Business is sold in a manner consistent with the Conditions and Obligations, in particular, if relevant, whether the Sale of the Divestment Business without one or more Assets or not all of the Personnel affects the viability of the Divestment Business after the Sale, taking account of the proposed purchaser.

Section E. Duties and Obligations of the Divestiture Trustee

9. With the commencement of the Trustee Divestiture Period, [X] hereby gives the Trustee an exclusive mandate to sell the Divestment Business to a purchaser according to the provisions of this section of the Mandate and the Commitments.

10. The purchaser shall fulfil the Purchaser Requirements and both the purchaser and the final sale and purchase agreement shall be approved by the Commission in accordance with the procedure laid down in paragraph [15] of the Commitments.

11. The Divestiture Trustee shall sell the Divestment Business at no minimum price and at such terms and conditions as it considers appropriate for an expedient sale in the Trustee Divestiture Period. In particular, the Divestiture Trustee may include in the sale and purchase agreement such customary representations and warranties and indemnities as are reasonably required to effect the Sale. At the same time, the Divestiture Trustee shall protect the legitimate financial interests of [X], subject to the Parties' unconditional obligation to divest at no minimum price in the Trustee Divestiture Period.

12. [X] grants a comprehensive and duly executed power of attorney to the Divestiture Trustee in Annex [Σ] to effect the Sale of the Divestment Business, the Closing and all actions and declarations which the Trustee considers necessary or appropriate for achieving the Sale of the Divestment Business or the Closing, including the power to appoint advisors to assist with the sale process. The power of attorney shall include the authority to grant sub-powers of attorney to members of the Trustee Team. If necessary to accomplish the Sale, [X] shall grant the Divestiture Trustee further powers of attorney, duly executed, or cause the documents required for the effecting of the Sale and the Closing to be duly executed. Any power of attorney granted by [X], including any sub-powers of attorney granted pursuant to them, shall expire on the earlier of the termination of this Mandate or the discharge of the Trustee.

13. The Trustee shall comply with the Commission's instructions as regards any aspects of the conduct or conclusion of the sale, in particular in ending negotiations with any prospective purchaser, if the Commission notifies the Trustee and [X] of the Commission's determination that the negotiations are being conducted with an unacceptable purchaser.

Section F. Reporting Obligations

14. Within 15 days of the end of each month or as otherwise agreed with the Commission, the Monitoring Trustee shall submit a written report to the Commission, sending [X] a non-confidential copy at the same time. The report shall cover the Monitoring Trustee's fulfilment of its obligations under the Mandate and the compliance of the Parties with the Conditions and Obligations. The reports shall cover in particular the following topics:
   - Operational and financial performance of the Divestment Business in the relevant period;
   - Any issues or problems which have arisen in the execution of the obligations as Monitoring Trustee, in particular any issues of non-compliance by [X] or the Divestment Business with the Conditions and Obligations;
   - Monitoring of the preservation of the economic viability, marketability and competitiveness of the Divestment Business and of [X's] compliance with the hold-separate and ring-fencing obligations as well as monitoring of the splitting of assets and of the allocation of

Personnel between the Divestment Business and the businesses retained by [X] or Affiliated Undertakings;

- Review and assessment of the progress of the divestiture process, including reporting on potential purchasers and all other information received from [X] regarding the divestiture;
- Any particular issues as set out in the Work-Plan;
- Estimated future timetable, including the date of next anticipated reporting;
- A proposal for a detailed Work-Plan in the first report as well as revisions in subsequent reports.

15. In the Trustee Divestiture Period, within 15 days after the end of every month, the Divestiture Trustee shall provide to the Commission, with a simultaneous copy to the Monitoring Trustee and a non-confidential copy to [X], a comprehensive report written in [*Indicate the language*] on the discharge of its obligations under the Mandate and the progress of the divestiture process, covering in particular the following information:
- List of potential purchasers and a preliminary assessment of each of them;
- State of negotiations with potential purchasers;
- Any issues or problems regarding the sale of the Divestment Business, including any issues and problems regarding the negotiation of the necessary agreement(s);
- Need for advisers for the sale of the Divestment Business and a list of advisers selected by the Trustee for this purpose;
- Any particular issues as set out in the Work-Plan;
- A proposal for a detailed Work-Plan in the first report as well as revisions in subsequent reports.

16. At any time, the Trustee will provide to the Commission, at its request (or on the Trustee's own initiative), a written or oral report on matters falling within the Trustee's Mandate. [X] shall receive simultaneously a non-confidential copy of such additional written reports and shall be informed promptly of the non-confidential content of any oral reports.

Section G. Duties and Obligations of [X]

17. [X] shall provide and shall cause its advisors to provide the Trustee with all such cooperation, assistance and information as the Trustee may reasonably require to perform its tasks. The Trustee shall have full and complete access to any of [X's] or the Divestment Business' books, records, documents, management or other personnel, facilities, sites and technical information necessary for fulfilling its duties under the Mandate and [X] and the Divestment Business shall provide the Trustee upon request with copies of any document. [X] and the Divestment Business shall make available to the Trustee one or more offices on their premises and shall be available for meetings in order to provide the Trustee with all information necessary for the performance of its tasks.

18. [X] shall provide the Monitoring Trustee with all managerial and administrative support that it may reasonably request on behalf of the management of the Divestment Business. This shall include all administrative support functions relating to the Divestment Business which are currently carried out at headquarters level. [X] shall provide and shall cause its advisors to provide the Monitoring Trustee, on request, with access to the information submitted to potential purchasers, in particular to the data room documentation and all other information granted to potential purchasers in the due diligence procedure. [X] shall inform the Monitoring Trustee on possible purchasers, submit a list of potential purchasers, and keep the Monitoring Trustee informed of all developments in the divestiture process. Once a purchaser has been chosen, [X] shall submit the fully documented and reasoned proposal, including a copy of the final agreement(s), to the Monitoring Trustee and allow the Monitoring Trustee to have confidential contacts with the proposed purchaser in order for the Monitoring Trustee to determine whether or not, in its opinion, it meets the Purchaser Criteria.

19. At the expense of [X], the Trustee may appoint advisors (in particular for corporate finance or legal advice), subject to [X's] approval (this approval not to be unreasonably withheld or delayed) if the Trustee considers the appointment of such advisors necessary or appropriate for the performance of its duties and obligations under the Mandate, provided that any fees and other expenses incurred by the Trustee are reasonable. Should [X] refuse to approve the advisors

proposed by the Trustee, the Commission may, after having heard [X], approve the appointment of such advisors instead. Only the Trustee shall be entitled to issue instructions to the advisors. Paragraph 25 of this Mandate shall apply to the advisors mutatis mutandis. In the Trustee Divestiture Period, the Divestiture Trustee may use advisors who served [X] during the First Divestiture Period if the Divestiture Trustee considers this in the best interest of an expedient sale.

Section H. Trustee Related Provisions

Conflict of Interests

20. The Trustee's, the Trustee Team's and the Trustee Partner Firms' current relationships with [X] and Affiliated Undertakings are disclosed in Annex [Σ] to this Mandate. On this basis, the Trustee confirms that, as of the date of this Mandate, the Trustee and each member of the Trustee Team is independent of [X] and Affiliated Undertakings and has no conflict of interest that impairs the Trustee's objectivity and independence in discharging its duties under the Mandate ("***Conflict of Interest***").

21. The Trustee undertakes not to create a Conflict of Interest during the term of the Mandate. The Trustee, members of the Trustee Team and the Trustee Partner Firms may therefore not during the term of this Mandate:

    (a) Have or accept any employment by or be or accept any appointment as Member of the Board or member of other management bodies of the Parties or Affiliated Undertakings other than appointments pertaining to the establishment and performance of the Mandate;

    (b) Have or accept any assignments or other business relationships with or financial interests in the Parties or Affiliated Undertakings that might lead to a Conflict of Interest. This affects neither assignments or other business relationships between the Trustee or Trustee Partner Firms and the Parties or Affiliated Undertakings nor investments by the Trustee or Trustee Partner Firms in the stock or securities of the Parties or Affiliated Undertakings if such assignments, business relationships or investments are in the normal course of business and are material neither to the Trustee or the Trustee Partner Firms nor to the undertaking concerned.

    Should the Trustee, the Trustee Partner Firms or members of the Trustee Team wish to undertake an assignment, business relationship or investment, such a person must seek the prior approval of the Commission. Should the Trustee become aware of a Conflict of Interest, the Trustee shall promptly inform [X] and the Commission, of such Conflict of Interest. In the event that [X] becomes aware that the Trustee or the Trustee Partner Firms have or may have a Conflict of Interest, [X] shall promptly notify the Trustee and the Commission, of such Conflict of Interest. Where a Conflict of Interest occurs during the term of the Mandate the Trustee undertakes to resolve it immediately. In case the Conflict of Interest cannot be resolved or is not resolved by the Trustee in a timely manner, the Mandate may be terminated in accordance with paragraph 30 below.

22. [*It is up to the Mandate Parties to insert suitable provisions regarding conflict of interests of the Trustee and the Trustee Partner Firms with (potential) purchasers.*]

23. The Trustee undertakes that, during the term of the Mandate and for a period of one year following termination of the Mandate, members of the Trustee Team shall not provide services to the Parties or Affiliated Undertakings without first obtaining the Commission's prior approval. Moreover, the Trustee undertakes to establish measures to ensure the independence and integrity of the Trustee Team and the Trustee's employees and agents directly assigned to the Trustee Team ("*Assigned Persons*") during the term of the Mandate and for a period of one year following termination of the Mandate, from any undue influence that might interfere with or in any way compromise the Trustee Team in the performance of its duties under the Mandate. In particular:

    (a) Access to confidential information shall be limited to the Trustee Team and Assigned Persons; and

    (b) The Trustee Team and Assigned Persons shall be prohibited from communicating any information relating to this Mandate to any other of the Trustee's personnel, except for information of a general nature (e.g. Trustee's appointment, fees, etc.), and except for information whose disclosure is required by law.

Remuneration

24. [*It is up to the Mandate Parties to agree on a suitable fee structure. As set out in the Standard Commitments Text, the Trustee shall be remunerated in such a way that it does not impede its*

independence and effectiveness in fulfilling the Mandate. Regarding the Divestiture Trustee, the Commission is in favour of fee structures that, at least to a significant part, are contingent on the Divestiture Trustee's accomplishing a timely divestiture. In particular, if the remuneration package includes a success premium linked to the final sale value of the Divestment Business, the fee should also be linked to a divestiture within the Trustee Divestiture Period as specified in the Commitments. It should be noted that the fee structure — as well as the entire Mandate — is subject to the Commission's approval.]

Indemnity

25. [X] shall indemnify the Trustee and its employees and agents (each an "***Indemnified Party***") and hold each Indemnified Party harmless against, and hereby agrees that an Indemnified Party shall have no liability to [X] for any liabilities arising out of the performance of the Mandate, except to the extent that such liabilities result from the wilful default, recklessness, gross negligence or bad faith of the Trustee, its employees, agents or advisors.

Confidentiality

26. [*It is up to the Mandate Parties to agree a suitable confidentiality provision prohibiting the use, or disclosure to anyone other than the Commission of any sensitive or proprietary information gained as a result of performing the Trustee role. As a matter of course, the Mandate cannot limit the disclosure of information by the Trustee vis-à-vis the Commission. However, the Trustee must not disclose certain information gained as a result of the Trustee role to the Parties. This in particular applies to information gained on the Divestment Business to which the ring-fencing provisions apply and to information received from (potential) purchasers of the Divestment Business.*]

Section I. Termination of the Mandate

27. The Mandate may only be terminated under the conditions set out in paragraphs 28–31.

Regular Termination of the Mandate

28. The Mandate shall automatically terminate if the Commission approves the discharge in writing of the Trustee from its obligations under this Mandate. The approval of the discharge of the Trustee may be requested after the Trustee has completed the performance of its obligations under the Mandate.

29. The Mandate Parties acknowledge that the Commission may at any time request the reappointment of the Trustee by [X] if it subsequently appears that the Conditions and Obligations might not have been fully and properly implemented. The Trustee hereby accepts such a reappointment in accordance with the terms and conditions of this Mandate.

Termination of the Mandate before the Discharge

30. [X] may only terminate the Mandate before the discharge of the Trustee in accordance with paragraph 31 of the Commitments. The Trustee may only terminate the Mandate for good cause by giving written notice to [X], with a copy to the Commission. The Trustee shall continue carrying out its functions under the Mandate until it has effected a full handover of all relevant information to a new trustee appointed by [X] pursuant to the procedure laid down in the Commitments.

Surviving Provisions

31. Paragraphs [23]–[26] shall survive the termination of the Mandate.

Section J. Additional Provisions

Amendments to the Mandate

32. The Mandate may only be amended in writing and with the Commission's prior approval. The Mandate Parties agree to amend this Mandate if required by the Commission, after consultation with the Mandate Parties, in order to secure compliance with the Commitments, in particular if the amendment is necessary in order to adapt the Mandate to amendments of the Commitments under the Review Clause.

<u>Governing Law and Dispute Resolution</u>

33. This Mandate shall be governed by, and construed in accordance with, the laws of [*Indicate the state by whose laws the Mandate shall be governed*].

34. In the event that a dispute arises concerning the Mandate Parties' obligations under the Mandate, such dispute shall be submitted to the non-exclusive jurisdiction of the [*Indicate the state whose courts shall have jurisdiction for disputes regarding the Mandate*] courts.

<u>Severability</u>

35. [*It is up to the Mandate Parties to agree on a suitable provision on severability, taking into account the rules under the governing law*].

<u>Notices</u>

36. All notices sent under this Mandate shall be made in writing and be deemed to have been duly given if served by personal delivery upon the party for whom it is intended or the Commission or delivered by registered or certified mail; return receipt requested, or if sent by fax, upon receipt of oral confirmation that such transmission has been received, to the person at the address set forth below:

If to [X], addressed as follows:

[Σ]

If to the Trustee, addressed as follows:

[Σ]

If to the Commission, addressed as follows:

To the attention of the Director
Director of Directorate B
European Commission
Directorate General for Competition
70 rue Joseph II / Jozef II-straat 70
B-1000 Brussels
Ref: Case No COMP/M . . . . . .
Fax: + 32 2 296 43 01

Or to any such other address or person as the relevant party may from time to time advise by notice in writing given pursuant to this section. The date of receipt of any such notice, request, consent, agreement or approval shall be deemed to be the date of delivery thereof.

[*Indicate place and date*]

_____

By:

Title:

_____

By:

Title:

Annex [Σ]

Power of Attorney, duly executed, for the exercise of [X's] rights as shareholder (pursuant to paragraph 6(d) of the Mandate)

Annex [Σ] Power of Attorney, duly executed, for the Divestiture Trustee (pursuant to paragraph 12 of the Mandate)

Annex [Σ] Disclosure of current relationships between the Trustee, the Trustee Team and the Trustees Partner Firm and [X] and Affiliated Undertakings.

D4

GUIDELINES ON THE ASSESSMENT OF HORIZONTAL MERGERS

under the Council Regulation on the control of concentrations between undertakings

(2004/C 31/03)

Official Journal C 31, 5.2.2004, p.5

Celex No: 52004XC0205(02)

EUR-Lex permanent link: <http://eur-lex.europa.eu/legal-content/EN/ALL/?uri=CELEX:52004X
C0205(02)&qid=1395770911476>

I. Introduction

1. Article 2 of Council Regulation (EC) No 139/2004 of 20 January 2004 on the control of concentrations between undertakings[1] (hereinafter: the "Merger Regulation") provides that the Commission has to appraise concentrations within the scope of the Merger Regulation with a view to establishing whether or not they are compatible with the common market. For that purpose, the Commission must assess, pursuant to Article 2(2) and (3), whether or not a concentration would significantly impede effective competition, in particular as a result of the creation or strengthening of a dominant position, in the common market or a substantial part of it.

Notes

[1] Council Regulation (EC) No 139/2004 of 20 January 2004 (OJ L 24, 29.1.2004, p.1).

---

2. Accordingly, the Commission must take into account any significant impediment to effective competition likely to be caused by a concentration. The creation or the strengthening of a dominant position is a primary form of such competitive harm. The concept of dominance was defined in the context of Council Regulation (EEC) No 4064/89 of 21 December 1989 on the control of concentrations between undertakings (hereinafter "Regulation No 4064/89") as:

"a situation where one or more undertakings wield economic power which would enable them to prevent effective competition from being maintained in the relevant market by giving them the opportunity to act to a considerable extent independently of their competitors, their customers and, ultimately, of consumers".[2]

769

Notes

2 Case T-102/96 *Gencor v Commission* [1999] ECR II-753, paragraph 200. See Joined Cases C-68/94 and C-30/95 *France and others v Commission* (hereinafter "*Kali and Salz*"), [1998] ECR I-1375, paragraph 221. In exceptional circumstances, a merger may give rise to the creation or the strengthening of a dominant position on the part of an undertaking which is not a party to the notified transaction (see Case IV/M.1383 – *Exxon/Mobil*, points 225–229; Case COMP/M.2434 – *Grupo Villar MIR/EnBW/Hidroelectrica del Cantabrico*, points 67–71).

Commentary
para 2: B&C: 8.203, F&N: 5.561

3. For the purpose of interpreting the concept of dominance in the context of Regulation No 4064/89, the Court of Justice referred to the fact that it "is intended to apply to all concentrations with a Community dimension insofar as they are likely, because of their effect on the structure of competition within the Community, to prove incompatible with the system of undistorted competition envisaged by the Treaty".[3]

Notes

3 See also Joined Cases C-68/94 and C-30/95, *Kali and Salz*, paragraph 170.

4. The creation or strengthening of a dominant position held by a single firm as a result of a merger has been the most common basis for finding that a concentration would result in a significant impediment to effective competition. Furthermore, the concept of dominance has also been applied in an oligopolistic setting to cases of collective dominance. As a consequence, it is expected that most cases of incompatibility of a concentration with the common market will continue to be based upon a finding of dominance. That concept therefore provides an important indication as to the standard of competitive harm that is applicable when determining whether a concentration is likely to impede effective competition to a significant degree, and hence, as to the likelihood of intervention.[4] To that effect, the present notice is intended to preserve the guidance that can be drawn from past decisional practice and to take full account of past case-law of the Community Courts.

Notes

4 See Recitals 25 and 26 of the Merger Regulation.

Commentary
para 4: B&C: 8.201, 8.203, 8.204

5. The purpose of this notice is to provide guidance as to how the Commission assesses concentrations[5] when the undertakings concerned are actual or potential competitors on the same relevant market.[6] In this notice such mergers will be denoted "horizontal mergers". While the notice presents the analytical approach used by the Commission in its appraisal of horizontal mergers it cannot provide details of all possible applications of this approach. The Commission applies the approach described in the notice to the particular facts and circumstances of each case.

Notes

5 The term "concentration" used in the Merger Regulation covers various types of transactions such as mergers, acquisitions, takeovers, and certain types of joint ventures. In the remainder of this notice, unless otherwise specified, the term "merger" will be used as a synonym for concentration and therefore cover all the above types of transactions.

6 The notice does not cover the assessment of the effects of competition that a merger has in other markets, including vertical and conglomerate effects. Nor does it cover the assessment of the effects of a joint venture as referred to in Article 2(4) of the Merger Regulation.

6. The guidance set out in this notice draws and elaborates on the Commission's evolving experience with the appraisal of horizontal mergers under Regulation No 4064/89 since its entry into force on 21 September 1990 as well as on the case-law of the Court of Justice and the Court of First Instance of the European Communities. The principles contained here will be applied and further developed and refined by the Commission in individual cases. The Commission may revise this notice from time to time in the light of future developments.

7. The Commission's interpretation of the Merger Regulation as regards the appraisal of horizontal mergers is without prejudice to the interpretation which may be given by the Court of Justice or the Court of First Instance of the European Communities.

II. Overview

8. Effective competition brings benefits to consumers, such as low prices, high quality products, a wide selection of goods and services, and innovation. Through its control of mergers, the Commission prevents mergers that would be likely to deprive customers of these benefits by significantly increasing the market power of firms. By "increased market power" is meant the ability of one or more firms to profitably increase prices, reduce output, choice or quality of goods and services, diminish innovation, or otherwise influence parameters of competition. In this notice, the expression "increased prices" is often used as shorthand for these various ways in which a merger may result in competitive harm.[7] Both suppliers and buyers can have market power. However, for clarity, market power will usually refer here to a supplier's market power. Where a buyer's market power is the issue, the term "buyer power" is employed.

Notes

[7] The expression should be understood to also cover situations where, for instance, prices are decreased less, or are less likely to decrease, than they otherwise would have without the merger and where prices are increased more, or are more likely to increase, than they otherwise would have without the merger.

Commentary
para 8: **B&C:** 8.207 **F&N:** 5.566, 5.831

9. In assessing the competitive effects of a merger, the Commission compares the competitive conditions that would result from the notified merger with the conditions that would have prevailed without the merger.[8] In most cases the competitive conditions existing at the time of the merger constitute the relevant comparison for evaluating the effects of a merger. However, in some circumstances, the Commission may take into account future changes to the market that can reasonably be predicted.[9] It may, in particular, take account of the likely entry or exit of firms if the merger did not take place when considering what constitutes the relevant comparison.[10]

Notes

[8] By analogy, in the case of a merger that has been implemented without having been notified, the Commission would assess the merger in the light of the competitive conditions that would have prevailed without the implemented merger.
[9] See, e.g. Commission Decision 98/526/EC in Case IV/M.950 – *Hoffmann La Roche/Boehringer Mannheim*, OJ L 234, 21.8.1998, p.14, point 13; Case IV/M.1846 – *Glaxo Wellcome/SmithKline Beecham*, points 70–72; Case COMP/M.2547 – *Bayer/Aventis Crop Science*, points 324 et seq.
[10] See, e.g. Case T-102/96 *Gencor v Commission* [1999] ECR II-753, paragraphs 247–263.

Commentary
para 9: **F&N:** 5.16, 5.560, 15.80

10. The Commission's assessment of mergers normally entails:
    (a) definition of the relevant product and geographic markets;
    (b) competitive assessment of the merger.
    The main purpose of market definition is to identify in a systematic way the immediate competitive constraints facing the merged entity. Guidance on this issue can be found in the Commission's Notice on the definition of the relevant market for the purposes of Community competition law.[11] Various considerations leading to the delineation of the relevant markets may also be of importance for the competitive assessment of the merger.

Notes

[11] OJ C 372, 9.12.1997, p.5.

Commentary
para 10: **B&C:** 4.001, 8.194

11. This notice is structured around the following elements:
    (a) The approach of the Commission to market shares and concentration thresholds (Section III).
    (b) The likelihood that a merger would have anti-competitive effects in the relevant markets, in the absence of countervailing factors (Section IV).
    (c) The likelihood that buyer power would act as a countervailing factor to an increase in market power resulting from the merger (Section V).
    (d) The likelihood that entry would maintain effective competition in the relevant markets (Section VI).
    (e) The likelihood that efficiencies would act as a factor counteracting the harmful effects on competition which might otherwise result from the merger (Section VII).
    (f) The conditions for a failing firm defence (Section VIII).

12. In order to assess the foreseeable impact[12] of a merger on the relevant markets, the Commission analyses its possible anti-competitive effects and the relevant countervailing factors such as buyer power, the extent of entry barriers and possible efficiencies put forward by the parties. In exceptional circumstances, the Commission considers whether the conditions for a failing firm defence are met.

Notes

[12] See Case T-102/96 *Gencor v Commission* [1999] ECR II-753, paragraph 262, and Case T-342/99 *Airtours v Commission* [2002] ECR II-2585, paragraph 280.

Commentary
para 12: **B&C:** 8.200

13. In the light of these elements, the Commission determines, pursuant to Article 2 of the Merger Regulation, whether the merger would significantly impede effective competition, in particular through the creation or the strengthening of a dominant position, and should therefore be declared incompatible with the common market. It should be stressed that these factors are not a "checklist" to be mechanically applied in each and every case. Rather, the competitive analysis in a particular case will be based on an overall assessment of the foreseeable impact of the merger in the light of the relevant factors and conditions. Not all the elements will always be relevant to each and every horizontal merger, and it may not be necessary to analyse all the elements of a case in the same detail.

III. Market Share and Concentration Levels

14. Market shares and concentration levels provide useful first indications of the market structure and of the competitive importance of both the merging parties and their competitors.

Commentary
para 14: **B&C:** 8.212 **F&N:** 5.680

15. Normally, the Commission uses current market shares in its competitive analysis.[13] However, current market shares may be adjusted to reflect reasonably certain future changes, for instance in the light of exit, entry or expansion.[14] Post-merger market shares are calculated on the assumption that the post-merger combined market share of the merging parties is the sum of their pre-merger market shares.[15] Historic data may be used if market shares have been volatile, for instance when the market is characterised by large, lumpy orders. Changes in historic market shares may provide useful information about the competitive process and the likely future importance of the various competitors, for instance, by indicating whether firms have been gaining or losing market shares. In any event, the Commission interprets market shares in the light of likely market conditions, for instance, if the market is highly dynamic in character and if the market structure is unstable due to innovation or growth.[16]

Notes

[13] As to the calculation of market shares, see also Commission Notice on the definition of the relevant market for the purposes of Community competition law, OJ C 372, 9.12.1997, p.3, paragraphs 54–55.
[14] See, e.g. Case COMP/M.1806 – *Astra Zeneca/Novartis*, points 150 and 415.

15 When relevant, market shares may be adjusted, in particular, to account for controlling interests in other firms (see, e.g. Case IV/M.1383 – *Exxon/Mobil*, points 446–458; Case COMP/M.1879 – *Boeing/Hughes*, points 60–79; Case COMP/JV 55 – *Hutchison/RCPM/ECT*, points 66–75), or for other arrangements with third parties (see, for instance, as regards sub-contractors, Commission Decision 2001/769/EC in Case COMP/M.1940 – *Framatome/Siemens/Cogema*, OJ L 289, 6.11.2001, p.8, point 142).

16 See, e.g. Case COMP/M.2256 – *Philips/Agilent Health Care Technologies*, points 31–32, and Case COMP/M.2609 – *HP/Compaq*, point 39.

Commentary
para 15: B&C: 8.213

16. The overall concentration level in a market may also provide useful information about the competitive situation. In order to measure concentration levels, the Commission often applies the Herfindahl-Hirschman Index (HHI).[17] The HHI is calculated by summing the squares of the individual market shares of all the firms in the market.[18] The HHI gives proportionately greater weight to the market shares of the larger firms. Although it is best to include all firms in the calculation, lack of information about very small firms may not be important because such firms do not affect the HHI significantly. While the absolute level of the HHI can give an initial indication of the competitive pressure in the market post-merger, the change in the HHI (known as the "delta") is a useful proxy for the change in concentration directly brought about by the merger.[19]

Notes

17 See, e.g. Case IV/M.1365 – *FCC/Vivendi*, point 40; Case COMP/JV 55 – *Hutchison/RCPM/ECT*, point 50. If appropriate, the Commission may also use other concentration measures such as, for instance, concentration ratios, which measure the aggregate market share of a small number (usually three or four) of the leading firms in a market.

18 For example, a market containing five firms with market shares of 40%, 20%, 15%, 15%, and 10%, respectively, has an HHI of 2550 ($40^2 + 20^2 + 15^2 + 15^2 + 10^2 = 2{,}550$). The HHI ranges from close to zero (in an atomistic market) to 10000 (in the case of a pure monopoly).

19 The increase in concentration as measured by the HHI can be calculated independently of the overall market concentration by doubling the product of the market shares of the merging firms. For example, a merger of two firms with market shares of 30% and 15% respectively would increase the HHI by 900 ($30 \times 15 \times 2 = 900$). The explanation for this technique is as follows: Before the merger, the market shares of the merging firms contribute to the HHI by their squares individually: $(a)^2 + (b)^2$. After the merger, the contribution is the square of their sum: $(a + b)^2$, which equals $(a)^2 + (b)^2 + 2ab$. The increase in the HHI is therefore represented by $2ab$.

Market share levels

17. According to well-established case law, very large market shares – 50% or more – may in themselves be evidence of the existence of a dominant market position.[20] However, smaller competitors may act as a sufficient constraining influence if, for example, they have the ability and incentive to increase their supplies. A merger involving a firm whose market share will remain below 50% after the merger may also raise competition concerns in view of other factors such as the strength and number of competitors, the presence of capacity constraints or the extent to which the products of the merging parties are close substitutes. The Commission has thus in several cases considered mergers resulting in firms holding market shares between 40% and 50%,[21] and in some cases below 40%,[22] to lead to the creation or the strengthening of a dominant position.

Notes

20 Case T-221/95 *Endemol v Commission*, [1999] ECR II-1299, paragraph 134, and Case T-102/96, *Gencor v Commission*, [1999] ECR II-753, paragraph 205. It is a distinct question whether a dominant position is created or strengthened as a result of the merger.

21 See, e.g. Case COMP/M.2337 – *Nestlé/Ralston Purina*, points 48–50.

22 See, e.g. Commission Decision 1999/674/EC in Case IV/M.1221 – *Rewe/Meinl*, OJ L 274, 23.10.1999, p.1, points 98–114; Case COMP/M.2337 – *Nestlé/Ralston Purina*, points 44–47.

Commentary
para 17: B&C: 8.214

18. Concentrations which, by reason of the limited market share of the undertakings concerned, are not liable to impede effective competition may be presumed to be compatible with the common market. Without prejudice to Articles [101] and [102] of the Treaty, an indication to this effect exists, in particular, where the market share of the undertakings concerned does not exceed 25%[23] either in the common market or in a substantial part of it.[24]

Notes

[23] The calculation of market shares depends critically on market definition. It must be emphasised that the Commission does not necessarily accept the parties' proposed market definition.

[24] Recital 32 of the Merger Regulation. However, such an indication does not apply to cases where the proposed merger creates or strengthens a collective dominant position involving the "undertakings concerned" and other third parties (see Joined Cases C-68/94 and C-30/95, *Kali and Salz*, [1998] ECR I-1375, paragraphs 171 et seq.; and Case T-102/96, *Gencor v Commission*, [1999] ECR II-753, paragraphs 134 et seq.).

Commentary
para 18: **B&C:** 8.213 **F&N:** 5.684

HHI levels

19. The Commission is unlikely to identify horizontal competition concerns in a market with a post-merger HHI below 1000. Such markets normally do not require extensive analysis.

Commentary
para 19: **B&C:** 8.213 **F&N:** 5.520, 5.684

20. The Commission is also unlikely to identify horizontal competition concerns in a merger with a post-merger HHI between 1000 and 2000 and a delta below 250, or a merger with a post-merger HHI above 2000 and a delta below 150, except where special circumstances such as, for instance, one or more of the following factors are present:
    (a) a merger involves a potential entrant or a recent entrant with a small market share;
    (b) one or more merging parties are important innovators in ways not reflected in market shares;
    (c) there are significant cross-shareholdings among the market participants;[25]
    (d) one of the merging firms is a maverick firm with a high likelihood of disrupting coordinated conduct;
    (e) indications of past or ongoing coordination, or facilitating practices, are present;
    (f) one of the merging parties has a pre-merger market share of 50% of more.[26]

Notes

[25] In markets with cross-shareholdings or joint ventures the Commission may use a modified HHI, which takes into account such share-holdings (see, e.g. Case IV/M.1383 – *Exxon/Mobil*, point 256).

[26] See paragraph 17.

Commentary
para 20: **B&C:** 8.213 **F&N:** 5.520, 5.684

21. Each of these HHI levels, in combination with the relevant deltas, may be used as an initial indicator of the absence of competition concerns. However, they do not give rise to a presumption of either the existence or the absence of such concerns.

Commentary
para 21: **F&N:** 12.101

IV. POSSIBLE ANTI-COMPETITIVE EFFECTS OF HORIZONTAL MERGERS

22. There are two main ways in which horizontal mergers may significantly impede effective competition, in particular by creating or strengthening a dominant position:
    (a) by eliminating important competitive constraints on one or more firms, which consequently would have increased market power, without resorting to coordinated behaviour (non-coordinated effects);

(b) by changing the nature of competition in such a way that firms that previously were not coordinating their behaviour, are now significantly more likely to coordinate and raise prices or otherwise harm effective competition. A merger may also make coordination easier, more stable or more effective for firms which were coordinating prior to the merger (coordinated effects).

Commentary
para 22: B&C: 8.210

---

23. The Commission assesses whether the changes brought about by the merger would result in any of these effects. Both instances mentioned above may be relevant when assessing a particular transaction.

Non-coordinated effects[27]

24. A merger may significantly impede effective competition in a market by removing important competitive constraints on one or more sellers, who consequently have increased market power. The most direct effect of the merger will be the loss of competition between the merging firms. For example, if prior to the merger one of the merging firms had raised its price, it would have lost some sales to the other merging firm. The merger removes this particular constraint. Non-merging firms in the same market can also benefit from the reduction of competitive pressure that results from the merger, since the merging firms' price increase may switch some demand to the rival firms, which, in turn, may find it profitable to increase their prices.[28] The reduction in these competitive constraints could lead to significant price increases in the relevant market.

Notes
[27] Also often called "unilateral" effects.
[28] Such expected reactions by competitors may be a relevant factor influencing the merged entity's incentives to increase prices.
Commentary
para 24: F&N: 5.700

---

25. Generally, a merger giving rise to such non-coordinated effects would significantly impede effective competition by creating or strengthening the dominant position of a single firm, one which, typically, would have an appreciably larger market share than the next competitor post-merger. Furthermore, mergers in oligopolistic markets[29] involving the elimination of important competitive constraints that the merging parties previously exerted upon each other together with a reduction of competitive pressure on the remaining competitors may, even where there is little likelihood of coordination between the members of the oligopoly, also result in a significant impediment to competition. The Merger Regulation clarifies that all mergers giving rise to such non-coordinated effects shall also be declared incompatible with the common market.[30]

Notes
[29] An oligopolistic market refers to a market structure with a limited number of sizeable firms. Because the behaviour of one firm has an appreciable impact on the overall market conditions, and thus indirectly on the situation of each of the other firms, oligopolistic firms are interdependent.
[30] Recital 25 of the Merger Regulation.
Commentary
para 25: B&C: 8.204, 8.215: F&N: 1.269

---

26. A number of factors, which taken separately are not necessarily decisive, may influence whether significant non-coordinated effects are likely to result from a merger. Not all of these factors need to be present for such effects to be likely. Nor should this be considered an exhaustive list.

Merging firms have large market shares

27. The larger the market share, the more likely a firm is to possess market power. And the larger the addition of market share, the more likely it is that a merger will lead to a significant increase in

market power. The larger the increase in the sales base on which to enjoy higher margins after a price increase, the more likely it is that the merging firms will find such a price increase profitable despite the accompanying reduction in output. Although market shares and additions of market shares only provide first indications of market power and increases in market power, they are normally important factors in the assessment.[31]

Notes

[31] See, in particular, paragraphs 17 and 18.

Merging firms are close competitors

28. Products may be differentiated[32] within a relevant market such that some products are closer substitutes than others.[33] The higher the degree of substitutability between the merging firms' products, the more likely it is that the merging firms will raise prices significantly.[34] For example, a merger between two producers offering products which a substantial number of customers regard as their first and second choices could generate a significant price increase. Thus, the fact that rivalry between the parties has been an important source of competition on the market may be a central factor in the analysis.[35] High pre-merger margins[36] may also make significant price increases more likely. The merging firms' incentive to raise prices is more likely to be constrained when rival firms produce close substitutes to the products of the merging firms than when they offer less close substitutes.[37] It is therefore less likely that a merger will significantly impede effective competition, in particular through the creation or strengthening of a dominant position, when there is a high degree of substitutability between the products of the merging firms and those supplied by rival producers.

Notes

[32] Products may be differentiated in various ways. There may, for example, be differentiation in terms of geographic location, based on branch or stores location; location matters for retail distribution, banks, travel agencies, or petrol stations. Likewise, differentiation may be based on brand image, technical specifications, quality or level of service. The level of advertising in a market may be an indicator of the firms' effort to differentiate their products. For other products, buyers may have to incur switching costs to use a competitor's product.

[33] For the definition of the relevant market, see the Commission's Notice on the definition of the relevant market for the purposes of Community competition law, cited above.

[34] See for example Case COMP/M.2817 – *Barilla/BPS/Kamps*, point 34; Commission Decision 2001/403/EC in Case COMP/M.1672 – *Volvo/Scania*, OJ L 143, 29.5.2001, p.74, points 107–148.

[35] See, e.g. Commission Decision 94/893/EC in Case IV/M.430 – *Procter & Gamble/VP Schickedanz (II)*, OJ L 354, 21.6.1994, p.32, Case T-290/94, *Kaysersberg v Commission*, [1997] II-2137, paragraph 153; Commission Decision 97/610/EC in Case IV/M.774 – *Saint-Gobain/Wacker-Chemie/NOM*, OJ L 247, 10.9.1997, p.1, point 179; Commission Decision 2002/156/EC in Case COMP/M.2097 – *SCA/Metsä Tissue*, OJ L 57, 27.2.2002, p.1, points 94– 108; Case T-310/01, *Schneider v Commission*, [2002] II-4071, paragraph 418.

[36] Typically, the relevant margin (m) is the difference between price (p) and the incremental cost (c) of supplying one more unit of output expressed as a percentage of price ($m = (p - c)p$).

[37] See, e.g. Case IV/M.1980 – *Volvo/Renault VI*, point 34; Case COMP/M.2256 – *Philips Agilent/Health Care Solutions*, points 33–35; Case COMP/M.2537 – *Philips/Marconi Medical Systems*, points 31–34.

Commentary

para 28: B&C: 8.216

29. When data are available, the degree of substitutability may be evaluated through customer preference surveys, analysis of purchasing patterns, estimation of the cross-price elasticities of the products involved,[38] or diversion ratios.[39] In bidding markets it may be possible to measure whether historically the submitted bids by one of the merging parties have been constrained by the presence of the other merging party.[40]

Notes

[38] The cross-price elasticity of demand measures the extent to which the quantity of a product demanded changes in response to a change in the price of some other product, all other things remaining equal. The own-price elasticity measures the extent to which demand for a product changes in response to the change in the price of the product itself.

[39] The diversion ratio from product A to product B measures the proportion of the sales of product A lost due to a price increase of A that are captured by product B.

[40] Commission Decision 97/816/EC in Case IV/M.877 – *Boeing/McDonnell Douglas*, OJ L 336, 8.12.1997, p.16, points 58 et seq.; Case COMP/M.3083 – *GE/Instrumentarium*, points 125 et seq.

Commentary
para 29: **B&C**: 4.004

30. In some markets it may be relatively easy and not too costly for the active firms to reposition their products or extend their product portfolio. In particular, the Commission examines whether the possibility of repositioning or product line extension by competitors or the merging parties may influence the incentive of the merged entity to raise prices. However, product repositioning or product line extension often entails risks and large sunk costs[41] and may be less profitable than the current line.

Notes
[41] Sunk costs are costs which are unrecoverable upon exit from the market.

Customers have limited possibilities of switching supplier

31. Customers of the merging parties may have difficulties switching to other suppliers because there are few alternative suppliers[42] or because they face substantial switching costs.[43] Such customers are particularly vulnerable to price increases. The merger may affect these customers' ability to protect themselves against price increases. In particular, this may be the case for customers that have used dual sourcing from the two merging firms as a means of obtaining competitive prices. Evidence of past customer switching patterns and reactions to price changes may provide important information in this respect.

Notes
[42] See e.g. Commission Decision 2002/156/EC in Case IV/M.877 – *Boeing/McDonnell Douglas*, OJ L 336, 8.12.1997, p.16, point 70.
[43] See, e.g. Case IV/M. 986 – *Agfa Gevaert/DuPont*, OJ L 211, 29.7.1998, p.22, points 63–71.

Commentary
para 31: **B&C**: 8.216 **F&N**: 5.736

Competitors are unlikely to increase supply if prices increase

32. When market conditions are such that the competitors of the merging parties are unlikely to increase their supply substantially if prices increase, the merging firms may have an incentive to reduce output below the combined pre-merger levels, thereby raising market prices.[44] The merger increases the incentive to reduce output by giving the merged firm a larger base of sales on which to enjoy the higher margins resulting from an increase in prices induced by the output reduction.

Notes
[44] See, e.g. Case COMP/M.2187 – *CVC/Lenzing*, points 162–170.

Commentary
para 32: **F&N**: 5.731

33. Conversely, when market conditions are such that rival firms have enough capacity and find it profitable to expand output sufficiently, the Commission is unlikely to find that the merger will create or strengthen a dominant position or otherwise significantly impede effective competition.

Commentary
para 33: **F&N**: 5.731

34. Such output expansion is, in particular, unlikely when competitors face binding capacity constraints and the expansion of capacity is costly[45] or if existing excess capacity is significantly more costly to operate than capacity currently in use.

Part D Mergers and Concentrations

Notes

45 When analysing the possible expansion of capacity by rivals, the Commission considers factors similar to those described in Section VI on entry. See, e.g. Case COMP/M.2187 – *CVC/Lenzing*, points 162–173.

35. Although capacity constraints are more likely to be important when goods are relatively homogeneous, they may also be important where firms offer differentiated products.

Merged entity able to hinder expansion by competitors

36. Some proposed mergers would, if allowed to proceed, significantly impede effective competition by leaving the merged firm in a position where it would have the ability and incentive to make the expansion of smaller firms and potential competitors more difficult or otherwise restrict the ability of rival firms to compete. In such a case, competitors may not, either individually or in the aggregate, be in a position to constrain the merged entity to such a degree that it would not increase prices or take other actions detrimental to competition. For instance, the merged entity may have such a degree of control, or influence over, the supply of inputs [46] or distribution possibilities[47] that expansion or entry by rival firms may be more costly. Similarly, the merged entity's control over patents[48] or other types of intellectual property (e.g. brands [49]) may make expansion or entry by rivals more difficult. In markets where interoperability between different infrastructures or platforms is important,[50] a merger may give the merged entity the ability and incentive to raise the costs or decrease the quality of service of its rivals.[51] In making this assessment the Commission may take into account, inter alia, the financial strength of the merged entity relative to its rivals.[52]

Notes

46 See, e.g. Case T-221/95 *Endemol v Commission* [1999] ECR II-1299, paragraph 167.

47 See, e.g. Case T-22/97 *Kesko v Commission* [1999], ECR II-3775, paragraphs 141 et seq.

48 See, e.g. Commission Decision 2001/684/EC in Case M.1671 – *Dow Chemical/Union Carbides* OJ L 245, 14.9.2001, p.1, points 107–114.

49 See, e.g. Commission Decision 96/435/EC in Case IV/M.623 – *Kimberly-Clark/Scott*, OJ L 183, 23.7.1996, p.1; Case T-114/02, *Babyliss SA v Commission* ("*Seb/Moulinex*"), [2003] ECR II-[1279], paragraphs 343 et seq.

50 This is, for example, the case in network industries such as energy, telecommunications and other communication industries.

51 Commission Decision 99/287/EC in Case IV/M.1069 – *Worldcom/MCI*, OJ L 116, 4.5.1999, p.1, points 117 et seq.; Case IV/M.1741 – *MCI Worldcom/Sprint*, points 145 et seq.; Case IV/M.1795 – *Vodafone Airtouch/Mannesmann*, points 44 et seq.

52 Case T-156/98 *RJB Mining v Commission* [2001] ECR II-337.

Commentary
para 36: B&C: 8.216   F&N: 5.738

Merger eliminates an important competitive force

37. Some firms have more of an influence on the competitive process than their market shares or similar measures would suggest. A merger involving such a firm may change the competitive dynamics in a significant, anti-competitive way, in particular when the market is already concentrated.[53] For instance, a firm may be a recent entrant that is expected to exert significant competitive pressure in the future on the other firms in the market.

Notes

53 Commission Decision 2002/156/EC in Case IV/M.877 – *Boeing/McDonnell Douglas*, OJ L 336, 8.12.1997, p.16, point 58; Case COMP/M.2568 – *Haniel/Ytong*, point 126.

Commentary
para 37: B&C: 8.216

38. In markets where innovation is an important competitive force, a merger may increase the firms' ability and incentive to bring new innovations to the market and, thereby, the competitive pressure on rivals to innovate in that market. Alternatively, effective competition may be significantly impeded by a merger between two important innovators, for instance between two companies

with "pipeline" products related to a specific product market. Similarly, a firm with a relatively small market share may nevertheless be an important competitive force if it has promising pipeline products.[54]

Notes

[54] For an example of pipeline products of one merging party likely to compete with the other party's pipeline or existing products, see, e.g. Case IV/M.1846 – *Glaxo Wellcome/SmithKline Beecham*, point 188.

Commentary
para 38: B&C: 4.006, 8.216

Coordinated effects

39. In some markets the structure may be such that firms would consider it possible, economically rational, and hence preferable, to adopt on a sustainable basis a course of action on the market aimed at selling at increased prices. A merger in a concentrated market may significantly impede effective competition, through the creation or the strengthening of a collective dominant position, because it increases the likelihood that firms are able to coordinate their behaviour in this way and raise prices, even without entering into an agreement or resorting to a concerted practice within the meaning of Article [101] of the Treaty.[55] A merger may also make coordination easier, more stable or more effective for firms, that were already coordinating before the merger, either by making the coordination more robust or by permitting firms to coordinate on even higher prices.

Notes

[55] Case T-102/96 *Gencor v Commission* [1999] ECR II-753, paragraph 277; Case T-342/99 *Airtours v Commission* [2002] ECR II-2585, paragraph 61. [Ed note: please see the Note on the Lisbon Treaty at p.xvii in regard to article renumbering introduced by the Lisbon Treaty.]

Commentary
para 39: F&N: 5.764

40. Coordination may take various forms. In some markets, the most likely coordination may involve keeping prices above the competitive level. In other markets, coordination may aim at limiting production or the amount of new capacity brought to the market. Firms may also coordinate by dividing the market, for instance by geographic area[56] or other customer characteristics, or by allocating contracts in bidding markets.

Notes

[56] This may be the case if the oligopolists have tended to concentrate their sales in different areas for historic reasons.

Commentary
para 40: B&C: 8.219 F&N: 5.779

41. Coordination is more likely to emerge in markets where it is relatively simple to reach a common understanding on the terms of coordination. In addition, three conditions are necessary for coordination to be sustainable. First, the coordinating firms must be able to monitor to a sufficient degree whether the terms of coordination are being adhered to. Second, discipline requires that there is some form of credible deterrent mechanism that can be activated if deviation is detected. Third, the reactions of outsiders, such as current and future competitors not participating in the coordination, as well as customers, should not be able to jeopardise the results expected from the coordination.[57]

Notes

[57] Case T-342/99, *Airtours v Commission*, [2002] ECR II-2585, paragraph 62.

Commentary
para 41: F&N: 1.223

42. The Commission examines whether it would be possible to reach terms of coordination and whether the coordination is likely to be sustainable. In this respect, the Commission considers

the changes that the merger brings about. The reduction in the number of firms in a market may, in itself, be a factor that facilitates coordination. However, a merger may also increase the likelihood or significance of coordinated effects in other ways. For instance, a merger may involve a "maverick" firm that has a history of preventing or disrupting coordination, for example by failing to follow price increases by its competitors, or has characteristics that gives it an incentive to favour different strategic choices than its coordinating competitors would prefer. If the merged firm were to adopt strategies similar to those of other competitors, the remaining firms would find it easier to coordinate, and the merger would increase the likelihood, stability or effectiveness of coordination.

Commentary
para 42: F&N: 5.783, 5.784

43. In assessing the likelihood of coordinated effects, the Commission takes into account all available relevant information on the characteristics of the markets concerned, including both structural features and the past behaviour of firms.[58] Evidence of past coordination is important if the relevant market characteristics have not changed appreciably or are not likely to do so in the near future.[59] Likewise, evidence of coordination in similar markets may be useful information.

Notes
[58] See Commission Decision 92/553/EC in Case IV/M.190 – *Nestlé/Perrier*, OJ L 356, 5.12.1992, p.1, points 117–118.
[59] See, e.g. Case IV/M.580 – *ABB/Daimler-Benz*, point 95.

Commentary
para 43: B&C: 8.219

Reaching terms of coordination

44. Coordination is more likely to emerge if competitors can easily arrive at a common perception as to how the coordination should work. Coordinating firms should have similar views regarding which actions would be considered to be in accordance with the aligned behaviour and which actions would not.

45. Generally, the less complex and the more stable the economic environment, the easier it is for the firms to reach a common understanding on the terms of coordination. For instance, it is easier to coordinate among a few players than among many. It is also easier to coordinate on a price for a single, homogeneous product, than on hundreds of prices in a market with many differentiated products. Similarly, it is easier to coordinate on a price when demand and supply conditions are relatively stable than when they are continuously changing.[60] In this context volatile demand, substantial internal growth by some firms in the market or frequent entry by new firms may indicate that the current situation is not sufficiently stable to make coordination likely.[61] In markets where innovation is important, coordination may be more difficult since innovations, particularly significant ones, may allow one firm to gain a major advantage over its rivals.

Notes
[60] See, e.g. Commission Decision 2002/156/EC in Case COMP/M.2097 – *SCA/Metsä Tissue*, OJ L 57, 27.2.2002, p.1, point 148.
[61] See, e.g. Case IV/M.1298 – *Kodak/Imation*, point 60.

46. Coordination by way of market division will be easier if customers have simple characteristics that allow the coordinating firms to readily allocate them. Such characteristics may be based on geography; on customer type or simply on the existence of customers who typically buy from one specific firm. Coordination by way of market division may be relatively straightforward if it is easy to identify each customer's supplier and the coordination device is the allocation of existing customers to their incumbent supplier.

47. Coordinating firms may, however, find other ways to overcome problems stemming from complex economic environments short of market division. They may, for instance, establish simple pricing rules that reduce the complexity of coordinating on a large number of prices. One example of

such a rule is establishing a small number of pricing points, thus reducing the coordination problem. Another example is having a fixed relationship between certain base prices and a number of other prices, such that prices basically move in parallel. Publicly available key information, exchange of information through trade associations, or information received through cross-shareholdings or participation in joint ventures may also help firms reach terms of coordination. The more complex the market situation is, the more transparency or communication is likely to be needed to reach a common understanding on the terms of coordination.

Commentary
para 47: B&C: 8.221

48. Firms may find it easier to reach a common understanding on the terms of coordination if they are relatively symmetric,[62] especially in terms of cost structures, market shares, capacity levels and levels of vertical integration.[63] Structural links such as cross-shareholding or participation in joint ventures may also help in aligning incentives among the coordinating firms.[64]

Notes

[62] Case T-102/96 *Gencor v Commission* [1999] ECR II-753, paragraph 222; Commission Decision 92/553/EC in Case IV/M.190 – *Nestlé/Perrier*, OJ L 356, 5.12.1992, p.1, points 63–123.

[63] In assessing whether or not a merger may increase the symmetry of the various firms present on the market, efficiency gains may provide important indications (see also paragraph 82 of the notice).

[64] See, e.g. Commission Decision 2001/519/EC in Case COMP/M.1673 – *VEBA/VIAG*, OJ L 188, 10.7.2001, p.1, point 226; Case COMP/M.2567 – *Nordbanken/Postgirot*, point 54.

Commentary
para 48: B&C: 6.059

Monitoring deviations

49. Coordinating firms are often tempted to increase their share of the market by deviating from the terms of coordination, for instance by lowering prices, offering secret discounts, increasing product quality or capacity or trying to win new customers. Only the credible threat of timely and sufficient retaliation keeps firms from deviating. Markets therefore need to be sufficiently transparent to allow the coordinating firms to monitor to a sufficient degree whether other firms are deviating, and thus know when to retaliate.[65]

Notes

[65] See, e.g. Case COMP/M.2389 – *Shell/DEA*, points 112 et seq.; and Case COMP/M.2533 – *BP/E.ON*, points 102 et seq.

50. Transparency in the market is often higher, the lower the number of active participants in the market. Further, the degree of transparency often depends on how market transactions take place in a particular market. For example, transparency is likely to be high in a market where transactions take place on a public exchange or in an open outcry auction.[66] Conversely, transparency may be low in a market where transactions are confidentially negotiated between buyers and sellers on a bilateral basis.[67] When evaluating the level of transparency in the market, the key element is to identify what firms can infer about the actions of other firms from the available information.[68] Coordinating firms should be able to interpret with some certainty whether unexpected behaviour is the result of deviation from the terms of coordination. For instance, in unstable environments it may be difficult for a firm to know whether its lost sales are due to an overall low level of demand or due to a competitor offering particularly low prices. Similarly, when overall demand or cost conditions fluctuate, it may be difficult to interpret whether a competitor is lowering its price because it expects the coordinated prices to fall or because it is deviating.

Notes

[66] See also Commission Decision 2000/42/EC in Case IV/M.1313 – *Danish Crown/Vestjyske Slagterier*, OJ L 20, 25.1.2000, p.1, points 176–179.

67 See, e.g. Case COMP/M.2640 – *Nestlé/Schöller*, point 37; Commission Decision 1999/641/EC in Case COMP/M.1225 – *Enso/Stora*, OJ L 254, 29.9.1999, p.9, points 67–68.
68 See, e.g. Case IV/M.1939 – *Rexam (PLM)/American National Can*, point 24.

51. In some markets where the general conditions may seem to make monitoring of deviations difficult, firms may nevertheless engage in practices which have the effect of easing the monitoring task, even when these practices are not necessarily entered into for such purposes. These practices, such as meeting-competition or most-favoured-customer clauses, voluntary publication of information, announcements, or exchange of information through trade associations, may increase transparency or help competitors interpret the choices made. Cross-directorships, participation in joint ventures and similar arrangements may also make monitoring easier.

Deterrent mechanisms

52. Coordination is not sustainable unless the consequences of deviation are sufficiently severe to convince coordinating firms that it is in their best interest to adhere to the terms of coordination. It is thus the threat of future retaliation that keeps the coordination sustainable.[69] However the threat is only credible if, where deviation by one of the firms is detected, there is sufficient certainty that some deterrent mechanism will be activated.[70]

Notes
69 See Case COMP/M.2389 – *Shell/DEA*, point 121, and Case COMP/M.2533 – *BP/E.ON*, point 111.
70 Although deterrent mechanisms are sometimes called "punishment" mechanisms, this should not be understood in the strict sense that such a mechanism necessarily punishes individually a firm that has deviated. The expectation that coordination may break down for a certain period of time, if a deviation is identified as such, may in itself constitute a sufficient deterrent mechanism.

53. Retaliation that manifests itself after some significant time lag, or is not certain to be activated, is less likely to be sufficient to offset the benefits from deviating. For example, if a market is characterised by infrequent, large-volume orders, it may be difficult to establish a sufficiently severe deterrent mechanism, since the gain from deviating at the right time may be large, certain and immediate, whereas the losses from being punished may be small and uncertain and only materialise after some time. The speed with which deterrent mechanisms can be implemented is related to the issue of transparency. If firms are only able to observe their competitors' actions after a substantial delay, then retaliation will be similarly delayed and this may influence whether it is sufficient to deter deviation.

54. The credibility of the deterrence mechanism depends on whether the other coordinating firms have an incentive to retaliate. Some deterrent mechanisms, such as punishing the deviator by temporarily engaging in a price war or increasing output significantly, may entail a short-term economic loss for the firms carrying out the retaliation. This does not necessarily remove the incentive to retaliate since the short-term loss may be smaller than the long-term benefit of retaliating resulting from the return to the regime of coordination.

55. Retaliation need not necessarily take place in the same market as the deviation.[71] If the coordinating firms have commercial interaction in other markets, these may offer various methods of retaliation.[72] The retaliation could take many forms, including cancellation of joint ventures or other forms of cooperation or selling of shares in jointly owned companies.

Notes
71 See, e.g. Commission Decision 2000/42/EC in Case IV/M.1313 – *Danish Crown/Vestjyske Slagterier*, OJ L 20, 25.1.2000, p.1, point 177.
72 See Case T-102/96 *Gencor v Commission* [1999] ECR II-753, paragraph 281.

Commentary
para 55: B&C: 8.224

Reactions of outsiders

56. For coordination to be successful, the actions of non-coordinating firms and potential competitors, as well as customers, should not be able to jeopardise the outcome expected from coordination. For example, if coordination aims at reducing overall capacity in the market, this will only hurt

consumers if non-coordinating firms are unable or have no incentive to respond to this decrease by increasing their own capacity sufficiently to prevent a net decrease in capacity, or at least to render the coordinated capacity decrease unprofitable.[73]

Notes

[73] These elements are analysed in a similar way to non-coordinated effects.

57. The effects of entry and countervailing buyer power of customers are analysed in later sections. However, special consideration is given to the possible impact of these elements on the stability of coordination. For instance, by concentrating a large amount of its requirements with one supplier or by offering long-term contracts, a large buyer may make coordination unstable by successfully tempting one of the coordinating firms to deviate in order to gain substantial new business.

Merger with a potential competitor

58. Concentrations where an undertaking already active on a relevant market merges with a potential competitor in this market can have similar anti-competitive effects to mergers between two undertakings already active on the same relevant market and, thus, significantly impede effective competition, in particular through the creation or the strengthening of a dominant position.

59. A merger with a potential competitor can generate horizontal anti-competitive effects, whether coordinated or non-coordinated, if the potential competitor significantly constrains the behaviour of the firms active in the market. This is the case if the potential competitor possesses assets that could easily be used to enter the market without incurring significant sunk costs. Anti-competitive effects may also occur where the merging partner is very likely to incur the necessary sunk costs to enter the market in a relatively short period of time after which this company would constrain the behaviour of the firms currently active in the market.[74]

Notes

[74] See, e.g. Case IV/M.1630 – *Air Liquide/BOC*, points 201 et seq. For an example of a case where entry by the other merging firm was not sufficiently likely in the short to medium term (Case T-158/00, *ARD v Commission*, [2003] ECR II-000, paragraphs 115–127).

60. For a merger with a potential competitor to have significant anti-competitive effects, two basic conditions must be fulfilled. First, the potential competitor must already exert a significant constraining influence or there must be a significant likelihood that it would grow into an effective competitive force. Evidence that a potential competitor has plans to enter a market in a significant way could help the Commission to reach such a conclusion.[75] Second, there must not be a sufficient number of other potential competitors, which could maintain sufficient competitive pressure after the merger.[76]

Notes

[75] Commission Decision 2001/98/EC in Case IV/M.1439 – *Telia/Telenor*, OJ L 40, 9.2.2001, p.1, points 330–331, and Case IV/M.1681 – *Akzo Nobel/Hoechst Roussel Vet*, point 64.

[76] Case IV/M.1630 – *Air Liquide/BOC*, point 219; Commission Decision 2002/164/EC in Case COMP/M. 1853 – *EDF/EnBW*, OJ L 59, 28.2.2002, p.1, points 54–64.

Commentary
para 60: B&C: 8.216

Mergers creating or strengthening buyer power in upstream markets

61. The Commission may also analyse to what extent a merged entity will increase its buyer power in upstream markets. On the one hand, a merger that creates or strengthens the market power of a buyer may significantly impede effective competition, in particular by creating or strengthening a dominant position. The merged firm may be in a position to obtain lower prices by reducing its purchase of inputs. This may, in turn, lead it also to lower its level of output in the final product market, and thus harm consumer welfare.[77] Such effects may in particular arise when upstream sellers are relatively fragmented. Competition in the downstream markets could also be adversely

affected if, in particular, the merged entity were likely to use its buyer power vis-à-vis its suppliers to foreclose its rivals.[78]

Notes
[77] See Commission Decision 1999/674/EC in Case M.1221 – *Rewe/Meinl*, OJ L 274, 23.10.1999, p.1, points 71–74.
[78] Case T-22/97, *Kesko v Commission*, [1999] ECR II-3775, paragraph 157; Commission Decision 2002/156/EC in Case M.877 – *Boeing/McDonnell Douglas*, OJ L 336, 8.12.1997, p.16, points 105–108.
Commentary
para 61: F&N: 5.756

62. On the other hand, increased buyer power may be beneficial for competition. If increased buyer power lowers input costs without restricting downstream competition or total output, then a proportion of these cost reductions are likely to be passed onto consumers in the form of lower prices.

Commentary
para 62: F&N: 5.755

63. In order to assess whether a merger would significantly impede effective competition by creating or strengthening buyer power, an analysis of the competitive conditions in upstream markets and an evaluation of the possible positive and negative effects described above are therefore required.

V. COUNTERVAILING BUYER POWER

64. The competitive pressure on a supplier is not only exercised by competitors but can also come from its customers. Even firms with very high market shares may not be in a position, post-merger, to significantly impede effective competition, in particular by acting to an appreciable extent independently of their customers, if the latter possess countervailing buyer power.[79] Countervailing buyer power in this context should be understood as the bargaining strength that the buyer has vis-à-vis the seller in commercial negotiations due to its size, its commercial significance to the seller and its ability to switch to alternative suppliers.

Notes
[79] See, e.g. Case IV/M.1882 – *Pirelli/BICC*, points 73–80.
Commentary
para 64: F&N: 5.878

65. The Commission considers, when relevant, to what extent customers will be in a position to counter the increase in market power that a merger would otherwise be likely to create. One source of countervailing buyer power would be if a customer could credibly threaten to resort, within a reasonable timeframe, to alternative sources of supply should the supplier decide to increase prices[80] or to otherwise deteriorate quality or the conditions of delivery. This would be the case if the buyer could immediately switch to other suppliers,[81] credibly threaten to vertically integrate into the upstream market or to sponsor upstream expansion or entry[82] for instance by persuading a potential entrant to enter by committing to placing large orders with this company. It is more likely that large and sophisticated customers will possess this kind of countervailing buyer power than smaller firms in a fragmented industry.[83] A buyer may also exercise countervailing buying power by refusing to buy other products produced by the supplier or, particularly in the case of durable goods, delaying purchases.

Notes
[80] See, e.g. Case IV/M.1245 – *Valeo/ITT Industries*, point 26.
[81] Even a small number of customers may not have sufficient buyer power if they are to a large extent "locked in" because of high switching costs (see Case COMP/M.2187 – *CVC/Lenzing*, point 223).
[82] Commission Decision 1999/641/EC in Case COMP/M.1225 – *Enso/Stora*, OJ L 254, 29.9.1999, p.9, points 89–91.

83 It may also be appropriate to compare the concentration existing on the customer side with the concentration on the supply side (Case COMP/JV 55 – *Hutchison/RCPM/ECT*, point 119, and Commission Decision 1999/641/EC in Case COMP/M.1225 – *Enso/Stora*, OJ L 254, 29.9.1999, p.9, point 97).

66. In some cases, it may be important to pay particular attention to the incentives of buyers to utilise their buyer power.[84] For example, a downstream firm may not wish to make an investment in sponsoring new entry if the benefits of such entry in terms of lower input costs could also be reaped by its competitors.

Notes

84 Case COMP/JV 55 – *Hutchison/RCPM/ECT*, points 129–130.

67. Countervailing buyer power cannot be found to sufficiently off-set potential adverse effects of a merger if it only ensures that a particular segment of customers,[85] with particular bargaining strength, is shielded from significantly higher prices or deteriorated conditions after the merger.[86] Furthermore, it is not sufficient that buyer power exists prior to the merger, it must also exist and remain effective following the merger. This is because a merger of two suppliers may reduce buyer power if it thereby removes a credible alternative.

Notes

85 Commission Decision 2002/156/EC in Case COMP/M.2097 – *SCA/Metsä Tissue*, OJ L 57, 27.2.2002, point 88. Price discrimination between different categories of customers may be relevant in some cases in the context of market definition (see the Commission's notice on the definition of the relevant market, cited above, at paragraph 43).

86 Accordingly, the Commission may assess whether the various purchasers will hold countervailing buyer power, see, e.g. Commission Decision 1999/641/EC in Case COMP/M.1225 – *Enso/Stora*, OJ L 254, 29.9.1999, p.9, points 84–97.

Commentary
para 67: **F&N:** 5.881

VI. ENTRY

68. When entering a market is sufficiently easy, a merger is unlikely to pose any significant anti-competitive risk. Therefore, entry analysis constitutes an important element of the overall competitive assessment. For entry to be considered a sufficient competitive constraint on the merging parties, it must be shown to be likely, timely and sufficient to deter or defeat any potential anti-competitive effects of the merger.

Commentary
para 68: **F&N:** 5.898, 5.904, 15.90

Likelihood of entry

69. The Commission examines whether entry is likely or whether potential entry is likely to constrain the behaviour of incumbents post-merger. For entry to be likely, it must be sufficiently profitable taking into account the price effects of injecting additional output into the market and the potential responses of the incumbents. Entry is thus less likely if it would only be economically viable on a large scale, thereby resulting in significantly depressed price levels. And entry is likely to be more difficult if the incumbents are able to protect their market shares by offering long-term contracts or giving targeted pre-emptive price reductions to those customers that the entrant is trying to acquire. Furthermore, high risk and costs of failed entry may make entry less likely. The costs of failed entry will be higher, the higher is the level of sunk cost associated with entry.[87]

Notes

87 Commission Decision 97/610/EC in Case IV/M.774 – *Saint-Gobain/Wacker-Chemie/NOM*, OJ L 247, 10.9.1997, p.1, point 184.

Part D **Mergers and Concentrations**

Commentary
para 69: F&N: 5.914

70. Potential entrants may encounter barriers to entry which determine entry risks and costs and thus have an impact on the profitability of entry. Barriers to entry are specific features of the market, which give incumbent firms advantages over potential competitors. When entry barriers are low, the merging parties are more likely to be constrained by entry. Conversely, when entry barriers are high, price increases by the merging firms would not be significantly constrained by entry. Historical examples of entry and exit in the industry may provide useful information about the size of entry barriers.

Commentary
para 70: F&N: 5.907

71. Barriers to entry can take various forms:
    (a) Legal advantages encompass situations where regulatory barriers limit the number of market participants by, for example, restricting the number of licences.[88] They also cover tariff and non-tariff trade barriers.[89]
    (b) The incumbents may also enjoy technical advantages, such as preferential access to essential facilities, natural resources,[90] innovation and R & D,[91] or intellectual property rights,[92] which make it difficult for any firm to compete successfully. For instance, in certain industries, it might be difficult to obtain essential input materials, or patents might protect products or processes. Other factors such as economies of scale and scope, distribution and sales networks,[93] access to important technologies, may also constitute barriers to entry.
    (c) Furthermore, barriers to entry may also exist because of the established position of the incumbent firms on the market. In particular, it may be difficult to enter a particular industry because experience or reputation is necessary to compete effectively, both of which may be difficult to obtain as an entrant. Factors such as consumer loyalty to a particular brand,[94] the closeness of relationships between suppliers and customers, the importance of promotion or advertising, or other advantages relating to reputation[95] will be taken into account in this context. Barriers to entry also encompass situations where the incumbents have already committed to building large excess capacity,[96] or where the costs faced by customers in switching to a new supplier may inhibit entry.

Notes

[88] Case IV/M.1430 – *Vodafone/Airtouch*, point 27; Case IV/M.2016 – *France Télécom/Orange*, point 33.

[89] Commission Decision 2002/174/EC in Case COMP/M.1693 – *Alcoa/Reynolds*, OJ L 58, 28.2.2002, point 87.

[90] Commission Decision 95/335/EC in Case IV/M.754 – *Anglo American Corp./Lonrho*, OJ L 149, 20.5.1998, p.21, points 118–119.

[91] Commission Decision 97/610/EC in Case IV/M.774 – *Saint-Gobain/Wacker-Chemie/NOM*, OJ L 247, 10.9.1997, p.1, points 184–187.

[92] Commission Decision 94/811/EC in Case IV/M.269 – *Shell/Montecatini*, OJ L 332, 22.12.1994, p.48, point 32.

[93] Commission Decision 98/327/EC in Case IV/M.833 – *The Coca-Cola Company/Carlsberg A/S*, OJ L 145, 15.5.1998, p.41, point 74.

[94] Commission Decision 98/327/EC in Case IV/M.833 – *The Coca-Cola Company/Carlsberg A/S*, OJ L 145, 15.5.1998, p.41, points 72–73.

[95] Commission Decision 2002/156/EC in Case COMP/M.2097 – *SCA/Metsä Tissue*, OJ L 57, 27.2.2002, p.1, points 83–84.

[96] Commission Decision 2001/432/EC in Case IV/M.1813 – *Industri Kapital Nordkem/Dyno*, OJ L 154, 9.6.2001, p.41, point 100.

Commentary
para 71: F&N: 5.901

72. The expected evolution of the market should be taken into account when assessing whether or not entry would be profitable. Entry is more likely to be profitable in a market that is expected to experience high growth in the future[97] than in a market that is mature or expected to decline.[98] Scale economies or network effects may make entry unprofitable unless the entrant can obtain a sufficiently large market share.[99]

Notes

[97] See, e.g. Commission Decision 98/475/EC in Case IV/M.986 – *Agfa-Gevaert/Dupont*, OJ L 211, 29.7.1998, p.22, points 84–85.

[98] Case T-102/96 *Gencor v Commission* [1999] ECR II-753, paragraph 237.

[99] See, e.g. Commission Decision 2000/718/EC in Case IV/M.1578 – *Sanitec/Sphinx*, OJ L 294, 22.11.2000, p.1, point 114.

73. Entry is particularly likely if suppliers in other markets already possess production facilities that could be used to enter the market in question, thus reducing the sunk costs of entry. The smaller the difference in profitability between entry and non-entry prior to the merger, the more likely such a reallocation of production facilities.

Timeliness

74. The Commission examines whether entry would be sufficiently swift and sustained to deter or defeat the exercise of market power. What constitutes an appropriate time period depends on the characteristics and dynamics of the market, as well as on the specific capabilities of potential entrants.[100] However, entry is normally only considered timely if it occurs within two years.

Notes

[100] See, e.g. Commission Decision 2002/174/EC in Case COMP/M.1693 – *Alcoa/Reynolds*, L 58, 28.2.2002, points 31–32, 38.

Commentary
para 74: F&N: 5.916

Sufficiency

75. Entry must be of sufficient scope and magnitude to deter or defeat the anti-competitive effects of the merger.[101] Small-scale entry, for instance into some market "niche", may not be considered sufficient.

Notes

[101] Commission Decision 91/535/EEC in Case IV/M.68 – *Tetra Pak/Alfa Laval*, OJ L 290, 22.10.1991, p.35, point 3.4.

Commentary
para 75: F&N: 5.920

VII. EFFICIENCIES

76. Corporate reorganisations in the form of mergers may be in line with the requirements of dynamic competition and are capable of increasing the competitiveness of industry, thereby improving the conditions of growth and raising the standard of living in the Community.[102] It is possible that efficiencies brought about by a merger counteract the effects on competition and in particular the potential harm to consumers that it might otherwise have.[103] In order to assess whether a merger would significantly impede effective competition, in particular through the creation or the strengthening of a dominant position, within the meaning of Article 2(2) and (3) of the Merger Regulation, the Commission performs an overall competitive appraisal of the merger. In making this appraisal, the Commission takes into account the factors mentioned in Article 2(1), including the development of technical and economic progress provided that it is to the consumers' advantage and does not form an obstacle to competition.[104]

Notes

[102] See Recital 4 of the Merger Regulation.

[103] See Recital 29 of the Merger Regulation.

[104] Cf. Article 2(1)(b) of the Merger Regulation.

77. The Commission considers any substantiated efficiency claim in the overall assessment of the merger. It may decide that, as a consequence of the efficiencies that the merger brings about,

there are no grounds for declaring the merger incompatible with the common market pursuant to Article 2(3) of the Merger Regulation. This will be the case when the Commission is in a position to conclude on the basis of sufficient evidence that the efficiencies generated by the merger are likely to enhance the ability and incentive of the merged entity to act pro-competitively for the benefit of consumers, thereby counteracting the adverse effects on competition which the merger might otherwise have.

78. For the Commission to take account of efficiency claims in its assessment of the merger and be in a position to reach the conclusion that as a consequence of efficiencies, there are no grounds for declaring the merger to be incompatible with the common market, the efficiencies have to benefit consumers, be merger-specific and be verifiable. These conditions are cumulative.

Commentary
para 78: F&N: 11.170

Benefit to consumers

79. The relevant benchmark in assessing efficiency claims is that consumers[105] will not be worse off as a result of the merger. For that purpose, efficiencies should be substantial and timely, and should, in principle, benefit consumers in those relevant markets where it is otherwise likely that competition concerns would occur.

Notes

[105] Pursuant to Article 2(1)(b), the concept of "consumers" encompasses intermediate and ultimate consumers, i.e. users of the products covered by the merger. In other words, consumers within the meaning of this provision include the customers, potential and/or actual, of the parties to the merger.

Commentary
para 79: F&N: 3.461, 5.943

80. Mergers may bring about various types of efficiency gains that can lead to lower prices or other benefits to consumers. For example, cost savings in production or distribution may give the merged entity the ability and incentive to charge lower prices following the merger. In line with the need to ascertain whether efficiencies will lead to a net benefit to consumers, cost efficiencies that lead to reductions in variable or marginal costs[106] are more likely to be relevant to the assessment of efficiencies than reductions in fixed costs; the former are, in principle, more likely to result in lower prices for consumers.[107] Cost reductions, which merely result from anti-competitive reductions in output, cannot be considered as efficiencies benefiting consumers.

Notes

[106] Variable costs should be viewed as those costs that vary with the level of production or sales over the relevant time period. Marginal costs are those costs associated with expanding production or sales at the margin.
[107] Generally, fixed cost savings are not given such weight as the relationship between fixed costs and consumer prices is normally less direct, at least in the short run.

81. Consumers may also benefit from new or improved products or services, for instance resulting from efficiency gains in the sphere of R & D and innovation. A joint venture company set up in order to develop a new product may bring about the type of efficiencies that the Commission can take into account.

82. In the context of coordinated effects, efficiencies may increase the merged entity's incentive to increase production and reduce prices, and thereby reduce its incentive to coordinate its market behaviour with other firms in the market. Efficiencies may therefore lead to a lower risk of coordinated effects in the relevant market.

Commentary
para 82: F&N: 5.790

83. In general, the later the efficiencies are expected to materialise in the future, the less weight the Commission can assign to them. This implies that, in order to be considered as a counteracting factor, the efficiencies must be timely.

84. The incentive on the part of the merged entity to pass efficiency gains on to consumers is often related to the existence of competitive pressure from the remaining firms in the market and from potential entry. The greater the possible negative effects on competition, the more the Commission has to be sure that the claimed efficiencies are substantial, likely to be realised, and to be passed on, to a sufficient degree, to the consumer. It is highly unlikely that a merger leading to a market position approaching that of a monopoly, or leading to a similar level of market power, can be declared compatible with the common market on the ground that efficiency gains would be sufficient to counteract its potential anti-competitive effects.

Commentary
para 84: F&N: 5.935, 5.949, 11.174

Merger specificity

85. Efficiencies are relevant to the competitive assessment when they are a direct consequence of the notified merger and cannot be achieved to a similar extent by less anticompetitive alternatives. In these circumstances, the efficiencies are deemed to be caused by the merger and thus, merger-specific.[108] It is for the merging parties to provide in due time all the relevant information necessary to demonstrate that there are no less anti-competitive, realistic and attainable alternatives of a non-concentrative nature (e.g. a licensing agreement, or a cooperative joint venture) or of a concentrative nature (e.g. a concentrative joint venture, or a differently structured merger) than the notified merger which preserve the claimed efficiencies. The Commission only considers alternatives that are reasonably practical in the business situation faced by the merging parties having regard to established business practices in the industry concerned.

Notes
[108] In line with the general principle set out in paragraph 9 of this notice.

Commentary
para 85: F&N: 5.952, 5.955

Verifiability

86. Efficiencies have to be verifiable such that the Commission can be reasonably certain that the efficiencies are likely to materialise, and be substantial enough to counteract a merger's potential harm to consumers. The more precise and convincing the efficiency claims are, the better the Commission can evaluate the claims. Where reasonably possible, efficiencies and the resulting benefit to consumers should therefore be quantified. When the necessary data are not available to allow for a precise quantitative analysis, it must be possible to foresee a clearly identifiable positive impact on consumers, not a marginal one. In general, the longer the start of the efficiencies is projected into the future, the less probability the Commission may be able to assign to the efficiencies actually being brought about.

Commentary
para 86: F&N: 5.956

87. Most of the information, allowing the Commission to assess whether the merger will bring about the sort of efficiencies that would enable it to clear a merger, is solely in the possession of the merging parties. It is, therefore, incumbent upon the notifying parties to provide in due time all the relevant information necessary to demonstrate that the claimed efficiencies are merger-specific and likely to be realised. Similarly, it is for the notifying parties to show to what extent the efficiencies are likely to counteract any adverse effects on competition that might otherwise result from the merger, and therefore benefit consumers.

Commentary
para 87: F&N: 5.957, 5.1187

88. Evidence relevant to the assessment of efficiency claims includes, in particular, internal documents that were used by the management to decide on the merger, statements from the management to

Part D Mergers and Concentrations

the owners and financial markets about the expected efficiencies, historical examples of efficiencies and consumer benefit, and pre-merger external experts' studies on the type and size of efficiency gains, and on the extent to which consumers are likely to benefit.

VIII. Failing Firm

89. The Commission may decide that an otherwise problematic merger is nevertheless compatible with the common market if one of the merging parties is a failing firm. The basic requirement is that the deterioration of the competitive structure that follows the merger cannot be said to be caused by the merger.[109] This will arise where the competitive structure of the market would deteriorate to at least the same extent in the absence of the merger.[110]

Notes

[109] Joined Cases C-68/94 and C-30/95 *Kali and Salz*, paragraph 110.

[110] Joined Cases C-68/94 and C-30/95 *Kali and Salz*, paragraph 114. See also Commission Decision 2002/365/EC in Case COMP/M.2314 – *BASF/Pantochim/Eurodiol*, OJ L 132, 17.5.2002, p.45, points 157–160. This requirement is linked to the general principle set out in paragraph 9 of this notice.

Commentary
para 89: F&N: 15.84

90. The Commission considers the following three criteria to be especially relevant for the application of a "failing firm defence". First, the allegedly failing firm would in the near future be forced out of the market because of financial difficulties if not taken over by another undertaking. Second, there is no less anti-competitive alternative purchase than the notified merger. Third, in the absence of a merger, the assets of the failing firm would inevitably exit the market. [111]

Notes

[111] The inevitability of the assets of the failing firm leaving the market in question may, in particular in a case of merger to monopoly, underlie a finding that the market share of the failing firm would in any event accrue to the other merging party. See Joined Cases C-68/94 and C-30/95 *Kali and Salz*, paragraphs 115–116.

Commentary
para 90: F&N: 15.84

91. It is for the notifying parties to provide in due time all the relevant information necessary to demonstrate that the deterioration of the competitive structure that follows the merger is not caused by the merger.

Commentary
para 91: F&N: 5.976, 5.1187, 15.84

D5

DG COMPETITION: BEST PRACTICES ON THE CONDUCT OF EC MERGER CONTROL PROCEEDINGS

Note

This document is published on the Europa website at: <http://ec.europa.eu/competition/mergers/legislation/legislation.html>

Commentary
Best Practices: F&N: 5.1161, 8.257, 17.422
paras 5–25: F&N: 5.365
paras 5–49: F&N: 5.341
paras 17–24: F&N: 2.43

1. Scope and Purpose of the Best Practices

1. The principal aim of these Best Practices is to provide guidance for interested parties on the day-to-day conduct of EC merger control proceedings. They are intended to foster and build upon a spirit of co-operation and better understanding between DG Competition and the legal and business community. In this regard, the Best Practices seek to increase understanding of the investigation process and thereby to further enhance the efficiency of investigations and to ensure a high degree of transparency and predictability of the review process. In particular, they aim at making the short time available in EC merger procedures as productive and efficient as possible for all parties concerned.

2. The Best Practices are built on the experience to date of DG Competition in the application of Council Regulation (EEC) No 4064/89[1] (the Merger Regulation) and replace the current Best Practices of 1999. They reflect the views and practice of DG Competition at the time of publication.[2]
The specificity of an individual case may require an adaptation of, or deviation from these Best Practices depending on the case at hand.

Notes

[1] Council Regulation No 4064/89, OJ L 395, 30.12.1989 p.1; corrigendum OJ L 257 of 21.9.1990, p.13; Regulation as last amended by Regulation (EC) No 1310/97 (OJ L 180, 9.7.1997, p.1, corrigendum OJ L 40, 13.2.1998, p.17).

[2] It is to be noted that a recast Merger Regulation replacing Regulation 4064/89 will apply from 1 May 2004. The Best Practices are equally applicable under Regulation 4064/89 and will continue to be applicable, possibly with further amendments, under the recast Merger Regulation. Appropriate references to the recast Merger Regulation are made throughout the Best Practices by means of footnotes. Those references will only become applicable from 1st of May 2004.

---

2. Relationship to Community Law

3. These Best Practices should not be taken as a full or comprehensive account of the relevant legislative, interpretative and administrative measures which govern Community merger control. They should be read in conjunction with such measures.

4. The Best Practices do not create or alter any rights or obligations as set out in the Treaty establishing the European Community, the Merger Regulation, its Implementing Regulation[3] as amended from time to time and as interpreted by the case-law of the Community Courts. Nor do they alter the Commission's interpretative notices. The Best Practices do not apply to proceedings under Council Regulation No 17,[4] to be replaced by Council Regulation No 1/2003[5] as of 1 May 2004, implementing Articles [101] and [102]* of the Treaty.

Notes

[3] Commission Regulation (EC) No 447/98 of 1 March 1998 on the notifications, time limits and hearings provided for in the Merger Regulation, OJ L 61, 2.3.1998, p.1.

[4] OJ P 013, 21/02/1962, p.204–211.

[5] Council Regulation (EC) No 1/2003 of 16 December 2002 on the implementation of the rules on competition laid down in Articles [101] and [102] of the Treaty, OJ L 1, 04.01.2003, pp.1–25.

* Ed note: please see the Note on the Lisbon Treaty at p.xvii in regard to article renumbering introduced by the Lisbon Treaty.

---

3. Pre-notification

Purpose of pre-notification contacts

5. In DG Competition's experience the pre-notification phase of the procedure is an important part of the whole review process. As a general rule, DG Competition finds it useful to have pre-notification contacts with notifying parties even in seemingly non-problematic cases. DG Competition will

therefore always give notifying parties and other involved parties the opportunity, if they so request, to discuss an intended concentration informally and in confidence prior to notification (cf. also Recital 10 Implementing Regulation).

6. Pre-notification contacts provide DG Competition and the notifying parties with the possibility, prior to notification, to discuss jurisdictional and other legal issues. They also serve to discuss issues such as the scope of the information to be submitted and to prepare for the upcoming investigation by identifying key issues and possible competition concerns (theories of harm) at an early stage.

7. Further, it is in the interests of DG Competition and the business and legal community to ensure that notification forms are complete from the outset so that declarations of incompleteness are avoided as far as possible. It is DG Competition's experience that in cases in which notifications have been declared incomplete, usually there were no or very limited pre-notification contacts. Accordingly, for this reason it is recommended that notifying parties contact DG Competition prior to notification.

8. Pre-notification discussions are held in strict confidence. The discussions are a voluntary part of the process and remain without prejudice to the handling and investigation of the case following formal notification. However, the mutual benefits for DG Competition and the parties of a fruitful pre-notification phase can only materialise if discussions are held in an open and co-operative atmosphere, where all potential issues are addressed in a constructive way.

9. In DG Competition's experience it is generally preferable that both legal advisers and business representatives, who have a good understanding of the relevant markets, are available for pre-notification discussions with the case-team. This normally results in more informed discussions on the business rationale for the transaction and the functioning of the markets in question.

Timing and extent of pre-notification contacts

10. Pre-notification contacts should preferably be initiated at least two weeks before the expected date of notification. The extent and format of the pre-notification contacts required is, however, linked to the complexity of the individual case in question. In more complex cases a more extended pre-notification period may be appropriate and in the interest of the notifying parties. In all cases it is advisable to make contact with DG Competition as soon as possible as this will facilitate planning of the case.

11. Pre-notification contacts should be launched with a submission that allows the selection of an appropriate DG Competition case-team.[6] This memorandum should provide a brief background to the transaction, a brief description of the relevant sector(s) and market(s) involved and the likely impact of the transaction on competition in general terms. It should also indicate the case language. In straightforward cases, the parties may chose to submit a draft Form CO as a basis for further discussions with DG Competition.

Notes

[6] Case teams for new cases are normally set up in weekly DG Competition's Merger Management Meetings.

---

12. After initial contacts have been made between the case-team and the notifying parties, it will be decided, whether it will suffice for DG Competition to make comments orally or in writing on the submissions made. This would typically be considered in straightforward cases. In more complex cases and cases that raise jurisdictional or other procedural issues, one or more pre-notification meetings are normally considered appropriate.

13. The first pre-notification meeting is normally held on the basis of a more substantial submission or a first draft Form CO. This allows for a more fruitful discussion about the proposed transaction in question or potential issue in point. Subsequent meetings may cover additional information submitted or outstanding issues.

14. Any submission sent to DG Competition should be provided sufficiently ahead of meetings or other contacts in order to allow for well prepared and fruitful discussions. In this regard, preparatory briefing memoranda/ draft Form COs sent in preparation of meetings should be filed in good time before the meeting (at least three working days) unless agreed otherwise with the case team.

In case of voluminous submissions and in less straightforward cases, this time may need to be extended to allow DG Competition to properly prepare for the meeting.

Commentary
para 14: F&N: 2.11

15. Irrespective of whether pre-notification meetings have taken place or not, it is advisable that the notifying parties systematically provide a substantially complete draft Form CO before filing a formal notification. DG Competition would thereafter normally require five working days to review the draft before being asked to comment, at a meeting or on the telephone, on the adequacy of the draft. In case of voluminous submissions, this time will normally be extended.

Commentary
para 15: F&N: 8.293, 8.317

Information to be provided / preparation of the Form CO

16. The format and the timing of all pre-notification submissions should be decided together with the case-team. Notifying parties are advised to fully and frankly disclose information relating to all potentially affected markets and possible competition concerns, even if they may ultimately consider that they are not affected and notwithstanding that they may take a particular view in relation to, for example, the issue of market definition. This will allow for an early market testing of alternative market definitions and/or the notifying parties' position on the market/s in question. In DG Competition's experience this approach minimises surprise submissions from third parties, and may avoid requests for additional information from the notifying parties at a late stage in the procedure and possible declarations of incompleteness under Article 4(2) of the Implementing Regulation or a decision under Article 11(5) of the Merger Regulation.

17. In addition, DG Competition recommends that notifying parties should, as early as possible in pre-notification, submit internal documents such as board presentations, surveys, analyses, reports and studies discussing the proposed concentration, the economic rationale for the concentration and competitive significance or the market context in which it takes place. Such documents provide DG Competition with an early and informed view of the transaction and its potential competitive impact and can thus allow for a productive discussion and finalisation of the Form CO.

Commentary
para 17: F&N: 2.231

18. Where appropriate, it is also recommended that notifying parties put forward, already at the pre-notification stage, any elements demonstrating that the merger leads to efficiency gains that they would like the Commission to take into account for the purposes of its competitive assessment of the proposed transaction. Such claims are likely to require extensive analysis. It is thus in the interests of the notifying parties to present these claims as early as possible to allow sufficient time for DG Competition to appropriately consider these elements in its assessment of a proposed transaction.

Commentary
para 18: F&N: 5.326

19. Pre-notification discussions provide the opportunity for the Commission and the notifying parties to discuss the amount of information to be provided in a notification. The notifying parties may in pre-notification request the Commission to waive the obligation to provide certain information that is not necessary for the examination of the case. All requests to omit any part of the information specified should be discussed in detail and any waiver has to be agreed with DG Competition prior to notification.[7]

Notes

7 See Article 3(2) Implementing Regulation. See also Commission Notice on a simplified procedure for treatment of certain concentrations under Council Regulation (EEC) No 4064/89, OJ C 217, 29.07.2000, p.32.

Commentary
para 19: F&N: 5.326

Completeness of the notification

20. Given that a notification is not considered effective until the information to be submitted in Form CO is complete in all material respects, the notifying parties and their advisers should ensure that the information contained in Form CO has been carefully prepared and verified: incorrect and misleading information is considered incomplete information.[8] In this regard, the notifying parties should take special care that the appropriate contact details are provided for customers, suppliers and competitors. If such information is not correct or provided in full it will significantly delay the investigation and therefore may lead to a declaration of incompleteness.

Notes

8 In addition, the Commission may impose fines on the notifying parties where they supply incorrect or misleading information in a notification under Article 14 (1)(b) Merger Regulation.

Commentary
para 20: F&N: 5.268, 5.407, 5.412

21. Further, to facilitate the effective and expeditious handling of their notification, notifying parties should also endeavour to provide the contact details required in Form CO electronically, at the latest on the day of notification, using the appropriate electronic form which can be provided by the case team.

Commentary
para 21: F&N: 5.407

22. Provided that the notifying parties follow the above described guidance, DG Competition will in principle, be prepared to confirm informally the adequacy of a draft notification at the pre-notification stage or, if appropriate, to identify in what material respects the draft Form CO is incomplete. However it has to be recognised that it will not be possible for DG Competition to exclude the fact that it may have to declare a notification incomplete in appropriate cases after notification.

23. In the event that DG Competition discovers omissions in the Form CO after formal notification, the notifying parties may be given an opportunity to urgently put right such omissions before a declaration of incompleteness is adopted. Due to the time constraints in merger procedures, the time allowed for such rectification is normally limited to 1 or 2 days. This opportunity will not be granted, however, in cases where DG Competition finds that the omissions immediately hinder the proper investigation of the proposed transaction.

Commentary
para 23: F&N: 5.414

Procedural questions and inter-agency co-operation

24. In addition to substantive issues, the notifying parties may in the pre-notification phase seek DG Competition's opinion on procedural matters such as jurisdictional questions.

25. Informal guidance may be provided if they are directly related to an actual, planned transaction and if sufficiently detailed background information is submitted by the notifying parties to properly assess the issue in question.[9] Further matters for pre-notification discussions include the possibility of referrals to or from national EU jurisdictions,[10] parallel proceedings in other non-EU jurisdictions and the issue of waivers on information sharing with other jurisdictions. As regards transactions likely to be reviewed in more than one jurisdiction,

DG Competition invites the notifying parties to discuss the timing of the case with a view to enhance efficiency of the respective investigations, to reduce burdens on the merging parties and third parties, and to increase overall transparency of the merger review process. In this regard, notifying parties should also have regard to the EU-US Best Practices on cooperation in merger investigations.[11]

Notes

[9] Such informal guidance cannot be regarded as creating legitimate expectations regarding the proper interpretation of applicable jurisdictional or other rules.

[10] Such jurisdictional discussions will become particularly pertinent under the recast Merger Regulation, which becomes applicable from 1 May 2004. Pursuant to Articles 4(4) and 4(5) of the recast Merger Regulation, notifying parties may, before notification, request on the basis of a reasoned submission, referral of a case to or from the Commission. DG Competition will be ready to discuss with notifying parties informally the possibility of such pre-notification referrals and to guide them through the pre-notification referral process.

[11] <http://europa.eu.int/comm/competition/mergers/others/eu_us.pdf>.

4. Fact Finding/Requests for Information

26. In carrying out its duties the Commission may obtain all necessary information from relevant persons, undertakings, associations of undertakings and competent authorities of Member States (see Article 11(1) Merger Regulation). That investigation normally starts after the notification of a proposed concentration. However, DG Competition may exceptionally decide that, in the interest of its investigation, market contacts could be initiated informally prior to notification. Such pre-notification contacts/enquiries would only take place if the existence of the transaction is in the public domain and once the notifying parties have had the opportunity to express their views on such measures.

27. The Commission's investigation is mainly conducted in the form of written Requests for Information (requests pursuant to Article 11 of the Merger Regulation) to customers, suppliers, competitors and other relevant parties. Such requests may also be addressed to the notifying parties. In addition to such Article 11 requests, the views of the notifying parties, other involved parties and third parties are also sought orally.

28. In the interest of an efficient investigation, DG Competition may consult the notifying parties, other involved parties or third parties on methodological issues regarding data and information gathering in the relevant economic sector. It may also seek external economic and/or industrial expertise and launch its own economic studies.

5. Communication and Meetings with the Notifying Parties, Other Involved Parties and 3rd Parties

29. One of the aims of these Best Practices is to enhance transparency in the day to day handling of merger cases and in particular, to ensure good communication between DG Competition, the merging parties and third parties. In this regard, DG Competition endeavours to give all parties involved in the proceeding ample opportunity for open and frank discussions and to make their points of view known throughout the procedure.

5.1. State of Play meetings with notifying parties

Aim and format of the State of Play meetings

30. The objective of the State of Play meetings is to contribute to the quality and efficiency of the decision-making process and to ensure transparency and communication between DG Competition and the notifying parties. As such these meetings should provide a forum for the mutual exchange of information between DG Competition and the notifying parties at key points in the procedure. They are entirely voluntary in nature.

31. State of Play meetings may be conducted in the form of meetings at the Commission's premises, or alternatively, if appropriate, by telephone or videoconference. In order for the meetings to operate properly they should be carefully prepared on the basis of an agenda agreed in advance. Further, senior DG Competition management will normally chair the meetings.

32. The State of Play meetings will not exclude discussions and exchanges of information between the notifying parties and DG Competition at other occasions throughout the procedure as appropriate. In this regard, notifying parties are advised to inform DG Competition, as soon as possible, about any important procedural or substantive developments that may be of relevance for the assessment of the proposed transaction. Such developments may include any remedy proposals the notifying parties are offering or are considering to offer in other jurisdictions, so as to facilitate co-ordination of the timing and substance of such remedy proposals. This also concerns matters already discussed at a State of Play meeting, in respect of which the parties consider it necessary to provide additional comments.

Timing of the State of Play meetings

33. Notifying parties will normally be offered the opportunity of attending a State of Play meeting at the following five different points in the Phase I and Phase II procedure:
    a) where it appears that "serious doubts" within the meaning of Article 6(1)(c) of the Merger Regulation are likely to be present a meeting will be offered before the expiry of 3 weeks[12] into Phase I. In addition to informing the notifying parties of the preliminary result of the initial investigation, this meeting provides an opportunity for the notifying parties to prepare the formulation of a possible remedy proposal in Phase I before expiry of the deadline provided in Article 18 of the Implementing Regulation.
    b) normally within 2 weeks following the adoption of the Article 6(1)(c) decision. In order to prepare for this meeting, the notifying parties should provide DG Competition with their comments on the Article 6(1)(c) decision and on any documents in the Commission's file, which they may have had the opportunity to review (see below section 7.2) by way of a written memorandum in advance of the meeting. The notifying parties should contact the case team to discuss an appropriate schedule for the filing of this memorandum. The main purpose of the post Article 6(1)(c) meeting is to facilitate the notifying parties' understanding of the Commission's concerns at an early stage of the Phase II proceedings. The meeting also serves to assist DG Competition in deciding the appropriate framework for its further investigation by discussing with the notifying parties matters such as the market definition and competition concerns outlined in the Article 6(1)(c) decision. The meeting is also intended to serve as a forum for mutually informing each other of any planned economic or other studies. The approximate timetable of the Phase II procedure may also be discussed.[13]
    c) before the issuing of a Statement of Objections (SO). This pre-SO meeting gives the notifying parties an opportunity to understand DG Competition's preliminary view on the outcome of the Phase II investigation and to be informed of the type of objections DG Competition may set out in the SO. The meeting may also be used by DG Competition to clarify certain issues and facts before it finalises its proposal on the issuing of a SO.
    d) following the reply to the SO and the Oral Hearing. This post-SO State of Play meeting provides the notifying parties with an opportunity to understand DG Competition's position after it has considered their reply and heard them at an Oral Hearing. If DG Competition indicates that it is minded to maintain some or all of its objections, the meeting may also serve as an opportunity to discuss the scope and timing of possible remedy proposals.[14]
    e) before the Advisory Committee meets. The primary purpose of this meeting is to enable the notifying parties to discuss with DG Competition its views on any proposed remedies and where relevant, the results of the market testing of such remedies. It also provides the notifying parties where necessary, with the opportunity to formulate improvements to their remedies proposal.[15]

Notes

[12] Fifteen working days under the recast Merger Regulation.

[13] Once the recast Merger Regulation becomes applicable, this post Article 6(1)(c) State of Play meeting will also serve to discuss the possibility of any extensions to the Phase II deadline pursuant to Article 10(3) of the recast Merger Regulation.

[14] It is to be noted that, under the recast Merger Regulation (Article 10(3)), the submission of remedies could lead to an automatic extension of the Phase II deadline.

[15] Modifications to remedies are only possible under those conditions set out in Article 18 of the Implementing Regulation and point 43 of the Commission's Notice on Remedies.

Commentary
para 33(a): F&N: 5.428, 5.1024
para 33(b): F&N: 5.446
para 33(c): F&N: 5.451, 5.488
para 33(d): F&N: 5.488

5.2. Involvement of third parties

34. According to Community merger control law, third parties considered as having a "sufficient interest" in the Commission's procedure include customers, suppliers, competitors, members of the administration or management organs of the undertakings concerned or recognised workers' representatives of those undertakings.[16] Their important role in the Commission's procedure is stressed in particular in Article 18(4) of the Merger Regulation and Articles 16(1) and (2) of the Implementing Regulation. In addition, the Commission also welcomes the views of any other interested third parties including consumer organisations.[17]

Notes

[16] See Article 11 of the Implementing Regulation.

[17] Article 16(3) Implementing Regulation. To this effect, DG Competition has appointed a Consumer Liaison Officer responsible for contacts with consumer organisations.

35. The primary way for third parties to contribute to the Commission's investigation is by means of replies to requests for information (Article 11 Merger Regulation).[18] However, DG Competition also welcomes any individual submission apart from direct replies to questionnaires, where third parties provide information and comments they consider relevant for the assessment of a given transaction. DG Competition may also invite third parties for meetings to discuss and clarify specific issues raised.

Notes

[18] Article 11(7) of the recast Merger Regulation expressly provides for the Commission's competence to interview any natural or legal person who consents to be interviewed for the purpose of collecting information relating to the subject-matter of an investigation.

36. In addition, DG Competition may in the interest of the investigation in appropriate cases provide third parties that have shown a sufficient interest in the procedure with an edited version of the SO from which business secrets have been removed, in order to allow them to make their views known on the Commission's preliminary assessment. In such cases, the SO is provided under strict confidentiality obligations and restrictions of use, which the third parties have to accept prior to receipt.

Commentary
para 36: F&N: 5.458

37. If third parties wish to express competition concerns as regards the transaction in question or to put forward views on key market data or characteristics that deviate from the notifying parties' position, it is essential that they are communicated as early as possible to DG Competition, so that they can be considered, verified and taken into account properly. Any point raised should be substantiated and supported by examples, documents and other factual evidence. Furthermore, in accordance with Article 17(2) of the Implementing Regulation, third parties should always provide the DG Competition with a non-confidential version of their submissions at the time of filing or shortly thereafter to facilitate access to the file and other measures intended to ensure transparency for the benefit of the decision making process (see further below section 7).

Commentary
para 37: F&N: 5.356

Part D Mergers and Concentrations

5.3. "Triangular" and other meetings

38. In addition to bilateral meetings between DG Competition and the notifying parties, other involved parties or third parties, DG Competition may decide to invite third parties and the notifying parties to a "triangular" meeting where DG Competition believes it is desirable, in the interests of the fact-finding investigation, to hear the views of the notifying parties and such third parties in a single forum. Such triangular meetings, which will be on a voluntary basis and which are not intended to replace the formal oral hearing, would take place in situations where two or more opposing views have been put forward as to key market data and characteristics and the effects of the concentration on competition in the markets concerned.

Commentary
para 38: F&N: 5.556, 5.448, 8.308

39. Triangular meetings should ideally be held as early in the investigation as possible in order to enable DG Competition to reach a more informed conclusion as to the relevant market characteristics and to clarify issues of substance before deciding on the issuing of an SO. Triangular meetings are normally chaired by senior DG Competition management. They are prepared in advance on the basis of an agenda established by DG Competition after consultation of all parties that agreed to attend the meeting. The preparation will normally include a mutual exchange of non-confidential submissions between the notifying parties and the third party in question sufficiently in advance of the meeting. The meeting will not require the disclosure of confidential information or business secrets, unless otherwise agreed by the parties.

Commentary
para 39: F&N: 3.356, 5.448, 8.308

6. REMEDIES DISCUSSIONS

40. As stated above, the State of Play meetings in both Phase I and Phase II, in addition to providing a forum for discussing issues related to the investigation, also serve to discuss possible remedy proposals. Detailed guidance on the requirements for such proposals is set out in the Commission Notice on remedies acceptable under Council Regulation (EEC) No 4064/89 and under Commission Regulation (EC) No 447/98[19] (the Remedies Notice). In particular, the Remedies Notice sets out the general principles applicable to remedies, the main types of commitments that have previously been accepted by the Commission, the specific requirements which proposals of remedies need to fulfil in both phases of the procedure, and guidance on the implementation of remedies. As regards the design of divestiture commitment proposals, the notifying parties are advised to take due account of the Commission's "Best Practice Guidelines on Divestiture Commitments".[20]

Notes
[19] OJ C 68, 02.03.2001, pp.3–11.
[20] Available under: <http://europa.eu.int/comm/competition/mergers/legislation/divestiture_commitments/>.

Commentary
para 40: F&N: 8.308

41. Although it is for the notifying parties to formulate suitable remedies proposals, DG Competition will provide guidance to the parties as to the general appropriateness of their draft proposal in advance of submission. In order to allow for such discussions, a notifying party should contact DG Competition in good time before the relevant deadline in Phase I or Phase II, in order to be able to address comments DG Competition may have on the draft proposal.[21]

Notes
[21] It is to be noted that under the recast Merger Regulation (Articles 10(1) and (3)), the submission of remedies could lead to an automatic extension of the Phase I and II deadlines.

7. Provision of Documents in the Commission's file/Confidentiality

7.1. Access to the file

42. According to Community law, the notifying parties have upon request a right to access the Commission's file after the Commission has issued an SO (see Article 18(3) of the Merger Regulation and Article 13(3) of the Implementing Regulation).

43. Further, the notifying parties will be given the opportunity to have access to documents received after the issuing of the SO up until the consultation of the Advisory Committee.

Commentary
para 43: F&N: 5.498

---

44. Access to the file will be provided subject to the legitimate interest of the protection of third parties' business secrets and other confidential information.

7.2. Review of key documents

45. DG Competition believes in the merits of an open exchange of views with ample opportunities for the notifying parties and third parties to make their points of view known throughout the procedure. This enables DG Competition to assess the main issues arising during the investigation with as much information at its disposal as possible. In this spirit, DG Competition's objective will be to provide the notifying parties with the opportunity of reviewing and commenting on "key documents" obtained by the Commission. Such documents would comprise substantiated submissions of third parties running counter to the notifying parties' own contentions received during Phase I and thereafter,[22] including key submissions to which specific reference is made in the Article 6(1)(c) decision and market studies.

Notes

[22] This would in particular include substantiated "complaints" contending that the notified transaction may give rise to competition concerns. The word "complaint" is to be understood in the non-technical sense of the term as no formal complaints procedure exists in merger cases.

Commentary
para 45: F&N: 5.445

---

46. DG Competition will use its best endeavours to provide notifying parties in a timely fashion, with the opportunity to review such documents following the initiation of proceedings and thereafter on an *ad hoc* basis. DG Competition will respect justified requests by third parties for non-disclosure of their submissions prior to the issuing of the SO relating to genuine concerns regarding confidentiality, including fears of retaliation and the protection of business secrets.

Commentary
para 46: F&N: 5.455

7.3. Confidentiality Rules

47. In accordance with Article [339 TFEU] and Article 17(1) of the Implementing Regulation, the Commission will, throughout its investigation, protect confidential information and business secrets contained in submissions provided by all parties involved in EC merger proceedings. Given the short legal deadlines of EC merger procedures, parties are encouraged to clarify as soon as possible any queries related to confidentiality claims with members of the case team. Guidance on what is considered to be business secrets or other confidential information is provided in the Commission's Notice on Access to file.[23]

Notes

23 OJ C 23, 23/01/97, p.3. [Ed note: see now Commission Notice of 13 December 2005 on the rules for access to the Commission file in cases pursuant to Articles [101 and 102 of the Treaty on the Functioning of the European Union], Articles 53, 54 and 57 of the EEA Agreement and Council Regulation (EC) No 139/2004, (2005/C 325/07), OJ C 225, 22.12.2005, p.7, reproduced in this volume at B10.]

Commentary
para 47: F&N: 17.528

8. Right to be Heard and Other Procedural Rights

48. The right of the parties concerned to be heard before a final decision affecting their interests is taken is a fundamental principle of Community law. That right is also set out in the Merger Regulation (Article 18) and the Implementing Regulation (Articles 14–16). These Best Practices do not alter any such rights under Community law.

Commentary
para 48: F&N: 5.426

49. Any issues related to the right to be heard and other procedural issues, including access to the file, time limits for replying to the SO and the objectivity of any enquiry conducted in order to assess the competition impact of commitments proposed in EC merger proceedings can be raised with the Hearing Officer, in accordance with Commission Decision of 23 May 2001 on the terms of reference of hearing officers in certain competition proceedings.[24]

Notes

24 Official Journal L 162, 19/06/2001 pp.21–24. The text can also be found at: <http://europa.eu.int/comm/competition/hearings/officers/>.

9. Future Review

50. These Best Practices may be revised to reflect changes to legislative, interpretative and administrative measures or due to case law of the European Courts, which govern EC merger control or any experience gained in applying such framework. DG Competition further intends to engage, on a regular basis, in a dialogue with the business and legal community on the experience gained through the application of the Merger Regulation in general, and these Best Practices in particular.

D6

COMMUNICATION FROM THE COMMISSION

Communication pursuant to Article 23(1) of Commission Regulation
(EC) No 802/2004[1] implementing Council Regulation (EC) No 139/2004[2]
on the control of concentrations between undertakings

(2004/C 139/02)

(Text with EEA relevance)

Official Journal C 139, 19.5.2004, p.2

Celex No: 52004XC0519(01)

EUR-Lex permanent link: <http://eur-lex.europa.eu/legal-content/EN/ALL/?uri=CELEX:52004X
C0519%2801%29&qid=1395771129404>

Notes

See also the information on merger correspondence published by the Directorate-General for Competition on the
Europa website at the following address: <http://ec.europa.eu/comm/competition/contacts/mergers_mail.html>. That
information is reproduced at D14.

Address of the Commission's Directorate General for Competition

European Commission

Directorate General for Competition

Merger Registry

Rue Joseph II / Jozef II Straat, 70

B-1000 Bruxelles / Brussel

Notes

[1] OJ L 133, 30.04.2004, pp.1–39.
[2] Council Regulation (EC) No 139/2004 of 20 January 2004 on the control of concentrations between undertakings,
OJ L 24, 29.01.2004, pp.1–22.

D7

COMMISSION NOTICE

on Case Referral in respect of concentrations

(2005/C 56/02)

(Text with EEA relevance)

Official Journal C 56, 5.3.2005, p.2

Celex No: 52005XC0305(01)

EUR-Lex permanent link: <http://eur-lex.europa.eu/legal-content/EN/ALL/?uri=CELEX:52005X C0305%2801%29&qid=1395770641765>

Commentary
Notice: B&C: 8.007, 8.096, 8.271
paras 8–14: B&C: 8.013
paras 25–32: F&N: 5.260
paras 46–82: F&N: 5.341

---

1. The purpose of this Notice is to describe in a general way the rationale underlying the case referral system in Article 4(4) and (5), Article 9 and Article 22 of Council Regulation (EC) No 139/2004 of 20 January 2004 on the control of concentrations between undertakings (the EC Merger Regulation)[1] (hereinafter "the Merger Regulation"), including the recent changes made to the system, to catalogue the legal criteria that must be fulfilled in order for referrals to be possible, and to set out the factors which may be taken into consideration when referrals are decided upon. The Notice also provides practical guidance regarding the mechanics of the referral system, in particular regarding the pre-notification referral mechanism provided for in Article 4(4) and (5) of the Merger Regulation. The guidance provided in this notice applies, *mutatis mutandis*, to the referral rules contained in the EEA Agreement.[2]

Notes

[1] OJ L 24, 29.1.2004, p.1. This Regulation has recast Council Regulation (EEC) No 4064/89 of 21 December 1989 on the control of concentrations between undertakings (OJ L 395, 30.12.1989, p.1. Corrected version in OJ L 257, 21.9.1990, p.13).

[2] See EEA Joint Committee Decision No 78/2004 of 8 June 2004 (OJ L 219, 8.6.2004, p.13).

I. INTRODUCTION

2. Community jurisdiction in the field of merger control is defined by the application of the turnover-related criteria contained in Articles 1(2) and 1(3) of the Merger Regulation. When dealing with concentrations, the Commission and Member States do not have concurrent jurisdiction. Rather, the Merger Regulation establishes a clear division of competence. Concentrations with a "Community dimension", i.e. those above the turnover thresholds in Article 1 of the Merger Regulation, fall within the exclusive jurisdiction of the Commission; Member States are precluded from applying national competition law to such concentrations by virtue of Article 21 of the Merger Regulation. Concentrations falling below the thresholds remain within the competence of the Member States; the Commission has no jurisdiction to deal with them under the Merger Regulation.

Commentary
para 2: F&N: 5.17

---

3. Determining jurisdiction exclusively by reference to fixed turnover-related criteria provides legal certainty for merging companies. While the financial criteria generally serve as effective proxies for the category of transactions for which the Commission is the more appropriate authority, Regulation (EEC) No 4064/89 complemented this "bright-line" jurisdictional scheme with a possibility for cases to be re-attributed by the Commission to Member States and vice versa, upon request and provided certain criteria were fulfilled.

4. When Regulation (EEC) No 4064/89 was first introduced, it was envisaged by the Council and Commission that case referrals would only be resorted to in "exceptional circumstances" and where "the interests in respect of competition of the Member State concerned could not be adequately protected in any other way".[3] There have, however, been a number of developments since the adoption of Regulation (EEC) No 4064/89. First, merger control laws have been introduced in almost all Member States. Second, the Commission has exercised its discretion to refer a number of cases to Member States pursuant to Article 9 in circumstances where it was felt that the Member State in question was in a better position to carry out the investigation than the Commission.[4] Likewise, in a number of cases,[5] several Member States decided to make a joint referral of a case pursuant to Article 22 in circumstances where it was felt that the Commission was the authority in a better position to carry out the investigation.[6] Third, there has been an increase in the number of transactions not meeting the thresholds in Article 1 of the Merger Regulation which must be filed in multiple Member State jurisdictions, a trend which is likely to continue in line with the Community's growing membership. Many of these transactions affect competition beyond the territories of individual Member States.[7]

Notes

[3] See the Notes on Council Regulation (EEC) No 4064/89 ["Merger Control in the European union", European Commission, Brussels-Luxembourg, 1998, at p.54]. See also Case T-119/02 *Philips v Commission* [2003] ECR II-1433 (Case M.2621 *SEB/Moulinex*) at paragraph 354.

[4] It is a fact that some concentrations of Community dimension affect competition in national or sub-national markets within one or more Member States.

[5] M.2698 *Promatech/Sulzer*; M.2738 *GE/Unison*; M.3136 *GE/AGFA*.

[6] In the same vein, Member States" competition authorities, in the context of the European Competition Authorities' association, have issued a recommendation designed to provide guidance as to the principles upon which national competition authorities should deal with cases eligible for joint referrals under Article 22 of the Merger Regulation – *Principles on the application, by National Competition Authorities within the ECA network, of Article 22 of the EC Merger Regulation.*

[7] While the introduction of Article 1(3) in 1997 has brought some such cases under the jurisdiction of the Merger Regulation, many are unaffected. See paragraph 21 et seq of the Commission's Green Paper of 11 December 2001 (COM(2001) 745 final).

5. The revisions made to the referral system in the Merger Regulation are designed to facilitate the reattribution of cases between the Commission and Member States, consistent with the principle of subsidiarity, so that the more appropriate authority or authorities for carrying out a particular merger investigation should in principle deal with the case. At the same time, the revisions are intended to preserve the basic features of the Community merger control system introduced in 1989, in particular the provision of a "one-stop-shop" for the competition scrutiny of mergers with a cross-border impact and an alternative to multiple merger control notifications within the Community.[8] Such multiple filings often entail considerable cost for competition authorities and businesses alike.

Notes

[8] See Recitals 11, 12 and 14 to the Merger Regulation.

Commentary
para 5: F&N: 5.19

6. The case re-attribution system now provides that a referral may also be triggered before a formal filing has been made in any Member State jurisdiction, thereby affording merging companies the possibility of ascertaining, at as early as possible a stage, where jurisdiction for scrutiny of their transaction will ultimately lie. Such pre-notification referrals have the advantage of alleviating the additional cost, notably in terms of time delay, associated with post-filing referral.

7. The revisions made to the referral system in Regulation (EC) No. 139/2004 were motivated by a desire that it should operate as a jurisdictional mechanism which is flexible[9] but which at the same time ensures effective protection of competition and limits the scope for "forum shopping" to the greatest extent possible. However, having regard in particular to the importance of legal certainty, it should be stressed that referrals remain a derogation from the general rules which determine jurisdiction based upon objectively determinable turnover thresholds. Moreover, the Commission and Member States retain a considerable margin of discretion in deciding whether to refer cases falling within their "original jurisdiction", or whether to accept to deal with cases not falling within their "original jurisdiction", pursuant to Article 4(4) and (5), Article 9(2)(a) and Article 22.[10] To that extent, the current Notice is intended to provide no more than general guidance regarding the appropriateness of particular cases or categories of cases for referral.

Notes

[9] See Recital 11 to the Merger Regulation.

[10] See, however, *infra*, footnote 14. It should moreover be noted that, pursuant to Article 4(5), the Commission has no discretion as to whether or not to accept a case not falling within its original jurisdiction.

II. REFERRAL OF CASES

Guiding principles

8. The system of merger control established by the Merger Regulation, including the mechanism for re-attributing cases between the Commission and Member States contained therein, is consistent with the principle of subsidiarity enshrined in the [Treaty on European Union].[11] Decisions taken with regard to the referral of cases should accordingly take due account of all aspects of the application of the principle of subsidiarity in this context, in particular which is the authority more appropriate for carrying out the investigation, the benefits inherent in a "one-stop-shop" system, and the importance of legal certainty with regard to jurisdiction.[12] These factors are inter-linked and the respective weight placed upon each of them will depend upon the specificities of a particular case. Above all, in considering whether or not to exercise their discretion to make or accede to a referral, the Commission and Member States should bear in mind the need to ensure effective protection of competition in all markets affected by the transaction.[13]

Notes

[11] See Article 5 of the [Treaty on European Union. [Ed note: please see the Note on the Lisbon Treaty at p.xvii in regard to article renumbering introduced by the Lisbon Treaty.]

[12] See Recitals 11 and 14 to the Merger Regulation.

[13] See Article 9(8) of the Merger Regulation; see also *Philips v Commission* (paragraph 343) where the Court of First Instance of the European Communities states that "...although the first subparagraph of Article 9(3) of Regulation (EEC) No 4064/89 confers on the Commission broad discretion as to whether or not to refer a concentration, it cannot decide to make such a referral if, when the Member State's request for referral is examined, it is clear, on the basis of a body of precise and coherent evidence, that such a referral cannot safeguard effective competition on the relevant market"; see also T-346/02 and T-347/02 *Cableuropa SA v Commission* of 30 September 2003, [[2003] ECR II-4251] (paragraph 215). Circumstances relevant for the purpose of the Commission assessment include, *inter alia*, the fact that a Member State: (i) has specific laws for the control of concentrations on competition grounds and specialised bodies to ensure that these laws are implemented under the supervision of the national courts; (ii) has accurately identified the competition concerns raised by the concentration on the relevant markets in that Member State (see paragraphs 346–347 of *Philips v Commission*, cited above).

Commentary

para 8: F&N: 5.19

More appropriate authority

9. In principle, jurisdiction should only be re-attributed to another competition authority in circumstances where the latter is the more appropriate for dealing with a merger, having regard to the specific characteristics of the case as well as the tools and expertise available to the authority. Particular regard should be had to the likely locus of any impact on competition resulting from the

merger. Regard may also be had to the implications, in terms of administrative effort, of any con-templated referral.[14]

[14] This may involve consideration of the relative cost, time delay, legal uncertainty and the risk of conflicting assessment which may be associated with the investigation, or a part of the investigation, being carried out by multiple authorities.

10. The case for re-attributing jurisdiction is likely to be more compelling where it appears that a particular transaction may have a significant impact on competition and thus may deserve careful scrutiny.

One-stop-shop

11. Decisions on the referral of cases should also have regard to the benefits inherent in a "one-stop-shop", which is at the core of the Merger Regulation.[15] The provision of a one-stop-shop is beneficial to competition authorities and businesses alike. The handling of a merger by a single competition authority normally increases administrative efficiency, avoiding duplication and fragmentation of enforcement effort as well as potentially incoherent treatment (regarding investigation, assessment and possible remedies) by multiple authorities. It normally also brings advantages to businesses, in particular to merging firms, by reducing the costs and burdens arising from multiple filing obligations and by eliminating the risk of conflicting decisions resulting from the concurrent assessment of the same transaction by a number of competition authorities under diverse legal regimes.

Notes

[15] See Recital 11 of the Merger Regulation.

12. Fragmentation of cases through referral should therefore be avoided where possible,[16] unless it appears that multiple authorities would be in a better position to ensure that competition in all markets affected by the transaction is effectively protected. Accordingly, while partial referrals are possible under Article 4(4) and Article 9, it would normally be appropriate for the whole of a case (or at least all connected parts thereof) to be dealt with by a single authority.[17]

Notes

[16] The Court of First Instance in *Philips v Commission* took the view, *obiter dictum*, that "fragmentation" of cases, while possible as a result of the application of Article 9, is "undesirable in view of the 'one-stop-shop' principle on which Regulation (EEC) No 4064/89 is based". Moreover, the Court, while recognising that the risk of "inconsistent, or even irreconcilable" decisions by the Commission and Member States "is inherent in the referral system established by Article 9", made it clear that this is not, in its view, desirable. (See paragraphs 350 and 380.)

[17] This is consistent with the Commission's decision in cases M.2389 *Shell/DEA* and M.2533 *BP/E.ON* to refer to Germany all of the markets for downstream oil products. The Commission retained the parts of the cases involving upstream markets. Likewise, in M.2706 *P&O Princess/Carnival*, the Commission exercised its discretion not to refer a part of the case to the United Kingdom, because it wished to avoid a fragmentation of the case. (See Commission press release of 11.4.2002, IP/02/552.)

Legal certainty

13. Due account should also be taken of the importance of legal certainty regarding jurisdiction over a particular concentration, from the perspective of all concerned.[18] Accordingly, referral should normally only be made when there is a compelling reason for departing from "original jurisdiction" over the case in question, particularly at the post-notification stage. Similarly, if a referral has been made prior to notification, a post-notification referral in the same case should be avoided to the greatest extent possible.[19]

Notes

[18] See Recital 11 of the Merger Regulation.

[19] See Recital 14 to the Merger Regulation. This is of course subject to the parties having made a full and honest disclosure of all relevant facts in their request for a pre-filing referral.

14. The importance of legal certainty should also be borne in mind with regard to the legal criteria for referral, and particularly – given the tight deadlines – at the pre-notification stage. Accordingly, pre-filing referrals should in principle be confined to those cases where it is relatively straightforward to establish, from the outset, the scope of the geographic market and/or the existence of a possible competitive impact, so as to be able to promptly decide upon such requests

Case referrals: legal requirements and other factors to be considered

Pre-notification referrals

15. The system of pre-notification referrals is triggered by a reasoned submission lodged by the parties to the concentration. When contemplating such a request, the parties to the concentration are required, first, to verify whether the relevant legal requirements set out in the Merger Regulation are fulfilled, and second, whether a pre-notification referral would be consistent with the guiding principles outlined above.

Referral of cases by the Commission to Member States under Article 4(4)

Legal requirements

16. In order for a referral to be made by the Commission to one or more Member States pursuant to Articles 4(4), two legal requirements must be fulfilled:
    (i) there must be indications *that the concentration may significantly affect competition* in a market or markets;
    (ii) the market(s) in question must be within a Member State and *present all the characteristics of a distinct market.*

17. As regards the *first criterion*, the requesting parties are in essence required to demonstrate that the transaction is liable to have a potential impact on competition on a distinct market in a Member State, which may prove to be significant, thus deserving close scrutiny. Such indications may be no more than preliminary in nature, and would be without prejudice to the outcome of the investigation. While the parties are not required to demonstrate that the effect on competition is likely to be an adverse one,[20] they should point to indicators which are generally suggestive of the existence of some competitive effects stemming from the transaction.[21]

Notes

[20] See Recital 16, which states that "the undertakings concerned should not . . . be required to demonstrate that the effects of the concentration would be detrimental to competition".

[21] The existence of "affected markets" within the meaning of Form RS would generally be considered sufficient to meet the requirements of Article 4(4). However, the parties can point to any factors which may be relevant for the competitive analysis of the case (market overlap, vertical integration, etc).

Commentary
para 17: **B&C:** 8.083 **F&N:** 5.227

---

18. As regards the *second criterion*, the requesting parties are required to show that a geographic market in which competition is affected by the transaction in the manner just described (paragraph 17) is national, or narrower than national in scope.[22]

Notes

[22] To this end, the requesting parties should consider those factors which are typically suggestive of national or narrower than national markets, such as, primarily, the product characteristics (e.g. low value of the product as opposed to significant costs of transport), specific characteristics of demand (e.g. end consumers sourcing in proximity to their centre of activity) and supply, significant variation of prices and market shares across countries national consumer habits, different regulatory frameworks, taxation or other legislation. Further guidance can be found in the Commission Notice on the definition of the relevant market for the purposes of Community competition law (OJ C 372, 9.12.1997, 5).

Commentary
para 18: **B&C:** 8.083, 8.095

Other factors to be considered

19. Other than verification of the legal requirements, in order to anticipate to the greatest extent possible the likely outcome of a referral request, merging parties contemplating a request should also consider whether referral of the case is likely to be considered appropriate. This will involve an examination of the application of the guiding principles referred to above (paragraphs 8 to 14), and in particular whether the competition authority or authorities to which they are contemplating requesting the referral of the case is the most appropriate authority for dealing with the case. To this end, consideration should be given in turn both to the likely locus of the competitive effects of the transaction and to how appropriate the national competition authority (NCA) would be for scrutinising the operation.

Commentary
para 19: B&C: 8.083 F&N: 5.230

20. Concentrations with a Community dimension which are likely to affect competition in markets that have a national or narrower than national scope, and the effects of which are likely to be confined to, or have their main economic impact in, a single Member State,[23] are the most appropriate candidate cases for referral to that Member State. This applies in particular to cases where the impact would occur on a distinct market which does not constitute a substantial part of the common market. To the extent that referral is made to one Member State only, the benefit of a "one-stop-shop" is also preserved.

Notes

[23] See, for example, the Commission's referral of certain distinct oil storage markets for assessment by the French authorities in Cases M.1021 *Compagnie Nationale de Navigation-SOGELF*, M.1464 *Total/Petrofina*, and Case M.1628 *Totalfina/Elf Aquitaine*, Case M.1030 *Lafarge/Redland*, Case M.1220 *Alliance Unichem/Unifarma*, Case M.2760 *Nehlsen/Rethmann/SWB/Bremerhavener Energiewirtschaft*, and Case M.2154 *C3D/Rhone/Go-ahead* ; Case M.2845 *Sogecable/Canal Satelite Digital/Vias Digital* .

21. The extent to which a concentration with a Community dimension which, despite having a potentially significant impact on competition in a nation-wide market, nonetheless potentially engenders substantial cross-border effects (e.g. because the effects of the concentration in one geographic market may have significant repercussions in geographic markets in other Member States, or because it may involve potential foreclosure effects and consequent fragmentation of the common market),[24] may be an appropriate candidate for referral will depend on the specific circumstances of the case. As both the Commission and Member States may be equally well equipped or be in an equally good position to deal with such cases, a considerable margin of discretion should be retained in deciding whether or not to refer such cases.

Notes

[24] See Case M.580 *ABB/Daimler Benz*, where the Commission did not accede to Germany's request for referral of a case under Article 9 in circumstances where, while the competition concerns were confined to German markets, the operation (which would create the largest supplier of railway equipment in the world) would have significant repercussions throughout Europe. See also Case M.2434 *Hidroelectrica del Cantabrico/EnBW/Grupo Vilar Mir*, where, despite a request by Spain to have the case referred under Article 9, the Commission pursued the investigation and adopted a decision pursuant to Article 8(2).

22. The extent to which concentrations with a Community dimension, and potentially affecting competition in a series of national or narrower than national markets in more than one Member State, may be appropriate candidates for referral to Member States will depend on factors specific to each individual case, such as the number of national markets likely to be significantly affected, the prospect of addressing any possible concerns by way of proportionate, non-conflicting remedies, and the investigative efforts that the case may require. To the extent that a case may engender competition concerns in a number of Member States, and require coordinated investigations and remedial action, this may militate in favour of the Commission retaining jurisdiction over the entirety of the case in question.[25] On the other hand, to the extent that the case gives rise to competition concerns

which, despite involving national markets in more than one Member State, do not appear to require coordinated investigation and/or remedial action, a referral may be appropriate. In a limited number of cases,[26] the Commission has even found it appropriate to refer a concentration to more than one Member State, in view of the significant differences in competitive conditions that characterised the affected markets in the Member States concerned. While fragmentation of the treatment of a case deprives the merging parties of the benefit of a one-stop-shop in such cases, this consideration is less pertinent at the pre-notification stage, given that the referral is triggered by a voluntary request from the merging parties.

Notes

[25] For some examples, see M.1383 *Exxon/Mobil*, where the Commission, despite the United Kingdom request to have the part of the concentration relating to the market for motor fuel retailing in North west of Scotland referred to it, pursued the investigation as the case required a single and coherent remedy package designed to address all the problematic issues in the sector concerned; see also M.2706 *P&O Princess/Carnival*, where, despite the fact that the UK authorities were assessing a rival bid by Royal Caribbean, the Commission did not accede to a request for a partial referral, so as to avoid a fragmentation of the case and secure a single investigation of the various national markets affected by the operation.

[26] See M. 2898, *Le Roy Merlin/Brico*, M.1030, *Redland/Lafarge*, M. 1684, *Carrefour/Promodes*.

Commentary
para 22: B&C: 8.083

23. Consideration should also, to the extent possible, be given to whether the NCA(s) to which referral of the case is contemplated may possess specific expertise concerning local markets,[27] or be examining, or about to examine, another transaction in the sector concerned.[28]

Notes

[27] In Case M.330 *MacCormick/CPC/Rabobank/Ostmann*, the Commission referred a case to Germany, because it was better placed to investigate local conditions in 85,000 sales points in Germany; a referral to the Netherlands was made in Case M.1060 *Vendex/KBB*, because it was better placed to assess local consumer tastes and habits; See also Case M.1555 *Heineken/Cruzcampo*, Case M.2621 *SEB/Moulinex* (where consumer preferences and commercial and marketing practices were specific to the French market); Case M.2639 *Compass/Restorama/Rail Gourmet/Gourmet*, and Case M.2662 *Danish-Crown/Steff-Houlberg* .

[28] In Case M.716 *Gehe/Lloyds Chemists*, for example, the Commission referred a case because Lloyds was also subject to another bid not falling under ECMR thresholds but being scrutinised by the UK authorities: the referral allowed both bids to be scrutinised by the same authority; in M.1001/M.1019 *Preussag/Hapag-Lloyd/TUI*, a referral was made to Germany of two transactions, which together with a third one notified in Germany, would present competition concerns: the referral ensured that all three operations were dealt with in like manner; in case M.2044 *Interbrew/Bass*, the Commission referred the case to the UK authorities, because they were at the same time assessing Interbrew's acquisition of another brewer, Whitbread, and because of their experience in recent investigations in the same markets; similarly, see also Cases M.2760 *Nehlsen/Rethmann/SWB/Bremerhavener Energiewirtschaft*, M.2234 *Metsalilitto Osuuskunta/Vapo Oy/JV*, M.2495 *Haniel/Fels*, M.2881 *Koninklijke BAM NBM/HBG*, and M.2857/M.3075-3080 *ECS/IEH* and six other acquisitions by Electrabel of local distributors. In M.2706 *P&O Princess/Carnival*, however, despite the fact that the UK authorities were already assessing a rival bid by Royal Caribbean, the Commission did not accede to a request for a partial referral. The Commission had identified preliminary competition concerns in other national markets affected by the merger and thus wished to avoid a fragmentation of the case (see Commission press release of 11.4.2002, IP/02/552).

Commentary
para 23: B&C: 8.083

Referral of cases from Member States to the Commission under Article 4(5)

Legal requirements

24. Under Article 4(5), only two legal requirements must be met in order for the parties to the transaction to request the referral of the case to the Commission: the transaction must be a concentration within the meaning of Article 3 of the Merger Regulation, and the concentration must be *capable of being reviewed under the national competition laws for the control of mergers of at least three Member States* (see also paragraphs 65 et seq and 70 et seq).

Other factors to be considered

25. Other than verification of the legal requirements, in order to anticipate to the greatest extent possible the likely outcome of a referral request, merging parties contemplating a request should also consider whether referral of the case is likely to be considered appropriate. This will involve an examination of the application of the guiding principles referred to above, and in particular whether the Commission is the more appropriate authority for dealing with the case.

26. In this regard, Recital 16 to the Merger Regulation states that "requests for pre-notification referrals to the Commission would be particularly pertinent in situations where the concentration would affect competition beyond the territory of one Member State." Particular consideration should therefore be given to the likely locus of any competitive effects resulting from the transaction, and to how appropriate it would be for the Commission to scrutinise the operation.

27. It should in particular be assessed whether the case is genuinely cross-border in nature, having regard to elements such as its likely effects on competition and the investigative and enforcement powers likely to be required to address any such effects. In this regard, particular consideration should be given to whether the case is liable to have a potential impact on competition in one or more markets affected by the concentration. In any case, indications of possible competitive impact may be no more than preliminary in nature,[29] and would be without prejudice to the outcome of the investigation. Nor would it be necessary for the parties to demonstrate that the effect on competition is likely to be an adverse one.

Notes

[29] The existence of "affected markets" within the meaning of Form RS would generally be considered sufficient. However, the parties can point to any factors which may be relevant for the competitive analysis of the case (market overlap, vertical integration, etc).

28. Cases where the market(s) in which there may be a potential impact on competition is/are wider than national in geographic scope,[30] or where some of the potentially affected markets are wider than national and the main economic impact of the concentration is connected to such markets, are the most appropriate candidate cases for referral to the Commission. In such cases, as the competitive dynamics extend over territories reaching beyond national boundaries, and may consequently require investigative efforts in several countries as well as appropriate enforcement powers, the Commission is likely to be in the best position to carry out the investigation.

Notes

[30] See the joint referral by seven Member States to the Commission of a transaction affecting worldwide markets in M.2738 *GE/Unison* , and the joint referral by seven Member States to the Commission of a transaction affecting a Western European market in M.2698 *Promatech/Sulzer* ; See also *Principles on the application, by National Competition Authorities within the ECA network, of Article 22 of the EC Merger Regulation*, a paper published by the European Competition Authorities (ECA), at paragraph 11.

29. The Commission may be more appropriately placed to treat cases (including investigation, assessment and possible remedial action) that give rise to potential competition concerns in a series of national or narrower than national markets located in a number of different Member States.[31] The Commission is likely to be in the best position to carry out the investigation in such cases, given the desirability of ensuring consistent and efficient scrutiny across the different countries, of employing appropriate investigative powers, and of addressing any competition concerns by way of coherent remedies.

Notes

[31] This may, for example, be the case in relation to operations where the affected markets, while national (or even narrower than national in scope for the purposes of a competition assessment), are nonetheless characterised by common Europe-wide or world-wide brands, by common Europe-wide or world-wide intellectual property rights, or by centralised manufacture or distribution – at least to the extent that such centralised manufacture or distribution would be likely to impact upon any remedial measures.

30. Similarly to what has been said above in relation to Article 4(4), the appropriateness of referring concentrations which, despite having a potentially significant impact on competition in a

nation-wide market, nonetheless potentially engender substantial cross-border effects, will depend on the specific circumstances of the case. As both the Commission and Member States may be in an equally good position to deal with such cases, a considerable margin of discretion should be retained in deciding whether or not to refer such cases.

31. Consideration should also, to the extent possible, be given to whether the Commission is particularly well equipped to properly scrutinise the case, in particular having regard to factors such as specific expertise, or past experience in the sector concerned. The greater a merger's potential to affect competition beyond the territory of one Member State, the more likely it is that the Commission will be better equipped to conduct the investigation, particularly in terms of fact finding and enforcement powers.

32. Finally, the parties to the concentration might submit that, despite the apparent absence of an effect on competition, there is a compelling case for having the operation treated by the Commission, having regard in particular to factors such as the cost and time delay involved in submitting multiple Member State filings.[32]

Notes

[32] See Recitals 12 and 16 of the Merger Regulation.

Post-notification referrals

Referrals from the Commission to Member States pursuant to Article 9

33. Under Article 9 there are two options for a Member State wishing to request referral of a case following its notification to the Commission: *Articles 9(2)(a) and 9(2)(b) respectively.*

Article 9(2)(a)

Legal requirements

34. In order for a referral to be made to a Member State or States pursuant to Article 9(2)(a), the following legal requirements must be fulfilled:
    (i) the concentration must *threaten to affect significantly competition in a market*; and
    (ii) the market in question must be *within the requesting Member State, and present all the characteristics of a distinct market.*

35. As regards the *first criterion*, in essence a requesting Member State is required to demonstrate that, based on a preliminary analysis, there is a real risk that the transaction may have a significant adverse impact on competition, and thus that it deserves close scrutiny. Such preliminary indications may be in the nature of *prima facie* evidence of such a possible significant adverse impact, but would be without prejudice to the outcome of a full investigation.

Commentary
para 35: B&C: 8.091 F&N: 5.242

---

36. As regards the *second criterion*, the Member State is required to show that a geographic market(s) in which competition is affected by the transaction in the manner just described (paragraph 35) is/are national, or narrower than national in scope.[33]

Notes

[33] See Commission notice on the definition of relevant market for the purposes of Community competition law (OJ C372, 9.12.1997, p.5).

Commentary
para 36: B&C: 8.083, 8.091, 8.095

Other factors to be considered

37. Other than verification of the legal requirements, other factors should also be considered in assessing whether referral of a case is likely to be considered appropriate. This will involve an examination of the application of the guiding principles referred to above, and in particular whether the competition authority or authorities requesting the referral of the case is/are in the

best position to deal with the case. To this end, consideration should be given in turn both to the likely locus of the competitive effects of the transaction and to how well equipped the NCA would be to scrutinise the operation (see above at paragraphs 19–23).

Article 9(2)(b)

Legal requirements

38. In order for a referral to be made to a Member State or States pursuant to Article 9(2)(b), the following legal requirements must be fulfilled:
   (i) the concentration *must affect competition in a market*; and
   (ii) the market in question must be *within the requesting Member State, present all the characteristics of a distinct market, and must not constitute a substantial part of the common market.*

39. As regards the *first criterion*, a requesting Member State is required to show, based on a preliminary analysis, that the concentration is liable to have an impact on competition in a market. Such preliminary indications may be in the nature of *prima facie* evidence of a possible adverse impact, but would be without prejudice to the outcome of a full investigation.

Commentary

para 39: **B&C:** 8.091 **F&N:** 5.245

---

40. As to the *second criterion*, a requesting Member State is required to show not only that the market in which competition is affected by the operation in the manner just described (paragraph 38) constitutes a distinct market within a Member State, but also that the market in question does not constitute a substantial part of the common market. In this respect, based on the past practice and case-law,[34] it appears that such situations are generally limited to markets with a narrow geographic scope, within a Member State.

Notes

[34] See Commission referrals granted under Article 9(2)(b) in: M.2446, *Govia/Connex South Central*, where the operation affected competition on specific railway routes in the London/Gatwick-Brighton area in the United Kingdom; in M.2730, *Connex/DNVBVG*, where the transaction affected competition in local public transport services in the Riesa area (Saxony, Germany); and in M. 3130, *Arla Foods/Express Diaries*, where the transaction affected competition in the market for the supply of bottled milk to doorstep deliverers in the London, Yorkshire and Lancashire regions of the United Kingdom. For the purpose of defining the notion of a non-substantial part of the common market, some guidance can also be found in the case-law relating to the application of Article 82 of EC Treaty. In that context, the Court of Justice has articulated quite a broad notion of what may constitute a substantial part of the common market, resorting *inter alia* to empirical evidence. In the case-law there can be found, for instance, indications essentially based on practical criteria such as "the pattern and volume of the production and consumption of the said product as well as the habits and economic opportunities of vendors and purchasers", see Case 40/73, *Suiker Unie v Commission*, [1975] ECR 1663. See also Case C-179/90, *Porto di Genova* [1991] ECR 5889, where the Port of Genova was considered as constituting a substantial part of the common market. In its case-law the Court has also stated that a series of separate markets may be regarded as together constituting a substantial part of the common market. See, for example, Case C-323/93, *Centre d'insémination de la Crespelle* [1994] ECR I-5077, paragraph. 17, where the Court stated "In this case, by making the operation of the insemination centres subject to authorization and providing that each centre should have the exclusive right to serve a defined area, the national legislation granted those centres exclusive rights. By thus establishing, in favour of those undertakings, a contiguous series of monopolies territorially limited but together covering the entire territory of a Member State, those national provisions create a dominant position, within the meaning of Article [106] of the Treaty, in a substantial part of the common market".

Commentary

para 40: **B&C:** 8.091, 8.096 **F&N:** 5.245

---

41. If these conditions are met, the Commission has an obligation to refer the case.

Referrals from Member States to the Commission pursuant to Article 22

Legal requirements

42. In order for a referral to be made by one or more Member States to the Commission pursuant to Article 22, two legal requirements must be fulfilled:
   (i) the concentration must *affect trade between Member States*; and

(ii) it must *threaten to significantly affect competition within the territory of the Member State or States making the request.*

43. As to the *first criterion*, a concentration fulfils this requirement to the extent that it is liable to have some discernible influence on the pattern of trade between Member States.[35]

Notes

[35] See also, by analogy, the Commission Notice – Guidelines on the effect on trade concept contained in Articles [101] and [102] of the Treaty (OJ C 101, 27.4.2004, p.81).

Commentary
para 43: F&N: 5.269

44. As to the *second criterion*, as under Article 9(2)(a), a referring Member State or States is/are required in essence to demonstrate that, based on a preliminary analysis, there is a real risk that the transaction may have a significant adverse impact on competition, and thus that it deserves close scrutiny. Such preliminary indications may be in the nature of *prima facie* evidence of such a possible significant adverse impact, but would be without prejudice to the outcome of a full investigation.

Commentary
para 44: F&N: 5.269

Other factors to be considered

45. As post-notification referrals to the Commission may entail additional cost and time delay for the merging parties, they should normally be limited to those cases which appear to present a real risk of negative effects on competition and trade between Member States, and where it appears that these would be best addressed at the Community level.[36] The categories of cases normally most appropriate for referral to the Commission pursuant to Article 22 are accordingly the following:
 — cases which give rise to serious competition concerns in one or more markets which are wider than national in geographic scope, or where some of the potentially affected markets are wider than national, and where the main economic impact of the concentration is connected to such markets,
 — cases which give rise to serious competition concerns in a series of national or narrower than national markets located in a number of Member States, in circumstances where coherent treatment of the case (regarding possible remedies, but also, in appropriate cases, the investigative efforts as such) is considered desirable, and where the main economic impact of the concentration is connected to such markets.

Notes

[36] See the joint referral by seven Member States to the Commission of a transaction affecting worldwide markets in M.2738 *GE/Unison*, and the joint referral by seven Member States to the Commission of a transaction affecting a Western European market in M.2698 *Promatech/Sulzer*; See also *Principles on the application, by National Competition Authorities within the ECA network, of Article 22 of the EC Merger Regulation*, a paper published by the European Competition Authorities (ECA), at paragraph 11.

Commentary
para 45: B&C: 8.100, 8.101 F&N: 5.271

III. Mechanics of the Referral System

A. overview of the referral system

46. The Merger Regulation sets out the relevant legal rules for the functioning of the referral system. The rules contained in Article 4(4) and (5), Article 9 and Article 22 set out in detail the various steps required for a case to be referred from the Commission to Member States and vice versa.

47. Each of the four relevant referral provisions establishes a self-contained mechanism for the referral of a given category of concentration. The provisions can be categorised in the following way:
    (a) Pre-notification referrals:

    (i) From the Commission to Member States (Article 4(4))
    (ii) From Member States to the Commission (Article 4(5))

    (b) Post-notification referrals:
    (i) From the Commission to Member States (Article 9)
    (ii) From Member States to the Commission (Article 22).
48. The flowcharts in Annex I to this Notice describe in graphical form the various procedural steps to be followed in the referral mechanisms set out in Articles 4(4) and (5), Article 9 and Article 22.

Pre-notification referrals

49. Pre-notification referrals can only be requested by the undertakings concerned.[37] It is for the undertakings concerned to verify whether the concentration meets the criteria specified in Article 4(4) (that the concentration has a Community dimension but may significantly affect competition in a distinct market within a Member State) or Article 4(5) (that the concentration does not have a Community dimension but is capable of being reviewed under the national competition laws of at least three Member States). The undertakings concerned may then decide to request a referral to or from the Commission by submitting a reasoned request on Form RS. The request is transmitted without delay by the Commission to all Member States. The remainder of the process differs under Article 4(4) and Article 4(5).
    — Under Article 4(4), the Member State or States concerned[38] have 15 working days from the date they receive the submission to express agreement or disagreement with the request. Silence on the part of a Member State is deemed to constitute agreement.[39] If the Member State or States concerned agree to the referral, the Commission has an additional period of approximately 10 working days (25 working days from the date the Commission received Form RS) in which it may decide to refer the case. Silence on the part of the Commission is deemed to constitute assent. If the Commission assents, the case (or one or more parts thereof) is referred to the Member States or States as requested by the undertakings concerned. If the referral is made, the Member State or States concerned apply their national law to the referred part of the case.[40] Articles 9(6) to 9(9) apply.
    — Under Article 4(5), the Member States concerned[41] have 15 working days from the date they receive the submission to express agreement or disagreement with the request. At the end of that period, the Commission checks whether any Member State competent to examine the concentration under its national competition law has expressed disagreement. If there is no expression of disagreement by any such competent Member State, the case is deemed to acquire a Community dimension and is thus referred to the Commission which has exclusive jurisdiction over it. It is then for the parties to notify the case to the Commission, using Form CO. On the other hand, if one or more competent Member States have expressed their disagreement, the Commission informs all Member States and the undertakings concerned without delay of any such expression of disagreement and the referral process ends. It is then for the parties to comply with any applicable national notification rules.

Notes

[37] The term "undertakings concerned" includes "persons" within the meaning of Article 3(1)(b).

[38] The Member State or States concerned are the ones identified in Form RS to which the case will be referred if the request is granted.

[39] This mechanism is an essential feature of all referral procedures set out in the Merger Regulation. The mechanism may be termed "positive silence" or non-opposition: that is to say that failure to take a decision on the part of the Commission or a Member State will be deemed to constitute the taking of a positive decision. This mechanism was already a feature of Regulation (EEC) No 4064/89, in Article 9(5). It is now included in Article 4(4) (second and fourth sub-paragraphs), Article 4(5) (fourth sub-paragraph), Article 9(5) and Article 22(3) (first sub-paragraph, last sentence) of the Merger Regulation. The positive silence mechanism is, however, not applicable with regard to decisions by Member States to join a request under Article 22(2).

Post-notification referrals

50. Pursuant to Article 9(2) and Article 22(1), post-notification referrals are triggered by Member States either on their own initiative or following an invitation by the Commission pursuant to Article 9(2) and Article 22(5) respectively. The procedures differ according to whether the referral is from or to the Commission.

    — Under Article 9, a Member State may request that the Commission refer to it a concentration with Community dimension, or a part thereof, which has been notified to the Commission and which threatens to significantly affect competition within a distinct market within that Member State (Article 9(2)(a)), or which affects such a distinct market not constituting a substantial part of the common market (Article 9(2)(b)). The request must be made within 15 working days from the date the Member State received a copy of Form CO. The Commission must first verify whether those legal criteria are met. It may then decide to refer the case, or a part thereof, exercising its administrative discretion. In the case of a referral request made pursuant to Article 9(2)(b), the Commission must (i.e. has no discretion) make the referral if the legal criteria are met. The decision must be taken within 35 working days from notification or, where the Commission has initiated proceedings, within 65 working days.[42] If the referral is made, the Member State concerned applies its own national competition law, subject only to Article 9(6) and (8).

    — Under Article 22, a Member State may request that the Commission examine a concentration which has no Community dimension but which affects trade between Member States and threatens to significantly affect competition within its territory. The request must be made within 15 working days from the date of national notification or, where no notification is required, the date when the concentration was "made known"[43] to the Member State concerned. The Commission transmits the request to all Member States. Any other Member States can decide to join the request[44] within a period of 15 working days from the date they receive a copy of the initial request. All national time limits relating to the concentration are suspended a decision has been taken as to where it will be examined; a Member State can re-start the national time limits before the expiry of the 15 working day period by informing the Commission and the merging parties that it does not wish to join the request. At the latest 10 working days following the expiry of the 15 working day period, the Commission must decide whether to accept the case from the requesting Member State(s). If the Commission accepts jurisdiction, national proceedings in the referring Member State(s) are terminated and the Commission examines the case pursuant to Article 22(4) of the Merger Regulation on behalf of the requesting State(s).[45] Non-requesting States can continue to apply national law.

by another Member State. Notwithstanding the Member State's ability to contact the merging parties in order to verify whether they are competent to review any particular transaction, the notifying parties are therefore strongly encouraged to file, where feasible, their notification to all competent Member States simultaneously.

[45] Where the Commission examines a concentration on behalf of one or more Member States pursuant to Article 22, it can adopt all the substantive decisions provided for in Articles 6 and 8 of the Merger Regulation. This is established in Article 22(4) of that Regulation. It is to be noted that the Commission examines the concentration upon the request of and on behalf of the requesting Member States. This provision should therefore be interpreted as requiring the Commission to examine the impact of the concentration within the territory of those Member States. The Commission will not examine the effects of the concentration in the territory of Member States which have not joined the request unless this examination is necessary for the assessment of the effects of the concentration within the territory of the requesting Member States (for example, where the geographic market extends beyond the territory/or territories of the requesting Member State(s).

Commentary
para 50: B&C: 8.099

51. The following section of the Notice focuses on a number of detailed elements of the system with the aim in particular of providing further guidance to undertakings contemplating making requests at the pre-notification stage, or who may be party to transactions subject to the possibility of post-notification referral.

B. DETAILS OF THE REFERRAL MECHANISM

52. This section of this Notice provides guidance regarding certain aspects of the functioning of the referral system set out in Article 4(4) and (5), Article 9 and Article 22 of the Merger Regulation.

1. The network of competition authorities

53. Article 19(2) of the Merger Regulation provides that the Commission is to carry out the procedures set out in that Regulation in close and constant liaison with the competent authorities of the Member States (the NCAs). Cooperation and dialogue between the Commission and the NCAs, and between the NCAs themselves, is particularly important in the case of concentrations which are subject to the referral system set out in the Merger Regulation.

54. According to Recital 14 to the Merger Regulation, "the Commission and the NCAs should form together a network of public authorities, applying their respective competences in close cooperation using efficient arrangements for information sharing and consultation with a view to ensuring that a case is dealt with by the most appropriate authority, in the light of the principle of subsidiarity, and with a view to ensuring that multiple notifications of a given concentration are avoided to the greatest extent possible".

55. The network should ensure the efficient re-attribution of concentrations according to the principles described in section II above. This involves facilitating the smooth operation of the pre-notification referral mechanism, as well as providing, to the extent foreseeable, a system whereby potential post-notification referral requests are identified as soon as possible.[46]

Notes
[46] Advance knowledge of the possibility of a referral request might, for example, be taken into account by the Commission in deciding not to accede to a request for derogation from the suspensive effect pursuant to Article 7(3) of the Merger Regulation.

56. Pursuant to Article 4(4) and (5), the Commission must transmit reasoned requests made by the undertakings concerned "without delay".[47] The Commission will endeavour to transmit such documents on the working day following that on which they are received or issued. Information within the network will be exchanged by various means, depending on the circumstances: e-mail, surface mail, courier, fax, telephone. It should be noted that for sensitive information or confidential information exchanges will be carried out by secure e-mail or by any other protected means of communication between these contact points.

Notes
[47] It should be noted that, as provided for in Article 19(1) of the Merger Regulation, the Commission is also under an obligation to transmit to the NCAs copies of notifications and of the most important documents lodged with or issued by the Commission.

57. All members of the network, including the Commission and all NCAs, their officials and other servants, and other persons working under the supervision of those authorities as well as officials and civil servants of other authorities of the Member States, will be bound by the professional secrecy obligations set out in Article 17 of the Merger Regulation. They must not disclose non-public information they have acquired through the application of the Merger Regulation, unless the natural or legal person who provided that information has consented to its disclosure.

58. Consultations and exchanges within the network is a matter between public enforcement agencies and do not alter any rights or obligations arising from Community or national law for companies. Each competition authority remains fully responsible for ensuring that due process is observed in the cases it deals with.

2. Triggering the pre-notification referral system; information to be provided by the requesting parties

59. For the referral system to work swiftly and smoothly, it is crucial that the requesting parties, provide complete and accurate information, whenever required, in a timely fashion and in the most efficient way possible. Legal requirements concerning the information to be provided and the consequences of providing incorrect, incomplete or misleading information are set out in the Merger Regulation, Regulation (EC) No 802/2004 (hereinafter "the Merger Implementing Regulation") and Form RS.[48]

Notes

[48] Form RS is annexed to Commission Regulation (EC) No 802/2004 of 7 April 2004 implementing Council Regulation (EC) No 139/2004 on the control of concentrations between undertakings (OJ L 133, 30.4.2004, 1).

60. Form RS states that all information submitted in a reasoned submission must be correct and complete. If parties submit incorrect or incomplete information, the Commission has the power to either adopt a decision pursuant to Article 6(1)(a) of the Merger Regulation (where failure to fulfil the conditions of Article 4(5) comes to its attention during the course of the investigation), or to revoke any decision it adopts pursuant to Article 6 or Article 8, following an Article 4(5) referral, pursuant to Article 6(3)(a) or 8(6)(a) of the Merger Regulation. Following the adoption of a decision pursuant to Article 6(1)(a) or following revocation, national competition laws would once again be applicable to the transaction. In the case of referrals under Article 4(4) made on the basis of incorrect or incomplete information, the Commission may require a notification pursuant to Article 4(1). In addition, the Commission has the power to impose fines under Article 14(1)(a) of the Merger Regulation. Finally, parties should also be aware that, if a referral is made on the basis of incorrect or incomplete information included in Form RS, the Commission and/or the Member States may consider making a post-notification referral reversing a pre-notification referral based on such incorrect or incomplete information.[49]

Notes

[49] This would be the appropriate "remedy" where the requesting parties have submitted incorrect or incomplete information not affecting fulfilment of the conditions of Article 4(5), which comes to the Commission's attention during the course of the investigation.

61. When providing information on Form RS or generally in making a request for a pre-notification referral, it is not envisaged or necessary for the undertakings concerned to show that their concentration will lead to detrimental effects on competition.[50] They should, however, provide as much information as possible showing clearly in what way the concentration meets the relevant legal criteria set out in Article 4(4) and (5) and why the concentration would be most appropriately dealt with by the competition authority or authorities specified in the request. The Merger Regulation does not require publication of the fact that a Form RS has been lodged, and it is not intended to do so. A non-public transaction can consequently be the subject of a pre-notification referral request.

Notes

[50] See Recital 16 to the Merger Regulation.

62. Even though, according to the Merger Implementing Regulation, the Commission will accept Form RS in any official Community language, undertakings concerned providing information which is to be distributed to the network are strongly encouraged to use a language which will be understood by all addressees of the information. This will facilitate Member State treatment of such requests. Moreover, as regards requests for referral to a Member State or States, the requesting parties are strongly encouraged to include a copy of the request in the language(s) of the Member State(s) to which the referral is being requested.

63. Beyond the legal requirements specified in Form RS, the undertakings concerned should be prepared to provide additional information, if required, and to discuss the matter with the Commission and the NCAs in a frank and open manner in order to enable the Commission and the NCAs to assess whether the concentration in question should be the subject of referral.

64. Informal contacts between merging parties contemplating lodging a pre-filing referral request, on the one hand, and the Commission and/or Member State authorities, on the other, are actively encouraged, even following the submission of Form RS. The Commission is committed to providing informal, early guidance to firms wishing to use the pre-notification referrals system set out in Article 4(4) and (5) of the Merger Regulation.[51]

Notes

[51] A request for derogation from the suspensive effect pursuant to Article 7(3) of the Merger Regulation would normally be inconsistent with an intention to make a pre-notification referral request pursuant to Article 4(4).

3. Concentrations eligible for referral

65. Only concentrations within the meaning of Article 3 of the Merger Regulation are eligible for referral pursuant to Article 4(5) and Article 22. Only concentrations falling within the ambit of the relevant national competition laws for the control of mergers are eligible for referral pursuant to Article 4(4) and Article 9.[52]

Notes

[52] By contrast, the reference to "national legislation on competition" in Article 21(3) and Article 22(3) should be understood as referring to all aspects of national competition law.

66. Pre-filing referral requests pursuant to Article 4(4) and (5) of the Merger Regulation must concern concentrations the plans for which are sufficiently concrete. In that regard, there must at least exist a good faith intention to merge on the part of the undertakings concerned, or, in the case of a public bid, at least a public announcement of an intention to make such a bid.[53]

Notes

[53] See Recital 34 to, and Article 4(1) of, the Merger Regulation.

Commentary
para 66: B&C: 8.089

4. The concept of "prior to notification" under Article 4(4) and (5)

67. Article 4(4) and (5) only apply at the pre-notification stage.

68. Article 4(4) specifies that the undertakings concerned may make a referral request by means of reasoned submission (Form RS), "prior to the notification of a concentration within the meaning of paragraph 1". This means that the request can only be made where no Form CO has been submitted pursuant to Article 4(1).

69. Likewise, Article 4(5) specifies that the request may be made "before any notification to the competent [national] authorities". This means that the concentration in question must not have been formally notified in any Member State jurisdiction for that provision to apply. Even one notification anywhere in the Community will preclude the undertakings concerned from triggering the mechanism of Article 4(5). In the Commission's view, no penalty should be imposed for non-notification of a transaction at the national level while a request pursuant to Article 4(5) is pending.

5. The concept of a "concentration capable of being reviewed under national competition law" and the concept of "competent Member State" in Article 4(5)

70. Article 4(5) enables the undertakings concerned to request a pre-notification referral of a concentration which does not have a Community dimension and which is "capable of being reviewed under the national competition laws of at least three Member States".

71. "Capable of being reviewed" or reviewable should be interpreted as meaning a concentration which falls within the jurisdiction of a Member State under its national competition law for the control of mergers. There is no need for a mandatory notification requirement, i.e. it is not necessary for the concentration to be required to be notified under national law.[54]

---

72. Pursuant to the third and fourth subparagraphs of Article 4(5), where at least one Member State "competent to examine the concentration under its national competition law" has expressed its disagreement with the referral, the case must not be referred. A "competent" Member State is one where the concentration is reviewable and which therefore has the power to examine the concentration under its national competition law.

73. All Member States, and not only those "competent" to review the case, receive a copy of the Form RS. However, only Member States "competent" to review the case are counted for the purposes of the third and fourth subparagraphs of Article 4(5). Pursuant to the third subparagraph of Article 4(5), "competent" Member States have 15 working days from the date they receive the Form RS to express their agreement or disagreement with the referral. If they all agree, the case will be deemed to acquire a Community dimension pursuant to the fifth subparagraph of Article 4(5). According to the fourth subparagraph of Article 4(5), by contrast, if even only one "competent" Member State disagrees, no referral will take place from any Member State.

74. Given the above mechanism, it is crucial to the smooth operation of Article 4(5) that *all* Member States where the case is reviewable under national competition law, and which are hence "competent" to examine the case under national competition law, are identified correctly. Form RS therefore requires the undertakings concerned to provide sufficient information to enable each and every Member State to identify whether or not it is competent to review the concentration pursuant to its own national competition law.

75. In situations where Form RS has been filled in correctly, no complications should arise. The undertakings concerned will have identified correctly all Member States which are competent to review the case. In situations, however, where the undertakings concerned have not filled in Form RS correctly, or where there is a genuine disagreement as to which Member States are "competent" to review the case, complications may arise.

— Within the period of 15 working days provided for in the third subparagraph of Article 4(5), a Member State which is not identified in Form RS as being competent may inform the Commission that it is competent and may, like any other competent Member State, express its agreement or disagreement with the referral.

— Likewise, within the period of 15 working days provided for in the third subparagraph of Article 4(5), a Member State which has been identified as competent in Form RS may inform the Commission that it is not "competent". That Member State would then be disregarded for the purposes of Article 4(5).

76. Once the period of 15 working days has expired without any disagreement having been expressed, the referral, will be considered valid. This ensures the validity of Commission decisions taken under Articles 6 or 8 of the Merger Regulation following an Article 4(5) referral.

77. This is not to say, however, that undertakings concerned can abuse the system by negligently or intentionally providing incorrect information, including as regards the reviewability of the concentration in the Member States, on Form RS. As noted at paragraph 60 above, the Commission may take measures to rectify the situation and to deter such violations. The undertakings concerned should also be aware that, in such circumstances, where a referral has been made on the basis of incorrect or incomplete information, a Member State which believes it was competent to

deal with the case but did not have the opportunity to veto the referral due to incorrect information being supplied, may request a post-notification referral.

6. Notification and Publication of Decisions

78. According to the fourth subparagraph of Article 4(4), the fourth subparagraph of Article 4(5), Article 9(1) and the second subparagraph of Article 22(3), the Commission is obliged to inform the undertakings or persons concerned and all Member States of any decision taken pursuant to those provisions as to the referral of a concentration.

79. The information will be provided by means of a letter addressed to the undertakings concerned (or for decisions adopted pursuant to Article 9(1) or Article 22(3), a letter addressed to the Member State concerned). All Member States will receive a copy thereof.

80. There is no requirement that such decisions be published in the *Official Journal of the European Union*.[55] The Commission will, however, give adequate publicity to such decisions on DG Competition's website, subject to confidentiality requirements.

Notes

[55] Pursuant to Article 20 of the Merger Regulation this is only required for decisions taken under Article 8(1)–(6) and Articles 14 and 15.

7. Article 9(6)

81. Article 9(6) provides that, when the Commission refers a notified concentration to a Member State in accordance with Article 4(4) or Article 9(3), the NCA concerned must deal with the case "without undue delay". Accordingly, the competent authority concerned should deal as expeditiously as possible with the case under national law.

82. In addition, Article 9(6) provides that the competent national authority must, within 45 working days after the Commission's referral or following receipt of a notification at the national level if requested inform the undertakings concerned of the result of the "preliminary competition assessment" and what "further action", if any, it proposes to take. Accordingly, within 45 working days after the referral or notification, as appropriate, the merging parties should be provided with sufficient information to enable them to understand the nature of any preliminary competition concerns the authority may have and be informed of the likely extent and duration of the investigation. The Member State concerned may only exceptionally suspend this time limit, where necessary information has not been provided to it by the undertakings concerned as required under its national competition law.

IV. Final Remarks

83. This Notice will be the subject of periodic review, in particular following any revision of the referral provisions in the Merger Regulation. In that regard, it should be noted that, according to Article 4(6) of the Merger Regulation, the Commission must report to the Council on the operation of the pre-notification referral provisions in Article 4(4) and (5), by 1 July 2009.

84. This Notice is without prejudice to any interpretation of the applicable Treaty and regulatory provisions by the Court of First Instance and the Court of Justice of the European Communities.

ANNEXES

REFERRAL CHARTS

Article 4(4)
Concentration with Community Dimension

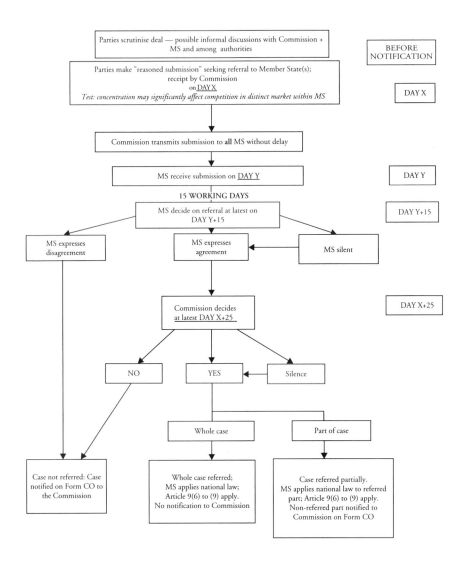

Article 4(5)
Concentration without Community Dimension
reviewable in at least three MS under national law

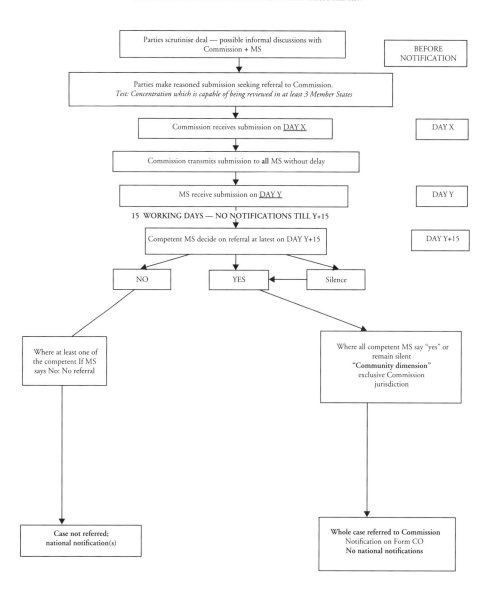

Article 9
Concentration with Community Dimension

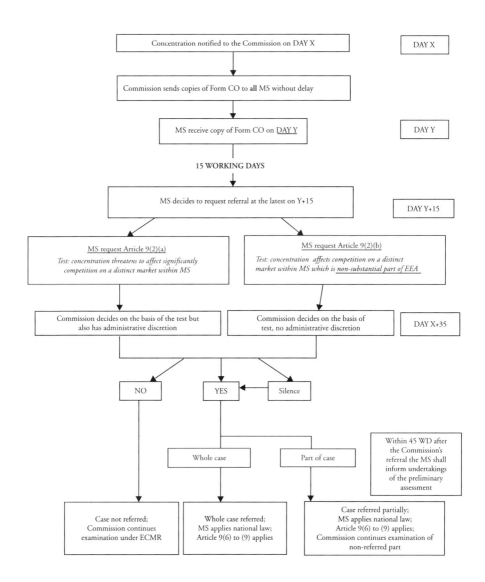

Article 22
Concentration without Community Dimension

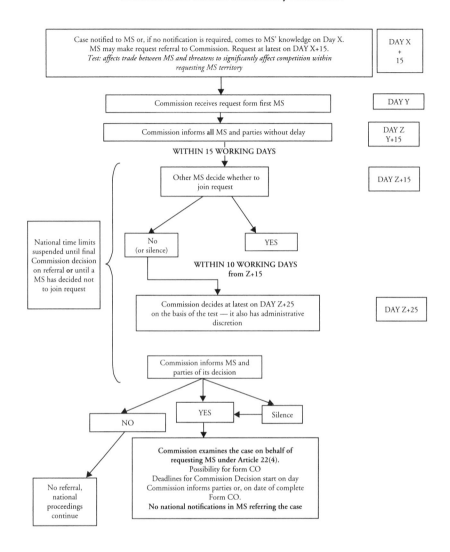

Case notified to MS or, if no notification is required, comes to MS' knowledge on Day X. MS may make request referral to Commission. Request at latest on DAY X+15. *Test: affects trade between MS and threatens to significantly affect competition within requesting MS territory*

DAY X + 15

Commission receives request form first MS

DAY Y

Commission informs **all** MS and parties without delay

DAY Z Y+15

WITHIN 15 WORKING DAYS

Other MS decide whether to join request

DAY Z+15

National time limits suspended until final Commission decision on referral **or** until a MS has decided not to join request

No (or silence)

YES

WITHIN 10 WORKING DAYS from Z+15

Commission decides at latest on DAY Z+25 on the basis of the test — it also has administrative discretion

DAY Z+25

Commission informs MS and parties of its decision

YES

Silence

NO

No referral, national proceedings continue

Commission examines the case on behalf of requesting MS under Article 22(4). Possibility for form CO Deadlines for Commission Decision start on day Commission informs parties or, on date of complete Form CO. **No national notifications in MS referring the case**

D8

COMMISSION NOTICE

on restrictions directly related and necessary to concentrations

(2005/C 56/03)

(Text with EEA relevance)

Official Journal C 56, 5.3.2005, p.24

Celex No: 52005XC0305(02)

EUR-Lex permanent link: <http://eur-lex.europa.eu/legal-content/EN/ALL/?uri=CELEX:52005X
C0305%2802%29&qid=1395771270553>

Commentary
Notice: **B&C:** 2.147, 2.151, 8.007, 8.273, 8.274, 8.279 **F&N:** 5.152, 12.92
paras 36–44: **B&C:** 2.151, 6.016

I. Introduction

1. Council Regulation (EC) No 139/2004 of 20 January 2004 on the control of concentrations between undertakings (the EC Merger Regulation)[1] provides in Article 6(1)(b), second subparagraph, in Article 8(1), second subparagraph and in Article 8(2), third subparagraph that a decision declaring a concentration compatible with the common market "*shall be deemed to cover restrictions directly related and necessary to the implementation of the concentration*".

Notes

[1] OJ L 24, 29.1.2004, p.1.

---

2. The amendment of the rules governing the assessment of restrictions directly related and necessary to the implementation of the concentration (hereinafter also referred to as "ancillary restraints") introduces a principle of self-assessment of such restrictions. This reflects the intention of the legislature not to oblige the Commission to assess and individually address ancillary restraints. The treatment of ancillary restraints under the EC Merger Regulation is further explained in recital 21 in the preamble to the EC Merger Regulation, which states that "*Commission decisions declaring concentrations compatible with the common market in application of this Regulation should automatically cover such restrictions, without the Commission having to assess such restrictions in individual cases*". While the Recital envisages that the Commission will exercise a residual function with regard to specific novel or unresolved issues giving rise to genuine uncertainty, it is in all other scenarios the task of the undertakings concerned to assess for themselves whether and to what extent their agreements can be regarded as ancillary to a transaction. Disputes as to whether restrictions are directly related and necessary to the implementation of the concentration, and thus automatically covered by the Commission's clearance decision, may be resolved before national courts.

Commentary
para 2: **B&C:** 8.273

---

3. The Commission's residual function is addressed in recital 21 of the Merger Regulation, where it is stated that the Commission should, at the request of the undertakings concerned, expressly assess the ancillary character of restrictions if a case presents "*novel and unresolved questions giving rise to genuine uncertainty*". The Recital subsequently defines a "novel or unresolved question giving rise to genuine uncertainty" as a question that is "*not covered by the relevant Commission notice in force or a published Commission decision.*"

4. In order to provide legal certainty to the undertakings concerned, this Notice provides guidance on the interpretation of the notion of ancillary restraints. The guidance given in the following sections reflects the essence of the Commission's practice, and sets out principles for assessing whether and to what extent the most common types of agreements are deemed to be ancillary restraints.

5. However, cases involving exceptional circumstances that are not covered by this Notice may justify departing from these principles. Parties may find further guidance in published Commission decisions[1] as to whether their agreements can be regarded as ancillary restraints or not. To the extent that cases involving exceptional circumstances have been previously addressed by the Commission in its published decisions,[2] they do not constitute "novel or unresolved questions" within the meaning of recital 21 of the Merger Regulation.

Notes

[1] For the purpose of this Notice, a decision is considered to be published when it is published in the *Official Journal of the European Union* or when it is made available to the public on the Commission's web site.

[2] See for example Commission Decision of 1 September 2000 (COMP/M.1980 – *Volvo/Renault V.I.*, paragraph 56) – *high degree of customer loyalty*; Commission Decision of 23 October 1998 (IV/M.1298 – *Kodak/Imation*, paragraph 73) – *long product life cycle*; Commission Decision of 13 March 1995 (IV/M.550 – *Union Carbide/ Enichem*, paragraph 99) – *limited number of alternative producers*; Commission Decision of 30 April 1992 (IV/M.197 – *Solvay-Laporte/ Interox*, paragraph 50) – *longer protection of know-how required*.

Commentary
para 5: B&C: 8.273 F&N: 5.152

6. Accordingly, a case presents a "novel and unresolved question giving rise to genuine uncertainty" if those restrictions are not covered by this Notice and have not been previously addressed by the Commission in its published decisions. As envisaged in recital 21 of the Merger Regulation, the Commission will, at the request of the parties, expressly assess such restrictions in these cases. Subject to confidentiality requirements, the Commission will provide adequate publicity as regards such assessments that further develop the principles set out in this Notice.

Commentary
para 6: F&N: 5.152

7. To the extent that restrictions are directly related and necessary to the implementation of the concentration, Article 21(1) of the Merger Regulation provides that this Regulation alone applies, to the exclusion of Council Regulations (EC) No 1/2003,[1] (EEC) No 1017/68[2] and (EEC) No 4056/86.[3] By contrast, for restrictions that cannot be regarded as directly related and necessary to the implementation of the concentration, Articles [101 and 102 TFEU]* remain potentially applicable. However, the mere fact that an agreement or arrangement is not deemed to be ancillary to a concentration is not, as such, prejudicial to the legal status thereof. Such agreements or arrangements are to be assessed in accordance with Article [101 and 102 TFEU] and the related regulatory texts and notices.[4] They may also be subject to any applicable national competition rules. Hence, agreements which contain a restriction on competition, but are not considered directly related and necessary to the implementation of the concentration pursuant to this notice, may nevertheless be covered by those provisions.

Notes

* Ed note: please see the Note on the Lisbon Treaty at p.xvii in regard to article renumbering introduced by the Lisbon Treaty.

[1] Council Regulation (EC) No 1/2003 of 16 December 2002 on the implementation of the rules on competition laid down in Articles 81 and 82 of the Treaty, OJ L 1, 4.1.2003, p.1; Regulation as last amended by Regulation (EC) No 411/2004 (OJ L 68, 6.3.2004, p.1).

[2] Council Regulation (EEC) No 1017/68 of 19 July 1968 applying rules of competition to transport by rail, road and inland waterway, OJ L 175, 23.7.1968, p.1; Regulation as last amended by Regulation (EC) No 1/2003. [Ed note: see now Regulation 169/2009/EC, OJ L 61, 5.3.2009, p.1, reproduced at E17.]

[3] Council Regulation (EEC) No 4056/86 of 22 December 1986 laying down detailed rules for the application of Articles [101] and [102] of the Treaty to maritime transport, OJ L 378, 31.12.1986, p.4; Regulation as last amended by Regulation (EC) No 1/2003. [Ed note: Regulation 4056/86/EEC was repealed by Regulation 1419/2006/EC. See also the Guidelines on the application of Article [101 TFEU] to maritime transport, C 245, 26.9.2008, p.2, which have themselves expired, and the note at E20.]

Part D Mergers and Concentrations

4 See, for example, for licence agreements Regulation (EC) No 772/2004 of 27 April 2004 on the application of Article [101](3) of the Treaty to categories of technology transfer agreements, OJ L 123, 27.4.2004, p.11; see for supply and purchase agreements, e.g. Commission Regulation (EC) No 2790/1999 of 22 December 1999 on the application of Article [101](3) of the Treaty to categories of vertical agreements and concerted practices, OJ L 336, 29.12.1999, p.21. [Ed note: see now Regulation 330/2010/EU on the application of Article 101(3) TFEU to categories of vertical agreements and concerted practices, OJ L 102, 23.4.2010, p.1, reproduced at C4.]

8. The Commission's interpretation of Article 6(1)(b), second subparagraph, and Article 8(1), second subparagraph, and (2), third subparagraph, of the Merger Regulation is without prejudice to the interpretation which may be given by the Court of Justice or the Court of First Instance of the European Communities.

9. This Notice replaces the Commission's previous Notice regarding restrictions directly related and necessary to concentrations.[1]

Notes

1 OJ C 188, 4.7.2001, p.5.

II. GENERAL PRINCIPLES

10. A concentration consists of contractual arrangements and agreements establishing control within the meaning of Article 3(2) of the Merger Regulation. All agreements which carry out the main object of the concentration,[1] such as those relating to the sale of shares or assets of an undertaking, are integral parts of the concentration. In addition to these arrangements and agreements, the parties to the concentration may enter into other agreements which do not form an integral part of the concentration but can restrict the parties' freedom of action in the market. If such agreements contain ancillary restraints, these are automatically covered by the decision declaring the concentration compatible with the Common Market.

Notes

1 See e.g. Commission Decision of 10 August 1992 (IV/M.206 – *Rhône-Poulenc/SNIA*, paragraph 8.3); Commission Decision of 19 December 1991 (IV/M.113 – *Courtaulds/SNIA*, paragraph 35); Commission Decision of 2 December 1991 (IV/M.102 – *TNT/Canada Post/DBP Postdienst/La Poste/PTT Poste & Sweden Post*, paragraph 46).

Commentary
para 10: B&C: 2.148, 8.274

11. The criteria of direct relation and necessity are objective in nature. Restrictions are not directly related and necessary to the implementation of a concentration simply because the parties regard them as such.

12. For restrictions to be considered "directly related to the implementation of the concentration", they must be closely linked to the concentration itself. It is not sufficient that an agreement has been entered into in the same context or at the same time as the concentration.[1] Restrictions which are directly related to the concentration are economically related to the main transaction and intended to allow a smooth transition to the changed company structure after the concentration.

Notes

1 Likewise, a restriction could, if all other requirements are fulfilled, be "directly related" even if it has not been entered into at the same time as the agreement carrying out the main object of the concentration.

Commentary
para 12: B&C: 2.148

13. Agreements must be "necessary to the implementation of the concentration",[1] which means that, in the absence of those agreements, the concentration could not be implemented or could only be implemented under considerably more uncertain conditions, at substantially higher cost, over an appreciably longer period or with considerably greater difficulty.[2] Agreements necessary to the implementation of a concentration are typically aimed at protecting the value transferred,[3] maintaining the continuity of supply after the break-up of a former economic entity,[4] or enabling the start-up of a new entity.[5] In determining whether a restriction is necessary, it is appropriate not only

to take account of its nature, but also to ensure that its duration, subject matter and geographical field of application does not exceed what the implementation of the concentration reasonably requires. If equally effective alternatives are available for attaining the legitimate aim pursued, the undertakings must choose the one which is objectively the least restrictive of competition.

Notes

[1] See European Court of Justice, Case 42/84 (*Remia*), [1985] ECR 2545, paragraph 20; Court of First Instance, Case T-112/99 (*Métropole Télévision – M6*), [2001] ECR II-2459, paragraph 106.

[2] Commission Decision of 18 December 2000 (COMP/M.1863 – *Vodafone/BT/Airtel JV*, paragraph 20).

[3] Commission Decision of 30 July 1998 (IV/M.1245 – *VALEO/ITT Industries*, paragraph 59); Commission Decision of 3 March 1999 (IV/M.1442 – *MMP/AFP*, paragraph 17); Commission Decision of 9 March 2001 (COMP/M.2330 – *Cargill/Banks*, paragraph 30); Commission Decision of 20 March 2001 (COMP/M.2227 – *Goldman Sachs/Messer Griesheim*, paragraph 11).

[4] Commission Decision of 25 February 2000 (COMP/M.1841 – *Celestica/IBM*, paragraph 21).

[5] Commission Decision of 30 March 1999 (IV/JV.15 – *BT/AT&T*, paragraphs 207–214); Commission Decision of 22 December 2000 (COMP/M.2243 – *Stora Enso/Assidoman/JV*, paragraphs 49, 56 and 57).

Commentary
para 13: **B&C:** 8.274

14. For concentrations which are carried out in stages, the contractual arrangements relating to the stages before the establishment of control within the meaning of Article 3(1) and (2) of the Merger Regulation cannot normally be considered directly related and necessary to the implementation of the concentration. However, an agreement to abstain from material changes in the target's business until completion is considered directly related and necessary to the implementation of the joint bid.[1] The same applies, in the context of a joint bid, to an agreement by the joint purchasers of an undertaking to abstain from making separate competing offers for the same undertaking, or otherwise acquiring control.

Notes

[1] Commission Decision of 27 July 1998 (IV/M.1226 – *GEC/GPTH*, paragraph 22); Commission Decision of 2 October 1997 (IV/M.984 – *Dupont/ICI*, paragraph 55); Commission Decision of 19 December 1997 (IV/M.1057 – *Terra Industries/ ICI*, paragraph 16); Commission Decision of 18 December 1996 (IV/M.861 – *Textron/Kautex*, paragraphs 19 and 22); Commission Decision of 7 August 1996 (IV/M.727 – *BP/Mobil*, paragraph 50).

Commentary
para 14: **B&C:** 8.127, 8.274

15. Agreements which serve to facilitate the joint acquisition of control are to be considered directly related and necessary to the implementation of the concentration. This will apply to arrangements between the parties for the joint acquisition of control aimed at implementing the division of assets in order to divide the production facilities or distribution networks among themselves, together with the existing trademarks of the undertaking acquired jointly.

Commentary
para 15: **B&C:** 8.274

16. To the extent that such a division involves the break-up of a pre-existing economic entity, arrangements that make the break-up possible under reasonable conditions are to be considered directly related and necessary to the implementation of the concentration, under the principles set out below.

Commentary
para 16: **B&C:** 8.274

III. Principles Applicable to Commonly Encountered Restrictions in Cases of Acquisition of an Undertaking

17. Restrictions agreed between the parties in the context of a transfer of an undertaking may be to the benefit of the purchaser or of the vendor. In general terms, the need for the purchaser to

Part D Mergers and Concentrations

benefit from certain protection is more compelling than the corresponding need for the vendor. It is the purchaser who needs to be assured that she/he will be able to acquire the full value of the acquired business. Thus, as a general rule, restrictions which benefit the vendor are either not directly related and necessary to the implementation of the concentration at all,[1] or their scope and/or duration need to be more limited than that of clauses which benefit the purchaser.[2]

Notes

[1] Commission Decision of 27 July 1998 (IV/M.1226 – *GEC/GPTH*, paragraph 24).

[2] See, for example, for a clause aiming at the protection of a part of the business remaining with the vendor: Commission Decision of 30 August 1993 (IV/M.319 – *BHF/CCF/Charterhouse*, paragraph 16).

A. Non-competition clauses

18. Non-competition obligations which are imposed on the vendor in the context of the transfer of an undertaking or of part of it can be directly related and necessary to the implementation of the concentration. In order to obtain the full value of the assets transferred, the purchaser must be able to benefit from some protection against competition from the vendor in order to gain the loyalty of customers and to assimilate and exploit the know-how. Such non-competition clauses guarantee the transfer to the purchaser of the full value of the assets transferred, which in general include both physical assets and intangible assets, such as the goodwill accumulated or the know-how[1] developed by the vendor. These are not only directly related to the concentration but are also necessary to its implementation because, without them, there would be reasonable grounds to expect that the sale of the undertaking or of part of it could not be accomplished.

Notes

[1] As defined in Article 1(1)(i) of Regulation (EC) No 772/2004.

19. However, such non-competition clauses are only justified by the legitimate objective of implementing the concentration when their duration, their geographical field of application, their subject matter and the persons subject to them do not exceed what is reasonably necessary to achieve that end.[1]

Notes

[1] See European Court of Justice, Case 42/84 (*Remia*), [1985] ECR 2545, paragraph 20; Court of First Instance, Case T-112/99 (*Métropole télévision – M6*), [2001] ECR II-2459, paragraph 106.

20. Non-competition clauses are justified for periods of up to three years,[1] when the transfer of the undertaking includes the transfer of customer loyalty in the form of both goodwill and know-how.[2] When only goodwill is included, they are justified for periods of up to two years.[3]

Notes

[1] See for exceptional cases in which longer periods may be justified, e.g. Commission Decision of 1 September 2000 (COMP/M.1980 – *Volvo/Renault V.I.*, paragraph 56); Commission Decision of 27 July 1995 (IV/M.612 – *RWE-DEA/Enichem Augusta*, paragraph 37); Commission decision of 23 October 1998 (IV/M.1298 – *Kodak/Imation*, paragraph 74).

[2] Commission Decision of 2 April 1998 (IV/M.1127 – *Nestlé/Dalgety*, paragraph 33); Commission Decision of 1 September 2000 (COMP/M.2077 – *Clayton Dubilier & Rice/Iteltel*, paragraph 15); Commission Decision of 2 March 2001 (COMP/M.2305 – *Vodafone Group PLC/EIRCELL*, paragraphs 21 and 22).

[3] Commission Decision of 12 April 1999 (IV/M.1482 – *KingFisher/Grosslabor*, paragraph 26); Commission Decision of 14 December 1997 (IV/M.884 – *KNP BT/Bunzl/Wilhelm Seiler*, paragraph 17).

Commentary

para 20: B&C: 8.276

21. By contrast, non-competition clauses cannot be considered necessary when the transfer is in fact limited to physical assets (such as land, buildings or machinery) or to exclusive industrial and commercial property rights (the holders of which could immediately take action against infringements by the transferor of such rights).

Commentary
para 21: B&C: 8.276

22. The geographical scope of a non-competition clause must be limited to the area in which the vendor has offered the relevant products or services before the transfer, since the purchaser does not need to be protected against competition from the vendor in territories not previously penetrated by the vendor.[1] That geographical scope can be extended to territories which the vendor was planning to enter at the time of the transaction, provided that he had already invested in preparing this move.

Notes

[1] Commission Decision of 14 December 1997 (IV/M.884 – *KNP BT/Bunzl/Wilhelm Seiler*, paragraph 17); Commission Decision of 12 April 1999 (IV/M.1482 – *KingFisher/Grosslabor*, paragraph 27); Commission Decision of 6 April 2001 (COMP/M.2355 – *Dow/Enichem Polyurethane*, paragraph 28); Commission Decision of 4 August 2000 (COMP/M.1979 – *CDC/Banco Urquijo/JV*, paragraph 18).

23. Similarly, non-competition clauses must remain limited to products (including improved versions or updates of products as well as successor models) and services forming the economic activity of the undertaking transferred. This can include products and services at an advanced stage of development at the time of the transaction, or products which are fully developed but not yet marketed. Protection against competition from the vendor in product or service markets in which the transferred undertaking was not active before the transfer is not considered necessary.[1]

Notes

[1] Commission Decision of 14 December 1997 (IV/M.884 – *KNP BT/Bunzl/Wilhelm Seiler*, paragraph 17); Commission Decision of 2 March 2001 (COMP/M.2305 – *Vodafone Group PLC/EIRCELL*, paragraph 22); Commission Decision of 6 April 2001 (COMP/M.2355 – *Dow/Enichem Polyurethane*, paragraph 28); Commission Decision of 4 August 2000 (COMP/M.1979 – *CDC/Banco Urquijo/JV*, paragraph 18).

24. The vendor may bind herself/himself, her/his subsidiaries and commercial agents. However, an obligation to impose similar restrictions on others would not be regarded as directly related and necessary to the implementation of the concentration. This applies, in particular, to clauses which would restrict the freedom of resellers or users to import or export.

25. Clauses which limit the vendor's right to purchase or hold shares in a company competing with the business transferred shall be considered directly related and necessary to the implementation of the concentration under the same conditions as outlined above for non-competition clauses, unless they prevent the vendor from purchasing or holding shares purely for financial investment purposes, without granting him/her, directly or indirectly, management functions or any material influence in the competing company.[1]

Notes

[1] Commission Decision of 4 February 1993 (IV/M.301 – *Tesco/Catteau*, paragraph 14); Commission Decision of 14 December 1997 (IV/M.884 – *KNP BT/Bunzl/Wilhelm Seiler*, paragraph 19); Commission Decision of 12 April 1999 (IV/M.1482 – *Kingfisher/Grosslabor*, paragraph 27); Commission Decision of 6 April 2000 (COMP/M.1832 – *Ahold/ICA Förbundet/Canica*, paragraph 26).

26. Non-solicitation and confidentiality clauses have a comparable effect and are therefore evaluated in a similar way to non-competition clauses.[1]

Notes

[1] Accordingly, confidentiality clauses on customer details, prices and quantities cannot be extended. By contrast, confidentiality clauses concerning technical know-how may exceptionally be justified for longer periods, see Commission Decision of 29 April 1998 (IV/M.1167 – *ICI/Williams*, paragraph 22); Commission Decision of 30 April 1992 (IV/M.197 – *Solvay-Laporte/Interox*, paragraph 50).

B. Licence agreements

27. The transfer of an undertaking or of part of it can include the transfer to the purchaser, with a view to the full exploitation of the assets transferred, of intellectual property rights or know-how. However, the vendor may remain the owner of the rights in order to exploit them for activities

other than those transferred. In these cases, the usual means for ensuring that the purchaser will have the full use of the assets transferred is to conclude licensing agreements in his/her favour. Likewise, where the vendor has transferred intellectual property rights with the business, she/he may still want to continue using some or all of these rights for activities other than those transferred; in such a case the purchaser will grant a licence to the vendor.

Commentary
para 27: B&C: 8.277

28. Licences of patents,[1] of similar rights, or of know-how,[2] can be considered necessary to the implementation of the concentration. They may equally be considered an integral part of the concentration and, in any event, need not be limited in time. These licences can be simple or exclusive and may be limited to certain fields of use, to the extent that they correspond to the activities of the undertaking transferred.

Notes

[1] Including patent applications, utility models, applications for registration of utility models, designs, topographies of semiconductor products, supplementary protection certificates for medicinal products or other products for which such supplementary protection certificates may be obtained and plant breeder's certificates (as referred to in Article 1(1)(h) of Regulation (EC) No 772/2004).
[2] As defined in Article 1(1)(i) of Regulation (EC) No 772/2004.

29. However, territorial limitations on manufacture reflecting the territory of the transferred activity are not necessary to the implementation of the operation. As regards licences granted by the seller of a business to the buyer, the seller can be made subject to territorial restrictions in the licence agreement under the same conditions as laid down for non-competition clauses in the context of the sale of a business.

30. Restrictions in licence agreements going beyond the above provisions, such as those which protect the licensor rather than the licensee, are not necessary to the implementation of the concentration.[1]

Notes

[1] To the extent that they fall within Article [101(1) TFEU], such agreements may nevertheless fall under Regulation (EC) No 772/2004, or other Community legislation.

Commentary
para 30: B&C: 8.277

31. Similarly, in the case of licences of trademarks, business names, design rights, copyrights or similar rights, there may be situations in which the vendor wishes to remain the owner of such rights in relation to activities retained, but the purchaser needs those rights in order to market the goods or services produced by the undertaking or part of the undertaking transferred. Here, the same considerations as above apply.[1]

Notes

[1] Commission Decision of 1 September 2000 (COMP/M.1980 – *Volvo/Renault V.I.*, paragraph 54).

C. Purchase and supply obligations

32. In many cases, the transfer of an undertaking or of part of it can entail the disruption of traditional lines of purchase and supply which have existed as a result of the previous integration of activities within the economic unity of the vendor. In order to enable the break-up of the economic unity of the vendor and the partial transfer of the assets to the purchaser under reasonable conditions, it is often necessary to maintain, for a transitional period, the existing or similar links between the vendor and the purchaser. This objective is normally attained by purchase and supply obligations for the vendor and/or the purchaser of the undertaking or of part of it. Taking into account the particular situation resulting from the break-up of the economic unity of the vendor, such obligations can be recognised as directly related and necessary to the implementation of the

concentration. They may be in favour of the vendor as well as the purchaser, depending on the particular circumstances of the case.

Commentary
para 32: B&C: 8.278

33. The aim of such obligations may be to ensure the continuity of supply to either of the parties of products necessary for carrying out the activities retained by the vendor or taken over by the purchaser. However, the duration of purchase and supply obligations must be limited to a period necessary for the replacement of the relationship of dependency by autonomy in the market. Thus, purchase or supply obligations aimed at guaranteeing the quantities previously supplied can be justified for a transitional period of up to five years.[1]

Notes

[1] Commission Decision of 5 February 1996 (IV/M.651 – *AT&T/Philips*, VII.); Commission Decision of 30 March 1999 (IV/JV.15 – *BT/AT&T*, paragraph 209); see for exceptional cases Commission Decision of 13 March 1995 (IV/M.550 – *Union Carbide/Enichem*, paragraph 99); Commission Decision of 27 July 1995 (IV/M.612 – *RWE-DEA/Enichem Augusta*, paragraph 45).

34. Both supply and purchase obligations providing for fixed quantities, possibly with a variation clause, are recognised as directly related and necessary to the implementation of the concentration. However, obligations providing for unlimited quantities,[1] exclusivity or conferring preferred-supplier or preferred-purchaser status,[2] are not necessary to the implementation of the concentration.

Notes

[1] In line with the principle of proportionality, obligations providing for fixed quantities with a variation clause are, in these cases, less restrictive on competition, see, e.g. Commission Decision of 18 September 1998 (IV/M.1292 – *Continental/ ITT*, paragraph 19).
[2] Commission Decision of 30 July 1998 (IV/M.1245 – *VALEO/ITT Industries*, paragraph 64); see for exceptional cases (e.g. absence of a market) Commission Decision of 13 March 1995 (IV/M.550 – *Union Carbide/Enichem*, paragraphs 92 to 96); Commission Decision of 27 July 1995 (IV/M.612 – *RWE-DEA/Enichem Augusta*, paragraphs 38 et seq.).

35. Service and distribution agreements are equivalent in their effect to supply arrangements; consequently the same considerations as above shall apply.

IV. Principles Applicable to Commonly Encountered Restrictions in Cases of Joint Ventures within the Meaning of Article 3(4) of the Merger Regulation

A. Non-competition obligations

36. A non-competition obligation between the parent undertakings and a joint venture may be considered directly related and necessary to the implementation of the concentration where such obligations correspond to the products, services and territories covered by the joint venture agreement or its bylaws. Such non-competition clauses reflect, *inter alia*, the need to ensure good faith during negotiations; they may also reflect the need to fully utilise the joint venture's assets or to enable the joint venture to assimilate know-how and goodwill provided by its parents; or the need to protect the parents' interests in the joint venture against competitive acts facilitated, *inter alia*, by the parents' privileged access to the know-how and goodwill transferred to or developed by the joint venture. Such non-competition obligations between the parent undertakings and a joint venture can be regarded as directly related and necessary to the implementation of the concentration for the lifetime of the joint venture.[1]

Notes

[1] Commission Decision of 15 January 1998 (IV/M.1042 – *Eastman Kodak/Sun Chemical*, paragraph 40); Commission Decision of 7 August 1996 (IV/M.727 – *BP/Mobil*, paragraph 51); Commission Decision of 3 July 1996 (IV/M.751 – *Bayer/Hüls*, paragraph 31); Commission Decision of 6 April 2000 (COMP/M.1832 – *Ahold/ICA Förbundet/Canica*, paragraph 26).

Commentary
para 36: B&C: 8.280

37. The geographical scope of a non-competition clause must be limited to the area in which the parents offered the relevant products or services before establishing the joint venture.[1] That geographical scope can be extended to territories which the parent companies were planning to enter at the time of the transaction, provided that they had already invested in preparing this move.

Notes

[1] Commission Decision of 29 August 2000 (COMP/M.1913 – *Lufthansa/Menzies/LGS/JV*; paragraph 18); Commission Decision of 22 December 2000 (COMP/M.2243 – *Stora Enso/Assidoman/JV*, paragraph 49, last sentence).

38. Similarly, non-competition clauses must be limited to products and services constituting the economic activity of the joint venture. This may include products and services at an advanced stage of development at the time of the transaction, as well as products and services which are fully developed but not yet marketed.

39. If the joint venture is set up to enter a new market, reference will be made to the products, services and territories in which it is to operate under the joint venture agreement or by-laws. However, the presumption is that one parent's interest in the joint venture does not need to be protected against competition from the other parent in markets other than those in which the joint venture will be active from the outset.

40. Additionally, non-competition obligations between non-controlling parents and a joint venture are not directly related and necessary to the implementation of the concentration.

41. The same principles as for non-competition clauses apply to non-solicitation and confidentiality clauses.

B. Licence agreements

42. A licence granted by the parent undertakings to the joint venture may be considered directly related and necessary to the implementation of the concentration. This applies regardless of whether or not the licence is an exclusive one and whether or not it is limited in time. The licence may be restricted to a particular field of use which corresponds to the activities of the joint venture.

Commentary
para 42: B&C: 8.281

43. Licences granted by the joint venture to one of its parents, or cross-licence agreements, can be regarded as directly related and necessary to the implementation of the concentration under the same conditions as in the case of the acquisition of an undertaking. Licence agreements between the parents are not considered directly related and necessary to the implementation of a joint venture.

Commentary
para 43: B&C: 8.281

C. Purchase and supply obligations

44. If the parent undertakings remain present in a market upstream or downstream of that of the joint venture, any purchase and supply agreements, including service and distribution agreements are subject to the principles applicable in the case of the transfer of an undertaking.

Commentary
para 44: B&C: 8.282

D9

COMMISSION NOTICE

on a simplified procedure for treatment of certain concentrations under
Council Regulation (EC) No 139/2004

(2005/C 56/04)

(Text with EEA relevance)

Official Journal C 56, 5.3.2005, p.32

Celex No: 52005XC0305(03)

EUR-Lex permanent link: <http://eur-lex.europa.eu/legal-content/EN/ALL/?uri=CELEX:52005X
C0305(03)&qid=1395771431899>

Commentary
Notice: **B&C**: 8.007, 8.122 **F&N**: 5.409, 5.507, 5.519
paras 6–11: **B&C**: 8.125
paras 15–18: **F&N**: 5.341

I. Introduction

1. This Notice sets out a simplified procedure under which the Commission intends to treat certain concentrations pursuant to Council Regulation (EC) No 139/2004 of 20 January 2004, on the control of concentrations between undertakings (the EC Merger Regulation)[1] on the basis that they do not raise competition concerns. This Notice replaces the Notice on a simplified procedure for treatment of certain concentrations under Council Regulation (EEC) No 4064/89.[2] The Commission's experience gained in applying Council Regulation (EEC) No 4064/89 of 21 December 1989 on the control of concentrations between undertakings[3] has shown that certain categories of notified concentrations are normally cleared without having raised any substantive doubts, provided that there were no special circumstances.

Notes

[1] OJ L 24, 29.1.2004, p.1.

[2] OJ C 217, 29.7.2000, p.32.

[3] OJ L 395, 30.12.1989, p.1; corrected version OJ L 257, 21.9.1990, p.13.

---

2. The purpose of this Notice is to set out the conditions under which the Commission usually adopts a short-form decision declaring a concentration compatible with the common market pursuant to the simplified procedure and to provide guidance in respect of the procedure itself. When all necessary conditions set forth at point 5 of this Notice are met and provided there are no special circumstances, the Commission adopts a short-form clearance decision within 25 working days from the date of notification, pursuant to Article 6(1)(b) of the EC Merger Regulation.[4]

Notes

[4] The notification requirements are set out in Annexes I and II to Commission Regulation (EC) No 802/2004 implementing Council Regulation (EC) No 139/2004 on the control of concentrations between undertakings.

---

3. However, if the safeguards or exclusions set forth at points 6 to 11 of this Notice are applicable, the Commission may launch an investigation and/or adopt a full decision under the EC Merger Regulation.

4. By following the procedure outlined in the following sections, the Commission aims to make Community merger control more focused and effective.

II. Categories of Concentrations Suitable for Treatment under the Simplified Procedure

Eligible concentrations

5. The Commission will apply the simplified procedure to the following categories of concentrations:

   (a) two or more undertakings acquire joint control of a joint venture, provided that the joint venture has no, or negligible, actual or foreseen activities within the territory of the European Economic Area (EEA). Such cases occur where:

      (i) the turnover[5] of the joint venture and/or the turnover of the contributed activities[6] is less than EUR 100 million in the EEA territory; and

      (ii) the total value of assets[7] transferred to the joint venture is less than EUR 100 million in the EEA territory;[8]

   (b) two or more undertakings merge, or one or more undertakings acquire sole or joint control of another undertaking, provided that none of the parties to the concentration are engaged in business activities in the same product and geographical market, or in a product market which is upstream or downstream of a product market in which any other party to the concentration is engaged;[9]

   (c) two or more undertakings merge, or one or more undertakings acquire sole or joint control of another undertaking and:

      (i) two or more of the parties to the concentration are engaged in business activities in the same product and geographical market (horizontal relationships) provided that their combined market share is less than 15%; or

      (ii) one or more of the parties to the concentration are engaged in business activities in a product market which is upstream or downstream of a product market in which any other party to the concentration is engaged (vertical relationships),[10] provided that none of their individual or combined market shares is at either level 25% or more;[11]

   (d) a party is to acquire sole control of an undertaking over which it already has joint control.

Notes

[5] The turnover of the joint venture should be determined according to the most recent audited accounts of the parent companies, or the joint venture itself, depending upon the availability of separate accounts for the resources combined in the joint venture.

[6] The expression "and/or" refers to the variety of situations covered; for example:

— in the case of a joint acquisition of a target company, the turnover to be taken into account is the turnover of this target (the joint venture),

— in the case of the creation of a joint venture to which the parent companies contribute their activities, the turnover to be taken into account is that of the contributed activities,

— in the case of entry of a new controlling party into an existing joint venture, the turnover of the joint venture and the turnover of the activities contributed by the new parent company (if any) must be taken into account.

[7] The total value of assets of the joint venture should be determined according to the last prepared and approved balance sheet of each parent company. The term "assets" includes: (1) all tangible and intangible assets that will be transferred to the joint venture (examples of tangible assets include production plants, wholesale or retail outlets, and inventory of goods; examples of intangible assets include intellectual property, goodwill, etc.), and (2) any amount of credit or any obligations of the joint venture which any parent company of the joint venture has agreed to extend or guarantee.

[8] Where the assets transferred generate turnover, then neither the value of the assets nor that of the turnover may exceed EUR 100 million.

[9] See Commission Notice on the definition of relevant market for the purposes of Community competition law (OJ C 372, 9.12.1997, p.5).

[10] See footnote 6.

[11] This means that only concentrations, which do not lead to affected markets, as defined in Section 6 III of Form CO, fall into this category. The thresholds for horizontal and vertical relationships apply to market shares both at national and at EEA levels and to any plausible alternative product market definition that may have to be considered in a given case. It is important that the underlying market definitions set out in the notification are precise enough to justify the assessment that these thresholds are not met, and that all plausible alternative market definitions are mentioned (including geographic markets narrower than national).

Commentary

para 5: B&C: 8.123 **F&N:** 5.510

para 5(a): **F&N:** 5.513
para 5(b): **F&N:** 5.514, 5.516, 5.521
para 5(c): **F&N:** 5.515, 5.516, 5.521
para 5(d): **F&N:** 5.99, 5.517

Safeguards and exclusions

6. In assessing whether a concentration falls into one of the categories referred to in point 5, the Commission will ensure that all relevant circumstances are established with sufficient clarity. Given that market definitions are likely to be a key element in this assessment, the parties should provide information on all plausible alternative market definitions during the pre-notification phase (see point 15). Notifying parties are responsible for describing all alternative relevant product and geographic markets on which the notified concentration could have an impact and for providing data and information relating to the definition of such markets.[12] The Commission retains the discretion to take the ultimate decision on market definition, basing its decision on an analysis of the facts of the case. Where it is difficult to define the relevant markets or to determine the parties' market shares, the Commission will not apply the simplified procedure. In addition, to the extent that concentrations involve novel legal issues of a general interest, the Commission would normally abstain from adopting short-form decisions, and would normally revert to a normal first phase merger procedure.

Notes

[12] As with all other notifications, the Commission may revoke the short-form decision if it is based on incorrect information for which one of the undertakings concerned is responsible (Article 6(3)(a), of the EC Merger Regulation).

7. While it can normally be assumed that concentrations falling into the categories referred to in point 5 will not raise serious doubts as to their compatibility with the common market, there may nonetheless be certain situations, which exceptionally require a closer investigation and/or a full decision. In such cases, the Commission may revert to a normal first phase merger procedure.

8. The following are indicative examples of types of cases which may be excluded from the simplified procedure. Certain types of concentrations may increase the parties' market power, for instance by combining technological, financial or other resources, even if the parties to the concentration do not operate in the same market. Concentrations where at least two parties to the concentration are present in closely related neighbouring markets[13] may also be unsuitable for the simplified procedure, in particular, where one or more of the parties to the concentration holds individually a market share of 25% or more in any product market in which there is no horizontal or vertical relationship between the parties but which is a neighbouring market to a market where another party is active. In other cases, it may not be possible to determine the parties' precise market shares. This is often the case when the parties operate in new or little developed markets. Concentrations in markets with high entry barriers, with a high degree of concentration[14] or other known competition problems may also be unsuitable.

Notes

[13] Product markets are closely related neighbouring markets when the products are complementary to each other or when they belong to a range of products that is generally purchased by the same set of customers for the same end use.
[14] See Guidelines on the assessment of horizontal mergers under the Council Regulation on the control of concentrations between undertakings OJ C 31, 5.2.2004, p.5, points 14–21.

Commentary
para 8: **F&N:** 5.516, 5.518

9. The Commission's experience to date has shown that a change from joint to sole control may exceptionally require closer investigation and/or a full decision. A particular competition concern could arise in circumstances where the former joint venture is integrated into the group or network of its remaining single controlling shareholder, whereby the disciplining constraints exercised by the potentially diverging incentives of the different controlling shareholders are removed and its strategic market position could be strengthened. For example, in a scenario in which undertaking

A and undertaking B jointly control a joint venture C, a concentration pursuant to which A acquires sole control of C may give rise to competition concerns in circumstances in which C is a direct competitor of A and where C and A will hold a substantial combined market position and where this removes a degree of independence previously held by C.[15] In cases where such scenarios require a closer analysis, the Commission may revert to a normal first phase merger procedure.[16]

Notes

[15] Case No. IV/M.1328 *KLM/Martinair*, XXIXth Report on Competition Policy 1999 – SEC(2000) 720 final, points 165–166.

[16] Case No COMP/M.2908 *Deutsche Post/DHL (II)*, Decision of 18.9.2002.

10. The Commission may also revert to a normal first phase merger procedure where neither the Commission nor the competent authorities of Member States have reviewed the prior acquisition of joint control of the joint venture in question.

11. Furthermore, the Commission may revert to a normal first phase merger procedure where an issue of coordination as referred to in Article 2(4) of the EC Merger Regulation arises.

Commentary
para 11: F&N: 5.516

12. If a Member State expresses substantiated concerns about the notified concentration within 15 working days of receipt of the copy of the notification, or if a third party expresses substantiated concerns within the time-limit laid down for such comments, the Commission will adopt a full decision. The time-limits set out in Article 10(1) of the EC Merger Regulation apply.

Commentary
para 12: B&C: 8.125

Referral requests

13. The simplified procedure will not be applied if a Member State requests the referral of a notified concentration pursuant to Article 9 of the EC Merger Regulation or if the Commission accepts a request from one or more Member States for referral of a notified concentration pursuant to Article 22 of the EC Merger Regulation.

Commentary
para 13: B&C: 8.125

Pre-notification referrals at the request of the notifying parties

14. Subject to the safeguards and exclusions set out in this Notice, the Commission may apply the simplified procedure to concentrations where:
    (i) following a reasoned submission pursuant to Article 4(4) of the EC Merger Regulation, the Commission decides not to refer the case to a Member State; or
    (ii) following a reasoned submission pursuant to Article 4(5) of the EC Merger Regulation the case is referred to the Commission.

III. PROCEDURAL PROVISIONS

Pre-notification contacts

15. The Commission has found pre-notification contacts between notifying parties and the Commission beneficial even in seemingly unproblematic cases.[17] The Commission's experience of the simplified procedure has shown that candidate cases for the simplified procedure may raise complex issues for instance, of market definition (see point 6) which should preferably be resolved prior to notification. Such contacts allow the Commission and the notifying parties to determine the precise amount of information to be provided in a notification. Pre-notification contacts should be initiated at least two weeks prior to the expected date of notification.

Notifying parties are therefore advised to engage in pre-notification contacts, particularly where they request the Commission to waive full-form notification in accordance with Article 3(1) of Commission Regulation (EC) No 802/2004 of 7 April 2004 implementing Council Regulation (EC) No 139/ 2004 on the control of concentrations between undertakings[18] on the grounds that the operation to be notified will not raise competition concerns.

Notes

[17] See DG Competition Best Practices on the conduct of EC merger control proceedings available at: <http://europa. eu.int/comm/competition/mergers/legislation/regulation/best_practices.pdf>.

[18] OJ L 133, 30.4.2004, p.1.

Commentary
para 15: **B&C:** 8.110

Publication of the fact of notification

16. The information to be published in the *Official Journal of the European Union* upon receipt of a notification[19] will include the names of the parties to the concentration, their country of origin, the nature of the concentration and the economic sectors involved, as well as an indication that, on the basis of the information provided by the notifying party, the concentration may qualify for a simplified procedure. Interested parties will then have the opportunity to submit observations, in particular on circumstances which might require an investigation.

Notes

[19] Article 4(3) of the EC Merger Regulation.

Short-form decision

17. If the Commission is satisfied that the concentration fulfils the criteria for the simplified procedure (see point 5), it will normally issue a short-form decision. This includes appropriate cases not giving rise to any competition concerns where it receives a full form notification. The concentration will thus be declared compatible with the common market, within 25 working days from the date of notification, pursuant to Article 10(1) and (6) of the EC Merger Regulation. The Commission will endeavour to issue a short-form decision as soon as practicable following expiry of the 15 working day period during which Member States may request referral of a notified concentration pursuant to Article 9 of the EC Merger Regulation. However, in the period leading up to the 25 working day deadline, the option of reverting to a normal first phase merger procedure and thus launching investigations and/or adopting a full decision remains open to the Commission, should it judge such action appropriate in the case in question.

Commentary
para 17: **B&C:** 8.122

Publication of the short-form decision

18. The Commission will publish a notice of the fact of the decision in the *Official Journal of the European Union* as it does for full clearance decisions. The public version of the decision will be made available on DG Competition's Internet website for a limited period. The short-form decision will contain the information about the notified concentration published in the Official Journal at the time of notification (names of the parties, their country of origin, nature of the concentration and economic sectors concerned) and a statement that the concentration is declared compatible with the common market because it falls within one or more of the categories described in this Notice, with the applicable category(ies) being explicitly identified.

Commentary
para 18: **B&C:** 8.122

IV. Ancillary Restrictions

19. The simplified procedure is not suited to cases in which the undertakings concerned request an express assessment of restrictions which are directly related to, and necessary for, the implementation of the concentration.

D10

COMMUNICATION FROM THE COMMISSION

Communication pursuant to Article 3(2) of Commission Regulation (EC) No 802/2004[1] implementing Council Regulation (EC) No 139/2004[2] on the control of concentrations between undertakings.

(2006/C 251/02)

(Text with EEA relevance)

Official Journal C 251, 17.10.2006, p.2

Celex No: 52006XC1017(01)

EUR-Lex permanent link: <http://eur-lex.europa.eu/legal-content/EN/ALL/?uri=CELEX:52006XC1017(01)&qid=1395771517216>

Notes

[1] OJ L 133, 30.4.2004, pp.1–39.
[2] OJ L 24, 29.1.2004, pp.1–22.

Commentary
Communication: B&C: 8.118

Introduction

The Commission hereby lays down, pursuant to Article 3(2) of Commission Regulation (EC) No 802/2004,[3] the format in which notifications and reasoned submissions should be delivered. Article 3(2) of Regulation 802/2004 requires notifications and reasoned submissions to be delivered in one original and 35 copies.

Notes

[3] Article 3(2) should be read together with Article 6(2) of Commission Regulation (EC) No 802/2004.

Notifications: Form CO and Short Form CO (Annexes I and II to Commission Regulation (EC) No 802/2004)

1) One signed original on paper.
2) Five paper copies of the entire Form CO or Short Form CO and its annexes ("notification").
3) Thirty copies of the notification in CD- or DVD-ROM format (the "medium"). The following specifications shall be adhered to:
   a) The files comprising the notification in this medium shall be in Portable Document Format (*.pdf) and should preferably not exceed 5 MB (mega-bytes) each in size. The copy of the notification may be contained on several CD- or DVD-ROMs. Documents which were originally produced in *.doc, *.xls and *.ppt format shall also be saved in this format in the same medium.

b) Files should be named in a way which allows easy identification of the section in the Form CO or Short Form CO they refer to.

c) A list of all files in the medium shall be delivered as a separate file in the medium.

d) Each file shall bear the number and name of the proceeding for which the notification is submitted.

Reasoned submissions:[4]— Form RS (Annex III to Commission Regulation (EC) No 802/2004)

1) One signed original on paper.

2) Five paper copies of the entire Form RS and its annexes ("Reasoned submission")

3) One CD- or DVD-ROM (the "medium") which contains the complete reasoned submission. The following specifications shall be adhered to:

a) The files comprising the reasoned submission in this medium shall be in Portable Document Format (*.pdf) and may not exceed 1 MB (mega-byte) each in size. Documents which were originally produced in *.doc, *.xls and *.ppt format shall also be saved in this format in the same medium.

b) Files should be named in a way which allows easy identification of the section in the Form RS they refer to.

c) A list of files in the medium shall be delivered as a separate file in the medium itself.

d) Each file shall bear the number and name of the proceeding for which the Reasoned submission is made.

4) If the files on the CD- or DVD-ROM cannot be kept under 1MB (mega-byte) each in size and/ or if the total size of the files on the CD- or DVD-ROM exceeds 5MB, the instructions for submitting Form CO should be followed instead, i.e. 30 copies in CD- or DVD-ROM format should be submitted.

Notes

4 Reasoned submissions within the meaning of Article 4(4) and 4(5) of Council Regulation (EC) No 139/2004.

Date of Applicability of this Communication

The instructions contained in this communication shall be applicable 20 days following the date of publication of this communication in the *Official Journal of the European Union*.

Notes

Date of applicability: 6 November 2006.

D11

COMMISSION CONSOLIDATED JURISDICTIONAL NOTICE

Under Council Regulation (EC) No 139/2004
on the control of concentrations between undertakings

(2008/C 95/01)

Official Journal C 95, 16.4.2008, p.1

Celex No: 52008XC0416(08)

EUR-Lex permanent link: <http://eur-lex.europa.eu/legal-content/EN/ALL/?uri=CELEX:52008X C0416(08)&qid=1395771668947>

Commentary

Notice: B&C: 6.005, 8.007, 8.042 F&N: 5.36, 11.71

paras 11–35: F&N: 5.37

paras 15–20: F&N: 5.91

paras 24–27: F&N: 5.62

paras 25–27: B&C: 8.027

paras 29–35: F&N: 5.69

paras 30–33: B&C: 8.047

paras 36–50: F&N: 5.37

paras 38–40: B&C: 8.047

paras 44–47: B&C: 8.044

paras 48–50: B&C: 8.065

paras 52–53: F&N: 5.37

paras 54–90: F&N: 5.37

paras 55–58: B&C: 8.028

paras 65–67: F&N: 5.90

paras 69–72: F&N: 5.91

paras 69–73: B&C: 8.037

paras 74–80: F&N: 5.93

paras 83–90: B&C: 8.040 F&N: 5.99

paras 85–90: B&C: 8.043 F&N: 5.115

paras 91–109: B&C: 8.054 F&N: 5.37, 7.254

paras 98–100: B&C: 8.057 F&N: 5.135

paras 104–109: F&N: 5.142

paras 106–108: B&C: 8.060 F&N: 5.118

paras 110–116: F&N: 5.37, 5.110

paras 117–121: F&N: 5.529

paras 117–123: F&N: 5.37

paras 122–123: B&C: 8.140

paras 124–128: F&N: 5.37

paras 129–153: B&C: 8.070 F&N: 5.37

paras 133–137: B&C: 8.070

paras 139–141: B&C: 8.070

paras 142–144: F&N: 5.169

paras 145–147: F&N: 5.169

paras 148–150: B&C: 8.072 F&N: 5.169, 5.183

paras 154–156: B&C: 8.111 F&N: 5.204

paras 157–160: F&N: 5.187

paras 157–220: F&N: 5.37

paras 158–160: B&C: 8.063

paras 161–163: F&N: 5.185

paras 169–171: F&N: 5.205

paras 169–174: B&C: 8.064

paras 172–174: F&N: 5.206

paras 176–184: B&C: 8.076

paras 179–181: F&N: 5.192

paras 189–191: B&C: 8.019 F&N: 5.195

A. Introduction

1. The purpose of this Notice is to provide guidance as to jurisdictional issues under Council Regulation (EC) No 139/2004, OJ L 24, 29.1.2003, page 1 (the "Merger Regulation").[1] This formal guidance should enable firms to establish more quickly, in advance of any contact with the Commission, whether and to what extent their operations may be covered by Community control of concentrations.

Notes

[1] Where it is necessary in this Notice to distinguish between Regulation 139/2004 and Council Regulation (EEC) No 4064/89 (OJ L 395, 30.12.1989, corrected version in OJ L 257, 21.9.1990, p.13, Regulation last amended by Regulation (EC) No 1310/97, OJ L 180, 9.7.1997, p.1, corrigendum in OJ L 40, 13.2.1998, p.17), the former will be referred to as the "recast Merger Regulation" whereas the latter will be referred to as the "former Merger Regulation". Articles without reference refer to the recast Merger Regulation.

2. This Notice replaces the Notice on the concept of concentration,[2] the Notice on the concept of full-function joint ventures,[3] the Notice on the concept of undertakings concerned[4] and the Notice on calculation of turnover.[5]

Notes

[2] OJ C 66, 02.03.1998, p.5.
[3] OJ C 66, 02.03.1998, p.1.
[4] OJ C 66, 02.03.1998, p.14.
[5] OJ C 66, 02.03.1998, p.25.

3. This Notice deals with the concepts of a concentration and of a full-function joint venture, undertakings concerned and the calculation of turnover as set out in Articles 1, 3 and 5 of the Merger Regulation. Issues concerning referrals are dealt with in the Notice on referrals.[6] The Commission's interpretation of Articles 1, 3 and 5 in the present Notice is without prejudice to the interpretation which may be given by the Court of Justice or by the Court of First Instance of the European Communities.

Notes

[6] OJ C 56, 05.03.2005, p.2.

4. The guidance set out in this Notice reflects the Commission's experience in applying the recast Merger Regulation and the former Merger Regulation since the latter entered into force on 21 September 1990. The general principles governing the issues dealt with in this Notice have not been changed by the entry into force of Regulation (EC) No 139/2004, but where changes have occurred, the Notice deals with them explicitly. The principles contained in the Notice will be applied and further developed by the Commission in individual cases.

5. According to Article 1, the Merger Regulation only applies to operations that satisfy two conditions. First, there must be a concentration of two or more undertakings within the meaning of Article 3 of the Merger Regulation. Secondly, the turnover of the undertakings concerned, calculated in accordance with Article 5, must satisfy the thresholds set out in Article 1 of the Regulation. The notion of a concentration (including the particular requirements for joint ventures), as the first condition, is dealt with under Part B; the identification of undertakings concerned and the calculation of their turnover as relevant for the second condition are dealt with under Part C.

Commentary

para 5: F&N: 5.32

6. The Commission addresses the question of its jurisdiction over a concentration in decisions according to Article 6 of the Merger Regulation.[7]

Notes

[7] See also opinion of AG Kokott in Case C-202/06, *Cementbouw v Commission* of 26 April 2007, paragraph 56 (not yet reported) [now [2007] ECR II-2129].

Commentary

para 6: F&N: 5.40

B. The Concept of Concentration

7. According to Article 3(1) of the Merger Regulation, a concentration only covers operations where a change of control in the undertakings concerned occurs on a lasting basis. Recital 20 in the preamble to the Merger Regulation further explains that the concept of concentration is intended to relate to operations which bring about a lasting change in the structure of the market. Because the test in Article 3 is centred on the concept of control, the existence of a concentration is to a great extent determined by qualitative rather than quantitative criteria.

Commentary

para 7: B&C: 8.014, 8.022 F&N: 5.33, 5.37, 5.51

8. Article 3(1) of the Merger Regulation defines two categories of concentrations: – those arising from a merger between previously independent undertakings (point (a)); –those arising from an acquisition of control (point (b)). These are treated respectively in Sections I and II below.

Commentary

para 8: B&C: 7.014 F&N: 5.33, 5.37, 5.154

I. Mergers between Previously Independent Undertakings

9. A merger within the meaning of Article 3(1)(a) of the Merger Regulation occurs when two or more independent undertakings amalgamate into a new undertaking and cease to exist as separate legal entities. A merger may also occur when an undertaking is absorbed by another, the latter retaining its legal identity while the former ceases to exist as a legal entity.[8]

Notes

[8] See, for example, Case COMP/M.1673 – *Veba/VIAG* of 13 June 2000; Case COMP/M.1806 – *AstraZeneca/Novartis* of 26 July 2000; Case COMP/M.2208 – *Chevron/Texaco* of 26 January 2001; and Case IV/M.1383 – *Exxon/Mobil* of 29 September 1999. A merger in the meaning of Article 3(1)(a) is not deemed to occur if a target company is merged with a subsidiary of the acquiring company to the effect that the parent company acquires control of the target undertaking under Article 3(1)(b), see Case COMP/M.2510 – *Cendant/Galileo* of 24 September 2001.

Commentary

para 9: B&C: 8.020 F&N: 5.37, 5.44

10. A merger within the meaning of Article 3(1)(a) may also occur where, in the absence of a legal merger, the combining of the activities of previously independent undertakings results in the creation of a single economic unit.[9] This may arise in particular where two or more undertakings, while retaining their individual legal personalities, establish contractually a common economic management[10] or the structure of a dual listed company.[11] If this leads to a *de facto* amalgamation of the undertakings concerned into a single economic unit, the operation is considered to be a merger. A prerequisite for the determination of such a *de facto* merger is the existence of a permanent, single economic management. Other relevant factors may include internal profit and loss

compensation or a revenue distribution as between the various entities within the group, and their joint liability or external risk sharing. The *de facto* amalgamation may be solely based on contractual arrangements,[12] but it can also be reinforced by cross-shareholdings between the undertakings forming the economic unit.

Notes

9 In determining the previous independence of undertakings, the issue of control may be relevant as the merger might otherwise only be an internal restructuring within the group. In this specific context, the assessment of control also follows the general concept set out below and includes *de jure* as well as *de facto* control.

10 This could apply for example in the case of a "Gleichordnungskonzern" in German law, certain "Groupements d'Intérêt Economique" in French law, and the amalgamation of partnerships, as in Case IV/M.1016 – *Price Waterhouse/Coopers&Lybrand* of 20 May 1998.

11 Case IV/M.660 – *RTZ/CRA* of 7 December 1995; Case COMP/M.3071 – *Carnival Corporation/P&O Princess II* of 24 July 2002.

12 See Case IV/M.1016 – *Price Waterhouse/Coopers&Lybrand* of 20 May 1998; Case COMP/M.2824 – *Ernst & Young/Andersen Germany* of 27 August 2002.

Commentary
para 10: **B&C:** 8.021 **F&N:** 5.37, 5.44, 5.155

II. Acquisition of Control

1. Concept of control

1.1. Person or undertaking acquiring control

11. Article 3(1)(b) provides that a concentration occurs in the case of an acquisition of control. Such control may be acquired by one undertaking acting alone or by several undertakings acting jointly.

Person controlling another undertaking

12. Control may also be acquired by a person in circumstances where that person already controls (whether solely or jointly) at least one other undertaking or, alternatively, by a combination of persons (which control another undertaking) and undertakings. The term "person" in this context extends to public bodies[13] and private entities, as well as natural persons. Acquisitions of control by natural persons are only considered to bring about a lasting change in the structure of the undertakings concerned if those natural persons carry out further economic activities on their own account or if they control at least one other undertaking.[14]

Notes

13 Including the State itself, e.g. Case IV/M.157 – *Air France/Sabena*, of 5 October 1992 in relation to the Belgian State, or other public bodies such as the Treuhandanstalt in Case IV/M.308 – *Kali und Salz/MDK/Treuhand*, of 14 December 1993. See, however, recital 22 of the Merger Regulation.

14 Case IV/M.82 – *Asko/Jakobs/Adia* of 16 May 1991 including a private individual as undertaking concerned.; Case COMP/M3762 – *Apax/Travelex* of 16 June 2005 in which a private individual acquiring joint control was not considered an undertaking concerned.

Commentary
para 12: **B&C:** 8.022 **F&N:** 5.53

Acquirer of control

13. Control is normally acquired by persons or undertakings which are the holders of the rights or are entitled to rights conferring control under the contracts concerned (Article 3(3)(a)). However, there are also situations where the formal holder of a controlling interest differs from the person or undertaking having in fact the real power to exercise the rights resulting from this interest. This may be the case, for example, where an undertaking uses another person or undertaking for the acquisition of a controlling interest and has the power to exercise the rights conferring control through this person or undertaking, i.e. the latter is formally the holder of the rights, but acts only as a vehicle. In such a situation, control is acquired by the undertaking which in reality is behind

the operation and in fact enjoys the power to control the target undertaking (Article 3(3)(b)). The Court of First Instance concluded from this provision that control held by commercial companies can be attributed to their exclusive shareholder, their majority shareholders or to those jointly controlling the companies since these companies comply in any event with the decisions of those shareholders.[15] A controlling shareholding which is held by different entities in a group is normally attributed to the undertaking exercising control over the different formal holders of the rights. In other cases, the evidence needed to establish this type of indirect control may include, either separately or in combination and to be assessed on a case-by-case basis, factors such as shareholdings, contractual relations, source of financing or family links.[16]

Notes

[15] Judgment in Case T-282/02 *Cementbouw v Commission*, paragraph 72, [2006] ECR II-319.

[16] See Case M.754 – *Anglo American Corporation/Lonrho* of 23 April 1997.

Commentary
para 13: B&C: 8.025 F&N: 5.53

Acquisition of control by investment funds

14. Specific issues may arise in the case of acquisitions of control by investment funds. The Commission will analyse structures involving investment funds on a case-by-case basis, but some general features of such structures can be set out on the basis of the Commission's past experience.

Commentary
para 14: B&C: 8.019 F&N: 5.56

15. Investment funds are often set up in the legal form of limited partnerships, in which the investors participate as limited partners and normally do not exercise control, either individually or collectively. The investment funds usually acquire the shares and voting rights which confer control over the portfolio companies. Depending on the circumstances, control is normally exercised by the investment company which has set up the fund as the fund itself is typically a mere investment vehicle; in more exceptional circumstances, control may be exercised by the fund itself. The investment company usually exercises control by means of the organisational structure, *e.g.* by controlling the general partner of fund partnerships, or by contractual arrangements, such as advisory agreements, or by a combination of both. This may be the case even if the investment company itself does not own the company acting as a general partner, but their shares are held by natural persons (who may be linked to the investment company) or by a trust. Contractual arrangements with the investment company, in particular advisory agreements, will become even more important if the general partner does not have any own resources and personnel for the management of the portfolio companies, but only constitutes a company structure whose acts are performed by persons linked to the investment company. In these circumstances, the investment company normally acquires indirect control within the meaning of Article 3(1)(b) and 3(3)(b) of the Merger Regulation, and has the power to exercise the rights which are directly held by the investment fund.[17]

Notes

[17] This structure also has an effect on how the turnover is calculated in situations involving investment funds, see paras 189ff.

Commentary
para 15: B&C: 8.019 F&N: 5.56

1.2. Means of control

16. Control is defined by Article 3(2) of the Merger Regulation as the possibility of exercising decisive influence on an undertaking. It is therefore not necessary to show that the decisive influence is or will be actually exercised. However, the possibility of exercising that influence must be effective.[18] Article 3(2) further provides that the possibility of exercising decisive influence on an undertaking can exist on the basis of rights, contracts or any other means, either separately or in

combination, and having regard to the considerations of fact and law involved. A concentration therefore may occur on a legal or a *de facto* basis, may take the form of sole or joint control, and extend to the whole or parts of one or more undertakings (cf Article 3(1)(b)).

Notes

[18] Judgment in Case T-282/02 *Cementbouw v Commission*, paragraph 58, [2006] ECR II-319

Commentary

para 16: B&C: 8.024, 8.036 **F&N:** 5.48

Control by the acquisition of shares or assets

17. Whether an operation gives rise to an acquisition of control therefore depends on a number of legal and/or factual elements. The most common means for the acquisition of control is the acquisition of shares, possibly combined with a shareholders' agreement in cases of joint control, or the acquisition of assets.

Commentary

para 17: F&N: 5.48

Control on a contractual basis

18. Control can also be acquired on a contractual basis. In order to confer control, the contract must lead to a similar control of the management and the resources of the other undertaking as in the case of acquisition of shares or assets. In addition to transferring control over the management and the resources, such contracts must be characterised by a very long duration (ordinarily without a possibility of early termination for the party granting the contractual rights). Only such contracts can result in a structural change in the market.[19] Examples of such contracts are organisational contracts under national company law [20] or other types of contracts, *e.g.* in the form of agreements for the lease of the business, giving the acquirer control over the management and the resources despite the fact that property rights or shares are not transferred. In this respect, Article 3(2)(a) specifies that control may also be constituted by a right to use the assets of an undertaking.[21] Such contracts may also lead to a situation of joint control if both the owner of the assets as well as the undertaking controlling the management enjoy veto rights over strategic business decisions.[22]

Notes

[19] In Case COMP/M.3858 – *Lehman Brothers/SCG/Starwood/Le Meridien* of 20 July 2005 the management agreements had a duration of 10–15 years; in Case COMP/M.2632 – *Deutsche Bahn/ECT International/United Depots/JV* of 11 February 2002 the contract had a duration of 8 years.

[20] Examples of such specific contracts under national company law are the "Beherrschungsvertrag" in German law or the "*Contrato de subordinação*" in Portuguese law; such contracts do not exist in all Member States.

[21] See Case COMP/M.2060 – *Bosch/Rexroth* of 12 January 2001 concerning a control contract (Beherrschungsvertrag) in combination with a business lease; Case COMP/M.3136 – *GE/Agfa NDT* of 5 December 2003 concerning a specific contract to transfer control over entrepreneurial resources, management and risks; Case COMP/M.2632 – *Deutsche Bahn/ECT International/United Depots/JV* of 11 February 2002 concerning a business lease.

[22] Case COMP/M.3858 – *Lehman Brothers/SCG/Starwood/Le Meridien* of 20 July 2005; see also case IV/M. 126 – *Accor/Wagon-Lits* of 28 April 1992 in the context of Article 5(4)(b) of the Merger Regulation.

Commentary

para 18: B&C: 8.023 **F&N:** 5.59

Control by other means

19. In line with these considerations, franchising agreements as such do not normally confer control over the franchisee's business on the franchisor. The franchisee usually exploits the entrepreneurial resources on its own account even if essential parts of the assets may belong to the franchisor.[23] Furthermore, purely financial agreements, such as sale-and-lease-back transactions with arrangements for a buyback of the assets at the end of the term, do not normally constitute a concentration as they do not change control over the management and the resources.

Notes

[23] Case M.940 – *UBS/Mister Minit*, in the context of Article 5(4)(b) of the Merger Regulation. For the treatment of franchising relationships in the competitive assessment, see Case COMP/M.4220 – *Food Service Project/ Tele Pizza* of 6 June 2006. The situation in Case IV/M.126 – *Accor/Wagon-Lits* of 28 April 1992 has to be distinguished from franchising agreements. In this case, again in the context of Article 5(4)(b), the hotel company had a right to manage also hotels in which it only owned a minority stake as it had entered into long-term hotel management agreements giving it decisive influence over the day-to-day operations of these hotels, including decisions on budgetary matters.

Commentary
para 19: F&N: 5.59

20. Furthermore, control can also be established by any other means. Purely economic relationships may play a decisive role for the acquisition of control. In exceptional circumstances, a situation of economic dependence may lead to control on a *de facto* basis where, for example, very important long-term supply agreements or credits provided by suppliers or customers, coupled with structural links, confer decisive influence.[24] In such a situation, the Commission will carefully analyse whether such economic links, combined with other links, are sufficient to lead to a change of control on a lasting basis.[25]

Notes

[24] See Case IV/M.794 – *Coca-Cola/Amalgamated Beverages GB* of 22 January 1997; Case IV/ESCS.1031 – *US/Sollac/ Bamesa* of 28 July 1993; Case IV/M.625 – *Nordic Capital/Transpool* of 23 August 1995; for the criteria see also Case IV/M.697 – *Lockheed Martin Corporation/Loral Corporation*, of 27 March 1996.
[25] See Case IV/M.258 – *CCIE/GTE*, of 25 September 1992 where the Commission did not find control due to the temporary nature of the commercial agreements involved.

Commentary
para 20: B&C 8.023

21. There may be an acquisition of control even if it is not the declared intention of the parties or if the acquirer is only passive and the acquisition of control is triggered by action of third parties. Examples are situations where the change of control results from the inheritance of a shareholder or where the exit of a shareholder triggers a change of control, in particular a change from joint to sole control.[26] Article 3(1)(b) covers such scenarios in specifying that control may also be acquired "by any other means".

Notes

[26] See Case COMP/M.3330 – *RTL/M6* of 12 March 2004; Case COMP/M.452 – *Avesta (II)* of 9 June 1994.

Commentary
para 21: F&N: 5.61

Control and national company law

22. National legislation within a Member State may provide specific rules on the structure of bodies representing the organization of decision-making within an undertaking. While such legislation may confer some power of control upon persons other than the shareholders, in particular on representatives of employees, the concept of control under the Merger Regulation is not related to such a means of influence as the Merger Regulation focuses on decisive influence enjoyed on the basis of rights, assets or contracts or equivalent de facto means. Restrictions in the articles of association or in general law concerning the persons eligible to sit on the board, such as a provisions requiring the appointment of independent members or excluding persons holding office or employment in the parent companies, do not exclude the existence of control as long as the shareholders decide the composition of the decision-making bodies.[27] Similarly, despite provisions of national law foreseeing that decisions of a company must be taken by its company organs in its interests, those persons holding the voting rights have the power to adopt those decisions and therefore have the possibility to exercise decisive influence on the company.[28]

Notes

27 Judgment in Case T-282/02 *Cementbouw v Commission*, paragraphs 70, 73, 74 [2006] ECR II-319.

28 Judgment in Case T-282/02 *Cementbouw v Commission*, paragraphs 79 [2006] ECR II-319.

Commentary
para 22: F&N: 5.49

Control in other areas of legislation

23. The concept of control under the Merger Regulation may be different from that applied in specific areas of Community and national legislation concerning, for example, prudential rules, taxation, air transport or the media. The interpretation of "control" in other areas is therefore not necessarily decisive for the concept of control under the Merger Regulation.

Commentary
para 23: B&C: 8.032   F&N: 5.49

1.3. Object of control

24. The Merger Regulation provides in Article 3(1)(b), (2) that the object of control can be one or more, or also parts of, undertakings which constitute legal entities, or the assets of such entities, or only some of these assets. The acquisition of control over assets can only be considered a concentration if those assets constitute the whole or a part of an undertaking, i.e. a business with a market presence, to which a market turnover can be clearly attributed.[29] The transfer of the client base of a business can fulfil these criteria if this is sufficient to transfer a business with a market turnover.[30] A transaction confined to intangible assets such as brands, patents or copyrights may also be considered to be a concentration if those assets constitute a business with a market turnover. In any case, the transfer of licences for brands, patents or copyrights, without additional assets, can only fulfil these criteria if the licences are exclusive at least in a certain territory and the transfer of such licences will transfer the turnover-generating activity.[31] For non-exclusive licences it can be excluded that they may constitute on their own a business to which a market turnover is attached.

Notes

29 See, e.g., Case COMP/M.3867 – *Vattenfall/Elsam and E2 Assets* of 22 December 2005.

30 Case COMP/M.2857 – *ECS/IEH* of 23 December 2002.

31 In addition, the granting of licences and the transfer of patent licences will only constitute a concentration if this is done on a lasting basis. In this respect, similar considerations as set out above in paragraph 18 for the acquisition of control by (long-term) agreements apply.

Commentary
para 24: B&C: 8.026   F&N: 5.65, 5.118, 5.123, 16.112

---

25. Specific issues arise in cases where an undertaking outsources in-house activities, such as the provision of services or the manufacturing of products, to a service provider. Typical cases are the outsourcing of IT services to specialised IT companies. Outsourcing contracts can take several forms; their common characteristic is that the outsourcing service supplier shall provide those services to the customer which the latter has performed in-house before. Cases of simple outsourcing do not involve any transfer of assets or employees to the outsourcing service suppliers, but it is usually the case that any assets or employees are retained by the customer. Such an outsourcing contract is akin to a normal service contract and even if the outsourcing service supplier acquires a right to direct those assets and employees of the customer, no concentration arises if the assets and employees will be used exclusively to service the customer.

26. The situation may be different if the outsourcing service supplier, in addition to taking over a certain activity which was previously provided internally, is transferred the associated assets and/or personnel. A concentration only arises in these circumstances if the assets constitute the whole or part of an undertaking, i.e. a business with access to the market. This requires that the assets previously dedicated to in-house activities of the seller will enable the outsourcing service

supplier to provide services not only to the outsourcing customer but also to third parties, either immediately or within a short period after the transfer. This will be the case if the transfer relates to an internal business unit or a subsidiary already engaged in the provision of services to third parties. If third parties are not yet supplied, the assets transferred in the case of manufacturing should contain production facilities, the product know-how (it is sufficient if the assets transferred allow the build-up of such capabilities in the near future) and, if there is no existing market access, the means for the purchaser to develop a market access within a short period of time (e.g. including existing contracts or brands).[32] As regards the provision of services, the assets transferred should include the required know-how (e.g. the relevant personnel and intellectual property) and those facilities which allow market access (such as, e.g., marketing facilities).[33] The assets transferred therefore have to include at least those core elements that would allow an acquirer to build up a market presence in a time-frame similar to the start-up period for joint ventures as set out below under paragraphs 97, 100. As in the case of joint ventures, the Commission will take account of substantiated business plans and general market features for assessing this.

Notes

[32] See Case COMP/M.1841 – *Celestica/IBM* of 25 February 2000; Case COMP/M.1849 – *Solectron/Ericsson* of 29 February 2000; Case COMP/M.2479 – *Flextronics/Alcatel* – of 29 June 2001; Case COMP/M.2629 – *Flextronics/Xerox* of 12 November 2001.

[33] See, in the context of joint ventures, Case IV/M.560 – *EDS/Lufthansa* of 11 May 1995; Case COMP/M.2478 – *IBM Italia/Business Solutions/JV* of 29 June 2001.

---

27. If the assets transferred do not allow the purchaser to at least develop a market presence, it is likely that they will be used only for providing services to the outsourcing customer. In such circumstances, the transaction will not result in a lasting change in the market structure and the outsourcing contract is again similar to a service contract. The transaction will not constitute a concentration. The specific requirements under which a joint venture for the provision of outsourcing services is qualified as a concentration are assessed in the present Notice in the section on full-function joint ventures.

1.4. Change of control on a lasting basis

28. Article 3(1) of the Merger Regulation defines the concept of a concentration in such a manner as to cover operations only if they bring about a lasting change in the control of the undertakings concerned and, as recital 20 adds, in the structure of the market. The Merger Regulation therefore does not deal with transactions resulting only in a temporary change of control. However, a change of control on a lasting basis is not excluded by the fact that the underlying agreements are entered into for a definite period of time, provided those agreements are renewable. A concentration may arise even in cases in which agreements envisage a definite end-date, if the period envisaged is sufficiently long to lead to a lasting change in the control of the undertakings concerned.[34]

Notes

[34] See, in cases of joint ventures, Case COMP/M.2903 – *DaimlerChrysler/Deutsche Telekom/JV* of 30 April 2003 where a period of 12 years was considered sufficient; Case COMP/M.2632 – *Deutsche Bahn/ECT International/United Depots/JV* of 11 February 2002 with a contract duration of 8 years. In Case COMP/M.3858 *Lehman Brothers/Starwood/Le Meridien* of 20 July 2005, the Commission considered a minimum period of 10–15 years sufficient, but not a period of three years. The acquisition of control by the acquisition of shares or assets is not normally confined to a definite period of time and is therefore assumed to lead to a change of control on a lasting basis. Only in the scenarios set out in paragraphs 29 ff., will an acquisition of control by shares or assets be exceptionally considered to be transitory in nature and thus not to lead to a lasting change in the control of the undertakings concerned.

Commentary
para 28: B&C: 8.014 F&N: 5.67

---

29. The question whether an operation results in a lasting change in the market structure is also relevant for the assessment of several operations occurring in succession, where the first transaction is only transitory in nature. Several scenarios can be distinguished in this respect.

30. In one scenario, several undertakings come together solely for the purpose of acquiring another company on the basis of an agreement to divide up the acquired assets according to a pre-existing plan immediately upon completion of the transaction. In such circumstances, in a first step, the acquisition of the entire target company is carried out by one or several undertakings. In a second step, the acquired assets are divided among several undertakings. The question is then whether the first transaction is to be considered as a separate concentration, involving an acquisition of sole control (in the case of a single purchaser) or of joint control (in the case of a joint purchase) of the entire target undertaking, or whether only the acquisitions in the second step constitute concentrations, whereby each of the acquiring undertakings acquires its relevant part of the target undertaking.

31. The Commission considers that the first transaction does not constitute a concentration, and examines the acquisitions of control by the ultimate acquirers, provided a number of conditions are met: First, the subsequent break-up must be agreed between the different purchasers in a legally binding way. Second, there must not be any uncertainty that the second step, the division of the acquired assets, will take place within a short time period after the first acquisition. The Commission considers that normally the maximum time-frame for the division of the assets should be one year.[35]

Notes

[35] See, e.g., Cases COMP/M. Case No COMP/M.3779 – *Pernod Ricard/Allied Domecq* of 24 June 2005 and COMP/M.3813 – *Fortune Brands/Allied Domecq* of 10 June 2005, where the split-up of the assets was foreseen to become effective within 6 months after the acquisition.

Commentary
para 31: **B&C:** 8.047

---

32. If both conditions are met, the first acquisition does not result in a structural change on a lasting basis. There is no effective concentration of economic power between the acquirer(s) and the target company as a whole since the acquired assets are not held in an undivided way on a lasting basis, but only for the time necessary to carry out the immediate split-up of the acquired assets. In those circumstances, only the acquisitions of the different parts of the undertaking in the second step will constitute concentrations, whereby each of these acquisitions by different purchasers will constitute a separate concentration. This is irrespective of whether the first acquisition is carried out by only one undertaking[36] or jointly by the undertakings which are also involved in the second step.[37] In any case, it must be noted that the scope of a clearance decision will only allow for a takeover of the entire target if the break-up can proceed within a short time-frame afterwards and the different parts of the target undertaking are directly sold on to the respective ultimate buyer.

Commentary
para 32: **B&C:** 8.047

---

33. However, if these conditions are not fulfilled, in particular if it is not certain that the second step will proceed within a short time-frame after the first acquisition, the Commission will consider the first transaction as a separate concentration, involving the entire target undertaking. This, *e.g.*, is the case if the first transaction may also proceed independently of the second transaction[38] or if a longer transitory period is needed to divide up the target undertaking.[39]

Notes

[36] For a first acquisition by only one undertaking see Case COMP/M.3779 – *Pernod Ricard/Allied Domecq* of 24 June 2005 and Case COMP/M.3813 – *Fortune Brands/Allied Domecq/Pernod Ricard* of 10 June 2005; Case COMP/M.2060 – *Bosch/Rexroth* of 12 January 2001.

[37] For a joint acquisition see Case COMP/M.1630 – *Air Liquide/BOC* of 18 January 2000; Case COMP/M.1922 – *Siemens/Bosch/Atecs* of 11 August 2000; Case COMP/M.2059 – *Siemens/Dematic/VDO Sachs* of 29 August 2000.

[38] See Case COMP/M.2498 – *UPM-Kymmene/Haindl* of 21 November 2001 and Case COMP/M.2499 – *Norske Skog/Parenco/Walsum* of 21 November 2001.

[39] Case COMP/M.3372 – *Carlsberg/Holsten* of 16 March 2004.

---

34. A second scenario is an operation leading to joint control for a starting-up period but, according to legally binding agreements, this joint control will be converted to sole control by one of the shareholders. As the joint control situation may not constitute a lasting change of control, the whole operation may be considered to be an acquisition of sole control. In the past, the Commission accepted that such a start-up period could last up to three years.[40] Such a period seems to be too long to exclude that the joint control scenario has an impact on the structure of the market. The period therefore should, in general, not exceed one year and the joint control period should be only transitory in nature.[41] Only such a relatively short period will make it unlikely that the joint control period will have a distinct impact on the market structure and can therefore be considered as not leading to a change in control on a lasting basis.

Notes

[40] Case IV/M.425 – *British Telecom/Santander* of 28 March 1994.
[41] See Case M.2389 – *Shell/DEA* of 20 December 2001 where the ultimate acquirer of sole control had a strong influence in the operational management during the joint control period; Case M.2854 – *RAG/Degussa* of 18 November 2002 where the transitional period was designed to facilitate internal post-merger restructuring.

Commentary
para 34: B&C: 8.059

35. In a third scenario, an undertaking is "parked" with an interim buyer, often a bank, on the basis of an agreement on the future onward sale of the business to an ultimate acquirer. The interim buyer generally acquires shares "on behalf" of the ultimate acquirer, which often bears the major part of the economic risks and may also be granted specific rights. In such circumstances, the first transaction is only undertaken to facilitate the second transaction and the first buyer is directly linked to the ultimate acquirer. Contrary to the situation described in the first scenario in paragraphs 30–33, no other ultimate acquirer is involved, the target business remains unchanged, and the sequence of transactions is initiated alone by the sole ultimate acquirer. From the date of the adoption of this Notice, the Commission will examine the acquisition of control by the ultimate acquirer, as provided for in the agreements entered into by the parties. The Commission will consider the transaction by which the interim buyer acquires control in such circumstances as the first step of a single concentration comprising the lasting acquisition of control by the ultimate buyer.

Commentary
para 35: B&C: 8.049, 8.050

1.5. Interrelated transactions

1.5.1. Relation between Article 3 and Article 5(2) second subparagraph

36. Several transactions can be treated as a single concentration under the Merger Regulation either according to the general rule of Article 3 – as the transactions are interdependent – or according to the specific provision of Article 5(2) second subparagraph.

Commentary
para 36: F&N: 5.140

37. Article 5(2) second subparagraph governs a different question from that referred to by Article 3 of the Merger Regulation. Article 3 defines the existence of a "concentration" in general and material terms, but does not directly determine the question of the Commission's competence in respect of concentrations. Article 5 intends to specify the scope of the Merger Regulation, in particular by defining the turnover to be taken into account for the purpose of determining whether a concentration has Community dimension, and Article 5(2) second subparagraph allows the Commission in this respect to consider two or more concentrative transactions to constitute a single concentration for the purposes of calculating the turnover of the undertakings concerned. The assessment whether, in application of Article 3, a number of transactions give rise to a single concentration or whether those transactions must be regarded as giving rise to a number of concentrations, is thereby logically precedent to the question addressed in Article 5(2) second subparagraph.[42]

Notes

⁴² Judgment in Case T-282/02 *Cementbouw v Commission*, paragraphs 113–119 [2006] ECR II-319.

Commentary
para 37: F&N: 5.140

1.5.2. Interdependent transactions under Article 3

38. The general and teleological definition of a concentration set out in Article 3(1) – the result being
control of one or more undertakings – implies that it makes no difference whether control was
acquired by one or several legal transactions, provided that the end result constitutes a single
concentration. Two or more transactions constitute a single concentration for the purposes of
Article 3 if they are unitary in nature. It should therefore be determined whether the result leads
to conferring one or more undertakings direct or indirect economic control over the activities of
one or more other undertakings. For the assessment, the economic reality underlying the transactions is to be identified and thus the economic aim pursued by the parties. In other words, in
order to determine the unitary nature of the transactions in question, it is necessary, in each
individual case, to ascertain whether those transactions are interdependent, in such a way that
one transaction would not have been carried out without the other.⁴³

Notes

⁴³ Judgment in Case T-282/02 *Cementbouw v Commission*, paragraphs 104–109 [2006] ECR II-319.

39. Recital 20 to the Merger Regulation explains in this respect that it is appropriate to treat as a
single concentration transactions that are closely connected in that they are linked by condition.
The requirement that the transactions are interdependent as set out by the Court of First Instance
in the *Cementbouw* judgment⁴⁴ thereby corresponds to the explanation set out in recital 20 that
the transactions are linked by condition.

Notes

⁴⁴ Judgment in Case T-282/02 *Cementbouw v Commission*, paragraphs 106–109 [2006] ECR II-319.

Commentary
para 39: F&N: 5.142

40. This general approach reflects, on the one hand, that under the Merger Regulation transactions
which stand or fall together according to the economic objectives pursued by the parties should also
be analysed in one procedure. In these circumstances, the change of the market structure is brought
about by these transactions together. On the other hand, if different transactions are not interdependent and if the parties would proceed with one of the transactions if the other ones would not succeed,
it seems appropriate to assess these transactions individually under the Merger Regulation.

41. However, several transactions, even if linked by condition upon each other, can only be treated
as a single concentration, if control is acquired ultimately by the same undertaking(s). Only in
these circumstances two or more transactions can be considered to be unitary in nature and
therefore to constitute a single concentration for the purposes of Article 3.⁴⁵ This excludes
de-mergers of joint ventures by which different parts of an undertaking are split between its former parent companies. The Commission will consider those transactions as separate concentra-
tions.⁴⁶ The same applies to transactions where two (or more) companies exchange assets in
transactions involving de-mergers of joint ventures or assets swaps. Although the parties will
normally consider those transactions as interdependent, the purpose of the Merger Regulation
requires a separate assessment of the results of each of the transactions: Several undertakings
acquire control of different assets; a separate combination of resources takes place for each of the
acquiring undertakings; and the impact on the market of each of those acquisitions of control
needs to be analysed separately under the Merger Regulation.

Notes

⁴⁵ This also covers situations where an undertaking sells a business to a purchaser and then acquirers the seller including
the business sold, see Case COMP/M.4521 – *LGI/Telenet* of 26 February 2007.

[46] See parallel cases COMP/M.3293 – *Shell/BEB* and COMP/M.3294 – *ExxonMobil/BEB* of 20 November 2003; case IV/M.197 – *Solvay/Laporte* of 30 April 1992.

Commentary
para 41: B&C: 8.043, 8.044, 8.046, 8.048 F&N: 5.143

42. The acquisition of different degrees of control (for example joint control of one business and sole control of another business) raises specific questions. An operation involving the acquisition of joint control of one part of an undertaking and sole control of another part is in principle regarded as two separate concentrations under the Merger Regulation.[47] Those transactions constitute only one concentration if they are interdependent and if the undertaking acquiring sole control is also acquiring joint control. In any case, such a scenario is considered to constitute one concentration where a corporate entity is acquired to which both the solely controlled and the jointly controlled undertaking belong. On the basis of the interpretation in recital 20, the situation where the same undertaking acquires sole and joint control of other undertakings based on interdependent agreements is not to be treated differently. These transactions, if they are interdependent, therefore constitute a single concentration.

Notes
[47] See Case IV/M.409 *ABB/Renault Automation* of 9 March 1994.

Commentary
para 42: B&C: 8.045 F&N: 5.143

Requirement of conditionality of transactions

43. The required conditionality implies that none of the transactions would take place without the others and they therefore constitute a single operation.[48] Such conditionality is normally demonstrated if the transactions are linked *de jure*, i.e. the agreements themselves are linked by mutual conditionality. If *de facto* conditionality can be satisfactorily demonstrated, it may also suffice for treating the transactions as a single concentration. This requires an economic assessment of whether each of the transactions necessarily depends on the conclusion of the others.[49] Further indications of the interdependence of several transactions may be the statements of the parties themselves or the simultaneous conclusion of the relevant agreements. A conclusion of *de facto* interconditionality of several transactions will be difficult to reach in the absence of their simultaneity. A pronounced lack of simultaneity of legally interconditional transactions may likewise put into doubt their true interdependence.

Notes
[48] Judgment in Case T-282/02 *Cementbouw v Commission*, paragraphs 127 et seq. [2006] ECR II-319.
[49] Judgment in Case T-282/02 *Cementbouw v Commission*, paragraphs 131 et seq. [2006] ECR II-319. See Case COMP/M.4521 – *LGI/Telenet* of 26 February 2007, where the interdependence was based on the fact that two transactions were decided and carried out simultaneously and that, according to the economic aims of the parties, each of the transactions would not have been carried out without the other.

Commentary
para 43: F&N: 5.142

44. The principle that several transactions can be treated as a single concentration under the mentioned conditions only applies if the result is that control of one or more undertakings is acquired by the same person(s) or undertaking(s). First, this may be the case if a single business or undertaking is acquired via several legal transactions. Second, also the acquisition of control of several undertakings – which could constitute concentrations in themselves – can be linked in such a way that it constitutes a single concentration. However, it is not possible under the Merger Regulation to link different legal transactions which only partly concern the acquisition of control of undertakings, but partly also the acquisition of other assets, such as non-controlling minority stakes in other companies. It would not be in line with the general framework and the purpose of the Merger Regulation if different transactions, linked by conditionality, were assessed as a whole under the Merger Regulations if only some of these transactions lead to a change in control of a given target.

Part D Mergers and Concentrations

Commentary
para 44: F&N: 5.100, 5.143

Acquisition of a single business

45. A single concentration may therefore exist if the same purchaser(s) acquire control of a single business, i.e. a single economic entity, via several legal transactions if those are inter-conditional. This is the case irrespective of whether the business is acquired in a corporate structure, consisting of one or several companies, or whether various assets are acquired which form a single business, i.e. a single economic entity managed for a common commercial purpose to which all the assets contribute. Such a business may comprise majority and minority stakes in companies as well as tangible and intangible assets. If several legal transactions which are interdependent are required to transfer such a business, these transactions constitute one concentration.[50]

Notes

[50] See Case IV/M.470 – *Gencor/Shell* of 29 August 1994; COMP/M.3410 – *Total/Gaz de France* of 8 October 2004; Case IV/M.957 – *L'Oreal/Procasa/Cosmetique Iberica/Albesa* of 19 September 1997; Case IV/M.861 – *Textron/Kautex* of 18 December 1996 where all the assets were also used in the same product market. The same considerations apply if a joint venture is created by several companies, forming a single business, see Case M.4048, *Sonae Industria/Tarkett* of 12 June 2006, where the interdependence of transactions establishing, respectively, a production and a distribution joint venture was necessary in order to demonstrate that there was a single concentration that would create a full-function joint venture.

Commentary
para 45: F&N: 5.145

Parallel and serial acquisitions of control

46. For the treatment of several acquisitions of control as a single concentration, several scenarios have arisen in the Commission's past decisional practice. One such scenario is a parallel acquisition of control, i.e. undertaking A acquires control of undertaking B and C in parallel from separate sellers on condition that A is not obliged to buy either and neither seller is obliged to sell, unless both transactions proceed.[51] Another scenario is a serial acquisition of control, i.e. undertaking A acquires control of undertaking B conditional on B's prior or simultaneous acquisition of undertaking C, as illustrated by the Kingfisher case.[52]

Notes

[51] Case COMP/M.2926 – *EQT/H&R/Dragoco* – of 16 September 2002; the same considerations apply to the question when several mergers constitute one concentration in the meaning of Article 3(1)(a), Case COMP/M.2824 – *Ernst & Young/Andersen Germany* of 27 August 2002.
[52] Case IV/M.1188 – *Kingfisher/Wegert/ProMarkt* of 18 June 1998; case COMP/M.2650 – *Haniel/Cementbouw/JV* (CVK) of 26 June 2002.

Commentary
para 46: F&N: 5.146, 5.147

Serial acquisition of sole/joint control

47. In the same way as the Kingfisher scenario, the Commission approaches cases where, in a serial transaction, an undertaking agrees to acquire first sole control of a target undertaking, with a view to directly selling on parts of the acquired stake in the target to another undertaking, finally resulting in joint control of both acquirers over the target company. If both acquisitions are inter-conditional, the two transactions constitute a single concentration and only the acquisition of joint control, as the final result of the transactions, will be considered by the Commission.[53]

Notes

[53] Case COMP/M.2420 – *Mitsui/CVRD/Caemi* of 30 October 2001.

1.5.3. Series of transactions in securities

48. Recital 20 of the Merger Regulation further explains that a single concentration will also arise in cases where control over one undertaking is acquired by a series of transactions in securities from one or several sellers taking place within a reasonably short period of time. The concentration in these scenarios is not limited to the acquisition of the "one and decisive" share, but will cover all the acquisitions of securities which take place in the reasonably short period of time.

Commentary
para 48: F&N: 5.148

1.5.4. Article 5(2) subparagraph 2

49. Article 5(2) subparagraph 2 provides a specific rule which allows the Commission. to consider successive transactions occurring in a fixed period of time a single concentration for the purposes of calculating the turnover of the undertakings concerned. The purpose of this provision is to ensure that the same persons do not break a transaction down into series of sales of assets over a period of time, with the aim of avoiding the competence conferred on the Commission by the Merger Regulation.[54]

Notes
[54] Judgment in Case T-282/02 *Cementbouw v Commission*, paragraph 118 [2006] ECR II-319.

50. If two or more transactions (each of them bringing about an acquisition of control) take place within a two-year period between the same persons or undertakings, they shall be qualified as a single concentration,[55] irrespective of whether or not those transactions relate to parts of the same business or concern the same sector. This does not apply where the same persons or undertakings are joined by other persons or undertakings for only some of the transactions involved. It is sufficient if the transactions, although not carried out between the same companies, are carried out between companies belonging to the same respective groups. The provision also applies to two or more transactions between the same persons or undertakings if they are carried out simultaneously. Whenever they lead to acquisitions of control by the same undertaking, such simultaneous transactions between the same parties form a single concentration even if they are not conditional upon each other.[56] However, Article 5(2) subparagraph 2 would not appear to apply to different transactions at least one of which involves an undertaking concerned which is distinct from the common seller(s) and buyer(s). In situations involving two transactions where one transaction results in sole control and the other in joint control, Article 5(2) subparagraph 2 therefore does not apply unless the other jointly controlling parent(s) in the latter transaction are the seller(s) of the solely controlling stake in the former transaction.

Notes
[55] See Case COMP/M.3173 – *E.ON/Fortum Burghausen/Smaland/Endenderry* of 13 June 2003. This also applies to situations where sole control is acquired whereby only parts of the undertaking were previously jointly controlled by the acquiring undertaking, Case COMP/M.2679 – *EdF/TXU/ Europe/24 Seven* of 20 December 2001.
[56] Case IV/M.1283 – *Volkswagen/RollsRoyce/Cosworth* of 24 August 1998.

Commentary
para 50: F&N: 5.140, 5.151

1.6. Internal restructuring

51. A concentration within the meaning of the Merger Regulation is limited to changes in control. An internal restructuring within a group of companies does not constitute a concentration. This applies, e.g., to increases in shareholdings not accompanied by changes of control or to restructuring operations such as a merger of a dual listed company into a single legal entity or a merger of subsidiaries. A concentration could only arise if the operation leads to a change in the quality of control of one undertaking and therefore is no longer purely internal.

Commentary
para 51: B&C: 8.016 F&N: 5.37, 5.73

1.7. Concentrations involving State-owned undertakings

52. An exceptional situation exists where both the acquiring and acquired undertakings are companies owned by the same State (or by the same public body or municipality). In this case, whether the operation is to be regarded as an internal restructuring depends in turn on the question whether both undertakings were formerly part of the same economic unit. Where the undertakings were formerly part of different economic units having an independent power of decision, the operation will be deemed to constitute a concentration and not an internal restructuring.[57] However, where the different economic units will continue to have an independent power of decision also after the operation, the operation is only to be regarded as an internal restructuring, even if the shares of the undertakings, constituting different economic units, should be held by a single entity, such as a pure holding company.[58]

Notes

[57] Case IV/M.097 – *Péchiney/Usinor*, of 24 June 1991; Case IV/M.216 – *CEA Industrie/France Telecom/SGS-Thomson*, of 22 February 1993; Case IV/M.931 – *Neste/IVO* of 2 June 1998. See also Recital 22 of the Merger Regulation.
[58] Specific issues concerning the calculation of turnover for state-owned companies are dealt with in paragraphs 192–194.

Commentary
para 52: B&C: 8.017 F&N: 5.75

53. However, the prerogatives exercised by a State acting as a public authority rather than as a shareholder, in so far as they are limited to the protection of the public interest, do not constitute control within the meaning of the Merger Regulation to the extent that they have neither the aim nor the effect of enabling the State to exercise a decisive influence over the activity of the undertaking.[59]

Notes

[59] Case IV/M.493 – *Tractebel/Distrigaz II*, of 1 September 1994.

Commentary
para 53: B&C: 8.017 F&N: 5.75

2. Sole control

54. Sole control is acquired if one undertaking alone can exercise decisive influence on an undertaking. Two general situations in which an undertaking has sole control can be distinguished. First, the solely controlling undertaking enjoys the power to determine the strategic commercial decisions of the other undertaking. This power is typically achieved by the acquisition of a majority of voting rights in a company. Second, a situation also conferring sole control exists where only one shareholder is able to veto strategic decisions in an undertaking, but this shareholder does not have the power, on his own, to impose such decisions (the so-called negative sole control). In these circumstances, a single shareholder possesses the same level of influence as that usually enjoyed by an individual shareholder which jointly-controls a company, i.e. the power to block the adoption of strategic decisions. In contrast to the situation in a jointly controlled company, there are no other shareholders enjoying the same level of influence and the shareholder enjoying negative sole control does not necessarily have to cooperate with specific other shareholders in determining the strategic behaviour of the controlled undertaking. Since this shareholder can produce a deadlock situation, the shareholder acquires decisive influence within the meaning of Article 3(2) and therefore control within the meaning of the Merger Regulation.[60]

Notes

[60] Since this shareholder is the only undertaking acquiring a controlling influence, only this shareholder is obliged to submit a notification under the Merger Regulation.

Commentary
para 54: B&C: 8.031 F&N: 5.78

55. Sole control can be acquired on a *de jure* and/or *de facto* basis.

De jure sole control

56. Sole control is normally acquired on a legal basis where an undertaking acquires a majority of the voting rights of a company. In the absence of other elements, an acquisition which does not include a majority of the voting rights does not normally confer control even if it involves the acquisition of a majority of the share capital. Where the company statutes require a supermajority for strategic decisions, the acquisition of a simple majority of the voting rights may not confer the power to determine strategic decisions, but may be sufficient to confer a blocking right on the acquirer and therefore negative control.

Commentary
para 56: B&C: 8.028

---

57. Even in the case of a minority shareholding, sole control may occur on a legal basis in situations where specific rights are attached to this shareholding. These may be preferential shares to which special rights are attached enabling the minority shareholder to determine the strategic commercial behaviour of the target company, such as the power to appoint more than half of the members of the supervisory board or the administrative board. Sole control can also be exercised by a minority shareholder who has the right to manage the activities of the company and to determine its business policy on the basis of the organisational structure (e.g. as a general partner in a limited partnership which often does not even have a shareholding).

Commentary
para 57: B&C: 8.029   F&N: 5.79

---

58. A typical situation of negative sole control occurs where one shareholder holds 50% in an undertaking whilst the remaining 50% is held by several other shareholders (assuming this does not lead to positive sole control on a *de facto* basis), or where there is a supermajority required for strategic decisions which in fact confers a veto right upon only one shareholder, irrespective of whether it is a majority or a minority shareholder.[61]

Notes
[61] See consecutive Cases COMP/M.3537 – *BBVA/BNL* of 20 August 2004 and M.3768 – *BBVA/BNL* of 27 April 2005; Case M.3198 – *VW-Audi/VW-Audi Vertriebszentren* of 29 July 2003; Case COMP/M.2777 – *Cinven Limited/ Angel Street Holdings* of 8 May 2002; Case IV/M.258 – *CCIE/GTE*, of 25 September 1992. In Case COMP/M. 3876 – *Diester Industrie/Bunge/JV* of 30 September 2005, there was the specific situation that a joint venture held a stake in a company by which it had negative sole control over this company.

Commentary
para 58: F&N: 5.79

De facto sole control

59. *A minority shareholder may also be deemed to have sole control on a de facto* basis. This is in particular the case where the shareholder is highly likely to achieve a majority at the shareholders'' meetings, given the level of its shareholding and the evidence resulting from the presence of shareholders in the shareholders' meetings in previous years.[62] Based on the past voting pattern, the Commission will carry out a prospective analysis and take into account foreseeable changes of the shareholders' presence which might arise in future following the operation.[63] The Commission will further analyse the position of other shareholders and assess their role. Criteria for such an assessment are in particular whether the remaining shares are widely dispersed, whether other important shareholders have structural, economic or family links with the large minority shareholder or whether other shareholders have a strategic or a purely financial interest in the target company; these criteria will be assessed on a case-by-case basis.[64] Where, on the basis of its shareholding, the historic voting pattern at the shareholders' meeting and the position of other shareholders, a minority shareholder is likely to have a stable majority of the votes at the shareholders' meeting, then that large minority shareholder is taken to have sole control.[65]

Notes

62 Case IV/M.343 – *Société Générale de Belgique/Générale de Banque*, of 3 August 1993; Case COMP/M.3330 – *RTL/ M6* of 12 March 2004; Case IV/M.159 – *Mediobanca/Generali* of 19 December 1991.

63 See Case COMP/M.4336 – *MAN/Scania* of 20 December 2007 as regards the question whether Volkswagen hat acquired control of MAN.

64 Case IV/M.754 – *Anglo American/Lonrho* of 23 April 1997; Case IV/M.025 – *Arjomari/Wiggins Teape*, of 10 February 1990.

65 See also Case COMP/M.2574 – *Pirelli/Edizione/Olivetti/Telecom Italia* of 20 September 2001; Case IV/M. 1519 – *Renault/Nissan* of 12 May 1999.

Commentary
para 59: B&C: 8.029 F&N: 5.80

60. An option to purchase or convert shares cannot in itself confer sole control unless the option will be exercised in the near future according to legally binding agreements.[66] However, in exceptional circumstances an option, together with other elements, may lead to the conclusion that there is *de facto* sole control.[67]

Notes

66 Judgment in Case T 2/93, *Air France v Commission* [1994] ECR II-323. Even though an option does normally not in itself lead to a concentration, it can be taken into account for the substantive assessment in a related concentration, see Case COMP/M.3696 – *E.ON/MOL* of 21 December 2005, at paragraphs 12–14, 480, 762 et subseq.

67 Case IV/M.397 – *Ford/Hertz* of 7 March 1994.

Commentary
para 60: B&C: 8.030, 8.031 F&N: 5.86

Sole control acquired by other means than voting rights

61. Apart from the acquisition of sole control on the basis of voting rights, the considerations outlined in section 1.2 concerning the acquisition of sole control by purchase of assets, by contract, or by any other means also apply.

Commentary
para 61: B&C: 8.032 F&N: 5.78

3. Joint control

62. Joint control exists where two or more undertakings or persons have the possibility of exercising decisive influence over another undertaking. Decisive influence in this sense normally means the power to block actions which determine the strategic commercial behaviour of an undertaking. Unlike sole control, which confers upon a specific shareholder the power to determine the strategic decisions in an undertaking, joint control is characterized by the possibility of a deadlock situation resulting from the power of two or more parent companies to reject proposed strategic decisions. It follows, therefore, that these shareholders must reach a common understanding in determining the commercial policy of the joint venture and that they are required to cooperate.[68]

Notes

68 See also Judgment in Case T-282/02 *Cementbouw v Commission*, paragraphs 42, 52, 67 [2006] ECR II-319.

Commentary
para 62: B&C: 8.024, 8.033 F&N: 5.87, 5.114, 8.532

63. As in the case of sole control, the acquisition of joint control can also be established on a *de jure* or *de facto* basis. There is joint control if the shareholders (the parent companies) must reach agreement on major decisions concerning the controlled undertaking (the joint venture).

Commentary
para 63: B&C: 8.033 F&N: 5.87, 5.114

3.1. Equality in voting rights or appointment to decision-making bodies

64. The clearest form of joint control exists where there are only two parent companies which share equally the voting rights in the joint venture. In this case, it is not necessary for a formal agreement to exist between them. However, where there is a formal agreement, it must be consistent with the principle of equality between the parent companies, by laying down, for example, that each is entitled to the same number of representatives in the management bodies and that none of the members has a casting vote.[69] Equality may also be achieved where both parent companies have the right to appoint an equal number of members to the decision-making bodies of the joint venture.

Notes

[69] Case COMP/M.3097 – *Maersk Data/Eurogate IT*; *Global Transport Solutions JV* of 12 March 2003; Case IV/M.272 – *Matra/CAP Gemini Sogeti*, of 17 March 1993.

Commentary
para 64: B&C: 8.034

3.2. Veto rights

65. Joint control may exist even where there is no equality between the two parent companies in votes or in representation in decision-making bodies or where there are more than two parent companies. This is the case where minority shareholders have additional rights which allow them to veto decisions which are essential for the strategic commercial behaviour of the joint venture.[70] These veto rights may be set out in the statute of the joint venture or conferred by agreement between its parent companies. The veto rights themselves may operate by means of a specific quorum required for decisions taken at the shareholders' meeting or by the board of directors to the extent that the parent companies are represented on this board. It is also possible that strategic decisions are subject to approval by a body, e.g. supervisory board, where the minority shareholders are represented and form part of the quorum needed for such decisions.

Notes

[70] Case T 2/93, *Air France v Commission* [1994] ECR II-323; Case IV/M.10 – *Conagra/Idea*, of 3 May 1991.

Commentary
para 65: B&C: 8.035

66. These veto rights must be related to strategic decisions on the business policy of the joint venture. They must go beyond the veto rights normally accorded to minority shareholders in order to protect their financial interests as investors in the joint venture. This normal protection of the rights of minority shareholders is related to decisions on the essence of the joint venture, such as changes in the statute, an increase or decrease in the capital or liquidation. A veto right, for example, which prevents the sale or winding-up of the joint venture does not confer joint control on the minority shareholder concerned.[71]

Notes

[71] Case IV/M.062 – *Eridania/ISI*, of 30 July 1991.

67. In contrast, veto rights which confer joint control typically include decisions on issues such as the budget, the business plan, major investments or the appointment of senior management. The acquisition of joint control, however, does not require that the acquirer has the power to exercise decisive influence on the day-to-day running of an undertaking. The crucial element is that the veto rights are sufficient to enable the parent companies to exercise such influence in relation to the strategic business behaviour of the joint venture. Moreover, it is not necessary to establish that an acquirer of joint control of the joint venture will actually make use of its decisive influence. The possibility of exercising such influence and, hence, the mere existence of the veto rights, is sufficient.

Commentary
para 67: B&C: 8.036

Part D Mergers and Concentrations

68. In order to acquire joint control, it is not necessary for a minority shareholder to have all the veto rights mentioned above. It may be sufficient that only some, or even one such right, exists. Whether or not this is the case depends upon the precise content of the veto right itself and also the importance of this right in the context of the specific business of the joint venture.

Commentary
para 68: **B&C:** 8.036 **F&N:** 5.114

Appointment of senior management and determination of budget

69. Very important are the veto rights concerning decisions on the appointment and dismissal of the senior management and the approval of the budget. The power to codetermine the structure of the senior management, such as the members of the board, usually confers upon the holder the power to exercise decisive influence on the commercial policy of an undertaking. The same is true with respect to decisions on the budget since the budget determines the precise framework of the activities of the joint venture and, in particular, the investments it may make.

Business plan

70. The business plan normally provides details of the aims of a company together with the measures to be taken in order to achieve those aims. A veto right over this type of business plan may be sufficient to confer joint control even in the absence of any other veto right. In contrast, where the business plan contains merely general declarations concerning the business aims of the joint venture, the existence of a veto right will be only one element in the general assessment of joint control but will not, on its own, be sufficient to confer joint control.

Commentary
para 70: **F&N:** 5.92

Investments

71. In the case of a veto right on investments, the importance of this right depends, first, on the level of investments which are subject to the approval of the parent companies and, secondly, on the extent to which investments constitute an essential feature of the market in which the joint venture is active. In relation to the first criterion, where the level of investments necessitating approval of the parent companies is extremely high, this veto right may be closer to the normal protection of the interests of a minority shareholder than to a right conferring a power of co-determination over the commercial policy of the joint venture. With regard to the second, the investment policy of an undertaking is normally an important element in assessing whether or not there is joint control. However, there may be some markets where investment does not play a significant role in the market behaviour of an undertaking.

Commentary
para 71: **B&C:** 8.037 **F&N:** 5.92

Market-specific rights

72. Apart from the typical veto rights mentioned above, there exist a number of other possible veto rights related to specific decisions which are important in the context of the particular market of the joint venture. One example is the decision on the technology to be used by the joint venture where technology is a key feature of the joint venture's activities. Another example relates to markets characterized by product differentiation and a significant degree of innovation. In such markets, a veto right over decisions relating to new product lines to be developed by the joint venture may also be an important element in establishing the existence of joint control.

Overall context

73. In assessing the relative importance of veto rights, where there are a number of them, these rights should not be evaluated in isolation. On the contrary, the determination of whether or not joint control exists is based upon an assessment of these rights as a whole. However, a veto right which does not relate either to strategic commercial policy, to the appointment of senior management or to the budget or business plan cannot be regarded as giving joint control to its owner.[72]

Notes

[72] Case IV/M.295 – *SITA-RPC/SCORI*, of 19 March 1993.

Commentary

para 73: **B&C:** 8.036 **F&N:** 5.92

3.3. Joint exercise of voting rights

74. Even in the absence of specific veto rights, two or more undertakings acquiring minority share-holdings in another undertaking may obtain joint control. This may be the case where the minority shareholdings together provide the means for controlling the target undertaking. This means that the minority shareholders, together, will have a majority of the voting rights; and they will act together in exercising these voting rights. This can result from a legally binding agreement to this effect, or it may be established on a *de facto* basis.

Commentary

para 74: **B&C:** 8.038

75. The legal means to ensure the joint exercise of voting rights can be in the form of a (jointly con-trolled) holding company to which the minority shareholders transfer their rights, or an agree-ment by which they undertake to act in the same way (pooling agreement).

Commentary

para 75: **B&C:** 8.038

76. Very exceptionally, collective action can occur on a de facto basis where strong common interests exist between the minority shareholders to the effect that they would not act against each other in exercising their rights in relation to the joint venture. The greater the number of parent com-panies involved in such a joint venture, however, the more remote is the likelihood of this situa-tion occurring.

Commentary

para 76: **B&C:** 8.038 **F&N:** 5.114

77. Indicative for such a commonality of interests is a high degree of mutual dependency as between the parent companies to reach the strategic objectives of the joint venture. This is in particular the case when each parent company provides a contribution to the joint venture which is vital for its operation (e.g. specific technologies, local know-how or supply agreements).[73] In these circum-stances, the parent companies may be able to block the strategic decisions of the joint venture and, thus, they can operate the joint venture successfully only with each other's agreement on the strategic decisions even if there is no express provision for any veto rights. The parent companies will therefore be required to cooperate.[74] Further factors are decision making procedures which are tailored in such a way as to allow the parent companies to exercise joint control even in the absence of explicit agreements granting veto rights or other links between the minority share-holders related to the joint venture.[75]

Notes

[73] Case COMP/JV.55 *Hutchinson/RCPM/ECT* of 3 July 2001; see also Case IV/M.553 – *RTL/Veronica/Endemol* of 20 September 1995.

[74] Judgment in Case T-282/02 *Cementbouw v Commission*, paragraphs 42, 52, 67 [2006] ECR II-319.

[75] Case COMP/JV.55 *Hutchinson/RCPM/ECT* of 3 July 2001. See also Case IV/M.553 – *RTL/Veronica/Endemol* of 20 September 1995.

Commentary

para 77: **B&C:** 8.038

78. Such a scenario may not only occur in a situation where two or more minority shareholders jointly control an undertaking on a *de facto* basis, but also where there is high degree of depend-ency of a majority shareholder on a minority shareholder. This may be the case where the joint venture economically and financially depends on the minority shareholder or where only the

minority shareholder has the required know-how for, and will play a major role in, the operation of the joint undertaking whereas the majority shareholder is a mere financial investor.[76] In such circumstances, the majority shareholder will not be able to enforce its position, but the joint venture partner may be able to block strategic decisions so that both parent undertakings will be required to cooperate permanently. This leads to a situation of *de facto* joint control which prevails over a pure *de jure* assessment according to which the majority shareholder could have been considered to have sole control.

Notes

[76] Case IV/M.967 – *KLM/Air UK* of 22 September 1997; Case COMP/M.4085 – *Arcelor/Oyak/Erdemir* of 13 February 2006.

Commentary
para 78: F&N: 5.93

79. These criteria apply to the formation of a new joint venture as well as to acquisitions of minority shareholdings, together conferring joint control. In case of acquisitions of shareholdings, there is a higher probability of a commonality of interests if the shareholdings are acquired by means of concerted action. However, an acquisition by way of a concerted action is not alone sufficient for the purposes of establishing *de facto* joint control. In general, a common interest as financial investors (or creditors) of a company in a return on investment does not constitute a commonality of interests leading to the exercise of *de facto* joint control.

Commentary
para 79: B&C: 8.038 F&N: 5.93, 5.114

80. In the absence of strong common interests such as those outlined above, the possibility of changing coalitions between minority shareholders will normally exclude the assumption of joint control. Where there is no stable majority in the decision-making procedure and the majority can on each occasion be any of the various combinations possible amongst the minority shareholders, it cannot be assumed that the minority shareholders (or a certain group thereof) will jointly control the undertaking.[77] In this context, it is not sufficient that there are agreements between two or more parties having an equal shareholding in the capital of an undertaking which establish identical rights and powers between the parties, where these fall short of strategic veto rights. For example, in the case of an undertaking where three shareholders each own one-third of the share capital and each elect one-third of the members of the Board of Directors, the shareholders do not have joint control since decisions are required to be taken on the basis of a simple majority.

Notes

[77] Case IV/JV.12 – *Ericsson/Nokia/Psion/Motorola* of 22 December 1998.

Commentary
para 80: B&C: 8.039

3.4. Other considerations related to joint control

Unequal role of the parent companies

81. Joint control is not incompatible with the fact that one of the parent companies enjoys specific knowledge of and experience in the business of the joint venture. In such a case, the other parent company can play a modest or even non-existent role in the daily management of the joint venture where its presence is motivated by considerations of a financial, long-term-strategy, brand image or general policy nature. Nevertheless, it must always retain the real possibility of contesting the decisions taken by the other parent company on the basis of equality in voting rights or rights of appointment to decision making bodies or of veto rights related to strategic issues. Without this, there would be sole control.

Commentary
para 81: B&C: 8.036 F&N: 5.90

Casting Vote

82. For joint control to exist, there should not be a casting vote for one parent company only as this would lead to sole control of the company enjoying the casting vote. However, there can be joint control when this casting vote is in practice of limited relevance and effectiveness. This may be the case when the casting vote can be exercised only after a series of stages of arbitration and attempts at reconciliation or in a very limited field or if the exercise of the casting vote triggers a put option implying a serious financial burden or if the mutual interdependence of the parent companies would make the exercise of the casting vote unlikely.[78]

Notes

[78] Case COMP/M.2574 – *Pirelli/Edizione/Olivetti/Telecom Italia* of 20 September 2001; Case IV/M.553 – *RTL/Veronica/Endemol* of 20 September 1995; Case IV/M.425 – *British Telecom/Banco Santander*, of 28 March 1994.

Commentary
para 82: B&C: 8.028 F&N: 5.94

III. Changes in the Quality of Control

83. The Merger Regulation covers operations resulting in the acquisition of sole or joint control, including operations leading to changes in the quality of control. First, such a change in the quality of control, resulting in a concentration, occurs if there is a change between sole and joint control. Second, a change in the quality of control occurs between joint control scenarios before and after the transaction if there is an increase in the number or a change in the identity of controlling shareholders. However, there is no change in the quality of control if a change from negative to positive sole control occurs. Such a change affects neither the incentives of the negatively controlling shareholder nor the nature of the control structure, as the controlling shareholder did not necessarily have to cooperate with specific shareholders at the time when it enjoyed negative control. In any case, mere changes in the level of shareholdings of the same controlling shareholders, without changes of the powers they hold in a company and of the composition of the control structure of the company, do not constitute a change in the quality of control and therefore are not a notifiable concentration.

Commentary
para 83: B&C: 8.042

84. These changes in the quality of control will be discussed in two categories: first, an entrance of one or more new controlling shareholders irrespective of whether or not they replace existing controlling shareholders and, second, a reduction of the number of controlling shareholders.

1. Entry of controlling shareholders

85. An entry of new controlling shareholders leading to a joint control scenario can either result from a change from sole to joint control, or from the entry of an additional shareholder or a replacement of an existing shareholder in an already jointly controlled undertaking.

86. A move from sole control to joint control is considered a notifiable operation as this changes the quality of control of the joint venture. First, there is a new acquisition of control for the shareholder entering the controlled undertaking. Second, only the new acquisition of control makes the controlled undertaking to a joint venture which changes decisively also the situation for the remaining controlling undertaking under the Merger Regulation: In the future, it has to take into account the interests of one or more other controlling shareholder(s) and it is required to cooperate permanently with the new shareholder(s). Before, it could either determine the strategic behaviour of the controlled undertaking alone (in the case of sole control) or was not forced to take into account the interests of specific other shareholders and was not forced to cooperate with those shareholders permanently.

87. The entry of a new shareholder in a jointly controlled undertaking – either in addition to the already controlling shareholders or in replacement of one of them – also constitutes a notifiable concentration, although the undertaking is jointly controlled before and after the operation.[79]

First, also in this scenario there is a shareholder newly acquiring control of the joint venture. Second, the quality of control of the joint venture is determined by the identity of all controlling shareholders. It lies in the nature of joint control that, since each shareholder alone has a blocking right concerning strategic decisions, the jointly controlling shareholders have to take into account each others interests and are required to cooperate for the determination of the strategic behaviour of the joint venture.[80] The nature of joint control therefore does not exhaust itself in a pure mathematical addition of the blocking rights exercised by several shareholders, but is determined by the composition of the jointly controlling shareholders. One of the most obvious scenarios leading to a decisive change in the nature of the control structure of a jointly controlled undertaking is a situation where in a joint venture, jointly controlled by a competitor of the joint venture and a financial investor, the financial investor is replaced by another competitor. In these circumstances, the control structure and the incentives of the joint venture may entirely change, not only because of the entry of the new controlling shareholder, but also due to the change in the behaviour of the remaining shareholder. The replacement of a controlling shareholder or the entry of a new shareholder in a jointly controlled undertaking therefore constitutes a change in the quality of control.[81]

Notes

[79] See, e.g. Case COMP/M.3440 – *ENI/EDP/GdP* of 9 December 2004.

[80] Judgment in Case T-282/02 *Cementbouw v Commission*, paragraph 67 [2006] ECR II-319.

[81] Generally, it should be noted that the Commission will not assess as a separate concentration the indirect replacement of a controlling shareholder in a joint control scenario which takes place via an acquisition of control of one of its parent undertakings. The Commission will assess any changes occurring in the competitive situation of the joint venture in the framework of the overall acquisition of control of its parent undertaking. In those circumstances, the other controlling shareholders in the joint venture will therefore not be undertakings concerned by the concentration which relates to its parent undertaking.

Commentary
para 87: B&C: 8.043

88. However, the entry of new shareholders only results in a notifiable concentration if one or several shareholders acquire sole or joint control by virtue of the operation. The entry of new shareholders may lead to a situation where joint control can neither be established on a *de jure* basis nor on a *de facto* basis as the entry of the new shareholder leads to the consequence that changing coalitions between minority shareholders are possible.[82]

Notes

[82] Case IV/JV.12 – *Ericsson/Nokia/Psion/Motorola* of 22 December 1998.

Commentary
para 88: B&C: 8.043

2. Reduction in the number of shareholders

89. A reduction in the number of controlling shareholders constitutes a change in the quality of control and is thus to be considered as a concentration if the exit of one or more controlling shareholders results in a change from joint to sole control. Decisive influence exercised alone is substantially different from decisive influence exercised jointly, since in the latter case the jointly controlling shareholders have to take into account the potentially different interests of the other party or parties involved.[83]

Notes

[83] See Case IV/M023 – *ICI/Tioxide*, of 28 November 1990; see also paragraph 5(d) of the Commission Notice on a simplified procedure for treatment of certain concentrations under Council Regulation (EC) No 139/2004.

Commentary
para 89: B&C: 8.041

90. Where the operation involves a reduction in the number of jointly controlling shareholders, without leading to a change from joint to sole control, the transaction will normally not lead to a notifiable concentration.

Commentary
para 90: **B&C:** 8.043

IV. Joint Ventures – the Concept of Full-Functionality

91. Article 3(1)(b) provides that a concentration shall be deemed to arise where control is acquired by *one or more* undertakings of the whole or parts of another undertaking. The new acquisition of another undertaking by several jointly controlling undertakings therefore constitutes a concentration under the Merger Regulation. As in the case of the acquisition of sole control of an undertaking, such an acquisition of joint control will lead to a structural change in the market even if, according to the plans of the acquiring undertakings, the acquired undertaking would no longer be considered full-function after the transaction (e.g. because it will sell exclusively to the parent undertakings in future). Thus, a transaction involving several undertakings acquiring joint control of another undertaking or parts of another undertaking, fulfilling the criteria set out in paragraph 24, from third parties will constitute a concentration according to Article 3(1) without it being necessary to consider the full-functionality criterion.[84]

Notes
[84] These considerations do not apply to Article 2(4) in the same way. Whereas the interpretation of Article 3, paragraphs (1) and (4) relates to the applicability of the Merger Regulation to joint ventures, Article 2(4) relates to the substantive analysis of joint ventures. The "creation of a joint venture constituting a concentration pursuant to Article 3", as provided for in Article 2(4), comprises the acquisition of joint control according to Article 3, paragraphs (1) and (4).

Commentary
para 91: **B&C:** 8.054 **F&N:** 5.122, 5.124, 5.126

92. Article 3(4) provides in addition that the creation of a joint venture performing on a lasting basis all the functions of an autonomous economic entity (so called full-function joint ventures) shall constitute a concentration within the meaning of the Merger Regulation. The full-functionality criterion therefore delineates the application of the Merger Regulation for the creation of joint ventures by the parties, irrespective of whether such a joint venture is created as a "greenfield operation" or whether the parties contribute assets to the joint venture which they previously owned individually. In these circumstances, the joint venture must fulfil the full-functionality criterion in order to constitute a concentration.

Commentary
para 92: **B&C:** 8.056 **F&N:** 5.33, 5.115, 5.121, 5.126, 5.128

93. The fact that a joint venture may be a full-function undertaking and therefore economically autonomous from an operational viewpoint does not mean that it enjoys autonomy as regards the adoption of its strategic decisions. Otherwise, a jointly controlled undertaking could never be considered a full-function joint venture and therefore the condition laid down in Article 3(4) would never be complied with.[85] It is therefore sufficient for the criterion of full-functionality if the joint venture is autonomous in operational respect.

Notes
[85] Judgment in Case T-282/02 *Cementbouw v Commission*, paragraph 62 [2006] ECR II-319.

Commentary
para 93: **F&N:** 5.129

1. Sufficient resources to operate independently on a market

94. Full function character essentially means that a joint venture must operate on a market, performing the functions normally carried out by undertakings operating on the same market. In order to do so the joint venture must have a management dedicated to its day-to-day operations and access to sufficient resources including finance, staff, and assets (tangible and intangible) in order to conduct on a lasting basis its business activities within the area provided for in the joint-venture agreement.[86] The personnel do not necessarily need to be employed by the joint venture itself. If it is standard practice in the industry where the joint venture is operating, it may be sufficient if third parties envisage the staffing under an operational agreement or if staff is assigned by an interim employment agency. The secondment of personnel by the parent companies may also be sufficient if this is done either only for a start-up period or if the joint venture deals with the parent companies in the same way as with third parties. The latter case requires that the joint venture deals with the parents at arm's length on the basis of normal commercial conditions and that the joint venture is also free to recruit its own employees or to obtain staff via third parties.

Notes

[86] Case IV/M.527 – *Thomson CSF/Deutsche Aerospace*, of 2 December 1994 – intellectual rights, Case IV/M.560 *EDS/Lufthansa* of 11 May 1995 – outsourcing, Case IV/M.585 – *Voest Alpine Industrieanlagenbau GmbH/Davy International Ltd*, of 7 September 1995 – joint venture's right to demand additional expertise and staff from its parent companies, Case IV/M.686 – *Nokia/Autoliv*, of 5 February 1996, joint venture able to terminate "service agreements" with parent company and to move from site retained by parent company, Case IV/M.791 – *British Gas Trading Ltd/Group 4 Utility Services Ltd*, of 7 October 1996, joint venture's intended assets will be transferred to leasing company and leased by joint venture.

Commentary
para 94: **B&C**: 8.055 **F&N**: 5.131

2. Activities beyond one specific function for the parents

95. A joint venture is not full-function if it only takes over one specific function within the parent companies' business activities without its own access to or presence on the market. This is the case, for example, for joint ventures limited to R&D or production. Such joint ventures are auxiliary to their parent companies' business activities. This is also the case where a joint venture is essentially limited to the distribution or sales of its parent companies' products and, therefore, acts principally as a sales agency. However, the fact that a joint venture makes use of the distribution network or outlet of one or more of its parent companies normally will not disqualify it as "full-function" as long as the parent companies are acting only as agents of the joint venture.[87]

Notes

[87] Case IV/M.102 – *TNT/Canada Post etc.* of 2 December 1991.

Commentary
para 95: **B&C**: 8.056 **F&N**: 5.132

96. A frequent example where this question arises are joint ventures involved in the holding of real estate property, which are typically set up for tax and other financial reasons. As long as the purpose of the joint venture is limited to the acquisition and/or holding of certain real estate for the parents and based on financial resources provided by the parents, it will not usually be considered to be full-function, as it lacks an autonomous, long term business activity on the market and will typically also lack the necessary resources to operate independently. This has to be distinguished from joint ventures that are actively managing a real estate portfolio and who act on their own behalf on the market, which typically indicates full-functionality.[88]

Notes

[88] See Case IV/M.929 – *DIA/Veba Immobilien/Deutschbau* of 23 June 1997; Case COMP/M.3325 – *Morgan Stanley/Glick/Canary Wharf* of 23 January 2004.

Commentary
para 96: **B&C:** 8.056 **F&N:** 5.132

3. Sale/purchase relations with the parents

97. The strong presence of the parent companies in upstream or downstream markets is a factor to be taken into consideration in assessing the full-function character of a joint venture where this presence results in substantial sales or purchases between the parent companies and the joint venture. The fact that, for an initial start-up period only, the joint venture relies almost entirely on sales to or purchases from its parent companies does not normally affect its full-function character. Such a start-up period may be necessary in order to establish the joint venture on a market. But the period will normally not exceed a period of three years, depending on the specific conditions of the market in question.[89]

Notes

[89] Case IV/M.560 – *EDS/Lufthansa* of 11 May 1995; Case IV/M.686 *Nokia/Autoliv* of 5 February 1996; to be contrasted with Case IV/M.904 – *RSB/Tenex/Fuel Logistics* of 2 April 1997 and Case IV/M.979 – *Preussag/Voest-Alpine* of 1 October 1997. A special case exists where sales by the joint venture to its parent are caused by a legal monopoly downstream of the joint venture, see Case IV/M.468 – *Siemens/Italtel* of 17 February 1995, or where the sales to a parent company consist of by-products, which are of minor importance to the joint venture, see Case IV/M.550 – *Union Carbide/Enichem* of 13 March 1995.

Commentary
para 97: **B&C:** 8.056 **F&N:** 5.134

Sales to the parents

98. Where sales from the joint venture to the parent companies are intended to be made on a lasting basis, the essential question is whether, regardless of these sales, the joint venture is geared to play an active role on the market and can be considered economically autonomous from an operational viewpoint. In this respect the relative proportion of sales made to its parents compared with the total production of the joint venture is an important factor. Due to the particularities of each individual case, it is impossible to define a specific turnover ratio which distinguishes full-function from other joint ventures. If the joint venture achieves more than 50% of its turnover with third parties, this will typically be an indication of full-functionality. Below this indicative threshold, a case-by-case analysis is required, whereby, for the finding of operational autonomy, the relationship between the joint venture and its parents must be truly commercial in character. For this purpose, it is to be demonstrated that the joint venture will supply its goods or services to the purchaser who values them most and will pay most and that the joint venture will also deal with its parents' companies at arm's length on the basis of normal commercial conditions.[90] Under these circumstances, i.e. if the joint venture will treat its parent companies in the same commercial way as third parties, it may be sufficient that at least 20% of the joint venture's predicted sales will go to third parties. However, the greater the proportion of sales likely to be made to the parents, the greater will be the need for clear evidence of the commercial character of the relationship.

Notes

[90] Case IV/M.556 – *Zeneca/Vanderhave* of 9 April 1996; Case IV/M.751 – *Bayer/Hüls* of 3 July 1996.

99. For the determination of the proportion between sales to the parents and to third parties, the Commission will take past accounts and substantiated business plans into account. However, especially where substantial third-party sales cannot be readily foreseen, the Commission will base its finding also on the general market structure. This may be a relevant factor as well for the assessment whether the joint venture will deal with its parents on an arm's length basis.

100. These issues frequently arise with regard to outsourcing agreements, where an undertaking creates a joint venture with a service provider[91] which will carry out functions that were previously dealt with by the undertaking in-house. The JV typically cannot be considered to be full-function in these scenarios: it provides its services exclusively to the client undertaking, and it is

dependent for its services on input from the service provider. The fact that the joint venture's business plan often at least does not exclude that the joint venture can provide its services to third parties does not alter this assessment, as in the typical outsourcing setup any third party revenues are likely to remain ancillary to the joint venture's main activities for the client undertaking. However, this general rule does not exclude that there are outsourcing situations where the joint venture partners, for example for reasons of economies of scale, set up a joint venture with the perspective of significant market access. This could qualify the joint venture as full function if significant third-party sales are foreseen and if the relationship between the joint venture and its parent will be truly commercial in character and if the joint venture deals with its parents on the basis of normal commercial conditions.

Notes

[91] The question under which circumstances an outsourcing arrangement qualifies as a concentration is dealt with in paragraphs 25ff. of this Notice.

Purchases from the parents

101. In relation to purchases made by the joint venture from its parent companies, the full-function character of the joint venture is questionable in particular where little value is added to the products or services concerned at the level of the joint venture itself. In such a situation, the joint venture may be closer to a joint sales agency.

Commentary
para 101: B&C: 8.058 F&N: 5.136

Trade markets

102. However, in contrast to this situation where a joint venture is active in a trade market and performs the normal functions of a trading company in such a market, it normally will not be an auxiliary sales agency but a full-function joint venture. A trade market is characterised by the existence of companies which specialise in the selling and distribution of products without being vertically integrated in addition to those which are integrated, and where different sources of supply are available for the products in question. In addition, many trade markets may require operators to invest in specific facilities such as outlets, stockholding, warehouses, depots, transport fleets and sales and service personnel. In order to constitute a full-function joint venture in a trade market, an undertaking must have the necessary facilities and be likely to obtain a substantial proportion of its supplies not only from its parent companies but also from other competing sources.[92]

Notes

[92] Case IV/M.788 – *AgrEVO/Marubeni* of 3 September 1996.

Commentary
para 102: F&N: 5.136

4. Operation on a lasting basis

103. Furthermore, the joint venture must be intended to operate on a lasting basis. The fact that the parent companies commit to the joint venture the resources described above normally demonstrates that this is the case. In addition, agreements setting up a joint venture often provide for certain contingencies, for example, the failure of the joint venture or fundamental disagreement as between the parent companies.[93] This may be achieved by the incorporation of provisions for the eventual dissolution of the joint venture itself or the possibility for one or more parent companies to withdraw from the joint venture. This kind of provision does not prevent the joint venture from being considered as operating on a lasting basis. The same is normally true where the agreement specifies a period for the duration of the joint venture where this period is sufficiently long in order to bring about a lasting change in the structure of the undertakings concerned,[94] or where the agreement provides for the possible continuation of the joint venture beyond this period.

Notes

[93] Case IV/M.891 – *Deutsche Bank/Commerzbank/JM Voith* of 23 April 1997.

[94] See Case COMP/M.2903 – *DaimlerChrysler/Deutsche Telekom/JV* of 30 April 2003 where a period of 12 years was considered sufficient; Case COMP/M.2632 – *Deutsche Bahn/ECT International/United Depots/JV* of 11 February 2002 with a contract duration of 8 years. In Case COMP/M.3858 *Lehman Brothers/Starwood/Le Meridien* of 20 July 2005, the Commission considered a minimum period of 10–15 years sufficient, but not a period of three years.

Commentary
para 103: B&C: 8.059 F&N: 5.137

---

104. By contrast, the joint venture will not be considered to operate on a lasting basis where it is established for a short finite duration. This would be the case, for example, where a joint venture is established in order to construct a specific project such as a power plant, but it will not be involved in the operation of the plant once its construction has been completed.

Commentary
para 104: B&C: 8.059 F&N: 5.137

---

105. A joint venture also lacks the sufficient operations on a lasting basis at a stage where there are decisions of third parties outstanding that are of an essential core importance for starting the joint venture's business activity. Only decisions that go beyond mere formalities and the award of which is typically uncertain qualify for these scenarios. Examples are the award of a contract (e.g., in public tenders), licences (e.g., in the telecoms sector) or access rights to property (e.g., exploration rights for oil and gas). Pending the decision on such factors, it is unclear whether the joint venture will become operational at all. Thus, at that stage the joint venture cannot be considered to perform economic functions on a lasting basis and consequently does not qualify as full function. However, once a decision has been taken in favour of the joint venture in question, this criterion is fulfilled and a concentration arises.[95]

Notes

[95] Subject to the other criteria mentioned in this chapter of the Notice.

Commentary
para 105: B&C: 8.059 F&N: 5.119, 5.138

---

5. Changes in the activities of the joint venture

106. The parents may decide to enlarge the scope of the activities of the joint venture in the course of its lifetime. This will be considered as a new concentration that may trigger a notification requirement if this enlargement entails the acquisition of the whole or part of another undertaking from the parents that would, considered in isolation, qualify as a concentration as explained in paragraph 24 of this Notice.[96]

Notes

[96] See Case COMP/M.3039 – *Soprol/Céréol/Lesieur* of 30 January 2003.

---

107. A concentration may also arise if the parent companies transfer significant additional assets, contracts, know-how or other rights to the joint venture and these assets and rights constitute the basis or nucleus of an extension of the activities of the joint venture into other product or geographic markets which were not the object of the original joint venture, and if the joint venture performs such activities on a full-function basis. As the transfer of the assets or rights shows that the parents are the real players behind the extension of the joint venture's scope, the enlargement of the activities of the joint venture can be considered in the same way as the creation of a new joint venture within the meaning of Article 3(4).[97]

Notes

[97] The triggering event for the notification in such a case will be the agreement or other legal act underlying the transfer of the assets, contracts, know-how or other rights.

Part D Mergers and Concentrations

108. If the scope of a joint venture is enlarged without additional assets, contracts, know-how or rights being transferred, no concentration will be deemed to arise.

109. A concentration arises if a change in the activity of an existing non-full-function joint venture occurs so that a full-function joint venture within the meaning of Article 3(4) is created. The following examples may be given: a change of the organisational structure of a joint venture so that it fulfils the full functionality criterion;[98] a joint venture that used to supply only the parent companies, which subsequently starts a significant activity on the market; or scenarios, as described in paragraph 105 above, where a joint venture can only start its activity on the market once it has essential input (such as a licence for a joint venture in the telecoms sector). Such a change in the activity of the joint venture will frequently require a decision by its shareholders or its management. Once the decision is taken that leads to the joint venture meeting the full functionality criterion, a concentration arises.

Notes
[98] Case COMP/M.2276 – *The Coca-Cola Company/Nestlé/JV* of 27 September 2001.

V. EXCEPTIONS

110. Article 3(5) sets out three exceptional situations where the acquisition of a controlling interest does not constitute a concentration under the Merger Regulation.

111. First, the acquisition of securities by companies whose normal activities include transactions and dealing in securities for their own account or for the account of others is not deemed to constitute a concentration if such an acquisition is made in the framework of these businesses and if the securities are held on only a temporary basis (Article 3(5)(a)). In order to fall within this exception, the following requirements must be fulfilled:
   — the acquiring undertaking must be a credit or other financial institution or insurance company the normal activities of which are described above;
   — the securities must be acquired with a view to their resale;
   — the acquiring undertaking must not exercise the voting rights with a view to determining the strategic commercial behaviour of the target company or must exercise these rights only with a view to preparing the total or partial disposal of the undertaking, its assets or the securities;
   — the acquiring undertaking must dispose of its controlling interest within one year of the date of the acquisition, that is, it must reduce its shareholding within this one-year period at least to a level which no longer confers control. This period, however, may be extended by the Commission where the acquiring undertaking can show that the disposal was not reasonably possible within the one-year period.

Commentary
para 111: B&C: 8.050

112. Second, there is no change of control, and hence no concentration within the meaning of the Merger Regulation, where control is acquired by an office-holder according to the law of a Member State relating to liquidation, winding-up, insolvency, cessation of payments, compositions or analogous proceedings (Article 3(5)(b));

Commentary
para 112: B&C: 8.052

113. Third, a concentration does not arise where a financial holding company within the meaning of Article 5(3) of the Council Directive 78/660/EEC[99] acquires control. The notion of "financial holding company" is thus limited to companies whose sole purpose it is to acquire holdings in other undertakings without involving themselves directly or indirectly in the management of those undertakings, the foregoing without prejudice to their rights as shareholders. Such investment companies must be further structured in a way that compliance with these limitations can be supervised by an administrative or judicial authority. The Merger Regulation

provides for an additional condition for this exception to apply: such companies may exercise the voting rights in the other undertakings only to maintain the full value of those investments and not to determine directly or indirectly the strategic commercial conduct of the controlled undertaking.

Notes

99 Fourth Council Directive 78/660/EEC of 25 July 1978 based on Article [50(2)(g)] of the Treaty on the annual accounts of certain types of companies, OJ L 222, 14.8.1978, p.11, as last amended by Directive 2003/51/EC of 18 June 2003, OJ L 178, 17.7.2003, p.16. Article 5(3) of this Directive defines financial holding companies as "those companies the sole objective of which is to acquire holdings in other undertakings, and to manage such holdings and turn them to profit, without involving themselves directly or indirectly in the management of those undertakings, the foregoing without prejudice to their rights as shareholders. The limitations imposed on the activities of these companies must be such that compliance with them can be supervised by an administrative or judicial authority".

Commentary
para 113: **F&N:** 5.109

114. The exceptions under Article 3(5) of the Merger Regulation only apply to a very limited field. First, these exceptions only apply if the operation would otherwise be a concentration in its own right, but not if the transaction is part of a broader, single concentration, in circumstances in which the ultimate acquirer of control would not fall within the terms of Article 3(5) (see e.g. paragraph 35 above). Second, the exceptions under Article 3(5)(a) and (c) only apply to acquisitions of control by way of purchase of securities, not to acquisitions of assets.

Commentary
para 114: **B&C:** 8.050, 8.051

115. The exceptions do not apply to typical investment fund structures. According to their objectives, these funds usually do not limit themselves in the exercise of the voting rights, but adopt decisions to appoint the members of the management and the supervisory bodies of the undertakings or to even restructure those undertakings. This would not be compatible with the requirement under both Article 3(5)(a) and (c) that the acquiring companies do not exercise the voting rights with a view to determine the competitive conduct of the other undertaking.[100]

Notes

100 Case IV/M.669 – *Charterhouse/Porterbrook*, of 11 December 1995.

116. The question may arise whether an operation to rescue an undertaking before or from insolvency proceedings constitutes a concentration under the Merger Regulation. Such a rescue operation typically involves the conversion of existing debt into a new company, through which a syndicate of banks may acquire joint control of the company concerned. Where such an operation meets the criteria for joint control, as outlined above, it will normally be considered to be a concentration.[101] Although the primary intention of the banks is to restructure the financing of the undertaking concerned for its subsequent resale, the exception set out in Article 3(5)(a) is normally not applicable to such an operation. In a similar way as set out for investment funds, the restructuring programme normally requires the controlling banks to determine the strategic commercial behaviour of the rescued undertaking. Furthermore, it is not normally a realistic proposition to transform a rescued company into a commercially viable entity and to resell it within the permitted one-year period. Moreover, the length of time needed to achieve this aim may be so uncertain that it would be difficult to grant an extension of the disposal period.

Notes

101 Case IV/M.116 – *Kelt/American Express*, of 28 August 1991.

Commentary
para 116: **B&C:** 8.050

VI. Abandonment of Concentrations

117. A concentration ceases to exist and the Merger Regulation ceases to be applicable if the undertakings concerned abandon the concentration.

118. In this respect, the revised Merger Regulation 139/2004 introduced a new provision related to the closure of procedures concerning the control of concentrations without a final decision after the Commission has initiated proceedings under Article 6(1)(c) 1st sentence. That sentence reads as follows: "Without prejudice to Article 9, such proceedings shall be closed by means of a decision as provided for in Article 8(1) to (4), unless the undertakings concerned have demonstrated to the satisfaction of the Commission that they have abandoned the concentration". Prior to the initiation of proceedings, such requirements do not apply.

119. As a general principle, the requirements for the proof of the abandonment must correspond in terms of legal form, intensity etc. to the initial act that was considered sufficient to make the concentration notifiable. In case the parties proceed from that initial act to a strengthening of their contractual links during the procedure, for example by concluding a binding agreement after the transaction was notified on the basis of a good faith intention, the requirements for the proof of the abandonment must correspond also to the nature of the latest act.

120. In line with this principle, in case of implementation of the concentration prior to a Commission decision, the re-establishment of the *status quo ante* has to be shown. The mere withdrawal of the notification is not considered as sufficient proof that the concentration has been abandoned in the sense of Article 6(1)(c). Likewise, minor modifications of a concentration which do not affect the change in control or the quality of that change, cannot be considered as an abandonment of the original concentration.[102]

   — Binding agreement: proof of the legally binding cancellation of the agreement in the form envisaged by the initial agreement (i.e. usually a document signed by all the parties) will be required. Expressions of intention to cancel the agreement or not to implement the notified concentration, as well as unilateral declarations by (one of) the parties will not be considered sufficient.[103]

   — Good faith intention to conclude an agreement: In case of a letter of intent or memorandum of understanding reflecting such good faith intention, documents proving that this basis for the good faith intention has been cancelled will be required. As for possible other forms that indicated the good faith intention, the abandonment must reverse this good faith intention and correspond in terms of form and intensity to the initial expression of intent.

   — Public announcement of a public bid or of the intention to make a public bid: a public announcement terminating the bidding procedure or renouncing to the intention to make a public bid will be required. The format and public reach of this announcement must be comparable to the initial announcement.

   — Implemented concentrations: In case the concentration has been implemented prior to a Commission decision, the parties will be required to show that the situation prevailing before the implementation of the concentration has been re-established.

Notes

102 This paragraph does not prejudge the assessment whether the modification requires submitting additional information to the Commission under Art. 5(3) Reg. 802/2004.

103 See Case COMP/M.4381 – *JCI/VB/FIAMM* of 10 May 2007, paragraph 15, where only one party did no longer wished to implement an agreement, whereas the other party still considered the agreement to be binding and enforceable.

---

121. It is for the parties to submit the necessary documentation to meet these requirements in due time.

VII. Changes of Transactions after a Commission Authorisation Decision

122. In some cases, parties may wish not to implement the concentration in the form foreseen after authorisation of the concentration by the Commission. The question arises whether the Commission's authorisation decision still covers the changed structure of the transaction.

Commentary
para 122: F&N: 5.531

123. Broadly speaking, if, before implementation of the authorised concentration, the transactional structure is changed from an acquisition of control, falling under Article 3(1)(b), to a merger according to Article 3(1)(a), or *vice versa*, then the change in the transactional structure is considered a different concentration under the Merger Regulation and a new notification is required.[104] However, less significant modifications of the transaction, for example minor changes in the shareholding percentages which do not affect the change in control or the quality of that change, changes in the offer price in the case of public bids or changes in the corporate structure by which the transaction is implemented without effects on the relevant control situation under the Merger Regulation, are considered as being covered by the Commission's authorisation decision.

Notes

[104] See cases COMP/M.2706 – *Carnival Corporation/P&O Princess* of 11 April 2002 and COMP/M.3071 – *Carnival Corporation/P&O Princess* of 10 February 2003. In such circumstances, the identity of the notifying parties changes, as both parties to a merger must notify, whereas only the party acquiring control must do so. However, if the parties implement an acquisition of control over a target company and only *subsequently* decide to merge with the newly acquired subsidiary, this would be regarded as an internal restructuring that does not give rise to a change in control and would thus not fall within the terms of Article 3 of the Merger Regulation.

Commentary
para 123: F&N: 5.531

C. Community Dimension

I. Thresholds

124. A two fold test defines the operations to which the Merger Regulation applies. The first test is that the operation must be a concentration within the meaning of Article 3. The second comprises the turnover thresholds contained in Article 1, designed to identify those operations which have an impact upon the Community and can be deemed to be of "Community dimension". Turnover is used as a proxy for the economic resources being combined in a concentration, and is allocated geographically in order to reflect the geographic distribution of those resources.

125. Two sets of thresholds are set out in Article 1 to establish whether the operation has a Community dimension. Article 1(2) establishes three different criteria: The worldwide turnover threshold is intended to measure the overall dimension of the undertakings concerned; the Community turnover threshold seek to determine whether the concentration involves a minimum level of activities in the Community; and the two-thirds rule aims to exclude purely domestic transactions from Community jurisdiction.

126. This second set of thresholds, contained in Article 1(3), is designed to tackle those concentrations which fall short of achieving Community dimension under Article 1(2), but would have a substantial impact in at least three Member States leading to multiple notifications under national competition rules of those Member States. For this purpose, Article 1(3) provides for lower turnover thresholds, both worldwide and Community-wide, and for a minimum level of activities of the undertakings concerned, jointly and individually, in at least three Member States. Similarly to Article 1(2), Article 1(3) also contains a two-thirds rule excluding predominantly domestic concentrations.[105]

Notes

[105] A concentration is further deemed to have a Community dimension if it is referred to the Commission under Article 4(5) of the Merger Regulation. These cases are dealt with in the Commission Notice on Case Referral in respect of concentrations, OJ C 56, 05.03.2005, p.2.

127. The thresholds as such are designed to govern jurisdiction and not to assess the market position of the parties to the concentration nor the impact of the operation. In so doing they include

turnover derived from, and thus the resources devoted to, all areas of activity of the parties, and not just those directly involved in the concentration. The thresholds are purely quantitative, since they are only based on turnover calculation instead of market share or other criteria. They pursue the objective to provide a simple and objective mechanism that can be easily handled by the companies involved in a merger in order to determine if their transaction has a Community dimension and is therefore notifiable.

128. Whereas Article 1 sets out the numerical thresholds to establish jurisdiction, the purpose of Article 5 is to explain how turnover should be calculated to ensure that the resulting figures are a true representation of economic reality.

Commentary
para 128: F&N: 5.205

II. Notion of Undertaking Concerned

1. General

129. From the point of view of determining jurisdiction, the undertakings concerned are those participating in a concentration, i.e. a merger or an acquisition of control as foreseen in Article 3(1). The individual and aggregate turnover of those undertakings will be decisive in determining whether the thresholds are met.

Commentary
para 129: F&N: 5.168

130. Once the undertakings concerned have been identified in a given transaction, their turnover for the purposes of determining jurisdiction is to be calculated according to the rules set out in Article 5. Article 5(4) sets out detailed criteria to identify undertakings whose turnover may be attributed to the undertaking concerned because of certain direct or indirect links with the latter. The legislator's intention was to lay down concrete rules which, seen together, can be taken to establish the notion of a "group" for the purposes of the turnover thresholds in the Merger Regulation. The term "group" will be used in the following sections exclusively to refer to the collection of undertakings whose relations with an undertaking concerned come within the terms of one or more of the sub-paragraphs of Article 5(4) of the Merger Regulation.

Commentary
para 130: B&C: 8.076

131. It is important, when referring to the various undertakings which may be involved in a procedure, not to confuse the concept of "undertakings concerned" under Articles 1 and 5 with the terminology used elsewhere in the Merger Regulation and in Commission Regulation (EC) No 802/2004 of 7 April 2004 implementing Council Regulation (EC) No 139/2004 on the control of concentrations between undertakings (hereinafter referred to as the "Implementing Regulation")[106] referring to the various undertakings which may be involved in a procedure. This terminology refers to the notifying parties, other involved parties, third parties and parties who may be subject to fines or periodic penalty payments, and they are defined in Chapter IV of the Implementing Regulation, along with their respective rights and duties.

Notes
[106] OJ L 133, 30 April 2004, p.1.

Commentary
para 131: B&C: 8.076 **F&N:** 5.168, 5.205

2. Mergers

132. In a merger the undertakings concerned are each of the merging entities.

Commentary
para 132: B&C: 8.070 F&N: 5.169

3. Acquisition of control

133. In the remaining cases, it is the concept of "acquiring control" that will determine which are the undertakings concerned. On the acquiring side, there can be one or more undertakings acquiring sole or joint control. On the acquired side, there can be one or more undertakings as a whole or parts thereof. As a general rule, each of these undertakings will be an undertaking concerned within the meaning of the Merger Regulation.

Commentary
para 133: B&C: 8.070 F&N: 5.173

Acquisition of sole control

134. Acquisition of sole control of the whole undertaking is the most straightforward case of acquisition of control. The undertakings concerned will be the acquiring undertaking and the target undertaking.

135. Where the target undertaking is acquired by a group through one of its subsidiaries, the undertakings concerned are the target undertaking and the acquiring subsidiary if this is not a mere acquisition vehicle. However, even though the subsidiary is normally the undertaking concerned for the purpose of calculating turnover, the turnover of all undertakings with which the undertaking concerned has the links as specified in Article 5(4) shall be included in the threshold calculations. In this respect, the group is considered to be a single economic unit and the different companies belonging to the same group cannot be considered as different undertakings concerned for jurisdictional purposes under the Merger Regulation. The actual notification can be made by the subsidiary concerned or by its parent company.

Acquisition of parts of an undertaking and staggered operations — Article 5(2)

136. The first subparagraph of Article 5(2) of the Merger Regulation provides that when the operation concerns the acquisition of parts of one or more undertakings, only those parts which are the subject of the transaction shall be taken into account with regard to the seller. The possible impact of the transaction on the market will depend only on the combination of the economic and financial resources that are the subject of the transaction with those of the acquirer and not on the remaining business of the seller. In this case, the undertakings concerned will be the acquirer(s) and the acquired part(s) of the target undertaking, but the remaining businesses of the seller will be ignored.

137. The second subparagraph of Article 5(2) includes a special provision on staggered operations or follow-up deals. The previous concentrations (within two years) involving the same parties become (re)notifiable with the most recent transaction, provided this constitutes a concentration, if the thresholds are met whether for one or more of the transactions taken in isolation or cumulatively. In this case, the undertakings concerned are the acquirer(s) and the different acquired part(s) of the target company taken as a whole.

Change from joint to sole control

138. If the acquisition of control occurs by way of a change from joint control to sole control, one shareholder normally acquires the stake previously held by the other shareholder(s). In this situation, the undertakings concerned are the acquiring shareholder and the joint venture. As is the case for any other seller, the "exiting" shareholder is not an undertaking concerned.[107]

Notes
[107] Case IV/M.023 – *ICI/Tioxide*, of 28 November 1990.

Commentary
para 138: B&C: 8.070

Part D Mergers and Concentrations

Acquisition of joint control

139. In the case of acquisition of joint control of a newly-created undertaking, the undertakings concerned are each of the companies acquiring control of the newly setup joint venture (which, as it does not yet exist, cannot be considered to be an undertaking concerned and moreover, as yet, has no turnover of its own). The same rule applies where one undertaking contributes a pre-existing subsidiary or a business (over which it previously exercised sole control) to a newly created joint venture. In these circumstances, each of the jointly-controlling undertakings is considered an undertaking concerned whereas any company or business contributed to the joint venture is not an undertaking concerned, and its turnover is part of the turnover of the initial parent company.

140. The situation is different if undertakings newly acquire joint control of a pre-existing undertaking or business. The undertakings concerned are each of the undertakings acquiring joint control on the one hand, and the pre-existing acquired undertaking or business on the other.

Commentary
para 140: F&N: 5.169

141. The acquisition of a company with a view to immediately split up the assets is, as explained above in paragraph 32, mostly not considered as an acquisition of joint control of the entire target company, but as the acquisition of sole control by each of the ultimate acquirers of the respective parts of the target company. In line with the considerations for the acquisition of sole control, undertakings concerned are the acquiring undertakings and the acquired parts in each of the transactions.

Commentary
para 141: B&C: 8.072 **F&N:** 5.169, 5.183

Changes of controlling shareholders in cases of joint control of an existing joint venture

142. A notifiable concentration may arise, as explained above, where a change in the quality of control occurs in a joint control structure due to the entrance of new controlling shareholders, irrespective of whether or not they replace existing controlling shareholders.

143. In the case where one or more shareholders acquire control, either by entry or by substitution of one or more shareholders, in a situation of joint control both before and after the operation, the undertakings concerned are the shareholders (both existing and new) who exercise joint control and the joint venture itself.[108] On the one hand, similar to the acquisition of joint control of an existing company, the joint venture itself can be considered as an undertaking concerned as it is an already pre-existing undertaking. On the other hand, as set out above, the entry of a new shareholder is not only in itself a new acquisition of control, but also leads to a change in the quality of control for the remaining controlling shareholders as the quality of control of the joint venture is determined by the identity and composition of the controlling shareholders and therefore also by the relationship between them. Furthermore, the Merger Regulation considers a joint venture as a combination of the economic resources of the parent companies, together with the joint venture if it already generates turnover on the market. For these reasons, the newly entering controlling shareholders are undertakings concerned alongside with the remaining controlling shareholders. Due to the change of the quality in control, all of them are considered to undertake an acquisition of control.

Notes
[108] See Case IV/M.376 – *Synthomer/Yule Catto*, of 22 October 1993.

144. As Article 4(2) first sentence of the Merger Regulation foresees that all acquisitions of joint control shall be notified jointly by the undertakings acquiring joint control, existing and new shareholders in principle have to notify concentrations arising from such changes in joint control scenarios jointly.

Commentary
para 144: F&N: 5.177

Acquisition of control by a joint venture

145. In transactions where a joint venture acquires control of another company, the question arises whether or not the joint venture should be regarded as the undertaking concerned (the turnover of which would include the turnover of its parent companies), or whether each of its parent companies should individually be regarded as undertakings concerned. This question may be decisive for jurisdictional purposes.[109] Whereas, in principle, the undertaking concerned is the joint venture as the direct participant in the acquisition of control, there may be circumstances where companies set up "shell" companies and the parent companies will individually be considered as undertakings concerned. In this type of situation, the Commission will look at the economic reality of the operation to determine which are the undertakings concerned.

Notes

[109] Assume the following scenario: The target company has an aggregate Community turnover of less than EUR 250 million, and the acquiring parties are two (or more) undertakings, each with a Community turnover exceeding EUR 250 million. If the target is acquired by a "shell" company set up between the acquiring undertakings, there would be only be one undertaking (the "shell" company) with a Community turnover exceeding EUR 250 million, and thus one of the cumulative threshold conditions for Community jurisdiction, namely, the existence of at least two undertakings with a Community turnover exceeding EUR 250 million, would not be fulfilled. Conversely, if instead of acting through a "shell" company, the acquiring undertakings acquire the target undertaking themselves, then the turnover threshold would be met and the Merger Regulation would apply to this transaction. The same considerations apply to the national turnover thresholds referred to in Article 1(3).

Commentary
para 145: B&C: 8.070 F&N: 5.176

146. Where the acquisition is carried out by a full-function joint venture, with the features set out above, and already operates on the same market, the Commission will normally consider the joint venture itself and the target undertaking to be the undertakings concerned (and not the joint venture's parent companies).

Commentary
para 146: B&C: 8.070

147. Conversely, where the joint venture can be regarded as a mere vehicle for an acquisition by the parent companies, the Commission will consider each of the parent companies themselves to be the undertakings concerned, rather than the joint venture, together with the target company. This is the case in particular where the joint venture is set up especially for the purpose of acquiring the target company or has not yet started to operate, where an existing joint venture has no full-function character as referred to above or where the joint venture is an association of undertakings. The same applies where there are elements which demonstrate that the parent companies are in fact the real players behind the operation. These elements may include a significant involvement by the parent companies themselves in the initiation, organisation and financing of the operation. In those cases, the parent companies are regarded as undertakings concerned.

Commentary
para 147: B&C: 8.070

Break-up of joint ventures and exchange of assets

148. When two (or more) undertakings break up a joint venture and split the assets (constituting businesses) between them, this will normally be considered as more than one acquisition of control, as explained above in paragraph 41. For example, undertakings A and B form a joint venture and subsequently split it up, in particular with a new asset configuration. The break-up of the joint venture involves a change from joint control over the joint venture's entire assets to sole control over the divided assets by each of the acquiring undertakings.[110]

Notes

110 See parallel cases COMP/M.3293 – *Shell/BEB* and COMP/M.3294 – *ExxonMobil/BEB* of 20 November 2003; Case IV/M.197 – *Solvay/Laporte* of 30 April 1992.

149. For each break-up operation, and in line with the consideration to the acquisition of sole control, the undertakings concerned will be, on the one hand, the acquiring party and, on the other, the assets that this undertaking will acquire.

150. Similar to the break-up scenario is the situation where two (or more) companies exchange assets constituting a business on each side. In this case, each acquisition of control is considered an independent acquisition of sole control. The undertakings concerned will be, for each transaction, the acquiring companies and the acquired undertaking or assets.

Acquisitions of control by natural persons

151. Control may also be acquired by natural persons, within the meaning of Article 3 of the Merger Regulation, if those persons themselves carry out further economic activities (and are therefore classified as economic undertakings in their own right) or if they control one or more other economic undertakings. In such a situation, the undertakings concerned are the target undertaking and the individual acquirer (with the turnover of the undertaking(s) controlled by that natural person being included in the calculation of the natural person's turnover to the extent that the terms of Article 5(4) are satisfied).[111]

Notes

111 See Case IV/M.082 – *Asko/Jacobs/Adia*, of 16 May 1991 where a private individual with other economic activities acquired joint control of an undertaking and was considered an undertaking concerned.

Commentary
para 151: **B&C**: 8.073 **F&N**: 5.169

152. An acquisition of control of an undertaking by its managers is also an acquisition by natural persons, and paragraph 151 above is also relevant. However, the managers may pool their interests through a "vehicle company", so that it acts with a single voice and also to facilitate decision-making. Such a vehicle company may be, but is not necessarily, an undertaking concerned. The general guidance given above in paragraphs 145–147 on acquisitions of control by a joint venture also applies here.

Commentary
para 152: **B&C**: 8.018, 8.074 **F&N**: 5.169

Acquisition of control by a State-owned undertaking

153. As described above, a merger or an acquisition of control arising between two undertakings owned by the same State (or the same public body) may constitute a concentration if the undertakings were formerly part of different economic units having an independent power of decision. If this is the case, both of them will qualify as undertakings concerned although both are owned by the same State.[112]

Notes

112 See recital 22 of the Merger Regulation, directly related to the calculation of turnover of a state-owned undertaking concerned in the context of Article 5(4).

Commentary
para 153: **B&C**: 8.075 **F&N**: 5.169

III. Relevant Date for Establishing Jurisdiction

154. The legal situation for establishing the Commission's jurisdiction has been changed under the recast Merger Regulation. Under the former Merger Regulation, the relevant date was the

triggering event for a notification according to Article 4(1) of this Regulation – the conclusion of a final agreement or the announcement of a public bid or the acquisition of a controlling interest – or, at the latest, the time when the parties were obliged to notify (i.e. one week after a triggering event for a notification).[113]

Notes

[113] See Case COMP/M.1741 –*MCI Worldcom/Sprint* of 28 June 2000.

155. Under the recast Merger Regulation, there is no longer an obligation for the parties to notify within a certain time-frame (provided the parties do not implement the planned concentration before notification). Moreover, according to Article 4(1) second subparagraph, the undertakings concerned can already notify the transaction on the basis of a good faith intention to conclude an agreement or, in the case of a public bid, where they have publicly announced an intention to make such a bid. At the time of the notification at the latest, the Commission – as well as national competition authorities – must be able to determine their jurisdiction. Article 4(1) subparagraph 1 of the Merger Regulation provides, generally, that concentrations shall be notified following the conclusion of the agreement, the announcement of the public bid, or the acquisition of a controlling interest. The dates of these events are therefore still decisive under the recast Merger Regulation in order to determine the relevant date for establishing jurisdiction, if a notification does not occur before such events on the basis of a good faith intention or an announced intention.[114]

Notes

[114] The alternative possibility that turnover should be defined on the latest date when the relevant parties are obliged to notify (seven days after the "triggering event" under the former Merger Regulation) cannot be retained under the recast merger Regulation, because there is no deadline for notification.

156. The relevant date for establishing Community jurisdiction over a concentration is therefore the date of the conclusion of the binding legal agreement, the announcement of a public bid or the acquisition of a controlling interest or the date of the first notification, whichever date is earlier.[115] Regarding the date of notification, a notification to either the Commission or to a Member State authority is relevant. The relevant date needs in particular to be considered for the question whether acquisitions or divestitures which occur after the period covered by the relevant account, but before the relevant date, require adaptations to those accounts according to the principles set out in paragraphs 172, 173.

Notes

[115] See also opinion of AG Kokott in Case C-202/06 *Cementbouw v Commission* of 26 April 2007, paragraph 46 (not yet reported) [now [2009] ECR II-2533]. Only the recast merger Regulation has provided for the possibility to take into account the first notification if this is earlier than the date of the conclusion of the binding legal agreement, the announcement of a public bid or the acquisition of a controlling interest, see footnote 35 of the opinion.

Commentary
para 156: F&N: 5.206

IV. Turnover

1. The concept of turnover

157. The concept of turnover as used in Article 5 of the Merger Regulation comprises "the amounts derived [...] from the sale of products and the provision of services". Those amounts generally appear in company accounts under the heading "sales". In the case of products, turnover can be determined without difficulty, namely by identifying each commercial act involving a transfer of ownership.

Commentary
para 157: B&C: 8.063

Part D Mergers and Concentrations

158. In the case of services, the method of calculating turnover in general does not differ from that used in the case of products: the Commission takes into consideration the total amount of sales. However, the calculation of the amounts derived from the provision of services may be more complex as this depends on the exact service provided and the underlying legal and economic arrangements in the sector in question. Where one undertaking provides the entire service directly to the customer, the turnover of the undertaking concerned consists of the total amount of sales for the provision of services in the last financial year.

159. In other areas, this general principle may have to be adapted to the specific conditions of the service provided. In certain sectors of activity (such as package holidays and advertising), the service may be sold through intermediaries.116 Even if the intermediary invoices the entire amount to the final customer, the turnover of the undertaking acting as an intermediary consists solely of the amount of its commission. For package holidays, the entire amount paid by the final customer is then allocated to the tour operator which uses the travel agency as distribution network. In the case of advertising, only the amounts received (without the commission) are considered to constitute the turnover of the TV channel or the magazine since media agencies, as intermediaries, do not constitute the distribution channel for the sellers of advertising space, but are chosen by the customers, i.e. those undertakings wishing to place advertising.

Notes

116 An undertaking will normally not act as an intermediary if it sells products via a commercial act which involves a transfer of ownership, Judgment in Case T-417/05, *Endesa v Commission*, paragraph 213, [2006] ECR II-2533.

Commentary
para 159: F&N: 5.187

160. The examples mentioned show that, due to the diversity of services, many different situations may arise and the underlying legal and economic relations have to be carefully analysed. Similarly, specific situations for the calculation of turnover may arise in the areas of credit, financial services and insurance. These issues will be dealt with in Section VI.

2. Ordinary activities

161. Article 5(1) provides that the amounts to be included in the calculation of turnover should correspond to the "ordinary activities" of the undertakings concerned. This is the turnover achieved from the sale of products or the provision of services in the normal course of its business. It generally excludes those items which are listed under the headers "financial income" or "extraordinary income" in the company's accounts. Such extraordinary income may be derived from the sale of businesses or of fixed assets. However, company accounts do not necessarily delineate the revenues derived from ordinary activities in the way required for the purposes of turnover calculation under the Merger Regulation. In some cases, the qualification of the items in the accounts may have to be adapted to the requirements of the Merger Regulation.117

Notes

117 In Case IV/M.126 – *Accor/Wagons-Lits*, of 28 April 1992, the Commission decided to consider certain income from car-hire activities as revenues from ordinary activities although they were included as "other operating proceeds" in Wagons-Lits' profit and loss account.

162. The revenues do not necessarily have to be derived from the customer of the products or services. With regard to aid granted to undertakings by public bodies, any aid has to be included in the calculation of turnover if the undertaking is itself the recipient of the aid and if the aid is directly linked to the sale of products and the provision of services by the undertaking. The aid is therefore an income of the undertaking from the sale of products or provision of services in addition to the price paid by the consumer.118

Notes

118 See Case IV/M.156 – *Cereol/Continentale Italiana* of 27 November 1991. In this case, the Commission excluded Community aid from the calculation of turnover because the aid was not intended to support the sale of products manufactured by one of the undertakings involved in the merger, but the producers of the raw materials (grain) used by the undertaking, which specialized in the crushing of grain.

163. Specific issues have arisen for the calculation of turnover of a business unit which only had internal revenues in the past. This may in particular apply for transactions involving the outsourcing of services by transfer of a business unit. If such a transaction constitutes a concentration on the basis of the considerations outlined in paragraphs 25 ff. of this Notice, the Commission's practice is that the turnover should normally be calculated on the basis of the previously internal turnover or of publicly quoted prices where such prices exist (e.g. in the oil industry). Where the previously internal turnover does not appear to correspond to a market valuation of the activities in question (and, thus, to the expected future turnover on the market), the forecast revenues to be received on the basis of an agreement with the former parent may be a suitable proxy.

3. "Net" turnover

164. The turnover to be taken into account is "net" turnover, after deduction of a number of components specified in the Regulation. The aim is to adjust turnover in such a way as to enable it to reflect the real economic strength of the undertaking.

3.1. Deduction of rebates and taxes

165. Article 5(1) provides for the "deduction of sales rebates and of value added tax and other taxes directly related to turnover". "Sales rebates" mean all rebates or discounts which are granted by the undertakings to their customers and which have a direct influence on the amounts of sales.

Commentary
para 165: F&N: 5.185

---

166. As regards the deduction of taxes, the Merger Regulation refers to VAT and "other taxes directly related to turnover". The concept of "taxes directly related to turnover" refers to indirect taxation linked to turnover, such as, for example, taxes on alcoholic beverages or cigarettes.

Commentary
para 166: F&N: 5.185

3.2. The treatment of "internal" turnover

167. The first subparagraph of Article 5(1) states that "the aggregate turnover of an undertaking concerned shall not include the sale of products or the provision of services between any of the undertakings referred to in paragraph 4", i.e. the group to which the undertaking concerned belongs. The aim is to exclude the proceeds of business dealings within a group so as to take account of the real economic weight of each entity in the form of market turnover. Thus, the "amounts" taken into account by the Merger Regulation reflect only the transactions which take place between the group of undertakings on the one hand and third parties on the other.

Commentary
para 167: B&C: 8.063 F&N: 5.197

---

168. Article 5(5)(a) of the Merger Regulation applies the principle that double counting is to be avoided specifically to the situation where two or more undertakings concerned in a concentration jointly have the rights or powers listed in Article 5(4)(b) in another company. According to this provision, the turnover resulting from the sale of products or the provision of services between the joint venture and each of the undertakings concerned (or any other undertaking connected with any one of them in the sense of Article 5(4)) should be excluded. As regards joint ventures between undertakings concerned and third parties, insofar as their turnover is taken into account according to Article 5(4)(b) as set out in paragraph 181 below, the turnover generated by sales between the joint venture and the undertaking concerned (as well as undertakings linked to the undertaking concerned in accordance with the criteria set out in Article 5(4)) is not taken into account according to Article 5(1).

Commentary
para 168: B&C: 8.078, 8.079 F&N: 5.198

4. Turnover calculation and financial accounts

4.1. The general rule

169. The Commission seeks to base itself upon the most accurate and reliable figures available. Generally, the Commission will refer to accounts which relate to the closest financial year to the date of the transaction and which are audited under the standard applicable to the undertaking in question and compulsory for the relevant financial year.[119] An adjustment of the audited figures should only take place if this is required by the provisions of the Merger Regulation, including the cases explained in more detail in paragraph 172.

Notes

[119] See Case COMP/M.3986 – *Gas Natural/Endesa* of 15 November 2005; confirmed by Judgment in Case T-417/05, *Endesa v Commission*, paragraphs 128, 131, [2006] ECR II-2533.

170. The Commission is reluctant to rely on management or any other form of provisional accounts in any but exceptional circumstances.[120] Where a concentration takes place within the first months of the year and audited accounts are not yet available for the most recent financial year, the figures to be taken into account are those relating to the previous year. Where there is a major divergence between the two sets of accounts, due to significant and permanent changes in the undertaking concerned, and, in particular, when the final draft figures for the most recent year have been approved by the board of management, the Commission may decide to take those figures into account.

Notes

[120] See Case COMP/M.3986 – *Gas Natural/Endesa* of 15 November 2005; confirmed by Judgment in Case T-417/05, *Endesa v Commission*, paragraphs 176,179, [2006] ECR II-2533.

171. Despite the general rule, in cases where major differences between the Community's accounting standards and those of a non-member country are observed, the Commission may consider it necessary to restate these accounts in accordance with Community standards in respect of turnover.

4.2. Adjustments after the date of the last audited accounts

172. Notwithstanding the foregoing paragraphs, an adjustment must always be made to account for permanent changes in the economic reality of the undertakings concerned, such as acquisitions or divestments which are not or not fully reflected in the audited accounts. Such changes have to be taken into account in order to identify the true resources being concentrated?and to better reflect the economic situation of the undertakings concerned. Those adjustments are only selective in nature and do not endanger the principle that there should be a simple and objective mechanism to determine the Commission's jurisdiction as they do not require a complete revision of the audited accounts.[121] First, this applies to acquisitions,?divestments or closure of part of its business subsequent to the date of the audited accounts. This is relevant if a company closes a transaction concerning the divestment and closure of part of its business at any time before the relevant date for establishing jurisdiction (see paragraph 154) or where such a divestment or closure of a business is a pre-condition for the operation.[122] In this case, the turnover to be attributed to that part of the business must be subtracted from the turnover of the notifying party as shown in its last audited accounts. If an agreement for the sale of part of its business is signed, but the closing of the sale (in other words, its legal implementation and the transfer of the legal title to the shares or assets acquired) has not yet occurred, such a change is not taken into account,[123] unless the sale is a pre-condition for the notified operation. Conversely, the turnover of those businesses whose acquisition has been closed subsequent to the preparation of the most recent audited accounts, but before the relevant date for establishing jurisdiction, must be added to a company's turnover for notification purposes.

Notes

121 Judgment in Case T-417/05, *Endesa v Commission*, paragraph 209, [2006] ECR II-2533.

122 See Judgment in Case T-3/93, *Air France v Commission*, [1994] ECR II-121 paragraphs 100 et seq. in relation to Case IV/M.278 – *British Airways/Dan Air*; Case IV/M.588 – *Ingersoll-Rand/Clark Equipment*.

123 Case IV/M.632 – *Rhône Poulenc Rorer/Fisons* of 21 September 1995; Case COMP/M.1741 – *MCI Worldcom/Sprint* of 28 June 2000.

Commentary
para 172: B&C: 8.064

173. Second, an adjustment may also be necessary for acquisitions, divestments or closure of part of the business which have taken place during the financial year for which the audited accounts are drawn up. If acquisitions, divestments or closure of part of the business within this period are made, the changes in the economic resources may only partly be reflected in the audited accounts of the undertaking concerned. As the turnover of the businesses acquired may be included in the accounts only from the time of their acquisition, this may not reflect the full annual turnover of the acquired business. Conversely, the turnover of the businesses divested or closed may still be included in the audited accounts up to the point in time of their actual divestment or closure. In these cases, adjustments have to be made to remove the turnover generated by the divested or closed businesses from the audited accounts until the time of deconsolidation and to add the turnover which the acquired businesses have generated in the year until the time they have been consolidated in the accounts. As a result, the turnover of the businesses divested or closed must be excluded in full and the full annual turnover of the businesses acquired must be included.

Commentary
para 173: B&C: 8.064

174. Other factors that may affect turnover on a temporary basis such as a decrease in orders for the product or a slow-down in the production process within the period prior to the transaction will be ignored for the purposes of calculating turnover. No adjustment to the definitive accounts will be made to incorporate them.

5. Attribution of turnover under Article 5(4)

5.1. Identification of undertakings whose turnover is taken into account

175. When an undertaking concerned by a concentration belongs to a group, not only the turnover of the undertaking concerned is considered, but the Merger Regulation requires to also take into account the turnover of those undertakings with which the undertaking concerned has links consisting in the rights or powers listed in Article 5(4) in order to determine whether the thresholds contained in Article 1 of the Merger Regulation are met. The aim is again to capture the total volume of the economic resources that are being combined through the operation irrespective of whether the economic activities are carried out directly by the undertaking concerned or whether they are undertaken indirectly via undertakings with which the undertaking concerned possesses the links described in Article 5(4).

Commentary
para 175: B&C: 8.076

176. The Merger Regulation does not delineate the concept of a group in a single abstract definition, but sets out in Article 5(4)(b) certain rights or powers. If an undertaking concerned directly or indirectly has such links with other companies, those are to be regarded as part of its group for purposes of turnover calculation under the Merger Regulation.

Commentary
para 176: F&N: 5.205

Part D Mergers and Concentrations

177. Article 5(4) of the Merger Regulation provides the following:

"Without prejudice to paragraph 2 [acquisitions of parts], the aggregate turnover of an undertaking concerned within the meaning of Article 1(2) and (3) shall be calculated by adding together the respective turnovers of the following:

(a) the undertaking concerned;

(b) those undertakings in which the undertaking concerned directly or indirectly:

  (i) owns more than half the capital or business assets, or

  (ii) has the power to exercise more than half the voting rights, or

  (iii) has the power to appoint more than half the members of the supervisory board, the administrative board or bodies legally representing the undertakings, or

  (iv) has the right to manage the undertaking's affairs;

(c) those undertakings which have in an undertaking concerned the rights or powers listed in (b);

(d) those undertakings in which an undertaking as referred to in (c) has the rights or powers listed in (b);

(e) those undertakings in which two or more undertakings as referred to in (a) to (d) jointly have the rights or powers listed in (b)."

An undertaking which has in another undertaking the rights and powers mentioned in Article 5(4)(b) will be referred to as the "parent" of the latter in the present section of this Notice dealing with the calculation of turnover, whereas the latter is referred to as "subsidiary" of the former. In short, Article 5(4) therefore provides that the turnover of the undertaking concerned by the concentration (point (a)) should include its subsidiaries (point (b)), its parent companies (point (c)), the other subsidiaries of its parent undertakings (point (d)) and any other subsidiary jointly held by two or more of the undertakings identified under (a)–(d) (point (e)).

178. A graphic example is as follows:

The undertaking concerned and its group:

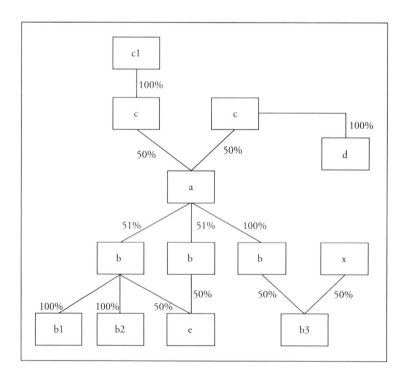

a: The undertaking concerned[124]

b: Its subsidiaries, jointly held companies together with third parties (b3) and their own subsidiaries (b1 and b2)

c: Its parent companies and their own parent companies (c1)

d: Other subsidiaries of the parent companies of the undertaking concerned

e: Companies jointly held by two (or more) companies of the group

x: Third party

Note: the letters a–e correspond to the relevant points of Article 5(4). Percentages set out in the graph relate to the percentage of voting rights held by the respective parent company.

Notes

[124] For the graph it is assumed that the joint venture itself is the undertaking concerned according to the criteria set out in paragraph 146 (acquisition by a full-function JV operating on the same market).

Commentary

para 178: F&N: 5.193

---

179. The rights or powers listed in Article 5(4)(b)(i)–(iii) can be identified in a rather straightforward way as they refer to quantitative thresholds. These thresholds are fulfilled if the undertaking concerned owns more than half of the capital or business assets of other undertakings, has more than half of the voting rights or has legally the power to appoint more than half of the board members in other undertakings. However, the thresholds are also met if the undertaking concerned *de facto* has the power to exercise more than half of the voting rights in the shareholders' assembly or the power to appoint more than half of the board members in other undertakings.[125]

Notes

[125] Case IV/M.187 – *Ifint/Exor* of 2 March 1992; Case IV/M.062 – *Eridania/ISI* of 30 July 1991.

Commentary

para 179: B&C: 8.077   F&N: 5.205

---

180. The provision contained in Article 5(4)(b)(iv) refers to the right to manage the undertaking's affairs. Such a right to manage exists under company law in particular on the basis of organisational contracts such as a "*Beherrschungsvertrag*" under German law, on the basis of business lease agreements or on the basis of the organisation structure for the general partner in a limited partnership.[126] However, the "right to manage" may also result from the holding of voting rights (alone or in combination with contractual arrangements, such as a shareholders' agreement) which enable, on a stable, *de jure* basis, to determine the strategic behaviour of an undertaking.

Notes

[126] Case IV/M.126 – *Accor/WagonLits* of 28 April 1992.

---

181. The right to manage also covers situations in which the undertaking concerned jointly has the right to manage an undertaking's affairs together with third parties.[127] The underlying consideration is that the undertakings exercising joint control have jointly the right to manage the controlled undertakings' affairs even if each of them individually may have those rights only in a negative sense, i.e. in the form of veto rights. In the example, the undertaking (b3) which is jointly controlled by the undertaking concerned (a) and a third party (x) is taken into account as both (a) and (x) have veto rights in (b3) on the basis of their equal shareholding in (b3).[128] Under Article 5(4)(b)(iv) the Commission only takes into account those joint ventures in which the undertaking concerned and third parties have *de jure* rights that give rise to a clear-cut right to manage. The inclusion of joint ventures is therefore limited to situations where the undertaking concerned and third parties have a joint *right* to manage on the basis of an agreement, *e.g.* a shareholders' agreement, or where the undertaking concerned and a third party have an equality of voting rights to the effect that they have the right to appoint an equal number of members to the decision-making bodies of the joint venture.

Part D Mergers and Concentrations

885

Notes

127 Case COMP/M.1741 – *MCI Worldcom/Sprint*; Case IV/M.187 – *Ifint/Exor*; Case IV/M.1046 – *Ameritech/Tele Danmark*.

128 However, only half of the turnover generated by b3 is taken into account, see paragraph 187.

Commentary
para 181: F&N: 5.198

182. In the same way, where two or more companies jointly control the undertaking concerned in the sense that the agreement of each and all of them is needed in order to manage the undertaking affairs, the turnover of all of them is included. In the example, the two parent companies (c) of the undertaking concerned (a) would be taken into account as well as their own parent companies (c1 in the example). This interpretation results from the referral from Article 5(4)(c), dealing with this case, to Article 5(4)(b), which is applicable to jointly controlled companies as set out in the preceding paragraph.

Commentary
para 182: B&C: 8.077

183. When any of the companies identified on the basis of Article 5(4) also has links as defined in Article 5(4) with other undertakings, these should also be brought into the calculation. In the example, one of the subsidiaries of the undertaking concerned a (called b) has in turn its own subsidiaries b1 and b2 and one of the parent companies (called c) has its own subsidiary (d).

184. Article 5(4) sets out specific criteria for identifying undertakings whose turnover can be attributed to the undertaking concerned. These criteria, including the "right to manage the undertaking's affairs", are not coextensive with the notion of "control" under Article 3(2). There are significant differences between Articles 3 and 5, as those provisions fulfil different roles. The differences are most apparent in the field of *de facto* control. Whereas under Article 3(2) even a situation of economic dependence may lead to control on a *de facto* basis (see in detail above), a solely controlled subsidiary is only taken into account on a *de facto* basis under Article 5(4)(b) if it is clearly demonstrated that the undertaking concerned has the power to exercise more than half of the voting rights or to appoint more than half of the board members. Concerning joint control scenarios, Article 5(4)(b)(iv) covers those scenarios where the controlling undertakings jointly have a right to manage on the basis of individual veto rights. However, Article 5(4) would not cover situations where joint control occurs on a *de facto* basis due to strong common interests between different minority shareholders of the joint venture company on the basis of shareholders' attendance. The difference is reflected in the fact that Article 5(4)(b)(iv) refers to the *right* to manage, and not a *power* (as in subparagraph (b)(ii) and (iii)) and is explained by the need for precision and certainty in the criteria used for calculating turnover so that jurisdiction can be readily verified. Under Article 3(3), however, the question whether a concentration arises can be much more comprehensively investigated. In addition, situations of negative sole control are only exceptionally covered (if the conditions of Article 5(4)(b)(i)–(iii) are met in the specific case); the "right to manage" under Article 5(4)(b)(iv) does not cover negative control scenarios. Finally, Article 5(4)(b)(i), for example, covers situations where "control" under Article 3(2) may not exist.

Commentary
para 184: B&C: 8.076 F&N: 5.190

5.2. Allocation of turnover of the undertakings identified

185. In general, as long as the test under Article 5(4)(b) is fulfilled, the whole turnover of the subsidiary in question will be taken into account regardless of the actual shareholding which the undertaking concerned holds in the subsidiary. In the chart, the whole turnover of the subsidiaries called b of the undertaking concerned a will be taken into account.

186. However, the Merger Regulation includes specific rules for joint ventures. Article 5(5)(b) provides that for joint ventures between two or more undertakings concerned, the turnover of the joint venture (as far as the turnover is generated from activities with third parties as set out above

in paragraph 168) should be apportioned equally amongst the undertakings concerned, irrespective of their share of the capital or the voting rights.

Commentary
para 186: B&C: 8.078

187. The principle contained in Article 5(5)(b) is followed by analogy for the allocation of turnover for joint ventures between undertakings concerned and third parties if their turnover is taken into account according to Article 5(4)(b) as set out above in paragraph 181. The Commission's practice has been to allocate to the undertaking concerned the turnover of the joint venture on a per capita basis according to the number of undertakings exercising joint control. In the example, half of the turnover of b3 is taken into account.

Commentary
para 187: B&C: 8.079 F&N: 5.195

188. The rules of Article 5(4) also have to be adapted in situations involving a change from joint to sole control in order to avoid double counting of the turnover of the joint venture. Even if the acquiring undertaking has rights or powers in the joint venture which satisfy the requirements of Article 5(4), the turnover of the acquiring shareholder has to be calculated without the turnover of the joint venture, and the turnover of the joint venture has to be taken without the turnover of the acquiring shareholder.

Commentary
para 188: F&N: 5.195

5.3. Allocation of turnover in case of investment funds

189. The investment company, as set out above in paragraph 15, normally acquires indirect control over portfolio companies held by an investment fund. In the same way, the investment company may be considered to indirectly have the powers and rights which are set out in Article 5(4)(b), in particular to indirectly have the power to exercise the voting rights held by the investment fund in the portfolio companies.

190. The same considerations, as set out above in the framework of Article 3 (paragraph 15), may also apply if an investment company sets up several investment funds with possibly different investors. Typically, on the basis of the organisational structure, in particular links between the investment company and the general partner(s) of the different funds organised as limited partnerships, or contractual arrangements, especially advisory agreements between the general partner or the investment fund and the investment company, the investment company will indirectly have the power to exercise the voting rights held by the investment fund in the portfolio companies or indirectly have one of the other powers or rights set out in Article 5(4)(b). In these circumstances, the investment company may exercise a common control structure over the different funds which it has set up and the common operation of the different funds by the investment company is often indicated by a common brand for the funds.

191. Consequently, such an organisation of the different funds by the investment company may lead to the result that the turnover of all portfolio companies held by different funds is taken into account for the purpose of assessing whether the turnover thresholds in Article 1 are met if the investment company acquires indirect control of a portfolio company via one of the funds.

5.4. Allocation of turnover for State-owned undertakings

192. As regards the calculation of turnover of State-owned undertakings, Article 5(4) should be read in conjunction with recital 22 of the Merger Regulation. This recital declares that, in order to avoid discrimination between the public and private sectors, "in the public sector, calculation of the turnover of an undertaking concerned in a concentration needs, therefore, to take account of undertakings making up an economic unit with an independent power of decision, irrespective of the way in which their capital is held or of the rules of administrative supervision applicable to them".[129]

Notes
129 See also Case IV/M.216 – *CEA Industrie/France Telecom/Finmeccanica/SGS-Thomson*, of 22 February 1993.

Commentary
para 192: B&C: 8.075

193. This recital clarifies that Member States (or other public bodies) are not considered as "undertakings" under Article 5(4) simply because they have interests in other undertakings which satisfy the conditions of Article 5(4). Therefore, for the purposes of calculating turnover of State-owned undertakings, account is only taken of those undertakings which belong to the same economic unit, having the same independent power of decision.

194. Thus, where a State-owned company is not subject to any coordination with other State-controlled holdings, it should be treated as independent for the purposes of Article 5, and the turnover of other companies owned by that State should not be taken into account. Where, however, several State-owned companies are under the same independent centre of commercial decision-making, then the turnover of those businesses should be considered part of the group of the undertaking concerned for the purposes of Article 5.

V. Geographic Allocation of Turnover

195. The thresholds concerning Community-wide and Member State turnover in Article 1(2) and (3) aim to identify cases which have sufficient turnover within the Community in order to be of Community interest and which are primarily cross-border in nature. They require turnover to be allocated geographically to the Community and to individual Member States. Since audited accounts often do not provide a geographical breakdown as required by the Merger Regulation, the Commission will rely on the best figures available provided by the undertakings. The second subparagraph of Article 5(1) provides that the location of turnover is determined by the location of the customer at the time of the transaction: "Turnover, in the Community or in a Member State, shall comprise products sold and services provided to undertakings or consumers, in the Community or in that Member State as the case may be."

Commentary
para 195: B&C: 8.067

General rule

196. The Merger Regulation does not discriminate between "products sold" and "services provided" for the geographic allocation of turnover. In both cases, the general rule is that turnover should be attributed to the place where the customer is located. The underlying principle is that turnover should be allocated to the location where competition with alternative suppliers takes place. This location is normally also the place where the characteristic action under the contract in question is to be performed, i.e. where the service is actually provided and the product is actually delivered. In the case of Internet transactions, it may be difficult for the undertakings to determine the location of the customer at the time when the contract is concluded via the Internet. If the product or the service itself is not supplied via the Internet, focusing on the place where the characteristic action under the contract is performed may avoid those difficulties. In the following, the sale of goods and the provision of services are dealt with separately as they exhibit certain different features in terms of allocation of turnover.

Sale of goods

197. For the sale of goods, particular situations may arise in situations in which the place where the customer was located at the time of concluding the purchase agreement is different from the billing address and/or the place of delivery. In these situations, the place where the purchase agreement was entered into and the place of delivery are more important than the billing address. As the delivery is in general the characteristic action for the sale of goods, the place of delivery may even be prevailing over the place where the customer was located at the time when the purchase agreement was concluded. This will depend on whether the place of delivery is to be considered the place where competition takes place for the sale of goods or whether competition

rather takes place at the residence of the customer. In the case of a sale of mobile goods, such as a motor car, to a final consumer, the place where the car is delivered to the customer is decisive even if the agreement was concluded via the phone or the Internet before.

198. A specific situation arises in cases where a multinational corporation has a Community buying strategy and sources all its requirements for a good from one location. As a central purchasing organisation can take different forms, it is necessary to consider its concrete form since this may determine how to allocate the turnover. Where goods are purchased by and delivered to the central purchasing organisation and are subsequently re-distributed internally to different plants in a variety of Member States, turnover is allocated only to the Member State where the central purchasing organisation is located. In this case, competition takes place at the location of the central purchasing organisation and this is also the place where the characteristic action under the sales contract is performed. The situation is different in case of direct links between the seller and the different subsidiaries. This comprises the case where the central purchasing organisation concludes a mere framework agreement, but the individual orders are placed by and the products are directly delivered to the subsidiaries in different Member States as well as the case where the individual orders are placed via the central purchasing organisation, but the products are directly delivered to the subsidiaries. In both cases, turnover is to be allocated to the different Member States in which the subsidiaries are located, irrespective of whether the central purchasing organisation or the subsidiaries receive the bills and effect the payment. The reason is that in both cases competition with alternative suppliers takes place for the delivery of products to the different subsidiaries even though the contract is concluded centrally. In the first case, in addition, the subsidiaries actually decide upon the quantities to be delivered and on an element essential for competition on their own.

Commentary
para 198: F&N: 5.202

Provision of services

199. For services, the Merger Regulation foresees that the place of their provision to the customer is relevant. Services containing cross-border elements can be considered to fall into three general categories. The first category comprises cases where the service provider travels, the second category cases where the customer travels. The third category comprises those cases where a service is provided without either the service provider or the customer having to travel. In the first two categories, the turnover generated is to be allocated to the place of destination of the traveller, i.e. the place where the service is actually provided to the customer. In the third category, the turnover is generally to be allocated to the location of the customer. For the central sourcing of services the above outlined principles for the central purchasing of goods apply in an analogous way.

Commentary
para 199: B&C: 8.070

---

200. An example of the first category would be a situation where a non-European company provides special airplane maintenance services to a carrier in a Member State. In this case, the service provider travels to the Community where the service is actually provided and where also competition for this service takes place. If a European tourist hires a car or books a hotel directly in the United States, this falls into the second category as the service is provided outside the Community and also competition takes place between hotels and rental car companies at the location chosen. However, the case is different for package holidays. For this kind of holiday, the service starts with the sale of the package through a travel agent at the customer's location and competition for the sale of holidays through travel agents takes place locally, as with retail shopping, even though parts of the service may be provided in a number of distant locations. The case therefore falls into the third category and the turnover generated is to be allocated to the customer's location. The third category also comprises cases like the supply of software or the distribution of films which are made outside the Community, but are supplied to a customer in a Member State so that the service is actually provided to the customer within the Community.

201. Cases concerning the transport of goods are different as the customer, to whom those services are provided, does not travel, but the transport service is provided to the customer at its location. Those cases fall into the third category and the location of the customer is the relevant criterion for the allocation of the turnover.

202. In telecom cases, the qualification of call termination services may raise problems. Although call termination would appear to fall into the third category, there are reasons to treat it differently. Call termination services are provided, *e.g.*, in situations where a call, originating from a European operator, is being terminated in the United States. Although neither the European nor the US operator travels, the signal travels and the service is provided by the US network to the European operator in the United States. This is also the place where competition takes place (if any). The turnover is therefore to be considered as non-Community turnover.[130]

Notes

[130] This does not affect the turnover which the European telephony operator generates vis-à-vis its own customer with this call.

Commentary
para 202: F&N: 5.202

Specific sectors

203. Certain sectors do, however, pose very particular problems with regard to the geographical allocation of turnover. These will be dealt with in Section VI below.

VI. Conversion of Turnover into Euro

204. When converting turnover figures into Euro great care should be taken with the exchange rate used. The annual turnover of a company should be converted at the average rate for the twelve months concerned. This average can be obtained via DG Competition's website.[131] The audited annual turnover figures should be converted as such and not be broken down into quarterly or monthly figures which would then be converted individually.

Notes

[131] See <http://europa.eu.int/comm/competition/mergers/others/exchange_rates.html#footnote_1>. The website makes reference to the European Central Bank's Monthly Bulletin.

Commentary
para 204: B&C: 8.063 F&N: 5.185

205. When a company has sales in a range of currencies, the procedure is no different. The total turnover given in the consolidated audited accounts and in that company's reporting currency is converted into Euros at the yearly average rate. Local currency sales should not be converted directly into Euros since these figures are not from the consolidated audited accounts of the company.

Commentary
para 205: B&C: 8.063 F&N: 5.185

VII. Provisions for Credit and Other Financial Institutions and Insurance Undertakings

1. Scope of application

206. Due to the specific nature of the sector, Article 5(3) contains specific rules for the calculation of turnover of credit and other financial institutions as well as insurance undertakings.

207. In order to define the terms "credit institutions and other financial institutions" under the Merger Regulation, the Commission in its practice has consistently adopted the definitions

provided in the applicable European regulation in the banking sector. The Directive on the taking up and pursuit of the business of credit institutions foresees that:[132]
— "Credit institution shall mean an undertaking whose business is to receive deposits or other repayable funds from the public and to grant credits for its own account."
— "Financial institution shall mean an undertaking other than a credit institution, the principal activity of which is to acquire holdings or to carry on one or more of the activities listed in points 2 to 12 of Annex I."

Notes

[132] The definitions are to be found in Article 1(1) and (5) of Directive 2000/12/EC of the European Parliament and of the Council of 20 March 2000 relating to the taking up and pursuit of the business of credit institutions (OJ L 126, 26.5.2000, p.1).

Commentary
para 207: B&C: 8.050 F&N: 11.71

208. Financial institutions within the meaning of Article 5(3) of the Merger Regulation are, accordingly, on the one hand holding companies and, on the other hand, undertakings which perform on a regular basis as a principal activity one or more activities expressly mentioned in points 2 to 12 of the Annex of the banking Directive. These activities include:
— lending (comprising activities such as consumer credit, mortgage credit, factoring);
— financial leasing;
— money transmission services;
— issuing and administering means of payment (e.g. credit cards, travellers' cheques and bankers' drafts);
— guarantees and commitments;
— trading for own account or for account of customers in money market instruments (cheques, bills, certificates of deposit, etc.), foreign exchange, financial futures and options, exchange and interest-rate instruments, transferable securities;
— participation in securities issues and the provision of services related to such issues;
— money broking;
— portfolio management and advice; and
— safekeeping and administration of securities.

2. Calculation of turnover

209. Article 5(3) of the Merger Regulation sets out the methods of calculation of turnover for credit and other financial institutions and for insurance undertakings. In the following Section, some supplementary questions related to turnover calculation for the abovementioned types of undertakings are addressed.

Commentary
para 209: F&N: 5.206

2.1. Calculation of turnover of credit and financial institutions (other than financial holding companies)

2.1.1. General

210. There are normally no particular difficulties in applying the banking income criterion for the definition of the worldwide turnover to credit institutions and other kinds of financial institutions. For the geographic allocation of turnover to the Community and to individual Member States, the specific provision of Article 5(3)(a) second subparagraph applies. It specifies that the turnover is to be allocated to the branch or division established in the Community or in the Member State which receives this income.

Commentary
para 210: B&C: 8.068 F&N: 5.202

Part D Mergers and Concentrations

2.1.2. Turnover of leasing companies

211. There is a fundamental distinction to be made between financial leases and operating leases. Basically, financial leases are made for longer periods than operating leases and ownership is generally transferred to the lessee at the end of the lease term by means of a purchase option included in the lease contract. Under an operating lease, on the contrary, ownership is not transferred to the lessee at the end of the lease term and the costs of maintenance, repair and insurance of the leased equipment are included in the lease payments. A financial lease therefore functions as a loan by the lessor to enable the lessee to purchase a given asset.

212. As already mentioned above, a company performing as its principal activity financial leasing is a financial institution within the meaning of Article 5(3)(a) and its turnover is to be calculated according to the specific rules set out in this provision. All payments on financial leasing contracts, except for the redemption part, are to be taken into account; a sale of future leasing payments at the beginning of the contract for refinancing purposes is not relevant.

213. Operational leasing activities are, however, not considered to be carried out by financial institutions, and therefore the general turnover calculation rules of Article 5(1) apply.[133]

Notes

[133] See Case IV/M.234 – *GECC/Avis Lease*, 15 July 1992.

2.2. Insurance undertakings

214. In order to measure the turnover of insurance undertakings, Article 5(3)(b) of the Merger Regulation provides that gross premiums written are taken into account. The gross premiums written are the sum of received premiums, including any received reinsurance premiums if the undertaking concerned has activities in the field of reinsurance. Outgoing or outward reinsurance premiums, i.e. all amounts paid and payable by the undertaking concerned to get reinsurance cover, are only costs related to the provision of insurance coverage and are not to be deducted from the gross premiums written.

215. The premiums to be taken into account are not only related to new insurance contracts made during the accounting year being considered but also to all premiums related to contracts made in previous years which remain in force during the period taken into consideration.

216. In order to constitute appropriate reserves allowing for the payment of claims, insurance undertakings, usually hold a portfolio of investments in shares, interest-bearing securities, land and property and other assets providing annual revenues. The annual revenues coming from those sources are not considered as turnover for insurance undertakings under Article 5(3)(b). However, a distinction has to be made between pure financial investments, which do not confer the rights and powers specified in Article 5(4) to the insurance undertaking in the undertakings in which the investment has been made, and those investments leading to the acquisition of an interest which meets the criteria specified in Article 5(4)(b). In the latter case, Article 5(4) of the Merger Regulation applies, and the turnover of this undertaking has to be added to the turnover of the insurance undertaking, as calculated according to Article 5(3)(b), for the determination of the thresholds laid down in the Merger Regulation.[134]

Notes

[134] See Case IV/M.18 – *AG/AMEV*, of 21 November 1990.

2.3. Financial holding companies

217. As an "other financial institution" within the meaning of Article 5(3)(a) of the Merger Regulation, the turnover of a financial holding company has to be calculated according to the specific rules set out in this provision. However, in the same way as mentioned above for insurance undertakings, Article 5(4) applies to those participations which meet the criteria specified in Article 5(4)(b). Thus, the turnover of a financial holding is to be basically calculated according

to Article 5(3), but it may be necessary to add turnover of undertakings falling within the categories set out in Article 5(4) ("Art. 5(4) companies").[135]

Notes

[135] The principles for financial holding companies may to a certain extent be applied to fund management companies.

218. In practice, the turnover of the financial holding company (non-consolidated) must first be taken into account. Then the turnover of the Art 5(4) companies must be added, whilst taking care to deduct dividends and other income distributed by those companies to the financial holdings. The following provides an example for this kind of calculation:

	EUR million
1. Turnover related to financial activities (from non-consolidated P&L)	3 000
2. Turnover related to insurance Art. 5(4) companies (gross premiums written)	300
3. Turnover of industrial Art. 5(4) companies	2 000
4. Deduct dividends and other income derived from Art. 5(4) companies 2 and 3	<200>
Total turnover financial holding and its group	5 100

219. In such calculations different accounting rules may need to be taken into consideration. Whilst this consideration applies to any type of undertaking concerned by the Merger Regulation, it is particularly important in the case of financial holding companies[136] where the number and the diversity of enterprises controlled and the degree of control the holding holds on its subsidiaries, affiliated companies and other companies in which it has shareholding requires careful examination.

Notes

[136] See, for example, Case IV/M.166 – *Torras/Sarrió*, of 24 February 1992.

220. Turnover calculation for financial holding companies as described above may in practice prove onerous. Therefore a strict and detailed application of this method will be necessary only in cases where it seems that the turnover of a financial holding company is likely to be close to the Merger Regulation thresholds; in other cases it may well be obvious that the turnover is far from the thresholds of the Merger Regulation, and therefore the published accounts are adequate for the establishment of jurisdiction.

Part D Mergers and Concentrations

D12

COMMISSION NOTICE

On the assessment of non-horizontal mergers under the Council Regulation
on the control of concentrations between undertakings

(2008/C 265/07)

Official Journal C 265, 18.10.2008, p.6

Celex No: 52008XC1018(03)

EUR-Lex permanent link: <http://eur-lex.europa.eu/legal-content/EN/ALL/?uri=CELEX:52008X
C1018%2803%29&qid=1395771814679>

I. Introduction

1. Article 2 of Council Regulation (EC) No 139/2004 of 20 January 2004 on the control of concentrations between undertakings[1] (hereinafter: the "Merger Regulation") provides that the Commission has to appraise concentrations within the scope of the Merger Regulation with a view to establishing whether or not they are compatible with the common market. For that purpose, the Commission must assess, pursuant to Article 2(2) and (3), whether or not a concentration would significantly impede effective competition, in particular as a result of the creation or strengthening of a dominant position, in the common market or a substantial part of it.

Notes

[1] Council Regulation (EC) No 139/2004 of 20 January 2004 (OJ L 24, 29.01.2004, p.1).

---

2. This document develops guidance as to how the Commission assesses concentrations[1] where the undertakings concerned are active on different relevant markets.[2] In this document, these concentrations will be called "non-horizontal mergers".

Notes

[1] The term *concentration* used in the Merger Regulation covers various types of transactions such as mergers, acquisitions, takeovers, and certain types of joint ventures. In the remainder of this Document, unless otherwise specified, the term "merger" will be used as a synonym for concentration and therefore cover all the above types of transactions.

[2] Guidance on the assessment of mergers involving undertakings which are actual or potential competitors on the same relevant market ("horizontal mergers") is given in the Commission Notice: Guidelines on the assessment of horizontal mergers under the Council Regulation on the control of concentrations between undertakings. OJ C 31, 5.2.2004, pp.5–18 ("Notice on Horizontal Mergers").

Commentary
para 2: F&N: 5.16

3. Two broad types of non-horizontal mergers can be distinguished: vertical mergers and conglomerate mergers.
4. Vertical mergers involve companies operating at different levels of the supply chain. For example, when a manufacturer of a certain product (the "upstream firm") merges with one of its distributors (the "downstream firm"), this is called a vertical merger.[1]

Notes

[1] In the present document, the terms "downstream" and "upstream" are used to describe the (potential) commercial relationship that the merging entities have with each other. Generally the commercial relationship is one where the "downstream" firm purchases the output from the "upstream" firm and uses it as an input in its own production, which it then sells on to its customers. The market where the former transactions take place is referred to as the intermediate market (upstream market). The latter market is referred to as the downstream market.

5. Conglomerate mergers are mergers between firms that are in a relationship which is neither horizontal (as competitors in the same relevant market) nor vertical (as suppliers or customers).[1] In practice, the focus of the present guidelines is on mergers between companies that are active in closely related markets (e.g. mergers involving suppliers of complementary products or products that belong to the same product range).

Notes

[1] The distinction between conglomerate mergers and horizontal mergers may be subtle, e.g. when a conglomerate merger involves products that are weak substitutes for each other. The same holds true for the distinction between conglomerate mergers and vertical mergers. For instance, products may be supplied by some companies with the inputs already integrated (vertical relationship), whereas other producers leave it to the customers to select and assemble the inputs themselves (conglomerate relationship).

6. The general guidance already given in the Notice on horizontal mergers is also relevant in the context of non-horizontal mergers. The purpose of the present document is to concentrate on the competition aspects that are relevant to the specific context of non-horizontal mergers. In addition, it will set out the Commission's approach to market shares and concentration thresholds in this context.
7. In practice, mergers may entail both horizontal and non-horizontal effects. This may for instance be the case where the merging firms are not only in a vertical or conglomerate relationship, but are also actual or potential competitors of each other in one or more of the relevant markets concerned.[1] In such a case, the Commission will appraise horizontal, vertical and/or conglomerate effects in accordance with the guidance set out in the relevant notices.[2]

Notes

[1] For instance, in certain markets upstream or downstream firms are often well-placed potential entrants. See, e.g. in the electricity and gas sector, Case COMP/M.3440 – EDP/ENI/GDP (2004). The same may hold for producers of complementary products. See, e.g. in the liquid packaging sector, Case COMP/M.2416 – TetraLaval/Sidel (2001).
[2] Guidance on the assessment of mergers with a potential competitor is given in the Notice on horizontal mergers, in particular at paragraphs 58 to 60 thereof.

8. The guidance set out in this document draws and elaborates on the Commission's evolving experience with the appraisal of non-horizontal mergers under Regulation (EEC) No 4064/89 since its entry into force on 21 September 1990, the Merger Regulation presently in force as well as on the case-law of the Court of Justice and the Court of First Instance of the European Communities. The principles contained here will be applied and further developed and refined by the Commission in individual cases. The Commission may revise the notice on non-horizontal mergers from time to time in the light of future developments and of evolving insight.
9. The Commission's interpretation of the Merger Regulation as regards the appraisal of non-horizontal mergers is without prejudice to the interpretation which may be given by the Court of Justice or the Court of First Instance of the European Communities.

II. Overview

10. Effective competition brings benefits to consumers, such as low prices, high quality products, a wide selection of goods and services, and innovation. Through its control of mergers, the Commission prevents mergers that would be likely to deprive customers of these benefits by significantly?increasing the market power of firms. An "increase in market power" in this context refers to the ability of one or more firms to profitably increase prices, reduce output, choice or quality of goods and services, diminish innovation, or otherwise influence parameters of competition.[1]

Notes

[1] In this document, the expression "increased prices" is often used as shorthand for these various ways in which a merger may result in competitive harm. The expression should be understood to also cover situations where, for instance, prices are decreased less, or are less likely to decrease, than they otherwise would have without the merger and where prices are increased more, or are more likely to increase, than they otherwise would have without the merger.

Commentary
para 10: B&C: 8.207 F&N: 5.563

11. Non-horizontal mergers are generally less likely to create competition concerns than horizontal mergers.

Commentary
para 11: B&C: 8.227

12. First, unlike horizontal mergers, vertical or conglomerate mergers do not entail the loss of direct competition between the merging firms in the same relevant market.[1] As a result, the main source of anti-competitive effect in horizontal mergers is absent from vertical and conglomerate mergers.

Notes

[1] Such a loss of direct competition can, nevertheless, arise where one of the merging firms is a potential competitor in the relevant market where the other merging firm operates. See paragraph 7 above.

Commentary
para 12: B&C: 8.227

13. Second, vertical and conglomerate mergers provide substantial scope for efficiencies. A characteristic of vertical mergers and certain conglomerate mergers is that the activities and/or the products of the companies involved are *complementary* to each other.[1] The integration of complementary activities or products within a single firm may produce significant efficiencies and be pro-competitive. In vertical relationships for instance, as a result of the complementarity, a decrease in mark-ups downstream will lead to higher demand also upstream. A part of the benefit of this increase in demand will accrue to the upstream suppliers. An integrated firm will take this benefit into account. Vertical integration may thus provide an increased incentive to seek to decrease prices and increase output because the integrated firm can capture a larger fraction of the benefits. This is often referred to as the "internalisation of double mark-ups". Similarly, other efforts to increase sales at one level (e.g. improve service or stepping up innovation) may provide a greater reward for an integrated firm that will take into account the benefits accruing at other levels.

Notes

[1] In this document, products or services are called "complementary" (or "economic complements") when they are worth more to a customer when used or consumed together than when used or consumed separately. Also a merger between upstream and downstream activities can be seen as a combination of complements which go into the final product. For instance, both production and distribution fulfil a complementary role in getting a product to the market.

Commentary
para 13: B&C: 8.277, 8.242 F&N: 5.856

14. Integration may also decrease transaction costs and allow for a better co-ordination in terms of product design, the organisation of the production process, and the way in which the products are sold. Similarly, mergers which involve products belonging to a range or portfolio of products that are generally sold to the same set of customers (be they complementary products or not) may give rise to customer benefits such as one-stop-shopping.

Commentary
para 14: **B&C:** 8.277

15. However, there are circumstances in which non-horizontal mergers may significantly impede effective competition, in particular as a result of the creation or strengthening of a dominant position. This is essentially because a non-horizontal merger may change the ability and incentive to compete on the part of the merging companies and their competitors in ways that cause harm to consumers.

Commentary
para 15: **B&C:** 8.227

16. In the context of competition law, the concept of "consumers" encompasses intermediate and ultimate consumers.[1] When intermediate customers are actual or potential competitors of the parties to the merger, the Commission focuses on the effects of the merger on the customers to which the merged entity and those competitors are selling. Consequently, the fact that a merger affects competitors is not in itself a problem. It is the impact on effective competition that matters, not the mere impact on competitors at some level of the supply chain.[1] In particular, the fact that rivals may be harmed because a merger creates efficiencies cannot in itself give rise to competition concerns.

Notes

[1] See Article 2(1)(b) of the Merger Regulation and paragraph 84 of the Communication from the Commission – Notice – Guidelines on the application of Article 81(3) of the Treaty (OJ C 101, 27.4.2004, p.97). [Ed note: please see the Note on the Lisbon Treaty at p.xvii in regard to article renumbering introduced by the Lisbon Treaty.]

[2] One example of this approach can be found in the case COMP/M.3653 Siemens/VA Tech (2005), in which the Commission assessed the effect of the transaction on the two complementary markets for electrical rail vehicles and electrical traction systems for rail vehicles, which combine into a full rail vehicle. While the merger allegedly reduced the independent supply of electrical traction systems, there would still be several integrated suppliers which could deliver the rail vehicle. The Commission thus concluded that even if the merger had negative consequences for independent suppliers of electrical rail vehicles "sufficient competition would remain in the relevant downstream market for rail vehicles".

Commentary
para 16: **F&N:** 5.23, 5.564, 5.833, 5.834

17. There are two main ways in which non-horizontal mergers may significantly impede effective competition: non-coordinated effects and coordinated effects.[1]

Notes
[1] See Section II of the Notice on Horizontal Mergers.

18. Non-coordinated effects may principally arise when non-horizontal mergers give rise to *foreclosure*. In this document, the term "foreclosure" will be used to describe any instance where actual or potential rivals' access to supplies or markets is hampered or eliminated as a result of the merger, thereby reducing these companies' ability and/or incentive to compete. As a result of such foreclosure, the merging companies – and, possibly, some of its competitors as well – may be able to profitably increase the price[1] charged to consumers. These instances give rise to a significant impediment to effective competition and are therefore referred to hereafter as "anticompetitive foreclosure".

Notes
[1] For the meaning of the expression "increased prices" see footnote 8.

Commentary
para 18: B&C: 8.228 F&N: 5.814

19. Coordinated effects arise where the merger changes the nature of competition in such a way that firms that previously were not coordinating their behaviour, are now significantly more likely to coordinate and raise prices or otherwise harm effective competition. A merger may also make coordination easier, more stable or more effective for firms which were coordinating prior to the merger.

Commentary
para 19: B&C: 8.229

20. In assessing the competitive effects of a merger, the Commission compares the competitive conditions that would result from the notified merger with the conditions that would have prevailed without the merger.[1] In most cases the competitive conditions existing at the time of the merger constitute the relevant comparison for evaluating the effects of a merger. However, in some circumstances, the Commission may take into account future changes to the market that can reasonably be predicted. It may, in particular, take account of the likely entry or exit of firms if the merger did not take place when considering what constitutes the relevant comparison. The Commission may take into account future market developments that result from expected regulatory changes.[2]

Notes

[1] By analogy, in the case of a merger that has been implemented without having been notified, the Commission would assess the merger in the light of the competitive conditions that would have prevailed without the implemented merger.

[2] This may be particularly relevant in cases where effective competition is expected to arise in the future as a result of market opening. See, e.g. Case COMP/M.3696 – *E.ON/MOL* (2005), at points 457 to 463.

Commentary
para 20: F&N: 5.16

21. In its assessment, the Commission will consider both the possible anti-competitive effects arising from the merger and the possible pro-competitive effects stemming from substantiated efficiencies benefiting consumers.[1] The Commission examines the various chains of cause and effect with a view to ascertaining which of them is the most likely. The more immediate and direct the perceived anti-competitive effects of a merger, the more likely the Commission is to raise competition concerns. Likewise, the more immediate and direct the pro-competitive effects of a merger, the more likely the Commission is to find that they counteract any anti-competitive effects.

Notes

[1] See Section VII on efficiencies in the Notice on Horizontal Mergers.

22. This document describes the main scenarios of competitive harm and sources of efficiencies in the context of vertical mergers and, subsequently, in the context of conglomerate mergers.

III. Market share and concentration levels

23. Non-horizontal mergers pose no threat to effective competition unless the merged entity has a significant degree of market power (which does not necessarily amount to dominance) in at least one of the markets concerned. The Commission will examine this issue before proceeding to assess the impact of the merger on competition.

Commentary
para 23: B&C: 8.204, 8.230 F&N: 5.861

24. Market shares and concentration levels provide useful first indications of the market power and the competitive importance of both the merging parties and their competitors.[1]

25. The Commission is unlikely to find concern in non-horizontal mergers, be it of a coordinated or of a non-coordinated nature, where the market share post-merger of the new entity in each of the markets concerned is below 30%[1] and where the post-merger HHI is below 2000.

26. In practice, the Commission will not extensively investigate such mergers, except where special circumstances such as, for instance, one or more of the following factors are present:
    (a) a merger involves a company that is likely to expand significantly in the near future, e.g. because of a recent innovation;
    (b) there are significant cross-shareholdings or cross-directorships among the market participants;
    (c) one of the merging firms is a firm with a high likelihood of disrupting coordinated conduct;
    (d) indications of past or ongoing coordination, or facilitating practices, are present.

27. The Commission will use the above market share thresholds and HHI levels as an initial indicator of the absence of competition concerns. However, these thresholds do not give rise to a legal presumption. The Commission is of the opinion that it is less appropriate in this context to present market share and concentration levels above which competition concerns would be deemed to be likely, as the existence of a significant degree of market power in at least one of the markets concerned is a necessary condition for competitive harm, but is not a sufficient condition.[1]

IV. VERTICAL MERGERS

28. This Section sets out the Commission's framework of analysis in the context of vertical mergers. In its assessment, the Commission will consider both the possible anti-competitive effects arising from vertical mergers and the pro-competitive effects stemming from efficiencies identified and substantiated by the parties.

A. Non-coordinated effects: foreclosure

29. A merger is said to result in foreclosure where actual or potential rivals' access to supplies or markets is hampered or eliminated as a result of the merger, thereby reducing these companies' ability and/or incentive to compete. Such foreclosure may discourage entry or expansion of rivals or encourage their exit. Foreclosure thus can be found even if the foreclosed rivals are not forced to exit the market: It is sufficient that the rivals are disadvantaged and consequently led to compete less effectively. Such foreclosure is regarded as anti-competitive where the merging companies – and, possibly, some of its competitors as well – are as a result able to profitably increase the price charged to consumers.[1]

Notes

1 For the meaning of the expression "increased prices" see footnote 8. For the meaning of "consumers", see paragraph 16.

30. Two forms of foreclosure can be distinguished. The first is where the merger is likely to raise the costs of downstream rivals by restricting their access to an important input (input foreclosure). The second is where the merger is likely to foreclose upstream rivals by restricting their access to a sufficient customer base (customer foreclosure).[1]

Notes

1 See Merger Regulation, Article 2(1)(b), referring to "access to supplies" and "access to [...] markets", respectively.

Commentary
para 30: B&C: 8.228

1. Input foreclosure

31. Input foreclosure arises where, post-merger, the new entity would be likely to restrict access to the products or services that it would have otherwise supplied absent the merger, thereby raising its downstream rivals' costs by making it harder for them to obtain supplies of the input under similar prices and conditions as absent the merger. This may lead the merged entity to profitably increase the price charged to consumers, resulting in a significant impediment to effective competition. As indicated above, for input foreclosure to lead to consumer harm, it is not necessary that the merged firm's rivals are forced to exit the market. The relevant benchmark is whether the increased input costs would lead to higher prices for consumers. Any efficiencies resulting from the merger may, however, lead the merged entity to reduce price, so that the overall likely impact on consumers is neutral or positive. A graphical presentation of this mechanism is provided in Figure 1.

Figure 1

Input foreclosure

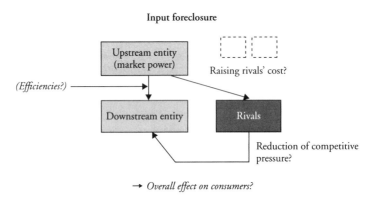

→ Overall effect on consumers?

Commentary
para 31: B&C: 8.231

32. In assessing the likelihood of an anticompetitive input foreclosure scenario, the Commission examines, first, whether the merged entity would have, post-merger, the ability to substantially foreclose access to inputs, second, whether it would have the incentive to do so, and third, whether a foreclosure strategy would have a significant detrimental effect on competition downstream.[1] In practice, these factors are often examined together since they are closely intertwined.

Notes

1 See e.g. Case COMP/M.4300 – Philips/Intermagnetics, COMP/M.4314 – Johnson & Johnson/Pfizer Consumer Healthcare, COMP/M.4389 – WLR/ BST, COMP/M.4403 – Thales/Finmeccanica/Alcatel Alenia Space and Telespazio, COMP/M.4494 – Evraz/Highveld, and COMP/M.4561 – GE/Smiths Aerospace.

Commentary
para 32: B&C: 5.836

A. Ability to foreclose access to inputs[1]

33. Input foreclosure may occur in various forms. The merged entity may decide not to deal with its actual or potential competitors in the vertically related market. Alternatively, the merged firm may decide to restrict supplies and/or to raise the price it charges when supplying competitors and/or to otherwise make the conditions of supply less favourable than they would have been absent the merger.[2] Further, the merged entity may opt for a specific choice of technology within the new firm which is not compatible with the technologies chosen by rival firms.[3] Foreclosure may also take more subtle forms, such as the degradation of the quality of input supplied.[4] In its assessment, the Commission may consider a series of alternative or complementary possible strategies.

Notes

[1] The term 'inputs' is used here as a generic term and may also cover services, access to infrastructure and access to intellectual property rights.

[2] See, e.g. Case COMP/M.1693 – Alcoa/Reynolds (2000), Case COMP/M.4403 – Thales/ Finmeccanica/ Alcatel Alenia Space/ Telespazio, points 257–260.

[3] See, e.g. Case COMP/M.2861 – Siemens/Drägerwerk/JV (2003), Case COMP/M.3998 Axalto, point 75.

[4] See, e.g. Case COMP/M.4314 – Johnson & Johnson/Pfizer Consumer Healthcare, points 127–130.

34. Input foreclosure may raise competition problems only if it concerns an important input for the downstream product.[1] This is the case, for example, when the input concerned represents a significant cost factor relative to the price of the downstream product. Irrespective of its cost, an input may also be sufficiently important for other reasons. For instance, the input may be a critical component without which the downstream product could not be manufactured or effectively sold on the market,[2] or it may represent a significant source of product differentiation for the downstream product.[3] It may also be that the cost of switching to alternative inputs is relatively high.

Notes

[1] See, e.g. Case COMP/M.3868 Dong/Elsam/Energi E2, Case COMP/M.4094 Ineos/ BP Dormagen, points 183–184, Case COMP/M.4561 GE/Smiths Aerospace, points 48–50.

[2] For instance, an engine starter can be considered a critical component to an engine (Case T-210/01, *General Electric v Commission* [2005] ECR II-000); see also, e.g. Case COMP/M.3410 – Total/GDF, points 53–54 and 60–61.

[3] For instance, personal computers are often sold with specific reference to the type of microprocessor they contain.

35. For input foreclosure to be a concern, the vertically integrated firm resulting from the merger must have market power in the upstream market. It is only in these circumstances that the merged firm can be expected to have a significant influence on the conditions of competition in the upstream market and thus, possibly, on prices and supply conditions in the downstream market.

36. The merged entity would only have the ability to foreclose downstream competitors if, by reducing access to its own upstream products or services, it could negatively affect the overall availability of inputs for the downstream market in terms of price or quality. This may be the case where the remaining upstream suppliers are less efficient, offer less preferred alternatives, or lack the ability to expand output in response to the supply restriction, for example because they face capacity constraints or, more generally, face decreasing returns to scale.[1] Also, the presence of exclusive contracts between the merged entity and independent input providers may limit the ability of downstream rivals to have adequate access to inputs.

Notes

[1] See, e.g. Case COMP/M.4494 Evraz/ Highveld, point 92 and points 97–112.

37. When determining the extent to which input foreclosure may occur, it must be taken into account that the decision of the merged entity to rely on its upstream division's supply of inputs may also

free up capacity on the part of the remaining input suppliers from which the downstream division used to purchase before. In fact, the merger may merely realign purchase patterns among competing firms.

38. When competition in the input market is oligopolistic, a decision of the merged entity to restrict access to its inputs reduces the competitive pressure exercised on remaining input suppliers, which may allow them to raise the input price they charge to nonintegrated downstream competitors. In essence, input foreclosure by the merged entity may expose its downstream rivals to non-vertically integrated suppliers with increased market power.[1] This increase in third-party market power will be greater the lower the degree of product differentiation between the merged entity and other upstream suppliers and the higher the degree of upstream concentration. However, the attempt to raise the input price may fail when independent input suppliers, faced with a reduction in the demand for their products (from the downstream division of the merged entity or from independent downstream firms), respond by pricing more aggressively.[2]

Notes

[1] The analysis of the likely effect of the removal of a competitive constraint is similar to the analysis of non-coordinated effects with horizontal mergers (See Section IV of the Notice on Horizontal Mergers).

[2] Also the nature of the supply contracts between upstream suppliers and the downstream independent firms may be important in this respect. For instance, when these contracts use a price system combining a fixed fee and a per-unit supply price, the effect on downstream competitors' marginal costs may be affected less than when these contracts involve only per-unit supply prices.

---

39. In its assessment, the Commission may consider, on the basis of the information available, whether there are effective and timely counter-strategies that the rival firms would be likely to deploy. Such counterstrategies include the possibility of changing their production process so as to be less reliant on the input concerned or sponsoring the entry of new suppliers upstream.

B. Incentive to foreclose access to inputs

40. The incentive to foreclose depends on the degree to which foreclosure would be profitable. The vertically integrated firm will take into account how its supplies of inputs to competitors downstream will affect not only the profits of its upstream division, but also of its downstream division. Essentially, the merged entity faces a trade-off between the profit lost in the upstream market due to a reduction of input sales to (actual or potential) rivals and the profit gain, in the short or longer term, from expanding sales downstream or, as the case may be, being able to raise prices to consumers.

41. The trade-off is likely to depend on the level of profits the merged entity obtains upstream and downstream.[1] Other things constant, the lower the margins upstream, the lower the loss from restricting input sales. Similarly, the higher the downstream margins, the higher the profit gain from increasing market share downstream at the expense of foreclosed rivals.[2]

Notes

[1] See, e.g. Case COMP/M.4300 – Philips/ Intermagnetics, points 56–62, Case COMP/M.4576 – AVR/ Van Gansewinkel, points 33–38.

[2] It has to be considered that upstream and downstream margins may change as a result of the merger. This may impact upon the merged entity's incentive to engage in foreclosure.

---

42. The incentive for the integrated firm to raise rivals' costs further depends on the extent to which downstream demand is likely to be diverted away from foreclosed rivals and the share of that diverted demand that the downstream division of the integrated firm can capture.[1] This share will normally be higher the less capacity constrained the merged entity will be relative to non-foreclosed downstream rivals and the more the products of the merged entity and foreclosed competitors are close substitutes. The effect on downstream demand will also be higher if the affected input represents a significant proportion of downstream rivals' costs or if the affected input represents a critical component of the downstream product.[2]

Notes

[1] See, e.g. Case COMP/M.3943 – Saint-Gobain/BPB (2005), point 78. The Commission noted that it would be very unlikely that BPB, the main supplier of plaster board in the UK, would cut back on supplies to rival distributors of Saint-Gobain, in part because expansion of Saint-Gobain's distribution capacity was difficult.

[2] Conversely, if the input accounts only for a small share of the downstream product and is not a critical component, even a high market share upstream may not give the merged entity the incentive to foreclose downstream rivals because few, if any, sales would be diverted to the integrated firm's downstream unit. See, e.g. Case COMP/M.2738 GEES/ Unison; Case COMP M.4561, GE/Smiths Aerospace, points 60–62.

43. The incentive to foreclose actual or potential rivals may also depend on the extent to which the downstream division of the integrated firm can be expected to benefit from higher price levels downstream as a result of a strategy to raise rivals' costs.[1] The greater the market shares of the merged entity downstream, the greater the base of sales on which to enjoy increased margins.[2]

Notes

[1] See, e.g. Case COMP/M.4314 – Johnson & Johnson/ Pfizer Consumer Healthcare, points 131–132.

[2] It must be noted that the less the merged firm can target a specific downstream market, the less it is likely to raise its prices for the input it supplies, as it would have to incur opportunity costs in other downstream markets. In this respect, the extent to which the merged entity can price discriminate when the merged entity supplies several downstream markets and/or ancillary markets may be taken into account (e.g. for spare parts).

44. An upstream monopolist that is already able to fully extract all available profits in vertically related markets may not have any incentive to foreclose rivals following a vertical merger. The ability to extract available profits from the consumers does not follow immediately from a very high market share.[1] Such a finding would require a more thorough analysis of the actual and future constraints under which the monopolist operates. When all available profits cannot be extracted, a vertical merger – even if it involves an upstream monopolist – may give the merged entity the incentive to raise the costs of downstream rivals, thereby reducing the competitive constraint they exert on the merged entity in the downstream market.

Notes

[1] One situation in which this may not be the case would be when the monopolist has a so-called commitment problem which it is unable to solve. For example, a downstream buyer may be willing to pay a high price to an upstream monopolist if the latter does not subsequently sell additional quantities to a competitor. But once the terms of supply are fixed with one downstream firm, the upstream supplier may have an incentive to increase its supplies to other downstream firms, thereby making the first purchase unprofitable. Since downstream firms will anticipate this kind of opportunistic behaviour, the upstream supplier will be unable to fully exploit its market power. Vertical integration may restore the upstream supplier's ability to commit not to expand input sales as this would harm its own downstream division. Another case in which the monopolist cannot obtain all available monopoly profits may arise when the company cannot differentiate its prices among customers.

45. In its assessment of the likely incentives of the merged firm, the Commission may take into account various considerations such as the ownership structure of the merged entity,[1] the type of strategies adopted on the market in the past[2] or the content of internal strategic documents such as business plans.

Notes

[1] For instance, in cases where two companies have joint control over a firm active in the upstream market, and only one of them is active downstream, the company without downstream activities may have little interest in foregoing input sales. In such cases, the incentive to foreclose is smaller than when the upstream company is fully controlled by a company with downstream activities. See, e.g. Case COMP/M.3440 – EDP/ENI/GDP (2004), Case COMP/M.4403 – Thales/ Finmeccanica/ Alcatel Alenia Space/ Telespazio, points 121 and 268.

[2] The fact that, in the past, a competitor with a similar market position as the merged entity has stopped supplying inputs may demonstrate that it is commercially rational to adopt such a strategy (See, e.g. Alcan/Pechiney, M. 3225 (2004), at point 40).

46. In addition, when the adoption of a specific course of conduct by the merged entity is an essential step in foreclosure, the Commission examines both the incentives to adopt such conduct and the factors liable to reduce, or even eliminate, those incentives, including the

possibility that the conduct is unlawful. Conduct may be unlawful *inter alia* because of competition rules or sector-specific rules at the EU or national levels. This appraisal, however, does not require an exhaustive and detailed examination of the rules of the various legal orders which might be applicable and of the enforcement policy practised within them.[1] Moreover, the illegality of a conduct may be likely to provide significant disincentives for the merged entity to engage in such conduct only in certain circumstances. In particular, the Commission will consider, on the basis of a summary analysis: (i) the likelihood that this conduct would be clearly, or highly probably, unlawful under Community law,[2] (ii) the likelihood that this illegal conduct could be detected,[3] and (iii) the penalties which could be imposed.

Notes

[1] Case C-12/03 P, *Commission v Tetra Laval BV* [2003] ECR I-000, paragraphs 74–76. Case T-210/01, *General Electric v Commission* [2005] ECR II-000, at paragraph 73.

[2] Case T-210/01, *General Electric v Commission* [2005] ECR II-000, specifically at points 74–75 and 311–312.

[3] For instance, in Case M.3696 E.ON/MOL (2005), points 433 and 443–446, the Commission attached importance to the fact that the national Hungarian regulator for the gas sector indicated that in a number of settings, although it has the right to control and to force market players to act without discrimination, it would not be able to obtain adequate information on the commercial behaviour of the operators. See also Case COMP/M.3440 – EDP/ENI/GDP (2004), point 424.

C. Overall likely impact on effective competition

47. A merger will raise competition concerns because of input foreclosure only if it would significantly impede effective competition in the downstream market.

48. First, anticompetitive foreclosure may occur when a vertical merger allows the merging parties to increase the costs of downstream rivals in the market thereby leading to an upward pressure on their sales prices. Significant harm to effective competition normally requires that the foreclosed firms play a sufficiently important role in the competitive process on the downstream market. The higher the proportion of rivals which would be foreclosed on the downstream market, the more likely the merger can be expected to result in a significant price increase in the downstream market and, therefore, to significantly impede effective competition therein.[1] Despite a relatively small market share compared to other players, a specific firm may play a significant competitive role compared to other players,[2] for instance because it is a close competitor of the vertically integrated firm or because it is a particularly aggressive competitor.

Notes

[1] See, e.g. Case COMP/M.4494 Evraz/ Highveld, points 97–112.

[2] See, e.g. Case COMP/M.3440 – EDP/ENI/GDP (2004).

49. Second, effective competition may be significantly impeded by raising barriers to entry to potential competitors.[1] A vertical merger may foreclose potential competition on the downstream market when the merged entity would be likely not to supply potential downstream entrants, or only on less favourable terms than absent the merger. The mere likelihood that the merged entity would carry out a foreclosure strategy post-merger may already create a strong deterrent effect on potential entrants.[2] Effective competition on the downstream market may be significantly impeded by raising barriers to entry, in particular if input foreclosure would entail for such potential competitors the need to enter at both the downstream and the upstream level in order to compete effectively on either market. The concern of raising entry barriers is particularly relevant in those industries that are opening up to competition or are expected to do so in the foreseeable future.[3]

Notes

[1] See, e.g. Case COMP/M.4180 Gaz de France/ Suez, points 876–931, Case COMP/M.4576 – AVR/ Van Gansewinkel, points 33–38.

[2] See Case COMP/M.3696 – E.ON/MOL (2005), at point 662 et seq.

[3] See paragraph 20. It is important that regulatory measures aimed at opening a market are not rendered ineffective through vertically-related incumbent companies merging and thereby closing off the market, or eliminating each other as potential entrants.

50. If there remain sufficient credible downstream competitors whose costs are not likely to be raised, for example because they are themselves vertically integrated[1] or they are capable of switching to adequate alternative inputs, competition from those firms may constitute a sufficient constraint on the merged entity and therefore prevent output prices from rising above pre-merger levels.

Notes

[1] See, e.g. Case COMP/M.3653 – Siemens/VA Tech (2005), at point 164.

51. The effect on competition on the downstream market must also be assessed in light of countervailing factors such as the presence of buyer power[1] or the likelihood that entry upstream would maintain effective competition.[2]

Notes

[1] See Section V on countervailing buyer power in the Notice on Horizontal Mergers.
[2] See Section VI on entry in the Notice on Horizontal Mergers.

52. Further, the effect on competition needs to be assessed in light of efficiencies substantiated by the merging parties.[1] The Commission may decide that, as a consequence of the efficiencies that the merger brings about, there are no grounds for declaring the merger incompatible with the common market pursuant to Article 2(3) of the Merger Regulation. This will be the case when the Commission is in a position to conclude on the basis of sufficient evidence that the efficiencies generated by the merger are likely to enhance the ability and incentive of the merged entity to act pro-competitively for the benefit of consumers, thereby counteracting the adverse effects on competition which the merger might otherwise have.

Notes

[1] See Section VII on efficiencies in the Notice on Horizontal Mergers.

53. When assessing efficiencies in the context of non-horizontal mergers, the Commission applies the principles already set out in Section VII of the Notice on Horizontal Mergers. In particular, for the Commission to take account of efficiency claims in its assessment of the merger, the efficiencies have to benefit consumers, be merger-specific and be verifiable. These conditions are cumulative.[1]

Notes

[1] See, more specifically, paragraphs 79 to 88 of the Notice on Horizontal Mergers.

54. Vertical mergers may entail some specific sources of efficiencies, the list of which is not exhaustive.

55. In particular, a vertical merger allows the merged entity to internalise any pre-existing double mark-ups resulting from both parties setting their prices independently pre-merger.[1] Depending on the market conditions, reducing the combined mark-up (relative to a situation where pricing decisions at both levels are not aligned) may allow the vertically integrated firm to profitably expand output on the downstream market.[2]

Notes

[1] See also paragraph 13 above.
[2] It is important to recognise, however, that the problem of double mark-ups is not always present or significant pre-merger, for instance because the merging parties had already concluded a supply agreement with a price mechanism providing for volume discounts eliminating the mark-up. The efficiencies associated with the elimination of double mark-ups may thus not always be merger specific because vertical cooperation or vertical agreements may, short of a merger, achieve similar benefits with less anti-competitive effects. In addition, a merger may not fully eliminate the double mark-up when the supply of the input is limited by capacity constraints and there is an equally profitable alternative use for the input. In such circumstances, the internal use of the input entails an opportunity cost for the vertically integrated company: using more of the input internally to increase output downstream means selling less in the alternative market. As a result, the incentive to use the input internally and increase output downstream is less than when there is no opportunity cost.

Commentary
para 55: F&N: 5.855

56. A vertical merger may further allow the parties to better coordinate the production and distribution process, and therefore to save on inventories costs.

57. More generally, a vertical merger may align the incentives of the parties with regard to investments in new products, new production processes and in the marketing of products. For instance, whereas before the merger, a downstream distributor entity might have been reluctant to invest in advertising and informing customers about the qualities of products of the upstream entity when such investment would also have benefited the sale of other downstream firms, the merged entity may reduce such incentive problems.

2. Customer foreclosure

58. Customer foreclosure may occur when a supplier integrates with an important customer in the downstream market.[1] Because of this downstream presence, the merged entity may foreclose access to a sufficient customer base to its actual or potential rivals in the upstream market (the input market) and reduce their ability or incentive to compete. In turn, this may raise downstream rivals' costs by making it harder for them to obtain supplies of the input under similar prices and conditions as absent the merger. This may allow the merged entity profitably to establish higher prices on the downstream market. Any efficiencies resulting from the merger, however, may lead the merged entity to reduce price, so that there is overall not a negative impact on consumers. For customer foreclosure to lead to consumer harm, it is thus not necessary that the merged firm's rivals are forced to exit the market. The relevant benchmark is whether the increased input costs would lead to higher prices for consumers. A graphical presentation of this mechanism is provided in Figure 2.

Figure 2

Customer foreclosure

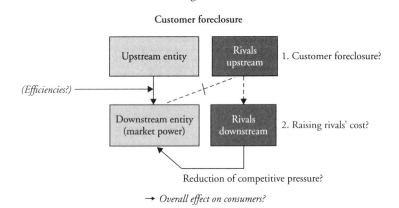

Notes
1 See footnote 4 for the definition of "downstream" and "upstream".

Commentary
para 58: B&C: 8.232

59. In assessing the likelihood of an anticompetitive customer foreclosure scenario, the Commission examines, first, whether the merged entity would have the ability to foreclose access to downstream markets by reducing its purchases from its upstream rivals, second, whether it would have the incentive to reduce its purchases upstream, and third, whether a foreclosure strategy would have a significant detrimental effect on consumers in the downstream market.[1]

Notes

[1] See, e.g. Case COMP/M.4389 – WLR/BST.

Commentary
para 59: F&N: 5.836

A. Ability to foreclose access to downstream markets

60. A vertical merger may affect upstream competitors by increasing their cost to access downstream customers or by restricting access to a significant customer base. Customer foreclosure may take various forms. For instance, the merged entity may decide to source all of its required goods or services from its upstream division and, as a result, may stop purchasing from its upstream competitors. It may also reduce its purchases from upstream rivals, or purchase from those rivals on less favourable terms than it would have done absent the merger.[1]

Notes

[1] For instance, in cases involving distribution, the merged entity may be less likely to grant access to its outlets under the same conditions as absent the merger.

61. When considering whether the merged entity would have the ability to foreclose access to downstream markets, the Commission examines whether there are sufficient economic alternatives in the downstream market for the upstream rivals (actual or potential) to sell their output.[1] For customer foreclosure to be a concern, it must be the case that the vertical merger involves a company which is an important customer with a significant degree of market power in the downstream market.[2] If, on the contrary, there is a sufficiently large customer base, at present or in the future, that is likely to turn to independent suppliers, the Commission is unlikely to raise competition concerns on that ground.[3]

Notes

[1] The loss of the integrated firm as a customer is normally less significant if that firm's pre-merger purchases from non-integrated firms are a small share of the available sales base for those firms. In that case, sufficient alternative customers are more likely to be available. The presence of exclusive contracts between the merged entity and other downstream firms may limit the ability of upstream rivals to reach a sufficient sales volume.

[2] See, e.g. Case COMP/M.2822 – ENBW/ENI/GVS (2002) at points 54–57.

[3] See, e.g. Case COMP/M.81 – VIAG/Continental Can (1991), point 51, See, e.g. Case COMP/M.4389 – WLR/BST, points 33–35.

Commentary
para 61: B&C: 8.232

62. Customer foreclosure can lead to higher input prices in particular if there are significant economies of scale or scope in the input market or when demand is characterised by network effects.[1] It is mainly in such circumstances that the ability to compete of upstream rivals, be they actual or potential, can be impaired.

Notes

[1] Economies of scale or scope exist when an increase in scale or scope of production leads to a reduction in average unit cost. Network effects occur when the value of a product for a customer increases when the number of other customers also using it increases. Examples include communication devices, specific software programmes, products requiring standardisation, and platforms bringing together buyers and sellers.

63. For instance, customer foreclosure can lead to higher input prices when existing upstream rivals operate at or close to their minimum efficient scale. To the extent that customer foreclosure and the corresponding loss of output for the upstream rivals increases their variable costs of production, this may result in an upward pressure on the prices they charge to their customers operating in the downstream market.

64. In the presence of economies of scale or scope, customer foreclosure may also render entry upstream by potential entrants unattractive by significantly reducing the revenue prospects of potential entrants. When customer foreclosure effectively results in entry deterrence, input prices

Part D Mergers and Concentrations

may remain at a higher level than otherwise would have been the case, thereby raising the cost of input supply to downstream competitors of the merged firm.

65. Further, when customer foreclosure primarily impacts upon the revenue streams of upstream rivals, it may significantly reduce their ability and incentive to invest in cost reduction, R & D and product quality.[1] This may reduce their ability to compete in the long run and possibly even cause their exit from the market.

Notes

[1] An input supplier foreclosed from an important customer may prefer to stay out of the market if it fails to reach some minimum viable scale following the investment. Such minimum viable scale may be achieved, however, if a potential entrant has access to a broader customer base including customers in other relevant markets. See Case No. COMP/M. 1879 – Boeing/Hughes (2000); Case No. COMP/M.2978 – Lagardère/Natexis/VUP (2003).

66. In its assessment, the Commission may take into account the existence of different markets corresponding to different uses for the input. If a substantial part of the downstream market is foreclosed, an upstream supplier may fail to reach efficient scale and may also operate at higher costs in the other market(s). Conversely, an upstream supplier may continue to operate efficiently if it finds other uses or secondary markets for its input without incurring significantly higher costs.

67. In its assessment, the Commission will consider, on the basis of the information available, whether there are effective and timely counter-strategies, sustainable over time, that the rival firms would be likely to deploy. Such counterstrategies include the possibility that upstream rivals decide to price more aggressively to maintain sales levels in the downstream market, so as to mitigate the effect of foreclosure.[1]

Notes

[1] For instance, in Case COMP/M.1879 – Boeing/Hughes (2000), point 100, it was considered, among several other factors, that in view of the high fixed costs involved, if competing satellite launch vehicle providers were to become less cost-competitive relative to the merged entity, they would try to cut prices in order to salvage volume and recoup at least part of their fixed costs rather than accept losing a contract and incur a higher loss. The most likely impact would therefore be greater price competition rather than market monopolisation.

B. Incentive to foreclose access to downstream markets

68. The incentive to foreclose depends on the degree to which it is profitable. The merged entity faces a trade-off between the possible costs associated with not procuring products from upstream rivals and the possible gains from doing so, for instance, because it allows the merged entity to raise price in the upstream or downstream markets.

69. The costs associated with reducing purchases from rival upstream suppliers are higher, when the upstream division of the integrated firm is less efficient than the foreclosed suppliers. Such costs are also higher if the upstream division of the merged firm is capacity constrained or rivals' products are more attractive due to product differentiation.

70. The incentive to engage in customer foreclosure further depends on the extent to which the upstream division of the merged entity can benefit from possibly higher price levels in the upstream market arising as a result of upstream rivals being foreclosed. The incentive to engage in customer foreclosure also becomes higher, the more the downstream division of the integrated firm can be expected to enjoy the benefits of higher price levels downstream resulting from the foreclosure strategy. In this context, the greater the market shares of the merged entity's downstream operations, the greater the base of sales on which to enjoy increased margins.[1]

Notes

[1] If the vertically integrated firm partially supplies inputs to downstream competitors it may benefit from the ability to expand sales, or as the case may be, to increase input prices.

71. When the adoption of a specific conduct by the merged entity is an essential step in foreclosure, the Commission examines both the incentives to adopt such conduct and the factors liable to reduce, or even eliminate, those incentives, including the possibility that the conduct is unlawful.[1]

C. Overall likely impact on effective competition

72. Foreclosing rivals in the upstream market may have an adverse impact in the downstream market and harm consumers. By denying competitive access to a significant customer base for the fore-closed rivals' (upstream) products, the merger may reduce their ability to compete in the foresee-able future. As a result, rivals downstream are likely to be put at a competitive disadvantage, for example in the form of raised input costs. In turn, this may allow the merged entity to profitably raise prices or reduce the overall output on the downstream market.

73. The negative impact on consumers may take some time to materialise when the primary impact of customer foreclosure is on the revenue streams of upstream rivals, reducing their incentives to make investments in cost reduction, product quality or in other competitive dimensions so as to remain competitive.

74. It is only when a sufficiently large fraction of upstream output is affected by the revenue decreases resulting from the vertical merger that the merger may significantly impede effective competition on the upstream market. If there remain a number of upstream competitors that are not affected, competition from those firms may be sufficient to prevent prices from rising in the upstream market and, consequently, in the downstream market. Sufficient competition from these non-foreclosed upstream firms requires that they do not face barriers to expansion e.g. through capacity constraints or product differentiation.[1] When the reduction of competition upstream affects a significant fraction of output downstream, the merger is likely, as with input foreclosure, to result in a significant increase of the price level in the downstream market and, therefore, to significantly impede effective competition.[2]

75. Effective competition on the upstream market may also be significantly impeded by raising bar-riers to entry to potential competitors. This may be so in particular if customer foreclosure would entail for such potential competitors the need to enter at both the downstream and the upstream level in order to compete effectively on either market. In such a context, customer foreclosure and input foreclosure may thus be part of the same strategy. The concern of raising entry barriers is particularly relevant in those industries that are opening up to competition or are expected to do so in the foreseeable future.[1]

76. The effect on competition must be assessed in light of countervailing factors such as the presence of countervailing buyer power[1] or the likelihood that entry would maintain effective competition in the upstream or downstream markets.[2]

77. Further, the effect on competition needs to be assessed in light of efficiencies substantiated by the merging parties.[1]

B. Other non-coordinated effects

78. The merged entity may, by vertically integrating, gain access to commercially sensitive information regarding the upstream or downstream activities of rivals.[1] For instance, by becoming the supplier of a downstream competitor, a company may obtain critical information, which allows it to price less aggressively in the downstream market to the detriment of consumers.[2] It may also put competitors at a competitive disadvantage, thereby dissuading them to enter or expand in the market.

Notes

[1] See Case COMP/M.1879 – Boeing/Hughes (2000); Case COMP/M.2510 – Cendant/Galileo, point 37; Case COMP/M.2738 – Gees/Unison, point 21; Case COMP/M.2925 – Charterhouse/CDC/Telediffusion de France, point 37–38; Case COMP/M.3440 – EDP/ENL/GDP (2004).

[2] See, e.g. Case COMP/M.2822 – ENBW/ENI/GVS (2002), at point 56; Case COMP/M.3440 – EDP/ENI/GDP (2004), points 368–379; Case COMP/M.3653 – Siemens/VA Tech (2005) points 159–164.

C. Coordinated effects

79. As set out in Section IV of the Notice on Horizontal Mergers, a merger may change the nature of competition in such a way that firms that previously were not coordinating their behaviour, are now significantly more likely to coordinate and raise prices or otherwise harm effective competition. A merger may also make coordination easier, more stable or more effective for firms which were coordinating prior to the merger.[1]

Notes

[1] See Case COMP/M.3101 – Accor/Hilton/Six Continents, points 23–28.

Commentary
para 79: B&C: 8.233

80. Market coordination may arise where competitors are able, without entering into an agreement or resorting to a concerted practice within the meaning of Article [101] of the Treaty, to identify and pursue common objectives, avoiding the normal mutual competitive pressure by a coherent system of implicit threats. In a normal competitive setting, each firm constantly has an incentive to compete. This incentive is ultimately what keeps prices low, and what prevents firms from jointly maximising their profits. Coordination involves a departure from normal competitive conditions in that firms are able to sustain prices in excess of what independent short term profit maximisation would yield. Firms will refrain from undercutting the high prices charged by their competitors in a coordinated way because they anticipate that such behaviour would jeopardise coordination in the future. For coordinated effects to arise, the profit that firms could make by competing aggressively in the short term ("deviating") has to be less than the expected reduction in revenues that this behaviour would entail in the longer term, as it would be expected to trigger an aggressive response by competitors ("a punishment").

81. Coordination is more likely to emerge in markets where it is relatively simple to reach a common understanding on the terms of coordination. In addition, three conditions are necessary for coordination to be sustainable. First, the coordinating firms must be able to monitor to a sufficient degree whether the terms of coordination are being adhered to. Second, discipline requires that there is some form of deterrent mechanism that can be activated if deviation is detected. Third, the reactions of outsiders, such as current and future competitors not participating in the coordination, as well as customers, should not be able to jeopardise the results expected from the coordination.[1]

Notes

[1] See Case T-342/99, *Airtours v Commission*, [2002] ECR II-2585, paragraph 62.

Reaching terms of coordination

82. A vertical merger may make it easier for the firms in the upstream or downstream market to reach a common understanding on the terms of coordination.[1]

Notes

[1] See, e.g. Case COMP/M.3314 – Air Liquide/Messer Targets, points 91–100.

83. For instance, when a vertical merger leads to foreclosure,[1] it results in a reduction in the number of effective competitors in the market. Generally speaking, a reduction in the number of players makes it easier to coordinate among the remaining market players.

Notes

[1] Foreclosure would have to be shown by the Commission along the lines of Part A of this Section.

84. Vertical mergers may also increase the degree of symmetry between firms active in the market.[1] This may increase the likelihood of coordination by making it easier to reach a common understanding on the terms of coordination. Likewise, vertical integration may increase the level of market transparency, making it easier to coordinate among the remaining market players.

Notes

[1] See Case COMP/M.2389 – Shell/DEA; Case COMP/M.2533 – BP/EON. Alternatively, vertical integration may also decrease the degree of symmetry between firms active in the market, rendering coordination more difficult.

85. Further, a merger may involve the elimination of a maverick in a market. A maverick is a supplier that for its own reasons is unwilling to accept the co-ordinated outcome and thus maintains aggressive competition. The vertical integration of the maverick may alter its incentives to such an extent that co-ordination will no longer be prevented.

Monitoring deviations

86. Vertical integration may facilitate coordination by increasing the level of market transparency between firms through access to sensitive information on rivals or by making it easier to monitor pricing. Such concerns may arise, for example, if the level of price transparency is higher downstream than upstream. This could be the case when prices to final consumers are public, while transactions at the intermediate market are confidential. Vertical integration may give upstream producers control over final prices and thus monitor deviations more effectively.

87. When it leads to foreclosure, a vertical merger may also induce a reduction in the number of effective competitors in a market. A reduction in the number of players may make it easier to monitor each other's actions in the market.

Deterrent mechanisms

88. Vertical mergers may affect coordinating firms' incentives to adhere to the terms of coordination. For instance, a vertically integrated company may be in a position to more effectively punish rival companies when they choose to deviate from the terms of coordination, because it is either a crucial customer or supplier to them.[1]

Notes

[1] For instance, in a case that was subsequently withdrawn (Case COMP/M.2322 – CRH/Addtek (2001)) the merger involved an upstream dominant supplier of cement and a downstream producer or pre-cast concrete products, both active in Finland. The Commission provisionally took the view in the administrative procedure that the new entity would be able to discipline the downstream rivals by using the fact that they would be highly dependent on cement supplies of the merged entity. As a result, the downstream entity would be able to increase the price of its pre-cast concrete products while making sure that the competitors would follow these price increases and avoiding that they turn to cement imports from the Baltic States and Russia.

Reactions of outsiders

89. Vertical mergers may reduce the scope for outsiders to destabilise the coordination by increasing barriers to enter the market or otherwise limiting the ability to compete on the part of outsiders to the coordination.

90. A vertical merger may also involve the elimination of a disruptive buyer in a market. If upstream firms view sales to a particular buyer as sufficiently important, they may be tempted to deviate

Part D Mergers and Concentrations

from the terms of co-ordination in an effort to secure their business. Similarly, a large buyer may be able to tempt the co-ordinating firms to deviate from these terms by concentrating a large amount of its requirements on one supplier or by offering long term contracts. The acquisition of such a buyer may increase the risk of co-ordination in a market.

V. CONGLOMERATE MERGERS

91. Conglomerate mergers are mergers between firms that are in a relationship which is neither purely horizontal (as competitors in the same relevant market) nor vertical (as supplier and customer). In practice, the focus is on mergers between companies that are active in closely related markets[1] (e.g. mergers involving suppliers of complementary products or of products which belong to a range of products that is generally purchased by the same set of customers for the same end use).

Notes

[1] See also Form CO, Section IV, 6.3 (c).

Commentary
para 91: B&C: 8.235

92. Whereas it is acknowledged that conglomerate mergers in the majority of circumstances will not lead to any competition problems, in certain specific cases there may be harm to competition. In its assessment, the Commission will consider both the possible anti-competitive effects arising from conglomerate mergers and the possible pro-competitive effects stemming from efficiencies substantiated by the parties.

A. Non-coordinated effects: foreclosure

93. The main concern in the context of conglomerate mergers is that of foreclosure. The combination of products in related markets may confer on the merged entity the ability and incentive to lever-age[1] a strong market position from one market to another by means of tying or bundling or other exclusionary practices.[2] Tying and bundling as such are common practices that often have no anticompetitive consequences. Companies engage in tying and bundling in order to provide their customers with better products or offerings in cost-effective ways. Nevertheless, in certain circumstances, these practices may lead to a reduction in actual or potential rivals' ability or incentive to compete. This may reduce the competitive pressure on the merged entity allowing it to increase prices.

Notes

[1] There is no received definition of "leveraging" but, in a neutral sense, it implies being able to increase sales of a product in one market (the "tied market" or "bundled market"), by virtue of the strong market position of the product to which it is tied or bundled (the "tying market" or "leveraging market").
[2] These concepts are defined further below.

Commentary
para 93: B&C: 8.235

94. In assessing the likelihood of such a scenario, the Commission examines, first, whether the merged firm would have the ability to foreclose its rivals, second, whether it would have the economic incentive to do so and, third, whether a foreclosure strategy would have a significant detrimental effect on competition, thus causing harm to consumers.[1] In practice, these factors are often examined together as they are closely intertwined.

Notes

[1] See Case T-210/01, *General Electric v Commission*, [2005], ECR II-000, paragraphs 327, 362–363, 405; Case COMP/M.3304 – GE/Amersham (2004), point 37, and Case COMP/M.4561 – GE/Smiths Aerospace, points 116–126.

Commentary
para 94: F&N: 5.836

A. Ability to foreclose

95. The most immediate way in which the merged entity may be able to use its market power in one market to foreclose competitors in another is by conditioning sales in a way that links the products in the separate markets together. This is done most directly either by tying or bundling.

96. "Bundling" usually refers to the way products are offered and priced by the merged entity. One can distinguish in this respect between pure bundling and mixed bundling. In the case of pure bundling the products are only sold jointly in fixed proportions. With mixed bundling the products are also available separately, but the sum of the stand-alone prices is higher than the bundled price.[1] Rebates, when made dependent on the purchase of other goods, may be considered a form of mixed bundling.

Notes

[1] The distinction between mixed bundling and pure bundling is not necessarily clear-cut. Mixed bundling may come close to pure bundling when the prices charged for the individual offerings are high.

97. "Tying" usually refers to situations where customers that purchase one good (the tying good) are required to also purchase another good from the producer (the tied good). Tying can take place on a technical or contractual basis. For instance, technical tying occurs when the tying product is designed in such a way that it only works with the tied product (and not with the alternatives offered by competitors). Contractual tying entails that the customer when purchasing the tying good undertakes only to purchase the tied product (and not the alternatives offered by competitors).

98. The specific characteristics of the products may be relevant for determining whether any of these means of linking sales between separate markets are available to the merged entity. For instance, pure bundling is very unlikely to be possible if products are not bought simultaneously or by the same customers.[1] Similarly, technical tying is only an option in certain industries.

Notes

[1] See, e.g. Case COMP.M.3304 – GE/Amersham (2004), point 35.

99. In order to be able to foreclose competitors, the new entity must have a significant degree of market power, which does not necessarily amount to dominance, in one of the markets concerned. The effects of bundling or tying can only be expected to be substantial when at least one of the merging parties' products is viewed by many customers as particularly important and there are few relevant alternatives for that product, e.g. because of product differentiation[1] or capacity constraints on the part of rivals.

Notes

[1] For instance, in the context of branded products, particularly important products are sometimes referred to as 'must stock' products. See, e.g. Case COMP/M.3732 – Procter & Gamble/Gillette (2005), point 110.

100. Further, for foreclosure to be a potential concern it must be the case that there is a large common pool of customers for the individual products concerned. The more customers tend to buy both products (instead of only one of the products), the more demand for the individual products may be affected through bundling or tying. Such a correspondence in purchasing behaviour is more likely to be significant when the products in question are complementary.

101. Generally speaking, the foreclosure effects of bundling and tying are likely to be more pronounced in industries where there are economies of scale and the demand pattern at any given point in time has dynamic implications for the conditions of supply in the market in the future. Notably, where a supplier of complementary goods has market power in one of the products (product A), the decision to bundle or tie may result in reduced sales by the non-integrated suppliers of the complementary good (product B). If further there are network externalities at play[1] this will significantly reduce these rivals' scope for expanding sales of product B in the future. Alternatively, where entry into the market for the complementary product is contemplated by potential entrants, the decision to bundle by the merged entity may have the effect of deterring such entry.

The limited availability of complementary products with which to combine may, in turn, discourage potential entrants to enter market A.

Notes

1 When a product features network externalities, this means that customers or producers derive benefit from the fact that other customers or producers are using the same products as well. Examples include communication devices, specific software programmes, products requiring standardisation, and platforms bringing together buyers and sellers.

102. It can also be noted that the scope for foreclosure tends to be smaller where the merging parties cannot commit to making their tying or bundling strategy a lasting one, for example through technical tying or bundling which is costly to reverse.

103. In its assessment, the Commission considers, on the basis of the information available, whether there are effective and timely counter-strategies that the rival firms may deploy. One such example is when a strategy of bundling would be defeated by single-product companies combining their offers so as to make them more attractive to customers.[1] Bundling is further less likely to lead to foreclosure if a company in the market would purchase the bundled products and profitably resell them unbundled. In addition, rivals may decide to price more aggressively to maintain market share, mitigating the effect of foreclosure.[2]

Notes

1 See, e.g. Case COMP/M.3304 – GE/Amersham (2004), point 39.
2 See, e.g. Case COMP/M.1879 – Boeing/Hughes (2000), point 100; Case COMP/M.3304 – GE/Amersham (2004), point 39. The resulting loss of revenues may, however, in certain circumstances, have an impact on the ability of rivals to compete. See Section C.

104. Customers may have a strong incentive to buy the range of products concerned from a single source (one-stop-shopping) rather than from many suppliers, e.g. because it saves on transaction costs. The fact that the merged entity will have a broad range or portfolio of products does not, as such, raise competition concerns.[1]

Notes

1 See, e.g. Case COMP/M.2608 – INA/ FAG, point 34.

B. Incentive to foreclose

105. The incentive to foreclose rivals through bundling or tying depends on the degree to which this strategy is profitable. The merged entity faces a trade-off between the possible costs associated with bundling or tying its products and the possible gains from expanding market shares in the market(s) concerned or, as the case may be, being able to raise price in those market(s) due to its market power.

106. Pure bundling and tying may entail losses for the merged company itself. For instance, if a significant number of customers are not interested in buying the bundle, but instead prefers to buy only one product (e.g. the product used to leverage), sales of that product (as contained in the bundle) may significantly fall. Furthermore, losses on the leveraging product may arise where customers who, before the merger, used to "mix and match" the leveraging product of a merging party with the product of another company, decide to purchase the bundle offered by rivals or no longer to purchase at all.[1]

Notes

1 See, e.g. Case COMP/M.3304 – GE/Amersham (2004), point 59.

107. In this context it may thus be relevant to assess the relative value of the different products. By way of example, it is unlikely that the merged entity would be willing to forego sales on one highly profitable market in order to gain market shares on another market where turnover is relatively small and profits are modest.

108. However, the decision to bundle and tie may also increase profits by gaining market power in the tied goods market, protecting market power in the tying goods market, or a combination of the two (see Section C below).

Commentary
para 108: F&N: 1.246

109. In its assessment of the likely incentives of the merged firm, the Commission may take into account other factors such as the ownership structure of the merged entity,[1] the type of strategies adopted on the market in the past or the content of internal strategic documents such as business plans.

Notes

[1] For instance, in cases where two companies have joint control over a firm active in one market, and only one of them is active on the neighbouring market, the company without activities on the latter market may have little interest in foregoing sales in the former market. See, e.g. Case T-210/01, *General Electric v Commission*, [2005], ECR II-000, paragraph 385 and Case COMP M.4561, GE/Smiths Aerospace, point 119.

110. When the adoption of a specific conduct by the merged entity is an essential step in foreclosure, the Commission examines both the incentives to adopt such conduct and the factors liable to reduce, or even eliminate, those incentives, including the possibility that the conduct is unlawful.[1]

Notes

[1] The analysis of these incentives will be conducted as set out in paragraph 46 above.

C. Overall likely impact on prices and choice

111. Bundling or tying may result in a significant reduction of sales prospects faced by single-component rivals in the market. The reduction in sales by competitors is not in and of itself a problem. Yet, in particular industries, if this reduction is significant enough, it may lead to a reduction in rivals' ability or incentive to compete. This may allow the merged entity to subsequently acquire market power (in the market for the tied or bundled good) and/or to maintain market power (in the market for the tying or leveraging good).

Commentary
para 111: F&N: 1.246

112. In particular, foreclosure practices may deter entry by potential competitors. They may do so for a specific market by reducing sales prospects for potential rivals in that market to a level below minimum viable scale. In the case of complementary products, deterring entry in one market through bundling or tying may also allow the merged entity to deter entry in another market if the bundling or tying forces potential competitors to enter both product markets at the same time rather than entering only one of them or entering them sequentially. The latter may have a significant impact in particular in those industries where the demand pattern at any given point in time has dynamic implications for the conditions of supply in the market in the future.

113. It is only when a sufficiently large fraction of market output is affected by foreclosure resulting from the merger that the merger may significantly impede effective competition. If there remain effective single-product players in either market, competition is unlikely to deteriorate following a conglomerate merger. The same holds when few single-product rivals remain, but these have the ability and incentive to expand output.

114. The effect on competition needs to be assessed in light of countervailing factors such as the presence of countervailing buyer power[1] or the likelihood that entry would maintain effective competition in the upstream or downstream markets.[2]

Notes

[1] See Section V on countervailing buyer power in the Notice on Horizontal Mergers.
[2] See, e.g. Case COMP/M.3732 – Procter & Gamble/Gillette (2005), point 131. See also Section VI on entry in the Notice on Horizontal Mergers.

Commentary
para 114: B&C: 8.209

115. Further, the effect on competition needs to be assessed in light of the efficiencies substantiated by the merging parties.[1]

Notes

[1] See Section VII on efficiencies in the Notice on Horizontal Mergers.

Commentary
para 115: B&C: 8.209

116. Many of the efficiencies identified in the context of vertical mergers may, mutatis mutandis, also apply to conglomerate mergers involving complementary products.

Commentary
para 116: B&C: 8.234

117. Notably, when producers of complementary goods are pricing independently, they will not take into account the positive effect of a drop in the price of their product on the sales of the other product. Depending on the market conditions, a merged firm may internalise this effect and may have a certain incentive to lower margins if this leads to higher overall profits (this incentive is often referred to as the "Cournot effect"). In most cases, the merged firm will make the most out of this effect by means of mixed bundling, i.e. by making the price drop conditional upon whether or not the customer buys both products from the merged entity.[1]

Notes

[1] It is important to recognise however that the problem of double mark-ups is not always present or significant pre-merger. In the context of mixed bundling, it must further be noted that while the merged entity may have an incentive to reduce the price for the bundle, the effect on the prices of the individual products is less clear cut. The incentive for the merged entity to raise its single product prices may come from the fact that it counts on selling more bundled products instead. The merged entity's bundle price and prices of the individually sold products (if any) will further depend on the price reactions of rivals in the market.

Commentary
para 117: F&N: 5.855

118. Specific to conglomerate mergers is that they may produce cost savings in the form of economies of scope (either on the production or the consumption side), yielding an inherent advantage to supplying the goods together rather than apart.[1] For instance, it may be more efficient that certain components are marketed together as a bundle rather than separately. Value enhancements for the customer can result from better compatibility and quality assurance of complementary components. Such economies of scope however are necessary but not sufficient to provide an efficiency justification for bundling or tying. Indeed, benefits from economies of scope frequently can be realised without any need for technical or contractual bundling.

Notes

[1] See, e.g. Case COMP/M.3732 – Procter & Gamble/Gillette (2005), point 131.

B. Co-ordinated effects

119. Conglomerate mergers may in certain circumstances facilitate anticompetitive coordination in markets, even in the absence of an agreement or a concerted practice within the meaning of Article [101] of the Treaty. The framework set out in Section IV of the Notice on Horizontal Mergers also applies in this context. In particular, coordination is more likely to emerge in markets where it is fairly easy to identify the terms of co-ordination and where such co-ordination is sustainable.

120. One way in which a conglomerate merger may influence the likelihood of a coordinated outcome in a given market is by reducing the number of effective competitors to such an extent that tacit coordination becomes a real possibility. Also when rivals are not excluded from the market, they may find themselves in a more vulnerable situation. As a result, foreclosed rivals may choose not

to contest the situation of co-ordination, but may prefer instead to live under the shelter of the increased price level.

121. Further, a conglomerate merger may increase the extent and importance of multi-market competition. Competitive interaction on several markets may increase the scope and effectiveness of disciplining mechanisms in ensuring that the terms of coordination are being adhered to.

D13

COMMISSION NOTICE ON REMEDIES ACCEPTABLE UNDER COUNCIL REGULATION (EC) NO 139/2004 AND UNDER COMMISSION REGULATION (EC) NO 802/2004

(Text with EEA relevance)

(2008/C 267/01)

OJ C 267, 22.10.2008, p.1

EUR-Lex permanent link: <http://eur-lex.europa.eu/legal-content/EN/ALL/?uri=uriserv:OJ.C_.2008.267.01.0001.01.ENG>

Notes

This document supersedes the draft notice on remedies published for consultation on 24 April 2007, included in previous editions of this work. [Ed note: please see the Note on the Lisbon Treaty at p.xvii in regard to article renumbering introduced by the Lisbon Treaty.]

Commentary

Notice: B&C: 8.007, 8.165, 8.166 F&N: 5.13, 5.409, 5.983, 12.232
paras 15–17: B&C: 8.171
paras 19–20: B&C: 8.165
paras 22–24: B&C: 8.172
paras 32–436: B&C: 8.172
paras 38–42: B&C: 8.171
paras 44–46: B&C: 8.173
paras 53–55: B&C: 8.173
paras 56–57: B&C: 8.173
paras 58–60: F&N: 5.1083
paras 61–69: B&C: 8.171
paras 71–76: B&C: 8.177 F&N: 5.1112
paras 77–94: F&N: 5.341
paras 97–127: F&N: 5.341
paras 108–112: B&C: 8.175
paras 117–120: B&C: 8.175
paras 117–121: F&N: 5.1104
paras 123–127: B&C: 8.175 F&N: 5.1104
paras 129–130: B&C: 8.171

I. Introduction

1. Council Regulation (EC) No 139/2004 of 20 January 2004 on the control of concentrations between undertakings[1] (hereinafter referred to as 'the Merger Regulation') in Articles 6 (2) and 8 (2) expressly provides that the Commission may decide to declare a concentration compatible with the common market following modification by the parties,[2] both before and after the initiation of proceedings. To that end, the Commission may attach to its decision conditions and obligations intended to ensure that the undertakings concerned comply with the commitments they have entered into vis-à-vis the Commission with a view to rendering the concentration compatible with the common market.[3]

Notes

[1] OJ L 24, 29.1.2004, pp.1–22.

[2] The references to 'parties' and 'merging parties' also cover situations with one notifying party.

[3] Articles 6 (2) and 8 (2), second subparagraphs respectively. See also Recital 30 of the Merger Regulation which states that 'where the undertakings concerned modify a notified concentration, in particular by offering commitments with a view to rendering the concentration compatible with the common market, the Commission should be able to declare the concentration, as modified, compatible with the common market. Such commitments should be proportionate to the competition problem and entirely eliminate it'. Recital 30 further explains that 'it is also appropriate to accept commitments before the initiation of proceedings where the competition problem is readily identifiable and can easily be remedied'.

2. The purpose of this Notice is to provide guidance on modifications to concentrations, in particular commitments by the undertakings concerned to modify a concentration. Such modifications are more commonly described as 'remedies' since their object is to eliminate the competition concerns[1] identified by the Commission. The guidance set out in this Notice reflects the Commission's evolving experience with the assessment, acceptance and implementation of remedies under the Merger Regulation since its entry into force on 21 September 1990.[2] The revision of the Commission's 2001 Notice on remedies[3] is entailed by the entry into force of the recast Merger Regulation (EC) No 139/2004[4] and of Commission Regulation (EC) No 802/2004 (the 'Implementing Regulation')[5] on 1 May 2004, case-law of the Court of Justice and the Court of First Instance, the conclusions drawn from the systematic ex post review of the Commission of past remedies case,[6] and decisional practice of the Commission in cases involving remedies in recent years. The principles contained herein will be applied and further developed and refined by the Commission in individual cases. The guidance provided in this Notice is without prejudice to the interpretation which may be given by the Court of Justice or by the Court of First Instance of the European Communities.

Notes

[1] Save where the contrary is indicated, in the following, the term 'competition concerns' corresponds, according to the stage of the procedure, to serious doubts or preliminary findings that the concentration is likely to significantly impede effective competition in the common market or in a substantial part of it, in particular as a result of the creation or strengthening of a dominant position.

[2] *Ex post* review under the Merger Remedies Study and experience acquired since the publication of the last Notice on remedies.

[3] Commission Notice on remedies acceptable under Council Regulation (EEC) No 4064/89 and under Commission Regulation (EC) No 447/98 (OJ C 68, 2.3.2001, p.3).

[4] Regulation replacing Council Regulation (EEC) No 4064/89 (OJ L 395, 30.12.1989, corrected version in OJ L 257, 21.9.1990, p.13).

[5] Commission Regulation (EC) No 802/2004 implementing Council Regulation (EC) No 139/2004 on the control of concentrations between undertakings, OJ L 133, 30.0.2004, p.1. This regulation replaces Commission Regulation (EC) No 447/98 implementing Council Regulation (EEC) No 4064/89 on the control of concentrations between undertakings, OJ L 61, 2.3.1998, p.1.

[6] DG COMP, Merger Remedies Study, October 2005.

3. This Notice sets out the general principles applicable to remedies acceptable to the Commission, the main types of commitments that may be accepted by the Commission in cases under the Merger Regulation, the specific requirements which proposals of commitments need to fulfil in both phases of the procedure, and the main requirements for the implementation of

commitments. In any case, the Commission will take due account of the particular circumstances of the individual case.

II. GENERAL PRINCIPLES

4. Under the Merger Regulation, the Commission assesses the compatibility of a notified concentration with the common market on the basis of its effect on the structure of competition in the Community.[1] The test for compatibility under Article 2(2) and (3) of the Merger Regulation is whether or not a concentration would significantly impede effective competition in the common market or a substantial part of it, in particular as a result of the creation or strengthening of a dominant position. A concentration that significantly impedes effective competition as described above is incompatible with the common market and the Commission is required to prohibit it. For the creation of a joint venture, the Commission will also examine the concentration under Article 2(4) of the Merger Regulation. The principles set out in this Notice will generally also apply to remedies submitted to eliminate competition concerns identified under Article 2(4).

Notes

[1] Recital 6 of the Merger Regulation.

5. Where a concentration raises competition concerns in that it could significantly impede effective competition, in particular as a result of the creation or strengthening of a dominant position, the parties may seek to modify the concentration in order to resolve the competition concerns and thereby gain clearance of their merger. Such modifications may be fully implemented in advance of a clearance decision. However, it is more common that the parties submit commitments with a view to rendering the concentration compatible with the common market and that those commitments are implemented following clearance.

6. Under the structure of the Merger Regulation, it is the responsibility of the Commission to show that a concentration would significantly impede competition.[1] The Commission communicates its competition concerns to the parties to allow them to formulate appropriate and corresponding remedies proposals.[2] It is then for the parties to the concentration to put forward commitments; the Commission is not in a position to impose unilaterally any conditions to an authorisation decision, but only on the basis of the parties' commitments.[3] The Commission will inform the parties about its preliminary assessment of remedies proposals. If, however, the parties do not validly propose remedies adequate to eliminate the competition concerns, the only option for the Commission will be to adopt a prohibition decision.[4]

Notes

[1] In phase I and before the issuance of a Statement of Objections, this corresponds to serious doubts as to the significant impediment to effective competition.

[2] The Merger Regulation provides for formal steps where the parties are informed of the competition concerns identified by the Commission (Article 6(1)(c) decision, Statement of Objections). In addition, the DG COMPETITION Best Practices on the conduct of EC merger control proceedings foresee that 'state of play' meetings will normally be offered at key stages of the procedure where the Commission will explain its concerns to the parties in order to allow them to respond with remedies proposals.

[3] Judgment of the CFI in Case T-210/01, *General Electric v Commission*, [2005] ECR II-5575, paragraph 52; see judgment of the CFI in Case T-87/05, *EDP v Commission*, [2005] ECR II-3745, paragraph 105.

[4] See Case COMP/M.2220 – *GE/Honeywell* of 3 July 2001, confirmed by judgment of the CFI in Case T-210/01 *General Electric v Commission* [2005] ECR II-5575, paragraph 555 et seq., 612 et seq.; Case COMP/M.3440 – *EDP/ ENI/GDP* of 9 December 2004, confirmed by judgment of the CFI in Case T-87/05 *EDP v Commission* [2005] ECR II-3745, paragraphs 63 et seq., 75 et seq.; Case IV/M.469 – *MSG Media Service* of 9 November 1994; Case IV/M. 490 – *Nordic Satellite Distribution* of 19 July 1995; Case IV/M.553 – *RTL/Veronica/Endemol* of 20 September 1995; Case IV/M.993 – *Bertelsmann/Kirch/Premiere* of 27 May 1998; Case IV/M.1027 – *Deutsche Telekom BetaResearch* of 27 May 1998; Case IV/M.774 – *St Gobain/Wacker Chemie* of 4 December 1996; Case IV/M.53 – *Aerospatiale/Alenia/De Havilland* of 2 October 1991; Case IV/M.619 – *Gencor/Lonrho* of 24 April 1996, confirmed by judgment of the CFI in Case T-102/96 *Gencor v Commission* [1999] ECR II-753.

Commentary
para 6: B&C: 5.985, 5.999

Part D Mergers and Concentrations

7. The Commission has to assess whether the proposed remedies, once implemented, would eliminate the competition concerns identified. Only the parties have all the relevant information necessary for such an assessment, in particular as to the feasibility of the commitments proposed and the viability and competitiveness of the assets proposed for divestiture. It is therefore the responsibility of the parties to provide all such information available that is necessary for the Commission's assessment of the remedies proposal. To this end, the Implementing Regulation obliges the notifying parties to provide, with the commitments, detailed information on the content of the commitments offered, the conditions for their implementation and showing their suitability to remove any significant impediment of effective competition, as set out in the annex to the Implementing Regulation ('Form RM'). For commitments consisting in the divestiture of a business, parties have to describe in detail in particular how the business to be divested is currently operated. This information will enable the Commission to assess the viability, competitiveness and marketability of the business by comparing its current operation to its proposed scope under the commitments. The Commission can adapt the precise requirements to the information necessary in the individual case at hand and will be available to discuss the scope of the information required with the parties in advance of submission of Form RM.

Commentary
para 7: **B&C**: 8.170 **F&N**: 5.987, 5.1100

8. Whereas the parties have to propose commitments sufficient to remove the competition concerns and submit the necessary information to assess them, it is for the Commission to establish whether or not a concentration, as modified by commitments validly submitted, must be declared incompatible with the common market because it leads, despite the commitments, to a significant impediment of effective competition. The burden of proof for a prohibition or authorisation of a concentration modified by commitments is therefore subject to the same criteria as an unmodified concentration.[1]

Notes
[1] See judgment of the CFI in Case T-87/05, *EDP v Commission*, [2005] ECR II-3745, paragraphs 62 ff.

Basic conditions for acceptable commitments

9. Under the Merger Regulation, the Commission only has power to accept commitments that are deemed capable of rendering the concentration compatible with the common market so that they will prevent a significant impediment of effective competition. The commitments have to eliminate the competition concerns entirely[1] and have to be comprehensive and effective from all points of view.[2] Furthermore, commitments must be capable of being implemented effectively within a short period of time as the conditions of competition on the market will not be maintained until the commitments have been fulfilled.

Notes
[1] See recital 30 of the Merger Regulation and judgment of the CFI in Case T-282/02, *Cementbouw v Commission*, [2006] ECR II-319, paragraph 307.
[2] CFI, Case T-210/01, *General Electrics v Commission*, [2005] ECR II-5575, paragraph 52; Case T-87/05, *EDP v Commission*, [2005] ECR II-3745, paragraph 105.

Commentary
para 9: **B&C**: 8.170, 5.1005, 5.1006

10. Structural commitments, in particular divestitures, proposed by the parties will meet these conditions only in so far as the Commission is able to conclude with the requisite degree of certainty that it will be possible to implement them and that it will be likely that the new commercial structures resulting from them will be sufficiently workable and lasting to ensure that the significant impediment to effective competition will not materialise.[1]

Notes

[1] CFI, Case T-210/01, *General Electric v Commission*, [2005] ECR II-5575, paragraphs 555, 612.

Commentary
para 10: F&N: 5.1010

11. The requisite degree of certainty concerning the implementation of the proposed commitments may in particular be affected by risks in relation to the transfer of a business to be divested, such as conditions attached by the parties to the divestiture, third party rights in relation to the business or the risks of finding a suitable purchaser, as well as risks in relation to the degradation of the assets until the divestiture has taken place. It is incumbent on the parties to remove such uncertainties as to the implementation of the remedy when submitting it to the Commission.[1]

Notes

[1] Depending on the nature of the risks, specific safeguards may aim at compensating for them. For example, the risk arising from third party rights in relation to the assets to be divested may be compensated by the proposal of an alternative divestiture. Such safeguards will be discussed in more detail below.

Commentary
para 11: F&N: 5.1059

12. In assessing the second condition, whether the proposed commitment are sufficiently workable and lasting to ensure that the commitments will likely eliminate the competition concerns identified, the Commission will consider all relevant factors relating to the proposed remedy itself, including, *inter alia,* the type, scale and scope of the remedy proposed, judged by reference to the structure and particular characteristics of the market in which the competition concerns arise, including the position of the parties and other players on the market.

Commentary
para 12: B&C: 8.170 F&N: 5.220, 5.998

13. In order for the commitments to comply with these principles, there has to be an effective implementation and ability to monitor the commitments.[1] Whereas divestitures, once implemented, do not require any further monitoring measures, other types of commitments require effective monitoring mechanisms in order to ensure that their effect is not reduced or even eliminated by the parties. Otherwise, such commitments would have to be considered as mere declarations of intentions by the parties and would not amount to binding obligations, as, due to the lack of effective monitoring mechanisms, any breach of them could not result in the revocation of the decision according to the provisions of the Merger Regulation.[2]

Notes

[1] CFI, Case T-177/04, *easyJet v Commission*, [2006] ECR II-1931, paragraph 188.
[2] CFI, Case T-177/04, *easyJet v Commission*, [2006] ECR II-1931, paragraph 186 et seq.; CFI, judgment in Case T-87/05, *EDP v Commission*, [2005] ECR II-3745, paragraph 72.

Commentary
para 13: B&C: 8.170 F&N: 5.1005, 5.1012, 5.1013

14. Where, however, the parties submit remedies proposals that are so extensive and complex that it is not possible for the Commission to determine, at the time of the Commission decision, with the requisite degree of certainty, at the time of its decision, that they will be fully implemented and that they are likely to maintain effective competition in the market, an authorisation decision cannot be granted.[1] The Commission may reject such remedies in particular on the grounds that the implementation of the remedies cannot be effectively monitored and that the lack of effective monitoring diminishes, or even eliminates, the effect of the commitments proposed.

Part D Mergers and Concentrations

Notes

1 See, as an example for such a complex and inappropriate remedy, Case COMP/M.3440 – *ENI/EDP/GDP* of 9 December 2004; confirmed by CFI, judgment in Case T-87/05 *EDP v Commission* of 21 September 2005, [2005] ECR-II-3745, paragraph 102; Case COMP/M.1672 – *Volvo/Scania* of 15 March 2000.

Commentary
para 14: B&C: 5.1005, 5.1013

Appropriateness of different types of remedies

15. According to the case law of the Court, the basic aim of commitments is to ensure competitive market structures.[1] Accordingly, commitments which are structural in nature, such as the commitment to sell a business unit, are, as a rule, preferable from the point of view of the Merger Regulation's objective, inasmuch as such commitments prevent, durably, the competition concerns which would be raised by the merger as notified, and do not, moreover, require medium or long-term monitoring measures. Nevertheless, the possibility cannot automatically be ruled out that other types of commitments may also be capable of preventing the significant impediment of effective competition.[2]

Notes

1 See recital 8 of the Merger Regulation; judgment of CFI in Case T-102/96, *Gencor v Commission*, [1999] ECR II-753, at paragraph 316; ECJ in Case C-12/03 P, *Commission v Tetra Laval*, [2005] ECR I-987, paragraph 86; judgment of CFI in Case T-158/00, *ARD v Commission*, [2003] ECR II-3825, at paragraphs 192 et seq.

2 ECJ, judgment in Case C-12/03 P, *Commission v Tetra Laval*, [2005] ECR I-987, paragraph 86; CFI, judgment of 25 March 1999 in Case T-102/96, *Gencor v Commission*, [1999] ECR II-753, paragraphs 319 et seq.; CFI; judgment of 30 September 2003 in Case T-158/00, *ARD v Commission*, [2003] ECR II-3825, paragraph 193; CFI in Case T-177/04, *easyJet v Commission*, [2006] ECR II-1931, paragraph 182; CFI, judgment in Case T-87/05, *EDP v Commission*, [2005] ECR II-3745, paragraph 101.

Commentary
para 15: B&C: 5.1010, 5.1050

16. The Commission stresses that the question of whether a remedy and, more specifically, which type of remedy is suitable to eliminate the competition concerns identified, has to be examined on a case-by-case basis.

17. Nevertheless, a general distinction can be made between divestitures, other structural remedies, such as granting access to key infrastructure or inputs on non-discriminatory terms, and commitments relating to the future behaviour of the merged entity. Divestiture commitments are the best way to eliminate competition concerns resulting from horizontal overlaps, and may also be the best means of resolving problems resulting from vertical or conglomerate concerns.[1] Other structural commitments may be suitable to resolve all types of concerns if those remedies are equivalent to divestitures in their effects, as explained in more detail below in paragraphs 61 et seq. Commitments relating to the future behaviour of the merged entity may be acceptable only exceptionally in very specific circumstances.[2] In particular, commitments in the form of undertakings not to raise prices, to reduce product ranges or to remove brands, etc., will generally not eliminate competition concerns resulting from horizontal overlaps. In any case, those types of remedies can only exceptionally be accepted if their workability is fully ensured by effective implementation and monitoring in line with the considerations set out in paragraphs 13–14, 66, 69, and if they do not risk leading to distorting effects on competition.[3]

Notes

1 See divestiture of storage facilities in Case COMP/M.3868 – *DONG/Elsam/Energi* E2 of 14 March 2006, paragraphs 170 et seq.; Case COMP/M.3696 – *E.ON/MOL* of 21 December 2005, paragraphs 735 et seq., for an example of 'ownership unbundling' to eliminate structural links between the parties in the gas storage sector; further Case COMP/M.4314 – *Johnson & Johnson/Pfizer* of 11 December 2006, Case COMP/M.4494 *Evraz/ Highveld* of 20 February 2007.

2 See, in relation to conglomerate effects of a concentration, ECJ, judgment of 15 February 2005 in Case C 12/03 P, *Commission v Tetra Laval*, [2005] ECR I-987, paragraphs 85, 89.

[3] For example, commitments regarding a certain pricing behaviour such as price caps which contain the risk to lead to an anticompetitive alignment of prices among competitors.

Commentary

para 17: F&N: 5.1010, 5.1014, 5.1049, 5.1053, 5.1058, 5.1095

Procedure

18. The Commission may accept commitments in either phase of the procedure.[1] However, given the fact that an in-depth market investigation is only carried out in phase II, commitments submitted to the Commission in phase I must be sufficient to clearly rule out 'serious doubts' within the meaning of Article 6(1)(c) of the Merger Regulation.[2] Pursuant to Article 10(2) of the Merger Regulation, the Commission has to take a clearance decision as soon as the serious doubts referred to in Article 6(1)(c) of the Merger Regulation are removed as a result of commitments submitted by the parties. This rule applies to commitments proposed in phase II-proceedings. After an in-depth investigation and where before the Commission issues a Statement of Objections.[3] If the Commission reaches the preliminary view that the merger leads to a significant impediment to effective competition and issues a Statement of Objections, the commitments must be sufficient to eliminate such a significant impediment to effective competition.

Notes

[1] As foreseen in recital 30 of the Merger Regulation, the Commission will ensure transparency and effective consultation of Member States in both phases of the procedure.

[2] Commitments in phase I can only be accepted in certain types of situations; see below in paragraph 81.

[3] See, *inter alia*, Case COMP/M.2972 – *DSM/Roche Vitamins* of 23 July 2003; Case COMP/M.2861 *Siemens/Drägerwerk/JV* of 30 April 2003; Case IV/JV.15 – *BT/AT & T* of 30 March 1999; Case IV/M.1532 – *BP Amoco/Arco* of 29 September 1999.

Commentary

para 18: B&C: 8.168 F&N: 5.1035, 5.1036

---

19. Whilst commitments have to be offered by the parties, the Commission will ensure the enforceability of commitments by making the authorisation of the merger subject to compliance with the commitments. A distinction must be made between conditions and obligations. The requirement for achievement of the structural change of the market is a condition – for example, that a business is to be divested. The implementing steps which are necessary to achieve this result are generally obligations on the parties, e.g. such as the appointment of a trustee with an irrevocable mandate to sell the business.

20. Where the undertakings concerned commit a breach of an obligation, the Commission may revoke clearance decisions issued either under Article 6(2) or Article 8(2) of the Merger Regulation, acting pursuant to Article 6(3) or Article 8(6), respectively. In case of a breach of an obligation, the parties may also be subject to fines and periodic penalty payments as provided in Article 14(2)(d) and 15(1)(c) respectively of the Merger Regulation. Where, however, a condition is breached, e.g. a business is not divested in the time-frame foreseen in the commitments or afterwards re-acquired, the compatibility decision is no longer applicable. In such circumstances, the Commission may, first, take interim measures appropriate to maintain conditions of effective competition pursuant to Article 8(5)(b) of the Merger Regulation. Second, it may, if the conditions of Article 8(4)(b) are met, order any appropriate measure to ensure that the undertakings concerned dissolve the concentration or take other restorative measures or, according to Article 8(7), take a decision pursuant to Article 8(1)(3). In addition, the parties may also be subject to fines as provided in Article 14(2)(d).

Commentary

para 20: B&C: 8.176 F&N: 5.990

Model Texts for divestiture commitments

21. The Commission services have issued Best Practice Guidelines for divestiture commitments, consisting of a Model Text for Divestiture Commitments and a Model Text for Trustee Mandates.[1]

Part D Mergers and Concentrations

These model texts are neither intended to provide an exhaustive coverage of all issues that may become relevant in all cases, nor are they legally binding upon parties in a merger procedure. They complement the present Notice as they outline the typical arrangements for divestiture commitments in a format which can be used by the parties. At the same time, the model texts leave the flexibility to adapt them to the requirements of the specific case.

Notes

[1] See website of DG COMP, released in May 2003, available at: <http://ec.europa.eu/comm/competition/mergers/legislation/legislation.html>. The model texts may be continuously up-dated and, if there should be a need, further best practice guidelines in the field of remedies may be issued.

III. Different types of remedies

1. Divestiture of a Business to a Suitable Purchaser

22. Where a proposed concentration threatens to significantly impede effective competition the most effective way to maintain effective competition, apart from prohibition, is to create the conditions for the emergence of a new competitive entity or for the strengthening of existing competitors via divestiture by the merging parties.

1.1. Divestiture of a viable and competitive business

23. The divested activities must consist of a viable business that, if operated by a suitable purchaser, can compete effectively with the merged entity on a lasting basis and that is divested as a going concern.[1] For the business to be viable, it may also be necessary to include activities which are related to markets where the Commission did not identify competition concerns if this is required to create an effective competitor in the affected markets.[2]

Notes

[1] This includes, under certain conditions, businesses that have to be carved out from a party's business or individual assets; see below paragraphs 35 ff.

[2] Case IV/M.913 – *Siemens/Elektrowatt* of 18 November 1997; Case IV/M.1578 – *Sanitec/Sphinx* of 1 December 1999, at paragraph 255; Case COMP/M.1802 – *Unilever/Amora-Maille* of 8 March 2000; Case COMP/M.1990 – *Unilever/Bestfoods* of 28 September 2000.

Commentary

para 23: F&N: 5.1059, 5.1060, 5.1062

24. In proposing a viable business for divestiture, it is necessary to take into account the uncertainties and risks related to the transfer of a business to a new owner. These risks may limit the competitive impact of the divested business, and, therefore, may lead to a market situation where the competition concerns at stake will not necessarily be eliminated.

Scope of the business to be divested

25. The business has to include all the assets which contribute to its current operation or which are necessary to ensure its viability and competitiveness and all personnel which is currently employed or which is necessary to ensure the business' viability and competitiveness.[1]

Notes

[1] Notifying parties will have to undertake in the commitments that the business to be divested includes all those assets and personnel. Where the detailed description of the business, to be provided by the parties as set out in paragraph 27, will at a later point in time appear to be incomplete in that respect and the parties do not complement the business with the necessary additional assets or personnel, the Commission may consider revoking the conditional clearance decision.

Commentary

para 25: F&N: 5.1064

26. Personnel and assets which are currently shared between the business to be divested and other businesses of the parties, but which contribute to the operation of the business or which are necessary to ensure its viability and competitiveness, also have to be included. Otherwise, the viability and competitiveness of the business to be divested would be endangered. Therefore, the divested business has to contain the personnel providing essential functions for the business such as, for instance, group R & D and information technology staff even where such personnel is currently employed by another business unit of the parties – at least in a sufficient proportion to meet the on-going needs of the divested business. In the same way shared assets have to be included even if those assets are owned by or allocated to another business unit.

27. In order for the Commission to be able to identify the scope of the business to be divested, the parties have to include a precise definition of the scope of the divested business in the commitments (the 'description of the business'). The description of the business has to be adapted to the individual case at hand and should contain all the elements that are part of the business to be divested: tangible (e.g., R & D, production, distribution, sales and marketing activities) and intangible assets (such as intellectual property rights, know-how and goodwill); licences, permits and authorisations by governmental organisations granted to the business; contracts, leases and commitments (e.g., arrangements with suppliers and customers) for the benefit of the business to be divested; and customer, credit and other records. In the description of the business, the parties have to include the personnel to be transferred in general terms, including staff seconded and temporary employees, and to insert a list of the key personnel, i.e. the personnel essential for the viability and competitiveness of the business. The transfer of those employees is without prejudice to the application of the Council Directives on collective redundancies;[1] on safeguarding employees' rights in the event of transfers of undertakings;[2] and on informing and consulting employees[3] as well as national provisions implementing those Directives and other national laws. The remedy has to include a non-solicitation commitment by the parties with regard to the key personnel.

Notes

[1] Council Directive 98/59/EC of 20 July 1998 on the approximation of the laws of the Member States relating to collective redundancies (OJ L 225, 12.8.1998, p.16).

[2] Council Directive 2001/23/EC of 2 March 2001 on the approximation of the laws of the Member States relating to the safeguarding of employees rights in the event of transfers of undertakings, businesses or parts of undertakings or businesses (OJ L 82, 22.3.2001, p.16).

[3] Council Directive 94/45/EC of 22 September 1994 on the establishment of a European Works Council or a procedure in Community-scale undertakings and Community-scale groups of undertakings for the purposes of informing and consulting employees (OJ L 254, 30.9.1994, p.64); Directive 2002/14/EC of the European Parliament and of the Council of 11 March 2002 establishing a general framework for informing and consulting employees in the European Community (OJ L 80, 23.3.2002, p.29).

Commentary
para 27: B&C: 8.172 **F&N:** 5.1064

28. In the description of the business, the parties also have to set out the arrangements for the supply of products and services by them to the divested business or by the divested business to them. Such on-going relationships of the divested business may be necessary to maintain the full economic viability and competitiveness of the divested business for a transitional basis. The Commission will only accept such arrangements if they do not affect the independence of the divested business from the parties.

29. In order to avoid any misunderstanding about the business to be divested, assets or personnel that are used within or employed by the business but that should not, according to the parties, be transferred with the divestiture, have to be expressly excluded by the parties in the commitments text. The Commission will only be able to accept such exclusion of assets or personnel if the parties can clearly show that this does not affect the viability and competitiveness of the business.

30. The business to be divested has to be viable as such. Therefore, the resources of a possible or even presumed future purchaser are not taken into account by the Commission at the stage of assessing the remedy. The situation is different if already during the procedure a sale and purchase agreement with a specific purchaser is concluded whose resources can be taken into account at the time

Part D Mergers and Concentrations

of the assessment of the commitment. This situation will be dealt with in more detail below in paragraphs 56 ff.

Commentary
para 30: F&N: 5.1063, 5.1081

31. Once a purchaser is identified after adoption of an authorisation decision, some of the assets or personnel included in the divested business may not be needed by the proposed purchaser. In the purchaser approval process, the Commission may, upon request by the parties, approve the divestiture of the business to the proposed purchaser without one or more assets or parts of the personnel if this does not affect the viability and competitiveness of the business to be divested after the sale, taking account of the resources of the proposed purchaser.

1.2. Stand-alone business and conditions for acceptability of alternatives

32. Normally, a viable business is a business that can operate on a stand-alone-basis, which means independently of the merging parties as regards the supply of input materials or other forms of cooperation other than during a transitory period.

33. The Commission has a clear preference for an existing stand-alone business. This may take the form of a pre-existing company or group of companies, or of a business division which was not previously legally incorporated as such.

Commentary
para 33: F&N: 5.1062

34. Where the competition concern results from a horizontal overlap, the parties may be able to choose between two businesses. In cases involving a hostile bid, a commitment to divest activities of the target company may, in such circumstances of limited information available to the notifying parties about the business to be divested, increase the risk that this business might not, after a divestiture, result in a viable competitor which could effectively compete in the market on a lasting basis. It may therefore be more appropriate for the parties to propose to divest activities of the acquiring company in such scenarios.

Carve-outs

35. Even though normally the divestiture of an existing viable stand-alone business is required, the Commission, taking into account the principle of proportionality, may also consider the divestiture of businesses which have existing strong links or are partially integrated with businesses retained by the parties and therefore need to be 'carved out' in those respects. In order to reduce the risks for the viability and competitiveness to a minimum in such circumstances, an option for the parties is to submit commitments proposing to carve out those parts of an existing business which do not necessarily have to be divested. In effect, an existing, stand-alone business is being divested in those circumstances although, by way of a 'reverse carve-out', the parties may carve-out the limited parts which they may keep.

36. In any case, the Commission will only be able to accept commitments which require the carve-out of a business if it can be certain that, at least at the time when the business is transferred to the purchaser, a viable business on a stand-alone basis will be divested and the risks for the viability and competitiveness caused by the carve-out will thereby be reduced to a minimum. The parties therefore have to ensure, as set out in detail below in paragraph 113, that the carve-out is started in the interim period, *i.e.* the period between the adoption of the Commission decision up to the completion of the divestiture (meaning the legal and factual transfer of the business to the purchaser). Consequently, at the end of this period, a viable business on a stand-alone basis will be divested. If this should not be possible or if the carve-out should be particularly difficult, parties may provide the requisite degree of certainty for the Commission by proposing an up-front buyer solution, as further detailed below in paragraph 55.

Commentary
para 36: F&N: 5.1067

Divestiture of assets, in particular of brands and licences

37. A divestiture consisting of a combination of certain assets which did not form a uniform and viable business in the past creates risks as to the viability and competitiveness of the resulting business. This is in particular the case if assets from more than one party are involved. Such an approach may be accepted by the Commission only if the viability of the business is ensured notwithstanding the fact that the assets did not form a uniform business in the past. This may be the case if the individual assets can already be considered a viable and competitive business.[1] Similarly, only in exceptional cases a divestiture package including only brands and supporting production and/or distribution assets may be sufficient to create the conditions for effective com-petition.[2] In such circumstances, the package consisting of brands and assets must be sufficient to allow the Commission to conclude that the resulting business will be immediately viable in the hands of a suitable purchaser.

Notes

[1] Case COMP/M.1806 – *AstraZeneca/Novartis* of 26 July 2000; COMP/M.1628 – *TotalFina/Elf* of 9 February 2000; Case IV/M.603 – *Crown Cork & Seal/ CarnaudMetalbox* of 14 November 1995.

[2] Case COMP/M.2544 – *Masterfoods/Royal Canin* of 15 February 2002; Case COMP/M.2337 – *Nestlé/Ralston Purina* of 27 July 2001; Case IV/M.623 – *Kimberly-Clark/Scott* Paper of 16 January 1996; Case COMP/M.3779 – *Pernod Ricard/Allied Domecq* of 24 June 2005.

Commentary
para 37: **B&C:** 8.171 **F&N:** 5.1066

38. Divestitures of a business generally appear preferable to the granting of licences to IP rights, as the granting of a licence involves more uncertainties, will not enable the licensee to compete immediately in the market, requires an on-going relationship with the parties which may allow the licensor to influence the licensee in its competitive behaviour and may give rise to disputes between the licensor and the licensee over the scope and the terms and conditions of the licence. The granting of a licence will therefore generally not be considered appropriate where a divestiture of a business seems feasible. Where the competition concerns arise from the market position held for such a technology or such IP rights, a divestiture of the technology or the IP rights is the preferable remedy as it eliminates a lasting relationship between the merged entity and its competitors.[1] However, the Commission may accept licensing arrangements as an alternative to divestiture where, for instance, a divestiture would impede efficient, on-going research or where a divestiture would be impossible due to the nature of the business.[2] Such licences will have to enable the licensee to compete effectively with the parties in a similar way as if a divestiture had taken place. They will normally be exclusive licences and have to be without any field-of-use and any geographical restrictions on the licensee. Where there might be any uncertainty as regards the scope of the licence or its terms and conditions, the parties will have to divest the underlying IP right, but may obtain a licence back. If there is uncertainty that the license will actually be granted to a suitable licensee, the parties may consider to propose an up-front licensee or a fix-it-first solution according to the considerations set out below in paragraphs 56, in order to enable the Commission to conclude with the requisite degree of certainty that the remedy will be implemented.[3]

Notes

[1] See Case COMP/M.2972 – *DSM/Roche Vitamins* of 23 July 2003; Case IV/M.1378 – *Hoechst/Rhône-Poulenc* of 9 August 1999; Case COMP/M.1601 – *Allied Signal/ Honeywell* of 1 December 1999; Case COMP/M.1671 – *Dow/ UCC* of 3 May 2000.

[2] Case COMP/M.2949 – *Finmeccanica/Alenia Telespazio* of 30 October 2002; Case COMP/M.3593 – *Apollo/ Bakelite* of 11 April 2005, commitment on carbon bond refractory licence; for cases from the pharmaceutical industry see Case COMP/M.2972 – *DSM/Roche Vitamins* of 23 July 2003; Case IV/M.555 – *Glaxo/Wellcome* of 28 February 1995.

[3] Case COMP/M.2972 – *DSM/Roche Vitamins* of 23 July 2003.

Commentary
para 38: **F&N:** 5.1066

Re-branding

39. In exceptional cases, the Commission has accepted commitments to grant an exclusive, time-limited licence for a brand with the purpose of allowing the licensee to re-brand the product in the period foreseen. After the first licence phase of these so-called re-branding commitments, the parties commit in a second phase to abstain from any use of the brand (blackout phase). The goal of such commitments is to allow the licensee to transfer the customers from the licensed brand to its own brand in order to create a viable competitor, without the licensed brand being permanently divested.

40. A re-branding remedy carries substantially higher risks for restoring effective competition than a divestiture, including the divestiture of a brand as there is considerable uncertainty whether the licensee will succeed in establishing itself as an active competitor in the market on the basis of the re-branded product. A re-branding remedy may be acceptable in circumstances where the brand at stake is widely used and a high proportion of its turnover is generated in markets outside those in which competition concerns have been identified.[1] In those circumstances, a re-branding remedy has to be defined in such a way as to ensure that the granting of the licence will effectively maintain competition in the market on a lasting basis and that the licensee will be an effective competitor after re-branding the products.

Notes

[1] However, even in these conditions a divestiture of the brand may be more appropriate, especially if the resulting split in the ownership of the brand corresponds to common practice in the industry, see for the pharmaceutical industry Case COMP/M.3544 – *Bayer Healthcare/Roche* (OTC) of 19 November 2004, paragraph 59 concerning the divestiture of the Desenex brand.

41. As the success of re-branding commitments is substantially linked to the viability of the licensed brand a number of preconditions have to be met for the design of such commitments. Firstly, the brand to be transferred must be well-known and one of considerable strength to guarantee both immediate viability of the licensed brand and its economic survival in the re-branding period. Secondly, part of the assets related to the production or the distribution of the products marketed under the licensed brand or the transfer of know-how may be necessary to ensure the viability of the remedy.[1] Thirdly, the licence has to be exclusive and normally comprehensive, i.e. not limited to a certain range of products within a specific market, and has to include the intellectual property rights to ensure that customers will acknowledge the familiarity of the re-branded product. The parties will not be allowed to use similar words or signs as this could undermine the effect of the re-branding exercise.[2] Fourthly, both the licence and the black-out period have to be sufficiently long, account being taken of the particularities of the case, so that the re-branding remedy is in its effects similar to a divestiture.[3]

Notes

[1] COMP/M.3149 *Procter&Gamble/Wella* paragraph 60; IV/M.623 – *Kimberly-Clark/Scott Paper* of 16 January 1996, paragraph 236 (i). This is particularly important during the licence phase in which the licensee has to prepare for the launch of a new competitive brand. Such a launch of a new brand appears to not be feasible if the purchaser had to spend considerable resources on the production process, marketing and distribution of the licensed brand; COMP/M.2337 – *Nestlé/Ralston Purina* of 27 July 2001, paragraphs 67 et seq.; COMP/M.2621 – *SEB/Moulinex* of 8 January 2002, paragraph 140.

[2] COMP/M.3149 – *Procter&Gamble/Wella* of 30 July 2003, paragraph 61; COMP/M.2337 – *Nestlé/Ralstone Purina* of 27 July 2001, paragraph 68; COMP/M.2621 – *SEB/Moulinex* of 8 January 2002, paragraph 141; IV/M. 623 – *Kimberly-Clark/Scott Paper* of 16 January 1996, paragraph 236 (ii).

[3] For example taking into account the life cycle of products, c.f. COMP/M.2621 – *SEB/Moulinex* of 8 January 2002, paragraph 141, where effectively the duration of the commitments covered a period equal to about three product life cycles; confirmed by judgment of CFI in Case T-119/02, *Royal Philips Electronics NV v Commission*, [2003] ECR II-1433, paragraphs 112 et seq.

42. The identity of the potential licensee will be a key factor for the success of the commitment. If there is uncertainty that a number of suitable licensees are available, being able and having strong incentives to carry out the re-branding exercise, the parties may consider proposing an up-front or fix-it-first solution, in line with the considerations set out below in paragraph 53 below.

1.3. Non-reacquisition clause

43. In order to maintain the structural effect of a remedy, the commitments have to foresee that the merged entity cannot subsequently acquire influence[1] over the whole or parts of the divested business. The commitments will normally have to foresee that no re-acquisition of material influence is possible for a significant period, generally of 10 years. However, the commitments can also provide for a waiver allowing the Commission to relieve the parties from this obligation if it subsequently finds that the structure of the market has changed to such an extent that the absence of influence over the divested business is no longer necessary to render the concentration compatible with the common market. Even in the absence of an explicit clause, a re-acquisition of the business would violate an implicit obligation on the parties under the commitments as this would affect the effectiveness of the remedies.

Notes

[1] An influence by the previous owner of the business in the competitive behaviour of the divested business risking to frustrate the objective of the remedy.

1.4. Alternative divestiture commitments: Crown Jewels

44. In certain cases, the implementation of the parties' preferred divestiture option (of a viable business solving the competition concerns) might be uncertain in view, for example, of third parties' pre-emption rights or uncertainty as to the transferability of key contracts, intellectual property rights, or the uncertainty of finding a suitable purchaser. Nevertheless, the parties may consider that they would be able to divest this business to a suitable purchaser within a very short time period.

45. In such circumstances, the Commission cannot take the risk that, in the end, effective competition will not be maintained. Accordingly, the Commission will only accept such divestiture commitments under the following conditions: (a) absent the uncertainty, the first divestiture proposed in the commitments would consist of a viable business, and (b) the parties will have to propose a second alternative divestiture which the parties will be obliged to implement if they are not able to implement the first commitment within the given time frame for the first divestiture.[1] Such an alternative commitment normally has to be a 'crown jewel',[2] *i.e.* it should be as least as good as the first proposed divestiture in terms of creating a viable competitor once implemented, it should not involve any uncertainties as to its implementation and it should be capable of being implemented quickly in order to avoid that the overall implementation period exceeds what would normally be regarded as acceptable in the conditions of the market in question. In order to limit the risks in the interim period, it is indispensable that interim preservation and holding separate measures apply to all assets included in both divestiture alternatives. Furthermore, the commitment has to establish clear criteria and a strict timetable as to how and when the alternative divestiture obligation will become effective and the Commission will require shorter periods for its implementation.

Notes

[1] See judgment of the CFI in Case T-210/01, *General Electric v Commission*, [2005] ECR II-5575, paragraph 617; COMP/M.1453 – *AXA/GRE* of 8 April 1999.

[2] The alternative may consist of an entirely different business or, in case of uncertainty as to finding a suitable buyer, of additional businesses and assets that are added to the initial package.

Commentary
para 45: F&N: 5.1072

46. If there is uncertainty as to the implementation of the divestiture due to third party rights or as to finding a suitable purchaser crown jewel commitments and up-front buyers as discussed below in paragraphs 54 address the same concerns, and the parties may therefore choose between both structures.

1.5. Transfer to a suitable purchaser

47. The intended effect of the divestiture will only be achieved if and once the business is transferred to a suitable purchaser in whose hands it will become an active competitive force in the market. The potential of a business to attract a suitable purchaser is an important element already of the Commission's assessment of the appropriateness of the proposed commitment.[1] In order to ensure that the business is divested to a suitable purchaser, the commitments have to include criteria to define its suitability which will allow the Commission to conclude that the divestiture of the business to such a purchaser will likely remove the competition concerns identified.

Notes

[1] Case IV/M.913 – *Siemens/Elektrowatt* of 18 November 1997.

(a) Suitability of a purchaser

48. The standard purchaser requirements are the following:
    — the purchaser is required to be independent of and unconnected to the parties,
    — the purchaser must possess the financial resources, proven relevant expertise and have the incentive and ability to maintain and develop the divested business as a viable and active competitive force in competition with the parties and other competitors, and
    — the acquisition of the business by a proposed purchaser must neither be likely to create new competition problems nor give rise to a risk that the implementation of the commitments will be delayed. Therefore, the proposed purchaser must reasonably be expected to obtain all necessary approvals from the relevant regulatory authorities for the acquisition of the business to be divested.

Commentary
para 48: F&N: 5.1014, 5.1076

49. The standard purchaser requirements may have to be supplemented on a case-by-case basis. An example is the requirement, where appropriate, that the purchaser should be an industrial, rather than a financial purchaser.[1] The commitments will normally contain such a clause where, due to the specific circumstances of the case, a financial buyer might not be able or might not have the incentives to develop the business as a viable and competitive force in the market even considering that it could obtain the necessary management expertise (*e.g.*, by recruiting managers experienced in the sector at stake) and therefore the acquisition by a financial buyer would not remove the competition concerns with sufficient certainty.

Notes

[1] See commitments in Case COMP/M.2621 – *SEB/Moulinex* of 8 January 2002, which foresee that the licensee needs to have its own trademark used in the sector concerned. Certain markets may require a sufficient degree of recognition by customers for a purchaser to be able to translate the business to be divested into a competitive force on the market.

Commentary
para 49: F&N: 5.1077

(b) Identification of a suitable purchaser

50. In general, there are three ways to ensure that the business is transferred to a suitable purchaser. First, the business is transferred within a fixed time-limit after adoption of the decision to a purchaser which is approved by the Commission on the basis of the purchaser requirements. Second, in addition to the conditions set out for the first category, the commitments foresee that the parties may not complete the notified operation before having entered into a binding agreement with a purchaser for the business, approved by the Commission (so-called 'up-front-buyer'). Third, the parties identify a purchaser for the business and enter into a binding agreement already during the Commission's procedure[1] (so-called 'fix-it-first'[2] remedy). The main difference between the two latter options is that in the case of an up-front buyer, the identity of the purchaser is not known to the Commission prior to the authorisation decision.

Notes
1 The transfer of the business may be implemented after the Commission decision.
2 This terminology might be used differently in other jurisdictions.

51. The choice of the category depends on the risks involved in the case and therefore on the measures which enable the Commission to conclude with the requisite degree of certainty that the commitment will be implemented. This will depend on the nature and the scope of the business to be divested, the risks of degradation of the business in the interim period up to divestiture and any uncertainties inherent in the transfer and implementation, in particular the risks of finding a suitable purchaser.

1. Sale of the divested business within a fixed time-limit after the decision

52. In the first category, the parties may proceed with the sale of the divested business on the basis of the purchaser requirements within a fixed time-limit after the adoption of the decision. This procedure is likely to be appropriate in the majority of cases, provided that a number of purchasers can be envisaged for a viable business and that no specific issues complicate or stand in the way of the divestiture. Where the purchaser needs to have special qualifications, this procedure may be appropriate if there are sufficient interested potential purchasers available which fulfil the specific purchaser requirements to be included in the commitments in such cases. In these circumstances the Commission may be able to conclude that the divestiture will be implemented and that there are no reasons for the implementation of the notified concentration to be suspended after the Commission decision.

2. Up-front buyer

53. There are cases where only the proposal of an up-front buyer will allow the Commission to conclude with the requisite degree of certainty that the business will be effectively divested to a suitable purchaser. The parties therefore have to undertake in the commitments that they are not going to complete the notified operation before having entered into a binding agreement with a purchaser for the divested business, approved by the Commission.[1]

54. First, this concerns cases where there are considerable obstacles for a divestiture, such as third party rights, or uncertainties as to finding a suitable purchaser.[1] In such cases, an up-front buyer will allow the Commission to conclude with the requisite degree of certainty that the commitments will be implemented, as such a commitment creates greater incentives for the parties to close the divestiture in order to be able to complete their own concentration. In these circumstances, parties may choose between proposing an up-front buyer and an alternative divestiture commitment, as set out above in paragraph 46.

55. Second, an up-front buyer may be necessary in cases which cause considerable risks of preserving the competitiveness and saleability of the divestment business in the interim period until divestiture. This category comprises cases where the risks of a degradation of the divestment business appear to be high, in particular due to a risk of losing employees being key for the business, or where the interim risks are increased as the parties are not able to undertake the carve-out process in the interim period, but the carve-out process can only take place once a sales and purchase agreement with a purchaser is entered into. The up-front buyer provision may accelerate the transfer of the business to be divested – given the increased incentives for the parties to close the divestiture in order to be able to complete their own concentration – to

such an extent that the commitments may allow the Commission to conclude with the requisite degree of certainty that those risks are limited and the divestiture will be effectively implemented.[1]

Notes

[1] See Case COMP/M.2060 – *Bosch/Rexroth* of 13 December 2000, paragraph 95.

3. Fix-it-first remedies

56. The third category involves cases where the parties identify and enter into a legally binding agreement with a buyer outlining the essentials of the purchase during the Commission procedure.[1] The Commission will be able to decide in the final decision whether the transfer of the divested business to the identified purchaser will remove the competition concerns. If the Commission authorises the notified concentration, no additional Commission decision for the purchaser approval will be needed and the closing of the sale of the divested business may take place shortly afterwards.

Notes

[1] Such agreements are normally conditional to the final Commission decision accepting the remedy in question.

Commentary
para 56: F&N: 5.1081

57. The Commission welcomes fix-it-first remedies in particular in cases where the identity of the purchaser is crucial for the effectiveness of the proposed remedy. This concerns cases where, given the circumstances, only very few potential purchasers can be considered suitable, in particular as the divested business is not a viable business in itself, but its viability will only be ensured by specific assets of the purchaser, or where the purchaser needs to have specific characteristics in order for the remedy to solve the competition concerns.[1] If the parties choose to enter into a binding agreement with a suitable purchaser during the procedure by way of a fix-it-first solution, the Commission can in those circumstances conclude with the requisite degree of certainty that the commitments will be implemented with a sale to a suitable purchaser. In these situations, an 'upfront buyer' solution containing specific requirements as to the suitability of a buyer will generally be considered equivalent and acceptable.

Notes

[1] See Case COMP/M.3916 – *T-Mobile Austria/tele.ring* of April 2006, the divestiture of certain mobile telephony sites and frequencies, not constituting a viable business, could only take place to a competitor which was likely to play a similar role in the market as tele.ring; Case COMP/M.4000 – *Inco/Falconbridge* of 4 July 2006, the divestiture of a nickel processing business could only take place to a competitor vertically integrated into the supply of nickel; Case COMP/M.4187 – *Metso/Aker Kvaerner* of 12 December 2006, only one purchaser was suitable for acquiring the businesses to be divested as it was the only one with the necessary know-how and the necessary presence in neighbouring markets; Case COMP/M. 3436 – *Continental/Phoenix* of 26 October 2004, only the partner in the distribution joint venture was able to render the divested business viable; Case COMP/M.3136 – *GE/Agfa* of 5 December 2003.

Commentary
para 57: F&N: 5.1081

2. Removal of Links with Competitors

58. Divestiture commitments may also be used for removing links between the parties and competitors in cases where these links contribute to the competition concerns raised by the merger. The divestiture of a minority shareholding in a joint venture may be necessary in order to sever a structural link with a major competitor,[1] or, similarly, the divestiture of a minority shareholding in a competitor.[2]

Notes

[1] Case IV/M.942 – VEBA/ Degussa of 3 December 1997.

[2] Case COMP/M. 3653 – Siemens/VA Tech of 13 July 2005, paragraphs 491, 493 ff.

59. Although the divestiture of such stakes is the preferable solution, the Commission may exception-ally accept the waiving of rights linked to minority stakes in a competitor where it can be excluded, given the specific circumstances of the case, that the financial gains derived from a minority shareholding in a competitor would in themselves raise competition concerns.[1] In such circum-stances, the parties have to waive all the rights linked to such a shareholding which were relevant for behaviour in terms of competition, such as representations on the board, veto rights and also information rights.[2] The Commission may only be able to accept such a severing of the link with a competitor if those rights are waived comprehensively and in a permanent way.[3]

Notes

[1] See Case COMP/M. 3653 – *Siemens/VA Tech* of 13 July 2005, paragraphs 327 ff., where effects from the minority stake in financial respect could be excluded as a put option for the sale of this stake had already been exercised.
[2] Case COMP/M.4153 – *Toshiba/Westinghouse* of 19 September 2006.
[3] See Case COMP/M.3440 – *ENI/EDP/GDP* of 9 December 2004, paragraphs 648 f., 672.

Commentary
para 59: **F&N:** 5.1085

60. Where competition concerns result from agreements with companies supplying the same prod-ucts or providing the same services, a suitable remedy may be the termination of the respective agreement, such as distribution agreements with competitors[1] or agreements resulting in the coordination of certain commercial behaviour.[2] However, the termination of a distribution agree-ment alone will only remove the competition concerns if it is ensured that the product of a com-petitor will also be distributed in the future and exercise effective competitive pressure on the parties.

Notes

[1] See for the termination of distribution agreements Case COMP/M.3779 – *Pernod Ricard/Allied Domecq* of 24 June 2005; Case COMP/M. 3658 – *Orkla/Chips* of 3 March 2005.
[2] See particularly the sea transport sector, Case COMP/M. 3829 – *Maersk/PONL* of 29 July 2005 and Case COMP/M.3863 – *TUI/CP* Ships of 12 October 2005. In those cases, the parties committed to withdraw from certain liner conferences and consortia.

Commentary
para 60: **F&N:** 5.1085

3. Other remedies

61. Whilst being the preferred remedy, divestitures or the removal of links with competitors are not the only remedy possible to eliminate certain competition concerns. However, divestitures are the benchmark for other remedies in terms of effectiveness and efficiency. The Commission therefore may accept other types of commitments, but only in circumstances where the other remedy pro-posed is at least equivalent in its effects to a divestiture.[1]

Notes

[1] Case COMP/M.3680 – *Alcatel/Finmeccanica/Alcatel Alenia Space & Telespazio* of 28 April 2005, where a divestiture was impossible.

Commentary
para 61: **F&N:** 5.1050, 5.1055

Access remedies

62. In a number of cases, the Commission has accepted remedies foreseeing the granting of access to key infrastructure, networks, key technology, including patents, know-how or other intellectual property rights, and essential inputs. Normally, the parties grant such access to third parties on a non-discriminatory and transparent basis.
63. Commitments granting access to infrastructure and networks may be submitted in order to facili-tate market entry by competitors. They may be acceptable to the Commission in circumstances where it is sufficiently clear that there will be actual entry of new competitors that would eliminate

any significant impediment to effective competition.[1] Other examples of access commitments are commitments granting access to pay-TV platforms,[2] and to energy via gas release programs.[3] Often, a sufficient reduction of entry barriers is not achieved by individual measures, but by a package comprising a combination of divestiture remedies and access commitments or a commitments package aimed at overall facilitating entry of competitors by a whole range of different measures. If those commitments actually make the entry of sufficient new competitors timely and likely, they can be considered to have a similar effect on competition in the market as a divestiture. If it cannot be concluded that the lowering of the entry barriers by the proposed commitments will likely lead to the entry of new competitors in the market, the Commission will reject such a remedies package.[4]

Notes

[1] See judgment of the CFI in Case T-177/04, *easyJet v Commission*, [2006] ECR II-1931, at paragraphs 197 et seq.

[2] See Case COMP/M.2876 – *Newscorp/Telepiù* of 2 April 2003, paragraphs 225 et seq., where the commitments package included access of competitors to all essential elements of a pay-TV network, such as 1. access to the necessary content, 2. access to the technical platform as well as 3. access to the necessary technical services. Similarly, in Case COMP/JV.37 – *BskyB/Kirch Pay TV* of 21 March 2000, confirmed by judgment of CFI in Case T-158/00, *ARD v Commission*, [2003] ECR II-3825, the Commission accepted a commitments package which allowed other operators comprehensive access to the pay-TV market.

[3] See Case COMP/M.3696 – *E.ON/MOL* of 21 December 2005; Case COMP/M.3868 – *DONG/Elsam/Energi E2* of 14 March 2006.

[4] In air transport mergers, a mere reduction of barriers to entry by a commitment of the parties to offer slots on specific airports may not always be sufficient to ensure the entry of new competitors on those routes where competition problems arise and to render the remedy equivalent in its effects to a divestiture.

Commentary
para 63: **F&N:** 5.1052, 5.1086

---

64. Commitments granting non-discriminatory access to infrastructure or networks of the merging parties may also be submitted in order to ensure that competition is not significantly impeded as a result of foreclosure. In past Commission decisions, commitments have foreseen the granting of access to pipelines[1] and to telecom or similar networks.[2] The Commission will only accept such commitments if it can be concluded that these commitments will be effective and competitors will likely use them so that foreclosure concerns will be eliminated. In specific cases, it may be appropriate to link such a commitment with an up-front or fix-it-first provision in order to allow the Commission to conclude with the requisite degree of certainty that the commitment will be implemented.[3]

Notes

[1] Case COMP/M.2533 – *BP/E.ON* of 20 December 2001, access to pipelines in addition to divestiture of shares in a pipeline company; Case COMP/M.2389 – *Shell/DEA* of 20 December 2001, access to an ethylene import terminal.

[2] For access to telecom networks, see Case COMP/M.2803 – *Telia/Sonera* of 10 July 2002; Case IV/M.1439 – *Telia/Telenor* of 13 October 1999; Case COMP/M.1795 – *Vodafone/ Mannesmann* of 12 April 2000. See also Case COMP/M.2903 – *DaimlerChrysler/Deutsche Telekom/JV* of 30 April 2003, where the Commission accepted a commitments package to grant third parties access to a telematics network and to reduce the entry barriers by allowing them to use parts of a telematics device, designed for toll collection, provided by the parties.

[3] See the 'qualitative moratorium' in Case COMP/M.2903 – *DaimlerChrysler/Deutsche Telekom/JV* of 30 April 2003, paragraph 76.

Commentary
para 64 **F&N:** 5.1086, 5.1088

---

65. Similarly, the control of key technology or IP rights may lead to concerns of foreclosure of competitors which depend on the technology or IP rights as essential input for the activities in a downstream market. This, for example, concerns cases where competition problems arise as the parties may withhold information necessary for the interoperability of different equipment. In such circumstances, commitments to grant competitors access to the necessary information may eliminate the competition concerns.[1] Similarly, in sectors where players commonly have to cooperate by licensing patents to each other, concerns that the merged entity would no longer have the incentive to provide licences to the same extent and under the same conditions as before may be

eliminated by commitments to grant licenses on the same basis also in the future.[2] In those cases, commitments should foresee non-exclusive licences or the disclosure of information on a non-exclusive basis to all third parties which depend on the IP rights or information for their activities. It has to be further ensured that the terms and conditions under which the licenses are granted do not impede the effective implementation of such a license remedy. If no clearly determined terms and conditions for the granting of licenses exist in the market at stake, the terms and conditions, including the pricing, should be clearly apparent from the commitments (e.g. by way of pricing formulas). An alternative solution may be to rely on royalty-free licences. Furthermore, depending on the case, the granting of licenses may also transmit sensitive information to the licensor on the competitive behaviour of the licensees which are active as competitors in the downstream market, e.g. by transmitting the number of licenses used in the downstream market. In such cases, in order for the remedy to be suitable, the commitments will have to exclude such confidentiality problems. Generally, as set out in the preceding paragraph, the Commission will only accept such commitments if it can be concluded that they will be effective and competitors will likely use them.

Notes

[1] Case COMP/M.3083 – *GE/Instrumentarium* of 2 September 2003; Case COMP/M.2861 – *Siemens/Draegerwerk* of 30 April 2003.

[2] See Case COMP/M. 3998 – *Axalto/Gemplus* of 19 May 2006.

Commentary
para 65: **B&C:** 9.050 **F&N:** 5.1052

66. Access commitments are often complex in nature and necessarily include general terms for determining the terms and conditions under which access is granted. In order to render them effective, those commitments have to contain the procedural requirements necessary for monitoring them, such as the requirement of separate accounts for the infrastructure in order to allow a review of the costs involved,[1] and suitable monitoring devices. Normally, such monitoring has to be done by the market participants themselves, e.g. by those undertakings wishing to benefit from the commitments. Measures allowing third parties themselves to enforce the commitments are in particular access to a fast dispute resolution mechanism via arbitration proceedings (together with trustees)[2] or via arbitration proceedings involving national regulatory authorities if existing for the markets concerned.[3] If the Commission can conclude that the mechanisms foreseen in the commitments will allow the market participants themselves to effectively enforce them in a timely manner, no permanent monitoring of the commitments by the Commission is required. In those cases, an intervention by the Commission would only be necessary in cases where the parties do not comply with the solutions found by those dispute resolution mechanisms.[4] However, the Commission will only be able to accept such commitments where the complexity does not lead to a risk of their effectiveness from the outset and where the monitoring devices proposed ensure that those commitments will be effectively implemented and the enforcement mechanism will lead to timely results.[5]

Notes

[1] See, e.g. Case COMP/M.2803 – *Telia/Sonera* of 10 July 2002; Case COMP/M.2903 – *DaimlerChrysler/Deutsche Telekom/JV* of 30 April 2003.

[2] As to the effects of arbitration clauses, see judgment of CFI in Case T-158/00, *ARD v Commission*, [2003] ECR II-3825, paragraphs 212, 295, 352; CFI judgment in Case T-177/04, *easyJet v Commission*, [2006] ECR II-1931, paragraph 186.

[3] See Case COMP/M.2876 – *Newscorp/Telepiù*; Case COMP/M.3916 – *T-Mobile Austria/tele.ring*.

[4] CFI, judgment in Case T-158/00, *ARD v Commission*, [2003] ECR II-3825, paragraphs 212, 295, 352.

[5] See judgments of the CFI in Case T-87/05, *EDP v Commission*, [2005] ECR II-3745, at paragraphs 102 et seq.; and Case T-177/04, *easyJet v Commission* [2006] ECR II-1931, at paragraph 188.

Commentary
para 66: **F&N:** 5.1089

Change of long-term exclusive contracts

67. The change in the market structure resulting from a proposed concentration can cause existing contractual arrangements to be inimical to effective competition. This is in particular true for exclusive long-term supply agreements if such agreements foreclose either, up-stream, the input for competitors or, down-stream, their access to customers. Where the merged entity will have the ability and the incentives to foreclose competitors in this way, the foreclosure effects resulting from existing exclusive agreements may contribute to significantly impeding effective competition.[1]

Notes

[1] See Commission Notice on non-horizontal mergers [...]; Case IV/M. 986 – *AGFA Gevaert/DuPont* of 11 February 1998.

68. In such circumstances, the termination or change of existing exclusive agreements may be considered appropriate to eliminate the competition concerns.[1] However, the available evidence must allow the Commission to clearly determine that no *de facto* exclusivity will be maintained. Furthermore, such change of long-term agreements will normally only be sufficient as part of a remedies package to remove the competition concerns identified.

Notes

[1] Case COMP/M.2876 – *Newscorp/Telepiù* of 2 April 2003, paragraphs 225 et seq., granting unilateral termination rights to suppliers of TV content, limiting the scope of the exclusivity clauses and limiting the duration of future exclusive agreements relating to supply of content; Case COMP/M. 2822 – *ENI/EnBW/GVS* of 17 December 2002, granting of early termination rights to all local gas distributors concerning long-term gas supply agreements; Case IV/M.1571 – *New Holland* of 28 October 1999; Case IV/M.1467 – *Rohm and Haas/Morton* of 19 April 1999.

Other non-divestiture remedies

69. As indicated above in paragraph 17, non-structural types of remedies, such as promises by the parties to abstain from certain commercial behaviour (e.g. bundling products), will generally not eliminate the competition concerns resulting from horizontal overlaps. In any case, it may be difficult to achieve the required degree of effectiveness of such a remedy due to the absence of effective monitoring of its implementation, as already set out above in paragraph 13(f).[1] Indeed, it may be impossible for the Commission to verify whether or not the commitment is complied with and even other market participants, such as competitors, may not be able to establish at all or with the requisite degree of certainty whether the parties meet the conditions of the commitment in practice. In addition, competitors may also not have an incentive to alert the Commission as they do not directly benefit from the commitments. Therefore, the Commission may examine other types of non-divestiture remedies, such as behavioural promises, only exceptionally in specific circumstances, such as in respect of competition concerns arising in conglomerate structures.[2]

Notes

[1] See, as an example for such remedies, Case COMP/M.3440 – *ENI/EDP/GDP* of 9 December 2004, paragraphs 663, 719.
[2] See, in relation to conglomerate effects of a concentration, ECJ, judgment of 15 February 2005 in Case C 12/03 P *Commission v Tetra Laval* [2005] ECR I-987, paragraphs 85, 89.

Commentary
para 69: F&N: 5.1010, 5.1095

Time limit for non-divestiture remedies

70. The Commission may accept that non-divestiture remedies are limited in their duration. The acceptability of a time limit and the duration will depend on the individual circumstances of the case and cannot be pre-defined in a general manner in the present Notice.

4. Review clause

71. Irrespective of the type of remedy, commitments will usually include a review clause.[1] This may allow the Commission, upon request by the parties showing good cause, to grant an extension of deadlines, in exceptional circumstances, to waive, modify or substitute the commitments.

Notes

[1] However, the review clause is of particular relevance for access remedies, which systematically should include such a clause; see below paragraph 74.

72. Modifying commitments by extending the deadlines is in particular relevant for divestiture commitments. Parties have to submit a request for an extension within the deadline. Where parties apply for an extension for the first divestiture period, the Commission will only accept that they have shown good cause if the parties were not able to meet the deadline for reasons outside their responsibility and if it can be expected that the parties subsequently will succeed in divesting the business within a short timeframe. Otherwise, the divestiture trustee may be better placed to undertake the divestiture and to fulfil the commitments for the parties.

Commentary
para 72: F&N: 5.1112

73. The Commission may grant waivers or accept modifications or substitutions of the commitments only in exceptional circumstances. This will very rarely be relevant for divestiture commitments. As divestiture commitments have to be implemented within a short time-frame after the decision, it is very unlikely that changes of market circumstances will have occurred in such a short time-frame and the Commission will normally not accept any modifications under the general review clause. For specific situations the commitments normally foresee more targeted review clauses.[1]

Notes

[1] As mentioned in paragraph 30, the Commission may approve a purchaser without some of the assets or personnel foreseen if this does not affect the competitiveness and viability of the divested business. Similarly, the non-requisition clause, as explained in paragraph 43, prohibits the re-acquisition of control over the assets divested only if the Commission has not previously found that that the market structure has changed to such an extent that the divestiture is no longer necessary.

Commentary
para 73: F&N: 5.1115

74. A waiver, modification or substitution of commitments may be more relevant for non-divestiture commitments, such as access commitments, which may be on-going for a number of years and for which not all contingencies can be predicted at the time of the adoption of the Commission decision. Exceptional circumstances justifying a waiver, modification or substitution may, first, be accepted for such commitments if parties show that market circumstances have changed significantly and on a permanent basis. For showing this, a sufficient long time-span, normally at least several years, between the Commission decision and a request by the parties is required. Second, exceptional circumstances may also be present if the parties can show that the experience gained in the application of the remedy demonstrates that the objective pursued with the remedy will be better achieved if modalities of the commitment are changed. For any waiver, modification or substitution of commitments, the Commission will also take into account the view of third parties and the impact a modification may have on the position of third parties and thereby on the overall effectiveness of the remedy. In this regard, the Commission will also consider whether modifications affect the right already acquired by third parties after implementation of the remedy.[1]

Notes

[1] See examples in judgment of CFI in Case T-119/02, *Royal Philips Electronics NV v Commission*, [2003] ECR II-1433, paragraph 184.

Commentary
para 74: F&N: 5.1115

75. If at the time of the adoption of the decision the Commission for particular reasons cannot anticipate all contingencies in relation to the implementation of such commitments, it may also be
appropriate for the parties to include a clause in the commitments allowing the Commission to
trigger a limited modification to the commitments. Such modifications may be necessary if the
original commitments do not achieve the envisaged results set out in those commitments, and
therefore do not effectively remove the competition concerns. Procedurally, the parties may be
obliged in such cases to propose a change to the commitments in order to achieve the result
defined in the commitments, or the Commission may itself, after hearing the parties, modify the
conditions and obligations to this end. This type of clause will typically be limited to cases where
specific modalities risk to jeopardise effective implementation of the commitments. Such clauses
have been used, for example, in relation to the modalities of gas release programs.[1]

Notes

[1] See Case COMP/M.3868 – *DONG/Elsam/Energi E2* of 14 March 2006, paragraph 24 of the Annex.

76. The Commission may, upon request, adopt a formal decision for any waiver, modification or
substitution of commitments or simply take note of satisfactory amendments of the remedy by
the parties, where such amendments improve the effectiveness of the remedy and result in legally
binding obligations of the parties, *e.g.* by contractual arrangements. A change of the commitments will normally only be effective *ex nunc*. Consequently, a modification of the commitments
will not heal retro actively any breach of the commitments which has been committed before the
time of the modification. The Commission may therefore, where appropriate, further pursue a
breach under Articles 14, 15 of the Merger Regulation.

IV. Aspects of Procedure for Submission of Commitments

1. Phase I

77. Pursuant to Article 6(2) of the Merger Regulation the Commission may declare a concentration
compatible with the common market also before the initiation of proceedings, where it is confi-
dent that following modification a notified concentration no longer raises serious doubts within
the meaning of paragraph 1(c).

78. Parties can submit proposals for commitments to the Commission on an informal basis, even
before notification. Parties have to submit commitments within not more than 20 working days
from the date of the receipt of the notification.[1] The Commission informs the parties about its
serious doubts in due time before that deadline.[2] Where the parties submit commitments, the
deadline for the Commission's decision pursuant to Article 6(1) of the Merger Regulation is
extended from 25 to 35 working days.[3]

Notes

[1] Article 19(1) of the Implementing Regulation.
[2] The notifying parties will normally be offered the opportunity of attending a state of play meeting in such circumstances, see point 33 of the DG COMPETITION Best Practices on the conduct of EC merger control proceedings.
[3] Article 10(1), subparagraph 2 of the Merger Regulation.

Commentary
para 78: B&C: 8.134, 8.168 F&N: 5.1022

79. In order to form the basis of a decision pursuant to Article 6(2), proposals for commitments must
meet the following requirements:
    (a) they shall fully specify the substantive and implementing commitments entered into by the
    parties;
    (b) they shall be signed by a person duly authorised to do so;
    (c) they shall be accompanied by the information on the commitments offered as provided for in
    the Implementing Regulation (as explained above in paragraph 7); and

(d) they shall be accompanied by a non-confidential version of the commitments[1] for the purposes of market testing them with third parties. The non-confidential version of the commitments must allow third parties to fully assess the workability and the effectiveness of the proposed remedies to remove the competition concerns.

Notes

[1] Article 20(2) of the Implementing Regulation.

Commentary

para 79: **B&C:** 8.166 **F&N:** 5.1018

80. Proposals submitted by the parties in accordance with these requirements will be assessed by the Commission. The Commission will consult the authorities of the Member States on the proposed commitments and, when considered appropriate, also third parties in the form of a market test, including in particular those third parties and the recognised representatives[1] of those employees whose positions are directly affected by the proposed remedies. In markets with national regulatory authorities the Commission may also, if appropriate, consult the competent national regulatory authorities.[2] In addition, in cases involving a geographic market that is wider than the European Economic Area ('EEA') or where, for reasons related to the viability of the business, the scope of the business to be divested is wider than the EEA territory, the non-confidential version of the proposed remedies may also be discussed with non-EEA competition authorities in the framework of the Community's bilateral cooperation agreements with these countries.

Notes

[1] Cf. Article 2(1)(c) of Council Directive 2001/23/EC of 12 March 2001 on the approximation of the laws of the Member States relating to the safeguarding of employees' rights in the event of transfers of undertakings, businesses or parts of undertakings or businesses (OJ L 82, 22.3.2001, p.16). See also Article 2(1)(g) of Council Directive 94/45/EC of 22 September 1994 on the establishment of a European Works Council or a procedure in Community-scale undertakings and Community-scale groups of undertakings for the purposes of informing and consulting employees (OJ L 254, 30.9.1994, p.64).

[2] For the role of national regulatory authorities in a dispute resolution mechanism, see paragraph 66.

Commentary

para 80: **B&C:** 8.166, 8.168

81. Commitments in phase I can only be accepted where the competition problem is readily identifiable and can easily be remedied.[1] The competition problem therefore needs to be so straightforward and the remedies so clear-cut that it is not necessary to enter into an in-depth investigation and that the commitments are sufficient to clearly rule out 'serious doubts' within the meaning of Article 6(1)(c) of the Merger Regulation.[2] Where the assessment confirms that the proposed commitments remove the grounds for serious doubts on this basis, the Commission clears the merger in phase I.

Notes

[1] See recital 30 of the Merger Regulation.

[2] See judgment of CFI in Case T-119/02, *Royal Philips Electronics NV v Commission*, [2003] ECR II-1433, paragraphs 79 et seq.

Commentary

para 81: **B&C:** 8.168 **F&N:** 5.1016

82. Due to the time-constraints in phase I, it is particularly important for the parties to submit in a timely manner to the Commission the information required in the Implementing Regulation to properly assess the content and workability of the commitments and their suitability to maintain conditions of effective competition in the common market on a permanent basis. If the parties do not comply with the obligation in the Implementing Regulation, the Commission may not be able to conclude that the proposed commitments will remove the grounds for serious doubts.

Part D Mergers and Concentrations

Commentary
para 82: F&N: 5.1023

83. Where the assessment shows that the commitments offered are not sufficient to remove the competition concerns raised by the concentration, the parties will be informed accordingly. Given that phase I remedies are designed to provide a clear-cut answer to a readily identifiable competition concern, only limited modifications can be accepted to the proposed commitments. Such modifications, presented as an immediate response to the result of the consultations, may include clarifications, refinements and/or other improvements designed to ensure that the commitments are workable and effective. However, such modifications may only be accepted in circumstances where it is ensured that the Commission can carry out a proper assessment of those commitments.[1]

Notes

[1] See recital 17 of the Implementing Regulation and judgment of the CFI, Case T-119/02, *Royal Philips Electronics NV v Commission*, [2003] ECR II-1433, paragraphs 237 et seq.

Commentary
para 83: B&C: 8.168 F&N: 5.1029, 5.1030

84. If the Commission's final assessment of a case shows that there are no competition concerns in one or more markets, the parties will be informed accordingly and may withdraw the unnecessary commitments for such markets. If the parties do not withdraw them, the Commission will normally ignore them in the decision. In any event, such commitment proposals do not constitute a condition for clearance.

Commentary
para 84: F&N: 5.992

85. Where the parties are informed that the Commission intends to maintain in its final decision that the transaction raises competition concerns for a specific market, it is for the parties to propose commitments. The Commission is not in a position to impose unilaterally any conditions to an authorisation decision, but only on the basis of the parties' commitments.[1] However, the Commission will review whether the commitments submitted by the parties are proportionate to the competition problem when assessing whether to attach them as conditions or obligations to its final decision.[2] Nevertheless, it has to be stressed that, in a commitments proposal, all those elements which are required to fulfil the basic conditions for acceptable commitments as set out above in paragraphs 9 et seq. will be considered necessary. This paragraph as well as the previous one also applies to commitments in phase II.

Notes

[1] See above paragraph 6.
[2] See judgment of ECJ of 18 December 2007 in Case C-202/06 P, *Cementbouw v Commission* [2007], paragraph 54.

86. If the Commission concludes that the commitments offered by the parties do not remove the serious doubts, it will issue an Article 6(1)(c) decision and open proceedings.

2. Phase II

87. Pursuant to Article 8(2) of the Merger Regulation, the Commission must declare a concentration compatible with the common market, where following modification a notified concentration does no longer significantly impede effective competition within the meaning of Article 2(3) of the Merger Regulation.

88. Commitments proposed to the Commission pursuant to Article 8(2) must be submitted to the Commission within not more than 65 working days from the day on which proceedings were initiated. Where the deadlines for the final decision have been extended according to Article 10(3) of the Merger Regulation, also the deadline for remedies is automatically extended by the same number of days.[1] Only in exceptional circumstances, the Commission may accept that commitments are submitted for the first time after the expiry of this period. The request by the parties for

an extension of the deadline must be received within the period and has to set forth the exceptional circumstances which, according to the parties, justify it. In addition to the existence of exceptional circumstances, an extension is only possible where there is sufficient time to make a proper assessment of the proposal by the Commission and to allow adequate consultation with Member States and third parties.[2]

Notes

[1] Article 19 (2) subparagraph 2 of the Implementing Regulation.

[2] Article 19 (2) subparagraph 3 of the Implementing Regulation. See Case COMP/M.1439 – *Telia/Telenor* of 13 October 1999; Case IV/M.754 – *Anglo American Corporation/Lonrho* of 23 April 1997.

Commentary
para 88: B&C: 8.169 **F&N:** 5.498

89. The question whether or not submitting remedies will extend the deadline for the Commission to take a final decision depends on the time in the procedure when the commitments are submitted. Where the parties submit commitments within less than 55 working days after the initiation of proceedings, the Commission has to take a final decision within not more than 90 working days of the date of initiation of proceedings.[1] Where the parties submit commitments on working day 55 or afterwards (even after working day 65, if those commitments should be acceptable due to exceptional circumstances as described above in paragraph 88), the period for the Commission to take a final decision is increased to 105 working days according to Article 10(3), subparagraph 2. Where the parties submit commitments within less than 55 working days, but submit a modified version on day 55 or thereafter, the period to take a final decision will also be extended to 105 working days.

Notes

[1] Where the deadlines for the final decision have been extended according to Article 10(3) subparagraph 2 of the Merger Regulation before working day 55, this period is also extended.

Commentary
para 89: B&C: 8.169 **F&N:** 5.1040

90. The Commission is available to discuss suitable commitments well in advance of the end of the 65 working day period. The parties are encouraged to submit draft proposals dealing with both substantive and implementation aspects which are necessary to ensure that the commitments are fully workable. If the parties are of the opinion that more time is needed for the investigation of the competition concerns and for the corresponding design of appropriate commitments, they may also suggest to the Commission to extend the final deadline under Article 10(3) subparagraph 1. Such a request will have to be made before the end of the 65 working day period. Indeed, the Commission will normally not extend the period for adopting a final decision according to Article 10(3), subparagraph 1 where the request for extension is presented after the deadline for submitting remedies foreseen in the Implementing Regulation, *i.e.* after working day 65.[1]

Notes

[1] The Court of First Instance confirmed that the Merger Regulation and the Implementing Regulation do not impose any obligations on the Commission to accept commitments which are submitted after the legal deadline, as set out below in paragraph 94, see Case T-87/05, *EDP v Commission*, [2005] ECR II-3745, at paragraph 161. Therefore, the Commission is not bound to consider any remedies which are submitted by the parties after the deadline for remedies, even if the parties were to agree to extend the final deadline. Moreover, this would not correspond to the purpose, as explained in recital 35 of the Merger Regulation, of the extensions foreseen in Article 10(3). The extension foreseen in Article 10(3), subparagraph 1 is to allow for sufficient time for the investigation of the competitive concerns, whereas it is the purpose of the extension laid down in Article 10(3), subparagraph 2 to allow for sufficient time for the analysis and market testing of commitments.

Commentary
para 90: B&C: 8.169

Part D Mergers and Concentrations

91. In order to meet the requirements for a decision pursuant to Article 8 (2), commitments must meet the following requirements:
    (a) they shall address all competition concerns raised by the concentration and shall fully specify the substantive and implementing commitments entered into by the parties;
    (b) they shall be signed by a person duly authorised to do so;
    (c) they shall by accompanied by the information on the commitments offered as provided for in the Implementing Regulation (as explained above in paragraph 7); and (d) they shall be accompanied by a non-confidential version of the commitments[1] for the purposes of market testing them with third parties, fulfilling the requirements set out above in paragraph 79.

Notes

[1] Article 20 (2) of the Implementing Regulation.

Commentary
para 91: **B&C:** 8.166 **F&N:** 5.1036, 5.1037

92. Proposals submitted by the parties in accordance with these requirements will be assessed by the Commission. If the assessment confirms that the proposed commitments remove the serious doubts (if no Statement of Objection has been issued yet by the Commission) or the competition concerns raised in the Statement of Objections, following the consultations as set out in paragraph 80 above, the Commission will adopt a conditional clearance decision.
93. Conversely, where the assessment leads to the conclusion that the proposed commitments appear not to be sufficient to resolve the competition concerns raised by the concentration, the parties will be informed accordingly.[1]

Notes

[1] See paragraphs 30ff of the DG Competition Best Practices on the conduct of EC merger proceedings which provide for several state of play meetings between the Commission and the parties throughout the procedure.

94. The Merger Regulation does not impose any obligation on the Commission to accept commitments after the legal deadline for remedies, unless the Commission voluntarily undertakes to assess commitments in specific circumstances.[1] In view of this, where parties subsequently modify the proposed commitments after the deadline of 65 working days, the Commission will only accept these modified commitments where it can clearly determine – on the basis of its assessment of information already received in the course of the investigation, including the results of prior market testing, and without the need for any other market test – that such commitments, once implemented, fully and unambiguously resolve the competition concerns identified and where there is sufficient time to allow for an adequate assessment by the Commission and for proper consultation with Member States.[2],[3] The Commission will normally reject modified commitments which do not fulfil those conditions.[4]

Notes

[1] See judgment of CFI in Case T-87/05, *EDP v Commission*, [2005] ECR II-3745, at paragraphs 161 et seq. See also judgement of CFI in case T-290/94 *Kaysersberg SA v Commission* [1997] ECR II-2137.

[2] Case COMP/M.3440 – *ENI/EDP/GDP* of 9 December 2004, paragraphs 855 et seq.; confirmed by Judgment of CFI in Case T-87/05, *EDP v Commission*, [2005] ECR II-3745, at paragraphs 162 et seq.; Case COMP/M.1628 – *TotalFina/Elf* of 9 March 2000, at paragraph 345.

[3] This consultation normally requires that the Commission has to be able to send a draft of the final decision, including an assessment of the modified commitments, to the Member States not less than 10 working days before the Advisory Committee with Member States. This period may only be shortened in exceptional circumstances (Article 19(5) of the Merger Regulation).

[4] See Case COMP/M.3440 – *ENI/EDP/GDP* of 9 December 2004, paragraph 913.

Commentary
para 94: **F&N:** 5.498, 5.1044

V. Requirements for Implementation of Commitments

95. Commitments are offered as a means of securing a clearance, with the implementation normally taking place after the decision. Commitments therefore require safeguards to ensure their effective and timely implementation. These implementing provisions will normally form part of the commitments entered into by the parties vis-à-vis the Commission.

96. In the following, detailed guidance is given on the implementation of divestiture commitments, as the most typical commitment. Afterwards, some aspects of the implementation of other types of commitments are discussed.

1. Divestiture process

97. The divestiture has to be completed within a fixed time period agreed between the parties and the Commission. In the Commission's practice, the total time period is divided into a period for entering into a final agreement and a further period for the closing, the transfer of legal title, of the transaction. The period for entering into a binding agreement is further normally divided into a first period in which the parties can look for a suitable purchaser (the 'first divestiture period') and, if the parties do not succeed to divest the business, a second period in which a divestiture trustee obtains the mandate to divest the business at no minimum price (the 'trustee divestiture period').

98. The Commission's experience has shown that short divestiture periods contribute largely to the success of the divestiture as, otherwise, the business to be divested will be exposed to an extended period of uncertainty. The time periods should therefore be as short as feasible. The Commission will normally consider a period of around six months for the first divestiture period and an additional period of three months for the trustee divestiture period as appropriate. A period of further three months is normally foreseen for closing the transaction. These periods may be modified on a case-by-case basis. In particular, they may have to be shortened if there is a high risk of degradation of the business' viability in the interim period.

Commentary
para 98: B&C: 8.174 F&N: 5.1008

99. The deadline for the divestiture shall normally start on the day of the adoption of the Commission decision. An exception might be justified for a transaction via public bid where the parties commit to divest a business belonging to the target. Where in such circumstances the parties cannot prepare for the divestiture of the target's business before closing of the notified concentration, the Commission might accept that the periods for such a divestiture only start with that date. Similarly, such a solution may be considered if the date of closing of the concentration is not under the control of the parties as it, *e.g.*, requires state approval.[1] In return, it may be appropriate to shorten the deadlines in order to reduce the time of uncertainty for the business to be divested.

Notes

[1] However, also in those circumstances, other provisions in the commitments, in particular the provisions establishing the safeguards in the interim period, should start running on the date of the adoption of the decision.

100. Whereas for up-front buyer solutions the above-described procedure applies, the procedure will be different for fix-it-first solutions. In general, a binding agreement with a purchaser will already be entered into during the procedure so that after the decision only a further period for the closing of the transaction has to be foreseen. If before the decision only a framework agreement has been concluded with the purchaser, the periods to be foreseen for entering into a full agreement and the closing afterwards will have to be decided on a case-by-case basis.[1]

Notes

[1] See Case COMP/M.3916 – *T-Mobile Austria/tele.ring* of 20 April 2006.

2. Approval of the Purchaser and of the Sale and Purchase Agreement

101. In order to ensure the effectiveness of the commitment, the sale to a proposed purchaser is subject to prior approval by the Commission. When the parties (or the divestiture trustee) have reached a final agreement with a purchaser, they have to submit a reasoned and documented proposal to

the Commission. The parties or the divestiture trustee, as the case may be, will be required to demonstrate to the satisfaction of the Commission that the proposed purchaser meets the purchaser requirements, and that the business is divested in a manner consistent with the Commission's decision and the commitments. Where the commitments allow that different purchasers are being proposed for different parts of the package, the Commission will assess whether each individual proposed purchaser is acceptable and that the total package solves the competition concern.

Commentary
para 101: B&C: 8.172

102. In assessing any proposed purchaser, the Commission will interpret the purchaser requirements in the light of the purpose of the commitments, to immediately maintain effective competition in the market where competition concerns had been found, and of the market circumstances as set out in the decision.[1] Generally, the basis for the Commission's assessment of the purchaser requirements will be the submission of the parties, the assessment of the monitoring trustee and, in particular, discussions with the proposed purchaser and its business plan. The Commission will further analyse whether the underlying assumptions of the purchaser appear plausible according to the market circumstances.

Notes
[1] See judgment of the CFI in Case T-342/00, *Petrolessence v Commission*, [2003] ECR II-1161.

103. The requirement that the purchaser has to have the necessary financial resources extends in particular to the way the acquisition is financed by the proposed purchaser. The Commission will normally not accept any financing of the divestiture by the seller, and, in particular, any seller financing if this were to give the seller a share in the profits of the divested business in the future.

104. In assessing whether the proposed purchaser threatens to create competition problems, the Commission will undertake a prima facie assessment in the light of the information available to the Commission in the purchaser approval process. Where the purchase results in a concentration that has a Community dimension, this new operation will have to be notified under the Merger Regulation and cleared under normal procedures.[1] Where this is not the case, the Commission's approval of a proposed purchaser is without prejudice to the merger control jurisdiction of national authorities. In addition, the proposed purchaser must be expected to obtain all other necessary approvals from the relevant regulatory authorities. Where it can be foreseen, in the light of the information available to the Commission, that difficulties in obtaining merger control clearance or other approvals may unduly delay the timely implementation of the commitment, it will be considered that the proposed purchaser does not meet the purchaser requirements. Otherwise, the competition concerns identified by the Commission would not be removed in the appropriate time-frame.

Notes
[1] Case IV/M.1383 – *Exxon/Mobil* of 29 September 1999 and the follow-up Cases COMP/M.1820 – *BP/JV Dissolution* of 2 February 2000 and COMP/M.1822 – *Mobil/JV Dissolution* of 2 February 2000.

Commentary
para 104: F&N: 5.1076

105. The requirement for an approval by the Commission does usually not only extend to the identity of the purchaser, but also to the sale and purchase agreement and any other agreement entered into between the parties and the proposed purchaser, including transitory agreements. The Commission will verify whether the divestiture according to the agreements is in line with the commitments.[1]

Notes
[1] As discussed above, the parties may apply to the Commission to approve the divestiture of the business to the proposed purchaser without one or more assets or parts of the personnel if this does not affect the viability and competitiveness of the Divestment Business after the sale, taking account of the resources of the proposed purchaser.

106. The Commission will communicate its view as to the suitability of the proposed purchaser to the parties. If the Commission concludes that the proposed purchaser does not meet the purchaser requirements, it will adopt a decision that the proposed purchaser is not a purchaser under the commitments.[1] If the Commission concludes that the sale and purchase agreement (or any ancillary agreements) does not foresee a divestiture in line with the commitments, the Commission will communicate this to the parties without necessarily rejecting the purchaser as such. If the Commission concludes that the purchaser is suitable under the commitments and that the contracts agree a divestiture in line with the commitments, the Commission will approve the divestiture to the proposed purchaser.[2] The Commission will issue the necessary approvals as expeditiously as possible.

Notes

[1] COMP/M.1628 – *TotalFina/Elf* of 9 February 2000, motorway service stations; confirmed by judgment of the CFI in Case T-342/00 *Petrolessence v Commission* [2003] ECR II-1161.

[2] The parties have to ensure, for example through appropriate provisions in the purchase agreement, that the purchaser will maintain the divested business as a competitive force in the market and will not sell on the business within a short time-span.

3. Obligations of the Parties in the Interim Period

107. Parties have to fulfil certain obligations in the interim period (as defined above in paragraph 36). The following should normally be included in the commitments in this respect: (i) safeguards for the interim preservation of the viability to the business; (ii) the necessary steps for a carve-out process, if relevant; and (iii) the necessary steps to prepare the divestiture of the business.

Interim preservation of the divested business

108. It is the parties' responsibility to reduce to the minimum any possible risk of loss of competitive potential of the business to be divested resulting from the uncertainties inherent in the transfer of a business. Up to the transfer of the business to the purchaser, the Commission will require the parties to offer commitments to maintain the independence, economic viability, marketability and competitiveness of the business. Only such commitments will allow the Commission to conclude with the requisite degree of certainty that the divestiture of the business will be implemented in the way as proposed by the parties in the commitments.

Commentary
para 108: F&N: 5.1100

109. Generally, these commitments should be designed to keep the business separate from the business retained by the parties, and to ensure that it is managed as a distinct and saleable business in its best interest, with a view to ensuring its continued economic viability, marketability and competitiveness and its independence from the businesses retained by the parties.

110. The parties will be required to ensure that all assets of the business are maintained, pursuant to good business practice and in the ordinary course of business, and that no acts which might have a significant adverse impact on the business are carried out. This relates in particular to the maintenance of fixed assets, know-how or commercial information of a confidential or proprietary nature, the customer base and the technical and commercial competence of the employees. Furthermore, the parties must maintain the business in the same conditions as before the concentration, in particular provide sufficient resources, such as capital or a line of credit, on the basis and continuation of existing business plans, the same administrative and management functions, or other factors relevant for maintaining competition in the specific sector. The commitments also have to foresee that the parties should take all reasonable steps, including appropriate incentive schemes, to encourage all key personnel to remain with the business, and that the parties may not solicit or move any personnel to their remaining businesses.

111. The parties should further hold the business separate from its retained business and ensure that the key personnel of the business to be divested do not have any involvement into the retained businesses and *vice versa*. If the business to be divested is in corporate form and a strict separation

of the corporate structure appears necessary, the parties' rights as shareholders, in particular the voting rights, should be exercised by the monitoring trustee which should also have the power to replace the board members appointed on behalf of the parties. In relation to information, the parties must ring-fence the business to be divested and take all necessary measures to ensure that the parties do not obtain any business secrets or other confidential information. Any documents or information confidential to the business obtained by the parties before adoption of the decision have to be returned to the business or destroyed.

112. The parties are further generally required to appoint a hold-separate manager with the necessary expertise, who will be responsible for the management of the business and the implementation of the hold-separate and ring-fencing obligations. The hold-separate manager should act under the supervision of the monitoring trustee who may issue instructions to the hold-separate manager. The commitments have to provide that the appointment should take place immediately after the adoption of the decision and even before the parties may close the notified concentration. Whereas the parties can appoint the hold-separate manager on their own, the commitments have to foresee that the monitoring trustee is able to remove the hold-separate manager if s/he does not act in line with the commitments or endangers their timely and proper implementation. A new appointment of a hold-separate manager afterwards will be subject to the approval of the monitoring trustee.

Commentary
para 112: B&C: F&N: 5.1102

Steps for a carve-out

113. As outlined above in paragraph 35, the Commission may accept in appropriate circumstances that the divestiture of a business which needs to be carved out from the remaining businesses of the parties can be considered a suitable remedy. Nevertheless, also in such circumstances only the transfer of a viable business to a purchaser which can maintain and develop this business as an active competitive force in the market will remove the Commission's competition concerns. Therefore, the parties have to commit to a result-oriented obligation to carry out, in the interim period, a carve-out of the assets that contribute to the divested business. The result has to be that a viable and competitive business, which is stand-alone and separate from the other businesses of the parties, can be transferred to a suitable purchaser at the end of the interim period. The parties will have to bear the costs and risks of such a carve-out in the interim period.

114. The carve-out will need to be carried out by the parties under the supervision of the trustee and in cooperation with the hold-separate manager. First, those assets and parts of the personnel which are shared between the business to be divested and remaining businesses of the parties have to be allocated to the business to the extent that this is not excluded in the commitments.[1] The allocation of the assets and the personnel will be monitored and has to be approved by the monitoring trustee. Second, the carve-out process may also require a replication for the business of assets held or functions performed by other parts of the parties' businesses if this is necessary to ensure the viability and competitiveness of the business to be divested. An example is the termination of the business' participation in a central information technology network and an installation of a separate IT system for the business. In general, the major steps of such a carve-out process and the functions to be replicated should be decided on a case-by-case basis and described in the commitments.

Notes
[1] See paragraph 26 above for the question how shared assets have to be dealt with in commitments.

115. At the same time, it has to be ensured that the viability of the business to be divested is not affected by such measures. In the interim period, the parties therefore have to maintain the use of shared assets by and to continue to provide services to the business to the same extent as in the past as long as the business is not yet viable on a stand-alone basis.

Specific obligations of the parties concerning the divestiture process

116. For the divestiture process, the commitments should foresee that potential purchasers can carry out a due diligence exercise and obtain, dependent on the stage of the procedure, sufficient information concerning the divested business to allow the purchaser to fully assess the value, scope and commercial potential of the business and have direct access to its personnel. The parties further have to submit periodic reports on potential purchasers and developments in the negotiations. The divestiture will only be implemented once the transaction is closed, that is the legal title has passed to the approved purchaser, and the assets have been actually transferred. At the end of the process, the parties will have to send a final report, confirming the closing and the transfer of the assets.

4. The Monitoring and the divestiture trustee

Role of the monitoring trustee

117. As the Commission cannot, on a daily basis, be directly involved in overseeing the implementation of the commitments, the parties have to propose the appointment of a trustee to oversee the parties' compliance with the commitments, in particular with their obligations in the interim period and the divestiture process (the so-called 'monitoring trustee'). Thereby, the parties guarantee the effectiveness of the commitments submitted by them and allow the Commission to ensure that the modification of the notified concentration, as proposed by the parties, will be carried out with the requisite degree of certainty.

118. The monitoring trustee will carry out its tasks under the supervision of the Commission and is to be considered the Commission's 'eyes and ears'. It shall be the guardian that the business is managed and kept properly on a stand-alone basis in the interim period. The Commission may therefore give any orders and instructions to the monitoring trustee in order to ensure compliance with the commitments, and the trustee may propose to the parties any measures it considers necessary for carrying out its tasks. The parties, however, may not issue any instructions to the trustee without approval by the Commission.

119. The Commitments will generally set out the tasks of the monitoring trustee. Its duties and obligations will be specified in detail in the trustee mandate, to be concluded between the parties and the trustee, and its tasks shall be further detailed in a work-plan. The tasks of the monitoring trustee will normally start immediately after the adoption of the Commission decision and last until the legal and actual transfer of the business to the approved purchaser. Five main, non-exhaustive tasks can be distinguished which the monitoring trustee should carry out under the supervision of the Commission:

— first, the monitoring trustee will be called upon to oversee the safeguards for the business to be divested in the interim period,

— second, in carve-out cases, the monitoring trustee has to monitor the splitting of assets and the allocation of the personnel between the divested business and retained businesses by the parties as well as the replication of assets and functions in the business previously provided by the parties,

— third, the monitoring trustee shall be responsible for overseeing the parties' efforts to find a potential purchaser and to transfer the business. In general, it shall review the progress of the divestiture process and the potential purchasers included in the process. It shall verify that potential purchasers receive sufficient information relating to the business – in particular by reviewing the information memorandum (if available), the data room or the due diligence process. Once a purchaser is proposed, the monitoring trustee shall submit to the Commission a reasoned opinion as to whether the proposed purchaser fulfils the purchaser requirements in the commitments and whether the business is sold in a manner consistent with the commitments. At the end of the process, the monitoring trustee has to oversee the legal and actual transfer of the business to the purchaser and make a final report, confirming the transfer,

— fourth, the monitoring trustee shall act as a contact point for any requests by third parties, in particular potential purchasers, in relation to the commitments. The parties shall inform interested third parties of the identity and the tasks of the monitoring trustee, including any potential purchasers. In case of disagreement between the parties and third parties in relation to matters dealt with by the commitments, the monitoring trustee shall discuss those matters with both sides and report to the Commission. In order to be able to carry out its role, the monitoring trustee will keep confidential any business secrets of the parties and third parties,

— fifth, the monitoring trustee shall report on these issues to the Commission in periodic compliance reports and shall also submit additional reports upon request by the Commission.

Commentary
para 119: F&N: 5.1107

120. The commitments will also comprehensively set out the monitoring trustee's needs for support by and cooperation with the parties; the Commission will supervise the relationship between the parties and the trustee also in this respect. In order to fulfil its tasks, the trustee shall have access to books and records of the parties and of the divested business, insofar and as long as this is relevant for the implementation of the commitments, may ask for managerial and administrative support by the parties, shall be informed of potential purchasers and all developments in the divestiture process, and shall be provided with the information submitted to potential purchasers. In addition, the parties shall indemnify the trustee and allow the trustee to appoint advisors, if appropriate for the fulfilment of its tasks under the commitments. The commitments will also enable the Commission to share the parties' information with the monitoring trustee in order to allow the monitoring trustee to fulfil its tasks. The monitoring trustee will be bound to keep this information confidential.

Role of the divestiture trustee

121. As for the monitoring trustee, the parties have to propose to appoint a divestiture trustee in order to make the commitments submitted by them effective and allow the Commission to ensure that the modification of the notified concentration, as proposed by them, will be carried out. If the parties do not succeed in finding a suitable purchaser within the first divestiture period, then in the trustee divestiture period, the divestiture trustee will be given an irrevocable and exclusive mandate to dispose of the business, under the supervision of the Commission, within a specific deadline at no minimum price to a suitable purchaser. The commitments shall allow the divestiture trustee to include in the sale and purchase agreement such terms and conditions as it considers appropriate for an expedient sale, in particular customary representations, warranties and indemnities. The sale of the business by the divestiture trustee is in the same way subject to the prior approval of the Commission as the sale by the parties.

Commentary
para 121: F&N: 5.1109

122. The commitments will set out that the parties shall support and inform the divestiture trustee and cooperate with the trustee in the same way as this is foreseen for the monitoring trustee. For the divestiture, the parties have to grant to the divestiture trustee comprehensive powers of attorney, covering all stages of the divestiture.

Commentary
para 122: F&N: 5.1110

Approval of the trustee and the trustee mandate

123. Depending on the commitment, the monitoring trustee may or may not be the same person or institution as the divestiture trustee. The parties shall propose one or several potential trustees to the Commission, including the full terms of the mandate and an outline of a work-plan. It is of the essence that the monitoring trustee is in place immediately after the Commission decision. Therefore, the parties should propose a suitable trustee immediately after the Commission decision[1] and the commitments normally have to foresee that the notified concentration can only be implemented once the monitoring trustee is appointed, after being approved by the

Commission.[2] The situation is different for the divestiture trustee who should be appointed well ahead of the end of the first divestiture period[3] so that its mandate can take effect with the beginning of the trustee divestiture period.

Notes

[1] Normally, the commitments should foresee that a monitoring trustee is proposed within two weeks of the date of the decision.

[2] See Case COMP/M.4180 – *GdF/Suez* of 14 November 2006; Case COMP/M.4187 – *Metso/Aker Kvaerner* of 12 December 2006; Case COMP/M.3916 – *T-Mobile/Tele.ring* of 20 April 2006.

[3] The Commission will normally require an appointment at least one month ahead of the end of the first divestiture period.

Commentary

para 123: F&N: 5.1104

124. Both types of trustees will be appointed by the parties on the basis of a trustee mandate, entered into by the parties and the trustee. The appointment and the mandate will be subject to the approval by the Commission which will have discretion in the selection of the trustee and will assess whether the proposed candidate is suitable for the tasks in the specific case. The trustee shall be independent of the parties, possess the necessary qualifications to carry out its mandate and shall not be, or become, exposed to a conflict of interests.

125. The Commission will assess the necessary qualifications in the light of the requirements of the specific case, including the geographic area and the sector concerned. According to the Commission's experience, auditing firms and other consulting firms may be particularly well placed to fulfil the tasks of a monitoring trustee. Individuals who have worked in the specific industry may also be suitable candidates for performing such a role if they have the necessary resources available to deal with the tasks at stake. Investment banks seem to be particularly suitable for the role of a divestiture trustee. The independence of the trustee is crucial in order to enable the trustee to properly fulfil its role of monitoring the parties' compliance for the Commission and to ensure its credibility vis-à-vis third parties. In particular, the Commission will not accept persons or institutions as trustees which are at the same time the parties' auditors or their investment advisors in the divestiture. However, no conflicts of interests will arise by relations of the trustee with the parties if those relations will not impair the Trustee's objectivity and independence in discharging its tasks. It is the parties' responsibility to supply the Commission with adequate information for it to verify that the trustee fulfils the requirements. The appointment of the trustee after approval by the parties is irrevocable unless the trustee is replaced with the approval of or upon request by the Commission.

126. The trustee mandate shall define the tasks as specified in the commitments further and shall include all provisions necessary to enable the trustee to fulfil its tasks under the commitments accepted by the Commission. The parties are responsible for remuneration of the trustee under the mandate, and the remuneration structure must be such as to not impede the trustee's independence and effectiveness in fulfilling the mandate. The Commission will approve a trustee only together with a suitable mandate. In appropriate cases, it may publish the identity of the trustee and a summary of its tasks.

127. When the specific commitments with which the trustee has been entrusted have been implemented—that is to say, when legal title for the business to be divested has passed, the assets have been actually transferred to the purchaser and specific arrangements which may continue post-divestiture have been fulfilled – the mandate will provide for the trustee to request the Commission for a discharge from further responsibilities. Even after the discharge has been given, it may be necessary for the Commission to require the reappointment of the trustee on the basis of the commitments, if it appears subsequently to the Commission that the relevant commitments might not have been fully and properly implemented.

5. Obligations of the parties following implementation of the divestiture

128. The Commitments also have to foresee that for a period of 10 years after the adoption of the decision accepting the commitments the Commission may request information from the parties. This will allow the Commission to monitor the effective implementation of the remedy.

6. Implementation of other commitments

129. Many of the principles discussed above for the implementation of divestiture commitments can equally be applied to other types of commitments if those commitments need to be implemented subsequent to the Commission decision. For example, if it is foreseen that the beneficiary of a licence needs to be approved by the Commission, the considerations regarding the purchaser approval can be applied. Given the wide range of non-divestiture commitments, no general and comprehensive requirements for the implementation of non-divestiture commitments can be set out.

130. However, given the long duration of non-divestiture commitments and their frequent complexity, they often require a very high monitoring effort and specific monitoring tools in order to allow the Commission to conclude that they will effectively be implemented. Therefore, the Commission will often require the involvement of a trustee to oversee the implementation of such commitments and the establishment of a fast-track arbitration procedure in order to provide for a dispute resolution mechanism and to render the commitments enforceable by the market participants themselves. In past cases, the Commission has often required both the appointment of a trustee and an arbitration clause.[1] In those circumstances, the trustee will oversee the implementation of the commitments, but will also be able to assist in arbitral proceedings to the effect that they may be finalised in a short period of time.

Notes

[1] Such an approach of combined monitoring by arbitration and a monitoring trustee was, *e.g.* used in Case COMP/M.2803 – *Telia/Sonera* of 10 July 2002; Case COMP/M.3083 – *GE/Instrumentarium* of 2 September 2003; and Case COMP/M.3225 – *Alcan/Pechiney II* of 29 September 2003.

D14

MERGER CORRESPONDENCE

Notes

This document is available on the Europa website at the following address:
<http://ec.europa.eu/comm/competition/contacts/mergers_mail.html>

In all your correspondence, please specify the name of the case and the case number

It is essential that the correspondents use only the fax numbers and/or addresses for any official communication relating to merger cases. This will facilitate and accelerate the treatment of your correspondence. Fax communications sent to other numbers/addresses may inevitably be treated with delay.

Addressee:	Merger Registry
Postal address:	European Commission Directorate-General for Competition Merger Registry B-1049 Brussels
Delivery by hand:	European Commission DG Competition Merger Registry rue Joseph II / Jozef II straat 70 1000 Brussels
Fax:	32-2-296.43.01

Delivery of merger-related documents

- Please note that the delivery at the above mentioned address is a legal obligation pursuant to Article 23(1) of Commission Regulation No (EC) 802/2004 implementing Council Regulation (EC) No 139/2004 on the control of concentrations between undertakings. (See the Commission Communication published in the Official Journal C 139, 19.05.2004, p.2)
- Security procedures :
  1. Prior to delivery, at Rue Joseph II / Jozef II straat 70 the law firm or the legal representative of the notifying company must call the Merger Registry (phone numbers: +32-2.296.55.77 or 32-2-295.68.27, fax number: ++32-2-296.43.01)
  2. An estimated delivery time and the name of the individual from the firm or company who will be making the delivery must be provided along with a description of the item to be delivered (number of envelopes, packages or boxes
  3. Packages and envelopes to be submitted must clearly indicate the name of the office delivering the filing
  4. The Registry will confirm the receipt of the items being delivered

[…]

For similar summaries of the notification requirements and procedure in other jurisdictions, please refer to the web-site of the International Competition Network, and to the information and links displayed there.

Email

For general queries only, you may also send an e-mail to the Merger Control, General Queries mailbox. Please note that notifications and all other case-related submissions may not be sent to this address and shall not be considered valid if sent to this address. They will also not be forwarded or registered.

Please do not send queries of a general nature falling outside the scope of EU Merger Control Policy to this mailbox as it is not to be used for general queries unrelated to EU Merger Control Policy.

[…]

Allocation of cases

In order for DG Competition to be able to allocate staff to cases in an efficient manner which best meets the requirements of individual cases, we kindly request that you use the standardised case allocation request which you will find below. Requests should be sent to the Merger Registry by email or by fax by 12 o' clock on Fridays at the latest. Items received after this time would risk being dealt with at a later Management Meeting.

[…]

D15

MERGER NOTIFICATION AND PROCEDURES TEMPLATE

NOTE

Note

This document was formerly (but is no longer) available on the Commission's website at the following address: <http://ec.europa.eu/comm/competition/mergers_mail.html>

It is no longer reproduced in this volume for reasons of space. It remains available on Oxford Competition Law.

Part D Mergers and Concentrations

D16

MERGER REGISTRY — INSTRUCTIONS FOR CASE ALLOCATION REQUEST

Notes
This document is available on the Europa website at the following addresses:
<http://ec.europa.eu/comm/competition/contacts/mergers_mail.html>
<http://ec.europa.eu/comm/competition/mergers/case_allocation_request.doc>

Case team allocation request - Mergers

**To be sent by email to COMP-MERGER-REGISTRY@ec.europa.eu
or by fax to +32-2-296.43.01**

Please indicate the information below:

1] Your contact details:

Name:

Company/law firm:

Telephone number:

Email:

2] Dossier type Pre-notification

☐ Form CO

☐ Form CO simplified

☐ Form RS Art. 4(4)

☐ Consultation

2) Extended level of confidentiality in the pre-notification phase

Information submitted in pre-notification is protected by Article 17 of the Merger Regulation and pre-notification contacts are kept confidential. Nevertheless, some highly market sensitive transactions may require additional protection. If this is the case, please indicate this below.

Where requests for an extended level of confidentiality are justified the Commission will use code names for the parties to the transaction.

An extended level of confidentiality is requested because:

☐ a) the transaction involves publicly traded companies, is not yet known to the market and is highly market sensitive

☐ b) other reason (please explain)

3] Companies involved country of origin, role and turnover[1]:

Companies	Country	Role[2]	Turnover (million EUR)		Year of turnover[3]
			World	Community	
-					
-					
-					
-					

4] Name the main product(s)/Economic activities

Name of product(s)/activities	NACE code

5] Brief description of the parties, the transaction, the markets involved and complexity of the case

6] Is case linked with or related to any other current or previous case?

☐ Yes, case number
☐ No

7] Expected date of first draft :

8] Expected date of notification :

11] Proposed case language

CS – DA - DE – ET - EL – EN - ES - FR - IT – LV – LT - HU – MT - NL – PL - PT – SK – SL - FI- SV *(please choose)*

13] Any other information you want to submit at this stage:

Notes

[1] For pre-notification, complete turnover if available.

[2] A/P = Acquirer/Parent(s)
A = Acquirer
T = Target
NC = Newly created company constituting a JV
MP = Merging Party

[3] If fiscal year does not fall together with calendar year, indicate end of fiscal year in full date format (dd/mm/yyyy).

D17

BEST PRACTICES ON COOPERATION BETWEEN EU NATIONAL COMPETITION AUTHORITIES IN MERGER REVIEW

Notes
This document was adopted by the EU Merger Working Group on 8 November 2011. It is available on the Commission's website at: <http://ec.europa.eu/competition/ecn/mergers.html>

Commentary
Best Practices: B&C: 1.071

---

1 Introduction

1.1 The national competition authorities of the EU who have responsibility for merger review ("NCAs") operate in compliance with different national legal systems. They believe, however, that it is desirable to cooperate in the review of some mergers which meet the requirements for notification or investigation in more than one Member State ("multi-jurisdictional mergers"), and have therefore decided jointly to publish an agreed set of Best Practices on Co-operation in Merger Review.

1.2 This document, which has been drawn up by the EU Merger Working Group,[1] sets out the Best Practices which the NCAs, to the extent consistent with their respective laws and enforcement priorities, aim to follow when they review the same merger transaction. It also sets out the steps that merging parties and third parties are encouraged to take in order to facilitate cooperation between NCAs. Cooperation extending beyond the existing ECA Notice system[2] is limited to NCAs who are reviewing the same merger transaction ("the NCAs concerned"). It is not intended that cooperation should provide a forum whereby NCAs not concerned will be involved in the review of a specific case.[3]

Notes

[1] The EU Merger Working Group ("the Working Group") was established in Brussels in January 2010. It consists of representatives of the European Commission and the national competition authorities ("NCAs") of the European Union ("EU") together with observers from the NCAs of the European Economic Area ("EEA"). The objective of the Working Group is to foster increased convergence and cooperation between the EU merger jurisdictions in order to ensure effective administration and enforcement of merger control laws.

[2] The European Competition Authorities ("ECA") Notice system is an information system among the NCAs of the EU and EEA EFTA States ("ECAs"). An ECA Notice is a notice which is distributed to all other ECAs by the first NCA to be notified of a multi-jurisdictional merger. It sets out the names of the merging parties, the sector/industry concerned and/or products concerned, the date of the notification, the name of the case handler, and the other member states concerned. See *ECA procedures guide on the exchange of information between members on multi-jurisdictional mergers* (2001); Available for example on http://ec.europa.eu/competition/ecn/eca_information_exchange_procedures_en.pdf.

[3] Some cooperation may, however, be necessary in order to determine the NCAs concerned. NCAs may also wish to consult non-involved NCAs about past experiences with similar mergers both as regards the substantive assessment and remedies, and these Best Practices do not preclude such discussions. For example, it may be helpful to exchange non-confidential information when assessing the effectiveness of a remedy, e.g. if the remedy concerns facilities or assets located in another Member State that is not reviewing the merger.

1.3 This document is intended to provide a non-binding reference for cooperation between NCAs. NCAs reserve their full discretion in the implementation of these Best Practices and nothing in this document is intended to create new rights or obligations which may fetter that discretion.

2 Objectives of cooperation

2.1 Cooperation is beneficial for the NCAs concerned, for the merging parties themselves and for third parties. The Best Practices are intended to provide clarity on how cooperation among NCAs will operate in multi-jurisdictional merger cases. Where the merging parties provide full and consistent information to NCAs concerned, cooperation can reduce burdens on merging parties and third parties by facilitating, where possible, the alignment of timing and the overall efficiency, transparency, effectiveness and timeliness of the merger review processes.

2.2 In cases where serious concerns or difficult analytical issues arise, cooperation can be invaluable in helping to reach informed and consistent or at least non-conflicting outcomes. In such cases, cooperation will ensure that NCAs are in a better position to exchange views on, for example, possible conceptual frameworks for the assessment of the transaction and theories of competitive harm, types of empirical evidence and so on.

2.3 Cooperation is also beneficial both for the NCAs concerned and for the merging parties in relation to any remedial action which may be necessary. Remedies in a merger that is reviewable in more than one jurisdiction may differ across jurisdictions depending on the competition concern identified in each one; indeed, remedies may not be necessary in every jurisdiction. Nevertheless, where the merger affects a market or markets in more than one jurisdiction, a remedy accepted in one jurisdiction may have an impact in another jurisdiction (see section 3.2(iii)). Cooperation can therefore contribute to avoiding inconsistent remedies and obtaining those that are more coherent.

2.4 These Best Practices are intended to promote the achievement of all these ends.

3 Scope of application of Best Practices

3.1 These Best Practices address cooperation in multi-jurisdictional merger cases. While it is always useful for NCAs to provide basic case information[4] to each other in merger cases which are notifiable in more than one Member State, further cooperation will not be necessary, or even efficient, in the case of every multi-jurisdictional merger. This is particularly the case where it is clear during the early stages of an investigation that the merger does not raise any significant competition or procedural issues in any Member State or that it does so only in one Member State, or where such issues are not decisive for the outcome of any of the different merger reviews. Close cooperation is not an end in itself: its benefits depend on the specific circumstances of each case.

Notes

[4] See model ECA notice (cf. Fn 2 above) as agreed in the ECA procedures guide on the exchange of information between members on multijurisdictional mergers (2001); available for example on http://ec.europa.eu/competition/ecn/eca_information_exchange_procedures_en.pdf.

3.2 Where multi-jurisdictional mergers raise similar or comparable issues in relation to jurisdictional or substantive questions, the NCAs concerned will decide on a case-by-case basis whether cooperation may be necessary or appropriate[5]. For example:

   (i) Cooperation may assist the NCAs in forming a view as to whether a transaction qualifies for notification or investigation under merger control laws in their respective jurisdictions. It is noted that although jurisdictional rules and practices may differ across jurisdictions, cooperation may assist the NCAs in reaching an informed view.

  (ii) Cooperation may assist the NCAs in relation to mergers which may have an impact on competition in more than one Member State, when markets affected by the transaction cover more than one Member State or when a merger affects national or sub-national markets in more than one Member State, if such national or subnational markets are the same or similar from the product standpoint.

 (iii) Cooperation may also be of value in relation to mergers where remedies need to be designed or examined in more than one Member State, such as in situations where the same remedy is designed to address competition issues in different Member States or where one remedy affects the effectiveness of a different remedy in another Member State.

Notes

5 Although the NCAs concerned will keep under review throughout the merger control process the need for cooperation, it will sometimes be possible for them to form a view in this regard at an early stage of the process, i.e. during pre-notification contacts (where such contacts take place) or following notification.

3.3 These Best Practices are without prejudice to the existing guidance on the system of reattribution of cases between the Member States and the Commission (see the Commission's referral notice and ECA's Principles on the application of Art. 4(5) and 22 of Regulation 139/2004).6 Nevertheless, the enhanced cooperation recommended in these Best Practices may also facilitate the smooth functioning of the reattribution mechanisms set out in Regulation (EC) 139/2004. In particular, where NCAs are contemplating an Article 22 referral request, contacts between them can facilitate the referral, and, if done before notification, can also assist merging parties in forming a view whether it is appropriate for them to speed up the referral process by themselves making an Art. 4(5) referral request (see further the description of pre-notification contacts in section 5.5).

Notes

6 Article 4(5) provides for referral of cases from the Member States to the Commission prior to notification with the purpose of providing a "one-stop-shop" review. Article 22 provides for referral from the Member States to the Commission after notification where it is considered that the Commission is better positioned to investigate a merger. See also Commission Notice on Case Referral in respect of concentrations (OJ C 56, 05.03.2005, p.2–23). See ECA principles on the application, by National Competition Authorities within the ECA, of Articles 4 (5) and 22 of the Merger Regulation (2005). Available for example on http://ec.europa.eu/competition/ecn/eca_referral_principles_en.pdf

4 Role of National Competition Authorities

4.1 In all cases that relate to a merger transaction that is reviewable in more than one EU Member State, the NCAs concerned will inform the other NCAs by means of the existing ECA Notice system, which involves the exchange of basic non-confidential case information after a notification in such a multi-jurisdictional merger case has been received.7

4.2 To facilitate cooperation, the NCAs concerned will aim to update the information contained in the ECA notice by informing the other NCAs about any decision to commence second phase proceedings/in-depth investigations, and any final decision, including a decision with remedies.

4.3 In cases where closer cooperation is necessary or appropriate (see paragraph 3.2 above), the NCAs, having due regard to confidentiality issues (see section 6 below), will aim to cooperate in particular in the following ways:

(i) The NCAs concerned will liaise with one another and keep one another appraised of their progress at key stages of their respective investigations. The key stages will vary depending on the procedural framework of each NCA concerned. The NCAs concerned will keep each other informed of the outcome of the first phase investigation, including, where relevant, the intention to open an in-depth investigation, and the outcome of the in-depth investigation. The NCAs concerned will also keep each other appraised of the launch and progress of any remedies discussions, if not conducted jointly.

(ii) Where it is helpful to do so, the NCAs concerned may discuss their respective jurisdictional and/or substantive analyses. Where necessary, having regard to the possible effects of the transaction on the national territories of the NCAs concerned, such discussions may relate to issues such as market definition, assessment of competitive effects, efficiencies, theories of competitive harm, and the empirical evidence needed to test those theories. NCAs concerned will also, where it is helpful to do so, exchange views on necessary remedial measures or submitted remedies.

5 Role of Merging Parties

5.1 Effective cooperation between NCAs requires the active assistance of the merging parties at all stages of the review process, both as regards the jurisdictional and/or substantive review and, where required, the assessment of remedies.

5.2 Parties to merger investigations play an important role with regard to cooperation between the NCAs concerned. They can contribute significantly to the alignment of the review proceedings in different Member States, taking into account, among other things, procedural requirements and review periods. Such alignment will be of benefit both to merging parties and to NCAs.

5.3 Therefore, where a transaction is expected to fulfil the requirements for notification or investigation in more than one jurisdiction, the merging parties are encouraged, unless it is clear and obvious from the outset that paragraph 3.2 above does not apply, to contact each of the NCAs concerned as soon as practicable and provide them with the following basic information:

    i. The name of each jurisdiction in which they intend to make a filing;

    ii. The date of the proposed filing in each jurisdiction;

    iii. The names and activities of the merging parties;

    iv. The geographic areas in which they carry on business;[8]

    v. The sector or sectors involved (short description and/or NACE code).

Notes

[8] The phrase "carry on business" does not include a situation where an undertaking is merely registered in a particular place.

5.4 It is important to note that the provision of this information by the parties will not of itself be a trigger for cooperation among the NCAs concerned. That will depend rather upon whether the case is one where cooperation is necessary or appropriate, as set out in paragraph 3.2 of these Best Practices. However, it will assist the NCAs concerned to decide at an early stage whether there might be a need for cooperation in the particular case.

5.5 Depending on the circumstances of the case it may be possible to provide much of this information at the pre-notification stage. For this purpose, and where it is permitted by law, it may be helpful for merging parties and the NCAs concerned to organize pre-notification contacts as early as possible. Such contacts can assist the parties and the NCAs concerned to align as far as possible the timing of parallel proceedings and can, ultimately, contribute to the reduction of the overall burden that falls on merging parties in the course of a multijurisdictional merger. It may at times, where circumstances permit, be useful for the merging parties and the NCAs concerned to engage in joint pre-notification contacts.

5.6 Merging parties have a crucial role in helping NCAs to ensure that remedies in different Member States do not lead to inconsistent or untenable results. As already stated above, remedies in a merger that is reviewable in more than one Member State may differ across Member States depending on the competition concern identified in each one; indeed, remedies may not be necessary in every Member State. Nevertheless, a remedy accepted in one Member State may have an impact on the effectiveness of remedies targeted at competition problems in another Member State. It is therefore clearly in the interest of the merging parties to coordinate the timing and substance of remedy proposals to the NCAs concerned, so as to ensure coherent remedies and to avoid inconsistent remedies. In certain cases, where circumstances permit, it might be appropriate for merging parties and the reviewing NCAs to engage in joint discussions on proposed remedies.

6 Confidential Information

6.1 It will often be helpful for the NCAs concerned to be able to exchange and discuss confidential information when reviewing the same merger. Therefore, while a certain degree of cooperation is feasible through the exchange of non-confidential information, waivers of confidentiality executed by merging parties can enable more effective communication between the NCAs concerned regarding evidence that is relevant to the investigation.

Part D Mergers and Concentrations

6.2 For that reason, the merging parties are encouraged to be proactive and to provide waivers of confidentiality to all NCAs concerned, including, where appropriate, at the pre-notification phase. The merging parties are encouraged to use the ICN model waiver provided in the Annex to these Best Practices.

6.3 For the same reasons, where appropriate, third parties are also encouraged to provide waivers of confidentiality to all NCAs concerned. Third parties are also encouraged to use the ICN model waiver provided in the Annex to these Best Practices.

6.4 NCAs are fully aware that it lies within the discretion of the merging or third parties whether to provide a waiver. The scope of the waiver to be provided may be adapted to the specific circumstances of the case, but is essential that the waiver should fulfil the purpose of allowing for an effective information exchange between the NCAs concerned.

6.5 Where a waiver has been provided the NCAs concerned will share the information covered by the waiver without further notice to the parties. NCAs will discuss with each other, prior to any exchange of confidential information as provided for in Sections 4 and 5, how it may best be protected. Confidential information and business secrets are protected under national law in all Member States.

6.6 Confidential information exchanged on the basis of a waiver will not be used for any purpose other than the review of the relevant merger, unless the national law provides otherwise (see paragraph 6.5).

APPENDIX A

ICN Model Waiver Form

[DATE]

[CONTACT NAME AT AGENCY A]
[ADDRESS]
Re: [CASE REFERENCE]
Dear -----:

On behalf of COMPANY A, I confirm that COMPANY A, subject to the conditions and limitations set forth herein, agrees to waive the confidentiality restrictions under [RELEVANT STATUTORY OR REGULATORY AUTHORITY] and other applicable laws and rules (collectively the "Confidentiality Obligations") that prevent AGENCY X from disclosing to FOREIGN AGENCY Y confidential information obtained from COMPANY A in connection with its proposed transaction with COMPANY B. Specifically, COMPANY A agrees that AGENCY X staff may share with FOREIGN AGENCY Y [any of COMPANY A's documents, statements, data and information, as well as AGENCY A's own internal analyses that contain or refer to COMPANY A's materials that would otherwise be foreclosed by the confidentiality Obligations].[18]

This waiver is granted only with respect to disclosures to FOREIGN AGENCY Y and only on the condition that FOREIGN AGENCY Y will treat as confidential information it obtains from AGENCY X in accordance with the terms of the attached letter from [CONTACT NAME] of FOREIGN AGENCY Y.[19] This agreement does not constitute a waiver by COMPANY A of its rights under the Confidentiality Obligations with respect to the protection afforded to COMPANY A against the direct or indirect disclosures of information to any third-party other than FOREIGN AGENCY Y.

COMPANY A submits this waiver under the condition and understanding that, with respect to information that AGENCY X obtains from COMPANY A and provides to the FOREIGN AGENCY Y pursuant to this waiver, AGENCY X should continue to protect the confidentiality of such information with respect to other outside parties in accordance with the Confidentiality Obligations.

A copy of this letter is being sent to [CONTACT PERSON AT FOREIGN AGENCY Y].

Sincerely,

[ATTORNEY FOR COMPANY A]
cc: [CONTACT FOR FOREIGN AGENCY Y]

Notes

18 NOTE: This model language is intended for those situations where a waiver with respect to any and all documents and information provided to Agency X is contemplated. There may be instances where such a broad waiver is not desired. In those cases, the parties may opt for a waiver limited in scope, such as to allow the agencies to discuss potential remedies that each is considering and the reasons for such remedies, or to discuss specific limited issues such as product market definition or barriers to entry. Parties and agency staff should consider the scope of the waiver that is desired to assist them in their investigation so as to not unnecessarily burden parties or other competition agencies.

19 NOTE: "Foreign Agency Y" should provide a letter describing the confidentiality protections provided by that country. (In some cases, the parties and Agency X staff may be satisfied if that letter is directed to that contact person by representatives of the parties, with a written confirmation that Foreign Agency Y agrees to the terms of that letter.) Attached to this model form at Appendix [D] are sample confidentiality letters.

D18

CASE REFERRAL UNDER THE EEA AGREEMENT

Notes

This document is published on the Europa website at:
<http://ec.europa.eu/comm/competition/mergers/legislation/regulation/regulation139/eea_referral.pdf>

Commentary
Notice: B&C: 8.081, 8.085

1. Introduction

When the Commission has jurisdiction to deal with a case under the Merger Regulation,[1] it is the sole competent authority in the EEA,[2] which means that it exercises its powers not only with respect to the EC Member States, but also with respect to the territories of the EFTA States.[3] The rules on referral of cases under the EEA Agreement are included in Protocol 24 to the EEA Agreement. These are based on the Merger Regulation's system for referral of cases, but have been subject to certain adaptations. Following the adoption of Council Regulation 139/2004, many of the new rules on referral (pre-notification and post-notification) of cases included in the Regulation have likewise been incorporated into the EEA Agreement.[4]

The referral rules in Protocol 24 of the EEA Agreement apply with regard to cases referred to or from the EFTA States. The referral rules in the Merger Regulation are applicable in parallel with regard to cases referred to or from the EC Member States. Thus, in a case which involves referrals involving both EFTA States and EC Member States, the two sets of rules are applicable. When a referral involves EFTA States only, the EEA Agreement alone applies. Similarly, when a referral involves exclusively EC Member States, only the rules of the Merger Regulation apply.

According to the referral rules in the EEA Agreement, there is a more limited scope for the EFTA States than for the EC Member States to request the referral of a case to the Commission. The rules on referral of cases from the Commission to the EFTA States are, however, essentially identical to those in the Merger Regulation.

Notes

1 Council Regulation (EC) No 139/2004 of 20 January 2004 on the control of concentrations between undertakings, OJ L 24/1, 29.1.2004.

2 This follows from Article 57(2) and Annex XIV to the EEA Agreement. The EEA Agreement and its Annexes and Protocols can be found of the web-site of the EFTA.

3 For the purpose of this note, the term EFTA States, which is the term used in the EEA Agreement, refers to Iceland, Liechtenstein and Norway, and not to Switzerland which has not ratified the EEA Agreement.

4 See the Commission's website:
<http://europa.eu.int/comm/competition/mergers/legislation/regulation/regulation139/>

2. Pre-notification referrals under the EEA Agreement

The EEA Agreement provides for pre-notification referrals from the EFTA States to the Commission, by allowing the parties to a concentration to request the Commission to examine a concentration which is "capable of being reviewed under the national competition laws of at least three EC Member States and at least one EFTA State".[5] Such a request is optional for the parties. It constitutes an "add-on" to a request for referral from three or more EC Member States under Article 4(5) of Regulation 139/2004. This means that if a case is capable of being reviewed under the competition laws of, e.g., France, Poland, and Norway, this is not sufficient for the case to be referred to the Commission; it is necessary that the case is reviewable also under the national law of a third EC Member State.

If one or more EFTA States vetoes the referral, the competent EFTA State(s) shall retain its/their competence to examine the case under its national competition law and the case shall not be referred from any EFTA State. However, a veto by an EFTA State has no impact on the fate of the request for referral from the EC Member States concerned and the Commission.

The parties can also request the pre-notification referral of a case from the Commission to a competent EFTA State. In this situation, the rules of the EEA Agreement are essentially identical to those of the Merger Regulation.[6] They provide that an undertaking concerned may inform the Commission by means of a reasoned submission that the "concentration may significantly affect competition in a market within an EFTA State, which presents all the characteristics of a distinct market and should therefore be examined, in whole or in part, by that EFTA State". In such circumstances, the rules applicable to the assessment of that request by the Commission and by the EFTA State(s) concerned are in substance the same as those set out in the Merger Regulation.

Notes

5 See Article 6(5) of Protocol 24 to the EEA Agreement, and Article 4(5) of the Merger Regulation. EEA referrals – 14/10/2004

6 See Article 6(4) of Protocol 24 to the EEA Agreement, and Article 4(4) of the Merger Regulation.

3. Post-notification referrals under the EEA Agreement

The EEA Agreement enables post-notification referral from the Commission to an EFTA State of a case or of a part or parts of a case.[7]

The Commission may refer a notified concentration to an EFTA State in two situations. First, a case may be referred where the concentration "threatens to affect significantly competition in a market within that EFTA State, which presents all the characteristics of a distinct market". Second, the Commission may refer a case to an EFTA State where the concentration "affects competition in a market within that EFTA State, which presents all the characteristics of a distinct market and which does not constitute a substantial part of the territory covered by the Agreement".[8]

As regards post-notification referral of cases to the Commission, an EFTA State may only join a referral request made by an EC Member State; it may not initiate such a request itself. This is consistent with the "two-pillar" system of the EEA-Agreement, and means that the powers of the EFTA States are in this regard somewhat more limited than those of the EC Member States.

Accordingly, where a concentration may affect trade between one or more EC Member States and one or more EFTA States, and it threatens to significantly affect competition in one or more EFTA States, that State or these States may join a request for referral put forward by one or more EC Member States.[9]

As under the Merger Regulation, the EEA Agreement provides that when the EFTA States receive the request by an EC Member State to refer a case to the Commission, all national time limits relating to the concentration shall be suspended in all the EFTA States competent to review the case until it has been decided whether the Commission will examine the case or not. Once an EFTA State has informed the Commission that it does not wish to join the request, that EFTA State retains its competence to examine the case and its national time limits start running anew. If the Commission decides to examine the referred concentration, the EFTA State or the EFTA States that joined the request are no longer competent to examine the case under their national competition law. An EFTA State that does not join the request can apply its national competition law to the concentration.

Notes

7 See Article 6(1) of Protocol 24 to the EEA Agreement.

8 These provisions closely correspond to the provisions in Article 9(2)(a) and 9(2)(b) of the Merger Regulation, but are not identical to them. In particular, it should be noted that the Commission has no discretion regarding a case meeting the requirements set out in Article 9(2)(b) of the Merger Regulation, but does enjoy discretion regarding referral of the corresponding category of cases under Article 6(1) of Protocol 24 to the EEA Agreement.

9 See Article 6(3) of Protocol 24 to the EEA Agreement. EEA referrals – 14/10/2004

4. *Calculation of time limits*

In general, the procedure governing referral requests including the EFTA States is the same as for requests applicable to requests involving only EC Member States. However, although the time limits are the same for the EFTA States as for the EC Member States, the manner in which they are calculated differs somewhat. The time limits start to run, for pre- and post notification referrals involving the EFTA States, upon receipt of the request for referral and other relevant documents by the EFTA Surveillance Authority, and not upon the receipt by the EFTA States of the documents in question.[10]

Notes

10 See Article 13 of Protocol 24 to the EEA Agreement.

5. *Submission of pre-notification referral requests*

As regards the submission of requests for pre-notification referrals, an unofficial version of the Form RS, which is intended to give guidance on the information undertakings may wish to provide should they seek a referral involving any of the EFTA States, has been published on the web site of DG Competition.[11] Merging parties are therefore encouraged to use this form.

According to Section D of that unofficial version of the Form RS, where a reasoned submission is made according to the EEA Agreement[12] in an official language of an EFTA State which is not an official language of the Community, the submission must simultaneously be supplemented by a translation into an official language of the Community.

Notes

11 <http://europa.eu.int/comm/competition/mergers/legislation/regulation/regulation139/form_rs_eea_en.pdf>.

12 See Article 12 of Protocol 24 to the EEA Agreement.

D19

US–EU MERGER WORKING GROUP: BEST PRACTICES ON COOPERATION IN MERGER INVESTIGATIONS

NOTE

Notes

This document was published on 14 October 2011 and is available on the Commission's website at: <http://ec.europa. eu/competition/mergers/legislation/international_cooperation.html>

For reasons of space, this document is no longer reproduced in this volume. It remains available on Oxford Competition Law.

Commentary

Best Practices: B&C: 8.007, 8.109, 8.293

PART E

SECTORAL REGIMES

E1

DIRECTIVE 2002/21/EC OF THE EUROPEAN PARLIAMENT AND OF THE COUNCIL

of 7 March 2002

on a common regulatory framework for electronic
communications networks and services (Framework Directive)

Official Journal L 108, 24.4.2002, p.33

Celex No: 32002L0021

EUR-Lex permanent link: <http://eur-lex.europa.eu/LexUriServ/LexUriServ.do?uri=CELEX:
32002L0021:EN:NOT>

Notes

EEA application: this Directive was adopted with appropriate adaptations by EEA Joint Committee Decision No
11/2004 (OJ No L 116, 22.4.2004, p.60 and EEA Supplement No 20, 22.4.2004, p.14): see EEA Agreement, Annex
XI, Point 5cl.

Commentary

Directive 2002/21/EC: B&C: 10.052, 12.005, 12.006, 12.008, 12.012, 12.013, 12.014, 12.016, 12.021, 12.027,
12.030, 12.034, 12.035, 12.043 **F&N:** 13.20, 13.22, 13.46, 13.50, 13.53, 13.211, 14.144, 14.151
Arts 14–16: B&C: 4.008

THE EUROPEAN PARLIAMENT AND THE COUNCIL OF THE EUROPEAN UNION,

Having regard to the [Treaty on the Functioning of the European Union], and in particular Article
[114]* thereof,

Having regard to the proposal from the Commission,[1]

Having regard to the opinion of the Economic and Social Committee,[2]

Acting in accordance with the procedure laid down in Article [294] of the Treaty,[3]

Notes

* Ed note: please see the Note on the Lisbon Treaty at p.xvii in regard to article renumbering introduced by the Lisbon Treaty.
[1] OJ C 365 E, 19.12.2000, p.198 and OJ C 270 E, 25.9.2001, p.199.
[2] OJ C 123, 25.4.2001, p.56.
[3] Opinion of the European Parliament of 1 March 2001 (OJ C 277, 1.10.2001, p.91), Council Common Position of
17 September 2001 (OJ C 337, 30.11.2001, p.34) and Decision of the European Parliament of 12 December 2001 [OJ
C 177 E, 25.7.2002, p.81]. Council Decision of 14 February 2002.

Whereas:

(1) The current regulatory framework for telecommunications has been successful in creating the
conditions for effective competition in the telecommunications sector during the transition from
monopoly to full competition.

(2) On 10 November 1999, the Commission presented a communication to the European Parliament, the Council, the Economic and Social Committee and the Committee of the Regions
entitled "Towards a new framework for electronic communications infrastructure and associated
services—the 1999 communications review". In that communication, the Commission reviewed
the existing regulatory framework for telecommunications, in accordance with its obligation
under Article 8 of Council Directive 90/387/EEC of 28 June 1990 on the establishment of the
internal market for telecommunications services through the implementation of open network

provision.[1] It also presented a series of policy proposals for a new regulatory framework for electronic communications infrastructure and associated services for public consultation.

Notes

[1] OJ L 192, 24.7.1990, p.1. Directive as amended by Directive 97/51/EC of the European Parliament and of the Council (OJ L 295, 29.10.1997, p.23).

(3) On 26 April 2000 the Commission presented a communication to the European Parliament, the Council, the Economic and Social Committee and the Committee of the Regions on the results of the public consultation on the 1999 communications review and orientations for the new regulatory framework. The communication summarised the public consultation and set out certain key orientations for the preparation of a new framework for electronic communications infrastructure and associated services.

(4) The Lisbon European Council of 23 and 24 March 2000 highlighted the potential for growth, competitiveness and job creation of the shift to a digital, knowledge-based economy. In particular, it emphasised the importance for Europe's businesses and citizens of access to an inexpensive, world-class communications infrastructure and a wide range of services.

(5) The convergence of the telecommunications, media and information technology sectors means all transmission networks and services should be covered by a single regulatory framework. That regulatory framework consists of this Directive and four specific Directives: Directive 2002/20/EC of the European Parliament and of the Council of 7 March 2002 on the authorisation of electronic communications networks and services (Authorisation Directive),[1] Directive 2002/19/EC of the European Parliament and of the Council of 7 March 2002 on access to, and interconnection of, electronic communications networks and associated facilities (Access Directive),[2] Directive 2002/22/EC of the European Parliament and of the Council of 7 March 2002 on universal service and users' rights relating to electronic communications networks and services (Universal Service Directive),[3] Directive 97/66/EC of the European Parliament and of the Council of 15 December 1997 concerning the processing of personal data and the protection of privacy in the telecommunications sector,[4] (hereinafter referred to as "the Specific Directives"). It is necessary to separate the regulation of transmission from the regulation of content. This framework does not therefore cover the content of services delivered over electronic communications networks using electronic communications services, such as broadcasting content, financial services and certain information society services, and is therefore without prejudice to measures taken at Community or national level in respect of such services, in compliance with Community law, in order to promote cultural and linguistic diversity and to ensure the defence of media pluralism. The content of television programmes is covered by Council Directive 89/552/EEC of 3 October 1989 on the coordination of certain provisions laid down by law, regulation or administrative action in Member States concerning the pursuit of television broadcasting activities.[5] The separation between the regulation of transmission and the regulation of content does not prejudice the taking into account of the links existing between them, in particular in order to guarantee media pluralism, cultural diversity and consumer protection.

Notes

[1] See [OJ L 108, 24.4.2002, p.21].
[2] See [OJ L 108, 24.4.2002, p.7].
[3] See [OJ L 108, 24.4.2002, p.51].
[4] OJ L 24, 30.1.1998, p.1.
[5] OJ L 298, 17.10.1989, p.23. Directive as amended by Directive 97/36/EC of the European Parliament and of the Council (OJ L 202, 30.7.1997, p.60).

Commentary
Recital 5: B&C: 12.005, 12.010, 12.011

(6) Audiovisual policy and content regulation are undertaken in pursuit of general interest objectives, such as freedom of expression, media pluralism, impartiality, cultural and linguistic diversity, social inclusion, consumer protection and the protection of minors. The Commission communication "Principles and guidelines for the Community's audio-visual policy in the digital age", and

the Council conclusions of 6 June 2000 welcoming this communication, set out the key actions to be taken by the Community to implement its audio-visual policy.

(7) The provisions of this Directive and the Specific Directives are without prejudice to the possibility for each Member State to take the necessary measures to ensure the protection of its essential security interests, to safeguard public policy and public security, and to permit the investigation, detection and prosecution of criminal offences, including the establishment by national regulatory authorities of specific and proportional obligations applicable to providers of electronic communications services.

Commentary
Recital 7: B&C: 12.012

(8) This Directive does not cover equipment within the scope of Directive 1999/5/EC of the European Parliament and of the Council of 9 March 1999 on radio equipment and telecommunications terminal equipment and the mutual recognition of their conformity,[1] but does cover consumer equipment used for digital television. It is important for regulators to encourage network operators and terminal equipment manufacturers to cooperate in order to facilitate access by disabled users to electronic communications services.

Notes
[1] OJ L 91, 7.4.1999, p.10.

(9) Information society services are covered by Directive 2000/31/EC of the European Parliament and of the Council of 8 June 2000 on certain legal aspects of information society services, in particular electronic commerce, in the internal market (Directive on electronic commerce).[1]

Notes
[1] OJ L 178, 17.7.2000, p.1.

(10) The definition of "information society service" in Article 1 of Directive 98/34/EC of the European Parliament and of the Council of 22 June 1998 laying down a procedure for the provision of information in the field of technical standards and regulations and of rules of information society services[1] spans a wide range of economic activities which take place on-line. Most of these activities are not covered by the scope of this Directive because they do not consist wholly or mainly in the conveyance of signals on electronic communications networks. Voice telephony and electronic mail conveyance services are covered by this Directive. The same undertaking, for example an Internet service provider, can offer both an electronic communications service, such as access to the Internet, and services not covered under this Directive, such as the provision of web-based content.

Notes
[1] OJ L 204, 21.7.1998, p.37. Directive as amended by Directive 98/48/EC (OJ L 217, 5.8.1998, p.18).

Commentary
Recital 10: B&C: 12.011

(11) In accordance with the principle of the separation of regulatory and operational functions, Member States should guarantee the independence of the national regulatory authority or authorities with a view to ensuring the impartiality of their decisions. This requirement of independence is without prejudice to the institutional autonomy and constitutional obligations of the Member States or to the principle of neutrality with regard to the rules in Member States governing the system of property ownership laid down in Article [345] of the Treaty. National regulatory authorities should be in possession of all the necessary resources, in terms of staffing, expertise, and financial means, for the performance of their tasks.

Commentary
Recital 11: B&C: 12.008

(12) Any party who is the subject of a decision by a national regulatory authority should have the right to appeal to a body that is independent of the parties involved. This body may be a court. Furthermore, any undertaking which considers that its applications for the granting of rights to install facilities have not been dealt with in accordance with the principles set out in this Directive should be entitled to appeal against such decisions. This appeal procedure is without prejudice to the division of competences within national judicial systems and to the rights of legal entities or natural persons under national law.

(13) National regulatory authorities need to gather information from market players in order to carry out their tasks effectively. Such information may also need to be gathered on behalf of the Commission, to allow it to fulfil its obligations under Community law. Requests for information should be proportionate and not impose an undue burden on undertakings. Information gathered by national regulatory authorities should be publicly available, except in so far as it is confidential in accordance with national rules on public access to information and subject to Community and national law on business confidentiality.

(14) Information that is considered confidential by a national regulatory authority, in accordance with Community and national rules on business confidentiality, may only be exchanged with the Commission and other national regulatory authorities where such exchange is strictly necessary for the application of the provisions of this Directive or the Specific Directives. The information exchanged should be limited to that which is relevant and proportionate to the purpose of such an exchange.

(15) It is important that national regulatory authorities consult all interested parties on proposed decisions and take account of their comments before adopting a final decision. In order to ensure that decisions at national level do not have an adverse effect on the single market or other Treaty objectives, national regulatory authorities should also notify certain draft decisions to the Commission and other national regulatory authorities to give them the opportunity to comment. It is appropriate for national regulatory authorities to consult interested parties on all draft measures which have an effect on trade between Member States. The cases where the procedures referred to in Articles 6 and 7 apply are defined in this Directive and in the Specific Directives. The Commission should be able, after consulting the Communications Committee, to require a national regulatory authority to withdraw a draft measure where it concerns definition of relevant markets or the designation or not of undertakings with significant market power, and where such decisions would create a barrier to the single market or would be incompatible with Community law and in particular the policy objectives that national regulatory authorities should follow. This procedure is without prejudice to the notification procedure provided for in Directive 98/34/EC and the Commission's prerogatives under the Treaty in respect of infringements of Community law.

(16) National regulatory authorities should have a harmonised set of objectives and principles to underpin, and should, where necessary, coordinate their actions with the regulatory authorities of other Member States in carrying out their tasks under this regulatory framework.

Commentary
Recital 16: B&C: 12.008

---

(17) The activities of national regulatory authorities established under this Directive and the Specific Directives contribute to the fulfilment of broader policies in the areas of culture, employment, the environment, social cohesion and town and country planning.

(18) The requirement for Member States to ensure that national regulatory authorities take the utmost account of the desirability of making regulation technologically neutral, that is to say that it neither imposes nor discriminates in favour of the use of a particular type of technology, does not preclude the taking of proportionate steps to promote certain specific services where this is justified, for example digital television as a means for increasing spectrum efficiency.

Commentary
Recital 18: B&C: 12.010

---

(19) Radio frequencies are an essential input for radio-based electronic communications services and, in so far as they relate to such services, should therefore be allocated and assigned by national

regulatory authorities according to a set of harmonised objectives and principles governing their action as well as to objective, transparent and non-discriminatory criteria, taking into account the democratic, social, linguistic and cultural interests related to the use of frequency. It is important that the allocation and assignment of radio frequencies is managed as efficiently as possible. Transfer of radio frequencies can be an effective means of increasing efficient use of spectrum, as long as there are sufficient safeguards in place to protect the public interest, in particular the need to ensure transparency and regulatory supervision of such transfers. Decision No 676/2002/EC of the European Parliament and of the Council of 7 March 2002 on a regulatory framework for radio spectrum policy in the European Community (Radio Spectrum Decision)[1] establishes a framework for harmonisation of radio frequencies, and action taken under this Directive should seek to facilitate the work under that Decision.

Notes
[1] See [OJ L 108, 24.4.2002, p.1].

(20) Access to numbering resources on the basis of transparent, objective and non-discriminatory criteria is essential for undertakings to compete in the electronic communications sector. All elements of national numbering plans should be managed by national regulatory authorities, including point codes used in network addressing. Where there is a need for harmonisation of numbering resources in the Community to support the development of pan-European services, the Commission may take technical implementing measures using its executive powers. Where this is appropriate to ensure full global interoperability of services, Member States should coordinate their national positions in accordance with the Treaty in international organisations and fora where numbering decisions are taken. The provisions of this Directive do not establish any new areas of responsibility for the national regulatory authorities in the field of Internet naming and addressing.

(21) Member States may use, *inter alia*, competitive or comparative selection procedures for the assignment of radio frequencies as well as numbers with exceptional economic value. In administering such schemes, national regulatory authorities should take into account the provisions of Article 8.

(22) It should be ensured that procedures exist for the granting of rights to install facilities that are timely, non-discriminatory and transparent, in order to guarantee the conditions for fair and effective competition. This Directive is without prejudice to national provisions governing the expropriation or use of property, the normal exercise of property rights, the normal use of the public domain, or to the principle of neutrality with regard to the rules in Member States governing the system of property ownership.

(23) Facility sharing can be of benefit for town planning, public health or environmental reasons, and should be encouraged by national regulatory authorities on the basis of voluntary agreements. In cases where undertakings are deprived of access to viable alternatives, compulsory facility or property sharing may be appropriate. It covers *inter alia*: physical co-location and duct, building, mast, antenna or antenna system sharing. Compulsory facility or property sharing should be imposed on undertakings only after full public consultation.

(24) Where mobile operators are required to share towers or masts for environmental reasons, such mandated sharing may lead to a reduction in the maximum transmitted power levels allowed for each operator for reasons of public health, and this in turn may require operators to install more transmission sites to ensure national coverage.

(25) There is a need for *ex ante* obligations in certain circumstances in order to ensure the development of a competitive market. The definition of significant market power in the Directive 97/33/EC of the European Parliament and of the Council of 30 June 1997 on interconnection in telecommunications with regard to ensuring universal service and interoperability through application of the principles of open network provision (ONP)[1] has proved effective in the initial stages of market opening as the threshold for *ex ante* obligations, but now needs to be adapted to suit more complex and dynamic markets. For this reason, the definition used in this Directive is equivalent to the concept of dominance as defined in the case law of the Court of Justice and the Court of First Instance of the European Communities.

Notes
1 OJ L 199, 26.7.1997, p.32. Directive as amended by Directive 98/61/EC (OJ L 268, 3.10.1998, p.37).

Commentary
Recital 25: B&C: 12.015

(26) Two or more undertakings can be found to enjoy a joint dominant position not only where there exist structural or other links between them but also where the structure of the relevant market is conducive to coordinated effects, that is, it encourages parallel or aligned anti-competitive behaviour on the market.

(27) It is essential that *ex ante* regulatory obligations should only be imposed where there is not effective competition, i.e. in markets where there are one or more undertakings with significant market power, and where national and Community competition law remedies are not sufficient to address the problem. It is necessary therefore for the Commission to draw up guidelines at Community level in accordance with the principles of competition law for national regulatory authorities to follow in assessing whether competition is effective in a given market and in assessing significant market power. National regulatory authorities should analyse whether a given product or service market is effectively competitive in a given geographical area, which could be the whole or a part of the territory of the Member State concerned or neighbouring parts of territories of Member States considered together. An analysis of effective competition should include an analysis as to whether the market is prospectively competitive, and thus whether any lack of effective competition is durable. Those guidelines will also address the issue of newly emerging markets, where *de facto* the market leader is likely to have a substantial market share but should not be subjected to inappropriate obligations. The Commission should review the guidelines regularly to ensure that they remain appropriate in a rapidly developing market. National regulatory authorities will need to cooperate with each other where the relevant market is found to be transnational.

Commentary
Recital 27: B&C: 12.016 F&N: 13.26

(28) In determining whether an undertaking has significant market power in a specific market, national regulatory authorities should act in accordance with Community law and take into the utmost account the Commission guidelines.

(29) The Community and the Member States have entered into commitments in relation to standards and the regulatory framework of telecommunications networks and services in the World Trade Organisation.

(30) Standardisation should remain primarily a market-driven process. However there may still be situations where it is appropriate to require compliance with specified standards at Community level to ensure interoperability in the single market. At national level, Member States are subject to the provisions of Directive 98/34/EC. Directive 95/47/EC of the European Parliament and of the Council of 24 October 1995 on the use of standards for the transmission of television signals[1] did not mandate any specific digital television transmission system or service requirement. Through the Digital Video Broadcasting Group, European market players have developed a family of television transmission systems that have been standardised by the European Telecommunications Standards Institute (ETSI) and have become International Telecommunication Union recommendations. Any decision to make the implementation of such standards mandatory should follow a full public consultation. Standardisation procedures under this Directive are without prejudice to the provisions of Directive 1999/5/EC, Council Directive 73/23/EEC of 19 February 1973 on the harmonisation of the laws of Member States relating to electrical equipment designed for use within certain voltage limits[2] and Council Directive 89/336/EEC of 3 May 1989 on the approximation of the laws of the Member States relating to electromagnetic compatibility.[3]

Notes
1 OJ L 281, 23.11.1995, p.51.
2 OJ L 77, 26.3.1973, p.29.
3 OJ L 139, 23.5.1989, p.19.

(31) Interoperability of digital interactive television services and enhanced digital television equipment, at the level of the consumer, should be encouraged in order to ensure the free flow of information, media pluralism and cultural diversity. It is desirable for consumers to have the capability of receiving, regardless of the transmission mode, all digital interactive television services, having regard to technological neutrality, future technological progress, the need to promote the take-up of digital television, and the state of competition in the markets for digital television services. Digital interactive television platform operators should strive to implement an open application program interface (API) which conforms to standards or specifications adopted by a European standards organisation. Migration from existing APIs to new open APIs should be encouraged and organised, for example by Memoranda of Understanding between all relevant market players. Open APIs facilitate interoperability, i.e. the portability of interactive content between delivery mechanisms, and full functionality of this content on enhanced digital television equipment. However, the need not to hinder the functioning of the receiving equipment and to protect it from malicious attacks, for example from viruses, should be taken into account.

(32) In the event of a dispute between undertakings in the same Member State in an area covered by this Directive or the Specific Directives, for example relating to obligations for access and interconnection or to the means of transferring subscriber lists, an aggrieved party that has negotiated in good faith but failed to reach agreement should be able to call on the national regulatory authority to resolve the dispute. National regulatory authorities should be able to impose a solution on the parties. The intervention of a national regulatory authority in the resolution of a dispute between undertakings providing electronic communications networks or services in a Member State should seek to ensure compliance with the obligations arising under this Directive or the Specific Directives.

(33) In addition to the rights of recourse granted under national or Community law, there is a need for a simple procedure to be initiated at the request of either party in a dispute, to resolve cross-border disputes which lie outside the competence of a single national regulatory authority.

(34) A single Committee should replace the "ONP Committee" instituted by Article 9 of Directive 90/387/EEC and the Licensing Committee instituted by Article 14 of Directive 97/13/EC of the European Parliament and of the Council of 10 April 1997 on a common framework for general authorisations and individual licences in the field of telecommunications services.[1]

Notes

[1] OJ L 117, 7.5.1997, p.15.

---

(35) National regulatory authorities and national competition authorities should provide each other with the information necessary to apply the provisions of this Directive and the Specific Directives, in order to allow them to cooperate fully together. In respect of the information exchanged, the receiving authority should ensure the same level of confidentiality as the originating authority.

(36) The Commission has indicated its intention to set up a European regulators group for electronic communications networks and services which would constitute a suitable mechanism for encouraging cooperation and coordination of national regulatory authorities, in order to promote the development of the internal market for electronic communications networks and services, and to seek to achieve consistent application, in all Member States, of the provisions set out in this Directive and the Specific Directives, in particular in areas where national law implementing Community law gives national regulatory authorities considerable discretionary powers in application of the relevant rules.

(37) National regulatory authorities should be required to cooperate with each other and with the Commission in a transparent manner to ensure consistent application, in all Member States, of the provisions of this Directive and the Specific Directives. This cooperation could take place, *inter alia*, in the Communications Committee or in a group comprising European regulators. Member States should decide which bodies are national regulatory authorities for the purposes of this Directive and the Specific Directives.

(38) Measures that could affect trade between Member States are measures that may have an influence, direct or indirect, actual or potential, on the pattern of trade between Member States in a manner

which might create a barrier to the single market. They comprise measures that have a significant impact on operators or users in other Member States, which include, *inter alia*: measures which affect prices for users in other Member States; measures which affect the ability of an undertaking established in another Member State to provide an electronic communications service, and in particular measures which affect the ability to offer services on a transnational basis; and measures which affect market structure or access, leading to repercussions for undertakings in other Member States.

(39) The provisions of this Directive should be reviewed periodically, in particular with a view to determining the need for modification in the light of changing technological or market conditions.

(40) The measures necessary for the implementation of this Directive should be adopted in accordance with Council Decision 1999/468/EC of 28 June 1999 laying down the procedures for the exercise of implementing powers conferred on the Commission.[1]

Notes

[1] OJ L 184, 17.7.1999, p.23.

(41) Since the objectives of the proposed action, namely achieving a harmonised framework for the regulation of electronic communications services, electronic communications networks, associated facilities and associated services cannot be sufficiently achieved by the Member States and can therefore, by reason of the scale and effects of the action, be better achieved at Community level, the Community may adopt measures in accordance with the principle of subsidiarity as set out in Article 5 of the [Treaty on European Union]. In accordance with the principle of proportionality, as set out in that Article, this Directive does not go beyond what is necessary for those objectives.

(42) Certain directives and decisions in this field should be repealed.

(43) The Commission should monitor the transition from the existing framework to the new framework, and may in particular, at an appropriate time, bring forward a proposal to repeal Regulation (EC) No 2887/2000 of the European Parliament and of the Council of 18 December 2000 on unbundled access to the local loop.[1]

Notes

[1] OJ L 336, 30.12.2000, p.4.

HAVE ADOPTED THIS DIRECTIVE:

CHAPTER I
SCOPE, AIM AND DEFINITIONS

Article 1

Scope and aim

[1. This Directive establishes a harmonised framework for the regulation of electronic communications services, electronic communications networks, associated facilities and associated services, and certain aspects of terminal equipment to facilitate access for disabled users. It lays down tasks of national regulatory authorities and establishes a set of procedures to ensure the harmonised application of the regulatory framework throughout the Community.]

2. This Directive as well as the Specific Directives are without prejudice to obligations imposed by national law in accordance with Community law or by Community law in respect of services provided using electronic communications networks and services.

3. This Directive as well as the Specific Directives are without prejudice to measures taken at Community or national level, in compliance with Community law, to pursue general interest objectives, in particular relating to content regulation and audio-visual policy.

[3a. Measures taken by Member States regarding end-users' access to, or use of, services and applications through electronic communications networks shall respect the fundamental rights and freedoms of natural persons, as guaranteed by the European Convention for the Protection of Human Rights and Fundamental Freedoms and general principles of Community law.

Any of these measures regarding end-users' access to, or use of, services and applications through electronic communications networks liable to restrict those fundamental rights or freedoms may only be imposed if they are appropriate, proportionate and necessary within a democratic society, and their implementation shall be subject to adequate procedural safeguards in conformity with the European Convention for the Protection of Human Rights and Fundamental Freedoms and with general principles of Community law, including effective judicial protection and due process. Accordingly, these measures may only be taken with due respect for the principle of the presumption of innocence and the right to privacy. A prior, fair and impartial procedure shall be guaranteed, including the right to be heard of the person or persons concerned, subject to the need for appropriate conditions and procedural arrangements in duly substantiated cases of urgency in conformity with the European Convention for the Protection of Human Rights and Fundamental Freedoms. The right to effective and timely judicial review shall be guaranteed.]

4. This Directive and the Specific Directives are without prejudice to the provisions of Directive 1999/5/EC.

[5. This Directive and the Specific Directive shall be without prejudice to any specific measure adapted for the regulation of international roaming on public mobile telephone networks within the Community.]

Notes

Article 1(5) was inserted as shown in square brackets by Regulation (EC) 717/2007 (OJ L 171 29.6.2007) with effect from 30 June 2007.

Article 1(1) was amended and Article 1(3a) was inserted as shown in square brackets by Directive 2009/140/EC (OJ L 337, 18.12.2009), p.37, with effect from 19 December 2009.

Commentary

Art 1: **B&C:** 12.012 **F&N:** 13.20
Art 1(2): **B&C:** 12.007
Art 1(3): **B&C:** 12.007
Art 1(4): **B&C:** 12.007

Article 2
Definitions

For the purposes of this Directive:

[(a) "electronic communications network" means transmission systems and, where applicable, switching or routing equipment and other resources, including network elements which are not active, which permit the conveyance of signals by wire, radio, optical or other electromagnetic means, including satellite networks, fixed (circuit- and packet-switched, including Internet) and mobile terrestrial networks, electricity cable systems, to the extent that they are used for the purpose of transmitting signals, networks used for radio and television broadcasting, and cable television networks, irrespective of the type of information conveyed;

(b) "transnational markets" means markets identified in accordance with Article 15(4) covering the Community or a substantial part thereof located in more than one Member State;]

(c) "electronic communications service" means a service normally provided for remuneration which consists wholly or mainly in the conveyance of signals on electronic communications networks, including telecommunications services and transmission services in networks used for broadcasting, but exclude services providing, or exercising editorial control over, content transmitted using electronic communications networks and services; it does not include information society services, as defined in Article 1 of Directive 98/34/EC, which do not consist wholly or mainly in the conveyance of signals on electronic communications networks;

[(d) "public communications network" means an electronic communications network used wholly or mainly for the provision of electronic communications services available to the public which support the transfer of information between network termination points;

(da) "network termination point (NTP)" means the physical point at which a subscriber is provided with access to a public communications network; in the case of networks involving switching or routing, the NTP is identified by means of a specific network address, which may be linked to a subscriber number or name;

(e) "associated facilities" means those associated services, physical infrastructures and other facilities or elements associated with an electronic communications network and/or an electronic communications service which enable and/or support the provision of services via that network and/or service or have the potential to do so, and include, inter alia, buildings or entries to buildings, building wiring, antennae, towers and other supporting constructions, ducts, conduits, masts, manholes, and cabinets;

(ea) "associated services" means those services associated with an electronic communications network and/or an electronic communications service which enable and/or support the provision of services via that network and/or service or have the potential to do so and include, inter alia, number translation or systems offering equivalent functionality, conditional access systems and electronic programme guides, as well as other services such as identity, location and presence service;]

(f) "conditional access system" means any technical measure and/or arrangement whereby access to a protected radio or television broadcasting service in intelligible form is made conditional upon subscription or other form of prior individual authorisation;

(g) "national regulatory authority" means the body or bodies charged by a Member State with any of the regulatory tasks assigned in this Directive and the Specific Directives;

(h) "user" means a legal entity or natural person using or requesting a publicly available electronic communications service;

(i) "consumer" means any natural person who uses or requests a publicly available electronic communications service for purposes which are outside his or her trade, business or profession;

(j) "universal service" means the minimum set of services, defined in Directive 2002/22/EC (Universal Service Directive), of specified quality which is available to all users regardless of their geographical location and, in the light of specific national conditions, at an affordable price;

(k) "subscriber" means any natural person or legal entity who or which is party to a contract with the provider of publicly available electronic communications services for the supply of such services;

[(l) "Specific Directives" means Directive 2002/20/EC (Authorisation Directive), Directive 2002/19/EC (Access Directive), Directive 2002/22/EC (Universal Service Directive) and Directive 2002/58/EC of the European Parliament and of the Council of 12 July 2002 concerning the processing of personal data and the protection of privacy in the electronic communications sector (Directive on privacy and electronic communications);[1]]

(m) "provision of an electronic communications network" means the establishment, operation, control or making available of such a network;

(n) "end-user" means a user not providing public communications networks or publicly available electronic communications services.

(o) "enhanced digital television equipment" means set-top boxes intended for connection to television sets or integrated digital television sets, able to receive digital interactive television services;

(p) "application program interface (API)" means the software interfaces between applications, made available by broadcasters or service providers, and the resources in the enhanced digital television equipment for digital television and radio services.

[(q) "spectrum allocation" means the designation of a given frequency band for use by one or more types of radio communications services, where appropriate, under specified conditions;

(r) "harmful interference" means interference which endangers the functioning of a radio navigation service or of other safety services or which otherwise seriously degrades, obstructs or repeatedly interrupts a radio communications service operating in accordance with the applicable international, Community or national regulations;

(s) "call" means a connection established by means of a publicly available electronic communications service allowing two-way voice communication.]

Notes

1 OJ L 2001, 31.7.2002, p.37]
Article 2 was amended as shown in square brackets by Directive 2009/140/EC (OJ L 337, 18.12.2009), p.37, with effect from 19 December 2009.

Commentary
Art 2: B&C: 12.010

CHAPTER II
NATIONAL REGULATORY AUTHORITIES

Article 3
National regulatory authorities

1. Member States shall ensure that each of the tasks assigned to national regulatory authorities in this Directive and the Specific Directives is undertaken by a competent body.

2. Member States shall guarantee the independence of national regulatory authorities by ensuring that they are legally distinct from and functionally independent of all organisations providing electronic communications networks, equipment or services. Member States that retain ownership or control of undertakings providing electronic communications networks and/or services shall ensure effective structural separation of the regulatory function from activities associated with ownership or control.

[3. Member States shall ensure that national regulatory authorities exercise their powers impartially, transparently and in a timely manner. Member States shall ensure that national regulatory authorities have adequate financial and human resources to carry out the task assigned to them.

3a. Without prejudice to the provisions of paragraphs 4 and 5, national regulatory authorities responsible for ex-ante market regulation or for the resolution of disputes between undertakings in accordance with Article 20 or 21 of this Directive shall act independently and shall not seek or take instructions from any other body in relation to the exercise of these tasks assigned to them under national law implementing Community law. This shall not prevent supervision in accordance with national constitutional law. Only appeal bodies set up in accordance with Article 4 shall have the power to suspend or overturn decisions by the national regulatory authorities. Member States shall ensure that the head of a national regulatory authority, or where applicable, members of the collegiate body fulfilling that function within a national regulatory authority referred to in the first subparagraph or their replacements may be dismissed only if they no longer fulfil the conditions required for the performance of their duties which are laid down in advance in national law. The decision to dismiss the head of the national regulatory authority concerned, or where applicable members of the collegiate body fulfilling that function shall be made public at the time of dismissal. The dismissed head of the national regulatory authority, or where applicable, members of the collegiate body fulfilling that function shall receive a statement of reasons and shall have the right to request its publication, where this would not otherwise take place, in which case it shall be published.

Member States shall ensure that national regulatory authorities referred to in the first subparagraph have separate annual budgets. The budgets shall be made public. Member States shall also ensure that national regulatory authorities have adequate financial and human resources to enable them to actively participate in and contribute to the Body of European Regulators for Electronic Communications (BEREC).1

3b. Member States shall ensure that the goals of BEREC of promoting greater regulatory coordination and coherence are actively supported by the respective national regulatory authorities.

3c. Member States shall ensure that national regulatory authorities take utmost account of opinions and common positions adopted by BEREC when adopting their own decisions for their national markets.]

4. Member States shall publish the tasks to be undertaken by national regulatory authorities in an easily accessible form, in particular where those tasks are assigned to more than one body. Member

States shall ensure, where appropriate, consultation and cooperation between those authorities, and between those authorities and national authorities entrusted with the implementation of competition law and national authorities entrusted with the implementation of consumer law, on matters of common interest. Where more than one authority has competence to address such matters, Member States shall ensure that the respective tasks of each authority are published in an easily accessible form.

5. National regulatory authorities and national competition authorities shall provide each other with the information necessary for the application of the provisions of this Directive and the Specific Directives. In respect of the information exchanged, the receiving authority shall ensure the same level of confidentiality as the originating authority.

6. Member States shall notify to the Commission all national regulatory authorities assigned tasks under this Directive and the Specific Directives, and their respective responsibilities.

Notes

[1] Regulation (EC) No 1211/2009 of the European Parliament and of the Council of 25 November 2009 establishing the Body of European Regulators for Electronic Communications (BEREC) and the Office.]
Article 3(3) was amended and Articles 3a, 3b and 3c were inserted as shown in square brackets by Directive 2009/140/EC (OJ L 337, 18.12.2009), p.37, with effect from 19 December 2009.

Commentary
Art 3: B&C: 12.008
Art 3(3): B&C: 12.009
Art 3(3a): B&C: 12.006, 12.009

Article 4
Right of appeal

[1. Member States shall ensure that effective mechanisms exist at national level under which any user or undertaking providing electronic communications networks and/or services who is affected by a decision of a national regulatory authority has the right of appeal against the decision to an appeal body that is independent of the parties involved. This body, which may be a court, shall have the appropriate expertise to enable it to carry out its functions effectively. Member States shall ensure that the merits of the case are duly taken into account and that there is an effective appeal mechanism.

Pending the outcome of the appeal, the decision of the national regulatory authority shall stand, unless interim measures are granted in accordance with national law.]

2. Where the appeal body referred to in paragraph 1 is not judicial in character, written reasons for its decision shall always be given. Furthermore, in such a case, its decision shall be subject to review by a court or tribunal within the meaning of Article [267] of the Treaty.

[3. Member States shall collect information on the general subject matter of appeals, the number of requests for appeal, the duration of the appeal proceedings and the number of decisions to grant interim measures. Member States shall provide such information to the Commission and BEREC after a reasoned request from either.]

Notes

Article 4(1) was amended and Article 4(3) was inserted by Directive 2009/140/EC (OJ L 337, 18.12.2009), p.37, with effect from 19 December 2009.

Commentary
Art 4: B&C: 12.008, 12.009

Article 5
Provision of information

[1. Member States shall ensure that undertakings providing electronic communications networks and services provide all the information, including financial information, necessary for national regulatory authorities to ensure conformity with the provisions of, or decisions made in accordance with, this Directive and the Specific Directives. In particular, national regulatory authorities shall have the power to require those undertakings to submit information concerning future network or service developments that could have an impact on the wholesale services that they make available to competitors. Undertakings with significant market power on wholesale markets may also be required to submit accounting data on the retail markets that are associated with those wholesale markets.

Undertakings shall provide such information promptly upon request and in conformity with the timescales and level of detail required by the national regulatory authority. The information requested by the national regulatory authority shall be proportionate to the performance of that task. The national regulatory authority shall give the reasons justifying its request for information and shall treat the information in accordance with paragraph 3.]

2. Member States shall ensure that national regulatory authorities provide the Commission, after a reasoned request, with the information necessary for it to carry out its tasks under the Treaty. The information requested by the Commission shall be proportionate to the performance of those tasks. Where the information provided refers to information previously provided by undertakings at the request of the national regulatory authority, such undertakings shall be informed thereof. To the extent necessary, and unless the authority that provides the information has made an explicit and reasoned request to the contrary, the Commission shall make the information provided available to another such authority in another Member State.

Subject to the requirements of paragraph 3, Member States shall ensure that the information submitted to one national regulatory authority can be made available to another such authority in the same or different Member State, after a substantiated request, where necessary to allow either authority to fulfil its responsibilities under Community law.

3. Where information is considered confidential by a national regulatory authority in accordance with Community and national rules on business confidentiality, the Commission and the national regulatory authorities concerned shall ensure such confidentiality.

4. Member States shall ensure that, acting in accordance with national rules on public access to information and subject to Community and national rules on business confidentiality, national regulatory authorities publish such information as would contribute to an open and competitive market.

5. National regulatory authorities shall publish the terms of public access to information as referred to in paragraph 4, including procedures for obtaining such access.

Notes

Article 5(1) was replaced as shown in square brackets by Directive 2009/140/EC (OJ L 337, 18.12.2009), p.37, with effect from 19 December 2009.

Commentary
Art 5: B&C: 12.008
Art 5(3): B&C: 12.009

[*Article 6*
Consultation and transparency mechanism

Except in cases falling within Articles 7(9), 20, or 21, Member States shall ensure that, where national regulatory authorities intend to take measures in accordance with this Directive or the Specific Directives, or where they intend to provide for restrictions in accordance with Article 9(3) and 9(4), which have a significant impact on the relevant market, they give interested parties the opportunity to comment on the draft measure within a reasonable period.

National regulatory authorities shall publish their national consultation procedures.

Member States shall ensure the establishment of a single information point through which all current consultations can be accessed.

The results of the consultation procedure shall be made publicly available by the national regulatory authority, except in the case of confidential information in accordance with Community and national law on business confidentiality.]

Notes

Article 6 was replaced as shown in square brackets by Directive 2009/140/EC (OJ L 337, 18.12.2009), p.37, with effect from 19 December 2009.

Commentary

Art 6: B&C: 12.009, 12.020, 12.026

[*Article 7*

Consolidating the internal market for electronic communications

1. In carrying out their tasks under this Directive and the Specific Directives, national regulatory authorities shall take the utmost account of the objectives set out in Article 8, including in so far as they relate to the functioning of the internal market.

2. National regulatory authorities shall contribute to the development of the internal market by working with each other and with the Commission and BEREC in a transparent manner so as to ensure the consistent application, in all Member States, of the provisions of this Directive and the Specific Directives. To this end, they shall, in particular, work with the Commission and BEREC to identify the types of instruments and remedies best suited to address particular types of situations in the marketplace.

3. Except where otherwise provided in recommendations or guidelines adopted pursuant to Article 7b upon completion of the consultation referred to in Article 6, where a national regulatory authority intends to take a measure which:

(a) falls within the scope of Articles 15 or 16 of this Directive, or Articles 5 or 8 of Directive 2002/19/ EC (Access Directive); and

(b) would affect trade between Member States;

it shall make the draft measure accessible to the Commission, BEREC, and the national regulatory authorities in other Member States, at the same time, together with the reasoning on which the measure is based, in accordance with Article 5(3), and inform the Commission, BEREC and other national regulatory authorities thereof. National regulatory authorities, BEREC and the Commission may make comments to the national regulatory authority concerned only within one month. The one-month period may not be extended.

4. Where an intended measure covered by paragraph 3 aims at:

(a) defining a relevant market which differs from those defined in the Recommendation in accordance with Article 15(1); or

(b) deciding whether or not to designate an undertaking as having, either individually or jointly with others, significant market power, under Article 16(3), (4) or (5);

and would affect trade between Member States, and the Commission has indicated to the national regulatory authority that it considers that the draft measure would create a barrier to the single market or if it has serious doubts as to its compatibility with Community law and in particular the objectives referred to in Article 8, the draft measure shall not be adopted for a further two months. This period may not be extended. The Commission shall inform other national regulatory authorities of its reservations in such a case.

5. Within the two-month period referred to in paragraph 4, the Commission may:

(a) take a decision requiring the national regulatory authority concerned to withdraw the draft measure; and/or

(b) take a decision to lift its reservations in relation to a draft measure referred to in paragraph 4.

The Commission shall take utmost account of the opinion of BEREC before issuing a decision. The decision shall be accompanied by a detailed and objective analysis of why the Commission considers that the draft measure should not be adopted, together with specific proposals for amending the draft measure.

6. Where the Commission has adopted a decision in accordance with paragraph 5, requiring the national regulatory authority to withdraw a draft measure, the national regulatory authority shall

amend or withdraw the draft measure within six months of the date of the Commission's decision. When the draft measure is amended, the national regulatory authority shall undertake a public consultation in accordance with the procedures referred to in Article 6, and shall re-notify the amended draft measure to the Commission in accordance with the provisions of paragraph 3.

7. The national regulatory authority concerned shall take the utmost account of comments of other national regulatory authorities, BEREC and the Commission and may, except in cases covered by paragraphs 4 and 5(a), adopt the resulting draft measure and, where it does so, shall communicate it to the Commission.

8. The national regulatory authority shall communicate to the Commission and BEREC all adopted final measures which fall under Article 7(3)(a) and (b).

9. In exceptional circumstances, where a national regulatory authority considers that there is an urgent need to act, in order to safeguard competition and protect the interests of users, by way of derogation from the procedure set out in paragraphs 3 and 4, it may immediately adopt proportionate and provisional measures. It shall, without delay, communicate those measures, with full reasons, to the Commission, the other national regulatory authority, and BEREC. A decision by the national regulatory authority to render such measures permanent or extend the time for which they are applicable shall be subject to the provisions of paragraphs 3 and 4].

Notes

Article 7 was replaced as shown in square brackets by Directive 2009/140/EC (OJ L 337, 18.12.2009), p.37, with effect from 19 December 2009.

Commentary

Art 7: **B&C:** 12.008, 12.020, 12.026, 12.034, 12.044 **F&N:** 2.67, 13.28, 13.31, 13.32, 13.33, 13.34, 13.35, 13.112

Art 7(3): **B&C:** 12.020

Art 7(4): **B&C:** 12.020

Art 7(4)(a): **F&N:** 13.28

Art 7(5): **B&C:** 12.017

[*Article 7a*

Procedure for the consistent application of remedies

1. Where an intended measure covered by Article 7(3) aims at imposing, amending or withdrawing an obligation on an operator in application of Article 16 in conjunction with Article 5 and Articles 9 to 13 of Directive 2002/19/EC (Access Directive), and Article 17 of Directive 2002/22/EC (Universal Service Directive), the Commission may, within the period of one month provided for by Article 7(3) of this Directive, notify the national regulatory authority concerned and BEREC of its reasons for considering that the draft measure would create a barrier to the single market or its serious doubts as to its compatibility with Community law. In such a case, the draft measure shall not be adopted for a further three months following the Commission's notification.

In the absence of such notification, the national regulatory authority concerned may adopt the draft measure, taking utmost account of any comments made by the Commission, BEREC or any other national regulatory authority.

2. Within the three month period referred to in paragraph 1, the Commission, BEREC and the national regulatory authority concerned shall cooperate closely to identify the most appropriate and effective measure in the light of the objectives laid down in Article 8, whilst taking due account of the views of market participants and the need to ensure the development of consistent regulatory practice.

3. Within six weeks from the beginning of the three month period referred to in paragraph 1, BEREC shall, acting by a majority of its component members, issue an opinion on the Commission's notification referred to in paragraph 1, indicating whether it considers that the draft measure should be amended or withdrawn and, where appropriate, provide specific proposals to that end. This opinion shall be reasoned and made public.

4. If in its opinion, BEREC shares the serious doubts of the Commission, it shall cooperate closely with the national regulatory authority concerned to identify the most appropriate and effective

measure. Before the end of the three month period referred in paragraph 1, the national regulatory authority may:

(a) amend or withdraw its draft measure taking utmost account of the Commission's notification referred to in paragraph 1 and of BEREC's opinion and advice;

(b) maintain its draft measure.

5. Where BEREC does not share the serious doubts of the Commission or does not issue an opinion, or where the national regulatory authority amends or maintains its draft measure pursuant to paragraph 4, the Commission may, within one month following the end of the three month period referred to in paragraph 1 and taking utmost account of the opinion of BEREC if any:

(a) issue a recommendation requiring the national regulatory authority concerned to amend or withdraw the draft measure, including specific proposals to that end and providing reasons justifying its recommendation, in particular where BEREC does not share the serious doubts of the Commission;

(b) take a decision to lift its reservations indicated in accordance with paragraph 1.

6. Within one month of the Commission issuing the recommendation in accordance with paragraph 5(a) or lifting its reservations in accordance with paragraph 5(b), the national regulatory authority concerned shall communicate to the Commission and BEREC the adopted final measure.

This period may be extended to allow the national regulatory authority to undertake a public consultation in accordance with Article 6.

7. Where the national regulatory authority decides not to amend or withdraw the draft measure on the basis of the recommendation issued under paragraph 5(a), it shall provide a reasoned justification.

8. The national regulatory authority may withdraw the proposed draft measure at any stage of the procedure.]

Notes

Article 7a was inserted as shown in square brackets by Directive 2009/140/EC (OJ L 337, 18.12.2009), p.37, with effect from 19 December 2009.

Commentary

Art 7a: **B&C:** 12.006, 12.008, 12.021, 12.026, 12.034
Art 7a(1): **B&C:** 12.021
Art 7a(2): **B&C:** 12.021
Art 7a(3): **B&C:** 12.021
Art 7a(4)–(8): **B&C:** 12.021

[*Article 7b*
Implementing provisions

1. After public consultation and consultation with national regulatory authorities and taking utmost account of the opinion of BEREC, the Commission may adopt recommendations and/or guidelines in relation to Article 7 that define the form, content and level of detail to be given in the notifications required in accordance with Article 7(3), the circumstances in which notifications would not be required, and the calculation of the time limits.

2. The measures referred to in paragraph 1 shall be adopted in accordance with the advisory procedure referred to in Article 22(2).]

Notes

Article 7b was inserted as shown in square brackets by Directive 2009/140/EC (OJ L 337, 18.12.2009), p.37, with effect from 19 December 2009.

Chapter III
Tasks of national regulatory authorities

Article 8
Policy objectives and regulatory principles

1. Member States shall ensure that in carrying out the regulatory tasks specified in this Directive and the Specific Directives, the national regulatory authorities take all reasonable measures which are aimed at achieving the objectives set out in paragraphs 2, 3 and 4. Such measures shall be proportionate to those objectives.

[Unless otherwise provided for in Article 9 regarding radio frequencies, Member States shall take the utmost account of the desirability of making regulations technologically neutral and shall ensure that, in carrying out the regulatory tasks specified in this Directive and the Specific Directives, in particular those designed to ensure effective competition, national regulatory authorities do likewise.]

National regulatory authorities may contribute within their competencies to ensuring the implementation of policies aimed at the promotion of cultural and linguistic diversity, as well as media pluralism.

2. The national regulatory authorities shall promote competition in the provision of electronic communications networks, electronic communications services and associated facilities and services by *inter alia*:

[(a) ensuring that users, including disabled users, elderly users, and users with special social needs derive maximum benefit in terms of choice, price, and quality;
(b) ensuring that there is no distortion or restriction of competition in the electronic communications sector, including the transmission of content;]
[ ]
(d) encouraging efficient use and ensuring the effective management of radio frequencies and numbering resources.

3. The national regulatory authorities shall contribute to the development of the internal market by *inter alia*:

(a) removing remaining obstacles to the provision of electronic communications networks, associated facilities and services and electronic communications services at European level;
(b) encouraging the establishment and development of trans-European networks and the interoperability of pan-European services, and end-to-end connectivity;
[ ]
[(d) cooperating with each other, with the Commission and BEREC so as to ensure the development of consistent regulatory practice and the consistent application of this Directive and the Specific Directives.]

4. The national regulatory authorities shall promote the interests of the citizens of the European Union by *inter alia*:

(a) ensuring all citizens have access to a universal service specified in Directive 2002/22/EC (Universal Service Directive);
(b) ensuring a high level of protection for consumers in their dealings with suppliers, in particular by ensuring the availability of simple and inexpensive dispute resolution procedures carried out by a body that is independent of the parties involved;
(c) contributing to ensuring a high level of protection of personal data and privacy;
(d) promoting the provision of clear information, in particular requiring transparency of tariffs and conditions for using publicly available electronic communications services;
[(e) addressing the needs of specific social groups, in particular disabled users, elderly users and users with special social needs;]
(f) ensuring that the integrity and security of public communications networks are maintained.
[(g) promoting the ability of end-users to access and distribute information or run applications and services of their choice;]

981

5. The national regulatory authorities shall, in pursuit of the policy objectives referred to in paragraphs 2, 3 and 4, apply objective, transparent, non-discriminatory and proportionate regulatory principles by, *inter alia*:

(a) promoting regulatory predictability by ensuring a consistent regulatory approach over appropriate review periods;

(b) ensuring that, in similar circumstances, there is no discrimination in the treatment of undertakings providing electronic communications networks and services;

(c) safeguarding competition to the benefit of consumers and promoting, where appropriate, infrastructure-based competition;

(d) promoting efficient investment and innovation in new and enhanced infrastructures, including by ensuring that any access obligation takes appropriate account of the risk incurred by the investing undertakings and by permitting various cooperative arrangements between investors and parties seeking access to diversify the risk of investment, whilst ensuring that competition in the market and the principle of non-discrimination are preserved;

(e) taking due account of the variety of conditions relating to competition and consumers that exist in the various geographic areas within a Member State;

(f) imposing ex-ante regulatory obligations only where there is no effective and sustainable competition and relaxing or lifting such obligations as soon as that condition is fulfilled.]

Notes

Article 8 was amended as shown in square brackets by Directive 2009/140/EC (OJ L 337, 18.12.2009), p.37, with effect from 19 December 2009.

Commentary

Art 8: B&C: 12.008, 12.009, 12.010, 12.043
Art 8(2): B&C: 12.009
Art 8(2)(d): B&C: 12.035
Art 8(4)(e): B&C: 12.043
Art 8(5)(f): F&N: 13.111

**[*Article 8a*
Strategic planning and coordination of radio spectrum policy**

1. Member States shall cooperate with each other and with the Commission in the strategic planning, coordination and harmonisation of the use of radio spectrum in the European Community. To this end, they shall take into consideration, inter alia, the economic, safety, health, public interest, freedom of expression, cultural, scientific, social and technical aspects of EU policies as well as the various interests of radio spectrum user communities with the aim of optimising the use of radio spectrum and avoiding harmful interference.

2. By cooperating with each other and with the Commission, Member States shall promote the coordination of radio spectrum policy approaches in the European Community and, where appropriate, harmonised conditions with regard to the availability and efficient use of radio spectrum necessary for the establishment and functioning of the internal market in electronic communications.

3. The Commission, taking utmost account of the opinion of the Radio Spectrum Policy Group (RSPG), established by Commission Decision 2002/622/EC of 26 July 2002 establishing a Radio Spectrum Policy Group [], may submit legislative proposals to the European Parliament and the Council for establishing multiannual radio spectrum policy programmes. Such programmes shall set out the policy orientations and objectives for the strategic planning and harmonisation of the use of radio spectrum in accordance with the provisions of this Directive and the Specific Directives.

4. Where necessary to ensure the effective coordination of the interests of the European Community in international organisations competent in radio spectrum matters, the Commission, taking utmost account of the opinion of the RSPG, may propose common policy objectives to the European Parliament and the Council.]

Notes
Article 8a was inserted as shown in square brackets by Directive 2009/140/EC (OJ L 337, 18.12.2009), p.37, with effect from 19 December 2009.

Commentary
Art 8a: B&C: 12.008, 12.035
Art 8a(3): F&N: 13.53

[*Article 9*
Management of radio frequencies for electronic communications services

[1. Taking due account of the fact that radio frequencies are a public good that has an important social, cultural and economic value, Member States shall ensure the effective management of radio frequencies for electronic communication services in their territory in accordance with Articles 8 and 8a. They shall ensure that spectrum allocation used for electronic communications services and issuing general authorisations or individual rights of use of such radio frequencies by competent national authorities are based on objective, transparent, non-discriminatory and proportionate criteria.

In applying this Article, Member States shall respect relevant international agreements, including the ITU Radio Regulations, and may take public policy considerations into account.

2. Member States shall promote the harmonisation of use of radio frequencies across the Community, consistent with the need to ensure effective and efficient use thereof and in pursuit of benefits for the consumer such as economies of scale and interoperability of services. In so doing, they shall act in accordance with Article 8a and with the Decision No 676/2002/EC (Radio Spectrum Decision).

3. Unless otherwise provided in the second subparagraph, Member States shall ensure that all types of technology used for electronic communications services may be used in the radio frequency bands, declared available for electronic communications services in their National Frequency Allocation Plan in accordance with Community law.

Member States may, however, provide for proportionate and non-discriminatory restrictions to the types of radio network or wireless access technology used for electronic communications services where this is necessary to:

(a) avoid harmful interference;
(b) protect public health against electromagnetic fields;
(c) ensure technical quality of service;
(d) ensure maximisation of radio frequency sharing;
(e) safeguard efficient use of spectrum; or
(f) ensure the fulfilment of a general interest objective in accordance with paragraph 4.

4. Unless otherwise provided in the second subparagraph, Member States shall ensure that all types of electronic communications services may be provided in the radio frequency bands, declared available for electronic communications services in their National Frequency Allocation Plan in accordance with Community law. Member States may, however, provide for proportionate and non-discriminatory restrictions to the types of electronic communications services to be provided, including, where necessary, to fulfil a requirement under the ITU Radio Regulations.

Measures that require an electronic communications service to be provided in a specific band available for electronic communications services shall be justified in order to ensure the fulfilment of a general interest objective as defined by Member States in conformity with Community law, such as, and not limited to:

(a) safety of life;
(b) the promotion of social, regional or territorial cohesion;
(c) the avoidance of inefficient use of radio frequencies; or
(d) the promotion of cultural and linguistic diversity and media pluralism, for example by the provision of radio and television broadcasting services.

A measure which prohibits the provision of any other electronic communications service in a specific band may only be provided for where justified by the need to protect safety of life services. Member

States may, exceptionally, also extend such a measure in order to fulfil other general interest objectives as defined by Member States in accordance with Community law.

5. Member States shall regularly review the necessity of the restrictions referred to in paragraphs 3 and 4, and shall make the results of these reviews public.

6. Paragraphs 3 and 4 shall apply to spectrum allocated to be used for electronic communications services, general authorisations issued and individual rights of use of radio frequencies granted after 25 May 2011.

Spectrum allocations, general authorisations and individual rights of use which existed by 25 May 2011 shall be subject to Article 9a.

7. Without prejudice to the provisions of the Specific Directives and taking into account the relevant national circumstances, Member States may lay down rules in order to prevent spectrum hoarding, in particular by setting out strict deadlines for the effective exploitation of the rights of use by the holder of the rights and by applying penalties, including financial penalties or the withdrawal of the rights of use in case of non-compliance with the deadlines. These rules shall be established and applied in a proportionate, non-discriminatory and transparent manner.]

Notes

Article 9 was replaced as shown in square brackets by Directive 2009/140/EC (OJ L 337, 18.12.2009), p.37, with effect from 19 December 2009.

Commentary

Art 9: **B&C:** 12.008
Art 9(1): **B&C:** 12.009, 12.035   **F&N:** 14.149
Art 9(2): **B&C:** 12.035
Art 9(3): **B&C:** 12.007, 12.035
Art 9(4): **B&C:** 12.010, 12.035

[*Article 9a*
Review of restrictions on existing rights

1. For a period of five years starting from 25 May 2011, Member States may allow holders of rights to use radio frequencies which were granted before that date and which will remain valid for a period of not less that five years after that date, to submit an application to the competent national authority for a reassessment of the restrictions on their rights in accordance with Article 9(3) and (4).

Before adopting its decision, the competent national authority shall notify the right holder of its reassessment of the restrictions, indicating the extent of the right after reassessment, and shall allow him a reasonable time limit to withdraw his application.

If the right holder withdraws his application, the right shall remain unchanged until its expiry or until the end of the five-year period, whichever is the earlier date.

2. After the five-year period referred to in paragraph 1, Member States shall take all appropriate measures to ensure that Article 9(3) and (4) apply to all remaining general authorisations or individual rights of use and spectrum allocations used for electronic communications services which existed on 25 May 2011.

3. In applying this Article, Member States shall take appropriate measures to promote fair competition.

4. Measures adopted in applying this Article do not constitute the granting of new rights of use and therefore are not subject to the relevant provisions of Article 5(2) of Directive 2002/20/EC (Authorisation Directive).]

Notes

Article 9a was inserted as shown in square brackets by Directive 2009/140/EC (OJ L 337, 18.12.2009), p.37, with effect from 19 December 2009.

[*Article 9b*
Transfer or lease of individual rights to use radio frequencies

1. Member States shall ensure that undertakings may transfer or lease to other undertakings in accordance with conditions attached to the rights of use of radio frequencies and in accordance with national procedures individual rights to use radio frequencies in the bands for which this is provided in the implementing measures adopted pursuant to paragraph 3.

In other bands, Member States may also make provision for undertakings to transfer or lease individual rights to use radio frequencies to other undertakings in accordance with national procedures.

Conditions attached to individual rights to use radio frequencies shall continue to apply after the transfer or lease, unless otherwise specified by the competent national authority.

Member States may also determine that the provisions of this paragraph shall not apply where the undertaking's individual right to use radio frequencies was initially obtained free of charge.

2. Member States shall ensure that an undertaking's intention to transfer rights to use radio frequencies, as well as the effective transfer thereof is notified in accordance with national procedures to the competent national authority responsible for granting individual rights of use and is made public. Where radio frequency use has been harmonised through the application of the Decision No 676/2002/EC (Radio Spectrum Decision) or other Community measures, any such transfer shall comply with such harmonised use.

3. The Commission may adopt appropriate implementing measures to identify the bands for which rights to use radio frequencies may be transferred or leased between undertakings. These measures shall not cover frequencies which are used for broadcasting.

These technical implementing measures, designed to amend non-essential elements of this Directive by supplementing it, shall be adopted in accordance with the regulatory procedure with scrutiny referred to in Article 22(3).]

Notes

Article 9b was inserted as shown in square brackets by Directive 2009/140/EC (OJ L 337, 18.12.2009), p.37, with effect from 19 December 2009.

Commentary
Art 9a: B&C: 12.008, 12.038
Art 9b: B&C: 12.008, 12.035

Article 10
Numbering, naming and addressing

[1. Member States shall ensure that national regulatory authorities control the granting of rights of use of all national numbering resources and the management of the national numbering plans. Member States shall ensure that adequate numbers and numbering ranges are provided for all publicly available electronic communications services. National regulatory authorities shall establish objective, transparent and non-discriminatory procedures for granting rights of use for national numbering resources.

2. National regulatory authorities shall ensure that national numbering plans and procedures are applied in a manner that gives equal treatment to all providers of publicly available electronic communications services. In particular, Member States shall ensure that an undertaking to which the right of use for a range of numbers has been granted does not discriminate against other providers of electronic communications services as regards the number sequences used to give access to their services.]

3. Member States shall ensure that the national numbering plans, and all subsequent additions or amendments thereto, are published, subject only to limitations imposed on the grounds of national security.

[4. Member States shall support the harmonisation of specific numbers or numbering ranges within the Community where it promotes both the functioning of the internal market and the development of pan-European services. The Commission may take appropriate technical implementing measures on this matter.

These measures designed to amend non-essential elements of this Directive by supplementing it, shall be adopted in accordance with the regulatory procedure with scrutiny referred to in Article 22(3).]

5. Where this is appropriate in order to ensure full global interoperability of services, Member States shall coordinate their positions in international organisations and forums in which decisions are taken on issues relating to the numbering, naming and addressing of electronic communications networks and services.

Notes

Article 10 was amended as shown in square brackets by Directive 2009/140/EC (OJ L 337, 18.12.2009), p.37, with effect from 19 December 2009.

Commentary
Art 10: B&C: 12.008
Art 10(1): B&C: 12.009

Article 11
Rights of way

1. Member States shall ensure that when a competent authority considers:
    — an application for the granting of rights to install facilities on, over or under public or private property to an undertaking authorised to provide public communications networks, or
    — an application for the granting of rights to install facilities on, over or under public property to an undertaking authorised to provide electronic communications networks other than to the public,

    the competent authority:

    [— acts on the basis of simple, efficient, transparent and publicly available procedures, applied without discrimination and without delay, and in any event makes its decision within six months of the application, except in cases of expropriation, and]
    — follows the principles of transparency and non-discrimination in attaching conditions to any such rights.

The abovementioned procedures can differ depending on whether the applicant is providing public communications networks or not.

[2. Member States shall ensure that where public or local authorities retain ownership or control of undertakings operating public electronic communications networks and/or publicly available electronic communications services, there is an effective structural separation of the function responsible for granting the rights referred to in paragraph 1 from the activities associated with ownership or control.]

3. Member States shall ensure that effective mechanisms exist to allow undertakings to appeal against decisions on the granting of rights to install facilities to a body that is independent of the parties involved.

Notes

Article 11 was amended as shown in square brackets by Directive 2009/140/EC (OJ L 337, 18.12.2009), p.37, with effect from 19 December 2009.

Commentary
Art 11: B&C: 12.008

[*Article 12*
Co-location and sharing of network elements and associated facilities for providers of electronic communications networks

1. Where an undertaking providing electronic communications networks has the right under national legislation to install facilities on, over or under public or private property, or may take advantage of

a procedure for the expropriation or use of property, national regulatory authorities shall, taking full account of the principle of proportionality, be able to impose the sharing of such facilities or property, including buildings, entries to buildings, building wiring, masts, antennae, towers and other supporting constructions, ducts, conduits, manholes, cabinets.

2. Member States may require holders of the rights referred to in paragraph 1 to share facilities or property (including physical co-location) or take measures to facilitate the coordination of public works in order to protect the environment, public health, public security or to meet town and country planning objectives and only after an appropriate period of public consultation, during which all interested parties shall be given an opportunity to express their views. Such sharing or coordination arrangements may include rules for apportioning the costs of facility or property sharing.

3. Member States shall ensure that national authorities, after an appropriate period of public consultation during which all interested parties are given the opportunity to state their views, also have the power to impose obligations in relation to the sharing of wiring inside buildings or up to the first concentration or distribution point where this is located outside the building, on the holders of the rights referred to in paragraph 1 and/or on the owner of such wiring, where this is justified on the grounds that duplication of such infrastructure would be economically inefficient or physically impracticable. Such sharing or coordination arrangements may include rules for apportioning the costs of facility or property sharing adjusted for risk where appropriate.

4. Member States shall ensure that competent national authorities may require undertakings to provide the necessary information, if requested by the competent authorities, in order for these authorities, in conjunction with national regulatory authorities, to be able to establish a detailed inventory of the nature, availability and geographical location of the facilities referred to in paragraph 1 and make it available to interested parties.

5. Measures taken by a national regulatory authority in accordance with this Article shall be objective, transparent, non-discriminatory, and proportionate. Where relevant, these measures shall be carried out in coordination with local authorities.]

Notes

Article 12 was replaced as shown in square brackets by Directive 2009/140/EC (OJ L 337, 18.12.2009), p.37, with effect from 19 December 2009.

Commentary
Art 12: **B&C:** 12.013

Article 13
Accounting separation and financial reports

1. Member States shall require undertakings providing public communications networks or publicly available electronic communications services which have special or exclusive rights for the provision of services in other sectors in the same or another Member State to:

(a) keep separate accounts for the activities associated with the provision of electronic communications networks or services, to the extent that would be required if these activities were carried out by legally independent companies, so as to identify all elements of cost and revenue, with the basis of their calculation and the detailed attribution methods used, related to their activities associated with the provision of electronic communications networks or services including an itemised breakdown of fixed asset and structural costs, or

(b) have structural separation for the activities associated with the provision of electronic communications networks or services.

Member States may choose not to apply the requirements referred to in the first subparagraph to undertakings the annual turnover of which in activities associated with electronic communications networks or services in the Member States is less than EUR 50 million.

2. Where undertakings providing public communications networks or publicly available electronic communications services are not subject to the requirements of company law and do not satisfy the small and medium-sized enterprise criteria of Community law accounting rules, their financial reports shall be drawn up and submitted to independent audit and published. The audit shall be carried out in accordance with the relevant Community and national rules.

This requirement shall also apply to the separate accounts required under paragraph 1(a).

Commentary
Art 13: B&C: 12.013

[Chapter IIIA
Security and Integrity of Networks and Services

Article 13a
Security and integrity

1. Member States shall ensure that undertakings providing public communications networks or publicly available electronic communications services take appropriate technical and organisational measures to appropriately manage the risks posed to security of networks and services. Having regard to the state of the art, these measures shall ensure a level of security appropriate to the risk presented. In particular, measures shall be taken to prevent and minimise the impact of security incidents on users and interconnected networks.

2. Member States shall ensure that undertakings providing public communications networks take all appropriate steps to guarantee the integrity of their networks, and thus ensure the continuity of supply of services provided over those networks.

3. Member States shall ensure that undertakings providing public communications networks or publicly available electronic communications services notify the competent national regulatory authority of a breach of security or loss of integrity that has had a significant impact on the operation of networks or services.

Where appropriate, the national regulatory authority concerned shall inform the national regulatory authorities in other Member States and the European Network and Information Security Agency (ENISA). The national regulatory authority concerned may inform the public or require the undertakings to do so, where it determines that disclosure of the breach is in the public interest.

Once a year, the national regulatory authority concerned shall submit a summary report to the Commission and ENISA on the notifications received and the action taken in accordance with this paragraph.

4. The Commission, taking the utmost account of the opinion of ENISA, may adopt appropriate technical implementing measures with a view to harmonising the measures referred to in paragraphs 1, 2, and 3, including measures defining the circumstances, format and procedures applicable to notification requirements. These technical implementing measures shall be based on European and international standards to the greatest extent possible, and shall not prevent Member States from adopting additional requirements in order to pursue the objectives set out in paragraphs 1 and 2.

These implementing measures, designed to amend non-essential elements of this Directive by supplementing it, shall be adopted in accordance with the regulatory procedure with scrutiny referred to in Article 22(3).

Notes

Chapter IIIA (Articles 13a and 13b) was inserted as shown in square brackets by Directive 2009/140/EC (OJ L 337, 18.12.2009), p.37, with effect from 19 December 2009.

Commentary
Art 13a: B&C: 12.006

Article 13b
Implementation and enforcement

1. Member States shall ensure that in order to implement Article 13a, competent national regulatory authorities have the power to issue binding instructions, including those regarding time limits for implementation, to undertakings providing public communications networks or publicly available electronic communications services.

2. Member States shall ensure that competent national regulatory authorities have the power to require undertakings providing public communications networks or publicly available electronic communications services to:

(a) provide information needed to assess the security and/or integrity of their services and networks, including documented security policies; and

(b) submit to a security audit carried out by a qualified independent body or a competent national authority and make the results thereof available to the national regulatory authority. The cost of the audit shall be paid by the undertaking.

3. Member States shall ensure that national regulatory authorities have all the powers necessary to investigate cases of non-compliance and the effects thereof on the security and integrity of the networks.

4. These provisions shall be without prejudice to Article 3 of this Directive.]

Notes

Chapter IIIA (Articles 13a and 13b) was inserted as shown in square brackets by Directive 2009/140/EC (OJ L 337, 18.12.2009), p.37, with effect from 19 December 2009.

Commentary
Art 13b: B&C: 12.006

Chapter IV
General provisions

Article 14
Undertakings with significant market power

1. Where the Specific Directives require national regulatory authorities to determine whether operators have significant market power in accordance with the procedure referred to in Article 16, paragraphs 2 and 3 of this Article shall apply.

2. An undertaking shall be deemed to have significant market power if, either individually or jointly with others, it enjoys a position equivalent to dominance, that is to say a position of economic strength affording it the power to behave to an appreciable extent independently of competitors, customers and ultimately consumers.

In particular, national regulatory authorities shall, when assessing whether two or more undertakings are in a joint dominant position in a market, act in accordance with Community law and take into the utmost account the guidelines on market analysis and the assessment of significant market power published by the Commission pursuant to Article 15. Criteria to be used in making such an assessment are set out in Annex II.

[3. Where an undertaking has significant market power on a specific market (the first market), it may also be designated as having significant market power on a closely related market (the second market), where the links between the two markets are such as to allow the market power held in the first market to be leveraged into the second market, thereby strengthening the market power of the undertaking. Consequently, remedies aimed at preventing such leverage may be applied in the second market pursuant to Articles 9, 10, 11 and 13 of Directive 2002/19/EC (Access Directive), and where such remedies prove to be insufficient, remedies pursuant to Article 17 of Directive 2002/22/EC (Universal Service Directive) may be imposed.]

Notes
Article 14 was amended as shown in square brackets by Directive 2009/140/EC (OJ L 337, 18.12.2009), p.37, with effect from 19 December 2009.
Commentary
Art 14(2): F&N: 13.112

Article 15
[Procedure for the identification and definition of markets]

[1. After public consultation including with national regulatory authorities and taking the utmost account of the opinion of BEREC, the Commission shall, in accordance with the advisory procedure referred to in Article 22(2), adopt a Recommendation on Relevant Product and Service Markets (the Recommendation). The Recommendation shall identify those product and service markets within the electronic communications sector the characteristics of which may be such as to justify the imposition of regulatory obligations set out in the Specific Directives, without prejudice to markets that may be defined in specific cases under competition law. The Commission shall define markets in accordance with the principles of competition law.]

The Commission shall regularly review the recommendation.

2. The Commission shall publish, at the latest on the date of entry into force of this Directive, guidelines for market analysis and the assessment of significant market power (hereinafter "the guidelines") which shall be in accordance with the principles of competition law.

[3. National regulatory authorities shall, taking the utmost account of the Recommendation and the Guidelines, define relevant markets appropriate to national circumstances, in particular relevant geographic markets within their territory, in accordance with the principles of competition law. National regulatory authorities shall follow the procedures referred to in Articles 6 and 7 before defining the markets that differ from those identified in the Recommendation.]

[4. After consultation including with national regulatory authorities the Commission may, taking the utmost account of the opinion of BEREC, adopt a Decision identifying transnational markets, acting in accordance with the regulatory procedure with scrutiny referred to in Article 22(3).]

Notes
Article 15 was amended as shown in square bracketsby Directive 2009/140/EC (OJ L 337, 18.12.2009), p.37, with effect from 19 December 2009.
Commentary
Art 15: B&C: 12.017, 12.044
Art 15(1): B&C: 12.044 F&N: 13.26, 13.27
Art 15(3): B&C: 12.017, 12.018 F&N: 13.112

Article 16
Market analysis procedure

[1. National regulatory authorities shall carry out an analysis of the relevant markets taking into account the markets identified in the Recommendation, and taking the utmost account of the Guidelines. Member States shall ensure that this analysis is carried out, where appropriate, in collaboration with the national competition authorities.

2. Where a national regulatory authority is required under paragraphs 3 or 4 of this Article, Article 17 of Directive 2002/22/EC (Universal Service Directive), or Article 8 of Directive 2002/19/EC (Access Directive) to determine whether to impose, maintain, amend or withdraw obligations on undertakings, it shall determine on the basis of its market analysis referred to in paragraph 1 of this Article whether a relevant market is effectively competitive.]

3. Where a national regulatory authority concludes that the market is effectively competitive, it shall not impose or maintain any of the specific regulatory obligations referred to in paragraph 2 of this Article. In cases where sector specific regulatory obligations already exist, it shall withdraw such

obligations placed on undertakings in that relevant market. An appropriate period of notice shall be given to parties affected by such a withdrawal of obligations.

[4. Where a national regulatory authority determines that a relevant market is not effectively competitive, it shall identify undertakings which individually or jointly have a significant market power on that market in accordance with Article 14 and the national regulatory authority shall on such undertakings impose appropriate specific regulatory obligations referred to in paragraph 2 of this Article or maintain or amend such obligations where they already exist.

5. In the case of transnational markets identified in the Decision referred to in Article 15(4), the national regulatory authorities concerned shall jointly conduct the market analysis taking the utmost account of the Guidelines and, in a concerted fashion, shall decide on any imposition, maintenance, amendment or withdrawal of regulatory obligations referred to in paragraph 2 of this Article.

6. Measures taken in accordance with the provisions of paragraphs 3 and 4 shall be subject to the procedures referred to in Articles 6 and 7. National regulatory authorities shall carry out an analysis of the relevant market and notify the corresponding draft measure in accordance with Article 7:

(a) within three years from the adoption of a previous measure relating to that market. However, exceptionally, that period may be extended for up to three additional years, where the national regulatory authority has notified a reasoned proposed extension to the Commission and the Commission has not objected within one month of the notified extension;

(b) within two years from the adoption of a revised Recommendation on relevant markets, for markets not previously notified to the Commission; or

(c) within two years from their accession, for Member States which have newly joined the Union.

7. Where a national regulatory authority has not completed its analysis of a relevant market identified in the Recommendation within the time limit laid down in paragraph 6, BEREC shall, upon request, provide assistance to the national regulatory authority concerned in completing the analysis of the specific market and the specific obligations to be imposed. With this assistance, the national regulatory authority concerned shall within six months notify the draft measure to the Commission in accordance with Article 7.]

Notes

Article 16 was amended as shown in square brackets by Directive 2009/140/EC (OJ L 337, 18.12.2009), p.37, with effect from 19 December 2009.

Commentary

Art 16: **B&C:** 12.014, 12.017

Art 16(3): **B&C:** 12.014

Article 17
Standardisation

1. The Commission, acting in accordance with the procedure referred to in Article 22(2), shall draw up and publish in the *Official Journal of the European Communities* a list of [non-compulsory standards] and/or specifications to serve as a basis for encouraging the harmonised provision of electronic communications networks, electronic communications services and associated facilities and services. Where necessary, the Commission may, acting in accordance with the procedure referred to in Article 22(2) and following consultation of the Committee established by Directive 98/34/EC, request that standards be drawn up by the European standards organisations (European Committee for Standardisation (CEN), European Committee for Electrotechnical Standardisation (CENELEC), and European Telecommunications Standards Institute (ETSI)).

2. Member States shall encourage the use of the standards and/or specifications referred to in paragraph 1, for the provision of services, technical interfaces and/or network functions, to the extent strictly necessary to ensure interoperability of services and to improve freedom of choice for users.

As long as standards and/or specifications have not been published in accordance with paragraph 1, Member States shall encourage the implementation of standards and/or specifications adopted by the European standards organisations.

[In the absence of such standards and/or specifications, Member States shall encourage the implementation of international standards or recommendations adopted by the International Telecommunication Union (ITU), the European Conference of Postal and Telecommunications Administrations (CEPT), the International Organisation for Standardisation (ISO) and the International Electrotechnical Commission (IEC).]

Where international standards exist, Member States shall encourage the European standards organisations to use them, or the relevant parts of them, as a basis for the standards they develop, except where such international standards or relevant parts would be ineffective.

3. If the standards and/or specifications referred to in paragraph 1 have not been adequately implemented so that interoperability of services in one or more Member States cannot be ensured, the implementation of such standards and/or specifications may be made compulsory under the procedure laid down in paragraph 4, to the extent strictly necessary to ensure such interoperability and to improve freedom of choice for users.

[4. Where the Commission intends to make the implementation of certain standards and/or specifications compulsory, it shall publish a notice in the Official Journal of the European Union and invite public comment by all parties concerned. The Commission shall take appropriate implementing measures and make implementation of the relevant standards compulsory by making reference to them as compulsory standards in the list of standards and/or specifications published in the Official Journal of the European Union.

5. Where the Commission considers that standards and/or specifications referred to in paragraph 1 no longer contribute to the provision of harmonised electronic communications services, or that they no longer meet consumers' needs or are hampering technological development, it shall, acting in accordance with the advisory procedure referred to in Article 22(2), remove them from the list of standards and/or specifications referred to in paragraph 1.]

6. Where the Commission considers that standards and/or specifications referred to in paragraph 4 no longer contribute to the provision of harmonised electronic communications services, or that they no longer meet consumers' needs or are hampering technological development, it shall [take the appropriate implementing measures and remove those standards and/or specifications from the list of standards and/or specifications referred to in paragraph 1].

[6a. The implementing measures designed to amend non-essential elements of this Directive by supplementing it, referred to in paragraphs 4 and 6, shall be adopted in accordance with the regulatory procedure with scrutiny referred to in Article 22(3).]

7. This Article does not apply in respect of any of the essential requirements, interface specifications or harmonised standards to which the provisions of Directive 1999/5/EC apply.

Notes

Article 17 was amended as shown in square brackets by Directive 2009/140/EC (OJ L 337, 18.12.2009), p.37, with effect from 19 December 2009.

Commentary
Art 17: **B&C**: 12.008

Article 18
Interoperability of digital interactive television services

1. In order to promote the free flow of information, media pluralism and cultural diversity, Member States shall encourage, in accordance with the provisions of Article 17(2):

(a) providers of digital interactive television services for distribution to the public in the Community on digital interactive television platforms, regardless of the transmission mode, to use an open API;

(b) providers of all enhanced digital television equipment deployed for the reception of digital interactive television services on interactive digital television platforms to comply with an open API in accordance with the minimum requirements of the relevant standards or specifications.

[(c) providers of digital TV services and equipment to cooperate in the provision of interoperable TV services for disabled end-users.]

2. Without prejudice to Article 5(1)(b) of Directive 2002/19/ EC (Access Directive), Member States shall encourage proprietors of APIs to make available on fair, reasonable and non-discriminatory terms, and against appropriate remuneration, all such information as is necessary to enable providers of digital interactive television services to provide all services supported by the API in a fully functional form.

[ ]

Notes

Article 18 was amended as shown in square brackets by Directive 2009/140/EC (OJ L 337, 18.12.2009), p.37, with effect from 19 December 2009.

Commentary
Art 18: B&C: 12.008

Article 19
Harmonisation procedures

1. Without prejudice to Article 9 of this Directive and Articles 6 and 8 of Directive 2002/20/EC (Authorisation Directive), where the Commission finds that divergences in the implementation by the national regulatory authorities of the regulatory tasks specified in this Directive and the Specific Directives may create a barrier to the internal market, the Commission may, taking the utmost account of the opinion of BEREC, issue a recommendation or a decision on the harmonised application of the provisions in this Directive and the Specific Directives in order to further the achievement of the objectives set out in Article 8.

2. Where the Commission issues a recommendation pursuant to paragraph 1, it shall act in accordance with the advisory procedure referred to in Article 22(2).

Member States shall ensure that national regulatory authorities take the utmost account of those recommendations in carrying out their tasks. Where a national regulatory authority chooses not to follow a recommendation, it shall inform the Commission, giving the reasons for its position.

3. The decisions adopted pursuant to paragraph 1 may include only the identification of a harmonised or coordinated approach for the purposes of addressing the following matters:

(a) the inconsistent implementation of general regulatory approaches by national regulatory authorities on the regulation of electronic communication markets in the application of Articles 15 and 16, where it creates a barrier to the internal market. Such decisions shall not refer to specific notifications issued by the national regulatory authorities pursuant to Article 7a;
In such a case, the Commission shall propose a draft decision only:

    — after at least two years following the adoption of a Commission Recommendation dealing with the same matter, and
    — taking utmost account of an opinion from BEREC on the case for adoption of such a decision, which shall be provided by BEREC within three months of the Commission's request;

(b) numbering, including number ranges, portability of numbers and identifiers, number and address translation systems, and access to 112 emergency services.

4. The decision referred to in paragraph 1, designed to amend non-essential elements of this Directive by supplementing it, shall be adopted in accordance with the regulatory procedure with scrutiny referred to in Article 22(3).

5. BEREC may on its own initiative advise the Commission on whether a measure should be adopted pursuant to paragraph 1.]

Notes

Article 19 was replaced as shown in square brackets by Directive 2009/140/EC (OJ L 337, 18.12.2009), p.37, with effect from 19 December 2009.

Commentary
Art 19: B&C: 12.008, 12.021

Article 20
Dispute resolution between undertakings

[1. In the event of a dispute arising in connection with existing obligations under this Directive or the Specific Directives between undertakings providing electronic communications networks or services in a Member State, or between such undertakings and other undertakings in the Member State benefiting from obligations of access and/or interconnection arising under this Directive or the Specific Directives, the national regulatory authority concerned shall, at the request of either party, and without prejudice to the provisions of paragraph 2, issue a binding decision to resolve the dispute in the shortest possible time frame and in any case within four months, except in exceptional circumstances. The Member State concerned shall require that all parties cooperate fully with the national regulatory authority.]

2. Member States may make provision for national regulatory authorities to decline to resolve a dispute through a binding decision where other mechanisms, including mediation, exist and would better contribute to resolution of the dispute in a timely manner in accordance with the provisions of Article 8. The national regulatory authority shall inform the parties without delay. If after four months the dispute is not resolved, and if the dispute has not been brought before the courts by the party seeking redress, the national regulatory authority shall issue, at the request of either party, a binding decision to resolve the dispute in the shortest possible time frame and in any case within four months.

3. In resolving a dispute, the national regulatory authority shall take decisions aimed at achieving the objectives set out in Article 8. Any obligations imposed on an undertaking by the national regulatory authority in resolving a dispute shall respect the provisions of this Directive or the Specific Directives.

4. The decision of the national regulatory authority shall be made available to the public, having regard to the requirements of business confidentiality. The parties concerned shall be given a full statement of the reasons on which it is based.

5. The procedure referred to in paragraphs 1, 3 and 4 shall not preclude either party from bringing an action before the courts.

Notes
Article 20 was amended as shown in square brackets by Directive 2009/140/EC (OJ L 337, 18.12.2009), p.37, with effect from 19 December 2009.

Commentary
Art 20: B&C: 12.009
Art 20(4): B&C: 12.009

[*Article 21*
Resolution of cross-border disputes

1. In the event of a cross-border dispute arising under this Directive or the Specific Directives between parties in different Member States, and where the dispute lies within the competence of national regulatory authorities from more than one Member State, the provisions set out in paragraphs 2, 3 and 4 shall be applicable.

2. Any party may refer the dispute to the national regulatory authorities concerned. The competent national regulatory authorities shall coordinate their efforts and shall have the right to consult BEREC in order to bring about a consistent resolution of the dispute, in accordance with the objectives set out in Article 8.

Any obligations imposed by the national regulatory authorities on undertakings as part of the resolution of a dispute shall comply with this Directive and the Specific Directives.

Any national regulatory authority which has competence in such a dispute may request BEREC to adopt an opinion as to the action to be taken in accordance with the provisions of the Framework Directive and/or the Specific Directives to resolve the dispute.

Where such a request has been made to BEREC, any national regulatory authority with competence in any aspect of the dispute shall await BEREC's opinion before taking action to resolve the dispute. This shall not preclude national regulatory authorities from taking urgent measures where necessary.

Any obligations imposed on an undertaking by the national regulatory authority in resolving a dispute shall respect the provisions of this Directive or the Specific Directives and take the utmost account of the opinion adopted by BEREC.

3. Member States may make provision for the competent national regulatory authorities jointly to decline to resolve a dispute where other mechanisms, including mediation, exist and would better contribute to resolving of the dispute in a timely manner in accordance with the provisions of Article 8.

They shall inform the parties without delay. If after four months the dispute is not resolved, where the dispute has not been brought before the courts by the party seeking redress and if either party requests it, the national regulatory authorities shall coordinate their efforts in order to resolve the dispute, in accordance with the provisions set out in Article 8 and taking the utmost account of any opinion adopted by BEREC.

4. The procedure referred to in paragraph 2 shall not preclude either party from bringing an action before the courts.]

Notes

Article 21 was replaced as shown in square brackets by Directive 2009/140/EC (OJ L 337, 18.12.2009), p.37, with effect from 19 December 2009.

[*Article 21a*
Penalties

Member States shall lay down rules on penalties applicable to infringements of national provisions adopted pursuant to this Directive and the Specific Directives and shall take all measures necessary to ensure that they are implemented. The penalties provided for must be appropriate, effective, proportionate and dissuasive. The Member States shall notify those provisions to the Commission by 25 May 2011 and shall notify it without delay of any subsequent amendment affecting them.]

Notes

Article 21a was inserted as shown in square brackets by Directive 2009/140/EC (OJ L 337, 18.12.2009), p.37, with effect from 19 December 2009.

Article 22
Committee

1. The Commission shall be assisted by a Committee ("the Communications Committee").

2. Where reference is made to this paragraph, Articles 3 and 7 of Decision 1999/468/EC shall apply, having regard to the provisions of Article 8 thereof.

[3. Where reference is made to this paragraph, Article 5a(1) to (4), and Article 7 of Decision 1999/468/EC shall apply, having regard to the provisions of Article 8 thereof.]

Notes

Article 22 was amended as shown in square brackets by Directive 2009/140/EC (OJ L 337, 18.12.2009), p.37, with effect from 19 December 2009.

Article 23
Exchange of information

1. The Commission shall provide all relevant information to the Communications Committee on the outcome of regular consultations with the representatives of network operators, service providers, users, consumers, manufacturers and trade unions, as well as third countries and international organisations.

2. The Communications Committee shall, taking account of the Community's electronic communications policy, foster the exchange of information between the Member States and between the Member States and the Commission on the situation and the development of regulatory activities regarding electronic communications networks and services.

Article 24
Publication of information

1. Member States shall ensure that up-to-date information pertaining to the application of this Directive and the Specific Directives is made publicly available in a manner that guarantees all interested parties easy access to that information. They shall publish a notice in their national official gazette describing how and where the information is published. The first such notice shall be published before the date of application referred to in Article 28(1), second subparagraph, and thereafter a notice shall be published whenever there is any change in the information contained therein.

2. Member States shall send to the Commission a copy of all such notices at the time of publication. The Commission shall distribute the information to the Communications Committee as appropriate.

Article 25
Review procedures

1. The Commission shall periodically review the functioning of this Directive and report to the European Parliament and to the Council, on the first occasion not later than three years after the date of application referred to in Article 28(1), second subparagraph. For this purpose, the Commission may request information from the Member States, which shall be supplied without undue delay.

Chapter V
Final provisions

Article 26
Repeal

The following Directives and Decisions are hereby repealed with effect from the date of application referred to in Article 28(1), second subparagraph:

— Directive 90/387/EEC,
— Council Decision 91/396/EEC of 29 July 1991 on the introduction of a single European emergency call number,[1]
— Council Directive 92/44/EEC of 5 June 1992 on the application of open network provision to leased lines,[2]
— Council Decision 92/264/EEC of 11 May 1992 on the introduction of a standard international telephone access code in the Community,[3]
— Directive 95/47/EC,
— Directive 97/13/EC,
— Directive 97/33/EC,
— Directive 98/10/EC of the European Parliament and of the Council of 26 February 1998 on the application of open network provision (ONP) to voice telephony and on universal service for telecommunications in a competitive environment.[4]

Notes

[1] OJ L 217, 6.8.1991, p.31.
[2] OJ L 165, 19.6.1992, p.27. Directive as last amended by Commission Decision 98/80/EC (OJ L 14, 20.1.1998, p.27).
[3] OJ L 137, 20.5.1992, p.21.
[4] OJ L 101, 1.4.1998, p.24.

[ ]

Notes

Article 27 was deleted by Directive 2009/140/EC (OJ L 337, 18.12.2009), p.37, with effect from 19 December 2009.

Commentary
Art 27: B&C: 12.007

Article 28
Transposition

1. Member States shall adopt and publish the laws, regulations and administrative provisions necessary to comply with this Directive not later than 24 July 2003. They shall forthwith inform the Commission thereof.

They shall apply those measures from 25 July 2003.

2. Then Member States adopt these measures, they shall contain a reference to this Directive or be accompanied by such a reference on the occasion of their official publication. The methods of making such a reference shall be laid down by the Member States.

3. Member States shall communicate to the Commission the text of the provisions of national law which they adopt in the field governed by this Directive and of any subsequent amendments to those provisions.

Notes

Measures to implement the amendments effected by Directive 2009/140/EC are required to be adopted and published by 25 May 2011 and applied from 26 May 2011: Directive 2009/140/EC, Article 5.

Article 29
Entry into force

This Directive shall enter into force on the day of its publication in the *Official Journal of the European Communities*.

Notes

Date of entry into force: 24 April 2002.

Article 30
Addressees

This Directive is addressed to the Member States.

Done at Brussels, 7 March 2002.

[]

Notes

Annex I was deleted by Directive 2009/140/EC (OJ L 337, 18.12.2009), p.37, with effect from 19 December 2009.

Annex II
Criteria to be Used by National Regulatory Authorities in Making an Assessment of Joint Dominance in Accordance with the Second Subparagraph of Article 14(2)

Two or more undertakings can be found to be in a joint dominant position within the meaning of Article 14 if, even in the absence of structural or other links between them, they operate in a market which is characterised by a lack of effective competition and in which no single undertaking has significant market power. In accordance with the applicable Community law and with the case-law of the Court of Justice of the European Communities on joint dominance, this is likely to be the case where the market is concentrated and exhibits a number of appropriate characteristics of which the following may be the most relevant in the context of electronic communications:

— low elasticity of demand,
— similar market shares,

— high legal or economic barriers to entry,
— vertical integration with collective refusal to supply,
— lack of countervailing buyer power,
— lack of potential competition.

The above is an indicative list and is not exhaustive, nor are the criteria cumulative. Rather, the list is intended to illustrate only the type of evidence that could be used to support assertions concerning the existence of joint dominance].

Notes

Annex II was replaced as shown in square brackets by Directive 2009/140/EC (OJ L 337, 18.12.2009), p.37, with effect from 19 December 2009.

Commentary
Annex II: F&N: 13.27

E2

DIRECTIVE 2002/19/EC OF THE EUROPEAN PARLIAMENT AND OF THE COUNCIL

of 7 March 2002

on access to, and interconnection of, electronic communications networks and associated facilities

(Access Directive)

Official Journal L 108, 24.4.2002, p.7

Celex No: 32002L0019

EUR-Lex permanent link: <http://eur-lex.europa.eu/LexUriServ/LexUriServ.do?uri=CELEX:3200 2L0019:EN:NOT>

Notes

EEA application: this Directive was adopted with appropriate adaptations by EEA Joint Committee Decision No 11/2004 (OJ No L 116, 22.4.2004, p.60 and EEA Supplement No 20, 22.4.2004, p.14): see EEA Agreement, Annex XI, Point 5cj.

Commentary
Directive 2002/19/EC: B&C: 12.005, 12.022, 12.023 F&N: 13.22, 14.144
Arts 8–13a: B&C: 12.026
Arts 9–13: F&N: 13.29
Arts 9–13a: B&C: 12.014, 12.019
Chap III: B&C: 12.026
Chap IV: B&C: 12.026

THE EUROPEAN PARLIAMENT AND THE COUNCIL OF THE EUROPEAN UNION,

Having regard to the Treaty establishing the European Community, and in particular Article [114]* thereof,

Having regard to the proposal from the Commission,[1]

Having regard to the opinion of the Economic and Social Committee,[2]

Acting in accordance with the procedure laid down in Article [294] of the Treaty,[3]

Notes

* Ed note: please see the Note on the Lisbon Treaty at p.xvii in regard to article renumbering introduced by the Lisbon Treaty.

[1] OJ C 365 E, 19.12.2000, p.215 and OJ C 270 E, 25.9.2001, p.161.

[2] OJ C 123, 25.4.2001, p.50.

[3] Opinion of the European Parliament of 1 March 2001 (OJ C 277, 1.10.2001, p.72), Council Common Position of 17 September 2001 (OJ C 337, 30.11.2001, p.1) and Decision of the European Parliament of 12 December 2001 [OJ C 177 E, 25.7.2002, p.82]. Council Decision of 14 February 2002.

Whereas:

(1) Directive 2002/21/EC of the European Parliament and of the Council of 7 March 2002 on a common regulatory framework for electronic communications networks and services (Framework Directive)[1] lays down the objectives of a regulatory framework to cover electronic communications networks and services in the Community, including fixed and mobile telecommunications networks, cable television networks, networks used for terrestrial broadcasting, satellite networks and Internet networks, whether used for voice, fax, data or images. Such networks may have been authorised by Member States under Directive 2002/20/EC of the European Parliament and of the Council of 7 March 2002 on the authorisation of electronic communications networks and services (Authorisation Directive)[2] or have been authorised under previous regulatory measures. The provisions of this Directive apply to those networks that are used for the provision of publicly available electronic communications services. This Directive covers access and interconnection arrangements between service suppliers. Non-public networks do not have obligations under this Directive except where, in benefiting from access to public networks, they may be subject to conditions laid down by Member States.

Notes

[1] See [OJ L 108, 24.4.2002, p.33].

[2] See [OJ L 108, 24.4.2002, p.21].

(2) Services providing content such as the offer for sale of a package of sound or television broadcasting content are not covered by the common regulatory framework for electronic communications networks and services.

(3) The term "access" has a wide range of meanings, and it is therefore necessary to define precisely how that term is used in this Directive, without prejudice to how it may be used in other Community measures. An operator may own the underlying network or facilities or may rent some or all of them.

(4) Directive 95/47/EC of the European Parliament and of the Council of 24 October 1995 on the use of standards for the transmission of television signals[1] did not mandate any specific digital television transmission system or service requirement, and this opened up an opportunity for the market actors to take the initiative and develop suitable systems. Through the Digital Video Broadcasting Group, European market actors have developed a family of television transmission systems that have been adopted by broadcasters throughout the world. These transmissions systems have been standardised by the European Telecommunications Standards Institute (ETSI) and have become International Telecommunication Union recommendations. In relation to wide-screen digital television, the 16:9 aspect ratio is the reference format for wide-format television services and programmes, and is now established in Member States' markets as a result of Council Decision 93/424/EEC of 22 July 1993 on an action plan for the introduction of advanced television services in Europe.[2]

Notes

[1] OJ L 281, 23.11.1995, p.51.

[2] OJ L 196, 5.8.1993, p.48.

(5) In an open and competitive market, there should be no restrictions that prevent undertakings from negotiating access and interconnection arrangements between themselves, in particular on cross-border agreements, subject to the competition rules of the Treaty. In the context of achieving a more efficient, truly pan-European market, with effective competition, more choice and competitive services to consumers, undertakings which receive requests for access or interconnection should in principle conclude such agreements on a commercial basis, and negotiate in good faith.

(6) In markets where there continue to be large differences in negotiating power between undertakings, and where some undertakings rely on infrastructure provided by others for delivery of their services, it is appropriate to establish a framework to ensure that the market functions effectively. National regulatory authorities should have the power to secure, where commercial negotiation fails, adequate access and interconnection and interoperability of services in the interest of end-users. In particular, they may ensure end-to-end connectivity by imposing proportionate obligations on undertakings that control access to end-users. Control of means of access may entail ownership or control of the physical link to the end-user (either fixed or mobile), and/or the ability to change or withdraw the national number or numbers needed to access an end-user's network termination point. This would be the case for example if network operators were to restrict unreasonably end-user choice for access to Internet portals and services.

Commentary
Recital 6: B&C: 12.024

(7) National legal or administrative measures that link the terms and conditions for access or interconnection to the activities of the party seeking interconnection, and specifically to the degree of its investment in network infrastructure, and not to the interconnection or access services provided, may cause market distortion and may therefore not be compatible with competition rules.

Commentary
Recital 7: B&C: 12.024

(8) Network operators who control access to their own customers do so on the basis of unique numbers or addresses from a published numbering or addressing range. Other network operators need to be able to deliver traffic to those customers, and so need to be able to interconnect directly or indirectly to each other. The existing rights and obligations to negotiate interconnection should therefore be maintained. It is also appropriate to maintain the obligations formerly laid down in Directive 95/47/EC requiring fully digital electronic communications networks used for the distribution of television services and open to the public to be capable of distributing wide-screen television services and programmes, so that users are able to receive such programmes in the format in which they were transmitted.

Commentary
Recital 8: B&C: 12.022

(9) Interoperability is of benefit to end-users and is an important aim of this regulatory framework. Encouraging interoperability is one of the objectives for national regulatory authorities as set out in this framework, which also provides for the Commission to publish a list of standards and/or specifications covering the provision of services, technical interfaces and/or network functions, as the basis for encouraging harmonisation in electronic communications. Member States should encourage the use of published standards and/or specifications to the extent strictly necessary to ensure interoperability of services and to improve freedom of choice for users.

(10) Competition rules alone may not be sufficient to ensure cultural diversity and media pluralism in the area of digital television. Directive 95/47/EC provided an initial regulatory framework for the nascent digital television industry which should be maintained, including in particular the obligation to provide conditional access on fair, reasonable and non-discriminatory terms, in order to make sure that a wide variety of programming and services is available. Technological and market developments make it necessary to review these obligations on a regular basis, either by a

Member State for its national market or the Commission for the Community, in particular to determine whether there is justification for extending obligations to new gateways, such as electronic programme guides (EPGs) and application program interfaces (APIs), to the extent that is necessary to ensure accessibility for end-users to specified digital broadcasting services. Member States may specify the digital broadcasting services to which access by end-users must be ensured by any legislative, regulatory or administrative means that they deem necessary.

Commentary
Recital 10: B&C: 12.043

(11) Member States may also permit their national regulatory authority to review obligations in relation to conditional access to digital broadcasting services in order to assess through a market analysis whether to withdraw or amend conditions for operators that do not have significant market power on the relevant market. Such withdrawal or amendment should not adversely affect access for end-users to such services or the prospects for effective competition.

(12) In order to ensure continuity of existing agreements and to avoid a legal vacuum, it is necessary to ensure that obligations for access and interconnection imposed under Articles 4, 6, 7, 8, 11, 12, and 14 of Directive 97/33/EC of the European Parliament and of the Council of 30 June 1997 on interconnection in telecommunications with regard to ensuring universal service and interoperability through application of the principles of open network provision (ONP),[1] obligations on special access imposed under Article 16 of Directive 98/10/EC of the European Parliament and of the Council of 26 February 1998 on the application of open network provision (ONP) to voice telephony and on universal service for telecommunications in a competitive environment,[2] and obligations concerning the provision of leased line transmission capacity under Council Directive 92/44/EEC of 5 June 1992 on the application of open network provision to leased lines,[3] are initially carried over into the new regulatory framework, but are subject to immediate review in the light of prevailing market conditions. Such a review should also extend to those organisations covered by Regulation (EC) No 2887/2000 of the European Parliament and of the Council of 18 December 2000 on unbundled access to the local loop.[4]

Notes
[1] OJ L 199, 26.7.1997, p.32. Directive as last amended by Directive 98/61/EC (OJ L 268, 3.10.1998, p.37).
[2] OJ L 101, 1.4.1998, p.24.
[3] OJ L 165, 19.6.1992, p.27. Directive as last amended by Commission Decision No 98/80/EC (OJ L 14, 20.1.1998, p.27).
[4] OJ L 366, 30.12.2000, p.4.

(13) The review should be carried out using an economic market analysis based on competition law methodology. The aim is to reduce *ex ante* sector specific rules progressively as competition in the market develops. However the procedure also takes account of transitional problems in the market such as those related to international roaming and of the possibility of new bottlenecks arising as a result of technological development, which may require *ex ante* regulation, for example in the area of broadband access networks. It may well be the case that competition develops at different speeds in different market segments and in different Member States, and national regulatory authorities should be able to relax regulatory obligations in those markets where competition is delivering the desired results. In order to ensure that market players in similar circumstances are treated in similar ways in different Member States, the Commission should be able to ensure harmonised application of the provisions of this Directive. National regulatory authorities and national authorities entrusted with the implementation of competition law should, where appropriate, coordinate their actions to ensure that the most appropriate remedy is applied. The Community and its Member States have entered into commitments on interconnection of telecommunications networks in the context of the World Trade Organisation agreement on basic telecommunications and these commitments need to be respected.

Commentary
Recital 13: B&C: 12.016

(14) Directive 97/33/EC laid down a range of obligations to be imposed on undertakings with significant market power, namely transparency, non-discrimination, accounting separation, access, and price control including cost orientation. This range of possible obligations should be maintained but, in addition, they should be established as a set of maximum obligations that can be applied to undertakings, in order to avoid over-regulation. Exceptionally, in order to comply with international commitments or Community law, it may be appropriate to impose obligations for access or interconnection on all market players, as is currently the case for conditional access systems for digital television services.

Commentary
Recital 14: B&C: 12.009

(15) The imposition of a specific obligation on an undertaking with significant market power does not require an additional market analysis but a justification that the obligation in question is appropriate and proportionate in relation to the nature of the problem identified.

(16) Transparency of terms and conditions for access and interconnection, including prices, serve to speed-up negotiation, avoid disputes and give confidence to market players that a service is not being provided on discriminatory terms. Openness and transparency of technical interfaces can be particularly important in ensuring interoperability. Where a national regulatory authority imposes obligations to make information public, it may also specify the manner in which the information is to be made available, covering for example the type of publication (paper and/or electronic) and whether or not it is free of charge, taking into account the nature and purpose of the information concerned.

(17) The principle of non-discrimination ensures that undertakings with market power do not distort competition, in particular where they are vertically integrated undertakings that supply services to undertakings with whom they compete on downstream markets.

(18) Accounting separation allows internal price transfers to be rendered visible, and allows national regulatory authorities to check compliance with obligations for non-discrimination where applicable. In this regard the Commission published Recommendation 98/322/EC of 8 April 1998 on interconnection in a liberalised telecommunications market (Part 2—accounting separation and cost accounting).[1]

Notes
[1] OJ L 141, 13.5.1998, p.6.

(19) Mandating access to network infrastructure can be justified as a means of increasing competition, but national regulatory authorities need to balance the rights of an infrastructure owner to exploit its infrastructure for its own benefit, and the rights of other service providers to access facilities that are essential for the provision of competing services. Where obligations are imposed on operators that require them to meet reasonable requests for access to and use of networks elements and associated facilities, such requests should only be refused on the basis of objective criteria such as technical feasibility or the need to maintain network integrity. Where access is refused, the aggrieved party may submit the case to the dispute resolutions procedure referred to in Articles 20 and 21 of Directive 2002/21/EC (Framework Directive). An operator with mandated access obligations cannot be required to provide types of access which are not within its powers to provide. The imposition by national regulatory authorities of mandated access that increases competition in the short-term should not reduce incentives for competitors to invest in alternative facilities that will secure more competition in the long-term. The Commission has published a Notice on the application of the competition rules to access agreements in the telecommunications sector[1] which addresses these issues. National regulatory authorities may impose technical and operational conditions on the provider and/or beneficiaries of mandated access in accordance with Community law. In particular the imposition of technical standards should comply with Directive 98/34/EC of the European Parliament and of the Council of 22 June 1998 laying down a procedure for the provision of information in the field of technical standards and regulations and of rules of Information Society Services.[2]

Notes

[1] OJ C 265, 22.8.1998, p.2.
[2] OJ L 204, 21.7.1998, p.37. Directive as amended by Directive 98/48/EC (OJ L 217, 5.8.1998, p.18).

(20) Price control may be necessary when market analysis in a particular market reveals inefficient competition. The regulatory intervention may be relatively light, such as an obligation that prices for carrier selection are reasonable as laid down in Directive 97/33/EC, or much heavier such as an obligation that prices are cost oriented to provide full justification for those prices where competition is not sufficiently strong to prevent excessive pricing. In particular, operators with significant market power should avoid a price squeeze whereby the difference between their retail prices and the interconnection prices charged to competitors who provide similar retail services is not adequate to ensure sustainable competition. When a national regulatory authority calculates costs incurred in establishing a service mandated under this Directive, it is appropriate to allow a reasonable return on the capital employed including appropriate labour and building costs, with the value of capital adjusted where necessary to reflect the current valuation of assets and efficiency of operations. The method of cost recovery should be appropriate to the circumstances taking account of the need to promote efficiency and sustainable competition and maximise consumer benefits.

(21) Where a national regulatory authority imposes obligations to implement a cost accounting system in order to support price controls, it may itself undertake an annual audit to ensure compliance with that cost accounting system, provided that it has the necessary qualified staff, or it may require the audit to be carried out by another qualified body, independent of the operator concerned.

(22) Publication of information by Member States will ensure that market players and potential market entrants understand their rights and obligations, and know where to find the relevant detailed information. Publication in the national gazette helps interested parties in other Member States to find the relevant information.

(23) In order to ensure that the pan-European electronic communications market is effective and efficient, the Commission should monitor and publish information on charges which contribute to determining prices to end-users.

(24) The development of the electronic communications market, with its associated infrastructure, could have adverse effects on the environment and the landscape. Member States should therefore monitor this process and, if necessary, take action to minimise any such effects by means of appropriate agreements and other arrangements with the relevant authorities.

(25) In order to determine the correct application of Community law, the Commission needs to know which undertakings have been designated as having significant market power and what obligations have been placed upon market players by national regulatory authorities. In addition to national publication of this information, it is therefore necessary for Member States to send this information to the Commission. Where Member States are required to send information to the Commission, this may be in electronic form, subject to appropriate authentication procedures being agreed.

(26) Given the pace of technological and market developments, the implementation of this Directive should be reviewed within three years of its date of application to determine if it is meeting its objectives.

(27) The measures necessary for the implementation of this Directive should be adopted in accordance with Council Decision 1999/468/EC of 28 June 1999 laying down the procedures for the exercise of implementing powers conferred on the Commission.[1]

Notes

[1] OJ L 184, 17.7.1999, p.23.

(28) Since the objectives of the proposed action, namely establishing a harmonised framework for the regulation of access to and interconnection of electronic communications networks and associated facilities, cannot be sufficiently achieved by the Member States and can therefore, by reason of the scale and effects of the action, be better achieved at Community level, the Community may adopt measures, in accordance with the principle of subsidiarity as set out in Article 5 of the [Treaty on

European Union]. In accordance with the principle of proportionality, as set out in that Article, this Directive does not go beyond what is necessary in order to achieve those objectives,

HAVE ADOPTED THIS DIRECTIVE:

CHAPTER I
SCOPE, AIM AND DEFINITIONS

Article 1
Scope and aim

1. Within the framework set out in Directive 2002/21/EC(Framework Directive), this Directive harmonises the way in which Member States regulate access to, and interconnection of, electronic communications networks and associated facilities. The aim is to establish a regulatory framework, in accordance with internal market principles, for the relationships between suppliers of networks and services that will result in sustainable competition, interoperability of electronic communications services and consumer benefits.

2. This Directive establishes rights and obligations for operators and for undertakings seeking interconnection and/or access to their networks or associated facilities. It sets out objectives for national regulatory authorities with regard to access and interconnection, and lays down procedures to ensure that obligations imposed by national regulatory authorities are reviewed and, where appropriate, withdrawn once the desired objectives have been achieved. Access in this Directive does not refer to access by end-users.

Commentary

Art 1
Art 1(1): **B&C:** 12.023
Art 1(2): **B&C:** 12.023

Article 2
Definitions

For the purposes of this Directive the definitions set out in Article 2 of Directive 2002/21/EC (Framework Directive) shall apply.

The following definitions shall also apply:

(a) "access" means the making available of facilities and/or services to another undertaking, under defined conditions, on either an exclusive or non-exclusive basis, for the purpose of providing electronic communications services, including when they are used for the delivery of information society services or broadcast content services. It covers inter alia: access to network elements and associated facilities, which may involve the connection of equipment, by fixed or non-fixed means (in particular this includes access to the local loop and to facilities and services necessary to provide services over the local loop); access to physical infrastructure including buildings, ducts and masts; access to relevant software systems including operational support systems; access to information systems or databases for pre-ordering, provisioning, ordering, maintaining and repair requests, and billing; access to number translation or systems offering equivalent functionality; access to fixed and mobile networks, in particular for roaming; access to conditional access systems for digital television services and access to virtual network services.]

(b) "interconnection" means the physical and logical linking of public communications networks used by the same or a different undertaking in order to allow the users of one undertaking to communicate with users of the same or another undertaking, or to access services provided by another undertaking. Services may be provided by the parties involved or other parties who have access to the network. Interconnection is a specific type of access implemented between public network operators;

(c) "operator" means an undertaking providing or authorised to provide a public communications network or an associated facility;

(d) "wide-screen television service" means a television service that consists wholly or partially of programmes produced and edited to be displayed in a full height wide-screen format. The 16:9 format is the reference format for wide-screen television services;

[(e) "local loop" means the physical circuit connecting the network termination point to a distribution frame or equivalent facility in the fixed public electronic communications network.]

Notes

Article 2 was amended as shown in square brackets by Directive 2009/140/EC (OJ L 337, 18.12.2009, p.37), with effect from 19 December 2009.

Commentary

Art 2(a): **B&C:** 12.022

Art 2(b): **B&C:** 12.022

Art 2(c): **B&C:** 12.024

Art 2(d): **B&C:** 12.023

CHAPTER II

GENERAL PROVISIONS

Article 3

General framework for access and interconnection

1. Member States shall ensure that there are no restrictions which prevent undertakings in the same Member State or in different Member States from negotiating between themselves agreements on technical and commercial arrangements for access and/or interconnection, in accordance with Community law. The undertaking requesting access or interconnection does not need to be -authorised to operate in the Member State where access or interconnection is requested, if it is not providing services and does not operate a network in that Member State.

2. Without prejudice to Article 31 of Directive 2002/22/EC of the European Parliament and of the Council of 7 March 2002 on universal service and users' rights relating to electronic communications networks and services (Universal Service Directive),[1] Member States shall not maintain legal or administrative measures which oblige operators, when granting access or interconnection, to offer different terms and conditions to different undertakings for equivalent services and/or imposing obligations that are not related to the actual access and interconnection services provided without prejudice to the conditions fixed in the Annex of Directive 2002/20/EC (Authorisation Directive).

Notes

[1] See [OJ L 108, 24.4.2002, p.51].

Commentary

Art 3: **B&C:** 12.024

Article 4

Rights and obligations for undertakings

[1. Operators of public communications networks shall have a right and, when requested by other undertakings so authorised in accordance with Article 4 of Directive 2002/20/EC (Authorisation Directive), an obligation to negotiate interconnection with each other for the purpose of providing publicly available electronic communications services, in order to ensure provision and interoperability of services throughout the Community. Operators shall offer access and interconnection to other undertakings on terms and conditions consistent with obligations imposed by the national regulatory authority pursuant to Articles 5 to 8.]

2. Public electronic communications networks established for the distribution of digital television services shall be capable of distributing wide-screen television services and programmes. Network operators that receive and redistribute wide-screen television services or programmes shall maintain that wide-screen format.

3. Without prejudice to Article 11 of Directive 2002/20/EC (Authorisation Directive), Member States shall require that undertakings which acquire information from another undertaking before, during or after the process of negotiating access or interconnection arrangements use that information solely for the purpose for which it was supplied and respect at all times the confidentiality of information transmitted or stored. The received information shall not be passed on to any other party, in particular other departments, subsidiaries or partners, for whom such information could provide a competitive advantage.

Notes

Article 4(1) was replaced as shown in square brackets by Directive 2009/140/EC (OJ L 337, 18.12.2009, p.37), with effect from 19 December 2009.

Commentary

Art 4: B&C: 12.026
Art 4(1): B&C: 12.025
Art 4(2): B&C: 12.023
Art 4(3): B&C: 12.025

Article 5

Powers and responsibilities of the national regulatory authorities with regard to access and interconnection

[1. National regulatory authorities shall, acting in pursuit of the objectives set out in Article 8 of Directive 2002/21/EC (Framework Directive), encourage and where appropriate ensure, in accordance with the provisions of this Directive, adequate access and interconnection, and the interoperability of services, exercising their responsibility in a way that promotes efficiency, sustainable competition, efficient investment and innovation, and gives the maximum benefit to end-users.]

In particular, without prejudice to measures that may be taken regarding undertakings with significant market power in accordance with Article 8, national regulatory authorities shall be able to impose:

   (a) to the extent that is necessary to ensure end-to-end connectivity, obligations on undertakings that control access to end-users, including in justified cases the obligation to interconnect their networks where this is not already the case;
   [(ab) in justified cases and to the extent that is necessary, the obligations on undertakings that control access to end-users to make their services interoperable.]
   (b) to the extent that is necessary to ensure accessibility for end-users to digital radio and television broadcasting services specified by the Member State, obligations on operators to provide access to the other facilities referred to in Annex I, Part II on fair, reasonable and non-discriminatory terms.

[2. Obligations and conditions imposed in accordance with paragraph 1 shall be objective, transparent, proportionate and non-discriminatory, and shall be implemented in accordance with the procedures referred to in Articles 6, 7 and 7a of Directive 2002/21/EC (Framework Directive).]

[ ]

[3. With regard to access and interconnection referred to in paragraph 1, Member States shall ensure that the national regulatory authority is empowered to intervene at its own initiative where justified in order to secure the policy objectives of Article 8 of Directive 2002/21/EC (Framework Directive), in accordance with the provisions of this Directive and the procedures referred to in Articles 6 and 7, 20 and 21 of Directive 2002/21/EC (Framework Directive).]

Notes

Article 5 was amended as shown in square brackets by Directive 2009/140/EC (OJ L 337, 18.12.2009, p.37), with effect from 19 December 2009.

Commentary

Art 5: B&C: 12.026
Art 5(1): B&C: 12.026, 12.043
Art 5(2): B&C: 12.019
Art 5(4): B&C: 12.026

CHAPTER III
OBLIGATIONS ON OPERATORS AND MARKET REVIEW PROCEDURES

Article 6
Conditional access systems and other facilities

1. Member States shall ensure that, in relation to conditional access to digital television and radio services broadcast to viewers and listeners in the Community, irrespective of the means of transmission, the conditions laid down in Annex I, Part I apply.

[2. In the light of market and technological developments, the Commission may adopt implementing measures to amend Annex I. The measures, designed to amend non-essential elements of this Directive, shall be adopted in accordance with the regulatory procedure with scrutiny referred to in Article 14(3).]

3. Notwithstanding the provisions of paragraph 1, Member States may permit their national regulatory authority, as soon as possible after the entry into force of this Directive and periodically thereafter, to review the conditions applied in accordance with this Article, by undertaking a market analysis in accordance with the first paragraph of Article 16 of Directive 2002/21/EC (Framework Directive) to determine whether to maintain, amend or withdraw the conditions applied.

Where, as a result of this market analysis, a national regulatory authority finds that one or more operators do not have significant market power on the relevant market, it may amend or withdraw the conditions with respect to those operators, in accordance with the procedures referred to in Articles 6 and 7 of Directive 2002/21/EC (Framework Directive), only to the extent that:

(a) accessibility for end-users to radio and television broadcasts and broadcasting channels and services specified in accordance with Article 31 of Directive 2002/22/EC (Universal Service Directive) would not be adversely affected by such amendment or withdrawal, and

(b) the prospects for effective competition in the markets for:

(i) retail digital television and radio broadcasting services, and
(ii) conditional access systems and other associated facilities,

would not be adversely affected by such amendment or withdrawal.

An appropriate period of notice shall be given to parties affected by such amendment or withdrawal of conditions.

4. Conditions applied in accordance with this Article are without prejudice to the ability of Member States to impose obligations in relation to the presentational aspect of electronic programme guides and similar listing and navigation facilities.

Notes
Article 6 was amended as shown in square brackets by Directive 2009/140/EC (OJ L 337, 18.12.2009, p.37), with effect from 19 December 2009.

Commentary
Art 6: B&C: 12.026

[ ]

Notes
Article 7 was deleted by Directive 2009/140/EC (OJ L 337, 18.12.2009, p.37), with effect from 19 December 2009.

Article 8
Imposition, amendment or withdrawal of obligations

1. Member States shall ensure that national regulatory authorities are empowered to impose the obligations identified in [Articles 9 to 13a].

2. Where an operator is designated as having significant market power on a specific market as a result of a market analysis carried out in accordance with Article 16 of Directive 2002/21/EC (Framework Directive), national regulatory authorities shall impose the obligations set out in Articles 9 to 13 of this Directive as appropriate.

3. Without prejudice to:

— the provisions of [Articles 5(1) and 6],
— the provisions of Articles 12 and 13 of Directive 2002/21/EC (Framework Directive), Condition 7 in Part B of the Annex to Directive 2002/20/EC (Authorisation Directive) as applied by virtue of Article 6(1) of that Directive, Articles 27, 28 and 30 of Directive 2002/22/EC (Universal Service Directive) and the relevant provisions of [Directive 2002/58/EC of the European Parliament and of the Council of 12 July 2002 concerning the processing of personal data and the protection of privacy in the electronic communications sector (Directive on privacy and electronic communications)[1]] containing obligations on undertakings other than those designated as having significant market power, or
— the need to comply with international commitments,

national regulatory authorities shall not impose the obligations set out in Articles 9 to 13 on operators that have not been designated in accordance with paragraph 2.

[In exceptional circumstances, when a national regulatory authority intends to impose on operators with significant market power obligations for access or interconnection other than those set out in Articles 9 to 13 in this Directive, it shall submit this request to the Commission. The Commission shall take utmost account of the opinion of the Body of European Regulators for Electronic Communications (BEREC).[2] The Commission, acting in accordance with Article 14(2), shall take a decision authorising or preventing the national regulatory authority from taking such measures.]

4. Obligations imposed in accordance with this Article shall be based on the nature of the problem identified, proportionate and justified in the light of the objectives laid down in Article 8 of Directive 2002/21/EC (Framework Directive). Such obligations shall only be imposed following consultation in accordance with Articles 6 and 7 of that Directive.

5. In relation to the third indent of the first subparagraph of paragraph 3, national regulatory authorities shall notify decisions to impose, amend or withdraw obligations on market players to the Commission, in accordance with the procedure referred to in Article 7 of Directive 2002/21/EC (Framework Directive).

Notes

[1] OJ L 201, 31.7.2002, p.37.
[2] Regulation (EC) No 1211/2009 of the European Parliament and of the Council of 25 November 2009 establishing the Body of European Regulators for Electronic Communications (BEREC) and the Office.]
Article 8 was amended as shown in square brackets by Directive 2009/140/EC (OJ L 337, 18.12.2009, p.37), with effect from 19 December 2009.

Commentary
Art 8(2): **B&C:** 12.009
Art 8(3): **F&N:** 13.29, 13.30, 13.38
Art 8(4): **B&C:** 12.019

Article 9
Obligation of transparency

[1. National regulatory authorities may, in accordance with the provisions of Article 8, impose obligations for transparency in relation to interconnection and/or access, requiring operators to make public specified information, such as accounting information, technical specifications, network characteristics, terms and conditions for supply and use, including any conditions limiting access to and/or use of services and applications where such conditions are allowed by Member States in conformity with Community law, and prices.]

2. In particular where an operator has obligations of non-discrimination, national regulatory authorities may require that operator to publish a reference offer, which shall be sufficiently unbundled to

ensure that undertakings are not required to pay for facilities which are not necessary for the service requested, giving a description of the relevant offerings broken down into components according to market needs, and the associated terms and conditions including prices. The national regulatory authority shall, *inter alia*, be able to impose changes to reference offers to give effect to obligations imposed under this Directive.

3. National regulatory authorities may specify the precise information to be made available, the level of detail required and the manner of publication.

[4. Notwithstanding paragraph 3, where an operator has obligations under Article 12 concerning wholesale network infrastructure access, national regulatory authorities shall ensure the publication of a reference offer containing at least the elements set out in Annex II.

5. The Commission may adopt the necessary amendments to Annex II in order to adapt it to technological and market developments. The measures, designed to amend non-essential elements of this Directive, shall be adopted in accordance with the regulatory procedure with scrutiny referred to in Article 14(3). In implementing the provisions of this paragraph, the Commission may be assisted by BEREC.]

Notes

Article 9 was amended as shown in square brackets by Directive 2009/140/EC (OJ L 337, 18.12.2009, p.37), with effect from 19 December 2009.

Commentary
Art 9: **B&C:** 12.019

Article 10
Obligation of non-discrimination

1. A national regulatory authority may, in accordance with the provisions of Article 8, impose obligations of non-discrimination, in relation to interconnection and/or access.

2. Obligations of non-discrimination shall ensure, in particular, that the operator applies equivalent conditions in equivalent circumstances to other undertakings providing equivalent services, and provides services and information to others under the same conditions and of the same quality as it provides for its own services, or those of it subsidiaries or partners.

Commentary
Art 10: **B&C:** 12.019

Article 11
Obligation of accounting separation

1. A national regulatory authority may, in accordance with the provisions of Article 8, impose obligations for accounting separation in relation to specified activities related to interconnection and/or access.

In particular, a national regulatory authority may require a vertically integrated company to make transparent its wholesale prices and its internal transfer prices *inter alia* to ensure compliance where there is a requirement for non-discrimination under Article 10 or, where necessary, to prevent unfair cross-subsidy. National regulatory authorities may specify the format and accounting methodology to be used.

2. Without prejudice to Article 5 of Directive 2002/21/EC (Framework Directive), to facilitate the verification of compliance with obligations of transparency and non-discrimination, national regulatory authorities shall have the power to require that accounting records, including data on revenues received from third parties, are provided on request. National regulatory authorities may publish such information as would contribute to an open and competitive market, while respecting national and Community rules on commercial confidentiality.

Commentary
Art 11: **B&C:** 12.019

Article 12
Obligations of access to, and use of, specific network facilities

1. A national regulatory authority may, in accordance with the provisions of Article 8, impose obligations on operators to meet reasonable requests for access to, and use of, specific network elements and associated facilities, *inter alia* in situations where the national regulatory authority considers that denial of access or unreasonable terms and conditions having a similar effect would hinder the emergence of a sustainable competitive market at the retail level, or would not be in the end-user's interest.

Operators may be required *inter alia*:

[(a) to give third parties access to specified network elements and/or facilities, including access to network elements which are not active and/or unbundled access to the local loop, to, inter alia, allow carrier selection and/or pre-selection and/or subscriber line resale offer;]
(b) to negotiate in good faith with undertakings requesting access;
(c) not to withdraw access to facilities already granted;
(d) to provide specified services on a wholesale basis for resale by third parties;
(e) to grant open access to technical interfaces, protocols or other key technologies that are indispensable for the interoperability of services or virtual network services;
[(f) to provide co-location or other forms of associated facilities sharing;]
(g) to provide specified services needed to ensure interoperability of end-to-end services to users, including facilities for intelligent network services or roaming on mobile networks;
(h) to provide access to operational support systems or similar software systems necessary to ensure fair competition in the provision of services;
(i) to interconnect networks or network facilities.
[(j) to provide access to associated services such as identity, location and presence service.]

National regulatory authorities may attach to those obligations conditions covering fairness, reasonableness and timeliness.

[2. When national regulatory authorities are considering the obligations referred in paragraph 1, and in particular when assessing how such obligations would be imposed proportionate to the objectives set out in Article 8 of Directive 2002/21/EC (Framework Directive), they shall take account in particular of the following factors:

(a) the technical and economic viability of using or installing competing facilities, in the light of the rate of market development, taking into account the nature and type of interconnection and/or access involved, including the viability of other upstream access products such as access to ducts;]
(b) the feasibility of providing the access proposed, in relation to the capacity available;
[(c) the initial investment by the facility owner, taking account of any public investment made and the risks involved in making the investment;
(d) the need to safeguard competition in the long term, with particular attention to economically efficient infrastructure-based competition;]
(e) where appropriate, any relevant intellectual property rights;
(f) the provision of pan-European services.

[3. When imposing obligations on an operator to provide access in accordance with the provisions of this Article, national regulatory authorities may lay down technical or operational conditions to be met by the provider and/or beneficiaries of such access where necessary to ensure normal operation of the network. Obligations to follow specific technical standards or specifications shall be in compliance with the standards and specifications laid down in accordance with Article 17 of Directive 2002/21/EC (Framework Directive).]

Notes
Article 12 was amended as shown in square brackets by Directive 2009/140/EC (OJ L 337, 18.12.2009, p.37), with effect from 19 December 2009.

Commentary
Art 12: B&C: 12.019, 12.031

Article 13
Price control and cost accounting obligations

[1. A national regulatory authority may, in accordance with the provisions of Article 8, impose obligations relating to cost recovery and price controls, including obligations for cost orientation of prices and obligations concerning cost accounting systems, for the provision of specific types of interconnection and/or access, in situations where a market analysis indicates that a lack of effective competition means that the operator concerned may sustain prices at an excessively high level, or may apply a price squeeze, to the detriment of end-users. To encourage investments by the operator, including in next generation networks, national regulatory authorities shall take into account the investment made by the operator, and allow him a reasonable rate of return on adequate capital employed, taking into account any risks specific to a particular new investment network project.]

2. National regulatory authorities shall ensure that any cost recovery mechanism or pricing methodology that is mandated serves to promote efficiency and sustainable competition and maximise consumer benefits. In this regard national regulatory authorities may also take account of prices available in comparable competitive markets.

3. Where an operator has an obligation regarding the cost orientation of its prices, the burden of proof that charges are derived from costs including a reasonable rate of return on investment shall lie with the operator concerned. For the purpose of calculating the cost of efficient provision of services, national regulatory authorities may use cost accounting methods independent of those used by the undertaking. National regulatory authorities may require an operator to provide full justification for its prices, and may, where appropriate, require prices to be adjusted.

4. National regulatory authorities shall ensure that, where implementation of a cost accounting system is mandated in order to support price controls, a description of the cost accounting system is made publicly available, showing at least the main categories under which costs are grouped and the rules used for the allocation of costs. Compliance with the cost accounting system shall be verified by a qualified independent body. A statement concerning compliance shall be published annually.

Notes

Article 13(1) was amended as shown in square brackets by Directive 2009/140/EC (OJ L 337, 18.12.2009, p.37), with effect from 19 December 2009.

Commentary
Art 13: B&C: 12.019
Art 13(a)–(b): F&N: 13.38

[Article 13a
Functional separation

1. Where the national regulatory authority concludes that the appropriate obligations imposed under Articles 9 to 13 have failed to achieve effective competition and that there are important and persisting competition problems and/or market failures identified in relation to the wholesale provision of certain access product markets, it may, as an exceptional measure, in accordance with the provisions of the second subparagraph of Article 8(3), impose an obligation on vertically integrated undertakings to place activities related to the wholesale provision of relevant access products in an independently operating business entity.

That business entity shall supply access products and services to all undertakings, including to other business entities within the parent company, on the same timescales, terms and conditions, including those relating to price and service levels, and by means of the same systems and processes.

2. When a national regulatory authority intends to impose an obligation for functional separation, it shall submit a proposal to the Commission that includes:

(a) evidence justifying the conclusions of the national regulatory authority as referred to in paragraph 1;

(b) a reasoned assessment that there is no or little prospect of effective and sustainable infrastructure-based competition within a reasonable time-frame;

(c) an analysis of the expected impact on the regulatory authority, on the undertaking, in particular on the workforce of the separated undertaking and on the electronic communications sector as a whole, and on incentives to invest in a sector as a whole, particularly with regard to the need to ensure social and territorial cohesion, and on other stakeholders including, in particular, the expected impact on competition and any potential entailing effects on consumers;

(d) an analysis of the reasons justifying that this obligation would be the most efficient means to enforce remedies aimed at addressing the competition problems/markets failures identified.

3. The draft measure shall include the following elements:

(a) the precise nature and level of separation, specifying in particular the legal status of the separate business entity;

(b) an identification of the assets of the separate business entity, and the products or services to be supplied by that entity;

(c) the governance arrangements to ensure the independence of the staff employed by the separate business entity, and the corresponding incentive structure;

(d) rules for ensuring compliance with the obligations;

(e) rules for ensuring transparency of operational procedures, in particular towards other stakeholders;

(f) a monitoring programme to ensure compliance, including the publication of an annual report.

4. Following the Commission's decision on the draft measure taken in accordance with Article 8(3), the national regulatory authority shall conduct a coordinated analysis of the different markets related to the access network in accordance with the procedure set out in Article 16 of Directive 2002/21/EC (Framework Directive). On the basis of its assessment, the national regulatory authority shall impose, maintain, amend or withdraw obligations, in accordance with Articles 6 and 7 of Directive 2002/21/EC (Framework Directive).

5. An undertaking on which functional separation has been imposed may be subject to any of the obligations identified in Articles 9 to13 in any specific market where it has been designated as having significant market power in accordance with Article 16 of Directive 2002/21/EC (Framework Directive), or any other obligations authorised by the Commission pursuant to Article 8(3).]

Notes
Article 13a was inserted by Directive 2009/140/EC (OJ L 337, 18.12.2009, p.37), with effect from 19 December 2009.

Commentary
Art 13a: B&C: 12.006, 12.019
Art 13a(1): B&C: 12.019

[*Article 13b*
Voluntary separation by a vertically integrated undertaking

1. Undertakings which have been designated as having significant market power in one or several relevant markets in accordance with Article 16 of Directive 2002/21/EC (Framework Directive) shall inform the national regulatory authority in advance and in a timely manner, in order to allow the national regulatory authority to assess the effect of the intended transaction, when they intend to transfer their local access network assets or a substantial part thereof to a separate legal entity under different ownership, or to establish a separate business entity in order to provide to all retail providers, including its own retail divisions, fully equivalent access products.

Undertakings shall also inform the national regulatory authority of any change of that intent as well as the final outcome of the process of separation.

2. The national regulatory authority shall assess the effect of the intended transaction on existing regulatory obligations under Directive 2002/21/EC (Framework Directive).

For that purpose, the national regulatory authority shall conduct a coordinated analysis of the different markets related to the access network in accordance with the procedure set out in Article 16 of Directive 2002/21/EC (Framework Directive).

On the basis of its assessment, the national regulatory authority shall impose, maintain, amend or withdraw obligations, in accordance with Articles 6 and 7 of Directive 2002/21/EC (Framework Directive).

3. The legally and/or operationally separate business entity may be subject to any of the obligations identified in Articles 9 to 13 in any specific market where it has been designated as having significant market power in accordance with Article 16 of Directive 2002/21/EC (Framework Directive), or any other obligations authorised by the Commission pursuant to Article 8(3).]

Notes

Article 13b was inserted by Directive 2009/140/EC (OJ L 337, 18.12.2009, p.37), with effect from 19 December 2009.

Commentary
Art 13b: B&C: 12.019

CHAPTER IV
PROCEDURAL PROVISIONS

Article 14
Committee

1. The Commission shall be assisted by the Communications Committee set up by Article 22 of Directive 2002/21/EC (Framework Directive).

2. Where reference is made to this paragraph, Articles 3 and 7 of Decision 1999/468/EC shall apply, having regard to the provisions of Article 8 thereof.

[3. Where reference is made to this paragraph, Article 5a(1) to (4) and Article 7 of Decision 1999/468/EC shall apply, having regard to the provisions of Article 8 thereof.]

[ ]

Notes

Article 14 was amended as shown in square brackets by Directive 2009/140/EC (OJ L 337, 18.12.2009, p.37), with effect from 19 December 2009.

Article 15
Publication of, and access to, information

1. Member States shall ensure that the specific obligations imposed on undertakings under this Directive are published and that the specific product/service and geographical markets are identified. They shall ensure that up-to-date information, provided that the information is not confidential and, in particular, does not comprise business secrets, is made publicly available in a manner that guarantees all interested parties easy access to that information.

2. Member States shall send to the Commission a copy of all such information published. The Commission shall make this information available in a readily accessible form, and shall distribute the information to the Communications Committee as appropriate.

Article 16
Notification

1. Member States shall notify to the Commission by at the latest the date of application referred to in Article 18(1) second subparagraph the national regulatory authorities responsible for the tasks set out in this Directive.

2. National regulatory authorities shall notify to the Commission the names of operators deemed to have significant market power for the purposes of this Directive, and the obligations imposed upon them under this Directive. Any changes affecting the obligations imposed upon undertakings or of the undertakings affected under the provisions of this Directive shall be notified to the Commission without delay.

Article 17
Review procedures

The Commission shall periodically review the functioning of this Directive and report to the European Parliament and to the Council, on the first occasion not later than three years after the date of application referred to in Article 18(1), second subparagraph. For this purpose, the Commission may request from the Member States information, which shall be supplied without undue delay.

Article 18
Transposition

1. Member States shall adopt and publish the laws, regulations and administrative provisions necessary to comply with this Directive by not later than 24 July 2003. They shall forthwith inform the Commission thereof.

They shall apply those measures from 25 July 2003.

When Member States adopt these measures, they shall contain a reference to this Directive or be accompanied by such a reference on the occasion of their official publication. The methods of making such reference shall be laid down by Member States.

2. Member States shall communicate to the Commission the text of the provisions of national law which they adopt in the field governed by this Directive and of any subsequent amendments to those provisions.

Notes

Measures to implement the amendments effected by Directive 2009/140/EC are required to be adopted and published by 25 May 2011 and applied from 26 May 2011: Directive 2009/140/EC, Article 5.

Article 19
Entry into force

This Directive shall enter into force on the day of its publication in the *Official Journal of the European Communities*.

Notes

Date of entry into force: 24 April 2002.

Article 20
Addressees

This Directive is addressed to the Member States.

Done at Brussels, 7 March 2002.

ANNEX I
CONDITIONS FOR ACCESS TO DIGITAL TELEVISION AND RADIO SERVICES BROADCAST TO VIEWERS AND LISTENERS IN THE COMMUNITY

Part I: Conditions for Conditional Access Systems to be Applied in Accordance with Article 6(1)

In relation to conditional access to digital television and radio services broadcast to viewers and listeners in the Community, irrespective of the means of transmission, Member States must ensure in accordance with Article 6 that the following conditions apply:

(a) conditional access systems operated on the market in the Community are to have the necessary technical capability for cost-effective transcontrol allowing the possibility for full control by network operators at local or regional level of the services using such conditional access systems;

(b) all operators of conditional access services, irrespective of the means of transmission, who provide access services to digital television and radio services and whose access services broadcasters depend on to reach any group of potential viewers or listeners are to:

— offer to all broadcasters, on a fair, reasonable and non-discriminatory basis compatible with Community competition law, technical services enabling the broadcasters" digitally-transmitted services to be received by viewers or listeners authorised by means of decoders administered by the service operators, and comply with Community competition law,

— keep separate financial accounts regarding their activity as conditional access providers.

(c) when granting licences to manufacturers of consumer equipment, holders of industrial property rights to conditional access products and systems are to ensure that this is done on fair, reasonable and non-discriminatory terms. Taking into account technical and commercial factors, holders of rights are not to subject the granting of licences to conditions prohibiting, deterring or discouraging the inclusion in the same product of:

— a common interface allowing connection with several other access systems, or

— means specific to another access system, provided that the licensee complies with the relevant and reasonable conditions ensuring, as far as he is concerned, the security of transactions of conditional access system operators.

Part II: Other Facilities to which Conditions may be Applied under Article 5(1)(b)

(a) Access to application program interfaces (APIs);

(b) Access to electronic programme guides (EPGs).

Commentary
Annex I, Part 2: B&C: 12.109

Annex II

[Minimum List of Items to Be Included in a Reference
Offer for Wholesale Network Infrastructure Access,
Including Shared or Fully Unbundled Access to the
Local Loop at a Fixed Location to be Published by Notified
Operators with Significant Market Power (smp)]

For the purposes of this Annex the following definitions apply:

[(a) "local sub-loop" means a partial local loop connecting the network termination point to a concentration point or a specified intermediate access point in the fixed public electronic communications network;]

(b) "unbundled access to the local loop" means full unbundled access to the local loop and shared access to the local loop; it does not entail a change in ownership of the local loop;

[(c) "full unbundled access to the local loop" means the provision to a beneficiary of access to the local loop or local sub-loop of the SMP operator allowing the use of the full capacity of the network infrastructure;]

[(d) "shared access to the local loop" means the provision to a beneficiary of access to the local loop or local sub-loop of the SMP operator, allowing the use of a specified part of the capacity of the network infrastructure such as a part of the frequency or an equivalent;]

A. Conditions for unbundled access to the local loop

[1. Network elements to which access is offered covering in particular the following elements together with appropriate associated facilities:

(a) unbundled access to local loops (full and shared);

(b) unbundled access to local sub-loops (full and shared), including, when relevant, access to network elements which are not active for the purpose of roll-out of backhaul networks;

(c) where relevant, duct access enabling the roll out of access networks.

2. Information concerning the locations of physical access sites including cabinets and distribution frames, availability of local loops, sub-loops and backhaul in specific parts of the access network and when relevant, information concerning the locations of ducts and the availability within ducts;

3. Technical conditions related to access and use of local loops and sub-loops, including the technical characteristics of the twisted pair and/or optical fibre and/or equivalent, cable distributors, and associated facilities and, when relevant, technical conditions related to access to ducts;]

4. Ordering and provisioning procedures, usage restrictions.

B. Co-location services

[1. Information on the SMP operator's existing relevant sites or equipment locations and planned update thereof.[1]]

2. Co-location options at the sites indicated under point 1 (including physical co-location and, as appropriate, distant co-location and virtual co-location).

3. Equipment characteristics: restrictions, if any, on equipment that can be co-located.

4. Security issues: measures put in place by notified operators to ensure the security of their locations.

5. Access conditions for staff of competitive operators.

6. Safety standards.

7. Rules for the allocation of space where co-location space is limited.

8. Conditions for beneficiaries to inspect the locations at which physical co-location is available, or sites where co-location has been refused on grounds of lack of capacity.

C. Information systems

Conditions for access to notified operator's operational support systems, information systems or databases for pre-ordering, provisioning, ordering, maintenance and repair requests and billing.

D. Supply conditions

1. Lead time for responding to requests for supply of services and facilities; service level agreements, fault resolution, procedures to return to a normal level of service and quality of service parameters.

2. Standard contract terms, including, where appropriate, compensation provided for failure to meet lead times.

3. Prices or pricing formulae for each feature, function and facility listed above.

Notes

[[1] Availability of this information may be restricted to interested parties only, in order to avoid public security concerns.] Annex II was amended as shown in square brackets by Directive 2009/140/EC (OJ L 337, 18.12.2009, p.37), with effect from 19 December 2009.

E3

DIRECTIVE 2002/20/EC OF THE EUROPEAN PARLIAMENT AND OF THE COUNCIL

of 7 March 2002

on the authorisation of electronic communications networks and services

(Authorisation Directive)

Official Journal L 108, 24.4.2002, p.21

Celex No: 32002L0020

EUR-Lex permanent link: <http://eur-lex.europa.eu/LexUriServ/LexUriServ.do?uri=CELEX:3200 2L0020:EN:NOT>

Notes

EEA application: this Directive was adopted with appropriate adaptations by EEA Joint Committee Decision No 11/2004 (OJ No L 116, 22.4.2004, p.60 and EEA Supplement No 20, 22.4.2004, p.14): see EEA Agreement, Annex XI, Point 5ck.

Commentary

Directive 2002/20/EC: B&C: 12.005, 12.006, 12.013, 12.024, 12.027, 12.035 **F&N:** 13.22, 13.50, 13.211, 14.144, 14.151

THE EUROPEAN PARLIAMENT AND THE COUNCIL OF THE EUROPEAN UNION,

Having regard to the Treaty establishing the European Community, and in particular Article [114]* thereof,

Having regard to the proposal from the Commission,[1]

Having regard to the opinion of the Economic and Social Committee,[2]

Acting in accordance with the procedure laid down in Article [294] of the Treaty,[3]

Notes

* Ed note: please see the Note on the Lisbon Treaty at p.xvii in regard to article renumbering introduced by the Lisbon Treaty.

[1] OJ C 365 E, 19.12.2000, p.230 and OJ C 270 E, 25.9.2001, p.182.

[2] OJ C 123, 25.4.2001, p.55.

[3] Opinion of the European Parliament of 1 March 2001 (OJ C 277, 1.10.2001, p.116), Council Common Position of 17 September 2001 (OJ C 337, 30.11.2001, p.18) and Decision of the European Parliament of 12 December 2001 [OJ C 177 E, 25.7.2002, p.82]. Council Decision of 14 February 2002.

Whereas:

(1) The outcome of the public consultation on the 1999 review of the regulatory framework for electronic communications, as reflected in the Commission communication of 26 April 2000, and the findings reported by the Commission in its communications on the fifth and sixth reports on the implementation of the telecommunications regulatory package, has confirmed the need for a more harmonised and less onerous market access regulation for electronic communications networks and services throughout the Community.

(2) Convergence between different electronic communications networks and services and their technologies requires the establishment of an authorisation system covering all comparable services in a similar way regardless of the technologies used.

(3) The objective of this Directive is to create a legal framework to ensure the freedom to provide electronic communications networks and services, subject only to the conditions laid down in this Directive and to any restrictions in conformity with Article 46(1) of the Treaty, in particular measures regarding public policy, public security and public health.

(4) This Directive covers authorisation of all electronic communications networks and services whether they are provided to the public or not. This is important to ensure that both categories of providers may benefit from objective, transparent, non-discriminatory and proportionate rights, conditions and procedures.

(5) This Directive only applies to the granting of rights to use radio frequencies where such use involves the provision of an electronic communications network or service, normally for remuneration. The self-use of radio terminal equipment, based on the non-exclusive use of specific radio frequencies by a user and not related to an economic activity, such as use of a citizen's band by radio amateurs, does not consist of the provision of an electronic communications network or service and is therefore not covered by this Directive. Such use is covered by the Directive 1999/5/EC of the European Parliament and of the Council of 9 March 1999 on radio equipment and telecommunications terminal equipment and the mutual recognition of their conformity.[1]

Notes

[1] OJ L 91, 7.4.1999, p.10.

Commentary

Recital 5: B&C: 12.027, 12.029

(6) Provisions regarding the free movement of conditional access systems and the free provision of protected services based on such systems are laid down in Directive 98/84/EC of the European Parliament and of the Council of 20 November 1998 on the legal protection of services based on, or consisting of, conditional access.[1] The authorisation of such systems and services therefore does not need to be covered by this Directive.

Notes
[1] OJ L 320, 28.11.1998, p.54.
Commentary
Recital 6: B&C: 12.027

(7) The least onerous authorisation system possible should be used to allow the provision of electronic communications networks and services in order to stimulate the development of new electronic communications services and pan-European communications networks and services and to allow service providers and consumers to benefit from the economies of scale of the single market.

Commentary
Recital 7: B&C: 12.028

(8) Those aims can be best achieved by general authorisation of all electronic communications networks and services without requiring any explicit decision or administrative act by the national regulatory authority and by limiting any procedural requirements to notification only. Where Member States require notification by providers of electronic communication networks or services when they start their activities, they may also require proof of such notification having been made by means of any legally recognised postal or electronic acknowledgement of receipt of the notification. Such acknowledgement should in any case not consist of or require an administrative act by the national regulatory authority to which the notification must be made.

Commentary
Recital 8: B&C: 12.013

(9) It is necessary to include the rights and obligations of undertakings under general authorisations explicitly in such authorisations in order to ensure a level playing field throughout the Community and to facilitate cross-border negotiation of interconnection between public communications networks.

Commentary
Recital 9: B&C: 12.027

(10) The general authorisation entitles undertakings providing electronic communications networks and services to the public to negotiate interconnection under the conditions of Directive 2002/19/EC of the European Parliament and of the Council of 7 March 2002 on access to, and interconnection of, electronic communication networks and associated facilities (Access Directive).[1] Undertakings providing electronic communications networks and services other than to the public can negotiate interconnection on commercial terms.

Notes
[1] See [OJ L 108, 24.4.2002, p.7].

(11) The granting of specific rights may continue to be necessary for the use of radio frequencies and numbers, including short codes, from the national numbering plan. Rights to numbers may also be allocated from a European numbering plan, including for example the virtual country code "3883" which has been attributed to member countries of the European Conference of Post and Telecommunications (CEPT). Those rights of use should not be restricted except where this is unavoidable in view of the scarcity of radio frequencies and the need to ensure the efficient use thereof.

Commentary
Recital 11: B&C: 12.112

(12) This Directive does not prejudice whether radio frequencies are assigned directly to providers of electronic communication networks or services or to entities that use these networks or services. Such entities may be radio or television broadcast content providers. Without prejudice to specific criteria and procedures adopted by Member States to grant rights of use for radio frequencies to providers of radio or television broadcast content services, to pursue general interest objectives in conformity with Community law, the procedure for assignment of radio frequencies should in any event be objective, transparent, non-discriminatory and proportionate. In accordance with case law of the Court of Justice, any national restrictions on the rights guaranteed by Article [56] of the Treaty should be objectively justified, proportionate and not exceed what is necessary to achieve general interest objectives as defined by Member States in conformity with Community law. The responsibility for compliance with the conditions attached to the right to use a radio frequency and the relevant conditions attached to the general authorisation should in any case lie with the undertaking to whom the right of use for the radio frequency has been granted.

(13) As part of the application procedure for granting rights to use a radio frequency, Member States may verify whether the applicant will be able to comply with the conditions attached to such rights. For this purpose the applicant may be requested to submit the necessary information to prove his ability to comply with these conditions. Where such information is not provided, the application for the right to use a radio frequency may be rejected.

(14) Member States are neither obliged to grant nor prevented from granting rights to use numbers from the national numbering plan or rights to install facilities to undertakings other than providers of electronic communications networks or services.

(15) The conditions, which may be attached to the general authorisation and to the specific rights of use, should be limited to what is strictly necessary to ensure compliance with requirements and obligations under Community law and national law in accordance with Community law.

(16) In the case of electronic communications networks and services not provided to the public it is appropriate to impose fewer and lighter conditions than are justified for electronic communications networks and services provided to the public.

Commentary
Recital 16: B&C: 12.028

(17) Specific obligations which may be imposed on providers of electronic communications networks and services in accordance with Community law by virtue of their significant market power as defined in Directive 2002/21/EC of the European Parliament and of the Council of 7 March 2002 on a common regulatory framework for electronic communications networks and services (Framework Directive)[1] should be imposed separately from the general rights and obligations under the general authorisation.

Notes
[1] See [OJ L 108, 24.4.2002, p.33].

(18) The general authorisation should only contain conditions which are specific to the electronic communications sector. It should not be made subject to conditions which are already applicable by virtue of other existing national law which is not specific to the electronic communications sector. Nevertheless, the national regulatory authorities may inform network operators and service providers about other legislation concerning their business, for instance through references on their websites.

(19) The requirement to publish decisions on the granting of rights to use frequencies or numbers may be fulfilled by making these decisions publicly accessible via a website.

(20) The same undertaking, for example a cable operator, can offer both an electronic communications service, such as the conveyance of television signals, and services not covered under this Directive, such as the commercialisation of an offer of sound or television broadcasting content services, and therefore additional obligations can be imposed on this undertaking in relation to its activity as a

content provider or distributor, according to provisions other than those of this Directive, without prejudice to the list of conditions laid in the Annex to this Directive.

Commentary
Recital 20: B&C: 12.027

---

(21) When granting rights of use for radio frequencies, numbers or rights to install facilities, the relevant authorities may inform the undertakings to whom they grant such rights of the relevant conditions in the general authorisation.

(22) Where the demand for radio frequencies in a specific range exceeds their availability, appropriate and transparent procedures should be followed for the assignment of such frequencies in order to avoid any discrimination and optimise use of those scarce resources.

(23) National regulatory authorities should ensure, in establishing criteria for competitive or comparative selection procedures, that the objectives in Article 8 of Directive 2002/21/EC (Framework Directive) are met. It would therefore not be contrary to this Directive if the application of objective, non-discriminatory and proportionate selection criteria to promote the development of competition would have the effect of excluding certain undertakings from a competitive or comparative selection procedure for a particular radio frequency.

(24) Where the harmonised assignment of radio frequencies to particular undertakings has been agreed at European level, Member States should strictly implement such agreements in the granting of rights of use of radio frequencies from the national frequency usage plan.

(25) Providers of electronic communications networks and services may need a confirmation of their rights under the general authorisation with respect to interconnection and rights of way, in particular to facilitate negotiations with other, regional or local, levels of government or with service providers in other Member States. For this purpose the national regulatory authorities should provide declarations to undertakings either upon request or alternatively as an automatic response to a notification under the general authorisation. Such declarations should not by themselves constitute entitlements to rights nor should any rights under the general authorisation or rights of use or the exercise of such rights depend upon a declaration.

(26) Where undertakings find that their applications for rights to install facilities have not been dealt with in accordance with the principles set out in Directive 2002/21/EC (Framework Directive) or where such decisions are unduly delayed, they should have the right to appeal against decisions or delays in such decisions in accordance with that Directive.

(27) The penalties for non-compliance with conditions under the general authorisation should be commensurate with the infringement. Save in exceptional circumstances, it would not be proportionate to suspend or withdraw the right to provide electronic communications services or the right to use radio frequencies or numbers where an undertaking did not comply with one or more of the conditions under the general authorisation. This is without prejudice to urgent measures which the relevant authorities of the Member States may need to take in case of serious threats to public safety, security or health or to economic and operational interests of other undertakings. This Directive should also be without prejudice to any claims between undertakings for compensation for damages under national law.

(28) Subjecting service providers to reporting and information obligations can be cumbersome, both for the undertaking and for the national regulatory authority concerned. Such obligations should therefore be proportionate, objectively justified and limited to what is strictly necessary. It is not necessary to require systematic and regular proof of compliance with all conditions under the general authorisation or attached to rights of use. Undertakings have a right to know the purposes for which the information they should provide will be used. The provision of information should not be a condition for market access. For statistical purposes a notification may be required from providers of electronic communication networks or services when they cease activities.

(29) This Directive should be without prejudice to Member States' obligations to provide any information necessary for the defence of Community interests within the context of international agreements. This Directive should also be without prejudice to any reporting obligations under legislation which is not specific to the electronic communications sector such as competition law.

(30) Administrative charges may be imposed on providers of electronic communications services in order to finance the activities of the national regulatory authority in managing the authorisation system and for the granting of rights of use. Such charges should be limited to cover the actual administrative costs for those activities. For this purpose transparency should be created in the income and expenditure of national regulatory authorities by means of annual reporting about the total sum of charges collected and the administrative costs incurred. This will allow undertakings to verify that administrative costs and charges are in balance.

(31) Systems for administrative charges should not distort competition or create barriers for entry into the market. With a general authorisation system it will no longer be possible to attribute administrative costs and hence charges to individual undertakings except for the granting of rights to use numbers, radio frequencies and for rights to install facilities. Any applicable administrative charges should be in line with the principles of a general authorisation system. An example of a fair, simple and transparent alternative for these charge attribution criteria could be a turnover related distribution key. Where administrative charges are very low, flat rate charges, or charges combining a flat rate basis with a turnover related element could also be appropriate.

(32) In addition to administrative charges, usage fees may be levied for the use of radio frequencies and numbers as an instrument to ensure the optimal use of such resources. Such fees should not hinder the development of innovative services and competition in the market. This Directive is without prejudice to the purpose for which fees for rights of use are employed. Such fees may for instance be used to finance activities of national regulatory authorities that cannot be covered by administrative charges. Where, in the case of competitive or comparative selection procedures, fees for rights of use for radio frequencies consist entirely or partly of a one-off amount, payment arrangements should ensure that such fees do not in practice lead to selection on the basis of criteria unrelated to the objective of ensuring optimal use of radio frequencies. The Commission may publish on a regular basis benchmark studies with regard to best practices for the assignment of radio frequencies, the assignment of numbers or the granting of rights of way.

(33) Member States may need to amend rights, conditions, procedures, charges and fees relating to general authorisations and rights of use where this is objectively justified. Such changes should be duly notified to all interested parties in good time, giving them adequate opportunity to express their views on any such amendments.

(34) The objective of transparency requires that service providers, consumers and other interested parties have easy access to any information regarding rights, conditions, procedures, charges, fees and decisions concerning the provision of electronic communications services, rights of use of radio frequencies and numbers, rights to install facilities, national frequency usage plans and national numbering plans. The national regulatory authorities have an important task in providing such information and keeping it up to date. Where such rights are administered by other levels of government the national regulatory authorities should endeavour to create a user-friendly instrument for access to information regarding such rights.

(35) The proper functioning of the single market on the basis of the national authorisation regimes under this Directive should be monitored by the Commission.

(36) In order to arrive at a single date of application of all elements of the new regulatory framework for the electronic communications sector, it is important that the process of national transposition of this Directive and of alignment of the existing licences with the new rules take place in parallel. However, in specific cases where the replacement of authorisations existing on the date of entry into force of this Directive by the general authorisation and the individual rights of use in accordance with this Directive would lead to an increase in the obligations for service providers operating under an existing authorisation or to a reduction of their rights, Member States may avail themselves of an additional nine months after the date of application of this Directive for alignment of such licences, unless this would have a negative effect on the rights and obligations of other undertakings.

(37) There may be circumstances under which the abolition of an authorisation condition regarding access to electronic communications networks would create serious hardship for one or more undertakings that have benefited from the condition. In such cases further transitional arrangements may be granted by the Commission, upon request by a Member State.

(38) Since the objectives of the proposed action, namely the harmonisation and simplification of electronic communications rules and conditions for the authorisation of networks and services cannot be sufficiently achieved by the Member States and can therefore, by reason of the scale and effects of the action, be better achieved at Community level, the Community may adopt measures in accordance with the principle of subsidiarity as set out in Article 5 of the [Treaty on European Union]. In accordance with the principle of proportionality, as set out in that Article, this Directive does not go beyond what is necessary for those objectives,

HAVE ADOPTED THIS DIRECTIVE:

Article 1
Objective and scope

1. The aim of this Directive is to implement an internal market in electronic communications networks and services through the harmonisation and simplification of authorisation rules and conditions in order to facilitate their provision throughout the Community.

2. This Directive shall apply to authorisations for the provision of electronic communications networks and services.

Commentary
Art 1: B&C: 12.027 F&N: 13.20

Article 2
Definitions

1. For the purposes of this Directive, the definitions set out in Article 2 of Directive 2002/21/EC (Framework Directive) shall apply.

[2. The following definition shall also apply:

"general authorisation" means a legal framework established by the Member State ensuring rights for the provision of electronic communications networks or services and laying down sector specific obligations that may apply to all or to specific types of electronic communications networks and services, in accordance with this Directive.]

Notes
Article 2(2) was amended as shown in square brackets by Directive 2009/140/EC (OJ L 337, 18.12.2009, p.37), with effect from 19 December 2009.

Article 3
General authorisation of electronic communications networks and services

1. Member States shall ensure the freedom to provide electronic communications networks and services, subject to the conditions set out in this Directive. To this end, Member States shall not prevent an undertaking from providing electronic communications networks or services, except where this is necessary for the reasons set out in Article [52] of the Treaty.

2. The provision of electronic communications networks or the provision of electronic communications services may, without prejudice to the specific obligations referred to in Article 6(2) or rights of use referred to in Article 5, only be subject to a general authorisation. The undertaking concerned may be required to submit a notification but may not be required to obtain an explicit decision or any other administrative act by the national regulatory authority before exercising the rights stemming from the authorisation. Upon notification, when required, an undertaking may begin activity, where necessary subject to the provisions on rights of use in Articles 5, 6 and 7.

[Undertakings providing cross-border electronic communications services to undertakings located in several Member States shall not be required to submit more than one notification per Member State concerned.]

3. The notification referred to in paragraph 2 shall not entail more than a declaration by a legal or natural person to the national regulatory authority of the intention to commence the provision of electronic communication networks or services and the submission of the minimal information which is required to allow the national regulatory authority to keep a register or list of providers of electronic communications networks and services. This information must be limited to what is necessary for the identification of the provider, such as company registration numbers, and the provider's contact persons, the provider's address, a short description of the network or service, and an estimated date for starting the activity.

Notes

Article 3 was amended as shown in square brackets by Directive 2009/140/EC (OJ L 337, 18.12.2009, p.37), with effect from 19 December 2009.

Commentary
Art 3: B&C: 12.027
Art 3(2): B&C: 12.027

Article 4
Minimum list of rights derived from the general authorisation

1. Undertakings authorised pursuant to Article 3, shall have the right to:

(a) provide electronic communications networks and services;
(b) have their application for the necessary rights to install facilities considered in accordance with Article 11 of Directive 2002/21/EC (Framework Directive).

2. When such undertakings provide electronic communications networks or services to the public the general authorisation shall also give them the right to:

(a) negotiate interconnection with and where applicable obtain access to or interconnection from other providers of publicly available communications networks and services covered by a general authorisation anywhere in the Community under the conditions of and in accordance with Directive 2002/19/EC (Access Directive);
(b) be given an opportunity to be designated to provide different elements of a universal service and/ or to cover different parts of the national territory in accordance with Directive 2002/22/EC of the European Parliament and of the Council of 7 March 2002 on universal service and users' rights relating to electronic communications networks and services (Universal Service Directive).[1]

Notes

[1] See [OJ L 108, 24.4.2002, p.51].

Commentary
Art 4: B&C: 12.025, 12.027

[Article 5
Rights of use for radio frequencies and numbers

1. Member States shall facilitate the use of radio frequencies under general authorisations. Where necessary, Member States may grant individual rights of use in order to:

— avoid harmful interference,
— ensure technical quality of service,
— safeguard efficient use of spectrum, or
— fulfil other objectives of general interest as defined by Member States in conformity with Community law.

2. Where it is necessary to grant individual rights of use for radio frequencies and numbers, Member States shall grant such rights, upon request, to any undertaking for the provision of networks or services under the general authorisation referred to in Article 3, subject to the provisions of Articles 6, 7 and 11(1)(c) of this Directive and any other rules ensuring the efficient use of those resources in accordance with Directive 2002/21/EC (Framework Directive).

Without prejudice to specific criteria and procedures adopted by Member States to grant rights of use of radio frequencies to providers of radio or television broadcast content services with a view to pursuing general interest objectives in conformity with Community law, the rights of use for radio frequencies and numbers shall be granted through open, objective, transparent, non-discriminatory and proportionate procedures, and, in the case of radio frequencies, in accordance with the provisions of Article 9 of Directive 2002/21/EC (Framework Directive). An exception to the requirement of open procedures may apply in cases where the granting of individual rights of use of radio frequencies to the providers of radio or television broadcast content services is necessary to achieve a general interest objective as defined by Member States in conformity with Community law.

When granting rights of use, Member States shall specify whether those rights can be transferred by the holder of the rights, and under which conditions. In the case of radio frequencies, such provision shall be in accordance with Articles 9 and 9b of Directive 2002/21/EC (Framework Directive).

Where Member States grant rights of use for a limited period of time, the duration shall be appropriate for the service concerned in view of the objective pursued taking due account of the need to allow for an appropriate period for investment amortisation.

Where individual rights to use radio frequencies are granted for 10 years or more and such rights may not be transferred or leased between undertakings pursuant to Article 9b of Directive 2002/21/EC (Framework Directive) the competent national authority shall ensure that the criteria to grant individual rights of use apply and are complied with for the duration of the licence, in particular upon a justified request of the holder of the right. If those criteria are no longer applicable, the individual right of use shall be changed into a general authorisation for the use of radio frequencies, subject to prior notice and after a reasonable period, or shall be made transferable or leaseable between undertakings in accordance with Article 9b of Directive 2002/21/EC (Framework Directive).

3. Decisions on the granting of rights of use shall be taken, communicated and made public as soon as possible after receipt of the complete application by the national regulatory authority, within three weeks in the case of numbers that have been allocated for specific purposes within the national numbering plan and within six weeks in the case of radio frequencies that have been allocated to be used by electronic communications services within the national frequency plan. The latter time limit shall be without prejudice to any applicable international agreements relating to the use of radio frequencies or of orbital positions.

4. Where it has been decided, after consultation with interested parties in accordance with Article 6 of Directive 2002/21/EC (Framework Directive), that rights for use of numbers of exceptional economic value are to be granted through competitive or comparative selection procedures, Member States may extend the maximum period of three weeks by up to a further three weeks.

With regard to competitive or comparative selection procedures for radio frequencies, Article 7 shall apply.

5. Member States shall not limit the number of rights of use to be granted except where this is necessary to ensure the efficient use of radio frequencies in accordance with Article 7.

6. Competent national authorities shall ensure that radio frequencies are efficiently and effectively used in accordance with Articles 8(2) and 9(2) of Directive 2002/21/EC (Framework Directive). They shall ensure competition is not distorted by any transfer or accumulation of rights of use of radio frequencies. For such purposes, Member States may take appropriate measures such as mandating the sale or the lease of rights to use radio frequencies.]

Notes

Article 5 was replaced as shown in square brackets by Directive 2009/140/EC (OJ L 337, 18.12.2009, p.37), with effect from 19 December 2009.

Commentary

Art 5: **B&C:** 12.026, 12.029
Art 5(2): **F&N:** 14.149

Article 6
Conditions attached to the general authorisation and to the rights of use for radio frequencies and for numbers, and specific obligations

[1. The general authorisation for the provision of electronic communications networks or services and the rights of use for radio frequencies and rights of use for numbers may be subject only to the conditions listed in the Annex. Such conditions shall be non-discriminatory, proportionate and transparent and, in the case of rights of use for radio frequencies, shall be in accordance with Article 9 of Directive 2002/21/EC (Framework Directive).]

2. Specific obligations which may be imposed on providers of electronic communications networks and services under Articles 5(1), 5(2), 6 and 8 of Directive 2002/19/EC (Access Directive) and [Article 17 of Directive 2002/22/EC (Universal Service Directive)] or on those designated to provide universal service under the said Directive shall be legally separate from the rights and obligations under the general authorisation. In order to achieve transparency for undertakings, the criteria and procedures for imposing such specific obligations on individual undertakings shall be referred to in the general authorisation.

3. The general authorisation shall only contain conditions which are specific for that sector and are set out in Part A of the Annex and shall not duplicate conditions which are applicable to undertakings by virtue of other national legislation.

4. Member States shall not duplicate the conditions of the general authorisation where they grant the right of use for radio frequencies or numbers.

Notes

Article 6 was amended as shown in square brackets by Directive 2009/140/EC (OJ L 337, 18.12.2009, p.37), with effect from 19 December 2009.

Commentary
Art 6(1): B&C: 12.028, 12.029
Art 6(2): B&C: 12.027

Article 7
Procedure for limiting the number of rights of use to be granted for radio frequencies

[1. Where a Member State is considering whether to limit the number of rights of use to be granted for radio frequencies or whether to extend the duration of existing rights other than in accordance with the terms specified in such rights, it shall *inter alia*:]

(a) give due weight to the need to maximise benefits for users and to facilitate the development of competition;

(b) give all interested parties, including users and consumers, the opportunity to express their views on any limitation in accordance with Article 6 of Directive 2002/21/EC (Framework Directive);

[(c) publish any decision to limit the granting of rights of use or the renewal of rights of use, stating the reasons therefor;]

(d) after having determined the procedure, invite applications for rights of use; and

(e) review the limitation at reasonable intervals or at the reasonable request of affected undertakings.

2. Where a Member State concludes that further rights of use for radio frequencies can be granted, it shall publish that conclusion and invite applications for such rights.

[3. Where the granting of rights of use for radio frequencies needs to be limited, Member States shall grant such rights on the basis of selection criteria which must be objective, transparent, non-discriminatory and proportionate. Any such selection criteria must give due weight to the achievement of the objectives of Article 8 of Directive 2002/21/EC (Framework Directive) and of the requirements of Article 9 of that Directive.]

4. Where competitive or comparative selection procedures are to be used, Member States may extend the maximum period of six weeks referred to in Article 5(3) for as long as necessary to ensure that such

procedures are fair, reasonable, open and transparent to all interested parties, but by no longer than eight months.

These time limits shall be without prejudice to any applicable international agreements relating to the use of radio frequencies and satellite coordination.

5. This Article is without prejudice to the transfer of rights of use for radio frequencies in accordance with [Article 9b] of Directive 2002/21/EC (Framework Directive).

Notes

Article 7 was amended as shown in square brackets by Directive 2009/140/EC (OJ L 337, 18.12.2009, p.37), with effect from 19 December 2009.

Commentary
Art 7: **B&C:** 12.029
Art 7(3): **F&N:** 14.149

Article 8
Harmonised assignment of radio frequencies

Where the usage of radio frequencies has been harmonised, access conditions and procedures have been agreed, and undertakings to which the radio frequencies shall be assigned have been selected in accordance with international agreements and Community rules, Member States shall grant the right of use for such radio frequencies in accordance therewith. Provided that all national conditions attached to the right to use the radio frequencies concerned have been satisfied in the case of a common selection procedure, Member States shall not impose any further conditions, additional criteria or procedures which would restrict, alter or delay the correct implementation of the common assignment of such radio frequencies.

Commentary
Art 8: **B&C:** 12.029
Art 8(1): **B&C:** 12.031, 12.032

Article 9
Declarations to facilitate the exercise of rights to install facilities and rights of interconnection

At the request of an undertaking, national regulatory authorities shall, within one week, issue standardised declarations, confirming, where applicable, that the undertaking has submitted a notification under Article 3(2) and detailing under what circumstances any undertaking providing electronic communications networks or services under the general authorisation has the right to apply for rights to install facilities, negotiate interconnection, and/or obtain access or interconnection in order to facilitate the exercise of those rights for instance at other levels of government or in relation to other undertakings. Where appropriate such declarations may also be issued as an automatic reply following the notification referred to in Article 3(2).

Commentary
Art 9: **B&C:** 12.027

Article 10
Compliance with the conditions of the general authorisation or of rights of use and with specific obligations

[1. National regulatory authorities shall monitor and supervise compliance with the conditions of the general authorisation or of rights of use and with the specific obligations referred to in Article 6(2), in accordance with Article 11.

National regulatory authorities shall have the power to require undertakings providing electronic communications networks or services covered by the general authorisation or enjoying rights of use for radio frequencies or numbers to provide all information necessary to verify compliance with the conditions of the general authorisation or of rights of use or with the specific obligations referred to in Article 6(2), in accordance with Article 11.

2. Where a national regulatory authority finds that an undertaking does not comply with one or more of the conditions of the general authorisation or of rights of use, or with the specific obligations referred to in Article 6(2), it shall notify the undertaking of those findings and give the undertaking the opportunity to state its views, within a reasonable time limit.

3. The relevant authority shall have the power to require the cessation of the breach referred to in paragraph 2 either immediately or within a reasonable time limit and shall take appropriate and proportionate measures aimed at ensuring compliance.

In this regard, Member States shall empower the relevant authorities to impose:

(a) dissuasive financial penalties where appropriate, which may include periodic penalties having retroactive effect; and

(b) orders to cease or delay provision of a service or bundle of services which, if continued, would result in significant harm to competition, pending compliance with access obligations imposed following a market analysis carried out in accordance with Article 16 of Directive 2002/21/EC (Framework Directive).

The measures and the reasons on which they are based shall be communicated to the undertaking concerned without delay and shall stipulate a reasonable period for the undertaking to comply with the measure.

4. Notwithstanding the provisions of paragraphs 2 and 3, Member States shall empower the relevant authority to impose financial penalties where appropriate on undertakings for failure to provide information in accordance with the obligations imposed under Article 11(1)(a) or (b) of this Directive and Article 9 of Directive 2002/19/EC (Access Directive) within a reasonable period stipulated by the national regulatory authority.

5. In cases of serious or repeated breaches of the conditions of the general authorisation or of the rights of use, or specific obligations referred to in Article 6(2), where measures aimed at ensuring compliance as referred to in paragraph 3 of this Article have failed, national regulatory authorities may prevent an undertaking from continuing to provide electronic communications networks or services or suspend or withdraw rights of use. Sanctions and penalties which are effective, proportionate and dissuasive may be applied to cover the period of any breach, even if the breach has subsequently been rectified.

6. Irrespective of the provisions of paragraphs 2, 3 and 5, where the relevant authority has evidence of a breach of the conditions of the general authorisation rights of use or of the specific obligations referred to in Article 6(2) that represents an immediate and serious threat to public safety, public security or public health or will create serious economic or operational problems for other providers or users of electronic communications networks or services or other users of the radio spectrum, it may take urgent interim measures to remedy the situation in advance of reaching a final decision. The undertaking concerned shall thereafter be given a reasonable opportunity to state its views and propose any remedies. Where appropriate, the relevant authority may confirm the interim measures, which shall be valid for a maximum of 3 months, but which may, in circumstances where enforcement procedures have not been completed, be extended for a further period of up to three months.]

7. Undertakings shall have the right to appeal against measures taken under this Article in accordance with the procedure referred to in Article 4 of Directive 2002/21/EC (Framework Directive).

Notes

Article 10 was amended as shown in square brackets by Directive 2009/140/EC (OJ L 337, 18.12.2009, p.37), with effect from 19 December 2009.

Commentary

Art 10: B&C: 12.019, 12.027

Article 11

**Information required under the general authorisation,
for rights of use and for the specific obligations**

1. Without prejudice to information and reporting obligations under national legislation other than the general authorisation, national regulatory authorities may only require undertakings to provide information under the general authorisation, for rights of use or the specific obligations referred to in Article 6(2) that is proportionate and objectively justified for:

[(a) systematic or case-by-case verification of compliance with conditions 1 and 2 of Part A, conditions 2 and 6 of Part B and conditions 2 and 7 of Part C of the Annex and of compliance with obligations as referred to in Article 6(2);]

(b) case-by-case verification of compliance with conditions as set out in the Annex where a complaint has been received or where the national regulatory authority has other reasons to believe that a condition is not complied with or in case of an investigation by the national regulatory authority on its own initiative;

(c) procedures for and assessment of requests for granting rights of use;

(d) publication of comparative overviews of quality and price of services for the benefit of consumers;

(e) clearly defined statistical purposes;

(f) market analysis for the purposes of Directive 2002/19/EC (Access Directive) or Directive 2002/22/EC (Universal Service Directive);

(g) safeguarding the efficient use and ensuring the effective management of radio frequencies;

(h) evaluating future network or service developments that could have an impact on wholesale services made available to competitors.

The information referred to in points (a), (b), (d), (e), (f), (g) and (h) of the first subparagraph may not be required prior to, or as a condition for, market access.]

2. Where national regulatory authorities require undertakings to provide information as referred to in paragraph 1, they shall inform them of the specific purpose for which this information is to be used.

Notes

Article 11 was amended as shown in square brackets by Directive 2009/140/EC (OJ L 337, 18.12.2009, p.37), with effect from 19 December 2009.

Commentary

Art 11: **B&C:** 12.019, 12.027

Article 12

Administrative charges

1. Any administrative charges imposed on undertakings providing a service or a network under the general authorisation or to whom a right of use has been granted shall:

(a) in total, cover only the administrative costs which will be incurred in the management, control and enforcement of the general authorisation scheme and of rights of use and of specific obligations as referred to in Article 6(2), which may include costs for international cooperation, harmonisation and standardisation, market analysis, monitoring compliance and other market control, as well as regulatory work involving preparation and enforcement of secondary legislation and administrative decisions, such as decisions on access and interconnection; and

(b) be imposed upon the individual undertakings in an objective, transparent and proportionate manner which minimises additional administrative costs and attendant charges.

2. Where national regulatory authorities impose administrative charges, they shall publish a yearly overview of their administrative costs and of the total sum of the charges collected. In the light of the difference between the total sum of the charges and the administrative costs, appropriate adjustments shall be made.

Commentary

Art 12: **B&C:** 12.027

1028

Article 13
Fees for rights of use and rights to install facilities

Member States may allow the relevant authority to impose fees for the rights of use for radio frequencies or numbers or rights to install facilities on, over or under public or private property which reflect the need to ensure the optimal use of these resources. Member States shall ensure that such fees shall be objectively justified, transparent, non-discriminatory and proportionate in relation to their intended purpose and shall take into account the objectives in Article 8 of Directive 2002/21/EC (Framework Directive).

Commentary
Art 13: B&C: 12.027

[Article 14
Amendment of rights and obligations

[1. Member States shall ensure that the rights, conditions and procedures concerning general authorisations and rights of use or rights to install facilities may only be amended in objectively justified cases and in a proportionate manner, taking into consideration, where appropriate, the specific conditions applicable to transferable rights of use for radio frequencies. Except where proposed amendments are minor and have been agreed with the holder of the rights or general authorisation, notice shall be given in an appropriate manner of the intention to make such amendments and interested parties, including users and consumers, shall be allowed a sufficient period of time to express their views on the proposed amendments, which shall be no less than four weeks except in exceptional circumstances.

2. Member States shall not restrict or withdraw rights to install facilities or rights of use for radio frequencies before expiry of the period for which they were granted except where justified and where applicable in conformity with the Annex and relevant national provisions regarding compensation for withdrawal of rights.]

Notes

Article 14 was replaced as shown in square brackets by Directive 2009/140/EC (OJ L 337, 18.12.2009, p.37), with effect from 19 December 2009.

Article 15
Publication of information

[1. Member States shall ensure that all relevant information on rights, conditions, procedures, charges, fees and decisions concerning general authorisations, rights of use and rights to install facilities is published and kept up to date in an appropriate manner so as to provide easy access to that information for all interested parties.]

2. Where information as referred to in paragraph 1 is held at different levels of government, in particular information regarding procedures and conditions on rights to install facilities, the national regulatory authority shall make all reasonable efforts, bearing in mind the costs involved, to create a user-friendly overview of all such information, including information on the relevant levels of government and the responsible authorities, in order to facilitate applications for rights to install facilities.

Notes

Article 15(1) was replaced as shown in square brackets by Directive 2009/140/EC (OJ L 337, 18.12.2009, p.37), with effect from 19 December 2009.

Article 16
Review procedures

The Commission shall periodically review the functioning of the national authorisation systems and the development of cross-border service provision within the Community and report to the European Parliament and to the Council on the first occasion not later than three years after the date of application of this Directive referred to in Article 18(1), second subparagraph. For this purpose, the Commission may request from the Member States information, which shall be supplied without undue delay.

Article 17

Existing authorisations

[1. Without prejudice to Article 9a of Directive 2002/21/EC (Framework Directive), Member States shall bring general authorisations and individual rights of use already in existence on 31 December 2009 into conformity with Articles 5, 6, 7, and the Annex of this Directive 19 December 2011 at the latest.

2. Where application of paragraph 1 results in a reduction of the rights or an extension of the general authorisations and individual rights of use already in existence, Member States may extend the validity of those authorisations and rights until 30 September 2012 at the latest, provided that the rights of other undertakings under Community law are not affected thereby. Member States shall notify such extensions to the Commission and state the reasons therefor.]

3. Where the Member State concerned can prove that the abolition of an authorisation condition regarding access to electronic communications networks, which was in force before the date of entry into force of this Directive, creates excessive difficulties for undertakings that have benefited from mandated access to another network, and where it is not possible for these undertakings to negotiate new agreements on reasonable commercial terms before the date of application referred to in Article 18(1), second subparagraph, Member States may request a temporary prolongation of the relevant condition(s). Such requests shall be submitted by the date of application referred to in Article 18(1), second subparagraph, at the latest, and shall specify the condition(s) and period for which the temporary prolongation is requested.

The Member State shall inform the Commission of the reasons for requesting a prolongation. The Commission shall consider such a request, taking into account the particular situation in that Member State and of the undertaking(s) concerned, and the need to ensure a coherent regulatory environment at a Community level. It shall take a decision on whether to grant or reject the request, and where it decides to grant the request, on the scope and duration of the prolongation to be granted. The Commission shall communicate its decision to the Member State concerned within six months after receipt of the application for a prolongation. Such decisions shall be published in the *Official Journal of the European Communities*.

Notes

Article 17 was amended as shown in square brackets by Directive 2009/140/EC (OJ L 337, 18.12.2009, p.37), with effect from 19 December 2009.

Article 18

Transposition

1. Member States shall adopt and publish the laws, regulations and administrative provisions necessary to comply with this Directive by 24 July 2003 at the latest. They shall forthwith inform the Commission thereof.

They shall apply those measures from 25 July 2003.

When Member States adopt these measures, they shall contain a reference to this Directive or be accompanied by such reference on the occasion of their official publication. The methods of making such reference shall be laid down by Member States.

2. Member States shall communicate to the Commission the text of the provisions of national law which they adopt in the field governed by this Directive and of any subsequent amendments to those provisions.

Notes

Measures to implement the amendments effected by Directive 2009/140/EC are required to be adopted and published by 25 May 2011 and applied from 26 May 2011: Directive 2009/140/EC, Article 5.

Article 19
Entry into force

This Directive shall enter into force on the day of its publication in the *Official Journal of the European Communities*.

Notes

Date of entry into force: 24 April 2002.

Article 20
Addressees

This Directive is addressed to the Member States.

Done at Brussels, 7 March 2002.

ANNEX

[The conditions listed in this Annex provide the maximum list of conditions which may be attached to general authorisations (Part A), rights to use radio frequencies (Part B) and rights to use numbers (Part C) as referred to in Article 6(1) and Article 11(1)(a), within the limits allowed under Articles 5, 6, 7, 8 and 9 of Directive 2002/21/EC (the Framework Directive).]

A. Conditions which may be attached to a general authorisation

1. Financial contributions to the funding of universal service in conformity with Directive 2002/22/EC (Universal Service Directive).

2. Administrative charges in accordance with Article 12 of this Directive.

3. Interoperability of services and interconnection of networks in conformity with Directive 2002/19/EC (Access Directive).

[4. Accessibility by end users of numbers from the national numbering plan, numbers from the European Telephone Numbering Space, the Universal International Freephone Numbers, and, where technically and economically feasible, from numbering plans of other Member States, and conditions in conformity with Directive 2002/22/EC (Universal Service Directive).]

5. Environmental and town and country planning requirements, as well as requirements and conditions linked to the granting of access to or use of public or private land and conditions linked to co-location and facility sharing in conformity with Directive 2002/22/EC (Framework Directive) and including, where applicable, any financial or technical guarantees necessary to ensure the proper execution of infrastructure works.

6. "Must carry" obligations in conformity with Directive 2002/22/EC (Universal Service Directive).

[7. Personal data and privacy protection specific to the electronic communications sector in conformity with Directive 2002/58/EC of the European Parliament and of the Council (Directive on privacy and electronic communications).[1]

8. Consumer protection rules specific to the electronic communications sector, including conditions in conformity with Directive 2002/22/EC (Universal Service Directive), and conditions on accessibility for users with disabilities in accordance with Article 7 of that Directive.]

9. Restrictions in relation to the transmission of illegal content, in accordance with Directive 2000/31/EC of the European Parliament and of the Council of 8 June 2000 on certain legal aspects of information society services, in particular electronic commerce, in the internal market[2] and restrictions in relation to the transmission of harmful content in accordance with Article 2a(2) of Council Directive 89/552/EEC of 3 October 1989 on the coordination of certain provisions laid down by law, regulation or administrative action in Member States concerning the pursuit of television broadcasting activities.[3]

10. Information to be provided under a notification procedure in accordance with Article 3(3) of this Directive and for other purposes as included in Article 11 of this Directive.

11. Enabling of legal interception by competent national authorities in conformity with [Directive 2002/58/EC] and Directive 95/46/EC of the European Parliament and of the Council of 24 October 1995 on the protection of individuals with regard to the processing of personal data and on the free movement of such data.[4]

[11a. Terms of use for communications from public authorities to the general public for warning the public of imminent threats and for mitigating the consequences of major catastrophes.]

[12. Terms of use during major disasters or national emergencies to ensure communications between emergency services and authorities.]

13. Measures regarding the limitation of exposure of the general public to electromagnetic fields caused by electronic communications networks in accordance with Community law.

14. Access obligations other than those provided for in Article 6(2) of this Directive applying to undertakings providing electronic communications networks or services, in conformity with Directive 2002/19/EC (Access Directive).

15. Maintenance of the integrity of public communications networks in accordance with Directive 2002/19/EC (Access Directive) and Directive 2002/22/EC (Universal Service Directive) including by conditions to prevent electromagnetic interference between electronic communications networks and/or services in accordance with Council Directive 89/336/EEC of 3 May 1989 on the approximation of the laws of the Member States relating to electromagnetic compatibility.[5]

[16. Security of public networks against unauthorised access according to Directive 2002/58/EC (Directive on Privacy and electronic communications).]

17. Conditions for the use of radio frequencies, in conformity with Article 7(2) of Directive 1999/5/EC, where such use is not made subject to the granting of individual rights of use in accordance with Article 5(1) of this Directive.

18. Measures designed to ensure compliance with the standards and/or specifications referred to in Article 17 of Directive 2002/21/EC (Framework Directive).

[19. Transparency obligations on public communications network providers providing electronic communications services available to the public to ensure end-to-end connectivity, in conformity with the objectives and principles set out in Article 8 of Directive 2002/21/EC (Framework Directive), disclosure regarding any conditions limiting access to and/or use of services and applications where such conditions are allowed by Member States in conformity with Community law, and, where necessary and proportionate, access by national regulatory authorities to such information needed to verify the accuracy of such disclosure.]

Notes

[[1] OJ L 201, 31.7.2002, p.37.]

[2] OJ L 178, 17.7.2000, p.1.

[3] OJ L 298, 17.10.1989, p.23. Directive as amended by Directive 97/36/EC of the European Parliament and of the Council (OJ L 202, 30.7.1997, p.60).

[4] OJ L 281, 23.11.1995, p.31.

[5] OJ L 139, 23.5.1989, p.19. Directive as last amended by Directive 93/68/EEC (OJ L 220, 30.8.1993, p.1).
Part A was amended as shown in square brackets by Directive 2009/140/EC (OJ L 337, 18.12.2009, p.37), with effect from 19 December 2009.

Commentary
Part A: B&C: 12.028

B. Conditions which may be attached to rights of use for radio frequencies

[1. Obligation to provide a service or to use a type of technology for which the rights of use for the frequency has been granted, including, where appropriate, coverage and quality requirements.]

[2. Effective and efficient use of frequencies in conformity with Directive 2002/21/EC (Framework Directive).]

3. Technical and operational conditions necessary for the avoidance of harmful interference and for the limitation of exposure of the general public to electromagnetic fields, where such conditions are different from those included in the general authorisation.

4. Maximum duration in conformity with Article 5 of this Directive, subject to any changes in the national frequency plan.

5. Transfer of rights at the initiative of the right holder and conditions for such transfer in conformity with Directive 2002/21/EC (Framework Directive).

6. Usage fees in accordance with Article 13 of this Directive.

7. Any commitments which the undertaking obtaining the usage right has made in the course of a competitive or comparative selection procedure.

8. Obligations under relevant international agreements relating to the use of frequencies.

[9. Obligations specific to an experimental use of radio frequencies.]

Notes

Part B was amended as shown in square brackets by Directive 2009/140/EC (OJ L 337, 18.12.2009, p.37), with effect from 19 December 2009.

Commentary
Part B: B&C: 12.026

C. Conditions which may be attached to rights of use for numbers

[1. Designation of service for which the number shall be used, including any requirements linked to the provision of that service and, for the avoidance of doubt, tariff principles and maximum prices that can apply in the specific number range for the purposes of ensuring consumer protection in accordance with Article 8(4)(b) of Directive 2002/21/EC (Framework Directive).]

2. Effective and efficient use of numbers in conformity with Directive 2002/21/EC (Framework Directive).

3. Number portability requirements in conformity with Directive 2002/22/EC (Universal Service Directive).

4. Obligation to provide public directory subscriber information for the purposes of Articles 5 and 25 of Directive 2002/22/EC (Universal Service Directive).

5. Maximum duration in conformity with Article 5 of this Directive, subject to any changes in the national numbering plan.

6. Transfer of rights at the initiative of the right holder and conditions for such transfer in conformity with Directive 2002/21/EC (Framework Directive).

7. Usage fees in accordance with Article 13 of this Directive.

8. Any commitments which the undertaking obtaining the usage right has made in the course of a competitive or comparative selection procedure.

9. Obligations under relevant international agreements relating to the use of numbers.

Notes

Part B was amended as shown in square brackets by Directive 2009/140/EC (OJ L 337, 18.12.2009, p.37), with effect from 19 December 2009.

Commentary
Part C: B&C: 12.112

E4

DIRECTIVE 2002/22/EC OF THE EUROPEAN PARLIAMENT AND OF THE COUNCIL

of 7 March 2002

on universal service and users' rights relating to
electronic communications networks and services

(Universal Service Directive)

Official Journal L 108, 24.4.2002, p.51

Celex No: 32002L0022

EUR-Lex permanent link: <http://eur-lex.europa.eu/LexUriServ/LexUriServ.do?uri=CELEX:3200
2L0022:EN:NOT>

Notes

EEA application: this Directive was adopted with appropriate adaptations by EEA Joint Committee Decision No
11/2004 (OJ No L 116, 22.4.2004, p.60 and EEA Supplement No 20, 22.4.2004, p.14): see EEA Agreement, Annex
XI, Point 5cm.

Commentary

Directive 2002/22/EC: **B&C:** 12.005, 12.019, 12.024, 12.030 **F&N:** 13.22, 13.211, 14.144, 17.341
Chap II: **B&C:** 12.031
Chap III: **B&C:** 12.031
Chap IV: **B&C:** 12.031
Chap V: **B&C:** 12.031
Arts 3–15: **B&C:** 12.031
Arts 20–31: **B&C:** 12.030, 12.031
Arts 32–40: **B&C:** 12.031

THE EUROPEAN PARLIAMENT AND THE COUNCIL OF THE EUROPEAN UNION,

Having regard to the [Treaty on the Functioning of the European Union], and in particular
Article [114]* thereof,

Having regard to the proposal from the Commission,[1]

Having regard to the opinion of the Economic and Social Committee,[2]

Having regard to the opinion of the Committee of the Regions,[3]

Acting in accordance with the procedure laid down in Article [294] of the Treaty,[4]

Notes

* Ed note: please see the Note on the Lisbon Treaty at p.xvii in regard to article renumbering introduced by the Lisbon Treaty.
[1] OJ C 365 E, 19.12.2000, p.238 and OJ C 332 E, 27.11.2001, p.292.
[2] OJ C 139, 11.5.2001, p.15.
[3] OJ C 144, 16.5.2001, p.60.
[4] Opinion of the European Parliament of 13 June 2001 [OJ C 53 E, 28.2.2002, p.133], Council Common Position of
17 September 2001 (OJ C 337, 30.11.2001, p.55) and Decision of the European Parliament of 12 December 2001 [OJ
C 177 E, 25.7.2002, p.83].

Whereas:

(1) The liberalisation of the telecommunications sector and increasing competition and choice for
communications services go hand in hand with parallel action to create a harmonised regulatory
framework which secures the delivery of universal service. The concept of universal service should

evolve to reflect advances in technology, market developments and changes in user demand. The regulatory framework established for the full liberalisation of the telecommunications market in 1998 in the Community defined the minimum scope of universal service obligations and established rules for its costing and financing.

(2) Under [Articles 12 and 169] of the Treaty, the Community is to contribute to the protection of consumers.

(3) The Community and its Member States have undertaken commitments on the regulatory framework of telecommunications networks and services in the context of the World Trade Organisation (WTO) agreement on basic telecommunications. Any member of the WTO has the right to define the kind of universal service obligation it wishes to maintain. Such obligations will not be regarded as anti-competitive per se, provided they are administered in a transparent, non-discriminatory and competitively neutral manner and are not more burdensome than necessary for the kind of universal service defined by the member.

(4) Ensuring universal service (that is to say, the provision of a defined minimum set of services to all end-users at an affordable price) may involve the provision of some services to some end-users at prices that depart from those resulting from normal market conditions. However, compensating undertakings designated to provide such services in such circumstances need not result in any distortion of competition, provided that designated undertakings are compensated for the specific net cost involved and provided that the net cost burden is recovered in a competitively neutral way.

Commentary
Recital 4: B&C: 12.030, 12.043

---

(5) In a competitive market, certain obligations should apply to all undertakings providing publicly available telephone services at fixed locations and others should apply only to undertakings enjoying significant market power or which have been designated as a universal service operator.

(6) The network termination point represents a boundary for regulatory purposes between the regulatory framework for electronic communication networks and services and the regulation of telecommunication terminal equipment. Defining the location of the network termination point is the responsibility of the national regulatory authority, where necessary on the basis of a proposal by the relevant undertakings.

(7) Member States should continue to ensure that the services set out in Chapter II are made available with the quality specified to all end-users in their territory, irrespective of their geographical location, and, in the light of specific national conditions, at an affordable price. Member States may, in the context of universal service obligations and in the light of national conditions, take specific measures for consumers in rural or geographically isolated areas to ensure their access to the services set out in the Chapter II and the affordability of those services, as well as ensure under the same conditions this access, in particular for the elderly, the disabled and for people with special social needs. Such measures may also include measures directly targeted at consumers with special social needs providing support to identified consumers, for example by means of specific measures, taken after the examination of individual requests, such as the paying off of debts.

(8) A fundamental requirement of universal service is to provide users on request with a connection to the public telephone network at a fixed location, at an affordable price. The requirement is limited to a single narrowband network connection, the provision of which may be restricted by Member States to the end-user's primary location/residence, and does not extend to the Integrated Services Digital Network (ISDN) which provides two or more connections capable of being used simultaneously. There should be no constraints on the technical means by which the connection is provided, allowing for wired or wireless technologies, nor any constraints on which operators provide part or all of universal service obligations. Connections to the public telephone network at a fixed location should be capable of supporting speech and data communications at rates sufficient for access to online services such as those provided via the public Internet. The speed of Internet access experienced by a given user may depend on a number of factors including the provider(s) of Internet connectivity as well as the given application for which a connection is

being used. The data rate that can be supported by a single narrowband connection to the public telephone network depends on the capabilities of the subscriber's terminal equipment as well as the connection. For this reason it is not appropriate to mandate a specific data or bit rate at Community level. Currently available voice band modems typically offer a data rate of 56 kbit/s and employ automatic data rate adaptation to cater for variable line quality, with the result that the achieved data rate may be lower than 56 kbit/s. Flexibility is required on the one hand to allow Member States to take measures where necessary to ensure that connections are capable of supporting such a data rate, and on the other hand to allow Member States where relevant to permit data rates below this upper limit of 56 kbits/s in order, for example, to exploit the capabilities of wireless technologies (including cellular wireless networks) to deliver universal service to a higher proportion of the population. This may be of particular importance in some accession countries where household penetration of traditional telephone connections remains relatively low. In specific cases where the connection to the public telephony network at a fixed location is clearly insufficient to support satisfactory Internet access, Member States should be able to require the connection to be brought up to the level enjoyed by the majority of subscribers so that it supports data rates sufficient for access to the Internet. Where such specific measures produce a net cost burden for those consumers concerned, the net effect may be included in any net cost calculation of universal service obligations.

(9) The provisions of this Directive do not preclude Member States from designating different undertakings to provide the network and service elements of universal service. Designated undertakings providing network elements may be required to ensure such construction and maintenance as are necessary and proportionate to meet all reasonable requests for connection at a fixed location to the public telephone network and for access to publicly available telephone services at a fixed location.

(10) Affordable price means a price defined by Member States at national level in the light of specific national conditions, and may involve setting common tariffs irrespective of location or special tariff options to deal with the needs of low-income users. Affordability for individual consumers is related to their ability to monitor and control their expenditure.

(11) Directory information and a directory enquiry service constitute an essential access tool for publicly available telephone services and form part of the universal service obligation. Users and consumers desire comprehensive directories and a directory enquiry service covering all listed telephone subscribers and their numbers (including fixed and mobile numbers) and want this information to be presented in a non-preferential fashion. Directive 97/66/EC of the European Parliament and of the Council of 15 December 1997 concerning the processing of personal data and the protection of privacy in the telecommunications sector[1] ensures the subscribers' right to privacy with regard to the inclusion of their personal information in a public directory.

Notes

[1] OJ L 24, 30.1.1998, p.1.

---

(12) For the citizen, it is important for there to be adequate provision of public pay telephones, and for users to be able to call emergency telephone numbers and, in particular, the single European emergency call number ("112") free of charge from any telephone, including public pay telephones, without the use of any means of payment. Insufficient information about the existence of "112" deprives citizens of the additional safety ensured by the existence of this number at European level especially during their travel in other Member States.

(13) Member States should take suitable measures in order to guarantee access to and affordability of all publicly available telephone services at a fixed location for disabled users and users with special social needs. Specific measures for disabled users could include, as appropriate, making available accessible public telephones, public text telephones or equivalent measures for deaf or speech-impaired people, providing services such as directory enquiry services or equivalent measures free of charge for blind or partially sighted people, and providing itemised bills in alternative format on request for blind or partially sighted people. Specific measures may also need to be taken to enable disabled users and users with special social needs to access emergency services "112" and to give them a similar possibility to choose between different operators or

service providers as other consumers. Quality of service standards have been developed for a range of parameters to assess the quality of services received by subscribers and how well undertakings designated with universal service obligations perform in achieving these standards. Quality of service standards do not yet exist in respect of disabled users. Performance standards and relevant parameters should be developed for disabled users and are provided for in Article 11 of this Directive. Moreover, national regulatory authorities should be enabled to require publication of quality of service performance data if and when such standards and parameters are developed. The provider of universal service should not take measures to prevent users from benefiting fully from services offered by different operators or service providers, in combination with its own services offered as part of universal service.

(14) The importance of access to and use of the public telephone network at a fixed location is such that it should be available to anyone reasonably requesting it. In accordance with the principle of subsidiarity, it is for Member States to decide on the basis of objective criteria which undertakings have universal service obligations for the purposes of this Directive, where appropriate taking into account the ability and the willingness of undertakings to accept all or part of the universal service obligations. It is important that universal service obligations are fulfilled in the most efficient fashion so that users generally pay prices that correspond to efficient cost provision. It is likewise important that universal service operators maintain the integrity of the network as well as service continuity and quality. The development of greater competition and choice provide more possibilities for all or part of the universal service obligations to be provided by undertakings other than those with significant market power. Therefore, universal service obligations could in some cases be allocated to operators demonstrating the most cost-effective means of delivering access and services, including by competitive or comparative selection procedures. Corresponding obligations could be included as conditions in authorisations to provide publicly available services.

(15) Member States should monitor the situation of consumers with respect to their use of publicly available telephone services and in particular with respect to affordability. The affordability of telephone service is related to the information which users receive regarding telephone usage expenses as well as the relative cost of telephone usage compared to other services, and is also related to their ability to control expenditure. Affordability therefore means giving power to consumers through obligations imposed on undertakings designated as having universal service obligations. These obligations include a specified level of itemised billing, the possibility for consumers selectively to block certain calls (such as high-priced calls to premium services), the possibility for consumers to control expenditure via pre-payment means and the possibility for consumers to offset up-front connection fees. Such measures may need to be reviewed and changed in the light of market developments. Current conditions do not warrant a requirement for operators with universal service obligations to alert subscribers where a predetermined limit of expenditure is exceeded or an abnormal calling pattern occurs. Review of the relevant legislative provisions in future should consider whether there is a possible need to alert subscribers for these reasons.

Commentary
Recital 15: B&C: 12.019

---

(16) Except in cases of persistent late payment or non-payment of bills, consumers should be protected from immediate disconnection from the network on the grounds of an unpaid bill and, particularly in the case of disputes over high bills for premium rate services, should continue to have access to essential telephone services pending resolution of the dispute. Member States may decide that such access may continue to be provided only if the subscriber continues to pay line rental charges.

(17) Quality and price are key factors in a competitive market and national regulatory authorities should be able to monitor achieved quality of service for undertakings which have been designated as having universal service obligations. In relation to the quality of service attained by such undertakings, national regulatory authorities should be able to take appropriate measures where they deem it necessary. National regulatory authorities should also be able to monitor the achieved

quality of services of other undertakings providing public telephone networks and/or publicly available telephone services to users at fixed locations.

(18) Member States should, where necessary, establish mechanisms for financing the net cost of universal service obligations in cases where it is demonstrated that the obligations can only be provided at a loss or at a net cost which falls outside normal commercial standards. It is important to ensure that the net cost of universal service obligations is properly calculated and that any financing is undertaken with minimum distortion to the market and to undertakings, and is compatible with the provisions of Articles [107] and [108] of the Treaty.

(19) Any calculation of the net cost of universal service should take due account of costs and revenues, as well as the intangible benefits resulting from providing universal service, but should not hinder the general aim of ensuring that pricing structures reflect costs. Any net costs of universal service obligations should be calculated on the basis of transparent procedures.

(20) Taking into account intangible benefits means that an estimate in monetary terms, of the indirect benefits that an undertaking derives by virtue of its position as provider of universal service, should be deducted from the direct net cost of universal service obligations in order to determine the overall cost burden.

(21) When a universal service obligation represents an unfair burden on an undertaking, it is appropriate to allow Member States to establish mechanisms for efficiently recovering net costs. Recovery via public funds constitutes one method of recovering the net costs of universal service obligations. It is also reasonable for established net costs to be recovered from all users in a transparent fashion by means of levies on undertakings. Member States should be able to finance the net costs of different elements of universal service through different mechanisms, and/or to finance the net costs of some or all elements from either of the mechanisms or a combination of both. In the case of cost recovery by means of levies on undertakings, Member States should ensure that that the method of allocation amongst them is based on objective and non-discriminatory criteria and is in accordance with the principle of proportionality. This principle does not prevent Member States from exempting new entrants which have not yet achieved any significant market presence. Any funding mechanism should ensure that market participants only contribute to the financing of universal service obligations and not to other activities which are not directly linked to the provision of the universal service obligations. Recovery mechanisms should in all cases respect the principles of Community law, and in particular in the case of sharing mechanisms those of non-discrimination and proportionality. Any funding mechanism should ensure that users in one Member State do not contribute to universal service costs in another Member State, for example when making calls from one Member State to another.

(22) Where Member States decide to finance the net cost of universal service obligations from public funds, this should be understood to comprise funding from general government budgets including other public financing sources such as state lotteries.

(23) The net cost of universal service obligations may be shared between all or certain specified classes of undertaking. Member States should ensure that the sharing mechanism respects the principles of transparency, least market distortion, non-discrimination and proportionality. Least market distortion means that contributions should be recovered in a way that as far as possible minimises the impact of the financial burden falling on end-users, for example by spreading contributions as widely as possible.

(24) National regulatory authorities should satisfy themselves that those undertakings benefiting from universal service funding provide a sufficient level of detail of the specific elements requiring such funding in order to justify their request. Member States' schemes for the costing and financing of universal service obligations should be communicated to the Commission for verification of compatibility with the Treaty. There are incentives for designated operators to raise the assessed net cost of universal service obligations. Therefore Member States should ensure effective transparency and control of amounts charged to finance universal service obligations.

(25) Communications markets continue to evolve in terms of the services used and the technical means used to deliver them to users. The universal service obligations, which are defined at a Community level, should be periodically reviewed with a view to proposing that the scope be changed or redefined. Such a review should take account of evolving social, commercial and

technological conditions and the fact that any change of scope should be subject to the twin test of services that become available to a substantial majority of the population, with a consequent risk of social exclusion for those who can not afford them. Care should be taken in any change of the scope of universal service obligations to ensure that certain technological choices are not artificially promoted above others, that a disproportionate financial burden is not imposed on sector undertakings (thereby endangering market developments and innovation) and that any financing burden does not fall unfairly on consumers with lower incomes. Any change of scope automatically means that any net cost can be financed via the methods permitted in this Directive. Member States are not permitted to impose on market players financial contributions which relate to measures which are not part of universal service obligations. Individual Member States remain free to impose special measures (outside the scope of universal service obligations) and finance them in conformity with Community law but not by means of contributions from market players.

(26) More effective competition across all access and service markets will give greater choice for users. The extent of effective competition and choice varies across the Community and varies within Member States between geographical areas and between access and service markets. Some users may be entirely dependent on the provision of access and services by an undertaking with significant market power. In general, for reasons of efficiency and to encourage effective competition, it is important that the services provided by an undertaking with significant market power reflect costs. For reasons of efficiency and social reasons, end-user tariffs should reflect demand conditions as well as cost conditions, provided that this does not result in distortions of competition. There is a risk that an undertaking with significant market power may act in various ways to inhibit entry or distort competition, for example by charging excessive prices, setting predatory prices, compulsory bundling of retail services or showing undue preference to certain customers. Therefore, national regulatory authorities should have powers to impose, as a last resort and after due consideration, retail regulation on an undertaking with significant market power. Price cap regulation, geographical averaging or similar instruments, as well as non-regulatory measures such as publicly available comparisons of retail tariffs, may be used to achieve the twin objectives of promoting effective competition whilst pursuing public interest needs, such as maintaining the affordability of publicly available telephone services for some consumers. Access to appropriate cost accounting information is necessary, in order for national regulatory authorities to fulfil their regulatory duties in this area, including the imposition of any tariff controls. However, regulatory controls on retail services should only be imposed where national regulatory authorities consider that relevant wholesale measures or measures regarding carrier selection or pre-selection would fail to achieve the objective of ensuring effective competition and public interest.

Commentary
Recital 26: B&C: 12.019, 12.043

---

(27) Where a national regulatory authority imposes obligations to implement a cost accounting system in order to support price controls, it may itself undertake an annual audit to ensure compliance with that cost accounting system, provided that it has the necessary qualified staff, or it may require the audit to be carried out by another qualified body, independent of the operator concerned.

(28) It is considered necessary to ensure the continued application of the existing provisions relating to the minimum set of leased line services in Community telecommunications legislation, in particular in Council Directive 92/44/EEC of 5 June 1992 on the application of open network provision to leased lines,[1] until such time as national regulatory authorities determine, in accordance with the market analysis procedures laid down in Directive 2002/21/EC of the European Parliament and of the Council of 7 March 2002 on a common regulatory framework for electronic communications networks and services (Framework Directive),[2] that such provisions are no longer needed because a sufficiently competitive market has developed in their territory. The degree of competition is likely to vary between different markets of leased lines in the minimum set, and in different parts of the territory. In undertaking the market analysis,

national regulatory authorities should make separate assessments for each market of leased lines in the minimum set, taking into account their geographic dimension. Leased lines services constitute mandatory services to be provided without recourse to any compensation mechanisms. The provision of leased lines outside of the minimum set of leased lines should be covered by general retail regulatory provisions rather than specific requirements covering the supply of the minimum set.

Notes
[1] OJ L 165, 19.6.1992, p.27. Directive as last amended by Commission Decision No 98/80/EC (OJ L 14, 20.1.1998, p.27).
[2] See [OJ L 108, 24.4.2002, p.33].

(29) National regulatory authorities may also, in the light of an analysis of the relevant market, require mobile operators with significant market power to enable their subscribers to access the services of any interconnected provider of publicly available telephone services on a call-by-call basis or by means of pre-selection.

(30) Contracts are an important tool for users and consumers to ensure a minimum level of transparency of information and legal security. Most service providers in a competitive environment will conclude contracts with their customers for reasons of commercial desirability. In addition to the provisions of this Directive, the requirements of existing Community consumer protection legislation relating to contracts, in particular Council Directive 93/13/EEC of 5 April 1993 on unfair terms in consumer contracts[1] and Directive 97/7/EC of the European Parliament and of the Council of 20 May 1997 on the protection of consumers in respect of distance contracts,[2] apply to consumer transactions relating to electronic networks and services. Specifically, consumers should enjoy a minimum level of legal certainty in respect of their contractual relations with their direct telephone service provider, such that the contractual terms, conditions, quality of service, condition for termination of the contract and the service, compensation measures and dispute resolution are specified in their contracts. Where service providers other than direct telephone service providers conclude contracts with consumers, the same information should be included in those contracts as well. The measures to ensure transparency on prices, tariffs, terms and conditions will increase the ability of consumers to optimise their choices and thus to benefit fully from competition.

Notes
[1] OJ L 95, 21.4.1993, p.29.
[2] OJ L 144, 4.6.1997, p.19.

(31) End-users should have access to publicly available information on communications services. Member States should be able to monitor the quality of services which are offered in their territories. National regulatory authorities should be able systematically to collect information on the quality of services offered in their territories on the basis of criteria which allow comparability between service providers and between Member States. Undertakings providing communications services, operating in a competitive environment, are likely to make adequate and up-to-date information on their services publicly available for reasons of commercial advantage. National regulatory authorities should nonetheless be able to require publication of such information where it is demonstrated that such information is not effectively available to the public.

(32) End-users should be able to enjoy a guarantee of interoperability in respect of all equipment sold in the Community for the reception of digital television. Member States should be able to require minimum harmonised standards in respect of such equipment. Such standards could be adapted from time to time in the light of technological and market developments.

(33) It is desirable to enable consumers to achieve the fullest connectivity possible to digital television sets. Interoperability is an evolving concept in dynamic markets. Standards bodies should do their utmost to ensure that appropriate standards evolve along with the technologies concerned. It is likewise important to ensure that connectors are available on television sets that are capable of passing all the necessary elements of a digital signal, including the audio and video streams, conditional access information, service information, application program interface (API)

information and copy protection information. This Directive therefore ensures that the functionality of the open interface for digital television sets is not limited by network operators, service providers or equipment manufacturers and continues to evolve in line with technological developments. For display and presentation of digital interactive television services, the realisation of a common standard through a market-driven mechanism is recognised as a consumer benefit. Member States and the Commission may take policy initiatives, consistent with the Treaty, to encourage this development.

(34) All end-users should continue to enjoy access to operator assistance services whatever organisation provides access to the public telephone network.

(35) The provision of directory enquiry services and directories is already open to competition. The provisions of this Directive complement the provisions of Directive 97/66/EC by giving subscribers a right to have their personal data included in a printed or electronic directory. All service providers which assign telephone numbers to their subscribers are obliged to make relevant information available in a fair, cost-oriented and non-discriminatory manner.

(36) It is important that users should be able to call the single European emergency number "112", and any other national emergency telephone numbers, free of charge, from any telephone, including public pay telephones, without the use of any means of payment. Member States should have already made the necessary organisational arrangements best suited to the national organisation of the emergency systems, in order to ensure that calls to this number are adequately answered and handled. Caller location information, to be made available to the emergency services, will improve the level of protection and the security of users of "112" services and assist the emergency services, to the extent technically feasible, in the discharge of their duties, provided that the transfer of calls and associated data to the emergency services concerned is guaranteed. The reception and use of such information should comply with relevant Community law on the processing of personal data. Steady information technology improvements will progressively support the simultaneous handling of several languages over the networks at a reasonable cost. This in turn will ensure additional safety for European citizens using the "112" emergency call number.

(37) Easy access to international telephone services is vital for European citizens and European businesses. "00" has already been established as the standard international telephone access code for the Community. Special arrangements for making calls between adjacent locations across borders between Member States may be established or continued. The ITU has assigned, in accordance with ITU Recommendation E.164, code "3883" to the European Telephony Numbering Space (ETNS). In order to ensure connection of calls to the ETNS, undertakings operating public telephone networks should ensure that calls using "3883" are directly or indirectly interconnected to ETNS serving networks specified in the relevant European Telecommunications Standards Institute (ETSI) standards. Such interconnection arrangements should be governed by the provisions of Directive 2002/19/EC of the European Parliament and of the Council of 7 March 2002 on access to, and interconnection of, electronic communications networks and associated facilities (Access Directive).[1]

Notes

[1] See [OJ L 108, 24.4.2002, p.7].

(38) Access by end-users to all numbering resources in the Community is a vital pre-condition for a single market. It should include freephone, premium rate, and other non-geographic numbers, except where the called subscriber has chosen, for commercial reasons, to limit access from certain geographical areas. Tariffs charged to parties calling from outside the Member State concerned need not be the same as for those parties calling from inside that Member State.

(39) Tone dialling and calling line identification facilities are normally available on modern telephone exchanges and can therefore increasingly be provided at little or no expense. Tone dialling is increasingly being used for user interaction with special services and facilities, including value added services, and the absence of this facility can prevent the user from making use of these services. Member States are not required to impose obligations to provide these facilities when they are already available. Directive 97/66/EC safeguards the privacy of users with regard to itemised billing, by giving them the means to protect their right to privacy when calling line

identification is implemented. The development of these services on a pan-European basis would benefit consumers and is encouraged by this Directive.

(40) Number portability is a key facilitator of consumer choice and effective competition in a competitive telecommunications environment such that end-users who so request should be able to retain their number(s) on the public telephone network independently of the organisation providing service. The provision of this facility between connections to the public telephone network at fixed and non-fixed locations is not covered by this Directive. However, Member States may apply provisions for porting numbers between networks providing services at a fixed location and mobile networks.

(41) The impact of number portability is considerably strengthened when there is transparent tariff information, both for end-users who port their numbers and also for end-users who call those who have ported their numbers. National regulatory authorities should, where feasible, facilitate appropriate tariff transparency as part of the implementation of number portability.

(42) When ensuring that pricing for interconnection related to the provision of number portability is cost-oriented, national regulatory authorities may also take account of prices available in comparable markets.

(43) Currently, Member States impose certain "must carry" obligations on networks for the distribution of radio or television broadcasts to the public. Member States should be able to lay down proportionate obligations on undertakings under their jurisdiction, in the interest of legitimate public policy considerations, but such obligations should only be imposed where they are necessary to meet general interest objectives clearly defined by Member States in conformity with Community law and should be proportionate, transparent and subject to periodical review. "Must carry" obligations imposed by Member States should be reasonable, that is they should be proportionate and transparent in the light of clearly defined general interest objectives, and could, where appropriate, entail a provision for proportionate remuneration. Such "must carry" obligations may include the transmission of services specifically designed to enable appropriate access by disabled users.

(44) Networks used for the distribution of radio or television broadcasts to the public include cable, satellite and terrestrial broadcasting networks. They might also include other networks to the extent that a significant number of end-users use such networks as their principal means to receive radio and television broadcasts.

(45) Services providing content such as the offer for sale of a package of sound or television broadcasting content are not covered by the common regulatory framework for electronic communications networks and services. Providers of such services should not be subject to universal service obligations in respect of these activities. This Directive is without prejudice to measures taken at national level, in compliance with Community law, in respect of such services.

(46) Where a Member State seeks to ensure the provision of other specific services throughout its national territory, such obligations should be implemented on a cost efficient basis and outside the scope of universal service obligations. Accordingly, Member States may undertake additional measures (such as facilitating the development of infrastructure or services in circumstances where the market does not satisfactorily address the requirements of end-users or consumers), in conformity with Community law. As a reaction to the Commission's e-Europe initiative, the Lisbon European Council of 23 and 24 March 2000 called on Member States to ensure that all schools have access to the Internet and to multimedia resources.

(47) In the context of a competitive environment, the views of interested parties, including users and consumers, should be taken into account by national regulatory authorities when dealing with issues related to end-users' rights. Effective procedures should be available to deal with disputes between consumers, on the one hand, and undertakings providing publicly available communications services, on the other. Member States should take full account of Commission Recommendation 98/257/EC of 30 March 1998 on the principles applicable to the bodies responsible for out-of-court settlement of consumer disputes.[1]

Notes
[1] OJ L 115, 17.4.1998, p.31.

(48) Co-regulation could be an appropriate way of stimulating enhanced quality standards and improved service performance. Co-regulation should be guided by the same principles as formal regulation, i.e. it should be objective, justified, proportional, non-discriminatory and transparent.

(49) This Directive should provide for elements of consumer protection, including clear contract terms and dispute resolution, and tariff transparency for consumers. It should also encourage the extension of such benefits to other categories of end-users, in particular small and medium-sized enterprises.

(50) The provisions of this Directive do not prevent a Member State from taking measures justified on grounds set out in Articles [36] and [52] of the Treaty, and in particular on grounds of public security, public policy and public morality.

(51) Since the objectives of the proposed action, namely setting a common level of universal service for telecommunications for all European users and of harmonising conditions for access to and use of public telephone networks at a fixed location and related publicly available telephone services and also achieving a harmonised framework for the regulation of electronic communications services, electronic communications networks and associated facilities, cannot be sufficiently achieved by the Member States and can therefore by reason of the scale or effects of the action be better achieved at Community level, the Community may adopt measures in accordance with the principles of subsidiarity as set out in Article 5 of the [Treaty on European Union]. In accordance with the principle of proportionality, as set out in that Article, this Directive does not go beyond what is necessary in order to achieve those objectives.

(52) The measures necessary for the implementation of this Directive should be adopted in accordance with Council Decision 1999/468/EC of 28 June 1999 laying down the procedures for the exercise of implementing powers conferred on the Commission,[1]

Notes

[1] OJ L 184, 17.7.1999, p.23.

HAVE ADOPTED THIS DIRECTIVE:

CHAPTER I
SCOPE, AIMS AND DEFINITIONS

[*Article 1*
Subject-matter and scope

1. Within the framework of Directive 2002/21/EC (Framework Directive), this Directive concerns the provision of electronic communications networks and services to end-users. The aim is to ensure the availability throughout the Community of good-quality publicly available services through effective competition and choice and to deal with circumstances in which the needs of end-users are not satisfactorily met by the market. The Directive also includes provisions concerning certain aspects of terminal equipment, including provisions intended to facilitate access for disabled end-users.

2. This Directive establishes the rights of end-users and the corresponding obligations of undertakings providing publicly available electronic communications networks and services. With regard to ensuring provision of universal service within an environment of open and competitive markets, this Directive defines the minimum set of services of specified quality to which all end-users have access, at an affordable price in the light of specific national conditions, without distorting competition. This Directive also sets out obligations with regard to the provision of certain mandatory services.

3. This Directive neither mandates nor prohibits conditions, imposed by providers of publicly available electronic communications and services, limiting end-users' access to, and/or use of, services and applications, where allowed under national law and in conformity with Community law, but lays down an obligation to provide information regarding such conditions. National measures regarding end-users' access to, or use of, services and applications through electronic communications networks shall respect the fundamental rights and freedoms of natural persons, including in relation to privacy

and due process, as defined in Article 6 of the European Convention for the Protection of Human Rights and Fundamental Freedoms.

4. The provisions of this Directive concerning end-users' rights shall apply without prejudice to Community rules on consumer protection, in particular Directives 93/13/EEC and 97/7/EC, and national rules in conformity with Community law.]

Notes

Article 1 was replaced as shown in square brackets by Directive 2009/136/EC of 25 November 2009 (OJ L 337, 18.12.2009, p.11), with effect from 19 December 2009.

Commentary
Art 1: F&N: 13.20
Art 1(1): B&C: 12.007, 12.030
Art 1(2): B&C: 12.030

Article 2
Definitions

For the purposes of this Directive, the definitions set out in Article 2 of Directive 2002/21/EC (Framework Directive) shall apply.

The following definitions shall also apply:

(a) "public pay telephone" means a telephone available to the general public, for the use of which the means of payment may include coins and/or credit/debit cards and/or pre-payment cards, including cards for use with dialling codes;

[ ]

[(c) "publicly available telephone service" means a service made available to the public for originating and receiving, directly or indirectly, national or national and international calls through a number or numbers in a national or international telephone numbering plan;

(d) "geographic number" means a number from the national telephone numbering plan where part of its digit structure contains geographic significance used for routing calls to the physical location of the network termination point (NTP);];

[ ]

[(f) "non-geographic number" means a number from the national telephone numbering plan that is not a geographic number. It includes, inter alia, mobile, freephone and premium rate numbers.];

Notes

Article 2 was amended as shown in square brackets by Directive 2009/136/EC of 25 November 2009 (OJ L 337, 18.12.2009, p.11), with effect from 19 December 2009.

CHAPTER II
UNIVERSAL SERVICE OBLIGATIONS INCLUDING SOCIAL OBLIGATIONS

Article 3
Availability of universal service

1. Member States shall ensure that the services set out in this Chapter are made available at the quality specified to all end-users in their territory, independently of geographical location, and, in the light of specific national conditions, at an affordable price.

2. Member States shall determine the most efficient and appropriate approach for ensuring the implementation of universal service, whilst respecting the principles of objectivity, transparency, non-discrimination and proportionality. They shall seek to minimise market distortions, in particular the provision of services at prices or subject to other terms and conditions which depart from normal commercial conditions, whilst safeguarding the public interest.

Commentary
Art 3: B&C: 12.030
Art 3(2): B&C: 12.019, 12.030

[*Article 4*

Provision of access at a fixed location and provision of telephone services

1. Member States shall ensure that all reasonable requests for connection at a fixed location to a public communications network are met by at least one undertaking.

2. The connection provided shall be capable of supporting voice, facsimile and data communications at data rates that are sufficient to permit functional Internet access, taking into account prevailing technologies used by the majority of subscribers and technological feasibility.

3. Member States shall ensure that all reasonable requests for the provision of a publicly available telephone service over the network connection referred to in paragraph 1 that allows for originating and receiving national and international calls are met by at least one undertaking.]

Notes

Article 4 was replaced as shown in square brackets by Directive 2009/136/EC of 25 November 2009 (OJ L 337, 18.12.2009, p.11), with effect from 19 December 2009.

Commentary

Art 4: **B&C:** 12.031

Article 5

Directory enquiry services and directories

1. Member States shall ensure that:

(a) at least one comprehensive directory is available to end-users in a form approved by the relevant authority, whether printed or electronic, or both, and is updated on a regular basis, and at least once a year;

(b) at least one comprehensive telephone directory enquiry service is available to all end-users, including users of public pay telephones.

[2. The directories referred to in paragraph 1 shall comprise, subject to the provisions of Article 12 of Directive 2002/58/EC of the European Parliament and of the Council of 12 July 2002 concerning the processing of personal data and the protection of privacy in the electronic communications sector (Directive on privacy and electronic communications) [], all subscribers of publicly available telephone services.]

3. Member States shall ensure that the undertaking(s) providing the services referred to in paragraph 1 apply the principle of non-discrimination to the treatment of information that has been provided to them by other undertakings.

Notes

Article 5(2) was replaced as shown in square brackets by Directive 2009/136/EC of 25 November 2009 (OJ L 337, 18.12.2009, p.11), with effect from 19 December 2009.

Commentary

Art 5: **B&C:** 12.031

Article 6

[Public pay telephones and other public voice telephony access points

1. Member States shall ensure that national regulatory authorities may impose obligations on undertakings in order to ensure that public pay telephones or other public voice telephony access points are provided to meet the reasonable needs of end-users in terms of the geographical coverage, the number of telephones or other access points, accessibility to disabled end-users and the quality of services.]

2. A Member State shall ensure that its national regulatory authority can decide not to impose obligations under paragraph 1 in all or part of its territory, if it is satisfied that these facilities or comparable services are widely available, on the basis of a consultation of interested parties as referred to in Article 33.

3. Member States shall ensure that it is possible to make emergency calls from public pay telephones using the single European emergency call number "112" and other national emergency numbers, all free of charge and without having to use any means of payment.

Notes

Article 6 was amended as shown in square brackets by Directive 2009/136/EC of 25 November 2009 (OJ L 337, 18.12.2009, p.11), with effect from 19 December 2009.

Commentary

Art 6: B&C: 12.031

[*Article 7*
Measures for disabled end-users

1. Unless requirements have been specified under Chapter IV which achieve the equivalent effect, Member States shall take specific measures to ensure that access to, and affordability of, the services identified in Article 4(3) and Article 5 for disabled end-users is equivalent to the level enjoyed by other end-users. Member States may oblige national regulatory authorities to assess the general need and the specific requirements, including the extent and concrete form of such specific measures for disabled end-users.

2. Member States may take specific measures, in the light of national conditions, to ensure that disabled end-users can also take advantage of the choice of undertakings and service providers available to the majority of end-users.

3. In taking the measures referred to in paragraphs 1 and 2, Member States shall encourage compliance with the relevant standards or specifications published in accordance with Articles 17 and 18 of Directive 2002/21/EC (Framework Directive).]

Notes

Article 7 was replaced as shown in square brackets by Directive 2009/136/EC of 25 November 2009 (OJ L 337, 18.12.2009, p.11), with effect from 19 December 2009.

Commentary

Art 7: B&C: 12.030, 12.031

Article 8
Designation of undertakings

1. Member States may designate one or more undertakings to guarantee the provision of universal service as identified in Articles 4, 5, 6 and 7 and, where applicable, Article 9(2) so that the whole of the national territory can be covered. Member States may designate different undertakings or sets of undertakings to provide different elements of universal service and/or to cover different parts of the national territory.

2. When Member States designate undertakings in part or all of the national territory as having universal service obligations, they shall do so using an efficient, objective, transparent and non-discriminatory designation mechanism, whereby no undertaking is a priori excluded from being designated. Such designation methods shall ensure that universal service is provided in a cost-effective manner and may be used as a means of determining the net cost of the universal service obligation in accordance with Article 12.

[3. When an undertaking designated in accordance with paragraph 1 intends to dispose of a substantial part or all of its local access network assets to a separate legal entity under different ownership, it shall inform in advance the national regulatory authority in a timely manner, in order to allow that authority to assess the effect of the intended transaction on the provision of access at a fixed location and of telephone services pursuant to Article 4. The national regulatory authority may impose, amend or withdraw specific obligations in accordance with Article 6(2) of Directive 2002/20/EC (Authorisation Directive).]

Notes

Article 8 was amended as shown in square brackets by Directive 2009/136/EC of 25 November 2009 (OJ L 337, 18.12.2009, p.11), with effect from 19 December 2009.

Commentary
Art 8(1): B&C: 12.031

Article 9
Affordability of tariffs

[1. National regulatory authorities shall monitor the evolution and level of retail tariffs of the services identified in Articles 4 to 7 as falling under the universal service obligations and either provided by designated undertakings or available on the market, if no undertakings are designated in relation to those services, in particular in relation to national consumer prices and income.

2. Member States may, in the light of national conditions, require that designated undertakings provide to consumers tariff options or packages which depart from those provided under normal commercial conditions, in particular to ensure that those on low incomes or with special social needs are not prevented from accessing the network referred to in Article 4(1) or from using the services identified in Article 4(3) and Articles 5, 6 and 7 as falling under the universal service obligations and provided by designated undertakings.]

3. Member States may, besides any provision for designated undertakings to provide special tariff options or to comply with price caps or geographical averaging or other similar schemes, ensure that support is provided to consumers identified as having low incomes or special social needs.

4. Member States may require undertakings with obligations under Articles 4, 5, 6 and 7 to apply common tariffs, including geographical averaging, throughout the territory, in the light of national conditions or to comply with price caps.

5. National regulatory authorities shall ensure that, where a designated undertaking has an obligation to provide special tariff options, common tariffs, including geographical averaging, or to comply with price caps, the conditions are fully transparent and are published and applied in accordance with the principle of non-discrimination. National regulatory authorities may require that specific schemes be modified or withdrawn.

Notes

Article 9 was amended as shown in square brackets by Directive 2009/136/EC of 25 November 2009 (OJ L 337, 18.12.2009, p.11), with effect from 19 December 2009.

Commentary
Art 9: B&C: 12.031
Art 9(5): B&C: 12.019

Article 10
Control of expenditure

1. Member States shall ensure that designated undertakings, in providing facilities and services additional to those referred to in Articles 4, 5, 6, 7 and 9(2), establish terms and conditions in such a way that the subscriber is not obliged to pay for facilities or services which are not necessary or not required for the service requested.

2. Member States shall ensure that designated undertakings with obligations under Articles 4, 5, 6, 7 and 9(2) provide the specific facilities and services set out in Annex I, Part A, in order that subscribers can monitor and control expenditure and avoid unwarranted disconnection of service.

3. Member States shall ensure that the relevant authority is able to waive the requirements of paragraph 2 in all or part of its national territory if it is satisfied that the facility is widely available.

Commentary
Art 10: B&C: 12.031

Article 11

Quality of service of designated undertakings

1. National regulatory authorities shall ensure that all designated undertakings with obligations under Articles 4, 5, 6, 7 and 9(2) publish adequate and up-to-date information concerning their performance in the provision of universal service, based on the quality of service parameters, definitions and measurement methods set out in Annex III. The published information shall also be supplied to the national regulatory authority.

2. National regulatory authorities may specify, inter alia, additional quality of service standards, where relevant parameters have been developed, to assess the performance of undertakings in the provision of services to disabled end-users and disabled consumers. National regulatory authorities shall ensure that information concerning the performance of undertakings in relation to these parameters is also published and made available to the national regulatory authority.

3. National regulatory authorities may, in addition, specify the content, form and manner of information to be published, in order to ensure that end-users and consumers have access to comprehensive, comparable and user-friendly information.

[4. National regulatory authorities shall be able to set performance targets for undertakings with universal service obligations. In so doing, national regulatory authorities shall take account of views of interested parties, in particular as referred to in Article 33.]

5. Member States shall ensure that national regulatory authorities are able to monitor compliance with these performance targets by designated undertakings.

6. Persistent failure by an undertaking to meet performance targets may result in specific measures being taken in accordance with Directive 2002/20/EC of the European Parliament and of the Council of 7 March 2002 on the authorisation of electronic communications networks and services (Authorisation Directive).[1] National regulatory authorities shall be able to order independent audits or similar reviews of the performance data, paid for by the undertaking concerned, in order to ensure the accuracy and comparability of the data made available by undertakings with universal service obligations.

Notes

[1] [OJ L 108, 24.4.2002, p.21].
Article 11 was amended as shown in square brackets by Directive 2009/136/EC of 25 November 2009 (OJ L 337, 18.12.2009, p.11), with effect from 19 December 2009.

Commentary
Art 11: **B&C:** 12.031

Article 12

Costing of universal service obligations

1. Where national regulatory authorities consider that the provision of universal service as set out in Articles 3 to 10 may represent an unfair burden on undertakings designated to provide universal service, they shall calculate the net costs of its provision.

For that purpose, national regulatory authorities shall:

(a) calculate the net cost of the universal service obligation, taking into account any market benefit which accrues to an undertaking designated to provide universal service, in accordance with Annex IV, Part A; or

(b) make use of the net costs of providing universal service identified by a designation mechanism in accordance with Article 8(2).

2. The accounts and/or other information serving as the basis for the calculation of the net cost of universal service obligations under paragraph 1(a) shall be audited or verified by the national regulatory authority or a body independent of the relevant parties and approved by the national regulatory authority. The results of the cost calculation and the conclusions of the audit shall be publicly available.

Commentary
Art 12: **B&C:** 12.032

Article 13
Financing of universal service obligations

1. Where, on the basis of the net cost calculation referred to in Article 12, national regulatory authorities find that an undertaking is subject to an unfair burden, Member States shall, upon request from a designated undertaking, decide:

(a) to introduce a mechanism to compensate that undertaking for the determined net costs under transparent conditions from public funds; and/or

(b) to share the net cost of universal service obligations between providers of electronic communications networks and services.

2. Where the net cost is shared under paragraph 1(b), Member States shall establish a sharing mechanism administered by the national regulatory authority or a body independent from the beneficiaries under the supervision of the national regulatory authority. Only the net cost, as determined in accordance with Article 12, of the obligations laid down in Articles 3 to 10 may be financed.

3. A sharing mechanism shall respect the principles of transparency, least market distortion, non-discrimination and proportionality, in accordance with the principles of Annex IV, Part B. Member States may choose not to require contributions from undertakings whose national turnover is less than a set limit.

4. Any charges related to the sharing of the cost of universal service obligations shall be unbundled and identified separately for each undertaking. Such charges shall not be imposed or collected from undertakings that are not providing services in the territory of the Member State that has established the sharing mechanism.

Commentary
Art 13: B&C: 12.032

Article 14
Transparency

1. Where a mechanism for sharing the net cost of universal service obligations as referred to in Article 13 is established, national regulatory authorities shall ensure that the principles for cost sharing, and details of the mechanism used, are publicly available.

2. Subject to Community and national rules on business confidentiality, national regulatory authorities shall ensure that an annual report is published giving the calculated cost of universal service obligations, identifying the contributions made by all the undertakings involved, and identifying any market benefits, that may have accrued to the undertaking(s) designated to provide universal service, where a fund is actually in place and working.

Article 15
Review of the scope of universal service

1. The Commission shall periodically review the scope of universal service, in particular with a view to proposing to the European Parliament and the Council that the scope be changed or redefined. A review shall be carried out, on the first occasion within two years after the date of application referred to in Article 38(1), second subparagraph, and subsequently every three years.

2. This review shall be undertaken in the light of social, economic and technological developments, taking into account, inter alia, mobility and data rates in the light of the prevailing technologies used by the majority of subscribers. The review process shall be undertaken in accordance with Annex V. The Commission shall submit a report to the European Parliament and the Council regarding the outcome of the review.

Chapter III
[Regulatory Controls on undertakings with significant market Power in specific Retail Markets]

[ ]

Notes

The title of Chapter III was replaced and Article 16 was deleted as shown in square brackets by Directive 2009/136/EC of 25 November 2009 (OJ L 337, 18.12.2009, p.11), with effect from 19 December 2009.

Commentary
Art 16: B&C: 12.031
Art 16(6): B&C: 12.014

Article 17
Regulatory controls on retail services

[1. Member States shall ensure that national regulatory authorities impose appropriate regulatory obligations on undertakings identified as having significant market power on a given retail market in accordance with Article 14 of Directive 2002/21/EC (Framework Directive) where:

(a) as a result of a market analysis carried out in accordance with Article 16 of Directive 2002/21/EC (Framework Directive), a national regulatory authority determines that a given retail market identified in accordance with Article 15 of that Directive is not effectively competitive; and

(b) the national regulatory authority concludes that obligations imposed under Articles 9 to 13 of Directive 2002/19/EC (Access Directive) would not result in the achievement of the objectives set out in Article 8 of Directive 2002/21/EC (Framework Directive).]

2. Obligations imposed under paragraph 1 shall be based on the nature of the problem identified and be proportionate and justified in the light of the objectives laid down in Article 8 of Directive 2002/21/EC (Framework Directive). The obligations imposed may include requirements that the identified undertakings do not charge excessive prices, inhibit market entry or restrict competition by setting predatory prices, show undue preference to specific end-users or unreasonably bundle services. National regulatory authorities may apply to such undertakings appropriate retail price cap measures, measures to control individual tariffs, or measures to orient tariffs towards costs or prices on comparable markets, in order to protect end-user interests whilst promoting effective competition.

[ ]

4. National regulatory authorities shall ensure that, where an undertaking is subject to retail tariff regulation or other relevant retail controls, the necessary and appropriate cost accounting systems are implemented. National regulatory authorities may specify the format and accounting methodology to be used. Compliance with the cost accounting system shall be verified by a qualified independent body. National regulatory authorities shall ensure that a statement concerning compliance is published annually.

5. Without prejudice to Article 9(2) and Article 10, national regulatory authorities shall not apply retail control mechanisms under paragraph 1 of this Article to geographical or user markets where they are satisfied that there is effective competition.

Notes

Article 17 was amended as shown in square brackets by Directive 2009/136/EC of 25 November 2009 (OJ L 337, 18.12.2009, p.11), with effect from 19 December 2009.

Commentary
Art 17: B&C: 12.014, 12.019, 12.031 **F&N:** 13.30
Art 17(1): B&C: 12.019
Art 17(2): B&C: 12.019

[ ]

Notes

Article 18 was deleted by Directive 2009/136/EC of 25 November 2009 (OJ L 337, 18.12.2009, p. 11), with effect from 19 December 2009.

Commentary
Art 18: B&C: 12.031 F&N: 13.30

[ ]

Notes
Article 19 was deleted by Directive 2009/136/EC of 25 November 2009 (OJ L 337, 18.12.2009, p.11), with effect from 19 December 2009.

Commentary
Art 19: B&C: 12.031 F&N: 13.30

CHAPTER IV
END-USER INTERESTS AND RIGHTS

[*Article 20*
Contracts

1. Member States shall ensure that, when subscribing to services providing connection to a public communications network and/or publicly available electronic communications services, consumers, and other end-users so requesting, have a right to a contract with an undertaking or undertakings providing such connection and/or services. The contract shall specify in a clear, comprehensive and easily accessible form at least:

(a) the identity and address of the undertaking;

(b) the services provided, including in particular,

   — whether or not access to emergency services and caller location information is being provided, and any limitations on the provision of emergency services under Article 26,

   — information on any other conditions limiting access to and/or use of services and applications, where such conditions are permitted under national law in accordance with Community law,

   — the minimum service quality levels offered, namely the time for the initial connection and, where appropriate, other quality of service parameters, as defined by the national regulatory authorities,

   — information on any procedures put in place by the undertaking to measure and shape traffic so as to avoid filling or overfilling a network link, and information on how those procedures could impact on service quality,

   — the types of maintenance service offered and customer support services provided, as well as the means of contacting these services,

   — any restrictions imposed by the provider on the use of terminal equipment supplied;

(c) where an obligation exists under Article 25, the subscriber's options as to whether or not to include his or her personal data in a directory, and the data concerned;

(d) details of prices and tariffs, the means by which up-to-date information on all applicable tariffs and maintenance charges may be obtained, payment methods offered and any differences in costs due to payment method;

(e) the duration of the contract and the conditions for renewal and termination of services and of the contract, including:

   — any minimum usage or duration required to benefit from promotional terms,

   — any charges related to portability of numbers and other identifiers,

   — any charges due on termination of the contract, including any cost recovery with respect to terminal equipment,

(f) any compensation and the refund arrangements which apply if contracted service quality levels are not met;

(g) the means of initiating procedures for the settlement of disputes in accordance with Article 34;

(h) the type of action that might be taken by the undertaking in reaction to security or integrity incidents or threats and vulnerabilities.

Member States may also require that the contract include any information which may be provided by the relevant public authorities for this purpose on the use of electronic communications networks and services to engage in unlawful activities or to disseminate harmful content, and on the means of protection against risks to personal security, privacy and personal data, referred to in Article 21(4) and relevant to the service provided.

2.   Member States shall ensure that subscribers have a right to withdraw from their contract without penalty upon notice of modification to the contractual conditions proposed by the undertakings providing electronic communications networks and/or services. Subscribers shall be given adequate notice, not shorter than one month, of any such modification, and shall be informed at the same time of their right to withdraw, without penalty, from their contract if they do not accept the new conditions. Member States shall ensure that national regulatory authorities are able to specify the format of such notifications.]

Notes

Article 20 was replaced as shown in square brackets by Directive 2009/136/EC of 25 November 2009 (OJ L 337, 18.12.2009, p.11), with effect from 19 December 2009.

Commentary
Art 20: B&C: 12.006, 12.039

[*Article 21*
Transparency and publication of information

1.   Member States shall ensure that national regulatory authorities are able to oblige undertakings providing public electronic communications networks and/or publicly available electronic communications services to publish transparent, comparable, adequate and up-to-date information on applicable prices and tariffs, on any charges due on termination of a contract and on standard terms and conditions in respect of access to, and use of, services provided by them to end-users and consumers in accordance with Annex II. Such information shall be published in a clear, comprehensive and easily accessible form. National regulatory authorities may specify additional requirements regarding the form in which such information is to be published.

2.   National regulatory authorities shall encourage the provision of comparable information to enable end-users and consumers to make an independent evaluation of the cost of alternative usage patterns, for instance by means of interactive guides or similar techniques. Where such facilities are not available on the market free of charge or at a reasonable price, Member States shall ensure that national regulatory authorities are able to make such guides or techniques available themselves or through third party procurement. Third parties shall have a right to use, free of charge, the information published by undertakings providing electronic communications networks and/or publicly available electronic communications services for the purposes of selling or making available such interactive guides or similar techniques.

3.   Member States shall ensure that national regulatory authorities are able to oblige undertakings providing public electronic communications networks and/or publicly available electronic communications services to inter alia:

(a)   provide applicable tariff information to subscribers regarding any number or service subject to particular pricing conditions; with respect to individual categories of services, national regulatory authorities may require such information to be provided immediately prior to connecting the call;

(b)   inform subscribers of any change to access to emergency services or caller location information in the service to which they have subscribed;

(c)   inform subscribers of any change to conditions limiting access to and/or use of services and applications, where such conditions are permitted under national law in accordance with Community law;

(d)   provide information on any procedures put in place by the provider to measure and shape traffic so as to avoid filling or overfilling a network link, and on how those procedures could impact on service quality;

(e) inform subscribers of their right to determine whether or not to include their personal data in a directory, and of the types of data concerned, in accordance with Article 12 of Directive 2002/58/EC (Directive on privacy and electronic communications); and

(f) regularly inform disabled subscribers of details of products and services designed for them.

If deemed appropriate, national regulatory authorities may promote self- or co-regulatory measures prior to imposing any obligation.

4. Member States may require that the undertakings referred to in paragraph 3 distribute public interest information free of charge to existing and new subscribers, where appropriate, by the same means as those ordinarily used by them in their communications with subscribers. In such a case, that information shall be provided by the relevant public authorities in a standardised format and shall, inter alia, cover the following topics:

(a) the most common uses of electronic communications services to engage in unlawful activities or to disseminate harmful content, particularly where it may prejudice respect for the rights and freedoms of others, including infringements of copyright and related rights, and their legal consequences; and

(b) the means of protection against risks to personal security, privacy and personal data when using electronic communications services.]

Notes

Article 21 was replaced as shown in square brackets by Directive 2009/136/EC of 25 November 2009 (OJ L 337, 18.12.2009, p.11), with effect from 19 December 2009.

Commentary

Art 21: B&C: 12.006, 12.039

[*Article 22*
Quality of service

1. Member States shall ensure that national regulatory authorities are, after taking account of the views of interested parties, able to require undertakings that provide publicly available electronic communications networks and/or services to publish comparable, adequate and up-to-date information for end-users on the quality of their services and on measures taken to ensure equivalence in access for disabled end-users. That information shall, on request, be supplied to the national regulatory authority in advance of its publication.

2. National regulatory authorities may specify, inter alia, the quality of service parameters to be measured and the content, form and manner of the information to be published, including possible quality certification mechanisms, in order to ensure that end-users, including disabled end-users, have access to comprehensive, comparable, reliable and user-friendly information. Where appropriate, the parameters, definitions and measurement methods set out in Annex III may be used.

3. In order to prevent the degradation of service and the hindering or slowing down of traffic over networks, Member States shall ensure that national regulatory authorities are able to set minimum quality of service requirements on an undertaking or undertakings providing public communications networks.

National regulatory authorities shall provide the Commission, in good time before setting any such requirements, with a summary of the grounds for action, the envisaged requirements and the proposed course of action. This information shall also be made available to the Body of European Regulators for Electronic Communications (BEREC). The Commission may, having examined such information, make comments or recommendations thereupon, in particular to ensure that the envisaged requirements do not adversely affect the functioning of the internal market. National regulatory authorities shall take the utmost account of the Commission's comments or recommendations when deciding on the requirements.]

Notes

Article 22 was replaced as shown in square brackets by Directive 2009/136/EC of 25 November 2009 (OJ L 337, 18.12.2009, p.11), with effect from 19 December 2009.

Commentary
Art 22: B&C: 12.039

[*Article 23*
Availability of services

Member States shall take all necessary measures to ensure the fullest possible availability of publicly available telephone services provided over public communications networks in the event of catastrophic network breakdown or in cases of force majeure. Member States shall ensure that undertakings providing publicly available telephone services take all necessary measures to ensure uninterrupted access to emergency services.]

Notes

Article 23 was replaced as shown in square brackets by Directive 2009/136/EC of 25 November 2009 (OJ L 337, 18.12.2009, p.11), with effect from 19 December 2009.

[*Article 23a*
Ensuring equivalence in access and choice for disabled end-users

1. Member States shall enable relevant national authorities to specify, where appropriate, requirements to be met by undertakings providing publicly available electronic communication services to ensure that disabled end-users:

(a) have access to electronic communications services equivalent to that enjoyed by the majority of end-users; and

(b) benefit from the choice of undertakings and services available to the majority of end-users.

2. In order to be able to adopt and implement specific arrangements for disabled end-users, Member States shall encourage the availability of terminal equipment offering the necessary services and functions.]

Notes

Article 23a was inserted as shown in square brackets by Directive 2009/136/EC of 25 November 2009 (OJ L 337, 18.12.2009, p.11), with effect from 19 December 2009.

Commentary
Art 23a: B&C: 12.006
Art 23a(2): B&C: 12.007

Article 24
Interoperability of consumer digital television equipment

In accordance with the provisions of Annex VI, Member States shall ensure the interoperability of the consumer digital television equipment referred to therein.

Commentary
Art 24: B&C: 12.007

Article 25
[Telephone directory enquiry services]

[1. Member States shall ensure that subscribers to publicly available telephone services have the right to have an entry in the publicly available directory referred to in Article 5(1)(a) and to have their information made available to providers of directory enquiry services and/or directories in accordance with paragraph 2.]

2. Member States shall ensure that all undertakings which assign telephone numbers to subscribers meet all reasonable requests to make available, for the purposes of the provision of publicly available directory enquiry services and directories, the relevant information in an agreed format on terms which are fair, objective, cost oriented and non-discriminatory.

[3. Member States shall ensure that all end-users provided with a publicly available telephone service can access directory enquiry services. National regulatory authorities shall be able to impose obligations and conditions on undertakings that control access of end-users for the provision of directory enquiry services in accordance with the provisions of Article 5 of Directive 2002/19/EC (Access Directive). Such obligations and conditions shall be objective, equitable, non-discriminatory and transparent.

4. Member States shall not maintain any regulatory restrictions which prevent end-users in one Member State from accessing directly the directory enquiry service in another Member State by voice call or SMS, and shall take measures to ensure such access in accordance with Article 28.

5. Paragraphs 1 to 4 shall apply subject to the requirements of Community legislation on the protection of personal data and privacy and, in particular, Article 12 of Directive 2002/58/EC (Directive on privacy and electronic communications).]

Notes

Article 25 was amended as shown in square brackets by Directive 2009/136/EC of 25 November 2009 (OJ L 337, 18.12.2009, p.11), with effect from 19 December 2009.

[*Article 26*
Emergency services and the single European emergency call number

1. Member States shall ensure that all end-users of the service referred to in paragraph 2, including users of public pay telephones, are able to call the emergency services free of charge and without having to use any means of payment, by using the single European emergency call number "112" and any national emergency call number specified by Member States.

2. Member States, in consultation with national regulatory authorities, emergency services and providers, shall ensure that undertakings providing end-users with an electronic communications service for originating national calls to a number or numbers in a national telephone numbering plan provide access to emergency services.

3. Member States shall ensure that calls to the single European emergency call number "112" are appropriately answered and handled in the manner best suited to the national organisation of emergency systems. Such calls shall be answered and handled at least as expeditiously and effectively as calls to the national emergency number or numbers, where these continue to be in use.

4. Member States shall ensure that access for disabled end-users to emergency services is equivalent to that enjoyed by other end-users. Measures taken to ensure that disabled end-users are able to access emergency services whilst travelling in other Member States shall be based to the greatest extent possible on European standards or specifications published in accordance with the provisions of Article 17 of Directive 2002/21/EC (Framework Directive), and they shall not prevent Member States from adopting additional requirements in order to pursue the objectives set out in this Article.

5. Member States shall ensure that undertakings concerned make caller location information available free of charge to the authority handling emergency calls as soon as the call reaches that authority. This shall apply to all calls to the single European emergency call number "112". Member States may extend this obligation to cover calls to national emergency numbers. Competent regulatory authorities shall lay down criteria for the accuracy and reliability of the caller location information provided.

6. Member States shall ensure that citizens are adequately informed about the existence and use of the single European emergency call number "112", in particular through initiatives specifically targeting persons travelling between Member States.

7. In order to ensure effective access to "112" services in the Member States, the Commission, having consulted BEREC, may adopt technical implementing measures. However, these technical implementing measures shall be adopted without prejudice to, and shall have no impact on, the organisation of emergency services, which remains of the exclusive competence of Member States.

Those measures, designed to amend non-essential elements of this Directive by supplementing it, shall be adopted in accordance with the regulatory procedure with scrutiny referred to in Article 37(2).]

Notes

Article 26 was replaced as shown in square brackets by Directive 2009/136/EC of 25 November 2009 (OJ L 337, 18.12.2009, p.11), with effect from 19 December 2009.

[*Article 27*
European telephone access codes

1. Member States shall ensure that the "00" code is the standard international access code. Special arrangements for making calls between locations adjacent to one another across borders between Member States may be established or continued. End-users in the locations concerned shall be fully informed of such arrangements.

2. A legal entity, established within the Community and designated by the Commission, shall have sole responsibility for the management, including number assignment, and promotion of the European Telephony Numbering Space (ETNS). The Commission shall adopt the necessary implementing rules.

3. Member States shall ensure that all undertakings that provide publicly available telephone services allowing international calls handle all calls to and from the ETNS at rates similar to those applied for calls to and from other Member States.]

Notes

Article 27 was replaced as shown in square brackets by Directive 2009/136/EC of 25 November 2009 (OJ L 337, 18.12.2009, p.11), with effect from 19 December 2009.

[*Article 27a*
Harmonised numbers for harmonised services of social value, including the missing children hotline number

1. Member States shall promote the specific numbers in the numbering range beginning with "116" identified by Commission Decision 2007/116/EC of 15 February 2007 on reserving the national numbering range beginning with "116" for harmonised numbers for harmonised services of social value [ ]. They shall encourage the provision within their territory of the services for which such numbers are reserved.

2. Member States shall ensure that disabled end-users are able to access services provided under the "116" numbering range to the greatest extent possible. Measures taken to facilitate disabled end-users' access to such services whilst travelling in other Member States shall be based on compliance with relevant standards or specifications published in accordance with Article 17 of Directive 2002/21/EC (Framework Directive).

3. Member States shall ensure that citizens are adequately informed of the existence and use of services provided under the "116" numbering range, in particular through initiatives specifically targeting persons travelling between Member States.

4. Member States shall, in addition to measures of general applicability to all numbers in the "116" numbering range taken pursuant to paragraphs 1, 2, and 3, make every effort to ensure that citizens have access to a service operating a hotline to report cases of missing children. The hotline shall be available on the number "116000".

5. In order to ensure the effective implementation of the "116" numbering range, in particular the missing children hotline number "116000", in the Member States, including access for disabled end-users when travelling in other Member States, the Commission, having consulted BEREC, may adopt technical implementing measures. However, these technical implementing measures shall be adopted without prejudice to, and shall have no impact on, the organisation of these services, which remains of the exclusive competence of Member States.

Those measures, designed to amend non-essential elements of this Directive by supplementing it, shall be adopted in accordance with the regulatory procedure with scrutiny referred to in Article 37(2).]

Notes

Article 27a was inserted as shown in square brackets by Directive 2009/136/EC of 25 November 2009 (OJ L 337, 18.12.2009, p.11), with effect from 19 December 2009.

[*Article 28*
Access to numbers and services

1. Member States shall ensure that, where technically and economically feasible, and except where a called subscriber has chosen for commercial reasons to limit access by calling parties located in specific geographical areas, relevant national authorities take all necessary steps to ensure that end-users are able to:

(a) access and use services using non-geographic numbers within the Community; and

(b) access all numbers provided in the Community, regardless of the technology and devices used by the operator, including those in the national numbering plans of Member States, those from the ETNS and Universal International Freephone Numbers (UIFN).

2. Member States shall ensure that the relevant authorities are able to require undertakings providing public communications networks and/or publicly available electronic communications services to block, on a case-by-case basis, access to numbers or services where this is justified by reasons of fraud or misuse and to require that in such cases providers of electronic communications services withhold relevant interconnection or other service revenues.]

Notes

Article 28 was replaced as shown in square brackets by Directive 2009/136/EC of 25 November 2009 (OJ L 337, 18.12.2009, p.11), with effect from 19 December 2009.

Article 29
Provision of additional facilities

[1. Without prejudice to Article 10(2), Member States shall ensure that national regulatory authorities are able to require all undertakings that provide publicly available telephone services and/or access to public communications networks to make available all or part of the additional facilities listed in Part B of Annex I, subject to technical feasibility and economic viability, as well as all or part of the additional facilities listed in Part A of Annex I.]

2. A Member State may decide to waive paragraph 1 in all or part of its territory if it considers, after taking into account the views of interested parties, that there is sufficient access to these facilities.

[ ]

Notes

Article 29 was amended as shown in square brackets by Directive 2009/136/EC of 25 November 2009 (OJ L 337, 18.12.2009, p.11), with effect from 19 December 2009.

[*Article 30*
Facilitating change of provider

1. Member States shall ensure that all subscribers with numbers from the national telephone numbering plan who so request can retain their number(s) independently of the undertaking providing the service in accordance with the provisions of Part C of Annex I.

2. National regulatory authorities shall ensure that pricing between operators and/or service providers related to the provision of number portability is cost-oriented, and that direct charges to subscribers, if any, do not act as a disincentive for subscribers against changing service provider.

3. National regulatory authorities shall not impose retail tariffs for the porting of numbers in a manner that would distort competition, such as by setting specific or common retail tariffs.

4. Porting of numbers and their subsequent activation shall be carried out within the shortest possible time. In any case, subscribers who have concluded an agreement to port a number to a new undertaking shall have that number activated within one working day.

Without prejudice to the first subparagraph, competent national authorities may establish the global process of porting of numbers, taking into account national provisions on contracts, technical feasibility and the need to maintain continuity of service to the subscriber. In any event, loss of service during the process of porting shall not exceed one working day. Competent national authorities shall also take into account, where necessary, measures ensuring that subscribers are protected throughout the switching process and are not switched to another provider against their will.

Member States shall ensure that appropriate sanctions on undertakings are provided for, including an obligation to compensate subscribers in case of delay in porting or abuse of porting by them or on their behalf.

5. Member States shall ensure that contracts concluded between consumers and undertakings providing electronic communications services do not mandate an initial commitment period that exceeds 24 months. Member States shall also ensure that undertakings offer users the possibility to subscribe to a contract with a maximum duration of 12 months.

6. Without prejudice to any minimum contractual period, Member States shall ensure that conditions and procedures for contract termination do not act as a disincentive against changing service provider.]

Notes

Article 30 was replaced as shown in square brackets by Directive 2009/136/EC of 25 November 2009 (OJ L 337, 18.12.2009, p.11), with effect from 19 December 2009.

Commentary
Art 30: B&C: 12.006

Article 31
"Must carry" obligations

[1. Member States may impose reasonable "must carry" obligations, for the transmission of specified radio and television broadcast channels and complementary services, particularly accessibility services to enable appropriate access for disabled end-users, on undertakings under their jurisdiction providing electronic communications networks used for the distribution of radio or television broadcast channels to the public where a significant number of end-users of such networks use them as their principal means to receive radio and television broadcast channels. Such obligations shall only be imposed where they are necessary to meet general interest objectives as clearly defined by each Member State and shall be proportionate and transparent.

The obligations referred to in the first subparagraph shall be reviewed by the Member States at the latest within one year of 25 May 2011, except where Member States have carried out such a review within the previous two years.

Member States shall review "must carry" obligations on a regular basis.]

2. Neither paragraph 1 of this Article nor Article 3(2) of Directive 2002/19/EC (Access Directive) shall prejudice the ability of Member States to determine appropriate remuneration, if any, in respect of measures taken in accordance with this Article while ensuring that, in similar circumstances, there is no discrimination in the treatment of undertakings providing electronic communications networks. Where remuneration is provided for, Member States shall ensure that it is applied in a proportionate and transparent manner.

Notes

Article 31(1) was replaced as shown in square brackets by Directive 2009/136/EC of 25 November 2009 (OJ L 337, 18.12.2009, p.11), with effect from 19 December 2009.

Chapter V
General and final provisions

Article 32
Additional mandatory services

Member States may decide to make additional services, apart from services within the universal service obligations as defined in Chapter II, publicly available in its own territory but, in such circumstances, no compensation mechanism involving specific undertakings may be imposed.

Article 33
Consultation with interested parties

[1. Member States shall ensure as far as appropriate that national regulatory authorities take account of the views of end-users, consumers (including, in particular, disabled consumers), manufacturers and undertakings that provide electronic communications networks and/or services on issues related to all end-user and consumer rights concerning publicly available electronic communications services, in particular where they have a significant impact on the market.

In particular, Member States shall ensure that national regulatory authorities establish a consultation mechanism ensuring that in their decisions on issues related to end-user and consumer rights concerning publicly available electronic communications services, due consideration is given to consumer interests in electronic communications.]

2. Where appropriate, interested parties may develop, with the guidance of national regulatory authorities, mechanisms, involving consumers, user groups and service providers, to improve the general quality of service provision by, inter alia, developing and monitoring codes of conduct and operating standards.

[3. Without prejudice to national rules in conformity with Community law promoting cultural and media policy objectives, such as cultural and linguistic diversity and media pluralism, national regulatory authorities and other relevant authorities may promote cooperation between undertakings providing electronic communications networks and/or services and sectors interested in the promotion of lawful content in electronic communication networks and services. That cooperation may also include coordination of the public interest information to be provided pursuant to Article 21(4) and the second subparagraph of Article 20(1).]

Notes

Article 33(1) was replaced and Article 33(3) was inserted as shown in square brackets by Directive 2009/136/EC of 25 November 2009 (OJ L 337, 18.12.2009, p.11), with effect from 19 December 2009.

Article 34
Out-of-court dispute resolution

[1. Member States shall ensure that transparent, non-discriminatory, simple and inexpensive out-of-court procedures are available for dealing with unresolved disputes between consumers and undertakings providing electronic communications networks and/or services arising under this Directive and relating to the contractual conditions and/or performance of contracts concerning the supply of those networks and/or services. Member States shall adopt measures to ensure that such procedures enable disputes to be settled fairly and promptly and may, where warranted, adopt a system of reimbursement and/or compensation. Such procedures shall enable disputes to be settled impartially and shall not deprive the consumer of the legal protection afforded by national law. Member States may extend these obligations to cover disputes involving other end-users.]

2. Member States shall ensure that their legislation does not hamper the establishment of complaints offices and the provision of on-line services at the appropriate territorial level to facilitate access to dispute resolution by consumers and end-users.

3. Where such disputes involve parties in different Member States, Member States shall coordinate their efforts with a view to bringing about a resolution of the dispute.

4. This Article is without prejudice to national court procedures.

Notes

Article 34(1) was replaced as shown in square brackets by Directive 2009/136/EC of 25 November 2009 (OJ L 337, 18.12.2009, p.11), with effect from 19 December 2009.

[*Article 35*
Adaptation of annexes

Measures designed to amend non-essential elements of this Directive and necessary to adapt Annexes I, II, III, and VI to technological developments or changes in market demand shall be adopted by the Commission in accordance with the regulatory procedure with scrutiny referred to in Article 37(2).]

Notes

Article 35 was replaced as shown in square brackets by Directive 2009/136/EC of 25 November 2009 (OJ L 337, 18.12.2009, p.11), with effect from 19 December 2009.

Article 36
Notification, monitoring and review procedures

1. National regulatory authorities shall notify to the Commission by at the latest the date of application referred to in Article 38(1), second subparagraph, and immediately in the event of any change thereafter in the names of undertakings designated as having universal service obligations under Article 8(1).

The Commission shall make the information available in a readily accessible form, and shall distribute it to the Communications Committee referred to in Article 37.

[2. National regulatory authorities shall notify to the Commission the universal service obligations imposed upon undertakings designated as having universal service obligations. Any changes affecting these obligations or of the undertakings affected under the provisions of this Directive shall be notified to the Commission without delay.]

3. The Commission shall periodically review the functioning of this Directive and report to the European Parliament and to the Council, on the first occasion not later than three years after the date of application referred to in Article 38(1), second subparagraph. The Member States and national regulatory authorities shall supply the necessary information to the Commission for this purpose.

Notes

Article 36(2) was replaced as shown in square brackets by Directive 2009/136/EC of 25 November 2009 (OJ L 337, 18.12.2009, p.11), with effect from 19 December 2009.

[*Article 37*
Committee procedure

1. The Commission shall be assisted by the Communications Committee set up under Article 22 of Directive 2002/21/EC (Framework Directive).

2. Where reference is made to this paragraph, Article 5a(1) to (4) and Article 7 of Decision 1999/468/EC shall apply, having regard to the provisions of Article 8 thereof.]

Notes

Article 37 was replaced as shown in square brackets by Directive 2009/136/EC of 25 November 2009 (OJ L 337, 18.12.2009, p.11), with effect from 19 December 2009.

Article 38
Transposition

1. Member States shall adopt and publish the laws, regulations and administrative provisions necessary to comply with this Directive by 24 July 2003 at the latest. They shall forthwith inform the Commission thereof.

They shall apply those measures from 25 July 2003.

2. When Member States adopt these measures, they shall contain a reference to this Directive or be accompanied by such a reference on the occasion of their official publication. The methods of making such a reference shall be laid down by the Member States.

3. Member States shall communicate to the Commission the text of the provisions of national law which they adopt in the field governed by this Directive and of any subsequent modifications to those provisions.

Notes

Measures to implement the amendments effected by Directive 2009/136/EC are required to be adopted and published by Member States by 25 May 2011 and applied from 26 May 2011: Directive 2009/136/EC, Article 45.

Article 39
Entry into force

This Directive shall enter into force on the day of its publication in the *Official Journal of the European Communities.*

Notes

Date of entry into force: 24 April 2002.

Article 40
Addressees

This Directive is addressed to the Member States.

Done at Brussels, 7 March 2002.

[ANNEX I
DESCRIPTION OF FACILITIES AND SERVICES REFERRED TO IN
ARTICLE 10 (CONTROL OF EXPENDITURE), ARTICLE 29
(ADDITIONAL FACILITIES) AND ARTICLE 30 (FACILITATING
CHANGE OF PROVIDER)

Part A: Facilities and services referred to in Article 10

(a) Itemised billing

Member States are to ensure that national regulatory authorities, subject to the requirements of relevant legislation on the protection of personal data and privacy, may lay down the basic level of itemised bills which are to be provided by undertakings to subscribers free of charge in order that they can:

(i) allow verification and control of the charges incurred in using the public communications network at a fixed location and/or related publicly available telephone services; and

(ii) adequately monitor their usage and expenditure and thereby exercise a reasonable degree of control over their bills.

Where appropriate, additional levels of detail may be offered to subscribers at reasonable tariffs or at no charge.

Calls which are free of charge to the calling subscriber, including calls to helplines, are not to be identified in the calling subscriber's itemised bill.

(b) Selective barring for outgoing calls or premium SMS or MMS, or, where technically feasible, other kinds of similar applications, free of charge

i.e. the facility whereby the subscriber can, on request to the designated undertaking that provides telephone services, bar outgoing calls or premium SMS or MMS or other kinds of similar applications of defined types or to defined types of numbers free of charge.

(c) Pre-payment systems

Member States are to ensure that national regulatory authorities may require designated undertakings to provide means for consumers to pay for access to the public communications network and use of publicly available telephone services on pre-paid terms.

(d) Phased payment of connection fees

Member States are to ensure that national regulatory authorities may require designated undertakings to allow consumers to pay for connection to the public communications network on the basis of payments phased over time.

(e) Non-payment of bills

Member States are to authorise specified measures, which are to be proportionate, non-discriminatory and published, to cover non-payment of telephone bills issued by undertakings. These measures are to ensure that due warning of any consequent service interruption or disconnection is given to the subscriber beforehand. Except in cases of fraud, persistent late payment or non-payment, these measures are to ensure, as far as is technically feasible that any service interruption is confined to the service concerned. Disconnection for non-payment of bills should take place only after due warning is given to the subscriber. Member States may allow a period of limited service prior to complete disconnection, during which only calls that do not incur a charge to the subscriber (e.g. "112" calls) are permitted.

(f) Tariff advice

i.e. the facility whereby subscribers may request the undertaking to provide information regarding alternative lower-cost tariffs, if available.

(g) Cost control

i.e. the facility whereby undertakings offer other means, if determined to be appropriate by national regulatory authorities, to control the costs of publicly available telephone services, including free-of-charge alerts to consumers in case of abnormal or excessive consumption patterns.

Part B: Facilities referred to in Article 29

(a) Tone dialling or DTMF (dual-tone multi-frequency operation)

i.e. the public communications network and/or publicly available telephone services supports the use of DTMF tones as defined in ETSI ETR 207 for end-to-end signalling throughout the network both within a Member State and between Member States.

(b) Calling-line identification

i.e. the calling party's number is presented to the called party prior to the call being established.

This facility should be provided in accordance with relevant legislation on protection of personal data and privacy, in particular Directive 2002/58/EC (Directive on privacy and electronic communications).

To the extent technically feasible, operators should provide data and signals to facilitate the offering of calling-line identity and tone dialling across Member State boundaries.

Part C: Implementation of the number portability provisions referred to in Article 30

The requirement that all subscribers with numbers from the national numbering plan, who so request can retain their number(s) independently of the undertaking providing the service shall apply:

(a) in the case of geographic numbers, at a specific location; and

(b) in the case of non-geographic numbers, at any location.

This Part does not apply to the porting of numbers between networks providing services at a fixed location and mobile networks.]

Notes

Annex I was replaced as shown in square brackets by Directive 2009/136/EC of 25 November 2009 (OJ L 337, 18.12.2009, p.11), with effect from 19 December 2009.

[ANNEX II
INFORMATION TO BE PUBLISHED IN ACCORDANCE WITH ARTICLE 21
(TRANSPARENCY AND PUBLICATION OF INFORMATION)

The national regulatory authority has a responsibility to ensure that the information in this Annex is published, in accordance with Article 21. It is for the national regulatory authority to decide which information is to be published by the undertakings providing public communications networks and/ or publicly available telephone services and which information is to be published by the national regulatory authority itself, so as to ensure that consumers are able to make informed choices.

1. Name(s) and address(es) of undertaking(s)

i.e. names and head office addresses of undertakings providing public communications networks and/ or publicly available telephone services.

2. Description of services offered

2.1. Scope of services offered

2.2. Standard tariffs indicating the services provided and the content of each tariff element (e.g. charges for access, all types of usage charges, maintenance charges), and including details of standard discounts applied and special and targeted tariff schemes and any additional charges, as well as costs with respect to terminal equipment.

2.3. Compensation/refund policy, including specific details of any compensation/refund schemes offered.

2.4. Types of maintenance service offered.

2.5. Standard contract conditions, including any minimum contractual period, termination of the contract and procedures and direct charges related to the portability of numbers and other identifiers, if relevant.

3. Dispute settlement mechanisms, including those developed by the undertaking.

4. Information about rights as regards universal service, including, where appropriate, the facilities and services mentioned in Annex I.]

Notes

Annex II was replaced as shown in square brackets by Directive 2009/136/EC of 25 November 2009 (OJ L 337, 18.12.2009, p.11), with effect from 19 December 2009.

[Annex III
Quality of Service Parameters

Quality-of-service Parameters, Definitions and Measurement
Methods Referred to in Articles 11 and 22

For undertakings providing access to a public communications network

Parameter (Note 1)	Definition	Measurement method
Supply time for initial connection	ETSI EG 202 057	ETSI EG 202 057
Fault rate per access line	ETSI EG 202 057	ETSI EG 202 057
Fault repair time	ETSI EG 202 057	ETSI EG 202 057
For undertakings providing a publicly available telephone service		
Call set up time (Note 2)	ETSI EG 202 057	ETSI EG 202 057
Response times for directory enquiry services	ETSI EG 202 057	ETSI EG 202 057
Proportion of coin and card operated public pay telephones in working order	ETSI EG 202 057	ETSI EG 202 057
Bill correctness complaints	ETSI EG 202 057	ETSI EG 202 057
Unsuccessful call ratio[2]	ETSI EG 202 057	ETSI EG 202 057
Version number of ETSI EG 202 057-1 is 1.3.1 (July 2008)		

Note 1

Parameters should allow for performance to be analysed at a regional level (i.e. no less than level 2 in the Nomenclature of Territorial Units for Statistics (NUTS) established by Eurostat).

Note 2

Member States may decide not to require up-to-date information concerning the performance for these two parameters to be kept if evidence is available to show that performance in these two areas is satisfactory.]

Notes

Annex III was replaced as shown in square brackets by Directive 2009/136/EC of 25 November 2009 (OJ L 337, 18.12.2009, p.11), with effect from 19 December 2009.

Annex IV
Calculating the Net Cost, if any, of Universal Service
Obligations and Establishing any Recovery or Sharing
Mechanism in Accordance with Articles 12 and 13

Part A: Calculation of net cost

Universal service obligations refer to those obligations placed upon an undertaking by a Member State which concern the provision of a network and service throughout a specified geographical area, including, where required, averaged prices in that geographical area for the provision of that service or provision of specific tariff options for consumers with low incomes or with special social needs.

National regulatory authorities are to consider all means to ensure appropriate incentives for undertakings (designated or not) to provide universal service obligations cost efficiently. In undertaking a calculation exercise, the net cost of universal service obligations is to be calculated as the difference between the net cost for a designated undertaking of operating with the universal service obligations and operating without the universal service obligations. This applies whether the network in a particular Member State is fully developed or is still undergoing development and expansion. Due attention is to be given to correctly assessing the costs that any designated undertaking would have chosen to avoid had there been no universal service obligation. The net cost calculation should assess the benefits, including intangible benefits, to the universal service operator.

The calculation is to be based upon the costs attributable to:

(i) elements of the identified services which can only be provided at a loss or provided under cost conditions falling outside normal commercial standards.

This category may include service elements such as access to emergency telephone services, provision of certain public pay telephones, provision of certain services or equipment for disabled people, etc;

(ii) specific end-users or groups of end-users who, taking into account the cost of providing the specified network and service, the revenue generated and any geographical averaging of prices imposed by the Member State, can only be served at a loss or under cost conditions falling outside normal commercial standards.

This category includes those end-users or groups of end-users which would not be served by a commercial operator which did not have an obligation to provide universal service.

The calculation of the net cost of specific aspects of universal service obligations is to be made separately and so as to avoid the double counting of any direct or indirect benefits and costs. The overall net cost of universal service obligations to any undertaking is to be calculated as the sum of the net costs arising from the specific components of universal service obligations, taking account of any intangible benefits. The responsibility for verifying the net cost lies with the national regulatory authority.

Part B: Recovery of any net costs of universal service obligations

The recovery or financing of any net costs of universal service obligations requires designated undertakings with universal service obligations to be compensated for the services they provide under non-commercial conditions. Because such a compensation involves financial transfers, Member States are to ensure that these are undertaken in an objective, transparent, non-discriminatory and proportionate manner. This means that the transfers result in the least distortion to competition and to user demand.

In accordance with Article 13(3), a sharing mechanism based on a fund should use a transparent and neutral means for collecting contributions that avoids the danger of a double imposition of contributions falling on both outputs and inputs of undertakings.

The independent body administering the fund is to be responsible for collecting contributions from undertakings which are assessed as liable to contribute to the net cost of universal service obligations in the Member State and is to oversee the transfer of sums due and/or administrative payments to the undertakings entitled to receive payments from the fund.

Annex V
Process for Reviewing the Scope of Universal Service in Accordance with Article 15

In considering whether a review of the scope of universal service obligations should be undertaken, the Commission is to take into consideration the following elements:

— social and market developments in terms of the services used by consumers,
— social and market developments in terms of the availability and choice of services to consumers,
— technological developments in terms of the way services are provided to consumers.

In considering whether the scope of universal service obligations be changed or redefined, the Commission is to take into consideration the following elements:

— are specific services available to and used by a majority of consumers and does the lack of availability or non-use by a minority of consumers result in social exclusion, and

— does the availability and use of specific services convey a general net benefit to all consumers such that public intervention is warranted in circumstances where the specific services are not provided to the public under normal commercial circumstances?

[ANNEX VI

INTEROPERABILITY OF DIGITAL CONSUMER
EQUIPMENT REFERRED TO IN ARTICLE 24

1. Common scrambling algorithm and free-to-air reception

All consumer equipment intended for the reception of conventional digital television signals (i.e. broadcasting via terrestrial, cable or satellite transmission which is primarily intended for fixed reception, such as DVB-T, DVB-C or DVB-S), for sale or rent or otherwise made available in the Community, capable of descrambling digital television signals, is to possess the capability to:

— allow the descrambling of such signals according to a common European scrambling algorithm as administered by a recognised European standards organisation, currently ETSI,

— display signals that have been transmitted in the clear provided that, in the event that such equipment is rented, the renter is in compliance with the relevant rental agreement.

2. Interoperability for analogue and digital television sets

Any analogue television set with an integral screen of visible diagonal greater than 42 cm which is put on the market for sale or rent in the Community is to be fitted with at least one open interface socket, as standardised by a recognised European standards organisation, e.g. as given in the Cenelec EN 50 049-1:1997 standard, permitting simple connection of peripherals, especially additional decoders and digital receivers.

Any digital television set with an integral screen of visible diagonal greater than 30 cm which is put on the market for sale or rent in the Community is to be fitted with at least one open interface socket (either standardised by, or conforming to a standard adopted by, a recognised European standards organisation, or conforming to an industry-wide specification) e.g. the DVB common interface connector, permitting simple connection of peripherals, and able to pass all the elements of a digital television signal, including information relating to interactive and conditionally accessed services.]

Notes

Annex VI was replaced as shown in square brackets by Directive 2009/136/EC of 25 November 2009 (OJ L 337, 18.12.2009, p.11), with effect from 19 December 2009.

[]

Notes

Annex VII was deleted by Directive 2009/136/EC of 25 November 2009 (OJ L 337, 18.12.2009, p.11), with effect from 19 December 2009.

E5

COMMISSION DIRECTIVE 2002/77/EC

of 16 September 2002

on competition in the markets for electronic communications networks and services

(Telecoms Competition Directive)

(Text with EEA relevance)

Official Journal L 249, 17.9.2002, p.21

Celex No: 32002L0077

EUR-Lex permanent link: <http://eur-lex.europa.eu/LexUriServ/LexUriServ.do?uri=CELEX:320 02L0077: EN:NOT>

Notes

EEA application: this Directive was adopted with appropriate adaptations by EEA Joint Committee Decision No 153/2003 (OJ No L 41, 12.02.2004, p.45 and EEA Supplement No 7, 12.02.2004, p.32): see EEA Agreement, Annex XIV, Chapter H, Point 13a.

Commentary

Directive 2002/77/EC: B&C: 12.005, 12.033 **F&N:** 6.38, 6.257, 13.21, 14.17, 14.143, 14.151
Recitals 1–6: B&C: 12.033
Arts 3–8: B&C: 12.033

THE COMMISSION OF THE EUROPEAN COMMUNITIES,

Having regard to the [Treaty on the Functioning of the European Union], and in particular Article [106(3)]* thereof,

---

Notes

* Ed note: please see the Note on the Lisbon Treaty at p.xvii in regard to article renumbering introduced by the Lisbon Treaty.

Whereas:

(1) Commission Directive 90/388/EEC of 28 June 1990 on competition in the markets for tel-ecommunications services,[1] as last amended by Directive 1999/64/EC,[2] has been substantially amended several times. Since further amendments are to be made, it should be recast in the inter-est of clarity.

Notes

[1] OJ L 192, 24.7.1990, p.10.
[2] OJ L 175, 10.7.1999, p.39.

---

(2) Article [106] of the Treaty entrusts the Commission with the task of ensuring that, in the case of public undertakings and undertakings enjoying special or exclusive rights, Member States com-ply with their obligations under Community law. Pursuant to Article [106(3)], the Commission can specify and clarify the obligations arising from that Article and, in that framework, set out the conditions which are necessary to allow the Commission to perform effectively the duty of sur-veillance imposed upon it by that paragraph.

(3) Directive 90/388/EEC required Member States to abolish special and exclusive rights for the provision of telecommunications services, initially for other services than voice telephony, satel-lite services and mobile radio communications, and then it gradually established full competition in the telecommunications market.

(4) A number of other Directives in this field have also been adopted under Article [114] of the Treaty by the European Parliament and the Council aiming, principally, at the establishment of an internal market for telecommunications services through the implementation of open network provision and the provision of a universal service in an environment of open and competitive markets. Those Directives should be repealed with effect from 25 July 2003 when the new regulatory framework for electronic communications networks and services is applied.

(5) The new electronic communications regulatory framework consists of one general Directive, Directive 2002/21/EC of the European Parliament and of the Council of 7 March 2002 on a common regulatory framework for electronic communications networks and services (Framework Directive)[1] and four specific Directives: Directive 2002/20/EC of the European Parliament and of the Council of 7 March 2002 on the authorisation of electronic communications networks and services (Authorisation Directive),[2] Directive 2002/19/EC of the European Parliament and of the Council of 7 March 2002 on access to, and interconnection of, electronic communications networks and associated facilities (Access Directive),[3] Directive 2002/22/EC of the European Parliament and of the Council of 7 March 2002 on universal service and users' rights relating to electronic communications networks and services (Universal Service Directive),[4] and Directive 2002/58/EC of the European Parliament and of the Council of 12 July 2002 concerning the processing of personal data and the protection of privacy in the electronic communications (Directive on privacy and electronic communications) sector.[5]

Notes

[1] OJ L 108, 24.4.2002, p.33.
[2] OJ L 108, 24.4.2002, p.21.
[3] OJ L 108, 24.4.2002, p.7.
[4] OJ L 108, 24.4.2002, p.51.
[5] OJ L 201, 31.7.2002, p.37.

(6) In the light of the developments which have marked the liberalisation process and the gradual opening of the telecommunications markets in Europe since 1990, certain definitions used in Directive 90/388/EEC and its amending acts should be adjusted in order to reflect the latest technological developments in the telecommunications field, or replaced in order to take account of the convergence phenomenon which has shaped the information technology, media and telecommunications industries over recent years. The wording of certain provisions should, where possible, be clarified in order to facilitate their application, taking into account, where appropriate, the relevant Directives adopted under Article [114] of the Treaty, and the experience acquired through the implementation of Directive 90/388/EEC as amended.

(7) This Directive makes reference to "electronic communications services" and "electronic communications networks" rather than the previously used terms "telecommunications services" and "telecommunications networks". These new definitions are indispensable in order to take account of the convergence phenomenon by bringing together under one single definition all electronic communications services and/or networks which are concerned with the conveyance of signals by wire, radio, optical or other electromagnetic means (i.e. fixed, wireless, cable television, satellite networks). Thus, the transmission and broadcasting of radio and television programmes should be recognised as an electronic communication service and networks used for such transmission and broadcasting should likewise be recognised as electronic communications networks. Furthermore, it should be made clear that the new definition of electronic communications networks also covers fibre networks which enable third parties, using their own switching or routing equipment, to convey signals.

Commentary
Recital 7: F&N: 14.144

(8) In this context, it should be made clear that Member States must remove (if they have not already done so) exclusive and special rights for the provision of all electronic communications networks, not just those for the provision of electronic communications services and should ensure that undertakings are entitled to provide such services without prejudice to the provisions of Directives

2002/19/EC, 2002/20/EC, 2002/21/EC and 2002/22/EC. The definition of electronic communications networks should also mean that Member States are not permitted to restrict the right of an operator to establish, extend and/or provide a cable network on the ground that such network could also be used for the transmission of radio and television programming. In particular, special or exclusive rights which amount to restricting the use of electronic communications networks for the transmission and distribution of television signals are contrary to Article [106(1)], read in conjunction with Article [49] (right of establishment) and/or Article [102(b)] of the [Treaty on the Functioning of the European Union] insofar as they have the effect of permitting a dominant undertaking to limit "production, markets or technical development to the prejudice of consumers". This is, however, without prejudice to the specific rules adopted by the Member States in accordance with Community law, and, in particular, in accordance with Council Directive 89/552/EEC of 3 October 1989,[1] on the coordination of certain provisions laid down by law, regulation or administrative action in Member States concerning the pursuit of television broadcasting activities, as amended by Directive 97/36/EC of the European Parliament and of the Council,[2] governing the distribution of audiovisual programmes intended for the general public.

Notes

[1] OJ L 298, 17.10.1989, p.23.

[2] OJ L 202, 30.7.1997, p.60.

(9) Pursuant to the principle of proportionality, Member States should no longer make the provision of electronic communications services and the establishment and provision of electronic communications networks subject to a licensing regime but to a general authorisation regime. This is also required by Directive 2002/20/EC, according to which electronic communications services or networks should be provided on the basis of a general authorisation and not on the basis of a license. An aggrieved party should have the right to challenge a decision preventing him from providing electronic communications services or networks before an independent body and, ultimately, before a court or a tribunal. It is a fundamental principle of Community law that an individual is entitled to effective judicial protection whenever a State measure violates rights conferred upon him by the provisions of a Directive.

(10) Public authorities may exercise a dominant influence on the behaviour of public undertakings, as a result either of the rules governing the undertaking or of the manner in which the shareholdings are distributed. Therefore, where Member States control vertically integrated network operators which operate networks which have been established under special or exclusive rights, those Member States should ensure that, in order to avoid potential breaches of the Treaty competition rules, such operators, when they enjoy a dominant position in the relevant market, do not discriminate in favour of their own activities. It follows that Member States should take all measures necessary to prevent any discrimination between such vertically integrated operators and their competitors.

(11) This Directive should also clarify the principle derived from Commission Directive 96/2/EC of 16 January 1996 amending Directive 90/388/EC with regard to mobile and personal communications,[1] by providing that Member States should not grant exclusive or special rights of use of radio frequencies and that the rights of use of those frequencies should be assigned according to objective, non-discriminatory and transparent procedures. This should be without prejudice to specific criteria and procedures adopted by Member States to grant such rights to providers of radio or television broadcast content services with a view to pursuing general interest objectives in conformity with Community law.

Notes

[1] OJ L 20, 26.1.1996, p.59.

(12) Any national scheme pursuant to Directive 2002/22/EC, serving to share the net cost of the provision of universal service obligations shall be based on objective, transparent and non-discriminatory criteria and shall be consistent with the principles of proportionality and of least market distortion. Least market distortion means that contributions should be recovered in

a way that as far as possible minimises the impact of the financial burden falling on end-users, for example by spreading contributions as widely as possible.

(13) Where rights and obligations arising from international conventions setting up international satellite organisations are not compatible with the competition rules of the Treaty, Member States should take, in accordance with Article [351] of the [Treaty on the Functioning of the European Union], all appropriate steps to eliminate such incompatibilities. This Directive should clarify this obligation because Article 3 of Directive 94/46/EC,[1] merely required Member States to "communicate to the Commission" the information they possessed on such incompatibilities. Article 11 of this Directive should clarify the obligation on Member States to remove any restrictions which could still be in force because of those international conventions.

Notes

[1] OJ L 268, 19.10.1994, p.15.

(14) This Directive should maintain the obligation imposed on Member States by Directive 1999/64/EC, so as to ensure that dominant providers of electronic communications networks and publicly available telephone services operate their public electronic communication network and cable television network as separate legal entities.

(15) This Directive should be without prejudice to obligations of the Member States concerning the time limits set out in Annex I, Part B, within which the Member States are to comply with the preceding Directives.

(16) Member States should supply to the Commission any information which is necessary to demonstrate that existing national implementing legislation reflects the clarifications provided for in this Directive as compared with Directives 90/388/EC, 94/46/EC, 95/51/EC,[1] 96/2/EC, 96/19/EC[2] and 1999/64/EC.

Notes

[1] OJ L 256, 26.10.1995, p.49.
[2] OJ L 74, 22.3.1996, p.13.

(17) In the light of the above, Directive 90/388/EC should be repealed,

HAS ADOPTED THIS DIRECTIVE:

Article 1
Definitions

For the purposes of this Directive the following definitions shall apply:

1. "electronic communications network" shall mean transmission systems and, where applicable, switching or routing equipment and other resources which permit the conveyance of signals by wire, by radio, by optical or by other electromagnetic means, including satellite networks, fixed (circuit - and packet - switched, including Internet) and mobile terrestrial networks, and electricity cable systems, to the extent that they are used for the purpose of transmitting signals, networks used for radio and television broadcasting, and cable television networks, irrespective of the type of information conveyed;

2. "public communications network" shall mean an electronic communications network used wholly or mainly for the provision of public electronic communications services;

3. "electronic communications services" shall mean a service normally provided for remuneration which consists wholly or mainly in the conveyance of signals on electronic communications networks, including telecommunications services and transmission services in networks used for broadcasting but exclude services providing or exercising editorial control over, content transmitted using electronic communications networks and services; it does not include information society services as defined in Article 1 of Directive 98/34/EC which do not consist wholly or mainly in the conveyance of signals on electronic communications networks;

4. "publicly available electronic communications services" shall mean electronic communications services available to the public;

5. "exclusive rights" shall mean the rights that are granted by a Member State to one undertaking through any legislative, regulatory or administrative instrument, reserving it the right to provide an electronic communications service or to undertake an electronic communications activity within a given geographical area;

6. "special rights" shall mean the rights that are granted by a Member State to a limited number of undertakings through any legislative, regulatory or administrative instrument which, within a given geographical area:

   (a) designates or limits to two or more the number of such undertakings authorised to provide an electronic communications service or undertake an electronic communications activity, otherwise than according to objective, proportional and non-discriminatory criteria, or

   (b) confers on undertakings, otherwise than according to such criteria, legal or regulatory advantages which substantially affect the ability of any other undertaking to provide the same electronic communications service or to undertake the same electronic communications activity in the same geographical area under substantially equivalent conditions;

7. "satellite earth station network" shall mean a configuration of two or more earth stations which interwork by means of a satellite;

8. "cable television networks" shall mean any mainly wire-based infrastructure established primarily for the delivery or distribution of radio or television broadcast to the public.

Commentary
Art 1: F&N: 14.148
Art 1(5): F&N: 6.34
Art 1(6): F&N: 6.38

Article 2
**Exclusive and special rights for electronic communications
networks and electronic communications services**

1. Member States shall not grant or maintain in force exclusive or special rights for the establishment and/or the provision of electronic communications networks, or for the provision of publicly available electronic communications services.

2. Member States shall take all measures necessary to ensure that any undertaking is entitled to provide electronic communications services or to establish, extend or provide electronic communications networks.

3. Member States shall ensure that no restrictions are imposed or maintained on the provision of electronic communications services over electronic communications networks established by the providers of electronic communications services, over infrastructures provided by third parties, or by means of sharing networks, other facilities or sites without prejudice to the provisions of Directives 2002/19/EC, 2002/20/EC, 2002/21/EC and 2002/22/EC.

4. Member States shall ensure that a general authorisation granted to an undertaking to provide electronic communications services or to establish and/or provide electronic communications networks, as well as the conditions attached thereto, shall be based on objective, non-discriminatory, proportionate and transparent criteria.

5. Reasons shall be given for any decision taken on the grounds set out in Article 3(1) of Directive 2002/20/EC preventing an undertaking from providing electronic communications services or networks.

Any aggrieved party should have the possibility to challenge such a decision before a body that is independent of the parties involved and ultimately before a court or a tribunal.

Commentary
Art 2(1): F&N: 14.145, 14.148
Art 2(2): F&N: 14.144, 14.145

Article 3
Vertically integrated public undertakings

In addition to the requirements set out in Article 2(2), and without prejudice to Article 14 of Directive 2002/21/EC, Member States, shall ensure that vertically integrated public undertakings which provide electronic communications networks and which are in a dominant position do not discriminate in favour of their own activities.

Article 4
Rights of use of frequencies

Without prejudice to specific criteria and procedures adopted by Member States to grant rights of use of radio frequencies to providers of radio or television broadcast content services with a view to pursuing general interest objectives in conformity with Community law:

1. Member States shall not grant exclusive or special rights of use of radio frequencies for the provision of electronic communications services.

2. The assignment of radio frequencies for electronic communication services shall be based on objective, transparent, non-discriminatory and proportionate criteria.

Commentary
Art 4(2): F&N: 14.144, 14.149, 14.154

Article 5
Directory services

Member States shall ensure that all exclusive and/or special rights with regard to the establishment and provision of directory services on their territory, including both the publication of directories and directory enquiry services, are abolished.

Article 6
Universal service obligations

1. Any national scheme pursuant to Directive 2002/22/EC, serving to share the net cost of the provision of universal service obligations shall be based on objective, transparent and non-discriminatory criteria and shall be consistent with the principle of proportionality and of least market distortion. In particular, where universal service obligations are imposed in whole or in part on public undertakings providing electronic communications services, this shall be taken into consideration in calculating any contribution to the net cost of universal service obligations.

2. Member States shall communicate any scheme of the kind referred to in paragraph 1 to the Commission.

Article 7
Satellites

1. Member States shall ensure that any regulatory prohibition or restriction on the offer of space segment capacity to any authorised satellite earth station network operator are abolished, and shall authorise within their territory any space-segment supplier to verify that the satellite earth station network for use in connection with the space segment of the supplier in question is in conformity with the published conditions for access to such person's space segment capacity.

2. Member States which are party to international conventions setting up international satellite organisations shall, where such conventions are not compatible with the competition rules of the EC Treaty, take all appropriate steps to eliminate such incompatibilities.

Article 8
Cable television networks

1. Each Member State shall ensure that no undertaking providing public electronic communications networks operates its cable television network using the same legal entity as it uses for its other public electronic communications network, when such undertaking:

(a) is controlled by that Member State or benefits from special rights; and

(b) is dominant in a substantial part of the common market in the provision of public electronic communications networks and publicly available telephone services; and

(c) operates a cable television network which has been established under special or exclusive right in the same geographic area.

2. The term "publicly available telephone services" shall be considered synonymous with the term "public voice telephony services" referred to in Article 1 of Directive 1999/64/EC.

3. Member States which consider that there is sufficient competition in the provision of local loop infrastructure and services in their territory shall inform the Commission accordingly.

Such information shall include a detailed description of the market structure. The information provided shall be made available to any interested party on demand, regard being had to the legitimate interest of undertakings in the protection of their business secrets.

4. The Commission shall decide within a reasonable period, after having heard the comments of these parties, whether the obligation of legal separation may be ended in the Member State concerned.

5. The Commission shall review the application of this Article not later than 31 December 2004.

Article 9

Member States shall supply to the Commission not later than 24 July 2003 such information as will allow the Commission to confirm that the provisions of this Directive have been complied with.

Article 10
Repeal

Directive 90/388/EC, as amended by the Directives listed in Annex I, Part A, is repealed with effect from 25 July 2003, without prejudice to the obligations of the Member States in respect of the time limits for transposition laid down in Annex I, Part B.

References to the repealed Directives shall be construed as references to this Directive and shall be read in accordance with the correlation table in Annex II.

Article 11

This Directive shall enter into force on the 20th day following that of its publication in the *Official Journal of the European Communities*.

Notes

Date of entry into force: 7 October 2002.

Article 12

This Directive is addressed to the Member States.

Done at Brussels, 16 September 2002.

ANNEX I

PART A
LIST OF DIRECTIVES TO BE REPEALED

Directive 90/388/EEC (OJ L 192, 24.7.1990, p.10)

Articles 2 and 3 of Directive 94/46/EC (OJ L 268, 19.1.1994, p.15)

Directive 95/51/EC (OJ L 256, 26.10.1995, p.49)

Directive 96/2/EC (OJ L 20, 26.1.1996, p.59)

Directive 96/19/EC (OJ L 74, 22.3.1996, p.13)

Directive 1999/64/EC (OJ L 175, 10.7.1999, p.39)

PART B
TRANSPOSITION DATES FOR THE ABOVE DIRECTIVES

Directive 90/388/EEC: transposition date:	31 December 1990
Directive 94/46/EC: transposition date:	8 August 1995
Directive 95/51/EC: transposition date:	1 October 1996
Directive 96/2/EC: transposition date:	15 November 1996
Directive 96/19/EC: transposition date:	11 January 1997
Directive 1999/64/EC: transposition date:	30 April 2000

ANNEX II
CORRELATION TABLE

This Directive	*Directive 90/388/EEC*
Article 1 (Definitions)	Article 1
Article 2 (withdrawal of exclusive/special rights)	Article 2
Article 3 (vertically integrated public undertakings)	Article 3(a)(ii)
Article 4 (rights of use of radio frequencies)	Article 3(b)
Article 5 (directory services)	Article 4(b)
Article 6 (universal service obligations)	Article 4(c)
Article 7 (satellites)	Article 3 of Directive 94/46/EC
Article 8 (cable networks)	Article 9

E6

COMMISSION RECOMMENDATION

of 17 December 2007

on relevant product and service markets within the electronic communications sector susceptible to *ex ante* regulation in accordance with Directive 2002/21/EC of the European Parliament and of the Council on a common regulatory framework for electronic communications networks and services

(notified under document number C(2007) 5406)

(Text with EEA relevance)

(2007/879/EC)

Official Journal L 344, 28.12.2007, p.65

Celex No: 32007H0879

EUR-Lex permanent link: <http://eur-lex.europa.eu/LexUriServ/LexUriServ.do?uri=CELEX:3200 3H0311:EN:NOT>

THE COMMISSION OF THE EUROPEAN COMMUNITIES,

Having regard to the [Treaty on the Functioning of the European Union]*,

Having regard to Directive 2002/21/EC of the European Parliament and of the Council of 7 March 2002 on a common regulatory framework for electronic communications networks and services[1], and in particular Article 15(1) thereof,

Notes

[1] OJ L 108, 24.4.2002, p.33.

Commentary

Recommendation: **B&C:** 12.017, 12.021, 12.070 **F&N:** 13.23, 13.25

* Ed note: please see the Note on the Lisbon Treaty at p.xvii in regard to article renumbering introduced by the Lisbon Treaty.

Recommendation

Whereas:

(1) Directive 2002/21/EC establishes a legislative framework for the electronic communications sector that seeks to respond to convergence trends by covering all electronic communications networks and services within its scope. The aim of the regulatory framework is to reduce ex ante sector-specific rules progressively as competition in the market develops.

(2) The purpose of this Recommendation is to identify those product and service markets in which ex ante regulation may be warranted in accordance with Article 15(1) of Directive 2002/21/EC. The objective of any ex ante regulatory intervention is ultimately to produce benefits for end-users by making retail markets competitive on a sustainable basis. The definition of relevant markets can and does change over time as the characteristics of products and services evolve and the possibilities for demand and supply substitution change. With the Recommendation 2003/311/EC having been in force for more than four years, it is now appropriate to revise the initial edition on the basis of market developments. Hence, this Recommendation replaces Commission Recommendation 2003/311/EC[1].

Notes

[1] OJ L 114, 8.5.2003, p.45.

(3) Article 15(1) of Directive 2002/21/EC requires the Commission to define markets in accordance with the principles of competition law. Competition law principles are therefore used in this Recommendation to set product market boundaries within the electronic communications sector, while the identification or selection of defined markets for ex ante regulation depends on those markets having characteristics which may be such as to justify the imposition of ex ante regulatory obligations. The terminology used in this Recommendation is based on terminology used in Directive 2002/21/EC and Directive 2002/22/EC; the Explanatory Note to this Recommendation describes the evolving technologies in relation to these markets. In accordance with Directive 2002/21/EC, it is for national regulatory authorities to define relevant markets appropriate to national circumstances, in particular relevant geographic markets within their territory.

(4) The starting point for the identification of markets in this Recommendation is the definition of retail markets from a forward-looking perspective, taking into account demand-side and supply-side substitutability. Having defined retail markets, it is then appropriate to identify relevant wholesale markets. If the downstream market is supplied by a vertically-integrated undertaking or undertakings, there may be no (merchant) wholesale market in the absence of regulation. Consequently, if the market warrants identification, it may be necessary to construct a notional upstream wholesale market. Markets in the electronic communications sector are often of a two-sided nature, in that they comprise services provided over networks or platforms that bring together users on either side of the market; for example end-users that exchange communications, or senders and receivers of information or content. These aspects need to be taken into account when considering the identification and definition of markets, as they can affect both the way markets are defined and whether they have the characteristics which may justify the imposition of ex ante regulatory obligations.

(5) In order to identify markets that are susceptible to ex ante regulation, it is appropriate to apply the following cumulative criteria. The first criterion is the presence of high and non-transitory barriers to entry. These may be of a structural, legal or regulatory nature. However, given the dynamic

character and functioning of electronic communications markets, possibilities to overcome barriers to entry within the relevant time horizon should also be taken into consideration when carrying out a prospective analysis to identify the relevant markets for possible ex ante regulation. Therefore the second criterion admits only those markets whose structure does not tend towards effective competition within the relevant time horizon. The application of this criterion involves examining the state of competition behind the barriers to entry. The third criterion is that application of competition law alone would not adequately address the market failure(s) concerned.

(6) The main indicators to be considered when assessing the first and second criteria are similar to those examined as part of a forward-looking market analysis, in particular, indicators of barriers to entry in the absence of regulation, (including the extent of sunk costs), market structure, market performance and market dynamics, including indicators such as market shares and trends, market prices and trends, and the extent and coverage of competing networks or infrastructures. Any market which satisfies the three criteria in the absence of ex ante regulation is susceptible to ex ante regulation.

(7) Newly emerging markets should not be subject to inappropriate obligations, even if there is a first mover advantage, in accordance with Directive 2002/21/EC. Newly emerging markets are considered to comprise products or services, where, due to their novelty, it is very difficult to predict demand conditions or market entry and supply conditions, and consequently difficult to apply the three criteria. The purpose of not subjecting newly emerging markets to inappropriate obligations is to promote innovation as required by Article 8 of the Directive 2002/21/EC; at the same time, foreclosure of such markets by the leading undertaking should be prevented, as also indicated in the Commission guidelines on market analysis and the assessment of significant market power under the Community regulatory framework for electronic communications and services[1]. Incremental upgrades to existing network infrastructure rarely lead to a new or emerging market. The lack of substitutability of a product has to be established from both demand and supply-side perspectives before it can be concluded that it is not part of an already existing market. The emergence of new retail services may give rise to a new derived wholesale market to the extent that such retail services cannot be provided using existing wholesale products.

Notes

[1] OJ C 165, 11.7.2002, p.6.

(8) As far as barriers to entry are concerned, two types are relevant for the purpose of this Recommendation: structural barriers and legal or regulatory barriers.

(9) Structural barriers to entry result from original cost or demand conditions that create asymmetric conditions between incumbents and new entrants impeding or preventing market entry of the latter. For instance, high structural barriers may be found to exist when the market is characterised by absolute cost advantages, substantial economies of scale and/or economies of scope, capacity constraints and high sunk costs. To date, such barriers can still be identified with respect to the widespread deployment and/or provision of local access networks to fixed locations. A related structural barrier can also exist where the provision of service requires a network component that cannot be technically duplicated or only duplicated at a cost that makes it uneconomic for competitors.

(10) Legal or regulatory barriers are not based on economic conditions, but result from legislative, administrative or other state measures that have a direct effect on the conditions of entry and/or the positioning of operators on the relevant market. An example of a legal or regulatory barrier preventing entry into a market is a limit on the number of undertakings that have access to spectrum for the provision of underlying services. Other examples of legal or regulatory barriers are price controls or other price-related measures imposed on undertakings, which affect not only entry but also the positioning of undertakings on the market. Legal or regulatory barriers, which can be removed within the relevant time horizon, should not normally be deemed to constitute an economic barrier to entry, such as to fulfil the first criterion.

(11) Barriers to entry may also become less relevant with regard to innovation-driven markets characterised by ongoing technological progress. In such markets, competitive constraints often come from innovative threats from potential competitors that are not currently in the market. In

innovation-driven markets, dynamic or longer-term competition can take place among firms that are not necessarily competitors in an existing "static" market. This Recommendation does not identify markets where barriers to entry are not expected to persist over a foreseeable period. In assessing whether barriers to entry are likely to persist in the absence of regulation, it is necessary to examine whether the industry has experienced frequent and successful entry and whether entry has been or is likely in the future to be sufficiently immediate and persistent to limit market power. The relevance of barriers to entry will depend inter alia on the minimum efficient scale of output and the costs which are sunk.

(12) Even when a market is characterised by high barriers to entry, other structural factors in that market may mean that the market tends towards an effectively competitive outcome within the relevant time horizon. Market dynamics may for instance be caused by technological developments, or by the convergence of products and markets which may give rise to competitive constraints being exercised between operators active in distinct product markets. This may also be the case in markets with a limited — but sufficient — number of undertakings having diverging cost structures and facing price-elastic market demand. There may also be excess capacity in a market that would normally allow rival firms to expand output very rapidly in response to any price increase. In such markets, market shares may change over time and/or falling prices may be observed. Where market dynamics are changing rapidly, care should be taken in choosing the relevant time horizon so as to reflect the pertinent market developments.

(13) The decision to identify a market as susceptible to ex ante regulation should also depend on an assessment of the sufficiency of competition law to address the market failures that result from the first two criteria being met. Competition law interventions are unlikely to be sufficient where the compliance requirements of an intervention to redress a market failure are extensive or where frequent and/or timely intervention is indispensable.

(14) The application of the three criteria should limit the number of markets within the electronic communications sector where ex ante regulatory obligations are imposed and thereby contribute to the aim of the regulatory framework to reduce ex ante sector-specific rules progressively as competition in the markets develops. These criteria should be applied cumulatively, so that failure to meet any one of them would indicate that a market should not be identified as susceptible to ex ante regulation.

(15) Regulatory controls on retail services should only be imposed where national regulatory authorities consider that relevant wholesale measures or measures regarding carrier selection or pre-selection would fail to achieve the objective of ensuring effective competition and the fulfilment of public interest objectives. By intervening at the wholesale level, including with remedies which may affect retail markets, Member States can ensure that as much of the value chain is open to normal competition processes as possible, thereby delivering the best outcomes for end-users. This Recommendation therefore mainly identifies wholesale markets, the appropriate regulation of which is intended to address a lack of effective competition that is manifest on end-user markets. Should a national regulatory authority demonstrate that wholesale interventions have been unsuccessful, the relevant retail market may be susceptible to ex ante regulation provided that the three criteria set out above are met.

(16) The process of identifying markets in this Recommendation is without prejudice to markets that may be defined in specific cases under competition law. Moreover, the scope of ex ante regulation is without prejudice to the scope of activities that may be analysed under competition law.

(17) The markets listed in the Annex have been identified on the basis of these three cumulative criteria. For markets not listed in this Recommendation national regulatory authorities should apply the three-criteria test to the market concerned. For the markets in the Annex to Recommendation 2003/311/EC of 11 February 2003, which are not listed in the Annex to this Recommendation, national regulatory authorities should have the power to apply the three-criteria test in order to assess whether, on the basis of national circumstances, a market is still susceptible to ex ante regulation. For markets listed in this Recommendation a national regulatory authority may choose not to carry out a market analysis procedure if it determines that the three criteria are not satisfied for the particular market. National regulatory authorities may identify markets that differ from those listed in this Recommendation, provided that they act in accordance with Article 7 of Directive 2002/21/EC. Failure to notify a draft measure which affects trade between

Member States as described in Recital 38 of Directive 2002/21/EC may result in infringement proceedings being taken. Markets other than those listed in this Recommendation should be defined on the basis of competition principles laid down in the Commission Notice on the definition of relevant market for the purposes of Community competition law [1] and be consistent with the Commission Guidelines on market analysis and the assessment of significant market power [2] whilst satisfying the three criteria set out above.

Notes

[1] OJ C 372, 9.12.1997, p.5.
[2] OJ C 165, 11.7.2002, p.6.

(18) The fact that this Recommendation identifies those product and service markets in which ex ante regulation may be warranted does not mean that regulation is always warranted or that these markets will be subject to the imposition of regulatory obligations set out in the specific Directives. In particular, regulation cannot be imposed or must be withdrawn if there is effective competition on these markets in the absence of regulation, that is to say, if no operator has significant market power within the meaning of Article 14 of Directive 2002/21/EC. Regulatory obligations must be appropriate and be based on the nature of the problem identified, proportionate and justified in the light of the objectives laid down in Directive 2002/21/EC, in particular maximising benefits for users, ensuring no distortion or restriction of competition, encouraging efficient investment in infrastructure and promoting innovation, and encouraging efficient use and management of radio frequencies and numbering resources.

(19) This Recommendation has been subject to a public consultation and to consultation with national regulatory authorities and national competition authorities,

HEREBY RECOMMENDS:

1. In defining relevant markets appropriate to national circumstances in accordance with Article 15(3) of Directive 2002/21/EC, national regulatory authorities should analyse the product and service markets identified in the Annex to this Recommendation.

2. When identifying markets other than those set out in the Annex, national regulatory authorities should ensure that the following three criteria are cumulatively met:

    (a) the presence of high and non-transitory barriers to entry. These may be of a structural, legal or regulatory nature;

    (b) a market structure which does not tend towards effective competition within the relevant time horizon. The application of this criterion involves examining the state of competition behind the barriers to entry;

    (c) the insufficiency of competition law alone to adequately address the market failure(s) concerned.

3. This Recommendation is without prejudice to market definitions, results of market analyses and regulatory obligations adopted by national regulatory authorities in accordance with Articles 15(3) and 16 of Directive 2002/21/EC prior to the date of adoption of this Recommendation.

4. This Recommendation is addressed to the Member States.
    Done at Brussels, 17 December 2007.

ANNEX

Retail level

1. Access to the public telephone network at a fixed location for residential and non-residential customers.

Wholesale level

2. Call origination on the public telephone network provided at a fixed location.
    For the purposes of this Recommendation, call origination is taken to include call conveyance, delineated in such a way as to be consistent, in a national context, with the delineated boundaries

for the market for call transit and for call termination on the public telephone network provided at a fixed location.

3. Call termination on individual public telephone networks provided at a fixed location.

For the purposes of this Recommendation, call termination is taken to include call conveyance, delineated in such a way as to be consistent, in a national context, with the delineated boundaries for the market for call origination and the market for call transit on the public telephone network provided at a fixed location.

4. Wholesale (physical) network infrastructure access (including shared or fully unbundled access) at a fixed location.

5. Wholesale broadband access.

This market comprises non-physical or virtual network access including "bit-stream" access at a fixed location. This market is situated downstream from the physical access covered by market 4 listed above, in that wholesale broadband access can be constructed using this input combined with other elements.

6. Wholesale terminating segments of leased lines, irrespective of the technology used to provide leased or dedicated capacity.

7. Voice call termination on individual mobile networks.

E7

GUIDELINES ON THE APPLICATION OF [EU]* COMPETITION RULES IN THE TELECOMMUNICATIONS SECTOR

(91/C 233/02)

Official Journal C 233, 6.9.1991, p.2

Celex No: 51991XC0906(02)

EUR-Lex permanent link: <http://eur-lex.europa.eu/LexUriServ/LexUriServ.do?uri=CELEX:51991XC0906(02):EN:NOT>

Notes

* Ed note: please see the Note on the Lisbon Treaty at p.xvii in regard to article renumbering introduced by the Lisbon Treaty.
EEA application: the EFTA Surveillance Authority has adopted a parallel notice under Article 5(2)(b) of the Surveillance and Court Agreement: OJ L 153, 18.6.1994, p.35 and EEA Supplement to the OJ No 15, 18.6.1994, p.34.

PREFACE

These guidelines aim at clarifying the application of Community competition rules to the market participants in the telecommunications sector. They must be viewed in the context of the special conditions of the telecommunications sector, and the overall Community telecommunications policy will be taken into account in their application. In particular, account will have to be taken of the actions the Commission will be in a position to propose for the telecommunications industry as a whole, actions deriving from the assessment of the state of play and issues at stake for this industry, as has already been the case for the European electronics and information technology industry in the communication of the Commission of 3 April 1991.[1]

A major political aim, as emphasized by the Commission, the Council, and the European Parliament, must be the development of efficient Europe-wide networks and services, at the lowest cost and of the highest quality, to provide the European user in the single market of 1992 with a basic infrastructure for efficient operation.

The Commission has made it clear in the past that in this context it is considered that liberalization and harmonization in the sector must go hand in hand.

Given the competition context in the telecommunications sector, the telecommunications operators should be allowed, and encouraged, to establish the necessary cooperation mechanisms, in order to create—or ensure—Community-wide full interconnectivity between public networks, and where required between services to enable European users to benefit from a wider range of better and cheaper telecommunications services.

This can and has to be done in compliance with, and respect of, EEC competition rules in order to avoid the diseconomies which otherwise could result. For the same reasons, operators and other firms that may be in a dominant market position should be made aware of the prohibition of abuse of such positions.

The guidelines should be read in the light of this objective. They set out to clarify, *inter alia*, which forms of cooperation amount to undesirable collusion, and in this sense they list what is *not* acceptable. They should therefore be seen as one aspect of an overall Community policy towards telecommunications, and notably of policies and actions to encourage and stimulate those forms of cooperation which promote the development and availability of advanced communications for Europe.

The full application of competition rules forms a major part of the Community's overall approach to telecommunications. These guidelines should help market participants to shape their strategies and arrangements for Europe-wide networks and services from the outset in a manner which allows them to be fully in line with these rules. In the event of significant changes in the conditions which prevailed when the guidelines were drawn up, the Commission may find it appropriate to adapt the guidelines to the evolution of the situation in the telecommunications sector.

Notes

[1] The European electronics and information technology industry: state of play, issues at stake and proposals for action, SEC(91) 565, 3 April 1991.

I. Summary

1. The Commission of the European Communities in its Green Paper on the development of the common market for telecommunications services and equipment (COM(87)290) dated 30 June 1987 proposed a number of Community positions. Amongst these, positions (H) and (I) are as follows:

   "(H) strict continuous review of operational (commercial) activities of telecommunications administrations according to Articles [101], [102] and [106] of the [Treaty on the Functioning of the European Union]. This applies in particular to practices of cross-subsidization of activities in the competitive services sector and of activities in manufacturing;
   (I) strict continuous review of all private providers in the newly opened sectors according to Articles [101] and [102], in order to avoid the abuse of dominant positions;".

2. These positions were restated in the Commission's document of 9 February 1988 "Implementing the Green Paper on the development of the common market for telecommunications services and equipment/state of discussions and proposals by the Commission" (COM(88)48). Among the areas where the development of concrete policy actions is now possible, the Commission indicated the following:

   "Ensuring fair conditions of competition:
   Ensuring an open competitive market makes continuous review of the telecommunications sector necessary.
   The Commission intends to issue guidelines regarding the application of competition rules to the telecommunications sector and on the way that the review should be carried out."
   This is the objective of this communication.

The telecommunications sector in many cases requires cooperation agreements, *inter alia*, between telecommunications organizations (TOs) in order to ensure network and services interconnectivity, one-stop shopping and one-stop billing which are necessary to provide for Europe-wide services and to offer optimum service to users. These objectives can be achieved, *inter alia*, by TOs cooperating— for example, in those areas where exclusive or special rights for provision may continue in accordance with Community law, including competition law, as well as in areas where optimum service will require certain features of cooperation. On the other hand the overriding objective to develop the conditions for the market to provide European users with a greater variety of telecommunications services, of better quality and at lower cost requires the introduction and safeguarding of a strong competitive structure. Competition plays a central role for the Community, especially in view of the completion of the single market for 1992. This role has already been emphasized in the Green Paper.

The single market will represent a new dimension for telecoms operators and users. Competition will give them the opportunity to make full use of technological development and to accelerate it, and encouraging them to restructure and reach the necessary economies of scale to become competitive not only on the Community market, but worldwide.

With this in mind, these guidelines recall the main principles which the Commission, according to its mandate under the Treaty's competition rules, has applied and will apply in the sector without prejudging the outcome of any specific case which will have to be considered on the facts.

The objective is, *inter alia*, to contribute to more certainty of [conditions] for investment in the sector and the development of Europe-wide services.

The mechanisms for creating certainty for individual cases (apart from complaints and ex-officio investigations) are provided for by the notification and negative clearance procedures provided under Regulation No 17, which give a formal procedure for clearing cooperation agreements in this area whenever a formal clearance is requested. This is set out in further detail in this communication.

II. Introduction

3. The fundamental technological development worldwide in the telecommunications sector[1] has caused considerable changes in the competition conditions. The traditional monopolistic administrations cannot alone take up the challenge of the technological revolution. New economic forces have appeared on the telecoms scene which are capable of offering users the numerous enhanced services generated by the new technologies. This has given rise to and stimulated a wide deregulation process propagated in the Community with various degrees of intensity.

This move is progressively changing the face of the European market structure. New private suppliers have penetrated the market with more and more transnational value-added services and equipment. The telecommunications administrations, although keeping a central role as public services providers, have acquired a business-like way of thinking. They have started competing dynamically with private operators in services and equipment. Wide restructuring, through mergers and joint ventures, is taking place in order to compete more effectively on the deregulated market through economies of scale and rationalization. All these events have a multiplier effect on technological progress.

Notes

[1] Telecommunications embraces any transmission, emission or reception of signs, signals, writing, images and sounds or intelligence of any nature by wire, radio, optical and other electromagnetic systems (Article 2 of WATTC Regulation of 9 December 1988).

4. In the light of this, the central role of competition for the Community appears clear, especially in view of the completion of the single market for 1992. This role has already been emphasized in the Green Paper.

5. In the application of competition rules the Commission endeavours to avoid the adopting of State measures or undertakings erecting or maintaining artificial barriers incompatible with the single market. But it also favours all forms of cooperation which foster innovation and economic

progress, as contemplated by competition law. Pursuing effective competition in telecoms is not a matter of political choice. The choice of a free market and a competition-oriented economy was already envisaged in the EEC Treaty, and the competition rules of the Treaty are directly applicable within the Community. The abovementioned fundamental changes make necessary the full application of competition law.

6. There is a need for more certainty as to the application of competition rules. The telecommunication administrations together with keeping their duties of public interest, are now confronted with the application of these rules practically without transition from a long tradition of legal protection. Their scope and actual implications are often not easily perceivable. As the technology is fast-moving and huge investments are necessary, in order to benefit from the new possibilities on the market-place, all the operators, public or private, have to take quick decisions, taking into account the competition regulatory framework.

7. This need for more certainty regarding the application of competition rules is already met by assessments made in several individual cases. However, assessments of individual cases so far have enabled a response to only some of the numerous competition questions which arise in telecommunications. Future cases will further develop the Commission's practice in this sector.

Purpose of these guidelines

8. These guidelines are intended to advise public telecommunications operators, other telecommunications service and equipment suppliers and users, the legal profession and the interested members of the public about the general legal and economic principles which have been and are being followed by the Commission in the application of competition rules to undertakings in the telecommunications sector, based on experience gained in individual cases in compliance with the rulings of the Court of Justice of the European Communities.

9. The Commission will apply these principles also to future individual cases in a flexible way, and taking the particular context of each case into account. These guidelines do not cover all the general principles governing the application of competition rules, but only those which are of specific relevance to telecommunication issues. The general principles of competition rules not specifically connected with telecommunications but entirely applicable to these can be found, inter alia, in the regulatory acts, the Court judgments and the Commission decisions dealing with the individual cases, the Commission's yearly reports on competition policy, press releases and other public information originating from the Commission.

10. These guidelines do not create enforceable rights. Moreover, they do not prejudice the application of EEC competition rules by the Court of Justice of the European Communities and by national authorities (as these rules may be directly applied in each Member State, by the national authorities, administrative or judicial).

11. A change in the economic and legal situation will not automatically bring about a simultaneous amendment to the guidelines. The Commission, however, reserves the possibility to make such an amendment when it considers that these guidelines no longer satisfy their purpose, because of fundamental and/or repeated changes in legal precedents, methods of applying competition rules, and the regulatory, economic and technical context.

12. These guidelines essentially concern the direct application of competition rules to undertakings, i.e. Articles [101 and 102 TFEU]. They do not concern those applicable to the Member States, in particular Articles [4, paragraph 3, TEU] and [106(1) and (3) TFEU]. Principles ruling the application of Article [106] in telecommunications are expressed in Commission Directives adopted under Article [106(3)] for the implementation of the Green Paper.[2]

Notes

[2] Commission Directive 88/301/EEC of 16 May 1988 on competition in the markets in telecommunications terminal equipment (OJ No L 131, 27.5.1988, p.73). [Ed note: see now Commission Directive 2008/63/EC of 20 June 2008 on competition in the markets in telecommunications terminal equipment (Codified version), (OJ L 162, 21.6.2008, p.20).]

Commission Directive 90/388/EEC of 28 June 1990 on competition in the markets for telecommunications services (OJ No L 192, 24.7.1990, p.10). [Directive 90/388/EEC was repealed by Commission Directive 2002/77/EC of 16 September 2002 (OJ L 249, 17.9.2002, p.21).]

*Relationship between competition rules applicable to undertakings and
those applicable to Member States*

13. The Court of Justice of the European Communities[3] has ruled that while it is true that Articles [101] and [102] of the Treaty concern the conduct of undertakings and not the laws or regulations of the Member States, by virtue of [Article 4, paragraph 3 of the Treaty on European Union], Member States must not adopt or maintain in force any measure which could deprive those provisions of their effectiveness. The Court has stated that such would be the case, in particular, if a Member State were to require or favour prohibited cartels or reinforce the effects thereof or to encourage abuses by dominant undertakings.

     If those measures are adopted or maintained in force *vis-à-vis* public undertakings or undertakings to which a Member State grants special or exclusive rights, Article [106] might also apply.

Notes

3 Judgment of 10.1.1985 in Case 229/83, *Leclerc/gasoline* [1985] ECR 17; Judgment of 11.7.1985 in Case 299/83, *Leclerc/books* [1985] ECR 2517; Judgment of 30.4.1986 in Cases from 209 to 213/84, *Ministère public v Asjes* [1986] ECR 1425; Judgment of 1.10.1987 in Case 311/85, *Vereniging van Vlaamse Reisbureaus v Sociale Dienst van de Plaatselijke en Gewestelijke Overheidsdiensten* [1987] ECR 3801.

14. When the conduct of a public undertaking or an undertaking to which a Member State grants special or exclusive rights arises entirely as a result of the exercise of the undertaking's autonomous behaviour, it can only be caught by Articles [101] and [102].

     When this behaviour is imposed by a mandatory State measure (regulative or administrative), leaving no discretionary choice to the undertakings concerned, Article [106] may apply to the State involved in association with Articles [101] and [102]. In this case Articles [101] and [102] apply to the undertakings' behaviour taking into account the constraints to which the undertakings are submitted by the mandatory State measure.

     Ultimately, when the behaviour arises from the free choice of the undertakings involved, but the State has taken a measure which encourages the behaviour or strengthens its effects, Articles [101] and/or [102] apply to the undertakings' behaviour and Article [106] may apply to the State measure. This could be the case, *inter alia*, when the State has approved and/or legally endorsed the result of the undertakings' behaviour (for instance tariffs).

     These guidelines and the Article [106] Directives complement each other to a certain extent in that they cover the principles governing the application of the competition rules: Articles [101] and [102] on the one hand, Article [106] on the other.

*Application of competition rules and other Community law, including
open network provision (ONP) rules*

15. Articles [101] and [102] and Regulations implementing those Articles in application of Article [103 TFEU] constitute law in force and enforceable throughout the Community. Conflicts should not arise with other Community rules because Community law forms a coherent regulatory framework. Other Community rules, and in particular those specifically governing the telecommunications sector, cannot be considered as provisions implementing Articles [101] and [102] in this sector. However it is obvious that Community acts adopted in the telecommunications sector are to be interpreted in a way consistent with competition rules, so to ensure the best possible implementation of all aspects of the Community telecommunications policy.

16. This applies, *inter alia*, to the relationship between competition rules applicable to undertakings and the ONP rules. According to the Council Resolution of 30 June 1988 on the development of the common market for telecommunications services and equipment up to 1992,[4] ONP comprises the "rapid definition, by Council Directives, of technical conditions, usage conditions, and tariff principles for open network provision, starting with harmonized conditions for the use of leased lines". The details of the ONP procedures have been fixed by Directive 90/387/EEC[5] on the establishment of the internal market for telecommunications services through the implementation of open network provision, adopted by Council on 28 June 1990 under Article [114 TFEU].

Notes

4 OJ No C 257, 4.10.1988, p.1.
5 OJ No L 192, 24.7.1990, p.1.

17. ONP has a fundamental role in providing European-wide access to Community-wide interconnected public networks. When ONP harmonization is implemented, a network user will be offered harmonized access conditions throughout the EEC, whichever country they address. Harmonized access will be ensured in compliance with the competition rules as mentioned above, as the ONP rules specifically provide.

    ONP rules cannot be considered as competition rules which apply to States and/or to undertakings" behaviour. ONP and competition rules therefore constitute two different but coherent sets of rules. Hence, the competition rules have full application, even when all ONP rules have been adopted.

18. Competition rules are and will be applied in a coherent manner with Community trade rules in force. However, competition rules apply in a non-discriminatory manner to EEC undertakings and to non-EEC ones which have access to the EEC market.

III. Common Principles of Application of Articles [101] and [102]

Equal application of Articles [101] and [102]

19. Articles [101] and [102] apply directly and throughout the Community to all undertakings, whether public or private, on equal terms and to the same extent, apart from the exception provided in Article [106(2)].[6]

    The Commission and national administrative and judicial authorities are competent to apply these rules under the conditions set out in Council Regulation No 17.[7]

Notes

6 Article [106(2)] states: "Undertakings entrusted with the operation of services of general economic interest or having the character of a revenue-producing monopoly shall be subject to the rules contained in [the Treaties], in particular to the rules on competition, in so far as the application of such rules does not obstruct the performance, in law or in fact, of the particular tasks assigned to them. The development of trade must not be affected to such an extent as would be contrary to the interests of the [Union]".
7 OJ No 13, 21.2.1962, p.204/62 (Special Edition 1959–62, p.87).

20. Therefore, Articles [101] and [102] apply both to private enterprises and public telecommunications operators embracing telecommunications administrations and recognized private operating agencies, hereinafter called "telecommunications organizations" (TOs).

    TOs are undertakings within the meaning of Articles [101] and [102] to the extent that they exert an economic activity, for the manufacturing and/or sale of telecommunications equipment and/or for the provision of telecommunications services, regardless of other facts such as, for example, whether their nature is economic or not and whether they are legally distinct entities or form part of the State organization.[8] Associations of TOs are associations of undertakings within the meaning of Article [101], even though TOs participate as undertakings in organizations in which governmental authorities are also represented.

    Articles [101] and [102] apply also to undertakings located outside the EEC when restrictive agreements are implemented or intended to be implemented or abuses are committed by those undertakings within the common market to the extent that trade between Member States is affected.[9]

Notes

8 See Judgment of the Court of 16.6.1987 in Case 118/85, *Commission v Italy—Transparency of Financial Relations between Member States and Public Undertakings* [1987] ECR 2599.
9 See Judgment of the Court of 27.9.1988 in Joined Cases 89, 104, 114, 116, 117, 125, 126, 127, 129/85, *Ålström & others v Commission ("Woodpulp")* [1988] ECR 5193.

Competition restrictions justified under Article [106(2)] or by essential requirements

21. The exception provided in Article [106(2)] may apply both to State measures and to practices by undertakings. The Services Directive 90/388/EEC, in particular in Article 3, makes provision for a Member State to impose specified restrictions in the licences which it can grant for the provision of certain telecommunications services. These restrictions may be imposed under Article [106(2)] or in order to ensure the compliance with State essential requirements specified in the Directive.

22. As far as Article [106(2)] is concerned, the benefit of the exception provided by this provision may still be invoked for a TO's behaviour when it brings about competition restrictions which its Member State did not impose in application of the Services Directive. However, the fact should be taken into account that in this case the State whose function is to protect the public and the general economic interest, did not deem it necessary to impose the said restrictions. This makes particularly hard the burden of proving that the Article [106(2)] exception still applies to an [undertaking's] behaviour involving these restrictions.

23. The Commission infers from the case law of the Court of Justice[10] that it has exclusive competence, under the control of the Court, to decide that the exception of Article [106(2)] applies. The national authorities including judicial authorities can assess that this exception does not apply, when they find that the competition rules clearly do not obstruct the performance of the task of general economic interest assigned to undertakings. When those authorities cannot make a clear assessment in this sense they should suspend their decision in order to enable the Commission to find that the conditions for the application of that provision are fulfilled.

Notes

[10] Case 10/71, *Mueller-Hein* [1971] ECR 723; Judgment of 11.4.1989 in Case 66/86, *Ahmed Saeed* [1989] ECR 803.

24. As to measures aiming at the compliance with "essential requirements" within the meaning of the Services Directive, under Article 1 of the latter,[11] they can only be taken by Member States and not by undertakings.

Notes

[11] "... the non-economic reasons in the general interest which may cause a Member State to restrict access to the public telecommunications network or public telecommunications services."

The relevant market

25. In order to assess the effects of an agreement on competition for the purposes of Article [101] and whether there is a dominant position on the market for the purposes of Article [102], it is necessary to define the relevant market(s), product or service market(s) and geographic market(s), within the domain of telecommunications. In a context of fast-moving technology the relevant market definition is dynamic and variable.

(a) The product market

26. A product market comprises the totality of the products which, with respect to their characteristics, are particularly suitable for satisfying constant needs and are only to a limited extent interchangeable with other products in terms of price, usage and consumer preference. An examination limited to the objective characteristics only of the relevant products cannot be sufficient: the competitive conditions and the structure of supply and demand on the market must also be taken into consideration.[12]

The Commission can precisely define these markets only within the framework of individual cases.

Notes

[12] Case 322/81, *Michelin v Commission*, 9 November 1983 [1983] ECR 3529, Ground 37.

27. For the guidelines' purpose it can only be indicated that distinct service markets could exist at least for terrestrial network provision, voice communication, data communication and satellites. With regard to the equipment market, the following areas could all be taken into account for the purposes of market definition: public switches, private switches, transmission systems and more

1085

particularly, in the field of terminals, telephone sets, modems, telex terminals, data transmission terminals and mobile telephones. The above indications are without prejudice to the definition of further narrower distinct markets. As to other services—such as value-added ones—as well as terminal and network equipment, it cannot be specified here whether there is a market for each of them or for an aggregate of them, or for both, depending upon the interchangeability existing in different geographic markets. This is mainly determined by the supply and the requirements in those markets.

28. Since the various national public networks compete for the installation of the telecommunication hubs of large users, market definition may accordingly vary. Indeed, large telecommunications users, whether or not they are service providers, locate their premises depending, *inter alia*, upon the features of the telecommunications services supplied by each TO. Therefore, they compare national public networks and other services provided by the TOs in terms of characteristics and prices.

29. As to satellite provision, the question is whether or not it is substantially interchangeable with terrestrial network provision:

    (a) communication by satellite can be of various kinds: fixed service (point to point communication), multipoint (point to multipoint and multipoint to multipoint), one-way or two-way;

    (b) satellites' main characteristics are: coverage of a wide geographic area not limited by national borders, insensitivity of costs to distance, flexibility and ease of networks deployment, in particular in the very small aperture terminals (VSAT) systems;

    (c) satellites' uses can be broken down into the following categories: public switched voice and data transmission, business value-added services and broadcasting;

    (d) a satellite provision presents a broad interchangeability with the terrestrial transmission link for the basic voice and data transmission on long distance. Conversely, because of its characteristics it is not substantially interchangeable but rather complementary to terrestrial transmission links for several specific voice and data transmission uses. These uses are: services to peripheral or lessdeveloped regions, links between non-contiguous countries, reconfiguration of capacity and provision of routing for traffic restoration. Moreover, satellites are not currently substantially interchangeable for direct broadcasting and multipoint private networks for value-added business services. Therefore, for all those uses satellites should constitute distinct product markets. Within satellites, there may be distinct markets.

30. In mobile communications distinct services seem to exist such as cellular telephone, paging, telepoint, cordless voice and cordless data communication. Technical development permits providing each of these systems with more and more enhanced features. A consequence of this is that the differences between all these systems are progressively blurring and their interchangeability increasing. Therefore, it cannot be excluded that in future for certain uses several of those systems be embraced by a single product market. By the same token, it is likely that, for certain uses, mobile systems will be comprised in a single market with certain services offered on the public switched network.

(b) The geographic market

31. A geographic market is an area:

    — where undertakings enter into competition with each other, and

    — where the objective conditions of competition applying to the product or service in question are similar for all traders.[13]

Notes

[13] Judgment of 14.2.1978 in Case 27/76, *United Brands v Commission* [1978] ECR 207, Ground 44. In the telecommunications sector: Judgment of 5.10.1988 in Case 247/86, *Alsatel-Novasam* [1988] ECR 5987.

---

32. Without prejudice to the definition of the geographic market in individual cases, each national territory within the EEC seems still to be a distinct geographic market as regards those relevant services or products, where:

    — the customer's needs cannot be satisfied by using a non-domestic service,

— there are different regulatory conditions of access to services, in particular special or exclusive rights which are apt to isolate national territories,

— as to equipment and network, there are no Community-common standards, whether mandatory or voluntary, whose absence could also isolate the national markets. The absence of voluntary Community-wide standards shows different national customers' requirements.

However, it is expected that the geographic market will progressively extend to the EEC territory at the pace of the progressive realization of a single EEC market.

33. It has also to be ascertained whether each national market or a part thereof is a substantial part of the common market. This is the case where the services of the product involved represent a substantial percentage of volume within the EEC. This applies to all services and products involved.

34. As to satellite uplinks, for cross-border communication by satellite the uplink could be provided from any of several countries. In this case, the geographic market is wider than the national territory and may cover the whole EEC.

As to space segment capacity, the extension of the geographic market will depend on the power of the satellite and its ability to compete with other satellites for transmission to a given area, in other words on its range. This can be assessed only case by case.

35. As to services in general as well as terminal and network equipment, the Commission assesses the market power of the undertakings concerned and the result for EEC competition of the undertakings' conduct, taking into account their interrelated activities and interaction between the EEC and world markets. This is even more necessary to the extent that the EEC market is progressively being opened. This could have a considerable effect on the structure of the markets in the EEC, on the overall competitivity of the undertakings operating in those markets, and in the long run, on their capacity to remain independent operators.

IV. Application of Article [101]

36. The Commission recalls that a major policy target of the Council Resolution of 30 June 1988 on the development of the common market for telecommunications services and equipment up to 1992 was that of:

> "...stimulating European cooperation at all levels, as far as compatible with Community competition rules, and particularly in the field of research and development, in order to secure a strong European presence on the telecommunications markets and to ensure the full participation of all Member States".

In many cases Europe-wide services can be achieved by TOs' cooperation—for example, by ensuring interconnectivity and interoperability

(i) in those areas where exclusive or special rights for provision may continue in accordance with Community law and in particular with the Services Directive 90/388/EEC; and

(ii) in areas where optimum service will require certain features of cooperation, such as so-called "one-stop shopping" arrangements, i.e. the possibility of acquiring Europe-wide services at a single sales point.

The Council is giving guidance, by Directives, Decisions, recommendations and resolutions on those areas where Europe-wide services are most urgently needed: such as by recommendation [90]/659/ EEC on the coordinated introduction of the integrated services digital network (ISDN) in the European Community[14] and by recommendation 87/371/EEC on the coordinated introduction of public pan-European cellular digital land-based mobile communications in the Community.[15]

The Commission welcomes and fully supports the necessity of cooperation particularly in order to promote the development of trans-European services and strengthen the competitivity of the EEC industry throughout the Community and in the world markets. However, this cooperation can only attain that objective if it complies with Community competition rules. Regulation No 17 provides well-defined clearing procedures for such cooperation agreements. The procedures foreseen by Regulation No 17 are:

(i) the application for negative clearance, by which the Commission certifies that the agreements are not caught by Article [101], because they do not restrict competition and/or do not affect trade between Member States; and

    (ii) the notification of agreements caught by Article [101] in order to obtain an exemption under Article [101(3)]. Although if a particular agreement is caught by Article [101], an exemption can be granted by the Commission under Article [101(3)], this is only so when the agreement brings about economic benefits—assessed on the basis of the criteria in the said paragraph 3—which outweigh its restrictions on competition. In any event competition may not be eliminated for a substantial part of the products in question. Notification is not an obligation; but if, for reasons of legal certainty, the parties decide to request an exemption pursuant to Article 4 of Regulation No 17 the agreements may not be exempted until they have been notified to the Commission.

Notes

14 OJ No L 382, 31.12.1986, p.36.

15 OJ No L 196, 17.7.1987, p.81.

37. Cooperation agreements may be covered by one of the Commission block exemption Regulations or Notices.[16] In the first case the agreement is automatically exempted under Article [101(3)]. In the latter case, in the Commission's view, the agreement does not appreciably restrict competition and trade between Member States and therefore does not justify a Commission action. In either case, the agreement does not need to be notified; but it may be notified in case of doubt. If the Commission receives a multitude of notifications of similar cooperation agreements in the telecommunications sector, it may consider whether a specific block exemption regulation for such agreements would be appropriate.

Notes

16 Reported in "Competition Law in the European Communities" Volume I (situation at 31.12.1989) published by the Commission.

38. The categories of agreements[17] which seem to be typical in telecommunications and may be caught by Article [101] are listed below. This list provides examples only and is, therefore, not exhaustive. The Commission is thereby indicating possible competition restrictions which could be caught by Article [101] and cases where there may be the possibility of an exemption.

Notes

17 For simplification's sake this term stands also for "decisions by associations" and "concerted practices" within the meaning of Article [101].

39. These agreements may affect trade between Member States for the following reasons:
    (i) services other than services reserved to TOs, equipment and spatial segment facilities are traded throughout the EEC; agreements on these services and equipment are therefore likely to affect trade. Although at present cross-frontier trade is limited, there is potentially no reason to suppose that suppliers of such facilities will in future confine themselves to their national market;
    (ii) as to reserved network services, one can consider that they also are traded throughout the Community. These services could be provided by an operator located in one Member State to customers located in other Member States, which decide to move their telecommunications hub into the first one because it is economically or qualitatively advantageous. Moreover, agreements on these matters are likely to affect EEC trade at least to the extent they influence the conditions under which the other services and equipment are supplied throughout the EEC.

40. Finally, to the extent that the TOs hold dominant positions in facilities, services and equipment markets, their behaviour leading to—and including the conclusion of—the agreements in question could also give rise to a violation of Article [102], if agreements have or are likely to have as their effect hindering the maintenance of the degree of competition still existing in the market or the growth of that competition, or causing the TOs to reap trading benefits which they would not have reaped if there had been normal and sufficiently effective competition.

A. Horizontal agreements concerning the provision of terrestrial facilities and reserved services

41. Agreements concerning terrestrial facilities (public switched network or leased circuits) or services (e.g. voice telephony for the general public) can currently only be concluded between TOs because of this legal regime providing for exclusive or special rights. The fact that the Services Directive recognizes the possibility for a Member State to reserve this provision to certain operators does not exempt those operators from complying with the competition rules in providing these facilities or services. These agreements may restrict competition within a Member State only where such exclusive rights are granted to more than one provider.

42. These agreements may restrict the competition between TOs for retaining or attracting large telecommunications users for their telecommunications centres. Such "hub competition" is substantially based upon favourable rates and other conditions, as well as the quality of the services. Member States are not allowed to prevent such competition since the Directive allows only the granting of exclusive and special rights by each Member State in its own territory.

43. Finally, these agreements may restrict competition in non-reserved services from third party undertakings, which are supported by the facilities in question, for example if they impose discriminatory or inequitable trading conditions on certain users.

44. (aa) *Price agreements*: all TOs' agreements on prices, discounting or collection charges for international services, are apt to restrict the hub competition to an appreciable extent. Coordination on or prohibition of discounting could cause particularly serious restrictions. In situations of public knowledge such as exists in respect of the tariff level, discounting could remain the only possibility of effective price competition.

45. In several cases the Court of Justice and the Commission have considered price agreements among the most serious infringements of Article [101].[18]

While harmonization of tariff structures may be a major element for the provision of Community-wide services, this goal should be pursued as far as compatible with Community competition rules and should include definition of efficient pricing principles throughout the Community. Price competition is a crucial, if not the principal, element of customer choice and is apt to stimulate technical progress. Without prejudice to any application for individual exemption that may be made, the justification of any price agreement in terms of Article [101(1)] would be the subject of very rigorous examination by the Commission.

Notes

18 *PVC*, Commission Decision 89/190/EEC, OJ No L 74, 17.3.1989, p.1; Case 123/85, *BNIC v Clair* [1985] ECR 391; Case 8/72, *Cementhandelaren v Commission* [1972] ECR 977; *Polypropylene*, Commission Decision 86/398/EEC (OJ No L 230/1, 18.8.1986, p.1) on appeal Case 179/86.

---

46. Conversely, where the agreements concern only the setting up of common tariff structures or principles, the Commission may consider whether this would not constitute one of the economic benefits under Article [101(3)] which outweigh the competition restriction. Indeed, this could provide the necessary transparency on tariff calculations and facilitate users' decisions about traffic flow or the location of headquarters or premises. Such agreements could also contribute to achieving one of the Green Paper's economic objectives—more cost-orientated tariffs.

In this connection, following the intervention of the Commission, the CEPT has decided to abolish recommendation PGT/10 on the general principles for the lease of international telecommunications circuits and the establishment of private international networks. This recommendation recommended, *inter alia*, the imposition of a 30% surcharge or an access charge where third-party traffic was carried on an international telecommunications leased circuit, or if such a circuit was interconnected to the public telecommunications network. It also recommended the application of uniform tariff coefficients in order to determine the relative price level of international telecommunications leased circuits. Thanks to the CEPT's cooperation with the Commission leading to the abolition of the recommendation, competition between telecoms operators for the supply of international leased circuits is re-established, to the benefit of users, especially suppliers of non-reserved services. The Commission had found that the recommendation amounted to a price agreement between undertakings under Article [101] of the Treaty which substantially restricted competition within the European Community.[19]

47. (ab) *Agreements on other conditions for the provision of facilities*

These agreements may limit hub competition between the partners. Moreover, they may limit the access of users to the network, and thus restrict third undertakings' competition as to non-reserved services. This applies especially to the use of leased circuits. The abolished CEPT recommendation PGT/10 on tariffs had also recommended restrictions on conditions of sale which the Commission objected to. These restrictions were mainly:

— making the use of leased circuits between the customer and third parties subject to the condition that the communication concern exclusively the activity for which the circuit has been granted,

— a ban on subleasing,

— authorization of private networks only for customers tied to each other by economic links and which carry out the same activity,

— prior consultation between the TOs for any approval of a private network and of any modification of the use of the network, and for any interconnection of private networks.

For the purpose of an exemption under Article [101(3)], the granting of special conditions for a particular facility in order to promote its development could be taken into account among other elements. This could foster technologies which reduce the costs of services and contribute to increasing competitiveness of European industry structures. Naturally, the other Article [101(3)] requirements should also be met.

48. (ac) *Agreements on the choice of telecommunication routes.*

These may have the following restrictive effects:

(i) to the extent that they coordinate the TOs' choice of the routes to be set up in international services, they may limit competition between TOs as suppliers to users' communications hubs, in terms of investments and production, with a possible effect on tariffs. It should be determined whether this restriction of their business autonomy is sufficiently appreciable to be caught by Article [101]. In any event, an argument for an exemption under Article [101(3)] could be more easily sustained if common routes designation were necessary to enable interconnections and, therefore, the use of a Europe-wide network;

(ii) to the extent that they reserve the choice of routes already set up to the TOs, and this choice concerns one determined facility, they could limit the use of other facilities and thus services provision possibly to the detriment of technological progress. By contrast, the choice of routes does not seem restrictive in principle to the extent that it constitutes a technical requirement.

49. (ad) *Agreements on the imposition of technical and quality standards on the services provided on the public network*

Standardization brings substantial economic benefits which can be relevant under Article [101(3)]. It facilitates *inter alia* the provision of pan-European telecommunications services. As set out in the framework of the Community's approach to standardization, products and services complying with standards may be used Community-wide. In the context of this approach, European standards institutions have developed in this field (ETSI and CEN-Cenelec). National markets in the EC would be opened up and form a Community market. Service and equipment markets would be enlarged, hence favouring economies of scale. Cheaper products and services are thus available to users. Standardization may also offer an alternative to specifications controlled by undertakings dominant in the network architecture and in non-reserved services. Standardization agreements may, therefore, lessen the risk of abuses by these undertakings which could block the access to the markets for non-reserved services and for equipment. However, certain standardization agreements can have restrictive effects on competition: hindering innovation, freezing a particular stage of technical development, blocking the network access of some users/service providers. This restriction could be appreciable, for example when deciding to what extent intelligence will in future be located in the network or continue to be permitted in customers' equipment. The imposition of specifications other than those provided for by Community law could have restrictive effects on competition. Agreements having these effects are, therefore, caught by Article [101].

The balance between economic benefits and competition restrictions is complex. In principle, an exemption could be granted if an agreement brings more openness and facilitates access to the market, and these benefits outweigh the restrictions caused by it.

50. Standards jointly developed and/or published in accordance with the ONP procedures carry with them the presumption that the cooperating TOs which comply with those standards fulfil the requirement of open and efficient access (see the ONP Directive mentioned in paragraph 16). This presumption can be rebutted, *inter alia*, if the agreement contains restrictions which are not foreseen by Community law and are not indispensable for the standardization sought.

51. One important Article [101(3)] requirement is that users must also be allowed a fair share of the resulting benefit. This is more likely to happen when users are directly involved in the standardization process in order to contribute to deciding what products or services will meet their needs. Also, the involvement of manufacturers or service providers other than TOs seems a positive element for Article [101(3)] purposes. However, this involvement must be open and widely representative in order to avoid competition restrictions to the detriment of excluded manufacturers or service providers. Licensing other manufacturers may be deemed necessary, for the purpose of granting an exemption to these agreements under Article [101(3)].

52. (ae) *Agreements foreseeing special treatment for TOs' terminal equipment or other companies' equipment for the interconnection or interoperation of terminal equipment with reserved services and facilities*

53. (af) *Agreements on the exchange of information*
A general exchange of information could indeed be necessary for the good functioning of international telecommunications services, and for cooperation aimed at ensuring interconnectivity or one-stop shopping and billing. It should not be extended to competition-sensitive information, such as certain tariff information which constitutes business secrets, discounting, customers and commercial strategy, including that concerning new products. The exchange of this information would affect the autonomy of each TO's commercial policy and it is not necessary to attain the said objectives.

B. Agreements concerning the provision of non-reserved services and terminal equipment

54. Unlike facilities markets, where only the TOs are the providers, in the services markets the actual or potential competitors are numerous and include, besides the TOs, international private companies, computer companies, publishers and others. Agreements on services and terminal equipment could therefore be concluded between TOs, between TOs and private companies, and between private companies.

55. The liberalizing process has led mostly to strategic agreements between (i) TOs, and (ii) TOs and other companies. These agreements usually take the form of joint ventures.

56. (ba) *Agreements between TOs*
The scope of these agreements, in general, is the provision by each partner of a value-added service including the management of the service. Those agreements are mostly based on the "one-stop shopping" principle, i.e. each partner offers to the customer the entire package of services which he needs. These managed services are called managed data network services (MDNS). An MDNS essentially consists of a broad package of services including facilities, value-added services and management. The agreements may also concern such basic services as satellite uplink.

57. *These agreements could restrict competition in the MDNS market and also in the markets for a service or a group of services included in the MDNS:*
(i) between the participating TOs themselves; and
(ii) vis-à-vis other actual or potential third-party providers.

58. (i) *Restrictions of competition between TOs*
Cooperation between TOs could limit the number of potential individual MDNS offered by each participating TO.

The agreements may affect competition at least in certain aspects which are contemplated as specific examples of prohibited practices under Article [101(1)(a) to (c)], in the event that:
— they fix or recommend, or at least lead (through the exchange of price information) to coordination of prices charged by each participant to customers,
— they provide for joint specification of MDNS products, quotas, joint delivery, specification of customers' systems; all this would amount to controlling production, markets, technical development and investments,
— they contemplate joint purchase of MDNS hardware and/or software, which would amount to sharing markets or sources of supply.

59. (ii) *Restrictive effects on third party undertakings*
Third parties' market entry could be precluded or hampered if the participating TOs:
— refuse to provide facilities to third party suppliers of services,
— apply usage restrictions only to third parties and not to themselves (e.g. a private provider is precluded from placing multiple customers on a leased line facility to obtain lower unit costs),
— favour their MDNS offerings over those of private suppliers with respect to access, availability, quality and price of leased circuits, maintenance and other services,
— apply especially low rates to their MDNS offerings, cross-subsidizing them with higher rates for monopoly services.
Examples of this could be the restrictions imposed by the TOs on private network operators as to the qualifications of the users, the nature of the messages to be exchanged over the network or the use of international private leased circuits.

60. Finally, as the participating TOs hold, individually or collectively, a dominant position for the creation and the exploitation of the network in each national market, any restrictive behaviour described in paragraph 59 could amount to an abuse of a dominant position under Article [102] (see V below).

61. On the other hand, agreements between TOs may bring economic benefits which could be taken into account for the possible granting of an exemption under Article [101(3)]. *Inter alia*, the possible benefits could be as follows:
— a European-wide service and "one-stop shopping" could favour business in Europe. Large multinational undertakings are provided with a European communication service using only a single point of contact,
— the cooperation could lead to a certain amount of European-wide standardization even before further EEC legislation on this matter is adopted,
— the cooperation could bring a cost reduction and consequently cheaper offerings to the advantage of consumers,
— a general improvement of public infrastructure could arise from a joint service provision.

62. Only by notification of the cases in question, in accordance with the appropriate procedures under Regulation No 17, will the Commission be able, where requested, to ascertain, on the merits, whether these benefits outweigh the competition restrictions. But in any event, restrictions on access for third parties seem likely to be considered as not indispensable and to lead to the elimination of competition for a substantial part of the products and services concerned within the meaning of Article [101(3)], thus excluding the possibility of an exemption. Moreover, if an MDNS agreement strengthens appreciably a dominant position which a participating TO holds in the market for a service included in the MDNS, this is also likely to lead to a rejection of the exemption.

63. The Commission has outlined the conditions for exempting such forms of cooperation in a case concerning a proposed joint venture between 22 TOs for the provision of a Europe-wide MDNS, later abandoned for commercial reasons,[20] The Commission considered that the MDNS project presented the risks of restriction of competition between the operators themselves and private service suppliers but it accepted that the project also offered economic benefits to telecommunications users such as access to Europe-wide services through a single operator. Such cooperation could also have accelerated European standardization, reduced costs and increased the quality of the services. The Commission had informed the participants that approval of the project would have to be subject to guarantees designed to prevent undue restriction of competition in the telecommunications services markets, such as discrimination against private services suppliers and

cross-subsidization. Such guarantees would be essential conditions for the granting of an exemption under the competition rules to cooperation agreements involving TOs. The requirement for an appropriate guarantee of non-discrimination and non-cross-subsidization will be specified in individual cases according to the examples of discrimination indicated in Section V below concerning the application of Article [102].

Notes

20 Commission press release IP(89) 948 of 14.12.1989.

64. (bb) *Agreements between TOs and other service providers*
    Cooperation between TOs and other operators is increasing in telecommunications services. It frequently takes the form of a joint venture. The Commission recognizes that it may have beneficial effects. However, this cooperation may also adversely affect competition and the opening up of services markets. Beneficial and harmful effects must therefore be carefully weighed.

65. Such agreements may restrict competition for the provision of telecommunications services:
    (i) between the partners; and
    (ii) from third parties.

66. (i) Competition between the partners may be restricted when these are actual or potential competitors for the relevant telecommunications service. This is generally the case, even when only the other partners and not the TOs are already providing the service. Indeed, TOs may have the required financial capacity, technical and commercial skills to enter the market for non-reserved services and could reasonably bear the technical and financial risk of doing it. This is also generally the case as far as private operators are concerned, when they do not yet provide the service in the geographical market covered by the cooperation, but do provide this service elsewhere. They may therefore be potential competitors in this geographic market.

67. (ii) The cooperation may restrict competition from third parties because:
    — there is an appreciable risk that the participant TO, i.e. the dominant network provider, will give more favourable network access to its cooperation partners than to other service providers in competition with the partners,
    — potential competitors may refrain from entering the market because of this objective risk or, in any event, because of the presence on the market-place of a cooperation involving the monopolist for the network provision. This is especially the case when market entry barriers are high: the market structure allows only few suppliers and the size and the market power of the partners are considerable.

68. On the other hand, the cooperation may bring economic benefits which outweigh its harmful effect and therefore justify the granting of an exemption under Article [101(3)]. The economic benefits can consist, *inter alia*, of the rationalization of the production and distribution of telecommunication services, in improvements in existing services or development of new services, or transfer of technology which improves the efficiency and the competitiveness of the European industrial structures.

69. In the absence of such economic benefits a complementarity between partners, i.e. between the provision of a reserved activity and that of a service under competition, is not a benefit as such. Considering it as a benefit would be equal to justifying an involvement through restrictive agreements of TOs in any non-reserved service provision. This would be to hinder a competitive structure in this market.
    In certain cases, the cooperation could consolidate or extend the dominant position of the TOs concerned to a non-reserved services market, in violation of Article [102].

70. The imposition or the proposal of cooperation with the service provider as a condition for the provision of the network may be deemed abusive (see paragraph 98(vi)).

71. (bc) *Agreements between service providers other than TOs*
    The Commission will apply the same principles indicated in (ba) and (bb) above also to agreements between private service providers, *inter alia*, agreements providing quotas, price fixing, market and/or customer allocation. In principle, they are unlikely to qualify for an exemption. The Commission will be particularly vigilant in order to avoid cooperation on services leading to a strengthening of dominant positions of the partners or restricting competition from third

parties. There is a danger of this occurring for example when an undertaking is dominant with regard to the network architecture and its proprietary standard is adopted to support the service contemplated by the cooperation. This architecture enabling interconnection between computer systems of the partners could attract some partners to the dominant partner. The dominant position for the network architecture will be strengthened and Article [102] may apply.

72. In any exemption of agreements between TOs and other services and/or equipment providers, or between these providers, the Commission will require from the partners appropriate guarantees of non-cross-subsidization and non-discrimination. The risk of cross-subsidization and discrimination is higher when the TOs or the other partners provide both services and equipment, whether within or outside the Community.

C. Agreements on research and development (R&D)

73. As in other high technology based sectors, R&D in telecommunications is essential for keeping pace with technological progress and being competitive on the market-place to the benefit of users. R&D requires more and more important financial, technical and human resources which only few undertakings can generate individually. Cooperation is therefore crucial for attaining the above objectives.

74. The Commission has adopted a Regulation for the block exemption under Article [101(3)] of R&D agreements in all sectors, including telecommunications.[21]

Notes

[21] Regulation (EEC) No 418/85, OJ No L 53, 22.2.1985, p.5. [Ed note: see now Commission Regulation (EU) No 1217/2010 (OJ L 335, 1812.210, p.36), reproduced at C6 above.]

---

75. Agreements which are not covered by this Regulation (or the other Commission block exemption Regulations) could still obtain an individual exemption from the Commission if Article [101(3)] requirements are met individually. However, not in all cases do the economic benefits of an R&D agreement outweigh its competition restrictions. In telecommunications, one major asset, enabling access to new markets, is the launch of new products or services. Competition is based not only on price, but also on technology. R&D agreements could constitute the means for powerful undertakings with high market shares to avoid or limit competition from more innovative rivals. The risk of excessive restrictions of competition increases when the cooperation is extended from R&D to manufacturing and even more to distribution.

76. The importance which the Commission attaches to R&D and innovation is demonstrated by the fact that it has launched several programmes for this purpose. The joint companies' activities which may result from these programmes are not automatically cleared or exempted as such in all aspects from the application of the competition rules. However, most of those joint activities may be covered by the Commission's block exemption Regulations. If not, the joint activities in question may be exempted, where required, in accordance with the appropriate criteria and procedures.

77. In the Commission's experience joint distribution linked to joint R&D which is not covered by the Regulation on R&D does not play the crucial role in the exploitation of the results of R&D. Nevertheless, in individual cases, provided that a competitive environment is maintained, the Commission is prepared to consider full-range cooperation even between large firms. This should lead to improving the structure of European industry and thus enable it to meet strong competition in the world market place.

V. Application of Article [102]

78. Article [102] applies when:
   (i) the undertaking concerned holds an individual or a joint dominant position;
   (ii) it commits an abuse of that dominant position; and
   (iii) the abuse may affect trade between Member States.

Dominant position

79. In each national market the TOs hold individually or collectively a dominant position for the creation and the exploitation of the network, since they are protected by exclusive or special rights

granted by the State. Moreover, the TOs hold a dominant position for some telecommunications services, in so far as they hold exclusive or special rights with respect to those services.[22]

Notes

[22] Commission Decision 82/861/EEC in the "*British Telecommunications*" case, point 26, OJ No L 360, 21.12.1982, p.36, confirmed in the Judgment of 20.3.1985 in Case 41/83, *Italian Republic v Commission* [1985] ECR 873, generally known as "*British Telecom*".

80. The TOs may also hold dominant positions on the markets for certain equipment or services, even though they no longer hold any exclusive rights on those markets. After the elimination of these rights, they may have kept very important market shares in this sector. When the market share in itself does not suffice to give the TOs a dominant position, it could do it in combination with the other factors such as the monopoly for the network or other related services and a powerful and wide distribution network. As to the equipment, for example terminal equipment, even if the TOs are not involved in the equipment manufacturing or in the services provision, they may hold a dominant position in the market as distributors.

81. Also, firms other than TOs may hold individual or collective dominant positions in markets where there are no exclusive rights. This may be the case especially for certain non-reserved services because of either the market shares alone of those undertakings, or because of a combination of several factors. Among these factors, in addition to the market shares, two of particular importance are the technological advance and the holding of the information concerning access protocols or interfaces necessary to ensure interoperability of software and hardware. When this information is covered by intellectual property rights this is a further factor of dominance.

82. Finally, the TOs hold, individually or collectively, dominant positions in the demand for some telecommunication equipment, works or software services. Being dominant for the network and other services provisions they may account for a purchaser's share high enough to give them dominance as to the demand, i.e. making suppliers dependent on them. Dependence could exist when the supplier cannot sell to other customers a substantial part of its production or change a production. In certain national markets, for example in large switching equipment, big purchasers such as the TOs face big suppliers. In this situation, it should be weighed up case by case whether the supplier or the customer position will prevail on the other to such an extent as to be considered dominant under Article [102].

With the liberalization of services and the expansion of new forces on the services markets, dominant positions of undertakings other than the TOs may arise for the purchasing of equipment.

Abuse

83. Commission's activity may concern mainly the following broad areas of abuses:

   A. *TOs' abuses*: in particular, they may take advantage of their monopoly or at least dominant position to acquire a foothold or to extend their power in non-reserved neighbouring markets, to the detriment of competitors and customers.

   B. *Abuses by undertaking other than TOs*: these may take advantage of the fundamental information they hold, whether or not covered by intellectual property rights, with the object and/or effect of restricting competition.

   C. *Abuses of a dominant purchasing position*: for the time being this concerns mainly the TOs, especially to the extent that they hold a dominant position for reserved activities in the national market. However, it may also increasingly concern other undertakings which have entered the market.

A. TOs' Abuses

84. The Commission has recognized in the Green Paper the central role of the TOs, which justifies the maintenance of certain monopolies to enable them to perform their public task. This public task consists in the provision and exploitation of a universal network or, where appropriate, universal service, i.e. one having general coverage and available to all users (including service providers and the TOs themselves) upon request on reasonable and non-discriminatory conditions. This fundamental obligation could justify the benefit of the exception provided in Article [106(2)] under certain circumstances, as laid down in the Services Directive.

85. In most cases, however, the competition rules, far from obstructing the fulfilment of this obligation, contribute to ensuring it. In particular, Article [102] can apply to behaviour of dominant
undertakings resulting in a refusal to supply, discrimination, restrictive tying clauses, unfair prices
or other inequitable conditions.

If one of these types of behaviour occurs in the provision of one of the monopoly services, the
fundamental obligation indicated above is not performed. This could be the case when a TO tries
to take advantage of its monopoly for certain services (for instance: network provision) in order
to limit the competition they have to face in respect of non-reserved services, which in turn are
supported by those monopoly services.

It is not necessary for the purpose of the application of Article [102] that competition be restricted
as to a service which is supported by the monopoly provision in question. It would suffice that the
behaviour results in an appreciable restriction of competition in whatever way. This means that an
abuse may occur when the company affected by the behaviour is not a service provider but an end
user who could himself be disadvantaged in competition in the course of his own business.

86. The Court of Justice has set out this fundamental principle of competition in telecommunications in one of its judgments.[23] An abuse within the meaning of Article [102] is committed where,
without any objective necessity, an undertaking holding a dominant position on a particular
market reserves to itself or to an undertaking belonging to the same group an ancillary activity
which might be carried out by another undertaking as part of its activities on a neighbouring but
separate market, with the possibility of eliminating all competition from such undertaking.

The Commission believes that this principle applies, not only when a dominant undertaking
monopolizes other markets, but also when by anti-competitive means it extends its activity to
other markets.

Hampering the provision of non-reserved services could limit production, markets and above all
the technical progress which is a key factor of telecommunications. The Commission has already
shown these adverse effects of usage restrictions on monopoly provision in its decision in the
"*British Telecom*" case.[24] In this Decision it was found that the restrictions imposed by British
Telecom on telex and telephone networks usage, namely on the transmission of international
messages on behalf of third parties:

  (i) limited the activity of economic operators to the detriment of technological progress;

  (ii) discriminated against these operators, thereby placing them at a competitive disadvantage
  vis-à-vis TOs not bound by these restrictions; and

  (iii) made the conclusion of the contracts for the supply of telex circuits subject to acceptance by
  the other parties of supplementary obligations which had no connection with such contracts.
  These were considered abuses of a dominant position identified respectively in Article
  [102(b), (c) and (d)].

This could be done:

(a) as above, by refusing or restricting the usage of the service provided under monopoly so as to
limit the provision of non-reserved services by third parties; or

(b) by predatory behaviour, as a result of cross-subsidization.

Notes

[23] Case 311/84, *Centre belge d'études de marché Télémarketing (CBEM) SA v Compagnie luxembourgeoise de télédiffusion
SA and Information Publicité Benelux SA*, 3 October 1985 [1985] ECR 3261, Grounds 26 and 27.
[24] See Note 22.

---

87. The separation of the TOs' regulatory power from their business activity is a crucial matter in the
context of the application of Article [102]. This separation is provided in the Article [106] Directives on terminals and on services mentioned in Note 2 above.

(a) Usage restrictions

88. Usage restrictions on provisions of reserved services are likely to correspond to the specific examples of abuses indicated in Article [102]. In particular:

  — they may limit the provision of telecommunications services in free competition, the investments and the technical progress, to the prejudice of telecommunications consumers (Article
  [102(b)]),

— to the extent that these usage restrictions are not applied to all users, including the TOs themselves as users, they may result in discrimination against certain users, placing them at a competitive disadvantage (Article [102(c)]),

— they may make the usage of the reserved services subject to the acceptance of obligations which have no connection with this usage (Article [102(d)]).

89. The usage restrictions in question mainly concern public networks (public switched telephone network (PSTN) or public switched data networks (PSDN)) and especially leased circuits. They may also concern other provisions such as satellite uplink, and mobile communication networks. The most frequent types of behaviour are as follows:

(i) *Prohibition imposed by TOs on third parties:*

(a) *to connect private leased circuits by means of concentrator, multiplexer or other equipment to the public switched network; and/or*

(b) *to use private leased circuits for providing services, to the extent that these services are not reserved, but under competition.*

90. To the extent that the user is granted a licence by State regulatory authorities under national law in compliance with EEC law, these prohibitions limit the user's freedom of access to the leased circuits, the provision of which is a public service. Moreover, it discriminates between users, depending upon the usage (Article [102(c)]). This is one of the most serious restrictions and could substantially hinder the development of international telecommunications services (Article [102(b)]).

91. When the usage restriction limits the provision of non-reserved service in competition with that provided by the TO itself the abuse is even more serious and the principles of the abovementioned "*Télémarketing*" judgment (Note 23 *supra*) apply.

92. In individual cases, the Commission will assess whether the service provided on the leased circuit is reserved or not, on the basis of the Community regulatory acts interpreted in the technical and economic context of each case. Even though a service could be considered reserved according to the law, the fact that a TO actually prohibits the usage of the leased circuit only to some users and not to others could constitute a discrimination under Article [102(c)].

93. The Commission has taken action in respect of the Belgian Régie des télégraphes et téléphones after receiving a complaint concerning an alleged abuse of dominant position from a private supplier of value-added telecommunications services relating to the conditions under which telecommunications circuits were being leased. Following discussions with the Commission, the RTT authorized the private supplier concerned to use the leased telecommunications circuits subject to no restrictions other than that they should not be used for the simple transport of data. Moreover, pending the possible adoption of new rules in Belgium, and without prejudice to any such rules, the RTT undertook that all its existing and potential clients for leased telecommunications circuits to which third parties may have access shall be governed by the same conditions as those which were agreed with the private sector supplier mentioned above.[25]

Notes

[25] Commission Press release IP(90) 67 of 29.1.1990.

(ii) *Refusal by TOs to provide reserved services (in particular the network and leased circuits) to third parties*

94. Refusal to supply has been considered an abuse by the Commission and the Court of Justice.[26] This behaviour would make it impossible or at least appreciably difficult for third parties to provide non-reserved services. This, in turn, would lead to a limitation of services and of technical development (Article [102(b)]) and, if applied only to some users, result in discrimination (Article [102(c)]).

Notes

[26] Cases 6 and 7/73 *Commercial Solvents v Commission* [1974] ECR 223;
United Brands v Commission (Note 13, above).

(iii)   Imposition of extra charges or other special conditions for certain usages of reserved services

95. An example would be the imposition of access charges to leased circuits when they are connected to the public switched network or other special prices and charges for service provision to third parties. Such access charges may discriminate between users of the same service (leased circuits provision) depending upon the usage and result in imposing unfair trading conditions. This will limit the usage of leased circuits and finally non-reserved service provision. Conversely, it does not constitute an abuse provided that it is shown, in each specific case, that the access charges correspond to costs which are entailed directly for the TOs for the access in question. In this case, access charges can be imposed only on an equal basis to all users, including TOs themselves.

96. Apart from these possible additional costs which should be covered by an extra charge, the interconnection of a leased circuit to the public switched network is already remunerated by the price related to the use of this network. Certainly, a leased circuit can represent a subjective value for a user depending on the profitability of the enhanced service to be provided on that leased circuit. However, this cannot be a criterion on which a dominant undertaking, and above all a public service provider, can base the price of this public service.

97. The Commission appreciates that the substantial difference between leased circuits and the public switched network causes a problem of obtaining the necessary revenues to cover the costs of the switched network. However, the remedy chosen must not be contrary to law, i.e. the EEC Treaty, as discriminatory pricing between customers would be.

(iv) Discriminatory price or quality of the service provided

98. This behaviour may relate, *inter alia*, to tariffs or to restrictions or delays in connection to the public switched network or leased circuits provision, in installation, maintenance and repair, in effecting interconnection of systems or in providing information concerning network planning, signalling protocols, technical standards and all other information necessary for an appropriate interconnection and interoperation with the reserved service and which may affect the interworking of competitive services or terminal equipment offerings.

   (v)   *Tying the provision of the reserved service to the supply by the TOs or others of terminal equipment to be interconnected or interoperated, in particular through imposition, pressure, offer of special prices or other trading conditions for the reserved service linked to the equipment.*

   (vi) *Tying the provision of the reserved service to the agreement of the user to enter into cooperation with the reserved service provider himself as to the non-reserved service to be carried on the network*

   (vii) *Reserving to itself for the purpose of non-reserved service provision or to other service providers information obtained in the exercise of a reserved service in particular information concerning users of a reserved services providers more favourable conditions for the supply of this information*

This latter information could be important for the provision of services under competition to the extent that it permits the targeting of customers of those services and the definition of business strategy. The behaviour indicated above could result in a discrimination against undertakings to which the use of this information is denied in violation of Article [102(c)]. The information in question can only be disclosed with the agreement of the users concerned and in accordance with relevant data protection legislation (see the proposal for a Council Directive concerning the protection of personal data and privacy in the context of public digital telecommunications networks, in particular the integrated services digital network (ISDN) and public digital mobile networks).[27]

Notes

[27] Commission document COM(90) 314 of 13.9.1990.

(viii) Imposition of unneeded reserved services by supplying reserved and/or non-reserved services when the former reserved services are reasonably separable from the others

99. The practices under (v) (vi) (vii) and (viii) result in applying conditions which have no connection with the reserved service, contravening Article [102(d)].

100. Most of these practices were in fact identified in the Services Directive as restrictions on the provision of services within the meaning of Article [56] and Article [102] of the Treaty brought about by State measures. They are therefore covered by the broader concept of "restrictions" which under Article 6 of the Directive have to be removed by Member States.

101. The Commission believes that the Directives on terminals and on services also clarify some principles of application of Articles [101] and [102] in the sector.

The Services Directive does not apply to important sectors such as mobile communications and satellites; however, competition rules apply fully to these sectors. Moreover, as to the services covered by the Directive it will depend very much on the degree of precision of the licences given by the regulatory body whether the TOs still have a discretionary margin for imposing conditions which should be scrutinized under competition rules. Not all the conditions can be regulated in licences: consequently, there could be room for discretionary action. The application of competition rules to companies will therefore depend very much on a case-by-case examination of the licences. Nothing more than a class licence can be required for terminals.

(b) Cross-subsidization

102. Cross-subsidization means that an undertaking allocates all or part of the costs of its activity in one product or geographic market to its activity in another product or geographic market. Under certain circumstances, cross-subsidization in telecommunications could distort competition, i.e. lead to beating other competitors with offers which are made possible not by efficiency and performance but by artificial means such as subsidies. Avoiding cross-subsidization leading to unfair competition is crucial for the development of service provision and equipment supply.

103. Cross-subsidization does not lead to predatory pricing and does not restrict competition when it is the costs of reserved activities which are subsidized by the revenue generated by other reserved activities since there is no competition possible as to these activities. This form of subsidization is even necessary, as it enables the TOs holders of exclusive rights to perform their obligation to provide a public service universally and on the same conditions to everybody. For instance, telephone provision in unprofitable rural areas is subsidized through revenues from telephone provision in profitable urban areas or long-distance calls. The same could be said of subsidizing the provision of reserved services through revenues generated by activities under competition. The application of the general principle of cost-orientation should be the ultimate goal, in order, *inter alia*, to ensure that prices are not inequitable as between users.

104. Subsidizing activities under competition, whether concerning services or equipment, by allocating their costs to monopoly activities, however, is likely to distort competition in violation of Article [102]. It could amount to an abuse by an undertaking holding a dominant position within the Community. Moreover, users of activities under monopoly have to bear unrelated costs for the provision of these activities. Cross-subsidization can also exist between monopoly provision and equipment manufacturing and sale. Cross-subsidization can be carried out through:

— funding the operation of the activities in question with capital remunerated substantially below the market rate;

— providing for those activities premises, equipment, experts and/or services with a remuneration substantially lower than the market price.

105. As to funding through monopoly revenues or making available monopoly material and intellectual means for the starting up of new activities under competition, this constitutes an investment whose costs should be allocated to the new activity. Offering the new product or service should normally include a reasonable remuneration of such investment in the long run. If it does not, the Commission will assess the case on the basis of the remuneration plans of the undertaking concerned and of the economic context.

106. Transparency in the TOs' accounting should enable the Commission to ascertain whether there is cross-subsidization in the cases in which this question arises. The ONP Directive provides in

this respect for the definition of harmonized tariff principles which should lessen the number of these cases.

This transparency can be provided by an accounting system which ensures the fully proportionate distribution of all costs between reserved and non-reserved activities. Proper allocation of costs is more easily ensured in cases of structural separation, i.e. creating distinct entities for running each of these two categories of activities.

An appropriate accounting system approach should permit the identification and allocation of all costs between the activities which they support. In this system all products and services should bear proportionally all the relevant costs, including costs of research and development, facilities and overheads. It should enable the production of recorded figures which can be verified by accountants.

107. As indicated above (paragraph 59), in cases of cooperation agreements involving TOs a guarantee of no cross-subsidization is one of the conditions required by the Commission for exemption under Article [101(3)]. In order to monitor properly compliance with that guarantee, the Commission now envisages requesting the parties to ensure an appropriate accounting system as described above, the accounts being regularly submitted to the Commission. Where the accounting method is chosen, the Commission will reserve the possibility of submitting the accounts to independent audit, especially if any doubt arises as to the capability of the system to ensure the necessary transparency or to detect any cross-subsidization. If the guarantee cannot be properly monitored, the Commission may withdraw the exemption.

108. In all other cases, the Commission does not envisage requiring such transparency of the TOs. However, if in a specific case there are substantial elements converging in indicating the existence of an abusive cross-subsidization and/or predatory pricing, the Commission could establish a presumption of such cross-subsidization and predatory pricing. An appropriate separate accounting system could be important in order to counter this presumption.

109. Cross-subsidization of a reserved activity by a non-reserved one does not in principle restrict competition. However, the application of the exception provided in Article [106(2)] to this non-reserved activity could not as a rule be justified by the fact that the financial viability of the TO in question rests on the non-reserved activity. Its financial viability and the performance of its task of general economic interest can only be ensured by the State where appropriate by the granting of an exclusive or special right and by imposing restrictions on activities competing with the reserved ones.

110. Also cross-subsidization by a public or private operator outside the EEC may be deemed abusive in terms of Article [102] if that operator holds a dominant position for equipment or non-reserved services within the EEC. The existence of this dominant position, which allows the holder to behave to an appreciable extent independently of its competitors and customers and ultimately of consumers, will be assessed in the light of all elements in the EEC and outside.

B. Abuses by undertakings other than the TOs

111. Further to the liberalization of services, undertakings other than the TOs may increasingly extend their power to acquire dominant positions in non-reserved markets. They may already hold such a position in some services markets which had not been reserved. When they take advantage of their dominant position to restrict competition and to extend their power, Article [102] may also apply to them. The abuses in which they might indulge are broadly similar to most of those previously described in relation to the TOs.

112. Infringements of Article [102] may be committed by the abusive exercise of industrial property rights in relation with standards, which are of crucial importance for telecommunications. Standards may be either the results of international standardization, or *de facto* standards and the property of undertakings.

113. Producers of equipment or suppliers of services are dependent on proprietary standards to ensure the interconnectivity of their computer resources. An undertaking which owns a dominant network architecture may abuse its dominant position by refusing to provide the necessary information for the interconnection of other architecture resources to its architecture products. Other possible abuses—similar to those indicated as to the TOs—are, *inter alia*, delays in providing the information, discrimination in the quality of the information, discriminatory

pricing or other trading conditions, and making the information provision subject to the acceptance by the producer, supplier or user of unfair trading conditions.

114. On 1 August 1984, the Commission accepted a unilateral undertaking from IBM to provide other manufacturers with the technical interface information needed to permit competitive products to be used with IBM's then most powerful range of computers, the System/370. The Commission thereupon suspended the proceedings under Article [102] which it had initiated against IBM in December 1980. The IBM Undertaking[28] also contains a commitment relating to SNA formats and protocols.

Notes

[28] Reproduced in full in EC Bulletin 10-1984 (point 3.4.1). As to its continued application, see Commission press release No IP(88) 814 of 15 December 1988.

115. The question how to reconcile copyrights on standards with the competition requirements is particularly difficult. In any event, copyright cannot be used unduly to restrict competition.

C. Abuses of dominant purchasing position

116. Article [102] also applies to behaviour of undertakings holding a dominant purchasing position. The examples of abuses indicated in that Article may therefore also concern that behaviour.

117. The Council Directive 90/531/EEC[29] based on Articles [53(2), 62, 114 and 207 TFEU] on the procurement procedures of entities operating in *inter alia* the telecommunications sector regulates essentially:
   (i) procurement procedures in order to ensure on a reciprocal basis non-discrimination on the basis of nationality; and
   (ii) for products or services for use in reserved markets, not in competitive markets. That Directive, which is addressed to States, does not exclude the application of Article [102] to the purchasing of products within the scope of the Directive. The Commission will decide case by case how to ensure that these different sets of rules are applied in a coherent manner.

Notes

[29] OJ No L 297, 29.10.1990, p.1.

118. Furthermore, both in reserved and competitive markets, practices other than those covered by the Directive may be established in violation of Article [102]. One example is taking advantage of a dominant purchasing position for imposing excessively favourable prices or other trading conditions, in comparison with other purchasers and suppliers (Article [102(a)]). This could result in discrimination under Article [102(c)]. Also obtaining, whether or not through imposition, an exclusive distributorship for the purchased product by the dominant purchaser may constitute an abusive extension of its economic power to other markets (see "*Télémarketing*" Court judgment (Note 23 *supra*)).

119. Another abusive practice could be that of making the purchase subject to licensing by the supplier of standards for the product to be purchased or for other products, to the purchaser itself, or to other suppliers (Article [102(d)]).

120. Moreover, even in competitive markets, discriminatory procedures on the basis of nationality may exist, because national pressures and traditional links of a non-economic nature do not always disappear quickly after the liberalization of the markets. In this case, a systematic exclusion or considerably unfavourable treatment of a supplier, without economic necessity, could be examined under Article [102], especially (b) (limitation of outlets) and (c) (discrimination). In assessing the case, the Commission will substantially examine whether the same criteria for awarding the contract have been followed by the dominant undertaking for all suppliers. The Commission will normally take into account criteria similar to those indicated in Article 27 (1) of the Directive.[30] The purchases in question being outside the scope of the Directive, the Commission will not require that transparent purchasing procedures be pursued.

Notes

30 (See Note 26) Article 27(1)(a) and (b). The criteria on which the contracting entities shall base the award of the contracts shall be: (a) the most economically advantageous tender involving various criteria such as delivery date, period for completion, running costs, cost-effectiveness, quality, aesthetic and functional characteristics, technical merit, after-sales services and technical assistance, commitments with regard to spare parts, security of supplies and price; or (b) the lowest price only.

D. Effect on trade between Member States

121. The same principle outlined regarding Article [101] applies here. Moreover, in certain circumstances, such as the case of the elimination of a competitor by an undertaking holding a dominant position, although trade between Member States is not directly affected, for the purposes of Article [102] it is sufficient to show that there will be repercussions on the competitive structure of the common market.

VI. APPLICATION OF ARTICLES [101] AND [102] IN THE FIELD OF SATELLITES

122. The development of this sector is addressed globally by the Commission in the "Green Paper on a common approach in the field of satellite communications in the European Community" of 20 November 1990 (Doc. COM(90) 490 final). Due to the increasing importance of satellites and the particular uncertainty among undertakings as to the application of competition rules to individual cases in this sector, it is appropriate to address the sector in a distinct section in these guidelines.

123. State regulations on satellites are not covered by the Commission Directives under Article [106 TFEU] respectively on terminals and services mentioned above except in the Directive on terminals which contemplates receive-only satellite stations not connected to a public network. The Commission's position on the regulatory framework compatible with the Treaty competition rules is stated in the Commission Green Paper on satellites mentioned above.

124. In any event the Treaty competition rules fully apply to the satellites domain, *inter alia*, Articles [101] and [102] to undertakings. Below is indicated how the principles set out above, in particular in Sections IV and V, apply to satellites.

125. Agreements between European TOs in particular within international conventions may play an important role in providing European satellites systems and a harmonious development of satellite services throughout the Community. These benefits are taken into consideration under competition rules, provided that the agreements do not contain restrictions which are not indispensable for the attainment of these objectives.

126. Agreements between TOs concerning the operation of satellite systems in the broadest sense may be caught by Article [101]. As to space segment capacity, the TOs are each other's competitors, whether actual or potential. In pooling together totally or partially their supplies of space segment capacity they may restrict competition between themselves. Moreover, they are likely to restrict competition vis-à-vis third parties to the extent that their agreements contain provisions with this object or effect: for instance provisions limiting their supplies in quality and/or quantity, or restricting their business autonomy by imposing directly or indirectly a coordination between these third parties and the parties to the agreements. It should be examined whether such agreements could qualify for an exemption under Article [101(3)] provided that they are notified. However, restrictions on third parties' ability to compete are likely to preclude such an exemption. It should also be examined whether such agreements strengthen any individual or collective dominant position of the parties, which also would exclude the granting of an exemption. This could be the case in particular if the agreement provides that the parties are exclusive distributors of the space segment capacity provided by the agreement.

127. Such agreements between TOs could also restrict competition as to the uplink with respect to which TOs are competitors. In certain cases the customer for satellite communication has the choice between providers in several countries, and his choice will be substantially determined by the quality, price and other sales conditions of each provider. This choice will be even ampler since uplink is being progressively liberalized and to the extent that the application of EEC rules to State

legislations will open up the uplink markets. Community-wide agreements providing directly or indirectly for coordination as to the parties' uplink provision are therefore caught by Article [101].

128. Agreements between TOs and private operators on space segment capacity may be also caught by Article [101], as that provision applies, *inter alia*, to cooperation, and in particular joint venture agreements. These agreements could be exempted if they bring specific benefits such as technology transfer, improvement of the quality of the service or enabling better marketing, especially for a new capacity, outweighing the restrictions. In any event, imposing on customers the bundled uplink and space segment capacity provision is likely to exclude an exemption since it limits competition in uplink provision to the detriment of the customer's choice, and in the current market situation will almost certainly strengthen the TOs' dominant position in violation of Article [102]. An exemption is unlikely to be granted also when the agreement has the effect of reducing substantially the supply in an oligopolistic market, and even more clearly when an effect of the agreement is to prevent the only potential competitor of a dominant provider in a given market from offering its services independently. This could amount to a violation of Article [102]. Direct or indirect imposition of any kind of agreement by a TO, for instance by making the uplink subject to the conclusion of an agreement with a third party, would constitute an infringement of Article [102].

VII. RESTRUCTURING IN TELECOMMUNICATIONS

129. Deregulation, the objective of a single market for 1992 and the fundamental changes in the telecommunications technology have caused wide strategic restructuring in Europe and throughout the world as well. They have mostly taken the form of mergers and joint ventures.

(a) Mergers

130. In assessing telecom mergers in the framework of Council Regulation (EEC) No 4064/89 on the control of concentrations between undertakings [31] the Commission will take into account, *inter alia*, the following elements.

Notes
[31] OJ No L 395, 30.12.1989, p.1; Corrigendum OJ No L 257, 21.9.1990, p.13.

---

131. Restructuring moves are in general beneficial to the European telecommunications industry. They may enable the companies to rationalize and to reach the critical mass necessary to obtain the economies of scale needed to make the important investments in research and development. These are necessary to develop new technologies and to remain competitive in the world market.

However, in certain cases they may also lead to the anti-competitive creation or strengthening of dominant positions.

132. The economic benefits resulting from critical mass must be demonstrated. The concentration operation could result in a mere aggregation of market shares, unaccompanied by restructuring measures or plans. This operation may create or strengthen Community or national dominant positions in a way which impedes competition.

133. When concentration operations have this sole effect, they can hardly be justified by the objective of increasing the competitivity of Community industry in the world market. This objective, strongly pursued by the Commission, rather requires competition in EEC domestic markets in order that the EEC undertakings acquire the competitive structure and attitude needed to operate in the world market.

134. In assessing concentration cases in telecommunications, the Commission will be particularly vigilant to avoid the strengthening of dominant positions through integration. If dominant service providers are allowed to integrate into the equipment market by way of mergers, access to this market by other equipment suppliers may be seriously hindered. A dominant service provider is likely to give preferential treatment to its own equipment subsidiary.

Moreover, the possibility of disclosure by the service provider to its subsidiary of sensitive information obtained from competing equipment manufacturers can put the latter at a competitive disadvantage.

The Commission will examine case by case whether vertical integration has such effects or rather is likely to reinforce the competitive structure in the Community.

135. The Commission has enforced principles on restructuring in a case concerning the GEC and Siemens joint bid for Plessey.[32]

Notes

[32] Commission Decision rejecting Plessey's complaint against the GEC-Siemens bid (Case IV/33.018 *GEC-Siemens/ Plessey*), OJ No C 239, 25.9.1990, p.2.

136. Article [101(1)] applies to the acquisition by an undertaking of a minority shareholding in a competitor where, *inter alia*, the arrangements involve the creation of a structure of cooperation between the investor and the other undertakings, which will influence these undertakings' competitive conduct.[33]

Notes

[33] *British American Tobacco Company Ltd and RJ Reynolds Industries Inc. v Commission* (Joined Cases 142 and 156/84) of 17.11.1987, [1987] ECR 4487.

(b) Joint ventures

137. A joint venture can be of a cooperative or a concentrative nature. It is of a cooperative nature when it has as its object or effect the coordination of the competitive behaviour of undertakings which remain independent. The principles governing cooperative joint ventures are to be set out in Commission guidelines to that effect. Concentrative joint ventures fall under Regulation (EEC) No 4064/89.[34]

Notes

[34] OJ No C 203, 14.8.1990, p.10.

138. In some of the latest joint venture cases the Commission granted an exemption under Article [101(3)] on grounds which are particularly relevant to telecommunications. Precisely in a decision concerning telecommunications, the "*Optical Fibres*" case,[35] the Commission considered that the joint venture enabled European companies to produce a high technology product, promoted technical progress, and facilitated technology transfer. Therefore, the joint venture permits European companies to withstand competition from non-Community producers, especially in the USA and Japan, in an area of fast-moving technology characterized by international markets. The Commission confirmed this approach in the " *Canon-Olivetti*" case.[36]

Notes

[35] Decision 86/405/EEC, OJ No L 236, 22.8.86, p.30.
[36] Decision 88/88/EEC, OJ No L 52, 26.2.1988, p.51.

VIII. Impact of the International Conventions on the Application of EEC Competition Rules to Telecommunications

139. International conventions (such as the Convention of International Telecommunication Union (ITU) or Conventions on Satellites) play a fundamental role in ensuring worldwide cooperation for the provision of international services. However, application of such international conventions on telecommunications by EEC Member States must not affect compliance with the EEC law, in particular with competition rules.

140. Article [351 TFEU] regulates this matter.[37] The relevant obligations provided in the various conventions or related Acts do not pre-date the entry into force of the Treaty. As to the ITU and World Administrative Telegraph and Telephone Conference (WATTC), whenever a revision or a new adoption of the ITU Convention or of the WATTC Regulations occurs, the ITU or WATTC members recover their freedom of action. The Satellites Conventions were adopted much later.

Moreover, as to all conventions, the application of EEC rules does not seem to affect the fulfilment of obligations of Member States vis-à-vis third countries. Article [351] does not protect obligations between EEC Member States entered into in international treaties. The purpose of Article [351] is to protect the right of third countries only and it is not intended to crystallize the acquired international treaty rights of Member States to the detriment of the EEC Treaty's objectives or of the Community interest. Finally, even if Article [351(1)] did apply, the Member States concerned would nevertheless be obliged to take all appropriate steps to eliminate incompatibility between their obligations vis-à-vis third countries and the EEC rules. This applies in particular where Member States acting collectively have the statutory possibility to modify the international convention in question as required, e.g. in the case of the Eutelsat Convention.

Notes

37 "The rights and obligations arising from agreements concluded before the entry into force of this Treaty between one or more Member States on the one hand and one or more third countries on the other, shall not be affected by the provisions of this Treaty. To the extent that such agreements are not compatible with this Treaty, the Member State or States concerned shall take all appropriate steps to eliminate the incompatibilities established. Member States shall, where necessary, assist each other to this end and shall, where appropriate, adopt a common attitude…"

141. As to the WATTC Regulations, the relevant provisions of the Regulations in force from 9 December 1988 are flexible enough to give the parties the choice whether or not to implement them or how to implement them.
     In any event, EEC Member States, by signing the Regulations, have made a joint declaration that they will apply them in accordance with their obligations under the EEC Treaty.

142. As to the International Telegraph and Telephone Consultative Committee (CCITT) recommendations, competition rules apply to them.

143. Members of the CCITT are, pursuant to Article 11(2) of the International Telecommunications Convention, "administrations" of the Members of the ITU and recognized private operating agencies ("RPOAs') which so request with the approval of the ITU members which have recognized them. Unlike the members of the ITU or the Administrative Conferences which are States, the members of the CCITT are telecommunications administrations and RPOAs. Telecommunications administrations are defined in Annex 2 to the International Telecommunications Conventions as "tout service ou département gouvernemental responsable des mesures à prendre pour exécuter les obligations de la Convention Internationale des télécommunications et des règlements" [any government service or department responsible for the measures to be taken to fulfil the obligations laid down in the International Convention on Telecommunications and Regulations]. The CCITT meetings are in fact attended by TOs. Article 11(2) of the International Telecommunications Convention clearly provides that telecommunications administrations and RPOAs are members of the CCITT by themselves. The fact that, because of the ongoing process of separation of the regulatory functions from the business activity, some national authorities participate in the CCITT is not in contradiction with the nature of undertakings of other members. Moreover, even if the CCITT membership became governmental as a result of the separation of regulatory and operational activities of the telecommunications administrations, Article [106] in association with Article [101] could still apply either against the State measures implementing the CCITT recommendations and the recommendations themselves on the basis of Article [106(1)], or if there is no such national implementing measure, directly against the telecommunications organizations which followed the recommendation.38

Notes

38 See Commission Decision 87/3/EEC *ENI/Montedison*, OJ No L 5, 7.1.1987, p.13.

144. In the Commission's view, the CCITT recommendations are adopted, *inter alia*, by undertakings. Such CCITT recommendations, although they are not legally binding, are agreements between undertakings or decisions by an association of undertakings. In any event, according to the case law of the Commission and the European Court of Justice39 a statutory body entrusted with certain public functions and including some members appointed by the government of a Member State may be an "association of undertakings' if it represents the trading interests of other members and takes decisions or makes agreements in pursuance of those interests.

The Commission draws attention to the fact that the application of certain provisions in the context of international conventions could result in infringements of the [EU] competition rules:

— As to the WATTC Regulations, this is the case for the respective provisions for mutual agreement between TOs on the supply of international telecommunications services (Article 1(5)), reserving the choice of telecommunications routes to the TOs (Article 3(3)), recommending practices equivalent to price agreements (Articles [6(1)(1), 6(1)(2)]), and limiting the possibility of special arrangements to activities meeting needs within and/or between the territories of the Members concerned (Article 9) and only where existing arrangements cannot satisfactorily meet the relevant telecommunications needs (Opinion PL A).

— CCITT recommendations D1 and D2 as they stand at the date of the adoption of these guidelines could amount to a collective horizontal agreement on prices and other supply conditions of international leased lines to the extent that they lead to a coordination of sales policies between TOs and therefore limit competition between them. This was indicated by the Commission in a CCITT meeting on 23 May 1990. The Commission reserves the right to examine the compatibility of other recommendations with Article [101].

— The agreements between TOs concluded in the context of the Conventions on Satellites are likely to limit competition contrary to Article [101] and/or [102] on the grounds set out in paragraphs 126 to 128 above.

Notes

39 See *Pabst & Richarz/BNIA*, OJ No L 231, 21.8.1976, p.24, *AROW/BNIC*, OJ No L 379, 31.12.1982, p.1, and Case 123/83 *BNIC v Clair* [1985] ECR 391.

E8

NOTICE ON THE APPLICATION OF THE COMPETITION RULES TO ACCESS AGREEMENTS IN THE TELECOMMUNICATIONS SECTOR

Framework, Relevant Markets and Principles (98/C 265/02)

(Text with EEA relevance)

Official Journal C 265, 22.8.1998, p.2

Celex No: 31998Y0822(01)

EUR-Lex permanent link: <http://eur-lex.europa.eu/LexUriServ/LexUriServ.do?uri=CELEX:31998Y0822(01):EN:NOT>

Commentary

Notice: B&C: 12.045, 12.070 **F&N:** 12.149
points 83–100: B&C: 12.075
points 89–97: B&C: 12.077
points 110–116: B&C: 10.070

points 113–115: **B&C:** 12.078
points 117–119: **B&C:** 10.115

PREFACE

In the telecommunications industry, access agreements are central in allowing market participants the benefits of liberalisation.

The purpose of this notice is threefold:

— to set out access principles stemming from Community competition law as shown in a large number of Commission decisions in order to create greater market certainty and more stable conditions for investment and commercial initiative in the telecoms and multimedia sectors;

— to define and clarify the relationship between competition law and sector specific legislation under the Article [114 TFEU]* framework (in particular this relates to the relationship between competition rules and open network provision legislation);

— to explain how competition rules will be applied in a consistent way across the sectors involved in the provision of new services, and in particular to access issues and gateways in this context.

Notes

* Ed note: please see the Note on the Lisbon Treaty at p.xvii in regard to article renumbering introduced by the Lisbon Treaty.

INTRODUCTION

1. The timetable for full liberalisation in the telecommunications sector has now been established, and most Member States had to remove the last barriers to the provision of telecommunications networks and services in a competitive environment to consumers by 1 January 1998.[1] As a result of this liberalisation a second set of related products or services will emerge as well as the need for access to facilities necessary to provide these services. In this sector, interconnection to the public switched telecommunications network is a typical, but not the only, example of such access.

   The Commission has stated that it will define the treatment of access agreements in the telecommunications sector under the competition rules.[2] This notice, therefore, addresses the issue of how competition rules and procedures apply to access agreements in the context of harmonised EC and national regulation in the telecommunications sector.

Notes

[1] According to Commission Directives 96/19/EC and 96/2/EC (cited in footnote 3), certain Member States may request a derogation from full liberalisation for certain limited periods. This notice is without prejudice to such derogations, and the Commission will take account of the existence of any such derogation when applying the competition rules to access agreements, as described in this notice.

See: Commission Decision 97/114/EC of 27 November 1996 concerning the additional implementation periods requested by Ireland for the implementation of Commission Directives 90/388/EEC and 96/2/EC as regards full competition in the telecommunications markets (OJ L 41, 12.2.1997, p.8); Commission Decision 97/310/EC of 12 February 1997 concerning the granting of additional implementation periods to the Portuguese Republic for the implementation of Commission Directives 90/388/EEC and 96/2/EC as regards full competition in the telecommunications markets (OJ L 133, 24.5.1997, p.19); Commission Decision 97/568/EC of 14 May 1997 on the granting of additional implementation periods to Luxembourg for the implementation of Directive 90/388/EEC as regards full competition in the telecommunications markets (OJ L 234, 26.8.1997, p.7); Commission Decision 97/603/EC of 10 June 1997 concerning the granting of additional implementation periods to Spain for the implementation of Commission Directive 90/388/EEC as regards full competition in the telecommunications markets (OJ L 243, 5.9.1997, p.48); Commission Decision 97/607/EC of 18 June 1997 concerning the granting of additional implementation periods to Greece for the implementation of Directive 90/388/EEC as regards full competition in the telecommunications markets (OJ L 245, 9.9.1997, p.6).

[2] Communication by the Commission of 3 May 1995 to the European Parliament and the Council, Consultation on the Green Paper on the liberalisation of telecommunications infrastructure and cable television networks, COM(95) 158 final.

2. The regulatory framework for the liberalisation of telecommunications consists of the liberalisation directives issued under Article [106] of the Treaty and the harmonisation Directives under

Article [114], including in particular the open network provision (ONP) framework. The ONP framework provides harmonised rules for access and interconnection to the telecommunications networks and the voice telephony services. The legal framework provided by the liberalisation and harmonisation legislation is the background to any action taken by the Commission in its application of the competition rules. Both the liberalisation legislation (the Article [106] Directives)[3] and the harmonisation legislation (the ONP Directives)[4] are aimed at ensuring the attainment of the objectives of the Community as laid out in Article 3 of the [EC] Treaty*, and specifically, the establishment of "a system ensuring that competition in the internal market is not distorted" and "an internal market characterised by the abolition, as between Member States, of obstacles to the free movement of goods, persons, services and capital".

Notes

* Ed note: see now Articles 3 to 6 TFEU.

3 Commission Directive 88/301/EEC of 16 May 1988, on competition in the markets in telecommunications terminal equipment (OJ L 131, 27.5.1988, p.73)[**]; Commission Directive 90/388/EEC of 28 June 1990 on competition in the markets for telecommunications services (OJ L 192, 24.7.1990, p.10) (the "Services Directive")[*]; Commission Directive 94/46/EC of 13 October 1994, amending Directive 88/301/EEC and Directive 90/388/EEC in particular with regard to satellite communications (OJ L 268, 19.10.1994, p.15); Commission Directive 95/51/EC of 18 October 1995 amending Directive 90/388/EEC with regard to the abolition of the restrictions on the use of cable television networks for the provision of already liberalised telecommunications services (OJ L 256, 26.10.1995, p.49) [*]; Commission Directive 96/2/EC of 16 January 1996 amending Directive 90/388/EEC with regard to mobile and personal communications (OJ L 20, 26.1.1996, p.59) [*]; Commission Directive 96/19/EC of 13 March 1996 amending Directive 90/388/EEC with regard to the implementation of full competition in the telecommunications markets (OJ L 74, 22.3.1996, p.13) (the "Full Competition Directive")[*].
[* Directive 90/388/EEC was repealed by Commission Directive 2002/77/EC of 16 September 2002 (OJ L 249, 17.9.2002).]
[** See now Commission Directive 2008/63/EC of 20 June 2008 on competition in the markets in telecommunications terminal equipment (Codified version), (OJ L 162, 21.6.2008, p.20).]

4 Interconnection agreements are the most significant form of access agreement in the telecommunications sector. A basic framework for interconnection agreements is set up by the rules on open network provision (ONP), and the application of competition rules must be seen against this background: Directive 97/13/EC of the European Parliament and of the Council of 10 April 1997 on a common framework for authorisations and individual licences in the field of telecommunications services (OJ L 117, 7.5.1997, p.15) (the "Licensing Directive")[*]; Directive 97/33/EC of the European Parliament and of the Council of 30 June 1997 on interconnection in Telecommunications with regard to ensuring universal service and interoperability through application of the principles of open network provision (ONP) (OJ L 199, 26.7.1997, p.32) (the "Interconnection Directive")[*]; Council Directive 90/387/EEC of 28 June 1990 on the establishment of the internal market for telecommunications services through the implementation of open network provision (OJ L 192, 24.7.1990, p.1) (the "Framework Directive")[*]; Council Directive 92/44/EEC of 5 June 1992 on the application of open network provision to leased lines (OJ L 165, 19.6.1992, p.27) (the "Leased Lines Directive")[*]; Directive 95/62/EEC of the European Parliament and of the Council of 13 December 1995 on the application of open network provision to voice telephony (OJ L 321, 30.12.1995, p.6) replaced by Directive 98/10/EC of the European Parliament and of the Council of 26 February 1998 on the application of open network provision (ONP) to voice telephony and on universal service for telecommunications in a competitive environment (OJ L 101, 1.4.1998, p.24) (the "Voice Telephony Directive")[*]; Directive 97/66/EC of the European Parliament and of the Council of 15 December 1997 concerning the processing of personal data and the protection of privacy in the telecommunications sector (OJ L 24, 30.1.1998, p.1) (the "Data Protection Directive").[**]
[* These Directives were repealed by Directive 2002/21/EC of 7 March 2002 on a common regulatory framework for electronic communications networks and services (Framework Directive) (OJ L 108, 24.4.2002).]
[** Directive 97/66/EC was repealed by Directive 2002/58/EC of 12 July 2002 concerning the processing of personal data and the protection of privacy in the electronic communications sector (Directive on privacy and electronic communications) (OJ L 201, 31.7.2002).]

3. The Commission has published Guidelines on the application of EEC competition rules in the telecommunications sector.[5] The present notice is intended to build on those Guidelines, which do not deal explicitly with access issues.

Notes

5 OJ C 233, 6.9.1991, p.2.

4. In the telecommunications sector, liberalisation and harmonisation legislation permit and simplify the task of Community firms in embarking on new activities in new markets and

consequently allow users to benefit from increased competition. These advantages must not be jeopardised by restrictive or abusive practices of undertakings: the Community's competition rules are therefore essential to ensure the completion of this development. New entrants must in the initial stages be guaranteed the right to have access to the networks of incumbent telecommunications operators (TOs). Several authorities, at the regional, national and Community levels, have a role in regulating this sector. If the competition process is to work well in the internal market, effective coordination between these institutions must be ensured.

5.   Part I of the notice sets out the legal framework and details how the Commission intends to avoid unnecessary duplication of procedures while safeguarding the rights of undertakings and users under the competition rules. In this context, the Commission's efforts to encourage decentralised application of the competition rules by national courts and national authorities aim at achieving remedies at a national level, unless a significant Community interest is involved in a particular case. In the telecommunications sector, specific procedures in the ONP framework likewise aim at resolving access problems in the first place at a decentralised, national level, with a further possibility for conciliation at Community level in certain circumstances. Part II defines the Commission's approach to market definition in this sector. Part III details the principles that the Commission will follow in the application of the competition rules: it aims to help telecommunications market participants shape their access agreements by explaining the competition law requirements. The principles set out in this Notice apply not only to traditional fixed line telecommunications, but also to all telecommunications, including areas such as satellite communications and mobile communications.

6.   The notice is based on the Commission's experience in several cases,[6] and certain studies into this area carried out on behalf of the Commission.[7] As this notice is based on the generally applicable competition rules, the principles set out in this Notice will, to extent that comparable problems arise, be equally applicable in other areas, such as access issues in digital communications sectors generally. Similarly, several of the principles contained in the Treaty will be of relevance to any company occupying a dominant position including those in fields other than telecommunications.

Notes

[6] In the telecommunications area, notably: Commission Decision 91/562/EEC of 18 October 1991, *Eirpage* (OJ L 306, 7.11.1991, p.22); Commission Decisions 96/546/EC and 96/547/EC of 17 July 1996, *Atlas and Phoenix* (OJ L 239, 19.9.1996, p.23 and p.57); and Commission Decision 97/780/EC of 29 October 1997, *Unisource* (OJ L 318, 20.11.1997, p.1). There are also a number of pending cases involving access issues.

[7] Competition aspects of interconnection agreements in the telecommunications sector, June 1995; Competition aspects of access by service providers to the resources of telecommunications operators, December 1995. See also Competition Aspects of Access Pricing, December 1995.

---

7.   The present notice is based on issues which have arisen during the initial stages of transition from monopolies to competitive markets. Given the convergence of the telecommunications, broadcasting and information technology sectors,[8] and the increased competition on these markets, other issues will emerge. This may make it necessary to adapt the scope and principles set out in this notice to these new sectors.

Notes

[8] See the Commission's Green Paper of 3 December 1997 on the Convergence of the Telecommunications, Media and Information Technology sectors and the implications for Regulation—Towards an information society approach (COM(97) 623).

---

8.   The principles set out in this document will apply to practices outside the Community to the extent that such practices have an effect on competition within the Community and affect trade between Member States. In applying the competition rules, the Commission is obliged to comply with the Community's obligations under the WTO telecommunications agreement.[9] The Commission also notes that there are continuing discussions with regard to the international accounting rates system in the context of the ITU. The present notice is without prejudice to the Commission's position in these discussions.

Notes

9 See Council Decision 97/838/EC of 28 November 1997 concerning the conclusion on behalf of the European Community, as regards matters within its competence, of the results of the WTO negotiations on basic telecommunications services (OJ L 347, 18.12.1997, p.45).

9. This notice does not in any way restrict the rights conferred on individuals or undertakings by Community law, and is without prejudice to any interpretation of the Community competition rules that may be given by the Court of Justice or the Court of First Instance of the European Communities. This notice does not purport to be a comprehensive analysis of all possible competition problems in this sector: other problems already exist and more are likely to arise in the future.

10. The Commission will consider whether the present notice should be amended or added to in the light of experience gained during the first period of a liberalised telecommunications environment.

PART I—FRAMEWORK

1. Competition rules and sector specific regulation

11. Access problems in the broadest sense of the word can be dealt with at different levels and on the basis of a range of legislative provisions, of both national and Community origin. A service provider faced with an access problem such as a TO's unjustified refusal to supply (or on reasonable terms) a leased line needed by the applicant to provide services to its customers could therefore contemplate a number of routes to seek a remedy. Generally speaking, aggrieved parties will experience a number of benefits, at least in an initial stage, in seeking redress at a national level. At a national level, the applicant has two main choices, namely (1) specific national regulatory procedures now established in accordance with Community law and harmonised under Open Network Provision (see footnote 4), and (2) an action under national and/or Community law before a national court or national competition authority.[10]

Notes

10 In the case of the ONP Leased Lines Directive[*], a first stage is foreseen which allows the aggrieved user to appeal to the National Regulatory Authority. This can offer a number of advantages. In the telecommunications areas where experience has shown that companies are often hesitant to be seen as complainants against the TO on which they heavily depend not only with respect to the specific point of conflict but also much broader and far-reaching sense, the procedures foreseen under ONP are an attractive option. ONP procedures furthermore can cover a broader range of access problems than could be approached on the basis of the competition rules. Finally, these procedures can offer users the advantage of proximity and familiarity with national administrative procedures; language is also a factor to be taken into account.

Under the ONP Leased Lines Directive, if a solution cannot be found at the national level, a second stage is organised at the European level (conciliation procedure). An agreement between the parties involved must then be reached within two months, with a possible extension of one month if the parties agree.

[* See note 4 above.]

12. Complaints made to the Commission under the competition rules in the place of or in addition to national courts, national competition authorities and/or to national regulatory authorities under ONP procedures will be dealt with according to the priority which they deserve in view of the urgency, novelty and transnational nature of the problem involved and taking into account the need to avoid duplicate proceedings (see points 23 *et seq.*).

13. The Commission recognises that national regulatory authorities (NRAs)[11] have different tasks, and operate in a different legal framework from the Commission when the latter is applying the competition rules. First, the NRAs operate under national law, albeit often implementing European law. Secondly, that law, based as it is on considerations of telecommunications policy, may have objectives different to, but consistent with, the objectives of Community competition policy. The Commission cooperates as far as possible with the NRAs, and NRAs also have to cooperate between themselves in particular when dealing with cross-border issues.[12] Under Community law, national authorities, including regulatory authorities and competition authorities, have a duty not to approve any practice or agreement contrary to Community competition law.

Notes

11 An NRA is a national telecommunications regulatory body created by a Member State in the context of the services directive as amended, and the ONP framework. The list of NRAs is published regularly in the Official Journal of the European Communities, and a copy of the latest list can be found at <http://www.ispo.cec.be>.

12 Articles 9 and 17 of the Interconnection Directive[*].[*See note 4 above.]

14. Community competition rules are not sufficient to remedy all of the various problems in the telecommunications sector. NRAs therefore have a significantly wider ambit and a significant and far-reaching role in the regulation of the sector. It should also be noted that as a matter of Community law, the NRAs must be independent.[13]

Notes

13 Article 7 of the Services Directive (see footnote 3), and Article 5a of the ONP Framework Directive (see footnote 4). See also Communication by the Commission to the European Parliament and the Council on the status and implementation of Directive 90/388/EEC on competition in the markets for telecommunications services (OJ C 275, 20.10.1995, p.2).
See also the judgment of the Court of Justice of the European Communities in Case C-91/94, *Thierry Tranchant and Telephones Stores* [1995] ECR I-3911.

15. It is also important to note that the ONP Directives impose on TOs having significant market power certain obligations of transparency and non-discrimination that go beyond those that would normally be imposed under Article [102] of the Treaty. ONP Directives lay down obligations relating to transparency, obligations to supply and pricing practices. These obligations are enforced by the NRAs, which also have jurisdiction to take steps to ensure effective competition.[14]

Notes

14 The Interconnection Directive cited in footnote 4, Article 9(3).

16. In relation to Article [102], this notice is written, for convenience, in most respects as if there was one telecommunications operator occupying a dominant position. This will not necessarily be the case in all Member States: for example new telecommunications networks offering increasingly wide coverage will develop progressively. These alternative telecommunications networks may, or may ultimately, be large and extensive enough to be partly or even wholly substitutable for the existing national networks, and this should be kept in mind. The existence and the position on the market of competing operators will be relevant in determining whether sole or joint dominant positions exist: references to the existence of a dominant position in this notice should be read with this in mind.

17. Given the Commission's responsibility for the Community's competition policy, the Commission must serve the Community's general interest. The administrative resources at the Commission's disposal to perform its task are necessarily limited and cannot be used to deal with all the cases brought to its attention. The Commission is therefore obliged, in general, to take all organisational measures necessary for the performance of its task and, in particular, to establish priorities.[15]

Notes

15 Judgments of the Court of First Instance of the European Communities: Case T-24/90, *Automec v Commission* [1992] ECR II-2223, at paragraph 77 and Case T-114/92 *BEMIM* [1995] ECR II-147.

18. The Commission has therefore indicated that it intends, in using its decision-making powers, to concentrate on notifications, complaints and own-initiative proceedings having particular political, economic or legal significance for the Community.[16] Where these features are absent in a particular case, notifications will not normally be dealt with by means of a formal decision, but rather a comfort letter (subject to the consent of the parties), and complaints should, as a rule, be handled by national courts or other relevant authorities. In this context, it should be noted that the competition rules are directly effective[17] so that Community competition law is enforceable in the national courts. Even where other Community legislation has been respected, this does not remove the need to comply with the Community competition rules.[18]

Notes

16 Notice on cooperation between national courts and the Commission in applying Articles [101] and [102] of the [Treaty on the Functioning of the European Union] (OJ C 39, 13.2.1993, p.6, at paragraph 14). [Ed note: see now Commission Notice on the co-operation between the Commission and the courts of the EU Member States in the application of Articles [101 and 102 TFEU] (OJ C 101, 27.4.2004, p.54), reproduced at B7.]
Notice on cooperation between national competition authorities and the Commission (OJ C 313, 15.10.1997, p.3). [Ed note: see now Commission Notice on cooperation within the Network of Competition Authorities (OJ C 101, 27.4.2004, p.43), reproduced at B6.]
17 Case 127/73, *BRT v SABAM* [1974] ECR 51.
18 Case 66/86, *Ahmed Saeed* [1989] ECR 838.

19. Other national authorities, in particular NRAs acting within the ONP framework, have jurisdiction over certain access agreements (which must be notified to them). However, notification of an agreement to an NRA does not make notification of an agreement to the Commission unnecessary. The NRAs must ensure that actions taken by them are consistent with Community competition law.[19] This duty requires them to refrain from action that would undermine the effective protection of Community law rights under the competition rules.[20] Therefore, they may not approve arrangements which are contrary to the competition rules.[21] If the national authorities act so as to undermine those rights, the Member State may itself be liable for damages to those harmed by this action.[22] In addition, NRAs have jurisdiction under the ONP directives to take steps to ensure effective competition.[23]

Notes

19 They must not, for example, encourage or reinforce or approve the results of anti-competitive behaviour:
— *Ahmed Saeed*, see footnote 18;
— Case 153/93, *Federal Republic of Germany v Delta Schiffahrtsges* [1994] ECR I-2517,
— Case 267/86, *Van Eycke* [1988] ECR 4769.
20 Case 13/77, GB-Inno-BM/ATAB [1977] ECR 2115, at paragraph 33:
"while it is true that Article [102] is directed at undertakings, nonetheless it is also true that the Treaty imposes a duty on Member States not to adopt or maintain in force any measure which could deprive the provision of its effectiveness."
21 For further duties of national authorities see: Case 103/88, *Fratelli Costanzo* [1989] ECR 1839. See *Ahmed Saeed*, cited in footnote 18:
"Articles [10] and [86] of the [EC] Treaty must be interpreted as (i) prohibiting the national authorities from encouraging the conclusion of agreements on tariffs contrary to Article [101(1)] or Article [102] of the Treaty, as the case may be; (ii) precluding the approval by those authorities of tariffs resulting from such agreements".
22 Joined Cases C-6/90, and C-9/90 *Francovich* [1991] ECR I-5357; Joined Cases C-46/93, *Brasserie de Pêcheur v Germany* and Case C-48/93, *R v Secretary of State for Transport ex parte Factortame and others* [1996] ECR I-1029.
23 For example, recital 18 of the Leased Lines Directive and Article 9(3) of the ONP Interconnection Directive, see footnote 4.

20. Access agreements in principle regulate the provision of certain services between independent undertakings and do not result in the creation of an autonomous entity which would be distinct from the parties to the agreements. Access agreements are thus generally outside the scope of the Merger Regulation.[24]

Notes

24 Council Regulation (EEC) No 4064/89 of 21 December 1989 on the control of concentrations between undertakings (OJ L 395, 30.12.1989, p.1); corrected version (OJ L 257, 21.9.1990, p.13). (Ed note: see now Council Regulation (EC) No 139/2004 (OJ L 24, 29.1.2004, p.1), reproduced at D1.]

21. Under Regulation No 17,[25] the Commission could be seised of an issue relating to access agreements by way of a notification of an access agreement by one or more of the parties involved,[26] by way of a complaint against a restrictive access agreement or against the behaviour of a dominant company in granting or refusing access,[27] by way of a Commission own-initiative procedure into such a grant or refusal, or by way of a sector inquiry.[28] In addition, a complainant may request that the Commission take interim measures in circumstances where there is an urgent risk of serious and irreparable harm to the complainant or to the public interest.[29] It should however, be noted in cases of great urgency that procedures before national courts can usually result more quickly in an order to end the infringements than procedures before the Commission.[30]

Notes

25 Council Regulation No 17 of 6 February 1962, First Regulation implementing Articles [101] and [102] of the Treaty (OJ 13, 21.2.1962, p.204). [Ed note: see now Council Regulation (EC) No 1/2003 (OJ L 1, 4.1.2003, p.1) reproduced at B2.]

26 Articles 2 and 4(1) of Regulation No 17.

27 Article 3 of Regulation No 17.

28 Articles 3 and 12 of Regulation No 17.

29 Case 792/79R, *Camera Care v Commission* [1980] ECR 119. See also Case T-44/90, *La Cinq v Commission* [1992] ECR II-1.

30 See point 16 of the Notice cited in footnote 16.

22. There are a number of areas where agreements will be subject to both the competition rules and national or European sector specific measures, most notably Internal Market measures. In the telecommunications sector, the ONP Directives aim at establishing a regulatory regime for access agreements. Given the detailed nature of ONP rules and the fact that they may go beyond the requirements of Article [102], undertakings operating in the telecommunications sector should be aware that compliance with the Community competition rules does not absolve them of their duty to abide by obligations imposed in the ONP context, and vice versa.

2. Commission action in relation to access agreements[31]

Notes

31 Article 2 or Article 4(1) of Regulation No 17.

23. Access agreements taken as a whole are of great significance, and it is therefore appropriate for the Commission to spell out as clearly as possible the Community legal framework within which these agreements should be concluded. Access agreements having restrictive clauses will involve issues under Article [101]. Agreements which involve dominant, or monopolist, undertakings involve Article [102] issues: concerns arising from the dominance of one or more of the parties will generally be of greater significance in the context of a particular agreement than those under Article [101].
Notifications

24. In applying the competition rules, the Commission will build on the ONP Directives which set a framework for action at the national level by the NRAs. Where agreements fall within Article [101(1)], they must be notified to the Commission if they are to benefit from an exemption under Article [101(3)]. Where agreements are notified, the Commission intends to deal with some notifications by way of formal decisions, following appropriate publicity in the Official Journal of the European Communities, and in accordance with the principles set out below. Once the legal principles have been clearly established, the Commission then proposes to deal by way of comfort letter with other notifications raising the same issues.

3. Complaints

25. Natural or legal persons with a legitimate interest may, under certain circumstances, submit a complaint to the Commission, requesting that the Commission by decision require that an infringement of Article [101] or Article [102] of the Treaty be brought to an end. A complainant may additionally request that the Commission take interim measures where there is an urgent risk of serious and irreparable harm.[32] A prospective complainant has other equally or even more effective options, such as an action before a national court. In this context, it should be noted that procedures before the national courts can offer considerable advantages for individuals and companies, such as in particular:[33]
   — national courts can deal with and award a claim for damages resulting from an infringement of the competition rules,
   — national courts can usually adopt interim measures and order the termination of an infringement more quickly than the Commission is able to do,
   — before national courts, it is possible to combine a claim under Community law with a claim under national law,
   — legal costs can be awarded to the successful applicant before a national court.

Furthermore, the specific national regulatory principles as harmonised under ONP Directives can offer recourse both at the national level and, if necessary, at the Community level.

Notes

32 *Camera Care* and *La Cinq*, referred to at footnote 29.
33 See point 16 of the Notice cited in footnote 16.

3.1. Use of national and ONP procedures

26. As referred to above[34] the Commission will take into account the Community interest of each case brought to its attention. In evaluating the Community interest, the Commission examines "…the significance of the alleged infringement as regards the functioning of the common market, the probability of establishing the existence of the infringement and the scope of the investigation required in order to fulfil, under the best possible conditions, its task of ensuring that Articles [101] and [102] are complied with…".[35]

Another essential element in this evaluation is the extent to which a national judge is in a position to provide an effective remedy for an infringement of Article [101] or [102]. This may prove difficult, for example, in cases involving extra-territorial elements.

Notes

34 See point 18.
35 See *Automec*, cited in footnote 15, at paragraph 86.

27. Article [101(1)] and Article [102] of the Treaty produce direct effects in relations between individuals which must be safeguarded by national courts.[36] As regards actions before the NRA, the ONP Interconnection Directive provides that such an authority has power to intervene and order changes in relation to both the existence and content of access agreements. NRAs must take into account "the need to stimulate a competitive market" and may impose conditions on one or more parties, inter alia, "to ensure effective competition".[37]

Notes

36 *BRT v SABAM*, cited in footnote 17.
37 Article 9(1) and (3) of the ONP Interconnection Directive[*]. [* See note 4 above.]

28. The Commission may itself be seised of a dispute either pursuant to the competition rules, or pursuant to an ONP conciliation procedure. Multiple proceedings might lead to unnecessary duplication of investigative efforts by the Commission and the national authorities. Where complaints are lodged with the Commission under Article 3 of Regulation No 17 while there are related actions before a relevant national or European authority or court, the Directorate-General for Competition will generally not initially pursue any investigation as to the existence of an infringement under Article [101] or [102] of the Treaty. This is subject, however, to the following points.

3.2. Safeguarding complainant's rights

29. Undertakings are entitled to effective protection of their Community law rights.[38] Those rights would be undermined if national proceedings were allowed to lead to an excessive delay of the Commission's action, without a satisfactory resolution of the matter at a national level. In the telecommunications sector, innovation cycles are relatively short, and any substantial delay in resolving an access dispute might in practice be equivalent to a refusal of access, thus prejudging the proper determination of the case.

Notes

38 Case 14/83, *Von Colson* [1984] ECR 1891.

30. The Commission therefore takes the view that an access dispute before an NRA should be resolved within a reasonable period of time, normally speaking not extending beyond six months of the matter first being drawn to the attention of that authority. This resolution could take the form of

either a final determination of the action or another form of relief which would safeguard the rights of the complainant. If the matter has not reached such a resolution then, *prima facie*, the rights of the parties are not being effectively protected, and the Commission would in principle, upon request by the complainant, begin its investigations into the case in accordance with its normal procedures, after consultation and in cooperation with the national authority in question. In general, the Commission will not begin such investigations where there is already an ongoing action under ONP conciliation procedures.

31. In addition, the Commission must always look at each case on its merits: it will take action if it feels that in a particular case, there is a substantial Community interest affecting, or likely to affect, competition in a number of Member States.

3.3. Interim measures

32. As regards any request for interim measures, the existence or possibility of national proceedings is relevant to the question of whether there is a risk of serious and irreparable harm. Such proceedings should, *prima facie*, remove the risk of such harm and it would therefore not be appropriate for the Commission to grant interim measures in the absence of evidence that the risk would nevertheless remain.

33. The availability of and criteria for interim injunctive relief is an important factor which the Commission must take into account in reaching this *prima facie* conclusion. If interim injunctive relief were not available, or if such relief was not likely adequately to protect the complainant's rights under Community law, the Commission would consider that the national proceedings did not remove the risk of harm, and could therefore commence its examination of the case.

4. Own-initiative investigation and sector inquiries

34. If it appears necessary, the Commission will open an own-initiative investigation. It can also launch a sector inquiry, subject to consultation of the Advisory Committee of Member State competition authorities.

5. Fines[*]

35. The Commission may impose fines of up to 10% of the annual worldwide turnover of undertakings which intentionally or negligently breach Article [101(1)] or Article [102].[39] Where agreements have been notified pursuant to Regulation No 17 for an exemption under Article [101(3)], no fine may be levied by the Commission in respect of activities described in the notification[40] for the period following notification. However, the Commission may withdraw the immunity from fines by informing the undertakings concerned that, after preliminary examination, it is of the opinion that Article [101(1)] of the Treaty applies and that application of Article [101(3)] is not justified.[41]

Notes

[39] Article 15(2) of Regulation No 17.
[40] Article 15(5) of Regulation No 17.
[41] Article 15(6) of Regulation No 17.
[* Ed note: see now Council Regulation (EC) No 1/2003 (OJ L 1, 4.1.2003, p.1), Article 23, reproduced at B2.]

36. The ONP Interconnection Directive has two particular provisions which are relevant to fines under the competition rules. First, it provides that interconnection agreements must be communicated to the relevant NRAs and made available to interested third parties, with the exception of those parts which deal with the commercial strategy of the parties.[42] Secondly, it provides that the NRA must have a number of powers which it can use to influence or amend the interconnection agreements.[43] These provisions ensure that appropriate publicity is given to the agreements, and provide the NRA with the opportunity to take steps, where appropriate, to ensure effective competition on the market.

Notes

[42] Article 6(c) of the ONP Interconnection Directive[*].
[43] Inter alia, at Article 9 of the ONP Interconnection Directive[*].
[* See note 4 above.]

37. Where an agreement has been notified to an NRA, but has not been notified to the Commission, the Commission does not consider it would be generally appropriate as a matter of policy to impose a fine in respect of the agreement, even if the agreement ultimately proves to contain conditions in breach of Article [101]. A fine would, however, be appropriate in some cases, for example where:

(a) the agreement proves to contain provisions in breach of Article [102]; and/or

(b) the breach of Article [101] is particularly serious.

The Commission has recently published Guidelines on how fines will be calculated.[44]

Notes

[44] Guidelines on the method of setting fines imposed pursuant to Article 15(2) of Regulation No 17 and Article 65(5) of the ECSC Treaty (OJ C 9, 14.1.1998, p.3). [Ed note: see now Guidelines on the method of setting fines imposed pursuant to Article 23(2)(a) of Regulation No 1/2003 (OJ C 210, 1.9.2006, p.2), reproduced at B11.]

38. Notification to the NRA is not a substitute for a notification to the Commission and does not limit the possibility for interested parties to submit a complaint to the Commission, or for the Commission to begin an own-initiative investigation into access agreements. Nor does such notification limit the rights of a party to seek damages before a national court for harm caused by anti-competitive agreements.[45]

Notes

[45] See footnote 22.

PART II—RELEVANT MARKETS

39. In the course of investigating cases within the framework set out in Part I above, the Commission will base itself on the approach to the definition of relevant markets set out in the Commission's Notice on the definition of the relevant market for the purposes of Community competition law.[46]

Notes

[46] OJ C 372, 9.12.1997, p.5.

40. Firms are subject to three main sources of competitive constraints; demand substitutability, supply substitutability and potential competition, with the first constituting the most immediate and effective disciplinary force on the suppliers of a given product or service. Demand substitutability is therefore the main tool used to define the relevant product market on which restrictions of competition for the purposes of Article [101(1)] and Article [102] can be identified.

41. Supply substitutability may in appropriate circumstances be used as a complementary element to define relevant markets. In practice it cannot be clearly distinguished from potential competition. Supply side substitutability and potential competition are used for the purpose of determining whether the undertaking has a dominant position or whether the restriction of competition is significant within the meaning of Article [101], or whether there is elimination of competition.

42. In assessing relevant markets it is necessary to look at developments in the market in the short term.

The following sections set out some basic principles of particular relevance to the telecommunications sector.

1. Relevant product market

43. Section 6 of Form A/B defines the relevant product market as follows:

"A relevant product market comprises all those products and/or services which are regarded as interchangeable or substitutable by the consumer, by reason of the products" characteristics, their prices and their intended use".

44. Liberalisation of the telecommunications sector will lead to the emergence of a second type of market, that of access to facilities which are currently necessary to provide these liberalised services. Interconnection to the public switched telecommunications network would be a typical

example of such access. Without interconnection, it will not be commercially possible for third parties to provide, for example, comprehensive voice telephony services.

45. It is clear, therefore, that in the telecommunications sector there are at least two types of relevant markets to consider—that of a service to be provided to end users and that of access to those facilities necessary to provide that service to end users (information, physical network, etc.). In the context of any particular case, it will be necessary to define the relevant access and services markets, such as interconnection to the public telecommunications network, and provision of public voice telephony services, respectively.

46. When appropriate, the Commission will use the test of a relevant market which is made by asking whether, if all the suppliers of the services in question raised their prices by 5 to 10%, their collective profits would rise. According to this test, if their profits would rise, the market considered is a separate relevant market.

47. The Commission considers that the principles under competition law governing these markets remain the same regardless of the particular market in question. Given the pace of technological change in this sector, any attempt to define particular product markets in this notice would run the risk of rapidly becoming inaccurate or irrelevant. The definition of particular product markets—for example, the determination of whether call origination and call termination facilities are part of the same facilities market—is best done in the light of a detailed examination of an individual case.

1.1. Services market

48. This can be broadly defined as the provision of any telecommunications service to users. Different telecommunications services will be considered substitutable if they show a sufficient degree of interchangeability for the end-user, which would mean that effective competition can take place between the different providers of these services.

1.2. Access to facilities

49. For a service provider to provide services to end-users it will often require access to one or more (upstream or downstream) facilities. For example, to deliver physically the service to end-users, it needs access to the termination points of the telecommunications network to which these end-users are connected. This access can be achieved at the physical level through dedicated or shared local infrastructure, either self provided or leased from a local infrastructure provider. It can also be achieved either through a service provider who already has these end-users as subscribers, or through an interconnection provider who has access directly or indirectly to the relevant termination points.

50. In addition to physical access, a service provider may need access to other facilities to enable it to market its service to end users: for example, a service provider must be able to make end-users aware of its services. Where one organisation has a dominant position in the supply of services such as directory information, similar concerns arise as with physical access issues.

51. In many cases, the Commission will be concerned with physical access issues, where what is necessary is access to the network facilities of the dominant TO.[47]

Notes

[47] Interconnection is defined in the Full Competition Directive as "...the physical and logical linking of the telecommunications facilities of organisations providing telecommunications networks and/or telecommunications services, in order to allow the users of one organisation to communicate with the users of the same or another organisation or to access services provided by third organisations."

In the Full Competition Directive and ONP Directives, telecommunications services are defined as "services, whose provision consists wholly or partly in the transmission and/or routing of signals on a telecommunications network."

It therefore includes the transmission of broadcasting signals and CATV networks."

A telecommunications network is itself defined as "...the transmission equipment and, where applicable, switching equipment and other resources which permit the conveyance of signals between defined termination points by wire, by radio, by optical or by other electromagnetic means".

---

52. Some incumbent TOs may be tempted to resist providing access to third party service providers or other network operators, particularly in areas where the proposed service will be in competition with a service provided by the TO itself. This resistance will often manifest itself as unjustified

delay in giving access, a reluctance to allow access or a willingness to allow it only under disadvantageous conditions. It is the role of the competition rules to ensure that these prospective access markets are allowed to develop, and that incumbent TOs are not permitted to use their control over access to stifle developments on the services markets.

53. It should be stressed that in the telecommunications sector, liberalisation can be expected to lead to the development of new, alternative networks which will ultimately have an impact on access market definition involving the incumbent telecommunications operator.

2. *Relevant geographic market*

54. Relevant geographic markets are defined in Form A/B as follows:
"The relevant geographic market comprises the area in which the undertakings concerned are involved in the supply and demand of products or services, in which the conditions of competition are sufficiently homogeneous and which can be distinguished from neighbouring areas because the conditions of competition are appreciably different in those areas."

55. As regards the provision of telecommunication services and access markets, the relevant geographic market will be the area in which the objective conditions of competition applying to service providers are similar, and competitors are able to offer their services. It will therefore be necessary to examine the possibility for these service providers to access an end-user in any part of this area, under similar and economically viable conditions. Regulatory conditions such as the terms of licences, and any exclusive or special rights owned by competing local access providers are particularly relevant.[48]

Notes

[48] Commission Decision 94/894/EC of 13 December 1994, *Eurotunnel* (OJ L 354, 21.12.1994, p.66).

Part III—Principles

56. The Commission will apply the following principles in cases before it.

57. The Commission has recognised that " Articles [101] and [102]…constitute law in force and enforceable throughout the Community. Conflicts should not arise with other Community rules because Community law forms a coherent regulatory framework…it is obvious that Community acts adopted in the telecommunications sector are to be interpreted in a way consistent with competition rules, so as to ensure the best possible implementation of all aspects of the Community telecommunications policy…This applies, inter alia, to the relationship between competition rules applicable to undertakings and the ONP rules".[49]

Notes

[49] See Guidelines cited in footnote 5, at paragraphs 15 and 16.

58. Thus, competition rules continue to apply in circumstances where other Treaty provisions or secondary legislation are applicable. In the context of access agreements, the internal market and competition provisions of Community law are both important and mutually reinforcing for the proper functioning of the sector. Therefore in making an assessment under the competition rules, the Commission will seek to build as far as possible on the principles established in the harmonisation legislation. It should also be borne in mind that a number of the competition law principles set out below are also covered by specific rules in the context of the ONP framework. Proper application of these rules should often avoid the need for the application of the competition rules.

59. As regards the telecommunications sector, attention should be paid to the cost of universal service obligations. Article [106(2)] of the Treaty may justify exceptions to the principles of Articles [101] and [102]. The details of universal service obligations are a regulatory matter. The field of application of Article [106(2)] has been specified in the Article [106] Directives in the telecommunications sector, and the Commission will apply the competition rules in this context.

60. Articles [101] and [102] of the Treaty apply in the normal manner to agreements or practices which have been approved or authorised by a national authority,[50] or where the national authority has required the inclusion of terms in an agreement at the request of one or more of the parties involved.

Notes

50 Commission Decision 82/896/EEC of 15 December 1982, *AROW/BNIC* (OJ L 379, 31.12.1982, p.19).

61. However, if a NRA were to require terms which were contrary to the competition rules, the undertakings involved would in practice not be fined, although the Member State itself would be in breach of Article 3(g)* [EC] and [Article 4, paragraph 3, TEU][51] and therefore subject to challenge by the Commission under Article [258]. Additionally, if an undertaking having special or exclusive rights within the meaning of Article [106], or a State-owned undertaking, were required or authorised by a national regulator to engage in behaviour constituting an abuse of its dominant position, the Member State would also be in breach of Article [106](1) and the Commission could adopt a decision requiring termination of the infringement.[52]

Notes

* Ed note: Article 3(1)(g) EC was repealed by the Treaty of Lisbon. Article 3(1) EC was replaced in substance by Articles 3 to 6 TFEU. The nearest to an equivalent provision to Article 3(1)(g) EC in the TFEU is Article 3(1)(b) TFEU ("The Union shall have exclusive competence in the following areas: . . . (b) the establishing of the competition rules necessary for the functioning of the internal market".

51 See footnote 18.

52 Joined Cases C-48 and 66/90 *Netherlands and others v Commission* [1992] ECR I-565.

62. NRAs may require strict standards of transparency, obligations to supply and pricing practices on the market, particularly where this is necessary in the early stages of liberalisation. When appropriate, legislation such as the ONP framework will be used as an aid in the interpretation of the competition rules.[53] Given the duty resting on NRAs to ensure that effective competition is possible, application of the competition rules is likewise required for an appropriate interpretation of the ONP principles. It should also be noted that many of the issues set out below are also covered by rules under the Full Competition Directive and the ONP Licensing and Data protection Directives: effective enforcement of this regulatory framework should prevent many of the competition issues set out below from arising.

Notes

53 See *Ahmed Saeed*, cited in footnote 18, where internal market legislation relating to pricing was used as an aid in determining what level of prices should be regarded as unfair for the purposes of Article [102].

1. Dominance (Article [102])

63. In order for an undertaking to provide services in the telecommunications services market, it may need to obtain access to various facilities. For the provision of telecommunications services, for example, interconnection to the public switched telecommunications network will usually be necessary. Access to this network will almost always be in the hands of a dominant TO. As regards access agreements, dominance stemming from control of facilities will be the most relevant to the Commission's appraisal.

Commentary
point 63: B&C: 12.069

64. Whether or not a company is dominant does not depend only on the legal rights granted to that company. The mere ending of legal monopolies does not put an end to dominance. Indeed, notwithstanding the liberalisation Directives, the development of effective competition from alternative network providers with adequate capacity and geographic reach will take time.

65. The judgment of the Court of Justice in *Tetra Pak* [54] is also likely to prove important in the telecommunications sector. The Court held that given the extremely close links between the dominated and non-dominated market, and given the extremely high market share on the dominated market, Tetra Pak was "in a situation comparable to that of holding a dominant position on the markets in question as a whole."

The *Tetra Pak* case concerned closely related horizontal markets: the analysis is equally applicable, however, to closely related vertical markets which will be common in the telecommunications sector. In the telecommunications sector, it is often the case that a particular operator has an extremely strong position on infrastructure markets, and on markets downstream of that infrastructure. Infrastructure costs also typically constitute the single largest cost of the downstream operations. Further, operators will often face the same competitors on both the infrastructure and downstream markets.

Notes

54 On each market, Tetra Pak was faced with the same potential customers and actual competitors. Case C-333/94 P, *Tetra Pak International SA v Commission* [1996] ECR I-5951.

66. It is therefore possible to envisage a number of situations where there will be closely related markets, together with an operator having a very high degree of market power on at least one of those markets.

67. It these circumstances are present, it may be appropriate for the Commission to find that the particular operator was in a situation comparable to that of holding a dominant position on the markets in question as a whole.

68. In the telecommunications sector, the concept of "essential facilities" will in many cases be of relevance in determining the duties of dominant TOs. The expression essential facility is used to describe a facility or infrastructure which is essential for reaching customers and/or enabling competitors to carry on their business, and which cannot be replicated by any reasonable means.55

Notes

55 See also the definition included in the "Additional commitment on regulatory principles by the European Communities and their Member States" used by the Group on basic telecommunications in the context of the World Trade Organisation (WTO) negotiations:

"Essential facilities mean facilities of a public telecommunications transport network and service that:

(a) are exclusively or predominantly provided by a single or limited number of suppliers; and

(b) cannot feasibly be economically or technically substituted in order to provide a service."

69. A company controlling the access to an essential facility enjoys a dominant position within the meaning of Article [102]. Conversely, a company may enjoy a dominant position pursuant to Article [102] without controlling an essential facility.

1.1. Services market

70. One of the factors used to measure the market power of an undertaking is the sales attributable to that undertaking, expressed as a percentage of total sales in the market for substitutable services in the relevant geographic area. As regards the services market, the Commission will assess, inter alia, the turnover generated by the sale of substitutable services, excluding the sale or internal usage of interconnection services and the sale or internal usage of local infrastructure,56 taking into consideration the competitive conditions and the structure of supply and demand on the market.

Notes

56 Case 6/72 *Continental Can* [1973] ECR 215.

1.2. Access to facilities

71. The concept of "access" as referred to in point 45 can relate to a range of situations, including the availability of leased lines enabling a service provider to build up its own network, and interconnection in the strict sense, that is interconnecting two telecommunication networks, for example mobile and fixed. In relation to access it is probable that the incumbent operator will remain dominant for some time after the legal liberalisation has taken place. The incumbent operator, which controls the facilities, is often also the largest service provider, and it has in the past not needed to distinguish between the conveyance of telecommunications services and the provision of these services to end-users. Traditionally, an operator who is also a service provider has not required its downstream operating arm to pay for access, and therefore it has not been easy to calculate the revenue to be allocated to the facility. In a case where an operator is providing both access and services it is necessary to separate so far as possible the revenues as the basis for the calculation of the company's share of whichever market is involved. Article 8(2) of

the Interconnection Directive addresses this issue by introducing a requirement for separate accounting for "activities related to interconnection—covering both interconnection services provided internally and interconnection services provided to others—and other activities". The proposed Commission Recommendation on Accounting Separation in the context of Interconnection will also be helpful in this regard.

72. The economic significance of obtaining access also depends on the coverage of the network with which interconnection is sought. Therefore, in addition to using turnover figures, the Commission will, where possible, also take into account the number of customers who have subscribed to services offered by the dominant company comparable with those which the service provider requesting access intends to provide. Accordingly, market power for a given undertaking will be measured partly by the number of subscribers who are connected to termination points of the telecommunications network of that undertaking expressed as a percentage of the total number of subscribers connected to termination points in the relevant geographic area.

Supply-side substitutability

73. As stated in point 41, supply-side substitutability is also relevant to the question of dominance. A market share of over 50%[57] is usually sufficient to demonstrate dominance although other factors will be examined. For example, the Commission will examine the existence of other network providers, if any, in the relevant geographic area to determine whether such alternative infrastructures are sufficiently dense to provide competition to the incumbent's network and the extent to which it would be possible for new access providers to enter the market.

Notes

[57] It should be noted in this context that under the ONP framework an organisation may be notified as having significant market power. The determination of whether an organisation does or does not have significant market power depends on a number of factors, but the starting presumption is that an organisation with a market share of more than 25% will normally be considered to have significant market power. The Commission will take account of whether an undertaking has been notified as having significant market power under the ONP rules in its appraisal under the competition rules. It is clear, however, that the notion of significant market power generally describes a position of economic power on a market less than that of dominance: the fact that an undertaking has significant market power under the ONP rules will generally therefore not lead to a presumption of dominance, although in a particular situation, this may prove to be the case. One important factor to be taken into consideration, however, will be whether the market definition used in the ONP procedures is appropriate for use in applying the competition rules.

Other relevant factors

74. In addition to market share data, and supply-side substitutability, in determining whether an operator is dominant the Commission will also examine whether the operator has privileged access to facilities which cannot reasonably be duplicated within an appropriate time frame, either for legal reasons or because it would cost too much.

75. As competing access providers appear and challenge the dominance of the incumbent, the scope of the rights they receive from Member States' authorities, and notably their territorial reach, will play an important part in the determination of market power. The Commission will closely follow market evolution in relation to these issues and will take account of any altered market conditions in its assessment of access issues under the competition rules.

1.3. Joint dominance

76. The wording of Article [102] makes it clear that the Article also applies when more than one company shares a dominant position. The circumstances in which a joint dominant position exists, and in which it is abused, have not yet been fully clarified by the case law of the Community judicature or the practice of the Commission, and the law is still developing.

77. The words of Article [102] ("abuse by one or more undertakings") describe something different from the prohibition of anti-competitive agreements or concerted practices in Article [101]. To hold otherwise would be contrary to the usual principles of interpretation of the Treaty, and would render the words pointless and without practical effect. This does not, however, exclude the parallel application of Articles [101] and [102] to the same agreement or practice, which has been upheld by the Commission and the Court in a number of cases,[58] nor is there anything to prevent the Commission from taking action only under one of the provisions, when both apply.

Notes
58 Case 85/76 *Hoffmann-La Roche* [1979] ECR 461. Commission Decision 89/113/EEC of 21 December 1988, *Decca Navigator System* (OJ L 43, 15.2.1989, p.27).

78. Two companies, each dominant in a separate national market, are not the same as two jointly dominant companies. For two or more companies to be in a joint dominant position, they must together have substantially the same position vis-à-vis their customers and competitors as a single company has if it is in a dominant position. With specific reference to the telecommunications sector, joint dominance could be attained by two telecommunications infrastructure operators covering the same geographic market.

79. In addition, for two or more companies to be jointly dominant it is necessary, though not sufficient, for there to be no effective competition between the companies on the relevant market. This lack of competition may in practice be due to the fact that the companies have links such as agreements for cooperation, or interconnection agreements. The Commission does not, however, consider that either economic theory or Community law implies that such links are legally necessary for a joint dominant position to exist.[59] It is a sufficient economic link if there is the kind of interdependence which often comes about in oligopolistic situations. There does not seem to be any reason in law or in economic theory to require any other economic link between jointly dominant companies. This having been said, in practice such links will often exist in the telecommunications sector where national TOs nearly inevitably have links of various kinds with one another.

Notes
59 Commission Decision 92/553/EEC of 22 July 1992, *Nestlé/Perrier* (OJ L 356, 5.12.1992, p.1).

Commentary
point 79: **B&C:** 10.050

80. To take as an example access to the local loop, in some Member States this could well be controlled in the near future by two operators—the incumbent TO and a cable operator. In order to provide particular services to consumers, access to the local loop of either the TO or the cable television operator is necessary. Depending on the circumstances of the case and in particular on the relationship between them, it is possible that neither operator holds a dominant position: together, however, they may hold a joint monopoly of access to these facilities. In the longer term, technological developments may lead to other local loop access mechanisms being viable, such as energy networks: the existence of such mechanisms will be taken into account in determining whether dominant positions or joint dominant positions exist.

2. Abuse of dominance

81. Application of Article [102] presupposes the existence of a dominant position and some link between the dominant position and the alleged abusive conduct. It will often be necessary in the telecommunications sector to examine a number of associated markets, one or more of which may be dominated by a particular operator. In these circumstances, there are a number of possible situations where abuses could arise:
   — conduct on the dominated market having effects on the dominated market,[60]
   — conduct on the dominated market having effects on markets other than the dominated market,[61]
   — conduct on a market other than the dominated market and having effects on the dominated market,[62]
   — conduct on a market other than the dominated market and having effects on a market other than the dominated market.[63]

Notes
60 The most common situation.
61 Joined Cases 6/73 and 7/73 *Commercial Solvents v Commission* [1974] ECR 223 and Case 311/84 *CBEM v CLT and IPB* [1985] ECR 3261.
62 Case C-62/86, *AKZO v Commission* [1991] ECR I-3359 and Case T-65/89 *BPB Industries and British Gypsum v Commission* [1993] ECR II-389.

63 Case C-333/94 P, *Tetra Pak International v Commission* [1996] ECR I-5951. In this fourth case, application of Article [102] can only be justified by special circumstances (*Tetra Pak*, at paragraphs 29 and 30).

82. Although the factual and economic circumstances of the telecommunications sector are often novel, in many cases it is possible to apply established competition law principles. When looking at competition problems in this sector, it is important to bear in mind existing case law and Commission decisional practice on, for example, leveraging market power, discrimination and bundling.

2.1. Refusal to grant access to facilities and application of unfavourable terms

83. A refusal to give access may be prohibited under Article [102] if the refusal is made by a company which is dominant because of its control of facilities, as incumbent TOs will usually be for the foreseeable future. A refusal may have "the effect of hindering the maintenance of the degree of competition still existing in the market or the growth of that competition".[64]

A refusal will only be abusive if it has exploitative or anti-competitive effects. Service markets in the telecommunications sector will initially have few competitive players and refusals will therefore generally affect competition on those markets. In all cases of refusal, any justification will be closely examined to determine whether it is objective.

Notes
64 Case 85/76, *Hoffmann-La Roche* [1979] ECR 461.

Commentary
point 83: B&C: 12.075

84. Broadly there are three relevant scenarios:
    (a) a refusal to grant access for the purposes of a service where another operator has been given access by the access provider to operate on that services market;
    (b) a refusal to grant access for the purposes of a service where no other operator has been given access by the access provider to operate on that services market;
    (c) a withdrawal of access from an existing customer.

Discrimination

85. As to the first of the above scenarios, it is clear that a refusal to supply a new customer in circumstances where a dominant facilities owner is already supplying one or more customers operating in the same downstream market would constitute discriminatory treatment which, if it would restrict competition on that downstream market, would be an abuse. Where network operators offer the same, or similar, retail services as the party requesting access, they may have both the incentive and the opportunity to restrict competition and abuse their dominant position in this way. There may, of course, be justifications for such refusal—for example, vis-à-vis applicants which represent a potential credit risk. In the absence of any objective justifications, a refusal would usually be an abuse of the dominant position on the access market.

86. In general terms, the dominant company's duty is to provide access in such a way that the goods and services offered to downstream companies are available on terms no less favourable than those given to other parties, including its own corresponding downstream operations.

Essential facilities

87. As to the second of the above situations, the question arises as to whether the access provider should be obliged to contract with the service provider in order to allow the service provider to operate on a new service market. Where capacity constraints are not an issue and where the company refusing to provide access to its facility has not provided access to that facility, either to its downstream arm or to any other company operating on that services market, then it is not clear what other objective justification there could be.

88. In the transport field,[65] the Commission has ruled that a firm controlling an essential facility must give access in certain circumstances.[66] The same principles apply to the telecommunications sector. If there were no commercially feasible alternatives to the access being requested, then unless access is granted, the party requesting access would not be able to operate on the service market. Refusal in this case would therefore limit the development of new markets, or new products on

those markets, contrary to Article [102(b)], or impede the development of competition on existing markets. A refusal having these effects is likely to have abusive effects.

Notes

65 Commission Decision 94/19/EC of 21 December 1993, *Sea Containers v. Stena Sealink*—Interim measure (OJ L 15, 18.1.1994, p.8). Commission Decision 94/119/EEC of 21 December 1993, *Port of Rødby (Denmark)* (OJ L 55, 26.2.1994, p.52).

66 See also (among others):

Judgments of the Court of Justice and the Court of First Instance: Cases 6 and 7/73 *Commercial Solvents v Commission* [1974] ECR 223; Case 311/84, *Télémarketing* [1985] ECR 3261; Case C-18/88 *RTT v GB-Inno* [1991] ECR I-5941; Case C-260/89, *Elliniki Radiophonia Teleorassi* [1991] ECR I-2925; Cases T-69, T-70 and T-76/89, *RTE, BBC and ITP v Commission* [1991] ECR II-485, 535, 575; Case C-271/90, *Spain v Commission* [1992] ECR I-5833; Cases C-241 and 242/91 P, *RTE and ITP Ltd v Commission* (Magill), [1995] ECR I-743.

Commission Decisions: Commission Decision 76/185/ECSC of 29 October 1975, *National Carbonising Company* (OJ L 35, 10.2.1976, p.6). Commission Decision 88/589/EEC of 4 November 1988, *London European/Sabena* (OJ L 317, 24.11.1988, p.47). Commission Decision 92/213/EEC of 26 February 1992, *British Midland v. Aer Lingus* (OJ L 96, 10.4.1992, p.34); *B&I v Sealink* [1992] 5 CMLR 255; EC Bulletin, No 6–1992, point 1.3.30.

89. The principle obliging dominant companies to contract in certain circumstances will often be relevant in the telecommunications sector. Currently, there are monopolies or virtual monopolies in the provision of network infrastructure for most telecom services in the Community. Even where restrictions have already been, or will soon be, lifted, competition in downstream markets will continue to depend upon the pricing and conditions of access to upstream network services that will only gradually reflect competitive market forces. Given the pace of technological change in the telecommunications sector, it is possible to envisage situations where companies would seek to offer new products or services which are not in competition with products or services already offered by the dominant access operator, but for which this operator is reluctant to provide access.

90. The Commission must ensure that the control over facilities enjoyed by incumbent operators is not used to hamper the development of a competitive telecommunications environment. A company which is dominant on a market for services and which commits an abuse contrary to Article [102] on that market may be required, in order to put an end to the abuse, to supply access to its facility to one or more competitors on that market. In particular, a company may abuse its dominant position if by its actions it prevents the emergence of a new product or service.

91. The starting point for the Commission's analysis will be the identification of an existing or potential market for which access is being requested. In order to determine whether access should be ordered under the competition rules, account will be taken of a breach by the dominant company of its duty not to discriminate (see below) or of the following elements, taken cumulatively:

(a) access to the facility in question is generally essential in order for companies to compete on that related market.[67]

The key issue here is therefore what is essential. It will not be sufficient that the position of the company requesting access would be more advantageous if access were granted—but refusal of access must lead to the proposed activities being made either impossible or seriously and unavoidably uneconomic.

Although, for example, alternative infrastructure may as from 1 July 1996 be used for liberalised services, it will be some time before this is in many cases a satisfactory alternative to the facilities of the incumbent operator. Such alternative infrastructure does not at present offer the same dense geographic coverage as that of the incumbent TO's network;

(b) there is sufficient capacity available to provide access;

(c) the facility owner fails to satisfy demand on an existing service or product market, blocks the emergence of a potential new service or product, or impedes competition on an existing or potential service or product market;

(d) the company seeking access is prepared to pay the reasonable and non-discriminatory price and will otherwise in all respects accept non-discriminatory access terms and conditions;

(e) there is no objective justification for refusing to provide access. Relevant justifications in this context could include an overriding difficulty of providing access to the requesting company, or the need for a facility owner which has undertaken investment aimed at the introduction of a new product or service to have sufficient time and opportunity to use the facility in order to place that new product or service on the market. However, although any justification will have to be examined carefully on a case-by-case basis, it is particularly important in the telecommunications sector that the benefits to end-users which will arise from a competitive environment are not undermined by the actions of the former State monopolists in preventing competition from emerging and developing.

Notes

[67] It would be insufficient to demonstrate that one competitor needed access to a facility in order to compete in the downstream market. It would be necessary to demonstrate that access is necessary for all except exceptional competitors in order for access to be made compulsory.

92. In determining whether an infringement of Article [102] has been committed, **account** will be taken both of the factual situation in that and other geographic areas, and, where relevant, the relationship between the access requested and the technical configuration of the facility.

93. The question of objective justification will require particularly close analysis in this area. In addition to determining whether difficulties cited in any particular case are serious enough to justify the refusal to grant access, the relevant authorities must also decide whether these difficulties are sufficient to outweigh the damage done to competition if access is refused or made more difficult and the downstream service markets are thus limited.

94. Three important elements relating to access which could be manipulated by the access provider in order, in effect, to refuse to provide access are timing, technical configuration and price.

95. Dominant TOs have a duty to deal with requests for access efficiently: undue and inexplicable or unjustified delays in responding to a request for access may constitute an abuse. In particular, however, the Commission will seek to compare the response to a request for access with:
    (a) the usual time frame and conditions applicable when the responding party grants access to its facilities to its own subsidiary or operating branch;
    (b) responses to requests for access to similar facilities in other Member States;
    (c) the explanations given for any delay in dealing with requests for access.

Commentary
point 95: F&N: 4.566

96. Issues of technical configuration will similarly be closely examined in order to determine whether they are genuine. In principle, competition rules require that the party requesting access must be granted access at the most suitable point for the requesting party, provided that this point is technically feasible for the access provider. Questions of technical feasibility may be objective justifications for refusing to supply—for example, the traffic for which access is sought must satisfy the relevant technical standards for the infrastructure—or there may be questions of capacity restraints, where questions of rationing may arise.[68]

Notes
[68] As noted in point 91.

97. Excessive pricing for access, as well as being abusive in itself,[69] may also amount to an effective refusal to grant access.

Notes
[69] See point 105.

98. There are a number of elements of these tests which require careful assessment. Pricing questions in the telecommunications sector will be facilitated by the obligations under ONP Directives to have transparent cost-accounting systems.

Commentary
point 98: B&C: 12.076

99. As to the third of the situations referred to in point 84, some previous Commission decisions and the case law of the Court have been concerned with the withdrawal of supply from downstream competitors. In Commercial Solvents, the Court held that "an undertaking which has a dominant position on the market in raw materials and which, with the object of reserving such raw material for manufacturing its own derivatives, refuses to supply a customer, which is itself a manufacturer of these derivatives, and therefore risks eliminating all competition on the part of this customer, is abusing its dominant position within the meaning of Article [102]".[70]

Notes

[70] Cases 6 and 7/73, *Commercial Solvents* [1974] ECR 223.

100. Although this case dealt with the withdrawal of a product, there is no difference in principle between this case and the withdrawal of access. The unilateral termination of access agreements raises substantially similar issues to those examined in relation to refusals. Withdrawal of access from an existing customer will usually be abusive. Again, objective reasons may be provided to justify the termination. Any such reasons must be proportionate to the effects on competition of the withdrawal.

2.2. Other forms of abuse

101. Refusals to provide access are only one form of possible abuse in this area. Abuses may also arise in the context of access having been granted. An abuse may occur inter alia where the operator is behaving in a discriminatory manner or the operator's actions otherwise limit markets or technical development. The following are non-exhaustive examples of abuse which can take place.

Network configuration

102. Network configuration by a dominant network operator which makes access objectively more difficult for service providers[71] could constitute an abuse unless it were objectively justifiable. One objective justification would be where the network configuration improves the efficiency of the network generally.

Notes

[71] That is to say, to use the network to reach their own customers.

Tying

103. This is of particular concern where it involves the tying of services for which the TO is dominant with those for which it is not.[72] Where the vertically integrated dominant network operator obliges the party requesting access to purchase one or more services[73] without adequate justification, this may exclude rivals of the dominant access provider from offering those elements of the package independently. This requirement could thus constitute an abuse under Article [102]. The Court has further held that "... even where tied sales of two products are in accordance with commercial usage or there is a natural link between the two products in question, such sales may still constitute abuse within the meaning of Article [102] unless they are objectively justified...".[74]

Notes

[72] This is also dealt with under the ONP framework: see Article 7(4) of the Interconnection Directive, Article 12(4) of the Voice telephony Directive and Annex II to the ONP Framework Directive.

[73] Including those which are superfluous to the party requesting access, or indeed those which may constitute services which that party itself would like to provide for its customers.

[74] *Tetra Pak International*, cited in footnote 63.

Commentary

point 103: B&C: 12.079

Pricing

104. In determining whether there is a pricing problem under the competition rules, it will be necessary to demonstrate that costs and revenues are allocated in an appropriate way. Improper allocation

of costs and interference with transfer pricing could be used as mechanisms for disguising excessive pricing, predatory pricing or a price squeeze.

Excessive pricing

105. Pricing problems in connection with access for service providers to a dominant operator's facilities will often revolve around excessively high prices:[75] In the absence of another viable alternative to the facility to which access is being sought by service providers, the dominant or monopolistic operator may be inclined to charge excessive prices.

Notes

[75] The Commission Communication of 27 November 1996 on Assessment Criteria for National Schemes for the Costing and Financing of Universal Service and Guidelines for the Operation of such Schemes will be relevant for the determination of the extent to which the universal service obligation can be used to justify additional charges related to the sharing of the net cost in the provision of universal service (COM(96) 608). See also the reference to the universal service obligation in point 59.

106. An excessive price has been defined by the Court of Justice as being "excessive in relation to the economic value of the service provided".[76] In addition the Court has made it clear that one of the ways this could be calculated is as follows:
    "This excess could, inter alia, be determined objectively if it were possible for it to be calculated by making a comparison between the selling price of the product in question and its cost of production".[77]

Notes

[76] Case 26/75, *General Motors Continental v Commission* [1975] ECR 1367, at paragraph 12.
[77] Case 27/76, *United Brands Company and United Brands Continental BV v Commission* [1978] ECR 207.

107. It is necessary for the Commission to determine what the actual costs for the relevant product are. Appropriate cost allocation is therefore fundamental to determining whether a price is excessive. For example, where a company is engaged in a number of activities, it will be necessary to allocate relevant costs to the various activities, together with an appropriate contribution towards common costs. It may also be appropriate for the Commission to determine the proper cost allocation methodology where this is a subject of dispute.

108. The Court has also indicated that in determining what constitutes an excessive price, account may be taken of Community legislation setting out pricing principles for the particular sector.[78]

Notes

[78] *Ahmed Saeed*, cited in footnote 18, at paragraph 43.

109. Further, comparison with other geographic areas can also be used as an indicator of an excessive price: the Court has held that if possible a comparison could be made between the prices charged by a dominant company, and those charged on markets which are open to competition.[79] Such a comparison could provide a basis for assessing whether or not the prices charged by the dominant company were fair.[80] In certain circumstances, where comparative data are not available, regulatory authorities have sought to determine what would have been the competitive price were a competitive market to exist.[81] In an appropriate case, such an analysis may be taken into account by the Commission in its determination of an excessive price.

Notes

[79] Case 30–87, Corinne Bodson v Pompes funèbres des régions libérées [1988] ECR 2479. See also: Joined Cases 110/88, 241/88 and 242/88 François Lucazeau and others v Société des Auteurs, Compositeurs et Editeurs de Musique (SACEM) and others [1989] ECR 2881, at paragraph 25: "When an undertaking holding a dominant position imposes scales of fees for its services which are appreciably higher than those charged in other Member States and where a comparison of the fee levels has been made on a consistent basis, that difference must be regarded as indicative of an abuse of a dominant position. In such a case it is for the undertaking in question to justify the difference by reference to objective dissimilarities between the situation in the Member State concerned and the situation prevailing in all the other Member States."

80 See ONP rules and Commission Recommendation on Interconnection in a liberalised telecommunications market (OJ L 73, 12.3.1998, p.42 (Text of Recommendation) and OJ C 84, 19.3.1998, p.3 (Communication on Recommendation)).
81 For example, in their calculation of interconnection tariffs.

Predatory pricing

110. Predatory pricing occurs, inter alia, where a dominant firm sells a good or service below cost for a sustained period of time, with the intention of deterring entry, or putting a rival out of business, enabling the dominant firm to further increase its market power and later its accumulated profits. Such unfairly low prices are in breach of Article [102(a)]. Such a problem could, for example, arise in the context of competition between different telecommunications infrastructure networks, where a dominant operator may tend to charge unfairly low prices for access in order to eliminate competition from other (emerging) infrastructure providers. In general a price is abusive if it is below the dominant company's average variable costs or if it is below average total costs and part of an anti-competitive plan.**82** In network industries a simple application of the above rule would not reflect the economic reality of network industries.

Notes
82 *AKZO*, cited in footnote 62.

111. This rule was established in the AKZO case where the Court of Justice defined average variable costs as "those which vary depending on the quantities produced"**83** and explained the reasoning behind the rule as follows:
"A dominant undertaking has no interest in applying such prices except that of eliminating competitors so as to enable it subsequently to raise its prices by taking advantage of its monopolistic position, since each sale generates a loss, namely the total amount of the fixed costs (that is to say, those which remain constant regardless of the quantities produced) and, at least, part of the variable costs relating to the unit produced."

Notes
83 *AKZO*, paragraph 71.

112. In order to trade a service or group of services profitably, an operator must adopt a pricing strategy whereby its total additional costs in providing that service or group of services are covered by the additional revenues earned as a result of the provision of that service or group of services. Where a dominant operator sets a price for a particular product or service which is below its average total costs of providing that service, the operator should justify this price in commercial terms: a dominant operator which would benefit from such a pricing policy only if one or more of its competitors was weakened would be committing an abuse.

113. As indicated by the Court of Justice in AKZO, the Commission must determine the price below which a company could only make a profit by weakening or eliminating one or more competitors. Cost structures in network industries tend to be quite different to most other industries since the former have much larger common and joint costs.

114. For example, in the case of the provision of telecommunications services, a price which equates to the variable cost of a service may be substantially lower than the price the operator needs in order to cover the cost of providing the service. To apply the AKZO test to prices which are to be applied over time by an operator, and which will form the basis of that operator's decisions to invest, the costs considered should include the total costs which are incremental to the provision of the service. In analysing the situation, consideration will have to be given to the appropriate time frame over which costs should be analysed. In most cases, there is reason to believe that neither the very short nor very long run are appropriate.

115. In these circumstances, the Commission will often need to examine the average incremental costs of providing a service, and may need to examine average incremental costs over a longer period than one year.

116. If a case arises, the ONP rules and Commission recommendations concerning accounting requirements and transparency will help to ensure the effective application of Article [102] in this context.

Price squeeze

117. Where the operator is dominant in the product or services market, a price squeeze could constitute an abuse. A price squeeze could be demonstrated by showing that the dominant company's own downstream operations could not trade profitably on the basis of the upstream price charged to its competitors by the upstream operating arm of the dominant company. A loss-making downstream arm could be hidden if the dominant operator has allocated costs to its access operations which should properly be allocated to the downstream operations, or has otherwise improperly determined the transfer prices within the organisation. The Commission Recommendation on Accounting Separation in the context of Interconnection addresses this issue by recommending separate accounting for different business areas within a vertically integrated dominant operator. The Commission may, in an appropriate case, require the dominant company to produce audited separated accounts dealing with all necessary aspects of the dominant company's business. However, the existence of separated accounts does not guarantee that no abuse exists: the Commission will, where appropriate, examine the facts on a case-by-case basis.

118. In appropriate circumstances, a price squeeze could also be demonstrated by showing that the margin between the price charged to competitors on the downstream market (including the dominant company's own downstream operations, if any) for access and the price which the network operator charges in the downstream market is insufficient to allow a reasonably efficient service provider in the downstream market to obtain a normal profit (unless the dominant company can show that its downstream operation is exceptionally efficient).[84]

Notes

[84] Commission Decision 88/518/EEC of 18 July 1988, *Napier Brown/British Sugar* (OJ L 284, 19.10.1988, p.41): the margin between industrial and retail prices was reduced to the point where the wholesale purchaser with packaging operations as efficient as those of the wholesale supplier could not profitably serve the retail market. See also *National Carbonising Company*, cited in footnote 66.

119. If either of these scenarios were to arise, competitors on the downstream market would be faced with a price squeeze which could force them out of the market.

Discrimination

120. A dominant access provider may not discriminate between the parties to different access agreements where such discrimination would restrict competition. Any differentiation based on the use which is to be made of the access rather than differences between the transactions for the access provider itself, if the discrimination is sufficiently likely to restrict or distort actual or potential competition, would be contrary to Article [102]. This discrimination could take the form of imposing different conditions, including the charging of different prices, or otherwise differentiating between access agreements, except where such discrimination would be objectively justified, for example on the basis of cost or technical considerations or the fact that the users are operating at different levels. Such discrimination could be likely to restrict competition in the downstream market on which the company requesting access was seeking to operate, in that it might limit the possibility for that operator to enter the market or expand its operations on that market.[85]

Notes

[85] However, when infrastructure capacity is under-utilised, charging a different price for access depending on the demand in the different downstream markets may be justified to the extent that such differentiation permits a better development of certain markets, and where such differentiation does not restrict or distort competition. In such a case, the Commission will analyse the global effects of such price differentiation on all of the downstream markets.

121. Such discrimination could similarly have an effect an competition where the discrimination was between operators on closely related downstream markets. Where two distinct downstream product markets exist, but one product would be regarded as substitutable for another save for the fact that there was a price difference between the two products, discriminating in the price charged to the providers of these two products could decrease existing or potential competition. For example, although fixed and mobile voice telephony services at present probably constitute

separate product markets, the markets are likely to converge. Charging higher interconnection prices to mobile operators as compared to fixed operators would tend to hamper this convergence, and would therefore have an effect on competition. Similar effects on competition are likely in other telecommunications markets.

Such discrimination would in any event be difficult to justify given the obligation to set cost-related prices.

122. With regard to price discrimination, Article [102(c)] prohibits unfair discrimination by a dominant firm between customers of that firm[86] including discriminating between customers on the basis of whether or not they agree to deal exclusively with that dominant firm.

Notes

[86] Case C-310/93 P, *BPB Industries und British Gypsum v Commission* [1995] ECR I-865, at p.904, applying to discrimination by BPB among customers in the related market for dry plaster.

123. Article 7 of the Interconnection Directive provides that "different tariffs, terms and conditions for interconnection may be set for different categories of organisations which are authorised to provide networks and services, where such differences can be objectively justified on the basis of the type of interconnection provided and/or the relevant national licensing conditions…" (provided that such differences do not result in distortions of competition).

124. A determination of whether such differences result in distortions of competition must be made in the particular case. It is important to remember that Articles [101] and [102] deal with competition and not regulatory matters. Article [102] cannot require a dominant company to treat different categories of customers differently, except where this is the result of market conditions and the principles of Article [102]. On the contrary, Article [102] prohibits dominant companies from discriminating between similar transactions where such a discrimination would have an effect on competition.

125. Discrimination without objective justification as regards any aspects or conditions of an access agreement may constitute an abuse. Discrimination may relate to elements such as pricing, delays, technical access, routing,[87] numbering, restrictions on network use exceeding essential requirements and use of customer network data. However, the existence of discrimination can only be determined on a case-by-case basis. Discrimination is contrary to Article [102] whether or not it results from or is apparent from the terms of a particular access agreement.

Notes

[87] That is to say, to a preferred list of correspondent network operators.

126. There is, in this context, a general duty on the network operator to treat independent customers in the same way as its own subsidiary or downstream service arm. The nature of the customer and its demands may play a significant role in determining whether transactions are comparable. Different prices for customers at different levels (for example, wholesale and retail) do not necessarily constitute discrimination.

127. Discrimination issues may arise in respect of the technical configuration of the access, given its importance in the context of access.

The degree of technical sophistication of the access: restrictions on the type or "level" in the network hierarchy of exchange involved in the access or the technical capabilities of this exchange are of direct competitive significance. These could be the facilities available to support a connection or the type of interface and signalling system used to determine the type of service available to the party requesting access (for example, intelligent network facilities).

The number and/or location of connection points: the requirement to collect and distribute traffic for particular areas at the switch which directly serves that area rather than at a higher level of the network hierarchy may be important. The party requesting access incurs additional expense by either providing links at a greater distance from its own switching centre or being liable to pay higher conveyance charges.

Equal access: the possibility for customers of the party requesting access to obtain the services provided by the access provider using the same number of dialled digits as are used by the customers of the latter is a crucial feature of competitive telecommunications.

Objective justifiction

128. Justifications could include factors relating to the actual operation of the network owned by the access provider, or licensing restrictions consistent with, for example, the subject matter of intellectual property rights.

2.3. Abuses of joint dominant positions

129. In the case of joint dominance (see points 76 *et seq.*) behaviour by one of several jointly dominant companies may be abusive even if others are not behaving in the same way.

130. In addition to remedies under the competition rules, if no operator was willing to grant access, and if there was no technical or commercial justification for the refusal, one would expect that the NRA would resolve the problem by ordering one or more of the companies to offer access, under the terms of the relevant ONP Directive or under national law.

3. Access agreements (Article [101])

131. Restrictions of competition included in or resulting from access agreements may have two distinct effects: restriction of competition between the two parties to the access agreement, or restriction of competition from third parties, for example through exclusivity for one or both of the parties to the agreement. In addition, where one party is dominant, conditions of the access agreement may lead to a strengthening of that dominant position, or to an extension of that dominant position to a related market, or may constitute an unlawful exploitation of the dominant position through the imposition of unfair terms.

132. Access agreements where access is in principle unlimited are not likely to be restrictive of competition within the meaning of Article [101(1)]. Exclusivity obligations in contracts providing access to one company are likely to restrict competition because they limit access to infrastructure for other companies. Since most networks have more capacity than any single user is likely to need, this will normally be the case in the telecommunications sector.

133. Access agreements can have significant pro-competitive effects as they can improve access to the downstream market. Access agreements in the context of interconnection are essential to interoperability of services and infrastructure, thus increasing competition in the downstream market for services, which is likely to involve higher added value than local infrastructure.

134. There is, however, obvious potential for anti-competitive effects of certain access agreements or clauses therein. Access agreements may, for example:
    (a) serve as a means of coordinating prices;
    (b) serve as a means of market sharing;
    (c) have exclusionary effects on third parties;[88]
    (d) lead to an exchange of commercially sensitive information between the parties.

Notes

[88] Commission Decision 94/663/EC of 21 September 1994, *Night Services* (OJ L 259, 7.10.1994, p.20); Commission Decision 94/894/EC, see footnote 48.

135. The risk of price coordination is particularly acute in the telecommunications sector since interconnection charges often amount to 50% or more of the total cost of the services provided, and where interconnection with a dominant operator will usually be necessary. In these circumstances, the scope for price competition is limited and the risk (and the seriousness) of price coordination correspondingly greater.

136. Furthermore, interconnection agreements between network operators may under certain circumstances be an instrument of market sharing between the network operator providing access and the network operator seeking access, instead of the emergence of network competition between them.

137. In a liberalised telecommunications environment, the above types of restrictions of competition will be monitored by the national authorities and the Commission under the competition rules. The right of parties who suffer from any type of anti-competitive behaviour to complain to the Commission is unaffected by national regulation.

Clauses falling within Article [101(1)]

138. The Commission has identified certain types of restriction which would potentially infringe Article [101(1)] of the Treaty and therefore require individual exemption. These clauses will most commonly relate to the commercial framework of the access.

139. In the telecommunications sector, it is inherent in interconnection that parties will obtain certain customer and traffic information about their competitors. This information exchange could in certain cases influence the competitive behaviour of the undertakings concerned, and could easily be used by the parties for collusive practices, such as market sharing.[89] The Interconnection Directive requires that information received from an organisation seeking interconnection be used only for the purposes for which it was supplied. In order to comply with the competition rules and the Interconnection Directives, operators will have to introduce safeguards to ensure that confidential information is only disclosed to those parts of the companies involved in making the interconnection agreements, and to ensure that the information is not used for anti-competitive purposes. Provided that these safeguards are complete and function correctly, there should be no reason in principle why simple interconnection agreements should be caught by Article [101(1)].

Notes

[89] Case T-34/92, *Fiatagri UK and New Holland Ford v Commission* [1994] ECR II-905; Case C-8/95 P, *New Holland Ford v Commission*, judgment of 28 May 1988, [[1998] ECR I-3175); Case T-35/92, *John Deere v Commission* [1994] ECR II-957; Case C-7/95 P, *John Deere v Commission*, judgment of 28 May 1988, [[1998] ECR I-3111] (Cases involving applications brought against Commission Decision 92/157/EEC of 17 February 1992, *UK Agricultural Tractor Registration Exchange*) (OJ L 68, 13.3.1992, p.19).

140. Exclusivity arrangements, for example where traffic would be conveyed exclusively through the telecommunications network of one or both parties rather than to the network of other parties with whom access agreements have been concluded will similarly require analysis under Article [101(3)]. If no justification is provided for such routing, such clauses will be prohibited. Such exclusivity clauses are not, however, an inherent part of interconnection agreements.

141. Access agreements that have been concluded with an anti-competitive object are extremely unlikely to fulfil the criteria for an individual exemption under Article [101(3)].

142. Furthermore, access agreements may have an impact on the competitive structure of the market. Local access charges will often account for a considerable portion of the total cost of the services provided to end-users by the party requesting access, thus leaving limited scope for price competition. Because of the need to safeguard this limited degree of competition, the Commission will therefore pay particular attention to scrutinising access agreements in the context of their likely effects on the relevant markets in order to ensure that such agreements do not serve as a hidden and indirect means for fixing or coordinating end-prices for end-users, which constitutes one of the most serious infringements of Article [101] of the Treaty.[90] This would be of particular concern in oligopolistic markets.

Notes

[90] Case 8/72, *Vereniging van Cementhandelaaren v Commission* [1972] ECR 977; Case 123/85, *Bureau National Interprofessionnel du Cognac v Clair* [1985] ECR 391.

143. In addition, clauses involving discrimination leading to the exclusion of third parties are similarly restrictive of competition. The most important is discrimination with regard to price, quality or other commercially significant aspects of the access to the detriment of the party requesting access, which will generally aim at unfairly favouring the operations of the access provider.

4. Effect on trade between Member States

144. The application of both Article [101] and Article [102] presupposes an effect on trade between Member States.

145. In order for an agreement to have an effect on trade between Member States, it must be possible for the Commission to "foresee with a sufficient degree of probability on the basis of a set of objective factors of law or of fact that the agreement in question may have an influence, direct or indirect, actual or potential, on the pattern of trade between Member States".[91]
It is not necessary for each of the restrictions of competition within the agreement to be capable of affecting trade,[92] provided the agreement as a whole does so.

91 Case 56/65, *STM* [1966] ECR 235, p.249.
92 Case 193/83, *Windsurfing International v Commission* [1986] ECR 611.

146. As regards access agreements in the telecommunications sector, the Commission will consider not only the direct effect of restrictions of competition on inter-state trade in access markets, but also the effects on inter-State trade in downstream telecommunications services. The Commission will also consider the potential of these agreements to foreclose a given geographic market which could prevent undertakings already established in other Member States from competing in this geographic market.

147. Telecommunications access agreements will normally affect trade between Member States as services provided over a network are traded throughout the Community and access agreements may govern the ability of a service provider or an operator to provide any given service. Even where markets are mainly national, as is generally the case at present given the stage of development of liberalisation, abuses of dominance will normally speaking affect market structure, leading to repercussions on trade between Member States.

148. Cases in this area involving issues under Article [102] are likely to relate either to abusive clauses in access agreements, or a refusal to conclude an access agreement on appropriate terms or at all. As such, the criteria listed above for determining whether an access agreement is capable of affecting trade between Member States would be equally relevant here.

Conclusions

149. The Commission considers that competition rules and sector specific regulation form a coherent set of measures to ensure a liberalised and competitive market environment for telecommunications markets in the Community.

150. In taking action in this sector, the Commission will aim to avoid unnecessary duplication of procedures, in particular competition procedures and national/Community regulatory procedures as set out under the ONP framework.

151. Where competition rules are invoked, the Commission will consider which markets are relevant and will apply Articles [101] and [102] in accordance with the principles set out above.

E9

COMMISSION GUIDELINES ON MARKET ANALYSIS AND THE ASSESSMENT OF SIGNIFICANT MARKET POWER

under the community regulatory framework for electronic communications networks and services (2002/C 165/03)*

(Text with EEA relevance)

Official Journal C 165, 11.7.2002, p.6

Celex No: 52002XC0711(02)

EUR-Lex permanent link: <http://eur-lex.europa.eu/LexUriServ/LexUriServ.do?uri=CELEX:52002XC0711(02):EN:NOT>

Notes

* Please see the Note on the Lisbon Treaty at p.xvii in regard to article renumbering introduced by the Lisbon Treaty.

Commentary

Guidelines: B&C: 4.010, 4.049, 10.028, 12.016, 12.018, 12.044, 12.045, 12.070, 12.071 F&N: 13.23, 13.27, 13.28
paras 24–28: B&C: 12.044
paras 26–27: B&C: 4.014
paras 72–106: B&C: 12.108
paras 83–85: B&C: 12.071
paras 86–101: B&C: 12.072
paras 102–106: B&C: 12.072

I. INTRODUCTION

1.1. Scope and purpose of the guidelines

1. These guidelines set out the principles for use by national regulatory authorities (NRAs) in the analysis of markets and effective competition under the new regulatory framework for electronic communications networks and services.

2. This new regulatory framework comprises five Directives: Directive 2002/21/EC of the European Parliament and of the Council of 7 March 2002 on a common regulatory framework for electronic communications networks and services,[1] hereinafter the framework Directive; Directive 2002/20/EC of the European Parliament and of the Council of 7 March 2002 on the authorisation of electronic communications networks and services,[2] hereinafter the authorisation Directive; Directive 2002/19/EC of the European Parliament and of the Council of 7 March 2002 on access to, and interconnection of, electronic communications networks and associated facilities,[3] hereinafter the access Directive; Directive 2002/22/EC of the European Parliament and of the Council of 7 March 2002 on universal service and users' rights relating to electronic communications networks and services,[4] hereinafter the universal service Directive; a Directive of the European Parliament and of the Council concerning the processing of personal data and the protection of privacy in the electronic communications sector.[5] However, until this last Directive is formally adopted, Directive 97/66/EC of the European Parliament and the Council concerning the processing of personal data and protection of privacy in the telecommunications sector,[6] hereinafter the data protection Directive, remains the relevant Directive.

Notes

[1] OJ L 108, 24.4.2002, p.33.
[2] OJ L 108, 24.4.2002, p.21.
[3] OJ L 108, 24.4.2002, p.7.
[4] OJ L 108, 24.4.2002, p.51.
[5] [Directive 2002/58/EC of the European Parliament and of the Council of 12 July 2002 concerning the processing of personal data and the protection of privacy in the electronic communications sector (Directive on privacy and electronic communications), OJ L 201, 31.7.2002, p.37.]
[6] OJ L 24, 30.1.1998, p.1.

3. Under the 1998 regulatory framework, the market areas of the telecommunications sector that were subject to *ex-ante* regulation were laid down in the relevant directives, but were not markets defined in accordance with the principles of competition law. In these areas defined under the 1998 regulatory framework, NRAs had the power to designate undertakings as having significant market power when they possessed 25% market share, with the possibility to deviate from this threshold taking into account the undertaking's ability to influence the market, its turnover relative to the size of the market, its control of the means of access to end-users, its access to financial resources and its experience in providing products and services in the market.

4. Under the new regulatory framework, the markets to be regulated are defined in accordance with the principles of European competition law. They are identified by the Commission in its recommendation on relevant product and service markets pursuant to Article 15(1) of the framework Directive (hereinafter "the Recommendation"). When justified by national circumstances, other

markets can also be identified by the NRAs, in accordance with the procedures set out in Articles 6 and 7 of the framework Directive. In case of transnational markets which are susceptible to *ex-ante* regulation, they will where appropriate be identified by the Commission in a decision on relevant transnational markets pursuant to Article 15(4) of the framework Directive (hereinafter "the Decision on transnational markets").

5. On all of these markets, NRAs will intervene to impose obligations on undertakings only where the markets are considered not to be effectively competitive[7] as a result of such undertakings being in a position equivalent to dominance within the meaning of Article [102 TFEU].[8] The notion of dominance has been defined in the case-law of the Court of Justice as a position of economic strength affording an undertaking the power to behave to an appreciable extent independently of competitors, customers and ultimately consumers. Therefore, under the new regulatory framework, in contrast with the 1998 framework, the Commission and the NRAs will rely on competition law principles and methodologies to define the markets to be regulated *ex-ante* and to assess whether undertakings have significant market power ("SMP") on those markets.

Notes

[7] Except where the new regulatory framework expressly permits obligations to be imposed independently of the competitive state of the market.

[8] Article 14 of the framework Directive.

6. These guidelines are intended to guide NRAs in the exercise of their new responsibilities for defining markets and assessing SMP. They have been adopted by the Commission in accordance with Article 15(2) of the framework Directive, after consultation of the relevant national authorities and following a public consultation, the results of which have been duly taken into account.

7. Under Article 15(3) of the framework Directive, NRAs should take the utmost account of these guidelines. This will be an important factor in any assessment by the Commission of the proportionality and legality of proposed decisions by NRAs, taking into account the policy objectives laid down in Article 8 of the framework Directive.

8. These guidelines specifically address the following subjects: (a) market definition; (b) assessment of SMP; (c) SMP designation; and (d) procedural issues related to all of these subjects.

9. The guidelines have been designed for NRAs to use as follows:
   — to define the geographical dimension of those product and service markets identified in the Recommendation. NRAs will not define the geographic scope of any transnational markets, as any Decision on transnational markets will define their geographic dimension,
   — to carry out, using the methodology set out in Section 3 of the guidelines, a market analysis of the conditions of competition prevailing in the markets identified in the Recommendation and Decision and by NRAs,
   — to identify relevant national or sub-national product and service markets which are not listed in the Recommendation when this is justified by national circumstances and following the procedures set out in Articles 6 and 7 of the framework Directive,
   — to designate, following the market analysis, undertakings with SMP in the relevant market and to impose proportionate *ex-ante* measures consistent with the terms of the regulatory framework as described in Sections 3 and 4 of the guidelines,
   — to assist Member States and NRAs in applying Article 11(1f) of the authorisation Directive, and Article 5(1) of the framework Directive, and thus ensure that undertakings comply with the obligation to provide information necessary for NRAs to determine relevant markets and assess significant market power thereon,
   — to guide NRAs when dealing with confidential information, which is likely to be provided by:
   — undertakings under Article 11(1f) of the authorisation Directive and Article 5(1) of the framework Directive,
   — national competition authorities (NCAs) as part of the cooperation foreseen in Article 3(5) of the framework Directive, and
   — the Commission and a NRA in another Member State as part of the cooperation foreseen in Article 5(2) of the framework Directive.

10. The guidelines are structured in the following way:

    Section 1 provides an introduction and overview of the background, purpose, scope and content of the guidelines. **Section 2** describes the methodology to be used by NRAs to define the geographic scope of the markets identified in the market Recommendation as well as to define relevant markets outside this Recommendation. **Section 3** describes the criteria for assessing SMP in a relevant market. **Section 4** outlines the possible conclusions that NRAs may reach in their market analyses and describes the possible actions that may result. **Section 5** describes the powers of investigation of NRAs, suggests procedures for coordination between NRAs and between NRAs and NCAs, and describes coordination and cooperation procedures between NRAs and the Commission. Finally, **Section 6** describes procedures for public consultation and publication of NRAs' proposed decisions.

11. The major objective of these guidelines is to ensure that NRAs use a consistent approach in applying the new regulatory framework, and especially when designating undertakings with SMP in application of the provisions of the regulatory framework.

12. By issuing these guidelines, the Commission also intends to explain to interested parties and undertakings operating in the electronic communications sector how NRAs should undertake their assessments of SMP under the framework Directive, thereby maximising the transparency and legal certainty of the application of the sector specific legislation.

13. The Commission will amend these guidelines, whenever appropriate, taking into account experience with the application of the regulatory framework and future developments in the jurisprudence of the Court of First Instance and the European Court of Justice.

14. These guidelines do not in any way restrict the rights conferred by Community law on individuals or undertakings. They are entirely without prejudice to the application of Community law, and in particular of the competition rules, by the Commission and the relevant national authorities, and to its interpretation by the European Court of Justice and the Court of First Instance. These guidelines do not prejudice any action the Commission may take or any guidelines the Commission may issue in the future with regard to the application of European competition law.

1.2. Principles and policy objectives behind sector specific measures

15. NRAs must seek to achieve the policy objectives identified in Article 8(2), (3) and (4) of the framework Directive. These fall into three categories:
    — promotion of an open and competitive market for electronic communications networks, services and associated facilities,
    — development of the internal market, and
    — promotion of the interests of European citizens.

16. The purpose of imposing *ex-ante* obligations on undertakings designated as having SMP is to ensure that undertakings cannot use their market power either to restrict or distort competition on the relevant market, or to leverage such market power onto adjacent markets.

17. These regulatory obligations should only be imposed on those electronic communications markets whose characteristics may be such as to justify sector-specific regulation and in which the relevant NRA has determined that one or more operators have SMP.

18. The product and service markets whose characteristics may be such as to justify sector-specific regulation are identified by the Commission in its Recommendation and, when the definition of different relevant markets is justified by national circumstances, by the NRAs following the procedures set out in Articles 6 and 7 of the framework Directive.[9] In addition, certain other markets are specifically identified in Article 6 of the access Directive and Articles 18 and 19 of the universal service Directive.

Notes

[9] In addition, transnational markets whose characteristics may be such as to justify sector-specific regulation may be identified by the Commission in a Decision on transnational markets.

---

19. In respect of each of these relevant markets, NRAs will assess whether the competition is effective. A finding that effective competition exists on a relevant market is equivalent to a finding that no operator enjoys a single or joint dominant position on that market. Therefore, for the purposes of applying the new regulatory framework, effective competition means that there is no undertaking

in the relevant market which holds alone or together with other undertakings a single or collective dominant position. When NRAs conclude that a relevant market is not effectively competitive, they will designate undertakings with SMP on that market, and will either impose appropriate specific obligations, or maintain or amend such obligations where they already exist, in accordance with Article 16(4) of the framework Directive.

20. In carrying out the market analysis under the terms of Article 16 of the framework Directive, NRAs will conduct a forward looking, structural evaluation of the relevant market, based on existing market conditions. NRAs should determine whether the market is prospectively competitive, and thus whether any lack of effective competition is durable,[10] by taking into account expected or foreseeable market developments over the course of a reasonable period. The actual period used should reflect the specific characteristics of the market and the expected timing for the next review of the relevant market by the NRA. NRAs should take past data into account in their analysis when such data are relevant to the developments in that market in the foreseeable future.

Notes
[10] Recital 27 of the framework Directive.
Commentary
para 20: B&C: 12.018

21. If NRAs designate undertakings as having SMP, they must impose on them one or more regulatory obligations, in accordance with the relevant Directives and taking into account the principle of proportionality. Exceptionally, NRAs may impose obligations for access and interconnection that go beyond those specified in the access Directive, provided this is done with the prior agreement of the Commission, as provided by Article 8(3) of that Directive.

22. In the exercise of their regulatory tasks under Article 15 and 16 of the framework Directive, NRAs enjoy discretionary powers which reflect the complexity of all the relevant factors that must be assessed (economic, factual and legal) when identifying the relevant market and determining the existence of undertakings with SMP. These discretionary powers remain subject, however, to the procedures provided for in Article 6 and 7 of the framework Directive.

Commentary
para 22: B&C: 12.018

23. Regulatory decisions adopted by NRAs pursuant to the Directives will have an impact on the development of the internal market. In order to prevent any adverse effects on the functioning of the internal market, NRAs must ensure that they implement the provisions to which these guidelines apply in a consistent manner. Such consistency can only be achieved by close coordination and cooperation with other NRAs, with NCAs and with the Commission, as provided in the framework Directive and as recommended in Section 5.3 of these guidelines.

1.3. Relationship with competition law

24. Under the regulatory framework, markets will be defined and SMP will be assessed using the same methodologies as under competition law. Therefore the definition of the geographic scope of markets identified in the Recommendation, the definition where necessary of relevant product/services markets outside the Recommendation, and the assessment of effective competition by NRAs should be consistent with competition case-law and practice. To ensure such consistency, these guidelines are based on (1) existing case-law of the Court of First Instance and the European Court of Justice concerning market definition and the notion of dominant position within the meaning of Article [102 TFEU] and Article 2 of the merger control Regulation;[11] (2) the "Guidelines on the application of EEC competition rules in the telecommunications sector';[12] (3) the "Commission notice on the definition of relevant markets for the purposes of Community competition law",[13] hereinafter the "Notice on market definition"; and (4) the "Notice on the application of competition rules to access agreements in the telecommunications sector",[14] hereinafter the "Access notice".

Notes

11 Regulation (EEC) No 4064/89 on the control of concentrations between undertakings (OJ L 395, 30.12.1989, p.1), as last amended by Regulation (EC) No 1310/97 of 30 June 1997 (OJ L 180, 9.7.1997, p.1) (hereafter the merger control Regulation). [Ed note: see now Council Regulation (EC) No 139/2004 (OJ L 24, 29.1.2004, p.1), reproduced at D1.]

12 Guidelines on the application of EEC competition rules in the telecommunications sector (OJ C 233, 6.9.1991, p.2).

13 Commission notice on the definition of relevant market for the purposes of Community competition law (OJ C 372, 9.12.1997, p.5).

14 Notice on the application of the competition rules to access agreements in the telecommunications sector (OJ C 265, 22.8.1998, p.2).

Commentary
para 24: B&C: 12.045

25. The use of the same methodologies ensures that the relevant market defined for the purpose of sector-specific regulation will in most cases correspond to the market definitions that would apply under competition law. In some cases, and for the reasons set out in Section 2 of these guidelines, markets defined by the Commission and competition authorities in competition cases may differ from those identified in the Recommendation and Decision, and/or from markets defined by NRAs under Article 15(3) of the framework Directive. Article 15(1) of the framework Directive makes clear that the markets to be defined by NRAs for the purpose of *ex-ante* regulation are without prejudice to those defined by NCAs and by the Commission in the exercise of their respective powers under competition law in specific cases.

26. For the purposes of the application of Community competition law, the Commission's Notice on market definition explains that the concept of the relevant market is closely linked to the objectives pursued under Community policies. Markets defined under Articles [101 and 102 TFEU] are generally defined on an ex-post basis. In these cases, the analysis will consider events that have already taken place in the market and will not be influenced by possible future developments. Conversely, under the merger control provisions of EC competition law, markets are generally defined on a forward-looking basis.

Commentary
para 26: B&C: 12.044

27. On the other hand, relevant markets defined for the purposes of sector-specific regulation will always be assessed on a forward looking basis, as the NRA will include in its assessment an appreciation of the future development of the market. However, NRAs' market analyses should not ignore, where relevant, past evidence when assessing the future prospects of the relevant market (see also Section 2, below). The starting point for carrying out a market analysis for the purpose of Article 15 of the framework Directive is not the existence of an agreement or concerted practice within the scope of Article [101 TFEU], nor a concentration within the scope of the Merger Regulation, nor an alleged abuse of dominance within the scope of Article [102 TFEU], but is based on an overall forward-looking assessment of the structure and the functioning of the market under examination. Although NRAs and competition authorities, when examining the same issues in the same circumstances and with the same objectives, should in principle reach the same conclusions, it cannot be excluded that, given the differences outlined above, and in particular the broader focus of the NRAs' assessment, markets defined for the purposes of competition law and markets defined for the purpose of sector-specific regulation may not always be identical.

Commentary
para 27: B&C: 12.018, 12.044

28. Although merger analysis is also applied *ex ante*, it is not carried out periodically as is the case with the analysis of the NRAs under the new regulatory framework. A competition authority does not, in principle, have the opportunity to conduct a periodic review of its decision in the light of market developments, whereas NRAs are bound to review their decisions periodically under Article 16(1) of the framework Directive. This factor can influence the scope and breadth of the market analysis and the competitive assessment carried out by NRAs, and for this reason, market

definitions under the new regulatory framework, even in similar areas, may in some cases, be different from those markets defined by competition authorities.

Commentary
para 28: B&C: 12.016

---

29. It is considered that markets which are not identified in the Recommendation will not warrant *ex-ante* sector specific regulation, except where the NRA is able to justify such regulation of an additional or different relevant market in accordance with the procedure in Article 7 of the framework Directive.

30. The designation of an undertaking as having SMP in a market identified for the purpose of *ex-ante* regulation does not automatically imply that this undertaking is also dominant for the purpose of Article [102 TFEU] or similar national provisions. Moreover, the SMP designation has no bearing on whether that undertaking has committed an abuse of a dominant position within the meaning of Article [102 TFEU] or national competition laws. It merely implies that, from a structural perspective, and in the short to medium term, the operator has and will have, on the relevant market identified, sufficient market power to behave to an appreciable extent independently of competitors, customers, and ultimately consumers, and this, solely for purposes of Article 14 of the framework Directive.

Commentary
para 30: F&N: 13.27

---

31. In practice, it cannot be excluded that parallel procedures under *ex-ante* regulation and competition law may arise with respect to different kinds of problems in relevant markets.[15] Competition authorities may therefore carry out their own market analysis and impose appropriate competition law remedies alongside any sector specific measures applied by NRAs. However, it must be noted that such simultaneous application of remedies by different regulators would address different problems in such markets. *Ex-ante* obligations imposed by NRAs on undertakings with SMP aim to fulfil the specific objectives set out in the relevant directives, whereas competition law remedies aim to sanction agreements or abusive behaviour which restrict or distort competition in the relevant market.

Notes
[15] It is expected that effective cooperation between NRAs and NCAs would prevent the duplication of procedures concerning identical market issues.

---

32. As far as emerging markets are concerned, recital 27 of the framework Directive notes that emerging markets, where *de facto* the market leader is likely to have a substantial market share, should not be subject to inappropriate *ex-ante* regulation. This is because premature imposition of *ex-ante* regulation may unduly influence the competitive conditions taking shape within a new and emerging market. At the same time, foreclosure of such emerging markets by the leading undertaking should be prevented. Without prejudice to the appropriateness of intervention by the competition authorities in individual cases, NRAs should ensure that they can fully justify any form of early, *ex-ante* intervention in an emerging market, in particular since they retain the ability to intervene at a later stage, in the context of the periodic re-assessment of the relevant markets.

2. Market Definition

2.1. Introduction

33. In the Competition guidelines issued in 1991,[16] the Commission recognised the difficulties inherent in defining the relevant market in an area of rapid technological change, such as the telecommunications sector. Whilst this statement still holds true today as far as the electronic communications sector is concerned, the Commission since the publication of those guidelines has gained considerable experience in applying the competition rules in a dynamic sector shaped by constant technological changes and innovation, as a result of its role in managing the transition

from monopoly to competition in this sector. It should however be recalled that the present guidelines do not purport to explain how the competition rules apply, generally, in the electronic communications sector, but focus only on issues related to (i) market definition; and (ii) the assessment of significant market power within the meaning of Article 14 of the framework Directive (hereafter SMP).

Notes

16 Guidelines on the application of EEC competition rules in the telecommunications sector (OJ C 233, 6.9.1991, p.2).

34. In assessing whether an undertaking has SMP, that is whether it "enjoys a position of economic strength affording it the power to behave to an appreciable extent independently of its competitors, customers and ultimately consumers",[17] the definition of the relevant market is of fundamental importance since effective competition can only be assessed by reference to the market thus defined.[18] The use of the term "relevant market" implies the description of the products or services that make up the market and the assessment of the geographical scope of that market (the terms "products" and "services" are used interchangeably throughout this text). In that regard, it should be recalled that relevant markets defined under the 1998 regulatory framework were distinct from those identified for competition-law purposes, since they were based on certain specific aspects of end-to-end communications rather than on the demand and supply criteria used in a competition law analysis.[19]

Notes

17 Article 14(2) of the framework Directive.
18 Case C-209/98, *Entreprenørforeningens Affalds* [2000] ECR I-3743, paragraph 57, and Case C-242/95 *GT-Link* [1997] ECR I-4449, paragraph 36. It should be recognised that the objective of market definition is not an end in itself, but part of a process, namely assessing the degree of a firm's market power.
19 See Directive 97/33/EC of the European Parliament and of the Council of 30 June 1997 on interconnection in telecommunications with regard to ensuring universal service and interoperability through application of the principles of open network provision (ONP) (OJ L 199, 26.7.1997, p.32) (the interconnection Directive); Council Directive 90/387/EEC of 28 June 1990 on the establishment of the internal market for telecommunications services through the implementation of open network provision (OJ L 192, 24.7.1990, p.1) (the ONP framework Directive); Council Directive 92/44/EEC of 5 June 1992 on the application of open network provision to leased lines (OJ L 165, 19.6.1992, p.27) (the leased lines Directive); Directive 95/62/EC of the European Parliament and of the Council of 13 December 1995 on the application of open network provision (ONP) to voice telephony (OJ L 321, 30.12.1995, p.6), replaced by Directive 98/10/EC of the European Parliament and of the Council of 26 February 1998 on the application of open network provision (ONP) to voice telephony and on universal service for telecommunications in a competitive environment (OJ L 101, 1.4.1998, p.24) (the ONP voice telephony Directive).

35. Market definition is not a mechanical or abstract process but requires an analysis of any available evidence of past market behaviour and an overall understanding of the mechanics of a given sector. In particular, a dynamic rather than a static approach is required when carrying out a prospective, or forward-looking, market analysis.[20] In this respect, any experience gained by NRAs, NCAs and the Commission through the application of competition rules to the telecommunication sector clearly will be of particular relevance in applying Article 15 of the framework Directive. Thus, any information gathered, any findings made and any studies or reports commissioned or relied upon by NRAs (or NCAs) in the exercise of their tasks, in relation to the conditions of competition in the telecommunications markets (provided of course that market conditions have since remained unchanged), should serve as a starting point for the purposes of applying Article 15 of the framework Directive and carrying out a prospective market analysis.[21]

Notes

20 Joined Cases C-68/94 and C-30/95, *France and Others v Commission* [1998] ECR I-1375. See, also, Notice on market definition, at paragraph 12.
21 To the extent that the electronic communications sector is technology and innovation-driven, any previous market definition may not necessarily be relevant at a later point in time.

36. The main product and service markets whose characteristics may be such as to justify the imposition of *ex-ante* regulatory obligations are identified in the Recommendation which the

Commission is required to adopt pursuant to Article 15(1) of the framework Directive, as well as any Decision on transnational markets which the Commission decides to adopt pursuant to Article 15(4) of the framework Directive. Therefore, in practice the task of NRAs will normally be to define the geographical scope of the relevant market, although NRAs have the possibility under Article 15(3) of the framework Directive to define markets other than those listed in the Recommendation in accordance with Article 7 of the framework Directive (see below, Section 6).

37. Whilst a prospective analysis of market conditions may in some cases lead to a market definition different from that resulting from a market analysis based on past behaviour,[22] NRAs should nonetheless seek to preserve, where possible, consistency in the methodology adopted between, on the one hand, market definitions developed for the purposes of *ex-ante* regulation, and on the other hand, market definitions developed for the purposes of the application of the competition rules. Nevertheless, as stated in Article 15(1) of the framework Directive and Section 1 of the guidelines, markets defined under sector-specific regulation are defined without prejudice to markets that may be defined in specific cases under competition law.

Notes

[22] Notice on market definition, paragraph 12.

Commentary
para 37: B&C: 4.020, 12.018

2.2. Main criteria for defining the relevant market

38. The extent to which the supply of a product or the provision of a service in a given geographical area constitutes the relevant market depends on the existence of competitive constraints on the price-setting behaviour of the producer(s) or service provider(s) concerned. There are two main competitive constraints to consider in assessing the behaviour of undertakings on the market, (i) demand-side; and (ii) supply-side substitution. A third source of competitive constraint on an operator's behaviour exists, namely potential competition. The difference between potential competition and supply-substitution lies in the fact that supply-side substitution responds promptly to a price increase whereas potential entrants may need more time before starting to supply the market. Supply substitution involves no additional significant costs whereas potential entry occurs at significant sunk costs.[23] The existence of potential competition should thus be examined for the purpose of assessing whether a market is effectively competitive within the meaning of the framework Directive, that is whether there exist undertakings with SMP.[24]

Notes

[23] See, also, Notice on market definition, paragraphs 20–23, Case IV/M.1225—*Enso/Stora*, (OJ L 254, 29.9.1999), paragraph 40.
[24] See Notice on market definition, paragraph 24. Distinguishing between supply-side substitution and potential competition in electronic communications markets may be more complicated than in other markets given the dynamic character of the former. What matters, however, is that potential entry from other suppliers is taken into consideration at some stage of the relevant market analysis, that is, either at the initial market definition stage or at the subsequent stage of the assessment of market power (SMP).

39. Demand-side substitutability is used to measure the extent to which consumers are prepared to substitute other services or products for the service or product in question,[25] whereas supply-side substitutability indicates whether suppliers other than those offering the product or services in question would switch in the immediate to short term their line of production or offer the relevant products or services without incurring significant additional costs.

Notes

[25] It is not necessary that all consumers switch to a competing product; it suffices that enough or sufficient switching takes place so that a relative price increase is not profitable. This requirement corresponds to the principle of "sufficient interchangeability" laid down in the case-law of the Court of Justice; see below, footnote 32.

40. One possible way of assessing the existence of any demand and supply-side substitution is to apply the so-called "hypothetical monopolist test".[26] Under this test, an NRA should ask what would happen if there were a small but significant, lasting increase in the price of a given product or service, assuming that the prices of all other products or services remain constant (hereafter, "relative price increase"). While the significance of a price increase will depend on each individual case, in practice, NRAs should normally consider customers" (consumers or undertakings) reactions to a permanent price increase of between 5 to 10%.[27] The responses by consumers or undertakings concerned will aid in determining whether substitutable products do exist and, if so, where the boundaries of the relevant product market should be delineated.[28]

Notes

[26] See, also, Access notice, paragraph 46, and Case T-83/91, *Tetra Pak v Commission*, [1994] ECR II-755, paragraph 68. This test is also known as "SSNIP" (small but significant non transitory increase in price). Although the SSNIP test is but one example of methods used for defining the relevant market and notwithstanding its formal econometric nature, or its margins for errors (the so-called "cellophane fallacy", see below), its importance lies primarily in its use as a conceptual tool for assessing evidence of competition between different products or services.

[27] See Notice on market definition, paragraphs 17–18.

[28] In other words, where the cross-price elasticity of demand between two products is high, one may conclude that consumers view these products as close substitutes. Where consumer choice is influenced by considerations other than price increases, the SSNIP test may not be an adequate measurement of product substitutability; see Case T-25/99, *Colin Arthur Roberts and Valerie Ann Roberts v Commission*, [2001] ECR II-1881.

41. As a starting point, an NRA should apply this test firstly to an electronic communications service or product offered in a given geographical area, the characteristics of which may be such as to justify the imposition of regulatory obligations, and having done so, add additional products or areas depending on whether competition from those products or areas constrains the price of the main product or service in question. Since a relative price increase of a set of products[29] is likely to lead to some sales being lost, the key issue is to determine whether the loss of sales would be sufficient to offset the increased profits which would otherwise be made from sales made following the price increase. Assessing the demand-side and supply-side substitution provides a way of measuring the quantity of the sales likely to be lost and consequently of determining the scope of the relevant market.

Notes

[29] Within the context of market definition under Article [102 TFEU], a competition authority or a court would estimate the "starting price" for applying the SSNIP on the basis of the price charged by the alleged monopolist. Likewise, under the prospective assessment of the effects which a merger may have on competition, the starting price would be based on the prevailing prices of the merging parties. However, where an NRA carries out a market analysis for the purposes of applying Article 14 of the framework Directive the service or product in question may be offered by several firms. In such a case, the starting price should be the industry "average price".

42. In principle, the "hypothetical monopolist test" is relevant only with regard to products or services, the price of which is freely determined and not subject to regulation. Thus, the working assumption will be that current prevailing prices are set at competitive levels. If, however, a service or product is offered at a regulated, cost-based price, then such price is presumed, in the absence of indications to the contrary, to be set at what would otherwise be a competitive level and should therefore be taken as the starting point for applying the "hypothetical monopolist test".[30] In theory, if the demand elasticity of a given product or service is significant, even at relative competitive prices, the firm in question lacks market power. If, however, elasticity is high even at current prices, that may mean only that the firm in question has already exercised market power to the point that further price increases will not increase its profits. In this case, the application of the hypothetical monopoly test may lead to a different market definition from that which would be produced if the prices were set at a competitive level.[31] Any assessment of market definition must therefore take into account this potential difficulty. However, NRAs should proceed on the basis that the prevailing price levels provide a reasonable basis from which to start the relevant analysis unless there is evidence that this is not in fact the case.

Notes

[30] It is worth noting that prices which result from price regulation which does not aim at ensuring that prices are cost-based, but rather at ensuring an affordable offer within the context of the provision of universal services, may not be presumed to be set at a competitive level, nor should they serve as a starting point for applying the SSNIP test.

[31] Indeed, one of the drawbacks of the application of the SSNIP test is that in some cases, a high-demand cross-price elasticity may mean that a firm has already exercised market power, a situation known in competition law and practice as the "cellophane fallacy". In such cases, the prevailing price does not correspond to a competitive price. Determining whether the prevailing price is set above the competitive level is admittedly one of the most difficult aspects of the SSNIP test. NRAs faced with such difficulties could rely on other criteria for assessing demand and supply substitution such as functionality of services, technical characteristics, etc. Clearly, if evidence exist to show that in the past a firm has engaged in anti-competitive behaviour (price-fixing) or has enjoyed market power, then this may serve as an indication that its prices are not under competitive constraint and accordingly are set above the competitive level.

Commentary
para 42: B&C: 4.024

43. If an NRA chooses to have recourse to the hypothetical monopolist test, it should then apply this test up to the point where it can be established that a relative price increase within the geographic and product markets defined will not lead consumers to switch to readily available substitutes or to suppliers located in other areas.

2.2.1. The relevant product/service market

44. According to settled case-law, the relevant product/service market comprises all those products or services that are sufficiently interchangeable or substitutable, not only in terms of their objective characteristics, by virtue of which they are particularly suitable for satisfying the constant needs of consumers, their prices or their intended use, but also in terms of the conditions of competition and/or the structure of supply and demand on the market in question.[32] Products or services which are only to a small, or relative degree interchangeable with each other do not form part of the same market.[33] NRAs should thus commence the exercise of defining the relevant product or service market by grouping together products or services that are used by consumers for the same purposes (end use).

Notes

[32] Case C-333/94 P, *Tetra Pak v Commission* [1996] ECR I-5951, paragraph 13, Case 31/80 *L'Oréal* [1980] ECR3775, paragraph 25, Case 322/81, *Michelin v Commission* [1983] ECR 3461, paragraph 37, Case C-62/86, *AkzoChemie v Commission* [1991] ECR I-3359, Case T-504/93, *Tiercé Ladbroke v Commission* [1997] ECR II-923, paragraph 81, T-65/96, *Kish Glass v Commission* [2000] ECR II-1885, paragraph 62, Case C-475/99, *Ambulanz Glöckner and Landkreis Südwestpfalz*, [2001] ECR I-[8089], paragraph 33. The test of sufficient substitutability or interchangeability was first laid down by the Court of Justice in Case 6/72, *Europemballage and Continental Can v Commission*, [1973] ECR 215, paragraph 32 and Case 85/76, *Hoffmann La-Roche v Commission* [1979] ECR 461, paragraph 23.

[33] Case C-333/94 P, *Tetra Pak v Commission* [1996] ECR I-5951, paragraph 13, Case 66/86, *Ahmed Saeed* [1989] ECR 803, paragraphs 39 and 40, Case *United Brands v Commission* [1978] ECR207, paragraphs 22 and 29, and 12; Case T-229/94, *Deutsche Bahn v Commission* [1997] ECR II-1689, paragraph 54. In *Tetra Pak*, the Court confirmed that the fact that demand for aseptic and non-aseptic cartons used for packaging fruit juice was marginal and stable over time relative to the demand for cartons used for packaging milk was evidence of a very little interchangeability between the milk and the non-milk packaging sector, idem, paragraphs 13 and 15.

45. Although the aspect of the end use of a product or service is closely related to its physical characteristics, different kind of products or services may be used for the same end. For instance, consumers may use dissimilar services such as cable and satellite connections for the same purpose, namely to access the Internet. In such a case, both services (cable and satellite access services) may be included in the same product market. Conversely, paging services and mobile telephony services, which may appear to be capable of offering the same service, that is, dispatching of two-way short messages, may be found to belong to distinct product markets in view of their different perceptions by consumers as regards their functionality and end use.

Commentary
para 45: B&C: 4.029

46. Differences in pricing models and offerings for a given product or service may also imply different groups of consumers. Thus, by looking into prices, NRAs may define separate markets for business and residential customers for essentially the same service. For instance, the ability of operators engaged in providing international retail electronic communications services to discriminate between residential and business customers, by applying different sets of prices and discounts, has led the Commission to decide that these two groups form separate markets as far as such services are concerned (see below). However, in order for products to be viewed as demand-side substitutes it is not necessary that they are offered at the same price. A low quality product or service sold at a low price could well be an effective substitute to a higher quality product sold at higher prices. What matters in this case is the likely responses of consumers following a relative price increase.[34]

Notes

[34] For example, in the case of a relative price increase, consumers of a lower quality/price service may switch to a higher quality/price service if the cost of doing so (the premium paid) is offset by the price increase. Conversely, consumers of a higher quality product may no longer accept a higher premium and switch to a lower quality service. In such cases, low and high quality products would appear to be effective substitutes.

47. Furthermore, product substitutability between different electronic communications services will arise increasingly through the convergence of various technologies. Use of digital systems leads to an increasing similarity in the performance and characteristics of network services using distinct technologies. A packet-switched network, for instance, such as Internet, may be used to transmit digitised voice signals in competition with traditional voice telephony services.[35]

Notes

[35] Communication from the Commission—Status of voice on the Internet under Community law, and in particular, under Directive 90/388/EEC—Supplement to the Communication by the Commission to the European Parliament and the Council on the status and implementation of Directive 90/388/EEC on competition in the markets for telecommunications services (OJ C 369, 22.12.2000, p.3). Likewise, it cannot be excluded that in the future xDSL technology and multipoint video distribution services based on wireless local loops may be used for the transmission of TV materials in direct competition with other existing TV delivery systems based on cable systems, direct-to-home satellite transmission and terrestrial analogue or digital transmission platforms.

48. In order, therefore, to complete the market-definition analysis, an NRA, in addition to considering products or services whose objective characteristics, prices and intended use make them sufficiently interchangeable, should also examine, where necessary, the prevailing conditions of demand and supply substitution by applying the hypothetical monopolist test.

Commentary
para 48: B&C: 4.011

2.2.1.1. Demand-side substitution

49. Demand-side substitution enables NRAs to determine the substitutable products or range of products to which consumers could easily switch in case of a relative price increase. In determining the existence of demand substitutability, NRAs should make use of any previous evidence of consumers' behaviour. Where available, an NRA should examine historical price fluctuations in potentially competing products, any records of price movements, and relevant tariff information. In such circumstances evidence showing that consumers have in the past promptly shifted to other products or services, in response to past price changes, should be given appropriate consideration. In the absence of such records, and where necessary, NRAs will have to seek and assess the likely response of consumers and suppliers to a relative price increase of the service in question.

50. The possibility for consumers to substitute a product or a service for another because of a small, but significant lasting price increase may, however, be hindered by considerable switching costs. Consumers who have invested in technology or made any other necessary investments in order to receive a service or use a product may be unwilling to incur any additional costs involved in switching to an otherwise substitutable service or product. In the same vein, customers of existing providers may also be "locked in" by long-term contracts or by the prohibitively high cost of switching terminals. Accordingly, in a situation where end users face significant switching costs in

order to substitute product A for product B, these two products should not be included in the same relevant market.[36]

Notes

[36] Switching costs which stem from strategic choices by undertakings rather than from exogenous factors should be considered, together with some other form of entry barriers, at the subsequent stage of SMP assessment. Where a market is still growing, total switching costs for already "captured" consumers may not be significant and may not thus deter demand or supply-side substitution.

51. Demand substitutability focuses on the interchangeable character of products or services from the buyer's point of view. Proper delineation of the product market may, however, require further consideration of potential substitutability from the supply side.

2.2.1.2. Supply-side substitution

52. In assessing the scope for supply substitution, NRAs may also take into account the likelihood that undertakings not currently active on the relevant product market may decide to enter the market, within a reasonable time frame,[37] following a relative price increase, that is, a small but significant, lasting price increase. In circumstances where the overall costs of switching production to the product in question are relatively negligible, then that product may be incorporated into the product market definition. The fact that a rival firm possesses some of the assets required to provide a given service is immaterial if significant additional investment is needed to market and offer profitably the services in question.[38] Furthermore, NRAs will need to ascertain whether a given supplier would actually use or switch its productive assets to produce the relevant product or offer the relevant service (for instance, whether their capacity is committed under long-term supply agreements, etc.). Mere hypothetical supply-side substitution is not sufficient for the purposes of market definition.

Notes

[37] The time frame to be used to assess the likely responses of other suppliers in case of a relative price increase will inevitably depend on the characteristics of each market and should be decided on a case-by-case basis.
[38] See, also, Case C-333/94, Tetra Pak v Commission, op. cit., paragraph 19. As mentioned above, the required investments should also be undertaken within a reasonable time frame.

53. Account should also be taken of any existing legal, statutory or other regulatory requirements which could defeat a time-efficient entry into the relevant market and as a result discourage supply-side substitution. For instance, delays and obstacles in concluding interconnection or co-location agreements, negotiating any other form of network access, or obtaining rights of ways for network expansion,[39] may render unlikely in the short term the provision of new services and the deployment of new networks by potential competitors.

Notes

[39] See, also, Case COMP/M.2574—*Pirelli/Edizione/Olivetti/Telecom Italia*, paragraph 58.

54. As can been seen from the above considerations, supply substitution may serve not only for defining the relevant market but also for identifying the number of market participants.

2.2.2. Geographic market

55. Once the relevant product market is identified, the next step to be undertaken is the definition of the geographical dimension of the market. It is only when the geographical dimension of the product or service market has been defined that a NRA may properly assess the conditions of effective competition therein.

56. According to established case-law, the relevant geographic market comprises an area in which the undertakings concerned are involved in the supply and demand of the relevant products or services, in which area the conditions of competition are similar or sufficiently homogeneous and which can be distinguished from neighbouring areas in which the prevailing conditions of competition are appreciably different.[40] The definition of the geographic market does not require the conditions of competition between traders or providers of services to be perfectly homogeneous.

It is sufficient that they are similar or sufficiently homogeneous, and accordingly, only those areas in which the conditions of competition are "heterogeneous" may not be considered to constitute a uniform market.[41]

Notes

[40] *United Brands*, op. cit., paragraph 44, *Michelin*, op. cit., paragraph 26, Case 247/86 *Alsatel v Novasam* [1988] ECR 5987, paragraph 15; *Tiercé Ladbroke v Commission*, op. cit., paragraph 102.

[41] *Deutsche Bahn v Commission*, op. cit., paragraph 92. Case T-139/98 *AAMS v Commission*, [2001] ECR [II-3413], paragraph 39.

57. The process of defining the limits of the geographic market proceeds along the same lines as those discussed above in relation to the assessment of the demand and supply-side substitution in response to a relative price increase.

58. Accordingly, with regard to demand-side substitution, NRAs should assess mainly consumers' preferences as well as their current geographic patterns of purchase. In particular, linguistic reasons may explain why certain services are not available or marketed in different language areas. As far as supply-side substitution is concerned, where it can be established that operators which are not currently engaged or present on the relevant market, will, however, decide to enter that market in the short term in the event of a relative price increase, then the market definition should be expanded to incorporate those "outside" operators.

59. In the electronic communications sector, the geographical scope of the relevant market has traditionally been determined by reference to two main criteria:[42]

    (a) the area covered by a network;[43] and

    (b) the existence of legal and other regulatory instruments.[44]

Notes

[42] See, for instance, Case IV/M.1025—*Mannesmann/Olivetti/Infostrada*, paragraph 17, and Case COMP/ JV.23—*Telefónica Portugal Telecom/Médi Telecom*.

[43] In practice, this area will correspond to the limits of the area in which an operator is authorised to operate. In Case COMP/M.1650—*ACEA/Telefónica*, the Commission pointed out that since the notified joint venture would have a licence limited to the area of Rome, the geographical market could be defined as local; at paragraph 16.

[44] The fact that mobile operators can provide services only in the areas where they have been authorised to and the fact that a network architecture reflects the geographical dimension of the mobile licences explains why mobile markets are considered to be national in scope. The extra connection and communications costs that consumers face when roaming abroad, coupled with the loss of certain additional service functionalities (i.e. lack of voice mail abroad) further supports this definition; see Case IV/M.1439—*Telia/Telenor*, paragraph 124, Case IV/M.1430—*Vodafone/Airtouch*, paragraphs 13–17, Case COMP/JV.17—*Mannesmann/Bell Atlantic/Omnitel*, paragraph 15.

60. On the basis of these two main criteria,[45] geographic markets can be considered to be local, regional, national or covering territories of two or more countries (for instance, pan-European, EEA-wide or global markets).

Notes

[45] Physical interconnection agreements may also be taken into consideration for defining the geographical scope of the market, Case IV/M.570—*TBT/BT/TeleDanmark/Telenor*, paragraph 35.

2.2.3. Other issues of market definition

61. For the purposes of *ex-ante* regulation, in certain exceptional cases, the relevant market may be defined on a route-by-route basis. In particular, when considering the dimension of markets for international retail or wholesale electronic communications services, it may be appropriate to treat paired countries or paired cities as separate markets.[46] Clearly, from the demand side, the delivery of a call to one country is not a substitute for the delivery of the same to another country. On the other hand, the question of whether indirect transmission services, that is, re-routing or transit of the same call via a third country, represent effective supply-side substitutes depends on the specificities of the market and should be decided on a case-by-case basis.[47] However, a market for the provision of services on a bilateral route would be national in scope since supply and

demand patterns in both ends of the route would most likely correspond to different market structures.[48]

Notes

[46] Case IV/M.856—*British Telecom/MCI (II)*, paragraph 19s., Case IV/JV.15—*BT/AT & T*, paragraph 84 and 92, Case COMP/M.2257—*France Telecom/Equant*, paragraph 32, It is highly unlikely that the provision of electronic communications services could be segmented on the basis of national (or local) bilateral routes.

[47] Reference may be made, for instance, to the market for backhaul capacity in international routes (i.e. cable station serving country A to country E) where a potential for substitution between cable stations serving different countries (i.e., cable stations connecting Country A to B, A to C and A to D) may exist where a supplier of backhaul capacity in relation to the route A to E is or would be constrained by the ability of consumers to switch to any of the other "routes", also able to deal with traffic from or to country E.

[48] Where a market is defined on the basis of a bilateral route, its geographical scope could be wider than national if suppliers are present in both ends of the market and can satisfy demand coming from both ends of the relevant route.

62. In its Notice on market definition, the Commission drew attention to certain cases where the boundaries of the relevant market may be expanded to take into consideration products or geographical areas which, although not directly substitutable, should be included in the market definition because of so-called "chain substitutability".[49] In essence, chain substitutability occurs where it can be demonstrated that although products A and C are not directly substitutable, product B is a substitute for both product A and product C and therefore products A and C may be in the same product market since their pricing might be constrained by the substitutability of product B. The same reasoning also applies for defining the geographic market. Given the inherent risk of unduly widening the scope of the relevant market, findings of chain substitutability should be adequately substantiated.[50]

Notes

[49] See Notice on market definition, paragraphs 57 and 58. For instance, chain substitutability could occur where an undertaking providing services at national level constraints the prices charged by undertakings providing services in separate geographical markets. This may be the case where the prices charged by undertakings providing cable networks in particular areas are constrained by a dominant undertaking operating nationally; see also, Case COMP/M.1628—*TotalFina/Elf* (OJ L 143, 29.5.2001, p.1), paragraph 188.

[50] Evidence should show clear price interdependence at the extremes of the chain and the degree of substitutability between the relevant products or geographical areas should be sufficiently strong.

2.3. The Commission's own practice

63. The Commission has adopted a number of decisions under Regulation No 17 and the merger control Regulation relating to the electronic communications sector. These decisions may be of particular relevance for NRAs with regard to the methodology applied by the Commission in defining the relevant market.[51] As stated above, however, in a sector characterised by constant innovation and rapid technological convergence, it is clear that any current market definition runs the risk of becoming inaccurate or irrelevant in the near future.[52] Furthermore, markets defined under competition law are without prejudice to markets defined under the new regulatory framework as the context and the timeframe within which a market analysis is conducted may be different.[53]

Notes

[51] The Commission has, inter alia, made references in its decisions to the existence of the following markets: international voice-telephony services (Case IV/M.856—*British Telecommunications/MCI* (II), OJ L 336, 8.12.1997), advanced telecommunications services to corporate users (Case IV/35.337, *Atlas*, OJ L 239, 19.9.1996, paragraphs 5–7, Case IV/35617, *Phoenix/Global/One*, OJ L 239, 19.9.1996, paragraph 6, Case IV/34.857, *BT-MCI (I)*, OJ L 223, 27.8.1994), standardised low-level packet-switched data-communications services, resale of international transmission capacity (Case IV/M.975—*Albacom/BT/ENI*, paragraph 24) audioconferencing (*Albacom/BT/ENI*, paragraph 17), satellite services (Case IV/350518—*Iridium*, OJ L 16, 18.1.1997), (enhanced) global telecommunications services (Case IV/JV.15—*BT/AT & T*, Case COMP/M.1741—*MCI WorldCom/Sprint*, paragraph 84, Case COMP/M.2257—*France Telecom/Equant*, paragraph 18), directory-assistance services (Case IV/M.2468—*SEAT Pagine Gialle/ENIRO*, paragraph 19, Case COMP/M.1957—*VIAG Interkom/Telenor Media*, paragraph 8), Internet-access services to end users (Case IV/M.1439—*Telia/Telenor*, Case COMP/JV.46—*Blackstone/CDPQ/Kabel Nordrhein/Westfalen*, paragraph 26, Case COMP/M.1838—*BT/Esat*, paragraph 7), top-level or universal Internet connectivity (Case

COMP/M.1741—*MCI WorldCom/Sprint*, paragraph 52), seamless pan-European mobile telecommunications services to internationally mobile customers (Case COMP/M.1975—*Vodafone Airtouch/Mannesmann*, Case COMP/M.2016—*France Telecom/Orange*, paragraph 15), wholesale roaming services (Case COMP/M.1863—*Vodafone/Airtel*, paragraph 17), and market for connectivity to the international signalling network (Case COMP/2598—*TDC/CMG/Migway JV*, paragraphs 17–18).
52 See, also, Joined Cases T-125/97 and T-127/97, *The Coca-Cola Company and Others v Commission* [2000] ECR II-1733, at paragraphs 81 and 82.
53 See, also, Article 15 of the framework Directive.

64. As stated in the Access notice, there are in the electronic communications sector at least two main types of relevant markets to consider, that of services provided to end users (services market) and that of access to facilities necessary to provide such services (access market).[54] Within these two broad market definitions further market distinctions may be made depending on demand and supply side patterns.

Notes
54 Access notice, paragraph 45.

65. In particular, in its decision-making practice, the Commission will normally make a distinction between the provision of services and the provision of underlying network infrastructure. For instance, as regards the provision of infrastructure, the Commission has identified separate markets for the provision of local loop, long distance and international infrastructure.[55] As regards fixed services, the Commission has distinguished between subscriber (retail) access to switched voice telephony services (local, long distance and international), operator (wholesale) access to networks (local, long distance and international) and business data communications services.[56] In the market for fixed telephony retail services, the Commission has also distinguished between the initial connection and the monthly rental.[57] Retail services are offered to two distinct classes of consumers, namely, residential and business users, the latter possibly being broken down further into a market for professional, small and medium sized business customers and another for large businesses.[58] With regard to fixed telephony retail services offered to residential users, demand and supply patterns seem to indicate that two main types of services are currently being offered, traditional fixed telephony services (voice and narrowband data transmissions) on the one hand, and high speed communications services (currently in the form of xDSL services) on the other hand.[59]

Notes
55 See Case COMP/M.1439—*Telia/Telenor*.
56 See *Telia/Telenor*, *BT/AT & T*, *France Télécom/Equant*, op. cit. See also Commission Decision of 20 May 1999, *Cégétel + 4* (OJ L 218, 18.8.1999), paragraph 22. With regard to the emerging market for "Global broadband data communications services—GBDS", the Commission has found that such services can be supported by three main network architectures: (i) terrestrial wireline systems; (ii) terrestrial wireless systems; and (iii) satellite-based systems, and that from a demand side, satellite-based GBDS can be considered as a separate market, Case COMP/M.1564—*Astrolink*, paragraphs 20–23.
57 Directive 96/19/EC, recital 20 (OJ L 74, 22.3.1996, p.13). See, also, communication from the Commission, "Unbundled access to the local loop: enabling the competitive provision of a full range of electronic communication services, including broadband multimedia and high speed Internet" (OJ C 272, 23.9.2000, p.55). Pursuant to point 3.2, "While categories of services have to be monitored closely, particularly given the speed of technological change, and regularly reassessed on a case-by-case basis, these services are presently normally not substitutable for one another, and would therefore be considered as forming different relevant markets".
58 The Commission has identified separate markets for services to large multinational corporations (MNCs) given the significant differences in the demand (and supply) of services to this group of customers compared to other retail (business) customers, see Case IV/JV.15—*BT/AT & T*, Case COMP/M.1741—*MCI WorldCom/Sprint*, Case COMP/M.2257—*France Télécom/Equant*.
59 See communication on "Unbundled access to the local loop", op.cit, point 3.2. The market for "high-speed" communications services could possibly be further divided into distinct segments depending on the nature of the services offered (i.e. Internet services, video-on-demand, etc.).

66. As regards the provision of mobile communications services, the Commission has found that, from a demand-side point of view, mobile telephony services and fixed telephony

services constitute separate markets.[60] Within the mobile market, evidence gathered from the Commission has indicated that the market for mobile communications services encompasses both GSM 900 and GSM 1800 and possibly analogue platforms.[61]

Notes

[60] Case COMP/M.2574—*Pirelli/Edizione/Olivetti/Telecom Italia*, paragraph 33. It could also be argued that dial-up access to the Internet via existing 2G mobile telephones is a separate market from dial-up access via the public switched telecommunications network. According to the Commission, accessing the Internet via a mobile phone is unlikely to be a substitute for existing methods of accessing the Internet via a PC due to difference in sizes of the screen and the format of the material that can be obtained through the different platforms; see Case COMP/M.1982—*Telia/Oracle/Drutt*, paragraph 15, and Case COMP/JV.48 *Vodafone/Vivendi/Canal+*.

[61] Case COMP/M.2469—*Vodafone/Airtel*, paragraph 7, Case IV/M.1430—*Vodafone/Airtouch*, Case IV/M.1669, *Deutsche Telecom/One2One*, paragraph 7. Whether this market can be further segmented into a carrier (network operator) market and a downstream service market should be decided on a case-by-case basis; see Case IV/M. 1760—*Mannesmann/Orange*, paragraphs 8–10, and Case COMP/M.2053—*Telenor/BellSouth/Sonofon*, paragraphs 9–10.

67. The Commission has found that with regard to the "access" market, the latter comprises all types of infrastructure that can be used for the provision of a given service.[62] Whether the market for network infrastructures should be divided into as many separate submarkets as there are existing categories of network infrastructure, depends clearly on the degree of substitutability among such (alternative) networks.[63] This exercise should be carried out in relation to the class of users to which access to the network is provided. A distinction should, therefore, be made between provision of infrastructure to other operators (wholesale level) and provision to end users (retail level).[64] At the retail level, a further segmentation may take place between business and residential customers.[65]

Notes

[62] For instance, in *British Interactive Broadcasting/Open*, the Commission noted that for the provision of basic voice services to consumers, the relevant infrastructure market included not only the traditional copper network of BT but also the cable networks of the cable operators, which were capable of providing basic telephony services, and possibly wireless fixed networks, Case IV/36.359, (OJ L 312, 6.12.1999, paragraphs 33–38). In Case IV/M.1113—*Nortel/ Norweb*, the Commission recognised that electricity networks using "digital power line" technology could provide an alternative to existing traditional local telecommunications access loop, paragraphs 28–29.

[63] In assessing the conditions of network competition in the Irish market that would ensue following full liberalisation, the Commission also relied on the existence of what, at that period of time, were perceived as potential alternative infrastructure providers, namely, cable TV and electricity networks, *Telecom Eireann*, cit., paragraph 30. The Commission left open the question whether the provision of transmission capacity by an undersea network infrastructure constitutes a distinct market from terrestrial or satellite transmissions networks, Case COMP/M.1926—*Telefonica/Tyco/JV*, at paragraph 8.

[64] Case COMP/M.1439, *Telia/Telenor*, paragraph 79. For instance, an emerging pan-European market for wholesale access (SMS) to mobile infrastructure has been identified by the Commission in Case COMP/2598—*TDC/CMG/ Migway* JV, at paragraphs 28–29.

[65] In applying these criteria, the Commission has found that, as far as the fixed infrastructure is concerned, demand for the lease of transmission capacity and the provision of related services to other operators occurs at wholesale level (the market for carrier's carrier services; see Case IV/M.683—*GTS-Hermes Inc./HIT Rail BV*, paragraph 14, Case IV/M.1069—*WorldCom/MCI* (OJ L 116, 4.5.1999, p.1), *Unisource* (OJ L 318, 20.11.1997, p.1), *Phoenix/Global One* (OJ L 239, 19.9.1996, p.57), Case IV/JV.2—*Enel/FT/DT*. In Case COMP/M.1439—*Telia/Telenor*, the Commission identified distinct patterns of demand for wholesale and retail (subscriber) access to network infrastructure (provision or access to the local loop, and provision or access to long distance and international network infrastructure), paragraphs 75–83.

68. When the service to be provided concerns only end users subscribed to a particular network, access to the termination points of that network may well constitute the relevant product market. This will not be the case if it can be established that the same services may be offered to the same class of consumers by means of alternative, easily accessible competing networks. For example, in its Communication on unbundling the local loop,[66] the Commission stated that although alternatives to the PSTN for providing high speed communications services to residential consumers exist (fibre optic networks, wireless local loops or upgradable TV networks), none of these

alternatives may be considered as a substitute to the fixed local loop infrastructure.[67] Future innovative and technological changes may, however, justify different conclusions.[68]

69. Access to mobile networks may also be defined by reference to two potentially separate markets, one for call origination and another for call termination. In this respect, the question whether the access market to mobile infrastructure relates to access to an individual mobile network or to all mobile networks, in general, should be decided on the basis of an analysis of the structure and functioning of the market.[69]

3. Assessing Significant Market Power (Dominance)

70. According to Article 14 of the framework Directive "an undertaking shall be deemed to have significant market power if, either individually or jointly with others, it enjoys a position equivalent to dominance, that is to say a position of economic strength affording it the power to behave to an appreciable extent independently of competitors customers and ultimately consumers". This is the definition that the Court of Justice case-law ascribes to the concept of dominant position in Article [102 TFEU].[70] The new framework has aligned the definition of SMP with the Court's definition of dominance within the meaning of Article [102 TFEU].[71] Consequently, in applying the new definition of SMP, NRAs will have to ensure that their decisions are in accordance with the Commission's practice and the relevant jurisprudence of the Court of Justice and the Court of First Instance on dominance.[72] However, the application of the new definition of SMP, *ex-ante*, calls for certain methodological adjustments to be made regarding the way market power is assessed. In particular, when assessing *ex-ante* whether one or more undertakings are in a dominant position in the relevant market, NRAs are, in principle, relying on different sets of assumptions and expectations than those relied upon by a competition authority applying Article [102], *ex post*, within a context of an alleged committed abuse.[73] Often, the lack of evidence or of records of past behaviour or conduct will mean that the market analysis will have to be based mainly on a prospective assessment. The accuracy of the market analysis carried out by NRAs will thus be conditioned by information and data existing at the time of the adoption of the relevant decision.

71. The fact that an NRA's initial market predictions do not finally materialise in a given case does not necessarily mean that its decision at the time of its adoption was inconsistent with the Directive. In applying *ex ante* the concept of dominance, NRAs must be accorded discretionary powers

correlative to the complex character of the economic, factual and legal situations that will need to be assessed. In accordance with the framework Directive, market assessments by NRAs will have to be undertaken on a regular basis. In this context, therefore, NRAs will have the possibility to react at regular intervals to any market developments and to take any measure deemed necessary.

3.1. Criteria for assessing SMP

72. As the Court has stressed, a finding of a dominant position does not preclude some competition in the market. It only enables the undertaking that enjoys such a position, if not to determine, at least to have an appreciable effect on the conditions under which that competition will develop, and in any case to act in disregard of any such competitive constraint so long as such conduct does not operate to its detriment.[74]

Notes

[74] Case 85/76, *Hoffmann-La Roche v Commission* [1979] ECR 461, paragraph 39. It should be stressed here that for the purposes of *ex-ante* regulation, if an undertaking has already been imposed regulatory obligations, the fact that competition may have been restored in the relevant market as a result precisely of the obligations thus imposed, this does not mean that that undertaking is no longer in a dominant position and that it should no longer continue being designated as having SMP.

Commentary
para 72: B&C: 10.026

73. In an *ex-post* analysis, a competition authority may be faced with a number of different examples of market behaviour each indicative of market power within the meaning of Article [102]. However, in an *ex-ante* environment, market power is essentially measured by reference of the power of the undertaking concerned to raise prices by restricting output without incurring a significant loss of sales or revenues.

74. The market power of an undertaking can be constrained by the existence of potential competitors.[75] An NRA should thus take into account the likelihood that undertakings not currently active on the relevant product market may in the medium term decide to enter the market following a small but significant non-transitory price increase. Undertakings which, in case of such a price increase, are in a position to switch or extend their line of production/services and enter the market should be treated by NRAs as potential market participants even if they do not currently produce the relevant product or offer the relevant service.

Notes

[75] The absence of any substitutable service or product may justify a finding of a situation of economic dependence which is characteristic of the existence of a dominant position. See Commission decisions, *Decca Navigator System* (OJ L 43, 15.2.1987, p.27) and *Magill TV Guide: ITP, BBC, RTE* (OJ L 78, 21.3.1989, p.43). See also, Case 22/78 *Hugin v Commission* [1979] ECR 1869, Case 226/84, *British Leyland v Commission* [1986] ECR 3263.

75. As explained in the paragraphs below, a dominant position is found by reference to a number of criteria and its assessment is based, as stated above, on a forward-looking market analysis based on existing market conditions. Market shares are often used as a proxy for market power. Although a high market share alone is not sufficient to establish the possession of significant market power (dominance), it is unlikely that a firm without a significant share of the relevant market would be in a dominant position. Thus, undertakings with market shares of no more than 25% are not likely to enjoy a (single) dominant position on the market concerned.[76] In the Commission's decision-making practice, single dominance concerns normally arise in the case of undertakings with market shares of over 40%, although the Commission may in some cases have concerns about dominance even with lower market shares,[77] as dominance may occur without the existence of a large market share. According to established case-law, very large market shares—in excess of 50%—are in themselves, save in exceptional circumstances, evidence of the existence of a dominant position.[78] An undertaking with a large market share may be presumed to have SMP, that is, to be in a dominant position, if its market share has remained stable over time.[79] The fact that an undertaking with a significant position on the market is gradually losing market share may well indicate that the market is becoming more competitive, but it does not preclude a finding of

significant market power. On the other hand, fluctuating market shares over time may be indicative of a lack of market power in the relevant market.

Notes

76 See, also, recital 15 of Council Regulation (EEC) No 4064/89.

77 *United Brands v Commission*, op. cit. The greater the difference between the market share of the undertaking in question and that of its competitors, the more likely will it be that the said undertaking is in a dominant position. For instance, in Case COMP/M.1741—*MCI WorldCom/Sprint* it was found that the merged entity would have in the market for the provision of top-level Internet connectivity an absolute combined market share of more than [35–45]%, several times larger than its closest competitor, enabling it to behave independently of its competitors and customers (see paragraphs 114, 123, 126, 146, 155 and 196).

78 Case C-62/86, *AKZO v Commission*, [1991] ECR I-3359, paragraph 60; Case T-228/97, *Irish Sugar v Commission*, [1999] ECR II-2969, paragraph 70, Case *Hoffmann-La Roche v Commission*, op. cit, paragraph 41, Case T-139/98, *AAMS and Others v Commission* [2001] ECR II-[3413], paragraph 51. However, large market shares can become accurate measurements only on the assumption that competitors are unable to expand their output by sufficient volume to meet the shifting demand resulting from a rival's price increase.

79 Case *Hoffmann-La Roche v Commission*, op. cit., paragraph 41, Case C-62/86, *Akzo v Commission* [1991] ECR I-3359, paragraphs 56, 59. "An undertaking which has a very large market share and holds it for some time, by means of the volume of production and the sale of the supply which it stands for—without holders of much smaller market shares being able to meet rapidly the demand from those who would like to break away from the undertaking which has largest market share—is by virtue of that share in a position of strength which makes it an unavoidable trading partner and which, because of this alone, secures for it, at the very least during relatively long periods, that freedom of action which is the special feature of a dominant position", Case *AAMS and Others v Commission*, op. cit., paragraph 51.

Commentary
para 75: B&C: 12.071

76. As regards the methods used for measuring market size and market shares, both volume sales and value sales provide useful information for market measurement.[80] In the case of bulk products preference is given to volume whereas in the case of differentiated products (i.e. branded products) sales in value and their associated market share will often be considered to reflect better the relative position and strength of each provider. In bidding markets the number of bids won and lost may also be used as approximation of market shares.[81]

Notes

80 Notice on market definition, op. cit., at p.5.

81 See Case COMP/M.1741—*MCI WorldCom/Sprint*, paragraph 239–240. In bidding markets, however, it is important not to rely only on market shares as they in themselves may not be representative of the undertakings actual position, for further discussion, see, also, Case COMP/M.2201—*MAN/Aüwarter*.

77. The criteria to be used to measure the market share of the undertaking(s) concerned will depend on the characteristics of the relevant market. It is for NRAs to decide which are the criteria most appropriate for measuring market presence. For instance, leased lines revenues, leased capacity or numbers of leased line termination points are possible criteria for measuring an undertaking's relative strength on leased lines markets. As the Commission has indicated, the mere number of leased line termination points does not take into account the different types of leased lines that are available on the market—ranging from analogue voice quality to high-speed digital leased lines, short distance to long distance international leased lines. Of the two criteria, leased lines revenues may be more transparent and less complicated to measure. Likewise, retail revenues, call minutes or numbers of fixed telephone lines or subscribers of public telephone network operators are possible criteria for measuring the market shares of undertakings operating in these markets.[82] Where the market defined is that of interconnection, a more realistic measurement parameter would be the revenues accrued for terminating calls to customers on fixed or mobile networks. This is so because the use of revenues, rather than for example call minutes, takes account of the fact that call minutes can have different values (i.e. local, long distance and international) and provides a measure of market presence that reflects both the number of customers and network coverage.[83] For the same reasons, the use of revenues for terminating calls to customers of mobile networks may be the most appropriate means to measure the market presence of mobile network operators.[84]

Notes

82 See, Determination of organisations with significant power (SMP) for the implementation of the ONP Directive, DG XIII, 1 March 1999, at <http://europa.eu.int/ISPO/infosoc/telecompolicy/en/SMPdeter.pdf>, at paragraph 3.2.
83 Idem, at paragraph 5.2.
84 With regard to the interconnection market of fixed and mobile networks, the termination traffic to be measured should include own network traffic and interconnection traffic received from all other fixed and mobile networks, national or international.

78. It is important to stress that the existence of a dominant position cannot be established on the sole basis of large market shares. As mentioned above, the existence of high market shares simply means that the operator concerned might be in a dominant position. Therefore, NRAs should undertake a thorough and overall analysis of the economic characteristics of the relevant market before coming to a conclusion as to the existence of significant market power. In that regard, the following criteria can also be used to measure the power of an undertaking to behave to an appreciable extent independently of its competitors, customers and consumers. These criteria include amongst others:
    — overall size of the undertaking,
    — control of infrastructure not easily duplicated,
    — technological advantages or superiority,
    — absence of or low countervailing buying power,
    — easy or privileged access to capital markets/financial resources,
    — product/services diversification (e.g. bundled products or services),
    — economies of scale,
    — economies of scope,
    — vertical integration,
    — a highly developed distribution and sales network,
    — absence of potential competition,
    — barriers to expansion.

Commentary
para 78: B&C: 12.071

79. A dominant position can derive from a combination of the above criteria, which taken separately may not necessarily be determinative.
80. A finding of dominance depends on an assessment of ease of market entry. In fact, the absence of barriers to entry deters, in principle, independent anti-competitive behaviour by an undertaking with a significant market share. In the electronic communications sector, barriers to entry are often high because of existing legislative and other regulatory requirements which may limit the number of available licences or the provision of certain services (i.e. GSM/DCS or 3G mobile services). Furthermore, barriers to entry exist where entry into the relevant market requires large investments and the programming of capacities over a long time in order to be profitable.[85] However, high barriers to entry may become less relevant with regard to markets characterised by on-going technological progress. In electronic communications markets, competitive constraints may come from innovative threats from potential competitors that are not currently in the market. In such markets, the competitive assessment should be based on a prospective, forward-looking approach.

Notes

85 *Hoffmann-La Roche v Commission*, op. cit., at paragraph 48. One of the most important types of entry barriers is sunk costs. Sunk costs are particularly relevant to the electronic communications sector in view of the fact that large investments are necessary to create, for instance, an efficient electronic communications network for the provision of access services and it is likely that little could be recovered if a new entrant decides to exit the market. Entry barriers are exacerbated by further economies of scope and density which generally characterise such networks. Thus, a large network is always likely to have lower costs than a smaller one, with the result that an entrant in order to take a large share of the market and be able to compete would have to price below the incumbent, making it thus difficult to recover sunk costs.

81. As regards the relevance of the notion of "essential facilities" for the purposes of applying the new definition of SMP, there is for the moment no jurisprudence in relation to the electronic communications sector. However, this notion, which is mainly relevant with regard to the existence of an abuse of a dominant position under Article [102 TFEU], is less relevant with regard to the *ex-ante* assessment of SMP within the meaning of Article 14 of the framework Directive. In particular, the doctrine of "essential facilities" is complementary to existing general obligations imposed on dominant undertaking, such as the obligation not to discriminate among customers and has been applied in cases under Article [102] in exceptional circumstances, such as where the refusal to supply or to grant access to third parties would limit or prevent the emergence of new markets, or new products, contrary to Article [102(b)] of the Treaty. It has thus primarily been associated with access issues or cases involving a refusal to supply or to deal under Article [102] of the Treaty, without the presence of any discriminatory treatment. Under existing case-law, a product or service cannot be considered "necessary" or "essential" unless there is no real or potential substitute. Whilst it is true that an undertaking which is in possession of an "essential facility" is by definition in a dominant position on any market for that facility, the contrary is not always true. The fact that a given facility is not "essential" or "indispensable" for an economic activity on some distinct market, within the meaning of the existing case-law[86] does not mean that the owner of this facility might not be in a dominant position. For instance, a network operator can be in a dominant position despite the existence of alternative competing networks if the size or importance of its network affords him the possibility to behave independently from other network operators.[87] In other words, what matters is to establish whether a given facility affords its owner significant market power in the market without thus being necessary to further establish that the said facility can also be considered "essential" or "indispensable" within the meaning of existing case-law.

Notes

86 Joined Cases C-241/91 P and C-242/91 P, *RTE and ITP v Commission*, [1995] ECR I-743, Case C-7/97, *Oscar Bronner* [1998] ECR I-7791, and Joined Cases T-374/94, T-375/94, T-384/94 and T-388/94, *European Night Services and others v Commission* [1998] ECR II-3141.
87 Case COMP/M.1741—*MCI WorldCom/Sprint*, paragraph 196.

82. It follows from the foregoing that the doctrine of the "essential facilities" is less relevant for the purposes of applying *ex ante* Article 14 of the framework Directive than applying ex-post Article [102 TFEU].

3.1.1. Leverage of market power

83. According to Article 14(3) of the framework Directive, "where an undertaking has significant market power on a specific market, it may also be deemed to have significant market power on a closely related market, where the links between the two markets are such as to allow the market power held in one market to be leveraged into the other market, thereby strengthening the market power of the undertaking".

84. This provision is intended to address a market situation comparable to the one that gave rise to the Court's judgment in *Tetra Pak II*.[88] In that case, the Court decided that an undertaking that had a dominant position in one market, and enjoyed a leading position on a distinct but closely associated market, was placed as a result in a situation comparable to that of holding a dominant position on the markets in question taken as a whole. Thanks to its dominant position on the first market, and its market presence on the associated, secondary market, an undertaking may thus leverage the market power which it enjoys in the first market and behave independently of its customers on the latter market.[89] Although in *Tetra Pak* the markets taken as a whole in which Tetra Pak was found to be dominant were horizontal, close associative links, within the meaning of the Court's case-law, will most often be found in vertically integrated markets. This is often the case in the telecommunications sector, where an operator often has a dominant position on the infrastructure market and a significant presence on the downstream, services market.[90] Under such circumstances, an NRA may consider it appropriate to find that such operator has SMP on both markets taken together. However, in practice, if an undertaking has been designated as having SMP on an upstream wholesale or access market, NRAs will normally be in a position to

prevent any likely spill-over or leverage effects downstream into the retail or services markets by imposing on that undertaking any of the obligations provided for in the access Directive which may be appropriate to avoid such effects. Therefore, it is only where the imposition of *ex-ante* obligations on an undertaking which is dominant in the (access) upstream market would not result in effective competition on the (retail) downstream market that NRAs should examine whether Article 14(3) may apply.

Notes

[88] Case C-333/94 P, *Tetra Pak v Commission* [1996] ECR I-5951.

[89] See, also, Case COMP/M.2146—*Tetra Laval/Sidel*, paragraphs 325–389, *subjudice*, T-5/02. [Ed note: see now Case T-5/02 *Tetra Level BV v Commission* [2002] ECR II-4381; case C-12/03 P *Commission v Tetra Level BV* [2005] ECR I-987.]

[90] See Access notice, paragraph 65.

85. The foregoing considerations are also relevant in relation to horizontal markets.[91] Moreover, irrespective of whether the markets under consideration are vertical or horizontal, both markets should be electronic communications markets within the meaning of Article 2 of the framework Directive and both should display such characteristics as to justify the imposition of *ex-ante* regulatory obligations.[92]

Notes

[91] In the case of horizontal markets, the market analysis should focus on establishing the existence of close associative links which will enable an undertaking dominant in one market to behave independently of its competitors in a neighbouring market. Such links may be found to exist by reference to the type of conduct of suppliers and users in the markets under consideration (same customers and/or suppliers in both markets, i.e. customers buying both retail voice calls and retail Internet access) or the fact that the input product or service is essentially the same (i.e. provision by a fixed operator of network infrastructure to ISPs for wholesale call origination and wholesale call termination); see, also, Case T-83/91, *Tetra Pak v Commission*, op. cit., paragraph 120 and Case COMP/M.2416—*Tetra Laval/Sidel*.

[92] Article 14(3) of the framework Directive is not intended to apply in relation to market power leveraged from a "regulated" market into an emerging, "non-regulated" market. In such cases, any abusive conduct in the "emerging" market would normally be dealt with under Article [102 TFEU].

3.1.2. Collective dominance

86. Under Article [102 TFEU], a dominant position can be held by one or more undertakings ("collective dominance"). Article 14(2) of the framework Directive also provides that an undertaking may enjoy significant market power, that is, it may be in a dominant position, either individually or jointly with others.

87. In the Access notice, the Commission had stated that, although at the time both its own practice and the case-law of the Court were still developing, it would consider two or more undertakings to be in a collective dominant position when they had substantially the same position vis-à-vis their customers and competitors as a single company has if it is in a dominant position, provided that no effective competition existed between them. The lack of competition could be due, in practice, to the existence of certain links between those companies. The Commission had also stated, however, that the existence of such links was not a prerequisite for a finding of joint dominance.[93]

Notes

[93] See Access notice, paragraph 79.

88. Since the publication of the Access notice, the concept of collective dominance has been tested in a number of decisions taken by the Commission under Regulation No 17 and under the merger control Regulation. In addition, both the Court of First Instance (CFI) and the Court of Justice of the European Communities (ECJ) have given judgments which have contributed to further clarifying the exact scope of this concept.

3.1.2.1. The jurisprudence of the CFI/ECJ

89. The expression "one or more undertakings" in Article [102 TFEU] implies that a dominant position may be held by two or more economic entities which are legally and economically independent of each other.[94]

Notes

94 Joined Cases C-395/96 P and C-396/96 P, *Compagnie maritime belge and others v Commission* [2000] ECR I-1365.

90. Until the ruling of the ECJ in *Compagnie maritime belge* **95** and the ruling of the CFI in *Gencor* **96** (see below), it might have been argued that a finding of collective dominance was based on the existence of economic links, in the sense of structural links, or other factors which could give rise to a connection between the undertakings concerned.**97** The question of whether collective dominance could also apply to an oligopolistic market, that is a market comprised of few sellers, in the absence of any kind of links among the undertakings present in such a market, was first raised in *Gencor*. The case concerned the legality of a decision adopted by the Commission under the merger control Regulation prohibiting the notified transaction on the grounds that it would lead to the creation of a duopoly market conducive to a situation of oligopolistic dominance.**98** Before the CFI, the parties argued that the Commission had failed to prove the existence of "links" between the members of the duopoly within the meaning of the existing case-law.

Notes

95 Idem, at paragraph 39.
96 Case T102/96, *Gencor v Commission* [1999] ECR II-753.
97 See Joined Cases T-68/89, T-77/89 and T-78/89, *SIV and Others v Commission* [1992] ECR II-1403, paragraph 358, Case C-393/92 *Almelo* [1994] ECR I-1477, paragraph 43, Case C-96/94, *Centro Servizi Spediporto* [1995] ECR I-2883, paragraph 33, Joined Cases C-140/94, 141/94, and C-142/94, *DIP*, [1995] ECR I-3257, paragraph 62, Case C-70/95, *Sodemare* [1997] ECR I-3395, paragraph 46, and Joined Cases C-68/94 and C-30/95 *France and Others v Commission* [1998] ECR I-1375, paragraph 221.
98 Case IV/M.619—*Gencor Lonhro* (OJ L 11, 14.1.1997, p.30).

91. The CFI dismissed the application by stating, *inter alia*, that there was no legal precedent suggesting that the notion of "economic links" was restricted to the notion of structural links between the undertakings concerned: According to the CFI, "there is no reason whatsoever in legal or economic terms to exclude from the notion of economic links the relationship of interdependence existing between the parties to a tight oligopoly within which, in a market with the appropriate characteristics, in particular in terms of market concentration, transparency and product homogeneity, those parties are in a position to anticipate one another's behaviour and are therefore strongly encouraged to align their conduct in the market, in particular in such a way as to maximise their joint profits by restricting production with a view to increasing prices. In such a context, each trader is aware that highly competitive action on its part designed to increase its market share (for example a price cut) would provoke identical action by the others, so that it would derive no benefit from its initiative. All the traders would thus be affected by the reduction in price *levels*".**99** As the Court pointed out, market conditions may be such that "each undertaking may become aware of common interests and, in particular, cause prices to increase without having to enter into an agreement or resort to concerted practice".**100**

Notes

99 *Gencor v Commission*, op. cit., at paragraph 276.
100 Idem, at paragraph 277.

92. The CFI's ruling in *Gencor* was later endorsed by the ECJ in *Compagnie maritime belge*, where the Court gave further guidance as to how the term of collective dominance should be understood and as to which conditions must be fulfilled before such finding can be made. According to the Court, in order to show that two or more undertakings hold a joint dominant position, it is necessary to consider whether the undertakings concerned together constitute a collective entity vis-à-vis their competitors, their trading partners and their consumers on a particular market.**101** This will be the case when (i) there is no effective competition among the undertakings in question; and (ii) the said undertakings adopt a uniform conduct or common policy in the relevant market.**102** Only when that question is answered in the affirmative, is it appropriate to consider whether the collective entity actually holds a dominant position.**103** In particular, it is necessary to ascertain whether economic links exist between the undertakings concerned which enable them to act independently of their competitors, customers and consumers. The Court recognised

that an implemented agreement, decision or concerted practice (whether or not covered by an exemption under Article [101(3)] of the Treaty) may undoubtedly result in the undertakings concerned being linked in a such way that their conduct on a particular market on which they are active results in them being perceived as a collective entity vis-à-vis their competitors, their trading partners and consumers.[104]

Notes

[101] *Compagnie maritime belge transports and Others*, op. cit., at paragraph 39, see, also, Case T-342/99 *Airtours/Commission* [2002] ECR II-[2585], paragraph 76.

[102] See, in particular, *France and Others v Commission*, op. cit., paragraph 221.

[103] *Compagnie maritime belge*, at paragraph 39.

[104] Idem at paragraph 44.

93. The mere fact, however, that two or more undertakings are linked by an agreement, a decision of associations of undertakings or a concerted practice within the meaning of Article [101(1)] of the Treaty does not, of itself, constitute a necessary basis for such a finding. As the Court stated, "a finding of a collective dominant position may also be based on other connecting factors and would depend on an economic assessment and, in particular, on an assessment of the structure of the market in question".[105]

Notes

[105] Idem at paragraph 45.

94. It follows from the *Gencor* and *Compagnie maritime belge* judgments that, although the existence of structural links can be relied upon to support a finding of a collective dominant position, such a finding can also be made in relation to an oligopolistic or highly concentrated market whose structure alone in particular, is conducive to coordinated effects on the relevant market.[106]

Notes

[106] The use here of the term "coordinated effects" is no different from the term "parallel anticompetitive behaviour" also used in Commission's decisions applying the concept of collective (oligopolistic) dominance.

3.1.2.2. The Commission's decision-making practice and Annex II of the framework Directive

95. In a number of decisions adopted under the merger control Regulation, the Commission considered the concept of collective dominance. It sought in those cases to ascertain whether the structure of the oligopolistic markets in question was conducive to coordinated effects on those markets.[107]

Notes

[107] See in particular, Cases COMP/M.2498—*UPM-Kymmene/Haindl*, and COMP/M.2499—*Norske Skog/Parenco/Walsum*, Case COMP/M.2201—*MAN/Auwärter*, Case COMP/M.2097—*SCA/Matsä Tissue*, Case COMP/M.1882—*Pirelli/BICC*, Case COMP/M.1741—*MCI WorldCom/Sprint, subjudice*, T-310/00 [Ed note: see now [2004] ECR II-3253] Case IV/M.1524—*Airtours/First Choice* (OJ L 93, 13.4.2000, p.1), *subjudice* T-342/99 [Ed note: see now [2002] ECR II-2585], Case IV/M.1383—*Exxon/Mobil*, Case IV/M.1313—*Danish Crown/Vestjyske Slagterier* (OJ L 20, 25.1.2000, p.1), Case IV/M.1225—*Enso/Stora* (OJ L 254, 29.9.1999, p.9), Case IV/M.1016—*Price Waterhouse/Coopers & Lybrand* (OJ L 50, 26.2.1999, p.27), Case IV/M.619—*Gencor/Lonrho*, cit., Case IV/M.308, *Kali + Salz/MdK/Treuhand* (OJ L 186, 21.7.1994, p.38) and Case IV/M.190—*Nestlé/Perrier* (OJ L 356, 5.12.1992, p.1).

96. When assessing *ex-ante* the likely existence or emergence of a market which is or could become conducive to collective dominance in the form of tacit coordination, NRAs, should analyse:
    (a) whether the characteristics of the market makes it conducive to tacit coordination; and
    (b) whether such form of coordination is sustainable that is, (i) whether any of the oligopolists have the ability and incentive to deviate from the coordinated outcome, considering the ability and incentives of the non-deviators to retaliate; and (ii) whether buyers/fringe competitors/potential entrants have the ability and incentive to challenge any anti-competitive coordinated outcome.[108]

97. This analysis is facilitated by looking at a certain number of criteria which are summarised in Annex II of the framework Directive, which have also been used by the Commission in applying the notion of collective dominance under the merger control Regulation. According to this Annex, "two or more undertakings can be found to be in a joint dominant position within the meaning of Article 14 if, even in the absence of structural or other links between them, they operate in a market, the structure of which is considered to be conducive to coordinated effects.[109] Without prejudice to the case-law of the Court of Justice on joint dominance, this is likely to be the case where the market satisfies a number of appropriate characteristics, in particular in terms of market concentration, transparency and other characteristics mentioned below:
    — mature market,
    — stagnant or moderate growth on the demand side,
    — low elasticity of demand,
    — homogeneous product,
    — similar cost structures,
    — similar market shares,
    — lack of technical innovation, mature technology,
    — absence of excess capacity,
    — high barriers to entry,
    — lack of countervailing buying power,
    — lack of potential competition,
    — various kind of informal or other links between the undertakings concerned,
    — retaliatory mechanisms,
    — lack or reduced scope for price competition".

98. Annex II of the framework Directive expressly states that the above is not an exhaustive list, nor are the criteria cumulative. Rather, the list is intended to illustrate the sorts of evidence that could be used to support assertions concerning the existence of a collective (oligopolistic) dominance in the form of tacit coordination.[110] As stated above, the list also shows that the existence of structural links among the undertakings concerned is not a prerequisite for finding a collective dominant position. It is however clear that where such links exist, they can be relied upon to explain, together with any of the other abovementioned criteria, why in a given oligopolistic market coordinated effects are likely to arise. In the absence of such links, in order to establish whether a market is conducive to collective dominance in the form of tacit coordination, it is necessary to consider a number of characteristics of the market. While these characteristics are often presented in the form of the abovementioned list, it is necessary to examine all of them and to make an overall assessment rather than mechanistically applying a "check list". Depending on the circumstances of the case, the fact that one or another of the structural elements usually associated with collective dominance may not be clearly established is not in itself decisive to exclude the likelihood of a coordinated outcome.[111]

99. In an oligopolistic market where most, if not all, of the abovementioned criteria are met, it should be examined whether, in particular, the market operators have a strong incentive to converge to a coordinated market outcome and refrain from reliance on competitive conduct. This will be the case where the long-term benefits of an anti-competitive conduct outweigh any short-term gains resulting from a resort to a competitive behaviour.

100. It must be stressed that a mere finding that a market is concentrated does not necessarily warrant a finding that its structure is conducive to collective dominance in the form of tacit coordination.[112]

Notes

[112] For instance, in Case COMP/M.2201—*MAN/Auwärter*, despite the fact that two of the parties present in the German city-bus market in Germany, MAN/Auwärter and EvoBus, would each supply just under half of that market, the Commission concluded that there was no risk of joint dominance. In particular, the Commission found that any tacit division of the market between EvoBus and MAN/Auwärter was not likely as there would be no viable coordination mechanism. Secondly, significant disparities between EvoBus and MAN/Auwärter, such as different cost structures, would make it likely that the companies would compete rather than collude. Likewise, in the *Alcoa/British Aluminium* case, the Commission found that despite the fact that two of the parties present in the relevant market accounted for almost 80% of the sales, the market could not be said to be conducive to oligopolistic dominance since (i) market shares were volatile and unstable; and (ii) demand was quite irregular making it difficult for the parties to be able to respond to each other's action in order to tacitly coordinate their behaviour. Furthermore, the market was not transparent in relation to prices and purchasers had significant countervailing power. The Commission's conclusions were further reinforced by the absence of any credible retaliation mechanism likely to sustain any tacit coordination and the fact that competition in the market was not only based on prices but depended to a large extent on technological innovation and after-sales follow-up, Case COMP/M.2111—*Alcoa/British Aluminium*.

101. Ultimately, in applying the notion of collective dominance in the form of tacit coordination, the criteria which will carry the most sway will be those which are critical to a coordinated outcome in the specific market under consideration. For instance, in Case COMP/M.2499—*Norske Skog/Parenco/Walsum*, the Commission came to the conclusion that even if the markets for newsprint and wood-containing magazine paper were concentrated, the products were homogeneous, demand was highly inelastic, buyer power was limited and barriers to entry were high, nonetheless the limited stability of market shares, the lack of symmetry in costs structures and namely, the lack of transparency of investments decisions and the absence of a credible retaliation mechanism rendered unlikely and unsustainable any possibility of tacit coordination among the oligopolists.[113]

Notes

[113] Likewise, in Case COMP/M.2348—*Outokumpu/Norzink*, the Commission found that even if the zinc market was composed of few players, entry barriers were high and demand growth perspectives low, the likelihood of the emergence of a market structure conducive to coordinated outcome was unlikely if it could be shown that (i) parties could not manipulate the formation of prices; (ii) producers had asymmetric cost structures and there was no credible retaliation mechanism in place.

3.1.2.3. Collective dominance and the telecommunications sector

102. In applying the notion of collective dominance, NRAs may also take into consideration decisions adopted under the merger control Regulation in the electronic communications sector, in which the Commission has examined whether any of the notified transactions could give rise to a finding of collective dominance.

103. In *MCI WorldCom/Sprint*, the Commission examined whether the merged entity together with Concert Alliance could be found to enjoy a collective dominant position on the market for global telecommunications services (GTS). Given that operators on that market competed on a bid basis where providers were selected essentially in the first instances of the bidding process on the basis of their ability to offer high quality, tailor-made sophisticated services, and not on the basis of prices, the Commission's investigation was focused on the incentives for market participants to engage in parallel behaviour as to who wins what bid (and who had won what bids).[114] After having examined in depth the structure of the market (homogenous product, high barriers of entry, customers countervailing power, etc.) the Commission concluded that it was not able to

show absence of competitive constraints from actual competitors, a key factor in examining whether parallel behaviour can be sustained, and thus decided not to pursue further its objections in relation to that market.[115]

Notes

[114] See Case COMP/M.1741—*MCI WorldCom/Sprint*, paragraph 263.

[115] Idem, paragraphs 257–302.

104. In *BT/Esat*,[116] one of the issues examined by the Commission was whether market conditions in the Irish market for dial-up Internet access lent themselves to the emergence of a duopoly consisting of the incumbent operator, Eircom, and the merged entity. The Commission concluded that this was not the case for the following reasons. First, market shares were not stable; second, demand was doubling every six months; third, internet access products were not considered homogeneous; and finally, technological developments were one of the main characteristics of the market.[117]

Notes

[116] Case COMP/M.1838—*BT/Esat*.

[117] Idem, paragraphs 10 to 14.

105. In *Vodafone/Airtouch*,[118] the Commission found that the merged entity would have joint control of two of the four mobile operators present on the German mobile market (namely D2 and E-Plus, the other two being T-Mobil and VIAG Interkom). Given that entry into the market was highly regulated, in the sense that licences were limited by reference to the amount of available radio frequencies, and that market conditions were transparent, it could not be ruled out that such factors could lead to the emergence of a duopoly conducive to coordinated effects.[119]

Notes

[118] Case IV/M.1430—*Vodafone/Airtouch*.

[119] Idem, at paragraph 28. The likely emergence of a duopolistic market concerned only the three largest mobile operators, that is D2 and E-Plus, on the one hand, and T-Mobil on the other hand, given that VIAG Interkom's market share was below 5%. The Commission's concerns were finally removed after the parties proposed to divest Vodafone's entire stake in E-Plus.

106. In *France Telecom/Orange* the Commission found that, prior to the entry of Orange into the Belgian mobile market, the two existing players, Proximus and Mobistar, were in a position to exercise joint dominance. As the Commission noted, for the four years preceding Orange's entry, both operators had almost similar and transparent pricing, their prices following exactly the same trends.[120] In the same decision the Commission further dismissed claims by third parties as to the risk of a collective dominant position of Vodafone and France Telecom in the market for the provision of pan-European mobile services to internationally mobile customers. Other than significant asymmetries between the market shares of the two operators, the market was considered to be emerging, characterised by an increasing demand and many types of different services on offer and on price.[121]

Notes

[120] Case COMP/M.2016—*France Telecom/Orange*, at paragraph 26.

[121] Idem, at paragraphs 39–40. In its working document "On the initial findings of the sector inquiry into mobile roaming charges", the Commission made reference to (i) the likely existence of a number of economic links between mobile operators, namely through their interconnection agreements, their membership of the GSM Association, the WAP and the UMTS forum, the fact that terms and conditions of roaming agreements were almost standardised; and (ii) the likely existence of high barriers to entry. In its preliminary assessment the Commission also stressed that the fact that the mobile market is, in general, technology driven, did not seem to have affected the conditions of competition prevailing on the wholesale international roaming market, see: <http://europa.eu.int/comm/competition/antitrust/others/sector_inquiries/roaming/>, at pages 24 and 25.

4. Imposition, Maintenance, Amendment or Withdrawal of Obligations under the Regulatory Framework

107. Section 3 of these guidelines dealt with the analysis of relevant markets that NRAs must carry out under Article 16 of the framework Directive to determine whether a market is effectively competitive, i.e. whether there are undertakings in that market who are in a dominant position. This section aims to provide guidance for NRAs on the action they should take following that analysis, i.e. the imposition, maintenance, amendment or withdrawal, as appropriate, of specific regulatory obligations on undertakings designated as having SMP. This section also describes the circumstances in which similar obligations than those that can be imposed on SMP operators may, exceptionally, be imposed on undertakings who have not been designated as having SMP.

108. The specific regulatory obligations which may be imposed on SMP undertakings can apply both to wholesale and retail markets. In principle, the obligations related to wholesale markets are set out in Articles 9 to 13 of the access Directive. The obligations related to retail markets are set out in Articles 17 to 19 of the universal service Directive.

109. The obligations set out in the access Directive are: transparency (Article 9); non-discrimination (Article 10); accounting separation (Article 11), obligations for access to and use of specific network facilities (Article 12), and price control and cost accounting obligations (Article 13). In addition, Article 8 of the access Directive provides that NRAs may impose obligations outside this list. In order to do so, they must submit a request to the Commission, which will take a decision, after seeking the advice of the Communications Committee, as to whether the NRA concerned is permitted to impose such obligations.

110. The obligations set out in the universal service Directive are: regulatory controls on retail services (Article 17), availability of the minimum set of leased lines (Article 18 and Annex VII) and carrier selection and preselection (Article 19).

111. Under the regulatory framework, these obligations should only be imposed on undertakings which have been designated as having SMP in a relevant market, except in certain defined cases, listed in Section 4.3.

4.1. Imposition, maintenance, amendment or withdrawal of obligations on SMP operators

112. As explained in Section 1, the notion of effective competition means that there is no undertaking with dominance on the relevant market. In other words, a finding that a relevant market is effectively competitive is, in effect, a determination that there is neither single nor joint dominance on that market. Conversely, a finding that a relevant market is not effectively competitive is a determination that there is single or joint dominance on that market.

113. If an NRA finds that a relevant market is subject to effective competition, it is not allowed to impose obligations on any operator on that relevant market under Article 16. If the NRA has previously imposed regulatory obligations on undertaking(s) in that market, the NRA must withdraw such obligations and may not impose any new obligation on that undertaking(s). As stipulated in Article 16(3) of the framework Directive, where the NRA proposes to remove existing regulatory obligations, it must give parties affected a reasonable period of notice.

114. If an NRA finds that competition in the relevant market is not effective because of the existence of an undertaking or undertakings in a dominant position, it must designate in accordance with Article 16(4) of the framework Directive the undertaking or undertakings concerned as having SMP and impose appropriate regulatory obligations on the undertaking(s) concerned. However, merely designating an undertaking as having SMP on a given market, without imposing any appropriate regulatory obligations, is inconsistent with the provisions of the new regulatory framework, notably Article 16(4) of the framework Directive. In other words, NRAs must impose at least one regulatory obligation on an undertaking that has been designated as having SMP. Where an NRA determines the existence of more than one undertaking with dominance, i.e. that a joint dominant position exists, it should also determine the most appropriate regulatory obligations to be imposed, based on the principle of proportionality.

115. If an undertaking was previously subject to obligations under the 1998 regulatory framework, the NRA must consider whether similar obligations continue to be appropriate under the new regulatory framework, based on a new market analysis carried out in accordance with these

guidelines. If the undertaking is found to have SMP in a relevant market under the new framework, regulatory obligations similar to those imposed under the 1998 regulatory framework may therefore be maintained. Alternatively, such obligations could be amended, or new obligations provided in the new framework might also be imposed, as the NRA considers appropriate.

116. Except where the Community's international commitments under international treaties prescribe the choice of regulatory obligation (see Section 4.4) or when the Directives prescribe particular remedies as under Article 18 and 19 of the universal service Directive, NRAs will have to choose between the range of regulatory obligations set out in the Directives in order to remedy a particular problem in a market found not to be effectively competitive. Where NRAs intend to impose other obligations for access and interconnection than those listed in the access Directive, they must submit a request for Commission approval of their proposed course of action. The Commission must seek the advice of the Communications Committee before taking its decision.

117. Community law, and in particular Article 8 of the framework Directive, requires NRAs to ensure that the measures they impose on SMP operators under Article 16 of the framework Directive are justified in relation to the objectives set out in Article 8 and are proportionate to the achievement of those objectives. Thus any obligation imposed by NRAs must be proportionate to the problem to be remedied. Article 7 of the framework Directive requires NRAs to set out the reasoning on which any proposed measure is based when they communicate that measure to other NRAs and to the Commission. Thus, in addition to the market analysis supporting the finding of SMP, NRAs need to include in their decisions a justification of the proposed measure in relation to the objectives of Article 8, as well as an explanation of why their decision should be considered proportionate.

118. Respect for the principle of proportionality will be a key criterion used by the Commission to assess measures proposed by NRAs under the procedure of Article 7 of framework Directive. The principle of proportionality is well-established in Community law. In essence, the principle of proportionality requires that the means used to attain a given end should be no more than what is appropriate and necessary to attain that end. In order to establish that a proposed measure is compatible with the principle of proportionality, the action to be taken must pursue a legitimate aim, and the means employed to achieve the aim must be both necessary and the least burdensome, i.e. it must be the minimum necessary to achieve the aim.

119. However, particularly in the early stages of implementation of the new framework, the Commission would not expect NRAs to withdraw existing regulatory obligations on SMP operators which have been designed to address legitimate regulatory needs which remain relevant, without presenting clear evidence that those obligations have achieved their purpose and are therefore no longer required since competition is deemed to be effective on the relevant market. Different remedies are available in the new regulatory framework to address different identified problems and remedies should be tailored to these specified problems.

120. The Commission, when consulted as provided for in Article 7(3) of the framework Directive, will also check that any proposed measure taken by the NRAs is in conformity with the regulatory framework as a whole, and will assess the impact of the proposed measure on the single market.

121. The Commission will assist NRAs to ensure that as far as possible they adopt consistent approaches in their choice of remedies where similar situations exist in different Member States. Moreover, as noted in Article 7(2) of the framework Directive, NRAs shall seek to agree on the types of remedies best suited to address particular situations in the marketplace.

4.2. Transnational markets: joint analysis by NRAs

122. Article 15(4) of the framework Directive gives the Commission the power to issue a Decision identifying product and service markets that are transnational, covering the whole of the Community or a substantial part thereof. Under the terms of Article 16(5) of the framework Directive, the NRAs concerned must jointly conduct the market analysis and decide whether obligations need to be imposed. In practice, the European Regulators Group is expected to provide a suitable forum for such a joint analysis.

123. In general, joint analysis by NRAs would follow similar procedures (e.g. for public consultation) to those required when a single national regulatory authority is conducting a market analysis. Precise arrangements for collective analysis and decision-making will need to be drawn up.

4.3. Imposition of certain specific regulatory obligations on non-SMP operators

124. The preceding parts of this section set out the procedures whereby certain specific obligations may be imposed on SMP undertakings, under Articles 7 and 8 of the access Directive and Article 16–19 of the universal service Directive. Exceptionally, similar obligations may be imposed on operators other than those that have been designated as having SMP, in the following cases, listed in Article 8(3) of the access Directive:

    — obligations covering *inter alia* access to conditional access systems, obligations to interconnect to ensure end-to-end interoperability, and access to application program interfaces and electronic programme guides to ensure accessibility to specified digital TV and radio broadcasting services (Article 5(1), 5(2) and 6 of the access Directive),

    — obligations that NRAs may impose for co-location where rules relating to environmental protection, health, security or town and country planning deprive other undertakings of viable alternatives to co-location (Article 12 of the framework Directive),

    — obligations for accounting separation on undertakings providing electronic communications services who enjoy special or exclusive rights in other sectors (Article 13 of the framework Directive),

    — obligations relating to commitments made by an undertaking in the course of a competitive or comparative selection procedure for a right of use of radio frequency (Condition B7 of the Annex to the authorisation Directive, applied via Article 6(1) of that Directive),

    — obligations to handle calls to subscribers using specific numbering resources and obligations necessary for the implementation of number portability (Articles 27, 28 and 30 of the universal service Directive),

    — obligations based on the relevant provisions of the data protection Directive, and

    — obligations to be imposed on non-SMP operators in order to comply with the Community's international commitments.

Commentary
para 124: F&N: 13.30

4.4. Relationship to WTO commitments

125. The EC and its Member States have given commitments in the WTO in relation to undertakings that are "major suppliers" of basic telecommunications services.[122] Such undertakings are subject to all of the obligations set out in the EC's and its Member States' commitments in the WTO for basic telecommunications services. The provisions of the new regulatory framework, in particular relating to access and interconnection, ensure that NRAs continue to apply the relevant obligations to undertakings that are major suppliers in accordance with the WTO commitments of the EC and its Member States.

Notes

[122] GATS commitments taken by EC on telecommunications: <http://gats-info.eu.int/gats-info/swtosvc.pl?&SECCODE=02.C>.

---

5. POWERS OF INVESTIGATION AND COOPERATION PROCEDURES FOR THE PURPOSE OF MARKET ANALYSIS

5.1. Overview

126. This section of the guidelines covers procedures in respect of an NRA's powers to obtain the information necessary to conduct a market analysis.

127. The regulatory framework contains provisions to enable NRAs to require undertakings that provide electronic communications networks and services to supply all the information, including confidential information, necessary for NRAs to assess the state of competition in the relevant markets and impose appropriate *ex-ante* obligations and thus to ensure compliance with the regulatory framework.

128. This section of the guidelines also includes guidance as to measures to ensure effective cooperation between NRAs and NCAs at national level, and among NRAs and between NRAs and the Commission at Community level. In particular this section deals with the exchange of information between those authorities.

129. Many electronic communication markets are fast-moving and their structures are changing rapidly. NRAs should ensure that the assessment of effective competition, the public consultation, and the designation of operators having SMP are all carried out within a reasonable period. Any unnecessary delay in the decision could have harmful effects on incentives for investment by undertakings in the relevant market and therefore on the interests of consumers.

5.2. Market analysis and powers of investigation

130. Under Article 16(1) of the framework Directive, NRAs must carry out an analysis of the relevant markets identified in the Recommendation and any Decision as soon as possible after their adoption or subsequent revision. The conclusions of the analysis of each of the relevant markets, together with the proposed regulatory action, must be published and a public consultation must be conducted, as described in Section 6.

131. In order to carry out their market analysis, NRAs will first need to collect all the information they consider necessary to assess market power in a given market. To the extent that such information needs to be obtained directly from undertakings, Article 11 of the authorisation Directive provides that undertakings are required by the terms of their general authorisation to supply the information necessary for NRAs to conduct a market analysis within the meaning of Article 16(2) of the framework Directive. This is reinforced by the more general obligation in Article 5(1) of the framework Directive which provides that Member States shall ensure that undertakings providing electronic communications networks and services provide all the information necessary for NRAs to ensure conformity with Community law.

132. When NRAs request information from an undertaking, they should state the reasons justifying the request and the time limit within which the information is to be provided. As provided for in Article 10(4) of the authorisation Directive, NRAs may be empowered to impose financial penalties on undertakings for failure to provide information.

133. In accordance with Article 5(4) of the framework Directive, NRAs must publish all information that would contribute to an open and competitive market, acting in accordance with national rules on public access to information and subject to Community and national rules on commercial confidentiality.

134. However, as regards information that is confidential in nature, the provisions of Article 5(3) of the framework Directive, require NRAs to ensure the confidentiality of such information in accordance with Community and national rules on business confidentiality. This confidentiality obligation applies equally to information that has been received in confidence from another public authority.

5.3. Cooperation procedures

Between NRAs and NCAs

135. Article 16(1) of the framework Directive requires NRAs to associate NCAs with the market analyses as appropriate. Member States should put in place the necessary procedures to guarantee that the analysis under Article 16 of the framework Directive is carried out effectively. As the NRAs conduct their market analyses in accordance with the methodologies of competition law, the views of NCAs in respect of the assessment of competition are highly relevant. Cooperation between NRAs and NCAs will be essential, but NRAs remain legally responsible for conducting the relevant analysis. Where under national law the tasks assigned under Article 16 of the framework Directive are carried out by two or more separate regulatory bodies, Member States should ensure clear division of tasks and set up procedures for consultation and cooperation between regulators in order to assure coherent analysis of the relevant markets.

136. Article 3(5) of the framework Directive requires NRAs and NCAs to provide each other with the information necessary for the application of the regulatory framework, and the receiving authority must ensure the same level of confidentiality as the originating authority. NCAs should therefore

provide NRAs with all relevant information obtained using the former's investigatory and enforcement powers, including confidential information.

137. Information that is considered confidential by an NCA, in accordance with Community and national rules on business confidentiality, should only be exchanged with NRAs where such exchange is necessary for the application of the provisions of the regulatory framework. The information exchanged should be limited to that which is relevant and proportionate to the purpose of such exchange.

Between the Commission and NRAs

138. For the regulatory framework to operate efficiently and effectively, it is vital that there is a high level of cooperation between the Commission and the NRAs. It is particularly important that effective informal cooperation takes place. The European Regulators Group will be of great importance in providing a framework for such cooperation, as part of its task of assisting and advising the Commission. Cooperation is likely to be of mutual benefit, by minimising the likelihood of divergences in approach between different NRAs, in particular divergent remedies to deal with the same problem.[123]

Notes

[123] The Communications Committee in Article 22 of the framework Directive also aims at ensuring effective cooperation between the Commission and the Member States.

---

139. In accordance with Article 5(2) of the framework Directive, NRAs must supply the Commission with information necessary for it to carry out its tasks under the Treaty. This covers information relating to the regulatory framework (to be used in verifying compatibility of NRA action with the legislation), but also information that the Commission might require, for example, in considering compliance with WTO commitments.

140. NRAs must ensure that, where they submit information to the Commission which they have requested undertakings to provide, they inform those undertakings that they have submitted it to the Commission.

141. The Commission can also make such information available to another NRA, unless the original NRA has made an explicit and reasoned request to the contrary. Although there is no legal requirement to do so, the Commission will normally inform the undertaking which originally provided the information that it has been passed on to another NRA.

Between NRAs

142. It is of the utmost importance that NRAs develop a common regulatory approach across Member States that will contribute to the development of a true single market for electronic communications. To this end, NRAs are required under Article 7(2) of the framework Directive to cooperate with each other and with the Commission in a transparent manner to ensure the consistent application, in all Member States, of the new regulatory framework. The European Regulators" Group is expected to serve as an important forum for cooperation.

143. Article 5(2) of the framework Directive also foresees that NRAs will exchange information directly between each other, as long as there is a substantiated request. This will be particularly necessary where a transnational market needs to be analysed, but it will also be required within the framework of cooperation in the European Regulators' Group. In all exchanges of information, the NRAs are required to maintain the confidentiality of information received.

6. PROCEDURES FOR CONSULTATION AND PUBLICATION OF PROPOSED NRA DECISIONS

6.1. Public consultation mechanism

144. Except in the urgent cases as explained below, an NRA that intends to take a measure which would have a significant impact on the relevant market should give the interested parties the opportunity to comment on the draft measure. To this effect, the NRA must hold a public consultation on its

proposed measure. Where the draft measure concerns a decision relating to an SMP designation or non-designation it should include the following:

— the market definition used and reasons therefor, with the exception of information that is confidential in accordance with European and national law on business confidentiality,

— evidence relating to the finding of dominance, with the exception of information that is confidential in accordance with European and national law on business confidentiality together with the identification of any undertakings proposed to be designated as having SMP,

— full details of the sector-specific obligations that the NRA proposes to impose, maintain, modify or withdraw on the abovementioned undertakings together with an assessment of the proportionality of that proposed measure.

145. The period of the consultation should be reasonable. However, NRAs' decisions should not be delayed excessively as this can impede the development of the market. For decisions related to the existence and designation of undertakings with SMP, the Commission considers that a period of two months would be reasonable for the public consultation. Different periods could be used in some cases if justified. Conversely, where a draft SMP decision is proposed on the basis of the results of an earlier consultation, the length of consultation period for these decisions may well be shorter than two months.

6.2. Mechanisms to consolidate the internal market for electronic communications

146. Where an NRA intends to take a measure which falls within the scope of the market definition or market analysis procedures of Articles 15 and 16 of the framework Directive, as well as when NRAs apply certain other specific Articles in the regulatory framework[124] and where the measures have an effect on trade between Member States, the NRAs must communicate the measures, together with their reasoning, to NRAs in other Member States and to the Commission in accordance with Article 7(3) of the framework Directive. It should do this at the same time as it begins its public consultation. The NRA must then give other NRAs and the Commission the chance to comment on the NRA's proposed measures, before adopting any final decision. The time available for other NRAs and the Commission to comment should be the same time period as that set by the NRA for its national public consultation, unless the latter is shorter than the minimum period of one month provided for in Article 7(3). The Commission may decide in justified circumstances to publish its comments.

Notes

124 The specific Articles covered are as follows: Articles 15 and 16 of the framework Directive (the latter of which refers to Articles 16–19 of the universal service Directive and Articles 7 and 8 of the access Directive), Articles 5 and 8 of the access Directive (the latter of which refers to the obligations provided for in Articles 9–13 of the access Directive) and Article 16 of the universal service Directive (which refers to Articles 17–19 of universal service Directive). In addition, Article 6 of the access Directive, although not explicitly referenced in Article 7 of the framework Directive, itself contains cross-reference to Article 7 of the framework Directive and is therefore covered by the procedures therein.

147. With regard to measures that could affect trade between Member States, this should be understood as meaning measures that may have an influence, direct or indirect, actual or potential, on the pattern of trade between Member States in a manner which might create a barrier to the single European market.[125] Therefore, the notion of an effect on trade between Member States is likely to cover a broad range of measures.

Notes

125 Recital 38 of the framework Directive.

148. NRAs must make public the results of the public consultation, except in the case of information that is confidential in accordance with Community and national law on business confidentiality.

149. With the exception of two specific cases, explained in the following paragraph, the NRA concerned may adopt the final measure after having taken account of views expressed during its mandatory consultation. The final measure must then be communicated to the Commission without delay.

6.3. Commission power to require the withdrawal of NRAs' draft measures

150. Under the terms of Article 7(4) of the framework Directive, there are two specific situations where the Commission has the possibility to require an NRA to withdraw a draft measure which falls within the scope of Article 7(3):
    — the draft measure concerns the definition of a relevant market which differs from that identified in the Recommendation, or
    — the draft measure concerns a decision as to whether to designate, or not to designate, an undertaking as having SMP, either individually or jointly with others.

151. In respect of the above two situations, where the Commission has indicated to the NRA in the course of the consultation process that it considers that the draft measure would create a barrier to the single European market or where the Commission has serious doubts as to the compatibility of the draft measure with Community law, the adoption of the measure must be delayed by a maximum of an additional two months.

152. During this two-month period, the Commission may, after consulting the Communications Committee following the advisory procedure,[126] take a decision requiring the NRA to withdraw the draft measure. The Commission's decision will be accompanied by a detailed and objective analysis of why it considers that the draft measure should not be adopted together with specific proposals for amending the draft measure. If the Commission does not take a decision within that period, the draft measure may be adopted by the NRA.

Notes

[126] As provided for in Article 3 of Council Decision 1999/468/EC laying the procedure for the exercising of implementing powers conferred on the Commission, the Commission shall take the utmost account of the opinion delivered by the Committee, but shall not be bound by the opinion.

6.4. Urgent cases

153. In exceptional circumstances, NRAs may act urgently in order to safeguard competition and protect the interest of users. An NRA may therefore, exceptionally, adopt proportionate and provisional measures without consulting either interested parties, the NRAs in other Member States, or the Commission. Where an NRA has taken such urgent action, it must, without delay, communicate these measures, with full reasons, to the Commission, and to the other NRAs. The Commission will verify the compatibility of those measures with Community law and in particular will assess their proportionality in relation to the policy objectives of Article 8 of the framework Directive.

154. If the NRA wishes to make the provisional measures permanent, or extends the time for which it is applicable, the NRA must go through the normal consultation procedure set out above. It is difficult to foresee any circumstances that would justify urgent action to define a market or designate an SMP operator, as such measure are not those that can be carried out immediately. The Commission therefore does not expect NRAs to use the exceptional procedures in such cases.

6.5. Adoption of the final decision

155. Once an NRA's decision has become final, NRAs should notify the Commission of the names of the undertakings that have been designated as having SMP and the obligations imposed on them, in accordance with the requirements of Article 36(2) of the universal service Directive and Articles 15(2) and 16(2) of the access Directive. The Commission will thereafter make this information available in a readily accessible form, and will transmit the information to the Communications Committee as appropriate.

156. Likewise, NRAs should publish the names of undertakings that they have designated as having SMP and the obligations imposed on them. They should ensure that up-to-date information is made publicly available in a manner that guarantees all interested parties easy access to that information.

E10

COUNCIL REGULATION (EEC) NO 1534/91

of 31 May 1991
on the application of Article [101](3)] of the [Treaty on the Functioning of the
European Union]* to certain categories of agreements, decisions and
concerted practices in the insurance sector

Official Journal L 143, 7.6.1991, p.1

Celex No: 31991R1534

EUR-Lex permanent link: <http://eur-lex.europa.eu/LexUriServ/LexUriServ.do?uri=CELEX:3199
1R1534:EN:NOT>

Notes

* Ed note: please see the Note on the Lisbon Treaty at p.xvii in regard to article renumbering introduced by the Lisbon Treaty.

Commentary

Regulation 1534/91/EEC: B&C: 1.025, 3.079, 12.122 F&N: 3.468, 11.189, 11.193, 11.217

THE COUNCIL OF THE EUROPEAN COMMUNITIES,

Having regard to the [Treaty on the Functioning of the European Union], and in particular Article [103] thereof,

Having regard to the proposal from the Commission,[1]

Having regard to the opinion of the European Parliament,[2]

Having regard to the opinion of the Economic and Social Committee,[3]

Notes

[1] OJ C 16, 23.1.1990, p.13.
[2] OJ C 260, 15.10.1990, p.57.
[3] OJ C 182, 23.7.1990, p.27.

---

[1] Whereas Article [101](1)] of the Treaty may, in accordance with Article [101](3)], be declared inapplicable to categories of agreements, decisions and concerted practices when satisfy the requirements of Article [101](3)];

[2] Whereas the detailed rules for the application of Article [101](3)] of the Treaty must be adopted by way of a Regulation based on Article [103] of the Treaty;

[3] Whereas cooperation between undertakings in the insurance sector is, to a certain extent, desirable to ensure the proper functioning of this sector and may at the same time promote consumers' interests;

[4] Whereas the application of Council Regulation (EEC) No 4064/89 of 21 December 1989 on the control of concentrations between undertakings[1] enables the Commission to exercise close supervision on issues arising from concentrations in all sectors, including the insurance sector;

Notes

[1] OJ L 395, 30.12.1989, p.1. [Ed note: see now Council Regulation (EC) No 139/2004 (OJ L 24, 29.1.2004, p.1), reproduced at D1.]

---

[5] Whereas exemptions granted under Article [101](3)] of the Treaty cannot themselves affect Community and national provisions safeguarding consumers' interests in this sector;

[6] Whereas agreements, decisions and concerted practices serving such aims may, in so far as they fall within the prohibition contained in Article [101](1) of the Treaty, be exempted therefrom under certain conditions; whereas this applies in particular to agreements, decisions and concerted practices relating to the establishment of common risk premium tariffs based on collectively ascertained statistics or the number of claims, the establishment of standard policy conditions, common coverage of certain types of risks, the settlement of claims, the testing and acceptance of security devices, and registers of, and information on, aggravated risks;

[7] Whereas in view of the large number of notifications submitted pursuant to Council Regulation No 17 of 6 February 1962: First Regulation implementing Articles [101] and [102] of the Treaty,[1] as last amended by the Act of Accession of Spain and Portugal, it is desirable that in order to facilitate the Commission's task, it should be enabled to declare, by way of Regulation, that the provisions of Article [101](1) of the Treaty are inapplicable to certain categories of agreements, decisions and concerted practices;

Notes

[1] OJ 13, 21.2.1962, p.204/62. [Ed note: see now Council Regulation (EC) No 1/2003 (OJ L 1, 4.1.2003, p.1), reproduced at B2.]

[8] Whereas it should be laid down under which conditions the Commission, in close and constant liaison with the competent authorities of the Member States, may exercise such powers;

[9] Whereas, in the exercise of such powers, the Commission will take account not only of the risk of competition being eliminated in a substantial part of the relevant market and of any benefit that might be conferred on policyholders resulting from the agreements, but also of the risk which the proliferation of restrictive clauses and the operation of accommodation companies would entail for policyholders;

[10] Whereas the keeping of registers and the handling of information on aggravated risks should be carried out subject to the proper protection of confidentiality;

[11] Whereas, under Article 6 of Regulation No 17, the Commission may provide that a decision taken in accordance with Article [101](3) of the Treaty shall apply with retroactive effect; whereas the Commission should also be able to adopt provisions to such effect in a Regulation;

[12] Whereas, under Article 7 of Regulation No 17, agreements, decisions and concerted practices may, by decision of the Commission, be exempted from prohibition, in particular if they are modified in such manner that they satisfy the requirements of Article [101](3) of the Treaty; whereas it is desirable that the Commission be enabled to grant by Regulation like exemption to such agreements, decisions and concerted practices if they are modified in such manner as to fall within a category defined in an exempting Regulation;

[13] Whereas it cannot be ruled out that, in specific cases, the conditions set out in Article [101](3) of the Treaty may not be fulfilled; whereas the Commission must have the power to regulate such cases pursuant to Regulation No 17 by way of a Decision having effect for the future,

HAS ADOPTED THIS REGULATION:

Article 1

1. Without prejudice to the application of Regulation No 17, the Commission may, by means of a Regulation and in accordance with Article [101](3) of the Treaty, declare that Article [101](1) shall not apply to categories of agreements between undertakings, decisions of associations of undertakings and concerted practices in the insurance sector which have as their object cooperation with respect to:

(a) the establishment of common risk premium tariffs based on collectively ascertained statistics or the number of claims;

(b) the establishment of common standard policy conditions;

(c) the common coverage of certain types of risks;

(d) the settlement of claims;

(e) the testing and acceptance of security devices;

(f) registers of, and information on, aggravated risks, provided that the keeping of these registers and the handling of this information is carried out subject to the proper protection of confidentiality.

2. The Commission Regulation referred to in paragraph 1, shall define the categories of agreements, decisions and concerted practices to which it applies and shall specify in particular:

(a) the restrictions or clauses which may, or may not, appear in the agreements, decisions and concerted practices;

(b) the clauses which must be contained in the agreements, decisions and concerted practices or the other conditions which must be satisfied.

Article 2

Any Regulation adopted pursuant to Article 1 shall be of limited duration.

It may be repealed or amended where circumstances have changed with respect to any of the facts which were essential to its being adopted; in such case, a period shall be fixed for modification of the agreements, decisions and concerted practices to which the earlier Regulation applies.

Article 3

A Regulation adopted pursuant to Article 1 may provide that it shall apply with retroactive effect to agreements, decisions and concerted practices to which, at the date of entry into force of the said Regulation, a Decision taken with retroactive effect pursuant to Article 6 of Regulation No 17 would have applied.

Article 4

1. A Regulation adopted pursuant to Article 1 may provide that the prohibition contained in Article [101](1) of the Treaty shall not apply, for such period as shall be fixed in that Regulation, to agreements, decisions and concerted practices already in existence on 13 March 1962 which do not satisfy the conditions of Article [101](3) where:

— within six months from the entry into force of the said Regulation, they are so modified as to satisfy the said conditions in accordance with the provisions of the said Regulation and

— the modifications are brought to the notice of the Commission within the time limit fixed by the said Regulation.

The provisions of the first subparagraph shall apply in the same way to those agreements, decisions and concerted practices existing at the date of accession of new Member States to which Article [101](1) of the Treaty applies by virtue of accession and which do not satisfy the conditions of Article [101](3).

2. Paragraph 1 shall apply to agreements, decisions and concerted practices which had to be notified before 1 February 1963, in accordance with Article 5 of Regulation No 17, only where they have been so notified before that date.

Paragraph 1 shall not apply to agreements, decisions and concerted practices existing at the date of accession of new Member States to which Article [101](1) of the Treaty applies by virtue of accession and which had to be notified within six months from the date of accession in accordance with Articles 5 and 25 of Regulation No 17, unless they have been so notified within the said period.

3. The benefit of provisions adopted pursuant to paragraph 1 may not be invoked in actions pending at the date of entry into force of a Regulation adopted pursuant to Article 1; neither may it be invoked as grounds for claims for damages against third parties.

Article 5

Where the Commission proposes to adopt a Regulation, it shall publish a draft thereof to enable all persons and organizations concerned to submit to it their comments within such time limit, being not less than one month, as it shall fix.

Article 6

1. The Commission shall consult the Advisory Committee on Restrictive Practices and Monopolies:

(a) before publishing a draft Regulation;

(b) before adopting a Regulation.

2. Article 10(5) and (6) of Regulation No 17, relating to consultation of the Advisory Committee, shall apply. However, joint meetings with the Commission shall take place not earlier than one month after dispatch of the notice convening them.

Article 7

[…]

Notes

Article 7 was repealed by Council Regulation (EC) No 1/2003 (OJ L 1, 4.1.2003, p.1), Article 40, with effect from 1 May 2004

Article 8

Not later than six years after the entry into force of the Commission Regulation provided for in Article 1, the Commission shall submit to the European Parliament and the Council a report on the functioning of this Regulation, accompanied by such proposals for amendments to this Regulation as may appear necessary in the light of experience. This Regulation shall be binding in its entirety and directly applicable in all Member States.

Done at Brussels, 31 May 1991.

E11

COMMISSION REGULATION (EU) NO 267/2010

of 24 March 2010

on the application of Article 101(3) of the Treaty on the Functioning of the European Union to certain categories of agreements, decisions and concerted practices in the insurance sector

(Text with EEA relevance)

Official Journal L 83, 30.3.2010, p.1

Celex No: 32010R0267

EUR-Lex permanent link: <http://eur-lex.europa.eu/LexUriServ/LexUriServ.do?uri=CELEX:32010R0267:EN:NOT>

Notes

EEA application: see EEA Agreement, Annex XIV, Chapter J, Point 15b, as amended by EEA Joint Committee Decision 52/2010, with effect from 1.4.2010.

THE EUROPEAN COMMISSION,

Having regard to the Treaty on the Functioning of the European Union,

Having regard to Council Regulation (EEC) No 1534/91 of 31 May 1991 on the application of Article [101(3)]* of the Treaty to certain categories of agreements, decisions and concerted practices in the insurance sector,[1] and in particular Article 1(1)(a), (b), (c) and (e) thereof,

Having published a draft of this Regulation,

After consulting the Advisory Committee on Restrictive Practices and Dominant Positions,

---

Notes

1 OJ L 143, 7.6.1991, p.1.

* Ed note: please see the Note on the Lisbon Treaty at p.xvii in regard to article renumbering introduced by the Lisbon Treaty.

Commentary

Regulation 267/2010/EU: **B&C:** 3.085, 3.096, 6.038, 12.122, 12.130 **F&N:** 7.435, 11.139, 11.191, 11.192, 11.202, 11.205, 11.206, 11.214

Chap. II: **F&N:** 11.197

recitals 9–12: **B&C:** 12.125

Whereas:

(1) Regulation (EEC) No 1534/91 empowers the Commission to apply Article 101(3) of the Treaty on the Functioning of the European Union[1] by regulation to certain categories of agreements, decisions and concerted practices in the insurance sector which have as their object cooperation with respect to:

— the establishment of common risk premium tariffs based on collectively ascertained statistics or the number of claims,

— the establishment of common standard policy conditions,

— the common coverage of certain types of risks,

— the settlement of claims,

— the testing and acceptance of security devices,

— registers of, and information on, aggravated risks.

Notes

1 With effect from 1 December 2009, Article 81 of the EC Treaty has become Article 101 of the Treaty on the Functioning of the European Union. The two articles are, in substance, identical. For the purposes of this Regulation, references to Article 101 of the Treaty on the Functioning of the European Union should be understood as references to Article 81 of the EC Treaty where appropriate.

---

(2) Pursuant to Regulation (EEC) No 1534/91, the Commission adopted Regulation (EC) No 358/2003 of 27 February 2003 on the application of Article [101(3)] of the Treaty to certain categories of agreements, decisions and concerted practices in the insurance sector.[1] Regulation (EC) No 358/2003 expires on 31 March 2010.

Notes

1 OJ L 53, 28.2.2003, p.8.

---

(3) Regulation (EC) No 358/2003 does not grant an exemption to agreements concerning the settlement of claims and registers of, and information on, aggravated risks. The Commission considered that it lacked sufficient experience in handling individual cases to make use of the power conferred by Regulation (EEC) No 1534/91 in those fields. That situation has not changed. Furthermore, although Regulation (EC) No 358/2003 granted an exemption for the establishment of standard policy conditions and the testing and acceptance of security devices, this Regulation should not do so since the Commission's review of the functioning of Regulation (EC) No 358/2003 revealed that it was no longer necessary to include such agreements in a sector specific block exemption regulation. In the context where those two categories of agreements are not specific to the insurance sector and, as the review showed, can also give rise to certain competition concerns, it is more appropriate that they be subject to self-assessment.

Commentary

recital 3: **B&C:** 12.122

---

(4) Following a public consultation launched on 17 April 2008, the Commission adopted a report to the European Parliament and the Council on the functioning of Regulation (EC) No 358/2003 (the Report)[1] on 24 March 2009. In the Report and its accompanying Working Document (the

Working Document) preliminary amendments of Regulation (EC) No 358/2003 were proposed. On 2 June 2009, the Commission held a public meeting with interested parties, including representatives of the insurance sector, consumer organisations and national competition authorities, on the findings and proposals in the Report and Working Document.

Notes

1 COM(2009) 138.

(5) This Regulation should ensure effective protection of competition while providing benefits to consumers and adequate legal security for undertakings. The pursuit of those objectives should take account of the Commission's experience in this field, and the results of the consultations leading up to the adoption of this Regulation.

(6) Regulation (EEC) No 1534/91 requires the exempting regulation of the Commission to define the categories of agreements, decisions and concerted practices to which it applies, to specify the restrictions or clauses which may, or may not, appear in the agreements, decisions and concerted practices, and to specify the clauses which must be contained in the agreements, decisions and concerted practices or the other conditions which must be satisfied.

(7) Nevertheless, it is appropriate to continue the approach taken in Regulation (EC) No 358/2003 of placing the emphasis on defining categories of agreements which are exempted up to a certain level of market share and on specifying the restrictions or clauses which are not to be contained in such agreements.

(8) The benefit of the block exemption established by this Regulation should be limited to those agreements which can be assumed with sufficient certainty to satisfy the conditions of Article 101(3) of the Treaty. For the application of Article 101(3) of the Treaty by regulation, it is not necessary to define those agreements which are capable of falling within Article 101(1) of the Treaty. At the same time, there is no presumption that agreements which do not benefit from this Regulation are either caught by Article 101(1) of the Treaty or that they fail to satisfy the conditions of Article 101(3) of the Treaty. In the individual assessment of agreements under Article 101(1) of the Treaty, account must be taken of several factors, and in particular the market structure on the relevant market.

(9) Collaboration between insurance undertakings or within associations of undertakings in the compilation of information (which may also involve some statistical calculations) allowing the calculation of the average cost of covering a specified risk in the past or, for life insurance, tables of mortality rates or of the frequency of illness, accident and invalidity, makes it possible to improve the knowledge of risks and facilitates the rating of risks for individual companies. This can in turn facilitate market entry and thus benefit consumers. The same applies to joint tudies on the probable impact of extraneous circumstances that may influence the frequency or scale of claims, or the yield of different types of investments. It is, however, necessary to ensure that such collaboration is only exempted to the extent to which it is necessary to attain these objectives. It is therefore appropriate to stipulate in particular that agreements on commercial premiums are not exempted. Indeed, commercial premiums may be lower than the amounts indicated by the compilations, tables or study results in question, since insurers can use the revenues from their investments in order to reduce their premiums. Moreover, the compilations, tables or studies in question should be non-binding and serve only for reference purposes. The exchange of information not necessary to attain the objectives set out in this recital should not be covered by this Regulation.

Commentary

recital 9: B&C: 6.038

(10) Moreover, the narrower the categories into which statistics on the cost of covering a specified risk in the past are grouped, the more leeway insurance undertakings have to differentiate their commercial premiums when they calculate them. It is therefore appropriate to exempt joint compilations of the past cost of risks on condition that the available statistics are provided with as much detail and differentiation as is actuarially adequate.

(11) Furthermore, access to the joint compilations, tables and study results is necessary both for insurance undertakings active on the geographic or product market in question and for those considering entering that market. Similarly access to such compilations, tables and study results may be of value to consumer organisations or customer organisations. Insurance undertakings not yet active on the market in question and consumer or customer organisations must be granted access to such compilations, tables and study results on reasonable, affordable and non-discriminatory terms, as compared with insurance undertakings already present on that market. Such terms might for example include a commitment from an insurance undertaking not yet present on the market to provide statistical information on claims, should it ever enter the market and might also include membership of the association of insurers responsible for producing the compilations. An exception to the requirement to grant access to consumer organisations and customer organisations should be possible on the grounds of public security, for example where the information relates to the security systems of nuclear plants or the weakness of flood prevention systems.

(12) The reliability of joint compilations, tables and studies becomes greater as the amount of statistics on which they are based is increased. Insurers with high market shares may generate sufficient statistics internally to be able to make reliable compilations, but those with small market shares may not be able to do so, and new entrants are even less likely to be able to generate such statistics. The inclusion in such joint compilations, tables and studies of information from all insurers on a market, including large ones, in principle promotes competition by helping smaller insurers, and facilitates market entry. Given this specificity of the insurance sector, it is not appropriate to subject any exemption for such joint compilations, tables and studies to market share thresholds.

(13) Co-insurance or co-reinsurance pools can, in certain limited circumstances, be necessary to allow the participating undertakings of a pool to provide insurance or reinsurance for risks for which they might only offer insufficient cover in the absence of the pool. Those types of pools do not generally give rise to a restriction of competition under Article 101(1) of the Treaty and are thus not prohibited by it.

(14) Co-insurance or co-reinsurance pools can allow insurers and reinsurers to provide insurance or reinsurance for risks even if pooling goes beyond what is necessary to ensure that such a risk is covered. However, such pools can involve restrictions of competition, such as the standardisation of policy conditions and even of amounts of cover and premiums. It is therefore appropriate to lay down the circumstances in which such pools can benefit from exemption.

(15) For genuinely new risks it is not possible to know in advance what subscription capacity is necessary to cover the risk, nor whether two or more pools could co-exist for the purposes of providing the specific type of insurance concerned. A pooling arrangement offering the co-insurance or co-reinsurance of such new risks can therefore be exempted for a limited period of time without a market share threshold. Three years should constitute an adequate period for the constitution of sufficient historical information on claims to assess the necessity or otherwise of a pool.

Commentary
recital 15: F&N: 11.205

---

(16) Risks which did not previously exist should be considered as new risks. However, in exceptional circumstances, a risk may be considered as a new risk where an objective analysis indicates that the nature of the risk has changed so materially that it is not possible to know in advance what subscription capacity is necessary in order to cover such a risk.

(17) For risks which are not new, co-insurance and co-reinsurance pools which involve a restriction of competition may, in certain limited circumstances, involve benefits so as to justify an exemption under Article 101(3) of the Treaty, even if they could be replaced by two or more competing insurance entities. They may, for example, allow their participating undertakings to gain the necessary experience of the sector of insurance involved, or they may allow cost savings, or reduction of commercial premiums through joint reinsurance on advantageous terms. However, any exemption should be limited to agreements which do not afford the undertakings involved the possibility of eliminating competition in respect of a substantial part of the products in question.

Consumers can benefit effectively from pools only if there is sufficient competition in the relevant markets in which the pools operate. This condition should be regarded as being met when the market share of a pool remains below a given threshold and can therefore be presumed to be subject to actual or potential competition from undertakings which are not participating in that pool.

(18) This Regulation should therefore grant an exemption to any such co-insurance or co-reinsurance pool which has existed for more than three years, or which is not created in order to cover a new risk, on condition that the combined market share held by the participating undertakings does not exceed certain thresholds. The threshold for co-insurance pools should be lower because co- insurance pools may involve uniform policy conditions and commercial premiums. For the assessment of whether a pool fulfils the market share condition, the overall market share of the participating undertakings should be aggregated. The market share of each participating undertaking is based on the overall gross premium income of that participating undertaking both within and outside that pool in the same relevant market. These exemptions however should only apply if the pool in question meets the further conditions laid down in this Regulation, which are intended to keep to a minimum the restrictions of competition between the participating undertakings of the pool. An individual analysis would be necessary in such cases, in order to determine whether or not the conditions set out in this Regulation are fulfilled.

(19) In order to facilitate the conclusion of agreements, some of which can involve significant investment decisions, the period of validity of this Regulation should be fixed at seven years.

(20) The Commission may withdraw the benefit of this Regulation, pursuant to Article 29(1) of Council Regulation (EC) No 1/2003 of 16 December 2002 on the implementation of the rules on competition laid down in Articles [101] and [102] of the Treaty,[1] where it finds in a particular case that an agreement to which the exemptions provided for in this Regulation apply nevertheless has effects which are incompatible with Article 101(3) of the Treaty.

Notes

[1] OJ L 1, 4.1.2003, p.1.

---

(21) The competition authority of a Member State may withdraw the benefit of this Regulation pursuant to Article 29(2) of Regulation (EC) No 1/2003 in respect of the territory of that Member State, or a part thereof where, in a particular case, an agreement to which the exemptions provided for in this Regulation apply nevertheless has effects which are incompatible with Article 101(3) of the Treaty in the territory of that Member State, or in a part thereof, and where such territory has all the characteristics of a distinct geographic market.

(22) In determining whether the benefit of this Regulation should be withdrawn pursuant to Article 29 of Regulation (EC) No 1/2003, the anti-competitive effects that may derive from the existence of links between a co- insurance or co-reinsurance pool and/or its participating undertakings and other pools and/or their participating undertakings on the same relevant market are of particular importance,

HAS ADOPTED THIS REGULATION:

CHAPTER I
DEFINITIONS

Article 1
Definitions

For the purposes of this Regulation, the following definitions shall apply:

1. "agreement" means an agreement, a decision of an association of undertakings or a concerted practice;

2. "participating undertakings" means undertakings party to the agreement and their respective connected undertakings;

3. "connected undertakings" means:

(a) undertakings in which a party to the agreement, directly or indirectly:
   (i) has the power to exercise more than half the voting rights; or
   (ii) has the power to appoint more than half the members of the supervisory board, board of management or bodies legally representing the undertaking; or
   (iii) has the right to manage the undertaking's affairs;
(b) undertakings which directly or indirectly have, over a party to the agreement, the rights or powers listed in point (a);
(c) undertakings in which an undertaking referred to in point (b) has, directly or indirectly, the rights or powers listed in point (a);
(d) undertakings in which a party to the agreement together with one or more of the undertakings referred to in points (a), (b) or (c), or in which two or more of the latter undertakings, jointly have the rights or powers listed in point (a);
(e) undertakings in which the rights or powers listed in point (a) are jointly held by:

   (i) parties to the agreement or their respective connected undertakings referred to in points (a) to (d); or
   (ii) one or more of the parties to the agreement or one or more of their connected undertakings referred to in points (a) to (d) and one or more third parties;

4. "co-insurance pools" means groups set up by insurance undertakings either directly or through brokers or authorised agents, with the exception of ad-hoc co-insurance agreements on the subscription market, whereby a certain part of a given risk is covered by a lead insurer and the remaining part of the risk is covered by follow insurers who are invited to cover that remainder, which:

(a) agree to underwrite, in the name and for the account of all the participants, the insurance of a specified risk category; or
(b) entrust the underwriting and management of the insurance of a specified risk category, in their name and on their behalf, to one of the insurance undertakings, to a common broker or to a common body set up for this purpose;

5. "co-reinsurance pools" means groups set up by insurance undertakings either directly or through broker or authorised agents, possibly with the assistance of one or more reinsurance undertakings, with the exception of ad-hoc co-reinsurance agreements on the subscription market, whereby a certain part of a given risk is covered by a lead insurer and the remaining part of this risk is covered by follow insurers who are then invited to cover that remainder in order to:

(a) reinsure mutually all or part of their liabilities in respect of a specified risk category;
(b) incidentally accept, in the name and on behalf of all the participants, the reinsurance of the same category of risks;

6. "new risks" means:

(a) risks which did not previously exist, and for which insurance cover requires the development of an entirely new insurance product, not involving an extension, improvement or replacement of an existing insurance product; or
(b) in exceptional cases, risks the nature of which has, on the basis of an objective analysis, changed so materially that it is not possible to know in advance what subscription capacity is necessary in order to cover such a risk;

7. "commercial premium" means the price which is charged to the purchaser of an insurance policy.

Commentary

Art 1(4): **B&C:** 12.123
Art 1(5): **B&C:** 12.123
Art 1(6): **B&C:** 12.128 **F&N:** 11.205
Art 1(6)(a): **F&N:** 11.205
Art 1(6)(b): **F&N:** 11.205
Art 1(7): **B&C:** 12.126

Chapter II
Joint Compilations, Tables, and Studies

Article 2
Exemption

Pursuant to Article 101(3) of the Treaty and subject to the provisions of this Regulation, Article 101(1) of the Treaty shall not apply to agreements entered into between two or more undertakings in the insurance sector with respect to:

(a) the joint compilation and distribution of information necessary for the following purposes:
  (i) calculation of the average cost of covering a specified risk in the past (hereinafter compilations);
  (ii) construction of mortality tables, and tables showing the frequency of illness, accident and invalidity in connection with insurance involving an element of capitalisation (hereinafter tables);

(b) the joint carrying-out of studies on the probable impact of general circumstances external to the interested undertakings, either on the frequency or scale of future claims for a given risk or risk category or on the profitability of different types of investment (hereinafter studies), and the distribution of the results of such studies.

Commentary
Art 2: B&C: 3.085, 6.038, 12.123, 12.125

Article 3
Conditions for exemption

1. The exemption provided for in Article 2(a) shall apply on condition that the compilations or tables:

(a) are based on the assembly of data, spread over a number of risk years chosen as an observation period, which relate to identical or comparable risks in sufficient numbers to constitute a base which can be handled statistically and which will yield figures on the following, amongst others:
  (i) the number of claims during the said period;
  (ii) the number of individual risks insured in each risk year of the chosen observation period;
  (iii) the total amounts paid or payable in respect of claims that have arisen during the said period;
  (iv) the total amount of capital insured for each risk year during the chosen observation period;

(b) include as detailed a breakdown of the available statistics as is actuarially adequate;

(c) do not include in any way elements for contingencies, income deriving from reserves, administrative or commercial costs or fiscal or parafiscal contributions, and take into account neither revenues from investments nor anticipated profits.

2. The exemptions provided for in Article 2 shall apply on condition that the compilations, tables or study results:

(a) do not identify the insurance undertakings concerned or any insured party;

(b) when compiled and distributed, include a statement that they are non-binding;

(c) do not contain any indication of the level of commercial premiums;

(d) are made available on reasonable, affordable and non- discriminatory terms, to any insurance undertaking which requests a copy of them, including insurance undertakings which are not active on the geographic or product market to which those compilations, tables or study results refer;

(e) except where non-disclosure is objectively justified on grounds of public security, are made available on reasonable, affordable and non-discriminatory terms, to consumer organisations or customer organisations which request access to them in specific and precise terms for a duly justified reason.

Commentary
Art 3: B&C: 12.125
Art 3(1): B&C: 12.126
Art 3(2): B&C: 12.126
Art 3(2)(a)–(e): F&N: 11.197
Art 3(2)(c): F&N: 11.198
Art 3(2)(d): F&N: 11.198

Article 4
Agreements not covered by the exemption

The exemptions provided for in Article 2 shall not apply where participating undertakings enter into an undertaking or commitment among themselves, or oblige other undertakings, not to use compilations or tables that differ from those referred to in Article 2(a), or not to depart from the results of the studies referred to in Article 2(b).

Commentary
Art 4: B&C: 12.126 F&N: 11.197

CHAPTER III
COMMON COVERAGE OF CERTAIN TYPES OF RISKS

Article 5
Exemption

Pursuant to Article 101(3) of the Treaty and subject to the provisions of this Regulation, Article 101(1) of the Treaty shall not apply to agreements entered into between two or more undertakings in the insurance sector with respect to the setting-up and operation of pools of insurance undertakings or of insurance undertakings and reinsurance undertakings for the common coverage of a specific category of risks in the form of co-insurance or co-reinsurance.

Commentary
Art 5: B&C: 12.125, 12.127

Article 6
Application of exemption and market share thresholds

1. As concerns co-insurance or co-reinsurance pools which are created in order exclusively to cover new risks, the exemption provided for in Article 5 shall apply for a period of three years from the date of the first establishment of the pool, regardless of the market share of the pool.

2. As concerns co-insurance or co-reinsurance pools which do not fall within the scope of paragraph 1, the exemption provided for in Article 5 shall apply as long as this Regulation remains in force, on condition that the combined market share held by the participating undertakings does not exceed:

(a) in the case of co-insurance pools, 20% of any relevant market;
(b) in the case of co-reinsurance pools, 25% of any relevant market.

3. In calculating the market share of a participating undertaking on the relevant market, account shall be taken of:

(a) the market share of the participating undertaking within the pool in question;
(b) the market share of the participating undertaking within another pool on the same relevant market as the pool in question, to which the participating undertaking is a party; and
(c) the market share of the participating undertaking on the same relevant market as the pool in question, outside any pool.

4. For the purposes of applying the market share thresholds provided for in paragraph 2, the following rules shall apply:

(a) the market share shall be calculated on the basis of gross premium income; if gross premium income data are not available, estimates based on other reliable market information, including insurance cover provided or insured risk value, may be used to establish the market share of the undertaking concerned;
(b) the market share shall be calculated on the basis of data relating to the preceding calendar year.

5. Where the market share referred to in paragraph 2(a) is initially not more than 20% but subsequently rises above that level without exceeding 25%, the exemption provided for in Article 5 shall continue to apply for a period of two consecutive calendar years following the year in which the 20% threshold was first exceeded.

6. Where the market share referred to in paragraph 2(a) is initially not more than 20% but subsequently rises above 25%, the exemption provided for in Article 5 shall continue to apply for a period of one calendar year following the year in which the level of 25% was first exceeded.

7. The benefit of paragraphs 5 and 6 may not be combined so as to exceed a period of two calendar years.

8. Where the market share referred to in paragraph 2(b) is initially not more than 25% but subsequently rises above that level without exceeding 30%, the exemption provided for in Article 5 shall continue to apply for a period of two consecutive calendar years following the year in which the 25% threshold was first exceeded.

9. Where the market share referred to in paragraph 2(b) is initially not more than 25% but subsequently rises above 30%, the exemption provided for in Article 5 shall continue to apply for a period of one calendar year following the year in which the level of 30% was first exceeded.

10. The benefit of paragraphs 8 and 9 may not be combined so as to exceed a period of two calendar years.

Commentary
Art 6(1): B&C: 12.128 F&N: 1.205
Art 6(2): B&C: 12.129 F&N: 11.206
Art 6(2)–(10): B&C: 12.129
Art 6(2)(a): B&C: 12.129
Art 6(2)(b): B&C: 12.129
Art 6(5): F&N: 11.206
Art 6(10): F&N: 11.06, 11.206

Article 7
Conditions for exemption

The exemption provided for in Article 5 shall apply on condition that:

(a) each participating undertaking having given a reasonable period of notice has the right to withdraw from the pool, without incurring any sanctions;

(b) the rules of the pool do not oblige any participating undertaking of the pool to insure or reinsure through the pool and do not restrict any participating undertaking of the pool from insuring or reinsuring outside the pool, in whole or in part, any risk of the type covered by the pool;

(c) the rules of the pool do not restrict the activity of the pool or its participating undertakings to the insurance or reinsurance of risks located in any particular geographical part of the Union;

(d) the agreement does not limit output or sales;

(e) the agreement does not allocate markets or customers; and

(f) the participating undertakings of a co-reinsurance pool do not agree on the commercial premiums which they charge for direct insurance.

Commentary
Art 7: B&C: 12.129 F&N: 11.207

Chapter IV
Final Provisions

Article 8
Transitional period

The prohibition laid down in Article 101(1) of the Treaty shall not apply during the period from 1 April 2010 to 30 September 2010 in respect of agreements already in force on 31 March 2010 which do not satisfy the conditions for exemption provided for in this Regulation but which satisfy the conditions for exemption provided for in Regulation (EC) No 358/2003.

Article 9
Period of validity

This Regulation shall enter into force on 1 April 2010.

It shall expire on 31 March 2017.

This Regulation shall be binding in its entirety and directly applicable in all Member States.

Done at Brussels, 24 March 2010.

E12

COMMUNICATION FROM THE COMMISSION

on the application of Article 101(3) of the Treaty on the Functioning
of the European Union to certain categories of agreements,
decisions and concerted practices in the insurance sector

(Text with EEA relevance)

(2010/C 82/02)

Official Journal C 82, 30.3.2010, p.20

Celex No: 52010XC0330(02)

EUR-Lex permanent link: <http://eur-lex.europa.eu/LexUriServ/LexUriServ.do?uri=CELEX:5201 0XC0330(02):EN:NOT>

Commentary
Communication: B&C: 3.005, 3.085, 12.122 F&N: 11.189, 11.215
paras 23–24: B&C: 12.131

---

1. Introduction and Background

1. Commission Regulation (EC) No 358/2003,[1] the previous Insurance Block Exemption Regulation (BER) which expired on 31 March 2010, applied Article 101(3) of the Treaty on the Functioning of the European Union[2] (the Treaty) to certain categories of agreements, decisions and concerted practices in the insurance sector.

Notes

[1] OJ L 53, 28.2.2003, p.8.

[2] With effect from 1 December 2009, Article 81 of the EC Treaty has become Article 101 of the Treaty on the Functioning of the European Union. The two Articles are, in substance, identical. For the purposes of this Communication, references to Article 101 of the Treaty on the Functioning of the European Union should be understood as references to Article 81 of the EC Treaty where appropriate. [Ed note: please see the Note on the Lisbon Treaty at p.xvii in regard to article renumbering introduced by the Lisbon Treaty.]

---

2. Following a lengthy review (the Review) of the functioning of Regulation (EC) No 358/2003, the Commission published its Report to the European Parliament and the Council on the functioning

of that Regulation[1] (the Report) as well as an accompanying Working Document[2] (the Working Document) on 24 March 2009.

Notes

[1] <http://eur-lex.europa.eu/LexUriServ/LexUriServ.do?uri=CELEX:52009DC0138:EN:NOT>.
[2] <http://ec.europa.eu/competition/sectors/financial_services/insurance_ber_working_document.pdf>.

3. As a result of its findings following the Review, the Commission has now adopted a new insurance BER which renews the exemptions for two of the four categories of agreements exempted in the previous BER; namely: (i) joint compilations, tables and studies; and (ii) common coverage of certain types of risks (pools).

2. First Principles Analysis

4. The Commission's original objective when it adopted Regulation (EC) No 358/2003 of reducing the number of notifications it received is no longer relevant since under Regulation (EC) No 1/2003 undertakings can no longer notify their agreements to the Commission, but now must conduct their own self-assessment. In this context, a specific legal instrument such as a BER should only be adopted if cooperation in the insurance sector is "special" and different to other sectors which do not benefit from a BER (i.e. most sectors currently). The Commission's analysis as to whether or not to renew the BER addressed three key questions in relation to each of the four categories of agreements exempted by the BER, namely:

(a) whether the business risks or other issues in the insurance sector make it "special" and different to other sectors such that this leads to an enhanced need for cooperation amongst insurers;

(b) if so, whether this enhanced need for cooperation requires a legal instrument such as the BER to protect or facilitate it; and

(c) if so, what is the most appropriate legal instrument (i.e. whether it is the current BER or whether partial renewal, amended renewal, or guidance would be more appropriate).

3. Renewed Exemptions

5. On the basis of its Review and consultation of stakeholders which was conducted over a 2-year period, the Commission adopted the new BER (Commission Regulation (EU) No 267/2010 of 24 March) renewing (with amendments) the exemptions for two forms of cooperation, namely (i) joint compilations, tables and studies; and (ii) common coverage of certain types of risks (pools).

6. When agreements falling within these categories of agreements do not meet all the conditions to benefit from the block exemption, an individual analysis under Article 101 of the Treaty is required. The analytical framework set out in the Commission's Guidelines on the applicability of Article [101 TFEU] to horizontal cooperation agreements[1] (the Horizontal Guidelines) will assist businesses in assessing the compatibility of agreements with Article 101 of the Treaty.[2]

Notes

[1] See paragraph 7 of Commission Notice of 6 January 2001: Guidelines on the applicability of Article [101 TFEU] to horizontal cooperation agreements, OJ C 3, 6.1.2001, p.2.
[2] The current Horizontal Guidelines are under review.

3.1. Joint compilations, tables and studies

7. Subject to certain conditions, the previous BER exempted agreements which relate to the joint establishment and distribution of (i) calculations of the average cost of covering a specified risk in the past, and (ii) mortality tables and tables showing the frequency of illness, accident and invalidity, in connection with insurance involving an element of capitalisation. It also exempted (subject to certain conditions) the joint carrying out of studies on the probable impact of general circumstances external to the interested undertakings, either on the frequency or scale of future claims for a given risk or risk category or on the profitability of different types of investment and the distribution of the results of such studies.

8. As summarised in the Report, the costs of insurance products are unknown at the time the price is agreed and the risk covered. Calculation of risk is a key issue in pricing all insurance products which appears to be a differentiating factor from other sectors including the banking sector. This makes access to past statistical data in order to technically price risks crucial. Therefore, the Commission considers that cooperation in this area is both specific to the insurance industry and necessary in order to price risks.

9. The Commission also considers that there are good reasons to protect and facilitate cooperation in this area with a BER and that it is appropriate that the BER be renewed for this category of agreements in order to avoid any reduction in such pro-competitive cooperation.

10. However, in renewing the exemption the Commission made the following key changes: (i) the term "joint calculations" was changed to "joint compilations" (which may also include some calculations); (ii) clarification that exchange of information is only allowed where it is necessary; and (iii) access to data shared is now also allowed for consumer organisations and customer organisations (as distinguished from individuals), with a public security exception.

3.2. Common coverage of certain types of risks (pools)

11. The previous BER exempted[1] the setting up and operation of co-(re)insurance pools for the common coverage of new risks as well as co-(re)insurance pools covering risks which are not new, subject to certain conditions, in particular to market share thresholds.

Notes

[1] For three years from the date of first establishment of the group, regardless of the market share of the group.

---

12. As a result of its Review, the Commission considers that risk sharing for certain types of risks (such as nuclear, terrorism and environmental risks), for which individual insurance companies are reluctant or unable to insure the entire risk alone, is crucial in order to ensure that all such risks can be covered. This makes the insurance sector different to other sectors and triggers an enhanced need for cooperation.[1] Therefore, the new BER also exempts pools under certain conditions.

Notes

[1] An alternative method of covering risks through co-(re)insurance is ad hoc co-(re)insurance agreements on the subscription market, which may be a less restrictive option depending on the analysis on a case-by-case basis.

---

13. In renewing the exemption, the Commission made the following key changes: (i) a change to the approach to market share calculation in order to bring it into line with other general and sector-specific competition rules so that not only gross premium income earned within the pool by the participating undertakings, but also outside the pool will be taken into account; and (ii) an amendment and expansion to the definition of "new risks".

14. In terms of self-assessment it is important to consider that there are three types of pools and determine into which category a particular pool falls: (i) pools which do not require a BER as a safe harbour because they do not give rise to a restriction of competition as long as the pooling is necessary to allow their members to provide a type of insurance that they could not provide alone; (ii) pools which fall under Article 101(1) of the Treaty and which do not comply with the conditions of the new BER but may benefit from an individual exception under Article 101(3) of the Treaty; (iii) pools which fall under Article 101(1) of the Treaty but which comply with the conditions of the BER.

15. For both types (ii) and (iii) it is necessary to carefully define the relevant product and geographic market, as market definition is a prerequisite in order to assess compliance with the market share thresholds.[1] The Commission's Notice on the definition of the relevant market for the purposes of Community competition law,[2] together with relevant Commission decisions and comfort letters in the insurance sector can be used as guidance in order for pools to determine the relevant market on which they operate.

Notes

[1] Concerns were also raised about the definition of "new risks".

[2] OJ C 372, 9.12.1997, p.5.

16. However, the Review showed that many insurers were incorrectly using the pool exemption in the BER as a "blanket" exemption, without carrying out the required careful legal assessment of a pool's compliance with the conditions of the BER.[1]

Notes

[1] In particular in relation to market share thresholds. Furthermore, it is crucial that any pools covering new risks and purporting to fall within the BER ensure that they are in fact covered by the precise definition of new risks in Article 1 of the new BER, as mentioned in the Report and Working Document.

17. Also, it should be remembered that ad hoc co-(re)insurance agreements on the subscription market[1] have never been covered by the BER and they remain outside the scope of the new BER. As mentioned in the Commission's Final Report on the Business Insurance Sector Inquiry of 25 September 2007,[2] practices involving an alignment of premium (between co-(re)insurers through ad hoc co-(re)insurance agreements) may fall within the scope of Article 101(1) of the Treaty, but may benefit from the exemption afforded by Article 101(3) of the Treaty.

Notes

[1] Whereby a certain part of a given risk is covered by a lead insurer and the remaining part of the risk is covered by follow insurers who are invited to cover the remainder.

[2] COM(2007) 556 final: Communication from the Commission to the European Parliament, the Council, the European Economic and Social Committee and the Committee of the Regions — Sector Inquiry under Article 17 of Regulation (EC) No 1/2003 on business insurance (Final Report).

18. The Commission intends to closely monitor, in cooperation with national competition authorities within the framework of the European Competition Network, the operation of pools to ensure that blanket applications of the BER or Article 101(3) of the Treaty are not occurring. This closer monitoring will be undertaken in line with enforcement cases where pools are found to fall foul of Article 101(1) of the Treaty and/or the BER.

4. Non-Renewed Exemptions

19. On the basis of the Commission's analysis set out in the Report and Working Document, as well as in its Impact Assessment of the new BER, two of the four exemptions in the previous BER, namely agreements on standard policy conditions (SPCs) and security devices have not been renewed by the new BER. This is primarily because they are not specific to the insurance sector and therefore their inclusion in such an exceptional legal instrument may result in unjustified discrimination against other sectors which do not benefit from a BER. In addition, although these two forms of cooperation may give rise to some benefits to consumers, the Review showed that they can also give rise to certain competition concerns. Therefore, it is more appropriate that they be subject to self-assessment.

20. Although non-renewal of the BER in relation to these two types of cooperation will inevitably result in slightly less legal certainty, it should be emphasised that the insurance sector will benefit in this regard from the same level of legal certainty as the other sectors which do not benefit from a BER. Furthermore, as outlined below the Commission plans to address both these forms of cooperation in its Horizontal Guidelines.

4.1. Standard Policy Conditions

21. The previous BER exempted the joint establishment and distribution of non-binding standard policy conditions (SPCs) for direct insurance.[1]

Notes

[1] Article 6(1)(a) to (k) of Regulation (EC) No 358/2003.

22. On the basis of the evidence found during its Review, the Commission no longer considers that a sector specific BER is necessary since cooperation on SPCs is not specific to the insurance sector, but common to many others, such as the banking sector, which do not benefit from a BER. As SPCs are not specific to the insurance sector it is appropriate that any guidance on SPCs is afforded to industry as a whole and in the form of a horizontal instrument.

23. The Commission considers that in many cases SPCs can give rise to positive effects for competition and consumers. For example, SPCs allow the comparison of insurance policies offered by different insurers, allowing customers to verify the content of guarantees more easily and facilitating switching between insurers and insurance products. However, whilst there is a need for comparability between insurance products for consumers, too much standardisation can be harmful for consumers and can lead to a lack of non-price competition. In addition, given that certain SPCs can be imbalanced, it is more appropriate that undertakings conduct their own assessment on the basis of Article 101(3) of the Treaty in the event that Article 101(1) of the Treaty is applicable in order to demonstrate that the cooperation they are part of gives rise to efficiency gains, a fair share of which benefit consumers.[1]

Notes

[1] Certain of the clauses listed in Article 6(1) of the previous BER, Regulation (EC) No 358/2003, would remain relevant for self-assessment of agreements under Article 101 of the Treaty, in particular those which have an impact on prices and product innovation. Of particular relevance are, for example, clauses which: (i) contain any indication of the level of commercial premiums; (ii) indicate the amount of cover or the part which the policyholder must pay himself; or (iii) impose comprehensive cover including risks to which a significant number of policyholders are not simultaneously exposed; (iv) require the policyholder to obtain cover from the same insurer for different risks.

---

24. Accordingly, the Commission is planning to expand its Horizontal Guidelines to also address SPCs for all sectors. These are currently under review and it is planned to publish a draft of the revised Horizontal Guidelines for stakeholder consultation in the first half of 2010.

4.2. Security devices

25. The previous BER exempted: (i) technical specifications, rules or codes of practice regarding security devices and procedures for assessing and approving their compliance with these standards as well as (ii) technical specifications, rules or codes of practice for the installation and maintenance of security devices and procedures for assessing and approving the compliance of undertakings which install or maintain security devices with such standards.

26. However, the Commission considers that the setting of technical standards falls into the general domain of standard setting, which is not unique to the insurance sector. As these kinds of agreements are not specific to the insurance sector, it is appropriate that any guidance is afforded to the industry as a whole and in the form of a horizontal instrument. This is already the case, as point 6 of the Horizontal Guidelines provides guidance on the compliance of technical standards with Article 101 of the Treaty. Moreover, the Horizontal Guidelines are currently under review and it is planned to publish a draft of the revised Horizontal Guidelines for stakeholder consultation during the first half of 2010.

27. In addition, these agreements were covered by the BER in so far as no harmonisation exists at Union level. The Commission's Review showed that there is reduced scope for the BER, since such harmonisation is now extensive. As regards the limited area where there is not yet Union harmonisation, detailed national rules result in fragmentation of the internal market, reduction of competition between producers of security devices across the Member States and less choice for consumers as consumers do not obtain insurance in the event that their security devices do not comply with standards commonly established by insurers.

28. The Commission has therefore not renewed the BER for these categories of agreements.

5. Conclusions

29. It will be necessary for undertakings to carefully assess their cooperation on joint compilations, tables and studies and pools under the conditions established by the BER, in order to avoid blanket application of the BER.

30. As regards self-assessment under Article 101(3) of the Treaty for cooperation on SPCs and security devices, undertakings benefit from two legal instruments, namely the Horizontal Guidelines (currently being revised) and the Guidelines on the application of Article [101(3)] of the Treaty.[1]

Notes

[1] OJ C 101, 27.4.2004, p.97.

E13

DIRECTIVE 97/67/EC OF THE EUROPEAN PARLIAMENT AND OF THE COUNCIL

of 15 December 1997
on common rules for the development of the internal market of Community postal services and the improvement of quality of service

Official Journal L 15, 21.1.1998, p.14

Celex No: 31997L0067

EUR-Lex permanent link: <http://eur-lex.europa.eu/LexUriServ/LexUriServ.do?uri=CELEX:31997L0067:EN:NOT>

Notes

Directive 97/67 was substantially amended by Directive 2008/6/EC of 20 February 2008 (OJ L 52, 27.2.2008, p.3) with effect from 27 February 2008. Member States were required to bring into force the laws, regulations and administrative provisions necessary to comply with Directive 2008/6/EC by 31 December 2010 (2008/6/EC Art 2), although certain member States may postpone implementation until 31 December 2012 (2008/6/EC Art 3). All B & C cross-references shown in the text are to Directive 96/67 as it stood immediately before its amendment on 27 February 2008.

Commentary

Directive 97/67: B&C: 12.137, 12.140, 12.143 **F&N:** 17.341
Arts 12–14: B&C: 12.140
Arts 16–19: B&C: 12.140

THE EUROPEAN PARLIAMENT AND THE COUNCIL OF THE EUROPEAN UNION,

Having regard to the [Treaty on the Functioning of the European Union], and in particular Articles [53(1)], [62] and [114]* thereof

Having regard to the proposal from the Commission,[1]

Having regard to the opinion of the Economic and Social Committee,[2]

Having regard to the opinion of the Committee of the Regions,[3]

Having regard to the resolution of the European Parliament of 22 January 1993 concerning the green paper on the development of the single market for postal services,[4]

Having regard to the Council resolution of 7 February 1994 on the development of Community postal services,[5]

Acting in accordance with the procedure laid down in Article [294] of the Treaty, in the light of the joint text approved by the Conciliation Committee on 7 November 1997,[6]

Notes

* Ed note: please see the Note on the Lisbon Treaty at p.xvii in regard to article renumbering introduced by the Lisbon Treaty.

[1] OJ C 322, 2.12.1995, p.22, and OJ C 300, 10.10.1996, p.22.

[2] OJ C 174, 17.6.1996, p.41.

[3] OJ C 337, 11.11.1996, p.28.

[4] OJ C 42, 15.2.1993, p.240.

[5] OJ C 48, 16.2.1994, p.3.

[6] Opinion of the European Parliament of 9 May 1996 (OJ C 152, 27.5.1996, p.20), Council Common Position of 29 April 1997 (OJ C 188, 19.6.1997, p.9) and Decision of the European Parliament of 16 September 1997 (OJ C 304, 6.10.1997, p.34); Decision of the European Parliament of 19 November 1997 and Decision of the Council of 1 December 1997.

(1) Whereas measures should be adopted with the aim of establishing the internal market in accordance with Article [26] of the Treaty; whereas this market comprises an area without internal frontiers in which the free movement of goods, persons, services and capital is ensured;

(2) Whereas the establishment of the internal market in the postal sector is of proven importance for the economic and social cohesion of the Community, in that postal services are an essential instrument of communication and trade;

(3) Whereas on 11 June 1992 the Commission presented a Green Paper on the development of the single market for postal services and, on 2 June 1993, a Communication on the guidelines for the development of Community postal services;

(4) Whereas the Commission has conducted wide-ranging public consultation on those aspects of postal services that are of interest to the Community and the interested parties in the postal sector have communicated their observations to the Commission;

(5) Whereas the current extent of the universal postal service and the conditions governing its provision vary significantly from one Member State to another; whereas, in particular, performance in terms of quality of services is very unequal amongst Member States;

(6) Whereas cross-border postal links do not always meet the expectations of users and European citizens, and performance, in terms of quality of service with regard to Community cross-border postal services, is at the moment unsatisfactory;

(7) Whereas the disparities observed in the postal sector have considerable implications for those sectors of activity which rely especially on postal services and effectively impede the progress towards internal Community cohesion, in that the regions deprived of postal services of sufficiently high quality find themselves at a disadvantage as regards both their letter service and the distribution of goods;

(8) Whereas measures seeking to ensure the gradual and controlled liberalisation of the market and to secure a proper balance in the application thereof are necessary in order to guarantee, throughout the Community, and subject to the obligations and rights of the universal service providers, the free provision of services in the postal sector itself;

(9) Whereas action at Community level to ensure greater harmonisation of the conditions governing the postal sector is therefore necessary and steps must consequently be taken to establish common rules;

(10) Whereas, in accordance with the principle of subsidiarity, a set of general principles should be adopted at Community level, whilst the choice of the exact procedures should be a matter for the Member States, which should be free to choose the system best adapted to their own circumstances;

(11) Whereas it is essential to guarantee at Community level a universal postal service encompassing a minimum range of services of specified quality to be provided in all Member States at

an affordable price for the benefit of all users, irrespective of their geographical location in the Community;

(12) Whereas the aim of the universal services is to offer all users easy access to the postal network through the provision, in particular, of a sufficient number of access points and by ensuring satisfactory conditions with regard to the frequency of collections and deliveries; whereas the provision of the universal service must meet the fundamental need to ensure continuity of operation, whilst at the same time remaining adaptable to the needs of users as well as guaranteeing them fair and non-discriminatory treatment;

(13) Whereas universal service must cover national services as well as cross-border services;

(14) Whereas users of the universal service must be given adequate information on the range of services offered, the conditions governing their supply and use, the quality of the services provided, and the tariffs;

(15) Whereas the provisions of this Directive relating to universal service provision are without prejudice to the right of universal service operators to negotiate contracts with customers individually;

(16) Whereas the maintenance of a range of those services that may be reserved, in compliance with the rules of the Treaty and without prejudice to the application of the rules on competition, appears justified on the grounds of ensuring the operation of the universal service under financially balanced conditions; whereas the process of liberalisation should not curtail the continuing supply of certain free services for blind and partially sighted persons introduced by the Member States;

(17) Whereas items of correspondence weighing 350 grammes and over represent less than 2% of letter volume and less than 3% of the receipts of the public operators; whereas the criteria of price (five times the basic tariff) will better permit the distinction between the reserved service and the express service, which is liberalised;

(18) Whereas, in view of the fact that the essential difference between express mail and universal postal services lies in the value added (whatever form it takes) provided by express services and perceived by customers, the most effective way of determining the extra value perceived is to consider the extra price that customers are prepared to pay, without prejudice, however, to the price limit of the reserved area which must be respected;

(19) Whereas it is reasonable to allow, on an interim basis, for direct mail and cross-border mail to continue to be capable of reservation within the price and weight limits provided; whereas, as a further step towards the completion of the internal market of postal services, a decision on the further gradual controlled liberalisation of the postal market, in particular with a view to the liberalisation of cross-border and direct mail as well as on a further review of the price and weight limits, should be taken by the European Parliament and the Council not later than 1 January 2000, on a proposal from the Commission following a review of the sector;

(20) Whereas, for reasons of public order and public security, Member States may have a legitimate interest in conferring on one or more entities designated by them the right to site on the public highway letter-boxes intended for the reception of postal items; whereas, for the same reasons, they are entitled to appoint the entity or entities responsible for issuing postage stamps identifying the country of origin and those responsible for providing the registered mail service used in the course of judicial or administrative procedures in accordance with their national legislation; whereas they may also indicate membership of the European Union by integrating the 12-star symbol;

(21) Whereas new services (services quite distinct from conventional services) and document exchange do not form part of the universal service and consequently there is no justification for their being reserved to the universal service providers; whereas this applies equally to self-provision (provision of postal services by the natural or legal person who is the originator of the mail, or collection and routing of these items by a third party acting solely on behalf of that person), which does not fall within the category of services;

(22) Whereas Member States should be able to regulate, by appropriate authorization procedures, on their territory, the provision of postal services which are not reserved to the universal service providers; whereas those procedures must be transparent, non-discriminatory, proportionate and based on objective criteria;

(23) Whereas the Member States should have the option of making the grant of licences subject to universal service obligations or contributions to a compensation fund intended to compensate the universal service provider for the provision of services representing an unfair financial burden; whereas Member States should be able to include in the authorisations an obligation that the authorised activities must not infringe the exclusive or special rights granted to the universal service providers for the reserved services; whereas an identification system for direct mail may be introduced for the purposes of supervision where direct mail is liberalised;

(24) Whereas measures necessary for the harmonisation of authorisation procedures laid down by the Member States governing the commercial provision to the public of non-reserved services will have to be adopted;

(25) Whereas, should this prove necessary, measures shall be adopted to ensure the transparency and non-discriminatory nature of conditions governing access to the public postal network in Member States;

(26) Whereas, in order to ensure sound management of the universal service and to avoid distortions of competition, the tariffs applied to the universal service should be objective, transparent, non-discriminatory and geared to costs;

(27) Whereas the remuneration for the provision of the intra-Community cross-border mail service, without prejudice to the minimum set of obligations derived from Universal Postal Union acts, should be geared to cover the costs of delivery incurred by the universal service provider in the country of destination; whereas this remuneration should also provide an incentive to improve or maintain the quality of the cross-border service through the use of quality-of-service targets; whereas this would justify suitable systems providing for an appropriate coverage of costs and related specifically to the quality of service achieved;

(28) Whereas separate accounts for the different reserved services and non-reserved services are necessary in order to introduce transparency into the actual costs of the various services and in order to ensure that cross-subsidies from the reserved sector to the non-reserved sector do not adversely affect the competitive conditions in the latter;

(29) Whereas, in order to ensure the application of the principles set out in the previous three recitals, universal service providers should implement, within a reasonable time limit, cost accounting systems, which can be independently verified, by which costs can be allocated to services as accurately as possible on the basis of transparent procedures; whereas such requirements can be fulfilled, for example, by implementation of the principle of fully distributed costing; whereas such cost accounting systems may not be required in circumstances where genuine conditions of open competition exist;

(30) Whereas consideration should be given to the interests of users, who are entitled to services of a high quality; whereas, therefore, every effort must be made to improve and enhance the quality of services provided at Community level; whereas such improvements in quality require Member States to lay down standards, to be attained or surpassed by the universal service providers, in respect of the services forming part of the universal service;

(31) Whereas the quality of service expected by users constitutes an essential aspect of the services provided; whereas the evaluation standards for this quality of service and the levels of quality achieved must be published in the interests of users; whereas it is necessary to have available harmonised quality-of-service standards and a common methodology for measurement in order to be able to evaluate the convergence of the quality of service throughout the Community;

(32) Whereas national quality standards consistent with Community standards must be determined by Member States; whereas, in the case of intra-Community cross-border services requiring the combined efforts of at least two universal service providers from two different Member States, quality standards must be defined at Community level;

(33) Whereas compliance with these standards must be independently verified at regular intervals and on a harmonised basis; whereas users must have the right to be informed of the results of this verification and Member States should ensure that corrective action is taken where those results demonstrate that the standards are not being met;

(34) Whereas Council Directive 93/13/EEC of 5 April 1993 on unfair terms in consumer contracts[1] applies to postal operators;

Notes

[1] OJ L 95, 21.4.1993, p.29.

(35) Whereas the need for improvement of quality of service means that disputes have to be settled quickly and efficiently; whereas, in addition to the forms of legal redress available under national and Community law, a procedure dealing with complaints should be provided, which should be transparent, simple and inexpensive and should enable all relevant parties to participate;

(36) Whereas progress in the interconnection of postal networks and the interests of users require that technical standardisation be encouraged; whereas technical standardisation is indispensable for the promotion of interoperability between national networks and for an efficient Community universal service;

(37) Whereas guidelines on European harmonisation provide for specialised technical standardisation activities to be entrusted to the European Committee for Standardisation;

(38) Whereas a committee should be established to assist the Commission with the implementation of this Directive, particularly in relation to the future work on the development of measures relating to the quality of Community cross-border service and technical standardisation;

(39) Whereas, in order to ensure the proper functioning of the universal service and to ensure undistorted competition in the non-reserved sector, it is important to separate the functions of the regulator, on the one hand, and the operator, on the other; whereas no postal operator may be both judge and interested party; whereas it is for the Member State to define the statute of one or more national regulatory authorities, which may be chosen from public authorities or independent entities appointed for that purpose;

(40) Whereas the effects of the harmonised conditions on the functioning of the internal market in postal services will need to be the subject of an assessment; whereas, therefore, the Commission will present a report to the European Parliament and the Council on the application of this Directive, including the appropriate information on developments in the sector, particularly concerning economic, social, employment and technological aspects, as well as on quality of service, three years following the date of its entry into force, and in any event no later than 31 December 2000;

(41) Whereas this Directive does not affect the application of the rules of the Treaty, and in particular its rules on competition and the freedom to provide services;

(42) Whereas nothing shall prevent Member States from maintaining in force or introducing measures for the postal sector which are more liberal than those provided for by this Directive, nor, should this Directive lapse, from maintaining in force measures which they have introduced in order to implement it, provided in each case that such measures are compatible with the Treaty;

(43) Whereas it is appropriate that this Directive should apply until 31 December 2004 unless otherwise decided by the European Parliament and the Council on the basis of a proposal from the Commission;

(44) Whereas this Directive does not apply to any activity which falls outside the scope of Community law, such as those provided for by Titles V and VI of the Treaty on European Union, and in any case to activities concerning public security, defence, State security (including the economic well-being of the State when the activities relate to State security matters) and the activities of the State in areas of criminal law;

(45) Whereas this Directive does not, in the case of undertakings which are not established in the Community, prevent the adoption of measures in accordance with both Community law and

existing international obligations designed to ensure that nationals of the Member States enjoy similar treatment in third countries; whereas Community undertakings should benefit in third countries from treatment and effective access that is comparable to the treatment and access to the market which is conferred on nationals of the countries concerned within the Community context,

HAVE ADOPTED THIS DIRECTIVE:

Chapter 1
Objective and scope

[Article 1

This Directive establishes common rules concerning:

— the conditions governing the provision of postal services,
— the provision of a universal postal service within the Community,
— the financing of universal services under conditions that guarantee the permanent provision of such services,
— tariff principles and transparency of accounts for universal service provision,
— the setting of quality standards for universal service provision and the setting-up of a system to ensure compliance with those standards,
— the harmonisation of technical standards,
— the creation of independent national regulatory authorities.];

Notes

Article 1 was substituted as shown in square brackets by Directive 2008/6/EC (OJ L 52, 27.2.2008), Article 1(1), with effect from 27 February 2008.

Article 2

For the purposes of this Directive, the following definitions shall apply:

[1. *postal services*: services involving the clearance, sorting, transport and distribution of postal items;]

[1a. *postal service provider*: undertaking that provides one or more postal services;]

2. *[postal network]*: the system of organisation and resources of all kinds used by the universal service provider(s) for the purposes in particular of:

— the clearance of postal items covered by a universal service obligation from access points throughout the territory,
— the routing and handling of those items from the postal network access point to the distribution centre,
— distribution to the addresses shown on items;

3. *access points*: physical facilities, including letter boxes provided for the public either on the public highway or at the premises of the postal service provider(s), where postal items may be deposited with the postal network by senders;]

[4. *clearance*: the operation of collecting postal items by a postal service provider;]

5. *distribution*: the process from sorting at the distribution centre to delivery of postal items to their addressees;

[6. *postal item*: an item addressed in the final form in which it is to be carried by a postal service provider. In addition to items of correspondence, such items also include for instance books, catalogues, newspapers, periodicals and postal parcels containing merchandise with or without commercial value;]

7. *item of correspondence*: a communication in written form on any kind of physical medium to be conveyed and delivered at the address indicated by the sender on the item itself or on its wrapping. Books, catalogues, newspapers and periodicals shall not be regarded as items of correspondence;

[…]

9. *registered item*: a service providing a flat-rate guarantee against risks of loss, theft or damage and supplying the sender, where appropriate upon request, with proof of the handing in of the postal item and/or of its delivery to the addressee;

10. *insured item*: a service insuring the postal item up to the value declared by the sender in the event of loss, theft or damage;

11. *cross-border mail*: mail from or to another Member State or from or to a third country;

[…]

[13. *universal service provider*: the public or private postal service provider providing a universal postal service or parts thereof within a Member State, the identity of which has been notified to the Commission in accordance with Article 4;]

[14. *authorisations*: any permission setting out rights and obligations specific to the postal sector and allowing undertakings to provide postal services and, where applicable, to establish and/or operate their networks for the provision of such services, in the form of a general authorisation or individual licence as defined below:

— "general authorisation": an authorisation, regardless of whether it is regulated by a "class licence" or under general law and regardless of whether such regulation requires registration or declaration procedures, which does not require the postal service provider concerned to obtain an explicit decision by the national regulatory authority before exercising the rights stemming from the authorisation,

— "individual licence": an authorisation which is granted by a national regulatory authority and which gives a postal service provider specific rights, or which subjects that undertaking's operations to specific obligations supplementing the general authorisation where applicable, where the postal service provider is not entitled to exercise the rights concerned until it has received the decision by the national regulatory authority;]

15. *terminal dues*: the remuneration of universal service providers for the distribution of incoming cross-border mail comprising postal items from another Member State or from a third country;

16. *sender*: a natural or legal person responsible for originating postal items;

[17. *user*: any natural or legal person benefiting from postal service provision as a sender or an addressee;]

18. *national regulatory authority*: the body or bodies, in each Member State, to which the Member State entrusts, inter alia, the regulatory functions falling within the scope of this Directive;

[19. *essential requirements*: general non-economic reasons which can induce a Member State to impose conditions on the supply of postal services. These reasons are the confidentiality of correspondence, security of the network as regards the transport of dangerous goods, respect for the terms and conditions of employment, social security schemes, laid down by law, regulation or administrative provision and/or by collective agreement negotiated between national social partners, in accordance with Community and national law and, where justified, data protection, environmental protection and regional planning. Data protection may include personal data protection, the confidentiality of information transmitted or stored and protection of privacy;]

[20. *Services provided at single piece tariff*: postal services for which the tariff is set in the general terms and conditions of universal service provider(s) for individual postal items.]

Notes

The amendments shown in square brackets were made by Directive 2008/6/EC (OJ L 52, 27.2.2008), Article 1(2), with effect from 27 February 2008.

CHAPTER 2
UNIVERSAL SERVICE

Article 3

1. Member States shall ensure that users enjoy the right to a universal service involving the permanent provision of a postal service of specified quality at all points in their territory at affordable prices for all users.

2. To this end, Member States shall take steps to ensure that the density of the points of contact and of the access points takes account of the needs of users.

[3. Member States shall take steps to ensure that the universal service is guaranteed not less than five working days a week, save in circumstances or geographical conditions deemed exceptional, and that it includes as a minimum:

— one clearance,

— one delivery to the home or premises of every natural or legal person or, by way of derogation, under conditions at the discretion of the national regulatory authority, one delivery to appropriate installations.]

Any exception or derogation granted by a national regulatory authority in accordance with this paragraph must be communicated to the Commission and to all national regulatory authorities.

4. Each Member State shall adopt the measures necessary to ensure that the universal service includes the following minimum facilities:

— the clearance, sorting, transport and distribution of postal items up to two kilograms,

— the clearance, sorting, transport and distribution of postal packages up to 10 kilograms,

— services for registered items and insured items.

[5. The national regulatory authorities may increase the weight limit of universal service coverage for postal parcels to any weight not exceeding 20 kilograms and may lay down special arrangements for the door-to-door delivery of such parcels.

Notwithstanding the weight limit of universal service coverage for postal parcels established by a given Member State, Member States shall ensure that postal parcels received from other Member States and weighing up to 20 kilograms are delivered within their territory.]

[6. The minimum and maximum dimensions for the postal items in question shall be those as laid down in the relevant provisions adopted by the Universal Postal Union.]

7. The universal service as defined in this Article shall cover both national and cross-border services.

Notes

The amendments shown in square brackets were made by Directive 2008/6/EC (OJ L 52, 27.2.2008), Article 1(3), with effect from 27 February 2008.

Commentary

Art 3: B&C: 12.140
Art 3(3): B&C: 12.140
Art 3(4): B&C: 12.140
Art 3(5): B&C: 12.140
[note: cross-references are to Art 3 before its amendment on 27 February 2008]

[Article 4

1. Each Member State shall ensure that the provision of the universal service is guaranteed and shall notify the Commission of the steps it has taken to fulfil this obligation. The Committee referred to in Article 21 shall be informed of the measures established by Member States to ensure the provision of the universal service.

2. Member States may designate one or more undertakings as universal service providers in order that the whole of the national territory can be covered. Member States may designate different undertakings to provide different elements of universal service and/or to cover different parts of the national territory. When they do so, they shall determine in accordance with Community law the obligations

and rights assigned to them and shall publish these obligations and rights. In particular, Member States shall take measures to ensure that the conditions under which universal services are entrusted are based on the principles of transparency, non-discrimination and proportionality, thereby guaranteeing the continuity of the universal service provision, by taking into account the important role it plays in social and territorial cohesion.

Member States shall notify the Commission of the identity of the universal service provider(s) they designate. The designation of a universal service provider shall be subject to a periodic review and be examined against the conditions and principles set out in this Article. However, Member States shall ensure that the duration of this designation provides a sufficient period for return on investments.]

Notes

Article 4 was substituted as shown in square brackets by Directive 2008/6/EC (OJ L 52, 27.2.2008), Article 1(4), with effect from 27 February 2008.

Commentary

Art 4(2): B&C: 12.140

Article 5

1. Each Member States shall take steps to ensure that universal service provision meets the following requirements:

— it shall offer a service guaranteeing compliance with the essential requirements,
— it shall offer an identical service to users under comparable conditions,
— it shall be made available without any form of discrimination whatsoever, especially without discrimination arising from political, religious or ideological considerations,
— it shall not be interrupted or stopped except in cases of force majeure,
— it shall evolve in response to the technical, economic and social environment and to the needs of users.

[2. The provisions of paragraph 1 shall not preclude measures which the Member States take in accordance with requirements relating to the public interest recognised in the Treaty, in particular Articles [36] and [52] thereof, concerning, inter alia, public morality, public security, including criminal investigations, and public policy.]

Notes

Article 5(2) was substituted as shown in square brackets by Directive 2008/6/EC (OJ L 52, 27.2.2008), Article 1(5), with effect from 27 February 2008.

Commentary

Art 5: B&C: 12.140

[Article 6

Member States shall take steps to ensure that users and postal service providers are regularly given sufficiently detailed and up-to-date information by the universal service provider(s) regarding the particular features of the universal service offered, with special reference to the general conditions of access to these services as well as to prices and quality standard levels. This information shall be published in an appropriate manner.

Member States shall notify the Commission, of how the information to be published in accordance with the first paragraph is to be made available.]

Notes

Article 6 was substituted as shown in square brackets by Directive 2008/6/EC (OJ L 52, 27.2.2008), Article 1(6), with effect from 27 February 2008.

Commentary

Art 6: B&C: 12.140 [note: cross-references are to Art 6 before its amendment on 27 February 2008]

CHAPTER 3

[FINANCING OF UNIVERSAL SERVICES]

[Article 7

1. Member States shall not grant or maintain in force exclusive or special rights for the establishment and provision of postal services. Member States may finance the provision of universal services in accordance with one or more of the means provided for in paragraphs 2, 3 and 4, or in accordance with any other means compatible with the Treaty.

2. Member States may ensure the provision of universal services by procuring such services in accordance with applicable public procurement rules and regulations, including, as provided for in Directive 2004/17/EC of the European Parliament and of the Council of 31 March 2004 coordinating the procurement procedures of entities operating in the water, energy, transport and postal services [ ], competitive dialogue or negotiated procedures with or without publication of a contract notice.

3. Where a Member State determines that the universal service obligations, as provided for in this Directive, entail a net cost, calculated taking into account Annex I, and represent an unfair financial burden on the universal service provider(s), it may introduce:

(a) a mechanism to compensate the undertaking(s) concerned from public funds; or
(b) a mechanism for the sharing of the net cost of the universal service obligations between providers of services and/or users.

4. Where the net cost is shared in accordance with paragraph 3(b), Member States may establish a compensation fund which may be funded by service providers and/or users' fees, and is administered for this purpose by a body independent of the beneficiary or beneficiaries. Member States may make the granting of authorisations to service providers under Article 9(2) subject to an obligation to make a financial contribution to that fund or to comply with universal service obligations. The universal service obligations of the universal service provider(s) set out in Article 3 may be financed in this manner.

5. Member States shall ensure that the principles of transparency, non-discrimination and proportionality are respected in establishing the compensation fund and when fixing the level of the financial contributions referred to in paragraphs 3 and 4. Decisions taken in accordance with paragraphs 3 and 4 shall be based on objective and verifiable criteria and be made public]

Notes

The heading of Chapter 3 and Article 7 were substituted as shown in square brackets by Directive 2008/6/EC (OJ L 52, 27.2.2008), Articles 1(7) and 1(8), with effect from 27 February 2008.

Commentary
Art 7: B&C: 12.139, 12.140
Art 7(1): B&C: 12.139

Article 8

The provisions of Article 7 shall be without prejudice to Member States' right to organise the siting of letter boxes on the public highway, the issue of postage stamps and the registered mail service used in the course of judicial or administrative procedures in accordance with their national legislation.

CHAPTER 4

[CONDITIONS GOVERNING THE PROVISION OF POSTAL SERVICES AND
ACCESS TO THE NETWORK]

[Article 9

1. For services which fall outside the scope of the universal service, Member States may introduce general authorisations to the extent necessary to guarantee compliance with the essential requirements.

2. For services which fall within the scope of the universal service, Member States may introduce authorisation procedures, including individual licences, to the extent necessary in order to guarantee compliance with the essential requirements and to ensure the provision of the universal service.

The granting of authorisations may:

— be made subject to universal service obligations,
— if necessary and justified, impose requirements concerning the quality, availability and performance of the relevant services,
— where appropriate, be subject to an obligation to make a financial contribution to the sharing mechanisms referred to in Article 7, if the provision of the universal service entails a net cost and represents an unfair burden on the universal service provider(s), designated in accordance with Article 4,
— where appropriate, be subject to an obligation to make a financial contribution to the national regulatory authority's operational costs referred to in Article 22,
— where appropriate, be made subject to or impose an obligation to respect working conditions laid down by national legislation.

Obligations and requirements referred to in the first indent and in Article 3 may only be imposed on designated universal service providers.

Except in the case of undertakings that have been designated as universal service providers in accordance with Article 4, authorisations may not:

— be limited in number,
— for the same elements of the universal service or parts of the national territory, impose universal service obligations and, at the same time, financial contributions to a sharing mechanism,
— duplicate conditions which are applicable to undertakings by virtue of other, non-sector-specific national legislation,
— impose technical or operational conditions other than those necessary to fulfil the obligations of this Directive.

3. The procedures, obligations and requirements referred to in paragraphs 1 and 2 shall be transparent, accessible, non-discriminatory, proportionate, precise and unambiguous, made public in advance and based on objective criteria. Member States shall ensure that the reasons for refusing or withdrawing an authorisation in whole or in part are communicated to the applicant and shall establish an appeal procedure.]

Notes

The heading of Chapter 4 and Article 9 were substituted as shown in square brackets by Directive 2008/6/EC (OJ L 52, 27.2.2008), Articles 1(9) and 1(10), with effect from 27 February 2008.

Commentary

Art 9(2): **B&C:** 12.141

Article 10

1. The European Parliament and the Council, acting on a proposal from the Commission and on the basis of Articles [53(1)], [62] and [114] of the Treaty, shall adopt the measures necessary for the harmonisation of the procedures referred to in Article 9 governing the commercial provision of postal services to the public.]

2. The harmonisation measures referred to in paragraph 1 shall concern, in particular, the criteria to be observed and the procedures to be followed by the postal operator, the manner of publication of those criteria and procedures, as well as the appeal procedures to be followed.

Notes

Article 10(1) was substituted as shown in square brackets by Directive 2008/6/EC (OJ L 52, 27.2.2008), Article 1(11), with effect from 27 February 2008.

[Article 11

The European Parliament and the Council, acting on a proposal from the Commission and on the basis of Articles [53(1)], [62] and [114] of the Treaty, shall adopt such harmonisation measures as are necessary to ensure that users and the postal service provider(s) have access to the postal network under conditions which are transparent and non-discriminatory.]

Notes

Article 11 was substituted as shown in square brackets by Directive 2008/6/EC (OJ L 52, 27.2.2008), Article 1(12), with effect from 27 February 2008.

[Article 11a

Whenever necessary to protect the interest of users and/or to promote effective competition, and in the light of national conditions and national legislation, Member States shall ensure that transparent, non-discriminatory access conditions are available to elements of postal infrastructure or services provided within the scope of the universal service, such as postcode system, address database, post office boxes, delivery boxes, information on change of address, re-direction service and return to sender service. This provision shall be without prejudice to the right of Member States to adopt measures to ensure access to the postal network under transparent, proportional and non-discriminatory conditions.]

Notes

Article 11a was inserted as shown in square brackets by Directive 2008/6/EC (OJ L 52, 27.2.2008), Article 1(13), with effect from 27 February 2008.

CHAPTER 5
TARIFF PRINCIPLES AND TRANSPARENCY OF ACCOUNTS

[Article 12

Member States shall take steps to ensure that the tariffs for each of the services forming part of the universal service comply with the following principles:

— prices shall be affordable and must be such that all users, independent of geographical location, and, in the light of specific national conditions, have access to the services provided. Member States may maintain or introduce the provision of a free postal service for the use of blind and partially-sighted persons,

— prices shall be cost-oriented and give incentives for an efficient universal service provision. Whenever necessary for reasons relating to the public interest, Member States may decide that a uniform tariff shall be applied, throughout their national territory and/or cross-border, to services provided at single piece tariff and to other postal items,

— the application of a uniform tariff shall not exclude the right of the universal service provider(s) to conclude individual agreements on prices with users,

— tariffs shall be transparent and non-discriminatory,

— whenever universal service providers apply special tariffs, for example for services for businesses, bulk mailers or consolidators of mail from different users, they shall apply the principles of transparency and non-discrimination with regard both to the tariffs and to the associated conditions. The tariffs, together with the associated conditions, shall apply equally both as between different third parties and as between third parties and universal service providers supplying equivalent services. Any such tariffs shall also be available to users, in particular individual users and small and medium-sized enterprises, who post under similar conditions.]

Notes

Article 12 was substituted as shown in square brackets by Directive 2008/6/EC (OJ L 52, 27.2.2008), Article 1(14), with effect from 27 February 2008.

Commentary

Art 12: B&C: 12.146

Article 13

1. In order to ensure the cross-border provision of the universal service, Member States shall encourage their universal service providers to arrange that in their agreements on terminal dues for intra-Community cross-border mail, the following principles are respected:

— terminal dues shall be fixed in relation to the costs of processing and delivering incoming cross-border mail,
— levels of remuneration shall be related to the quality of service achieved,
— terminal dues shall be transparent and non-discriminatory.

2. The implementation of these principles may include transitional arrangements designed to avoid undue disruption on postal markets or unfavourable implications for economic operators provided there is agreement between the operators of origin and receipt; such arrangements shall, however, be restricted to the minimum required to achieve these objectives.

Article 14

[1. Member States shall take the measures necessary to ensure that the accounting of the universal service providers is conducted in accordance with the provisions of this Article.]

[2. The universal service provider(s) shall keep separate accounts within their internal accounting systems in order to clearly distinguish between each of the services and products which are part of the universal service and those which are not. This accounting separation shall be used as an input when Member States calculate the net cost of the universal service. Such internal accounting systems shall operate on the basis of consistently applied and objectively justifiable cost accounting principles.]

[3. The accounting systems referred to in paragraph 2 shall, without prejudice to paragraph 4, allocate costs in the following manner:

(a) costs which can be directly assigned to a particular service or product shall be so assigned;
(b) common costs, that is costs which cannot be directly assigned to a particular service, shall be allocated as follows:

  (i) whenever possible, common costs shall be allocated on the basis of direct analysis of the origin of the costs themselves;
  (ii) when direct analysis is not possible, common cost categories shall be allocated on the basis of an indirect linkage to another cost category or group of cost categories for which a direct assignment or allocation is possible; the indirect linkage shall be based on comparable cost structures;
  (iii) when neither direct nor indirect measures of cost allocation can be found, the cost category shall be allocated on the basis of a general allocator computed by using the ratio of all expenses directly or indirectly assigned or allocated, on the one hand, to each of the universal services and, on the other hand, to the other services;
  (iv) common costs, which are necessary for the provision of both universal services and non-universal services, shall be allocated appropriately; the same cost drivers must be applied to both universal services and non-universal services.]

4. Other cost accounting systems may be applied only if they are compatible with paragraph 2 and have been approved by the national regulatory authority. The Commission shall be informed prior to their application.

5. National regulatory authorities shall ensure that compliance with one of the cost accounting systems described in paragraphs 3 or 4 is verified by a competent body which is independent of the universal service provider. Member States shall ensure that a statement concerning compliance is published periodically.

6. The national regulatory authority shall keep available, to an adequate level of detail, information on the cost accounting systems applied by a universal service provider, and shall submit such information to the Commission on request.

7. On request, detailed accounting information arising from these systems shall be made available in confidence to the national regulatory authority and to the Commission.

[8. Where a given Member State has not used a financing mechanism for the provision of the universal service, as permitted under Article 7, and where the national regulatory authority is satisfied that none of the designated universal service providers in that Member State is in receipt of State assistance, hidden or otherwise, and that competition in the market is fully effective, the national regulatory authority may decide not to apply the requirements of this Article.]

[9. This Article may, however, be applied to the universal service provider designated before the final date for Full Market Opening as long as no other universal service provider(s) have been designated. The national regulatory authority shall inform the Commission in advance of any such decision.]

[10. Member States may require those postal service providers which are obliged to contribute to a compensation fund to introduce an appropriate accounting separation to ensure the functioning of the fund.]

Notes

Articles 14(1), (2), (3) and (8) were substituted, and Articles 14(9) and (10) were inserted, all as shown in square brackets, by Directive 2008/6/EC (OJ L 52, 27.2.2008), Article 1(15), with effect from 27 February 2008.

Article 15

The financial accounts of all universal service providers shall be drawn up, submitted to audit by an independent auditor and published in accordance with the relevant Community and national legislation to commercial undertakings.

CHAPTER 6
QUALITY OF SERVICES

Article 16

Member States shall ensure that quality-of-service standards are set and published in relation to universal service in order to guarantee a postal service of good quality.

Quality standards shall focus, in particular, on routing times and on the regularity and reliability of services.

These standards shall be set by:

— the Member States in the case of national services,
[— the European Parliament and the Council in the case of intra-Community cross-border services (see Annex II). Future adjustment of these standards to technical progress or market developments shall be made in accordance with the regulatory procedure with scrutiny referred to in Article 21(2).]

[Independent performance monitoring shall be carried out at least once a year by external bodies having no links with the universal service providers under standardised conditions to be specified in accordance with the regulatory procedure with scrutiny referred to in Article 21(2) and shall be the subject of reports published at least once a year.]

Notes

The amendments shown in square brackets were made by Directive 2008/6/EC (OJ L 52, 27.2.2008), Article 1(16), with effect from 27 February 2008.

Article 17

Member States shall day down quality standards for national mail and shall ensure that they are compatible with those laid down for intra-Community cross-border services.

Member States shall notify their quality standards for national services to the Commission, who will publish them in the same manner as the standards for intra-Community cross-border services referred to in Article 18.

National regulatory authorities shall ensure that independent performance monitoring is carried out in accordance with the fourth subparagraph of Article 16, that the results are justified, and that corrective action is taken where necessary.

Article 18

[1. In accordance with Article 16, quality standards for intra-Community cross-border services are laid down in Annex II.]

[2. Where exceptional situations relating to infrastructure or geography so require, the national regulatory authorities may determine exemptions from the quality standards provided for in Annex II. Where national regulatory authorities determine exemptions in this manner, they shall notify the Commission forthwith. The Commission shall submit an annual report of the notifications received during the previous 12 months to the Committee referred to in Article 21 for its information.]

3. The Commission shall publish in the *Official Journal of the European Communities* any adjustments made to the quality standards for intra-Community cross-border services and shall take steps to ensure the regular independent monitoring and the publication of performance levels certifying compliance with these standards and the progress accomplished. National regulatory authorities shall ensure that corrective action is taken where necessary.

Notes

Articles 18(1) and 18(2) were substituted as shown in square brackets by Directive 2008/6/EC (OJ L 52, 27.2.2008), Article 1(17), with effect from 27 February 2008.

[Article 19

1. Member States shall ensure that transparent, simple and inexpensive procedures are made available by all postal service providers for dealing with postal users' complaints, particularly in cases involving loss, theft, damage or non-compliance with service quality standards (including procedures for determining where responsibility lies in cases where more than one operator is involved), without prejudice to relevant international and national provisions on compensation schemes.

Member States shall adopt measures to ensure that the procedures referred to in the first subparagraph enable disputes to be settled fairly and promptly with provision, where warranted, for a system of reimbursement and/or compensation.

Member States shall also encourage the development of independent out-of-court schemes for the resolution of disputes between postal service providers and users.

2. Without prejudice to other possibilities of appeal or means of redress under national and Community legislation, Member States shall ensure that users, acting individually or, where permitted by national law, jointly with organisations representing the interests of users and/or consumers, may bring before the competent national authority cases where users' complaints to undertakings providing postal services within the scope of the universal service have not been satisfactorily resolved.

In accordance with Article 16, Member States shall ensure that the universal service providers and, wherever appropriate, undertakings providing services within the scope of the universal service, publish, together with the annual report on the monitoring of their performance, information on the number of complaints and the manner in which they have been dealt with.]

Notes

Article 19 was substituted as shown in square brackets by Directive 2008/6/EC (OJ L 52, 27.2.2008), Article 1(18), with effect from 27 February 2008.

CHAPTER 7
HARMONISATION OF TECHNICAL STANDARDS

Article 20

The harmonisation of technical standards shall be continued, taking into account in particular the interests of users.

The European Committee for Standardisation shall be entrusted with drawing up technical standards applicable in the postal sector on the basis of remits to it pursuant to the principles set out in Council Directive 83/189/EEC of 28 March 1983 laying down a procedure for the provision of information in the field of technical standards and regulations.[1]

This work shall take account of the harmonisation measures adopted at international level and in particular those decided upon within the Universal Postal Union.

The standards applicable shall be published in the Official Journal of the European Communities once a year.

Member States shall ensure that universal service providers refer to the standards published in the Official Journal where necessary in the interests of users and in particular when they supply the information referred to in Article 6.

The Committee provided for in Article 21 shall be kept informed of the discussions within the European Committee for Standardisation and the progress achieved in this area by that body.

Notes

[1] OJ L 109, 26.4.1983, p.8. Directive as last amended by Commission Decision 96/139/EC (OJ L 32, 10.2.1996, p.31).

CHAPTER 8
THE COMMITTEE

[Article 21

1. The Commission shall be assisted by a committee.

2. Where reference is made to this paragraph, Articles 5a(1) to (4) and Article 7 of Decision 1999/468/EC shall apply, having regard to the provisions of Article 8 thereof.]

Notes

Article 21 was substituted as shown in square brackets by Directive 2008/6/EC (OJ L 52, 27.2.2008), Article 1(19), with effect from 27 February 2008.

CHAPTER 9
THE NATIONAL REGULATORY AUTHORITY

[Article 22

1. Each Member State shall designate one or more national regulatory authorities for the postal sector that are legally separate from and operationally independent of the postal operators. Member States that retain ownership or control of postal service providers shall ensure effective structural separation of the regulatory functions from activities associated with ownership or control.

Member States shall inform the Commission which national regulatory authorities they have des-ignated to carry out the tasks arising from this Directive. They shall publish the tasks to be under-taken by national regulatory authorities in an easily accessible form, in particular where those tasks are assigned to more than one body. Member States shall ensure, where appropriate, consultation and cooperation between those authorities and national authorities entrusted with the implementation of competition law and consumer protection law on matters of common interest.

2. The national regulatory authorities shall have as a particular task ensuring compliance with the obligations arising from this Directive, in particular by establishing monitoring and regulatory procedures to ensure the provision of the universal service. They may also be charged with ensuring compliance with competition rules in the postal sector.

The national regulatory authorities shall work in close collaboration and shall provide mutual assistance in order to facilitate the application of this Directive within the appropriate existing bodies.

3. Member States shall ensure that effective mechanisms exist at national level under which any user or postal service provider affected by a decision of a national regulatory authority has the right to appeal against the decision to an appeal body which is independent of the parties involved. Pending the outcome of any such appeal, the decision of the national regulatory authority shall stand, unless the appeal body decides otherwise.]

Notes

Article 22 was substituted as shown in square brackets by Directive 2008/6/EC (OJ L 52, 27.2.2008), Article 1(20), with effect from 27 February 2008.

Commentary

Art 22: B&C: 12.138 [note: cross-references are to Art 22 before its replacement on 27 February 2008]

[CHAPTER 9A
PROVISION OF INFORMATION

Article 22a

1. Member States shall ensure that postal service providers provide all the information, in particular to the national regulatory authorities, including financial information and information concerning the provision of the universal service, namely for the following purposes:

(a) for national regulatory authorities to ensure conformity with the provisions of, or decisions made in accordance with this Directive,

(b) for clearly defined statistical purposes.

2. Postal service providers shall provide such information promptly on request and in confidence, where necessary, within the timescales and to the level of detail required by the national regulatory authority. The information requested by the national regulatory authority shall be proportionate to the performance of its tasks. The national regulatory authority shall give the reasons justifying its request for information.

3. Member States shall ensure that national regulatory authorities provide the Commission, upon request, with appropriate and relevant information necessary for it to carry out its tasks under this Directive.

4. Where information is considered confidential by a national regulatory authority, in accordance with Community and national business confidentiality rules, the Commission and the national regulatory authorities concerned shall preserve such confidentiality.]

Notes

Chapter 9a was inserted as shown in square brackets by Directive 2008/6/EC (OJ L 52, 27.2.2008), Article 1(21), with effect from 27 February 2008.

CHAPTER 10
FINAL PROVISIONS

[Article 23

Every four years, on the first occasion no later than 31 December 2013, the Commission shall submit a report to the European Parliament and the Council on the application of this Directive, including appropriate information on developments in the sector, particularly concerning economic, social, employment patterns and technological aspects, as well as on quality of service. The report shall be accompanied, where appropriate, by proposals to the European Parliament and the Council.]

Notes
Article 23 was substituted as shown in square brackets by Directive 2008/6/EC (OJ L 52, 27.2.2008), Article 1(22), with effect from 27 February 2008.
Commentary
Art 23: B&C: 12.137 [note: cross-references are to Art 23 before its amendment on 27 February 2008]

[*Article 23a*

The Commission shall provide assistance to the Member States on the implementation of this Directive, including on the calculation of any net cost of the universal service.]

Notes
Article 23a was inserted as shown in square brackets by Directive 2008/6/EC (OJ L 52, 27.2.2008), Article 1(23), with effect from 27 February 2008.

[…]

Notes
Articles 24, 25, 26 and 27 were deleted by Directive 2008/6/EC (OJ L 52, 27.2.2008), Article 1(24), with effect from 27 February 2008.

Article 28

This Directive is addressed to the Member States.

Done at Brussels, 15 December 1997.

[ANNEX I
Guidance on calculating the net cost, if any, of universal service

Part A: Definition of the universal service obligations

Universal service obligations refer to the obligations referred to in Article 3 placed upon a postal service provider by a Member State which concern the provision of a postal service throughout a specified geographical area, including, where required, uniform prices in that geographical area for the provision of that service or provision of certain free services for blind and partially-sighted persons.

Those obligations may include, among others, the following:

— a number of days of delivery, superior to those set in this Directive,
— accessibility to access points, in order to satisfy the universal service obligations,
— the tariffs affordability of the universal service,
— uniform prices for universal service,
— the provision of certain free services for blind and partially-sighted persons.

Part B: Calculation of net cost

National regulatory authorities are to consider all means to ensure appropriate incentives for postal service providers (designated or not) to provide universal service obligations cost efficiently.

The net cost of universal service obligations is any cost related to and necessary for the operation of the universal service provision. The net cost of universal service obligations is to be calculated, as the difference between the net cost for a designated universal service provider of operating with the universal service obligations and the same postal service provider operating without the universal service obligations.

The calculation shall take into account all other relevant elements, including any intangible and market benefits which accrue to a postal service provider designated to provide universal service, the entitlement to a reasonable profit and incentives for cost efficiency.

Due attention is to be given to correctly assessing the costs that any designated universal service provider would have chosen to avoid, had there been no universal service obligation. The net cost calculation should assess the benefits, including intangible benefits, to the universal service operator.

The calculation is to be based upon the costs attributable to:

(i) elements of the identified services which can only be provided at a loss or provided under cost conditions falling outside normal commercial standards. This category may include service elements such as the services defined in Part A;

(ii) specific users or groups of users who, taking into account the cost of providing the specified service, the revenue generated and any uniform prices imposed by the Member State, can only be served at a loss or under cost conditions falling outside normal commercial standards.

This category includes those users or groups of users that would not be served by a commercial operator that did not have an obligation to provide universal service.

The calculation of the net cost of specific aspects of universal service obligations is to be made separately and so as to avoid the double counting of any direct or indirect benefits and costs. The overall net cost of universal service obligations to any designated universal service provider is to be calculated as the sum of the net costs arising from the specific components of universal service obligations, taking account of any intangible benefits. The responsibility for verifying the net cost lies with the national regulatory authority. The universal service provider(s) shall cooperate with the national regulatory authority to enable it to verify the net cost.

Part C: Recovery of any net costs of universal service obligations

The recovery or financing of any net costs of universal service obligations may require designated universal service providers to be compensated for the services that they provide under non-commercial conditions. As such compensation involves financial transfers, Member States have to ensure that they are undertaken in an objective, transparent, non-discriminatory and proportionate manner. This means that the transfers result as far as possible in the least distortion to competition and to user demand.

A sharing mechanism based on a fund referred to in Article 7(4) should use a transparent and neutral mechanism for collecting contributions that avoids a double imposition of contributions falling on both outputs and inputs of undertakings.

The independent body administering the fund is to be responsible for collecting contributions from undertakings, which are assessed as liable to contribute to the net cost of universal service obligations in the Member State and is to oversee the transfer of sums due to the undertakings entitled to receive payments from the fund.]

Notes

Annex I was inserted by Directive 2008/6/EC (OJ L 52, 27.2.2008), Article 1(25), with effect from 27 February 2008.

[*ANNEX II*]
Quality standards for intra-Community cross-border mail

The quality standards for intra-Community cross-border mail in each country are to be established in relation to the time limit for routing measured from end to end* for postal items of the fastest standard category according to the formula D + n, where D represents the date of deposit** and n the number of working days which elapse between that date and that delivery to the addressee.

Quality standards for intra-Community cross-border mail

Time limit	Objective
D + 3	85% of items
D + 5	97% of items

The standards must be achieved not only for the entirety of intra-Community traffic but also for each of the bilateral flows between two Member States.

Notes

* End-to-end routing is measured from the access point to the network to the point of delivery to the addressee.

** The date of deposit to be taken into account shall be the same day as that on which the item is deposited, provided that deposit occurs before the last collection time notified from the access point to the network in question. When deposit takes place after this time limit, the date of deposit to be taken into consideration will be that of the following day of collection.

This annex became Annex II following amendment of the title by Directive 2008/6/EC (OJ L 52, 27.2.2008), Article 1(26), with effect from 27 February 2008.

E14

NOTICE FROM THE COMMISSION

on the application of the competition rules to the postal sector and on the assessment of certain State measures relating to postal services*

(98/C 39/02)

(Text with EEA relevance)

Official Journal C 39, 6.2.1998, p.2

Celex No: 31998Y0206(01)

EUR-Lex permanent link: <http://eur-lex.europa.eu/LexUriServ/LexUriServ.do?uri=CELEX:3199 8Y0206(01):EN:NOT>

Commentary
Notice: B&C: 12.142, 17.062 F&N: 17.326
Ed note: please see the Note on the Lisbon Treaty at p.xvii in regard to article renumbering introduced by the Lisbon Treaty.

Preface

Subsequent to the submission by the Commission of a Green Paper on the development of the single market for postal services[1] and of a communication to the European Parliament and the Council, setting out the results of the consultations on the Green Paper and the measures advocated by the Commission,[2] a substantial discussion has taken place on the future regulatory environment for the postal sector in the Community. By Resolution of 7 February 1994 on the development of Community postal services,[3] the Council invited the Commission to propose measures defining a harmonised universal service and the postal services which could be reserved. In July 1995, the Commission proposed a package of measures concerning postal services which consisted of a proposal for a Directive of the European Parliament and the Council on common rules for the development of Community postal services and the improvement of quality of service[4] and a draft of the present Notice on the application of the competition rules.[5]

Notes
1 COM(91) 476 final.
2 "Guidelines for the development of Community postal services" (COM(93) 247 of 2 June 1993).

3 OJ C 48, 16.2.1994, p.3.
4 OJ C 322, 2.12.1995, p.22.
5 OJ C 322, 2.12.1995, p.3.

This notice, which complements the harmonisation measures proposed by the Commission, builds on the results of those discussions in accordance with the principles established in the Resolution of 7 February 1994. It takes account of the comments received during the public consultation on the draft of this notice published in December 1995, of the European Parliament's resolution[6] on this draft adopted on 12 December 1996, as well as of the discussions on the proposed Directive in the European Parliament and in Council.

Notes

6 OJ C 20, 20.1.1997, p.159.

The Commission considers that because they are an essential vehicle of communication and trade, postal services are vital for all economic and social activities. New postal services are emerging and market certainty is needed to favour investment and the creation of new employment in the sector. As recognized by the Court of Justice of the European Communities, Community law, and in particular the competition rules of the EC Treaty, apply to the post sector.[7] The Court stated that "in the case of public undertakings to which Member States grant special or exclusive rights, they are neither to enact nor to maintain in force any measure contrary to the rules contained in the Treaty with regard to competition' and that those rules "must be read in conjunction with Article [106(2)] which provides that undertakings entrusted with the operation of services of general economic interest are to be subject to the rules on competition in so far as the application of such rules does not obstruct the performance, in law or in fact, of the particular tasks assigned to them." Questions are therefore frequently put to the Commission on the attitude it intends to take, for purposes of the implementation of the competition rules contained in the Treaty, with regard to the behaviour of postal operators and with regard to State measures relating to public undertakings and undertakings to which the Member States grant special or exclusive rights in the postal sector.

Notes

7 In particular in Joined Cases C-48/90 and C-66/90, *Netherlands and Koninklijke PTT Nederland and PTT Post BV v Commission* [1992] ECR I-565 and Case C-320/91 *Procureur du Roi v Paul Corbeau* [1993] ECR I-2533.

This notice sets out the Commission's interpretation of the relevant Treaty provisions and the guiding principles according to which the Commission intends to apply the competition rules of the Treaty to the postal sector in individual cases, while maintaining the necessary safeguards for the provision of a universal service, and gives to enterprises and Member States clear guidelines so as to avoid infringements of the Treaty. This Notice is without prejudice to any interpretation to be given by the Court of Justice of the European Communities.

Furthermore, this Notice sets out the approach the Commission intends to take when applying the competition rules to the behaviour of postal operators and when assessing the compatibility of State measures restricting the freedom to provide service and/or to compete in the postal markets with the competition rules and other rules of the Treaty. In addition, it addresses the issue of non-discriminatory access to the postal network and the safeguards required to ensure fair competition in the sector.

Especially on account of the development of new postal services by private and public operators, certain Member States have revised, or are revising, their postal legislation in order to restrict the monopoly of their postal organisations to what is considered necessary for the realisation of the public-interest objective. At the same time, the Commission is faced with a growing number of complaints and cases under competition law on which it must take position. At this stage, a notice is therefore the appropriate instrument to provide guidance to Member States and postal operators, including those enjoying special or exclusive rights, to ensure correct implementation of the competition rules. This Notice, although it cannot be exhaustive, aims to provide the necessary guidance for the correct interpretation, in particular, of Articles [56], [101], [102], [106], and [107] of the Treaty in individual cases. By issuing the present notice, the Commission is taking steps to bring transparency and to facilitate investment decisions of all postal operators, in the interest of the users of postal services in the European Union.

As the Commission explained in its communication of 11 September 1996 on "Services of general interest in Europe",[8] solidarity and equal treatment within a market economy are fundamental Community objectives. Those objectives are furthered by services of general interest. Europeans have come to expect high-quality services at affordable prices, and many of them even view services of general interest as social rights.

Notes

[8] COM(96) 443 final.

As regards, in particular, the postal sector, consumers are becoming increasingly assertive in exercising their rights and wishes. Worldwide competition is forcing companies using such services to seek out better price deals comparable to those enjoyed by their competitors. New technologies, such as fax or electronic mail, are putting enormous pressures on the traditional postal services. Those developments have given rise to worries about the future of those services accompanied by concerns over employment and economic and social cohesion. The economic importance of those services is considerable. Hence the importance of modernising and developing services of general interest, since they contribute so much to European competitiveness, social solidarity and quality of life.

The Community's aim is to support the competitiveness of the European economy in an increasingly competitive world and to give consumers more choice, better quality and lower prices, while at the same time helping, through its policies, to strengthen economic and social cohesion between the Member States and to reduce certain inequalities. Postal services have a key role to play here. The Community is committed to promoting their functions of general economic interest, as solemnly confirmed in the new Article [14], introduced by the Amsterdam Treaty, while improving their efficiency. Market forces produce a better allocation of resources and greater effectiveness in the supply of services, the principal beneficiary being the consumer, who gets better quality at a lower price. However, those mechanisms sometimes have their limits; as a result the potential benefits might not extend to the entire population and the objective of promoting social and territorial cohesion in the Union may not be attained. The public authority must then ensure that the general interest is taken into account.

The traditional structures of some services of general economic interest, which are organised on the basis of national monopolies, constitute a challenge for European economic integration. This includes postal monopolies, even where they are justified, which may obstruct the smooth functioning of the market, in particular by sealing off a particular market sector.

The real challenge is to ensure smooth interplay between the requirements of the single market in terms of free movement, economic performance and dynamism, free competition, and the general interest objectives. This interplay must benefit individual citizens and society as a whole. This is a difficult balancing act, since the goalposts are constantly moving: the single market is continuing to expand and public services, far from being fixed, are having to adapt to new requirements.

The basic concept of universal service, which was originated by the Commission,[9] is to ensure the provision of high-quality service to all prices everyone can afford. Universal service is defined in terms of principles: equality, universality, continuity and adaptability; and in terms of sound practices: openness in management, price-setting and funding and scrutiny by bodies independent of those operating the services. Those criteria are not always all met at national level, but where they have been introduced using the concept of European universal service, there have been positive effects for the development of general interest services. Universal service is the expression in Europe of the requirements and special features of the European model of society in a policy which combines a dynamic market, cohesion and solidarity.

Notes

[9] See footnote 8.

High-quality universal postal services are of great importance for private and business customers alike. In view of the development of electronic commerce their importance will even increase in the very near future. Postal services have a valuable role to play here.

As regards the postal sector, Directive 97/67/EC has been adopted by the European Parliament and the Council (hereinafter referred to as "the Postal Directive"). It aims to introduce common rules for developing the postal sector and improving the quality of service, as well as gradually opening up the markets in a controlled way.

The aim of the Postal Directive is to safeguard the postal service as a universal service in the long term. It imposes on Member States a minimum harmonised standard of universal services including a high-quality service countrywide with regular guaranteed deliveries at prices everyone can afford. This involves the collection, transport, sorting and delivery of letters as well as catalogues and parcels within certain price and weight limits. It also covers registered and insured (valeur déclarée) items and applies to both domestic and cross-border deliveries. Due regard is given to considerations of continuity, confidentiality, impartiality and equal treatment as well as adaptability.

To guarantee the funding of the universal service, a sector may be reserved for the operators of this universal service. The scope of the reserved sector has been harmonised in the Postal Directive According to the Postal Directive, Member States can only grant exclusive rights for the provision of postal services to the extent that this is necessary to guarantee the maintenance of the universal service. Moreover, the Postal Directive establishes the maximum scope that Member States may reserve in order to achieve this objective. Any additional funding which may be required for the universal service may be found by writing certain obligations into commercial operator's franchises; for example, they may be required to make financial contributions to a compensation fund administered for this purpose by a body independent of the beneficiary or beneficiaries, as foreseen in Article 9 of the Postal Directive.

The Postal Directive lays down a minimum common standard of universal services and establishes common rules concerning the reserved area. It therefore increases legal certainty as regards the legality of some exclusive and special rights in the postal sector. There are, however State measures that are not dealt with in it and that can be in conflict with the Treaty rules addressed to Member States. The autonomous behaviour of the postal operators also remains subject to the competition rules in the Treaty.

Article [106(2)] of the Treaty provides that suppliers of services of general interest may be exempted from the rules in the Treaty, to the extent that the application of those rules would obstruct the performance of the general interest tasks for which they are responsible. That exemption from the Treaty rules is however subject to the principle of proportionality. That principle is designed to ensure the best match between the duty to provide general interest services and the way in which the services are actually provided, so that the means used are in proportion to the ends pursued. The principle is formulated to allow for a flexible and context-sensitive balance that takes account of the technical and budgetary constraints that may vary from one sector to another. It also makes for the best possible interaction between market efficiency and general interest requirements, by ensuring that the means used to satisfy the requirements do not unduly interfere with the smooth running of the single European market and do not affect trade to an extent that would be contrary to the Community interest.[10]

Notes

[10] See judgment of 23 October 1997 in Cases C-157/94 to C-160/94 *"Member State Obligations—Electricity" Commission v Netherlands* (157/94), *Italy* (158/94), *France* (154/94), *Spain* (160/94).

The application of the Treaty rules, including the possible application of the Article [106(2)] exemption, as regards both behaviour of undertakings and State measures can only be done on a case-by-case basis. It seems, however, highly desirable, in order to increase legal certainty as regards measures not covered by the Postal Directive, to explain the Commission's interpretation of the Treaty and the approach that it aims to follow in its future application of those rules. In particular, the Commission considers that, subject to the provisions of Article [106(2)] in relation to the provision of the universal service, the application of the Treaty rules would promote the competitiveness of the undertakings active in the postal sector, benefit consumers and contribute in a positive way to the objectives of general interest.

The postal sector in the European Union is characterised by areas which Member States have reserved in order to guarantee universal service and which are now being harmonised by the Postal Directive in order to limit distortive effects between Member States. The Commission must, according to the Treaty, ensure that postal monopolies comply with the rules of the Treaty, and in particular the competition rules, in order to ensure maximum benefit and limit any distortive effects for the consumers. In pursuing this objective by applying the competition rules to the sector on a case-by-case-basis, the Commission will ensure that monopoly power is not used for extending a protected dominant position into liberalised activities or for unjustified discrimination in favour of big accounts at the expense of small users. The Commission will also ensure that postal monopolies granted in the area of cross-border services are not used for creating or maintaining illicit price cartels harming the interest of companies and consumers in the European Union.

This notice explains to the players on the market the practical consequences of the applicability of the competition rules to the postal sector, and the possible derogations from the principles. It sets out the position the Commission would adopt, in the context set by the continuing existence of special and exclusive rights as harmonised by the Postal Directive, in assessing individual cases or before the Court of Justice in cases referred to the Court by national courts under Article [267] of the Treaty.

1. Definitions

In the context of this notice, the following definitions shall apply:[11]

"*postal services*": services involving the clearance, sorting, transport and delivery of postal items;

"*public postal network*": the system of organisation and resources of all kinds used by the universal service provider(s) for the purposes in particular of:

— the clearance of postal items covered by a universal service obligation from access points throughout the territory,

— the routing and handling of those items from the postal network access point to the distribution centre,

— distribution to the addresses shown on items;

"*access points*": physical facilities, including letter boxes provided for the public either on the public highway or at the premises of the universal service provider, where postal items may be deposited with the public postal network by customers;

"*clearance*": the operation of collecting postal items deposited at access points;

"*distribution*": the process from sorting at the distribution centre to delivery of postal items to their addresses;

"*postal item*": an item addressed in the final form in which it is to be carried by the universal service provider. In addition to items of correspondence, such items also include for instance books, catalogues, newspapers, periodicals and postal packages containing merchandise with or without commercial value;

"*item of [correspondence]*": a communication in written form on any kind of physical medium to be conveyed and delivered at the address indicated by the sender on the item itself or on its wrapping. Books, catalogues, newspapers and periodicals shall not be regarded as items of correspondence;

"*direct mail*": a communication consisting solely of advertising, marketing or publicity material and comprising an identical message, except for the addressee's name, address and identifying number as well as other modifications which do not alter the nature of the message, which is sent to a significant number of addresses, to be conveyed and delivered at the address indicated by the sender on the item itself or on its wrapping. The National Regulatory Authority should interpret the term "significant number of addressees" within each Member State and publish an appropriate definition. Bills, invoices, financial statements and other non-identical messages should not be regarded as direct mail. A communication combining direct mail with other items within the same wrapping should not be regarded as direct mail. Direct mail includes cross-border as well as domestic direct mail;

"document exchange": provision of means, including the supply of *ad hoc* premises as well as transportation by a third party, allowing self-delivery by mutual exchange of postal items between users subscribing to this service;

"express mail service": a service featuring, in addition to greater speed and reliability in the collection, distribution, and delivery of items, all or some of the following supplementary facilities: guarantee of delivery by a fixed date; collection from point of origin; personal delivery to addressee; possibility of changing the destination and address in transit; confirmation to sender of receipt of the item dispatched; monitoring and tracking of items dispatched; personalised service for customers and provision of an *à la carte service*, as and when required. Customers are in principle prepared to pay a higher price for this service;

"universal service provider": the public or private entity providing a universal postal service or parts thereof within a Member State, the identity of which has been notified to the Commission;

"exclusive rights": rights granted by a Member State which reserve the provision of postal services to one undertaking through any legislative, regulatory or administrative instrument and reserve to it the right to provide a postal service, or to undertake an activity, within a given geographical area;

"special rights": rights granted by a Member State to a limited number of undertakings through any legislative, regulatory or administrative instrument which, within a given geographical area:

— limits, on a discretionary basis, to two or more the number of such undertakings authorised to provide a service or undertake an activity, otherwise than according to objective, proportional and non-discriminatory criteria, or

— designates, otherwise than according to such criteria, several competing undertakings as undertakings authorised to provide a service or undertake an activity, or

— confers on any undertaking or undertakings, otherwise than according to such criteria, legal or regulatory advantages which substantially affect the ability of any other undertaking to provide the same service or undertake the same activity in the same geographical area under substantially comparable conditions;

"terminal dues": the remuneration of universal service providers for the distribution of incoming cross-border mail comprising postal items from another Member State or from a third country;

"intermediary": any economical operator who acts between the sender and the universal service provider, by clearing, routing and/or pre-sorting postal items, before channelling them into the public postal network of the same or of another country;

"national regulatory authority": the body or bodies, in each Member State, to which the Member State entrusts, inter alia, the regulatory functions falling within the scope of the Postal Directive;

"essential requirements" general non-economic reasons which can induce a Member State to impose conditions on the supply of postal services.[12] These reasons are: the confidentiality of correspondence, security of the network as regards the transport of dangerous goods and, where justified, data protection, environmental protection and regional planning.

Data protection may include personal data protection, the confidentiality of information transmitted or stored and protection of privacy.

Notes

[11] The definitions will be interpreted in the light of the Postal Directive and any changes resulting from review of that Directive.

[12] The meaning of this important phrase in the context of Community competition law is explained in paragraph 5.3.

---

2. MARKET DEFINITION AND POSITION ON THE POSTAL MARKET

(a) Geographical and product market definition

2.1. Articles [101] and [102] of the Treaty prohibit as incompatible with the common market any conduct by one or more undertakings that may negatively affect trade between Member States which involves the prevention, restriction, or distortion of competition and/or an abuse of a dominant position within the common market or a substantial part of it. The territories of the Member States constitute separate geographical markets with regard to the delivery of domestic mail and also with regard to the domestic delivery of inward cross-border mail, owing primarily to the exclusive rights of the operators referred to in point 4.2 and to the restrictions imposed on the provision of postal services. Each of the geographical markets constitutes a substantial part of the common market. For the determination of "relevant market", the country of origin of inward cross-border mail is immaterial.

2.2. As regards the product markets, the differences in practice between Member States demonstrate that recognition of several distinct markets is necessary in some cases. Separation of different product-markets is relevant, among, other things, to special or exclusive rights granted. In its assessment of individual cases on the basis of the different market and regulatory situations in the Member States and on the basis of a harmonised framework provided by the Postal Directive, the Commission will in principle consider that a number of distinct product markets exist, like the clearance, sorting, transport and delivery of mail, and for example direct mail, and cross-border mail. The Commission will take into account the fact that these markets are wholly or partly liberalised in a number of Member States. The Commission will consider the following markets when assessing individual cases.

2.3. The general letter service concerns the delivery of items of correspondence to the addresses shown on the items.

It does not include self-provision, that is the provision of postal services by the natural or legal person (including a sister or subsidiary organisation) who is the originator of the mail.

Also excluded, in accordance with practice in many Member States, are such postal items as are not considered items of correspondence, since they consist of identical copies of the same written communication and have not been altered by additions, deletions or indications other than the name of the addressee and his address. Such items are magazines, newspapers, printed periodicals catalogues, as well as goods or documents accompanying and relating to such items.

Direct mail is covered by the definition of items of correspondence. However, direct mail items do not contain personalised messages. Direct mail addresses the needs of specific operators for commercial communications services, as a complement to advertising in the media. Moreover, the senders of direct mail do not necessarily require the same short delivery times, priced at first-class letter tariffs, asked for by customers requesting services on the market as referred to above. The fact that both services are not always directly interchangeable indicates the possibility of distinct markets.

2.4. Other distinct markets include, for example, the express mail market, the document exchange market, as well as the market for new services (services quite distinct from conventional services). Activities combining the new telecommunications technologies and some elements of the postal services may be, but are not necessarily, new services within the meaning of the Postal Directive. Indeed, they may reflect the adaptability of traditional services.

A document exchange differs from the market referred to in point 2.3 since it does not include the collection and the delivery to the addressee of the postal items transported. It involves only means, including the supply of ad hoc premises as well as transportation by a third party, allowing self-delivery by mutual exchange of postal items between users subscribing to this service. The users of a document exchange are members of a closed user group.

The express mail service also differs from the market referred to in point 2.3 owing to the value added by comparison with the basic postal service.[13] In addition to faster and more reliable collection, transportation and delivery of the postal items, an express mail service is characterised by the provision of some or all of the following supplementary services: guarantee of delivery by a given date; collection from the sender's address; delivery to the addressee in person; possibility of a change of destination and addressee in transit; conformation to the sender of delivery; tracking and tracing; personalised treatment for customers and the offer of a range of services according to requirements. Customers are in principle prepared to pay a higher price for this service. The reservable services as defined in the Postal Directive may include accelerated delivery of items of domestic correspondence falling within the prescribed price and weight limits.

Notes

13 Commission Decisions 90/16/EEC (OJ L 10, 12.1.1990, p.47) and 90/456/EEC (OJ L 233, 28.8.1990, p.19).

2.5. Without prejudice to the definition of reservable services given in the Postal Directive, different activities can be recognised, within the general letter service, which meet distinct needs and should in principle be considered as different markets; the markets for the clearance and for the sorting of mail, the market for the transport of mail and, finally, the delivery of mail (domestic or inward cross-border). Different categories of customers must be distinguished in this respect. Private customers demand the distinct products or services as one integrated service. However, business customers, which represent most of the revenues of the operators referred to in point 4.2, actively pursue the possibilities of sub-stituting for distinct components of the final service alternative solutions (with regard to quality of service levels and/or costs incurred) which are in some cases provided by, or sub-contracted to, different operators. Business customers want to balance the advantages and disadvantages of self-provision versus provision by the postal operator. The existing monopolies limit the external supply of those individual services, but they would otherwise limit the external supply of those individual according to market conditions. That market reality supports the opinion that clearance, sorting, transport and delivery of postal items constitute different markets.[14] From a competition-law point of view, the distinction between the four markets may be relevant.

That is the case for cross-border mail where the clearance and transport will be done by a postal operator other than the one providing the distribution. This is also the case as regards domestic mail, since most postal operators permit major customers to undertake sorting of bulk traffic in return for discounts, based on their public tariffs. The deposit and collection of mail and method of payment also vary in these circumstances. Mail rooms of larger companies are now often operated by intermediaries, which prepare and pre-sort mail before handing it over to the postal operator for final distribution. Moreover, all postal operators allow some kind of downstream access to distribution. Moreover, all postal operators allow some kind of downstream access to their postal network, for instance by allowing or even demanding (sorted) mail to be deposited at an expediting or sorting centre. This permits in many cases a higher reliability (quality of service) by bypassing any sources of failure in the postal network upstream.

Notes

[14] See Commission Notice on the definition of the relevant market for the purpose of the application of Community competition law (OJ C 372, 9.12.1997, p.5).

(b) Dominant position

2.6. Since in most Member States the operator referred to in point 4.2 is, by virtue of the exclusive rights granted to him, the only operator controlling a public postal network covering the whole territory of the Member State, such an operator has a dominant position within the meaning of Article [102] of the Treaty on the national market for the distribution of items of correspondence. Distribution is the service to the user which allows for important economies of scale, and the operator providing this service is in most cases also dominant on the markets for the clearance, sorting and transport of mail. In addition, the enterprise which provides distribution, particularly if it also operates post office premises, has the important advantage of being regarded by the users as the principal postal enterprise, because it is the most conspicuous one, and is therefore the natural first choice. Moreover, this dominant position also includes, in most Member States, services such as registered mail or special delivery services, and/or some sectors of the parcels market.

(c) Duties of dominant postal operators

2.7. According to point (b) of the second paragraph of Article [102] of the Treaty, an abuse may consist in limiting the performance of the relevant service to the prejudice of its consumers. Where a Member State grants exclusive rights to an operator referred to in point 4.2 for services which it does not offer, or offers in conditions not satisfying the needs of customers in the same way as the services which competitive economic operators would have offered, the Member State induces those operators, by the simple exercise of the exclusive right which has been conferred on them, to limit the supply of the relevant service, as the effective exercise of those activities by private companies is, in this case, impossible. This is particularly the case where measures adopted to protect the postal service restrict the provision of other distinct services on distinct or neighbouring markets such as the express mail market. The Commission has requested several Member States to abolish restrictions resulting from exclusive rights regarding the provision of express mail services by international couriers.[15]

Another type of possible abuse involves providing a seriously inefficient service and failing to take advantage of technical developments. This harms customers who are prevented from choosing between alternative suppliers. For instance, a report prepared for the Commission[16] in 1994 showed that, where they have not been subject to competition, the public postal operators in the Member States have not made any significant progress since 1990 in the standardisation of dimensions and weights. The report also showed that some postal operators practised hidden cross-subsidies between reserved and non-reserved services (see points 3.1 and 3.4), which explained, according to that study, most of the price disparities between Member States in 1994, especially penalising residential users who do not qualify for any discounts schemes, since they make use of reserved services that are priced at a higher level than necessary.

The examples given illustrate the possibility that, where they are granted special or exclusive rights, postal operators may let the quality of the service decline[17] and omit to take necessary steps to improve service quality. In such cases, the Commission may be induced to act taking account of the conditions explained in point 8.3.

As regards cross-border postal services, the study referred to above showed that the quality of those services needed to be improved significantly in order to meet the needs of customers, and in particular of residential customers who cannot afford to use the services of courier companies or facsimile transmission instead. Independent measurements carried out in 1995 and 1996 show an improvement of quality of service since 1994. However, those measurements only concern first class mail, and the most recent measurements show that the quality has gone down slightly again.

The majority of Community public postal operators have notified an agreement on terminal dues to the Commission for assessment under the competition rules of the Treaty. The parties to the agreement have explained that their aim is to establish fair compensation for the delivery of cross-border mail reflecting more closely the real costs incurred and to improve the quality of cross-border mail services.

Notes

[15] See footnote 13.

[16] UFC—Que Choisir, Postal services in the European Union, April 1994.

[17] In many Member States users could, some decades ago, still rely on this service to receive in the afternoon, standard letters posted in the morning. Since then, a continuous decline in the quality of the service has been observed, and in particular of the number of daily rounds of the postmen, which were reduced from five to one (or two in some cities of the European Union). The exclusive rights of the postal organisations favoured a fall in quality, since they prevented other companies from entering the market. As a consequence the postal organisations failed to compensate for wage increases and reduction of the working hours by introducing modern technology, as was done by enterprises in industries open to competition.

2.8. Unjustified refusal to supply is also an abuse prohibited by Article [102] of the Treaty. Such behaviour would lead to a limitation of services within the meaning of Article [102], second paragraph, (b) and, if applied only to some users, result in discrimination contrary to Article [102], second paragraph, (c), which requires that no dissimilar conditions be applied to equivalent transactions. In most of the Member States, the operators referred to in point 4.2 provide access at various access points of their postal networks to intermediaries. Conditions of access, and in particular the tariffs applied, are however, often confidential and may facilitate the application of discriminatory conditions, Member States should ensure that their postal legislation does not encourage postal operators to differentiate unjustifiably as regards the conditions applied or to exclude certain companies.

2.9. While a dominant firm is entitled to defend its position by competing with rivals, it has a special responsibility not to further diminish the degree of competition remaining on the market. Exclusionary practices may be directed against existing competitors on the market or intended to impede market access by new entrants. Examples of such illegal behaviour include: refusal to deal as a means of eliminating a competitor by a firm which is the sole or dominant source of supply of a product or controls access to an essential technology or infrastructure; predatory pricing and selective price cutting (see section 3); exclusionary dealing agreements; discrimination as part of a wider pattern of monopolizing conduct designed to exclude competitors; and exclusionary rebate schemes.

3. Cross-subsidisation

(a) Basic principles

3.1. Cross-subsidisation means that an undertaking bears or allocates all or part of the costs of its activity in one geographical or product market to its activity in another geographical or product market. Under certain circumstances, cross-subsidisation in the postal sector, where nearly all operators provide reserved and non-reserved services, can distort competition and lead to competitors being beaten by offers which are made possible not by efficiency (including economies of scope) and performance but by cross-subsidies. Avoiding cross-subsidisation leading to unfair competition is crucial for the development of the postal sector.

3.2. Cross-subsidisation does not distort competition when the costs of reserved activities are subsidised by the revenue generated by other reserved services since there is no competition possible as to these services. This form of subsidisation may sometimes be necessary, to enable the operators referred to in point 4.2 to perform their obligation to provide a service universally, and on the same conditions to everybody.[18] For instance, unprofitable mail delivery in rural areas is subsidised through revenues from profitable mail delivery in urban areas. The same could be said of subsidising the provision of reserved services through revenues generated by activities open to competition. Moreover, cross-subsidisation between non-reserved activities is not in itself abusive.

Notes

[18] See [the] Postal Directive, recitals 16 and 28, and Chapter 5.

3.3. By contrast, subsidising activities open to competition by allocating their costs to reserved services is likely to distort competition in breach of Article [102]. It could amount to an abuse by an undertaking holding a dominant position within the Community. Moreover, users of activities covered by a monopoly would have to bear costs which are unrelated to the provision of those activities. Nonetheless, dominant companies too [may] compete on price, or improve their cash flow and obtain only partial contribution to their fixed (overhead) costs, unless the prices are predatory or go against relevant national or Community regulations.

(b) Consequences

3.4. A reference to cross-subsidisation was made in point 2.7; duties of dominant postal operators. The operators referred to in point 4.2 should not use the income from the reserved area to cross-subsidise activities in areas open to competition. Such a practice could prevent, restrict or distort competition in the non-reserved area. However, in some justified cases, subject to the provisions of Article [106(2)], cross-subsidisation can be regarded as lawful, for example for cultural mail,[19] as long as it is applied in a non discriminatory manner, or for particular services to the socially, medically and economically disadvantaged. When necessary, the Commission will indicate what other exemptions the Treaty would allow to be made. In all other cases, taking into account the indications given in point 3.3, the price of competitive services offered by the operator referred to in point 4.2 should, because of the difficulty of allocating common costs, in principle be at least equal to the average total costs of provision. This means covering the direct costs plus an appropriate proportion of the common and overhead costs of the operator. Objective criteria, such as volumes, time (labour) usage, or intensity of usage, should be used to determine the appropriate proportion. When using the turnover generated by the services involved as a criterion in a case of cross-subsidisation, allowance should be made for the fact that in such a scenario the turnover of the relevant activity is being kept artificially low. Demand-influenced factors, such as revenues or profits, are themselves influenced by predation. If services were offered systematically and selectively at a price below average total cost, the Commission would, on a case-by-case basis, investigate the matter under Article [102], or under Article [102] and Article [106(1)] or under Article [107].

Notes

[19] Referred to by UPU as "work of the mind", comprising books, newspapers, periodicals and journals.

4. Public Undertakings and Special or Exclusive Rights

4.1. The treaty obliges the Member States, in respect of public undertakings and undertakings to which they grant special or exclusive rights, neither to enact nor maintain in force any measures contrary to the Treaty rules (Article [106(1)]). The expression "undertaking" includes every person or legal entity exercising an economic activity, irrespective of the legal status of the entity and the way in which it is financed. The clearance, sorting, transportation and distribution of postal items constitute economic activities, and these services are normally supplied for reward.

The term "public undertaking" includes every undertaking over which the public authorities may exercise directly or indirectly a dominant influence by virtue of ownership of it, their financial participation in it or the rules which govern it.[20] A dominant influence on the part of the public authorities may in particular be presumed when the public authorities hold, directly or indirectly, the majority of the subscribed capital of the undertaking, control the majority of the voting rights attached to shares issued by the undertaking or can appoint more than half of the members of the administrative, managerial or supervisory body. Bodies which are part of the Member State's administration and which provide in an organised manner postal services for third parties against remuneration are to be regarded as such undertakings. Undertakings to which special or exclusive rights are granted can, according to Article [106(1)], be public as well as private.

Notes

[20] Commission Directive 80/723/EEC on the transparency of financial relations between Member States and public undertakings, OJ L 195, 29.7.1980, p.35.

4.2. National regulations concerning postal operators to which the Member States have granted special or exclusive rights to provide certain postal services are "measures" within the meaning of Article [106(1)] of the Treaty and must be assessed under the Treaty provisions to which that Article refers.

In addition to Member States' obligations under Article [106(1)], public undertakings and undertakings that have been granted special or exclusive rights are subject to Articles [101] and [102].

4.3. In most Member States, special and exclusive rights apply to services such as the clearance, transportation and distribution of certain postal items, as well as the way in which those services are provided, such as the exclusive right to place letter boxes along the public highway or to issue stamps bearing the name of the country in question.

Commentary
point 4: B&C: 11.011

5. Freedom to Provide Services

(a) Basic principles

5.1. The granting of special or exclusive rights to one or more operators referred to in point 4.2 to carry out the clearance, including public collection, transport and distribution of certain categories of postal items inevitably restricts the provision of such services, both by companies established in other Member States and by undertakings established in the Member State concerned. This restriction has a trans-border character when the addresses or the senders of the postal items handled by those undertakings are established in other Member States. In practice, restrictions on the provision of postal services, within the meaning of Article [56] of the Treaty,[21] comprise prohibiting the conveyance of certain categories of postal items to other Member States including by intermediaries, as well as the prohibition on distributing gross-border mail. The Postal Directive lays down the justified restrictions on the provision of postal services.

Notes

[21] For a general explanation of the principles deriving from Article [56], see Commission interpretative communication concerning the free movement of services cross frontiers (OJ C 334, 9.12.1993, p.3).

5.2. Article [62], read in conjunction with Article [51] and [52] of the Treaty, sets out exceptions from Article [56]. Since they are exceptions to a fundamental principle, they must be interpreted restrictively. As regards postal services, the exception under Article [51] only applies to the conveyance and distribution of a special kind of mail, that is mail generated in the curse of judicial or administrative procedures, connected, even occasionally, with the exercise of official authority, in particular notifications in pursuance of any judicial or administrative procedures. The conveyance and distribution of such items on a Member State's territory may therefore be subjected at a licensing requirement (see point 5.5) in order to protect the public interest. The conditions of the other derogations from the Treaty listed in those provisions will not normally be fulfilled in relation to postal services. Such services cannot, in themselves, threaten public policy and cannot affect public health.

5.3. The case-law of the Court of Justice allows, in principle, further derogations on the basis of mandatory requirements, provided that they fulfil non-economic essential requirements in the general interest, are applied without discrimination, and are appropriate and proportionate to the objective to be achieved. As regards postal services, the essential requirements which the Commission would consider as justifying restrictions on the freedom to provide postal services are data protection subject to approximation measures taken in this field, the confidentiality of correspondence, security of the network as regards the transport of dangerous goods, as well as, where justified under the provisions of the Treaty, environmental protection and regional planning. Conversely, the Commission would not consider it justified to impose restrictions on the freedom to provide postal services for reasons of consumer protection since this general interest requirement can be met by the general legislation on fair trade practices and consumer protection. Benefits to consumers are enhanced by the freedom to provide postal services, provided that universal service obligations are well defined on the basis of the Postal Directive and can be fulfilled.

5.4. The Commission therefore considers that the maintenance of any special or exclusive right which limits cross-border provision of postal services needs to be justified in the light of Articles [106] and [56] of the Treaty. At present, the special or exclusive rights whose scope does not go beyond the reserved services as defined in the Postal Directive are prima facie justified under Article [106(2)]. Outward cross-border mail is de jure or de facto liberalised in some Member States, such as Denmark, the Netherlands, Finland, Sweden, and the United Kingdom.

(b) Consequences

5.5. The adoption of the measures contained in the Postal Directive requires Member States to regulate postal services. Where Member States restrict postal services to ensure the achievement of universal service and essential requirements, the content of such regulation must correspond to the objective pursued. Obligations should, as a general rule, be enforced within the framework of class licences and declaration procedures by which operators of postal services supply their name, legal form, title and address as well as a short description of the services they offer to the public. Individual licensing should only be applied for specific postal services, where it is demonstrated that less restrictive procedures cannot ensure those objectives. Member States may be invited, on a case-by-case basis, to notify the measures they adopt to the Commission to enable it to assess their proportionality.

6. Measures Adopted by Member States

(a) Basic principles

6.1. Member States have the freedom to define what are general interest services, to grant the special or exclusive rights that are necessary for providing them, to regulate their management and, where appropriate, to fund them. However, under Article [106(1)] of the Treaty, Member States must, in the case of public undertakings and undertakings to which they have granted special or exclusive rights, neither enact nor maintain in force any measure contrary to the Treaty rules, and in particular its competition rules.

(b) Consequences

6.2. The operation of a universal clearance and distribution network confers significant advantages on the operator referred to in point 4.2 in offering not only reserved or liberalised services falling within the definition of universal service, but also other (non-universal postal) services. The prohibition under Article [106(1)], read in conjunction with Article [102](b), applies to the use, without objective justification, of a dominant position on one market to obtain market power on related or neighbouring markets which are distinct from the former, at the risk of eliminating competition on those markets. In countries where local delivery of items of correspondence is liberalised, such as Spain, and the monopoly is limited to inter-city transport and delivery, the use of a dominant position to extend the monopoly from the latter market to the former would therefore be incompatible with the Treaty provisions, in the absence of specific justification, if the functioning of services in the general economic interest was not previously endangered. The Commission considers that it would be appropriate for Member States to inform the Commission of any extension of special or exclusive rights and of the justification therefor.

6.3. There is a potential effect on the trade between Member States from restrictions on the provision of postal services, since the postal services offered by operators other than the operators referred to in point 4.2 can cover mailings to or from other Member States, and restrictions may impede cross-border activities of operators in other Member States.

6.4. As explained in point 8(b)(vii), Member States must monitor access conditions and the exercise of special and exclusive rights. They need not necessarily set up new bodies to do this but they should not give to their operator[22] as referred to in point 4.2, or to a body which is related (legally, administratively and structurally) to that operator, the power of supervision of the exclusive rights granted and of the activities of postal operators generally. An enterprise in a dominant position must not be allowed to have such a power over its competitors. The independence, both in theory and in practice, of the supervisory authority from all the enterprise supervised is essential. The system of undistorted competition required by the Treaty can only be ensured if equal opportunities for the different economic operators, including confidentiality of sensitive business information, are guaranteed. To allow an operator to check the declarations of its competitors or to assign to an undertaking the power to supervise the activities of its competitors or to be associated in the granting of licences means that such undertaking is given commercial information about its competitors and thus has the opportunity to influence the activity of those competitors.

Notes

[22] See in particular, Case C-18/88 *RTT v GB-Inno-BM* [1991] ECR I-5981, paragraphs 25 to 28.

7. POSTAL OPERATORS AND STATE AID

(a) Principles

While a few operators referred to in point 4.2 are highly profitable, the majority appear to be operating either in financial deficit or at close to break-even in postal operations, although information on underlying financial performance is limited, as relatively few operators publish relevant information of an auditable standard on a regular basis. However, direct financial support in the form of subsidies or indirect support such as tax exemptions is being given to fund some postal services, even if the actual amounts are often not transparent.

The Treaty makes the Commission responsible for enforcing Article [107], which declares State aid that affects trade between Member States of the Community to be incompatible with the common market except in certain circumstances where an exemption is, or may be, granted. Without prejudice to Article [106(2)], Articles [107] and [108] are applicable to postal services.[23]

Pursuant to Article [108(3)], Member States are required to notify to the Commission for approval all plans to grant aid or to alter existing aid arrangements. Moreover, the Commission is required to monitor aid which it has previously authorised or which dates from before the entry into force of the Treaty or before the accession of the Member State concerned.

All universal service providers currently fall within the scope of Commission Directive 80/723/EEC of 25 June 1980 on the transparency of financial relations between Member States and public undertakings,[24] as last amended by Directive 93/84/EEC.[25] In addition to the general transparency requirement for the accounts of operators referred to in point 4.2 as discussed in point 8(b)(vi), Member States must therefore ensure that financial relations between them and those operators are transparent as required by the Directive, so that the following are clearly shown:

(a) public funds made available directly, including tax exemptions or reductions;
(b) public funds made available through other public undertakings or financial institutions;
(c) the use to which those public funds are actually put.

The Commission regards, in particular, the following as making available public funds:

(a) the setting-off of operating losses;
(b) the provision of capital;
(c) non-refundable grants or loans on privileged terms;
(d) the granting of financial advantages by forgoing profits or the recovery of sums due;
(e) the forgoing of a normal return on public funds used;
(f) compensation for financial burdens imposed by the public authorities.

Notes

23 Case C-387/92 *Banco de Credito Industrial v Ayuntamiento Valencia* [1994] ECR I-877.

24 OJ L 195, 29.7.1980, p.35.

25 OJ L 254, 12.10.1993, p.16. [Ed note: see now Commission Directive 2006/111/EC of 16 November 2006 on the transparency of financial relations between Member States and public undertakings as well as on financial transparency within certain undertakings (OJ L 318, 17.11.2006, p.17), reproduced at F1 below.]

(b) Application of Articles [106] and [107]

The Commission has been called upon to examine a number of tax advantages granted to a postal operator on the basis of Article [107] in connection with Article [106] of the Treaty. The Commission sought to check whether that privileged tax treatment could be used to cross-subsidize that operator's operations in sectors open to competition. At that time, the postal operator did not have an analytical cost-accounting system serving to enable the Commission to distinguish between the reserved activities and the competitive ones. Accordingly, the Commission, on the basis of the findings of studies carried out in that area, assessed the additional costs due to universal-service obligations borne by that postal operator and compared those costs with the tax advantages. The Commission concluded that the costs exceeded those advantages and therefore decided that the tax system under examination could not lead to cross-subsidization of that operator's operations in the competitive areas.[26]

It is worth noting that in its decision the Commission invited the Member State concerned to make sure that the postal operator adopted an analytical cost-accounting system and requested an annual report which would allow the monitoring of compliance with Community law.

The Court of First Instance has endorsed the Commission's decision and has stated that the tax advantages to that postal operator are State aid which benefit from an exemption from the prohibition set out in Article [107(1)] on the basis of Article [106(2)].[27]

Notes

26 Case NN 135/92, OJ C 262, 7.10.1995, p.11.

27 Case T-106/95 *FFSA v Commission* [1997] ECR II-229.

---

8. SERVICE OF GENERAL ECONOMIC INTEREST

(a) Basic principles

8.1. Article [106(2)] of the Treaty allows an exception from the application of the Treaty rules where the application of those rules obstructs, in law or in fact, the performance of the particular task assigned to the operators referred to in point 4.2 for the provision of a service of general economic interest. Without prejudice to the rights of the Member States to define particular requirements of services of general interest, that task consists primarily in the provision and the maintenance of a universal public postal service, guaranteeing at affordable, cost-effective and transparent tariffs nationwide access to the public postal network within a reasonable distance and during adequate opening hours, including the clearance of postal items from accessible postal boxes or collection points throughout the territory and the timely delivery of such items to the address indicated, as well as associated services entrusted by measures of a regulatory nature to those operators for universal delivery at a specified quality. The universal service is to evolve in response to the social, economical and technical environment and to the demands of users.

The general interest involved requires the availability in the Community of a genuinely integrated public postal network, allowing efficient circulation of information and thereby fostering, on the one hand, the competitiveness of European industry and the development of trade and greater cohesion between the regions and Member States, and on the other, the improvement of social contacts between the citizens of the Union. The definition of the reserved area has to take into account the financial resources necessary for the provision of the service of general economic interest.

8.2. The financial resources for the maintenance and improvement of that public network still derive mainly from the activities referred to in point 2.3. Currently, and in the absence of harmonisation at Community level, most Member States have fixed the limits of the monopoly by reference to the weight of the item. Some Member States apply a combined weight and price limit whereas one Member State applies a price limit only. Information collected by the Commission on the revenues obtained from mail flows in the Member States seems to indicate that the maintenance of special or exclusive rights with regard to this market could, in the absence of exceptional circumstances, be sufficient to guarantee the improvement an maintenance of the public postal network.

The service for which Member States can reserve exclusive or special rights, to the extent necessary to ensure the maintenance of the universal service, is harmonised in the Postal Directive. To the extent to which Member States grant special or exclusive rights for this service, the service is to be considered a separate product-market in the assessment of individual cases in particular with regard to direct mail, the distribution of inward cross-border mail, outward cross-border mail, as well as with regard to the collection, sorting and transport of mail. The Commission will take account of the fact that those markets are wholly or partly liberalised in a number of Member States.

8.3. When applying the competition rules and other relevant Treaty rules to the postal sector, the Commission, acting upon a complaint or upon its own initiative, will take account of the harmonized definition set out in the Postal Directive in assessing whether the scope of the reserved area can be justified under Article [106(2)]. The point of departure will be a presumption that, to the extent that they fall within the limits of the reserved area as defined in the Postal Directive, the special or exclusive rights will be prima facie justified under Article [106(2)]. That presumption can, however, be rebutted if the facts in a case show that a restriction does not fulfil the conditions of Article [106(2)].[28]

Notes

[28] In relation to the limits on the application of the exception set out in Article [106(2)], see the position taken by the Court of Justice in the following cases: Case C-179/90 Merci convenzionali porto di Genova v Siderurgica Gabrielli [1991] ECR I-1979; Case C-41/90 Klaus Höfner and Fritz Elser v Macroton [1991] ECR I-5889.

8.4. The direct mail market is still developing at a different pace from one Member State to the other, which makes it difficult for the Commission, at this stage, to specify in a general way the obligations of the Member States regarding that service. The two principal issues in relation to direct mail are potential abuse by customers of its tariffication and of its liberalisation (reserved items being delivered by an alternative operators as if they were non-reserved direct mail items) so as to circumvent the reserved services referred to in point 8.2. Evidence from the Member States which do not restrict direct mail services, such as Spain, Italy, the Netherlands, Austria, Sweden and Finland, is still inconclusive and does not yet allow a definitive general assessment. In view of that uncertainty, it is considered appropriate to proceed temporarily on a case-by-case basis. If particular circumstances make it necessary, and without prejudice to point 8.3, Member States may maintain certain existing restrictions on direct mail services or introduce licensing in order to avoid artificial traffic distortions and substantial destabilization of revenues.

8.5. As regards the distribution of inward cross-border mail, the system of terminal dues received by the postal operator of the Member State of delivery of cross-border mail from the operator of the

Member State of origin is currently under revision to adapt terminal dues, which are in many cases too low, to actual costs of delivery.

Without prejudice to point 8.3, Member States may maintain certain existing restrictions on the distribution of inward cross-border mail,[29] so as to avoid artificial diversion of traffic, which would inflate the share of cross-border mail in Community traffic. Such restrictions may only concern items falling under the reservable area of services. In assessing the situation in the framework of individual cases, the Commission will take into account the relevant, specific circumstances in the Member States.

Notes

[29] This may in particular concern mail from one State which has been conveyed by commercial companies to another State to be introduced in the public postal network via a postal operator of that other State.

8.6. The clearance, sorting and transport of postal items has been or is currently increasingly being opened up to third parties by postal operators in a number of Member States. Given that the revenue effects of such opening up may vary according to the situation in the different Member States, certain Member States may, if particular circumstances make it necessary, and without prejudice to point 8.3, maintain certain existing restrictions on the clearance, sorting and transport of postal items by intermediaries,[30] so as to allow for the necessary restructuring of the operator referred to in point 4.2. However, such restrictions should in principle be applied only to postal items covered by the existing monopolies, should not limit what is already accepted in the Member State concerned, and should be compatible with the principle of non-discriminatory access to the postal network as set out in point 8(b)(vii).

Notes

[30] Even in a monopoly situation, senders will have the freedom to make use of particular services provided by an intermediary, such as (pre-)sorting before deposit with the postal operator.

(b) Conditions for the application of Article [106(2)] to the postal sector

The following conditions should apply with regard to the exception under Article [106(2)]:

(i) Liberalisation of other postal services

Except for those services for which reservation is necessary, and which the Postal Directive allows to be reserved, Member States should withdraw all special or exclusive rights for the supply of postal services to the extent that the performance of the particular task assigned to the operators referred to in point 4.2 for the provision of a service of a general economic interest is not obstructed in law or in fact, with the exception of mail connected to the exercise of official authority, and they should take all necessary measures to guarantee the right of all economic operators to supply postal services.

This does not prevent Member States from making, where necessary, the supply of such services subject to declaration procedures or class licences and, when necessary, to individual licensing procedures aimed at the enforcement of essential requirements and at safeguarding the universal service. Member States should, in that event, ensure that the conditions set out in those procedures are transparent, objective, and without discriminatory effect, and that there is an efficient procedure of appealing to the courts against any refusal.

(ii) Absence of less restrictive means to ensure the services in the general economic interest

Exclusive rights may be granted or maintained only where they are indispensable for ensuring the functioning of the tasks of general economic interest. In many areas the entry of new companies into the market could, on the basis of their specific skills and expertise, contribute to the realisation of the services of general economic interest.

If the operator referred to in point 4.2 fails to provide satisfactorily all of the elements of the universal service required by the Postal Directive (such as the possibility of every citizen in the Member State concerned, and in particular those living in remote areas, to have access to newspapers, magazines and books), even with the benefit of a universal postal network and of special or exclusive rights, the

Member State concerned must take action.[31] Instead of extending the rights already granted, Member States should create the possibility that services are provided by competitors and for this purpose may impose obligations on those competitors in addition to essential requirements. All of those obligations should be objective, non-discriminatory and transparent.

Notes

[31] According to Article 3 of the Postal Directive, Member States are to ensure that users enjoy the right to a universal service.

(iii) Proportionality

Member States should moreover ensure that the scope of any special and exclusive rights granted is in proportion to the general economic interest which is pursued through those rights. Prohibiting self-delivery, that is the provision of postal services by the natural or legal person (including a sister or subsidiary organisation) who is the originator of the mail, or collection and transport of such items by a third party acting solely on its behalf, would for example not be proportionate to the objective of guaranteeing adequate resources for the public postal network. Member States must also adjust the scope of those special or exclusive rights, according to changes in the needs and the conditions under which postal services are provided and taking account of any State aid granted to the operator referred to in point 4.2.

(iv) Monitoring by an independent regulatory body

The monitoring of the performance of the public-service tasks of the operators referred to in point 4.2 and of open access to the public postal network and, where applicable, the grant of licences or the control of declarations as well as the observance by economic operators of the special or exclusive rights of operators referred to in point 4.2 should be ensured by a body or bodies independent of the latter.[32]

That body should in particular ensure: that contracts for the provision of reserved services are made fully transparent, are separately invoiced and distinguished from non-reserved services, such as printing, labelling and enveloping; that terms and conditions for services which are in part reserved and in part liberalised are separate; and that the reserved element is open to all postal users, irrespective of whether or not the non-reserved component is purchased.

Notes

[32] See in particular Articles 9 and 22 of the Postal Directive.

(v) Effective monitoring of reserved services

The tasks excluded from the scope of competition should be effectively monitored by the Member State according to published service targets and performance levels and there should be regular and public reporting on their fulfilment.

(vi) Transparency of accounting

Each operator referred to in point 4.2 uses a single postal network to compete in a variety of markets. Price and service discrimination between or within classes of customers can easily be practised by operators running a universal postal network, given the significant overheads which cannot be fully and precisely assigned to any one service in particular. It is therefore extremely difficult to determine cross-subsidies within them, both between the different stages of the handling of postal items in the public postal network and between the reserved services and the services provided under conditions of competition. Moreover, a number of operators offer preferential tariffs for cultural items which clearly do not cover the average total costs. Member States are obliged by Article [4, paragraph 3, TEU] and [106] to ensure that Community law is fully complied with. The Commission considers that the most appropriate way of fulfilling that obligation would be for Member States to require operators referred to in point 4.2 to keep separate financial records, identifying separately, inter alia, costs and revenues associated with the provision of the services supplied under their exclusive rights and those provided under competitive conditions, and making it possible to assess fully the conditions applied at the various access points of the public postal network. Services made up of elements falling within the reserved and competitive services should also distinguish between the costs of each element. Internal accounting systems should operate on the basis of consistently applied and objectively justified cost-accounting principles. The financial accounts should be drawn up, audited by an independent auditor, which may be appointed by the National Regulatory Authority, and be published in accordance with the relevant Community and national legislation applying to commercial organisations.

(vii) Non-discriminatory access to the postal network

Operators should provide the universal postal service by affording non-discriminatory access to customers or intermediaries at appropriate public points of access, in accordance with the needs of those users. Access conditions including contracts (when offered) should be transparent, published in an appropriate manner and offered on a non-discriminatory basis.

Preferential tariffs appear to be offered by some operators to particular groups of customers in a non-transparent fashion. Member States should monitor the access conditions to the network with a view to ensuring that there is no discrimination either in the conditions of use or in the charges payable. It should in particular be ensured that intermediaries, including operators from other Member States, can choose from amongst available access points to the public postal network and obtain access within a reasonable period at price conditions based on costs, that take into account the actual services required.

The obligation to provide non-discriminatory access to the public postal network does not mean that Member States are required to ensure access for items of correspondence from its territory, which were conveyed by commercial companies to another State, in breach of a postal monopoly, to be introduced in the public postal network via a postal operator of that other State, for the sole purpose of taking advantage of lower postal tariffs. Other economic reasons, such as production costs and facilities, added values or the level of service offered in other Member States are not regarded as improper. Fraud can be made subject to penalties by the independent regulatory body.

At present cross-border access to postal networks is occasionally rejected, or only allowed subject to conditions, for postal items whose production process includes cross-border data transmission before those postal items were given physical form. Those cases are usually called non-physical remail. In the present circumstances there may indeed be an economic problem for the postal operator that delivers the mail, due to the level of terminal dues applied between postal operators. The operators seek to resolve this problem by the introduction of an appropriate terminal dues system.

The Commission may request Member States, in accordance with the first paragraph of Article [10] of the Treaty, to inform the Commission of the conditions of access applied and of the reasons for them. The Commission is not to disclose information acquired as a result of such requests to the extent that it is covered by the obligation of professional secrecy.

9. REVIEW

This notice is adopted at Community level to facilitate the assessment of certain behaviour of undertakings and certain State measures relating to postal services. It is appropriate that after a certain period of development, possibly by the year 2000, the Commission should carry out an evaluation of the postal sector with regard to the Treaty rules, to establish whether modifications of the views set out in this notice are required on the basis of social, economic or technological considerations and on the basis of experience with cases in the postal sector. In due time the Commission will carry out a global evaluation of the situation in the postal sector in the light of the aims of this notice.

E15

[COUNCIL REGULATION (EC) NO 1184/2006

of 24 July 2006
**applying certain rules of competition to the production of and trade in
certain agricultural products]**

Official Journal L 214, 4.8.2006, p.7

Celex No: 32006R1184

EUR-Lex permanent link: <http://eur-lex.europa.eu/LexUriServ/LexUriServ.do?uri=CELEX:3200
6R1184:EN:NOT>

Notes

The title was substituted as shown in square brackets by Council Regulation (EC) No 1234/2007 of 22 October 2007
(Single CMO Regulation) (OJ L 299, 16.11.2007, p.1), Article 200(1), with effect from 1 January 2008.

Commentary

Regulation 1184/2006: B&C: 3.097, 12.151, 12.153, 16.008

THE COUNCIL OF THE EUROPEAN UNION,

Having regard to the [Treaty on the Functioning of the European Union], and in particular Articles
[42] and [43]* thereof,

Having regard to the proposal from the Commission,

Having regard to the opinion of the European Parliament.[1]

Notes

* Ed note: please see the Note on the Lisbon Treaty at p.xvii in regard to article renumbering introduced by the Lisbon Treaty.
[1] Opinion of the European Parliament of 27 April 2006 (not yet published in the Official Journal).

Whereas:

(1) The content of Council Regulation No 26 of 4 April 1962 applying certain rules of competition
to production of and trade in agricultural products[1] has been amended.[2] In the interests of clarity
and rationality the said Regulation should be codified.

Notes

[1] OJ 30, 20.4.1962, p.993/62. Regulation as amended by Regulation No 49 (OJ 53, 1.7.1962, p.1571/62).
[2] See Annex I.

---

(2) By virtue of Article [42] of the Treaty one of the matters to be decided under the common agricultural policy is whether the rules on competition laid down in the Treaty are to apply to the
production of, and trade in, agricultural products. Accordingly, the provisions of this Regulation
should be supplemented in the light of developments in that policy.

(3) The rules on competition relating to the agreements, decisions and practices referred to in
Article [101] of the Treaty and to the abuse of dominant positions are to be applied to the production of, and trade in, agricultural products, in so far as their application does not impede the
functioning of national organisations of agricultural markets or jeopardise attainment of the
objectives of the common agricultural policy.

(4) Special attention is warranted in the case of farmers' organisations the particular objective of
which is the joint production or marketing of agricultural products or the use of joint facilities, unless such joint action excludes competition or jeopardises attainment of the objectives of
Article [39] of the Treaty.

(5) In order both to avoid compromising the development of a common agricultural policy and to ensure certainty in the law and non-discriminatory treatment of the undertakings concerned, the Commission should have sole power, subject to review by the Court of Justice, to determine whether the conditions provided for in the two preceding recitals are fulfilled as regards the agreements, decisions and practices referred to in Article [101] of the Treaty.

(6) In order to implement, as part of the development of the common agricultural policy, the rules on aid for production of, or trade in, agricultural products, the Commission should be in a position to draw up a list of existing, new or proposed types of aid, to make appropriate observations to the Member States and to propose suitable measures to them,

HAS ADOPTED THIS REGULATION:

[*Article 1*

This Regulation shall lay down the rules to be applied as regards the applicability of Articles [101] to [106] and certain provisions of Article [108] of the Treaty in relation to production of, or trade in, the products listed in Annex I to the Treaty with the exception of the products covered by Council Regulation (EC) No 1234/2007 of 22 October 2007 establishing a common organisation of agricultural markets and on specific provisions for certain agricultural products (Single CMO Regulation).[1]]

Notes

[1 OJ L 299, 16.11.2007, p.1.]

Article 1 was replaced as shown in square brackets by Council Regulation (EC) No 491/2008 of 25 May 2009 (OJ L 154, 17.6.2009, p.1), Article 2, with effect from 1 August 2009.

[*Article 1a*

Articles [101] to [106] of the Treaty and provisions made for their implementation shall, subject to Article 2 of this Regulation, apply to all agreements, decisions and practices referred to in Articles [101(1)] and [102] of the Treaty which relate to the production of, or trade in, the products referred to in Article 1.]

Notes

Article 1a was inserted as shown in square brackets by Council Regulation (EC) No 1234/2007 of 22 October 2007 (Single CMO Regulation) (OJ L 299, 16.11.2007, p.1), Article 200(1), with effect from 1 January 2008.

Commentary

Art 1a: B&C: 12.154

Article 2

[1. Article [101(1)] of the Treaty shall not apply to those agreements, decisions and practices referred to in Article 1a of this Regulation which form an integral part of a national market organisation or are necessary for attainment of the objectives set out in Article [39] of the Treaty.]

In particular, it shall not apply to agreements, decisions and practices of farmers, farmers' associations, or associations of such associations belonging to a single Member State which concern the production or sale of agricultural products or the use of joint facilities for the storage, treatment or processing of agricultural products, and under which there is no obligation to charge identical prices, unless the Commission finds that competition is thereby excluded or that the objectives of Article [39] of the Treaty are jeopardised.

2. After consulting the Member States and hearing the undertakings or associations of undertakings concerned and any other natural or legal person that it considers should be heard, the Commission shall have sole power, subject to review by the Court of Justice, to determine, by decision which shall be published, which agreements, decisions and practices fulfil the conditions specified in paragraph 1.

The Commission shall so determine either on its own initiative or at the request of a competent authority of a Member State or of an interested undertaking or association of undertakings.

3. The publication shall state the names of the parties and the main content of the decision. It shall have regard to the legitimate interest of undertakings in the protection of their business secrets.

Notes

Article 2(1) was substituted as shown in square brackets by Council Regulation (EC) No 1234/2007 of 22 October 2007 (Single CMO Regulation) (OJ L 299, 16.11.2007, p.1), Article 200(2), with effect from 1 January 2008.

Commentary

Art 2: B&C: 12.154
Art 2(1): B&C: 12.154, 12.155, 12.157, 12.158, 12.159, 16.008
Art 2(2): B&C: 12.158
Art 2(3): B&C: 12.158

[*Article 3*

Article [108(1)] and the first sentence of Article [108(3)] of the Treaty shall apply to aid granted for the production of, or trade in, the products referred to in Article 1.]

Notes

Article 3 was substituted as shown in square brackets by Council Regulation (EC) No 1234/2007 of 22 October 2007 (Single CMO Regulation) (OJ L 299, 16.11.2007, p.1), Article 200(3), with effect from 1 January 2008.

Article 4

Regulation No 26 shall be repealed.

References to the repealed Regulation shall be construed as references to this Regulation and shall be read in accordance with the correlation table in Annex II.

Article 5

This Regulation shall enter into force on the 20th day following its publication in the Official Journal of the European Union.

Notes

Date of entry into force: 24 August 2006.

This Regulation shall be binding in its entirety and directly applicable in all Member States.

Done at Brussels, 24 July 2006.

ANNEX I
REPEALED REGULATION WITH ITS AMENDMENT

Council Regulation No 26   (OJ 30, 20.4.1962, p.993/62)

Council Regulation No 49   (OJ 53, 1.7.1962, p.1571/62) Only Article 1(1)(g)

ANNEX II
CORRELATION TABLE

Regulation No 26	This Regulation
Article 1	Article 1
Article 2(1)	Article 2(1)
Article 2(2)	Article 2(2), first subparagraph
Article 2(3)	Article 2(2), second subparagraph

Regulation No 26	*This Regulation*
Article 2(4)	Article 2(3)
Article 3	—
Article 4	Article 3
—	Article 4
Article 5	Article 5
—	Annex I
—	Annex II

E16

COUNCIL REGULATION (EC) NO 1234/2007

of 22 October 2007
establishing a common organisation of agricultural markets and on specific
provisions for certain agricultural products (Single CMO Regulation)

Official Journal L 299, 16.11.2007, p.1

Celex No: 32007R1234

EUR-Lex permanent link: <http://eur-lex.europa.eu/LexUriServ/LexUriServ.do?uri=CELEX:3200 7R1234:EN:NOT>

Notes

For reasons of space and relevance, this document is reproduced in part only. The State aid provisions in Articles 180 to 182a are not reproduced in this volume.

* Ed note: please see the Note on the Lisbon Treaty at p.xvii in regard to article renumbering introduced by the Lisbon Treaty.

Commentary

Regulation 1234/2007/EC: B&C: 3.079, 12.151, 12.153, 12.154, 16.008

THE COUNCIL OF THE EUROPEAN UNION,

Having regard to the [Treaty on the Functioning of the European Union], and in particular Articles [42] and [43] thereof,

Having regard to the proposal from the Commission,

Having regard to the opinion of the European Parliament[1],

Notes

OJ L 214, 4.8.2006, p.7.

Whereas:

[…]

(83) In accordance with Article [42] of the Treaty the provisions of the chapter of the Treaty relating to rules on competition shall apply to production of and trade in agricultural products only to the

extent determined by the Council within the framework of Article [43(2) and (3)] of the Treaty and in accordance with the procedure laid down therein. In the various CMOs the provisions on state aid had been largely declared applicable. The application in particular of the Treaty rules applying to undertakings was furthermore defined in Council Regulation (EC) No 1184/2006 of 24 July 2006 applying certain rules on competition to the production of, and trade in, agricultural products[1]. In line with the objective of creating one comprehensive set of market policy rules it is appropriate to incorporate the provisions concerned in this Regulation.

(84) The rules on competition relating to the agreements, decisions and practices referred to in Article [101] of the Treaty and to the abuse of dominant positions should be applied to the production of, and trade in, agricultural products, in so far as their application does not impede the functioning of national organisations of agricultural markets or jeopardise the attainment of the objectives of the CAP.

(85) A special approach is warranted in the case of farmers' organisations the particular objective of which is the joint production or marketing of agricultural products or the use of joint facilities, unless such joint action excludes competition or jeopardises the attainment of the objectives of Article [39] of the Treaty.

(86) In order both to avoid compromising the development of a CAP and to ensure legal certainty and non-discriminatory treatment of the undertakings concerned, the Commission should have the sole power, subject to review by the Court of Justice, to determine whether agreements, decisions and practices referred to in Article [101] of the Treaty are compatible with the objectives of the CAP.

(87) The proper working of the single market based on common prices would be jeopardised by the granting of national aid. Therefore, the provisions of the Treaty governing State aid should, as a general rule, apply to the products covered by this Regulation. In certain situations exceptions should be allowed. Where such exceptions apply, the Commission should, however, be in a position to draw up a list of existing, new or proposed national aids, to make appropriate observations to the Member States and to propose suitable measures to them.

[…]

(95) It is appropriate to provide, under certain conditions and for certain products, for measures to be taken in cases where disturbances are occurring or are likely to occur due to significant changes in the internal market prices or as regards quotations or prices on the world market.

[…]

(100) In order to avoid abuse of any of the advantages provided for in this Regulation, such advantages should not be granted or, as the case may be, should be withdrawn, in cases where it is found that the conditions for obtaining any of those advantages have been created artificially, contrary to the objectives of this Regulation.

[…]

(104) This Regulation incorporates provisions concerning the applicability of the competition rules under the Treaty. Such provisions have, so far, been dealt with in Regulation (EC) No 1184/2006. The scope of that Regulation should be amended so that its provisions only apply to products listed in Annex I to the Treaty that are not covered by this Regulation.

[…]

HAS ADOPTED THIS REGULATION:

PART I

INTRODUCTORY PROVISIONS

Article 1
Scope

1. This Regulation establishes a common organisation of the markets for the products of the following sectors, as provided further in Annex I:

(a) cereals, Part I of Annex I;
(b) rice, Part II of Annex I;
(c) sugar, Part III of Annex I;
(d) dried fodder, Part IV of Annex I;
(e) seeds, Part V of Annex I;
(f) hops, Part VI of Annex I;
(g) olive oil and table olives, Part VII of Annex I;
(h) flax and hemp, Part VIII of Annex I;
(i) fruit and vegetables, Part IX of Annex I;
(j) processed fruit and vegetables, Part X of Annex I;
(k) bananas, Part XI of Annex I;
(l) wine, Part XII of Annex I;
(m) live plants and products of floriculture, Part XIII of Annex I (hereinafter referred to as the live plants sector);
(n) raw tobacco, Part XIV of Annex I;
(o) beef and veal, Part XV of Annex I;
(p) milk and milk products, Part XVI of Annex I;
(q) pigmeat, Part XVII of Annex I;
(r) sheepmeat and goatmeat, Part XVIII of Annex I;
(s) eggs, Part XIX of Annex I;
(t) poultrymeat, Part XX of Annex I;
(u) other products, Part XXI of Annex I.

3. This Regulation establishes specific measures for the following sectors as listed and, as the case may be, as further defined in Annex II:

(a) ethyl alcohol of agricultural origin, Part I of Annex II (hereinafter referred to as the agricultural ethyl alcohol sector);
(b) apiculture products, Part II of Annex II (hereinafter referred to as the apiculture sector);
(c) silkworms, Part III of Annex II.

[…]

Notes

For reasons of space, the Annexes to Regulation 1234/2007 are not reproduced in this volume.

PART IV

COMPETITION RULES

CHAPTER I
Rules applying to undertakings

[*Article 175*
Application of Articles [101] to [106] of the Treaty

Save as otherwise provided for in this Regulation, Articles [101] to [106] of the Treaty and implementation provisions thereof shall, [subject to Articles 176 to 177a of this Regulation][2], apply to all agreements, decisions and practices referred to in Articles [101(1)] and [102] of the Treaty which relate to the production of, or trade in, the products covered by this Regulation.][1]

Notes

[1] Article 175 was replaced as shown in square brackets by Council Regulation (EC) No 491/2008 of 25 May 2009 (OJ L 154, 17.6.2009, p.1), Article 2, with effect from 1 August 2009.

[2] The amendment in square brackets was made by Regulation (EU) No 261/2012 of 14 March 2012 (OJ L 94, 30.3.2012, p.38), with effect from 30 March 2012.

Commentary
Art 175: B&C: 12.154

Article 176
Exceptions

1. Article [101(1)] of the Treaty shall not apply to the agreements, decisions and practices referred to in Article 175 of this Regulation which are an integral part of a national market organisation or are necessary for the attainment of the objectives set out in Article [39] of the Treaty.

In particular, Article [101(1)] of the Treaty shall not apply to agreements, decisions and practices of farmers, farmers' associations, or associations of such associations belonging to a single Member State which concern the production or sale of agricultural products or the use of joint facilities for the storage, treatment or processing of agricultural products, and under which there is no obligation to charge identical prices, unless the Commission finds that competition is thereby excluded or that the objectives of Article [39] of the Treaty are jeopardised.

2. After consulting the Member States and hearing the undertakings or associations of undertakings concerned and any other natural or legal person that it considers appropriate, the Commission shall have sole power, subject to review by the Court of Justice, to determine, by a decision which shall be published, which agreements, decisions and practices fulfil the conditions specified in paragraph 1.

The Commission shall undertake such determination either on its own initiative or at the request of a competent authority of a Member State or of an interested undertaking or association of undertakings.

3. The publication of the decision referred to in the first subparagraph of paragraph 2 shall state the names of the parties and the main content of the decision. It shall have regard to the legitimate interest of undertakings in the protection of their business secrets.

Commentary
Art 176: B&C: 12.154
Art 176(1): B&C: 12.154, 12.155, 12.157, 16.008
Art 176(2): B&C: 12.158
Art 176(3): B&C: 12.158

[Article 176a
Agreements and concerted practices in the fruit and vegetables sector

1. Article [101(1)] of the Treaty shall not apply to the agreements, decisions and concerted practices of recognised interbranch organisations with the object of carrying out the activities referred to in Article 123(3)(c) of this Regulation.

2. Paragraph 1 shall apply only provided that:

(a) the agreements, decisions and concerted practices have been notified to the Commission;

(b) within two months of receipt of all the details required the Commission has not found that the agreements, decisions or concerted practices are incompatible with Community rules.

3. The agreements, decisions and concerted practices may not be put into effect before the lapse of the period referred to in paragraph 2(b).

4. The following agreements, decisions and concerted practices shall in any case be declared incompatible with Community rules:

(a) agreements, decisions and concerted practices which may lead to the partitioning of markets in any form within the Community;

(b) agreements, decisions and concerted practices which may affect the sound operation of the market organisation;

(c) agreements, decisions and concerted practices which may create distortions of competition which are not essential to achieving the objectives of the common agricultural policy pursued by the interbranch organisation activity;

(d) agreements, decisions and concerted practices which entail the fixing of prices, without prejudice to activities carried out by interbranch organisations in the application of specific Community rules;

(e) agreements, decisions and concerted practices which may create discrimination or eliminate competition in respect of a substantial proportion of the products in question.

5. If, following expiry of the two-month period referred to in paragraph 2(b), the Commission finds that the conditions for applying paragraph 1 have not been met, it shall take a Decision declaring that Article [101(1)] of the Treaty applies to the agreement, decision or concerted practice in question.

That Commission Decision shall not apply earlier than the date of its notification to the interbranch organisation concerned, unless that interbranch organisation has given incorrect information or abused the exemption provided for in paragraph 1.

6. In the case of multiannual agreements, the notification for the first year shall be valid for the subsequent years of the agreement. However, in that event, the Commission may, on its own initiative or at the request of another Member State, issue a finding of incompatibility at any time.]

Notes

[1] Article 176a was inserted as shown in square brackets by Council Regulation (EC) No 361/2008 of 14 April 2008 (OJ L 121, 7.5.2008, p.1) with effect from 7 May 2008.

Article 177
Agreements and concerted practices in the tobacco sector

1. Article [101(1)] of the Treaty shall not apply to the agreements and concerted practices of recognised interbranch organisations in the tobacco sector, intended to implement the aims referred to in Article 123(c) of this Regulation provided that:

(a) the agreements and concerted practices have been notified to the Commission;

(b) the Commission, acting within three months of receipt of all the details required, has not found that those agreements or concerted practices are incompatible with Community competition rules.

The agreements and concerted practices may not be implemented during that three-month period.

2. Agreements and concerted practices shall be declared contrary to Community competition rules in the following cases where:

(a) they may lead to the partitioning of markets in any form within the Community;

(b) they may affect the sound operation of the market organisation;

(c) they may create distortions of competition which are not essential to achieving the objectives of the common agricultural policy pursued by the interbranch organisation measure;

(d) they entail the fixing of prices or quotas, without prejudice to measures taken by interbranch organisations in the application of specific provisions of Community rules;

(e) they may create discrimination or eliminate competition in respect of a substantial proportion of the products in question.

3. If, following expiry of the three-month period referred to in point (b) of paragraph 1, the Commission finds that the conditions for applying this Chapter have not been met, it shall without the assistance of the Committee referred to in Article 195(1), take a decision declaring that Article [101(1)] of the Treaty applies to the agreement or concerted practice in question.

That decision shall not apply earlier than the date of notification to the interbranch organisation concerned, unless that interbranch organisation has given incorrect information or misused the exemption provided for in paragraph 1.

Commentary
Art 177: **B&C:** 12.154

[Article 177a
Agreements, decisions and concerted practices in the milk and milk products sector

1. Article 101(1) TFEU shall not apply to the agreements, decisions and concerted practices of recognised interbranch organisations for the purpose of carrying out the activities referred to in Article 123(4)(c) of this Regulation.

2. Paragraph 1 shall only apply if:

(a) the agreements, decisions and concerted practices have been notified to the Commission; and
(b) within 3 months of receipt of all the details required, the Commission, without applying the procedure referred to in Article 195(2) or Article 196b(2), has not found that the agreements, decisions or concerted practices are incompatible with Union rules.

3. The agreements, decisions and concerted practices may not be put into effect before the period referred to in point (b) of paragraph 2 elapses.

4. Agreements, decisions and concerted practices shall in any case be declared incompatible with Union rules if they:

(a) may lead to the partitioning of markets in any form within the Union;
(b) may affect the sound operation of the market organisation;
(c) may create distortions of competition and are not essential to achieving the objectives of the common agricultural policy pursued by the interbranch organisation activity;
(d) entail the fixing of prices;
(e) may create discrimination or eliminate competition in respect of a substantial proportion of the products in question.

5. If, after the period referred to in point (b) of paragraph 2 has expired, the Commission finds that the conditions for applying paragraph 1 have not been met, it shall, without applying the procedure referred to in Article 195(2) or Article 196b(2), take a decision declaring that Article 101(1) TFEU applies to the agreement, decision or concerted practice in question.

That Commission decision shall not apply earlier than the date of its notification to the interbranch organisation concerned, unless that interbranch organisation has given incorrect information or has abused the exemption provided for in paragraph 1 of this Article.

6. In the case of multiannual agreements, the notification for the first year shall be valid for the subsequent years of the agreement. However, the Commission may, on its own initiative or at the request of another Member State, issue a finding of incompatibility at any time.

7. The Commission may adopt implementing acts laying down measures necessary for the uniform application of this Article. Those implementing acts shall be adopted in accordance with the examination procedure referred to in Article 196b(2).][1]

Notes

[1] Article 177a inserted as shown in square brackets by Regulation (EU) No 261/2012 of 14 March 2012 (OJ L 94, 30.3.2012, p.38), with effect from 30 March 2012.

Article 178
Binding effect of agreements and concerted practices on non-members in the tobacco sector

1. Interbranch organisations in the tobacco sector may request that certain of their agreements or concerted practices be made binding for a limited period on individuals and groups in the economic sector concerned which are not members of the trade branches which they represent, in the areas in which the branches operate.

In order for their rules to be extended, interbranch organisations shall represent at least two thirds of the production and/or the trade concerned. Where the proposed extension of the rules is of inter-regional scope, the interbranch organisations shall prove they possess a minimum degree of representativeness, in respect of each of the grouped branches, in each region covered.

2. The rules for which an extension of scope is requested shall have been in force for at least one year and shall relate to one of the following objectives:

(a) knowledge of production and the market;

(b) definition of minimum qualities;

(c) use of cultivation methods compatible with the protection of the environment;

(d) definition of minimum standards of packing and presentation;

(e) use of certified seed and monitoring of product quality.

3. Extension of the rules shall be subject to approval by the Commission.

[*Article 179*

Implementing rules in respect of agreements and concerted practices in the fruit and vegetables and tobacco sectors

The Commission may adopt the detailed rules for the application of Articles 176a, 177 and 178, including the rules concerning notification and publication.]

Notes

[1] Article 179 was replaced as shown in square brackets by Council Regulation (EC) No 361/2008 of 14 April 2008 (OJ L 121, 7.5.2008, p.1) with effect from 7 May 2008.

E17

COUNCIL REGULATION (EC) NO 169/2009

of 26 February 2009
applying rules of competition to transport by rail, road and
inland waterway (Codified version)

(Text with EEA relevance)

Official Journal L 61, 5.3.2009, p.1

Celex No: 32009R0169

EUR-Lex permanent link: <http://eur-lex.europa.eu/LexUriServ/LexUriServ.do?uri=CELEX:32009R0169:EN:NOT>

Notes

Regulation 169/2009 repealed Council Regulation (EEC) No 1017/68 with effect from 25 March 2009, with the exception of Article 13(3), which continues to apply to decisions adopted pursuant to Article 5 of Regulation 1017/68 prior to 1 May 2004 until the date of expiration of those decisions (Regulation 169/2009, Article 4).

Commentary

Regulation 169/2009 (ex 1017/68): B&C: 1.025, 3.002, 3.079, 3.086, 3.096, 12.165, 12.168 **F&N:** 15.243, 15.244, 15.246

THE COUNCIL OF THE EUROPEAN UNION,

Having regard to the [Treaty on the Functioning of the European Union], and in particular Article [103]* thereof,

Having regard to the proposal from the Commission,

Having regard to the opinion of the European Parliament[1]

Having regard to the opinion of the European Economic and Social Committee,[2]

Notes

* Ed note: please see the Note on the Lisbon Treaty at p.xvii in regard to article renumbering introduced by the Lisbon Treaty.
1 OJ C 219 E, 28.8.2008, p.67.
2 OJ C 161, 13.7.2007, p.100.

Whereas:

(1) Regulation (EEC) No 1017/68 of the Council of 19 July 1968 applying rules of competition totransport by rail, road and inland waterway[1] has been substantially amended several times.[2] Inthe interests of clarity and rationality the said Regulation should be codified.

Notes

1 OJ L 175, 23.7.1968, p.1.
2 See Annex I.

(2) Rules of competition for transport by rail, road and inland waterway are part of the common transport policy and of general economic policy.

(3) Rules of competition for those sectors should take account of the distinctive features of transport.

(4) Since the rules of competition for transport derogate from the general rules of competition, it should be made possible for undertakings to ascertain what rules apply in any particular case.

(5) The system of rules on competition for transport should apply equally to the joint financing or acquisition of transport equipment for the joint operation of services by certain groupings of undertakings, and also to certain operations in connection with transport by rail, road or inland waterway of providers of services ancillary to transport.

(6) In order to ensure that trade between Member States is not affected or competition within the internal market distorted, it is necessary to prohibit in principle for the three modes of transport specified above all agreements between undertakings, decisions of associations of undertakings and concerted practices between undertakings and all instances of abuse of a dominant position within the internal market which could have such effects.

(7) Certain types of agreement, decision and concerted practice in the transport sector the object and effect of which is merely to apply technical improvements or to achieve technical co-operation may be exempted from the prohibition on restrictive agreements since they contribute to improving productivity. In the light of experience following application of this Regulation, the Council may, on a proposal from the Commission, amend the list of such types of agreement.

(8) In order that an improvement may be fostered in the sometimes too dispersed structure of the industry in the road and inland waterway sectors, exemption from the prohibition on restrictive agreements should also be granted in the case of those agreements, decisions and concerted practices providing for the creation and operation of groupings of undertakings in these two transport sectors whose object is the carrying on of transport operations, including the joint financing or acquisition of transport equipment for the joint operation of services. Such overall exemption can be granted only on condition that the total carrying capacity of a grouping does not exceed a fixed maximum, and that the individual capacity of undertakings belonging to the grouping does not exceed certain limits so fixed as to ensure that no one undertaking can hold a dominant position within the grouping. The Commission should, however, have power to intervene if, in specific cases, such agreements should have effects incompatible with the conditions under which a restrictive agreement may be recognised as lawful, and should constitute an abuse of the exemption. Nevertheless, the fact that a grouping has a total carrying capacity greater than the fixed maximum, or cannot claim the overall exemption because of the individual capacity of the undertakings belonging to the grouping, does not in itself prevent such a grouping from constituting a lawful agreement, decision or concerted practice if it satisfies the relevant conditions laid down in this Regulation.

(9) It is for the undertakings themselves, in the first instance, to judge whether the predominant effects of their agreements, decisions or concerted practices are the restriction of competition or the economic benefits acceptable as justification for such restriction and to decide accordingly, on their own responsibility, as to the illegality or legality of such agreements, decisions or concerted practices.

(10) Therefore, undertakings should be allowed to conclude or operate agreements without declaring them. This exposes such agreements to the risk of being declared void with retroactive effect should they be examined following a complaint or on the Commission's own initiative, but does not prevent their being retroactively declared lawful in the event of such subsequent examination,

HAS ADOPTED THIS REGULATION:

Article 1
Scope

The provisions of this Regulation shall, in the field of transport by rail, road and inland waterway, apply both to all agreements, decisions and concerted practices which have as their object or effect the fixing of transport rates and conditions, the limitation or control of the supply of transport, the sharing of transport markets, the application of technical improvements or technical co-operation, or the joint financing or acquisition of transport equipment or supplies where such operations are directly related to the provision of transport services and are necessary for the joint operation of services by a grouping within the meaning of Article 3 of road or inland waterway transport undertakings, and to the abuse of a dominant position on the transport market. These provisions shall apply also to operations of providers of services ancillary to transport which have any of those objects or effects.

Commentary

Art 1 (ex Art 1, Regulation 1017/68): B&C: 12.165

Article 2
Exception for technical agreements

1. The prohibition in Article [101(1)] of the Treaty shall not apply to agreements, decisions or concerted practices the object and effect of which is to apply technical improvements or to achieve technical co-operation by means of:

(a) the standardisation of equipment, transport supplies, vehicles or fixed installations;
(b) the exchange or pooling, for the purpose of operating transport services, of staff, equipment, vehicles or fixed installations;
(c) the organisation and execution of successive, complementary, substitute or combined transport operations, and the fixing and application of inclusive rates and conditions for such operations, including special competitive rates;
(d) the use, for journeys by a single mode of transport, of the routes which are most rational from the operational point of view;
(e) the co-ordination of transport timetables for connecting routes;
(f) the grouping of single consignments;
(g) the establishment of uniform rules as to the structure of tariffs and their conditions of application, provided such rules do not lay down transport rates and conditions.

2. The Commission shall, where appropriate, submit proposals to the Council with a view to extending or reducing the list in paragraph 1.

Commentary

Art 2 (ex Art 3, Regulation 1017/68/EEC): B&C: 12.166 F&N: 15.247, 15.248, 15.249

Article 3
Exemption for groups of small and medium-sized undertakings

1. Agreements, decisions and concerted practices as referred to in Article [101(1)] of the Treaty shall be exempt from the prohibition in that Article where their purpose is:

(a) the constitution and operation of groupings of road or inland waterway transport undertakings with a view to carrying on transport activities;
(b) the joint financing or acquisition of transport equipment or supplies, where these operations are directly related to the provision of transport services and are necessary for the joint operations of

the aforesaid groupings;always provided that the total carrying capacity of any grouping does not exceed:

(i) 10,000 metric tons in the case of road transport;

(ii) 500,000 metric tons in the case of transport by inland waterway.

The individual capacity of each undertaking belonging to a grouping shall not exceed 1,000 metric tons in the case of road transport or 50,000 metric tons in the case of transport by inland waterway.

2. If the implementation of any agreement, decision or concerted practice covered by paragraph 1 has, in a given case, effects which are incompatible with the requirements of Article [101(3)] of the Treaty, undertakings or associations of undertakings may be required to make such effects cease.

Commentary

Art 3 (ex Art 4, Regulation 1017/68/EEC): B&C: 12.165, 12.167 F&N: 15.249, 15.253, 15.256

Article 4
Repeal

Regulation (EEC) No 1017/68, as amended by the Regulation listed in Annex I, Part A, is repealed, with the exception of Article 13(3), which continues to apply to decisions adopted pursuant to Article 5 of Regulation (EEC) No 1017/68 prior to 1 May 2004 until the date of expiration of those decisions. References to the repealed Regulation shall be construed as references to this Regulation and shall be read in accordance with the correlation table in Annex II.

Commentary

Art 4(2): B&C: 3.086

Article 5
Entry into force, existing agreements

1. This Regulation shall enter into force on the 20th following its publication in the *Official Journal of the European Union.*

2. The prohibition in Article [101(1)] of the Treaty shall not apply to agreements, decisions and concerted practices which were in existence at the date of accession of Austria, Finland and Sweden or at the date of accession of the Czech Republic, Estonia, Cyprus, Latvia, Lithuania, Hungary, Malta, Poland, Slovenia and Slovakia and which, by reason of accession, fall within the scope of Article [101(1)] of the Treaty if, within six months from the date of accession, they are so amended that they comply with the conditions laid down in Article 3 of this Regulation. This paragraph does not apply to agreements, decisions and concerted practices which at the date of accession already fall under Article 53(1) of the EEA Agreement.

This Regulation shall be binding in its entirety and directly applicable in all Member States.

Done at Brussels, 26 February 2009

ANNEX I

PART A

Repealed Regulation with its successive amendment (referred to in Article 4)

Regulation (EEC) No 1017/68 of the Council	except Article 13(3) (OJ L 175, 23.7.1968, p.1)
Council Regulation (EC) No 1/2003	Article 36 only (OJ L 1, 4.1.2003, p.1)

PART B

Non-repealed successive amendments

1972 Act of Accession
1979 Act of Accession
1994 Act of Accession
2003 Act of Accession

ANNEX II

Correlation Table

Regulation (EEC) No 1017/68	This Regulation
Article 1	Article 1
Article 3	Article 2
Article 4(1), first subparagraph, first	Article 3(1), first subparagraph, first introductory phrase, first indent introductory phrase, (a)
Article 4(1), first subparagraph, first	Article 3(1), first subparagraph, introductory phrase, second indent first introductory phrase, (b)
Article 4(1), first subparagraph, second	Article 3(1), first subparagraph, introductory phrase, first indent second introductory phrase, (i)
Article 4(1), first subparagraph, second	Article 3(1), first subparagraph, introductory phrase, second indent second introductory phrase, (ii)
Article 4(1), second subparagraph	Article 3(1), second subparagraph
Article 4(2)	Article 3(2)
—	Article 4
Article 30(1)	Article 5(1)
Article 30(3), second subparagraph	Article 5(2)
Article 31	—
—	Annex I
—	Annex II

E18

COUNCIL REGULATION (EC) NO 246/2009

of 26 February 2009

on the application of Article [101(3)] of the [Treaty on the Functioning of the
European Union]* to certain categories of agreements, decisions and
concerted practices between liner shipping companies (consortia)

(Codified version)

Official Journal L 79, 25.3.2009, p.1

Celex No: 32009R0246

EUR-Lex permanent link: <http://eur-lex.europa.eu/LexUriServ/LexUriServ.do?uri=CELEX:3200
9R0246:EN:NOT>

Notes

* Ed note: please see the Note on the Lisbon Treaty at p.xvii in regard to article renumbering introduced by the Lisbon Treaty.

Commentary

Regulation 246/2009 (ex Regulation 479/92): **B&C:** 1.025, 3.079, 12.181 **F&N:** 13.46

THE COUNCIL OF THE EUROPEAN UNION,

Having regard to the [Treaty on the Functioning of the European Union], and in particular Article [103] thereof,

Having regard to the proposal from the Commission,

Having regard to the opinion of the European Parliament,[1]

Notes

[1] Opinion of the European Parliament of 23 April 2008 (not yet published in the Official Journal).

Whereas:

(1) Council Regulation (EEC) No 479/92 of 25 February 1992 on the application of Article [105(3)] of the Treaty to certain categories of agreements, decisions and concerted practices between liner shipping companies (consortia)[1] has been substantially amended several times.[2] In the interests of clarity and rationality the said Regulation should be codified.

Notes

[1] OJ L 55, 29.2.1992, p.3.

[2] See Annex I.

---

(2) Article [101(1)] of the Treaty may in accordance with Article [101(3)] thereof be declared inapplicable to categories of agreements, decisions and concerted practices which fulfil the conditions contained in Article [101(3)].

(3) Pursuant to Article [103] of the Treaty, the provisions for the application of Article [101(3)] of the Treaty should be adopted by way of Regulation or Directive. According to Article [103(2)(b)], these provisions must lay down detailed rules for the application of Article [101(3)], taking into account the need to ensure effective supervision, on the one hand, and to simplify administration to the greatest possible extent on the other. According to Article [103(2)(d)], these provisions are required to define the respective functions of the Commission and of the Court of Justice.

(4) Liner shipping is a capital intensive industry. Containerisation has increased pressures for cooperation and rationalisation. The Community shipping industry should attain the necessary economies of scale in order to compete successfully on the world liner shipping market.

(5) Joint-service agreements between liner shipping companies with the aim of rationalising their operations by means of technical, operational and/or commercial arrangements (described in shipping circles as consortia) can help to provide the necessary means for improving the productivity of liner shipping services and promoting technical and economic progress.

(6) Maritime transport is important for the development of the Community's trade and the consortia agreements may play a role in this respect, taking account of the special features of international liner shipping. The legalisation of these agreements is a measure which can make a positive contribution to improving the competitiveness of shipping in the Community.

(7) Users of the shipping services offered by consortia can obtain a share of the benefits resulting from the improvements in productivity and service, by means of, inter alia, regularity, cost reductions derived from higher levels of capacity utilisation, and better service quality stemming from improved vessels and equipment.

(8) The Commission should be enabled to declare by way of Regulation that the provisions of Article [101(1)] of the Treaty do not apply to certain categories of consortia agreements, decisions and concerted practices, in order to make it easier for undertakings to cooperate in ways which are economically desirable and without adverse effect from the point of view of competition policy. The Commission, in close and constant liaison with the competent authorities of the Member States, should be able to define precisely the scope of these exemptions and the conditions attached to them.

(9) Consortia in liner shipping are a specialised and complex type of joint venture. There is a great variety of different consortia agreements operating in different circumstances. The scope, parties, activities or terms of consortia are frequently altered. The Commission should therefore be given the responsibility of defining from time to time the consortia to which a group exemption should apply.

(10) In order to ensure that all the conditions of Article [101(3)] of the Treaty are met, conditions should be attached to group exemptions to ensure in particular that a fair share of the benefits will be passed on to shippers and that competition is not eliminated,

HAS ADOPTED THIS REGULATION:

Article 1

1. The Commission may by Regulation and in accordance with Article [101(3)] of the Treaty, declare that Article [101(1)] of the Treaty shall not apply to certain categories of agreements between undertakings, decisions of associations of undertakings and concerted practices that have as an object to promote or establish cooperation in the joint operation of maritime transport services between liner shipping companies, for the purpose of rationalising their operations by means of technical, operational or commercial arrangements with the exception of price fixing (consortia).

2. Such Regulation adopted pursuant to paragraph 1 of this article shall define the categories of agreements, decisions and concerted practices to which it applies and shall specify the conditions and obligations under which, pursuant to Article [101(3)] of the Treaty, they shall be considered exempted from the application of Article [101(1)] of the Treaty.

Article 2

1. The Regulation adopted pursuant to Article 1 shall apply for a period of five years, calculated as from the date of its entry into force.

2. The Regulation adopted pursuant to Article 1 may be repealed or amended where circumstances have changed with respect to any of the facts which were basic to its adoption.

Article 3

The Regulation adopted pursuant to Article 1 may include a provision stating that it applies with retroactive effect to agreements, decisions and concerted practices which were in existence at the date of entry into force of such Regulation, provided they comply with the conditions established in that Regulation.

Article 4

The Regulation adopted pursuant to Article 1 may stipulate that the prohibition contained in Article [101(1)] of the Treaty shall not apply, for such a period as fixed by that Regulation, to agreements, decisions and concerted practices already in existence at 1 January 1995, to which Article [101(1)] applies by virtue of the accession of Austria, Finland and Sweden and which do not satisfy the conditions of Article [101(3)]. However, this Article shall not apply to agreements, decisions and concerted practices which, as at 1 January 1995, already fell under Article 53(1) of the EEA Agreement.

Article 5

Before adopting the Regulation referred to in Article 1, the Commission shall publish a draft thereof to enable all the persons and organisations concerned to submit their comments within such reasonable time limit as the Commission shall fix, but in no case less than one month.

Article 6

Before publishing the draft Regulation and before adopting the Regulation pursuant to Article 1, the Commission shall consult the Advisory Committee on Restrictive Practices and Dominant Positions referred to in Article 14 of Council Regulation (EC) No 1/2003 of 16 December 2002 on the implementation of the rules on competition laid down in Articles [101] and [102] of the Treaty.[1]

Notes

[1] OJ L 1, 4.1.2003, p.1.

Article 7

Regulation (EEC) No 479/92, as amended by the acts listed in Annex I, is repealed. References to the repealed Regulation shall be construed as references to this Regulation and shall be read in accordance with the correlation table in Annex II.

Article 8

This Regulation shall enter into force on the 20th day following that of its publication in the *Official Journal of the European Union*.

Notes

Date of entry into force: 14 April 2009

This Regulation shall be binding in its entirety and directly applicable in all Member States.

Done at Brussels, 26 February 2009.

ANNEX I
REPEALED REGULATION WITH LIST OF ITS SUCCESSIVE AMENDMENTS

(referred to in Article 7)

Council Regulation (EEC) No 479/92

(OJ L 55, 29.2.1992, p.3)

Council Regulation (EC) No 1/2003

(OJ L 1, 4.1.2003, p.1) Article 42 only

1994 Act of Accession, Article 29 and Annex I, point IIIA.4

(OJ C 241, 29.8.1994, p.56)

ANNEX II
CORRELATION TABLE

Regulation (EEC) No 479/92	This Regulation
Articles 1, 2 and 3	Articles 1, 2 and 3
Article 3a	Article 4
Article 4	Article 5
Article 5	Article 6
—	Article 7
Article 7	Article 8
—	Annex I
—	Annex II

E19

COMMISSION REGULATION (EC) NO 906/2009

of 28 September 2009

on the application of [Article 101(3)_of the Treaty on the Functioning of the European Union]* to certain categories of agreements, decisions and concerted practices between liner shipping companies (consortia)

(Text with EEA relevance)

Official Journal L 256, 29.9.2009, p.31

Celex No: 32009R0906

EUR-Lex permanent link: <http://eur-lex.europa.eu/LexUriServ/LexUriServ.do?uri=CELEX:32009R0906:EN:NOT>

Notes

* Ed note: please see the Note on the Lisbon Treaty at p.xvii in regard to article renumbering introduced by the Lisbon Treaty.
EEA application: see EEA Agreement, Annex XIV, Chapter G, Point 11(c), as amended by EEA Joint Committee Decision 51/2010 of 30 April 2010 (OJ L 18, 15.7.2010, p.19) with effect from 26.4.2010.

Commentary
Regulation 906/2009/EC: B&C: 3.087, 3.096, 12.181, 12.182, 15.153 **F&N:** 2.12, 15.153, 15.155, 15.156, 15.161, 15.168, 15.169, 15.171

THE COMMISSION OF THE EUROPEAN COMMUNITIES,

Having regard to the [Treaty on the Functioning of the European Union],

Having regard to Council Regulation (EC) No 246/2009 of 26 February 2009 on the application of Article [101(3)] of the Treaty to certain categories of agreements, decisions and concerted practices between liner shipping companies (consortia),[1] and in particular Article 1 thereof,

Having published a draft of this Regulation,[2]

After consulting the Advisory Committee on Restrictive Practices and Dominant Positions,

Notes

1 OJ L 79, 25.3.2009, p.1.
2 OJ C 266, 21.10.2008, p.1.

Whereas:

(1) Regulation (EEC) No 479/92 empowers the Commission to apply Article [101(3)] of the Treaty by regulation to certain categories of agreements, decisions and concerted practices between shipping companies (consortia) relating to the joint operation of liner transport services, which, through the cooperation they bring about between the shipping companies that are parties thereto, are liable to restrict competition within the common market and to affect trade between Member States and may therefore be caught by the prohibition contained in Article [101(1)] of the Treaty.

(2) The Commission has made use of its power by adopting Commission Regulation (EC) No 823/2000 of 19 April 2000 on the application of Article [101(3)] of the Treaty to certain categories of agreements, decisions and concerted practices between liner shipping companies (consortia),[1] which will expire on 25 April 2010. On the basis of the Commission's experience to date it can be concluded that the justifications for a block exemption for liner consortia are still valid. However, certain changes are necessary in order to remove references to Council Regulation (EEC) No 4056/86 of 22 December 1986 laying down detailed rules for the application of Articles [101] and [102] of the Treaty to maritime transport[2] which allowed liner shipping lines to fix prices and capacity, but has now been repealed. Modifications are also necessary to ensure a greater convergence with other block exemption regulations for horizontal cooperation in force whilst taking into account current market practices in the liner industry.

Notes

1 OJ L 100, 20.4.2000, p.24.
2 OJ L 378, 31.12.1986, p.4.

(3) Consortium agreements vary significantly ranging from those that are highly integrated, requiring a high level of investment for example due to the purchase or charter by their members of vessels specifically for the purpose of setting up the consortium and the setting up of joint operations centres, to flexible slot exchange agreements. For the purposes of this Regulation a consortium agreement consists of one or a set of separate but interrelated agreements between liner shipping companies under which the parties operate the joint service. The legal form of the arrangements is less important than the underlying economic reality that the parties provide a joint service.

Commentary
Recital 3: F&N: 15.172

(4) The benefit of the block exemption should be limited to those agreements for which it can be assumed with a sufficient degree of certainty that they satisfy the conditions of Article [101(3)] of the Treaty. However, there is no presumption that consortia which do not benefit from this Regulation fall within the scope of Article [101(1)] of the Treaty or, if they do, that they do not satisfy the conditions of Article [101(3)] of the Treaty. When conducting a self-assessment of the compatibility of their agreement with Article [101] of the Treaty, parties to such consortia may consider the specific features of markets with small volumes carried or situations where the market share threshold is exceeded as a result of the presence in the consortium of a small carrier without important resources and whose increment to the overall market share of the consortium is only insignificant.

(5) Consortia, as defined in this Regulation, generally help to improve the productivity and quality of available liner shipping services by reason of the rationalisation they bring to the activities of member companies and through the economies of scale they allow in the operation of vessels and utilisation of port facilities. They also help to promote technical and economic progress by facilitating and encouraging greater utilisation of containers and more efficient use of vessel capacity. For the purpose of establishing and running a joint service, an essential feature inherent in consortia is the ability to make capacity adjustments in response to fluctuations in supply and demand.

By contrast, unjustified limitation of capacity and sales as well as the joint fixing of freight rates or market and customer allocation are unlikely to bring any efficiency. Therefore, the exemption provided for in this Regulation should not apply to consortium agreements that involve such activities, irrespective of the market power of the parties.

(6) A fair share of the benefits resulting from the efficiencies should be passed on to transport users. Users of the shipping services provided by consortia may benefit from the improvements in productivity which consortia can bring about. Those benefits may also take the form of an improvement in the frequency of sailings and port calls, or an improvement in scheduling as well as better quality and personalised services through the use of more modern vessels and other equipment, including port facilities.

(7) Users can benefit effectively from consortia only if there is sufficient competition in the relevant markets in which the consortia operate. This condition should be regarded as being met when a consortium remains below a given market share threshold and can therefore be presumed to be subject to effective actual or potential competition from carriers that are not members of that consortium. In order to assess the relevant market, account should be taken not only of direct trade between the ports served by a consortium but also of any competition from other liner services sailing from ports which may be substituted for those served by the consortium and, where appropriate, of other modes of transport.

Commentary
Recital 7: F&N: 15.167

(8) This Regulation should not exempt agreements containing restrictions of competition which are not indispensable to the attainment of the objectives justifying the grant of the exemption. To that end, severely anti-competitive restraints (hardcore restrictions) relating to the fixing of prices charged to third parties, the limitation of capacity or sales and the allocation of markets or customers should be excluded from the benefit of this Regulation. Other than the activities which are expressly exempted by this Regulation, only ancillary activities which are directly related to the operation of the consortium, necessary for its implementation and proportionate to it should be covered by this Regulation.

(9) The market share threshold and the other conditions set out in this Regulation, as well as the exclusion of certain conduct from its benefit, should normally ensure that the agreements to which the block exemption applies do not give the companies concerned the possibility of eliminating competition in a substantial part of the relevant market in question.

Commentary
Recital 9: F&N: 15.167

(10) For the assessment of whether a consortium fulfils the market share condition, the overall market shares of the consortium members should be added up. The market share of each member should take into account the overall volumes it carries within and outside the consortium. In the latter case account should be taken of all volumes carried by a member within another consortium or in relation to any service provided individually by the member, be it on its own vessels or on third party vessels pursuant to contractual arrangements such as slot charters.

(11) In addition, the benefit of the block exemption should be subject to the right of each consortium member to withdraw from the consortium provided that it gives reasonable notice. However, provision should be made for a longer notice period and a longer initial lock-in period in the case of highly integrated consortia in order to take account of the higher investments undertaken to set them up and the more extensive reorganisation entailed in the event of a member leaving.

(12) In particular cases in which the agreements falling under this Regulation nevertheless have effects incompatible with Article [101(3)] of the Treaty, the Commission may withdraw the benefit of the block exemption, on the basis of Council Regulation (EC) No 1/2003 of 16 December 2002 on the implementation of the rules on competition laid down in Articles [101] and [102] of the Treaty.[1] In that respect, the negative effects that may derive from the existence of links between

the consortium and/or its members and other consortia and/or liner carriers on the same relevant market are of particular importance.

Notes
[1] OJ L 1, 4.1.2003, p.1

(13) Furthermore, where agreements have effects which are incompatible with Article [101(3)] of the Treaty in the territory of a Member State, or in a part thereof, which has all the characteristics of a distinct geographic market, the competition authority of that Member State may withdraw the benefit of the block exemption in respect of that territory pursuant to Regulation (EC) No 1/2003.

Commentary
Recital 13: F&N: 15.171

(14) This Regulation is without prejudice to the application of Article [102] of the Treaty.

(15) In view of the expiry of Regulation (EC) No 823/2000, it is appropriate to adopt a new Regulation renewing the block exemption,

HAS ADOPTED THIS REGULATION:

CHAPTER I
SCOPE AND DEFINITIONS

Article 1
Scope

This Regulation shall apply to consortia only in so far as they provide international liner transport services from or to one or more Community ports.

Article 2
Definitions

For the purposes of this Regulation the following definitions shall apply:

1. 'consortium' means an agreement or a set of interrelated agreements between two or more vessel-operating carriers which provide international liner shipping services exclusively for the carriage of cargo, chiefly by container, relating to one or more trades, and the object of which is to bring about cooperation in the joint operation of a maritime transport service, and which improves the service that would be offered individually by each of its members in the absence of the consortium, in order to rationalise their operations by means of technical, operational and/or commercial arrangements;

2. 'liner shipping' means the transport of goods on a regular basis on a particular route or routes between ports and in accordance with timetables and sailing dates advertised in advance and available, even on an occasional basis, to any transport user against payment;

3. 'transport user' means any undertaking (such as shipper, consignee, forwarder) or its representative organisations which has entered into, or demonstrated an intention to enter into, a contractual agreement with a consortium (or one of its members) for the shipment of goods;

4. 'commencement of the service' means the date on which the first vessel sails on the service or, whenthere has been substantial new investment, the date on which the first vessel sails under the conditions directly arising from that substantial new investment;

Commentary
Art 2(1): B&C: 12.182

Chapter II
Exemptions

Article 3
Exempted agreements

Pursuant to Article [101(3)] of the Treaty and subject to the conditions and obligations laid down in this Regulation, it is hereby declared that Article [101(1)] of the Treaty shall not apply to the following activities of a consortium:

1. the joint operation of liner shipping services including any of the following activities:

(a) the coordination and/or joint fixing of sailing timetables and the determination of ports of call;
(b) the exchange, sale or cross-chartering of space or slots on vessels;
(c) the pooling of vessels and/or port installations;
(d) the use of one or more joint operations offices;
(e) the provision of containers, chassis and other equipment and/or the rental, leasing or purchase contracts for such equipment;

2. capacity adjustments in response to fluctuations in supply and demand;

3. the joint operation or use of port terminals and related services (such as lighterage or stevedoring services);

4. any other activity ancillary to those referred to in points 1, 2 and 3 which is necessary for their implementation, such as:

(a) the use of a computerised data exchange system;
(b) an obligation on members of a consortium to use in the relevant market or markets vessels allocated to the consortium and to refrain from chartering space on vessels belonging to third parties;
(c) an obligation on members of a consortium not to assign or charter space to other vessel-operating carriers in the relevant market or markets except with the prior consent of the other members of the consortium.

Commentary
Art 3: **B&C:** 12.183 **F&N:** 15.162

Article 4
Hardcore restrictions

The exemption provided for in Article 3 shall not apply to a consortium which, directly or indirectly, in isolation or in combination with other factors under the control of the parties, has as its object:

1. the fixing of prices when selling liner shipping services to third parties;

2. the limitation of capacity or sales except for the capacity adjustments referred to in Article 3(2);

3. the allocation of markets or customers.

Commentary
Art 4: **B&C:** 12.184 **F&N:** 15.157, 15.162

Chapter III
Conditions for Exemption

Article 5
Conditions relating to market share

1. In order for a consortium to qualify for the exemption provided for in Article 3, the combined market share of the consortium members in the relevant market upon which the consortium operates shall not exceed 30% calculated by reference to the total volume of goods carried in freight tonnes or 20-foot equivalent units.

2. For the purpose of establishing the market share of a consortium member the total volumes of goods carried by it in the relevant market shall be taken into account irrespective of whether those volumes are carried:

(a) within the consortium in question;

(b) within another consortium to which the member is a party; or

(c) outside a consortium on the member's own or on third party vessels.

3. The exemption provided for in Article 3 shall continue to apply if the market share referred to in paragraph 1 of this Article is exceeded during any period of two consecutive calendar years by not more than one tenth.

4. Where one of the limits specified in paragraphs 1 and 3 of this Article is exceeded, the exemption provided for in Article 3 shall continue to apply for a period of six months following the end of the calendar year during which it was exceeded. That period shall be extended to 12 months if the excess is due to the withdrawal from the market of a carrier which is not a member of the consortium.

Commentary
Art 5: B&C: 12.184
Art 5(4): B&C: 12.184

Article 6
Other conditions

In order to qualify for the exemption provided for in Article 3, the consortium must give members the right to withdraw without financial or other penalty such as, in particular, an obligation to cease all transport activity in the relevant market or markets in question, whether or not coupled with the condition that such activity may be resumed after a certain period has elapsed. That right shall be subject to a maximum period of notice of six months. The consortium may, however, stipulate that such notice can only be given after an initial period of a maximum of 24 months starting from the date of entry into force of the agreement or, if later, from the commencement of the service.

In the case of a highly integrated consortium the maximum period of notice may be extended to 12 months and the consortium may stipulate that such notice can only be given after an initial period of a maximum of 36 months starting from the date of entry into force of the agreement or, if later, from the commencement of the service.

Commentary
Art 6: B&C: 12.184

Chapter IV
Final Provisions

Article 7
Entry into force

This Regulation shall enter into force on 26 April 2010.

It shall apply until 25 April 2015.

This Regulation shall be binding in its entirety and directly applicable in all Member States.

Done at Brussels, 28 September 2009.

Commentary
Art 7: B&C: 3.087

E20

COMMISSION GUIDELINES

on the application of [Article 101] of the [Treaty on the Functioning of the
European Union]* to maritime transport services

[NOTE]

(2008/C 245/02)

Official Journal C 245, 26.9.2008, p.2

Celex No: 52008SC2151

EUR-Lex permanent link: <http://eur-lex.europa.eu/LexUriServ/LexUriServ.do?uri=CELEX:52008
XC0926%2801%29:EN:NOT>

Notes

* Ed note: please see the Note on the Lisbon Treaty at p.xvii in regard to article renumbering introduced by the Lisbon Treaty.
On 19 February 2013, the European Commission announced they would not prolong or renew a set of specific guidelines on
the application of Article 101 TFEU to maritime transport services. The maritime guidelines therefore expired on 26 September
2013. They are not reproduced in this volume but remain available on the Oxford Competition Law website.
EEA application: on 16 December 2009, the EFTA Surveillance Authority adopted corresponding Guidelines on the
application to maritime transport services of European Economic Area rules on restrictive business practices (Article 53
of the EEA Agreement).

Commentary
Guidelines: B&C: 3.005, 3.087, 12.174, 12.175, 12.176, 12.177, 12.180 F&N: 15.174, 15.175, 15.177, 15.178
paras 9–12: B&C: 12.175
paras 18–19: B&C: 12.176
paras 22–30: B&C: 12.177
paras 31–32: B&C: 12.177
paras 68–71: B&C: 12.180
paras 72–77: B&C: 12.180

E21

COUNCIL REGULATION (EC) NO 487/2009

of 25 May 2009
on the application of [Article 101(3)] of the [Treaty on the Functioning of the
European Union]* to certain categories of agreements and concerted
practices in the air transport sector

(Codified version)

[NOTE]

(Text with EEA relevance)

Official Journal L 148, 11.6.09, p.1

Celex No: 32009R0487

EUR-Lex permanent link: <http://eur-lex.europa.eu/LexUriServ/LexUriServ.do?uri=CELEX:3200
9R0487:EN:NOT>

Notes

* Ed note: please see the Note on the Lisbon Treaty at p.xvii in regard to article renumbering introduced by the Lisbon Treaty. For reasons of space, this regulation is not reproduced in this volume. It remains available on Oxford Competiton Law. No block exemption regulation made under this regulation is currently in force.

Commentary

Regulation 487/2009/EC: B&C: 1.025, 3.079, 3.088, 12.188, 12.192, 12.193

PART F

PUBLIC UNDERTAKINGS

F1

COMMISSION DIRECTIVE 2006/111/EC

of 16 November 2006

on the transparency of financial relations between Member States and public undertakings as well as on financial transparency within certain undertakings*

(Text with EEA relevance)

(Codified version)

Official Journal L 318, 17.11.2006, p.17

Celex No: 32006L0111

EUR-Lex permanent link: <http://eur-lex.europa.eu/LexUriServ/LexUriServ.do?uri=CELEX:3200 6L0111:EN:NOT>

---

* Ed note: please see the Note on the Lisbon Treaty at p.xvii in regard to article renumbering introduced by the Lisbon Treaty.

Commentary

Directive 2006/111: B&C: 11.011, 17.017, 17.019, 17.029, 17.073

THE COMMISSION OF THE EUROPEAN COMMUNITIES,

Having regard to the [Treaty on the Functioning of the European Union], and in particular Article [106(3)] thereof,

Whereas:

(1) Commission Directive 80/723/EEC of 25 June 1980 on the transparency of financial relations between Member States and public undertakings as well as on financial transparency within certain undertakings[1] has been substantially amended several times.[2] In the interests of clarity and rationality the said Directive should be codified.

Notes

[1] OJ L 195, 29.7.1980, p.35. Directive as last amended by Directive 2005/81/EC (OJ L 312, 29.11.2005, p.47).

[2] See Annex I, Part A.

---

(2) Public undertakings play a substantial role in the national economy of the Member States.

(3) Member States sometimes grant special or exclusive rights to particular undertakings, or make payments or give some other kind of compensation to particular undertakings entrusted with the operation of services of general economic interest. These undertakings are often also in competition with other undertakings.

(4) Article [345] of the Treaty provides that the Treaty is in no way to prejudice the rules in Member States governing the system of property ownership. There should be no unjustified discrimination between public and private undertakings in the application of the rules on competition. This Directive should apply to both public and private undertakings.

(5) The Treaty requires the Commission to ensure that Member States do not grant undertakings, public or private, aids incompatible with the common market.

(6) However, the complexity of the financial relations between national public authorities and public undertakings tends to hinder the performance of this duty.

(7) A fair and effective application of the aid rules in the Treaty to both public and private undertakings will be possible only if these financial relations are made transparent.

(8) Such transparency applied to public undertakings should enable a clear distinction to be made between the role of the State as public authority and its role as proprietor.

(9) Article [106(1)] of the Treaty imposes obligations on Member States in the case of public undertakings and undertakings to which Member States grant special or exclusive rights. Article [106(2)] of the Treaty applies to undertakings entrusted with the operation of services of general economic interest. Article [106(3)] of the Treaty requires the Commission to ensure the application of the provisions of that Article and provides it with the requisite means to this end. In order to ensure the application of the provisions of Article [106] of the Treaty the Commission must have the necessary information. This entails defining the conditions for ensuring such transparency.

(10) It should be made clear what is to be understood by the terms "public authorities" and "public undertakings".

(11) The Member States have differing administrative territorial structures. This Directive should cover public authorities at all levels in each Member State.

(12) Public authorities may exercise a dominant influence on the behaviour of public undertakings not only where they are the proprietor or have a majority participation but also by virtue of powers they hold in management or supervisory bodies as a result either of the rules governing the undertaking or of the manner in which the shareholdings are distributed.

(13) The provision of public funds to public undertakings may take place either directly or indirectly. Transparency must be achieved irrespective of the manner in which such provision of public funds is made. It may also be necessary to ensure that adequate information is made available as regards the reasons for such provision of public funds and their actual use.

(14) Complex situations linked to the diverse forms of public and private undertakings granted special or exclusive rights or entrusted with the operation of services of general economic interest as well as the range of activities that might be carried on by a single undertaking and the different degrees of market liberalisation in the various Member States could complicate application of the competition rules, and particularly Article [106] of the Treaty. It is therefore necessary for Member States and the Commission to have detailed data about the internal and financial and organisational structure of such undertakings, in particular separate and reliable accounts relating to different activities carried on by the same undertaking.

(15) The accounts should show the distinction between different activities, the costs and revenues associated with each activity and the methods of cost and revenue assignment and allocation. Such separate accounts should be available in relation to, on the one hand, products and services in respect of which the Member State has granted a special or exclusive right or entrusted the undertaking with the operation of a service of general economic interest, as well as, on the other hand, for each other product or service in respect of which the undertaking is active. The obligation of separation of accounts should not apply to undertakings whose activities are limited to the provision of services of general economic interest and which do not operate activities outside the scope of these services of general economic interest. It does not seem necessary to require separation of accounts within the area of services of general economic interest or within the area of the special or exclusive rights, as far as this is not necessary for the cost and revenue allocation between these services and products and those outside the services of general economic interest or the special or exclusive rights.

(16) Requiring Member States to ensure that the relevant undertakings maintain such separate accounts is the most efficient means by which fair and effective application of the rules of competition to such undertakings can be assured. In 1996 the Commission adopted a Communication on services of general interest in Europe,[1] which was supplemented by another Communication in 2001,[2] in which it emphasised the importance of such services. It is necessary to take account of the importance of the sectors concerned, which may involve services of general interest, the strong market position that the relevant undertakings may have and the vulnerability of emerging competition in the sectors being liberalised. In accordance with the principle of proportionality it is necessary and appropriate for the achievement of the basic objective of transparency to lay down rules on such separate accounts. This Directive does not go beyond what is necessary in order to achieve the objectives pursued, in accordance with the provisions of the third paragraph of Article 5 of the [Treaty on European Union].

Notes

[1] OJ C 281, 26.9.1996, p.3.
[2] OJ C 17, 19.1.2001, p.4.

(17) In certain sectors provisions adopted by the Community require Member States and certain undertakings to maintain separate accounts. It is necessary to ensure an equal treatment for all economic activities throughout the Community and to extend the requirement to maintain separate accounts to all comparable situations. This Directive should not amend specific rules established for the same purpose in other Community provisions and should not apply to activities of undertakings covered by those provisions.

(18) Certain undertakings should be excluded from the application of this Directive by virtue of the size of their turnover. This applies to those public undertakings whose business is not conducted on such a scale as to justify the administrative burden of ensuring transparency. In view of the limited potential for an effect on trade between Member States, it is not necessary, at this time, to require separate accounts in relation to the supply of certain categories of services.

(19) This Directive is without prejudice to other provisions of the Treaty, notably Articles [106(2)], 88 and 296, and to any other rules concerning the provision of information by Member States to the Commission.

(20) In cases where the compensation for the fulfilment of services of general economic interest has been fixed for an appropriate period following an open, transparent and non-discriminatory procedure it does not seem necessary to require such undertakings to maintain separate accounts.

(21) The undertakings in question being in competition with other undertakings, information acquired should be covered by the obligation of professional secrecy.

(22) A reporting system based on *ex post facto* checks of the financial flows between public authorities and public undertakings operating in the manufacturing sector will enable the Commission to fulfil its obligations. That system of control must cover specific financial information.

(23) In order to limit the administrative burden on Member States, the reporting system should make use of both publicly available data and information available to majority shareholders. The presentation of consolidated reports is to be permitted. Incompatible aid to major undertakings operating in the manufacturing sector will have the greatest distortive effect on competition in the common market. Therefore, such a reporting system may at present be limited to undertakings with a yearly turnover of more than EUR 250 million.

(24) This Directive should be without prejudice to the obligations of the Member States relating to the time-limits for transposition into national law of the Directives set out in Annex I, Part B,

HAS ADOPTED THIS DIRECTIVE:

Article 1

1. The Member States shall ensure that financial relations between public authorities and public undertakings are transparent as provided in this Directive, so that the following emerge clearly:

(a) public funds made available directly by public authorities to the public undertakings concerned;
(b) public funds made available by public authorities through the intermediary of public undertakings or financial institutions;
(c) the use to which these public funds are actually put.

2. Without prejudice to specific provisions laid down by the Community the Member States shall ensure that the financial and organisational structure of any undertaking required to maintain separate accounts is correctly reflected in the separate accounts, so that the following emerge clearly:

(a) the costs and revenues associated with different activities;
(b) full details of the methods by which costs and revenues are assigned or allocated to different activities.

Commentary
Art 1(2): F&N: 6.256

Article 2

For the purpose of this Directive:

(a) "public authorities" means all public authorities, including the State and regional, local and all other territorial authorities;

(b) "public undertakings" means any undertaking over which the public authorities may exercise directly or indirectly a dominant influence by virtue of their ownership of it, their financial participation therein, or the rules which govern it.

A dominant influence on the part of the public authorities shall be presumed when these authorities, directly or indirectly in relation to an undertaking:

   (i) hold the major part of the undertaking's subscribed capital; or

   (ii) control the majority of the votes attaching to shares issued by the undertakings; or

   (iii) can appoint more than half of the members of the undertaking's administrative, managerial or supervisory body;

(c) "public undertakings operating in the manufacturing sector" means all undertakings whose principal area of activity, defined as being at least 50% of total annual turnover, is in manufacturing. These undertakings are those whose operations fall under Section D — Manufacturing being subsection DA up to and including subsection DN of the NACE (Rev.1) classification;[1]

(d) "undertaking required to maintain separate accounts" means any undertaking that enjoys a special or exclusive right granted by a Member State pursuant to Article [106(1)] of the Treaty or is entrusted with the operation of a service of general economic interest pursuant to Article [106(2)] of the Treaty, that receives public service compensation in any form whatsoever in relation to such service and that carries on other activities;

(e) "different activities" means, on the one hand, all products or services in respect of which a special or exclusive right is granted to an undertaking or all services of general economic interest with which an undertaking is entrusted and, on the other hand, each other separate product or service in respect of which the undertaking is active;

(f) "exclusive rights" means rights that are granted by a Member State to one undertaking through any legislative, regulatory or administrative instrument, reserving it the right to provide a service or undertake an activity within a given geographical area;

(g) "special rights" means rights that are granted by a Member State to a limited number of undertakings, through any legislative, regulatory or administrative instrument, which, within a given geographical area:

   (i) limits to two or more the number of such undertakings, authorised to provide a service or undertake an activity, otherwise than according to objective, proportional and non-discriminatory criteria; or

   (ii) designates, otherwise than according to such criteria, several competing undertakings, as being authorised to provide a service or undertake an activity; or

   (iii) confers on any undertaking or undertakings, otherwise than according to such criteria, any legal or regulatory advantages which substantially affect the ability of any other undertaking to provide the same service or to operate the same activity in the same geographical area under substantially equivalent conditions.

Notes

[1] OJ L 83, 3.4.1993, p.1.

Commentary

Art 2(b): F&N: 6.27

Art 2(f): B&C: 11.013 F&N: 6.34

Article 3

The transparency referred to in Article 1(1) shall apply in particular to the following aspects of financial relations between public authorities and public undertakings:

(a) the setting-off of operating losses;

(b) the provision of capital;

(c) non-refundable grants, or loans on privileged terms;

(d) the granting of financial advantages by forgoing profits or the recovery of sums due;

(e) the forgoing of a normal return on public funds used;

(f) compensation for financial burdens imposed by the public authorities.

Article 4

1. To ensure the transparency referred to in Article 1(2), the Member States shall take the measures necessary to ensure that for any undertaking required to maintain separate accounts:

(a) the internal accounts corresponding to different activities are separate;

(b) all costs and revenues are correctly assigned or allocated on the basis of consistently applied and objectively justifiable cost accounting principles;

(c) the cost accounting principles according to which separate accounts are maintained are clearly established. 2. Paragraph 1 shall only apply to activities which are not covered by specific provisions laid down by the Community and shall not affect any obligations of Member States or undertakings arising from the Treaty or from such specific provisions.

Article 5

1. As far as the transparency referred to in Article 1(1) is concerned, this Directive shall not apply to financial relations between the public authorities and:

(a) public undertakings, as regards services the supply of which is not liable to affect trade between Member States to an appreciable extent;

(b) central banks;

(c) public credit institutions, as regards deposits of public funds placed with them by public authorities on normal commercial terms;

(d) public undertakings whose total annual net turnover over the period of the two financial years preceding that in which the funds referred to in Article 1(1) are made available or used has been less than EUR 40 million. However, for public credit institutions the corresponding threshold shall be a balance sheet total of EUR 800 million.

2. As far as the transparency referred to in Article 1(2) is concerned, this Directive shall not apply:

(a) to undertakings, as regards services the supply of which is not liable to affect trade between Member States to an appreciable extent;

(b) to undertakings whose total annual net turnover over the period of the two financial years preceding any given year in which it enjoys a special or exclusive right granted by a Member State pursuant to Article [106(1)] of the Treaty, or in which it is entrusted with the operation of a service of general economic interest pursuant to Article [106(2)] of the Treaty is less than EUR 40 million; however, for public credit institutions the corresponding threshold shall be a balance sheet total of EUR 800 million;

(c) to undertakings which have been entrusted with the operation of services of general economic interest pursuant to Article [106(2)] of the Treaty if the compensation they receive, in any form whatsoever, was fixed for an appropriate period following an open, transparent and non-discriminating procedure.

Article 6

1. Member States shall ensure that information concerning the financial relations referred to in Article 1(1) be kept at the disposal of the Commission for five years from the end of the financial year in which the public funds were made available to the public undertakings concerned. However, where the same funds are used during a later financial year, the five-year time limit shall run from the end of that financial year.

2. Member States shall ensure that information concerning the financial and organisational structure of undertakings referred to in Article 1(2) be kept at the disposal of the Commission for five years from the end of the financial year to which the information refers.

3. Member States shall, where the Commission considers it necessary so to request, supply to it the information referred to in paragraphs 1 and 2, together with any necessary background information, notably the objectives pursued.

Commentary

Art 6: B&C: 11.028

Article 7

The Commission shall not disclose such information supplied to it pursuant to Article 6(3) as is of a kind covered by the obligation of professional secrecy. The first paragraph shall not prevent publication of general information or surveys which do not contain information relating to particular public undertakings to which this Directive applies.

Article 8

1. Member States whose public undertakings operate in the manufacturing sector shall supply the financial information as set out in paragraphs 2 and 3 to the Commission on an annual basis within the timetable contained in paragraph 5.

2. The financial information required for each public undertaking operating in the manufacturing sector and in accordance with paragraph 4 shall be the annual report and annual accounts, in accordance with the definition of Council Directive 78/660/EEC.[1] The annual accounts and annual report include the balance sheet and profit/loss account, explanatory notes, together with accounting policies, statements by directors, segmental and activity reports. Moreover, notices of shareholders' meetings and any other pertinent information shall be provided.

The reports required shall be provided for each individual public undertaking separately, as well as for the holding or subholding company which consolidates several public undertakings in so far as the consolidated sales of the holding or subholding company lead to its being classified as "manufacturing".

3. The following details, in so far as not disclosed in the annual report and annual accounts of each public undertaking, shall be provided in addition to the information referred to in paragraph 2:

(a) the provision of any share capital or quasi-capital funds similar in nature to equity, specifying the terms of its or their provision (whether ordinary, preference, deferred or convertible shares and interest rates; the dividend or conversion rights attaching thereto);

(b) non-refundable grants, or grants which are only refundable in certain circumstances;

(c) the award to the enterprise of any loans, including overdrafts and advances on capital injections, with a specification of interest rates and the terms of the loan and its security, if any, given to the lender by the enterprise receiving the loan;

(d) guarantees given to the enterprise by public authorities in respect of loan finance (specifying terms and any charges paid by enterprises for these guarantees);

(e) dividends paid out and profits retained;

(f) any other forms of State intervention, in particular, the forgoing of sums due to the State by a public undertaking, including *inter alia* the repayment of loans, grants, payment of corporate or social taxes or any similar charges.

The share capital referred to in (a) shall include share capital contributed by the State directly and any share capital received contributed by a public holding company or other public undertaking, including financial institutions, whether inside or outside the same group, to a given public undertaking. The relationship between the provider of the finance and the recipient shall always be specified.

4. The information required by paragraphs 2 and 3 shall be provided for all public undertakings whose turnover for the most recent financial year was more than EUR 250 million. The information required above shall be supplied separately for each public undertaking including those located in other Member States, and shall include, where appropriate, details of all intra- and inter-group transactions between different public undertakings, as well as transactions conducted directly between public undertakings and the State.

Certain public enterprises split their activities into several legally distinct undertakings. For such enterprises the Commission is willing to accept one consolidated report. The consolidation should reflect the economic reality of a group of enterprises operating in the same or closely related sectors. Consolidated reports from diverse, and purely financial, holdings shall not be sufficient.

5. The information required under paragraphs 2 and 3 shall be supplied to the Commission on an annual basis.

The information shall be provided within 15 working days of the date of publication of the annual report of the public undertaking concerned. In any case, and specifically for undertakings which do not publish an annual report, the required information shall be submitted not later than nine months following the end of the undertaking's financial year.

6. In order to assess the number of companies covered by this reporting system, Member States shall supply to the Commission a list of the companies covered by this Article and their turnover. The list is to be updated by 31 March of each year.

7. Member States will furnish the Commission with any additional information that it deems necessary in order to complete a thorough appraisal of the data submitted.

Notes
1 OJ L 222, 14.8.1978, p.11.

Commentary
Art 8: B&C: 11.028, 17.015

Article 9

The Commission shall regularly inform the Member States of the results of the operation of this Directive.

Article 10

Directive 80/723/EEC, as amended by the Directives listed in Annex I, Part A, is repealed, without prejudice to the obligations of the Member States relating to the time-limits for transposition into national law of the Directives set out in Annex I, Part B.

References to the repealed Directive shall be construed as references to this Directive and shall be read in accordance with the correlation table in Annex II.

Commentary
Art 10: B&C: 11.028

Article 11

This Directive shall enter into force on 20 December 2006.

Article 12

This Directive is addressed to the Member States.

Done at Brussels, 16 November 2006.

ANNEX I

PART A
REPEALED DIRECTIVE WITH ITS SUCCESSIVE AMENDMENTS

(referred to in Article 10)

Commission Directive 80/723/EEC	(OJ L 195, 29.7.1980, p.35)
Commission Directive 85/413/EEC	(OJ L 229, 28.8.1985, p.20)
Commission Directive 93/84/EEC	(OJ L 254, 12.10.1993, p.16)
Commission Directive 2000/52/EC	(OJ L 193, 29.7.2000, p.75)
Commission Directive 2005/81/EC	(OJ L 312, 29.11.2005, p.47)

PART B

LIST OF TIME LIMITS FOR TRANSPOSITION INTO NATIONAL LAW

(referred to in Article 10)

Directive	Time limit for transposition
80/723/EEC	31 December 1981
85/413/EEC	1 January 1986
93/84/EEC	1 November 1993
2000/52/EC	31 July 2001
2005/81/EC	19 December 2006

ANNEX II

CORRELATION TABLE

Directive 80/723/EEC	*This Directive*
Article 1	Article 1
Article 2(1), introductory sentence	Article 2, introductory sentence
Article 2(1), point (a)	Article 2, point (a)
Article 2(1), point (b)	Article 2, point (b), first subparagraph
Article 2(1), points (c) to (f)	Article 2, points (c) to (f)
Article 2(1), point (g), introductory words	Article 2, point (g), introductory words
Article 2(1), point (g), first indent	Article 2, point (g)(i)
Article 2(1), point (g), second indent	Article 2, point (g)(ii)
Article 2(1), point (g), third indent	Article 2, point (g)(iii)
Article 2(2), introductory sentence	Article 2, point (b), second subparagraph, introductory sentence
Article 2(2), point (a)	Article 2, point (b), second subparagraph, point (i)
Article 2(2), point (b)	Article 2, point (b), second subparagraph, point (ii)
Article 2(2), point (c)	Article 2, point (b), second subparagraph, point (iii)
Article 3	Article 3
Article 3a	Article 4
Article 4	Article 5
Article 5	Article 6
Article 5a(1)	Article 8(1)
Article 5a(2), first subparagraph, introductory sentence	Article 8(2), first subparagraph
Article 5a(2), first subparagraph, point (i)	Article 8(2), first subparagraph

Directive 80/723/EEC	This Directive
Article 5a(2), second subparagraph,	Article 8(3), first subparagraph, introductory sentence
Article 5a(2), second subparagraph, point (ii)	Article 8(3), first subparagraph, point (a)
Article 5a(2), second subparagraph, point (iii)	Article 8(3), first subparagraph, point(b)
Article 5a(2), second subparagraph, point (iv)	Article 8(3), first subparagraph, point (c)
Article 5a(2), second subparagraph, point (v)	Article 8(3), first subparagraph, point(d)
Article 5a(2), second subparagraph, point (vi)	Article 8(3), first subparagraph, point (e)
Article 5a(2), second subparagraph, point (vii)	Article 8(3), first subparagraph, point (f)
Article 5a(3), first subparagraph	Article 8(4), first subparagraph
Article 5a(3), second subparagraph, first sentence	Article 8(4), second subparagraph
Article 5a(3), second subparagraph, second sentence	Article 8(3), second subparagraph, first sentence
Article 5a(3), second subparagraph, third sentence	Article 8(3), second subparagraph, second sentence
Article 5a(3), second subparagraph, last sentence	Article 8(2), second subparagraph
Article 5a(3), third subparagraph	Article 8(4), third subparagraph
Article 5a(4), first subparagraph	Article 8(5), first subparagraph
Article 5a(4), second subparagraph	Article 8(5), second subparagraph
Article 5a(4), third subparagraph	Article 8(6)
Article 5a(5)	—
Article 5a(6)	Article 8(7)
Article 6(1)	Article 7, first paragraph
Article 6(2)	Article 7, second paragraph
Article 7	Article 9
Article 8	—
—	Article 10
—	Article 11
Article 9	Article 12
—	Annex I
—	Annex II

Commentary

Annex II: B&C: 11.028

F2

COMMISSION DECISION

of 20 December 2011

on the application of Article 106(2) of the Treaty on the Functioning of the European Union to
State aid in the form of public service compensation granted to certain undertakings entrusted
with the operation of services of general economic interest

(notified under document C(2011) 9380)

(Text with EEA relevance)

(2012/21/EU)

Official Journal OJ L 7, 11.1.2012, p.3

Celex No : 32012D0021

EUR-Lex permanent link: <http://eur-lex.europa.eu/LexUriServ/LexUriServ.do?uri=CELEX:3201
2D0021:EN:NOT>

Notes
* Ed note: please see the Note on the Lisbon Treaty at p.xvii in regard to article renumbering introduced by the Lisbon Treaty.
Commentary
B&C: 11.048, 11.060, 17.073, 17.080 F&N: 6.166, 6.258, 17.185

THE EUROPEAN COMMISSION,

Having regard to the Treaty on the Functioning of the European Union, and in particular Article
106(3) thereof,

Whereas:

(1) Article 14 of the Treaty requires the Union, without prejudice to Articles 93, 106 and 107 of the
Treaty, to use its powers in such a way as to make sure that services of general economic interest
operate on the basis of principles and conditions which enable them to fulfil their missions.

(2) For certain services of general economic interest to operate on the basis of principles and under
conditions which enable them to fulfil their missions, financial support from the State may prove
necessary to cover some or all of the specific costs resulting from the public service obligations. In
accordance with Article 345 of the Treaty, as interpreted by the Court of Justice of the European
Union, it is irrelevant whether such services of general economic interest are operated by public or
private undertakings.

(3) Article 106(2) of the Treaty states in this respect that undertakings entrusted with the operation
of services of general economic interest or having the character of a revenue-producing monopoly
are subject to the rules contained in the Treaty, in particular to the rules on competition, in so far
as the application of these rules does not obstruct, in law or in fact, the performance of the tasks
entrusted. This should however not affect the development of trade to such an extent as would be
contrary to the interests of the Union.

(4) In its judgment in *Altmark*[1], the Court of Justice held that public service compensation does not
constitute State aid within the meaning of Article 107 of the Treaty provided that four cumulative
criteria are met. First, the recipient undertaking must actually have public service obligations to
discharge, and the obligations must be clearly defined. Second, the parameters on the basis of
which the compensation is calculated must be established in advance in an objective and transparent manner. Third, the compensation must not exceed what is necessary to cover all or part of the

costs incurred in the discharge of the public service obligations, taking into account the relevant receipts and a reasonable profit. Finally, where the undertaking that is to discharge public service obligations, in a specific case, is not chosen pursuant to a public procurement procedure which would allow for the selection of the tenderer capable of providing those services at the least cost to the community, the level of compensation needed must be determined on the basis of an analysis of the costs that a typical undertaking, well-run and adequately provided with the relevant means, would have incurred.

Notes

[1] Case C-280/00 *Altmark Trans and Regierungspräsidium Magdeburg v Nahverkehrsgesellschaft Altmark* [2003] ECR I-7747.

---

(5) Where those criteria are not fulfilled and the general conditions for the applicability of Article 107(1) of the Treaty are met, public service compensation constitutes State aid and is subject to Articles 93, 106, 107 and 108 of the Treaty.

(6) In addition to this Decision, three instruments are relevant for the application of the State aid rules to compensation granted for the provision of services of general economic interest:

   (a) a new Communication on the application of the European Union State aid rules to compensation granted for the provision of services of general economic interest[1] clarifies the application of Article 107 of the Treaty and the criteria set by the *Altmark* ruling to such compensation;

   (b) a new Regulation, which the Commission intends to adopt, on the application of Articles 107 and 108 of the Treaty to *de minimis* aid for the provision of SGEI lays down certain conditions — including the amount of the compensation — under which public service compensations shall be deemed not to meet all the criteria of Article 107(1);

   (c) a revised framework for State aid in the form of public service compensation[2] specifies how the Commission will analyse cases that are not covered by this Decision and therefore have to be notified to the Commission.

Notes

[1] OJ C 8, 11.1.2012, p.4.
[2] OJ C 8, 11.1.2012, p.15.

---

(7) Commission Decision 2005/842/EC of 28 November 2005 on the application of Article [106 TFEU] to State aid in the form of public service compensation granted to certain undertakings entrusted with the operation of services of general economic interest[1] specifies the meaning and extent of the exception pursuant to Article 106(2) of the Treaty and sets out rules intended to enable effective monitoring of the fulfilment of the criteria set out in that provision. This Decision replaces Decision 2005/842/EC and lays down the conditions under which State aid in the form of compensation for a service of general economic interest is not subject to the prior notification requirement of Article 108(3) of the Treaty as it can be deemed compatible with Article 106(2) of the Treaty.

Notes

[1] OJ L 312, 29.11.2005, p.67.

---

(8) Such aid may be deemed compatible only if it is granted in order to ensure the provision of services of general economic interest as referred to in Article 106(2) of the Treaty. It is clear from the case-law that, in the absence of sectoral Union rules governing the matter, Member States have a wide margin of discretion in the definition of services that could be classified as being services of general economic interest. Thus the Commission's task is to ensure that there is no manifest error as regards the definition of services of general economic interest.

(9) Provided a number of conditions are met, limited amounts of compensation granted to undertakings entrusted with the provision of services of general economic interest do not affect the development of trade and competition to such an extent as would be contrary to the interests of the Union. An individual State aid notification should therefore not be required for compensation below a specified annual amount of compensation provided the requirements of this Decision are met.

(10) Given the development of intra-Union trade in the provision of services of general economic interest, demonstrated for instance by the strong development of multi-national providers in a number of sectors which are of great importance for the development of the internal market, it is appropriate to set a lower limit for the amount of compensation which can be exempted from the notification requirement in accordance with this Decision than what was set by Decision 2005/842/EC, while allowing for that amount to be computed as an annual average over the entrustment period.

(11) Hospitals and undertakings in charge of social services, which are entrusted with tasks of general economic interest, have specific characteristics that need to be taken into consideration. In particular, account should be taken of the fact that, in the present economic conditions and at the current stage of development of the internal market, social services may require an amount of aid beyond the threshold in this Decision to compensate for the public service costs. A larger amount of compensation for social services does thus not necessarily produce a greater risk of distortions of competition. Accordingly, undertakings in charge of social services, including the provision of social housing for disadvantaged citizens or socially less advantaged groups, who due to solvency constraints are unable to obtain housing at market conditions, should also benefit from the exemption from notification provided for in this Decision, even if the amount of compensation they receive exceeds the general compensation threshold laid down in this Decision. The same should apply to hospitals providing medical care, including, where applicable, emergency services and ancillary services directly related to their main activities, in particular in the field of research. In order to benefit from the exemption from notification, social services should be clearly identified services, meeting social needs as regards health and long-term care, childcare, access to and reintegration into the labour market, social housing and the care and social inclusion of vulnerable groups.

(12) The extent to which a particular compensation measure affects trade and competition depends not only on the average amount of compensation received per year and the sector concerned, but also on the overall duration of the period of entrustment. Unless a longer period is justified due to the need for a significant investment, for example in the area of social housing, the application of this Decision should therefore be limited to periods of entrustment not exceeding 10 years.

(13) In order for Article 106(2) of the Treaty to apply, the undertaking in question must have been specifically entrusted by the Member State with the operation of a particular service of general economic interest.

(14) In order to ensure that the criteria set out in Article 106(2) of the Treaty are met, it is necessary to lay down more precise conditions that must be fulfilled in respect of the entrustment of the operation of services of general economic interest. The amount of compensation can be properly calculated and checked only if the public service obligations incumbent on the undertakings and any obligations incumbent on the State are clearly set out in one or more acts of the competent public authorities in the Member State concerned. The form of the instrument may vary from one Member State to another but it should specify, at least, the undertakings concerned, the precise content and duration of and, where appropriate, the territory concerned by the public service obligations imposed, the granting of any exclusive or special rights, and describe the compensation mechanism and the parameters for determining the compensation and avoiding and recovering any possible overcompensation. In order to ensure transparency in relation to the application of this Decision, the act of entrustment should also include a reference to it.

(15) In order to avoid unjustified distortions of competition, the compensation should not exceed what is necessary to cover the net costs incurred by the undertaking in operating the service, including a reasonable profit.

(16) Compensation in excess of what is necessary to cover the net costs incurred by the undertaking concerned in operating the service is not necessary for the operation of the service of general economic interest, and consequently constitutes incompatible State aid that should be repaid to the State. Compensation granted for the operation of a service of general economic interest but actually used by the undertaking concerned to operate on another market for purposes other than those specified in the act of entrustment is not necessary for the operation of the service of general economic interest, and may consequently also constitute incompatible State aid that should be repaid.

(17) The net cost to be taken into account should be calculated as the difference between the cost incurred in operating the service of general economic interest and the revenue earned from the service of general economic interest or, alternatively, as the difference between the net cost of operating with the public service obligation and the net cost or profit operating without the public service obligation. In particular, if the public service obligation leads to a reduction of the revenue, for instance due to regulated tariffs, but does not affect the costs, it should be possible to determine the net cost incurred in discharging the public service obligation on the basis of the foregone revenue. In order to avoid unjustified distortions of competition, all revenues earned from the service of general economic interest, that is to say, any revenues that the provider would not have obtained had it not been entrusted with the obligation should be taken into account for the purposes of calculating the amount of compensation. If the undertaking in question holds special or exclusive rights linked to activities, other than the service of general economic interest for which the aid is granted, that generate profits in excess of the reasonable profit, or benefits from other advantages granted by the State, these should be included in its revenue, irrespective of their classification for the purposes of Article 107 of the Treaty.

(18) Reasonable profit should be determined as a rate of return on capital that takes into account the degree of risk, or absence of risk, incurred. The rate of return on capital should be defined as the internal rate of return that the undertaking obtains on its invested capital over the duration of the period of entrustment.

(19) Profit not exceeding the relevant swap rate plus 100 basis points should not be regarded as unreasonable. In this context, the relevant swap rate is viewed as an appropriate rate of return for a risk-free investment. The premium of 100 basis points serves, inter alia, to compensate for liquidity risk related to the provision of capital which is committed for the operation of the service during the period of entrustment.

(20) In cases where the undertaking entrusted with a service of general economic interest does not bear a substantial degree of commercial risk, for instance because the costs it incurs in the operation of the service are compensated in full, profits exceeding the benchmark of the relevant swap rate plus 100 basis points should not be viewed as reasonable.

(21) Where, by reason of specific circumstances, it is not appropriate to use the rate of return on capital, Member States should be able to rely on other profit level indicators to determine what the reasonable profit should be, such as the average return on equity, return on capital employed, return on assets or return on sales.

(22) In determining what constitutes a reasonable profit, the Member States should be able to introduce incentive criteria relating, in particular, to the quality of service provided and gains in productive efficiency. Efficiency gains should not reduce the quality of the service provided. For instance, Member States should be able to define productive efficiency targets in the entrustment act whereby the level of compensation is made dependent upon the extent to which the targets have been met. The entrustment act may provide that if the undertaking does not meet the objectives, the compensation is to be reduced by applying a calculation method specified in the entrustment act, whereas if the undertaking exceeds the objectives, the compensation may be increased by applying a method specified in the entrustment act. Any rewards linked to productive efficiency gains should be set at a level such as to allow balanced sharing of those gains between the undertaking and the Member State and/or the users.

(23) Article 93 of the Treaty constitutes a *lex specialis* with regard to Article 106(2) of the Treaty. It lays down the rules applicable to public service compensation in the land transport sector. Article 93 has been interpreted by Regulation (EC) No 1370/2007 of the European Parliament and of the Council of 23 October 2007 on public passenger transport services by rail and by road and repealing Council Regulations (EEC) Nos 1191/69 and 1107/70[1], which lays down the rules applicable to the compensation of public service obligations in public passenger traffic. Its application to inland waterway passenger traffic is at the discretion of the Member States. Regulation (EC) No 1370/2007 exempts from notification pursuant to Article 108(3) of the Treaty all compensation in the land transport sector that fulfils the conditions of that Regulation. In accordance with the judgment in *Altmark*, compensation in the land transport sector that does not comply with the provisions of Article 93 of the Treaty cannot be declared compatible with the Treaty on the basis of Article 106(2) of the Treaty, or on the basis of any other Treaty provision. Consequently, this Decision does not apply to the land transport sector.

Notes
1 OJ L 315, 3.12.2007, p.1.
Commentary
recital 23: B&C: 17.073

(24) Unlike land transport, the maritime and air transport sectors are subject to Article 106(2) of the Treaty. Certain rules applicable to public service compensation in the air and maritime transport sectors are to be found in Regulation (EC) No 1008/2008 of the European Parliament and of the Council of 24 September 2008 on common rules for the operation of air services in the Community[1] and in Council Regulation (EEC) No 3577/92 of 7 December 1992 applying the principle of freedom to provide services to maritime transport within Member States (maritime cabotage)[2]. However, unlike Regulation (EC) No 1370/2007, those Regulations do not refer to the compatibility of the possible State aid elements, nor do they provide for an exemption from the obligation to notify pursuant to Article 108(3) of the Treaty. This Decision should therefore apply to public service compensation in the air and maritime transport sectors provided that, in addition to fulfilling the conditions set out in this Decision, such compensation also complies with the sectoral rules contained in Regulations (EC) No 1008/2008 and (EEC) No 3577/92 where applicable.

Notes
1 OJ L 293, 31.10.2008, p.3.
2 OJ L 364, 12.12.1992, p.7.

(25) In the specific cases of public service compensation for air or maritime links to islands and for airports and ports which constitute services of general economic interest as referred to in Article 106(2) of the Treaty, it is appropriate to provide thresholds based on the average annual number of passengers as this more accurately reflects the economic reality of these activities and their character of services of general economic interest.

(26) Exemption from the requirement of prior notification for certain services of general economic interest does not rule out the possibility for Member States to notify a specific aid project. In the event of such a notification, or if the Commission assesses the compatibility of a specific aid measure following a complaint or *ex officio*, the Commission will assess whether the conditions of this Decision are met. If that is not the case, the measure will be assessed in accordance with the principles contained in the Commission Communication on a framework for State aid in the form of public service compensation.

(27) This Decision should apply without prejudice to the provisions of Commission Directive 2006/111/EC of 16 November 2006 on the transparency of financial relations between Member States and public undertakings as well as on financial transparency within certain undertakings[1].

Notes
1 OJ L 318, 17.11.2006, p.17.

(28) This Decision should apply without prejudice to the Union provisions in the field of competition, in particular Articles 101 and 102 of the Treaty.

(29) This Decision should apply without prejudice to the Union provisions in the field of public procurement.

(30) This Decision should apply without prejudice to stricter provisions relating to public service obligations that are contained in sectoral Union legislation.

(31) Transitional provisions should be laid down for individual aid that was granted before the entry into force of this Decision. Aid schemes put into effect in accordance with Decision 2005/842/ EC before the entry into force of this Decision should continue to be compatible with the internal market and exempt from the notification requirement for a further period of 2 years. Aid put into effect before the entry into force of this Decision that was not awarded in accordance with Decision 2005/842/EC but fulfils the conditions laid down in this Decision should be compatible with the internal market and exempt from the notification requirement.

(32) The Commission intends to carry out a review of this Decision 5 years after its entry into force,

HAS ADOPTED THIS DECISION:

Article 1
Subject matter

This Decision sets out the conditions under which State aid in the form of public service compensation granted to certain undertakings entrusted with the operation of services of general economic interest is compatible with the internal market and exempt from the requirement of notification laid down in Article 108(3) of the Treaty.

Article 2
Scope

1. This Decision applies to State aid in the form of public service compensation, granted to undertakings entrusted with the operation of services of general economic interest as referred to in Article 106(2) of the Treaty, which falls within one of the following categories:

(a) compensation not exceeding an annual amount of EUR 15 million for the provision of services of general economic interest in areas other than transport and transport infrastructure;
where the amount of compensation varies over the duration of the entrustment, the annual amount shall be calculated as average of the annual amounts of compensation expected to be made over the entrustment period;

(b) compensation for the provision of services of general economic interest by hospitals providing medical care, including, where applicable, emergency services; the pursuit of ancillary activities directly related to the main activities, notably in the field of research, does not, however, prevent the application of this paragraph;

(c) compensation for the provision of services of general economic interest meeting social needs as regards health and long term care, childcare, access to and reintegration into the labour market, social housing and the care and social inclusion of vulnerable groups;

(d) compensation for the provision of services of general economic interest as regards air or maritime links to islands on which the average annual traffic during the 2 financial years preceding that in which the service of general economic interest was assigned does not exceed 300 000 passengers;

(e) compensation for the provision of services of general economic interest as regards airports and ports for which the average annual traffic during the 2 financial years preceding that in which the service of general economic interest was assigned does not exceed 200 000 passengers, in the case of airports, and 300 000 passengers, in the case of ports.

2. This Decision only applies where the period for which the undertaking is entrusted with the operation of the service of general economic interest does not exceed 10 years. Where the period of entrustment exceeds 10 years, this Decision only applies to the extent that a significant investment is required from the service provider that needs to be amortised over a longer period in accordance with generally accepted accounting principles.

3. If during the duration of the entrustment the conditions for the application of this Decision cease to be met, the aid shall be notified in accordance with Article 108(3) of the Treaty.

4. In the field of air and maritime transport, this Decision only applies to State aid in the form of public service compensation, granted to undertakings entrusted with the operation of services of general economic interest as referred to in Article 106(2) of the Treaty, which complies with Regulation (EC) No 1008/2008 and, respectively, Regulation (EEC) No 3577/92 where applicable.

5. This Decision does not apply to State aid in the form of public service compensation granted to undertakings in the field of land transport.

Commentary
Art 2(1): **B&C:** 17.073
Art 2(4): **B&C:** 17.073
Art 2(5): **B&C:** 17.073

Article 3

Compatibility and exemption from notification

State aid in the form of public service compensation that meets the conditions laid down in this Decision shall be compatible with the internal market and shall be exempt from the prior notification obligation provided for in Article 108(3) of the Treaty provided that it also complies with the requirements flowing from the Treaty or from sectoral Union legislation.

Article 4

Entrustment

Operation of the service of general economic interest shall be entrusted to the undertaking concerned by way of one or more acts, the form of which may be determined by each Member State. The act or acts shall include, in particular:

(a) the content and duration of the public service obligations;
(b) the undertaking and, where applicable, the territory concerned;
(c) the nature of any exclusive or special rights assigned to the undertaking by the granting authority;
(d) a description of the compensation mechanism and the parameters for calculating, controlling and reviewing the compensation;
(e) the arrangements for avoiding and recovering any overcompensation; and
(f) a reference to this Decision.

Commentary
Art 4: **B&C:** 17.073

Article 5

Compensation

1. The amount of compensation shall not exceed what is necessary to cover the net cost incurred in discharging the public service obligations, including a reasonable profit.

2. The net cost may be calculated as the difference between costs as defined in paragraph 3 and revenues as defined in paragraph 4. Alternatively, it may be calculated as the difference between the net cost for the undertaking of operating with the public service obligation and the net cost or profit of the same undertaking operating without the public service obligation.

3. The costs to be taken into consideration shall comprise all the costs incurred in operating the service of general economic interest. They shall be calculated on the basis of generally accepted cost accounting principles, as follows:

(a) where the activities of the undertaking in question are confined to the service of general economic interest, all its costs may be taken into consideration;
(b) where the undertaking also carries out activities falling outside the scope of the service of general economic interest, only the costs related to the service of general economic interest shall be taken into consideration;
(c) the costs allocated to the service of general economic interest may cover all the direct costs incurred in operating the service of general economic interest and an appropriate contribution to costs common to both the service of general economic interest and other activities;
(d) the costs linked with investments, notably concerning infrastructure, may be taken into account when necessary for the operation of the service of general economic interest.

4. The revenue to be taken into consideration shall include at least the entire revenue earned from the service of general economic interest, regardless of whether the revenue is classified as State aid within the meaning of Article 107 of the Treaty. If the undertaking in question holds special or exclusive rights linked to activities, other than the service of general economic interest for which the aid is granted, that generate profits in excess of the reasonable profit, or benefits from other advantages granted by the State, these shall be included in its revenue, irrespective of their classification for the purposes of Article 107 of the Treaty. The Member State concerned may decide

that the profits accruing from other activities outside the scope of the service of general economic interest in question are to be assigned in whole or in part to the financing of the service of general economic interest.

5. For the purposes of this Decision, 'reasonable profit' means the rate of return on capital that would be required by a typical undertaking considering whether or not to provide the service of general economic interest for the whole period of entrustment, taking into account the level of risk. The 'rate of return on capital' means the internal rate of return that the undertaking makes on its invested capital over the duration of the period of entrustment. The level of risk depends on the sector concerned, the type of service and the characteristics of the compensation.

6. In determining what constitutes a reasonable profit, Member States may introduce incentive criteria relating, in particular, to the quality of service provided and gains in productive efficiency. Efficiency gains shall not reduce the quality of the service provided. Any rewards linked to productive efficiency gains shall be set at a level such as to allow balanced sharing of those gains between the undertaking and the Member State and/or the users.

7. For the purposes of this Decision, a rate of return on capital that does not exceed the relevant swap rate plus a premium of 100 basis points shall be regarded as reasonable in any event. The relevant swap rate shall be the swap rate the maturity and currency of which correspond to the duration and currency of the entrustment act. Where the provision of the service of general economic interest is not connected with a substantial commercial or contractual risk, in particular when the net cost incurred in providing the service of general economic interest is essentially compensated *ex post* in full, the reasonable profit may not exceed the relevant swap rate plus a premium of 100 basis points.

8. Where, by reasons of specific circumstances, it is not appropriate to use the rate of return on capital, Member States may rely on profit level indicators other than the rate of return on capital to determine what the reasonable profit should be, such as the average return on equity, return on capital employed, return on assets or return on sales. The 'return' means the earnings before interests and taxes in that year. The average return is computed using the discount factor over the life of the contract as specified by the Communication from the Commission on the revision of the method for setting the reference and discount rates[1]. Whatever indicator is chosen, the Member State shall be able to provide the Commission upon request with evidence that the profit does not exceed what would be required by a typical undertaking considering whether or not to provide the service, for instance by providing references to returns achieved on similar types of contracts awarded under competitive conditions.

9. Where an undertaking carries out activities falling both inside and outside the scope of the service of general economic interest, the internal accounts shall show separately the costs and receipts associated with the service of general economic interest and those of other services, as well as the parameters for allocating costs and revenues. The costs linked to any activities outside the scope of the service of general economic interest shall cover all the direct costs, an appropriate contribution to the common costs and an adequate return on capital. No compensation shall be granted in respect of those costs.

10. Member States shall require the undertaking concerned to repay any overcompensation received.

Notes

[1] OJ C 14, 19.1.2008, p.6.

Article 6
Control of overcompensation

1. Member States shall ensure that the compensation granted for the operation of the service of general economic interest meets the requirements set out in this Decision and in particular that the undertaking does not receive compensation in excess of the amount determined in accordance with Article 5. They shall provide evidence upon request from the Commission. They shall carry out regular checks, or ensure that such checks are carried out, at least every 3 years during the period of entrustment and at the end of that period.

2. Where an undertaking has received compensation in excess of the amount determined in accordance with Article 5, the Member State shall require the undertaking concerned to repay

any overcompensation received. The parameters for the calculation of the compensation shall be updated for the future. Where the amount of overcompensation does not exceed 10% of the amount of the average annual compensation, such overcompensation may be carried forward to the next period and deducted from the amount of compensation payable in respect of that period.

Article 7
Transparency

For compensation above EUR 15 million granted to an undertaking which also has activities outside the scope of the service of general economic interest, the Member State concerned shall publish the following information on the Internet or by other appropriate means:

(a) the entrustment act or a summary which includes the elements listed in Article 4;
(b) the amounts of aid granted to the undertaking on a yearly basis.

Commentary
Art 7: B&C: 17.073

Article 8
Availability of information

The Member States shall keep available, during the period of entrustment and for at least 10 years from the end of the period of entrustment, all the information necessary to determine whether the compensation granted is compatible with this Decision.

On written request by the Commission, Member States shall provide the Commission with all the information that the latter considers necessary to determine whether the compensation measures in force are compatible with this Decision.

Article 9
Reports

Each Member State shall submit a report on the implementation of this Decision to the Commission every 2 years. The reports shall provide a detailed overview of the application of this Decision for the different categories of services referred to in Article 2(1), including:

(a) a description of the application of this Decision to the services falling within its scope, including in-house activities;
(b) the total amount of aid granted in accordance with this Decision, with a breakdown by the economic sector of the beneficiaries;
(c) an indication of whether, for a particular type of service, the application of this Decision has given rise to difficulties or complaints by third parties; and
(d) any other information concerning the application of this Decision required by the Commission and to be specified in due time before the report is to be submitted.

The first report shall be submitted by 30 June 2014.

Article 10
Transitional provisions

This Decision shall apply to individual aid and aid schemes as follows:

(a) any aid scheme put into effect before the entry into force of this Decision that was compatible with the internal market and exempted from the notification requirement in accordance with Decision 2005/842/EC shall continue to be compatible with the internal market and exempt from the notification requirement for a further period of 2 years;
(b) any aid put into effect before the entry into force of this Decision that was not compatible with the internal market nor exempted from the notification requirement in accordance with Decision 2005/842/EC but fulfils the conditions laid down in this Decision shall be compatible with the internal market and exempt from the requirement of prior notification.

Article 11
Repeal

Decision 2005/842/EC is hereby repealed.

Article 12
Entry into force

This Decision shall enter into force on 31 January 2012.

Article 13
Addressees

This Decision is addressed to the Member States.

Done at Brussels, 20 December 2011.

F3

COMMISSION COMMUNICATION TO THE MEMBER STATES

Application of Articles [107] and [108] of the [Treaty on the Functioning of the European Union]* and of Article 5 of Commission Directive 80/723/EEC to public undertakings in the manufacturing sector

Official Journal C 307, 13.11.1993, p.3

Celex No: 31993Y1113(01)

EUR-Lex permanent link: <http://eur-lex.europa.eu/LexUriServ/LexUriServ.do?uri=CELEX:3199 3Y1113(01):EN:NOT>

Notes

* Ed note: please see the Note on the Lisbon Treaty at p.xvii in regard to article renumbering introduced by the Lisbon Treaty. Directive 80/723/EEC was repealed with effect from 20 December 2006 by Commission Directive 2006/111/EC of 16 November 2006 on the transparency of financial relations between Member States and public undertakings as well as on financial transparency within certain undertakings (Codified version), OJ L318, 17.11.2006, p.17. Article 10 of Directive 2006/111/EC provides that references to the repealed Directive shall be construed as references to Directive 2006/111/EC and shall be read in accordance with the correlation table in Annex II to Directive 2006/111/EC. Unless otherwise indicated, Article numbers in the new Directive are the same as in the old Directive.

EEA application: for the corresponding EEA provision, see the EFTA Surveillance Authority's Procedural and Substantive Rules in the Field of State Aid (Guidelines on the application and interpretation of Articles 61 and 62 of the EEA Agreement and Article 1 of Protocol 3 to the Surveillance and Court Agreement), Part IV, Chapter 20 (OJ L 231, 03.09.1994, and EEA Supplement No 32).

Commentary
Communication: B&C: 11.028, 17.014

I. Introduction

1. A reinforced application of policy towards State aid is necessary for the successful completion of the internal market. One of the areas identified as worthy of attention in this respect is public

undertakings. There is need for both increased transparency and development of policy for public undertakings because they have not been sufficiently covered by State aid disciplines:

— in many cases only capital injections and not other forms of public funds have been fully included in aid disciplines for public undertakings;

— in addition, these disciplines in general only cover loss-making public undertakings;

— finally it also appears that there is a considerable volume of aid to public undertakings given other than through approved aid schemes (which are also available to private undertakings) which have not been notified under Article [108(3)].

2. This communication is designed to remedy this situation. In the first place it explains the legal background of the Treaty and outlines the aid policy and case-law of the Council, Parliament, Commission and Court of Justice for public enterprises. This will, in particular, focus, on the one hand, on Directive 80/723/EC[*] on the transparency of the financial relationship between public undertakings and the State, and, on the other hand, it will develop the well established principle that where the State provides finances to a company in circumstances that would not be acceptable to an investor operating under normal market economy conditions, State aid is involved. The communication then explains how the Commission intends to increase transparency by applying this principle to all forms of public funds and to companies in all situations.

Notes

[* See now Directive 2006/111/EC, OJ L 318, 17.11.2006, p.17.]

3. This communication does not deal with the question of the compatibility under one of the derogations provided for in the EEC Treaty because no change is envisaged in this policy. Finally, this communication is limited to the manufacturing sector. This will not, however, preclude the Commission from using the approach described by this communication in individual cases or sectors outside manufacturing to the extent that the principles in this communication apply in these excluded sectors and where it feels that it is essential to determine if State aid is involved.

II. Public Undertakings and the Rules of Competition

4. Article [345] states: "This Treaty shall in no way prejudice the rules in Member States governing the system of property ownership". In other words the Treaty is neutral in the choice a Member State may make between public and private ownership and does not prejudice a Member State's right to run a mixed economy. However, these rights do not absolve public undertakings from the rules of competition because the institution of a system ensuring that competition in the common market is not distorted is one of the bases on which the Treaty is built (Article [3(1)(g)EC]*). The Treaty also provides the general rules for ensuring such a system (Articles [101] to [109]). In addition the Treaty lays down that these general rules of competition shall apply to public undertakings (Article [106(1)]). There is a specific derogation in Article [106(2)] from the general rule of Article [106(1)] in that the rules of competition apply to all public undertakings including those entrusted with the operation of services of general economic interest or having the character of a revenue-producing monopoly in so far as the application of such rules does not obstruct the performance in law or in fact of the particular tasks assigned to them. The development of trade must not be affected to such an extent as would be contrary to the interests of the Community. In the context of the State aid rules (Articles [107] to [109]), this means that aid granted to public undertakings must, like any other State aid to private undertakings, be notified in advance to the Commission (Article [108(3)]) to ascertain whether or not it falls within the scope of Article [107(1)], i.e. aid that affects trade and competition between Member States. If it falls within Article [107(1)], it is for the Commission to determine whether one of the general derogations provided for in the Treaty is applicable such that the aid becomes compatible with the common market. It is the Commission's role to ensure that there is no discrimination against either public or private undertakings when it applies the rules of competition.

Notes

* Ed note: Article 3(1)(g) EC was repealed by the Treaty of Lisbon. Article 3(1) EC was replaced in substance by Articles 3 to 6 TFEU. The nearest to an equivalent provision to Article 3(1)(g) EC in the TFEU is Article 3(1)(b) TFEU ("The

Union shall have exclusive competence in the following areas: ... (b) the establishing of the competition rules necessary for the functioning of the internal market".

5. It was to ensure this principle of non-discrimination, or neutrality of treatment that, in 1980, the Commission adopted a Directive on the transparency of financial relations between Member States and public undertakings.[1] The Commission was motivated by the fact that the complexity of the financial relations between national public authorities and public undertakings tended to hinder its duty of ensuring that aid incompatible with the common market was not granted. It further considered that the State aid rules could only be applied fairly to both public and private undertakings when the financial relations between public authorities and public undertakings were made transparent.

Notes

[1] Directive 80/723/EEC (OJ L 195, 29.7.1980, p.35) as amended by Directive 85/413/EEC (OJ L 229, 28.8.1985, p.20) which included previously excluded sectors. [See now Commission Directive 2006/111/EC of 16 November 2006 on the transparency of financial relations between Member States and public undertakings as well as on financial transparency within certain undertakings (Codified version), OJ L318, 17.11.2006, p.17.]

6. The Directive obliged Member States to ensure that the flow of all public funds to public undertakings and the uses to which these funds are put are made transparent (Article 1). Member States shall, when the Commission considers it necessary so to request, supply to it the information referred to in Article 1, together with any necessary background information, notably the objectives pursued (Article 5 [*]). Although the transparency in question applied to all public funds, the following were particularly mentioned as falling within its scope:
    — the setting-off of operating losses,
    — the provision of capital,
    — non-refundable grants or loans on privileged terms,
    — the granting of financial advantages by forgoing profits or the recovery of sums due,
    — the forgoing of a normal return on public funds used,
    — compensation for financial burdens imposed by the public authorities.

Notes

[* See now Directive 2006/111/EC (OJ L 318, 17.11.2006, p.17), Article 6.]

7. The Commission further considered that transparency of public funds must be achieved irrespective of the manner in which such provision of public funds is made. Thus, not only were the flows of funds directly from public authorities to public enterprises deemed to fall within the scope of the transparency Directive but also the flows of funds indirectly from other public undertakings over which the public authority holds a dominant influence (Article 2).

8. The legality of the transparency Directive was upheld by the Court of Justice in its judgment of 6 July 1982.[2]

Notes

[2] Joined Cases 188 to 190/80 *France, Italy and the United Kingdom v Commission* [1982] ECR 2545.

8.1. On the argument that there was no necessity for the Directive and that it infringed the rule of proportionality, the Court held as follows (paragraph 18): "In view of the diverse forms of public undertakings in the various Member States and the ramifications of their activities, it is inevitable that their financial relations with public authorities should themselves be very diverse, often complex and therefore difficult to supervise, even with the assistance of the sources of published information to which the applicant governments have referred. In those circumstances there is an undeniable need for the Commission to seek additional information on those relations by establishing common criteria for all the Member States and for all the undertakings in question".

8.2. On the argument that the Directive in question infringed the principle of neutrality of Article [345] of the Treaty, the Court held that (paragraph 21), "it should be borne in mind that the principle of equality, to which the governments refer in connection with the relationship between public and private undertakings in general, presupposes that the two are in comparable situations.... private undertakings determine their industrial and commercial strategy by taking into account, in particular, requirements of profitability. Decisions of public undertakings, on the other hand, may be affected by factors of a different kind within the framework of the pursuit of objectives of public interest by public authorities which may exercise an influence over those decisions. The economic and financial consequences of the impact of such factors lead to the establishment between those undertakings and public authorities of financial relations of a special kind which differ from those existing between public authorities and private undertakings. As the Directive concerns precisely those special financial relations, the submission relating to discrimination cannot be accepted."

8.3. On the argument that the Directive's list of public funds to be made transparent (Article 3) was an attempt to define the notion of aid within the meaning of Articles [107] and [108], the Court stated as follows (paragraph 23): "In relation to the definition contained in Article 3 of the financial relations which are subject to the rules contained in the Directive, it is sufficient to state that it is not an attempt by the Commission to define the concept of aid which appears in Articles [107] and [108] of the Treaty, but only a statement of the financial transactions of which the Commission considers that it must be informed in order to check whether a Member State has granted aids to the undertakings in question, without complying with its obligation to notify the Commission under Article [108(3)]".

8.4. On the argument that the public enterprises on which information was to be provided (Article 2) was an attempt to define the notion of public undertakings within the meaning of Article [106] of the Treaty, the Court stated that (paragraph 24), "it should be emphasized that the object of those provisions is not to define the concept as it appears in Article [106] of the Treaty, but to establish the necessary criteria to delimit the group of undertakings whose financial relations with the public authorities are to be subject to the duty laid down by the Directive to supply information". It continued in paragraph 25 as follows: "According to Article 2 of the Directive, the expression "public undertakings" means any undertaking over which the public authorities may exercise directly or indirectly a dominant influence. According to the second paragraph, such influence is not to be presumed when the public authorities directly or indirectly hold the major part of the undertaking's subscribed capital, control the majority of the votes, or can appoint more than half of the members of its administrative, managerial of supervisory body". It continued in paragraph 26 as follows: "As the Court has already stated, the reason for the inclusion in the Treaty of the provisions of Article [106] is precisely the influence which the public authorities are able to exert over the commercial decisions of public undertakings. That influence may be exerted on the basis of financial participation or of rules governing the management of the undertaking. By choosing the same criteria to determine the financial relations on which it must be able to obtain information in order to perform its duty of surveillance under Article [106(3)], the Commission has remained within the limits of the discretion conferred upon it by that provision".

9. The principles developed by the Court of Justice with respect to the transparency Directive are now part of the established jurisprudence and of particular importance is the fact that the Court has confirmed that:
— making financial relations transparent and the provision, on request, of information under the Directive is necessary and respects the principle of proportionality;
— the Directive respects the principle of neutrality of treatment of public and private undertakings;
— for the purposes of monitoring compliance with Articles [107] and [108] the Commission has a legitimate interest to be informed of all the types of flows of public funds to public enterprises;
— for the purposes of monitoring compliance with Articles [107] and [108] the Commission has a legitimate interest in the flows of public funds to public undertakings that come either directly from the public authorities or indirectly from other public undertakings.

III. Principles to be Used in Determining Whether Aid is Involved

10. Having established over which enterprises and over which funds the Commission has a legitimate interest for the purposes of Articles [107] and [108], it is necessary to examine the

principles to be used in determining whether any aid is involved. Only if aid is involved is there any question of any prior notification. Where aid is involved it is necessary to then examine whether any of the derogations provided for in the Treaty are applicable.[3] This analysis of determining on the one hand whether aid is involved and on the other whether the aid is compatible under one of the derogations of the Treaty, must be kept as a two stage process if full transparency is to be assured.

Notes

[3] See also points 32 and 33 below.

11. When public undertakings, just like private ones, benefit from monies granted under transparent aid schemes approved by the Commission, then it is clear that aid is involved and under what conditions the Commission has authorized its approval. However, the situation with respect to the other forms of public funds listed in the transparency Directive is not always so clear. In certain circumstances public enterprises can derive an advantage from the nature of their relationship with public authorities through the provision of public funds when this latter provides funds in circumstances that go beyond its simple role as proprietor. To ensure respect for the principle of neutrality the aid must be assessed as the difference between the terms on which the funds were made available by the State to the public enterprise, and the terms which a private investor would find acceptable in providing funds to a comparable private undertaking when the private investor is operating under normal market economy conditions (hereinafter "market economy investor principle"). As the Commission points out in its communication on Industrial policy in an open and competitive environment (COM (90) 556) "competition is becoming ever more global and more intense both on the world and on Community markets". This trend has many implications for European companies, for example with regards to R&D, investment strategies and their financing. Both public and private enterprises in similar sectors and in comparable economic and financial situations must be treated equally with respect to this financing. However, if any public funds are provided on terms more favourable (i.e. in economic terms more cheaply) than a private owner would provide them to a private undertaking in a comparable financial and competitive position, then the public undertaking is receiving an advantage not available to private undertakings from their proprietors. Unless the more favourable provision of public funds is treated as aid, and evaluated with respect to one of the derogations of the Treaty, then the principle of neutrality of treatment between public and private undertakings is infringed.

12. This principle of using an investor operating under normal market conditions as a benchmark to determine both whether aid is involved and if so to quantify it, has been adopted by the *Council* and the *Commission* in the steel and shipbuilding sectors, and has been endorsed by the *Parliament* in this context. In addition the Commission has adopted and applied this principle in numerous individual cases. The principle has also been accepted by the *Court* in every case submitted to it as a yardstick for the determination of whether aid was involved.

13. In 1981 the Council adopted the principle of the market economy investor principle on two occasions. Firstly it approved unanimously the Commission decision establishing Community rules for aid to the steel industry,[4] and secondly it approved, by a qualified majority, the shipbuilding code.[5] In both cases the Council stated that the concept of aid includes any aid elements contained in the financing measures taken by Member States in respect of the steel/shipbuilding undertakings which they *directly or indirectly control* and which do not count as the provision of equity capital *according to standard company practice in a market economy*. Thus not only did the Council approve or adopt the market economy principle, it went along the same lines as the Commission in the abovementioned transparency Directive, which brought within its scope not only the direct provision of funds but also their indirect provision.

Notes

[4] Decision 81/2320/ECSC of 7 August 1981 (OJ L 228, 13.8.1981, p.14.). See, in particular, the second recital and Article 1.

[5] Council Directive 81/363/EEC of 28 April 1981 (OJ L 137, 23.5.1981, p.39). See, in particular, the last recital and Article 1(e).

14. The Council has maintained this general principle, most recently in 1989 in the case of steel,[6] and in 1990 in the case of shipbuilding.[7] In fact in the 1989 steel aid code the Council agreed to prior notification of all provisions of capital or similar financing in order to allow the Commission to decide whether they constituted aid, i.e. could "be regarded as a genuine provision of risk capital *according to usual investment practice in a market economy*" (Article 1(2)). The Council also reaffirmed and approved unanimously this principle in Commission Decision 89/218/ECSC concerning new aid to Finsider/ILVA.[8]

Notes

[6] Commission Decision 322/89/ECSC of 1 February 1989 (OJ L 38, 10.2.1989, p.8).

[7] Council Directive 90/684/EEC of 21 December 1990, (OJ L 380, 31.12.1990, p.27).

[8] OJ L 86, 31.3.1989, p.76.

15. The Parliament has been called upon to give its opinion on the market economy investor principle contained in the shipbuilding Directives. For these Directives the Parliament agreed to the Commission drafts which included this principle.[9]

Notes

[9] See, for example, OJ C 28, 9.2.1981, p.23, and OJ C 7, 12.1.1987, p.320.

16. The Commission adopted the same market economy investor principle when it laid down its position in general on public holdings in company capital which still remains valid.[10] It stated "where it is apparent that a public authority which injects capital . . . in a company is not merely providing equity capital under normal market economy conditions, the case has to be assessed in the light of Article [107] of the [EC] Treaty" (paragraph 1). It considered in particular that State aid was involved "where the financial position of the company and particularly the structure and volume of its debts, is such that a normal return (in dividends or capital gains) cannot be expected within a reasonable time from the capital invested".

Notes

[10] Communication to the Member States concerning public authorities holdings in company capital. (Bul. EC 9 1984).

17. The Commission has moreover applied this market economy investor principle in many individual cases to determine whether any aid was involved. The Commission examined in each case the financial circumstances of the company which received the public funds to see if a market economy investor would have made the monies available on similar terms. In the Leeuwarden Decision the Commission established that the capital injections constituted aid because "the overcapacity in the . . . industry constituted handicaps indicating that the firm would *probably* have been unable to raise on the private capital market the funds essential to its survival. The situation on the market provides *no reasonable grounds* for hope that a firm urgently needing large-scale restructuring could generate sufficient cash flow to finance the replacement investment necessary . . . ".[11] This policy has been applied consistently over a number of years. More recently in the CDF v Orkem decision,[12] the Commission established that the public authority "injected capital into an undertaking in conditions that are not those of a market economy". In fact, the company in question "had very little chance of obtaining sufficient capital from the private market to ensure its survival and long-term stability". In the ENI/Lanerossi Decision,[13] the Commission stated that "finance was granted in circumstances that would not be acceptable to a private investor operating under normal market economy conditions, as in the present case the financial and economic position of these factories, particularly in view of the duration and volumes of their losses, was such that a normal return in dividends or capital gains could not be expected for the capital invested".[14] There have also been a number of cases where the Commission has clearly stated that capital injections by the State have not constituted aid because a reasonable return by way of dividends or capital growth could normally be expected.[15]

Notes

[11] OJ L 277, 29.9.1982, p.15.

[12] OJ C 198, 7.8.1990, p.2.

13 OJ L 16, 20.1.1989, p.52.
14 Decisions *Meura* (OJ L 276, 19.10.1984, p.34), *Leeuwarden* (OJ L 277, 29.9.1982, p.15), *Intermills I* (OJ L 280, 2.10.1982, p.30), *Boch/Noviboch* (OJ L 59, 27.2.1985, p.21), *Boussac* (OJ L 352, 15.12.1987, p.42), *Alfa-Fiat* (OJ L 394, 31.5.1989, p.9), *Pinault-Isoroy* (OJ L 119, 7.5.1988, p.38), *Fabelta* (OJ L 62, 3.3.1984, p.18) *Ideal Spun* (OJ L 283, 27.10.1984, p.42), *Renault* (OJ L 220, 11.8.1988, p.30), *Veneziana Vetro* (OJ L 166, 16.6.1989, p.60), *Quimigal* (OJ C 188, 28.7.1990, p.3) and *IOR/Finalp* [OJ L 183, 3.7.1992, p.30] where the same reasoning can be found.
15 Decisions *CDF/Orkem*, in parts, (op. cit.), *Quimigal*, in parts, (op. cit.), *Intermills II* (Bulletin EC 4-1990, point 1.1.34) and *Ernaelsteen* (Eighteenth Competition Report, points 212 and 213).

18. The Commission has also applied the market economy investor principle to many individual cases under the shipbuilding Directives and steel aid codes. In shipbuilding, for example in Bremer Vulkan,[16] the Commission considered that a bridging loan and the purchase of new shares constituted State aid because it did "not accept the argument put forward by the German Government that [it] ... only acted like a private investor who happened to be better at foreseeing future market developments than anyone else." In steel, for example, it took decisions in several individual cases where capital injections were considered as aid.[17]

Notes

16 [OJ L 185, 28.7.1993, p.43.]
17 OJ L 227, 19.8.1983, p.1. See also, in particular, cases relating to *Arbed, Sidmar, ALZ, Hoogovens, Irish Steel, Sacilor v Usinor and British Steel* where the same reasoning can be found. In all these steel cases the aid was held to be compatible. More recently, the Council unanimously approved this principle in the *Finsider/ILVA* case — see point 26 below.

19. It is noteworthy that in many of the above described cases the capital injected into the public undertakings came not directly from the State but indirectly from State holding companies or other public undertakings.

20. The Court has been called upon to examine a number of cases decided by the Commission in its application of the market economy investor principle set out in the 1984 guidelines. In each case submitted to it, the Court accepted the principle as an appropriate one to be used to determine whether or not aid was involved. It then examined whether the Commission decision sufficiently proved its application in the specific circumstances of the case in question. For example, in its judgment in Case 40/85[18] (*Boch*), the Court stated (paragraph 13):

"An appropriate way of establishing whether [the] measure is a State aid is to apply the criterion, which was mentioned in the Commission's decision and, moreover, was not contested by the Belgian Government, of determining to what extent the undertaking would be able to obtain the sums in question on the private capital markets. In the case of an undertaking whose capital is almost entirely held by the public authorities, the test is, in particular, whether in similar circumstances a private shareholder, having regard to the foreseeability of obtaining a return and leaving aside all social, regional policy and sectoral considerations, would have subscribed the capital in question".

The Court has recently reaffirmed this principle in the *Boussac* judgment,[19] where it stated (paragraphs 39 and 40): "In order to determine if the measures constitute State aid, it is necessary to apply the criterion in the Commission's decision, which was not contested by the French Government, whether it would have been possible for the undertaking to obtain the funds on the private capital market", and "the financial situation of the company was such that it would not expect an acceptable return on the investment within a reasonable time period and that Boussac would not have been able to find the necessary funds on the market" (unofficial translation).[20]

The Court has recently further refined the market economy investor principle by making a distinction between a private investor whose time horizon is a short-term even speculative one, and that of a private holding group with a longer-term perspective (*Alfa/Fiat and Lanerossi*).[21] "It is necessary to make clear that the behaviour of a private investor with which the intervention of the public investor ... must be compared, while not necessarily that of an ordinary investor placing his capital with a more or less short-term view of its profitability, must at least be that of a private holding or group of enterprises which pursue a structural, global or sectoral policy and which are guided by a longer-term view of profitability". On the basis of the facts of the case "the Commission was able to correctly conclude that a private investor, even if taking decisions at the level of the whole group in a wider economic context, would not, under normal market economy conditions, have been able to expect an acceptable rate of profitability (even in the long term) on the capital invested..." (unofficial translation). "A private investor may well inject new capital to ensure the survival of a company experiencing temporary difficulties, but which after, if necessary, a restructuring will become profitable again. A parent company may also, during a limited time, carry the losses of a subsidiary in order to allow this latter to withdraw from the sector under the most favourable conditions. Such decisions can be motivated not only by the possibility to get a direct profit, but also by other concerns such as maintaining the image of the whole group or to redirect its activities. However, when the new injections of capital are divorced from all possibility of profitability, even in the long term, these injections must be considered as aid..." (unofficial translation).

Notes

18 *Belgium v Commission* [1986] ECR 2321.
19 Case C-301/87 [1990] ECR I-307].
20 See also *Intermills* Case 323/82, *Leeuwarden* Joined Cases 296/318/82, *Meura* Case 234/84 where the same reasoning can be found.
21 Cases C-305/89 [[1991] ECR I-1603] and C-303/88 [[1991] ECR I-1433] respectively [...].

21. The fact that in many of the cases decided by the Court the injections came indirectly from State holding companies or from other public undertakings and not directly from the State, did not alter the aid character of the monies in question. The Court has always examined the economic reality of the situation to determine whether State resources were involved. In the *Steinicke* and *Weinlig* judgment,[22] the Court stated that "...save for the reservation in Article [106(2)] of the Treaty, Article [107] covers all private and public undertakings and all their production" and that "in applying Article [107] regard must primarily be had to the effects of aid on the undertakings or producers favoured and not the status of the institutions entrusted with the distribution and administration of the aid". More recently in the *Crédit Agricole* judgment,[23] the Court confirmed this and added that "...aid need not necessarily be financed from State resources to be classified as State aid...there is no necessity to draw any distinction according to whether the aid is granted directly by the State or by public or private bodies established or appointed by it to administer aid."

Notes

22 Case 78/76.
23 Case 290/83.

IV. INCREASED TRANSPARENCY OF POLICY

22. To date most but by no means all of the cases which have come before the Council, the Commission and the Court where the market economy investor principle has been applied have concerned capital injections in loss-making or even near-bankrupt companies. One of the aims of this communication is to increase transparency by more systematically applying aid disciplines:
   — to public undertakings in all situations, not just those making losses as is the case at present,
   — to all the forms of public funds mentioned in the transparency Directive (Article 3 — see points 6 and 8.3 above), in particular, for loans, guarantees and the rate of return, not just for capital injections as is the case at present.

23. This increased transparency of policy is to be brought about by clearly applying the market economy investor principle to public undertakings in all situations and all public funds covered by the transparency Directive. The market economy investor principle is used because:
   — it is an appropriate yardstick both for measuring any financial advantage a public undertaking may enjoy over an equivalent private one and for ensuring neutrality of treatment between public and private undertakings;
   — it has proved itself practical to the Commission in numerous cases;
   — it has been confirmed by the Court (see particularly points 20 and 21 above), and
   — it has been approved by the Council in the steel and shipbuilding sector.

1274

Unless this clarification is implemented there is a danger not only of lack of transparency, but also of discrimination against private undertakings which do not have the same links with the public authorities nor the same access to public funds. The current communication is a logical development of existing policy rather than any radical new departure and is necessary to explain the application of the principle to a wider number of situations and a wider range of funds. In fact the Court, the Commission and the Council have already applied the principle of the market economy investor in a limited number of cases to the forms of public funds other than equity which are also the object of this communication — i.e. guarantees, loans, return on capital.[24]

Notes

[24] It should be noted that this is not an exhaustive list of the different forms of financing which may entail aid. The Commission will act against the provision of any other advantages to public undertakings in a tangible or intangible form that may constitute aid.

24. Guarantee. In *IOR/Finalp* (op. cit.) the Commission considered that when a State holding company became the one and only owner of an ailing company (thereby exposing it to unlimited liability under Italian commercial law) this was equivalent to taking extra risk by giving, in effect, an open-ended guarantee. The Commission using its well established principle stated that a market economy investor would normally be reluctant to become the one and only shareholder of a company if as a consequence he must assume unlimited liability for it; he will make sure that this additional risk is outweighed by additional gains.

25. Loan. In *Boch* (op. cit.) the Court stated (paragraphs 12 and 13): "By virtue of Article [87] (1) ... the provisions of the Treaty concerning State aid apply to aid granted by a Member State or through State resources in any form whatsoever. It follows ... that no distinction can be drawn between aid granted in the form of *loans* and aid granted in the form of a subscription of capital of an undertaking. An appropriate way of establishing whether such a measure is a State aid is to apply the criterion ... of determining to what extent the undertaking would be able to obtain the sums in question on the private capital markets."

26. Return on capital. When it opened the Article 88 procedure of the ECSC Treaty (letter to the Italian Government of 6 May 1988) in the *Finsider/ILVA* case, the Commission considered that the loans granted by State credit institutions were not granted to the undertaking in question under conditions acceptable to a private investor operating under normal market conditions, but were dependent on an *(implicit)guarantee* of the State and as such constituted State aid. In fact at a later date this implicit guarantee was made explicit when the debts were honoured. The opening of the procedure led to a decision with the unanimous approval of the Council[25] which imposed conditions on the enterprise in question to ensure that its *viability* would be re-established, and a *minimum return on capital* should be earned.

Notes

[25] OJ L 86, 31.3.1989, p.76. See also the Commission communication to the Council of 25 October 1988 — SEC(88) 1485 final, and point 207 of the Fourteenth Competition Report. In fact, the whole aim of the steel code for all Member States was to restore viability through a minimum return and self-financing according to market principles.

V. Practicality of the Market Economy Investor Principle

27. The practical experience gained by the Commission from the application of State aid rules to public enterprises and the general support among the Community institutions for the basic themes of the market economy investor principle confirm the Commission's view that it is, as such, an appropriate yardstick to determine whether, or not aid exists. However, it is noted that the majority of cases to which the mechanism has been applied have been of a particular nature and the wider application of the mechanism may appear to cause certain difficulties. Some further explanations are therefore warranted. In addition, the fear has been expressed that the application of the market economy investor principle could lead to the Commission's judgment replacing the investor and his appreciation of investment projects. In the first place this criticism can be refuted by the fact that this principle has already shown itself to be both an appropriate and practical yardstick for determining which public funds constitute aid in numerous

individual cases. Secondly it is not the aim of the Commission in the future, just as it has not been in the past, to replace the investor's judgment. Any requests for extra finance naturally call for public undertakings and public authorities, just as they do for private undertakings and the private providers of finance, to analyse the risk and the likely outcome of the project.

In turn, the Commission realizes that this analysis of risk requires public undertakings, like private undertakings, to exercise entrepreneurial skills, which by the very nature of the problem implies a wide margin of judgment on the part of the investor. Within that wide margin the exercise of judgment by the investor cannot be regarded as involving State aid. It is in evaluation of the justification for the provision of funds that the Member State has to decide if a notification is necessary in conformity with its obligation under Article [88](3). In this context, it is useful to recall the arrangements of the 1984 communication on public authorities' holdings which stated that where there is a presumption that a financial flow from the State to a public holding constitutes aid, the Commission shall be informed in advance. On the basis of an examination of the information received it will decide within 15 working days whether the information should be regarded as notification for the purposes of Article [88](3) (point 4.4.2). Only where there are no objective grounds to reasonably expect that an investment will give an adequate rate of return that would be acceptable to a private investor in a comparable private undertaking operating under normal market conditions, is State aid involved even when this is financed wholly or partially by public funds. It is not the Commission's intention to analyse investment projects on an *ex-ante* basis (unless notification is received in advance in conformity with Article [88](3)).

Commentary
para 27: B&C: 17.014

28. There is no question of the Commission using the benefit of hindsight to state that the provision of public funds constituted State aid on the sole basis that the outturn rate of return was not adequate. Only projects where the Commission considers that there were no objective or bona fide grounds to reasonably expect an adequate rate of return in a comparable private undertaking *at the moment the investment/financing* decision is made can be treated as State aid. It is only in such cases that funds are being provided more cheaply than would be available to a private undertaking, i.e. a subsidy is involved. It is obvious that, because of the inherent risks involved in any investment, not all projects will be successful and certain investments may produce a subnormal rate of return or even be a complete failure. This is also the case for private investors whose investment can result in subnormal rates of return or failures. Moreover such an approach makes no discrimination between projects which have short or long-term payback periods, as long as the risk are adequately and objectively assessed and discounted at the time the decision to invest is made, in the way that a private investor would.

Commentary
para 28: B&C: 17.014

29. This communication, by making clearer how the Commission applies the market economy investor principle and the criteria used to determine when aid is involved, will reduce uncertainty in this field. It is not the Commission's intention to apply the principles in this communication (in what is necessarily a complex field) in a dogmatic or doctrinaire fashion. It understands that a wide margin of judgment must come into entrepreneurial investment decisions. The principles have however to be applied when it is beyond reasonable doubt that there is no other plausible explanation for the provision of public funds other than considering them as State aid. This approach will also have to be applied to any cross-subsidization by a profitable part of a public group of undertakings of an unprofitable part. This happens in private undertakings when either the undertaking in question has a strategic plan with good hopes of long-term gain, or that the cross-subsidy has a net benefit to the group as a whole. In cases where there is cross-subsidization in public holding companies the Commission will take account of similar strategic goals. Such cross-subsidization will be considered as aid only where the Commission considers that there is no other reasonable explanation to explain the flow of funds other than that they constituted aid. For fiscal or other reasons certain enterprises, be they public or private, are often split into several

legally distinct subsidiaries. However, the Commission will not normally ask for information of the flow of funds between such legally distinct subsidiaries of companies for which one consolidated report is required.

30. The Commission is also aware of the differences in approach a market economy investor may have between his minority holding in a company on the one hand and full control of a large group on the other hand. The former relationship may often be characterized as more of a speculative or even short-term interest, whereas the latter usually implies a longer-term interest. Therefore, where the public authority controls an individual public undertaking or group of undertakings it will normally be less motivated by purely short-term profit considerations than if it had merely a minority/non-controlling holding and its time horizon will accordingly be longer. The Commission will take account of the nature of the public authorities' holding in comparing their behaviour with the benchmark of the equivalent market economy investor. This remark is also valid for the evaluation of calls for extra funds to financially restructure a company as opposed to calls for funds required to finance specific projects.[26] In addition the Commission is also aware that a market economy investor's attitude is generally more favourably disposed towards calls for extra finance when the undertaking or group requiring the extra finance has a good record of providing adequate returns by way of dividends or capital accumulation on past investments. Where a company has underperformed in this respect in comparison with equivalent companies, this request for finance will normally be examined more sceptically by the private investor/owner called upon to provide the extra finance. Where this call for finance is necessary to protect the value of the whole investment the public authority like a private investor can be expected to take account of this wider context when examining whether the commitment of new funds is commercially justified. Finally where a decision is made to abandon a line of activity because of its lack of medium/long-term commercial viability, a public group, like a private group, can be expected to decide the timing and scale of its run down in the light of the impact on the overall credibility and structure of the group.

Part F Public Undertakings

Notes

[26] This may be particularly important for public undertakings that have been deliberately undercapitalized by the public authority owner for reasons extraneous to commercial justifications (e.g. public expenditure restrictions).

Commentary
para 30: B&C: 17.014

31. In evaluating any calls for extra finance a shareholder would typically have at his disposal the information necessary to judge whether he is justified in responding to these calls for additional finance. The extent and detail of the information provided by the undertaking requiring finance may vary according to the nature and volume of the funding required, to the relationship between the undertaking and the shareholder and even to the past performance of the undertaking in providing an adequate return.[27] A market economy investor would not usually provide any additional finance without the appropriate level of information. Similar considerations would normally apply to public undertakings seeking finance. This financial information in the form of the relevant documentation should be made available at the specific request of the Commission if it is considered that it would help in evaluating the investment proposals from the point of view of deciding whether or not their financing constitutes aid.[28] The Commission will not disclose, information supplied to it as it is covered by the obligation of professional secrecy. Therefore, investment projects will not be scrutinized by the Commission in advance except where aid is involved and prior notification in conformity with Article [88](3) is required. However, where it has reasonable grounds to consider that aid may be granted in the provision of finance to public undertakings, the Commission, pursuant to its responsibilities under Articles [107] and [108], may ask for the information from Member States necessary to determine whether aid is involved in the specific case in question.

Notes

[27] Minority shareholders who have no "inside" information on the running of the company may require a more formal justification for providing funds than a controlling owner who may in fact be involved at board level in formulating strategies and is already party to detailed information on the undertaking's financial situation.

---

28 The provision of this information on request falls within scope of the Commission's powers of investigation of aid under Articles [107] and [108] in combination with Article [10] of the [EC] Treaty and under Article 1(c) of the Transparency Directive which states that the use to which public funds are put should be made transparent.

VI. Compatibility of Aid

32. Each Member State is free to choose the size and nature of its public sector and to vary it over time. The Commission recognizes that when the State decides to exercise its right to public ownership, commercial objectives are not always the essential motivation. Public enterprises are sometimes expected to fulfil non-commercial functions alongside, or in addition to, their basic commercial activities. For example, in some Member States public companies may be used as a locomotive for the economy, as part of efforts to counter recession, to restructure troubled industries or to act as catalysts for regional development. Public companies may be expected to locate in less developed regions where costs are higher or to maintain employment at levels beyond purely commercial levels. The Treaty enables the Commission to take account of such considerations where they are justified in the Community interest. In addition the provision of some services may entail a public service element, which may even be enforced by political or legal constraints. These non-commercial objectives/functions (i.e. social goods) have a cost which ultimately has to be financed by the State (i.e. taxpayers) either in the form of new finance (e.g. capital injections) or a reduced rate of return on capital invested. This aiding of the provision of public services can, in certain circumstances, distort competition. Unless one of the derogations of the Treaty is applicable, public undertakings are not exempted from the rules of competition by the imposition of these non-commercial objectives.

33. If the Commission is to carry out its duties under the Treaty, it must have the information available to determine whether the financial flows to public undertakings constitute aid, to quantify such aid and then to determine if one of the derogations provided for in the Treaty is applicable. This communication limits itself to the objective of increasing transparency for the financial flows in question which is an essential first step. To decide, as a second step, whether any aid that is identified is compatible, is a question which is not dealt with because such a decision will be in accordance with the well known principles used by the Commission in the area to which no change is envisaged. (It should be stressed that the Commission is concerned with aid only when it has an impact on intra-Community trade and competition. Thus, if aid is granted for a non-commercial purpose to a public undertaking which has no impact on intra-Community trade and competition, Article [107(1)] is not applicable.) This obligation of submitting to Community control all aid having a Community dimension is the necessary counterpart to the right of Member States being able to export freely to other Member States and is the basis of a common market.

VII. Different Forms of State Intervention

34. In deciding whether any public funds to public undertakings constitute aid, the Commission must take into account the factors discussed below for each type of intervention covered by this communication — capital injections, guarantees, loans, return on investment.29 These factors are given as a guide to Member States of the likely Commission attitude in individual cases. In applying this policy the Commission will bear in mind the practicability of the market economy investor principle described above. This communication takes over the definition of public funds and public undertakings used in the transparency Directive. This is given as guidance for Member States as to the general attitude of the Commission. However, the Commission will obviously have to prove in individual cases of application of this policy that public undertakings within the meaning of Article [106] and State resources within the meaning of Article [107(1)] are involved, just as it has in individual cases in the past. As far as any provision of information under the transparency Directive is concerned, these definitions have been upheld by the Court for the purposes of the Directive and there is no further obligation on the Commission to justify them.

Notes

29 This list is not exhaustive.

Capital injections

35. A capital injection is considered to be an aid when it is made in circumstances which would not be acceptable to an investor operating under normal market conditions. This is normally taken to mean a situation where the structure and future prospects for the company are such that a normal return (by way of dividend payments or capital appreciation) by reference to a comparable private enterprise cannot be expected within a reasonable time. Thus, the 1984 communication on capital injections remains valid.

     A market economy investor would normally provide equity finance if the present value[30] of expected future cash flows from the intended project (accruing to the investor by way of dividend payments and/or capital gains and adjusted for risk) exceed the new outlay. The context within which this will have to be interpreted was explained above in paragraphs 27 to 31.

Notes

30 Future cash flows discounted at the company's cost of capital (in-house discount rate).

36. In certain Member States investors are obliged by law to contribute additional equity to firms whose capital base has been eroded by continuous losses to below a predetermined level. Member States have claimed that these capital injections cannot be considered as aid as they are merely fulfilling a legal obligation. However, this "obligation" is more apparent than real. Commercial investors faced with such a situation must also consider all other options including the possibility of liquidating or otherwise running down their investment. If this liquidation or running down proves to be the more financially sound option taking into account the impact on the group and is not followed, then any subsequent capital injection or any other State intervention has to be considered as constituting aid.

37. When comparing the actions of the State and those of a market economy investor in particular when a company is not making a loss, the Commission will evaluate the financial position of the company at the time it is/was proposed to inject additional capital. On the basis of an evaluation of the following items the Commission will examine whether there is an element of aid contained in the amount of capital invested. This aid element consists in the cost of the investment less the value of the investment, appropriately discounted. It is stressed that the items listed below are indispensable to any analysis but not necessarily sufficient since account must also be taken of the principles set out in paragraphs 27 to 31 above and of the question whether the funds required are for investment projects or a financial restructuring.

37.1. *Profit and loss situation.* An analysis of the results of the company spread over several years. Relevant profitability ratios would be extracted and the underlying trends subject to evaluation.

37.2. *Financial indicators.* The debt/equity ratio (gearing of the company) would be compared with generally accepted norms, industry-sector averages and those of close competitors, etc. The calculation of various liquidity and solvency ratios would be undertaken to ascertain the financial standing of the company (this is particularly relevant in relation to the assessment of the loan finance potential of a company operating under normal market conditions). The Commission is aware of the difficulties involved in making such comparisons between Member States due in particular to different accounting practices or standards. It will bear this in mind when choosing the appropriate reference points to be used as a comparison with the public undertakings receiving funds.

37.3. *Financial projections.* In cases where funding is sought to finance an investment programme then obviously this programme and the assumptions upon which it is based have to be studied in detail to see if the investment is justified.

37.4. *Market situation.* Market trends (past performance and most importantly future prospects) and the company's market share over a reasonable time period should be examined and future projections subjected to scrutiny.

Guarantees

38. The position currently adopted by the Commission in relation to loan guarantees has recently been communicated to Member States.[31] It regards all guarantees given by the State directly or by way of delegation through financial institutions as falling within the scope of Article [107(1)] of the [EC] Treaty. It is only if guarantees are assessed at the granting stage that all the distortions or potential distortions of competition can be detected. The fact that a firm receives a guarantee even if it is never called in may enable it to continue trading, perhaps forcing competitors who do not enjoy such facilities to go out of business. The firm in question has therefore received support which has disadvantaged its competitors i.e. it has been aided and this has had an effect on competition. An assessment of the aid element of guarantees will involve an analysis of the borrower's financial situation (see point 37 above). The aid element of these guarantees would be the difference between the rate which the borrower would pay in a free market and that actually obtained with the benefit of the guarantee, net of any premium paid for the guarantee. Creditors can only safely claim against a government guarantee where this is made and given explicitly to either a public or a private undertaking. If this guarantee is deemed incompatible with the common market following evaluation with respect to the derogations under the Treaty, reimbursement of the value of any aid will be made by the undertaking to the government even if this means a declaration of bankruptcy but creditors' claims will be honoured. These provisions apply equally to public and private undertakings and no additional special arrangements are necessary for public enterprises other than the remarks made below.

Notes

31 Communication to all Member States dated 5 April 1989, as amended by letter of 12 October 1989.

38.1. Public enterprises whose legal status does not allow bankruptcy are in effect in receipt of permanent aid on all borrowings equivalent to a guarantee when such status allows the enterprises in question to obtain credit on terms more favourable than would otherwise be available.

38.2. Where a public authority takes a hold in a public undertaking of a nature such that it is exposed to unlimited liability instead of the normal limited liability, the Commission will treat this as a guarantee on all the funds which are subject to unlimited liability.[32] It will then apply the above described principles to this guarantee.

Notes

32 See point 24 above.

Loans

39. When a lender operating under normal market economy conditions provides loan facilities for a client, he is aware of the inherent risk involved in any such venture. The risk is of course that the client will be unable to repay the loan. The potential loss extends to the full amount advanced (the capital) and any interest due but unpaid at the time of default. The risk attached to any loan arrangement is usually reflected in two distinct parameters:
    (a) the interest rate charged;
    (b) the security sought to cover the loan.

40. Where the perceived risk attached to the loan is high then *ceteris paribus* both (a) and (b) above can be expected to reflect this fact. It is when this does not take place in practice that the Commission will consider that the firm in question has had an advantage conferred on it, i.e. has been aided. Similar considerations apply where the assets pledged by a fixed or floating charge on the company would be insufficient to repay the loan in full. The Commission will in future examine carefully the security used to cover loan finance. This evaluation process would be similar to that proposed for capital injections (see point 37 above).

41. The aid element amounts to the difference between the rate which the firm should pay (which itself is dependent on its financial position and the security which it can offer on foot of the loan) and that actually paid. (This one-stage analysis of the loan is based on the presumption that in the event of default the lender will exercise his legal right to recover any monies due to him). In the

extreme case, i.e. where an unsecured loan is given to a company which under normal circumstances would be unable to obtain finance (for example because its prospects of repaying the loan are poor) then the loan effectively equates a grant payment and the Commission would evaluate it as such.

42. The situation would be viewed from the point of view of the lender at the moment the loan is approved. If he chooses to lend (or is directly or indirectly forced to do so as may be the case with State-controlled banks) on conditions which could not be considered as normal in banking terms, then there is an element of aid involved which has to be quantified. These provisions would of course also apply to private undertakings obtaining loans from public financial institutions.

Return on investments

43. The State, in common with any other market economy investor, should expect a normal return obtained by comparable private undertakings on its capital investments by way of dividends or capital appreciation.[33] The rate of return will be measured by the profit (after depreciation but before taxation and disposals) expressed as a percentage of assets employed. It is therefore a measure that is neutral with respect to the form of finance used in each undertaking (i.e. debt or equity) which for public undertakings may be decided for reasons extraneous to purely commercial considerations. If this normal return is neither forthcoming beyond the short term nor is likely to be forthcoming in the long term (with the uncertainty of this longer-term future gain not appropriately accounted for) and no remedial action has been taken by the public undertaking to rectify the situation, then it can be assumed that the entity is being indirectly aided as the State is foregoing the benefit which a market economy investor would expect from a similar investment. A normal rate of return will be defined with reference where possible being made to comparable private companies. The Commission is aware of the difficulties involved in making such comparisons between Member States — see particularly point 37. In addition the difference in capital markets, currency fluctuations and interest rates between Member States further complicate international comparisons of such ratios. Where accounting practices even within a single Member State make accurate asset valuation hazardous, thereby undermining rate of return calculations, the Commission will examine the possibility of using either adjusted valuations or other simpler criteria such as operating cash flow (after depreciation but before disposals) as a proxy of economic performance.

When faced with an inadequate rate of return a private undertaking would either take action to remedy the situation or be obliged to do so by its shareholders. This would normally involve the preparation of a detailed plan to increase overall profitability. If a public undertaking has an inadequate rate of return, the Commission could consider that this situation contains elements of aid, which should be analysed with respect to Article [87]. In these circumstances, the public undertaking is effectively getting its capital cheaper than the market rate, i.e. equivalent to a subsidy.

Notes

[33] The foregoing of a normal return on public funds falls within the scope of the Transparency Directive.

44. Similarly, if the State forgoes dividend income from a public undertaking and the resultant retained profits do not earn a normal rate of return as defined above then the company in question is effectively being subsidized by the State. It may well be that the State sees it as preferable for reasons not connected with commercial considerations to forgo dividends (or accept reduced dividend payments) rather than make regular capital injections into the company. The end result is the same and this regular "funding" has to be treated in the same way as new capital injections and evaluated in accordance with the principles set out above.

45. **Duration**

After an initial period of five years, the Commission will review the application of the policy described in this communication. On the basis of this review, and after consulting Member States, the Commission may propose any modifications which it considers appropriate.

F4

COMMUNICATION FROM THE COMMISSION ON THE APPLICATION OF THE EUROPEAN UNION STATE AID RULES TO COMPENSATION GRANTED FOR THE PROVISION OF SERVICES OF GENERAL ECONOMIC INTEREST

(Text with EEA relevance)

(2012/C 8/02)

Official Journal C 8, 11.1.12, p.4

Celex No : 52012XC0111(02)

EUR-Lex permanent link: <http://eur-lex.europa.eu/legal-content/EN/ALL/?uri=CELEX:52012X C0111(02)&qid=1395773445177>

Notes

* Ed note: please see the Note on the Lisbon Treaty at p.xvii in regard to article renumbering introduced by the Lisbon Treaty. **EEA application:** see EFTA Surveillance Authority Decision No 12/12/COL of 25 January 2012 amending, for the eighty-fourth time, the procedural and substantive rules in the field of state aid by introducing new chapters on the application of state aid rules to compensation granted for the provision of services of general economic interest and on the framework for state aid in the form of public service compensation, OJ L 161, 13.6.2013, p.12.

Commentary

B&C: 11.048 F&N: 6.166, 6.178, 17.368
paras 54–59: F&N: 17.374
paras 71–77: F&N: 17.376

---

1. PURPOSE AND SCOPE OF THE COMMUNICATION

1. Services of general economic interest (SGEIs) are not only rooted in the shared values of the Union but also play a central role in promoting social and territorial cohesion. The Union and the Member States, each within their respective powers, must take care that such services operate on the basis of principles and conditions which enable them to fulfil their missions.

2. Certain SGEIs can be provided by public or private undertakings[1] without specific financial support from Member States' authorities. Other services can only be provided if the authority concerned offers financial compensation to the provider. In the absence of specific Union rules, Member States are generally free to determine how their SGEIs should be organised and financed.

Notes

[1] In accordance with Article 345 of the Treaty, the Treaties in no way prejudice the rules in Member States governing the system of property ownership. Consequently, the competition rules do not discriminate against companies based on whether they are in public or private ownership.

---

3. The purpose of this Communication is to clarify the key concepts underlying the application of the State aid rules to public service compensation[1]. It will therefore focus on those State aid requirements that are most relevant for public service compensation.

Notes

[1] Further guidance is contained in the Guide to the application of the European Union rules on State aid, public procurement and the internal market to services of general economic interest, and in particular to social services of general interest, SEC(2010) 1545 final, 7 December 2010.

4. In parallel with this Communication, the Commission envisages adopting an SGEI-specific *de minimis* Regulation clarifying that certain compensation measures do not constitute State aid within the meaning of Article 107 of the Treaty[1], and is issuing a Decision[2], which declares certain types of SGEI compensation constituting State aid to be compatible with the Treaty pursuant to Article 106(2) of the Treaty and exempts them from the notification obligation under Article 108(3) of the Treaty, and a Framework[3], which sets out the conditions under which State aid for SGEIs not covered by the Decision can be declared compatible under Article 106(2) of the Treaty.

Notes

[1] See [OJ C 8, 11.1.12, p.23].
[2] Commission Decision 2012/21/EU of 21 December 2011 on the application of Article 106(2) of the Treaty on the Functioning of the European Union to State aid in the form of public service compensation granted to certain undertakings entrusted with the operation of services of general economic interest (OJ L 7, 11.1.2012, p.3).
[3] See [OJ C 8, 11.1.12, p.15].

5. This Communication is without prejudice to the application of other provisions of Union law, in particular those relating to public procurement and requirements flowing from the Treaty and from sectoral Union legislation. Where a public authority chooses to entrust a third party with the provision of a service, it is required to comply with Union law governing public procurement, stemming from Articles 49 to 56 of the Treaty, the Union Directives on public procurement (Directive 2004/17/EC of the European Parliament and of the Council of 31 March 2004 coordinating the procurement procedures of entities operating in the water, energy, transport and postal services sectors[1] and Directive 2004/18/EC of the European Parliament and of the Council of 31 March 2004 on the coordination of procedures for the award of public works contracts, public supply contracts and public service contracts[2] and sectoral rules[3]. Also in cases where the Directives on public procurement are wholly or partially inapplicable (for example, for service concessions and service contracts listed in Annex IIB to Directive 2004/18/EC, including different types of social services), the award may nevertheless have to meet Treaty requirements of transparency, equality of treatment, proportionality and mutual recognition[4].

Notes

[1] OJ L 134, 30.4.2004, p.1.
[2] OJ L 134, 30.4.2004, p.114.
[3] See for example, Regulation (EC) No 1370/2007 of the European Parliament and of the Council of 23 October 2007 on public passenger transport services by rail and by road and repealing Council Regulations (EEC) Nos 1191/69 and 1107/70 (OJ L 315, 3.12.2007, p.1).
[4] Case C-324/98 *Telaustria Verlags GmbH and Telefonadress GmbH v Telekom Austria AG* [2000] ECR I-10745, paragraph 60 and Commission interpretative communication on the Community law applicable to contract awards not or not fully subject to the provisions of the Public Procurement Directives (OJ C 179, 1.8.2006, p.2).

6. In addition to the issues addressed in this Communication, the Decision 2012/21/EU and the Communication from the Commission on EU Framework for State aid in the form of public service compensation (2011), the Commission will answer individual questions that arise in the context of the application of the State aid rules to SGEIs. It will do so *inter alia* through its Interactive Information Service on Services of General Interest, which is accessible on the Commission's website[1].

Notes

[1] http://ec.europa.eu/services_general_interest/registration/form_en.html

7. This Communication is without prejudice to the relevant case-law of the Court of Justice of the European Union.

2. GENERAL PROVISIONS RELATING TO THE CONCEPT OF STATE AID

2.1. Concepts of undertaking and economic activity

8. Based on Article 107(1) of the Treaty, the State aid rules generally only apply where the recipient is an 'undertaking'. Whether or not the provider of a service of general interest is to be regarded as an undertaking is therefore fundamental for the application of the State aid rules.

2.1.1. *General principles*

9. The Court of Justice has consistently defined undertakings as entities engaged in an economic activity, regardless of their legal status and the way in which they are financed[1]. The classification of a particular entity as an undertaking thus depends entirely on the nature of its activities. This general principle has three important consequences:

First, the status of the entity under national law is not decisive. For example, an entity that is classified as an association or a sports club under national law may nevertheless have to be regarded as an undertaking within the meaning of Article 107(1) of the Treaty. The only relevant criterion in this respect is whether it carries out an economic activity.

Second, the application of the State aid rules as such does not depend on whether the entity is set up to generate profits. Based on the case-law of the Court of Justice and the General Court, non-profit entities can offer goods and services on a market too[2]. Where this is not the case, non-profit providers remain of course entirely outside of State aid control.

Third, the classification of an entity as an undertaking is always relative to a specific activity. An entity that carries out both economic and non-economic activities is to be regarded as an undertaking only with regard to the former.

Notes

[1] Joined Cases C-180/98 to C-184/98 *Pavlov and Others* [2000] ECR I-6451.
[2] Joined Cases 209/78 to 215/78 and 218/78 *Van Landewyck* [1980] ECR 3125, paragraph 21; Case C-244/94 *FFSA and Others* [1995] ECR I-4013; Case C-49/07 *MOTOE* [2008] ECR I-4863, paragraphs 27 and 28.

10. Two separate legal entities may be considered to form one economic unit for the purposes of the application of State aid rules. That economic unit is then considered to be the relevant undertaking. In this respect, the Court of Justice looks at the existence of a controlling share or functional, economic and organic links[1]. On the other hand, an entity that in itself does not provide goods or services on a market is not an undertaking for the simple fact of holding shares, even a majority shareholding, when the shareholding gives rise only to the exercise of the rights attached to the status of shareholder or member as well as, if appropriate, the receipt of dividends, which are merely the fruits of the ownership of an asset[2].

Notes

[1] Case C-480/09 P *AceaElectrabel Produzione SpA v Commission* [2010] ECR paragraphs 47 to 55; Case C-222/04 *Ministero dell'Economia e delle Finanze v Cassa di Risparmio di Firenze SpA and Others* [2006] ECR I-289, paragraph 112.
[2] Case C-222/04 *Ministero dell'Economia e delle Finanze v Cassa di Risparmio di Firenze SpA and Others* [2006] ECR I-289, paragraphs 107–118 and 125.

11. To clarify the distinction between economic and non-economic activities, the Court of Justice has consistently held that any activity consisting in offering goods and services on a market is an economic activity[1].

Notes

[1] Case 118/85 *Commission v Italy* [1987] ECR 2599, paragraph 7; Case C-35/96 *Commission v Italy* [1998] ECR I-3851, paragraph 36; Joined Cases C-180/98 to C-184/98 *Pavlov and Others*, paragraph 75.

12. The question whether a market exists for certain services may depend on the way those services are organised in the Member State concerned[1]. The State aid rules only apply where a certain activity is provided in a market environment. The economic nature of certain services can therefore differ from one Member State to another. Moreover, due to political choice or economic developments, the classification of a given service can change over time. What is not a market activity today may turn into one in the future, and vice versa.

Notes

[1] Joined Cases C-159/91 and C-160/91 *Poucet and Pistre* [1993] ECR I-637.

13. The decision of an authority not to allow third parties to provide a certain service (for example, because it wishes to provide the service in-house) does not rule out the existence of an economic activity. In spite of such market closure, an economic activity can exist where other operators would be willing and able to provide the service in the market concerned. More generally, the fact that a particular service is provided in-house[1] has no relevance for the economic nature of the activity[2].

Notes

[1] See Opinion of Mr Advocate General Geelhoed in Case C-295/05 *Asociación Nacional de Empresas Forestales (Asemfo) v Transformación Agraria SA (Tragsa) and Administración del Estado* [2007] ECR I-2999, paragraphs 110 to 116; Regulation (EC) No 1370/2007 of the European Parliament and of the Council of 23 October 2007 on public passenger transport services by rail and by road and repealing Council Regulations (EEC) Nos 1191/69 and 1107/70, OJ L 315, 3.12.2007, p.1, Articles 5(2) and 6(1); Commission Decision 2011/501/EU of 23 February 2011 on State aid C 58/06 (ex NN 98/05) implemented by Germany for Bahnen der Stadt Monheim (BSM) and Rheinische Bahngesellschaft (RBG) in the Verkehrsverbund Rhein-Ruhr, OJ L 210, 17.8.2011, p.1, paragraphs 208–209.

[2] Neither has it any relevance for the question whether the service can be defined as SGEI; see section 3.2.

14. Since the distinction between economic and non-economic services depends on political and economic specificities in a given Member State, it is not possible to draw up an exhaustive list of activities that *a priori* would never be economic. Such a list would not provide genuine legal certainty and would thus be of little use. The following paragraphs instead seek to clarify the distinction with respect to a number of important areas.

Commentary
para 14: F&N:17.418

15. In the absence of a definition of economic activity in the Treaties, the case-law appears to offer different criteria for the application of internal market rules and for the application of competition law[1].

Notes

[1] Case C-519/04 P *David Meca-Medina and Igor Majcen v Commission* [2006] ECR I-6991, paragraphs 30 to 33; Case C-350/07 *Kattner Stahlbau* [2009] ECR I-1513, paragraphs 66, 72, 74 and 75; Opinion of Mr Advocate General Poiares Maduro delivered on 10 November 2005 in Case C-205/03 P *FENIN* [2006] ECR I-6295, paragraphs 50 and 51.

2.1.2. *Exercise of public powers*

16. It follows from the Court of Justice case-law that Article 107 of the Treaty does not apply where the State acts 'by exercising public power'[1] or where authorities emanating from the State act 'in their capacity as public authorities'[2]. An entity may be deemed to act by exercising public powers where the activity in question is a task that forms part of the essential functions of the State or is connected with those functions by its nature, its aim and the rules to which it is subject[3]. Generally speaking, unless the Member State concerned has decided to introduce market mechanisms, activities that intrinsically form part of the prerogatives of official authority and are performed by the State do not constitute economic activities. Examples are activities related to:

(a) the army or the police;
(b) air navigation safety and control[4];
(c) maritime traffic control and safety[5];

(d) anti-pollution surveillance[6]; and

(e) the organisation, financing and enforcement of prison sentences[7].

Notes

[1] Case C-118/85 *Commission v Italy*, paragraphs 7 and 8.

[2] Case C-30/87 *Bodson/Pompes funèbres des régions libérées* [1988] ECR I-2479, paragraph 18.

[3] See, in particular, Case C-364/92 *SAT/Eurocontrol* [1994] ECR I-43, paragraph 30.

[4] Case C-364/92 *SAT/Eurocontrol*, paragraph 27; Case C-113/07 P *Selex Sistemi Integrati v Commission* [2009] ECR I-2207, paragraph 71.

[5] Commission Decision of 16 October 2002 in Case N 438/02 — *Belgium — Aid to port authorities*, OJ C 284, 21.11.2002.

[6] Case C-343/95 *Calì & Figli* [1997] ECR I-1547, paragraph 22.

[7] Commission Decision in Case N 140/06 — *Lithuania — Allotment of subsidies to the State Enterprises at the Correction Houses*, OJ C 244, 11.10.2006.

2.1.3. Social security

17. Whether schemes in the area of social security are to be classified as involving an economic activity depends on the way they are set up and structured. In essence, the Court of Justice and the General Court distinguish between schemes based on the principle of solidarity and economic schemes.

Commentary
para 17: F&N:17.382

---

18. The Court of Justice and the General Court use a range of criteria to determine whether a social security scheme is solidarity-based and therefore does not involve an economic activity. A bundle of factors can be relevant in this respect:

(a) whether affiliation with the scheme is compulsory[1];

(b) whether the scheme pursues an exclusively social purpose[2];

(c) whether the scheme is non-profit[3];

(d) whether the benefits are independent of the contributions made[4];

(e) whether the benefits paid are not necessarily proportionate to the earnings of the person insured[5]; and

(f) whether the scheme is supervised by the State[6].

Notes

[1] Joined Cases C-159/91 and C-160/91 *Poucet and Pistre* [1993] ECR I-637, paragraph 13.

[2] Case C-218/00 *Cisal and INAIL* [2002] ECR I-691, paragraph 45.

[3] Joined Cases C-264/01, C-306/01, C-354/01 and C-355/01 *AOK Bundesverband* [2004] ECR I-2493, paragraphs 47 to 55.

[4] Joined Cases C-159/91 and C-160/91 *Poucet and Pistre*, paragraphs 15 to 18.

[5] Case C-218/00 *Cisal and INAIL*, paragraph 40.

[6] Joined Cases C-159/91 and C-160/91 *Poucet and Pistre*, paragraph 14; Case C-218/00 *Cisal and INAIL*, paragraphs 43 to 48; Joined Cases C-264/01, C-306/01, C-354/01 and C-355/01 *AOK Bundesverband*, paragraphs 51 to 55.

---

19. Such solidarity-based schemes must be distinguished from economic schemes[1]. In contrast with solidarity-based schemes, economic schemes are regularly characterised by:

(a) optional membership[2];

(b) the principle of capitalisation (dependency of entitlements on the contributions paid and the financial results of the scheme)[3];

(c) their profit-making nature[4]; and

(d) the provision of entitlements which are supplementary to those under a basic scheme[5].

Notes

[1] See, in particular, Case C-244/94 *FFSA and Others*, paragraph 19.

[2] Case C-67/96 *Albany* [1999] ECR I-5751, paragraphs 80–87.
[3] Case C-244/94 *FFSA and Others*, paragraphs 9 and 17 to 20; Case C-67/96 *Albany*, paragraphs 81 to 85; see also Joined Cases C-115/97 to C-117/97 *Brentjens* [1999] ECR I-6025, paragraphs 81 to 85, Case C-219/97 *Drijvende Bokken* [1999] ECR I-6121, paragraphs 71 to 75, and Joined Cases C-180/98 to C-184/98 *Pavlov and Others*, paragraphs 114 and 115.
[4] Joined Cases C-115/97 to C-117/97 *Brentjens*.
[5] Joined Cases C-180/98 to C-184/98 *Pavlov and Others*.

20. Some schemes combine features of both categories. In such cases, the classification of the scheme depends on an analysis of different elements and their respective importance[1].

Notes

[1] Case C-350/07 *Kattner Stahlbau* [2009] ECR I-1513.

2.1.4. Health care

21. In the Union, the health care systems differ significantly between Member States. The degree to which different health care providers compete with each other in a market environment largely depends on these national specificities.

22. In some Member States, public hospitals are an integral part of a national health service and are almost entirely based on the principle of solidarity[1]. Such hospitals are directly funded from social security contributions and other State resources and provide their services free of charge to affiliated persons on the basis of universal coverage[2]. The Court of Justice and the General Court have confirmed that, where such a structure exists, the relevant organisations do not act as undertakings[3].

Notes

[1] Based on the case-law of the European Courts, a prominent example is the Spanish National Health System (see Case T-319/99 *FENIN* [2003] ECR II-357).
[2] Depending on the overall characteristics of the system, charges which only cover a small fraction of the true cost of the service may not affect its classification as non-economic.
[3] Case T-319/99 *FENIN* [2003] ECR II-357, paragraph 39.

23. Where that structure exists, even activities that in themselves could be of an economic nature, but are carried out merely for the purpose of providing another non-economic service, are not of an economic nature. An organisation that purchases goods — even in large quantities — for the purpose of offering a non-economic service does not act as an undertaking simply because it is a purchaser in a given market[1].

Notes

[1] Case T-319/99 *FENIN*, paragraph 40.

24. In many other Member States, hospitals and other health care providers offer their services for remuneration, be it directly from patients or from their insurance[1]. In such systems, there is a certain degree of competition between hospitals concerning the provision of health care services. Where this is the case, the fact that a health service is provided by a public hospital is not sufficient for the activity to be classified as non-economic.

Notes

[1] See, for example, Case C-244/94 *FFSA*, Case C-67/96 *Albany*, Joined Cases C-115/97, C-116/97 and C-117/97 *Brentjens*, and Case C-219/97 *Drijvende Bokken*.

25. The Court of Justice and the General Court have also clarified that health care services which independent doctors and other private practitioners provide for remuneration at their own risk are to be regarded as an economic activity[1]. The same principles would apply as regards independent pharmacies.

Notes

[1] See Joined Cases C-180 to C-184/98 *Pavlov and Others*, paragraphs 75 and 77.

2.1.5. Education

26. Case-law of the Union has established that public education organised within the national educational system funded and supervised by the State may be considered as a non- economic activity. In this regard, the Court of Justice has indicated that the State:

> 'by establishing and maintaining such a system of public education and financed entirely or mainly by public funds and not by pupils or their parents ... does not intend to become involved in activities for remuneration, but carries out its task towards its population in the social, cultural and educational areas'[1].

Notes

[1] See, among others, Case C-318/05 *Commission v Germany* [2007] ECR I-6957, paragraph 68. See also Decision of the Commission of 25 April 2001, N 118/00 *Subvention publiques aux clubs sportifs professionnels* and decision of the EFTA Surveillance Authority in Case 68123 *Norway Nasjonal digital laeringsarena*, 12.10.2011, p.9.

27. According to the same case-law, the non-economic nature of public education is in principle not affected by the fact that pupils or their parents sometimes have to pay tuition or enrolment fees which contribute to the operating expenses of the system. Such financial contributions often only cover a fraction of the true costs of the service and can thus not be considered as remuneration for the service provided. They therefore do not alter the non-economic nature of a general education service predominantly funded by the public purse[1]. These principles can cover public educational services such as vocational training[2], private and public primary schools[3] and kindergartens[4], secondary teaching activities in universities[5] and the provision of education in universities[6].

Notes

[1] Judgment of the EFTA Court of 21 February 2008 in Case E-5/07.
[2] Case 263/86 *Humbel* [1988] ECR-5365.
[3] Case C-318/05 *Commission v Germany* [2007] ECR I-6957; Case C-76/05 *Schwartz* [2007] ECR-6849.
[4] Judgment of the EFTA Court of 21 February 2008 in Case E-5/07.
[5] Case C-281/06 *Jundt* [2007] ECR I-12231.
[6] Case 109/92 *Wirth* [1993] ECR I-6447.

28. Such public provision of educational services must be distinguished from services financed predominantly by parents or pupils or commercial revenues. For example, commercial enterprises offering higher education financed entirely by students clearly fall within the latter category. In certain Member States public institutions can also offer educational services which, due to their nature, financing structure and the existence of competing private organisations, are to be regarded as economic.

29. In the Community Framework for State aid for research and development and innovation[1], the Commission has clarified that certain activities of universities and research organisations fall outside the ambit of the State aid rules. This concerns the primary activities of research organisations, namely:

(a) education for more and better skilled human resources;
(b) the conduct of independent research and development for more knowledge and better understanding, including collaborative research and development; and
(c) the dissemination of research results.

Notes

[1] See Community Framework for State aid for research and development and innovation, OJ C 323, 30.12.2006, p.1.

30. The Commission has also clarified that technology transfer activities (licensing, spin-off creation or other forms of management of knowledge created by the research organisation) are non-economic

where those activities are of an internal nature[1] and all income is reinvested in the primary activities of the research organisations concerned[2].

Notes

[1] According to footnote 25 of the Community Framework for State aid for research and development and innovation, 'internal nature' means a situation where the management of the knowledge of the research organisation is conducted either by a department or a subsidiary of the research organisation or jointly with other research organisations. Contracting the provision of specific services to third parties by way of open tenders does not jeopardise the internal nature of such activities.

[2] See paragraphs 3.1.1 and 3.1.2 of the Community Framework for State aid for research and development and innovation.

2.2. State resources

31. Only advantages granted directly or indirectly through State resources can constitute State aid within the meaning of Article 107 of the Treaty[1]. Advantages financed from private resources may have the effect of strengthening the position of certain undertakings but do not fall within the scope of Article 107 of the Treaty.

Notes

[1] Joined Cases C-52/97 to C-54/97 *Viscido and Others* [1998] ECR I-2629, paragraph 13, and Case C-53/00 *Ferring* [2001] ECR I-9067, paragraph 16. See also Case C-379/98, *PreussenElektra v Schleswag* [2001] ECR I-2099.

32. This transfer of State resources may take many forms such as direct grants, tax credits and benefits in kind. In particular, the fact that the State does not charge market prices for certain services constitutes a waiver of State resources. In its judgment in Case C-482/99 *France v Commission*[1], the Court of Justice also confirmed that the resources of a public undertaking constitute State resources within the meaning of Article 107 of the Treaty because the public authorities are capable of controlling these resources. In cases where an undertaking entrusted with the operation of an SGEI is financed by resources provided by a public undertaking and this financing is imputable to the State, such financing is thus capable of constituting State aid.

Notes

[1] [2002] ECR I-4397.

33. The granting, without tendering, of licences to occupy or use public domain, or of other special or exclusive rights having an economic value, may imply a waiver of State resources and create an advantage for the beneficiaries[1].

Notes

[1] Case C-462/99 *Connect Austria Gesellschaft für Telekommunikation GmbH v Telekom-Control-Kommission, and Mobilkom Austria AG* [2003] ECR I-05197, paragraphs 92 and 93; Case T-475/04 *Bouygues and Bouygues Télécom SA v Commission* [2007] ECR II-02097, paragraphs 101, 104, 105 and 111.

34. Member States may, in some instances, finance an SGEI from charges or contributions paid by certain undertakings or users, the revenue from which is transferred to the undertakings entrusted with the operation of that SGEI. This type of financing arrangement has been examined by the Court of Justice, in particular in its judgment in Case 173/73 Italy v Commission[1], in which it held that:

'As the funds in question are financed through compulsory contributions imposed by State legislation and as, as this case shows, they are managed and apportioned in accordance with the provisions of that legislation, they must be regarded as State resources within the meaning of Article (107 of the Treaty), even if they are administered by institutions distinct from the public authorities.'

Notes

[1] Case 173/73 *Italy v Commission* [1974] ECR 709, paragraph 16. See also Case 78/79 *Steinike* [1977] ECR 595, paragraph 21, Case C206/06, *Essent Netwerk* [2008] 5497, paragraphs 47, 57 and 96.

35. Similarly, in its judgment in Joined Cases C-78/90 to C-83/90 Compagnie Commerciale de l'Ouest[1], the Court of Justice confirmed that measures financed through parafiscal charges constitute measures financed through State resources.

Notes

[1] *Compagnie Commerciale de l'Ouest and others v Receveur Principal des Douanes de La Pallice Port* [1992] ECR I-1847, paragraph 35. See also Joined Cases C-34/01 to C-38/01 *Enirisorse SpA v Ministero delle Finanze* [2003] ECR I-14243, paragraph 26.

36. Accordingly, compensatory payments for the operation of SGEIs which are financed through parafiscal charges or compulsory contributions imposed by the State and managed and apportioned in accordance with the provisions of the legislation are compensatory payments made through State resources.

2.3. Effect on trade

37. In order to be caught by Article 107 of the Treaty, public service compensation must affect or threaten to affect trade between Member States. Such an effect generally presupposes the existence of a market open to competition. Therefore, where markets have been opened up to competition either by Union or national legislation or *de facto* by economic development, State aid rules apply. In such situations Member States retain their discretion as to how to define, organise and finance SGEIs, subject to State aid control where compensation is granted to the SGEI provider, be it private or public (including in-house). Where the market has been reserved for a single undertaking (including an in-house provider), the compensation granted to that undertaking is equally subject to State aid control. In fact, where economic activity has been opened up to competition, the decision to provide the SGEI by methods other than through a public procurement procedure that ensures the least cost to the community may lead to distortions in the form of preventing entry by competitors or making easier the expansion of the beneficiary in other markets. Distortions may also occur in the input markets. Aid granted to an undertaking operating on a non-liberalised market may affect trade if the recipient undertaking is also active on liberalised markets[1].

Notes

[1] Joined Cases T-298/97, T-312/97, T-313/97, T-315/97, T-600/97 to T-607/97, T-1/98, T-3/98 to T-6/98 and T-23/98, *Mauro Alzetta and others v Commission* [2000] ECR II-2319, paragraphs 143–147.

38. Aid measures can also have an effect on trade where the recipient undertaking does not itself participate in cross-border activities. In such cases, domestic supply may be maintained or increased, with the consequence that the opportunities for undertakings established in other Member States to offer their services in that Member State are reduced[1].

Notes

[1] See, in particular, Case C-280/00 *Altmark Trans GmbH and Regierungspräsidium Magdeburg v Nahverkehrsgesellschaft Altmark GmbH* [2003] ECR I-7747.

39. According to the case-law of the Court of Justice, there is no threshold or percentage below which trade between Member States can be regarded as not having been affected[1]. The relatively small amount of aid or the relatively small size of the recipient undertaking does not *a priori* mean that trade between Member States may not be affected.

Notes

[1] Case C-280/00 *Altmark Trans GmbH and Regierungspräsidium Magdeburg v Nahverkehrsgesellschaft Altmark GmbH*, paragraph 81.

40. On the other hand, the Commission has in several cases concluded that activities had a purely local character and did not affect trade between Member States. Examples are:

(a) swimming pools to be used predominantly by the local population[1];

(b) local hospitals aimed exclusively at the local population[2];

(c) local museums unlikely to attract cross-border visitors[3]; and

(d) local cultural events, whose potential audience is restricted locally[4].

Notes

[1] Commission Decision in Case N 258/00 — *Germany — Leisure Pool Dorsten*, OJ C 172, 16.6.2001, p.16.

[2] Commission Decision in Case N 543/01 — *Ireland — Capital allowances for hospitals*, OJ C 154, 28.6.2002, p.4.

[3] Commission Decision in Case N 630/03 — *Italy — Local museums — Sardinia*, OJ C 275, 8.12.2005, p.3.

[4] Commission Decision in Case N 257/07 — *Spain — Grants for theatrical productions in the Basque Country*, OJ C 173, 26.7.2007, p.2.

41. Finally, the Commission does not have to examine all financial support granted by Member States. Regulation (EC) No 1998/2006 of 15 December 2006 on the application of Articles [107] and [108] of the Treaty to *de minimis* aid[1] stipulates that aid amounting to less than EUR 200 000 per undertaking over any period of three years is not caught by Article 107(1) of the Treaty. Specific *de minimis* thresholds apply in the transport, fisheries and agricultural sectors[6] and the Commission envisages adopting a Regulation with a specific *de minimis* threshold for local services of general economic interest.

Notes

[1] Commission Regulation (EC) No 1998/2006 of 15 December 2006 on the application of Articles [107] and [108] of the [Treaty on the Functioning of the European Union] to *de minimis* aid, OJ L 379, 28.12.2006, p.5.

[2] See Article 2(2) of Regulation (EC) No 1998/2006 for transport; Commission Regulation (EC) No 875/2007 of 24 July 2007 on the application of Articles [107] and [108] of the Treaty to *de minimis* aid in the fisheries sector and amending Regulation (EC) No 1860/2004 (OJ L 193, 25.7.2007, p.6); and Commission Regulation (EC) No 1535/2007 of 20 December 2007 on the application of Articles [107] and [108] of the [Treaty on the Functioning of the European Union] to *de minimis* aid in the sector of agricultural production (OJ L 337, 21.12.2007, p.35).

3. CONDITIONS UNDER WHICH PUBLIC SERVICE COMPENSATION DOES NOT CONSTITUTE STATE AID

3.1. The criteria established by the Court of Justice

42. The Court of Justice, in its Altmark judgment[1], provided further clarification regarding the conditions under which public service compensation does not constitute State aid owing to the absence of any advantage.

Notes

[1] Case C-280/00 *Altmark Trans GmbH and Regierungspräsidium Magdeburg v Nahverkehrsgesellschaft Altmark GmbH.*

43. According to the Court of Justice,

'Where a State measure must be regarded as compensation for the services provided by the recipient undertakings in order to discharge public service obligations, so that those undertakings do not enjoy a real financial advantage and the measure thus does not have the effect of putting them in a more favourable competitive position than the undertakings competing with them, such a measure is not caught by Article (107(1) of the Treaty). However, for such compensation to escape qualification as State aid in a particular case, a number of conditions must be satisfied.

— . . . First, the recipient undertaking must actually have public service obligations to discharge, and the obligations must be clearly defined. . . .

— . . . Second, the parameters on the basis of which the compensation is calculated must be established in advance in an objective and transparent manner, to avoid it conferring an economic advantage which may favour the recipient undertaking over competing undertakings. . . . Payment by a Member State of compensation for the loss incurred by an undertaking without the parameters of such compensation having been established beforehand, where it turns out after the event that the operation of certain services in connection with the discharge of public service obligations was not economically viable, therefore constitutes a financial measure which falls within the concept of State aid within the meaning of Article (107(1) of the Treaty).

— ...Third, the compensation cannot exceed what is necessary to cover all or part of the costs incurred in the discharge of public service obligations, taking into account the relevant receipts and a reasonable profit...

— ...Fourth, where the undertaking which is to discharge public service obligations, in a specific case, is not chosen pursuant to a public procurement procedure which would allow for the selection of the tenderer capable of providing those services at the least cost to the community, the level of compensation needed must be determined on the basis of an analysis of the costs which a typical undertaking, well run and adequately provided with means of transport so as to be able to meet the necessary public service requirements, would have incurred in discharging those obligations, taking into account the relevant receipts and a reasonable profit for discharging the obligations' [1].

Notes

[1] Case C-280/00 *Altmark Trans GmbH and Regierungspräsidium Magdeburg v Nahverkehrsgesellschaft Altmark GmbH*, paragraphs 87 to 93.

44. Sections 3.2 to 3.6 will address the different requirements established in the *Altmark* case-law, namely the concept of a service of general economic interest for the purposes of Article 106 of the Treaty[1], the need for an entrustment act[2], the obligation to define the parameters of compensation[3], the principles concerning the avoidance of overcompensation[4] and the principles concerning the selection of the provider[5].

Notes

[1] See section 3.2.
[2] See section 3.3.
[3] See section 3.4.
[4] See section 3.5.
[5] See section 3.6.

3.2. Existence of a service of general economic interest

45. The concept of service of general economic interest is an evolving notion that depends, among other things, on the needs of citizens, technological and market developments and social and political preferences in the Member State concerned. The Court of Justice has established that SGEIs are services that exhibit special characteristics as compared with those of other economic activities[1].

Notes

[1] Cases C-179/90 *Merci convenzionali porto di Genova* [1991] ECR I-5889, paragraph 27; Case C-242/95 *GT-Link A/S* [1997] ECR I-4449, paragraph 53; and Case C-266/96, *Corsica Ferries France SA* [1998] ECR I-3949, paragraph 45.

46. In the absence of specific Union rules defining the scope for the existence of an SGEI, Member States have a wide margin of discretion in defining a given service as an SGEI and in granting compensation to the service provider. The Commission's competence in this respect is limited to checking whether the Member State has made a manifest error when defining the service as an SGEI[1] and to assessing any State aid involved in the compensation. Where specific Union rules exist, the Member States' discretion is further bound by those rules, without prejudice to the Commission's duty to carry out an assessment of whether the SGEI has been correctly defined for the purpose of State aid control.

Notes

[1] Case T-289/03 *BUPA and Others v Commission* [2008] ECR II-81, paragraphs 166–169 and 172; Case T-17/02 *Fred Olsen* [2005] ECR II-2031, paragraph 216.

47. The first Altmark criterion requires the definition of an SGEI task. This requirement coincides with that of Article 106(2) of the Treaty[1]. It transpires from Article 106(2) of the Treaty that undertakings entrusted with the operation of SGEIs are undertakings entrusted with 'a particular task'[2]. Generally speaking, the entrustment of a 'particular public service task' implies the supply of services which, if it were considering its own commercial interest, an undertaking would not assume or would not assume to the same extent or under the same conditions[3]. Applying a general interest criterion, Member States or the Union may attach specific obligations to such services.

Notes

[1] Case T-289/03 *British United Provident Association Ltd (BUPA) v Commission* [2008], ECR II-81, paragraphs. 171 and 224.

[2] See, in particular, Case C-127/73 *BRT v SABAM* [1974] ECR-313.

[3] See, in particular, Article 2 of Regulation (EC) No 1370/2007 of the European Parliament and of the Council of 23 October 2007 on public passenger transport services by rail and by road and repealing Council Regulations (EEC) Nos 1191/69 and 1107/70 (OJ L 315, 3.12.2007, p.1).

48. The Commission thus considers that it would not be appropriate to attach specific public service obligations to an activity which is already provided or can be provided satisfactorily and under conditions, such as price, objective quality characteristics, continuity and access to the service, consistent with the public interest, as defined by the State, by undertakings operating under normal market conditions[1]. As for the question of whether a service can be provided by the market, the Commission's assessment is limited to checking whether the Member State has made a manifest error.

Notes

[1] Case C-205/99 *Analir* [2001] ECR I-1271, paragraph 71.

Commentary

para 48: F&N:17.370

49. An important example of this principle is the broadband sector, for which the Commission has already given clear indications as to the types of activities that can be regarded as SGEIs. Most importantly, the Commission considers that in areas where private investors have already invested in broadband network infrastructure (or are in the process of expanding further their network infrastructure) and are already providing competitive broadband services with adequate coverage, setting up parallel broadband infrastructure should not be considered as an SGEI. In contrast, where investors are not in a position to provide adequate broadband coverage, SGEI compensation may be granted under certain conditions[1].

Notes

[1] For more detailed provisions see paragraphs 24 to 30 of the Communication from the Commission — Community Guidelines for the application of State aid rules in relation to rapid deployment of broadband networks (OJ C 235, 30.9.2009, p.7).

50. The Commission also considers that the services to be classified as SGEIs must be addressed to citizens or be in the interest of society as a whole.

3.3. Entrustment act

51. For Article 106(2) of the Treaty to apply, the operation of an SGEI must be entrusted to one or more undertakings. The undertakings in question must therefore have been entrusted with a special task by the State[1]. Also the first Altmark criterion requires that the undertaking has a public service obligation to discharge. Accordingly, in order to comply with the Altmark case-law, a public service assignment is necessary that defines the obligations of the undertakings in question and of the authority.

Notes

[1] See, in particular, Case C-127/73 *BRT v SABAM* [1974] ECR-313.

52. The public service task must be assigned by way of an act that, depending on the legislation in Member States, may take the form of a legislative or regulatory instrument or a contract. It may also be laid down in several acts. Based on the approach taken by the Commission in such cases, the act or series of acts must at least specify:

(a) the content and duration of the public service obligations;
(b) the undertaking and, where applicable, the territory concerned;
(c) the nature of any exclusive or special rights assigned to the undertaking by the authority in question;
(d) the parameters for calculating, controlling and reviewing the compensation; and
(e) the arrangements for avoiding and recovering any overcompensation.

Commentary
para 52: F&N:17.371

53. The involvement of the service provider in the process by which it is entrusted with a public service task does not mean that that task does not derive from an act of public authority, even if the entrustment is issued at the request of the service provider[1]. In some Member States, it is not uncommon for authorities to finance services which were developed and proposed by the provider itself. However, the authority has to decide whether it approves the provider's proposal before it may grant any compensation. It is irrelevant whether the necessary elements of the entrustment act are inserted directly into the decision to accept the provider's proposal or whether a separate legal act, for example, a contract with the provider, is put in place.

Notes
[1] Case T-17/02 *Fred Olsen*, paragraph 188.

3.4. Parameters of compensation

54. The parameters that serve as the basis for calculating compensation must be established in advance in an objective and transparent manner in order to ensure that they do not confer an economic advantage that could favour the recipient undertaking over competing undertakings.

55. The need to establish the compensation parameters in advance does not mean that the compensation has to be calculated on the basis of a specific formula (for example, a certain price per day, per meal, per passenger or per number of users). What matters is only that it is clear from the outset how the compensation is to be determined.

56. Where the authority decides to compensate all cost items of the provider, it must determine at the outset how those costs will be determined and calculated. Only the costs directly associated with the provision of the SGEI can be taken into account in that context. All the revenue accruing to the undertaking from the provision of the SGEI must be deducted.

57. Where the undertaking is offered a reasonable profit as part of its compensation, the entrustment act must also establish the criteria for calculating that profit.

58. Where a review of the amount of compensation during the entrustment period is provided for, the entrustment act must specify the arrangements for the review and any impact it may have on the total amount of compensation.

59. If the SGEI is assigned under a tendering procedure, the method for calculating the compensation must be included in the information provided to all the undertakings wishing to take part in the procedure.

3.5. Avoidance of overcompensation

60. According to the third Altmark criterion, the compensation must not exceed what is necessary to cover all or part of the costs incurred in the discharge of public service obligations, taking into account the relevant receipts and a reasonable profit. Therefore any mechanism concerning the selection of the

service provider must be decided in such a way that the level of compensation is determined on the basis of these elements.

61. Reasonable profit should be taken to mean the rate of return on capital[1] that would be required by a typical company considering whether or not to provide the service of general economic interest for the whole duration of the period of entrustment, taking into account the level of risk. The level of risk depends on the sector concerned, the type of service and the characteristics of the compensation mechanism. The rate should be determined where possible by reference to the rate of return on capital that is achieved on similar types of public service contracts under competitive conditions (for example, contracts awarded under a tender). In sectors where there is no undertaking comparable to the undertaking entrusted with the operation of the service of general economic interest, reference can be made to comparable undertakings situated in other Member States, or if necessary, in other sectors, provided that the particular characteristics of each sector are taken into account. In determining what constitutes a reasonable profit, the Member States may introduce incentive criteria relating, in particular, to the quality of service provided and gains in productive efficiency. Efficiency gains cannot be achieved at the expense of the quality of the service provided.

Notes

[1] The rate of return on capital means the Internal Rate of Return (IRR) that the undertaking makes on its invested capital over the lifetime of the project, that is to say the IRR over the cash flows of the contract.

3.6. Selection of provider

62. In accordance with the fourth Altmark criterion, the compensation offered must either be the result of a public procurement procedure which allows for selection of the tenderer capable of providing those services at the least cost to the community, or the result of a benchmarking exercise with a typical undertaking, well run and adequately provided with the necessary means.

3.6.1. *Amount of compensation where the SGEI is assigned under an appropriate tendering procedure*

63. The simplest way for public authorities to meet the fourth Altmark criterion is to conduct an open, transparent and non-discriminatory public procurement procedure in line with Directive 2004/17/EC of the European Parliament and of the Council of 31 March 2004 coordinating the procurement procedures of entities operating in the water, energy, transport and postal services sectors[1] and Directive 2004/18/EC of the European Parliament and of the Council of 31 March 2004 on the coordination of procedures for the award of public works contracts, public supply contracts and public service contracts[2], as specified below[3]. As indicated in paragraph 5, the conduct of such a public procurement procedure is often a mandatory requirement under existing Union rules.

Notes

[1] OJ L 134, 30.4.2004, p.114.

[2] OJ L 134, 30.4.2004, p.1.

[3] The Commission intends to amend this Communication once new Union rules on public procurement have been adopted in order to clarify the relevance for State aid purposes of the use of the procedures foreseen in those new rules.

64. Also in cases where it is not a legal requirement, an open, transparent and non-discriminatory public procurement procedure is an appropriate method to compare different potential offers and set the compensation so as to exclude the presence of aid.

65. Based on the case law of the Court of Justice, a public procurement procedure only excludes the existence of State aid where it allows for the selection of the tenderer capable of providing the service at 'the least cost to the community'.

66. Concerning the characteristics of the tender, an open[1] procedure in line with the requirement of the public procurement rules is certainly acceptable, but also a restricted[2] procedure can satisfy the fourth Altmark criterion, unless interested operators are prevented to tender without valid reasons.

On the other hand, a competitive dialogue[3] or a negotiated procedure with prior publication[4] confer a wide discretion upon the adjudicating authority and may restrict the participation of interested operators. Therefore, they can only be deemed sufficient to satisfy the fourth *Altmark* criterion in exceptional cases. The negotiated procedure without publication of a contract notice[5] cannot ensure that the procedure leads to the selection of the tenderer capable of providing those services at the least cost to the community.

Notes

[1] Article 1(11)(a) of Directive 2004/18EC, Article 1(9)(a) of Directive 2004/17/EC.

[2] Article 1(11)(b) of Directive 2004/18EC, Article 1(9)(b) of Directive 2004/17/EC.

[3] Article 29 of Directive 2004/18/EC.

[4] Article 30 of Directive 2004/18/EC, Article 1(9)(a) of Directive 2004/17/EC.

[5] Article 31 of Directive 2004/18/EC. See also Article 40(3) of Directive 2004/17/EC.

---

67. As to the award criteria, the 'lowest price'[1] obviously satisfies the fourth *Altmark* criterion. Also the 'most economically advantageous tender'[2] is deemed sufficient, provided that the award criteria, including environmental[3] or social ones, are closely related to the subject-matter of the service provided and allow for the most economically advantageous offer to match the value of the market[4]. Where such circumstances occur, a claw-back mechanism may be appropriate to minimise the risk of overcompensation ex ante. The awarding authority is not prevented from setting qualitative standards to be met by all economic operators or from taking qualitative aspects related to the different proposals into account in its award decision.

Notes

[1] Article 53(1)(b) of Directive 2004/18/EC, Article 55 (1)(b) of Directive 2004/17/EC.

[2] Article 53(1)(a) of Directive 2004/18/EC, Article 55(1)(a) of Directive 2004/17/EC; Case 31/87 *Beentjes* [1988] ECR 4635 and Case C-225/98 *Commission v France* [2000] ECR I-7445; Case C-19/00 *SIAC Construction* [2001] ECR I-7725.

[3] See for example a new edition of 'Buying Green! A Handbook on Green public procurement', available at: http://ec.europa.eu/environment/gpp/buying_handbook_en.htm

[4] In other words, the criteria should be defined in such a way as to allow for an effective competition that minimises the advantage for the successful bidder.

Commentary

para 67: F&N:17.375

---

68. Finally, there can be circumstances where a procurement procedure cannot allow for the least cost to the community as it does not give rise to a sufficient open and genuine competition. This could be the case, for example, due to the particularities of the service in question, existing intellectual property rights or necessary infrastructure owned by a particular service provider. Similarly, in the case of procedures where only one bid is submitted, the tender cannot be deemed sufficient to ensure that the procedure leads to the least cost for the community.

3.6.2. *Amount of compensation where the SGEI is not assigned under a tendering procedure*

69. Where a generally accepted market remuneration exists for a given service, that market remuneration provides the best benchmark for the compensation in the absence of a tender[1].

Notes

[1] See for example Commission Decision in Case C 49/06 — *Italy — State aid scheme implemented by Italy to remunerate Poste Italiane for distributing postal savings certificates* (OJ L 189, 21.7.2009, p.3).

Commentary

para 69: F&N:17.376

---

70. Where no such market remuneration exists, the amount of compensation must be determined on the basis of an analysis of the costs that a typical undertaking, well run and adequately provided with material means so as to be able to meet the necessary public service requirements, would have incurred

in discharging those obligations, taking into account the relevant receipts and a reasonable profit for discharging those obligations. The aim is to ensure that the high costs of an inefficient undertaking are not taken as the benchmark.

Commentary
para 70: F&N:17.376

71. As regards the concept of 'well run undertaking' and in the absence of any official definition, the Member States should apply objective criteria that are economically recognised as being representative of satisfactory management. The Commission considers that simply generating a profit is not a sufficient criterion for deeming an undertaking to be 'well run'. Account should also be taken of the fact that the financial results of undertakings, particularly in the sectors most often concerned by SGEIs, may be strongly influenced by their market power or by sectoral rules.

72. The Commission takes the view that the concept of 'well run undertaking' entails compliance with the national, Union or international accounting standards in force. The Member States may base their analysis, among other things, on analytical ratios representative of productivity (such as turnover to capital employed, total cost to turnover, turnover per employee, value added per employee or staff costs to value added). Member States can also use analytical ratios relating to the quality of supply as compared with user expectations. An undertaking entrusted with the operation of an SGEI that does not meet the qualitative criteria laid down by the Member State concerned does not constitute a well run undertaking even if its costs are low.

73. Undertakings with such analytical ratios representative of efficient management may be regarded as representative typical undertakings. However, the analysis and comparison of the cost structures must take into account the size of the undertaking in question and the fact that in certain sectors undertakings with very different cost structures may exist side by side.

74. The reference to the costs of a 'typical' undertaking in the sector under consideration implies that there are a sufficient number of undertakings whose costs may be taken into account. Those undertakings may be located in the same Member State or in other Member States. However, the Commission takes the view that reference cannot be made to the costs of an undertaking that enjoys a monopoly position or receives public service compensation granted on conditions that do not comply with Union law, as in both cases the cost level may be higher than normal. The costs to be taken into consideration are all the costs relating to the SGEI, that is to say, the direct costs necessary to discharge the SGEI and an appropriate contribution to the indirect costs common to both the SGEI and other activities.

75. If the Member State can show that the cost structure of the undertaking entrusted with the operation of the SGEI corresponds to the average cost structure of efficient and comparable undertakings in the sector under consideration, the amount of compensation that will allow the undertaking to cover its costs, including a reasonable profit, is deemed to comply with the fourth *Altmark* criterion.

76. The expression 'undertaking adequately provided with material means' should be taken to mean an undertaking which has the resources necessary for it to discharge immediately the public service obligations incumbent on the undertaking to be entrusted with the operation of the SGEI.

77. 'Reasonable profit' should be taken to mean the rate of return on capital[1] that would be required by a typical company considering whether or not to provide the service of general economic interest for the whole duration of the period of entrustment, taking into account the level of risk, as provided in section 3.5.

Notes

[1] The rate of return on capital means the Internal Rate of Return (IRR) that the undertaking makes on its invested capital over the lifetime of the project, that is to say the IRR over the cash flows of the contract.

F5

COMMUNICATION FROM THE COMMISSION — EUROPEAN UNION FRAMEWORK FOR STATE AID IN THE FORM OF PUBLIC SERVICE COMPENSATION (2011)

(Text with EEA relevance)

(2012/C 8/03)

Official Journal C 8, 11.1.2012, p.15

Celex No: 52012XC0111(03)

EUR-Lex permanent link: <http://eur-lex.europa.eu/legal-content/EN/ALL/?uri=CELEX:52012X C0111(03)&qid=1395773545645>

Notes

* Ed note: please see the Note on the Lisbon Treaty at p.xvii in regard to article renumbering introduced by the Lisbon Treaty. **EEA Application:** see EFTA Surveillance Authority Decision No 12/12/COL of 25 January 2012 amending, for the eighty-fourth time, the procedural and substantive rules in the field of state aid by introducing new chapters on the application of state aid rules to compensation granted for the provision of services of general economic interest and on the framework for state aid in the form of public service compensation, OJ L 161, 13.6.2013, p.12.

Commentary
B&C: 11.048, 17.073 F&N: 17.368

---

1. PURPOSE AND SCOPE

1. For certain services of general economic interest (SGEIs) to operate on the basis of principles and under conditions that enable them to fulfil their missions, financial support from the public authorities may prove necessary where revenues accruing from the provision of the service do not allow the costs resulting from the public service obligation to be covered.

2. It follows from the case-law of the Court of Justice of the European Union[1] that public service compensation does not constitute State aid within the meaning of Article 107(1) of the Treaty on the Functioning of the European Union if it fulfils a certain number of conditions[2]. Where those conditions are met, Article 108 of the Treaty does not apply.

Notes

[1] Judgments in Case C-280/00 *Altmark Trans GmbH and Regierungspräsidium Magdeburg v Nahverkehrsgesellschaft Altmark GmbH ('Altmark')* [2003] ECR I-7747 and Joined Cases C-34/01 to C-38/01 *Enirisorse SpA v Ministero delle Finanze* [2003] ECR I-14243.

[2] In its judgment in *Altmark*, the Court of Justice held that public service compensation does not constitute State aid if four cumulative criteria are met. First, the recipient undertaking must actually have public service obligations to discharge, and the obligations must be clearly defined. Second, the parameters on the basis of which the compensation is calculated must be established in advance in an objective and transparent manner. Third, the compensation cannot exceed what is necessary to cover all or part of the costs incurred in the discharge of the public service obligations, taking into account the relevant receipts and a reasonable profit. Finally, where the undertaking which is to discharge public service obligations, in a specific case, is not chosen pursuant to a public procurement procedure which would allow for the selection of the tenderer capable of providing those services at the least cost to the community, the level of compensation needed must be determined on the basis of an analysis of the costs which a typical undertaking, well run and adequately provided with the relevant means, would have incurred.

3. Where public service compensation does not meet those conditions, and to the extent the general criteria for the applicability of Article 107(1) of the Treaty are satisfied, such compensation constitutes State aid and is subject to Articles 106, 107 and 108 of the Treaty.

4. In its Communication on the application of the European Union State aid rules to compensation granted for the provision of services of general economic interest[1], the Commission has clarified the conditions under which public service compensation is to be regarded as State aid. Furthermore, in its Commission Regulation on the application of Articles 107 and 108 of the Treaty on the Functioning of the European Union to *de minimis* aid granted to undertakings providing services of general economic interest[2], the Commission will set out the conditions under which small amounts of public service compensation should be deemed not to affect trade between Member States and/or not to distort or threaten to distort competition. In those circumstances, compensation is not caught by Article 107(1) of the Treaty and consequently does not fall under the notification procedure provided for in Article 108(3) of the Treaty.

Notes
[1] See [OJ C 8, 11.1.12, p.23].
[2] See [OJ C 8, 11.1.12, p.4].

5. Article 106(2) of the Treaty provides the legal basis for assessing the compatibility of State aid for SGEIs. It states that undertakings entrusted with the operation of SGEIs or having the character of a revenue-producing monopoly are subject to the rules contained in the Treaty, in particular to the rules on competition. However, Article 106(2) of the Treaty provides for an exception from the rules contained in the Treaty insofar as the application of the competition rules would obstruct, in law or in fact, the performance of the tasks assigned. This exception only applies where the development of trade is not affected to such an extent as would be contrary to the interests of the Union.

6. Commission Decision 2012/21/EU[1] on the application of Article 106(2) of the Treaty on the Functioning of the European Union to State aid in the form of public service compensation granted to certain undertakings entrusted with the operation of services of general economic interest[2] lays down the conditions under which certain types of public service compensation are to be regarded as compatible with the internal market pursuant to Article 106(2) of the Treaty and exempt from the requirement of prior notification under Article 108(3) of the Treaty.

Notes
[1] OJ L 7, 11.1.2012, p.3.
[2] OJ L 7, 11.1.2012.

7. The principles set out in this Communication apply to public service compensation only in so far as it constitutes State aid not covered by Decision 2012/21/EU. Such compensation is subject to the prior notification requirement under Article 108(3) of the Treaty. This Communication spells out the conditions under which such State aid can be found compatible with the internal market pursuant to Article 106(2) of the Treaty. It replaces the Community framework for State aid in the form of public service compensation[1].

Notes
[1] OJ C 297, 29.11.2005, p.4.

8. The principles set out in this Communication apply to public service compensation in the field of air and maritime transport, without prejudice to stricter specific provisions contained in sectoral Union legislation. They apply neither to the land transport sector, nor to the public service broadcasting sector, which is covered by the Communication from the Commission on the application of State aid rules to public service broadcasting[1].

Notes
[1] OJ C 257, 27.10.2009, p.1.

9. Aid for providers of SGEIs in difficulty will be assessed under the Community guidelines on State aid for rescuing and restructuring firms in difficulty[1].

Notes
1 OJ C 244, 1.10.2004, p.2.

10. The principles set out in this Communication apply without prejudice to:

(a) requirements imposed by Union law in the field of competition (in particular Articles 101 and 102 of the Treaty);

(b) requirements imposed by Union law in the field of public procurement;

(c) the provisions of the Commission Directive 2006/111/EC of 16 November 2006 on the transparency of financial relations between Member States and public undertakings as well as on financial transparency within certain undertakings[1];

(d) additional requirements flowing from the Treaty or from sectoral Union legislation.

Notes
1 OJ L 318, 17.11.2006, p.17.

2. CONDITIONS GOVERNING THE COMPATIBILITY OF PUBLIC SERVICE COMPENSATION THAT CONSTITUTES STATE AID

2.1. General provisions

11. At the current stage of development of the internal market, State aid falling outside the scope of Decision 2012/21/EU may be declared compatible with Article 106(2) of the Treaty if it is necessary for the operation of the service of general economic interest concerned and does not affect the development of trade to such an extent as to be contrary to the interests of the Union. The conditions set out in sections 2.2 to 2.10 must be met in order to achieve that balance.

2.2. Genuine service of general economic interest as referred to in Article 106 of the Treaty

12. The aid must be granted for a genuine and correctly defined service of general economic interest as referred to in Article 106(2) of the Treaty.

13. In its Communication on the application of the European Union State aid rules to compensation granted for the provision of services of general economic interest, the Commission has provided guidance on the requirements concerning the definition of a service of general economic interest. In particular, Member States cannot attach specific public service obligations to services that are already provided or can be provided satisfactorily and under conditions, such as price, objective quality characteristics, continuity and access to the service, consistent with the public interest, as defined by the State, by undertakings operating under normal market conditions. As for the question of whether a service can be provided by the market, the Commission's assessment is limited to checking whether the Member State's definition is vitiated by a manifest error, unless provisions of Union law provide a stricter standard.

14. For the scope of application of the principles set out in this Communication, Member States should show that they have given proper consideration to the public service needs supported by way of a public consultation or other appropriate instruments to take the interests of users and providers into account. This does not apply where it is clear that a new consultation will not bring any significant added value to a recent consultation.

2.3. Need for an entrustment act specifying the public service obligations and the methods of calculating compensation

15. Responsibility for the operation of the SGEI must be entrusted to the undertaking concerned by way of one or more acts, the form of which may be determined by each Member State. The term 'Member State' covers the central, regional and local authorities.

16. The act or acts must include, in particular:

(a) the content and duration of the public service obligations;

(b) the undertaking and, where applicable, the territory concerned;

1300

(c) the nature of any exclusive or special rights assigned to the undertaking by the granting authority;

(d) the description of the compensation mechanism and the parameters for calculating, monitoring and reviewing the compensation; and

(e) the arrangements for avoiding and recovering any overcompensation.

2.4. Duration of the period of entrustment

17. The duration of the period of entrustment should be justified by reference to objective criteria such as the need to amortise non-transferable fixed assets. In principle, the duration of the period of entrustment should not exceed the period required for the depreciation of the most significant assets required to provide the SGEI.

2.5. Compliance with the Directive 2006/111/EC

18. Aid will be considered compatible with the internal market on the basis of Article 106(2) of the Treaty only where the undertaking complies, where applicable, with Directive 2006/111/EC[1]. Aid that does not comply with that Directive is considered to affect the development of trade to an extent that would be contrary to the interest of the Union within the meaning of Article 106(2) of the Treaty.

Notes

[1] Directive 2006/111/EC on the transparency of financial relations between Member States and public undertakings as well as on financial transparency within certain undertakings.

2.6. Compliance with Union public procurement rules

19. Aid will be considered compatible with the internal market on the basis of Article 106(2) of the Treaty only where the responsible authority, when entrusting the provision of the service to the undertaking in question, has complied or commits to comply with the applicable Union rules in the area of public procurement. This includes any requirements of transparency, equal treatment and non-discrimination resulting directly from the Treaty and, where applicable, secondary Union law. Aid that does not comply with such rules and requirements is considered to affect the development of trade to an extent that would be contrary to the interests of the Union within the meaning of Article 106(2) of the Treaty.

2.7. Absence of discrimination

20. Where an authority assigns the provision of the same SGEI to several undertakings, the compensation should be calculated on the basis of the same method in respect of each undertaking.

2.8. Amount of compensation

21. The amount of compensation must not exceed what is necessary to cover the net cost[1] of discharging the public service obligations, including a reasonable profit.

Notes

[1] In this context, net cost means net cost as determined in paragraph 25 or costs minus revenues where the net avoided cost methodology cannot be applied.

22. The amount of compensation can be established on the basis of either the expected costs and revenues, or the costs and revenues actually incurred, or a combination of the two, depending on the efficiency incentives that the Member State wishes to provide from the outset, in accordance with paragraphs 40 and 41.

23. Where the compensation is based, in whole or in part, on expected costs and revenues, they must be specified in the entrustment act. They must be based on plausible and observable parameters concerning the economic environment in which the SGEI is being provided. They must rely, where appropriate, on the expertise of sector regulators or of other entities independent from the undertaking. Member States must indicate the sources on which these expectations are based[1]. The cost

estimation must reflect the expectations of efficiency gains achieved by the SGEI provider over the lifetime of the entrustment.

Notes

1 Public sources of information, cost levels incurred by the SGEI provider in the past, cost levels of competitors, business plans, industry reports, etc.

Net cost necessary to discharge the public service obligations

24. The net cost necessary, or expected to be necessary, to discharge the public service obligations should be calculated using the net avoided cost methodology where this is required by Union or national legislation and in other cases where this is possible.

Net avoided cost methodology

25. Under the net avoided cost methodology, the net cost necessary, or expected to be necessary, to discharge the public service obligations is calculated as the difference between the net cost for the provider of operating with the public service obligation and the net cost or profit for the same provider of operating without that obligation. Due attention must be given to correctly assessing the costs that the service provider is expected to avoid and the revenues it is expected not to receive, in the absence of the public service obligation. The net cost calculation should assess the benefits, including intangible benefits as far as possible, to the SGEI provider.

26. Annex IV to Directive 2002/22/EC of the European Parliament and of the Council of 7 March 2002 on universal service and users' rights relating to electronic communications networks and services[1], and Annex I to Directive 97/67/EC of the European Parliament and of the Council of 15 December 1997 on common rules for the development of the internal market of Community postal services and the improvement of quality of service[2], contain more detailed guidance on how to apply the net avoided cost methodology.

Notes

1 OJ L 108, 24.4.2002, p.51.
2 OJ L 15, 21.1.1998, p.14.

27. Although the Commission regards the net avoided cost methodology as the most accurate method for determining the cost of a public service obligation, there may be cases where the use of that methodology is not feasible or appropriate. In such cases, where duly justified, the Commission can accept alternative methods for calculating the net cost necessary to discharge the public service obligations, such as the methodology based on cost allocation.

Methodology based on cost allocation

28. Under the cost allocation methodology, the net cost necessary to discharge the public service obligations can be calculated as the difference between the costs and the revenues for a designated provider of fulfilling the public service obligations, as specified and estimated in the entrustment act.

29. The costs to be taken into consideration include all the costs necessary to operate the SGEI.

30. Where the activities of the undertaking in question are confined to the SGEI, all its costs may be taken into consideration.

31. Where the undertaking also carries out activities falling outside the scope of the SGEI, the costs to be taken into consideration may cover all the direct costs necessary to discharge the public service obligations and an appropriate contribution to the indirect costs common to both the SGEI and other activities. The costs linked to any activities outside the scope of the SGEI must include all the direct costs and an appropriate contribution to the common costs. To determine the appropriate contribution to the common costs, market prices for the use of the resources, where available, can be taken as a benchmark[1]. In the absence of such market prices, the appropriate contribution to the common costs can be determined by reference to the level of reasonable profit[2] the undertaking is expected to make on the activities falling outside the scope of the SGEI or by other methodologies where more appropriate.

Notes

[1] In *Chronopost* (Joined Cases C-83/01 P, C-93/01 P and C-94/01 P *Chronopost SA* [2003] ECR I-6993), the European Court of Justice referred to 'normal market conditions': 'In the absence of any possibility of comparing the situation of La Poste with that of a private group of undertakings not operating in a reserved sector, "normal market conditions", which are necessarily hypothetical, must be assessed by reference to the objective and verifiable elements which are available'.

[2] The reasonable profit will be assessed from an *ex ante* perspective (based on expected profits rather than on realised profits) in order not to remove the incentives for the undertaking to make efficiency gains when operating activities outside the SGEI.

Revenue

32. The revenue to be taken into account must include at least the entire revenue earned from the SGEI, as specified in the entrustment act, and the excessive profits generated from special or exclusive rights even if linked to other activities as provided in paragraph 45, regardless of whether those excessive profits are classified as State aid within the meaning of Article 107(1) of the Treaty.

Reasonable profit

33. Reasonable profit should be taken to mean the rate of return on capital[1] that would be required by a typical company considering whether or not to provide the service of general economic interest for the whole duration of the entrustment act, taking into account the level of risk. The level of risk depends on the sector concerned, the type of service and the characteristics of the compensation mechanism.

Notes

[1] The rate of return on capital is defined here as the Internal Rate of Return (IRR) that the company makes on its invested capital over the lifetime of the project, that is to say the IRR on the cash flows of the contract.

34. Where duly justified, profit level indicators other than the rate of return on capital can be used to determine what the reasonable profit should be, such as the average return on equity[1] over the entrustment period, the return on capital employed, the return on assets or the return on sales.

Notes

[1] In any given year the accounting measure return on equity (ROE) is defined as the ratio between earnings before interests and taxes (EBIT) and equity capital in that year. The average annual return should be computed over the lifetime of the entrustment by applying as discount factor either the company's cost of capital or the rate set by the Commission Reference rate Communication, whatever more appropriate.

35. Whatever indicator is chosen, the Member State must provide the Commission with evidence that the projected profit does not exceed what would be required by a typical company considering whether or not to provide the service, for instance by providing references to returns achieved on similar types of contracts awarded under competitive conditions.

36. A rate of return on capital that does not exceed the relevant swap rate[1] plus a premium of 100 basis points[2] is regarded as reasonable in any event. The relevant swap rate is the swap rate whose maturity and currency correspond to the duration and currency of the entrustment act.

Notes

[1] The swap rate is the longer maturity equivalent to the Inter-Bank Offered Rate (IBOR rate). It is used in the financial markets as a benchmark rate for establishing the funding rate.

[2] The premium of 100 basis points serves, inter alia, to compensate for liquidity risk related to the fact that an SGEI provider that invests capital in an SGEI contract commits that capital for the duration of the entrustment act and will be unable to sell its stake as rapidly and at as low a cost as is the case with a widely held and liquid risk-free asset.

37. Where the provision of the SGEI is connected with a substantial commercial or contractual risk, for instance because the compensation takes the form of a fixed lump sum payment covering expected net costs and a reasonable profit and the undertaking operates in a competitive environment, the reasonable profit may not exceed the level that corresponds to a rate of return on capital that

is commensurate with the level of risk. That rate should be determined where possible by reference to the rate of return on capital that is achieved on similar types of public service contracts awarded under competitive conditions (for example, contracts awarded under a tender). Where it is not possible to apply that method, other methods for establishing a return on capital may also be used, upon justification[1].

Notes

[1] For instance, by comparing the return with the weighted average cost of capital (WACC) of the company in relation to the activity in question, or with the average return on capital for the sector in recent years, taking into account whether historical data can be appropriate for forward-looking purposes.

38. Where the provision of the SGEI is not connected with a substantial commercial or contractual risk, for instance because the net cost incurred in providing the service of general economic interest is essentially compensated *ex post* in full, the reasonable profit may not exceed the level that corresponds to the level specified in paragraph 36. Such a compensation mechanism provides no efficiency incentives for the public service provider. Hence its use is strictly limited to cases where the Member State is able to justify that it is not feasible or appropriate to take into account productive efficiency and to have a contract design which gives incentives to achieve efficiency gains.

Efficiency incentives

39. In devising the method of compensation, Member States must introduce incentives for the efficient provision of SGEI of a high standard, unless they can duly justify that it is not feasible or appropriate to do so.

40. Efficiency incentives can be designed in different ways to best suit the specificity of each case or sector. For instance, Member States can define upfront a fixed compensation level which anticipates and incorporates the efficiency gains that the undertaking can be expected to make over the lifetime of the entrustment act.

41. Alternatively, Member States can define productive efficiency targets in the entrustment act whereby the level of compensation is made dependent upon the extent to which the targets have been met. If the undertaking does not meet the objectives, the compensation should be reduced following a calculation method specified in the entrustment act. In contrast, if the undertaking exceeds the objectives, the compensation should be increased following a method specified in the entrustment act. Rewards linked to productive efficiency gains are to be set at a level such as to allow balanced sharing of those gains between the undertaking and the Member State and/or the users.

42. Any such mechanism for incentivising efficiency improvements must be based on objective and measurable criteria set out in the entrustment act and subject to transparent *ex post* assessment carried out by an entity independent from the SGEI provider.

43. Efficiency gains should be achieved without prejudice to the quality of the service provided and should meet the standards laid down in Union legislation.

Provisions applicable to undertakings also carrying out activities outside the scope of the SGEI or providing several SGEIs

44. Where an undertaking carries out activities falling both inside and outside the scope of the SGEI, the internal accounts must show separately the costs and revenues associated with the SGEI and those of the other services in line with the principles set out in paragraph 31. Where an undertaking is entrusted with the operation of several SGEIs because the granting authority or the nature of the SGEI is different, the undertaking's internal accounts must make it possible to verify whether there has been any overcompensation at the level of each SGEI.

45. If the undertaking in question holds special or exclusive rights linked to activities, other than the SGEI for which aid is granted, that generate profits in excess of the reasonable profit, or benefits from other advantages granted by the State, these must be taken into consideration, irrespective of their classification for the purposes of Article 107(1) of the Treaty, and added to the undertaking's revenue. The reasonable profit on the activities for which the undertaking holds special or exclusive rights has to be assessed from an *ex ante* perspective, in the light of the risk, or the absence of risk, incurred by the

undertaking in question. That assessment also has to take into account the efficiency incentives that the Member State has introduced in relation to the provision of the services in question.

46. The Member State may decide that the profits accruing from other activities outside the scope of the SGEI, in particular those activities which rely on the infrastructure necessary to provide the SGEI, must be allocated in whole or in part to the financing of the SGEI.

Overcompensation

47. Overcompensation should be understood as compensation that the undertaking receives in excess of the amount of aid as defined in paragraph 21 for the whole duration of the contract. As stated in paragraphs 39 to 42, a surplus that results from higher than expected efficiency gains may be retained by the undertaking as additional reasonable profit as specified in the entrustment act[1].

Notes

[1] Similarly, a deficit which results from efficiency gains lower than expected should be partially borne by the undertaking when stipulated in the entrustment act.

---

48. Since overcompensation is not necessary for the operation of the SGEI, it constitutes incompatible State aid.

49. Member States must ensure that the compensation granted for operating the SGEI meets the requirements set out in this Communication and in particular that undertakings are not receiving compensation in excess of the amount determined in accordance with this the requirements set out in this section. They must provide evidence upon request from the Commission. They must carry out regular checks, or ensure that such checks are carried out, at the end of the period of entrustment and, in any event, at intervals of not more than three years. For aid granted by means other than a public procurement procedure with publication[1], checks should normally be made at least every two years.

Notes

[1] Such as aid granted in relation to in-house contracts, concessions with no competitive allocation, public procurement procedures with no prior publication.

---

50. Where the Member State has defined upfront a fixed compensation level which adequately anticipates and incorporates the efficiency gains that the public service provider can be expected to make over the period of entrustment, on the basis of a correct allocation of costs and revenues and of reasonable expectations as described in this section, the overcompensation check is in principle confined to verifying that the level of profit to which the provider is entitled in accordance with the entrustment act is indeed reasonable from an *ex ante* perspective.

2.9. Additional requirements which may be necessary to ensure that the development of trade is not affected to an extent contrary to the interests of the Union

51. The requirements set out in sections 2.1 to 2.8 are usually sufficient to ensure that aid does not distort competition in a way that is contrary to the interests of the Union.

52. It is conceivable, however, that in some exceptional circumstances, serious competition distortions in the internal market could remain unaddressed and the aid could affect trade to such an extent as would be contrary to the interest of the Union.

53. In such a case, the Commission will examine whether such distortions can be mitigated by requiring conditions or requesting commitments from the Member State.

54. Serious competition distortions such as to be contrary to the interests of the Union are only expected to occur in exceptional circumstances. The Commission will restrict its attention to those distortions where the aid has significant adverse effects on other Member States and the functioning of the internal market, for example, because they deny undertakings in important sectors of the economy the possibility to achieve the scale of operations necessary to operate efficiently.

55. Such distortions may arise, for instance, where the entrustment either has a duration which cannot be justified by reference to objective criteria (such as the need to amortise non-transferable fixed assets) or bundles a series of tasks (typically subject to separate entrustments with no loss of social

benefit and no additional costs in terms of efficiency and effectiveness in the provision of the services). In such a case, the Commission would examine whether the same public service could equally well be provided in a less distortive manner, for instance by way of a more limited entrustment in terms of duration or scope or through separate entrustments.

56. Another situation in which a more detailed assessment may be necessary is where the Member State entrusts a public service provider, without a competitive selection procedure, with the task of providing an SGEI in a non-reserved market where very similar services are already being provided or can be expected to be provided in the near future in the absence of the SGEI. Those adverse effects on the development of trade may be more pronounced where the SGEI is to be offered at a tariff below the costs of any actual or potential provider, so as to cause market foreclosure. The Commission, while fully respecting the Member State's wide margin of discretion to define the SGEI, may therefore require amendments, for instance in the allocation of the aid, where it can reasonably show that it would be possible to provide the same SGEI at equivalent conditions for the users, in a less distortive manner and at lower cost for the State.

57. Closer scrutiny is also warranted where the entrustment of the service obligation is connected with special or exclusive rights that seriously restrict competition in the internal market to an extent contrary to the interest of the Union. While the primary route for apprehending such a case remains Article 106(1) of the Treaty, the State aid may not be deemed compatible where the exclusive right provides for advantages that could not be properly assessed, quantified or apprehended according to the methodologies to calculate the net costs of the SGEI described in section 2.8.

58. The Commission will also pay attention to situations where the aid allows the undertaking to finance the creation or use of an infrastructure that is not replicable and enables it to foreclose the market where the SGEI is provided or related relevant markets. Where this is the case, it may be appropriate to require that competitors are given fair and non-discriminatory access to the infrastructure under appropriate conditions.

59. If distortions of competition are a consequence of the entrustment hindering effective implementation or enforcement of Union legislation aimed at safeguarding the proper functioning of the internal market, the Commission will examine whether the public service could equally well be provided in a less distortive manner, for instance by fully implementing the sectoral Union legislation.

2.10. Transparency

60. For each SGEI compensation falling within the scope of this Communication, the Member State concerned must publish the following information on the internet or by other appropriate means:

(a) the results of the public consultation or other appropriate instruments referred to in paragraph 14;
(b) the content and duration of the public service obligations;
(c) the undertaking and, where applicable, the territory concerned;
(d) the amounts of aid granted to the undertaking on a yearly basis.

2.11. Aid which meets the conditions laid down in Article 2(1) of Decision 2012/21/EU

61. The principles set out in paragraphs 14, 19, 20, 24, 39, 51 to 59 and 60(a) do not apply to aid which meets the conditions laid down in Article 2(1) of Decision 2012/21/EU.

3. REPORTING AND EVALUATION

62. Member States shall report to the Commission on the compliance with this Communication every two years. The reports must provide an overview of the application of this Communication to the different sectors of service providers, including:

(a) a description of the application of the principles set out in this Communication to the services falling within its scope, including in-house activities;
(b) the total amount of aid granted to undertakings falling within the scope of this Communication with a breakdown by the economic sector of the beneficiaries;

(c) an indication of whether, for a particular type of service, the application of the principles set out in this Communication has given rise to difficulties or complaints by third parties; and

(d) any other information concerning the application of the principles set out in this Communication required by the Commission and to be specified in due time before the report is to be submitted.

The first report shall be submitted by 30 June 2014.

63. In addition, in accordance with the requirements of Council Regulation (EC) No 659/1999 of 22 March 1999 laying down detailed rules for the application of Article [108] of the [Treaty on the Functioning of the European Union]¹ […]and Commission Regulation (EC) No 794/2004 of 21 April 2004 implementing Council Regulation (EC) No 659/1999 laying down detailed rules for the application of Article [108] of the [Treaty on the Functioning of the European Union]², Member States must submit annual reports to the Commission on the aid granted following a decision of the Commission based on this Communication.

Notes

1 OJ L 83, 27.3.1999, p.1.
2 OJ L 140, 30.4.2004, p.1.

---

64. The reports will be published on the internet site of the Commission.

65. The Commission intends to carry out a review of this Communication by 31 January 2017.

4. CONDITIONS AND OBLIGATIONS ATTACHED TO COMMISSION DECISIONS

66. Pursuant to Article 7(4) of Regulation (EC) No 659/1999, the Commission may attach to a positive decision conditions subject to which aid may be considered compatible with the internal market, and lay down obligations to enable compliance with the decision to be monitored. In the field of SGEI, conditions and obligations may be necessary in particular to ensure that aid granted to the undertakings concerned does not lead to undue distortions of competition and trade in the internal market. In this context, periodic reports or other obligations may be necessary, in the light of the specific situation of each service of general economic interest.

5. APPLICATION

67. The Commission will apply the provisions of this Communication from 31 January 2012.

68. The Commission will apply the principles set out in this Communication to all aid projects notified to it and will take a decision on those projects in accordance with those principles, even if the projects were notified prior to 31 January 2012.

69. The Commission will apply the principles set out in this Communication to unlawful aid on which it takes a decision after 31 January 2012 even if the aid was granted before this date. However, where the aid was granted before 31 January 2012, the principles set out in paragraphs 14, 19, 20, 24, 39 and 60 do not apply.

6. APPROPRIATE MEASURES

70. The Commission proposes as appropriate measures for the purposes of Article 108(1) of the Treaty that Member States publish the list of existing aid schemes regarding public service compensation which have to be brought into line with this Communication by 31 January 2013, and that they bring those aid schemes into line with this Communication by 31 January 2014.

71. Member States should confirm to the Commission by 29 February 2012 that they agree to the appropriate measures proposed. In the absence of any reply, the Commission will take it that the Member State concerned does not agree.

Part G

STATE AIDS

Horizontal Rules

Specific Aid Instruments

Reference/Discount Rates and Recovery Interest Rates

G1

[COUNCIL REGULATION (EC) No 659/1999

of 22 March 1999
laying down detailed rules for the application of Article 108 of the Treaty
on the Functioning of the European Union]*

Official Journal L 83, 27.3.1999, p.1

Celex No: 31999R0659

EUR-Lex permanent link: <http://eur-lex.europa.eu/LexUriServ/LexUriServ.do?uri=CELEX:3199
9R0659:EN:NOT>

Notes

* Ed note: The title of the Regulation was replaced as shown in square brackets by Council Regulation (EU) No 734/2013 of 22 July 2013 (OJ L 204, 31.7.13, p.15), Article 1(1), with effect from 20 August 2013. Please see also the Note on the Lisbon Treaty at p.xvii in regard to article renumbering introduced by the Lisbon Treaty. Unless otherwise stated, all Treaty article numbers are the new numbers of the Treaty on the Functioning of the European Union (TFEU) (and the Treaty on European Union (TEU)).

EEA application: this Regulation was adopted with appropriate adaptations by an agreement between EFTA States of 10 December 2001 amending Protocol 3 to the Surveillance and Court Agreement, with effect from 28 August 2003. See also EEA Agreement, Protocol 26, Article 2, Point 1 (as amended by EEA Joint Committee Decision No 164/2001 (OJ L 65, 7.3.2002, p.46 and EEA Supplement No 13, 7.3.2002, p.26) and Decision No 123/2005 (OJ L 339, 22.12.2005, p.32, and EEA Supplement No 66, 22.12.2005, p.18)). The EFTA Surveillance Authority's State Aid Guidelines are available at <http://www.eftasurv.int/state-aid/legal-framework/state-aid-guidelines/>.

Commentary

Regulation 659/99/EC: **B&C:** 1.028, 17.075 **F&N:** 17.395, 17.448, 17.450, 17.521, 17.536, 17.546

THE COUNCIL OF THE EUROPEAN UNION,

Having regard to the [Treaty on the Functioning of the European Union], and in particular Article [109] thereof,

Having regard to the proposal from the Commission,[1]

Having regard to the opinion of the European Parliament,[2]

Having regard to the opinion of the Economic and Social Committee,[3]

Notes

[1] OJ C 116, 16.4.1998, p.13.
[2] Opinion delivered on 14 January 1999 (not yet published in the Official Journal).
[3] OJ C 284, 14.9.1998, p.10.

---

(1) Whereas, without prejudice to special procedural rules laid down in regulations for certain sectors, this Regulation should apply to aid in all sectors; whereas, for the purpose of applying Articles [93] and [107] of the Treaty, the Commission has specific competence under Article [108] thereof to decide on the compatibility of State aid with the common market when reviewing existing aid, when taking decisions on new or altered aid and when taking action regarding non-compliance with its decisions or with the requirement as to notification;

(2) Whereas the Commission, in accordance with the case-law of the Court of Justice of the European Communities, has developed and established a consistent practice for the application of Article [108] of the Treaty and has laid down certain procedural rules and principles in a number of communications; whereas it is appropriate, with a view to ensuring effective and efficient procedures pursuant to Article [108] of the Treaty, to codify and reinforce this practice by means of a regulation;

(3) Whereas a procedural regulation on the application of Article [108] of the Treaty will increase transparency and legal certainty;

(4) Whereas, in order to ensure legal certainty, it is appropriate to define the circumstances under which aid is to be considered as existing aid; whereas the completion and enhancement of the internal market is a gradual process, reflected in the permanent development of State aid policy; whereas, following these developments, certain measures, which at the moment they were put into effect did not constitute State aid, may since have become aid;

(5) Whereas, in accordance with Article [108(3)] of the Treaty, any plans to grant new aid are to be notified to the Commission and should not be put into effect before the Commission has authorised it;

(6) Whereas, in accordance with [Article 4, paragraph 3 TEU], Member States are under an obligation to cooperate with the Commission and to provide it with all information required to allow the Commission to carry out its duties under this Regulation;

(7) Whereas the period within which the Commission is to conclude the preliminary examination of notified aid should be set at two months from the receipt of a complete notification or from the receipt of a duly reasoned statement of the Member State concerned that it considers the notification to be complete because the additional information requested by the Commission is not available or has already been provided; whereas, for reasons of legal certainty, that examination should be brought to an end by a decision;

(8) Whereas in all cases where, as a result of the preliminary examination, the Commission cannot find that the aid is compatible with the common market, the formal investigation procedure should be opened in order to enable the Commission to gather all the information it needs to assess the compatibility of the aid and to allow the interested parties to submit their comments; whereas the rights of the interested parties can best be safeguarded within the framework of the formal investigation procedure provided for under Article [108(2)] of the Treaty;

(9) Whereas, after having considered the comments submitted by the interested parties, the Commission should conclude its examination by means of a final decision as soon as the doubts have been removed; whereas it is appropriate, should this examination not be concluded after a period of 18 months from the opening of the procedure, that the Member State concerned has the opportunity to request a decision, which the Commission should take within two months;

(10) Whereas, in order to ensure that the State aid rules are applied correctly and effectively, the Commission should have the opportunity of revoking a decision which was based on incorrect information;

(11) Whereas, in order to ensure compliance with Article [108] of the Treaty, and in particular with the notification obligation and the standstill clause in Article [108(3)], the Commission should examine all cases of unlawful aid; whereas, in the interests of transparency and legal certainty, the procedures to be followed in such cases should be laid down; whereas when a Member State has not respected the notification obligation or the standstill clause, the Commission should not be bound by time limits;

(12) Whereas in cases of unlawful aid, the Commission should have the right to obtain all necessary information enabling it to take a decision and to restore immediately, where appropriate, undistorted competition; whereas it is therefore appropriate to enable the Commission to adopt interim measures addressed to the Member State concerned; whereas the interim measures may take the form of information injunctions, suspension injunctions and recovery injunctions; whereas the Commission should be enabled in the event of non-compliance with an information injunction, to decide on the basis of the information available and, in the event of non-compliance with suspension and recovery injunctions, to refer the matter to the Court of Justice direct, in accordance with the second subparagraph of Article [108(2)] of the Treaty;

(13) Whereas in cases of unlawful aid which is not compatible with the common market, effective competition should be restored; whereas for this purpose it is necessary that the aid, including interest, be recovered without delay; whereas it is appropriate that recovery be

effected in accordance with the procedures of national law; whereas the application of those procedures should not, by preventing the immediate and effective execution of the Commission decision, impede the restoration of effective competition; whereas to achieve this result, Member States should take all necessary measures ensuring the effectiveness of the Commission decision;

(14) Whereas for reasons of legal certainty it is appropriate to establish a period of limitation of 10 years with regard to unlawful aid, after the expiry of which no recovery can be ordered;

(15) Whereas misuse of aid may have effects on the functioning of the internal market which are similar to those of unlawful aid and should thus be treated according to similar procedures; whereas unlike unlawful aid, aid which has possibly been misused is aid which has been previously approved by the Commission; whereas therefore the Commission should not be allowed to use a recovery injunction with regard to misuse of aid;

(16) Whereas it is appropriate to define all the possibilities in which third parties have to defend their interests in State aid procedures;

(17) Whereas in accordance with Article [108(1)] of the Treaty, the Commission is under an obligation, in cooperation with Member States, to keep under constant review all systems of existing aid; whereas in the interests of transparency and legal certainty, it is appropriate to specify the scope of cooperation under that Article;

(18) Whereas, in order to ensure compatibility of existing aid schemes with the common market and in accordance with Article [108(1)] of the Treaty, the Commission should propose appropriate measures where an existing aid scheme is not, or is no longer, compatible with the common market and should initiate the procedure provided for in Article [108(2)] of the Treaty if the Member State concerned declines to implement the proposed measures;

(19) Whereas, in order to allow the Commission to monitor effectively compliance with Commission decisions and to facilitate cooperation between the Commission and Member States for the purpose of the constant review of all existing aid schemes in the Member States in accordance with Article [108(1)] of the Treaty, it is necessary to introduce a general reporting obligation with regard to all existing aid schemes;

(20) Whereas, where the Commission has serious doubts as to whether its decisions are being complied with, it should have at its disposal additional instruments allowing it to obtain the information necessary to verify that its decisions are being effectively complied with; whereas for this purpose on-site monitoring visits are an appropriate and useful instrument, in particular for cases where aid might have been misused; whereas therefore the Commission must be empowered to undertake on-site monitoring visits and must obtain the cooperation of the competent authorities of the Member States where an undertaking opposes such a visit;

(21) Whereas, in the interests of transparency and legal certainty, it is appropriate to give public information on Commission decisions while, at the same time, maintaining the principle that decisions in State aid cases are addressed to the Member State concerned; whereas it is therefore appropriate to publish all decisions which might affect the interests of interested parties either in full or in a summary form or to make copies of such decisions available to interested parties, where they have not been published or where they have not been published in full; whereas the Commission, when giving public information on its decisions, should respect the rules on professional secrecy, in accordance with Article [339] of the Treaty;

(22) Whereas the Commission, in close liaison with the Member States, should be able to adopt implementing provisions laying down detailed rules concerning the procedures under this Regulation; whereas, in order to provide for cooperation between the Commission and the competent authorities of the Member States, it is appropriate to create an Advisory Committee on State aid to be consulted before the Commission adopts provisions pursuant to this Regulation,

HAS ADOPTED THIS REGULATION:

Part G State Aids

CHAPTER I
GENERAL

Article 1
Definitions

For the purpose of this Regulation:

(a) 'aid' shall mean any measure fulfilling all the criteria laid down in Article [107(1)] of the Treaty;

(b) 'existing aid' shall mean:

[(i) without prejudice to Articles 144 and 172 of the Act of Accession of Austria, Finland and Sweden, to Annex IV, point 3 and the Appendix to said Annex of the Act of Accession of the Czech Republic, Estonia, Cyprus, Latvia, Lithuania, Hungary, Malta, Poland, Slovenia and Slovakia, to Annex V, point 2 and 3(b) and the Appendix to said Annex of the Act of Accession of Bulgaria and Romania, and to Annex IV, points 2 and 3(b) and the Appendix to said Annex of the Act of Accession of Croatia, all aid which existed prior to the entry into force of the Treaty in the respective Member States, that is to say, aid schemes and individual aid which were put into effect before, and are still applicable after, the entry into force of the Treaty;].

(ii) authorised aid, that is to say, aid schemes and individual aid which have been authorised by the Commission or by the Council;

(iii) aid which is deemed to have been authorised pursuant to Article 4(6) of this Regulation or prior to this Regulation but in accordance with this procedure;

(iv) aid which is deemed to be existing aid pursuant to Article 15;

(v) aid which is deemed to be an existing aid because it can be established that at the time it was put into effect it did not constitute an aid, and subsequently became an aid due to the evolution of the common market and without having been altered by the Member State. Where certain measures become aid following the liberalisation of an activity by Community law, such measures shall not be considered as existing aid after the date fixed for liberalisation;

(c) 'new aid' shall mean all aid, that is to say, aid schemes and individual aid, which is not existing aid, including alterations to existing aid;

(d) 'aid scheme' shall mean any act on the basis of which, without further implementing measures being required, individual aid awards may be made to undertakings defined within the act in a general and abstract manner and any act on the basis of which aid which is not linked to a specific project may be awarded to one or several undertakings for an indefinite period of time and/or for an indefinite amount;

(e) 'individual aid' shall mean aid that is not awarded on the basis of an aid scheme and notifiable awards of aid on the basis of an aid scheme;

(f) 'unlawful aid' shall mean new aid put into effect in contravention of Article [108(3)] of the Treaty;

(g) 'misuse of aid' shall mean aid used by the beneficiary in contravention of a decision taken pursuant to Article 4(3) or Article 7(3) or (4) of this Regulation;

(h) 'interested party' shall mean any Member State and any person, undertaking or association of undertakings whose interests might be affected by the granting of aid, in particular the beneficiary of the aid, competing undertakings and trade associations.

Notes

Article 1(b)(i) as shown in square brackets was inserted by Council Regulation (EU) No 519/2013 of 21 February 2013 adapting certain regulations and decisions by reason of the accession of Croatia (OJ L 158, 10.6.2013, p.74), with effect from 1 July 2013.

Commentary
Art 1(a): **B&C:** 17.080
Art 1(b)(i): **F&N:** 17.500
Art 1(b)(i)–(v): **B&C:** 17.076
Art 1(c): **B&C:** 17.080 **F&N:** 17.508
Art 1(d): **B&C:** 17.076
Art 1(e): **B&C:** 17.076

CHAPTER II
PROCEDURE REGARDING NOTIFIED AID

Article 2
Notification of new aid

1. Save as otherwise provided in regulations made pursuant to Article [109] of the Treaty or to other relevant provisions thereof, any plans to grant new aid shall be notified to the Commission in sufficient time by the Member State concerned. The Commission shall inform the Member State concerned without delay of the receipt of a notification.

2. In a notification, the Member State concerned shall provide all necessary information in order to enable the Commission to take a decision pursuant to Articles 4 and 7 (hereinafter referred to as 'complete notification').

Article 3
Standstill clause

Aid notifiable pursuant to Article 2(1) shall not be put into effect before the Commission has taken, or is deemed to have taken, a decision authorising such aid.

Article 4
Preliminary examination of the notification and decisions of the Commission

1. The Commission shall examine the notification as soon as it is received. Without prejudice to Article 8, the Commission shall take a decision pursuant to paragraphs 2, 3 or 4.

2. Where the Commission, after a preliminary examination, finds that the notified measure does not constitute aid, it shall record that finding by way of a decision.

3. Where the Commission, after a preliminary examination, finds that no doubts are raised as to the compatibility with the common market of a notified measure, in so far as it falls within the scope of Article [107(1)] of the Treaty, it shall decide that the measure is compatible with the common market (hereinafter referred to as a 'decision not to raise objections'). The decision shall specify which exception under the Treaty has been applied.

4. Where the Commission, after a preliminary examination, finds that doubts are raised as to the compatibility with the common market of a notified measure, it shall decide to initiate proceedings pursuant to Article [108(2)] of the Treaty (hereinafter referred to as a 'decision to initiate the formal investigation procedure').

5. The decisions referred to in paragraphs 2, 3 and 4 shall be taken within two months. That period shall begin on the day following the receipt of a complete notification. The notification will be considered as complete if, within two months from its receipt, or from the receipt of any additional information requested, the Commission does not request any further information. The period can be extended with the consent of both the Commission and the Member State concerned. Where appropriate, the Commission may fix shorter time limits.

6. Where the Commission has not taken a decision in accordance with paragraphs 2, 3 or 4 within the period laid down in paragraph 5, the aid shall be deemed to have been authorised by the Commission.

The Member State concerned may thereupon implement the measures in question after giving the Commission prior notice thereof, unless the Commission takes a decision pursuant to this Article within a period of 15 working days following receipt of the notice.

Commentary
Art 4(1): B&C: 17.084
Art 4(2): B&C: 17.086 F&N: 17.256
Art 4(2)–(4): B&C: 17.084
Art 4(3): B&C: 17.086, 17.097 F&N: 17.526
Art 4(4): B&C: 17.086, 17.125
Art 4(5): B&C: 17.084, 17.125 F&N: 17.423
Art 4(6): B&C: 17.085 F&N: 17.423

Article 5
[Request for information made to the notifying Member State]

1. Where the Commission considers that information provided by the Member State concerned with regard to a measure notified pursuant to Article 2 is incomplete, it shall request all necessary additional information. Where a Member State responds to such a request, the Commission shall inform the Member State of the receipt of the response.

2. Where the Member State concerned does not provide the information requested within the period prescribed by the Commission or provides incomplete information, the Commission shall send a reminder, allowing an appropriate additional period within which the information shall be provided.

3. The notification shall be deemed to be withdrawn if the requested information is not provided within the prescribed period, unless before the expiry of that period, either the period has been extended with the consent of both the Commission and the Member State concerned, or the Member State concerned, in a duly reasoned statement, informs the Commission that it considers the notification to be complete because the additional information requested is not available or has already been provided. In that case, the period referred to in Article 4(5) shall begin on the day following receipt of the statement. If the notification is deemed to be withdrawn, the Commission shall inform the Member State thereof.

Notes

The title of Article 5 was replaced as shown in square brackets by Council Regulation (EU) No 734/2013 of 22 July 2013 (OJ L 204, 31.7.13, p.15), Article 1(2), with effect from 20 August 2013.

Commentary
Art 5: B&C: 17.081 F&N: 17.425, 17.524
Art 5(1): B&C: 17.100
Art 5(2): B&C: 17.100

Article 6
Formal investigation procedure

1. The decision to initiate the formal investigation procedure shall summarise the relevant issues of fact and law, shall include a preliminary assessment of the Commission as to the aid character of the proposed measure and shall set out the doubts as to its compatibility with the common market. The decision shall call upon the Member State concerned and upon other interested parties to submit comments within a prescribed period which shall normally not exceed one month. In duly justified cases, the Commission may extend the prescribed period.

2. The comments received shall be submitted to the Member State concerned. If an interested party so requests, on grounds of potential damage, its identity shall be withheld from the Member State concerned. The Member State concerned may reply to the comments submitted within a prescribed period which shall normally not exceed one month. In duly justified cases, the Commission may extend the prescribed period.

Commentary
Art 6: F&N: 17.427, 17.522, 17.523, 17.544
Art 6(1): B&C: 17.087
Art 6(2): B&C: 17.089

[*Article 6a*
Request for information made to other sources

1. After the initiation of the formal investigation procedure provided for in Article 6, in particular as regards technically complex cases subject to substantive assessment, the Commission may, if the information provided by a Member State concerned during the course of the preliminary investigation is not sufficient, request any other Member State, an undertaking or an association of undertakings to provide all market information necessary to enable the Commission to complete its assessment of the measure at stake taking due account of the principle of proportionality, in particular for small and medium-sized enterprises.

2. The Commission may request information only:

(a) if it is limited to formal investigation procedures that have been identified by the Commission as being ineffective to date; and

(b) in so far as aid beneficiaries are concerned, if the Member State concerned agrees to the request.

3. The undertakings or associations of undertakings providing information following a Commission's request for market information based on paragraphs 6 and 7 shall submit their answer simultaneously to the Commission and to the Member State concerned, to the extent that the documents provided do not include information that is confidential vis-á-vis that Member State.

The Commission shall steer and monitor the information transmission between the Member States, undertakings or associations of undertakings concerned, and verify the purported confidentiality of the information transmitted.

4. The Commission shall request only information that is at the disposal of the Member State, undertaking or association of undertakings concerned by the request.

5. Member States shall provide the information on the basis of a simple request and within a time limit prescribed by the Commission which should normally not exceed one month. Where a Member State does not provide the information requested within that period or provides incomplete information, the Commission shall send a reminder.

6. The Commission may, by simple request, require an undertaking or an association of undertakings to provide information. Where the Commission sends a simple request for information to an undertaking or an association of undertakings, it shall state the legal basis and the purpose of the request, specify what information is required and prescribe a proportionate time limit within which the information is to be provided. It shall also refer to the fines provided for in Article 6b(1) for supplying incorrect or misleading information.

7. The Commission may, by decision, require an undertaking or an association of undertakings to provide information. Where the Commission, by decision, requires an undertaking or an association of undertakings to supply information, it shall state the legal basis, the purpose of the request, specify what information is required and prescribe a proportionate time limit within which the information is to be provided. It shall also indicate the fines provided for in Article 6b(1) and shall indicate or impose the periodic penalties payments provided for in Article 6b(2), as appropriate. In addition, it shall indicate the right of the undertaking or association of undertakings to have the decision reviewed by the Court of Justice of the European Union.

8. When issuing a request under paragraph 1 or 6, or adopting a decision under paragraph 7, the Commission shall also simultaneously provide the Member State concerned with a copy thereof. The Commission shall indicate the criteria by which it selected the recipients of the request or decision.

9. The owners of the undertakings or their representatives, or, in the case of legal persons, companies, firms or associations having no legal personality, the persons authorised to represent them by law or by their constitution, shall supply on their behalf the information requested or required. Persons duly authorised to act may supply the information on behalf of their clients. The latter shall nevertheless be held fully responsible if the information supplied is incorrect, incomplete or misleading.

Article 6b
Fines and periodic penalty payments

1. The Commission may, if deemed necessary and proportionate, impose by decision on undertakings or associations of undertakings fines not exceeding 1 % of their total turnover in the preceding business year where they, intentionally or through gross negligence:

(a) supply incorrect or misleading information in response to a request made pursuant to Article 6a(6);

(b) supply incorrect, incomplete or misleading information in response to a decision adopted pursuant to Article 6a(7), or do not supply the information within the prescribed time limit.

2. The Commission may, by decision, impose on undertakings or associations of undertakings periodic penalty payments where an undertaking or association of undertakings fails to supply complete and correct information as requested by the Commission by decision adopted pursuant to Article 6a(7).

The periodic penalty payments shall not exceed 5 % of the average daily turnover of the undertaking or association concerned in the preceding business year for each working day of delay, calculated from the date established in the decision, until it supplies complete and correct information as requested or required by the Commission.

3. In fixing the amount of the fine or periodic penalty payment, regard shall be had to the nature, gravity and duration of the infringement, taking due account of the principles of proportionality and appropriateness, in particular for small and medium-sized enterprises.

4. Where the undertakings or associations of undertakings have satisfied the obligation which the periodic penalty payment was intended to enforce, the Commission may reduce the definitive amount of the periodic penalty payment compared to that under the original decision imposing periodic penalty payments. The Commission may also waive any periodic penalty payment.

5. Before adopting any decision in accordance with paragraph 1 or 2, the Commission shall set a final deadline of two weeks to receive the missing market information from the undertakings or associations of undertakings concerned and also give them the opportunity of making known their views.

6. The Court of Justice of the European Union shall have unlimited jurisdiction within the meaning of Article 261 of the TFEU to review fines or periodic penalty payments imposed by the Commission It may cancel, reduce or increase the fine or periodic penalty payment imposed.]

Notes

Articles 6(a) and 6(b) were inserted by Council Regulation (EU) No 734/2013 of 22 July 2013 (OJ L 204, 31.7.13, p.15), Article 1(3), with effect from 20 August 2013.

Article 7
Decisions of the Commission to close the formal investigation procedure

1. Without prejudice to Article 8, the formal investigation procedure shall be closed by means of a decision as provided for in paragraphs 2 to 5 of this Article.

2. Where the Commission finds that, where appropriate following modification by the Member State concerned, the notified measure does not constitute aid, it shall record that finding by way of a decision.

3. Where the Commission finds that, where appropriate following modification by the Member State concerned, the doubts as to the compatibility of the notified measure with the common market have been removed, it shall decide that the aid is compatible with the common market (hereinafter referred to as a 'positive decision'). That decision shall specify which exception under the Treaty has been applied.

4. The Commission may attach to a positive decision conditions subject to which an aid may be considered compatible with the common market and may lay down obligations to enable compliance with the decision to be monitored (hereinafter referred to as a 'conditional decision').

5. Where the Commission finds that the notified aid is not compatible with the common market, it shall decide that the aid shall not be put into effect (hereinafter referred to as a 'negative decision').

6. Decisions taken pursuant to paragraphs 2, 3, 4 and 5 shall be taken as soon as the doubts referred to in Article 4(4) have been removed. The Commission shall as far as possible endeavour to adopt a decision within a period of 18 months from the opening of the procedure. This time limit may be extended by common agreement between the Commission and the Member State concerned.

7. Once the time limit referred to in paragraph 6 has expired, and should the Member State concerned so request, the Commission shall, within two months, take a decision on the basis of the information available to it. If appropriate, where the information provided is not sufficient to establish compatibility, the Commission shall take a negative decision.

[8. Before adopting any decision in accordance with paragraphs 2 to 5, the Commission shall give the Member State concerned the opportunity of making known its views, within a time-limit that shall not normally exceed one month, on the information received by the Commission and provided to the Member State concerned pursuant to Article 6a(3).

9. The Commission shall not use confidential information provided by respondents, which cannot be aggregated or otherwise be anonymised, in any decision taken in accordance with paragraphs 2 to 5, unless it has obtained their agreement to disclose that information to the Member State concerned. The Commission may take a reasoned decision, which shall be notified to the undertaking or association of undertakings concerned, finding that information provided by a respondent and marked as confidential is not protected, and setting a date after which the information will be disclosed. That period shall not be less than one month.

10. The Commission shall take due account of the legitimate interests of undertakings in the protection of their business secrets and other confidential information. An undertaking or an association of undertakings providing information pursuant to Article 6a, and which is not a beneficiary of the State aid measure in question may request, on grounds of potential damage, that its identity be withheld from the Member State concerned.]

Notes

Paragraphs 8, 9 and 10 were added by Council Regulation (EU) No 734/2013 of 22 July 2013 (OJ L 204, 31.7.13, p.15), Article 1(4), with effect from 20 August 2013.

Commentary

Art 7: **B&C:** 17.097
Art 7(1): **B&C:** 17.089
Art 7(2): **B&C:** 17.091
Art 7(3): **B&C:** 17.091
Art 7(4): **B&C:** 17.092
Art 7(5): **B&C:** 17.091
Art 7(6): **B&C:,** 17.089, 17.125 **F&N:** 17.429
Art 7(7): **B&C:** 17.089

Article 8
Withdrawal of notification

1. The Member State concerned may withdraw the notification within the meaning of Article 2 in due time before the Commission has taken a decision pursuant to Article 4 or 7.

2. In cases where the Commission initiated the formal investigation procedure, the Commission shall close that procedure.

Article 9
Revocation of a decision

The Commission may revoke a decision taken pursuant to Article 4(2) or (3), or Article 7(2), (3), (4), after having given the Member State concerned the opportunity to submit its comments, where the decision was based on incorrect information provided during the procedure which was a determining factor for the decision. Before revoking a decision and taking a new decision, the Commission shall open the formal investigation procedure pursuant to Article 4(4). Articles 6, 7 and 10, Article 11(1), Articles 13, 14 and 15 shall apply *mutatis mutandis*.

Commentary
Art 9: F&N: 17.442

CHAPTER III
PROCEDURE REGARDING UNLAWFUL AID

Article 10
Examination, request for information and information injunction

[1. Without prejudice to Article 20, the Commission may on its own initiative examine information regarding alleged unlawful aid from whatever source.

The Commission shall examine without undue delay any complaint submitted by any interested party in accordance with Article 20(2) and shall ensure that the Member State concerned is kept fully and regularly informed of the progress and outcome of the examination.

2. If necessary, the Commission shall request information from the Member State concerned. Article 2(2) and Article 5(1) and (2) shall apply *mutatis mutandis*.

After the initiation of the formal investigation procedure, the Commission may also request information from any other Member State, from an undertaking, or association of undertakings in accordance with Article 6a and 6b, which shall apply *mutatis mutandis*.];

3. Where, despite a reminder pursuant to Article 5(2), the Member State concerned does not provide the information requested within the period prescribed by the Commission, or where it provides incomplete information, the Commission shall by decision require the information to be provided (hereinafter referred to as an 'information injunction'). The decision shall specify what information is required and prescribe an appropriate period within which it is to be supplied.

Notes

Paragraphs 1 and 2 were replaced as shown in square brackets by Council Regulation (EU) No 734/2013 of 22 July 2013 (OJ L 204, 31.7.13, p.15), Article 1(5), with effect from 20 August 2013.

Commentary
Art 10: B&C: 17.078
Art 10(1): B&C: 17.097
Art 10(2): B&C: 17.100
Art 10(3): B&C: 17.083, 17.100 F&N: 17.448

Article 11
Injunction to suspend or provisionally recover aid

1. The Commission may, after giving the Member State concerned the opportunity to submit its comments, adopt a decision requiring the Member State to suspend any unlawful aid until the Commission has taken a decision on the compatibility of the aid with the common market (hereinafter referred to as a 'suspension injunction').

2. The Commission may, after giving the Member State concerned the opportunity to submit its comments, adopt a decision requiring the Member State provisionally to recover any unlawful aid until the Commission has taken a decision on the compatibility of the aid with the common market (hereinafter referred to as a 'recovery injunction'), if the following criteria are fulfilled:

— according to an established practice there are no doubts about the aid character of the measure concerned
   and

— there is an urgency to act
   and

— there is a serious risk of substantial and irreparable damage to a competitor.

Recovery shall be effected in accordance with the procedure set out in Article 14(2) and (3). After the aid has been effectively recovered, the Commission shall take a decision within the time limits applicable to notified aid.

The Commission may authorise the Member State to couple the refunding of the aid with the payment of rescue aid to the firm concerned.

The provisions of this paragraph shall be applicable only to unlawful aid implemented after the entry into force of this Regulation.

Commentary
Art 11: B&C: 17.078, 17.100
Art 11(1): B&C: 17.083, 17.101
Art 11(2): B&C: 17.083, 17.102 F&N: 17.449

Article 12
Non-compliance with an injunction decision

If the Member State fails to comply with a suspension injunction or a recovery injunction, the Commission shall be entitled, while carrying out the examination on the substance of the matter on the basis of the information available, to refer the matter to the Court of Justice of the European Communities direct and apply for a declaration that the failure to comply constitutes an infringement of the Treaty.

Commentary
Art 12: B&C: 17.119, 17.131

Article 13
Decisions of the Commission

1. The examination of possible unlawful aid shall result in a decision pursuant to Article 4(2), (3) or (4). In the case of decisions to initiate the formal investigation procedure, proceedings shall be closed by means of a decision pursuant to Article 7. If a Member State fails to comply with an information injunction, that decision shall be taken on the basis of the information available.

2. In cases of possible unlawful aid and without prejudice to Article 11(2), the Commission shall not be bound by the time-limit set out in Articles 4(5), 7(6) and 7(7).

3. Article 9 shall apply *mutatis mutandis*.

Commentary
Art 13: B&C: 17.100
Art 13(1): B&C: 17.100 F&N: 17.526
Art 13(2): B&C: 17.084 F&N: 17.448

Article 14
Recovery of aid

1. Where negative decisions are taken in cases of unlawful aid, the Commission shall decide that the Member State concerned shall take all necessary measures to recover the aid from the beneficiary (hereinafter referred to as a 'recovery decision'). The Commission shall not require recovery of the aid if this would be contrary to a general principle of Community law.

2. The aid to be recovered pursuant to a recovery decision shall include interest at an appropriate rate fixed by the Commission. Interest shall be payable from the date on which the unlawful aid was at the disposal of the beneficiary until the date of its recovery.

3. Without prejudice to any order of the Court of Justice of the European Communities pursuant to Article [278] of the Treaty, recovery shall be effected without delay and in accordance with the procedures under the national law of the Member State concerned, provided that they allow the immediate and effective execution of the Commission's decision. To this effect and in the event of a

procedure before national courts, the Member States concerned shall take all necessary steps which are available in their respective legal systems, including provisional measures, without prejudice to Community law.

Commentary
Art 14: B&C: 17.104 **F&N:** 17.451, 17.455, 17.474
Art 14(1): B&C: 17.104, 17.127
Art 14(2): B&C: 17.106 **F&N:** 17.467
Art 14(3): B&C: 17.108, 17.133 **F&N:** 17.459

[CHAPTER IIIA
LIMITATION PERIODS]

Article 15
[Limitation period for the recovery of aid]

1. The powers of the Commission to recover aid shall be subject to a limitation period of ten years.

2. The limitation period shall begin on the day on which the unlawful aid is awarded to the beneficiary either as individual aid or as aid under an aid scheme. Any action taken by the Commission or by a Member State, acting at the request of the Commission, with regard to the unlawful aid shall interrupt the limitation period. Each interruption shall start time running afresh. The limitation period shall be suspended for as long as the decision of the Commission is the subject of proceedings pending before the Court of Justice of the European Communities.

3. Any aid with regard to which the limitation period has expired, shall be deemed to be existing aid.

Notes
The chapter heading was inserted and the title of Article 15 was replaced as shown in square brackets by Council Regulation (EU) No 734/2013 of 22 July 2013 (OJ L 204, 31.7.13, p.15), Articles 1(6) and 1(7), with effect from 20 August 2013.

Commentary
Art 15: B&C: 17.076, 17.107

[*Article 15a*
Limitation period for the imposition of fines and periodic penalty payments

1. The powers conferred on the Commission by Article 6b shall be subject to a limitation period of three years.

2. The period provided for in paragraph 1 shall start on the day on which the infringement referred to in Article 6b is committed. However, in the case of continuing or repeated infringements, the period shall begin on the day on which the infringement ceases.

3. Any action taken by the Commission for the purpose of the investigation or proceedings in respect of an infringement referred to in Article 6b shall interrupt the limitation period for the imposition of fines or periodic penalty payments, with effect from the date on which the action is notified to the undertaking or association of undertakings concerned.

4. After each interruption, the limitation period shall start running afresh. However, the limitation period shall expire at the latest on the day on which a period of six years has elapsed without the Commission having imposed a fine or a periodic penalty payment. That period shall be extended by the time during which the limitation period is suspended in accordance with paragraph 5.

5. The limitation period for the imposition of fines or periodic penalty payments shall be suspended for as long as the decision of the Commission is the subject of proceedings pending before the Court of Justice of the European Union.

Article 15b
Limitation periods for the enforcement of fines and periodic penalty payments

1. The powers of the Commission to enforce decisions adopted pursuant to Article 6b shall be subject to a limitation period of five years.

2. The period provided for in paragraph 1 shall start on the day on which the decision taken pursuant to Article 6b becomes final.

3. The limitation period provided for in paragraph 1 shall be interrupted:

(a) by notification of a decision modifying the original amount of the fine or periodic penalty payment or refusing an application for modification;

(b) by any action of a Member State, acting at the request of the Commission, or of the Commission, intended to enforce payment of the fine or periodic penalty payment.

4. After each interruption, the limitation period shall start running afresh.

5. The limitation period provided for in paragraph 1 shall be suspended for so long as:

(a) the respondent is allowed time to pay;

(b) the enforcement of payment is suspended pursuant to a decision of the Court of Justice of the European Union.]

Notes

Articles 15(a) and (b) were inserted by Council Regulation (EU) No 734/2013 of 22 July 2013 (OJ L 204, 31.7.13, p.15), Article 1(8), with effect from 20 August 2013.

CHAPTER IV
PROCEDURE REGARDING MISUSE OF AID

[Article 16
Misuse of aid

Without prejudice to Article 23, the Commission may, in cases of misuse of aid, initiate the formal investigation procedure pursuant to Article 4(4). Articles 6, 6a, 6b, 7, 9 and 10, Article 11(1) and Articles 12 to 15 shall apply *mutatis mutandis.*];.

Notes

Article 16 was replaced as shown in square brackets by Council Regulation (EU) No 734/2013 of 22 July 2013 (OJ L 204, 31.7.13, p.15), Article 1(9), with effect from 20 August 2013.

Commentary

Art 16: B&C: 17.092, 17.099, 17.100, 17.101

CHAPTER V
PROCEDURE REGARDING EXISTING AID SCHEMES

Article 17
Cooperation pursuant to Article [108(1)] of the Treaty

1. The Commission shall obtain from the Member State concerned all necessary information for the review, in cooperation with the Member State, of existing aid schemes pursuant to Article [108(1)] of the Treaty.

2. Where the Commission considers that an existing aid scheme is not, or is no longer, compatible with the common market, it shall inform the Member State concerned of its preliminary view and give the Member State concerned the opportunity to submit its comments within a period of one month. In duly justified cases, the Commission may extend this period.

Commentary
Art 17:   F&N: 17.511
Art 17(1):   B&C: 17.077
Art 17(2):   B&C: 17.079

Article 18
Proposal for appropriate measures

Where the Commission, in the light of the information submitted by the Member State pursuant to Article 17, concludes that the existing aid scheme is not, or is no longer, compatible with the common market, it shall issue a recommendation proposing appropriate measures to the Member State concerned. The recommendation may propose, in particular:

(a) substantive amendment of the aid scheme,
   or

(b) introduction of procedural requirements,
   or

(c) abolition of the aid scheme.

Commentary
Art 18:   B&C: 17.079, 17.118   F&N: 17.512, 17.514, 17.518

Article 19
Legal consequences of a proposal for appropriate measures

1. Where the Member State concerned accepts the proposed measures and informs the Commission thereof, the Commission shall record that finding and inform the Member State thereof. The Member State shall be bound by its acceptance to implement the appropriate measures.

2. Where the Member State concerned does not accept the proposed measures and the Commission, having taken into account the arguments of the Member State concerned, still considers that those measures are necessary, it shall initiate proceedings pursuant to Article 4(4). Articles 6, 7 and 9 shall apply *mutatis mutandis*.

Commentary
Art 19:   F&N: 17.513
Art 19(1):   B&C: 17.079
Art 19(2):   B&C: 17.079

CHAPTER VI
INTERESTED PARTIES

Article 20
Rights of interested parties

1. Any interested party may submit comments pursuant to Article 6 following a Commission decision to initiate the formal investigation procedure. Any interested party which has submitted such comments and any beneficiary of individual aid shall be sent a copy of the decision taken by the Commission pursuant to Article 7.

[2. Any interested party may submit a complaint to inform the Commission of any alleged unlawful aid or any alleged misuse of aid. To that effect, the interested party shall duly complete a form that has been defined in an implementing provision referred to in Article 27 and shall provide the mandatory information requested therein.

Where the Commission considers that the interested party does not comply with the compulsory complaint form, or that the facts and points of law put forward by the interested party do not provide sufficient grounds to show, on the basis of a *prima facie* examination, the existence of unlawful aid or misuse of aid, it shall inform the interested party thereof and call upon it to submit comments within a prescribed period which shall not normally exceed one month. If the interested party fails to make known its views within the prescribed period, the complaint shall be deemed to have been withdrawn. The Commission shall inform the Member State concerned when a complaint has been deemed to have been withdrawn.

The Commission shall send a copy of the decision on a case concerning the subject matter of the complaint to the complainant.]

3. At its request, any interested party shall obtain a copy of any decision pursuant to Articles 4 and 7, Article 10(3) and Article 11.

Notes

Paragraph 2 was replaced as shown in square brackets by Council Regulation (EU) No 734/2013 of 22 July 2013 (OJ L 204, 31.7.13, p.15), Article 1(10), with effect from 20 August 2013.

Commentary

Art 20: F&N: 17.537, 17.540
Art 20(1): B&C: 16.297, 16.387, 16.388 **F&N:** 17.522, 17.523
Art 20(2): B&C: 17.118 **F&N:** 17.524, 17.525, 17.526, 17.527, 17.550

[CHAPTER VIA
INVESTIGATIONS INTO SECTORS OF THE ECONOMY AND INTO AID INSTRUMENTS

Article 20a
Investigations into sectors of the economy and into aid instruments

1. Where the information available substantiates a reasonable suspicion that State aid measures in a particular sector or based on a particular aid instrument may materially restrict or distort competition within the internal market in several Member States, or that existing aid measures in a particular sector in several Member States are not, or no longer, compatible with the internal market, the Commission may conduct an inquiry across various Member States into the sector of the economy or the use of the aid instrument concerned. In the course of that inquiry, the Commission may request the Member States and/or the undertakings or associations of undertakings concerned to supply the necessary information for the application of Articles 107 and 108 of the TFEU, taking due account of the principle of proportionality.

The Commission shall state the reasons for the inquiry and for the choice of addressees in all requests for information sent under this Article.

The Commission shall publish a report on the results of its inquiry into particular sectors of the economy or particular aid instruments across various Member States and shall invite the Member States and any undertakings or associations of undertakings concerned to submit comments.

2. Information obtained from sector inquiries may be used in the framework of procedures under this Regulation.

3. Articles 5, 6a and 6b shall apply *mutatis mutandis.*]

Notes

Chapter VIA was inserted as shown in square brackets by Council Regulation (EU) No 734/2013 of 22 July 2013 (OJ L 204, 31.7.13, p.15), Article 1(11), with effect from 20 August 2013.

CHAPTER VII
MONITORING

Article 21
Annual reports

1. Member States shall submit to the Commission annual reports on all existing aid schemes with regard to which no specific reporting obligations have been imposed in a conditional decision pursuant to Article 7(4).

2. Where, despite a reminder, the Member State concerned fails to submit an annual report, the Commission may proceed in accordance with Article 18 with regard to the aid scheme concerned.

Commentary
Art 21: **B&C:** 17.095

Article 22
On-site monitoring

1. Where the Commission has serious doubts as to whether decisions not to raise objections, positive decisions or conditional decisions with regard to individual aid are being complied with, the Member State concerned, after having been given the opportunity to submit its comments, shall allow the Commission to undertake on-site monitoring visits.

2. The officials authorised by the Commission shall be empowered, in order to verify compliance with the decision concerned:

(a) to enter any premises and land of the undertaking concerned;
(b) to ask for oral explanations on the spot;
(c) to examine books and other business records and take, or demand, copies.

The Commission may be assisted if necessary by independent experts.

3. The Commission shall inform the Member State concerned, in good time and in writing, of the on-site monitoring visit and of the identities of the authorised officials and experts. If the Member State has duly justified objections to the Commission's choice of experts, the experts shall be appointed in common agreement with the Member State. The officials of the Commission and the experts authorised to carry out the on-site monitoring shall produce an authorisation in writing specifying the subject-matter and purpose of the visit.

4. Officials authorised by the Member State in whose territory the monitoring visit is to be made may be present at the monitoring visit.

5. The Commission shall provide the Member State with a copy of any report produced as a result of the monitoring visit.

6. Where an undertaking opposes a monitoring visit ordered by a Commission decision pursuant to this Article, the Member State concerned shall afford the necessary assistance to the officials and experts authorised by the Commission to enable them to carry out the monitoring visit. To this end the Member States shall, after consulting the Commission, take the necessary measures within eighteen months after the entry into force of this Regulation.

Commentary
Art 22(1): **B&C:** 17.095
Art 22(6): **B&C:** 17.095

Article 23
Non-compliance with decisions and judgments

1. Where the Member State concerned does not comply with conditional or negative decisions, in particular in cases referred to in Article 14, the Commission may refer the matter to the Court of Justice of the European Communities direct in accordance with Article [108(2)] of the Treaty.

2. If the Commission considers that the Member State concerned has not complied with a judgment of the Court of Justice of the European Communities, the Commission may pursue the matter in accordance with Article [260] of the Treaty.

Commentary
Art 23: **B&C:** 17.119

[CHAPTER VIIA
COOPERATION WITH NATIONAL COURTS

Article 23a
Cooperation with national courts

1. For the application of Article 107(1) and Article 108 of the TFEU, the courts of the Member States may ask the Commission to transmit to them information in its possession or its opinion on questions concerning the application of State aid rules.

2. Where the coherent application of Article 107(1) or Article 108 of the TFEU so requires, the Commission, acting on its own initiative, may submit written observations to the courts of the Member States that are responsible for applying the State aid rules. It may, with the permission of the court in question, also make oral observations.

The Commission shall inform the Member State concerned of its intention to submit observations before formally doing so.

For the exclusive purpose of preparing its observations, the Commission may request the relevant court of the Member State to transmit documents at the disposal of the court, necessary for the Commission's assessment of the matter.]

Notes

Chapter VIIA was inserted as shown in square brackets by Council Regulation (EU) No 734/2013 of 22 July 2013 (OJ L 204, 31.7.13, p.15), Article 1(12), with effect from 20 August 2013.

CHAPTER VIII
COMMON PROVISIONS

Article 24
Professional secrecy

The Commission and the Member States, their officials and other servants, including independent experts appointed by the Commission, shall not disclose information which they have acquired through the application of this Regulation and which is covered by the obligation of professional secrecy.

[*Article 25*
Addressee of decisions

1. The decisions taken pursuant to Article 6a(7), Article 6b(1) and (2), and Article 7(9) shall be addressed to the undertaking or association of undertakings concerned. The Commission shall notify the decision to the addressee without delay and shall give the addressee the opportunity to indicate to the Commission which information it considers to be covered by the obligation of professional secrecy.

2. All other decisions of the Commission taken pursuant to Chapters II, III, IV, V and VII shall be addressed to the Member State concerned. The Commission shall notify them to the Member State concerned without delay and shall give that Member State the opportunity to indicate to the Commission which information it considers to be covered by the obligation of professional secrecy.]

Notes

Article 25 was replaced as shown in square brackets by Council Regulation (EU) No 734/2013 of 22 July 2013 (OJ L 204, 31.7.13, p.15), Article 1(13), with effect from 20 August 2013.

Article 26
Publication of decisions

1. The Commission shall publish in the *Official Journal of the European Communities* a summary notice of the decisions which it takes pursuant to Article 4(2) and (3) and Article 18 in conjunction with Article 19(1). The summary notice shall state that a copy of the decision may be obtained in the authentic language version or versions.

2. The Commission shall publish in the *Official Journal of the European Communities* the decisions which it takes pursuant to Article 4(4) in their authentic language version. In the Official Journal published in languages other than the authentic language version, the authentic language version will be accompanied by a meaningful summary in the language of that Official Journal.

[2a. The Commission shall publish in the Official Journal of the European Union the decisions which it takes pursuant to Article 6b(1) and (2).]

3. The Commission shall publish in the *Official Journal of the European Communities* the decisions which it takes pursuant to Article 7.

4. In cases where Article 4(6) or Article 8(2) applies, a short notice shall be published in the *Official Journal of the European Communities*.

5. The Council, acting unanimously, may decide to publish decisions pursuant to the third subparagraph of Article [108(2)] of the Treaty in the *Official Journal of the European Communities*.

Notes

Paragraph 2a was inserted as shown in square brackets by Council Regulation (EU) No 734/2013 of 22 July 2013 (OJ L 204, 31.7.13, p.15), Article 1(14), with effect from 20 August 2013.

Commentary
Art 26: B&C: 17.095

[*Article 27*
Implementing provisions

The Commission, acting in accordance with the procedure laid down in Article 29, shall have the power to adopt implementing provisions concerning:

(a) the form, content and other details of notifications;
(b) the form, content and other details of annual reports;
(c) the form, content and other details of complaints submitted in accordance with Article 10(1) and Article 20(2);
(d) details of time-limits and the calculation of time-limits; and
(e) the interest rate referred to in Article 14(2).]

Notes

Article 27 was replaced as shown in square brackets by Council Regulation (EU) No 734/2013 of 22 July 2013 (OJ L 204, 31.7.13, p.15), Article 1(27), with effect from 20 August 2013.

Commentary
Art 27: F&N: 17.396, 17.407

Article 28
Advisory Committee on State aid

An Advisory Committee on State aid (hereinafter referred to as the 'Committee') shall be set up. It shall be composed of representatives of the Member States and chaired by the representative of the Commission.

Article 29
Consultation of the Committee

1. The Commission shall consult the Committee before adopting any implementing provision pursuant to Article 27.

2. Consultation of the Committee shall take place at a meeting called by the Commission. The drafts and documents to be examined shall be annexed to the notification. The meeting shall take place no earlier than two months after notification has been sent. This period may be reduced in the case of urgency.

3. The Commission representative shall submit to the Committee a draft of the measures to be taken. The Committee shall deliver an opinion on the draft, within a time-limit which the chairman may lay down according to the urgency of the matter, if necessary by taking a vote.

4. The opinion shall be recorded in the minutes; in addition, each Member State shall have the right to ask to have its position recorded in the minutes. The Committee may recommend the publication of this opinion in the *Official Journal of the European Communities*.

5. The Commission shall take the utmost account of the opinion delivered by the Committee. It shall inform the Committee on the manner in which its opinion has been taken into account.

Article 30
Entry into force

This Regulation shall enter into force on the twentieth day following that of its publication in the *Official Journal of the European Communities.*

Notes

Date of entry in force: 16 April 1999.

This Regulation shall be binding in its entirety and directly applicable in all Member States.

Done at Brussels, 22 March 1999.

G2

COMMISSION REGULATION (EC) NO 794/2004

of 21 April 2004

implementing Council Regulation (EC) No 659/1999 laying down detailed rules for the application of Article [108* of the Treaty on the Functioning of the European Union]*

Official Journal L 140, 30.4.2004, p.1

Celex No: 32004R0794

EUR-Lex permanent link: <http://eur-lex.europa.eu/LexUriServ/LexUriServ.do?uri=CELEX: 32004R0794:EN:NOT>

Notes

This regulation is reproduced as corrected by the corrigenda published at OJ L 25, 28.1.2005, p.75 and OJ L 131, 25.5.2005, p.45.

*Ed note: please see the Note on the Lisbon Treaty at p.xvii in regard to article renumbering introduced by the Lisbon Treaty. Unless otherwise stated, all Treaty article numbers are the new numbers of the Treaty on the Functioning of the European Union (TFEU) and the Treaty on European Union (TEU).

EEA application: the EFTA Surveillance Authority has adopted a corresponding instrument under Article 5(2)(b) of the Surveillance and Court Agreement: see EFTA Surveillance Authority Decision No 195/04/COL (OJ L 139, 25.5.2006, p.37) as subsequently amended by Decision No 319/05/COL of 14 December 2005 (OJ L 113, 27.4.2006, p.24) and Decision No 387/06/COL of 13 December 2006 (OJ L 148, 11.6.09, p.35). See also EEA Agreement, Protocol 26, Article 2, Point 2 (as amended by EEA Joint Committee Decision No 164/2001 (OJ L 65, 7.3.2002, p.46 and EEA Supplement No 13, 7.3.2002, p.26) Decision No 123/2005 (OJ L 339, 22.12.2005, p.32, and EEA Supplement No 66, 22.12.2005, p.18)) and Decision No 119/2009 (OJ L 334, 17.12.2009, p.23).

Commentary

Regulation 794/2004/EC: B&C: 17.075, 17.080, 17.097 **F&N:** 17.396, 17.525
Chap V: B&C: 17.106

THE COMMISSION OF THE EUROPEAN COMMUNITIES,

Having regard to the [Treaty on the Functioning of the European Union],

Having regard to Council Regulation (EC) No 659/1999 of 22 March 1999 laying down detailed rules for the application of Article [108] of the [Treaty on the Functioning of the European Union],[1] and in particular Article 27 thereof,

After consulting the Advisory Committee on State Aid,

Notes
1 OJ L 83, 27.3.1999, p.1. Regulation as amended by the 2003 Act of Accession.

Whereas:
(1) In order to facilitate the preparation of State aid notifications by Member States, and their assessment by the Commission, it is desirable to establish a compulsory notification form. That form should be as comprehensive as possible.
(2) The standard notification form as well as the summary information sheet and the supplementary information sheets should cover all existing guidelines and frameworks in the state aid field. They should be subject to modification or replacement in accordance with the further development of those texts.
(3) Provision should be made for a simplified system of notification for certain alterations to existing aid. Such simplified arrangements should only be accepted if the Commission has been regularly informed on the implementation of the existing aid concerned.
(4) In the interests of legal certainty it is appropriate to make it clear that small increases of up to 20% of the original budget of an aid scheme, in particular to take account of the effects of inflation, should not need to be notified to the Commission as they are unlikely to affect the Commission's original assessment of the compatibility of the scheme, provided that the other conditions of the aid scheme remain unchanged.
(5) Article 21 of Regulation (EC) No 659/1999 requires Member States to submit annual reports to the Commission on all existing aid schemes or individual aid granted outside an approved aid scheme in respect of which no specific reporting obligations have been imposed in a conditional decision.
(6) For the Commission to be able to discharge its responsibilities for the monitoring of aid, it needs to receive accurate information from Member States about the types and amounts of aid being granted by them under existing aid schemes. It is possible to simplify and improve the arrangements for the reporting of State aid to the Commission which are currently described in the joint procedure for reporting and notification under the [Treaty on the Functioning of the European Union] and under the World Trade Organisation (WTO) Agreement set out in the Commission's letter to Member States of 2 August 1995. The part of that joint procedure relating to Member States reporting obligations for subsidy notifications under Article 25 of the WTO Agreement on Subsidies and Countervailing measures and under Article XVI of GATT 1994, adopted on 21 July 1995 is not covered by this Regulation.
(7) The information required in the annual reports is intended to enable the Commission to monitor overall aid levels and to form a general view of the effects of different types of aid on competition. To this end, the Commission may also request Member States to provide, on an ad hoc basis, additional data for selected topics. The choice of subject matter should be discussed in advance with Member States.
(8) The annual reporting exercise does not cover the information, which may be necessary in order to verify that particular aid measures respect Community law. The Commission should therefore retain the right to seek undertakings from Member States, or to attach to decisions conditions requiring the provision of additional information.
(9) It should be specified that time-limits for the purposes of Regulation (EC) No 659/1999 should be calculated in accordance with Regulation (EEC, Euratom) No 1182/71 of the Council of 3 June 1971 determining the rules applicable to periods, dates and time limits,1 as supplemented by the specific rules set out in this Regulation. In particular, it is necessary to identify the events, which determine the starting point for time-limits applicable in State aid procedures. The rules set out in this Regulation should apply to pre-existing time-limits which will continue to run after the entry into force of this Regulation.

Notes
1 OJ L 124, 8.6.1971, p.1.

(10) The purpose of recovery is to re-establish the situation existing before aid was unlawfully granted. To ensure equal treatment, the advantage should be measured objectively from the moment when the aid is available to the beneficiary undertaking, independently of the outcome of any commercial decisions subsequently made by that undertaking.

(11) In accordance with general financial practice it is appropriate to fix the recovery interest rate as an annual percentage rate.

(12) The volume and frequency of transactions between banks results in an interest rate that is consistently measurable and statistically significant, and should therefore form the basis of the recovery interest rate. The inter-bank swap rate should, however, be adjusted in order to reflect general levels of increased commercial risk outside the banking sector. On the basis of the information on inter-bank swap rates the Commission should establish a single recovery interest rate for each Member State. In the interest of legal certainty and equal treatment, it is appropriate to fix the precise method by which the interest rate should be calculated, and to provide for the publication of the recovery interest rate applicable at any given moment, as well as relevant previously applicable rates.

(13) A State aid grant may be deemed to reduce a beneficiary undertaking's medium-term financing requirements. For these purposes, and in line with general financial practice, the medium-term may be defined as five years. The recovery interest rate should therefore correspond to an annual percentage rate fixed for five years.

(14) Given the objective of restoring the situation existing before the aid was unlawfully granted, and in accordance with general financial practice, the recovery interest rate to be fixed by the Commission should be annually compounded. For the same reasons, the recovery interest rate applicable in the first year of the recovery period should be applied for the first five years of the recovery period, and the recovery interest rate applicable in the sixth year of the recovery period for the following five years.

(15) This Regulation should apply to recovery decisions notified after the date of entry into force of this Regulation,

HAS ADOPTED THIS REGULATION:

CHAPTER I
SUBJECT MATTER AND SCOPE

Article 1
Subject matter and scope

1. This Regulation sets out detailed provisions concerning the form, content and other details of notifications and annual reports referred to in Regulation (EC) No 659/1999. It also sets out provisions for the calculation of time limits in all procedures concerning State aid and of the interest rate for the recovery of unlawful aid.

2. This Regulation shall apply to aid in all sectors.

CHAPTER II
NOTIFICATIONS

Article 2
Notification forms

Without prejudice to Member States' obligations to notify state aids in the coal sector under Commission Decision 2002/871/CE,[1] notifications of new aid pursuant to Article 2(1) of Regulation (EC) No 659/1999, other than those referred to in Article 4(2), shall be made on the notification form set out in Part I of Annex I to this Regulation.

Supplementary information needed for the assessment of the measure in accordance with regulations, guidelines, frameworks and other texts applicable to State aid shall be provided on the supplementary information sheets set out in Part III of Annex I.

Whenever the relevant guidelines or frameworks are modified or replaced, the Commission shall adapt the corresponding forms and information sheets.

Notes
1 OJ L 300, 5.11.2002, p.42.

[Article 3
Transmission of notifications

1. The notification shall be transmitted to the Commission by means of the electronic validation carried out by the person designated by the Member State. Such validated notification shall be considered as sent by the Permanent Representative.

2. The Commission shall address its correspondence to the Permanent Representative of the Member State concerned, or to any other address designated by that Member State.

3. As from 1 July 2008, notifications shall be transmitted electronically via the web application State Aid Notification Interactive (SANI).

All correspondence in connection with a notification shall be transmitted electronically via the secured e-mail system Public Key Infrastructure (PKI).

4. In exceptional circumstances and upon the agreement of the Commission and the Member State concerned, an agreed communication channel other than those referred to in paragraph 3 may be used for submission of a notification or any correspondence in connection with a notification.

In the absence of such an agreement, any notification or correspondence in connection with a notification sent to the Commission by a Member State through a communication channel other than those referred to in paragraph 3 shall not be considered as submitted to the Commission.

5. Where the notification or correspondence in connection with a notification contains confidential information, the Member State concerned shall clearly identify such information and give reasons for its classification as confidential.

6. The Member States shall refer to the State aid identification number allocated to an aid scheme by the Commission in each grant of aid to a final beneficiary.

The first subparagraph shall not apply to aid granted through fiscal measures.]

Notes

Article 3 was substituted as shown in square brackets by Commission Regulation (EC) No 271/2008 (OJ L 82, 25.3.2008, p.1), Article 1(1), with effect from 14 April 2008.

Article 4
Simplified notification procedure for certain alterations to existing aid

1. For the purposes of Article 1(c) of Regulation (EC) No 659/1999, an alteration to existing aid shall mean any change, other than modifications of a purely formal or administrative nature which cannot affect the evaluation of the compatibility of the aid measure with the common market. However an increase in the original budget of an existing aid scheme by up to 20% shall not be considered an alteration to existing aid.

2. The following alterations to existing aid shall be notified on the simplified notification form set out in Annex II:

(a) increases in the budget of an authorised aid scheme exceeding 20%;
(b) prolongation of an existing authorised aid scheme by up to six years, with or without an increase in the budget;
(c) tightening of the criteria for the application of an authorised aid scheme, a reduction of aid intensity or a reduction of eligible expenses.

The Commission shall use its best endeavours to take a decision on any aid notified on the simplified notification form within a period of one month.

3. The simplified notification procedure shall not be used to notify alterations to aid schemes in respect of which Member States have not submitted annual reports in accordance with Article 5, 6, and 7, unless the annual reports for the years in which the aid has been granted are submitted at the same time as the notification.

CHAPTER III
ANNUAL REPORTS

Article 5
Form and content of annual reports

1. Without prejudice to the second and third subparagraphs of this Article and to any additional specific reporting requirements laid down in a conditional decision adopted pursuant to Article 7(4) of Regulation (EC) No 659/1999, or to the observance of any undertakings provided by the Member State concerned in connection with a decision to approve aid, Member States shall compile the annual reports on existing aid schemes referred to in Article 21(1) of Regulation (EC) No 659/1999 in respect of each whole or part calendar year during which the scheme applies in accordance with the standardised reporting format set out in Annex IIIA.

Annex IIIB sets out the format for annual reports on existing aid schemes relating to the production, processing and marketing of agricultural products listed in Annex I of the Treaty.

Annex IIIC sets out the format for annual reports on existing aid schemes for state aid relating to the production, processing or marketing of fisheries products listed in Annex I of the Treaty.

2. The Commission may ask Member States to provide additional data for selected topics, to be discussed in advance with Member States.

Article 6
Transmission and publication of annual reports

1. Each Member State shall transmit its annual reports to the Commission in electronic form no later than 30 June of the year following the year to which the report relates.

In justified cases Member States may submit estimates, provided that the actual figures are transmitted at the very latest with the following year's data.

2. Each year the Commission shall publish a State aid synopsis containing a synthesis of the information contained in the annual reports submitted during the previous year.

Article 7
Status of annual reports

The transmission of annual reports shall not be considered to constitute compliance with the obligation to notify aid measures before they are put into effect pursuant to Article [108] of the Treaty, nor shall such transmission in any way prejudice the outcome of an investigation into allegedly unlawful aid in accordance with the procedure laid down in Chapter III of Regulation (EC) No 659/1999.

CHAPTER IV
TIME-LIMITS

Article 8
Calculation of time-limits

1. Time-limits provided for in Regulation (EC) No 659/1999 and in this Regulation or fixed by the Commission pursuant to Article [108] of the Treaty shall be calculated in accordance with Regulation (EEC, Euratom) No 1182/71, and the specific rules set out in paragraphs 2 to 5 of this Article. In case of conflict, the provisions of this regulation shall prevail.

2. Time limits shall be specified in months or in working days.

[3. With regard to time-limits for action by the Commission, the receipt of the notification or subsequent correspondence in accordance with Article 3(1) and Article 3(3) of this Regulation shall be the relevant event for the purpose of Article 3(1) of Regulation (EEC, Euratom) No 1182/71.]

[4. With regard to time-limits for action by Member States, the receipt of the relevant notification or correspondence from the Commission in accordance with Article 3(2) of this Regulation shall be the relevant event for the purposes of Article 3(1) of Regulation (EEC, Euratom) No 1182/71.]

5. With regard to the time-limit for the submission of comments following initiation of the formal investigation procedure referred to in [Article] 6(1) of Regulation (EC) No 659/1999 by third parties and those Member States which are not directly concerned by the procedure, the publication of the notice of initiation in the *Official Journal of the European Union* shall be the relevant event for the purposes of Article 3(1) of Regulation (EEC, Euratom) No 1182/71.

6. Any request for the extension of a time-limit shall be duly substantiated, and shall be submitted in writing to the address designated by the party fixing the time-limit at least two working days before expiry.

Notes

Articles 8(3) and 8(4) were substituted as shown in square brackets by Commission Regulation (EC) No 271/2008 (OJ L 82, 25.3.2008, p.1), Article 1(2), with effect from 14 April 2008.

CHAPTER V

INTEREST RATE FOR THE RECOVERY OF UNLAWFUL AID

[*Article 9*

Method for fixing the interest rate

1. Unless otherwise provided for in a specific decision, the interest rate to be used for recovering State aid granted in breach of Article [108(3)] of the Treaty shall be an annual percentage rate which is fixed by the Commission in advance of each calendar year.

2. The interest rate shall be calculated by adding 100 basis points to the one-year money market rate. Where those rates are not available, the three-month money market rate will be used, or in the absence thereof, the yield on State bonds will be used.

3. In the absence of reliable money market or yield on stock bonds or equivalent data or in exceptional circumstances the Commission may, in close co-operation with the Member State(s) concerned, fix a recovery rate on the basis of a different method and on the basis of the information available to it.

4. The recovery rate will be revised once a year. The base rate will be calculated on the basis of the one-year money market recorded in September, October and November of the year in question. The rate thus calculated will apply throughout the following year.

5. In addition, to take account of significant and sudden variations, an update will be made each time the average rate, calculated over the three previous months, deviates more than 15% from the rate in force. This new rate will enter into force on the first day of the second month following the months used for the calculation.]

Notes

Article 9 was substituted as shown in square brackets by Commission Regulation (EC) No 271/2008 (OJ L 82, 25.3.2008, p.1), Article 1(3), with effect from 14 April 2008.

Article 10

Publication

The Commission shall publish current and relevant historical State aid recovery interest rates in the *Official Journal of the European Union* and for information on the Internet.

Article 11

Method for applying interest

1. The interest rate to be applied shall be the rate applicable on the date on which unlawful aid was first put at the disposal of the beneficiary.

2. The interest rate shall be applied on a compound basis until the date of the recovery of the aid. The interest accruing in the previous year shall be subject to interest in each subsequent year.

[3. The interest rate referred to in paragraph 1 shall be applied throughout the whole period until the date of recovery. However, if more than one year has elapsed between the date on which the unlawful aid was first put at the disposal of the beneficiary and the date of the recovery of the aid, the interest rate shall be recalculated at yearly intervals, taking as a basis the rate in force at the time of recalculation.]

Notes

Article 11(3) was substituted as shown in square brackets by Commission Regulation (EC) No 271/2008 (OJ L 82, 25.3.2008, p.1), Article 1(4), with effect from 14 April 2008.

Chapter VI
Final provisions

Article 12
Review

The Commission shall in consultation with the Member States, review the application of this Regulation within four years after its entry into force.

Article 13
Entry into force

This Regulation shall enter into force on the twentieth day following that of its publication in the *Official Journal of the European Union*.

Chapter II shall apply only to those notifications transmitted to the Commission more than five months after the entry into force of this Regulation.

Chapter III shall apply to annual reports covering aid granted from 1 January 2003 onwards.

Chapter IV shall apply to any time limit, which has been fixed but which has not yet expired on the date of entry into force of this Regulation.

Articles 9 and 11 shall apply in relation to any recovery decision notified after the date of entry into force of this Regulation.

This Regulation shall be binding in its entirety and be directly applicable in all Member States.

Done at Brussels, 21 April 2004.

Notes

Date of entry into force: 20 May 2004.

Annex I
Standard Form for Notification of State Aids Pursuant to Article [108(3) TFEU] and for the Provision of Information on Unlawful Aid

Notes

Owing to the length of the Standard Form, Annex I is not reproduced in this volume. Annex I was amended by Commission Regulation (EC) No 271/2008 of 30 January 2008 (OJ L 82, 25.3.2008, p.1) with effect from 14 April 2008, which replaced Part I (General Information), deleted Part II, amended Supplementary Information sheet 6a and replaced Supplementary Information sheets 6b and 11; by Commission Regulation (EC) No 1147/2008 of 31 October 2008 (OJ L 313, 22.11.2008, p.1) which replaced Part III.10 of Annex 1 (supplementary information sheet on state aid for environmental protection) with effect from 22 November 2008; by Commission Regulation (EC) No 257/2009 of 24 March 2009 (OJ L 81, 27.3.2009, p.15), which replaced Part III.14 of Annex I (supplementary information sheet for notification of aid to fisheries and aquaculture) with effect from 16 April 2009; and by Commission Regulation (EC) No 1125/2009 of 23 November 2009 (OJ L 308, 24.11.2009, p.5) which replaced Part III.2 and Part III.3 of Annex I and amended question 2.3 of Part III.7a, with effect from 24 November 2011.

Electronic versions of Annex I (including those parts amended by Commission Regulation (EC) 271/2008) are available on the Europa website at the following address: <http://ec.europa.eu/comm/competition/state_aid/legislation/forms.html>

[ANNEX II
SIMPLIFIED NOTIFICATION FORM]

Notes

Annex II was substituted as shown below in square brackets by Commission Regulation (EC) No 271/2008 (OJ L 82, 25.3.2008, p.1) with effect from 14 April 2008. An electronic version of Annex II as substituted is available on the Europa website at the following address:
<http://ec.europa.eu/comm/competition/state_aid/legislation/forms.html>

[This form may be used for the simplified notification pursuant to Article 4(2) of Commission Regulation (EC) No 794/2004 implementing Council Regulation (EC) No 659/1999 laying down detailed rules for the application of Article [108 TFEU].[1]

1. *Prior approved aid scheme*[2]

    1.1. Aid number allocated by the Commission:

    1.2. Title:

    1.3. Date of approval [by reference to the letter of the Commission SG(..)D/...]:

    1.4. Publication in the *Official Journal of the European Union*:

    1.5. Primary objective (please specify one):

    1.6. Legal basis:

    1.7. Overall budget:

    1.8. Duration:

2. *Instrument subject to notification*

    ❏ New budget (please specify the overall as well as the annual budget in the respective national currency):

    ❏ New duration (please specify the starting date from which the aid may be granted and the last date until which the aid may be granted):

    ❏ Tightening of criteria (please indicate if the amendment concerns a reduction of aid intensity or eligible expenses and specify details):

3. *Validity of commitments*

    ❏ Please confirm that the commitments provided by the Member State for the purposes of the prior approved aid scheme are valid in their entirety also for the new notified measure.

Please attach a copy (or a web link) of the relevant extracts of the final text(s) of the legal basis.]

Notes

[1 Commission Regulation (EC) No 794/2004 of 21 April 2004 implementing Council Regulation (EC) No 659/1999 laying down detailed rules for the application of Article [108 TFEU] (OJ L 140, 20.4.2004, p.1). Regulation as last amended by Regulation No 1935/2006 (OJ L 407, 30.12.2006, p.1).

2 If the aid scheme has been notified to the Commission on more than one occasion, please provide details for the latest complete notification that has been approved by the Commission]

ANNEX IIIA
STANDARDISED REPORTING FORMAT FOR EXISTING STATE AID

(This format covers all sectors except agriculture)

Notes

For reasons of space, Annex IIIA is not reproduced in this volume. An electronic version of Annex IIIA is available on the Europa website at the following address:
<http://ec.europa.eu/comm/competition/state_aid/legislation/forms.html>

ANNEX IIIB
STANDARDISED REPORTING FORMAT FOR EXISTING STATE AID

(This format covers the agricultural sector)

Notes

For reasons of space, Annex IIIB is not reproduced in this volume. An electronic version of Annex IIIB is published on the Europa website at the following address:

<http://ec.europa.eu/comm/competition/state_aid/legislation/forms.html>

ANNEX IIIC
INFORMATION TO BE CONTAINED IN THE ANNUAL REPORT TO BE PROVIDED TO THE COMMISSION

Notes

For reasons of space, Annex IIIC is not reproduced in this volume. An electronic version of Annex IIIC is available on the Europa website at the following address:

<http://ec.europa.eu/comm/competition/state_aid/legislation/forms.html>

G3

COMMISSION NOTICE

on the determination of the applicable rules for the assessment of unlawful
State aid (notified under document number C(2002) 458)

(2002/C 119/12)

Text with EEA relevance

Official Journal C 119, 22.5.2002, p.22

Celex No: 52002XC0522(04)

EUR-Lex permanent link: <http://eur-lex.europa.eu/LexUriServ/LexUriServ.do?uri=CELEX:5200
2XC0522(04):EN:NOT>

[NOTE]

Commentary
Notice: F&N: 17.219

G4

COMMISSION COMMUNICATION
C(2003) 4582

of 1 December 2003
on professional secrecy in state aid decisions

(2003/C 297/03)

Official Journal C 297, 9.12.2003, p.6

Celex No: 52003XC1209(02)

EUR-Lex permanent link: <http://eur-lex.europa.eu/LexUriServ/LexUriServ.do?uri=CELEX:5200
3XC1209(02):EN:NOT>

Notes

EEA application: for the corresponding EEA provision, see the EFTA Surveillance Authority's Procedural and Substantive Rules in the Field of State Aid (Guidelines on the application and interpretation of Articles 61 and 62 of the EEA Agreement and Article 1 of Protocol 3 to the Surveillance and Court Agreement), Part II, Chapter 9C (as added by EFTA Surveillance Authority Decision No 15/04/COL of 18 February 2004 (OJ L 154, 8.6.2006, p.27)).

Commentary
Communication: B&C: 17.081

---

1. Introduction

(1) This Communication sets out how the Commission intends to deal with requests by Member States, as addressees of State aid decisions, to consider parts of such decisions as covered by the obligation of professional secrecy and thus not to be disclosed when the decision is published.

(2) This involves two aspects, namely:
   (a) the identification of the information which might be covered by the obligation of professional secrecy; and
   (b) the procedure to be followed for dealing with such requests.

2. Legal Framework

(3) Article [339]* of the Treaty states that: 'The members of the institutions of the Community, the members of committees, and the officials and other servants of the Community shall be required, even after their duties have ceased, not to disclose information of the kind covered by the obligation of professional secrecy, in particular information about undertakings, their business relations or their cost components'.

(4) This is also reflected in Articles 24 and 25 of Council Regulation (EC) No 659/1999 of 22 March 1999 laying down detailed rules for the application of Article [108 TFEU].[1]

Notes

* Ed note: please see the Note on the Lisbon Treaty at p.xvii in regard to article renumbering introduced by the Lisbon Treaty. Unless otherwise stated, all Treaty article numbers are the new numbers of the Treaty on the Functioning of the European Union (TFEU) and the Treaty on European Union (TEU).

[1] OJ L 83, 27.3.1999, p.1.

---

(5) Article [296] of the Treaty states: 'Regulations, directives and decisions adopted jointly by the European Parliament and the Council, and such acts adopted by the Council or the Commission, shall state the reasons on which they are based and shall refer to any proposals or opinions which were required to be obtained pursuant to this Treaty'.

(6) Article 6(1), first sentence of Regulation (EC) No 659/1999 further stipulates with regard to decisions to initiate the formal investigation procedures: 'The decision to initiate the formal investigation procedure shall summarise the relevant issues of fact and law, shall include a pre-liminary assessment of the Commission as to the aid character of the proposed measure and shall set out the doubts as to its compatibility with the common market [...]'.

3. IDENTIFICATION OF INFORMATION WHICH CAN BE COVERED BY PROFESSIONAL SECRECY

(7) The Court of Justice has established that although Article [339] of the Treaty primarily refers to information gathered from undertakings, the expression 'in particular' shows that the principle in question is a general one which applies also to other confidential information.[1]

Notes

[1] Case 145/83 *Adams v Commission* [1985] ECR 3539, paragraph 34, and Case T-353/94 *Postbank v Commission* [1996] ECR II-921, paragraph 86.

(8) It follows that professional secrecy covers both business secrets and other confidential information.

(9) There is no reason why the notions of business secret and other confidential information should be interpreted differently from the meaning given to these terms in the context of antitrust and merger procedures. The fact that in antitrust and merger procedures the addressees of the Commission decision are undertakings, while in State aid procedures the addressees are Member States, does not constitute an obstacle to a uniform approach as to the identification of what can constitute business secrets or other confidential information.

3.1. Business secrets

(10) Business secrets can only concern information relating to a business which has actual or potential economic value, the disclosure or use of which could result in economic benefits for other companies. Typical examples are methods of assessing manufacturing and distri-bution costs, production secrets (that is to say, a secret, commercially valuable plan, for-mula, process or device that is used for the making, preparing, compounding, or processing of trade commodities and that can be said to be the end product of either innovation or substantial effort) and processes, supply sources, quantities produced and sold, market shares, customer and distributor lists, marketing plans, cost price structure, sales policy, and information on the internal organisation of the undertaking.

Commentary
point 10: F&N: 2.198

(11) It would appear that in principle business secrets can only relate to the beneficiary of the aid (or other third party) and can only concern information submitted by the Member State (or third party). Hence, statements from the Commission itself (for example, expressing doubts about feasibility of a restructuring plan) cannot be covered by the obligation of professional secrecy.

(12) The simple fact that disclosure of information might cause harm to the company is not of itself sufficient grounds to consider that such information should be considered as business secret. For example, a Commission decision to initiate the formal investigation procedure in the case of a restructuring aid may cast doubt on certain aspects of the restructuring plan in the light of information the Commission has received. Such a decision could (further) affect the credit-position of that company. However, that would not necessarily lead to the conclusion that the information on which that decision was based must be considered as business secrets.

(13) In general, the Commission will apply the following non-exhaustive list of criteria to deter-mine whether information can be deemed to constitute business secrets:
   (a) the extent to which the information is known outside the company;
   (b) the extent to which measures have been taken to protect the information within the com-pany, for example, through non compete clauses or non-disclosure agreements imposed on employees or agents, etc;

(c) the value of the information for the company and its competitors;

(d) the effort or investment which the undertaking had to undertake to acquire the information;

(e) the effort which others would need to undertake to acquire or copy the information;

(f) the degree of protection offered to such information under the legislation of the Member State concerned.

Commentary
point 13: F&N: 2.200

---

(14) In principle, the Commission considers that the following information would not normally be covered by the obligation of professional secrecy:

(a) information which is publicly available, including information available only upon payment through specialised information services or information which is common knowledge among specialists in the field (for example common knowledge among engineers or medical doctors). Likewise, turnover is not normally considered as a business secret, as it is a figure published in the annual accounts or otherwise known to the market. Reasons must be given for requests for confidentiality concerning turnover figures which are not in the public domain and the requests must be evaluated on a case-by-case basis. The fact that information is not publicly available does not necessarily mean that the information can be regarded as a business secret;

(b) historical information, in particular information at least five years old;

(c) statistical or aggregate information;

(d) names of aid recipients, sector of activity, purpose and amount of the aid, etc.

(15) Detailed reasons must be given for any request to derogate from these principles in exceptional cases.

3.2. Other confidential information

(16) In antitrust and merger cases, confidential information includes certain types of information communicated to the Commission on condition that confidentiality is observed (for example a market study commissioned by an undertaking which is party to the procedure and forming part of its property). It seems that a similar approach could be retained for State aid decisions.

(17) In the field of State aid, there may, however, be some forms of confidential information, which would not necessarily be present in antitrust and merger procedures, referring specifically to secrets of the State or other confidential information relating to its organisational activity. Generally, in view of the Commission's obligation to state the reasons for its decisions and the transparency requirement, such information can only in very exceptional circumstances be covered by the obligation of professional secrecy. For example, information regarding the organisation and costs of public services will not normally be considered 'other confidential information' (although it may constitute a business secret, if the criteria laid down in section 3.1 are met).

4. APPLICABLE PROCEDURE

4.1. General principles

(18) The Commission's main task is to reconcile two opposing obligations, namely the requirement to state the reasons for its decisions under Article [296] of the Treaty and therefore ensure that its decisions contain all the essential elements on which they are based, and that of safeguarding the obligation of professional secrecy.

(19) Besides the basic obligation to state the reasons for its decisions, the Commission has to take into account the need for effective application of the State aid rules (inter alia, by giving Member States, beneficiaries and interested parties the possibility to comment on or challenge its decisions) and for transparency of its policy. There is therefore an overriding interest in making public the full substance of its decisions. As a general principle, requests for

confidential treatment can only be granted where strictly necessary to protect business secrets or other confidential information meriting similar protection.

(20) Business secrets and other confidential information do not enjoy an absolute protection: this means for example that they could be divulged when they are essential for the Commission's statement of the reasons for its decisions. This means that information necessary for the identification of an aid measure and its beneficiary cannot normally be covered by the obligation of professional secrecy. Similarly, information necessary to demonstrate that the conditions of Article [107(1)] of the Treaty are met, cannot normally be covered by the obligation of professional secrecy. However, the Commission will have to consider carefully whether the need for publication is more important, given the specific circumstances of a case, than the prejudice that might be generated for that Member State or undertaking involved.

(21) The public version of a Commission decision can only feature deletions from the adopted version for reasons of professional secrecy. Paragraphs cannot be moved, and no sentence can be added or altered. Where the Commission considers that certain information cannot be disclosed, a footnote may be added, paraphrasing the non-disclosed information or indicating a range of magnitude or size, if useful to assure the comprehensibility and coherence of the decision.

(22) Requests not to disclose the full text of a decision or substantial parts of it which would undermine the understanding of the Commission's statement of reasons cannot be accepted.

(23) If there is a complainant involved, the Commission will take into account the complainant's interest in ascertaining the reasons why the Commission adopted a certain decision, without the need to have recourse to Court proceedings.[1] Hence, requests by Member States for parts of the decision which address concerns of complainants to be covered by the obligation of professional secrecy will need to be particularly well reasoned and persuasive. On the other hand, the Commission will not normally be inclined to disclose information alleged to be of the kind covered by the obligation of professional secrecy where there is a suspicion that the complaint has been lodged primarily to obtain access to the information.

Notes

[1] Case C-367/95 P P *Commission v Sytraval* [ECR] 1998 I-1719, paragraph 64.

(24) Member States cannot invoke professional secrecy to refuse to provide information to the Commission which the Commission considers necessary for the examination of aid measures. In this respect, reference is made to the procedure set out in Regulation (EC) No 659/1999 (in particular Articles 2(2), 5, 10 and 16).

4.2. Procedure

(25) The Commission currently notifies its decisions to the Member State concerned without delay and gives the latter the opportunity to indicate, normally within a time period of 15 working days, which information it considers to be covered by the obligation of professional secrecy. This time period may be extended by agreement between the Commission and the Member State concerned.

(26) Where the Member State concerned does not indicate which information it considers to be covered by the obligation of professional secrecy within the period prescribed by the Commission, the decision will normally be disclosed in full.

(27) Where the Member State concerned wishes certain information to be covered by the obligation of professional secrecy, it must indicate the parts it considers to be covered and provide a justification in respect of each part for which non-disclosure is requested.

(28) The Commission will then examine the request from the Member State without delay. If the Commission does not accept that certain parts of the decision are covered by the obligation of professional secrecy, it will state the reasons why in its view those parts cannot be left out of the public version of the decision. In the absence of an acceptable justification by the Member State for its request (i.e. reasoning which is not manifestly irrelevant or manifestly

wrong), the Commission need not further specify the reasons why those parts cannot be left out of the public version of the decision other than by referring to the absence of justification.

(29) If the Commission decides to accept that certain parts are covered by the obligation of professional secrecy without agreeing in full with the Member State's request, it will notify its decision with a new draft to the Member State indicating the parts which have been omitted. If the Commission accepts that the parts indicated by the Member State are covered by the obligation of professional secrecy, the text of the decision will be published pursuant to Article 26 of Regulation (EC) No 659/1999, with the omission of the parts covered by the obligation of professional secrecy. Such omissions will be indicated in the text.[1]

Notes

[1] Using square brackets [...] and indicating in a footnote 'covered by the obligation of professional secrecy'.

---

(30) The Member State will have 15 working days following receipt of the Commission's decision stating the reasons for its refusal to accept the non-disclosure of certain parts, to react and provide additional elements to justify its request.

(31) If the Member State concerned does not react further within the period prescribed by the Commission, the Commission will normally publish the decision as indicated in its reply to the original request made by the Member State.

(32) If the Member State concerned does submit any additional elements within the prescribed period, those elements will be examined by the Commission without delay. If the Commission accepts that the parts indicated by the Member State are covered by the obligation of professional secrecy, the text of the decision will be published as set out in paragraph (29).

(33) In the event that it is not possible to reach agreement, the Commission will proceed with the publication of its decision to initiate the formal investigation procedure forthwith. Such decisions must summarise the relevant issues of fact and law, include a preliminary assessment of the aid character of the proposed measure and set out the doubts as to its compatibility with the common market. Clearly certain essential information must be included in order to enable third parties and the other Member States to comment usefully. The duty of the Commission to provide such essential information will normally prevail over any claim to the protection of business secrets or other confidential information. Furthermore, it is in the interest of the beneficiary as well as interested parties to have access to such a decision as quickly as possible. Permitting any delay in this respect would jeopardise the process of State aid control.

(34) In the event that it is not possible to reach agreement on requests for certain information in decisions not to raise objections and decisions to close the formal investigation procedure to be covered by the obligation of professional secrecy, the Commission will notify its final decision to the Member State together with the text it intends to publish, giving the Member State another 15 working days to react. In the absence of an answer which the Commission considers pertinent, the Commission will normally proceed with the publication of the text.

(35) The Commission is currently reviewing its State aid notification forms. In order to avoid unnecessary correspondence with Member States and delay in the publication of decisions, it intends, in the future, to include in the form a question asking whether the notification contains information which should not be published, and the reasons for non-publication. Only if that question is answered in the affirmative will the Commission enter into correspondence with the Member State in respect of specific cases. Similarly, if additional information is required by the Commission, the Member State will have to indicate at the moment it provides the information requested whether such information should not be published, and the reasons for non-publication. If the Commission uses the information thus identified by the Member State in its decision, it will communicate the adopted decision to the Member State, stating the reasons why in its view these

parts cannot be left out from the public version of the decision as laid down in paragraph (28).

(36) Once the Commission has decided what text it will publish and notified the Member State of its final decision, it is for the Member State to decide whether or not to make use of any judicial procedures available to it, including any interim measures, within the time limits provided for in Article [263 TFEU].

4.3. Third parties

(37) Where third parties other than the Member State concerned (for example, complainants, other Member States or the beneficiary) submit information in the context of State aid procedures, these guidelines will be applied mutatis mutandis.

4.4. Application in time

(38) These guidelines cannot establish binding legal rules and do not purport to do so. They merely set out in advance, in the interests of sound administration, the manner in which the Commission intends to address the issue of confidentiality in State aid procedures. As a rule, if agreement cannot be reached, the Commission's decision to publish may be the subject of specific judicial review proceedings. As these guidelines merely pertain to procedural matters (and to a large extent set out existing practice), they will be applied with immediate effect, including for decisions not to raise objections[1] adopted before the entry into force of Regulation (EC) No 659/1999 to which third parties seek access.

Notes

[1] Decisions to initiate the formal investigation procedure and final decisions adopted before that date were already published in full in the Official Journal of the European Communities. Prior to publication, Member States could indicate whether any information was covered by the obligation of professional secrecy.

G5

NOTICE FROM THE COMMISSION

towards an effective implementation of commission decisions ordering member states
to recover unlawful and incompatible state aid

(2007/C 272/05)

Official Journal C 272, 15.11.2007, p.4

Celex No: 52007XC1115(01)

EUR-Lex permanent link: <http://eur-lex.europa.eu/LexUriServ/LexUriServ.do?uri=CELEX:52007XC1115(01):EN:NOT>

Notes

EEA application: for the corresponding EEA measure, see EFTA Surveillance Authority Decision No 788/08/COL of 17 December 2008 amending, for the 67th time, the procedural and substantive rules in the field of State aid by amending the existing chapters on reference and discount rates and on State aid granted in the form of guarantees and by introducing a new chapter on recovery of unlawful and incompatible State aid, on State aid to cinematographic and other audiovisual works and State aid for railway undertakings, OJ L 105, 21.4.2011, p.32.

Commentary

Notice: B&C: 17.108, 17.116

1. INTRODUCTION

1. In 2005, the Commission presented its road map for State aid reform in its State Aid Action Plan.[1] The programme of reform will improve the effectiveness, transparency and credibility of the EU State aid regime. At the heart of the Action Plan is the principle of 'less and better targeted State aid'. The central objective is to encourage Member States to reduce their overall aid levels, whilst redirecting State aid resources at objectives having a clear Community interest. To achieve this, the Commission is committed to continue taking a strict approach towards the most distortive types of of aid, in particular towards unlawful and incompatible aid.

Notes

[1] State Aid action plan: Less and better targeted State aid: a roadmap for State aid reform 2005–2009.

2. In recent years, the Commission has demonstrated that it is prepared to take a strong stance against unlawful aid. Ever since the entry into force of the Council Regulation (EC) No 659/1999[2] ('the Procedural Regulation'), it has systematically ordered Member States to recover any unlawful aid found to be incompatible with the common market, unless it considered that this would be contrary to a principle of Community law. Since 2000, it has adopted 110 such recovery decisions.

Notes

[2] Council Regulation (EC) No 659/1999 of 22 March 1999 laying down detailed rules for the application of Article [108 TFEU]* (OJ L 83, 27.3.1999, p.1).

* Ed note: please see the Note on the Lisbon Treaty at p.xvii in regard to article renumbering introduced by the Lisbon Treaty.

3. It is essential for the integrity of the State aid regime that these Commission decisions ordering Member States to recover unlawful State aid (hereafter 'recovery decisions') are enforced in an effective and immediate manner. The information collected by the Commission in recent years shows that there is cause for real concern in this respect. Experience shows that there is practically not a single case in which recovery was completed within the deadline set out in the recovery decision. Recent editions of the State aid Scoreboard also show that 45% of all recovery decisions adopted in 2000–2001 had still not been implemented by June 2006.

4. In 2004, the Commission ordered a comparative study on the enforcement of EU State aid policy in different Member States[3] (hereinafter referred to as the 'Enforcement Study'). One of the objectives of the study was to assess the effectiveness of recovery procedures and practices in a number of Member States. The authors of the Study found that the 'excessive length of recovery proceedings is a recurring theme in all country reports'. They recognised that the implementation of recovery decisions had somewhat improved in recent years, but concluded that the recovery of unlawful and incompatible aid still faces a number of obstacles in most of the Member States surveyed.

Notes

[3] Study on the enforcement of State aid law at national level, Competition studies 6, Luxembourg, Office for Official Publications of the European Communities: <http://ec.europa.eu/comm/competition/state_aid/overview/studies.html>.

5. In its State aid Action Plan, the Commission stresses the need for an effective enforcement of recovery decisions. It is clear that the implementation of such decisions is a shared responsibility between the Commission and the Member States and will require considerable efforts by both in order to be successful.

6. The purpose of the present communication is to explain the Commission's policy towards the implementation of recovery decisions. It shall not examine the consequences that national courts may draw from the non respect of the notification and standstill obligation of Article [108(3) TFEU]. The Commission considers there is a need to clarify the measures it intends to take to facilitate the execution of recovery decisions and to set out actions Member States could take to ensure that they reach full compliance with the rules and principles as established by the body of European law and, in particular, the case law of the Community Courts. To this end, the notice will first recall the purpose of recovery and the basic principles underlying the implementation of recovery decisions. It will then present the practical implications of these basic principles for each of the actors involved in the recovery process.

2. The Principles of Recovery Policy

2.1. A short history of recovery policy

7. Article [108(3) TFEU] states that 'the Commission shall be informed in sufficient time to enable it to submit its comments, of any plans to grant or alter aid. [...] The Member State concerned shall not put its proposed measures into effect until this procedure has resulted in a final decision.'

8. In cases where Member States do not notify the Commission of its plans to grant or alter aid prior to such aid being put into effect, the aid is unlawful in relation to Community law from the time that it is granted.

9. In its 'Kohlegesetz' judgment[4] of 1973, the European Court of Justice (ECJ) confirmed for the first time that the Commission had the power to order the recovery of unlawful and incompatible State aid. The Court held that the Commission was competent to decide that a Member State must alter or abolish a State aid that was incompatible with the common market. It should therefore also be entitled to require repayment of this aid. On the basis of this judgment and subsequent case law,[5] the Commission informed the Member States in a Communication published in 1983 that it had decided to use all measures at its disposal to ensure that Member States' obligations under Article [108(3) TFEU] are fulfilled, including the requirement, that Member States recover incompatible aid granted unlawfully from the recipient.[6]

Notes

4 Case 70/72, *Commission v Germany*, [1973] ECR 813, paragraph 13.

5 Case 121/73, *Markmann KG v Germany and Land of Schleswig-Holstein*, [1973] ECR 01495, Case 122/73, *Nordsee, Deutsche Hochseefischerei GmbH v Germany and Land Rheinland-Pfalz*, [1973] ECR 01511, and Case 141/73, *Fritz Lohrey v Germany and the Land Hessen*, [1973] ECR 01527.

6 OJ C 318, 24.11.1983, p.3.

10. In the second half of the 1980s and in the 1990s, the Commission started to order the recovery of unlawful and incompatible aid more systematically. In 1999, basic rules on recovery were included in the Procedural Regulation. Further implementing provisions on recovery were included in Commission Regulation (EC) No 794/2004[7] ('the Implementing Regulation').

Notes

7 Commission Regulation (EC) No 794/2004 of 21 April 2004 implementing Council Regulation (EC) No 659/1999 laying down detailed rules for the application of Article [108(3) TFEU] (OJ L 140, 30.4.2004, p.1).

11. **Article 14(1)** of the Procedural Regulation confirms the constant case law of the Community Courts[8] and establishes an obligation on the Commission to order recovery of unlawful and incompatible aid unless this would be contrary to a general principle of law. This Article also provides that the Member State concerned shall take all necessary measures to recover unlawful aid that is found to be incompatible. **Article 14(2)** establishes that the aid is to be recovered, including interest from the date on which the unlawful aid was at the disposal of the beneficiary until the date of its effective recovery. The Implementing Regulation elaborates the methods to be used for the calculation of recovery interest. Finally, **Article 14(3)** of the Procedural Regulation states, that 'recovery shall be effected without delay and in accordance with the procedures under the national law of the Member State concerned, provided that they allow for the immediate and effective execution of the Commission decision'.

Notes

8 Case C-301/87, *France v Commission*, [1990] ECR I-307.

12. In a number of recent judgments, the ECJ further clarified the scope and interpretation of Article 14(3) of the Procedural Regulation, thereby emphasising the need for an immediate and effective execution of recovery decisions.[9] In addition, the Commission has also started to apply Deggendorf case law[10] in a more systematic manner. This case law enables the Commission, if certain conditions have been satisfied, to order Member States to suspend the payment of a new

compatible aid to a company until that company has reimbursed old unlawful and incompatible aid that is subject to a recovery decision.

Notes

9 Case C-415/03, *Commission v Greece*, ('Olympic Airways'), [2005] ECR I-03875 and Case C-232/05, *Commission v France* ('Scott'), [2006], judgment of 5 October 2006.

10 Case C-188/92, *TWD Textilwerke Deggendorf GmbH v Germany*, ('Deggendorf') ECR [1994], I-00833.

2.2. Purpose and principles of recovery policy

2.2.1 Purpose of recovery

13. The ECJ has held on several occasions that the purpose of recovery is to re-establish the situation that existed on the market prior to the granting of the aid. This is necessary to ensure that the level-playing field in the internal market is maintained, in accordance with Article 3(g) of the EC Treaty*. In this context, the ECJ underlined that the recovery of unlawful and incompatible aid is not a penalty,[11] but the logical consequence of the finding that it is unlawful.[12] It can therefore not be regarded as disproportionate to the objectives of the Treaty with regards to State Aid.[13]

Notes

11 Case C-75/97, *Belgium v Commission*, [1999] ECR I-03671, paragraph 65.

12 Case C-183/91, *Commission v Greece*, [1993] ECR I-3131, paragraph 16.

13 Joined Cases C-278/92, C-279/92 and C-280/92, *Spain v Commission*, [1994] ECR I-04103, paragraph 75.

* Ed note: Article 3(1)(g) EC was repealed by the Treaty of Lisbon. Article 3(1) EC was replaced in substance by Articles 3 to 6 TFEU. The nearest to an equivalent provision to Article 3(1)(g) EC in the TFEU is Article 3(1)(b) TFEU ("The Union shall have exclusive competence in the following areas: ... (b) the establishing of the competition rules necessary for the functioning of the internal market").

14. According to the ECJ, the 're-establishment of the previously existing situation is obtained once the unlawful and incompatible aid is repaid by the recipient who thereby forfeits the advantage which he enjoyed over his competitors in the market, and the situation as it existed prior to the granting of the aid is restored'.[14] In order to eliminate any financial advantages incidental to unlawful aid, interest is to be recovered on the sums unlawfully granted. Such interest must be equivalent to the financial advantage arising from the availability of the funds in question, free of charge, over a given period.[15]

Notes

14 Case C-348/93, *Commission v Italy*, [1995] ECR I-673, paragraph 27.

15 Case T-459/93, *Siemens v Commission*, [1995] ECR II-1675, paragraph 97 to 101.

15. Furthermore, the ECJ has insisted that in order for a Commission recovery decision to be fully executed, the actions undertaken by a Member State must produce concrete effects as regards recovery[16] and that recovery must be immediate.[17] For recovery to reach its objective, it is indeed essential that the repayment of the aid takes place without delay.

Notes

16 Case C-415/03, *Commission v Greece*, cited above footnote 9.

17 Case C-232/05, *Commission v France*, cited above footnote 9.

2.2.2. The obligation to recover unlawful and incompatible State aid and its exceptions

16. Article 14(1) of the Procedural Regulation specifies that 'where negative decisions are taken in cases of unlawful aid, the Commission shall decide that the Member State concerned shall take all necessary measures to recover the aid from the beneficiary'.

17. The Procedural Regulation imposes two limits on the Commission's power to order recovery of unlawful and incompatible aid. Article 14(1) of the Procedural Regulation provides that the Commission shall not require recovery of the aid if this would be contrary to a **general principle of law**. The general principles of law most often invoked in this context are the principles of the protection of legitimate expectation[18] and of legal certainty.[19] It is important to note that the ECJ has given a

very restrictive interpretation to these principles in the context of recovery. Article 15 of the Procedural Regulation states that the powers of the Commission to recover aid shall be subject to a limitation period of 10 years (the so-called '**prescription period**'). The limitation period shall begin on the day on which the unlawful aid is awarded to the beneficiary either as individual aid or as aid under an aid scheme. Any action taken by the Commission[20] or by a Member State, acting at the request of the Commission, with regard to the unlawful aid, shall interrupt the limitation period.

Notes

[18] On the principle of the protection of the legitimate expectations, please see Case C-24/95, *Alcan*, [1997] ECR I-1591, paragraph 25, Case C-5/89, *BUG-Alutechnik*, [1990] ECR I-3437, paragraphs 13 and 14. For an example where the ECJ recognised the existence of legitimate expectations on the side of the beneficiary, please see Case C-223/85, *RSV*, [1987] ECR 4617.

[19] On the principle of legal certainty, please see T-115/94, *Opel Austria GmbH v Council*, [1997] ECR II-00039 and Case C-372/97, *Italy v Commission*, [2004] ECR I-3679, paragraphs 116 to 118, Joined Cases C-74/00 P and C-75/00, *P Falck and Acciaierie di Bolzano v Commission*, [2002] ECR I-7869, paragraph 140. See also Case T-308/00, *Saltzgitter v Commission*, [2004] ECR II-01933, paragraph 166.

[20] For an interpretation of 'any Commission action', please see Case T-369/00, *Département du Loiret v Commission*, [2003] ECR II-01789.

18. Under Article [288 TFEU], decisions are binding in their entirety upon those to whom they are addressed. Therefore, the Member State to which a recovery decision is addressed is obliged to execute this decision.[21] The ECJ has recognised only one exception to this obligation for a Member State to implement a recovery decision addressed to it, namely the existence of exceptional circumstances that would make it **absolutely impossible** for the Member State to execute the decision properly.[22]

Notes

[21] Case 94/87, *Commission v Germany*, [1989] ECR 175.

[22] Case C-404/00, *Commission v Spain*, [2003] ECR I-6695.

19. According to the Community Courts, absolute impossibility can however not be merely supposed. The Member State must demonstrate that it attempted, in good faith, to recover unlawful aid and it must cooperate with the Commission in accordance with Article [4, paragraph 3 TEU], with a view to overcoming the difficulties encountered.[23]

Notes

[23] Case C-280/95, *Commission v Italy*, [1998] ECR I-259.

20. A review of the jurisprudence shows that the Community Courts have interpreted the concept of 'absolute impossibility' in a very restrictive manner. The Courts have confirmed on several occasions that a Member State may not plead requirements of its national law, such as national prescription rules[24] or the absence of a recovery title under national law,[25] in order to justify its failure to comply with a recovery decision.[26] In the same way, the ECJ held that the obligation to recover is not affected by circumstances linked to the economic situation of the beneficiary. It clarified that a company in financial difficulties does not constitute proof that recovery was impossible.[27] In such circumstances, the court pointed out that the absence of any recoverable assets is the only way for a Member State to show the absolute impossibility of recovering the aid.[28] In a number of cases, the Member State argued that they had not been able to execute the recovery decision, because of the administrative or technical difficulties involved (e.g. the very high number of beneficiaries involved). The Court consistently refused to accept that such difficulties constitute an absolute impossibility to recover.[29] Finally, the apprehension of even insurmountable internal difficulties cannot justify a failure by a Member State to fulfil its obligations under Community law.[30]

Notes

[24] Case C-24/95, *Alcan*, [1997] ECR 1591, paragraph 34–37.

[25] Case C-303/88, *Italy v Commission*, [1991] ECR I-1433.

[26] Case C-52/84, *Commission v Belgium*, [1986] ECR 89, paragraph 9.

[27] Case C-52/84, *Commission v Belgium*, cited above footnote 26, paragraph 14.

28 Case C-499/99, *Commission v Spain*, [2002] ECR I-06301.
29 Case C-280/95, *Commission v Italy*, cited above footnote 23.
30 Case C-6/97, *Italy v Commission*, [1999] ECR I-2981, paragraph 34.

2.2.3. *The use of national procedures and the necessity of an immediate and effective execution*

21. Article 14(3) of the Procedural Regulation specifies that 'recovery shall be effected without delay and in accordance with the procedures under the national law of the Member State concerned, provided that they allow the immediate and effective execution of the Commission's decision.'

22. If Member States are free to choose, according to their national law, the means by which they implement recovery decisions, the measures chosen should give full effect to the recovery decision. It is therefore necessary that the national measures taken by Member States lead to an **effective and immediate** execution of the Commission decision.

23. In its Olympic Airways judgment,[31] the ECJ underlined that the implementation measures taken by the Member State must be **effective** and produce a concrete outcome in terms of recovery. The actions undertaken by the Member State must result in the actual recovery of the sums owed by the beneficiary. In its recent Scott judgment,[32] the ECJ confirmed that line and emphasised that national procedures which do not fulfil the conditions laid down in Article 14(3) of the Procedural Regulation should be left unapplied. It refuted, in particular, the Member State's argument that it had taken all steps available in its national system and insisted that these steps should also lead to a concrete outcome in terms of recovery, and this within the deadline set by the Commission.

Notes

31 Case C-415/03, *Commission v Greece*, cited above footnote 9.
32 Case C-232/05, *Commission v France*, cited above footnote 9.

24. Article 14(3) of the Procedural Regulation requires that recovery decisions are implemented in a way that is both effective and **immediate**. In the Scott case, the ECJ stressed the importance of the time-dimension in the recovery process. The Court specified that the application of national procedures should not impede the restoration of effective competition by preventing the immediate and effective execution of the Commission's decision. National procedures, which prevent the immediate restoration of the previously existing situation and prolong the unfair competitive advantage resulting from unlawful and incompatible aid, do not fulfil the conditions laid down in Article 14(3) of the Procedural Regulation.

25. In this context it is important to recall that an action for annulment of a recovery decision brought under Article [263 TFEU] does not have a suspensive effect. In the context of such an action, the beneficiary of the aid may however apply for the suspension of the execution of the recovery decision pursuant of Article [278 TFEU]. Applications for suspension, must state the circumstances giving rise to urgency and must contain the pleas of fact and law establishing a prima facie case for the interim measures being applied for. The ECJ or the CFI may then, if they consider that circumstances so require, order that application of the contested Commission decision be suspended.

2.2.4. *The principle of loyal cooperation*

26. [Article 4, paragraph 3 TEU] obliges Member States to facilitate the achievement of the Community tasks and imposes mutual duties of cooperation on the EU institutions and Member States, with a view to attaining the objectives of the Treaty.

27. In the context of the implementation of recovery decisions, the Commission and the Member States' authorities must therefore cooperate to attain the objective of the restoration of competitive conditions in the internal market.

28. If a Member State encounters unforeseen or unforeseeable difficulties in executing the recovery decision within the required time-limit or perceives consequences overlooked by the Commission, it should submit those problems for consideration to the Commission, together with proposals for suitable amendments.[33] In such a case, the Commission and the Member State concerned must work together in good faith to overcome the difficulties whilst fully observing the [Treaty on the Functioning of the European Union] provisions.[34] Likewise the principle of loyal cooperation requires that the Member States provide the Commission with all the

information enabling it to establish that the means chosen constitutes an adapted implementation of the decision.[35]

Notes

[33] Case C-404/00, *Commission v Spain*, cited above footnote 22.

[34] Case C-94/87, *Commission v Germany* [1989] ECR 175, paragraph 9, Case C-348/93, *Commission v Italy*, cited above footnote 14, paragraph 17.

[35] For an illustration of proposals for implementation see Case C-209/00, *Commission v Germany*, [2002] ECR I-11695.

29. Informing the Commission of the technical and legal difficulties involved in implementing a recovery decision does however not relieve Member States from the duty to take all necessary steps possible to recover the aid from the undertaking in question and to propose to the Commission any suitable arrangements for implementing the decision.[36]

Notes

[36] Case 94/87, *Commission v Germany* cited above footnote 34, paragraph 10.

3. Implementing Recovery Policy

30. Both the Commission and the Member States have an essential role to play in the implementation of recovery decisions and may contribute to [an] effective enforcement of recovery policy.

3.1. The role of the Commission

31. The Commission's recovery decision imposes a recovery obligation upon the Member State concerned. It requires the Member State concerned to recover a certain amount of aid from a beneficiary or a number of beneficiaries within a given time frame. Experience shows that the speed with which a recovery decision is executed is affected by the degree of precision or the completeness of that decision. The Commission will therefore continue its efforts to ensure that recovery decisions provide a clear indication of the amount(s) of aid to be recovered, the undertaking(s) liable to recovery and the deadline within which the recovery should be completed.

Identification of the undertakings from whom the aid must be recovered

32. *The unlawful and incompatible aid must be recovered from the undertakings that actually benefited from it.*[37] The Commission will continue its present practice of identifying in its recovery decisions, where possible, the identity of the undertaking(s) from whom the aid must be recovered. If, at the stage of the implementation, it appears that the aid was transferred to other entities, the Member State may have to extend recovery to encompass all effective beneficiaries to ensure that the recovery obligation is not circumvented.

Notes

[37] Case C-303/88, *Italy v Commission*, [1991] ECR I-1433, paragraph 57; Case C-277/00, *Germany v Commission* ('SMI'), [2004] ECR I-3925, paragraph 75.

33. The Community Courts have given some guidance on the conditions under which the recovery obligation must be extended to companies other than the original beneficiary of the unlawful and incompatible aid. According to the ECJ, a transfer of the undue advantage may occur when the assets of the original aid beneficiary are transferred to a third party at a price that is lower than their market value sometimes to a successor company set up in order to circumvent the recovery order. If the Commission can prove that assets have been sold at a price that is lower than their market value, especially to a successor company set up to circumvent the recovery order, the ECJ considers that the recovery order can be extended to that third party.[38] Typical cases of circumvention are cases where the transfer does not reflect any economic logic other than the invalidation of the recovery order.[39]

Notes

[38] Case C-277/00, *Germany v Commission*, cited above footnote 37.

[39] Case C-328/99 and C-399/00, *Italy and SMI 2 Multimedia Spa v Commission*. For another example of circumvention, see Case C-415/03, *Commission v Greece*, cited above footnote 9.

34. As regards transfer of shares of a company that has to reimburse an illegal and incompatible aid (share deals), the ECJ held[40] that the sale of shares in such a company to a third party does not affect the obligation of the beneficiary to reimburse such aid.[41] When it can be established that the buyer of the shares paid the prevailing market price for the shares of that company, it cannot be regarded as having benefited from an advantage that could constitute a State Aid.[42]

Notes

[40] Case C-328/99 and C-399/00, *Italy and SIM 2 Multimedia v Commission*, [2003] I-4035, paragraph 83.

[41] In the event of a privatisation of a company that received State aid declared compatible by the Commission, the Member State can introduce a liability clause in the privatisation agreement to protect the buyer of the company against the risk that the initial Commission decision approving the aid would be overturned by the Community Courts and replaced by a Commission decision ordering the recovery of that aid from the beneficiary. Such a clause could provide for an adjustment of the price paid by the buyer for the privatised company to take due account of the new recovery liability.

[42] Case C-277/00, *Germany v Commission*, cited above footnote 37, paragraph 80.

35. When it adopts a recovery decision regarding aid schemes, the Commission is normally not in a position to identify, in the decision itself, all the undertakings that have received unlawful and incompatible aid. This will have to be done at the start of the implementation process by the Member State concerned, who will have to look at the individual situation of each undertaking concerned.[43]

Notes

[43] Case C-310/99, *Italy v Commission*, [2002] ECR I-2289, paragraph 91.

Determination of the amount to be recovered

36. The purpose of recovery is achieved 'once the aid in question, together where appropriate with default interest, has been repaid by the recipient or, in other words, by the undertakings which actually benefited from it. By repaying the aid, the recipient forfeits the advantage which it had enjoyed over its competitors on the market, and the situation prior to payment of the aid is restored'.[44]

Notes

[44] Case C-277/00, *Germany v Commission*, cited above footnote 37, paragraphs 74–76.

37. As it has done in the past, the Commission will clearly identify the unlawful and incompatible aid measures that are subject to recovery in its recovery decisions. When it has the necessary data at its disposal, the Commission will also endeavour to quantify the precise amount of aid to be recovered. It is clear, though, that the Commission cannot and is legally not required to fix the exact amount to be recovered. It is sufficient for the Commission's decision to include information enabling the Member State to determine the amount, without too much difficulty.[45]

Notes

[45] Case C-480/98, *Spain v Commission*, [2000] ECR I-8717, paragraph 25 and Joint Cases C-67/85, C-68/85 and C-70/85, *Kwekerij van der Kooy BV and others v Commission*, [1988] ECR 219.

38. In the case of an unlawful and incompatible aid scheme, the Commission is not able to quantify the amount of incompatible aid to be recovered from each beneficiary. This would require a detailed analysis by the Member State of the aid granted in each individual case on the basis of the scheme in question. The Commission therefore indicates in its decision that Member States will have to recover all aid, unless it has been granted to a specific project, which, at the time of granting, fulfilled all conditions of the block exemption regulations or in an aid scheme approved by the Commission.

39. According to Article 14(2) of the Procedural Regulation, the aid to be recovered pursuant to a recovery decision shall include interest at an appropriate level to be fixed by the Commission. Interest shall be payable from the time the unlawful aid was at the disposal of the beneficiary until the date of its recovery.[46] The Implementing Regulation establishes that the interest rate shall be applied on a compound basis until the date of the recovery of the aid.

Notes

46 See in that context, the exception of Case C-480/98, *Spain v Commission*, cited above footnote 45, paragraphs 36 and following.

Timetable for the implementation of the decision

40. In the past, the Commission's recovery decisions specified a single time-limit of two months, within which the Member State concerned was required to communicate to the Commission, the measures it had taken to comply with a given decision. The Court acknowledged that this deadline is to be regarded as the deadline for the execution of the Commission decision itself.[47]

Notes

47 Case C-207/05, *Commission v Italy*, [2006] ECR I-00070, paragraph 31–36; see also Case C-378/98, *Commission v Belgium*, [2001] ECR I-5107, paragraph 28 and Case C-232/05, *Commission v France*, cited above footnote 9.

41. The Court further concluded that contacts and negotiations between the Commission and the Member State, in the context of the execution of the Commission decision, could not relieve the Member State from the duty to take all necessary measures to execute the decision within the prescribed time-limit.[48]

Notes

48 Case C-5/86, *Commission v Belgium*, [1987] ECR 1773.

42. The Commission recognizes that the two months deadline for the execution of the Commission decisions is too short in the majority of cases. Therefore, it decided to prolong to four months the deadline for the execution of the recovery decisions. From now on, the Commission will specify two time limits in its decisions: — a first time-limit of two months following the entry into force of the decision, within which the Member State must *inform* the Commission of the measures planned or taken, — a second time-limit of four months following the entry into force of the decision, within which the Commission decision must have been *executed*.

43. If a Member State encounters serious difficulties preventing it from respecting either one of these deadlines, it must inform the Commission of these difficulties, providing an appropriate justification. The Commission may then prolong the deadline in accordance with the principle of loyal cooperation.[49]

Notes

49 Case C-207/05, *Commission v Italy*, [2006], judgement of 1 June 2006.

3.2. The role of the Member States: implementing the recovery decisions

3.2.1. Who is responsible for the implementation of the recovery decision?

44. The Member State is responsible for the implementation of the recovery decision. Article 14(1) of the Procedural Regulation provides that the Member State concerned is to take all necessary measures to recover the aid from the beneficiary.

45. In this context, it is important to keep in mind that the ECJ has recalled on several occasions that a Commission decision addressed to a Member State is binding on all the organs of that State, including the Courts of that State.[50] This implies that each organ of the Member State involved in the implementation of a recovery decision must take all necessary measures to secure the immediate and effective application of such a decision.

Notes

50 Case 249/85, *Albako Margarinefabrik Maria von der Linde GmbH & Co. KG v Bundesanstalt für landwirtschaftliche Marktordnung*, [1987] ECR 02345.

46. Community law does not prescribe which organ of the Member State should be in charge of the practical implementation of a recovery decision. It is for the domestic legal system of each Member State to designate the bodies that will be responsible for the implementation of the recovery decision. The authors of the Enforcement Study note that 'a principle common to all countries

reviewed is that recovery must be effected by the authority that granted the aid. This leads to the involvement of a variety of central, regional and local bodies, in the recovery process'.[51] They also point out that some Member States have charged one central body with the task to control and oversee the recovery process. This body normally has ongoing contact with the Commission. The authors of the Enforcement Study conclude that the existence of such a central body appears to contribute to a more efficient implementation of recovery decisions.

3.2.2. Implementation of the recovery obligation

47. Article 14(3) of the Procedural Regulation obliges the Member State to initiate recovery proceedings without any delay. As mentioned in section 3.1 above, the recovery decision will specify a time-limit within which the Member State is to submit precise information on the measures it has taken and planned to execute the decision. In particular, the Member State will be required to provide complete information on the identity of the beneficiaries of the unlawful and incompatible aid, the amounts of aid involved and the national procedure applied to obtain recovery. In addition, the Member State will be required to provide documentation showing that it notified the beneficiary of its obligation to repay the aid.

Identification of the aid beneficiary and the amount to be recovered

48. The recovery decision will not always contain complete information on the identity of the beneficiaries, nor on the amounts of aid to be recovered. In such cases, the Member State must identify without any delay the undertakings concerned by the decision and quantify the precise amount of aid to be recovered from each of them.

49. In the case of an unlawful and incompatible aid scheme, the Member State will be required to carry out a detailed analysis of each individual aid granted on the basis of the scheme in question. To quantify the precise amount of aid to be recovered from each individual beneficiary under the scheme, it will need to determine the extent to which the aid has been granted to a specific project, which, at the time of granting, fulfilled all conditions of the block exemption regulations or in an aid scheme approved by the Commission. In such cases, the Member State may also apply the substantive De Minimis criteria applicable at the time of the granting of the unlawful and incompatible [aid] that is subject to the recovery decision.

50. National authorities are allowed to take into account the incidence of the tax system in order to determine the amount to be reimbursed. Where a beneficiary of unlawful and incompatible aid has paid tax on the aid received, the national authorities may, in accordance with their national tax rules, take account of the earlier payment of tax by recovering only the net amount received by the beneficiary.[52] The Commission considers that in such cases, the national authorities will need to ensure that the beneficiary will not be able to enjoy a further tax deduction by claiming that the reimbursement has reduced his taxable income, since this would mean that the net amount of the recovery was lower than the net amount initially received.

The applicable recovery procedure

51. The authors of the Enforcement Study provide ample evidence of the fact that recovery procedures vary significantly between Member States. The Study also shows that, even within one single Member State, several procedures can be applied to pursue the recovery of unlawful and incompatible aid. In most Member States, the applicable recovery procedure is normally determined by nature of the measure underlying the granting of the aid. Administrative procedures, on the whole, tend to be much more efficient than civil procedures, because administrative recovery orders are or can be made immediately enforceable.[53]

52. Community law does not prescribe which procedure the Member State should apply to execute a recovery decision. However, Member States should be aware that the choice and application of a national procedure is subject to the condition that such procedure allows for the immediate and effective execution of the Commission's decision. This implies that the authorities responsible should carefully consider the full range of recovery instruments available under national law and select the procedure most likely to secure the immediate execution of the decision.[54] They should use fast-track procedures where possible under national law. According to the principle of equivalence and effectiveness, these procedures must not be less favourable than those governing similar domestic actions, and that they should not render practically impossible or excessively difficult the exercise of rights conferred by Community law.[55]

53. More generally, Member States should not be able to place any obstacles in the way of carrying out a Commission recovery decision.[56] Consequently, Member State authorities are under an obligation to set aside any provisions of national law, which might impede the immediate execution of the Commission decision.[57]

The notification and enforcement of recovery orders

54. Once the beneficiary, the amount to be recovered and the applicable procedure have been determined, recovery orders should be sent to the beneficiaries of the unlawful and incompatible aid without delay and within the deadline prescribed by the Commission decision. The authorities responsible for carrying out the recovery must ensure that these recovery orders are enforced and that recovery is completed within the time-limit specified in the decision. Where a beneficiary does not comply with the recovery order, Member States should seek the immediate enforcement of its recovery claims under national law.

3.2.3. Litigation before national courts

55. The implementation of recovery decisions can give rise to litigation in national courts. Although there are very significant differences in the judicial traditions and systems of Member States, two main categories of recovery-related litigation can be distinguished: actions brought by the recovering authority seeking a court order to force an unwilling recipient to refund the unlawful and incompatible aid and actions brought by beneficiaries contesting the recovery order.

56. The analysis carried out in the context of the Enforcement Study provides evidence that the execution of a recovery decision can be delayed for many years when the national measures taken for the implementation of a recovery decision are challenged in court. This is even more the case when the recovery decision is itself challenged before Community courts and when national judges are asked to suspend the implementation of national measures until the Community Courts have ruled on the validity of the recovery decision.

57. The ECJ has ruled that the beneficiary of an aid who could without any doubt have challenged a Commission recovery decision under Article [263 TFEU] before a European Court can no longer challenge the validity of the decision in proceedings before the national court on the ground that the decision was unlawful.[58] It derives from this that the beneficiary of an aid who could have asked for interim relief before the Community Courts in accordance with Articles [278 and 279 TFEU] and has failed to do so cannot ask for a suspension of the measures taken by the national authorities for implementing that decision on grounds linked to the validity of the decision. This question is reserved for the Community Courts.[59]

Notes

[58] Case C-188/92, *TWD Textilwerke Deggendorf GmbH v Germany*, cited above footnote 10.
[59] As reaffirmed in the Case C-232/05, *Commission v France*, cited above footnote 9.

58. On the other hand, in cases where it is not self-evident that an action for annulment brought against the contested decision by the beneficiary of the aid would have been admissible, an adequate legal protection must be offered to the aid beneficiary. In the event that the aid beneficiary challenges the implementation of the decision in proceedings before the national court on the ground that such recovery decision was unlawful, the national judge must make a request for a preliminary ruling on the validity of such decision to the ECJ in accordance with Article [267 TFEU].[60]

Notes

[60] Case C-346/03, *Atzeni a.o.*, [2006], page I-01875, paragraph 30–34.

59. In case the beneficiary also asks for interim relief of the national measures adopted to implement the recovery decision because of an alleged illegality of the Commission's recovery decision, the national judge has to assess whether the case at hand fulfils the conditions established by the ECJ in the cases Zuckerfabrik[61] and Atlanta.[62] According to settled case-law, interim relief can be ordered by the national court only if:
   1. that court entertains serious doubts as to the validity of the Community act and, if the validity of the contested act is not already in issue before the Court of Justice, itself refers the question to the Court of Justice;
   2. there is urgency, in that the interim relief is necessary to avoid serious and irreparable damage being caused to the party seeking the relief;
   3. the court takes due account of the Community interest; and
   4. in its assessment of all those conditions, it respects any decisions of the Court of Justice or the Court of First Instance ruling on the lawfulness of the Community act or on an application for interim measures seeking similar interim relief at Community level.[63]

Notes

[61] Joined Cases C-143/88 and C-92/89, *Zuckerfabrik Süderdithmarschen A.G. a.o.*, [1991] ECR I-415, paragraphs 23 and following.
[62] Case C-465/93, *Atlanta Fruchthandelsgesellschaft mbH a.o.*, [1995] ECR I-3761, paragraph 51.
[63] Case C-465/93, *Atlanta Fruchthandelsgesellschaft mbH a.o.,* cited above footnote 61, paragraph 51.

3.2.4. The specific case of insolvent beneficiaries

60. As a preliminary observation, it is important to recall that the ECJ has consistently held that the fact that a beneficiary is insolvent or subject to bankruptcy proceedings has no effect on its obligation to repay unlawful and incompatible aid.[64]

Notes

[64] Case C-42–93, *Spain v Commission* ('Merco'), [1994] ECR I-4175.

61. In the majority of cases involving an insolvent aid beneficiary, it will not be possible to recover the full amount of unlawful and incompatible aid (including interests), as the beneficiary's assets will be insufficient to satisfy all creditors' claims. Consequently, it is not possible to fully re-establish the ex-ante situation in the traditional manner. Since the ultimate objective of recovery is to end the distortion of competition, the ECJ has stated that the liquidation of the beneficiary can be regarded as an acceptable

option to recovery in such cases.[65] The Commission is therefore of the view that a decision ordering the Member State to recover unlawful and incompatible aid from an insolvent beneficiary may be considered to be properly executed either when full recovery is completed or, in case of partial recovery, when the company is liquidated and its assets are sold under market conditions.

Notes

[65] Case C-52/84, *Commission v Belgium*, [1986] ECR p.89.

62. When implementing recovery decisions concerning insolvent beneficiaries, Member State authorities should ensure that due account is taken throughout the insolvency proceedings of the Community interest, and more in particular of the need to end immediately the distortion of competition caused by the granting of unlawful and incompatible aid.

63. However, the Commission's experience has shown that the sole registration of claims in bankruptcy proceedings may not always be sufficient to ensure the immediate and effective implementation of the Commission's recovery decisions. The application of certain provisions of national bankruptcy laws may frustrate the effect of recovery decisions by allowing the company to operate despite the absence of full recovery, thus allowing the distortion of competition to continue. Based on its experience in dealing with cases of recovery from insolvent beneficiaries, the Commission considers that there is a need to define the obligations of Member States at the different steps of bankruptcy proceedings.

64. The Member State should immediately register its claims in the bankruptcy proceedings[66] According to the ECJ case law, recovery will be done according to national bankruptcy rules.[67] The recovery debt will thus be refunded by virtue of the status given to it by national law.

Notes

[66] C-142/87, *Commission v Belgium*, [1990] ECR I-959, paragraph 62.

[67] Case C-142/87, *ibid.* Case C-499/99, *Commission v Spain* ('Magefesa') [2002], ECR I-603, paragraphs 28–44.

65. In the past, there have been cases in which the insolvency administrator refused to register a recovery claim in the bankruptcy proceedings, and this because of the form of the illegal and incompatible aid granted (for example when the aid had been granted in the form of a capital injection). The Commission considers that this situation is problematic, especially if such a refusal would deprive the authorities responsible for the execution of the recovery decision of any means to ensure that due account is taken of the Community interest in the course of the insolvency proceedings. Therefore the Commission considers that the Member State should dispute the refusal by the insolvency administrator to register its claims.[68]

Notes

[68] Please see in that context, the judgment of the Commercial Chamber of the Amberg Court of 23 July 2001 in relation to the aid granted by Germany to 'Neue Maxhütte Stahlwerke GmbH' (Commission Decision 96/178/ECSC (OJ L 53, 2.3.1996, p.41). In that case, the German court over-ruled the refusal of the insolvency administrator to register a recovery claim resulting from an illegal and incompatible aid granted in the form of a capital injection, as this would render the execution of the recovery decision impossible.

66. To ensure the immediate and effective implementation of the Commission's recovery decision, the Commission is of the view that the authorities responsible for the execution of the recovery decision should also appeal any decision by the insolvency administrator or the insolvency court to allow a continuation of the insolvent beneficiary's activity beyond the time limits set in the recovery decision. Likewise, national courts, when faced with such a request, should take the Community interest fully into account, and more in particular the need to ensure that the execution of the Commission's decision is immediate and that the distortion of competition caused by the unlawful and incompatible aid is ended as soon as possible. The Commission considers that they should therefore not allow for a continuation of an insolvent beneficiary's activity in the absence of full recovery.

67. In the case where a continuation plan is proposed to the creditors' committee implying a continuation of the activity of the beneficiary, the national authorities responsible for the execution of the

recovery decision can only support this plan if it ensures that the aid is repaid in full within the time limits foreseen in the Commission's recovery decision. In particular, the Member State cannot waive part of its recovery claim, nor can it accept any other solution that would not result in the immediate ending of the activity of the beneficiary. In the absence of a full and immediate repayment of the unlawful and incompatible aid, the authorities responsible for the execution of the recovery decision should take all measures available to oppose the adoption of a continuation plan and should insist on the ending of the activity of the beneficiary within the time limit set in the recovery decision.

68. In the case of liquidation, and as long as the aid has not been fully recovered, the Member State should oppose any transfer of assets that is not carried out on market terms and/or that is organised so as to circumvent the recovery decision. To achieve a 'correct transfer of assets', the Member State has to ensure that the undue advantage created by the aid is not transferred to the acquirer of the assets. This may be the case if the assets of the original aid beneficiary are transferred to a third party at a price that is lower than their market value or to a successor company set up in order to circumvent the recovery order. In such a case, the recovery order needs to be extended to that third party.[69]

Notes

[69] Case C-277/00, *Germany v Commission*, cited above footnote 37.

4. Consequences of the Failure to Implement the Commission Recovery Decisions

69. A Member State is deemed to comply with the recovery decision when the aid has been fully reimbursed within the prescribed time limit or, in the case of an insolvent beneficiary, when the company is liquidated under market conditions.

70. The Commission may also accept, in duly justified cases, a provisional implementation of the decision when it is subject to litigation before the national or the Community Courts (e.g. the payment of the full amount of unlawful and incompatible aid into a blocked account).[70] The Member State must ensure that the advantage linked to the unlawful and incompatible aid leaves the company.[71] The Member State should submit, for approval by the Commission, a justification for the adoption of such provisional measures and a full description of the provisional measure envisaged.

Notes

[70] In practical terms, the payment of the total amount of aid and the interests on a blocked account may be ruled by a specific contract, signed by the bank and the beneficiary, and by which the parties agree that the sum will be released in favour of one or the other party once the litigation has come to an end.

[71] Contrary to the constitution of a blocked account, the use of bank guarantees may not be considered as an adequate provisional measure since the total amount of the aid is still at the recipient's disposal.

71. Where the Member State concerned has not complied with the recovery decision, and where it has not been able to demonstrate the existence of absolute impossibility, the Commission may initiate infringement proceedings. In addition, if certain conditions are satisfied, it may require the Member State concerned to suspend the payment of a new compatible aid to the beneficiary or beneficiaries concerned in application of the Deggendorf principle.

4.1. Infringement proceedings

— Actions on the basis of Article [108(2) TFEU]

72. If the Member State concerned does not comply with the recovery decision within the prescribed time limit and if it has not been able to demonstrate absolute impossibility, the Commission, as it has already done, or any other interested State, may refer the matter directly to the ECJ pursuant to with Article [108(2)] of the Treaty. The Commission may then invoke arguments concerning the behaviour of the executive, legislative or judicial organs of the Member State concerned, as the Member State should be considered in its entirety.[72]

Notes

72 Case C-224/01, *Köbler*, [2003] ECR I-10239, paragraphs 31–33; Case C-173/03, *Traghetti del Mediterraneo*, [2003] page I-05177, paragraphs 30–33.

— Actions on the basis of Article [260 TFEU]

73. In the event that that the ECJ condemns the Member State for non compliance with a Commission decision and if the Commission considers that the Member State concerned has not complied with the judgment of the ECJ, the Commission may pursue the matter in accordance with Article [260(2)] of the Treaty. In such a case, after giving the Member State the opportunity to submit its observations, the Commission delivers a reasoned opinion specifying the points on which the Member State concerned was non-compliant with the judgment of the ECJ.

74. If the Member State concerned fails to take the necessary measures to comply with the ECJ's judgment within the time limit laid down in the reasoned opinion, the Commission may further refer the matter to the ECJ, pursuant to Article [260(2) TFEU]. The Commission will then request the ECJ to impose a penalty payment on the Member State concerned. This *penalty payment* will be fixed in accordance with the Commission communication on the application of Article [260 TFEU],73 and be calculated on the basis of three criteria: the seriousness of the infringement, its duration, and the need to ensure that the penalty itself is a deterrent to further infringements. According to the same communication, the Commission will also ask for the payment of a *lump sum* penalising the continuation of the infringement between the first judgement of non-compliance and the judgement delivered under Article [260 TFEU]. In view of the fact that the failure to implement the Commission recovery decision prolongs the distortion of competition caused by the granting of illegal and incompatible aid, the Commission will not hesitate to make use of this possibility if it appears necessary to ensure the respect of the State aid rules.

Notes

73 Communication from the Commission on the application of Article [260 TFEU] — SEC/2005/1658 (OJ C 126, 7.6.2007, p.15).

4.2. Applying the Deggendorf case-law

75. In its judgment on the Deggendorf case, the CFI has held that, 'when the Commission considers the compatibility of a State aid with the common market, it must take all the relevant factors into account, including, where relevant, the circumstances already considered in a prior decision and the obligations which that previous decision may have imposed on a Member State. It follows that the Commission has the power to take into consideration, first, any accumulated effect of the old [...] aid and the new [...] aid and, secondly, the fact that the [old] aid declared unlawful [...] had not been repaid'.74 In application of this judgment, and to avoid a distortion of competition contrary to the common interest, the Commission may order a Member State to suspend the payment of a new compatible aid to an undertaking that has at its disposal an unlawful and incompatible aid subject to an earlier recovery decision, and this until the Member State has reassured itself that the undertaking concerned has reimbursed the old unlawful and incompatible aid.

Notes

74 Case T-244/93 and T-486/93, *TWD Deggendorf v Commission*, [1995] ECR II-2265, paragraph 56.

76. The Commission has been applying the so-called Deggendorf principle in a more systematic manner for a few years now. In practice, in the course of the preliminary investigation of a new aid measure, the Commission will request a commitment from the Member State to suspend the payment of new aid to any beneficiary that still needs to reimburse an unlawful and incompatible aid subject to an earlier recovery decision. If the Member State does not give this commitment and/or in the absence of clear data on the aid measures involved75 preventing the Commission to assess the global impact of the old and the new aid on competition, the Commission will take a final conditional decision on the basis of Article 7(4) of the Procedural Regulation, requiring the

Member State concerned to suspend payment of the new aid until it is satisfied that the beneficiary concerned has reimbursed the old unlawful and incompatible aid, including any recovery interests due.

Notes

75 E.g. in the case of illegal and incompatible schemes where the amount and the beneficiaries are not known to the Commission.

77. The Deggendorf principle has meanwhile been integrated in the Community Guidelines on State aid for rescuing and restructuring firms in difficulty[76] and in recent Block Exemption Regulations.[77] The Commission intends to integrate this principle into all forthcoming State aid rules and decisions.

Notes

76 OJ C 244, 1.10.2004, p.2, paragraph 23.
77 Commission Regulation (EC) No 1628/2006 of 24 October 2006 on the application of Articles [107 and 108] of the Treaty to national regional investment aid (OJ L 302, 1.11.2006, p.29).

78. Finally, the Commission welcomes the initiative of Italy to insert a specific 'Deggendorf' provision in its 'Legge Finanziaria 2007', which provides that beneficiaries of new State aid measures should declare that they do not have at their disposal any illegal or incompatible State aid.[78]

Notes

78 *Legge 27 dicembre 2006, n. 296, art. 1223.*

5. CONCLUSION

79. The maintenance of a system of free and undistorted competition is one of the cornerstones of the European Community. As part of the European competition policy, State aid discipline is essential to ensure that the internal market remains a level playing field in all economic sectors in Europe. In this key task, the Commission and the Member States have the joint responsibility to ensure a proper enforcement of State aid discipline and in particular of recovery decisions.

80. By issuing this communication, the Commission is willing to increase the awareness of the principles of recovery policy as defined by the Community Courts and to clarify the Commission practice as regards its recovery policy. The Commission commits itself to abide by these recalled principles and invites Member States to ask for advice when facing difficulties in implementing recovery decisions. The services of the Commission remain at the disposal of the Member States to provide further guidance and assistance if required.

81. In return, the Commission expects Member States to abide to the principles of recovery policy. It is only through a joint effort of both Commission and Member States that State aid discipline will be ensured and produce its desired objective, i.e. the maintenance of undistorted competition within the internal market.

G6

COMMISSION NOTICE ON THE ENFORCEMENT OF STATE AID LAW BY NATIONAL COURTS

(2009/C 85/01)

Official Journal C 85, 9.4.2009, p.1

Celex No: 52009XC0409(01)

EUR-Lex permanent link: <http://eur-lex.europa.eu/LexUriServ/LexUriServ.do?uri=CELEX:5200
9XC0409(01):EN:NOT>

Notes

EEA application: on 10 June 2009 the EFTA Surveillance Authority adopted a new chapter of its State Aid Guidelines on enforcement of state aid law by national courts. The new chapter corresponds to this Notice except for necessary adjustments based on particularities of the EEA Agreement. See EFTA Surveillance Authority Decision No 254/09/COL of 10 June 2009 amending, for the 71st time, the procedural and substantive rules in the field of state aid by introducing a new chapter on enforcement of state aid law by national courts, OJ L 115, 5.5.2011, p.13.

Commentary

Notice: **B&C:** 17.003, 17.117 **F&N:** 17.556

I. INTRODUCTION

1. In 2005, the Commission adopted a road map for State aid reform, the State Aid Action Plan[1] ('the SAAP'), to improve the effectiveness, transparency, credibility and predictability of the State aid regime under the [Treaty on the Functioning of the European Union]*. Based on the principle of 'less and better targeted State aid', the central objective of the SAAP is to encourage Member States to reduce their overall aid, whilst redirecting State aid resources to horizontal common interest objectives. In this context, the Commission has reaffirmed its commitment to a strict approach towards unlawful and incompatible aid. The SAAP highlighted the need for better targeted enforcement and monitoring as regards State aid granted by Member States and stressed that private litigation before national courts could contribute to this aim by ensuring increased discipline in the field of State aid.[2]

Notes

[1] State Aid Action Plan: Less and better targeted State aid: a roadmap for State aid reform 2005–2009, COM(2005) 107 final.

[2] SAAP, paragraphs 55 and 56.

* Ed note: please see the Note on the Lisbon Treaty at p.xvii in regard to renaming and article renumbering introduced by the Lisbon Treaty.

2. Prior to the adoption of the SAAP, the Commission had already addressed the role of national courts in the Notice on cooperation between national courts and the Commission in the State aid field, published in 1995[3] ('the 1995 Cooperation Notice'). The 1995 Cooperation Notice introduced mechanisms for cooperation and exchange of information between the Commission and national courts.

Notes

[3] OJ C 312, 23.11.1995, p.8.

3. In 2006, the Commission commissioned a study on the enforcement of State aid law at national level[4] ('the Enforcement Study'). This study was aimed at providing a detailed analysis of private State aid enforcement in different Member States. The Enforcement Study concluded that, in the period between 1999 and 2006, State aid litigation at Member State level had increased significantly.[5]

Notes

[4] Available at <http://ec.europa.eu/comm/competition/state_aid/studies_reports/studies_reports.cfm>.
The study only covered EU-15.
[5] A total increase from 116 cases to 357 cases.

4. However, the Enforcement Study also revealed that a large number of the legal proceedings at Member State level were not aimed at reducing the anticompetitive effect of the underlying State aid measures. This was because almost two thirds of the judgments analysed concerned actions brought by taxpayers who sought relief from the allegedly discriminatory imposition of a (tax) burden[6] and actions brought by beneficiaries to challenge the recovery of unlawful and incompatible State aid.[7] The number of legal challenges aimed at enforcing compliance with the State aid rules was relatively small: actions by competitors against a Member State authority for damages, recovery and/or injunctive measures based on Article [108(3)] of the Treaty accounted for only 19% of the judgments analysed, whilst direct actions by competitors against beneficiaries accounted for only 6% of the judgments.

Notes

[6] 51% of all judgments.
[7] 12% of all judgments.

5. In spite of the fact that, as highlighted in the Enforcement Study, genuine private enforcement before national courts has played a relatively limited role in State aid to date, the Commission considers that private enforcement actions can offer considerable benefits for State aid policy. Proceedings before national courts give third parties the opportunity to address and resolve many State aid related concerns directly at national level. In addition, based on the jurisprudence of the Court of Justice of the European Communities ('ECJ'), national courts can offer claimants very effective remedies in the event of a breach of the State aid rules. This can in turn contribute to stronger overall State aid discipline.

6. Accordingly, the main purpose of this Notice is to inform national courts and third parties about the remedies available in the event of a breach of State aid rules and to provide them with guidance as to the practical application of those rules. In addition, the Commission seeks to develop its cooperation with national courts by introducing more practical tools for supporting national judges in their daily work.

7. This Notice replaces the 1995 Cooperation Notice and is without prejudice to any interpretation of the applicable Treaty and regulatory provisions by the Community courts. Additional information aimed at national courts will be made available on the Commission's website.

2. ROLE OF NATIONAL COURTS IN STATE AID ENFORCEMENT

2.1. General issues

2.1.1. Identifying State aid

8. The first issue facing national courts and potential claimants when applying Articles [107 and 108] of the Treaty is whether the measure concerned actually constitutes State aid within the meaning of the Treaty.

9. Article [107(1)] of the Treaty covers '*any aid granted by a Member State or through State resources in any form whatsoever which distorts or threatens to distort competition by favouring certain undertakings or the production of certain goods, in so far as it affects trade between Member States*'.

10. The ECJ has explicitly stated that, as is the case for the Commission, national courts have powers to interpret the notion of State aid.[8]

Notes

8 Case 78/76, *Steinike & Weinlig*, [1977] ECR 595, paragraph 14; Case C-39/94, *SFEI and Others*, [1996] ECR I-3547, paragraph 49; Case C-354/90, *Fédération Nationale du Commerce Extérieur des Produits Alimentaires and Others v France* [1991] ECR I-5505, paragraph 10; and Case C-368/04, *Transalpine Ölleitung in Österreich*, [2006] ECR I-9957, paragraph 39.

11. The notion of State aid is not limited to subsidies.[9] It also comprises, *inter alia*, tax concessions and investments from public funds made in circumstances where a private investor would have withheld his support.[10] Whether the aid is granted directly by the State or by public or private bodies established or appointed by it to administer the aid is immaterial in this respect.[11] But, for public support to be considered State aid, the aid needs to favour certain undertakings or the production of certain goods ('selectivity'), as opposed to general measures to which Article [107(1)] of the Treaty does not apply.[12] In addition, the aid must distort or threaten to distort competition and must have an effect on trade between Member States.[13]

Notes

 9 Case C-308/01, *GIL Insurance and Others*, [2004] ECR I-4777, paragraph 69; Case C-387/92, *Banco Exterior de España v Ayuntamiento de Valencia*, [1994] ECR I-877, paragraph 13; Case C-295/97, *Piaggio*, [1999] ECR I-3735, paragraph 34; Case C-39/94, *SFEI*, cited above footnote 8 paragraph 58; Case C-237/04, *Enirisorse*, [2006] ECR I-2843, paragraph 42; and Case C-66/02, *Italy v Commission*, [2005] ECR I-10901, paragraph 77.

 10 Cf. Advocate General Jacobs' Opinion in Joined Cases C-278/92, C-279/92 and C-280/92, *Spain v Commission*, [1994] ECR I-4103, paragraph 28: 'State aid is granted whenever a Member State makes available to an undertaking funds which in the normal course of events would not be provided by a private investor applying normal commercial criteria and disregarding other considerations of a social, political or philanthropic nature'.

 11 Case 290/83, *Commission v France*, [1985] ECR 439, paragraph 14; and Case C-482/99, *France v Commission*, [2002] ECR I-4397, paragraphs 36 to 42.

 12 A clear analysis of this distinction is to be found in Advocate General Darmon's Opinion in Joined Cases C-72/91 and C-73/91, *Sloman Neptun v Bodo Ziesemer*, [1993] ECR I-887.

 13 See, *inter alia*, Joined Cases C-393/04 and C-41/05, *Air Liquide Industries Belgium*, [2006] ECR I-5293, paragraphs 33 to 36; Case C-222/04, *Cassa di Risparmio di Firenze and Others*, [2006] ECR I-289, paragraphs 139 to 141; and Case C-310/99, *Italy v Commission*, [2002] ECR I-2289, paragraphs 84 to 86.

12. The case law of the Community courts[14] and decisions taken by the Commission have frequently addressed the question of whether certain measures qualify as State aid. In addition, the Commission has issued detailed guidance on a series of complex issues, such as the application of the private investor principle[15] and of the private creditor test,[16] the circumstances under which State guarantees must be regarded as State aid,[17] the treatment of public land sales,[18] privatisation and assimilated State actions,[19] aid below the *de minimis* thresholds,[20] export credit insurance,[21] direct business taxation,[22] risk capital investments,[23] and State aid for research, development and innovation.[24] Case law, Commission guidance and decision making practice can provide valuable assistance to national courts and potential claimants concerning State aid.

Notes

 14 A good example is the *Altmark* ruling of the ECJ, Case C-280/00, *Altmark Trans GmbH and Regierungspräsidium Magdeburg v Nahverkehrsgesellschaft Altmark GmbH*, [2003] ECR I-7747.

 15 On the private investor test in general, see Case C-142/87, *Belgium v Commission (Tubemeuse)* [1990] ECR I-959; Case C-305/89, *Italy v Commission (Alfa Romeo)*, [1991] ECR I-1603 paragraphs 19 and 20. As to its detailed reasoning, see Joined Cases T-228/99 and T-233/99, *Westdeutsche Landesbank Girozentrale v Commission*, [2003] ECR II-435, paragraph 245 et seq. See also Bulletin EC 9–1984, reproduced in 'Competition law in the European Communities', Volume IIA, and Communication of the Commission on the application of Articles [107 and 108 TFEU] and of [Article 6 of Commission Directive 2006/111/EC] to public undertakings in the manufacturing sector, (OJ C 307, 13.11.1993, p.3). As regards the application of this principle in relation to the financing of airports, see Community guidelines on financing of airports and start-up aid to airlines departing from regional airports (OJ C 312, 9.12.2005, paragraphs 42 to 52, p.1).

 16 Case C-342/96, *Spain v Commission*, [1999] ECR I-2459, paragraph 34; and Case C-256/97, *DM Transport* [1999] ECR I-3913, paragraph 25.

 17 Commission Notice on the application of Articles [107 and 108 TFEU] to State aid in the form of guarantees (OJ C 155, 20.6.2008, p.10).

18 Commission Communication on State aid elements in sales of land and buildings by public authorities (OJ C 209, 10.7.1997, p.3).

19 XXIII Report on Competition Policy, paragraphs 401 to 402 and Case C-278/92, *Spain v Commission*, [1994] ECR I- 4103.

20 Commission Regulation (EC) No 1998/2006 of 15 December 2006 on the application of Articles [107 and 108 TFEU] to *de minimis* aid (OJ L 379, 28.12.2006, p.5); Commission Regulation (EC) No 875/2007 of 24 July 2007 on the application of Articles [107 and 108 TFEU] to *de minimis* aid in the fisheries sector and amending Regulation (EC) No 1860/2004 (OJ L 193, 25.7.2007, p.6); and Commission Regulation (EC) No 1535/2007 of 20 December 2007 on the application of Articles [107 and 108 TFEU] to *de minimis* aid in the sector of agricultural production (OJ L 337, 21.12.2007, p.35).

21 Communication of the Commission to the Member States pursuant to Article [108(1) TFEU] applying Articles [107 and 108 TFEU] of the Treaty to short-term export-credit insurance (OJ C 281, 17.9.1997, p.4), as last amended by the Communication of the Commission to Member States amending the communication pursuant to Article [108(1) TFEU] applying Articles [107 and 108 TFEU] of the Treaty to short-term export-credit insurance (OJ C 325, 22.12.2005, p.22).

22 Commission Notice on the application of the State aid rules to measures relating to direct business taxation (OJ C 384, 10.12.1998, p.3).

23 Community Guidelines on State aid to promote risk capital investments in small and medium-sized enterprises (OJ C 194, 18.8.2006, p.2).

24 Community Framework for State aid for research and development and innovation (OJ C 323, 30.12.2006, p.1).

13. Where doubts exist as to the qualification of State aid, national courts may ask for a Commission opinion under section 3 of this Notice. This is without prejudice to the possibility or the obligation for a national court to refer the matter to the ECJ for a preliminary ruling under Article [267] of the Treaty.

2.1.2. *The standstill obligation*

14. According to Article [108(3)] of the Treaty, Member States may not implement State aid measures without the prior approval of the Commission ('standstill obligation'):

> '*The Commission shall be informed, in sufficient time to enable it to submit its comments, of any plans to grant or alter aid. If it considers that any such plan is not compatible with the common market having regard to Article [107], it shall without delay initiate the procedure provided for in paragraph 2. The Member State concerned shall not put its proposed measures into effect until this procedure has resulted in a final decision*'.[25]

Notes

25 The Standstill Obligation is reiterated in Article 3 of Council Regulation (EC) No 659/1999 of 22 March 1999 laying down detailed rules for the application of Article [109 TFEU] (OJ L 83, 27.3.1999, p.1) ('the Procedural Regulation'). As regards the exact time of the granting of an aid, see Commission Regulation (EC) No 1998/2006 of 15 December 2006 on the application of Articles [107 and 108 TFEU] to *de minimis* aid (OJ L 379, 28.12.2006, p.5) at recital 10.

15. However, there are a number of circumstances in which State aid can be lawfully implemented without Commission approval:
    (a) Where the measure is covered by a Block Exemption Regulation issued under the framework of Council Regulation (EC) No 994/98 of 7 May 1998 on the application of Articles [107 and 108 TFEU] to certain categories of horizontal State aid[26] ('the Enabling Regulation'). Where a measure meets all the requirements of a Block Exemption Regulation, the Member State is relieved of its obligation to notify the planned aid measure and the standstill obligation does not apply. Based on the Enabling Regulation, the Commission originally adopted several Block Exemption Regulations,[27] some of which have in the meantime been replaced by Commission Regulation (EC) No 800/2008 of 6 August 2008 declaring certain categories of aid compatible with the common market in application of Articles [107 and 108 TFEU] (General block exemption Regulation).[28]
    (b) Similarly, existing aid[29] is not subject to the standstill obligation. This includes, amongst others, aid granted under a scheme which existed before a Member State's accession to the European Union or under a scheme previously approved by the Commission.[30]

Notes

26 OJ L 142, 14.5.1998, p.1.

27 Commission Regulation (EC) No 68/2001 of 12 January 2001 on the application of Articles [107 and 108 TFEU] to training aid (OJ L 10, 13.1.2001, p.20); Commission Regulation (EC) No 70/2001 of 12 January 2001 on the application of Articles [107 and 108 TFEU] to State aid to small and medium-sized enterprises (OJ L 10, 13.1.2001, p.33); Commission Regulation (EC) No 2204/2002 of 12 December 2002 on the application of Articles [107 and 108 TFEU] to State aid for employment (OJ L 337, 13.12.2002, p.3) and Commission Regulation (EC) No 1628/2006 of 24 October 2006 on the application of Articles [107 and 108 TFEU] to national regional investment aid (OJ L 302, 1.11.2006, p.29). The SME, training and employment Block Exemption Regulation were prolonged until 30 June 2008 by Commission Regulation (EC) No 1976/2006 of 20 December 2006 amending Regulations (EC) No 2204/2002, (EC) No 70/2001 and (EC) No 68/2001 as regards the extension of the periods of application (OJ L 368, 23.12.2006, p.85). Specific Block Exemption Regulations apply in the fisheries and agricultural sector. See Commission Regulation (EC) No 736/2008 of 22 July 2008 on the application of Articles [107 and 108 TFEU] to State aid to small and medium-sized enterprises active in the production, processing and marketing of fisheries products (OJ L 201, 30.7.2008, p.16); and Commission Regulation (EC) No 1857/2006 of 15 December 2006 on the application of Articles [107 and 108 TFEU] to State aid to small and medium-sized enterprises active in the production of agricultural products and amending Regulation (EC) No 70/2001 (OJ L 358, 16.12.2006, p.3).

28 OJ L 214, 9.8.2008, p.3. The General Block Exemption Regulation entered into force on 29 August 2008. The rules governing the transition to the new regime are contained in its Article 44.

29 See Article 1 (b) of Council Regulation (EC) No 659/1999 of 22 March 1999 laying down detailed rules for the application of Article [108 TFEU] (OJ L 83, 27.3.1999, p.1).

30 This does not apply where the scheme itself foresees an individual notification requirement for certain types of aid. On the notion of existing aid, see also Case C-44/93 *Namur-Les assurances du crédit v Office national du ducroire and Belgian State* [1994] ECR I-3829, paragraphs 28 to 34.

16. National court proceedings in State aid matters may sometimes concern the applicability of a Block Exemption Regulation or an existing or approved aid scheme, or both. Where the applicability of such a Regulation or scheme is at stake, the national court can only assess whether all the conditions of the Regulation or scheme are met. It cannot assess the compatibility of an aid measure where this is not the case, since that assessment is the exclusive responsibility of the Commission.[31]

Notes

31 See paragraph 20.

17. If the national court needs to determine whether the measure falls under an approved aid scheme, it can only verify whether all conditions of the approval decision are met. Where the issues raised at national level concern the validity of a Commission decision, the national court has no jurisdiction to declare acts of Community institutions invalid.[32] Where the issue of validity arises, the national court may, or in some cases must, refer the matter to the ECJ for a preliminary ruling.[33] Based on the principle of legal certainty as interpreted by the ECJ, even the possibility of questioning the validity of the underlying Commission decision by way of a preliminary ruling is no longer available where the claimant could undoubtedly have challenged the Commission decision before the Community courts under Article [263] of the Treaty, but failed to do so.[34]

Notes

32 See Case C-119/05 *Lucchini* [2007] ECR I-6199, paragraph 53.

33 Case T-330/94, *Salt Union v Commission*, [1996] ECR II-1475, paragraph 39.

34 Case C-188/92, *TWD Textilwerke Deggendorf v Germany*, [1994] ECR I-833, paragraphs 17, 25 and 26; see also Joined Cases C-346/03 and C-529/03, *Atzeni and Others*, [2006] ECR I-1875, paragraph 31; and Case C-232/05, *Commission v France*, ('Scott'), [2006] ECR I-10071, paragraph 59.

18. The national court may ask the Commission for an opinion under section 3 of the present Notice if it has doubts concerning the applicability of a Block Exemption Regulation or an existing or approved aid scheme.

2.1.3. Respective roles of the Commission and national courts

19. The ECJ has repeatedly confirmed that both national courts and the Commission play essential, but distinct roles in the context of State aid enforcement.[35]

Notes

35 Case C-368/04, *Transalpine Ölleitung in Österreich*, cited above footnote 8, paragraph 37; Joined Cases C-261/01 and C-262/01, *Van Calster and Cleeren*, [2003] ECR I-12249, paragraph 74; and Case C-39/94, *SFEI and Others*, cited above footnote 8, paragraph 41.

20. The Commission's main role is to examine the compatibility of proposed aid measures with the common market, based on the criteria laid down in Article [107(2) and (3)] of the Treaty. This compatibility assessment is the exclusive responsibility of the Commission, subject to review by the Community courts. According to settled ECJ jurisprudence, national courts do not have the power to declare a State aid measure compatible with Article [107(2) or (3)] of the Treaty.[36]

Notes

36 Case C-199/06, *CELF and Ministre de la Culture et de la Communication*, [2008] ECR I-469, paragraph 38; Case C-17/91, *Lornoy and Others v Belgian State*, [1992] ECR I-6523, paragraph 30; and Case C-354/90, *Fédération Nationale du Commerce Extérieur des Produits Alimentaires and Others v France*, cited above footnote 8, paragraph 14.

21. The role of the national court depends on the aid measure at issue and whether that measure has been duly notified and approved by the Commission:
    (a) National courts are often asked to intervene in cases where a Member State authority[37] has granted aid without respecting the standstill obligation. This situation arises either because the aid was not notified at all, or because the authority implemented it before getting the Commission's approval. The role of national courts in such cases is to protect the rights of individuals affected by the unlawful implementation of the aid.[38]
    (b) National courts also play an important role in the enforcement of recovery decisions adopted under Article 14(1) of Council Regulation (EC) No 659/1999 of 22 March 1999 laying down detailed rules for the application of Article [108 TFEU][39] ('the Procedural Regulation'), where the Commission's assessment concludes that aid granted unlawfully is incompatible with the common market and enjoins the Member State concerned to recover the incompatible aid from the beneficiary. The involvement of national courts in such cases usually arises from actions brought by beneficiaries for review of the legality of the repayment request issued by national authorities. However, depending on national procedural law, other types of legal action may be possible (such as actions by Member State authorities against the beneficiary aimed at the full implementation of a Commission recovery decision).

Notes

37 This includes authorities at national, regional and local level.
38 Case C-368/04, *Transalpine Ölleitung in Österreich*, cited above footnote 8, paragraphs 38 and 44; Joined Cases C-261/01 and C-262/01, *Van Calster and Cleeren*, cited above footnote 35, paragraph 75; and Case C-295/97, *Piaggio*, cited above footnote 9, paragraph 31.
39 OJ L 83, 27.3.1999, p.1.

22. When preserving the interests of individuals, national courts must take full account of the effectiveness and direct effect[40] of Article [108(3)] of the Treaty and the interests of the Community.[41]

Notes

40 Case C-354/90, *Fédération Nationale du Commerce Extérieur des Produits Alimentaires and Others v France*, cited above footnote 8, paragraphs 11 and 12; and Case C-39/94, *SFEI and Others*, cited above footnote 8, paragraphs 39 and 40.
41 Case C-368/04, *Transalpine Ölleitung in Österreich*, cited above footnote 8, paragraph 48.

23. The role of national courts in such settings is set out in more detail under sections 2.2 and 2.3.

2.2. Role of national courts in enforcing Article [108(3) TFEU] – Unlawful State Aid

24. Like Articles [101 and 102 TFEU], the standstill obligation laid down in Article [108(3)] of the Treaty gives rise to directly effective individual rights of affected parties (such as the competitors of the beneficiary). These affected parties can enforce their rights by bringing legal action before competent national courts against the granting Member State. Dealing with such legal actions and thus protecting competitor's rights under Article [108(3)] of the Treaty is one of the most important roles of national courts in the State aid field.

25. The essential role played by national courts in this context also stems from the fact that the Commission's own powers to protect competitors and other third parties against unlawful aid are limited. Most importantly, as the ECJ held in its 'Boussac'[42] and 'Tubemeuse'[43] judgments, the Commission cannot adopt a final decision ordering recovery merely because the aid was not notified in accordance with Article [108(3)] of the Treaty. The Commission must therefore conduct a full compatibility assessment, regardless of whether the standstill obligation has been respected or not.[44] This assessment can be time-consuming and the Commission's powers to issue preliminary recovery injunctions are subject to very strict legal requirements.[45]

Notes

[42] Case C-301/87, *France v Commission*, ('Boussac'), [1990] ECR I-307.

[43] Case C-142/87, *Belgium v Commission*, ('Tubemeuse'), [1990] ECR I-959.

[44] Case C-301/87, *France v Commission*, ('Boussac'), cited above footnote 42, paragraphs 17 to 23; Case C-142/87, *Belgium v Commission*, ('Tubemeuse'), cited above footnote 43, paragraphs 15 to 19; Case C-354/90, *Fédération Nationale du Commerce Extérieur des Produits Alimentaires and Others v France*, cited above footnote 8, paragraph 14; and Case C-199/06, *CELF and Ministre de la Culture et de la Communication*, cited above footnote 36, paragraph 38.

[45] Cf. Article 11(2) of the Procedural Regulation, which requires that there are no doubts about the aid character of the measure concerned, that there is an urgency to act and that there is a serious risk of substantial and irreparable damage to a competitor.

26. As a result, actions before national courts offer an important means of redress for competitors and other third parties affected by unlawful State aid. Remedies available before national courts include:
    (a) preventing the payment of unlawful aid;
    (b) recovery of unlawful aid (regardless of compatibility);
    (c) recovery of illegality interest;
    (d) damages for competitors and other third parties; and
    (e) interim measures against unlawful aid.

27. Each of these remedies is set out in more detail in sections 2.2.1 to 2.2.6.

2.2.1. Preventing the payment of unlawful aid

28. National courts are obliged to protect the rights of individuals affected by violations of the standstill obligation. National courts must therefore draw all appropriate legal consequences, in accordance with national law, where an infringement of Article [108(3)] of the Treaty has occurred.[46] However, the national courts obligations are not limited to unlawful aid already disbursed. They also extend to cases where an unlawful payment is about to be made. As part of their duties under Article [108(3)] of the Treaty, national courts must safeguard the rights of individuals against possible disregard of those rights.[47] Where unlawful aid is about to be disbursed, the national court is therefore obliged to prevent this payment from taking place.

Notes

[46] Case C-354/90, *Fédération Nationale du Commerce Extérieur des Produits Alimentaires and Others v France*, cited above footnote 8, paragraph 12; Case C-39/94, *SFEI and Others*, cited above footnote 8, paragraph 40; Case C-368/04, *Transalpine Ölleitung in Österreich*, cited above footnote 8, paragraph 47; and Case C-199/06, *CELF and Ministre de la Culture et de la Communication*, cited above footnote 36, paragraph 41.

[47] See references cited in footnote 38.

29. The national courts obligation to prevent the payment of unlawful aid can arise in a variety of procedural settings, depending on different types of actions available under national law. Very often, the claimant will seek to challenge the validity of the national act granting the unlawful State aid. In such cases, preventing the unlawful payment will usually be the logical consequence of finding that the granting act is invalid as a result of the Member State's breach of Article [108(3)] of the Treaty.[48]

Notes

[48] On the invalidity of the granting act in cases where the Member State has violated Article [108(3) TFEU], see Case C-354/90, *Fédération Nationale du Commerce Extérieur des Produits Alimentaires and Others v France*, cited above footnote 8, paragraph 12; see also, as an illustration, German Federal Court of Justice ('Bundesgerichtshof'), judgment of 4 April 2003, V ZR 314/02, VIZ 2003, 340, and judgment of 20 January 2004, XI ZR 53/03, NVwZ 2004, 636.

2.2.2. *Recovery of unlawful aid*

30. Where a national court is confronted with unlawfully granted aid, it must draw all legal consequences from this unlawfulness under national law. The national court must therefore in principle order the full recovery of unlawful State aid from the beneficiary.[49] Ordering the full recovery of unlawful aid is part of the national courts obligation to protect the individual rights of the claimant (such as the competitor) under Article [108(3)] of the Treaty. The recovery obligation of the national court is thus not dependent on the compatibility of the aid measure with Article [107(2) or (3)] of the Treaty.

Notes

[49] Case C-71/04, *Xunta de Galicia*, [2005] ECR I-7419, paragraph 49; Case C-39/94, *SFEI and Others*, cited above footnote 8, paragraphs 40 and 68; and Case C-354/90, *Fédération Nationale du Commerce Extérieur des Produits Alimentaires and Others v France*, cited above footnote 8, paragraph 12.

31. Since national courts must order the full recovery of unlawful aid regardless of its compatibility, recovery can be swifter before a national court than through a complaint with the Commission. Indeed, unlike the Commission,[50] the national court can and must limit itself to determining whether the measure constitutes State aid and whether the standstill obligation applies to it.

Notes

[50] Which needs to conduct a compatibility analysis before ordering recovery, see references cited in footnote 44.

32. However, the national courts recovery obligation is not absolute. According to the 'SFEI' jurisprudence,[51] there can be exceptional circumstances in which the recovery of unlawful State aid would not be appropriate. The legal standard to be applied in this context should be similar to the one applicable under Articles 14 and 15 of the Procedural Regulation.[52] In other words, circumstances which would not stand in the way of a recovery order by the Commission cannot justify a national court refraining from ordering full recovery under Article[108(3)] of the Treaty. The standard which the Community courts apply in this respect is very strict.[53] In particular, the ECJ has consistently held that, in principle, a beneficiary of unlawful aid cannot plead legitimate expectation against a Commission recovery order.[54] This is because a diligent businessman would have been able to verify whether the aid he received was notified or not.[55]

Notes

[51] Case C-39/94, *SFEI and Others*, cited above footnote 8, paragraphs 70 and 71, referring to Advocate General Jacobs' Opinion in this case, paragraphs 73 to 75; see also Case 223/85, *RSV v Commission*, [1987] ECR 4617, paragraph 17; and Case C-5/89, *Commission v Germany*, [1990] ECR I-3437, paragraph 16.

[52] On the standard applied in this respect, see Advocate General Jacobs' Opinion in Case C-39/94, *SFEI and Others*, cited above footnote 8, paragraph 75.

[53] Article 14 only provides for an exemption from the Commissions recovery obligation where a recovery would contravene general principles of Community law. The only case in which a Member State can refrain from implementing a recovery decision by the Commission is where such recovery would be objectively impossible, cf. Case C-177/06, *Commission v Spain*, [2007] ECR I-7689, paragraph 46. Also see paragraph 17 of the Notice from the Commission towards an effective implementation of Commission decisions ordering Member States to recover unlawful and incompatible aid (OJ C 272, 15.11.2007, p.4).

[54] Case C-5/89, *Commission v Germany*, cited above footnote 51, paragraph 14; Case C-169/95, *Spain v Commission*, [1997] ECR I-135, paragraph 51; and Case C-148/04, *Unicredito Italiano*, [2005] ECR I-11137, paragraph 104.

[55] Case C-5/89, *Commission v Germany*, cited above footnote 51, paragraph 14; Case C-24/95, *Alcan Deutschland*, [1997] ECR I-1591, paragraph 25; and Joined Cases C-346/03 and C-529/03, *Atzeni and Others*, cited above footnote 34, paragraph 64.

33. To justify the national court not ordering recovery under Article [108(3)] of the Treaty, a specific and concrete fact must therefore have generated legitimate expectation on the beneficiary's part.[56] This can be the case if the Commission itself has given precise assurances that the measure in question does not constitute State aid, or that it is not covered by the standstill obligation.[57]

Notes

[56] Cf. Advocate General Jacobs' Opinion in Case C-39/94, *SFEI and Others*, cited above footnote 8, paragraph 73; and Case 223/85, *RSV v Commission*, cited above footnote 51, paragraph 17.

[57] Joined Cases C-182/03 and C-217/03 *Belgium and Forum 187 v Commission* [2006] ECR I-5479, paragraph 147.

34. In its 'CELF' judgment,[58] the ECJ clarified that the national court's obligation to order full recovery of unlawful State aid ceases if, by the time the national court renders its judgment, the Commission has already decided that the aid is compatible with the common market. Since the purpose of the standstill obligation is to ensure that only compatible aid can be implemented, this purpose can no longer be frustrated where the Commission has already confirmed compatibility.[59] Therefore, the national court's obligation to protect individual rights under Article [108(3)] of the Treaty remains unaffected where the Commission has not yet taken a decision, regardless of whether a Commission procedure is pending or not.[60]

Notes

[58] Case C-199/06, *CELF and Ministre de la Culture et de la Communication*, cited above footnote 36, paragraphs 45, 46 and 55; and Case C-384/07, *Wienstrom*, judgment of 11 December 2008, [[2008] ECR I- 393], paragraph 28.

[59] Case C-199/06, *CELF and Ministre de la Culture et de la Communication*, cited above footnote 36, paragraph 49.

[60] The judgment explicitly confirms the recovery obligation imposed by the ECJ in its previous jurisprudence, cf. Case C-199/06, *CELF and Ministre de la Culture et de la Communication*, cited above footnote 36, paragraph 41.

35. While after a positive Commission decision the national court is no longer under a *Community law* obligation to order full recovery, the ECJ also explicitly recognises that a recovery obligation may exist under *national law*.[61] However, where such a recovery obligation exists, this is without prejudice to the Member State's right to re-implement the aid subsequently.

Notes

[61] Case C-199/06, *CELF and Ministre de la Culture et de la Communication*, cited above footnote 36, paragraphs 53 and 55.

36. Once the national court has decided that unlawful aid has been disbursed in violation of Article [108(3)] of the Treaty, it must quantify the aid in order to determine the amount to be recovered. The case law of the Community courts on the application of Article [107(1)] of the Treaty and the Commission's guidance and decision making practice should assist the court in this respect. Should the national court encounter difficulties in calculating the aid amount, it may request the Commission's support, as further set out in section 3 of this Notice.

2.2.3. Recovery of interest

37. The economic advantage of unlawful aid is not limited to its nominal amount. In addition, the beneficiary obtains a financial advantage resulting from the premature implementation of the aid. This is due to the fact that, had the aid been notified to the Commission, payment would (if at all) have taken place later. This would have obliged the beneficiary to borrow the relevant funds on the capital markets, including interest at market rates.

38. This undue time advantage is the reason why, if recovery is ordered by the Commission, Article 14(2) of the Procedural Regulation requires not only recovery of the nominal aid amount, but also recovery of interest from the day the unlawful aid was put at the disposal of the beneficiary to the day when it is effectively recovered. The interest rate to be applied in this context is defined in Article 9 of Commission Regulation (EC) No 794/2004 of 21 April 2004 implementing Council Regulation (EC) No 659/1999 laying down detailed rules for the application of Article [108] of the Treaty ('the Implementing Regulation').[62]

Notes

[62] OJ L 140, 30.4.2004, p.1. On the method for setting the reference and discount rates, see the Communication from the Commission on the revision of the method for setting the reference and discount rates (OJ C 14, 19.1.2008, p.6) ('The Reference Rate Communication').

39. In its 'CELF' judgment, the ECJ clarified that the need to recover the financial advantage resulting from premature implementation of the aid (hereinafter referred to as 'illegality interest') is part of the national courts obligation under Article [108(3)] of the Treaty. This is because the premature implementation of unlawful aid will at least cause competitors to suffer depending on the circumstances earlier than they would have to, in competition terms, from the effects of the aid. The beneficiary has therefore obtained an undue advantage.[63]

Notes

63 Case C-199/06, *CELF and Ministre de la Culture et de la Communication*, cited above footnote 36, paragraphs 50 to 52 and 55.

40. The national court's obligation to order the recovery of illegality interest can arise in two different settings:

    (a) The national court must normally order full recovery of unlawful aid under Article [108(3)] of the Treaty. Where this is the case, illegality interest needs to be added to the original aid amount when determining the total recovery amount.

    (b) However, the national court must also order the recovery of illegality interest in circumstances in which, exceptionally, there is no obligation to order full recovery. As confirmed in 'CELF', the national court's obligation to order recovery of illegality interest therefore remains in place even after a positive Commission decision.[64] This can be of central importance to potential claimants, since it also offers a successful remedy in cases where the Commission has already declared the aid compatible with the common market.

Notes

64 Case C-199/06, *CELF and Ministre de la Culture et de la Communication*, cited above footnote 36, paragraphs 52 and 55.

41. In order to comply with their recovery obligation as regards illegality interest, national courts need to determine the interest amount to be recovered. The following principles apply in this respect:

    (a) The starting point is the nominal aid amount.[65]

    (b) When determining the applicable interest rate and calculation method, national courts should take account of the fact that recovery of illegality interest by a national court serves the same purpose as the Commissions interest recovery under Article 14 of the Procedural Regulation. In addition, claims for the recovery of illegality interest are Community law claims based directly on Article [108(3)] of the Treaty.[66] The principles of equivalence and effectiveness described under section 2.4.1 of this Notice therefore apply to these claims.

    (c) In order to ensure consistency with Article 14 of the Procedural Regulation and to comply with the effectiveness requirement, the Commission considers that the method of interest calculation used by the national court may not be less strict than that foreseen in the Implementing Regulation.[67] Consequently, illegality interest must be calculated on a compound basis and the applicable interest rate may not be lower than the reference rate.[68]

    (d) Moreover, in the Commission's view, it follows from the principle of equivalence that, where the interest rate calculation under national law is stricter than that laid down in the Implementing Regulation, the national court will have to apply the stricter national rules also to claims based on Article [108(3)] of the Treaty.

    (e) The start date for the interest calculation will always be the day on which the unlawful aid was put at the disposal of the beneficiary. The end date depends on the situation at the time of the national judgment. If, as was the case in 'CELF', the Commission has already approved the aid, the end date is the date of the Commission decision. Otherwise, illegality interest accumulates for the whole period of unlawfulness until the date of actual repayment of the aid by the beneficiary. As was confirmed in 'CELF', illegality interest also needs to be applied for the period between the adoption of a positive Commission decision and the subsequent annulment of this decision by the Community courts.[69]

Notes

65 See paragraph 36. Taxes paid on the nominal aid amount can be deducted for the purposes of recovery, see Case T-459/93 *Siemens v Commission* [1995] ECR II-1675, paragraph 83.
66 Case C-199/06, *CELF and Ministre de la Culture et de la Communication*, cited above footnote 36, paragraphs 52 and 55.
67 See chapter V of the Implementing Regulation.
68 See footnote 62.
69 Case C-199/06, *CELF and Ministre de la Culture et de la Communication*, cited above footnote 36, paragraph 69.

42. In case of doubt, the national court may ask the Commission for support under section 3 of this Notice.

2.2.4. Damages claims

43. As part of their role under Article [108(3)] of the Treaty, national courts may also be required to uphold claims for compensation for damage caused to competitors of the beneficiary and to other third parties by the unlawful State aid.[70] Such damages actions are usually directed at the State aid granting authority. They can be particularly important for the claimant, since, contrary to actions aimed at mere recovery, a successful damages action provides the claimant with direct financial compensation for suffered loss.

Notes

[70] Case C-199/06, *CELF and Ministre de la Culture et de la Communication*, cited above footnote 36, paragraphs 53 and 55; Case C-368/04, *Transalpine Ölleitung in Österreich*, cited above footnote 8, paragraph 56; and Case C-334/07 P, *Commission v Freistaat Sachsen*, judgment of 11 December 2008, [[2008] ECR I- 9465], paragraph 54.

44. The ECJ has repeatedly held that affected third parties can bring such damages actions under *national law*.[71] Such challenges are obviously dependent on national legal rules. Therefore, the legal bases on which claimants have relied in the past vary significantly across the Community.

Notes

[71] Case C-199/06, *CELF and Ministre de la Culture et de la Communication*, cited above footnote 36, paragraphs 53 and 55; Case C-368/04, *Transalpine Ölleitung in sterreich*, cited above footnote 8, paragraph 56; and Case C-39/94, *SFEI and Others*, cited above footnote 8, paragraph 75.

45. Irrespective of the possibility to claim damages under national law, breaches of the standstill obligation have direct and binding consequences under *Community law*. This is because the standstill obligation under Article [108(3)] of the Treaty is a directly applicable rule of Community law which is binding on all Member State authorities.[72] Breaches of the standstill obligation can therefore, in principle, give rise to damages claims based on the 'Francovich'[73] and 'Brasserie du Pêcheur'[74] jurisprudence of the ECJ.[75] This jurisprudence confirms that Member States are required to compensate for loss and damage caused to individuals as a result of breaches of Community law for which the State is responsible.[76] Such liability exists where: (i) the rule of law infringed is intended to confer rights on individuals; (ii) the breach is sufficiently serious; and (iii) there is a direct causal link between the breach of the Member State's obligation and the damage suffered by the injured parties.[77]

Notes

[72] Case 6/64, *Costa v E.N.E.L.*, [1964] ECR 1141; Case 120/73, *Lorenz GmbH v Bundesrepublik Deutschland and Others*, [1973] ECR 1471, paragraph 8; and Case C-354/90, *Fédération Nationale du Commerce Extérieur des Produits Alimentaires and Others v France*, cited above footnote 8, paragraph 11.

[73] Joined Cases C-6/90 and C-9/90, *Francovich and Bonifaci v Italy*, [1991] ECR I-5357.

[74] Joined Cases C-46/93 and C-48/93, *Brasserie du Pêcheur and Factortame*, [1996] ECR I-1029.

[75] The fact that violations of the State aid rules can give rise to Member State liability directly on the basis of Community law has been confirmed in Case C-173/03, *Traghetti del Mediterraneo v Italy*, [2006] ECR I-5177, paragraph 41.

[76] Joined Cases C-6/90 and C-9/90, *Francovich and Bonifaci v Italy*, cited above footnote 73, paragraphs 31 to 37; and Joined Cases C-46/93 and C-48/93, *Brasserie du Pêcheur and Factortame*, cited above footnote 74, paragraph 31.

[77] See Case C-173/03, *Traghetti del Mediterraneo v Italy*, cited above footnote 75, paragraph 45.

46. The first requirement (Community law obligation aimed at protecting individual rights) is met in relation to violations of Article [108(3)] of the Treaty. The ECJ has not only repeatedly confirmed the existence of individual rights under Article [108(3)] of the Treaty but has also clarified that the protection of these individual rights is the genuine role of national courts.[78]

Notes

[78] Case C-354/90, *Fédération Nationale du Commerce Extérieur des Produits Alimentaires and Others v France*, cited above footnote 8, paragraphs 12 to 14; Joined Cases C-261/01 and C-262/01, *Van Calster and Cleeren*, cited above footnote 35, paragraph 53; and Case C-199/06, *CELF and Ministre de la Culture et de la Communication*, cited above footnote 36, paragraph 38.

47. The requirement of a sufficiently serious breach of Community law will also generally be met as regards Article [108(3)] of the Treaty. When determining whether or not a breach of Community law is sufficiently serious, the ECJ lays strong emphasis on the amount of discretion enjoyed by the authorities concerned.[79] Where the authority in question has no discretion, the mere infringement of Community law may be sufficient to establish the existence of a sufficiently serious breach.[80] However, with regard to Article [108(3)] of the Treaty, Member State authorities have no discretion not to notify State aid measures. They are, in principle, under an absolute obligation to notify all such measures prior to their implementation. Although the ECJ sometimes takes the excusability of the relevant breach of Community law into account,[81] in the presence of State aid, Member State authorities cannot normally argue that they were not aware of the standstill obligation. This is because there is a large body of case law and Commission guidance on the application of Articles [107(1)] and [108(3)] of the Treaty. In case of doubt, Member States can always notify the measure to the Commission for reasons of legal certainty.[82]

Notes

[79] Joined Cases C-46/93 and C-48/93, *Brasserie du Pêcheur and Factortame*, cited above footnote 74, paragraph 55.

[80] Case C-278/05, *Robins and Others*, [2007] ECR I-1053, paragraph 71; Case C-424/97, *Haim*, [2000] ECR I-5123, paragraph 38; and Case C-5/94, *Hedley Lomas*, [1996] ECR I-2553, paragraph 28.

[81] Joined Cases C-46/93 and C-48/93, *Brasserie du Pêcheur and Factortame*, cited above footnote 74, paragraph 56.

[82] Although breaches of Article [108(3) TFEU] must therefore generally be regarded as sufficiently serious, there can be exceptional circumstances which stand in the way of a damages claim. In such circumstances, the requirement of a sufficiently serious breach may not be met. See paragraphs 32 and 33.

---

48. The third requirement that the breach of Community law must have caused an actual and certain financial damage to the claimant can be met in various ways.

49. The claimant will often argue that the aid was directly responsible for a loss of profit. When confronted with such a claim, the national court should take account of the following considerations:

   (a) By virtue of the Community law requirements of equivalence and effectiveness,[83] national rules may not exclude a Member State's liability for loss of profit.[84] Damage under Community law can exist regardless of whether the breach caused the claimant to lose an asset or whether it prevented the claimant from improving his asset position. Should national law contain such an exclusion, the national court would need to leave the provision unapplied as regards damages claims under Article [108(3)] of the Treaty.

   (b) Determining the actual amount of lost profit will be easier where the unlawful aid enabled the beneficiary to win over a contract or a specific business opportunity from the claimant. The national court can then calculate the revenue which the claimant was likely to generate under this contract. In cases where the contract has already been fulfilled by the beneficiary, the national court would also take account of the actual profit generated.

   (c) More complicated damage assessments are necessary where the aid merely leads to an overall loss of market share. One possible way for dealing with such cases could be to compare the claimant's actual income situation (based on the profit and loss account) with the hypothetical income situation had the unlawful aid not been granted.

   (d) There may be circumstances where the damage suffered by the claimant exceeds the lost profit. This could, for example, be the case where, as a consequence of the unlawful aid, the claimant is forced out of business (through insolvency for example).

Notes

[83] See section 2.4.1.

[84] Joined Cases C-46/93 and C-48/93, *Brasserie du Pêcheur and Factortame*, cited above footnote 74, paragraphs 87 and 90.

---

50. The possibility to claim damages is, in principle, independent of any parallel Commission investigation concerning the same aid measure. Such an ongoing investigation does not release the national court from its obligation to safeguard individual rights under Article [108(3)] of the Treaty.[85] Since the claimant may be able to demonstrate that he suffered loss due to the premature implementation of the aid, and, more specifically, as a result of the beneficiary's illegal time

advantage, successful damages claims are also not ruled out where the Commission has already approved the aid by the time the national court decides.[86]

Notes

[85] Case C-39/94, *SFEI and Others*, cited above footnote 8, paragraph 44.
[86] Case C-199/06, *CELF and Ministre de la Culture et de la Communication*, cited above footnote 36, paragraphs 53 and 55.

51. National procedural rules will sometimes allow the national court to rely on reasonable estimates for the purpose of determining the actual amount of damages to be granted to the claimant. Where that is the case, and provided the principle of effectiveness[87] is respected, the use of such estimates would also be possible in relation to damages claims arising under Article [108(3)] of the Treaty. This can be a useful tool for national courts which face difficulties in relation to the calculation of damages.

Notes
[87] See Section 2.4.1.

52. The legal prerequisites for damages claims under Community law and issues of damages calculation can also form the basis of requests for Commission assistance under section 3 of the present Notice.

2.2.5. Damages claims against the beneficiary

53. Potential claimants are entitled to bring damages claims against the State aid granting authority. However, there may be circumstances in which the claimant prefers to claim damages directly from the beneficiary.
54. In the 'SFEI' judgment, the ECJ explicitly addressed the question whether direct damages actions can be brought against the beneficiary under Community law. It concluded that, because Article [108(3)] of the Treaty does not impose any direct obligations on the beneficiary, there is no sufficient *Community law* basis for such claims.[88]

Notes
[88] Case C-39/94, *SFEI and Others*, cited above footnote 8, paragraphs 72 to 74.

55. However, this does not in any way prejudice the possibility of a successful damages action against the beneficiary on the basis of substantive *national law*. In that context, the ECJ specifically referred to the possibility for potential claimants to rely on national rules governing non-contractual liability.[89]

Notes

[89] Case C-39/94, *SFEI and Others*, cited above footnote 8, paragraph 75. In situations involving a conflict of laws, the law applicable is determined by Regulation (EC) No 864/2007 of the European Parliament and the Council on the law applicable to non-contractual obligations (Rome II) (OJ L 199, 31.7.2007, p.40).

2.2.6. Interim measures

56. The duty of national courts to draw the necessary legal consequences from violations of the standstill obligation is not limited to their final judgments. As part of their role under Article [108(3)] of the Treaty, national courts are also required to take interim measures where this is appropriate to safeguard the rights of individuals[90] and the effectiveness of Article [108(3)] of the Treaty.

Notes

[90] Case C-354/90, *Fédération Nationale du Commerce Extérieur des Produits Alimentaires and Others v France*, cited above footnote 8, paragraph 12; Case C-39/94, *SFEI and Others*, cited above footnote 8, paragraph 52; and Case C-368/04, *Transalpine Ölleitung in Österreich*, cited above footnote 8, paragraph 46.

57. The power of national courts to adopt interim measures can be of central importance to interested parties where fast relief is required. Because of their ability to act swiftly against unlawful aid, their proximity and the variety of measures available to them, national courts are very well placed to take interim measures where unlawful aid has already been paid or is about to be paid.

Part G State Aids

58. The most straightforward cases are those where unlawful aid has not yet been disbursed, but where there is a risk that such payments will be made during the course of national court proceedings. In such cases, the national courts obligation to prevent violations of Article [108(3)] of the Treaty[91] can require it to issue an interim order preventing the illegal disbursement until the substance of the matter is resolved.

Notes

[91] See section 2.2.1.

59. Where the illegal payment has already been made, the role of national courts under Article [108(3)] of the Treaty usually requires them to order full recovery (including illegality interest). Because of the principle of effectiveness,[92] the national court may not postpone this by unduly delaying proceedings. Such delays would not only affect the individual rights which Article [108(3)] of the Treaty protects, but also directly increase the competitive harm which stems from the unlawfulness of the aid.

Notes

[92] See section 2.4.1.

60. However, in spite of this general obligation, there may nevertheless be circumstances in which the final judgment for the national court is delayed. In such cases, the obligation to protect the individual rights under Article [108(3)] of the Treaty requires the national court to use all interim measures available to it under the applicable national procedural framework to at least terminate the anti-competitive effects of the aid on a provisional basis ('interim recovery').[93] The application of national procedural rules in this context is subject to the requirements of equivalence and effectiveness.[94]

Notes

[93] See also Case C-39/94, *SFEI and Others*, cited above footnote 8, paragraph 52; and Case C-368/04, *Transalpine Ölleitung in Österreich*, cited above footnote 8, paragraph 46.
[94] See section 2.4.1.

61. Where, based on the case law of the Community courts and the practice of the Commission, the national judge has reached a reasonable *prima facie* conviction that the measure at stake involves unlawful State aid, the most expedient remedy will, in the Commission's view and subject to national procedural law, be to order the unlawful aid *and* the illegality interest to be put on a blocked account until the substance of the matter is resolved. In its final judgment, the national court would then either order the funds on the blocked account to be returned to the State aid granting authority, if the unlawfulness is confirmed, or order the funds to be released to the beneficiary.

62. Interim recovery can also be a very effective instrument in cases where national court proceedings run parallel to a Commission investigation.[95] An ongoing Commission investigation does not release the national court from its obligation to protect individual rights under Article [108(3)] of the Treaty.[96] The national court may therefore not simply suspend its own proceedings until the Commission has decided and leave the rights of the claimant under Article [108(3)] of the Treaty unprotected in the meantime. Where the national court wishes to await the outcome of the Commission's compatibility assessment before adopting a final and irreversible recovery order, it should therefore adopt appropriate interim measures. Here again, ordering the placement of the funds on a blocked account would seem an appropriate remedy. In cases where:
    (a) the Commission declares the aid incompatible, the national court would order the funds on the blocked account to be returned to the State aid granting authority (aid plus illegality interest);
    (b) the Commission declares the aid compatible, this would release the national court from its Community law obligation to order full recovery.[97] The court may therefore, subject to national law,[98] order the actual aid amount to be released to the beneficiary. However, as described in section 2.2.3, the national court remains under a Community law obligation to

order the recovery of illegality interest.[99] This illegality interest will therefore have to be paid to the State aid granting authority.

2.3. Role of national courts in the implementation of negative Commission decisions ordering recovery

63. National courts can also face State aid issues in cases where the Commission has already ordered recovery. Although most cases will be actions for the annulment of a national recovery order, third parties can also claim damages from national authorities for failure to implement a Commission recovery decision.

2.3.1. Challenging the validity of a national recovery order

64. According to Article 14(3) of the Procedural Regulation, Member States must implement recovery decisions without delay. Recovery takes place according to the procedures available under national law, provided they allow for immediate and effective execution of the recovery decision. Where a national procedural rule prevents immediate and/or effective recovery, the national court must leave this provision unapplied.[100]

65. The validity of recovery orders issued by national authorities to implement a Commission recovery decision is sometimes challenged before a national court. The rules governing such actions are set out in detail in the Commission's 2007 Recovery Notice,[101] the main principles of which are summarised in this section.

66. In particular, national court actions cannot challenge the validity of the underlying Commission decision where the claimant could have challenged this decision directly before the Community courts.[102] This also means that, where a challenge under Article [263] of the Treaty would have been possible, the national court may not suspend the execution of the recovery decision on grounds linked to the validity of the Commission decision.[103]

67. Where it is not clear that the claimant can bring an annulment action under Article [263] of the Treaty (for example where the measure was an aid scheme with a wide coverage for which the claimant may not be able to demonstrate an individual concern), the national court must, in principle, offer legal protection. However, even in those circumstances, the national judge must request a preliminary ruling under Article [267] of the Treaty where the legal action concerns the validity and lawfulness of the Commission decision.[104]

68. Granting interim relief in such circumstances is subject to the very strict legal requirements defined in the 'Zuckerfabrik'[105] and 'Atlanta'[106] jurisprudence: a national court may only suspend recovery orders under the following conditions (i) the court has serious doubts as regards the validity of the Community act. If the validity of the contested act is not already in issue before the ECJ, it must itself refer the question to the ECJ; (ii) there must be urgency in the sense that the interim relief is necessary to avoid serious and irreparable damage to the party seeking relief; and (iii) the court has to take due account of the Community interest. In its assessment of all those conditions, the national court must respect any ruling by the Community courts on the lawfulness of the Commission decision or on an application for interim relief at Community level.[107]

Notes

105 Joined Cases C-143/88 and C-92/89, *Zuckerfabrik Süderdithmarschen and Zuckerfabrik Soest v Hauptzollamt Itzehoe and Hauptzollamt Paderborn*, [1991] ECR I-415, paragraph 33.

106 Case C-465/93, *Atlanta Fruchthandelsgesellschaft and Others v Bundesamt für Ernährung und Forstwirtschaft*, [1995] ECR I- 3761, paragraph 51.

107 For further guidance, cf. 2007 Recovery Notice, paragraph 59.

2.3.2. *Damages for failure to implement a recovery decision*

69. Like violations of the standstill obligation, failure by the Member State authorities to comply with a Commission recovery decision under Article 14 of the Procedural Regulation can give rise to damages claims under the 'Francovich' and 'Brasserie du Pêcheur' jurisprudence.[108] In the Commission's view, the treatment of such damages claims mirrors the principles as regards violations of the standstill obligation.[109] This is because, (i) the Member States recovery obligation is aimed at protecting the same individual rights as the standstill obligation, and (ii) the Commission's recovery decisions do not leave national authorities any discretion; breaches of the recovery obligation are thus, in principle, to be regarded as sufficiently serious. Consequently, the success of a damages claim for non-implementation of a Commission recovery decision will again depend on whether the claimant can demonstrate that he suffered loss directly as a result of the delayed recovery.[110]

Notes

108 See references cited in footnote 77.

109 See section 2.2.4.

110 See paragraphs 48 to 51.

2.4. Procedural rules and legal standing before national courts

2.4.1. *General principles*

70. National courts are obliged to enforce the standstill obligation and protect the rights of individuals against unlawful State aid. In principle, national procedural rules apply to such proceedings.[111] However, based on general principles of Community law, the application of national law in these circumstances is subject to two essential conditions: (a) national procedural rules applying to claims under Article [108(3)] of the Treaty may not be less favourable than those governing claims under domestic law (principle of equivalence);[112] and (b) national procedural rules may not render excessively difficult or practically impossible the exercise of the rights conferred by Community law (principle of effectiveness).[113]

Notes

111 Case C-368/04, *Transalpine Ölleitung in Österreich*, cited above footnote 8, paragraph 45; and Case C-526/04, *Laboratoires Boiron*, [2006] ECR I-7529, paragraph 51.

112 Case C-368/04, *Transalpine Ölleitung in Österreich*, cited above footnote 8, paragraph 45; Joined Cases C-392/04 and C-422/04, i-21 *Germany*, [2006] ECR I-8559, paragraph 57; and Case 33/76, *Rewe*, [1976] ECR 1989, paragraph 5.

113 Case C-368/04, *Transalpine Ölleitung in Österreich*, cited above footnote 8, paragraph 45; Case C-174/02, *Streekgewest*, [2005] ECR I-85, paragraph 18; and Case 33/76, *Rewe*, cited above footnote 112, paragraph 5.

71. Given the supremacy of Community law, national courts must leave national procedural rules unapplied if doing otherwise would violate the principles set out in paragraph 70.[114]

Notes

[114] Case 106/77, *Amministrazione delle finanze dello Stato v Simmenthal*, [1978] ECR 629, paragraphs 21 and 24.

2.4.2. Legal standing

72. The principle of effectiveness has a direct impact on the standing of possible claimants before national courts under Article [108(3)] of the Treaty. In this respect, Community law requires that national rules on legal standing do not undermine the right to effective judicial protection.[115] National rules cannot therefore limit legal standing only to the competitors of the beneficiary.[116] Third parties who are not affected by the distortion of competition resulting from the aid measure can also have a sufficient legal interest of a different character (as has been recognised in tax cases) in bringing proceedings before a national court.[117]

Notes

[115] Case C-174/02, *Streekgewest*, cited above footnote 113, paragraph 18.
[116] Case C-174/02, *Streekgewest*, cited above footnote 113, paragraphs 14 to 21.
[117] Case C-174/02, *Streekgewest*, cited above footnote 113, paragraph 19.

2.4.3. Standing issues in tax cases

73. The jurisprudence cited in paragraph 72 is particularly relevant for State aid granted in the form of exemptions from taxes and other financial liabilities. In such cases, it is not uncommon for persons who do not benefit from the same exemption to challenge their own tax burden based on Article [108(3)] of the Treaty.[118]

Notes

[118] See statistics in paragraph 3. The imposition of an exceptional tax burden on specific sectors or producers can also amount to State aid in favour of other companies, see Case C-487/06 P *British Aggregates Association v Commission*, judgment of 22 December 2008, [[2008] ECR I- 10515], paragraphs 81 to 86.

74. However, based on the jurisprudence of the Community courts, third party tax payers may only rely on the standstill obligation where their own tax payment forms an integral part of the unlawful State aid measure.[119] This is the case where, under the relevant national rules, the tax revenue is reserved exclusively for funding the unlawful State aid and has a direct impact on the amount of State aid granted in violation of Article [108(3)] of the Treaty.[120]

Notes

[119] Case C-174/02, *Streekgewest*, cited above footnote 113, paragraph 19.
[120] Joined Cases C-393/04 and C-41/05, *Air Liquide*, cited above footnote 13, paragraph 46; Joined Cases C-266/04 to C-270/04, C-276/04 and C-321/04 to C-325/04, *Casino France and Others*, [2005] ECR I-9481, paragraph 40; and Case C-174/02, *Streekgewest*, cited above footnote 113, paragraph 26.

75. If exemptions have been granted from general taxes, these criteria are usually not met. An undertaking liable to pay such taxes therefore cannot generally claim that someone else's tax exemption is unlawful under Article [108(3)] of the Treaty.[121] It also results from settled case law that extending an illegal tax exemption to the claimant is no appropriate remedy for breaches of Article [108(3)] of the Treaty. Such a measure would not eliminate the anticompetitive effects of unlawful aid, but on the contrary, strengthen them.[122]

Notes

[121] Joined Cases C-393/04 and C-41/05, *Air Liquide*, cited above footnote 13, paragraph 48; and Joined Cases C-266/04 to C-270/04, C-276/04 and C-321/04 to C-325/04, *Casino France and Others*, cited above footnote 120, paragraphs 43 and 44.
[122] Joined Cases C-393/04 and C-41/05, *Air Liquide*, cited above footnote 13, paragraph 45.

Part G State Aids

2.4.4. *Gathering evidence*

76. The principle of effectiveness can also influence the process of gathering evidence. For example, where the burden of proof as regards a particular claim makes it impossible or excessively difficult for a claimant to substantiate its claim (for example where the necessary documentary evidence is not in its possession), the national court is required to use all means available under national procedural law to give the claimant access to this evidence. This can include, where provided for under national law, the obligation for the national court to order the defendant or a third party to make the necessary documents available to the claimant.[123]

Notes

[123] Case C-526/04, *Laboratoires Boiron*, cited above footnote 111, paragraphs 55 and 57.

3. COMMISSION SUPPORT FOR NATIONAL COURTS

77. According to Article [4, paragraph 3 TEU], the institutions of the Community and Member States have a mutual duty of loyal cooperation with a view to attaining the objectives of the [TEU and TFEU]. Article [4, paragraph 3 TEU] thus implies that the Commission must assist national courts when they apply Community law.[124] Conversely, national courts may be obliged to assist the Commission in the fulfilment of its tasks.[125]

Notes

[124] Case C-39/94, *SFEI and Others*, cited above footnote 8, paragraph 50; Order of 13 July 1990 in Case C-2/88 Imm., *Zwartveld and Others*, [1990] ECR I-3365, paragraphs 16 to 22; and Case C-234/89, *Delimitis v Henninger Bräu*, [1991] ECR I-935, paragraph 53.
[125] Case C-94/00, *Roquette Frères*, [2002] ECR I-9011, paragraph 31.

78. Given the key role which national courts play in the enforcement of the State aid rules, the Commission is committed to helping national courts where the latter find such assistance necessary for their decision on a pending case. Whilst the 1995 Cooperation Notice already offered national courts the possibility to ask the Commission for assistance, this possibility has not been used regularly by national courts. The Commission therefore wishes to make a fresh attempt at establishing closer cooperation with national courts by providing more practical and user-friendly support mechanisms. In doing so, it draws inspiration from the Antitrust Cooperation Notice.[126]

Notes

[126] Commission Notice on the cooperation between the Commission and the courts of the EU Member States in the application of Articles [101 and 102 TFEU] (OJ C 101, 27.4.2004, p.54), paragraphs 15 to 30.

79. Commission support to national courts can take two different forms:
    (a) The national court may ask the Commission to transmit to it relevant information in its possession (see section 3.1).
    (b) The national court may ask the Commission for an opinion concerning the application of the State aid rules (see section 3.2).
80. When supporting national courts, the Commission must respect its duty of professional secrecy and safeguard its own functioning and independence.[127] In fulfilling its duty under Article [4 paragraph 3 TEU] towards national courts, the Commission is therefore committed to remaining neutral and objective. Since the Commission's assistance to national courts is part of its duty to defend the public interest, the Commission has no intention to serve the private interests of the parties involved in the case pending before the national court. The Commission will therefore not hear any of the parties involved in the national proceedings about its assistance to the national court.

Notes

[127] Order of 6 December 1990 in Case C-2/88 Imm., *Zwartveld and Others*, [1990] ECR I-4405, paragraphs 10 and 11; and Case T-353/94, *Postbank v Commission*, [1996] ECR II-921, paragraph 93.

81. The support offered to national courts under this Notice is voluntary and without prejudice to the possibility or obligation[128] for the national court to ask the ECJ for a preliminary ruling regarding the interpretation or the validity of Community law in accordance with Article [267] of the Treaty.

Notes

[128] Based on Article [267 TFEU], a national court whose decision is not subject to further judicial review is under an obligation to initiate a preliminary reference to the ECJ in certain circumstances.

3.1. Transmission of information to national courts

82. The Commission's duty to assist national courts in the application of State aid rules comprises the obligation to transmit relevant information in its possession to national courts.[129]

Notes

[129] Case C-39/94, *SFEI and Others*, cited above footnote 8, paragraph 50; Order of 13 July 1990 in Case C-2/88 Imm., *Zwartveld and Others*, cited above footnote 124, paragraphs 17 to 22; Case C-234/89, *Delimitis v Henninger Bräu*, cited above footnote 124, paragraph 53; and Case T-353/94, *Postbank v Commission*, cited above footnote 127, paragraphs 64 and 65.

83. A national court may, *inter alia*, ask the Commission for the following types of information:
    (a) Information concerning a pending Commission procedure; this can, *inter alia*, include information on whether a procedure regarding a particular aid measure is pending before the Commission, whether a certain aid measure has been duly notified in accordance with Article [108(3)] of the Treaty, whether the Commission has initiated a formal investigation, and whether the Commission has already taken a decision.[130] In the absence of a decision, the national court may ask the Commission to clarify when this is likely to be adopted.
    (b) In addition, national courts may ask the Commission to transmit documents in its possession. This can include copies of existing Commission decisions to the extent that these decisions are not already published on the Commission's website, factual data, statistics, market studies and economic analysis.

Notes

[130] Upon receipt of this information, the national court may ask for regular updates on the state of play.

84. In order to ensure efficiency in its cooperation with national courts, requests for information will be processed as quickly as possible. The Commission will endeavour to provide the national court with the requested information within one month from the date of the request. Where the Commission needs to ask the national court for further clarifications, this one-month period starts to run from the moment the clarification is received. Where the Commission has to consult third parties who are directly affected by the transmission of the information, the one-month period starts from the conclusion of this consultation. This could, for example, be the case for certain types of information submitted by a private person,[131] or where information submitted by one Member State is being requested by a court in a different Member State.

Notes

[131] Case T-353/94, *Postbank v Commission*, cited above footnote 127, paragraph 91.

85. In transmitting information to national courts, the Commission needs to uphold the guarantees given to natural and legal persons under Article [339] of the Treaty.[132] Article [339] of the Treaty prevents members, officials and other servants of the Commission from disclosing information which is covered by the obligation of professional secrecy. This can include confidential information and business secrets.

Notes

[132] Case C-234/89, *Delimitis v Henninger Bräu*, cited above footnote 124, paragraph 53; and Case T-353/94, *Postbank v Commission*, cited above footnote 127, paragraph 90.

86. Articles [4, paragraph 3 TEU] and [339 TFEU] do not lead to an absolute prohibition for the Commission to transmit to national courts information covered by professional secrecy. As confirmed by the Community courts, the duty of loyal cooperation requires the Commission to provide the national court with whatever information the latter may seek.[133] This also includes information covered by the obligation of professional secrecy.

Notes

[133] Case T-353/94, *Postbank v Commission*, cited above footnote 127, paragraph 64; and Order of 13 July 1990 in Case C-2/88 Imm., *Zwartveld and Others*, cited above footnote 124, paragraphs 16 to 22.

87. Where it intends to provide information covered by professional secrecy to a national court, the Commission will therefore remind the court of its obligations under Article [339] of the Treaty. It will ask the national court whether it can and will guarantee the protection of such confidential information and business secrets. Where the national court cannot offer such a guarantee, the Commission will not transmit the information concerned.[134] Where, on the other hand, the national court has offered such a guarantee, the Commission will transmit the information requested.

Notes

[134] Case T-353/94, *Postbank v Commission*, cited above footnote 127, paragraph 93; and Order of 6 December 1990 in Case C-2/88 Imm., *Zwartveld and Others*, cited above footnote 127, paragraphs 10 and 11.

88. There are further scenarios where the Commission may be prevented from disclosing information to a national court. In particular, the Commission may refuse to transmit information to a national court where such transmission would interfere with the functioning and independence of the Communities. This would be the case where disclosure would jeopardise the accomplishment of the tasks entrusted to the Commission[135] (for example, information concerning the Commission's internal decision making process).

Notes

[135] Order of 6 December 1990 in Case C-2/88 Imm., *Zwartveld and Others*, cited above footnote 127, paragraph 11; Case C-275/00, *First and Franex*, [2002] ECR I-10943, paragraph 49; and Case T-353/94, *Postbank v Commission*, cited above footnote 127, paragraph 93.

3.2. Opinions on questions concerning the application of State aid rules

89. When called upon to apply State aid rules to a case pending before it, a national court must respect any relevant Community rules in the area of State aid and the existing case law of the Community courts. In addition, a national court may seek guidance in the Commission's decision-making practice and in the notices and guidelines concerning the application of the State aid rules issued by the Commission. However, there may be circumstances in which these tools do not offer the national court sufficient guidance on the issues at stake. In the light of its obligations under Article [4, paragraph 3 TEU] and given the important and complex role which national courts play in State aid enforcement, the Commission therefore gives national courts the opportunity to request the Commission's opinion on relevant issues concerning the application of the State aid rules.[136]

Notes

[136] See Case C-39/94, *SFEI and Others*, cited above footnote 8, paragraph 50.

90. Such Commission opinions may, in principle, cover all economic, factual or legal matters which arise in the context of the national proceedings.[137] Matters concerning the interpretation of Community law can obviously also lead the national court to ask for a preliminary ruling of the ECJ under Article [267] of the Treaty. Where no further judicial remedy exists against the court's decision under national law, the use of this preliminary reference procedure is, in principle, mandatory.[138]

Notes

[137] However, please note paragraph 92.

[138] Where the interpretation of EC law may be clearly deduced from existing case-law or where it leaves no scope for reasonable doubt, a court against whose decisions there is no judicial remedy under national law is not required to refer the case

for a preliminary ruling by the Court of Justice, although it is free to do so. See Case 283/81 *Cilfit and others* [1982] ECR 3415, paragraphs 14 to 20, and Joined Cases C-428/06 to C-434/06 *Unión General de Trabajadores de la Rioja* [2008] ECR I-0000, judgment of 11 September 2008, not yet reported, [now [2008] ECR I-6747] paragraphs 42 and 43.

91. Possible subject matters for Commission opinions include, *inter alia*:
    (a) Whether a certain measure qualifies as State aid within the meaning of Article [107] of the Treaty and, if so, how the exact aid amount is to be calculated. Such opinions can relate to each of the criteria under Article [107] of the Treaty (namely, the existence of an advantage, granted by a Member State or through State resources, possible distortion of competition and effect on trade between Member States).
    (b) Whether a certain aid measure meets a certain requirement of a Block Exemption Regulation so that no individual notification is necessary and the standstill obligation under Article [108(3)] of the Treaty does not apply.
    (c) Whether a certain aid measure falls under a specific aid scheme which has been notified and approved by the Commission or otherwise qualifies as existing aid. Also in such cases, the standstill obligation under Article [108(3)] of the Treaty does not apply.
    (d) Whether exceptional circumstances (as referred to in the 'SFEI' judgment[139] exist which would prevent the national court from ordering full recovery under Community law.
    (e) Where the national court is required to order the recovery of interest, it can ask the Commission for assistance as regards the interest calculation and the interest rate to be applied.
    (f) The legal prerequisites for damages claims under Community law and issues concerning the calculation of the damage incurred.

Notes
[139] See references cited in footnote 51.

92. As stated in paragraph 20, the assessment of the compatibility of an aid measure with the common market pursuant to Article [107(2)] and [107(3)] of the Treaty falls within the exclusive competence of the Commission. National courts are not competent to assess the compatibility of an aid measure. Whilst the Commission cannot, therefore, provide opinions on compatibility, this does not prevent the national court from requesting procedural information as to whether the Commission is already assessing the compatibility of a certain aid measure (or intends to do so) and, if so, when its decision is likely to be adopted.[140]

Notes
[140] See paragraph 83.

93. When giving its opinion, the Commission will limit itself to providing the national court with the factual information or the economic or legal clarification sought, without considering the merits of the case pending before the national court. Moreover, unlike the authoritative interpretation of Community law by the Community courts, the opinion of the Commission does not legally bind the national court.
94. In the interest of making its cooperation with national courts as effective as possible, requests for Commission opinions will be processed as quickly as possible. The Commission will endeavour to provide the national court with the requested opinion within four months from the date of the request. Where the Commission needs to ask the national court for further clarifications concerning its request, this four-month period starts to run from the moment when the clarification is received.
95. In this context, it should be noted, however, that the general obligation of national courts to protect individual rights under Article [108(3)] of the Treaty also applies during the period in which the Commission prepares the requested opinion. This is because, as set out in paragraph 62, the national courts obligation to protect individual rights under Article [108(3)] of the Treaty applies irrespective of whether a statement from the Commission is still awaited or not.[141]

Notes
[141] This can include interim measures as outlined in section 2.2.6.

96. As already indicated in paragraph 80, the Commission will not hear the parties before providing its opinion to the national court. The introduction of the Commission's opinion to the national proceeding is subject to the relevant national procedural rules, which have to respect the general principles of Community law.

3.3. Practical issues

97. In order to further contribute to more effective cooperation and communication between the Commission and national courts, the Commission has decided to establish a single contact point, to which national courts can address all requests for support under sections 3.1 and 3.2, and any other written or oral questions about State aid policy that may arise in their daily work.
European Commission
Secretariat General
B-1049 Brussels
Belgium
Telephone 0032 2 29 76271
Fax 0032 2 29 98330
Email ec-amicus-state-aid@ec.europa.eu

98. The Commission will publish a summary concerning its cooperation with national courts pursuant to this Notice in its annual Report on Competition Policy. It may also make its opinions and observations available on its website.

4. FINAL PROVISIONS

99. This Notice is issued in order to assist national courts in the application of the State aid rules. It does not bind the national courts or affect their independence. The Notice also does not affect the rights and obligations of Member States and natural or legal persons under Community law.

100. This Notice replaces the 1995 Cooperation Notice.

101. The Commission intends to carry out a review of this Notice five years after its adoption.

G7

NOTICE FROM THE COMMISSION ON A SIMPLIFIED PROCEDURE FOR TREATMENT OF CERTAIN TYPES OF STATE AID

(Text with EEA relevance)

(2009/C 136/03)

Official Journal C 136, 16.6.2009, p.3

Celex No: 52009XC0616(01)

EUR-Lex permanent link: <http://eur-lex.europa.eu/LexUriServ/LexUriServ.do?uri=CELEX:52009XC0616(01):EN:NOT>

Notes
EEA application: on 16 December the EFTA Surveillance Authority adopted parallel guidelines concerning best practice for the conduct of state aid control procedures and simplified procedure for treatment of certain types of state aid.

Commentary
Notice: B&C: 17.003, 17.082

1. Introduction

1. This Notice sets out a simplified procedure under which the Commission intends, in close coop-eration with the Member State concerned, to examine within an accelerated time frame certain types of State support measures which only require the Commission to verify that the measure is in accordance with existing rules and practices without exercising any discretionary powers. The Commission's experience gained in applying Article [107 of the Treaty on the Functioning of the European Union]* and the regulations, frameworks, guidelines and notices adopted on the basis of Article [107],[1] has shown that certain categories of notified aid are normally approved without raising any doubts as to their compatibility with the common market, provided that there are no special circumstances. These categories of aid are described in Section 2. Other aid measures noti-fied to the Commission will be subject to the appropriate procedures[2] and normally to the Code of Best Practice for the conduct of State aid control procedures.[3]

Notes

* Ed note: please see the Note on the Lisbon Treaty at p.xvii in regard to article renumbering introduced by the Lisbon Treaty. Unless otherwise stated, all Treaty article numbers are the new numbers of the Treaty on the Functioning of the European Union (TFEU) and the Treaty on European Union (TEU).

[1] See, in particular, the Community framework for State aid for research and development and innovation, OJ C 323, 30.12.2006, p.1, hereinafter referred to as the 'Framework for Research and Development and Innovation'; the Community Guidelines on State aid to promote risk capital investments in small and medium-sized enterprises, OJ C 194, 18.8.2006, p.2, hereinafter the 'Risk Capital Guidelines'; the Community Guidelines on State aid for environmen-tal protection, OJ C 82, 1.4.2008, p.1, hereinafter the 'Environmental Aid Guidelines'; the Guidelines on national regional aid for 2007-2013, OJ C 54, 4.3.2006, p.13, hereinafter the 'Regional Aid Guidelines'; the Commission com-munication concerning the prolongation of the Framework on State aid to shipbuilding, OJ C 260, 28.10.2006, p.7, hereinafter the 'Shipbuilding Framework'; the Commission Communication concerning the prolongation of the appli-cation of the Communication on the follow-up to the Commission communication on certain legal aspects relating to cinematographic and other audiovisual works, OJ C 134, 16.6.2007, p.5, hereinafter the 'Cinema Communication'; Commission Regulation (EC) No 800/2008 of 6 August 2008 declaring certain categories of aid compatible with the common market in application of Articles [107 and 108 TFEU] (General block exemption Regulation), OJ L 214, 9.8.2008, p.3.

[2] Measures notified to the Commission in the context of the current financial crisis pursuant to the Communications from the Commission entitled 'The application of State aid rules to measures taken in relation to financial institutions in the context of the current global financial crisis' (OJ C 270, 25.10.2008, p.8) and the 'Temporary Community framework for State aid measures to support access to finance in the current financial and economic crisis' (OJ C 16, 22.1.2009, p.1) and State aid measures implementing the European Recovery Plan (Communication from the Commission to the European Council, A European Economic Recovery Plan, COM(2008) 800 final of 26 November 2008) will not be subject to the simplified procedure set out in this Notice. Specific ad hoc arrangements have been put in place in order to deal swiftly with those cases.

[3] See page 13 of this Official Journal. [OJ C 136, 16.6.2009, p.13]

2. The purpose of this Notice is to set out the conditions under which the Commission will usually adopt a short-form decision declaring certain types of State support measures compatible with the common market under the simplified procedure and to provide guidance in respect of the proced-ure itself. When all the conditions set out in this Notice are met, the Commission will use its best endeavours to adopt a short-form decision that the notified measure does not constitute aid or not to raise objections within 20 working days from the date of notification, in accordance with Article 4(2) or Article 4(3) of Council Regulation (EC) No 659/1999 of 22 March 1999 laying down detailed rules for the application of Article [108 TFEU].[1]

Notes

[1] OJ L 83, 27.3.1999, p.1.

3. However, if any of the safeguards or exclusions set out in points 6 to 12 of this Notice are applica-ble, the Commission will revert to the normal procedure regarding notified aid described in Chap-ter II of Regulation (EC) No 659/1999 and will then adopt a full-form decision pursuant to Article 4 and/or Article 7 of that Regulation. In any case, the only legally enforceable time limits are those set out in Article 4(5) and Article 7(6) of Regulation (EC) No 659/1999.

4. By following the procedure outlined in this Notice, the Commission aims to make Community State Aid control more predictable and efficient, pursuant to the general principles set out in the State Aid Action Plan: Less and Better Targeted State Aid: A Roadmap for State Aid Reform 2005-2009.[1] This Notice thereby also contributes to the simplification strategy launched by the Commission in October 2005.[2] No part of this Notice should be interpreted as implying that a support measure which does not qualify as State aid within the meaning of Article [107] of the Treaty must be notified to the Commission, although Member States remain free to notify such support measures for reasons of legal certainty.

Notes

[1] COM(2005) 107 final.
[2] Implementing the Community Lisbon programme: A strategy for the simplification of the regulatory environment COM(2005) 535 final.

2. Categories of State Aid Suitable for Treatment Under the Simplified Procedure

Eligible categories of State aid

5. The following categories of measures are in principle suitable for treatment under the simplified procedure:

(a) Category 1: Aid measures falling within the 'standard assessment' sections of existing frameworks or guidelines

Aid measures falling within the 'standard assessment' (so-called 'safe harbour' sections)[1] or equivalent types of assessment[2] in horizontal guidelines and frameworks, which are not covered by the General block exemption Regulation, are in principle suitable for treatment under the simplified procedure.

The simplified procedure will only be applied in cases where the Commission is satisfied, after the pre-notification phase (see points 13 to 16), that all the substantive and procedural requirements laid down in the applicable sections of the respective instruments are fulfilled. This implies that the pre-notification phase confirms that the notified aid measure prima facie meets the relevant conditions, as further detailed in each of the applicable horizontal instruments, concerning:

— type of beneficiaries,
— eligible costs,
— aid intensities and bonuses,
— individual notification ceiling or maximum aid amount,
— type of aid instrument used,
— cumulation,
— incentive effect,
— transparency,
— exclusion of beneficiaries which are subject to an outstanding recovery order.[3]

The types of measures for which the Commission is prepared to consider applying the simplified procedure within this category include in particular the following:

(i) risk capital measures taking a form other than a participation into a private equity investment fund and meeting all other conditions of Section 4 of the Risk Capital Guidelines;[4]

(ii) environmental investment aid meeting the conditions of Section 3 of the Environmental Aid Guidelines:

— the eligible cost basis of which is determined on the basis of a full cost calculation methodology in line with point 82 of the Environmental Aid Guidelines,[5] or

— including an eco-innovation bonus demonstrated to be in line with point 78 of the Environmental Aid Guidelines;[6]

(iii) aid for young innovative enterprises granted in accordance with Section 5.4 of the Framework for Research and Development and Innovation and the innovative character of which is determined on the basis of Section 5.4(b)(i) of the Framework;[7]

> (iv) aid for innovation clusters granted in accordance with Sections 5.8 and 7.1 of the Framework for Research and Development and Innovation;
>
> (v) aid for process and organisational innovation in services granted in accordance with Section 5.5 of the Framework for Research and Development and Innovation;
>
> (vi) ad hoc regional aid which is below the individual notification threshold laid down in point 64 of the Regional Aid Guidelines;[8]
>
> (vii) rescue aid in the manufacturing and services sectors (except in the financial sector) meeting all substantive conditions of Sections 3.1.1 and 3.1.2 of the Rescue and Restructuring Guidelines;[9]
>
> (viii) rescue and restructuring schemes for small enterprises meeting all conditions of Section 4 of the Rescue and Restructuring Guidelines;[10]
>
> (ix) ad hoc restructuring aid for small and medium enterprises, provided it meets all the conditions laid down in Section 3 of the Rescue and Restructuring Guidelines;[11]
>
> (x) export credits in the shipbuilding sector meeting all the conditions of Section 3.3.4 of the Shipbuilding Framework;[12]
>
> (xi) audiovisual support schemes meeting all the conditions set out in Section 2.3 of the Cinema Communication as regards the development, production, distribution and promotion of audiovisual works.[13]

The above list is illustrative and may evolve on the basis of future revisions of the currently applicable instruments or the adoption of new instruments. The Commission may review this list from time to time to keep it in line with applicable State aid rules.

Notes

[1] Such as Section 5 of the Framework for Research and Development and Innovation or Section 3 of the Environmental Aid Guidelines, and Section 4 of the Risk Capital Guidelines.

[2] Regional Aid Guidelines; Section 3.1.2 of the Community Guidelines on State aid for rescuing and restructuring firms in difficulty, OJ C 244, 1.10.2004, p.2, hereinafter the 'Rescue and Restructuring Guidelines'.

[3] The Commission will revert to the normal procedure where the notified aid measure could benefit an undertaking which is subject to an outstanding recovery order following a previous Commission decision declaring an aid unlawful and incompatible with the common market (so-called *Deggendorf* issue). See Case C-188/92 *TWD Textilwerke Deggendorf* [1994] ECR I-833.

[4] Including cases where the financial institutions of the European Union act as holding fund to the extent the risk capital measure at stake falls under Section 4 of the Risk Capital Guidelines.

[5] Article 18(5) of the General block exemption Regulation foresees a simplified cost calculation methodology.

[6] The General block exemption Regulation does not exempt eco-innovation bonuses.

[7] Only aid to young innovative enterprises meeting the conditions laid down in point 5.4(b)(ii) of the Framework for Research and Development and Innovation are subject to the General block exemption Regulation.

[8] In such cases, the information to be provided by the Member State will need to demonstrate upfront that: (i) the aid amount remains below the notification threshold (without sophisticated net present value calculations); (ii) the aid concerns a new investment (no replacement investment); and (iii) the beneficial effects of the aid on regional development manifestly outweigh the distortions of competition it creates. See for example the Commission's Decision in case N 721/2007 (Poland, 'Reuters Europe SA').

[9] See for example the Commission's Decision in cases N 28/2006 (Poland, Techmatrans), N 258/2007 (Germany, Rettungsbeihilfe zugunsten der Erich Rohde KG) and N 802/2006 (Italy, rescue aid to Sandretto Industrie).

[10] See for example the Commission's Decisions in cases N 85/2008 (Austria, Guarantee scheme for small and medium-sized enterprises in the region of Salzburg), N 386/2007 (France, Rescue and restructuring scheme for small and medium-sized enterprises), N 832/2006 (Italy, Rescue and restructuring scheme Valle d'Aosta). This approach is in line with Article 1(7) of the General block exemption Regulation.

[11] See for example the Commission's Decisions in cases N 92/2008 (Austria, Restructuring aid for Der Bäcker Legat) and N 289/2007 (Italy, Restructuring aid to Fiem SRL).

[12] See for example the Commission's Decisions in cases N 76/2008 (Germany, Prolongation of CIRR financing scheme for the export of ships), N 26/2008 (Denmark, Changes to financing scheme for the export of ships) and N 760/2006 (Spain, Extension of export financing scheme — Spanish shipbuilding).

[13] Although the Communication's criteria apply directly only to the activity of production, in practice, they are also applied by analogy to assess the compatibility of the activities of pre- and post-production of audiovisual works, as well as the principles of necessity and proportionality under Articles [107(3)(d)] and [167] of the Treaty. See for example the Commission's Decisions in cases N 233/2008 (Latvian film support scheme), N 72/2008 (Spain, Scheme for the promotion of films in Madrid), N 60/2008 (Italy, Film support in the Sardinia region) and N 291/2007 (Netherlands Film Fund).

Part G State Aids

(b) Category 2: Measures corresponding to well-established Commission decision-making practice
Aid measures with features corresponding to those of aid measures approved in at least three earlier Commission decisions (hereinafter 'precedent decisions'), the assessment of which can thus be immediately carried out on the basis of this established Commission decision-making practice, are in principle suitable for treatment under the simplified procedure. Only Commission decisions adopted within the last ten years preceding the date of pre-notification (see point 14) may qualify as 'precedent decisions'.

The simplified procedure will only be applied in cases where the Commission is satisfied, after the pre-notification phase (see points 13–16), that the relevant substantive and procedural conditions which governed the precedent decisions are met, in particular as regards the objectives and overall set-up of the measure, the types of beneficiaries, eligible costs, individual notification ceilings, aid intensities and (where applicable) bonuses, cumulation provisions, incentive effect, and transparency requirements. In addition, as pointed out in point 11, the Commission will revert to the normal procedure where the notified aid measure could benefit an undertaking which is subject to an outstanding recovery order following a previous Commission decision declaring an aid unlawful and incompatible with the common market (so-called *Deggendorf* issue).

The types of measures for which the Commission is prepared to consider applying the simplified procedure within this category include in particular the following:

(i) aid measures for the preservation of national cultural heritage related to activities linked to historic, ancient sites or national monuments, provided that the aid is limited to 'heritage conservation' within the meaning of Article [107(3)(d)] of the Treaty;[1]

(ii) aid schemes for theatre, dance and music activities;[2]

(iii) aid schemes for the promotion of minority languages;[3]

(iv) aid measures in favour of the publishing industry;[4]

(v) aid measures in favour of broadband connectivity in rural areas;[5]

(vi) guarantee schemes for shipbuilding finance;[6]

(vii) aid measures fulfilling all other applicable provisions of the General block exemption Regulation, but excluded from its application merely because:

— the measures constitute 'ad hoc aid',[7]

— the measures are provided in an untransparent form (Article 5 of the General block exemption Regulation), but their gross grant equivalent is calculated on the basis of a methodology approved by the Commission in three individual decisions adopted after 1 January 2007;

(viii) measures supporting the development of local infrastructure not constituting State aid within the meaning of Article [107(1)] of the Treaty in view of the fact that, having regard to the specificities of the case, the measure in question will not have any effect on intra-Community trade;[8]

(ix) the prolongation and/or modification of existing schemes outside the scope of the simplified procedure foreseen in Commission Regulation (EC) No 794/2004 of 21 April 2004 implementing Council Regulation (EC) No 659/1999 laying down detailed rules for the application of Article [108 TFEU][9] (see category 3 below), for example as regards the adaptation of existing schemes to new horizontal guidelines.[10]

This list is illustrative, since the exact scope of this category may evolve in line with Commission decision-making practice. The Commission may review this illustrative list from time to time to keep it in line with evolving practice.

Notes

[1] See for example the Commission's Decisions in cases N 393/2007 (Netherlands, Subsidy to NV Bergkwartier), N 106/2005 (Poland, Hala Ludowa in Wroclaw) and N 123/2005 (Hungary, Earmarked scheme for tourism and culture in Hungary).

[2] See for example the Commission's Decisions in cases N 340/2007 (Spain, Aid for theatre, dance, music and audiovisual activities in the Basque country), N 257/2007 (Spain, Promotion of theatre production in the Basque country) and N 818/99 (France; Parafiscal tax on spectacles and concerts).

3 See for example the Commission's Decisions in cases N 776/2006 (Spain, Aid for the promotion of the Basque Language), N 49/2007 (Spain, Aid for the promotion of the Basque Language) and N 161/2008 (Spain, Aid to the Basque Language).

4 See for example the Commission's Decisions in cases N 687/2006 (Slovak Republic, Aid to Kalligram s.r.o. in favour of a periodical), N 1/2006 (Slovenia, Promotion of the publishing industry in Slovenia) and N 268/2002 (Italy, Aid in favour of the publishing industry in Sicily).

5 See for example the Commission's Decisions in cases N 264/2006 (Italy, Broadband for rural Tuscany), N 473/2007 (Italy, Broadband connections for Alto Adige) and N 115/2008 (Broadband in rural areas of Germany).

6 See for example the Commission's Decisions in cases N 325/2006 (Germany, prolongation of the guarantee schemes for shipbuilding finance), N 35/2006 (France, Guarantee scheme for ship financing and bonding) and N 253/2005 (Netherlands, Guarantee scheme for ship financing).

7 Ad hoc aid is often excluded from the scope of the General block exemption Regulation. This exclusion applies to all large enterprises (Article 1(6) of the General block exemption Regulation), as well as, in certain instances, to small and medium-sized enterprises (see Articles 13 and 14 concerning regional aid, Article 16 concerning female entrepreneurship, Article 29 concerning aid in the form of risk capital and Article 40 concerning aid for the recruitment of disadvantaged workers). As regards the specific conditions governing ad hoc regional investment aid, see footnote 14 above. Moreover this Notice is without prejudice to any Commission communication or guidance paper laying down detailed economic assessment criteria for the compatibility analysis of cases subject to individual notification.

8 See the Commission's Decisions in cases N 258/2000 (Germany, leisure pool Dorsten), N 486/2002 (Sweden, Aid in favour of a congress hall in Visby), N 610/2001 (Germany, Tourism infrastructure program Baden-Württemberg), N 377/2007 (The Netherlands, Support to *Bataviawerf*— Reconstruction of a vessel from the 17th century). In order for the measure concerned to be considered as not having any effect on intra-Community trade, these four precedent decisions require, most prominently, a demonstration by the Member State of the following features: 1. that the aid does not lead to investments being attracted in the region concerned; and 2. that the goods/services produced by the beneficiary are purely local and/or have a geographically limited attraction zone; and 3. that there is no more than marginal effect on consumers from neighbouring Member States; and 4. that the market share of the beneficiary is minimal on any relevant market definition used and that the beneficiary does not belong to a wider group of undertakings. These features should be highlighted in the draft notification form referred to in point 14 of this Notice.

9 OJ L 140, 30.4.2004, p.1.

10 See for example the Commission's Decisions in cases N 585/2007 (United Kingdom, Prolongation of Yorkshire R&D scheme), N 275/2007 (Germany, Prolongation of rescue and restructuring scheme for small and medium-sized enterprises in Bremen), N 496/2007 (Italy (Lombardia) Guarantee Fund for the development of risk capital) and N 625/2007 (Latvia, Aid to risk capital to small and medium-sized enterprises).

(c) Category 3: Prolongation or extension of existing schemes

Article 4 of Regulation (EC) No 794/2004 foresees a simplified notification procedure for certain alterations to existing aid. Under that Article, the '[…] following alterations to existing aid shall be notified on the simplified notification form set out in Annex II:

(a) increases in the budget of an authorised aid scheme exceeding 20%;

(b) prolongation of an existing authorised aid scheme by up to six years, with or without an increase in the budget;

(c) tightening of the criteria for the application of an authorised aid scheme, a reduction of aid intensity or a reduction of eligible expenses'. The possibility of applying Article 4 of Regulation (EC) No 794/2004 remains unaffected by this Notice. However, the Commission invites the notifying Member State to proceed in accordance with this Notice, including pre-notification of the aid measures concerned, while using the simplified notification form annexed to Regulation (EC) No 794/2004. The Commission will, in the context of this procedure, also invite the Member State concerned to agree on the publication on the Commission's website of the summary of its notification.

Safeguards and exclusions

6. Since the simplified procedure applies only to aid notified on the basis of Article [108(3)] of the Treaty, unlawful aids are excluded. Moreover, due to the specificities of the sectors concerned the simplified procedure will not apply to aid favouring activities in the fishery and aquaculture sectors, activities in the primary production of agricultural products or activities in the processing or marketing of agricultural products. In addition, the simplified procedure will not be applied retroactively to measures pre-notified before 1 September 2009.

7. In assessing whether a notified aid measure falls into one of the eligible categories set out in point 5, the Commission will ensure that the applicable frameworks or guidelines and/or established Commission decision-making practice on the basis of which the notified aid measure is to be assessed, as well as all relevant factual circumstances, are established with sufficient clarity. Given that the completeness of the notification constitutes a key element for determining whether the simplified procedure is to be applied, the notifying Member State is invited to provide all relevant information, including the precedent decisions relied upon, if appropriate, at the outset of the pre-notification phase (see point 14).

8. Where the notification form is not complete or contains misleading or incorrect information, the Commission will not apply the simplified procedure. In addition, to the extent that the notification involves novel legal issues of a general interest, the Commission will not normally apply the simplified procedure.

9. While it can normally be assumed that aid measures falling into the categories set out in point 5 will not raise doubts as to their compatibility with the common market, there may nonetheless be special circumstances which require a closer investigation. In such cases, the Commission may revert to the normal procedure at any time.

10. Such special circumstances may include in particular: certain forms of aid as yet untested in the Commission's decision-making practice, precedent decisions which the Commission may be in the course of reassessing in the light of recent case-law or developments of the common market, novel technical issues, or concerns as regards the measure's compatibility with other provisions of the Treaty (for example, non-discrimination, the four freedoms, etc.).

11. The Commission will revert to the normal procedure where the notified aid measure could benefit an undertaking which is subject to an outstanding recovery order following a previous Commission decision declaring an aid unlawful and incompatible with the common market (so-called *Deggendorf* issue).

12. Finally, if a third party expresses substantiated concerns about the notified aid measure within the time-limit laid down in point 21 of this Notice, the Commission will revert to the normal procedure[1] and will inform the Member State to that effect.

Notes

[1] This does not imply any increase of third parties' rights in view of the case law of the Community Courts. See Case T-95/03 *Asociación de Empresarios de Estaciones de Servicio de la Comunidad Autónoma de Madrid and Federación Catalana de Estaciones de Servicio v Commission* [2006] ECR II-4739, paragraph 139 and Case T-73/98 *Prayon-Rupel v Commission* [2001] ECR II-867, paragraph 45.

3. Procedural Provisions

Pre-notification contacts

13. The Commission has found pre-notification contacts with the notifying Member State beneficial even in seemingly unproblematic cases. Such contacts allow the Commission and the Member States, in particular, to determine at an early stage the relevant Commission instruments or precedent decisions, the degree of complexity which the Commission's assessment is likely to involve and the scope and depth of the information required for the Commission to make a full assessment of the case.

14. In view of the time constraints of the simplified procedure, the assessment of a State support measure under the simplified procedure is conditional upon the Member State holding pre-notification contacts with the Commission. In this context, the Member State is invited to submit a draft notification form with the necessary supplementary information sheets provided for in Article 2 of Regulation (EC) No 794/2004, and the relevant precedent decisions if appropriate, via the Commission's established IT application. The Member State may also request, at this stage, that the Commission waive the completion of certain parts of the notification form. The Member State and the Commission may also agree, in the context of the pre-notification contact, that the Member State does not need to provide a draft notification form and accompanying information in the pre-notification phase. Such an agreement may be appropriate, for instance, due to the repetitive nature of certain aid measures (for instance the category of aid set out in point 5(c) of this Notice). In this context, the Member State may be invited to proceed directly with the notification where detailed discussion about the envisaged aid measures is not considered necessary by the Commission.

15. Within two weeks from the receipt of the draft notification form, the Commission services will organise a first pre-notification contact. The Commission will promote the holding of contacts via email or conference calls or, at the specific request of the Member State concerned, organise meetings. Within 5 working days after the last pre-notification contact, the Commission services will inform the Member State concerned whether it considers that the case qualifies prima facie for treatment under the simplified procedure, which information still needs to be provided for the measure to qualify for treatment under that procedure, or whether the case will remain subject to the normal procedure.

16. The indication by the Commission services that the case concerned can be treated under the simplified procedure implies that the Member State and the Commission services agree prima facie that the information provided in the pre-notification context would, if submitted as a formal notification, constitute a complete notification. The Commission would thus, in principle, be in a position to approve the measure, once formally notified on the basis of a notification form embodying the result of the pre-notification contacts, without a further request for information.

Notification

17. The Member State must notify the aid measure(s) concerned no later than 2 months after it is informed by the Commission services that the measure qualifies prima facie for treatment under the simplified procedure. If the notification includes any changes as compared to the information presented in the pre-notification documents, such changes must be highlighted prominently in the context of the notification form.

18. The submission of the notification by the Member State concerned triggers the start of the period referred to in point 2.

19. The simplified procedure does not provide for a specific simplified notification form. Except as regards cases which fall within the category of aid set out in point 5(c) of this Notice, the notification is to be carried out on the basis of the standard notification forms in Regulation (EC) No 794/2004.

Publication of a summary of the notification

20. The Commission will publish on its website a summary of the notification, based on the information provided by the Member State, in the standard form set out in the Annex to this Notice. The standard form contains an indication that, on the basis of the information provided by the Member State, the aid measure may qualify for the application of a simplified procedure. By requesting the Commission to treat a notified measure under this Notice, the Member State concerned will be considered to agree that the information provided in its notification, which is to be published on the website in the form set out in the Annex to this Notice, is non-confidential in nature. Furthermore, Member States are invited to clearly indicate whether the notification contains any business secrets.

21. Interested parties will then have 10 working days to submit observations (including a non-confidential version), in particular on circumstances which might require a more thorough investigation. In cases where substantiated competition concerns are raised by interested parties with respect to the notified measure, the Commission will revert to the normal procedure and inform the Member State and the interested party or parties concerned to that effect. The Member State concerned will also be informed of any substantiated concerns and will be given the opportunity to comment on them.

Short-form decision

22. If the Commission is satisfied that the notified measure fulfils the criteria for the simplified procedure (see, in particular, point 5), it will issue a short-form decision. The Commission will thus use its best endeavours to adopt a decision that the notified measure does not constitute aid or a decision not to raise objections pursuant to Article 4(2) or (3) of Regulation (EC) No 659/1999 within 20 working days from the date of notification, unless any safeguard or exclusion referred to in points 6 to 12 of this Notice is applicable.

Publication of the short-form decision

23. In accordance with Article 26(1) of Regulation (EC) No 659/1999 the Commission will publish a summary notice of the decision in the Official Journal of the European Union. The short-form decision will be made available on the Commission's website. It will contain a reference to the summary information about the notification as published on the Commission's website at the

Part G State Aids

time of notification, a standard assessment of the measure under Article [107(1)] of the Treaty and, where applicable, a statement that the aid measure is declared compatible with the common market because it falls within one or more of the categories set out in point 5 of this Notice, with the applicable category or categories being explicitly identified and a reference to the applicable horizontal instruments and/or precedent decisions included.

4. FINAL PROVISIONS

24. Upon request of the Member State concerned, the Commission will apply the principles set out in this Notice to measures notified pursuant to point 17 as from 1 September 2009.

25. The Commission may review this Notice on the basis of important competition policy considerations or in order to take account of the evolution of State aid law and decision-making practice. The Commission intends to carry out a first review of this Notice at the latest four years after its publication. In this context, the Commission will examine the extent to which specific simplified notification forms should be developed in order to facilitate the implementation of this Notice.

ANNEX
SUMMARY OF NOTIFICATION: INVITATION TO THIRD
PARTIES TO SUBMIT COMMENTS

NOTIFICATION OF A STATE AID MEASURE

On ... the Commission received a notification of an aid measure pursuant to [Article 108 TFEU]. On preliminary examination, the Commission finds that the notified measure could fall within the scope of the Commission Notice on a simplified procedure for treatment of certain types of State aid (OJ C [136], 16.6.2009, p.[3]).

The Commission invites interested third parties to submit their possible observations on the proposed measure to the Commission.

The main features of the aid measure are the following:

Reference number of the aid: N ...

Member State:

Member State reference number:

Region:

Granting authority:

Title of the aid measure:

National legal basis:

Proposed Community basis for assessment: ... guidelines or established Commission practice as highlighted in Commission Decision (1, 2 and 3).

Type of measure: Aid scheme/Ad hoc aid

Amendment of an existing aid measure:

Duration (scheme):

Date of granting:

Economic sector(s) concerned:

Type of beneficiary (SMEs/large enterprises):

Budget:

Aid instrument (grant, interest rate subsidy, ...):

Observations raising competition issues relating to the notified measure must reach the Commission no later than 10 working days following the date of this publication and include a non-confidential version of these observations to be provided to the Member State concerned and/or other interested parties. Observations can be sent to the Commission by fax, by post or email under reference number N ... to the following address:

European Commission
Directorate-General for Competition
State Aid Registry
1049 Bruxelles/Brussels
BELGIQUE/BELGIË
Fax +32 22961242
Email: stateaidgreffe@ec.europa.eu

G8

CODE OF BEST PRACTICE FOR THE CONDUCT OF STATE AID CONTROL PROCEDURES

(2009/C 136/04)

Official Journal C 136, 16.6.2009, p.13

Celex No: 52009XC0616(02)

EUR-Lex permanent link: <http://eur-lex.europa.eu/LexUriServ/LexUriServ.do?uri=CELEX:52009XC0616(02):EN:NOT>

Notes

EEA application: on 16 December the EFTA Surveillance Authority adopted parallel guidelines concerning best practice for the conduct of state aid control procedures and simplified procedure for treatment of certain types of state aid.

Commentary

Notice: B&C: 17.003, 17.082 **F&N:** 17.397, 17.422, 17.425, 17.529, 17.536
Chap 7: F&N: 17.528

---

1. Scope and Purpose of this Code

1. In 2005, the Commission adopted the State Aid Action Plan: Less and better targeted State aid: a roadmap for State aid reform 2005–2009 ('the SAAP')[1] to improve the effectiveness, transparency, credibility and predictability of the State aid regime under the [Treaty on the Functioning of the European Union]. Based on the principle of less and better targeted State aid, the central objective of the SAAP is to encourage Member States to reduce their overall aid levels, whilst redirecting State resources to horizontal common interest objectives. To support this objective, the SAAP also calls for more effective, simple and predictable procedures in the State aid field.

Notes

[1] COM(2005) 107 final.

---

2. The Commission wishes to reaffirm that commitment by issuing this Code of Best Practice to make procedures as productive and efficient as possible for all parties concerned. This Code is built on the experience acquired in the application of Council Regulation (EC) No 659/1999 of 22 March 1999 laying down detailed rules for the application of Article [108 TFEU][1] and on internal Commission studies on the duration of the different steps of the State aid procedure, the treatment of complaints and information gathering tools. The principal aim of this Code is to

provide guidance on the day-to-day conduct of State aid procedures, thereby fostering a spirit of better co-operation and mutual understanding between the Commission services, Member State authorities and the legal and business community.

Notes

[1] OJ L 83, 27.3.1999, p.1. [Ed note: please see the Note on the Lisbon Treaty at p.xvii in regard to article renumbering introduced by the Lisbon Treaty.]

3. A successful improvement of State aid procedures requires discipline on both sides and a mutual commitment from the Commission and the Member States. While the Commission cannot be held responsible for the consequences of a lack of cooperation from Member States and interested parties, it will work to improve the conduct of its investigations and its internal decision-making process, in order to ensure greater transparency, predictability and efficiency of State aid procedures.

4. In line with modern State aids architecture, this Code is the final part of a simplification package comprising the Notice from the Commission on a simplified procedure for treatment of certain types of State aid[1] and the Commission Notice on the enforcement of State aid law by national courts[2] which contributes to more predictable and transparent procedures.

Notes

[1] See page 3 of this Official Journal. [OJ C 136, 16.6.2009, p.3]
[2] OJ C 85, 9.4.2009, p.1.

5. The specific features of an individual case may however require an adaptation of, or deviation from, this Code.[1]

Notes

[1] In the context of the 2008 banking crisis, the Commission has taken appropriate steps to ensure the swift adoption of decisions upon complete notification, if necessary within 24 hours and over a weekend. See Communication from the Commission — The application of State aid rules to measures taken in relation to financial institutions in the context of the current global financial crisis (OJ C 270, 25.10.2008, p.8). As regards the real economy, see Communication from the Commission — Temporary Community framework for State aid measures to support access to finance in the current financial and economic crisis (OJ C 83, 7.4.2009, p.1).

6. The specificities of the fishery and aquaculture sectors and of the activities in the primary production, marketing or processing of agricultural products may also justify a deviation from this Code.

2. RELATIONSHIP TO COMMUNITY LAW

7. This Code is not intended to provide a full or comprehensive account of the relevant legislative, interpretative and administrative measures which govern Community State aid control. It should be read in conjunction with and as a supplement to the basic rules governing State aid procedures.

8. This Code therefore does not create or alter any rights or obligations as set out in the [Treaty on the Functioning of the European Union], Regulation (EC) No 659/1999 and Commission Regulation (EC) No 794/2004 of 21 April 2004,[1] which implements Regulation (EC) No 659/1999, as interpreted by the case-law of the Community Courts.

Notes

[1] OJ L 140, 30.4.2004, p.1.

9. This Code sets out day-to-day Best Practices to contribute to speedier, more transparent and more predictable State aid procedures at each step of the investigation of a notified or non-notified case or a complaint.

3. PRE-NOTIFICATION CONTACTS

10. The Commission's experience demonstrates the added value of pre-notification contacts, even in seemingly standard cases. Pre-notification contacts provide the Commission services and the notifying Member State with the possibility to discuss the legal and economic aspects of a

proposed project informally and in confidence prior to notification, and thereby enhance the quality and completeness of notifications. In this context, the Member State and the Commission services can also jointly develop constructive proposals for amending problematic aspects of a planned measure. This phase thus paves the way for a more speedy treatment of notifications, once formally submitted to the Commission. Successful pre-notifications should effectively allow the Commission to adopt decisions pursuant to Article 4(2), (3) and (4) of Regulation (EC) No 659/1999 within two months from the date of notification.[1]

Notes

[1] This time limit cannot be respected where the Commission's services have to issue several requests for information due to incomplete notifications.

11. Pre-notification contacts are strongly recommended for cases where there are particular novelties or specific features which would justify informal prior discussions with the Commission services but informal guidance will be provided whenever a Member State calls for it.

3.1. Content

12. The pre-notification phase offers the possibility to discuss and provide guidance to the Member State concerned about the scope of the information to be submitted in the notification form to ensure it is complete as from the date of notification. A fruitful pre-notification phase will also allow discussions, in an open and constructive atmosphere, of any substantive issues raised by a planned measure. This is particularly important as regards projects which could not be accepted as such and should thus be withdrawn or significantly amended. It can also comprise an analysis of the availability of other legal bases or the identification of relevant precedents. In addition, a successful pre-notification phase will allow the Commission services and the Member State to address key competition concerns, economic analysis and, where appropriate, external expertise required to demonstrate the compatibility of a planned project with the common market. The notifying Member State may thus also request the Commission services, in pre-notification, to waive the obligation to provide certain information foreseen in the notification form which in the specific circumstances of the case is not necessary for its examination. Finally, the pre-notification phase is decisive to determine whether a case qualifies *prima facie* for treatment under the simplified procedure.[1]

Notes

[1] See Notice from the Commission on a simplified procedure for treatment of certain types of State aid.

3.2. Scope and timing

13. In order to allow for a constructive and efficient pre-notification phase, it is in the interest of the Member State concerned to provide the Commission with the information necessary for the assessment of a planned State aid project, on the basis of a draft notification form. In order to facilitate swift treatment of the case, contacts by emails or conference calls will in principle be favoured rather than meetings. Within two weeks from the receipt of the draft notification form, the Commission services will normally organise a first pre-notification contact.

14. As a general rule, pre-notification contacts should not last longer than 2 months and should be followed by a complete notification. Should pre-notification contacts not bring the desired results, the Commission services may declare the pre-notification phase closed. However, since the timing and format of pre-notification contacts depend on the complexity of the individual case, pre-notification contacts may last several months. The Commission therefore recommends that, in cases which are particularly complex (for example, rescue aid, large research and development aid, large individual aid or particularly large or complex aid schemes), Member States launch pre-notification contacts as early as possible to allow for meaningful discussions.

15. In the Commission's experience, involving the aid beneficiary in the pre-notification contacts is very useful, particularly for cases with major technical, financial and project-related implications. The Commission therefore recommends that beneficiaries of individual aid be involved in the pre-notification contacts.

16. Except in particularly novel or complex cases, the Commission services will endeavour to provide the Member State concerned with an informal preliminary assessment of the project at the end of the pre-notification phase. That non-binding assessment will not be an official position of the Commission, but informal guidance from the Commission services on the completeness of the draft notification and the *prima facie* compatibility of the planned project with the common market. In particularly complex cases, the Commission services may also provide written guidance, at the Member State's request, on the information still to be provided.

17. Pre-notification contacts are held in strict confidence. The discussions take place on a voluntary basis and remain without prejudice to the handling and investigation of the case following formal notification.

18. In order to enhance the quality of notifications, the Commission services will endeavour to meet requests for training sessions by Member States. The Commission will also maintain regular contacts with Member States to discuss further improvements of the State aid procedure, in particular as regards the scope and content of the applicable notification forms.

4. Mutually Agreed Planning

19. In cases which are particularly novel, technically complex or otherwise sensitive, or which have to be examined as a matter of absolute urgency, the Commission services will offer mutually agreed planning to the notifying Member State to increase the transparency and predictability of the likely duration of a State aid investigation.

4.1. Content

20. Mutually agreed planning is a form of structured cooperation between the Member State and the Commission services, based on a joint planning and understanding of the likely course of the investigation and its expected time frame.

21. In this context, the Commission services and the notifying Member State could in particular agree on:
    — the priority treatment of the case concerned, in return for the Member State formally accepting the suspension of the examination[1] of other notified cases originating from the same Member State, should this be necessary for planning or resource purposes,[2]
    — the information to be provided by the Member State and/or the beneficiary concerned, including studies or external expertise, or unilateral information-gathering by the Commission services, and
    — the likely form and duration of the assessment of the case by the Commission services, once notified.

Notes

[1] See Article 4(5) of Regulation (EC) No 659/1999.
[2] For instance, in cases where the financial institutions of the European Union act as holding fund.

---

22. In return for the Member State's efforts in providing all the necessary information in a timely manner and as agreed in the context of mutually agreed planning, the Commission services will endeavour to respect the mutually agreed time frame for the further investigation of the case, unless the information provided by the Member State or interested parties raises unexpected issues.

4.2. Scope and timing

23. Mutually agreed planning will in principle be reserved for cases which are so novel, technically complex or otherwise sensitive that a clear preliminary assessment of the case by the Commission services proves impossible at the end of the pre-notification phase. In such cases, mutually agreed planning will take place at the end of the pre-notification phase, and be followed by the formal notification.

24. However, the Commission services and the Member State concerned may also agree, at the latter's request, on mutually agreed planning for the further treatment of the case at the outset of the formal investigation procedure.

5. THE PRELIMINARY EXAMINATION OF NOTIFIED MEASURES

5.1. Requests for information

25. In order to streamline the course of the investigation, the Commission services will endeavour to group requests for information during the preliminary examination phase. In principle, there will therefore only be one comprehensive information request, normally to be sent within 4–6 weeks after the date of notification. Unless otherwise agreed in mutually agreed planning, pre-notification should enable Member States to submit a complete notification thereby reducing the need for additional information. However, the Commission may subsequently raise questions most notably on points that have been raised by the Member States' answers, although this does not necessarily indicate that the Commission is experiencing serious difficulties in assessing the case.

26. Should the Member State fail to provide the requested information within the prescribed period, Article 5(3) of Regulation (EC) No 659/1999 will, after one reminder, normally be applied, and the Member State will be informed that the notification is deemed to have been withdrawn. The formal investigation procedure will normally be initiated whenever the necessary conditions are met, and generally after two rounds of questions at most.

5.2. Agreed suspension of the preliminary examination

27. In certain circumstances, the course of the preliminary examination may be suspended if a Member State so requests to amend its project and bring it in line with State aid rules, or otherwise by common agreement. Suspension may only be granted for a period agreed in advance. Should the Member State fail to submit a complete, *prima facie* compatible project at the end of the suspension period, the Commission will resume the procedure from the point at which it was halted. The Member State concerned will normally be informed that the notification is deemed to have been withdrawn, or the formal investigation procedure opened without delay in case of serious doubts.

5.3. State of play contacts

28. At their request, notifying Member States will be informed of the state of play of an ongoing preliminary examination. Member States are invited to involve the beneficiary of an individual aid in these contacts.

6. THE FORMAL INVESTIGATION PROCEDURE

29. In the light of the general complexity of cases subject to formal investigation, the Commission is committed to improving the transparency, predictability and efficiency of this phase as a matter of utmost priority, to contribute to meaningful decision-making in line with the needs of modern business. The Commission will therefore streamline the conduct of formal investigations through efficient use of all the procedural means available to it under Regulation (EC) No 659/1999.

6.1. Publication of the decision and meaningful summary

30. Where the Member State concerned does not request the removal of confidential information, the Commission will endeavour to publish its decision to open the formal investigation procedure, including the meaningful summaries, within two months from the date of adoption of that decision.

31. Where there is disagreement concerning confidentiality issues, the Commission will apply the principles of its Communication of 1 December 2003 on professional secrecy in State aid decisions[1] and use its best endeavours to proceed with publication of the decision within the shortest possible time frame following its adoption. The same will apply to the publication of all final decisions.

Notes

[1] OJ C 297, 9.12.2003, p.6.

32. To improve the transparency of the procedure, the Member State, the beneficiary and other stakeholders (in particular potential complainants) will be informed of all delays triggered by disagreements concerning confidentiality issues.

6.2. Comments from interested parties

33. According to Article 6 of Regulation (EC) No 659/1999, interested parties must submit comments within a prescribed period which must normally not exceed one month following the publication of the decision to initiate the formal investigation procedure. That time limit will not normally be extended, and the Commission services will thus usually not accept any belated submission of information from interested parties, including the beneficiary of the aid.[1] Extensions may be granted only in exceptional duly justified cases, such as the provision of particularly voluminous factual information or following contact between the Commission services and the interested party concerned.

Notes

[1] Without prejudice to Article 10(1) of Regulation (EC) No 659/1999.

34. In order to improve the factual basis of the investigation of particularly complex cases, the Commission services may send a copy of the decision to initiate the formal investigation procedure to identified interested parties including trade or business associations, and invite them to comment on specific aspects of the case.[1] Interested parties' cooperation in this context is purely voluntary, but if an interested party chooses to provide comments, it is in its interest to submit those comments in a timely manner so that the Commission will be able to take them into account. Therefore, the Commission will invite interested parties to react within one month from the date on which the copy of the decision is sent to them. The Commission will not wait any further for those comments to be submitted. In order to ensure equal treatment between interested parties the Commission will send the same invitation to comment to the aid beneficiary. In order to respect the Member State's right of defence, it will forward to the Member State a non-confidential version of any comments received from interested parties and invite the Member State to reply within one month.

Notes

[1] According to settled case-law, the Commission is entitled to send the decision to open the formal investigation to identified third parties; see for example, Case T-198/01, *Technische Glaswerke Ilmenau v Commission*, [2004] ECR II-2717, paragraph 195; T-198/01R, *Technische Glaswerke Ilmenau v Commission*, [2002] ECR II-2153; Joined Cases C-74/00 P and C-75/00 P, *Falck Spa and others v Commission*, [2002] ECR I-7869, paragraph 83.

35. In order to ensure transmission of all comments from interested parties to the Member State concerned in the most expedient manner, Member States will, as far as possible, be invited to accept transmission of those comments in their original language. If a Member State so requests, the Commission services will provide a translation, which may have implications as regards the expediency of procedures.

36. Member States will also be informed of the absence of any comments from interested parties.

6.3. Member States' comments

37. To ensure timely completion of the formal investigation procedure, the Commission will rigorously enforce all time limits applicable to this phase under Regulation (EC) No 659/1999. If a Member State fails to submit its comments on the Commission's decision to initiate the formal investigation procedure and on interested parties' comments within the one-month time limit set in Article 6(1) of Regulation (EC) No 659/1999, the Commission services will immediately send a reminder granting the Member State concerned an additional period of one month and informing the Member State that no further extension will be granted, save in exceptional circumstances. In the absence of a meaningful reply by the Member State concerned, the Commission will take a decision on the basis of the information available to it, in accordance with Article 7(7) and Article 13(1) of Regulation (EC) No 659/1999.

38. In the case of unlawful aid, and in the absence of comments from the Member State on the decision to initiate the formal investigation procedure, the Commission will, pursuant to Article 10 of Regulation (EC) No 659/1999, issue an information injunction. Should the Member State fail to reply to that injunction within the time limit set therein, the Commission will take a decision on the basis of the information available to it.

6.4. Request for additional information

39. It cannot be excluded that, in particularly complex cases, the information submitted by the Member State in response to the decision to initiate the formal investigation procedure may require the

Commission services to send a further request for information. A time limit of one month will be set for the Member State to reply.

40. Should the Member State not reply within the time limit, the Commission services will immediately send a reminder setting a final deadline of 15 working days and informing the Member State concerned that the Commission will thereafter take a decision on the basis of the information available to it, or issue an information injunction in the case of unlawful aid.

6.5. Justified suspension of the formal investigation

41. Only in exceptional circumstances and by common agreement between the Commission services and the Member State concerned may the formal investigation be suspended. Suspension could, for example, occur if the Member State formally requests a suspension in order to bring its project in line with State aid rules, or if there is pending litigation before the Community courts regarding similar issues, the outcome of which is likely to have an impact on the assessment of the case.

42. Suspension will normally only be granted once, and for a period agreed in advance between the Commission services and the Member State concerned.

6.6. Adoption of the final decision and justified extension of the formal investigation

43. In accordance with Article 7(6) of Regulation (EC) No 659/1999, the Commission will as far as possible endeavour to adopt a decision within a period of 18 months from the opening of the procedure. That time limit may be extended by common agreement between the Commission and the Member State concerned. An extension of the duration of the investigation may in particular be appropriate in cases concerning novel projects or raising novel legal issues.

44. In order to ensure effective implementation of Article 7(6) of Regulation (EC) No 659/1999, the Commission will endeavour to adopt the final decision no later than 4 months after the submission of the last information by the Member State, or the expiry of the last time limit without information having been received.

7. Complaints

45. The efficient and transparent handling by the Commission services of complaints brought before them is of considerable importance to all stakeholders in State aid procedures. The Commission therefore proposes the following Best Practices, designed to contribute to that joint objective.

7.1. The complaint form

46. The Commission services will systematically invite complainants to use the new complaints form available on DG's Competition website (http://ec.europa.eu/comm/competition/forms/sa_complaint_en.html) and, at the same time, to submit a non-confidential version of the complaint. The submission of complete forms will normally allow complainants to enhance the quality of their submissions.

7.2. Indicative time frame and outcome of the investigation of a complaint

47. The Commission will use its best endeavours to investigate a complaint within an indicative time frame of twelve months from its receipt. That time limit does not constitute a binding commitment. Depending on the circumstances of the individual case, the possible need to request complementary information from the complainant, the Member State or interested parties may extend the investigation of a complaint.

Commentary
para 47: F&N: 17.528

---

48. The Commission is entitled to give different degrees of priority to the complaints brought before it,[1] depending for instance on the scope of the alleged infringement, the size of the beneficiary, the economic sector concerned or the existence of similar complaints. In the light of its workload and its right to set the priorities for investigations,[2] it can thus postpone dealing with a measure which is not a priority. Within twelve months, the Commission will, therefore, in principle, endeavour to:
(a) adopt a decision for priority cases pursuant to Article 4 of Regulation (EC) No 659/1999, with a copy addressed to the complainant;

(b) send an initial administrative letter to the complainant setting out its preliminary views on non-priority cases. The administrative letter is not an official position of the Commission, but only a preliminary view of the Commission services, based on the information available and pending any additional comments the complainant might wish to make within one month from the date of the letter. If further comments are not provided within the prescribed period, the complaint will be deemed to be withdrawn.

Notes

1 Case C-119/97, *Ufex and Others v Commission*,[1999] ECR I-1341, paragraph 88.
2 Case T-475/04, *Bouygues SA v Commission*, [2007] ECR II-2097, paragraphs 158 and 159.

Commentary
para 48: F&N: 17.528, 17.532, 17.536

49. As a matter of transparency, the Commission services will use their best endeavours to inform the complainant of the priority status of its submission, within two months from the date of receipt of the complaint. In the case of unsubstantiated complaints, the Commission services will inform the complainant within two months from receipt of the complaint that there are insufficient grounds for taking a view on the case, and that the complaint will be deemed to be withdrawn if further substantive comments are not provided within one month. As regards complaints which refer to approved aid, the Commission services will also endeavour to reply to the complainant within 2 months from receipt of the complaint.

50. In the case of unlawful aid, complainants will be reminded of the possibility to initiate proceedings before national courts, which can order the suspension or recovery of such aid.[1]

Notes

1 See Commission Notice on the enforcement of State aid law by national courts.

51. When necessary, the non-confidential version of a complaint will be transmitted to the Member State concerned for comments. Member States and the complainants will systematically be kept informed of the closure or other processing of a complaint. In return, Member States will be invited to respect the time limits for commenting and providing information on complaints transmitted to them. They will also be invited to accept, as far as possible, transmission of complaints in their original language. If a Member State so requests, the Commission services will provide a translation, which may have implications as regards the expediency of procedures.

8. INTERNAL DECISION MAKING PROCEDURES

52. The Commission is committed to streamlining and further improving its internal decision-making process, in order to contribute to an overall shortening of State aid procedures.

53. To this effect, internal decision-making procedures will be applied as efficiently as possible. The Commission will also review its current internal legal framework to optimise its decision-making procedures.

54. The Commission services will keep their internal decision-making practice under constant review and adapt it if necessary.

9. FUTURE REVIEW

55. Procedural Best Practices can only be effective if they are based on a shared commitment by the Commission and Member States to diligently pursue State aid investigations, respect applicable time limits and thereby ensure the necessary transparency and predictability of procedures. This Code and the Best Practices enshrined therein are a first contribution to this joint commitment.

56. The Commission will apply this Code to measures which have been notified to the Commission or otherwise brought to the Commission's attention as from 1 September 2009.

57. This Code may be revised to reflect changes to legislative, interpretative and administrative measures or the case-law of the European Courts, which govern State Aid procedure or any experience gained in its application. The Commission further intends to engage, on a regular basis, in a dialogue with the Member States and other stakeholders on the experience gained in the application of Regulation (EC) No 659/1999 in general, and this Code of Best Practice in particular.

G9

[COUNCIL REGULATION (EC) NO 994/98

of 7 May 1998
on the application of Articles 107 and 108 of the Treaty on the Functioning of the
European Union to certain categories of horizontal State aid]*

Official Journal L 142, 14.5.1998, p.1

Celex No: 31998R0994

EUR-Lex permanent link: <http://eur-lex.europa.eu/legal-content/EN/ALL/?uri=CELEX:31998R
0994&qid=1395777517381>

Notes

* Ed note: the title of the Regulation was replaced as shown in square brackets by Council Regulation (EU) No
733/2013 of 22 July 2013 (OJ L 204, 31.7.13, p.11), Article 1(1), with effect from 20 August 2013.
Please see also the Note on the Lisbon Treaty at p.xvii in regard to article renumbering introduced by the Lisbon Treaty.
Unless otherwise stated, all Treaty article numbers are the new numbers of the Treaty on the Functioning of the European
Union (TFEU) and the Treaty on European Union (TEU).

Commentary
Regulation 994/98/EC: B&C: 1.027, 1.028, 1.073, 17.096 F&N: 17.148, 17.387

THE COUNCIL OF THE EUROPEAN UNION,

Having regard to the [Treaty on the Functioning of the European Union], and in particular Article
[109] thereof,

Having regard to the proposal from the Commission,[1]

After consulting the European Parliament,[2]

Having regard to the opinion of the Economic and Social Committee,[3]

Notes

[1] OJ C 262, 28.8.1997, p.6.
[2] OJ C 138, 4.5.1998.
[3] OJ C 129, 27.4.1998, p.70.

---

(1) Whereas, pursuant to Article [109] of the Treaty, the Council may make any appropriate regulations
for the application of Articles [107 and 108] and may, in particular, determine the conditions in
which Article [108(3)] shall apply and the categories of aid exempted from this procedure;

(2) Whereas, under the Treaty, the assessment of compatibility of aid with the common market essentially rests with the Commission;

(3) Whereas the proper functioning of the internal market requires strict and efficient application of
the rules of competition with regard to State aids;

(4) Whereas the Commission has applied Articles [107 and 108] of the Treaty in numerous decisions
and has also stated its policy in a number of communications; whereas, in the light of the Commission's considerable experience in applying Articles [107 and 108] of the Treaty and the general
texts issued by the Commission on the basis of those provisions, it is appropriate, with a view to
ensuring efficient supervision and simplifying administration, without weakening Commission
monitoring, that the Commission should be enabled to declare by means of regulations, in areas
where the Commission has sufficient experience to define general compatibility criteria, that
certain categories of aid are compatible with the common market pursuant to one or more of the
provisions of Article [107(2)] and (3) of the Treaty and are exempted from the procedure provided
for in Article [108(3)] thereof;

(5) Whereas group exemption regulations will increase transparency and legal certainty; whereas they can be directly applied by national courts, without prejudice to Articles [4, paragraph 3 TEU] and [267 TFEU];

(6) Whereas it is appropriate that the Commission, when it adopts regulations exempting categories of aid from the obligation to notify provided for in Article [108(3)] of the Treaty, specifies the purpose of the aid, the categories of beneficiaries and thresholds limiting the exempted aid, the conditions governing the cumulation of aid and the conditions of monitoring, in order to ensure the compatibility with the common market of aid covered by this Regulation;

(7) Whereas it is appropriate to enable the Commission, when it adopts regulations exempting certain categories of aid from the obligation to notify in Article [108(3)] of the Treaty, to attach further detailed conditions in order to ensure the compatibility with the common market of aid covered by this Regulation;

(8) Whereas it may be useful to set thresholds of other appropriate conditions requiring the notification of awards of aid in order to allow the Commission to examine individually the effect of certain aid on competition and trade between Member States and its compatibility with the common market;

(9) Whereas the Commission, having regard to the development and the functioning of the common market, should be enabled to establish by means of a regulation that certain aid does not fulfil all the criteria of Article [107(1)] of the Treaty and is therefore exempted from the notification procedure laid down in Article [108(3)], provided that aid granted to the same undertaking over a given period of time does not exceed a certain fixed amount;

Commentary
Recital 9: F&N: 17.148

---

(10) Whereas in accordance with Article [108(1)] of the Treaty the Commission is under an obligation, in cooperation with Member States, to keep under constant review all systems of existing aid; whereas for this purpose and in order to ensure the largest possible degree of transparency and adequate control it is desirable that the Commission ensures the establishment of a reliable system of recording and storing information about the application of the regulations it adopts, to which all Member States have access, and that it receives all necessary information from the Member States on the implementation of aid exempted from notification to fulfil this obligation, which may be examined and evaluated with the Member States within the Advisory Committee; whereas for this purpose it is also desirable that the Commission may require such information to be supplied as is necessary to ensure the efficiency of such review;

(11) Whereas the control of the granting of aid involves factual, legal and economic issues of a very complex nature and great variety in a constantly evolving environment; whereas the Commission should therefore regularly review the categories of aid which should be exempted from notification; whereas the Commission should be able to repeal or amend regulations it has adopted pursuant to this Regulation where circumstances have changed with respect to any important element which constituted grounds for their adoption or where the progressive development or the functioning of the common market so requires;

(12) Whereas the Commission, in close and constant liaison with the Member States, should be able to define precisely the scope of these regulations and the conditions attached to them; whereas, in order to provide for cooperation between the Commission and the competent authorities of the Member States, it is appropriate to set up an advisory committee on State aid to be consulted before the Commission adopts regulations pursuant to this Regulation,

HAS ADOPTED THIS REGULATION:

Article 1
Group exemptions

1. The Commission may, by means of regulations adopted in accordance with the procedures laid down in Article 8 of this Regulation and in accordance with Article [107] of the Treaty, declare that

the following categories of aid should be compatible with the common market and shall not be subject to the notification requirements of Article [108(3)] of the Treaty:

[(a) aid in favour of:

> (i) small and medium-sized enterprises;
>
> (ii) research, development and innovation;
>
> (iii) environmental protection;
>
> (iv) employment and training;
>
> (v) culture and heritage conservation;
>
> (vi) making good the damage caused by natural disasters;
>
> (vii) making good the damage caused by certain adverse weather conditions in fisheries;
>
> (viii) forestry;
>
> (ix) promotion of food sector products not listed in Annex I of the TFEU;
>
> (x) conservation of marine and freshwater biological resources;
>
> (xi) sports;
>
> (xii) residents of remote regions, for transport, when this aid has a social character and is granted without discrimination related to the identity of the carrier;
>
> (xiii) basic broadband infrastructure, small individual infrastructure measures covering next-generation access networks, broadband-related civil engineering works and passive broadband infrastructure, in areas where there is either no such infrastructure or where no such infrastructure is likely to be developed in the near future;
>
> (xiv) infrastructure in support of the objectives listed in (i) to (xiii) and in point (b) of this paragraph and in support of other objectives of common interest, in particular the Europe 2020 objectives.].

(b) aid that complies with the map approved by the Commission for each Member State for the grant of regional aid.

2. The Regulations referred to in paragraph 1 shall specify for each category of aid:

(a) the purpose of the aid;

(b) the categories of beneficiaries;

[(c) thresholds expressed in terms of aid intensities in relation to a set of eligible costs or in terms of maximum aid amounts or, for certain types of aid where it may be difficult to identify the aid intensity or amount of aid precisely, in particular financial engineering instruments or risk capital investments or those of a similar nature, in terms of the maximum level of State support in or related to that measure, without prejudice to the qualification of the measures concerned in the light of Article 107(1) of the TFEU;]

(d) the conditions governing the cumulation of aid;

(e) the conditions of monitoring as specified in Article 3.

3. In addition, the regulations referred to in paragraph 1 may, in particular:

(a) set thresholds or other conditions for the notification of awards of individual aid;

(b) exclude certain sectors from their scope;

(c) attach further conditions for the compatibility of aid exempted under such regulations.

Notes

Paragraphs 1(a) and 2(c) were replaced as shown in square brackets by Council Regulation (EU) No 733/2013 of 22 July 2013 (OJ L 204, 31.7.13, p.11), Article 1(2)(a) and (b), with effect from 20 August 2013.

Article 2

De minimis

1. The Commission may, by means of a Regulation adopted in accordance with the procedure laid down in Article 8 of this Regulation, decide that, having regard to the development and functioning of the common market, certain aids do not meet all the criteria of Article [108(1)] and that they are therefore exempted from the notification procedure provided for in Article [108(3)], provided that aid granted to the same undertaking over a given period of time does not exceed a certain fixed amount.

Part G State Aids

2. At the Commission's request, Member States shall, at any time, communicate to it any additional information relating to aid exempted under paragraph 1.

Commentary
Art 2: B&C: 17.027, 17.074

Article 3
Transparency and monitoring

1. When adopting regulations pursuant to Article 1, the Commission shall impose detailed rules upon Member States to ensure transparency and monitoring of the aid exempted from notification in accordance with those regulations. Such rules shall consist, in particular, of the requirements laid down in paragraphs 2, 3 and 4.

[2. Upon implementing aid systems or individual aids granted outside any system, which have been exempted pursuant to regulations referred to in Article 1(1), Member States shall forward to the Commission, with a view to publication on the website of the Commission, summaries of the information regarding such systems of aid or such individual aids as are not covered by exempted aid systems.]

3. Member States shall record and compile all the information regarding the application of the group exemptions. If the Commission has information which leads it to doubt that an exemption regulation is being applied properly, the Member States shall forward to it any information it considers necessary to assess whether an aid complies with that regulation.

4. At least once a year, Member States shall supply the Commission with a report on the application of group exemptions, in accordance with the Commission's specific requirements, preferably in computerised form. The Commission shall make access to those reports available to all the Member States. The Advisory Committee referred to in Article 7 shall examine and evaluate those reports once a year.

Notes

Article 3(2) was replaced as shown in square brackets by Council Regulation (EU) No 733/2013 of 22 July 2013 (OJ L 204, 31.7.13, p.11), Article 1(3), with effect from 20 August 2013.

Article 4
Period of validity and amendment of regulations

1. Regulations adopted pursuant to Articles 1 and 2 shall apply for a specific period. Aid exempted by a regulation adopted pursuant to Articles 1 and 2 shall be exempted for the period of validity of that regulation and for the adjustment period provided for in paragraphs 2 and 3.

2. Regulations adopted pursuant to Articles 1 and 2 may be repeated or amended where circumstances have changed with respect to any important element that constituted grounds for their adoption or where the progressive development or the functioning of the common market so requires. In that case the new regulation shall set a period of adjustment of six months for the adjustment of aid covered by the previous regulation.

3. Regulations adopted pursuant to Articles 1 and 2 shall provide for a period as referred to in paragraph 2, should their application not be extended when they expire.

Commentary
Art 4: B&C: 17.070

Article 5
Evaluation report

Every five years the Commission shall submit a report to the European Parliament and to the Council on the application of this Regulation. It shall submit a draft report for consideration by the Advisory Committee referred to in Article 7.

Article 6
Hearing of interested parties

Where the Commission intends to adopt a regulation, it shall publish a draft thereof to enable all interested persons and organisations to submit their comments to it within a reasonable time limit to be fixed by the Commission and which may not under any circumstances be less than one month.

Article 7
Advisory committee

An advisory committee, hereinafter referred to as the Advisory Committee on State Aid, shall be set up. It shall be composed of representatives of the Member States and chaired by the representative of the Commission.

Article 8
Consultation of the Advisory Committee

1. The Commission shall consult the Advisory Committee on State Aid:

[(a) at the same time as publishing any draft regulation in accordance with Article 6;]
(b) before adopting any regulation.

2. Consultation of the Committee shall take place at a meeting called by the Commission. [The drafts and documents to be examined shall be annexed to the notification and may be published on the Commission website.] The meeting shall take place no earlier than two months after notification has been sent.

This period may be reduced in the case of the consultations referred to in paragraph 1(b), when urgent or for simple extension of a regulation.

3. The representative of the Commission shall submit to the Committee a draft of the measures to be taken. The Committee shall deliver its opinion on the draft, within a time limit which the Chairman may lay down according to the urgency of the matter, if necessary by taking a vote.

4. The opinion shall be recorded in the minutes; in addition, each Member State shall have the right to ask to have its position recorded in the minutes. The Advisory Committee may recommend publication of the opinion in the *Official Journal of the European Communities*.

5. The Commission shall take the utmost account of the opinion delivered by the Committee. It shall inform the Committee of the manner in which its opinion has been taken into account.

Notes

Paragraphs 1(a) and 2 were amended as shown in square brackets by Council Regulation (EU) No 733/2013 of 22 July 2013 (OJ L 204, 31.7.13, p.11), Article 1(4)(a) and (b), with effect from 20 August 2013.

Article 9
Final provisions

This Regulation shall enter into force on the day following its publication in the *Official Journal of the European Communities*.

This Regulation shall be binding in its entirety and directly applicable in all Member States.

Done at Brussels, 7 May 1998.

Notes

Date of entry into force: 15 May 1998.

G10

COMMISSION REGULATION (EC) NO 1998/2006

of 15 December 2006 on the application of Articles [107 and 108]* of the
Treaty to de minimis aid

Official Journal L 379, 28.12.2006, p.5

Celex No: 32006R1998

EUR-Lex permanent link: <http://eur-lex.europa.eu/LexUriServ/LexUriServ.do?uri=CELEX:3200
6R1998EN:NOT>

Notes

* Ed note: please see the Note on the Lisbon Treaty at p.xvii in regard to article renumbering introduced by the Lisbon
Treaty. Unless otherwise stated, all Treaty article numbers are the new numbers of the Treaty on the Functioning of the
European Union (TFEU) and the Treaty on European Union (TEU).

Regulation 1998/2006 expired on 31 December 2013. With effect from 1 January 2014, it was superseded by
Commission Regulation 1407/2013 of 18 December 2013 on the application of Articles 107 and 108 TFEU to de
minimis aid (OJ L 352, 24.12.2013, p.1). It has not been possible to include the new regulation in this volume.
Regulation 1407/2013 is available at http://eur-lex.europa.eu/legal-content/EN/ALL/?uri=CELEX:32013R1407&
qid=1395777703201.

THE COMMISSION OF THE EUROPEAN COMMUNITIES,

Having regard to the [Treaty on the Functioning of the European Union],

Having regard to Council Regulation (EC) No 994/98 of 7 May 1998 on the application of Articles
[107 and 108] of the [Treaty on the Functioning of the European Union] to certain categories of
horizontal State aid,[1] and in particular Article 2 thereof,

Having published a draft of this Regulation,[2]

Having consulted the Advisory Committee on State aid,

Notes

[1] OJ L 142, 14.5.1998, p.1.
[2] OJ C 137, 10.6.2006, p.4.

Commentary

Regulation 1998/2006/EC: B&C: 1.120, 17.003, 17.027, 17.074 **F&N:** 17.150, 17.152, 17.153, 17.154, 17.157,
  17.161, 17.165, 17.170, 17.171, 17.172, 17.174, 17.175, 17.177, 17.181, 17.182, 17.377

Whereas:

(1) Regulation (EC) No 994/98 empowers the Commission to set out in a Regulation a threshold
under which aid measures are deemed not to meet all the criteria of Article [107(1)] of the Treaty
and therefore do not fall under the notification procedure provided for in Article [108(3)] of the
Treaty.

(2) The Commission has applied Articles [107 and 108 TFEU] and has, in particular, clarified in
numerous decisions the notion of aid within the meaning of Article [107(1)] of the Treaty. The
Commission has also stated its policy with regard to a *de minimis* ceiling, below which Article
[107(1)] can be considered not to apply, initially in its notice on the *de minimis* rule for State aid[1]
and subsequently in Commission Regulation (EC) No 69/2001 of 12 January 2001 on the application of Articles [107 and 108 TFEU] to *de minimis* aid.[2] In the light of the experience gained in
applying that Regulation and in order to take account of the evolution of inflation and gross

domestic product in the Community up to and including 2006 and of the likely developments through the period of validity of this Regulation, it appears appropriate to revise some of the conditions laid down in Regulation (EC) No 69/2001 and to replace that Regulation.

Notes
[1] OJ C 68, 6.3.1996, p.9.
[2] OJ L 10, 13.1.2001, p.30.

Commentary
Recital 2: F&N: 17.150

(3) In view of the special rules which apply in the sectors of primary production of agricultural products, fisheries and aquaculture and of the risk that smaller amounts of aid than those set out in this Regulation could fulfil the criteria of Article [107(1)] of the Treaty in those sectors, this Regulation should not apply to those sectors. Given the evolution of the transport sector, in particular the restructuring of many transport activities following their liberalisation, it is no longer appropriate to exclude the transport sector from the scope of the *de minimis* Regulation. The scope of this Regulation should therefore be extended to the whole of the transport sector. The general *de minimis* ceiling should however be adapted in order to take account of the average small size of undertakings active in the road freight and passengers transport sector. For the same reasons, and also in view of the overcapacity of the sector and of the objectives of transport policy as regards road congestion and freight transports, aid for the acquisition of road freight transport vehicles by undertakings performing road freight transport for hire and reward should be excluded. This does not call into question the Commission's favourable approach with regard to State aid for cleaner and more environmentally friendly vehicles in Community instruments other than this Regulation. In view of Council Regulation (EC) No 1407/2002 of 23 July 2002 on State aid to the coal industry,[1] this Regulation should not apply to the coal sector.

Notes
[1] OJ L 205, 02.08.2002, p.1.

Commentary
Recital 3: F&N: 17.153

(4) Considering the similarities between the processing and marketing of agricultural products, on the one hand, and of non-agricultural products, on the other hand, this Regulation should apply to the processing and marketing of agricultural products, provided that certain conditions are met. Neither on-farm activities necessary for preparing a product for the first sale, such as harvesting, cutting and threshing of cereals, packing of eggs etc., nor the first sale to resellers or processors should be considered as processing or marketing in this respect. As from the entry into force of this Regulation, aid granted in favour of undertakings active in the processing or marketing of agricultural products should no longer be subject to Commission Regulation (EC) No 1860/2004 of 6 October 2004 on the application of Articles [107 and 108 TFEU] to *de minimis* aid in the agriculture and fisheries sector.[1] Regulation (EC) No 1860/2004 should therefore be amended accordingly.

Notes
[1] OJ L 325, 28.10.2004, p.4.

(5) The Court of Justice of the European Communities has established that, once the Community has legislated for the establishment of a common organisation of the market in a given sector of agriculture, Member States are under an obligation to refrain from taking any measure which might undermine or create exceptions to it. For this reason, this Regulation should not apply to aid, the amount of which is fixed on the basis of price or quantity of products purchased or put on the market. Nor should it apply to *de minimis* support which is linked to an obligation to share the aid with primary producers.

(6) This Regulation should not apply to *de minimis* export aid or *de minimis* aid favouring domestic over imported products. In particular, it should not apply to aid financing the establishment and

operation of a distribution network in other countries. Aid towards the cost of participating in trade fairs, or of studies or consultancy services needed for the launch of a new or existing product on a new market does not normally constitute export aid.

Commentary
Recital 6: F&N: 17.153

(7) This Regulation should not apply to undertakings in difficulty within the meaning of the Community guidelines on State aid for rescuing and restructuring firms in difficulty[1] in view of the difficulties linked to determining the gross grant equivalent of aid granted to this type of undertaking.

Notes
[1] OJ C 244, 1.10.2004, p.2.

Commentary
Recital 7: F&N: 17.153

(8) In the light of the Commission's experience, it can be established that aid not exceeding a ceiling of EUR 200,000 over any period of three years does not affect trade between Member States and/or does not distort or threaten to distort competition and therefore does not fall under Article [107(1)] of the Treaty. As regards undertakings active in the road transport sector, this ceiling should be set at EUR 100 000.

(9) The years to take into account for this purpose are the fiscal years as used for fiscal purposes by the undertaking in the Member State concerned. The relevant period of three years should be assessed on a rolling basis so that, for each new grant of *de minimis* aid, the total amount of *de minimis* aid granted in the fiscal year concerned, as well as during the previous two fiscal years, needs to be determined. Aid granted by a Member State should be taken into account for this purpose even when financed entirely or partly by resources of Community origin. It should not be possible for aid measures exceeding the *de minimis* ceiling to be broken down into a number of smaller parts in order to bring such parts within the scope of this Regulation.

(10) In accordance with the principles governing aid falling within Article [107(1)] of the Treaty, *de minimis* aid should be considered to be granted at the moment the legal right to receive the aid is conferred on the undertaking under the applicable national legal regime.

Commentary
Recital 10: F&N: 17.163

(11) In order to avoid circumvention of maximum aid intensities provided in different Community instruments, *de minimis* aid should not be cumulated with State aid in respect of the same eligible costs if such cumulation would result in an aid intensity exceeding that fixed in the specific circumstances of each case by a block exemption Regulation or Decision adopted by the Commission.

(12) For the purposes of transparency, equal treatment and the correct application of the *de minimis* ceiling, all Member States should apply the same method of calculation. In order to facilitate this calculation and in accordance with the present practice of application of the *de minimis* rule, aid amounts not taking the form of a cash grant should be converted into their gross grant equivalent. Calculation of the grant equivalent of transparent types of aid other than grants or of aid payable in several instalments requires the use of market interest rates prevailing at the time of granting such aid. With a view to a uniform, transparent and simple application of the State aid rules, the market rates for the purposes of this Regulation should be deemed to be the reference rates periodically fixed by the Commission on the basis of objective criteria and published in the *Official Journal of the European Union* or on the Internet. It may, however, be necessary to add additional basis points on top of the floor rate in view of the securities provided or the risk associated with the beneficiary.

(13) For the purposes of transparency, equal treatment and effective monitoring, this Regulation should apply only to *de minimis* aid which is transparent. Transparent aid is aid for which it is

possible to calculate precisely the gross grant equivalent *ex ante* without a need to undertake a risk assessment. Such precise calculation can, for instance, be realised as regards grants, interest rate subsidies and capped tax exemptions. Aid comprised in capital injections should not be considered as transparent *de minimis* aid, unless the total amount of the public injection is lower than the *de minimis* ceiling. Aid comprised in risk capital measures as referred to in the Community guidelines on State aid to promote risk capital investments in small and medium-sized enterprises[1] should not be considered as transparent *de minimis* aid, unless the risk capital scheme concerned provides capital only up to the *de minimis* ceiling to each target undertaking. Aid comprised in loans should be treated as transparent *de minimis* aid when the gross grant equivalent has been calculated on the basis of market interest rates prevailing at the time of grant.

Notes

1 OJ C 194, 18.8.2006, p.2.

(14) This Regulation does not exclude the possibility that a measure, adopted by a Member State, might not be considered as State aid within the meaning of Article [107(1)] of the Treaty on the basis of other grounds than those set out in this Regulation, for instance, in the case of capital injections, because such measure has been decided in conformity with the market investor principle.

(15) It is necessary to provide legal certainty for guarantee schemes which do not have the potential to affect trade and distort competition and in respect of which sufficient data is available to assess any potential effects reliably. This Regulation should therefore transpose the general *de minimis* ceiling of EUR 200,000 into a guarantee-specific ceiling based on the guaranteed amount of the individual loan underlying such guarantee. It is appropriate to calculate this specific ceiling using a methodology assessing the State aid amount included in guarantee schemes covering loans in favour of viable undertakings. The methodology and the data used to calculate the guarantee-specific ceiling should exclude undertakings in difficulty as referred to in the Community guidelines on State aid for rescuing and restructuring firms in difficulty. This specific ceiling should therefore not apply to ad hoc individual aid granted outside the scope of a guarantee scheme, to aid granted to undertakings in difficulty, or to guarantees on underlying transactions not constituting a loan, such as guarantees on equity transactions. The specific ceiling should be determined on the basis of the fact that taking account of a cap rate (net default rate) of 13%, representing a worst case scenario for guarantee schemes in the Community, a guarantee amounting to EUR 1,500,000 can be considered as having a gross grant equivalent identical to the general *de minimis* ceiling. This amount should be reduced to EUR 750,000 as regards undertakings active in the road transport sector. Only guarantees covering up to 80% of the underlying loan should be covered by these specific ceilings. A methodology accepted by the Commission following notification of such methodology on the basis of a Commission Regulation in the State aid area, like Commission Regulation (EC) No 1628/2006 of 24 October 2006 on the application of Articles [107 and 108 TFEU] to national regional investment aid,[1] may also be used by Member States for the purpose of assessing the gross grant equivalent contained in a guarantee, if the approved methodology explicitly addresses the type of guarantees and the type of underlying transactions at stake in the context of the application of the present Regulation.

Notes

1 OJ L 302, 1.11.2006, p.29.

(16) Upon notification by a Member State, the Commission may examine whether an aid measure which does not consist in a grant, loan, guarantee, capital injection or risk capital measure leads to a gross grant equivalent that does not exceed the *de minimis* ceiling and could therefore be covered by the provisions of this Regulation.

(17) The Commission has a duty to ensure that State aid rules are respected and in particular that aid granted under the *de minimis* rules adheres to the conditions thereof. In accordance with the cooperation principle laid down in Article [4, paragraph 3 TEU], Member States should facilitate the achievement of this task by establishing the necessary machinery in order to ensure that

the total amount of *de minimis* aid, granted to the same undertaking under the *de minimis* rule, does not exceed the ceiling of EUR 200,000 over a period of three fiscal years. To that end, when granting a *de minimis* aid, Member States should inform the undertaking concerned of the amount of the aid and of its *de minimis* character, by referring to this Regulation. Moreover, prior to granting such aid the Member State concerned should obtain from the undertaking a declaration about other *de minimis* aid received during the fiscal year concerned and the two previous fiscal years and carefully check that the *de minimis* ceiling will not be exceeded by the new *de minimis* aid. Alternatively it should be possible to ensure that the ceiling is respected by means of a central register, or, in the case of guarantee schemes set up by the European Investment Fund, the latter may establish itself a list of beneficiaries and require Member States to inform the beneficiaries of the *de minimis* aid received.

(18) Regulation (EC) No 69/2001 expires on 31 December 2006. This Regulation should therefore apply from 1 January 2007. In view of the fact that Regulation (EC) No 69/2001 did not apply to the transport sector, which was not subject to *de minimis* so far; given also the very limited *de minimis* amount applicable in the sector of processing and marketing of agricultural products, and provided that certain conditions are met, this Regulation should apply to aid granted before its entry into force to undertakings active in the transport sector, and in the sector of processing and marketing of agricultural products. Moreover, any individual aid granted in accordance with Regulation (EC) No 69/2001 during the period of application of that Regulation should remain unaffected by this Regulation.

(19) Having regard to the Commission's experience and in particular the frequency with which it is generally necessary to revise State aid policy, it is appropriate to limit the period of application of this Regulation. Should this Regulation expire without being extended, Member States should have an adjustment period of six months with regard to *de minimis* aid covered by this Regulation,

HAS ADOPTED THIS REGULATION:

Article 1
Scope

1. This Regulation applies to aid granted to undertakings in all sectors, with the exception of:

(a) aid granted to undertakings active in the fishery and aquaculture sectors, as covered by Council Regulation (EC) No 104/2000;[1]

(b) aid granted to undertakings active in the primary production of agricultural products as listed in Annex I to the Treaty;

(c) aid granted to undertakings active in the processing and marketing of agricultural products as listed in Annex I to the Treaty, in the following cases:

   (i) when the amount of the aid is fixed on the basis of the price or quantity of such products purchased from primary producers or put on the market by the undertakings concerned,

   (ii) when the aid is conditional on being partly or entirely passed on to primary producers;

(d) aid to export-related activities towards third countries or Member States, namely aid directly linked to the quantities exported, to the establishment and operation of a distribution network or to other current expenditure linked to the export activity;

(e) aid contingent upon the use of domestic over imported goods;

(f) aid granted to undertakings active in the coal sector, as defined in Regulation (EC) No 1407/2002;

(g) aid for the acquisition of road freight transport vehicles granted to undertakings performing road freight transport for hire or reward;

(h) aid granted to undertakings in difficulty.

2. For the purposes of this Regulation:

(a) "agricultural products" means products listed in Annex I to the [Treaty on the Functioning of the European Union], with the exception of fishery products;

(b) "processing of agricultural products" means any operation on an agricultural product resulting in a product which is also an agricultural product, except on farm activities necessary for preparing an animal or plant product for the first sale;

(c) "marketing of agricultural products" means holding or display with a view to sale, offering for sale, delivery or any other manner of placing on the market, except the first sale by a primary producer to resellers or processors and any activity preparing a product for such first sale; a sale by a primary producer to final consumers shall be considered as marketing if it takes place in separate premises reserved for that purpose.

Notes
[1] OJ L 17, 21.1.2000, p.22.

Commentary
Art 1(b): F&N: 17.153

Article 2
De minimis aid

1. Aid measures shall be deemed not to meet all the criteria of Article [107(1)] of the Treaty and shall therefore be exempt from the notification requirement of Article [108(3)] of the Treaty, if they fulfil the conditions laid down in paragraphs 2 to 5 of this Article.

2. The total *de minimis* aid granted to any one undertaking shall not exceed EUR 200 000 over any period of three fiscal years. The total *de minimis* aid granted to any one undertaking active in the road transport sector shall not exceed EUR 100,000 over any period of three fiscal years. These ceilings shall apply irrespective of the form of the *de minimis* aid or the objective pursued and regardless of whether the aid granted by the Member State is financed entirely or partly by resources of Community origin. The period shall be determined by reference to the fiscal years used by the undertaking in the Member State concerned.

When an overall aid amount provided under an aid measure exceeds this ceiling, that aid amount cannot benefit from this Regulation, even for a fraction not exceeding that ceiling. In such a case, the benefit of this Regulation cannot be claimed for this aid measure either at the time the aid is granted or at any subsequent time.

3. The ceiling laid down in paragraph 2 shall be expressed as a cash grant. All figures used shall be gross, that is, before any deduction of tax or other charge. Where aid is awarded in a form other than a grant, the aid amount shall be the gross grant equivalent of the aid.

Aid payable in several instalments shall be discounted to its value at the moment of its being granted. The interest rate to be used for discounting purposes and to calculate the gross grant equivalent shall be the reference rate applicable at the time of grant.

4. This Regulation shall apply only to aid in respect of which it is possible to calculate precisely the gross grant equivalent of the aid *ex ante* without need to undertake a risk assessment ("transparent aid"). In particular:

(a) Aid comprised in loans shall be treated as transparent *de minimis* aid when the gross grant equivalent has been calculated on the basis of market interest rates prevailing at the time of the grant.

(b) Aid comprised in capital injections shall not be considered as transparent *de minimis* aid, unless the total amount of the public injection does not exceed the *de minimis* ceiling.

(c) Aid comprised in risk capital measures shall not be considered as transparent *de minimis* aid, unless the risk capital scheme concerned provides capital only up to the *de minimis* ceiling to each target undertaking.

(d) Individual aid provided under a guarantee scheme to undertakings which are not undertakings in difficulty shall be treated as transparent *de minimis* aid when the guaranteed part of the underlying loan provided under such scheme does not exceed EUR 1 500 000 per undertaking. Individual aid provided under a guarantee scheme in favour of undertakings active in the road transport sector which are not undertakings in difficulty shall be treated as transparent *de minimis* aid when the guaranteed part of the underlying loan provided under such scheme does not exceed EUR 750 000 per undertaking. If the guaranteed part of the underlying loan only accounts for a given proportion of this ceiling, the gross grant equivalent of that guarantee shall be deemed to correspond to the same proportion of the applicable ceiling laid down in Article 2(2). The guarantee shall not exceed 80% of the underlying loan. Guarantee schemes shall also be considered as transparent if (i) before the implementation of the scheme, the methodology to calculate the gross grant equivalent of the guarantees has been accepted following notification of this methodology to the Commission under another Regulation adopted by the Commission in the State aid area and (ii) the approved methodology explicitly addresses the type of guarantees and the type of underlying transactions at stake in the context of the application of this Regulation.

5. *De minimis* aid shall not be cumulated with State aid in respect of the same eligible costs if such cumulation would result in an aid intensity exceeding that fixed in the specific circumstances of each case by a block exemption Regulation or Decision adopted by the Commission.

Commentary

Art 2(3): F&N: 17.158, 17.159
Art 2(4): F&N: 17.161

Article 3
Monitoring

1. Where a Member State intends to grant *de minimis* aid to an undertaking, it shall inform that undertaking in writing of the prospective amount of the aid (expressed as gross grant equivalent) and of its *de minimis* character, making express reference to this Regulation, and citing its title and publication reference in the *Official Journal of the European Union*. Where the *de minimis* aid is granted to different undertakings on the basis of a scheme and different amounts of individual aid are granted to those undertakings under the scheme, the Member State concerned may choose to fulfil this obligation by informing the undertakings of a fixed sum corresponding to the maximum aid amount to be granted under the scheme. In such case, the fixed sum shall be used for determining whether the ceiling laid down in Article 2(2) is met. Prior to granting the aid, the Member State shall also obtain a declaration from the undertaking concerned, in written or electronic form, about any other *de minimis* aid received during the previous two fiscal years and the current fiscal year.

The Member State shall only grant the new *de minimis* aid after having checked that this will not raise the total amount of *de minimis* aid received by the undertaking during the period covering the fiscal year concerned, as well as the previous two fiscal years in that Member State, to a level above the ceiling laid down in Article 2(2).

2. Where a Member State has set up a central register of *de minimis* aid containing complete information on all *de minimis* aid granted by any authority within that Member State, the first subparagraph of paragraph 1 shall cease to apply from the moment the register covers a period of three years.

Where an aid is provided by a Member State on the basis of a guarantee scheme providing a guarantee which is financed from the EU budget under mandate through the European Investment Fund, the first subparagraph of paragraph 1 of this Article may cease to apply.

In such cases, the following monitoring system shall apply:

(a) the European Investment Fund shall establish, on a yearly basis, on the basis of information that financial intermediaries must provide to the EIF, a list of beneficiaries of aid and of the gross grant equivalent received by each of them. The European Investment Fund shall send this information to the Member State concerned and to the Commission; and

(b) the Member State concerned shall disseminate that information to the final beneficiaries within three months of receipt of such information from the European Investment Fund; and

(c) the Member State concerned shall obtain a declaration from each beneficiary that the overall *de minimis* aid it has received does not exceed the ceiling laid down in Article 2(2). In case the ceiling is exceeded with respect to one or more beneficiaries, the Member State concerned shall ensure that the aid measure leading to the ceiling being exceeded is either notified to the Commission or recovered from the beneficiary.

3. Member States shall record and compile all the information regarding the application of this Regulation. Such records shall contain all information necessary to demonstrate that the conditions of this Regulation have been complied with. Records regarding individual *de minimis* aid shall be

maintained for 10 years from the date on which it was granted. Records regarding a *de minimis* aid scheme shall be maintained for 10 years from the date on which the last individual aid was granted under such scheme. On written request the Member State concerned shall provide the Commission, within a period of 20 working days, or such longer period as may be fixed in the request, with all the information that the Commission considers necessary for assessing whether the conditions of this Regulation have been complied with, in particular the total amount of *de minimis* aid received by any undertaking.

Commentary
Art 3(1): F&N: 17.166
Art 3(3): F&N: 17.169

Article 4
Amendment

Article 2 of Regulation (EC) No 1860/2004 is amended as follows:

(a) in point 1, the words "processing and marketing" are deleted;
(b) point 3 is deleted.

Article 5
Transitional measures

1. This Regulation shall apply to aid granted before its entry into force to undertakings active in the transport sector and undertakings active in the processing and marketing of agricultural products if the aid fulfils all the conditions laid down in Articles 1 and 2. Any aid which does not fulfil those conditions will be assessed by the Commission in accordance with the relevant frameworks, guidelines, communications and notices.

2. Any individual *de minimis* aid granted between 2 February 2001 and 30 June 2007, which fulfils the conditions of Regulation (EC) No 69/2001, shall be deemed not to meet all the criteria of Article [107(1)] of the Treaty and shall therefore be exempt from the notification requirement of Article [108(3)] of the Treaty.

3. At the end of the period of validity of this Regulation, any *de minimis* aid which fulfils the conditions of this Regulation may be validly implemented for a further period of six months.

Article 6
Entry into force and period of validity

1. This Regulation shall enter into force on the 20th day following that of its publication in the *Official Journal of the European Union.*

It shall apply from 1 January 2007 until 31 December 2013.

2. This Regulation shall be binding in its entirety and directly applicable in all Member States.

Done at Brussels, 15 December 2006.

Notes
Date of entry into force: 29 December 2006.

Commentary
Art 6: F&N: 17.164

G11

COMMISSION REGULATION (EC) NO 800/2008

of 6 August 2008

declaring certain categories of aid compatible with the common market in application
of [107 and 108 of the Treaty on the Functioning of the European Union]*
(General block exemption Regulation)

Official Journal L 214, 9.8.2008, p.3

Celex No: 32008R0800

EUR-Lex permanent link: <http://eur-lex.europa.eu/LexUriServ/LexUriServ.do?uri=CELEX:3200
8R0800EN:NOT>

Notes

* Ed note: please see the Note on the Lisbon Treaty at p.xvii in regard to article renumbering introduced by the Lisbon Treaty. Unless otherwise stated, all Treaty article numbers are the new numbers of the Treaty on the Functioning of the European Union (TFEU) and the Treaty on European Union (TEU).

Commission Regulation (EC) No 800/2008 ('GBER') was adopted by the Commission on 7 July 2008. It came into force on 29 August 2008 (see Article 45). It repeals Regulation (EC) No 1628/2006 and replaces Regulation (EC) No 68/2001, Regulation (EC) No 70/2001 and Regulation (EC) No 2204/2002 following their expiration, subject to the transitional provisions contained in Article 44.

The GBER was due to expire on 31 December 2013. On 24 July 2013, the Commission announced its intention to prepare a consolidated proposal for a revised GBER, for consultation in late 2013. On 29 November 2013, its validity was extended to 30 June 2014 by Commission Regulation (EU) No 224/2013 (OJ L320, 30.11.2013, p.20).

EEA Application: see Decision of the EEA Joint Committee No 120/2008 of 7 November 2008 amending Annex XV (State aid) to the EEA Agreement (OJ L 339, 18.12.2008, p.111). Decision No 120/2008 incorporates the GBER into Annex XV (point 1j) of the EEA Agreement, with appropriate adaptations, and deletes the texts of points 1d (Commission Regulation (EC) No 68/2001), 1f (Commission Regulation (EC) No 70/2001), 1g (Commission Regulation (EC) No 2204/2002) and 1i (Commission Regulation (EC) No 1628/2006), including the related headings, with effect from 1 January 2009.

THE COMMISSION OF THE EUROPEAN COMMUNITIES

Having regard to the [Treaty on the Functioning of the European Union],

Having regard to Council Regulation (EC) 994/98 of 7 May 1998 on the application of [107 and 108] of the [Treaty on the Functioning of the European Union] to certain categories of horizontal State aid,[1] and in particular Article 1 points (a) and (b) thereof,

Having published a draft of this Regulation,[2]

After consulting the Advisory Committee on State Aid,

Notes

[1] OJ L 142, 14.5.1998, p.1.
[2] OJ C 210, 8.9.2007, p.14.

Commentary

Regulation 800/2008/EC: B&C: 17.003, 17.054, 17.070 F&N: 17.387–17.393

Whereas:

(1) Regulation (EC) No 994/98 empowers the Commission to declare, in accordance with Article [107] of the Treaty that under certain conditions aid to small and medium-sized enterprises ("SMEs"), aid in favour of research and development, aid in favour of environmental protection, employment and training aid, and aid that complies with the map approved by the Commission for each Member State for the grant of regional aid is compatible with the common market and not subject to the notification requirement of Article [107(3)] of the Treaty.

(2) The Commission has applied Articles [107 and 108 TFEU] in numerous decisions and gained sufficient experience to define general compatibility criteria as regards aid in favour of SMEs, in the form of investment aid in and outside assisted areas, in the form of risk capital schemes and in the area of research, development and innovation, in particular in the context of the implementation of Commission Regulation (EC) No 70/2001 of 12 January 2001 on the application of Articles [107 and 108 TFEU] to State aid to small and medium-sized enterprises,[1] and as regards the extension of the scope of that Regulation to include aid for research and development, the implementation of Commission Regulation (EC) No 364/2004 of 25 February 2004 amending Regulation (EC) No 70/2001,[2] the implementation of the Commission communication on State aid and risk capital[3] and the Community guidelines on State aid to promote risk capital investments in small and medium-sized enterprises,[4] as well as the implementation of the Community framework for State aid for research and development and innovation.[5]

Notes

[1] OJ L 10, 13.1.2001, p.33.
[2] OJ L 63, 28.2.2004, p.22.
[3] OJ C 235, 21.08.2001, p.3
[4] OJ C 194, 18.8.2006, p.2.
[5] OJ C 323, 30.12.2006, p.1.

(3) The Commission has also gained sufficient experience in the application of Articles [107 and 108 TFEU] in the fields of training aid, employment aid, environmental aid, research and development and innovation aid and regional aid with respect to both SMEs and large enterprises, in particular in the context of the implementation of Commission Regulation (EC) No 68/2001 of 12 January 2001 on the application of Articles [107 and 108 TFEU] to training aid,[1] Commission Regulation (EC) No 2204/2002 of 12 December 2002 on the application of Articles [107 and 108 TFEU] to State aid for employment,[2] Commission Regulation (EC) No 1628/2006 of 24 October 2006 on the application of Articles [107 and 108 TFEU] to national regional investment aid[3] the Community framework for State aid for research and development,[4] the Community Framework for State aid for research and development and innovation, the 2001 Community guidelines on State for environmental protection,[5] the 2008 Community guidelines on State aid for environmental protection[6] and the Guidelines on national regional aid for 2007–2013.[7]

Notes

[1] OJ L 10, 13.1.2001, p.20. Regulation as last amended by Regulation (EC) No 1976/2006.
[2] OJ L 337, 13.12.2002, p.3. Regulation as last amended by Regulation (EC) No 1976/2006.
[3] OJ L 302, 1.11.2006, p.29.
[4] OJ C 45, 17.2.1996, p.5.
[5] OJ C 37, 3.2.2001, p.3.
[6] OJ C 82, 1.4.2008, p.1.
[7] OJ C 54, 4.3.2006, p.13.

(4) In the light of this experience, it is necessary to adapt some of the conditions laid down in Regulations (EC) Nos 68/2001, 70/2001, 2204/2002 and 1628/2006. For reasons of simplification and to ensure more efficient monitoring of aid by the Commission, those Regulations should be replaced by a single Regulation. Simplification should result from, amongst other things, a set of common harmonised definitions and common horizontal provisions laid down in Chapter I of this Regulation. In order to ensure the coherence of State aid legislation, the definitions of aid and aid scheme should be identical to the definitions provided for these concepts in Council Regulation (EC) No 659/1999 of 22 March 1999 laying down detailed rules for the application of

Article [108 TFEU].[1] Such simplification is essential in order to ensure that the Lisbon Strategy for Growth and Jobs yields results, especially for SMEs.

Notes
[1] OJ L 83, 27.3.1999, p.1. Regulation as last amended by Regulation (EC) No 1791/2006 (OJ L 363, 20.12.2006, p.1).

(5) This Regulation should exempt any aid that fulfils all the relevant conditions of this Regulation, and any aid scheme, provided that any individual aid that could be granted under such scheme fulfils all the relevant conditions of this Regulation. In order to ensure transparency, as well as more efficient monitoring of aid, any individual aid measure granted under this Regulation should contain an express reference to the applicable provision of Chapter II and to the national law on which the individual aid is based.

(6) In order to monitor the implementation of this Regulation, the Commission should also be in a position to obtain all necessary information from Member States concerning the measures implemented under this Regulation. A failure of the Member State to provide information within a reasonable deadline on these aid measures may therefore be considered to be an indication that the conditions of this Regulation are not being respected. Such failure may therefore lead the Commission to decide that this Regulation, or the relevant part of this Regulation, should be withdrawn, for the future, as regards the Member State concerned and that all subsequent aid measures, including new individual aid measures granted on the basis of aid schemes previously covered by this Regulation, need to be notified to the Commission in accordance with Article [108 TFEU]. As soon as the Member State has provided correct and complete information, the Commission should allow the Regulation to be fully applicable again.

(7) State aid within the meaning of Article [107(1)] of the Treaty not covered by this Regulation should remain subject to the notification requirement of Article [108(3)] of the Treaty. This Regulation should be without prejudice to the possibility for Member States to notify aid the objectives of which correspond to objectives covered by this Regulation. Such aid will be assessed by the Commission in particular on the basis of the conditions set out in this Regulation and in accordance with the criteria laid down in specific guidelines or frameworks adopted by the Commission wherever the aid measure at stake falls within the scope of application of such specific instrument.

(8) This Regulation should not apply to export aid or aid favouring domestic over imported products. In particular, it should not apply to aid financing the establishment and operation of a distribution network in other countries. Aid towards the cost of participating in trade fairs, or of studies or consultancy services needed for the launch of a new or existing product on a new market should not normally constitute export aid.

(9) This Regulation should apply across virtually all sectors. In the sector of fisheries and aquaculture, this Regulation should only exempt aid in the fields of research and development and innovation, aid in the form of risk capital, training aid and aid for disadvantaged and disabled workers.

(10) In the agricultural sector, in view of the special rules which apply in the primary production of agricultural products, this Regulation should exempt only aid in the fields of research and development, aid in the form of risk capital, training aid, environmental aid and aid for disadvantaged and disabled workers to the extent that these categories of aid are not covered by Commission Regulation (EC) No 1857/2006 of 15 December 2006 on the application of Articles [107 and 108 TFEU] to State aid to small and medium-sized enterprises active in the production of agricultural products and amending Regulation (EC) No 70/2001.[1]

Notes
[1] OJ L 358, 16.12.2006, p.3.

(11) In view of the similarities between the processing and marketing of agricultural products and of non-agricultural products this Regulation should apply to the processing and marketing of agricultural products, provided that certain conditions are met.

(12) Neither on-farm activities necessary for preparing a product for the first sale, nor the first sale to resellers or processors should be considered processing or marketing for the purposes of this Regulation. The Court of Justice of the European Communities has established that, once the Community has legislated for the establishment of a common organisation of the market in a given sector of agriculture, Member States are under an obligation to refrain from taking any measure which might undermine or create exceptions to it. This Regulation should therefore not apply to aid, the amount of which is fixed on the basis of price or quantity of products purchased or put on the market, nor should it apply to aid which is linked to an obligation to share it with primary producers.

(13) In view of Council Regulation (EC) No 1407/2002 of 23 July 2002 on State aid to the coal industry,[1] this Regulation should not apply to aid favouring activities in the coal sector with the exception of training aid, research, development and innovation aid and environmental aid.

Notes

[1] OJ L 205, 2.8.2002, p.1. Regulation as last amended by Regulation (EC) No 1791/2006 (OJ L 363, 20.12.2006, p.1).

(14) Where a regional aid scheme purports to realise regional objectives, but is targeted at particular sectors of the economy, the objective and likely effects of the scheme may be sectorial rather than horizontal. Therefore, regional aid schemes targeted at specific sectors of economic activity, as well as regional aid granted for activities in the steel sector, in the shipbuilding sector, as foreseen in the Commission communication concerning the prolongation of the Framework on State aid to shipbuilding,[1] and in the synthetic fibres sector, should not be covered by the exemption from notification. However, the tourism sector plays an important role in national economies and in general has a particularly positive effect on regional development. Regional aid schemes aimed at tourism activities should therefore be exempt from the notification requirement.

Notes

[1] OJ C 260, 28.10.2006, p.7.

(15) Aid granted to undertakings in difficulty within the meaning of the Community guidelines on State aid for rescuing and restructuring firms in difficulty[1] should be assessed under those Guidelines in order to avoid their circumvention. Aid to such undertakings should therefore be excluded from the scope of this Regulation. In order to reduce the administrative burden for Member States, when granting aid covered by this Regulation to SMEs, the definition of what is to be considered an undertaking in difficulty should be simplified as compared to the definition used in those Guidelines. Moreover, SMEs which have been incorporated for less than three years should not be considered, for the purposes of this Regulation, to be in difficulty with regard to that period, unless they fulfil the criteria under the relevant national law for being the subject of collective insolvency proceedings. That simplification should be without prejudice to the qualification of those SMEs under those Guidelines with regard to aid not covered by this Regulation and without prejudice to the qualification as undertakings in difficulty of large enterprises, under this Regulation, which remain subject to the full definition provided in those Guidelines.

Notes

[1] OJ C 244, 1.10.2004, p.2.

(16) The Commission has to ensure that authorised aid does not alter trading conditions in a way contrary to the general interest. Therefore, aid in favour of a beneficiary which is subject to an outstanding recovery order following a previous Commission Decision declaring an aid illegal and incompatible with the common market, should be excluded from the scope of this Regulation. As a consequence, any ad hoc aid paid out to such a beneficiary and any aid scheme not containing a provision explicitly excluding such beneficiaries remains subject to the notification requirements of Article [108(3)] of the Treaty. That provision should not affect the legitimate expectations of beneficiaries of aid schemes which are not subject to outstanding recovery orders.

(17) In order to ensure the consistent application of Community State aid rules, as well as for reasons of administrative simplification, the definitions of terms which are relevant to the different categories of aid covered by this Regulation should be harmonised.

(18) For the purposes of calculating aid intensity, all figures used should be taken before any deduction of tax or other charge. For the purpose of calculating aid intensities, aid payable in several instalments should be discounted to its value at the moment of granting. The interest rate to be used for discounting purposes and for calculating the aid amount in aid not taking the form of a grant, should be the reference rate applicable at the time of grant, as laid down in the Communication from the Commission on the revision of the method for setting the reference and discount rates.[1]

Notes
[1] OJ C 14, 19.1.2008, p.6.

(19) In cases where aid is awarded by means of tax exemptions or reductions on future taxes due, subject to the respect of a certain aid intensity defined in gross grant equivalent, discounting of aid tranches should take place on the basis of the reference rates applicable at the various times the tax advantages become effective. In the case of tax exemptions or reductions on future taxes, the applicable reference rate and the exact amount of the aid tranches may not be known in advance. In such a case, Member States should set in advance a cap on the discounted value of the aid respecting the applicable aid intensity. Subsequently, when the amount of the aid tranche in a given year becomes known, discounting can take place on the basis of the reference rate applicable at that time. The discounted value of each aid tranche should be deducted from the overall amount of the cap.

(20) For the purposes of transparency, equal treatment and effective monitoring, this Regulation should apply only to aid which is transparent. Transparent aid is aid for which it is possible to calculate precisely the gross grant equivalent ex ante without a need to undertake a risk assessment. Aid comprised in loans, in particular, should be considered transparent where the gross grant equivalent has been calculated on the basis of the reference rate as laid down in the Communication from the Commission on the revision of the method for setting the reference and discount rates. Aid comprised in fiscal measures should be considered transparent where the measure provides for a cap ensuring that the applicable threshold is not exceeded. In the case of reductions in environmental taxes, which are not subject to an individual notification threshold under this Regulation, no cap needs to be included for the measure to be considered transparent.

(21) Aid comprised in guarantee schemes should be considered transparent when the methodology to calculate the gross grant equivalent has been approved following notification of this methodology to the Commission, and, in the case of regional investment aid, also when the Commission has approved such methodology after adoption of Commission Regulation (EC) No 1628/2006. The Commission will examine such notifications on the basis of the Commission Notice on the application of Articles [107 and 108 TFEU] to State aid in the form of guarantees.[1] Aid comprised in guarantee schemes should also be considered transparent where the beneficiary is an SME and the gross grant equivalent has been calculated on the basis of the safe-harbour premiums laid down in points 3.3 and 3.5 of that Notice.

Notes
[1] OJ C 155, 20.6.2008, p.10.

(22) In view of the difficulty in calculating the grant equivalent of aid in the form of repayable advances, such aid should be covered by this Regulation only if the total amount of the repayable advance is inferior to the applicable individual notification threshold and the maximum aid intensities provided under this Regulation.

(23) Due to the higher risk of distortion of competition, large amounts of aid should continue to be assessed by the Commission on an individual basis. Thresholds should therefore be set for each category of aid within the scope of this Regulation, at a level which takes into account the

category of aid concerned and its likely effects on competition. Any aid granted above those thresholds remains subject to the notification requirement of Article [108(3)] of the Treaty.

(24) With a view to ensuring that aid is proportionate and limited to the amount necessary, thresholds should, whenever possible, be expressed in terms of aid intensities in relation to a set of eligible costs. Because it is based on a form of aid for which eligible costs are difficult to identify, the threshold with regard to aid in the form of risk capital should be formulated in terms of maximum aid amounts.

(25) The thresholds in terms of aid intensity or aid amount should be fixed, in the light of the Commission's experience, at a level that strikes the appropriate balance between minimising distortions of competition in the aided sector and tackling the market failure or cohesion issue concerned. With respect to regional investment aid, this threshold should be set at a level taking into account the allowable aid intensities under the regional aid maps.

(26) In order to determine whether the individual notification thresholds and the maximum aid intensities laid down in this Regulation are respected, the total amount of public support for the aided activity or project should be taken into account, regardless of whether that support is financed from local, regional, national or Community sources.

(27) Moreover, this Regulation should specify the circumstances under which different categories of aid covered by this Regulation may be cumulated. As regards cumulation of aid covered by this Regulation with State aid not covered by this Regulation, regard should be had to the Decision of the Commission approving the aid not covered by this Regulation, as well as to the State aid rules on which this decision is based. Special provisions should apply in respect of cumulation of aid for disabled workers with other categories of aid, notably with investment aid, which can be calculated on the basis of the wage costs concerned. This Regulation should also make provision for cumulation of aid measures with identifiable eligible costs and aid measures without identifiable eligible costs.

(28) In order to ensure that the aid is necessary and acts as an incentive to develop further activities or projects, this Regulation should not apply to aid for activities in which the beneficiary would already engage under market conditions alone. As regards any aid covered by this Regulation granted to an SME, such incentive should be considered present when, before the activities relating to the implementation of the aided project or activities are initiated, the SME has submitted an application to the Member State. As regards aid in the form of risk capital in favour of SMEs, the conditions laid down in this Regulation notably with respect to the size of the investment tranches per target enterprise, the degree of involvement of private investors and consideration of the size of the company and the business stage financed ensure that the risk capital measure will have an incentive effect.

(29) As regards any aid covered by this Regulation granted to a beneficiary which is a large enterprise, the Member State should, in addition to the conditions applying to SMEs, also ensure that the beneficiary has analysed, in an internal document, the viability of the aided project or activity with aid and without aid. The Member State should verify that this internal document confirms a material increase in size or scope of the project/activity, a material increase in the total amount spent by the beneficiary on the subsidised project or activity or a material increase in the speed of completion of the project/activity concerned. As regards regional aid, incentive effect may also be established on the basis of the fact that the investment project would not have been carried out as such in the assisted region concerned in the absence of the aid.

(30) As regards aid for disadvantaged or disabled workers, an incentive effect should be considered to be present by the fact that the aid measure concerned leads to a net increase in the number of disadvantaged or disabled workers hired by the undertaking concerned or leads to additional costs in favour of facilities or equipment devoted to disabled workers. Where the beneficiary of an aid for the employment of disabled workers in the form of wage subsidies was already benefiting from aid for employing disabled workers, which either fulfilled the conditions of Regulation (EC) No 2204/2002 or had been individually approved by the Commission, it is presumed that the condition of a net increase in the number of disabled workers, which was fulfilled for the pre-existing aid measures, continues to be fulfilled for the purpose of this Regulation.

(31) Fiscal aid measures should be subject to specific conditions of incentive effect, in view of the fact that they are provided on the basis of different procedures than other categories of aid.

Reductions in environmental taxes fulfilling the conditions of Council Directive 2003/96/EC of 27 October 2003 restructuring the Community framework for the taxation of energy products and electricity[1] and covered by this Regulation should be presumed to have an incentive effect in view of fact that these reduced rates contribute at least indirectly to an improvement of environmental protection by allowing the adoption or the continuation of the overall tax scheme concerned, thereby incentivising the undertakings subject to the environmental tax to reduce their level of pollution.

Notes

[1] OJ L 283, 31.10.2003, p.51. Directive as last amended by Directive 2004/75/EC (OJ L 157, 30.4.2004, p.100).

(32) Moreover, as the incentive effect of ad hoc aid granted to large enterprises is considered to be difficult to establish, this form of aid should be excluded from the scope of application of this Regulation. The Commission will examine the existence of such incentive effect in the context of the notification of the aid concerned on the basis of the criteria established in the applicable guidelines, frameworks or other Community instruments.

(33) In order to ensure transparency and effective monitoring in accordance with Article 3 of Regulation (EC) No 994/98, it is appropriate to establish a standard form to be used by Member States to provide the Commission with summary information whenever, in pursuance of this Regulation, an aid scheme or ad hoc aid is implemented. The summary information form should be used for the publication of the measure in the *Official Journal of the European Union* and on the internet. The summary information should be sent to the Commission in electronic format making use of the established IT application. The Member State concerned should publish on the internet the full text of such aid measure. In the case of ad hoc aid measures, business secrets may be deleted. The name of the beneficiary and the amount of aid should however not be considered a business secret. Member States should ensure that such text remains accessible on the internet as long as the aid measure is in force. With the exception of aid taking the form of fiscal measures, the act granting the aid should also contain a reference to the specific provision(s) of Chapter II of this Regulation relevant to such an act.

(34) In order to ensure transparency and effective monitoring, the Commission should establish specific requirements as regards the form and the content of the annual reports to be submitted to the Commission by Member States. Moreover, it is appropriate to establish rules concerning the records that Member States should keep regarding the aid schemes and individual aid exempted by this Regulation, in view of the provisions of Article 15 of Regulation (EC) No 659/1999.

(35) It is necessary to establish further conditions that should be fulfilled by any aid measure exempted by this Regulation. Having regard to Articles [107(3)(a)] and [107(3)(c)] of the Treaty, such aid should be proportionate to the market failures or handicaps that have to be overcome in order to be in the Community interest. It is therefore appropriate to limit the scope of this Regulation, as far as it concerns investment aid to aid granted in relation to certain tangible and intangible investments. In the light of Community overcapacity and the specific problems of distortion of competition in the road freight and air transport sectors, so far as undertakings having their main economic activity in those transport sectors are concerned, transport means and equipment should not be regarded as eligible investment costs. Special provisions should apply as regards the definition of tangible assets for the purpose of environmental aid.

(36) Consistent with the principles governing the aid falling within Article [107(1)] of the Treaty, aid should be considered to be granted at the moment the legal right to receive the aid is conferred on the beneficiary under the applicable national legal regime.

(37) In order not to favour the capital factor of an investment over the labour factor, provision should be made for the possibility of measuring aid to investment in favour of SMEs and regional aid on the basis of either the costs of the investment or the costs of employment directly created by an investment project.

(38) Environmental aid schemes in the form of tax reductions, aid for disadvantaged workers, regional investment aid, aid for newly created small enterprises, aid for enterprises newly created by female entrepreneurs or aid in the form of risk capital granted to a beneficiary on an ad hoc

basis may have a major impact on competition in the relevant market because it favours the beneficiary over other undertakings which have not received such aid. Because it is granted only to a single undertaking, ad hoc aid is likely to have only a limited positive structural effect on the environment, the employment of disabled and disadvantaged workers regional cohesion or the risk capital market failure. For this reason, aid schemes concerning these categories of aid should be exempted under this Regulation, whilst ad hoc aid should be notified to the Commission. This Regulation should however exempt ad hoc regional aid when this ad hoc aid is used to supplement aid granted on the basis of a regional investment aid scheme, with a maximum limit for the ad hoc component of 50% of the total aid to be granted for the investment.

(39) The provisions of this Regulation relating to SME investment and employment aid should not provide, as was the case in Regulation (EC) No 70/2001, any possibility for increasing the maximum aid intensities by means of a regional bonus. However, it should be possible for the maximum aid intensities laid down in the provisions concerning regional investment aid to be granted also to SMEs, as long as the conditions for granting regional investment and employment aid are fulfilled. Similarly, the provisions relating to environmental investment aid should not provide any possibility for increasing the maximum aid intensities by means of a regional bonus. It should also be possible for the maximum aid intensities laid down in the provisions concerning regional investment aid to be applied to projects which have a positive impact on the environment, as long as the conditions for granting regional investment aid are fulfilled.

(40) By addressing the handicaps of the disadvantaged regions, national regional aid promotes the economic, social and territorial cohesion of Member States and the Community as a whole. National regional aid is designed to assist the development of the most disadvantaged regions by supporting investment and job creation in a sustainable context. It promotes the setting-up of new establishments, the extension of existing establishments, the diversification of the output of an establishment into new additional products or a fundamental change in the overall production process of an existing establishment.

(41) In order to prevent large regional investment projects from being artificially divided into sub-projects, thereby escaping the notification thresholds provided under this Regulation, a large investment project should be considered to be a single investment project if the investment is undertaken within a period of three years by the same undertaking or undertakings and consists of fixed assets combined in an economically indivisible way. To assess whether an investment is economically indivisible, Member States should take into account the technical, functional and strategic links and the immediate geographical proximity. The economic indivisibility should be assessed independently from ownership. This means that to establish whether a large investment project constitutes a single investment project, the assessment should be the same irrespective of whether the project is carried out by one undertaking, by more than one undertaking sharing the investment costs or by more undertakings bearing the costs of separate investments within the same investment project (for example in the case of a joint venture).

(42) In contrast to regional aid, which should be confined to assisted areas, SME investment and employment aid should be able to be granted both in assisted and in non-assisted areas. The Member States should thus be able to provide, in assisted areas, investment aid as long as they respect either all conditions applying to regional investment and employment aid or all conditions applying to SME investment and employment aid.

(43) The economic development of the assisted regions is hindered by relatively low levels of entrepreneurial activity and in particular by even lower than average rates of business start-ups. It is therefore necessary to include in this Regulation a category of aid, which can be granted in addition to regional investment aid, in order to provide incentives to support business start-ups and the early stage development of small enterprises in the assisted areas. In order to ensure that this aid for newly created enterprises in assisted regions is effectively targeted, this category of aid should be graduated in accordance with the difficulties faced by each category of region. Furthermore, in order to avoid an unacceptable risk of distortions of competition, including the risk of crowding-out existing enterprises, the aid should be strictly limited to small enterprises, limited in amount and degressive. Granting aid designed exclusively for newly created small enterprises or enterprises newly created by female entrepreneurs may produce perverse incentives for existing small enterprises to close down and re-open in order to receive this category of

aid. Member States should be aware of this risk and should design aid schemes in such a way as to avoid this problem, for example by placing limits on applications from owners of recently closed firms.

(44) The economic development of the Community may be hindered by low levels of entrepreneurial activity by certain categories of the population who suffer certain disadvantages, such as getting access to finance. The Commission has reviewed the possibility of market failure in this respect as regards a variety of categories of persons, and is at this stage in a position to conclude that women, in particular have lower than average rates of business start-ups as compared to men, as is evidenced, amongst others, by statistical data of Eurostat. It is therefore necessary to include in this Regulation a category of aid providing incentives for the creation of enterprises by female entrepreneurs in order to tackle the specific market failures women encounter most notably with respect to access to finance. Women also face particular difficulties linked to bearing caring costs for family members. Such aid should allow the achievement of substantive rather than formal equality between men and women by reducing de facto inequalities existing in the area of entrepreneurship, in line with the requirements of the case-law of the Court of Justice of the European Communities. At the expiry of this Regulation the Commission will have to reconsider whether the scope of this exemption and the categories of beneficiaries concerned remain justified.

(45) Sustainable development is one of the main pillars in the Lisbon Strategy for Growth and Jobs, together with competitiveness and security of energy supplies. Sustainable development is based, amongst other things, on a high level of protection and improvement of the quality of the environment. Promoting environmental sustainability and combating climate change leads as well to increasing security of supply and ensuring the competitiveness of European economies and the availability of affordable energy. The area of environmental protection is often confronted with market failures in the form of negative externalities. Under normal market conditions, undertakings may not necessarily have an incentive to reduce their pollution since such reduction may increase their costs. When undertakings are not obliged to internalise the costs of pollution, society as a whole bears these costs. This internalisation of environmental costs can be ensured by imposing environmental regulation or taxes. The lack of full harmonization of environmental standards at Community level creates an uneven playing field. Furthermore, an even higher level of environmental protection can be achieved by the initiatives to go beyond the mandatory Community standards, which may harm the competitive position of the undertakings concerned.

(46) In view of the sufficient experience gathered in the application of the Community guidelines on State aid for environmental protection, investment aid enabling undertakings to go beyond Community standards for environmental protection or increase the level of environmental protection in the absence of Community standards, aid for the acquisition of transport vehicles which go beyond Community standards or which increase the level of environmental protection in the absence of Community standards, aid for early adaptation to future Community standards by SMEs, environmental aid for investment in energy saving, environmental aid for investment in high efficiency cogeneration, environmental aid for investments to promote renewable energy sources including investment aid relating to sustainable biofuels, aid for environmental studies and certain aid in the form of reductions in environmental taxes should be exempt from the notification requirement.

(47) Aid in the form of tax reductions favouring environmental protection covered by this Regulation, should, in line with the Community guidelines on State aid for environmental protection, be limited to a period of 10 years. After this period, Member States should re-evaluate the appropriateness of the tax reductions concerned. This should be without prejudice to the possibility for Member States of re-adopting these measures or similar measures under this Regulation after having realised such reevaluation.

(48) A correct calculation of the extra investment or production costs to achieve environmental protection is essential to determine whether or not aid is compatible with Article [107(3)] of the Treaty. As outlined in the Community guidelines on State aid for environmental protection, eligible costs should be limited to the extra investment costs necessary to achieve a higher level of environmental protection.

(49) In view of the difficulties which may arise, in particular, with respect to the deduction of benefits?deriving from extra investment, provision should be made for a simplified method of calculation of the extra investment costs. Therefore these costs should, for the purpose of applying this Regulation, be calculated without taking into account operating benefits, cost savings or additional ancillary production and without taking into account operating costs engendered during the life of the investment. The maximum aid intensities provided under this Regulation for the different categories of environmental investment aid concerned have therefore been reduced systematically as compared to the maximum aid intensities provided for by the Community guidelines on State aid for environmental protection.

(50) As regards environmental aid for investment in energy saving measures it is appropriate to allow Member States to choose either the simplified method of calculation or the full cost calculation, identical to the one provided for in the Community guidelines on State aid for environmental protection. In view of the particular practical difficulties which may arise when applying the full cost calculation method, those cost calculations should be certified by an external auditor.

(51) As regards environmental aid for investment in cogeneration and environmental aid for investments to promote renewable energy sources, the extra costs should, for the purpose of the application of this Regulation, be calculated without taking into account other support measures granted for the same eligible costs, with the exception of other environmental investment aid.

(52) With regard to investments related to hydropower installations it should be noted that their environmental impact can be twofold. In terms of low greenhouse gas emissions they certainly provide potential. On the other hand, such installations might also have a negative impact, for example on water systems and biodiversity.

(53) In order to eliminate differences that might give rise to distortions of competition and to facilitate coordination between different Community and national initiatives concerning SMEs, as well as for reasons of administrative clarity and legal certainty, the definition of SME used for the purpose of this Regulation should be based on the definition in Commission Recommendation 2003/361/EC of 6 May 2003 concerning the definition of micro, small and medium sized enterprises.[1]

Notes

[1] OJ L 124, 20.5.2003, p.36.

(54) SMEs play a decisive role in job creation and, more generally, act as a factor of social stability and economic drive. However, their development may be limited by market failures, leading to these SMEs suffering from typical handicaps. SMEs often have difficulties in obtaining capital, risk capital or loans, given the risk-averse nature of certain financial markets and the limited collateral that they may be able to offer. Their limited resources may also restrict their access to information, notably regarding new technology and potential markets. In order to facilitate the development of the economic activities of SMEs, this Regulation should therefore exempt certain categories of aid when they are granted in favour of SMEs. Consequently, it is justified to exempt such aid from prior notification and to consider that, for the purposes of the application of this Regulation only, when a beneficiary falls within the SME definition provided for in this Regulation, that SME can be presumed, when the aid amount does not exceed the applicable notification threshold, to be limited in its development by the typical SME handicaps prompted by market failures.

(55) Having regard to the differences between small enterprises and medium-sized enterprises, different basic aid intensities and different bonuses should be set for small enterprises and for medium-sized enterprises. Market failures affecting SMEs in general, including difficulties of access to finance, result in even greater obstacles to the development of small enterprises as compared to medium-sized enterprises.

(56) On the basis of the experience gained in applying the Community guidelines on State aid to promote risk capital investments in small and medium-sized enterprises there appear to be a number of specific risk capital market failures in the Community in respect of certain types of investments at certain stages of undertakings' development. These market failures result from an imperfect matching of supply and demand of risk capital. As a result, the level of risk capital

provided in the market may be too restricted, and undertakings do not obtain funding despite having a valuable business model and growth prospects. The main source of market failure relevant to risk capital markets, which particularly affects access to capital by SMEs and which may justify public intervention, relates to imperfect or asymmetric information. Consequently, risk capital schemes taking the form of commercially managed investment funds in which a sufficient proportion of the funds are provided by private investors in the form of private equity promoting profit-driven risk capital measures in favour of target enterprises should be exempt from the notification requirement under certain conditions. The conditions that the investment funds should be commercially managed and that the ensuing risk capital measures be profit driven should not prevent the investment funds from targeting their activities and particular market segments, such as enterprises created by female entrepreneurs. This Regulation should not affect the status of the European Investment Fund and the European Investment Bank, as defined in the Community guidelines on risk capital.

(57) Aid for research, development and innovation can contribute to economic growth, strengthening competitiveness and boosting employment. On the basis of its experience with the application of Regulation (EC) No 364/2004, the Community framework for State aid for research and development and the Community Framework for State aid for research and development and innovation, it appears that given the available research and development capabilities of both SMEs and large enterprises, market failures may prevent the market from reaching the optimal output and lead to an inefficient outcome. Such inefficient outcomes generally relate to positive externalities/knowledge spill-overs, public goods/knowledge spill-overs, imperfect and asymmetric information and coordination and network failures.

(58) Aid for research, development and innovation is of particular importance, especially for SMEs because one of the structural disadvantages of SMEs lies in the difficulty they may experience in gaining access to new technological developments, technology transfers or highly qualified personnel. Therefore, aid for research and development projects, aid for technical feasibility studies and aid to cover industrial property rights costs for SMEs, as well as aid for young innovative small enterprises, aid for innovation advisory services and for innovation support services and aid for the loan of highly qualified personnel should be exempt from the requirement of prior notification, under certain conditions.

(59) As regards project aid for research and development, the aided part of the research project should completely fall within the categories of fundamental research, industrial research or experimental development. When a project encompasses different tasks, each task should be qualified as falling under the categories of fundamental research, industrial research or experimental development or as not falling under any of those categories at all. That qualification need not necessarily follow a chronological approach, moving sequentially over time from fundamental research to activities closer to the market. Accordingly, a task which is carried out at a late stage of a project may be qualified as industrial research. Similarly, it is not excluded that an activity carried out at an earlier stage of the project may constitute experimental development.

(60) In the agricultural sector certain aid for research and development should be exempted if conditions similar to those provided in the specific provisions laid down for the agricultural sector in the Community framework for State aid for research and development and innovation are fulfilled. If those specific conditions are not fulfilled, it is appropriate to provide for the aid to be exempted if it fulfils the conditions set out in the general provisions related to research and development in this Regulation.

(61) The promotion of training and the recruitment of disadvantaged and disabled workers and compensation of additional costs for the employment of disabled workers constitute a central objective of the economic and social policies of the Community and of its Member States.

(62) Training usually has positive externalities for society as a whole since it increases the pool of skilled workers from which other firms may draw, improves the competitiveness of Community industry and plays an important role in the Community employment strategy. Training, including e-learning, is also essential for the constitution, the acquisition and the diffusion of knowledge, a public good of primary importance. In view of the fact that undertakings in the Community generally underinvest in the training of their workers, especially when this training is general in nature and does not lead to an immediate and concrete advantage for the undertaking

concerned, State aid can help to correct this market failure. Therefore such aid should be exempt, under certain conditions, from prior notification. In view of the particular handicaps with which SMEs are confronted and the higher relative costs that they have to bear when they invest in training, the intensities of aid exempted by this Regulation should be increased for SMEs. The characteristics of training in the maritime transport sector justify a specific approach for that sector.

(63) A distinction can be drawn between general and specific training. The permissible aid intensities should differ in accordance with the type of training provided and the size of the undertaking. General training provides transferable qualifications and substantially improves the employability of the trained worker. Aid for this purpose has less distortive effects on competition, meaning that higher intensities of aid can be exempted from prior notification. Specific training, which mainly benefits the undertaking, involves a greater risk of distortion of competition and the intensity of aid which can be exempted from prior notification should therefore be much lower. Training should be considered to be general in nature also when it relates to environmental management, eco-innovation or corporate social responsibility and thereby increases the capacity of the beneficiary to contribute to general objectives in the environment field.

(64) Certain categories of disabled or disadvantaged workers still experience particular difficulty in entering the labour market. For this reason there is a justification for public authorities to apply measures providing incentives to undertakings to increase their levels of employment, in particular of workers from these disadvantaged categories. Employment costs form part of the normal operating costs of any undertaking. It is therefore particularly important that aid for the employment of disabled and disadvantaged workers should have a positive effect on employment levels of those categories of workers and should not merely enable undertakings to reduce costs which they would otherwise have to bear. Consequently, such aid should be exempt from prior notification when it is likely to assist those categories of workers in re-entering the job market or, as regards disabled workers, re-entering and staying in the job market.

(65) Aid for the employment of disabled workers in the form of wage subsidies may be calculated on the basis of the specific degree of disability of the disabled worker concerned or may be provided as a lump sum provided that neither method leads to the aid exceeding the maximum aid intensity for each individual worker concerned.

(66) It is appropriate to lay down transitional provisions for individual aid which was granted before the entry into force of this Regulation and was not notified in breach of the obligation provided for in Article [108(3)] of the Treaty. With the repeal of Regulation (EC) No 1628/2006, the existing regional investment schemes, as exempted, should be allowed to continue being implemented under the conditions foreseen by that Regulation, in line with Article 9(2), second subparagraph, of that Regulation.

(67) In the light of the Commission's experience in this area, and in particular the frequency with which it is generally necessary to revise State aid policy, it is appropriate to limit the period of application of this Regulation. Should this Regulation expire without being extended, aid schemes already exempted by this Regulation should continue to be exempted for a further period of six months, in order to give Member States time to adapt.

(68) Regulation (EC) No 70/2001, Regulation (EC) No 68/2001 and Regulation (EC) No 2204/2002 expired on 30 June 2008 and Regulation (EC) No 1628/2006 should be repealed.

HAS ADOPTED THIS REGULATION:

TABLE OF CONTENTS

Chapter I
Common Provisions

Article 1
Scope

1. This Regulation shall apply to the following categories of aid:

(a) regional aid;
(b) SME investment and employment aid
(c) aid for the creation of enterprises by female entrepreneurs;
(d) aid for environmental protection;
(e) aid for consultancy in favour of SMEs and SME participation in fairs
(f) aid in the form of risk capital;
(g) aid for research, development and innovation;
(h) training aid;
(i) aid for disadvantaged or disabled workers.

2. It shall not apply to:

(a) aid to export-related activities, namely aid directly linked to the quantitie s exported, to the establishment and operation of a distribution network or to other current costs linked to the export activity;
(b) aid contingent upon the use of domestic over imported goods.

3. This Regulation shall apply to aid in all sectors of the economy with the exception of the following:

(a) aid favouring activities in the fishery and aquaculture sectors, as covered by Council Regulation (EC) No 104/2000,[1] except for training aid, aid in the form of risk capital, aid for research and development and innovation and aid for disadvantaged and disabled workers;
(b) aid favouring activities in the primary production of agricultural products, except for training aid, aid in the form of risk capital, aid for research and development, environmental aid, and aid for disadvantaged and disabled workers to the extent that these categories of aid are not covered by Commission Regulation (EC) No 1857/2006;

(c) aid favouring activities in the processing and marketing of agricultural products, in the following cases:

    (i) when the amount of the aid is fixed on the basis of the price or quantity of such products purchased from primary producers or put on the market by the undertakings concerned; or

    (ii) when the aid is conditional on being partly or entirely passed on to primary producers;

(d) aid favouring activities in the coal sector with the exception of training aid, research and development and innovation aid and environmental aid;

(e) regional aid favouring activities in the steel sector;

(f) regional aid favouring activities in the shipbuilding sector;

(g) regional aid favouring activities in the synthetic fibres sector.

4. This Regulation shall not apply to regional aid schemes which are targeted at specific sectors of economic activity within manufacturing or services. Schemes aimed at tourism activities are not considered targeted at specific sectors.

5. This Regulation shall not apply to ad hoc aid granted to large enterprises, except as provided for in Article 13(1).

6. This Regulation shall not apply to the following aid:

(a) aid schemes which do not explicitly exclude the payment of individual aid in favour of an undertaking which is subject to an outstanding recovery order following a previous Commission Decision declaring an aid illegal and incompatible with the common market;

(b) ad hoc aid in favour of an undertaking which is subject to an outstanding recovery order following a previous Commission Decision declaring an aid illegal and incompatible with the common market;

(c) aid to undertakings in difficulty.

7. For the purposes of point (c) of paragraph 6, an SME shall be considered to be an undertaking in difficulty if it fulfils the following conditions:

(a) in the case of a limited liability company, where more than half of its registered capital has disappeared and more than one quarter of that capital has been lost over the preceding 12 months; or

(b) in the case of a company where at least some members have unlimited liability for the debt of the company, where more than half of its capital as shown in the company accounts has disappeared and more than one quarter of that capital has been lost over the preceding 12 months; or

(c) whatever the type of company concerned, where it fulfils the criteria under its domestic law for being the subject of collective insolvency proceedings.

An SME which has been incorporated for less than three years shall not be considered, for the purposes of this Regulation, to be in difficulty with regard to that period unless it meets the condition set out in point (c) of the first subparagraph.

Notes
1 OJ L 17, 21.1.2000, p.22.

Article 2
Definitions

For the purposes of this Regulation the following definitions shall apply:

1. "aid" means any measure fulfilling all the criteria laid down in Article [107(1)] of the Treaty;

2. 'aid scheme' means any act on the basis of which, without further implementing measures being required, individual aid awards may be made to undertakings defined within the act in a general and abstract manner and any act on the basis of which aid which is not linked to a specific project may be awarded to one or several undertakings for an indefinite period of time and/or for an indefinite amount;

3. 'individual aid' means:

    (a) ad hoc aid; and

    (b) notifiable awards of aid on the basis of an aid scheme;

4. 'ad hoc aid' means individual aid not awarded on the basis of an aid scheme;

5. 'aid intensity' means the aid amount expressed as a percentage of the eligible costs;

6. 'transparent aid' means aid in respect of which it is possible to calculate precisely the gross grant equivalent ex ante without need to undertake a risk assessment;

7. 'small and medium-sized enterprises' or 'SMEs' means undertakings fulfilling the criteria laid down in Annex I;

8. 'large enterprises' means undertakings not fulfilling the criteria laid down in Annex I;

9. 'assisted areas' means regions eligible for regional aid, as determined in the approved regional aid map for the Member State concerned for the period 2007–2013;

10. 'tangible assets' means, without prejudice to Article 17(12), assets relating to land, buildings and plant, machinery and equipment; in the transport sector transport means and transport equipment are considered eligible assets, except with regard to regional aid and except for road freight and air transport;

11. 'intangible assets' means assets entailed by the transfer of technology through the acquisition of patent rights, licences, know-how or unpatented technical knowledge;

12. 'large investment project' means an investment in capital assets with eligible costs above EUR 50 million, calculated at prices and exchange rates on the date when the aid is granted;

13. 'number of employees' means the number of annual labour units (ALU), namely the number of persons employed full time in one year, part-time and seasonal work being ALU fractions;

14. 'employment directly created by an investment project' means employment concerning the activity to which the investment relates, including employment created following an increase in the utilisation rate of the capacity created by the investment;

15. 'wage cost' means the total amount actually payable by the beneficiary of the aid in respect of the employment concerned, comprising:
    (a) the gross wage, before tax; and
    (b) the compulsory contributions, such as social security charges;
    (c) child care and parent care costs;

16. 'SME investment and employment aid' means aid fulfilling the conditions laid down in Article 15;

17. 'investment aid' means, regional investment and employment aid under Article 13, SME investment and employment aid under Article 15 and investment aid for environmental protection under Articles 18 to 23;

18. 'disadvantaged worker' means any person who:
    (a) has not been in regular paid employment for the previous 6 months; or
    (b) has not attained an upper secondary educational or vocational qualification (ISCED 3); or
    (c) is over the age of 50 years; or
    (d) lives as a single adult with one or more dependents; or
    (e) works in a sector or profession in a Member State where the gender imbalance is at least 25% higher than the average gender imbalance across all economic sectors in that Member State, and belongs to that underrepresented gender group; or
    (f) is a member of an ethnic minority within a Member State and who requires development of his or her linguistic, vocational training or work experience profile to enhance prospects of gaining access to stable employment;

19. 'severely disadvantaged worker' means any person who has been unemployed for 24 months or more;

20. 'disabled worker' means any person:
    (a) recognised as disabled under national law; or
    (b) having a recognised limitation which results from physical, mental or psychological impairment;

Part G State Aids

21. 'sheltered employment' means employment in an undertaking where at least 50% of workers are disabled;

22. "agricultural product" means:
    (a) the products listed in Annex I to the Treaty, except fishery and aquaculture products covered by Regulation (EC) No 104/2000;
    (b) products falling under CN codes 4502, 4503 and 4504 (cork products);
    (c) products intended to imitate or substitute milk and milk products, as referred to in Council Regulation (EC) No 1234/2007;[1]

23. 'processing of agricultural products' means any operation on an agricultural product resulting in a product which is also an agricultural product, except on-farm activities necessary for preparing an animal or plant product for the first sale;

24. 'marketing of agricultural products' means holding or display with a view to sale, offering for sale, delivery or any other manner of placing on the market, except the first sale by a primary producer to resellers or processors and any activity preparing a product for such first sale; a sale by a primary producer to final consumers shall be considered to be marketing if it takes place in separate premises reserved for that purpose;

25. 'tourism activities' means the following activities in terms of NACE Rev. 2:
    (a) NACE 55: Accommodation;
    (b) NACE 56: Food and beverage service activities;
    (c) NACE 79: Travel agency, tour operator reservation service and related activities;
    (d) NACE 90: Creative, arts and entertainment activities;
    (e) NACE 91: Libraries, archives, museums and other cultural activities;
    (f) NACE 93: Sports activities and amusement and recreation activities;

26. 'repayable advance' means a loan for a project which is paid in one or more instalments and the conditions for the reimbursement of which depend on the outcome of the research and development and innovation project;

27. 'risk capital' means finance provided through equity and quasi-equity financing to undertakings during their early-growth stages (seed, start-up and expansion phases);

28. 'enterprise newly created by female entrepreneurs' means a small enterprise fulfilling the following conditions:
    (a) one or more women own at least 51% of the capital of the small enterprise concerned or are the registered owners of the small enterprise concerned; and
    (b) a woman is in charge of the management of the small enterprise;

29. 'steel sector' means all activities related to the production of one or more of the following products:
    (a) pig iron and ferro-alloys:
        pig iron for steelmaking, foundry and other pig iron, spiegeleisen and high-carbon ferro-manganese, not including other ferro-alloys;
    (b) crude and semi finished products of iron, ordinary steel or special steel:
        liquid steel cast or not cast into ingots, including ingots for forging semi finished products: blooms, billets and slabs; sheet bars and tinplate bars; hot-rolled wide coils, with the exception of production of liquid steel for castings from small and medium-sized foundries;
    (c) hot finished products of iron, ordinary steel or special steel:
        rails, sleepers, fishplates, soleplates, joists, heavy sections 80 mm and over, sheet piling, bars and sections of less than 80 mm and flats of less than 150 mm, wire rod, tube rounds and squares, hot-rolled hoop and strip (including tube strip), hot-rolled sheet (coated or uncoated), plates and sheets of 3 mm thickness and over, universal plates of 150 mm and over, with the exception of wire and wire products, bright bars and iron castings;
    (d) cold finished products:
        tinplate, terneplate, blackplate, galvanized sheets, other coated sheets, colled-rolled sheets, electrical sheets and strip for tinplate, cold-rolled plate, in coil and in strip;
    (e) tubes:
        all seamless steel tubes, welded steel tubes with a diameter of over 406.4 mm;

30. 'synthetic fibres sector' means:

    (a) extrusion/texturisation of all generic types of fibre and yarn based on polyester, polyamide, acrylic or polypropylene, irrespective of their end-uses; or

    (b) polymerisation (including polycondensation) where it is integrated with extrusion in terms of the machinery used; or

    (c) any ancillary process linked to the contemporaneous installation of extrusion/texturisation capacity by the prospective beneficiary or by another company in the group to which it belongs and which, in the specific business activity concerned, is normally integrated with such capacity in terms of the machinery used.

Notes

1 OJ L 299, 16.11.2007, p.1.

Article 3
Conditions for exemption

1. Aid schemes fulfilling all the conditions of Chapter I of this Regulation, as well as the relevant provisions of Chapter II of this Regulation, shall be compatible with the common market within the meaning of Article [107(3)] of the Treaty and shall be exempt from the notification requirement of Article [108(3)] of the Treaty provided that any individual aid awarded under such scheme fulfils all the conditions of this Regulation, and the scheme contains an express reference to this Regulation, by citing its title and publication reference in the *Official Journal of the European Union*.

2. Individual aid granted under a scheme referred to in paragraph 1 shall be compatible with the common market within the meaning of Article [107(3)] of the Treaty and shall be exempt from the notification requirement of Article [108(3)] of the Treaty provided that the aid fulfils all the conditions of Chapter I of this Regulation, as well as the relevant provisions of Chapter II of this Regulation, and that the individual aid measure contains an express reference to the relevant provisions of this Regulation, by citing the relevant provisions, the title of this Regulation and its publication reference in the *Official Journal of the European Union*.

3. Ad hoc aid fulfilling all the conditions of Chapter I of this Regulation, as well as the relevant provisions of Chapter II of this Regulation, shall be compatible with the common market within the meaning of Article [107(3)] of the Treaty and shall be exempt from the notification requirement of Article [108(3)] of the Treaty provided that the aid contains an express reference to the relevant provisions of this Regulation, by citing the relevant provisions, the title of this Regulation and its publication reference in the *Official Journal of the European Union*.

Article 4
Aid intensity and eligible costs

Aid intensity and eligible costs

1. For the purposes of calculating aid intensity, all figures used shall be taken before any deduction of tax or other charge. Where aid is awarded in a form other than a grant, the aid amount shall be the grant equivalent of the aid. Aid payable in several instalments shall be discounted to its value at the moment of granting. The interest rate to be used for discounting purposes shall be the reference rate applicable at the time of grant.

2. In cases where aid is awarded by means of tax exemptions or reductions on future taxes due, subject to the respect of a certain aid intensity defined in gross grant equivalent, discounting of aid tranches shall take place on the basis of the reference rates applicable at the various times the tax advantages become effective.

3. The eligible costs shall be supported by documentary evidence which shall be clear and itemised.

Article 5
Transparency of aid

1. This Regulation shall apply only to transparent aid.

In particular, the following types of aid shall be considered to be transparent:

(a) aid comprised in grants and interest rate subsidies;

(b) aid comprised in loans, where the gross grant equivalent has been calculated on the basis of the reference rate prevailing at the time of the grant;

(c) aid comprised in guarantee schemes:

    (i) where the methodology to calculate the gross grant equivalent has been accepted following notification of this methodology to the Commission in the context of the application of this Regulation or Regulation (EC) No 1628/2006 and the approved methodology explicitly addresses the type of guarantees and the type of underlying transactions at stake; or

    (ii) where the beneficiary is a small or medium-sized enterprise and the gross grant equivalent has been calculated on the basis of the safe-harbour premiums laid down in the Commission Notice on the application of Articles [107 and 108 TFEU] to State aid in the form of guarantees;

(d) aid comprised in fiscal measures, where the measure provides for a cap ensuring that the applicable threshold is not exceeded.

2. The following categories of aid shall not be considered to be transparent:

(a) aid comprised in capital injections, without prejudice to the specific provisions concerning risk capital;

(b) aid comprised in risk capital measures, with the exception of aid fulfilling the conditions of Article 29.

3. Aid in the form of repayable advances shall be considered to be transparent aid only if the total amount of the repayable advance does not exceed the applicable thresholds under this Regulation. If the threshold is expressed in terms of aid intensity, the total amount of the repayable advance, expressed as a percentage of the eligible costs, shall not exceed the applicable aid intensity.

Commentary
Art 5: **B&C:** 17.070

Article 6
Individual notification thresholds

1. This Regulation shall not apply to any individual aid, whether granted ad hoc or on the basis of a scheme, the gross grant equivalent of which exceeds the following thresholds:

(a) SME investment and employment aid: EUR 7,5 million per undertaking per investment project;

(b) investment aid for environmental protection: EUR 7,5 million per undertaking per investment project;

(c) aid for consultancy in favour of SMEs: EUR 2 million per undertaking per project;

(d) aid for SME participation in fairs: EUR 2 million per undertaking per project;

(e) research and development project aid and feasibility studies:

    (i) if the project is predominantly fundamental research EUR 20 million per undertaking, per project/feasibility study;

    (ii) if the project is predominantly industrial research, EUR 10 million per undertaking, per project/feasibility study;

    (iii) for all other projects, EUR 7,5 million per undertaking, per project/feasibility study;

    (iv) if the project is a EUREKA project twice the amounts laid down in points (i), (ii) and (iii) respectively.

(f) aid for industrial property rights costs for SMEs: EUR 5 million per undertaking per project;

(g) training aid: EUR 2 million per training project;

(h) aid for the recruitment of disadvantaged workers: EUR 5 million per undertaking per year;

(i) aid for the employment of disabled workers in the form of wage costs: EUR 10 million per undertaking per year;

(j) aid compensating for additional costs of employing disabled workers: EUR 10 million per undertaking per year.

For the purposes of determining the appropriate threshold applicable to research and development project aid and feasibility studies pursuant to point (e), a project shall be considered to consist 'predominantly' of fundamental research or 'predominantly' of industrial research, if more than 50% of the eligible project costs are incurred through activities which fall within the category of fundamental research or industrial research respectively. In cases where the predominant character of the project cannot be established, the lower threshold shall apply.

2. Regional investment aid awarded in favour of large investment projects shall be notified to the Commission if the total amount of aid from all sources exceeds 75% of the maximum amount of aid an investment with eligible costs of EUR 100 million could receive, applying the standard aid threshold in force for large enterprises in the approved regional aid map on the date the aid is to be granted.

Commentary
Art 6: B&C: 17.070

Article 7
Cumulation

1. In determining whether the individual notification thresholds laid down in Article 6 and the maximum aid intensities laid down in Chapter II are respected, the total amount of public support measures for the aided activity or project shall be taken into account, regardless of whether that support is financed from local, regional, national or Community sources.

2. Aid exempted by this Regulation may be cumulated with any other aid exempted under this Regulation as long as those aid measures concern different identifiable eligible costs.

3. Aid exempted by this Regulation shall not be cumulated with any other aid exempted under this Regulation or de minimis aid fulfilling the conditions laid down in Commission Regulation (EC) No 1998/2006[1] or with other Community funding in relation to the same — partly or fully overlapping — eligible costs if such cumulation would result in exceeding the highest aid intensity or aid amount applicable to this aid under this Regulation.

4. By way of derogation from paragraph 3, aid in favour of disabled workers, as provided for in Articles 41 and 42, may be cumulated with aid exempted under this Regulation in relation to the same eligible costs above the highest applicable threshold under this Regulation, provided that such cumulation does not result in an aid intensity exceeding 100% of the relevant costs over any period for which the workers concerned are employed.

5. As regards the cumulation of aid measures exempted under this Regulation with identifiable eligible costs and aid measures exempted under this Regulation without identifiable eligible costs, the following conditions shall apply:

(a) where a target undertaking has received capital under a risk capital measure under Article 29 and subsequently applies, during the first three years after the first risk capital investment, for aid within the scope of this Regulation, the relevant aid thresholds or maximum eligible amounts under this Regulation shall be reduced by 50% in general and by 20% for target undertakings located in assisted areas; the reduction shall not exceed the total amount of risk capital received; this reduction shall not apply to aid for research, development and innovation exempted under Articles 31 to 37;

(b) during the first 3 years after being granted, aid for young innovative enterprises may not be cumulated with other aid exempted under this Regulation, with the only exception of aid exempted under Article 29 and aid exempted under Articles 31 to 37.

Notes
[1] OJ L 379, 28.12.2006, p.5.

Commentary
Art 7(3): F&N: 17.28, 17.185, 17.389

Part G State Aids

Article 8
Incentive effect

1. This Regulation shall exempt only aid which has an incentive effect.

2. Aid granted to SMEs, covered by this Regulation, shall be considered to have an incentive effect if, before work on the project or activity has started, the beneficiary has submitted an application for the aid to the Member State concerned.

3. Aid granted to large enterprises, covered by this Regulation, shall be considered to have an incentive effect if, in addition to fulfilling the condition laid down in paragraph 2, the Member State has verified, before granting the individual aid concerned, that documentation prepared by the beneficiary establishes one or more of the following criteria:

(a) a material increase in the size of the project/activity due to the aid;
(b) a material increase in the scope of the project/activity due to the aid;
(c) a material increase in the total amount spent by the beneficiary on the project/activity due to the aid;
(d) a material increase in the speed of completion of the project/activity concerned;
(e) as regards regional investment aid referred to in Article 13, that the project would not have been carried out as such in the assisted region concerned in the absence of the aid.

4. The conditions laid down in paragraphs 2 and 3 shall not apply in relation to fiscal measures if the following conditions are fulfilled:

(a) the fiscal measure establishes a legal right to aid in accordance with objective criteria and without further exercise of discretion by the Member State; and
(b) the fiscal measure has been adopted before work on the aided project or activity has started; this condition shall not apply in the case of fiscal successor schemes.

5. As regards aid compensating for the additional costs of employing disabled workers, as referred to in Article 42, the conditions laid down in paragraphs 2 and 3 of this Article shall be considered to be met if the conditions laid down in Article 42(3) are fulfilled.

As regards aid for the recruitment of disadvantaged workers in the form of wage subsidies and aid for the employment of disabled workers in the form of wage subsidies, as referred to in Articles 40 and 41, the conditions laid down in paragraphs 2 and 3 of this Article shall be considered to be met if the aid leads to a net increase in the number of disadvantaged/disabled workers employed.

As regards aid in the form of reductions in environmental taxes, as referred to in Article 25, the conditions laid down in paragraphs 2, 3 and 4 of this Article shall be considered to be met.

As regards aid in the form of risk capital, as referred to in Article 29, the conditions laid down in paragraph 2 of this Article shall be considered to be met.

6. If the conditions of paragraphs 2 and 3 are not fulfilled, the entire aid measure shall not be exempted under this Regulation.

Commentary
Art 8: B&C: 17.070

Article 9
Transparency

1. Within 20 working days following the entry into force of an aid scheme or the awarding of an ad hoc aid, which has been exempted pursuant to this Regulation, the Member State concerned shall forward to the Commission a summary of the information regarding such aid measure. That summary shall be provided in electronic form, via the established Commission IT application and in the form laid down in Annex III. The Commission shall acknowledge receipt of the summary without delay.

The summaries shall be published by the Commission in the *Official Journal of the European Union* and on the Commission's website.

2. Upon the entry into force of an aid scheme or the awarding of an ad hoc aid, which has been exempted pursuant to this Regulation, the Member State concerned shall publish on the internet the full text of such aid measure. In the case of an aid scheme, this text shall set out the conditions laid down in national law which ensure that the relevant provisions of this Regulation are complied with. The Member State concerned shall ensure that the full text of the aid measure is accessible on the internet as long as the aid measure concerned is in force. The summary information provided by the Member State concerned pursuant to paragraph 1 shall specify an internet address leading directly to the full text of the aid measure.

3. When granting individual aid exempted pursuant to this Regulation, with the exception of aid taking the form of fiscal measures, the act granting the aid shall contain an explicit reference to the specific provisions of Chapter II concerned by that act, to the national law which ensures that the relevant provisions of this Regulation are complied with and to the internet address leading directly to the full text of the aid measure.

4. Without prejudice to the obligations contained in paragraphs 1, 2 and 3, whenever individual aid is granted under an existing aid scheme for research and development projects covered by Article 31 and the individual aid exceeds EUR 3 million and whenever individual regional investment aid is granted, on the basis of an existing aid scheme for large investment projects, which is not individually notifiable pursuant to Article 6, the Member States shall, within 20 working days from the day on which the aid is granted by the competent authority, provide the Commission with the summary information requested in the standard form laid down in Annex II, via the established Commission IT application.

Commentary
Art 9: B&C: 17.070

Article 10
Monitoring

1. The Commission shall regularly monitor aid measures of which it has been informed pursuant to Article 9.

2. Member States shall maintain detailed records regarding any individual aid or aid scheme exempted under this Regulation. Such records shall contain all information necessary to establish that the conditions laid down in this Regulation are fulfilled, including information on the status of any undertaking whose entitlement to aid or a bonus depends on its status as an SME, information on the incentive effect of the aid and information making it possible to establish the precise amount of eligible costs for the purpose of applying this Regulation.

Records regarding individual aid shall be maintained for 10 years from the date on which the aid was granted. Records regarding an aid scheme shall be maintained for 10 years from the date on which the last aid was granted under such scheme.

3. On written request, the Member State concerned shall provide the Commission within a period of 20 working days or such longer period as may be fixed in the request, with all the information which the Commission considers necessary to monitor the application of this Regulation.

Where the Member State concerned does not provide the information requested within the period prescribed by the Commission or within a commonly agreed period, or where the Member State provides incomplete information, the Commission shall send a reminder setting a new deadline for the submission of the information. If, despite such reminder, the Member State concerned does not provide the information requested, the Commission may, after having provided the Member State concerned with the possibility to make its views known, adopt a decision stating that all or part of the future aid measures to which this Regulation applies are to be notified to the Commission in accordance with Article [108(3)] of the Treaty.

Article 11
Annual reporting

In accordance with Chapter III of Commission Regulation (EC) No 794/2004,[1] Member States shall compile a report in electronic form on the application of this Regulation in respect of each whole year or each part of the year during which this Regulation applies. The internet address leading directly to the full text of the aid measures shall also be included in such annual report.

Article 12
Specific conditions applicable to investment aid

1. In order to be considered an eligible cost for the purposes of this Regulation, an investment shall consist of the following:

(a) an investment in tangible and/or intangible assets relating to the setting-up of a new establishment, the extension of an existing establishment, diversification of the output of an establishment into new additional products or a fundamental change in the overall production process of an existing establishment; or

(b) the acquisition of the capital assets directly linked to an establishment, where the establishment has closed or would have closed had it not been purchased, and the assets are bought by an independent investor; in the case of business succession of a small enterprise in favour of family of the original owner(s) or in favour of former employees, the condition that the assets shall be bought by an independent investor shall be waived.

The sole acquisition of the shares of an undertaking shall not constitute investment.

2. In order to be considered eligible costs for the purposes of this Regulation, intangible assets shall fulfil all the following conditions:

(a) they must be used exclusively in the undertaking receiving the aid; as regards regional investment aid, they must be used exclusively in the establishment receiving the aid;

(b) they must be regarded as amortizable assets;

(c) they must be purchased from third parties under market conditions, without the acquirer being in a position to exercise control, within the meaning of Article 3 of Council Regulation (EC) No 139/2004 1, on the seller, vice versa; or

(d) in the case of SME investment aid, they must be included in the assets of the undertaking for at least three years; in the case of regional investment aid, they must be included in the assets of the undertaking and remain in the establishment receiving the aid for at least five years or, in the case of SMEs, at least three years.

3. In order to be considered an eligible cost for the purposes of this Regulation, employment directly created by an investment project shall fulfil all the following conditions:

(a) employment shall be created within three years of completion of the investment;

(b) the investment project shall lead to a net increase in the number of employees in the establishment concerned, compared with the average over the previous 12 months;

(c) the employment created shall be maintained during a minimum period of five years in the case of large enterprise and a minimum period of three years in case of SMEs.

Chapter II
Specific Provisions For The Different Categories of Aid

Section i
Regional Aid

Article 13
Regional investment and employment aid

1. Regional investment and employment aid schemes shall be compatible with the common market within the meaning of Article [107(3)] of the Treaty and shall be exempt from the notification requirement of Article [108(3)] of the Treaty, provided that the conditions laid down in this Article are fulfilled.

Ad hoc aid which is only used to supplement aid granted on the basis of regional investment and employment aid schemes and which does not exceed 50% of the total aid to be granted for the investment, shall be compatible with the common market within the meaning of Article [107(3)] of the Treaty and shall be exempt from the notification requirement of Article [108(3)] of the Treaty provided that the ad hoc aid awarded fulfils all the conditions of this Regulation.

2. The aid shall be granted in regions eligible for regional aid, as determined in the approved regional aid map for the Member State concerned for the period 2007–2013. The investment must be maintained in the recipient region for at least five years, or three years in the case of SMEs, after the whole investment has been completed. This shall not prevent the replacement of plant or equipment which has become outdated due to rapid technological change, provided that the economic activity is retained in the region concerned for the minimum period.

3. The aid intensity in present gross grant equivalent shall not exceed the regional aid threshold which is in force at the time the aid is granted in the assisted region concerned.

4. With the exception of aid granted in favour of large investment projects and regional aid for the transport sector, the thresholds fixed in paragraph 3 may be increased by 20 percentage points for aid awarded to small enterprises and by 10 percentage points for aid awarded to medium-sized enterprises.

5. The thresholds fixed in paragraph 3 shall apply to the intensity of the aid calculated either as a percentage of the investment's eligible tangible and intangible costs or as a percentage of the estimated wage costs of the person hired, calculated over a period of two years, for employment directly created by the investment project or a combination thereof, provided that the aid does not exceed the most favourable amount resulting from the application of either calculation.

6. Where the aid is calculated on the basis of tangible or intangible investment costs, or of acquisition costs in case of takeovers, the beneficiary must provide a financial contribution of at least 25% of the eligible costs, either through its own resources or by external financing, in a form which is free of any public support. However, where the maximum aid intensity approved under the national regional aid map for the Member State concerned, increased in accordance with paragraph 4, exceeds 75%, the financial contribution of the beneficiary is reduced accordingly. If the aid is calculated on the basis of tangible or intangible investment costs, the conditions set out in paragraph 7 shall also apply.

7. In the case of acquisition of an establishment, only the costs of buying assets from third parties shall be taken into consideration, provided that the transaction has taken place under market conditions. Where the acquisition is accompanied by other investment, the costs relating to the latter shall be added to the cost of the purchase.

Costs related to the acquisition of assets under lease, other than land and buildings, shall be taken into consideration only if the lease takes the form of financial leasing and contains an obligation to purchase the asset at the expiry of the term of the lease. For the lease of land and buildings, the lease must continue for at least five years after the anticipated date of the completion of the investment project or three years in the case of SMEs.

Except in the case of SMEs and takeovers, the assets acquired shall be new. In the case of takeovers, assets for the acquisition of which aid has already been granted prior to the purchase shall be deducted. For SMEs, the full costs of investments in intangible assets may also be taken into consideration. For large enterprises, such costs are eligible only up to a limit of 50% of the total eligible investment costs for the project.

8. Where the aid is calculated on the basis of wage costs, the employment shall be directly created by the investment project.

9. By way of derogation from paragraphs 3 and 4, the maximum aid intensities for investments in the processing and marketing of agricultural products may be set at:

(a) 50% of eligible investments in regions eligible under Article [107(3)(a)] of the Treaty and 40% of eligible investments in other regions eligible for regional aid, as determined in the regional aid map approved for the Member States concerned for the period 2007–2013, if the beneficiary is an SME;

(b) 25% of eligible investments in regions eligible under Article [107(3)(a)] of the Treaty and 20% of eligible investments in other regions eligible for regional aid, as determined in the regional aid map approved for the Member States concerned for the period 2007–2013, if the beneficiary has less than 750 employees and/or less than EUR 200 million turnover, calculated in accordance with Annex I to this Regulation.

10. In order to prevent a large investment being artificially divided into sub-projects, a large investment project shall be considered to be a single investment project when the investment is undertaken within a period of three years by the same undertaking or undertakings and consists of fixed assets combined in an economically indivisible way.

Article 14
Aid for newly created small enterprises

1. Aid schemes in favour of newly created small enterprises shall be compatible with the common market within the meaning of Article [107(3)] of the Treaty and shall be exempt from the notification requirement of Article [108(3)] of the Treaty, provided that the conditions laid down in paragraphs 2, 3 and 4 of this Article are fulfilled.

2. The beneficiary shall be a small enterprise.

3. The aid amount shall not exceed:

(a) EUR 2 million for small enterprises with their economic activity in regions eligible for the derogation provided for in Article [107(3)(a)] of the Treaty;

(b) EUR 1 million for small enterprises with their economic activity in regions eligible for the derogation provided for in Article [107(3)(c)] of the Treaty.

Annual amounts of aid per undertaking shall not exceed 33% of the amounts of aid laid down in points (a) and (b).

4. The aid intensity shall not exceed:

(a) in regions covered by Article [107(3)(a)] of the Treaty, 35% of eligible costs incurred in the first three years after the creation of the undertaking, and 25% in the two years thereafter;

(b) in regions covered by Article [107(3)(c)] of the Treaty, 25% of eligible costs incurred in the first three years after the creation of the undertaking, and 15% in the two years thereafter.

These intensities may be increased by 5% in regions covered by Article [107(3)(a)] of the Treaty with a gross domestic product (GDP) per capita of less than 60% of the EU-25 average, in regions with a population density of less than 12.5 inhabitants/km2 and in small islands with a population of less than 5 000 inhabitants, and other communities of the same size suffering from similar isolation.

5. The eligible costs shall be legal, advisory, consultancy and administrative costs directly related to the creation of the small enterprise, as well as the following costs, insofar as they are actually incurred within the first five years after the creation of the undertaking:

(a) interest on external finance and a dividend on own capital employed not exceeding the reference rate;

(b) fees for renting production facilities/equipment;

(c) energy, water, heating, taxes (other than VAT and corporate taxes on business income) and administrative charges;

(d) depreciation, fees for leasing production facilities/equipment as well as wage costs, provided that the underlying investments or job creation and recruitment measures have not benefited from other aid.

6. Small enterprises controlled by shareholders of undertakings that have closed down in the previous 12 months cannot benefit from aid under this Article if the enterprises concerned are active in the same relevant market or in adjacent markets.

SECTION 2
SME Investment and Employment Aid

Article 15
SME investment and employment aid

1. SME investment and employment aid shall be compatible with the common market within the meaning of Article [107(3)] of the Treaty and shall be exempt from the notification requirement of Article [108(3)] of the Treaty, provided that the conditions laid down in paragraphs 2, 3 and 4 of this Article are fulfilled.

2. The aid intensity shall not exceed:

(a) 20% of the eligible costs in the case of small enterprises;
(b) 10% of the eligible costs in the case of medium-sized enterprises.

3. The eligible costs shall be the following:

(a) the costs of investment in tangible and intangible assets; or
(b) the estimated wage costs of employment directly created by the investment project, calculated over a period of two years.

4. Where the investment concerns the processing and marketing of agricultural products, the aid intensity shall not exceed:

(a) 75% of eligible investments in the outermost regions;
(b) 65% of eligible investments in the smaller Aegean Islands within the meaning of Council Regulation (EC) No 1405/2006;[1]
(c) 50% of eligible investments in regions eligible under Article [107(3)(a)] of the Treaty;
(d) 40% of eligible investments in all other regions.

Notes
[1] OJ L 265, 26.9.2006, p.1.

SECTION 3
Aid for Female Entrepreneurship

Article 16
Aid for small enterprises newly created by female entrepreneurs

1. Aid schemes in favour of small enterprises newly created by female entrepreneurs shall be compatible with the common market within the meaning of Article [107(3)] of the Treaty and shall be exempt from the notification requirement of Article [108(3)] of the Treaty, provided that the conditions laid down in paragraphs 2 to 5 of this Article are fulfilled.

2. The beneficiaries shall be small enterprises newly created by female entrepreneurs.

3. The aid amount shall not exceed EUR 1 million per undertaking.

Annual amounts of aid per undertaking shall not exceed 33% of the amounts of aid laid down in the first subparagraph.

4. The aid intensity shall not exceed 15% of eligible costs incurred in the first five years after the creation of the undertaking.

5. The eligible costs shall be legal, advisory, consultancy and administrative costs directly related to the creation of the small enterprise, as well as the following costs, insofar as they are actually incurred within the first five years of the creation of the undertaking:

(a) interest on external finance and a dividend on own capital employed not exceeding the reference rate;

(b) fees for renting production facilities/equipment;

(c) energy, water, heating, taxes (other than VAT and corporate taxes on business income) and administrative charges;

(d) depreciation, fees for leasing production facilities/equipment as well as wage costs, provided that the underlying investments or job creation and recruitment measures have not benefited from other aid;

(e) child care and parent care costs including, where applicable, costs relating to parental leave.

6. Small enterprises controlled by shareholders of undertakings that have closed down in the previous 12 months cannot benefit from aid under this Article if the enterprises concerned are active in the same relevant market or in adjacent markets.

SECTION 4

Aid for Environmental Protection

Article 17

Definitions

For the purposes of this Section, the following definitions shall apply:

1. 'environmental protection' means any action designed to remedy or prevent damage to physical surroundings or natural resources by the beneficiary's own activities, to reduce risk of such damage or to lead to a more efficient use of natural resources, including energy saving measures and the use of renewable sources of energy;

2. 'energy saving measures' mean action which enables undertakings to reduce the amount of energy used notably in their production cycle;

3. 'Community standard' means:
   (a) a mandatory Community standard setting the levels to be attained in environmental terms by individual undertakings; or
   (b) the obligation under Directive 2008/1/EC of the European Parliament and of the Council[1] to use the best available techniques as set out in the most recent relevant information published by the Commission pursuant to Article 17(2) of that Directive;

4. 'renewable energy sources' means the following renewable non fossil energy sources: wind, solar, geothermal, wave, tidal, hydropower installations, biomass, landfill gas, sewage treatment plant gas and biogases;

5. 'biofuels' means liquid or gaseous fuel for transport produced from biomass;

6. 'sustainable biofuels' means biofuels fulfilling the sustainability criteria set out in Article 15 of the proposal for a Directive of the European Parliament and the Council on the promotion of the use of energy from renewable sources;[2] once the Directive has been adopted by the European Parliament and the Council and published in the *Official Journal of the European Union*, the sustainability criteria laid down in the Directive shall apply;

7. 'energy from renewable energy sources' means energy produced by plants using only renewable energy sources, as well as the share in terms of calorific value of energy produced from renewable energy sources in hybrid plants C which also use conventional energy sources; it includes renewable electricity used for filling storage systems, but excludes electricity produced as a result of storage systems;

8. 'cogeneration' means the simultaneous generation in one process of thermal energy and electrical and/or mechanical energy;

9. 'high efficiency cogeneration' means cogeneration meeting the criteria of Annex III to Directive 2004/8/EC of the European Parliament and of the Council[3] and satisfying the harmonised efficiency reference values established by Commission Decision 2007/74/EC;[4]

10. 'environmental tax' means a tax whose specific tax base has a clear negative effect on the environment or which seeks to tax certain activities, goods or services so that the environmental costs may be included in their price and/or so that producers and consumers are oriented towards activities which better respect the environment;

1436

11. 'Community minimum tax level' means the minimum level of taxation provided for in Community legislation; for energy products and electricity, the Community minimum tax level means the minimum level of taxation laid down in Annex I to Directive 2003/96/EC;
12. 'tangible assets' means investments in land which are strictly necessary in order to meet environmental objectives, investments in buildings, plant and equipment intended to reduce or eliminate pollution and nuisances, and investments to adapt production methods with a view to protecting the environment.

Notes
[1] OJ L 24, 29.1.2008, p.8.
[2] COM(2008) 19 final.
[3] OJ L 52, 21.2.2004, p.50.
[4] OJ L 32, 6.2.2007, p.183.

Article 18
Investment aid enabling undertakings to go beyond Community standards for environmental protection or increase the level of environmental protection in the absence of Community standards

1. Investment aid enabling undertakings to go beyond Community standards for environmental protection or increase the level of environmental protection in the absence of Community standards shall be compatible with the common market within the meaning of Article [107(3)] of the Treaty and shall be exempt from the notification requirement of Article [108(3)] of the Treaty, provided that the conditions laid down in paragraphs 2 to 8 of this Article are fulfilled.

2. The aided investment shall fulfil one of the following conditions:

(a) the investment shall enable the beneficiary to increase the level of environmental protection resulting from its activities by going beyond the applicable Community standards, irrespective of the presence of mandatory national standards that are more stringent than the Community standards;
(b) the investment shall enable the beneficiary to increase the level of environmental protection resulting from its activities in the absence of Community standards.

3. Aid may not be granted where improvements are to ensure that companies comply with Community standards already adopted and not yet in force.

4. The aid intensity shall not exceed 35% of the eligible costs.

However, the aid intensity may be increased by 20 percentage points for aid awarded to small enterprises and by 10 percentage points for aid awarded to medium sized enterprises.

5. The eligible costs shall be the extra investment costs necessary to achieve a level of environmental protection higher than the level required by the Community standards concerned, without taking account of operating benefits and operating costs.

6. For the purposes of paragraph 5, the cost of the investment directly related to environmental protection shall be established by reference to the counterfactual situation:

(a) where the cost of investing in environmental protection can be easily identified in the total investment cost, this precise environmental protection related cost shall constitute the eligible costs;
(b) in all other cases, the extra investment costs shall be established by comparing the investment with the counterfactual situation in the absence of State aid; the correct counterfactual shall be the cost of a technically comparable investment that provides a lower degree of environmental protection (corresponding to mandatory Community standards, if they exist) and that would credibly be realised without aid ('reference investment'); technically comparable investment means an investment with the same production capacity and all other technical characteristics (except those directly related to the extra investment for environmental protection); in addition, such a reference investment must, from a business point of view, be a credible alternative to the investment under assessment.

7. The eligible investment shall take the form of investment in tangible assets and/or in intangible assets.

Part G State Aids

8. In the case of investments aiming at obtaining a level of environmental protection higher than Community standards, the counterfactual shall be chosen as follows:

(a) where the undertaking is adapting to national standards adopted in the absence of Community standards, the eligible costs shall consist of the additional investment costs necessary to achieve the level of environmental protection required by the national standards;

(b) where the undertaking adapts to or goes beyond national standards which are more stringent than the relevant Community standards or goes beyond Community standards, the eligible costs shall consist of the additional investment costs necessary to achieve a level of environmental protection higher than the level required by the Community standards. The cost of investments needed to reach the level of protection required by the Community standards shall not be eligible;

(c) where no standards exist, the eligible costs shall consist of the investment costs necessary to achieve a higher level of environmental protection than that which the undertaking or undertakings in question would achieve in the absence of any environmental aid.

9. Aid for investments relating to the management of waste of other undertakings shall not be exempted under this Article.

Article 19
Aid for the acquisition of new transport vehicles which go beyond Community standards or which increase the level of environmental protection in the absence of Community standards

1. Investment aid for the acquisition of new transport vehicles enabling undertakings active in the transport sector to go beyond Community standards for environmental protection or increase the level of environmental protection in the absence of Community standards shall be compatible with the common market within the meaning of Article [107(3)] of the Treaty and shall be exempt from the notification requirement of Article [108(3)] of the Treaty, provided that the conditions laid down in paragraphs 2, 3 and 4 of this Article are fulfilled.

2. The aided investment shall fulfil the condition laid down in Article 18(2).

3. Aid for the acquisition of new transport vehicles for road, railway, inland waterway and maritime transport complying with adopted Community standards shall be exempted, when such acquisition occurs before these Community standards enter into force and where, once mandatory, they do not apply retroactively to vehicles already purchased.

4. Aid for retrofitting operations of existing transport vehicles with an environmental protection objective shall be exempted if the existing means of transport are upgraded to environmental standards that were not yet in force at the date of entry into operation of those means of transport or if the means of transport are not subject to any environmental standards.

5. The aid intensity shall not exceed 35% of the eligible costs.

However, the aid intensity may be increased by 20 percentage points for aid awarded to small enterprises and by 10 percentage points for aid awarded to medium sized enterprises.

6. The eligible costs shall be the extra investment costs necessary to achieve a level of environmental protection higher than the level required by the Community standards.

The eligible costs shall be calculated as set out in Article 18(6) and (7) and without taking account of operating benefits and operating costs.

Article 20
Aid for early adaptation to future Community standards for SMEs

1. Aid allowing SMEs to comply with new Community standards which increase the level of environmental protection and are not yet in force shall be compatible with the common market within the meaning of Article [107(3)] of the Treaty and shall be exempt from the notification requirement of Article [108(3)] of the Treaty, provided that the conditions laid down in paragraphs 2, 3 and 4 of this Article are fulfilled.

2. The Community standards shall have been adopted and the investment shall be implemented and finalised at least one year before the date of entry into force of the standard concerned.

3. The aid intensity shall not exceed 15% of the eligible costs for small enterprises and 10% of the eligible costs for medium sized enterprises if the implementation and finalisation take place more than three years before the date of entry into force of the standard and 10% for small enterprises if the implementation and finalisation take place between one and three years before the date of entry into force of the standard.

4. The eligible costs shall be the extra investment costs necessary to achieve the level of environmental protection required by the Community standard compared to the existing level of environmental protection required prior to the entry into force of this standard.

The eligible costs shall be calculated as set out in Article 18(6) and (7) and without taking account of operating benefits and operating costs.

Article 21
Environmental investment aid for energy saving measures

1. Environmental investment aid enabling undertakings to achieve energy savings shall be compatible with the common market within the meaning of Article [107(3)] of the Treaty and shall be exempt from the notification requirement of Article [108(3)] of the Treaty, provided that it meets:

(a) the conditions laid down in paragraphs 2 and 3 of this Article; or
(b) the conditions laid down in paragraphs 4 and 5 thereof.

2. The aid intensity shall not exceed 60% of the eligible costs.

However, the aid intensity may be increased by 20 percentage points for aid awarded to small enterprises and by 10 percentage points for aid awarded to medium sized enterprises.

3. The eligible costs shall be the extra investment costs necessary to achieve energy savings beyond the level required by the Community standards.

The eligible costs shall be calculated as set out in Article 18(6) and (7).

The eligible costs shall be calculated net of any operating benefits and costs related to the extra investment for energy saving and arising during the first three years of the life of this investment in the case of SMEs, the first four years in the case of large undertakings that are not part of the EU CO_2 Emission Trading System and the first five years in the case of large undertakings that are part of the EU CO_2 Emission Trading System. For large undertakings this period may be reduced to the first three years of the life of this investment where the depreciation time of the investment can be demonstrated not to exceed three years.

The eligible cost calculations shall be certified by an external auditor.

4. The aid intensity shall not exceed 20% of the eligible costs.

However, the aid intensity may be increased by 20 percentage points for aid awarded to small enterprises and by 10 percentage points for aid awarded to medium sized enterprises.

5. The eligible costs shall be calculated as set out in Article 18(6) and (7) and without taking account of operating benefits and operating costs.

Article 22
Environmental investment aid for high efficiency cogeneration

1. Environmental investment aid for high efficiency cogeneration shall be compatible with the common market within the meaning of Article [107(3)] of the Treaty and shall be exempt from the notification requirement of Article [108(3)] of the Treaty, provided that the conditions laid down in paragraphs 2, 3 and 4 of this Article are fulfilled.

2. The aid intensity shall not exceed 45% of the eligible costs.

However, the aid intensity may be increased by 20 percentage points for aid awarded to small enterprises and by 10 percentage points for aid awarded to medium sized enterprises.

3. The eligible costs shall be the extra investment costs necessary to realise a high efficiency cogeneration plant as compared to the reference investment. The eligible costs shall be calculated as set out in Article 18(6) and (7) and without taking account of operating benefits and operating costs.

4. A new cogeneration unit shall overall make primary energy savings compared to separate production as provided for by Directive 2004/8/EC and Decision 2007/74/EC. The improvement of an existing cogeneration unit or conversion of an existing power generation unit into a cogeneration unit shall result in primary energy savings compared to the original situation.

Article 23
Environmental investment aid for the promotion of energy from renewable energy sources

1. Environmental investment aid for the promotion of energy from renewable energy sources shall be compatible with the common market within the meaning of Article [107(3)] of the Treaty and shall be exempt from the notification requirement of Article [108(3)] of the Treaty, provided that the conditions laid down in paragraphs 2, 3 and 4 of this Article are fulfilled.

2. The aid intensity shall not exceed 45% of the eligible costs.

However, the aid intensity may be increased by 20 percentage points for aid awarded to small enterprises and by 10 percentage points for aid awarded to medium sized enterprises.

3. The eligible costs shall be the extra costs borne by the beneficiary compared with a conventional power plant or with a conventional heating system with the same capacity in terms of the effective production of energy.

The eligible costs shall be calculated as set out in Article 18(6) and (7) and without taking account of operating benefits and operating costs.

4. Environmental investment aid for the production of biofuels shall be exempted only to the extent the aided investments are used exclusively for the production of sustainable biofuels.

Article 24
Aid for environmental studies

1. Aid for studies directly linked to investments referred to in Article 18, investments in energy saving measures under the conditions set out in Article 21 and investments for the promotion of energy from renewable energy sources under the conditions set out in Article 23 shall be compatible with the common market within the meaning of Article [107(3)] of the Treaty and shall be exempt from the notification requirement of Article [108(3)] of the Treaty provided that the conditions laid down in paragraphs 2 and 3 of this Article are fulfilled.

2. The aid intensity shall not exceed 50% of the eligible costs.

However, the aid intensity may be increased by 20 percentage points for studies undertaken on behalf of small enterprises and by 10 percentage points for studies undertaken on behalf of medium sized enterprises.

3. The eligible costs shall be the costs of the study.

Article 25
Aid in the form of reductions in environmental taxes

1. Environmental aid schemes in the form of reductions in environmental taxes fulfilling the conditions of Directive 2003/96/EC shall be compatible with the common market within the meaning of Article [107(3)] of the Treaty and shall be exempt from the notification requirement of Article [108(3)] of the Treaty, provided the conditions laid down in paragraphs 2 and 3 of this Article are fulfilled.

2. The beneficiaries of the tax reduction shall pay at least the Community minimum tax level set by Directive 2003/96/EC.

3. Tax reductions shall be granted for maximum periods of ten years. After such 10 year period, Member States shall reevaluate the appropriateness of the aid measures concerned.

Section 5
Aid for Consultancy in Favour of SMEs and SME participation in Fairs

Article 26
Aid for consultancy in favour of SMEs

1. Aid for consultancy in favour of SMEs shall be compatible with the common market within the meaning of Article [107(3)] of the Treaty and shall be exempt from the notification requirement of Article [108(3)] of the Treaty, provided that the conditions laid down in paragraphs 2 and 3 of this Article are fulfilled.

2. The aid intensity shall not exceed 50% of the eligible costs.

3. The eligible costs shall be the consultancy costs of services provided by outside consultants.

The services concerned shall not be a continuous or periodic activity nor relate to the undertaking's usual operating costs, such as routine tax consultancy services, regular legal services or advertising.

Article 27
Aid for SME participation in fairs

1. Aid to SMEs for participation in fairs shall be compatible with the common market within the meaning of Article [107(3)] of the Treaty and shall be exempt from the notification requirement of Article [108(3)] of the Treaty provided the conditions laid down in paragraphs 2 and 3 of this Article are fulfilled.

2. The aid intensity shall not exceed 50% of the eligible costs.

3. The eligible costs shall be the costs incurred for renting, setting up and running the stand for the first participation of an undertaking in any particular fair or exhibition.

Section 6
Aid in the Form of Risk Capital

Article 28
Definitions

For the purposes of this section, the following definitions shall apply:

1. 'equity' means ownership interest in an undertaking, represented by the shares issued to investors;

2. 'quasi equity' means financial instruments whose return for the holder is predominantly based on the profits or losses of the underlying target undertaking and which are unsecured in the event of default;

3. 'private equity' means private — as opposed to public — equity or quasi equity investment in undertakings not listed on a stock market, including venture capital;

4. 'seed capital' means financing provided to study, assess and develop an initial concept, preceding the start up phase;

5. 'start up capital' means financing provided to undertakings, which have not sold their product or service commercially and are not yet generating a profit for product development and initial marketing;

6. 'expansion capital' means financing provided for the growth and expansion of an undertaking, which may or may not break even or trade profitably, for the purposes of increasing production capacity, market or product development or the provision of additional working capital;

7. 'exit strategy' means a strategy for the liquidation of holdings by a venture capital or private equity fund in accordance with a plan to achieve maximum return, including trade sale, write offs, repayment of preference shares/loans, sale to another venture capitalist, sale to a financial institution and sale by public offering, including Initial Public Offerings;

8. 'target undertaking' means an undertaking in which an investor or investment fund is considering investing.

Article 29
Aid in the form of risk capital

1. Risk capital aid schemes in favour of SMEs shall be compatible with the common market within the meaning of Article [107(3)] of the Treaty and shall be exempt from the notification requirement of Article [108(3)] of the Treaty, provided the conditions laid down in paragraphs 2 to 8 of this Article are fulfilled.

2. The risk capital measure shall take the form of participation into a profit driven private equity investment fund, managed on a commercial basis.

3. The tranches of investment to be made by the investment fund shall not exceed EUR 1,5 million per target undertaking over any period of twelve months.

4. For SMEs located in assisted areas, as well as for small enterprises located in non assisted areas, the risk capital measure shall be restricted to providing seed capital, start up capital and/or expansion capital. For medium sized enterprises located in non assisted areas, the risk capital measure shall be restricted to providing seed capital and/or start up capital, to the exclusion of expansion capital.

5. The investment fund shall provide at least 70% of its total budget invested into target SMEs in the form of equity or quasiequity.

6. At least 50% of the funding of the investment funds shall be provided by private investors. In the case of investment funds targeting exclusively SMEs located in assisted areas, at least 30% of the funding shall be provided by private investors.

7. To ensure that the risk capital measure is profit driven, the following conditions shall be fulfilled:

(a) a business plan shall exist for each investment, containing details of product, sales and profitability development and establishing the ex ante viability of the project; and

(b) a clear and realistic exit strategy shall exist for each investment.

8. To ensure that the investment fund is managed on a commercial basis, the following conditions shall be fulfilled:

(a) there shall be an agreement between a professional fund manager and participants in the fund, providing that the manager's remuneration is linked to performance and setting out the objectives of the fund and proposed timing of investments; and

(b) private investors shall be represented in decision making, such as through an investors' or advisory committee; and

(c) best practices and regulatory supervision shall apply to the management of funds.

Section 7
Aid for Research and Development and Innovation

Article 30
Definitions

For the purposes of this section, the following definitions shall apply:

1. 'research organisation' means an entity, such as a university or research institute, irrespective of its legal status (organised under public or private law) or way of financing, whose primary goal is to conduct fundamental research, industrial research or experimental development and to disseminate their its results by way of teaching, publication or technology transfer; all profits must be reinvested in these activities, the dissemination of their results or teaching; undertakings that can exert influence upon such an organisation, for instance in their capacity as shareholders or members of the organisation, shall enjoy no preferential access to the research capacities of such an organisation or to the research results generated by it;

2. 'fundamental research' means experimental or theoretical work undertaken primarily to acquire new knowledge of the underlying foundations of phenomena and observable facts, without any direct practical application or use in view;

3. 'industrial research' means the planned research or critical investigation aimed at the acquisition of new knowledge and skills for developing new products, processes or services or for bringing about a

significant improvement in existing products, processes or services. It comprises the creation of components parts to complex systems, which is necessary for the industrial research, notably for generic technology validation, to the exclusion of prototypes;

4. 'experimental development' means the acquiring, combining, shaping and using existing scientific, technological, business and other relevant knowledge and skills for the purpose of producing plans and arrangements or designs for new, altered or improved products, processes or services. These may also include, for instance, other activities aiming at the conceptual definition, planning and documentation of new products, processes or services. Those activities may comprise producing drafts, drawings, plans and other documentation, provided that they are not intended for commercial use;

The development of commercially usable prototypes and pilot projects is also included where the prototype is necessarily the final commercial product and where it is too expensive to produce for it to be used only for demonstration and validation purposes. In case of a subsequent commercial use of demonstration or pilot projects, any revenue generated from such use must be deducted from the eligible costs.

The experimental production and testing of products, processes and services shall also be eligible, provided that these cannot be used or transformed to be used in industrial applications or commercially.

Experimental development shall not include routine or periodic changes made to products, production lines, manufacturing processes, existing services and other operations in progress, even if such changes may represent improvements;

5. 'highly qualified personnel' means researchers, engineers, designers and marketing managers with tertiary education degree and at least 5 years of relevant professional experience; doctoral training may count as relevant professional experience;

6. 'secondment' means temporary employment of personnel by a beneficiary during a period of time, after which the personnel has the right to return to its previous employer.

Article 31
Aid for research and development projects

1. Aid for research and development projects shall be compatible with the common market within the meaning of Article [107(3)] of the Treaty and shall be exempt from the notification requirement of Article [108(3)] of the Treaty provided that the conditions laid down in paragraphs 2 to 5 of this Article are fulfilled.

2. The aided part of the research and development project shall completely fall within one or more of the following research categories:

(a) fundamental research;
(b) industrial research;
(c) experimental development.

When a project encompasses different tasks, each task shall be qualified as falling under one of the categories listed in the first subparagraph or as not falling under any of those categories.

3. The aid intensity shall not exceed:

(a) 100% of the eligible costs for fundamental research;
(b) 50% of the eligible costs for industrial research;
(c) 25% of the eligible costs for experimental development.

The aid intensity shall be established for each beneficiary of aid, including in a collaboration project, as provided in paragraph 4(b)(i).

In the case of aid for a research and development project being carried out in collaboration between research organisations and undertakings, the combined aid deriving from direct government support for a specific project and, where they constitute aid, contributions from research organisations to that project may not exceed the applicable aid intensities for each beneficiary undertaking.

4. The aid intensities set for industrial research and experimental development in paragraph 3 may be increased as follows:

(a) where the aid is granted to SMEs, the aid intensity may be increased by 10 percentage points for medium sized enterprises and by 20 percentage points for small enterprises; and

(b) a bonus of 15 percentage points may be added, up to a maximum aid intensity of 80% of the eligible costs, if:

    (i) the project involves effective collaboration between at least two undertakings which are independent of each other and the following conditions are fulfilled:

        — no single undertaking bears more than 70% of the eligible costs of the collaboration project,

        — the project involves collaboration with at least one SME or is carried out in at least two different Member States, or

    (ii) the project involves effective collaboration between an undertaking and a research organisation and the following conditions are fulfilled:

        — the research organisation bears at least 10% of the eligible project costs, and

        — the research organisation has the right to publish the results of the research projects insofar as they stem from research carried out by that organisation, or

    (iii) in the case of industrial research, the results of the project are widely disseminated through technical and scientific conferences or through publication in scientific or technical journals or in open access repositories (databases where raw research data can be accessed by anyone), or through free or open source software.

For the purposes of point (b)(i) and (ii) of the first subparagraph, subcontracting shall not be considered to be effective collaboration.

5. The eligible costs shall be the following:

(a) personnel costs (researchers, technicians and other supporting staff to the extent employed on the research project);

(b) costs of instruments and equipment to the extent and for the period used for the research project; if such instruments and equipment are not used for their full life for the research project, only the depreciation costs corresponding to the life of the research project, as calculated on the basis of good accounting practice, shall be considered eligible;

(c) costs for buildings and land, to the extent and for the duration used for the research project; with regard to buildings, only the depreciation costs corresponding to the life of the research project, as calculated on the basis of good accounting practice shall be considered eligible; for land, costs of commercial transfer or actually incurred capital costs shall be eligible;

(d) cost of contractual research, technical knowledge and patents bought or licensed from outside sources at market prices, where the transaction has been carried out at arm's length and there is no element of collusion involved, as well as costs of consultancy and equivalent services used exclusively for the research activity;

(e) additional overheads incurred directly as a result of the research project;

(f) other operating costs, including costs of materials, supplies and similar products incurred directly as a result of the research activity.

6. All eligible costs shall be allocated to a specific category of research and development.

Article 32
Aid for technical feasibility studies

1. Aid for technical feasibility studies preparatory to industrial research or experimental development activities shall be compatible with the common market within the meaning of Article [107(3)] of the Treaty and shall be exempt from the notification requirement of Article [108(3)] of the Treaty, provided that the conditions laid down in paragraphs 2 and 3 of this Article are fulfilled.

2. The aid intensity shall not exceed:

(a) for SMEs, 75% of the eligible costs for studies preparatory to industrial research activities and 50% of the eligible costs for studies preparatory to experimental development activities;

(b) for large enterprises, 65% of the eligible costs for studies preparatory to industrial research activities and 40% of the eligible costs for studies preparatory to experimental development activities.

3. The eligible costs shall be the costs of the study.

Article 33
Aid for industrial property rights costs for SMEs

1. Aid to SMEs for the costs associated with obtaining and validating patents and other industrial property rights shall be compatible with the common market within the meaning of Article [107(3)] of the Treaty and shall be exempt from the notification requirement of Article [108(3)] of the Treaty, provided the conditions laid down in paragraphs 2 and 3 of this Article are fulfilled.

2. The aid intensity shall not exceed the intensity for research and development project aid laid down in Article 31(3) and (4), in respect of the research activities which first led to the industrial property rights concerned.

3. The eligible costs shall be the following:

(a) all costs preceding the grant of the right in the first jurisdiction, including costs relating to the preparation, filing and prosecution of the application as well as costs incurred in renewing the application before the right has been granted;

(b) translation and other costs incurred in order to obtain the granting or validation of the right in other legal jurisdictions;

(c) costs incurred in defending the validity of the right during the official prosecution of the application and possible opposition proceedings, even if such costs occur after the right is granted.

Article 34
Aid for research and development in the agricultural and fisheries sectors

1. Aid for research and development concerning products listed in Annex I to the Treaty shall be compatible with the common market within the meaning of Article [107(3)] of the Treaty and shall be exempt from the notification requirement of Article [108(3)] of the Treaty, provided that the conditions laid down in paragraphs 2 to 7 of this Article are fulfilled.

2. The aid shall be of interest to all operators in the particular sector or sub sector concerned.

3. Information that research will be carried out, and with which goal, shall be published on the internet, prior to the commencement of the research. An approximate date of expected results and their place of publication on the internet, as well as a mention that the result will be available at no cost, must be included.

The results of the research shall be made available on internet, for a period of at least 5 years. They shall be published no later than any information which may be given to members of any particular organisation.

4. Aid shall be granted directly to the research organisation and must not involve the direct granting of non research related aid to a company producing, processing or marketing agricultural products, nor provide price support to producers of such products.

5. The aid intensity shall not exceed 100% of the eligible costs.

6. The eligible costs shall be those provided in Article 31(5).

7. Aid for research and development concerning products listed in Annex I to the Treaty and not fulfilling the conditions laid down in this Article shall be compatible with the common market within the meaning of Article [107(3)(c)] of the Treaty and shall be exempt from the notification requirement of Article [108(3)] of the Treaty, provided the conditions laid down in Articles 30, 31 and 32 of this Regulation are fulfilled.

Article 35
Aid to young innovative enterprises

1. Aid to young innovative enterprises shall be compatible with the common market within the meaning of Article [107(3)] of the Treaty and shall be exempt from the notification requirement of

Article [108(3)] of the Treaty, provided that the conditions laid down in paragraphs 2 to 5 of this Article are fulfilled.

2. The beneficiary shall be a small enterprise that has been in existence for less than 6 years at the time when the aid is granted.

3. The research and development costs of the beneficiary shall represent at least 15% of its total operating costs in at least one of the three years preceding the granting of the aid or, in the case of a start up enterprise without any financial history, in the audit of its current fiscal period, as certified by an external auditor.

4. The aid amount shall not exceed EUR 1 million.

However, the aid amount shall not exceed EUR 1,5 million in regions eligible for the derogation provided for in Article [107(3)(a)] of the Treaty, and EUR 1,25 million in regions eligible for the derogation provided for in Article [107(3)(c)] of the Treaty.

5. The beneficiary may receive the aid only once during the period in which it qualifies as a young innovative enterprise.

Article 36
Aid for innovation advisory services and for innovation support services

1. Aid for innovation advisory services and for innovation support services shall be compatible with the common market within the meaning of Article [107(3)] of the Treaty and shall be exempt from the notification requirement of Article [108(3)] of the Treaty, provided that the conditions laid down in paragraphs 2 to 6 of this Article are fulfilled.

2. The beneficiary shall be an SME.

3. The aid amount shall not exceed a maximum of EUR 200 000 per beneficiary within any three year period.

4. The service provider shall benefit from a national or European certification. If the service provider does not benefit from a national or European certification, the aid intensity shall not exceed 75% of the eligible costs.

5. The beneficiary must use the aid to buy the services at market price, or if the service provider is a non for profit entity, at a price which reflects its full costs plus a reasonable margin.

6. The eligible costs shall be the following:

(a) as regards innovation advisory services, the costs relating to: management consulting, technological assistance, technology transfer services, training, consultancy for acquisition, protection and trade in Intellectual Property Rights and for licensing agreements, consultancy on the use of standards;

(b) as regards innovation support services, the costs relating to: office space, data banks, technical libraries, market research, use of laboratory, quality labelling, testing and certification.

Article 37
Aid for the loan of highly qualified personnel

1. Aid for the loan of highly qualified personnel seconded from a research organisation or a large enterprise to an SME shall be compatible with the common market within the meaning of Article [107(3)] of the Treaty and shall be exempt from the notification requirement of Article [108(3)] of the Treaty, provided that the conditions laid down in paragraphs 2 to 5 of this Article are fulfilled.

2. The seconded personnel must not be replacing other personnel, but must be employed in a newly created function within the beneficiary undertaking and must have been employed for at least two years in the research organisation or the large enterprise, which is sending the personnel on secondment.

The seconded personnel must work on research and development and innovation activities within the SME receiving the aid.

3. The aid intensity shall not exceed 50% of the eligible costs, for a maximum of 3 years per undertaking and per person borrowed.

4. The eligible costs shall be all personnel costs for borrowing and employing highly qualified personnel, including the costs of using a recruitment agency and of paying a mobility allowance for the seconded personnel.

5. This Article shall not apply to consultancy costs as referred to in Article 26.

SECTION 8
Training Aid

Article 38
Definitions

For the purposes of this Section, the following definitions shall apply:

1. 'specific training' means training involving tuition directly and principally applicable to the employee's present or future position in the undertaking and providing qualifications which are not or only to a limited extent transferable to other undertakings or fields of work;

2. 'general training' means training involving tuition which is not applicable only or principally to the employee's present or future position in the undertaking, but which provides qualifications that are largely transferable to other undertakings or fields of work. Training shall be considered 'general' if, for example:

(a) it is jointly organised by different independent undertakings or where employees of different undertakings may avail themselves of the training;

(b) it is recognised, certified or validated by public authorities or bodies or by other bodies or institutions on which a Member State or the Community has conferred the necessary powers.

Article 39
Training aid

1. Training aid shall be compatible with the common market within the meaning of Article [107(3)] of the Treaty and shall be exempt from the notification requirement of Article [108(3)] of the Treaty, provided that the conditions laid down in paragraphs 2, 3 and 4 of this Article are fulfilled.

2. The aid intensity shall not exceed:

(a) 25% of the eligible costs for specific training; and
(b) 60% of the eligible costs for general training.

However, the aid intensity may be increased, up to a maximum aid intensity of 80% of the eligible costs, as follows:

(a) by 10 percentage points if the training is given to disabled or disadvantaged workers;
(b) by 10 percentage points if the aid is awarded to medium-sized enterprises and by 20 percentage points if the aid is awarded to small enterprises.

Where the aid is granted in the maritime transport sector, it may reach an intensity of 100% of the eligible costs, whether the training project concerns specific or general training, provided that the following conditions are met:

(a) the trainee shall not be an active member of the crew but shall be supernumerary on board; and
(b) the training shall be carried out on board ships entered on Community registers.

3. In cases where the aid project involves both specific and general training components which cannot be separated for the calculation of the aid intensity, and in cases where the specific or general character of the training aid project cannot be established, the aid intensities applicable to specific training shall apply.

4. The eligible costs of a training aid project shall be:

(a) trainers' personnel costs;
(b) trainers' and trainees' travel expenses, including accommodation;
(c) other current expenses such as materials and supplies directly related to the project;

(d) depreciation of tools and equipment, to the extent that they are used exclusively for the training project;

(e) cost of guidance and counselling services with regard to the training project;

(f) trainees' personnel costs and general indirect costs (administrative costs, rent, overheads) up to the amount of the total of the other eligible costs referred to in points (a) to (e). As regards the trainees' personnel costs, only the hours during which the trainees actually participate in the training, after deduction of any productive hours, may be taken into account.

SECTION 9

Aid for Disadvantaged and Disabled Workers

Article 40

Aid for the recruitment of disadvantaged workers in the form of wage subsidies

1. Aid schemes for the recruitment of disadvantaged workers in the form of wage subsidies shall be compatible with the common market within the meaning of Article [107(3)] of the Treaty and shall be exempt from the notification requirement of Article [108(3)] of the Treaty, provided the conditions laid down in paragraphs 2 to 5 of this Article are fulfilled.

2. The aid intensity shall not exceed 50% of the eligible costs.

3. Eligible costs shall be the wage costs over a maximum period of 12 months following recruitment.

However, where the worker concerned is a severely disadvantaged worker, eligible costs shall be the wage costs over a maximum period of 24 months following recruitment.

4. Where the recruitment does not represent a net increase, compared with the average over the previous twelve months, in the number of employees in the undertaking concerned, the post or posts shall have fallen vacant following voluntary departure, disability, retirement on grounds of age, voluntary reduction of working time or lawful dismissal for misconduct and not as a result of redundancy.

5. Except in the case of lawful dismissal for misconduct, the disadvantaged worker shall be entitled to continuous employment for a minimum period consistent with the national legislation concerned or any collective agreements governing employment contracts.

If the period of employment is shorter than 12 months or, as the case may be 24 months, the aid shall be reduced pro rata accordingly.

Article 41

Aid for the employment of disabled workers in the form of wage subsidies

1. Aid for the employment of disabled workers in the form of wage subsidies shall be compatible with the common market within the meaning of Article [107(3)] of the Treaty and shall be exempt from the notification requirement of Article [108(3)] of the Treaty, provided the conditions laid down in paragraphs 2 to 5 of this Article are fulfilled.

2. The aid intensity shall not exceed 75% of the eligible costs.

3. Eligible costs shall be the wage costs over any given period during which the disabled worker is being employed.

4. Where the recruitment does not represent a net increase, compared with the average over the previous twelve months, in the number of employees in the undertaking concerned, the post or posts shall have fallen vacant following voluntary departure, disability, retirement on grounds of age, voluntary reduction of working time or lawful dismissal for misconduct and not as a result of redundancy.

5. Except in the case of lawful dismissal for misconduct the workers shall be entitled to continuous employment for a minimum period consistent with the national legislation concerned or any collective agreements governing employment contracts.

If the period of employment is shorter than 12 months, the aid shall be reduced pro rata accordingly.

Article 42
Aid for compensating the additional costs of employing disabled workers

1. Aid for compensating the additional costs of employing disabled workers shall be compatible with the common market within the meaning of Article [107(3)] of the Treaty and shall be exempt from the notification requirement of Article [108(3)] of the Treaty, provided the conditions laid down in paragraphs 2 and 3 of this Article are fulfilled.

2. The aid intensity shall not exceed 100% of the eligible costs.

3. Eligible costs shall be costs other than wage costs covered by Article 41, which are additional to those which the undertaking would have incurred if employing workers who are not disabled, over the period during which the worker concerned is being employed.

The eligible costs shall be the following:

(a) costs of adapting premises;
(b) costs of employing staff for time spent solely on the assistance of the disabled workers;
(c) costs of adapting or acquiring equipment, or acquiring and validating software for use by disabled workers, including adapted or assistive technology facilities, which are additional to those which the beneficiary would have incurred if employing workers who are not disabled;
(d) where the beneficiary provides sheltered employment, the costs of constructing, installing or expanding the establishment concerned, and any costs of administration and transport which result directly from the employment of disabled workers.

CHAPTER III
FINAL PROVISIONS

Article 43
Repeal

Any references to the repealed Regulation and to Regulation (EC) No 68/2001, Regulation (EC) No 70/2001 and Regulation (EC) No 2204/2002 shall be construed as references to this Regulation.

Article 44
Transitional provisions

1. This Regulation shall apply to individual aid granted before its entry into force, if the aid fulfils all the conditions laid down in this Regulation, with the exception of Article 9.

2. Any aid granted before 31 December 2008, which does not fulfil the conditions laid down in this Regulation but fulfils the conditions laid down in Regulation (EC) No 68/2001, Regulation (EC) No 70/2001, Regulation (EC) No 2204/2002 or Regulation (EC) No 1628/2006 shall be compatible with the common market and exempt from the notification requirement of Article [108(3)] of the Treaty.

Any other aid granted before the entry into force of this Regulation, which fulfils neither the conditions laid down in this Regulation nor the conditions laid down in one of the Regulations referred to in the first subparagraph, shall be assessed by the Commission in accordance with the relevant frameworks, guidelines, communications and notices.

3. At the end of the period of validity of this Regulation, any aid schemes exempted under this Regulation shall remain exempted during an adjustment period of six months, with the exception of regional aid schemes. The exemption of regional aid schemes shall expire at the date of expiry of the approved regional aid maps.

Article 45
Entry into force and applicability

This Regulation shall enter into force on the twentieth day following that of its publication in the *Official Journal of the European Union.*

It shall apply until 31 December 2013.

This Regulation shall be binding in its entirety and directly applicable in all Member States.

Done at Brussels, 6 August 2008.

ANNEX I

Definition of SME

Article 1

Enterprise

An enterprise is considered to be any entity engaged in an economic activity, irrespective of its legal form. This includes, in particular, self employed persons and family businesses engaged in craft or other activities, and partnerships or associations regularly engaged in an economic activity.

Article 2

Staff headcount and financial thresholds determining enterprise categories

1. The category of micro, small and medium sized enterprises ('SMEs') is made up of enterprises which employ fewer than 250 persons and which have an annual turnover not exceeding EUR 50 million, and/or an annual balance sheet total not exceeding EUR 43 million.

2. Within the SME category, a small enterprise is defined as an enterprise which employs fewer than 50 persons and whose annual turnover and/or annual balance sheet total does not exceed EUR 10 million.

3. Within the SME category, a micro enterprise is defined as an enterprise which employs fewer than 10 persons and whose annual turnover and/or annual balance sheet total does not exceed EUR 2 million.

Article 3

Types of enterprise taken into consideration in calculating staff numbers and financial amounts

1. An 'autonomous enterprise' is any enterprise which is not classified as a partner enterprise within the meaning of paragraph 2 or as a linked enterprise within the meaning of paragraph 3.

2. 'Partner enterprises' are all enterprises which are not classified as linked enterprises within the meaning of paragraph 3 and between which there is the following relationship: an enterprise (upstream enterprise) holds, either solely or jointly with one or more linked enterprises within the meaning of paragraph 3, 25% or more of the capital or voting rights of another enterprise (downstream enterprise).

However, an enterprise may be ranked as autonomous, and thus as not having any partner enterprises, even if this 25% threshold is reached or exceeded by the following investors, provided that those investors are not linked, within the meaning of paragraph 3, either individually or jointly to the enterprise in question:

(a) public investment corporations, venture capital companies, individuals or groups of individuals with a regular venture capital investment activity who invest equity capital in unquoted businesses (business angels), provided the total investment of those business angels in the same enterprise is less than EUR 1 250 000;

(b) universities or non profit research centres;

(c) institutional investors, including regional development funds;

(d) autonomous local authorities with an annual budget of less than EUR 10 million and less than 5 000 inhabitants.

3. 'Linked enterprises' are enterprises which have any of the following relationships with each other:

(a) an enterprise has a majority of the shareholders' or members' voting rights in another enterprise;

(b) an enterprise has the right to appoint or remove a majority of the members of the administrative, management or supervisory body of another enterprise;

(c) an enterprise has the right to exercise a dominant influence over another enterprise pursuant to a contract entered into with that enterprise or to a provision in its memorandum or articles of association;

(d) an enterprise, which is a shareholder in or member of another enterprise, controls alone, pursuant to an agreement with other shareholders in or members of that enterprise, a majority of shareholders' or members' voting rights in that enterprise.

There is a presumption that no dominant influence exists if the investors listed in the second subparagraph of paragraph 2 are not involving themselves directly or indirectly in the management of the enterprise in question, without prejudice to their rights as shareholders.

Enterprises having any of the relationships described in the first subparagraph through one or more other enterprises, or any one of the investors mentioned in paragraph 2, are also considered to be linked.

Enterprises which have one or other of such relationships through a natural person or group of natural persons acting jointly are also considered linked enterprises if they engage in their activity or in part of their activity in the same relevant market or in adjacent markets.

An 'adjacent market' is considered to be the market for a product or service situated directly upstream or downstream of the relevant market.

4. Except in the cases set out in paragraph 2, second subparagraph, an enterprise cannot be considered an SME if 25% or more of the capital or voting rights are directly or indirectly controlled, jointly or individually, by one or more public bodies.

5. Enterprises may make a declaration of status as an autonomous enterprise, partner enterprise or linked enterprise, including the data regarding the thresholds set out in Article 2. The declaration may be made even if the capital is spread in such a way that it is not possible to determine exactly by whom it is held, in which case the enterprise may declare in good faith that it can legitimately presume that it is not owned as to 25% or more by one enterprise or jointly by enterprises linked to one another. Such declarations are made without prejudice to the checks and investigations provided for by national or Community rules.

Article 4
Data used for the staff headcount and the financial amounts and reference period

1. The data to apply to the headcount of staff and the financial amounts are those relating to the latest approved accounting period and calculated on an annual basis. They are taken into account from the date of closure of the accounts. The amount selected for the turnover is calculated excluding value added tax (VAT) and other indirect taxes.

2. Where, at the date of closure of the accounts, an enterprise finds that, on an annual basis, it has exceeded or fallen below the headcount or financial thresholds stated in Article 2, this will not result in the loss or acquisition of the status of medium sized, small or micro enterprise unless those thresholds are exceeded over two consecutive accounting periods.

3. In the case of newly established enterprises whose accounts have not yet been approved, the data to apply is to be derived from a bona fide estimate made in the course of the financial year.

Article 5
Staff headcount

The headcount corresponds to the number of annual work units (AWU), i.e. the number of persons who worked full time within the enterprise in question or on its behalf during the entire reference year under consideration. The work of persons who have not worked the full year, the work of those who have worked part time, regardless of duration, and the work of seasonal workers are counted as fractions of AWU. The staff consists of:

(a) employees;
(b) persons working for the enterprise being subordinated to it and deemed to be employees under national law;
(c) owner managers;
(d) partners engaging in a regular activity in the enterprise and benefiting from financial advantages from the enterprise.

Apprentices or students engaged in vocational training with an apprenticeship or vocational training contract are not included as staff. The duration of maternity or parental leaves is not counted.

Establishing the data of an enterprise

1. In the case of an autonomous enterprise, the data, including the number of staff, are determined exclusively on the basis of the accounts of that enterprise.

2. The data, including the headcount, of an enterprise having partner enterprises or linked enterprises are determined on the basis of the accounts and other data of the enterprise or, where they exist, the consolidated accounts of the enterprise, or the consolidated accounts in which the enterprise is included through consolidation.

To the data referred to in the first subparagraph are added the data of any partner enterprise of the enterprise in question situated immediately upstream or downstream from it. Aggregation is proportional to the percentage interest in the capital or voting rights (whichever is greater). In the case of cross holdings, the greater percentage applies.

To the data referred to in the first and second subparagraph are added 100% of the data of any enterprise, which is linked directly or indirectly to the enterprise in question, where the data were not already included through consolidation in the accounts.

3. For the application of paragraph 2, the data of the partner enterprises of the enterprise in question are derived from their accounts and their other data, consolidated if they exist. To these are added 100% of the data of enterprises which are linked to these partner enterprises, unless their accounts data are already included through consolidation.

For the application of the same paragraph 2, the data of the enterprises which are linked to the enterprise in question are to be derived from their accounts and their other data, consolidated if they exist. To these are added, pro rata, the data of any possible partner enterprise of that linked enterprise, situated immediately upstream or downstream from it, unless it has already been included in the consolidated accounts with a percentage at least proportional to the percentage identified under the second subparagraph of paragraph 2.

4. Where in the consolidated accounts no staff data appear for a given enterprise, staff figures are calculated by aggregating proportionally the data from its partner enterprises and by adding the data from the enterprises to which the enterprise in question is linked.

ANNEX II
Form for the Provision of Summary Information for Research and Development Under the Extended Reporting Obligation Laid Down in Article 9(4)

Notes

For reasons of space, Annex II is not reproduced in this volume.

ANNEX III
Form for the Provision of Summary Information Under the Reporting Obligation Laid Down in Article 9(1)

Notes

For reasons of space, Annex III is not reproduced in this volume. An electronic version of Annex III is available on the Europa website at the following address:
<http://ec.europa.eu/comm/competition/state_aid/legislation/forms.cfm#forms_gber>

G12

COMMISSION REGULATION (EU) NO 360/2012

of 25 April 2012
on the application of Articles 107 and 108 of the Treaty on the
Functioning of the European Union to de minimis aid granted to undertakings
providing services of general economic interest

(Text with EEA relevance)

Official Journal L 114, 26.4.2012, p.8

Celex No:32012R0360

EUR-Lex permanent link: <http://eur-lex.europa.eu/LexUriServ/LexUriServ.do?uri=CELEX:3201
2R0360:EN:NOT>

EEA Application: this instrument was incorporated into the EEA Agreement as point 1(ha) of Annex XV by EEA Joint
Committee Decision 225/2012 of 7 December 2012 (OJ L 81, 21.3.2013, p.27).

Commentary
B&C: 17.003, 17.027, 17.074, F&N: 17.179, 17.182, 17.368

THE EUROPEAN COMMISSION,

Having regard to the Treaty on the Functioning of the European Union,

Having regard to Council Regulation (EC) No 994/98 of 7 May 1998 on the application of Articles
[107] and [108] of the [Treaty on the Functioning of the European Union] to certain categories of
horizontal State aid[1], and in particular Article 2(1) thereof,*

Having published a draft of this Regulation[2],

After consulting the Advisory Committee on State Aid,

Notes

[1] OJ L 142, 14.5.1998, p.1.
[2] OJ C 8, 11.1.2012, p.23.
* Ed note: please see the Note on the Lisbon Treaty at p.xvii in regard to article renumbering introduced by the Lisbon Treaty.

Whereas:
(1) Regulation (EC) No 994/98 empowers the Commission to set out in a Regulation a threshold
    below which aid measures are considered not to meet all the criteria laid down in Article 107(1)
    of the Treaty and therefore do not fall under the notification procedure provided for in Article
    108(3) of the Treaty.
(2) On the basis of that Regulation, the Commission has adopted, in particular, Regulation (EC) No
    1998/2006 of 15 December 2006 on the application of Articles [107] and [108] of the Treaty to
    de minimis aid[1], which sets a general *de minimis* ceiling of EUR 200 000 per beneficiary over a
    period of three fiscal years.

Notes
[1] OJ L 379, 28.12.2006, p.5.

---

(3) The Commission's experience in applying the State aid rules to undertakings providing services of
    general economic interest within the meaning of Article 106(2) of the Treaty has shown that the
    ceiling below which advantages granted to such undertakings may be deemed not to affect trade
    between Member States and/or not to distort or threaten to distort competition can, in some
    cases, differ from the general *de minimis* ceiling established in Regulation (EC) No 1998/2006.

Indeed, at least some of those advantages are likely to constitute compensation for additional costs linked to the provision of services of general economic interest. Moreover, many activities qualifying as the provision of services of general economic interest have a limited territorial scope. It is therefore appropriate to introduce, alongside Regulation (EC) No 1998/2006, a Regulation containing specific *de minimis* rules for undertakings providing services of general economic interest. A ceiling should be established for the amount of *de minimis* aid each undertaking may receive over a specific period of time.

(4) In the light of the Commission's experience, aid granted to undertakings providing a service of general economic interest should be deemed not to affect trade between Member States and/or not to distort or threaten to distort competition provided that the total amount of aid granted for the provision of services of general economic interest received by the beneficiary undertaking does not exceed EUR 500 000 over any period of three fiscal years. In view of the development of the road passenger transport sector and of the mostly local nature of services of general economic interest in this field, it is not appropriate to apply a lower ceiling to this sector and the ceiling of EUR 500 000 should apply.

(5) The years to be taken into account for the purpose of determining whether that ceiling is met should be the fiscal years as used for fiscal purposes by the undertaking in the Member State concerned. The relevant period of three years should be assessed on a rolling basis so that, for each new grant of *de minimis* aid, the total amount of *de minimis* aid granted in the fiscal year concerned, as well as during the previous two fiscal years, needs to be determined. Aid granted by a Member State should be taken into account for this purpose even when financed entirely or partly by resources of Union origin. It should not be possible for aid measures exceeding the *de minimis* ceiling to be broken down into a number of smaller parts in order to bring such parts within the scope of this Regulation.

(6) This Regulation should apply only to aid granted for the provision of a service of general economic interest. The beneficiary undertaking should therefore be entrusted in writing with the service of general economic interest in respect of which the aid is granted. While the entrustment act should inform the undertaking of the service of general economic interest in respect of which it is granted, it must not necessarily contain all the detailed information as set out in Commission Decision 2012/21/EU of 20 December 2011 on the application of Article 106(2) of the Treaty on the Functioning of the European Union to State aid in the form of public service compensation granted to certain undertakings entrusted with the operation of services of general economic interest[1].

Notes
[1] OJ L 7, 11.1.2012, p.3.

---

(7) In view of the special rules which apply in the sectors of primary production of agricultural products, fisheries, aquaculture and road freight transport, of the fact that undertakings in those sectors are rarely entrusted with services of general economic interest, and of the risk that amounts of aid below the ceiling set out in this Regulation could fulfil the criteria of Article 107(1) of the Treaty in those sectors, this Regulation should not apply to those sectors. However, if undertakings are active in the sectors of primary production of agricultural products, fisheries, aquaculture or road freight transport as well as in other sectors or activities, this Regulation should apply to those other sectors or activities (such as for example collection of litter at sea) provided that Member States ensure that the activities in the excluded sectors do not benefit from the *de minimis* aid under this Regulation, by appropriate means such as separation of activities or distinction of costs. Member States can fulfill this obligation, in particular, by limiting the amount of *de minimis* aid to the compensation of the costs of the provision of the service, including a reasonable profit. This Regulation should not apply to the coal sector, in view of its special characteristics and of fact that undertakings in those sectors are rarely entrusted with services of general economic interest.

(8) Considering the similarities between the processing and marketing of agricultural products, on the one hand, and of non-agricultural products, on the other, this Regulation should apply to the processing and marketing of agricultural products, provided that certain conditions are met. Neither on-farm activities necessary for preparing a product for the first sale, such as harvesting,

cutting and threshing of cereals, or packing of eggs, nor the first sale to resellers or processors should be considered as processing or marketing in this respect.

(9) The Court of Justice has established[1] that, once the Union has legislated for the establishment of a common organisation of the market in a given sector of agriculture, Member States are under an obligation to refrain from taking any measure which might undermine or create exceptions to it. For this reason, this Regulation should not apply to aid the amount of which is set on the basis of the price or quantity of products purchased or put on the market. Nor should it apply to *de minimis* support which is linked to an obligation to share the aid with primary producers.

Notes

[1] Case C-456/00 *French Republic* v *Commission of the European Communities* [2002] I-11949.

---

(10) This Regulation should not apply to *de minimis* export aid or *de minimis* aid favouring domestic over imported products.

(11) This Regulation should not apply to undertakings in difficulty within the meaning of the Community guidelines on State aid for rescuing and restructuring firms in difficulty[1] since it is not appropriate to grant operating aid to firms in difficulty outside of a restructuring concept and there are difficulties linked to determining the gross grant equivalent of aid granted to undertakings of this type.

Notes

[1] OJ C 244, 1.10.2004, p.2.

---

(12) In accordance with the principles governing aid falling within Article 107(1) of the Treaty, *de minimis* aid should be considered to be granted at the moment the legal right to receive the aid is conferred on the undertaking under the applicable national legal regime.

(13) In order to avoid circumvention of maximum aid intensities laid down in different Union instruments, *de minimis* aid should not be cumulated with State aid in respect of the same eligible costs if such cumulation would result in an aid intensity exceeding that specified in the particular circumstances of each case by a block exemption regulation or decision adopted by the Commission.

(14) This Regulation should not restrict the application of Regulation (EC) No 1998/2006 to undertakings providing services of general economic interest. Member States should remain free to rely either on this Regulation or on Regulation (EC) No 1998/2006 as regards aid granted for the provision of services of general economic interest.

Commentary

recital 14: **B&C:** 17.074

---

(15) The Court of Justice, in its *Altmark* judgment[1], has identified a number of conditions which must be fulfilled in order for compensation for the provision of a service of general economic interest not to constitute State aid. Those conditions ensure that compensation limited to the net costs incurred by efficient undertakings for the provision of a service of general economic interest does not constitute State aid within the meaning of Article 107(1) of the Treaty. Compensation in excess of those net costs constitutes State aid which may be declared compatible on the basis of the applicable Union rules. In order to avoid this Regulation being applied to circumvent the conditions identified in the *Altmark* judgment, and in order to avoid *de minimis* aid granted under this Regulation affecting trade due to its cumulation with other compensation for the same service of general economic interest, *de minimis* aid under this Regulation should not be cumulated with any other compensation in respect of the same service, regardless of whether or not it constitutes State aid under the *Altmark* judgment or compatible State aid under Decision 2012/21/EU or under the Communication from the Commission — European Union framework for State aid in the form of public service compensation (2011)[2]. Therefore, this Regulation should not apply to compensation received for the provision of a service of general economic interest in respect of which other types of compensation are also being granted, except where that other compensation constitutes *de minimis* aid according to other *de minimis* regulations and the cumulation rules set out in this Regulation are complied with.

Notes

1 Case C-280/00 *Altmark Trans GmbH and Regierungspräsidium Magdeburg* v *Nahverkehrsgesellschaft Altmark GmbH, and Oberbundesanwalt beim Bundesverwaltungsgericht* [2003] ECR I-7747.
2 OJ C 8, 11.1.2012, p.15.

Commentary
recital 15: B&C: 17.074

(16) For the purposes of transparency, equal treatment and correct application of the *de minimis* ceiling, all Member States should apply the same method of calculation. In order to facilitate such calculation and in accordance with present practice in applying the *de minimis* rule, aid amounts not taking the form of a cash grant should be converted into their gross grant equivalent. Calculation of the grant equivalent of transparent types of aid other than grants and of aid payable in several instalments requires the use of market rates prevailing at the time of granting such aid. With a view to uniform, transparent and simple application of the State aid rules, the market rates for the purposes of this Regulation should be deemed to be the reference rates, as currently set out in the Communication from the Commission on the revision of the method for setting the reference and discount rates[1].

Notes
1 OJ C 14, 19.1.2008, p.6.

(17) For the purposes of transparency, equal treatment and effective monitoring, this Regulation should apply only to *de minimis* aid which is transparent. Transparent aid is aid for which it is possible to calculate precisely the gross grant equivalent *ex ante* without a need to undertake a risk assessment. Such a precise calculation can, for instance, be made for grants, interest rate subsidies and capped tax exemptions. Aid comprised in capital injections should not be considered as transparent *de minimis* aid, unless the total amount of the public injection is lower than the *de minimis* ceiling. Aid comprised in risk capital measures as referred to in the Community guidelines on State aid to promote risk capital investments in small and medium-sized enterprises[1] should not be considered as transparent *de minimis* aid, unless the risk capital scheme concerned provides capital only up to the *de minimis* ceiling to each target undertaking. Aid comprised in loans should be treated as transparent *de minimis* aid when the gross grant equivalent has been calculated on the basis of market interest rates prevailing at the time of grant.

Notes
1 OJ C 194, 18.8.2006, p.2.

(18) Legal certainty needs to be provided for guarantee schemes which do not have the potential to affect trade and distort competition and in respect of which sufficient data are available to assess any potential effects reliably. This Regulation should therefore transpose the *de minimis* ceiling of EUR 500 000 into a guarantee-specific ceiling based on the guaranteed amount of the individual loan underlying such guarantee. This specific ceiling should be calculated using a methodology assessing the State aid amount included in guarantee schemes covering loans in favour of viable undertakings. The methodology and the data used to calculate the guarantee-specific ceiling should exclude undertakings in difficulty as referred to in the Community guidelines on State aid for rescuing and restructuring firms in difficulty. This specific ceiling should therefore not apply to individual aid granted outside the scope of a guarantee scheme, to aid granted to undertakings in difficulty, or to guarantees on underlying transactions not constituting a loan, such as guarantees on equity transactions. The specific ceiling should be determined on the basis of the fact that taking account of a cap rate (net default rate) of 13%, representing a worst case scenario for guarantee schemes in the Union, a guarantee amounting to EUR 3 750 000 can be considered as having a gross grant equivalent identical to the EUR 500 000 *de minimis* ceiling. Only guarantees covering up to 80% of the underlying loan should be covered by these specific ceilings. A methodology accepted by the Commission following notification of such methodology on the basis of a Commission regulation in the State aid area may also be used by Member States for the purpose of assessing the gross grant equivalent contained in a guarantee, if the

approved methodology explicitly addresses the type of guarantees and the type of underlying transactions at stake in the context of the application of this Regulation.

(19) Upon notification by a Member State, the Commission may examine whether an aid measure which does not consist in a grant, loan, guarantee, capital injection, risk capital measure or capped tax exemption leads to a gross grant equivalent that does not exceed the *de minimis* ceiling and could therefore be covered by the provisions of this Regulation.

(20) The Commission has a duty to ensure that State aid rules are complied with and in particular that aid granted under the *de minimis* rules adheres to the conditions thereof. In accordance with the cooperation principle laid down in Article 4(3) of the Treaty on European Union, Member States should facilitate the fulfilment of this task by establishing the necessary tools in order to ensure that the total amount of *de minimis* aid granted to the same undertaking for the provision of services of general economic interest does not exceed the overall permissible ceiling. To that end and to ensure compliance with the provisions on cumulation with *de minimis* aid under other *de minimis* regulations, when granting *de minimis* aid under this Regulation, Member States should inform the undertaking concerned of the amount of the aid and of its *de minimis* character by referring to this Regulation. Moreover, prior to granting such aid the Member State concerned should obtain from the undertaking a declaration about other *de minimis* aid covered by this Regulation or by other *de minimis* regulations received during the fiscal year concerned and the two previous fiscal years. Alternatively, the Member State should have the possibility to ensure that the ceiling is observed by means of a central register.

(21) This Regulation should apply without prejudice to the requirements of Union law in the area of public procurement or of additional requirements flowing from the Treaty or from sectoral Union legislation.

(22) This Regulation should apply to aid granted before its entry into force to undertakings providing services of general economic interest.

(23) The Commission intends to carry out a review of this Regulation five years after its entry into force,

HAS ADOPTED THIS REGULATION:

Article 1
Scope and definitions

1. This Regulation applies to aid granted to undertakings providing a service of general economic interest within the meaning of Article 106(2) of the Treaty.

2. This Regulation does not apply to:

(a) aid granted to undertakings active in the fishery and aquaculture sectors, as covered by Council Regulation (EC) No 104/2000[1];

(b) aid granted to undertakings active in the primary production of agricultural products;

(c) aid granted to undertakings active in the processing and marketing of agricultural products, in the following cases:

(i) when the amount of the aid is fixed on the basis of the price or quantity of such products purchased from primary producers or put on the market by the undertakings concerned,

(ii) when the aid is conditional on being partly or entirely passed on to primary producers;

(d) aid to export-related activities towards third countries or Member States, namely aid directly linked to the quantities exported, to the establishment and operation of a distribution network or to other current expenditure linked to the export activity;

(e) aid contingent upon the use of domestic over imported goods;

(f) aid granted to undertakings active in the coal sector, as defined in Council Decision 2010/787/EU[2];

(g) aid granted to undertakings performing road freight transport for hire or reward;

(h) aid granted to undertakings in difficulty.

If undertakings are active in the sectors referred to in points (a), (b), (c) or (g) of the first subparagraph as well as in sectors not excluded from the scope of application of this Regulation, this Regulation applies only to aid granted in respect of those other sectors or activities, provided that Member States ensure that the activities in the excluded sectors do not benefit from the de minimis aid under this Regulation, by appropriate means such as separation of activities or distinction of costs.

3. For the purposes of this Regulation:

(a) 'agricultural products' means products listed in Annex I to the Treaty, with the exception of fishery products;

(b) 'processing of agricultural products' means any operation on an agricultural product resulting in a product which is also an agricultural product, except on-farm activities necessary for preparing an animal or plant product for the first sale;

(c) 'marketing of agricultural products' means holding or display with a view to sale, offering for sale, delivery or any other manner of placing on the market, except the first sale by a primary producer to resellers or processors and any activity preparing a product for such first sale; a sale by a primary producer to final consumers shall be considered as marketing if it takes place in separate premises reserved for that purpose.

Notes
1 OJ L 17, 21.1.2000, p.22.
2 OJ L 336, 21.12.2010, p.24.

Article 2
De minimis aid

1. Aid granted to undertakings for the provision of a service of general economic interest shall be deemed not to meet all the criteria of Article 107(1) of the Treaty and shall therefore be exempt from the notification requirement of Article 108(3) of the Treaty if it fulfils the conditions laid down in paragraphs 2 to 8 of this Article.

2. The total amount of *de minimis* aid granted to any one undertaking providing services of general economic interest shall not exceed EUR 500 000 over any period of three fiscal years.

This ceiling shall apply irrespective of the form of the *de minimis* aid and regardless of whether the aid granted by the Member State is financed entirely or partly by resources of Union origin. The period shall be determined by reference to the fiscal years used by the undertaking in the Member State concerned.

3. The ceiling laid down in paragraph 2 shall be expressed as a cash grant. All figures used shall be gross, that is, before any deduction of tax or other charges. Where aid is awarded in a form other than a grant, the aid amount shall be the gross grant equivalent of the aid.

Aid payable in several instalments shall be discounted to its value at the moment of it being granted. The interest rate to be used for discounting purposes shall be the discount rate applicable at the time of grant.

4. This Regulation shall apply only to aid in respect of which it is possible to calculate precisely the gross grant equivalent of the aid *ex ante* without need to undertake a risk assessment ('transparent aid'). In particular:

(a) aid comprised in loans shall be considered as transparent *de minimis* aid when the gross grant equivalent has been calculated on the basis of the reference rate applicable at the time of the grant;

(b) aid comprised in capital injections shall not be considered as transparent *de minimis* aid, unless the total amount of the public injection does not exceed the *de minimis* ceiling;

(c) aid comprised in risk capital measures shall not be considered as transparent *de minimis* aid, unless the risk capital scheme concerned provides capital only up to the *de minimis* ceiling to each target undertaking;

(d) individual aid provided under a guarantee scheme to undertakings which are not undertakings in difficulty shall be treated as transparent *de minimis* aid when the guaranteed part of the underlying loan provided under such scheme does not exceed EUR 3 750 000 per undertaking. If the guaranteed part of the underlying loan only accounts for a given proportion of this ceiling, the gross grant equivalent of that guarantee shall be deemed to correspond to the same proportion of the ceiling laid down in paragraph 2. The guarantee shall not exceed 80% of the underlying loan. Guarantee schemes shall also be considered as transparent if:

(i) before the implementation of the scheme, the methodology to calculate the gross grant equivalent of the guarantees has been accepted following notification of this methodology to the Commission under a regulation adopted by the Commission in the State aid area, and

(ii) the approved methodology explicitly addresses the type of guarantees and the type of underlying transactions at stake in the context of the application of this Regulation.

5. Where the overall amount of *de minimis* aid under this Regulation granted to an undertaking for the provision of services of general economic interest exceeds the ceiling laid down in paragraph 2, that amount may not benefit from this Regulation, even for a fraction not exceeding that ceiling. In such a case, the benefit of this Regulation may not be claimed for this aid measure.

6. *De minimis* aid under this Regulation shall not be cumulated with State aid in respect of the same eligible costs if such cumulation would result in an aid intensity exceeding that stipulated in the specific circumstances of each case by a block exemption regulation or decision adopted by the Commission.

7. *De minimis* aid under this Regulation may be cumulated with *de minimis* aid under other *de minimis* regulations up to the ceiling laid down in paragraph 2.

8. *De minimis* aid under this Regulation shall not be cumulated with any compensation in respect of the same service of general economic interest, regardless of whether or not it constitutes State aid.

Commentary
Art 2: F&N: 17.377
Art 2(3): B&C: 17.074
Art 2(6): B&C: 17.074

Article 3
Monitoring

1. Where a Member State intends to grant *de minimis* aid under this Regulation to an undertaking, it shall inform that undertaking in writing of the prospective amount of the aid expressed as gross grant equivalent, of the service of general economic interest in respect of which it is granted and of the *de minimis* character of the aid, making express reference to this Regulation and citing its title and publication reference in the *Official Journal of the European Union*. Where *de minimis* aid under this Regulation is granted to different undertakings on the basis of a scheme and different amounts of individual aid are granted to those undertakings under that scheme, the Member State concerned may choose to fulfil that obligation by informing the undertakings of a fixed sum corresponding to the maximum aid amount to be granted under that scheme. In such case, the fixed sum shall be used for determining whether the ceiling laid down in Article 2(2) is met. Prior to granting the aid, the Member State shall also obtain a declaration from the undertaking providing the service of general economic interest, in written or electronic form, about any other *de minimis* aid received under this Regulation or under other *de minimis* regulations during the previous two fiscal years and the current fiscal year.

The Member State shall grant the new *de minimis* aid under this Regulation only after having checked that this will not raise the total amount of *de minimis* aid granted to the undertaking concerned to a level above the ceiling laid down in Article 2(2) and that the cumulation rules in Article 2(6), (7) and (8) are complied with.

2. Where a Member State has set up a central register of *de minimis* aid containing complete information on all *de minimis* aid granted to undertakings providing services of general economic interest by any authority within that Member State, the first subparagraph of paragraph 1 shall cease to apply from the moment the register covers a period of three years.

3. Member States shall record and compile all the information regarding the application of this Regulation. Such records shall contain all information necessary to demonstrate that the conditions of this Regulation have been complied with. Records regarding individual *de minimis* aid shall be

maintained for 10 fiscal years from the date on which the aid was granted. Records regarding a *de minimis* aid scheme shall be maintained for 10 years from the date on which the last individual aid was granted under such a scheme. On written request, the Member State concerned shall provide the Commission, within a period of 20 working days or such longer period as may be fixed in the request, with all the information that the Commission considers necessary for assessing whether the conditions of this Regulation have been complied with, and in particular the total amount of *de minimis* aid under this Regulation and under other *de minimis* regulations received by any undertaking.

Article 4
Transitional provisions

This Regulation shall apply to *de minimis* aid granted for the provision of services of general economic interest before its entry into force, provided that such aid fulfils the conditions laid down in Articles 1 and 2. Any aid for the provision of services of general economic interest which does not fulfil those conditions shall be assessed in accordance with the relevant decisions, frameworks, guidelines, communications and notices.

At the end of the period of validity of this Regulation, any *de minimis* aid which fulfils the conditions of this Regulation may be validly implemented for a further period of six months.

Article 5
Entry into force and period of validity

This Regulation shall enter into force on the third day following that of its publication in the *Official Journal of the European Union*.

It shall apply until 31 December 2018.

This Regulation shall be binding in its entirety and directly applicable in all Member States.

Done at Brussels, 25 April 2012.

G13

COMMUNITY GUIDELINES ON STATE AID FOR RESCUING AND RESTRUCTURING FIRMS IN DIFFICULTY

(2004/C 244/02)

Text with EEA relevance

Official Journal C 244, 1.10.2004, p.2

Celex No: 52004XC1001(01)

EUR-Lex permanent link: <http://eur-lex.europa.eu/LexUriServ/LexUriServ.do?uri=CELEX: 5200 4XC1001(01)EN:NOT>

Notes

In 2009, the validity of the 2004 Guidelines was extended until 9 October 2012: see Commission communication concerning the prolongation of the community guidelines on State aid for rescuing and restructuring firms in difficulty (OJ C 156, 9.7.09, p.3). On 28 September 2012, the Commission decided to continue to apply the 2004 guidelines until such time as they are replaced by new rules on State aid for rescuing and restructuring firms in difficulty following the Commission's review process in the context of the EU State aid modernisation programme launched in May 2012: see Commission communication concerning the prolongation of the application of the Community guidelines on State aid for rescuing and restructuring firms in difficulty of 1 October 2004 (OJ C 296, 2.10.2011, p.3).

EEA application: for the corresponding EEA provision, see the EFTA Surveillance Authority's Procedural and Substantive Rules in the Field of State Aid (Guidelines on the application and interpretation of Articles 61 and 62 of the EEA Agreement and Article 1 of Protocol 3 to the Surveillance and Court Agreement), Part III, Chapter 16 (as amended by EFTA Surveillance Authority Decision No 305/04/COL of 1 December 2004 (OJ L 97, 15.4.2005, p.41)). On 28 November 2012 the EFTA Surveillance Authority extended the validity of the Chapter in its State Aid Guidelines on State Aid for Rescuing and Restructuring Firms in Difficulty until it is replaced by new rules: see EFTA Surveillance Authority Decision No 438/12/COL of 28 November 2012 amending for the eighty-sixth time the procedural and substantive rules in the field of state aid (OJ L 190, 11.7.2013, p.91).

Commentary
Guidelines: **B&C:** 17.064, 17.083 **F&N:** 17.153, 17.492
points 38–39: **B&C:** 17.066
points 43–44: **B&C:** 17.066
points 55–56: **B&C:** 17.067
points 72–73: **B&C:** 17.066

1. Introduction

1. The Commission adopted its original Community Guidelines on State aid for rescuing and restructuring firms in difficulty[1] in 1994. In 1997, the Commission added specific rules for agriculture.[2] A new version of the guidelines was adopted in 1999[3] and will expire on 9 October 2004*.

Notes
[1] OJ C 368, 23.12.1994, p.12.
[2] OJ C 283, 19.9.1997, p.2. See also the footnote relating to the heading of Chapter 5.
[3] OJ C 288, 9.10.1999, p.2.
[* Ed note: see above regarding the extension of the guidelines.]

2. The Commission wishes through this version of the Guidelines, the text of which builds on previous versions, to make certain changes and clarifications prompted by a number of factors.

3. First, in the light of conclusions of the meetings of the European Councils of Stockholm on 23 and 24 March 2001 and of Barcelona on 15 and 16 March 2002, which called on Member States to continue to reduce State aid as a percentage of gross domestic product while redirecting it towards more horizontal objectives of common interest including cohesion objectives, closer scrutiny of the distortion created by allowing aid for rescue and restructuring operations seems warranted. This is also consistent with the conclusions of the European Council held in Lisbon on 23 and 24 March 2000 aimed at increasing the competitiveness of the European economy.

4. The exit of inefficient firms is a normal part of the operation of the market. It cannot be the norm that a company which gets into difficulties is rescued by the State. Aid for rescue and restructuring operations has given rise to some of the most controversial State aid cases in the past and is among the most distortive types of State aid. Hence, the general principle of the prohibition of State aid as laid down in the Treaty should remain the rule and derogation from that rule should be limited.

Commentary
point 4: **B&C:** 17.064

5. The "one time, last time" principle is further reinforced, to avoid the use of repeated rescue or restructuring aids to keep firms artificially alive.

6. The 1999 guidelines made a distinction between rescue aid and restructuring aid, whereby rescue aid was defined as temporary assistance to keep an ailing firm afloat for the time needed to work out a restructuring and/or a liquidation plan. In principle, restructuring measures financed through State aid could not be undertaken during this phase. However, such strict distinction between rescue and restructuring has given rise to difficulties. Firms in difficulty may already need to take certain urgent structural measures to halt or reduce a worsening of the financial situation

Part G State Aids

in the rescue phase. These guidelines therefore widen the concept of "rescue aid" in order to allow the beneficiary to undertake urgent measures, even of a structural nature, such as an immediate closure of a branch or other form of abandonment of loss-making activities. Given the urgent character of such aids, the Member States should be given the opportunity to opt for a simplified procedure to obtain their approval.

7. As regards restructuring aids, building on the 1994 guidelines, the 1999 guidelines continued to require a substantial contribution from the beneficiary to the restructuring. Within this revision, it is appropriate to reaffirm with greater clarity the principle that this contribution must be real and free of aid. The beneficiary's contribution has a twofold purpose: on the one hand, it will demonstrate that the markets (owners, creditors) believe in the feasibility of the return to viability within a reasonable time period. On the other hand, it will ensure that restructuring aid is limited to the minimum required to restore viability while limiting distortion of competition. In this respect the Commission will also request compensatory measures to minimise the effect on competitors.

8. The provision of rescue or restructuring aid to firms in difficulty may only be regarded as legitimate subject to certain conditions. It may be justified, for instance, by social or regional policy considerations, by the need to take into account the beneficial role played by small and medium-sized enterprises (SMEs) in the economy or, exceptionally, by the desirability of maintaining a competitive market structure when the demise of firms could lead to a monopoly or to a tight oligopolistic situation. On the other hand, it would not be justified to keep a firm artificially alive in a sector with long-term structural overcapacity or when it can only survive as a result of repeated State interventions.

2. Definitions and Scope of the Guidelines and Links with Other Texts on State Aid

2.1. Meaning of "a firm in difficulty"

9. There is no Community definition of what constitutes "a firm in difficulty". However, for the purposes of these Guidelines, the Commission regards a firm as being in difficulty where it is unable, whether through its own resources or with the funds it is able to obtain from its owner/shareholders or creditors, to stem losses which, without outside intervention by the public authorities, will almost certainly condemn it to going out of business in the short or medium term.

Commentary
point 9: B&C: 17.064

---

10. In particular, a firm is, in principle and irrespective of its size, regarded as being in difficulty for the purposes of these Guidelines in the following circumstances:

   (a) in the case of a limited liability company,[1] where more than half of its registered capital has disappeared[2] and more than one quarter of that capital has been lost over the preceding 12 months;

   (b) in the case of a company where at least some members have unlimited liability for the debt of the company,[3] where more than half of its capital as shown in the company accounts has disappeared and more than one quarter of that capital has been lost over the preceding 12 months;

   (c) whatever the type of company concerned, where it fulfils the criteria under its domestic law for being the subject of collective insolvency proceedings.

Notes

[1] This refers in particular to the types of company mentioned in the first subparagraph of Article 1(1) of Council Directive 78/660/EEC (OJ L 222, 14.8.1978, p.11) as last amended by Directive 2003/51/EC of the European Parliament and of the Council (OJ L 178, 17.7.2003, p.16).

[2] By analogy with the provisions of Article 17 of Council Directive 77/91/EEC (OJ L 26, 30.1.1977, p.1) as last amended by the 2003 Act of Accession.

[3] This refers in particular to the types of company mentioned in the second subparagraph of Article 1(1) of Council Directive 78/660/EEC.

11. Even when none of the circumstances set out in point 10 are present, a firm may still be considered to be in difficulties, in particular where the usual signs of a firm being in difficulty are present, such as increasing losses, diminishing turnover, growing stock inventories, excess capacity, declining cash flow, mounting debt, rising interest charges and falling or nil net asset value. In acute cases the firm may already have become insolvent or may be the subject of collective insolvency proceedings brought under domestic law. In the latter case, these Guidelines apply to any aid granted in the context of such proceedings which leads to the firm's continuing in business. In any event, a firm in difficulty is eligible only where, demonstrably, it cannot recover through its own resources or with the funds it obtains from its owners/shareholders or from market sources.

12. For the purposes of these Guidelines, a newly created firm is not eligible for rescue or restructuring aid even if its initial financial position is insecure. This is the case, for instance, where a new firm emerges from the liquidation of a previous firm or merely takes over such firm's assets. A firm will in principle be considered as newly created for the first three years following the start of operations in the relevant field of activity. Only after that period will it become eligible for rescue or restructuring aid, provided that:

    (a) it qualifies as a firm in difficulty within the meaning of these Guidelines, and

    (b) it does not form part of a larger business group[1] except under the conditions laid down in point 13.

Notes

[1] To determine whether a company is independent or forms part of a group, the criteria laid down in Annex I to Commission Regulation (EC) No 68/2001 (OJ L 10, 13.1.2001, p.20), as amended by Regulation (EC) No 363/2004 (OJ L 63, 28.2.2004, p.20) will be taken into account.

Commentary
point 12: B&C: 17.066

---

13. A firm belonging to or being taken over by a larger business group is not normally eligible for rescue or restructuring aid, except where it can be demonstrated that the firm's difficulties are intrinsic and are not the result of an arbitrary allocation of costs within the group, and that the difficulties are too serious to be dealt with by the group itself. Where a firm in difficulty creates a subsidiary, the subsidiary, together with the firm in difficulty controlling it, will be regarded as a group and may receive aid under the conditions laid down in this point.

2.2. Definition of "rescue and restructuring aid"

14. Rescue aid and restructuring aid are covered by the same set of guidelines, because in both cases the public authorities are faced with a firm in difficulty and the rescue and restructuring are often two parts of a single operation, even if they involve different processes.

15. Rescue aid is by nature temporary and reversible assistance. Its primary objective is to make it possible to keep an ailing firm afloat for the time needed to work out a restructuring or liquidation plan. The general principle is that rescue aid makes it possible temporarily to support a company confronted with an important deterioration of its financial situation reflected by an acute liquidity crisis or technical insolvency. Such temporary support should allow time to analyse the circumstances which gave rise to the difficulties and to develop an appropriate plan to remedy those difficulties. Moreover, the rescue aid must be limited to the minimum necessary. In other words, rescue aid offers a short respite, not exceeding six months, to a firm in difficulty. The aid must consist of reversible liquidity support in the form of loan guarantees or loans, with an interest rate at least comparable to those observed for loans to healthy firms and in particular the reference rates adopted by the Commission. Structural measures which do not require immediate action, such as, the irremediable and automatic participation of the State in the own funds of the firm, cannot be financed through rescue aid.

Commentary
point 15: B&C: 17.065

---

16. Once a restructuring or liquidation plan for which aid has been requested has been established and is being implemented, all further aid will be considered as restructuring aid. Measures which

need to be implemented immediately to stem losses, including structural measures (for example, immediate withdrawal from a loss-making field of activity), can be undertaken with the rescue aid, subject to the conditions mentioned in Section 3.1 for individual aids and section 4.3 for aid schemes. Except where use is made of the simplified procedure set out in section 3.1.2, a Member State will need to demonstrate that such structural measures must be undertaken immediately. Rescue aid cannot normally be granted for financial restructuring.

Commentary
point 16: B&C: 17.065

17. Restructuring, on the other hand, will be based on a feasible, coherent and far-reaching plan to restore a firm's long-term viability. Restructuring usually involves one or more of the following elements: the reorganisation and rationalisation of the firm's activities on to a more efficient basis, typically involving the withdrawal from loss-making activities, the restructuring of those existing activities that can be made competitive again and, possibly, diversification in the direction of new and viable activities. Financial restructuring (capital injections, debt reduction) usually has to accompany the physical restructuring. Restructuring operations within the scope of these Guidelines cannot, however, be limited to financial aid designed to make good past losses without tackling the reasons for those losses.

2.3. Scope

18. These Guidelines apply to firms in all sectors, except to those operating in the coal[1] or steel sector,[2] without prejudice to any specific rules relating to firms in difficulty in the sector concerned.[3] With the exception of point 79,[4] they apply to the fisheries and aquaculture sector, subject to compliance with the specific rules laid down in the Guidelines for the examination of State aid to fisheries and aquaculture.[5] Chapter 5 contains some additional rules for agriculture.

Notes
[1] Article 3 of Council Regulation (EC) No 1407/2002 (OJ L 205, 2.8.2002, p.1), as amended by the 2003 Act of Accession.
[2] Point 19 of the Communication from the Commission concerning certain aspects of the treatment of competition cases resulting from the expiry of the ECSC Treaty (OJ C 152, 26.6.2002, p.5). Point 1 of the communication from the Commission on rescue and restructuring aid and closure aid for the steel sector (OJ C 70, 19.3.2002, p.21). Appropriate measures adopted in the context of the Multisectoral Framework on regional aid for large investment projects (OJ C 70, 19.3.2002, p.8).
[3] Specific rules of this nature exist for the aviation sector (OJ C 350, 10.12.1994, p.5).
[4] In other words, awards of aid to SMEs that do not fulfil the conditions set out in this point 0 may nevertheless be exempted from individual notification.
[5] OJ C 19, 20.1.2001, p.7.

2.4. Compatibility with the common market

19. Article [107(2) and (3)]* of the Treaty provide for the possibility that aid falling within the scope of Article [107(1)] will be regarded as compatible with the common market. Apart from cases of aid envisaged by Article [107(2)], in particular aid to make good the damage caused by natural disasters or exceptional occurrences, which are not covered here, the only basis on which aid for firms in difficulty can be deemed compatible is Article [107(3)(c)]. Under that provision the Commission has the power to authorise "aid to facilitate the development of certain economic activities (…) where such aid does not adversely affect trading conditions to an extent contrary to the common interest." In particular, this could be the case where the aid is necessary to correct disparities caused by market failures or to ensure economic and social cohesion.

20. Given that its very existence is in danger, a firm in difficulty cannot be considered an appropriate vehicle for promoting other public policy objectives until such time as its viability is assured. Consequently, the Commission considers that aid to firms in difficulty may contribute to the development of economic activities without adversely affecting trade to an extent contrary to the Community interest only if the conditions set out in these Guidelines are met. Where the firms which are to receive rescue or restructuring aid are located in assisted areas, the Commission will

take the regional considerations referred to in Article [107(3)(a) and (c)] of the Treaty into account as described in points 55 and 56.

Commentary
point 20: F&N: 17.201

21. The Commission will pay particular attention to the need to prevent the use of these Guidelines to circumvent the principles laid down in existing frameworks and Guidelines.
22. The assessment of rescue or restructuring aid should not be affected by changes in the ownership of the business aided.

Notes
* Ed note: please see the Note on the Lisbon Treaty at p.xvii in regard to article renumbering introduced by the Lisbon Treaty. Unless otherwise stated, all Treaty article numbers are the new numbers of the Treaty on the Functioning of the European Union (TFEU) and the Treaty on European Union (TEU).

2.5. Recipients of previous unlawful aid

23. Where unlawful aid has previously been granted to the firm in difficulty, in respect of which the Commission has adopted a negative decision with a recovery order, and where no such recovery has taken place in compliance with Article 14 of Council Regulation (EC) No 659/1999 of 22 March 1999 laying down detailed rules for the application of Article [108 TFEU],[1] the assessment of any rescue and restructuring aid to be granted to the same undertaking shall take into account, first, the cumulative effect of the old aid and of the new aid and, secondly, the fact that the old aid has not been repaid.[2]

Notes
[1] OJ L 83, 27.3.1999, p.1. Regulation as amended by the 2003 Act of Accession.
[2] Case C-355/95 P, *Textilwerke Deggendorf v Commission and others* [1997] ECR I-2549.

3. GENERAL CONDITIONS FOR THE AUTHORISATION OF RESCUE AND/OR RESTRUCTURING AID NOTIFIED INDIVIDUALLY TO THE COMMISSION

24. This Chapter deals exclusively with aid measures that are notified individually to the Commission. Under certain conditions, the Commission may authorise rescue or restructuring aid schemes: those conditions are set out in Chapter 4.

3.1. Rescue aid

3.1.1. Conditions

25. In order to be approved by the Commission, rescue aid as defined in point 15 must:
    (a) consist of liquidity support in the form of loan guarantees or loans;[1] in both cases, the loan must be granted at an interest rate at least comparable to those observed for loans to healthy firms, and in particular the reference rates adopted by the Commission; any loan must be reimbursed and any guarantee must come to an end within a period of not more than six months after the disbursement of the first instalment to the firm;
    (b) be warranted on the grounds of serious social difficulties and have no unduly adverse spillover effects on other Member States;
    (c) be accompanied, on notification, by an undertaking given by the Member State concerned to communicate to the Commission, not later than six months after the rescue aid measure has been authorised, a restructuring plan or a liquidation plan or proof that the loan has been reimbursed in full and/or that the guarantee has been terminated; in the case of non-notified aid the Member State must communicate, no later than six months after the first implementation of a rescue aid measure, a restructuring plan or a liquidation plan or proof that the loan has been reimbursed in full and /or that the guarantee has been terminated;

(d) be restricted to the amount needed to keep the firm in business for the period during which the aid is authorised; such an amount may include aid for urgent structural measures in accordance with point 16; the amount necessary should be based on the liquidity needs of the company stemming from losses; in determining that amount regard will be had to the outcome of the application of the formula set out in the Annex; any rescue aid exceeding the result of that calculation will need to be duly explained;

(e) respect the condition set out in section 3.3 (one time, last time).

Notes

[1] An exception may be made in the case of rescue aid in the banking sector, in order to enable the credit institution in question to continue temporarily carrying on its banking business in accordance with the prudential legislation in force (Directive 2000/12/EC of the European Parliament and of the Council, OJ L 126, 26.5.2000, p.1). At any rate, aid granted in a form other than loan guarantees or loans fulfilling the conditions set out in point (a), should fulfil the general principles of rescue aid and cannot consist in structural financial measures related to the bank's own funds. Any aid granted in a form other than loan guarantees or loans fulfilling the conditions set out in point (a), will be taken into account when any compensatory measures under a restructuring plan are examined in accordance with points 38 to 42.

Commentary
point 25(b): B&C: 17.065

26. Where the Member State has submitted a restructuring plan within six months of the date of authorisation or, in the case of non-notified aid, of implementation of the measure, the deadline for reimbursing the loan or for putting an end to the guarantee is extended until the Commission reaches its decision on the plan, unless the Commission decides that such an extension is not justified.

27. Without prejudice to Article 23 of Regulation (EC) No 659/1999 and to the possibility of an action before the Court of Justice, in accordance with the second subparagraph of Article [108(2)] of the Treaty, the Commission will initiate proceedings under Article [108(2)] of the Treaty if the Member State fails to communicate:

(a) a credible and substantiated restructuring plan or a liquidation plan, or

(b) proof that the loan has been reimbursed in full and/or that the guarantee has been terminated before the six-month deadline has expired.

28. In any event, the Commission may decide to initiate such proceedings, without prejudice to Article 23 of Regulation (EC) No 659/1999 and to the possibility of an action before the Court of Justice in accordance with the second subparagraph of Article [108(2)] of the Treaty, if it considers that the loan or the guarantee has been misused, or that, after the six-month deadline has expired, the failure to reimburse the aid is no longer justified.

29. The approval of rescue aid does not necessarily mean that aid under a restructuring plan will subsequently be approved; such aid will have to be assessed on its own merits.

3.1.2. Simplified procedure

30. The Commission will as far as possible endeavour to take a decision within a period of one month in respect of rescue aids fulfilling all conditions set out in section 3.1.1 and the following cumulative requirements:

(a) the firm concerned satisfies at least one of the three criteria set out in point 10;

(b) the rescue aid is limited to the amount resulting from the application of the formula set out in the Annex and does not exceed EUR 10 million.

Commentary
point 30: B&C: 17.065

3.2. Restructuring aid

3.2.1. Basic principle

31. Aid for restructuring raises particular competition concerns as it can shift an unfair share of the burden of structural adjustment and the attendant social and economic problems onto other producers who are managing without aid, and to other Member States. The general principle

should therefore be to allow the grant of restructuring aid only in circumstances in which it can be demonstrated that it does not run counter to the Community interest. This will only be possible if strict criteria are met, and if it is certain that any distortions of competition will be offset by the benefits flowing from the firm's survival (for instance, where it is clear that the net effect of redundancies resulting from the firm's going out of business, combined with the effects on its suppliers, would exacerbate employment problems or, exceptionally, where the firm's disappearance would result in a monopoly or tight oligopolistic situation) and that, in principle, there are adequate compensatory measures in favour of competitors.

Commentary
point 31: B&C: 17.065

3.2.2. Conditions for the authorisation of aid

32. Subject to the special provisions for assisted areas, SMEs and the agricultural sector (see points 55, 56, 57, 59 and Chapter 5), the Commission will approve aid only under the following conditions:

Eligibility of the firm

33. The firm must qualify as a firm in difficulty within the meaning of these Guidelines (see points 9 to 13).

Restoration of long-term viability

34. The grant of the aid must be conditional on implementation of the restructuring plan which must be endorsed by the Commission in all cases of individual aid, except in the case of SMEs, as laid down in section 3.2.5.

35. The restructuring plan, the duration of which must be as short as possible, must restore the long-term viability of the firm within a reasonable timescale and on the basis of realistic assumptions as to future operating conditions. Restructuring aid must therefore be linked to a viable restructuring plan to which the Member State concerned commits itself. The plan must be submitted in all relevant detail to the Commission and include, in particular, a market survey. The improvement in viability must derive mainly from internal measures contained in the restructuring plan; it may be based on external factors such as variations in prices and demand over which the company has no great influence, but only if the market assumptions made are generally acknowledged. Restructuring must involve the abandonment of activities which would remain structurally loss-making even after restructuring.

36. The restructuring plan must describe the circumstances that led to the company's difficulties, thereby providing a basis for assessing whether the proposed measures are appropriate. It must take account, inter alia, of the present state of and future prospects for supply and demand on the relevant product market, with scenarios reflecting best-case, worst-case and intermediate assumptions and the firm's specific strengths and weaknesses. It must enable the firm to progress towards a new structure that offers it prospects for long-term viability and enables it to stand on its own feet.

37. The plan must provide for a turnaround that will enable the company, after completing its restructuring, to cover all its costs including depreciation and financial charges. The expected return on capital must be enough to enable the restructured firm to compete in the marketplace on its own merits. Where the firm's difficulties stem from flaws in its corporate governance system, appropriate adaptations will have to be introduced.

Avoidance of undue distortions of competition

38. In order to ensure that the adverse effects on trading conditions are minimized as much as possible, so that the positive effects pursued outweigh the adverse ones, compensatory measures must be taken. Otherwise, the aid will be regarded as "contrary to the common interest" and therefore incompatible with the common market. The Commission will have regard to the objective of restoring the long-term viability in determining the adequacy of the compensatory measures.

39. These measures may comprise divestment of assets, reductions in capacity or market presence and reduction of entry barriers on the markets concerned. When assessing whether the compensatory

measures are appropriate the Commission will take account of the market structure and the conditions of competition to ensure that any such measure does not lead to a deterioration in the structure of the market, for example by having the indirect effect of creating a monopoly or a tight oligopolistic situation. If a Member State is able to prove that such a situation would arise, the compensatory measures should be construed in such a way to avoid this situation.

40. The measures must be in proportion to the distortive effects of the aid and, in particular, to the size[1] and the relative importance of the firm on its market or markets. They should take place in particular in the market(s) where the firm will have a significant market position after restructuring. The degree of reduction must be established on a case-by-case basis. The Commission will determine the extent of the measures necessary on the basis of the market survey attached to the restructuring plan and, where appropriate on the basis of any other information at the disposal of the Commission including that supplied by interested parties. The reduction must be an integral part of the restructuring as laid down in the restructuring plan. This principle applies irrespective of whether the divestitures take place before or after the granting of the State aid, as long as they are part of the same restructuring. Write-offs and closure of loss-making activities which would at any rate be necessary to restore viability will not be considered reduction of capacity or market presence for the purpose of the assessment of the compensatory measures. Such an assessment will take account of any rescue aid granted beforehand.

Notes

[1] In this respect the Commission may also take into account whether the company in question is a medium-sized enterprise or a large one.

41. However, this condition will not normally apply to small enterprises, since it can be assumed that ad hoc aid to small enterprises does not normally distort competition to an extent contrary to the common interest, except where otherwise provided by rules on State aid in a particular sector or when the beneficiary is active in a market suffering from long-term overcapacity.

42. When the beneficiary is active in a market suffering from long-term structural overcapacity, as defined in the context of the Multisectoral framework on regional aid for large investments,[1] the reduction in the company's capacity or market presence may have to be as high as 100%.[2]

Notes

[1] OJ C 70, 19.3.2002, p.8.
[2] In such cases, the Commission will only allow aid to alleviate the social costs of the restructuring, in line with section 3.2.6 and environmental aid to clean up polluted sites which might otherwise be abandoned.

Aid limited to the minimum: real contribution, free of aid

43. The amount and intensity of the aid must be limited to the strict minimum of the restructuring costs necessary to enable restructuring to be undertaken in the light of the existing financial resources of the company, its shareholders or the business group to which it belongs. Such assessment will take account of any rescue aid granted beforehand. Aid beneficiaries will be expected to make a significant contribution to the restructuring plan from their own resources, including the sale of assets that are not essential to the firm's survival, or from external financing at market conditions. Such contribution is a sign that the markets believe in the feasibility of the return to viability. Such contribution must be real, i.e., actual, excluding all future expected profits such as cash flow, and must be as high as possible.

44. The Commission will normally consider the following contributions[1] to the restructuring to be appropriate: at least 25% in the case of small enterprises, at least 40%, for medium-sized enterprises and at least 50% for large firms. In exceptional circumstances and in cases of particular hardship, which must be demonstrated by the Member State, the Commission may accept a lower contribution.

Notes

[1] See point 7. This minimum contribution must not contain any aid. This is not the case, for instance, where a loan carries an interest-rate subsidy or is backed by government guarantees containing elements of aid.

45. To limit the distortive effect, the amount of the aid or the form in which it is granted must be such as to avoid providing the company with surplus cash which could be used for aggressive, market-distorting activities not linked to the restructuring process. The Commission will accordingly examine the level of the firm's liabilities after restructuring, including the situation after any postponement or reduction of its debts, particularly in the context of its continuation in business following collective insolvency proceedings brought against it under national law.[1] None of the aid should go to finance new investment that is not essential for restoring the firm's viability.

Notes
[1] See point 10(c).

Specific conditions attached to the authorisation of aid

46. In addition to the compensatory measures described in points 38 to 42, the Commission may impose any conditions and obligations it considers necessary in order to ensure that the aid does not distort competition to an extent contrary to the common interest, in the event that the Member State concerned has not given a commitment that it will adopt such provisions. For example, it may require the Member State:
    (a) to take certain measures itself (for example, to open up certain markets directly or indirectly linked to the company's activities to other Community operators with due respect to Community law);
    (b) to impose certain obligations on the recipient firm;
    (c) to refrain from granting other types of aid to the recipient firm during the restructuring period.

Full implementation of restructuring plan and observance of conditions

47. The company must fully implement the restructuring plan and must discharge any other obligations laid down in the Commission decision authorising the aid. The Commission will regard any failure to implement the plan or to fulfil the other obligations as misuse of the aid, without prejudice to Article 23 of Regulation (EC) No 659/1999 and to the possibility of an action before the Court of Justice in accordance with the second subparagraph of Article [108(2)] of the Treaty.
48. Where restructuring operations cover several years and involve substantial amounts of aid, the Commission may require payment of the restructuring aid to be split into instalments and may make payment of each instalment subject to:
    (i) confirmation, prior to each payment, of the satisfactory implementation of each stage in the restructuring plan, in accordance with the planned timetable; or
    (ii) its approval, prior to each payment, after verification that the plan is being satisfactorily implemented.

Monitoring and annual report

49. The Commission must be put in a position to make certain that the restructuring plan is being implemented properly, through regular detailed reports communicated by the Member State concerned.
50. In the case of aid to large firms, the first of these reports will normally have to be submitted to the Commission not later than six months after approval of the aid. Reports will subsequently have to be sent to the Commission at least once a year, at a fixed date, until the objectives of the restructuring plan can be deemed to have been achieved. They must contain all the information the Commission needs in order to be able to monitor the implementation of the restructuring programme, the timetable for payments to the company and its financial position and the observance of any conditions or obligations laid down in the decision approving the aid. They must in particular include all relevant information on any aid for any purpose which the company has received, either on an individual basis or under a general scheme, during the restructuring period (see points 68 to 71). Where the Commission needs prompt confirmation of certain key items of information, for example, on closures or capacity reductions, it may require more frequent reports.

Part G State Aids

51. In the case of aid to SMEs, transmission each year of a copy of the recipient firm's balance sheet and profit-and-loss account will normally be sufficient, except where stricter conditions have been laid down in the decision approving the aid.

3.2.3. Amendment of the restructuring plan

52. Where restructuring aid has been approved, the Member State concerned may, during the restructuring period, ask the Commission to agree to changes to the restructuring plan and the amount of the aid. The Commission may allow such changes where they meet the following conditions:

    (a) the revised plan must still show a return to viability within a reasonable time scale;
    (b) if the amount of the aid is increased, any requisite compensatory measures must be more extensive than those initially imposed;
    (c) if the proposed compensatory measures are smaller than those initially planned, the amount of the aid must be correspondingly reduced;
    (d) the new timetable for implementation of the compensatory measures may be delayed with respect to the timetable initially adopted only for reasons outside the company's or the Member State's control: if that is not the case, the amount of the aid must be correspondingly reduced.

53. If the conditions imposed by the Commission or the commitments given by the Member State are relaxed, the amount of aid must be correspondingly reduced or other conditions may be imposed.

54. Should the Member State introduce changes to an approved restructuring plan without duly informing the Commission, the Commission will initiate proceedings under Article [108(2)] of the Treaty, as provided for by Article 16 of Regulation (EC) No 659/1999 (misuse of aid), without prejudice to Article 23 of Regulation (EC) No 659/1999 and to the possibility of an action before the Court of Justice in accordance with the second subparagraph of Article [108(2)] of the Treaty.

3.2.4. Restructuring aid in assisted areas

55. Economic and social cohesion being a priority objective of the Community under Article [174] of the Treaty and other policies being required to contribute to this objective under Article [175],[1] the Commission must take the needs of regional development into account when assessing restructuring aid in assisted areas. The fact that an ailing firm is located in an assisted area does not, however, justify a permissive approach to aid for restructuring: in the medium to long term it does not help a region to prop up companies artificially. Furthermore, in order to promote regional development it is in the region's own best interest to apply its resources to develop as soon as possible activities that are viable and sustainable. Finally, distortions of competition must be minimised even in the case of aid to firms in assisted areas. In this context, regard must also be had to possible harmful spill-over effects which could take place in the area concerned and other assisted areas.

Notes

[1] Article [175 TFEU] provides, inter alia, that "the formulation and implementation of the [Union's] policies and actions and the implementation of the internal market shall take into account the objectives set out in Article [174] and shall contribute to their achievement".

---

56. Thus, the criteria listed in points 32 to 54 are equally applicable to assisted areas, even when the needs of regional development are considered. In assisted areas, however, and unless otherwise stipulated in rules on State aid in a particular sector, the conditions for authorising aid may be less stringent as regards the implementation of compensatory measures and the size of the beneficiary's contribution. If needs of regional development justify it, in cases in which a reduction of capacity or market presence appear to be the most appropriate measure to avoid undue distortions of competition, the required reduction will be smaller in assisted areas than in non-assisted areas. In those cases, which need to be demonstrated by the Member State concerned, a distinction will be drawn between areas eligible for regional aid under Article [107(3)(a)] of the Treaty and those eligible under Article [107(3)(c)] so as to take account of the greater severity of the regional problems in the former areas.

3.2.5. Aid for restructuring SMEs

57. Aid to small enterprises[1] tends to affect trading conditions less than that granted to medium-sized and large firms. This also applies to aid to help restructuring, so that the conditions laid down in points 32 to 54 are applied less strictly in the following respects:

    (a) the grant of restructuring aid to small enterprises will not usually be linked to compensatory measures (see point 41), unless this is otherwise stipulated in rules on State aid in a particular sector.

    (b) the requirements regarding the content of reports will be less stringent for SMEs (see points 49, 50 and 51).

Notes

[1] As defined in the Commission Recommendation 2003/361/EC (OJ L 124, 20.5.2003, p.36). Until 31 December 2004, the relevant definition is to be found in the Commission Recommendation 96/280/EC (OJ L 107, 30.4.1996, p.4).

58. However, the "one time, last time" principle (section 3.3) applies in full to SMEs.

59. For SMEs the restructuring plan does not need to be endorsed by the Commission. However, the plan must meet the requirements laid down in points 35, 36 and 37 and be approved by the Member State concerned and communicated to the Commission. The grant of aid must be conditional on full implementation of the restructuring plan. The obligation to verify that these conditions are fulfilled lies with the Member State.

3.2.6. Aid to cover the social costs of restructuring

60. Restructuring plans normally entail reductions in or abandonment of the affected activities. Such retrenchments are often necessary in the interests of rationalisation and efficiency, quite apart from any capacity reductions that may be required as a condition for granting aid. Whatever the reason for them, such measures will generally lead to reductions in the company's workforce.

61. Member States' labour legislation may comprise general social security schemes under which redundancy benefits and early retirement pensions are paid direct to redundant employees. Such schemes are not to be regarded as State aid falling within the scope of Article [107(1)] of the Treaty.

62. Besides direct redundancy benefit and early retirement provision for employees, general social support schemes frequently provide for the government to cover the cost of benefits which the company grants to redundant workers and which go beyond its statutory or contractual obligations. Where such schemes are available generally without sectoral limitations to any worker meeting predefined and automatic eligibility conditions, they are not deemed to involve aid under Article [107(1)] for firms undertaking restructuring. On the other hand, if the schemes are used to support restructuring in particular industries, they may well involve aid because of the selective way in which they are used.[1]

Notes

[1] In its judgment in Case C-241/94 *France v Commission* [1996] ECR I-4551 (Kimberly Clark Sopalin), the Court of Justice confirmed that the system of financing on a discretionary basis by the French authorities, through the National Employment Fund, was liable to place certain firms in a more favourable situation than others and thus to qualify as aid within the meaning of Article [107(1)] of the Treaty. (The Court's judgment did not call into question the Commission's conclusion that the aid was compatible with the common market.)

63. The obligations a company itself bears under employment legislation or collective agreements with trade unions, to provide redundancy benefits and/or early retirement pensions are part of the normal costs of a business which a firm has to meet from its own resources. That being so, any contribution by the State to these costs must be counted as aid. This is true regardless of whether the payments are made direct to the firm or are administered through a government agency to the employees.

64. The Commission has no a priori objection to such aid when it is granted to firms in difficulty, for it brings economic benefits above and beyond the interests of the firm concerned, facilitating structural change and reducing hardship.

65. Besides meeting the cost of redundancy payments and early retirement, aid is commonly provided in connection with a particular restructuring scheme for training, counselling and practical help with finding alternative employment, assistance with relocation, and professional training and assistance for employees wishing to start new businesses. The Commission consistently takes a favourable view of such aid when it is granted to firms in difficulty.

66. The type of aid described in points 62 to 65 must be clearly identified in the restructuring plan, since aid for social measures exclusively for the benefit of redundant employees is disregarded for the purposes of determining the extent of the compensatory measures referred to in points 38 to 42.

67. In the common interest, the Commission will ensure in the context of the restructuring plan that social effects of the restructuring in Member States other than the one granting aid are kept to the minimum.

3.2.7. Need to inform the Commission of any aid granted to the recipient firm during the restructuring period

68. Where restructuring aid received by a large or medium-sized enterprise is examined under these Guidelines, the grant of any other aid during the restructuring period, even in accordance with a scheme that has already been authorised, is liable to influence the Commission's assessment of the extent of the compensatory measures required.

69. Notifications of aid for restructuring a large or medium-sized enterprise must indicate all other aid of any kind which is planned to be granted to the recipient firm during the restructuring period, unless it is covered by the de minimis rule or by exemption regulations. The Commission shall take such aid into account when assessing the restructuring aid.

70. Any aid actually granted to a large or medium-sized enterprise during the restructuring period, including aid granted in accordance with an approved scheme, must be notified individually to the Commission to the extent that the latter was not informed thereof at the time of its decision on the restructuring aid.

71. The Commission shall ensure that the grant of aid under approved schemes is not liable to circumvent the requirements of these Guidelines.

3.3. "One time, last time"

72. Rescue aid is a one-off operation primarily designed to keep a company in business for a limited period, during which its future can be assessed. It should not be possible to allow repeated granting of rescue aids that would merely maintain the status quo, postpone the inevitable and in the meantime shift economic and social problems on to other, more efficient producers or other Member States. Hence, rescue aid should be granted only once (one time, last time condition). In accordance with the same principle, in order to prevent firms from being unfairly assisted when they can only survive thanks to repeated State support, restructuring aid should be granted once only. Finally, if rescue aid is granted to a firm that has already received restructuring aid, it can be considered that the beneficiary's difficulties are of a recurrent nature and that repeated State interventions give rise to distortions of competition that are contrary to the common interest. Such repeated State interventions should not be permitted.

73. When planned rescue or restructuring aid is notified to the Commission, the Member State must specify whether the firm concerned has already received rescue or restructuring aid in the past, including any such aid granted before the date of application of these Guidelines and any unnotified aid.[1] If so, and where less than 10 years have elapsed since the rescue aid was granted or the restructuring period came to an end or implementation of the restructuring plan has been halted (whichever is the latest), the Commission will not allow further rescue or restructuring aid. Exceptions to that rule are permitted in the following cases:

(a) where restructuring aid follows the granting of rescue aid as part of a single restructuring operation;

(b) where rescue aid has been granted in accordance with the conditions in section [3.1], and this aid was not followed by a State supported restructuring, if:

(i) the firm could reasonably be believed to be viable in the long-term following the granting of rescue aid, and

(ii) new rescue or restructuring aid becomes necessary after at least five years due to unforeseeable circumstances[2] for which the company is not responsible;

(c) in exceptional and unforeseeable circumstances for which the company is not responsible.

In the cases set out in points (b) and (c), the simplified procedure mentioned in section 3.1.2 cannot be used.

Notes

[1] With regard to unnotified aid, the Commission will take account in its appraisal of the possibility that the aid could have been declared compatible with the common market other than as rescue or restructuring aid.

[2] An unforeseeable circumstance is one which could in no way be anticipated by the company's management when the restructuring plan was drawn up and which is not due to negligence or errors of the company's management or decisions of the group to which it belongs.

---

74. The application of this rule will in no way be affected by any changes in ownership of the recipient firm following the grant of aid or by any judicial or administrative procedure which has the effect of putting its balance sheet on a sounder footing, reducing its liabilities or wiping out its previous debts where it is the same firm that is continuing in business.

75. Where a business group has received rescue or restructuring aid, the Commission will normally not allow further rescue or restructuring aid to the group itself or any of the entities belonging to the group unless 10 years have elapsed since the rescue aid was granted or the restructuring period came to an end or implementation of the restructuring plan has been halted, whichever is the latest. Where an entity belonging to a business group has received rescue or restructuring aid, the group as a whole as well as the other entities of the group remain eligible for rescue or restructuring aid (subject to compliance with the other provisions of these Guidelines), with the exception of the earlier beneficiary of the aid. Member States must ensure that no aid will be passed on from the group or other group entities to the earlier beneficiary of the aid.

76. Where a firm takes over assets of another firm, and in particular one that has been the subject of one of the procedures referred to in point 74 or of collective insolvency proceedings brought under national law and has already received rescue or restructuring aid, the purchaser is not subject to the "one time, last time" requirement, provided that the following cumulative conditions are met:

(a) the purchaser is clearly separate from the old firm;

(b) the purchaser has acquired the old firm's assets at market prices;

(c) the winding-up or court-supervised administration and purchase of the old company are not merely devices aimed at evading application of the "one time, last time" principle: the Commission may determine that this was the case if, for example, the difficulties encountered by the purchaser were clearly foreseeable when it took over the assets of the old company.

77. It should, however, be stressed here that, since it constitutes aid for initial investment, aid for the purchase of the assets cannot be authorised under these Guidelines.

4. Aid Schemes for SMEs

4.1. General principles

78. The Commission will authorise schemes for providing rescue and/or restructuring aid to small or medium-sized enterprises in difficulty only where the firms concerned correspond to the Community definition of SMEs. Subject to the following specific provisions, the compatibility of such schemes will be assessed in the light of the conditions set out in Chapters 2 and 3, with the exception of Section 3.1.2 which does not apply to aid schemes. Any aid which is granted under a scheme but does not meet any of those conditions must be notified individually and approved in advance by the Commission.

4.2. Eligibility

79. Unless otherwise stipulated in rules on State aid in a particular sector, awards of aid under schemes authorised from the date of application of these Guidelines, to small or medium-sized enterprises will be exempted from individual notification only where the enterprise concerned meets at least

one of the three criteria set out in point 10. Aid to enterprises that do not meet any of those three criteria must be notified individually to the Commission so that it can assess whether they qualify as firms in difficulty. Aid to enterprises active in a market suffering from long-term structural overcapacity, irrespective of the size of the beneficiary, must also be notified individually to the Commission so that it can assess the application of point 42.

Commentary
point 79: B&C: 17.064

4.3. Conditions for the authorisation of rescue aid schemes

80. In order to be approved by the Commission, rescue aid schemes must satisfy the conditions set out in points (a), (b), (d) and (e) of point 25. Furthermore, rescue aid may not be granted for more than six months, during which time an analysis must be made of the firm's position. Before the end of that period the Member State must either approve a restructuring plan or a liquidation plan, or demand reimbursement of the loan and the aid corresponding to the risk premium from the beneficiary.

81. Any rescue aid granted for longer than six months or not reimbursed after six months must be individually notified to the Commission.

4.4. Conditions for the authorisation of restructuring aid schemes

82. The Commission will authorise restructuring aid schemes only if the grant of aid is conditional on full implementation by the recipient of a restructuring plan that has been approved by the Member State concerned and meets the following conditions:

(a) restoration of viability: the criteria set out in points 34 to 37 apply;

(b) avoidance of undue distortions of competition: since aid to small enterprises tends to distort competition less, the principle set out in points 38 to 42 does not apply unless it is otherwise stipulated in rules on State aid in a particular sector; schemes should nevertheless provide that recipient firms must not increase their capacity during the restructuring; for medium-sized enterprises points 38 to 42 apply;

(c) aid limited to the minimum necessary: the principles set out in points 43, 44 and 45 apply;

(d) amendment of the restructuring plan: any changes to the plan must comply with the rules set out in points 52, 53 and 54.

4.5. Common conditions for the authorisation of rescue and/ or restructuring aid schemes

83. Schemes must specify the maximum amount of aid that can be awarded to any one firm as part of an operation to provide rescue and/or restructuring aid, including where the plan is modified. Any aid exceeding that amount must be notified individually to the Commission. The maximum amount of aid granted for the combined rescue and restructuring aid of any one firm may not be more than EUR 10 million, including any aid obtained from other sources or under other schemes.

84. In addition, the "one time, last time" principle must be respected. The rule laid down in section 3.3 applies.

85. Member States must also notify measures individually to the Commission where one firm takes over assets of another firm which has itself already received rescue or restructuring aid.

4.6. Monitoring and annual reports

86. Points 49, 50 and 51 do not apply to aid schemes. However, it will be a condition of approval that reports are presented on the scheme's operation, normally on an annual basis, containing the information specified in the Commission's instructions on standardised reports.[1] The reports must also include a list of all beneficiary companies, indicating for each of them:

(a) 'company name;

(b) the company's sectoral code, using the NACE[2] three-digit sectoral classification codes;

    (c) number of employees;

    (d) annual turnover and balance sheet value;

    (e) amount of aid granted;

    (f) amount and form of the beneficiary's contribution;

    (g) where appropriate, the form and the degree of the compensatory measures;

    (h) where appropriate, any restructuring aid, or other support treated as such, which it has received in the past;

    (i) whether or not the beneficiary company has been wound up or subject to collective insolvency proceedings before the end of the restructuring period.

Notes

1 See Annex III. A and B (standardised reporting format for existing State aid) to Commission Regulation (EC) No 794/2004 of 21 April 2004 adopting provisions for the implementation of Council Regulation (EC) No 659/1999 laying down detailed rules for the application of Article [108 TFEU] (OJ L 140, 30.4.2004, p.1).

2 Statistical classification of economic activities in the European Community, published by the Statistical Office of the European Communities.

5. PROVISIONS APPLICABLE TO AID FOR RESTRUCTURING IN THE AGRICULTURAL SECTOR[1]

Notes

1 This covers, for the purpose of these Guidelines, all operators involved in the primary production of agricultural products of Annex I to the Treaty (farming). Aid measures in favour of enterprises processing and marketing agricultural products are not covered by this Chapter. Aid to processing and marketing companies is to be assessed in line with the general rules of these Guidelines. Fisheries and aquaculture are not covered by this chapter.

5.1. Compensatory measures

87. Points 38 to 42, and 57 and 82(b) provide that the requirement for compensatory measures is not normally applied in the case of small enterprises, unless otherwise stipulated in sector-specific State aid rules. In the agricultural sector, the Commission will normally require compensatory measures, in accordance with the principles set out in points 38 to 42, to be carried out by all recipients of restructuring aid, whatever their size.

5.2. Definition of excess capacity

88. For the purposes of these Guidelines, structural excess capacity in the agricultural sector will be defined by the Commission on a case-by-case basis taking account in particular of the extent and trend for the relevant product category over the past three years, of market stabilisation measures, especially export refunds and withdrawals from the market, of development of world market prices, and of the presence of sectoral limits in Community legislation.

5.3. Eligibility for rescue and restructuring aid schemes

89. By way of derogation from point 79, the Commission may also exempt aid to SMEs from individual notification if the SME concerned does not meet at least one of the three criteria set out in point 10.

5.4. Capacity reductions

90. Where there is a structural excess of production capacity, the requirement of irreversibly reducing or closing capacity set out in points 38 to 42 applies. Open farmland may be re-used after 15 years following effective capacity closure. Until then, it has to be maintained in good agricultural and environmental condition for land no longer used for production purposes, in accordance with Article 5 of Council Regulation (EC) No 1782/2003 of 29 September 2003 establishing common rules for direct support schemes under the common agricultural policy and establishing certain support schemes for farmers,[1] and with the relevant implementation rules.

Notes
1 OJ L 270, 21.10. 2003, p.1. Regulation as last amended by Regulation (EC) No 864/2004 (OJ L 161, 30.4.2004, p.48).

91. Where the aid measure is targeted on particular products or operators, the production capacity reduction must attain at least 10% of that for which the restructuring aid is effectively granted. For measures not so targeted, the production capacity reduction must attain at least 5%. For restructuring aid granted in less favoured areas,[1] the capacity reduction requirement will be reduced by two percentage points. The Commission will waive these capacity reduction requirements where the decisions to grant restructuring aid taken in favour of beneficiaries in a given sector over any consecutive 12-month period do not together involve more than 1% of the production capacity of that sector in the Member State concerned. This rule may be applied at regional level in the case of an aid regime limited to a given region.

Notes
1 As defined in Articles 13 and following of Council Regulation (EC) No 1257/1999 (OJ L 160, 26.6.1999, p.80), as last amended by Regulation (EC) No 583/2004 (OJ L 91, 30.3.2004, p.1).

92. The requirement of irreversibly reducing capacity may be achieved at the relevant market level (not necessarily involving reductions by the beneficiaries of the restructuring aid). Subject to compliance with common agricultural policy provisions, Member States may choose whatever capacity reduction system they wish.

93. The Member State must demonstrate that the capacity reduction would be supplementary to any reduction which would be applied in the absence of the restructuring aid.

94. Where the capacity reduction is not sought at the level of the beneficiary of the aid, measures to achieve the reduction must be implemented no later than one year after the aid has been granted.

95. In order to ensure the effectiveness of the closure of capacity undertaken at the relevant market level, the Member State must give a commitment not to grant State aid for capacity increases in the sector concerned. This commitment shall remain in force for a period of five years from the date where the required capacity reduction actually has been achieved.

96. In determining eligibility for and amounts of restructuring aid, no account shall be taken of the burdens of compliance with Community quota and related provisions at the level of individual operators.

5.5. "One time, last time" condition

97. The principle that rescue or restructuring aid should be granted once only also applies to the agricultural sector. However, instead of the period of 10 years set out in section 3.3 a five-year period will apply.

5.6. Monitoring and annual report

98. The rules set out in Chapters 3 and 4 apply to monitoring and annual reports in the agricultural sector, except for the obligation to supply a list of all aid beneficiaries and certain items of information on each of them (see point 86). Where recourse has been had to the provisions of points 90 to 96, the report must also include data showing the production capacity which has effectively benefited from restructuring aid and the capacity reduction achieved.

6. Appropriate Measures as Referred to in Article [108(1)]

99. The Commission will propose, by separate letter, pursuant to Article [108(1)] of the Treaty, that the Member States adopt appropriate measures as set out in points 100 and 101, with regard to their existing aid schemes. The Commission will make authorisation of any future scheme conditional on compliance with those provisions.

100. Member States which have accepted the Commission's proposal must adapt their existing aid schemes which are to remain in operation after 9 October 2004 within six months in order to bring them into line with these Guidelines.

101. Member States must indicate their acceptance of these appropriate measures within one month following receipt of said letter proposing appropriate measures.

7. DATE OF APPLICATION AND DURATION

102. The Commission will apply these Guidelines with effect from 10 October 2004 until 9 October 2009.

Notes

The validity of the 2004 Guidelines has been extended until 9 October 2012: see Commission communication concerning the prolongation of the community guidelines on State aid for rescuing and restructuring firms in difficulty (OJ C 156, 9.7.09, p.3)

103. Notifications registered by the Commission prior to 10 October 2004 will be examined in the light of the criteria in force at the time of notification.

104. The Commission will examine the compatibility with the common market of any rescue or restructuring aid granted without its authorisation and therefore in breach of Article [108(3)] of the Treaty on the basis of these Guidelines if some or all of the aid is granted after their publication in the *Official Journal of the European Union*.

In all other cases it will conduct the examination on the basis of the Guidelines which apply at the time the aid is granted.

ANNEX

Formula[1] to calculate maximum amount of rescue aid to qualify for the simplified procedure:

$$\frac{\text{EBIT}_t + \text{depreciation}_t + (\text{working capital}_t - \text{working capital}_{t-1})}{2}$$

The formula is based on the operating results of the company (EBIT, earnings before interest and taxes) recorded in the year before granting/notifying the aid (indicated as t). To this amount depreciation has been added. Then changes in working capital must be added to the total. The change in working capital is calculated as the difference between the current assets and current liabilities[2] for the latest closed accounting periods. Similarly, if there would be provisions at the level of the operating result, this will need to be clearly indicated and the result should not include such provisions.

The formula aims at estimating the negative operating cash flow of the company in the year preceding the application for the aid (or before the award of the aid in case of non-notified aids). Half of this amount should keep the company in business for a six-month period. Thus the result of the formula has to be divided by 2.

This formula can only be applied where the result is a negative amount.

In case the formula leads to a positive result, a detailed explanation will need to be submitted demonstrating that the firm is in difficulty as defined in points 10 and 11.

Example:

Earnings before interest and taxes (EUR million)	(12)	
Depreciation (EUR million)	(2)	
Balance sheet (EUR million)	December 31, X	December 31, XO
Current assets		
Cash or equivalents	10	5
Accounts receivable	30	20
Inventories	50	45

Prepaid expenses	20	10
Other current assets	20	20
Total current assets	130	100
Current liabilities		
Accounts payable	20	25
Accrued expenses	15	10
Deferred income	5	5
Total current liabilities	40	40
Working capital	90	60
Change in working capital	(30)	

Maximum amount of rescue aid = [–12 + 2 + (–30)] / 2 = –EUR 20 million.

As the outcome of the formula is higher than EUR 10 million, the simplified procedure described in point 30 cannot be used. If this limit is exceeded, the Member State should provide an explanation of how the future cash-flow needs of the company and the amount of rescue aid have been determined.

Notes

[1] EBIT (earnings before interest and taxes as set out in the annual accounts of the year before the application, indicated as t) must be increased with depreciation in the same period plus the changes in working capital over a two-year period (year before the application and preceding year), divided by two to determine an amount over six months, i.e. normal period for permitting rescue aid.

[2] Current assets: liquid funds, receivables (client and debtor accounts), other current assets and prepaid expenses, inventories. Current liabilities: financial debt, trade accounts payable (supplier and creditor accounts) and other current liabilities, deferred income, other accrued liabilities, tax liabilities.

G14

GUIDELINES ON NATIONAL REGIONAL AID FOR 2007–2013

(2006/C 54/08)

(Text with EEA relevance)

Official Journal C 54, 4.3.2006, p.13

Celex No: 52006XC0304(02)

EUR-Lex permanent link: <http://eur-lex.europa.eu/LexUriServ/LexUriServ.do?uri=CELEX:52006XC0304(02)EN:NOT>

Notes

On 28 June 2013, new Guidelines on regional State aid for 2014–2020 were adopted (OJ C 209, 23.7.2013, p.1). The new Guidelines will apply to aid granted from 1 July 2014. The current regional aid rules, which were due to expire at the end of 2013, are extended until 30 June 2014.

For reasons of space, the new Guidelines are not reproduced in this edition of the Materials. It is hoped they will be included in the next edition and are already available on Oxford Competition Law. They are also available on EUR-Lex at <http://eur-lex.europa.eu/LexUriServ/LexUriServ.do?uri=CELEX:52013XC0723%2803%29:EN:NOT>.

EEA application: for the corresponding EEA provision, see the EFTA Surveillance Authority's Procedural and Substantive Rules in the Field of State Aid (Guidelines on the application and interpretation of Articles 61 and 62 of the EEA Agreement and Article 1 of Protocol 3 to the Surveillance and Court Agreement), Part VI, Chapter 25B (as introduced by EFTA Surveillance Authority Decision No. 85/06/COL of 6 April 2006, OJ L 54, 28.2.2008, p.1).

Commentary
Guidelines: B&C: 17.049 F&N: 17.221, 17.225, 17.228, 17.230
paras 1–3: B&C: 17.049
paras 21–32: B&C: 17.052, 17.059
paras 60–70: B&C: 17.053
paras 84–91: B&C: 17.053
paras 99–107: B&C: 17.053

1. Introduction

1. On the basis of Article [107(3)(a) and (c)]* of the Treaty, State aid granted to promote the economic development of certain disadvantaged areas within the European Union may be considered to be compatible with the common market by the Commission. This kind of State aid is known as national regional aid. National regional aid consists of aid for investment granted to large companies, or in certain limited circumstances, operating aid, which in both cases are targeted on specific regions in order to redress regional disparities. Increased levels of investment aid granted to small and medium-sized enterprises located within the disadvantaged regions over and above what is allowed in other areas are also considered as regional aid.

2. By addressing the handicaps of the disadvantaged regions, national regional aid promotes the economic, social and territorial cohesion of Member States and the European Union as a whole. This geographical specificity distinguishes regional aid from other forms of horizontal aid, such as aid for research, development and innovation, employment, training or the environment, which pursue other objectives of common interest in accordance with Article [107(3)] of the Treaty, albeit sometimes with higher rates of aid in the disadvantaged areas in recognition of the specific difficulties which they face.[1]

Notes
* Ed note: please see the Note on the Lisbon Treaty at p.xvii in regard to article renumbering introduced by the Lisbon Treaty. Unless otherwise stated, all Treaty article numbers are the new numbers of the Treaty on the Functioning of the European Union (TFEU) and the Treaty on European Union (TEU).
[1] Regional top-ups for aid granted for such purposes are therefore not considered as regional aid.

3. National regional investment aid is designed to assist the development of the most disadvantaged regions by supporting investment and job creation. It promotes the expansion and diversification of the economic activities of enterprises located in the less-favoured regions, in particular by encouraging firms to set up new establishments there.

4. The criteria applied by the Commission when examining the compatibility of national regional aid with the common market under Articles [107(3)(a) and 107(3)(c) TFEU] have been codified in the 1998 guidelines on national regional aid[2] which cover the period 2000–2006.[3] The specific rules governing aid for large investment projects have been codified in the 2002 Multisectoral Framework.[4] However, important political and economic developments since 1998, including the enlargement of the European Union on 1 May 2004, the anticipated accession of Bulgaria and Romania and the accelerated process of integration following the introduction of the single currency, have created the need for a comprehensive review in order to prepare new guidelines which will apply from 2007 to 2013.

Notes
[2] OJ C 74 10.3.1998, p.9, modified in OJ C 288 9.10.1999, p.2, and OJ C 285 9.9.2000, p.5.
[3] Point 4.4 of the regional aid guidelines was amended by the Community Guidelines on State aid for rescuing and restructuring firms in difficulty, OJ C 288, 9.10.1999, p.2.
[4] OJ C 70, 19.3.2002, p.8, as amended in OJ C 263, 1.11.2003, p.3.

5. Regional aid can only play an effective role if it is used sparingly and proportionately and is concentrated on the most disadvantaged regions of the European Union. In particular the permissible aid ceilings should reflect the relative seriousness of the problems affecting the development of the regions concerned. Furthermore, the advantages of the aid in terms of the development of a less-favoured region must outweigh the resulting distortions of competition.[5] The weight given to the advantages of the aid is likely to vary according to the derogation applied, so that a greater distortion of competition can be accepted in the case of the most disadvantaged regions covered by Article [107(3)(a)] than in those covered by Article [107(3)(c)].[6]

Notes

[5] See in this respect the judgment of the Court of Justice in Case 730/79, *Philip Morris* [1980] ECR 2671, paragraph 17 and in Case C-169/95, *Spain v Commission* [1997] ECR I-135, paragraph 20.
[6] See in this respect the judgment of the Court of First Instance in T-380/94, *AIUFFASS and AKT* [1996] ECR II-2169, paragraph 54.

Commentary
para 5: B&C: 17.048

6. In certain very limited, well-defined cases, the structural handicaps of a region may be so severe that regional investment aid, together with a comprehensive horizontal aid regime may not be sufficient to trigger a process of regional development. Only in such cases may regional investment aid be supplemented by regional operating aid.

7. An increasing body of evidence suggests that there are significant barriers to the formation of new enterprises in the Community which are more acute inside the disadvantaged regions. The Commission has therefore decided to introduce a new aid instrument in these guidelines to encourage small business start-ups in disadvantaged regions with differentiated aid ceilings according to the regions concerned.

2. Scope

8. The Commission will apply these Guidelines to regional aid granted in every sector of the economy apart from the fisheries sector and the coal industry[7] which are subject to special rules laid down by specific legal instruments. In the agricultural sector, these guidelines do not apply to the production of agricultural products listed in Annex I of the Treaty. They do apply to the processing and marketing of such products, but only to the extent laid down in the Community guidelines for State aid in the agriculture sector,[8] or any replacement Guidelines. In addition, some other sectors are also subject to specific rules which take account of the particular situation of the sectors concerned and which may totally or partially derogate from these guidelines.[9] As regards the steel industry, in accordance with its long-established practice, the Commission considers that regional aid to the steel industry as defined in Annex I is not compatible with the common market. This incompatibility also applies to large individual aid grants made in this sector to small and medium-sized enterprises within the meaning of Article 6 of Regulation (EC) No 70/2001,[10] or any successor regulation, which are not exempted by the same Regulation. In addition, due to its specific characteristics, no regional investment aid may be granted in the synthetic fibres sector as defined in Annex II.

Notes

[7] For the purposes of these guidelines "coal" means high-grade, medium-grade and low-grade category A and B coal within the meaning of the international codification system for coal laid down by the United Nations Economic Commission for Europe.
[8] OJ C 28 of 1.2.2000, p.2. Corrigendum OJ C 232 12.8.2000, p.17.
[9] The sectors covered by special rules over and above those set out here are currently: transport and shipbuilding.
[10] OJ L 10, 13.1.2001, p.33. Regulation as amended by Regulation (EC) No 364/2004 (OJ L 63, 28.2.2004, p.22). [Ed note: see now Commission Regulation (EC) No 800/2008 of 6 August 2008 declaring certain categories of aid compatible with the common market in application of Articles [107 and 108 TFEU] (General block exemption Regulation) (OJ L 214, 9.8.2008, p.3), reproduced above at G11.]

9. Aid may only be granted to firms in difficulties within the meaning of the Community guidelines on State aid for rescuing and restructuring firms in difficulty[11] in accordance with the latter guidelines.[12]

Notes
¹¹ OJ C 244, 1.10.2004, p.2.
¹² In particular, aid granted to large or medium-sized enterprises during the restructuring period must always be notified individually to the Commission, even if it is granted as part of an approved scheme.

10. As a general rule, regional aid should be granted under a multi-sectoral aid scheme which forms an integral part of a regional development strategy with clearly defined objectives. Such a scheme may also enable the competent authorities to prioritise investment projects according to their interest for the region concerned. Where, exceptionally, it is envisaged to grant individual ad hoc aid to a single firm, or aid confined to one area of activity, it is the responsibility of the Member State to demonstrate that the project contributes towards a coherent regional development strategy and that, having regard to the nature and size of the project, it will not result in unacceptable distortions of competition. If aid granted under a scheme appears to be unduly concentrated on a particular sector of activity, the Commission may review the scheme pursuant to Article 17 of Regulation (EC) No 659/1999 of 22 March 1999 on modalities for the application of Article [108 TFEU]¹³ and may propose, in line with Article 18 (c) of this Regulation, to abolish the scheme.

Notes
¹³ OJ L 83, 27.3.1999, p.1.

Commentary
para 10: B&C: 17.048

11. Member States do not have to notify national regional aid schemes which fulfil all the conditions laid down in the group exemption Regulations adopted by the Commission pursuant to Article 1 of Council Regulation (EC) No 994/98 of 7 May 1998 on the application of Articles [107 and 108 TFEU] to certain categories of horizontal State aid.¹⁴

Notes
¹⁴ OJ L 142, 14.5.1998, p.1.

3. Demarcation of regions

3.1. *Population coverage eligible for regional aid, 2007–2013*

12. In the light of the principle of the exceptional nature of regional aid, the Commission considers that the total population coverage of assisted regions in the Community must be substantially less than that of unassisted regions.

13. Having regard to the conclusions of different European Councils calling for a reduction in overall levels of State aid, and in view of the widely shared concerns about the distortive effects of investment aid for large companies, the Commission considers that the overall population coverage of the regional aid guidelines for 2007–2013 should be limited to that which is necessary to allow coverage of the most disadvantaged regions, as well as a limited number of regions which are disadvantaged in relation to the national average in the Member State concerned. Accordingly, it has decided to fix the limit for the overall population coverage to 42% of the population of the current Community of 25 Member States, which is similar to the limit fixed on the basis of a Community of 15 members in 1998. This limit will provide for an appropriate level of concentration of regional aid in EU-25, while allowing a sufficient degree of flexibility for the accession of Bulgaria and Romania, the entire territory of which will normally be eligible for regional aid.¹⁵

Notes
¹⁵ This 42% limit is estimated to rise to 45.5% on an EU-27 basis following the Accession of Bulgaria and Romania.

14. This notwithstanding, in order to ensure a sufficient degree of continuity for the existing Member States, the Commission has also decided to apply an additional safety net to ensure that no Member State loses more than 50% of the coverage of its population covered during the period 2000–2006.¹⁶

Notes
16 Application of the safety net will lead to a total population coverage of about 43.1% on an EU-25 basis, or 46.6% on an EU-27 basis.

3.2. *The derogation in Article [107(3)(a)]*

15. Article [107(3)(a)] provides that aid to promote the economic development of areas where the standard of living is abnormally low or where there is serious underemployment may be considered compatible with the common market. As the Court of Justice of the European Communities has held, "the use of the words "abnormally" and "serious" in the exemption contained in Article [107(3)(a)] shows that it concerns only areas where the economic situation is extremely unfavourable in relation to the Community as a whole".[17]

Notes
17 Case 248/84, *Germany v Commission* [1987] ECR 4013, paragraph 19.

16. The Commission accordingly considers that the conditions laid down are fulfilled if the region, being a NUTS[18] level II geographical unit, has a per capita gross domestic product (GDP), measured in purchasing power standards (PPS), of less than 75% of the Community average.[19] The GDP per capita[20] of each region and the Community average to be used in the analysis are determined by the Statistical Office of the European Communities. In the interest of ensuring the maximum possible coherence between the designation of regions eligible for the derogation under Article [107(3)(a)] under the regional aid guidelines, and the regions eligible for the convergence objective under the structural fund regulations, the Commission has used the same GDP per capita data to designate the Article [107(3)(a)] regions as that used to designate the convergence regions under the structural fund regulations.[21]

Notes
18 Regulation (EC) No 1059/2003 of the European Parliament and of the Council of 26 May 2003 on the establishment of a common classification of territorial units for statistics (NUTS) OJ L 154, 21.6.2003, p.1. The NUTS nomenclature is used by EUROSTAT as a reference for the collection, development and harmonisation of EU regional statistics and for socio-economic analyses of the regions.
19 The underlying assumption being that the GDP indicator is capable of reflecting synthetically both the phenomena mentioned.
20 In this, and all subsequent references to GDP per capita in these guidelines, GDP is measured in terms of purchasing power standards.
21 The data cover the period 2000–2002.
Commentary
para 16: B&C: 17.048

17. In recognition of the special handicaps which they face by reason of their remoteness and specific constraints in integrating into the internal market, the Commission considers that regional aid for the outermost regions covered by [Article 349 TFEU][22] also falls within the scope of the derogation in Article [107(3)(a)], whether or not the regions concerned have a GDP per capita of less than 75% of the Community average.

Notes
22 Azores, Madeira, Canary Islands, Guadeloupe, Martinique, Réunion and French Guyana.

3.3. *Phasing out arrangements for the "statistical effect" regions*

18. For certain regions, the GDP per capita exceeds 75% of the Community average solely because of the statistical effect of enlargement. These are regions at NUTS II level which have a GDP per capita of more than 75% of the EU-25 average, but less than 75% of the EU-15 average.[23] [24]

Notes
23 In practice, 75% of the average EU-15 GDP per capita corresponds to 82.2% of the average EU-25 GDP per capita.
24 These regions are subsequently referred to as the "statistical effect" regions.

19. In order to ensure that the past progress of these regions is not undermined by too rapid change, in terms of aid intensities and the availability of operating aid, the Commission considers that they should continue to remain eligible for the derogation in Article [107(3)(a)] on a transitional basis until 31 December 2010.

20. In 2010 the Commission will review the position of these regions on the basis of the three-year average of the most recent GDP data available from Eurostat. If the relative GDP per capita of any of the regions has declined below 75% of the EU-25 average, the regions concerned will continue to be eligible for the derogation under Article [107(3)(a)]. Otherwise the statistical effect regions will become eligible for aid under the derogation of Article [107(3)(c)] from 1 January 2011.

3.4. *The derogation in Article [107(3)(c)]*

21. The Court of Justice, in Case 248/84,[25] has expressed its views on the range of problems covered by this derogation and the reference framework for the analysis as follows: "The exemption in [Article [107](3)(c)], on the other hand, is wider in scope inasmuch as it permits the development of certain areas without being restricted by the economic conditions laid down in Article [107(3)(a)], provided such aid "does not adversely affect trading conditions to an extent contrary to the common interest". That provision gives the Commission power to authorize aid intended to further the economic development of areas of a Member State which are disadvantaged in relation to the national average".

Notes

[25] Footnote 17, supra.

---

22. The regional aid covered by the derogation in Article [107(3)(c)] must, however, form part of a well-defined regional policy of the Member State and adhere to the principle of geographical concentration. Inasmuch as it is intended for regions which are less disadvantaged than those to which Article [107(3)(a)] relates, both the geographic scope of the exception and the aid intensity allowed must be strictly limited. This being so, only a small part of the national territory of a Member State may normally qualify for the aid in question.

23. So as to afford national authorities sufficient latitude when it comes to choosing eligible regions without jeopardizing the effectiveness of the system of checks and balances operated by the Commission in respect of this type of aid and the equal treatment of all Member States, the selection of the regions eligible under the derogation in question should be undertaken by a two-step process which consists, first, of the determination by the Commission of the maximum population coverage for each Member State[26] for such aid, and, secondly, of the selection of eligible regions.

Notes

[26] With the exception of Member States whose entire territory is eligible for the derogation under Article [107(3)(a)].

3.4.1. Determination of eligible national population coverage

24. As a first step, the determination of the national population coverage eligible for aid under the derogation in Article [107(3)(c)] must be made by a method which is objective, fair and transparent. Furthermore, the final outcome must remain within the overall limit for coverage of regional aid determined by the Commission under section 3.1, taking account also of the safety net. In order to achieve this, the Commission determines the population ceiling for each Member State on the basis of the following method.

25. First, Member States automatically receive an allocation equivalent to the population of any regions which were eligible for aid under the derogation in Article [107(3)(a)] of the Treaty but which no longer meet the conditions for eligibility under that Article and which are not covered by the arrangements for the statistical effect regions described in section 3.3. These are the regions which had a GDP per capita of less than 75% on an EU-15 basis when the 1998 regional aid guidelines were adopted, but which as a result of their economic development no longer meet that condition on an EU-15 basis. Since these regions[27] have previously benefited from a

relatively high level of aid, the Commission considers it necessary to allow Member States the flexibility, if they so wish, to continue to support these regions for the duration of these guidelines, under the derogation in Article [107(3)(c)].[28]

Notes

[27] Subsequently referred to as the "economic development" regions.

[28] Although it was not eligible for aid pursuant to Article [107(3)(a)], Northern Ireland has in fact benefited during the period 2000–2006 from the same aid intensities as many of the Article [107(3)(a)] regions. Accordingly, Northern Ireland should also be considered as an economic development region for the purposes of these Guidelines.

26. Second, in order to allow for the continued support of low population density regions, the Member States concerned also receive an allocation based on the population of low population density regions.[29]

Notes

[29] Calculated on the basis of the NUTS III option of paragraph 30(b) of these guidelines.

27. After deducting the population coverage resulting from the application of the objective criteria set out in sections 3.2 and 3.3, as well as the allocations referred to in the two preceding paragraphs from the upper limit of 42% of EU-25 population determined in section 3.1, the balance is available for distribution between the Member States using a distribution key that takes account of variations in GDP per capita and unemployment between the regions, both in a national and a Community context. The detailed formula is set out in Annex IV.[30]

Notes

[30] The same method was used by the Commission in its 1998 Guidelines on national regional aid: Annex 3, paragraphs 4–7.

28. Finally, as indicated in section 3.1, a safety net is applied to ensure that no Member State loses more than 50% of the coverage of its population under the 1998 guidelines.

29. The resulting allocations are set out in Annex V, together with the lists of regions eligible for support under Article [107(3)(a)], the statistical effect regions and the economic development regions.

3.4.2. Selection of eligible regions[31]

30. The eligibility criteria for the selection of regions by the Member States must be sufficiently flexible to allow for the wide diversity of situations in which the granting of national regional aid may potentially be justified but at the same time they must be transparent and provide sufficient safeguards that the award of regional aid will not distort trade and competition to an extent contrary to the common interest. Accordingly, the Commission considers that the following regions may be eligible for selection by the Member States concerned for the award of regional investment aid pursuant to the derogation under Article [107(3)(c)]:[32]

(a) the "economic development" regions;

(b) the low population density regions: such areas are made up essentially of NUTS-II geographic regions with a population density of less than 8 inhabitants per km^2, or NUTS-III geographic regions with a population density of less than 12.5 inhabitants per km^2.[33] However, a certain flexibility is allowed in the selection of these areas, subject to the following limitations:

   — flexibility in the selection of areas must not mean an increase in the population covered;

   — the NUTS III parts qualifying for flexibility must have a population density of less than 12.5 inhabitants per square kilometre;

   — they must be contiguous with NUTS III regions which satisfy the low population density test;

(c) regions which form contiguous zones with a minimum population of at least 100,000 and which are located within either NUTS-II or NUTS-III regions which have either a GDP per capita of less than the EU-25 average, **or** which have an unemployment rate which is higher than 115% of the national average, (both calculated on the average of the most recent 3 years of Eurostat data);

(d) NUTS-III regions with less than 100,000 population which have either a GDP per capita of less than the EU-25 average **or** which have an unemployment rate which is higher than 115% of the national average, (both calculated on the average of the most recent three years of Eurostat data);

(e) islands and other regions categorised by similar geographical isolation[34] which have either a GDP per capita of less than the EU-25 average, **or** which have an unemployment rate which is higher than 115% of the national average, (both calculated on the average of the most recent three years of Eurostat data);

(f) islands with fewer than 5,000 inhabitants and other communities with fewer than 5,000 inhabitants categorised by similar geographical isolation;

(g) NUTS-III regions or parts thereof adjacent to a region which is eligible for support under Article [107(3)(a)] as well as NUTS-III regions or parts thereof which share a land border, or a sea border of less than 30 kilometres with a country which is not a Member State of the European Economic Area or EFTA.

(h) In duly justified cases, Member States may also designate other regions which form contiguous zones with a minimum population of at least 50,000 which are undergoing major structural change, or are in serious relative decline, when compared with other comparable regions. It will be the task of Member States which wish to use this possibility to demonstrate that the award of regional investment aid in the region concerned is justified, using recognised economic indicators and comparisons with the situation at Community level.

Notes

31 Those statistical effect regions which from 1 January 2011 are not eligible for the derogation under Article [107(3)(a)] are automatically eligible under Article [107(3)(c)].

32 Taking account of their small size, for Cyprus and Luxembourg it is sufficient that the regions designated have either a GDP per capita which is less than the EU average, or an unemployment rate which is higher than 115% of the national average, and have a minimum population of 10,000 inhabitants.

33 In order to prevent double counting, this criterion should be applied on a residual basis, after taking account of the relative wealth of the regions concerned.

34 For example peninsulas and mountainous regions.

31. In addition, in order to allow Member States greater flexibility to target very localised regional disparities, below the NUTS-III level, Member States may also designate other smaller areas which do not meet the conditions described above provided they have a minimum population of 20,000.[35] It will be the task of Member States which wish to use this possibility to demonstrate that the areas proposed are relatively more in need of economic development than other areas in that region, using recognised economic indicators such as GDP per capita, employment or unemployment levels, local productivity or skills indicators. Regional aid will be approved by the Commission in these areas for SMEs, and the relevant SME bonus will also apply. However, because of the potential distortion of competition resulting from the spill-over effect into the more prosperous surrounding regions, the Commission will not approve aid for investments by large companies in these areas, or aids for investments with eligible expenses exceeding EUR 25 million.

Notes

35 This minimum limit may be reduced in the case of islands and other areas categorised by similar geographical isolation.

32. Compliance with the total coverage allowed for each Member State will be determined by the actual population of the regions concerned, on the basis of the most recent recognised statistical information available.

4. Regional investment aid

4.1. Form of aid and aid ceilings

4.1.1. Form of aid

33. Regional investment aid is aid awarded for an initial investment project.

34. *Initial investment* means an investment in material and immaterial assets relating to:
    — the setting-up of a new establishment;
    — the extension of an existing establishment;
    — diversification of the output of an establishment into new, additional products;
    — a fundamental change in the overall production process of an existing establishment.

    "Material assets" means assets relating to land, buildings and plant/machinery. In case of acquisition of an establishment, only the costs of buying assets from third parties should be taken into consideration, provided the transaction has taken place under market conditions.
    "Immaterial assets" means assets entailed by the transfer of technology through the acquisition of patent rights, licences, know-how or unpatented technical knowledge.
    Replacement investment which does not meet any of these conditions is thus excluded from the concept.[36]

Notes

[36] Replacement investment may however qualify as operating aid under certain conditions as set out in section 5.

35. The acquisition of the assets directly linked to an establishment may also be regarded as initial investment provided the establishment has closed or would have closed had it not been purchased, and is bought by an independent investor.[37]

Notes

[37] Consequently, the sole acquisition of the shares of the legal entity of an enterprise does not qualify as initial investment.

36. Regional investment aid is calculated either in reference to material and immaterial investment costs resulting from the initial investment project or to (estimated) wage costs for jobs directly created by the investment project.[38]

Notes

[38] A job is deemed to be directly created by an investment project if it concerns the activity to which the investment relates and is created within three years of completion of the investment, including jobs created following an increase in the utilisation rate of the capacity created by the investment.

37. The form of the aid is variable. It may, for example, take the form of grants, low-interest loans or interest rebates, state guarantees, the purchase of a share-holding or an alternative provision of capital on favourable terms, exemptions or reductions in taxes, social security or other compulsory charges, or the supply of land, goods or services at favourable prices.

38. It is important to ensure that regional aid produces a real incentive effect to undertake investments which would not otherwise be made in the assisted areas. Therefore aid may only be granted under aid schemes if the beneficiary has submitted an application for aid and the authority responsible for administering the scheme has subsequently confirmed in writing[39] that, subject to detailed verification, the project in principle meets the conditions of eligibility laid down by the scheme before the start of work on the project.[40] An express reference to both conditions must also be included in all aid schemes.[41] In the case of ad hoc aid, the competent authority must have issued a letter of intent, conditional on Commission approval of the measure, to award aid before work starts on the project. If work begins before the conditions laid down in this paragraph are fulfilled, the whole project will not be eligible for aid.

Notes

[39] In the case of aid which is subject to individual notification to and approval by the Commission, confirmation of eligibility must be made conditional on the Commission decision approving the aid.
[40] "Start of work" means either the start of construction work or the first firm commitment to order equipment, excluding preliminary feasibility studies.

39. Where the aid is calculated on the basis of material or immaterial investment costs, or of acquisition costs in the case referred to in paragraph 35, to ensure that the investment is viable and sound and respecting the applicable aid ceilings, the beneficiary must provide a financial contribution of at least 25% of the eligible costs, either through its own resources or by external financing, in a form which is free of any public support.[42]

Notes

42 This is for example not the case for a subsidised loan, public equity-capital loans or public participations which do not meet the market economy investor principle, state guarantees containing elements of aid, as well as public support granted within the scope of the *de minimis* rule.

40. Furthermore, in order to ensure that the investment makes a real and sustained contribution to regional development, aid must be made conditional, through the conditions attached to the aid, or its method of payment, on the maintenance of the investment in question in the region concerned for a minimum period of at least five years after its completion.[43] In addition, where the aid is calculated on the basis of wage costs, the posts must be filled within three years of the completion of the works. Each of the jobs created through the investment must be maintained within the region concerned for a period of five years from the date the post was first filled. In the case of SMEs, Member States may reduce these five-year periods for the maintenance of an investment or jobs created to a minimum of three years.

Notes

43 This rule shall not prevent the replacement of plant or equipment which has become out-dated within this five year period due to rapid technological change, provided the economic activity is retained in the region concerned for the minimum period.

41. The level of the aid is defined in terms of intensity compared with reference costs. All aid intensities must be calculated in terms of gross grant equivalents (GGE).[44] The aid intensity in gross grant equivalent is the discounted value of the aid expressed as a percentage of the discounted value of the eligible costs. For aid which is individually notified to the Commission, the gross grant equivalent is calculated at the moment of notification. In other cases, the eligible investment costs are discounted to their value at the moment of the granting of the aid. Aid payable in several instalments shall be discounted to its value at the moment of its being notified or granted, as appropriate. The interest rate to be used for discounting purposes and to calculate the aid amount in a soft loan is the reference rate applicable at the time of grant. In cases where aid is awarded by means of tax exemptions or reductions on future taxes due, discounting of aid tranches takes place on the basis of the reference rates applicable at the various times the tax advantages become effective.

Notes

44 The Commission is discontinuing its former practice of converting regional aid notified by Member States into net grant equivalents in order to take account of the judgment of the Court of First Instance of 15 June 2000 in Case T-298/97, *Alzetta*. In that case the Court of First Instance ruled: "The Commission is not empowered, under the State aid monitoring system established by the Treaty, to take into consideration the incidence of tax on the amount of financial aid allocated when it assesses whether it is compatible with the Treaty. Such charges are not levied specifically on the aid itself but are levied downstream, and apply to the aid in question in the same way as to any income received. They cannot therefore be relevant when assessing the specific effect of the aid on trade and competition and, in particular, when estimating the benefit obtained by the recipients of such aid by comparison with competing undertakings which have not received such aid and whose income is also liable to tax." Furthermore, the Commission considers that the use of GGEs, which are also used to calculate the intensities of other types of State aid, will contribute to increasing the simplicity and transparency of the State aid control system, and also takes account of the increased proportion of State aid which is awarded in the form of tax exemptions.

Commentary
point 41: B&C: 17.051

4.1.2. Aid ceilings (maximum aid intensities) for aid to large companies

42. The intensity of the aid must be adapted to take account of the nature and intensity of the regional problems that are being addressed. This means that the admissible aid intensities are from the outset less high in regions qualifying for exemption under Article [107(3)(c)] than in those qualifying under Article [107(3)(a)].

43. The Commission must also take account of the fact that following recent enlargements the disparities in the relative wealth of the regions qualifying under Article [107(3)(a)] have increased substantially. In fact, a significant number of regions and indeed entire Member States now have a per capita GDP of below 45% of the EU-25 average, which was not the case in 1998. The existence of these greater disparities of wealth within the Community requires the Commission to introduce a greater categorisation of the regions concerned.

44. In the case of regions falling under Article [107(3)(a)], the Commission thus considers that the intensity of regional aid must not exceed:
    — 30% GGE for regions with less than 75% of average EU-25 GDP per capita, for outermost regions with higher GDP per capita and until 1 January 2011 statistical effect regions;
    — 40% GGE for regions with less than 60% of average EU-25 GDP per capita;
    — 50% GGE for regions with less than 45% of average EU-25 GDP per capita.

Commentary
para 44: B&C: 17.051

45. In recognition of their specific handicaps, the outermost regions will be eligible for a further bonus of 20% GGE if their GDP per capita falls below 75% of the EU-25 average and 10% GGE in other cases.

46. The statistical effect regions which fall under the derogation under Article [107(3)(c)] from 1 January 2011 will be eligible for an aid intensity of 20%.

47. In the other Article [107(3)(c)] regions, the ceiling on regional aid must not exceed 15% GGE. This is reduced to 10% GGE in the case of regions with both more than 100% of average EU-25 GDP per capita and a lower unemployment rate than the EU-25 average, measured at NUTS-III level (based on averages for the last three years, using Eurostat data).[45]

Notes

[45] By way of exception, a higher aid intensity may be permitted in the case of a NUTS-III region, or smaller, adjacent to an Article [107(3)(a)] region if this is necessary to ensure that the differential between the two regions does not exceed 20 percentage points.

Commentary
para 47: B&C: 17.052, 17.059

48. However, the low population density regions and regions (corresponding to NUTS-III level or smaller) adjoining a region with Article [107(3)(a)] status selected by Member States for coverage under Article [107(3)(c)], as well as NUTS-III regions or parts thereof which share a land border with a country which is not a Member State of the European Economic Area or EFTA, are always eligible for an aid intensity of 15% GGE.

Commentary
para 48: B&C: 17.059

4.1.3. Bonuses for small and medium-sized enterprises

49. In the case of aid awarded to small and medium-sized enterprises,[46] the ceilings in section 4.1.2 may be increased by 20% GGE for aid granted to small enterprises and by 10% GGE for aid granted to medium-sized enterprises.[47]

Notes

[46] Annex I of Commission Regulation (EC) No 364/2004 of 25 February 2004 amending Regulation (EC) No 70/2001, OJ L 63, 28.2.2004, p.22, or any successor regulation.
[47] These bonuses do not apply to aid awarded in the transport sector.

Commentary
para 49: B&C: 17.053

4.2. Eligible expenses

4.2.1. Aid calculated on the basis of investment costs

50. Expenditures on land, buildings and plant/machinery[48] are eligible for aid for initial investment.

Notes

[48] In the transport sector, expenditure on the purchase of transport equipment (movable assets) is not eligible for aid for initial investment.

51. For SMEs, the costs of preparatory studies and consultancy costs linked to the investment may also be taken into account up to an aid intensity of 50% of the actual costs incurred.

52. In the event of an acquisition of the type referred to in paragraph 35, only the costs of buying assets[49] from third parties should be taken into consideration.[50] The transaction must take place under market conditions.

Notes

[49] Where the acquisition is accompanied by other initial investment, the expenditure relating to the latter should be added to the cost of the purchase.

[50] In exceptional cases, the aid may alternatively be calculated by reference to the (estimated) wage costs for the jobs safeguarded or newly created by the acquisition. These cases have to be individually notified to the Commission.

53. Costs related to the acquisition of assets other than land and buildings under lease can only be taken into consideration if the lease takes the form of financial leasing and contains an obligation to purchase the asset at the expiry of the term of the lease. For the lease of land and buildings, the lease must continue for at least five years after the anticipated date of the completion of the investment project for large companies, and three years for SMEs.

54. Except in the case of SMEs and takeovers, the assets acquired should be new. In the case of takeovers, assets for whose acquisition aid has already been granted prior to the purchase should be deducted.

55. For SMEs, the full costs of investments in intangible assets by the transfer of technology through the acquisition of patent rights, licences, know-how or unpatented technical knowledge may always be taken into consideration. For large companies, such costs are eligible only up to a limit of 50% of the total eligible investment expenditure for the project.

56. In all cases, eligible intangible assets will be subject to the necessary conditions for ensuring that they remain associated with the recipient region eligible for the regional aid and, consequently, that they are not the subject of a transfer benefiting other regions, especially other regions not eligible for regional aid. To this end, eligible intangible assets will have to satisfy the following conditions in particular:

— they must be used exclusively in the establishment receiving the regional aid;

— they must be regarded as amortizable assets;

— they must be purchased from third parties under market conditions;

— they must be included in the assets of the firm and remain in the establishment receiving the regional aid for at least five years (three years for SMEs).

4.2.2. Aid calculated on the basis of wage costs

57. As was indicated in section 4.1.1, regional aid may also be calculated by reference to the expected wage costs[51] arising from job creation as a result of an initial investment project.

Notes

[51] The wage cost means the total amount actually payable by the beneficiary of the aid in respect of the employment concerned, comprising the gross wage, before tax, and the compulsory social security contributions.

58. *Job creation* means a *net* increase in the number of employees[52] directly employed in a particular establishment compared with the average over the previous 12 months. Any jobs lost during that

Part G State Aids

12 month period must therefore be deducted from the apparent number of jobs created during the same period.[53]

Notes

[52] The number of employees means the number of annual labour units, namely the number of persons employed full time in one year, part-time and seasonal work being ALU fractions.

[53] Such a definition holds true as much for an existing establishment as for a new establishment.

---

59. The amount of aid must not exceed a certain percentage of the wage cost of the person hired, calculated over a period of two years. The percentage is equal to the intensity allowed for investment aid in the area in question.

4.3. Aid for large investment projects

60. For the purpose of these guidelines, a "*large investment project*" is an "initial investment" as defined by these guidelines with an eligible expenditure above EUR 50 million.[54] In order to prevent that a large investment project being artificially divided into sub-projects in order to escape the provisions of these guidelines, a large investment project will be considered to be a single investment project when the initial investment is undertaken in a period of three years by one or more companies and consists of fixed assets combined in an economically indivisible way.[55]

Notes

[54] The EUR 50 million must be calculated at prices and exchange rates on the date when the aid is granted, or in the case of large investment projects where individual notification is required, at prices and exchange rates at the date of the notification.

[55] To assess whether an initial investment is economically indivisible, the Commission will take into account the technical, functional and strategic links and the immediate geographical proximity. The economic indivisibility will be assessed independently from ownership. This implies that to establish whether a large investment project constitutes a single investment project, the assessment should be the same irrespective of whether the project is carried out by one undertaking, by more than one undertakings sharing the investment costs or by more undertakings bearing the costs of separate investments within the same investment project (for example in the case of a joint venture).

---

61. To calculate whether the eligible expenditure for large investment projects reaches the various thresholds in these guidelines, the eligible expenditure to be taken into account is either the traditional investment costs or the wage cost, whichever is the higher.

62. In two successive Multisectoral frameworks on regional aid for large investment projects in 1998[56] and 2002,[57] the Commission reduced the maximum aid intensities for large investment projects to limit distortions of competition. In the interests of simplification and transparency, the Commission has decided to integrate the provisions of the 2002 Multisectoral framework (MSF-2002) into the Regional aid guidelines for the period 2007–13.

Notes

[56] OJ C 107, 7.4.1998, p.7.

[57] OJ C 70, 19.3.2002, p.8 as amended by OJ C 263, 1.11.2003, p.1.

---

63. MSF-2002 will therefore cease to apply to aid awarded or notified[58] after 31 December 2006 and will be replaced by these guidelines.[59]

Notes

[58] Individually notifiable investment projects will be assessed in accordance with the rules in force at the time of notification.

[59] Given the wide general scope of these guidelines, the Commission decided that it is not technically feasible to proceed with the establishment of a list of sectors where serious structural difficulties prevail.

4.3.1. Increased transparency and monitoring of large investment projects

64. Member States are required to notify individually to the Commission any aid to be awarded to investment projects under an existing aid scheme if the aid proposed from all sources is more than the maximum allowable amount of aid that an investment with eligible expenditure EUR 100 million can receive under the scale and the rules laid down in paragraph 67.[60] The

notification thresholds for different regions with the most commonly encountered aid intensities under these guidelines are summarised in the table below.

Aid intensity	10%	15%	20%	30%	40%	50%
Notification threshold	EUR 7.5 million	EUR 11.25 million	EUR 15.0 million	EUR 22.5 million	EUR 30.0 million	EUR 37.5 million

Notes

[60] Ad hoc individual aid must always be notified to the Commission. Because of its clear effect on the conditions of trade and competition, the need for a specific justification for the link with regional development applies with greater force to ad hoc individual aid for large individual investment projects.

Commentary
para 64: B&C: 17.080

65. Whenever regional aid is granted on the basis of existing aid schemes for non-notifiable large investments projects, Member States must, within 20 working days starting from the granting of the aid by the competent authority, provide the Commission with the information requested in the standard form laid down in Annex III. The Commission will make summary information available to the public through its website (http://europa.eu.int/comm/competition/).

66. Member States must maintain detailed records regarding the granting of aid for all large investment projects. Such records, which must contain all information necessary to establish that the maximum allowable aid intensity has been observed, must be maintained for 10 years from the date on which the aid was granted.

4.3.2. Rules for the assessment of large investment projects

67. Regional investment aid for large investment projects is subject to an adjusted regional aid ceiling,[61] on the basis of the following scale:

Eligible expenditure	Adjusted aid ceiling
Up to EUR 50 million	100% of regional ceiling
For the part between EUR 50 million and EUR 100 million	50% of regional ceiling
For the part exceeding EUR 100 million	34% of regional ceiling

Thus, the allowable aid amount for a large investment project will be calculated according to the following formula: maximum aid amount = $R \times (50 + 0.50 \times B + 0.34 \times C)$, where R is the unadjusted regional aid ceiling, B is the eligible expenditure between EUR 50 million and EUR 100 million, and C is the eligible expenditure above EUR 100 million. This is calculated on the basis of the official exchange rates prevailing on the date of the grant of aid, or in the case of aid subject to individual notification, on the date of notification.

Notes

[61] The starting point for the calculation of the adjusted aid ceiling is always the maximum aid intensity allowed for aid for large enterprises in accordance with section 4.1.2 above. No SME bonuses may be granted to large investment projects.

68. Where the total amount of aid from all sources exceeds 75% of the maximum amount of aid an investment with eligible expenditure of EUR 100 million could receive, applying the standard aid ceiling in force for large enterprises in the approved regional aid map on the date the aid is to be granted, and where

(a) the aid beneficiary accounts for more than 25% of the sales of the product(s) concerned on the market(s) concerned before the investment or will account for more than 25% after the investment, or

(b) the production capacity created by the project is more than 5% of the market measured using apparent consumption data[62] for the product concerned, unless the average annual growth rate of its apparent consumption over the last five years is above the average annual growth rate of the European Economic Area's GDP, the Commission will approve regional investment aid only after a detailed verification, following the opening of the procedure provided for in Article [108(2)] of the Treaty, that the aid is necessary to provide an incentive effect for the investment and that the benefits of the aid measure outweigh the resulting distortion of competition and effect on trade between Member States.[63]

Notes

[62] Apparent consumption of the product concerned is production plus imports minus exports.
[63] Before the entry into force of these guidelines the Commission will draw up further guidance on the criteria it will take into account during this assessment.

69. The product concerned is normally the product covered by the investment project.[64] When the project concerns an intermediate product and a significant part of the output is not sold on the market, the product concerned may be the downstream product. The relevant product market includes the product concerned and its substitutes considered to be such either by the consumer (by reason of the product's characteristics, prices and intended use) or by the producer (through flexibility of the production installations).

Notes

[64] Where an investment project involves the production of several different products, each of the products needs to be considered.

70. The burden of proof that the situations to which paragraphs 68(a) and (b) refer do not apply, lies with the Member State.[65] For the purpose of applying points (a) and (b), sales and apparent consumption will be defined at the appropriate level of the Prodcom classification,[66] normally in the EEA, or, if such information is not available or relevant, on the basis of any other generally accepted market segmentation for which statistical data are readily available.

Notes

[65] If the Member State demonstrates that the aid beneficiary creates a new product market, the tests laid down in paragraph 68(a) and (b) do not need to be carried out, and the aid will be authorised under the scale in paragraph 67.
[66] Council Regulation (EEC) No 3924/91 of 19 December 1991 on the establishment of a Community survey of industrial production (OJ L 374, 31.12.1991, p.1).

4.4. Rules on the cumulation of aid

71. The aid intensity ceilings laid down in sections 4.1 and 4.3 above apply to the total aid:
    — where assistance is granted concurrently under several regional schemes or in combination with ad hoc aid;
    — whether the aid comes from local, regional, national or Community sources.
72. Where aid calculated on the basis of material or immaterial investment costs is combined with aid calculated on the basis of wage costs, the intensity ceiling laid down for the region concerned must be respected.[67]

Notes

[67] This condition is deemed to be met if the sum of the aid for the initial investment, expressed as a percentage of the investment, and of the job creation aid, expressed as a percentage of wage costs, does not exceed the most favourable amount resulting from application of either the ceiling set for the region in accordance with the criteria indicated at section 4.1 or the ceiling set for the region in accordance with the criteria indicated at section 4.3.

73. Where the expenditure eligible for regional aid is eligible in whole or in part for aid for other purposes, the common portion will be subject to the most favourable ceiling under the applicable rules.

74. Where the Member State lays down that State aid under one scheme may be combined with aid under other schemes, it must specify, in each scheme, the method by which it will ensure compliance with the conditions listed above.

75. Regional investment aid shall not be cumulated with *de minimis* support in respect of the same eligible expenses in order to circumvent the maximum aid intensities laid down in these guidelines.

5. Operating aid[68]

76. Regional aid aimed at reducing a firm's current expenses (operating aid) is normally prohibited. Exceptionally, however, such aid may be granted in regions eligible under the derogation in Article [107(3)(a)] provided that (i) it is justified in terms of its contribution to regional development and its nature and (ii) its level is proportional to the handicaps it seeks to alleviate.[69] It is for the Member State to demonstrate the existence and importance of any handicaps.[70] In addition, certain specific forms of operating aid can be accepted in the low population density regions and the least populated areas.

Notes
[68] Like other forms of regional aid, the granting of operating aid is always subject to the specific rules which may apply in particular sectors.
[69] Operating aid takes the form in particular of tax exemptions or reductions in social security contributions which are not linked to eligible investment costs.
[70] The Commission is currently studying the feasibility of establishing a methodology for evaluating the additional costs in the outermost regions.

Commentary
para 76: B&C: 17.053

77. Operating aid should in principle only be granted in respect of a predefined set of eligible expenditures or costs [71] and limited to a certain proportion of those costs.

Notes
[71] For example, replacement investments, transport costs or labour costs.

78. Because of the specific nature of financial and intra-group activities, as defined in Section J (codes 65, 66 and 67) and intra-group activities falling within the scope of Section K (code 74) of the NACE code, operating aid granted for these activities has only a very limited likelihood of promoting regional development but a very high risk of distorting competition, as stated in the Commission notice on the application of the State aid rules to measures relating to direct business taxation.[72] The Commission will therefore not approve any operating aid to the financial services sector, or for intra-group activities under these guidelines unless such aid is granted under general schemes which are open to all sectors and which are designed to offset additional transport or employment costs. Operating aid intended to promote exports is likewise excluded.

Notes
[72] OJ C 384, 10.12.1998, p.3.

79. Because it is intended to overcome delays and bottlenecks in regional development, except as provided for in paragraphs 80 and 81, operating aid should always be temporary and reduced over time, and should be phased out when the regions concerned achieve real convergence with the wealthier areas of the EU.[73]

Notes
[73] This principle of degressivity must also be respected when new operating aid schemes are notified to replace existing ones. However, flexibility as regards the application of this principle may be permitted in the case of operating aid schemes designed to address the geographical handicaps of particular areas located within Article [107(3)(a)] regions.

80. In derogation from the previous paragraph, operating aid which is not both progressively reduced and limited in time may only be authorised:

Part G State Aids

1493

—	in the outermost regions, in so far as it is intended to offset the additional costs arising in the pursuit of economic activity from the factors identified in Article [349] of the Treaty, the permanence and combination of which severely restrain the development of such regions (remoteness, insularity, small size, difficult topography and climate, and economic dependence on a few products);[74]

—	in the least populated regions, in so far as it is intended to prevent or reduce the continuing depopulation of these regions.[75] The least populated regions represent or belong to regions at NUTS-II level with a population density of 8 inhabitants per km2 or less and extend to adjacent and contiguous smaller areas meeting the same population density criterion.

Notes

[74] In view of the constraints faced by the outermost regions, except in the cases referred to in paragraph 78, the Commission considers that operating aid of up to 10% of the turnover of the beneficiary may be awarded without the need for specific justification. It is the task of the Member State to demonstrate that any proposed aid above this amount is justified in terms of its contribution to regional development, and that its level is proportional to the additional costs linked to the factors identified in Article 299(2) which it is intended to offset.

[75] It is the task of the Member State to demonstrate that the aid proposed is necessary and appropriate to prevent or reduce continuing depopulation.

Commentary
para 80: B&C: 17.053

81.	In addition, in the outermost regions and low population density regions, aid which is not both progressively reduced and limited in time and which is intended partly to offset additional transport costs may be authorized under the following conditions:

—	aid may serve only to compensate for the additional cost of transport, taking into account other schemes of assistance to transport. While the amount of aid may be calculated on a representative basis, systematic overcompensation must be avoided;

—	aid may be given only in respect of the extra cost of transport of goods produced in the outermost regions and low population density regions inside the national borders of the country concerned. It must not be allowed to become export aid. No aid may be given towards the transport or transmission of the products of businesses without an alternative location (products of the extractive industries, hydroelectric power stations, etc.);

—	for the outermost regions only, aid may also cover the cost of transporting primary commodities, raw materials or intermediate products from the place of their production to the place of final processing in the region concerned;

—	the aid must be objectively quantifiable in advance, on the basis of an aid-per-passenger or aid per-ton/kilometre ratio, and there must be an annual report drawn up which, among other things, shows the operation of the ratio or ratios;

—	the estimate of additional cost must be based on the most economical form of transport and the shortest route between the place of production or processing and commercial outlets using that form of transport; external costs to the environment should also be taken into account.

Commentary
para 81: B&C: 17.053

82.	In all cases, the need for and level of operating aid should be regularly re-examined to ensure its long-term relevance to the region concerned. The Commission will therefore only approve operating aid schemes for the duration of these guidelines.

83.	In order to verify the effects on trade and competition of operating aid schemes, Member States will be required to provide each year a single report in respect of each NUTS-II region in which operating aid is granted which provides a breakdown of total expenditure, or estimated income forgone, for each operating aid scheme approved in the region concerned and identifies the ten largest beneficiaries of operating aid in the region concerned,[76] specifying the sector(s) of activity of the beneficiaries and the amount of aid received by each.

Notes

76 In terms of the amount of aid received.

6. Aid for newly created small enterprises

84. While newly created small enterprises encounter difficulties throughout the EU, it appears that the economic development of the assisted regions is hindered by relatively low levels of entrepreneurial activity and in particular by even lower than average rates of business start-ups. It therefore appears necessary to introduce a new form of aid, which can be granted in addition to regional investment aid, in order to provide incentives to support business start-ups and the early stage development of small enterprises in the assisted areas.

85. In order to ensure that it is effectively targeted, it appears that this type of aid should be graduated according to the difficulties faced by each category of region. Furthermore, in order to avoid an unacceptable risk of distortions of competition, including the risk of crowding-out existing enterprises, the aid should, for an initial period at least, be strictly limited to small enterprises, limited in amount and degressive.

86. The Commission will accordingly approve aid schemes which provide aid of up to a total of EUR 2 million per enterprise[77] for small enterprises with their economic activity in regions eligible for the derogation in Article [107(3)(a)], and up to EUR 1 million per enterprise for small enterprises with their economic activity in regions eligible for the derogation in Article [107(3)(c)]. Annual amounts of aid awarded for newly created small enterprises must not exceed 33% of the abovementioned total amounts of aid per enterprise.

Notes

77 Eligible enterprises are small enterprises within the meaning of Article 2 of Annex I to Commission Regulation (EC) No 364/2004 or any successor regulation, which are autonomous within the meaning of Article 3 of the Annex to Commission Regulation (EC) No 364/2004 and which have been created less than five years ago.

87. The eligible expenses are legal, advisory, consultancy and administrative costs directly related to the creation of the enterprise, as well as the following costs, insofar as they are actually incurred within the first five years of the creation of the enterprise thereafter:[78]
    — interests on external finance and a dividend on own capital employed not exceeding the reference rate;
    — fees for renting production facilities/equipment;
    — energy, water, heating, taxes (other than VAT and corporate taxes on business income) and administrative charges;
    — depreciation, fees for leasing production facilities/equipment as well as wage costs including compulsory social charges may also be included provided that the underlying investments or job creation and recruitment measures have not benefited from other forms of aid.

Notes

78 VAT and direct business profit/income taxes are not included in the eligible expenses.

88. The aid intensity may not exceed
    — in Article [107(3)(a)] regions, 35% of eligible expenses incurred in the first three years after the creation of the enterprise, and 25% in the two years thereafter;
    — in Article [107(3)(c)] regions, 25% of eligible expenses incurred in the first three years after the creation of the enterprise, and 15% in the two years thereafter.

89. These intensities are increased by 5% in Article [107(3)(a)] regions with a GDP per capita of less than 60% of the EU-25 average, in regions with a population density of less than 12.5 inhabitants/km^2 and in small islands with a population of less than 5,000, and other communities of the same size suffering from similar isolation.

90. The Member State shall put in place the necessary system to ensure that the upper limits for the amount of aid and the relevant aid intensity in relation to the eligible costs concerned are not exceeded. In particular, the aid provided for in this chapter shall not be cumulated with other public support (including *de minimis* support) in order to circumvent the maximum aid intensities or amounts laid down.

91. Granting aid designed exclusively for newly created small enterprises may produce perverse incentives for existing small enterprises to close down and re-open in order to receive this type of aid. Member States should be aware of this risk and should design aid schemes in such a way as to avoid this problem, for example by placing limits on applications from owners of recently closed firms.

7. Transitional arrangements

7.1. Reductions of aid intensities for regions remaining within Article [107(3)(a)] on 1 January 2007

92. Where the implementation of these guidelines will result in a reduction in maximum aid intensities of more than 15 percentage points, net to gross,[79] the reduction may be implemented in two stages with the initial reduction of a minimum of 10 percentage points being applied on 1 January 2007, and the balance on 1 January 2011.

Notes

[79] I.e. from 50% net grant equivalent to 30% gross grant equivalent.

7.2. Reductions of aid intensities in the economic development regions

93. Provided the areas concerned are proposed by the Member State as eligible for regional aid under Article [107(3)(c)] for the whole period 2007–2013, the reduction of aid intensities for the economic development regions may take place in two stages. A reduction of at least 10 percentage points net to gross shall be applied on 1 January 2007. As necessary to meet the new aid intensities allowed under these guidelines, a final reduction shall be applied at the latest on 1 January 2011.[80]

Notes

[80] Since Northern Ireland benefited from a specific provision in the regional aid guidelines for the period 2000–2006, the application of the same transitional arrangement is also justified.

7.3. Phasing-out of operating aid

94. For regions which lose their capacity to grant operating aid as a result of the loss of eligibility under Article [107(3)(a)], the Commission can accept a linear phasing out of operating aid schemes over a two-year period from the date of the loss of eligibility to grant such aid.

7.4. Phasing out of Article [107(3)(c)] regions

95. Following the entry into force of these guidelines, a number of regions will lose their eligibility for regional investment aid. In order to facilitate the smooth transition of these regions to the reformed horizontal State aid regime which is progressively being put in place through the implementation of the State aid action plan, Member States may exceptionally designate additional regions to be eligible for regional aid under Article [107(3)(c)] until 1 January 2009, provided that the following conditions are met:
   — the regions concerned were eligible for regional aid under Article [107(3)(c)] on 31 December 2006;
   — the combined total population of the regions eligible for regional investment aid under Article [107(3)(c)] pursuant to the allocation of population coverages referred to in paragraphs 27 and 28 and those designated in accordance with this provision shall not exceed 66% of the national population eligible for regional aid under Article [107(3)(c)] on 31 December 2006;[81]
   — the maximum aid intensity permitted in the additional regions designated in accordance with this provision shall not exceed 10%.

Notes

[81] After exclusion of those regions which were eligible for regional aid under Article [107(3)(c)] on 31 December 2006 and which qualify for aid under the present guidelines by virtue of other provisions (statistical effect regions, economic development regions, low population density regions). The resulting allocations are set out in Annex V.

8. Regional aid maps and declaration of compatibility

96. The regions of a Member State eligible for regional investment aid under the derogations and the ceilings on the intensity of aid for initial investment[82] approved for each region together form a Member State's regional aid map. The regional aid map also defines the regions eligible to grant enterprise aid. Operating aid schemes are not covered by the regional aid maps, and are assessed on a case by case basis on the basis of a notification by the Member State concerned pursuant to Article [108(3)] of the Treaty.

Notes

[82] As adjusted in accordance with paragraph 67 in the case of individually notifiable aid for large investment projects.

97. The Court of Justice has ruled that the "decisions" by which the Commission adopts the regional aid maps for each Member State should be construed as forming an integral part of the guidelines on regional aid and as having binding force only on condition that they have been accepted by Member States.[83]

Notes

[83] Judgment of 18 June 2002 in Case C-242/00 *Germany v Commission*.

98. Furthermore, it should be recalled that the regional aid maps also define the scope of any group exemption exempting regional aid from the notification obligation under Article [108(3)] of the Treaty, whether such aid is granted on the basis of Regulation (EC) No 70/2001,[84] or on the basis of a possible future exemption regulation for other forms of regional aid. Article 1(1)(b) of Regulation (EC) No 994/98[85] provides only for the exemption of "aid that complies with the map approved by the Commission for each Member State for the grant of regional aid".

Notes

[84] Commission Regulation (EC) No 70/2001 of 12 January 2001 on the application of Articles [107 and 108 TFEU] to State aid to small and medium-sized enterprises (OJ L 10, 13.1.2001, p.33), as amended by Commission Regulation (EC) No 364/2004 of 25 February 2004 amending Regulation (EC) No 70/2001 as regards the extension of its scope to include aid for research and development (OJ L 63, 28.2.2004, p.22). [Ed note: see now Commission Regulation (EC) No 800/2008 of 6 August 2008 declaring certain categories of aid compatible with the common market in application of Articles [107 and 108 TFEU] (General block exemption Regulation) (OJ L 214, 9.8.2008, p.3), reproduced above at G11.]
[85] Council Regulation (EC) No 994/98 of 7 May 1998 on the application of Articles [107 and 108 TFEU] to certain categories of horizontal State aid OJ L 142, 14.5.1998, p.1.

99. Under these guidelines, depending on the socio-economic situation of the Member States, the regional aid map will include:
    (1) regions which can be identified on the basis of the criteria set out in these guidelines and in respect of which maximum aid intensities are defined by these guidelines. These are the regions eligible for the derogation under Article [107(3)(a)] and the statistical effect regions.
    (2) regions which are to be designated by Member States for eligibility for regional aid in accordance with Article [107(3)(c)] up to the limit for population coverage determined in accordance with section 3.4.1.

100. Of course, provided they respect the conditions set out in these guidelines, it is the responsibility of the Member States themselves to decide whether they wish to grant regional investment aid and up to what level. As soon as possible after the publication of these guidelines, each Member State should accordingly notify to the Commission, in accordance with Article [108(3)] of the Treaty, a single regional aid map covering its entire national territory.

101. The Commission will examine the notifications in accordance with the procedure set out in Article [108(3)] of the Treaty. At the conclusion of its examination, it will publish the approved regional aid maps in the *Official Journal of the European Union*. These maps will take effect on 1 January 2007, or their date of publication if later, and will be considered an integral part of the present guidelines.

102. The notification should clearly identify the regions proposed for eligibility under Article [107(3) (a) or (c)], and the aid intensities envisaged for large companies, taking account of adjustments in the regional aid ceiling for large investment projects. Where for certain regions, transitional

rules will apply, or where a change of aid intensity is anticipated, the relevant periods and aid intensities should be detailed.

103. Given that the regions eligible for support under Article [107(3)(a)] and the statistical effect regions are determined exogenously at the NUTS-II level, it will not normally be necessary to provide detailed supporting socio-economic data. On the other hand detailed supporting information should be given to explain the designation of the Article [107(3)(c)] regions, other than the economic development, the low population density and the border regions, including the detailed identification of the regions concerned, population data, information on GDP and unemployment levels in the regions concerned, and any other relevant information.

104. In order to ensure continuity, which is essential for long-term regional development, the list of regions notified by Member States should in principle apply throughout the period 2007–2013. It may, however, be subject to a mid-term review in 2010. Any Member State wishing to amend the list of regions eligible for aid under Article [107(3)(c)] or the applicable aid intensities must submit a notification to the Commission before 1 April 2010 at the latest. Any changes of region in this context may not exceed 50% of the total coverage allowed for the Member State under Article [107(3)(c)]. With the exception of the statistical effect regions, regions which loose their eligibility for regional aid coverage as a result of this mid-term review will not be eligible for any transitional support. Moreover, Member States may at any time notify to the Commission a request to add further regions to the list until such time as the relevant population coverage is reached.

9. Entry into force, implementation, transparency and review

105. The Commission intends to apply these guidelines to all regional aid to be granted after 31 December 2006. Regional aid awarded or to be granted before 2007 will be assessed in accordance with the 1998 guidelines on national regional aid.

106. Since they must be coherent with the regional aid map, notifications of regional aid schemes, or ad hoc aid to be granted after 31 December 2006, cannot normally be considered complete until the regional aid map has been adopted for the Member State concerned in accordance with the arrangements described in section 8. Accordingly, the Commission will not normally examine notifications of regional aid schemes which are to apply after 31 December 2006, or ad hoc aid to be granted after that date, until the adoption of the regional aid map for the Member State concerned.[86] The same applies to aid schemes for newly created small enterprises covered by section 6 of these guidelines.

Notes

[86] The Commission informs the Member States that in order to reduce that burden of the obligation of notification to the maximum extent possible, it intends to make use of the powers conferred on it by Regulation (EC) No 994/98 to exempt from notification under Article [108(3)] of the Treaty all transparent regional investment aid schemes which comply with the national regional aid map approved for the Member State concerned. Ad hoc individual aid and operating aid schemes will not be exempt from notification. Moreover, the information and individual notification requirements for large individual aid projects set out in section 4.3 of these guidelines will continue to apply, including in the case of aid which is granted under exempted schemes.

---

107. The Commission considers that the implementation of these guidelines will lead to substantial changes in the rules applicable to regional aid throughout the Community. Furthermore, in the light of the changed economic and social conditions prevailing in the EU, it appears necessary to review the continuing justification for and effectiveness of all regional aid schemes, including both investment aid and operating aid schemes. For these reasons, the Commission will propose the following appropriate measures to Member States pursuant to Article [108(1)] of the Treaty:

— without prejudice to Article 10(2) of Regulation (EC) No 70/2001[87] on the application of Articles [107 and 108 TFEU] to State aid for small and medium-sized enterprises, as amended by Regulation (EC) No 364/2004[88] and to Article 11(2) of Regulation (EC) No 2204/2002 on the application of Articles [107 and 108 TFEU] to State aid for employment,[89] Member States shall limit the application in time of all existing regional aid schemes to aid to be granted on or before 31 December 2006;

— where environment aid schemes allow regional investment aid to be granted for environmental investments pursuant to footnote 29 of the Community guidelines on State aid for environmental protection,[90] Member States shall amend the relevant schemes in order to ensure that aid may only be granted after 31 December 2006 if it complies with the regional aid map in force on the date the aid is granted;

— Member States shall as necessary amend other existing aid schemes in order to ensure that any regional bonuses such as those allowed for training aid, aid for research and development or environment aid may only be granted after 31 December 2006 in areas which are eligible for support under Article [107(3)(a) or (c)] in accordance with the regional aid map adopted by the Commission in force on the date the aid is granted.

The Commission will invite Member States to confirm their acceptance of these proposals within one month.

Notes

[87] OJ L 10, 13.1.2001, p.33. [Ed note: see now Commission Regulation (EC) No 800/2008 of 6 August 2008 declaring certain categories of aid compatible with the common market in application of Articles [107 and 108 TFEU] (General block exemption Regulation) (OJ L 214, 9.8.2008, p.3)]

[88] OJ L 63, 28.2.2004, p.22.

[89] OJ L 337, 13.12.2002, p.3. [Ed note: see now Commission Regulation (EC) No 800/2008 of 6 August 2008 declaring certain categories of aid compatible with the common market in application of Articles [107 and 108 TFEU] (General block exemption Regulation) (OJ L 214, 9.8.2008, p.3)]

[90] OJ C 37, 3.2.2001, p.3. [Ed note: see now the 2008 Community guidelines on State aid for environmental protection (OJ C 82, 1.4.2008, p.1), reproduced at G17 below.]

108. In addition, the Commission considers that further measures are necessary to improve the transparency of regional aid in an enlarged union. In particular, it appears necessary to ensure that the Member States, economic operators, interested parties and indeed the Commission itself should have easy access to the full text of all applicable regional aid schemes in the EU. The Commission considers that this can easily be achieved through the establishment of linked internet sites. For this reason, when examining regional aid schemes, the Commission will systematically seek an undertaking from the Member State that the full text of the final aid scheme will be published on the internet and that the internet address of the publication will be communicated to the Commission. Projects for which expenses were incurred before the date of publication of the scheme will not be eligible for regional aid.

109. The Commission may decide to review or amend these guidelines at any time if this should be necessary for reasons associated with competition policy or in order to take account of other Community policies and international commitments.

Annex I
Definition of the Steel Industry

Annex II
Definition of the Synthetic Fibres Industry

Annex III
Form for the Provision of Summary Information for Aid for Large Investment Projects Requested in Paragraph 65

Annex IV
Method for Allocation of Population Shares in Assisted Article [107(3)(c)] Areas Across Member States

Annex V
Regional Aid Coverage, 2007–2013

Notes

For reasons of space, Annexes I to V are no longer reproduced in this volume. They remain available on Oxford Competition Law.

G15

COMMUNITY GUIDELINES ON STATE AID TO PROMOTE RISK CAPITAL INVESTMENTS IN SMALL AND MEDIUM-SIZED ENTERPRISES

(2006/C 194/02)

(Text with EEA relevance)

Official Journal C 194, 18.8.2006, p.2

Celex No: 52006XC0818(01)

EUR-Lex permanent link: <http://eur-lex.europa.eu/LexUriServ/LexUriServ.do?uri=CELEX: 52006XC0818(01)EN:NOT>

Notes

EEA application: for the corresponding EEA provision, see the EFTA Surveillance Authority's Procedural and Substantive Rules in the Field of State Aid (Guidelines on the application and interpretation of Articles 61 and 62 of the EEA Agreement and Article 1 of Protocol 3 to the Surveillance and Court Agreement), Part III, Chapter 10A (as substituted by EFTA Surveillance Authority Decision of 25 October 2006 (OJ L 184, 16.7.09, p.18)).

Commentary
Guidelines: B&C: 17.063 **F&N:** 17.326

---

1. Introduction

1.1. Risk capital as a Community objective

Risk capital relates to the equity financing of companies with perceived high-growth potential during their early growth stages. The demand for risk capital typically comes from companies with growth potential that do not have sufficient access to capital markets, while the offer of risk capital comes from investors ready to take high risk in exchange of potentially above average returns from the equity invested. In its Communication to the Spring European Council, Working together for growth and jobs — A new start for the Lisbon strategy,[1] the Commission has recognised the insufficient level of risk capital available for start-up, innovative young businesses. The Commission has taken initiatives, like the Joint European Resources for Micro- to Medium Enterprises (JEREMIE) which is a joint initiative of the Commission and the European Investment Fund to tackle the lack of risk capital for small and medium-sized enterprises in some regions. Building on the experience gained with the financial instruments under the multiannual programme for enterprise and entrepreneurship, and in particular for small and medium-sized enterprises (MAP) adopted by Council Decision 2000/819/EC[2] the Commission has proposed a High Growth and Innovative SME Facility (GIF) under the Competitiveness and Innovation Programme (CIP), which is currently being adopted and will cover the period 2007–2013.[3] The Facility will increase the supply of equity to innovative SMEs by investing on market terms into venture capital funds focused on SMEs in their early stages and in the expansion phase.

The Commission addressed the issue of risk capital financing in its Communication on "Financing SME Growth — Adding European Value" adopted on 29 June 2006.[4] The Commission has also stressed the importance of reducing and redirecting State aids to address market failures in order to increase economic efficiency and to stimulate research, development and innovation. In this context, the Commission has undertaken to reform the State aid rules, inter alia, with the aim of facilitating access to finance and risk capital.

In fulfilment of its commitment, the Commission published the "State Aid Action Plan — Less and better targeted State aid: A roadmap for State aid reform 2005–2009 ("the State Aid Action Plan")"[5] in June 2005. The State Aid Action Plan has highlighted the importance of improving the business climate and facilitating the rapid start-up of new enterprises. In this context, the State Aid Action Plan announced the review of the Communication on State aid and risk capital[6] to tackle the market failures affecting the provision of risk capital to start-ups and young, innovative small and medium-sized enterprises ("SMEs"), in particular by increasing the flexibility of the rules contained in the Communication on State aid and risk capital.

While it is the primary role of the market to provide sufficient risk capital in the Community, there is an "equity gap" in the risk capital market, a persistent capital market imperfection preventing supply from meeting demand at a price acceptable to both sides, which negatively affects European SMEs. The gap concerns mainly high-tech innovative and mostly young firms with high growth potential. However, a wider range of firms of different ages and in different sectors with smaller growth potential that cannot find financing for their expansion projects without external risk capital may also be affected. The existence of the equity gap may justify the granting of State aid in certain limited circumstances. If properly targeted, State aid in support of risk capital provision can be an effective means to alleviate the identified market failures in this field and to leverage private capital.

These guidelines replace the Communication on State aid and risk capital by setting out the conditions under which State aid supporting risk capital investments may be considered compatible with the common market. The guidelines explain the conditions under which State aid is present in accordance with Article [107(1) TFEU]* and the criteria that the Commission will apply in the compatibility assessment of the risk capital measures in accordance with Article [107(3) TFEU].

Note

1 COM(2005) 24.

2 OJ L 333, 29.12.2000, p.84. Decision as last amended by Decision No 1776/2005/EC of the European Parliament and of the Council (OJ L 289, 3.11.2005, p.14).

3 COM(2005) 121 final.

4 COM(2006) 349.

5 COM(2005) 107 final – SEC(2005) 795.

6 OJ C 235, 21.8.2001, p.3.

* Ed note: please see the Note on the Lisbon Treaty at p.xvii in regard to article renumbering introduced by the Lisbon Treaty. Unless otherwise stated, all Treaty article numbers are the new numbers of the Treaty on the Functioning of the European Union (TFEU) and the Treaty on European Union (TEU).

1.2. Experience in the field of State aid to risk capital

These guidelines have been prepared in the light of the experience gained in the application of the Communication on State aid and risk capital. Comments from public consultations of Member States and stakeholders on the revision of the Communication on State aid and risk capital, on the State aid Action Plan and on the Communication on State aid to innovation[1] have also been taken into account.

The experience of the Commission and the comments received in the consultations have shown that the Communication on State aid and risk capital has generally worked well in practice, but also revealed a need to increase the flexibility in the application of the rules and to adjust the rules to reflect the changed situation of the risk capital market. In addition, experience has shown that for some types of risk capital investments in some areas it was not always possible to fulfil the conditions set out in the Communication on State aid and risk capital, and, as a result, risk capital could not be adequately supported with State aid in these cases. Furthermore, experience has also shown a low overall profitability of the aided risk capital funds.

To remedy these problems, these guidelines adopt a more flexible approach in certain circumstances so as to allow Member States to better target their risk capital measures to the relevant market failure. These guidelines also set out a refined economic approach for the assessment of the compatibility of risk capital measures with the [Treaty on the Functioning of the European Union]. Under the Communication on State aid and risk capital the assessment of the compatibility of schemes was already based on a relatively sophisticated economic analysis focussing on the size of the market failure and the targeting of the measure. Hence, the Communication on State aid and risk capital already reflected the key focus of a refined economic approach. However, some fine-tuning was still needed in respect of some of the criteria to ensure that the measure better target the relevant market failure. In particular, the guidelines contain elements to ensure that profit-driven and professional investment decisions are strengthened in order to further encourage private investors to co-invest with the State. Finally, an effort has been made to provide clarity where the experience with the Communication on State aid and risk capital has shown that this was needed.

Note
1 COM(2005) 436 final.

1.3. The balancing test for State aid supporting risk capital investments

1.3.1. The State Aid Action Plan and the balancing test

In the State Aid Action Plan the Commission underlined the importance of strengthening the economic approach to State aid analysis. This translates into a balancing the potential positive effects of the measure in reaching an objective of common interest against its potential negative effects in terms of distortion of competition and trade. The balancing test, as outlined in the State Aid Action Plan, is composed of three steps, the first two relating to the positive effects and the last one to the negative effects and the resulting balance:

(1) Is the aid measure aimed at a well-defined objective of common interest, such as growth, employment, cohesion and environment?
(2) Is the aid well designed to deliver the objective of common interest, that is does the proposed aid address the market failure or other objective?
   (i) Is State aid an appropriate policy instrument?
   (ii) Is there an incentive effect, i.e. does the aid change the behaviour of firms and/or investors?
   (iii) Is the aid measure proportional, i.e. could the same change in behaviour be obtained with less aid?
(3) Are the distortions of competition and effect on trade limited, so that the overall balance is positive?

The balancing test is equally relevant for the design of State aid rules and for the assessment of cases falling within their scope.

1.3.2. Market failures

On the basis of the experience gained in applying the Communication on State aid and risk capital, the Commission considers that there is no general risk capital market failure in the Community. It does, however, accept that there are market gaps for some types of investments at certain stages of enterprises" development. These gaps result from an imperfect matching of supply and demand of risk capital and can generally be described as an equity gap.

The provision of equity finance, in particular to smaller businesses, presents numerous challenges both to the investor and to the enterprise invested in. On the supply side, the investor needs to make a careful analysis not merely of any collateral being offered (as is the case of a lender) but of the entire business strategy in order to estimate the possibilities of making a profit on the investment and the risks associated with it. The investor also needs to be able to monitor that the business strategy is well implemented by the enterprise's managers. The investor finally needs to plan and execute an exit strategy, in order to generate a risk-adjusted return on investment from selling its equity stake in the company in which the investment is made.

On the demand side, the enterprise must understand the benefits and risks associated with external equity investment to pursue the venture and to prepare sound business plans to secure the necessary resources and mentoring. Owing to a lack of internal capital or the collateral needed to obtain debt funding and/or a solid credit history, the enterprise may face very tight funding constraints. In addition, the enterprise must share control with an outside investor, who usually has an influence over company decisions in addition to a portion of the equity.

As a result, the matching of supply and demand of risk capital may be inefficient so that the level of risk capital provided in the market is too restricted, and enterprises do not obtain funding despite having a valuable business model and growth prospects. The Commission considers that the main source of market failure relevant to risk capital markets, which particularly affects access to capital by SMEs and companies at the early stages of their development and which may justify public intervention, relates to imperfect or asymmetric information. Imperfect or asymmetric information may result notably in:

(a) Transaction and agency costs: potential investors face more difficulties in gathering reliable information on the business prospects of an SME or a new company and subsequently in monitoring and supporting the enterprise's development. This is in particular the case for highly innovative projects or risky projects. Furthermore, small deals are less attractive to investment funds due to relatively high costs for investment appraisal and other transaction costs.

(b) Risk aversion: investors may become more reluctant to provide risk capital to SMEs, the more the provision of risk capital is subject to imperfect of asymmetric information. In other words, imperfect or asymmetric information tends to exacerbate risk aversion.

1.3.3. *Appropriateness of the instrument*

The Commission considers that State aid to risk capital measures may constitute an appropriate instrument within the limits and conditions set out in these guidelines. However, it must be borne in mind that risk capital provision is essentially a commercial activity involving commercial decisions. In this context, more general structural measures not constituting State aid may also contribute to an increase in the provision of risk capital, such as promoting a culture of entrepreneurship, introducing a more neutral taxation of the different forms of SME financing (for example new equity, retained earnings and debt), fostering market integration, and easing regulatory constraints, including limitations on investments by certain types of financial institutions (for example, pension funds) and administrative procedures for setting up companies.

1.3.4. *Incentive effect and necessity*

State aid for risk capital must result in a net increase in the availability of risk capital to SMEs, in particular by leveraging investments by private investors. The risk of "dead weight", or lack of incentive effect, means that some enterprises funded through publicly supported measures would have obtained finance on the same terms even in the absence of State aid (crowding out). There is evidence of this happening, although such evidence is inevitably anecdotal. In those circumstances public resources are ineffective.

The Commission considers that aid in the form of risk capital satisfying the conditions laid down in these guidelines ensures the presence of an incentive effect. The need to provide incentives depends on the size of the market failure related to the different types of measures and beneficiaries. Therefore different criteria are expressed in terms of size of investment tranches per target enterprise, degree of involvement of private investors, and consideration of notably the size of the company and the business stage financed.

1.3.5. *Proportionality of aid*

The need to provide incentives depends on the size of the market failure related to the different types of measures, beneficiaries and development stage of the SMEs. A risk capital measure is well designed if the aid is necessary in all its elements to create the incentives to provide equity to SMEs in their seed, start-up and early stages. State aid will be inefficient if it goes beyond what is needed to induce more risk capital provision. In particular, to ensure that aid is limited to the minimum, it is crucial that there is significant private participation and that the investments are profit-driven and are managed on a commercial basis.

1.3.6. *Negative effects and overall balance*

The [Treaty on the Functioning of the European Union] requires the Commission to control State aid within the Community. This is why the Commission has to be vigilant in order to ensure that measures are well targeted and to avoid severe distortions of competition. When deciding whether the grant of public funds for measures designed to promote risk capital is compatible with the common market, the Commission will seek to limit as far as possible the following categories of risk:

(a) the risk of "crowding out". The presence of publicly supported measures may discourage other potential investors from providing capital. This could, over the longer term, further discourage private investment in young SMEs and thus end up widening the equity gap, while at the same time creating the need for additional public funding;

(b) the risk that advantages to the investors and/or investment funds create an undue distortion of competition in the venture capital market relative to their competitors that do not receive the same advantages;

(c) the risk that an oversupply of public risk capital for target enterprises not invested according to a commercial logic could help inefficient firms stay afloat and could cause an artificial inflation of their valuations, making it all the less attractive for private investors to supply risk capital to these firms.

1.4. Approach for State aid control in the area of risk capital

Provision of risk capital funding to enterprises cannot be linked to the traditional concept of "eligible costs" used for State aid control, which relies on certain specified costs for which aid is allowed and the setting of maximum aid intensities. The diversity of possible models for risk capital measures devised by Member States also means that the Commission is not in a position to define rigid criteria by which to determine whether such measures are compatible with the common market. The assessment of risk capital therefore implies a departure from the traditional way in which State aid control is carried out.

However, since the Communication on State aid and risk capital has proved to work well in practice in the area of risk capital, the Commission has decided to continue and thereby ensure continuity with the approach of the Communication.

2. Scope and Definitions

2.1. Scope

These guidelines only apply to risk capital schemes targeting SMEs. They are not intended to constitute the legal basis for declaring an ad hoc measure providing capital to an individual enterprise compatible with the common market.

Nothing in these guidelines should be taken to call into question the compatibility of State aid measures which meet the criteria laid down in any other guidelines, frameworks or regulations adopted by the Commission. The Commission will pay particular attention to the need to prevent the use of these guidelines to circumvent the principles laid down in existing frameworks, guidelines and Regulations. Risk capital measures must specifically exclude the provision of aid to enterprises:

(a) in difficulty, within the meaning of the Community guidelines on State aid for rescuing and restructuring firms in difficulty;[1]

(b) in the shipbuilding,[2] coal[3] and steel industry.[4]

These Guidelines do not apply to aid to export-related activities, namely aid directly linked to the quantities exported, to the establishment and operation of a distribution network or to other current expenditure linked to the export activity, as well as aid contingent upon the use of domestic in preference to imported goods.

Notes

[1] OJ C 244, 1.10.2004, p.2.

[2] For the purpose of these Guidelines, the definitions laid down in the Framework on State aid to shipbuilding OJ C317, 30.12.2003, p.11, apply.

[3] For the purpose of these Guidelines, "coal" means high-grade, medium-grade and low–grade category A and B coal within the meaning of the international codification system for coal laid down by the United Nations Economic Commission for Europe.

[4] For the purpose of these Guidelines, the definition laid down in Annex I in the Guidelines on national regional aid for 2007–2013 (OJ C 54, 4.3.2006, p.13) applies.

2.2. Definitions

For the purposes of these guidelines, the following definitions shall apply:

(a) "**equity**" means ownership interest in a company, represented by the shares issued to investors;

(b) "**private equity**" means private (as opposed to public) equity investment in companies not listed on a stock-market, including venture capital, replacement capital and buy-outs;

(c) "**quasi-equity investment instruments**" means instruments whose return for the holder (investor/lender) is predominantly based on the profits or losses of the underlying target company, are unsecured in the event of default. This definition is based on a substance over form approach;

(d) "**debt investment instruments**" means loans and other funding instruments which provide the lender/investor with a predominant component of fixed minimum remuneration and are at least partly secured. This definition is based on a substance over form approach;

(e) "**seed capital**" means financing provided to study, assess and develop an initial concept, preceding the start-up phase;

(f) "**start-up capital**" means financing provided to companies, which have not sold their product or service commercially and are not yet generating a profit, for product development and initial marketing;

(g) "**early-stage capital**" means seed and start-up capital;

(h) "**expansion capital**" means financing provided for the growth and expansion of a company, which may or may not break even or trade profitably, for the purposes of increasing production capacity, market or product development or the provision of additional working capital;

(i) "**venture capital**" means investment in unquoted companies by investment funds (venture capital funds) that, acting as principals, manage individual, institutional or in-house money and includes early-stage and expansion financing, but not replacement finance and buy-outs;

(j) "**replacement capital**" means the purchase of existing shares in a company from another private equity investment organisation or from another shareholder or shareholders. Replacement capital is also called secondary purchase;

(k) "**risk capital**" means equity and quasi-equity financing to companies during their early-growth stages (seed, start-up and expansion phases), including informal investment by business angels, venture capital and alternative stock markets specialised in SMEs including high-growth companies (hereafter referred to as investment vehicles);

(l) "**risk capital measures**" means schemes to provide or promote aid in the form of risk capital;

(m) "**Initial Public Offering**" ("**IPO**") means the process of launching the sale or distribution of a company's shares to the public for the first time;

(n) "**follow-on investment**" means an additional investment in a company subsequent to an initial investment;

(o) "**buyout**" means the purchase of at least a controlling percentage of a company's equity from the current shareholders to take over its assets and operations through negotiation or a tender offer;

(p) "**exit strategy**" means a strategy for the liquidation of holdings by a venture capital or private equity fund according to a plan to achieve maximum return, including trade sale, write-offs, repayment of preference shares/loans, sale to another venture capitalist, sale to a financial institution and sale by public offering (including Initial Public Offerings);

(q) "**small and medium-sized enterprises**" ("**SMEs**") means small enterprises and medium-sized enterprises within the meaning of Commission Regulation (EC) No 70/2001 of 12 January 2001 on the application of Articles [107 and 108 TFEU] to State aid to small and medium-sized enterprises[1] or any Regulation replacing that Regulation;

(r) "**target enterprise or company**" means an enterprise or company in which an investor or investment fund is considering investing;

(s) "**business angels**" means wealthy private individuals who invest directly in young new and growing unquoted business (seed finance) and provide them with advice, usually in return for an equity stake in the business, but may also provide other long-term finance;

(t) "**assisted areas**" means regions falling within the scope of the derogations contained in Article [107(3)(a) or (c) TFEU];

Notes

[1] OJ L 10, 13.1.2001, p.33: Regulation as last amended by Regulation (EC) No 1040/2006 (OJ L 187, 8.7.2006, p.8). [Ed note: see now Commission Regulation (EC) No 800/2008 of 6 August 2008 declaring certain categories of aid compatible with the common market in application of Articles [107 and 108 TFEU] (General block exemption Regulation) (OJ L 214, 9.8.2008, p.3), reproduced above at G11.]

3. Applicability of Article [107(1)] in the Field of Risk Capital

3.1. General applicable texts

There are already a number of published Commission texts which provide interpretation on whether individual measures fall within the definition of State aid and which may be relevant to risk capital measures. These include the 1984 communication on government capital injections,[1] the 1998 notice on the application of the State aid rules to measures relating to direct business taxation[2] and the notice on the application of Articles [107 and 108 TFEU] to State aid in the form of guarantees.[3] The Commission will continue to apply these texts, when assessing whether risk capital measures constitute State aid.

Notes

[1] Bulletin EC 9–1984, reproduced in "Competition law in the European Communities", Volume IIA, p.133.

[2] OJ C 384, 10.12.1998, p.3.

[3] OJ C 71, 11.3.2000, p.14. [Ed note: see now the 2008 Commission Notice on the application of Articles [107 and 108 TFEU] to State aid in the form of guarantees (OJ C 155, 20.6.2008, p.10).]

3.2. Presence of aid at three levels

Risk capital measures often involve complex constructions devised to promote risk capital because the public authorities create incentives for one set of economic operators (investors) in order to provide finance to another set (target SMEs). Depending on the design of the measure, and even if the intention of the public authorities may be only to provide benefits to the latter group, enterprises at either or both levels may benefit from State aid. Moreover, in most cases the measure provides for the creation of a fund or other investment vehicle which has an existence separate from that of the investors and the enterprises in which the investment is made. In such cases it is also necessary to consider whether the fund or vehicle can be considered to be an enterprise benefiting from State aid.

In this context, funding with resources, which are not State resources within the meaning of Article [107(1) TFEU], is considered to be provided by private investors. This is, in particular, the case for funding by the European Investment Bank and the European Investment fund.

The Commission will take into account the following specific factors in determining whether State aid is present at each of the different levels.[1]

Aid to investors. Where a measure allows private investors to effect equity or quasi-equity investments into a company or set of companies on terms more favourable than public investors, or than if they had undertaken such investments in the absence of the measure, then those private investors will be considered to receive an advantage. Such advantage may take different forms, as specified in section 4.2 of these guidelines. This remains the case even if the private investor is persuaded by the measure to confer an advantage on the company or companies concerned. In contrast, the Commission will consider the investment to be effected *pari passu* between public and private investors, and thus not to constitute State aid, where its terms would be acceptable to a normal economic operator in a market economy in the absence of any State intervention. This is assumed to be the case only if public and private investors share exactly the same upside and downside risks and rewards and hold the same level of subordination, and normally where at least 50 percent of the funding of the measure is provided by private investors, which are independent from the companies in which they invest.

Aid to an investment fund, investment vehicle and/or its manager. In general, the Commission considers that an investment fund or an investment vehicle is an intermediary vehicle for the transfer of aid to investors and/or enterprises in which investment is made, rather than being a beneficiary of aid itself. However, measures such as fiscal measures or other measures involving direct transfers in favour of an investment vehicle or an existing fund with numerous and diverse investors with the character of an independent enterprise may constitute aid unless the investment is made on terms which would be acceptable to a normal economic operator in a market economy and therefore provide no advantage to the beneficiary. Likewise, aid to the fund's managers or the management company will be considered to be present if their remuneration does not fully reflect the current market remuneration in comparable situations.

On the other hand, there is a presumption of no aid if the managers or management company are chosen through an open and transparent public tender procedure or if they do not receive any other advantages granted by the State.

Aid to the enterprises in which investment is made. In particular, where aid is present at the level of the investors, the investment vehicle or the investment fund, the Commission will normally consider that it is at least partly passed on to the target enterprises and thus that it is also present at their level. This is the case even where investment decisions are being taken by the managers of the fund with a purely commercial logic.

In cases where the investment is made on terms which would be acceptable to a private investor in a market economy in the absence of any State intervention the enterprises in which the investment is made will not be considered as aid recipients. For this purpose, the Commission will consider whether such investment decisions are exclusively profit-driven and are linked to a reasonable business plan and projections, as well as to a clear and realistic exit strategy. Also important will be the choice and investment mandate of the fund's managers or the management company as well as the percentage and degree of involvement of private investors.

Notes

[1] It should, however, be noted that guarantees granted by the State in favour of investments in risk capital are more likely to include an element of aid to the investor than is the case with traditional loan guarantees, which are normally considered to constitute aid to the borrower rather than to the lender.

3.3. *De minimis* amounts

Where all financing in the form of risk capital provided to beneficiaries is *de minimis* within the meaning of Commission Regulation (EC) No 69/2001 of 12 January 2001 on the application of Articles [107 and 108 TFEU] to de minimis aid[1] and Commission Regulation (EC) No 1860/2004 on the application of Articles [107 and 108 TFEU] to de minimis aid in the agriculture and fisheries sectors,[2] then it is deemed not to fall under Article [107(1) TFEU]. In risk capital measures the application of the *de minimis* rule is made more complicated by difficulties in the calculation of the aid and also by the fact that measures may provide aid not only to the target enterprises but also to other investors. Where these difficulties can be overcome, however, the *de minimis* rule remains applicable. Therefore, if a scheme provides public capital only up to the relevant *de minimis* threshold to each enterprise over a three-year period, then it is certain that any aid to these enterprises and/or the investors is within the prescribed limits.

Notes

[1] OJ L 10, 13.1.2001, p.30.
[2] OJ L 325, 28.10.2004, p.4.

---

4. Assessment of the Compatibility of Risk Capital Aid Under Article [107(3)(c) TFEU]

4.1. General principles

Article [107(3)(c) TFEU] provides that aid to facilitate the development of certain economic activities may be considered to be compatible with the common market where such aid does not adversely affect trading conditions to an extent contrary to the common interest. On the basis of the balancing test set out in section 1.3, the Commission will declare a risk capital measure compatible only if it concludes that the aid measure leads to an increased provision of risk capital without adversely affecting trading conditions to an extent contrary to the common interest. This section sets out a set of conditions under which the Commission will consider that aid in the form of risk capital is compatible with Article [107(3)(c)].

Where the Commission is in possession of a complete notification which shows that all the conditions laid down in this section are met, it will try to make a rapid assessment of the aid within the time limits laid down in Council Regulation (EC) No 659/1999 of 22 March 1999 laying down detailed rules for the application of Article [108 TFEU].[1] For certain types of measures which do not fulfil all the conditions set out in this section, the Commission will undertake a more detailed assessment of the risk capital measure as set out in detail in section 5.

Where there is also aid at the level of target enterprises and the provision of risk capital is linked to costs which are eligible for aid under another regulation or framework or other guidelines, that text may be applied to consider whether the aid is compatible with the common market.

Notes
[1] OJ L 83, 27.3.1999, p.1.

4.2. Form of aid

The choice of form of an aid measure lies in general with the Member State and this applies equally to risk capital measures. However, the Commission's assessment of such measures will include whether they encourage market investors to provide risk capital to the target enterprises and are likely to result in investment decisions being taken on a commercial (that is, a profit-driven) basis, as further explained in section 4.3.

The Commission believes that the types of measure capable of producing this result include the following:

(a) constitution of investment funds ("venture capital funds") in which the State is a partner, investor or participant, even if on less advantageous terms than other investors;
(b) guarantees to risk capital investors or to venture capital funds against a proportion of investment losses, or guarantees given in respect of loans to investors/funds for investment in risk capital, provided the public cover for the potential underlying losses does not exceed 50% of the nominal amount of the investment guaranteed;
(c) other financial instruments in favour of risk capital investors or venture capital funds to provide extra capital for investment;
(d) fiscal incentives to investment funds and/or their managers, or to investors to undertake risk capital investment.

4.3. Conditions for compatibility

To ensure that the incentive effect and the necessity of aid as set out in section 1.3.4 are present in a risk capital measure a number of indicators are relevant. The rationale is that State aid must target a specific market failure for the existence of which there is sufficient evidence. For this purpose, these guidelines lay down specific safe-harbour thresholds relating to tranches of investment in target SMEs in their early stages of business activity. Furthermore, so that aid is limited to the minimum necessary, it is crucial that aided investments into target SMEs are profit-driven and are managed on a commercial basis. The Commission will consider that the incentive effect, the necessity and proportionality of aid are present in a risk capital measure and that the overall balance is positive where all the following conditions are met. Measures specifically involving investment vehicles will be assessed under section 5 of these guidelines and not under the conditions in this section.

[4.3.1. Maximum level of investment tranches

The risk capital measure must provide for tranches of finance, whether wholly or partly financed through State aid, not exceeding EUR 2.5 million per target SME over each period of 12 months.][1]

Notes
[1] Text in square brackets as substituted by the Communication from the Commission amending the Community guidelines on State aid to promote risk capital investments in small and medium-sized enterprises, OJ C 329, 7.12.2010, p.4, with effect from 1 January 2011.

4.3.2. Restriction to seed, start-up and expansion financing

The risk capital measure must be restricted to provide financing up to the expansion stage for small enterprises, or for medium-sized enterprises located in assisted areas. It must be restricted to provide financing up to the start-up stage for medium-sized enterprises located in non-assisted areas.

4.3.3. Prevalence of equity and quasi-equity investment instruments

The risk capital measure must provide at least 70% of its total budget in the form of equity and quasi-equity investment instruments into target SMEs. In assessing the nature of such instruments, the Commission will have regard to the economic substance of the instrument rather than to its name and the qualification attributed to it by the investors. In particular, the Commission will take into account the degree of risk in the target company's venture borne by the investor, the potential losses borne by the investor, the predominance of profit-dependent remuneration versus fixed remuneration, and the level of subordination of the investor in the event of the company's bankruptcy. The Commission may also take into account the treatment applicable to the investment instrument under the prevalent domestic legal, regulatory, financial, and accounting rules, if these are consistent and relevant for the qualification.

4.3.4. Participation by private investors

At least 50% of the funding of the investments made under the risk capital measure must be provided by private investors, or for at least 30% in the case of measures targeting SMEs located in assisted areas.

4.3.5. Profit-driven character of investment decisions

The risk capital measure must ensure that decisions to invest into target companies are profit-driven. This is the case where the motivation to effect the investment is based on the prospects of a significant profit potential and constant assistance to target companies for this purpose. This criterion is considered to be met if all the following conditions are fulfilled:

(a) the measures have significant involvement of private investors as described in section 4.3.4, providing investments on a commercial basis (that is, only for profit) directly or indirectly in the equity of the target enterprises; and

(b) a business plan exists for each investment containing details of product, sales and profitability development and establishing the *ex ante* viability of the project; and

(c) a clear and realistic exit strategy exists for each investment.

4.3.6. Commercial management

The management of a risk capital measure or fund must be effected on a commercial basis. The management team must behave as managers in the private sector, seeking to optimise the return for their investors. This criterion is considered to be present where all the following conditions are fulfilled:

(a) there is an agreement between a professional fund manager or a management company and participants in the fund, providing that the manager's remuneration is linked to performance and setting out the objectives of the fund and proposed timing of investments; and

(b) private market investors are represented in decision-making, such as through an investors' or advisory committee; and

(c) best practices and regulatory supervision apply to the management of funds.

4.3.7. Sectoral focus

To the extent that many private sector funds focus on specific innovative technologies or even sectors (such as health, information technology, biotechnology) the Commission may accept a sectoral focus for risk capital measures, provided the measure falls within the scope of these guidelines as set out in section 2.1.

5. COMPATIBILITY OF RISK CAPITAL AID MEASURES SUBJECT TO A DETAILED ASSESSMENT

This section applies to risk capital measures which do not satisfy all the conditions laid down in section 4. A more detailed compatibility assessment based on the balancing test outlined in section 1.3 is necessary for these measures due to the need to ensure the targeting of the relevant market failure and due to the higher risks of potential crowding-out of private investors and of distortion of competition.

The analysis of compatibility of the measures with the [Treaty on the Functioning of the European Union] will be based on a number of positive and negative elements. No single element is determinant, nor can any set of elements be regarded as sufficient on its own to ensure compatibility. In some cases their applicability, and the weight attached to them, may depend on the form of the measure. Member States will have to provide all the elements and the evidence they consider useful for the assessment of a measure. The level of evidence required and the Commission assessment will depend on the features of each case and will be proportionate to the level of market failure tackled and to the risk of crowding out private investment.

5.1. Aid measures subject to a detailed assessment

The following types of risk capital measures not complying with one or more of the conditions set out in section 4 will be subject to a more detailed assessment given the less obvious evidence of a market failure and the higher potential for crowding out of private investment and/or distortion of competition.

[(a) Measures providing for investment tranches beyond the safe-harbour threshold of EUR 2.5 million per target SME over each period of 12 months

The Commission is aware of the constant fluctuation of the risk capital market and of the equity gap over time, as well as of the different degree by which enterprises are affected by the market failure depending on their size, on their stage of business development, and on their economic sector. Therefore, the Commission is prepared to consider declaring risk capital measures providing for investment tranches exceeding the threshold of EUR 2.5 million per enterprise per year compatible with the common market, provided the necessary evidence of the market failure is submitted.][1]

Notes

[1] Text in square brackets as substituted by the Communication from the Commission amending the Community guidelines on State aid to promote risk capital investments in small and medium-sized enterprises, OJ C 329, 7.12.2010, p.4, with effect from 1 January 2011.

(b) Measures providing finance for the expansion stage for medium-sized enterprises in non-assisted areas

The Commission recognises that certain medium-sized enterprises in non-assisted areas may have insufficient access to risk capital even in their expansion stage despite the availability of finance to enterprises having a significant turnover and/or total balance. Therefore, the Commission is prepared to consider declaring measures partly covering the expansion stage of medium-sized enterprises compatible with the common market in certain cases, provided the necessary evidence is submitted.

(c) Measures providing for follow-on investments into target companies that already received aided capital injections to fund subsequent financing rounds even beyond the general safe-harbour thresholds and the companies' early-growth financing

The Commission recognises the importance of follow-on investments into target companies that already received aided capital injections in their early stages to finance financing rounds even beyond the maximum safe-harbour investment tranches and the companies" early-growth financing up to the exit of the initial investment. This may be necessary to avoid dilution of the public participation in these financing rounds while ensuring continuity of financing for the target enterprises so that both public and private investors can fully benefit from the risky investments. In these circumstances and taking into account the specificities of the targeted sector and enterprises, the Commission is prepared to consider declaring follow-on investment compatible with the common market provided the amount of this investment is consistent with the initial investment and with the size of the fund.

(d) Measures providing for a participation by private investors below 50% in non-assisted areas or below 30% in assisted areas

In the Community the level of development of the private risk capital market varies to a significant extent in the various Member States. In some cases, it might be difficult to find private investors, and therefore the Commission is prepared to consider declaring measures with a private participation below the thresholds set out in section 4.3.4 compatible with the common market, if Member States submit the necessary evidence.

This problem may be even greater for risk capital measures targeting SMEs in assisted areas. In these cases there may be an additional shortage of capital available for them given their remote location from venture capital centres, the lower population density, and the increased risk-aversion of private investors. These SMEs may also be affected by demand-side issues such as the difficulty in drawing up a viable, investment-ready business proposition, a more limited equity culture, and particular reluctance to lose management control as a result of venture capital intervention.

(e) Measures providing seed capital to small enterprises which may foresee (i) less or no private participation by private investors, and/or (ii) predominance of debt investment instruments as opposed to equity and quasi-equity

The market failures affecting enterprises in their seed stage are more pronounced due to the high degree of risk involved by the potential investment and the need to closely mentor the entrepreneur in this crucial phase. This is also reflected by the reluctance and near absence of private investors to provide seed capital, which implies no or very limited risk of crowding-out. Furthermore, there is reduced potential for distortion of competition due to the significant distance from the market of these small-size enterprises. These reasons may justify a more favourable stance of the Commission towards measures targeting the seed stage, also in light of their potentially crucial importance to generate growth and jobs in the Community.

(f) Measures specifically involving an investment vehicle

An investment vehicle may facilitate the matching between investors and target SMEs for which it may therefore improve the access to risk capital. In case of market failures related to the enterprises targeted by the vehicle, the vehicle may not function efficiently without financial incentives. For instance, investors may not find the type of investments targeted by the vehicle attractive compared to investments of higher tranches of investments or investments in more established enterprises or more established market places, despite a clear potential for profitability of the target enterprises. Therefore, the Commission is prepared to consider declaring measures specifically involving an investment vehicle compatible with the common market, provided the necessary evidence for a clearly defined market failure is submitted.

(g) Costs linked to the first screening of companies in view of the conclusion of the investments, up to the due diligence phase ("scouting costs")

Risk capital funds or their managers may incur "scouting costs" in identifying SMEs, prior to the due diligence phase. Grants covering part of these scouting costs must encourage the funds or their managers to carry out more "scouting" activities than would otherwise be the case. This may also be beneficial for the SMEs concerned, even if the search does not lead to an investment, since it enables those SMEs to acquire more experience with risk capital financing. These reasons may justify a more favourable stance of the Commission towards grants covering part of the scouting costs of risk capital funds or their managers, subject to the following conditions: The eligible costs must be limited to the scouting costs related to SMEs mainly in their seed or start-up stage, where such costs do not lead to investment, and the costs must exclude legal and administrative costs of the funds. In addition, the grant must not exceed 50% of the eligible costs.

5.2. Positive effects of the aid

[5.2.1. Existence and evidence of market failure

For risk capital measures envisaging investment tranches into target enterprises beyond the conditions laid down in Section 4, in particular those providing for tranches above EUR 2.5 million per target SME over each period of 12 months, follow-on investments or financing of the expansion stage for medium-sized enterprises in non-assisted areas as well as for measures specifically involving an investment vehicle, the Commission will require additional evidence of the market failure being tackled at each level where aid may be present before declaring the proposed risk capital measure compatible with the common market. Such evidence must be based on a study showing the level of the "equity gap" with regard to the enterprises and sectors targeted by the risk capital measure. The relevant information concerns the supply of risk capital and the fundraising capital, as well as the significance of the venture capital industry in the local economy. It should ideally be provided for periods of three to five years preceding the implementation of the measure and also for the future, on the basis of reasonable projections, if available. The evidence submitted could also include the following elements:][1]

(a) development of the fundraising over the past five years, also in comparison with the correspondent national and/or European averages;

(b) the current overhang of money;

(c) the share of government aided investment programs in the total venture capital investment over the preceding three to five years;

(d) the percentage of new start-ups receiving venture capital;

(e) the distribution of investments by categories of amount of investment;

(f) a comparison of the number of business plans presented with the number of investments made by segment (amount of investment, sector, round of financing, etc.).

For measures targeting SMEs located in assisted areas, the relevant information must be supplemented by any other relevant evidence proving the regional specificities which justify the features of the measure envisaged.

The following elements may be relevant:

(a) estimation of the additional size of the equity gap caused by the peripherality and other regional specificities, in particular in terms of total amount of risk capital invested, number of funds or investment vehicles present in the territory or at a short distance, availability of skilled managers, number of deals and average and minimum size of deals if available;

(b) specific local economic data, social and/or historic reasons for an underprovision of risk capital, in comparison with the relevant average data and/or situation at national and/or Community level as appropriate;

(c) any other relevant indicator showing an increased degree of market failure. Member States may resubmit the same evidence several times provided that the underlying market conditions have not changed. The Commission reserves the right to question the validity of the submitted evidence.

Notes

[1] Text in square brackets as substituted by the Communication from the Commission amending the Community guidelines on State aid to promote risk capital investments in small and medium-sized enterprises, OJ C 329, 7.12.2010, p.4, with effect from 1 January 2011.

5.2.2. Appropriateness of the instrument

An important element in the balancing test is whether and to what extent State aid in the field of risk capital can be considered as an appropriate instrument to encourage private risk capital investment. This assessment is closely related to the assessment of the incentive effect and the necessity of aid, as set out in section 5.2.3.

In its detailed assessment, the Commission will take particular account of any impact assessment of the proposed measure which the Member State has made. Where the Member State has considered other policy options and the advantages of using a selective instrument such as State aid have been established and submitted to the Commission, the measures concerned are considered to constitute an appropriate instrument. The Commission will also assess evidence of other measures taken or to be taken to address the "equity gap" notably *ex post* evaluations and both supply and demand side issues affecting the targeted SMEs, to see how they would interact with the proposed risk capital measure.

5.2.3. Incentive effect and necessity of aid

The incentive effect of the risk capital aid measures plays a crucial role in the compatibility assessment. The Commission believes that the incentive effect is present for measures meeting all the conditions in section 4. However, as for the measures covered in this section the presence of the incentive effect becomes less obvious. Therefore, the Commission will also take into account the following additional criteria showing the profit-driven character of investment decisions and the commercial management of the measure, where relevant.

5.2.3.1. Commercial management

In addition to the conditions laid down in section 4.3.6 the Commission will consider it positively that the risk capital measure or fund is managed by professionals from the private sector or by independent professionals chosen according to a transparent, non-discriminatory procedure, preferably an open tender, with proven experience and a track record in capital market investments ideally in the same sector(s) targeted by the fund, as well as an understanding of the relevant legal and accounting background for the investment.

5.2.3.2. Presence of an investment committee

A further positive element would be the existence of an investment committee, independent of the fund management company and composed of independent experts coming from the private sector with significant experience in the targeted sector, and preferably also of representatives of investors, or independent experts chosen according to a transparent, non-discriminatory procedure, preferably an open tender. These experts would provide the managers or management company with analyses of the existing and the expected future market situation and would scrutinise and propose to them potential target enterprises with good investment prospects.

5.2.3.3. Size of the measure/fund

The Commission will consider it positively where a risk capital measure has a budget for investments into target SMEs of a sufficient size to take advantage of economies of scale in administering a fund and the possibility of diversifying risk via a pool of a sufficient number of investments. The size of the fund should be such as to ensure the possibility of absorbing the transaction costs and/or financing the later more profitable financing stages of target companies. Larger funds will be considered positively also taking into account the sector targeted, and provided the risks of crowding-out private investment and distorting competition are minimised.

5.2.3.4. Presence of business angels

For measures targeting seed capital, in view of the more pronounced level of market failure that can be perceived in this phase, the Commission will consider positively the direct or indirect involvement of business angels in investments in the seed stage. In such circumstances, it is therefore prepared to consider declaring measures compatible with the common market even if they foresee a predominance of debt instruments, including a higher degree of subordination of the State funds and a right of first profit for business angels or higher remuneration for their provision of capital and active involvement in the management of the measure/fund and/or of the target enterprises.

5.2.4. Proportionality

Compatibility requires that the aid amount is limited to the minimum necessary. The way to achieve this aspect of proportionality will necessarily depend on the form of the measure in question. However in the absence of any mechanism to check that investors are not overcompensated, or a measure where the risk of losses is borne entirely by the public sector and/or where the benefits flow entirely to the other investors, the measure will not be considered proportionate.

The Commission will consider that the following elements positively influence the assessment of proportionality as they represent a best-practice approach:

(a) **Open tender for managers.** A transparent, non-discriminatory open tender for the choice of the managers or management company ensuring the best combination of quality and value for money will be considered positively, as it will limit the cost (and possibly aid) level at the minimum necessary and will also minimise distortion of competition.

(b) **Call for tender or public invitation to investors.** A call for tender for the establishment of any "preferential terms" given to investors, or the availability of any such terms to other investors. This availability might take the form of a public invitation to investors at the launch of an investment fund or investment vehicle, or might take the form of a scheme (such as a guarantee scheme) which remained open to new entrants over an extended period.

5.3 Negative effects of the aid

The Commission will balance the potential negative effects in terms of distortion of competition and risk of crowding-out private investment against the positive effects when assessing the compatibility of risk capital measures. These potentially negative effects will have to be analysed at each of the three levels where aid may be present. Aid to investors, to investment vehicles and to investment funds may negatively affect competition in the market for the provision of risk capital. Aid to target enterprises may negatively affect the product markets on which these enterprises compete.

5.3.1. Crowding-out

At the level of the market for the provision of risk capital, State aid may result in crowding out private investment. This might reduce the incentives of private investors to provide funding for target SMEs and encourage them to wait until the State provides aid for such investments. This risk becomes more relevant, the higher the amount of an investment tranche invested into an enterprise, the larger the size of an enterprise, and the later the business stage, as private risk capital becomes progressively available in these circumstances. Therefore, the Commission will require specific evidence regarding the risk of crowding-out for measures providing for larger investment tranches in target SMEs, for follow-on investments or for financing of the expansion stage in medium-sized enterprises in non-assisted areas or for measures with low participation by private investors or measures involving specifically an investment vehicle. In addition, Member States will have to provide evidence to show that there is no risk of crowding-out, specifically concerning the targeted segment, sector and/or industry structure. The following elements may be relevant:

(a) the number of venture capital firms/funds/investment vehicles present at national level or in the area in case of a regional fund and the segments in which they are active;
(b) the targeted enterprises in terms of size of companies, growth stage, and business sector;
(c) the average deal size and possibly the minimum deal size the funds or investors would scrutinise;
(d) the total amount of venture capital available for the target enterprises, sector and stage targeted by the relevant measure.

5.3.2. Other distortions of competition

As most target SMEs are recently established, at the level of the market where they are present, it is unlikely that these SMEs will have significant market power and thus that there will be a significant distortion of competition in this respect. However, it can not be excluded that risk capital measures might have the effect of keeping inefficient firms or sectors afloat, which would otherwise disappear. Furthermore, an over-supply of risk capital funding to inefficient enterprises may artificially increase their valuation and thus distort the risk capital market at the level of fund providers, which would have to pay higher prices to buy these enterprises. Sector specific aid may also maintain production in non-competitive sectors, whereas region-specific aid may build up an inefficient allocation of production factors between regions.

In its analysis of these risks, the Commission will examine, in particular, the following factors:

(a) overall profitability of the firms invested in over time and prospects of future profitability;
(b) rate of enterprise failure targeted by the measure;
(c) maximum size of investment tranche envisaged by the measure as compared to the turnover and costs of the target SMEs;
(d) over-capacity of the sector benefiting from the aid.

5.4. Balancing and decision

In the light of the above positive and negative elements, the Commission will balance the effects of the risk capital measure and determine whether the resulting distortions adversely affect trading conditions to an extent contrary to the common interest. The analysis in each particular case will be based on an overall assessment of the foreseeable positive and negative impact of the State aid. For that purpose the Commission will not use the criteria set out in these guidelines mechanically but will make an overall assessment of their relative importance.

The Commission may raise no objections to the notified aid measure without entering into the formal investigation procedure or, following the formal investigation procedure laid down in Article 6 of

Regulation (EC) No 659/1999, it may close the procedure with a decision pursuant to Article 7 of that Regulation. If it adopts a conditional decision pursuant to Article 7(4) of Regulation (EC) No 659/1999 closing a formal investigation procedure, it may in particular attach the following conditions to limit the potential distortion of competition and ensure proportionality:

(a) if higher thresholds of investment tranches per target enterprise are foreseen, it may lower the maximum amount proposed per investment tranche or set an overall maximum amount of finance per target enterprise;

(b) if investments in the expansion stage in medium-sized enterprises in non-assisted areas are foreseen, it may limit investments predominantly to the seed and start-up stage and/or limit the investments to one or two rounds and/or limit the tranches to a maximum threshold per target enterprise;

(c) if follow-on investment is foreseen, it may set specific limits to the maximum amount to be invested into each target enterprise, to the investment stage eligible for intervention, and/or to the period during which aid may be granted, having also regard to the sector concerned and to the size of the fund;

(d) if a lower participation of private investors is foreseen, it may require a progressive increase of the participation of private investors over the life of the fund, having particular regard to the business stage, the sector, the respective levels of profit-sharing and subordination, and possibly the localisation in assisted areas of the target enterprises;

(e) for measures providing seed capital only, it may require Member States to ensure that the State receives an adequate return on its investment commensurate with the risks incurred for these investments, in particular where the State finances the investment in the form of quasi-equity or debt instruments, the return on which should, for instance, be linked to potential rights of exploitation (for example, royalties) generated by intellectual property rights created as a result of the investment;

(f) require a different balancing between respective profit- and loss-sharing arrangements and level of subordination between the State and private investors;

(g) require more stringent commitments as regards cumulation of risk capital aid with aid granted under other State aid regulations or frameworks, by way of derogation from section 6.

6. Cumulation

Where capital provided to a target enterprise under a risk capital measure covered by these guidelines is used to finance initial investment or other costs eligible for aid under other block exemption regulations, guidelines, frameworks, or other State aid documents, the relevant aid ceilings or maximum eligible amounts will be reduced by 50% in general and by 20% for target enterprises located in assisted areas during the first three years of the first risk capital investment and up to the total amount received. This reduction does not apply to aid intensities provided for in the Community Framework for State aid for Research and Development[1] or any successor framework or block exemption regulation in this field.

Notes
[1] OJ C 45, 17.2.1996, p.5.

7. Final Provisions

7.1. Monitoring and reporting

Regulation (EC) No 659/1999 and Commission Regulation (EC) No 794/2004 of 21 April 2004 implementing Council Regulation (EC) No 659/1999 laying down detailed rules for the application of Article [108 TFEU][1] require Member States to submit annual reports to the Commission. In respect of risk capital measures the reports must contain a summary table with a breakdown of the investments effected by the fund or under the risk capital measure including a list of all the enterprise beneficiaries of risk capital measures. The report must also give a brief description of the activity of investments funds with details of potential deals scrutinised and of the transactions actually undertaken as well as the performance of investment vehicles with aggregate information about the amount of capital raised through the vehicle. The Commission may request additional information regarding the aid granted, to check whether the conditions of the Commission's decision approving the aid measure have been respected.

The annual reports will be published on the internet site of the Commission.

In addition, the Commission considers that further measures are necessary to improve the transparency of State aid in the Community. In particular, it appears necessary to ensure that the Member States, economic operators, interested parties and the Commission itself have easy access to the full text of all applicable risk capital aid schemes. This can easily be achieved through the establishment of linked internet sites. For this reason, when examining risk capital aid schemes, the Commission will systematically require the Member State concerned to publish the full text of all final aid schemes on the internet and to communicate the internet address of the publication to the Commission. The scheme must not be applied before the information is published on the internet. Member States must maintain detailed records regarding the granting of aid for all risk capital measures. Such records must contain all information necessary to establish that the conditions laid down in the guidelines have been observed, notably as regards the size of the tranche, the size of the company (small or medium-sized), the development stage of the company (seed, start-up or expansion), its sector of activity (preferably at 4 digit level of the NACE classification) as well as information on the management of the funds and on the other criteria mentioned in these guidelines. This information must be maintained for 10 years from the date on which the aid is granted.

The Commission will ask Member States to provide this information in order to carry out an impact assessment of these guidelines three years after their entry into force.

Notes
1 OJ L 140, 30.4.2004, p.1.

7.2. Entry into force and validity

The Commission will apply these guidelines from the date of their publication in the *Official Journal of the European Union*. These guidelines will replace the 2001 Communication on State aid and risk capital. These guidelines will cease to be valid on 31 December 2013. After consulting Member States, the Commission may amend it before that date on the basis of important competition policy or risk capital policy considerations or in order to take account of other Community policies or international commitments.

Where this would be helpful the Commission may also provide further clarifications of its approach to particular issues. The Commission intends to carry out a review of these guidelines three years after their entry into force.

The Commission will apply these guidelines to all notified risk capital measures in respect of which it must take a decision after the guidelines are published in the *Official Journal of the European Union*, even where the measures were notified prior to the publication of the guidelines. In accordance with the Commission notice on the determination of the applicable rules for the assessment of unlawful State aid ("*consecutio legis*"),1 the Commission will apply the following in respect of non-notified aid:

(a) these guidelines, if the aid was granted after their publication in the *Official Journal of the European Union*;

(b) the Communication on State aid and risk capital in all other cases.

Notes
1 OJ C 119, 22.5.2002, p.22.

7.3. Appropriate Measures

The Commission hereby proposes to Member States, on the basis of Article [108(1) TFEU], the following appropriate measures concerning their respective existing risk capital measures. Member States should amend, where necessary, their existing risk capital measures in order to bring them into line with these guidelines within twelve months after the publication of the guidelines. The Member States are invited to give their explicit unconditional agreement to these proposed appropriate measures within two months from the date of publication of these guidelines. In the absence of any reply, the Commission will assume that the Member State in question does not agree with the proposed measures.

G16

COMMUNITY FRAMEWORK FOR STATE AID FOR RESEARCH AND DEVELOPMENT AND INNOVATION

(2006/C 323/01)

Official Journal C 323, 30.12.2006, p.1

Celex No: 52006XC1230(01)

EUR-Lex permanent link: <http://eur-lex.europa.eu/legal-content/EN/ALL/?uri=
CELEX:52006XC1230%2801%29&qid=1395778597989>

Notes

The Commission has extended the validity of this instrument until 30 June 2014: Communication from the Commission concerning the prolongation of the application of the Community framework for State aid for research and development and innovation (2013/C 360/01), OJ C 360, 10.12.2013, p.1.

EEA application: for the corresponding EEA provision, see the EFTA Surveillance Authority's Procedural and Substantive Rules in the Field of State Aid (Guidelines on the application and interpretation of Articles 61 and 62 of the EEA Agreement and Article 1 of Protocol 3 to the Surveillance and Court Agreement), Part III, Chapter 14 (as substituted by EFTA Surveillance Authority Decision of 7 February 2007 (not yet published)).

Commentary

Communication: B&C: 17.063, 17.077

---

1. Introduction

    1.1. Objectives of State aid for Research and Development and Innovation

    1.2. State aid policy and R&D&I

    1.3. The balancing test and its application to aid to Research and Development and Innovation

        1.3.1. The State Aid Action Plan: less and better targeted aid, balancing test for the assessment of aid

        1.3.2. The objective of common interest addressed by the framework

        1.3.3. Appropriate instrument

        1.3.4. Incentive effect and necessity of aid

        1.3.5. Proportionality of the aid

        1.3.6. Negative effects of the aid to R&D&I must be limited so that the overall balance is positive

    1.4. Implementing the balancing test: legal presumptions and need for more specific assessment

    1.5. Motivation for specific measures covered by this framework

2. Scope of application and definitions

    2.1. Scope of application of the framework

    2.2. Definitions

3. State aid within the meaning of Article [107(1) TFEU]

Part G   State Aids

1. Introduction

1.1. Objectives of State aid for Research and Development and Innovation

Promoting Research and Development and Innovation (hereinafter: R&D&I) is an important object-ive of common interest. Article [179 TFEU]* stipulates that "The Community shall have the objective of strengthening the scientific and technological bases of Community industry and encouraging it to become more competitive at international level, while promoting all the research activities deemed necessary…". Articles [180 to 190 TFEU] determine the activities to be carried out in this respect and the scope and implementation of the multi-annual framework programme.

When meeting in Barcelona in March 2002, the European Council adopted a clear goal for the future development of research spending. It agreed that overall spending on Research and Development (hereinafter: R&D) and innovation in the Community should be increased with the aim of approach-ing 3% of gross domestic product by 2010. It further clarified that two-thirds of this new investment should come from the private sector. To reach this objective, research investment should grow at an average rate of 8% every year, shared between a 6% growth rate for public expenditure[1] and a 9% yearly growth rate for private investment.[2]

The objective is through State aid to enhance economic efficiency[3] and thereby, contribute to sustain-able growth and jobs. Therefore, State aid for R&D&I shall be compatible if the aid can be expected to lead to additional R&D&I and if the distortion of competition is not considered to be contrary to the common interest, which the Commission equates for the purposes of this framework with economic efficiency. The aim of this framework is to ensure this objective and in particular, to make it easier for Member States to better target the aid to the relevant market failures.[4]

Article [107(1) TFEU] lays down the principle that State aid is prohibited. In certain cases, how-ever, such aid may be compatible with the common market on the basis of Article [107(2) and (3)]. Aid for R&D&I will primarily be justified on the basis of Article [107(3)(b)] and [107(3)(c)]. In this framework the Commission lays down rules which it will apply in the assessment of aid noti-fied to it, thereby exercising its discretion and increasing legal certainty and transparency of its decision-making.

Notes

* Ed note: please see the Note on the Lisbon Treaty at p.xvii in regard to article renumbering introduced by the Lisbon Treaty. Unless otherwise stated, all Treaty article numbers are the new numbers of the Treaty on the Functioning of the European Union (TFEU) and the Treaty on European Union (TEU).

[1] It must be kept in mind that only a part of the public expenditure on R&D will qualify as State aid.

[2] Cf. "Investing in research: an action plan for Europe": Communication from the Commission to the Council, the European Parliament, the European Economic and Social Committee and the Committee of the Regions, COM(2003)226 final, p.7.

[3] In economics, the term "efficiency" (or "economic efficiency") refers to the extent to which total welfare is optimised in a particular market or in the economy at large. Additional R&D&I increases economic efficiency by shifting market demand towards new or improved products, processes or services, which is equivalent to a decrease in the quality adjusted price of these goods.

[4] A "market failure" is said to exist when the market, if left to its own devices, does not lead to an economically efficient outcome. It is in those circumstances that state intervention, including state aid, has the potential to improve the market outcome in terms of prices, output and use of resources.

1.2. State aid policy and R&D&I

In the context of the Lisbon strategy the level of R&D&I is considered not to be optimal for the economy in the Community, implying that an increase in the level of R&D&I would lead to higher growth in the Community. The Commission considers that the existing rules for State aid to R&D have to be modernised and enhanced to meet this challenge.

First, the Commission, in this framework, expands the existing possibilities of aid to R&D to new activities supporting innovation. Innovation is related to a process connecting knowledge and tech-nology with the exploitation of market opportunities for new or improved products, services and business processes compared to those already available on the common market, and encompassing a certain degree of risk. For the purpose of State aid rules, the Commission considers however that State aid for innovation should be authorised not on the basis of an abstract definition of innovation but only to the extent that it relates to precise activities, which clearly address the market failures that are hampering innovation and for which the benefits of State aid are likely to outweigh any possible harm to competition and trade

Second, the Commission aims at supporting a better administration of State aid to R&D&I. It intends to extend the scope of the block-exemption for R&D, which is currently limited to aid to small and medium-sized enterprises (hereafter: SMEs).[5] A future general block exemption regulation (hereafter: BER) will cover the less problematic aid measures in the area of R&D&I. This framework will continue to apply for all measures notified to the Commission whether because the measure is not covered by the BER, because of an obligation in the BER to notify aid individually, or because the Member State decides to notify a measure which could in principle have been exempted under the BER, as well as for the assessment of all non-notified aid.

Third, in order to better focus the Commission's scrutiny, this framework provides, for the assessment of measures falling within its scope, not only rules on the compatibility of certain aid measure (Chapter 5 below) but also, due to the increased risk of certain aid measures distorting competition and trade, additional elements concerning the analysis of the incentive effect and necessity of aid (Chapter 6 below) and an additional methodology to be applied in case of detailed assessment (Chapter 7 below).

In this context the Commission underlines that competitive markets should in principle, on their own, lead to the most efficient outcome in terms of R&D&I. However, this may not always be the case in the field of R&D&I and government intervention might then improve the outcome. Undertakings will invest more in research only to the extent that they can draw concrete commercial benefits from the results and are aware of the possibilities to do so. There are many reasons for low levels of R&D&I, which are partly due to structural barriers, and partly to the presence of market failures. Structural barriers should preferably be handled by structural measures,[6] whereas State aid may play a role in counter-weighing inefficiencies due to market failures. Furthermore, empirical evidence indicates that for State aid to be efficient it must be accompanied by favourable framework conditions, such as adequate intellectual property right systems, a competitive environment with research and innovation-friendly regulations and supportive financial markets.

However, State aid also distorts competition, and strong competition is at the same time a crucial factor for the market-driven stimulation of investment in R&D&I. Therefore, State aid measures must be carefully designed in order to limit the distortions. Otherwise, State aid can become counterproductive and reduce the overall level of R&D&I and economic growth.

The main concern related to R&D&I aid to undertakings is that rival undertakings' dynamic incentives to invest are distorted and possibly reduced. When an undertaking receives aid, this generally strengthens its position on the market and reduces the return on investment for other undertakings. When the reduction is significant enough, it is possible that rivals will cut back on their R&D&I activity. In addition, when the aid results in a soft budget constraint for the beneficiary, it may also reduce the incentive to innovate at the level of the beneficiary. Furthermore, the aid can support inefficient undertakings or enable the beneficiary to enhance exclusionary practices or market power.

Notes

5 State Aid Action Plan. Less and better targeted State aid: a roadmap for State aid reform 2005–2009. COM(2005) 107 final — SEC (2005) 795: adopted on 7 June 2005.

6 Including: university education, research programmes and public research facilities, IPR rules favouring innovation, attractive framework conditions for undertakings to do R&D&I.

1.3. The balancing test and its application to aid to Research and Development and Innovation

1.3.1. The State Aid Action Plan: less and better targeted aid, balancing test for the assessment of aid

In the State Aid Action Plan,[7] the Commission announced that "to best contribute to the re-launched Lisbon Strategy for growth and jobs, the Commission will, when relevant, strengthen its economic approach to State aid analysis. An economic approach is an instrument to better focus and target certain State aid towards the objectives of the re-launched Lisbon Strategy". In assessing whether an aid measure can be deemed compatible with the common market, the Commission balances the positive impact of the aid measure in reaching an objective of common interest against its potentially negative side effects by distortion of trade and competition. The State Aid Action Plan, building on existing practice, has formalised this balancing exercise in what has been termed a "balancing test".[8] It operates in three steps to decide upon the approval of a State aid measure; the first two steps are addressing the positive effects of State aid and the third is addressing the negative effects and resulting balancing of the positive and negative effects:

(1) Is the aid measure aimed at a well-defined objective of common interest (e.g. growth, employment, cohesion, environment)?

(2) Is the aid well designed to deliver the objective of common interest i.e. does the proposed aid address the market failure or other objective?

  (i) Is State aid an appropriate policy instrument?
  (ii) Is there an incentive effect, i.e. does the aid change the behaviour of firms?
  (iii) Is the aid measure proportional, i.e. could the same change in behaviour be obtained with less aid?

(3) Are the distortions of competition and effect on trade limited, so that the overall balance is positive?

This balancing test is applicable to the design of State aid rules as well as for the assessment of cases.

For a block exemption regulation, the State aid is compatible if the conditions laid down are fulfilled. The same applies in general to most cases addressed in this framework. However, for the individual aid measures which may have a high distortive potential due to high aid amounts, the Commission will make an overall assessment of the positive and negative effects of the aid based on the proportionality principle.

Notes
[7] State aid Action Plan (footnote), paragraph 21.
[8] Cf. State Aid Action Plan (footnote 5), paragraph 11 and 20, as elaborated in more detail already in the Communication on Innovation, COM(2005) 436 final of 21 September 2005.

1.3.2. The objective of common interest addressed by the framework

This framework addresses the objective of common interest of promoting Research and Development and Innovation. It aims at enhancing economic efficiency by tackling well defined market failures, which prevent the economy in the Community from reaching the optimal level of R&D&I.

To establish rules ensuring that aid measures achieve this objective, it is, first of all, necessary to identify the market failures hampering R&D&I. R&D&I takes place through a series of activities, which are upstream to a number of product markets, and which exploit available R&D&I capabilities to develop new or improved products[9] and processes in these product markets, thus fostering growth in the economy. However, given the available R&D&I capabilities, market failures may prevent the market from reaching the optimal output and lead to an inefficient outcome for the following reasons:

— **Positive externalities/knowledge spill-overs**: R&D&I often generate benefits for society in the form of knowledge spill-overs. However, left to the market, a number of projects may have an unattractive rate of return from a private perspective, even though the projects would be beneficial for society because profit seeking undertakings neglect the external effects of their actions when deciding how much R&D&I they should undertake. Consequently, projects in the common interest may not be pursued unless the government intervenes.

— **Public good/knowledge spill-overs**: For the creation of general knowledge, like fundamental research, it is impossible to prevent others from using the knowledge (public good), whereas more specific knowledge related to production can be protected, for example through patents allowing the inventor a higher return on their invention. To find the appropriate policy to support R&D&I, it is important to distinguish between creation of general knowledge and knowledge that can be protected. Undertakings tend to free ride on the general knowledge created by others, which makes undertakings unwilling to create the knowledge themselves. In fact, the market may not only be inefficient but completely absent. If more general knowledge was produced, the whole society could benefit from the knowledge spill-overs throughout the economy. For this purpose, governments may have to support the creation of knowledge by undertakings. In the case of fundamental research, they may have to pay fully for companies' efforts to conduct fundamental research.

— **Imperfect and asymmetric information**: R&D&I are characterised by a high degree of risk and uncertainty. Due to imperfect and/or asymmetric information, private investors may be reluctant to finance valuable projects; highly-qualified personnel may be unaware of recruitment possibilities in innovative undertakings. As a result, the allocation of human resources and financial resources may not be adequate in these markets and valuable projects for the economy may not be carried out.

— **Coordination and network failures**. The ability of undertakings to coordinate with each other or at least interact, and thus deliver R&D&I may be impaired. Problems may arise for various reasons, including difficulties in coordinating R&D and finding adequate partners.

Notes

9 This includes services.

1.3.3. Appropriate instrument

It is important to keep in mind that there may be other, better placed instruments to increase the level of R&D&I in the economy, for example regulation, increase in funding of universities, general tax measures in favour of R&D&I.[10] The appropriateness of a policy instrument in a given situation is normally linked to the main reasons behind the problem. Reducing market barriers may be more appropriate than State aid to deal with the difficulty of a new entrant to appropriate R&D&I results. Increased investment in universities may be more appropriate to deal with a lack of qualified R&D&I personnel than granting State aid to R&D&I projects. Member States should therefore choose State aid when it is an appropriate instrument on the basis of the problem they are trying to address. This means it is necessary to clearly identify the market failure they intend to target with the aid measure.

Notes

10 See the Notice on the application of the State aid rules to measures relating to direct business taxation: OJ C 384, 10.12.1998, p.3.

1.3.4. Incentive effect and necessity of aid

State aid for R&D&I must lead to the recipient of aid changing its behaviour so that it increases its level of R&D&I activity and R&D&I projects or activities take place which would not otherwise be carried out, or which would be carried out in a more restricted manner. The Commission considers that as a result of aid, R&D&I activity should be increased in size, scope, amount spent or speed. Incentive effect is identified by counterfactual analysis, comparing the levels of intended activity with aid and without aid. Member States must clearly demonstrate how they intend to ensure that the incentive effect is present.

1.3.5. Proportionality of the aid

Aid is considered to be proportional only if the same result could not be reached with a less distortive aid measure. In particular, the amount and intensity of the aid must be limited to the minimum needed for the aided R&D&I activity to take place.

1.3.6. Negative effects of the aid to R&D&I must be limited so that the overall balance is positive

The possible distortions of competition resulting from State aid for R&D&I can be categorised as:

— disrupting the dynamic incentives of undertakings and crowding out;

— supporting inefficient production;

— exclusionary practices and enhancing market power;

— effects on the localisation of economic activities across Member States;
— effects on trade flows within the internal market.

The negative effects are normally higher for higher aid amounts and for aid granted to activities which are close to commercialisation of the product or the service. Therefore aid intensities should generally be lower for activities linked to development and innovation than for research related activities. Furthermore, in the definition of eligible costs it is important to ensure that costs that can be considered to cover routine company activities are not eligible for aid. Also, characteristics of the beneficiary and the relevant markets have an influence on the level of distortion. Such aspects will be taken into account in more detail for the cases which will undergo a detailed assessment.

1.4. Implementing the balancing test: legal presumptions and need for more specific assessment

This framework will be used for the assessment of aid for research and development and innovation which is notified to the Commission. The Commission's compatibility assessment will be conducted on the basis of the balancing test presented in Chapter 1. Accordingly, a measure will only be approved if, considering each of the elements in the balancing test, this leads to an overall positive evaluation. However, the Commission's assessment may differ in the way this evaluation is conducted, as in each case the risks for competition and trade associated with certain types of measures may differ. Without prejudice to Articles 4 to 7 of Council Regulation (EC) No 659/1999 of 22 March 1999 laying down detailed rules for the application of Article [108 TFEU],[11] the Commission applies different legal presumptions according to the type of State aid measure notified.

All notified aid will be assessed first under the provisions in Chapter 5. In that chapter, the Commission has identified a series of measures for which it considers *a priori* that State aid targeting these measures will address a specific market failure hampering R&D&I. The Commission has furthermore elaborated a series of conditions and parameters, which aim at ensuring that State aid targeting these measures actually presents an incentive effect, is proportionate and has a limited negative impact on competition and trade. Chapter 5 thus contains parameters in respect of the aided activity, aid intensities and conditions attached to compatibility. In principle, only measures which fulfil the criteria specified in Chapter 5 are eligible for compatibility under Article [107(3)(c) TFEU] on the basis of this framework.

In Chapter 6, the Commission presents more specifically how it will assess the necessity and incentive effect of the aid.

In Chapter 7, the Commission presents more specifically in which cases and how it will conduct a detailed assessment. This translates into different levels of assessment described in more detail below. For the first level, the Commission considers that it is in principle sufficient that the measures concerned are in line with the conditions described in Chapter 5, provided that the conditions in Chapter 6 to presume the incentive effect are fulfilled. For all other measures, the Commission considers that additional scrutiny is necessary, because of higher risks for competition and trade, due to the activity, aid amount, or type of beneficiary. The additional scrutiny will generally consist in further and more detailed factual analysis of the case in line with the provisions set out in Chapter 6 in respect of necessity and incentive effect or in Chapter 7, in respect of the assessment for aid exceeding the threshold set in section 7.1. of this framework. As a result of this additional scrutiny, the Commission may approve the aid, declare it incompatible with the common market or declare that it is compatible with the common market subject to conditions.

Firstly, the Commission considers that for certain aid measures, fulfilling the provisions set out in Chapters 5 and 6 will generally be sufficient for securing compatibility, as it is presumed that for such a measure the result of the application of the balancing test would be positive. Whether a measure falls into this category depends upon the type of beneficiary, the activity aided and the amount of aid granted. The Commission considers that the following measures will be declared compatible on the basis of Chapters 5 and 6 if (i) they fulfil all the conditions and parameters mentioned in Chapter 5 and (ii) the aid is only granted after the aid application has been made to the national authorities:

— project aid and feasibility studies where the aid beneficiary is an SME and where the aid amount is below EUR 7.5 million per SME for a project (project aid plus aid for feasibility study);
— aid for industrial property rights costs for SMEs;
— aid for young innovative enterprises;

— aid for innovation advisory services; aid for innovation support services;
— aid for the loan of highly qualified personnel.

For the measures listed above, Chapter 6 clarifies that the incentive effect is presumed to be present if the condition mentioned above in (ii) is fulfilled.

Second, for notified aid **below** the thresholds set in section 7.1. of this framework, the additional scrutiny consists in a demonstration of the incentive effect and necessity as set out in Chapter 6. Such measures will therefore be declared compatible on the basis of Chapter 5 and Chapter 6 only if (i) they fulfil all the conditions and parameters mentioned in Chapter 5 and (ii) the incentive effect and necessity have been demonstrated in accordance with Chapter 6. Third, for notified aid **above** the thresholds set in section 7.1. of this framework, the additional scrutiny consists in a detailed assessment according to Chapter 7. These measures will therefore be declared compatible on the basis of Chapters 5, 6 and 7 only if (i) they fulfil all the conditions and parameters mentioned in Chapter 5 and (ii) the balancing test pursuant to Chapter 7 results in an overall positive evaluation.

Notes
11 OJ L 83, 27.3.1999, p.1.

1.5. Motivation for specific measures covered by this framework

Applying these criteria to R&D&I, the Commission has identified a series of measures for which State aid may, under specific conditions, be compatible with Article [107(3)(c) TFEU].

Aid for projects covering fundamental and industrial research and experimental development is mainly targeted at the market failure related to positive externalities (knowledge spillovers), including public goods. The Commission considers it useful to maintain different categories of R&D&I activities regardless of the fact that the activities may follow an interactive model of innovation rather than a linear model. Different aid intensities reflect different sizes of market failures and how close the activity is to commercialisation. Furthermore, compared to the previous State aid rules in this field, certain innovation activities have been included in experimental development. In addition, the bonus system has been simplified. Due to expected larger implications of market failures and expected higher positive externalities, bonuses appear justified for SMEs, collaboration by and collaboration with SMEs, cross-border collaboration as well as public-private partnerships (collaborations of undertakings with public research organisations).

Aid for technical feasibility studies related to R&D&I projects aims at overcoming the market failure related to imperfect and asymmetric information. These studies are considered to be further away from the market than the project itself, and therefore relatively high aid intensities can be accepted.

Aid for industrial property rights costs for SMEs is targeted at the market failure related to positive externalities (knowledge spillovers). The aim is to increase the possibilities for SMEs to sufficiently appropriate returns, thereby giving them greater incentive to undertake R&D&I.

Aid for young innovative enterprises has been introduced to deal with the market failures linked with imperfect and asymmetric information, which harm these undertakings in a particularly acute way, damaging their ability to receive appropriate funding for innovative ventures.

Aid for process and organisational innovation in services targets the market failures linked to imperfect information and positive externalities. It is meant to tackle the problem that innovation in services activities may not fit in the R&D categories. Innovation in service activities often results from interactions with customers and confrontation with the market, rather than from the exploitation and use of existing scientific, technological or business knowledge. Furthermore, innovation in service activities tends to be based on new processes and organisation rather than technological development. To that extent, process and organisational innovation in services is not properly covered by R&D project aid and requires an additional and specific aid measure to address the market failures that hamper it.

Aid for advisory services and innovation support services, provided by innovation intermediaries, targets market failures linked with insufficient information dissemination, externalities and lack of coordination. State aid is an appropriate solution to change the incentives for SMEs to buy such services and to increase the supply and demand of the services provided by innovation intermediaries.

Aid for the loan of highly qualified personnel addresses the market failure linked with imperfect information in the labour market in the Community. Highly qualified personnel in the Community are more likely to be hired by large undertakings, because they tend to perceive large undertakings as offering better working conditions, and more secure and more attractive careers. By contrast, SMEs could benefit from important knowledge transfer and from increased innovation capabilities, if they were able to recruit highly qualified personnel to conduct R&D&I activities. Creating bridges between large undertakings or universities and SMEs may also contribute to addressing coordination market failures, and supporting clustering.

Aid for innovation clusters aims at tackling market failures linked with coordination problems hampering the development of clusters, or limiting the interaction and knowledge flows within clusters. State aid could contribute in two ways to this problem: first by supporting the investment in open and shared infrastructures for innovation clusters, and secondly by supporting cluster animation, so that collaboration, networking and learning is enhanced.

2. Scope of Application and Definitions

2.1. Scope of application of the framework

This framework applies to State aid for research and development and innovation. It will be applied in accordance with other Community policies on State aid, other provisions of the Treaties founding the European Communities and legislation adopted pursuant to those Treaties.

According to general Treaty principles, State aid cannot be approved if the aid measure is discriminatory to an extent not justified by its State aid character. With regard to R&D&I, it should in particular be underlined that the Commission will not approve an aid measure which excludes the possibility of exploitation of R&D&I results in other Member States.

Public authorities may commission R&D from companies or buy the results of R&D from them. If such R&D is not procured at market price, this will normally involve State aid within the meaning of Article Article [107(1) TFEU]. If, on the other hand, these contracts are awarded according to market conditions, an indication for which may be that a tender procedure in accordance with the applicable directives on public procurement, in particular Directive 2004/17/EC of the European Parliament and of the Council of 31 March 2004 coordinating the procurement procedures of entities operating in the water, energy, transport and postal services sectors[12] and Directive 2004/18/EC of the European Parliament and of the Council of 31 March 2004 on the coordination of procedures for the award of public works contracts, public supply contracts and public service contracts[13] has been carried out, the Commission will normally consider that no State aid within the meaning of Article Article [107(1) TFEU] is involved.

This framework applies to aid to support research and development and innovation in all sectors governed by the [Treaty on the Functioning of the European Union]. It also applies to those sectors which are subject to specific Community rules on State aid, unless such rules provide otherwise.[14]

This framework applies to State aid for R&D&I in the environmental field,[15] as there are many synergies to exploit between innovation for quality and performance and innovation to optimise energy use, waste and safety.

Following the entry into force of Commission Regulation (EC) No 364/2004 of 25 February 2004 amending Regulation (EC) No 70/2001 as regards the extension of its scope to include aid for research and development,[16] aid for research and development to SMEs is exempt from the notification requirement under the conditions stipulated in Commission Regulation (EC) No 70/2001 of 12 January 2001 on the application of Articles [107 and 108 TFEU] to State aid to small and medium-sized enterprises.[17] Member States, however, remain free to notify such aid. If they decide to do so, this framework will continue to be used for the assessment of such notified aid.

While personnel costs are eligible in several of the measures covered by this framework and a measure on aid for the loan of highly qualified personnel has been introduced, general employment and training aid for researchers continue to fall under the specific State aid instruments for employment and training aid, currently Commission Regulation (EC) No 68/2001 of 12 January 2001 on the application of Articles [107 and 108 TFEU] to training aid[18] and Commission Regulation (EC) No 2204/ 2002 of 12 December 2002 on the application of Articles [107 and 108 TFEU] to State aid for employment.[19] Aid for research and development and innovation for undertakings in difficulty within the meaning of the Community Guidelines on State aid for rescue and restructuring undertakings in difficulty[20] is excluded from the scope of this framework.

Notes

12 OJ L 134, 30.4.2004, p.1.

13 OJ L 134, 30.4.2004, p.114.

14 For example, Article 3 of Regulation (EEC) No 1107/70 of the Council of 4 June 1970 on the granting of aids for transport by rail, road and inland waterway provides special rules for the compatibility of State aid to R&D in the sector of transport by rail, road and inland waterway.

15 See current Community guidelines on State aid for environmental protection, OJ C 37, 3.2.2001, p.3, point 7. In addition, in the context of the revision of the environmental guidelines, the Commission will consider the opportunity to integrate new measures that can also cover eco-innovation. [Ed note: see now the 2008 Community guidelines on State aid for environmental protection (OJ C 82, 1.4.2008, p.1).]

16 OJ L 63, 28.2.2004, p.22.

17 OJ L 10, 13.1.2001, p.33. Regulation as amended by Regulation (EC) No 364/2004. [Ed note: see now Commission Regulation (EC) No 800/2008 of 6 August 2008 declaring certain categories of aid compatible with the common market in application of Articles [107 and 108 TFEU] (General block exemption Regulation) (OJ L 214, 9.8.2008, p.3), reproduced above at G11.]

18 OJ L 10, 13.1.2001, p.20. Regulation as amended by Regulation (EC) No 363/2004 (OJ L 63, 28.2.2004, p.20). [Ed note: see now Commission Regulation (EC) No 800/2008 of 6 August 2008 declaring certain categories of aid compatible with the common market in application of Articles [107 and 108 TFEU] (General block exemption Regulation) (OJ L 214, 9.8.2008, p.3), reproduced above at G11.]

19 OJ L 337, 13.12.2002, p.3. [Ed note: see now Commission Regulation (EC) No 800/2008 of 6 August 2008 declaring certain categories of aid compatible with the common market in application of Articles [107 and 108 TFEU] (General block exemption Regulation) (OJ L 214, 9.8.2008, p.3), reproduced above at G11.]

20 Currently OJ C 244, 1.10.2004, p.2.

2.2. Definitions

For the purpose of this framework the following definitions apply:

(a) "**small and medium-sized enterprises**", or "**SMEs**", "**small enterprises**" and "**medium-sized enterprises**" means such undertakings within the meaning of Regulation (EC) No 70/2001, or any regulation replacing that regulation;

(b) "**large enterprises**" means undertakings not coming under the definition of small and medium-sized enterprises;

(c) "**aid intensity**" means the gross aid amount expressed as a percentage of the project's eligible costs. All figures used shall be taken before any deduction of tax or other charge. Where aid is awarded in a form other than a grant, the aid amount shall be the grant equivalent of the aid. Aid payable in several instalments shall be discounted to its value at the moment of granting. The interest rate to be used for discounting purposes and for calculating the aid amount in a soft loan shall be the reference rate applicable at the time of grant. The aid intensity is calculated per beneficiary;

(d) "**research organisation**" means an entity, such as university or research institute, irrespective of its legal status (organised under public or private law) or way of financing, whose primary goal is to conduct fundamental research, industrial research or experimental development and to disseminate their results by way of teaching, publication or technology transfer; all profits are reinvested in these activities, the dissemination of their results or teaching; undertakings that can exert influence upon such an entity, in the quality of, for example, shareholders or members, shall enjoy no preferential access to the research capacities of such an entity or to the research results generated by it;

(e) "**fundamental research**" means experimental or theoretical work undertaken primarily to acquire new knowledge of the underlying foundations of phenomena and observable facts, without any direct practical application or use in view;

(f) "**industrial research**" means the planned research or critical investigation aimed at the acquisition of new knowledge and skills for developing new products, processes or services or for bringing about a significant improvement in existing products, processes or services. It comprises the creation of components of complex systems, which is necessary for the industrial research, notably for generic technology validation, to the exclusion of prototypes as covered by point (g);

(g) "**experimental development**" means the acquiring, combining, shaping and using of existing scientific, technological, business and other relevant knowledge and skills for the purpose of producing plans and arrangements or designs for new, altered or improved products, processes or services. These may also include, for example, other activities aiming at the conceptual definition, planning and documentation of new products, processes and services. The activities may comprise producing drafts, drawings, plans and other documentation, provided that they are not intended for commercial use.

The development of commercially usable prototypes and pilot projects is also included where the prototype is necessarily the final commercial product and where it is too expensive to produce for it to be used only for demonstration and validation purposes. In case of a subsequent commercial use of demonstration or pilot projects, any revenue generated from such use must be deducted from the eligible costs.

The experimental production and testing of products, processes and services are also eligible, provided that these cannot be used or transformed to be used in industrial applications or commercially.

Experimental development does not include the routine or periodic changes made to products, production lines, manufacturing processes, existing services and other operations in progress, even if such changes may represent improvements;

(h) "**repayable advance**" means a loan for a project which is paid in one or more instalments and the conditions for the reimbursement of which depend on the outcome of the R&D&I project,

(i) "**process innovation**"[21] means the implementation of a new or significantly improved production or delivery method (including significant changes in techniques, equipment and/or software). Minor changes or improvements, an increase in production or service capabilities through the addition of manufacturing or logistical systems which are very similar to those already in use, ceasing to use a process, simple capital replacement or extension, changes resulting purely from changes in factor prices, customisation, regular seasonal and other cyclical changes, trading of new or significantly improved products are not considered innovations;

(j) "**organisational innovation**"[22] means the implementation of a new organisational method in the undertaking's business practices, workplace organisation or external relations. Changes in business practices, workplace organisation or external relations that are based on organisational methods already in use in the undertaking, changes in management strategy, mergers and acquisitions, ceasing to use a process, simple capital replacement or extension, changes resulting purely from changes in factor prices, customisation, regular seasonal and other cyclical changes, trading of new or significantly improved products are not considered innovations;

(k) "**highly qualified personnel**" means researchers, engineers, designers and marketing managers with tertiary education degree and at least 5 years of relevant professional experience. Doctoral training may count as relevant professional experience;

(l) "**secondment**" means temporary employment of personnel by a beneficiary during a period of time, after which the personnel has the right to return to its previous employer;

(m) "**innovation clusters**" means groupings of independent undertakings — innovative start-ups, small, medium and large undertakings as well as research organisations — operating in a particular sector and region and designed to stimulate innovative activity by promoting intensive interactions, sharing of facilities and exchange of knowledge and expertise and by contributing effectively to technology transfer, networking and information dissemination among the undertakings in the cluster. Preferably, the Member State should intend to create a proper balance of SMEs and large undertakings in the cluster, to achieve a certain critical mass, notably through specialisation in a certain area of R&D&I and taking into account existing clusters in the Member State and at Community-level.

Notes

[21] Cf. definition in the OSLO manual, Guidelines for Collecting and Interpreting Innovation Data, 3rd Edition, Organisation for Economic Co-operation and Development, 2005, page 49.

[22] Cf. definition in the OSLO manual, page 51.

---

3. State Aid within the Meaning of Article [107(1) TFEU]

Generally, any funding meeting the criteria of Article [107(1) TFEU] will be considered to be State aid. For the sake of providing further guidance, situations typically arising in the field of Research, Development and Innovation activities are considered below.

3.1. Research organisations and innovation intermediaries as recipients of State aid within the meaning of Article [107(1) TFEU]

The question whether research organisations are recipients of State aid must be answered in accordance with general State aid principles.

In line with Article [107(1) TFEU] and the case-law of the Court, public financing of R&D&I activities by research organisations will qualify as State aid, if all conditions of Article [107(1) TFEU] are fulfilled. In accordance with the case-law, this requires inter alia that the research organisation qualifies as an undertaking within the meaning of Article [107(1) TFEU]. This does not depend upon its legal status (organized under public or private law) or economic nature (i.e. profit making or not). What is decisive for its qualification as an undertaking is whether the research organisation carries out an economic activity, which is an activity consisting of offering goods and/or services on a given market.[23] Accordingly, any public funding of economic activities falls under Article [107(1) TFEU], should all other conditions be fulfilled.

Note

[23] Case 118/85 *Commission v Italy* [1987] ECR 2599, paragraph 7, Case C-35/96 *Commission v Italy* [1998] ECR I-3851, CNSD, paragraph 36: Case C-309/99 *Wouters* [2002] ECR I-1577 paragraph 46.

3.1.1. *Public funding of non-economic activities*

If the same entity carries out activities of both economic and non-economic nature, in order to avoid cross-subsidisation of the economic activity, the public funding of the non-economic activities will not fall under Article [107(1) TFEU], if the two kinds of activities and their costs and funding can be clearly separated.[24] Evidence that the costs have been allocated correctly can consist of annual financial statements of the universities and research organisations.

The Commission nevertheless considers that the primary activities of research organisations are normally of a non-economic character, notably:

— education for more and better skilled human resources;
— the conduct of independent R&D for more knowledge and better understanding, including collaborative R&D;
— the dissemination of research results.

The Commission furthermore considers that technology transfer activities (licensing, spin-off creation or other forms of management of knowledge created by the research organisation) are of non-economic character if these activities are of an internal nature[25] and all income from these activities is reinvested in the primary activities of the research organisations.[26]

Notes

[24] Economic activities comprise in particular research carried out under contract with industry, the renting out of research infrastructure and consultancy work.

[25] By internal nature, the Commission means a situation where the management of the knowledge of the research organisation(s) is conducted either by a department or a subsidiary of the research organisation or jointly with other research organisations. Contracting the provision of specific services to third parties by way of open tenders does not jeopardise the internal nature of such activities.

[26] For all remaining kinds of technology transfer receiving State funding, the Commission does not consider itself in a position, on the basis of its current knowledge, to decide in a general manner upon the State aid character of the funding of such activities. It underlines the obligation of the Member States under Article [108(3)] of the [Treaty on the Functioning of the European Union] to assess the character of such measures in each case and to notify them to the Commission, in case they consider them to represent State aid.

3.1.2. *Public funding of economic activities*

If research organisations or other not-for-profit innovation intermediaries (for example, technology centres, incubators, chambers of commerce) perform economic activities, such as renting out infrastructures, supplying services to business undertakings or performing contract research, this should be done on normal market conditions, and public funding of these economic activities will generally entail State aid.

However, if the research organisation or not-for-profit innovation intermediary can prove that the totality of the State funding that it received to provide certain services has been passed on to the final recipient, and that there is no advantage granted to the intermediary, the intermediary organisation may not be recipient of State aid.

For aid to the final recipients, normal State aid rules apply.

3.2. Indirect State aid within the meaning of Article [107(1) TFEU] to undertakings through publicly funded research organisations

This section is intended to clarify under which conditions undertakings obtain an advantage within the meaning of Article [107(1) TFEU] in cases of contract research by a research organisation or collaboration with a research organisation. As far as the other elements of Article [107(1) TFEU] are concerned, the normal rules apply. In particular, it will have to be assessed in accordance with the relevant case-law whether the behaviour of the research organisation can be attributed to the State.[27]

Notes

[27] Cf. Case C-482/99 *France v Commission* [2002] ECR I-4397, on the issue of imputability to the State.

3.2.1. *Research on behalf of undertakings (Contract research or research services)*

This point concerns the situation in which a project is carried out by a research organisation on behalf of an undertaking. The research organisation, acting as an agent, renders a service to the undertaking acting as principal in situations where (i) the agent receives payment of an adequate remuneration for its service and (ii) the principal specifies the terms and conditions of this service. Typically, the principal will own the results of the project and carry the risk of failure. When a research organisation carries out such a contract, there will normally be no State aid passed to the undertaking through the research organisation, if one of the following conditions is fulfilled:

(1) the research organisation provides its service at market price; or

(2) if there is no market price, the research organisation provides its service at a price which reflects its full costs plus a reasonable margin.

3.2.2. *Collaboration of undertakings and research organisations*

In a collaboration project, at least two partners participate in the design of the project, contribute to its implementation and share the risk and the output of the project.

In the case of collaboration projects carried out jointly by undertakings and research organisations, the Commission considers that no indirect State aid is granted to the industrial partner through the research organisation due to the favourable conditions of the collaboration if one of the following conditions is fulfilled:

(1) the participating undertakings bear the full cost of the project.

(2) the results which do not give rise to intellectual property rights may be widely disseminated and any intellectual property rights to the R&D&I results which result from the activity of the research organisation are fully allocated[28] to the research organisation.

(3) the research organisation receives from the participating undertakings compensation equivalent to the market price for the intellectual property rights[29] which result from the activity of the research organisation carried out in the project and which are transferred to the participating undertakings. Any contribution of the participating undertakings to the costs of the research organisation shall be deducted from such compensation.

If none of the previous conditions are fulfilled, the Member State may rely on an individual assessment of the collaboration project.[30] There may also be no State aid where the assessment of the contractual agreement between the partners leads to the conclusion that any intellectual property rights to the R&D&I results as well as access rights to the results are allocated to the different partners of the collaboration and adequately reflect their respective interests, work packages, and financial and other contributions to the project. If conditions (1), (2) and (3) are not fulfilled and the individual assessment of the collaboration project does not lead to the conclusion that there is no State aid, the Commission will consider the full value of the contribution of the research organisation to the project as aid to undertakings.

Notes

[28] "Full allocation" means that the research organisation enjoys the full economic benefit of those rights by retaining full disposal of them, notably the right of ownership and the right to license. These conditions may also be fulfilled if the organisation decides to conclude further contracts concerning these rights including licensing them to the collaboration partner.

[29] "Compensation equivalent to the market price for the intellectual property rights" refers to compensation for the full economic benefit of those rights. In line with general State aid principles and given the inherent difficulty to establish objectively the market price for intellectual property rights, the Commission will consider this condition fulfilled if the research organisation as seller negotiates in order to obtain the maximum benefit at the moment when the contract is concluded.

[30] This provision does not intend to modify the obligation of the Member States to notify certain measures on the basis of Article [108(3)] of the [Treaty on the Functioning of the European Union].

---

4.   COMPATIBILITY OF AID UNDER ARTICLE [107(3)(B) TFEU]

Aid for R&D&I to promote the execution of an important project of common European interest may be considered to be compatible with the common market pursuant to Article [107(3)(b) TFEU].

The Commission will conclude that Article [107(3)(b) TFEU] applies if the following cumulative conditions are fulfilled:

(1)   the aid proposal concerns a project which is clearly defined in respect of the terms of its implementation including its participants as well as its objectives. The Commission may also consider a group of projects as together constituting a project.

(2)   the project must be in the common European interest: the project must contribute in a concrete, clear and identifiable manner to the Community interest. The advantage achieved by the objective of the project must not be limited to one Member State or the Member States implementing it, but must extend to the Community as a whole. The project must present a substantive leap forward for the Community objectives, for instance by being of great importance for the European Research Area or being a lead project for European industry. The fact that the project is carried out by undertakings in different countries is not sufficient. The positive effects of the aid could be shown for example by important spill-overs for society, through the contribution of the measure to the improvement of the Community situation regarding R&D&I in the international context, through creation of new markets or the development of new technologies. The benefits of the project should not be confined to the industry directly concerned but its results should be of wider relevance and application to the economy within the Community (up- or downstream markets, alternative uses in other sectors, etc.).

(3)   the aid is necessary to achieve the defined objective of common interest and presents an incentive for the execution of the project, which must also involve a high level of risk. This could be shown by looking at the level of profitability of the project, at the amount of investment and time path of cash flows and at feasibility studies, risk assessments and expert opinions.

(4)   the project is of great importance with respect to its character and its volume: it must be a meaningful project with regard to its objective and a project of substantial size.

The Commission will consider notified projects more favourably if they include a significant own contribution of the beneficiary to the project. It will equally consider more favourably notified projects involving undertakings or research entities from a significant number of Member States.

Part G   State Aids

In order to allow for the Commission to properly assess the case, the common European interest must be demonstrated in practical terms: for example, it must be demonstrated that the project enables significant progress to be made towards achieving specific Community objectives.

5. Compatibility of Aid under Article [107(3)(c) TFEU]

State aid for research and development and innovation shall be compatible with the common market within the meaning of Article [107(3)(c) TFEU], if, on the basis of the balancing test, it leads to increased R&D&I-activities without adversely affecting trading conditions to an extent contrary to the common interest. The Commission will view favourably notifications of aid measures which are supported by rigorous evaluations of similar past aid measures demonstrating the incentive effect of the aid. The following measures are eligible for compatibility under Article [107(3)(c) TFEU].

5.1. Aid for R&D projects

Aid for R&D projects will be considered compatible with the common market within the meaning of Article [107(3)(c) TFEU] provided that the conditions set out in this section are fulfilled.

5.1.1. Research categories

The aided part of the research project must completely fall within one or more of the following research categories: fundamental research, industrial research, experimental development.

When classifying different activities, the Commission will refer to its own practice as well as the specific examples and explanations provided in the Frascati Manual on the Measurement of Scientific and technological Activities, Proposed Standard Practice for Surveys on Research and Experimental Development.[31]

When a project encompasses different tasks, each task must be qualified as falling under the categories of fundamental research, industrial research or experimental development or as not falling under any of those categories at all.

This qualification need not necessarily follow a chronological approach, moving sequentially over time from fundamental research to activities closer to the market. Accordingly, nothing will prevent the Commission from qualifying a task which is carried out at a late stage of a project as industrial research, while finding that an activity carried out at an earlier stage of the project constitutes experimental development or is not research at all.

Notes

[31] Organisation for Economic Co-operation and Development, 2002.

5.1.2. Basic aid intensities

The aid intensity, as calculated on the basis of the eligible costs of the project, shall not exceed:

(a) 100% for fundamental research;
(b) 50% for industrial research;
(c) 25% for experimental development.

The aid intensity must be established for each beneficiary of aid, including in a collaboration project.

In the case of State aid for an R&D project being carried out in collaboration between research organisations and undertakings, the combined aid deriving from direct government support for a specific research project and, where they constitute aid (see section), contributions from research organisations to that project may not exceed the applicable aid intensities for each benefiting undertaking.

5.1.3. Bonuses

The ceilings fixed for industrial research and experimental development may be increased as follows:

(a) where the aid is to be given to SMEs, the aid intensity may be increased by 10 percentage points for medium-sized enterprises and by 20 percentage points for small enterprises;
(b) up to a maximum aid intensity of 80%, a bonus of 15 percentage points may be added if:[32]

(i) the project involves effective collaboration between at least two undertakings which are independent of each other and the following conditions are fulfilled:

— no single undertaking must bear more than 70% of the eligible costs of the collaboration project;

— the project must involve collaboration with at least one SME or be cross-border, that is to say, the research and development activities are carried out in at least two different Member States.

(ii) the project involves effective collaboration between an undertaking and a research organisation, particularly in the context of co-ordination of national R&D policies, and the following conditions are fulfilled:

— the research organisation bears at least 10% of the eligible project costs;

— the research organisation has the right to publish the results of the research projects insofar as they stem from research implemented by that organisation.

(iii) only in case of industrial research, if the results of the project are widely disseminated through technical and scientific conferences or published in scientific or technical journals or in open access repositories (databases where raw research data can be accessed by anyone), or through free or open source software.

For the purposes of points (i) and (ii) subcontracting is not considered to be effective collaboration. In case of collaboration between an undertaking and a research organisation, the maximum aid intensities and bonuses specified in this Framework do not apply to the research organisation.

Table illustrating the aid intensities:

	Small enterprise	Medium sized enterprise	Large Enterprise
Fundamental research	100%	100%	100%
Industrial research	70%	60%	50%
Industrial research	80%	75%	65%
Subject to:			
— collaboration between undertakings; for large undertakings: cross-border or with at least one SME			
or			
— collaboration of an undertaking with a research organisation			
or			
— dissemination of results			
Experimental development	45%	35%	25%
Experimental development	60%	50%	40%
subject to			
— collaboration between undertakings; for large undertakings: cross-border or at least one SME			
or			
— collaboration of an undertaking with a research organisation			

Notes

32 Projects funded under the Framework programme of the European Community for research, technological development and demonstration activities will automatically qualify for a bonus for collaboration due to the minimum conditions for participation in such projects.

5.1.4. Eligible costs

The aid intensity will be calculated on the basis of the costs of the research project to the extent that they can be considered as eligible. All eligible costs must be allocated to a specific category of R&D.

The following costs shall be eligible:

(a) personnel costs (researchers, technicians and other supporting staff to the extent employed on the research project);

(b) costs of instruments and equipment to the extent and for the period used for the research project. If such instruments and equipment are not used for their full life for the research project, only the depreciation costs corresponding to the life of the research project, as calculated on the basis of good accounting practice, are considered as eligible;

(c) costs for building and land, to the extent and for the duration used for the research project. With regard to buildings, only the depreciation costs corresponding to the life of the research project, as calculated on the basis of good accounting practice are considered as eligible. For land, costs of commercial transfer or actually incurred capital costs are eligible;

(d) cost of contractual research, technical knowledge and patents bought or licensed from outside sources at market prices, where the transaction has been carried out at arm's length and there is no element of collusion involved, as well as costs of consultancy and equivalent services used exclusively for the research activity;

(e) additional overheads incurred directly as a result of the research project;

(f) other operating expenses, including costs of materials, supplies and similar products incurred directly as a result of the research activity.

5.1.5. Repayable advance

If a Member State grants a repayable advance which qualifies as State aid within the meaning of Article [107(1) TFEU], the following rules shall apply.

Where a Member State can demonstrate, on the basis of a valid methodology based on sufficient verifiable data, that it is possible to calculate the gross grant equivalent of such aid granted in the form of a repayable advance and to accordingly design a scheme where this gross grant equivalent fulfils the conditions on maximum intensities in this section, it may notify this scheme and the associated methodology to the Commission. If the Commission accepts the methodology and deems the scheme compatible, the aid may be granted on the basis of the gross grant equivalent of the repayable advance, up to the aid intensities permissible under this section.

In all other cases, the repayable advance is expressed as a percentage of the eligible costs; it may then exceed the rates indicated in this section. provided that the following rules are fulfilled.

In order to allow the Commission to assess the measure, it must provide for detailed provisions on the repayment in case of success and clearly define what will be considered as a successful outcome of the research activities. All these elements must be notified to the Commission. The Commission will examine that the definition of a successful outcome has been established on the basis of a reasonable and prudent hypothesis. In case of a successful outcome, the measure must provide that the advance is repaid with an interest rate at least equal to the applicable rate resulting from the application of the Commission notice on the method for setting the reference and discount rates.[33]

In case of a success exceeding the outcome defined as successful, the Member State concerned should be entitled to request payments beyond repayment of the advance amount including interest according to the reference rate foreseen by the Commission.

In case the project fails, the advance does not have to be fully repaid. In case of partial success, the Commission will normally require that the repayment secured is in proportion to the degree of success achieved.

The advance may cover up to a maximum of 40% of the eligible costs for the experimental development phase of the project and up to 60% for the industrial research phase, to which bonuses can be added.

Notes

33 OJ C 273, 9.9.1997, p.3. Also published under:
<http://ec.europa.eu/comm/competition/state_aid/legislation/reference.html>. [Ed note: see now the 2008 Communication from the Commission on the revision of the method for setting the reference and discount rates (OJ C 14, 19.1.2008, p.6).]

5.1.6. Fiscal measures

On the basis of evaluation studies[34] provided by Member States in the notification, the Commission will consider that R&D&I fiscal aid schemes have an incentive effect by stimulating higher R&D&I-spending by undertakings.

The aid intensity of an R&D&I fiscal State aid measure can be calculated either on the basis of individual R&D&I projects or, at the level of an undertaking, as the ratio between the overall tax relief and the sum of all eligible R&D&I costs incurred in a period not exceeding three consecutive fiscal years. In the latter case, the R&D&I fiscal State aid measure may apply without distinction to all eligible R&D&I activities; the applicable aid intensity for experimental development must then not be exceeded.[35]

At the time of notification, the Member State must provide an estimate of the number of beneficiaries.

Notes

34 Even though this may not be possible *ex ante* for a newly introduced fiscal State aid measure, Member States will be expected to provide evaluation studies on the incentive effects of their own fiscal measures.
35 Conversely, where an R&D&I fiscal State aid measure distinguishes between different R&D&I categories, the relevant aid intensities must not be exceeded.

5.1.7. Matching clause

In order to address actual or potential direct or indirect distortions of international trade, higher intensities than generally permissible under this section may be authorized if — directly or indirectly — competitors located outside the Community have received (in the last three years) or are going to receive, aid of an equivalent intensity for similar projects, programmes, research, development or technology. However, where distortions of international trade are likely to occur after more than three years, given the particular nature of the sector in question, the reference period may be extended accordingly.

If at all possible, the Member State concerned will provide the Commission with sufficient information to enable it to assess the situation, in particular regarding the need to take account of the competitive advantage enjoyed by a third-country competitor. If the Commission does not have evidence concerning the granted or proposed aid, it may also base its decision on circumstantial evidence.

5.2. Aid for technical feasibility studies

Aid for technical feasibility studies preparatory to industrial research or experimental development activities shall be compatible with the common market within the meaning of Article [107(3)(c) TFEU] provided that the aid intensity, as calculated on the basis of the study costs, does not exceed the following aid intensities:

(a) for SMEs, 75% for studies preparatory to industrial research activities and 50% for studies preparatory to experimental development activities,
(b) for large undertakings, 65% for studies preparatory to industrial research activities and 40% for studies preparatory to experimental development activities.

5.3. Aid for industrial property rights costs for SMEs

Aid to SMEs for the costs associated with obtaining and validating patents and other industrial property rights shall be compatible with the common market within the meaning of Article [107(3)(c)

TFEU] up to the same level of aid as would have qualified as R&D aid in respect of the research activities which first led to the industrial property rights concerned.

Eligible costs are:

(a) all costs preceding the grant of the right in the first legal jurisdiction, including costs relating to the preparation, filing and prosecution of the application as well as costs incurred in renewing the application before the right has been granted;

(b) translation and other costs incurred in order to obtain the granting or validation of the right in other legal jurisdictions;

(c) costs incurred in defending the validity of the right during the official prosecution of the application and possible opposition proceedings, even if such costs occur after the right is granted.

5.4. Aid for young innovative enterprises

Aid to young innovative enterprises shall be compatible with the common market within the meaning of Article [107(3)(c) TFEU] if the following conditions are fulfilled:[36]

(a) the beneficiary is a small enterprise that has been of existence for less than 6 years at the time when the aid is granted and

(b) the beneficiary is an innovative enterprise, on the basis that:

  (i) the Member State can demonstrate, by means of an evaluation carried out by an external expert, notably on the basis of a business plan, that the beneficiary will in the foreseeable future develop products, services or processes which are technologically new or substantially improved compared to the state of the art in its industry in the Community, and which carry a risk of technological or industrial failure, or

  (ii) the R&D expenses of the beneficiary represent at least 15% of its total operating expenses in at least one of the three years preceding the granting of the aid or in the case of a start-up enterprise without any financial history, in the audit of its current fiscal period, as certified by an external auditor.

(c) the aid is not higher than EUR 1 million. This aid may not exceed EUR 1.5 million in regions eligible for the derogation in Article [107(3)(a) TFEU], and EUR 1.25 million in regions eligible for the derogation in Article [107(3)(c) TFEU].

The beneficiary may receive the aid only once during the period in which it qualifies as a young innovative enterprise This aid may be cumulated with other aid under this framework, with aid for research and development and innovation exempted by Regulation (EC) No 364/2004 or any successor regulation and with aid approved by the Commission under the risk capital guidelines.

The beneficiary may receive State aid other than R&D&I aid and risk capital aid only 3 years after the granting of the young innovative enterprise aid.

Note

[36] This is without prejudice to the application of the Guidelines on national regional aid for 2007–2013, OJ C 54, 4.3.2006, p.13, and notably the granting of aid for newly created small enterprises up to a total of EUR 2 million per small enterprise located in regions eligible for the derogation in Article [107(3)(a)] of the Treaty.

5.5. Aid for process and organisational innovation in services

Innovation in services may not always fall within the research categories defined in section 5.1 but is typically less systematic and stems frequently from customer interaction, market demand, adoption of business and organisational models and practices from more innovative sectors or from other similar sources.

Aid for process and organisational innovation in services shall be compatible with the common market within the meaning of Article [107(3)(c) TFEU] with a maximum aid intensity of 15% for large enterprises, 25% for medium enterprises and 35% for small enterprises. Large enterprises are only eligible for such aid if they collaborate with SMEs in the aided activity, whereby the collaborating SMEs must incur at least 30% of the total eligible costs.

Routine or periodic changes made to products, production lines, manufacturing processes, existing services and other operations in progress, even if such changes may represent improvements, do not qualify for State aid.

The following conditions must be fulfilled:

(a) organisational innovation must always be related to the use and exploitation of Information and Communication Technologies (ICT) to change the organisation;

(b) the innovation must be formulated as a project with an identified and qualified project manager, as well as identified project costs;

(c) the result of the aided project must be the development of a standard, of a business model, methodology or concept, which can be systematically reproduced, possibly certified, and possibly patented;

(d) the process or organisational innovation must be new or substantially improved compared to the state of the art in its industry in the Community. The novelty could be demonstrated by the Member States for instance on the basis of a precise description of the innovation, comparing it with state of the art process or organisational techniques used by other undertakings in the same industry;

(e) the process or organisational innovation project must entail a clear degree of risk. This risk could be demonstrated by the Member State for instance in terms of: project costs in relation to company turnover, time required to develop the new process, expected gains from the process innovation by comparison with the project costs, probability of failure. Eligible costs are the same as for aid to R&D projects (cf. section). In case of organisational innovation, however, costs of instruments and equipment cover costs of ICT instruments and equipment only.

5.6. Aid for innovation advisory services and for innovation support services

Aid for innovation advisory services and for innovation support services shall be compatible with the common market within the meaning of Article [107(3)(c) TFEU] if each of the following conditions are fulfilled:

(1) the beneficiary is an SME;

(2) the aid does not exceed a maximum of EUR 200 000 per beneficiary within any three year period;[37]

(3) the service provider benefits from a national or European certification. If the service provider does not benefit from a national or European certification, the aid may not cover more than 75% of the eligible costs;

(4) the beneficiary must use the State aid to buy the services at market price (or if the service provider is a non-for-profit entity, at a price which reflects its full costs plus a reasonable margin).

The following costs shall be eligible:

— as regards innovation advisory services the following costs: management consulting; technological assistance; technology transfer services; training; consultancy for acquisition, protection and trade in Intellectual Property Rights and for licensing agreements; consultancy on the use of standards[;]

— as regards innovation support services the following costs: office space; data banks; technical libraries; market research; use of laboratory; quality labelling, testing and certification.

If the service provider is a not-for-profit entity, the aid may be given in the form of a reduced price, as the difference between the price paid and the market price (or a price which reflects full costs plus a reasonable margin). In such a case, the Member States shall set up a system ensuring transparency about the full costs of the innovation advisory and innovation support services provided, as well as about the price paid by the beneficiary, so that the aid received can be measured and monitored.

Note

37 Without prejudice to the possibility of also receiving *de minimis* aid in respect of other eligible expenses.

5.7. Aid for the loan of highly qualified personnel

Aid for the loan of highly qualified personnel seconded from a research organisation or a large enterprise to an SME shall be compatible with the common market within the meaning of Article [107(3) (c) TFEU], provided the following conditions are fulfilled:

The seconded personnel must not be replacing other personnel, but must be employed in a newly created function within the beneficiary undertaking and must have been employed for at least two years in the research organisation or the large enterprise, which is sending the personnel on secondment. The seconded personnel must work on R&D&I activities within the SME receiving the aid.

Eligible costs are all personnel costs for borrowing and employing highly qualified personnel, including the costs of using a recruitment agency, as well as a mobility allowance for the seconded personnel. The maximum aid intensity shall be 50% of the eligible costs, for a maximum of 3 years per undertaking and per person borrowed.

This provision does not allow covering consultancy costs (payment of the service rendered by the expert, without employing the expert in the undertaking) as such, which are covered under the rules for SME-aid.[38]

Notes

[38] Currently Regulation (EC) No 70/2001. [Ed note: see now Commission Regulation (EC) No 800/2008 of 6 August 2008 declaring certain categories of aid compatible with the common market in application of Articles [107 and 108 TFEU] (General block exemption Regulation) (OJ L 214, 9.8.2008, p.3), reproduced above at G11.]

5.8. Aid for innovation clusters

Investment aid may be granted for the setting up, expansion and animation of innovation clusters exclusively to the legal entity operating the innovation cluster. This entity shall be in charge of managing the participation and access to the cluster's premises, facilities and activities. Access to the cluster's premises, facilities and activities must not be restricted and the fees charged for using the cluster's facilities and for participating in the cluster's activities should reflect their costs. Such aid may be granted for the following facilities:

— facilities for training and research centre;
— open-access research infrastructures: laboratory, testing facility;
— broadband network infrastructures.

The maximum aid intensity is 15%. In the case of regions falling under Article [107(3)(a) TFEU], the Commission considers that the intensity must not exceed:

— 30% for regions with less than 75% of average EU-25 GDP per capita, for outermost regions with higher GDP per capita and until 1 January 2011 statistical effect regions,[39]
— 40% for regions with less than 60% of average EU-25 GDP per capita,
— 50% for regions with less than 45% of average EU-25 GDP per capita.

In recognition of their specific handicaps, the outermost regions will be eligible for a further bonus of 20% if their GDP per capita falls below 75% of the EU-25 average and 10% in other cases.

The statistical effect regions which fall under the derogation under Article [107(3)(c) TFEU] from 1 January 2011 will be eligible for an aid intensity of 20%.

In the case of aid being granted to an SME, the maximum intensities shall be increased by 20 percentage points for aid granted to a small enterprise and by 10 percentage points for aid granted to a medium-sized enterprise.

The eligible costs shall be the costs relating to investment in land, buildings, machinery and equipment.

Operating aid for cluster animation may be granted to the legal entity operating the innovation cluster. Such aid must be temporary and, as a general rule, must be abolished over time, so as to provide an incentive for prices to reflect costs reasonably rapidly.

Such aid may be granted for a limited duration of five years where the aid is degressive. Its intensity may amount to 100% the first year but must have fallen in a linear fashion to zero by the end of the fifth year. In the case of non-degressive aid, its duration is limited to five years and its intensity must not exceed 50% of the eligible costs. In duly justified cases, and on the basis of convincing evidence provided by the notifying Member State, aid for cluster animation may be granted for a longer period of time, not exceeding 10 years.

The eligible costs shall be the personnel and administrative costs relating to the following activities:

— marketing of the cluster to recruit new companies to take part in the cluster,
— management of the cluster's open-access facilities,
— organisation of training programmes, workshops and conferences to support knowledge sharing and networking between the members of the cluster.

When notifying investment aid or aid for cluster animation, the Member State must provide an analysis of the technological specialisation of the innovation cluster, existing regional potential, existing research capacity, presence of clusters in the Community with similar purposes and potential market volumes of the activities in the cluster.

Cases where Member States fund innovation infrastructure to be operated on an open access basis within not for profit research organisations should be assessed using the provisions set out in section 3.1.

Notes
[39] Cf. Guidelines on national regional aid for 2007–2013, para. 18–20.

---

6. INCENTIVE EFFECT AND NECESSITY OF AID

State aid must have an incentive effect, i.e. result in the recipient changing its behaviour so that it increases its level of R&D&I activity. As a result of the aid, the R&D&I activity should be increased in size, scope, amount spent or speed. The Commission considers that the aid does not present an incentive for the beneficiary in all cases in which the R&D&I activity[40] has already commenced prior to the aid application by the beneficiary to the national authorities. If the aided R&D&I-project has not started before the application, the Commission considers that the incentive effect is **automatically met** for the following aid measures:

— project aid and feasibility studies where the aid beneficiary is an SME and where the aid amount is below EUR 7.5 million for a project per SME,
— aid for industrial property rights costs for SMEs,
— aid for young innovative enterprises,
— aid for innovation advisory services and innovation support services,
— aid for the loan of highly qualified personnel.

For all other measures,[41] the Commission will require that an incentive effect is demonstrated by the notifying Member States.

In order to verify that the planned aid will induce the aid recipient to change its behaviour so that it increases its level of R&D&I activity, the Member States shall provide an *ex-ante* evaluation of the increased R&D&I activity **for all individual measures assessed by the Commission**, on the basis of an analysis comparing a situation without aid and a situation with aid being granted. The following criteria may be used, together with other relevant quantitative and/or qualitative factors submitted by the Member State that made the notification:

increase in project size: increase in the total project costs (without decreased spending by the aid beneficiary by comparison with a situation without aid); increase in the number of people assigned to R&D&I activities;

increase in scope: increase in the number of the expected deliverables from the project; more ambitious project illustrated by a higher probability of a scientific or technological breakthrough or a higher risk of failure (notably linked to the higher risk involved in the research project, to the long-term nature of the project and uncertainty about its results);

increase in speed: shorter time before completion of the project as compared to the same project being carried out without aid;

increase in total amount spent on R&D&I: increase in total R&D&I spending by the aid beneficiary; changes in the committed budget for the project (without corresponding decrease in the budget of other projects); increase in R&D&I spending by the aid beneficiary as a proportion of total turnover.

If a significant effect on *at least one* of these elements can be demonstrated, taking account of the normal behaviour of an undertaking in the respective sector, the Commission will normally conclude that the aid proposal has an incentive effect.

If the Commission undertakes a **detailed assessment** of an individual measure, these indicators may not be considered sufficient demonstration of an incentive effect, and the Commission may need to be provided with complementary evidence.

When **assessing an aid scheme**, the conditions relating to the incentive effect shall be deemed to be satisfied if the Member State has committed itself to grant individual aid under the approved aid scheme only after it has verified that an incentive effect is present and to submit annual reports on the implementation of the approved aid scheme. In the annual reports, the Member State must demonstrate how it has assessed the incentive effect of the aid before granting the aid through the use of the quantitative and qualitative indicators given above.

Notes

[40] If the aid proposal is to grant aid for an R&D&I-project, this does not exclude that the potential beneficiary has already carried out feasibility studies which are not covered by the request for State aid.

[41] I.e. project aid for large undertakings and for SMEs for aid exceeding EUR 7.5 million: aid for process and organisational innovation in services and aid for innovation clusters.

---

7. COMPATIBILITY OF AID SUBJECT TO A DETAILED ASSESSMENT

The Commission considers that an increase in the level of R&D&I activity in the Community is in the common interest of the Community as it can be expected to significantly contribute to growth, prosperity and sustainable development. In this context, the Commission recognises that State aid has a positive role to play when it is well targeted and creates the right incentive for undertakings to increase R&D&I. Nevertheless, State aid may also lead to significant distortions of competition which must be taken into consideration.

7.1. Measures subject to a detailed assessment

For the following measures, due to the higher risk of distortion of competition, the Commission will carry out a more detailed assessment.

For measures covered by a BER

— for all cases notified to the Commission following **a duty to notify aid individually** as prescribed in the BER.

For measures covered by this framework

Where the aid amount exceeds:

— for **project aid**[42] and **feasibility studies**:
— if the project is predominantly fundamental research,[43] EUR 20 million per undertaking, per project/feasibility study;
— if the project is predominantly industrial research,[44] EUR 10 million per undertaking, per project/feasibility study;
— for all other projects, EUR 7.5 million per undertaking, per project/feasibility study.
— for **process or organisational innovation** in services activities, EUR 5 million per project per undertaking;
— for innovation clusters (per cluster), EUR 5 million.

The purpose of this detailed assessment is to ensure that high amounts of aid for R&D&I do not distort competition to an extent contrary to the common interest, but actually contribute to the common interest. This happens when the benefits of State aid in terms of additional R&D&I outweigh the harm for competition and trade.

The detailed assessment is a proportionate assessment, depending on the distortion potential of the case. Accordingly, the fact that a detailed assessment will be carried out does not necessarily imply the need to open a formal investigation procedure, although this may be the case for certain measures.

Provided Member States ensure full co-operation and provide adequate information in a timely manner, the Commission will use its best endeavours to conduct the investigation in a timely manner.

Notes

42 For EUREKA projects, this ceiling is set at twice the amount.

43 A project is considered to consist "predominantly" of fundamental research, if more than half of the eligible project costs is incurred through activities which fall within the category of fundamental research.

44 A project is considered to consist "predominantly" of industrial research, if more than half of the eligible project costs is incurred through activities which fall within the categories of industrial research or fundamental research.

7.2. Methodology of the detailed assessment: R&D&I criteria for economic assessment of certain individual cases

Below, the Commission presents guidance as to the kind of information it may require and the methodology it would follow for measures subject to a detailed assessment. This guidance is intended to make the Commission's decisions and their reasoning transparent and foreseeable in order to create predictability and legal certainty.

Detailed assessment will be conducted on the basis of the following positive and negative elements which will apply in addition to the criteria set out in Chapter 5. In some cases, the applicability and the weight attached to these elements may depend on the form or objective of the aid. The level of the Commission's assessment will be proportional to the risk of distortion of competition. This means that the scope of the analysis will depend on the nature of the case. State aid for activities that are far away from the market is therefore less likely to give rise to very extensive scrutiny.

Member States are invited to provide all the elements that they consider useful for the assessment of the case. The Member States are, in particular, invited to rely on evaluations of past State aid schemes or measures, impact assessments made by the granting authority, risk assessments, financial reports, internal business plans that any company should realise for important projects, expert opinions and other studies related to R&D&I.

7.3. Positive effects of the aid

The fact that the aid induces undertakings to pursue R&D&I in the Community which they would not otherwise have pursued constitutes the main positive element to take into consideration when assessing the compatibility of the aid.

In this context, the Commission will notably pay attention to the following elements:

— the net increase of R&D&I conducted by the undertaking,
— the contribution of the measure to the global improvement of the sector concerned as regards the level of R&D&I,
— the contribution of the measure to the improvement of the Community situation regarding R&D&I in the international context.

7.3.1. Existence of a market failure

As indicated in Chapter 1, State aid may be necessary to increase R&D&I in the economy only to the extent that the market, on its own, fails to deliver an optimal outcome. It is established that certain market failures hamper the overall level of R&D&I in the Community. However, not all undertakings and sectors in the economy are confronted to these market failures to the same extent. Consequently, as regards measures subject to a detailed assessment, the Member State should provide adequate information whether the aid refers to a general market failure regarding R&D&I in the Community, or to a specific market failure. Depending on the specific market failure addressed, the Commission will take into consideration the following elements:

— **Knowledge spillovers**: the level of information dissemination foreseen; the specificity of the knowledge created; the availability of IPR protection.

— **Imperfect and asymmetric information**: level of risk and complexity of research; need for external finance; characteristics of the aid beneficiary to receive external finance.

— **Coordination failures**: number of collaborating undertakings; intensity of collaboration; diverging interest between collaborating partners; problems in designing contracts; problems of third parties to coordinate collaboration.

For State aid targeting R&D&I projects or activities located in assisted areas, the Commission will take into account: (i) disadvantages caused by the peripherality and other regional specificities, (ii) specific local economic data, social and/or historic reasons for a low level of R&D&I activity in comparison with the relevant average data and/or situation at national and/or Community level as appropriate; and (iii) any other relevant indicator showing an increased degree of market failure.

7.3.2. Appropriate Instrument

State aid for R&D&I can be authorised under Article [107(3)(c) TFEU] when it is necessary to achieve an objective of common interest, as an exception to the general prohibition of State aid. An important element in the balancing test is whether and to what extent State aid for R&D&I can be considered an appropriate instrument to increase R&D&I activities, given that other less distortive instruments may achieve the same results.

In its compatibility analysis, the Commission will take particular account of any impact assessment of the proposed measure which the Member State has made. Measures for which the Member State has considered other policy options and for which the advantages of using a selective instrument such as State aid are established and submitted to the Commission, are considered to constitute an appropriate instrument.

7.3.3. Incentive effect and necessity of aid

Analysing the incentive effect of the aid measure is the most important condition in analysing State aid for R&D&I. Identifying the incentive effect **translates** into assessing whether the planned aid will induce undertakings to pursue R&D&I which they would not otherwise have pursued.

Chapter 6 provides a series of indicators that can be used by Member States to demonstrate an incentive effect. However, when a measure undergoes a detailed assessment, the Commission will require that the incentive effect of the aid is substantiated more precisely, to avoid undue distortions of competition.

In its analysis, the Commission will, in addition to the indicators mentioned in Chapter 6, take into consideration the following elements:

— **Specification of intended change**: the intended change in behaviour State aid aims at in the notified case has to be well specified (new project triggered, size, scope or speed of a project enhanced).

— **Counterfactual analysis**: the change of behaviour has to be identified by counterfactual analysis: what would be the level of intended activity with and without aid? The difference of the two scenarios is considered to be the impact of the aid measure and describes the incentive effect.

— **Level of profitability**: if a project would not, in itself, be profitable to undertake for a private undertaking, but would generate important benefits for society, it is more likely that the aid has an incentive effect. To evaluate the overall profitability (or lack thereof) of the project, evaluation methodologies can be used which are standard practice in the particular industry concerned.[45]

— **Amount of investment and time path of cash flows**: High start-up investment, low level of appropriable cash flows and a significant fraction of cash flows arising in the very far future will be considered positive elements in assessing the incentive effect.

— **Level of risk involved in the research project**: On the basis of e.g. feasibility studies, risk assessments and expert opinions, the assessment of risk will in particular take into account the irreversibility of the investment, the probability of commercial failure, the risk that the project will be less productive than expected, the risk that conducting the project would undermine other activities and the risk that the project costs undermine the undertaking's financial viability. For State aid targeting R&D&I projects or activities located in assisted areas, the Commission will take into account disadvantages caused by the peripherality and other regional specificities, which negatively impact on the level of risk in the research project.

— **Continuous evaluation**: measures for which (low scale) pilot projects are foreseen, or which define well specified milestones resulting in termination of the project in case of failure and where a publicly available *ex post* monitoring is foreseen will be considered more positively as regards the assessment of the incentive effect.

Notes

45 These may include methods to evaluate the Net Present Value of the project (that is to say, the sum of the discounted expected cash flow resulting from the investment minus the investment cost), the internal rate of return (IRR) or the return of capital employed (ROCE). Financial reports and internal business plans containing information on demand forecasts: cost forecasts: financial forecasts (for example, NPV, IRR, ROCE), documents that are submitted to an investment committee and that elaborate on various investment scenarios or documents provided to the financial markets could serve as evidence.

7.3.4. Proportionality of the aid

Independently of the criteria mentioned in Chapter 5, the Member State concerned should provide the additional following information:

— **Open selection process**: Where there are multiple (potential) candidates for undertaking the R&D&I project in a Member State, the proportionality requirement is more likely to be met if the project has been allocated on the basis of transparent, objective and non-discriminatory criteria.
— **Aid to the minimum**: Member States have to explain how the amount given has been calculated to ensure that it is limited to the minimum necessary.

7.4. Analysis of the distortion of competition and trade

State aid for R&D&I may impact on competition at two levels: (i) competition in the innovation process, i.e. competition in terms of R&D&I which takes place upstream of product markets and (ii) competition in the product markets where the results of the R&D&I activities are exploited.

In assessing the negative effects of the aid measure, the Commission will focus its analysis of the distortions of competition on the foreseeable impact the R&D&I aid has on competition between undertakings in the product markets concerned. The Commission will give more weight to risks for competition and trade that arise in a predictable future and with particular likelihood.

The impact on competition in the innovation process will be relevant insofar as it has a foreseeable impact on the outcome of future product market competition. In certain cases the results of R&D&I, for example, in the form of intellectual property rights, are themselves traded in so-called technology markets, for instance through patent licensing. In these cases, the Commission may also consider the effect of the aid on competition in the technology markets.

The impact of R&D&I on product markets is largely dynamic and the analysis will therefore be of a forward-looking nature. Frequently, the same innovative activity will be associated with multiple future product markets. If so, the impact of State aid will be looked upon on the set of markets concerned.

There are three distinct ways in which R&D&I aid can distort competition in product markets:

(1) R&D&I aid can distort the dynamic incentives of market players to invest (crowding out effect);
(2) R&D&I aid can create or maintain positions of market power;
(3) R&D&I aid can maintain an inefficient market structure.

State aid may also have a negative effect on trade in the common market. In particular where R&D&I aid leads to the crowding out of competitors, the aid measures may essentially result in a shift of trade flows and location of economic activity.

7.4.1. Distorting dynamic incentives

The main concern related to R&D&I aid to undertakings is that competitors' dynamic incentives to invest are distorted. When an undertaking receives aid, this generally increases the likelihood of successful R&D&I on the part of this undertaking leading to an increased presence on the product

Part G State Aids

market(s) in the future. This increased presence may lead competitors to reduce the scope of their original investment plans (crowding out effect).

In its analysis, the Commission will consider the following elements:

— **Aid amount**. Aid measures which involve significant amounts of aid are more likely to lead to significant crowding out effects. The significance of the aid amount will be measured with reference to total private R&D expenditure in the sector, and the amount spent by the main players.

— **Closeness to the market/category of the aid**. The more the aid measure is aimed at R&D&I activity close to the market, the more it is liable to develop significant crowding out effects.

— **Open selection process**: Where the grant is given on the basis of objective and non-discriminatory criteria, the Commission will take a more positive stance.

— **Exit barriers**: Competitors are more likely to maintain (or even to increase) their investment plans when exit barriers to the innovation process are high. This may be the case when many of the competitors" past investments are locked in to a particular R&D&I trajectory.

— **Incentives to compete for a future market**: R&D&I aid may lead to a situation where competitors to the aid beneficiary renounce competing for a future market, because the advantage provided by the aid (in terms of the degree of technological advance or in terms of timing) reduces the possibility for them to profitably enter this future market.

— **Product differentiation and intensity of competition**: Where product innovation is rather about developing differentiated products (related, for example, to distinct brands, standards, technologies, consumer groups) competitors are less likely to be affected. The same is true if there are many effective competitors in the market.

7.4.2. Creating market power

Aid in support of R&D&I may have distortive effects in terms of increasing or maintaining the degree of market power in product markets. Market power is the power to influence market prices, output, the variety or quality of goods and services, or other parameters of competition on the market for a significant period of time, to the detriment of consumers. The Commission will assess the market power before the aid is granted, and the change in market power, which can be expected as a result of the aid.

The Commission is concerned mainly about those R&D&I measures allowing the aid beneficiary to transfer or strengthen market power held on existing product markets to future product markets. The Commission is therefore unlikely to identify competition concerns related to market power in markets where each aid beneficiary has a market share below 25% and in markets having a market concentration with Herfindahl-Hirschman Index (HHI) below 2 000. In its analysis, the Commission will consider the following elements:

— **Market power of aid beneficiary and market structure**: Where the recipient is already dominant on a product market, the aid measure may reinforce this dominance by further weakening the competitive constraint that competitors can exert on the recipient undertaking. Similarly, State aid measures may have significant impact in oligopolistic markets where only a few players are active.

— **Level of entry barriers**: In the field of R&D&I, significant entry barriers may exist for new entrants. These barriers include legal entry barriers (in particular intellectual property rights), economies of scale and scope, access barriers to networks and infrastructure, and other strategic barriers to entry or expansion.

— **Buyer power**: The market power of an undertaking may also be limited by the market position of the buyers. The presence of strong buyers can serve to counter a finding of a strong market position if it is likely that the buyers will seek to preserve sufficient competition in the market.

— **Selection process**: Aid measures which allow undertakings with a strong market position to influence the selection process, for example, by having the right to recommend undertakings in the selection process or influencing the research path in a way which disfavours alternatives path on unjustified grounds, is liable to raise concern by the Commission.

7.4.3. Maintaining inefficient market structures

R&D&I aid may, if not correctly targeted, support inefficient undertakings and hence lead to market structures where many market players operate significantly below efficient scale. In its analysis, the

Commission will consider whether the aid is granted in markets featuring overcapacity, in declining industries or in sensitive sectors. Concerns are less likely in situations where State aid for R&D&I aims at changing the growth dynamics of the sector, notably by introducing new technologies.

7.5. Balancing and decision

In the light of these positive and negative elements, the Commission balances the effects of the measure and determines whether the resulting distortions adversely affect trading conditions to an extent contrary to the common interest. The analysis in each particular case will be based on an overall assessment of the foreseeable positive and negative impacts of the State aid. For that purpose the Commission will not use the criteria set out in sections 7.3 and 7.4 mechanically but will make an overall assessment based on the proportionality principle.

The Commission may raise no objections to the notified aid measure without entering into the formal investigation procedure or, following the formal investigation procedure laid down in Article 6 of Regulation (EC) No 659/1999, decide to close the procedure with a decision pursuant to Article 7 of that Regulation. If it takes a conditional decision within the meaning of Article 7(4) of Regulation (EC) No 659/1999, it may in particular consider attaching the following conditions, which must reduce the resulting distortions or effect on trade and be proportionate:

— lower aid intensities than the maximum intensities allowed in Chapter 5, including claw-back mechanisms and different conditions for repaying reimbursable advances,
— diffusion of results, collaboration and other behavioural commitments,
— separation of accounts in order to avoid cross-subsidization from one market to another market, when the beneficiary is active in multiple markets,
— no discrimination against other potential beneficiaries (reduce selectivity).

8. Cumulation

As regards cumulation, the aid ceilings fixed under this framework shall apply regardless of whether the support for the aided project is financed entirely from State resources or is partly financed by the Community, except in the specific and limited context of the conditions established for Community funding under the RTD Framework Programmes, adopted respectively in accordance with Title [XIX] of the [Treaty on the Functioning of the European Union] or Title II of the Euratom Treaty.

Where the expenditure eligible for aid for R&D&I is eligible in whole or in part for aid for other purposes, the common portion will be subject to the most favourable ceiling under the applicable rules. This limitation does not apply to aid granted in accordance with the Community guidelines on State aid to promote risk capital investments in SME.[46]

Aid for R&D&I shall not be cumulated with *de minimis* support in respect of the same eligible expenses in order to circumvent the maximum aid intensities laid down in this framework.

Notes
[46] OJ C 194, 18.8.2006, p.2.

9. Special Rules for Agriculture and Fisheries

As regards R&D aid concerning products listed in Annex I to the [Treaty on the Functioning of the European Union], and by way of derogation from aid intensity limitations or supplements specified elsewhere in this framework, the Commission will continue to allow an aid intensity of up to 100%, subject to fulfilment in each case of the four following conditions:

— it is of general interest to the particular sector or sub-sector concerned;
— information that research will be carried out, and with which goal, is published on the internet, prior to the commencement of the research. An approximate date of expected results and their place of publication on the internet, as well as a mention that the result will be available at no cost, must be included;

— the results of the research are made available on internet, for a period of at least 5 years. This information on the internet shall be published no later than any which may be given to members of any particular organisation;

— aid shall be granted directly to the researching institution or body and must not involve the direct granting of non-research related aid to a company producing, processing or marketing agricultural products, nor provide price support to producers of such products.

The Commission will allow State aid for cooperation pursuant to Article 29 of Council Regulation (EC) No 1698/2005 of 20 September 2005 on support for rural development by the European Agricultural Fund for Rural Development (EAFRD)[47] if such cooperation has been approved for Community co-financing under that Article and/or the State aid is granted as additional financing pursuant to Article 89 of Regulation (EC) No 1698/2005 under the same conditions and at the same intensity as the co-financing.

Cases of R&D aid for products listed in Annex I to the [Treaty on the Functioning of the European Union] not fulfilling the conditions in this chapter are to be examined under the normal rules of this framework.

Notes

[47] OJ L 277, 21.10.2005, p.1. Regulation as amended by Regulation (EC) No 1463/2006 (OJ L 277, 9.10.2006, p.1).

10. Final Provisions

10.1. Reporting and monitoring

10.1.1. Annual reports

In line with the requirements of Regulation (EC) No 659/1999 and Commission Regulation (EC) No 794/2004 of 21 April 2004 implementing Council Regulation (EC) No 659/1999 laying down detailed rules for the application of Article [108 TFEU],[48] Member States must submit annual reports to the Commission.

Beyond the requirements stipulated in those provisions, annual reports for R&D&I-aid measures shall contain for each measure, including the granting of aid under an approved scheme, the following information:

— the name of the beneficiary,
— the aid amount per beneficiary,
— the aid intensity,
— the sectors of activity where the aided projects are undertaken.

In case of fiscal aid, the Member State must only provide a list of those beneficiaries who have received an annual tax relief in excess of 200 000 EUR.

In case of clusters, the report must also give a brief description of the activity of the cluster and its effectiveness in attracting R&D&I activity. The Commission may request additional information regarding the aid granted, to check whether the conditions of the Commission's decision approving the aid measure have been respected.

The annual reports will be published on the internet site of the Commission.

For all aid granted under an approved scheme to large undertakings, Member States must also explain in the annual report how the incentive effect has been respected for aid given to such undertakings, notably using the indicators and criteria mentioned in Chapter 6 above.

Notes

[48] OJ L 140, 30.4.2004, p.1. Regulation as amended by Regulation (EC) No 1627/2006 (OJ L 302, 1.11.2006, p.10).

10.1.2. Access to full text of schemes

The Commission considers that further measures are necessary to improve the transparency of State aid in the Community. In particular, it appears necessary to ensure that the Member States, economic operators, interested parties and the Commission itself have easy access to the full text of all applicable R&D&I aid schemes.

This can easily be achieved through the establishment of linked internet sites. For this reason, when examining R&D&I aid schemes, the Commission will systematically require the Member State concerned to publish the full text of all final aid schemes on the internet and to communicate the internet address of the publication to the Commission. The scheme must not be applied before the information is published on the internet.

10.1.3. Information sheets

Besides, whenever aid for R&D&I is granted on the basis of aid schemes without falling under the duty for individual notification, and exceeds EUR 3 million, Member States must, within 20 working days starting from the granting of the aid by the competent authority, provide the Commission with the information requested in the standard form laid down in the Annex to this framework. The Commission will make summary information available to the public through its website (http://ec.europa.%20eu/comm/competition/index_en.html).

Member States must ensure that detailed records regarding the granting of aid for all R&D&I measures are maintained. Such records, which must contain all information necessary to establish that the eligible costs and maximum allowable aid intensity have been observed, must be maintained for 10 years from the date on which the aid was granted.

The Commission will ask Member States to provide this information in order to carry out an impact assessment of this framework three years after its entry into force.[49]

Notes
[49] In that process, Member States may want to support the Commission by providing their own *ex post* assessment of schemes and individual measures.

10.2. Appropriate Measures

The Commission herewith proposes to Member States, on the basis of Article [108(1) TFEU], the following appropriate measures concerning their respective existing research and development aid schemes:

In order to comply with the provisions of this framework, Member States should amend, where necessary, such schemes in order to bring them into line with this framework within twelve months after its entry into force, with the following exceptions:

— Member States have twenty four months to introduce amendments regarding the provisions covered in point 3.1.1 of this framework;

— the new threshold for large individual projects will apply as from the entry into force of this framework;

— the duty to provide more detailed annual reports pursuant to point 10.1.1. and the duty to submit information sheets pursuant to point 10.1.3. will apply to existing aid schemes six months after the entry into force of this framework.

The Member States are invited to give their explicit unconditional agreement to these proposed appropriate measures within two months from the date of publication of this framework. In the absence of any reply, the Commission will assume that the Member State in question does not agree with the proposed measures.

10.3. Entry into force, validity and revision

This framework will enter into force on 1 January 2007 or, if it has not been published in the *Official Journal of the European Union* before that date, on the first day following its publication therein and will replace the Community Framework for State aid for Research and Development.

This framework will be applicable until 31 December 2013. After consulting the Member States, the Commission may amend it before that date on the basis of important competition policy or research policy considerations or in order to take account of other Community policies or international

Part G State Aids

commitments. The Commission intends to carry out a review of the framework 3 years after its entry into force.

The Commission will apply this framework to all aid projects notified in respect of which it is called upon to take a decision after the framework is published in the *Official Journal*, even where the projects were notified prior to its publication. This includes individual aid granted under approved aid schemes and notified to the Commission following an obligation to notify such aid individually.

In line with the Commission notice on the determination of the applicable rules for the assessment of unlawful State aid,[50] the Commission will apply in the case of non-notified aid,

— this framework if the aid was granted after its entry into force,
— the framework in force when the aid was granted in all other cases.

Notes
[50] OJ C 119 of 22.5.2002, p.22.

ANNEX

FORM FOR THE PROVISION OF SUMMARY INFORMATION FOR AID UNDER THE EXTENDED REPORTING OBLIGATION (SECTION 10.1)

(1) Aid in favour of (name of the undertaking/undertakings receiving the aid, SME or not):..........
....

(2) Aid scheme reference (Commission reference of the existing scheme or schemes under which the aid is awarded):..

(3) Public entity/entities providing the assistance (name and co-ordinates of the granting authority or authorities):..

(4) Member State where the aided project or measure is carried out:...

(5) Type of project or measure: ....

(6) Short description of project or measure: ....
....
....
....

(7) Where applicable, eligible costs (in EUR):..

(8) Discounted aid amount (gross) in EUR:...

(9) Aid intensity (% in gross grant equivalent): ....

(10) Conditions attached to the payment of the proposed aid (if any):...

(11) Planned start and end date of the project or measure:...

(12) Date of award of the aid:...

G17

COMMUNITY GUIDELINES ON STATE AID FOR ENVIRONMENTAL PROTECTION

(Text with EEA relevance)

(2008/C 82/01)

Official Journal C 82, 1.4.2008, p.1

Celex No: 52008XC0401(03)

EUR-Lex permanent link: <http://eur-lex.europa.eu/LexUriServ/LexUriServ.do?uri=CELEX:5200 8XC0401(03):EN:NOT>

Notes

The 2008 Community guidelines on State aid for environmental protection replaced the Community Guidelines on State aid for environmental protection of 3 February 2001 (OJ C 37, 3.2.2001, p.3,) with effect from 2 April 2008 (see paragraph 202). The Commission will continue to apply the 2001 guidelines to non-notified aid granted during the period of their validity: see Article 205.

EEA application: on 15 July 2008 the EFTA Surveillance Authority adopted parallel Guidelines on State aid for environmental protection, with necessary adjustments based on particularities of the EEA Agreement. See EFTA Surveillance Authority Decision No. 500/08/COL of 16 July 2008 amending, for the sixty-fifth time, the procedural and substantive rules in the field of State aid by introducing a new chapter on State aid for environmental protection, OJ L 144, 10.6.2010, p.1.

Commentary
Guidelines: B&C: 17.003, 17.045, 17.063, 17.077

---

1. **Introduction**

1. INTRODUCTION

1.1. State aid policy and Energy Policy for Europe

(1) The spring 2007 European Council called on Member States and EU institutions to pursue actions to develop a sustainable integrated European climate and energy policy. The Council stated among other things: 'Given that energy production and use are the main sources for greenhouse gas emissions, an integrated approach to climate and energy policy is needed to realise this objective. Integration should be achieved in a mutually supportive way. With this in mind, the Energy Policy for Europe (EPE) will pursue the following three objectives, fully respecting Member States' choice of energy mix and sovereignty over primary energy sources and underpinned by a spirit of solidarity amongst Member States:

— increasing security of supply,

— ensuring the competitiveness of European economies and the availability of affordable energy,

— promoting environmental sustainability and combating climate change.'

(2) As a milestone in the creation of this Energy Policy for Europe, the European Council supported a comprehensive Energy Action Plan for the period 2007–2009 and invited in particular the Commission to submit the proposals requested in the Action Plan as speedily as possible. One of these proposals relates to the review of the Community guidelines on State aid for environmental protection.

(3) The European Council made a firm independent commitment for the EU to achieve at least a 20% reduction in greenhouse gas emissions by 2020 compared to 1990. It also stressed the need to increase energy efficiency in the EU so as to achieve the objective of saving 20% of the EU's energy consumption compared to projections for 2020, and endorsed a binding target of a 20% share of renewable energies in overall EU energy consumption by 2020 as well as a 10% binding minimum target to be achieved by all Member States for the share of biofuels in overall EU transport petrol and diesel consumption by 2020.

(4) These new guidelines constitute one of the instruments to implement the Action Plan and the environmental aspects of the energy- and climate change-related targets decided by the European Council.

1.2. State aid policy and environmental protection

(5) In the 'State Aid Action Plan — Less and better targeted State aid: A roadmap for State aid reform 2005–2009'[1] (hereafter referred to as the 'State Aid Action Plan') the Commission noted that State aid measures can sometimes be effective tools for achieving objectives of common interest. Under some conditions, State aid can correct market failures, thereby improving the functioning of markets and enhancing competitiveness. It can also help to promote sustainable development, irrespective of the correction of market failures.[2] The State Aid Action Plan also stressed that environmental protection can provide opportunities for innovation, create new markets and increase competitiveness through resource efficiency and new investment opportunities. Under some conditions, State aid can be conducive to these objectives, thus contributing to the core Lisbon strategy objectives of more sustainable growth and jobs. Decision No 1600/2002/EC of the European Parliament and of the Council of 22 July 2002 laying down the Sixth Community Environment Action Programme[3] (hereafter referred to as the 'Sixth Environment Action Programme') identifies the priority areas for actions to protect the environment.[4]

Notes

[1] COM(2005) 107 final.

[2] See State Aid Action Plan, para. 10.

[3] OJ L 242, 10.9.2002, p.1.

[4] The priority areas are: climate change, nature and biodiversity, environment and health and natural resources and waste. Health is not covered by these guidelines.

(6) The primary objective of State aid control in the field of environmental protection is to ensure that State aid measures will result in a higher level of environmental protection than would occur without the aid and to ensure that the positive effects of the aid outweigh its negative effects in terms of

distortions of competition, taking account of the polluter pays principle (hereafter 'PPP') established by Article [191 TFEU]*.

(7) Economic activities can harm the environment not least through pollution. In certain cases, in the absence of government intervention, undertakings can avoid bearing the full cost of the environmental harm arising from their activities. As a result, the market fails to allocate resources in an efficient manner, since the (negative) external effects of production are not taken into account by the producer, but are borne by society as a whole.

(8) According to the PPP, these negative externalities can be tackled by ensuring that the polluter pays for its pollution, which implies full internalisation of environmental costs by the polluter. This is intended to ensure that the private costs (borne by the undertaking) reflect the true social costs of the economic activity. Full implementation of the PPP would thus lead to correction of the market failure. The PPP can be implemented either by setting mandatory environmental standards or by market-based instruments.[5] Some of the market-based instruments may involve the granting of State aid to all or some of the undertakings which are subject to them.

(9) Although there are currently limits to the application of the PPP, this regulatory failure should not prevent Member States from imposing requirements for environmental protection that go beyond Community requirements and from reducing negative externalities to the greatest possible extent.

(10) In order to increase the level of environmental protection, Member States may want to use State aid to create incentives on an individual level (at the level of the undertaking) to achieve a higher level of environmental protection than required by Community standards or to increase the environmental protection in the absence of Community standards. They may also set national standards or environmental taxation at a higher level than required by Community legislation or they may use environmental taxation to implement PPP unilaterally in the absence of Community legislation.

(11) The Commission considers that it is necessary to revise the State aid guidelines on environmental protection in order to meet the objectives set out in the State Aid Action Plan, in particular to ensure better targeted aid, improved economic analysis and more effective procedures. Furthermore, the Commission considers it necessary to take into account developments in environmental policy and environmental technologies and to adjust the rules in the light of experience.

(12) The Commission will apply these Guidelines in the assessment of environmental aid, thereby increasing legal certainty and the transparency of its decision-making. Aid for environmental protection will primarily be justified on the basis of Article [107(3)(c) TFEU]. These Guidelines replace the Community guidelines on State aid for environmental protection[6] that came into force in 2001.

(13) Guidelines are given for two types of assessments: a standard assessment for measures involving aid under a certain threshold or aid granted to installations with a production capacity below a certain threshold (Chapter 3) and a detailed assessment for measures involving aid above that threshold or aid granted to installations with a production capacity above that threshold as well as for aid granted to new plants producing renewable energy where the aid amount is based on a calculation of the external costs avoided (Chapter 5).

(14) These Guidelines will be applied to all measures notified to the Commission (either because the measure is not covered by a block exemption regulation (hereafter 'BER') or a BER imposes an obligation to notify aid individually, or because the Member State concerned decides to notify a measure which could in principle have been exempted under a BER), as well as in the assessment of all non-notified aid after the publication of these Guidelines.

1.3. The balancing test and its application to aid for environmental protection

1.3.1. The State Aid Action Plan: less and better targeted aid, balancing test for the assessment of aid

(15) In the State Aid Action Plan, the Commission announced that 'to best contribute to the re-launched Lisbon Strategy for growth and jobs, the Commission will, when relevant, strengthen its economic approach to State aid analysis. An economic approach is an instrument to better focus and target certain State aid towards the objectives of the re-launched Lisbon Strategy'.

(16) In assessing whether an aid measure can be deemed compatible with the common market, the Commission balances the positive impact of the aid measure in reaching an objective of common interest against its potentially negative side effects, such as distortion of trade and competition. The State Aid Action Plan, building on existing practice, has formalised this balancing exercise in what has been termed a 'balancing test'.[7] It operates in three steps; the first two steps address the positive effects of the State aid and the third addresses the negative effects and resulting balancing of the positive and negative effects. The balancing test is structured as follows:

1) Is the aid measure aimed at a well-defined objective of common interest? (for example: growth, employment, cohesion, environment, energy security). In the context of these Guidelines, the relevant common interest objective is the protection of the environment.
2) Is the aid well designed to deliver the objective of common interest that is to say, does the proposed aid address the market failure or other objective?
   a) is State aid an appropriate policy instrument?
   b) is there an incentive effect, namely does the aid change the behaviour of undertakings?
   c) is the aid measure proportional, namely could the same change in behaviour be obtained with less aid?
3) Are the distortions of competition and effect on trade limited, so that the overall balance is positive?

Notes

[7] Cf. State Aid Action Plan, para. 11 and 20, as elaborated in more detail in the Communication on innovation (COM(2005) 436 final 21.9.2005).

(17) This balancing test is applicable to the design of State aid rules as well as to the assessment of cases.

1.3.2. The objective of common interest addressed by the Guidelines

(18) The first indent of Article[3] of the Treaty on European Union stipulates that sustainable development is one of the objectives in the European Union. This should be based on economic prosperity, social cohesion and a high level of protection of the environment. Promoting environmental protection is thus an important objective of common interest. In addition, Article [11 TFEU] mentions the need to integrate protection of the environment into all Community policies and Article [191(2) TFEU] states that environment policy is to be based on the principles of precaution, prevention, rectifying pollution[8] at source and 'polluter pays'.

Notes

[8] This can include activities such as the release of chemical pollutants into the environment, or for instance physically altering the aquatic environment, and thereby causing disturbances of ecosystems or activities having a negative impact on the status of water resources.

(19) These Guidelines lay down the conditions for authorising the granting of State aid to address those market failures which lead to a sub-optimal level of environmental protection.

(20) The most common market failure in the field of environmental protection is related to negative externalities. Undertakings acting in their own interest have no incentive to take the negative externalities arising from production into account either when they decide on a particular production technology or when they decide on the production level. In other words, the production costs that are borne by the undertaking are lower than the costs borne by society. Therefore undertakings have no incentive to reduce their level of pollution or to take individual measures to protect the environment.

Part G State Aids

(21) Governments confronted with this market failure tend to use regulation in order to ensure that the negative externalities arising from production are accounted for. Through the introduction of standards, taxation, economic instruments and other regulation, the undertakings producing pollution have to pay for the cost to society of pollution in accordance with the PPP. Internalising these negative externalities will consequently raise the private costs borne by those undertakings, thereby negatively affecting their revenue. Moreover, since the generation of pollution is unevenly spread among industries and undertakings, the costs of any environmentally friendly regulation tend to be differentiated, not only between undertakings, but also between Member States. Member States may furthermore have a different appreciation of the need to introduce high environmental targets.

(22) In the absence of Community standards and market-based instruments fully reflecting the PPP level (regulatory failure), Member States may thus decide unilaterally to pursue a higher level of environmental protection. This may in turn create additional costs for the undertakings active in their territory. For that reason, in addition to regulation, Member States may use State aid as a positive incentive to achieve higher levels of environmental protection. They can do this in two ways:

— **positive individual incentives to reduce pollution and other negative impacts on the environment**: First, Member States can create positive incentives on an individual level (at the level of the undertaking) to go beyond Community standards. In this case, the aid beneficiary reduces pollution because it receives aid to change its behaviour, and not because it has to pay for the costs of this pollution. The objective of State aid here is to address directly the market failure linked with the negative effects of pollution;
— **positive incentives to introduce national environmental regulation going beyond Community standards**: Second, Member States can impose national regulation going beyond the Community standards. However, this may lead to additional costs for certain undertakings, and thus affect their competitive conditions. Moreover, such costs may not represent the same burden for all undertakings given their size, market position, technology and other specificities. In this case, State aid may be necessary, to lessen the burden on the most affected undertakings and thereby enable Member States to adopt national environmental regulation that is stricter than Community standards.

1.3.3. Appropriate instrument

(23) There is a role for government intervention to ensure more adequate environmental protection. Regulation and market-based instruments are the most important tools to achieve environmental objectives. Soft instruments, such as voluntary eco-labels, and the diffusion of environmentally friendly technologies may also play an important role. However, even if finding the optimal mix of policy instruments can be complicated, the existence of market failures or political objectives does not automatically justify the use of State aid.

(24) According to the PPP, the polluter should pay all the costs of its pollution, including the indirect costs borne by society. For this purpose, environmental regulation can be a useful instrument to increase the burden on the polluter. Respect for the PPP ensures, in theory, that the market failure linked to negative externalities will be rectified. Consequently, if the PPP were fully implemented, further government intervention would not be necessary to ensure a market-efficient outcome. The PPP remains the main rule and State aid is in fact a second-best option. Using State aid in the context of the PPP would relieve the polluter of the burden of paying the cost of its pollution. Therefore, State aid may not be an appropriate instrument in such cases.

(25) However, on account, in particular, of incomplete implementation of the PPP, the existing level of environmental protection is often considered to be unsatisfactory for the following reasons:

a) first, the exact cost of pollution is not easy to establish. It is technically complicated to calculate the extra costs for society for all types of production, and it may sometimes be inefficient to take account of the fact that different producers have different levels of pollution if the associated administrative costs are very high. Different sensitivities towards changes in consumer prices (price elasticity) also play a role. Furthermore, the valuation of the cost of pollution can differ among individuals and societies, depending on societal choices as regards, for instance, the effect of current policies on future generations. In addition, some costs are difficult to express without some uncertainty in monetary terms, such as shorter life expectancy or environmental damage. There will therefore always be a degree of uncertainty involved in calculating the costs of pollution.

b) second, raising the price of a series of (industrial) products too abruptly in order to internalise the cost of pollution may act as an external shock and create disturbances in the economy. Governments may therefore consider it more desirable to progress with moderation towards integrating the full price of pollution into certain production processes.

(26) In the context of an unsatisfactory level of environmental protection, State aid, although it does not resolve all the above-mentioned problems, may provide positive incentives for undertakings to carry out activities or make investments which are not mandatory and would otherwise not be undertaken by profit-seeking companies. In addition, State aid may be an appropriate instrument to enable Member States to adopt national environmental regulation going beyond Community standards, by lowering the burden on the undertakings most affected by that regulation, and thus making the regulation possible.

1.3.4. Incentive effect and necessity of aid

(27) State aid for environmental protection must result in the recipient of the aid changing its behaviour so that the level of environmental protection will be higher than if the aid had not been granted. However, investments which increase the level of environmental protection may at the same time increase revenues[9] and/or decrease costs[10] and thus be economically attractive in their own right. Therefore, it needs to be verified that the investment concerned would not have been undertaken without any State aid.

Notes

[9] More environmentally friendly production may result, for example, in more possibilities for recycling waste materials, thus generating additional revenues. It may also be possible to increase the price or the sales of products that are perceived as more environmentally-friendly and thus more appealing to consumers.

[10] More environmentally friendly production may result notably in reduced consumption of energy and input materials.

---

(28) The objective is to be sure that undertakings would not, without the aid, engage in the same activity because of its intrinsic benefits. The incentive effect is identified through counterfactual analysis, comparing the levels of intended activity with aid and without aid. Correct identification of the counterfactual scenario is key to determining whether or not State aid has an incentive effect. It is also essential for the calculation of the extra investment or production costs incurred to achieve the higher level of environmental protection.

(29) Investment may be necessary in order to meet mandatory Community standards. Since the company would have to comply with those standards in any event, State aid to meet mandatory Community standards that are already in force cannot be justified.

1.3.5. Proportionality of the aid

(30) Aid is considered to be proportional only if the same result could not be achieved with less aid. In addition, proportionality may also depend on the degree of selectivity of a measure.

(31) In particular, the aid amount must be limited to the minimum needed to achieve the environmental protection sought. Therefore, eligible costs for investment aid are based on the notion of the extra (net) cost necessary to meet the environmental objectives. This concept implies that, in order to establish how much aid can be granted, all the economic benefits which the investment gives the company must in principle be subtracted from the additional investment costs.

(32) However, it is difficult to fully take into account all economic benefits which a company will derive from an additional investment. For example, according to the methodology for calculating eligible costs set out in points 80 to 84, operating benefits are not taken into account beyond a certain initial period following the investment. Likewise, certain kinds of benefits which are not always easy to measure — such as the 'green image' enhanced by an environmental investment — are not taken into account in this context either. Consequently, in order for the aid to be proportionate, the Commission

considers that the aid amount must normally be less than the eligible investment costs, see Annex. It is only in cases where investment aid is granted in a genuinely competitive bidding process on the basis of clear, transparent and non discriminatory criteria — effectively ensuring that the aid is limited to the minimum necessary for achieving the environmental gain — that the aid amount may reach 100% of the eligible investment cost. This is because under such circumstances it can be assumed that the respective bids reflect all possible benefits that might flow from the additional investment.

(33) Moreover, for some measures, it is not possible to calculate the amount of aid on the basis of the extra costs; this is the case for aid in the form of environmental tax exemptions or reductions and aid in the form of tradable permit schemes. In those cases, proportionality has to be ensured through conditions and criteria for granting the exemptions and reductions, which ensure that the beneficiary does not receive excessive advantages, and that the selectivity of the measure is limited to the strict minimum.

(34) The cost of achieving environmental protection is often higher for small and medium-sized enterprises in relative terms compared to the size of their activity. In addition, the ability of small and medium-sized enterprises to bear such costs is often restricted by capital market imperfections. For this reason, and in view of the reduced risk of serious distortions of competition when the beneficiary is a small or medium-sized enterprise, a bonus can be justified for such enterprises for some types of aid.

(35) In addition, Member States are encouraged to ensure cost effectiveness in achieving environmental benefits, for example by choosing measures for which the external costs avoided are significant in relation to the amount of aid. However, since there is no direct link between the external costs avoided and the cost incurred by the undertaking, only in exceptional cases may external costs avoided be used as a basis to determine State aid amounts. Normally, in order to ensure an adequate incentive for the undertaking to change its behaviour, the aid amount must be linked directly to the cost borne by the undertaking.

1.3.6. Negative effects of environmental aid must be limited so that the overall balance is positive

(36) If environmental State aid measures are well targeted to counterweigh only the actual extra costs linked to a higher level of environmental protection, the risk that the aid will unduly distort competition is normally rather limited. Consequently, it is crucial that environmental State aid measures are well targeted. In cases where aid is not necessary or proportionate to achieve its intended objective it will harm competition. This may in particular be the case if aid leads to:

a) maintaining inefficient firms afloat;
b) distorting dynamic incentives/crowding out;
c) creating market power or exclusionary practices;
d) artificially altering trade flows or the location of production.

(37) In some cases, the purpose of the measure is to intervene in the functioning of the market with a view to favouring, to the overall benefit of the environment, certain environmentally friendly productions at the expense of other, more polluting ones. As a result of such measures, the producers of the environmentally friendly products concerned will be able to improve their market position in relation to competitors offering environmentally less beneficial products. In such cases, the Commission will take into account the overall environmental effect of the measure when looking at its negative impact on the market position, and thus on the profits, of non-aided firms. The lower the expected environmental effect of the measure in question, the more important the verification of its effect on market shares and profits of competing products.

1.4. Implementing the balancing test: legal presumptions and need for more detailed assessment

(38) Without prejudice to Articles 4 to 7 of Council Regulation (EC) No 659/1999 of 22 March 1999 laying down detailed rules for the application of Article [108 TFEU],[11] the legal presumptions applied by the Commission differ according to the type of State aid measure notified.

Note

11 OJ L 83, 27.3.1999, p.1. Regulation as last amended by Regulation (EC) No 1791/2006 (OJ L 363, 20.12. 2006, p.1).

(39) In Chapter 3 of these Guidelines, the Commission has identified a series of measures in respect of which it considers *a priori* that State aid will address a market failure hampering environmental protection or improve on the level of environmental protection. The Commission also sets out a series of conditions and parameters, which are intended to ensure that State aid actually has an incentive effect, is proportionate and has a limited negative impact on competition and trade. Chapter 3 thus contains parameters in respect of the aided activity, aid intensities and conditions attached to compatibility.

(40) However, for aid amounts above certain thresholds as well as for certain specific situations, additional scrutiny is necessary, because of higher risks of distortion of competition and trade. The additional scrutiny will generally consist in further and more detailed factual analysis of the measure in accordance with Chapter 5. These measures will be declared compatible if the balancing test pursuant to Chapter 5 results in an overall positive evaluation. In the context of this analysis, no compatibility criteria will be presumed to be fulfilled at the outset. Tax exemptions and reductions from environmental taxes will be subject only to the assessment laid down in Chapter 4.[12]

Notes

12 Aid granted in the form of fiscal aid in accordance with Chapter 3 will be subject to a detailed assessment if the thresholds in Chapter 5 are exceeded.

(41) As a result of this detailed assessment, the Commission may approve the aid, declare it incompatible with the common market or take a compatibility decision subject to conditions.

1.5. Reasons for specific measures covered by these Guidelines

(42) The Commission has identified a series of measures for which State aid may, under specific conditions, be compatible with Article [107(3)(c) TFEU].

1.5.1. *Aid for undertakings which go beyond Community standards or which increase the level of environmental protection in the absence of Community standards*

(43) This type of aid provides individual incentives to companies to achieve higher environmental protection. Normally, an undertaking does not have an incentive to go beyond mandatory standards if the cost of doing so exceeds the benefit for the undertaking. In such cases State aid may be granted to give an incentive to undertakings to improve environmental protection. In accordance with the Community objective to support eco-innovation, more favourable treatment can be accepted for eco-innovation projects that address the double market failure linked to the higher risks of innovation, coupled with the environmental aspect of the project. Aid for eco-innovation thus aims to accelerate the market diffusion of eco-innovations.

1.5.2. *Aid for the acquisition of new transport vehicles which go beyond Community standards or which increase the level of environmental protection in the absence of Community standards*

(44) Transport is responsible for a large share of overall greenhouse gas emissions (approximately 30%), as well as for local pollution by dust, particulates, NOx and SOx. Hence, it is important to encourage clean modes of transport, both in order to fight global climate change and in order to reduce local pollution, in particular in cities. In this context, it is particularly important to encourage the acquisition of clean transport vehicles (including clean ships).

1.5.3. *Aid for early adaptation to future Community standards*

(45) These Guidelines do not authorise aid to assist undertakings to comply with Community standards already in force, because such aid would not lead to a higher level of environmental protection. However, State aid may ensure significantly quicker implementation of newly adopted Community standards which are not yet in force and thereby contribute to reducing pollution at a faster pace than would have been the case without the aid. In such situations, State aid may therefore create individual incentives for enterprises to counterbalance the effects of the negative externalities linked to pollution.

1.5.4. Aid for environmental studies

(46) Aid to companies for studies on investments aimed at achieving a level of environmental protection going beyond Community standards or increasing the level of environmental protection in the absence of Community standards, as well as studies on energy saving and production of renewable energy, addresses the market failure linked to asymmetric information. Often undertakings underestimate the possibilities and benefits related to energy saving and renewable energy, which leads to under-investment.

1.5.5. Aid for energy saving

(47) This type of aid addresses the market failure linked to negative externalities by creating individual incentives to attain environmental targets for energy saving and for the reduction of greenhouse gas emissions. At Community level, in the Communication from the Commission to the European Council and the European Parliament — an Energy Policy for Europe[13] the aim has been set to achieve at least a 20% reduction in greenhouse gas emissions by 2020 compared to 1990, as endorsed by the European Council of 8 and 9 March 2007. Furthermore, Member States are obliged to adopt and aim to achieve an overall national indicative energy savings target of 9% over nine years in accordance with Directive 2006/32/EC of the European Parliament and of the Council of 5 April 2006 on energy end-use efficiency and energy services and repealing Council Directive 93/76/EEC.[14] State aid may be appropriate where the investments resulting in energy savings are not compulsory pursuant to applicable Community standards and where they are not profitable, that is to say where the cost of energy saving is higher than the related private economic benefit. In the case of small and medium-sized enterprises, more favourable support may be needed to take into account the fact that these enterprises often under-estimate the benefits related to energy savings over long periods, which leads to their under-investment in energy-saving measures.

Notes
[13] COM(2007) 1 final.
[14] OJ L 114, 27.4.2006, p.64.

1.5.6. Aid for renewable energy sources

(48) This type of aid addresses the market failure linked to negative externalities by creating individual incentives to increase the share of renewable sources of energy in total energy production. Increased use of renewable energy sources is one of the Community's environmental priorities as well as an economic and energy-related priority. It is expected to play an important role in meeting the targets for the reduction of greenhouse gas emissions. At Community level, in the Communication from the Commission to the European Council and the European Parliament — an energy policy for Europe the target has been set for renewable energy to account for 20% of overall EU energy consumption by 2020. State aid may be justified if the cost of production of renewable energy is higher than the cost of production based on less environmentally friendly sources and if there is no mandatory Community standard concerning the share of energy from renewable sources for individual undertakings. The high cost of production of some types of renewable energy does not allow undertakings to charge competitive prices on the market and thus creates a market-access barrier for renewable energy. However, due to technological developments in the field of renewable energy and to gradually increasing internalisation of environmental externalities (resulting, for example, from Directive 2008/1/EC of the European Parliament and of the Council of 15 January 2008 concerning integrated pollution prevention and control,[15] air quality legislation and the emissions trading scheme), the cost difference has shown a decreasing trend over the past years, thus reducing the need for aid.

Notes
[15] OJ L 24, 29.1.2008, p.8.

(49) In addition, as highlighted in the Biofuel Progress Report,[16] biofuel promotion should benefit both security of supply and climate change policy in a sustainable way. Therefore, State aid may be an appropriate instrument only for those uses of renewable energy sources where the environmental

benefit and sustainability is evident. More particularly, biofuels not fulfilling the sustainability criteria set out in Article 15 of the proposal for a Directive of the European Parliament and the Council on the promotion of the use of energy from renewable sources[17] will not be considered eligible for State aid. When designing their support systems, Member States may encourage the use of biofuels which give additional benefits — including the benefits of diversification offered by biofuels made from wastes, residues, cellulosic and ligno-cellulosic material — by taking due account of the different costs of producing energy from traditional biofuels, on the one hand, and of those biofuels which give additional benefits, on the other hand.

Notes

[16] COM(2006) 845 final.

[17] COM(2008) 19 final. Once the Directive has been adopted by the European Parliament and the Council, the Commission will apply the sustainability criteria in the final text.

---

(50) With regard to hydropower installations it should be noted that their environmental impact can be twofold. In terms of low greenhouse gas emissions they certainly provide potential. Therefore, they can play an important part in the overall energy mix. On the other hand, such installations might also have a negative impact, for example on water systems and biodiversity.[18]

Notes

[18] Directive 2000/60/EC of the European Parliament and of the Council of 23 October 2000 establishing a framework for Community action in the field of water policy (OJ L 327, 22.12.2000, p.1). Directive as last amended by Decision No 2455/2001/EC (OJ L 331, 15.12.2001, p.1). In particular Article 4(7) lays down criteria in relation to allowing new modifications of bodies of water.

1.5.7. Aid for cogeneration and aid for district heating (DH)

(51) These types of aid address market failure linked to negative externalities by creating individual incentives to meet environmental targets in the field of energy savings. Cogeneration of heat and electricity (hereafter 'CHP') is the most efficient way of producing electricity and heat simultaneously. By producing both electricity and heat together, less energy is wasted in production. The Community strategy outlined in the Commission's cogeneration strategy of 1997 sets an overall indicative target of doubling the share of electricity production from cogeneration to 18% by 2010. Since then the importance of CHP for the EU energy strategy has been underlined by the adoption of Directive 2004/8/EC of the European Parliament and of the Council of 11 February 2004 on the promotion of cogeneration based on a useful heat demand in the internal energy market and amending Directive 92/42/EEC[19] and by a chapter on cogeneration in the Commission Action Plan for Energy Efficiency: Realising the Potential.[20] The latter document also points to the potential of waste heat, for example from industry or utilities, for useful applications, for example in district heating (hereafter 'DH'). Further, DH may be more energy-efficient than individual heating and may provide a significant improvement in urban air quality. Therefore, provided that DH is shown to be less polluting and more energy efficient in the generation process and the distribution of the heat, but more costly than individual heating, State aid can be granted with a view to giving incentives to attain environmental targets. However, as in the case of renewable energies, the progressive internalisation of environmental externalities in the costs of other technologies can be expected to reduce the need for aid by bringing about a gradual convergence of these costs with those of CHP and DH.

Notes

[19] OJ L 52, 21.2.2004, p.50.

[20] COM(2006) 545 final.

1.5.8. Aid for waste management

(52) This type of aid aims to give individual incentives to reach environmental targets linked to waste management.[21] The Sixth Environment Action Programme identifies waste prevention and management as one of the four top priorities. Its primary objective is to separate waste generation from

economic activity, so that EU growth will not lead to more and more waste. In this context, State aid may be granted to the producer of the waste (under section 3.1.1) as well as to undertakings managing or recycling waste created by other undertakings (under section 3.1.9). However, the positive effects on the environment must be ensured, the PPP must not be circumvented and the normal functioning of secondary materials markets should not be distorted.

Notes
21 Waste management includes re-utilisation, recycling and recovery.

1.5.9. *Aid for the remediation of contaminated sites*

(53) This type of aid is intended to create an individual incentive to counterbalance the effects of negative externalities, where it is not possible to identify the polluter and make it pay for repairing the environmental damage it has caused. In such cases, State aid may be justified if the cost of remediation is higher than the resulting increase in the value of the site.

1.5.10. *Aid for the relocation of undertakings*

(54) This type of investment aid aims to create individual incentives to reduce negative externalities by relocating undertakings that create major pollution to areas where such pollution will have a less damaging effect, which will reduce external costs. In line with the precautionary principle, these Guidelines introduce the possibility of granting aid for the relocation of *high risk establishments* in accordance with Council Directive 96/82/EC of 9 December 1996 on the control of major-accident hazards involving dangerous substances[22] (hereafter the 'Seveso II Directive'). Past accidents have shown that the location of an establishment covered by the Seveso II Directive is of crucial importance as regards both the prevention of accidents and limitation of the consequences of accidents on people and the environment. State aid may therefore be justified if the relocation is made for environmental reasons. To ensure that aid is not granted for relocation for other purposes, an administrative or judicial decision of a competent public authority or an agreement between the competent public authority and the undertaking to relocate the firm is required. The eligible costs must take into account any advantages that the firm may obtain due to the relocation.

Notes
22 OJ L 10, 14.1.1997, p.13. Directive as last amended by Regulation (EC) No 1882/2003 of the European Parliament and of the Council (OJ L 284, 31.10.2003, p.1).

1.5.11. *Aid involved in tradable permit schemes*

(55) Tradable permit schemes may involve State aid in various ways, for example, when Member States grant permits and allowances below their market value and this is imputable to Member States. This type of aid may be used to target negative externalities by allowing market-based instruments targeting environmental objectives to be introduced. If the global amount of permits granted by the Member State is lower than the global expected needs of undertakings, the overall effect on the level of environmental protection will be positive. At the individual level of each undertaking, if the allowances granted do not cover the totality of expected needs of the undertaking, the undertaking must either reduce its pollution, thus contributing to the improvement of the level of environmental protection, or buy supplementary allowances on the market, thus paying a compensation for its pollution. To limit the distortion of competition, no over-allocation of allowances can be justified and provision must be made to avoid undue barriers to entry.

(56) The criteria set out in point 55 form the basis for the Commission's assessment of situations arising during the trading period ending on 31 December 2012. With respect to situations arising during the trading period after that date, the Commission will assess the measures according to whether they are both necessary and proportional. Finally, this will inform the revision of these Guidelines taking into account, in particular, the new Directive on the EU CO_2 Emission Trading System, for the trading period after 31 December 2012.

1.5.12. *Aid in the form of reductions of or exemptions from environmental taxes*

(57) Reductions of and exemptions from environmental taxes concerning certain sectors or categories of undertakings may make it feasible to adopt higher taxes for other undertakings, thus resulting in an overall improvement of cost internalisation, and to create further incentives to improve on environmental protection. Accordingly, this type of aid may be necessary to target negative externalities indirectly by facilitating the introduction or maintenance of relatively high national environmental taxation. For aid to be compatible, it must be shown that the exemptions or reductions are necessary for all the suggested categories of beneficiaries and that they are proportional in size. This is assumed to be the case if beneficiaries pay at least the Community minimum tax level set by the applicable Directive, if any. Otherwise, the necessity will depend on the extent to which the national tax impacts on production costs as well as on the possibility to pass on the tax to consumers and reduce profit margins. Proportionality will depend on the extent to which the beneficiaries can further reduce their consumption or emission, pay a part of the national tax or enter into environmental agreements to reduce pollution.[23]

Notes

[23] The Commission may re-evaluate the approach towards this kind of aid when Directive 2003/96/EC is reviewed.

2. Scope of Application and Definitions

2.1. Scope of application of the Guidelines

(58) These Guidelines apply to State aid for environmental protection. They will be applied in accordance with other Community policies on State aid, other provisions of the [Treaty on the Functioning of the European Union] and the Treaty on European Union and legislation adopted pursuant to those Treaties.

(59) These Guidelines apply to aid[24] to support environmental protection in all sectors governed by the [Treaty on the Functioning of the European Union]. They also apply to those sectors which are subject to specific Community rules on State aid (steel processing, shipbuilding, motor vehicles, synthetic fibres, transport, coal agriculture and fisheries) unless such specific rules provide otherwise.

Notes

[24] These guidelines do not discuss the concept of State aid, which derives from Article Article [107(1) TFEU] and from the case law of the Court of Justice of the European Communities.

(60) The design and manufacture of environmentally friendly products, machines or means of transport with a view to operating with fewer natural resources and action taken within plants or other production units with a view to improving safety or hygiene are not covered by these Guidelines.

(61) For agriculture and fisheries, these Guidelines apply to aid for environmental protection in favour of undertakings active in the processing and marketing of products. For undertakings active in the processing and marketing of fisheries products, if the aid concerns expenses eligible under Council Regulation (EC) No 1198/2006 of 27 July 2006 on the European Fisheries Fund,[25] the maximum aid rate allowed is the higher of the aid rate provided for in these Guidelines and the aid rate laid down in that Regulation. In the field of agricultural primary production, these Guidelines apply only to measures which are not already governed by the Community guidelines for State aid in the agriculture and forestry sector 2007 to 2013,[26] and in the field of fisheries and aquaculture primary production, they apply only where no specific provisions dealing with environmental aid exist.

Notes

[25] OJ L 223, 15.8.2006, p.1.
[26] OJ C 319, 27.12.2006, p.1.

(62) The financing of environmental protection measures relating to air, road, railway, inland waterway and maritime transport infrastructure, including any project of common interest as identified

in Decision No 1692/96/EC of the European Parliament and of the Council of 23 July 1996 on Community guidelines for the development of the trans-European transport network[27] is not covered by these Guidelines.

Notes

[27] OJ L 228, 9.9.1996, p.1. Decision as last amended by Council Regulation (EC) No 1791/2006 (OJ L 363, 20.12.2006, p.1).

(63) State aid for research, development and innovation in the environmental field is subject to the rules set out in the Community framework for State aid for research and development and innovation.[28] However, the market diffusion stage of eco-innovation (acquisition of an eco-innovation asset) is covered by these Guidelines.

Notes

[28] OJ C 323, 30.12.2006, p.1.

(64) The characteristics of aid for environmental training activities do not justify separate rules to those on aid for training activities generally, and the Commission will therefore examine such aid in accordance with Commission Regulation (EC) No 68/2001 of 12 January 2001 on the application of Articles [107 and 108 TFEU] to training aid.[29]

Notes

[29] OJ L 10, 13.1.2001, p.20. Regulation as last amended by Regulation (EC) No 1976/2006 (OJ L 368, 23.12.2006, p.85). When the new block exemption regulation covering training aid is adopted, the new regulation will apply. [Ed note: see now Commission Regulation (EC) No 800/2008 of 6 August 2008 declaring certain categories of aid compatible with the common market in application of Articles [107 and 108 TFEU] (General block exemption Regulation) (OJ L 214, 9.8.2008, p.3), reproduced in this volume at G11 above.]

(65) Consultancy services play an important role in helping small and medium-sized enterprises to make progress in environmental protection. In particular, they can be used to conduct eco-audits or to evaluate the economic benefits of an environmentally friendly investment for the undertaking and thus give an incentive to those enterprises to undertake the investment supporting environmental protection. Aid to small and medium-sized enterprises for advisory/consultancy services in the environmental field may be granted under Commission Regulation (EC) No 70/2001 of 12 January 2001 on the application of Articles [107 and 108 TFEU] to State aid for small and medium-sized enterprises.[30]

Notes

[30] OJ L 10, 13.1.2001, p.33. Regulation as last amended by Regulation (EC) No 1976/2006. When the new block exemption regulation covering aid to SMEs is adopted, the new regulation will apply. [Ed note: see now Commission Regulation (EC) No 800/2008 of 6 August 2008 declaring certain categories of aid compatible with the common market in application of Articles [107 and 108 TFEU] (General block exemption Regulation) (OJ L 214, 9.8.2008, p.3), reproduced in this volume at G11 above.]

(66) These Guidelines do not apply to stranded costs as defined in the Commission Communication relating to the methodology for analysing State aid linked to stranded costs.[31]

Notes

[31] Adopted by the Commission on 26 July 2001 and communicated to Member States by letter ref. SG(2001) D/290869, 6 August 2001.

(67) Furthermore, to the extent that the provisions relating to energy saving set out in section 3.1.5 are not applicable, these Guidelines do not apply to State aid to investments in infrastructure related to district heating, which will be assessed under Article [107(3)(c) TFEU].

(68) In some Member States, companies may be subject to environmental taxes and, at the same time, participate in tradable permit schemes. The Commission has not gathered sufficient experience in assessing the compatibility of reductions of environmental taxes in such situations. Consequently, it is too early for the Commission to provide general guidance thereon. Instead, the assessment of such

cases, to the extent that they constitute State aid within the meaning of Article [107(1) TFEU], will take place on the basis of Article [107(3)(c) TFEU].

(69) Finally, some of the means to support fossil fuel power plants or other industrial installations equipped with CO_2 capture, transport and storage facilities, or individual elements of the Carbon Capture Storage chain, envisaged by Member States, could constitute State aid but, in view of the lack of experience, it is too early to lay down guidelines relating to the authorisation of any such aid. Given the strategic importance of this technology for the Community in terms of energy security, reduction of greenhouse gas emissions and achievement of its agreed long-term objective to limit climate change to 2 °C above pre-industrial levels and given also the Commission's stated support for the construction of industrial-scale demonstration plants up to 2015, provided that they are environmentally safe and contribute to environmental protection, the Commission will have a generally positive attitude towards State aid for such projects.[32] Projects could be assessed under Article [107(3)(c) TFEU] or be eligible as important projects of common European interest under the conditions set out in Article [107(3)(b)] of the Treaty and point 147 of these Guidelines.

Notes
[32] See Commission proposal for a Directive of the European Parliament and of the Council on the geological storage of carbon dioxide COM(2008) 18 final.

2.2. Definitions

(70) For the purpose of these Guidelines the following definitions shall apply:

1) *environmental protection* means any action designed to remedy or prevent damage to physical surroundings or natural resources by a beneficiary's own activities, to reduce the risk of such damage or to lead to more efficient use of natural resources, including energy-saving measures and the use of renewable sources of energy;[33]
2) *energy-saving measure* means any action which enables undertakings to reduce the amount of energy used in particular in their production cycle;
3) *Community standard* means
   i) a mandatory Community standard setting the levels to be attained in environmental terms by individual undertakings,[34] or
   ii) the obligation under Directive 2008/1/EC to use the best available techniques as set out in the most recent relevant information published by the Commission pursuant to Article 17(2) of that Directive;
4) *eco-innovation* means all forms of innovation activities resulting in or aimed at significantly improving environmental protection. Eco-innovation includes new production processes, new products or services, and new management and business methods, whose use or implementation is likely to prevent or substantially reduce the risks for the environment, pollution and other negative impacts of resources use, throughout the life cycle of related activities. The following are not considered innovations:
   i) minor changes or improvements;
   ii) an increase in production or service capabilities through the addition of manufacturing or logistical systems which are very similar to those already in use;
   iii) changes in business practices, workplace organisation or external relations that are based on organisational methods already in use in the undertaking;
   iv) changes in management strategy;
   v) mergers and acquisitions;
   vi) ceasing to use a process;
   vii) simple capital replacement or extension;
   viii) changes resulting purely from changes in factor prices, customisation, regular seasonal and other cyclical changes;
   ix) trading of new or significantly improved products;

Part G State Aids

5) *renewable energy sources* means the following renewable non-fossil energy sources: wind, solar, geothermal, wave, tidal, hydropower installations, biomass, landfill gas, sewage treatment plant gas and biogases;

6) *biomass* means the biodegradable fraction of products, waste and residues from agriculture (including vegetal and animal substances), forestry and related industries, as well as the biodegradable fraction of industrial and municipal waste;

7) *biofuels* means liquid or gaseous fuel for transport produced from biomass;

8) *sustainable biofuels* means biofuels fulfilling the sustainability criteria set out in Article 15 of the proposal for a Directive of the European Parliament and the Council on the promotion of the use of energy from renewable sources;[35]

9) *energy from renewable energy sources* means energy produced by plants using only renewable energy sources, as well as the share in terms of calorific value of energy produced from renewable energy sources in hybrid plants which also use conventional energy sources. It includes renewable electricity used for filling storage systems, but excludes electricity produced as a result of storage systems;

10) *cogeneration* means the simultaneous generation in one process of thermal energy and electrical and/or mechanical energy;

11) *high-efficiency cogeneration* means cogeneration meeting the criteria of Annex III to Directive 2004/8/EC and satisfying the harmonised efficiency reference values established by Commission Decision 2007/74/EC of 21 December 2006 establishing harmonised efficiency reference values for separate production of electricity and heat in application of Directive 2004/8/EC of the European Parliament and of the Council;[36]

12) *district heating* means the supply of heat, either in the form of steam or hot water, from a central source of production through a transmission and distribution system to multiple buildings, for the purpose of heating;

13) *energy-efficient district heating* means district heating which, with regard to generation, either complies with the criteria for high-efficiency cogeneration or, in the case of heat-only boilers, meets the reference values for separate heat production laid down in Decision 2007/74/EC;

14) *environmental tax* means a tax whose specific tax base has a clear negative effect on the environment or which seeks to tax certain activities, goods or services so that the environmental costs may be included in their price and/or so that producers and consumers are oriented towards activities which better respect the environment;

15) *Community minimum tax level* means the minimum level of taxation provided for in Community legislation. For energy products and electricity, the Community minimum tax level means the minimum level of taxation laid down in Annex I to Council Directive 2003/96/EC of 27 October 2003 restructuring the Community framework for the taxation of energy products and electricity;[37]

16) *small and medium-sized enterprises* (hereafter 'SMEs'), *small enterprises* and *medium-sized enterprises* (or 'undertakings') mean such enterprises within the meaning of Regulation (EC) No 70/2001 or any regulation replacing it;

17) *large enterprises* and *large undertakings* means enterprises which are not within the definition of small and medium-sized enterprises;

18) *aid* means any measure fulfilling all the criteria laid down in Article Article [107(1) TFEU];

19) *aid intensity* means the gross aid amount expressed as a percentage of the eligible costs. All figures used must be taken before any deduction of tax or other charge. Where aid is awarded in a form other than a grant, the aid amount must be the grant equivalent of the aid. Aid payable in several instalments must be calculated at its value at the moment of granting. The interest rate to be used for discounting purposes and for calculating the aid amount in a soft loan must be the reference rate applicable at the time of grant. The aid intensity is calculated per beneficiary;

20) *operating benefits* means, for the purposes of calculating eligible costs, in particular cost savings or additional ancillary production directly linked to the extra investment for environmental protection and, where applicable, benefits accruing from other support measures whether or not they constitute State aid (operating aid granted for the same eligible costs, feed-in tariffs or other support measures). By contrast, proceeds flowing from the sale by the undertaking of tradable

permits issued under the European Trading System will not be deemed to constitute operating benefits;

21) *operating costs* means, for the purposes of calculating eligible costs, in particular additional production costs flowing from the extra investment for environmental protection;

22) *tangible assets* means, for the purposes of calculating eligible costs, investments in land which are strictly necessary in order to meet environmental objectives, investments in buildings, plant and equipment intended to reduce or eliminate pollution and nuisances, and investments to adapt production methods with a view to protecting the environment;

23) *intangible assets* means, for the purposes of calculating eligible costs, spending on technology transfer through the acquisition of operating licences or of patented and non-patented know-how where the following conditions are complied with:

   i) the intangible asset concerned must be regarded as a depreciable asset,

   ii) it must be purchased on market terms, from an undertaking in which the acquirer has no power of direct or indirect control,

   iii) it must be included in the assets of the undertaking, and remain in the establishment of the recipient of the aid and be used there for at least five years. This condition does not apply if the intangible asset is technically out of date. If it is sold during those five years, the yield from the sale must be deducted from the eligible costs and all or part of the amount of aid must, where appropriate, be reimbursed;

24) *internalisation of costs* means the principle that all costs associated with the protection of the environment should be included in the polluting undertakings' production costs;

25) *the polluter pays principle* means that the costs of measures to deal with pollution should be borne by the polluter who causes the pollution, unless the person responsible for the pollution cannot be identified or cannot be held liable under Community or national legislation or may not be made to bear the costs of remediation. Pollution in this context is the damage caused by the polluter by directly or indirectly damaging the environment, or by creating conditions leading to such damage,[38] to physical surroundings or natural resources;

26) *polluter* means someone who directly or indirectly damages the environment or who creates conditions leading to such damage;[39]

27) *contaminated site* means a site where there is a confirmed presence, caused by man, of dangerous substances of such a level that they pose a significant risk to human health or the environment taking into account current and approved future use of the land.

Notes

[33] See in particular the Sixth Environment Action Programme.

[34] Consequently, standards or targets set at Community level which are binding for Member States but not for individual undertakings are not deemed to be 'Community standards'.

[35] COM(2008) 19 final. Once the Directive has been adopted by the European Parliament and the Council, the Commission will apply the sustainability criteria in the final text.

[36] OJ L 32, 6.2.2007, p.183.

[37] OJ L 283, 31.10.2003, p.51. Directive as last amended by Directive 2004/75/EC (OJ L 157, 30.4.2004, p.100).

[38] Council Recommendation of 3 March 1975 regarding cost allocation and action by public authorities on environmental matters (OJ L 194, 25.7.1975, p.1).

[39] Recommendation of 3 March 1975 regarding cost allocation and action by public authorities on environmental matters.

---

3. Compatibility of Aid under Article [107(3) TFEU]

3.1. Compatibility of aid under Article [107(3)(c) TFEU]

(71) State aid for environmental protection is compatible with the common market within the meaning of Article [107(3)(c) TFEU] if, on the basis of the balancing test, it leads to increased environmental protection activities without adversely affecting trading conditions to an extent contrary to the common interest. In this context, the duration of aid schemes should be subject to reasonable time limits, without prejudice to the possibility for a Member State to re-notify a measure after the time limit set by the Commission decision has passed. Member States may support notifications of

aid measures by rigorous evaluations of similar past aid measures demonstrating the incentive effect of the aid.

(72) The measures described in points 73 to 146 may be found to be compatible under Article [107(3)(c)].

3.1.1. Aid for undertakings which go beyond Community standards or which increase the level of environmental protection in the absence of Community standards

(73) Investment aid enabling undertakings to go beyond Community standards for environmental protection or to increase the level of environmental protection in the absence of Community standards will be considered compatible with the common market within the meaning of Article [107(3)(c) TFEU] provided that the conditions set out in points 74 to 84 and section 3.2 are fulfilled.

(74) The aided investment must fulfil one of the following two conditions:

   a) the investment enables the beneficiary to increase the level of environmental protection resulting from its activities by going beyond the applicable Community standards, irrespective of the presence of mandatory national standards that are more stringent than the Community standard, or
   b) the investment enables the beneficiary to increase the level of environmental protection resulting from its activities in the absence of Community standards.

(75) Aid may not be granted where improvements bring undertakings into compliance with Community standards already adopted and not yet in force.[40]

Notes

[40] However, aid for early adaptation to future standards and for the acquisition of new transport vehicles is possible under the conditions developed in sections 3.1.3 and 3.1.2.

Aid intensity

(76) The aid intensity must not exceed 50% of the eligible investment cost as defined in points 80 to 84.

(77) Where the investment aid is granted in a genuinely competitive bidding process on the basis of clear, transparent and non discriminatory criteria, effectively ensuring that the aid is limited to the minimum necessary for achieving the environmental gain, the aid intensity may amount to up to 100% of the eligible investment cost as defined in points 80 to 84. Such a bidding process must be non-discriminatory and provide for the participation of a sufficient number of undertakings. In addition, the budget related to the bidding process must be a binding constraint in the sense that not all participants can receive aid. Finally, the aid must be granted on the basis of the initial bid submitted by the bidder, thus excluding subsequent negotiations.

(78) Where the investment concerns the acquisition of an eco-innovation asset or the launching of an eco-innovation project, the aid intensity may be increased by 10 percentage points, provided that following conditions are fulfilled:

a) the eco-innovation asset or project must be new or substantially improved compared to the state of the art in its industry in the Community. The novelty could, for example, be demonstrated by the Member States on the basis of a precise description of the innovation and of market conditions for its introduction or diffusion, comparing it with state-of-the-art processes or organisational techniques generally used by other undertakings in the same industry;
b) the expected environmental benefit must be significantly higher than the improvement resulting from the general evolution of the state of the art in comparable activities;[41]
c) the innovative character of these assets or projects involves a clear degree of risk, in technological, market or financial terms, which is higher than the risk generally associated with comparable non-innovative assets or projects. This risk could be demonstrated by the Member State for instance in terms of: costs in relation to the undertaking's turnover, time required for the development, expected gains from the eco-innovation in comparison with the costs, probability of failure.

41 When assessing point 78(b), if quantitative parameters can be used to compare eco-innovative activities with standard, non-innovative activities, 'significantly higher' means that the marginal improvement expected from eco-innovative activities, in terms of reduced environmental risk or pollution, or improved efficiency in energy or resources, should be at least twice as high as the marginal improvement expected from the general evolution of comparable non-innovative activities. Where the proposed approach is not appropriate for a given case, or if no quantitative comparison is possible, the application file for State aid should contain a detailed description of the method used to assess this criterion, ensuring a standard comparable to that of the proposed method.

(79) Where the investment aid for undertakings going beyond Community standards or increasing the level of environmental protection in the absence of such Community standards is to be given to SMEs, the aid intensity may be increased by 10 percentage points for medium-sized enterprises and by 20 percentage points for small enterprises, as set out in the table.

	Aid intensity for aid to undertakings going beyond Community standards or increasing the level of environmental protection in the absence of Community standards *except for eco-innovation*	Aid intensity for aid to undertakings going beyond Community standards or increasing the level of environmental protection in the absence of Community standards *in the field of eco-innovation*
Small enterprises	70%	80%
Medium-sized enterprises	60%	70%
Large enterprises	50%	60%

Calculation of eligible costs — methodology

(80) Eligible costs must be limited to the extra investment costs necessary to achieve a higher level of environmental protection than required by the Community standards and will be calculated in two steps. First, the cost of the investment directly related to environmental protection will be established by reference to the counterfactual situation, where appropriate. Second, operating benefits will be deducted and operating costs will be added.

(81) Identifying the part of the investment directly related to environmental protection:

a) where the cost of investing in environmental protection can be easily identified in the total investment cost, this precise environmental protection-related cost constitutes the eligible costs; **42**

b) in all other cases the extra investment costs must be established by comparing the investment with the counterfactual situation in the absence of State aid. The correct counterfactual is the cost of a technically comparable investment that provides a lower degree of environmental protection (corresponding to mandatory Community standards, if they exist) and that would credibly be realised without aid ('reference investment'). Technically comparable investment means an investment with the same production capacity and all other technical characteristics (except those directly related to the extra investment for environmental protection). In addition, such a reference investment must, from a business point of view, be a credible alternative to the investment under assessment.

42 This could be the case, for example, where an existing production process is up-graded and where the very parts which improve the environmental performance can be clearly identified.

(82) Identifying operating benefits/costs: eligible costs must, unless specified otherwise in this chapter, be calculated net of any operating benefits and operating costs related to the extra investment for environmental protection and arising during the first five years of the life of the investment concerned. This means that such operating benefits must be deducted and such operating costs may be added to the extra investment costs.

(83) The eligible investment may take the form of investment in tangible assets and/or in intangible assets.

(84) In the case of investments aiming at obtaining a level of environmental protection higher than Community standards the counterfactual should be chosen as follows:

a) **where the undertaking is adapting to national standards** adopted in the absence of Community standards, the eligible costs consist of the additional investment costs necessary to achieve the level of environmental protection required by the national standards;

b) **where the undertaking is adapting to, or goes beyond, national standards which are more stringent than the relevant Community standards or goes beyond Community standards,** the eligible costs consist of the additional investment costs necessary to achieve a level of environmental protection higher than the level required by the Community standards. The cost of investments needed to reach the level of protection required by the Community standards is not eligible;

c) **where no standards exist,** eligible costs consist of the investment costs necessary to achieve a higher level of environmental protection than that which the undertaking or undertakings in question would achieve in the absence of any environmental aid.

3.1.2. *Aid for the acquisition of new transport vehicles which go beyond Community standards or which increase the level of environmental protection in the absence of Community standards*

(85) The general rules set out in points 73 to 84 apply to aid for undertakings improving on Community standards or increasing the level of environmental protection in the absence of Community standards in the transport sector. By derogation from point 75, aid for acquisition of new transport vehicles for road, railway, inland waterway and maritime transport complying with adopted Community standards is permissible, when such acquisition occurs before their entry into force and where the new Community standards, once mandatory, will not apply retroactively to already purchased vehicles.

(86) For retrofitting operations with an environmental protection objective in the transport sector the eligible costs are the total extra net costs involved according to the methodology of calculating eligible costs set out in points 80 to 84 if the existing means of transport are upgraded to environmental standards that were not yet in force at the date of entry into operation of those means of transport or if the means of transport are not subject to any environmental standards.

3.1.3. *Aid for early adaptation to future Community standards*

(87) Aid for complying with new Community standards which increase the level of environmental protection and are not yet in force will be considered compatible with the common market within the meaning of Article [107(3)(c) TFEU] if the Community standards have been adopted, provided that the investment is implemented and finalised at least one year before the entry into force of the standard.

Aid intensity

(88) The maximum aid intensities are 25% for small enterprises, 20% for medium-sized enterprises and 15% for large enterprises if the implementation and finalisation take place more than three years before the mandatory date of transposition or date of entry into force. The aid intensity is 20% for small enterprises, 15% for medium-sized enterprises and 10% for large enterprises if the implementation and finalisation take place between one and three years before the mandatory date of transposition or date of entry into force.

Eligible costs

(89) Eligible costs must be limited to the extra investment costs necessary to achieve the level of environmental protection required by the Community standard compared to the existing level of environmental protection required prior to the entry into force of this standard.

(90) Eligible costs must be calculated net of any operating benefits and operating costs related to the extra investment and arising during the first five years of the life of this investment, as set out in points 81, 82 and 83.

3.1.4. *Aid for environmental studies*

(91) Aid to companies for studies directly linked to investments for the purposes of achieving standards under the conditions set out in section 3.1.1, of achieving energy saving under the conditions set out in section 3.1.5, of producing renewable energy under the conditions set out in section 3.1.6 will be considered compatible with the common market within the meaning of Article [107(3)(c) TFEU] if the conditions set out in this chapter are fulfilled. This will also apply in cases where, following the findings of a preparatory study, the investment under investigation is not undertaken.

(92) The aid intensity must not exceed 50% of the costs of the study.

(93) Where the study is undertaken on behalf of an SME, the aid intensity may be increased by 10 percentage points for medium-sized enterprises and by 20 percentage points for small enterprises, as set out in the table.

	Environmental studies
Small enterprises	70%
Medium-sized enterprises	60%
Large enterprises	50%

3.1.5. *Aid for energy saving*

(94) Investment and/or operating aid enabling undertakings to achieve energy savings will be considered compatible with the common market within the meaning of Article [107(3)(c) TFEU], if the following conditions are fulfilled:

3.1.5.1. Investment aid

Aid intensity

(95) The aid intensity must not exceed 60% of the eligible investment costs.

(96) Where the investment aid for energy saving is to be given to SMEs, the aid intensity may be increased by 10 percentage points for medium-sized enterprises and by 20 percentage points for small enterprises, as set out in the table.

	Aid intensity for energy saving
Small enterprises	80%
Medium-sized enterprises	70%
Large enterprises	60%

(97) Where the investment aid is granted in a genuinely competitive bidding process on the basis of clear, transparent and non discriminatory criteria, effectively ensuring that the aid is limited to the minimum necessary for achieving the maximum energy saving, the aid intensity may amount to up to 100% of the eligible investment cost as defined in point 98. Such a bidding process must be non-discriminatory and must provide for the participation of a sufficient number of undertakings. In addition, the budget related to the bidding process must be a binding constraint in the sense that not all participants can receive aid. Finally, the aid must be granted on the basis of the initial bid submitted by the bidder, thus excluding subsequent negotiations.

Eligible costs

(98) Eligible costs must be limited to the extra investment costs necessary to achieve energy savings beyond the level required by the Community standards.

The calculation of extra costs must respect the following rules:

a) *the part of the investment directly related to energy saving* must be identified in accordance with the rules laid down in points 81 and 83 of these Guidelines;

b) *a level of energy saving higher than Community standards* must be identified in accordance with the rules laid down in point 84 of these Guidelines;

c) *identifying operating benefits/costs*: eligible costs must be calculated net of any operating benefits and operating costs related to the extra investment for energy saving and arising during the first three years of the life of this investment in the case of SMEs, the first four years in the case of large undertakings that are not part of the EU CO_2 Emission Trading System and the first five years in the case of large undertakings that are part of the EU CO_2 Emission Trading System. For large undertakings this period can be reduced to the first three years of the life of this investment where the depreciation time of the investment can be demonstrated not to exceed three years.

3.1.5.2. Operating aid

(99) Operating aid for energy saving shall be granted only if the following conditions are met:

a) the aid is limited to compensating for net extra production costs resulting from the investment, taking account of benefits resulting from energy saving.[43] In determining the amount of operating aid, any investment aid granted to the undertaking in question in respect of the new plant must be deducted from production costs;

b) the aid is subject to a limited duration of five years.

Notes

[43] The concept of production costs must be understood as being net of any aid but inclusive of a normal level of profit.

---

(100) In the case of aid which is gradually reduced, the aid intensity must not exceed 100% of the extra costs in the first year but must have fallen in a linear fashion to zero by the end of the fifth year. In the case of aid which does not decrease gradually, the aid intensity must not exceed 50% of the extra costs.

3.1.6. Aid for renewable energy sources

(101) Environmental investment and operating aid for the promotion of energy from renewable sources will be considered compatible with the common market within the meaning of Article [107(3)(c) TFEU], if the conditions in points 102 to 111 are fulfilled. State aid may be justified if there is no mandatory Community standard concerning the share of energy from renewable sources for individual undertakings. Aid for investment and/or operating aid for the production of biofuels shall be allowed only with regard to sustainable biofuels.

3.1.6.1. Investment aid

Aid intensity

(102) The aid intensity must not exceed 60% of the eligible investment costs.

(103) Where the investment aid for renewable energy sources is to be given to SMEs, the aid intensity may be increased by 10 percentage points for medium-sized enterprises and by 20 percentage points for small enterprises, as set out in the table.

(104) Where the investment aid is granted in a genuinely competitive bidding process on the basis of clear, transparent and non discriminatory criteria, effectively ensuring that the aid is limited to the minimum necessary for delivering maximum renewable energy, the aid intensity may amount to up to 100% of the eligible investment cost as defined in points 105 and 106. Such a bidding process must be non-discriminatory and must provide for the participation of a sufficient number of undertakings. In addition, the budget related to the bidding process must be a binding constraint in the sense that not all participants can receive aid. Finally, the aid must be granted on the basis of the initial bid submitted by the bidder, thus excluding subsequent negotiations.

Eligible costs

(105) For renewable energy, eligible investment costs must be limited to the extra investment costs borne by the beneficiary compared with a conventional power plant or with a conventional heating system with the same capacity in terms of the effective production of energy.

(106) Eligible costs must be calculated net of any operating benefits and operating costs related to the extra investment for renewable sources of energy and arising during the first five years of the life of this investment, as set out in points 81, 82 and 83.

<u>3.1.6.2. Operating aid</u>

(107) Operating aid for the production of renewable energy may be justified in order to cover the difference between the cost of producing energy from renewable energy sources and the market price of the form of energy concerned. That applies to the production of renewable energy for the purposes of subsequently selling it on the market as well as for the purposes of the undertaking's own consumption.

(108) Member States may grant aid for renewable energy sources as follows:

(109) **Option 1**

a) Member States may grant operating aid to compensate for the difference between the cost of producing energy from renewable sources, including depreciation of extra investments for environmental protection, and the market price of the form of energy concerned. Operating aid may then be granted until the plant has been fully depreciated according to normal accounting rules. Any further energy produced by the plant will not qualify for any assistance. However, the aid may also cover a normal return on capital.

b) Where aid is granted in accordance with point (a) any investment aid granted to the undertaking in question in respect of the new plant must be deducted from production costs when determining the amount of operating aid. When notifying aid schemes to the Commission, Member States must state the precise support mechanisms and in particular the methods of calculating the amount of aid.

c) Unlike most other renewable sources of energy, biomass requires relatively low investment costs, but higher operating costs. The Commission will, therefore, be amenable to operating aid for the production of renewable energy from biomass exceeding the amount of investment where Member States can show that the aggregate costs borne by the undertakings after plant depreciation are still higher than the market prices of the energy.

(110) **Option 2**

a) Member States may also grant support for renewable energy sources by using market mechanisms such as green certificates or tenders. These market mechanisms allow all renewable energy producers to benefit indirectly from guaranteed demand for their energy, at a price above the market price for conventional power. The price of these green certificates is not fixed in advance but depends on supply and demand.

b) Where the market mechanisms constitute State aid, they may be authorised by the Commission if Member States can show that support is essential to ensure the viability of the renewable energy sources concerned, does not in the aggregate result in overcompensation and does not dissuade renewable energy producers from becoming more competitive. The Commission will authorise such aid systems for a period of ten years.

(111) **Option 3**

Furthermore, Member States may grant operating aid in accordance with the provisions set out in point 100.

3.1.7. Aid for cogeneration

(112) Environmental investment and operating aid for cogeneration will be considered compatible with the common market within the meaning of Article [107(3)(c) TFEU], provided that the cogeneration unit satisfies the definition of high-efficiency cogeneration set out in point 70(11), and provided that for investment aid:

(a) a new cogeneration unit will overall make primary energy savings compared to separate production as defined by Directive 2004/8/EC and Decision 2007/74/EC;

(b) improvement of an existing cogeneration unit or conversion of an existing power generation unit into a cogeneration unit will result in primary energy savings compared to the original situation.

Part G State Aids

(113) For operating aid, an existing cogeneration must satisfy both the definition of high-efficiency cogeneration set out in point 70(11) and the requirement that there are overall primary energy savings compared to separate production as defined by Directive 2004/8/EC and Decision 2007/74/EC.

3.1.7.1. Investment aid

Aid intensity

(114) The aid intensity must not exceed 60% of the eligible investment costs.

	Aid intensity for high-efficiency cogeneration
Small enterprises	80%
Medium-sized enterprises	70%
Large enterprises	60%

(115) Where the investment aid for cogeneration is to be given to SMEs, the aid intensity may be increased by 10 percentage points for medium-sized enterprises and by 20 percentage points for small enterprises, as set out in the table.

(116) Where the investment aid is granted in a genuinely competitive bidding process on the basis of clear, transparent and non discriminatory criteria, effectively ensuring that the aid is limited to the minimum necessary for achieving the maximum energy saving, the aid intensity may amount to up to 100% of the eligible investment cost as defined in points 117 and 118. Such a bidding process must be non-discriminatory and must provide for the participation of a sufficient number of companies. In addition, the budget related to the bidding process must be a binding constraint in a sense that not all participants can receive aid. Finally, the aid must be granted on the basis of the initial bid submitted by the bidder, thus excluding subsequent negotiations.

Eligible costs

(117) Eligible costs must be limited to the extra investment costs necessary to realise a high-efficiency cogeneration plant as compared to the reference investment.

(118) Eligible costs must be calculated net of any operating benefits and operating costs related to the extra investment and arising during the first five years of the life of this investment, as set out in points 81 to 83.

3.1.7.2. Operating aid

(119) Operating aid for high-efficiency cogeneration may be granted in accordance with the rules for operating aid for renewable energy laid down in section 3.1.6.2:

a) to undertakings distributing electric power and heat to the public where the costs of producing such electric power or heat exceed its market price. The decision as to whether the aid is necessary will take account of the costs and revenue resulting from the production and sale of the electric power or heat;

b) for the industrial use of the combined production of electric power and heat where it can be shown that the production cost of one unit of energy using that technique exceeds the market price of one unit of conventional energy. The production cost may include the plant's normal return on capital, but any gains by the undertaking in terms of heat production must be deducted from production costs.

3.1.8. Aid for energy-efficient district heating

(120) Environmental investment aid in energy-efficient district heating installations[44] will be considered compatible with the common market within the meaning of Article [107(3)(c) TFEU], provided that it leads to primary energy savings and that the beneficiary district heating installation satisfies the definition of energy-efficient district heating set out in point 70(13) and that:

a) the combined operation of the generation of heat (as well as electricity in the case of cogeneration) and the distribution of heat will result in primary energy savings; or

b)   the investment is meant for the use and distribution of waste heat for district heating purposes.

Note
44   To the exclusion of district heating infrastructure the financing of which does not fall within the scope of the present Guidelines but which will be assessed only under Article [107(3)(c)].

Aid intensity

(121)   The aid intensity for district heating installations must not exceed 50% of the eligible investment costs. If the aid is intended solely for the generation part of a district heating installation, energy-efficient district heating installations using renewable sources of energy or cogeneration will be covered by the rules set out in sections 3.1.6 and 3.1.7 respectively.

(122)   Where the investment aid for energy-efficient district heating is to be given to SMEs, the aid intensity may be increased by 10 percentage points for medium-sized enterprises and by 20 percentage points for small enterprises, as set out in the table.

	Aid intensity for energy-efficient district heating using conventional sources of energy
Small enterprises	70%
Medium-sized enterprises	60%
Large enterprises	50%

(123)   Where the investment aid is granted in a genuinely competitive bidding process on the basis of clear, transparent and non discriminatory criteria, effectively ensuring that the aid is limited to the minimum necessary for achieving the maximum energy saving, the aid intensity may amount to up to 100% of the eligible investment cost as defined in points 124 and 125. Such a bidding process must be non-discriminatory and must provide for the participation of a sufficient number of undertakings. In addition, the budget related to the bidding process must be a binding constraint in the sense that not all participants can receive aid. Finally, the aid must be granted on the basis of the initial bid submitted by the bidder, thus excluding subsequent negotiations.

Eligible costs

(124)   Eligible costs must be limited to the extra investment costs necessary to realise an investment leading to energy-efficient district heating as compared to the reference investment.

(125)   Eligible costs must be calculated net of any operating benefits and operating costs related to the extra investment and arising during the first five years of the life of this investment, as set out in points 81 to 83.

3.1.9. Aid for waste management

(126)   Environmental investment aid for the management of waste of other undertakings, including activities of re-utilisation, recycling and recovery, will be considered compatible with the common market within the meaning of Article [107(3)(c) TFEU], provided that such management is in accordance with the hierarchical classification of the principles of waste management45 and is in accordance with the conditions set out in point 127.

Notes
45   Classification given in the Communication from the Commission on the review of the Community Strategy for Waste Management (COM(96) 399 final, 30.7.1996). In that communication, the Commission stresses that waste management is a priority objective for the Community in order to reduce the risks to the environment. The concept of waste treatment must be looked at from three angles: re-utilisation, recycling and recovery. Waste whose production is unavoidable must be treated and eliminated without danger. In its Communication on a Thematic Strategy for the prevention and recycling of waste (COM(2005) 666), the Commission reiterated its commitment to these principles and allows for concrete measures towards promoting prevention, such as eco-design of processes and products or incentives to SMEs to put in place waste prevention measures, and recycling.

Part G State Aids

(127) Investment aid for waste management shall be granted only if each of the following conditions are met:

a) the investment is aimed at reducing pollution generated by other undertakings ('polluters') and does not extend to pollution generated by the beneficiary of the aid;

b) the aid does not indirectly relieve the polluters from a burden that should be borne by them under Community law, or from a burden that should be considered a normal company cost for the polluters;

c) the investment goes beyond the 'state of the art'[46] or uses conventional technologies in an innovative manner;

d) the materials treated would otherwise be disposed of, or be treated in a less environmentally friendly manner;

e) the investment does not merely increase demand for the materials to be recycled without increasing collection of those materials.

Notes

[46] 'State of the art' shall mean a process in which the use of a waste product to manufacture an end product is economically profitable normal practice. Where appropriate, the concept of 'state of the art' must be interpreted from a Community technological and common market perspective.

Aid intensity

(128) The aid intensity must not exceed 50% of the eligible investment costs.

(129) Where the investment aid for waste management is to be given to SMEs, the aid intensity may be increased by 10 percentage points for medium-sized enterprises and by 20 percentage points for small enterprises, as set out in the table.

	Aid intensity for waste management
Small enterprises	70%
Medium-sized enterprises	60%
Large enterprises	50%

Eligible costs

(130) Eligible costs must be limited to the extra investment costs necessary to realise an investment leading to waste management and borne by the beneficiary compared to the reference investment, that is to say, a conventional production not involving waste management with the same capacity. The cost of such reference investment must be deducted from the eligible cost.

(131) Eligible costs must be calculated net of any operating benefits and operating costs related to the extra investment for waste management and arising during the first five years of the life of this investment,[47] as set out in points 81 to 83.

Notes

[47] If the investment is concerned solely with environmental protection without any other economic benefits, no additional reduction will be applied in determining the eligible costs.

3.1.10. Aid for the remediation of contaminated sites

(132) Investment aid to undertakings repairing environmental damage by remediating contaminated sites will be considered compatible with the common market within the meaning of Article [107(3)(c) TFEU][48] provided that it leads to an improvement of environmental protection. The environmental damage concerned covers damage to the quality of the soil or of surface water or groundwater.

Where the polluter is clearly identified, that person must finance the remediation in accordance with the 'polluter pays' principle, and no State aid may be granted. In this context, 'polluter' refers to the person liable under the law applicable in each Member State, without prejudice to the adoption of Community rules in the matter.

Where the polluter is not identified or cannot be made to bear the costs, the person responsible for the work may receive aid.

Notes
48 Remediation work carried out by public authorities on their own land is not as such subject to Article [107] of the Treaty. Problems of State aid may, however, arise if the land is sold after remediation at a price below its market value. In this respect, the Commission Communication on State aid elements in sales of land and buildings by public authorities (OJ C 209, 10.7.1997, p.3) is still applicable.

Aid intensity

(133) Aid for the remediation of contaminated sites may amount to up to 100% of the eligible costs.

The total amount of aid may under no circumstances exceed the actual expenditure incurred by the undertaking.

Eligible costs

(134) The eligible costs are equal to the cost of the remediation work less the increase in the value of the land. All expenditure incurred by an undertaking in remediating its site, whether or not such expenditure can be shown as a fixed asset on its balance sheet, ranks as eligible investment in the case of the remediation of contaminated sites.

3.1.11. Aid for the relocation of undertakings

(135) Investment aid for relocation of undertakings to new sites for environmental protection reasons will be considered compatible with the common market within the meaning of Article [107(3)(c) TFEU] provided that the following conditions are met:

a) the change of location must be dictated by environmental protection or prevention grounds and must have been ordered by the administrative or judicial decision of a competent public authority or agreed between the undertaking and the competent public authority;

b) the undertaking must comply with the strictest environmental standards applicable in the new region where it is located.

(136) The beneficiary can be:

a) an undertaking established in an urban area or in a special area of conservation designated under Council Directive 92/43/EEC of 21 May 1992 on the conservation of natural habitats and of wild fauna and flora,[49] which lawfully carries out (that is to say, it complies with all legal requirements including all environmental standards applicable to it) an activity that creates major pollution and must, on account of that location, move from its place of establishment to a more suitable area; or

b) an establishment or installation falling within the scope of the Seveso II Directive.

Notes
49 OJ L 206, 22.7.1992, p.7. Directive as last amended by Directive 2006/105/EC (OJ L 363, 20.12.2006, p.368)

Aid intensity

(137) The aid intensity must not exceed 50% of the eligible investment costs. The aid intensity may be increased by 10 percentage points for medium-sized enterprises and by 20 percentage points for small enterprises, as set out in the table.

	Aid intensity for relocation
Small enterprises	70%
Medium-sized enterprises	60%
Large enterprises	50%

Part G State Aids

Eligible costs

(138) In order to determine the amount of eligible costs in the case of relocation aid, the Commission will take into account, in particular:

a) the following benefits:
    i) the yield from the sale or renting of the plant or land abandoned;
    ii) the compensation paid in the event of expropriation;
    iii) any other gains connected with the transfer of the plant, notably gains resulting from an improvement, on the occasion of the transfer, in the technology used and accounting gains associated with better use of the plant;
    iv) investments relating to any capacity increase;
b) the following costs:
    i) the costs connected with the purchase of land or the construction or purchase of new plant of the same capacity as the plant abandoned;
    ii) any penalties imposed on the undertaking for having terminated the contract for the renting of land or buildings, if the administrative or judicial decision ordering the change of location results in the early termination of this contract.

3.1.12. *Aid involved in tradable permit schemes*

(139) Tradable permit schemes may involve State aid in various ways, for example when permits and allowances are granted for less than their market value and such granting is imputable to Member States.

(140) State aid involved in tradable permit schemes may be declared compatible with the common market within the meaning of Article [107(3)(c) TFEU], provided that the conditions in points (a) to (d) of this point and point 141 are fulfilled. By derogation point 141 does not apply for the trading period ending on 31 December 2012 for tradable permit schemes in accordance with Directive 2003/87/EC of the European Parliament and of the Council of 13 October 2003 establishing a scheme for greenhouse gas emission allowance trading within the Community and amending Council Directive 96/61/EC[50] (hereafter 'EU ETS'):[51]

a) the tradable permit schemes must be set up in such a way as to achieve environmental objectives beyond those intended to be achieved on the basis of Community standards that are mandatory for the undertakings concerned;
b) the allocation must be carried out in a transparent way, based on objective criteria and on data sources of the highest quality available, and the total amount of tradable permits or allowances granted to each undertaking for a price below their market value must not be higher than its expected needs as estimated for the situation in absence of the trading scheme;
c) the allocation methodology must not favour certain undertakings or certain sectors, unless this is justified by the environmental logic of the scheme itself or where such rules are necessary for consistency with other environmental policies;
d) in particular, new entrants shall not in principle receive permits or allowances on more favourable conditions than existing undertakings operating on the same markets. Granting higher allocations to existing installations compared to new entrants should not result in creating undue barriers to entry.

Notes

[50] OJ L 275, 25.10.2003, p.32. Directive as last amended by Directive 2004/101/EC (OJ L 338, 13.11.2004, p.18).
[51] The Commission has assessed the State aid involved in the National Allocation Plans under the EU ETS for the trading period ending on 31 December 2012 on the basis of the criteria set out in point 140.

---

(141) The Commission will assess the necessity and the proportionality of State aid involved in a tradable permit scheme according to the following criteria:

a) the choice of beneficiaries must be based on objective and transparent criteria, and the aid must be granted in principle in the same way for all competitors in the same sector/relevant market if they are in a similar factual situation;

b) full auctioning must lead to a substantial increase in production costs for each sector or category of individual beneficiaries;

c) the substantial increase in production costs cannot be passed on to customers without leading to important sales reductions. This analysis may be conducted on the basis of estimations of *inter alia* the product price elasticity of the sector concerned. These estimations will be made in the relevant geographic market. To evaluate whether the cost increase from the tradable permit scheme cannot be passed on to customers, estimates of lost sales as well as their impact on the profitability of the company may be used;

d) it is not possible for individual undertakings in the sector to reduce emission levels in order to make the price of the certificates bearable. Irreducible consumption may be demonstrated by providing the emission levels derived from best performing technique in the European Economic Area (hereafter 'EEA') and using it as a benchmark. Any undertaking reaching the best performing technique can benefit at most from an allowance corresponding to the increase in production cost from the tradable permit scheme using the best performing technique, and which cannot be passed on to customers. Any undertaking having a worse environmental performance shall benefit from a lower allowance, proportionate to its environmental performance.

3.2. Incentive effect and necessity of aid

(142) State aid must have an incentive effect. State aid for environmental protection must result in the aid recipient changing its behaviour so that the level of environmental protection is increased.

(143) The Commission considers that aid does not present an incentive effect for the beneficiary in all cases in which the project has already started prior to the aid application by the beneficiary to the national authorities.

(144) If the aided project has not started before the aid application, the requirement of incentive effect is presumed to be automatically met for all categories of aid granted to an SME, except in cases where the aid must be assessed in accordance with the detailed assessment in chapter 5.

(145) For all other aided projects, the Commission will require that the incentive effect is demonstrated by the notifying Member State.

(146) To demonstrate the incentive effect, the Member State concerned must prove that without the aid, that is to say, in the counterfactual situation, the more environmentally friendly alternative would not have been retained. For this purpose, the Member State concerned must provide information demonstrating:

a) that the counterfactual situation is credible;

b) that the eligible costs have been calculated in accordance with the methodology set out in points 81, 82 and 83, and

c) that the investment would not be sufficiently profitable without aid, due account being taken of the benefits associated with the investment without aid, including the value of tradable permits which may become available to the undertaking concerned following the environmentally friendly investment.

3.3. Compatibility of aid under Article [107(3)(b) TFEU]

(147) Aid to promote the execution of important projects of common European interest which are an environmental priority may be considered compatible with the common market according to Article [107(3)(b) TFEU] provided that the following conditions are fulfilled:

a) the aid proposal concerns a project which is specific and clearly defined in respect of the terms of its implementation including its participants, its objectives and effects and the means to achieve the objectives. The Commission may also consider a group of projects as together constituting a project;

b) the project must be in the common European interest: the project must contribute in a concrete, exemplary and identifiable manner to the Community interest in the field of environmental protection, such as by being of great importance for the environmental strategy of the European Union. The advantage achieved by the objective of the project must not be limited to the Member State or the Member States implementing it, but must extend to the Community as a whole. The project must present a substantive contribution to the Community objectives. The fact that the project is carried out by undertakings in different Member States is not sufficient;

c) the aid is necessary and presents an incentive for the execution of the project, which must involve a high level of risk;

d) the project is of great importance with regard to its volume: it must be substantial in size and produce substantial environmental effects.

(148) In order to allow the Commission to properly assess such projects, the common European interest must be demonstrated in practical terms: for example, it must be demonstrated that the project enables significant progress to be made towards achieving specific environmental objectives of the Community.

(149) The Commission will consider notified projects more favourably if they include a significant own contribution of the beneficiary to the project. It will equally consider more favourably notified projects involving undertakings from a significant number of Member States.

(150) When the aid is considered to be compatible with the common market in accordance with Article [107(3)(b) TFEU], the Commission may authorise aid at higher rates than otherwise laid down in these Guidelines.

4. Aid in the form of Reductions of or Exemptions from Environmental Taxes

(151) Aid in the form of reductions of or exemptions from environmental taxes will be considered compatible with the common market within the meaning of Article [107(3)(c) TFEU] provided that it contributes at least indirectly to an improvement of the level of environmental protection and that the tax reductions and exemptions do not undermine the general objective pursued.

(152) In order to be approved under Article [107 TFEU], reductions of or exemptions from harmonised taxes, in particular those harmonised through Directive 2003/96/EC, must be compatible with the relevant applicable Community legislation and comply with the limits and conditions set out therein.

(153) Aid in the form of tax reductions and exemptions from harmonised environmental taxes is considered to be compatible with the common market within the meaning of Article [107(3)(c) TFEU] for a period of 10 years provided the beneficiaries pay at least the Community minimum tax level set by the relevant applicable Directive.[52]

Notes

[52] See point 70(15).

---

(154) Aid in the form of reductions of or exemptions from environmental taxes other than those referred to in point 153[53] is considered to be compatible with the common market within the meaning of Article [107(3)(c) TFEU] for a period of 10 years provided that the conditions set out in points 155 to 159 are fulfilled.

Notes

[53] For example, reductions of or exemptions from taxes which are not covered by Community legislation or which are below the Community minimum tax level.

---

(155) When analysing tax schemes which include elements of State aid in the form of reductions of or exemptions from such tax, the Commission will analyse in particular the necessity and proportionality of the aid and its effects at the level of the economic sectors concerned.

(156) For this purpose the Commission will rely on information provided by Member States. Information should include, on the one hand, the respective sector(s) or categories of beneficiaries covered by the exemptions/reductions and, on the other hand, the situation of the main beneficiaries in each sector concerned and how the taxation may contribute to environmental protection. The exempted sectors should be properly described and a list of the largest beneficiaries for each sector should be provided (considering notably turnover, market shares and size of the tax base). For each

sector, information should be provided as to the best performing techniques within the EEA regarding the reduction of the environmental harm targeted by the tax.

(157) In addition, aid in the form of reductions of or exemptions from environmental taxes must be necessary and proportional.

(158) The Commission will consider the aid to be necessary if the following cumulative conditions are met:

a) the choice of beneficiaries must be based on objective and transparent criteria, and the aid must be granted in principle in the same way for all competitors in the same sector/relevant market[54] if they are in a similar factual situation;

b) the environmental tax without reduction must lead to a substantial increase in production costs for each sector or category of individual beneficiaries;[55]

c) the substantial increase in production costs cannot be passed on to customers without leading to important sales reductions. In this respect, Member States may provide estimations of *inter alia* the product price elasticity of the sector concerned in the relevant geographic market[56] as well as estimates of lost sales and/or reduced profits for the companies in the sector/category concerned.

Notes

[54] As defined in the Commission notice on the definition of the relevant market for the purposes of Community competition law (OJ C 372, 9.12.1997, p.5).
[55] With regard to energy products and electricity, 'energy-intensive business' as defined in Article 17(1)(a) of Directive 2003/96/EC shall be regarded as fulfilling this criterion as long as that provision remains in force.
[56] As defined in the Commission notice on the definition of the relevant market for the purposes of Community competition law.

---

(159) The Commission will consider the aid to be proportional if one of the following conditions is met:

a) the scheme lays down criteria ensuring that each individual beneficiary pays a proportion of the national tax level which is broadly equivalent to the environmental performance of each individual beneficiary compared to the performance related to the best performing technique within the EEA. Under the aid scheme any undertaking reaching the best performing technique can benefit, at most, from a reduction corresponding to the increase in production costs from the tax, using the best performing technique, and which cannot be passed on to customers. Any undertaking having a worse environmental performance shall benefit from a lower reduction, proportionate to its environmental performance;

b) aid beneficiaries pay at least 20% of the national tax, unless a lower rate can be justified in view of a limited distortion of competition;

c) the reductions or exemptions are conditional on the conclusion of agreements between the Member State and the recipient undertakings or associations of undertakings whereby the undertakings or associations of undertakings commit themselves to achieve environmental protection objectives which have the same effect as if point (a) or (b) or the Community minimum tax level were applied. Such agreements or commitments may relate, among other things, to a reduction in energy consumption, a reduction in emissions or any other environmental measure and must satisfy the following conditions:

  i) the substance of the agreements must be negotiated by each Member State and must specify in particular the targets and fix a time schedule for reaching the targets;

  ii) Member States must ensure independent[57] and timely monitoring of the commitments concluded in these agreements;

  iii) these agreements must be revised periodically in the light of technological and other developments and stipulate effective penalty arrangements applicable if the commitments are not met.

Notes

[57] It is irrelevant for these purposes whether the monitoring is done by a public or a private body.

5. Compatibility of Aid Subject to a Detailed Assessment

5.1. Measures subject to a detailed assessment

(160) In order to enable the Commission to carry out a more detailed assessment of any substantial amounts of aid granted under authorised schemes and to decide whether such aid is compatible with the common market, Member States must notify it in advance of any individual case of investment or operating aid granted under an authorised scheme or individually where the aid satisfies the following conditions:[58]

a) **for measures covered by a BER**: all cases notified to the Commission pursuant to *a duty to notify aid individually* as prescribed in the BER;

b) **for individual measures covered by these Guidelines**:[59] all the following cases:

i) *investment aid*: where the aid amount exceeds EUR 7.5 million for one undertaking (even if part of an approved aid scheme);

ii) *operating aid for energy saving*: where the aid *amount* exceeds EUR 5 million per undertaking for five years;

iii) *operating aid for the production of renewable electricity and/or combined production of renewable heat*: when the aid is granted to renewable electricity installations in sites where the resulting renewable electricity generation capacity exceeds 125 MW;

iv) *operating aid for the production of biofuel*: when the aid is granted to a biofuel production installation in sites where the resulting production exceeds 150 000 t per year;

v) *operating aid for cogeneration*: where aid is granted to cogeneration installation with the resulting cogeneration electricity capacity exceeding 200 MW. Aid for the production of heat from cogeneration will be assessed in the context of notification based on electricity capacity.

Notes

[58] This also applies irrespective of whether the individual beneficiary benefits at the same time from a tax exemption or reduction assessed under chapter 4.

[59] Tax exemptions and reductions from environmental taxes falling under chapter 4 of these guidelines will not be subject to a detailed assessment. However, aid granted in accordance with chapter 3 in the form of fiscal aid will be subject to a detailed assessment if the thresholds in this point are exceeded.

---

(161) Member States may grant operating aid to new plants producing renewable energy on the basis of a calculation of the external costs avoided. Where this method is used to determine the aid amount, the measure must be notified and be subject to detailed assessment, regardless of the thresholds in point 160(b)(iii). The external costs avoided represent a monetary quantification of the additional socio-environmental damage that society would experience if the same quantity of energy were produced by a production plant operating with conventional forms of energy. They will be calculated on the basis of the difference between, on the one hand, the external costs produced and not paid by renewable energy producers and, on the other hand, the external costs produced and not paid by non-renewable energy producers. To carry out these calculations, the Member State will have to use a method of calculation that is internationally recognised and has been validated by the Commission. It will have to provide among other things a reasoned and quantified comparative cost analysis, together with an assessment of competing energy producers' external costs, so as to demonstrate that the aid does genuinely compensate for external costs avoided.

(162) In any event, the amount of aid granted to producers that exceeds the amount of aid resulting from option 1 set out in point 109 for operating aid for renewable sources of energy must be reinvested by the firms in renewable sources of energy in accordance with section 3.1.6.1.

(163) Provided that Member States ensure full cooperation and supply adequate information in a timely manner, the Commission will use its best endeavours to conduct the investigation in a timely manner. Member States are invited to provide all the elements that they consider useful for the assessment of the case. The Member States may, in particular, rely on evaluations of past State aid schemes or measures, impact assessments made by the granting authority and other studies related to environmental protection.

(164) The detailed assessment is a proportionate assessment, depending on the distortion potential of the case. Accordingly, the fact that a detailed assessment is carried out does not necessarily mean that a formal investigation procedure needs to be opened, although this may be the case for certain measures.

5.2. Criteria for economic assessment of individual cases

(165) The detailed assessment will be conducted on the basis of the positive and negative elements specified in sections 5.2.1 and 5.2.2 which will be used in addition to the criteria set out in Chapter 3. The aid intensities set out therein must in any event not be exceeded. Furthermore, the detailed assessment will be conducted on the basis of the specific positive and negative elements, when they are relevant for the type or form of aid.

5.2.1. Positive effects of the aid

(166) The fact that the aid induces undertakings to pursue environmental protection which they would not otherwise have pursued constitutes the main positive element to be taken into consideration when assessing the compatibility of the aid.

5.2.1.1. Existence of a market failure

(167) The Commission will in general not question whether there are negative externalities related to certain types of conduct or the use of certain goods which have harmful effects on the environment. However, the Commission will verify whether the State aid is targeted at this market failure by having a substantial impact on environmental protection. In this context, the Commission will pay attention in particular to the expected contribution of the measure to environmental protection (in quantifiable terms) and the level of environmental protection targeted, as compared to existing Community standards and/or standards in other Member States.

(168) The Commission will also examine the considerations that may justify aid for adapting to national standards going beyond Community standards. The Commission will take into account in particular the nature, type and location of the main competitors of the aid beneficiary, the cost of implementation of the national standards (or tradable permit schemes) for the aid beneficiary had no aid been given, and the comparative costs of implementation of those standards for the main competitors of the aid beneficiary.

5.2.1.2. Appropriate instrument

(169) Account will be taken of whether State aid is an appropriate instrument to obtain the objective of environmental protection, given that other less distortive instruments may achieve the same results and since State aid may breach the PPP.

(170) In its compatibility analysis, the Commission will in particular take account of any impact assessment of the proposed measure which the Member State may have made, including considerations of using policy options other than State aid, and take account of evidence that the PPP will be respected.

5.2.1.3. Incentive effect and necessity of aid

(171) State aid must always have an incentive effect, when it is provided for environmental purposes, that is to say it must result in the recipient changing its behaviour to increase the level of environmental protection. Aid cannot be considered necessary solely because the level of environmental protection is increased. The advantages of new investments or production methods are normally not limited to their environmental effects.

(172) In addition to the calculation of extra costs outlined in Chapter 3, the Commission will take into account the following elements in its analysis:

a) **counterfactual situation:** evidence must be provided about the specific action(s) that would not have been taken by the undertaking without the aid, for instance, a new investment, a more environmentally friendly production process and/or a new product that is more environmentally friendly;

b) **expected environmental effect linked to the change in behaviour:** at least one of the following elements must be present:

   i) *increase in the level of environmental protection*: reduction of a specific type of pollution that would not be reduced without the aid;

   ii) *increase in speed of the implementation of future standards*: reduction in pollution starting at an earlier point in time owing to the aid;

c) **production advantages:** if there are other advantages linked to the investment in terms of increased capacity, productivity, cost reductions or quality, the incentive effect is normally lower. This is in particular the case if the benefits over the life time of the investment are substantial, possibly to the extent that the extra environmental costs can be recouped even without aid;

d) **market conditions:** in some markets, notably due to product image and the labelling of production methods, there may be competitive pressure to maintain a high level of environmental protection. If there is evidence that the level of environmental protection resulting from the aid goes beyond the normal behaviour in the market, it is more likely that the aid has an incentive effect;

e) **possible future mandatory standards:** if there are negotiations at Community level to introduce new or higher mandatory standards which the measure concerned would seek to target, the incentive effect of aid is normally lower;

f) **level of risk:** if there is a particular risk that the investment will be less productive than expected, the incentive effect of aid will normally be higher;

g) **level of profitability:** if the level of profitability of the action pursued is negative over the time horizon by which the investment is fully depreciated or the operating aid is intended to be in force, account being taken of all the advantages and risks identified in this point, aid will normally have an incentive effect.

(173) Where the undertaking is adapting to a national standard going beyond Community standards or adopted in the absence of Community standards, the Commission will verify that the aid beneficiary would have been affected substantially in terms of increased costs and would not have been able to bear the costs associated with the immediate implementation of national standards.

5.2.1.4. Proportionality of the aid

(174) The Member State should provide evidence that the aid is necessary, that the amount is kept to the minimum and that the selection process is proportional. In its analysis the Commission will consider the following elements:

a) **accurate calculation of the eligible costs:** evidence that the eligible costs are indeed limited to the extra costs necessary to achieve the level of environmental protection;

b) **selection process:** the selection process should be conducted in a non-discriminatory, transparent and open manner, without unnecessarily excluding companies that may compete with projects to address the same environmental objective. The selection process should lead to the selection of beneficiaries that can address the environmental objective using the least amount of aid or in the most cost-effective way;

c) **aid limited to the minimum:** evidence that the aid amount does not exceed the expected lack of profitability including a normal return over the time horizon for which the investment is fully depreciated.

5.2.2. Analysis of the distortion of competition and trade

(175) In assessing the negative effects of the aid measure, the Commission will focus its analysis of the distortions of competition on the foreseeable impact the environmental aid has on competition between undertakings in the product markets affected.[60]

Notes

[60] A number of markets may be affected by the aid, because the impact of the aid may not be restricted to the market corresponding to the activity that is supported but may extend to other markets, which are connected to that market either because they are upstream, downstream or complementary, or because the beneficiary is already present on them or may be so present in the near future.

(176) If the aid is proportional, notably if the calculation of the extra investment or operating costs has taken into account all advantages to the undertaking, the negative impact of the aid is likely to be limited. However, as mentioned in section 1.3.6 even where aid is necessary and proportional for the specific undertaking to increase the environmental protection, the aid may result in a change in behaviour of the beneficiary which distorts competition. A profit-seeking undertaking will normally only increase the level of environmental protection beyond mandatory requirements if it considers that this will result at least marginally in some sort of advantage for the undertaking.

(177) As a starting point, the Commission will assess the likelihood that the beneficiary will be able to increase or maintain sales as a result of the aid. The Commission will in particular consider the following elements:

a) **reduction in or compensation of production unit costs:** if the new equipment[61] will lead to reduced costs per unit produced compared to the situation without the aid or if the aid compensates a part of the operating cost, it is likely that the beneficiary will increase its sales. The more price elastic the product, the greater the competition distortion;

b) **more environmentally friendly production process:** if the beneficiary obtains a more environmentally friendly production process and if it is common through labelling or image to differentiate the product towards consumers on the basis of the level of environmental protection, it is likely that the beneficiary can increase its sales. The greater the consumer preference for environmental product characteristics, the greater the competition distortion;

c) **new product:** if the beneficiary obtains a new or higher quality product it is likely that it will increase its sales and possibly gain a 'first mover' advantage. The greater the consumer preference for environmental product characteristics, the greater the competition distortion.

Notes

61 The calculation of extra costs may not fully capture all operating benefits, since the benefits are not deducted over the life time of the investment. In addition, certain types of benefits, for example linked to increased productivity and increased production with unaltered capacity, may be difficult to take into account.

5.2.2.1. Dynamic incentives/crowding out

(178) State aid for environmental protection may be used strategically to promote innovative environmentally friendly technologies with the aim of giving domestic producers a 'first mover' advantage. Consequently, the aid may distort the dynamic incentives and crowd out investments in the specific technology in other Member States and lead to a concentration of this technology in one Member State. This effect is higher the more competitors reduce their innovative effort as compared to the no-aid counterfactual.

(179) In its analysis, the Commission will consider the following elements:

a) **amount of aid:** the higher the amount of aid, the more likely it is that part of the aid can be used to distort competition. This is in particular the case if the aid amount is high compared to the size of the general activity of the beneficiary;

b) **frequency of aid:** if an undertaking receives aid repeatedly, it is more likely that this will distort dynamic incentives;

c) **duration of the aid:** if operating aid is granted for a long period, this is more likely to distort competition;

d) **gradual decrease of aid:** if operating aid is reduced over time, the undertaking will have an incentive to improve efficiency and the distortion of dynamic incentives will therefore be reduced over time;

e) **readiness to meet future standards:** if the aid will enable the undertaking concerned to meet new Community standards expected to be adopted in the foreseeable future, the aided investment will reduce the costs of investments that the undertaking would have had to make in any event;

f) **level of the regulatory standards in relation to the environmental objectives:** the lower the level of mandatory requirements the higher the risk that aid to go beyond mandatory requirements is not necessary and will crowd out investments or be used in a way that distorts dynamic incentives;

g) **risk of cross-subsidisation**: where the undertaking produces a wide range of products or produces the same product using a conventional and an environmentally friendly process, the risk of cross-subsidisation is higher;

h) **technological neutrality**: where a measure focuses on one technology only, the risk of distorting dynamic incentives is higher;

i) **competing innovation**: where foreign competitors develop competing technologies (innovation competition), the more likely the aid will distort dynamic incentives.

5.2.2.2. Maintaining inefficient firms afloat

(180) State aid for environmental protection may be justified as a transitional mechanism to move towards a full allocation of environmentally negative externalities. It should not be used to grant unnecessary support to undertakings which are unable to adapt to more environmentally friendly standards and technologies because of their low levels of efficiency. In its analysis, the Commission will consider the following elements:

a) **type of beneficiaries**: where the beneficiary has a relatively low level of productivity and is in poor financial health, it is more likely that the aid will contribute to artificially maintaining the undertaking in the market;

b) **overcapacity in the sector targeted by the aid**: in sectors where there is overcapacity, the risk is higher that investment aid will sustain the overcapacity and maintain inefficient market structures;

c) **normal behaviour in the sector targeted by the aid**: if other undertakings in the sector have reached the same level of environmental protection without aid, it is more likely that the aid will serve to maintain inefficient market structures. Thus, the weaker the evidence that PPP is respected by the beneficiary and the greater the fraction of external environmental cost internalised by the beneficiary's competitors, the more significant the competition distortion;

d) **relative importance of the aid**: the greater the reduction/compensation to variable production costs, the greater the competition distortion;

e) **selection process**: if the selection process is conducted in a non-discriminatory, transparent and open manner it is less likely that the aid will contribute to artificially maintaining the undertaking in the market. The more extensive (in terms of relevant market coverage) and the more competitive (in terms of auctioning/procurement) the allocation of a subsidy, the lower the competition distortion;

f) **selectivity**: if the measure under which the aid is granted covers a relatively high number of potential beneficiaries, if it covers all undertakings in the relevant market and if it does not exclude companies that could address the same environmental objective, it is less likely that the aid will maintain inefficient firms in the market.

5.2.2.3. Market power/exclusionary behaviour

(181) Aid for environmental protection given to a beneficiary may be used to strengthen or maintain its market power in the given product market. The Commission will assess the market power of the beneficiary concerned before the aid is granted, and the change in market power which can be expected as a result of the aid. Aid for environmental protection given to a beneficiary with substantial market power may be used by this beneficiary to strengthen or maintain its market power, by further differentiating its products or excluding rivals. The Commission is unlikely to identify competition concerns related to market power in markets where each aid beneficiary has a market share below 25% and in markets whose Herfindahl-Hirschman Index of market concentration is below 2,000.

(182) In its analysis, the Commission will consider the following elements:

a) **market power of aid beneficiary and market structure**: Where the recipient is already dominant on the affected market,[62] the aid measure may reinforce this dominance by further weakening the competitive constraint that competitors can exert on the recipient undertaking;

b) **new entry**: where the aid concerns product markets or technologies that compete with products where the aid recipient is an incumbent and has market power, the aid may be used strategically to prevent new entry. Thus, if the aid is not available to potential new entrants, the risk that the aid distorts competition is higher;

c) **product differentiation and price discrimination**: the aid may have the negative effect of facilitating product differentiation and price discrimination by the aid recipient, to the detriment of consumers;

d) **buyer power**: where there are strong buyers in the market, it is less likely that an aid beneficiary with market power can increase prices vis-à-vis the strong buyers. Thus, the stronger the buyer power the less likely it is that the aid will harm consumers.

Notes

62 A number of markets may be affected by the aid, because the impact of the aid may not be restricted to the market corresponding to the activity that is supported but may extend to other markets, which are connected to that market either because they are upstream, downstream or complementary, or because the beneficiary is already present on them or may be present in the near future.

5.2.2.4. Effects on trade and location

(183) State aid for environmental protection may result in some territories benefiting from more favourable production conditions, notably because of comparatively lower production costs as a result of the aid or because of higher production standards achieved through the aid. This may result in companies re-locating to the aided territories, or to displacement of trade flows towards the aided area.

(184) Consequently, the aid will shift profits to the Member State in the product market concerned by the aid as well as in input markets.

(185) In its analysis, the Commission will consider whether there is evidence that the beneficiary had considered other locations for its investment, in which case it is more likely that the aid significantly distorts competition.

5.2.3. *Balancing and decision*

(186) In the light of these positive and negative elements, the Commission will balance the effects of the measure and determine whether the resulting distortions adversely affect trading conditions to an extent contrary to the common interest. Ideally, the positive effects and the negative effects should be expressed using the same referential (for example external cost avoided versus the loss of competitor's profits in monetary unit).

(187) In general, the higher the environmental benefit and the more clearly it is established that the aid amount is limited to the minimum necessary, the more likely a positive appraisal. On the other hand, the larger the indication that the aid will significantly distort competition, the less likely a positive appraisal. If the expected positive effects are extensive and the distortions are likely to be very significant, the appraisal will depend on the extent to which the positive effects are considered to outweigh the negative effects.

(188) The Commission may raise no objections to the notified aid measure without initiating the formal investigation procedure or, following the formal investigation procedure laid down in Article 6 of Regulation (EC) No 659/1999, may decide to close the procedure with a decision in accordance with Article 7 of that Regulation. Where it takes a conditional decision within the meaning of Article 7(4) of that Regulation, it may, for instance, consider attaching the following conditions, which must reduce the resulting distortions or effect on trade and be proportionate:

a) **lower aid intensities** than the maximum intensities allowed in Chapter 3;
b) **separation of accounts** in order to avoid cross-subsidisation from one market to another market, when the beneficiary is active in multiple markets;
c) **additional requirements to be met to improve the environmental effect** of the measure;
d) **no discrimination** against other potential beneficiaries (reduced selectivity).

Part G State Aids

6. CUMULATION

(189) The aid ceilings fixed under these Guidelines shall apply regardless of whether the support for the aided project is financed entirely from State resources or is partly financed by the Community.

(190) Aid authorised under these Guidelines may not be combined with other State aid within the meaning of Article Article [107(1) TFEU] or with other forms of Community financing if such overlapping results in an aid intensity higher than that laid down in these Guidelines. However, where the expenditure eligible for aid for environmental protection is eligible in whole or in part for aid for other purposes, the common portion will be subject to the most favourable aid ceiling under the applicable rules.

(191) Aid for environmental protection must not be cumulated with *de minimis* aid in respect of the same eligible costs if such cumulation would result in an aid intensity exceeding that fixed in these Guidelines.

7. FINAL PROVISIONS

7.1. Annual reporting

(192) In accordance with the requirements of Regulation (EC) No 659/1999 and Commission Regulation (EC) No 794/2004 of 21 April 2004 implementing Council Regulation (EC) No 659/1999 laying down detailed rules for the application of Article [108 TFEU],[63] Member States must submit annual reports to the Commission.

Notes

[63] OJ L 140, 30.4.2004, p.1. Regulation as last amended by Regulation (EC) No 1935/2006 (OJ L 407, 30.12.2006, p.1).

---

(193) Beyond the requirements stipulated in those provisions, annual reports for environmental aid measures must contain, for each approved scheme, the following information as regards large undertakings:
— the names of the beneficiaries,
— the aid amount per beneficiary,
— the aid intensity,
— a description of the objective of the measure and of what type of environmental protection it is intended to promote,
— the sectors of activity where the aided projects are undertaken,
— an explanation of how the incentive effect has been respected, notably using the indicators and criteria mentioned in Chapter 5.

(194) In the case of tax exemptions or reductions, the Member State need provide only the legislative and/or regulatory text(s) establishing the aid and details of the categories of undertakings benefiting from tax reductions or exemptions and the sectors of the economy most affected by those tax exemptions/reductions.

(195) The annual reports will be published on the internet site of the Commission.

7.2. Transparency

(196) The Commission considers that further measures are necessary to improve the transparency of State aid in the Community. In particular, it is necessary to ensure that the Member States, economic operators, interested parties and the Commission itself have easy access to the full text of all applicable environmental aid schemes.

(197) This can easily be achieved through the establishment of linked internet sites. For this reason, when examining environmental aid schemes, the Commission will systematically require the Member State concerned to publish the full text of all final aid schemes on the internet and to communicate the internet address of the publication to the Commission. The scheme must not be applied before the information is published on the internet.

7.3. Monitoring and evaluation

(198) Member States must ensure that detailed records regarding the granting of aid for all environmental measures are maintained. Such records, which must contain all information necessary to establish that the eligible costs and maximum allowable aid intensity have been observed, must be maintained for 10 years from the date on which the aid was granted and be provided to the Commission upon request.

(199) The Commission will ask Member States to provide this information in order to carry out an evaluation of these Guidelines four years after their publication.[64]

Notes

[64] In that process, Member States may want to assist the Commission by providing their own ex post assessment of schemes and individual measures.

7.4. Appropriate measures

(200) The Commission herewith proposes to Member States, on the basis of Article [108(1) TFEU], the following appropriate measures concerning their respective existing environmental aid schemes:

Member States should amend, where necessary, such schemes in order to bring them into line with these Guidelines within 18 months after their publication, with the following exceptions:

  i) Member States should amend, where necessary, schemes concerning aid in the form of tax reduction or exemption covered by Directive 2003/96/EC before 31 December 2012;
  ii) the new thresholds mentioned in point 160 for individual projects will apply as from the first day following the publication of these Guidelines in the *Official Journal of the European Union*;
  iii) the duty to provide more detailed annual reports will apply to aid granted under existing aid schemes as of 1 January 2009.

(201) The Member States are invited to give their explicit unconditional agreement to these proposed appropriate measures within two months from the date of publication of these Guidelines in the *Official Journal of the European Union*. In the absence of any reply, the Commission will assume that the Member State in question does not agree with the proposed measures.

7.5. Application, validity and revision

(202) These Guidelines will be applied from the first day following their publication in the *Official Journal of the European Union* and will replace the Community Guidelines on State aid for environmental protection of 3 February 2001.[65]

Notes

[65] OJ C 37, 3.2.2001, p.3.

(203) These Guidelines will be applicable until 31 December 2014. After consulting the Member States, the Commission may amend them before that date on the basis of important competition policy or environmental policy considerations or in order to take account of other Community policies or international commitments. Such amendments might in particular be necessary in the light of future international agreements in the area of climate change and future European climate change legislation. Four years after the date of their publication, the Commission will undertake an evaluation of these Guidelines based on factual information and the results of wide consultations conducted by the Commission on the basis, notably, of data provided by the Member States. The results of the evaluation will be made available to the European Parliament, the Committee of the Regions and the European Economic and Social Committee and to the Member States.

(204) The Commission will apply these Guidelines to all notified aid measures in respect of which it is called upon to take a decision after the Guidelines are published in the *Official Journal*, even where the projects were notified prior to their publication. This includes individual aid granted under approved aid schemes and notified to the Commission pursuant to an obligation to notify such aid individually.

(205) In accordance with the Commission notice on the determination of the applicable rules for the assessment of unlawful State aid,[66] the Commission will apply, in the case of non-notified aid,

a) these Guidelines, if the aid was granted after their publication;

b) the guidelines applicable when the aid was granted, in all other cases.

Notes

[66] OJ C 119, 22.5.2002, p.22.

ANNEX

TABLE ILLUSTRATING THE AID INTENSITIES FOR INVESTMENT AID AS A PART OF ELIGIBLE COSTS

	Small enterprise	Medium-sized enterprise	Large enterprise
Aid for undertakings going beyond Community standards or increasing the level of environmental protection in the absence of Community standards	70% 80% if eco-innovation 100% if bidding process	60% 70% if eco-innovation 100% if bidding process	50% 60% if eco-innovation 100% if bidding process
Aid for environmental studies	70%	60%	50%
Aid for early adaptation to future Community standards —more than 3 years —between 1 and 3 years before the entry into force	25% 20%	20% 15%	15% 10%
Aid for waste management	70%	60%	50%
Aid for renewable energies	80% 100% if bidding process	70% 100% if bidding process	60% 100% if bidding process
Aid for energy savingAid for cogeneration installations	80% 100% if bidding process	70% 100% if bidding process	60% 100% if bidding process
Aid for district heating using conventional energy	70% 100% if bidding process	60% 100% if bidding process	50% 100% if bidding process
Aid the remediation of contaminated sites	100%	100%	100%
Aid for relocation of undertakings	70%	60%	50%

G18

COMMUNICATION FROM THE COMMISSION

Criteria for the analysis of the compatibility of State aid for
training subject to individual notification

(2009/C 188/01)

[NOTE]

Official Journal C 188, 11.8.2009, p.1

Celex No: 52009XC0811(01)

EUR-Lex permanent link: <http://eur-lex.europa.eu/LexUriServ/LexUriServ.do?uri=CELEX:5200
9XC0811(01):EN:NOT>

Notes

For reasons of space, this instrument is no longer reproduced in this volume. It remains available on Oxford Competition
Law.

EEA application: See EFTA Surveillance Authority Decision No 471/09/COL of 25 November 2009 amending, for the
74th time, the procedural and substantive rules in the field of State aid by introducing a new Chapter on criteria for the
analysis of the compatibility of State aid for training subject to individual notification, OJ L 231, 8.9.2011, p.23.

Commentary

Communication: F&N: 17.326

G19

COMMUNICATION FROM THE COMMISSION

Criteria for the analysis of the compatibility of State aid for the employment of
disadvantaged and disabled workers subject to individual notification

(2009/C 188/02)

[NOTE]

Official Journal C 188, 11.8.2006, p.6

Celex No: 52009XC0811(02)

EUR-Lex permanent link: <http://eur-lex.europa.eu/LexUriServ/LexUriServ.do?uri=CELEX:5200
9XC0811(02):EN:NOT>

Notes

For reasons of space, this instrument is no longer reproduced in this volume. It remains available on Oxford Competition Law.

EEA application: on 16 December 2009 the EFTA Surveillance Authority adopted parallel guidelines, available at the
following address:
<http://www.eftasurv.int/media/state-aid-guidelines/Criteria-for-the-analysis-of-the-compatibility-of-state-aid-
for-the-employment-of-disadvantaged-and-disabled-workers-subject-to-individual-notification.pdf>.

Commentary

Communication: F&N: 17.326

G20

COMMUNICATION FROM THE COMMISSION CONCERNING THE CRITERIA FOR AN IN-DEPTH ASSESSMENT OF REGIONAL AID TO LARGE INVESTMENT PROJECTS

(2009/C 223/02)

Official Journal C 223, 16.9.2009, p.3

Celex No: 52009XC0916(02)

EUR-Lex permanent link: <http://eur-lex.europa.eu/LexUriServ/LexUriServ.do?uri=CELEX:52009 XC0916%2802%29:EN:NOT>

Notes

On 28 June 2013, new Guidelines on regional State aid for 2014–2020 were adopted (OJ C 209, 23.7.2013, p.1).The new Guidelines will apply to aid granted from 1 July 2014. The current regional aid rules, which were due to expire at the end of 2013, are extended until 30 June 2014.

The new Guidelines are available on Oxford Competition Law and at <http://eur-lex.europa.eu/LexUriServ/LexUriServ. do?uri=CELEX:52013XC0723%2803%29:EN:NOT>.

EEA application: see EFTA Surveillance Authority Decision No 98/10/COL of 24 March 2010 amending, for the 81st time, the procedural and substantive rules in the field of State aid by introducing a new chapter on the criteria for an in-depth assessment of regional aid to large investment projects (OJ L 206, 2.8.2012, p.13).

Commentary

Communication: B&C: 4.008, 17.053

---

1. INTRODUCTION

1.1. General rules for regional aid measures

1. The Commission Guidelines on national regional aid for 2007–2013[1] ('RAG') clarify the general approach of the Commission regarding regional State aid. In accordance with the conditions laid down in the RAG, and notwithstanding the negative effects that regional State aid may have on trade and competition, the Commission may consider State aid compatible with the common market if it is granted to promote the economic development of certain disadvantaged regions within the European Union.

Notes

[1] OJ C 54, 4.3.2006.

---

2. In general, the RAG take account of the relative seriousness of the problems affecting the development of the regions concerned by introducing specific regional aid ceilings. These maximum aid intensities are graduated between 10% and 50% of eligible costs, based primarily on the GDP per capita of the regions concerned, but also allowing Member States some flexibility to take account of local conditions. The regional aid maps for each Member State are published on the Europa site.[1] These graduated aid intensities reflect, in essence, the balancing exercise which the Commission must perform between, on the one hand, the positive effects that regional investment aid can have, in particular in terms of promoting cohesion through attracting investment to disadvantaged areas, and, on the other hand, limiting the potential negative effects that can occur when granting such aid to individual undertakings, for example the negative impact for other economic operators and for regions whose relative competitive advantage is correspondingly diminished.

Notes
1 <http://ec.europa.eu/comm/competition/state_aid/regional_aid/regional_aid.html>.

3. A large investment project is an initial investment with an eligible expenditure above EUR 50 million.[1] Large investment projects are less affected by the handicaps that characterise disadvantaged areas than investment projects of a lesser scale. There is an increased risk that trade will be affected by large investment projects and thus a risk of a stronger distortion effect vis-à-vis competitors in other regions. Large investments also run the risk of the amount of aid exceeding the minimum necessary to compensate for the regional disadvantages, and there is the risk that State aid for these projects would lead to perverse effects such as inefficient location choices, higher distortion of competition and, since aid is a costly transfer from taxpayers in favour of aid recipients, net welfare losses, i.e. the cost of the aid exceeds the benefits to consumers and producers.

Notes
1 As defined in paragraph 60 and footnotes 54 and 55 of the RAG.

4. The RAG foresee specific rules for regional aid to large investment projects.[1] The RAG provide for the automatic, progressive scaling-down of regional aid ceilings for these large investment projects to limit distortions of competition to a level which can generally be assumed to be compensated by their benefits in terms of development of the regions concerned.[2]

Notes
1 Cf. section 4.3 of the RAG.
2 Cf. paragraph 67 of the RAG.

5. Moreover, Member States have to notify individually any aid for investment projects if the aid proposed is more than the maximum allowable amount of aid that an investment with eligible expenditure of EUR 100 million can receive under the applicable rules (notification threshold).[1] For these notified cases, the Commission verifies in particular the aid intensities, the compatibility with the general criteria of the RAG and whether the notified investment represents a major increase of production capacities, while at the same time addressing an underperforming or even declining market, or benefits firms with high market shares.

Notes
1 Cf. paragraph 64 of the RAG.

1.2. Regional aid measures subject to an in-depth assessment

6. Despite the automatic scaling-down, certain large amounts of regional aid for large investment projects could still have significant effects on trade, and may lead to substantive distortions of competition. For this reason, it was formerly Commission policy not to authorise aid for large investment projects above the following thresholds:[1]

— the aid beneficiary accounts for more than 25% of the sales of the product(s) concerned on the market(s) concerned, or

— the production capacity created by the project exceeds 5% of the market, while the growth rate of the market concerned is below the EEA GDP growth rate.

Notes
1 Cf. paragraph 24 of the 2002 Multisectoral framework on regional aid for large investment projects (OJ C 70, 19.3.2002, p.8, as amended in OJ C 263, 1.11.2003, p.3).

7. However, under the current RAG, the Commission has opted for a more individualised approach, which allows the cohesion and other benefits that can be derived from such projects to be taken into consideration, in as concrete a fashion as possible. Any such benefits must, however, be weighed against the likely negative effects on trade and competition, which should also be identified in as

Part G State Aids

concrete a manner as possible. Therefore, paragraph 68 of the RAG foresees that the Commission will conduct a formal investigation procedure pursuant to Article [108(2) TFEU]* for cases above the notification threshold and meeting one or both of the conditions set out in points (a) and (b) of paragraph 68 of the RAG (the in-depth assessment thresholds which are the same as the thresholds described in paragraph 6 of this communication). In these cases, the objective of the formal investigation is to carry out a detailed verification 'that the aid is necessary to provide an incentive effect for the investment and that the benefits of the aid measure outweigh the resulting distortion of competition and effect on trade between Member States'.[1]

Notes

* Ed note: please see the Note on the Lisbon Treaty at p.xvii in regard to article renumbering introduced by the Lisbon Treaty. Unless otherwise stated, all Treaty article numbers are the new numbers of the Treaty on the Functioning of the European Union (TFEU) and the Treaty on European Union (TEU).
[1] Cf. paragraph 68 of the RAG.

8. In footnote 63 of the RAG, the Commission announced its intention to 'draw up further guidance on the criteria it will take into account during this assessment'. Below, the Commission presents guidance as to the kind of information it may require and the methodology it will follow for measures subject to a detailed assessment. In line with the State Aid Action Plan,[1] the Commission will carry out an overall evaluation of the aid based on a balance of its positive and negative effects in order to determine whether, as a whole, the aid measure can be approved.

Notes
[1] Cf. paragraphs 11 and 20 of the SAAP (COM(2005) 107 final).

9. The detailed assessment should be proportionate to the potential distortions which may be created by the aid. This means that the scope of the analysis will depend on the nature of the case. Therefore, the nature and the level of the evidence required will also depend on the features of each individual case. Also, while respecting the provisions governing the conduct of the formal investigation as set out in Articles 6 and 7 of Council Regulation (EC) No 659/1999 of 22 March 1999 laying down detailed rules for the application of Article [108 TFEU],[1] the Commission may, inter alia, ask the Member State to provide independent studies to confirm the information contained in the notification, or seek input from other economic operators active in the relevant markets or from experts in regional development. Moreover, comments by interested parties are welcomed during formal investigations. The Commission will identify the key issues on which it is seeking input in the opening of the procedure.

Notes
[1] OJ L 83, 27.3.1999, p.1.

10. The present communication is intended to ensure the transparency and predictability of the Commission decision-making process and equal treatment of Member States. The Commission reserves the possibility to amend and review this guidance in the light of case experience.

2. POSITIVE EFFECTS OF THE AID

2.1. *Objective of the aid*

11. Regional aid has an objective of common interest which reflects equity considerations, namely furthering economic cohesion by helping to reduce the gap between the development levels of the various regions of the Community. Paragraph 2 of the RAG sets out that: 'By addressing the handicaps of the disadvantaged regions, national regional aid promotes the economic, social and territorial cohesion of Member States and the European Union as a whole'. Paragraph 3 of the RAG adds that: 'Regional investment aid is designed to assist the development of the most disadvantaged regions by supporting investment and job creation. It promotes the expansion and diversification of the economic activities of enterprises located in the less-favoured regions, in particular by encouraging firms to set up new establishments there'.

12. For those large investment projects that meet the in-depth assessment thresholds, the Member State will be requested to demonstrate that the aid will address the equity objective in question. The Member State will therefore need to substantiate the contribution of the investment project to the development of the region concerned.

13. While the primary objective of regional aid is to foster equity concerns as economic cohesion, regional aid may also address issues of market failure. Regional handicaps may be linked to market failures such as imperfect information, co-ordination problems, difficulties for the beneficiary to appropriate investments in public goods or externalities from investments. Where, apart from equity objectives, regional aid also addresses efficiency concerns, the overall positive effect of the aid will be considered greater.

14. The following non-exhaustive list of indicative criteria can be used to demonstrate the regional contribution of the aid, in so far as it leads to attracting additional investment and activity in the region. These positive effects of the aid can be both direct (e.g. direct jobs created) and indirect (e.g. local innovation).

    — The number of direct *jobs* created by the investment is an important indicator of the contribution to regional development. The quality of the jobs created and the required skill level should also be considered.

    — An even higher number of new jobs might be created in the local (sub-)supplier network, helping to better integrate the investment in the region concerned and ensuring more widespread spillover effects. The number of *indirect jobs* created will therefore also be taken into account.

    — A commitment by the beneficiary to enter into widespread *training* activities to improve the skills (general and specific) of its workforce will be considered as a factor that contributes to regional development. Emphasis will also be put on training that improves the knowledge and employability of workers outside the firm. General or specific training for which training aid is approved will not be counted as a positive effect of the regional aid to avoid double counting.

    — External economies of scale or other benefits from a regional development viewpoint may arise as a result of proximity (*clustering effect*). Clustering of firms in the same industry allows individual plants to specialise more which leads to increased efficiency. Physical proximity facilitates the exchange of information, ideas and knowledge between firms. A concentration of economic activities attracts many job seekers, which assures a large pool of workers with different skills available to firms. Access to legal and commercial services is ensured which enhances productivity. In general, a concentration of economic activities may again attract other investments which in turn increase the positive spillover effects (virtuous circle).

    — Investments embody technical knowledge and can be the source of a significant *transfer of technology (knowledge spillovers)*. Investments taking place in technology intensive industries are more likely to involve technology transfer to the recipient region. The level and the specificity of the knowledge dissemination are also important in this regard.

    — The projects' contribution to the region's ability to create new technology through local innovation can also be considered. Co-operation of the new production facility with *local higher education institutions* can be considered positively in this respect.

    — The *duration* of the investment and possible future follow-on investments are an indication of a durable engagement of a company in the region.

15. The Member States are, in particular, invited to rely on evaluations of past State aid schemes or measures, impact assessments made by the granting authorities, expert opinions and other possible studies related to the investment project under assessment. The business plan of the aid beneficiary could provide information on the number of jobs created, salaries paid (increase in household wealth as spill-over effect), volume of sales from local producers, turnover generated by the investment and benefiting the region possibly through additional tax revenues.

16. If relevant, the relationship between the planned investment project and the national strategic reference framework, as well as the relationship between the project and the operational programmes co-financed by the structural funds, also have to be considered. In this regard, the Commission might specifically take account of any Commission Decision relating to the measure in the context of the analysis of major projects under the structural funds or the

Cohesion Fund.[1] Such a decision is, among other elements, based on 'a cost-benefit analysis, including a risk assessment and the foreseeable impact on the sector concerned and on the social-economic situation of the Member State and/or the region and, when possible and where appropriate, of other regions of the Community'.

Notes

[1] Cf. section 2 of Council Regulation (EC) No 1083/2006 of 11 July 2006 laying down general provisions on the ERDF, the European Social Fund and the Cohesion Fund and repealing Regulation (EC) No 1260/1999 (OJ L 210, 31.7.2006, p.25).

2.2. Appropriateness of the aid instrument

17. State aid in the form of investment subsidies is not the only policy instrument available to Member States to support investment and job creation in disadvantaged regions. Member States can use general measures such as infrastructure development, enhancing the quality of education and training, or improvements in the general business environment.

18. Measures for which the Member State considered other policy options, and for which the advantages of using a selective instrument such as State aid for a specific company are established, are considered to constitute an appropriate instrument. The Commission will in particular take account of any impact assessment of the proposed measure the Member State may have made.

2.3. Incentive effect

19. Analysing the incentive effect of the aid measure is one of the most important elements in the in-depth assessment of regional aid to large investment projects. The Commission will assess whether the proposed aid is necessary to produce 'a real incentive effect to undertake investments which would not otherwise be made in the assisted areas'.[1] This assessment will take place at two levels: first, at a general, procedural level, and, second, at a more detailed, economic level.

Notes

[1] Cf. paragraph 38 of the RAG.

20. In paragraph 38, the RAG contain general criteria to provide a formal assessment of the incentive effect of regional aid. These criteria apply to all regional aid, not only regional aid for large investment projects.

21. In the case of regional aid to large investment projects covered by this communication, the Commission will verify in detail 'that the aid is necessary to provide an incentive effect for the investment'.[1] The objective of this detailed assessment is to determine whether the aid actually contributes to changing the behaviour of the beneficiary, so that it undertakes (additional) investment in the assisted region concerned. There are many valid reasons for a company to locate in a certain region, even without any aid being granted.

Notes

[1] Cf. paragraph 68 of the RAG.

22. Having regard to the equity objective deriving from cohesion policy and as far as the aid contributes to achieving this objective, an incentive effect can be proven in two possible scenarios:

1. The aid gives an incentive to adopt a positive investment decision because an investment that would otherwise not be profitable for the company at any location can take place in the assisted region.[1]

2. The aid gives an incentive to opt to locate a planned investment in the relevant region rather than elsewhere because it compensates for the net handicaps and costs linked to a location in the assisted region.

Notes

[1] Such investments may create conditions allowing further investments that are able to survive without additional aid.

23. The Member State should demonstrate to the Commission the existence of an incentive effect of the aid. It will need to provide clear evidence that the aid effectively has an impact on the investment choice or the location choice. It will have to specify which scenario applies. In order to permit a comprehensive assessment, the Member State will have to provide not only information concerning the aided project but also a comprehensive description of the counterfactual scenario, in which no aid would be granted by the Member State to the beneficiary.

24. In scenario 1, the Member State could provide proof of the incentive effect of the aid by providing company documents that show that the investment would not be profitable without the aid and that no other location than the assisted region concerned could be envisaged.

25. In scenario 2, the Member State could provide proof of the incentive effect of the aid by providing company documents that show a comparison has been made between the costs and benefits of locating in the assisted region concerned with an alternative region. Such comparative scenarios will have to be considered to be realistic by the Commission.

26. The Member States are, in particular, invited to rely on risk assessments (including the assessment of location-specific risks), financial reports, internal business plans, expert opinions and other studies related to the investment project under assessment. Documents containing information on demand forecasts, cost forecasts, financial forecasts, documents that are submitted to an investment committee and that elaborate on various investment scenarios, or documents provided to the financial markets could help to verify the incentive effect.

27. In this context, and in particular in scenario 1, the level of profitability can be evaluated by reference to methodologies which are standard practice in the particular industry concerned, and which may include: methods to evaluate the net present value of the project (NPV), the internal rate of return (IRR) or the return on capital employed (ROCE).

28. If the aid does not change the behaviour of the beneficiary by stimulating (additional) investment in the assisted region concerned, there is a lack of incentive effect to achieve the regional objective. If the aid has no incentive effect to achieve the regional objective, such aid can be considered as free money for the company. Therefore, in an in-depth assessment of regional aid to large investment projects, aid will not be approved in cases where it appears that the same investment would take place in the region even without the aid.

2.4. Proportionality of the aid

29. For the regional aid to be proportional, the amount and intensity of the aid must be limited to the minimum needed for the investment to take place in the assisted region.

30. The RAG generally ensure that regional aid is proportional to the seriousness of the problems affecting the assisted regions by applying regional aid ceilings in general and an automatic, progressive scaling-down of these regional aid ceilings for large investment projects (see paragraphs 1 and 3).

31. For regional aid cases that require an in-depth assessment, a more detailed verification of this general principle of proportionality contained in the RAG is necessary.

32. In scenario 1, for an investment incentive, the aid will generally be considered proportionate if, because of the aid, the return on investment is in line with the normal rate of return applied by the company in other investment projects, with the cost of capital of the company as a whole or with returns commonly observed in the industry concerned.

33. In scenario 2, for a location incentive, the aid will generally be considered proportionate if it equals the difference between the net costs for the beneficiary company to invest in the assisted region and the net costs to invest in the alternative region(s). All such costs and benefits need to be taken into account, including for example administrative costs, transport costs, training costs not covered by training aid and also wage differences.

34. Ultimately, these net costs which are considered to be related to the regional handicaps result in a lower profitability of the investment. For that reason, calculations used for the analysis of the incentive effect, can also be used to evaluate whether the aid is proportionate.

35. The Member State needs to demonstrate the proportionality on the basis of appropriate documentation such as that mentioned in paragraph 26.

36. In no case can the aid intensity be higher than the regional aid ceilings corrected by the scaling-down mechanism, as indicated in the RAG.

3. NEGATIVE EFFECTS OF THE AID

37. To assess market shares and potential overcapacity in a market in structural decline, the Commission needs to define the relevant product market and geographic market. Thus, usually,[1] the relevant markets will already have been defined for regional aid measures subject to an in-depth assessment.

Notes

[1] Where doubts remain as to the appropriate definition of the relevant markets, the Commission will identify these in the decision to initiate the formal investigation procedure pursuant to Article [108(2) TFEU].

38. Two main indicators of potential negative effects arising from the aid are already identified in paragraph 68 of the RAG, namely high market shares and potential overcapacity in a market in structural decline. They are linked to two theories of harm in a competition context, respectively the creation of market power and the creation or maintenance of inefficient market structures. A prima facie measurement of these two indicators will already have taken place before the opening of the investigation procedure. In order to provide all the elements for the final balancing exercise, the assessment of the two indicators will be refined in the in-depth assessment. A third indicator of potential negative effects arising from the aid that will be assessed in depth is the influence of the aid on trade. Although these three indicators are considered as the main negative effects potentially arising from regional aid to a large investment project, the Commission does not exclude that other indicators might also be relevant in specific cases.

39. The Commission will place particular emphasis on the negative effects linked with the notion of market power and overcapacity in cases where the aid gives an incentive to change the investment decision, so that without the aid no investment would take place (scenario 1 of the incentive effect).

40. If, however, the counterfactual analysis suggests that without the aid the investment would have gone ahead in any case, albeit possibly in another location (scenario 2), and if the aid is proportional, possible indications of distortions such as a high market share and an increase in capacity in an underperforming market would in principle be the same regardless of the aid.

3.1. Crowding-out of private investment

3.1.1. Market power

41. When establishing its optimum investment level, in markets with a limited number of market players (a situation typical for large investment projects) each firm takes into account the investment carried out by its competitors. If aid induces a particular company to invest more, competitors may react by reducing their own expenditure in that area. In that case aid leads to a crowding-out of private investment. If, as a result, such competitors are weakened or even have to exit, the aid distorts competition. In this regard, as discussed in paragraph 38, the RAG distinguishes between cases where the aid beneficiary has market power and cases where the aid leads to a significant capacity expansion in a declining market.

42. In general, any aid to one beneficiary in a concentrated market is more likely to distort competition, since the decision of each firm is likely to affect its competitors more directly. This is especially the case if a dominant market player is subsidised. As a result, if, due to the aid, the beneficiary can maintain or increase its market power,[1] regional aid for large investment projects may have a deterrent effect on competitors' investment decisions and thereby generate distortions of competition. This would be to the detriment of consumers. Therefore, the Commission wants to limit State aid to companies with market power.

Notes

[1] Market power is the power to influence market prices, output, the variety or quality of goods and services, or other parameters of competition on the market for a significant period of time.

43. For all regional aid cases that trigger the notification threshold (paragraph 64 of the RAG), the Commission needs to assess (paragraph 68(a) of the RAG) the share of the aid beneficiary (or the group to which it belongs) of the sales of the product or products concerned on the relevant

product market(s) and geographic market(s). However, market shares can only give a preliminary indication of possible problems. Therefore, in an in-depth assessment, the Commission will also take account of other factors, where relevant, including for example the market structure by looking at the concentration in the market,[1] possible barriers to entry,[2] buyer power[3] and barriers to exit.

Notes

[1] For this purpose, the Commission may consider the Herfindahl-Hirschman index (HHI). This index provides a basic analysis of the market structure. In a market with few market players where several of them have a relatively high market share, a high market share of the beneficiary might be less of a concern for competition.

[2] These entry barriers include legal barriers (in particular intellectual property rights), economies of scale and scope, access barriers to networks and infrastructure. Where the aid concerns a market where the aid beneficiary is an incumbent, possible barriers to entry may exacerbate the potential market power wielded by the aid beneficiary and thus the possible negative effects of that market power.

[3] Where there are strong buyers in the market, it is less likely that an aid beneficiary can increase prices vis-à-vis these strong buyers.

44. The Commission will take account of the market shares and other related factors before and after the investment (normally the year before the investment starts and the year after full production is reached). When assessing negative effects in detail, the Commission will take into account that, while some investment projects are carried out over a relatively short time-scale of one or two years, most large investment projects have a much longer duration. Therefore, in most cases, long-term analyses of the evolution of markets are necessary. However, the Commission will acknowledge the fact that those long-term analyses are more speculative, particularly in the case of volatile markets or markets undergoing rapid technological change. Therefore, the more long-term and thus the more speculative the analysis is, the less weight will be attached to the possible negative effect of market power or the possibility of exclusionary behaviour.

3.1.2. Creating or maintaining inefficient market structures

45. It is a sign of effective competition if inefficient firms are forced to exit a market. In the long term, this process fosters technological progress and an efficient use of scarce resources in the economy. However, a substantial capacity expansion induced by State aid in an underperforming market might unduly distort competition as the overcapacity could lead to a squeeze on profit margins and a reduction of competitors' capacity or even their exit from the market. This might lead to a situation where competitors that would otherwise be able to stay on are forced out of the market as a consequence of State aid. It may also prevent low cost firms from entering and it may weaken incentives for competitors to innovate. This results in inefficient market structures which are also harmful to consumers in the long run.

46. In order to evaluate whether the aid may serve to create or maintain inefficient market structures, as pointed out above, the Commission will take into account the additional production capacity created by the project and whether the market is underperforming.[1] According to the RAG, additional capacity will only be considered problematic if it is created in an underperforming market and if the additional capacity is more than five per cent of the market concerned.

Notes

[1] In this context, a market is meant to be 'underperforming' if its average annual growth rate in the reference period does not exceed the growth rate of EEA's GDP.

47. Since capacity created in a market in absolute decline will normally be more distortive than capacity created in a market in relative decline, the Commission will distinguish between cases for which, from a long-term perspective, the relevant market is structurally in decline (i.e. shows a negative growth rate), and cases for which the relevant market is in relative decline (i.e. shows a positive growth rate, but does not exceed a benchmark growth rate (see paragraph 48)). Where the capacity created by the project takes place in a market which is structurally in absolute decline, the Commission will consider it to be a negative element in the balancing test that is unlikely to be compensated by any positive elements. The long term benefit for the region concerned is also more doubtful in such a case.

48. Underperformance of the market will normally be measured compared to the EEA GDP over the last five years before the start of the project (benchmark rate). Data on past performance are more readily available and less speculative then future projections. Nevertheless, in the in-depth assessment, the Commission may also take into account expected future trends since the increase in capacity will exert its effect in the years following the investment. Indicators could be the foreseeable future growth of the market concerned and the resulting expected capacity utilisation rates, as well as the likely impact of the capacity increase on competitors through its effects on prices and profit margins.

49. Experience also shows that, in some cases, considering the growth of the product concerned in the EEA may not be the appropriate benchmark to assess the effects of aid, in particular if the market is considered to be worldwide and there is only limited production or consumption of the products concerned within the EEA. In such cases, the Commission will take a broader view of the effect of the aid on market structures, having regard, in particular, to its potential to crowd out EEA producers.

3.2. Negative effects on trade

50. As explained in paragraph 2 of the RAG, the geographical specificity of regional aid distinguishes it from other forms of horizontal aid. It is a particular characteristic of regional aid that it is intended to influence the choice made by investors about where to locate investment projects. When regional aid is off-setting the additional costs stemming from the regional handicaps and supports additional investment in assisted areas, it is contributing not only to the development of the region, but also to cohesion and ultimately benefits the whole Community.[1] With regard to the potential negative location effects of regional aid, these are already recognised and restricted to a degree by RAG and the regional aid maps, which define exhaustively the areas eligible to grant regional aid, taking account of the equity and cohesion policy objectives, and the eligible aid intensities. Aid may not be granted to attract investments outside of these areas. When appraising large investment projects subject to this guidance, the Commission should have all necessary information to consider whether State aid would result in a substantial loss of jobs in existing locations within the Community.

Notes

[1] In particular, additional activity or increased standard of living in the assisted area may increase demand for products and services originating from other parts of the Community.

51. More concretely, when investments adding production capacity in a market are made possible because of State aid, there is a risk that production or investment in other regions of the Community may be negatively affected. This is particularly likely if the capacity increase exceeds market growth, which will generally be the case for large investment projects meeting the second criteria of paragraph 68 of the RAG. The negative effects on trade, corresponding to the lost economic activity in the regions affected by the aid, may be felt through lost jobs in the market concerned, at the level of subcontractors[1] and as a result of lost positive externalities (e.g. clustering effect, knowledge spill-overs, education and training, etc.).

Notes

[1] Especially if they operate in local markets in the region.

4. BALANCING THE EFFECTS OF THE AID

52. Having established that the aid is necessary as an incentive to carry out the investment in the region concerned, the Commission will balance the positive effects of the regional investment aid to a large investment project with its negative effects. Careful consideration will be given to the overall effects of the aid on cohesion within the Community. The Commission will not use the criteria set out in this communication mechanically but will make an overall assessment of their relative importance. In this balancing exercise, no single element is determinant, nor can any set of elements be regarded as sufficient on its own to ensure compatibility.

53. In particular, the Commission considers that attracting an investment to a poorer region (as defined by the higher regional aid ceiling) is more beneficial for cohesion within the Community than if the same investment is located in a more advantaged region. Thus, under scenario 2, where evidence has to be given of an alternative location, an assessment that without aid the investment would have been located to a poorer region (more regional handicaps — higher maximum regional aid intensity) or to a region that is considered to have the same regional handicaps as the target region (same maximum regional aid intensity) will constitute a negative element in the overall balancing test that is unlikely to be compensated by any positive elements because it runs counter to the very rationale of regional aid. On the other hand, the positive effects of regional aid which merely compensate for the difference in net costs relative to a more developed alternative investment location (and thus fulfils the proportionality test above, in addition to the 'positive effect' requirements as to objective, appropriateness and incentive effect), will normally be considered, under the balancing test, to outweigh any negative effects in the alternative location for new investment.

54. However, where there is credible evidence that the State aid would result in a substantial loss of jobs in existing locations within the European Union, which would otherwise have been likely to be preserved in the medium term, the social and economic effects on that existing location will have to be taken into account in the balancing exercise.

55. The Commission may, following the formal investigation procedure laid down in Article 6 of Regulation (EC) No 659/1999, close the procedure with a decision pursuant to Article 7 of that Regulation.

56. The Commission may decide either to approve, condition or prohibit the aid.[1] If it adopts a conditional decision pursuant to Article 7(4) of that Regulation, it may attach conditions to limit the potential distortion of competition and ensure proportionality. In particular, it may reduce the notified amount of aid or aid intensity to a level considered to be proportional and thus compatible with the common market.

Notes

[1] When the aid is granted on the basis of an existing regional aid scheme, it is however to be noted that the Member State retains the possibility to grant such aid up to the level which corresponds to the maximum allowable amount that an investment with eligible expenditure of EUR 100 million can receive under the applicable rules.

G21

COMMISSION COMMUNICATION

on State aid elements in sales of land and buildings by public authorities

(97/C 209/03)

(Text with EEA relevance)

Official Journal C 209, 10.7.1997, p.3

Celex No: 31997Y0710(01)

EUR-Lex permanent link: <http://eur-lex.europa.eu/LexUriServ/LexUriServ.do?uri=CELEX:3199 7Y0710(01):EN:NOT>

Notes

EEA application: for the corresponding EEA provision, see the EFTA Surveillance Authority's Procedural and Substantive Rules in the Field of State Aid (Guidelines on the application and interpretation of Articles 61 and 62 of the

EEA Agreement and Article 1 of Protocol 3 to the Surveillance and Court Agreement), Part III, Chapter 18B (as introduced by EFTA Surveillance Authority Decision No 275/99/COL of 17 November 1999 (OJ L 137, 8.6.2000, p.28 and EEA Supplement No 26, 8.6.2000)).

Commentary
Communication: **B&C:** 17.036, 17.063 **F&N:** 17.80

1. INTRODUCTION

On a number of occasions in recent years the Commission has investigated sales of publicly owned land and buildings in order to establish whether there was an element of State aid in favour of the buyers. The Commission has drawn up general guidance to Member States in order to make its general approach with regard to the problem of State aid through sales of land and buildings by public authorities transparent and to reduce the number of cases it has to examine.

The following guidance to Member States:

— describes a simple procedure that allows Member States to handle sales of land and buildings in a way that automatically precludes the existence of State aid,

— specifies clearly cases of sales of land and buildings that should be notified to the Commission to allow for assessment of whether or not a certain transaction contains aid and, if so, whether or not the aid is compatible with the common market,

— enables the Commission to deal expeditiously with any complaints or submissions from third parties drawing its attention to cases of alleged aid connected to sales of land and buildings.

This guidance takes account of the fact that in most Member States budgetary provisions exist to ensure that public property is in principle not sold below its value. Therefore, the procedural precautions recommended to avoid State aid rules coming into play are formulated in a way that should normally allow Member States to comply with the guidance without changing their domestic procedures.

The guidance concerns only sales of publicly owned land and buildings. It does not concern the public acquisition of land and buildings or the letting or leasing of land and buildings by public authorities. Such transactions may also include State aid elements.

The guidance does not affect specific provisions or practices of Member States intended to promote the quality of and access to private housing.

2. PRINCIPLES

1. Sale through an unconditional bidding procedure

A sale of land and buildings following a sufficiently well-publicized, open and unconditional bidding procedure, comparable to an auction, accepting the best or only bid is by definition at market value and consequently does not contain State aid. The fact that a different valuation of the land and buildings existed prior to the bidding procedure, e.g. for accounting purposes or to provide a proposed initial minimum bid, is irrelevant.

(a) An offer is "sufficiently well-publicized" when it is repeatedly advertised over a reasonably long period (two months or more) in the national press, estate gazettes or other appropriate publications and through real-estate agents addressing a broad range of potential buyers, so that it can come to the notice of all potential buyers. The intended sale of land and buildings, which in view of their high value or other features may attract investors operating on a Europe-wide or international scale, should be announced in publications which have a regular international circulation. Such offers should also be made known through agents addressing clients on a Europe-wide or international scale.

(b) An offer is "unconditional" when any buyer, irrespective of whether or not he runs a business or of the nature of his business, is generally free to acquire the land and buildings and to use it for his own purposes, Restrictions may be imposed for the prevention of public nuisance, for reasons of environmental protection or to avoid purely speculative bids. Urban and regional planning restrictions imposed on the owner pursuant to domestic law on the use of the land and buildings do not affect the unconditional nature of an offer.

(c) If it is a condition of the sale that the future owner is to assume special obligations — other than those arising from general domestic law or decision of the planning authorities or those relating to the general protection and conservation of the environment and to public health — for the benefit of the public authorities or in the general public interest, the offer is to be regarded as "unconditional" within the meaning of the above definition only if all potential buyers would have to, and be able to, meet that obligation, irrespective of whether or not they run a business or of the nature of their business.

2. Sale without an unconditional bidding procedure

(a) Independent expert evaluation

If public authorities intend not to use the procedure described under 1, an independent evaluation should be carried out by one or more independent asset valuers prior to the sale negotiations in order to establish the market value on the basis of generally accepted market indicators and valuation standards. The market price thus established is the minimum purchase price that can be agreed without granting State aid.

An "asset valuer" is a person of good repute who:

— has obtained an appropriate degree at a recognized centre of learning or an equivalent academic qualification,
— has suitable experience and is competent in valuing land and buildings in the location and of the category of the asset.

If in any Member State there are not appropriate established academic qualifications, the asset valuer should be a member of a recognized professional body concerned with the valuation of land and buildings and either:

— be appointed by the courts or an authority of equivalent status,
— have as a minimum a recognized certificate of secondary education and sufficient level of training with at least three years post-qualification practical experience in, and with knowledge of, valuing land and buildings in that particular locality.

The valuer should be independent in the carrying out of his tasks, i.e. public authorities should not be entitled to issue orders as regards the result of the valuation. State valuation offices and public officers or employees are to be regarded as independent provided that undue influence on their findings is effectively excluded.

"Market value" means the price at which land and buildings could be sold under private contract between a willing seller and an arm's length buyer on the date of valuation, it being assumed that the property is publicly exposed to the market, that market conditions permit orderly disposal and that a normal period, having regard to the nature of the property, is available for the negotiation of the sale.[1]

Notes
[1] Article 49(2) of Council Directive 91/674/EEC (OJ No L 374, 31.12.1991, p.7).

(b) Margin

If, after a reasonable effort to sell the land and buildings at the market value, it is clear that the value set by the valuer cannot be obtained, a divergence of up to 5% from that value can be deemed to be in line with market conditions. If, after a further reasonable time, it is clear that the land and buildings cannot be sold at the value set by the valuer less this 5% margin, a new valuation may be carried out which is to take account of the experience gained and of the offers received.

(c) Special obligations

Special obligations that relate to the land and buildings and not to the purchaser or his economic activities may be attached to the sale in the public interest provided that every potential buyer is required, and in principle is able, to fulfil them, irrespective of whether or not he runs a business or of the nature of his business. The economic disadvantage of such obligations should be evaluated separately by independent valuers and may be set off against the purchase price. Obligations whose fulfilment would at least partly be in the buyer's own interest should be evaluated with that fact in mind: there may, for example, be an advantage in terms of advertising, sport or arts sponsorship, image, improvement of the buyer's own environment, or recreational facilities for the buyer's own staff.

The economic burden related to obligations incumbent on all landowners under the ordinary law are not to be discounted from the purchase price (these would include, for example, care and maintenance of the land and buildings as part of the ordinary social obligations of property ownership or the payment of taxes and similar charges).

(d) Cost to the authorities

The primary cost to the public authorities of acquiring land and buildings is an indicator for the market value unless a significant period of time elapsed between the purchase and the sale of the land and buildings. In principle, therefore, the market value should not be set below primary costs during a period of at least three years after acquisition unless the independent valuer specifically identified a general decline in market prices for land and buildings in the relevant market.

3. Notification

Member States should consequently notify to the Commission, without prejudice to the *de minimis* rule,[2] the following transactions to allow it to establish whether State aid exists and, if so, to assess its compatibility with the common market.

(a) any sale that was not concluded on the basis of an open and unconditional bidding procedure, accepting the best or only bid; and

(b) any sale that was, in the absence of such procedure, conducted at less than market value as established by independent valuers.

Notes
[2] OJ No C 68, 6.3.1996, p.9.

---

4. Complaints

When the Commission receives a complaint or other submission from third parties alleging that there was a State aid element in an agreement for the sale of land and buildings by public authorities, it will assume that no State aid is involved if the information supplied by the Member State concerned shows that the above principles were observed.

Commentary
Section II(2): **B&C:** 17.036

G22

COMMUNICATION OF THE COMMISSION TO THE MEMBER STATES

pursuant to Article [108(1) of the Treaty on the Functioning of the European Union] applying Articles [107 and 108] of the Treaty to short-term export-credit insurance

(97/C 281/03)

[NOTE]

(Text with EEA relevance)

Official Journal C 281, 17.9.1997, p.4

Celex No: 31997Y0917(01)

EUR-Lex permanent link: <http://eur-lex.europa.eu/LexUriServ/LexUriServ.do?uri=CELEX:31997Y0917(01):EN:NOT>

Notes

With effect from 1 January 2013, this Communication has been superseded by the 2012 Communication from the Commission to the Member States on the application of Articles 107 and 108 of the Treaty on the Functioning of the European Union to short-term export-credit insurance, OJ C 392, 19.12.2012, p.1. The 2012 Communication is reproduced at G24A.

EEA application: for the corresponding EEA provision, see the EFTA Surveillance Authority's Procedural and Substantive Rules in the Field of State Aid (Guidelines on the application and interpretation of Articles 61 and 62 of the EEA Agreement and Article 1 of Protocol 3 to the Surveillance and Court Agreement), Part III, Chapter 17A and Annex XI (as introduced by EFTA Surveillance Authority Decision No 45/98/COL of 4 March 1998 (OJ L 120, 23.4.1998, p.27 and EEA Supplement No 16), as subsequently re-enacted and amended).

Commentary

Communication: B&C: 17.063

G23

COMMISSION NOTICE

on the application of the State aid rules to measures relating to direct business taxation

(98/C 384/03)

(Text with EEA relevance)

Official Journal C 384, 10.12.1998, p.3

Celex No: 31998Y1210(01)

EUR-Lex permanent link: <http://eur-lex.europa.eu/LexUriServ/LexUriServ.do?uri= CELEX: 31998Y1210(01)EN:NOT>

Notes

EEA application: for the corresponding EEA provision, see the EFTA Surveillance Authority's Procedural and Substantive Rules in the Field of State Aid (Guidelines on the application and interpretation of Articles 61 and 62 of the EEA Agreement and Article 1 of Protocol 3 to the Surveillance and Court Agreement), Part III, Chapter 17B (as introduced by EFTA Surveillance Authority Decision No 149/99/COL of 30 June 1999 (OJ L 137, 8.6.2000, p.20 and EEA Supplement No 26, 8.6.2000)).

Commentary
Notice: B&C: 17.019, 17.063 F&N: 17.91, 17.102

INTRODUCTION

1. On 1 December 1997, following a wide-ranging discussion on the need for coordinated action at Community level to tackle harmful tax competition, the Council (Ecofin) adopted a series of conclusions and agreed a resolution on a code of conduct for business taxation (hereinafter "code of conduct").[1] On that occasion, the Commission undertook to draw up guidelines on the application of Articles [107 and 108]* of the Treaty to measures relating to direct business taxation and committed itself "to the strict application of the aid rules concerned". The code of conduct aims to improve transparency in the tax area through a system of information exchanges between Member States and of assessment of any tax measures that may be covered by it. For their part, the State aid provisions of the Treaty will also contribute through their own mechanism to the objective of tackling harmful tax competition.

Notes

* Ed note: please see the Note on the Lisbon Treaty at p.xvii in regard to article renumbering introduced by the Lisbon Treaty.
[1] OJ C 2, 6.1.1998, p.1.

2. The Commission's undertaking regarding State aid in the form of tax measures forms part of the wider objective of clarifying and reinforcing the application of the State aid rules in order to reduce distortions of competition in the single market. The principle of incompatibility with the common market and the derogations from that principle apply to aid "in any form whatsoever", including certain tax measures. However, the question whether a tax measure can be qualified as aid under Article [107(1)] of the Treaty calls for clarification which this notice proposes to provide. Such clarification is particularly important in view of the procedural requirements that stem from designation as aid and of the consequences where Member States fail to comply with such requirements.

Commentary
para 2: B&C: 17.037

3. Following the completion of the single market and the liberalisation of capital movements, it has also become apparent that there is a need to examine the particular effects of aid granted in the form of tax measures and to spell out the consequences as regards assessment of the aid's compatibility with the common market.[2] The establishment of economic and monetary union and the consolidation of national budgets which it entails will make it even more essential to have strict control of State aid in whatever form it may take. Similarly, account must also be taken, in the common interest, of the major repercussions which some aid granted through tax systems may have on the revenue of other Member States.

Notes
[2] See action plan for the single market, CSE(97) 1, 4 June 1997, strategic target 2, action 1.

4. In addition to the objective of ensuring that Commission decisions are transparent and predictable, this notice also aims to ensure consistency and equality of treatment between Member States. The Commission intends, as the code of conduct notes, to examine or re-examine case by case, on the basis of this notice, the tax arrangements in force in the Member States.

A. Community powers of action

5. The Treaty empowers the Community to take measures to eliminate various types of distortion that harm the proper functioning of the common market. It is thus essential to distinguish between the different types of distortion.

6. Some general tax measures may impede the proper functioning of the internal market. In the case of such measures, the Treaty provides, on the one hand, for the possibility of harmonising Member States' tax provisions on the basis of Article [115] (Council directives, adopted unanimously). On the other, some disparities between planned or existing general provisions in Member States may distort competition and create distortions that need to be eliminated on the basis of Articles [116] and [117] (consultation of the relevant Member States by the Commission; if necessary, Council directives adopted by a qualified majority).

7. The distortions of competition deriving from State aid fall under a system of prior Commission authorisation, subject to review by the Community judicature. Pursuant to Article [108(3)], State aid measures must be notified to the Commission. Member States may not put their proposed aid measures into effect until the Commission has approved them. The Commission examines the compatibility of aid not in terms of the form which it may take, but in terms of its effect. It may decide that the Member State must amend or abolish aid which the Commission finds to be incompatible with the common market. Where aid has already been implemented in breach of the procedural rules, the Member State must in principle recover it from the recipient(s).

B. Application of Article [107(1) TFEU] to tax measures

8. Article [107(1)] states that "any aid granted by a Member State or through State resources in any form whatsoever which distorts or threatens to distort competition by favouring certain undertakings or the production of certain goods shall, in so far as it affects trade between Member States, be incompatible with the common market". In applying the Community rules on State aid, it is irrelevant whether the measure is a tax measure, since Article [107] applies to aid measures "in any form whatsoever". To be termed aid, within the meaning of Article [107], a measure must meet the cumulative criteria described below.

9. Firstly, the measure must confer on recipients an advantage which relieves them of charges that are normally borne from their budgets. The advantage may be provided through a reduction in the firm's tax burden in various ways, including:
— a reduction in the tax base (such as special deductions, special or accelerated depreciation arrangements or the entering of reserves on the balance sheet),
— a total or partial reduction in the amount of tax (such as exemption or a tax credit),
— deferment, cancellation or even special rescheduling of tax debt.

Commentary
para 9: **B&C:** 17.031

10. Secondly, the advantage must be granted by the State or through State resources. A loss of tax revenue is equivalent to consumption of State resources in the form of fiscal expenditure. This criterion also applies to aid granted by regional or local bodies in the Member States.[3] Furthermore, State support may be provided just as much through tax provisions of a legislative, regulatory or administrative nature as through the practices of the tax authorities.

Notes
3 Judgment of the Court of Justice in Case 248/84 *Germany v Commission* [1987] ECR 4013.

11. Thirdly, the measure must affect competition and trade between Member States. This criterion presupposes that the beneficiary of the measure exercises an economic activity, regardless of the beneficiary's legal status or means of financing. Under settled case-law, for the purposes of this provision, the criterion of trade being affected is met if the recipient firm carries on an economic activity involving trade between Member States. The mere fact that the aid strengthens the firm's position compared with that of other firms which are competitors in intra-Community trade is enough to allow the conclusion to be drawn that intra-Community trade is affected. Neither the

Part G State Aids

fact that aid is relatively small in amount,[4] nor the fact that the recipient is moderate in size or its share of the Community market very small,[5] nor indeed the fact that the recipient does not carry out exports[6] or exports virtually all its production outside the Community[7] do anything to alter this conclusion.

Notes

[4] With the exception, however, of aid meeting the tests of the *de minimis* rule. See the Commission notice published in OJ C 68, 6.3.1996, p.9. [Ed note: see now Commission Regulation (EC) No 1998/2006 of 15 November 2006 on the application of Articles [107 and 108 TFEU] to *de minimis* aid (OJ L 379 28.12.2006, p.5)

[5] Joined Cases C-278/92, C-279/92 and C-280/92 *Spain v Commission* [1994] ECR I-4103.

[6] Case 102/87 *France v Commission* [1998] ECR 4067.

[7] Case C-142/87 *Belgium v Commission* [1990] ECR I-959.

12. Lastly, the measure must be specific or selective in that it favours "certain undertakings or the production of certain goods". The selective advantage involved here may derive from an exception to the tax provisions of a legislative, regulatory or administrative nature or from a discretionary practice on the part of the tax authorities. However, the selective nature of a measure may be justified by "the nature or general scheme of the system".[8] If so, the measure is not considered to be aid within the meaning of Article [107(1)] of the Treaty. These various aspects are looked at below.

Notes

[8] Case 173/73 *Italy v Commission* [1974] ECR 709.

Distinction between State aid and general measures

13. Tax measures which are open to all economic agents operating within a Member State are in principle general measures. They must be effectively open to all firms on an equal access basis, and they may not *de facto* be reduced in scope through, for example, the discretionary power of the State to grant them or through other factors that restrict their practical effect. However, this condition does not restrict the power of Member States to decide on the economic policy which they consider most appropriate and, in particular, to spread the tax burden as they see fit across the different factors of production. Provided that they apply without distinction to all firms and to the production of all goods, the following measures do not constitute State aid:
   — tax measures of a purely technical nature (for example, setting the rate of taxation, depreciation rules and rules on loss carry-overs; provisions to prevent double taxation or tax avoidance),
   — measures pursuing general economic policy objectives through a reduction of the tax burden related to certain production costs (research and development (R&D), the environment, training, employment).

14. The fact that some firms or some sectors benefit more than others from some of these tax measures does not necessarily mean that they are caught by the competition rules governing State aid. Thus, measures designed to reduce the taxation of labour for all firms have a relatively greater effect on labour-intensive industries than on capital-intensive industries, without necessarily constituting State aid. Similarly, tax incentives for environmental, R&D or training investment favour only the firms which undertake such investment, but again do not necessarily constitute State aid.

Commentary

point 14: F&N: 17.106

15. In a judgment delivered in 1974,[9] the Court of Justice held that any measure intended partially or wholly to exempt firms in a particular sector from the charges arising from the normal application of the general system "without there being any justification for this exemption on the basis of the nature or general scheme of this system" constituted State aid. The judgment also states that "Article [107] does not distinguish between the measures of State intervention concerned by reference to their causes or aims but defines them in relation to their effects". The

judgment also points out that the fact that the measure brings charges in the relevant sector more into line with those of its competitors in other Member States does not alter the fact that it is aid. Such divergences between tax systems, which, as pointed out above, are covered by Articles [115] to [117], cannot be corrected by unilateral measures that target the firms which are most affected by the disparities between tax systems.

Notes
9 See footnote 8.

16. The main criterion in applying Article [107(1)] to a tax measure is therefore that the measure provides in favour of certain undertakings in the Member State an exception to the application of the tax system. The common system applicable should thus first be determined. It must then be examined whether the exception to the system or differentiations within that system are justified "by the nature or general scheme" of the tax system, that is to say, whether they derive directly from the basic or guiding principles of the tax system in the Member State concerned. If this is not the case, then State aid is involved.

The selectivity or specificity criterion

17. The Commission's decision-making practice so far shows that only measures whose scope extends to the entire territory of the State escape the specificity criterion laid down in Article [107(1)]. Measures which are regional or local in scope may favour certain undertakings, subject to the principles outlined in paragraph 16. The Treaty itself qualifies as aid measures which are intended to promote the economic development of a region. Article [107(3)](a) and (c) explicitly provides, in the case of this type of aid, for possible derogations from the general principle of incompatibility laid down in Article [107(1)].

18. The Treaty clearly provides that a measure which is sectorally specific is caught by Article [107(1)]. Article [107(1)] expressly includes the phrase "the production of certain goods" among the criteria determining whether there is aid that is subject to Commission monitoring. According to well-established practice and case-law, a tax measure whose main effect is to promote one or more sectors of activity constitutes aid. The same applies to a measure that favours only national products which are exported.[10] Furthermore, the Commission has taken the view that a measure which targets all of the sectors that are subject to international competition constitutes aid.[11] A derogation from the base rate of corporation tax for an entire section of the economy therefore constitutes, except for certain cases,[12] State aid, as the Commission decided for a measure concerning the whole of the manufacturing sector.[13]

Notes
10 Joined Cases 6 and 11/69 *Commission v. France* [1969] ECR 561.
11 Commission Decision 97/239/EC of 4 December 1996 in the "*Maribel bis/ter*" case (OJ L 95, 10.4.1997, p.25) (currently *sub judice*, Case C-75/97). [Ed note: see now Case C-75/97 *Belgium v Commission* [1999] ECR I- 3671.]
12 In particular, agriculture and fisheries, see paragraph 27.
13 Commission decision of 22 July 1998 in the "Irish corporation tax" case (SG(98) D/7209) not yet published. [Ed note: see also OJ C 395, 18.12.1998, p.19.]

19. In several Member States, different tax rules apply depending on the status of the undertakings. Some public undertakings, for example, are exempt from local taxes or from company taxes. Such rules, which accord preferential treatment to undertakings having the legal status of public undertaking and carrying out an economic activity, may constitute State aid within the meaning of Article [107] of the Treaty.

20. Some tax benefits are on occasion restricted to certain types of undertaking, to some of their functions (intra-group services, intermediation or coordination) or to the production of certain goods. In so far as they favour certain undertakings or the production of certain goods, they may constitute State aid as referred to in Article [107(1)].

Discretionary administrative practices

21. The discretionary practices of some tax authorities may also give rise to measures that are caught by Article [107]. The Court of Justice acknowledges that treating economic agents on a

discretionary basis may mean that the individual application of a general measure takes on the features of a selective measure, in particular where exercise of the discretionary power goes beyond the simple management of tax revenue by reference to objective criteria.[14]

Notes

[14]   Case C-241/94 *France v Commission (Kimberly Clark Sopalin)* [1996] ECR I-4551.

Commentary
point 21: F&N: 17.113

22. If in daily practice tax rules need to be interpreted, they cannot leave room for a discretionary treatment of undertakings. Every decision of the administration that departs from the general tax rules to the benefit of individual undertakings in principle leads to a presumption of State aid and must be analysed in detail. As far as administrative rulings merely contain an interpretation of general rules, they do not give rise to a presumption of aid. However, the opacity of the decisions taken by the authorities and the room for manoeuvre which they sometimes enjoy support the presumption that such is at any rate their effect in some instances. This does not make Member States any less able to provide their taxpayers with legal certainty and predictability on the application of general tax rules.

Justification of a derogation by "the nature or general scheme of the system"

23. The differential nature of some measures does not necessarily mean that they must be considered to be State aid. This is the case with measures whose economic rationale makes them necessary to the functioning and effectiveness of the tax system.[15] However, it is up to the Member State to provide such justification.

Notes

[15]   Commission decision 96/369/EC of 13 March 1996 concerning fiscal aid given to German airlines in the form of a depreciation facility (OJ L 146, 20.6.1996, p.42).

Commentary
point 23: F&N: 17.115

24. The progressive nature of an income tax scale or profit tax scale is justified by the redistributive purpose of the tax. Calculation of asset depreciation and stock valuation methods vary from one Member State to another, but such methods may be inherent in the tax systems to which they belong. In the same way, the arrangements for the collection of fiscal debts can differ from one Member State to the other. Lastly, some conditions may be justified by objective differences between taxpayers. However, if the tax authority has discretionary freedom to set different depreciation periods or different valuation methods, firm by firm, sector by sector, there is a presumption of aid. Such a presumption also exists when the fiscal administration handles fiscal debts on a case by case basis with an objective different from the objective of optimising the recovery of tax debts from the enterprise concerned.

25. Obviously, profit tax cannot be levied if no profit is earned. It may thus be justified by the nature of the tax system that non-profit-making undertakings, such as foundations or associations, are specifically exempt from the taxes on profits if they cannot actually earn any profits. Furthermore, it may also be justified by the nature of the tax system that cooperatives which distribute all their profits to their members are not taxed at the level of the cooperative when tax is levied at the level of their members.

Commentary
point 25: F&N: 17.117

26. A distinction must be made between, on the one hand, the external objectives assigned to a particular tax scheme (in particular, social or regional objectives) and, on the other, the objectives which are inherent in the tax system itself. The whole purpose of the tax system is to collect revenue to finance State expenditure. Each firm is supposed to pay tax once only. It is therefore inherent in the logic of the tax system that taxes paid in the State in which the firm is resident for

tax purposes should be taken into account. Certain exceptions to the tax rules are, however, difficult to justify by the logic of a tax system. This is, for example, the case if non-resident companies are treated more favourably than resident ones or if tax benefits are granted to head offices or to firms providing certain services (for example, financial services) within a group.

27. Specific provisions that do not contain discretionary elements, allowing for example tax to be determined on a fixed basis (for example, in the agriculture or fisheries sectors), may be justified by the nature and general scheme of the system where, for example, they take account of specific accounting requirements or of the importance of land in assets which are specific to certain sectors; such provisions do not therefore constitute State aid. Lastly, the logic underlying certain specific provisions on the taxation of small and medium-sized enterprises (including small agricultural enterprises)[16] is comparable to that underlying the progressiveness of a tax scale.

Notes
[16] Operators in the agricultural sector with no more than 10 annual work units.

C. Compatibility with the Common Market of State Aid in the Form of Tax Measures

28. If a tax measure constitutes aid that is caught by Article [107(1)], it can nevertheless, like aid granted in other forms, qualify for one of the derogations from the principle of incompatibility with the common market provided for in Article [107(2)] and (3). Furthermore, where the recipient, whether a private or public undertaking, has been entrusted by the State with the operation of services of general economic interest, the aid may also qualify for application of the provisions of Article [106] of the Treaty.[17]

Notes
[17] Judgment of the Court of First Instance in Case T-106/95 *FFSA and others v Commission* [1997] ECR II-229. Order of the Court of Justice in Case C-174/97 P [1998] I-1303.

29. The Commission could not, however, authorise aid which proved to be in breach both of the rules laid down in the Treaty, particularly those relating to the ban on discrimination and to the right of establishment, and of the provisions of secondary law on taxation.[18] Such aspects may, in parallel, be the object of a separate procedure on the basis of Article [258]. As is clear from case-law, those aspects of aid which are indissolubly linked to the object of the aid and which contravene specific provisions of the Treaty other than Articles [107] and [108] must however be examined in the light of the procedure under Article [108] as part of an overall examination of the compatibility or the incompatibility of the aid.

Notes
[18] Case 74/76 *Iannelli v Meroni* [1977] ECR 557. See also Cases 73/79 "*Sovraprezzo*" [1980] ECR 1533, T-49/93 "*SIDE*" [1995] ECR II-2501 and Joined Cases C 142 and 143/80 "*Salengo*" [1981] ECR 1413.

30. The qualification of a tax measure as harmful under the code of conduct does not affect its possible qualification as a State aid. However the assessment of the compatibility of fiscal aid with the common market will have to be made, taking into account, *inter alia*, the effects of aid that are brought to light in the application of the code of conduct.

31. Where a fiscal aid is granted in order to provide an incentive for firms to embark on certain specific projects (investment in particular) and where its intensity is limited with respect to the costs of carrying out the project, it is no different from a subsidy and may be accorded the same treatment. Nevertheless, such arrangements must lay down sufficiently transparent rules to enable the benefit conferred to be quantified.

32. In most cases, however, tax relief provisions are general in nature: they are not linked to the carrying-out of specific projects and reduce a firm's current expenditure without it being possible to assess the precise volume involved when the Commission carries out its ex ante examination. Such measures constitute "operating aid". Operating aid is in principle prohibited. The Commission authorises it at present only in exceptional cases and subject to certain conditions, for example in shipbuilding, certain types of environmental protection aid[19] and in regions, including ultra-peripheral regions, covered by the Article [107(3)](a) aid derogation provided that they are

duly justified and their level is proportional to the handicaps they are intended to offset.[20] It must in principle (with the exception of the two categories of aid mentioned below) be degressive and limited in time. At present, operating aid can also be authorised in the form of transport aid in ultra-peripheral regions and in certain Nordic regions that are sparsely populated and are seriously handicapped in terms of accessibility. Operating aid may not be authorised where it represents aid for exports between Member States. As for State aid in favour of the maritime transport sector the specific rules for that sector apply.[21]

Notes

[19] Community guidelines on State aid for environmental protection (OJ C 72, 10.3.1994, p.3). [Ed note: see now the 2008 Community guidelines on State aid for environmental protection (OJ C 82, 1.4.2008, p.1).]

[20] Guidelines on national regional aid (OJ C 74, 10.3.1998, p.9). [See Guidelines on National Regional Aid for 2007–2013 (OJ C 54, 4.3.2006, p.13).]

[21] Community guidelines on State aid to maritime transport (OJ C 205, 5.7.1997, p.5). [Ed note: see now Commission communication C(2004) 43 — Community guidelines on State aid to maritime transport (OJ C 13, 17.1.2004, p.3).]

33. If it is to be considered by the Commission to be compatible with the common market, State aid intended to promote the economic development of particular areas must be "in proportion to, and targeted at, the aims sought'. For the examination of regional aid the criteria allow account to be taken of other possible effects, in particular of certain effects brought to light by the code of conduct. Where a derogation is granted on the basis of regional criteria, the Commission must ensure in particular that the relevant measures:

— contribute to regional development and relate to activities having a local impact. The establishment of off-shore activities does not, to the extent that their externalities on the local economy are low, normally provide satisfactory support for the local economy,

— relate to real regional handicaps. It is open to question whether there are any real regional handicaps for activities for which the additional costs have little incidence, such as for example the transport costs for financing activities, which lend themselves to tax avoidance,

— are examined in a Community context.[22] The Commission must in this respect take account of any negative effects which such measures may have on other Member States.

Notes

[22] Case 730/79 *Philip Morris v Commission* [1980] ECR 2671.

D. Procedures

34. Article [108(3)] requires Member States to notify the Commission of all their "plans to grant or alter aid" and provides that any proposed measures may not be put into effect without the Commission's prior approval. This procedure applies to all aid, including tax aid.

35. If the Commission finds that State aid which has been put into effect in breach of this rule does not qualify for any of the exemptions provided for in the Treaty and is therefore incompatible with the common market, it requires the Member State to recover it, except where that would be contrary to a general principle of Community law, in particular legitimate expectations to which the Commission's behaviour can give rise. In the case of State aid in the form of tax measures, the amount to be covered is calculated on the basis of a comparison between the tax actually paid and the amount which should have been paid if the generally applicable rule had been applied. Interest is added to this basic amount. The interest rate to be applied is equivalent to the reference rate used to calculate the grant equivalent of regional aid.

36. Article [108(1)] states that the Commission "shall in cooperation with Member States, keep under constant review all systems of aid existing in those States". Such review extends to State aid in the form of tax measures. So as to allow such review to be carried out, the Member States are required to submit to the Commission every year reports on their existing State aid systems. In the case of tax relief or full or partial tax exemption, the reports must provide an estimate of budgetary revenue lost. Following its review, the Commission may, if it considers that the scheme is not or is no longer compatible with the common market, propose that the Member State amend or abolish it.

E. Implementation

37. The Commission will, on the basis of the guidelines set out in this notice and as from the time of its publication, examine the plans for tax aid notified to it and tax aid illegally implemented in the Member States and will review existing systems. This notice is published for guidance purposes and is not exhaustive. The Commission will take account of all the specific circumstances in each individual case.

38. The Commission will review the application of this notice two years after its publication.

G24

COMMISSION NOTICE

on the application of Articles [107 and 108 of the Treaty on the Functioning of the European Union]* to State aid in the form of guarantees

(2008/C 155/02)

Official Journal C 155, 20.6.2008, p.10

Celex No: 52008XC0620(02)

EUR-Lex permanent link: <http://eur-lex.europa.eu/LexUriServ/LexUriServ.do?uri= CELEX: 52008XC0620(02)EN:NOT>

Notes

* Ed note: please see the Note on the Lisbon Treaty at p.xvii in regard to article renumbering introduced by the Lisbon Treaty. Unless otherwise stated, all Treaty article numbers are the new numbers of the Treaty on the Functioning of the European Union (TFEU) and the Treaty on European Union (TEU).

EEA application: for the corresponding EEA measure, see EFTA Surveillance Authority Decision No 788/08/COL of 17 December 2008 amending, for the 67th time, the procedural and substantive rules in the field of State aid by amending the existing chapters on reference and discount rates and on State aid granted in the form of guarantees and by introducing a new chapter on recovery of unlawful and incompatible State aid, on State aid to cinematographic and other audiovisual works and State aid for railway undertakings (OJ L 105, 21.4.2011, p.32).

Commentary
Notice: **B&C:** 17.003 **F&N:** 17.77

This Notice replaces the Commission Notice on the application of Articles [107 and 108 TFEU] to State aid in the form of guarantees (OJ C 71, 11.3.2000, p.14).

1. INTRODUCTION

1.1. Background

This Notice updates the Commission's approach to State aid granted in the form of guarantees and aims to give Member States more detailed guidance about the principles on which the Commission intends to base its interpretation of Articles [107 and 108] and their application to State guarantees. These principles are currently laid down in the Commission Notice on the application of Articles [107 and 108 TFEU] to State aid in the form of guarantees.[1] Experience gained in the application of this Notice since 2000 suggests that the Commission's policy in this area should be reviewed. In this connection, the Commission wishes to recall for instance its recent practice in various specific decisions[2] with respect to the need to undertake an individual assessment of the risk of losses related to each guarantee in the case of schemes. The Commission intends to further make its policy in this area as transparent as possible so that its decisions are predictable and that equal treatment is ensured. In particular, the Commission wishes to provide small and medium-sized enterprises (hereafter 'SMEs') and Member States with safe-harbours predetermining, for a given company and on the basis of its financial rating, the minimum margin that should be charged for a State guarantee in order to be deemed as not constituting aid within the scope of Article [107(1)] of the Treaty. Likewise, any shortfall in the premium charged in comparison with that level could be deemed as the aid element.

Notes

1 OJ C 71, 11.3.2000, p.14.

2 For example: Commission Decision 2003/706/EC of 23 April 2003 on the aid scheme implemented by Germany entitled 'Guarantee schemes of the Land of Brandenburg for 1991 and 1994' — State aid C 45/98 (ex NN 45/97) (OJ L 263, 14.10.2003, p.1); Commission Decision of 16 December 2003 on the guarantee schemes in ship financing — Germany (N 512/03) (OJ C 62, 11.3.2004, p.3); Commission Decision 2006/599/EC of 6 April 2005 on the aid scheme which Italy is planning to implement for ship financing (OJ L 244, 7.9.2006, p.17).

1.2. Types of guarantee

In their most common form, guarantees are associated with a loan or other financial obligation to be contracted by a borrower with a lender; they may be granted as individual guarantees or within guarantee schemes.

However, various forms of guarantee may exist, depending on their legal basis, the type of transaction covered, their duration, etc. Without the list being exhaustive, the following forms of guarantee can be identified:

— general guarantees, i.e. guarantees provided to undertakings as such as opposed to guarantees linked to a specific transaction, which may be a loan, an equity investment, etc.,

— guarantees provided by a specific instrument as opposed to guarantees linked to the status of the undertaking itself,

— guarantees provided directly or counter guarantees provided to a first level guarantor,

— unlimited guarantees as opposed to guarantees limited in amount and/or time. The Commission also regards as aid in the form of a guarantee the more favourable funding terms obtained by enterprises whose legal form rules out bankruptcy or other insolvency procedures or provides an explicit State guarantee or coverage of losses by the State. The same applies to the acquisition by a State of a holding in an enterprise if unlimited liability is accepted instead of the usual limited liability,

— guarantees clearly originating from a contractual source (such as formal contracts, letters of comfort) or another legal source as opposed to guarantees whose form is less visible (such as side letters, oral commitments), possibly with various levels of comfort that can be provided by this guarantee.

Especially in the latter case, the lack of appropriate legal or accounting records often leads to very poor traceability. This is true both for the beneficiary and for the State or public body providing it and, as a result, for the information available to third parties.

1.3. Structure and scope of the Notice

For the purpose of this Notice:

(a) 'guarantee scheme' means any tool on the basis of which, without further implementing measures being required, guarantees can be provided to undertakings respecting certain conditions of duration, amount, underlying transaction, type or size of undertakings (such as SMEs);

(b) 'individual guarantee' means any guarantee provided to an undertaking and not awarded on the basis of a guarantee scheme.

Sections 3 and 4 of this Notice are designed to be directly applicable to guarantees linked to a specific financial transaction such as a loan. The Commission considers that, owing to their frequency and the fact that they can usually be quantified, these are the cases where guarantees most need to be classed as constituting State aid or otherwise.

As in most cases the transaction covered by a guarantee would be a loan, the Notice will further refer to the principal beneficiary of the guarantee as the 'borrower' and to the body whose risk is diminished by the State guarantee as the 'lender'. The use of these two specific terms also aims to facilitate understanding of the rationale underpinning the text, since the basic principle of a loan is broadly understood. However, it does not ensue that Sections 3 and 4 are only applicable to a loan guarantee. They apply to all guarantees where a similar transfer of risk takes place such as an investment in the form of equity, provided the relevant risk profile (including the possible lack of collateralisation) is taken into account.

The Notice applies to all economic sectors, including the agriculture, fisheries and transport sectors without prejudice to specific rules relating to guarantees in the sector concerned.

This Notice does not apply to export credit guarantees.

1.4. Other types of guarantee

Where certain forms of guarantee (see point 1.2) involve a transfer of risk to the guarantor and where they do not display one or more of the specific features referred to in point 1.3, for instance insurance guarantees, a case-by-case analysis will have to be made for which, as far as is necessary, the applicable Sections or methodologies described in this Notice will be applied.

1.5. Neutrality

This Notice applies without prejudice to Article [345] of the Treaty and thus does not prejudice the rules in Member States governing the system of property ownership. The Commission is neutral as regards public and private ownership.

In particular, the mere fact that the ownership of an undertaking is largely in public hands is not sufficient in itself to constitute a State guarantee provided there are no explicit or implicit guarantee elements.

2. APPLICABILITY OF ARTICLE [107(1)]

2.1. General remarks

Article [107(1)] of the Treaty states that any aid granted by a Member State or through State resources in any form whatsoever which distorts or threatens to distort competition by favouring certain undertakings or the production of certain goods shall, in so far as it affects trade between Member States, be incompatible with the common market.

These general criteria equally apply to guarantees. As for other forms of potential aid, guarantees given directly by the State, namely by central, regional or local authorities, as well as guarantees given through State resources by other State-controlled bodies such as undertakings and imputable to public authorities,[3] may constitute State aid.

In order to avoid any doubts, the notion of State resources should thus be clarified as regards State guarantees. The benefit of a State guarantee is that the risk associated with the guarantee is carried by the State. Such risk-carrying by the State should normally be remunerated by an appropriate premium. Where the State forgoes all or part of such a premium, there is both a benefit for the undertaking and a drain on the resources of the State. Thus, even if it turns out that no payments are ever made by the State under a guarantee, there may nevertheless be State aid under Article [107(1)] of the Treaty. The aid is granted at the moment when the guarantee is given, not when the guarantee is invoked nor when payments are made under the terms of the guarantee. Whether or not a guarantee constitutes State aid, and, if so, what the amount of that State aid may be, must be assessed at the moment when the guarantee is given. In this context the Commission points out that the analysis under State aid rules does not prejudge the compatibility of a given measure with other Treaty provisions.

Notes

3 See Case C-482/99, *France v Commission* (Stardust) [2002] ECR I-4397.

2.2. Aid to the borrower

Usually, the aid beneficiary is the borrower. As indicated under point 2.1, risk-carrying should normally be remunerated by an appropriate premium. When the borrower does not need to pay the premium, or pays a low premium, it obtains an advantage. Compared to a situation without guarantee, the State guarantee enables the borrower to obtain better financial terms for a loan than those normally available on the financial markets. Typically, with the benefit of the State guarantee, the borrower can obtain lower rates and/or offer less security. In some cases, the borrower would not, without a State guarantee, find a financial institution prepared to lend on any terms. State guarantees may thus facilitate the creation of new business and enable certain undertakings to raise money in order to pursue new activities. Likewise, a State guarantee may help a failing firm remain active instead of being eliminated or restructured, thereby possibly creating distortions of competition.

2.3. Aid to the lender

2.3.1. Even if usually the aid beneficiary is the borrower, it cannot be ruled out that under certain circumstances the lender, too, will directly benefit from the aid. In particular, for example, if a State guarantee is given ex post in respect of a loan or other financial obligation already entered into without the terms of this loan or financial obligation being adjusted, or if one guaranteed loan is used to pay back another, non-guaranteed loan to the same credit institution, then there may also be aid to the lender, in so far as the security of the loans is increased. Where the guarantee contains aid to the lender, attention should be drawn to the fact that such aid might, in principle, constitute operating aid.

2.3.2. Guarantees differ from other State aid measures, such as grants or tax exemptions, in that, in the case of a guarantee, the State also enters into a legal relationship with the lender. Therefore, consideration has to be given to the possible consequences for third parties of State aid that has been illegally granted. In the case of State guarantees for loans, this concerns mainly the lending financial institutions. In the case of guarantees for bonds issued to obtain financing for undertakings, this concerns the financial institutions involved in the issuance of the bonds. The question whether the illegality of the aid affects the legal relations between the State and third parties is a matter which has to be examined under national law. National courts may have to examine whether national law prevents the guarantee contracts from being honoured, and in that assessment the Commission considers that they should take account of the breach of Community law. Accordingly, lenders may have an interest in verifying, as a standard precaution, that the Community rules on State aid have been observed whenever guarantees are granted. The Member State should be able to provide a case number issued by the Commission for an individual case or a scheme and possibly a non-confidential copy of the Commission's decision together with the relevant reference to the Official Journal of the European Union. The Commission for its part will do its utmost to make available in a transparent manner information on cases and schemes approved by it.

3. Conditions Ruling out the Existence of Aid

3.1. General considerations

If an individual guarantee or a guarantee scheme entered into by the State does not bring any advantage to an undertaking, it will not constitute State aid.

In this context, in order to determine whether an advantage is being granted through a guarantee or a guarantee scheme, the Court has confirmed in its recent judgments[4] that the Commission should base its assessment on the principle of an investor operating in a market economy (hereafter referred to as the 'market economy investor principle'). Account should therefore be taken of the effective possibilities for a beneficiary undertaking to obtain equivalent financial resources by having recourse to the capital market. State aid is not involved where a new funding source is made available on conditions which would be acceptable for a private operator under the normal conditions of a market economy.[5]

In order to facilitate the assessment of whether the market economy investor principle is fulfilled for a given guarantee measure, the Commission sets out in this Section a number of sufficient conditions for the absence of aid. Individual guarantees are covered in point 3.2 with a simpler option for SMEs in point 3.3. Guarantee schemes are covered in point 3.4 with a simpler option for SMEs in point 3.5.

Notes

4 See Case C-482/99 referred to in footnote 3.

5 See Commission Communication on the application of Article [107 and 108 TFEU] to public shareholdings (Bulletin of the European Communities No 9-1984); Joined Cases 296/82 and 318/82, *Netherlands and Leeuwarder Papierwarenfabriek BV v Commission* [1985] ECR 809, paragraph 17. Commission Communication on the application of Articles [107 and 108 TFEU] and Article 61 of the EEA Agreement to State aid in the aviation sector (OJ C 350, 10.12.1994, p.5), points 25 and 26.

3.2. Individual guarantees

Regarding an individual State guarantee, the Commission considers that the fulfilment of all the following conditions will be sufficient to rule out the presence of State aid.

(a) The borrower is not in financial difficulty. In order to decide whether the borrower is to be seen as being in financial difficulty, reference should be made to the definition set out in the Community guidelines on State aid for rescuing and restructuring firms in difficulty.[6] SMEs which have been incorporated for less than three years shall not be considered as being in difficulty for that period for the purposes of this Notice.

(b) The extent of the guarantee can be properly measured when it is granted. This means that the guarantee must be linked to a specific financial transaction, for a fixed maximum amount and limited in time.

(c) The guarantee does not cover more than 80% of the outstanding loan or other financial obligation; this limitation does not apply to guarantees covering debt securities.[7] The Commission considers that if a financial obligation is wholly covered by a State guarantee, the lender has less incentive to properly assess, secure and minimise the risk arising from the lending operation, and in particular to properly assess the borrower's creditworthiness. Such risk assessment might, due to lack of means, not always be taken over by the State guarantor. This lack of incentive to minimise the risk of non-repayment of the loan might encourage lenders to contract loans with a greater than normal commercial risk and could thus increase the amount of higher-risk guarantees in the State's portfolio. This limitation of 80% does not apply to a public guarantee granted to finance a company whose activity is solely constituted by a properly entrusted Service of General Economic Interest (SGEI)[8] and when this guarantee has been provided by the public authority having put in place this entrustment. The limitation of 80% applies if the company concerned provides other SGEIs or other economic activities. In order to ensure that the lender effectively bears part of the risk, due attention must be given to the following two aspects:

— when the size of the loan or of the financial obligation decreases over time, for instance because the loan starts to be reimbursed, the guaranteed amount has to decrease proportionally, in such a way that at each moment in time the guarantee does not cover more than 80% of the outstanding loan or financial obligation,

— losses have to be sustained proportionally and in the same way by the lender and the guarantor. In the same manner, net recoveries (i.e. revenues excluding costs for claim handling) generated from the recuperation of the debt from the securities given by the borrower have to reduce proportionally the losses borne by the lender and the guarantor. First-loss guarantees, where losses are first attributed to the guarantor and only then to the lender, will be regarded as possibly involving aid. If a Member State wishes to provide a guarantee above the 80% threshold and claims that it does not constitute aid, it should duly substantiate the claim, for instance on the basis of the arrangement of the whole transaction, and notify it to the Commission so that the guarantee can be properly assessed with regards to its possible State aid character.

(d) A market-oriented price is paid for the guarantee. As indicated under point 2.1, risk-carrying should normally be remunerated by an appropriate premium on the guaranteed or counter-guaranteed amount. When the price paid for the guarantee is at least as high as the corresponding guarantee premium benchmark that can be found on the financial markets, the guarantee does not contain aid. If no corresponding guarantee premium benchmark can be found on the financial markets, the total financial cost of the guaranteed loan, including the interest rate of the loan and the guarantee premium, has to be compared to the market price of a similar non-guaranteed loan. In both cases, in order to determine the corresponding market price, the characteristics of the guarantee and of the underlying loan should be taken into consideration. This includes: the amount and duration of the transaction; the security given by the borrower and other experience affecting the recovery rate evaluation; the probability of default of the borrower due to its financial position, its sector of activity and prospects; as well as other economic conditions. This analysis should notably allow the borrower to be classified by means of a risk rating. This classification may be provided by an internationally recognised rating agency or, where available, by the internal rating used by the bank providing the underlying loan. The Commission points to the link between rating and default rate made by international financial institutions, whose work is also publicly available.[9] To assess whether the premium is in line with the market prices the Member State can carry out a comparison of prices paid by similarly rated undertakings on the market. The Commission will therefore not accept that the guarantee premium is set at a single rate deemed to correspond to an overall industry standard.

Notes

[6] OJ C 244, 1.10.2004, p.2.

[7] For the definition of 'debt securities', see Article 2(1)(b) of Directive 2004/109/EC of the European Parliament and of the Council of 15 December 2004 on the harmonisation of transparency requirements in relation to information about issuers whose securities are admitted to trading on a regulated market and amending Directive 2001/34/EC (OJ L 390, 31.12.2004, p.38). Directive as last amended by Directive 2008/22/EC (OJ L 76, 19.3.2008, p.50).

[8] Such an SGEI must comply with Community rules such as Commission Decision 2005/842/EC of 28 November 2005 on the application of Article [106(2) TFEU] to State aid in the form of public service compensation granted to certain undertakings entrusted with the operation of services of general economic interest (OJ L 312, 29.11.2005, p.67), and the Community framework for State aid in the form of public service compensation (OJ C 297, 29.11.2005, p.4).

[9] Such as Table 1 on agencies' credit ratings to be found in the Bank for International Settlements Working Paper No 207, available at: <http://www.bis.org/publ/work207.pdf>.

Commentary

section 3.2: F&N: 17.77

3.3. Valuation of individual guarantees for SMEs

As an exception, if the borrower is an SME,[10] the Commission can by way of derogation from point 3.2(d) accept a simpler evaluation of whether or not a loan guarantee involves aid. In that case, and provided all the other conditions laid down in points 3.2(a), (b) and (c) are met, a State guarantee would be deemed as not constituting aid if the minimum annual premium ('safe-harbour premium')[11] set out in the following table is charged on the amount effectively guaranteed by the State, based on the rating of the borrower:[12]

The safe-harbour premiums apply to the amount effectively guaranteed or counter-guaranteed by the State at the beginning of each year concerned. They must be considered as the minimum to be applied with respect to a company whose credit rating is at least equal to those given in the table.[13]

Credit quality	Standard & Poor's	Fitch	Moody's	Annual safe-harbour premium
Highest quality	AAA	AAA	Aaa	0,4%
Very strong payment capacity	AA+ AA AA-	AA+ AA AA-	Aa 1 Aa 2 Aa 3	0,4%
Strong payment capacity	A+ A A-	A+ A A-	A 1 A 2 A 3	0,55%
Adequate payment capacity	BBB+ BBB BBB-	BBB+ BBB BBB-	Baa 1 Baa 2 Baa 3	0,8%

Credit quality	Standard & Poor's	Fitch	Moody's	Annual safe-harbour premium
Payment capacity is vulnerable to adverse conditions	BB+ BB BB- B+	BB+ BB BB- B+	Ba 1 Ba 2 Ba 3 B 1	2,0% 3,8%
Payment capacity is likely to be impaired by adverse condition	B B-	B B-	B 2 B 3	6,3%
Payment capacity is dependent upon sustained favourable conditions	CCC+ CCC CCC- CC	CCC+ CCC CCC- CC C	Caa 1 Caa 2 Caa 3	No safe-harbour annual premium can be provided
In or near default	SD D	DDD DD D	Ca C	No safe-harbour annual premium can be provided

In the case of a single upfront guarantee premium, the loan guarantee is deemed to be free of aid if it is at least equal to the present value of the future guarantee premiums as indicated above, the discount rate used being the corresponding reference rate.[14]

As outlined in the table above, companies with a rating corresponding to CCC/Caa or worse cannot benefit from this simplified methodology.

For SMEs which do not have a credit history or a rating based on a balance sheet approach, such as certain special purpose companies or start-up companies, the safe-harbour premium is set at 3,8% but this can never be lower than the premium which would be applicable to the parent company or companies.

These margins may be revised from time to time to take account of the market situation.

Notes

[10] 'SMEs' refer to small and medium-sized enterprises as defined in Annex I to Regulation (EC) No 70/2001 on the application of Articles [107 and 108 TFEU] to State aid to small and medium-sized enterprises (OJ L 10, 13.1.2001, p.33). Regulation as last amended by Regulation (EC) No 1976/2006 (OJ L 368, 23.12.2006, p.85). [Ed note: see now Commission Regulation (EC) No 800/2008 of 6 August 2008 declaring certain categories of aid compatible with the common market in application of Articles [107 and 108 TFEU] (General block exemption Regulation) (OJ L 214, 9.8.2008, p.3), reproduced above at G11.]

[11] These safe-harbour premiums are established in line with the margins determined for loans to similarly rated undertakings in the Communication from the Commission on the revision of the method for setting the reference and discount rates (OJ C 14, 19.1.2008, p. 6). Following the study commissioned by the Commission on that topic: (<http://ec.europa.eu/comm/competition/state_aid/studies_reports/full_report.pdf>, see pages 23 and 156–159 of the study), a general reduction of 20 basis points has been taken into account. This reduction corresponds to the difference in margin for a similar risk between a loan and a guarantee in order to take into account the additional costs specifically linked to loans.

[12] The table refers to the rating classes of Standard & Poor's, Fitch and Moody's, which are the rating agencies most frequently used by the banking sector in order to link their own rating system, as described in point 3.2(d). However, ratings do not need to be obtained from those specific rating agencies. National rating systems or rating systems used by banks to reflect default rates are equally acceptable provided they supply the one-year probability of default as this figure is used by rating agencies to rank companies. Other systems should allow for a similar classification through this ranking key.

[13] For example, a company to which a bank assigns a credit rating corresponding to BBB-/Baa3 should be charged a yearly guarantee premium of at least 0,8% on the amount effectively guaranteed by the State at the beginning of each year.

[14] See the Communication referred to in footnote 11 providing that: '*The reference rate is also to be used as a discount rate, for calculating present values. To that end, in principle, the base rate increased by a fixed margin of 100 basis points will be used*' (p.4).

[Ed. The table is reproduced as corrected by the corrigendum published at OJ C 244, 25.9.2008, p.32]

3.4. Guarantee schemes

For a State guarantee scheme, the Commission considers that the fulfilment of all the following conditions will rule out the presence of State aid:

(a) the scheme is closed to borrowers in financial difficulty (see details in point 3.2(a));

(b) the extent of the guarantees can be properly measured when they are granted. This means that the guarantees must be linked to specific financial transactions, for a fixed maximum amount and limited in time;

(c) the guarantees do not cover more than 80% of each outstanding loan or other financial obligation (see details and exceptions in point 3.2(c));

(d) the terms of the scheme are based on a realistic assessment of the risk so that the premiums paid by the beneficiaries make it, in all probability, self-financing. The self-financing nature of the scheme and the proper risk orientation are viewed by the Commission as indications that the guarantee premiums charged under the scheme are in line with market prices. This entails that the risk of each new guarantee has to be assessed, on the basis of all the relevant factors (quality of the borrower, securities, duration of the guarantee, etc). On the basis of this risk analysis, risk classes[15] have to be defined, the guarantee has to be classified in one of these risk classes and the corresponding guarantee premium has to be charged on the guaranteed or counter-guaranteed amount;

(e) in order to have a proper and progressive evaluation of the self-financing aspect of the scheme, the adequacy of the level of the premiums has to be reviewed at least once a year on the basis of the effective loss rate of the scheme over an economically reasonable time horizon, and premiums adjusted accordingly if there is a risk that the scheme may no longer be self-financing. This adjustment may concern all issued and future guarantees or only the latter;

(f) in order to be viewed as being in line with market prices, the premiums charged have to cover the normal risks associated with granting the guarantee, the administrative costs of the scheme, and a yearly remuneration of an adequate capital, even if the latter is not at all or only partially constituted.

As regards administrative costs, these should include at least the specific initial risk assessment as well as the risk monitoring and risk management costs linked to the granting and administration of the guarantee.

As regards the remuneration of the capital, the Commission observes that usual guarantors are subject to capital requirement rules and, in accordance with these rules, are forced to constitute equity in order not to go bankrupt when there are variations in the yearly losses related to the guarantees. State guarantee schemes are normally not subject to these rules and thus do not need to constitute such reserves. In other words, each time the losses stemming from the guarantees exceed the revenues from the guarantee premiums, the deficit is simply covered by the State budget. This State guarantee to the scheme puts the latter in a more favourable situation than a usual guarantor. In order to avoid this disparity and to remunerate the State for the risk it is taking, the Commission considers that the guarantee premiums have to cover the remuneration of an adequate capital.

The Commission considers that this capital has to correspond to 8%[16] of the outstanding guarantees. For guarantees granted to undertakings whose rating is equivalent to AAA/AA- (Aaa/Aa3), the amount of capital to be remunerated can be reduced to 2% of the outstanding guarantees. Meanwhile, with regard to guarantees granted to undertakings whose rating is equivalent to A+/A- (A1/A3), the amount of capital to be remunerated can be reduced to 4% of the outstanding guarantees.

The normal remuneration of this capital is made up of a risk premium, possibly increased by the risk-free interest rate.

The risk premium must be paid to the State on the adequate amount of capital in all cases. Based on its practice, the Commission considers that a normal risk premium for equity amounts to at least 400 basis points and that such risk premium should be included in the guarantee premium charged to the beneficiaries.[17]

If, as in most State guarantee schemes, the capital is not provided to the scheme and therefore there is no cash contribution by the State, the risk-free interest rate does not have to be taken into account. Alternatively, if the underlying capital is effectively provided by the State, the State has to incur borrowing costs and the scheme benefits from this cash by possibly investing it. Therefore the risk-free interest rate has to be paid to the State on the amount provided. Moreover, this charge should be taken from the financial income of the scheme and does not necessarily have to impact the guarantee premiums.[18] The Commission considers that the yield of the 10-year government bond may be used as a suitable proxy for the risk-free rate taken as normal return on capital;

(g) in order to ensure transparency, the scheme must provide for the terms on which future guarantees will be granted, such as eligible companies in terms of rating and, when applicable, sector and size, maximum amount and duration of the guarantees.

Notes

[15] See further details in footnote 12.

[16] Corresponding to the capital requirements laid down in Article 75 of Directive 2006/48/EC of the European Parliament and of the Council of 14 June 2006 relating to the taking up and pursuit of the business of credit institutions (OJ L 177, 30.6.2006, p.1) read in conjunction with Annex VI (paragraph 41 onwards) thereto.

[17] For a guarantee to a BBB rated company amounting to 100, the reserves to be constituted thus amount to 8. Applying 400 basis points (or 4%) to this amount results in annual capital costs of $8\% \times 4\% = 0,32\%$ of the guaranteed amount, which will impact the price of the guarantee accordingly. If the one-year default rate anticipated by the scheme for this company is, for instance, 0,35% and the yearly administrative costs are estimated at 0,1%, the price of the guarantee deemed as non-aid will be 0,77% per year.

[18] In that case, and provided the risk-free rate is deemed to be 5%, the annual cost of the reserves to be constituted will be, for the same guarantee of 100 and reserves of 8 to be constituted, $8\% \times (4\% + 5\%) = 0,72\%$ of the guaranteed amount. Under the same assumptions (default rate of 0,35% and administrative costs of 0,1%), the price of the guarantee would be 0,77% per year and an additional charge of 0,4% should be paid by the scheme to the State.

3.5. Valuation of guarantee schemes for SMEs

In view of the specific situation of SMEs and in order to facilitate their access to finance, especially through the use of guarantee schemes, two specific possibilities exist for such companies:

— the use of safe-harbour premiums as defined for individual guarantees to SMEs,
— the valuation of guarantee schemes as such by allowing the application of a single premium and avoiding the need for individual ratings of beneficiary SMEs.

The conditions of use of both rules are defined as follows:

Use of safe-harbour premiums in guarantee schemes for SMEs

In line with what is proposed for simplification purposes in relation to individual guarantees, guarantee schemes in favour of SMEs can also, in principle, be deemed self-financing and not constitute State aid if the minimum safe-harbour premiums set out in point 3.3 and based on the ratings of undertakings are applied.[19] The other conditions set out in points 3.4(a), (b) and (c) as well as in point 3.4(g) still have to be fulfilled, and the conditions set out in points 3.4(d), (e) and (f) are deemed to be fulfilled by the use of the minimum annual premiums set out in point 3.3.

Use of single premiums in guarantee schemes for SMEs

The Commission is aware that carrying out an individual risk assessment of each borrower is a costly process, which may not be appropriate where a scheme covers a large number of small loans for which it represents a risk pooling tool.

Consequently, where a scheme only relates to guarantees for SMEs and the guaranteed amount does not exceed a threshold of EUR 2,5 million per company in that scheme, the Commission may accept, by way of derogation from point 3.4(d), a single yearly guarantee premium for all borrowers. However, in order for the guarantees granted under such a scheme to be regarded as not constituting State aid, the scheme has to remain self-financing and all the other conditions set out in points 3.4(a), (b) and (c) as well as in points 3.4(e), (f) and (g) still have to be fulfilled.

Notes

[19] This includes the provision whereby for SMEs which do not have a credit history or a rating based on a balance sheet approach, the safe-harbour premium is set at 3,8% but this can never be lower than the premium which would be applicable to the parent companies.

3.6. No automatic classification as State aid

Failure to comply with any one of the conditions set out in points 3.2 to 3.5 does not mean that the guarantee or guarantee scheme is automatically regarded as State aid. If there is any doubt as to whether a planned guarantee or guarantee scheme constitutes State aid, it should be notified to the Commission.

4. Guarantees with an Aid Element

4.1. General

Where an individual guarantee or a guarantee scheme does not comply with the market economy investor principle, it is deemed to entail State aid. The State aid element therefore needs to be quantified in order to check whether the aid may be found compatible under a specific State aid exemption. As a matter of principle, the State aid element will be deemed to be the difference between the appropriate market price of the guarantee provided individually or through a scheme and the actual price paid for that measure.

The resulting yearly cash grant equivalents should be discounted to their present value using the reference rate, then added up to obtain the total grant equivalent.

When calculating the aid element in a guarantee, the Commission will devote special attention to the following elements:

(a) whether in the case of individual guarantees the borrower is in financial difficulty. Whether in the case of guarantee schemes, the eligibility criteria of the scheme provide for exclusion of such undertakings (see details in point 3.2(a)). The Commission notes that for companies in difficulty, a market guarantor, if any, would, at the time the guarantee is granted charge a high premium given the expected rate of default. If the likelihood that the borrower will not be able to repay the loan becomes particularly high, this market rate may not exist and in exceptional circumstances the aid element of the guarantee may turn out to be as high as the amount effectively covered by that guarantee;

(b) whether the extent of each guarantee can be properly measured when it is granted. This means that the guarantees must be linked to a specific financial transaction, for a fixed maximum amount and limited in time. In this connection the Commission considers in principle that unlimited guarantees are incompatible with Article [107] of the Treaty;

(c) whether the guarantee covers more than 80% of each outstanding loan or other financial obligation (see details and exceptions in point 3.2(c)). In order to ensure that the lender has a real incentive to properly assess, secure and minimise the risk arising from the lending operation, and in particular to assess properly the borrower's creditworthiness, the Commission considers that a percentage of at least 20% not covered by a State guarantee should be carried by the lender[20] to properly secure its loans and to minimise the risk associated with the transaction. The Commission will therefore, in general, examine more thoroughly any guarantee or guarantee scheme covering the entirety (or nearly the entirety) of a financial transaction except if a Member State duly justifies it, for instance, by the specific nature of the transaction;

(d) whether the specific characteristics of the guarantee and loan (or other financial obligation) have been taken into account when determining the market premium of the guarantee, from which the aid element is calculated by comparing it with the premium actually paid (see details in point 3.2(d)).

Notes

[20] This is based on the assumption that the corresponding level of security is provided by the company to the State and the credit institution.

4.2. Aid element in individual guarantees

For an individual guarantee the cash grant equivalent of a guarantee should be calculated as the difference between the market price of the guarantee and the price actually paid.

Where the market does not provide guarantees for the type of transaction concerned, no market price for the guarantee is available. In that case, the aid element should be calculated in the same way as the grant equivalent of a soft loan, namely as the difference between the specific market interest rate this company would have borne without the guarantee and the interest rate obtained by means of the State guarantee after any premiums paid have been taken into account. If there is no market interest rate and if the Member State wishes to use the reference rate as a proxy, the Commission stresses that the conditions laid down in the communication on reference rates[21] are valid to calculate the aid intensity of an individual guarantee. This means that due attention must be paid to the top-up to be added to the base rate in order to take into account the relevant risk profile linked to the operation covered, the undertaking guaranteed and the collaterals provided.

Notes

21 See the Communication referred to in footnote 11.

4.3. Aid element in individual guarantees for SMEs

For SMEs, the simplified evaluation system outlined in point 3.3 can also be applied. In that case, if the premium for a given guarantee does not correspond to the value set as a minimum for its rating class, the difference between this minimum level and the premium charged will be regarded as aid. If the guarantee lasts more than a year, the yearly shortfalls are discounted using the relevant reference rate.[22]

Only in cases clearly evidenced and duly justified by the Member State concerned may the Commission accept a deviation from these rules. A risk-based approach still has to be respected in such cases.

Notes

22 See further details in footnote 14.

4.4. Aid element in guarantee schemes

For guarantee schemes, the cash grant equivalent of each guarantee within the scheme is the difference between the premium effectively charged (if any) and the premium that should be charged in an equivalent non-aid scheme set up in accordance with the conditions laid down in point 3.4. The aforementioned theoretical premiums from which the aid element is calculated have therefore to cover the normal risks associated with the guarantee as well as the administrative and capital costs.[23] This way of calculating the grant equivalent is aimed at ensuring that, also over the medium and long term, the total aid granted under the scheme is equal to the money injected by the public authorities to cover the deficit of the scheme.

Since, in the case of State guarantee schemes, the specific features of the individual cases may not be known at the time when the scheme is to be assessed, the aid element must be assessed by reference to the provisions of the scheme.

Aid elements in guarantee schemes can also be calculated through methodologies already accepted by the Commission following their notification under a regulation adopted by the Commission in the field of State aid, such as Commission Regulation (EC) No 1628/2006 of 24 October 2006 on the application of Articles [107 and 108 TFEU] to national regional investment aid[24] or Commission Regulation (EC) No 1857/2006 of 15 December 2006 on the application of Articles [107 and 108 TFEU] to State aid to small and medium-sized enterprises active in the production of agricultural products and amending Regulation (EC) No 70/2001,[25] provided that the approved methodology explicitly addresses the type of guarantees and the type of underlying transactions at stake.

Only in cases clearly evidenced and duly justified by the Member State concerned may the Commission accept a deviation from these rules. A risk-based approach still has to be respected in such cases.

Notes

23 This calculation can be summarised, for each risk class, as the difference between (a) the outstanding sum guaranteed, multiplied by the risk factor of the risk class ('risk' being the probability of default after inclusion of administrative and capital costs), which represents the market premium, and (b) any premium paid, i.e. (guaranteed sum × risk) – premium paid.

Part G State Aids

24 OJ L 302, 1.11.2006, p.29. [Ed note: see now Commission Regulation (EC) No 800/2008 of 6 August 2008 declaring certain categories of aid compatible with the common market in application of Articles [107 and 108 TFEU] (General block exemption Regulation) (OJ L 214, 9.8.2008, p.3), reproduced above at G11.]
25 OJ L 358, 16.12.2006, p.3.

4.5. Aid element in guarantee schemes for SMEs

The two simplification tools outlined in point 3.5 and relating to guarantee schemes for SMEs can also be used for aid calculation purposes. The conditions of use of both rules are defined as follows:

Use of safe-harbour premiums in guarantee schemes for SMEs

For SMEs, the simplified evaluation system outlined above in point 3.5 can also be applied. In that case, if the premium for a given category in a guarantee scheme does not correspond to the value set as a minimum for its rating class,[26] the difference between this minimum level and the premium charged will be regarded as aid.[27] If the guarantee lasts more than a year, the yearly shortfalls are discounted using the reference rate.[28]

Use of single premiums in guarantee schemes for SMEs

In view of the more limited distortion of competition that may be caused by State aid provided in the framework of a guarantee scheme for SMEs, the Commission considers that if an aid scheme only relates to guarantees for SMEs, where the guaranteed amount does not exceed a threshold of EUR 2,5 million per company in this given scheme, the Commission may accept, by way of derogation from point 4.4, a valuation of the aid intensity of the scheme as such, without the need to carry out a valuation for each individual guarantee or risk class within the scheme.[29]

Notes

26 This includes the possibility whereby SMEs which do not have a credit history or a rating based on a balance sheet approach, the safe-harbour premium is set at 3,8% but this can never be lower than the premium which would be applicable to the parent company or companies.
27 This calculation can be summarised, for each risk class, as the outstanding sum guaranteed multiplied by the difference between (a) the safe-harbour premium percentage of that risk class and (b) the premium percentage paid, i.e. guaranteed sum × (safe-harbour premium – premium paid).
28 See further details in footnote 11.
29 This calculation can be summarised, irrespective of the risk class, as the difference between (a) the outstanding sum guaranteed, multiplied by the risk factor of the scheme ('risk' being the probability of default after inclusion of administrative and capital costs), and (b) any premium paid, i.e. (guaranteed sum × risk) – premium paid.

5. COMPATIBILITY WITH THE COMMON MARKET OF STATE AID IN THE FORM OF GUARANTEES

5.1. General

State guarantees within the scope of Article [107(1)] of the Treaty must be examined by the Commission with a view to determining whether or not they are compatible with the common market. Before such assessment of compatibility can be made, the beneficiary of the aid must be identified.

5.2. Assessment

Whether or not this aid is compatible with the common market will be examined by the Commission according to the same rules as are applied to aid measures taking other forms. The concrete criteria for the compatibility assessment have been clarified and detailed by the Commission in frameworks and guidelines concerning horizontal, regional and sectoral aid.[30] The examination will take into account, in particular, the aid intensity, the characteristics of the beneficiaries and the objectives pursued.

Notes

30 See Competition law applicable to State aid in the European Community: <http://ec.europa.eu/comm/competition/state_aid/legislation/legislation.html>. For sector specific State aid legislation, see for agriculture: <http://ec.europa.eu/agriculture/stateaid/leg/index_en.htm> and for transport: <http://ec.europa.eu/dgs/energy_transport/state_aid/transport_en.htm>.

5.3. Conditions

The Commission will accept guarantees only if their mobilisation is contractually linked to specific conditions which may go as far as the compulsory declaration of bankruptcy of the beneficiary undertaking, or any similar procedure. These conditions will have to be agreed between the parties when the guarantee is initially granted. In the event that a Member State wants to mobilise the guarantee under conditions other than those initially agreed to at the granting stage, then the Commission will regard the mobilisation of the guarantee as creating new aid which has to be notified under Article [108(3)] of the Treaty.

6. Reports to be Presented to the Commission by the Member States

In accordance with general monitoring obligations,[31] in order to further monitor new developments on the financial markets and since the value of State guarantees is difficult to assess and changes over time, the constant review, pursuant to Article [108(1)] of the Treaty, of State guarantee schemes approved by the Commission is of particular importance. Member States shall therefore submit reports to the Commission.

For aid guarantee schemes, these reports will have to be presented at least at the end of the period of validity of the guarantee scheme and for the notification of an amended scheme. The Commission may however consider it appropriate to request reports on a more frequent basis, depending on the case.

For guarantee schemes, for which the Commission has taken a non-aid decision, and especially when no solid historic data exists for the scheme, the Commission may request, when taking its non-aid decision for such reports to be presented, thereby clarifying on a case-by-case basis the frequency and the content of the reporting requirement. Reports should include at least the following information:

(a) the number and amount of guarantees issued;
(b) the number and amount of guarantees outstanding at the end of the period;
(c) the number and value of defaulted guarantees (displayed individually) on a yearly basis;
(d) the yearly income:

1. income from the premiums charged;
2. income from recoveries;
3. other revenues (e.g. interest received on deposits or investments);

(e) the yearly costs:

1. administrative costs;
2. indemnifications paid on mobilised guarantees;

(f) the yearly surplus or shortfall (difference between income and costs); and
(g) the accumulated surplus or shortfall since the beginning of the scheme.[32]

For individual guarantees, the relevant information, mainly that referred to in points (d) to (g), should be similarly reported.

In all cases, the Commission draws the attention of Member States to the fact that correct reporting at a remote date presupposes correct collection of the necessary data from the beginning of the use of the scheme and their aggregation on a yearly basis.

The attention of Member States is also drawn to the fact that for non-aid guarantees provided individually or under a scheme, although no notification obligation exists, the Commission may have to verify that the guarantee or scheme does not entail aid elements, for instance following a complaint. In that case, the Commission will request information similar to that set out above for reports from the Member State concerned.

Where reports already have to be presented following specific reporting obligations established by block exemption regulations, guidelines or frameworks applicable in the State aid field, those specific reports will replace the reports to be presented under the present guarantee reporting obligation provided the information listed above is included.

Notes

[31] Such as those laid down in particular by Commission Regulation (EC) No 794/2004 of 21 April 2004 implementing Council Regulation (EC) No 659/1999 laying down detailed rules for the application of Article [108 TFEU] (OJ L 140, 30.4.2004, p.1). Regulation as last amended by Regulation (EC) No 271/2008 (OJ L 82, 25.3.2008, p.1).

[32] If the scheme has been active for more than 10 years, only the last 10 annual amounts of shortfall or surplus are to be provided.

7. Implementing Measures

The Commission invites Member States to adjust their existing guarantee measures to the stipulations of the present Notice by 1 January 2010 as far as new guarantees are concerned.

G24A

COMMUNICATION FROM THE COMMISSION

to the Member States on the application of Articles 107 and 108 of the Treaty on the Functioning of the European Union to short-term export-credit insurance

(Text with EEA relevance)

(2012/C 392/01)

Official Journal C 392, 19.12.2012, p.1

Celex No: 52012XC1219(01)

EUR-Lex permanent link: <http://eur-lex.europa.eu/legal-content/EN/ALL/?uri=CELEX:52012X C1219(01)&qid=1395779012611>

Notes

EEA application: on 30.1.2013 the EFTA Surveillance Authority adopted corresponding Guidelines on Short-term export-credit insurance. These are available at the following address: <http://www.eftasurv.int/media/state-aid-guidelines/Part-V---Short-term-export-credit-insurance.pdf>

Commentary
Communication: F&N: 17.326

1. Introduction

1. Export subsidies can adversely affect competition in the marketplace among potential rival suppliers of goods and services. That is why the Commission, as the guardian of competition under the Treaty, has always strongly condemned export aid for intra-Union trade and for exports outside the Union. To prevent Member States' support for export-credit insurance from distorting competition, its assessment under Union State aid rules needs to be clarified.

2. The Commission has used its power to regulate State aid in the area of short-term export-credit insurance to address actual or potential distortions of competition in the internal market, not only among exporters in different Member States (in trade within and outside the Union), but also among export-credit insurers operating in the Union. In 1997, the Commission laid down the principles for State intervention in its Communication to the Member States pursuant to Article

93(1) of the EC Treaty applying Articles 92 and 93 of the Treaty to short-term export-credit insurance ¹ ('the 1997 Communication'). The 1997 Communication was to be applied for a period of five years from 1 January 1998. It was subsequently amended and its period of application was prolonged in 2001 ², 2004 ³, 2005 ⁴ and 2010 ⁵. It now applies until 31 December 2012.

Notes

1 OJ C 281, 17.9.1997, p.4.
2 OJ C 217, 2.8.2001, p.2.
3 OJ C 307, 11.12.2004, p.12.
4 OJ C 325, 22.12.2005, p.22.
5 OJ C 329, 7.12.2010, p.6.

3. Experience gained in applying the 1997 Communication, in particular during the financial crisis between 2009 and 2011, suggests that the Commission's policy in this area should be reviewed.

4. The rules set out in this Communication will help to ensure that State aid does not distort competition among private and public or publicly supported export-credit insurers and to create a level-playing field among exporters.

5. It aims to give Member States more detailed guidance about the principles on which the Commission intends to base its interpretation of Articles 107 and 108 of the Treaty and their application to short-term export-credit insurance. It should make the Commission's policy in this area as transparent as possible and ensure predictability and equal treatment. To that end, it lays down a set of conditions that must be fulfilled when State insurers wish to enter the short-term export- credit insurance market for marketable risks.

6. Risks that are in principle non-marketable are outside the scope of this Communication.

7. Section 2 describes the scope of this Communication and the definitions used in it. Section 3 deals with the applicability of Article 107(1) of the Treaty and the general prohibition of State aid for the export-credit insurance of marketable risks. Finally, Section 4 provides for some exceptions from the definition of marketable risks and specifies the conditions for State intervention in the insurance of temporarily non-marketable risks.

2. Scope of the Communication and Definitions

2.1. Scope

8. The Commission will apply the principles set out in this Communication only to export-credit insurance with a risk period of less than two years. All other export finance instruments are excluded from the scope of this Communication.

2.2. Definitions

9. For the purposes of this Communication the following definitions will apply:

'co-insurance' means the percentage of each insured loss that is not indemnified by the insurer but is borne by another insurer;

'credit period' means the period of time given to the buyer to pay for the delivered goods and services under an export-credit transaction;

'commercial risks' means risks including, in particular:

— arbitrary repudiation of a contract by a buyer, that is to say any arbitrary decision made by a non-public buyer to interrupt or terminate the contract without a legitimate reason,

— arbitrary refusal of a non-public buyer to accept the goods covered by the contract without a legitimate reason,

— insolvency of a non-public buyer and its guarantor,

— protracted default, that is to say non-payment by a non-public buyer and by its guarantor of a debt resulting from the contract, 'export-credit insurance' means an insurance product whereby the insurer provides insurance against a commercial and political risk related to payment obligations in an export transaction;

'manufacturing period' means the period between the date of an order and the delivery of the goods or services;

'marketable risks' means commercial and political risks with a maximum risk period of less than two years, on public and non-public buyers in the countries listed in the Annex; all other risks are considered non-marketable for the purposes of this Communication.

'political risks' means risks including, in particular:

— the risk that a public buyer or country prevents the completion of a transaction or does not pay on time,

— a risk that is beyond the scope of an individual buyer or falls outside the individual buyer's responsibility,

— the risk that a country fails to transfer to the country of the insured the money paid by buyers domiciled in that country,

— the risk that a case of force majeure occurs outside the country of the insurer, which could include warlike events, in so far as its effects are not otherwise insured,

'private credit insurer' means a company or organisation other than a State insurer that provides export-credit insurance;

'quota-share' means reinsurance that requires the insurer to transfer, and the reinsurer to accept, a given percentage of every risk within a defined category of business written by the insurer;

'reinsurance' means insurance that is purchased by an insurer from another insurer to manage risk by lowering its own risk;

'risk period' means the manufacturing period plus the credit period;

'single-risk cover' means cover for all sales to one buyer or for a single contract with one buyer;

'State insurer' means a company or other organisation that provides export-credit insurance with the support of, or on behalf of, a Member State, or a Member State that provides export-credit insurance;

'top-up cover' means additional cover over a credit limit established by another insurer;

'whole turnover policy' means a credit insurance policy other than single risk-cover; that is to say, a credit insurance policy that covers all or most of the credit sales of the insured as well as payment receivables from sales to multiple buyers.

3. APPLICABILITY OF ARTICLE 107(1) OF THE TREATY

3.1. General principles

10. Article 107(1) of the Treaty states that 'any aid granted by a Member State or through State resources in any form whatsoever which distorts or threatens to distort competition by favouring certain undertakings or the production of certain goods shall, in so far as it affects trade between Member States, be incompatible with the internal market'.

11. If export-credit insurance is provided by State insurers, it involves State resources. The involvement of the State may give the insurers and/or the exporters a selective advantage and could thereby distort or threaten to distort competition and affect trade between Member States. The following principles are designed to provide guidance on how such measures will be assessed under State aid rules.

3.2. Aid for insurers

12. If State insurers have certain advantages compared to private credit insurers, State aid may be involved. The advantages can take different forms and might include, for example:
    (a) State guarantees of borrowing and losses;
    (b) exemption from the requirement to constitute adequate reserves and the other requirements stemming from the exclusion of export-credit insurance operations for the account of or

guaranteed by the State from First Council Directive 73/239/EEC of 24 July 1973 on the coordination of laws, regulations and administrative provisions relating to the taking-up and pursuit of the business of direct insurance other than life assurance[1];

(c) relief or exemption from taxes normally payable (such as company taxes and taxes levied on insurance policies);

(d) awards of aid or provisions of capital by the State or other forms of financing that are not in accordance with the market economy investor principle;

(e) provision by the State of services in kind, such as access to and use of State infrastructure, facilities or privileged information, on terms that do not reflect their market value;

(f) direct reinsurance by the State or a direct State reinsurance guarantee on terms more favourable than those available on the private reinsurance market, leading to under-pricing of the reinsurance cover or to the artificial creation of capacity that would not be forthcoming from the private market.

Notes

[1] OJ L 228, 16.8.1973, p.3.

3.3. Prohibition of State aid for export credits

13. The advantages for State insurers listed in point 12 with regard to marketable risks affect intra-Union trade in credit insurance services. They lead to variations in the insurance cover available for marketable risks in different Member States. This distorts competition among insurers in different Member States and has secondary effects on intra-Union trade regardless of whether intra-Union exports or exports outside the Union are concerned[1]. It is necessary to define the conditions under which State insurers can operate if they have such advantages compared to private credit insurers, in order to ensure they do not benefit from State aid. This requires that they should not be able to insure marketable risks.

Notes

[1] In its judgment in Case C-142/87 *Kingdom of Belgium* v *Commission of the European Communities*, the Court held that not only aid for intra-Union exports, but also aid for exports outside the Union, can influence intra-Union competition and trade. Both types of operation are insured by export-credit insurers and aid for both can therefore affect intra-Union competition and trade.

14. Advantages for State insurers are also sometimes passed on to exporters, at least in part. Such advantages may distort competition and trade and constitute State aid within the meaning of Article 107(1) of the Treaty. However, if the conditions for the provision of export-credit insurance for marketable risks, as set out in section 4.3 of this Communication, are fulfilled, the Commission will consider that no undue advantage has been passed on to exporters.

4. CONDITIONS FOR PROVIDING EXPORT-CREDIT INSURANCE FOR TEMPORARILY NON-MARKETABLE RISKS

4.1. General principles

15. As stated in point 13, if State insurers have any advantages compared to private credit insurers, as described in point 12, they must not insure marketable risks. If State insurers or their subsidiaries wish to insure marketable risks, it must be ensured that in so doing, they do not directly or indirectly benefit from State aid. To this end, they must have a certain amount of own funds (a solvency margin, including a guarantee fund) and technical provisions (an equalisation reserve) and must have obtained the required authorisation in accordance with Directive 73/239/EEC. They must also at least keep a separate administration account and separate accounts for their insurance of marketable risks and non-marketable risks for the account of or guaranteed by the State, to show that they do not receive State aid for their insurance of marketable risks. The accounts for businesses insured on the insurer's own account should comply with Council Directive 91/674/EEC of 19 December 1991 on the annual accounts and consolidated accounts of insurance undertakings[1].

Notes
[1] OJ L 374, 31.12.1991, p.7.

16. Member States providing reinsurance cover to an export- credit insurer by way of participation or involvement in private sector reinsurance treaties covering marketable and non-marketable risks, must be able to demonstrate that the arrangements do not involve State aid as referred to in point 12(f).

17. State insurers may provide export-credit insurance for temporarily non-marketable risks, subject to the conditions set out in this Communication.

4.2. Exceptions to the definition of marketable risks: temporarily non-marketable risks

18. Notwithstanding the definition of marketable risks, certain commercial and political risks on buyers established in the countries listed in the Annex, are considered temporarily non-marketable in the following cases:

   (a) if the Commission decides to temporarily remove one or more countries from the list of marketable risk countries in the Annex, by means of the mechanism described in Section 5.2, because the capacity of the private insurance market in is insufficient to cover all economically justifiable risks in the country or countries concerned;

   (b) if the Commission, after having received a notification from a Member State, decides that the risks incurred by small and medium-sized enterprises as defined by the Commission Recommendation of 6 May 2003 concerning the definition of micro, small and medium-sized enterprises[1], with a total annual export turnover not exceeding EUR 2 million, are temporarily non-marketable for exporters in the notifying Member State;

   (c) if the Commission, after having received a notification from a Member State, decides that single-risk cover with a risk period at least 181 days and less than two years is temporarily non-marketable for exporters in the notifying Member State;

   (d) if the Commission, after having received a notification from a Member State, decides that due to a shortage of export-credit insurance, certain risks are temporarily non-marketable for exporters in the notifying Member State.

Notes
[1] OJ L 124, 20.5.2003, p.36.

19. To minimise distortions of competition in the internal market, risks which are considered temporarily non- marketable in accordance with point 18 can be covered by State insurers, provided they fulfil the conditions in section 4.3.

4.3. Conditions for providing cover for temporarily non-marketable risks

4.3.1. Quality of cover

20. The quality of cover offered by State insurers must be consistent with market standards. In particular, only economically justified risks, that is to say, risks that are acceptable on the basis of sound underwriting principles, can be covered. The maximum percentage of cover must be 95 % for commercial risks and political risks and the claims waiting period must be a minimum of 90 days.

4.3.2. Underwriting principles

21. Sound underwriting principles must always be applied to the assessment of risks. Accordingly, the risk of financially unsound transactions must not be eligible for cover under publicly supported schemes. With regard to such principles, risk acceptance criteria must be explicit. If a business relationship already exists, exporters must have a positive trading and/or payment experience. Buyers must have a clean claims record, the probability of the buyers' default must be acceptable and their internal and/or external financial ratings must also be acceptable.

4.3.3. Adequate pricing

22. Risk-carrying in the export-credit insurance contract must be remunerated by an adequate premium. To minimise the crowding out of private credit insurers, average premiums under publicly supported schemes must be higher than the average premiums charged by private credit insurers for similar risks. This requirement ensures the phasing out of State intervention, because the higher premium will ensure that exporters return to private credit insurers as soon as market conditions allow them to do so and the risk becomes marketable again.

23. Pricing is considered adequate if the minimum premium [1] ('safe-harbour premium') for the relevant buyers' risk category [2] as set out in the following table is charged. The safe-harbour premium applies unless Member States provide evidence that these rates are inadequate for the risk in question. For a whole turnover policy, the risk category must correspond to the average risk of buyers covered by the policy.

Notes

[1] For each relevant risk category, the safe-harbour risk premium range was established on the basis of one-year Credit Default Swap (CDS) spreads, based on a composite rating including ratings of all three main credit rating agencies (Standard & Poor, Moody's and Fitch), for the past five years (2007–2011), assuming that average recovery ratios for short-term export-credit insurance are 40 %. The ranges were subsequently made continuous to better cater for the fact that risk premiums do not remain constant over time.

[2] The buyers' risk categories are based on credit ratings. Ratings do not need to be obtained from specific rating agencies. National rating systems or rating systems used by banks are equally acceptable. For firms without a public rating, a rating based on verifiable information could be applied.

Risk category	Annual risk premium[1] (% of insured volume)
Excellent[2]	0.2–0.4
Good[3]	0.41–0.9
Satisfactory[4]	0.91–2.3
Weak[5]	2.31–4.5

Notes

[1] Safe harbour for a 30-day insurance contract can be obtained by dividing the annual risk premium by 12.

[2] The excellent risk category includes risks equivalent to AAA, AA+, AA, AA-, A+, A, A- in Standard and Poor's credit ratings.

[3] The good risk category includes risks equivalent to BBB+, BBB or BBB- in Standard and Poor's credit ratings.

[4] The satisfactory risk category includes risks equivalent to BB+, BB or BB- in Standard and Poor's credit ratings.

[5] The weak risk category includes risks equivalent to B+, B or B- in Standard and Poor's credit ratings.

24. For co-insurance, quota share and top-up cover, pricing is considered adequate only if the premium charged is at least 30 % higher than the premium for the (original) cover provided by a private credit insurer.

25. An administration fee must be added to the risk premium regardless of the term of the contract in order for pricing to be considered adequate.

4.3.4 Transparency and reporting

26. Member States must publish the schemes put in place for risks which are considered temporarily non-marketable in accordance with point 18 on the websites of State insurers, specifying all applicable conditions.

27. They must submit annual reports to the Commission on risks which are considered temporarily non-marketable in accordance with point 18 and are covered by State insurers. They must do so at the latest on 31 July of the year following the intervention.

28. The report must contain information on use of each scheme, including in particular the total volume of credit limits granted, turnover insured, premiums charged, claims registered and paid, amounts recovered and the administrative costs of the scheme. The Commission will publish the reports on its website.

5. Procedural Issues

5.1. General principles

29. The risks specified in point 18(a) can be covered by State insurers, subject to the conditions in section 4.3. The Commission does not have to be notified in such cases.

30. The risks specified in point 18(b), (c) and (d) can be covered by State insurers, subject to the conditions in section 4.3 and following notification to and approval by the Commission.

31. Failure to fulfil any one of the conditions set out in Section 4.3 does not mean that the export-credit insurance or insurance scheme is automatically prohibited. If a Member States wishes to deviate from any of the conditions or if there is any doubt about whether a planned export-credit insurance scheme fulfils the conditions set out in this Communication, the Member State must notify the scheme to the Commission.

32. Analysis under State aid rules does not prejudge the compatibility of a given measure with other Treaty provisions.

5.2. Modification of the list of marketable risk countries

33. When determining whether the lack of sufficient private capacity justifies the temporary removal of a country from the list of marketable risk countries, as referred to in point 18(a), the Commission will take the following factors into account, in order of priority:

    (a) contraction of private credit insurance capacity: in particular, the decision of a major credit insurer not to cover risks on buyers in the country concerned, a significant decrease in total insured amounts or a significant decrease in acceptance ratios for the country concerned within a six-month period;

    (b) deterioration of sovereign sector ratings: in particular, sudden changes in credit ratings within a six-month period, for example multiple downgrading by independent rating agencies, or a big increase in Credit Default Swap spreads;

    (c) deterioration of corporate sector performance: in particular, a sharp increase in insolvencies in the country concerned within a six-month period.

34. When market capacity becomes insufficient to cover all economically justifiable risks, the Commission may revise the list of marketable risk countries at the written request of at least three Member States or on its own initiative.

35. If the Commission intends to modify the list of marketable risk countries in the Annex, it will consult and seek information from Member States, private credit insurers and interested parties. The consultation and the type of information sought will be announced on the Commission's website. The consultation period will usually not be longer than 20 working days. When, on the basis of the information gathered, the Commission decides to modify the list of marketable risk countries, it will inform Member States in writing and announce the decision on its website.

36. The temporary removal of a country from the list of marketable risk countries will be valid for no less than 12 months. Insurance policies relating to the temporarily removed country which are signed during that period may be valid for a maximum of 180 days after the date on which the temporary removal ceases. New insurance policies may not be signed after that date. Three months before the temporary removal ceases, the Commission will consider whether to prolong the removal of the country concerned from the list. If the Commission determines that market capacity is still insufficient to cover all economically justifiable risks, taking into account the factors set out in point 33, it may prolong the temporary removal of the country from the list, in accordance with point 35.

5.3. Notification obligation for exceptions in point 18(b) and (c)

37. The evidence currently available to the Commission suggests that there is a market gap as regards the risks specified in point 18(b) and (c) and that those risks are therefore non-marketable. It must be borne in mind, however, that the lack of cover does not exist in every Member State and that the situation could change over time, as the private sector might become interested in this segment of the market. State intervention should only be allowed for risks which the market would otherwise not cover.

38. For these reasons, if a Member State wants to cover the risks specified in point 18(b) or (c), it must make a notification to the Commission pursuant to Article 108(3) of the Treaty and demonstrate in its notification that it has contacted the main credit insurers and brokers in that Member State [1] and given them an opportunity to provide evidence that cover for the risks concerned is available there. If the credit insurers concerned do not give the Member State or the Commission information about the conditions of cover and insured volumes for the type of risks the Member State wants to cover within 30 days of receiving a request from the Member State to do so, or if the information provided does not demonstrate that cover for the risks concerned is available in that Member State, the Commission will consider the risks temporarily non-marketable.

Notes

1 The contacted credit insurers and brokers should be representative in terms of the products offered (for example, specialised providers for single risks) and the size of the market they cover (for example, representing jointly a minimum share of 50 % of the market).

5.4. Notification obligation in other cases

39. As regards the risks specified in point 18(d), the Member State concerned must, in its notification to the Commission pursuant to Article 108(3) of the Treaty, demonstrate that cover is unavailable for exporters in that particular Member State due to a supply shock in the private insurance market, in particular the withdrawal of a major credit insurer from the Member State concerned, reduced capacity or a limited range of products compared to other Member States.

6. Date of Application and Duration

40. The Commission will apply the principles in this Communication from 1 January 2013 until 31 December 2018, except for point 18(a) and section 5.2, which will be applied from the date of adoption of this Communication.

Annex

[List of marketable risk countries

All Member States with the exception of Greece

Australia

Canada

Iceland

Japan

New Zealand

Norway

Switzerland

United States of America]

Notes

The annex is reproduced as replaced by the Communication from the Commission amending the Annex to the Communication from the Commission to the Member States on the application of Articles 107 and 108 of the Treaty on the Functioning of the European Union to short-term export-credit insurance (OJ C 398, 22.12.2012, p.6). The amendment will apply from 1 January 2013 until 31 December 2013.

G25

COMMUNICATION FROM THE COMMISSION

on the revision of the method for setting the reference and discount rates

(2008/C 14/02)

Official Journal C 14, 19.1.2008, p.6

Celex No: 52008XC0119(01)

EUR-Lex permanent link: <http://eur-lex.europa.eu/LexUriServ/LexUriServ.do?uri=CELEX: 52008 XC0119(01)EN:NOT>

Notes

EEA application: Base rates are calculated in accordance with the Chapter on the method for setting reference and discount rates of the EFTA Surveillance Authority's State aid Guidelines as amended by the EFTA Surveillance Authority's Decision No 788/08/COL of 17 December 2008 (OJ L 105, 21.4.2011, p.32).

Commentary
Communication: B&C: 17.028 **F&N**: 17.77, 17.459, 17.468

(This communication replaces the previous notices on the method for setting the reference and discount rates)

REFERENCE AND DISCOUNT RATES

Within the framework of the Community control of State aid, the Commission makes use of reference and discount rates. The reference and discount rates are applied as a proxy for the market rate and to measure the grant equivalent of aid, in particular when it is disbursed in several instalments and to calculate the aid element resulting from interest subsidy schemes. They are also used to check compliance with the *de minimis* rule and block exemption regulations.

BACKGROUND TO THE REFORM

The main reason for re-examining the methodology for setting reference and discount rates is that the required financial parameters are not always available in all Member States, especially in the new ones.[1] In addition, the current method could be improved in order to take account of the debtor's creditworthiness and collaterals.

Therefore, this Communication presents a revised method for setting reference and discount rates. The proposed approach builds on the current arrangement, which is accepted by all Member States and practical to apply, to develop a new method that mitigates some of the current shortcomings, is compatible with the various financial systems in the EU (in particular in the new Member States) and remains simple to implement.

Notes

[1] The current reference rates for these Member States are those communicated by the Member States as reflecting a suitable market rate. The methodology for arriving at these rates diverges from one Member State to another.

A study by Deloitte & Touche,[2] commissioned by DG Competition, proposes a system based on two pillars: a 'standard' approach and an 'advanced' approach.

Notes

2 Available on the website of DG Competition: <http://ec.europa.eu/comm/competition/state_aid/others/>.

Standard approach

In this approach, the Commission publishes, each quarter, a base rate calculated on several maturities — 3 months, 1 year, 5 years and 10 years — and for various currencies. IBOR rates[1] and ask swap rates are used or, in the absence of these parameters, government bond rates. The premium applied to obtain the reference rate for a loan is calculated according to the borrower's creditworthiness and collaterals. According to the rating category of the company ('rating' provided by rating agencies in the case of major companies or by banks in the case of SMEs), the margin applicable to the default case (normal rating and normal collateralisation)[2] represents 220 basis points. The increase could be up to 1 650 in the case of 'low' creditworthiness and low collateralisation.

Notes

1 Inter-bank offered rate on the money market.
2 Cases where the recipient shows a satisfactory rating (BB) and a loss given default rate between 31% and 59%.

Advanced approach

This approach would allow Member States to appoint an independent calculation agent — a central bank for instance — in charge of publishing regularly a fair reference interest rate, for a higher number of maturities and on a more frequent basis than the standard approach. This approach would be justified by the knowledge and proximity of the financial and banking data available to this institution in comparison with the Commission. In that case, the Commission and an external auditor would validate calculation methods. In this approach, opting out, in certain cases, could be considered.

Weaknesses

Despite the economic relevance of the two methods, certain difficulties can be underlined.

Standard approach:
— it does not solve the problem of the lack of financial data in the new Member States and adds new, not readily accessible parameters,
— this standard method could favour large companies to the detriment of SMEs for which either no rating is available, or a less advantageous one exists (in particular because of information asymmetry with respect to the lender). It could give rise to multiple disputes on the subject of calculation methods for the premium to be applied according to creditworthiness and the level of collaterals,
— it does not simplify the task of Member States, in particular regarding calculations to check compliance with the *de minimis* rule and the block exemption regulations.

Advanced method:
— the advanced method could prove problematic when applied to aid schemes: the volatility of market rates might make the difference between the underlying rate of a loan scheme and the then valid reference rate so advantageous to the borrower that some measures would become incompatible with the State aid rules,
— a quarterly adjustment of the rates would complicate the handling of cases as the calculated aid amounts may vary considerably between the beginning of the assessment phase and the date of the final decision taken by the Commission,
— these arrangements seem overly complicated and may fail to ensure consistently fair treatment across Member States.

NEW METHODOLOGY

NEW METHODOLOGY

To avoid these difficulties, the Commission proposes a method that:
— is easy to apply (in particular for the Member States when dealing with measures falling under the *de minimis* or block exemption regulations),
— ensures equal treatment across Member States with minimum deviations from current practice and facilitating the application of reference rates for the new Member States,
— uses simplified criteria taking into account firms' creditworthiness instead of the mere size of undertakings, which seems a too simplistic criterion.

Moreover, this method makes it possible to avoid adding uncertainty and complexity to calculation methods in a changing banking and financial environment due to the implementation of the Basel II framework, which could have a significant impact on the allocation of capital as well as on banks' behaviour. The Commission will continue to monitor this changing environment and, if necessary, provide further guidance.

COMMISSION NOTICE

The main reason for re-examining the methodology for setting reference and discount rates is that the required financial parameters are not always available in all Member States. In addition, the current method can be improved in order to take account of the debtor's creditworthiness and collaterals. The Commission therefore adopts the following methodology for setting the reference rates:

— Calculation basis: 1-year IBOR
The base rate is based on 1-year money market rates, available in almost all Member States, the Commission reserving the right to use shorter or longer maturities adapted to certain cases.
Where those rates are not available, the 3-month money market rate will be used.
In the absence of reliable or equivalent data or in exceptional circumstances the Commission may, in close cooperation with the Member State(s) concerned and in principle based on data from that Member State's Central Bank, determine another calculation basis.
— Margins[1]
The following margins are to be applied in principle depending on the rating of the undertaking concerned and the collateral[2] offered.

Loan margins in basis points			
Rating category	Collateralisation		
	High	Normal	Low
Strong (AAA-A)	60	75	100
Good (BBB)	75	100	220
Satisfactory(BB)	100	220	400
Weak (B)	220	400	650
Bad/Financial difficulties (CCC and below)	400	650	1 000[1]

[1] Subject to the application of the specific provisions for rescue and restructuring aid, as currently lain down in the Community guidelines on state aid for rescuing and restructuring firms in difficulty (OJ C 244, 1.10.2004, p.2) and in particular point 25(a), which refers to 'a rate at least comparable with the rates observed for loans to healthy companies, and in particular at the reference rates adopted by the Commission'. Hence, for rescue aid cases, the 1-year IBOR increased with at least 100 basis points shall be applied.

Normally, 100 basis points are added to the base rate. This assumes (i) loans to undertakings with satisfactory rating and high collateral; or (ii) loans to undertakings with good rating and normal collateral.

For borrowers that do not have a credit history or a rating based on a balance sheet approach, such as certain special-purpose companies or start-up companies, the base rate should be increased by at least 400 basis points (depending on the available collaterals) and the margin can never be lower than the one which would be applicable to the parent company.

Ratings do not need to be obtained from specific rating agencies — national rating systems or rating systems used by banks to reflect default rates are equally acceptable.[3]

The above margins may be revised from time to time to take account of the market situation.

— Update

An update of the reference rate will be carried out every year. The base rate will thus be calculated on the basis of the 1-year IBOR recorded in September, October and November of the previous year. The then fixed base rate will be in force as from the first of January. For the period from 1 July 2008 until 31 December 2008, the reference rate will exceptionally be calculated on the basis of the 1-year IBOR recorded in February, March and April 2008, subject to the application of the next paragraph.

In addition, to take account of significant and sudden variations, an update will be made each time the average rate, calculated over the previous three months, deviates by more than 15% from the rate in force. This new rate will enter into force on the first day of the second month following the months used for the calculation.

— Discount rate: Calculation of net present value

The reference rate is also to be used as a discount rate, for calculating present values. To that end, in principle, the base rate increased by a fixed margin of 100 basis points will be used.

— The present methodology will enter into force as of 1 July 2008.

Notes

1 As follows from the study, the margin is largely independent of the maturity of the loan.

2 Normal collateral should be understood as the level of collateral normally required by financial institutions as a guarantee for their loan. The level of collaterals can be measured as the Loss Given Default (LGD), which is the expected loss in percentage of the debtor's exposure taking into account recoverable amounts from collateral and the bankruptcy assets; as a consequence the LGD is inversely proportional to the validity of collaterals. For the present communication it is assumed that 'High' collateralisation implies an LGD below or equal to 30%, 'Normal' collateralisation an LGD between 31% and 59%, and 'Low' collateralisation an LGD above or equal to 60%. For more details, on the notion LGD, see Basel II: International Convergence of Capital Measurement and Capital Standards: A Revised Framework — Comprehensive Version, available on: <http://www.bis.org/publ/bcbs128.pdf>.

3 For a comparison between the most commonly used credit rating mechanisms, see e.g. Table 1 in Working Paper No 207 of the Bank for International settlements: <http://www.bis.org/publ/work207.pdf>.